$\mathcal{P}$resented to:

···

$\mathcal{F}$rom

···

$\mathcal{D}$ate

···

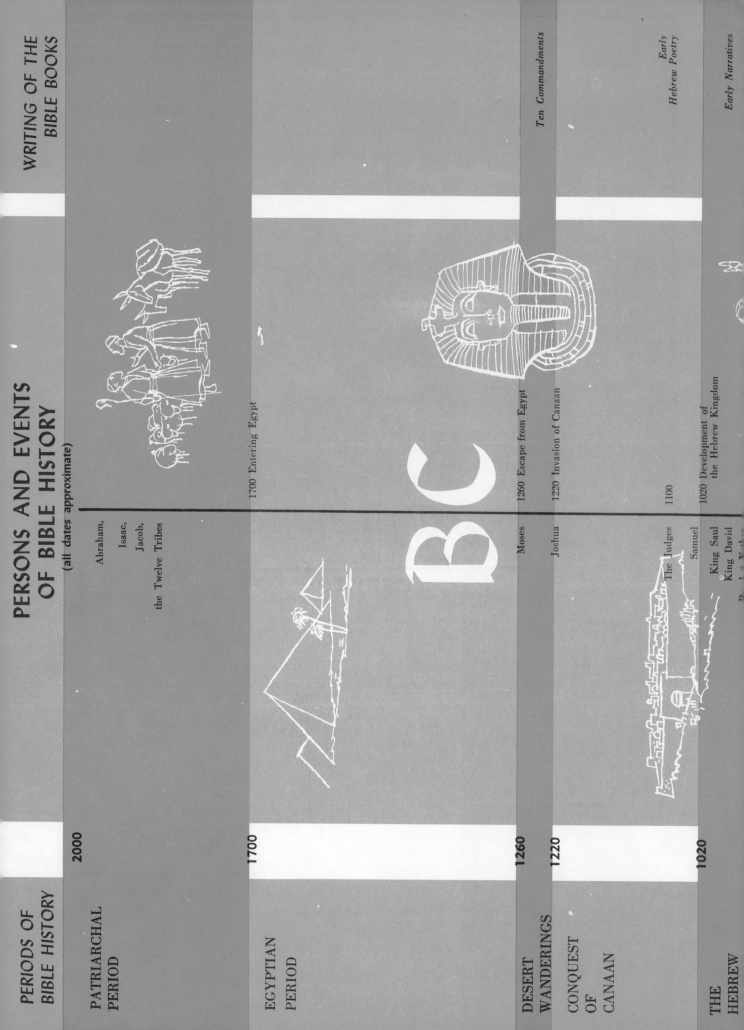

PERSONS AND EVENTS OF BIBLE HISTORY

(all dates approximate)

PERIODS OF BIBLE HISTORY	PERSONS AND EVENTS OF BIBLE HISTORY	WRITING OF THE BIBLE BOOKS
2000 PATRIARCHAL PERIOD	Abraham, Isaac, Jacob, the Twelve Tribes	
1700 EGYPTIAN PERIOD	1700 Entering Egypt	
1260 DESERT WANDERINGS	Moses — 1260 Escape from Egypt	*Ten Commandments*
1220 CONQUEST OF CANAAN	Joshua — 1220 Invasion of Canaan	
	The Judges 1100 Samuel	*Early Hebrew Poetry*
1020 THE HEBREW	King Saul, King David — 1020 Development of the Hebrew Kingdom	*Early Narratives*

BC

THE OLD TESTAMENT AND NEW TESTAMENT TIMELINE

Judean Records	Israelite Records
	Amos
	Hosea
Isaiah 1-39	
Micah	
Deuteronomy	
Zephaniah, Nahum	
Habakkuk	
Jeremiah, Obadiah	
Ezekiel	
Joshua, Judges, I & II Samuel	
I & II Kings, Isaiah 40-66	

Job
Haggai, Zechariah
Malachi
Joel, Ruth
Genesis, Exodus
Leviticus, Numbers
Deuteronomy completed
Jonah
I & II Chronicles
Nehemiah, Ezra

Song of Solomon
Lamentations completed

Proverbs completed

Ecclesiastes

Daniel
Esther
Psalms completed
Books of Apocrypha
being written

I & II Thessalonians, Galatians
I & II Corinthians, Romans
Philippians, Colossians, Philemon
I Peter, Mark, Matthew, Luke, Acts
Ephesians, Hebrews, Revelation
Gospel of John, I, II, III John
I, II Timothy, Titus, James
Jude, II Peter

KINGDOM OF ISRAEL

King Jeroboam
Prophet Elijah
Prophet Elisha
Prophet Amos
Prophet Hosea
760 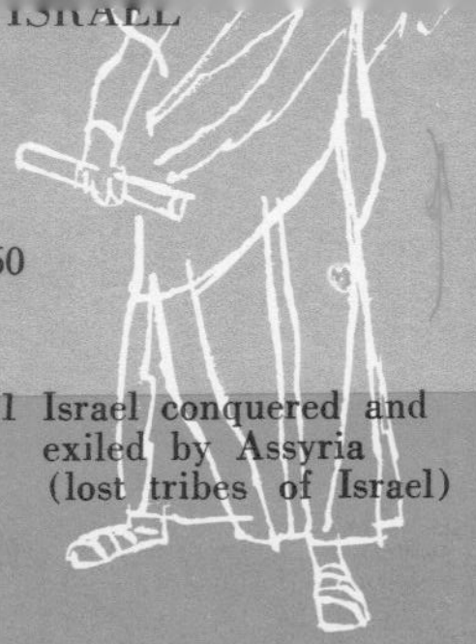
721 Israel conquered and exiled by Assyria (lost tribes of Israel)

KINGDOM OF JUDAH

King Rehoboam
740 King Azariah (Uzziah) / Prophet Isaiah
715 King Hezekiah / Prophet Micah
690 King Manasseh
650 Prophet Zephaniah
626 King Josiah
621 Reform of Josiah and discovery of Deuteronomy

605 Assyria conquered by Babylonia
597 Fall of Jerusalem
586 Jews deported to Babylonia
Prophets Jeremiah, Nahum, Habakkuk, Obadiah, Ezekiel, Isaiah of Babylon

538 Babylonia conquered by Persia, Jews freed to return to Judah
516 Second Temple dedicated
Prophets Haggai, Zechariah

440 Rebuilding walls of Jerusalem
398 Ezra reads the Law
Prophet Malachi
Statesmen Nehemiah, Ezra
Prophet Joel

333 Persia and Palestine conquered by Alexander
The Ptolemies rule Palestine

250 Old Testament books translated from Hebrew into Greek. This translation was called *The Septuagint.*

198 Seleucid Kings rule Syria and Palestine
165 Jews revolt from Syria under the Maccabees (Hasmonean kings)

63 B.C. Jerusalem captured by Rome

END OF OLD TESTAMENT ERA — BEGINNING OF CHRISTIAN ERA

A.D.

Birth of Jesus
30 Crucifixion and Resurrection
33 Conversion of Paul
50-63 Writing of Paul's Letters
63 Death of Paul
65-150 Writing of Gospels and other New Testament books
150 New Testament completed

DIVIDED KINGDOM

ASSYRIAN PERIOD — 721

BABYLONIAN PERIOD — 610

PERSIAN PERIOD — 538

GREEK PERIOD — 333

MACCABEAN PERIOD — 165

ROMAN PERIOD — 63

YOUNG READERS BIBLE

THE HOLY BIBLE

REVISED STANDARD VERSION

Containing
The Old and New Testaments
Translated from the Original Languages
Being the Version Set Forth A.D. 1611
Revised A.D. 1881-1885 and A.D. 1901
Compared with the Most Ancient Authorities
and Revised A.D. 1946–1952

Second Edition of the New Testament A.D. 1971

Study Helps for Each Book of the Bible and
Additional Materials Prepared by
The Rev. Henry M. Bullock, Ph.D.
Former Editor of Church School Publications
The Board of Education of The Methodist Church
and
The Rev. Edward C. Peterson, Ed.D.
Former Editor of Children's Publications
The Board of Education of The Methodist Church

Published
by
A. J. Holman Co.
Philadelphia

Distributed by

Nashville • Cokesbury

Table of Contents

What Is Special About This Book? ...... ⑤
What Is the Bible? .... ⑦
How We Got Our Bible .... ⑧
How to Use the Bible .... ⑩
About the Bible .... ⑫
How to Find a Bible Passage .... ⑬
Ways to Use the Bible .... ⑭
A Plan for Reading the Bible .... ⑭
Where to Find Some Great Bible Passages .. ⑮
Preface .... ⑯

OLD TESTAMENT

Genesis 1
Exodus 40
Leviticus 68
Numbers 83
Deuteronomy 107
Joshua 130
Judges 146
Ruth 163
1 Samuel (1 Kingdoms in Greek) 167
2 Samuel (2 Kingdoms in Greek) 192
1 Kings (3 Kingdoms in Greek) 214
2 Kings (4 Kingdoms in Greek) 237
1 Chronicles (1 Paralipomenon in Greek) 261
2 Chronicles (2 Paralipomenon in Greek) 277
Ezra ..... ⎡ 303
Nehemiah ⎢ = Esdras B in Greek ⎥ 311
Esther 321
Job 327
Psalms 352
Proverbs 420
Ecclesiastes 441
Song of Solomon 448
Isaiah 453
Jeremiah 505
Lamentations 555
Ezekiel 562
Daniel 598
Hosea 610
Joel 619
Amos 623
Obadiah 630
Jonah 632
Micah 635
Nahum 641
Habakkuk 644
Zephaniah 647

Haggai 650
Zechariah 652
Malachi 659

NEW TESTAMENT

Matthew 663
Mark 687
Luke 703
John 730
The Acts 749
Romans 775
1 Corinthians 786
2 Corinthians 797
Galatians 805
Ephesians 809
Philippians 813
Colossians 816
1 Thessalonians 819
2 Thessalonians 822
1 Timothy 824
2 Timothy 827
Titus 830
Philemon 832
Hebrews 834
James 843
1 Peter 846
2 Peter 849
1 John 852
2 John 855
3 John 856
Jude 857
Revelation 859

FULL COLOR MAPS

Biblical World in the Time of the Patriarchs
The Kingdoms of Israel and Judah
The Route of the Exodus and the Conquest of
    Canaan
The Assyrian Empire
Great Empires of the Sixth Century
The Empire of Alexander the Great
            and
The Kingdoms of Alexander's Successors
The Roman World in the Time of Caesar
Palestine in the Time of Christ
The Missionary Journeys of Paul
The Spread of Christianity
The Near East Today
The Mediterranean World Today

Alphabetical Arrangement
of the Names
of the
Books of the Old and New Testaments

Book	Page
Acts, The	749
Amos	623
1 Chronicles	261
2 Chronicles	277
Colossians	816
1 Corinthians	786
2 Corinthians	797
Daniel	598
Deuteronomy	107
Ecclesiastes	441
Ephesians	809
Esther	321
Exodus	40
Ezekiel	562
Ezra	303
Galatians	805
Genesis	1
Habakkuk	644
Haggai	650
Hebrews	834
Hosea	610
Isaiah	453
James	843
Jeremiah	505
Job	327
Joel	619
John	730
1 John	852
2 John	855
3 John	856
Jonah	632
Joshua	130
Jude	857

Book	Page
Judges	146
1 Kings	214
2 Kings	237
Lamentations	555
Leviticus	68
Luke	703
Malachi	659
Mark	687
Matthew	663
Micah	635
Nahum	641
Nehemiah	311
Numbers	83
Obadiah	630
1 Peter	846
2 Peter	849
Philemon	832
Philippians	813
Proverbs	420
Psalms	352
Revelation	859
Romans	775
Ruth	163
1 Samuel	167
2 Samuel	192
Song of Solomon	448
1 Thessalonians	819
2 Thessalonians	822
1 Timothy	824
2 Timothy	827
Titus	830
Zechariah	652
Zephaniah	647

What You Should Know About Your Bible

WHAT IS SPECIAL ABOUT THIS BOOK?

The Bible in your hands is the result of a big dream come true. The dream was to publish the Bible in such a way that it would be easier for new Bible readers to use than traditional Bibles. What would a Bible be like that was really planned for young readers? The answer is in your hands.

The special features of your Bible are especially planned to help you learn about and use the Holy Scriptures.

The many new special features of this edition of the Bible are included for important reasons. This Book has been designed to make the reading of your Bible more meaningful and pleasurable.

THIS BIBLE:

- Includes the whole uncut text of the Holy Bible (unabridged).
- Is the translation used officially in the church school curriculum of most Protestant denominations.
- Uses several sizes of type to indicate special kinds of content.
    - ✓ Introductory helps are set in an easy-to-read type size. The columns of all interpretive helps run the full width of the page. The long reading line tells the reader "These helps have been added to the Bible text itself to explain something about what you are reading."
    - ✓ The basic text of the Bible is set in another easy-to-read type size in two column widths on the page. The shorter line allows for easier reading of each line.
    - ✓ A third easy-to-read type size, but smaller, is used in two columns to make for easiest reading of long lists of names. The smallest type tells you that the text printed in that way is either:
        - long lists of names (genealogies, lists of ancestors)
        - long lists of the rules of the ancient Hebrews (such as food laws and directions for the priests)
        - long lists of materials, sizes and rules for the building of the ancient temple in Jerusalem (temple specifications).
- Includes four kinds of illustrations placed right by the text they explain. The skillful use of color makes each page beautiful and more easy to read.
    1. *Action Pictures* hint at the story the words tell about.
    2. *Pictures that Explain the Text*—where Bible terms or customs may not be clear, illustrations have been included to add information and to interpret (illustrations to amplify).
    3. *Church Symbols*—most of the picture language of the church had its origin in the Bible. Many of these picture symbols are identified by the Bible verses that have suggested them.

4. *Maps*—that show where specific events took place are pinpointed on simple maps right by the words that tell about them. More complete color maps are included at the back.

INTRODUCTORY HELPS

—have been moved to where they will be most helpful; immediately before the text they introduce.

- Helps to understanding the whole Bible appear on the first pages.
- Introductions to each individual book appear immediately before each book.
- General reference maps are on the back pages.

An Outline of Each Book

—has been inserted into the text itself in the form of headings.

—Such headings were not included by the first Bible editors. This new outline has been added to the text of this edition to help the reader see the main subjects of each book and to follow its important ideas, to find passages easier. The outlines and headings for this *Young Readers Bible* have been adapted from the book outlines of *The Interpreter's Bible* (a scholarly and authoritative Bible commentary published by Abingdon Press)

Easy to Find Numbers

—Chapters and verses have been put in easy-to-read type in vertical columns in the margins to help the reader find references easily. (The first known chapter and verse numbers were added to the whole Bible text in the year 1555, by Robert Stephens of Paris, France, in a Bible published in Latin, called the Vulgate, to make it easier to find particular passages.)

—The paragraphing of Bible content helps keep ideas together and is an important feature of the Revised Standard Version. The verse numbers have been removed from the text itself in this edition to speed individual and classroom study.

New Large Page Size

↗ The untraditional page size for this Bible with its sturdy attractive binding has made possible a Bible truly designed for the reader and student. Pocket editions must either leave out important text or use type unsuitable for comfortable reading; leave out important guides to reading.

↗ Quick reference thumb tabs on the first page of each Bible book help make each section more easy to find.

↗ Modern skills of making attractive books have been applied in the production of this volume of the Holy Scriptures. The religious educators who have designed this volume have kept before them the importance of the word of God and the needs of those who would learn from it.

↗ Modern forms of transportation have changed our ideas of what is easy to carry. This volume is larger than traditional small but somber and unused Bibles. Its unique features bring to fulfillment the dream of religious educators. It will be carried more and used more because of the very features its untraditional size makes possible.

WHAT IS THE BIBLE?

What is the Bible? The word Bible simply means "book," but this a very special book. It is often called the Scriptures, meaning "writings." Because Christians believe that through the Bible we can learn about God and his will, it is for us the most important book in the world.

We believe that God inspired the men who wrote the Bible. The more like God these men were, the more clearly they were able to tell others of God's thoughts and his will for men.

Really, the Bible is not just one book but a whole library of sixty-six books. The Old Testament contains thirty-nine books telling about the years before Jesus. The New Testament contains twenty-seven books telling about Jesus Christ and the beginning of the church.

The Old Testament story begins in Genesis with the creation of the world. It then tells of God's dealings with the Hebrew people as they developed into a nation. It tells of their victories and defeats, their sinful men and their righteous men. The story ends in the Book of Nehemiah when the people were trying to rebuild their nation and their religion after they had returned from many years as prisoners in a foreign land.

The rest of the Old Testament is composed of sermons, short stories, hymns, and other writings by great Hebrew leaders during various periods of Hebrew history. God spoke through the Old Testament writers. As we read them, we realize God wanted us to know more of himself. This is why Jesus came into the world—to give a more complete revelation of God.

The New Testament begins with four books called Gospels. Gospels because they tell the good news about God's Son, Jesus Christ. Following the Gospels is a book called the Acts of the Apostles, which tells how the Christian faith spread and the church began.

The rest of the New Testament, except the Book of Revelation, is made up of interesting letters, some quite long and some very short. All these were written by great leaders whom God inspired to tell the good news about Jesus Christ or to help men be faithful to Christ and his Way.

The different books in the Bible were written at different times by many different men. Some wrote history; some, stories; some, poetry; some, biographies; some, letters; and some, sermons. This edition of the Bible has at the beginning of each book an introduction that tells something about who wrote that book, for whom it was written, when and why it was written, and sometimes where it was written. Then there is an outline of what is in the book itself. You will enjoy and understand each book more fully if you read the introduction first.

As we read these wonderful writings—in both the Old Testament and the New Testament—God will speak to us, guide, and help us today.

HOW WE GOT OUR BIBLE

Long before any of the Bible was written down, men who were striving to live godly lives were telling their children and grandchildren stories and singing songs about the struggles of the Hebrew people as they tried to know and serve God. These poems and stories were eventually written down so the people would not forget them.

The Old Testament books were written by the Hebrews—or Jews, as they later came to be

called. They were first written in the Hebrew language; later they were translated into Greek. The New Testament books were written in Greek.

Of course these ancient books did not look like our books. They were hand-lettered because the printing press had not been invented. Instead of being fastened together at one side so they could be turned, the pages were sewed into long strips of paper or sheepskin and rolled up. The rolls or scrolls were kept in the synagogues where the people worshiped and where the children went to school.

The Jews thought that the first five books of the Old Testament—Genesis, Exodus, Leviticus, Numbers, and Deuteronomy—were the most important; they called them the Law, or the Torah. Another group of writings containing mainly history and sermons they called the Prophets. The third group, containing books of stories, Psalms, and Proverbs, they called the Writings.

By the time Jesus was a boy all the books that are now in our Old Testament were familiar to most Jews, along with other religious writings. About a hundred years after Jesus' birth a meeting

of Jewish leaders in the city of Jamnia selected the books that were to make up their official Bible.

After Jesus Christ came and his followers gathered together into the church, Christians began to write about the life and meaning of Jesus Christ. They also wrote about how the church began and how Christians spread the good news about Jesus Christ and his Way. By A.D. 150 the books that are now in the New Testament were widely known and loved among most of the Christian churches. The earliest list of Christian writings we have found that agrees with our New Testament is one prepared in A.D. 367 by a great Christian leader named Athanasius, who lived in the city of Alexandria, Egypt.

More than a thousand years passed between the writings of the earliest parts of the Bible and the completion of the most recent letters of the New Testament. The Bible was written by hundreds of authors and editors who lived on three continents. It was written in two major languages about all kinds of people and problems, but always God and his will are the important concerns.

When Rome became one of the strong centers of the Christian church, both the Old Testament and the New Testament were translated into the Latin language from the original Hebrew and Greek. This meant that more people could then read the Bible. Bibles in Latin were preserved and recopied when they wore out from use in the churches and in monasteries where monks lived and studied. Few private citizens could afford the costly books.

As Christianity was taken to other lands by missionaries, now and then someone would translate part of the Bible into a new language so still more people could understand. We find it hard to believe now, but some church leaders opposed this practice. They wanted to keep the Bible in the Latin language, which few of the people but the priests could read. Some men were put in prison or even killed because they dared to translate the Bible into the language the people spoke. It was about 1,200 years from the completion of the Bible until it was first translated into the English language.

Even though some opposed it at first, the Bible has now been translated into almost every language in the world. Today we are thankful for the heroic men who risked their lives to give us the Word of God in a language we can understand.

Perhaps the most famous English translation of the Bible is called the King James Version. It was finished in A.D. 1611 by order of King James I of England. Some people criticized the new version severely. They loved the older, familiar translations and did not want them replaced. They falsely accused the translators of the new version of being disloyal to the king and unfaithful to God. The King James Version required nearly fifty years before it finally won approval.

The same kind of objection was raised again in 1952 when the translation you now have in your hands, the Revised Standard Version, was published. This translation was needed because the everyday language of England in 1611, 341 years before, was not always easily understood by Americans in the twentieth century. Its translators were attacked by some people who thought that a new translation could not possibly be as good as the King James Version. In recent years there have been many other translations of the Bible into English and into many other languages. God can and does speak to men through any faithful translation of the Bible—his Word.

Use your Bible faithfully. Many have suffered and died and even more have labored long and hard to put this volume into your hands. As you read it, seek to learn God's will for your own life, and respond to him in faith and love.

HOW TO USE THE BIBLE

Sometimes you will hear a person say, "God speaks to us through the Bible." This statement does not mean that we can hear an actual voice with our ears. It means that when we read the Bible and think about what we are reading, we learn what God is like and become aware of him and what he wants our lives to be.

The Bible contains the writings of the long-ago Hebrews, telling about their experiences with God and showing God's patient love as he helped them know better how to love, serve, and obey him.

The Bible tells about all of life. It tells about times of success and victory. It also tells about times of defeat and failure. It shows the sin and evil in men as well as what is godly, true, and good.

The most important part of the Bible tells about Jesus Christ and his first followers. Here we also read about the beginning of the church—groups of Christ's followers led by God's Spirit. These early Christians carefully collected the books now included in the New Testament and saved them for others to read. They made new Bibles, copying by hand every letter and word on every page. Other men of God translated the words into our language. Because of their careful work of copying and translating long ago, today we have Bibles like this one that we can read ourselves.

Here are some ways to read the Bible that will help you enjoy it and help you understand God's message in it:

1. Learn all you can about the writer of each book and why he wrote that part of the Bible. As you begin to read in some book of the Bible, try to find out who wrote it, to whom he wrote it, and when, where, and why it was written. Such information is found in the introduction at the beginning of each book in this Bible. When you have finished reading the introduction to a book, try to imagine you are the person for whom it was written. Then, as you read, you will understand the book better.

2. Test ideas and teachings in the Bible by comparing them with Jesus Christ. More clearly than any other person, Jesus showed us what God is like and how God wants us to live. Don't be surprised when you discover that the Bible includes some teachings, stories, and ideas about God which do not seem as good as the teachings and ideas we learn from Jesus Christ. In the Bible

we read how God was making himself known to many men over thousands of years. Not all ideas are of the same importance or truth just because they are included in the Bible.

God has always been seeking to make himself known to his people, but men have not always understood when God spoke. A few great men listened and understood God and in turn tried to help other people understand God's will. The Bible tells of such great prophets and leaders. It also tells about other men who did not understand as well and taught false ideas about God.

The Bible teaches us by these bad examples as well as by the good examples.

When you wonder who is right, turn to the life and teachings of Jesus; there you will find the standard or example by which to test everything in the Bible and in life itself. Jesus is God's Word in human form. Jesus once talked about a wrong idea he had read in the Old Testament part of the Bible. Then he corrected it. He said, "You have heard that it was said, 'You shall love your neighbor and hate your enemy.' But I say to you, Love your enemies . . ." (Matthew 5. 43-44a). You can check ideas in the Bible by comparing them with the way Jesus lived and the things he said.

3. Read large parts of the Bible at one time. Read a whole psalm, a whole section, or maybe

a whole book at a time. This is better than reading a verse or two from one part of the Bible one day and a verse or two from another part another day. Start where you left off last time, and continue until you finish the whole book or section.

In this edition of the Bible you may turn past the portions printed in small type without missing the main ideas of that section. The small type includes old lists of rules for priests, long lists of many names, or directions for the builders of the ancient Temple in Jerusalem. These sections are important for scholars but are not likely to be interesting for beginning readers.

4. Let God speak to you when you read the Bible. The Bible is a collection of written accounts of times when men felt God was speaking. The main reason the Bible was written was to have a record of these times when men felt God's Spirit leading and helping them. So when you read the Bible, try to let God's Spirit help you know God's love and his will for your life.

The Bible also tells about people and events. It is interesting to learn about Bible people and happenings. But the important thing is the way God made himself known in these events and in the lives of the people.

Sometimes the Bible refers to ancient science and other matters, but it is a mistake to try to use the Bible to understand modern science. The Bible is not a book of science; it tells us about God and his will for his children.

ABOUT THE BIBLE

Here are some ideas to remember that will help you enjoy the Bible and understand God's message in it.

1. The Bible was written because men felt God's Spirit at work in them and in the events around them. Sometimes we say the Bible is inspired by God. Inspired means "breathed into." The writers felt God near and helping them. It was as if his Spirit had "breathed into" them and helped them understand the ideas or happenings they wrote about.

When you read the Bible, you are reading about times when men felt God's Spirit guiding them and encouraging them. The Bible is about God, his ways with men, and his plan for our lives.

2. You can grow up in your use of the Bible as you grow older and learn to use the Bible better. The early Christian, the apostle Paul, in a letter he wrote to the church at Corinth, reminds us that babies have to be fed milk, but more grown-up persons can eat meat (1 Corinthians 3. 1-2). We must grow as Christians just as we grow in our bodies. As you use your Bible, ideas that are hard to understand now will later come to have important meaning for you, if you keep reading and studying it and asking God to help you understand it.

3. Don't be surprised or worried when you find things you cannot understand. If you try to understand and follow what you do understand, you can expect to grow.

But there may always be unsolved mysteries about the Bible, no matter how much you read it. The ideas you can clearly understand are all God asks you to follow now if you are truly trying to grow in understanding.

4. Learn to enjoy and appreciate Bible poetry, because a great deal of the Old Testament is poetry.

Psalms and Proverbs are collections of poems, but most of the other books of the Old Testament contain poetry. Many of the prophets or preachers wrote their sermons in poetry.

Hebrew poems do not rhyme. The chief trait of Hebrew poetry is that it states an idea in one line and then says about the same thing in a different way in another line. For instance, one of the Psalms begins:

"The heavens are telling the glory of God;
and the firmament proclaims his handiwork" (Psalms 19. 1).

Sometimes a Hebrew poem states an idea in one line and then emphasizes its truth by stating the opposite idea in the next line. Here is one example from the Book of Proverbs.

"A soft answer turns away wrath,
but a harsh word stirs up anger" (Proverbs 15. 1).

Sometimes a poet would repeat an idea not just twice but eight, nine, or even more times to make it very emphatic. Obadiah 12-18 illustrates this.

HOW TO FIND A BIBLE PASSAGE

The Bible has so much to read that we need to know just how to find the story or the verses we want. Remember that the Bible is divided into two major sections—the Old Testament and the New Testament. If you will memorize the names of the books of the Old Testament and of the New Testament, you can soon find your way around in this wonderful library of books. Each Testament is made up of a group of books. All but the shortest books are divided into chapters, and each chapter is divided into verses. The books have names, and the chapters and verses have numbers. The numbers help us find Bible passages more quickly.

The information we need to find a passage is often called a Bible "reference." In your church school books you frequently find a reference like this: Luke 2. 52. Luke is the short name we use for the Gospel of Luke. Now look in the table of contents in the front of your Bible and find Luke. Notice the page number on which it begins and turn in the Bible to that page. Now read the number next to the word Luke. That number is 2, and it tells you that the passage we are looking for is in Chapter 2. Now look at the number following the period (.). This number is 52, and it tells you to look for verse 52 in Chapter 2.

Sometimes you may want to find a passage of several verses. The reference may read like this: Luke 2. 41-52. This means that you begin to read at verse 41 and read all the verses to the end of verse 52. Sometimes you will see a reference like Luke 2. 1, 35. This comma means that you read verse 1 and then skip all the other verses until you come to verse 35. A hyphen (-) means, Read all the verses between the two numbers. The comma means, Do not read the verses between.

Sometimes if you are not to read all of a verse, the reference will say, Luke 2. 43a. This means to read in Luke, Chapter 2, verse 43, until you finish the first part of the verse. Or the reference might read, Luke 2. 43b. This would mean that you would read the second part of the verse.

When two books of the Bible have the same name, we distinguish between them by numbering them. Thus we refer to the First Book of Samuel or, more simply, First Samuel. In giving a reference in one of these books, we use the numeral, like this: 1 Samuel. References in the Second Book of Samuel are written 2 Samuel. Other examples are 1 and 2 Kings, 1 and 2 Peter, and 1, 2, and 3 John. Notice, however, that the Gospel of John is called simply John with no number before it.

If a Bible passage begins in one chapter and runs over into the next one or into several chapters, it is written like this: Genesis 44. 1 through 45. 3. Sometimes the word "through" is left out and a dash (—) takes its place: 44. 1—45. 3. These both mean that the passage goes all the way from the first verse of Chapter 44 through the third verse of Chapter 45 in the Book of Genesis.

When the passage you are looking for is a complete chapter, the reference usually gives only the chapter number. For example, if the reference is Romans 12, find Chapter 12 of the Letter to the Romans, and read all twenty-one verses. In similar fashion, if your reference is Galatians 1 and 2 (or Galatians 1—2), read all the verses in the first two chapters of the Letter to the Galatians. If your reference is John 13 through 17 (or John 13—17), find Chapter 13 of the Gospel of John, start reading with the first verse, and read all the way through the last verse of Chapter 17.

The shortest books in the Bible have not been divided into chapters. In referring to passages in these books we can give only verse numbers. Thus, in 2 John 5, the number 5 refers to a verse, not a chapter. To find this reference, look up the Second Letter of John (Second John is the short name we use), and read the fifth verse. If the reference is Jude 24-25, find the Letter of Jude, and read verses 24 and 25.

If you practice finding references, you can soon do it very quickly. Here are a few practice references for you to look up: John 3. 16; Genesis 8. 22; Matthew 7. 12; Psalms 122. 1; Ephesians 4. 25 through 5. 2.

WAYS TO USE THE BIBLE

Your church through its church school literature began to introduce you to some of the most wonderful parts of the Bible when you were quite small. You have heard many stories from the Bible and have heard parts of it read at home and at church. This is a good way to begin to get

acquainted with this wonderful book. Be sure to look up and read the passages from the Bible you are asked to read for your church school classes.

Now that you are older, you can also begin to use the Bible for yourself. In your church and church school you will continue to learn much about the Bible. Here is a plan to help you discover more wonderful things in your Bible for yourself.

A PLAN FOR READING THE BIBLE

How do you read a library? You do not read the first book on the shelf and continue book by book until you finish. The Bible is a library of books.

One of the best ways to read the Bible is to begin with one of the books that tells about Jesus. The Gospel of Mark is the shortest Gospel, but Matthew and Luke also give the main events we know about Jesus' life. After you have read a Gospel, possibly Mark, then read about the early Christians and the beginning of the church in the Book of Acts. When you have read these, you will enjoy the other writings of the New Testament more fully.

After you have read what one of the Gospels tells about Jesus, you will realize that there is much more to be learned and enjoyed in the Old Testament books. The Old Testament will help you understand Jesus Christ much better.

The best way to read the Old Testament is to begin with the books that tell the main story. Start with Genesis and read through Second Kings. Then First Chronicles tells again the stories from Second Samuel. Second Chronicles retells what was in First and Second Kings. The story moves forward again in Ezra and Nehemiah. After you have read these books, you will be ready to read other books of the Old Testament, and you will realize that the world needed a savior so badly that God sent Jesus Christ.

Some Bible passages are so wonderful that you will want to read them many times. The list that follows includes some of the most loved passages.

WHERE TO FIND SOME GREAT BIBLE PASSAGES

The Ten Commandments—Exodus 20; Deuteronomy 5.

The Shepherd Psalm—Psalms 23.

The Birth of Jesus (Christmas story)—Matthew 1 and 2; Luke 2. 1-38.

The Boy Jesus at the Temple—Luke 2. 41-52.

The Sermon on the Mount—Matthew 5 through 7.

The Beatitudes—Matthew 5. 3-12.

Jesus' Crucifixion and Resurrection—Matthew 26 through 28; Mark 14 through 16; Luke 22 through 24; John 13 through 21.

The Golden Rule—Matthew 7. 12; Luke 6. 31.

The Little Gospel—John 3. 16-17.

The Great Commandment—Matthew 22. 34-40; Mark 12. 28-34; Luke 10. 27.

The Great Commission—Matthew 28. 19-20; Mark 16. 15.

Paul's Chapter on Love—1 Corinthians 13.

The Parable of the Sower—Matthew 13. 3-9, 18-23; Mark 4. 3-9, 13-20; Luke 8. 5-8, 11-15.

The Parable of the Good Samaritan—Luke 10. 29-37.

The Parable of the Prodigal Son—Luke 15. 11-32.

PREFACE

THE REVISED STANDARD VERSION of the Bible is an authorized revision of the American Standard Version, published in 1901, which was a revision of the King James Version, published in 1611.

The first English version of the Scriptures made by direct translation from the original Hebrew and Greek, and the first to be printed, was the work of William Tyndale. He met bitter opposition. He was accused of willfully perverting the meaning of the Scriptures, and his New Testaments were ordered to be burned as "untrue translations." He was finally betrayed into the hands of his enemies, and in October 1536, was publicly executed and burned at the stake.

Yet Tyndale's work became the foundation of subsequent English versions, notably those of Coverdale, 1535; Thomas Matthew (probably a pseudonym for John Rogers), 1537; the Great Bible, 1539; the Geneva Bible, 1560; and the Bishops' Bible, 1568. In 1582 a translation of the New Testament, made from the Latin Vulgate by Roman Catholic scholars, was published at Rheims.

The translators who made the King James Version took into account all of these preceding versions; and comparison shows that it owes something to each of them. It kept felicitous phrases and apt expressions, from whatever source, which had stood the test of public usage. It owed most, especially in the New Testament, to Tyndale.

The King James Version had to compete with the Geneva Bible in popular use; but in the end it prevailed, and for more than two and a half centuries no other authorized translation of the Bible into English was made. The King James Version became the "Authorized Version" of the English-speaking peoples.

The King James Version has with good reason been termed "the noblest monument of English prose." Its revisers in 1881 expressed admiration for "its simplicity, its dignity, its power, its happy turns of expression . . . the music of its cadences, and the felicities of its rhythm." It entered, as no other book has, into the making of the personal character and the public institutions of the English-speaking peoples. We owe to it an incalculable debt.

Yet the King James Version has grave defects. By the middle of the nineteenth century, the development of biblical studies and the discovery of many manuscripts, more ancient than those upon which the King James Version was based, made it manifest that these defects are so many and so serious as to call for revision of the English translation. The task was undertaken, by authority of the Church of England, in 1870. The English Revised Version of the Bible was published in 1881–1885; and the American Standard Version, its variant embodying the preferences of the American scholars associated in the work, was published in 1901.

Because of unhappy experience with unauthorized publications in the two decades between 1881 and 1901, which tampered with the text of the English Revised Version in the supposed interest of the American public, the American Standard Version was copyrighted, to protect the text from unauthorized changes. In 1928 this copyright was acquired by the International Council of Religious Education, and thus passed into the ownership of the churches of the United States and Canada which were associated in this council through their boards of education and publication.

The council appointed a committee of scholars to have charge of the text of the American Standard Version and to undertake inquiry as to whether further revision was necessary. For more than two years the committee worked upon the problem of whether or not revision should be undertaken; and if so, what should be its nature and extent. In the end the decision was reached that there is need for a thorough revision of the version of 1901, which will stay as close to the Tyndale-King James tradition as it can in the light of our present knowledge of the Hebrew and Greek texts and their meaning on the one hand, and our present understanding of English on the other.

In 1937 the revision was authorized by vote of the council, which directed that the resulting version should "embody the best results of modern scholarship as to the meaning of the Scriptures, and express this meaning in English diction which is designed for use in public and private worship and preserves those qualities which have given to the King James Version a supreme place in English literature."

Thirty-two scholars have served as members of the committee charged with making the revision, and they have secured the review and counsel of an Advisory Board of fifty representatives of the cooperating denominations. The committee has worked in two sections, one dealing with the Old Testament and one with the New Testament. Each section has submitted its work to the scrutiny of the members of the other section; and the charter of the committee requires that all changes be agreed upon by a two-thirds vote of the total membership of the committee. The Revised Standard Version of the New Testament was published in 1946. The publication of the Revised Standard Version of the Bible, containing the Old and New Testaments, was authorized by vote of the National Council of the Churches of Christ in the U.S.A. in 1951.

The problem of establishing the correct Hebrew and Aramaic text of the Old Testament is very different from the corresponding problem in the New Testament. For the New Testament we have a large number of Greek manuscripts, preserving many variant forms of the text. Some of them were made only two or three centuries later than the original composition of the books. For the Old Testament only late manuscripts survive, all (with the exception of the Dead Sea texts of Isaiah and Habakkuk and some fragments of other books) based on a standardized form of the text established many centuries after the books were written.

The present revision is based on the consonantal Hebrew and Aramaic text as fixed early in the Christian era and revised by Jewish scholars (the "Masoretes") of the sixth to ninth centuries. The vowel signs, which were added by the Masoretes, are accepted also in the main, but where a more probable and convincing reading can be ordained by assuming different vowels, this has been done. No notes are given in such cases, because the vowel points are less ancient and reliable than the consonants.

Departures from the consonantal text of the best manuscripts have been made only where it seems clear that errors in copying had been made before the text was standardized. Most of the corrections adopted are based on the ancient versions (translations into Greek, Aramaic, Syriac, and Latin), which were made before the time of the Masoretic revision and therefore reflect earlier forms of the text. In every such instance a footnote specifies the version or versions from which the correction has been derived, and also gives a translation of the Masoretic Text.

Sometimes it is evident that the text has suffered in transmission, but none of the versions provides a satisfactory restoration. Here we can only follow the best judgment of competent scholars as to the most probable reconstruction of the original text. Such corrections are indicated in the footnotes by the abbreviation *Cn*, and a translation of the Masoretic Text is added.

The discovery of the meaning of the text, once the best readings have been established, is aided by many new resources for understanding the original languages. Much progress has been made in the historical and comparative study of these languages. A vast quantity of writings in related Semitic languages, some of them only recently discovered, has greatly enlarged our knowledge of the vocabulary and grammar of biblical Hebrew and Aramaic. Sometimes the present translation will be found to render a Hebrew word in a sense quite different from that of the traditional interpretation. It has not been felt necessary in such cases to attach a footnote, because no change in the text is involved and it may be assumed that the new rendering was not adopted without convincing evidence. The analysis of religious texts from the ancient Near East has made clearer the significance of ideas and practices recorded in the Old Testament. Many difficulties and obscurities, of course, remain. Where the choice between two meanings is particularly difficult or doubtful, we have given an alternative rendering in a footnote. If in the judgment of the committee the meaning of a passage is quite uncertain or obscure, either because of corruption in the text or because of the inadequacy of our present knowledge of the language, that fact is indicated by a note. It should not be assumed, however, that the committee was entirely sure or unanimous concerning every rendering not so indicated. To record all minority views was obviously out of the question.

A major departure from the practice of the American Standard Version is the rendering of the Divine Name, the "Tetragrammaton." The American Standard Version used the term "Jehovah"; the King James version had employed this in four places, but everywhere else, except in three cases where it was employed as part of a proper name, used the English word Lord (or in certain cases God) printed in capitals. The present revision returns to the procedure of the King James Version, which follows the precedent of the ancient Greek and Latin translators and the long established practice in the reading of the Hebrew scriptures in the synagogue. While it is almost if not quite certain that the Name was originally pronounced "Yahweh," this pronunciation was not indicated when the Masoretes added vowel signs to the consonantal Hebrew text. To the four consonants YHWH of the Name, which had come to be regarded as too sacred to be pronounced, they attached vowel signs indicat-

ing that in its place should be read the Hebrew word *Adonai* meaning "Lord" (or *Elohim* meaning "God"). The ancient Greek translators substituted the word *Kyrios* (Lord) for the Name. The Vulgate likewise used the Latin word *Dominus*. The form "Jehovah" is of late medieval origin; it is a combination of the consonants of the Divine Name and the vowels attached to it by the Masoretes but belonging to an entirely different word. The sound of Y is represented by J and the sound of W by V, as in Latin. For two reasons the committee has returned to the more familiar usage of the King James Version: (1) the word "Jehovah" does not accurately represent any form of the Name ever used in Hebrew; and (2) the use of any proper name for the one and only God, as though there were other gods from whom he had to be distinguished, was discontinued in Judaism before the Christian era is entirely inappropriate for the universal faith of the Christian Church.

The King James Version of the New Testament was based upon a Greek text that was marred by mistakes, containing the accumulated errors of fourteen centuries of manuscript copying. It was essentially the Greek text of the New Testament as edited by Beza, 1589, who closely followed that published by Erasmus, 1516-1535, which was based upon a few medieval manuscripts. The earliest and best of the eight manuscripts which Erasmus consulted was from the tenth century, and he made the least use of it because it differed most from the commonly received text; Beza had access to two manuscripts of great value, dating from the fifth and sixth centuries, but he made very little use of them because they differed from the text published by Erasmus.

We now possess many more ancient manuscripts of the New Testament, and are far better equipped to seek to recover the original wording of the Greek text. The evidence for the text of the books of the New Testament is better than for any other ancient book, both in the number of extant manuscripts and in the nearness of the date of some of these manuscripts to the date when the book was originally written.

The revisers in the 1870s had most of the evidence that we now have for the Greek text, though the most ancient of all extant manuscripts of the Greek New Testament were not discovered until 1931. But they lacked the resources which discoveries within the past eighty years have afforded for understanding the vocabulary, grammar, and idioms of the Greek New Testament. An amazing body of Greek papyri has been unearthed in Egypt since the 1870s—private letters, official reports, wills, business accounts, petitions, and other such trivial, everyday recordings of the activities of human beings. In 1895 appeared the first of Adolph Deissmann's studies of these ordinary materials. He proved that many words which had hitherto been assumed to belong to what was called "biblical Greek" were current in the spoken vernacular of the first century A.D. The New Testament was written in the Koine, the common Greek which was spoken and understood practically everywhere throughout the Roman Empire in the early centuries of the Christian era. This development in the study of New Testament Greek has come since the work on the English Revised Version and the American Standard Version was done, and at many points sheds new light upon the meaning of the Greek text.

A major reason for revision of the King James Version, which is valid for both the Old Testament and the New Testament, is the change since 1611 in English usage. Many forms of expression have become archaic, while still generally intelligible—the use of thou, thee, thy, thine, and the verb endings -est and -edst, the verb endings -eth and -th, it came to pass that, whosoever, whatsoever, insomuch that, because that, for that, unto, howbeit, peradventure, holden, aforetime, must needs, would fain, behooved, to you-ward, etc. Other words are obsolete and no longer understood by the common reader. The greatest problem, however, is presented by the English words which are still in constant use but now convey a different meaning from that which they had in 1611 and in the King James Version. These words were once accurate translations of the Hebrew and Greek Scriptures; but now, having changed in meaning, they have become misleading. They no longer say what the King James translators meant them to say. Thus, the King James Version uses the word "let" in the sense of "hinder," "prevent" to mean "precede," "allow" in the sense of "approve," "communicate" for "share," "conversation" for "conduct," "comprehend" for "overcome," "ghost" for "spirit," "wealth" for "well-being," "allege" for "prove," "demand" for "ask," "take no thought" for "be not anxious," etc.

The Revised Standard Version of the Bible, containing the Old and New Testaments, was published on September 30, 1952, and has met with wide acceptance. This preface does not undertake to set forth in detail the lines along which the revision proceeded. That is done in pamphlets entitled *An Introduction to the Revised Standard Version of the Old Testament* and *An Introduction to the Revised Standard Version of the New Testament*, written by members of the committee and designed to help the general public to understand the main principles which have guided this comprehensive revision of the King James and American Standard versions.

These principles were reaffirmed by the committee in 1959 in connection with a study of criticisms and suggestions from various readers. As a result, a few changes were authorized for subsequent editions, most of them corrections of punctuation, capitalization, or footnotes. Some of them are changes of words or phrases made in the interest of consistency, clarity, or accuracy of translation.

The Revised Standard Version Bible Committee is a continuing body, holding its meetings at regular intervals. It has become both ecumenical and international, with Protestant and Catholic active members, who come from Great Britain, Canada, and the United States.

The Second Edition of the translation of the New Testament (1971) profits from textual and linguistic studies published since the Revised Standard Version New Testament was first issued in 1946. Many proposals for modification were submitted to the committee by individuals and by two denominational committees. All of these were given careful attention by the committee.

Two passages, the longer ending of Mark (16.9-20) and the account of the woman caught in adultery (John 7.53-8.11), are restored to the text, separated from it by a blank space and accompanied by informative notes describing the various arrangements of the text in the ancient authorities. With new manuscript support two passages, Luke 22.19b-20 and 24.51b, are restored to the text, and one passage, Luke 22.43-44, is placed in the note, as is a phrase in Luke 12.39. Notes are added which indicate significant variations, additions, or omissions in the ancient authorities (Matthew 9.34; Mark 3.16; 7.4; Luke 24.32, 51, etc.). Among the new notes are those giving the equivalence of ancient coinage with the contemporary day's or year's wages of a laborer (Matthew 18.24, 28; 20.2, etc.). Some of the revisions clarify the meaning through rephrasing or reordering the text (see Mark 5.42; Luke 22.29-30; John 10.33; I Corinthians 3.9; 2 Corinthians 5.19; Hebrews 13.13). Even when the changes appear to be largely matters of English style, they have the purpose of presenting to the reader more adequately the meaning of the text (see Matthew 10.8; 12.1; 15.29; 17.20; Luke 7.36; 11.17; 12.40; John 16.9; Romans 10.16; 1 Corinthians 12.24; 2 Corinthians 2.3; 3.5, 6; etc.).

The Revised Standard Version Bible seeks to preserve all that is best in the English Bible as it has been known and used through the years. It is intended for use in public and private worship, not merely for reading and instruction. We have resisted the temptation to use phrases that are merely current usage, and have sought to put the message of the Bible in simple, enduring words that are worthy to stand in the great Tyndale-King James tradition. We are glad to say, with the King James translators: "Truly (good Christian Reader) we never thought from the beginning, that we should need to make a new Translation, nor yet to make of a bad one a good one . . . but to make a good one better."

The Bible is more than a historical document to be preserved. And it is more than a classic of English literature to be cherished and admired. It is a record of God's dealing with men, of God's revelation of himself and his will. It records the life and work of him in whom the Word of God became flesh and dwelt among men. The Bible carries its full message, not to those who regard it simply as a heritage of the past or praise its literary style, but to those who read it that they may discern and understand God's Word to men. That Word must not be disguised in phrases that are no longer clear, or hidden under words that have changed or lost their meaning. It must stand forth in language that is direct and plain and meaningful to people today. It is our hope and our earnest prayer that this Revised Standard Version of the Bible may be used by God to speak to men in these momentous times, and to help them to understand and believe and obey his Word.

OLD TESTAMENT

INTRODUCTION TO

GENESIS

People have always wondered about how the world began. Among the Hebrew people many hundreds of years ago there were devoted men who tried hard to serve God. As they thought about how our world began, God helped them understand that he had planned and made the world and had created human beings to live good lives as his children. For hundreds of years stories and teachings that are now in Genesis were told around the campfires of the Hebrews.

The people wanted these accounts to be handed down to their grandchildren and great-grand-children. So about nine hundred years before Jesus Christ men who had thought and prayed about it finally began to write down what they had been told around their campfires. At different times (during the next several hundred years) other men added to the writings, and the entire narrative was finally finished about four hundred years before Christ. It made such a long story that it was divided up into the books of Genesis, Exodus, Leviticus, Numbers, and Deuteronomy. These are now the first five books of the Old Testament.

The Book of Genesis means the "book of beginnings." It opens by telling that God made the earth and everything in it. He made men and women to be his human family. God loved his human family, but in the story of Adam and Eve we see that men began to disobey God. Because of human selfishness and sin, all sorts of trouble and evil began.

Genesis tells about many men of long ago. Particularly it tells about the large family of the first great leader of the Hebrews, who was named Abraham. The book ends with the fascinating story of Joseph and his brothers, who all went to Egypt.

Sometimes in Genesis and in other books of the Bible the same story is told more than once. This is because the writer who gathered the stories from different groups of Hebrews decided to include two or more versions of the same event.

An illustration of two versions of the same story is to be found right at the beginning of Genesis. Chapters 1. 1 through 2. 3 gives the account of creation as told in the northern kingdom of Israel, where the name "Elohim" was used for God. Chapter 2. 4-24 gives the account of creation as told in the southern kingdom of Judah where the people called God "Yahweh" or "the Lord."

As you read Genesis—and, in fact, all the Bible—remember that the Bible is a library of books about God's plan and his mighty acts. These books tell of God's help and guidance for men of old. This Bible library also helps us learn about God and his purposes for us. It helps us live as faithful members of God's family. We believe that God inspired its writing, and we call the Bible the Word of God.

THE BOOK OF

GENESIS

BEGINNINGS
The Creation

1 In the beginning God created[a] the heavens and the
2 earth. The earth was without form and void, and
darkness was upon the face of the deep; and the Spirit[b]
of God was moving over the face of the waters.

3 And God said, "Let there be light"; and there was light.
4 And God saw that the light was good; and God separated
5 the light from the darkness. God called the light Day,
and the darkness he called Night. And there was evening
and there was morning, one day.

6 And God said, "Let there be a firmament in the midst
of the waters, and let it separate the waters from the

7 waters." And God made the firmament and separated the
waters which were under the firmament from the waters
8 which were above the firmament. And it was so. And God
called the firmament Heaven. And there was evening and
there was morning, a second day.

9 And God said, "Let the waters under the heavens be
gathered together into one place, and let the dry land
10 appear." And it was so. God called the dry land Earth,
and the waters that were gathered together he called Seas.
11 And God saw that it was good. And God said, "Let the
earth put forth vegetation, plants yielding seed, and fruit
trees bearing fruit in which is their seed, each according
12 to its kind, upon the earth." And it was so. The earth
brought forth vegetation, plants yielding seed according
to their own kinds, and trees bearing fruit in which is
their seed, each according to its kind. And God saw that
13 it was good. And there was evening and there was morning, a third day.

14 And God said, "Let there be lights in the firmament of
the heavens to separate the day from the night; and let
them be for signs and for seasons and for days and years,
15 and let them be lights in the firmament of the heavens to
16 give light upon the earth." And it was so. And God made
the two great lights, the greater light to rule the day,
and the lesser light to rule the night; he made the stars

17 also. And God set them in the firmament of the heavens to
18 give light upon the earth, to rule over the day and over
the night, and to separate the light from the darkness.
19 And God saw that it was good. And there was evening
and there was morning, a fourth day.

20 And God said, "Let the waters bring forth swarms of
living creatures, and let birds fly above the earth across
21 the firmament of the heavens." So God created the great
sea monsters and every living creature that moves, with
which the waters swarm, according to their kinds, and
every winged bird according to its kind. And God saw
22 that it was good. And God blessed them, saying, "Be
fruitful and multiply and fill the waters in the seas, and
23 let birds multiply on the earth." And there was evening
and there was morning, a fifth day.

24 And God said, "Let the earth bring forth living
creatures according to their kinds: cattle and creeping
things and beasts of the earth according to their kinds."
25 And it was so. And God made the beasts of the earth
according to their kinds and the cattle according to their
kinds, and everything that creeps upon the ground according to its kind. And God saw that it was good.

26 Then God said, "Let us make man in our image, after
our likeness; and let them have dominion over the fish
of the sea, and over the birds of the air, and over the
cattle, and over all the earth, and over every creeping
27 thing that creeps upon the earth." So God created man in
his own image, in the image of God he created him; male
28 and female he created them. And God blessed them, and
God said to them, "Be fruitful and multiply, and fill the
earth and subdue it; and have dominion over the fish
of the sea and over the birds of the air and over every
29 living thing that moves upon the earth." And God said,
"Behold, I have given you every plant yielding seed which
is upon the face of all the earth, and every tree with seed
30 in its fruit; you shall have them for food. And to every
beast of the earth, and to every bird of the air, and to
everything that creeps on the earth, everything that has
the breath of life, I have given every green plant for
31 food." And it was so. And God saw everything that he
had made, and behold, it was very good. And there was
evening and there was morning, a sixth day.

2 Thus the heavens and the earth were finished, and
2 the host of them. And on the seventh day God finished
his work which he had done, and he rested on the seventh
3 day from all his work which he had done. So God blessed
the seventh day and hallowed it, because on it God rested

[a] Or When God began to create   [b] Or wind

from all his work which he had done in creation.

4 These are the generations of the heavens and the earth when they were created.

The Creation of Man

In the day that the LORD God made the earth and the
5 heavens, when no plant of the field was yet in the earth and no herb of the field had yet sprung up—for the LORD God had not caused it to rain upon the earth, and there
6 was no man to till the ground; but a mist c went up from the earth and watered the whole face of the ground—
7 then the LORD God formed man of dust from the ground, and breathed into his nostrils the breath of life; and man
8 became a living being. And the LORD God planted a garden in Eden, in the east; and there he put the man
9 whom he had formed. And out of the ground the LORD God made to grow every tree that is pleasant to the sight and good for food, the tree of life also in the midst of the garden, and the tree of the knowledge of good and evil.
10 A river flowed out of Eden to water the garden, and
11 there it divided and became four rivers. The name of the first is Pishon; it is the one which flows around the whole
12 land of Hav'i-lah, where there is gold; and the gold of
13 that land is good; bdellium and onyx stone are there. The name of the second river is Gihon; it is the one which
14 flows around the whole land of Cush. And the name of the third river is Tigris, which flows east of Assyria. And the fourth river is the Eu-phra'tes.
15 The LORD God took the man and put him in the garden
16 of Eden to till it and keep it. And the LORD God commanded the man, saying, "You may freely eat of every
17 tree of the garden; but of the tree of the knowledge of good and evil you shall not eat, for in the day that you eat of it you shall die."
18 Then the LORD God said, "It is not good that the man should be alone; I will make him a helper fit for him."
19 So out of the ground the LORD God formed every beast of the field and every bird of the air, and brought them to the man to see what he would call them; and whatever the man called every living creature, that was its name.
20 The man gave names to all cattle, and to the birds of the air, and to every beast of the field; but for the man there
21 was not found a helper fit for him. So the LORD God caused a deep sleep to fall upon the man, and while he slept took one of his ribs and closed up its place with
22 flesh; and the rib which the LORD God had taken from the man he made into a woman and brought her to the
23 man. Then the man said,

"This at last is bone of my bones and flesh of my flesh;
she shall be called Woman,d

because she was taken out of Man." e

24 Therefore a man leaves his father and his mother and
25 cleaves to his wife, and they become one flesh. And the

c Or flood   d Heb ishshah   e Heb ish

man and his wife were both naked, and were not ashamed.

Man's Alienation From God

3 Now the serpent was more subtle than any other wild creature that the LORD God had made. He said to the woman, "Did God say, 'You shall not eat of any tree
2 of the garden'?" And the woman said to the serpent, "We
3 may eat of the fruit of the trees of the garden; but God said, 'You shall not eat of the fruit of the tree which is in the midst of the garden, neither shall you touch it, lest
4 you die.'" But the serpent said to the woman, "You will
5 not die. For God knows that when you eat of it your eyes will be opened, and you will be like God, knowing good
6 and evil." So when the woman saw that the tree was good for food, and that it was a delight to the eyes, and that the tree was to be desired to make one wise, she took of its fruit and ate; and she also gave some to her husband,
7 and he ate. Then the eyes of both were opened, and they knew that they were naked; and they sewed fig leaves together and made themselves aprons.

8 And they heard the sound of the LORD God walking in the garden in the cool of the day, and the man and his wife hid themselves from the presence of the LORD God
9 among the trees of the garden. But the LORD God called
10 to the man, and said to him, "Where are you?" And he said, "I heard the sound of thee in the garden, and I was
11 afraid, because I was naked; and I hid myself." He said, "Who told you that you were naked? Have you eaten of
12 the tree of which I commanded you not to eat?" The man said, "The woman whom thou gavest to be with me, she

13 gave me fruit of the tree, and I ate." Then the LORD God said to the woman, "What is this that you have done?" The woman said, "The serpent beguiled me, and
14 I ate." The LORD God said to the serpent,

"Because you have done this,
cursed are you above all cattle, and above all wild animals;
upon your belly you shall go,
and dust you shall eat all the days of your life.
15 I will put enmity between you and the woman,
and between your seed and her seed;
he shall bruise your head,

and you shall bruise his heel."

16 To the woman he said,

"I will greatly multiply your pain in childbearing;
   in pain you shall bring forth children,
yet your desire shall be for your husband,
   and he shall rule over you."

17 And to Adam he said,

"Because you have listened to the voice of your wife,
   and have eaten of the tree
of which I commanded you,
   'You shall not eat of it,'
cursed is the ground because of you;
   in toil you shall eat of it all the days of your life;

18 thorns and thistles it shall bring forth to you;
   and you shall eat the plants of the field.

19 In the sweat of your face
   you shall eat bread
till you return to the ground,
   for out of it you were taken;
you are dust,
   and to dust you shall return."

20 The man called his wife's name Eve,[f] because she was
21 the mother of all living. And the LORD God made for Adam and for his wife garments of skins, and clothed them.

22 Then the LORD God said, "Behold, the man has become like one of us, knowing good and evil; and now, lest he put forth his hand and take also of the tree of life, and eat,
23 and live for ever"—therefore the LORD God sent him forth from the garden of Eden, to till the ground from
24 which he was taken. He drove out the man; and at the east of the garden of Eden he placed the cherubim, and a flaming sword which turned every way, to guard the way to the tree of life.

Beginnings of Civilization

4 Now Adam knew Eve his wife, and she conceived and bore Cain, saying, "I have gotten[g] a man with the
2 help of the LORD." And again, she bore his brother Abel. Now Abel was a keeper of sheep, and Cain a tiller of the
3 ground. In the course of time Cain brought to the LORD
4 an offering of the fruit of the ground, and Abel brought of the firstlings of his flock and of their fat portions.
5 And the LORD had regard for Abel and his offering, but for Cain and his offering he had no regard. So Cain was very
6 angry, and his countenance fell. The LORD said to Cain, "Why are you angry, and why has your countenance
7 fallen? If you do well, will you not be accepted? And if you do not do well, sin is couching at the door; its desire is for you, but you must master it."
8 Cain said to Abel his brother, "Let us go out to the field."[h] And when they were in the field, Cain rose up
9 against his brother Abel, and killed him. Then the LORD

said to Cain, "Where is Abel your brother?" He said,
10 "I do not know; am I my brother's keeper?" And the LORD said, "What have you done? The voice of your
11 brother's blood is crying to me from the ground. And now you are cursed from the ground, which has opened its mouth to receive your brother's blood from your hand.
12 When you till the ground, it shall no longer yield to you its strength; you shall be a fugitive and a wanderer on
13 the earth." Cain said to the LORD, "My punishment is
14 greater than I can bear. Behold, thou hast driven me this day away from the ground; and from thy face I shall be hidden; and I shall be a fugitive and a wanderer on the
15 earth, and whoever finds me will slay me." Then the LORD said to him, "Not so![i] If any one slays Cain, vengeance

shall be taken on him sevenfold." And the LORD put a mark on Cain, lest any who came upon him should kill
16 him. Then Cain went away from the presence of the LORD, and dwelt in the land of Nod,[j] east of Eden.

17 Cain knew his wife, and she conceived and bore Enoch; and he built a city, and called the name of the city after
18 the name of his son, Enoch. To Enoch was born Irad; and Irad was the father of Me-hu'ja-el, and Me-hu'ja-el the father of Me-thu'sha-el, and Me-thu'sha-el the father of
19 Lamech. And Lamech took two wives; the name of the
20 one was Adah, and the name of the other Zillah. Adah bore Jabal; he was the father of those who dwell in tents
21 and have cattle. His brother's name was Jubal; he was
22 the father of all those who play the lyre and pipe. Zillah bore Tubal-cain; he was the forger of all instruments of bronze and iron. The sister of Tubal-cain was Na'amah.
23 Lamech said to his wives:

"Adah and Zillah, hear my voice;
   you wives of Lamech, hearken to what I say:
I have slain a man for wounding me,
   a young man for striking me.
24 If Cain is avenged sevenfold,
   truly Lamech seventy-sevenfold."

25 And Adam knew his wife again, and she bore a son and called his name Seth, for she said, "God has appointed for me another child instead of Abel, for Cain
26 slew him." To Seth also a son was born, and he called his name Enosh. At that time men began to call upon the name of the LORD.

---

f The name in Hebrew resembles the word for *living*   g Heb *qanah*, get

h Sam Gk Syr Compare Vg: Heb lacks *Let us go out to the field*   i Gk Syr Vg: Heb *Therefore*   j That is *Wandering*

DESCENDANTS OF ADAM

5 ² This is the book of the generations of Adam. When God created man, he made him in the likeness of God. Male and female he created them, and he blessed them and named them ³ Man when they were created. When Adam had lived a hundred and thirty years, he became the father of a son in his own ⁴ likeness, after his image, and named him Seth. The days of Adam after he became the father of Seth were eight hundred ⁵ years; and he had other sons and daughters. Thus all the days that Adam lived were nine hundred and thirty years; and he died.

⁶ When Seth had lived a hundred and five years, he became ⁷ the father of Enosh. Seth lived after the birth of Enosh eight hundred and seven years, and had other sons and daughters. ⁸ Thus all the days of Seth were nine hundred and twelve years; and he died.

⁹ When Enosh had lived ninety years, he became the father of ¹⁰ Kenan. Enosh lived after the birth of Kenan eight hundred ¹¹ and fifteen years, and had other sons and daughters. Thus all the days of Enosh were nine hundred and five years; and he died.

¹² When Kenan had lived seventy years, he became the father ¹³ of Ma-hal′alel. Kenan lived after the birth of Ma-hal′alel eight hundred and forty years, and had other sons and daughters. ¹⁴ Thus all the days of Kenan were nine hundred and ten years; and he died.

¹⁵ When Ma-hal′alel had lived sixty-five years, he became the ¹⁶ father of Jared. Ma-hal′alel lived after the birth of Jared eight hundred and thirty years, and had other sons and daughters. ¹⁷ Thus all the days of Ma-hal′alel were eight hundred and ninety-five years; and he died.

¹⁸ When Jared had lived a hundred and sixty-two years he be- ¹⁹ came the father of Enoch. Jared lived after the birth of Enoch ²⁰ eight hundred years, and had other sons and daughters. Thus all the days of Jared were nine hundred and sixty-two years; and he died.

²¹ When Enoch had lived sixty-five years, he became the father ²² of Methu′selah. Enoch walked with God after the birth of Methu′selah three hundred years, and had other sons and ²³ daughters. Thus all the days of Enoch were three hundred and ²⁴ sixty-five years. Enoch walked with God; and he was not, for God took him.

²⁵ When Methu′selah had lived a hundred and eighty-seven ²⁶ years, he became the father of Lamech. Methu′selah lived after the birth of Lamech seven hundred and eighty-two years, and ²⁷ had other sons and daughters. Thus all the days of Methu′selah were nine hundred and sixty-nine years; and he died.

BEGINNING OF AGRICULTURE

²⁸ When Lamech had lived a hundred and eighty-two years, he ²⁹ became the father of a son, and called his name Noah, saying, "Out of the ground which the LORD has cursed this one shall bring us relief from our work and from the toil of our hands." ³⁰ Lamech lived after the birth of Noah five hundred and ninety- ³¹ five years, and had other sons and daughters. Thus all the days of Lamech were seven hundred and seventy-seven years; and he died.

³² After Noah was five hundred years old, Noah became the father of Shem, Ham, and Japheth.

Sons of God and Daughters of Men

6 When men began to multiply on the face of the ² ground, and daughters were born to them, the sons of God saw that the daughters of men were fair; and they ³ took to wife such of them as they chose. Then the LORD said, "My spirit shall not abide in man for ever, for he is flesh, but his days shall be a hundred and twenty years." ⁴ The Nephilim were on the earth in those days, and also afterward, when the sons of God came in to the daughters of men, and they bore children to them. These were the mighty men that were of old, the men of renown.

ᵏ Or *window*

NOAH AND THE FLOOD
Making of the Ark

⁵ The LORD saw that the wickedness of man was great in the earth, and that every imagination of the thoughts of ⁶ his heart was only evil continually. And the LORD was sorry that he had made man on the earth, and it grieved ⁷ him to his heart. So the LORD said, "I will blot out man whom I have created from the face of the ground, man and beast and creeping things and birds of the air, for I ⁸ am sorry that I have made them." But Noah found favor in the eyes of the LORD.

⁹ These are the generations of Noah. Noah was a right-eous man, blameless in his generation; Noah walked with ¹⁰ God. And Noah had three sons, Shem, Ham, and Japheth.

¹¹ Now the earth was corrupt in God's sight, and the earth ¹² was filled with violence. And God saw the earth, and behold, it was corrupt; for all flesh had corrupted their ¹³ way upon the earth. And God said to Noah, "I have determined to make an end of all flesh; for the earth is filled with violence through them; behold, I will destroy ¹⁴ them with the earth. Make yourself an ark of gopher wood; make rooms in the ark, and cover it inside and out ¹⁵ with pitch. This is how you are to make it: the length of the ark three hundred cubits, its breadth fifty cubits, and ¹⁶ its height thirty cubits. Make a roof ᵏ for the ark, and finish it to a cubit above; and set the door of the ark in ¹⁷ its side; make it with lower, second, and third decks. For behold, I will bring a flood of waters upon the earth, to destroy all flesh in which is the breath of life from under ¹⁸ heaven; everything that is on the earth shall die. But I will establish my covenant with you; and you shall come into the ark, you, your sons, your wife, and your sons' ¹⁹ wives with you. And of every living thing of all flesh, you shall bring two of every sort into the ark, to keep them ²⁰ alive with you; they shall be male and female. Of the birds according to their kinds, and of the animals according to their kinds, of every creeping thing of the ground according to its kind, two of every sort shall come in to ²¹ you, to keep them alive. Also take with you every sort of food that is eaten, and store it up; and it shall serve as ²² food for you and for them." Noah did this; he did all that God commanded him.

The Flood Comes

7 Then the LORD said to Noah, "Go into the ark, you and all your household, for I have seen that you ² are righteous before me in this generation. Take with you seven pairs of all clean animals, the male and his mate; and a pair of the animals that are not clean, the male and ³ his mate; and seven pairs of the birds of the air also, male and female, to keep their kind alive upon the face of all ⁴ the earth. For in seven days I will send rain upon the earth forty days and forty nights; and every living thing

that I have made I will blot out from the face of the
5 ground." And Noah did all that the LORD had commanded
him.

6 Noah was six hundred years old when the flood of
7 waters came upon the earth. And Noah and his sons and
his wife and his sons' wives with him went into the ark,
8 to escape the waters of the flood. Of clean animals, and of
animals that are not clean, and of birds, and of everything
9 that creeps on the ground, two and two, male and female,
went into the ark with Noah, as God had commanded
10 Noah. And after seven days the waters of the flood came
upon the earth.

11 In the six hundredth year of Noah's life, in the second
month, on the seventeenth day of the month, on that day
all the fountains of the great deep burst forth, and the
12 windows of the heavens were opened. And rain fell upon
13 the earth forty days and forty nights. On the very same
day Noah and his sons, Shem and Ham and Japheth, and
Noah's wife and the three wives of his sons with them
14 entered the ark, they and every beast according to its
kind, and all the cattle according to their kinds, and every
creeping thing that creeps on the earth according to its
kind, and every bird according to its kind, every bird of
15 every sort. They went into the ark with Noah, two and
two of all flesh in which there was the breath of life.
16 And they that entered, male and female of all flesh, went
in as God had commanded him; and the LORD shut him
in.

17 The flood continued forty days upon the earth; and
the waters increased, and bore up the ark, and it rose
18 high above the earth. The waters prevailed and increased
greatly upon the earth; and the ark floated on the face
19 of the waters. And the waters prevailed so mightily upon
the earth that all the high mountains under the whole
20 heaven were covered; the waters prevailed above the
21 mountains, covering them fifteen cubits deep. And all
flesh died that moved upon the earth, birds, cattle, beasts,
all swarming creatures that swarm upon the earth, and
22 every man; everything on the dry land in whose nostrils
23 was the breath of life died. He blotted out every living
thing that was upon the face of the ground, man and
animals and creeping things and birds of the air; they
were blotted out from the earth. Only Noah was left, and
24 those that were with him in the ark. And the waters prevailed upon the earth a hundred and fifty days.

The Waters Recede

8 But God remembered Noah and all the beasts and
all the cattle that were with him in the ark. And God
made a wind blow over the earth, and the waters sub-
2 sided; the fountains of the deep and the windows of the
heavens were closed, the rain from the heavens was re-
3 strained, and the waters receded from the earth continu-

ally. At the end of a hundred and fifty days the waters
4 had abated; and in the seventh month, on the seventeenth
day of the month, the ark came to rest upon the mountains
5 of Ar'arat. And the waters continued to abate until the
tenth month; in the tenth month, on the first day of the
month, the tops of the mountains were seen.

6 At the end of forty days Noah opened the window of
7 the ark which he had made, and sent forth a raven; and
it went to and fro until the waters were dried up from
8 the earth. Then he sent forth a dove from him, to see
if the waters had subsided from the face of the ground;
9 but the dove found no place to set her foot, and she returned to him to the ark, for the waters were still on the
face of the whole earth. So he put forth his hand and
10 took her and brought her into the ark with him. He waited
another seven days, and again he sent forth the dove out
11 of the ark; and the dove came back to him in the evening,
and lo, in her mouth a freshly plucked olive leaf; so Noah
12 knew that the waters had subsided from the earth. Then
he waited another seven days, and sent forth the dove;
and she did not return to him any more.

Noah's Sacrifice

13 In the six hundred and first year, in the first month,
the first day of the month, the waters were dried from off
the earth; and Noah removed the covering of the ark, and
looked, and behold, the face of the ground was dry.
14 In the second month, on the twenty-seventh day of the
15 month, the earth was dry. Then God said to Noah,
16 "Go forth from the ark, you and your wife, and your sons
17 and your sons' wives with you. Bring forth with you
every living thing that is with you of all flesh—birds and
animals and every creeping thing that creeps on the earth
—that they may breed abundantly on the earth, and be
18 fruitful and multiply upon the earth." So Noah went forth,
and his sons and his wife and his sons' wives with him.
19 And every beast, every creeping thing, and every bird,
everything that moves upon the earth, went forth by
families out of the ark.

20 Then Noah built an altar to the LORD, and took of every
clean animal and of every clean bird, and offered burnt
21 offerings on the altar. And when the LORD smelled the
pleasing odor, the LORD said in his heart, "I will never
again curse the ground because of man, for the imagination of man's heart is evil from his youth; neither will I
ever again destroy every living creature as I have done.
22 While the earth remains, seedtime and harvest, cold and
heat, summer and winter, day and night, shall not cease."

9 And God blessed Noah and his sons, and said to
them, "Be fruitful and multiply, and fill the earth.
2 The fear of you and the dread of you shall be upon every
beast of the earth, and upon every bird of the air, upon
everything that creeps on the ground and all the fish of

3 the sea; into your hand they are delivered. Every moving
thing that lives shall be food for you; and as I gave you
4 the green plants, I give you everything. Only you shall not
5 eat flesh with its life, that is, its blood. For your lifeblood
I will surely require a reckoning; of every beast I will
require it and of man; of every man's brother I will
6 require the life of man. Whoever sheds the blood of man,

by man shall his blood be shed; for God made man in
7 his own image. And you, be fruitful and multiply, bring
forth abundantly on the earth and multiply in it."

The Covenant With Noah

8 Then God said to Noah and to his sons with him,
9 "Behold, I establish my covenant with you and your de-
10 scendants after you, and with every living creature that
is with you, the birds, the cattle, and every beast of the
11 earth with you, as many as came out of the ark.[1] I establish my covenant with you, that never again shall all flesh
be cut off by the waters of a flood, and never again shall
12 there be a flood to destroy the earth." And God said,
"This is the sign of the covenant which I make between
me and you and every living creature that is with you,
13 for all future generations: I set my bow in the cloud, and
it shall be a sign of the covenant between me and the
14 earth. When I bring clouds over the earth and the bow
15 is seen in the clouds, I will remember my covenant which
is between me and you and every living creature of all
flesh; and the waters shall never again become a flood to
16 destroy all flesh. When the bow is in the clouds, I will
look upon it and remember the everlasting covenant between God and every living creature of all flesh that is
17 upon the earth." God said to Noah, "This is the sign of
the covenant which I have established between me and
all flesh that is upon the earth."

18 The sons of Noah who went forth from the ark were
Shem, Ham, and Japheth. Ham was the father of Canaan.
19 These three were the sons of Noah; and from these the
whole earth was peopled.

Last Days of Noah

20 Noah was the first tiller of the soil. He planted a vine-
21 yard; and he drank of the wine, and became drunk, and
22 lay uncovered in his tent. And Ham, the father of Canaan,
saw the nakedness of his father, and told his two brothers
23 outside. Then Shem and Japheth took a garment, laid it
upon both their shoulders, and walked backward and
covered the nakedness of their father; their faces were
turned away, and they did not see their father's naked-
24 ness. When Noah awoke from his wine and knew what
25 his youngest son had done to him, he said,
"Cursed be Canaan;
      a slave of slaves shall he be to his brothers."
26 He also said,
"Blessed by the Lord my God be Shem; [m]
      and let Canaan be his slave.
27 God enlarge Japheth,
      and let him dwell in the tents of Shem;
      and let Canaan be his slave."

28 After the flood Noah lived three hundred and fifty
29 years. All the days of Noah were nine hundred and fifty
years; and he died.

DESCENDANTS OF NOAH

10 These are the generations of the sons of Noah, Shem,
Ham, and Japheth; sons were born to them after the flood.
2 The sons of Japheth: Gomer, Magog, Madai, Javan, Tubal,
3 Meshech, and Tiras. The sons of Gomer: Ash'kenaz, Riphath,
4 and Togar'mah. The sons of Javan: Eli'shah, Tarshish, Kittim,
5 and Do'danim. From these the coastland peoples spread. These
are the sons of Japheth [n] in their lands, each with his own
language, by their families, in their nations.
6, 7 The sons of Ham: Cush, Egypt, Put, and Canaan. The sons
of Cush: Seba, Hav'ilah, Sabtah, Ra'amah, and Sab'teca. The
8 sons of Ra'amah: Sheba and Dedan. Cush became the father of
9 Nimrod; he was the first on earth to be a mighty man. He was a
mighty hunter before the Lord; therefore it is said, "Like Nim-
10 rod a mighty hunter before the Lord." The beginning of his
kingdom was Babel, Erech, and Accad, all of them in the land
11 of Shinar. From that land he went into Assyria, and built
12 Nin'eveh, Reho'both-Ir, Calah, and Resen between Nin'eveh
13 and Calah; that is the great city. Egypt became the father of
14 Ludim, An'amim, Leha'bim, Naph-tu'him, Pathru'sim, Caslu'-
him (whence came the Philistines), and Caph'torim.
15 Canaan became the father of Sidon his first-born, and Heth,
16, 17 and the Jeb'usites, the Amorites, the Gir'gashites, the Hivites,
18 the Arkites, the Sinites, the Ar'vadites, the Zem'arites, and the
Ha'mathites. Afterward the families of the Canaanites spread
19 abroad. And the territory of the Canaanites extended from
Sidon, in the direction of Gerar, as far as Gaza, and in the
direction of Sodom, Gomor'rah, Admah, and Zeboi'im, as far
20 as Lasha. These are the sons of Ham, by their families, their
languages, their lands, and their nations.
21 To Shem also, the father of all the children of Eber, the elder
22 brother of Japheth, children were born. The sons of Shem:
23 Elam, Asshur, Arpach'shad, Lud, and Aram. The sons of Aram:
24 Uz, Hul, Gether, and Mash. Arpach'shad became the father of
25 Shelah; and Shelah became the father of Eber. To Eber were
born two sons: the name of the one was Peleg,[o] for in his days
the earth was divided, and his brother's name was Joktan.
26 Joktan became the father of Almo'dad, Sheleph, Hazarma'veth,
27, 28 Jerah, Hador'am, Uzal, Diklah, Obal, Abim'a-el, Sheba,
29 Ophir, Hav'i-lah, and Jobab; all these were the sons of Joktan.
30 The territory in which they lived extended from Mesha in the
31 direction of Sephar to the hill country of the east. These are
the sons of Shem, by their families, their languages, their lands,
and their nations.
32 These are the families of the sons of Noah, according to their
genealogies, in their nations; and from these the nations spread
abroad on the earth after the flood.

---

[1] Gk: Heb repeats *every beast of the earth*   [m] Or *Blessed be the* Lord, *the God of Shem*
[n] Compare verses 20, 31. Heb lacks *These are the sons of Japheth*   [o] That is *Division*

The Confusion of Tongues

11 Now the whole earth had one language and few
2 words. And as men migrated from the east, they
3 found a plain in the land of Shinar and settled there. And
they said to one another, "Come, let us make bricks, and
burn them thoroughly." And they had brick for stone,
4 and bitumen for mortar. Then they said, "Come, let us
build ourselves a city, and a tower with its top in the
heavens, and let us make a name for ourselves, lest we be
5 scattered abroad upon the face of the whole earth." And
the LORD came down to see the city and the tower, which
6 the sons of men had built. And the LORD said, "Behold,
they are one people, and they have all one language; and
this is only the beginning of what they will do; and
nothing that they propose to do will now be impossible
7 for them. Come, let us go down, and there confuse their
language, that they may not understand one another's
8 speech." So the LORD scattered them abroad from there
over the face of all the earth, and they left off building
9 the city. Therefore its name was called Babel, because
there the LORD confused[p] the language of all the earth;
and from there the LORD scattered them abroad over the
face of all the earth.

DESCENDANTS OF SHEM

10 These are the descendants of Shem. When Shem was a hundred years old, he became the father of Arpach'shad two years
11 after the flood; and Shem lived after the birth of Arpach'shad
five hundred years, and had other sons and daughters.
12 When Arpach'shad had lived thirty-five years, he became
13 the father of Shelah; and Arpach'shad lived after the birth of
Shelah four hundred and three years, and had other sons and
daughters.
14 When Shelah had lived thirty years, he became the father of
15 Eber, and Shelah lived after the birth of Eber four hundred
and three years, and had other sons and daughters.
16 When Eber had lived thirty-four years, he became the father
17 of Peleg; and Eber lived after the birth of Peleg four hundred
and thirty years, and had other sons and daughters.
18 When Peleg had lived thirty years, he became the father of
19 Re'u; and Peleg lived after the birth of Re'u two hundred and
nine years, and had other sons and daughters.
20 When Re'u had lived thirty-two years, he became the father
21 of Serug; and Re'u lived after the birth of Serug two hundred
and seven years, and had other sons and daughters.
22 When Serug had lived thirty years, he became the father of
23 Nahor; and Serug lived after the birth of Nahor two hundred
years, and had other sons and daughters.
24 When Nahor had lived twenty-nine years, he became the
25 father of Terah; and Nahor lived after the birth of Terah a
hundred and nineteen years, and had other sons and daughters.

26 When Terah had lived seventy years, he became the
father of Abram, Nahor, and Haran.

ABRAHAM'S LIFE AND TIMES

Genealogy of Abraham

27 Now these are the descendants of Terah. Terah was the
father of Abram, Nahor, and Haran; and Haran was
28 the father of Lot. Haran died before his father Terah in
29 the land of his birth, in Ur of the Chal'deans. And Abram
and Nahor took wives; the name of Abram's wife was
Sar'ai, and the name of Nahor's wife, Milcah, the daughter
30 of Haran the father of Milcah and Iscah. Now Sar'ai was
barren; she had no child.
31 Terah took Abram his son and Lot the son of Haran,
his grandson, and Sar'ai his daughter-in-law, his son
Abram's wife, and they went forth together from Ur of
the Chal'deans to go into the land of Canaan; but when
32 they came to Haran, they settled there. The days of Terah
were two hundred and five years; and Terah died in
Haran.

The Call of Abraham

12 Now the LORD said to Abram, "Go from your
country and your kindred and your father's house
2 to the land that I will show you. And I will make of you
a great nation, and I will bless you, and make your name
3 great, so that you will be a blessing. I will bless those who
bless you, and him who curses you I will curse; and by
you all the families of the earth shall bless themselves."[q]
4 So Abram went, as the LORD had told him; and Lot
went with him. Abram was seventy-five years old when he
5 departed from Haran. And Abram took Sar'ai his wife,
and Lot his brother's son, and all their possessions which
they had gathered, and the persons that they had gotten in
Haran; and they set forth to go to the land of Canaan.
6 When they had come to the land of Canaan, Abram
passed through the land to the place at Shechem, to the
oak[r] of Moreh. At that time the Canaanites were in the

7 land. Then the LORD appeared to Abram, and said, "To
your descendants I will give this land." So he built there
8 an altar to the LORD, who had appeared to him. Thence he
removed to the mountain on the east of Bethel, and
pitched his tent, with Bethel on the west and Ai on the
east; and there he built an altar to the LORD and called
9 on the name of the LORD. And Abram journeyed on, still
going toward the Negeb.

Abraham in Egypt

10 Now there was a famine in the land. So Abram went
down to Egypt to sojourn there, for the famine was severe
11 in the land. When he was about to enter Egypt, he said
to Sar'ai his wife, "I know that you are a woman beauti-
12 ful to behold; and when the Egyptians see you, they will
say, 'This is his wife'; then they will kill me, but they will
13 let you live. Say you are my sister, that it may go well
with me because of you, and that my life may be spared
14 on your account." When Abram entered Egypt the Egyp-
15 tians saw that the woman was very beautiful. And when
the princes of Pharaoh saw her, they praised her to
Pharaoh. And the woman was taken into Pharaoh's house.
16 And for her sake he dealt well with Abram; and he had

[p] Compare Heb *balal*, confuse [q] Or *in you all the families of the earth shall be blessed* [r] Or *terebinth*

sheep, oxen, he-asses, menservants, maidservants, she-asses, and camels.

17 But the LORD afflicted Pharaoh and his house with great
18 plagues because of Sar'ai, Abram's wife. So Pharaoh called Abram, and said, "What is this you have done to me? Why did you not tell me that she was your wife?
19 Why did you say, 'She is my sister,' so that I took her for my wife? Now then, here is your wife, take her, and
20 be gone." And Pharaoh gave men orders concerning him; and they set him on the way, with his wife and all that he had.

13 So Abram went up from Egypt, he and his wife, and all that he had, and Lot with him, into the Negeb.

Abraham and Lot

2 Now Abram was very rich in cattle, in silver, and in
3 gold. And he journeyed on from the Negeb as far as Bethel, to the place where his tent had been at the begin-
4 ning, between Bethel and Ai, to the place where he had made an altar at the first; and there Abram called on the
5 name of the LORD. And Lot, who went with Abram, also
6 had flocks and herds and tents, so that the land could not support both of them dwelling together; for their posses-
7 sions were so great that they could not dwell together, and there was strife between the herdsmen of Abram's cattle and the herdsmen of Lot's cattle. At that time the Canaanites and the Per'izzites dwelt in the land.

8 Then Abram said to Lot, "Let there be no strife between you and me, and between your herdsmen and my
9 herdsmen; for we are kinsmen. Is not the whole land before you? Separate yourself from me. If you take the left hand, then I will go to the right; or if you take the
10 right hand, then I will go to the left." And Lot lifted up his eyes, and saw that the Jordan valley was well watered everywhere like the garden of the LORD, like the land of Egypt, in the direction of Zo'ar; this was before the LORD
11 destroyed Sodom and Gomor'rah. So Lot chose for himself all the Jordan valley, and Lot journeyed east; thus
12 they separated from each other. Abram dwelt in the land of Canaan, while Lot dwelt among the cities of the valley
13 and moved his tent as far as Sodom. Now the men of Sodom were wicked, great sinners against the LORD.

14 The LORD said to Abram, after Lot had separated from him, "Lift up your eyes, and look from the place where you are, northward and southward and eastward and
15 westward; for all the land which you see I will give to
16 you and to your descendants for ever. I will make your descendants as the dust of the earth; so that if one can count the dust of the earth, your descendants also can
17 be counted. Arise, walk through the length and the
18 breadth of the land, for I will give it to you." So Abram moved his tent, and came and dwelt by the oaks⁸ of

⁸ Or *terebinths*

Mamre, which are at Hebron; and there he built an altar to the LORD.

The War of the Kings

14 In the days of Am'raphel king of Shinar, Ar'ioch king of Ella'sar, Ched-or-lao'mer king of Elam, and
2 Tidal king of Goi'im, these kings made war with Bera king of Sodom, Birsha king of Gomor'rah, Shinab king of Admah, Sheme'ber king of Zeboi'im, and the king of
3 Bela (that is, Zo'ar). And all these joined forces in the
4 Valley of Siddim (that is, the Salt Sea). Twelve years they had served Ched-or-lao'mer, but in the thirteenth

5 year they rebelled. In the fourteenth year Ched-or-lao'mer and the kings who were with him came and subdued the Reph'aim in Ash'teroth-karna'im, the Zuzim in Ham, the
6 Emim in Sha'veh-kiriatha'im, and the Horites in their Mount Se'ir as far as El-paran on the border of the wil-
7 derness; then they turned back and came to En-mish'pat (that is, Kadesh), and subdued all the country of the Amal'ekites, and also the Amorites who dwelt in Haz'-
8 azon-ta'mar. Then the king of Sodom, the king of Gomor'rah, the king of Admah, the king of Zeboi'im, and the king of Bela (that is, Zo'ar) went out, and they
9 joined battle in the Valley of Siddim with Ched-or-lao'mer king of Elam, Tidal king of Goi'im, Am'raphel king of Shinar, and Ar'ioch king of Ella'sar, four kings against
10 five. Now the Valley of Siddim was full of bitumen pits; and as the kings of Sodom and Gomor'rah fled, some
11 fell into them, and the rest fled to the mountain. So the enemy took all the goods of Sodom and Gomor'rah, and
12 all their provisions, and went their way; they also took Lot, the son of Abram's brother, who dwelt in Sodom, and his goods, and departed.

13 Then one who had escaped came, and told Abram the Hebrew, who was living by the oaks⁸ of Mamre the Amorite, brother of Eshcol and of Aner; these were allies
14 of Abram. When Abram heard that his kinsman had been taken captive, he led forth his trained men, born in his house, three hundred and eighteen of them, and went
15 in pursuit as far as Dan. And he divided his forces against them by night, he and his servants, and routed them and pursued them to Hobah, north of Damascus.

16 Then he brought back all the goods, and also brought back his kinsman Lot with his goods, and the women and the people.

17 After his return from the defeat of Ched-or-lao'mer and the kings who were with him, the king of Sodom went out to meet him at the Valley of Shaveh (that is, 18 the King's Valley). And Mel-chiz'edek king of Salem brought out bread and wine; he was priest of God Most 19 High. And he blessed him and said,

"Blessed be Abram by God Most High,
maker of heaven and earth;
20 and blessed be God Most High.

who has delivered your enemies into your hand!"

21 And Abram gave him a tenth of everything. And the king of Sodom said to Abram, "Give me the persons, but

22 take the goods for yourself." But Abram said to the king of Sodom, "I have sworn to the LORD God Most High, 23 maker of heaven and earth, that I would not take a thread or a sandal-thong or anything that is yours, lest you 24 should say, 'I have made Abram rich.' I will take nothing but what the young men have eaten, and the share of the men who went with me; let Aner, Eshcol, Mamre take their share."

The Covenant With Abraham

15 After these things the word of the LORD came to Abram in a vision, "Fear not, Abram, I am your 2 shield; your reward shall be very great." But Abram said, "O Lord GOD, what wilt thou give me, for I continue childless, and the heir of my house is Elie'zer of 3 Damascus?" And Abram said, "Behold, thou hast given me no offspring; and a slave born in my house will be 4 my heir." And behold, the word of the LORD came to him, "This man shall not be your heir; your own son shall 5 be your heir." And he brought him outside and said, "Look toward heaven, and number the stars, if you are able to number them." Then he said to him, "So shall 6 your descendants be." And he believed the LORD; and he reckoned it to him as righteousness.

7 And he said to him, "I am the LORD who brought you from Ur of the Chal'deans, to give you this land to 8 possess." But he said, "O Lord GOD, how am I to know 9 that I shall possess it?" He said to him, "Bring me a heifer three years old, a she-goat three years old, a ram 10 three years old, a turtledove, and a young pigeon." And he brought him all these, cut them in two, and laid each

half over against the other; but he did not cut the birds 11 in two. And when birds of prey came down upon the carcasses, Abram drove them away.

12 As the sun was going down, a deep sleep fell on Abram; 13 and lo, a dread and great darkness fell upon him. Then the LORD said to Abram, "Know of a surety that your descendants will be sojourners in a land that is not theirs, and will be slaves there, and they will be oppressed for 14 four hundred years; but I will bring judgment on the nation which they serve, and afterward they shall come 15 out with great possessions. As for yourself, you shall go to your fathers in peace; you shall be buried in a good 16 old age. And they shall come back here in the fourth generation; for the iniquity of the Amorites is not yet complete."

17 When the sun had gone down and it was dark, behold, a smoking fire pot and a flaming torch passed between 18 these pieces. On that day the LORD made a covenant with Abram, saying, "To your descendants I give this land, from the river of Egypt to the great river, the river 19 Eu-phra'tes, the land of the Ken'ites, the Ken'izzites, the 20 Kad'mo-nites, the Hittites, the Per'izzites, the Reph'aim, 21 the Amorites, the Canaanites, the Gir'gashites and the Jeb'usites."

Abraham and Hagar

16 Now Sar'ai, Abram's wife, bore him no children. She had an Egyptian maid whose name was Hagar; 2 and Sar'ai said to Abram, "Behold now, the LORD has prevented me from bearing children; go in to my maid; it may be that I shall obtain children by her." And 3 Abram hearkened to the voice of Sar'ai. So, after Abram had dwelt ten years in the land of Canaan, Sar'ai, Abram's wife, took Hagar the Egyptian, her maid, and gave her 4 to Abram her husband as a wife. And he went in to Hagar, and she conceived; and when she saw that she had conceived, she looked with contempt on her mistress. 5 And Sar'ai said to Abram, "May the wrong done to me be on you! I gave my maid to your embrace, and when she saw that she had conceived, she looked on me with 6 contempt. May the LORD judge between you and me!" But Abram said to Sar'ai, "Behold, your maid is in your power; do to her as you please." Then Sar'ai dealt harshly with her, and she fled from her.

7 The angel of the LORD found her by a spring of water 8 in the wilderness, the spring on the way to Shur. And he said, "Hagar, maid of Sar'ai, where have you come from and where are you going?" She said, "I am fleeing 9 from my mistress Sar'ai." The angel of the LORD said to 10 her, "Return to your mistress, and submit to her." The angel of the LORD also said to her, "I will so greatly multiply your descendants that they cannot be numbered 11 for multitude." And the angel of the LORD said to her,

"Behold, you are with child, and shall bear a son; you shall call his name Ish′mael; [t] because the LORD has given [12] heed to your affliction. He shall be a wild ass of a man, his hand against every man and every man's hand against [13] him; and he shall dwell over against all his kinsmen." So she called the name of the LORD who spoke to her, "Thou

art a God of seeing"; for she said, "Have I really seen [14] God and remained alive after seeing him?" [u] Therefore the well was called Beer-la′hai-roi; [v] it lies between Kadesh and Bered.

[15] And Hagar bore Abram a son; and Abram called the [16] name of his son, whom Hagar bore, Ish′mael. Abram was eighty-six years old when Hagar bore Ish′mael to Abram.

The Covenant of Circumcision

17 When Abram was ninety-nine years old the LORD appeared to Abram, and said to him, "I am God [2] Almighty; [w] walk before me, and be blameless. And I will make my covenant between me and you, and will [3] multiply you exceedingly." Then Abram fell on his face; [4] and God said to him, "Behold, my covenant is with you, [5] and you shall be the father of a multitude of nations. No longer shall your name be Abram, [x] but your name shall be Abraham; [y] for I have made you the father of a mul- [6] titude of nations. I will make you exceedingly fruitful and I will make nations of you, and kings shall come [7] forth from you. And I will establish my covenant between me and you and your descendants after you throughout their generations for an everlasting covenant, to be God [8] to you and to your descendants after you. And I will give to you, and to your descendants after you, the land of your sojournings, all the land of Canaan, for an ever-lasting possession; and I will be their God."

[9] And God said to Abraham, "As for you, you shall keep my covenant, you and your descendants after you through- [10] out their generations. This is my covenant, which you shall keep, between me and you and your descendants after you: Every male among you shall be circumcised. [11] You shall be circumcised in the flesh of your foreskins, and it shall be a sign of the covenant between me and [12] you. He that is eight days old among you shall be cir-cumcised; every male throughout your generations, whether born in your house, or bought with your money [13] from any foreigner who is not of your offspring, both he that is born in your house and he that is bought with your money, shall be circumcised. So shall my covenant be in

[14] your flesh an everlasting covenant. Any uncircumcised male who is not circumcised in the flesh of his foreskin shall be cut off from his people; he has broken my covenant."

[15] And God said to Abraham, "As for Sar′ai your wife, you shall not call her name Sar′ai, but Sarah shall be her [16] name. I will bless her, and moreover I will give you a son by her; I will bless her, and she shall be a mother of [17] nations; kings of peoples shall come from her." Then Abraham fell on his face and laughed, and said to him-self, "Shall a child be born to a man who is a hundred years old? Shall Sarah, who is ninety years old, bear a [18] child?" And Abraham said to God, "O that Ish′mael [19] might live in thy sight!" God said, "No, but Sarah your wife shall bear you a son, and you shall call his name Isaac. [z] I will establish my covenant with him as an ever- [20] lasting covenant for his descendants after him. As for Ish′mael, I have heard you; behold, I will bless him and make him fruitful and multiply him exceedingly; he shall be the father of twelve princes, and I will make him a [21] great nation. But I will establish my covenant with Isaac, whom Sarah shall bear to you at this season next year." [22] When he had finished talking with him, God went up [23] from Abraham. Then Abraham took Ish′mael his son and all the slaves born in his house or bought with his money, every male among the men of Abraham's house, and he circumcised the flesh of their foreskins that very day, as [24] God had said to him. Abraham was ninety-nine years old when he was circumcised in the flesh of his foreskin. [25] And Ish′mael his son was thirteen years old when he was

[26] circumcised in the flesh of his foreskin. That very day [27] Abraham and his son Ish′mael were circumcised; and all the men of his house, those born in the house and those bought with money from a foreigner, were circumcised with him.

The Lord's Visit to Hebron

18 And the LORD appeared to him by the oaks [a] of Mamre, as he sat at the door of his tent in the heat [2] of the day. He lifted up his eyes and looked, and behold, three men stood in front of him. When he saw them, he ran from the tent door to meet them, and bowed himself [3] to the earth, and said, "My lord, if I have found favor in [4] your sight, do not pass by your servant. Let a little water be brought, and wash your feet, and rest yourselves under

---

[t] That is *God hears* [u] Cn: Heb *have I even here seen after him who sees me?* [v] That is *the well of one who sees and lives*
[w] Heb *El Shaddai* [x] That is *exalted father* [y] Here taken to mean *father of a multitude* [z] That is *he laughs*
[a] Or *terebinths*

5 the tree, while I fetch a morsel of bread, that you may refresh yourselves, and after that you may pass on—since you have come to your servant." So they said, "Do as 6 you have said." And Abraham hastened into the tent to Sarah, and said, "Make ready quickly three measures b of 7 fine meal, knead it, and make cakes." And Abraham ran to the herd, and took a calf, tender and good, and gave it 8 to the servant, who hastened to prepare it. Then he took curds, and milk, and the calf which he had prepared, and set it before them; and he stood by them under the tree while they ate.

9 They said to him, "Where is Sarah your wife?" And 10 he said, "She is in the tent." The LORD said, "I will surely return to you in the spring, and Sarah your wife shall have a son." And Sarah was listening at the tent door 11 behind him. Now Abraham and Sarah were old, advanced in age; it had ceased to be with Sarah after the manner 12 of women. So Sarah laughed to herself, saying, "After I have grown old, and my husband is old, shall I have 13 pleasure?" The LORD said to Abraham, "Why did Sarah laugh, and say, 'Shall I indeed bear a child, now that I 14 am old?' Is anything too hard c for the LORD? At the appointed time I will return to you, in the spring, and Sarah 15 shall have a son." But Sarah denied, saying, "I did not laugh"; for she was afraid. He said, "No, but you did laugh."

16 Then the men set out from there, and they looked toward Sodom; and Abraham went with them to set them 17 on their way. The LORD said, "Shall I hide from Abraham 18 what I am about to do, seeing that Abraham shall become a great and mighty nation, and all the nations of 19 the earth shall bless themselves by him? d No, for I have chosen e him, that he may charge his children and his household after him to keep the way of the LORD by doing righteousness and justice; so that the LORD may bring to 20 Abraham what he has promised him." Then the LORD said, "Because the outcry against Sodom and Gomor'rah 21 is great and their sin is very grave, I will go down to see whether they have done altogether according to the outcry which has come to me; and if not, I will know." 22 So the men turned from there, and went toward Sod- 23 om; but Abraham still stood before the LORD. Then Abraham drew near, and said, "Wilt thou indeed destroy the 24 righteous with the wicked? Suppose there are fifty righteous within the city; wilt thou then destroy the place and 25 not spare it for the fifty righteous who are in it? Far be it from thee to do such a thing, to slay the righteous with the wicked, so that the righteous fare as the wicked! Far be that from thee! Shall not the Judge of all the earth do 26 right?" And the LORD said, "If I find at Sodom fifty righteous in the city, I will spare the whole place for their 27 sake." Abraham answered, "Behold, I have taken upon myself to speak to the Lord, I who am but dust and ashes.

28 Suppose five of the fifty righteous are lacking? Wilt thou destroy the whole city for lack of five?" And he said, "I 29 will not destroy it if I find forty-five there." Again he spoke to him, and said, "Suppose forty are found there." He answered, "For the sake of forty I will not do it." 30 Then he said, "Oh let not the Lord be angry, and I will speak. Suppose thirty are found there." He answered, "I 31 will not do it, if I find thirty there." He said, "Behold, I have taken upon myself to speak to the Lord. Suppose twenty are found there." He answered, "For the sake of 32 twenty I will not destroy it." Then he said, "Oh let not the Lord be angry, and I will speak again but this once. Suppose ten are found there." He answered, "For the 33 sake of ten I will not destroy it." And the LORD went his way, when he had finished speaking to Abraham; and Abraham returned to his place.

Destruction of Sodom and Gomorrah

19 The two angels came to Sodom in the evening; and Lot was sitting in the gate of Sodom. When Lot saw them, he rose to meet them, and bowed himself with 2 his face to the earth, and said, "My lords, turn aside, I pray you, to your servant's house and spend the night, and wash your feet; then you may rise up early and go on your way." They said, "No; we will spend the night in 3 the street." But he urged them strongly; so they turned aside to him and entered his house; and he made them a 4 feast, and baked unleavened bread, and they ate. But before they lay down, the men of the city, the men of Sodom, both young and old, all the people to the last man, 5 surrounded the house; and they called to Lot, "Where are the men who came to you tonight? Bring them out 6 to us, that we may know them." Lot went out of the door 7 to the men, shut the door after him, and said, "I beg you, 8 my brothers, do not act so wickedly. Behold, I have two daughters who have not known man; let me bring them out to you, and do to them as you please; only do nothing to these men, for they have come under the shelter of my 9 roof." But they said, "Stand back!" And they said, "This fellow came to sojourn, and he would play the judge! Now we will deal worse with you than with them." Then they pressed hard against the man Lot, and drew near to 10 break the door. But the men put forth their hands and brought Lot into the house to them, and shut the door. 11 And they struck with blindness the men who were at the door of the house, both small and great, so that they wearied themselves groping for the door.

12 Then the men said to Lot, "Have you any one else here? Sons-in-law, sons, daughters, or any one you have 13 in the city, bring them out of the place; for we are about to destroy this place, because the outcry against its people has become great before the LORD, and the LORD has sent 14 us to destroy it." So Lot went out and said to his sons-in-

b Heb seahs   c Or wonderful   d Or in him all the nations of the earth shall be blessed   e Heb known

law, who were to marry his daughters, "Up, get out of this place; for the LORD is about to destroy the city." But he seemed to his sons-in-law to be jesting.

15 When morning dawned, the angels urged Lot, saying, "Arise, take your wife and your two daughters who are here, lest you be consumed in the punishment of the city."
16 But he lingered; so the men seized him and his wife and his two daughters by the hand, the LORD being merciful to him, and they brought him forth and set him outside
17 the city. And when they had brought them forth, they ᶠ

said, "Flee for your life; do not look back or stop anywhere in the valley; flee to the hills, lest you be con-
18 sumed." And Lot said to them, "Oh, no, my lords;
19 behold, your servant has found favor in your sight, and you have shown me great kindness in saving my life; but I cannot flee to the hills, lest the disaster overtake me, and
20 I die. Behold, yonder city is near enough to flee to, and it is a little one. Let me escape there—is it not a little
21 one?—and my life will be saved!" He said to him, "Behold, I grant you this favor also, that I will not over-
22 throw the city of which you have spoken. Make haste, escape there; for I can do nothing till you arrive there."
23 Therefore the name of the city was called Zo'ar.ᵍ The sun had risen on the earth when Lot came to Zo'ar.

24 Then the LORD rained on Sodom and Gomor'rah brim-
25 stone and fire from the LORD out of heaven; and he over-threw those cities, and all the valley, and all the inhabi-
26 tants of the cities, and what grew on the ground. But Lot's wife behind him looked back, and she became a
27 pillar of salt. And Abraham went early in the morning to
28 the place where he had stood before the LORD; and he looked down toward Sodom and Gomor'rah and toward all the land of the valley, and beheld, and lo, the smoke of the land went up like the smoke of a furnace.

29 So it was that, when God destroyed the cities of the

valley, God remembered Abraham, and sent Lot out of the midst of the overthrow, when he overthrew the cities in which Lot dwelt.

Origin of Moab and Ammon

30 Now Lot went up out of Zo'ar, and dwelt in the hills with his two daughters, for he was afraid to dwell in Zo'ar; so he dwelt in a cave with his two daughters.
31 And the first-born said to the younger, "Our father is old, and there is not a man on earth to come in to us
32 after the manner of all the earth. Come, let us make our father drink wine, and we will lie with him, that we may
33 preserve offspring through our father." So they made their father drink wine that night; and the first-born went in, and lay with her father; he did not know when
34 she lay down or when she arose. And on the next day, the first-born said to the younger, "Behold, I lay last night with my father; let us make him drink wine tonight also; then you go in and lie with him, that we may preserve
35 offspring through our father." So they made their father drink wine that night also; and the younger arose, and lay with him; and he did not know when she lay down
36 or when she arose. Thus both the daughters of Lot were
37 with child by their father. The first-born bore a son, and called his name Moab; he is the father of the Moabites
38 to this day. The younger also bore a son, and called his name Ben-ammi; he is the father of the Ammonites to this day.

Abraham and Isaac

20 From there Abraham journeyed toward the territory of the Negeb, and dwelt between Kadesh and
2 Shur; and he sojourned in Gerar. And Abraham said of Sarah his wife, "She is my sister." And Abim'elech king
3 of Gerar sent and took Sarah. But God came to Abim'-elech in a dream by night, and said to him, "Behold, you are a dead man, because of the woman whom you have
4 taken; for she is a man's wife." Now Abim'elech had not approached her; so he said, "Lord, wilt thou slay an in-
5 nocent people? Did he not himself say to me, 'She is my sister'? And she herself said, 'He is my brother.' In the integrity of my heart and the innocence of my hands I
6 have done this." Then God said to him in the dream, "Yes, I know that you have done this in the integrity of your heart, and it was I who kept you from sinning
7 against me; therefore I did not let you touch her. Now then restore the man's wife; for he is a prophet, and he will pray for you, and you shall live. But if you do not restore her, know that you shall surely die, you, and all that are yours."

8 So Abim'elech rose early in the morning, and called all his servants, and told them all these things; and the
9 men were very much afraid. Then Abim'elech called Abra-

ᶠ Gk Syr Vg: Heb *he*   ᵍ That is *Little*

ham, and said to him, "What have you done to us? And
how have I sinned against you, that you have brought on
me and my kingdom a great sin? You have done to me
¹⁰ things that ought not to be done." And Abim'elech said
to Abraham, "What were you thinking of, that you did
¹¹ this thing?" Abraham said, "I did it because I thought,
There is no fear of God at all in this place, and they will
¹² kill me because of my wife. Besides she is indeed my
sister, the daughter of my father but not the daughter of
¹³ my mother; and she became my wife. And when God
caused me to wander from my father's house, I said to
her, 'This is the kindness you must do me: at every place
¹⁴ to which we come, say of me, He is my brother.' " Then
Abim'elech took sheep and oxen, and male and female
slaves, and gave them to Abraham, and restored Sarah
¹⁵ his wife to him. And Abim'elech said, "Behold, my land
¹⁶ is before you; dwell where it pleases you." To Sarah he
said, "Behold, I have given your brother a thousand
pieces of silver; it is your vindication in the eyes of all
who are with you; and before every one you are righted."
¹⁷ Then Abraham prayed to God; and God healed Abim'-
elech, and also healed his wife and female slaves so that
¹⁸ they bore children. For the LORD had closed all the wombs
of the house of Abim'elech because of Sarah, Abraham's
wife.

21 The LORD visited Sarah as he had said, and the
² LORD did to Sarah as he had promised. And Sarah
conceived, and bore Abraham a son in his old age at the
³ time of which God had spoken to him. Abraham called
the name of his son who was born to him, whom Sarah
⁴ bore him, Isaac. And Abraham circumcised his son Isaac
when he was eight days old, as God had commanded
⁵ him. Abraham was a hundred years old when his son
⁶ Isaac was born to him. And Sarah said, "God has made
laughter for me; every one who hears will laugh over
⁷ me." And she said, "Who would have said to Abraham
that Sarah would suckle children? Yet I have borne him
a son in his old age."

Hagar and Ishmael

⁸ And the child grew, and was weaned; and Abraham
made a great feast on the day that Isaac was weaned.

⁹ But Sarah saw the son of Hagar the Egyptian, whom she
had borne to Abraham, playing with her son Isaac.ʰ
¹⁰ So she said to Abraham, "Cast out this slave woman with
her son; for the son of this slave woman shall not be
¹¹ heir with my son Isaac." And the thing was very dis-
¹² pleasing to Abraham on account of his son. But God said
to Abraham, "Be not displeased because of the lad and
because of your slave woman; whatever Sarah says to
you, do as she tells you, for through Isaac shall your
¹³ descendants be named. And I will make a nation of the
son of the slave woman also, because he is your off-
¹⁴ spring." So Abraham rose early in the morning, and took
bread and a skin of water, and gave it to Hagar, putting
it on her shoulder, along with the child, and sent her
away. And she departed, and wandered in the wilderness
of Beer-sheba.

¹⁵ When the water in the skin was gone, she cast the child
¹⁶ under one of the bushes. Then she went, and sat down
over against him a good way off, about the distance of a
bowshot; for she said, "Let me not look upon the death
of the child." And as she sat over against him, the child
¹⁷ lifted up his voice ⁱ and wept. And God heard the voice
of the lad; and the angel of God called to Hagar from
heaven, and said to her, "What troubles you, Hagar?
Fear not; for God has heard the voice of the lad where
¹⁸ he is. Arise, lift up the lad, and hold him fast with your
¹⁹ hand; for I will make him a great nation." Then God
opened her eyes, and she saw a well of water; and she
went, and filled the skin with water, and gave the lad a
²⁰ drink. And God was with the lad, and he grew up; he
lived in the wilderness, and became an expert with the
²¹ bow. He lived in the wilderness of Paran; and his mother
took a wife for him from the land of Egypt.

Abraham's Dispute With Abimelech

²² At that time Abim'elech and Phicol the commander of
his army said to Abraham, "God is with you in all that
²³ you do; now therefore swear to me here by God that you
will not deal falsely with me or with my offspring or with
my posterity, but as I have dealt loyally with you, you
will deal with me and with the land where you have
²⁴ sojourned." And Abraham said, "I will swear."

²⁵ When Abraham complained to Abim'elech about a
well of water which Abim'elech's servants had seized,
²⁶ Abim'elech said, "I do not know who has done this thing;
you did not tell me, and I have not heard of it until
²⁷ today." So Abraham took sheep and oxen and gave them
to Abim'elech, and the two men made a covenant.
²⁸, ²⁹ Abraham set seven ewe lambs of the flock apart. And
Abim'elech said to Abraham, "What is the meaning of
³⁰ these seven ewe lambs which you have set apart?" He
said, "These seven ewe lambs you will take from my
hand, that you may be a witness for me that I dug this

ʰ Gk Vg: Heb lacks *with her son Isaac*   ⁱ Gk: Heb *she lifted up her voice*

³¹ well." Therefore that place was called Beer-sheba; ʲ be-
³² cause there both of them swore an oath. So they made
a covenant at Beer-sheba. Then Abim'elech and Phicol the
commander of his army rose up and returned to the land
³³ of the Philistines. Abraham planted a tamarisk tree in
Beer-sheba, and called there on the name of the LORD, the
³⁴ Everlasting God. And Abraham sojourned many days
in the land of the Philistines.

Testing of Abraham

22 After these things God tested Abraham, and said
to him, "Abraham!" And he said, "Here am I."
² He said, "Take your son, your only son Isaac, whom you
love, and go to the land of Mori'ah, and offer him there
as a burnt offering upon one of the mountains of which
³ I shall tell you." So Abraham rose early in the morning,
saddled his ass, and took two of his young men with him,
and his son Isaac; and he cut the wood for the burnt
offering, and arose and went to the place of which God
⁴ had told him. On the third day Abraham lifted up his
⁵ eyes and saw the place afar off. Then Abraham said to
his young men, "Stay here with the ass; I and the lad
⁶ will go yonder and worship, and come again to you." And
Abraham took the wood of the burnt offering and laid it
on Isaac his son; and he took in his hand the fire and the
⁷ knife. So they went both of them together. And Isaac
said to his father Abraham, "My father!" And he said,
"Here am I, my son." He said, "Behold, the fire and the
wood; but where is the lamb for a burnt offering?"
⁸ Abraham said, "God will provide himself the lamb for a
burnt offering, my son." So they went both of them
together.
⁹ When they came to the place of which God had told
him, Abraham built an altar there, and laid the wood
in order, and bound Isaac his son, and laid him on
¹⁰ the altar, upon the wood. Then Abraham put forth
¹¹ his hand, and took the knife to slay his son. But the angel
of the LORD called to him from heaven, and said, "Abra-
¹² ham, Abraham!" And he said, "Here am I." He said,
"Do not lay your hand on the lad or do anything to
him; for now I know that you fear God, seeing you have
¹³ not withheld your son, your only son, from me." And
Abraham lifted up his eyes and looked, and behold,
behind him was a ram, caught in a thicket by his horns;
and Abraham went and took the ram, and offered it up as
¹⁴ a burnt offering instead of his son. So Abraham called
the name of that place The LORD will provide; ᵏ as it is
said to this day, "On the mount of the LORD it shall be
provided." ˡ
¹⁵ And the angel of the LORD called to Abraham a second
¹⁶ time from heaven, and said, "By myself I have sworn,
says the LORD, because you have done this, and have not
¹⁷ withheld your son, your only son, I will indeed bless you,

and I will multiply your descendants as the stars of
heaven and as the sand which is on the seashore. And
your descendants shall possess the gate of their enemies,
¹⁸ and by your descendants shall all the nations of the earth
bless themselves, because you have obeyed my voice."
¹⁹ So Abraham returned to his young men, and they arose
and went together to Beer-sheba; and Abraham dwelt at
Beer-sheba.

Descendants of Nahor

²⁰ Now after these things it was told Abraham, "Behold,
Milcah also has borne children to your brother Nahor:
²¹ Uz the first-born, Buz his brother, Kemu'el the father of
²² Aram, Chesed, Hazo, Pildash, Jidlaph, and Bethu'el."
²³ Bethu'el became the father of Rebekah. These eight
²⁴ Milcah bore to Nahor, Abraham's brother. Moreover, his
concubine, whose name was Reumah, bore Tebah, Gaham,
Tahash, and Ma'acah.

Burial of Sarah

23 Sarah lived a hundred and twenty-seven years;
² these were the years of the life of Sarah. And Sarah
died at Kir'iath-ar'ba (that is, Hebron) in the land of
Canaan; and Abraham went in to mourn for Sarah and
³ to weep for her. And Abraham rose up from before his
⁴ dead, and said to the Hittites, "I am a stranger and a
sojourner among you; give me property among you for
a burying place, that I may bury my dead out of my
⁵,⁶ sight." The Hittites answered Abraham, "Hear us, my
lord; you are a mighty prince among us. Bury your dead
in the choicest of our sepulchres; none of us will withhold
from you his sepulchre, or hinder you from burying your
⁷ dead." Abraham rose and bowed to the Hittites, the peo-
⁸ ple of the land. And he said to them, "If you are willing
that I should bury my dead out of my sight, hear me,
⁹ and entreat for me Ephron the son of Zohar, that he may
give me the cave of Mach-pe'lah, which he owns; it is
at the end of his field. For the full price let him give it to
me in your presence as a possession for a burying place."
¹⁰ Now Ephron was sitting among the Hittites; and Ephron
the Hittite answered Abraham in the hearing of the
¹¹ Hittites, of all who went in at the gate of his city, "No,
my lord, hear me; I give you the field, and I give you
the cave that is in it; in the presence of the sons of my
¹² people I give it to you; bury your dead." Then Abraham
¹³ bowed down before the people of the land. And he said
to Ephron in the hearing of the people of the land, "But

ʲ That is *Well of seven* or *Well of the oath*   ᵏ Or *see*   ˡ Or *he will be seen*

if you will, hear me; I will give the price of the field; accept it from me, that I may bury my dead there."

14, 15 Ephron answered Abraham, "My lord, listen to me; a piece of land worth four hundred shekels of silver, what
16 is that between you and me? Bury your dead." Abraham agreed with Ephron; and Abraham weighed out for Ephron the silver which he had named in the hearing of the Hittites, four hundred shekels of silver, according to the weights current among the merchants.
17 So the field of Ephron in Mach-pe'lah, which was to the east of Mamre, the field with the cave which was in it and all the trees that were in the field, throughout its whole
18 area, was made over to Abraham as a possession in the presence of the Hittites, before all who went in at the gate
19 of his city. After this, Abraham buried Sarah his wife in the cave of the field of Mach-pe'lah east of Mamre (that
20 is, Hebron) in the land of Canaan. The field and the cave that is in it were made over to Abraham as a possession for a burying place by the Hittites.

Choice of a Wife for Isaac

24 Now Abraham was old, well advanced in years; and the LORD had blessed Abraham in all things.
2 And Abraham said to his servant, the oldest of his house, who had charge of all that he had, "Put your hand under
3 my thigh, and I will make you swear by the LORD, the God of heaven and of the earth, that you will not take a wife for my son from the daughters of the Canaanites,
4 among whom I dwell, but will go to my country and
5 to my kindred, and take a wife for my son Isaac." The servant said to him, "Perhaps the woman may not be willing to follow me to this land; must I then take your
6 son back to the land from which you came?" Abraham said to him, "See to it that you do not take my son back
7 there. The LORD, the God of heaven, who took me from my father's house and from the land of my birth, and who spoke to me and swore to me, 'To your descendants I will give this land,' he will send his angel before you,
8 and you shall take a wife for my son from there. But if the woman is not willing to follow you, then you will be free from this oath of mine; only you must not take my
9 son back there." So the servant put his hand under the thigh of Abraham his master, and swore to him concerning this matter.
10 Then the servant took ten of his master's camels and departed, taking all sorts of choice gifts from his master; and he arose, and went to Mesopota'mia, to the city of
11 Nahor. And he made the camels kneel down outside the city by the well of water at the time of evening, the time
12 when women go out to draw water. And he said, "O LORD, God of my master Abraham, grant me success today, I pray thee, and show steadfast love to my master Abraham.
13 Behold, I am standing by the spring of water, and the daughters of the men of the city are coming out to draw
14 water. Let the maiden to whom I shall say, 'Pray let down your jar that I may drink,' and who shall say, 'Drink, and I will water your camels'—let her be the one whom thou hast appointed for thy servant Isaac. By this I shall know that thou hast shown steadfast love to my master."

15 Before he had done speaking, behold, Rebekah, who was born to Bethu'el the son of Milcah, the wife of Nahor, Abraham's brother, came out with her water jar
16 upon her shoulder. The maiden was very fair to look upon, a virgin, whom no man had known. She went down
17 to the spring, and filled her jar, and came up. Then the servant ran to meet her, and said, "Pray give me a little
18 water to drink from your jar." She said, "Drink, my lord"; and she quickly let down her jar upon her hand,
19 and gave him a drink. When she had finished giving him a drink, she said, "I will draw for your camels also, until
20 they have done drinking." So she quickly emptied her jar into the trough and ran again to the well to draw, and
21 she drew for all his camels. The man gazed at her in silence to learn whether the LORD had prospered his journey or not.
22 When the camels had done drinking, the man took a gold ring weighing a half shekel, and two bracelets for
23 her arms weighing ten gold shekels, and said, "Tell me whose daughter you are. Is there room in your father's
24 house for us to lodge in?" She said to him, "I am the daughter of Bethu'el the son of Milcah, whom she bore
25 to Nahor." She added, "We have both straw and prov-
26 ender enough, and room to lodge in." The man bowed his
27 head and worshiped the LORD, and said, "Blessed be the LORD, the God of my master Abraham, who has not forsaken his steadfast love and his faithfulness toward my master. As for me, the LORD has led me in the way to the house of my master's kinsmen."
28 Then the maiden ran and told her mother's household
29 about these things. Rebekah had a brother whose name was Laban; and Laban ran out to the man, to the spring.
30 When he saw the ring, and the bracelets on his sister's arms, and when he heard the words of Rebekah his sister, "Thus the man spoke to me," he went to the man;

and behold, he was standing by the camels at the spring. [31] He said, "Come in, O blessed of the LORD; why do you stand outside? For I have prepared the house and a place [32] for the camels." So the man came into the house; and Laban ungirded the camels, and gave him straw and provender for the camels, and water to wash his feet and the [33] feet of the men who were with him. Then food was set before him to eat; but he said, "I will not eat until I have told my errand." He said, "Speak on."

[34, 35] So he said, "I am Abraham's servant. The LORD has greatly blessed my master, and he has become great; he has given him flocks and herds, silver and gold, menserv- [36] ants and maidservants, camels and asses. And Sarah my master's wife bore a son to my master when she was old; [37] and to him he has given all that he has. My master made me swear, saying, 'You shall not take a wife for my son from the daughters of the Canaanites, in whose land I [38] dwell; but you shall go to my father's house and to my [39] kindred, and take a wife for my son.' I said to my master, [40] 'Perhaps the woman will not follow me.' But he said to me, 'The LORD, before whom I walk, will send his angel with you and prosper your way; and you shall take a wife for my son from my kindred and from my father's house; [41] then you will be free from my oath, when you come to my kindred; and if they will not give her to you, you will be free from my oath.'

[42] "I came today to the spring, and said, 'O LORD, the God of my master Abraham, if now thou wilt prosper [43] the way which I go, behold, I am standing by the spring of water; let the young woman who comes out to draw, to whom I shall say, "Pray give me a little water from [44] your jar to drink," and who will say to me, "Drink, and

I will draw for your camels also," let her be the woman whom the LORD has appointed for my master's son.'

[45] "Before I had done speaking in my heart, behold, Rebekah came out with her water jar on her shoulder; and she went down to the spring, and drew. I said to her, [46] 'Pray let me drink.' She quickly let down her jar from her shoulder, and said, 'Drink, and I will give your camels drink also.' So I drank, and she gave the camels [47] drink also. Then I asked her, 'Whose daughter are you?'

She said, 'The daughter of Bethu'el, Nahor's son, whom Milcah bore to him.' So I put the ring on her nose, and [48] the bracelets on her arms. Then I bowed my head and worshiped the LORD, and blessed the LORD, the God of my master Abraham, who had led me by the right way to take the daughter of my master's kinsman for his son. [49] Now then, if you will deal loyally and truly with my master, tell me; and if not, tell me; that I may turn to the right hand or to the left."

[50] Then Laban and Bethu'el answered, "The thing comes from the LORD; we cannot speak to you bad or good. [51] Behold, Rebekah is before you, take her and go, and let her be the wife of your master's son, as the LORD has spoken."

[52] When Abraham's servant heard their words, he bowed [53] himself to the earth before the LORD. And the servant brought forth jewelry of silver and of gold, and raiment, and gave them to Rebekah; he also gave to her brother [54] and to her mother costly ornaments. And he and the men who were with him ate and drank, and they spent the night there. When they arose in the morning, he said, [55] "Send me back to my master." Her brother and her mother said, "Let the maiden remain with us a while, at least ten [56] days; after that she may go." But he said to them, "Do not delay me, since the LORD has prospered my way; let [57] me go that I may go to my master." They said, "We will [58] call the maiden, and ask her." And they called Rebekah, and said to her, "Will you go with this man?" She said, [59] "I will go." So they sent away Rebekah their sister and [60] her nurse, and Abraham's servant and his men. And they blessed Rebekah, and said to her, "Our sister, be the mother of thousands of ten thousands; and may your descendants possess the gate of those who hate them!" [61] Then Rebekah and her maids arose, and rode upon the camels and followed the man; thus the servant took Rebekah, and went his way.

[62] Now Isaac had come from [n] Beer-la'hai-roi, and was [63] dwelling in the Negeb. And Isaac went out to meditate in the field in the evening; and he lifted up his eyes and [64] looked, and behold, there were camels coming. And Rebekah lifted up her eyes, and when she saw Isaac, she [65] alighted from the camel, and said to the servant, "Who is the man yonder, walking in the field to meet us?" The servant said, "It is my master." So she took her veil and [66] covered herself. And the servant told Isaac all the things [67] that he had done. Then Isaac brought her into the tent,[o] and took Rebekah, and she became his wife; and he loved her. So Isaac was comforted after his mother's death.

The Sons of Keturah

[25] Abraham took another wife, whose name was [2] Ketu'rah. She bore him Zimran, Jokshan, Medan, [3] Mid'ian, Ishbak, and Shuah. Jokshan was the father of

[n] Syr Tg: Heb *from coming to*   [o] Heb adds *Sarah his mother*

Sheba and Dedan. The sons of Dedan were As-shu'rim, 4 Letu'shim, and Le-um'mim. The sons of Mid'ian were Ephah, Epher, Hanoch, Abi'da, and Elda'ah. All these 5 were the children of Ketu'rah. Abraham gave all he had 6 to Isaac. But to the sons of his concubines Abraham gave gifts, and while he was still living he sent them away from his son Isaac, eastward to the east country.

Death of Abraham

7 These are the days of the years of Abraham's life, a 8 hundred and seventy-five years. Abraham breathed his last and died in a good old age, an old man and full of 9 years, and was gathered to his people. Isaac and Ish'mael his sons buried him in the cave of Mach-pe'lah, in the field of Ephron the son of Zohar the Hittite, east of 10 Mamre, the field which Abraham purchased from the Hittites. There Abraham was buried, with Sarah his wife. 11 After the death of Abraham God blessed Isaac his son. And Isaac dwelt at Beer-la'hai-roi.

DESCENDANTS OF ISHMAEL

12 These are the descendants of Ish'mael, Abraham's son, whom 13 Hagar the Egyptian, Sarah's maid, bore to Abraham. These are the names of the sons of Ish'mael, named in the order of their birth: Neba'ioth, the first-born of Ish'mael; and Kedar, 14, 15 Adbeel, Mibsam, Mishma, Dumah, Massa, Hadad, Tema, 16 Jetur, Naphish, and Ked'emah. These are the sons of Ish'mael and these are their names, by their villages and by their en- 17 campments, twelve princes according to their tribes. (These are the years of the life of Ish'mael, a hundred and thirty-seven years; he breathed his last and died, and was gathered to his 18 kindred.) They dwelt from Hav'ilah to Shur, which is opposite Egypt in the direction of Assyria; he settled p over against all his people.

ISAAC AND HIS SONS, ESAU AND JACOB
Jacob and Esau

19 These are the descendants of Isaac, Abraham's son: 20 Abraham was the father of Isaac, and Isaac was forty years old when he took to wife Rebekah, the daughter of Bethu'el the Aramean of Paddan-aram, the sister of 21 Laban the Aramean. And Isaac prayed to the Lord for his wife, because she was barren; and the Lord granted 22 his prayer, and Rebekah his wife conceived. The children struggled together within her; and she said, "If it is thus, why do I live?" q So she went to inquire of the Lord. 23 And the Lord said to her,

"Two nations are in your womb,
 and two peoples, born of you, shall be divided;
the one shall be stronger than the other,
 the elder shall serve the younger."

24 When her days to be delivered were fulfilled, behold, 25 there were twins in her womb. The first came forth red, all his body like a hairy mantle; so they called his name 26 Esau. Afterward his brother came forth, and his hand had taken hold of Esau's heel; so his name was called Jacob.r Isaac was sixty years old when she bore them. 27 When the boys grew up, Esau was a skilful hunter, a man of the field, while Jacob was a quiet man, dwelling 28 in tents. Isaac loved Esau, because he ate of his game; but Rebekah loved Jacob.

29 Once when Jacob was boiling pottage, Esau came in 30 from the field, and he was famished. And Esau said to Jacob, "Let me eat some of that red pottage, for I am famished!" (Therefore his name was called Edom.s) 31, 32 Jacob said, "First sell me your birthright." Esau said, "I am about to die; of what use is a birthright to me?" 33 Jacob said, "Swear to me first." t So he swore to him, 34 and sold his birthright to Jacob. Then Jacob gave Esau bread and pottage of lentils, and he ate and drank, and rose and went his way. Thus Esau despised his birthright.

Isaac, Rebekah, and Abimelech

26 Now there was a famine in the land, besides the former famine that was in the days of Abraham. And Isaac went to Gerar, to Abim'elech king of the 2 Philistines. And the Lord appeared to him, and said, "Do not go down to Egypt; dwell in the land of which I shall 3 tell you. Sojourn in this land, and I will be with you, and will bless you; for to you and to your descendants I will give all these lands, and I will fulfil the oath which I 4 swore to Abraham your father. I will multiply your descendants as the stars of heaven, and will give to your descendants all these lands; and by your descendants all 5 the nations of the earth shall bless themselves: because Abraham obeyed my voice and kept my charge, my commandments, my statutes, and my laws."

6, 7 So Isaac dwelt in Gerar. When the men of the place asked him about his wife, he said, "She is my sister"; for he feared to say, "My wife," thinking, "lest the men of the place should kill me for the sake of Rebekah"; be- 8 cause she was fair to look upon. When he had been there a long time, Abim'elech king of the Philistines looked out of a window and saw Isaac fondling Rebekah his wife. 9 So Abim'elech called Isaac, and said, "Behold, she is your wife; how then could you say, 'She is my sister'?" Isaac said to him, "Because I thought, 'Lest I die because 10 of her.'" Abim'elech said, "What is this you have done to us? One of the people might easily have lain with your wife, and you would have brought guilt upon us." 11 So Abim'elech warned all the people, saying, "Whoever touches this man or his wife shall be put to death."

Dispute Concerning the Wells

12 And Isaac sowed in that land, and reaped in the same 13 year a hundredfold. The Lord blessed him, and the man became rich, and gained more and more until he 14 became very wealthy. He had possessions of flocks and herds, and a great household, so that the Philistines en- 15 vied him. (Now the Philistines had stopped and filled with earth all the wells which his father's servants had

p Heb fell   q Syr: Heb obscure   r That is He takes by the heel or He supplants   s That is Red   t Heb today

16 dug in the days of Abraham his father.) And Abim'elech said to Isaac, "Go away from us; for you are much mightier than we."

17 So Isaac departed from there, and encamped in the
18 valley of Gerar and dwelt there. And Isaac dug again the wells of water which had been dug in the days of Abraham his father; for the Philistines had stopped them after the death of Abraham; and he gave them the names
19 which his father had given them. But when Isaac's servants dug in the valley and found there a well of springing
20 water, the herdsmen of Gerar quarreled with Isaac's herdsmen, saying, "The water is ours." So he called the name of the well Esek,u because they contended with him.
21 Then they dug another well, and they quarreled over that
22 also; so he called its name Sitnah.v And he moved from

35 daughter of Elon the Hittite; and they made life bitter for Isaac and Rebekah.

Jacob Seeks His Father's Blessing

27 When Isaac was old and his eyes were dim so that he could not see, he called Esau his older son, and said to him, "My son"; and he answered, "Here I am."
2 He said, "Behold, I am old; I do not know the day of my
3 death. Now then, take your weapons, your quiver and your bow, and go out to the field, and hunt game for me,
4 and prepare for me savory food, such as I love, and bring it to me that I may eat; that I may bless you before I die."
5 Now Rebekah was listening when Isaac spoke to his son Esau. So when Esau went to the field to hunt for

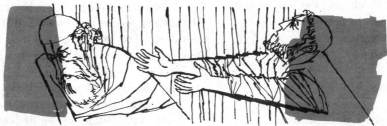

there and dug another well, and over that they did not quarrel; so he called its name Reho'both,w saying, "For now the LORD has made room for us, and we shall be fruitful in the land."
23, 24 From there he went up to Beer-sheba. And the LORD appeared to him the same night and said, "I am the God of Abraham your father; fear not, for I am with you and will bless you and multiply your descendants for my
25 servant Abraham's sake." So he built an altar there and called upon the name of the LORD, and pitched his tent there. And there Isaac's servants dug a well.
26 Then Abim'elech went to him from Gerar with Ahuz'-zath his adviser and Phicol the commander of his army.
27 Isaac said to them, "Why have you come to me, seeing that you hate me and have sent me away from you?"
28 They said, "We see plainly that the LORD is with you; so we say, let there be an oath between you and us, and
29 let us make a covenant with you, that you will do us no harm, just as we have not touched you and have done to you nothing but good and have sent you away in peace.
30 You are now the blessed of the LORD." So he made them
31 a feast, and they ate and drank. In the morning they rose early and took oath with one another; and Isaac set them on their way, and they departed from him in peace.
32 That same day Isaac's servants came and told him about the well which they had dug, and said to him, "We have
33 found water." He called it Shibah; therefore the name of the city is Beer-sheba to this day.
34 When Esau was forty years old, he took to wife Judith the daughter of Be-e'ri the Hittite, and Bas'emath the

6 game and bring it, Rebekah said to her son Jacob, "I
7 heard your father speak to your brother Esau, 'Bring me game, and prepare for me savory food, that I may eat it,
8 and bless you before the LORD before I die.' Now there-
9 fore, my son, obey my word as I command you. Go to the flock, and fetch me two good kids, that I may prepare from them savory food for your father, such as he loves;
10 and you shall bring it to your father to eat, so that he
11 may bless you before he dies." But Jacob said to Rebekah his mother, "Behold, my brother Esau is a hairy man,
12 and I am a smooth man. Perhaps my father will feel me, and I shall seem to be mocking him, and bring a curse
13 upon myself and not a blessing." His mother said to him, "Upon me be your curse, my son; only obey my word,
14 and go, fetch them to me." So he went and took them and brought them to his mother; and his mother prepared
15 savory food, such as his father loved. Then Rebekah took the best garments of Esau her older son, which were with her in the house, and put them on Jacob her younger son;
16 and the skins of the kids she put upon his hands and
17 upon the smooth part of his neck; and she gave the savory food and the bread, which she had prepared, into the hand of her son Jacob.
18 So he went in to his father, and said, "My father";
19 and he said, "Here I am; who are you, my son?" Jacob said to his father, "I am Esau your first-born. I have done as you told me; now sit up and eat of my game, that
20 you may bless me." But Isaac said to his son, "How is it that you have found it so quickly, my son?" He answered,
21 "Because the LORD your God granted me success." Then

---

u That is *Contention*   v That is *Enmity*   w That is *Broad places* or *Room*

Isaac said to Jacob, "Come near, that I may feel you, my son, to know whether you are really my son Esau or 22 not." So Jacob went near to Isaac his father, who felt him and said, "The voice is Jacob's voice, but the hands 23 are the hands of Esau." And he did not recognize him, because his hands were hairy like his brother Esau's 24 hands; so he blessed him. He said, "Are you really my 25 son Esau?" He answered, "I am." Then he said, "Bring it to me, that I may eat of my son's game and bless you." So he brought it to him, and he ate; and he brought him 26 wine, and he drank. Then his father Isaac said to him, 27 "Come near and kiss me, my son." So he came near and kissed him; and he smelled the smell of his garments, and blessed him, and said,

"See, the smell of my son
　is as the smell of a field which the LORD has blessed!
28 May God give you of the dew of heaven,
　and of the fatness of the earth,
　and plenty of grain and wine.
29 Let peoples serve you,
　and nations bow down to you.
Be lord over your brothers,
　and may your mother's sons bow down to you.
Cursed be every one who curses you,
　and blessed be every one who blesses you!"

30 As soon as Isaac had finished blessing Jacob, when Jacob had scarcely gone out from the presence of Isaac his father, Esau his brother came in from his hunting. 31 He also prepared savory food, and brought it to his father. And he said to his father, "Let my father arise, and eat of his son's game, that you may bless me." 32 His father Isaac said to him, "Who are you?" He an- 33 swered, "I am your son, your first-born, Esau." Then Isaac trembled violently, and said, "Who was it then that hunted game and brought it to me, and I ate it all x before you came, and I have blessed him?—yes, and he shall be 34 blessed." When Esau heard the words of his father, he cried out with an exceedingly great and bitter cry, and said to his father, "Bless me, even me also, O my father!" 35 But he said, "Your brother came with guile, and he has 36 taken away your blessing." Esau said, "Is he not rightly named Jacob? For he has supplanted me these two times. He took away my birthright; and behold, now he has taken away my blessing." Then he said, "Have you not 37 reserved a blessing for me?" Isaac answered Esau, "Be- hold, I have made him your lord, and all his brothers I have given to him for servants, and with grain and wine I have sustained him. What then can I do for you, my 38 son?" Esau said to his father, "Have you but one bless- ing, my father? Bless me, even me also, O my father." And Esau lifted up his voice and wept.

39 Then Isaac his father answered him:

"Behold, away from y the fatness of the earth shall your dwelling be,
　and away from y the dew of heaven on high.
40 By your sword you shall live,
　and you shall serve your brother;
but when you break loose
　you shall break his yoke from your neck."

Esau's Hatred of Jacob

41 Now Esau hated Jacob because of the blessing with which his father had blessed him, and Esau said to him- self, "The days of mourning for my father are approach- 42 ing; then I will kill my brother Jacob." But the words of Esau her older son were told to Rebekah; so she sent and called Jacob her younger son, and said to him, "Behold, your brother Esau comforts himself by planning to kill 43 you. Now therefore, my son, obey my voice; arise, flee to 44 Laban my brother in Haran, and stay with him a while, 45 until your brother's fury turns away; until your brother's anger turns away, and he forgets what you have done to him; then I will send, and fetch you from there. Why should I be bereft of you both in one day?"

46 Then Rebekah said to Isaac, "I am weary of my life because of the Hittite women. If Jacob marries one of the Hittite women such as these, one of the women of the **28** land, what good will my life be to me?" Then Isaac called Jacob and blessed him, and charged him, 2 "You shall not marry one of the Canaanite women. Arise, go to Paddan-aram to the house of Bethu'el your mother's father; and take as wife from there one of the daughters 3 of Laban your mother's brother. God Almighty z bless you and make you fruitful and multiply you, that you 4 may become a company of peoples. May he give the bless- ing of Abraham to you and to your descendants with you, that you may take possession of the land of your 5 sojournings which God gave to Abraham!" Thus Isaac sent Jacob away; and he went to Paddan-aram to Laban, the son of Bethu'el the Aramean, the brother of Rebekah, Jacob's and Esau's mother.

6 Now Esau saw that Isaac had blessed Jacob and sent him away to Paddan-aram to take a wife from there, and that as he blessed him he charged him, "You shall not 7 marry one of the Canaanite women," and that Jacob had obeyed his father and his mother and gone to Paddan- 8 aram. So when Esau saw that the Canaanite women did 9 not please Isaac his father, Esau went to Ish'mael and took to wife, besides the wives he had, Ma'ha-lath the daughter of Ish'mael Abraham's son, the sister of Neba'ioth.

Jacob at Bethel

10, 11 Jacob left Beer-sheba, and went toward Haran. And he came to a certain place, and stayed there that night, because the sun had set. Taking one of the stones of the

---

x Cn: Heb of all　　　y Or of　　　z Heb El Shaddai

place, he put it under his head and lay down in that place
12 to sleep. And he dreamed that there was a ladder set up on the earth, and the top of it reached to heaven; and behold, the angels of God were ascending and descending
13 on it! And behold, the LORD stood above it[a] and said, "I am the LORD, the God of Abraham your father and the God of Isaac; the land on which you lie I will give to you
14 and to your descendants; and your descendants shall be like the dust of the earth, and you shall spread abroad to the west and to the east and to the north and to the south; and by you and your descendants shall all the families of
15 the earth bless themselves.[b] Behold, I am with you and will keep you wherever you go, and will bring you back to this land; for I will not leave you until I have done
16 that of which I have spoken to you." Then Jacob awoke from his sleep and said, "Surely the LORD is in this place;
17 and I did not know it." And he was afraid, and said, "How awesome is this place! This is none other than the house of God, and this is the gate of heaven."
18 So Jacob rose early in the morning, and he took the stone which he had put under his head and set it up for
19 a pillar and poured oil on the top of it. He called the name of that place Bethel; [c] but the name of the city was Luz
20 at the first. Then Jacob made a vow, saying, "If God will be with me, and will keep me in this way that I go, and
21 will give me bread to eat and clothing to wear, so that I come again to my father's house in peace, then the LORD
22 shall be my God, and this stone, which I have set up for a pillar, shall be God's house; and of all that thou givest me I will give the tenth to thee."

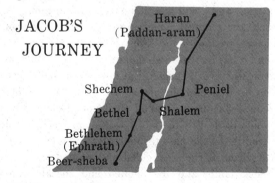

JACOB'S JOURNEY

Haran (Paddan-aram)
Shechem
Peniel
Bethel
Shalem
Bethlehem (Ephrath)
Beer-sheba

Jacob at Paddan-aram

29 Then Jacob went on his journey, and came to
2 the land of the people of the east. As he looked, he saw a well in the field, and lo, three flocks of sheep lying beside it; for out of that well the flocks were watered.
3 The stone on the well's mouth was large, and when all the flocks were gathered there, the shepherds would roll the stone from the mouth of the well, and water the sheep, and put the stone back in its place upon the mouth of the well.
4 Jacob said to them, "My brothers, where do you come
5 from?" They said, "We are from Haran." He said to

them, "Do you know Laban the son of Nahor?" They
6 said, "We know him." He said to them, "Is it well with him?" They said, "It is well; and see, Rachel his
7 daughter is coming with the sheep!" He said, "Behold, it is still high day, it is not time for the animals to be gathered together; water the sheep, and go, pasture them."
8 But they said, "We cannot until all the flocks are gathered together, and the stone is rolled from the mouth of the well; then we water the sheep."
9 While he was still speaking with them, Rachel came with
10 her father's sheep; for she kept them. Now when Jacob saw Rachel the daughter of Laban his mother's brother, and the sheep of Laban his mother's brother, Jacob went up and rolled the stone from the well's mouth, and watered
11 the flock of Laban his mother's brother. Then Jacob
12 kissed Rachel, and wept aloud. And Jacob told Rachel that he was her father's kinsman, and that he was Rebekah's son; and she ran and told her father.
13 When Laban heard the tidings of Jacob his sister's son, he ran to meet him, and embraced him and kissed him, and brought him to his house. Jacob told Laban all these
14 things, and Laban said to him, "Surely you are my bone and my flesh!" And he stayed with him a month.
15 Then Laban said to Jacob, "Because you are my kinsman, should you therefore serve me for nothing? Tell me,
16 what shall your wages be?" Now Laban had two daughters; the name of the older was Leah, and the name
17 of the younger was Rachel. Leah's eyes were weak, but
18 Rachel was beautiful and lovely. Jacob loved Rachel; and he said, "I will serve you seven years for your younger
19 daughter Rachel." Laban said, "It is better that I give her to you than that I should give her to any other man; stay
20 with me." So Jacob served seven years for Rachel, and they seemed to him but a few days because of the love he had for her.
21 Then Jacob said to Laban, "Give me my wife that I
22 may go in to her, for my time is completed." So Laban gathered together all the men of the place, and made a
23 feast. But in the evening he took his daughter Leah and
24 brought her to Jacob; and he went in to her (Laban gave his maid Zilpah to his daughter Leah to be her maid.)
25 And in the morning, behold, it was Leah; and Jacob said to Laban, "What is this you have done to me? Did I not serve with you for Rachel? Why then have you deceived
26 me?" Laban said, "It is not so done in our country, to
27 give the younger before the first-born. Complete the week of this one, and we will give you the other also in return
28 for serving me another seven years." Jacob did so, and completed her week; then Laban gave him his daughter
29 Rachel to wife. (Laban gave his maid Bilhah to his
30 daughter Rachel to be her maid.) So Jacob went in to Rachel also, and he loved Rachel more than Leah, and served Laban for another seven years.

[a] Or *beside him*   [b] Or *be blessed*   [c] That is *The house of God*

Jacob's Family

31 When the LORD saw that Leah was hated, he opened
32 her womb; but Rachel was barren. And Leah conceived and bore a son, and she called his name Reuben; [d] for she said, "Because the LORD has looked upon my affliction;
33 surely now my husband will love me." She conceived again and bore a son, and said, "Because the LORD has heard [e] that I am hated, he has given me this son also";
34 and she called his name Simeon. Again she conceived and bore a son, and said, "Now this time my husband will be joined [f] to me, because I have borne him three sons";
35 therefore his name was called Levi. And she conceived again and bore a son, and said, "This time I will praise [g] the LORD"; therefore she called his name Judah; then she ceased bearing.

30 When Rachel saw that she bore Jacob no children, she envied her sister; and she said to Jacob,
2 "Give me children, or I shall die!" Jacob's anger was kindled against Rachel, and he said, "Am I in the place of God, who has withheld from you the fruit of the
3 womb?" Then she said, "Here is my maid Bilhah; go in to her, that she may bear upon my knees, and even I
4 may have children through her." So she gave him her
5 maid Bilhah as a wife; and Jacob went in to her. And
6 Bilhah conceived and bore Jacob a son. Then Rachel said, "God has judged me, and has also heard my voice and given me a son"; therefore she called his name Dan.[h]
7 Rachel's maid Bilhah conceived again and bore Jacob
8 a second son. Then Rachel said, "With mighty wrestlings I have wrestled [i] with my sister, and have prevailed"; so she called his name Naph'tali.
9 When Leah saw that she had ceased bearing children, she took her maid Zilpah and gave her to Jacob as a
10, 11 wife. Then Leah's maid Zilpah bore Jacob a son. And Leah said, "Good fortune!" so she called his name Gad.[j]
12, 13 Leah's maid Zilpah bore Jacob a second son. And Leah said, "Happy am I! For the women will call me happy"; so she called his name Asher.[k]
14 In the days of wheat harvest Reuben went and found mandrakes in the field, and brought them to his mother Leah. Then Rachel said to Leah, "Give me, I pray, some
15 of your son's mandrakes." But she said to her, "Is it a small matter that you have taken away my husband? Would you take away my son's mandrakes also?" Rachel said, "Then he may lie with you tonight for your son's
16 mandrakes." When Jacob came from the field in the evening, Leah went out to meet him, and said, "You must come in to me; for I have hired you with my son's
17 mandrakes." So he lay with her that night. And God hearkened to Leah, and she conceived and bore Jacob a
18 fifth son. Leah said, "God has given me my hire [l] because I gave my maid to my husband"; so she called his name
19 Is'sachar. And Leah conceived again, and she bore Jacob

20 a sixth son. Then Leah said, "God has endowed me with a good dowry; now my husband will honor [m] me, because I have borne him six sons"; so she called his name Zeb'u-
21 lun. Afterwards she bore a daughter, and called her name
22 Dinah. Then God remembered Rachel, and God hearkened
23 to her and opened her womb. She conceived and bore a
24 son, and said, "God has taken away my reproach"; and she called his name Joseph,[n] saying, "May the LORD add to me another son!"

Jacob Outwits Laban

25 When Rachel had borne Joseph, Jacob said to Laban, "Send me away, that I may go to my own home and
26 country. Give me my wives and my children for whom I have served you, and let me go; for you know the service
27 which I have given you." But Laban said to him, "If you will allow me to say so, I have learned by divination that
28 the LORD has blessed me because of you; name your
29 wages, and I will give it." Jacob said to him, "You yourself know how I have served you, and how your cattle
30 have fared with me. For you had little before I came, and it has increased abundantly; and the LORD has blessed you wherever I turned. But now when shall I provide for
31 my own household also?" He said, "What shall I give you?" Jacob said, "You shall not give me anything; if you will do this for me, I will again feed your flock and
32 keep it: let me pass through all your flock today, removing from it every speckled and spotted sheep and every black lamb, and the spotted and speckled among the
33 goats; and such shall be my wages. So my honesty will answer for me later, when you come to look into my wages with you. Every one that is not speckled and spotted among the goats and black among the lambs, if found
34 with me, shall be counted stolen." Laban said, "Good!
35 Let it be as you have said." But that day Laban removed the he-goats that were striped and spotted, and all the she-goats that were speckled and spotted, every one that had white on it, and every lamb that was black, and put
36 them in charge of his sons; and he set a distance of three days' journey between himself and Jacob; and Jacob fed the rest of Laban's flock.

---

[d] That is *See, a son*   [e] Heb *shama*   [f] Heb *lawah*   [g] Heb *hodah*   [h] That is *He judged*
[i] Heb *niphtal*   [j] That is *Fortune*   [k] That is *Happy*   [l] Heb *sakar*   [m] Heb *zabal*
[n] That is *He adds*

37 Then Jacob took fresh rods of poplar and almond and plane, and peeled white streaks in them exposing the
38 white of the rods. He set the rods which he had peeled in front of the flocks in the runnels, that is, the watering troughs, where the flocks came to drink. And since they
39 bred when they came to drink, the flocks bred in front of the rods and so the flocks brought forth striped,
40 speckled, and spotted. And Jacob separated the lambs, and set the faces of the flocks toward the striped and all

the black in the flock of Laban; and he put his own droves apart, and did not put them with Laban's flock.
41 Whenever the stronger of the flock were breeding Jacob laid the rods in the runnels before the eyes of the flock,
42 that they might breed among the rods, but for the feebler of the flock he did not lay them there; so the feebler were
43 Laban's, and the stronger Jacob's. Thus the man grew exceedingly rich, and had large flocks, maidservants and menservants, and camels and asses.

Jacob's Decision to Return Home

31 Now Jacob heard that the sons of Laban were saying, "Jacob has taken all that was our father's; and from what was our father's he has gained all this
2 wealth." And Jacob saw that Laban did not regard him
3 with favor as before. Then the Lord said to Jacob, "Return to the land of your fathers and to your kindred, and
4 I will be with you." So Jacob sent and called Rachel and
5 Leah into the field where his flock was, and said to them, "I see that your father does not regard me with favor as he did before. But the God of my father has been with
6 me. You know that I have served your father with all my
7 strength; yet your father has cheated me and changed my wages ten times, but God did not permit him to harm
8 me. If he said, 'The spotted shall be your wages,' then all the flock bore spotted; and if he said, 'The striped shall be
9 your wages' then all the flock bore striped. Thus God has taken away the cattle of your father, and given them to
10 me. In the mating season of the flock I lifted up my eyes, and saw in a dream that the he-goats which leaped upon
11 the flock were striped, spotted, and mottled. Then the angel of God said to me in the dream, 'Jacob,' and I said,
12 'Here I am!' And he said, 'Lift up your eyes and see, all the goats that leap upon the flock are striped, spotted, and mottled; for I have seen all that Laban is doing to you.
13 I am the God of Bethel, where you anointed a pillar and made a vow to me. Now arise, go forth from this land,

14 and return to the land of your birth.' " Then Rachel and Leah answered him, "Is there any portion or inheritance
15 left to us in our father's house? Are we not regarded by him as foreigners? For he has sold us, and he has been
16 using up the money given for us. All the property which God has taken away from our father belongs to us and to our children; now then, whatever God has said to you, do."

Jacob's Flight from Laban

17 So Jacob arose, and set his sons and his wives on
18 camels; and he drove away all his cattle, all his livestock which he had gained, the cattle in his possession which he had acquired in Paddan-aram, to go to the land of Canaan
19 to his father Isaac. Laban had gone to shear his sheep,
20 and Rachel stole her father's household gods. And Jacob outwitted Laban the Aramean, in that he did not tell him
21 that he intended to flee. He fled with all that he had, and arose and crossed the Eu-phra'tes, and set his face toward the hill country of Gilead.
22 When it was told Laban on the third day that Jacob
23 had fled, he took his kinsmen with him and pursued him for seven days and followed close after him into the hill
24 country of Gilead. But God came to Laban the Aramean in a dream by night, and said to him, "Take heed that you say not a word to Jacob, either good or bad."
25 And Laban overtook Jacob. Now Jacob had pitched his tent in the hill country, and Laban with his kinsmen
26 encamped in the hill country of Gilead. And Laban said to Jacob, "What have you done, that you have cheated me, and carried away my daughters like captives of the
27 sword? Why did you flee secretly, and cheat me, and did not tell me, so that I might have sent you away with mirth
28 and songs, with tambourine and lyre? And why did you not permit me to kiss my sons and my daughters fare-
29 well? Now you have done foolishly. It is in my power to do you harm; but the God of your father spoke to me last night, saying, 'Take heed that you speak to Jacob
30 neither good nor bad.' And now you have gone away because you longed greatly for your father's house, but
31 why did you steal my gods?" Jacob answered Laban, "Because I was afraid, for I thought that you would take
32 your daughters from me by force. Any one with whom you find your gods shall not live. In the presence of our kinsmen point out what I have that is yours, and take it." Now Jacob did not know that Rachel had stolen them.
33 So Laban went into Jacob's tent, and into Leah's tent, and into the tent of the two maidservants, but he did not find them. And he went out of Leah's tent, and entered
34 Rachel's. Now Rachel had taken the household gods and put them in the camel's saddle, and sat upon them. Laban
35 felt all about the tent, but did not find them. And she said to her father, "Let not my lord be angry that I can-

not rise before you, for the way of women is upon me." So he searched, but did not find the household gods.

36 Then Jacob became angry, and upbraided Laban; Jacob said to Laban, "What is my offense? What is my
37 sin, that you have hotly pursued me? Although you have felt through all my goods, what have you found of all your household goods? Set it here before my kinsmen and your
38 kinsmen, that they may decide between us two. These twenty years I have been with you; your ewes and your she-goats have not miscarried, and I have not eaten the
39 rams of your flocks. That which was torn by wild beasts I did not bring to you; I bore the loss of it myself; of my hand you required it, whether stolen by day or stolen
40 by night. Thus I was; by day the heat consumed me, and the cold by night, and my sleep fled from my eyes.
41 These twenty years I have been in your house; I served you fourteen years for your two daughters, and six years for your flock, and you have changed my wages ten times.
42 If the God of my father, the God of Abraham and the Fear of Isaac, had not been on my side, surely now you would have sent me away empty-handed. God saw my affliction and the labor of my hands, and rebuked you last night."

43 Then Laban answered and said to Jacob, "The daughters are my daughters, the children are my children, the flocks are my flocks, and all that you see is mine. But what can I do this day to these my daughters, or to their
44 children whom they have borne? Come now, let us make a covenant, you and I; and let it be a witness between you
45 and me." So Jacob took a stone, and set it up as a
46 pillar. And Jacob said to his kinsmen, "Gather stones," and they took stones, and made a heap; and they ate there
47 by the heap. Laban called it Je′gar-sahadu′tha:° but
48 Jacob called it Galeed.ᵖ Laban said, "This heap is a wit-

ness between you and me today." Therefore he named it
49 Galeed, and the pillar ᑫ Mizpah,ʳ for he said, "The LORD watch between you and me, when we are absent one from
50 the other. If you ill-treat my daughters, or if you take wives besides my daughters, although no man is with us, remember, God is witness between you and me."
51 Then Laban said to Jacob, "See this heap and the
52 pillar, which I have set between you and me. This heap is a witness, and the pillar is a witness, that I will not pass over the heap to you, and you will not pass over this
53 heap and this pillar to me, for harm. The God of Abra-

ham and the God of Nahor, the God of their father, judge between us." So Jacob swore by the Fear of his
54 father Isaac, and Jacob offered a sacrifice on the mountain and called his kinsmen to eat bread; and they ate bread and tarried all night on the mountain.
55 ˢ Early in the morning Laban arose, and kissed his grandchildren and his daughters and blessed them; then he departed and returned home.

Jacob Prepares to Meet Esau

32 Jacob went on his way and the angels of God
2 met him; and when Jacob saw them he said, "This is God's army!" So he called the name of that place Mahana′im.ᵗ
3 And Jacob sent messengers before him to Esau his
4 brother in the land of Se′ir, the country of Edom, instructing them, "Thus you shall say to my lord Esau: Thus says your servant Jacob, 'I have sojourned with Laban,
5 and stayed until now; and I have oxen, asses, flocks, menservants, and maidservants; and I have sent to tell my lord, in order that I may find favor in your sight.'"
6 And the messengers returned to Jacob, saying, "We came to your brother Esau, and he is coming to meet you,
7 and four hundred men with him." Then Jacob was greatly afraid and distressed; and he divided the people that were with him, and the flocks and herds and camels, into
8 two companies, thinking, "If Esau comes to the one company and destroys it, then the company which is left will escape."
9 And Jacob said, "O God of my father Abraham and God of my father Isaac, O LORD who didst say to me, 'Return to your country and to your kindred, and I will
10 do you good,' I am not worthy of the least of all the steadfast love and all the faithfulness which thou hast shown to thy servant, for with only my staff I crossed this Jordan; and now I have become two companies.
11 Deliver me, I pray thee, from the hand of my brother, from the hand of Esau, for I fear him, lest he come and
12 slay us all, the mothers with the children. But thou didst say, 'I will do you good, and make your descendants as the sand of the sea, which cannot be numbered for multitude.'"
13 So he lodged there that night, and took from what he
14 had with him a present for his brother Esau, two hun-

° In Aramaic *The heap of witness*   ᵖ In Hebrew *The heap of witness*   ᑫ Compare Sam: Heb lacks *the pillar*
ʳ That is *Watchpost*   ˢ Ch 32.1 in Heb   ᵗ Here taken to mean *Two armies*

dred she-goats and twenty he-goats, two hundred ewes
15 and twenty rams, thirty milch camels and their colts, forty cows and ten bulls, twenty she-asses and ten he-asses.
16 These he delivered into the hand of his servants, every drove by itself, and said to his servants, "Pass on before
17 me, and put a space between drove and drove." He instructed the foremost, "When Esau my brother meets you, and asks you, 'To whom do you belong? Where are you
18 going? And whose are these before you?' then you shall say, 'They belong to your servant Jacob; they are a present sent to my lord Esau; and moreover he is behind
19 us.'" He likewise instructed the second and the third and all who followed the droves, "You shall say the same
20 thing to Esau when you meet him, and you shall say, 'Moreover your servant Jacob is behind us.'" For he thought, "I may appease him with the present that goes before me, and afterwards I shall see his face; perhaps
21 he will accept me." So the present passed on before him; and he himself lodged that night in the camp.
22 The same night he arose and took his two wives, his two maids, and his eleven children, and crossed the ford
23 of the Jabbok. He took them and sent them across the
24 stream, and likewise everything that he had. And Jacob was left alone; and a man wrestled with him until the
25 breaking of the day. When the man saw that he did not prevail against Jacob, he touched the hollow of his thigh; and Jacob's thigh was put out of joint as he wrestled
26 with him. Then he said, "Let me go, for the day is breaking." But Jacob said, "I will not let you go, unless you
27 bless me." And he said to him, "What is your name?"
28 And he said, "Jacob." Then he said, "Your name shall no more be called Jacob, but Israel,[u] for you have striven
29 with God and with men, and have prevailed." Then Jacob asked him, "Tell me, I pray, your name." But he said, "Why is it that you ask my name?" And there he blessed
30 him. So Jacob called the name of the place Peni'el,[v]

Jacob's Meeting With Esau

33 And Jacob lifted up his eyes and looked, and behold, Esau was coming, and four hundred men with him. So he divided the children among Leah and
2 Rachel and the two maids. And he put the maids with their children in front, then Leah with her children, and
3 Rachel and Joseph last of all. He himself went on before them, bowing himself to the ground seven times, until he came near to his brother.
4 But Esau ran to meet him, and embraced him, and fell
5 on his neck and kissed him, and they wept. And when Esau raised his eyes and saw the women and children, he said, "Who are these with you?" Jacob said, "The children whom God has graciously given your servant."
6 Then the maids drew near, they and their children, and
7 bowed down; Leah likewise and her children drew near and bowed down; and last Joseph and Rachel drew near,
8 and they bowed down. Esau said, "What do you mean by all this company which I met?" Jacob answered, "To find
9 favor in the sight of my lord." But Esau said, "I have enough, my brother; keep what you have for yourself."
10 Jacob said, "No, I pray you, if I have found favor in your sight, then accept my present from my hand; for truly to see your face is like seeing the face of God, with
11 such favor have you received me. Accept, I pray you, my gift that is brought to you, because God has dealt graciously with me, and because I have enough." Thus he urged him, and he took it.
12 Then Esau said, "Let us journey on our way, and I
13 will go before you." But Jacob said to him, "My lord knows that the children are frail, and that the flocks and herds giving suck are a care to me; and if they are over-
14 driven for one day, all the flocks will die. Let my lord pass on before his servant, and I will lead on slowly, according to the pace of the cattle which are before me and according to the pace of the children, until I come to

saying, "For I have seen God face to face, and yet my
31 life is preserved." The sun rose upon him as he passed
32 Penu'el, limping because of his thigh. Therefore to this day the Israelites do not eat the sinew of the hip which is upon the hollow of the thigh, because he touched the hollow of Jacob's thigh on the sinew of the hip.

my lord in Se'ir."
15 So Esau said, "Let me leave with you some of the men who are with me." But he said, "What need is there? Let
16 me find favor in the sight of my lord." So Esau returned
17 that day on his way to Se'ir. But Jacob journeyed to Succoth,[w] and built himself a house, and made booths

---

[u] That is *He who strives with God* or *God strives*   [v] That is *The face of God*   [w] That is *Booths*

for his cattle; therefore the name of the place is called Succoth.

Jacob and His Family

18 And Jacob came safely to the city of Shechem, which is in the land of Canaan, on his way from Paddan-aram; 19 and he camped before the city. And from the sons of Hamor, Shechem's father, he bought for a hundred pieces of money [x] the piece of land on which he had pitched his

20 tent. There he erected an altar and called it El-El'ohe-Israel.[y]

34 Now Dinah the daughter of Leah, whom she had borne to Jacob, went out to visit the women of the 2 land; and when Shechem the son of Hamor the Hivite, the prince of the land, saw her, he seized her and lay 3 with her and humbled her. And his soul was drawn to Dinah the daughter of Jacob; he loved the maiden and 4 spoke tenderly to her. So Shechem spoke to his father 5 Hamor, saying, "Get me this maiden for my wife." Now Jacob heard that he had defiled his daughter Dinah; but his sons were with his cattle in the field, so Jacob held 6 his peace until they came. And Hamor the father of 7 Shechem went out to Jacob to speak with him. The sons of Jacob came in from the field when they heard of it; and the men were indignant and very angry, because he had wrought folly in Israel by lying with Jacob's daughter, for such a thing ought not to be done.

8 But Hamor spoke with them, saying, "The soul of my son Shechem longs for your daughter; I pray you, give 9 her to him in marriage. Make marriages with us; give your daughters to us, and take our daughters for your- 10 selves. You shall dwell with us; and the land shall be open to you; dwell and trade in it, and get property in 11 it." Shechem also said to her father and to her brothers, "Let me find favor in your eyes, and whatever you say 12 to me I will give. Ask of me ever so much as marriage present and gift, and I will give according as you say to me; only give me the maiden to be my wife."

13 The sons of Jacob answered Shechem and his father Hamor deceitfully, because he had defiled their sister 14 Dinah. They said to them, "We cannot do this thing, to give our sister to one who is uncircumcised, for that 15 would be a disgrace to us. Only on this condition will we

consent to you: that you will become as we are and every 16 male of you be circumcised. Then we will give our daughters to you, and we will take your daughters to ourselves, and we will dwell with you and become one 17 people. But if you will not listen to us and be circumcised, then we will take our daughter, and we will be gone."

18 Their words pleased Hamor and Hamor's son Shechem. 19 And the young man did not delay to do the thing, because he had delight in Jacob's daughter. Now he was 20 the most honored of all his family. So Hamor and his son Shechem came to the gate of their city and spoke to 21 the men of their city, saying, "These men are friendly with us; let them dwell in the land and trade in it, for behold, the land is large enough for them; let us take their daughters in marriage, and let us give them our 22 daughters. Only on this condition will the men agree to dwell with us, to become one people: that every male 23 among us be circumcised as they are circumcised. Will not their cattle, their property and all their beasts be ours? Only let us agree with them, and they will dwell 24 with us." And all who went out of the gate of his city hearkened to Hamor and his son Shechem; and every male was circumcised, all who went out of the gate of his city.

25 On the third day, when they were sore, two of the sons of Jacob, Simeon and Levi, Dinah's brothers, took their swords and came upon the city unawares, and killed 26 all the males. They slew Hamor and his son Shechem with the sword, and took Dinah out of Shechem's house, and 27 went away. And the sons of Jacob came upon the slain, and plundered the city, because their sister had been 28 defiled; they took their flocks and their herds, their asses, 29 and whatever was in the city and in the field; all their wealth, all their little ones and their wives, all that was 30 in the houses, they captured and made their prey. Then Jacob said to Simeon and Levi, "You have brought trouble on me by making me odious to the inhabitants of the land, the Canaanites and the Per'izzites; my numbers are few, and if they gather themselves against me and attack me, I shall be destroyed, both I and my house- 31 hold." But they said, "Should he treat our sister as a harlot?"

Jacob's Return to Bethel

35 God said to Jacob, "Arise, go up to Bethel, and dwell there; and make there an altar to the God who appeared to you when you fled from your brother Esau." 2 So Jacob said to his household and to all who were with him, "Put away the foreign gods that are among you, 3 and purify yourselves, and change your garments; then let us arise and go up to Bethel, that I may make there an altar to the God who answered me in the day of my

[x] Heb *a hundred qesitah*   [y] That is *God, the God of Israel*

distress and has been with me wherever I have gone."

4 So they gave to Jacob all the foreign gods that they had, and the rings that were in their ears; and Jacob hid them under the oak which was near Shechem.

5 And as they journeyed, a terror from God fell upon the cities that were round about them, so that they did not

6 pursue the sons of Jacob. And Jacob came to Luz (that is, Bethel), which is in the land of Canaan, he and all the

7 people who were with him, and there he built an altar, and called the place El-bethel,[z] because there God had revealed himself to him when he fled from his brother.

8 And Deb'orah, Rebekah's nurse, died, and she was buried under an oak below Bethel; so the name of it was called Al'lon-bacuth.[a]

9 God appeared to Jacob again, when he came from

10 Paddan-aram, and blessed him. And God said to him, "Your name is Jacob; no longer shall your name be called Jacob, but Israel shall be your name." So his name was

11 called Israel. And God said to him, "I am God Almighty:[b] be fruitful and multiply; a nation and a company of nations shall come from you, and kings shall

12 spring from you. The land which I gave to Abraham and Isaac I will give to you, and I will give the land to

13 your descendants after you." Then God went up from

14 him in the place where he had spoken with him. And Jacob set up a pillar in the place where he had spoken with him, a pillar of stone; and he poured out a drink

15 offering on it, and poured oil on it. So Jacob called the name of the place where God had spoken with him, Bethel.

16 Then they journeyed from Bethel; and when they were still some distance from Ephrath, Rachel travailed, and

17 she had hard labor. And when she was in her hard labor, the midwife said to her, "Fear not; for now you will

18 have another son." And as her soul was departing (for she died), she called his name Ben-o'ni;[c] but his father

19 called his name Benjamin.[d] So Rachel died, and she was

20 buried on the way to Ephrath (that is, Bethlehem), and Jacob set up a pillar upon her grave; it is the pillar of

21 Rachel's tomb, which is there to this day. Israel journeyed on, and pitched his tent beyond the tower of Eder.

22 While Israel dwelt in that land Reuben went and lay with Bilhah his father's concubine; and Israel heard of it.

23 Now the sons of Jacob were twelve. The sons of Leah: Reuben (Jacob's first-born), Simeon, Levi, Judah, Is'-

24 sachar, and Zeb'ulun. The sons of Rachel: Joseph and

25 Benjamin. The sons of Bilhah, Rachel's maid: Dan and

26 Naph'tali. The sons of Zilpah, Leah's maid: Gad and Asher. These were the sons of Jacob who were born to him in Paddan-aram.

Death of Isaac

27 And Jacob came to his father Isaac at Mamre, or Kir'-iath-ar'ba (that is, Hebron), where Abraham and Isaac

28 had sojourned. Now the days of Isaac were a hundred and

29 eighty years. And Isaac breathed his last; and he died and was gathered to his people, old and full of days; and his sons Esau and Jacob buried him.

DESCENDANTS OF ESAU

36 2 These are the descendants of Esau (that is, Edom). Esau took his wives from the Canaanites: Adah the daughter of Elon the Hittite, Oholiba'mah the daughter of Anah the son[e]

3 of Zibeon the Hivite, and Bas'emath, Ish'mael's daughter, the

4 sister of Neba'ioth. And Adah bore to Esau, El'iphaz; Bas'emath

5 bore Reu'el; and Oholiba'mah bore Je'ush, Jalam, and Korah. These are the sons of Esau who were born to him in the land of Canaan.

6 Then Esau took his wives, his sons, his daughters, and all the members of his household, his cattle, all his beasts, and all his property which he had acquired in the land of Canaan; and he

7 went into a land away from his brother Jacob. For their possessions were too great for them to dwell together; the land of their sojournings could not support them because of their cattle.

8 So Esau dwelt in the hill country of Se'ir; Esau is Edom.

9 These are the descendants of Esau the father of the E'domites

10 in the hill country of Se'ir. These are the names of Esau's sons:• El'iphaz the son of Adah the wife of Esau, Reu'el the son of

11 Bas'emath the wife of Esau. The sons of El'iphaz were Teman,

12 Omar, Zepho, Gatam, and Kenaz. (Timna was a concubine of El'iphaz, Esau's son; she bore Am'alek to El'iphaz.) These are

13 the sons of Adah, Esau's wife. These are the sons of Reu'el: Nahath, Zerah, Shammah, and Mizzah. These are the sons of

14 Bas'emath, Esau's wife. These are the sons of Oholiba'mah the daughter of Anah the son[f] of Zib'eon, Esau's wife: she bore to Esau Je'ush, Jalam, and Korah.

15 These are the chiefs of the sons of Esau. The sons of El'iphaz the firstborn of Esau: the chiefs Teman, Omar, Zepho, Kenaz,

16 Korah, Gatam, and Am'alek; these are the chiefs of El'iphaz in

17 the land of Edom; they are the sons of Adah. These are the sons of Reu'el, Esau's son: the chiefs Nahath, Zerah, Shammah, and Mizzah; these are the chiefs of Reu'el in the land of Edom; they

18 are the sons of Bas'emath, Esau's wife. These are the sons of Oholiba'mah, Esau's wife: the chiefs Je'ush, Jalam, and Korah; these are the chiefs born of Oholiba'mah the daughter of Anah,

19 Esau's wife. These are the sons of Esau (that is, Edom), and these are their chiefs.

20 These are the sons of Se'ir the Horite, the inhabitants of the

21 land: Lotan, Shobal, Zib'eon, Anah, Dishon, Ezer, and Dishan; these are the chiefs of the Horites, the sons of Se'ir in the land

22 of Edom. The sons of Lotan were Hori and Heman; and Lotan's

23 sister was Timna. These are the sons of Shobal: Alvan, Man'-

24 ahath, Ebal, Shepho, and Onam. These are the sons of Zib'eon: A'iah and Anah; he is the Anah who found the hot springs in the wilderness, as he pastured the asses of Zib'eon his father.

25 These are the children of Anah: Dishon and Oholiba'mah the

26 daughter of Anah. These are the sons of Dishon: Hemdan,

27 Eshban, Ithran, and Cheran. These are the sons of Ezer: Bilhan,

28 Za'avan, and Akan. These are the sons of Dishan: Uz and Aran.

29 These are the chiefs of the Horites: the chiefs Lotan, Shobal,

30 Zib'eon, Anah, Dishon, Ezer, and Dishan; these are the chiefs

---

[z] That is God of Bethel   [a] That is Oak of weeping   [b] Heb El Shaddai   [c] That is Son of my sorrow
[d] That is Son of the right hand or Son of the South   [e] Sam Gk Syr: Heb daughter   [f] Gk Syr: Heb daughter

of the Horites, according to their clans in the land of Se'ir.

31 These are the kings who reigned in the land of Edom, before 32 any king reigned over the Israelites. Bela the son of Be'or 33 reigned in Edom, the name of his city being Din'habah. Bela died, and Jobab the son of Zerah or Bozrah reigned in his 34 stead. Jobab died, and Husham of the land of the Te'manites 35 reigned in his stead. Husham died, and Hadad the son of Bedad, who defeated Mid'ian in the country of Moab, reigned in his 36 stead, the name of his city being Avith. Hadad died, and 37 Samlah of Masre'kah reigned in his stead. Samlah died, and Shaul of Reho'both on the Eu-phra'tes reigned in his stead. 38 Shaul died, and Ba'al-ha'nan the son of Achbor reigned in his 39 stead. Ba'al-ha'nan the son of Achbor died, and Hadar reigned in his stead, the name of his city being Pau; his wife's name was Mehet'abel, the daughter of Matred, daughter of Mez'ahab. 40 These are the names of the chiefs of Esau, according to their families and their dwelling places, by their names: the 41 chiefs Timna, Alvah, Jetheth, Oholiba'mah, Elah, Pinon, 42, 43 Kenaz, Teman, Mibzar, Mag'diel, and Iram; these are the chiefs of Edom (that is, Esau, the father of Edom), according to their dwelling places in the land of their possession.

JOSEPH
Joseph Comes to Egypt

37 Jacob dwelt in the land of his father's sojournings, 2 in the land of Canaan. This is the history of the family of Jacob.

Joseph, being seventeen years old, was shepherding the flock with his brothers; he was a lad with the sons of Bilhah and Zilpah, his father's wives; and Joseph brought 3 an ill report of them to their father. Now Israel loved Joseph more than any other of his children, because he was the son of his old age; and he made him a long robe 4 with sleeves. But when his brothers saw that their father loved him more than all his brothers, they hated him, and could not speak peaceably to him.

5 Now Joseph had a dream, and when he told it to his 6 brothers they only hated him the more. He said to them, 7 "Hear this dream which I have dreamed: behold, we were binding sheaves in the field, and lo, my sheaf arose and stood upright; and behold, your sheaves gathered round 8 it, and bowed down to my sheaf." His brothers said to him, "Are you indeed to reign over us? Or are you indeed to have dominion over us?" So they hated him yet 9 more for his dreams and for his words. Then he dreamed another dream, and told it to his brothers, and said, "Behold, I have dreamed another dream; and behold, the sun, the moon, and eleven stars were bowing down to 10 me." But when he told it to his father and to his brothers his father rebuked him, and said to him, "What is this dream that you have dreamed? Shall I and your mother and your brothers indeed come to bow ourselves to the 11 ground before you?" And his brothers were jealous of him, but his father kept the saying in mind.

12 Now his brothers went to pasture their father's flock 13 near Shechem. And Israel said to Joseph, "Are not your brothers pasturing the flock at Shechem? Come, I will send you to them." And he said to him, "Here I am." 14 So he said to him, "Go now, see if it is well with your brothers, and with the flock; and bring me word again."

So he sent him from the valley of Hebron, and he came 15 to Shechem. And a man found him wandering in the fields; and the man asked him, "What are you seeking?" 16 "I am seeking my brothers," he said, "tell me, I pray 17 you, where they are pasturing the flock." And the man said, "They have gone away, for I heard them say, 'Let us go to Dothan.'" So Joseph went after his brothers, and 18 found them at Dothan. They saw him afar off, and before he came near to them they conspired against him to kill 19 him. They said to one another, "Here comes this dreamer. 20 Come now, let us kill him and throw him into one of the pits; then we shall say that a wild beast has devoured him, 21 and we shall see what will become of his dreams." But when Reuben heard it, he delivered him out of their 22 hands, saying, "Let us not take his life." And Reuben said to them, "Shed no blood; cast him into this pit here in the wilderness, but lay no hand upon him"—that he might rescue him out of their hand, to restore him to 23 his father. So when Joseph came to his brothers, they stripped him of his robe, the long robe with sleeves that 24 he wore; and they took him and cast him into a pit. The pit was empty, there was no water in it.

25 Then they sat down to eat; and looking up they saw a caravan of Ish'maelites coming from Gilead, with their camels bearing gum, balm, and myrrh, on their way to 26 carry it down to Egypt. Then Judah said to his brothers, "What profit is it if we slay our brother and conceal his 27 blood? Come, let us sell him to the Ish'maelites, and let not our hand be upon him, for he is our brother, our own 28 flesh." And his brothers heeded him. Then Mid'ianite traders passed by; and they drew Joseph up and lifted him out of the pit, and sold him to the Ish'maelites for twenty shekels of silver; and they took Joseph to Egypt.

29 When Reuben returned to the pit and saw that Joseph 30 was not in the pit, he rent his clothes and returned to his brothers, and said, "The lad is gone; and I, where shall 31 I go?" Then they took Joseph's robe, and killed a goat, 32 and dipped the robe in the blood; and they sent the long robe with sleeves and brought it to their father, and said, "This we have found; see now whether it is your son's 33 robe or not." And he recognized it, and said, "It is my son's robe; a wild beast has devoured him; Joseph is 34 without doubt torn to pieces." Then Jacob rent his garments, and put sackcloth upon his loins, and mourned 35 for his son many days. All his sons and all his daughters rose up to comfort him; but he refused to be comforted, and said, "No, I shall go down to Sheol to my son, 36 mourning." Thus his father wept for him. Meanwhile the Mid'ianites had sold him in Egypt to Pot'i-phar, an officer of Pharaoh, the captain of the guard.

JUDAH AND TAMAR

38 It happened at that time that Judah went down from his brothers, and turned in to a certain Adullamite, whose

²name was Hirah. There Judah saw the daughter of a certain Canaanite whose name was Shua; he married her and went in
³to her, and she conceived and bore a son, and he called his
⁴name Er. Again she conceived and bore a son, and she called
⁵his name Onan. Yet again she bore a son, and she called his
⁶name Shelah. She ᵍ was in Chezib when she bore him. And Judah took a wife for Er his first-born, and her name was
⁷Tamar. But Er, Judah's first-born, was wicked in the sight of
⁸the LORD; and the LORD slew him. Then Judah said to Onan, "Go in to your brother's wife, and perform the duty of a brother-in-law to her, and raise up offspring for your brother."
⁹But Onan knew that the offspring would not be his; so when he went in to his brother's wife he spilled the semen on the ground,
¹⁰lest she should give offspring to his brother. And what he did was displeasing in the sight of the LORD, and he slew him also.

¹¹Then Judah said to Tamar his daughter-in-law, "Remain a widow in your father's house, till Shelah my son grows up" —for he feared that he would die, like his brothers. So Tamar went and dwelt in her father's house.
¹²In course of time the wife of Judah, Shua's daughter, died; and when Judah was comforted, he went up to Timnah to his
¹³sheepshearers, he and his friend Hirah the Adullamite. And when Tamar was told, "Your father-in-law is going up to
¹⁴Timnah to shear his sheep," she put off her widow's garments, put on a veil, wrapping herself up, and sat at the entrance to Enaim, which is on the road to Timnah; for she saw that Shelah was grown up, and she had not been given to him
¹⁵in marriage. When Judah saw her, he thought her to be a
¹⁶harlot, for she had covered her face. He went over to her at the road side, and said, "Come, let me come in to you," for he did not know that she was his daughter-in-law. She said, "What
¹⁷will you give me, that you may come in to me?" He answered, "I will send you a kid from the flock." And she said,
¹⁸"Will you give me a pledge, till you send it?" He said, "What pledge shall I give you?" She replied, "Your signet and your cord, and your staff that is in your hand." So he gave them to
¹⁹her, and went in to her, and she conceived by him. Then she arose and went away, and taking off her veil she put on the garments of her widowhood.
²⁰When Judah sent the kid by his friend the Adullamite, to receive the pledge from the woman's hand, he could not find
²¹her. And he asked the men of the place, "Where is the harlot ʰ who was at Enaim by the wayside?" And they said, "No harlot ʰ
²²has been here." So he returned to Judah, and said, "I have not found her; and also the men of the place said, 'No harlot ʰ
²³has been here.'" And Judah replied, "Let her keep the things as her own, lest we be laughed at; you see, I sent this kid, and you could not find her."
²⁴About three months later Judah was told, "Tamar your daughter-in-law has played the harlot; and moreover she is with child by harlotry." And Judah said, "Bring her out, and
²⁵let her be burned." As she was being brought out, she sent word to her father-in-law, "By the man to whom these belong, I am with child." And she said, "Mark, I pray you, whose these
²⁶are, the signet and the cord and the staff." Then Judah acknowledged them and said, "She is more righteous than I, inasmuch as I did not give her to my son Shelah." And he did not lie with her again.
²⁷When the time of her delivery came, there were twins in
²⁸her womb. And when she was in labor, one put out a hand; and the midwife took and bound on his hand a scarlet thread,
²⁹saying, "This came out first." But as he drew back his hand, behold, his brother came out; and she said, "What a breach you have made for yourself!" Therefore his name was called
³⁰Perez. ⁱ Afterward his brother came out with the scarlet thread upon his hand; and his name was called Zerah.

Joseph in Egypt

39 Now Joseph was taken down to Egypt, and Pot'i-phar, an officer of Pharaoh, the captain of the guard, an Egyptian, bought him from the Ish'maelites who had
²brought him down there. The LORD was with Joseph, and he became a successful man; and he was in the house of
³his master the Egyptian, and his master saw that the LORD was with him, and that the LORD caused all that he did to
⁴prosper in his hands. So Joseph found favor in his sight and attended him, and he made him overseer of his house
⁵and put him in charge of all that he had. From the time that he made him overseer in his house and over all that he had the LORD blessed the Egyptian's house for Joseph's sake; the blessing of the LORD was upon all that he had,
⁶in house and field. So he left all that he had in Joseph's charge; and having him he had no concern for anything but the food which he ate.
⁷Now Joseph was handsome and good-looking. And after a time his master's wife cast her eyes upon Joseph,
⁸and said, "Lie with me." But he refused and said to his master's wife, "Lo, having me my master has no concern about anything in the house, and he has put everything
⁹that he has in my hand; he is not greater in this house than I am; nor has he kept back anything from me except yourself, because you are his wife; how then can I do this
¹⁰great wickedness, and sin against God?" And although she spoke to Joseph day after day, he would not listen
¹¹to her, to lie with her or to be with her. But one day, when he went into the house to do his work and none of
¹²the men of the house was there in the house, she caught him by his garment, saying, "Lie with me." But he left his garment in her hand, and fled and got out of the
¹³house. And when she saw that he had left his garment in
¹⁴her hand, and had fled out of the house, she called to the men of her household and said to them, "See, he has brought among us a Hebrew to insult us; he came in to me to lie with me, and I cried out with a loud voice;
¹⁵and when he heard that I lifted up my voice and cried, he left his garment with me, and fled and got out of the
¹⁶house." Then she laid up his garment by her until his
¹⁷master came home, and she told him the same story, saying, "The Hebrew servant, whom you have brought among
¹⁸us, came in to me to insult me; but as soon as I lifted up my voice and cried, he left his garment with me, and fled out of the house."
¹⁹When his master heard the words which his wife spoke to him, "This is the way your servant treated me," his
²⁰anger was kindled. And Joseph's master took him and put him into the prison, the place where the king's
²¹prisoners were confined, and he was there in prison. But the LORD was with Joseph and showed him steadfast love, and gave him favor in the sight of the keeper of the
²²prison. And the keeper of the prison committed to

ᵍ Gk: Heb He   ʰ Or *cult prostitute*   ⁱ That is *A breach*

Joseph's care all the prisoners who were in the prison; and whatever was done there, he was the doer of it; 23 the keeper of the prison paid no heed to anything that was in Joseph's care, because the LORD was with him; and whatever he did, the LORD made it prosper.

Interpreter of Dreams

40 Some time after this, the butler of the king of Egypt and his baker offended their lord the king of 2 Egypt. And Pharaoh was angry with his two officers, the 3 chief butler and the chief baker, and he put them in custody in the house of the captain of the guard, in the 4 prison where Joseph was confined. The captain of the guard charged Joseph with them, and he waited on them; 5 and they continued for some time in custody. And one night they both dreamed—the butler and the baker of the king of Egypt, who were confined in the prison—each his own dream, and each dream with its own meaning. 6 When Joseph came to them in the morning and saw them, 7 they were troubled. So he asked Pharaoh's officers who were with him in custody in his master's house, "Why 8 are your faces downcast today?" They said to him, "We have had dreams, and there is no one to interpret them." And Joseph said to them, "Do not interpretations belong to God? Tell them to me, I pray you." 9 So the chief butler told his dream to Joseph, and said 10 to him, "In my dream there was a vine before me, and on the vine there were three branches; as soon as it budded, its blossoms shot forth, and the clusters ripened 11 into grapes. Pharaoh's cup was in my hand; and I took

the grapes and pressed them into Pharaoh's cup, and 12 placed the cup in Pharaoh's hand." Then Joseph said to him, "This is its interpretation: the three branches are 13 three days; within three days Pharaoh will lift up your head and restore you to your office; and you shall place Pharaoh's cup in his hand as formerly, when you were 14 his butler. But remember me, when it is well with you, and do me the kindness, I pray you, to make mention of 15 me to Pharaoh, and so get me out of this house. For I was indeed stolen out of the land of the Hebrews; and here also I have done nothing that they should put me into the dungeon." 16 When the chief baker saw that the interpretation was favorable, he said to Joseph, "I also had a dream: there

j Gk: Heb them

17 were three cake baskets on my head, and in the uppermost basket there were all sorts of baked food for Pharaoh, but the birds were eating it out of the basket on my 18 head." And Joseph answered, "This is its interpretation: 19 the three baskets are three days; within three days Pharaoh will lift up your head—from you!—and hang you on a tree; and the birds will eat the flesh from you."

20 On the third day, which was Pharaoh's birthday, he made a feast for all his servants, and lifted up the head of the chief butler and the head of the chief baker among 21 his servants. He restored the chief butler to his butlership, 22 and he placed the cup in Pharaoh's hand; but he hanged 23 the chief baker, as Joseph had interpreted to them. Yet the chief butler did not remember Joseph, but forgot him.

Joseph's Rise to Power

41 After two whole years, Pharaoh dreamed that he 2 was standing by the Nile, and behold, there came up out of the Nile seven cows sleek and fat, and they fed in 3 the reed grass. And behold, seven other cows, gaunt and thin, came up out of the Nile after them, and stood by the 4 other cows on the bank of the Nile. And the gaunt and thin cows ate up the seven sleek and fat cows. And 5 Pharaoh awoke. And he fell asleep and dreamed a second time; and behold, seven ears of grain, plump and good, 6 were growing on one stalk. And behold, after them sprouted seven ears, thin and blighted by the east wind. 7 And the thin ears swallowed up the seven plump and full ears. And Pharaoh awoke, and behold, it was a dream. 8 So in the morning his spirit was troubled; and he sent and called for all the magicians of Egypt and all its wise men; and Pharaoh told them his dream, but there was none who could interpret it j to Pharaoh.

9 Then the chief butler said to Pharaoh, "I remember my 10 faults today. When Pharaoh was angry with his servants, and put me and the chief baker in custody in the house 11 of the captain of the guard, we dreamed on the same night, he and I, each having a dream with its own 12 meaning. A young Hebrew was there with us, a servant of the captain of the guard; and when we told him, he interpreted our dreams to us, giving an interpretation to 13 each man according to his dream. And as he interpreted to us, so it came to pass; I was restored to my office, and the baker was hanged."

14 Then Pharaoh sent and called Joseph, and they brought him hastily out of the dungeon; and when he had shaved himself and changed his clothes, he came in before 15 Pharaoh. And Pharoah said to Joseph, "I have had a dream, and there is no one who can interpret it; and I have heard it said of you that when you hear a dream you 16 can interpret it." Joseph answered Pharaoh, "It is not in 17 me; God will give Pharaoh a favorable answer." Then Pharaoh said to Joseph, "Behold, in my dream I was

18 standing on the banks of the Nile; and seven cows, fat and sleek, came up out of the Nile and fed in the reed
19 grass; and seven other cows came up after them, poor and very gaunt and thin, such as I had never seen in all
20 the land of Egypt. And the thin and gaunt cows ate up
21 the first seven fat cows, but when they had eaten them no one would have known that they had eaten them, for they were still as gaunt as at the beginning. Then I awoke.
22 I also saw in my dream seven ears growing on one stalk,
23 full and good; and seven ears, withered, thin, and
24 blighted by the east wind, sprouted after them, and the thin ears swallowed up the seven good ears. And I told it to the magicians, but there was no one who could explain it to me."

25 Then Joseph said to Pharaoh, "The dream of Pharaoh is one; God has revealed to Pharaoh what he is about to
26 do. The seven good cows are seven years, and the seven
27 good ears are seven years; the dream is one. The seven lean and gaunt cows that came up after them are seven years, and the seven empty ears blighted by the east wind
28 are also seven years of famine. It is as I told Pharaoh,
29 God has shown to Pharaoh what he is about to do. There will come seven years of great plenty throughout all the
30 land of Egypt, but after them there will arise seven years of famine, and all the plenty will be forgotten in the land
31 of Egypt; the famine will consume the land, and the plenty will be unknown in the land by reason of that famine which will follow, for it will be very grievous.
32 And the doubling of Pharaoh's dream means that the thing is fixed by God, and God will shortly bring it to
33 pass. Now therefore let Pharaoh select a man discreet and
34 wise, and set him over the land of Egypt. Let Pharaoh proceed to appoint overseers over the land, and take the fifth part of the produce of the land of Egypt during the
35 seven plenteous years. And let them gather all the food of these good years that are coming, and lay up grain under the authority of Pharaoh for food in the cities, and
36 let them keep it. That food shall be a reserve for the land against the seven years of famine which are to befall the land of Egypt, so that the land may not perish through the famine."

37 This proposal seemed good to Pharaoh and to all his
38 servants. And Pharaoh said to his servants, "Can we find such a man as this, in whom is the Spirit of God?"
39 So Pharaoh said to Joseph, "Since God has shown you all this, there is none so discreet and wise as you are;
40 you shall be over my house, and all my people shall order themselves as you command; only as regards the throne
41 will I be greater than you." And Pharaoh said to Joseph,
42 "Behold, I have set you over all the land of Egypt." Then Pharaoh took his signet ring from his hand and put it on Joseph's hand, and arrayed him in garments of fine linen,
43 and put a gold chain about his neck; and he made him to

ride in his second chariot; and they cried before him, "Bow the knee!" k Thus he set him over all the land of
44 Egypt. Moreover Pharaoh said to Joseph, "I am Pharaoh, and without your consent no man shall lift up hand or
45 foot in all the land of Egypt." And Pharaoh called Joseph's name Zaph'enath-pane'ah; and he gave him in marriage As'enath, the daughter of Poti'phera priest of On. So Joseph went out over the land of Egypt.

46 Joseph was thirty years old when he entered the service of Pharaoh king of Egypt. And Joseph went out from the presence of Pharaoh, and went through all the land of
47 Egypt. During the seven plenteous years the earth brought
48 forth abundantly, and he gathered up all the food of the seven years when there was plenty [1] in the land of Egypt,

and stored up food in the cities; he stored up in every
49 city the food from the fields around it. And Joseph stored up grain in great abundance, like the sand of the sea, until he ceased to measure it, for it could not be measured.
50 Before the year of famine came, Joseph had two sons, whom As'enath, the daughter of Poti'phera priest of On,
51 bore to him. Joseph called the name of the first-born Manas'seh,[m] "For," he said, "God has made me forget
52 all my hardship and all my father's house." The name of the second he called E'phraim,[n] "For God has made me fruitful in the land of my affliction."
53 The seven years of plenty that prevailed in the land of
54 Egypt came to an end; and the seven years of famine began to come, as Joseph had said. There was famine in all lands; but in all the land of Egypt there was bread.
55 When all the land of Egypt was famished, the people cried to Pharaoh for bread; and Pharaoh said to all the Egyptians, "Go to Joseph; what he says to you, do."
56 So when the famine had spread over all the land, Joseph opened all the storehouses,[o] and sold to the Egyptians, for
57 the famine was severe in the land of Egypt. Moreover, all the earth came to Egypt to Joseph to buy grain, because the famine was severe over all the earth.

Joseph and His Brothers in Egypt

42 When Jacob learned that there was grain in Egypt, he said to his sons, "Why do you look at
2 one another?" And he said, "Behold, I have heard that there is grain in Egypt; go down and buy grain for us
3 there, that we may live, and not die." So ten of Joseph's
4 brothers went down to buy grain in Egypt. But Jacob did not send Benjamin, Joseph's brother, with his brothers,

k Abrek, probably an Egyptian word similar in sound to the Hebrew word meaning to kneel
m That is Making to forget   n From a Hebrew word meaning to be fruitful
o Gk Vg Compare Syr: Heb all that was in them

l Sam Gk: Heb which were

31

5 for he feared that harm might befall him. Thus the sons of Israel came to buy among the others who came, for the famine was in the land of Canaan.

6 Now Joseph was governor over the land; he it was who sold to all the people of the land. And Joseph's brothers came, and bowed themselves before him with their faces 7 to the ground. Joseph saw his brothers, and knew them, but he treated them like strangers and spoke roughly to them. "Where do you come from?" he said. They said, 8 "From the land of Canaan, to buy food." Thus Joseph 9 knew his brothers, but they did not know him. And Joseph remembered the dreams which he had dreamed of them; and he said to them, "You are spies, you have 10 come to see the weakness of the land." They said to him, "No, my lord, but to buy food have your servants come. 11 We are all sons of one man, we are honest men, your 12 servants are not spies." He said to them, "No, it is the 13 weakness of the land that you have come to see." And they said, "We, your servants, are twelve brothers, the sons of one man in the land of Canaan; and behold, the youngest is this day with our father, and one is no more." 14 But Joseph said to them, "It is as I said to you, you are 15 spies. By this you shall be tested: by the life of Pharaoh, you shall not go from this place unless your youngest 16 brother comes here. Send one of you, and let him bring your brother, while you remain in prison, that your words may be tested, whether there is truth in you; or else, by 17 the life of Pharaoh, surely you are spies." And he put them all together in prison for three days.

18 On the third day Joseph said to them, "Do this and you 19 will live, for I fear God: if you are honest men, let one of your brothers remain confined in your prison, and let the rest go and carry grain for the famine of your house- 20 holds, and bring your youngest brother to me; so your words will be verified, and you shall not die." And they 21 did so. Then they said to one another, "In truth we are guilty concerning our brother, in that we saw the distress of his soul, when he besought us and we would not listen; 22 therefore is this distress come upon us." And Reuben answered them, "Did I not tell you not to sin against the lad? But you would not listen. So now there comes a 23 reckoning for his blood." They did not know that Joseph understood them, for there was an interpreter between 24 them. Then he turned away from them and wept; and he returned to them and spoke to them. And he took Simeon 25 from them and bound him before their eyes. And Joseph gave orders to fill their bags with grain, and to replace every man's money in his sack, and to give them provisions for the journey. This was done for them.

The Brothers' Return to Canaan

26 Then they loaded their asses with their grain, and de- 27 parted. And as one of them opened his sack to give his ass provender at the lodging place, he saw his money in 28 the mouth of his sack; and he said to his brothers, "My money has been put back; here it is in the mouth of my sack!" At this their hearts failed them, and they turned trembling to one another, saying, "What is this that God has done to us?"

29 When they came to Jacob their father in the land of Canaan, they told him all that had befallen them, saying, 30 "The man, the lord of the land, spoke roughly to us, and 31 took us to be spies of the land. But we said to him, 'We 32 are honest men, we are not spies; we are twelve brothers, sons of our father; one is no more, and the youngest is 33 this day with our father in the land of Canaan.' Then the man, the lord of the land, said to us, 'By this I shall know that you are honest men: leave one of your brothers with me, and take grain for the famine of your households, 34 and go your way. Bring your youngest brother to me; then I shall know that you are not spies but honest men, and I will deliver to you your brother, and you shall trade in the land.' "

35 As they emptied their sacks, behold, every man's bundle of money was in his sack; and when they and their father 36 saw their bundles of money, they were dismayed. And Jacob their father said to them, "You have bereaved me of my children: Joseph is no more, and Simeon is no more, and now you would take Benjamin; all this has 37 come upon me." Then Reuben said to his father, "Slay

my two sons if I do not bring him back to you; put him 38 in my hands, and I will bring him back to you." But he said, "My son shall not go down with you, for his brother is dead, and he only is left. If harm should befall him on the journey that you are to make, you would bring down my gray hairs with sorrow to Sheol."

The Brothers' Second Journey to Egypt

43 Now the famine was severe in the land. And when they had eaten the grain which they had brought from Egypt, their father said to them, "Go again, buy us

3 a little food." But Judah said to him, "The man solemnly warned us, saying, 'You shall not see my face, unless your 4 brother is with you.' If you will send our brother with us, 5 we will go down and buy you food; but if you will not send him, we will not go down, for the man said to us, 'You shall not see my face, unless your brother is with 6 you.'" Israel said, "Why did you treat me so ill as to 7 tell the man that you had another brother?" They replied, "The man questioned us carefully about ourselves and our kindred, saying, 'Is your father still alive? Have you another brother?' What we told him was in answer to these questions; could we in any way know that he would say, 8 'Bring your brother down'?" And Judah said to Israel his father, "Send the lad with me, and we will arise and go, that we may live and not die, both we and you and 9 also our little ones. I will be surety for him; of my hand you shall require him. If I do not bring him back to you and set him before you, then let me bear the blame for 10 ever; for if we had not delayed, we would now have returned twice."

11 Then their father Israel said to them, "If it must be so, then do this: take some of the choice fruits of the land in your bags, and carry down to the man a present, a little balm and a little honey, gum, myrrh, pistachio nuts, and 12 almonds. Take double the money with you; carry back with you the money that was returned in the mouth of 13 your sacks; perhaps it was an oversight. Take also your 14 brother, and arise, go again to the man; may God Almighty ᴾ grant you mercy before the man, that he may send back your other brother and Benjamin. If I am 15 bereaved of my children, I am bereaved." So the men took the present, and they took double the money with them, and Benjamin; and they arose and went down to Egypt, and stood before Joseph.

Joseph's Meeting With Benjamin

16 When Joseph saw Benjamin with them, he said to the steward of his house, "Bring the men into the house, and slaughter an animal and make ready, for the men are to 17 dine with me at noon." The man did as Joseph bade him, 18 and brought the men to Joseph's house. And the men were afraid because they were brought to Joseph's house, and they said, "It is because of the money, which was replaced in our sacks the first time, that we are brought in, so that he may seek occasion against us and fall upon us, to make 19 slaves of us and seize our asses." So they went up to the steward of Joseph's house, and spoke with him at the door 20 of the house, and said, "Oh, my lord, we came down the 21 first time to buy food; and when we came to the lodging place we opened our sacks, and there was every man's money in the mouth of his sack, our money in full 22 weight; so we have brought it again with us, and we have brought other money down in our hand to buy

ᴾ Heb *El Shaddai*

food. We do not know who put our money in our 23 sacks." He replied, "Rest assured, do not be afraid; your God and the God of your father must have put treasure in your sacks for you; I received your money." Then he 24 brought Simeon out to them. And when the man had brought the men into Joseph's house, and given them water, and they had washed their feet, and when he had 25 given their asses provender, they made ready the present for Joseph's coming at noon, for they heard that they should eat bread there.

26 When Joseph came home, they brought into the house to him the present which they had with them, and bowed 27 down to him to the ground. And he inquired about their welfare, and said, "Is your father well, the old man of 28 whom you spoke? Is he still alive?" They said, "Your servant our father is well, he is still alive." And they 29 bowed their heads and made obeisance. And he lifted up his eyes, and saw his brother Benjamin, his mother's son, and said, "Is this your youngest brother, of whom you 30 spoke to me? God be gracious to you, my son!" Then Joseph made haste, for his heart yearned for his brother, and he sought a place to weep. And he entered his 31 chamber and wept there. Then he washed his face and came out; and controlling himself he said, "Let food be 32 served." They served him by himself, and them by themselves, and the Egyptians who ate with him by themselves, because the Egyptians might not eat bread with the Hebrews, for that is an abomination to the Egyptians. 33 And they sat before him, the first-born according to his birthright and the youngest according to his youth; and the men looked at one another in amazement. 34 Portions were taken to them from Joseph's table, but Benjamin's portion was five times as much as any of theirs. So they drank and were merry with him.

Benjamin in Jeopardy

44 Then he commanded the steward of his house, "Fill the men's sacks with food, as much as they can carry, and put each man's money in the mouth of 2 his sack, and put my cup, the silver cup, in the mouth of the sack of the youngest, with his money for the grain." 3 And he did as Joseph told him. As soon as the morning 4 was light, the men were sent away with their asses. When they had gone but a short distance from the city, Joseph said to his steward, "Up, follow after the men; and when

you overtake them, say to them, 'Why have you returned evil for good? Why have you stolen my silver cup? q
5 Is it not from this that my lord drinks, and by this that he divines? You have done wrong in so doing.' "
6 When he overtook them, he spoke to them these words.
7 They said to him, "Why does my lord speak such words as these? Far be it from your servants that they should
8 do such a thing! Behold, the money which we found in the mouth of our sacks, we brought back to you from

the land of Canaan; how then should we steal silver or
9 gold from your lord's house? With whomever of your servants it be found, let him die, and we also will be my
10 lord's slaves." He said, "Let it be as you say: he with whom it is found shall be my slave, and the rest of you
11 shall be blameless." Then every man quickly lowered his sack to the ground, and every man opened his sack.
12 And he searched, beginning with the eldest and ending with the youngest; and the cup was found in Benjamin's
13 sack. Then they rent their clothes, and every man loaded his ass, and they returned to the city.
14 When Judah and his brothers came to Joseph's house, he was still there; and they fell before him to the ground.
15 Joseph said to them, "What deed is this that you have done? Do you not know that such a man as I can indeed
16 divine?" And Judah said, "What shall we say to my lord? What shall we speak? Or how can we clear ourselves? God has found out the guilt of your servants; behold, we are my lord's slaves, both we and he also in
17 whose hand the cup has been found." But he said, "Far be it from me that I should do so! Only the man in whose hand the cup was found shall be my slave; but as for you, go up in peace to your father."
18 Then Judah went up to him and said, "O my lord, let your servant, I pray you, speak a word in my lord's ears, and let not your anger burn against your servant; for you
19 are like Pharaoh himself. My lord asked his servants,
20 saying, 'Have you a father, or a brother?' And we said to my lord, 'We have a father, an old man, and a young brother, the child of his old age; and his brother is dead, and he alone is left of his mother's children; and his
21 father loves him.' Then you said to your servants, 'Bring
22 him down to me, that I may set my eyes upon him.' We said to my lord, 'The lad cannot leave his father, for if
23 he should leave his father, his father would die.' Then you said to your servants, 'Unless your youngest brother

q Gk Compare Vg: Heb lacks Why have you stolen my silver cup?

comes down with you, you shall see my face no more.'
24 When we went back to your servant my father we told
25 him the words of my lord. And when our father said, 'Go
26 again, buy us a little food,' we said, 'We cannot go down. If our youngest brother goes with us, then we will go down; for we cannot see the man's face unless our young-
27 est brother is with us.' Then your servant my father said
28 to us, 'You know that my wife bore me two sons; one left me, and I said, Surely he has been torn to pieces; and I
29 have never seen him since. If you take this one also from me, and harm befalls him, you will bring down my gray
30 hairs in sorrow to Sheol.' Now therefore, when I come to your servant my father, and the lad is not with us, then,
31 as his life is bound up in the lad's life, when he sees that the lad is not with us, he will die; and your servants will bring down the gray hairs of your servant our father
32 with sorrow to Sheol. For your servant became surety for the lad to my father, saying, 'If I do not bring him back to you, then I shall bear the blame in the sight of my
33 father all my life.' Now therefore, let your servant, I pray you, remain instead of the lad as a slave to my lord; and
34 let the lad go back with his brothers. For how can I go back to my father if the lad is not with me? I fear to see the evil that would come upon my father."

Joseph Reveals His Identity

45 Then Joseph could not control himself before all those who stood by him; and he cried, "Make every one go out from me." So no one stayed with him when
2 Joseph made himself known to his brothers. And he wept aloud, so that the Egyptians heard it, and the household
3 of Pharaoh heard it. And Joseph said to his brothers, "I am Joseph; is my father still alive?" But his brothers could not answer him, for they were dismayed at his presence.
4 So Joseph said to his brothers, "Come near to me, I pray you." And they came near. And he said, "I am
5 your brother, Joseph, whom you sold into Egypt. And now do not be distressed, or angry with yourselves, because you sold me here; for God sent me before you to
6 preserve life. For the famine has been in the land these two years; and there are yet five years in which there
7 will be neither plowing nor harvest. And God sent me before you to preserve for you a remnant on earth, and to
8 keep alive for you many survivors. So it was not you who sent me here, but God; and he has made me a father to Pharaoh, and lord of all his house and ruler over all
9 the land of Egypt. Make haste and go up to my father and say to him, 'Thus says your son Joseph, God has made me lord of all Egypt; come down to me, do not tarry;
10 you shall dwell in the land of Goshen, and you shall be near me, you and your children and your children's children, and your flocks, your herds, and all that you

11 have; and there I will provide for you, for there are yet five years of famine to come; lest you and your house-
12 hold, and all that you have, come to poverty.' And now your eyes see, and the eyes of my brother Benjamin see,
13 that it is my mouth that speaks to you. You must tell my father of all my splendor in Egypt, and of all that you have seen. Make haste and bring my father down here."
14 Then he fell upon his brother Benjamin's neck and wept;
15 and Benjamin wept upon his neck. And he kissed all his brothers and wept upon them; and after that his brothers talked with him.
16 When the report was heard in Pharaoh's house, "Joseph's brothers have come," it pleased Pharaoh and
17 his servants well. And Pharaoh said to Joseph, "Say to your brothers, 'Do this: load your beasts and go back to
18 the land of Canaan; and take your father and your house-holds, and come to me, and I will give you the best of the land of Egypt, and you shall eat the fat of the land.'
19 Command them r also, 'Do this: take wagons from the land of Egypt for your little ones and for your wives,
20 and bring your father, and come. Give no thought to your goods, for the best of all the land of Egypt is yours.' "
21 The sons of Israel did so; and Joseph gave them wagons, according to the command of Pharaoh, and gave
22 them provisions for the journey. To each and all of them he gave festal garments; but to Benjamin he gave three
23 hundred shekels of silver and five festal garments. To his father he sent as follows: ten asses loaded with the good things of Egypt, and ten she-asses loaded with grain,
24 bread, and provision for his father on the journey. Then he sent his brothers away, and as they departed, he said
25 to them, "Do not quarrel on the way." So they went up

out of Egypt, and came to the land of Canaan to their
26 father Jacob. And they told him, "Joseph is still alive, and he is ruler over all the land of Egypt." And his heart
27 fainted, for he did not believe them. But when they told him all the words of Joseph, which he had said to them, and when he saw the wagons which Joseph had sent to
28 carry him, the spirit of their father Jacob revived; and Israel said, "It is enough; Joseph my son is still alive; I will go and see him before I die."

Jacob in Egypt

46 So Israel took his journey with all that he had, and came to Beer-sheba, and offered sacrifices to
2 the God of his father Isaac. And God spoke to Israel in visions of the night, and said, "Jacob, Jacob." And he
3 said, "Here am I." Then he said, "I am God, the God of your father; do not be afraid to go down to Egypt; for I
4 will there make of you a great nation. I will go down with you to Egypt; and I will also bring you up again; and
5 Joseph's hand shall close your eyes." Then Jacob set out from Beer-sheba; and the sons of Israel carried Jacob their father, their little ones, and their wives, in the
6 wagons which Pharaoh had sent to carry him. They also took their cattle and their goods, which they had gained in the land of Canaan, and came into Egypt, Jacob and all
7 his offspring with him, his sons, and his sons' sons with him, his daughters, and his sons' daughters; all his off-spring he brought with him into Egypt.

Jacob's Family

8 Now these are the names of the descendants of Israel, who came into Egypt, Jacob and his sons. Reuben, Jacob's first-born,
9 and the sons of Reuben: Hanoch, Pallu, Hezron, and Carmi.
10 The sons of Simeon: Jemu'el, Jamin, Ohad, Jachin, Zohar, and
11 Shaul, the son of a Canaanitish woman. The sons of Levi:
12 Gershon, Kohath, and Merar'i. The sons of Judah: Er, Onan, Shelah, Perez, and Zerah (but Er and Onan died in the land of Canaan); and the sons of Perez were Hezron and Hamul.
13, 14 The sons of Is'sachar: Tola, Puvah, Iob, and Shimron. The
15 sons of Zeb'ulun: Sered, Elon, and Jah'leel (these are the sons of Leah, whom she bore to Jacob in Paddan-aram, together with his daughter Dinah; altogether his sons and his daughters
16 numbered thirty-three). The sons of Gad: Ziph'ion, Haggi,
17 Shuni, Ezbon, Eri, Aro'di, and Are'li. The sons of Asher: Imnah, Ishvah, Ishvi, Beri'ah, with Serah their sister. And the
18 sons of Beri'ah: Heber and Mal'chiel (these are the sons of Zilpah, whom Laban gave to Leah his daughter; and these she
19 bore to Jacob—sixteen persons). The sons of Rachel, Jacob's
20 wife: Joseph and Benjamin. And to Joseph in the land of Egypt were born Manas'seh and E'phraim, whom As'enath, the daugh-
21 ter of Poti'phera the priest of On, bore to him. And the sons of Benjamin: Bela, Becher, Ashbel, Gera, Na'aman, Ehi, Rosh,
22 Muppim, Huppim, and Ard (these are the sons of Rachel, who
23 were born to Jacob—fourteen persons in all). The sons of Dan:
24 Hushim. The sons of Naph'tali: Jahzeel, Guni, Jezer, and
25 Shillem (these are the sons of Bilhah, whom Laban gave to Rachel his daughter, and these she bore to Jacob—seven persons
26 in all). All the persons belonging to Jacob who came into Egypt, who were his own offspring, not including Jacob's sons'
27 wives, were sixty-six persons in all; and the sons of Joseph, who were born to him in Egypt, were two; all the persons of the house of Jacob, that came into Egypt, were seventy.

Jacob Settles in Goshen

28 He sent Judah before him to Joseph, to appear s before him in Goshen; and they came into the land of Goshen.
29 Then Joseph made ready his chariot and went up to meet Israel his father in Goshen; and he presented himself to him, and fell on his neck, and wept on his neck a good
30 while. Israel said to Joseph, "Now let me die, since I have
31 seen your face and know that you are still alive." Joseph said to his brothers and to his father's household, "I will go up and tell Pharaoh, and will say to him, 'My brothers and my father's household, who were in the land of

---

r Compare Gk Vg: Heb *you are commanded*   s Sam Syr Compare Gk Vg: Heb *to show the way*

32 Canaan, have come to me; and the men are shepherds, for they have been keepers of cattle; and they have brought their flocks, and their herds, and all that they 33 have.' When Pharaoh calls you, and says, 'What is your 34 occupation?' you shall say, 'Your servants have been keepers of cattle from our youth even until now, both we and our fathers,' in order that you may dwell in the land of Goshen; for every shepherd is an abomination to the Egyptians."

47 So Joseph went in and told Pharaoh, "My father and my brothers, with their flocks and herds and all that they possess, have come from the land of Canaan; 2 they are now in the land of Goshen." And from among his brothers he took five men and presented them to Pharaoh. 3 Pharaoh said to his brothers, "What is your occupation?" And they said to Pharaoh, "Your servants are shepherds, 4 as our fathers were." They said to Pharaoh, "We have come to sojourn in the land; for there is no pasture for your servants' flocks, for the famine is severe in the land of Canaan; and now, we pray you, let your servants dwell 5 in the land of Goshen." Then Pharaoh said to Joseph, 6 "Your father and your brothers have come to you. The land of Egypt is before you; settle your father and your brothers in the best of the land; let them dwell in the land of Goshen; and if you know any able men among them, put them in charge of my cattle."

7 Then Joseph brought in Jacob his father, and set him 8 before Pharaoh, and Jacob blessed Pharaoh. And Pharaoh said to Jacob, "How many are the days of the years 9 of your life?" And Jacob said to Pharaoh, "The days of the years of my sojourning are a hundred and thirty years; few and evil have been the days of the years of my life, and they have not attained to the days of the years of the life of my fathers in the days of their sojourn- 10 ing." And Jacob blessed Pharaoh, and went out from the 11 presence of Pharaoh. Then Joseph settled his father and his brothers, and gave them a possession in the land of Egypt, in the best of the land, in the land of Ram'eses, as 12 Pharaoh had commanded. And Joseph provided his father, his brothers, and all his father's household with food, according to the number of their dependents.

Joseph's Agrarian Policy

13 Now there was no food in all the land; for the famine was very severe, so that the land of Egypt and the land 14 of Canaan languished by reason of the famine. And Joseph gathered up all the money that was found in the land of Egypt and in the land of Canaan, for the grain which they bought; and Joseph brought the money into 15 Pharaoh's house. And when the money was all spent in the land of Egypt and in the land of Canaan, all the Egyptians came to Joseph, and said, "Give us food; why should we die before your eyes? For our money is gone."

16 And Joseph answered, "Give your cattle, and I will give you food in exchange for your cattle, if your money is 17 gone." So they brought their cattle to Joseph; and Joseph gave them food in exchange for the horses, the flocks, the herds, and the asses: and he supplied them with food 18 in exchange for all their cattle that year. And when that year was ended, they came to him the following year, and said to him, "We will not hide from my lord that our money is all spent; and the herds of cattle are my lord's; there is nothing left in the sight of my lord but our bodies 19 and our lands. Why should we die before your eyes, both we and our land? Buy us and our land for food, and we with our land will be slaves to Pharaoh; and give us seed, that we may live, and not die, and that the land may not be desolate."

20 So Joseph bought all the land of Egypt for Pharaoh; for all the Egyptians sold their fields, because the famine was severe upon them. The land became Pharaoh's; 21 and as for the people, he made slaves of them [t] from one 22 end of Egypt to the other. Only the land of the priests he did not buy; for the priests had a fixed allowance from Pharaoh, and lived on the allowance which Pharaoh gave 23 them; therefore they did not sell their land. Then Joseph

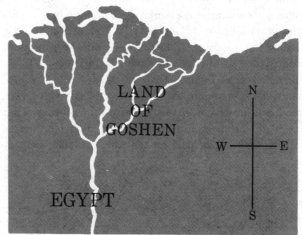

said to the people, "Behold, I have this day bought you and your land for Pharaoh. Now here is seed for you, 24 and you shall sow the land. And at the harvests you shall give a fifth to Pharaoh, and four fifths shall be your own, as seed for the field and as food for yourselves and your 25 households, and as food for your little ones." And they said, "You have saved our lives; may it please my lord, we 26 will be slaves to Pharaoh." So Joseph made it a statute concerning the land of Egypt, and it stands to this day, that Pharaoh should have the fifth; the land of the priests alone did not become Pharaoh's.

Jacob's Last Words to Joseph

27 Thus Israel dwelt in the land of Egypt, in the land of Goshen; and they gained possessions in it, and were fruit-

---

t Sam Gk Compare Vg: Heb *he removed them to the cities*

28 ful and multiplied exceedingly. And Jacob lived in the land of Egypt seventeen years; so the days of Jacob, the years of his life, were a hundred and forty-seven years.

29 And when the time drew near that Israel must die, he called his son Joseph and said to him, "If now I have found favor in your sight, put your hand under my thigh, and promise to deal loyally and truly with me. Do not 30 bury me in Egypt, but let me lie with my fathers; carry me out of Egypt and bury me in their burying place." He 31 answered, "I will do as you have said." And he said, "Swear to me"; and he swore to him. Then Israel bowed himself upon the head of his bed.

48 After this Joseph was told, "Behold, your father is ill"; so he took with him his two sons, Manas'seh 2 and E'phraim. And it was told to Jacob, "Your son Joseph has come to you"; then Israel summoned his strength, 3 and sat up in bed. And Jacob said to Joseph, "God Almighty u appeared to me at Luz in the land of Canaan 4 and blessed me, and said to me, 'Behold, I will make you fruitful, and multiply you, and I will make of you a company of peoples, and will give this land to your de-5 scendants after you for an everlasting possession.' And now your two sons, who were born to you in the land of Egypt before I came to you in Egypt, are mine; E'phraim and Manas'seh shall be mine, as Reuben and Simeon are. 6 And the offspring born to you after them shall be yours; they shall be called by the name of their brothers in their 7 inheritance. For when I came from Paddan, Rachel to my sorrow died in the land of Canaan on the way, when there was still some distance to go to Ephrath; and I buried her there on the way to Ephrath (that is, Bethlehem)."

8 When Israel saw Joseph's sons, he said, "Who are 9 these?" Joseph said to his father, "They are my sons, whom God has given me here." And he said, "Bring 10 them to me, I pray you, that I may bless them." Now the eyes of Israel were dim with age, so that he could not see. So Joseph brought them near him; and he kissed 11 them and embraced them. And Israel said to Joseph, "I had not thought to see your face; and lo, God has let me 12 see your children also." Then Joseph removed them from his knees, and he bowed himself with his face to the earth. 13 And Joseph took them both, E'phraim in his right hand toward Israel's left hand, and Manas'seh in his left hand toward Israel's right hand, and brought them near him. 14 And Israel stretched out his right hand and laid it upon the head of E'phraim, who was the younger, and his left hand upon the head of Manas'seh, crossing his hands, for 15 Manas'seh was the first-born. And he blessed Joseph, and said,

"The God before whom my fathers Abraham and Isaac walked,
the God who has led me all my life long to this day,

16 the angel who has redeemed me from all evil, bless the lads;
and in them let my name be perpetuated, and the name of my fathers Abraham and Isaac;
and let them grow into a multitude in the midst of the earth."

17 When Joseph saw that his father laid his right hand upon the head of E'phraim, it displeased him; and he took his father's hand, to remove it from E'phraim's head to 18 Manas'seh's head. And Joseph said to his father, "Not so, my father; for this one is the first-born; put your right 19 hand upon his head." But his father refused, and said, "I know, my son, I know; he also shall become a people, and he also shall be great; nevertheless his younger brother shall be greater than he, and his descendants shall become 20 a multitude of nations." So he blessed them that day, saying,

"By you Israel will pronounce blessings, saying,
'God make you as E'phraim and as Manas'seh' ";

21 and thus he put E'phraim before Manas'seh. Then Israel said to Joseph, "Behold, I am about to die, but God will be with you, and will bring you again to the land of your 22 fathers. Moreover I have given to you rather than to your brothers one mountain slope v which I took from the hand of the Amorites with my sword and with my bow."

Jacob Blesses His Sons and Dies

49 Then Jacob called his sons, and said, "Gather yourselves together, that I may tell you what shall befall you in days to come.
2 Assemble and hear, O sons of Jacob,
and hearken to Israel your father.

3 Reuben, you are my first-born,
my might, and the first fruits of my strength,
pre-eminent in pride and pre-eminent in power.
4 Unstable as water, you shall not have pre-eminence
because you went up to your father's bed;
then you defiled it—you w went up to my couch!

5 Simeon and Levi are brothers;
weapons of violence are their swords.
6 O my soul, come not into their council;
O my spirit,x be not joined to their company;
for in their anger they slay men,
and in their wantonness they hamstring oxen.
7 Cursed be their anger, for it is fierce;
and their wrath, for it is cruel!
I will divide them in Jacob
and scatter them in Israel.

8 Judah, your brothers shall praise you;
your hand shall be on the neck of your enemies;

u Heb El Shaddai   v Heb shekem, shoulder   w Gk Syr Tg: Heb he   x Or glory

your father's sons shall bow down before you.
⁹ Judah is a lion's whelp;
    from the prey, my son, you have gone up.
He stooped down, he couched as a lion,
    and as a lioness; who dares rouse him up?
¹⁰ The scepter shall not depart from Judah,
    nor the ruler's staff from between his feet,
until he comes to whom it belongs; ʸ
    and to him shall be the obedience of the peoples.
¹¹ Binding his foal to the vine
    and his ass's colt to the choice vine,
he washes his garments in wine
    and his vesture in the blood of grapes;
¹² his eyes shall be red with wine,
    and his teeth white with milk.

¹³ Zeb'ulun shall dwell at the shore of the sea;
    he shall become a haven for ships,
    and his border shall be at Sidon.

¹⁴ Is'sachar is a strong ass,
    crouching between the sheepfolds;
¹⁵ he saw that a resting place was good,
    and that the land was pleasant;
so he bowed his shoulder to bear,
    and became a slave at forced labor.

¹⁶ Dan shall judge his people
    as one of the tribes of Israel.
¹⁷ Dan shall be a serpent in the way,
    a viper by the path,
that bites the horse's heels
    so that his rider falls backward.
¹⁸ I wait for thy salvation, O Lord.

¹⁹ Raiders ᶻ shall raid Gad,
    but he shall raid at their heels.

²⁰ Asher's food shall be rich,
    and he shall yield royal dainties.

²¹ Naph'tali is a hind let loose,
    that bears comely fawns.ᵃ

²² Joseph is a fruitful bough,
    a fruitful bough by a spring;
    his branches run over the wall.
²³ The archers fiercely attacked him,
    shot at him, and harassed him sorely;
²⁴ yet his bow remained unmoved,
    his arms ᵇ were made agile
by the hands of the Mighty One of Jacob
    (by the name of the Shepherd, the Rock of Israel),
²⁵ by the God of your father who will help you,
    by God Almighty ᵘ who will bless you
with blessings of heaven above,
    blessings of the deep that couches beneath,
    blessings of the breasts and of the womb.
²⁶ The blessings of your father
    are mighty beyond the blessings of the eternal moun-
        tains,ᶜ
    the bounties of the everlasting hills;
may they be on the head of Joseph,
    and on the brow of him who was separate from his
        brothers.

²⁷ Benjamin is a ravenous wolf,
    in the morning devouring the prey,
    and at even dividing the spoil."

²⁸   All these are the twelve tribes of Israel; and this is
what their father said to them as he blessed them, bless-
²⁹ ing each with the blessing suitable to him. Then he
charged them, and said to them, "I am to be gathered to
my people; bury me with my fathers in the cave that is
³⁰ in the field of Ephron the Hittite, in the cave that is in
the field at Mach-pe'lah, to the east of Mamre, in the land
of Canaan, which Abraham bought with the field from
³¹ Ephron the Hittite to possess as a burying place. There
they buried Abraham and Sarah his wife; there they
buried Isaac and Rebekah his wife; and there I buried
³² Leah—the field and the cave that is in it were purchased
³³ from the Hittites." When Jacob finished charging his
sons, he drew up his feet into the bed, and breathed his
last, and was gathered to his people.

Burial of Jacob

50   Then Joseph fell on his father's face, and wept
² over him, and kissed him. And Joseph commanded his servants the physicians to embalm his father.
³ So the physicians embalmed Israel; forty days were required for it, for so many are required for embalming.
And the Egyptians wept for him seventy days.
⁴   And when the days of weeping for him were past,
Joseph spoke to the household of Pharaoh, saying, "If
now I have found favor in your eyes, speak, I pray you,
⁵ in the ears of Pharaoh, saying, My father made me swear,
saying, 'I am about to die: in my tomb which I hewed

ʸ Syr Compare Tg: Heb *until Shiloh comes* or *until he comes to Shiloh*
ᵃ Or *who gives beautiful words*   ᵇ Heb *the arms of his hands*

ᶻ Heb *gedud,* a raiding troop
ᶜ Compare Gk: Heb *of my progenitors to*

out for myself in the land of Canaan, there shall you bury me.' Now therefore let me go up, I pray you, and bury 6 my father; then I will return." And Pharaoh answered, "Go up, and bury your father, as he made you swear." 7 So Joseph went up to bury his father; and with him went up all the servants of Pharaoh, the elders of his house- 8 hold, and all the elders of the land of Egypt, as well as all the household of Joseph, his brothers, and his father's household; only their children, their flocks, and their 9 herds were left in the land of Goshen. And there went up with him both chariots and horsemen; it was a very great 10 company. When they came to the threshing floor of Atad, which is beyond the Jordan, they lamented there with a very great and sorrowful lamentation; and he made a 11 mourning for his father seven days. When the inhabitants of the land, the Canaanites, saw the mourning on the threshing floor of Atad, they said, "This is a grievous mourning to the Egyptians." Therefore the place was 12 named A'bel-mizraim; d it is beyond the Jordan. Thus 13 his sons did for him as he had commanded them; for his sons carried him to the land of Canaan, and buried him in the cave of the field at Mach-pe'lah, to the east of Mamre, which Abraham bought with the field from 14 Ephron the Hittite, to possess as a burying place. After he had buried his father, Joseph returned to Egypt with his brothers and all who had gone up with him to bury his father.

15 When Joseph's brothers saw that their father was dead, they said, "It may be that Joseph will hate us and pay us 16 back for all the evil which we did to him." So they sent a message to Joseph, saying, "Your father gave this com- 17 mand before he died, 'Say to Joseph, Forgive, I pray you, the transgression of your brothers and their sin, because they did evil to you.' And now, we pray you, forgive the transgression of the servants of the God of your father." 18 Joseph wept when they spoke to him. His brothers also came and fell down before him, and said, "Behold, we 19 are your servants." But Joseph said to them, "Fear not, 20 for am I in the place of God? As for you, you meant evil against me; but God meant it for good, to bring it about that many people should be kept alive, as they are today. 21 So do not fear; I will provide for you and your little ones." Thus he reassured them and comforted them.

Death of Joseph

22 So Joseph dwelt in Egypt, he and his father's house; 23 and Joseph lived a hundred and ten years. And Joseph saw E'phraim's children of the third generation; the chil- dren also of Machir the son of Manas'seh were born upon 24 Joseph's knees. And Joseph said to his brothers, "I am about to die; but God will visit you, and bring you up out of this land to the land which he swore to Abraham, 25 to Isaac, and to Jacob." Then Joseph took an oath of the sons of Israel, saying, "God will visit you, and you shall 26 carry up my bones from here." So Joseph died, being a hundred and ten years old; and they embalmed him, and he was put in a coffin in Egypt.

d That is *meadow* (or *mourning*) *of Egypt*

INTRODUCTION TO

EXODUS

The word "exodus" means "going out." This book tells of the going out, or deliverance, of the Hebrews from Egypt, where they had become slaves. Abraham's descendants had moved to Egypt to escape a great famine. Joseph helped them prosper in Egypt, and they grew in number. The Egyptians became worried over the number of Hebrews and made them slaves so they could control them. The kings or pharaohs of Egypt became cruel masters, and the Hebrews prayed to God to be free.

Exodus tells the thrilling story of how God prepared a great man, Moses, to be the leader of the slaves. In answer to their prayers God helped Moses bring the Hebrews out of their slavery in Egypt to the freedom of the land promised to Abraham.

This book tells how Moses worshiped God truly and listened to him faithfully. Through Moses God gave to mankind his great rules for living that we call the Ten Commandments (Exodus 20. 1-7).

The Book of Exodus was completed by about 400 B.C. during the time Genesis and several other books of the Old Testament were being finished. Be sure to read the introduction to Genesis on page 1 so that you can understand better how God helped men write Exodus and other Old Testament books.

THE BOOK OF

EXODUS

ISRAEL ENSLAVED

1 These are the names of the sons of Israel who came to Egypt with Jacob, each with his household:
2, 3 Reuben, Simeon, Levi, and Judah, Is'sachar, Zeb'ulun,
4, 5 and Benjamin, Dan and Naph'tali, Gad and Asher. All the offspring of Jacob were seventy persons; Joseph was al-
6 ready in Egypt. Then Joseph died, and all his brothers,
7 and all that generation. But the descendants of Israel were fruitful and increased greatly; they multiplied and grew exceedingly strong; so that the land was filled with them.
8 Now there arose a new king over Egypt, who did not
9 know Joseph. And he said to his people, "Behold, the people of Israel are too many and too mighty for us.
10 Come, let us deal shrewdly with them, lest they multiply, and, if war befall us, they join our enemies and fight
11 against us and escape from the land." Therefore they set taskmasters over them to afflict them with heavy burdens; and they built for Pharaoh store-cities, Pithom and Ra-
12 am'ses. But the more they were oppressed, the more they multiplied and the more they spread abroad. And the
13 Egyptians were in dread of the people of Israel. So they
14 made the people of Israel serve with rigor, and made their lives bitter with hard service, in mortar and brick, and in all kinds of work in the field; in all their work they made them serve with rigor.
15 Then the king of Egypt said to the Hebrew midwives, one of whom was named Shiph'rah and the other Pu'ah,
16 "When you serve as midwife to the Hebrew women, and see them upon the birthstool, if it is a son, you shall kill
17 him; but if it is a daughter, she shall live." But the midwives feared God, and did not do as the king of Egypt
18 commanded them, but let the male children live. So the

king of Egypt called the midwives, and said to them, "Why have you done this, and let the male children live?" ¹⁹ The midwives said to Pharaoh, "Because the Hebrew women are not like the Egyptian women; for they are vigorous and are delivered before the midwife comes to ²⁰ them." So God dealt well with the midwives; and the ²¹ people multiplied and grew very strong. And because the ²² midwives feared God he gave them families. The Pharaoh commanded all his people, "Every son that is born to the Hebrews[a] you shall cast into the Nile, but you shall let every daughter live."

GOD PROVIDES FOR A LEADER

2 Now a man from the house of Levi went and took ² to wife a daughter of Levi. The woman conceived and bore a son; and when she saw that he was a goodly ³ child, she hid him three months. And when she could hide him no longer she took for him a basket made of bulrushes, and daubed it with bitumen and pitch; and she put the child in it and placed it among the reeds at ⁴ the river's brink. And his sister stood at a distance, to ⁵ know what would be done to him. Now the daughter of Pharaoh came down to bathe at the river, and her maidens walked beside the river; she saw the basket among the ⁶ reeds and sent her maid to fetch it. When she opened it she saw the child; and lo, the babe was crying. She took pity on him and said, "This is one of the Hebrews' chil- ⁷ dren." Then his sister said to Pharaoh's daughter, "Shall I go and call you a nurse from the Hebrew women to ⁸ nurse the child for you?" And Pharaoh's daughter said to her, "Go." So the girl went and called the child's ⁹ mother. And Pharaoh's daughter said to her, "Take this child away, and nurse him for me, and I will give you your wages." So the woman took the child and nursed ¹⁰ him. And the child grew, and she brought him to Pharaoh's daughter, and he became her son; and she named him Moses,[b] for she said, "Because I drew him out[c] of the water."

Moses Flees to Midian

¹¹ One day, when Moses had grown up, he went out to his people and looked on their burdens; and he saw ¹² an Egyptian beating a Hebrew, one of his people. He looked this way and that, and seeing no one he killed ¹³ the Egyptian and hid him in the sand. When he went out the next day, behold, two Hebrews were struggling together; and he said to the man that did the wrong, "Why ¹⁴ do you strike your fellow?" He answered, "Who made you a prince and a judge over us? Do you mean to kill me as you killed the Egyptian?" Then Moses was afraid, ¹⁵ and thought, "Surely the thing is known." When Pharaoh heard of it, he sought to kill Moses.

But Moses fled from Pharaoh, and stayed in the land

¹⁶ of Mid'ian; and he sat down by a well. Now the priest of Mid'ian had seven daughters; and they came and drew water, and filled the troughs to water their father's flock. ¹⁷ The shepherds came and drove them away; but Moses ¹⁸ stood up and helped them, and watered their flock. When they came to their father Reu'el, he said, "How is it that ¹⁹ you have come so soon today?" They said, "An Egyptian delivered us out of the hand of the shepherds, and even ²⁰ drew water for us and watered the flock." He said to his daughters, "And where is he? Why have you left the ²¹ man? Call him, that he may eat bread." And Moses was content to dwell with the man, and he gave Moses his ²² daughter Zippo'rah. She bore a son, and he called his name Gershom; for he said, "I have been a sojourner[d] in a foreign land."

²³ In the course of those many days the king of Egypt died. And the people of Israel groaned under their bondage, and cried out for help, and their cry under bondage ²⁴ came up to God. And God heard their groaning, and God remembered his covenant with Abraham, with Isaac, and ²⁵ with Jacob. And God saw the people of Israel, and God knew their condition.

The Calling and Commission of Moses

3 Now Moses was keeping the flock of his father-in-law, Jethro, the priest of Mid'ian; and he led his flock to the west side of the wilderness, and came to Horeb, ² the mountain of God. And the angel of the LORD appeared to him in a flame of fire out of the midst of a bush; and he looked, and lo, the bush was burning, yet it was not ³ consumed. And Moses said, "I will turn aside and see ⁴ this great sight, why the bush is not burnt." When the

LORD saw that he turned aside to see, God called to him out of the bush, "Moses, Moses!" And he said, "Here ⁵ am I." Then he said, "Do not come near; put off your shoes from your feet, for the place on which you are ⁶ standing is holy ground." And he said, "I am the God of your father, the God of Abraham, the God of Isaac, and the God of Jacob." And Moses hid his face, for he was afraid to look at God.

⁷ Then the LORD said, "I have seen the affliction of my people who are in Egypt, and have heard their cry be- ⁸ cause of their taskmasters; I know their sufferings, and

[a] Sam Gk Tg: Heb lacks *to the Hebrews*   [b] Heb *Mosheh*   [c] Heb *mashah*   [d] Heb *ger*

I have come down to deliver them out of the hand of the Egyptians, and to bring them up out of that land to a good and broad land, a land flowing with milk and honey, to the place of the Canaanites, the Hittites, the Amorites, 9 the Per'izzites, the Hivites, and the Jeb'usites. And now, behold, the cry of the people of Israel has come to me, and I have seen the oppression with which the Egyptians 10 oppress them. Come, I will send you to Pharaoh that you may bring forth my people, the sons of Israel, out of

11 Egypt." But Moses said to God, "Who am I that I should go to Pharaoh, and bring the sons of Israel out of 12 Egypt?" He said, "But I will be with you; and this shall be the sign for you, that I have sent you: when you have brought forth the people out of Egypt, you shall serve God upon this mountain."

13 Then Moses said to God, "If I come to the people of Israel and say to them, 'The God of your fathers has sent me to you,' and they ask me, 'What is his name?' 14 what shall I say to them?" God said to Moses, "I AM WHO I AM." e And he said, "Say this to the people of 15 Israel, 'I AM has sent me to you.'" God also said to Moses, "Say this to the people of Israel, 'The LORD, f the God of your fathers, the God of Abraham, the God of Isaac, and the God of Jacob, has sent me to you': this is my name for ever, and thus I am to be remembered 16 throughout all generations. Go and gather the elders of Israel together, and say to them, 'The LORD, the God of your fathers, the God of Abraham, of Isaac, and of Jacob, has appeared to me, saying, "I have observed 17 you and what has been done to you in Egypt; and I promise that I will bring you up out of the affliction of Egypt, to the land of the Canaanites, the Hittites, the Amorites, the Per'izzites, the Hivites, and the Jeb'usites, 18 a land flowing with milk and honey."' And they will hearken to your voice; and you and the elders of Israel shall go to the king of Egypt and say to him, 'The LORD, the God of the Hebrews, has met with us; and now, we pray you, let us go a three days' journey into the wilder-19 ness, that we may sacrifice to the LORD our God.' I know that the king of Egypt will not let you go unless compelled 20 by a mighty hand. g So I will stretch out my hand and smite Egypt with all the wonders which I will do in it; 21 after that he will let you go. And I will give this people favor in the sight of the Egyptians; and when you go, 22 you shall not go empty, but each woman shall ask of her

neighbor, and of her who sojourns in her house, jewelry of silver and of gold, and clothing, and you shall put them on your sons and on your daughters; thus you shall despoil the Egyptians."

4 Then Moses answered, "But behold, they will not believe me or listen to my voice, for they will say, 2 'The LORD did not appear to you.'" The LORD said to him, "What is that in your hand?" He said, "A rod." 3 And he said, "Cast it on the ground." So he cast it on the ground, and it became a serpent; and Moses fled from 4 it. But the LORD said to Moses, "Put out your hand, and take it by the tail"—so he put out his hand and caught it, 5 and it became a rod in his hand—"that they may believe that the LORD, the God of their fathers, the God of Abraham, the God of Isaac, and the God of Jacob, has ap-6 peared to you." Again, the LORD said to him, "Put your hand into your bosom." And he put his hand into his bosom; and when he took it out, behold, his hand was 7 leprous, as white as snow. Then God said, "Put your hand back into your bosom." So he put his hand back into his bosom; and when he took it out, behold, it was 8 restored like the rest of his flesh. "If they will not believe you," God said, "or heed the first sign, they may believe 9 the latter sign. If they will not believe even these two signs or heed your voice, you shall take some water from the Nile and pour it upon the dry ground; and the water which you shall take from the Nile will become blood upon the dry ground."

Aaron Becomes Spokesman

10 But Moses said to the LORD, "Oh, my Lord, I am not eloquent, either heretofore or since thou hast spoken to thy servant; but I am slow of speech and of tongue." 11 Then the LORD said to him, "Who has made man's mouth? Who makes him dumb, or deaf, or seeing, or 12 blind? Is it not I, the LORD? Now therefore go, and I will be with your mouth and teach you what you shall 13 speak." But he said, "Oh, my Lord, send, I pray, some 14 other person." Then the anger of the LORD was kindled against Moses and he said, "Is there not Aaron, your brother, the Levite? I know that he can speak well; and behold, he is coming out to meet you, and when he sees 15 you he will be glad in his heart. And you shall speak to him and put the words in his mouth; and I will be with your mouth and with his mouth, and will teach you 16 what you shall do. He shall speak for you to the people; and he shall be a mouth for you, and you shall be to 17 him as God. And you shall take in your hand this rod, with which you shall do the signs."

Moses Returns to Egypt

18 Moses went back to Jethro his father-in-law and said to him, "Let me go back, I pray, to my kinsmen in Egypt

e Or I AM WHAT I AM or I WILL BE WHAT I WILL BE
f The word LORD when spelled with capital letters, stands for the divine name, YHWH, which is here connected with the verb hayah, to be
g Gk Vg: Heb no, not by a mighty hand

and see whether they are still alive." And Jethro said to
19 Moses, "Go in peace." And the LORD said to Moses in
Mid'ian, "Go back to Egypt; for all the men who were
20 seeking your life are dead." So Moses took his wife and
his sons and set them on an ass, and went back to the
land of Egypt; and in his hand Moses took the rod of
God.

21 And the LORD said to Moses, "When you go back to
Egypt, see that you do before Pharaoh all the miracles
which I have put in your power; but I will harden his
22 heart, so that he will not let the people go. And you shall
say to Pharaoh, 'Thus says the LORD, Israel is my first-
23 born son, and I say to you "Let my son go that he may
serve me"; if you refuse to let him go, behold, I will
slay your first-born son.'"

24 At a lodging place on the way the LORD met him and
25 sought to kill him. Then Zippo'rah took a flint and cut
off her son's foreskin, and touched Moses' feet with it,
and said, "Surely you are a bridegroom of blood to me!"
26 So he let him alone. Then it was that she said, "You
are a bridegroom of blood," because of the circumcision.

27 The LORD said to Aaron, "Go into the wilderness to
meet Moses." So he went, and met him at the mountain
28 of God and kissed him. And Moses told Aaron all the
words of the LORD with which he had sent him, and all
29 the signs which he had charged him to do. Then Moses
and Aaron went and gathered together all the elders of the
30 people of Israel. And Aaron spoke all the words which
the LORD had spoken to Moses, and did the signs in the
31 sight of the people. And the people believed; and when
they heard that the LORD had visited the people of Israel
and that he had seen their affliction, they bowed their
heads and worshiped.

4 us with pestilence or with the sword." But the king of
Egypt said to them, "Moses and Aaron, why do you take
the people away from their work? Get to your burdens."
5 And Pharaoh said, "Behold, the people of the land are
now many and you make them rest from their burdens!"
6 The same day Pharaoh commanded the taskmasters of
7 the people and their foremen, "You shall no longer give
the people straw to make bricks, as heretofore; let them
8 go and gather straw for themselves. But the number of
bricks which they made heretofore you shall lay upon
them, you shall by no means lessen it; for they are idle;
therefore they cry, 'Let us go and offer sacrifice to our
9 God.' Let heavier work be laid upon the men that they
may labor at it and pay no regard to lying words."

10 So the taskmasters and the foremen of the people went
out and said to the people, "Thus says Pharaoh, 'I will
11 not give you straw. Go yourselves, get your straw wherever you can find it; but your work will not be lessened
12 in the least.'" So the people were scattered abroad
throughout all the land of Egypt, to gather stubble for
13 straw. The taskmasters were urgent, saying, "Complete
your work, your daily task, as when there was straw."
14 And the foremen of the people of Israel, whom Pharaoh's
taskmasters had set over them, were beaten, and were
asked, "Why have you not done all your task of making
bricks today, as hitherto?"

15 Then the foremen of the people of Israel came and
cried to Pharaoh, "Why do you deal thus with your ser-
16 vants? No straw is given to your servants, yet they say to
us, 'Make bricks!' And behold, your servants are beaten;
17 but the fault is in your own people." But he said, "You
are idle, you are idle; therefore you say, 'Let us go and
18 sacrifice to the LORD.' Go now, and work; for no straw
shall be given you, yet you shall deliver the same number

The Pharaoh Scorns the Lord

5 Afterward Moses and Aaron went to Pharaoh and
said, "Thus says the LORD, the God of Israel, 'Let my
people go, that they may hold a feast to me in the wilder-
2 ness.'" But Pharaoh said, "Who is the LORD, that I
should heed his voice and let Israel go? I do not know
3 the LORD, and moreover I will not let Israel go." Then
they said, "The God of the Hebrews has met with us;
let us go, we pray, a three days' journey into the wilderness, and sacrifice to the LORD our God, lest he fall upon

19 of bricks." The foremen of the people of Israel saw that
they were in evil plight, when they said, "You shall by
20 no means lessen your daily number of bricks." They
met Moses and Aaron, who were waiting for them, as
21 they came forth from Pharaoh; and they said to them,
"The LORD look upon you and judge, because you have
made us offensive in the sight of Pharaoh and his servants, and have put a sword in their hand to kill us."

22 Then Moses turned again to the LORD and said, "O
LORD, why hast thou done evil to this people? Why didst

23 thou ever send me? For since I came to Pharaoh to speak in thy name, he has done evil to this people, and
16 thou hast not delivered thy people at all." But the LORD said to Moses, "Now you shall see what I will do to Pharaoh; for with a strong hand he will send them out, yea, with a strong hand he will drive them out of his land."

GOD DISCLOSES HIS PLAN

2,3 And God said to Moses, "I am the LORD. I appeared to Abraham, to Isaac, and to Jacob, as God Almighty,[h] but by my name the LORD I did not make myself known
4 to them. I also established my covenant with them, to give them the land of Canaan, the land in which they
5 dwelt as sojourners. Moreover I have heard the groaning of the people of Israel whom the Egyptians hold in
6 bondage and I have remembered my covenant. Say therefore to the people of Israel, 'I am the LORD, and I will bring you out from under the burdens of the Egyptians, and I will deliver you from their bondage, and I will redeem you with an outstretched arm and with great
7 acts of judgment, and I will take you for my people, and I will be your God; and you shall know that I am the LORD your God, who has brought you out from under
8 the burdens of the Egyptians. And I will bring you into the land which I swore to give to Abraham, to Isaac, and to Jacob; I will give it to you for a possession. I am the
9 LORD.' " Moses spoke thus to the people of Israel; but they did not listen to Moses, because of their broken spirit and their cruel bondage.
10,11 And the LORD said to Moses, "Go in, tell Pharaoh king of Egypt to let the people of Israel go out of his
12 land." But Moses said to the LORD, "Behold, the people of Israel have not listened to me; how then shall Pharaoh listen to me, who am a man of uncircumcised lips?"
13 But the LORD spoke to Moses and Aaron, and gave them a charge to the people of Israel and to Pharaoh king of Egypt to bring the people of Israel out of the land of Egypt.

THE GENEALOGY OF MOSES AND AARON

14 These are the heads of their fathers' houses: the sons of Reuben, the first-born of Israel: Hanoch, Pallu, Hezron, and
15 Carmi; these are the families of Reuben. The sons of Simeon: Jemu'el, Jamin, Ohad, Jachin, Zohar, and Shaul, the son of a
16 Canaanite woman; these are the families of Simeon. These are the names of the sons of Levi according to their generations: Gershon, Kohath, and Merar'i, the years of the life of Levi
17 being a hundred and thirty-seven years. The sons of Gershon:
18 Libni and Shimei, by their families. The sons of Kohath: Amram, Izhar, Hebron, and Uz'ziel, the years of the life of
19 Kohath being a hundred and thirty-three years. The sons of Merar'i: Mahli and Mushi. These are the families of the Levites
20 according to their generations. Amram took to wife Joch'ebed his father's sister and she bore him Aaron and Moses, the years of the life of Amram being one hundred and thirty-seven years.
21,22 The sons of Izhar: Korah, Nepheg, and Zichri. And the sons
23 of Uz'ziel: Mi'sha-el, Elza'phan, and Sithri. Aaron took to wife Eli'sheba, the daughter of Ammin'adab and the sister of Nahshon; and she bore him Nadab, Abi'hu, Elea'zar, and
24 Ith'amar. The sons of Korah: Assir, Elka'nah, and Ebi'asaph;

25 these are the families of the Ko'rahites. Elea'zar, Aaron's son, took to wife one of the daughters of Pu'ti-el; and she bore him Phin'ehas. These are the heads of the fathers' houses of the Levites by their families.
26 These are the Aaron and Moses to whom the LORD said: "Bring out the people of Israel from the land of Egypt by their
27 hosts." It was they who spoke to Pharaoh king of Egypt about bringing out the people of Israel from Egypt, this Moses and this Aaron.

THE PROMISES OF GOD

28 On the day when the LORD spoke to Moses in the land
29 of Egypt, the LORD said to Moses, "I am the LORD; tell
30 Pharaoh king of Egypt all that I say to you." But Moses said to the LORD, "Behold, I am of uncircumcised lips;
17 how then shall Pharaoh listen to me?" And the LORD said to Moses, "See, I make you as God to Pharaoh;
2 and Aaron your brother shall be your prophet. You shall speak all that I command you; and Aaron your brother shall tell Pharaoh to let the people of Israel go out of his
3 land. But I will harden Pharaoh's heart, and though I
4 multiply my signs and wonders in the land of Egypt, Pharaoh will not listen to you; then I will lay my hand upon Egypt and bring forth my hosts, my people the sons of Israel, out of the land of Egypt by great acts of judg-
5 ment. And the Egyptians shall know that I am the LORD, when I stretch forth my hand upon Egypt and bring out
6 the people of Israel from among them." And Moses and Aaron did so; they did as the LORD commanded them.
7 Now Moses was eighty years old, and Aaron eighty-three years old, when they spoke to Pharaoh.
8,9 And the LORD said to Moses and Aaron, "When Pharaoh says to you, 'Prove yourselves by working a miracle,' then you shall say to Aaron, 'Take your rod and cast it down before Pharaoh, that it may become a serpent.' "
10 So Moses and Aaron went to Pharaoh and did as the LORD commanded; Aaron cast down his rod before Pha-
11 raoh and his servants, and it became a serpent. Then Pharaoh summoned the wise men and the sorcerers; and they also, the magicians of Egypt, did the same by their
12 secret arts. For every man cast down his rod, and they became serpents. But Aaron's rod swallowed up their
13 rods. Still Pharaoh's heart was hardened, and he would not listen to them; as the LORD had said.

GOD REVEALS HIS POWER

14 Then the LORD said to Moses, "Pharaoh's heart is
15 hardened, he refuses to let the people go. Go to Pharaoh in the morning, as he is going out to the water; wait for him by the river's brink, and take in your hand the
16 rod which was turned into a serpent. And you shall say to him, 'The LORD, the God of the Hebrews, sent me to you, saying, "Let my people go, that they may serve me in the
17 wilderness; and behold, you have not yet obeyed." Thus says the LORD, "By this you shall know that I am the LORD: behold, I will strike the water that is in the Nile with the rod that is in my hand, and it shall be turned to

[h] Heb El Shaddai

18 blood, and the fish in the Nile shall die, and the Nile shall become foul, and the Egyptians will loathe to drink 19 water from the Nile." ' " And the Lord said to Moses, "Say to Aaron, 'Take your rod and stretch out your hand over the waters of Egypt, over their rivers, their canals, and their ponds, and all their pools of water, that they may become blood; and there shall be blood throughout all the land of Egypt, both in vessels of wood and in

vessels of stone.' "

20 Moses and Aaron did as the Lord commanded; in the sight of Pharaoh and in the sight of his servants, he lifted up the rod and struck the water that was in the Nile, and all the water that was in the Nile turned to 21 blood. And the fish in the Nile died; and the Nile became foul, so that the Egyptians could not drink water from the Nile; and there was blood throughout all the land of 22 Egypt. But the magicians of Egypt did the same by their secret arts; so Pharaoh's heart remained hardened, and he would not listen to them; as the Lord had said. 23 Pharaoh turned and went into his house, and he did 24 not lay even this to heart. And all the Egyptians dug round about the Nile for water to drink, for they could not drink the water of the Nile.

The Plague of Frogs

25 Seven days passed after the Lord[i] had struck the Nile. 1 **8** Then the Lord said to Moses, "Go in to Pharaoh and say to him, 'Thus says the Lord, "Let my people 2 go, that they may serve me. But if you refuse to let them go, behold, I will plague all your country with frogs; 3 the Nile shall swarm with frogs which shall come up into your house, and into your bedchamber and on your bed, and into the houses of your servants and of your people,[j] and into your ovens and your kneading bowls; 4 the frogs shall come up on you and on your people and 5 on all your servants." ' " [k] And the Lord said to Moses, "Say to Aaron, 'Stretch out your hand with your rod over the rivers, over the canals, and over the pools, and cause 6 frogs to come upon the land of Egypt!' " So Aaron stretched out his hand over the waters of Egypt; and the

7 frogs came up and covered the land of Egypt. But the magicians did the same by their secret arts, and brought frogs upon the land of Egypt.

8 Then Pharaoh called Moses and Aaron, and said, "Entreat the Lord to take away the frogs from me and from my people; and I will let the people go to sacrifice 9 to the Lord." Moses said to Pharaoh, "Be pleased to command me when I am to entreat, for you and for your servants and for your people, that the frogs be destroyed from you and your houses and be left only in 10 the Nile." And he said, "Tomorrow." Moses said, "Be it as you say, that you may know that there is no one 11 like the Lord our God. The frogs shall depart from you and your houses and your servants and your people; they 12 shall be left only in the Nile." So Moses and Aaron went out from Pharaoh; and Moses cried to the Lord con-13 cerning the frogs, as he had agreed with Pharaoh.[l] And the Lord did according to the word of Moses; the frogs died out of the houses and courtyards and out of the 14 fields. And they gathered them together in heaps, and 15 the land stank. But when Pharaoh saw that there was a respite, he hardened his heart, and would not listen to them; as the Lord had said.

The Plague of Gnats

16 Then the Lord said to Moses, "Say to Aaron, 'Stretch out your rod and strike the dust of the earth, that it may become gnats throughout all the land of Egypt.' " 17 And they did so; Aaron stretched out his hand with his rod, and struck the dust of the earth, and there came gnats on man and beast; all the dust of the earth became 18 gnats throughout all the land of Egypt. The magicians tried by their secret arts to bring forth gnats, but they 19 could not. So there were gnats on man and beast. And the magicians said to Pharaoh, "This is the finger of God." But Pharaoh's heart was hardened, and he would not listen to them; as the Lord had said.

The Plague of Flies

20 Then the Lord said to Moses, "Rise up early in the morning and wait for Pharaoh, as he goes out to the water, and say to him, 'Thus says the Lord, "Let my 21 people go, that they may serve me. Else, if you will not let my people go, behold, I will send swarms of flies on you and your servants and your people, and into your houses; and the houses of the Egyptians shall be filled with swarms of flies, and also the ground on which they 22 stand. But on that day I will set apart the land of Goshen, where my people dwell, so that no swarms of flies shall be there; that you may know that I am the Lord in the 23 midst of the earth. Thus I will put a division[m] between my people and your people. By tomorrow shall this sign 24 be." ' " And the Lord did so; there came great swarms

i Ch 7. 26 in Heb   j Gk: Heb *upon your people*   k Ch 8. 1 in Heb   l Or *which he had brought upon Pharaoh*
m Gk Vg: Heb *set redemption*

of flies into the house of Pharaoh and into his servants' houses, and in all the land of Egypt the land was ruined by reason of the flies.

25 Then Pharaoh called Moses and Aaron, and said, "Go, 26 sacrifice to your God within the land." But Moses said, "It would not be right to do so; for we shall sacrifice to the LORD our God offerings abominable to the Egyptians. If we sacrifice offerings abominable to the Egyptians be-27 fore their eyes, will they not stone us? We must go three days' journey into the wilderness and sacrifice to the 28 LORD our God as he will command us." So Pharaoh said, "I will let you go, to sacrifice to the LORD your God in the wilderness; only you shall not go very far away. 29 Make entreaty for me." Then Moses said, "Behold, I am going out from you and I will pray to the LORD that the swarms of flies may depart from Pharaoh, from his servants, and from his people, tomorrow; only let not Pharaoh deal falsely again by not letting the people go to 30 sacrifice to the LORD." So Moses went out from Pharaoh 31 and prayed to the LORD. And the LORD did as Moses asked, and removed the swarms of flies from Pharaoh, from his servants, and from his people; not one re-32 mained. But Pharaoh hardened his heart this time also, and did not let the people go.

The Plague on Cattle

9 Then the LORD said to Moses, "Go in to Pharaoh, and say to him, 'Thus says the LORD, the God of the 2 Hebrews, "Let my people go, that they may serve me. For 3 if you refuse to let them go and still hold them, behold, the hand of the LORD will fall with a very severe plague upon your cattle which are in the field, the horses, the

4 asses, the camels, the herds, and the flocks. But the LORD will make a distinction between the cattle of Israel and the cattle of Egypt, so that nothing shall die of all that 5 belongs to the people of Israel." ' " And the LORD set a time, saying, "Tomorrow the LORD will do this thing in 6 the land." And on the morrow the LORD did this thing; all the cattle of the Egyptians died, but of the cattle of the 7 people of Israel not one died. And Pharaoh sent, and behold, not one of the cattle of the Israelites was dead. But the heart of Pharaoh was hardened, and he did not let the people go.

The Plague of Boils

8 And the LORD said to Moses and Aaron, "Take handfuls of ashes from the kiln, and let Moses throw them toward 9 heaven in the sight of Pharaoh. And it shall become fine dust over all the land of Egypt, and become boils breaking out in sores on man and beast throughout all the 10 land of Egypt." So they took ashes from the kiln, and stood before Pharaoh, and Moses threw them toward heaven, and it became boils breaking out in sores on 11 man and beast. And the magicians could not stand before Moses because of the boils, for the boils were upon the 12 magicians and upon all the Egyptians. But the LORD hardened the heart of Pharaoh, and he did not listen to them; as the LORD had spoken to Moses.

The Hail

13 Then the LORD said to Moses, "Rise up early in the morning and stand before Pharaoh, and say to him, 'Thus says the LORD, the God of the Hebrews, "Let my 14 people go, that they may serve me. For this time I will send all my plagues upon your heart, and upon your servants and your people, that you may know that there 15 is none like me in all the earth. For by now I could have put forth my hand and struck you and your people with pestilence, and you would have been cut off from the 16 earth; but for this purpose have I let you live, to show you my power, so that my name may be declared through-17 out all the earth. You are still exalting yourself against 18 my people, and will not let them go. Behold, tomorrow about this time I will cause very heavy hail to fall, such as never has been in Egypt from the day it was founded 19 until now. Now therefore send, get your cattle and all that you have in the field into safe shelter; for the hail shall come down upon every man and beast that is in the field and is not brought home, and they shall die." ' " 20 Then he who feared the word of the LORD among the servants of Pharaoh made his slaves and his cattle flee 21 into the houses; but he who did not regard the word of the LORD left his slaves and his cattle in the field.

22 And the LORD said to Moses, "Stretch forth your hand toward heaven, that there may be hail in all the land of Egypt, upon man and beast and every plant of the field, 23 throughout the land of Egypt." Then Moses stretched forth his rod toward heaven; and the LORD sent thunder and hail, and fire ran down to the earth. And the LORD 24 rained hail upon the land of Egypt; there was hail, and fire flashing continually in the midst of the hail, very heavy hail, such as had never been in all the land of 25 Egypt since it became a nation. The hail struck down everything that was in the field throughout all the land of Egypt, both man and beast; and the hail struck down every plant of the field, and shattered every tree of the 26 field. Only in the land of Goshen, where the people of Israel were, there was no hail.

Then Pharaoh sent, and called Moses and Aaron, and said to them, "I have sinned this time; the LORD is in the right, and I and my people are in the wrong. Entreat the LORD; for there has been enough of this thunder and hail; I will let you go, and you shall stay no longer." Moses said to him, "As soon as I have gone out of the city, I will stretch out my hands to the LORD; the thunder will cease, and there will be no more hail, that you may know that the earth is the LORD's. But as for you and your servants, I know that you do not yet fear the LORD God." (The flax and the barley were ruined, for the barley was in the ear and the flax was in bud. But the wheat and the spelt were not ruined, for they are late in coming up.) So Moses went out of the city from Pharaoh, and stretched out his hands to the LORD; and the thunder and the hail ceased, and the rain no longer poured upon the earth. But when Pharaoh saw that the rain and the hail and the thunder had ceased, he sinned yet again, and hardened his heart, he and his servants. So the heart of Pharaoh was hardened, and he did not let the people of Israel go; as the LORD had spoken through Moses.

The Plague of Locusts

10 Then the LORD said to Moses, "Go in to Pharaoh; for I have hardened his heart and the heart of his servants, that I may show these signs of mine among them, and that you may tell in the hearing of your son and of your son's son how I have made sport of the Egyptians and what signs I have done among them; that you may know that I am the LORD."

So Moses and Aaron went in to Pharaoh, and said to him, "Thus says the LORD, the God of the Hebrews, 'How long will you refuse to humble yourself before me? Let my people go, that they may serve me. For if you refuse to let my people go, behold, tomorrow I will bring locusts into your country, and they shall cover the face of the land, so that no one can see the land; and they shall eat what is left to you after the hail, and they shall eat every tree of yours which grows in the field, and they shall fill your houses, and the houses of all your servants and of all the Egyptians; as neither your fathers nor your grandfathers have seen, from the day they came on earth to this day.'" Then he turned and went out from Pharaoh.

And Pharaoh's servants said to him, "How long shall this man be a snare to us? Let the men go, that they may serve the LORD their God; do you not yet understand that Egypt is ruined?" So Moses and Aaron were brought back to Pharaoh; and he said to them, "Go, serve the LORD your God; but who are to go?" And Moses said, "We will go with our young and our old; we will go with our sons and daughters and with our flocks and herds, for we must hold a feast to the LORD." And he said to them, "The LORD be with you, if ever I let you and your little ones go! Look, you have some evil purpose in mind.ⁿ No! Go, the men among you, and serve the LORD, for that is what you desire." And they were driven out from Pharaoh's presence.

Then the LORD said to Moses, "Stretch out your hand over the land of Egypt for the locusts, that they may come upon the land of Egypt, and eat every plant in the land, all that the hail has left." So Moses stretched forth

his rod over the land of Egypt, and the LORD brought an east wind upon the land all that day and all that night; and when it was morning the east wind had brought the locusts. And the locusts came up over all the land of Egypt, and settled on the whole country of Egypt, such a dense swarm of locusts as had never been before, nor ever shall be again. For they covered the face of the whole land, so that the land was darkened, and they ate all the plants in the land and all the fruit of the trees which the hail had left; not a green thing remained, neither tree nor plant of the field, through all the land of Egypt. Then Pharaoh called Moses and Aaron in haste, and said, "I have sinned against the LORD your God, and against you. Now therefore, forgive my sin, I pray you, only this once, and entreat the LORD your God only to remove this death from me." So he went out from Pharaoh, and entreated the LORD. And the LORD turned a very strong west wind, which lifted the locusts and drove them into the Red Sea; not a single locust was left in all the country of Egypt. But the LORD hardened Pharaoh's heart, and he did not let the children of Israel go.

The Plague of Darkness

Then the LORD said to Moses, "Stretch out your hand toward heaven that there may be darkness over the land of Egypt, a darkness to be felt." So Moses stretched out his hand toward heaven, and there was thick darkness in all the land of Egypt three days; they did not see one another, nor did any rise from his place for three days; but all the people of Israel had light where they dwelt. Then Pharaoh called Moses, and said, "Go, serve the

ⁿ Heb *before your face*

LORD; your children also may go with you; only let your
25 flocks and your herds remain behind." But Moses said,
"You must also let us have sacrifices and burnt offerings,
26 that we may sacrifice to the LORD our God. Our cattle also
must go with us; not a hoof shall be left behind, for we
must take of them to serve the LORD our God, and we do
not know with what we must serve the LORD until we
27 arrive there." But the LORD hardened Pharaoh's heart,
28 and he would not let them go. Then Pharaoh said to him,
"Get away from me; take heed to yourself; never see
my face again; for in the day you see my face you shall
29 die." Moses said, "As you say! I will not see your face
again."

The Plague of Death

11 The LORD said to Moses, "Yet one plague more I
will bring upon Pharaoh and upon Egypt; afterwards he will let you go hence; when he lets you go, he
2 will drive you away completely. Speak now in the hearing
of the people, that they ask, every man of his neighbor
and every woman of her neighbor, jewelry of silver and
3 of gold." And the LORD gave the people favor in the sight
of the Egyptians. Moreover, the man Moses was very
great in the land of Egypt, in the sight of Pharaoh's
servants and in the sight of the people.
4 And Moses said, "Thus says the LORD: About midnight
5 I will go forth in the midst of Egypt; and all the first-
born in the land of Egypt shall die, from the first-born of
Pharaoh who sits upon his throne, even to the first-born
of the maidservant who is behind the mill; and all the
6 first-born of the cattle. And there shall be a great cry
throughout all the land of Egypt, such as there has never
7 been, nor ever shall be again. But against any of the
people of Israel, either man or beast, not a dog shall
growl; that you may know that the LORD makes a dis-
8 tinction between the Egyptians and Israel. And all these
your servants shall come down to me, and bow down
to me, saying, 'Get you out, and all the people who follow
you.' And after that I will go out." And he went out from
9 Pharaoh in hot anger. Then the LORD said to Moses,
"Pharaoh will not listen to you; that my wonders may be
multiplied in the land of Egypt."
10 Moses and Aaron did all these wonders before Pharaoh; and the LORD hardened Pharaoh's heart, and he did
not let the people of Israel go out of his land.

THE LORD'S PASSOVER

12 The LORD said to Moses and Aaron in the land of
2 Egypt, "This month shall be for you the beginning
of months; it shall be the first month of the year for you.
3 Tell all the congregation of Israel that on the tenth day
of this month they shall take every man a lamb according
4 to their fathers' houses, a lamb for a household; and if

the household is too small for a lamb, then a man and his
neighbor next to his house shall take according to the
number of persons; according to what each can eat you
5 shall make your count for the lamb. Your lamb shall be
without blemish, a male a year old; you shall take it from
6 the sheep or from the goats; and you shall keep it until
the fourteenth day of this month, when the whole assembly of the congregation of Israel shall kill their lambs in
7 the evening.° Then they shall take some of the blood, and
put it on the two doorposts and the lintel of the houses
8 in which they eat them. They shall eat the flesh that night,
roasted; with unleavened bread and bitter herbs they
9 shall eat it. Do not eat any of it raw or boiled with water,
but roasted, its head with its legs and its inner parts.

10 And you shall let none of it remain until the morning,
anything that remains until the morning you shall burn.
11 In this manner you shall eat it: your loins girded, your
sandals on your feet, and your staff in your hand; and
12 you shall eat it in haste. It is the LORD's passover. For I
will pass through the land of Egypt that night, and I will
smite all the first-born in the land of Egypt, both man
and beast; and on all the gods of Egypt I will execute
13 judgments: I am the LORD. The blood shall be a sign
for you, upon the houses where you are; and when I see
the blood, I will pass over you, and no plague shall fall
upon you to destroy you, when I smite the land of Egypt.
14 "This day shall be for you a memorial day, and you
shall keep it as a feast to the LORD; throughout your
generations you shall observe it as an ordinance for ever.
15 Seven days you shall eat unleavened bread; on the first
day you shall put away leaven out of your houses, for if
any one eats what is leavened, from the first day until the
seventh day, that person shall be cut off from Israel.
16 On the first day you shall hold a holy assembly, and on
the seventh day a holy assembly; no work shall be done
on those days; but what every one must eat, that only
17 may be prepared by you. And you shall observe the feast

° Heb *between the two evenings*

of unleavened bread, for on this very day I brought your hosts out of the land of Egypt: therefore you shall observe this day, throughout your generations, as an ordinance for ever. In the first month, on the fourteenth day of the month at evening, you shall eat unleavened bread, and so until the twenty-first day of the month at evening. For seven days no leaven shall be found in your houses; for if any one eats what is leavened, that person shall be cut off from the congregation of Israel, whether he is a sojourner or a native of the land. You shall eat nothing leavened; in all your dwellings you shall eat unleavened bread."

21 Then Moses called all the elders of Israel, and said to them, "Select lambs for yourselves according to your families, and kill the passover lamb. Take a bunch of hyssop and dip it in the blood which is in the basin, and touch the lintel and the two doorposts with the blood which is in the basin; and none of you shall go out of the door of his house until the morning. For the LORD will pass through to slay the Egyptians; and when he sees the blood on the lintel and on the two doorposts, the LORD will pass over the door, and will not allow the destroyer to enter your houses to slay you. You shall observe this rite as an ordinance for you and for your sons for ever. And when you come to the land which the LORD will give you, as he has promised, you shall keep this service. And when your children say to you, 'What do you mean by this service?' you shall say, 'It is the sacrifice of the LORD's passover, for he passed over the houses of the people of Israel in Egypt, when he slew the

Egyptians but spared our houses.'" And the people bowed their heads and worshiped.

28 Then the people of Israel went and did so; as the LORD had commanded Moses and Aaron, so they did.

29 At midnight the LORD smote all the first-born in the land of Egypt, from the first-born of Pharaoh who sat on his throne to the first-born of the captive who was in the dungeon, and all the first-born of the cattle. And Pharaoh rose up in the night, he, and all his servants, and all the Egyptians; and there was a great cry in Egypt, for there was not a house where one was not dead. And he summoned Moses and Aaron by night, and said, "Rise up, go forth from among my people, both you and the people

of Israel; and go, serve the LORD, as you have said. Take your flocks and your herds, as you have said, and be gone; and bless me also!"

33 And the Egyptians were urgent with the people, to send them out of the land in haste; for they said, "We are all dead men." So the people took their dough before it was leavened, their kneading bowls being bound up in their mantles on their shoulders. The people of Israel had also done as Moses told them, for they had asked of the Egyptians jewelry of silver and of gold, and clothing; and the LORD had given the people favor in the sight of the Egyptians, so that they let them have what they asked. Thus they despoiled the Egyptians.

37 And the people of Israel journeyed from Ram'eses to Succoth, about six hundred thousand men on foot, besides women and children. A mixed multitude also went up with them, and very many cattle, both flocks and herds. And they baked unleavened cakes of the dough which they had brought out of Egypt, for it was not leavened, because they were thrust out of Egypt and could not tarry, neither had they prepared for themselves any provisions.

40 The time that the people of Israel dwelt in Egypt was four hundred and thirty years. And at the end of four hundred and thirty years, on that very day, all the hosts of the LORD went out from the land of Egypt. It was a night of watching by the LORD, to bring them out of the land of Egypt; so this same night is a night of watching kept to the LORD by all the people of Israel throughout their generations.

ORDINANCE OF THE PASSOVER

43 And the LORD said to Moses and Aaron, "This is the ordinance of the passover: no foreigner shall eat of it; but every slave that is bought for money may eat of it after you have circum-45, 46 cised him. No sojourner or hired servant may eat of it. In one house shall it be eaten; you shall not carry forth any of the flesh outside the house; and you shall not break a bone of it. 47, 48 All the congregation of Israel shall keep it. And when a stranger shall sojourn with you and would keep the passover to the LORD, let all his males be circumcised, then he may come near and keep it; he shall be as a native of the land. But no uncircumcised person shall eat of it. There shall be one law for the native and for the stranger who sojourns among you."

50 Thus did all the people of Israel; as the LORD commanded Moses and Aaron, so they did. And on that very day the LORD brought the people of Israel out of the land of Egypt by their hosts.

Dedication of First-born

13 The LORD said to Moses, "Consecrate to me all the first-born; whatever is the first to open the womb among the people of Israel, both of man and of beast, is mine."

3 And Moses said to the people, "Remember this day, in which you came out from Egypt, out of the house of bondage, for by strength of hand the LORD brought you out from this place; no leavened bread shall be eaten. This day you are to go forth, in the month of Abib. And when the LORD brings you into the land of the Canaanites, the Hittites, the Amorites, the Hivites, and the Jeb'usites, which he swore to your fathers to give you, a land flowing with milk and honey, you shall keep this service in this month. Seven days you shall eat unleavened bread, and on the seventh day there shall be a feast to the LORD. Unleavened bread shall be eaten for seven days; no leavened bread shall be seen with you, and no leaven shall be seen with you

8 in all your territory. And you shall tell your son on that day,
'It is because of what the LORD did for me when I came out of
9 Egypt.' And it shall be to you as a sign on your hand and as
a memorial between your eyes, that the law of the LORD may
be in your mouth; for with a strong hand the LORD has brought
10 you out of Egypt. You shall therefore keep this ordinance at
its appointed time from year to year.
11 "And when the LORD brings you into the land of the Canaanites, as he swore to you and your fathers, and shall give it to
12 you, you shall set apart to the LORD all that first opens the
womb. All the firstlings of your cattle that are males shall be
13 the LORD's. Every firstling of an ass you shall redeem with a
lamb, or if you will not redeem it you shall break its neck.
Every first-born of man among your sons you shall redeem.
14 And when in time to come your son asks you, 'What does this
mean?' you shall say to him, 'By strength of hand the LORD
15 brought us out of Egypt, from the house of bondage. For when
Pharaoh stubbornly refused to let us go, the LORD slew all the
first-born in the land of Egypt, both the first-born of man and
the first-born of cattle. Therefore I sacrifice to the LORD all the

males that first open the womb; but all the first-born of my
16 sons I redeem.' It shall be as a mark on your hand or frontlets
between your eyes; for by a strong hand the LORD brought us
out of Egypt."

GOD LEADS ISRAEL OUT OF EGYPT

17 When Pharaoh let the people go, God did not lead them
by way of the land of the Philistines, although that was
near; for God said, "Lest the people repent when they
18 see war, and return to Egypt." But God led the people
round by the way of the wilderness toward the Red Sea.
And the people of Israel went up out of the land of Egypt
19 equipped for battle. And Moses took the bones of Joseph
with him; for Joseph had solemnly sworn the people of
Israel, saying, "God will visit you; then you must carry
20 my bones with you from here." And they moved on from
Succoth, and encamped at Etham, on the edge of the
21 wilderness. And the LORD went before them by day in a
pillar of cloud to lead them along the way, and by night
in a pillar of fire to give them light, that they might travel
22 by day and by night; the pillar of cloud by day and the
pillar of fire by night did not depart from before the
people.

Crossing the Red Sea

2
14 Then the LORD said to Moses, "Tell the people
of Israel to turn back and encamp in front of Pi-
ha-hi'roth, between Migdol and the sea, in front of
Ba'al-zephon; you shall encamp over against it, by the
3 sea. For Pharaoh will say of the people of Israel, 'They
are entangled in the land; the wilderness has shut them
4 in.' And I will harden Pharaoh's heart, and he will pursue
them and I will get glory over Pharaoh and all his host;
and the Egyptians shall know that I am the LORD." And
they did so.

p Gk: Heb *and it lit up the night*

5 When the king of Egypt was told that the people had
fled, the mind of Pharaoh and his servants was changed
toward the people, and they said, "What is this we have
6 done, that we have let Israel go from serving us?" So he
7 made ready his chariot and took his army with him, and
took six hundred picked chariots and all the other chariots
8 of Egypt with officers over all of them. And the LORD
hardened the heart of Pharaoh king of Egypt and he
pursued the people of Israel as they went forth defiantly.
9 The Egyptians pursued them, all Pharaoh's horses and
chariots and his horsemen and his army, and overtook
them encamped at the sea, by Pi-ha-hi'roth, in front of
Ba'al-zephon.
10 When Pharaoh drew near, the people of Israel lifted
up their eyes, and behold, the Egyptians were marching
after them; and they were in great fear. And the people
11 of Israel cried out to the LORD; and they said to Moses,
"Is it because there are no graves in Egypt that you have
taken us away to die in the wilderness? What have you
12 done to us, in bringing us out of Egypt? Is not this what
we said to you in Egypt, 'Let us alone and let us serve
the Egyptians'? For it would have been better for us to
13 serve the Egyptians than to die in the wilderness." And
Moses said to the people, "Fear not, stand firm, and see
the salvation of the LORD, which he will work for you
today; for the Egyptians whom you see today, you shall
14 never see again. The LORD will fight for you, and you
15 have only to be still." The LORD said to Moses, "Why do
you cry to me? Tell the people of Israel to go forward.
16 Lift up your rod, and stretch out your hand over the sea
and divide it, that the people of Israel may go on dry
17 ground through the sea. And I will harden the hearts of
the Egyptians so that they shall go in after them, and I
will get glory over Pharaoh and all his host, his chariots,
18 and his horsemen. And the Egyptians shall know that
I am the LORD, when I have gotten glory over Pharaoh,
his chariots, and his horsemen."
19 Then the angel of God who went before the host of
Israel moved and went behind them; and the pillar of
cloud moved from before them and stood behind them,
20 coming between the host of Egypt and the host of Israel.
And there was the cloud and the darkness; and the night
passed p without one coming near the other all night.
21 Then Moses stretched out his hand over the sea; and
the LORD drove the sea back by a strong east wind all
night, and made the sea dry land, and the waters were
22 divided. And the people of Israel went into the midst of
the sea on dry ground, the waters being a wall to them
23 on their right hand and on their left. The Egyptians pursued, and went in after them into the midst of the sea, all
24 Pharaoh's horses, his chariots, and his horsemen. And in
the morning watch the LORD in the pillar of fire and of
cloud looked down upon the host of the Egyptians, and

25 discomfited the host of the Egyptians, clogging q their chariot wheels so that they drove heavily; and the Egyptians said, "Let us flee from before Israel; for the LORD fights for them against the Egyptians."

26 Then the LORD said to Moses, "Stretch out your hand over the sea, that the water may come back upon the Egyptians, upon their chariots, and upon their horsemen."

27 So Moses stretched forth his hand over the sea, and the sea returned to its wonted flow when the morning appeared; and the Egyptians fled into it, and the LORD

28 routed r the Egyptians in the midst of the sea. The waters returned and covered the chariots and the horsemen and all the host s of Pharaoh that had followed them into the

29 sea; not so much as one of them remained. But the people of Israel walked on dry ground through the sea, the waters being a wall to them on their right hand and on their left.

30 Thus the LORD saved Israel that day from the hand of the Egyptians; and Israel saw the Egyptians dead upon the

31 seashore. And Israel saw the great work which the LORD did against the Egyptians, and the people feared the LORD; and they believed in the LORD and in his servant Moses.

HYMNS IN PRAISE OF THE LORD

15 Then Moses and the people of Israel sang this song to the LORD, saying,

"I will sing to the LORD, for he has triumphed gloriously;
    the horse and his rider t he has thrown into the sea.
2 The LORD is my strength and my song,
    and he has become my salvation;
  this is my God, and I will praise him,
    my father's God, and I will exalt him.
3 The LORD is a man of war;
    the LORD is his name.

4 "Pharaoh's chariots and his host he cast into the sea;
    and his picked officers are sunk in the Red Sea.

thou sendest forth thy fury, it consumes them like stubble.
8 At the blast of thy nostrils the waters piled up,
    the floods stood up in a heap;
    the deeps congealed in the heart of the sea.
9 The enemy said, 'I will pursue, I will overtake,
    I will divide the spoil, my desire shall have its fill of them.
    I will draw my sword, my hand shall destroy them.'
10 Thou didst blow with thy wind, the sea covered them;
    they sank as lead in the mighty waters.

11 "Who is like thee, O LORD, among the gods?
    Who is like thee, majestic in holiness,
    terrible in glorious deeds, doing wonders?
12 Thou didst stretch out thy right hand,
    the earth swallowed them.

13 "Thou hast led in thy steadfast love the people whom thou hast redeemed,
    thou hast guided them by thy strength to thy holy abode.
14 The peoples have heard, they tremble;
    pangs have seized on the inhabitants of Philistia.
15 Now are the chiefs of Edom dismayed;
    the leaders of Moab, trembling seizes them;
    all the inhabitants of Canaan have melted away.
16 Terror and dread fall upon them;
    because of the greatness of thy arm, they are as still as a stone,
  till thy people, O LORD, pass by,
    till the people pass by whom thou hast purchased.
17 Thou wilt bring them in, and plant them on thy own mountain,
    the place, O LORD, which thou hast made for thy abode,
    the sanctuary, O LORD, which thy hands have established.

5 The floods cover them;
    they went down into the depths like a stone.
6 Thy right hand, O LORD, glorious in power,
    thy right hand, O LORD, shatters the enemy.
7 In the greatness of thy majesty thou overthrowest thy adversaries;

18 The LORD will reign for ever and ever."

19 For when the horses of Pharaoh with his chariots and his horsemen went into the sea, the LORD brought back the waters of the sea upon them; but the people of Israel

20 walked on dry ground in the midst of the sea. Then

---

q Or binding. Sam Gk Syr: Heb removing   r Heb shook off   s Gk Syr: Heb to all the host   t Or its chariot

Miriam, the prophetess, the sister of Aaron, took a timbrel in her hand; and all the women went out after her with
21 timbrels and dancing. And Miriam sang to them:

"Sing to the LORD, for he has triumphed gloriously;
the horse and his rider he has thrown into the sea."

THE PILGRIMAGE TO SINAI

22 Then Moses led Israel onward from the Red Sea, and they went into the wilderness of Shur; they went three
23 days in the wilderness and found no water. When they came to Marah, they could not drink the water of Marah
24 because it was bitter; therefore it was named Marah.u And the people murmured against Moses, saying, "What shall
25 we drink?" And he cried to the LORD; and the LORD showed him a tree, and he threw it into the water, and the water became sweet.

There the LORDv made for them a statute and an
26 ordinance and there he proved them, saying, "If you will diligently hearken to the voice of the LORD your God, and do that which is right in his eyes, and give heed to his commandments and keep all his statutes, I will put none of the diseases upon you which I put upon the Egyptians; for I am the LORD, your healer."
27 Then they came to Elim, where there were twelve springs of water and seventy palm trees; and they encamped there by the water.

Quail and Manna

16 They set out from Elim, and all the congregation of the people of Israel came to the wilderness of Sin, which is between Elim and Sinai, on the fifteenth day of the second month after they had departed from
2 the land of Egypt. And the whole congregation of the people of Israel murmured against Moses and Aaron in
3 the wilderness, and said to them, "Would that we had died by the hand of the LORD in the land of Egypt, when we sat by the fleshpots and ate bread to the full; for you have brought us out into this wilderness to kill this whole assembly with hunger."
4 Then the LORD said to Moses, "Behold, I will rain bread from heaven for you; and the people shall go out and gather a day's portion every day, that I may prove them,
5 whether they will walk in my law or not. On the sixth day, when they prepare what they bring in, it will be
6 twice as much as they gather daily." So Moses and Aaron said to all the people of Israel, "At evening you shall know that it was the LORD who brought you out of the land of
7 Egypt, and in the morning you shall see the glory of the LORD, because he has heard your murmurings against the LORD. For what are we, that you murmur against us?"
8 And Moses said, "When the LORD gives you in the evening flesh to eat and in the morning bread to the full, because

the LORD has heard your murmurings which you murmur against him—what are we? Your murmurings are not against us but against the LORD."
9 And Moses said to Aaron, "Say to the whole congregation of the people of Israel, 'Come near before the LORD,
10 for he has heard your murmurings.'" And as Aaron spoke to the whole congregation of the people of Israel, they looked toward the wilderness, and behold, the glory of
11 the LORD appeared in the cloud. And the LORD said to
12 Moses, "I have heard the murmurings of the people of Israel; say to them, 'At twilight you shall eat flesh, and in the morning you shall be filled with bread; then you shall know that I am the LORD your God.'"

13 In the evening quails came up and covered the camp; and in the morning dew lay round about the camp.
14 And when the dew had gone up, there was on the face of the wilderness a fine, flake-like thing, fine as hoarfrost
15 on the ground. When the people of Israel saw it, they said to one another, "What is it?"w For they did not know what it was. And Moses said to them, "It is the
16 bread which the LORD has given you to eat. This is what the LORD has commanded: Gather of it, every man of you, as much as he can eat; you shall take an omer apiece, according to the number of the persons whom each of
17 you has in his tent.'" And the people of Israel did so;
18 they gathered, some more, some less. But when they measured it with an omer, he that gathered much had nothing over, and he that gathered little had no lack;
19 each gathered according to what he could eat. And Moses said to them, "Let no man leave any of it till the morn-
20 ing." But they did not listen to Moses; some left part of it till the morning, and it bred worms and became foul;
21 and Moses was angry with them. Morning by morning they gathered it, each as much as he could eat; but when the sun grew hot, it melted.

Institution of the Sabbath

22 On the sixth day they gathered twice as much bread, two omers apiece; and when all the leaders of the congre-
23 gation came and told Moses, he said to them, "This is what the LORD has commanded: 'Tomorrow is a day of solemn rest, a holy sabbath to the LORD; bake what you will bake and boil what you will boil, and all that is left
24 over lay by to be kept till the morning.'" So they laid it by till the morning, as Moses bade them; and it did not

u That is *Bitterness*   v Heb *he*   w Or "*It is manna.*" Heb *man hu*

25 become foul, and there were no worms in it. Moses said, "Eat it today, for today is a sabbath to the LORD; today 26 you will not find it in the field. Six days you shall gather it; but on the seventh day, which is a sabbath, there will 27 be none." On the seventh day some of the people went out 28 to gather, and they found none. And the LORD said to Moses, "How long do you refuse to keep my command- 29 ments and my laws? See! The LORD has given you the sabbath, therefore on the sixth day he gives you bread for two days; remain every man of you in his place, let 30 no man go out of his place on the seventh day." So the people rested on the seventh day.

31 Now the house of Israel called its name manna; it was like coriander seed, white, and the taste of it was like 32 wafers made with honey. And Moses said, "This is what the LORD has commanded: 'Let an omer of it be kept throughout your generations, that they may see the bread with which I fed you in the wilderness, when I brought 33 you out of the land of Egypt.'" And Moses said to Aaron, "Take a jar, and put an omer of manna in it, and place it before the LORD, to be kept throughout your genera-

34 tions." As the LORD commanded Moses, so Aaron placed 35 it before the testimony, to be kept. And the people of Israel ate the manna forty years, till they came to a habitable land; they ate the manna, till they came to the 36 border of the land of Canaan. (An omer is the tenth part of an ephah.)

Water from the Rock

17 All the congregation of the people of Israel moved on from the wilderness of Sin by stages, according to the commandment of the LORD, and camped at Reph'- idim; but there was no water for the people to drink. 2 Therefore the people found fault with Moses, and said, "Give us water to drink." And Moses said to them, "Why do you find fault with me? Why do you put the LORD 3 to the proof?" But the people thirsted there for water, and the people murmured against Moses, and said, "Why did you bring us up out of Egypt, to kill us and our 4 children and our cattle with thirst?" So Moses cried to the LORD, "What shall I do with this people? They are 5 almost ready to stone me." And the LORD said to Moses, "Pass on before the people, taking with you some of the elders of Israel; and take in your hand the rod with which 6 you struck the Nile, and go. Behold, I will stand before you there on the rock at Horeb; and you shall strike the

rock, and water shall come out of it, that the people may drink." And Moses did so, in the sight of the elders of 7 Israel. And he called the name of the place Massah x and Mer'ibah,y because of the faultfinding of the children

of Israel, and because they put the LORD to the proof by saying, "Is the LORD among us or not?"

8 Then came Am'alek and fought with Israel at Reph'- 9 idim. And Moses said to Joshua, "Choose for us men, and go out, fight with Am'alek; tomorrow I will stand on the top of the hill with the rod of God in my hand." 10 So Joshua did as Moses told him, and fought with Am'- alek; and Moses, Aaron, and Hur went up to the top of 11 the hill. Whenever Moses held up his hand, Israel pre- vailed; and whenever he lowered his hand, Am'alek 12 prevailed. But Moses' hands grew weary; so they took a stone and put it under him, and he sat upon it, and Aaron and Hur held up his hands, one on one side, and the other on the other side; so his hands were steady 13 until the going down of the sun. And Joshua mowed down Am'alek and his people with the edge of the sword.

14 And the LORD said to Moses, "Write this as a memorial in a book and recite it in the ears of Joshua, that I will utterly blot out the remembrance of Am'alek from under 15 heaven." And Moses built an altar and called the name of 16 it, The LORD is my banner, saying, "A hand upon the banner of the LORD! z The LORD will have war with Am'alek from generation to generation."

Jethro Visits Moses

18 Jethro, the priest of Mid'ian, Moses' father-in-law, heard of all that God had done for Moses and for Israel his people, how the LORD had brought Israel out of 2 Egypt. Now Jethro, Moses' father-in-law, had taken 3 Zippo'rah, Moses' wife, after he had sent her away, and her two sons, of whom the name of the one was Gershom (for he said, "I have been a sojourner a in a foreign 4 land"), and the name of the other, Elie'zer b (for he said, "The God of my father was my help, and delivered me 5 from the sword of Pharaoh"). And Jethro, Moses' father- in-law, came with his sons and his wife to Moses in the wilderness where he was encamped at the mountain of 6 God. And when one told Moses, "Lo,c your father-in-law Jethro is coming to you with your wife and her two 7 sons with her," Moses went out to meet his father-in-law,

x That is *Proof*   y That is *Contention*   z Cn: Heb obscure   a Heb *ger*   b Heb *Eli*, my God, *ezer*, help
c Sam Gk Syr: Heb *I*

and did obeisance and kissed him; and they asked each
8 other of their welfare, and went into the tent. Then Moses
told his father-in-law all that the LORD had done to Pharaoh and to the Egyptians for Israel's sake, all the hardship that had come upon them in the way, and how the
9 LORD had delivered them. And Jethro rejoiced for all
the good which the LORD had done to Israel, in that he
had delivered them out of the hand of the Egyptians.
10 And Jethro said, "Blessed be the LORD, who has delivered you out of the hand of the Egyptians and out of
11 the hand of Pharaoh. Now I know that the LORD is greater
than all gods, because he delivered the people from under
the hand of the Egyptians,d when they dealt arrogantly
12 with them." And Jethro, Moses' father-in-law, offerede a
burnt offering and sacrifices to God; and Aaron came
with all the elders of Israel to eat bread with Moses'
father-in-law before God.
13 On the morrow Moses sat to judge the people, and the
people stood about Moses from morning till evening.
14 When Moses' father-in-law saw all that he was doing for
the people, he said, "What is this that you are doing for
the people? Why do you sit alone, and all the people
15 stand about you from morning till evening?" And Moses
said to his father-in-law, "Because the people come to me
16 to inquire of God; when they have a dispute, they come
to me and I decide between a man and his neighbor, and
I make them know the statutes of God and his decisions."
17 Moses' father-in-law said to him, "What you are doing is
18 not good. You and the people with you will wear yourselves out, for the thing is too heavy for you; you are
19 not able to perform it alone. Listen now to my voice; I
will give you counsel, and God be with you! You shall
represent the people before God, and bring their cases
20 to God; and you shall teach them the statutes and the
decisions, and make them know the way in which they
21 must walk and what they must do. Moreover choose able
men from all the people, such as fear God, men who are
trustworthy and who hate a bribe; and place such men
over the people as rulers of thousands, of hundreds, of
22 fifties, and of tens. And let them judge the people at all
times; every great matter they shall bring to you, but any
small matter they shall decide themselves; so it will be
easier for you, and they will bear the burden with you.
23 If you do this, and God so commands you, then you will
be able to endure, and all this people also will go to their
place in peace."
24 So Moses gave heed to the voice of his father-in-law
25 and did all that he had said. Moses chose able men out
of all Israel, and made them heads over the people, rulers
26 of thousands, of hundreds, of fifties, and of tens. And
they judged the people at all times; hard cases they
brought to Moses, but any small matter they decided
27 themselves. Then Moses let his father-in-law depart, and
he went his way to his own country.

---

d Transposing the last clause of v. 10 to v. 11   e Syr Tg Vg: Heb took

THE COVENANT

19 On the third new moon after the people of Israel
had gone forth out of the land of Egypt, on that
2 day they came into the wilderness of Sinai. And when
they set out from Reph'idim and came into the wilderness
of Sinai, they encamped in the wilderness; and there
3 Israel encamped before the mountain. And Moses went
up to God, and the LORD called to him out of the mountain, saying, "Thus you shall say to the house of Jacob,
4 and tell the people of Israel: You have seen what I did to
the Egyptians, and how I bore you on eagles' wings and
5 brought you to myself. Now therefore, if you will obey
my voice and keep my covenant, you shall be my own
possession among all peoples; for all the earth is mine,
6 and you shall be to me a kingdom of priests and a holy
nation. These are the words which you shall speak to the
children of Israel."
7 So Moses came and called the elders of the people, and
set before them all these words which the LORD had com-
8 manded him. And all the people answered together and
said, "All that the LORD has spoken we will do." And
9 Moses reported the words of the people to the LORD. And
the LORD said to Moses, "Lo, I am coming to you in a
thick cloud, that the people may hear when I speak with
you, and may also believe you for ever."
Then Moses told the words of the people to the LORD.
10 And the LORD said to Moses, "Go to the people and
consecrate them today and tomorrow, and let them wash
11 their garments, and be ready by the third day; for on
the third day the LORD will come down upon Mount Sinai
12 in the sight of all the people. And you shall set bounds
for the people round about, saying, 'Take heed that you
do not go up into the mountain or touch the border of it;
13 whoever touches the mountain shall be put to death; no
hand shall touch him, but he shall be stoned or shot;
whether beast or man, he shall not live.' When the
trumpet sounds a long blast, they shall come up to the
14 mountain." So Moses went down from the mountain to
the people, and consecrated the people; and they washed
15 their garments. And he said to the people, "Be ready by
the third day; do not go near a woman."
16 On the morning of the third day there were thunders
and lightnings, and a thick cloud upon the mountain, and
a very loud trumpet blast, so that all the people who were
17 in the camp trembled. Then Moses brought the people
out of the camp to meet God; and they took their stand
18 at the foot of the mountain. And Mount Sinai was
wrapped in smoke, because the LORD descended upon it
in fire; and the smoke of it went up like the smoke of a
19 kiln, and the whole mountain quaked greatly. And as the
sound of the trumpet grew louder and louder, Moses
20 spoke, and God answered him in thunder. And the LORD
came down upon Mount Sinai, to the top of the mountain;
and the LORD called Moses to the top of the mountain,

²¹ and Moses went up. And the LORD said to Moses, "Go down and warn the people, lest they break through to the ²² LORD to gaze and many of them perish. And also let the priests who come near to the LORD consecrate themselves, ²³ lest the LORD break out upon them." And Moses said to the LORD, "The people cannot come up to Mount Sinai; for thou thyself didst charge us, saying, 'Set bounds about ²⁴ the mountain, and consecrate it.'" And the LORD said to him, "Go down, and come up bringing Aaron with you; but do not let the priests and the people break through to come up to the LORD, lest he break out against them." ²⁵ So Moses went down to the people and told them.

COMMANDMENTS FROM THE LORD

20 And God spoke all these words, saying,
² "I am the LORD your God, who brought you out of the land of Egypt, out of the house of bondage.
³ "You shall have no other gods before ͨ me.

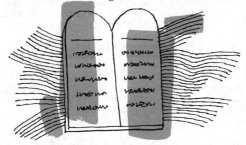

⁴ "You shall not make for yourself a graven image, or any likeness of anything that is in heaven above, or that is in the earth beneath, or that is in the water under the ⁵ earth; you shall not bow down to them or serve them; for I the LORD your God am a jealous God, visiting the iniquity of the fathers upon the children to the third and ⁶ the fourth generation of those who hate me, but showing steadfast love to thousands of those who love me and keep my commandments.

⁷ "You shall not take the name of the LORD your God in vain; for the LORD will not hold him guiltless who takes his name in vain.

⁸,⁹ "Remember the sabbath day, to keep it holy. Six days ¹⁰ you shall labor, and do all your work; but the seventh day is a sabbath to the LORD your God; in it you shall not do any work, you, or your son, or your daughter, your manservant, or your maidservant, or your cattle, or the ¹¹ sojourner who is within your gates; for in six days the LORD made heaven and earth, the sea, and all that is in them, and rested the seventh day; therefore the LORD blessed the sabbath day and hallowed it.

¹² "Honor your father and your mother, that your days may be long in the land which the LORD your God gives you.

¹³ "You shall not kill.

¹⁴ "You shall not commit adultery.

¹⁵ "You shall not steal.

¹⁶ "You shall not bear false witness against your neighbor.

¹⁷ "You shall not covet your neighbor's house; you shall not covet your neighbor's wife, or his manservant, or his maidservant, or his ox, or his ass, or anything that is your neighbor's."

The People's Fear of God

¹⁸ Now when all the people perceived the thunderings and the lightnings and the sound of the trumpet and the mountain smoking, the people were afraid and trembled; and ¹⁹ they stood afar off, and said to Moses, "You speak to us, and we will hear; but let not God speak to us, lest we ²⁰ die." And Moses said to the people, "Do not fear; for God has come to prove you, and that the fear of him may be before your eyes, that you may not sin."

²¹ And the people stood afar off, while Moses drew near to the thick darkness where God was.

THE LAWS OF THE COVENANT

²² And the LORD said to Moses, "Thus you shall say to the people of Israel: 'You have seen for yourselves that I have talked ²³ with you from heaven. You shall not make gods of silver to be ²⁴ with me, nor shall you make for yourselves gods of gold. An altar of earth you shall make for me and sacrifice on it your burnt offerings and your peace offerings, your sheep and your oxen; in every place where I cause my name to be remembered ²⁵ I will come to you and bless you. And if you make me an altar of stone, you shall not build it of hewn stones; for if you wield ²⁶ your tool upon it you profane it. And you shall not go up by steps to my altar, that your nakedness be not exposed on it.'

Civil and Criminal Laws

21 "Now these are the ordinances which you shall set ² before them. When you buy a Hebrew slave, he shall serve six years, and in the seventh he shall go out free, for ³ nothing. If he comes in single, he shall go out single; if he ⁴ comes in married, then his wife shall go out with him. If his master gives him a wife and she bears him sons or daughters, the wife and her children shall be her master's and he shall ⁵ go out alone. But if the slave plainly says, 'I love my master, ⁶ my wife, and my children; I will not go out free,' then his master shall bring him to God, and he shall bring him to the door or the doorpost; and his master shall bore his ear through with an awl; and he shall serve him for life.

⁷ "When a man sells his daughter as a slave, she shall not go ⁸ out as the male slaves do. If she does not please her master, who has designated her ᵍ for himself, then he shall let her be redeemed; he shall have no right to sell her to a foreign people, ⁹ since he has dealt faithlessly with her. If he designates her for ¹⁰ his son, he shall deal with her as with a daughter. If he takes another wife to himself, he shall not diminish her food, her ¹¹ clothing, or her marital rights. And if he does not do these three things for her, she shall go out for nothing, without payment of money.

¹² "Whoever strikes a man so that he dies shall be put to death. ¹³ But if he did not lie in wait for him, but God let him fall into his hand, then I will appoint for you a place to which he may ¹⁴ flee. But if a man willfully attacks another to kill him treacherously, you shall take him from my altar, that he may die.

¹⁵ "Whoever strikes his father or his mother shall be put to death.

¹⁶ "Whoever steals a man, whether he sells him or is found in possession of him, shall be put to death.

¹⁷ "Whoever curses his father or his mother shall be put to death.

¹⁸ "When men quarrel and one strikes the other with a stone or with his fist and the man does not die but keeps his bed, ¹⁹ then if the man rises again and walks abroad with his staff, he that struck him shall be clear; only he shall pay for the

---

ᶠ Or *besides*   ᵍ Another reading is *so that he has not designated her*

loss of his time, and shall have him thoroughly healed.

20 "When a man strikes his slave, male or female, with a rod
21 and the slave dies under his hand, he shall be punished. But if the slave survives a day or two, he is not to be punished; for the slave is his money.

22 "When men strive together, and hurt a woman with child, so that there is a miscarriage, and yet no harm follows, the one who hurt her shall[h] be fined, according as the woman's husband shall lay upon him; and he shall pay as the judges
23 determine. If any harm follows, then you shall give life for
24 life, eye for eye, tooth for tooth, hand for hand, foot for foot,
25 burn for burn, wound for wound, stripe for stripe.

26 "When a man strikes the eye of his slave, male or female, and destroys it, he shall let the slave go free for the eye's
27 sake. If he knocks out the tooth of his slave, male or female, he shall let the slave go free for the tooth's sake.

28 "When an ox gores a man or a woman to death, the ox shall be stoned, and its flesh shall not be eaten; but the owner of
29 the ox shall be clear. But if the ox has been accustomed to gore in the past, and its owner has been warned but has not kept it in, and it kills a man or a woman, the ox shall be
30 stoned, and its owner also shall be put to death. If a ransom is laid on him, then he shall give for the redemption of his
31 life whatever is laid upon him. If it gores a man's son or daughter, he shall be dealt with according to this same rule.
32 If the ox gores a slave, male or female, the owner shall give to their master thirty shekels of silver, and the ox shall be stoned.

33 "When a man leaves a pit open, or when a man digs a pit
34 and does not cover it, and an ox or an ass falls into it, the owner of the pit shall make it good; he shall give money to its owner, and the dead beast shall be his.

35 "When one man's ox hurts another's, so that it dies, then they shall sell the live ox and divide the price of it; and the dead
36 beast also they shall divide. Or if it is known that the ox has been accustomed to gore in the past, and its owner has not kept it in, he shall pay ox for ox, and the dead beast shall be his.

22[i] "If a man steals an ox or a sheep, and kills it or sells it, he shall pay five oxen for an ox, and four sheep for a sheep. [j] He shall make restitution; if he has nothing, then he
4 shall be sold for his theft. If the stolen beast is found alive in his possession, whether it is an ox or an ass or a sheep, he shall pay double.

2 [k] "If a thief is found breaking in, and is struck so that he
3 dies, there shall be no bloodguilt for him; but if the sun has risen upon him, there shall be bloodguilt for him.

5 "When a man causes a field or vineyard to be grazed over, or lets his beast loose and it feeds in another man's field, he shall make restitution from the best in his own field and in his own vineyard.

6 "When fire breaks out and catches in thorns so that the stacked grain or the standing grain or the field is consumed, he that kindled the fire shall make full restitution.

7 "If a man delivers to his neighbor money or goods to keep, and it is stolen out of the man's house, then, if the thief is
8 found, he shall pay double. If the thief is not found, the owner of the house shall come near to God, to show whether or not he has put his hand to his neighbor's goods.

9 "For every breach of trust, whether it is for ox, for ass, for sheep, for clothing, or for any kind of lost thing, of which one says, 'This is it,' the case of both parties shall come before God; he whom God shall condemn shall pay double to his neighbor.

10 "If a man delivers to his neighbor an ass or an ox or a sheep or any beast to keep, and it dies or is hurt or is driven away,
11 without any one seeing it, an oath by the LORD shall be between them both to see whether he has not put his hand to his neighbor's property; and the owner shall accept the oath,
12 and he shall not make restitution. But if it is stolen from him,
13 he shall make restitution to its owner. If it is torn by beasts, let him bring it as evidence; he shall not make restitution for what has been torn.

14 "If a man borrows anything of his neighbor, and it is hurt or dies, the owner not being with it, he shall make full restitu-
15 tion. If the owner was with it, he shall not make restitution; if it was hired, it came for its hire.[l]

16 "If a man seduces a virgin who is not betrothed, and lies

with her, he shall give the marriage present for her, and make
17 her his wife. If her father utterly refuses to give her to him, he shall pay money equivalent to the marriage present for virgins.

Moral and Religious Laws

18 "You shall not permit a sorceress to live.
19 "Whoever lies with a beast shall be put to death.
20 "Whoever sacrifices to any god, save to the LORD only, shall be utterly destroyed.
21 "You shall not wrong a stranger or oppress him, for you
22 were strangers in the land of Egypt. You shall not afflict any
23 widow or orphan. If you do afflict them, and they cry out to
24 me, I will surely hear their cry; and my wrath will burn, and I will kill you with the sword, and your wives shall become widows and your children fatherless.

25 "If you lend money to any of my people with you who is poor, you shall not be to him as a creditor, and you shall not
26 exact interest from him. If ever you take your neighbor's garment in pledge, you shall restore it to him before the sun
27 goes down; for that is his only covering, it is his mantle for his body; in what else shall he sleep? And if he cries to me, I will hear, for I am compassionate.

28 "You shall not revile God, nor curse a ruler of your people.
29 "You shall not delay to offer from the fulness of your harvest and from the outflow of your presses.
30 "The first-born of your sons you shall give me. You shall do likewise with your oxen and with your sheep: seven days it shall be with its dam; on the eighth day you shall give it to me.
31 "You shall be men consecrated to me; therefore you shall not eat any flesh that is torn by beasts in the field; you shall cast it to the dogs.

23 "You shall not utter a false report. You shall not join hands with a wicked man, to be a malicious witness.
2 You shall not follow a multitude to do evil; nor shall you bear witness in a suit, turning aside after a multitude, so as to
3 pervert justice; nor shall you be partial to a poor man in his suit.
4 "If you meet your enemy's ox or his ass going astray, you
5 shall bring it back to him. If you see the ass of one who hates you lying under its burden, you shall refrain from leaving him with it, you shall help him to lift it up.[m]
6 "You shall not pervert the justice due to your poor in his
7 suit. Keep far from a false charge, and do not slay the innocent
8 and righteous, for I will not acquit the wicked. And you shall take no bribe, for a bribe blinds the officials, and subverts the cause of those who are in the right.
9 "You shall not oppress a stranger; you know the heart of a stranger, for you were strangers in the land of Egypt.
10 "For six years you shall sow your land and gather in its
11 yield; but the seventh year you shall let it rest and lie fallow, that the poor of your people may eat; and what they leave the wild beasts may eat. You shall do likewise with your vineyard, and with your olive orchard.
12 "Six days you shall do your work, but on the seventh day you shall rest; that your ox and your ass may have rest, and the son of your bondmaid, and the alien, may be refreshed.
13 Take heed to all that I have said to you; and make no mention of the names of other gods, nor let such be heard out of your mouth.
14 "Three times in the year you shall keep a feast to me.
15 You shall keep the feast of unleavened bread; as I commanded you, you shall eat unleavened bread for seven days at the appointed time in the month of Abib, for in it you came out
16 of Egypt. None shall appear before me empty-handed. You shall keep the feast of harvest, of the first fruits of your labor, of what you sow in the field. You shall keep the feast of ingathering at the end of the year, when you gather in from the
17 field the fruit of your labor. Three times in the year shall all your males appear before the Lord GOD.
18 "You shall not offer the blood of my sacrifice with leavened bread, or let the fat of my feast remain until the morning.
19 "The first of the first fruits of your ground you shall bring into the house of the LORD your God.

"You shall not boil a kid in its mother's milk.

20 "Behold, I send an angel before you, to guard you on the way and to bring you to the place which I have prepared.
21 Give heed to him and hearken to his voice, do not rebel against

---

[h] Heb *he shall* [i] Ch 21. 37 in Heb [j] Restoring the second half of verse 3 with 4 to their place immediately following verse 1
[k] Ch 22. 1 in Heb [l] Or *it is reckoned in* (Heb *comes into*) *its hire* [m] Gk: Heb obscure

him, for he will not pardon your transgression; for my name is in him.

22 "But if you hearken attentively to his voice and do all that I say, then I will be an enemy to your enemies and an adversary to your adversaries.

23 "When my angel goes before you, and brings you in to the Amorites, and the Hittites, and the Per'izzites, and the Canaanites, the Hivites, and the Jeb'usites, and I blot them out,

24 you shall not bow down to their gods, nor serve them, nor do according to their works, but you shall utterly overthrow

25 them and break their pillars in pieces. You shall serve the LORD your God, and I[n] will bless your bread and your water;

26 and I will take sickness away from the midst of you. None shall cast her young or be barren in your land; I will fulfil

27 the number of your days. I will send my terror before you, and will throw into confusion all the people against whom you shall come, and I will make all your enemies turn their backs

28 to you. And I will send hornets before you, which shall drive

29 out Hivite, Canaanite, and Hittite from before you. I will not drive them out from before you in one year, lest the land become desolate and the wild beasts multiply against you.

30 Little by little I will drive them out from before you, until

31 you are increased and possess the land. And I will set your bounds from the Red Sea to the sea of the Philistines, and from the wilderness to the Eu-phra'tes; for I will deliver the inhabitants of the land into your hand, and you shall drive

32 them out before you. You shall make no covenant with them

33 or with their gods. They shall not dwell in your land, lest they make you sin against me; for if you serve their gods, it will surely be a snare to you."

9 Then Moses and Aaron, Nadab, and Abi'hu, and

10 seventy of the elders of Israel went up, and they saw the God of Israel; and there was under his feet as it were a pavement of sapphire stone, like the very heaven for

11 clearness. And he did not lay his hand on the chief men of the people of Israel; they beheld God, and ate and drank.

12 The LORD said to Moses, "Come up to me on the mountain, and wait there; and I will give you the tables of stone, with the law and the commandment, which I

13 have written for their instruction." So Moses rose with his servant Joshua, and Moses went up into the mountain

14 of God. And he said to the elders, "Tarry here for us, until we come to you again; and, behold, Aaron and Hur are with you; whoever has a cause, let him go to them."

15 Then Moses went up on the mountain, and the cloud

16 covered the mountain. The glory of the LORD settled on Mount Sinai, and the cloud covered it six days; and on the seventh day he called to Moses out of the midst of

THE LORD'S COVENANT WITH ISRAEL

24 And he said to Moses, "Come up to the LORD, you and Aaron, Nadab, and Abi'hu, and seventy

2 of the elders of Israel, and worship afar off. Moses alone shall come near to the LORD; but the others shall not come near, and the people shall not come up with him."

3 Moses came and told the people all the words of the LORD and all the ordinances; and all the people answered with one voice, and said, "All the words which the LORD

4 has spoken we will do." And Moses wrote all the words of the LORD. And he rose early in the morning, and built an altar at the foot of the mountain, and twelve pillars,

5 according to the twelve tribes of Israel. And he sent young men of the people of Israel, who offered burnt offerings

6 and sacrificed peace offerings of oxen to the LORD. And Moses took half of the blood and put it in basins, and

7 half of the blood he threw against the altar. Then he took the book of the covenant, and read it in the hearing of the people; and they said, "All that the LORD has spoken

8 we will do, and we will be obedient." And Moses took the blood and threw it upon the people, and said, "Behold the blood of the covenant which the LORD has made with you in accordance with all these words."

[n] Gk Vg: Heb *he*

17 the cloud. Now the appearance of the glory of the LORD was like a devouring fire on the top of the mountain in

18 the sight of the people of Israel. And Moses entered the cloud, and went up on the mountain. And Moses was on the mountain forty days and forty nights.

25 The LORD said to Moses, "Speak to the people of Israel, that they take for me an offering; from every man whose heart makes him willing you shall receive the

3 offering for me. And this is the offering which you shall

4 receive from them: gold, silver, and bronze, blue and purple and scarlet stuff and fine twined linen, goats' hair,

5,6 tanned rams' skins, goatskins, acacia wood, oil for the lamps, spices for the anointing oil and for the fragrant

7 incense, onyx stones, and stones for setting, for the ephod

8 and for the breastpiece. And let them make me a sanc

9 tuary, that I may dwell in their midst. According to all that I show you concerning the pattern of the tabernacle, and of all its furniture, so you shall make it.

THE PATTERN OF THE TABERNACLE

10 "They shall make an ark of acacia wood; two cubits and a half shall be its length, a cubit and a half its breadth, and a

11 cubit and a half its height. And you shall overlay it with pure gold, within and without shall you overlay it, and you shall

12 make upon it a molding of gold round about. And you shall

cast four rings of gold for it and put them on its four feet, two rings on the one side of it, and two rings on the other side of

13 it. You shall make poles of acacia wood, and overlay them with

14 gold. And you shall put the poles into the rings on the sides

15 of the ark, to carry the ark by them. The poles shall remain

16 in the rings of the ark; they shall not be taken from it. And you shall put into the ark the testimony which I shall give you.

17 Then you shall make a mercy seat° of pure gold; two cubits and a half shall be its length, and a cubit and half its breadth.

18 And you shall make two cherubim of gold; of hammered work

19 shall you make them, on the two ends of the mercy seat. Make one cherub on the one end, and one cherub on the other end; of one piece with the mercy seat shall you make the cherubim

20 on its two ends. The cherubim shall spread out their wings above, overshadowing the mercy seat with their wings, their faces one to another; toward the mercy seat shall the faces of

21 the cherubim be. And you shall put the mercy seat on the top of the ark; and in the ark you shall put the testimony that I

22 shall give you. There I will meet with you, and from above the mercy seat, from between the two cherubim that are upon the ark of the testimony, I will speak with you of all that I will give you in commandment for the people of Israel.

23 "And you shall make a table of acacia wood; two cubits shall be its length, a cubit its breadth, and a cubit and a half its

24 height. You shall overlay it with pure gold, and make a mold-

25 ing of gold around it. And you shall make around it a frame a handbreadth wide, and a molding of gold around the frame.

26 And you shall make for it four rings of gold, and fasten the

27 rings to the four corners at its four legs. Close to the frame the

28 rings shall lie, as holders for the poles to carry the table. You shall make the poles of acacia wood, and overlay them with

29 gold, and the table shall be carried with these. And you shall make its plates and dishes for incense, and its flagons and bowls with which to pour libations; of pure gold you shall

30 make them. And you shall set the bread of the Presence on the table before me always.

31 "And you shall make a lampstand of pure gold. The base and the shaft of the lampstand shall be made of hammered work; its cups, its capitals, and its flowers shall be of one piece

32 with it; and there shall be six branches going out of its sides, three branches of the lampstand out of one side of it and three

33 branches of the lampstand out of the other side of it; three cups made like almonds, each with capital and flower, on one branch, and three cups made like almonds, each with capital and flower, on the other branch—so for the six branches

34 going out of the lampstand; and on the lampstand itself four

35 cups made like almonds, with their capitals and flowers, and a capital of one piece with it under each pair of the six branches

36 going out from the lampstand. Their capitals and their branches shall be of one piece with it, the whole of it one piece of

37 hammered work of pure gold. And you shall make the seven lamps for it; and the lamps shall be set up so as to give light

38 upon the space in front of it. Its snuffers and their trays shall

39 be of pure gold. Of a talent of pure gold shall it be made,

40 with all these utensils. And see that you make them after the pattern for them, which is being shown you on the mountain.

26 "Moreover you shall make the tabernacle with ten curtains of fine twined linen and blue and purple and scarlet stuff; with cherubim skilfully worked shall you make

2 them. The length of each curtain shall be twenty-eight cubits, and the breadth of each curtain four cubits; all the curtains

3 shall have one measure. Five curtains shall be coupled to one another; and the other five curtains shall be coupled to one

4 another. And you shall make loops of blue on the edge of the outmost curtain in the first set; and likewise you shall make loops on the edge of the outmost curtain in the second set.

5 Fifty loops you shall make on the one curtain, and fifty loops you shall make on the edge of the curtain that is in the second

6 set; the loops shall be opposite one another. And you shall make fifty clasps of gold, and couple the curtains one to the other with the clasps, that the tabernacle may be one whole.

7 "You shall also make curtains of goats' hair for a tent over

8 the tabernacle; eleven curtains shall you make. The length of each curtain shall be thirty cubits, and the breadth of each curtain four cubits; the eleven curtains shall have the same

9 measure. And you shall couple five curtains by themselves, and six curtains by themselves, and the sixth curtain you shall

10 double over at the front of the tent. And you shall make fifty loops on the edge of the curtain that is outmost in one set,

and fifty loops on the edge of the curtain which is outmost in the second set.

11 "And you shall make fifty clasps of bronze, and put the clasps into the loops, and couple the tent together that it may

12 be one whole. And the part that remains of the curtains of the tent, the half curtain that remains, shall hang over the back

13 of the tabernacle. And the cubit on the one side, and the cubit on the other side, of what remains in the length of the curtains of the tent shall hang over the sides of the tabernacle, on this

14 side and that side, to cover it. And you shall make for the tent a covering of tanned rams' skins and goatskins.

15 "And you shall make upright frames for the tabernacle of

16 acacia wood. Ten cubits shall be the length of a frame, and

17 a cubit and a half the breadth of each frame. There shall be two tenons in each frame, for fitting together; so shall you do

18 for all the frames of the tabernacle. You shall make the frames

19 for the tabernacle: twenty frames for the south side; and forty bases of silver you shall make under the twenty frames, two bases under one frame for its two tenons, and two bases under

20 another frame for its two tenons; and for the second side of

21 the tabernacle, on the north side twenty frames, and their forty bases of silver, two bases under one frame, and two bases

22 under another frame; and for the rear of the tabernacle west-

23 ward you shall make six frames. And you shall make two

24 frames for corners of the tabernacle in the rear; they shall be separate beneath, but joined at the top, at the first ring; thus shall it be with both of them; they shall form the two corners.

25 And there shall be eight frames, with their bases of silver, sixteen bases; two bases under one frame, and two bases under another frame.

26 "And you shall make bars of acacia wood, five for the frames

27 of the one side of the tabernacle, and five bars for the frames of the other side of the tabernacle, and five bars for the frames of the side of the tabernacle at the rear westward.

28 The middle bar, halfway up the frames, shall pass through

29 from end to end. You shall overlay the frames with gold, and shall make their rings of gold for holders for the bars; and you

30 shall overlay the bars with gold. And you shall erect the tabernacle according to the plan for it which has been shown you on the mountain.

31 "And you shall make a veil of blue and purple and scarlet stuff and fine twined linen; in skilled work shall it be made,

32 with cherubim; and you shall hang it upon four pillars of acacia overlaid with gold, with hooks of gold, upon four bases

33 of silver. And you shall hang the veil from the clasps, and bring the ark of the testimony in thither within the veil; and the veil shall separate for you the holy place from the most

34 holy. You shall put the mercy seat upon the ark of the

35 testimony in the most holy place. And you shall set the table outside the veil, and the lampstand on the south side of the tabernacle opposite the table; and you shall put the table on the north side.

36 "And you shall make a screen for the door of the tent, of blue and purple and scarlet stuff and fine twined linen, em-

37 broidered with needlework. And you shall make for the screen five pillars of acacia, and overlay them with gold; their hooks shall be of gold, and you shall cast five bases of bronze for them.

27 "You shall make the altar of acacia wood, five cubits long and five cubits broad; the altar shall be square, and

2 its height shall be three cubits. And you shall make horns for it on its four corners; its horns shall be of one piece with

3 it, and you shall overlay it with bronze. You shall make pots for it to receive its ashes, and shovels and basins and forks

4 and firepans; all its utensils you shall make of bronze. You shall also make for it a grating, a network of bronze; and upon the net you shall make four bronze rings at its four

5 corners. And you shall set it under the ledge of the altar so

6 that the net shall extend halfway down the altar. And you shall make poles for the altar, poles of acacia wood, and over-

7 lay them with bronze; and the poles shall be put through the rings, so that the poles shall be upon the two sides of the

8 altar, when it is carried. You shall make it hollow, with boards; as it has been shown you on the mountain, so shall it be made.

9 "You shall make the court of the tabernacle. On the south side the court shall have hangings of fine twined linen a

10 hundred cubits long for one side; their pillars shall be twenty and their bases twenty, of bronze, but the hooks of the pillars

11 and their fillets shall be of silver. And likewise for its length
on the north side there shall be hangings a hundred cubits
long, their pillars twenty and their bases twenty, of bronze,
but the hooks of the pillars and their fillets shall be of silver.
12 And for the breadth of the court on the west side there shall
be hangings for fifty cubits, with ten pillars and ten bases.
13 The breadth of the court on the front to the east shall be fifty
14 cubits. The hangings for the one side of the gate shall be
15 fifteen cubits, with three pillars and three bases. On the other
side the hangings shall be fifteen cubits, with three pillars
16 and three bases. For the gate of the court there shall be a
screen twenty cubits long, of blue and purple and scarlet stuff
and fine twined linen, embroidered with needlework; it shall
17 have four pillars and with them four bases. All the pillars
around the court shall be filleted with silver; their hooks shall
18 be of silver, and their bases of bronze. The length of the court
shall be a hundred cubits, the breadth fifty, and the height
five cubits, with hangings of fine twined linen and bases of
19 bronze. All the utensils of the tabernacle for every use, and all
its pegs and all the pegs of the court, shall be of bronze.
20 "And you shall command the people of Israel that they bring
to you pure beaten olive oil for the light, that a lamp may be
21 set up to burn continually. In the tent of meeting, outside the
veil which is before the testimony, Aaron and his sons shall
tend it from evening to morning before the LORD. It shall be a
statute for ever to be observed throughout their generations by
the people of Israel.

THE GARMENTS FOR THE PRIESTS

28 "Then bring near to you Aaron your brother, and his
sons with him, from among the people of Israel, to serve
me as priests—Aaron and Aaron's sons, Nadab and Abi'hu,
2 Elea'zar and Ith'amar. And you shall make holy garments for
3 Aaron your brother, for glory and for beauty. And you shall
speak to all who have ability, whom I have endowed with an
able mind, that they make Aaron's garments to consecrate him
4 for my priesthood. These are the garments which they shall
make: a breastpiece, an ephod, a robe, a coat of checker work,
a turban, and a girdle; they shall make holy garments for
Aaron your brother and his sons to serve me as priests.
5 "They shall receive gold, blue and purple and scarlet stuff,
6 and fine twined linen. And they shall make the ephod of gold,
of blue and purple and scarlet stuff, and of fine twined linen,
7 skilfully worked. It shall have two shoulder-pieces attached
8 to its two edges, that it may be joined together. And the skilfully woven band upon it, to gird it on, shall be of the same
workmanship and materials, of gold, blue and purple and
9 scarlet stuff, and fine twined linen. And you shall take two
onyx stones, and engrave on them the names of the sons of
10 Israel, six of their names on the one stone, and the names of
the remaining six on the other stone, in the order of their
11 birth. As a jeweler engraves signets, so shall you engrave the
two stones with the names of the sons of Israel; you shall
12 enclose them in settings of gold filigree. And you shall set the
two stones upon the shoulder-pieces of the ephod, as stones of
remembrance for the sons of Israel; and Aaron shall bear their
names before the LORD upon his two shoulders for remembrance.
13, 14 And you shall make settings of gold filigree, and two chains
of pure gold, twisted like cords; and you shall attach the corded
chains to the settings.
15 "And you shall make a breastpiece of judgment, in skilled
work; like the work of the ephod you shall make it; of gold,
blue and purple and scarlet stuff, and fine twined linen shall
16 you make it. It shall be square and double, a span its length
17 and a span its breadth. And you shall set in it four rows of
stones. A row of sardius, topaz, and carbuncle shall be the
18 first row; and the second row an emerald, a sapphire, and a
19 diamond; and the third row a jacinth, an agate, and an
20 amethyst; and the fourth row a beryl, an onyx, and a jasper;
21 they shall be set in gold filigree. There shall be twelve stones
with their names according to the names of the sons of Israel;
they shall be like signets, each engraved with its name, for the
22 twelve tribes. And you shall make for the breastpiece twisted
23 chains like cords, of pure gold; and you shall make for the
breastpiece two rings of gold, and put the two rings on the two
24 edges of the breastpiece. And you shall put the two cords of
25 gold in the two rings at the edges of the breastpiece; the two
ends of the two cords you shall attach to the two settings of
filigree, and so attach it in front to the shoulder-pieces of the
26 ephod. And you shall make two rings of gold, and put them
at the two ends of the breastpiece, on its inside edge next to
27 the ephod. And you shall make two rings of gold, and attach
them in front to the lower part of the two shoulder-pieces of
the ephod, at its joining above the skilfully woven band of the
28 ephod. And they shall bind the breastpiece by its rings to the
rings of the ephod with a lace of blue, that it may lie upon
the skilfully woven band of the ephod, and that the breast-
29 piece shall not come loose from the ephod. So Aaron shall
bear the names of the sons of Israel in the breastpiece of judgment upon his heart, when he goes into the holy place, to
30 bring them to continual remembrance before the LORD. And in
the breastpiece of judgment you shall put the Urim and the
Thummim, and they shall be upon Aaron's heart, when he
goes in before the LORD; thus Aaron shall bear the judgment
of the people of Israel upon his heart before the LORD continually.
31 "And you shall make the robe of the ephod all of blue.
32 It shall have in it an opening for the head, with a woven binding around the opening, like the opening in a garment,[p] that it
33 may not be torn. On its skirts you shall make pomegranates of
blue and purple and scarlet stuff, around its skirts, with bells
34 of gold between them, a golden bell and a pomegranate, a
golden bell and a pomegranate, round about on the skirts of
35 the robe. And it shall be upon Aaron when he ministers, and
its sound shall be heard when he goes into the holy place
before the LORD, and when he comes out, lest he die.
36 "And you shall make a plate of pure gold, and engrave on it,
37 like the engraving of a signet, 'Holy to the LORD.' And you
shall fasten it on the turban by a lace of blue; it shall be on
38 the front of the turban. It shall be upon Aaron's forehead, and
Aaron shall take upon himself any guilt incurred in the holy
offering which the people of Israel hallow as their holy gifts;
it shall always be upon his forehead, that they may be accepted
before the LORD.
39 "And you shall weave the coat in checker work of fine linen,
and you shall make a turban of fine linen, and you shall make
a girdle embroidered with needlework.
40 "And for Aaron's sons you shall make coats and girdles and
41 caps; you shall make them for glory and beauty. And you shall
put them upon Aaron your brother, and upon his sons with
him, and shall anoint them and ordain them and consecrate
42 them, that they may serve me as priests. And you shall make
for them linen breeches to cover their naked flesh; from the
43 loins to the thighs they shall reach; and they shall be upon
Aaron and upon his sons when they go into the tent of
meeting, or when they come near the altar to minister in the
holy place; lest they bring guilt upon themselves and die. This
shall be a perpetual statute for him and for his descendants
after him.

THE ORDINATION OF THE PRIESTS

29 "Now this is what you shall do to them to consecrate
them, that they may serve me as priests. Take one young
2 bull and two rams without blemish, and unleavened bread,
unleavened cakes mixed with oil, and unleavened wafers
spread with oil. You shall make them of fine wheat flour.
3 And you shall put them in one basket and bring them in the
4 basket, and bring the bull and the two rams. You shall bring
Aaron and his sons to the door of the tent of meeting, and
5 wash them with water. And you shall take the garments, and
put on Aaron the coat and the robe of the ephod, and the
ephod, and the breastpiece, and gird him with the skilfully
6 woven band of the ephod; and you shall set the turban on his
7 head, and put the holy crown upon the turban. And you shall
take the anointing oil, and pour it on his head and anoint him.
8, 9 Then you shall bring his sons, and put coats on them, and you
shall gird them with girdles[q] and bind caps on them; and the
priesthood shall be theirs by a perpetual statute. Thus you shall
ordain Aaron and his sons.

Sacrifices

10 "Then you shall bring the bull before the tent of meeting.
Aaron and his sons shall lay their hands upon the head of the
11 bull, and you shall kill the bull before the LORD, at the door
12 of the tent of meeting, and shall take part of the blood of the
bull and put it upon the horns of the altar with your finger,
and the rest of[r] the blood you shall pour out at the base of
13 the altar. And you shall take all the fat that covers the entrails,
and the appendage of the liver, and the two kidneys with the

[p] The Hebrew word is of uncertain meaning [q] Gk: Heb *girdles, Aaron and his sons* [r] Heb *all*

14 fat that is on them, and burn them upon the altar. But the flesh of the bull, and its skin, and its dung, you shall burn with fire outside the camp; it is a sin offering.

15 "Then you shall take one of the rams, and Aaron and his
16 sons shall lay their hands upon the head of the ram, and you shall slaughter the ram, and shall take its blood and throw it
17 against the altar round about. Then you shall cut the ram into pieces, and wash its entrails and its legs, and put them with
18 its pieces and its head, and burn the whole ram upon the altar; it is a burnt offering to the LORD; it is a pleasing odor, an offering by fire to the LORD.

19 "You shall take the other ram; and Aaron and his sons shall
20 lay their hands upon the head of the ram, and you shall kill the ram, and take part of its blood and put it upon the tip of the right ear of Aaron and upon the tips of the right ears of his sons, and upon the thumbs of their right hands, and upon the great toes of their right feet, and throw the rest of the
21 blood against the altar round about. Then you shall take part of the blood that is on the altar, and of the anointing oil, and sprinkle it upon Aaron and his garments, and upon his sons and his sons' garments with him; and he and his garments shall be holy, and his sons and his sons' garments with him.

22 "You shall also take the fat of the ram, and the fat tail, and the fat that covers the entrails, and the appendage of the liver, and the two kidneys with the fat that is on them, and the
23 right thigh (for it is a ram of ordination), and one loaf of bread, and one cake of bread with oil, and one wafer, out
24 of the basket of unleavened bread that is before the LORD; and you shall put all these in the hands of Aaron and in the hands of his sons, and wave them for a wave offering before the
25 LORD. Then you shall take them from their hands, and burn them on the altar in addition to the burnt offering, as a pleasing odor before the LORD; it is an offering by fire to the LORD.

26 "And you shall take the breast of the ram of Aaron's ordi-
27 nation and wave it for a wave offering before the LORD; and it shall be your portion. And you shall consecrate the breast of the wave offering, and the thigh of the priests' portion, which is waved, and which is offered from the ram of ordina-
28 tion, since it is for Aaron and for his sons. It shall be for Aaron and his sons as a perpetual due from the people of Israel, for it is the priests' portion to be offered by the people of Israel from their peace offerings; it is their offering to the LORD.

29 "The holy garments of Aaron shall be for his sons after him,
30 to be anointed in them and ordained in them. The son who is priest in his place shall wear them seven days, when he comes into the tent of meeting to minister in the holy place.

31 "You shall take the ram of ordination, and boil its flesh in
32 a holy place; and Aaron and his sons shall eat the flesh of the ram and the bread that is in the basket, at the door of the tent
33 of meeting. They shall eat those things with which atonement was made, to ordain and consecrate them, but an outsider
34 shall not eat of them, because they are holy. And if any of the flesh for the ordination, or of the bread, remain until the morning, then you shall burn the remainder with fire; it shall not be eaten, because it is holy.

35 "Thus you shall do to Aaron and to his sons, according to all that I have commanded you; through seven days shall you
36 ordain them, and every day you shall offer a bull as a sin offering for atonement. Also you shall offer a sin offering for the altar, when you make atonement for it, and shall anoint it,
37 to consecrate it. Seven days you shall make atonement for the altar, and consecrate it, and the altar shall be most holy; whatever touches the altar shall become holy.

38 "Now this is what you shall offer upon the altar: two lambs
39 a year old day by day continually. One lamb you shall offer in the morning, and the other lamb you shall offer in the eve-
40 ning; and with the first lamb a tenth measure of fine flour mingled with a fourth of a hin of beaten oil, and a fourth of
41 a hin of wine for a libation. And the other lamb you shall offer in the evening, and shall offer with it a cereal offering and its libation, as in the morning, for a pleasing odor, an
42 offering by fire to the LORD. It shall be a continual burnt offering throughout your generations at the door of the tent of meeting before the LORD, where I will meet with you, to speak
43 there to you. There I will meet with the people of Israel, and
44 it shall be sanctified by my glory; I will consecrate the tent of meeting and the altar. Aaron also and his sons I will con-
45 secrate, to serve me as priests. And I will dwell among the
46 people of Israel, and will be their God. And they shall know

that I am the LORD their God, who brought them forth out of the land of Egypt that I might dwell among them; I am the LORD their God.

THE ALTAR OF INCENSE

30 "You shall make an altar to burn incense upon; of acacia
2 wood shall you make it. A cubit shall be its length, and a cubit its breadth; it shall be square and two cubits shall
3 be its height; its horns shall be of one piece with it. And you shall overlay it with pure gold, its top and its sides round about
4 and its horns; and you shall make for it a molding of gold round about. And two golden rings shall you make for it; under its molding on two opposite sides of it shall you make them, and they shall be holders for poles with which to carry
5 it. You shall make the poles of acacia wood, and overlay them
6 with gold. And you shall put it before the veil that is by the ark of the testimony, before the mercy seat that is over the
7 testimony, where I will meet with you. And Aaron shall burn fragrant incense on it; every morning when he dresses the
8 lamps he shall burn it, and when Aaron sets up the lamps in the evening, he shall burn it, a perpetual incense before the
9 LORD throughout your generations. You shall offer no unholy incense thereon, nor burnt offering, nor cereal offering; and
10 you shall pour no libation thereon. Aaron shall make atonement upon its horns once a year; with the blood of the sin offering of atonement he shall make atonement for it once in the year throughout your generations; it is most holy to the LORD."

11, 12 The LORD said to Moses, "When you take the census of the people of Israel, then each shall give a ransom for himself to the LORD when you number them, that there be no plague
13 among them when you number them. Each who is numbered in the census shall give this: half a shekel according to the shekel of the sanctuary (the shekel is twenty gerahs), half a
14 shekel as an offering to the LORD. Every one who is numbered in the census, from twenty years old and upward, shall give
15 the LORD's offering. The rich shall not give more, and the poor shall not give less, than the half shekel, when you give the
16 LORD's offering to make atonement for yourselves. And you shall take the atonement money from the people of Israel, and shall appoint it for the service of the tent of meeting; that it may bring the people of Israel to remembrance before the LORD, so as to make atonement for yourselves."

17, 18 The LORD said to Moses, "You shall also make a laver of bronze, with its base of bronze, for washing. And you shall put it between the tent of meeting and the altar, and you shall
19 put water in it, with which Aaron and his sons shall wash
20 their hands and their feet. When they go into the tent of meeting, or when they come near the altar to minister, to burn an offering by fire to the LORD, they shall wash with water, lest
21 they die. They shall wash their hands and their feet, lest they die: it shall be a statute for ever to them, even to him and to his descendants throughout their generations."

22, 23 Moreover, the LORD said to Moses, "Take the finest spices: of liquid myrrh five hundred shekels, and of sweet-smelling cinnamon half as much, that is, two hundred and fifty, and
24 of aromatic cane two hundred and fifty, and of cassia five hundred, according to the shekel of the sanctuary, and of
25 olive oil a hin; and you shall make of these a sacred anointing oil blended as by the perfumer; a holy anointing oil it shall be.
26 And you shall anoint with it the tent of meeting and the ark
27 of the testimony, and the table and all its utensils, and the
28 lampstand and its utensils, and the altar of incense, and the altar of burnt offering with all its utensils and the laver and
29 its base; you shall consecrate them, that they may be most
30 holy; whatever touches them will become holy. And you shall anoint Aaron and his sons, and consecrate them, that they may
31 serve me as priests. And you shall say to the people of Israel, 'This shall be my holy anointing oil throughout your genera-
32 tions. It shall not be poured upon the bodies of ordinary men, and you shall make no other like it in composition; it is holy,
33 and it shall be holy to you. Whoever compounds any like it or whoever puts any of it on an outsider shall be cut off from his people.'"

34 And the LORD said to Moses, "Take sweet spices, stacte, and onycha, and galbanum, sweet spices with pure frankincense
35 (of each there shall be an equal part), and make an incense blended as by the perfumer, seasoned with salt, pure and holy;
36 and you shall beat some of it very small, and put part of it before the testimony in the tent of meeting where I shall meet

³⁷ with you; it shall be for you most holy. And the incense which you shall make according to its composition, you shall not make for yourselves; it shall be for you holy to the LORD.
³⁸ Whoever makes any like it to use as perfume shall be cut off from his people."

² 31 The LORD said to Moses, "See, I have called by name Bez'alel the son of Uri, son of Hur, of the tribe of Judah:
³ and I have filled him with the Spirit of God, with ability and
⁴ intelligence, with knowledge and all craftsmanship, to devise
⁵ artistic designs, to work in gold, silver, and bronze, in cutting stones for setting, and in carving wood, for work in every
⁶ craft. And behold, I have appointed with him Oho'liab, the son of Ahis'amach, of the tribe of Dan; and I have given to all able men ability, that they may make all that I have com-
⁷ manded you: the tent of meeting, and the ark of the testimony, and the mercy seat that is thereon, and all the furnishings of
⁸ the tent, the table and its utensils, and the pure lampstand with
⁹ all its utensils, and the altar of incense, and the altar of burnt
¹⁰ offering with all its utensils, and the laver and its base, and the finely worked garments, the holy garments for Aaron the priest and the garments of his sons, for their service as priests,
¹¹ and the anointing oil and the fragrant incense for the holy place. According to all that I have commanded you they shall do."

^{12, 13} And the LORD said to Moses, "Say to the people of Israel, 'You shall keep my sabbaths, for this is a sign between me and you throughout your generations, that you may know
¹⁴ that I, the LORD, sanctify you. You shall keep the sabbath, because it is holy for you; every one who profanes it shall be put to death; whoever does any work on it, that soul shall
¹⁵ be cut off from among his people. Six days shall work be done, but the seventh day is a sabbath of solemn rest, holy to the LORD; whoever does any work on the sabbath day shall be put
¹⁶ to death. Therefore the people of Israel shall keep the sabbath, observing the sabbath throughout their generations, as a per-
¹⁷ petual covenant. It is a sign for ever between me and the people of Israel that in six days the LORD made heaven and earth, and on the seventh day he rested, and was refreshed.' "
¹⁸ And he gave to Moses, when he had made an end of speaking with him upon Mount Sinai, the two tables of the testimony, tables of stone, written with the finger of God.

AARON MAKES A GOLDEN CALF

32 When the people saw that Moses delayed to come down from the mountain, the people gathered themselves together to Aaron, and said to him, "Up, make us gods, who shall go before us; as for this Moses, the man who brought us up out of the land of Egypt, we do not
² know what has become of him." And Aaron said to them, "Take off the rings of gold which are in the ears of your wives, your sons, and your daughters, and bring
³ them to me." So all the people took off the rings of gold which were in their ears, and brought them to Aaron.
⁴ And he received the gold at their hand, and fashioned it with a graving tool, and made a molten calf; and they said, "These are your gods, O Israel, who brought you
⁵ up out of the land of Egypt!" When Aaron saw this, he built an altar before it; and Aaron made proclamation
⁶ and said, "Tomorrow shall be a feast to the LORD." And they rose up early on the morrow, and offered burnt offerings and brought peace offerings; and the people sat down to eat and drink, and rose up to play.
⁷ And the LORD said to Moses, "Go down; for your people, whom you brought up out of the land of Egypt,
⁸ have corrupted themselves; they have turned aside quickly out of the way which I commanded them; they have made for themselves a molten calf, and have worshiped

it and sacrificed to it, and said, 'These are your gods, O Israel, who brought you up out of the land of Egypt!' "
⁹ And the LORD said to Moses, "I have seen this people,
¹⁰ and behold, it is a stiff-necked people; now therefore let me alone, that my wrath may burn hot against them and I may consume them; but of you I will make a great nation."
¹¹ But Moses besought the LORD his God, and said, "O LORD, why does thy wrath burn hot against thy people, whom thou hast brought forth out of the land of Egypt
¹² with great power and with a mighty hand? Why should the Egyptians say, 'With evil intent did he bring them forth, to slay them in the mountains, and to consume them from the face of the earth'? Turn from thy fierce
¹³ wrath, and repent of this evil against thy people. Remember Abraham, Isaac, and Israel, thy servants, to whom thou didst swear by thine own self, and didst say to them, 'I will multiply your descendants as the stars of heaven, and all this land that I have promised I will give to your
¹⁴ descendants, and they shall inherit it for ever.' " And the LORD repented of the evil which he thought to do to his people.

¹⁵ And Moses turned, and went down from the mountain with the two tables of the testimony in his hands, tables that were written on both sides; on the one side and on
¹⁶ the other were they written. And the tables were the work of God, and the writing was the writing of God,
¹⁷ graven upon the tables. When Joshua heard the noise of the people as they shouted, he said to Moses, "There
¹⁸ is a noise of war in the camp." But he said, "It is not the sound of shouting for victory, or the sound of the cry of defeat, but the sound of singing that I hear."
¹⁹ And as soon as he came near the camp and saw the calf and the dancing, Moses' anger burned hot, and he threw the tables out of his hands and broke them at the foot of
²⁰ the mountain. And he took the calf which they had made, and burnt it with fire, and ground it to powder, and scattered it upon the water, and made the people of Israel drink it.

21 And Moses said to Aaron, "What did this people do to you that you have brought a great sin upon them?" 22 And Aaron said, "Let not the anger of my lord burn hot; you know the people, that they are set on evil. 23 For they said to me, 'Make us gods, who shall go before us; as for this Moses, the man who brought us up out of the land of Egypt, we do not know what has become 24 of him.' And I said to them, 'Let any who have gold take it off'; so they gave it to me, and I threw it into the fire, and there came out this calf."

25 And when Moses saw that the people had broken loose (for Aaron had let them break loose, to their shame 26 among their enemies), then Moses stood in the gate of the camp, and said, "Who is on the LORD's side? Come to me." And all the sons of Levi gathered themselves 27 together to him. And he said to them, "Thus says the LORD God of Israel, 'Put every man his sword on his side, and go to and fro from gate to gate throughout the camp, and slay every man his brother, and every 28 man his companion, and every man his neighbor.'" And the sons of Levi did according to the word of Moses; and there fell of the people that day about three thousand 29 men. And Moses said, "Today you have ordained your-selves [s] for the service of the LORD, each one at the cost

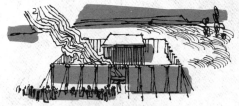

of his son and of his brother, that he may bestow a blessing upon you this day."

30 On the morrow Moses said to the people, "You have sinned a great sin. And now I will go up to the LORD; 31 perhaps I can make atonement for your sin." So Moses returned to the LORD and said, "Alas, this people have sinned a great sin; they have made for themselves gods 32 of gold. But now, if thou wilt forgive their sin—and if not, blot me, I pray thee, out of thy book which thou hast 33 written." But the LORD said to Moses, "Whoever has 34 sinned against me, him will I blot out of my book. But now go, lead the people to the place of which I have spoken to you; behold, my angel shall go before you. Nevertheless, in the day when I visit, I will visit their sin upon them."

35 And the LORD sent a plague upon the people, because they made the calf which Aaron made.

THE PROMISE OF GOD'S PRESENCE

33 The LORD said to Moses, "Depart, go up hence, you and the people whom you have brought up out of the land of Egypt, to the land of which I swore to Abraham, Isaac, and Jacob, saying, 'To your descendants

[s] Gk Vg See Tg: Heb *ordain yourselves*

2 I will give it.' And I will send an angel before you, and I will drive out the Canaanites, the Amorites, the Hittites, 3 the Per'izzites, the Hivites, and the Jeb'usites. Go up to a land flowing with milk and honey; but I will not go up among you, lest I consume you in the way, for you are a stiff-necked people."

4 When the people heard these evil tidings, they 5 mourned; and no man put on his ornaments. For the LORD had said to Moses, "Say to the people of Israel, 'You are a stiff-necked people; if for a single moment I should go up among you, I would consume you. So now put off your ornaments from you, that I may know 6 what to do with you.'" Therefore the people of Israel stripped themselves of their ornaments, from Mount Horeb onward.

The Tent of Meeting

7 Now Moses used to take the tent and pitch it outside the camp, far off from the camp; and he called it the tent of meeting. And every one who sought the LORD would go out to the tent of meeting, which was outside 8 the camp. Whenever Moses went out to the tent, all the people rose up, and every man stood at his tent door, and looked after Moses, until he had gone into the tent. 9 When Moses entered the tent, the pillar of cloud would descend and stand at the door of the tent, and the LORD 10 would speak with Moses. And when all the people saw the pillar of cloud standing at the door of the tent, all the people would rise up and worship, every man at his 11 tent door. Thus the LORD used to speak to Moses face to face, as a man speaks to his friend. When Moses turned again into the camp, his servant Joshua the son of Nun, a young man, did not depart from the tent.

12 Moses said to the LORD, "See, thou sayest to me, 'Bring up this people'; but thou hast not let me know whom thou wilt send with me. Yet thou hast said, 'I know you by name, and you have also found favor in my sight.' 13 Now therefore, I pray thee, if I have found favor in thy sight, show me now thy ways, that I may know thee and find favor in thy sight. Consider too that this nation is 14 thy people." And he said, "My presence will go with you, 15 and I will give you rest." And he said to him, "If thy presence will not go with me, do not carry us up from 16 here. For how shall it be known that I have found favor in thy sight, I and thy people? Is it not in thy going with us, so that we are distinct, I and thy people, from all other people that are upon the face of the earth?"

17 And the LORD said to Moses, "This very thing that you have spoken I will do; for you have found favor in 18 my sight, and I know you by name." Moses said, "I pray 19 thee, show me thy glory." And he said, "I will make all my goodness pass before you, and will proclaim before you my name 'The LORD'; and I will be gracious to whom I will be gracious, and will show mercy on whom

²⁰ I will show mercy. But," he said, "you cannot see my
²¹ face; for man shall not see me and live." And the LORD
said, "Behold, there is a place by me where you shall
²² stand upon the rock; and while my glory passes by I will
put you in a cleft of the rock, and I will cover you with
²³ my hand until I have passed by; then I will take away
my hand, and you shall see my back; but my face shall
not be seen."

THE RENEWAL OF THE COVENANT

34 The LORD said to Moses, "Cut two tables of stone
like the first; and I will write upon the tables the
words that were on the first tables, which you broke.
² Be ready in the morning, and come up in the morning
to Mount Sinai, and present yourself there to me on the
³ top of the mountain. No man shall come up with you,
and let no man be seen throughout all the mountain; let
⁴ no flocks or herds feed before that mountain." So Moses
cut two tables of stone like the first; and he rose early
in the morning and went up on Mount Sinai, as the LORD
had commanded him, and took in his hand two tables
⁵ of stone. And the LORD descended in the cloud and stood
with him there, and proclaimed the name of the LORD.
⁶ The LORD passed before him, and proclaimed, "The LORD,
the LORD, a God merciful and gracious, slow to anger, and
⁷ abounding in steadfast love and faithfulness, keeping
steadfast love for thousands, forgiving iniquity and
transgression and sin, but who will by no means clear
the guilty, visiting the iniquity of the fathers upon the
children and the children's children, to the third and
⁸ the fourth generation." And Moses made haste to bow
⁹ his head toward the earth, and worshiped. And he said,
"If now I have found favor in thy sight, O LORD, let the
LORD, I pray thee, go in the midst of us, although it is a
stiff-necked people; and pardon our iniquity and our
sin, and take us for thy inheritance."

¹⁰ And he said, "Behold, I make a covenant. Before all
your people I will do marvels, such as have not been
wrought in all the earth or in any nation; and all the
people among whom you are shall see the work of the
LORD; for it is a terrible thing that I will do with you.

¹¹ "Observe what I command you this day. Behold, I
will drive out before you the Amorites, the Canaanites,
the Hittites, the Per'izzites, the Hivites, and the Jeb'usites.
¹² Take heed to yourself, lest you make a covenant with the
inhabitants of the land whither you go, lest it become a

¹³ snare in the midst of you. You shall tear down their
altars, and break their pillars, and cut down their Ashe'-
¹⁴ rim (for you shall worship no other god, for the LORD,
¹⁵ whose name is Jealous, is a jealous God), lest you make
a covenant with the inhabitants of the land, and when
they play the harlot after their gods and sacrifice to their
¹⁶ gods and one invites you, you eat of his sacrifice, and
you take of their daughters for your sons, and their
daughters play the harlot after their gods and make your
sons play the harlot after their gods.

¹⁷ "You shall make for yourself no molten gods.

¹⁸ "The feast of unleavened bread you shall keep. Seven
days you shall eat unleavened bread, as I commanded
you, at the time appointed in the month Abib; for in
¹⁹ the month Abib you came out from Egypt. All that opens
the womb is mine, all your male[x] cattle, the firstlings of

²⁰ cow and sheep. The firstling of an ass you shall redeem
with a lamb, or if you will not redeem it you shall break
its neck. All the first-born of your sons you shall redeem.
And none shall appear before me empty.

²¹ "Six days you shall work, but on the seventh day you
shall rest; in plowing time and in harvest you shall rest.
²² And you shall observe the feast of weeks, the first fruits
of wheat harvest, and the feast of ingathering at the
²³ year's end. Three times in the year shall all your males
²⁴ appear before the LORD God, the God of Israel. For I
will cast out nations before you, and enlarge your borders; neither shall any man desire your land, when you
go up to appear before the LORD your God three times in
the year.

²⁵ "You shall not offer the blood of my sacrifice with
leaven; neither shall the sacrifice of the feast of the
²⁶ passover be left until the morning. The first of the first
fruits of your ground you shall bring to the house of the
LORD your God. You shall not boil a kid in its mother's
milk."

²⁷ And the LORD said to Moses, "Write these words; in
accordance with these words I have made a covenant
²⁸ with you and with Israel." And he was there with the
LORD forty days and forty nights; he neither ate bread
nor drank water. And he wrote upon the tables the words
of the covenant, the ten commandments.[t]

²⁹ When Moses came down from Mount Sinai, with the two
tables of the testimony in his hand as he came down from

^x Gk Theodotion Vg Tg: Heb uncertain   ^t Heb *words*

the mountain, Moses did not know that the skin of his
30 face shone because he had been talking with God. And
when Aaron and all the people of Israel saw Moses, behold, the skin of his face shone, and they were afraid to
31 come near him. But Moses called to them; and Aaron
and all the leaders of the congregation returned to him,
32 and Moses talked with them. And afterward all the people
of Israel came near, and he gave them in commandment
all that the LORD had spoken with him in Mount Sinai.
33 And when Moses had finished speaking with them, he
34 put a veil on his face; but whenever Moses went in before
the LORD to speak with him, he took the veil off, until he
came out; and when he came out, and told the people of
35 Israel what he was commanded, the people of Israel saw
the face of Moses, that the skin of Moses' face shone; and
Moses would put the veil upon his face again, until he
went in to speak with him.

THE OFFERING TO THE LORD

35 Moses assembled all the congregation of the people of
Israel, and said to them, "These are the things which the
2 LORD has commanded you to do. Six days shall work be done,
but on the seventh day you shall have a holy sabbath of
solemn rest to the LORD; whoever does any work on it shall be
3 put to death; you shall kindle no fire in all your habitations
on the sabbath day."
4 Moses said to all the congregation of the people of Israel,
5 "This is the thing which the LORD has commanded. Take from
among you an offering to the LORD; whoever is of a generous
heart, let him bring the LORD's offering: gold, silver, and
6 bronze; blue and purple and scarlet stuff and fine twined
7 linen; goats' hair, tanned rams' skins, and goatskins; acacia
8 wood, oil for the light, spices for the anointing oil and for the
9 fragrant incense, and onyx stones and stones for setting, for the
ephod and for the breastpiece.
10 "And let every able man among you come and make all
11 that the LORD has commanded: the tabernacle, its tent and its
covering, its hooks and its frames, its bars, its pillars, and its
12 bases; the ark with its poles, the mercy seat, and the veil of the
13 screen; the table with its poles and all its utensils, and the
14 bread of the Presence; the lampstand also for the light, with
15 its utensils and its lamps, and the oil for the light; and the
altar of incense, with its poles, and the anointing oil and
the fragrant incense, and the screen for the door, at the door of
16 the tabernacle; the altar of burnt offering, with its grating of
bronze, its poles, and all its utensils, the laver and its base;
17 the hangings of the court, its pillars and its bases, and the
18 screen for the gate of the court; the pegs of the tabernacle and
19 the pegs of the court, and their cords; the finely wrought
garments for ministering in the holy place, the holy garments
for Aaron the priest, and the garments of his sons, for their
service as priests."
20 Then all the congregation of the people of Israel departed
21 from the presence of Moses. And they came, every one whose
heart stirred him, and every one whose spirit moved him, and
brought the LORD's offering to be used for the tent of meeting,
22 and for all its service, and for the holy garments. So they
came, both men and women; all who were of a willing heart
brought brooches and earrings and signet rings and armlets,
all sorts of gold objects, every man dedicating an offering of
23 gold to the LORD. And every man with whom was found blue
or purple or scarlet stuff or fine linen or goats' hair or tanned
24 rams' skins or goatskins, brought them. Every one who could
make an offering of silver or bronze brought it as the LORD's
offering; and every man with whom was found acacia wood
25 of any use in the work, brought it. And all women who had
ability spun with their hands, and brought what they had
spun in blue and purple and scarlet stuff and fine twined linen;
26 all the women whose hearts were moved with ability spun the
27 goats' hair. And the leaders brought onyx stones and stones to
28 be set, for the ephod and for the breastpiece, and spices and oil

29 for the light, and for the anointing oil, and for the fragrant incense. All the men and women, the people of Israel, whose
heart moved them to bring anything for the work which the
LORD had commanded by Moses to be done, brought it as their
freewill offering to the LORD.

THE CRAFTSMEN

30 And Moses said to the people of Israel, "See, the LORD has
called by name Bez'alel the son of Uri, son of Hur, of the tribe
31 of Judah; and he has filled him with the Spirit of God, with
ability, with intelligence, with knowledge, and with all crafts-
32 manship, to devise artistic designs, to work in gold and silver
33 and bronze, in cutting stones for setting, and in carving wood,
34 for work in every skilled craft. And he has inspired him to
teach, both him and Oho'liab the son of Ahis'amach of the tribe
35 of Dan. He has filled them with ability to do every sort of
work done by a craftsman or by a designer or by an embroiderer in blue and purple and scarlet stuff and fine twined
linen, or by a weaver—by any sort of workman or skilled de-
36 signer. Bez'alel and Oho'liab and every able man in whom
the LORD has put ability and intelligence to know how to
do any work in the construction of the sanctuary shall work
in accordance with all that the LORD has commanded."
2 And Moses called Bez'alel and Oho'liab and every able man
in whose mind the LORD had put ability, every one whose heart
3 stirred him up to come to do the work; and they received
from Moses all the freewill offering which the people of Israel
had brought for doing the work on the sanctuary. They still
4 kept bringing him freewill offerings every morning, so that all
the able men who were doing every sort of task on the
5 sanctuary came, each from the task that he was doing, and
said to Moses, "The people bring much more than enough for
doing the work which the LORD has commanded us to do."
6 So Moses gave command, and word was proclaimed throughout the camp, "Let neither man nor woman do anything more
for the offering for the sanctuary." So the people were re-
7 strained from bringing; for the stuff they had was sufficient to
do all the work, and more.

THE MAKING OF THE TABERNACLE

8 And all the able men among the workmen made the tabernacle with ten curtains; they were made of fine twined linen
and blue and purple and scarlet stuff, with cherubim skilfully
9 worked. The length of each curtain was twenty-eight cubits,
and the breadth of each curtain four cubits; all the curtains
had the same measure.
10 And he coupled five curtains to one another, and the other
11 five curtains he coupled to one another. And he made loops
of blue on the edge of the outmost curtain of the first set;
likewise he made them on the edge of the outmost curtain of
12 the second set; he made fifty loops on the one curtain, and
he made fifty loops on the edge of the curtain that was in the
13 second set; the loops were opposite one another. And he made
fifty clasps of gold, and coupled the curtains one to the other
with clasps; so the tabernacle was one whole.
14 He also made curtains of goats' hair for a tent over the
15 tabernacle; he made eleven curtains. The length of each curtain
was thirty cubits, and the breadth of each curtain four cubits;
16 the eleven curtains had the same measure. He coupled five
17 curtains by themselves, and six curtains by themselves. And
he made fifty loops on the edge of the outmost curtain of the
one set, and fifty loops on the edge of the other connecting
18 curtain. And he made fifty clasps of bronze to couple the tent
19 together that it might be one whole. And he made for the tent
a covering of tanned rams' skins and goatskins.
20 Then he made the upright frames for the tabernacle of acacia
21 wood. Ten cubits was the length of a frame, and a cubit and a
22 half the breadth of each frame. Each frame had two tenons,
for fitting together; he did this for all the frames of the taber-
23 nacle. The frames for the tabernacle he made thus: twenty
24 frames for the south side; and he made forty bases of silver
under the twenty frames, two bases under one frame for its
two tenons, and two bases under another frame for its two
25 tenons. And for the second side of the tabernacle, on the north
26 side, he made twenty frames and their forty bases of silver,
two bases under one frame and two bases under another
27 frame. And for the rear of the tabernacle westward he made
28 six frames. And he made two frames for corners of the taber-
29 nacle in the rear. And they were separate beneath, but joined
at the top, at the first ring; he made two of them thus, for the

30 two corners. There were eight frames with their bases of silver:
31 sixteen bases, under every frame two bases. And he made bars of acacia wood, five for the frames of
32 the one side of the tabernacle, and five bars for the frames of
the other side of the tabernacle, and five bars for the frames
33 of the tabernacle at the rear westward. And he made the middle
bar to pass through from end to end halfway up the frames.
34 And he overlaid the frames with gold, and made their rings
of gold for holders for the bars, and overlaid the bars with
gold.
35 And he made the veil of blue and purple and scarlet stuff
and fine twined linen; with cherubim skilfully worked he
36 made it. And for it he made four pillars of acacia, and overlaid them with gold; their hooks were of gold, and he cast
37 for them four bases of silver. He also made a screen for the
door of the tent, of blue and purple and scarlet stuff and fine
38 twined linen, embroidered with needlework; and its five pillars
with their hooks. He overlaid their capitals, and their fillets
were of gold, but their five bases were of bronze.

The Ark and the Table

37 Bez'alel made the ark of acacia wood; two cubits and a
half was its length, a cubit and a half its breadth, and a
2 cubit and a half its height. And he overlaid it with pure gold
within and without, and made a molding of gold around it.
3 And he cast for it four rings of gold for its four corners, two
4 rings on its one side and two rings on its other side. And
he made poles of acacia wood, and overlaid them with gold,
5 and put the poles into the rings on the sides of the ark, to
6 carry the ark. And he made a mercy seat of pure gold; two
cubits and a half was its length, and a cubit and a half its
7 breadth. And he made two cherubim of hammered gold; on
8 the two ends of the mercy seat he made them, one cherub on
the one end, and one cherub on the other end; of one piece with
9 the mercy seat he made the cherubim on its two ends. The
cherubim spread out their wings above, overshadowing the
mercy seat with their wings, with their faces one to another;
toward the mercy seat were the faces of the cherubim.
10 He also made the table of acacia wood; two cubits was its
length, a cubit its breadth, and a cubit and a half its height;
11 and he overlaid it with pure gold, and made a molding of
12 gold around it. And he made around it a frame a handbreadth
13 wide, and made a molding of gold around the frame. He cast
for it four rings of gold, and fastened the rings to the four
14 corners at its four legs. Close to the frame were the rings, as
15 holders for the poles to carry the table. He made the poles
of acacia wood to carry the table, and overlaid them with gold.
16 And he made the vessels of pure gold which were to be upon
the table, its plates and dishes for incense, and its bowls and
flagons with which to pour libations.
17 He also made the lampstand of pure gold. The base and the
shaft of the lampstand were made of hammered work; its cups,
18 its capitals, and its flowers were of one piece with it. And there
were six branches going out of its sides, three branches of
the lampstand out of one side of it and three branches
19 of the lampstand out of the other side of it; three cups
made like almonds, each with capital and flower, on one
branch, and three cups made like almonds, each with capital
and flower, on the other branch—so for the six branches
20 going out of the lampstand. And on the lampstand itself were
four cups made like almonds, with their capitals and flowers,
21 and a capital of one piece with it under each pair of the six
22 branches going out of it. Their capitals and their branches were
of one piece with it; the whole of it was one piece of ham-
23 mered work of pure gold. And he made its seven lamps and its
24 snuffers and its trays of pure gold. He made it and all its
utensils of a talent of pure gold.
25 He made the altar of incense of acacia wood; its length was
a cubit, and its breadth was a cubit; it was square, and two
cubits was its height; its horns were of one piece with it.
26 He overlaid it with pure gold, its top, and its sides round about,
and its horns; and he made a molding of gold round about it,
27 and made two rings of gold on it under its molding, on two
opposite sides of it, as holders for the poles with which to
28 carry it. And he made the poles of acacia wood, and overlaid
them with gold.
29 He made the holy anointing oil also, and the pure fragrant
incense, blended as by the perfumer.

The Altar of Burnt Offering

38 He made the altar of burnt offering also of acacia wood;
five cubits was its length, and five cubits its breadth; it
2 was square, and three cubits was its height. He made horns
for it on its four corners; its horns were of one piece with it,
3 and he overlaid it with bronze. And he made all the utensils
of the altar, the pots, the shovels, the basins, the forks, and
4 the firepans: all its utensils he made of bronze. And he made
for the altar a grating, a network of bronze, under its ledge,
5 extending halfway down. He cast four rings on the four
6 corners of the bronze grating as holders for the poles; he
made the poles of acacia wood, and overlaid them with bronze.
7 And he put the poles through the rings on the sides of the
altar, to carry it with them; he made it hollow, with boards.
8 And he made the laver of bronze and its base of bronze, from
the mirrors of the ministering women who ministered at the
door of the tent of meeting.

The Court of the Tabernacle

9 And he made the court; for the south side the hangings of
10 the court were of fine twined linen, a hundred cubits; their
pillars were twenty and their bases twenty, of bronze, but the
11 hooks of the pillars and their fillets were of silver. And for the
north side a hundred cubits, their pillars twenty, their bases
twenty, of bronze, but the hooks of the pillars and their fillets
12 were of silver. And for the west side were hangings of fifty
cubits, their pillars ten, and their sockets ten; the hooks of the
13 pillars and their fillets were of silver. And for the front to the
14 east, fifty cubits. The hangings for one side of the gate were
15 fifteen cubits, with three pillars and three bases. And so for the
other side; on this hand and that hand by the gate of the court
were hangings of fifteen cubits, with three pillars and three
16 bases. All the hangings round about the court were of fine
17 twined linen. And the bases for the pillars were of bronze, but
the hooks of the pillars and their fillets were of silver; the
overlaying of their capitals was also of silver, and all the
18 pillars of the court were filleted with silver. And the screen
for the gate of the court was embroidered with needlework in
blue and purple and scarlet stuff and fine twined linen; it
was twenty cubits long and five cubits high in its breadth,
19 corresponding to the hangings of the court. And their pillars
were four; their four bases were of bronze, their hooks of
silver, and the overlaying of their capitals and their fillets of
20 silver. And all the pegs for the tabernacle and for the court
round about were of bronze.
21 This is the sum of the things for the tabernacle, the tabernacle
of the testimony, as they were counted at the commandment
of Moses, for the work of the Levites under the direction of
22 Ith'amar the son of Aaron the priest. Bez'alel the son of Uri,
son of Hur, of the tribe of Judah, made all that the Lord
23 commanded Moses; and with him was Oho'liab the son of Ahis'-
amach, of the tribe of Dan, a craftsman and designer and
embroiderer in blue and purple and scarlet stuff and fine
twined linen.
24 All the gold that was used for the work, in all the construction of the sanctuary, the gold from the offering, was
twenty-nine talents and seven hundred and thirty shekels, by
25 the shekel of the sanctuary. And the silver from those of the
congregation who were numbered was a hundred talents and a
thousand seven hundred and seventy-five shekels, by the
26 shekel of the sanctuary: a beka a head (that is, half a shekel,
by the shekel of the sanctuary), for every one who was numbered in the census, from twenty years old and upward, for
six hundred and three thousand, five hundred and fifty men.
27 The hundred talents of silver were for casting the bases of the
sanctuary, and the bases of the veil; a hundred bases for the
28 hundred talents, a talent for a base. And of the thousand seven
hundred and seventy-five shekels he made hooks for the pil-
29 lars, and overlaid their capitals and made fillets for them. And
the bronze that was contributed was seventy talents, and two
30 thousand and four hundred shekels; with it he made the bases
for the door of the tent of meeting, the bronze altar and its
31 bronze grating for it and all the utensils of the altar, the bases
round about the court, and the bases of the gate of the court, all
the pegs of the tabernacle, and all the pegs round about the
court.

The Ephod and Breastpiece

39 And of the blue and purple and scarlet stuff they made
finely wrought garments, for ministering in the holy place;

they made the holy garments for Aaron; as the Lord had commanded Moses.

2 And he made the ephod of gold, blue and purple and scarlet 3 stuff, and fine twined linen. And gold leaf was hammered out and cut into threads to work into the blue and purple and the scarlet stuff, and into the fine twined linen, in skilled design. 4 They made for the ephod shoulder-pieces, joined to it at its 5 two edges. And the skilfully woven band upon it, to gird it on, was of the same materials and workmanship, of gold, blue and purple and scarlet stuff, and fine twined linen; as the Lord had commanded Moses.

6 The onyx stones were prepared, enclosed in settings of gold filigree and engraved like the engravings of a signet, according 7 to the names of the sons of Israel. And he set them on the shoulder-pieces of the ephod, to be stones of remembrance for the sons of Israel; as the Lord had commanded Moses.

8 He made the breastpiece, in skilled work, like the work of the ephod, of gold, blue and purple and scarlet stuff, and fine 9 twined linen. It was square; the breastpiece was made double, 10 a span its length and a span its breadth when doubled. And they set in it four rows of stones. A row of sardius, topaz, and 11 carbuncle was the first row; and the second row, an emerald, a 12 sapphire, and a diamond; and the third row, a jacinth, an agate, 13 and an amethyst; and the fourth row, a beryl, an onyx, and a 14 jasper; they were enclosed in settings of gold filigree. There were twelve stones with their names according to the names of the sons of Israel; they were like signets, each engraved with 15 its name, for the twelve tribes. And they made on the breast- 16 piece twisted chains like cords, of pure gold; and they made two settings of gold filigree and two gold rings, and put the two 17 rings on the two edges of the breastpiece; and they put the two cords of gold in the two rings at the edges of the breast- 18 piece. Two ends of the two cords they had attached to the two settings of filigree; thus they attached it in front to the 19 shoulder-pieces of the ephod. Then they made two rings of gold, and put them at the two ends of the breastpiece, on its 20 inside edge next to the ephod. And they made two rings of gold, and attached them in front to the lower part of the two shoulder-pieces of the ephod, at its joining above the skilfully 21 woven band of the ephod. And they bound the breastpiece by its rings to the rings of the ephod with a lace of blue, so that it should lie upon the skilfully woven band of the ephod, and that the breastpiece should not come loose from the ephod; as the Lord had commanded Moses.

22 He also made the robe of the ephod woven all of blue; 23 and the opening of the robe in it was like the opening in a garment, with a binding around the opening, that it might not 24 be torn. On the skirts of the robe they made pomegranates of 25 blue and purple and scarlet stuff and fine twined linen. They also made bells of pure gold, and put the bells between the pomegranates upon the skirts of the robe around about, be- 26 tween the pomegranates; a bell and a pomegranate, a bell and a pomegranate round about upon the skirts of the robe for ministering; as the Lord had commanded Moses.

27 They also made the coats, woven of fine linen, for Aaron 28 and his sons, and the turban of fine linen, and the caps of 29 fine linen, and the linen breeches of fine twined linen, and the girdle of fine twined linen and of blue and purple and scarlet stuff, embroidered with needlework; as the Lord had commanded Moses.

30 And they made the plate of the holy crown of pure gold, and wrote upon it an inscription, like the engraving of a signet, 31 "Holy to the Lord." And they tied to it a lace of blue, to fasten it on the turban above; as the Lord had commanded Moses.

THE TABERNACLE FINISHED

32 Thus all the work of the tabernacle of the tent of meeting was finished; and the people of Israel had done according to all that the Lord had commanded Moses; 33 so had they done. And they brought the tabernacle to Moses, the tent and all its utensils, its hooks, its frames, 34 its bars, its pillars, and its bases; the covering of tanned rams' skins and goatskins, and the veil of the screen; 35 the ark of the testimony with its poles and the mercy 36 seat; the table with all its utensils, and the bread of the 37 Presence; the lampstand of pure gold and its lamps with the lamps set and all its utensils, and the oil for the 38 light; the golden altar, the anointing oil and the fragrant 39 incense, and the screen for the door of the tent; the bronze altar, and its grating of bronze, its poles, and all 40 its utensils; the laver and its base; the hangings of the court, its pillars, and its bases, and the screen for the gate of the court, its cords, and its pegs; and all the utensils for the service of the tabernacle, for the tent of 41 meeting; the finely worked garments for ministering in the holy place, the holy garments for Aaron the priest, 42 and the garments of his sons to serve as priests. According to all that the Lord had commanded Moses, so the 43 people of Israel had done all the work. And Moses saw all the work, and behold, they had done it; as the Lord had commanded, so had they done it. And Moses blessed them.

The Erection of the Tabernacle

2 40 The Lord said to Moses, "On the first day of the first month you shall erect the tabernacle of the tent 3 of meeting. And you shall put in it the ark of the testi- 4 mony, and you shall screen the ark with the veil. And you shall bring in the table, and set its arrangements in order; and you shall bring in the lampstand, and set up 5 its lamps. And you shall put the golden altar for incense before the ark of the testimony, and set up the screen 6 for the door of the tabernacle. You shall set the altar of burnt offering before the door of the tabernacle of the 7 tent of meeting, and place the laver between the tent of 8 meeting and the altar, and put water in it. And you shall set up the court round about, and hang up the screen for 9 the gate of the court. Then you shall take the anointing oil, and anoint the tabernacle and all that is in it, and consecrate it and all its furniture; and it shall become 10 holy. You shall also anoint the altar of burnt offering and all its utensils, and consecrate the altar; and the 11 altar shall be most holy. You shall also anoint the laver 12 and its base, and consecrate it. Then you shall bring Aaron and his sons to the door of the tent of meeting, 13 and shall wash them with water, and put upon Aaron the holy garments, and you shall anoint him and consecrate 14 him, that he may serve me as priest. You shall bring his 15 sons also and put coats on them, and anoint them, as you anointed their father, that they may serve me as priests: and their anointing shall admit them to a perpetual priest- hood throughout their generations."

16 Thus did Moses; according to all that the Lord com- 17 manded him, so he did. And in the first month in the second year, on the first day of the month, the tabernacle 18 was erected. Moses erected the tabernacle; he laid its bases, and set up its frames, and put in its poles, and

19 raised up its pillars; and he spread the tent over the tabernacle, and put the covering of the tent over it, as the
20 LORD had commanded Moses. And he took the testimony and put it into the ark, and put the poles on the ark,
21 and set the mercy seat above on the ark; and he brought the ark into the tabernacle, and set up the veil of the screen, and screened the ark of the testimony; as the LORD
22 had commanded Moses. And he put the table in the tent of meeting, on the north side of the tabernacle, outside
23 the veil, and set the bread in order on it before the LORD;
24 as the LORD had commanded Moses. And he put the lampstand in the tent of meeting, opposite the table on the
25 south side of the tabernacle, and set up the lamps before
26 the LORD; as the LORD had commanded Moses. And he put the golden altar in the tent of meeting before the
27 veil, and burnt fragrant incense upon it; as the LORD
28 had commanded Moses. And he put in place the screen
29 for the door of the tabernacle. And he set the altar of burnt offering at the door of the tabernacle of the tent of meeting, and offered upon it the burnt offering and the cereal offering; as the LORD had commanded Moses.
30 And he set the laver between the tent of meeting and the
31 altar, and put water in it for washing, with which Moses and Aaron and his sons washed their hands and their
32 feet; when they went into the tent of meeting, and when

they approached the altar, they washed; as the LORD
33 commanded Moses. And he erected the court round the tabernacle and the altar, and set up the screen of the gate of the court. So Moses finished the work.

THE GLORY OF THE LORD

34 Then the cloud covered the tent of meeting, and
35 the glory of the LORD filled the tabernacle. And Moses was not able to enter the tent of meeting, because the cloud abode upon it, and the glory of the LORD filled the
36 tabernacle. Throughout all their journeys, whenever the cloud was taken up from over the tabernacle, the people
37 of Israel would go onward; but if the cloud was not taken up, then they did not go onward till the day that it was
38 taken up. For throughout all their journeys the cloud of the LORD was upon the tabernacle by day, and fire was in it by night, in the sight of all the house of Israel.

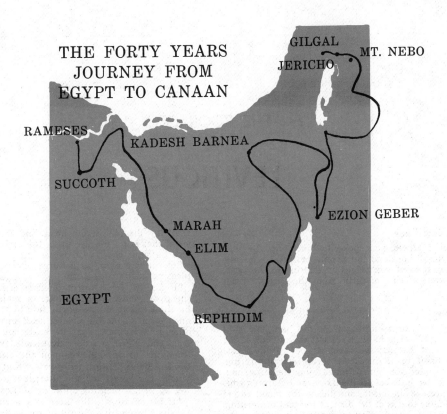

THE FORTY YEARS JOURNEY FROM EGYPT TO CANAAN

LEVITICUS

Leviticus gets its name from the Levites, who were the Hebrew priests. It contains detailed directions for the conduct of worship and other priestly tasks.

Leviticus tells about these priests and their work. It tells how they were to kill certain animals and offer them as sacrifices to God. Such a custom seems strange to us today, but in those days the Hebrews thought it was the way to show God they were thankful or to ask God's help. This book tells which animals could be used and describes many other rules and customs of the long-ago religion of the Hebrews.

This book also contains some rules about cleanliness and about how people should act toward one another. Moreover, it tells what punishment was to be given to those who broke the rules. These laws helped govern the people.

Jesus was familiar with this and other books of the Old Testament. He was quoting from Leviticus when he said, "You shall love your neighbor as yourself" (Leviticus 19.18). This rule for living is as good today as when it was first given to the people.

Parts of this book were written about 600 B.C., a few years before many Hebrews were taken as prisoners to Babylonia, whose armies had captured them. Leviticus was not finished until about 400 B.C. when Genesis and several other books of the Old Testament were completed.

Turn now to the introduction to Genesis on page 1 to learn more about how God inspired men to write these books.

THE BOOK OF

LEVITICUS

Worship and Sacrifices

1 The LORD called Moses, and spoke to him from the tent
2 of meeting, saying, "Speak to the people of Israel, and say to them, When any man of you brings an offering to the LORD, you shall bring your offering of cattle from the herd or from the flock.

Law of Burnt Offerings

3 "If his offering is a burnt offering from the herd, he shall offer a male without blemish; he shall offer it at the door of the tent of meeting, that he may be accepted before the LORD;
4 he shall lay his hand upon the head of the burnt offering, and it shall be accepted for him to make atonement for him.
5 Then he shall kill the bull before the LORD; and Aaron's sons the priests shall present the blood, and throw the blood round about against the altar that is at the door of the tent of meeting.
6 And he shall flay the burnt offering and cut it into pieces;
7 and the sons of Aaron the priest shall put fire on the altar, and
8 lay wood in order upon the fire; and Aaron's sons the priests shall lay the pieces, the head, and the fat, in order upon the
9 wood that is on the fire upon the altar; but its entrails and its legs he shall wash with water. And the priest shall burn the whole on the altar, as a burnt offering, an offering by fire, a pleasing odor to the LORD.
10 "If his gift for a burnt offering is from the flock, from the
11 sheep or goats, he shall offer a male without blemish; and he shall kill it on the north side of the altar before the LORD, and Aaron's sons the priests shall throw its blood against the
12 altar round about. And he shall cut it into pieces, with its head and its fat, and the priest shall lay them in order upon the
13 wood that is on the fire upon the altar; but the entrails and the legs he shall wash with water. And the priest shall offer the whole, and burn it on the altar; it is a burnt offering, an offering by fire, a pleasing odor to the LORD.
14 "If his offering to the LORD is a burnt offering of birds, then he shall bring his offering of turtledoves or of young pigeons.
15 And the priest shall bring it to the altar and wring off its head, and burn it on the altar; and its blood shall be drained

16 out on the side of the altar; and he shall take away its crop
with the feathers, and cast it beside the altar on the east side,
17 in the place for ashes; he shall tear it by its wings, but shall
not divide it asunder. And the priest shall burn it on the altar,
upon the wood that is on the fire; it is a burnt offering, an
offering by fire, a pleasing odor to the LORD.

Law of Cereal Offerings

2 "When any one brings a cereal offering as an offering to
the LORD, his offering shall be of fine flour; he shall pour
2 oil upon it, and put frankincense on it, and bring it to Aaron's
sons the priests. And he shall take from it a handful of the
fine flour and oil, with all of its frankincense; and the priest
shall burn this as its memorial portion upon the altar, an offer-
3 ing by fire, a pleasing odor to the LORD. And what is left of
the cereal offering shall be for Aaron and his sons; it is a most
holy part of the offerings by fire to the LORD.
4 "When you bring a cereal offering baked in the oven as an
offering, it shall be unleavened cakes of fine flour mixed with
5 oil, or unleavened wafers spread with oil. And if your offering
is a cereal offering baked on a griddle, it shall be of fine flour
6 unleavened, mixed with oil; you shall break it in pieces, and
7 pour oil on it; it is a cereal offering. And if your offering is a
cereal offering cooked in a pan, it shall be made of fine flour
8 with oil. And you shall bring the cereal offering that is made
of these things to the LORD; and when it is presented to the
9 priest, he shall bring it to the altar. And the priest shall take
from the cereal offering its memorial portion and burn this on
the altar, an offering by fire, a pleasing odor to the LORD.
10 And what is left of the cereal offering shall be for Aaron and
his sons; it is a most holy part of the offerings by fire to the
LORD.
11 "No cereal offering which you bring to the LORD shall be
made with leaven; for you shall burn no leaven nor any honey
12 as an offering by fire to the LORD. As an offering of first fruits
you may bring them to the LORD, but they shall not be offered
13 on the altar for a pleasing odor. You shall season all your cereal
offerings with salt; you shall not let the salt of the covenant
with your God be lacking from your cereal offering; with all
your offerings you shall offer salt.
14 "If you offer a cereal offering of first fruits to the LORD, you
shall offer for the cereal offering of your first fruits crushed
15 new grain from fresh ears, parched with fire. And you shall put
oil upon it, and lay frankincense on it; it is a cereal offering.
16 And the priest shall burn as its memorial portion part of the
crushed grain and of the oil with all of its frankincense; it is
an offering by fire to the LORD.

Law of Peace Offerings

3 "If a man's offering is a sacrifice of peace offering, if he
offers an animal from the herd, male or female, he shall
2 offer it without blemish before the LORD. And he shall lay his
hand upon the head of his offering and kill it at the door of
the tent of meeting; and Aaron's sons the priests shall throw
3 the blood against the altar round about. And from the sacrifice
of the peace offering, as an offering by fire to the LORD, he shall
offer the fat covering the entrails and all the fat that is on
4 the entrails, and the two kidneys with the fat that is on
them at the loins, and the appendage of the liver which he
5 shall take away with the kidneys. Then Aaron's sons shall burn
it on the altar upon the burnt offering, which is upon the wood
on the fire; it is an offering by fire, a pleasing odor to the
LORD.
6 "If his offering for a sacrifice of peace offering to the LORD
is an animal from the flock, male or female, he shall offer it
7 without blemish. If he offers a lamb for his offering, then he
8 shall offer it before the LORD, laying his hand upon the head
of his offering and killing it before the tent of meeting; and
Aaron's sons shall throw its blood against the altar round about.
9 Then from the sacrifice of the peace offering as an offering by
fire to the LORD he shall offer its fat, the fat tail entire, taking
it away close by the backbone, and the fat that covers the
10 entrails, and all the fat that is on the entrails, and the two
kidneys with the fat that is on them at the loins, and the
appendage of the liver which he shall take away with the
11 kidneys. And the priest shall burn it on the altar as food
offered by fire to the LORD.
12 "If his offering is a goat, then he shall offer it before the
13 LORD, and lay his hand upon its head, and kill it before the

tent of meeting; and the sons of Aaron shall throw its blood
14 against the altar round about. Then he shall offer from it, as
his offering for an offering by fire to the LORD, the fat covering
15 the entrails, and all the fat that is on the entrails, and the
two kidneys with the fat that is on them at the loins, and the
appendage of the liver which he shall take away with the
16 kidneys. And the priest shall burn them on the altar as food
17 offered by fire for a pleasing odor. All fat is the LORD's. It shall
be a perpetual statute throughout your generations, in all your
dwelling places, that you eat neither fat nor blood."

Law of Sin Offerings

2 And the LORD said to Moses, "Say to the people of Israel,
4 If any one sins unwittingly in any of the things which the
LORD has commanded not to be done, and does any one of
3 them, if it is the anointed priest who sins, thus bringing guilt
on the people, then let him offer for the sin which he has committed a young bull without blemish to the LORD for a sin offer-
4 ing. He shall bring the bull to the door of the tent of meeting
before the LORD, and lay his hand on the head of the bull, and
5 kill the bull before the LORD. And the anointed priest shall take
some of the blood of the bull and bring it to the tent of
6 meeting; and the priest shall dip his finger in the blood and
sprinkle part of the blood seven times before the LORD in front
7 of the veil of the sanctuary. And the priest shall put some of
the blood on the horns of the altar of fragrant incense before
the LORD which is in the tent of meeting, and the rest of the
blood of the bull he shall pour out at the base of the altar of
burnt offering which is at the door of the tent of meeting.
8 And all the fat of the bull of the sin offering he shall take
from it, the fat that covers the entrails and all the fat that is
9 on the entrails, and the two kidneys with the fat that is on
them at the loins, and the appendage of the liver which he
10 shall take away with the kidneys (just as these are taken
from the ox of the sacrifice of peace offerings), and the
11 priest shall burn them upon the altar of burnt offering. But the
skin of the bull and all its flesh, with its head, its legs, its
12 entrails, and its dung, the whole bull he shall carry forth
outside the camp to a clean place, where the ashes are poured
out, and shall burn it on a fire of wood; where the ashes are
poured out it shall be burned.
13 "If the whole congregation of Israel commits a sin unwittingly
and the thing is hidden from the eyes of the assembly, and they
do any one of the things which the LORD has commanded not
14 to be done and are guilty; when the sin which they have
committed becomes known, the assembly shall offer a young
bull for a sin offering and bring it before the tent of meeting;
15 and the elders of the congregation shall lay their hands upon
the head of the bull before the LORD, and the bull shall be
16 killed before the LORD. Then the anointed priest shall bring
17 some of the blood of the bull to the tent of meeting, and the
priest shall dip his finger in the blood and sprinkle it seven
18 times before the LORD in front of the veil. And he shall put
some of the blood on the horns of the altar which is in the
tent of meeting before the LORD; and the rest of the blood he
shall pour out at the base of the altar of burnt offering which
19 is at the door of the tent of meeting. And all its fat he shall
20 take from it and burn upon the altar. Thus shall he do with the
bull; as he did with the bull of the sin offering, so shall he do
with this; and the priest shall make atonement for them, and
21 they shall be forgiven. And he shall carry forth the bull outside
the camp, and burn it as he burned the first bull; it is the sin
offering for the assembly.
22 "When a ruler sins, doing unwittingly any one of all the
things which the LORD his God has commanded not to be done,
23 and is guilty, if the sin which he has committed is made known
to him, he shall bring as his offering a goat, a male without
24 blemish, and shall lay his hand upon the head of the goat,
and kill it in the place where they kill the burnt offering before
25 the LORD; it is a sin offering. Then the priest shall take some
of the blood of the sin offering with his finger and put it on
the horns of the altar of burnt offering, and pour out the rest
26 of its blood at the base of the altar of burnt offering. And all
its fat he shall burn on the altar, like the fat of the sacrifice of
peace offerings; so the priest shall make atonement for him
for his sin, and he shall be forgiven.
27 "If any one of the common people sins unwittingly in doing
any one of the things which the LORD has commanded not to
28 be done, and is guilty, when the sin which he has committed

Lv

is made known to him he shall bring for his offering a goat, a female without blemish, for his sin which he has committed.

29 And he shall lay his hand on the head of the sin offering, and kill the sin offering in the place of burnt offering.
30 And the priest shall take some of its blood with his finger and put it on the horns of the altar of burnt offering, and pour out
31 the rest of its blood at the base of the altar. And all its fat he shall remove, as the fat is removed from the peace offerings, and the priest shall burn it upon the altar for a pleasing odor to the Lord; and the priest shall make atonement for him, and he shall be forgiven.
32 "If he brings a lamb as his offering for a sin offering, he shall
33 bring a female without blemish, and lay his hand upon the head of the sin offering, and kill it for a sin offering in the
34 place where they kill the burnt offering. Then the priest shall take some of the blood of the sin offering with his finger and put it on the horns of the altar of burnt offering, and pour
35 out the rest of its blood at the base of the altar. And all its fat he shall remove as the fat of the lamb is removed from the sacrifice of peace offerings, and the priest shall burn it on the altar, upon the offerings by fire to the Lord; and the priest shall make atonement for him for the sin which he has committed, and he shall be forgiven.

5 "If any one sins in that he hears a public adjuration to testify and though he is a witness, whether he has seen or come to know the matter, yet does not speak, he shall bear
2 his iniquity. Or if any one touches an unclean thing, whether the carcass of an unclean beast or a carcass of unclean cattle or a carcass of unclean swarming things, and it is hidden from
3 him, and he has become unclean, he shall be guilty. Or if he touches human uncleanness, of whatever sort the uncleanness may be with which one becomes unclean, and it is hidden
4 from him, when he comes to know it he shall be guilty. Or if any one utters with his lips a rash oath to do evil or to do good, any sort of rash oath that men swear, and it is hidden from him, when he comes to know it he shall in any of these
5 be guilty. When a man is guilty of any of these, he shall confess
6 the sin he has committed, and he shall bring his guilt offering to the Lord for the sin which he has committed, a female from the flock, a lamb or a goat, for a sin offering; and the priest shall make atonement for him for his sin.
7 "But if he cannot afford a lamb, then he shall bring, as his guilt offering to the Lord for the sin which he has committed, two turtledoves or two young pigeons, one for a sin offering
8 and the other for a burnt offering. He shall bring them to the priest, who shall offer first the one for the sin offering; he shall
9 wring its head from its neck, but shall not sever it, and he shall sprinkle some of the blood of the sin offering on the side of the altar, while the rest of the blood shall be drained out
10 at the base of the altar; it is a sin offering. Then he shall offer the second for a burnt offering according to the ordinance; and the priest shall make atonement for him for the sin which he has committed, and he shall be forgiven.
11 "But if he cannot afford two turtledoves or two young pigeons, then he shall bring, as his offering for the sin which he has committed, a tenth of an ephah of fine flour for a sin offering; he shall put no oil upon it, and shall put no frankin-
12 cense on it, for it is a sin offering. And he shall bring it to the priest, and the priest shall take a handful of it as its memorial portion and burn this on the altar, upon the offerings
13 by fire to the Lord; it is a sin offering. Thus the priest shall make atonement for him for the sin which he has committed in any one of these things, and he shall be forgiven. And the remainder shall be for the priest, as in the cereal offering."

Law of the Trespass Offering

14, 15 The Lord said to Moses, "If any one commits a breach of faith and sins unwittingly in any of the holy things of the Lord, he shall bring, as his guilt offering to the Lord, a ram without blemish out of the flock, valued by you in shekels of silver, according to the shekel of the sanctuary; it is a guilt
16 offering. He shall also make restitution for what he has done amiss in the holy thing, and shall add a fifth to it and give it to the priest; and the priest shall make atonement for him with the ram of the guilt offering, and he shall be forgiven.
17 "If any one sins, doing any of the things which the Lord has commanded not to be done, though he does not know it, yet he
18 is guilty and shall bear his iniquity. He shall bring to the priest a ram without blemish out of the flock, valued by you at the price for a guilt offering, and the priest shall make atonement

for him for the error which he committed unwittingly, and he
19 shall be forgiven. It is a guilt offering; he is guilty before the Lord."

2 6[a] The Lord said to Moses, "If any one sins and commits a breach of faith against the Lord by deceiving his neighbor in a matter of deposit or security, or through robbery, or if he
3 has oppressed his neighbor or has found what was lost and lied about it, swearing falsely—in any of all the things which
4 men do and sin therein, when one has sinned and become guilty, he shall restore what he took by robbery, or what he got by oppression, or the deposit which was committed to him,
5 or the lost thing which he found, or anything about which he has sworn falsely; he shall restore it in full, and shall add a fifth to it, and give it to him to whom it belongs, on the day
6 of his guilt offering. And he shall bring to the priest his guilt offering to the Lord, a ram without blemish out of the flock,
7 valued by you at the price for a guilt offering; and the priest shall make atonement for him before the Lord, and he shall be forgiven for any of the things which one may do and thereby become guilty."

INSTRUCTIONS FOR THE PRIESTS

8b, 9 The Lord said to Moses, "Command Aaron and his sons, saying, This is the law of the burnt offering. The burnt offering shall be on the hearth upon the altar all night until the morn-
10 ing, and the fire of the altar shall be kept burning on it. And the priest shall put on his linen garment, and put his linen breeches upon his body, and he shall take up the ashes to which the fire has consumed the burnt offering on the altar, and
11 put them beside the altar. Then he shall put off his garments, and put on other garments, and carry forth the ashes outside
12 the camp to a clean place. The fire on the altar shall be kept burning on it, it shall not go out; the priest shall burn wood on it every morning, and he shall lay the burnt offering in order upon it, and shall burn on it the fat of the peace offerings.
13 Fire shall be kept burning upon the altar continually; it shall not go out.
14 "And this is the law of the cereal offering. The sons of Aaron
15 shall offer it before the Lord, in front of the altar. And one shall take from it a handful of the fine flour of the cereal offering with its oil and all the frankincense which is on the cereal offering, and burn this as its memorial portion on the
16 altar, a pleasing odor to the Lord. And the rest of it Aaron and his sons shall eat; it shall be eaten unleavened in a holy place;
17 in the court of the tent of meeting they shall eat it. It shall not be baked with leaven. I have given it as their portion of my offerings by fire; it is most holy, like the sin offer-
18 ing and the guilt offering. Every male among the children of Aaron may eat of it, as decreed for ever throughout your generations, from the Lord's offerings by fire; whoever touches them shall become holy."
19, 20 The Lord said to Moses, "This is the offering which Aaron and his sons shall offer to the Lord on the day when he is anointed: a tenth of an ephah of fine flour as a regular cereal
21 offering, half of it in the morning and half in the evening. It shall be made with oil on a griddle; you shall bring it well mixed, in baked [c] pieces like a cereal offering, and offer it for
22 a pleasing odor to the Lord. The priest from among Aaron's sons, who is anointed to succeed him, shall offer it to the
23 Lord as decreed for ever; the whole of it shall be burned. Every cereal offering of a priest shall be wholly burned; it shall not be eaten."
24, 25 The Lord said to Moses, "Say to Aaron and his sons, This is the law of the sin offering. In the place where the burnt offering is killed shall the sin offering be killed before the
26 Lord; it is most holy. The priest who offers it for sin shall eat it; in a holy place it shall be eaten, in the court of the tent
27 of meeting. Whatever [d] touches its flesh shall be holy; and when any of its blood is sprinkled on a garment, you shall
28 wash that on which it was sprinkled in a holy place. And the earthen vessel in which it is boiled shall be broken; but if it is boiled in a bronze vessel, that shall be scoured, and rinsed
29 in water. Every male among the priests may eat of it; it is
30 most holy. But no sin offering shall be eaten from which any blood is brought into the tent of meeting to make atonement in the holy place; it shall be burned with fire.

2 7 "This is the law of the guilt offering. It is most holy; in the place where they kill the burnt offering they shall kill the guilt offering, and its blood shall be thrown on the altar

---

[a] Ch 5. 20 in Heb   [b] Ch 6. 1 in Heb   [c] Meaning of Heb is uncertain   [d] Or *Whoever*

³ round about. And all its fat shall be offered, the fat tail, the
⁴ fat that covers the entrails, the two kidneys with the fat that
is on them at the loins, and the appendage of the liver which
⁵ he shall take away with the kidneys; the priest shall burn
them on the altar as an offering by fire to the Lᴏʀᴅ; it is a
⁶ guilt offering. Every male among the priests may eat of it; it
⁷ shall be eaten in a holy place; it is most holy. The guilt offering is like the sin offering, there is one law for them; the
⁸ priest who makes atonement with it shall have it. And the
priest who offers any man's burnt offering shall have for him-
⁹ self the skin of the burnt offering which he has offered. And
every cereal offering baked in the oven and all that is prepared on a pan or a griddle shall belong to the priest who
¹⁰ offers it. And every cereal offering, mixed with oil or dry, shall
be for all the sons of Aaron, one as well as another.

Peace Offerings

¹¹ "And this is the law of the sacrifice of peace offerings which
¹² one may offer to the Lᴏʀᴅ. If he offers it for a thanksgiving,
then he shall offer with the thank offering unleavened cakes
mixed with oil, unleavened wafers spread with oil, and cakes
¹³ of fine flour well mixed with oil. With the sacrifice of his peace
offerings for thanksgiving he shall bring his offering with
¹⁴ cakes of leavened bread. And of such he shall offer one cake
from each offering, as an offering to the Lᴏʀᴅ; it shall belong
to the priest who throws the blood of the peace offerings.
¹⁵ And the flesh of the sacrifice of his peace offerings for thanksgiving shall be eaten on the day of his offering; he shall not
¹⁶ leave any of it until the morning. But if the sacrifice of his
offering is a votive offering or a freewill offering, it shall be
eaten on the day that he offers his sacrifice, and on the morrow
¹⁷ what remains of it shall be eaten, but what remains of the
flesh of the sacrifice on the third day shall be burned with fire.
¹⁸ If any of the flesh of the sacrifice of his peace offering is eaten
on the third day, he who offers it shall not be accepted, neither
shall it be credited to him; it shall be an abomination, and he
who eats of it shall bear his iniquity.
¹⁹ "Flesh that touches any unclean thing shall not be eaten;
it shall be burned with fire. All who are clean may eat flesh,
²⁰ but the person who eats of the flesh of the sacrifice of the
Lᴏʀᴅ's peace offerings while an uncleanness is on him, that
²¹ person shall be cut off from his people. And if any one touches
an unclean thing, whether the uncleanness of man or an unclean beast or any unclean abomination, and then eats of the
flesh of the sacrifice of the Lᴏʀᴅ's peace offerings, that person
shall be cut off from his people."
²², ²³ The Lᴏʀᴅ said to Moses, "Say to the people of Israel, You
²⁴ shall eat no fat, of ox, or sheep, or goat. The fat of an animal
that dies of itself, and the fat of one that is torn by beasts,
may be put to any other use, but on no account shall you eat
²⁵ it. For every person who eats of the fat of an animal of which
an offering by fire is made to the Lᴏʀᴅ shall be cut off from his
²⁶ people. Moreover you shall eat no blood whatever, whether of
²⁷ fowl or of animal, in any of your dwellings. Whoever eats any
blood, that person shall be cut off from his people."
²⁸, ²⁹ The Lᴏʀᴅ said to Moses, "Say to the people of Israel, He that
offers the sacrifice of his peace offerings to the Lᴏʀᴅ shall bring
his offering to the Lᴏʀᴅ; from the sacrifice of his peace offerings
³⁰ he shall bring with his own hands the offerings by fire to the
Lᴏʀᴅ; he shall bring the fat with the breast, that the breast
³¹ may be waved as a wave offering before the Lᴏʀᴅ. The priest
shall burn the fat on the altar, but the breast shall be for
³² Aaron and his sons. And the right thigh you shall give to the
priest as an offering from the sacrifice of your peace offerings;
³³ he among the sons of Aaron who offers the blood of the peace
offerings and the fat shall have the right thigh for a portion.
³⁴ For the breast that is waved and the thigh that is offered I
have taken from the people of Israel, out of the sacrifices of
their peace offerings, and have given them to Aaron the priest
and to his sons, a perpetual due from the people of Israel.
³⁵ This is the portion of Aaron and of his sons from the offerings
made by fire to the Lᴏʀᴅ, consecrated to them on the day they
³⁶ were presented to serve as priests of the Lᴏʀᴅ; the Lᴏʀᴅ commanded this to be given them by the people of Israel, on the
day that they were anointed; it is a perpetual due throughout
their generations."
³⁷ This is the law of the burnt offering, of the cereal offering, of
the sin offering, of the guilt offering, of the consecration, and
³⁸ of the peace offerings, which the Lᴏʀᴅ commanded Moses on
Mount Sinai, on the day that he commanded the people of

Israel to bring their offerings to the Lᴏʀᴅ, in the wilderness of
Sinai.

THE PRIESTHOOD

²
8 The Lᴏʀᴅ said to Moses, "Take Aaron and his sons with
him, and the garments, and the anointing oil, and the bull
of the sin offering, and the two rams, and the basket of un-
³ leavened bread; and assemble all the congregation at the door
⁴ of the tent of meeting." And Moses did as the Lᴏʀᴅ commanded
him; and the congregation was assembled at the door of the
tent of meeting.
⁵ And Moses said to the congregation, "This is the thing which
⁶ the Lᴏʀᴅ has commanded to be done." And Moses brought
⁷ Aaron and his sons, and washed them with water. And he put

on him the coat, and girded him with the girdle, and clothed
him with the robe, and put the ephod upon him, and girded
him with the skilfully woven band of the ephod, binding it to
⁸ him therewith. And he placed the breastpiece on him, and in
⁹ the breastpiece he put the Urim and the Thummim. And he
set the turban upon his head, and on the turban, in front, he
set the golden plate, the holy crown, as the Lᴏʀᴅ commanded
Moses.

Consecration of Aaron and Sons

¹⁰ Then Moses took the anointing oil, and anointed the taber-
¹¹ nacle and all that was in it, and consecrated them. And he
sprinkled some of it on the altar seven times, and anointed
the altar and all its utensils, and the laver and its base, to
¹² consecrate them. And he poured some of the anointing oil on
¹³ Aaron's head, and anointed him, to consecrate him. And Moses
brought Aaron's sons, and clothed them with coats, and girded
them with girdles, and bound caps on them, as the Lᴏʀᴅ commanded Moses.
¹⁴ Then he brought the bull of the sin offering; and Aaron and
his sons laid their hands upon the head of the bull of the sin
¹⁵ offering. And Moses killed it, and took the blood, and with
his finger put it on the horns of the altar round about, and
purified the altar, and poured out the blood at the base of the
¹⁶ altar, and consecrated it, to make atonement for it. And he
took all the fat that was on the entrails, and the appendage
of the liver, and the two kidneys with their fat, and Moses
¹⁷ burned them on the altar. But the bull, and its skin, and its
flesh, and its dung, he burned with fire outside the camp, as
the Lᴏʀᴅ commanded Moses.
¹⁸ Then he presented the ram of the burnt offering; and Aaron
¹⁹ and his sons laid their hands on the head of the ram. And
Moses killed it, and threw the blood upon the altar round
²⁰ about. And when the ram was cut into pieces, Moses burned
²¹ the head and the pieces and the fat. And when the entrails
and the legs were washed with water, Moses burned the whole
ram on the altar, as a burnt offering, a pleasing odor, an
offering by fire to the Lᴏʀᴅ, as the Lᴏʀᴅ commanded Moses.
²² Then he presented the other ram, the ram of ordination;
and Aaron and his sons laid their hands on the head of the
²³ ram. And Moses killed it, and took some of its blood and put
it on the tip of Aaron's right ear and on the thumb of his
²⁴ right hand and on the great toe of his right foot. And Aaron's
sons were brought, and Moses put some of the blood on the
tips of their right ears and on the thumbs of their right hands
and on the great toes of their right feet; and Moses threw the
²⁵ blood upon the altar round about. Then he took the fat, and
the fat tail, and all the fat that was on the entrails, and the
appendage of the liver, and the two kidneys with their fat,
²⁶ and the right thigh; and out of the basket of unleavened bread
which was before the Lᴏʀᴅ he took one unleavened cake, and
one cake of bread with oil, and one wafer, and placed them on
²⁷ the fat and on the right thigh; and he put all these in the hands
of Aaron and in the hands of his sons, and waved them as a

28 wave offering before the LORD. Then Moses took them from their hands, and burned them on the altar with the burnt offering, as an ordination offering, a pleasing odor, an offering 29 by fire to the LORD. And Moses took the breast, and waved it for a wave offering before the LORD; it was Moses' portion of the ram of ordination, as the LORD commanded Moses.

30 Then Moses took some of the anointing oil and of the blood which was on the altar, and sprinkled it upon Aaron and his garments, and also upon his sons and his sons' garments; so he consecrated Aaron and his garments, and his sons and his sons' garments with him.

31 And Moses said to Aaron and his sons, "Boil the flesh at the door of the tent of meeting, and there eat it and the bread that is in the basket of ordination offerings, as I commanded, saying, 32 'Aaron and his sons shall eat it'; and what remains of the flesh 33 and the bread you shall burn with fire. And you shall not go out from the door of the tent of meeting for seven days, until the days of your ordination are completed, for it will take seven 34 days to ordain you. As has been done today, the LORD has 35 commanded to be done to make atonement for you. At the door of the tent of meeting you shall remain day and night for seven days, performing what the LORD has charged, lest you 36 die; for so I am commanded." And Aaron and his sons did all the things which the LORD commanded by Moses.

Ceremonies of Installation

9 On the eighth day Moses called Aaron and his sons and 2 the elders of Israel; and he said to Aaron, "Take a bull calf for a sin offering, and a ram for a burnt offering, both without 3 blemish, and offer them before the LORD. And say to the people of Israel, 'Take a male goat for a sin offering, and a calf and a lamb, both a year old without blemish, for a burnt offering, 4 and an ox and a ram for peace offerings, to sacrifice before the LORD, and a cereal offering mixed with oil; for today the LORD 5 will appear to you.'" And they brought what Moses commanded before the tent of meeting; and all the congregation 6 drew near and stood before the LORD. And Moses said, "This is the thing which the LORD commanded you to do; and the glory 7 of the LORD will appear to you." Then Moses said to Aaron, "Draw near to the altar, and offer your sin offering and your burnt offering, and make atonement for yourself and for the people; and bring the offering of the people, and make atonement for them; as the LORD has commanded."

8 So Aaron drew near to the altar, and killed the calf of the 9 sin offering, which was for himself. And the sons of Aaron presented the blood to him, and he dipped his finger in the blood and put it on the horns of the altar, and poured out the 10 blood at the base of the altar; but the fat and the kidneys and the appendage of the liver from the sin offering he burned upon 11 the altar, as the LORD commanded Moses. The flesh and the skin he burned with fire outside the camp.

12 And he killed the burnt offering; and Aaron's sons delivered to him the blood, and he threw it on the altar round about. 13 And they delivered the burnt offering to him, piece by piece, 14 and the head; and he burned them upon the altar. And he washed the entrails and the legs, and burned them with the burnt offering on the altar.

15 Then he presented the people's offering, and took the goat of the sin offering which was for the people, and killed it, 16 and offered it for sin, like the first sin offering. And he presented the burnt offering, and offered it according to the 17 ordinance. And he presented the cereal offering, and filled his hand from it, and burned it upon the altar, besides the burnt offering of the morning.

18 He killed the ox also and the ram, the sacrifice of peace offerings for the people; and Aaron's sons delivered to him the 19 blood, which he threw upon the altar round about, and the fat of the ox and of the ram, the fat tail, and that which covers the entrails, and the kidneys, and the appendage of the liver; 20 and they put the fat upon the breasts, and he burned the fat 21 upon the altar, but the breasts and the right thigh Aaron waved for a wave offering before the LORD; as Moses commanded.

22 Then Aaron lifted up his hands toward the people and blessed them; and he came down from offering the sin offering 23 and the burnt offering and the peace offerings. And Moses and Aaron went into the tent of meeting; and when they came out they blessed the people, and the glory of the LORD appeared to 24 all the people. And fire came forth from before the LORD and consumed the burnt offering and the fat upon the altar; and

when all the people saw it, they shouted, and fell on their faces.

Nadab and Abihu

10 Now Nadab and Abi'hu, the sons of Aaron, each took his censer, and put fire in it, and laid incense on it, and offered unholy fire before the LORD, such as he had not com- 2 manded them. And fire came forth from the presence of the 3 LORD and devoured them, and they died before the LORD. Then Moses said to Aaron, "This is what the LORD has said, 'I will show myself holy among those who are near me, and before all the people I will be glorified.'" And Aaron held his peace.

4 And Moses called Mish'a-el and Elza'phan, the sons of Uz'ziel the uncle of Aaron, and said to them, "Draw near, carry your 5 brethren from before the sanctuary out of the camp." So they drew near, and carried them in their coats out of the camp, as 6 Moses had said. And Moses said to Aaron and to Elea'zar and Ith'amar, his sons, "Do not let the hair of your heads hang loose, and do not rend your clothes, lest you die, and lest wrath come upon all the congregation; but your brethren, the whole house of Israel, may bewail the burning which the LORD has 7 kindled. And do not go out from the door of the tent of meeting, lest you die; for the anointing oil of the LORD is upon you." And they did according to the word of Moses.

8, 9 And the LORD spoke to Aaron, saying, "Drink no wine nor strong drink, you nor your sons with you, when you go into the tent of meeting, lest you die; it shall be a statute for ever 10 throughout your generations. You are to distinguish between the holy and the common, and between the unclean and the 11 clean; and you are to teach the people of Israel all the statutes which the LORD has spoken to them by Moses."

12 And Moses said to Aaron and to Elea'zar and Ith'amar, his sons who were left, "Take the cereal offering that remains of the offerings by fire to the LORD, and eat it unleavened beside 13 the altar, for it is most holy; you shall eat it in a holy place, because it is your due and your sons' due, from the offerings 14 by fire to the LORD; for so I am commanded. But the breast that is waved and the thigh that is offered you shall eat in any clean place, you and your sons and your daughters with you; for they are given as your due and your sons' due, from the 15 sacrifices of the peace offerings of the people of Israel. The thigh that is offered and the breast that is waved they shall bring with the offerings by fire of the fat, to wave for a wave offering before the LORD, and it shall be yours, and your sons' with you, as a due for ever; as the LORD has commanded."

16 Now Moses diligently inquired about the goat of the sin offering, and behold, it was burned! And he was angry with Elea'zar and Ith'amar, the sons of Aaron who were left, saying, 17 "Why have you not eaten the sin offering in the place of the sanctuary, since it is a thing most holy and has been given to you that you may bear the iniquity of the congregation, to 18 make atonement for them before the LORD? Behold, its blood was not brought into the inner part of the sanctuary. You certainly ought to have eaten it in the sanctuary, as I com- 19 manded." And Aaron said to Moses, "Behold, today they have offered their sin offering and their burnt offering before the LORD; and yet such things as these have befallen me! If I had eaten the sin offering today, would it have been acceptable in 20 the sight of the LORD?" And when Moses heard that, he was content.

LAWS OF PURIFICATION

11 And the LORD said to Moses and Aaron, "Say to the 2 people of Israel, These are the living things which you 3 may eat among all the beasts that are on the earth. Whatever parts the hoof and is cloven-footed and chews the cud, among 4 the animals, you may eat. Nevertheless among those that chew the cud or part the hoof, you shall not eat these: The camel, because it chews the cud but does not part the hoof, is unclean 5 to you. And the rock badger, because it chews the cud but 6 does not part the hoof, is unclean to you. And the hare, because it chews the cud but does not part the hoof, is unclean to you. 7 And the swine, because it parts the hoof and is cloven-footed 8 but does not chew the cud, is unclean to you. Of their flesh you shall not eat, and their carcasses you shall not touch; they are unclean to you.

9 "These you may eat, of all that are in the waters. Everything in the waters that has fins and scales, whether in the seas 10 or in the rivers, you may eat. But anything in the seas or the rivers that has not fins and scales, of the swarming creatures in

the waters and of the living creatures that are in the waters, is
11 an abomination to you. They shall remain an abomination to you; of their flesh you shall not eat, and their carcasses you shall
12 have in abomination. Everything in the waters that has not fins and scales is an abomination to you.

13 "And these you shall have in abomination among the birds, they shall not be eaten, they are an abomination: the eagle,
14 the vulture, the osprey, the kite, the falcon according to its
15, 16 kind, every raven according to its kind, the ostrich, the
17 nighthawk, the sea gull, the hawk according to its kind, the
18 owl, the cormorant, the ibis, the water hen, the pelican, the
19 carrion vulture, the stork, the heron according to its kind, the hoopoe, and the bat.

20 "All winged insects that go upon all fours are an abomina-
21 tion to you. Yet among the winged insects that go on all fours you may eat those which have legs above their feet, with
22 which to leap on the earth. Of them you may eat: the locust according to its kind, the bald locust according to its kind, the cricket according to its kind, and the grasshopper according
23 to its kind. But all other winged insects which have four feet are an abomination to you.

24 "And by these you shall become unclean; whoever touches
25 their carcass shall be unclean until the evening, and whoever carries any part of their carcass shall wash his clothes and be
26 unclean until the evening. Every animal which parts the hoof but is not cloven-footed or does not chew the cud is unclean
27 to you; every one who touches them shall be unclean. And all that go on their paws, among the animals that go on all fours, are unclean to you; whoever touches their carcass shall
28 be unclean until the evening, and he who carries their carcass shall wash his clothes and be unclean until the evening; they are unclean to you.

29 "And these are unclean to you among the swarming things that swarm upon the earth: the weasel, the mouse, the great
30 lizard according to its kind, the gecko, the land crocodile, the
31 lizard, the sand lizard, and the chameleon. These are unclean to you among all that swarm; whoever touches them when
32 they are dead shall be unclean until the evening. And anything upon which any of them falls when they are dead shall be unclean, whether it is an article of wood or a garment or a skin or a sack, any vessel that is used for any purpose; it must be put into water, and it shall be unclean until the evening;
33 then it shall be clean. And if any of them falls into any earthen vessel, all that is in it shall be unclean, and you shall break it.
34 Any food in it which may be eaten, upon which water may come, shall be unclean; and all drink which may be drunk from
35 every such vessel shall be unclean. And everything upon which any part of their carcass falls shall be unclean; whether oven or stove, it shall be broken in pieces; they are unclean, and
36 shall be unclean to you. Nevertheless a spring or a cistern holding water shall be clean; but whatever touches their carcass
37 shall be unclean. And if any part of their carcass falls upon
38 any seed for sowing that is to be sown, it is clean; but if water is put on the seed and any part of their carcass falls on it, it is unclean to you.

39 "And if any animal of which you may eat dies, he who
40 touches its carcass shall be unclean until the evening, and he who eats of its carcass shall wash his clothes and be unclean until the evening; he also who carries the carcass shall wash his clothes and be unclean until the evening.
41 "Every swarming thing that swarms upon the earth is an
42 abomination; it shall not be eaten. Whatever goes on its belly, and whatever goes on all fours, or whatever has many feet, all the swarming things that swarm upon the earth, you shall
43 not eat; for they are an abomination. You shall not make yourselves abominable with any swarming thing that swarms; and you shall not defile yourselves with them, lest you become
44 unclean. For I am the Lord your God; consecrate yourselves therefore, and be holy, for I am holy. You shall not defile yourselves with any swarming thing that crawls upon the
45 earth. For I am the Lord who brought you up out of the land of Egypt, to be your God; you shall therefore be holy, for I am holy."

46 This is the law pertaining to beast and bird and every living
47 creature that moves through the waters and every creature that swarms upon the earth, to make a distinction between the unclean and the clean and between the living creature that may be eaten and the living creature that may not be eaten.

12 The Lord said to Moses, "Say to the people of Israel, If
2 a woman conceives, and bears a male child, then she shall be unclean seven days; as at the time of her menstruation, she
3 shall be unclean. And on the eighth day the flesh of his fore-
4 skin shall be circumcised. Then she shall continue for thirty-three days in the blood of her purifying; she shall not touch any hallowed thing, nor come into the sanctuary, until
5 the days of her purifying are completed. But if she bears a female child, then she shall be unclean two weeks, as in her menstruation; and she shall continue in the blood of her purifying for sixty-six days.
6 "And when the days of her purifying are completed, whether for a son or for a daughter, she shall bring to the priest at the door of the tent of meeting a lamb a year old for a burnt offering and a young pigeon or a turtledove for a sin offering,
7 and he shall offer it before the Lord, and make atonement for her; then she shall be clean from the flow of her blood. This is the law for her who bears a child, either male or female.
8 And if she cannot afford a lamb, then she shall take two turtledoves or two young pigeons, one for a burnt offering and the other for a sin offering; and the priest shall make atonement for her, and she shall be clean."

Diagnosis of Leprosy

13 The Lord said to Moses and Aaron, "When a man has
2 on the skin of his body a swelling or an eruption or a spot, and it turns into a leprous disease on the skin of his body, then he shall be brought to Aaron the priest or to one
3 of his sons the priests, and the priest shall examine the diseased spot on the skin of his body; and if the hair in the diseased spot has turned white and the disease appears to be deeper than the skin of his body, it is a leprous disease; when the priest has examined him he shall pronounce him unclean.
4 But if the spot is white in the skin of his body, and appears no deeper than the skin, and the hair in it has not turned white, the priest shall shut up the diseased person for seven
5 days; and the priest shall examine him on the seventh day, and if in his eyes the disease is checked and the disease has not spread in the skin, then the priest shall shut him up seven
6 days more; and the priest shall examine him again on the seventh day, and if the diseased spot is dim and the disease has not spread in the skin, then the priest shall pronounce him clean; it is only an eruption; and he shall wash his clothes, and
7 be clean. But if the eruption spreads in the skin, after he has shown himself to the priest for his cleansing, he shall appear
8 again before the priest; and the priest shall make an examination, and if the eruption has spread in the skin, then the priest shall pronounce him unclean; it is leprosy.
9 "When a man is afflicted with leprosy, he shall be brought to
10 the priest; and the priest shall make an examination, and if there is a white swelling in the skin, which has turned the
11 hair white, and there is quick raw flesh in the swelling, it is a chronic leprosy in the skin of his body, and the priest shall pronounce him unclean; he shall not shut him up, for he is
12 unclean. And if the leprosy breaks out in the skin, so that the leprosy covers all the skin of the diseased person from head
13 to foot, so far as the priest can see, then the priest shall make an examination, and if the leprosy has covered all his body, he shall pronounce him clean of the disease; it has all turned
14 white, and he is clean. But when raw flesh appears on him, he
15 shall be unclean. And the priest shall examine the raw flesh, and pronounce him unclean; raw flesh is unclean, for it is
16 leprosy. But if the raw flesh turns again and is changed to
17 white, then he shall come to the priest, and the priest shall examine him, and if the disease has turned white, then the priest shall pronounce the diseased person clean; he is clean.
18 "And when there is in the skin of one's body a boil that has
19 healed, and in the place of the boil there comes a white swelling or a reddish-white spot, then it shall be shown to the
20 priest; and the priest shall make an examination, and if it appears deeper than the skin and its hair has turned white, then the priest shall pronounce him unclean; it is the disease
21 of leprosy, it has broken out in the boil. But if the priest examines it, and the hair on it is not white and it is not deeper than the skin, but is dim, then the priest shall shut him up
22 seven days; and if it spreads in the skin, then the priest shall
23 pronounce him unclean; it is diseased. But if the spot remains in one place and does not spread, it is the scar of the boil; and the priest shall pronounce him clean.
24 "Or, when the body has a burn on its skin and the raw flesh
25 of the burn becomes a spot, reddish-white or white, the priest shall examine it, and if the hair in the spot has turned white

and it appears deeper than the skin, then it is leprosy; it has broken out in the burn, and the priest shall pronounce him

26 unclean; it is a leprous disease. But if the priest examines it, and the hair in the spot is not white and it is no deeper than the skin, but is dim, the priest shall shut him up seven days,

27 and the priest shall examine him the seventh day; if it is spreading in the skin, then the priest shall pronounce him

28 unclean; it is a leprous disease. But if the spot remains in one place and does not spread in the skin, but is dim, it is a swelling from the burn, and the priest shall pronounce him clean; for it is the scar of the burn.

29 "When a man or woman has a disease on the head or the

30 beard, the priest shall examine the disease; and if it appears deeper than the skin, and the hair in it is yellow and thin, then the priest shall pronounce him unclean; it is an itch, a

31 leprosy of the head or the beard. And if the priest examines the itching disease, and it appears no deeper than the skin and there is no black hair in it, then the priest shall shut up

32 the person with the itching disease for seven days; and on the seventh day the priest shall examine the disease; and if the itch has not spread, and there is in it no yellow hair, and the

33 itch appears to be no deeper than the skin, then he shall shave himself, but the itch he shall not shave; and the priest shall shut up the person with the itching disease for seven days

34 more; and on the seventh day the priest shall examine the itch, and if the itch has not spread in the skin and it appears to be no deeper than the skin, then the priest shall pronounce

35 him clean; and he shall wash his clothes, and be clean. But

36 if the itch spreads in the skin after his cleansing, then the priest shall examine him, and if the itch has spread in the skin,

37 the priest need not seek for the yellow hair; he is unclean. But if in his eyes the itch is checked, and black hair has grown in it, the itch is healed, and he is clean; and the priest shall pronounce him clean.

38 "When a man or a woman has spots on the skin of the

39 body, white spots, the priest shall make an examination, and if the spots on the skin of the body are of a dull white, it is tetter that has broken out in the skin; he is clean.

40 "If a man's hair has fallen from his head, he is bald but he is

41 clean. And if a man's hair has fallen from his forehead and

42 temples, he has baldness of the forehead but he is clean. But if there is on the bald head or the bald forehead a reddish-white diseased spot, it is leprosy breaking out on his bald head or his

43 bald forehead. Then the priest shall examine him, and if the diseased swelling is reddish-white on his bald head or on his

bald forehead, like the appearance of leprosy in the skin of the

44 body, he is a leprous man, he is unclean; the priest must pronounce him unclean; his disease is on his head.

45 "The leper who has the disease shall wear torn clothes and let the hair of his head hang loose, and he shall cover his upper

46 lip and cry, 'Unclean, unclean.' He shall remain unclean as long as he has the disease; he is unclean; he shall dwell alone in a habitation outside the camp.

47 "When there is a leprous disease in a garment, whether a

48 woolen or a linen garment, in warp or woof of linen or wool,

49 or in a skin or in anything made of skin, if the disease shows greenish or reddish in the garment, whether in warp or woof or in skin or in anything made of skin, it is a leprous disease

50 and shall be shown to the priest. And the priest shall examine the disease, and shut up that which has the disease for seven

51 days; then he shall examine the disease on the seventh day. If the disease has spread in the garment, in warp or woof, or in the skin, whatever be the use of the skin, the disease is

52 a malignant leprosy; it is unclean. And he shall burn the garment, whether diseased in warp or woof, woolen or linen,

or anything of skin, for it is a malignant leprosy; it shall be burned in the fire.

53 "And if the priest examines, and the disease has not spread in the garment in warp or woof or in anything of skin,

54 then the priest shall command that they wash the thing in which is the disease, and he shall shut it up seven days more;

55 and the priest shall examine the diseased thing after it has been washed. And if the diseased spot has not changed color, though the disease has not spread, it is unclean; you shall burn it in the fire, whether the leprous spot is on the back or on the front.

56 "But if the priest examines, and the disease is dim after it is washed, he shall tear the spot out of the garment or the skin

57 or the warp or woof; then if it appears again in the garment, in warp or woof, or in anything of skin, it is spreading; you

58 shall burn with fire that in which is the disease. But the garment, warp or woof, or anything of skin from which the disease departs when you have washed it, shall then be washed a second time, and be clean."

59 This is the law for a leprous disease in a garment of wool or linen, either in warp or woof, or in anything of skin, to decide whether it is clean or unclean.

Treatment of Leprosy

14 The Lord said to Moses, "This shall be the law of the

2 leper for the day of his cleansing. He shall be brought to

3 the priest; and the priest shall go out of the camp, and the priest shall make an examination. Then, if the leprous disease is

4 healed in the leper, the priest shall command them to take for him who is to be cleansed two living clean birds and cedar-

5 wood and scarlet stuff and hyssop; and the priest shall command them to kill one of the birds in an earthen vessel over

6 running water. He shall take the living bird with the cedarwood and the scarlet stuff and the hyssop, and dip them and the living bird in the blood of the bird that was killed over the

7 running water; and he shall sprinkle it seven times upon him who is to be cleansed of leprosy; then he shall pronounce him

8 clean, and shall let the living bird go into the open field. And he who is to be cleansed shall wash his clothes, and shave off all his hair, and bathe himself in water, and he shall be clean; and after that he shall come into the camp, but shall dwell

9 outside his tent seven days. And on the seventh day he shall shave all his hair off his head; he shall shave off his beard and his eyebrows, all his hair. Then he shall wash his clothes, and bathe his body in water, and he shall be clean.

10 "And on the eighth day he shall take two male lambs without blemish, and one ewe lamb a year old without blemish, and a cereal offering of three tenths of an ephah of fine flour

11 mixed with oil, and one log of oil. And the priest who cleanses him shall set the man who is to be cleansed and these things

12 before the Lord, at the door of the tent of meeting. And the priest shall take one of the male lambs, and offer it for a guilt offering, along with the log of oil, and wave them for a wave

13 offering before the Lord; and he shall kill the lamb in the place where they kill the sin offering and the burnt offering, in the holy place; for the guilt offering, like the sin offering, belongs

14 to the priest; it is most holy. The priest shall take some of the blood of the guilt offering, and the priest shall put it on the tip of the right ear of him who is to be cleansed, and on the thumb of his right hand, and on the great toe of his right foot.

15 Then the priest shall take some of the log of oil, and pour it

16 into the palm of his own left hand, and dip his right finger in the oil that is in his left hand, and sprinkle some oil with

17 his finger seven times before the Lord. And some of the oil that remains in his hand the priest shall put on the tip of the right ear of him who is to be cleansed, and on the thumb of his right hand, and on the great toe of his right foot, upon the

18 blood of the guilt offering; and the rest of the oil that is in the priest's hand he shall put on the head of him who is to be cleansed. Then the priest shall make atonement for him before

19 the Lord. The priest shall offer the sin offering, to make atonement for him who is to be cleansed from his uncleanness. And

20 afterward he shall kill the burnt offering; and the priest shall offer the burnt offering and the cereal offering on the altar. Thus the priest shall make atonement for him, and he shall be clean.

21 "But if he is poor and cannot afford so much, then he shall take one male lamb for a guilt offering to be waved, to make atonement for him, and a tenth of an ephah of fine flour

22 mixed with oil for a cereal offering, and a log of oil; also two turtledoves or two young pigeons, such as he can afford; the

one shall be a sin offering and the other a burnt offering.
23 And on the eighth day he shall bring them for his cleansing to the priest, to the door of the tent of meeting, before the Lord;
24 and the priest shall take the lamb of the guilt offering, and the log of oil, and the priest shall wave them for a wave offering
25 before the Lord. And he shall kill the lamb of the guilt offering; and the priest shall take some of the blood of the guilt offering, and put it on the tip of the right ear of him who is to be cleansed, and on the thumb of his right hand, and on the great
26 toe of his right foot. And the priest shall pour some of the oil
27 into the palm of his own left hand; and shall sprinkle with his right finger some of the oil that is in his left hand seven
28 times before the Lord; and the priest shall put some of the oil that is in his hand on the tip of the right ear of him who is to be cleansed, and on the thumb of his right hand, and the great toe of his right foot, in the place where the blood of the guilt
29 offering was put; and the rest of the oil that is in the priest's hand he shall put on the head of him who is to be cleansed,
30 to make atonement for him before the Lord. And he shall offer,
31 of the turtledoves or young pigeons such as he can afford, one ˣ for a sin offering and the other for a burnt offering, along with a cereal offering; and the priest shall make atonement before
32 the Lord for him who is being cleansed. This is the law for him in whom is a leprous disease, who cannot afford the offerings for his cleansing."

33, 34 The Lord said to Moses and Aaron, "When you come into the land of Canaan, which I give you for a possession, and I put a leprous disease in a house in the land of your possession,
35 then he who owns the house shall come and tell the priest, 'There seems to me to be some sort of disease in my house.'
36 Then the priest shall command that they empty the house before the priest goes to examine the disease, lest all that is in the house be declared unclean; and afterward the priest shall
37 go in to see the house. And he shall examine the disease; and if the disease is in the walls of the house with greenish or reddish spots, and if it appears to be deeper than the surface,
38 then the priest shall go out of the house to the door of the
39 house, and shut up the house seven days. And the priest shall come again on the seventh day, and look; and if the disease
40 has spread in the walls of the house, then the priest shall command that they take out the stones in which is the disease and
41 throw them into an unclean place outside the city; and he shall cause the inside of the house to be scraped round about, and the plaster that they scrape off they shall pour into an
42 unclean place outside the city; then they shall take other stones and put them in the place of those stones, and he shall take other plaster and plaster the house.
43 "If the disease breaks out again in the house, after he has taken out the stones and scraped the house and plastered it,
44 then the priest shall go and look; and if the disease has spread in the house, it is a malignant leprosy in the house; it is unclean.
45 And he shall break down the house, its stones and timber and all the plaster of the house; and he shall carry them forth out
46 of the city to an unclean place. Moreover he who enters the house while it is shut up shall be unclean until the evening;
47 and he who lies down in the house shall wash his clothes; and he who eats in the house shall wash his clothes.
48 "But if the priest comes and makes an examination, and the disease has not spread in the house after the house was plastered, then the priest shall pronounce the house clean, for the
49 disease is healed. And for the cleansing of the house he shall take two small birds, with cedarwood and scarlet stuff and
50 hyssop, and shall kill one of the birds in an earthen vessel
51 over running water, and shall take the cedarwood and the hyssop and the scarlet stuff, along with the living bird, and dip them in the blood of the bird that was killed and in the run-
52 ning water, and sprinkle the house seven times. Thus he shall cleanse the house with the blood of the bird, and with the running water, and with the living bird, and with the cedar-
53 wood and hyssop and scarlet stuff; and he shall let the living bird go out of the city into the open field; so he shall make atonement for the house, and it shall be clean."
54, 55 This is the law for any leprous disease: for an itch, for
56 leprosy in a garment or in a house, and for a swelling or an
57 eruption or a spot, to show when it is unclean and when it is clean. This is the law for leprosy.

Personal Cleanliness

15 2 The Lord said to Moses and Aaron, "Say to the people of Israel, When any man has a discharge from his body,

3 his discharge is unclean. And this is the law of his uncleanness for a discharge: whether his body runs with his discharge, or his body is stopped from discharge, it is uncleanness in him.
4 Every bed on which he who has the discharge lies shall be
5 unclean; and everything on which he sits shall be unclean. And any one who touches his bed shall wash his clothes, and bathe himself in water, and be unclean until the evening.
6 And whoever sits on anything on which he who has the discharge has sat shall wash his clothes, and bathe himself in
7 water, and be unclean until the evening. And whoever touches the body of him who has the discharge shall wash his clothes, and bathe himself in water, and be unclean until the evening.
8 And if he who has the discharge spits on one who is clean, then he shall wash his clothes, and bathe himself in water, and
9 be unclean until the evening. And any saddle on which he
10 who has the discharge rides shall be unclean. And whoever touches anything that was under him shall be unclean until the evening; and he who carries such a thing shall wash his clothes, and bathe himself in water, and be unclean until the
11 evening. Any one whom he that has the discharge touches without having rinsed his hands in water shall wash his clothes, and bathe himself in water, and be unclean until the
12 evening. And the earthen vessel which he who has the discharge touches shall be broken; and every vessel of wood shall be rinsed in water.
13 "And when he who has a discharge is cleansed of his discharge, then he shall count for himself seven days for his cleansing, and wash his clothes; and he shall bathe his body
14 in running water, and shall be clean. And on the eighth day he shall take two turtledoves or two young pigeons, and come before the Lord to the door of the tent of meeting, and give
15 them to the priest; and the priest shall offer them, one for a sin offering and the other for a burnt offering; and the priest shall make atonement for him before the Lord for his discharge.
16 "And if a man has an emission of semen, he shall bathe his
17 whole body in water, and be unclean until the evening. And every garment and every skin on which the semen comes shall be washed with water, and be unclean until the evening.
18 If a man lies with a woman and has an emission of semen, both of them shall bathe themselves in water, and be unclean until the evening.
19 "When a woman has a discharge of blood which is her regular discharge from her body, she shall be in her impurity for seven days, and whoever touches her shall be unclean until
20 the evening. And everything upon which she lies during her impurity shall be unclean; everything also upon which she
21 sits shall be unclean. And whoever touches her bed shall wash his clothes, and bathe himself in water, and be unclean until
22 the evening. And whoever touches anything upon which she sits shall wash his clothes, and bathe himself in water, and be
23 unclean until the evening; whether it is the bed or anything upon which she sits, when he touches it he shall be unclean
24 until the evening. And if any man lies with her, and her impurity is on him, he shall be unclean seven days; and every bed on which he lies shall be unclean.
25 "If a woman has a discharge of blood for many days, not at the time of her impurity, or if she has a discharge beyond the time of her impurity, all the days of the discharge she shall continue in uncleanness; as in the days of her impurity,
26 she shall be unclean. Every bed on which she lies, all the days of her discharge, shall be to her as the bed of her impurity; and everything on which she sits shall be unclean, as
27 in the uncleanness of her impurity. And whoever touches these things shall be unclean, and shall wash his clothes, and bathe himself in water, and be unclean until the evening.
28 But if she is cleansed of her discharge, she shall count for
29 herself seven days, and after that she shall be clean. And on the eighth day she shall take two turtledoves or two young pigeons, and bring them to the priest, to the door of the tent of
30 meeting. And the priest shall offer one for a sin offering and the other for a burnt offering; and the priest shall make atonement for her before the Lord for her unclean discharge.
31 "Thus you shall keep the people of Israel separate from their uncleanness, lest they die in their uncleanness by defiling my tabernacle that is in their midst."
32 This is the law for him who has a discharge and for him who has an emission of semen, becoming unclean thereby;
33 also for her who is sick with her impurity; that is, for any one, male or female, who has a discharge, and for the man who lies with a woman who is unclean.

ˣ Gk Syr: Heb *afford,* ³¹ *such as he can afford, one*

THE RITUAL OF ATONEMENT

16 The LORD spoke to Moses, after the death of the two sons of Aaron, when they drew near before the LORD and ² died; and the LORD said to Moses, "Tell Aaron your brother not to come at all times into the holy place within the veil, before the mercy seat which is upon the ark, lest he die; ³ I will appear in the cloud upon the mercy seat. But thus shall Aaron come into the holy place: with a young bull for a sin ⁴ offering and a ram for a burnt offering. He shall put on the holy linen coat, and shall have the linen breeches on his body, be girded with the linen girdle, and wear the linen turban; these are the holy garments. He shall bathe his body in water, and ⁵ then put them on. And he shall take from the congregation of the people of Israel two male goats for a sin offering, and one ram for a burnt offering.

⁶ "And Aaron shall offer the bull as a sin offering for himself, ⁷ and shall make atonement for himself and for his house. Then he shall take the two goats, and set them before the LORD at ⁸ the door of the tent of meeting; and Aaron shall cast lots upon the two goats, one lot for the LORD and the other lot for Aza′- ⁹ zel. And Aaron shall present the goat on which the lot fell ¹⁰ for the LORD, and offer it as a sin offering; but the goat on which the lot fell for Aza′zel shall be presented alive before the LORD to make atonement over it, that it may be sent away into the wilderness to Aza′zel.

¹¹ "Aaron shall present the bull as a sin offering for himself, and shall make atonement for himself and for his house; he ¹² shall kill the bull as a sin offering for himself. And he shall take a censer full of coals of fire from the altar before the LORD, and two handfuls of sweet incense beaten small; and he shall ¹³ bring it within the veil and put the incense on the fire before the LORD, that the cloud of the incense may cover the mercy ¹⁴ seat which is upon the testimony, lest he die; and he shall take some of the blood of the bull, and sprinkle it with his finger on the front of the mercy seat, and before the mercy seat he shall sprinkle the blood with his finger seven times.

¹⁵ "Then he shall kill the goat of the sin offering which is for the people, and bring its blood within the veil, and do with its blood as he did with the blood of the bull, sprinkling it ¹⁶ upon the mercy seat and before the mercy seat; thus he shall make atonement for the holy place, because of the unclean-nesses of the people of Israel, and because of their transgres-sions, all their sins; and so he shall do for the tent of meeting, which abides with them in the midst of their uncleannesses. ¹⁷ There shall be no man in the tent of meeting when he enters to make atonement in the holy place until he comes out and has made atonement for himself and for his house and for all the ¹⁸ assembly of Israel. Then he shall go out to the altar which is before the LORD and make atonement for it, and shall take some of the blood of the bull and of the blood of the goat, and put ¹⁹ it on the horns of the altar round about. And he shall sprinkle some of the blood upon it with his finger seven times, and cleanse it and hallow it from the uncleannesses of the people of Israel.

²⁰ "And when he has made an end of atoning for the holy place and the tent of meeting and the altar, he shall present ²¹ the live goat; and Aaron shall lay both his hands upon the head of the live goat, and confess over him all the iniquities of the people of Israel, and all their transgressions, all their sins; and he shall put them upon the head of the goat, and send him away into the wilderness by the hand of a man who ²² is in readiness. The goat shall bear all their iniquities upon him to a solitary land; and he shall let the goat go in the wilderness.

²³ "Then Aaron shall come into the tent of meeting, and shall put off the linen garments which he put on when he went into ²⁴ the holy place, and shall leave them there; and he shall bathe his body in water in a holy place, and put on his garments, and come forth, and offer his burnt offering and the burnt offering of the people, and make atonement for himself and ²⁵ for the people. And the fat of the sin offering he shall burn ²⁶ upon the altar. And he who lets the goat go to Aza′zel shall wash his clothes and bathe his body in water, and afterward ²⁷ he may come into the camp. And the bull for the sin offering and the goat for the sin offering, whose blood was brought in to make atonement in the holy place, shall be carried forth out-side the camp; their skin and their flesh and their dung shall ²⁸ be burned with fire. And he who burns them shall wash his clothes and bathe his body in water, and afterward he may come into the camp.

²⁹ "And it shall be a statute to you for ever that in the seventh month, on the tenth day of the month, you shall afflict your-selves, and shall do no work, either the native or the stranger ³⁰ who sojourns among you; for on this day shall atonement be made for you, to cleanse you; from all your sins you shall be ³¹ clean before the LORD. It is a sabbath of solemn rest to you, and you shall afflict yourselves; it is a statute for ever. ³² And the priest who is anointed and consecrated as priest in his father's place shall make atonement, wearing the holy linen ³³ garments; he shall make atonement for the sanctuary, and he shall make atonement for the tent of meeting and for the altar, and he shall make atonement for the priests and for all the ³⁴ people of the assembly. And this shall be an everlasting statute for you, that atonement may be made for the people of Israel once in the year because of all their sins." And Moses did as the LORD commanded him.

LAW OF HOLINESS

17 And the LORD said to Moses, ² "Say to Aaron and his sons, and to all the people of Israel, This is the thing ³ which the LORD has commanded. If any man of the house of Israel kills an ox or a lamb or a goat in the camp, or kills ⁴ it outside the camp, and does not bring it to the door of the tent of meeting, to offer it as a gift to the LORD before the tabernacle of the LORD, bloodguilt shall be imputed to that man; he has shed blood; and that man shall be cut off from ⁵ among his people. This is to the end that the people of Israel may bring their sacrifices which they slay in the open field, that they may bring them to the LORD, to the priest at the door of the tent of meeting, and slay them as sacrifices of peace ⁶ offerings to the LORD; and the priest shall sprinkle the blood on the altar of the LORD at the door of the tent of meeting, and ⁷ burn the fat for a pleasing odor to the LORD. So they shall no more slay their sacrifices for satyrs, after whom they play the harlot. This shall be a statute for ever to them throughout their generations.

⁸ "And you shall say to them, Any man of the house of Israel, or of the strangers that sojourn among them, who offers a burnt ⁹ offering or sacrifice, and does not bring it to the door of the tent of meeting, to sacrifice it to the LORD; that man shall be cut off from his people.

¹⁰ "If any man of the house of Israel or of the strangers that sojourn among them eats any blood, I will set my face against that person who eats blood, and will cut him off from among ¹¹ his people. For the life of the flesh is in the blood; and I have given it for you upon the altar to make atonement for your souls; for it is the blood that makes atonement, by reason of ¹² the life. Therefore I have said to the people of Israel, No person among you shall eat blood, neither shall any stranger ¹³ who sojourns among you eat blood. Any man also of the people of Israel, or of the strangers that sojourn among them, who takes in hunting any beast or bird that may be eaten shall pour out its blood and cover it with dust.

¹⁴ "For the life of every creature is the blood of it; ᵉ therefore I have said to the people of Israel, You shall not eat the blood of any creature, for the life of every creature is its blood; ¹⁵ whoever eats it shall be cut off. And every person that eats what dies of itself or what is torn by beasts, whether he is a native or a sojourner, shall wash his clothes, and bathe himself in water, and be unclean until the evening; then he shall be ¹⁶ clean. But if he does not wash them or bathe his flesh, he shall bear his iniquity."

Incest Forbidden

18 And the LORD said to Moses, ² "Say to the people of Israel, ³ I am the LORD your God. You shall not do as they do in the land of Egypt, where you dwelt, and you shall not do as they do in the land of Canaan, to which I am bringing you. ⁴ You shall not walk in their statutes. You shall do my ordi-nances and keep my statutes and walk in them. I am the LORD ⁵ your God. You shall therefore keep my statutes and my ordinances, by doing which a man shall live: I am the LORD. ⁶ "None of you shall approach any one near of kin to him to ⁷ uncover nakedness. I am the LORD. You shall not uncover the nakedness of your father, which is the nakedness of your mother; she is your mother, you shall not uncover her naked- ⁸ ness. You shall not uncover the nakedness of your father's ⁹ wife; it is your father's nakedness. You shall not uncover the nakedness of your sister, the daughter of your father or the daughter of your mother, whether born at home or born ¹⁰ abroad. You shall not uncover the nakedness of your son's

ᵉ Gk Syr Compare Vg: Heb *for the life of all flesh, its blood is in its life* daughter or of your daughter's daughter, for their nakedness ¹¹ is your own nakedness. You shall not uncover the nakedness of your father's wife's daughter, begotten by your father, ¹² since she is your sister. You shall not uncover the nakedness of your father's sister; she is your father's near kinswoman. ¹³ You shall not uncover the nakedness of your mother's sister, ¹⁴ for she is your mother's near kinswoman. You shall not uncover the nakedness of your father's brother, that is, you shall ¹⁵ not approach his wife; she is your aunt. You shall not uncover the nakedness of your daughter-in-law; she is your son's wife, ¹⁶ you shall not uncover her nakedness. You shall not uncover the nakedness of your brother's wife; she is your brother's ¹⁷ nakedness. You shall not uncover the nakedness of a woman and of her daughter, and you shall not take her son's daughter or her daughter's daughter to uncover her nakedness; they are ¹⁸ your ^f near kinswomen; it is wickedness. And you shall not take a woman as a rival wife to her sister, uncovering her nakedness while her sister is yet alive.

¹⁹ "You shall not approach a woman to uncover her nakedness ²⁰ while she is in her menstrual uncleanness. And you shall not lie carnally with your neighbor's wife, and defile yourself ²¹ with her. You shall not give any of your children to devote them by fire to Molech, and so profane the name of your God: ²² I am the LORD. You shall not lie with a male as with a ²³ woman; it is an abomination. And you shall not lie with any beast and defile yourself with it, neither shall any woman give herself to a beast to lie with it: it is perversion.

²⁴ "Do not defile yourselves by any of these things, for by all these the nations I am casting out before you defiled them- ²⁵ selves; and the land became defiled, so that I punished its ²⁶ iniquity, and the land vomited out its inhabitants. But you shall keep my statutes and my ordinances and do none of these abominations, either the native or the stranger who sojourns ²⁷ among you (for all of these abominations the men of the land did, who were before you, so that the land became defiled); ²⁸ lest the land vomit you out, when you defile it, as it vomited ²⁹ out the nation that was before you. For whoever shall do any of these abominations, the persons that do them shall be cut ³⁰ off from among their people. So keep my charge never to practice any of these abominable customs which were practiced before you, and never to defile yourselves by them: I am the LORD your God."

Holiness of Behavior

19 ² And the LORD said to Moses, "Say to all the congregation of the people of Israel, You shall be holy; for I the ³ LORD your God am holy. Every one of you shall revere his mother and his father, and you shall keep my sabbaths: I am ⁴ the LORD your God. Do not turn to idols or make for yourselves molten gods: I am the LORD your God.

⁵ "When you offer a sacrifice of peace offerings to the LORD, you ⁶ shall offer it so that you may be accepted. It shall be eaten the same day you offer it, or on the morrow; and anything left ⁷ over until the third day shall be burned with fire. If it is eaten at all on the third day, it is an abomination; it will not be ac- ⁸ cepted, and every one who eats it shall bear his iniquity, because he has profaned a holy thing of the LORD; and that person shall be cut off from his people.

⁹ "When you reap the harvest of your land, you shall not reap your field to its very border, neither shall you ¹⁰ gather the gleanings after your harvest. And you shall not strip your vineyard bare, neither shall you gather the fallen grapes of your vineyard; you shall leave them

for the poor and for the sojourner: I am the LORD your God.

¹¹ "You shall not steal, nor deal falsely, nor lie to one ¹² another. And you shall not swear by my name falsely, and so profane the name of your God: I am the LORD.

¹³ "You shall not oppress your neighbor or rob him. The wages of a hired servant shall not remain with you ¹⁴ all night until the morning. You shall not curse the deaf or put a stumbling block before the blind, but you shall fear your God: I am the LORD.

¹⁵ "You shall do no injustice in judgment; you shall not be partial to the poor or defer to the great, but in righ- ¹⁶ teousness shall you judge your neighbor. You shall not go up and down as a slanderer among your people, and you shall not stand forth against the life ^g of your neighbor: I am the LORD.

¹⁷ "You shall not hate your brother in your heart, but you shall reason with your neighbor, lest you bear sin ¹⁸ because of him. You shall not take vengeance or bear any grudge against the sons of your own people, but you shall love your neighbor as yourself: I am the LORD.

¹⁹ "You shall keep my statutes. You shall not let your cattle breed with a different kind; you shall not sow your field with two kinds of seed; nor shall there come upon you a garment of cloth made of two kinds of stuff.

²⁰ "If a man lies carnally with a woman who is a slave, betrothed to another man and not yet ransomed or given her freedom, an inquiry shall be held. They shall not be put to ²¹ death, because she was not free; but he shall bring a guilt offering for himself to the LORD, to the door of the tent of ²² meeting, a ram for a guilt offering. And the priest shall make atonement for him with the ram of the guilt offering before the LORD for his sin which he has committed; and the sin which he has committed shall be forgiven him.

²³ "When you come into the land and plant all kinds of trees for food, then you shall count their fruit as forbidden; ^h three ²⁴ years it shall be forbidden to you, it must not be eaten. And in the fourth year all their fruit shall be holy, an offering of ²⁵ praise to the LORD. But in the fifth year you may eat of their fruit, that they may yield more richly for you: I am the LORD your God.

²⁶ "You shall not eat any flesh with the blood in it. You shall ²⁷ not practice augury or witchcraft. You shall not round off the hair on your temples or mar the edges of your beard. ²⁸ You shall not make any cuttings in your flesh on account of the dead or tattoo any marks upon you: I am the LORD.

²⁹ "Do not profane your daughter by making her a harlot, lest the land fall into harlotry and the land become full of ³⁰ wickedness. You shall keep my sabbaths and reverence my sanctuary: I am the LORD.

³¹ "Do not turn to mediums or wizards; do not seek them out, to be defiled by them: I am the LORD your God.

³² "You shall rise up before the hoary head, and honor the face of an old man, and you shall fear your God: I am the LORD.

³³ "When a stranger sojourns with you in your land, you ³⁴ shall not do him wrong. The stranger who sojourns with you shall be to you as the native among you, and you shall love him as yourself; for you were strangers in the land of Egypt: I am the LORD your God.

³⁵ "You shall do no wrong in judgment, in measures of length ³⁶ or weight or quantity. You shall have just balances, just weights, a just ephah, and a just hin: I am the LORD your God, ³⁷ who brought you out of the land of Egypt. And you shall observe all my statutes and all my ordinances, and do them: I am the LORD."

---

^f Gk: Heb lacks *your*   ^g Heb *blood*   ^h Heb *their uncircumcision*

Penalties for Pagan Practices

20 ² The LORD said to Moses, "Say to the people of Israel, Any man of the people of Israel, or of the strangers that sojourn in Israel, who gives any of his children to Molech shall be put to death; the people of the land shall stone him with ³ stones. I myself will set my face against that man, and will cut him off from among his people, because he has given one of his children to Molech, defiling my sanctuary and profaning ⁴ my holy name. And if the people of the land do at all hide their eyes from that man, when he gives one of his children ⁵ to Molech, and do not put him to death, then I will set my face against that man and against his family, and will cut them off from among their people, him and all who follow him in playing the harlot after Molech.

⁶ "If a person turns to mediums and wizards, playing the harlot after them, I will set my face against that person, and ⁷ will cut him off from among his people. Consecrate yourselves ⁸ therefore, and be holy; for I am the LORD your God. Keep my ⁹ statutes, and do them; I am the LORD who sanctify you. For every one who curses his father or his mother shall be put to death; he has cursed his father or his mother, his blood is upon him.

¹⁰ "If a man commits adultery with the wife of ¹ his neighbor, ¹¹ both the adulterer and the adulteress shall be put to death. The man who lies with his father's wife has uncovered his father's nakedness; both of them shall be put to death, their ¹² blood is upon them. If a man lies with his daughter-in-law, both of them shall be put to death; they have committed incest, ¹³ their blood is upon them. If a man lies with a male as with a woman, both of them have committed an abomination; they ¹⁴ shall be put to death, their blood is upon them. If a man takes a wife and her mother also, it is wickedness; they shall be burned with fire, both he and they, that there may be no ¹⁵ wickedness among you. If a man lies with a beast, he shall be ¹⁶ put to death; and you shall kill the beast. If a woman approaches any beast and lies with it, you shall kill the woman and the beast; they shall be put to death, their blood is upon them.

¹⁷ "If a man takes his sister, a daughter of his father or a daughter of his mother, and sees her nakedness, and she sees his nakedness, it is a shameful thing, and they shall be cut off in the sight of the children of their people; he has uncovered his sister's nakedness, he shall bear his iniquity. ¹⁸ If a man lies with a woman having her sickness, and uncovers her nakedness, he has made naked her fountain, and she has uncovered the fountain of her blood; both of them shall be cut ¹⁹ off from among their people. You shall not uncover the nakedness of your mother's sister or of your father's sister, for that is to make naked one's near kin; they shall bear their iniquity. ²⁰ If a man lies with his uncle's wife, he has uncovered his uncle's nakedness; they shall bear their sin, they shall die childless. ²¹ If a man takes his brother's wife, it is impurity; he has uncovered his brother's nakedness, they shall be childless.

²² "You shall therefore keep all my statutes and all my ordinances, and do them; that the land where I am bringing you ²³ to dwell may not vomit you out. And you shall not walk in the customs of the nation which I am casting out before you; for ²⁴ they did all these things, and therefore I abhorred them. But I have said to you, 'You shall inherit their land, and I will give it to you to possess, a land flowing with milk and honey.' I am the LORD your God, who have separated you from the ²⁵ peoples. You shall therefore make a distinction between the clean beast and the unclean, and between the unclean bird and the clean; you shall not make yourselves abominable by beast or by bird or by anything with which the ground teems, ²⁶ which I have set apart for you to hold unclean. You shall be holy to me; for I the LORD am holy, and have separated you from the peoples, that you should be mine.

²⁷ "A man or a woman who is a medium or a wizard shall be put to death; they shall be stoned with stones, their blood shall be upon them."

Rules for Priests

21 And the LORD said to Moses, "Speak to the priests, the sons of Aaron, and say to them that none of them shall ² defile himself for the dead among his people, except for his nearest of kin, his mother, his father, his son, his daughter, his ³ brother, or his virgin sister (who is near to him because she ⁴ has had no husband; for her he may defile himself). He shall not defile himself as a husband among his people and so

⁵ profane himself. They shall not make tonsures upon their heads, nor shave off the edges of their beards, nor make any ⁶ cuttings in their flesh. They shall be holy to their God, and not profane the name of their God; for they offer the offerings by fire to the LORD, the bread of their God; therefore they shall ⁷ be holy. They shall not marry a harlot or a woman who has been defiled; neither shall they marry a woman divorced from ⁸ her husband; for the priest is holy to his God. You shall consecrate him, for he offers the bread of your God; he shall be ⁹ holy to you; for I the LORD, who sanctify you, am holy. And the daughter of any priest, if she profanes herself by playing the harlot, profanes her father; she shall be burned with fire.

¹⁰ "The priest who is chief among his brethren, upon whose head the anointing oil is poured, and who has been consecrated to wear the garments, shall not let the hair of his head hang ¹¹ loose, nor rend his clothes; he shall not go in to any dead body, nor defile himself, even for his father or for his mother; ¹² neither shall he go out of the sanctuary, nor profane the sanctuary of his God; for the consecration of the anointing oil of his ¹³ God is upon him: I am the LORD. And he shall take a wife in ¹⁴ her virginity. A widow, or one divorced, or a woman who has been defiled, or a harlot, these he shall not marry; but he shall ¹⁵ take to wife a virgin of his own people, that he may not profane his children among his people; for I am the LORD who sanctify him."

^{16, 17} And the LORD said to Moses, "Say to Aaron, None of your descendants throughout their generations who has a blemish ¹⁸ may approach to offer the bread of his God. For no one who has a blemish shall draw near, a man blind or lame, or one ¹⁹ who has a mutilated face or a limb too long, or a man who ²⁰ has an injured foot or an injured hand, or a hunchback, or a dwarf, or a man with a defect in his sight or an itching ²¹ disease or scabs or crushed testicles; no man of the descendants of Aaron the priest who has a blemish shall come near to offer the LORD's offerings by fire; since he has a blemish, he shall ²² not come near to offer the bread of his God. He may eat the bread of his God, both of the most holy and of the holy things, ²³ but he shall not come near the veil or approach the altar, because he has a blemish, that he may not profane my sanc- ²⁴ tuaries; for I am the LORD who sanctify them." So Moses spoke to Aaron and to his sons and to all the people of Israel.

22 ² And the LORD said to Moses, "Tell Aaron and his sons to keep away from the holy things of the people of Israel, which they dedicate to me, so that they may not profane my ³ holy name: I am the LORD. Say to them, 'If any one of all your descendants throughout your generations approaches the holy things, which the people of Israel dedicate to the LORD, while he has an uncleanness, that person shall be cut off from my ⁴ presence: I am the LORD. None of the line of Aaron who is a leper or suffers a discharge may eat of the holy things until he is clean. Whoever touches anything that is unclean through contact with the dead or a man who has had an emission of ⁵ semen, and whoever touches a creeping thing by which he may be made unclean or a man from whom he may take un- ⁶ cleanness, whatever his uncleanness may be—the person who touches any such shall be unclean until the evening and shall not eat of the holy things unless he has bathed his body in ⁷ water. When the sun is down he shall be clean; and afterward ⁸ he may eat of the holy things, because such are his food. That which dies of itself or is torn by beasts he shall not eat, ⁹ defiling himself by it: I am the LORD.' They shall therefore keep my charge, lest they bear sin for it and die thereby when they profane it: I am the LORD who sanctify them.

¹⁰ "An outsider shall not eat of a holy thing. A sojourner of the ¹¹ priest's or a hired servant shall not eat of a holy thing; but if a priest buys a slave as his property for money, the slave may eat of it; and those that are born in his house may eat of his ¹² food. If a priest's daughter is married to an outsider she shall not ¹³ eat of the offering of the holy things. But if a priest's daughter is a widow or divorced, and has no child, and returns to her father's house, as in her youth, she may eat of her father's ¹⁴ food; yet no outsider shall eat of it. And if a man eats of a holy thing unwittingly, he shall add the fifth of its value to ¹⁵ it, and give the holy thing to the priest. The priests shall not profane the holy things of the people of Israel, which they ¹⁶ offer to the LORD, and so cause them to bear iniquity and guilt, by eating their holy things: for I am the LORD who sanctify them."

^{17, 18} And the LORD said to Moses, "Say to Aaron and his sons and all the people of Israel, When any one of the house of

¹ Heb repeats *if a man commits adultery with the wife of*

Israel or of the sojourners in Israel presents his offering, whether in payment of a vow or as a freewill offering which
19 is offered to the LORD as a burnt offering, to be accepted you shall offer a male without blemish, of the bulls or the sheep or
20 the goats. You shall not offer anything that has a blemish, for
21 it will not be acceptable for you. And when any one offers a sacrifice of peace offerings to the LORD, to fulfil a vow or as a freewill offering, from the herd or from the flock, to be accepted it must be perfect; there shall be no blemish in it.
22 Animals blind or disabled or mutilated or having a discharge or an itch or scabs, you shall not offer to the LORD or make
23 of them an offering by fire upon the altar to the LORD. A bull or a lamb which has a part too long or too short you may present for a freewill offering; but for a votive offering it
24 cannot be accepted. Any animal which has its testicles bruised or crushed or torn or cut, you shall not offer to the LORD or
25 sacrifice within your land; neither shall you offer as the bread of your God any such animals gotten from a foreigner. Since there is a blemish in them, because of their mutilation, they will not be accepted for you."
26, 27 And the LORD said to Moses, "When a bull or sheep or goat is born, it shall remain seven days with its mother; and from the eighth day on it shall be acceptable as an offering by fire
28 to the LORD. And whether the mother is a cow or a ewe, you
29 shall not kill both her and her young in one day. And when you sacrifice a sacrifice of thanksgiving to the LORD, you shall
30 sacrifice it so that you may be accepted. It shall be eaten on the same day, you shall leave none of it until morning: I am the LORD.
31 "So you shall keep my commandments and do them: I am the
32 LORD. And you shall not profane my holy name, but I will be hallowed among the people of Israel; I am the LORD who
33 sanctify you, who brought you out of the land of Egypt to be your God: I am the LORD."

SACRED CALENDAR

2 **23** The LORD said to Moses, "Say to the people of Israel, The appointed feasts of the LORD which you shall proclaim
3 as holy convocations, my appointed feasts, are these. Six days shall work be done; but on the seventh day is a sabbath of solemn rest, a holy convocation; you shall do no work; it is a sabbath to the LORD in all your dwellings.
4 "These are the appointed feasts of the LORD, the holy convocations, which you shall proclaim at the time appointed for them.
5 In the first month, on the fourteenth day of the month in the
6 evening,ʲ is the LORD's passover. And on the fifteenth day of the same month is the feast of unleavened bread to the LORD;
7 seven days you shall eat unleavened bread. On the first day you shall have a holy convocation; you shall do no laborious
8 work. But you shall present an offering by fire to the LORD seven days; on the seventh day is a holy convocation; you shall do no laborious work."

9, 10 And the LORD said to Moses, "Say to the people of Israel, When you come into the land which I give you and reap its harvest, you shall bring the sheaf of the first
11 fruits of your harvest to the priest; and he shall wave the sheaf before the LORD, that you may find acceptance; on the morrow after the sabbath the priest shall wave it.
12 And on the day when you wave the sheaf, you shall offer a male lamb a year old without blemish as a burnt offer-
13 ing to the LORD. And the cereal offering with it shall be two tenths of an ephah of fine flour mixed with oil, to be offered by fire to the LORD, a pleasing odor; and the drink offering with it shall be of wine, a fourth of a hin.
14 And you shall eat neither bread nor grain parched or fresh until this same day, until you have brought the offering of your God: it is a statute for ever throughout your generations in all your dwellings.

15 "And you shall count from the morrow after the sabbath, from the day that you brought the sheaf of the wave offering;
16 seven full weeks shall they be, counting fifty days to the morrow after the seventh sabbath; then you shall present a
17 cereal offering of new grain to the LORD. You shall bring from your dwellings two loaves of bread to be waved, made of two tenths of an ephah; they shall be of fine flour, they shall be
18 baked with leaven, as first fruits to the LORD. And you shall present with the bread seven lambs a year old without blemish, and one young bull, and two rams; they shall be a burnt offering to the LORD, with their cereal offering and their drink
19 offerings, an offering by fire, a pleasing odor to the LORD. And you shall offer one male goat for a sin offering, and two
20 male lambs a year old as a sacrifice of peace offerings. And the priest shall wave them with the bread of the first fruits as a wave offering before the LORD, with the two lambs; they shall
21 be holy to the LORD for the priest. And you shall make proclamation on the same day; you shall hold a holy convocation; you shall do no laborious work: it is a statute for ever in all your dwellings throughout your generations.
22 "And when you reap the harvest of your land, you shall not reap your field to its very border, nor shall you gather the gleanings after your harvest; you shall leave them for the poor and for the stranger: I am the LORD your God."
23, 24 And the LORD said to Moses, "Say to the people of Israel, In the seventh month, on the first day of the month, you shall observe a day of solemn rest, a memorial proclaimed with
25 blast of trumpets, a holy convocation. You shall do no laborious work; and you shall present an offering by fire to the LORD."

26, 27 And the LORD said to Moses, "On the tenth day of this seventh month is the day of atonement; it shall be for you a time of holy convocation, and you shall afflict yourselves and present an offering by fire to the LORD.
28 And you shall do no work on this same day; for it is a day of atonement, to make atonement for you before the
29 LORD your God. For whoever is not afflicted on this same
30 day shall be cut off from his people. And whoever does any work on this same day, that person I will destroy from
31 among his people. You shall do no work: it is a statute for ever throughout your generations in all your dwellings.
32 It shall be to you a sabbath of solemn rest, and you shall afflict yourselves; on the ninth day of the month beginning at evening, from evening to evening shall you keep your sabbath."

33, 34 And the LORD said to Moses, "Say to the people of Israel, On the fifteenth day of this seventh month and for seven days
35 is the feast of boothsᵏ to the LORD. On the first day shall be
36 a holy convocation; you shall do no laborious work. Seven days you shall present offerings by fire to the LORD; on the eighth day you shall hold a holy convocation and present an offering by fire to the LORD; it is a solemn assembly; you shall do no laborious work.
37 "These are the appointed feasts of the LORD, which you shall proclaim as times of holy convocation, for presenting to the LORD offerings by fire, burnt offerings and cereal offerings,
38 sacrifices and drink offerings, each on its proper day; besides the sabbaths of the LORD, and besides your gifts, and besides all your votive offerings, and besides all your freewill offerings, which you give to the LORD.

39 "On the fifteenth day of the seventh month, when you have gathered in the produce of the land, you shall keep the feast of the LORD seven days; on the first day shall be a solemn rest, and on the eighth day shall be a solemn
40 rest. And you shall take on the first day the fruit of goodly trees, branches of palm trees, and boughs of leafy trees, and willows of the brook; and you shall rejoice
41 before the LORD your God seven days. You shall keep it as a feast to the LORD seven days in the year; it is a

ʲ Heb *between the two evenings*   ᵏ Or *tabernacles*

statute for ever throughout your generations; you shall
⁴² keep it in the seventh month. You shall dwell in booths
for seven days; all that are native in Israel shall dwell in
⁴³ booths, that your generations may know that I made the
people of Israel dwell in booths when I brought them out
of the land of Egypt: I am the LORD your God."

RULES ON RITUAL AND BLASPHEMY

⁴⁴ Thus Moses declared to the people of Israel the appointed
feasts of the LORD.

²**24** The LORD said to Moses, "Command the people of Israel
to bring you pure oil from beaten olives for the lamp, that
³ a light may be kept burning continually. Outside the veil of
the testimony, in the tent of meeting, Aaron shall keep it in
order from evening to morning before the LORD continually; it

shall be a sabbath of solemn rest for the land, a sabbath to the
LORD; you shall not sow your field or prune your vineyard.
⁵ What grows of itself in your harvest you shall not reap, and
the grapes of your undressed vine you shall not gather; it shall
⁶ be a year of solemn rest for the land. The sabbath of the land
shall provide food for you, for yourself and for your male
and female slaves and for your hired servant and the so-
⁷ journer who lives with you; for your cattle also and for the
beasts that are in your land all its yield shall be for food.
⁸ "And you shall count seven weeks ¹ of years, seven times
seven years, so that the time of the seven weeks of years shall
⁹ be to you forty-nine years. Then you shall send abroad the
loud trumpet on the tenth day of the seventh month; on the
day of atonement you shall send abroad the trumpet through-
¹⁰ out all your land. And you shall hallow the fiftieth year, and
proclaim liberty throughout the land to all its inhabitants;
it shall be a jubilee for you, when each of you shall return
¹¹ to his property and each of you shall return to his family. A

⁴ shall be a statute for ever throughout your generations. He
shall keep the lamps in order upon the lampstand of pure
gold before the LORD continually.
⁵ "And you shall take fine flour, and bake twelve cakes of it;
⁶ two tenths of an ephah shall be in each cake. And you shall
set them in two rows, six in a row, upon the table of pure
⁷ gold. And you shall put pure frankincense with each row, that
it may go with the bread as a memorial portion to be offered by
⁸ fire to the LORD. Every sabbath day Aaron shall set it in order
before the LORD continually on behalf of the people of Israel
⁹ as a covenant for ever. And it shall be for Aaron and his sons,
and they shall eat it in a holy place, since it is for him a most
holy portion out of the offerings by fire to the LORD, a perpetual due."
¹⁰ Now an Israelite woman's son, whose father was an Egyptian,
went out among the people of Israel; and the Israelite woman's
¹¹ son and a man of Israel quarreled in the camp, and the Israelite woman's son blasphemed the Name, and cursed. And they
brought him to Moses. His mother's name was Shelo'mith, the
¹² daughter of Dibri, of the tribe of Dan. And they put him in
custody, till the will of the LORD should be declared to them.
¹³, ¹⁴ And the LORD said to Moses, "Bring out of the camp him
who cursed; and let all who heard him lay their hands upon
¹⁵ his head, and let all the congregation stone him. And say to the
people of Israel, Whoever curses his God shall bear his sin.
¹⁶ He who blasphemes the name of the LORD shall be put to death;
all the congregation shall stone him; the sojourner as well as
the native, when he blasphemes the Name, shall be put to
¹⁷, ¹⁸ death. He who kills a man shall be put to death. He who kills
¹⁹ a beast shall make it good, life for life. When a man causes a
disfigurement in his neighbor, as he has done it shall be done
²⁰ to him, fracture for fracture, eye for eye, tooth for tooth; as
²¹ he has disfigured a man, he shall be disfigured. He who kills
a beast shall make it good; and he who kills a man shall be
²² put to death. You shall have one law for the sojourner and for
²³ the native; for I am the LORD your God." So Moses spoke to the
people of Israel; and they brought him who had cursed out of
the camp, and stoned him with stones. Thus the people of
Israel did as the LORD commanded Moses.

SABBATH AND JUBILEE YEAR

²**25** The LORD said to Moses on Mount Sinai, "Say to the
people of Israel, When you come into the land which I
³ give you, the land shall keep a sabbath to the LORD. Six years
you shall sow your field, and six years you shall prune your
⁴ vineyard, and gather in its fruits; but in the seventh year there

jubilee shall that fiftieth year be to you; in it you shall neither
sow, nor reap what grows of itself, nor gather the grapes
¹² from the undressed vines. For it is a jubilee; it shall be holy
to you; you shall eat what it yields out of the field.
¹³ "In this year of jubilee each of you shall return to his
¹⁴ property. And if you sell to your neighbor or buy from your
¹⁵ neighbor, you shall not wrong one another. According to the
number of years after the jubilee, you shall buy from your
neighbor, and according to the number of years for crops he
¹⁶ shall sell to you. If the years are many you shall increase the
price, and if the years are few you shall diminish the price,
for it is the number of the crops that he is selling to you.
¹⁷ You shall not wrong one another, but you shall fear your God;
for I am the LORD your God.
¹⁸ "Therefore you shall do my statutes, and keep my ordinances
and perform them; so you will dwell in the land securely.
¹⁹ The land will yield its fruit, and you will eat your fill, and
²⁰ dwell in it securely. And if you say, 'What shall we eat in the
²¹ seventh year, if we may not sow or gather in our crop?' I will
command my blessing upon you in the sixth year, so that it
²² will bring forth fruit for three years. When you sow in the
eighth year, you will be eating old produce; until the ninth
²³ year, when its produce comes in, you shall eat the old. The
land shall not be sold in perpetuity, for the land is mine; for
²⁴ you are strangers and sojourners with me. And in all the
country you possess, you shall grant a redemption of the land.
²⁵ "If your brother becomes poor, and sells part of his property,
then his next of kin shall come and redeem what his brother
²⁶ has sold. If a man has no one to redeem it, and then himself
becomes prosperous and finds sufficient means to redeem it,
²⁷ let him reckon the years since he sold it and pay back the
overpayment to the man to whom he sold it; and he shall return
²⁸ to his property. But if he has not sufficient means to get it
back for himself, then what he sold shall remain in the hand
of him who bought it until the year of jubilee; in the jubilee
it shall be released, and he shall return to his property.
²⁹ "If a man sells a dwelling house in a walled city, he may
redeem it within a whole year after its sale; for a full year he
³⁰ shall have the right of redemption. If it is not redeemed within
a full year, then the house that is in the walled city shall be
made sure in perpetuity to him who bought it, throughout his
³¹ generations; it shall not be released in the jubilee. But the
houses of the villages which have no wall around them shall
be reckoned with the fields of the country; they may be re-
³² deemed, and they shall be released in the jubilee. Nevertheless
the cities of the Levites, the houses in the cities of their pos-

¹ Or *sabbaths*

[33] session, the Levites may redeem at any time. And if one of the Levites does not exercise [m] his right of redemption, then the house that was sold in a city of their possession shall be released in the jubilee; for the houses in the cities of the Levites [34] are their possession among the people of Israel. But the fields of common land belonging to their cities may not be sold; for that is their perpetual possession.

[35] "And if your brother becomes poor, and cannot maintain himself with you, you shall maintain him; as a stranger and a [36] sojourner he shall live with you. Take no interest from him or increase, but fear your God; that your brother may live [37] beside you. You shall not lend him your money at interest, nor [38] give him your food for profit. I am the Lord your God, who brought you forth out of the land of Egypt to give you the land of Canaan, and to be your God.

[39] "And if your brother becomes poor beside you, and sells himself to you, you shall not make him serve as a slave: [40] he shall be with you as a hired servant and as a sojourner. He [41] shall serve with you until the year of the jubilee; then he shall go out from you, he and his children with him, and go back to his own family, and return to the possession of his [42] fathers. For they are my servants, whom I brought forth out [43] of the land of Egypt; they shall not be sold as slaves. You shall not rule over him with harshness, but shall fear your God. [44] As for your male and female slaves whom you may have: you may buy male and female slaves from among the nations that [45] are round about you. You may also buy from among the strangers who sojourn with you and their families that are with you, who have been born in your land; and they may be [46] your property. You may bequeath them to your sons after you, to inherit as a possession for ever; you may make slaves of them, but over your brethren the people of Israel you shall not rule, one over another, with harshness.

[47] "If a stranger or sojourner with you becomes rich, and your brother beside him becomes poor and sells himself to the stranger or sojourner with you, or to a member of the [48] stranger's family, then after he is sold he may be redeemed; [49] one of his brothers may redeem him, or his uncle, or his cousin may redeem him, or a near kinsman belonging to his family may redeem him; or if he grows rich he may redeem [50] himself. He shall reckon with him who bought him from the year when he sold himself to him until the year of jubilee, and the price of his release shall be according to the number of years; the time he was with his owner shall be rated as the [51] time of a hired servant. If there are still many years, according to them he shall refund out of the price paid for him the price [52] for his redemption. If there remain but a few years until the year of jubilee, he shall make a reckoning with him; according to the years of service due from him he shall refund the [53] money for his redemption. As a servant hired year by year shall he be with him; he shall not rule with harshness over [54] him in your sight. And if he is not redeemed by these means, then he shall be released in the year of jubilee, he and his [55] children with him. For to me the people of Israel are servants, they are my servants whom I brought forth out of the land of Egypt: I am the Lord your God.

BLESSINGS OF OBEDIENCE

26 "You shall make for yourselves no idols and erect no graven image or pillar, and you shall not set up a figured stone in your land, to bow down to them; for I am the Lord [2] your God. You shall keep my sabbaths and reverence my sanctuary: I am the Lord.

[3] "If you walk in my statutes and observe my command- [4] ments and do them, then I will give you your rains in their season, and the land shall yield its increase, and the [5] trees of the field shall yield their fruit. And your threshing shall last to the time of vintage, and the vintage shall last to the time for sowing; and you shall eat your bread to the full, and dwell in your land securely.

[6] And I will give peace in the land, and you shall lie down, and none shall make you afraid; and I will remove evil beasts from the land, and the sword shall not go through your land. [7] And you shall chase your enemies, and they shall fall before

[8] you by the sword. Five of you shall chase a hundred, and a hundred of you shall chase ten thousand; and your enemies [9] shall fall before you by the sword. And I will have regard for you and make you fruitful and multiply you, and will confirm [10] my covenant with you. And you shall eat old store long kept, [11] and you shall clear out the old to make way for the new. And I will make my abode among you, and my soul shall not abhor [12] you. And I will walk among you, and will be your God, and [13] you shall be my people. I am the Lord your God, who brought you forth out of the land of Egypt, that you should not be their slaves; and I have broken the bars of your yoke and made you walk erect.

PUNISHMENTS OF DISOBEDIENCE

[14] "But if you will not hearken to me, and will not do all these [15] commandments, if you spurn my statutes, and if your soul abhors my ordinances, so that you will not do all my command- [16] ments, but break my covenant, I will do this to you: I will appoint over you sudden terror, consumption, and fever that waste the eyes and cause life to pine away. And you shall [17] sow your seed in vain, for your enemies shall eat it; I will set my face against you, and you shall be smitten before your enemies; those who hate you shall rule over you, and you [18] shall flee when none pursues you. And if in spite of this you will not hearken to me, then I will chastise you again sevenfold [19] for your sins, and I will break the pride of your power, and I will make your heavens like iron and your earth like brass; [20] and your strength shall be spent in vain, for your land shall not yield its increase, and the trees of the land shall not yield their fruit.

[21] "Then if you walk contrary to me, and will not hearken to me, I will bring more plagues upon you, sevenfold as many [22] as your sins. And I will let loose the wild beasts among you, which shall rob you of your children, and destroy your cattle, and make you few in number, so that your ways shall become desolate.

[23] "And if by this discipline you are not turned to me, but [24] walk contrary to me, then I also will walk contrary to you, [25] and I myself will smite you sevenfold for your sins. And I will bring a sword upon you, that shall execute vengeance for the covenant; and if you gather within your cities I will send pestilence among you, and you shall be delivered into the [26] hand of the enemy. When I break your staff of bread, ten women shall bake your bread in one oven, and shall deliver your bread again by weight; and you shall eat, and not be satisfied.

[27] "And if in spite of this you will not hearken to me, but walk [28] contrary to me, then I will walk contrary to you in fury, and [29] chastise you myself sevenfold for your sins. You shall eat the flesh of your sons, and you shall eat the flesh of your [30] daughters. And I will destroy your high places, and cut down your incense altars, and cast your dead bodies upon the dead [31] bodies of your idols; and my soul will abhor you. And I will lay your cities waste, and will make your sanctuaries desolate, [32] and I will not smell your pleasing odors. And I will devastate the land, so that your enemies who settle in it shall be [33] astonished at it. And I will scatter you among the nations, and I will unsheathe the sword after you; and your land shall be a desolation, and your cities shall be a waste.

[34] "Then the land shall enjoy [n] its sabbaths as long as it lies desolate, while you are in your enemies' land; then the land [35] shall rest, and enjoy [n] its sabbaths. As long as it lies desolate it shall have rest, the rest which it had not in your sabbaths [36] when you dwelt upon it. And as for those of you that are left, I will send faintness into their hearts in the lands of their enemies; the sound of a driven leaf shall put them to flight, and they shall flee as one flees from the sword, and they shall [37] fall when none pursues. They shall stumble over one another, as if to escape a sword, though none pursues; and you shall [38] have no power to stand before your enemies. And you shall perish among the nations, and the land of your enemies shall [39] eat you up. And those of you that are left shall pine away in your enemies' lands because of their iniquity; and also because of the iniquities of their fathers they shall pine away like them.

[40] "But if they confess their iniquity and the iniquity of their fathers in their treachery which they committed against me, [41] and also in walking contrary to me, so that I walked contrary to them and brought them into the land of their enemies; if then their uncircumcised heart is humbled and they make [42] amends for their iniquity; then I will remember my covenant

[m] Compare Vg: Heb *exercises*   [n] Or *pay for*

with Jacob, and I will remember my covenant with Isaac and my covenant with Abraham, and I will remember the land.
43 But the land shall be left by them, and enjoy [n] its sabbaths while it lies desolate without them; and they shall make amends for their iniquity, because they spurned my ordinances,
44 and their soul abhorred my statutes. Yet for all that, when they are in the land of their enemies, I will not spurn them, neither will I abhor them so as to destroy them utterly and break my covenant with them; for I am the LORD their God;
45 but I will for their sake remember the covenant with their forefathers, whom I brought forth out of the land of Egypt in the sight of the nations, that I might be their God: I am the LORD."
46 These are the statutes and ordinances and laws which the LORD made between him and the people of Israel on Mount Sinai by Moses.

VOWS AND TITHES

27 The LORD said to Moses, "Say to the people of Israel, When a man makes a special vow of persons to the LORD
3 at your valuation, then your valuation of a male from twenty years old up to sixty years old shall be fifty shekels of silver,
4 according to the shekel of the sanctuary. If the person is a
5 female, your valuation shall be thirty shekels. If the person is from five years old up to twenty years old, your valuation shall be for a male twenty shekels, and for a female ten
6 shekels. If the person is from a month old up to five years old, your valuation shall be for a male five shekels of silver, and for a female your valuation shall be three shekels of silver.
7 And if the person is sixty years old and upward, then your valuation for a male shall be fifteen shekels, and for a female
8 ten shekels. And if a man is too poor to pay your valuation, then he shall bring the person before the priest, and the priest shall value him; according to the ability of him who vowed the priest shall value him.
9 "If it is an animal such as men offer as an offering to the
10 LORD, all of such that any man gives to the LORD is holy. He shall not substitute anything for it or exchange it, a good for a bad, or a bad for a good; and if he makes any exchange of beast for beast, then both it and that for which it is exchanged
11 shall be holy. And if it is an unclean animal such as is not offered as an offering to the LORD, then the man shall bring
12 animal before the priest, and the priest shall value it as either
13 good or bad; as you, the priest, value it, so it shall be. But if he wishes to redeem it, he shall add a fifth to the valuation.
14 "When a man dedicates his house to be holy to the LORD, the priest shall value it as either good or bad; as the priest values
15 it, so it shall stand. And if he who dedicates it wishes to re-

deem his house, he shall add a fifth of the valuation in money to it, and it shall be his.
16 "If a man dedicates to the LORD part of the land which is his by inheritance, then your valuation shall be according to the seed for it; a sowing of a homer of barley shall be valued at
17 fifty shekels of silver. If he dedicates his field from the year of
18 jubilee, it shall stand at your full valuation; but if he dedicates his field after the jubilee, then the priest shall compute the money-value for it according to the years that remain until the year of jubilee, and a deduction shall be made from your
19 valuation. And if he who dedicates the field wishes to redeem it, then he shall add a fifth of the valuation in money to it,
20 and it shall remain his. But if he does not wish to redeem the field, or if he has sold the field to another man, it shall not be
21 redeemed any more; but the field, when it is released in the jubilee, shall be holy to the LORD, as a field that has been
22 devoted; the priest shall be in possession of it. If he dedicates to the LORD a field which he has bought, which is not a part
23 of his possession by inheritance, then the priest shall compute the valuation for it up to the year of jubilee, and the man shall give the amount of the valuation on that day as a holy thing
24 to the LORD. In the year of jubilee the field shall return to him from whom it was bought, to whom the land belongs as
25 a possession by inheritance. Every valuation shall be according to the shekel of the sanctuary: twenty gerahs shall make a shekel.
26 "But a firstling of animals, which as a firstling belongs to the LORD, no man may dedicate; whether ox or sheep, it is the
27 LORD's. And if it is an unclean animal, then he shall buy it back at your valuation, and add a fifth to it; or, if it is not redeemed, it shall be sold at your valuation.
28 "But no devoted thing that a man devotes to the LORD, of anything that he has, whether of man or beast, or of his inherited field, shall be sold or redeemed; every devoted thing
29 is most holy to the LORD. No one devoted, who is to be utterly destroyed from among men, shall be ransomed; he shall be put to death.
30 "All the tithe of the land, whether of the seed of the land or of the fruit of the trees, is the LORD's; it is holy to the LORD.
31 If a man wishes to redeem any of his tithe, he shall add a
32 fifth to it. And all the tithe of herds and flocks, every tenth animal of all that pass under the herdsman's staff, shall be holy
33 to the LORD. A man shall not inquire whether it is good or bad, neither shall he exchange it; and if he exchanges it, then both it and that for which it is exchanged shall be holy; it shall not be redeemed."
34 These are the commandments which the LORD commanded Moses for the people of Israel on Mount Sinai.

INTRODUCTION TO

NUMBERS

The Book of Numbers gets its name from the "numbering" or the census of the Hebrews that was taken not long after they escaped from Egypt, where they had been slaves. It includes many stories from the early days of the Hebrew people. This book was completed about 400 B.C. along with Genesis, Exodus, Leviticus, and Deuteronomy, but it tells of events that happened long before.

Numbers tells many adventures of the Hebrews as they continued to wander in the Wilderness of Zin, the desert south of Palestine, tending their sheep and goats. One of the most familiar stories is that about how Moses sent spies into Canaan, the land promised to Abraham. Most of the spies came back discouraged and afraid, but Joshua and Caleb came back saying that with God's help they could conquer the land. Numbers shows how God led the people through many trials until they learned to depend on him.

Turn to the introduction to Genesis on page 1 to learn more about how God helped men write these books.

THE BOOK OF

NUMBERS

CENSUS TAKEN

1 The LORD spoke to Moses in the wilderness of Sinai, in the tent of meeting, on the first day of the second month, in the second year after they had come out of the land of ² Egypt, saying, "Take a census of all the congregation of the people of Israel, by families, by fathers' houses, according to

³ the number of names, every male, head by head; from twenty years old and upward, all in Israel who are able to go forth to war, you and Aaron shall number them, company by com- ⁴ pany. And there shall be with you a man from each tribe, each ⁵ man being the head of the house of his fathers. And these are the names of the men who shall attend you. From Reuben, ⁶ Eli'zur the son of Shed'eur; from Simeon, Shelu'mi-el the son of ⁷ Zurishad'dai; from Judah, Nahshon the son of Ammin'adab; ⁸, ⁹ from Is'sachar, Nethan'el the son of Zu'ar; from Zeb'ulun, ⁹ Eli'ab the son of Helon; from the sons of Joseph, from E'phraim, ¹⁰ Elish'ama the son of Ammi'hud, and from Manas'seh, Gama'liel ¹¹ the son of Pedah'zur; from Benjamin, Ab'idan the son of ¹², ¹³ Gideo'ni; from Dan, Ahi-e'zer the son of Ammishad'dai; from

¹⁴ Asher, Pa'giel the son of Ochran; from Gad, Eli'asaph the son ¹⁵, ¹⁶ of Deu'el; from Naph'tali, Ahi'ra the son of Enan." These were the ones chosen from the congregation, the leaders of their ancestral tribes, the heads of the clans of Israel.
¹⁷ Moses and Aaron took these men who have been named, ¹⁸ and on the first day of the second month, they assembled the whole congregation together, who registered themselves by families, by fathers' houses, according to the number of names ¹⁹ from twenty years old and upward, head by head, as the LORD commanded Moses. So he numbered them in the wilderness of Sinai.
²⁰ The people of Reuben, Israel's first-born, their generations, by their families, by their fathers' houses, according to the number of names, head by head, every male from twenty years ²¹ old and upward, all who were able to go forth to war: the number of the tribe of Reuben was forty-six thousand five hundred.
²² Of the people of Simeon, their generations, by their families, by their fathers' houses, those of them that were numbered, according to the number of names, head by head, every male from twenty years old and upward, all who were able to go ²³ forth to war: the number of the tribe of Simeon was fifty-nine thousand three hundred.
²⁴ Of the people of Gad, their generations, by their families, by their fathers' houses, according to the number of the names, from twenty years old and upward, all who were able to go ²⁵ forth to war: the number of the tribe of Gad was forty-five thousand six hundred and fifty.

26 Of the people of Judah, their generations, by their families, by their fathers' houses, according to the number of names, from twenty years old and upward, every man able to go 27 forth to war: the number of the tribe of Judah was seventy-four thousand six hundred.

28 Of the people of Is'sachar, their generations, by their families, by their fathers' houses, according to the number of names, from twenty years old and upward, every man able to go 29 forth to war: the number of the tribe of Is'sachar was fifty-four thousand four hundred.

30 Of the people of Zeb'ulun, their generations, by their families, by their fathers' houses, according to the number of names, from twenty years old and upward, every man able to 31 go forth to war: the number of the tribe of Zeb'ulun was fifty-seven thousand five hundred.

32 Of the people of Joseph, namely, of the people of E'phraim, their generations, by their families, by their fathers' houses, according to the number of names, from twenty years old and 33 upward, every man able to go forth to war: the number of the tribe of E'phraim was forty thousand five hundred.

34 Of the people of Manas'seh, their generations, by their families, by their fathers' houses, according to the number of names, from twenty years old and upward, every man able to 35 go forth to war: the number of the tribe of Manas'seh was thirty-two thousand two hundred.

36 Of the people of Benjamin, their generations, by their families, by their fathers' houses, according to the number of names, from twenty years old and upward, every man able to 37 go forth to war: the number of the tribe of Benjamin was thirty-five thousand four hundred.

38 Of the people of Dan, their generations, by their families, by their fathers' houses, according to the number of names, from twenty years old and upward, every man able to go forth to 39 war: the number of the tribe of Dan was sixty-two thousand seven hundred.

40 Of the people of Asher, their generations, by their families, by their fathers' houses, according to the number of names, from twenty years old and upward, every man able to go 41 forth to war: the number of the tribe of Asher was forty-one thousand five hundred.

42 Of the people of Naph'tali, their generations, by their families, by their fathers' houses, according to the number of names, from twenty years old and upward, every man able to go forth 43 to war: the number of the tribe of Naph'tali was fifty-three thousand four hundred.

44 These are those who were numbered, whom Moses and Aaron numbered with the help of the leaders of Israel, twelve 45 men, each representing his fathers' house. So the whole number of the people of Israel, by their fathers' houses, from twenty years old and upward, every man able to go forth to war in 46 Israel—their whole number was six hundred and three thousand five hundred and fifty.

47 But the Levites were not numbered by their ancestral tribe 48, 49 along with them. For the LORD said to Moses, "Only the tribe of Levi you shall not number, and you shall not take a census 50 of them among the people of Israel; but appoint the Levites over the tabernacle of the testimony, and over all its furnishings, and over all that belongs to it; they are to carry the tabernacle and all its furnishings, and they shall tend it, and 51 shall encamp around the tabernacle. When the tabernacle is to set out, the Levites shall take it down; and when the tabernacle is to be pitched, the Levites shall set it up. And if any 52 one else comes near, he shall be put to death. The people of Israel shall pitch their tents by their companies, every man by 53 his own camp and every man by his own standard; but the Levites shall encamp around the tabernacle of the testimony, that there may be no wrath upon the congregation of the people of Israel; and the Levites shall keep charge of the tabernacle 54 of the testimony." Thus did the people of Israel; they did according to all that the LORD commanded Moses.

Marching Positions

2 2 The LORD said to Moses and Aaron, "The people of Israel shall encamp each by his own standard, with the ensigns of their fathers' houses; they shall encamp facing the tent of 3 meeting on every side. Those to encamp on the east side toward the sunrise shall be of the standard of the camp of Judah by their companies, the leader of the people of Judah 4 being Nahshon the son of Ammin'adab, his host as numbered 5 being seventy-four thousand six hundred. Those to encamp

next to him shall be the tribe of Is'sachar, the leader of the 6 people of Is'sachar being Nethan'el the son of Zu'ar, his host 7 as numbered being fifty-four thousand four hundred. Then the tribe of Zeb'ulun, the leader of the people of Zeb'ulun being 8 Eli'ab the son of Helon, his host as numbered being fifty-seven 9 thousand four hundred. The whole number of the camp of Judah, by their companies, is a hundred and eighty-six thousand four hundred. They shall set out first on the march.

10 "On the south side shall be the standard of the camp of Reuben by their companies, the leader of the people of Reuben 11 being Eli'zur the son of Shed'eur, his host as numbered being 12 forty-six thousand five hundred. And those to encamp next to him shall be the tribe of Simeon, the leader of the people 13 of Simeon being Shelu'mi-el the son of Zurishad'dai, his host 14 as numbered being fifty-nine thousand three hundred. Then the tribe of Gad, the leader of the people of Gad being Eli'- 15 asaph the son of Reu'el, his host as numbered being forty-five 16 thousand six hundred and fifty. The whole number of the camp of Reuben, by their companies, is a hundred and fifty-one thousand four hundred and fifty. They shall set out second.

17 "Then the tent of meeting shall set out, with the camp of the Levites in the midst of the camps; as they encamp, so shall they set out, each in position, standard by standard.

18 "On the west side shall be the standard of the camp of E'phraim by their companies, the leader of the people of 19 E'phraim being Elish'ama the son of Ammi'hud, his host as 20 numbered being forty thousand five hundred. And next to him shall be the tribe of Manas'seh, the leader of the people of 21 Manas'seh being Gama'liel the son of Pedah'zur, his host as 22 numbered being thirty-two thousand two hundred. Then the tribe of Benjamin, the leader of the people of Benjamin being 23 Abi'dan the son of Gideo'ni, his host as numbered being thirty- 24 five thousand four hundred. The whole number of the camp of E'phraim, by their companies, is a hundred and eight thousand one hundred. They shall set out third on the march.

25 "On the north side shall be the standard of the camp of Dan by their companies, the leader of the people of Dan being 26 Ahi-e'zer the son of Ammishad'dai, his host as numbered being 27 sixty-two thousand seven hundred. And those to encamp next to him shall be the tribe of Asher, the leader of the people of 28 Asher being Pa'giel the son of Ochran, his host as numbered 29 being forty-one thousand five hundred. Then the tribe of Naph'tali, the leader of the people of Naph'tali being Ahi'ra the 30 son of Enan, his host as numbered being fifty-three thousand 31 four hundred. The whole number of the camp of Dan is a hundred and fifty-seven thousand six hundred. They shall set out last, standard by standard."

32 These are the people of Israel as numbered by their fathers' houses; all in the camps who were numbered by their companies were six hundred and three thousand five hundred and 33 fifty. But the Levites were not numbered among the people of Israel, as the LORD commanded Moses.

34 Thus did the people of Israel. According to all that the LORD commanded Moses, so they encamped by their standards, and so they set out, every one in his family, according to his fathers' house.

Positions of the Levites

3 3 These are the generations of Aaron and Moses at the time 2 when the LORD spoke with Moses on Mount Sinai. These are the names of the sons of Aaron: Nadab the first-born, and 3 Abi'hu, Elea'zar, and Ith'amar; these are the names of the sons of Aaron, the anointed priests, whom he ordained to 4 minister in the priest's office. But Nadab and Abi'hu died before the LORD when they offered unholy fire before the LORD in the wilderness of Sinai; and they had no children. So Elea'zar and Ith'amar served as priests in the lifetime of Aaron their father.

5, 6 And the LORD said to Moses, "Bring the tribe of Levi near, and set them before Aaron the priest, that they may minister 7 to him. They shall perform duties for him and for the whole congregation before the tent of meeting, as they minister at 8 the tabernacle; they shall have charge of all the furnishings of the tent of meeting, and attend to the duties for the people of 9 Israel as they minister at the tabernacle. And you shall give the Levites to Aaron and his sons; they are wholly given to 10 him from among the people of Israel. And you shall appoint Aaron and his sons, and they shall attend to their priesthood; but if any one else comes near, he shall be put to death."

11, 12 And the LORD said to Moses, "Behold, I have taken the

Levites from among the people of Israel instead of every first-born that opens the womb among the people of Israel. The
13 Levites shall be mine, for all the first-born are mine; on the day that I slew all the first-born in the land of Egypt, I consecrated for my own all the first-born in Israel, both of man and of beast; they shall be mine: I am the LORD."

14 And the LORD said to Moses in the wilderness of Sinai,
15 "Number the sons of Levi, by fathers' houses and by families; every male from a month old and upward you shall number."
16 So Moses numbered them according to the word of the LORD,
17 as he was commanded. And these were the sons of Levi by
18 their names: Gershon and Kohath and Merar'i. And these are the names of the sons of Gershon by their families: Libni and
19 Shim'e-ites. And the sons of Kohath by their families: Amram,
20 Izhar, Hebron, and Uz'ziel. And the sons of Merar'i by their families: Mahli and Mushi. These are the families of the Levites, by their fathers' houses.

21 Of Gershon were the family of the Libnites and the family of the Shim'e-ites; these were the families of the Gershonites.
22 Their number according to the number of all the males from a month old and upward was [a] seven thousand five hundred.
23 The families of the Gershonites were to encamp behind the
24 tabernacle on the west, with Eli'asaph, the son of La'el as head
25 of the fathers' house of the Gershonites. And the charge of the sons of Gershon in the tent of meeting was to be the tabernacle, the tent with its covering, the screen for the door
26 of the tent of meeting, the hangings of the court, the screen for the door of the court which is around the tabernacle and the altar, and its cords; all the service pertaining to these.

27 Of Kohath were the family of the Amramites, and the family of the Izhar'ites, and the family of the He'bronites, and the family of the Uz'zi-elites; these are the families of the Ko'-
28 hathites. According to the number of all the males, from a month old and upward, there were eight thousand six hundred,
29 attending to the duties of the sanctuary. The families of the
30 sons of Kohath were to encamp on the south side of the tabernacle, with Eliz'aphan the son of Uz'ziel as head of the fathers'
31 house of the families of the Ko'hathites. And their charge was to be the ark, the table, the lampstand, the altars, the vessels of the sanctuary with which the priests minister, and the screen;
32 all the service pertaining to these. And Elea'zar the son of Aaron the priest was to be chief over the leaders of the Levites, and to have oversight of those who had charge of the sanctuary.

33 Of Merar'i were the family of the Mahlites and the family
34 of the Mushites: these are the families of Merar'i. Their number according to the number of all the males from a month old
35 and upward was six thousand two hundred. And the head of the fathers' house of the families of Merar'i was Zu'riel the son of Abiha'il; they were to encamp on the north side of the
36 tabernacle. And the appointed charge of the sons of Merar'i was to be the frames of the tabernacle, the bars, the pillars, the bases, and all their accessories; all the service pertaining to
37 these; also the pillars of the court round about, with their bases and pegs and cords.

38 And those to encamp before the tabernacle on the east, before the tent of meeting toward the sunrise, were Moses and Aaron and his sons, having charge of the rites within the sanctuary, whatever had to be done for the people of Israel; and any one
39 else who came near was to be put to death. All who were numbered of the Levites, whom Moses and Aaron numbered at the commandment of the LORD, by families, all the males from a month old and upward, were twenty-two thousand.

40 And the LORD said to Moses, "Number all the first-born males of the people of Israel, from a month old and upward, taking
41 their number by names. And you shall take the Levites for me —I am the LORD—instead of all the first-born among the people of Israel, and the cattle of the Levites instead of all the first-
42 lings among the cattle of the people of Israel." So Moses numbered all the first-born among the people of Israel, as the LORD
43 commanded him. And all the first-born males, according to the number of names, from a month old and upward as numbered were twenty-two thousand two hundred and seventy-three.

44,45 And the LORD said to Moses, "Take the Levites instead of all the first-born among the people of Israel, and the cattle of the Levites instead of their cattle, and the Levites shall be
46 mine: I am the LORD. And for the redemption of the two hundred and seventy-three of the first-born of the people of
47 Israel, over and above the number of the male Levites, you shall take five shekels apiece; reckoning by the shekel of the

[a] Heb their number was

sanctuary, the shekel of twenty gerahs, you shall take them,
48 and give the money by which the excess number of them is
49 redeemed to Aaron and his sons." So Moses took the redemption money from those who were over and above those
50 redeemed by the Levites; from the first-born of the people of Israel he took the money, one thousand three hundred and sixty-five shekels, reckoned by the shekel of the sanctuary;
51 and Moses gave the redemption money to Aaron and his sons, according to the word of the LORD, as the LORD commanded Moses.

Levites Counted, Duties

2 4 The LORD said to Moses and Aaron, "Take a census of the sons of Kohath from among the sons of Levi, by their
3 families and their fathers' houses, from thirty years old up to fifty years old, all who can enter the service, to do the work in
4 the tent of meeting. This is the service of the sons of Kohath
5 in the tent of meeting: the most holy things. When the camp is to set out, Aaron and his sons shall go in and take down the veil of the screen, and cover the ark of the testimony with it;
6 then they shall put on it a covering of goatskin, and spread
7 over that a cloth all of blue, and shall put in its poles. And over the table of the bread of the Presence they shall spread a cloth of blue, and put upon it the plates, the dishes for incense, the bowls, and the flagons for the drink offering; the
8 continual bread also shall be on it; then they shall spread over them a cloth of scarlet, and cover the same with a covering of
9 goatskin, and shall put in its poles. And they shall take a cloth of blue, and cover the lampstand for the light, with its lamps, its snuffers, its trays, and all the vessels for oil with
10 which it is supplied: and they shall put it with all its utensils in a covering of goatskin and put it upon the carrying frame.
11 And over the golden altar they shall spread a cloth of blue, and cover it with a covering of goatskin, and shall put in its
12 poles; and they shall take all the vessels of the service which are used in the sanctuary, and put them in a cloth of blue, and cover them with a covering of goatskin, and put them on
13 the carrying frame. And they shall take away the ashes from
14 the altar, and spread a purple cloth over it; and they shall put on it all the utensils of the altar, which are used for the service there, the firepans, the forks, the shovels, and the basins, all the utensils of the altar; and they shall spread upon
15 it a covering of goatskin, and shall put in its poles. And when Aaron and his sons have finished covering the sanctuary and all the furnishings of the sanctuary, as the camp sets out, after that the sons of Kohath shall come to carry these, but they must not touch the holy things, lest they die. These are the things of the tent of meeting which the sons of Kohath are to carry.

16 "And Elea'zar the son of Aaron the priest shall have charge of the oil for the light, the fragrant incense, the continual cereal offering, and the anointing oil, with the oversight of all the tabernacle and all that is in it, of the sanctuary and its vessels."

17,18 The LORD said to Moses and Aaron, "Let not the tribe of the families of the Ko'hathites be destroyed from among the
19 Levites; but deal thus with them, that they may live and not die when they come near to the most holy things: Aaron and his sons shall go in and appoint them each to his task and to
20 his burden, but they shall not go in to look upon the holy things even for a moment, lest they die."

21,22 The LORD said to Moses, "Take a census of the sons of
23 Gershon also, by their families and their fathers' houses; from thirty years old up to fifty years old, you shall number them, all who can enter for service, to do the work in the tent of
24 meeting. This is the service of the families of the Gershonites,
25 in serving and bearing burdens: they shall carry the curtains of the tabernacle, and the tent of meeting with its covering, and the covering of goatskin that is on top of it, and the screen
26 for the door of the tent of meeting, and the hangings of the court, and the screen for the entrance of the gate of the court which is around the tabernacle and the altar, and their cords, and all the equipment for their service; and they shall do all
27 that needs to be done with regard to them. All the service of the sons of the Gershonites shall be at the command of Aaron and his sons, in all that they are to carry, and in all that they have to do; and you shall assign to their charge all that they
28 are to carry. This is the service of the families of the sons of the Gershonites in the tent of meeting, and their work is to be under the oversight of Ith'amar the son of Aaron the priest.

29 "As for the sons of Merar'i, you shall number them by their
30 families and their fathers' houses; from thirty years old up to fifty years old, you shall number them, every one that can enter the service, to do the work of the tent of meeting.
31 And this is what they are charged to carry, as the whole of their service in the tent of meeting: the frames of the tabernacle,
32 with its bars, pillars, and bases, and the pillars of the court round about with their bases, pegs, and cords, with all their equipment and all their accessories; and you shall assign by
33 name the objects which they are required to carry. This is the service of the families of the sons of Merar'i, the whole of their service in the tent of meeting, under the hand of Ith'amar the son of Aaron the priest."

34 And Moses and Aaron and the leaders of the congregation numbered the sons of the Ko'hathites, by their families and
35 their fathers' houses, from thirty years old up to fifty years old, every one that could enter the service, for work in the
36 tent of meeting; and their number by families was two thou-
37 sand seven hundred and fifty. This was the number of the families of the Ko'hathites, all who served in the tent of meeting, whom Moses and Aaron numbered according to the commandment of the LORD by Moses.

38 The number of the sons of Gershon, by their families and
39 their fathers' houses, from thirty years old up to fifty years old, every one that could enter the service for work in the tent of
40 meeting—their number by their families and their fathers'
41 houses was two thousand six hundred and thirty. This was the number of the families of the sons of Gershon, all who served in the tent of meeting, whom Moses and Aaron numbered according to the commandment of the LORD.

42 The number of the families of the sons of Merar'i, by their
43 families and their fathers' houses, from thirty years old up to fifty years old, every one that could enter the service, for
44 work in the tent of meeting—their number by families was
45 three thousand two hundred. These are those who were numbered of the families of the sons of Merar'i, whom Moses and Aaron numbered according to the commandment of the LORD by Moses.

46 All those who were numbered of the Levites, whom Moses and Aaron and the leaders of Israel numbered, by their fam-
47 ilies and their fathers' houses, from thirty years old up to fifty years old, every one that could enter to do the work of
48 service and the work of bearing burdens in the tent of meeting, those who were numbered of them were eight thousand five
49 hundred and eighty. According to the commandment of the LORD through Moses they were appointed, each to his task of serving or carrying; thus they were numbered by him, as the LORD commanded Moses.

Laws and Regulations

5 2 The LORD said to Moses, "Command the people of Israel that they put out of the camp every leper, and every one having a discharge, and every one that is unclean through
3 contact with the dead; you shall put out both male and female, putting them outside the camp, that they may not defile their
4 camp, in the midst of which I dwell." And the people of Israel did so, and drove them outside the camp; as the LORD said to Moses, so the people of Israel did.

5, 6 And the LORD said to Moses, "Say to the people of Israel, When a man or woman commits any of the sins that men commit by breaking faith with the LORD, and that person is
7 guilty, he shall confess his sin which he has committed; and he shall make full restitution for his wrong, adding a fifth to it,
8 and giving it to him to whom he did the wrong. But if the man has no kinsman to whom restitution may be made for the wrong, the restitution for wrong shall go to the LORD for the priest, in addition to the ram of atonement with which atone-
9 ment is made for him. And every offering, all the holy things of the people of Israel, which they bring to the priest, shall be his;
10 and every man's holy things shall be his; whatever any man gives to the priest shall be his."

11, 12 And the LORD said to Moses, "Say to the people of Israel, If any man's wife goes astray and acts unfaithfully against
13 him, if a man lies with her carnally, and it is hidden from the eyes of her husband, and she is undetected though she has defiled herself, and there is no witness against her, since she
14 was not taken in the act; and if the spirit of jealousy comes upon him, and he is jealous of his wife who has defiled herself; or if the spirit of jealousy comes upon him, and he is jealous of
15 his wife, though she has not defiled herself; then the man shall

bring his wife to the priest, and bring the offering required of her, a tenth of an ephah of barley meal; he shall pour no oil upon it and put no frankincense on it, for it is a cereal offering of jealousy, a cereal offering of remembrance, bringing iniquity to remembrance.
16 "And the priest shall bring her near, and set her before the
17 LORD; and the priest shall take holy water in an earthen vessel, and take some of the dust that is on the floor of the tabernacle
18 and put it into the water. And the priest shall set the woman before the LORD, and unbind the hair of the woman's head, and place in her hands the cereal offering of remembrance, which is the cereal offering of jealousy. And in his hand the priest
19 shall have the water of bitterness that brings the curse. Then the priest shall make her take an oath, saying, 'If no man has lain with you, and if you have not turned aside to uncleanness, while you were under your husband's authority, be free from this
20 water of bitterness that brings the curse. But if you have gone astray, though you are under your husband's authority, and if you have defiled yourself, and some man other than your
21 husband has lain with you, then' (let the priest make the woman take the oath of the curse, and say to the woman) 'the LORD make you an execration and an oath among your people, when the LORD makes your thigh fall away and your
22 body swell; may this water that brings the curse pass into your bowels and make your body swell and your thigh fall away.' And the woman shall say, 'Amen, Amen.'
23 "Then the priest shall write these curses in a book, and wash
24 them off into the water of bitterness; and he shall make the woman drink the water of bitterness that brings the curse, and the water that brings the curse shall enter into her and cause
25 bitter pain. And the priest shall take the cereal offering of jealousy out of the woman's hand, and shall wave the cereal
26 offering before the LORD and bring it to the altar; and the priest shall take a handful of the cereal offering, as its memorial portion, and burn it upon the altar, and afterward shall
27 make the woman drink the water. And when he has made her drink the water, then, if she has defiled herself and has acted unfaithfully against her husband, the water that brings the curse shall enter into her and cause bitter pain, and her body shall swell, and her thigh shall fall away, and the
28 woman shall become an execration among her people. But if the woman has not defiled herself and is clean, then she shall be free and shall conceive children.
29 "This is the law in cases of jealousy, when a wife, though under her husband's authority, goes astray and defiles herself,
30 or when the spirit of jealousy comes upon a man and he is jealous of his wife; then he shall set the woman before the
31 LORD, and the priest shall execute upon her all this law. The man shall be free from iniquity, but the woman shall bear her iniquity."

6 2 And the LORD said to Moses, "Say to the people of Israel, When either a man or a woman makes a special vow, the
3 vow of a Nazirite,[b] to separate himself to the LORD, he shall separate himself from wine and strong drink; he shall drink no vinegar made from wine or strong drink, and shall not drink
4 any juice of grapes or eat grapes, fresh or dried. All the days of his separation[c] he shall eat nothing that is produced by the grapevine, not even the seeds or the skins.
5 "All the days of his vow of separation no razor shall come upon his head; until the time is completed for which he separates himself to the LORD, he shall be holy; he shall let the locks of hair of his head grow long.
6 "All the days that he separates himself to the LORD he shall
7 not go near a dead body. Neither for his father nor for his mother, nor for brother or sister, if they die, shall he make himself unclean; because his separation to God is upon his
8 head. All the days of his separation he is holy to the LORD.
9 "And if any man dies very suddenly beside him, and he defiles his consecrated head, then he shall shave his head on the day of his cleansing; on the seventh day he shall shave it.
10 On the eighth day he shall bring two turtledoves or two young
11 pigeons to the priest to the door of the tent of meeting, and the priest shall offer one for a sin offering and the other for a burnt offering, and make atonement for him, because he sinned by reason of the dead body. And he shall consecrate his head
12 that same day, and separate himself to the LORD for the days of his separation, and bring a male lamb a year old for a guilt offering; but the former time shall be void, because his separation was defiled.
13 "And this is the law for the Nazirite, when the time of his

b That is *one separated* or *one consecrated*   c Or *Naziriteship*

separation has been completed: he shall be brought to the
14 door of the tent of meeting, and he shall offer his gift to the LORD, one male lamb a year old without blemish for a burnt offering, and one ewe lamb a year old without blemish as a sin offering, and one ram without blemish as a peace offering,
15 and a basket of unleavened bread, cakes of fine flour mixed with oil, and unleavened wafers spread with oil, and their
16 cereal offering and their drink offerings. And the priest shall present them before the LORD and offer his sin offering and his
17 burnt offering, and he shall offer the ram as a sacrifice of peace offering to the LORD, with the basket of unleavened bread; the priest shall offer also its cereal offering and its drink offering.
18 And the Nazirite shall shave his consecrated head at the door of the tent of meeting, and shall take the hair from his consecrated head and put it on the fire which is under the
19 sacrifice of the peace offering. And the priest shall take the shoulder of the ram, when it is boiled, and one unleavened cake out of the basket, and one unleavened wafer, and shall put them upon the hands of the Nazirite, after he has shaven
20 the hair of his consecration, and the priest shall wave them for a wave offering before the LORD; they are a holy portion for the priest, together with the breast that is waved and the thigh that is offered; and after that the Nazirite may drink wine.
21 "This is the law for the Nazirite who takes a vow. His offering to the LORD shall be according to his vow as a Nazirite, apart from what else he can afford; in accordance with the vow which he takes, so shall he do according to the law for his separation as a Nazirite."

The Benediction

22, 23   The LORD said to Moses, "Say to Aaron and his sons, Thus you shall bless the people of Israel: you shall say to them,

24 The LORD bless you and keep you:

25 The LORD make his face to shine upon you, and be gracious to you:

26 The LORD lift up his countenance upon you, and give you peace.

27   "So shall they put my name upon the people of Israel, and I will bless them."

The Princes' Offerings

7   On the day when Moses had finished setting up the tabernacle, and had anointed and consecrated it with all its furnishings, and had anointed and consecrated the altar with
2 all its utensils, the leaders of Israel, heads of their fathers' houses, the leaders of the tribes, who were over those who
3 were numbered, offered and brought their offerings before the LORD, six covered wagons and twelve oxen, a wagon for every two of the leaders, and for each one an ox; they offered
4 them before the tabernacle. Then the LORD said to Moses,
5 "Accept these from them, that they may be used in doing the service of the tent of meeting, and give them to the Levites,
6 to each man according to his service." So Moses took the
7 wagons and the oxen, and gave them to the Levites. Two wagons and four oxen he gave to the sons of Gershon, ac-
8 cording to their service; and four wagons and eight oxen he gave to the sons of Merar'i, according to their service, under
9 the direction of Ith'amar the son of Aaron the priest. But to the sons of Kohath he gave none, because they were charged with the care of the holy things which had to be carried on
10 the shoulder. And the leaders offered offerings for the dedication of the altar on the day it was anointed; and the leaders
11 offered their offering before the altar. And the LORD said to

Moses, "They shall offer their offerings, one leader each day, for the dedication of the altar."
12 He who offered his offering the first day was Nahshon the
13 son of Ammin'adab, of the tribe of Judah; and his offering was one silver plate whose weight was a hundred and thirty shekels, one silver basin of seventy shekels, according to the shekel of the sanctuary, both of them full of fine flour mixed with oil
14 for a cereal offering; one golden dish of ten shekels, full of
15 incense; one young bull, one ram, one male lamb a year old,
16, 17 for a burnt offering; one male goat for a sin offering; and for the sacrifice of peace offerings, two oxen, five rams, five male goats, and five male lambs a year old. This was the offering of Nahshon the son of Ammin'adab.
18 On the second day Nethan'el the son of Zu'ar, the leader of
19 Is'sachar, made an offering; he offered for his offering one silver plate, whose weight was a hundred and thirty shekels, one silver basin of seventy shekels, according to the shekel of the sanctuary, both of them full of fine flour mixed with oil
20 for a cereal offering; one golden dish of ten shekels, full of
21 incense; one young bull, one ram, one male lamb a year old,
22, 23 for a burnt offering; one male goat for a sin offering; and for the sacrifice of peace offerings, two oxen, five rams, five male goats, and five male lambs a year old. This was the offering of Nethan'el the son of Zu'ar.
24 On the third day Eli'ab the son of Helon, the leader of the
25 men of Zeb'ulun: his offering was one silver plate, whose weight was a hundred and thirty shekels, one silver basin of seventy shekels, according to the shekel of the sanctuary, both of them full of fine flour mixed with oil for a cereal offering;
26, 27 one golden dish of ten shekels, full of incense; one young bull, one ram, one male lamb a year old, for a burnt offering;
28, 29 one male goat for a sin offering; and for the sacrifice of peace offerings, two oxen, five rams, five male goats, and five male lambs a year old. This was the offering of Eli'ab the son of Helon.
30 On the fourth day Eli'zur the son of Shed'eur, the leader of
31 the men of Reuben: his offering was one silver plate whose weight was a hundred and thirty shekels, one silver basin of seventy shekels, according to the shekel of the sanctuary, both of them full of fine flour mixed with oil for a cereal offering;
32, 33 one golden dish of ten shekels, full of incense; one young bull, one ram, one male lamb a year old, for a burnt offering;
34, 35 one male goat for a sin offering; and for the sacrifice of peace offerings, two oxen, five rams, five male goats, and five male lambs a year old. This was the offering of Eli'zur the son of Shed'eur.
36 On the fifth day Shelu'mi-el the son of Zurishad'dai, the
37 leader of the men of Simeon: his offering was one silver plate whose weight was a hundred and thirty shekels, one silver basin of seventy shekels, according to the shekel of the sanctuary, both of them full of fine flour mixed with oil for
38 a cereal offering; one golden dish of ten shekels, full of incense;
39 one young bull, one ram, one male lamb a year old, for a burnt
40, 41 offering; one male goat for a sin offering; and for the sacrifice of peace offerings, two oxen, five rams, five male goats, and five male lambs a year old. This was the offering of Shelu'mi-el the son of Zurishad'dai.
42 On the sixth day Eli'asaph the son of Deu'el, the leader of
43 the men of Gad: his offering was one silver plate, whose weight was a hundred and thirty shekels, one silver basin of seventy shekels, according to the shekel of the sanctuary, both of them
44 full of fine flour mixed with oil for a cereal offering; one golden
45 dish of ten shekels, full of incense; one young bull, one ram,
46 one male lamb a year old, for a burnt offering; one male goat
47 for a sin offering; and for the sacrifice of peace offerings, two oxen, five rams, five male goats, and five male lambs a year old. This was the offering of Eli'asaph the son of Deu'el.
48 On the seventh day Elish'ama the son of Ammi'hud, the
49 leader of the men of E'phraim: his offering was one silver plate, whose weight was a hundred and thirty shekels, one silver basin of seventy shekels, according to the shekel of the sanctuary, both of them full of fine flour mixed with oil for
50 a cereal offering; one golden dish of ten shekels, full of incense;
51 one young bull, one ram, one male lamb a year old, for a
52, 53 burnt offering; one male goat for a sin offering; and for the sacrifice of peace offerings, two oxen, five rams, five male goats, and five male lambs a year old. This was the offering of Elish'ama the son of Ammi'hud.
54 On the eighth day Gama'liel the son of Pedah'zur, the leader
55 of the men of Manas'seh: his offering was one silver plate,

whose weight was a hundred and thirty shekels, one silver basin of seventy shekels, according to the shekel of the sanctuary, both of them full of fine flour mixed with oil for 56 a cereal offering; one golden dish of ten shekels, full of incense; 57 one young bull, one ram, one male lamb a year old, for a burnt 58, 59 offering; one male goat for a sin offering; and for the sacrifice of peace offerings, two oxen, five rams, five male goats, and five male lambs a year old. This was the offering of Gama′liel the son of Pedah′zur.

60 On the ninth day A-bi′dan the son of Gideo′ni, the leader 61 of the men of Benjamin: his offering was one silver plate, whose weight was a hundred and thirty shekels, one silver basin of seventy shekels, according to the shekel of the sanctuary, both of them full of fine flour mixed with oil for 62 a cereal offering; one golden dish of ten shekels, full of incense; 63 one young bull, one ram, one male lamb a year old, for a burnt 64, 65 offering; one male goat for a sin offering; and for the sacrifice of peace offerings, two oxen, five rams, five male goats, and five male lambs a year old. This was the offering of A-bi′dan the son of Gideo′ni.

66 On the tenth day Ahie′zer the son of Ammishad′dai, the 67 leader of the men of Dan: his offering was one silver plate, whose weight was a hundred and thirty shekels, one silver basin of seventy shekels, according to the shekel of the sanctuary, both of them full of fine flour mixed with oil for a 68 cereal offering; one golden dish of ten shekels, full of incense; 69 one young bull, one ram, one male lamb a year old, for a 70, 71 burnt offering; one male goat for a sin offering; and for the sacrifice of peace offerings, two oxen, five rams, five male goats, and five male lambs a year old. This was the offering of Ahie′zer the son of Ammishad′dai.

72 On the eleventh day Pa′giel the son of Ochran, the leader 73 of the men of Asher: his offering was one silver plate, whose weight was a hundred and thirty shekels, one silver basin of seventy shekels, according to the shekel of the sanctuary, both of them full of fine flour mixed with oil for a cereal offering; 74, 75 one golden dish of ten shekels, full of incense; one young bull, one ram, one male lamb a year old, for a burnt offering; 76, 77 one male goat for a sin offering; and for the sacrifice of peace offerings, two oxen, five rams, five male goats, and five male lambs a year old. This was the offering of Pa′giel the son of Ochran.

78 On the twelfth day Ahi′ra the son of Enan, the leader of the 79 men of Naph′tali: his offering was one silver plate, whose weight was a hundred and thirty shekels, one silver basin of seventy shekels, according to the shekel of the sanctuary, both of them full of fine flour mixed with oil for a cereal offering; 80, 81 one golden dish of ten shekels, full of incense; one young bull, 82 one ram, one male lamb a year old, for a burnt offering; one 83 male goat for a sin offering; and for the sacrifice of peace offerings, two oxen, five rams, five male goats, and five male lambs a year old. This was the offering of Ahi′ra the son of Enan.

84 This was the dedication offering for the altar, on the day when it was anointed, from the leaders of Israel: twelve silver 85 plates, twelve silver basins, twelve golden dishes, each silver plate weighing a hundred and thirty shekels and each basin seventy, all the silver of the vessels two thousand four hundred 86 shekels according to the shekel of the sanctuary, the twelve golden dishes, full of incense, weighing ten shekels apiece according to the shekel of the sanctuary, all the gold of the dishes 87 being a hundred and twenty shekels; all the cattle for the burnt offering twelve bulls, twelve rams, twelve male lambs a year old, with their cereal offering; and twelve male goats 88 for a sin offering; and all the cattle for the sacrifice of peace offerings twenty-four bulls, the rams sixty, the male goats sixty, the male lambs a year old sixty. This was the dedication offering for the altar, after it was anointed.

89 And when Moses went into the tent of meeting to speak with the Lord, he heard the voice speaking to him from above the mercy seat that was upon the ark of the testimony, from between the two cherubim; and it spoke to him.

8 2 Now the Lord said to Moses, "Say to Aaron, When you set up the lamps, the seven lamps shall give light in front 3 of the lampstand." And Aaron did so; he set up its lamps to give light in front of the lampstand, as the Lord commanded 4 Moses. And this was the workmanship of the lampstand, hammered work of gold; from its base to its flowers, it was hammered work; according to the pattern which the Lord had shown Moses, so he made the lampstand.

Purification of the Levites

5, 6 And the Lord said to Moses, "Take the Levites from among 7 the people of Israel, and cleanse them. And thus you shall do to them, to cleanse them: sprinkle the water of expiation upon them, and let them go with a razor over all their body, and 8 wash their clothes and cleanse themselves. Then let them take a young bull and its cereal offering of fine flour mixed with oil, and you shall take another young bull for a sin offering. 9 And you shall present the Levites before the tent of meeting, and assemble the whole congregation of the people of Israel. 10 When you present the Levites before the Lord, the people of 11 Israel shall lay their hands upon the Levites, and Aaron shall offer the Levites before the Lord as a wave offering from the people of Israel, that it may be theirs to do the service of the 12 Lord. Then the Levites shall lay their hands upon the heads of the bulls; and you shall offer the one for a sin offering and the other for a burnt offering to the Lord, to make atonement 13 for the Levites. And you shall cause the Levites to attend Aaron and his sons, and shall offer them as a wave offering to the Lord.

14 "Thus you shall separate the Levites from among the people 15 of Israel, and the Levites shall be mine. And after that the Levites shall go in to do service at the tent of meeting, when you have cleansed them and offered them as a wave offering. 16 For they are wholly given to me from among the people of Israel; instead of all that open the womb, the first-born of all 17 the people of Israel, I have taken them for myself. For all the first-born among the people of Israel are mine, both of man 18 and of beast; on the day that I slew all the first-born in the land of Egypt I consecrated them for myself, and I have taken the Levites instead of all the first-born among the people of 19 Israel. And I have given the Levites as a gift to Aaron and his sons from among the people of Israel, to do the service for the people of Israel at the tent of meeting, and to make atonement for the people of Israel, that there may be no plague among the people of Israel in case the people of Israel should come near the sanctuary."

20 Thus did Moses and Aaron and all the congregation of the people of Israel to the Levites; according to all that the Lord commanded Moses concerning the Levites, the people of Israel 21 did to them. And the Levites purified themselves from sin, and washed their clothes; and Aaron offered them as a wave offering before the Lord, and Aaron made atonement for them 22 to cleanse them. And after that the Levites went in to do their service in the tent of meeting in attendance upon Aaron and his sons; as the Lord had commanded Moses concerning the Levites, so they did to them.

23, 24 And the Lord said to Moses, "This is what pertains to the Levites: from twenty-five years old and upward they shall go in to perform the work in the service of the tent of meeting; 25 and from the age of fifty years they shall withdraw from the 26 work of the service and serve no more, but minister to their brethren in the tent of meeting, to keep the charge, and they shall do no service. Thus shall you do to the Levites in assigning their duties."

9 And the Lord spoke to Moses in the wilderness of Sinai, in the first month of the second year after they had come out 2 of the land of Egypt, saying, "Let the people of Israel keep 3 the passover at its appointed time. On the fourteenth day of this month, in the evening, you shall keep it at its appointed time; according to all its statutes and all its ordinances you 4 shall keep it." So Moses told the people of Israel that they 5 should keep the passover. And they kept the passover in the first month, on the fourteenth day of the month, in the evening, in the wilderness of Sinai; according to all that the Lord com- 6 manded Moses, so the people of Israel did. And there were certain men who were unclean through touching the dead body of a man, so that they could not keep the passover on that day; and they came before Moses and Aaron on that day; 7 and those men said to him, "We are unclean through touching the dead body of a man; why are we kept from offering the Lord's offering at its appointed time among the people of 8 Israel?" And Moses said to them, "Wait, that I may hear what the Lord will command concerning you."

9, 10 The Lord said to Moses, "Say to the people of Israel, If any man of you or of your descendants is unclean through touching a dead body, or is afar off on a journey, he shall still keep 11 the passover to the Lord. In the second month on the fourteenth day in the evening they shall keep it; they shall eat it with 12 unleavened bread and bitter herbs. They shall leave none of it

until the morning, nor break a bone of it; according to all the
¹³ statute for the passover they shall keep it. But the man who is clean and is not on a journey, yet refrains from keeping the passover, that person shall be cut off from his people, because he did not offer the LORD's offering at its appointed time; that
¹⁴ man shall bear his sin. And if a stranger sojourns among you, and will keep the passover to the LORD, according to the statute of the passover and according to its ordinance, so shall he do; you shall have one statute, both for the sojourner and for the native."

LEAVING SINAI

¹⁵ On the day that the tabernacle was set up, the cloud covered the tabernacle, the tent of the testimony; and at evening it was over the tabernacle like the appearance of
¹⁶ fire until morning. So it was continually; the cloud covered it by day,[d] and the appearance of fire by night.
¹⁷ And whenever the cloud was taken up from over the tent, after that the people of Israel set out; and in the place where the cloud settled down, there the people of Israel
¹⁸ encamped. At the command of the LORD the people of Israel set out, and at the command of the LORD they encamped; as long as the cloud rested over the tabernacle,
¹⁹ they remained in camp. Even when the cloud continued over the tabernacle many days, the people of Israel kept
²⁰ the charge of the LORD, and did not set out. Sometimes the cloud was a few days over the tabernacle, and according to the command of the LORD they remained in camp; then according to the command of the LORD they set out.
²¹ And sometimes the cloud remained from evening until morning; and when the cloud was taken up in the morning, they set out, or if it continued for a day and a night,
²² when the cloud was taken up they set out. Whether it was two days, or a month, or a longer time, that the cloud continued over the tabernacle, abiding there, the people of Israel remained in camp and did not set out; but when
²³ it was taken up they set out. At the command of the LORD they encamped, and at the command of the LORD they set out; they kept the charge of the LORD, at the command of the LORD by Moses.

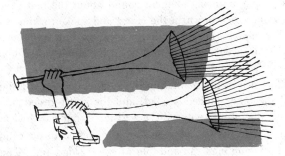

²,10 The LORD said to Moses, "Make two silver trumpets; of hammered work you shall make them; and you shall use them for summoning the congregation,
³ and for breaking camp. And when both are blown, all the congregation shall gather themselves to you at the entrance
⁴ of the tent of meeting. But if they blow only one, then the leaders, the heads of the tribes of Israel, shall gather them-

⁵ selves to you. When you blow an alarm, the camps that
⁶ are on the east side shall set out. And when you blow an alarm the second time, the camps that are on the south side shall set out. An alarm is to be blown whenever they
⁷ are to set out. But when the assembly is to be gathered together, you shall blow, but you shall not sound an alarm.
⁸ And the sons of Aaron, the priests, shall blow the trumpets. The trumpets shall be to you for a perpetual
⁹ statute throughout your generations. And when you go to war in your land against the adversary who oppresses you, then you shall sound an alarm with the trumpets, that you may be remembered before the LORD your God,
¹⁰ and you shall be saved from your enemies. On the day of your gladness also, and at your appointed feasts, and at the beginnings of your months, you shall blow the trumpets over your burnt offerings and over the sacrifices of your peace offerings; they shall serve you for remembrance before your God: I am the LORD your God."

March from Sinai to Paran

¹¹ In the second year, in the second month, on the twentieth day of the month, the cloud was taken up from
¹² over the tabernacle of the testimony, and the people of Israel set out by stages from the wilderness of Sinai; and
¹³ the cloud settled down in the wilderness of Paran. They set out for the first time at the command of the LORD by
¹⁴ Moses. The standard of the camp of the men of Judah set out first by their companies; and over their host was
¹⁵ Nahshon the son of Ammin'adab. And over the host of the tribe of the men of Is'sachar was Nethan'el the son of
¹⁶ Zu'ar. And over the host of the tribe of the men of Zeb'ulun was Eli'ab the son of Helon.
¹⁷ And when the tabernacle was taken down, the sons of Gershon and the sons of Merar'i, who carried the taber-
¹⁸ nacle, set out. And the standard of the camp of Reuben set out by their companies; and over their host was Eli'zur
¹⁹ the son of Shed'eur. And over the host of the tribe of the men of Simeon was Shelu'mi-el the son of Zurishad'dai.
²⁰ And over the host of the tribe of the men of Gad was Eli'asaph the son of Deu'el.
²¹ Then the Ko'hathites set out, carrying the holy things,
²² and the tabernacle was set up before their arrival. And the standard of the camp of the men of E'phraim set out by their companies; and over their host was Elish'ama the
²³ son of Ammi'hud. And over the host of the tribe of the men of Manas'seh was Gama'liel the son of Pedah'zur.
²⁴ And over the host of the tribe of the men of Benjamin was A-bi'dan the son of Gideo'ni.
²⁵ Then the standard of the camp of the men of Dan, acting as the rear guard of all the camps, set out by their companies; and over their host was Ahie'zer the son of
²⁶ Ammishad'dai. And over the host of the tribe of the men
²⁷ of Asher was Pa'giel the son of Ochran. And over the host of the tribe of the men of Naph'tali was Ahi'ra the son of

[d] Gk Syr Vg: Heb lacks *by day*

28 Enan. This was the order of march of the people of Israel according to their hosts, when they set out.

29 And Moses said to Hobab the son of Reu'el the Mid'-ianite, Moses' father-in-law, "We are setting out for the place of which the LORD said, 'I will give it to you'; come with us, and we will do you good; for the LORD has
30 promised good to Israel." But he said to him, "I will not go; I will depart to my own land and to my kindred."
31 And he said, "Do not leave us, I pray you, for you know how we are to encamp in the wilderness, and you will
32 serve as eyes for us. And if you go with us, whatever good the LORD will do to us, the same will we do to you."

33 So they set out from the mount of the LORD three days' journey; and the ark of the covenant of the LORD went before them three days' journey, to seek out a resting
34 place for them. And the cloud of the LORD was over them by day, whenever they set out from the camp.
35 And whenever the ark set out, Moses said, "Arise, O LORD, and let thy enemies be scattered; and let them that
36 hate thee flee before thee." And when it rested, he said, "Return, O LORD, to the ten thousand thousands of Israel."

Discontent

11 And the people complained in the hearing of the LORD about their misfortunes; and when the LORD heard it, his anger was kindled, and the fire of the LORD burned among them, and consumed some outlying parts
2 of the camp. Then the people cried to Moses; and Moses
3 prayed to the LORD, and the fire abated. So the name of that place was called Tab'erah,e because the fire of the LORD burned among them.

4 Now the rabble that was among them had a strong craving; and the people of Israel also wept again, and
5 said, "O that we had meat to eat! We remember the fish we ate in Egypt for nothing, the cucumbers, the melons,
6 the leeks, the onions, and the garlic; but now our strength is dried up, and there is nothing at all but this manna to look at."

7 Now the manna was like coriander seed, and its ap-
8 pearance like that of bdellium. The people went about and gathered it, and ground it in mills or beat it in mortars, and boiled it in pots, and made cakes of it; and the taste of it was like the taste of cakes baked with oil.
9 When the dew fell upon the camp in the night, the manna fell with it.

10 Moses heard the people weeping throughout their fami-lies, every man at the door of his tent; and the anger of
11 the LORD blazed hotly, and Moses was displeased. Moses said to the LORD, "Why hast thou dealt ill with thy servant? And why have I not found favor in thy sight, that thou dost lay the burden of all this people upon me?
12 Did I conceive all this people? Did I bring them forth, that thou shouldst say to me, 'Carry them in your bosom, as a nurse carries the sucking child, to the land which

13 thou didst swear to give their fathers?' Where am I to get meat to give to all this people? For they weep before
14 me and say, 'Give us meat, that we may eat.' I am not able to carry all this people alone, the burden is too heavy
15 for me. If thou wilt deal thus with me, kill me at once, if I find favor in thy sight, that I may not see my wretched-ness."

16 And the LORD said to Moses, "Gather for me seventy men of the elders of Israel, whom you know to be the elders of the people and officers over them; and bring them to the tent of meeting, and let them take their stand
17 there with you. And I will come down and talk with you there; and I will take some of the spirit which is upon you and put it upon them; and they shall bear the burden of the people with you, that you may not bear it yourself
18 alone. And say to the people, 'Consecrate yourselves for tomorrow, and you shall eat meat; for you have wept in the hearing of the LORD, saying, "Who will give us meat to eat? For it was well with us in Egypt." Therefore the
19 LORD will give you meat, and you shall eat. You shall not eat one day, or two days, or five days, or ten days, or
20 twenty days, but a whole month, until it comes out at your nostrils and becomes loathsome to you, because you have rejected the LORD who is among you, and have wept before him, saying, "Why did we come forth out of
21 Egypt?"'" But Moses said, "The people among whom I am number six hundred thousand on foot; and thou hast said, 'I will give them meat, that they may eat a whole
22 month!' Shall flocks and herds be slaughtered for them, to suffice them? Or shall all the fish of the sea be
23 gathered together for them, to suffice them?" And the LORD said to Moses, "Is the LORD's hand shortened? Now you shall see whether my word will come true for you or not."

24 So Moses went out and told the people the words of the LORD; and he gathered seventy men of the elders of
25 the people, and placed them round about the tent. Then the LORD came down in the cloud and spoke to him, and took some of the spirit that was upon him and put it upon the seventy elders; and when the spirit rested upon them, they prophesied. But they did so no more.
26 Now two men remained in the camp, one named Eldad, and the other named Medad, and the spirit rested upon them; they were among those registered, but they had not gone out to the tent, and so they prophesied in the camp.
27 And a young man ran and told Moses, "Eldad and Medad
28 are prophesying in the camp." And Joshua the son of Nun, the minister of Moses, one of his chosen men, said,
29 "My lord Moses, forbid them." But Moses said to him, "Are you jealous for my sake? Would that all the LORD's people were prophets, that the LORD would put his spirit
30 upon them!" And Moses and the elders of Israel re-turned to the camp.

e That is Burning

31 And there went forth a wind from the LORD, and it brought quails from the sea, and let them fall beside the camp, about a day's journey on this side and a day's journey on the other side, round about the camp, and
32 about two cubits above the face of the earth. And the people rose all that day, and all night, and all the next day, and gathered the quails; he who gathered least gathered ten homers; and they spread them out for them-
33 selves all around the camp. While the meat was yet between their teeth, before it was consumed, the anger of the LORD was kindled against the people, and the LORD smote
34 the people with a very great plague. Therefore the name of that place was called Kib'roth-hatta'avah,f because there
35 they buried the people who had the craving. From Kib'-roth-hatta'avah the people journeyed to Haze'roth; and they remained at Haze'roth.

Miriam, Aaron, and Moses

12 Miriam and Aaron spoke against Moses because of the Cushite woman whom he had married, for
2 he had married a Cushite woman; and they said, "Has the LORD indeed spoken only through Moses? Has he not
3 spoken through us also?" And the LORD heard it. Now the man Moses was very meek, more than all men that
4 were on the face of the earth. And suddenly the LORD said to Moses and to Aaron and Miriam, "Come out, you three, to the tent of meeting." And the three of them
5 came out. And the LORD came down in a pillar of cloud, and stood at the door of the tent, and called Aaron and
6 Miriam; and they both came forward. And he said, "Hear my words: If there is a prophet among you, I the LORD make myself known to him in a vision, I speak with him
7 in a dream. Not so with my servant Moses; he is en-
8 trusted with all my house. With him I speak mouth to mouth, clearly, and not in dark speech; and he beholds the form of the LORD. Why then were you not afraid to speak against my servant Moses?"
9 And the anger of the LORD was kindled against them,
10 and he departed; and when the cloud removed from over the tent, behold, Miriam was leprous, as white as snow. And Aaron turned towards Miriam, and behold, she was
11 leprous. And Aaron said to Moses, "Oh, my lord, do not g punish us because we have done foolishly and have sinned.
12 Let her not be as one dead, of whom the flesh is half con-
13 sumed when he comes out of his mother's womb." And Moses cried to the LORD, "Heal her, O God, I beseech
14 thee." But the LORD said to Moses, "If her father had but spit in her face, should she not be shamed seven days? Let her be shut up outside the camp seven days, and after
15 that she may be brought in again." So Miriam was shut up outside the camp seven days; and the people did not set out on the march till Miriam was brought in again.
16 After that the people set out from Haze'roth, and encamped in the wilderness of Paran.

SOJOURN IN PARAN

13 The LORD said to Moses, "Send men to spy out
2 the land of Canaan, which I give to the people of Israel; from each tribe of their fathers shall you send a
3 man, every one a leader among them." So Moses sent them from the wilderness of Paran, according to the command of the LORD, all of them men who were heads of the
4 people of Israel. And these were their names: From the
5 tribe of Reuben, Sham'mu-a the son of Zaccur; from the
6 tribe of Simeon, Shaphat the son of Hori; from the tribe
7 of Judah, Caleb the son of Jephun'neh; from the tribe of
8 Is'sachar, Igal the son of Joseph; from the tribe of
9 E'phraim, Hoshe'a the son of Nun; from the tribe of
10 Benjamin, Palti the son of Raphu; from the tribe of Zeb'-
11 ulun, Gad'diel the son of Sodi; from the tribe of Joseph (that is from the tribe of Manas'seh), Gaddi the son of
12 Susi; from the tribe of Dan, Am'miel the son of Gemal'li;
13, 14 from the tribe of Asher, Sethur the son of Michael; from
15 the tribe of Naph'tali, Nahbi the son of Vophsi; from the
16 tribe of Gad, Geu'el the son of Machi. These were the names of the men whom Moses sent to spy out the land. And Moses called Hoshe'a the son of Nun Joshua.

Spies Sent to Canaan

17 Moses sent them to spy out the land of Canaan, and said to them, "Go up into the Negeb yonder, and go up
18 into the hill country, and see what the land is, and whether the people who dwell in it are strong or weak, whether
19 they are few or many, and whether the land that they dwell in is good or bad, and whether the cities that they
20 dwell in are camps or strongholds, and whether the land

is rich or poor, and whether there is wood in it or not. Be of good courage, and bring some of the fruit of the land." Now the time was the season of the first ripe grapes.
21 So they went up and spied out the land from the wilder-
22 ness of Zin to Rehob, near the entrance of Hamath. They went up into the Negeb, and came to Hebron; and Ahi'-man, Sheshai, and Talmai, the descendants of Anak, were there. (Hebron was built seven years before Zo'an in
23 Egypt.) And they came to the Valley of Eshcol, and cut down from there a branch with a single cluster of grapes, and they carried it on a pole between two of them; they
24 brought also some pomegranates and figs. That place was called the Valley of Eshcol,h because of the cluster which the men of Israel cut down from there.
25 At the end of forty days they returned from spying

---

f That is *Graves of craving*   g Heb *lay not sin upon us*   h That is *Cluster*

26 out the land. And they came to Moses and Aaron and to all the congregation of the people of Israel in the wilderness of Paran, at Kadesh; they brought back word to them and to all the congregation, and showed them the 27 fruit of the land. And they told him, "We came to the land to which you sent us; it flows with milk and honey, 28 and this is its fruit. Yet the people who dwell in the land are strong, and the cities are fortified and very large; and 29 besides, we saw the descendants of Anak there. The Amal'ekites dwell in the land of the Negeb; the Hittites, the Jeb'usites, and the Amorites dwell in the hill country; and the Canaanites dwell by the sea, and along the Jordan."

30 But Caleb quieted the people before Moses, and said, "Let us go up at once, and occupy it; for we are well able 31 to overcome it." Then the men who had gone up with him said, "We are not able to go up against the people; 32 for they are stronger than we." So they brought to the people of Israel an evil report of the land which they had spied out, saying, "The land, through which we have gone, to spy it out, is a land that devours its inhabitants; and all the people that we saw in it are men of great stature. 33 And there we saw the Nephilim (the sons of Anak, who come from the Nephilim); and we seemed to ourselves like grasshoppers, and so we seemed to them."

14 Then all the congregation raised a loud cry; and 2 the people wept that night. And all the people of Israel murmured against Moses and Aaron; the whole congregation said to them, "Would that we had died in the land of Egypt! Or would that we had died in this 3 wilderness! Why does the LORD bring us into this land, to fall by the sword? Our wives and our little ones will become a prey; would it not be better for us to go back to Egypt?"

4 And they said to one another, "Let us choose a captain, 5 and go back to Egypt." Then Moses and Aaron fell on their faces before all the assembly of the congregation of 6 the people of Israel. And Joshua the son of Nun and Caleb the son of Jephun'neh, who were among those who had 7 spied out the land, rent their clothes, and said to all the congregation of the people of Israel, "The land, which we passed through to spy it out, is an exceedingly good land. 8 If the LORD delights in us, he will bring us into this land and give it to us, a land which flows with milk and honey. 9 Only, do not rebel against the LORD; and do not fear the people of the land, for they are bread for us; their protection is removed from them, and the LORD is with us; 10 do not fear them." But all the congregation said to stone them with stones.

Then the glory of the LORD appeared at the tent of 11 meeting to all the people of Israel. And the LORD said to Moses, "How long will this people despise me? And how long will they not believe in me, in spite of all the signs 12 which I have wrought among them? I will strike them with the pestilence and disinherit them, and I will make of you a nation greater and mightier than they."

Moses' Intercession

13 But Moses said to the LORD, "Then the Egyptians will hear of it, for thou didst bring up this people in thy might 14 from among them, and they will tell the inhabitants of this land. They have heard that thou, O LORD, art in the midst of this people; for thou, O LORD, art seen face to face, and thy cloud stands over them and thou goest before them, in a pillar of cloud by day and in a pillar of fire by 15 night. Now if thou dost kill this people as one man, then 16 the nations who have heard thy fame will say, 'Because the LORD was not able to bring this people into the land which he swore to give to them, therefore he has slain 17 them in the wilderness.' And now, I pray thee, let the power of the LORD be great as thou hast promised, say- 18 ing, 'The LORD is slow to anger, and abounding in steadfast love, forgiving iniquity and transgression, but he will by no means clear the guilty, visiting the iniquity of fathers upon children, upon the third and upon the fourth 19 generation.' Pardon the iniquity of this people, I pray thee, according to the greatness of thy steadfast love, and according as thou hast forgiven this people, from Egypt even until now."

20 Then the LORD said, "I have pardoned, according to 21 your word; but truly, as I live, and as all the earth shall 22 be filled with the glory of the LORD, none of the men who have seen my glory and my signs which I wrought in Egypt and in the wilderness, and yet have put me to the proof these ten times and have not hearkened to my voice, 23 shall see the land which I swore to give to their fathers; 24 and none of those who despised me shall see it. But my servant Caleb, because he has a different spirit and has followed me fully, I will bring into the land into which 25 he went, and his descendants shall possess it. Now, since the Amal'ekites and the Canaanites dwell in the valleys, turn tomorrow and set out for the wilderness by the way to the Red Sea."

Disobedience and Defeat

26, 27 And the LORD said to Moses and to Aaron, "How long shall this wicked congregation murmur against me? I have heard the murmurings of the people of Israel, which 28 they murmur against me. Say to them, 'As I live,' says the LORD, 'what you have said in my hearing I will do to 29 you: your dead bodies shall fall in this wilderness; and of all your number, numbered from twenty years old and 30 upward, who have murmured against me, not one shall come into the land where I swore that I would make you dwell, except Caleb the son of Jephun'neh and Joshua the 31 son of Nun. But your little ones, who you said would become a prey, I will bring in, and they shall know the

32 land which you have despised. But as for you, your dead
33 bodies shall fall in this wilderness. And your children shall be shepherds in the wilderness forty years, and shall suffer for your faithlessness, until the last of your dead
34 bodies lies in the wilderness. According to the number of the days in which you spied out the land, forty days, for every day a year, you shall bear your iniquity, forty
35 years, and you shall know my displeasure.' I, the LORD, have spoken; surely this will I do to all this wicked congregation that are gathered together against me: in this wilderness they shall come to a full end, and there they shall die."

36 And the men whom Moses sent to spy out the land, and who returned and made all the congregation to murmur against him by bringing up an evil report against
37 the land, the men who brought up an evil report of the
38 land, died by plague before the LORD. But Joshua the son of Nun and Caleb the son of Jephun'neh remained alive, of those men who went to spy out the land.

39 And Moses told these words to all the people of Israel,
40 and the people mourned greatly. And they rose early in the morning, and went up to the heights of the hill country, saying, "See, we are here, we will go up to the place which the LORD has promised; for we have sinned."
41 But Moses said, "Why now are you transgressing the
42 command of the LORD, for that will not succeed? Do not go up lest you be struck down before your enemies, for
43 the LORD is not among you. For there the Amal'ekites and the Canaanites are before you, and you shall fall by the sword; because you have turned back from following
44 the LORD, the LORD will not be with you." But they presumed to go up to the heights of the hill country, although neither the ark of the covenant of the LORD, nor
45 Moses, departed out of the camp. Then the Amal'ekites and the Canaanites who dwelt in that hill country came down, and defeated them and pursued them, even to Hormah.

SUPPLEMENTARY LAWS

2 **15** The LORD said to Moses, "Say to the people of Israel, When you come into the land you are to inhabit, which I
3 give you, and you offer to the LORD from the herd or from the flock an offering by fire or a burnt offering or a sacrifice, to fulfil a vow or as a freewill offering or at your appointed
4 feasts, to make a pleasing odor to the LORD, then he who brings his offering shall offer to the LORD a cereal offering of a tenth of an ephah of fine flour, mixed with a fourth of a hin of oil;
5 and wine for the drink offering, a fourth of a hin, you shall prepare with the burnt offering, or for the sacrifice, for
6 each lamb. Or for a ram, you shall prepare for a cereal offering two tenths of an ephah of fine flour mixed with a
7 third of a hin of oil; and for the drink offering you shall offer a third of a hin of wine, a pleasing odor to the LORD.
8 And when you prepare a bull for a burnt offering, or for a
9 sacrifice, to fulfil a vow, or for peace offerings to the LORD, then one shall offer with the bull a cereal offering of three tenths
10 of an ephah of fine flour, mixed with half a hin of oil, and you shall offer for the drink offering half a hin of wine, as an offering by fire, a pleasing odor to the LORD.
11 "Thus it shall be done for each bull or ram, or for each of the
12 male lambs or the kids. According to the number that you prepare, so shall you do with every one according to their
13 number. All who are native shall do these things in this way, in offering an offering by fire, a pleasing odor to the LORD.
14 And if a stranger is sojourning with you, or any one is among you throughout your generations, and he wishes to offer an offering by fire, a pleasing odor to the LORD, he shall do as you
15 do. For the assembly, there shall be one statute for you and for the stranger who sojourns with you, a perpetual statute throughout your generations; as you are, so shall the sojourner
16 be before the LORD. One law and one ordinance shall be for you and for the stranger who sojourns with you."
17, 18 The LORD said to Moses, "Say to the people of Israel, When
19 you come into the land to which I bring you and when you eat of the food of the land, you shall present an offering to the
20 LORD. Of the first of your coarse meal you shall present a cake as an offering; as an offering from the threshing floor,
21 so shall you present it. Of the first of your coarse meal you shall give to the LORD an offering throughout your generations.
22 "But if you err, and do not observe all these commandments
23 which the LORD has spoken to Moses, all that the LORD has commanded you by Moses, from the day that the LORD gave com-
24 mandment, and onward throughout your generations, then if it was done unwittingly without the knowledge of the congregation, all the congregation shall offer one young bull for a burnt offering, a pleasing odor to the LORD, with its cereal offering and its drink offering, according to the ordinance, and
25 one male goat for a sin offering. And the priest shall make atonement for all the congregation of the people of Israel, and they shall be forgiven; because it was an error, and they have brought their offering, an offering by fire to the LORD, and their
26 sin offering before the LORD, for their error. And all the congregation of the people of Israel shall be forgiven, and the stranger who sojourns among them, because the whole population was involved in the error.
27 "If one person sins unwittingly, he shall offer a female goat
28 a year old for a sin offering. And the priest shall make atonement before the LORD for the person who commits an error, when he sins unwittingly, to make atonement for him; and he
29 shall be forgiven. You shall have one law for him who does anything unwittingly, for him who is native among the people of Israel, and for the stranger who sojourns among them.
30 But the person who does anything with a high hand, whether he is native or a sojourner, reviles the LORD, and that person
31 shall be cut off from among his people. Because he has despised the word of the LORD, and has broken his commandment, that person shall be utterly cut off; his iniquity shall be upon him."
32 While the people of Israel were in the wilderness, they found
33 a man gathering sticks on the sabbath day. And those who found him gathering sticks brought him to Moses and Aaron,
34 and to all the congregation. They put him in custody, because it had not been made plain what should be done to him.
35 And the LORD said to Moses, "The man shall be put to death;

all the congregation shall stone him with stones outside the
36 camp." And all the congregation brought him outside the camp, and stoned him to death with stones, as the LORD commanded Moses.
37, 38 The LORD said to Moses, "Speak to the people of Israel, and bid them to make tassels on the corners of their garments throughout their generations, and to put upon the tassel of each
39 corner a cord of blue; and it shall be to you a tassel to look upon and remember all the commandments of the LORD, to do them, not to follow after your own heart and your own eyes,
40 which you are inclined to go after wantonly. So you shall remember and do all my commandments, and be holy to your
41 God. I am the LORD your God, who brought you out of the land of Egypt, to be your God: I am the LORD your God."

Rebellion Against Moses and Aaron

16 Now Korah the son of Izhar, son of Kohath, son of Levi, and Dathan and Abi'ram the sons of Eli'ab, ² and On the son of Peleth, sons of Reuben, took men; and they rose up before Moses, with a number of the people of Israel, two hundred and fifty leaders of the congregation, chosen from the assembly, well-known men; ³ and they assembled themselves together against Moses and against Aaron, and said to them, "You have gone too far! For all the congregation are holy, every one of them, and the LORD is among them; why then do you exalt yourselves above the assembly of the LORD?" ⁴ When Moses heard it, he fell on his face; ⁵ and he said to Korah and all his company, "In the morning the LORD will show who is his, and who is holy, and will cause him to come near to him; him whom he will choose he will cause to come near to him. ⁶ Do this: take censers, Korah and all his company; ⁷ put fire in them and put incense upon them before the LORD tomorrow, and the man whom the LORD chooses shall be the holy one. You have gone too far, sons of Levi!" ⁸ And Moses said to Korah, "Hear now, you sons of Levi: ⁹ is it too small a thing for you that the God of Israel has separated you from the congregation of Israel, to bring you near to himself, to do service in the tabernacle of the LORD, and to stand before the congregation to minister to them; ¹⁰ and that he has brought you near him, and all your brethren the sons of Levi with you? And would you seek the priesthood also? ¹¹ Therefore it is against the LORD that you and all your company have gathered together; what is Aaron that you murmur against him?"

¹² And Moses sent to call Dathan and Abi'ram the sons of Eli'ab; and they said, "We will not come up. ¹³ Is it a small thing that you have brought us up out of a land flowing with milk and honey, to kill us in the wilderness, that you must also make yourself a prince over us? ¹⁴ Moreover you have not brought us into a land flowing with milk and honey, nor given us inheritance of fields and vineyards. Will you put out the eyes of these men? We will not come up."

¹⁵ And Moses was very angry, and said to the LORD, "Do not respect their offering. I have not taken one ass from them, and I have not harmed one of them." ¹⁶ And Moses said to Korah, "Be present, you and all your company, before the LORD, you and they, and Aaron, tomorrow; ¹⁷ and let every one of you take his censer, and put incense upon it, and every one of you bring before the LORD his censer, two hundred and fifty censers; you also, and Aaron, each his censer." ¹⁸ So every man took his censer, and they put fire in them and laid incense upon them, and they stood at the entrance of the tent of meeting with Moses ¹⁹ and Aaron. Then Korah assembled all the congregation against them at the entrance of the tent of meeting. And

the glory of the LORD appeared to all the congregation. ²⁰, ²¹ And the LORD said to Moses and to Aaron, "Separate yourselves from among this congregation, that I may consume them in a moment." ²² And they fell on their faces, and said, "O God, the God of the spirits of all flesh, shall one man sin, and wilt thou be angry with all the congregation?" ²³, ²⁴ And the LORD said to Moses, "Say to the congregation, Get away from about the dwelling of Korah, Dathan, and Abi'ram."

²⁵ Then Moses rose and went to Dathan and Abi'ram; ²⁶ and the elders of Israel followed him. And he said to the congregation, "Depart, I pray you, from the tents of these wicked men, and touch nothing of theirs, lest you ²⁷ be swept away with all their sins." So they got away from about the dwelling of Korah, Dathan, and Abi'ram; and Dathan and Abi'ram came out and stood at the door of their tents, together with their wives, their sons, and ²⁸ their little ones. And Moses said, "Hereby you shall know that the LORD has sent me to do all these works, and that ²⁹ it has not been of my own accord. If these men die the common death of all men, or if they are visited by the ³⁰ fate of all men, then the LORD has not sent me. But if the LORD creates something new, and the ground opens its mouth, and swallows them up, with all that belongs to them, and they go down alive into Sheol, then you shall know that these men have despised the LORD."

³¹ And as he finished speaking all these words, the ground ³² under them split asunder; and the earth opened its mouth and swallowed them up, with their households and all the ³³ men that belonged to Korah and all their goods. So they and all that belonged to them went down alive into Sheol; and the earth closed over them, and they perished from ³⁴ the midst of the assembly. And all Israel that were round about them fled at their cry; for they said, "Lest the earth ³⁵ swallow us up!" And fire came forth from the LORD, and consumed the two hundred and fifty men offering the incense.

³⁶, i³⁷ Then the LORD said to Moses, "Tell Elea'zar the son of Aaron the priest to take up the censers out of the blaze; then scatter the fire far and wide. For they are ³⁸ holy, the censers of these men who have sinned at the cost of their lives; so let them be made into hammered plates as a covering for the altar, for they offered them before the LORD; therefore they are holy. Thus they shall ³⁹ be a sign to the people of Israel." So Elea'zar the priest took the bronze censers, which those who were burned had offered; and they were hammered out as a covering ⁴⁰ for the altar, to be a reminder to the people of Israel, so that no one who is not a priest, who is not of the descendants of Aaron, should draw near to burn incense before the LORD, lest he become as Korah and as his company—as the LORD said to Elea'zar through Moses.

⁴¹ But on the morrow all the congregation of the people

ⁱ Ch 17. 1 in Heb

of Israel murmured against Moses and against Aaron,
42 saying, "You have killed the people of the LORD." And
when the congregation had assembled against Moses and
against Aaron, they turned toward the tent of meeting;
and behold, the cloud covered it, and the glory of the
43 LORD appeared. And Moses and Aaron came to the front
44, 45 of the tent of meeting, and the LORD said to Moses, "Get
away from the midst of this congregation, that I may
consume them in a moment." And they fell on their faces.
46 And Moses said to Aaron, "Take your censer, and put
fire therein from off the altar, and lay incense on it, and
carry it quickly to the congregation, and make atonement for them; for wrath has gone forth from the LORD,
47 the plague has begun." So Aaron took it as Moses said,
and ran into the midst of the assembly; and behold, the
plague had already begun among the people; and he put
48 on the incense, and made atonement for the people. And
he stood between the dead and the living; and the plague
49 was stopped. Now those who died by the plague were
fourteen thousand seven hundred, besides those who died
50 in the affair of Korah. And Aaron returned to Moses at
the entrance of the tent of meeting, when the plague was
stopped.

Aaron's Rod

2 **17**ʲ The LORD said to Moses, "Speak to the people of
Israel, and get from them rods, one for each fathers'
house, from all their leaders according to their fathers'
houses, twelve rods. Write each man's name upon his
3 rod, and write Aaron's name upon the rod of Levi. For
there shall be one rod for the head of each fathers' house.
4 Then you shall deposit them in the tent of meeting before

5 the testimony, where I meet with you. And the rod of the
man whom I choose shall sprout; thus I will make to
cease from me the murmurings of the people of Israel,
6 which they murmur against you." Moses spoke to the
people of Israel; and all their leaders gave him rods, one
for each leader, according to their fathers' houses, twelve
7 rods; and the rod of Aaron was among their rods. And
Moses deposited the rods before the LORD in the tent of
the testimony.
8   And on the morrow Moses went into the tent of the
testimony; and behold, the rod of Aaron for the house
of Levi had sprouted and put forth buds, and produced
9 blossoms, and it bore ripe almonds. Then Moses brought
out all the rods from before the LORD to all the people of

10 Israel; and they looked, and each man took his rod. And
the LORD said to Moses, "Put back the rod of Aaron before the testimony, to be kept as a sign for the rebels,
that you may make an end of their murmurings against
11 me, lest they die." Thus did Moses; as the LORD commanded him, so he did.
12   And the people of Israel said to Moses, "Behold, we
13 perish, we are undone, we are all undone. Every one who
comes near, who comes near to the tabernacle of the LORD,
shall die. Are we all to perish?"

DUTIES OF PRIESTS AND LEVITES

18 So the LORD said to Aaron, "You and your sons and your
fathers' house with you shall bear iniquity in connection
with the sanctuary; and you and your sons with you shall bear
2 iniquity in connection with your priesthood. And with you
bring your brethren also, the tribe of Levi, the tribe of your
father, that they may join you, and minister to you while you
and your sons with you are before the tent of the testimony.
3 They shall attend you and attend to all duties of the tent; but
shall not come near to the vessels of the sanctuary or to the
4 altar, lest they, and you, die. They shall join you, and attend
to the tent of meeting, for all the service of the tent; and no
5 one else shall come near you. And you shall attend to the
duties of the sanctuary and the duties of the altar, that there
6 be wrath no more upon the people of Israel. And behold, I
have taken your brethren the Levites from among the people
of Israel; they are a gift to you, given to the LORD, to do the
7 service of the tent of meeting. And you and your sons with
you shall attend to your priesthood for all that concerns the
altar and that is within the veil; and you shall serve. I give
your priesthood as a gift,ᵏ and any one else who comes near
shall be put to death."
8   Then the LORD said to Aaron, "And behold, I have given you
whatever is kept of the offerings made to me, all the consecrated things of the people of Israel; I have given them to
9 you as a portion, and to your sons as a perpetual due. This
shall be yours of the most holy things, reserved from the fire;
every offering of theirs, every cereal offering of theirs and
every sin offering of theirs and every guilt offering of theirs,
which they render to me, shall be most holy to you and
10 to your sons. In a most holy place shall you eat of it;
11 every male may eat of it; it is holy to you. This also is
yours, the offering of their gift, all the wave offerings of
the people of Israel; I have given them to you, and to
your sons and daughters with you, as a perpetual due; every
12 one who is clean in your house may eat of it. All the best of
the oil, and all the best of the wine and of the grain, the first
13 fruits of what they give to the LORD, I give to you. The first
ripe fruits of all that is in their land, which they bring to the
LORD, shall be yours; every one who is clean in your house
14 may eat of it. Every devoted thing in Israel shall be yours.
15 Everything that opens the womb of all flesh, whether man or
beast, which they offer to the LORD, shall be yours; nevertheless the first-born of man you shall redeem, and the firstling
16 of unclean beasts you shall redeem. And their redemption price
(at a month old you shall redeem them) you shall fix at five
shekels in silver, according to the shekel of the sanctuary,
17 which is twenty gerahs. But the firstling of a cow, or the firstling of a sheep, or the firstling of a goat, you shall not redeem;
they are holy. You shall sprinkle their blood upon the altar,
and shall burn their fat as an offering by fire, a pleasing odor
18 to the LORD; but their flesh shall be yours, as the breast that
19 is waved and as the right thigh are yours. All the holy offerings which the people of Israel present to the LORD I give to
you, and to your sons and daughters with you, as a perpetual
due; it is a covenant of salt for ever before the LORD for you
20 and for your offspring with you." And the LORD said to Aaron,
"You shall have no inheritance in their land, neither shall you
have any portion among them; I am your portion and your
inheritance among the people of Israel.
21   "To the Levites I have given every tithe in Israel for an
inheritance, in return for their service which they serve, their
22 service in the tent of meeting. And henceforth the people of
Israel shall not come near the tent of meeting, lest they bear

ʲ Ch 17. 16 in Heb   ᵏ Heb *service of gift*

95

23 sin and die. But the Levites shall do the service of the tent of meeting, and they shall bear their iniquity; it shall be a perpetual statute throughout your generations; and among the 24 people of Israel they shall have no inheritance. For the tithe of the people of Israel, which they present as an offering to the LORD, I have given to the Levites for an inheritance; therefore I have said of them that they shall have no inheritance among the people of Israel."

25, 26 And the LORD said to Moses, "Moreover you shall say to the Levites, 'When you take from the people of Israel the tithe which I have given you from them for your inheritance, then you shall present an offering from it to the LORD, a tithe of the 27 tithe. And your offering shall be reckoned to you as though it were the grain of the threshing floor, and as the fulness of 28 the wine press. So shall you also present an offering to the LORD from all your tithes, which you receive from the people of Israel; and from it you shall give the LORD's offering to 29 Aaron the priest. Out of all the gifts to you, you shall present every offering due to the LORD, from all the best of them, 30 giving the hallowed part from them.' Therefore you shall say to them, 'When you have offered from it the best of it, then the rest shall be reckoned to the Levites as produce of the 31 threshing floor, and as produce of the wine press; and you may eat it in any place, you and your households; for it is your 32 reward in return for your service in the tent of meeting. And you shall bear no sin by reason of it, when you have offered the best of it. And you shall not profane the holy things of the people of Israel, lest you die.'"

The Red Heifer

19 Now the LORD said to Moses and to Aaron, "This is the statute of the law which the LORD has commanded: Tell the people of Israel to bring you a red heifer without defect, in which there is no blemish, and upon which a yoke has never 3 come. And you shall give her to Elea'zar the priest, and she shall be taken outside the camp and slaughtered before him; 4 and Elea'zar the priest shall take some of her blood with his finger, and sprinkle some of her blood toward the front of 5 the tent of meeting seven times. And the heifer shall be burned in his sight; her skin, her flesh, and her blood, with her dung, 6 shall be burned; and the priest shall take cedarwood and hyssop and scarlet stuff, and cast them into the midst of the 7 burning of the heifer. Then the priest shall wash his clothes and bathe his body in water, and afterwards he shall come into the camp; and the priest shall be unclean until evening. 8 He who burns the heifer shall wash his clothes in water and bathe his body in water, and shall be unclean until evening. 9 And a man who is clean shall gather up the ashes of the heifer, and deposit them outside the camp in a clean place; and they shall be kept for the congregation of the people of Israel for 10 the water for impurity, for the removal of sin. And he who gathers the ashes of the heifer shall wash his clothes, and be unclean until evening. And this shall be to the people of Israel, and to the stranger who sojourns among them, a perpetual statute.

11 "He who touches the dead body of any person shall be un-12 clean seven days; he shall cleanse himself with the water on the third day and on the seventh day, and so be clean; but if he does not cleanse himself on the third day and on the seventh 13 day, he will not become clean. Whoever touches a dead person, the body of any man who has died, and does not cleanse himself, defiles the tabernacle of the LORD, and that person shall be cut off from Israel; because the water for impurity was not thrown upon him, he shall be unclean; his uncleanness is still on him.

14 "This is the law when a man dies in a tent: every one who comes into the tent, and every one who is in the tent, shall be 15 unclean seven days. And every open vessel, which has no 16 cover fastened upon it, is unclean. Whoever in the open field touches one who is slain with a sword, or a dead body, or a 17 bone of a man, or a grave, shall be unclean seven days. For the unclean they shall take some ashes of the burnt sin offering, 18 and running water shall be added in a vessel; then a clean person shall take hyssop, and dip it in the water, and sprinkle it upon the tent, and upon all the furnishings, and upon the persons who were there, and upon him who touched the bone, 19 or the slain, or the dead, or the grave; and the clean person shall sprinkle upon the unclean on the third day and on the seventh day; thus on the seventh day he shall cleanse him, and

he shall wash his clothes and bathe himself in water, and at evening he shall be clean.
20 "But the man who is unclean and does not cleanse himself, that person shall be cut off from the midst of the assembly, since he has defiled the sanctuary of the LORD; because the water for impurity has not been thrown upon him, he is 21 unclean. And it shall be a perpetual statute for them. He who sprinkles the water for impurity shall wash his clothes; and he who touches the water for impurity shall be unclean until 22 evening. And whatever the unclean person touches shall be unclean; and any one who touches it shall be unclean until evening."

WANDERING IN THE WILDERNESS
March from Kadesh for Moab

20 And the people of Israel, the whole congregation, came into the wilderness of Zin in the first month, and the people stayed in Kadesh; and Miriam died there, and was buried there.

Water from the Rock

2 Now there was no water for the congregation; and they assembled themselves together against Moses and 3 against Aaron. And the people contended with Moses, and said, "Would that we had died when our brethren 4 died before the LORD! Why have you brought the assembly of the LORD into this wilderness, that we should 5 die here, both we and our cattle? And why have you made us come up out of Egypt, to bring us to this evil place? It is no place for grain, or figs, or vines, or 6 pomegranates; and there is no water to drink." Then Moses and Aaron went from the presence of the assembly to the door of the tent of meeting, and fell on their faces. 7 And the glory of the LORD appeared to them, and the

8 LORD said to Moses, "Take the rod, and assemble the congregation, you and Aaron your brother, and tell the rock before their eyes to yield its water; so you shall bring water out of the rock for them; so you shall give 9 drink to the congregation and their cattle." And Moses took the rod from before the LORD, as he commanded him.

10 And Moses and Aaron gathered the assembly together before the rock, and he said to them, "Hear now, you rebels; shall we bring forth water for you out of this 11 rock?" And Moses lifted up his hand and struck the rock with his rod twice; and water came forth abundantly, and 12 the congregation drank, and their cattle. And the LORD said to Moses and Aaron, "Because you did not believe in me, to sanctify me in the eyes of the people of Israel,

therefore you shall not bring this assembly into the land 13 which I have given them." These are the waters of Mer'-ibah,[1] where the people of Israel contended with the LORD, and he showed himself holy among them.

14 Moses sent messengers from Kadesh to the king of Edom, "Thus says your brother Israel: You know all the 15 adversity that has befallen us: how our fathers went down to Egypt, and we dwelt in Egypt a long time; and the 16 Egyptians dealt harshly with us and our fathers; and when we cried to the LORD, he heard our voice, and sent an angel and brought us forth out of Egypt; and here we 17 are in Kadesh, a city on the edge of your territory. Now let us pass through your land. We will not pass through field or vineyard, neither will we drink water from a well; we will go along the King's Highway, we will not turn aside to the right hand or to the left, until we have passed 18 through your territory." But Edom said to him, "You shall not pass through, lest I come out with the sword 19 against you." And the people of Israel said to him, "We will go up by the highway; and if we drink of your water, I and my cattle, then I will pay for it; let me only 20 pass through on foot, nothing more." But he said, "You shall not pass through." And Edom came out against 21 them with many men, and with a strong force. Thus Edom refused to give Israel passage through his territory; so Israel turned away from him.

Death of Aaron

22 And they journeyed from Kadesh, and the people of Israel, the whole congregation, came to Mount Hor. 23 And the LORD said to Moses and Aaron at Mount Hor, 24 on the border of the land of Edom, "Aaron shall be gathered to his people; for he shall not enter the land which I have given to the people of Israel, because you rebelled against my command at the waters of Mer'ibah. 25 Take Aaron and Elea'zar his son, and bring them up to 26 Mount Hor, and strip Aaron of his garments, and put them upon Elea'zar his son; and Aaron shall be gathered 27 to his people, and shall die there." Moses did as the LORD commanded; and they went up Mount Hor in the sight 28 of all the congregation. And Moses stripped Aaron of his garments, and put them upon Elea'zar his son; and Aaron died there on the top of the mountain. Then Moses 29 and Elea'zar came down from the mountain. And when all the congregation saw that Aaron was dead, all the house of Israel wept for Aaron thirty days.

The Bronze Serpent

21 When the Canaanite, the king of Arad, who dwelt in the Negeb, heard that Israel was coming by the way of Atharim, he fought against Israel, and took some 2 of them captive. And Israel vowed a vow to the LORD, and said, "If thou wilt indeed give this people into my 3 hand, then I will utterly destroy their cities." And the LORD hearkened to the voice of Israel, and gave over the Canaanites; and they utterly destroyed them and their cities; so the name of the place was called Hormah.[m]

4 From Mount Hor they set out by the way to the Red Sea, to go around the land of Edom; and the people be- 5 came impatient on the way. And the people spoke against God and against Moses, "Why have you brought us up out of Egypt to die in the wilderness? For there is no food and no water, and we loathe this worthless food." 6 Then the LORD sent fiery serpents among the people, and they bit the people, so that many people of Israel died. 7 And the people came to Moses, and said, "We have sinned, for we have spoken against the LORD and against you; pray to the LORD, that he take away the serpents 8 from us." So Moses prayed for the people. And the LORD said to Moses, "Make a fiery serpent, and set it on a pole; and every one who is bitten, when he sees it, shall live." 9 So Moses made a bronze serpent, and set it on a pole; and if a serpent bit any man, he would look at the bronze serpent and live.

10 And the people of Israel set out, and encamped in 11 Oboth. And they set out from Oboth, and encamped at I'-ye-ab'arim, in the wilderness which is opposite Moab, to- 12 ward the sunrise. From there they set out, and encamped 13 in the Valley of Zered. From there they set out, and en- camped on the other side of the Arnon, which is in the wilderness, that extends from the boundary of the Amorites; for the Arnon is the boundary of Moab, be- 14 tween Moab and the Amorites. Wherefore it is said in the Book of the Wars of the LORD,
"Waheb in Suphah,
    and the valleys of the Arnon,
15 and the slope of the valleys
    that extends to the seat of Ar,
    and leans to the border of Moab."

16 And from there they continued to Beer;[n] that is the well of which the LORD said to Moses, "Gather the people 17 together, and I will give them water." Then Israel sang this song:
"Spring up, O well!—Sing to it!—
18 the well which the princes dug,
    which the nobles of the people delved,
    with the scepter and with their staves."

19 And from the wilderness they went on to Mat'tanah, and from Mat'tanah to Nahal'iel, and from Nahal'iel to 20 Bamoth, and from Bamoth to the valley lying in the region of Moab by the top of Pis'gah which looks down upon the desert.[o]

21 Then Israel sent messengers to Sihon king of the 22 Amorites, saying, "Let me pass through your land; we will not turn aside into field or vineyard; we will not drink the water of a well; we will go by the King's High- 23 way, until we have passed through your territory." But

---

[1] That is *Contention*   [m] Heb *Destruction*   [n] That is *Well*   [o] Or *Jeshimon*

Sihon would not allow Israel to pass through his territory. He gathered all his men together, and went out against Israel to the wilderness, and came to Jahaz, and fought 24 against Israel. And Israel slew him with the edge of the sword, and took possession of his land from the Arnon to the Jabbok, as far as to the Ammonites; for Jazer was 25 the boundary of the Ammonites.p And Israel took all these cities, and Israel settled in all the cities of the 26 Amorites, in Heshbon, and in all its villages. For Heshbon was the city of Sihon the king of the Amorites, who had fought against the former king of Moab and taken all 27 his land out of his hand, as far as the Arnon. Therefore the ballad singers say,

"Come to Heshbon, let it be built, let the city of Sihon be established.

28 For fire went forth from Heshbon, flame from the city of Sihon.

It devoured Ar of Moab,
the lords of the heights of the Arnon.

29 Woe to you, O Moab!
You are undone, O people of Chemosh!
He has made his sons fugitives,
and his daughters captives,
to an Amorite king, Sihon.

30 So their posterity perished from Heshbon,q as far as Dibon,
and we laid waste until fire spread to Med′eba.r"

31, 32 Thus Israel dwelt in the land of the Amorites. And Moses sent to spy out Jazer; and they took its villages, 33 and dispossessed the Amorites that were there. Then they turned and went up by the way to Bashan; and Og the king of Bashan came out against them, he and all his 34 people, to battle at Ed′re-i. But the LORD said to Moses, "Do not fear him; for I have given him into your hand, and all his people, and his land; and you shall do to him as you did to Sihon king of the Amorites, who dwelt at 35 Heshbon." So they slew him, and his sons, and all his people, until there was not one survivor left to him; and they possessed his land.

THE STORY OF BALAAM

22 Then the people of Israel set out, and encamped in the plains of Moab beyond the Jordan at Jericho. 2 And Balak the son of Zippor saw all that Israel had done 3 to the Amorites. And Moab was in great dread of the people, because they were many; Moab was overcome 4 with fear of the people of Israel. And Moab said to the elders of Mid′ian, "This horde will now lick up all that is round about us, as the ox licks up the grass of the field." So Balak the son of Zippor, who was king of Moab 5 at that time, sent messengers to Balaam the son of Be′or at Pethor, which is near the River, in the land of Amaw to call him, saying, "Behold, a people has come out of Egypt; they cover the face of the earth, and they are 6 dwelling opposite me. Come now, curse this people for

me, since they are too mighty for me; perhaps I shall be able to defeat them and drive them from the land; for I know that he whom you bless is blessed, and he whom you curse is cursed."

7 So the elders of Moab and the elders of Mid′ian departed with the fees for divination in their hand; and they came to Balaam, and gave him Balak's message. 8 And he said to them, "Lodge here this night, and I will bring back word to you, as the LORD speaks to me"; so 9 the princes of Moab stayed with Balaam. And God came 10 to Balaam and said, "Who are these men with you?" And Balaam said to God, "Balak the son of Zippor, king of 11 Moab, has sent to me, saying, 'Behold, a people has come out of Egypt, and it covers the face of the earth; now come, curse them for me; perhaps I shall be able to fight 12 against them and drive them out.' " God said to Balaam, "You shall not go with them; you shall not curse the 13 people, for they are blessed." So Balaam rose in the morning, and said to the princes of Balak, "Go to your own land; for the LORD has refused to let me go with 14 you." So the princes of Moab rose and went to Balak, and said, "Balaam refuses to come with us."

15 Once again Balak sent princes, more in number and 16 more honorable than they. And they came to Balaam and said to him, "Thus says Balak the son of Zippor: 17 'Let nothing hinder you from coming to me; for I will surely do you great honor, and whatever you say to me 18 I will do; come, curse this people for me.' " But Balaam answered and said to the servants of Balak, "Though Balak were to give me his house full of silver and gold, I could not go beyond the command of the LORD my God, 19 to do less or more. Pray, now, tarry here this night also, 20 that I may know what more the LORD will say to me." And God came to Balaam at night and said to him, "If the men have come to call you, rise, go with them; but only what I bid you, that shall you do."

21 So Balaam rose in the morning, and saddled his ass, 22 and went with the princes of Moab. But God's anger was kindled because he went; and the angel of the LORD took his stand in the the way as his adversary. Now he was 23 riding on the ass, and his two servants were with him. And the ass saw the angel of the LORD standing in the road, with a drawn sword in his hand; and the ass turned aside out of the road, and went into the field; and Balaam 24 struck the ass, to turn her into the road. Then the angel of the LORD stood in a narrow path between the vine-25 yards, with a wall on either side. And when the ass saw the angel of the LORD, she pushed against the wall, and pressed Balaam's foot against the wall; so he struck her 26 again. Then the angel of the LORD went ahead, and stood in a narrow place, where there was no way to turn either 27 to the right or to the left. When the ass saw the angel of the LORD, she lay down under Balaam; and Balaam's anger was kindled, and he struck the ass with his staff.

p Gk: Heb the boundary of the Ammonites was strong   q Gk: Heb we have shot at them. Heshbon has perished
r Compare Sam and Gk: Heb we have laid waste to Nophah which to Medebah

28 Then the LORD opened the mouth of the ass, and she said to Balaam, "What have I done to you, that you have 29 struck me these three times?" And Balaam said to the ass, "Because you have made sport of me. I wish I had a 30 sword in my hand, for then I would kill you." And the ass said to Balaam, "Am I not your ass, upon which you have ridden all your life long to this day? Was I ever accustomed to do so to you?" And he said, "No." 31 Then the LORD opened the eyes of Balaam, and he saw the angel of the LORD standing in the way, with his drawn sword in his hand; and he bowed his head, and fell on 32 his face. And the angel of the LORD said to him, "Why have you struck your ass these three times? Behold, I have come forth to withstand you, because your way is 33 perverse before me; and the ass saw me, and turned aside before me these three times. If she had not turned aside from me, surely just now I would have slain you and let 34 her live." Then Balaam said to the angel of the LORD, "I have sinned, for I did not know that thou didst stand in the road against me. Now therefore, if it is evil in thy 35 sight, I will go back again." And the angel of the LORD said to Balaam, "Go with the men; but only the word which I bid you, that shall you speak." So Balaam went on with the princes of Balak.

36 When Balak heard that Balaam had come, he went out to meet him at the city of Moab, on the boundary formed by the Arnon, at the extremity of the boundary. 37 And Balak said to Balaam, "Did I not send to you to call you? Why did you not come to me? Am I not able 38 to honor you?" Balaam said to Balak, "Lo, I have come to you! Have I now any power at all to speak anything? The word that God puts in my mouth, that must I speak." 39 Then Balaam went with Balak, and they came to Kir'- 40 iath-hu′zoth. And Balak sacrificed oxen and sheep, and sent to Balaam and to the princes who were with him.

Balaam's Oracles
41 And on the morrow Balak took Balaam and brought him up to Bamoth-ba′al; and from there he saw the 1 **23** nearest of the people. And Balaam said to Balak, "Build for me here seven altars, and provide for me 2 here seven bulls and seven rams." Balak did as Balaam had said; and Balak and Balaam offered on each altar a bull 3 and a ram. And Balaam said to Balak, "Stand beside your burnt offering, and I will go; perhaps the LORD will come to meet me; and whatever he shows me I will tell you." 4 And he went to a bare height. And God met Balaam; and Balaam said to him, "I have prepared the seven altars, and I have offered upon each altar a bull and a ram." 5 And the LORD put a word in Balaam's mouth, and said, 6 "Return to Balak, and thus you shall speak." And he returned to him, and lo, he and all the princes of Moab 7 were standing beside his burnt offering. And Balaam took up his discourse, and said,

"From Aram Balak has brought me, the king of Moab
    from the eastern mountains:
'Come, curse Jacob for me,
    and come, denounce Israel!'
8 How can I curse whom God has not cursed?
    How can I denounce whom the LORD has not de-
        nounced?
9 For from the top of the mountains I see him,
    from the hills I behold him;
lo, a people dwelling alone,
    and not reckoning itself among the nations!
10 Who can count the dust of Jacob,
    or number the fourth part ⁵ of Israel?
Let me die the death of the righteous,
    and let my end be like his!"

11 And Balak said to Balaam, "What have you done to me? I took you to curse my enemies, and behold, you 12 have done nothing but bless them." And he answered, "Must I not take heed to speak what the LORD puts in my mouth?"

13 And Balak said to him, "Come with me to another place, from which you may see them; you shall see only the nearest of them, and shall not see them all; then curse 14 them for me from there." And he took him to the field of Zophim, to the top of Pisgah, and built seven altars, and 15 offered a bull and a ram on each altar. Balaam said to Balak, "Stand here beside your burnt offering, while I 16 meet the LORD yonder." And the LORD met Balaam, and put a word in his mouth, and said, "Return to Balak, and 17 thus shall you speak." And he came to him, and, lo, he was standing beside his burnt offering, and the princes of Moab with him. And Balak said to him, "What has the 18 LORD spoken?" And Balaam took up his discourse, and said,

"Rise, Balak, and hear;
    hearken to me, O son of Zippor:
19 God is not man, that he should lie,
    or a son of man, that he should repent.
Has he said, and will he not do it?
    Or has he spoken, and will he not fulfil it?
20 Behold, I received a command to bless:
    he has blessed, and I cannot revoke it.
21 He has not beheld misfortune in Jacob;
    nor has he seen trouble in Israel.
The LORD their God is with them,
    and the shout of a king is among them.
22 God brings them out of Egypt;
    they have as it were the horns of the wild ox.
23 For there is no enchantment against Jacob,
    no divination against Israel;
now it shall be said of Jacob and Israel,
    'What has God wrought!'
24 Behold, a people! As a lioness it rises up

⁵ Or *dust clouds*

and as a lion it lifts itself;
it does not lie down till it devours the prey,
and drinks the blood of the slain."

25 And Balak said to Balaam, "Neither curse them at all,
26 nor bless them at all." But Balaam answered Balak, "Did
I not tell you, 'All that the LORD says, that I must do'?"
27 And Balak said to Balaam, "Come now, I will take you
to another place; perhaps it will please God that you may
28 curse them for me from there." So Balak took Balaam to
29 the top of Pe'or, that overlooks the desert.ᵗ And Balaam
said to Balak, "Build for me here seven altars, and provide
30 for me here seven bulls and seven rams." And Balak did
as Balaam had said, and offered a bull and a ram on
each altar.

24 When Balaam saw that it pleased the LORD to
bless Israel, he did not go, as at other times, to look
2 for omens, but set his face toward the wilderness. And
Balaam lifted up his eyes, and saw Israel encamping tribe
3 by tribe. And the Spirit of God came upon him, and he
took up his discourse, and said,
"The oracle of Balaam the son of Be'or,
the oracle of the man whose eye is opened,ᵘ
4 the oracle of him who hears the words of God,
who sees the vision of the Almighty,
falling down, but having his eyes uncovered:
5 how fair are your tents, O Jacob,
your encampments, O Israel!
6 Like valleys that stretch afar,
like gardens beside a river,
like aloes that the LORD has planted,
like cedar trees beside the waters.
7 Water shall flow from his buckets,
and his seed shall be in many waters,
his king shall be higher than Agag,
and his kingdom shall be exalted.
8 God brings him out of Egypt;
he has as it were the horns of the wild ox,
he shall eat up the nations his adversaries,
and shall break their bones in pieces,
and pierce them through with his arrows.
9 He couched, he lay down like a lion,
and like a lioness; who will rouse him up?
Blessed be every one who blesses you,
and cursed be every one who curses you."

10 And Balak's anger was kindled against Balaam, and
he struck his hands together; and Balak said to Balaam,
"I called you to curse my enemies, and behold, you have
11 blessed them these three times. Therefore now flee to
your place; I said, 'I will certainly honor you,' but the
12 LORD has held you back from honor." And Balaam said
to Balak, "Did I not tell your messengers whom you sent
13 to me, 'If Balak should give me his house full of silver
and gold, I would not be able to go beyond the word of

LORD, to do either good or bad of my own will; what the
14 LORD speaks, that will I speak'? And now, behold, I am
going to my people; come, I will let you know what this
15 people will do to your people in the latter days." And he
took up his discourse, and said,
"The oracle of Balaam the son of Be'or,
the oracle of the man whose eye is opened,ᵛ

16 the oracle of him who hears the words of God,
and knows the knowledge of the Most High,
who sees the vision of the Almighty,
falling down, but having his eyes uncovered:
17 I see him, but not now;
I behold him, but not nigh:
a star shall come forth out of Jacob,
and a scepter shall rise out of Israel;
it shall crush the foreheadʷ of Moab,
and break down all the sons of Sheth.
18 Edom shall be dispossessed,
Se'ir also, his enemies, shall be dispossessed,
while Israel does valiantly.
19 By Jacob shall dominion be exercised,
and the survivors of cities be destroyed!"
20 Then he looked on Am'a·lek, and took up his discourse,
and said,
"Am'a·lek was the first of the nations,
but in the end he shall come to destruction."
21 And he looked on the Kenite, and took up his discourse,
and said,
"Enduring is your dwelling place,
and your nest is set in the rock;
22 nevertheless Kain shall be wasted.
How long shall Asshur take you away captive?"
23 And he took up his discourse, and said,
"Alas, who shall live when God does this?
24 But ships shall come from Kittim
and shall afflict Asshur and Eber;
and he also shall come to destruction."
25 Then Balaam rose, and went back to his place; and
Balak also went his way.

INCIDENTS AND LAWS
Israel Bows Before Baal
25 While Israel dwelt in Shittim the people began
to play the harlot with the daughters of Moab.

ᵗ Or *Jeshimon*   ᵘ Or *closed* or *perfect*   ᵛ Or *closed* or *perfect*   ʷ Heb *corners* (of the head)

2 These invited the people to the sacrifices of their gods,
3 and the people ate, and bowed down to their gods. So Israel yoked himself to Ba′al of Pe′or. And the anger of
4 the LORD was kindled against Israel; and the LORD said to Moses, "Take all the chiefs of the people, and hang them in the sun before the LORD, that the fierce anger
5 of the LORD may turn away from Israel." And Moses said to the judges of Israel, "Every one of you slay his men who have yoked themselves to Ba′al of Pe′or."

6 And behold, one of the people of Israel came and brought a Mid′ianite woman to his family, in the sight of Moses and in the sight of the whole congregation of the people of Israel, while they were weeping at the door of
7 the tent of meeting. When Phin′ehas the son of Elea′zar, son of Aaron the priest, saw it, he rose and left the congre-
8 gation, and took a spear in his hand and went after the man of Israel into the inner room, and pierced both of them, the man of Israel and the woman, through her body. Thus the plague was stayed from the people of
9 Israel. Nevertheless those that died by the plague were twenty-four thousand.

10, 11 And the LORD said to Moses, "Phine′has the son of Elea′zar, son of Aaron the priest, has turned back my wrath from the people of Israel, in that he was jealous with my jealousy among them, so that I did not consume
12 the people of Israel in my jealousy. Therefore say, 'Be-
13 hold, I give to him my covenant of peace; and it shall be to him, and to his descendants after him, the covenant of a perpetual priesthood, because he was jealous for his God, and made atonement for the people of Israel.'"

14 The name of the slain man of Israel, who was slain with the Mid′ianite woman, was Zimri the son of Salu,
15 head of a fathers' house belonging to the Simeonites. And the name of the Mid′ianite woman who was slain was Cozbi the daughter of Zur, who was the head of the people of a fathers' house in Mid′ian.

16, 17 And the LORD said to Moses, "Harass the Mid′ianites,
18 and smite them; for they have harassed you with their wiles, with which they beguiled you in the matter of Pe′or, and in the matter of Cozbi, the daughter of the prince of Mid′ian, their sister, who was slain on the day of the plague on account of Pe′or."

SECOND CENSUS

26 After the plague the LORD said to Moses and to Elea′zar
2 the son of Aaron, the priest, "Take a census of all the congregation of the people of Israel, from twenty years old and upward, by their fathers' houses, all in Israel who are
3 able to go forth to war." And Moses and Elea′zar the priest spoke with them in the plains of Moab by the Jordan at
4 Jericho, saying, "Take a census of the people,ˣ from twenty years old and upward," as the LORD commanded Moses. The people of Israel, who came forth out of the land of Egypt, were:
5 Reuben, the first-born of Israel; the sons of Reuben: of Hanoch, the family of the Ha′nochites; of Pallu, the family of
6 the Pal′luites; of Hezron, the family of the Hez′ronites; of
7 Carmi, the family of the Carmites. These are the families of the Reubenites; and their number was forty-three thousand
8 seven hundred and thirty. And the sons of Pallu: Eli′ab.

ˣ Supplying *take a census of the people* Compare verse 2

9 The sons of Eli′ab: Nem′u-el, Dathan, and Abi′ram. These are the Dathan and Abi′ram, chosen from the congregation, who contended against Moses and Aaron in the company of Korah,
10 when they contended against the LORD, and the earth opened its mouth and swallowed them up together with Korah, when that company died, when the fire devoured two hundred and
11 fifty men; and they became a warning. Notwithstanding, the sons of Korah did not die.

12 The sons of Simeon according to their families: of Nem′u-el, the family of the Nem′uelites; of Jamin, the family of the
13 Ja′minites; of Jachin, the family of the Ja′chinites; of Zerah, the family of the Zer′ahites; of Sha′ul, the family of the
14 Sha′ulites. These are the families of the Simeonites, twenty-two thousand two hundred.

15 The sons of Gad according to their families: of Zephon, the family of the Ze′phonites; of Haggi, the family of the Haggites;
16 of Shuni, the family of the Shunites; of Ozni, the family of the
17 Oznites; of Eri, the family of the Erites; of Ar′od, the family
18 of the Ar′odites; of Are′li, the family of the Are′lites. These are the families of the sons of Gad according to their number, forty thousand five hundred.

19 The sons of Judah were Er and Onan; and Er and Onan died
20 in the land of Canaan. And the sons of Judah according to their families were: of Shelah, the family of the Shela′nites; of Perez, the family of the Per′ezites; of Zerah, the family of the
21 Zer′ahites. And the sons of Perez were: of Hezron, the family of the Hez′ronites; of Hamul, the family of the Hamu′lites.
22 These are the families of Judah according to their number, seventy-six thousand five hundred.

23 The sons of Is′sachar according to their families: of Tola, the family of the To′laites; of Puvah, the family of the Punites;
24 of Jashub, the family of the Jash′ubites; of Shimron, the family
25 of the Shim′ronites. These are the families of Is′sachar according to their number, sixty-four thousand three hundred.

26 The sons of Zeb′ulun, according to their families: of Sered, the family of the Ser′edites; of Elon, the family of the E′lonites;
27 of Jahleel, the family of the Jah′leelites. These are the families of the Zebu′lunites according to their number, sixty thousand five hundred.

28 The sons of Joseph according to their families: Manas′seh and
29 E′phraim. The sons of Manas′seh: of Machir, the family of the Ma′chirites; and Machir was the father of Gilead; of Gilead,
30 the family of the Gil′eadites. These are the sons of Gilead: of Ie′zer, the family of the Ie′zerites; of Helek, the family of the
31 He′lekites; and of As′riel, the family of the As′rielites; and of
32 Shechem, the family of the She′chemites; and of Shemi′da, the family of the Shemi′daites; and of Hepher, the family of the
33 He′pherites. Now Zelo′phehad the son of Hepher had no sons, but daughters: and the names of the daughters of Zelo′phehad
34 were Mahlah, Noah, Hoglah, Milcah, and Tirzah. These are the families of Manas′seh; and their number was fifty-two thousand seven hundred.

35 These are the sons of E′phraim according to their families: of Shu′thelah, the family of the Shu′thela′hites; of Becher, the family of the Be′cherites; of Tahan, the family of the Ta′hanites.
36 And these are the sons of Shu′thelah: of Eran, the family of
37 the E′ranites. These are the families of the sons of E′phraim according to their number, thirty-two thousand five hundred. These are the sons of Joseph according to their families.

38 The sons of Benjamin according to their families: of Bela, the family of the Be′la-ites; of Ashbel, the family of the
39 Ash′belites; of Ahi′ram, the family of the Ahi′ramites; of Shephu′pham, the family of the Shu′phamites; of Hupham, the
40 family of the Hu′phamites. And the sons of Bela were Ard and Na′aman: of Ard, the family of the Ard′ites; of Na′aman, the
41 family of the Na′amites. These are the sons of Benjamin according to their families; and their number was forty-five thousand six hundred.

42 These are the sons of Dan according to their families: of Shuham, the family of the Shu′hamites. These are the families
43 of Dan according to their families. All the families of the Shu′hamites, according to their number, were sixty-four thousand four hundred.

44 The sons of Asher according to their families: of Imnah, the family of the Imnites; of Ishvi, the family of the Ishvites; of
45 Beri′ah, the family of the Beri′ites. Of the sons of Beri′ah: of Heber, the family of the He′berites; of Mal′chi-el, the family
46 of the Mal′chi-elites. And the name of the daughter of Asher
47 was Serah. These are the families of the sons of Asher according to their number, fifty-three thousand four hundred.

48 The sons of Naph'tali according to their families: of Jahzeel, the family of the Jah'zeelites; of Guni, the family of the 49 Gunites; of Jezer, the family of the Je'zerites; of Shillem, the 50 family of the Shil'lemites. These are the families of Naph'tali according to their families; and their number was forty-five thousand four hundred.

51 This was the number of the people of Israel, six hundred and one thousand seven hundred and thirty.

52, 53 The LORD said to Moses: "To these the land shall be divided 54 for inheritance according to the number of names. To a large tribe you shall give a large inheritance, and to a small tribe you shall give a small inheritance; every tribe shall be given 55 its inheritance according to its numbers. But the land shall be divided by lot; according to the names of the tribes of their 56 fathers they shall inherit. Their inheritance shall be divided according to lot between the larger and the smaller."

57 These are the Levites as numbered according to their families: of Gershon, the family of the Gershonites; of Kohath, the family of the Ko'hathites; of Merar'i, the family of the Merar'- 58 ites. These are the families of Levi: the family of the Libnites, the family of the He'bronites, the family of the Mahlites, the family of the Mushites, the family of the Ko'rahites. And 59 Kohath was the father of Amram. The name of Amram's wife was Joch'ebed the daughter of Levi, who was born to Levi in Egypt; and she bore to Amram Aaron and Moses and Miriam 60 their sister. And to Aaron were born Nadab, Abi'hu, Elea'zar 61 and Ith'amar. But Nadab and Abi'hu died when they offered 62 unholy fire before the LORD. And those numbered of them were twenty-three thousand, every male from a month old and upward; for they were not numbered among the people of Israel, because there was no inheritance given to them among the people of Israel.

63 These were those numbered by Moses and Elea'zar the priest, who numbered the people of Israel in the plains of Moab by 64 the Jordan at Jericho. But among these there was not a man of those numbered by Moses and Aaron the priest, who had 65 numbered the people of Israel in the wilderness of Sinai. For the LORD had said of them, "They shall die in the wilderness." There was not left a man of them, except Caleb the son of Jephun'neh and Joshua the son of Nun.

Law of Female Inheritance

27 Then drew near the daughters of Zelo'phehad the son of Hepher, son of Gilead, son of Machir, son of Manas'seh, from the families of Manas'seh the son of Joseph. The names of his daughters were: Mahlah, Noah, Hoglah, Milcah, and 2 Tirzah. And they stood before Moses, and before Elea'zar the priest, and before the leaders and all the congregation, at the 3 door of the tent of meeting, saying, "Our father died in the wilderness; he was not among the company of those who gathered themselves together against the LORD in the company 4 of Korah, but died for his own sin; and he had no sons. Why should the name of our father be taken away from his family, because he had no son? Give to us a possession among our father's brethren."

5, 6 Moses brought their case before the LORD. And the LORD said 7 to Moses, "The daughters of Zelo'phehad are right; you shall give them possession of an inheritance among their father's brethren and cause the inheritance of their father to pass to 8 them. And you shall say to the people of Israel, 'If a man dies, and has no son, then you shall cause his inheritance to pass 9 to his daughter. And if he has no daughter, then you shall 10 give his inheritance to his brothers. And if he has no brothers, then you shall give his inheritance to his father's brothers. 11 And if his father has no brothers, then you shall give his inheritance to his kinsman that is next to him of his family, and he shall possess it. And it shall be to the people of Israel a statute and ordinance, as the LORD commanded Moses.'"

Appointment of Joshua

12 The LORD said to Moses, "Go up into this mountain of Ab'arim, and see the land which I have given to the people 13 of Israel. And when you have seen it, you also shall be gathered to your people, as your brother Aaron was 14 gathered, because you rebelled against my word in the wilderness of Zin during the strife of the congregation, to sanctify me at the waters before their eyes." (These are the waters of Mer'ibah of Kadesh in the wilderness of 15, 16 Zin.) Moses said to the LORD, "Let the LORD, the God of the spirits of all flesh, appoint a man over the congre- 17 gation, who shall go out before them and come in before them, who shall lead them out and bring them in; that the congregation of the LORD may not be as sheep which 18 have no shepherd." And the LORD said to Moses, "Take Joshua the son of Nun, a man in whom is the spirit, and 19 lay your hand upon him; cause him to stand before Elea'zar the priest and all the congregation, and you shall 20 commission him in their sight. You shall invest him with some of your authority, that all the congregation of the 21 people of Israel may obey. And he shall stand before Elea'zar the priest, who shall inquire for him by the judgment of the Urim before the LORD; at his word they shall go out, and at his word they shall come in, both he and all the people of Israel with him, the whole congregation." 22 And Moses did as the LORD commanded him; he took Joshua and caused him to stand before Elea'zar the priest 23 and the whole congregation, and he laid his hands upon him, and commissioned him as the LORD directed through Moses.

LAWS OF PUBLIC WORSHIP

2 28 The LORD said to Moses, "Command the people of Israel, and say to them, 'My offering, my food for my offerings by fire, my pleasing odor, you shall take heed to offer to me 3 in its due season.' And you shall say to them, This is the offering by fire which you shall offer to the LORD: two male lambs a year old without blemish, day by day, as a continual 4 offering. The one lamb you shall offer in the morning, and the 5 other lamb you shall offer in the evening; also a tenth of an ephah of fine flour for a cereal offering, mixed with a fourth 6 of a hin of beaten oil. It is a continual burnt offering, which was ordained at Mount Sinai for a pleasing odor, an offering 7 by fire to the LORD. Its drink offering shall be a fourth of a hin for each lamb; in the holy place you shall pour out a drink 8 offering of strong drink to the LORD. The other lamb you shall offer in the evening; like the cereal offering of the morning, and like its drink offering, you shall offer it as an offering by fire, a pleasing odor to the LORD.

9 "On the sabbath day two male lambs a year old without blemish, and two tenths of an ephah of fine flour for a cereal 10 offering, mixed with oil, and its drink offering: this is the burnt offering of every sabbath, besides the continual burnt offering and its drink offering.

11 "At the beginnings of your months you shall offer a burnt offering to the LORD: two young bulls, one ram, seven male 12 lambs a year old without blemish; also three tenths of an ephah of fine flour for a cereal offering, mixed with oil, for each bull; and two tenths of fine flour for a cereal offering, mixed with 13 oil, for the one ram; and a tenth of fine flour mixed with oil as a cereal offering for every lamb; for a burnt offering of 14 pleasing odor, an offering by fire to the LORD. Their drink offerings shall be half a hin of wine for a bull, a third of a hin for a ram, and a fourth of a hin for a lamb; this is the burnt offering of each month throughout the months of the 15 year. Also one male goat for a sin offering to the LORD; it shall be offered besides the continual burnt offering and its drink offering.

16 "On the fourteenth day of the first month is the LORD's 17 passover. And on the fifteenth day of this month is a feast; 18 seven days shall unleavened bread be eaten. On the first day there shall be a holy convocation: you shall do no laborious 19 work, but offer an offering by fire, a burnt offering to the LORD: two young bulls, one ram, and seven male lambs a year 20 old; see that they are without blemish; also their cereal offering of fine flour mixed with oil; three tenths of an ephah 21 shall you offer for a bull, and two tenths for a ram; a tenth

22 shall you offer for each of the seven lambs; also one male goat
23 for a sin offering, to make atonement for you. You shall offer
these besides the burnt offering of the morning, which is for a
24 continual burnt offering. In the same way you shall offer
daily, for seven days, the food of an offering by fire, a pleasing
odor to the LORD; it shall be offered besides the continual burnt
25 offering and its drink offering. And on the seventh day you
shall have a holy convocation; you shall do no laborious work.
26 "On the day of the first fruits, when you offer a cereal offering of new grain to the LORD at your feast of weeks, you shall
27 have a holy convocation; you shall do no laborious work, but
offer a burnt offering, a pleasing odor to the LORD: two young
28 bulls, one ram, seven male lambs a year old; also their cereal
offering of fine flour mixed with oil, three tenths of an ephah
29 for each bull, two tenths for one ram, a tenth for each of the
30 seven lambs; with one male goat, to make atonement for you.
31 Besides the continual burnt offering and its cereal offering, you
shall offer them and their drink offering. See that they are
without blemish.

29 "On the first day of the seventh month you shall have a
holy convocation; you shall do no laborious work. It is a
2 day for you to blow the trumpets, and you shall offer a burnt
offering, a pleasing odor to the LORD: one young bull, one ram,
3 seven male lambs a year old without blemish; also their cereal
offering of fine flour mixed with oil, three tenths of an ephah
4 for the bull, two tenths for the ram, and one tenth for each of
5 the seven lambs; with one male goat for a sin offering, to make
6 atonement for you; besides the burnt offering of the new
moon, and its cereal offering, and the continual burnt offering
and its cereal offering, and their drink offering, according to
the ordinance for them, a pleasing odor, an offering by fire to
the LORD.
7 "On the tenth day of this seventh month you shall have a
holy convocation, and afflict yourselves; you shall do no work,
8 but you shall offer a burnt offering to the LORD, a pleasing
odor: one young bull, one ram, seven male lambs a year old;
9 they shall be to you without blemish; and their cereal offering
of fine flour mixed with oil, three tenths of an ephah for the
10 bull, two tenths for the one ram, a tenth for each of the seven
11 lambs: also one male goat for a sin offering, besides the sin
offering of atonement, and the continual burnt offering and its
cereal offering, and their drink offerings.
12 "On the fifteenth day of the seventh month you shall have a
holy convocation; you shall do no laborious work, and you
13 shall keep a feast to the LORD seven days; and you shall offer
a burnt offering, an offering by fire, a pleasing odor to the
LORD, thirteen young bulls, two rams, fourteen male lambs a
14 year old; they shall be without blemish; and their cereal offering of fine flour mixed with oil, three tenths of an ephah for
each of the thirteen bulls, two tenths for each of the two rams,
15, 16 and a tenth for each of the fourteen lambs; also one male goat
for a sin offering, besides the continual burnt offering, its cereal
offering and its drink offering.
17 "On the second day twelve young bulls, two rams, fourteen
18 male lambs a year old without blemish, with the cereal offering
and the drink offerings for the bulls, for the rams, and for the
19 lambs, by number, according to the ordinance; also one male
goat for a sin offering, besides the continual burnt offering
and its cereal offering, and their drink offerings.
20 "On the third day eleven bulls, two rams, fourteen male
21 lambs a year old without blemish, with the cereal offering and
the drink offerings for the bulls, for the rams, and for the
22 lambs, by number, according to the ordinance; also one male
goat for a sin offering, besides the continual burnt offering
and its cereal offering and its drink offering.
23 "On the fourth day ten bulls, two rams, fourteen male lambs
24 a year old without blemish, with the cereal offering and the
drink offerings for the bulls, for the rams, and for the lambs,
25 by number, according to the ordinance; also one male goat for
a sin offering, besides the continual burnt offering, its cereal
offering and its drink offering.
26 "On the fifth day nine bulls, two rams, fourteen male lambs
27 a year old without blemish, with the cereal offering and the
drink offerings for the bulls, for the rams, and for the lambs,
28 by number, according to the ordinance; also one male goat for
a sin offering; besides the continual burnt offerings and its
cereal offering and its drink offering.
29 "On the sixth day eight bulls, two rams, fourteen male lambs
30 a year old without blemish, with the cereal offering and the
drink offerings for the bulls, for the rams, and for the lambs,

31 by number, according to the ordinance; also one male goat for
a sin offering; besides the continual burnt offering, its cereal
offering, and its drink offerings.
32 "On the seventh day seven bulls, two rams, fourteen male
33 lambs a year old without blemish, with the cereal offering and
the drink offerings for the bulls, for the rams, and for the
34 lambs, by number, according to the ordinance; also one male
goat for a sin offering; besides the continual burnt offering, its
cereal offering, and its drink offering.
35 "On the eighth day you shall have a solemn assembly: you
36 shall do no laborious work, but you shall offer a burnt offering,
an offering by fire, a pleasing odor to the LORD: one bull, one
37 ram, seven male lambs a year old without blemish, and the
cereal offering and the drink offerings for the bull, for the ram,
and for the lambs, by number, according to the ordinance;
38 also one male goat for a sin offering; besides the continual
burnt offering and its cereal offering and its drink offering.
39 "These you shall offer to the LORD at your appointed feasts,
in addition to your votive offerings and your freewill offerings,
for your burnt offerings, and for your cereal offerings, and for
your drink offerings, and for your peace offerings."
40 y And Moses told the people of Israel everything just as the
LORD had commanded Moses.

THE LAW ON WOMAN'S VOWS

30 Moses said to the heads of the tribes of the people of
2 Israel, "This is what the LORD has commanded. When a
man vows a vow to the LORD, or swears an oath to bind himself by a pledge, he shall not break his word; he shall do
3 according to all that proceeds out of his mouth. Or when a
woman vows a vow to the LORD, and binds herself by a pledge,
4 while within her father's house, in her youth, and her father
hears of her vow and of her pledge by which she has bound
herself, and says nothing to her; then all her vows shall stand,
and every pledge by which she has bound herself shall stand.
5 But if her father expresses disapproval to her on the day that
he hears of it, no vow of hers, no pledge by which she has
bound herself, shall stand; and the LORD will forgive her, be-
6 cause her father opposed her. And if she is married to a husband, while under her vows or any thoughtless utterance of
7 her lips by which she has bound herself, and her husband hears
of it, and says nothing to her on the day that he hears; then
her vows shall stand, and her pledges by which she has bound
8 herself shall stand. But if, on the day that her husband comes
to hear of it, he expresses disapproval, then he shall make
void her vow which was on her, and the thoughtless utterance
of her lips, by which she bound herself; and the LORD will
9 forgive her. But any vow of a widow or of a divorced woman,
anything by which she has bound herself, shall stand against
10 her. And if she vowed in her husband's house, or bound herself
11 by a pledge with an oath, and her husband heard of it, and
said nothing to her, and did not oppose her; then all her vows
shall stand, and every pledge by which she bound herself shall
12 stand. But if her husband makes them null and void on the
day that he hears them, then whatever proceeds out of her
lips concerning her vows, or concerning her pledge of herself,
shall not stand: her husband has made them void, and the
13 LORD will forgive her. Any vow and any binding oath to afflict
herself, her husband may establish, or her husband may make
14 void. But if her husband says nothing to her from day to day,
then he establishes all her vows, or all her pledges, that are
upon her; he has established them, because he said nothing to
15 her on the day that he heard of them. But if he makes them
null and void after he has heard of them, then he shall bear
her iniquity."
16 These are the statutes which the LORD commanded Moses, as
between a man and his wife, and between a father and his
daughter, while in her youth, within her father's house.

SPOILS OF WAR

2 31 The LORD said to Moses, "Avenge the people of Israel
on the Mid′ianites; afterward you shall be gathered to
3 your people." And Moses said to the people, "Arm men from
among you for the war, that they may go against Mid′ian, to
4 execute the LORD's vengeance on Mid′ian. You shall send a thou-
5 sand from each of the tribes of Israel to the war." So there were
provided, out of the thousands of Israel, a thousand from each
6 tribe, twelve thousand armed for war. And Moses sent them to
the war, a thousand from each tribe, together with Phin′ehas

y Ch 30. 1 in Heb

the son of Elea'zar the priest, with the vessels of the sanctuary ⁷ and the trumpets for the alarm in his hand. They warred against Mid'ian, as the LORD commanded Moses, and slew every ⁸ male. They slew the kings of Mid'ian with the rest of their slain, Evi, Rekem, Zur, Hur, and Reba, the five kings of Mid'ian; and they also slew Balaam the son of Be'or with the ⁹ sword. And the people of Israel took captive the women of Mid'ian and their little ones; and they took as booty all their ¹⁰ cattle, their flocks, and all their goods. All their cities in the places where they dwelt, and all their encampments, they ¹¹ burned with fire, and took all the spoil and all the booty, both ¹² of man and of beast. Then they brought the captives and the booty and the spoil to Moses, and to Elea'zar the priest, and to the congregation of the people of Israel, at the camp on the plains of Moab by the Jordan at Jericho.

¹³ Moses, and Elea'zar the priest, and all the leaders of the congregation, went forth to meet them outside the camp. ¹⁴ And Moses was angry with the officers of the army, the commanders of thousands and the commanders of hundreds, who ¹⁵ had come from service in the war. Moses said to them, "Have ¹⁶ you let all the women live? Behold, these caused the people of Israel, by the counsel of Balaam, to act treacherously against the LORD in the matter of Pe'or, and so the plague came among ¹⁷ the congregation of the LORD. Now therefore, kill every male among the little ones, and kill every woman who has known ¹⁸ man by lying with him. But all the young girls who have not known man by lying with him, keep alive for yourselves. ¹⁹ Encamp outside the camp seven days; whoever of you has killed any person, and whoever has touched any slain, purify yourselves and your captives on the third day and on the ²⁰ seventh day. You shall purify every garment, every article of skin, all work of goats' hair, and every article of wood."

²¹ And Elea'zar the priest said to the men of war who had gone to battle: "This is the statute of the law which the LORD has ²² commanded Moses: only the gold, the silver, the bronze, the ²³ iron, the tin, and the lead, everything that can stand the fire, you shall pass through the fire, and it shall be clean. Nevertheless it shall also be purified with the water of impurity; and whatever cannot stand the fire, you shall pass through the ²⁴ water. You must wash your clothes on the seventh day, and you shall be clean; and afterward you shall come into the camp."

²⁵, ²⁶ The LORD said to Moses, "Take the count of the booty that was taken, both of man and of beast, you and Elea'zar the priest and the heads of the fathers' houses of the congregation; ²⁷ and divide the booty into two parts, between the warriors who ²⁸ went out to battle and all the congregation. And levy for the LORD a tribute from the men of war who went out to battle, one out of five hundred, of the persons and of the oxen and ²⁹ of the asses and of the flocks; take it from their half, and give ³⁰ it to Elea'zar the priest as an offering to the LORD. And from the people of Israel's half you shall take one drawn out of every fifty, of the persons, of the oxen, of the asses, and of the flocks, of all the cattle, and give them to the Levites who ³¹ have charge of the tabernacle of the LORD." And Moses and Elea'zar the priest did as the LORD commanded Moses.

³² Now the booty remaining of the spoil that the men of war took was: six hundred and seventy-five thousand sheep, ³³, ³⁴, ³⁵ seventy-two thousand cattle, sixty-one thousand asses, and thirty-two thousand persons in all, women who had not known ³⁶ man by lying with him. And the half, the portion of those who had gone out to war, was in number three hundred and thirty-³⁷ seven thousand five hundred sheep, and the LORD's tribute of ³⁸ sheep was six hundred and seventy-five. The cattle were thirty-six thousand, of which the LORD's tribute was seventy-two. ³⁹ The asses were thirty thousand five hundred, of which the ⁴⁰ LORD's tribute was sixty-one. The persons were sixteen thousand, ⁴¹ of which the LORD's tribute was thirty-two persons. And Moses gave the tribute, which was the offering for the LORD, to Elea'zar the priest, as the LORD commanded Moses.

⁴² From the people of Israel's half, which Moses separated from ⁴³ that of the men who had gone to war—now the congregation's half was three hundred and thirty-seven thousand five hundred ⁴⁴, ⁴⁵ sheep, thirty-six thousand cattle, and thirty thousand five ⁴⁶, ⁴⁷ hundred asses, and sixteen thousand persons—from the people of Israel's half Moses took one of every fifty, both of persons and of beasts, and gave them to the Levites who had charge of the tabernacle of the LORD; as the LORD commanded Moses.

⁴⁸ Then the officers who were over the thousands of the army, the captains of thousands and the captains of hundreds, came ⁴⁹ near to Moses, and said to Moses, "Your servants have counted the men of war who are under our command, and there is not ⁵⁰ a man missing from us. And we have brought the LORD's offering, what each man found, articles of gold, armlets and bracelets, signet rings, earrings, and beads, to make atonement ⁵¹ for ourselves before the LORD." And Moses and Elea'zar the ⁵² priest received from them the gold, all wrought articles. And all the gold of the offering that they offered to the LORD, from the commanders of thousands and the commanders of hundreds, was sixteen thousand seven hundred and fifty shekels. ⁵³ (The men of war had taken booty, every man for himself.) ⁵⁴ And Moses and Elea'zar the priest received the gold from the commanders of thousands and of hundreds, and brought it into the tent of meeting, as a memorial for the people of Israel before the LORD.

SETTLEMENT OF TRIBES

32 Now the sons of Reuben and the sons of Gad had a very great multitude of cattle; and they saw the land of Jazer and the land of Gilead, and behold, the place was a place for ² cattle. So the sons of Gad and the sons of Reuben came and said to Moses and to Elea'zar the priest and to the leaders of ³ the congregation, "At'aroth, Dibon, Jazer, Nimrah, Heshbon, ⁴ Elea'leh, Sebam, Nebo, and Be'on, the land which the LORD smote before the congregation of Israel, is a land for cattle; ⁵ and your servants have cattle." And they said, "If we have found favor in your sight, let this land be given to your servants for a possession; do not take us across the Jordan." ⁶ But Moses said to the sons of Gad and to the sons of Reuben, ⁷ "Shall your brethren go to the war while you sit here? Why will you discourage the heart of the people of Israel from ⁸ going over into the land which the LORD has given them? Thus did your fathers, when I sent them from Ka'desh-bar'nea to ⁹ see the land. For when they went up to the Valley of Eshcol, and saw the land, they discouraged the heart of the people of Israel from going into the land which the LORD had given them. ¹⁰ And the LORD's anger was kindled on that day, and he swore, ¹¹ saying, 'Surely none of the men who came up out of Egypt, from twenty years old and upward, shall see the land which I swore to give to Abraham, to Isaac, and to Jacob, because ¹² they have not wholly followed me; none except Caleb the son of Jephun'neh the Ken'izzite and Joshua the son of Nun, ¹³ for they have wholly followed the LORD.' And the LORD's anger was kindled against Israel, and he made them wander in the wilderness forty years, until all the generation that had done ¹⁴ evil in the sight of the LORD was consumed. And behold, you have risen in your fathers' stead, a brood of sinful men, to increase still more the fierce anger of the LORD against Israel! ¹⁵ For if you turn away from following him, he will again abandon them in the wilderness; and you will destroy all this people."

¹⁶ Then they came near to him, and said, "We will build sheep-¹⁷ folds here for our flocks, and cities for our little ones, but we will take up arms, ready to go before the people of Israel, until we have brought them to their place; and our little ones shall ¹⁸ live in the fortified cities because of the inhabitants of the land. We will not return to our homes until the people of ¹⁹ Israel have inherited each his inheritance. For we will not inherit with them on the other side of the Jordan and beyond; because our inheritance has come to us on this side of the ²⁰ Jordan to the east." So Moses said to them, "If you will do this, if you will take up arms to go before the LORD for the ²¹ war, and every armed man of you will pass over the Jordan before the LORD, until he has driven out his enemies from ²² before him and the land is subdued before the LORD; then after that you shall return and be free of obligation to the LORD and to Israel; and this land shall be your possession before the ²³ LORD. But if you will not do so, behold, you have sinned against ²⁴ the LORD; and be sure your sin will find you out. Build cities for your little ones, and folds for your sheep; and do what you ²⁵ have promised." And the sons of Gad and the sons of Reuben said to Moses, "Your servants will do as my lord commands. ²⁶ Our little ones, our wives, our flocks, and all our cattle, shall ²⁷ remain there in the cities of Gilead; but your servants will pass over, every man who is armed for war, before the LORD to battle, as my lord orders."

²⁸ So Moses gave command concerning them to Elea'zar the priest, and to Joshua the son of Nun, and to the heads of the ²⁹ fathers' houses of the tribes of the people of Israel. And Moses said to them, "If the sons of Gad and the sons of Reuben,

every man who is armed to battle before the LORD, will pass with you over the Jordan and the land shall be subdued before you, then you shall give them the land of Gilead for a posses-
30 sion; but if they will not pass over with you armed, they shall
31 have possessions among you in the land of Canaan." And the sons of Gad and the sons of Reuben answered, "As the LORD
32 has said to your servants, so we will do. We will pass over armed before the LORD into the land of Canaan, and the possession of our inheritance shall remain with us beyond the Jordan."
33 And Moses gave to them, to the sons of Gad and to the sons of Reuben and to the half-tribe of Manas'seh the son of Joseph, the kingdom of Sihon king of the Amorites and the kingdom of Og king of Bashan, the land and its cities with their terri-
34 tories, the cities of the land throughout the country. And the
35 sons of Gad built Dibon, At'aroth, Aro'er, At'roth-sho'phan,
36 Jazer, Jog'behah, Beth-nim'rah and Beth-har'an, fortified cities,
37 and folds for sheep. And the sons of Reuben built Heshbon,
38 Elea'leh, Kiriatha'im, Nebo, and Ba'al-me'on (their names to be changed), and Sibmah; and they gave other names to the
39 cities which they built. And the sons of Machir the son of Manas'seh went to Gilead and took it, and dispossessed the
40 Amorites who were in it. And Moses gave Gilead to Machir
41 the son of Manas'seh, and he settled in it. And Ja'ir the son of Manas'seh went and took their villages, and called them
42 Hav'voth-ja'ir.ᶻ And Nobah went and took Kenath and its villages, and called it Nobah, after his own name.

RECAPITULATION
Route from Egypt to Canaan

33 These are the stages of the people of Israel, when they went forth out of the land of Egypt by their hosts under
2 the leadership of Moses and Aaron. Moses wrote down their starting places, stage by stage, by command of the LORD; and
3 these are their stages according to their starting places. They set out from Ram'eses in the first month, on the fifteenth day of the first month; on the day after the passover the people of Israel went out triumphantly in the sight of all the Egyp-
4 tians, while the Egyptians were burying all their first-born, whom the LORD had struck down among them; upon their gods also the LORD executed judgments.
5 So the people of Israel set out from Ram'eses, and encamped
6 at Succoth. And they set out from Succoth, and encamped at
7 Etham, which is on the edge of the wilderness. And they set out from Etham, and turned back to Pi-hahi'roth, which is east
8 of Ba'al-ze'phon; and they encamped before Migdol. And they set out from before Hahi'roth, and passed through the midst of the sea into the wilderness, and they went a three days' journey in the wilderness of Etham, and encamped at Marah.
9 And they set out from Marah, and came to Elim; at Elim there were twelve springs of water and seventy palm trees,
10 and they encamped there. And they set out from Elim, and en-
11 camped by the Red Sea. And they set out from the Red Sea, and
12 encamped in the wilderness of Sin. And they set out from the
13 wilderness of Sin, and encamped at Dophkah. And they set out
14 from Dophkah, and encamped at Alush. And they set out from Alush, and encamped at Reph'idim, where there was no
15 water for the people to drink. And they set out from Reph'idim,
16 and encamped in the wilderness of Sinai. And they set out from the wilderness of Sinai, and encamped at Kib'roth-hatta'-
17 avah. And they set out from Kib'roth-hatta'avah, and encamped
18 at Haze'roth. And they set out from Haze'roth, and encamped
19 at Rithmah. And they set out from Rithmah, and encamped at
20 Rim'mon-per'ez. And they set out from Rim'mon-per'ez, and
21 encamped at Libnah. And they set out from Libnah, and en-
22 camped at Rissah. And they set out from Rissah, and encamped
23 at Kehela'thah. And they set out from Kehela'thah, and en-
24 camped at Mount Shepher. And they set out from Mount
25 Shepher, and encamped at Hara'dah. And they set out from
26 Hara'dah, and encamped at Makhe'loth. And they set out from
27 Makhe'loth, and encamped at Tahath. And they set out from
28 Tahath, and encamped at Terah. And they set out from Terah,
29 and encamped at Mithkah. And they set out from Mithkah,
30 and encamped at Hashmo'nah. And they set out from Hashmo'-
31 nah, and encamped at Mose'roth. And they set out from Mose'-
32 roth, and encamped at Bene-ja'akan. And they set out from
33 Bene-ja'akan, and encamped at Hor-haggid'gad. And they set
34 out from Hor-haggid'gad, and encamped at Jot'bathah. And
35 they set out from Jot'bathah, and encamped at Abro'nah. And

they set out from Abro'nah, and encamped at E'zion-ge'ber.
36 And they set out from E'zion-ge'ber, and encamped in the
37 wilderness of Zin (that is, Kadesh). And they set out from Kadesh, and encamped at Mount Hor, on the edge of the land of Edom.
38 And Aaron the priest went up Mount Hor at the command of the LORD, and died there, in the fortieth year after the people of Israel had come out of the land of Egypt, on the first day

39 of the fifth month. And Aaron was a hundred and twenty-three years old when he died on Mount Hor.
40 And the Canaanite, the king of Arad, who dwelt in the Negeb in the land of Canaan, heard of the coming of the people of Israel.
41 And they set out from Mount Hor, and encamped at Zalmo'-
42 nah. And they set out from Zalmo'nah, and encamped at
43 Punon. And they set out from Punon, and encamped at Oboth.
44 And they set out from Oboth, and encamped at I'ye-ab'arim, in
45 the territory of Moab. And they set out from I'yim, and en-
46 camped at Dibon-gad. And they set out from Dibon-gad, and
47 encamped at Al'mon-diblatha'im. And they set out from Al'-mon-diblatha'im, and encamped in the mountains of Ab'arim,
48 before Nebo. And they set out from the mountains of Ab'arim, and encamped in the plains of Moab by the Jordan at Jericho;
49 they encamped by the Jordan from Beth-jes'himoth as far as Abel-shittim in the plains of Moab.

Israel's Duty to Canaan

50 And the LORD said to Moses in the plains of Moab by the
51 Jordan at Jericho, "Say to the people of Israel, When you pass
52 over the Jordan into the land of Canaan, then you shall drive out all the inhabitants of the land from before you, and destroy all their figured stones, and destroy all their molten images,
53 and demolish all their high places; and you shall take possession of the land and settle in it, for I have given the land to you
54 to possess it. You shall inherit the land by lot according to your families; to a large tribe you shall give a large inheritance, and to a small tribe you shall give a small inheritance; wherever the lot falls to any man, that shall be his; according to
55 the tribes of your fathers you shall inherit. But if you do not drive out the inhabitants of the land from before you, then those of them whom you let remain shall be as pricks in your eyes and thorns in your sides, and they shall trouble you in
56 the land where you dwell. And I will do to you as I thought to do to them."

Tribal Boundaries in Canaan

2 **34** The LORD said to Moses, "Command the people of Israel, and say to them, When you enter the land of Canaan (this is the land that shall fall to you for an inheritance, the
3 land of Canaan in its full extent), your south side shall be from the wilderness of Zin along the side of Edom, and your southern boundary shall be from the end of the Salt Sea on
4 the east; and your boundary shall turn south of the ascent of Akrab'bim, and cross to Zin, and its end shall be south of Ka'desh-bar'nea; then it shall go on to Ha'zar-ad'dar, and pass
5 along to Azmon; and the boundary shall turn from Azmon to the Brook of Egypt, and its termination shall be at the sea.
6 "For the western boundary, you shall have the Great Sea and its ᵃ coast; this shall be your western boundary.
7 "This shall be your northern boundary: from the Great Sea
8 you shall mark out your line to Mount Hor; from Mount Hor you shall mark it out to the entrance of Hamath, and the end
9 of the boundary shall be at Zedad; then the boundary shall extend to Ziphron, and its end shall be at Hazar-enan; this shall be your northern boundary.
10 "You shall mark out your eastern boundary from Hazar-enan
11 to Shepham; and the boundary shall go down from Shepham to Riblah on the east side of A'in; and the boundary shall go

ᶻ That is the villages of Jair   ᵃ Syr: Heb lacks its

down, and reach to the shoulder of the sea of Chin'nereth on
12 the east; and the boundary shall go down to the Jordan, and its end shall be at the Salt Sea. This shall be your land with its boundaries all round."
13 Moses commanded the people of Israel, saying, "This is the land which you shall inherit by lot, which the LORD has com-
14 manded to give to the nine tribes and to the half-tribe; for the tribe of the sons of Reuben by fathers' houses and the tribe of the sons of Gad by their fathers' houses have received
15 their inheritance, and also the half-tribe of Manas'seh; the two tribes and the half-tribe have received their inheritance beyond the Jordan at Jericho eastward, toward the sunrise."
16, 17 The LORD said to Moses, "These are the names of the men who shall divide the land to you for inheritance: Elea'zar the
18 priest and Joshua the son of Nun. You shall take one leader
19 of every tribe, to divide the land for inheritance. These are the names of the men: Of the tribe of Judah, Caleb the son
20 of Jephun'neh. Of the tribe of the sons of Simeon, Shemu'el
21 the son of Ammi'hud. Of the tribe of Benjamin, Eli'dad the
22 son of Chislon. Of the tribe of the sons of Dan a leader, Bukki
23 the son of Jogli. Of the sons of Joseph: of the tribe of the
24 sons of Manas'seh a leader, Han'niel the son of Ephod. And of the tribe of the sons of E'phraim a leader, Kemu'el the son of
25 Shiphtan. Of the tribe of the sons of Zeb'ulun a leader, Eliz'-
26 aphan the son of Parnach. Of the tribe of the sons of Is'sachar
27 a leader, Pal'tiel the son of Azzan. And of the tribe of the sons
28 of Asher a leader, Ahi'hud the son of Shelo'mi. Of the tribe of the sons of Naph'tali a leader, Pedah'el the son of Ammi'hud.
29 These are the men whom the LORD commanded to divide the inheritance for the people of Israel in the land of Canaan."

Cities for Levites

35 The LORD said to Moses in the plains of Moab by the
2 Jordan at Jericho, "Command the people of Israel, that they give to the Levites, from the inheritance of their posses-sion, cities to dwell in; and you shall give to the Levites
3 pasture lands round about the cities. The cities shall be theirs to dwell in, and their pasture lands shall be for their cattle and
4 for their livestock and for all their beasts. The pasture lands of the cities, which you shall give to the Levites, shall reach from
5 the wall of the city outward a thousand cubits all round. And you shall measure, outside the city, for the east side two thousand cubits, and for the south side two thousand cubits, and for the west side two thousand cubits, and for the north side two thousand cubits, the city being in the middle; this
6 shall belong to them as pasture land for their cities. The cities which you give to the Levites shall be the six cities of refuge, where you shall permit the manslayer to flee, and in addition
7 to them you shall give forty-two cities. All the cities which you give to the Levites shall be forty-eight, with their pasture
8 lands. And as for the cities which you shall give from the pos-session of the people of Israel, from the larger tribes you shall take many, and from the smaller tribes you shall take few; each, in proportion to the inheritance which it inherits, shall give of its cities to the Levites."

Cities of Refuge

9, 10 And the LORD said to Moses, "Say to the people of Israel,
11 When you cross the Jordan into the land of Canaan, then you shall select cities to be cities of refuge for you, that the man-
12 slayer who kills any person without intent may flee there. The cities shall be for you a refuge from the avenger, that the manslayer may not die until he stands before the congregation
13 for judgment. And the cities which you give shall be your
14 six cities of refuge. You shall give three cities beyond the Jordan, and three cities in the land of Canaan, to be cities of
15 refuge. These six cities shall be for refuge for the people of Israel, and for the stranger and for the sojourner among them, that any one who kills any person without intent may flee there.
16 "But if he struck him down with an instrument of iron, so that he died, he is a murderer; the murderer shall be put to
17 death. And if he struck him down with a stone in the hand, by which a man may die, and he died, he is a murderer; the
18 murderer shall be put to death. Or if he struck him down with a weapon of wood in the hand, by which a man may die, and he died, he is a murderer; the murderer shall be put to death.
19 The avenger of blood shall himself put the murderer to death;
20 when he meets him, he shall put him to death. And if he stabbed him from hatred, or hurled at him, lying in wait, so

21 that he died, or in enmity struck him down with his hand, so that he died, then he who struck the blow shall be put to death; he is a murderer; the avenger of blood shall put the murderer to death, when he meets him.
22 "But if he stabbed him suddenly without enmity, or hurled
23 anything on him without lying in wait, or used a stone, by which a man may die, and without seeing him cast it upon him, so that he died, though he was not his enemy, and did not
24 seek his harm; then the congregation shall judge between the manslayer and the avenger of blood, in accordance with these
25 ordinances; and the congregation shall rescue the manslayer from the hand of the avenger of blood, and the congregation shall restore him to his city of refuge, to which he had fled, and he shall live in it until the death of the high priest who was
26 anointed with the holy oil. But if the manslayer shall at any time go beyond the bounds of his city of refuge to which he
27 fled, and the avenger of blood finds him outside the bounds of his city of refuge, and the avenger of blood slays the man-
28 slayer, he shall not be guilty of blood. For the man must remain in his city of refuge until the death of the high priest; but after the death of the high priest the manslayer may return to the land of his possession.
29 "And these things shall be for a statute and ordinance to you
30 throughout your generations in all your dwellings. If any one kills a person, the murderer shall be put to death on the evidence of witnesses; but no person shall be put to death on
31 the testimony of one witness. Moreover you shall accept no ransom for the life of a murderer, who is guilty of death; but
32 he shall be put to death. And you shall accept no ransom for him who has fled to his city of refuge, that he may return to
33 dwell in the land before the death of the high priest. You shall not thus pollute the land in which you live; for blood pollutes the land, and no expiation can be made for the land, for the blood that is shed in it, except by the blood of him who shed
34 it. You shall not defile the land in which you live, in the midst of which I dwell; for I the LORD dwell in the midst of the people of Israel."

Inheritance of Daughters

36 The heads of the fathers' houses of the families of the sons of Gilead the son of Machir, son of Manas'seh, of the fathers' houses of the sons of Joseph, came near and spoke before Moses and before the leaders, the heads of the fathers'
2 houses of the people of Israel; they said, "The LORD commanded my lord to give the land for inheritance by lot to the people of Israel; and my lord was commanded by the LORD to give the
3 inheritance of Zelo'phehad our brother to his daughters. But if they are married to any of the sons of the other tribes of the people of Israel then their inheritance will be taken from the inheritance of our fathers, and added to the inheritance of the tribe to which they belong; so it will be taken away
4 from the lot of our inheritance. And when the jubilee of the people of Israel comes, then their inheritance will be added to the inheritance of the tribe to which they belong; and their inheritance will be taken from the inheritance of the tribe of our fathers."
5 And Moses commanded the people of Israel according to the word of the LORD, saying, "The tribe of the sons of Joseph is
6 right. This is what the LORD commands concerning the daughters of Zelo'phehad, 'Let them marry whom they think best; only, they shall marry within the family of the tribe of their father.
7 The inheritance of the people of Israel shall not be transferred from one tribe to another; for every one of the people of Israel
8 shall cleave to the inheritance of the tribe of his fathers. And every daughter who possesses an inheritance in any tribe of the people of Israel shall be wife to one of the family of the tribe of her father, so that every one of the people of Israel
9 may possess the inheritance of his fathers. So no inheritance shall be transferred from one tribe to another; for each of the tribes of the people of Israel shall cleave to its own in-heritance.' "
10 The daughters of Zelo'phehad did as the LORD commanded
11 Moses; for Mahlah, Tirzah, Hoglah, Milcah, and Noah, the daughters of Zelo'phehad, were married to sons of their father's
12 brothers. They were married into the families of the sons of Manas'seh the son of Joseph, and their inheritance remained in the tribe of the family of their father.
13 These are the commandments and the ordinances which the LORD commanded by Moses to the people of Israel in the plains of Moab by the Jordan at Jericho.

INTRODUCTION TO

DEUTERONOMY

The Book of Deuteronomy gets its name from two Greek words that mean "second law" because Deuteronomy states again the Ten Commandments, which had already been written down in the Book of Exodus.

Deuteronomy continues the story of the wanderings of the Hebrews in the desert. It tells how Moses finally had to give up as leader and send his people on their journey without him. Because Moses was their greatest hero and lawgiver, this entire second law book is written as if it were a long farewell speech of Moses to his people just before they went into Canaan, their "promised land."

The great men who wrote this book were devout worshipers of God. They remembered how they had been inspired by the courageous preaching of the prophets Amos, Hosea, Isaiah, and Micah. This Book of Deuteronomy was intended to apply the inspired teachings of these great prophets to the everyday life of the nation. Naturally it gives many new rules by which the Hebrews were to live.

Evidently Deuteronomy was lost sight of for many years after it was written. Second Kings 22 and 23 tells how it was found when repairs were being made on the Temple in Jerusalem in 621 B.C. The discovery of the scrolls of the second law helped King Josiah and the people correct some of their sinful ways and begin a reform of their country.

This book contains a famous statement of the great law that the people should be loyal to the one true God. This passage was quoted by Jesus as the first and great commandment: "Hear, O Israel: The Lord our God is one Lord; and you shall love the Lord your God with all your heart, and with all your soul, and with all your might" (Deuteronomy 6. 4-5).

Part of the Book of Deuteronomy was written about 650 B.C. and it was probably revised and enlarged about 400 B.C. when Genesis and several other Old Testament books were completed. Turn now to the introduction to Genesis on page 1 to learn more about how God inspired men to write these books.

THE BOOK OF

DEUTERONOMY

AN ADDRESS TO THE PEOPLE
What God Has Done

1 These are the words that Moses spoke to all Israel beyond the Jordan in the wilderness, in the Arabah over against Suph, between Paran and Tophel, Laban, 2 Haze′roth, and Di′zahab. It is eleven days' journey from 3 Horeb by the way of Mount Se′ir to Ka′desh-bar′nea. And in the fortieth year, on the first day of the eleventh month, Moses spoke to the people of Israel according to all that the LORD had given him in commandment to 4 them, after he had defeated Sihon the king of the Amorites, who lived in Heshbon, and Og the king of 5 Bashan, who lived in Ash′taroth and in Ed′re-i. Beyond the Jordan, in the land of Moab, Moses undertook to 6 explain this law, saying, "The LORD our God said to us in Horeb, 'You have stayed long enough at this mountain; 7 turn and take your journey, and go to the hill country of the Amorites, and to all their neighbors in the Arabah, in the hill country and in the lowland, and in the Negeb, and by the seacoast, the land of the Canaanites, and Lebanon, as far as the great river, the river Euphra′tes. 8 Behold, I have set the land before you; go in and take possession of the land which the LORD swore to your fathers, to Abraham, to Isaac, and to Jacob, to give to them and to their descendants after them.'

9 "At that time I said to you, 'I am not able alone to 10 bear you; the LORD your God has multiplied you, and behold, you are this day as the stars of heaven for multi- 11 tude. May the LORD, the God of your fathers, make you a thousand times as many as you are, and bless you, as 12 he has promised you! How can I bear alone the weight 13 and burden of you and your strife? Choose wise, under-standing, and experienced men, according to your tribes, 14 and I will appoint them as your heads.' And you an-swered me, 'The thing that you have spoken is good for 15 us to do.' So I took the heads of your tribes, wise and experienced men, and set them as heads over you, com-manders of thousands, commanders of hundreds, com-manders of fifties, commanders of tens, and officers,

16 throughout your tribes. And I charged your judges at that time, 'Hear the cases between your brethren, and judge righteously between a man and his brother or the 17 alien that is with him. You shall not be partial in judg-ment; you shall hear the small and the great alike; you shall not be afraid of the face of man, for the judgment is God's; and the case that is too hard for you, you shall 18 bring to me, and I will hear it.' And I commanded you at that time all the things that you should do.

19 "And we set out from Horeb, and went through all that great and terrible wilderness which you saw, on the way to the hill country of the Amorites, as the LORD our God commanded us; and we came to Ka′desh-bar′nea. 20 And I said to you, 'You have come to the hill country of the Amorites, which the LORD our God gives us. 21 Behold, the LORD your God has set the land before you; go up, take possession, as the LORD, the God of your 22 fathers, has told you; do not fear or be dismayed.' Then all of you came near me, and said, 'Let us send men be-fore us, that they may explore the land for us, and bring us word again of the way by which we must go up and 23 the cities into which we shall come.' The thing seemed good to me, and I took twelve men of you, one man for 24 each tribe; and they turned and went up into the hill country, and came to the Valley of Eshcol and spied it 25 out. And they took in their hands some of the fruit of the land and brought it down to us, and brought us word again, and said, 'It is a good land which the LORD our God gives us.'

26 "Yet you would not go up, but rebelled against the 27 command of the LORD your God; and you murmured in your tents, and said, 'Because the LORD hated us he has brought us forth out of the land of Egypt, to give us into 28 the hand of the Amorites, to destroy us. Whither are we going up? Our brethren have made our hearts melt, say-ing, "The people are greater and taller than we; the cities are great and fortified up to heaven; and moreover we 29 have seen the sons of the Anakim there." ' Then I said to 30 you, 'Do not be in dread or afraid of them. The LORD

your God who goes before you will himself fight for you,
31 just as he did for you in Egypt before your eyes, and in the wilderness, where you have seen how the LORD your God bore you, as a man bears his son, in all the way that
32 you went until you came to this place.' Yet in spite of
33 this word you did not believe the LORD your God, who went before you in the way to seek you out a place to pitch your tents, in fire by night, to show you by what way you should go, and in the cloud by day.

34 "And the LORD heard your words, and was angered,
35 and he swore, 'Not one of these men of this evil generation shall see the good land which I swore to give to your
36 fathers, except Caleb the son of Jephun'neh; he shall see it, and to him and to his children I will give the land upon which he has trodden, because he has wholly fol-
37 lowed the LORD!' The LORD was angry with me also on your account, and said, 'You also shall not go in there;
38 Joshua the son of Nun, who stands before you, he shall enter; encourage him, for he shall cause Israel to inherit
39 it. Moreover your little ones, who you said would become a prey, and your children, who this day have no knowl-edge of good or evil, shall go in there, and to them I will
40 give it, and they shall possess it. But as for you, turn, and journey into the wilderness in the direction of the Red Sea.'

41 "Then you answered me, 'We have sinned against the LORD; we will go up and fight, just as the LORD our God commanded us.' And every man of you girded on his weapons of war, and thought it easy to go up into the
42 hill country. And the LORD said to me, 'Say to them, Do not go up or fight, for I am not in the midst of you;
43 lest you be defeated before your enemies.' So I spoke to you, and you would not hearken; but you rebelled against the command of the LORD, and were presumptuous and
44 went up into the hill country. Then the Amorites who lived in that hill country came out against you and chased you as bees do and beat you down in Se'ir as far
45 as Hormah. And you returned and wept before the LORD; but the LORD did not hearken to your voice or give ear to
46 you. So you remained at Kadesh many days, the days that you remained there.

2 "Then we turned, and journeyed into the wilderness in the direction of the Red Sea, as the LORD told me;
2 and for many days we went about Mount Se'ir. Then the
3 LORD said to me, 'You have been going about this moun-
4 tain country long enough; turn northward. And command the people, You are about to pass through the territory of your brethren the sons of Esau, who live in Se'ir; and
5 they will be afraid of you. So take good heed; do not contend with them; for I will not give you any of their land, no, not so much as for the sole of the foot to tread on, because I have given Mount Se'ir to Esau as a pos-
6 session. You shall purchase food from them for money,

that you may eat; and you shall also buy water of them
7 for money, that you may drink. For the LORD your God has blessed you in all the work of your hands; he knows your going through this great wilderness; these forty years the LORD your God has been with you; you have
8 lacked nothing.' So we went on, away from our brethren the sons of Esau who live in Se'ir, away from the Arabah road from Elath and E'zi-on-ge'ber.

"And we turned and went in the direction of the wilder-
9 ness of Moab. And the LORD said to me, 'Do not harass Moab or contend with them in battle, for I will not give you any of their land for a possession, because I have
10 given Ar to the sons of Lot for a possession.' (The Emim formerly lived there, a people great and many, and tall
11 as the Anakim; like the Anakim they are also known as
12 Reph'aim, but the Moabites call them Emim. The Horites also lived in Se'ir formerly, but the sons of Esau dispos-sessed them, and destroyed them from before them, and settled in their stead; as Israel did to the land of their
13 possession, which the LORD gave to them.) 'Now rise up, and go over the brook Zered.' So we went over the brook
14 Zered. And the time from our leaving Ka'desh-bar'nea until we crossed the brook Zered was thirty-eight years, until the entire generation, that is, the men of war, had perished from the camp, as the LORD has sworn to them.
15 For indeed the hand of the LORD was against them, to destroy them from the camp, until they had perished.

16 "So when all the men of war had perished and were
17, 18 dead from among the people, the LORD said to me, 'This day you are to pass over the boundary of Moab at Ar;
19 and when you approach the frontier of the sons of Am-mon, do not harass them or contend with them, for I will not give you any of the land of the sons of Ammon as a possession, because I have given it to the sons of Lot for a
20 possession.' (That also is known as a land of Reph'aim; Reph'aim formerly lived there, but the Ammonites call
21 them Zamzum'mim, a people great and many, and tall as the Anakim; but the LORD destroyed them before them;
22 and they dispossessed them, and settled in their stead; as he did for the sons of Esau, who live in Se'ir, when he destroyed the Horites before them, and they dispossessed
23 them, and settled in their stead even to this day. As for the Avvim, who lived in villages as far as Gaza, the Caph'-torim, who came from Caphtor, destroyed them and settled
24 in their stead.) Rise up, take your journey, and go over the valley of the Arnon; behold, I have given into your hand Sihon the Amorite, king of Heshbon, and his land; begin to take possession, and contend with him in battle.
25 This day I will begin to put the dread and fear of you upon the peoples that are under the whole heaven, who shall hear the report of you and shall tremble and be in anguish because of you.'

26 "So I sent messengers from the wilderness of Ked'-

emoth to Sihon the king of Heshbon, with words of peace,
27 saying, 'Let me pass through your land; I will go only
by the road, I will turn aside neither to the right nor to
28 the left. You shall sell me food for money, that I may eat,
give me water for money, that I may drink; only let me
29 pass through on foot, as the sons of Esau who live in
Se'ir and the Moabites who live in Ar did for me, until
I go over the Jordan into the land which the LORD our
30 God gives to us.' But Sihon the king of Heshbon would
not let us pass by him; for the LORD your God hardened
his spirit and made his heart obstinate, that he might
31 give him into your hand, as at this day. And the LORD
said to me, 'Behold, I have begun to give Sihon and his
land over to you; begin to take possession, that you may
32 occupy his land.' Then Sihon came out against us, he and
33 all his people, to battle at Jahaz. And the LORD our God
gave him over to us; and we defeated him and his sons
34 and all his people. And we captured all his cities at that
time and utterly destroyed every city, men, women, and
35 children; we left none remaining; only the cattle we took
as spoil for ourselves, with the booty of the cities which
36 we captured. From Aro'er, which is on the edge of the
valley of the Arnon, and from the city that is in the valley,
as far as Gilead, there was not a city too high for us;
37 the LORD our God gave all into our hands. Only to the
land of the sons of Ammon you did not draw near, that
is, to all the banks of the river Jabbok and the cities of
the hill country, and wherever the LORD our God forbade
us.

3 "Then we turned and went up the way to Bashan;
and Og the king of Bashan came out against us, he
2 and all his people, to battle at Ed're-i. But the LORD said
to me, 'Do not fear him; for I have given him and all
his people and his land into your hand; and you shall do
to him as you did to Sihon the king of the Amorites, who
3 dwelt at Heshbon.' So the LORD our God gave into our
hand Og also, the king of Bashan, and all his people; and
4 we smote him until no survivor was left to him. And we
took all his cities at that time—there was not a city which
we did not take from them—sixty cities, the whole region
5 of Argob, the kingdom of Og in Bashan. All these were
cities fortified with high walls, gates, and bars, besides
6 very many unwalled villages. And we utterly destroyed
them, as we did to Sihon the king of Heshbon, destroying
7 every city, men, women, and children. But all the cattle
8 and the spoil of the cities we took as our booty. So we
took the land at that time out of the hand of the two
kings of the Amorites who were beyond the Jordan, from
9 the valley of the Arnon to Mount Hermon (the Sido'nians
call Hermon Si'rion, while the Amorites call it Senir),
10 all the cities of the tableland and all Gilead and all Bashan,
as far as Sal'ecah and Ed're-i, cities of the kingdom of Og
11 in Bashan. (For only Og the king of Bashan was left of
the remnant of the Reph'aim; behold, his bedstead was a

bedstead of iron; is it not in Rabbah of the Ammonites?
Nine cubits was its length, and four cubits its breadth,
according to the common cubit.[a])
12 "When we took possession of this land at that time, I
gave to the Reubenites and the Gadites the territory beginning at Aro'er, which is on the edge of the valley of
the Arnon, and half the hill country of Gilead with its
13 cities; the rest of Gilead, and all Bashan, the kingdom of
Og, that is, all the region of Argob, I gave to the half-
tribe of Manas'seh. (The whole of that Bashan is called
14 the land of Reph'aim. Ja'ir the Manas'site took all the
region of Argob, that is, Bashan, as far as the border of
the Gesh'urites and the Ma-ac'athites, and called the villages after his own name, Hav'voth-ja'ir, as it is to this
15, 16 day.) To Machir I gave Gilead, and to the Reubenites
and the Gadites I gave the territory from Gilead as far
as the valley of the Arnon, with the middle of the valley
as a boundary, as far over as the river Jabbok, the bound-
17 ary of the Ammonites; the Arabah also, with the Jordan
as the boundary, from Chin'nereth as far as the sea of
the Arabah, the Salt Sea, under the slopes of Pisgah on
the east.
18 "And I commanded you at that time, saying, 'The LORD
your God has given you this land to possess; all your
men of valor shall pass over armed before your brethren
19 the people of Israel. But your wives, your little ones, and
your cattle (I know that you have many cattle) shall re-
20 main in the cities which I have given you, until the LORD
gives rest to your brethren, as to you, and they also occupy the land which the LORD your God gives them beyond the Jordan; then you shall return every man to his
21 possession which I have given you.' And I commanded
Joshua at that time, 'Your eyes have seen all that the LORD
your God has done to these two kings; so will the LORD
do to all the kingdoms into which you are going over.
22 You shall not fear them; for it is the LORD your God who
fights for you.'
23, 24 "And I besought the LORD at that time, saying, 'O
Lord GOD, thou hast only begun to show thy servant thy
greatness and thy mighty hand; for what god is there in
heaven or on earth who can do such works and mighty
25 acts as thine? Let me go over, I pray, and see the good
land beyond the Jordan, that goodly hill country, and
26 Lebanon.' But the LORD was angry with me on your account, and would not hearken to me; and the LORD said
to me, 'Let it suffice you; speak no more to me of this
27 matter. Go up to the top of Pisgah, and lift up your eyes
westward and northward and southward and eastward,
and behold it with your eyes; for you shall not go over
28 this Jordan. But charge Joshua, and encourage and
strengthen him; for he shall go over at the head of this
people, and he shall put them in possession of the land
29 which you shall see.' So we remained in the valley opposite Beth-pe'or.

[a] Heb *cubit of a man*

What Israel Should Do

4 "And now, O Israel, give heed to the statutes and the ordinances which I teach you, and do them; that you may live, and go in and take possession of the land 2 which the LORD, the God of your fathers, gives you. You shall not add to the word which I command you, nor take from it; that you may keep the commandments of the LORD 3 your God which I command you. Your eyes have seen what the LORD did at Ba'al-pe'or; for the LORD your God destroyed from among you all the men who followed the 4 Ba'al of Pe'or; but you who held fast to the LORD your 5 God are all alive this day. Behold, I have taught you statutes and ordinances, as the LORD my God commanded me, that you should do them in the land which you are 6 entering to take possession of it. Keep them and do them; for that will be your wisdom and your understanding in the sight of the peoples, who, when they hear all these statutes, will say, 'Surely this great nation is a wise and 7 understanding people.' For what great nation is there that has a god so near to it as the LORD our God is to us, 8 whenever we call upon him? And what great nation is there, that has statutes and ordinances so righteous as all this law which I set before you this day?

9 "Only take heed, and keep your soul diligently, lest you forget the things which your eyes have seen, and lest they depart from your heart all the days of your life; make them known to your children and your children's 10 children—how on the day that you stood before the LORD your God at Horeb, the LORD said to me, 'Gather the people to me, that I may let them hear my words, so that they may learn to fear me all the days that they live upon the earth, and that they may teach their children 11 so.' And you came near and stood at the foot of the mountain, while the mountain burned with fire to the heart of heaven, wrapped in darkness, cloud, and gloom. 12 Then the LORD spoke to you out of the midst of the fire; you heard the sound of words, but saw no form; there 13 was only a voice. And he declared to you his covenant, which he commanded you to perform, that is, the ten commandments;[b] and he wrote them upon two tables of 14 stone. And the LORD commanded me at that time to teach you statutes and ordinances, that you might do them in the land which you are going over to possess.

15 "Therefore take good heed to yourselves. Since you saw no form on the day that the LORD spoke to you at 16 Horeb out of the midst of the fire, beware lest you act corruptly by making a graven image for yourselves, in 17 the form of any figure, the likeness of male or female, the likeness of any beast that is on the earth, the likeness of 18 any winged bird that flies in the air, the likeness of anything that creeps on the ground, the likeness of any fish 19 that is in the water under the earth. And beware lest you lift up your eyes to heaven, and when you see the sun and the moon and the stars, all the host of heaven, you

be drawn away and worship them and serve them, things which the LORD your God has allotted to all the peoples 20 under the whole heaven. But the LORD has taken you, and brought you forth out of the iron furnace, out of Egypt, 21 to be a people of his own possession, as at this day. Furthermore the LORD was angry with me on your account, and he swore that I should not cross the Jordan, and that I should not enter the good land which the LORD your 22 God gives you for an inheritance. For I must die in this land, I must not go over the Jordan; but you shall go 23 over and take possession of that good land. Take heed to yourselves, lest you forget the covenant of the LORD your God, which he made with you, and make a graven image in the form of anything which the LORD your God has 24 forbidden you. For the LORD your God is a devouring fire, a jealous God.

25 "When you beget children and children's children, and have grown old in the land, if you act corruptly by making a graven image in the form of anything, and by doing what is evil in the sight of the LORD your God, so as to 26 provoke him to anger, I call heaven and earth to witness against you this day, that you will soon utterly perish from the land which you are going over the Jordan to possess; you will not live long upon it, but will be utterly 27 destroyed. And the LORD will scatter you among the peoples, and you will be left few in number among the na- 28 tions where the LORD will drive you. And there you will serve gods of wood and stone, the work of men's hands, 29 that neither see, nor hear, nor eat, nor smell. But from there you will seek the LORD your God, and you will find him, if you search after him with all your heart and with 30 all your soul. When you are in tribulation, and all these things come upon you in the latter days, you will return 31 to the LORD your God and obey his voice, for the LORD your God is a merciful God; he will not fail you or destroy you or forget the covenant with your fathers which he swore to them.

32 "For ask now of the days that are past, which were before you, since the day that God created man upon the earth, and ask from one end of heaven to the other, whether such a great thing as this has ever happened or 33 was ever heard of. Did any people ever hear the voice of a god speaking out of the midst of the fire, as you have 34 heard, and still live? Or has any god ever attempted to go and take a nation for himself from the midst of another nation, by trials, by signs, by wonders, and by war, by a mighty hand and an outstretched arm, and by great terrors, according to all that the LORD your God did for 35 you in Egypt before your eyes? To you it was shown, that you might know that the LORD is God; there is no 36 other besides him. Out of heaven he let you hear his voice, that he might discipline you; and on earth he let you see his great fire, and you heard his words out of the 37 midst of the fire. And because he loved your fathers and

[b] Heb words

chose their descendants after them, and brought you out of Egypt with his own presence, by his great power, 38 driving out before you nations greater and mightier than yourselves, to bring you in, to give you their land for an 39 inheritance, as at this day; know therefore this day, and lay it to your heart, that the LORD is God in heaven above 40 and on the earth beneath; there is no other. Therefore you shall keep his statutes and his commandments, which I command you this day, that it may go well with you, and with your children after you, and that you may prolong your days in the land which the LORD your God gives you for ever."

41 Then Moses set apart three cities in the east beyond 42 the Jordan, that the manslayer might flee there, who kills his neighbor unintentionally, without being at enmity with him in time past, and that by fleeing to one of these 43 cities he might save his life: Bezer in the wilderness on the tableland for the Reubenites, and Ramoth in Gilead for the Gadites, and Golan in Bashan for the Manas'sites.

AN ADDRESS ABOUT THE LAW OF GOD

44 This is the law which Moses set before the children of 45 Israel; these are the testimonies, the statutes, and the ordinances, which Moses spoke to the children of Israel 46 when they came out of Egypt, beyond the Jordan in the valley opposite Beth-pe'or, in the land of Sihon the king of the Amorites, who lived at Heshbon, whom Moses and the children of Israel defeated when they came out of 47 Egypt. And they took possession of his land and the land of Og the king of Bashan, the two kings of the Amorites, 48 who lived to the east beyond the Jordan; from Aro'er, which is on the edge of the valley of the Arnon, as far as 49 Mount Sirion c (that is, Hermon), together with all the Arabah on the east side of the Jordan as far as the Sea of the Arabah, under the slopes of Pisgah.

The Covenant of Faith

5 And Moses summoned all Israel, and said to them, "Hear, O Israel, the statutes and the ordinances which I speak in your hearing this day, and you shall learn them 2 and be careful to do them. The LORD our God made a 3 covenant with us in Horeb. Not with our fathers did the LORD make this covenant, but with us, who are all of us 4 here alive this day. The LORD spoke with you face to face 5 at the mountain, out of the midst of the fire, while I stood between the LORD and you at that time, to declare to you the word of the LORD; for you were afraid because of the fire, and you did not go up into the mountain. He said:

The Ten Commandments

6 " 'I am the LORD your God, who brought you out of the land of Egypt, out of the house of bondage.

7 " 'You shall have no other gods before d me.

c Syr: Heb Sion   d Or besides

8 " 'You shall not make for yourself a graven image, or any likeness of anything that is in heaven above, or that is on the earth beneath, or that is in the water under the 9 earth; you shall not bow down to them or serve them; for I the LORD your God am a jealous God, visiting the iniquity of the fathers upon the children to the third and 10 fourth generation of those who hate me, but showing steadfast love to thousands of those who love me and keep my commandments.

11 " 'You shall not take the name of the LORD your God in vain: for the LORD will not hold him guiltless who takes his name in vain.

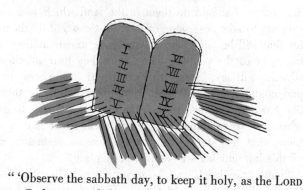

12 " 'Observe the sabbath day, to keep it holy, as the LORD 13 your God commanded you. Six days you shall labor, and 14 do all your work; but the seventh day is a sabbath to the LORD your God; in it you shall not do any work, you, or your son, or your daughter, or your manservant, or your maidservant, or your ox, or your ass, or any of your cattle, or the sojourner who is within your gates, that your manservant and your maidservant may rest as well 15 as you. You shall remember that you were a servant in the land of Egypt, and the LORD your God brought you out thence with a mighty hand and an outstretched arm; therefore the LORD your God commanded you to keep the sabbath day.

16 " 'Honor your father and your mother, as the LORD your God commanded you; that your days may be prolonged, and that it may go well with you, in the land which the LORD your God gives you.

17 " 'You shall not kill.

18 " 'Neither shall you commit adultery.

19 " 'Neither shall you steal.

20 " 'Neither shall you bear false witness against your neighbor.

21 " 'Neither shall you covet your neighbor's wife; and you shall not desire your neighbor's house, his field, or his manservant, or his maidservant, his ox, or his ass, or anything that is your neighbor's.'

22 "These words the LORD spoke to all your assembly at the mountain out of the midst of the fire, the cloud, and the thick darkness, with a loud voice; and he added no more. And he wrote them upon two tables of stone, and

23 gave them to me. And when you heard the voice out of the midst of the darkness, while the mountain was burning with fire, you came near to me, all the heads of your
24 tribes, and your elders; and you said, 'Behold, the LORD our God has shown us his glory and greatness, and we have heard his voice out of the midst of the fire; we have this day seen God speak with man and man still live.
25 Now therefore why should we die? For this great fire will consume us; if we hear the voice of the LORD our God
26 any more, we shall die. For who is there of all flesh, that has heard the voice of the living God speaking out of the
27 midst of fire, as we have, and has still lived? Go near, and hear all that the LORD our God will say; and speak to us all that the LORD our God will speak to you; and we will hear and do it.'
28 "And the LORD heard your words, when you spoke to me; and the LORD said to me, 'I have heard the words of this people, which they have spoken to you; they have
29 rightly said all that they have spoken. Oh that they had such a mind as this always, to fear me and to keep all my commandments, that it might go well with them and with
30 their children for ever! Go and say to them, "Return to
31 your tents." But you, stand here by me, and I will tell you all the commandment and the statutes and the ordinances which you shall teach them, that they may do
32 them in the land which I give them to possess.' You shall be careful to do therefore as the LORD your God has commanded you; you shall not turn aside to the right hand
33 or to the left. You shall walk in all the way which the LORD your God has commanded you, that you may live, and that it may go well with you, and that you may live long in the land which you shall possess.

6 "Now this is the commandment, the statutes and the ordinances which the LORD your God commanded me to teach you, that you may do them in the land to which
2 you are going over, to possess it; that you may fear the LORD your God, you and your son and your son's son, by keeping all his statutes and his commandments, which I command you, all the days of your life; and that your
3 days may be prolonged. Hear therefore, O Israel, and be careful to do them; that it may go well with you, and that you may multiply greatly, as the LORD, the God of your fathers, has promised you, in a land flowing with milk and honey.
4 "Hear, O Israel: The LORD our God is one LORD; e

5 and you shall love the LORD your God with all your heart,
6 and with all your soul, and with all your might. And these words which I command you this day shall be upon your
7 heart; and you shall teach them diligently to your children, and shall talk of them when you sit in your house, and when you walk by the way, and when you lie down,
8 and when you rise. And you shall bind them as a sign upon your hand, and they shall be as frontlets between
9 your eyes. And you shall write them on the doorposts of your house and on your gates.
10 "And when the LORD your God brings you into the land which he swore to your fathers, to Abraham, to Isaac, and to Jacob, to give you, with great and goodly
11 cities, which you did not build, and houses full of all good things, which you did not fill, and cisterns hewn out, which you did not hew, and vineyards and olive trees, which you did not plant, and when you eat and are full,
12 then take heed lest you forget the LORD who brought you
13 out of the land of Egypt, out of the house of bondage. You shall fear the LORD your God; you shall serve him; and
14 swear by his name. You shall not go after other gods, of
15 the gods of the peoples who are round about you; for the LORD your God in the midst of you is a jealous God; lest the anger of the LORD your God be kindled against you, and he destroy you from off the face of the earth.
16 "You shall not put the LORD your God to the test, as
17 you tested him at Massah. You shall diligently keep the commandments of the LORD your God, and his testimonies, and his statutes, which he has commanded you.
18 And you shall do what is right and good in the sight of the LORD, that it may go well with you, and that you may go in and take possession of the good land which the
19 LORD swore to give to your fathers by thrusting out all your enemies from before you, as the LORD has promised.
20 "When your son asks you in time to come, 'What is the meaning of the testimonies and the statutes and the ordinances which the LORD our God has commanded
21 you?' then you shall say to your son, 'We were Pharaoh's slaves in Egypt; and the LORD brought us out of Egypt
22 with a mighty hand; and the LORD showed signs and wonders, great and grievous, against Egypt and against
23 Pharaoh and all his household, before our eyes; and he brought us out from there, that he might bring us in and give us the land which he swore to give to our fathers.
24 And the LORD commanded us to do all these statutes, to fear the LORD our God, for our good always, that he might
25 preserve us alive, as at this day. And it will be righteousness for us, if we are careful to do all this commandment before the LORD our God, as he has commanded us.'
7 "When the LORD your God brings you into the land which you are entering to take possession of it, and clears away many nations before you, the Hittites, the Gir'gashites, the Amorites, the Canaanites, the Per'-

e Or the LORD our God, the LORD is one; Or the LORD is our God, the LORD is one; Or the LORD is our God, the LORD alone

izzites, the Hivites, and the Jeb'usites, seven nations
2 greater and mightier than yourselves, and when the LORD your God gives them over to you, and you defeat them; then you must utterly destroy them; you shall make no
3 covenant with them, and show no mercy to them. You shall not make marriages with them, giving your daughters to their sons or taking their daughters for your sons.
4 For they would turn away your sons from following me, to serve other gods; then the anger of the LORD would be kindled against you, and he would destroy you quickly.
5 But thus shall you deal with them: you shall break down their altars, and dash in pieces their pillars, and hew down their Ashe'rim, and burn their graven images with fire.
6 "For you are a people holy to the LORD your God; the LORD your God has chosen you to be a people for his own possession, out of all the peoples that are on the face
7 of the earth. It was not because you were more in number than any other people that the LORD set his love upon you and chose you, you were the fewest of all peoples;
8 but it is because the LORD loves you, and is keeping the oath which he swore to your fathers, that the LORD has brought you out with a mighty hand, and redeemed you from the house of bondage, from the hand of Pharaoh
9 king of Egypt. Know therefore that the LORD your God is God, the faithful God who keeps covenant and steadfast love with those who love him and keep his command-
10 ments, to a thousand generations, and requites to their face those who hate him, by destroying them; he will not be slack with him who hates him, he will requite him to
11 his face. You shall therefore be careful to do the commandment, and the statutes, and the ordinances, which I command you this day.
12 "And because you hearken to these ordinances, and keep and do them, the LORD your God will keep with you the covenant and the steadfast love which he swore to
13 your fathers to keep; he will love you, bless you, and multiply you; he will also bless the fruit of your body and the fruit of your ground, your grain and your wine and your oil, the increase of your cattle and the young of your flock, in the land which he swore to your fathers
14 to give you. You shall be blessed above all peoples; there shall not be male or female barren among you, or among
15 your cattle. And the LORD will take away from you all sickness; and none of the evil diseases of Egypt, which you knew, will he inflict upon you, but he will lay them
16 upon all who hate you. And you shall destroy all the peoples that the LORD your God will give over to you, your eye shall not pity them; neither shall you serve their gods, for that would be a snare to you.
17 "If you say in your heart, 'These nations are greater
18 than I; how can I dispossess them?' you shall not be afraid of them, but you shall remember what the LORD
19 your God did to Pharaoh and to all Egypt, the great trials

which your eyes saw, the signs, the wonders, the mighty hand, and the outstretched arm, by which the LORD your God brought you out; so will the LORD your God do to
20 all the peoples of whom you are afraid. Moreover the LORD your God will send hornets among them, until those who are left and hide themselves from you are destroyed.
21 You shall not be in dread of them; for the LORD your God is in the midst of you, a great and terrible God.
22 The LORD your God will clear away these nations before you little by little; you may not make an end of them at once,[f] lest the wild beasts grow too numerous for you.
23 But the LORD your God will give them over to you, and throw them into great confusion, until they are destroyed.
24 And he will give their kings into your hand, and you shall make their name perish from under heaven; not a man shall be able to stand against you, until you have de-
25 stroyed them. The graven images of their gods you shall burn with fire; you shall not covet the silver or the gold that is on them, or take it for yourselves, lest you be ensnared by it; for it is an abomination to the LORD your
26 God. And you shall not bring an abominable thing into your house, and become accursed like it; you shall utterly detest and abhor it; for it is an accursed thing.

8 "All the commandment which I command you this day you shall be careful to do, that you may live and multiply, and go in and possess the land which the LORD
2 swore to give to your fathers. And you shall remember all the way which the LORD your God has led you these forty years in the wilderness, that he might humble you, testing you to know what was in your heart, whether you would
3 keep his commandments, or not. And he humbled you and let you hunger and fed you with manna, which you did not know, nor did your fathers know; that he might make you know that man does not live by bread alone, but that man lives by everything that proceeds out of the
4 mouth of the LORD. Your clothing did not wear out upon
5 you, and your foot did not swell, these forty years. Know then in your heart that, as a man disciplines his son, the
6 LORD your God disciplines you. So you shall keep the commandments of the LORD your God, by walking in his
7 ways and by fearing him. For the LORD your God is bringing you into a good land, a land of brooks of water, of fountains and springs, flowing forth in valleys and hills,
8 a land of wheat and barley, of vines and fig trees and
9 pomegranates, a land of olive trees and honey, a land in which you will eat bread without scarcity, in which you will lack nothing, a land whose stones are iron, and out of
10 whose hills you can dig copper. And you shall eat and be full, and you shall bless the LORD your God for the good land he has given you.
11 "Take heed lest you forget the LORD your God, by not keeping his commandments and his ordinances and his
12 statutes, which I command you this day: lest, when you have eaten and are full, and have built goodly houses and

f Or *quickly*

live in them, and when your herds and flocks multiply, and your silver and gold is multiplied, and all that you [14] have is multiplied, then your heart be lifted up, and you forget the LORD your God, who brought you out of the [15] land of Egypt, out of the house of bondage, who led you through the great and terrible wilderness, with its fiery serpents and scorpions and thirsty ground where there was no water, who brought you water out of the flinty [16] rock, who fed you in the wilderness with manna which your fathers did not know, that he might humble you and [17] test you, to do you good in the end. Beware lest you say in your heart, 'My power and the might of my hand [18] have gotten me this wealth.' You shall remember the LORD your God, for it is he who gives you power to get wealth; that he may confirm his covenant which he swore to your [19] fathers, as at this day. And if you forget the LORD your God and go after other gods and serve them and worship them, I solemnly warn you this day that you shall surely [20] perish. Like the nations that the LORD makes to perish before you, so shall you perish, because you would not obey the voice of the LORD your God.

9 "Hear, O Israel; you are to pass over the Jordan this day, to go in to dispossess nations greater and mightier than yourselves, cities great and fortified up to [2] heaven, a people great and tall, the sons of the Anakim, whom you know, and of whom you have heard it said, [3] 'Who can stand before the sons of Anak?' Know therefore this day that he who goes over before you as a devouring fire is the LORD your God; he will destroy them and subdue them before you; so you shall drive them out, and make them perish quickly, as the LORD has promised you.

[4] "Do not say in your heart, after the LORD your God has thrust them out before you, 'It is because of my righteousness that the LORD has brought me in to possess this land'; whereas it is because of the wickedness of these nations [5] that the LORD is driving them out before you. Not because of your righteousness or the uprightness of your heart are you going in to possess their land; but because of the wickedness of these nations the LORD your God is driving them out from before you, and that he may confirm the word which the LORD swore to your fathers, to Abraham, to Isaac, and to Jacob.

[6] "Know therefore, that the LORD your God is not giving you this good land to possess because of your righteous- [7] ness; for you are a stubborn people. Remember and do not forget how you provoked the LORD your God to wrath in the wilderness; from the day you came out of the land of Egypt, until you came to this place, you have been [8] rebellious against the LORD. Even at Horeb you provoked the LORD to wrath, and the LORD was so angry with you [9] that he was ready to destroy you. When I went up the mountain to receive the tables of stone, the tables of the covenant which the LORD made with you, I remained on the mountain forty days and forty nights; I neither ate [10] bread nor drank water. And the LORD gave me the two tables of stone written with the finger of God; and on them were all the words which the LORD had spoken with you on the mountain out of the midst of the fire on the [11] day of the assembly. And at the end of forty days and forty nights the LORD gave me the two tables of stone, [12] the tables of the covenant. Then the LORD said to me, 'Arise, go down quickly from here; for your people whom you have brought from Egypt have acted corruptly; they have turned aside quickly out of the way which I commanded them; they have made themselves a molten image.' [13] "Furthermore the LORD said to me, 'I have seen this [14] people, and behold, it is a stubborn people; let me alone, that I may destroy them and blot out their name from under heaven; and I will make of you a nation mightier [15] and greater than they.' So I turned and came down from the mountain, and the mountain was burning with fire; and the two tables of the covenant were in my two hands. [16] And I looked, and behold, you had sinned against the LORD your God; you had made yourselves a molten calf; you had turned aside quickly from the way which the [17] LORD had commanded you. So I took hold of the two tables, and cast them out of my two hands, and broke [18] them before your eyes. Then I lay prostrate before the LORD as before, forty days and forty nights; I neither ate bread nor drank water, because of all the sin which you had committed, in doing what was evil in the sight [19] of the LORD, to provoke him to anger. For I was afraid of the anger and hot displeasure which the LORD bore against you, so that he was ready to destroy you. But [20] the LORD hearkened to me that time also. And the LORD was so angry with Aaron that he was ready to destroy [21] him; and I prayed for Aaron also at the same time. Then I took the sinful thing, the calf which you had made, and burned it with fire and crushed it, grinding it very small, until it was as fine as dust; and I threw the dust of it into the brook that descended out of the mountain.

[22] "At Tab'erah also, and at Massah, and at Kib'roth- [23] hatta'avah, you provoked the LORD to wrath. And when the LORD sent you from Ka'desh-bar'ne-a, saying, 'Go up and take possession of the land which I have given you,' then you rebelled against the commandment of the LORD your God, and did not believe him or obey his voice. [24] You have been rebellious against the LORD from the day that I knew you.

[25] "So I lay prostrate before the LORD for these forty days and forty nights, because the LORD had said he would [26] destroy you. And I prayed to the LORD, 'O Lord God, destroy not thy people and thy heritage, whom thou hast redeemed through thy greatness, whom thou hast brought [27] out of Egypt with a mighty hand. Remember thy servants, Abraham, Isaac, and Jacob; do not regard the stubbornness of this people, or their wickedness, or their sin,

28 lest the land from which thou didst bring us say, "Because the LORD was not able to bring them into the land which he promised them, and because he hated them, he has 29 brought them out to slay them in the wilderness." For they are thy people and thy heritage, whom thou didst bring out by thy great power and by thy outstretched arm.'

10 "At that time the LORD said to me, 'Hew two tables of stone like the first, and come up to me on the 2 mountain, and make an ark of wood. And I will write on the tables the words that were on the first tables which 3 you broke, and you shall put them in the ark.' So I made an ark of acacia wood, and hewed two tables of stone like the first, and went up the mountain with the two 4 tables in my hand. And he wrote on the tables, as at the first writing, the ten commandments g which the LORD had spoken to you on the mountain out of the midst of the fire on the day of the assembly; and the LORD gave them 5 to me. Then I turned and came down from the mountain, and put the tables in the ark which I had made; and there they are, as the LORD commanded me.

6 (The people of Israel journeyed from Be-er'oth Bene-ja'a-kan h to Mose'rah. There Aaron died, and there he was buried; and his son Elea'zar ministered as priest in 7 his stead. From there they journeyed to Gud'godah, and from Gud'godah to Jot'bathah, a land with brooks of 8 water. At that time the LORD set apart the tribe of Levi to carry the ark of the covenant of the LORD, to stand before the LORD to minister to him and to bless in his 9 name, to this day. Therefore Levi has no portion of inheritance with his brothers; the LORD is his inheritance, as the LORD your God said to him.)

10 "I stayed on the mountain, as at the first time, forty days and forty nights, and the LORD hearkened to me that 11 time also; the LORD was unwilling to destroy you. And the LORD said to me, 'Arise, go on your journey at the head of the people, that they may go in and possess the land, which I swore to their fathers to give them.'

12 "And now, Israel, what does the LORD your God require of you, but to fear the LORD your God, to walk in all his ways, to love him, to serve the LORD your God with all 13 your heart and with all your soul, and to keep the commandments and statutes of the LORD, which I command 14 you this day for your good? Behold, to the LORD your God belong heaven and the heaven of heavens, the earth 15 with all that is in it; yet the LORD set his heart in love upon your fathers and chose their descendants after them, 16 you above all peoples, as at this day. Circumcise therefore the foreskin of your heart, and be no longer stubborn. 17 For the LORD your God is God of gods and Lord of lords, the great, the mighty, and the terrible God, who 18 is not partial and takes no bribe. He executes justice for the fatherless and the widow, and loves the sojourner, 19 giving him food and clothing. Love the sojourner therefore; 20 for you were sojourners in the land of Egypt. You

shall fear the LORD your God; you shall serve him and 21 cleave to him, and by his name you shall swear. He is your praise; he is your God, who has done for you these great and terrible things which your eyes have seen. 22 Your fathers went down to Egypt seventy persons; and now the LORD your God has made you as the stars of heaven for multitude.

11 "You shall therefore love the LORD your God, and keep his charge, his statutes, his ordinances, and his 2 commandments always. And consider this day (since I am not speaking to your children who have not known or seen it), consider the discipline i of the LORD your God, his greatness, his mighty hand and his outstretched arm, 3 his signs and his deeds which he did in Egypt to Pharaoh 4 the king of Egypt and to all his land; and what he did to the army of Egypt, to their horses and to their chariots; how he made the water of the Red Sea overflow them as they pursued after you, and how the LORD has destroyed 5 them to this day; and what he did to you in the wilder- 6 ness, until you came to this place; and what he did to Dathan and Abi'ram the sons of Eli'ab, son of Reuben; how the earth opened its mouth and swallowed them up, with their households, their tents, and every living thing 7 that followed them, in the midst of all Israel; for your eyes have seen all the great work of the LORD which he did.

8 "You shall therefore keep all the commandment which I command you this day, that you may be strong, and go in and take possession of the land which you are going 9 over to possess, and that you may live long in the land which the LORD swore to your fathers to give to them and to their descendants, a land flowing with milk and honey. 10 For the land which you are entering to take possession of it is not like the land of Egypt, from which you have come, where you sowed your seed and watered it with 11 your feet, like a garden of vegetables; but the land which you are going over to possess is a land of hills and valleys, 12 which drinks water by the rain from heaven, a land which the LORD your God cares for; the eyes of the LORD your God are always upon it, from the beginning of the year to the end of the year.

13 "And if you will obey my commandments which I command you this day, to love the LORD your God, and to serve him with all your heart and with all your soul, 14 he j will give the rain for your land in its season, the early rain and the later rain, that you may gather in your grain 15 and your wine and your oil. And he j will give grass in your fields for your cattle, and you shall eat and be full. 16 Take heed lest your heart be deceived, and you turn aside 17 and serve other gods and worship them, and the anger of the LORD be kindled against you, and he shut up the heavens, so that there be no rain, and the land yield no fruit, and you perish quickly off the good land which the LORD gives you.

g Heb words   h Or the wells of the Bene-jaakan   i Or instruction   j Sam Gk Vg: Heb I

18 "You shall therefore lay up these words of mine in your heart and in your soul; and you shall bind them as a sign upon your hand, and they shall be as frontlets 19 between your eyes. And you shall teach them to your children, talking of them when you are sitting in your house, and when you are walking by the way, and when 20 you lie down, and when you rise. And you shall write them upon the doorposts of your house and upon your 21 gates, that your days and the days of your children may be multiplied in the land which the LORD swore to your fathers to give them, as long as the heavens are above the 22 earth. For if you will be careful to do all this commandment which I command you to do, loving the LORD your 23 God, walking in all his ways, and cleaving to him, then the LORD will drive out all these nations before you, and you will dispossess nations greater and mightier than 24 yourselves. Every place on which the sole of your foot treads shall be yours; your territory shall be from the wilderness and Lebanon and from the River, the river 25 Eu-phra'tes, to the western sea. No man shall be able to stand against you; the LORD your God will lay the fear of you and the dread of you upon all the land that you shall tread, as he promised you.

26 "Behold, I set before you this day a blessing and a 27 curse: the blessing, if you obey the commandments of 28 the LORD your God, which I command you this day, and the curse, if you do not obey the commandments of the LORD your God, but turn aside from the way which I command you this day, to go after other gods which you 29 have not known. And when the LORD your God brings you into the land which you are entering to take possession of it, you shall set the blessing on Mount Ger'izim 30 and the curse on Mount Ebal. Are they not beyond the Jordan, west of the road, toward the going down of the sun, in the land of the Canaanites who live in the Arabah, 31 over against Gilgal, beside the oak k of Moreh? For you are to pass over the Jordan to go in to take possession of the land which the LORD your God gives you; and when 32 you possess it and live in it, you shall be careful to do all the statutes and the ordinances which I set before you this day.

LAWS TO OBEY

12 "These are the statutes and ordinances which you shall be careful to do in the land which the LORD, the God of your fathers, has given you to possess, all the days that you 2 live upon the earth. You shall surely destroy all the places where the nations whom you shall dispossess served their gods, upon the high mountains and upon the hills and under every 3 green tree; you shall tear down their altars, and dash in pieces their pillars, and burn their Ashe'rim with fire; you shall hew down the graven images of their gods, and destroy their 4 name out of that place. You shall not do so to the LORD your 5 God. But you shall seek the place which the LORD your God will choose out of all your tribes to put his name and make his 6 habitation there: thither you shall go, and thither you shall bring your burnt offerings and your sacrifices, your tithes and the offering that you present, your votive offerings, your freewill offerings, and the firstlings of your herd and of your flock;

7 and there you shall eat before the LORD your God, and you shall rejoice, you and your households, in all that you under- 8 take, in which the LORD your God has blessed you. You shall not do according to all that we are doing here this day, every 9 man doing whatever is right in his own eyes; for you have not as yet come to the rest and to the inheritance which the LORD 10 your God gives you. But when you go over the Jordan, and live in the land which the LORD your God gives you to inherit, and when he gives you rest from all your enemies round about, 11 so that you live in safety, then to the place which the LORD your God will choose, to make his name dwell there, thither you shall bring all that I command you: your burnt offerings and your sacrifices, your tithes and the offering that you present, and all your votive offerings which you vow to the LORD. 12 And you shall rejoice before the LORD your God, you and your sons and your daughters, your menservants and your maidservants, and the Levite that is within your towns, since he has 13 no portion or inheritance with you. Take heed that you do not 14 offer your burnt offerings at every place that you see; but at the place which the LORD will choose in one of your tribes, there you shall offer your burnt offerings, and there you shall do all that I am commanding you.

15 "However, you may slaughter and eat flesh within any of your towns, as much as you desire, according to the blessing of the LORD your God which he has given you; the unclean and the clean may eat of it, as of the gazelle and as of the hart. 16 Only you shall not eat the blood; you shall pour it out upon 17 the earth like water. You may not eat within your towns the tithe of your grain or of your wine or of your oil, or the firstlings of your herd or of your flock, or any of your votive offerings which you vow, or your freewill offerings, or the 18 offering that you present; but you shall eat them before the LORD your God in the place which the LORD your God will choose, you and your son and your daughter, your manservant and your maidservant, and the Levite who is within your towns; and you shall rejoice before the LORD your God in all 19 that you undertake. Take heed that you do not forsake the Levite as long as you live in your land.

20 "When the LORD your God enlarges your territory, as he has promised you, and you say, 'I will eat flesh,' because you crave 21 flesh, you may eat as much flesh as you desire. If the place which the LORD your God will choose to put his name there is too far from you, then you may kill any of your herd or your flock, which the LORD has given you, as I have commanded you; and you may eat within your towns as much as you desire. 22 Just as the gazelle or the hart is eaten, so you may eat of it; 23 the unclean and the clean alike may eat of it. Only be sure that you do not eat the blood; for the blood is the life, and 24 you shall not eat the life with the flesh. You shall not eat it; 25 you shall pour it out upon the earth like water. You shall not eat it; that all may go well with you and with your children after you, when you do what is right in the sight of the LORD. 26 But the holy things which are due from you, and your votive offerings, you shall take, and you shall go to the place which 27 the LORD will choose, and offer your burnt offerings, the flesh and the blood, on the altar of the LORD your God; the blood of your sacrifices shall be poured out on the altar of the LORD your 28 God, but the flesh you may eat. Be careful to heed all these words which I command you, that it may go well with you and with your children after you for ever, when you do what is good and right in the sight of the LORD your God.

29 "When the LORD your God cuts off before you the nations whom you go in to dispossess, and you dispossess them and 30 dwell in their land, take heed that you be not ensnared to follow them, after they have been destroyed before you, and that you do not inquire about their gods, saying, 'How did these 31 nations serve their gods?—that I also may do likewise.' You shall not do so to the LORD your God; for every abominable thing which the LORD hates they have done for their gods; for they even burn their sons and their daughters in the fire to their gods.

32 1 "Everything that I command you you shall be careful to do; you shall not add to it or take from it.

13 "If a prophet arises among you, or a dreamer of dreams, 2 and gives you a sign or a wonder, and the sign or wonder which he tells you comes to pass, and if he says, 'Let us go after other gods,' which you have not known, 'and let us serve 3 them,' you shall not listen to the words of that prophet or to that dreamer of dreams; for the LORD your God is testing you, to know whether you love the LORD your God with all your

k Gk Syr: See Gn 12. 6. Heb *oaks* or *terebinths*   1 Ch 13. 1 in Heb

4 heart and with all your soul. You shall walk after the LORD your God and fear him, and keep his commandments and obey 5 his voice, and you shall serve him and cleave to him. But that prophet or that dreamer of dreams shall be put to death, because he has taught rebellion against the LORD your God, who brought you out of the land of Egypt and redeemed you out of the house of bondage, to make you leave the way in which the LORD your God commanded you to walk. So you shall purge the evil from the midst of you.

6 "If your brother, the son of your mother, or your son, or your daughter, or the wife of your bosom, or your friend who is as your own soul, entices you secretly, saying, 'Let us go and serve other gods,' which neither you nor your fathers have known, 7 some of the gods of the peoples that are round about you, whether near you or far off from you, from the one end of the 8 earth to the other, you shall not yield to him or listen to him, nor shall your eye pity him, nor shall you spare him, nor shall 9 you conceal him; but you shall kill him; your hand shall be first against him to put him to death, and afterwards the hand 10 of all the people. You shall stone him to death with stones, because he sought to draw you away from the LORD your God, who brought you out of the land of Egypt, out of the house 11 of bondage. And all Israel shall hear, and fear, and never again do any such wickedness as this among you.

12 "If you hear in one of your cities, which the LORD your God 13 gives you to dwell there, that certain base fellows have gone out among you and have drawn away the inhabitants of the city, saying, 'Let us go and serve other gods,' which you have 14 not known, then you shall inquire and make search and ask diligently; and behold, if it be true and certain that such an 15 abominable thing has been done among you, you shall surely put the inhabitants of that city to the sword, destroying it utterly, all who are in it and its cattle, with the edge of the 16 sword. You shall gather all its spoil into the midst of its open square, and burn the city and all its spoil with fire, as a whole burnt offering to the LORD your God; it shall be a heap for 17 ever, it shall not be built again. None of the devoted things shall cleave to your hand; that the LORD may turn from the fierceness of his anger, and show you mercy, and have compassion on you, and multiply you, as he swore to your fathers, 18 if you obey the voice of the LORD your God, keeping all his commandments which I command you this day, and doing what is right in the sight of the LORD your God.

14 "You are the sons of the LORD your God; you shall not cut yourselves or make any baldness on your foreheads for 2 the dead. For you are a people holy to the LORD your God, and the LORD has chosen you to be a people for his own possession, out of all the peoples that are on the face of the earth.

3, 4 "You shall not eat any abominable thing. These are the 5 animals you may eat: the ox, the sheep, the goat, the hart, the gazelle, the roebuck, the wild goat, the ibex, the antelope, and 6 the mountain-sheep. Every animal that parts the hoof and has the hoof cloven in two, and chews the cud, among the animals, 7 you may eat. Yet of those that chew the cud or have the hoof cloven you shall not eat these: the camel, the hare, and the rock badger, because they chew the cud but do not part the 8 hoof, are unclean for you. And the swine, because it parts the hoof but does not chew the cud, is unclean for you. Their flesh you shall not eat, and their carcasses you shall not touch.

9 "Of all that are in the waters you may eat these: whatever 10 has fins and scales you may eat. And whatever does not have fins and scales you shall not eat; it is unclean for you.

11, 12 "You may eat all clean birds. But these are the ones which 13 you shall not eat: the eagle, the vulture, the osprey, the buzz-14 ard, the kite, after their kinds; every raven after its kind; 15 the ostrich, the nighthawk, the sea gull, the hawk, after their 16, 17 kinds; the little owl and the great owl, the water hen and the 18 pelican, the carrion vulture and the cormorant, the stork, the 19 heron, after their kinds; the hoopoe and the bat. And all winged 20 insects are unclean for you; they shall not be eaten. All clean winged things you may eat.

21 "You shall not eat anything that dies of itself; you may give it to the alien who is within your towns, that he may eat it, or you may sell it to a foreigner; for you are a people holy to the LORD your God.

"You shall not boil a kid in its mother's milk.

22 "You shall tithe all the yield of your seed, which comes forth 23 from the field year by year. And before the LORD your God, in the place which he will choose, to make his name dwell there, you shall eat the tithe of your grain, of your wine, and of your oil, and the firstlings of your herd and flock; that you may 24 learn to fear the LORD your God always. And if the way is too long for you, so that you are not able to bring the tithe, when the LORD your God blesses you, because the place is too far from you, which the LORD your God chooses, to set his name 25 there, then you shall turn it into money, and bind up the money in your hand, and go to the place which the LORD your God 26 chooses, and spend the money for whatever you desire, oxen, or sheep, or wine or strong drink, whatever your appetite craves; and you shall eat there before the LORD your God and 27 rejoice, you and your household. And you shall not forsake the Levite who is within your towns, for he has no portion or inheritance with you.

28 "At the end of every three years you shall bring forth all the tithe of your produce in the same year, and lay it up within 29 your towns; and the Levite, because he has no portion or inheritance with you, and the sojourner, the fatherless, and the widow, who are within your towns, shall come and eat and be filled; that the LORD your God may bless you in all the work of your hands that you do.

15 "At the end of every seven years you shall grant a 2 release. And this is the manner of the release: every creditor shall release what he has lent to his neighbor; he shall not exact it of his neighbor, his brother, because the LORD's 3 release has been proclaimed. Of a foreigner you may exact it; but whatever of yours is with your brother your hand shall 4 release. But there will be no poor among you (for the LORD will bless you in the land which the LORD your God gives you 5 for an inheritance to possess), if only you will obey the voice of the LORD your God, being careful to do all this command-6 ment which I command you this day. For the LORD your God will bless you, as he promised you, and you shall lend to many nations, but you shall not borrow; and you shall rule over many nations, but they shall not rule over you.

7 "If there is among you a poor man, one of your brethren, in any of your towns within your land which the LORD your God gives you, you shall not harden your heart or shut your hand 8 against your poor brother, but you shall open your hand to him, and lend him sufficient for his need, whatever it may be. 9 Take heed lest there be a base thought in your heart, and you say, 'The seventh year, the year of release is near,' and your eye be hostile to your poor brother, and you give him nothing, and he cry to the LORD against you, and it be sin in you. 10 You shall give to him freely, and your heart shall not be grudging when you give to him; because for this the LORD your God will bless you in all your work and in all that you under-11 take. For the poor will never cease out of the land; therefore I command you, You shall open wide your hand to your brother, to the needy and to the poor, in the land.

12 "If your brother, a Hebrew man, or a Hebrew woman, is sold to you, he shall serve you six years, and in the seventh year 13 you shall let him go free from you. And when you let him go 14 free from you, you shall not let him go empty-handed; you shall furnish him liberally out of your flock, out of your threshing floor, and out of your wine press; as the LORD your God has 15 blessed you, you shall give to him. You shall remember that you were a slave in the land of Egypt, and the LORD your God 16 redeemed you; therefore I command you this today. But if he says to you, 'I will not go out from you,' because he loves you 17 and your household, since he fares well with you, then you shall take an awl, and thrust it through his ear into the door, and he shall be your bondman for ever. And to your bond-18 woman you shall do likewise. It shall not seem hard to you, when you let him go free from you; for at half the cost of a hired servant he has served you six years. So the LORD your God will bless you in all that you do.

19 "All the firstling males that are born of your herd and flock you shall consecrate to the LORD your God; you shall do no work with the firstling of your herd, nor shear the firstling 20 of your flock. You shall eat it, you and your household, before the LORD your God year by year at the place which the LORD 21 will choose. But if it has any blemish, if it is lame or blind, or has any serious blemish whatever, you shall not sacrifice it 22 to the LORD your God. You shall eat it within your towns; the unclean and the clean alike may eat it, as though it were a 23 gazelle or a hart. Only you shall not eat its blood; you shall pour it out on the ground like water.

16 "Observe the month of Abib, and keep the passover to the LORD your God; for in the month of Abib the LORD 2 your God brought you out of Egypt by night. And you shall

offer the passover sacrifice to the LORD your God, from the flock or the herd, at the place which the LORD will choose, to ³ make his name dwell there. You shall eat no leavened bread with it; seven days you shall eat it with unleavened bread, the bread of affliction—for you came out of the land of Egypt in hurried flight—that all the days of your life you may remember ⁴ the day when you came out of the land of Egypt. No leaven shall be seen with you in all your territory for seven days; nor shall any of the flesh which you sacrifice on the evening ⁵ of the first day remain all night until morning. You may not offer the passover sacrifice within any of your towns which the ⁶ LORD your God gives you; but at the place which the LORD your God will choose, to make his name dwell in it, there you shall offer the passover sacrifice, in the evening at the going down ⁷ of the sun, at the time you came out of Egypt. And you shall boil it and eat it at the place which the LORD your God will choose; and in the morning you shall turn and go to your tents. ⁸ For six days you shall eat unleavened bread; and on the seventh day there shall be a solemn assembly to the LORD your God; you shall do no work on it.

⁹ "You shall count seven weeks; begin to count the seven weeks from the time you first put the sickle to the standing ¹⁰ grain. Then you shall keep the feast of weeks to the LORD your God with the tribute of a freewill offering from your hand, which you shall give as the LORD your God blesses you; ¹¹ and you shall rejoice before the LORD your God, you and your son and your daughter, your manservant and your maidservant, the Levite who is within your towns, the sojourner, the fatherless, and the widow who are among you, at the place which the LORD your God will choose, to make his name dwell there. ¹² You shall remember that you were a slave in Egypt; and you shall be careful to observe these statutes.

¹³ "You shall keep the feast of booths seven days, when you make your ingathering from your threshing floor and your wine ¹⁴ press; you shall rejoice in your feast, you and your son and your daughter, your manservant and your maidservant, the Levite, the sojourner, the fatherless, and the widow who are ¹⁵ within your towns. For seven days you shall keep the feast to the LORD your God at the place which the LORD will choose; because the LORD your God will bless you in all your produce and in all the work of your hands, so that you will be altogether ¹⁶ joyful.

"Three times a year all your males shall appear before the LORD your God at the place which he will choose: at the feast of unleavened bread, at the feast of weeks, and at the feast of booths. They shall not appear before the LORD empty-handed; ¹⁷ every man shall give as he is able, according to the blessing of the LORD your God which he has given you.

¹⁸ "You shall appoint judges and officers in all your towns which the LORD your God gives you, according to your tribes; and ¹⁹ they shall judge the people with righteous judgment. You shall not pervert justice; you shall not show partiality; and you shall not take a bribe, for a bribe blinds the eyes of the wise and ²⁰ subverts the cause of the righteous. Justice, and only justice, you shall follow, that you may live and inherit the land which the LORD your God gives you.

²¹ "You shall not plant any tree as an Ashe'rah beside the altar ²² of the LORD your God which you shall make. And you shall not set up a pillar, which the LORD your God hates.

17 "You shall not sacrifice to the LORD your God an ox or a sheep in which is a blemish, any defect whatever; for that is an abomination to the LORD your God.

² "If there is found among you, within any of your towns which the LORD your God gives you, a man or woman who does what is evil in the sight of the LORD your God, in transgressing ³ his covenant, and has gone and served other gods and worshiped them, or the sun or the moon or any of the host of heaven, ⁴ which I have forbidden, and it is told you and you hear of it; then you shall inquire diligently, and if it is true and certain that such an abominable thing has been done in Israel, ⁵ then you shall bring forth to your gates that man or woman who has done this evil thing, and you shall stone that man ⁶ or woman to death with stones. On the evidence of two witnesses or of three witnesses he that is to die shall be put to death; a person shall not be put to death on the evidence of ⁷ one witness. The hand of the witnesses shall be first against him to put him to death, and afterward the hand of all the people. So you shall purge the evil from the midst of you.

⁸ "If any case arises requiring decision between one kind of homicide and another, one kind of legal right and another, or one kind of assault and another, any case within your towns which is too difficult for you, then you shall arise and go up ⁹ to the place which the LORD your God will choose, and coming to the Levitical priests, and to the judge who is in office in those days, you shall consult them, and they shall declare to ¹⁰ you the decision. Then you shall do according to what they declare to you from that place which the LORD will choose; and you shall be careful to do according to all that they direct you; ¹¹ according to the instructions which they give you, and according to the decision which they pronounce to you, you shall do; you shall not turn aside from the verdict which they declare ¹² to you, either to the right hand or to the left. The man who acts presumptuously, by not obeying the priest who stands to minister there before the LORD your God, or the judge, and that man ¹³ shall die; so you shall purge the evil from Israel. And all the people shall hear, and fear, and not act presumptuously again.

¹⁴ "When you come to the land which the LORD your God gives you, and you possess it and dwell in it, and then say, 'I will set a king over me, like all the nations that are round about me'; ¹⁵ you may indeed set as king over you him whom the LORD your God will choose. One from among your brethren you shall set as king over you; you may not put a foreigner over you, who is ¹⁶ not your brother. Only he must not multiply horses for himself, or cause the people to return to Egypt in order to multiply horses, since the LORD has said to you, 'You shall never return ¹⁷ that way again.' And he shall not multiply wives for himself, lest his heart turn away; nor shall he greatly multiply for himself silver and gold.

¹⁸ "And when he sits on the throne of his kingdom, he shall write for himself in a book a copy of this law, from that which ¹⁹ is in charge of the Levitical priests; and it shall be with him, and he shall read in it all the days of his life, that he may learn to fear the LORD his God, by keeping all the words of ²⁰ this law and these statutes, and doing them; that his heart may not be lifted up above his brethren, and that he may not turn aside from the commandment, either to the right hand or to the left; so that he may continue long in his kingdom, he and his children, in Israel.

18 "The Levitical priests, that is, all the tribe of Levi, shall have no portion or inheritance with Israel; they shall eat ² the offerings by fire to the LORD, and his rightful dues. They shall have no inheritance among their brethren; the LORD is ³ their inheritance, as he promised them. And this shall be the priests' due from the people, from those offering a sacrifice, whether it be ox or sheep: they shall give to the priest the ⁴ shoulder and the two cheeks and the stomach. The first fruits of your grain, of your wine and of your oil, and the first of the ⁵ fleece of your sheep, you shall give him. For the LORD your God has chosen him out of all your tribes, to stand and minister in the name of the LORD, him and his sons for ever.

⁶ "And if a Levite comes from any of your towns out of all Israel, where he lives—and he may come when he desires—to ⁷ the place which the LORD will choose, then he may minister in the name of the LORD his God, like all his fellow-Levites who ⁸ stand to minister there before the LORD. They shall have equal portions to eat, besides what he receives from the sale of his patrimony.ᵐ

⁹ "When you come into the land which the LORD your God gives you, you shall not learn to follow the abominable prac- ¹⁰ tices of those nations. There shall not be found among you any one who burns his son or his daughter as an offering,ⁿ any one who practices divination, a soothsayer, or an augur, or a ¹¹ sorcerer, or a charmer, or a medium, or a wizard, or a necro- ¹² mancer. For whoever does these things is an abomination to the LORD; and because of these abominable practices the LORD ¹³ your God is driving them out before you. You shall be blame- ¹⁴ less before the LORD your God. For these nations, which you are about to dispossess, give heed to soothsayers and to diviners; but as for you, the LORD your God has not allowed you so to do.

¹⁵ "The LORD your God will raise up for you a prophet like me from among you, from your brethren—him you shall heed— ¹⁶ just as you desired of the LORD your God at Horeb on the day of the assembly; when you said, 'Let me not hear again the voice of the LORD my God, or see this great fire any more, lest ¹⁷ I die.' And the LORD said to me, 'They have rightly said all ¹⁸ that they have spoken. I will raise up for them a prophet like you from among their brethren; and I will put my words in his mouth, and he shall speak to them all that I command him. ¹⁹ And whoever will not give heed to my words which he shall ²⁰ speak in my name, I myself will require it of him. But the

ᵐ Heb obscure   ⁿ Heb *makes his son or his daughter pass through the fire*

prophet who presumes to speak a word in my name which I have not commanded him to speak, or who speaks in the name
21 of other gods, that same prophet shall die.' And if you say in your heart, 'How may we know the word which the LORD has
22 not spoken?'—when a prophet speaks in the name of the LORD, if the word does not come to pass or come true, that is a word which the LORD has not spoken; the prophet has spoken it presumptuously, you need not be afraid of him.

19 "When the LORD your God cuts off the nations whose land the LORD your God gives you, and you dispossess
2 them and dwell in their cities and in their houses, you shall set apart three cities for you in the land which the LORD your
3 God gives you to possess. You shall prepare the roads, and divide into three parts the area of the land which the LORD your God gives you as a possession, so that any manslayer can flee to them.

4 "This is the provision for the manslayer, who by fleeing there may save his life. If any one kills his neighbor unintentionally
5 without having been at enmity with him in time past—as when a man goes into the forest with his neighbor to cut wood, and his hand swings the axe to cut down a tree, and the head slips from the handle and strikes his neighbor so that he dies—he
6 may flee to one of these cities and save his life; lest the avenger of blood in hot anger pursue the manslayer and overtake him, because the way is long, and wound him mortally, though the man did not deserve to die, since he was not at enmity with
7 his neighbor in time past. Therefore I command you, You shall
8 set apart three cities. And if the LORD your God enlarges your border, as he has sworn to your fathers, and gives you all the
9 land which he promised to give to your fathers—provided you are careful to keep all this commandment, which I command you this day, by loving the LORD your God and by walking ever in his ways—then you shall add three other cities to these three,
10 lest innocent blood be shed in your land which the LORD your God gives you for an inheritance, and so the guilt of bloodshed be upon you.

11 "But if any man hates his neighbor, and lies in wait for him, and attacks him, and wounds him mortally so that he dies, and
12 the man flees into one of these cities, then the elders of his city shall send and fetch him from there, and hand him over to the
13 avenger of blood, so that he may die. Your eye shall not pity him, but you shall purge the guilt of innocent blood° from Israel, so that it may be well with you.

14 "In the inheritance which the LORD your God gives you to possess, in the land that the LORD your God gives you to possess, you shall not remove your neighbor's landmark, which the men of old have set.

15 "A single witness shall not prevail against a man for any crime or for any wrong in connection with any offense that he has committed; only on the evidence of two witnesses, or of
16 three witnesses, shall a charge be sustained. If a malicious witness rises against any man to accuse him of wrongdoing,
17 then both parties to the dispute shall appear before the LORD, before the priests and the judges who are in office in those
18 days; the judges shall inquire diligently, and if the witness is
19 a false witness and has accused his brother falsely, then you shall do to him as he had meant to do to his brother; so you
20 shall purge the evil from the midst of you. And the rest shall hear, and fear, and shall never again commit any such evil
21 among you. Your eye shall not pity; it shall be life for life, eye for eye, tooth for tooth, hand for hand, foot for foot.

20 "When you go forth to war against your enemies, and see horses and chariots and an army larger than your own, you shall not be afraid of them; for the LORD your God is
2 with you, who brought you up out of the land of Egypt. And when you draw near to the battle, the priest shall come forward
3 and speak to the people, and shall say to them, 'Hear, O Israel, you draw near this day to battle against your enemies: let not your heart faint; do not fear, or tremble, or be in dread of
4 them; for the LORD your God is he that goes with you, to fight
5 for you against your enemies, to give you the victory.' Then the officers shall speak to the people, saying, 'What man is there that has built a new house and has not dedicated it? Let him go back to his house, lest he die in the battle and another
6 man dedicate it. And what man is there that has planted a vineyard and has not enjoyed its fruit? Let him go back to his house, lest he die in the battle and another man enjoy its
7 fruit. And what man is there that has betrothed a wife and has not taken her? Let him go back to his house, lest he die
8 in the battle and another man take her.' And the officers shall speak further to the people, and say, 'What man is there that

° Or *the blood of the innocent*

is fearful and fainthearted? Let him go back to his house, lest
9 the heart of his fellows melt as his heart.' And when the officers have made an end of speaking to the people, then commanders shall be appointed at the head of the people.
10 "When you draw near to a city to fight against it, offer terms
11 of peace to it. And if its answer to you is peace and it opens to you, then all the people who are found in it shall do forced
12 labor for you and shall serve you. But if it makes no peace with you, but makes war against you, then you shall besiege it;
13 and when the LORD your God gives it into your hand you shall
14 put all its males to the sword, but the women and the little ones, the cattle, and everything else in the city, all its spoil, you shall take as booty for yourselves; and you shall enjoy the spoil of your enemies, which the LORD your God has given you.
15 Thus you shall do to all the cities which are very far from you,
16 which are not cities of the nations here. But in the cities of these peoples that the LORD your God gives you for an inheri-
17 tance, you shall save alive nothing that breathes, but you shall utterly destroy them, the Hittites and the Amorites, the Canaanites and the Per'izzites, the Hivites and the Jeb'usites, as the
18 LORD your God has commanded; that they may not teach you to do according to all their abominable practices which they have done in the service of their gods, and so to sin against the LORD your God.
19 "When you besiege a city for a long time, making war against it in order to take it, you shall not destroy its trees by wielding an axe against them; for you may eat of them, but you shall not cut them down. Are the trees in the field men that they
20 should be besieged by you? Only the trees which you know are not trees for food you may destroy and cut down that you may build siegeworks against the city that makes war with you, until it falls.

21 "If in the land which the LORD your God gives you to possess, any one is found slain, lying in the open country,
2 and it is not known who killed him, then your elders and your judges shall come forth, and they shall measure the distance to
3 the cities which are around him that is slain; and the elders of the city which is nearest to the slain man shall take a heifer which has never been worked and which has not pulled in the
4 yoke. And the elders of that city shall bring the heifer down to a valley with running water, which is neither plowed nor sown, and shall break the heifer's neck there in the valley.
5 And the priests the sons of Levi shall come forward, for the LORD your God has chosen them to minister to him and to bless in the name of the LORD, and by their word every dispute
6 and every assault shall be settled. And all the elders of that city nearest to the slain man shall wash their hands over the heifer
7 whose neck was broken in the valley; and they shall testify, 'Our hands did not shed this blood, neither did our eyes see it
8 shed. Forgive, O LORD, thy people Israel, whom thou hast redeemed, and set not the guilt of innocent blood in the midst of thy people Israel; but let the guilt of blood be forgiven
9 them.' So you shall purge the guilt of innocent blood from your midst, when you do what is right in the sight of the LORD.
10 "When you go forth to war against your enemies, and the

LORD your God gives them into your hands, and you take them
11 captive, and see among the captives a beautiful woman, and you have desire for her and would take her for yourself as
12 wife, then you shall bring her home to your house, and she
13 shall shave her head and pare her nails. And she shall put off her captive's garb, and shall remain in your house and bewail her father and her mother a full month; after that you may go in to her, and be her husband, and she shall be your wife.
14 Then, if you have no delight in her, you shall let her go where she will; but you shall not sell her for money, you shall not

treat her as a slave, since you have humiliated her.
15 "If a man has two wives, the one loved and the other disliked, and they have borne him children, both the loved and
16 the disliked, and if the first-born son is hers that is disliked, then
on the day when he assigns his possessions as an inheritance to
his sons, he may not treat the son of the loved as the first-born
in preference to the son of the disliked, who is the first-born,
17 but he shall acknowledge the first-born, the son of the disliked,
by giving him a double portion of all that he has, for he is the
first issue of his strength; the right of the first-born is his.
18 "If a man has a stubborn and rebellious son, who will not
obey the voice of his father or the voice of his mother, and,
19 though they chastise him, will not give heed to them, then his
father and his mother shall take hold of him and bring him out
to the elders of his city at the gate of the place where he lives,
20 and they shall say to the elders of his city, 'This our son is
stubborn and rebellious, he will not obey our voice; he is a
21 glutton and a drunkard.' Then all the men of the city shall stone
him to death with stones; so you shall purge the evil from your
midst; and all Israel shall hear, and fear.
22 "And if a man has committed a crime punishable by death
23 and he is put to death, and you hang him on a tree, his body
shall not remain all night upon the tree, but you shall bury
him the same day, for a hanged man is accursed by God; you
shall not defile your land which the LORD your God gives you
for an inheritance.
22 "You shall not see your brother's ox or his sheep go
astray, and withhold your help[p] from them; you shall
2 take them back to your brother. And if he is not near you, or
if you do not know him, you shall bring it home to your house,
and it shall be with you until your brother seeks it; then you
3 shall restore it to him. And so you shall do with his ass; so you
shall do with his garment; so you shall do with any lost thing
of your brother's, which he loses and you find; you may not
4 withhold your help. You shall not see your brother's ass or his
ox fallen down by the way, and withhold your help[p] from
them; you shall help him to lift them up again.
5 "A woman shall not wear anything that pertains to a man,
nor shall a man put on a woman's garment; for whoever does
these things is an abomination to the LORD your God.
6 "If you chance to come upon a bird's nest, in any tree or
on the ground, with young ones or eggs and the mother sitting
upon the young or upon the eggs, you shall not take the mother
7 with the young; you shall let the mother go, but the young
you may take to yourself; that it may go well with you, and
that you may live long.
8 "When you build a new house, you shall make a parapet for
your roof, that you may not bring the guilt of blood upon your
house, if any one fall from it.
9 "You shall not sow your vineyard with two kinds of seed,
lest the whole yield be forfeited to the sanctuary,[q] the crop
10 which you have shown and the yield of the vineyard. You shall
11 not plow with an ox and an ass together. You shall not wear a
mingled stuff, wool and linen together.
12 "You shall make yourself tassels on the four corners of your
cloak with which you cover yourself.
13 "If any man takes a wife, and goes in to her, and then spurns
14 her, and charges her with shameful conduct, and brings an
evil name upon her, saying, 'I took this woman, and when I
came near her, I did not find in her the tokens of virginity,'
15 then the father of the young woman and her mother shall take
and bring out the tokens of her virginity to the elders of the
16 city in the gate; and the father of the young woman shall say
to the elders, 'I gave my daughter to this man to wife, and he
17 spurns her; and lo, he has made shameful charges against her,
saying, "I did not find in your daughter the tokens of virginity." And yet these are the tokens of my daughter's virginity.' And they shall spread the garment before the elders
18 of the city. Then the elders of that city shall take the man and
19 whip him; and they shall fine him a hundred shekels of silver,
and give them to the father of the young woman, because he
has brought an evil name upon a virgin of Israel; and she shall
20 be his wife; he may not put her away all his days. But if the
thing is true, that the tokens of virginity were not found in the
21 young woman, then they shall bring out the young woman to
the door of her father's house, and the men of her city shall
stone her to death with stones, because she has wrought folly
in Israel by playing the harlot in her father's house; so you shall
purge the evil from the midst of you.
22 "If a man is found lying with the wife of another man, both
of them shall die, the man who lay with the woman, and the
woman; so you shall purge the evil from Israel.
23 "If there is a betrothed virgin, and a man meets her in the
24 city and lies with her, then you shall bring them both out
to the gate of that city, and you shall stone them to death
with stones, the young woman because she did not cry for help
though she was in the city, and the man because he violated his
neighbor's wife; so you shall purge the evil from the midst
of you.
25 "But if in the open country a man meets a young woman who
is betrothed, and the man seizes her and lies with her, then
26 only the man who lay with her shall die. But to the young
woman you shall do nothing; in the young woman there is no
offense punishable by death, for this case is like that of a man
27 attacking and murdering his neighbor; because he came upon
her in the open country, and though the betrothed young
woman cried for help there was no one to rescue her.
28 "If a man meets a virgin who is not betrothed, and seizes
29 her and lies with her, and they are found, then the man who
lay with her shall give to the father of the young woman fifty
shekels of silver, and she shall be his wife, because he has
violated her; he may not put her away all his days.
30 [r] "A man shall not take his father's wife, nor shall he uncover
her who is his father's.[s]
23 "He whose testicles are crushed or whose male member
is cut off shall not enter the assembly of the LORD.
2 "No bastard shall enter the assembly of the LORD; even to the
tenth generation none of his descendants shall enter the assembly of the LORD.
3 "No Ammonite or Moabite shall enter the assembly of the
LORD; even to the tenth generation none belonging to them shall
4 enter the assembly of the LORD for ever; because they did not
meet you with bread and with water on the way, when you
came forth out of Egypt, and because they hired against you
Balaam the son of Be'or from Pethor of Mesopota'mia, to curse
5 you. Nevertheless the LORD your God would not hearken to
Balaam; but the LORD your God turned the curse into a blessing
6 for you, because the LORD your God loved you. You shall not
seek their peace or their prosperity all your days for ever.
7 "You shall not abhor an E'domite, for he is your brother; you
shall not abhor an Egyptian, because you were a sojourner in
8 his land. The children of the third generation that are born to
them may enter the assembly of the LORD.
9 "When you go forth against your enemies and are in camp,
then you shall keep yourself from every evil thing.
10 "If there is among you any man who is not clean by reason
of what chances to him by night, then he shall go outside the
11 camp, he shall not come within the camp; but when evening
comes on, he shall bathe himself in water, and when the sun is
down, he may come within the camp.
12 "You shall have a place outside the camp and you shall go
13 out to it; and you shall have a stick with your weapons; and
when you sit down outside, you shall dig a hole with it, and
14 turn back and cover up your excrement. Because the LORD your
God walks in the midst of your camp, to save you and to give
up your enemies before you, therefore your camp must be
holy, that he may not see anything indecent among you, and
turn away from you.
15 "You shall not give up to his master a slave who has escaped
16 from his master to you; he shall dwell with you, in your midst,
in the place which he shall choose within one of your towns,
where it pleases him best; you shall not oppress him.
17 "There shall be no cult prostitute of the daughters of Israel,
neither shall there be a cult prostitute of the sons of Israel.
18 You shall not bring the hire of a harlot, or the wages of a
dog,[t] into the house of the LORD your God in payment for any
vow; for both of these are an abomination to the LORD your
God.
19 "You shall not lend upon interest to your brother, interest on
money, interest on victuals, interest on anything that is lent for
20 interest. To a foreigner you may lend upon interest, but to your
brother you shall not lend upon interest; that the LORD your
God may bless you in all that you undertake in the land which
you are entering to take possession of it.
21 "When you make a vow to the LORD your God, you shall not
be slack to pay it; for the LORD your God will surely require it
22 of you, and it would be sin in you. But if you refrain from
23 vowing, it shall be no sin in you. You shall be careful to perform what has passed your lips, for you have voluntarily

[p] Heb *hide yourself* [q] Heb *become holy* [r] Ch 23. 1 in Heb [s] Heb *uncover his father's skirt* [t] Or *sodomite*

vowed to the Lord your God what you have promised with your mouth.

24 "When you go into your neighbor's vineyard, you may eat your fill of grapes, as many as you wish, but you shall not put 25 any in your vessel. When you go into your neighbor's standing grain, you may pluck the ears with your hand, but you shall not put a sickle to your neighbor's standing grain.

24 "When a man takes a wife and marries her, if then she finds no favor in his eyes because he has found some indecency in her, and he writes her a bill of divorce and puts it in her hand and sends her out of his house, and she departs 2 out of his house, and if she goes and becomes another man's 3 wife, and the latter husband dislikes her and writes her a bill of divorce and puts it in her hand and sends her out of his house, or if the latter husband dies, who took her to be his 4 wife, then her former husband, who sent her away, may not take her again to be his wife, after she has been defiled; for that is an abomination before the Lord, and you shall not bring guilt upon the land which the Lord your God gives you for an inheritance.

5 "When a man is newly married, he shall not go out with the army or be charged with any business; he shall be free at home one year, to be happy with his wife whom he has taken.

6 "No man shall take a mill or an upper millstone in pledge; for he would be taking a life in pledge.

7 "If a man is found stealing one of his brethren, the people of Israel, and if he treats him as a slave or sells him, then that thief shall die; so you shall purge the evil from the midst of you.

8 "Take heed, in an attack of leprosy, to be very careful to do according to all that the Levitical priests shall direct you; as I 9 commanded them, so you shall be careful to do. Remember what the Lord your God did to Miriam on the way as you came forth out of Egypt.

10 "When you make your neighbor a loan of any sort, you shall 11 not go into his house to fetch his pledge. You shall stand outside, and the man to whom you make the loan shall bring the 12 pledge out to you. And if he is a poor man, you shall not sleep 13 in his pledge; when the sun goes down, you shall restore to him the pledge that he may sleep in his cloak and bless you; and it shall be righteousness to you before the Lord your God.

14 "You shall not oppress a hired servant who is poor and needy, whether he is one of your brethren or one of the sojourners 15 who are in your land within your towns; you shall give him his hire on the day he earns it, before the sun goes down (for he is poor, and sets his heart upon it); lest he cry against you to the Lord, and it be sin in you.

16 "The fathers shall not be put to death for the children, nor shall the children be put to death for the fathers; every man shall be put to death for his own sin.

17 "You shall not pervert the justice due to the sojourner or to 18 the fatherless, or take a widow's garment in pledge; but you shall remember that you were a slave in Egypt and the Lord your God redeemed you from there; therefore I command you to do this.

19 "When you reap your harvest in your field, and have forgotten a sheaf in the field, you shall not go back to get it; it shall be for the sojourner, the fatherless, and the widow; that the Lord your God may bless you in all the work of your hands. 20 When you beat your olive trees, you shall not go over the boughs again; it shall be for the sojourner, the fatherless, and 21 the widow. When you gather the grapes of your vineyard, you shall not glean it afterward; it shall be for the sojourner, the 22 fatherless, and the widow. You shall remember that you were a slave in the land of Egypt; therefore I command you to do this.

25 "If there is a dispute between men, and they come into court, and the judges decide between them, acquitting the 2 innocent and comdemning the guilty, then if the guilty man deserves to be beaten, the judge shall cause him to lie down and be beaten in his presence with a number of stripes in pro- 3 portion to his offense. Forty stripes may be given him, but not more; lest, if one should go on to beat him with more stripes than these, your brother be degraded in your sight.

4 "You shall not muzzle an ox when it treads out the grain.

5 "If brothers dwell together, and one of them dies and has no son, the wife of the dead shall not be married outside the family to a stranger; her husband's brother shall go in to her, and take her as his wife, and perform the duty of a husband's 6 brother to her. And the first son whom she bears shall succeed

u Heb *its name*

to the name of his brother who is dead, that his name may not 7 be blotted out of Israel. And if the man does not wish to take his brother's wife, then his brother's wife shall go up to the gate to the elders, and say, 'My husband's brother refuses to

perpetuate his brother's name in Israel; he will not perform the 8 duty of a husband's brother to me.' Then the elders of his city shall call him, and speak to him: and if he persists, saying, 'I 9 do not wish to take her,' then his brother's wife shall go up to him in the presence of the elders, and pull his sandal off his foot, and spit in his face; and she shall answer and say, 'So shall it be done to the man who does not build up his brother's 10 house.' And the name of his house u shall be called in Israel, The house of him that had his sandal pulled off.

11 "When men fight with one another, and the wife of the one draws near to rescue her husband from the hand of him who is beating him, and puts out her hand and seizes him by the 12 private parts, then you shall cut off her hand; your eye shall have no pity.

13 "You shall not have in your bag two kinds of weights, a large 14 and a small. You shall not have in your house two kinds of 15 measures, a large and a small. A full and just weight you shall have, a full and just measure you shall have; that your days may be prolonged in the land which the Lord your God gives 16 you. For all who do such things, all who act dishonestly, are an abomination to the Lord your God.

17 "Remember what Am'alek did to you on the way as you 18 came out of Egypt, how he attacked you on the way, when you were faint and weary, and cut off at your rear all who lagged 19 behind you; and he did not fear God. Therefore when the Lord your God has given you rest from all your enemies round about, in the land which the Lord your God gives you for an inheritance to possess, you shall blot out the remembrance of Am'alek from under heaven; you shall not forget.

26 "When you come into the land which the Lord your God gives you for an inheritance, and have taken possession of 2 it, and live in it, you shall take some of the first of all the fruit of the ground, which you harvest from your land that the Lord your God gives you, and you shall put it in a basket, and you shall go to the place which the Lord your God will choose, 3 to make his name to dwell there. And you shall go to the priest who is in office at that time, and say to him, 'I declare this day to the Lord your God that I have come into the land which 4 the Lord swore to our fathers to give us.' Then the priest shall take the basket from your hand, and set it down before the altar of the Lord your God.

5 "And you shall make response before the Lord your God, 'A wandering Aramean was my father; and he went down into Egypt and sojourned there, few in number; and there he 6 became a nation, great, mighty, and populous. And the Egyptians treated us harshly, and afflicted us, and laid upon us 7 hard bondage. Then we cried to the Lord the God of our fathers, and the Lord heard our voice, and saw our affliction, 8 our toil, and our oppression; and the Lord brought us out of Egypt with a mighty hand and an outstretched arm, with great 9 terror, with signs and wonders; and he brought us into this place and gave us this land, a land flowing with milk and 10 honey. And behold, now I bring the first of the fruit of the ground, which thou, O Lord, hast given me.' And you shall set

it down before the LORD your God, and worship before the
[11] LORD your God; and you shall rejoice in all the good which the
LORD your God has given to you and to your house, you, and
the Levite, and the sojourner who is among you.

[12] "When you have finished paying all the tithe of your produce
in the third year, which is the year of tithing, giving it to the
Levite, the sojourner, the fatherless, and the widow, that they
[13] may eat within your towns and be filled, then you shall say
before the LORD your God, 'I have removed the sacred portion
out of my house, and moreover I have given it to the Levite,
the sojourner, the fatherless, and the widow, according to all
thy commandment which thou hast commanded me; I have
not transgressed any of thy commandments, neither have I
[14] forgotten them; I have not eaten of the tithe while I was
mourning, or removed any of it while I was unclean, or offered
any of it to the dead; I have obeyed the voice of the LORD my
God, I have done according to all that thou hast commanded
[15] me. Look down from thy holy habitation, from heaven, and
bless thy people Israel and the ground which thou hast given
us, as thou didst swear to our fathers, a land flowing with
milk and honey.'

[16] "This day the LORD your God commands you to do these
statutes and ordinances; you shall therefore be careful to do
[17] them with all your heart and with all your soul. You have
declared this day concerning the LORD that he is your God, and
that you will walk in his ways, and keep his statutes and his
commandments and his ordinances, and will obey his voice;
[18] and the LORD has declared this day concerning you that you
are a people for his own possession, as he has promised you,
[19] and that you are to keep all his commandments, that he will
set you high above all nations that he has made, in praise and
in fame and in honor, and that you shall be a people holy to
the LORD your God, as he has spoken."

Altars and Ceremonies

27 Now Moses and the elders of Israel commanded
the people, saying, "Keep all the commandment
[2] which I command you this day. And on the day you pass
over the Jordan to the land which the LORD your God
gives you, you shall set up large stones, and plaster them
[3] with plaster; and you shall write upon them all the words
of this law, when you pass over to enter the land which
the LORD your God gives you, a land flowing with milk
and honey, as the LORD, the God of your fathers, has
[4] promised you. And when you have passed over the
Jordan, you shall set up these stones, concerning which
I command you this day, on Mount Ebal, and you shall
[5] plaster them with plaster. And there you shall build an
altar to the LORD your God, an altar of stones; you shall
[6] lift up no iron tool upon them. You shall build an altar
to the LORD your God of unhewn [v] stones; and you shall
[7] offer burnt offerings on it to the LORD your God; and you
shall sacrifice peace offerings, and shall eat there; and
[8] you shall rejoice before the LORD your God. And you shall
write upon the stones all the words of this law very
plainly."

[9] And Moses and the Levitical priests said to all Israel,
"Keep silence and hear, O Israel: this day you have
[10] become the people of the LORD your God. You shall therefore obey the voice of the LORD your God, keeping his
commandments and his statutes, which I command you
this day."

[11, 12] And Moses charged the people the same day, saying, "When
you have passed over the Jordan, these shall stand upon

Mount Ger'izim to bless the people: Simeon, Levi, Judah, Is'-
[13] sachar, Joseph, and Benjamin. And these shall stand upon
Mount Ebal for the curse: Reuben, Gad, Asher, Zeb'ulun, Dan,
[14] and Naph'tali. And the Levites shall declare to all the men of
Israel with a loud voice:

[15] "'Cursed be the man who makes a graven or molten image,
an abomination to the LORD, a thing made by the hands of a
craftsman, and sets it up in secret.' And all the people shall
answer and say, 'Amen.'

[16] "'Cursed be he who dishonors his father or his mother.' And
all the people shall say, 'Amen.'

[17] "'Cursed be he who removes his neighbor's landmark.' And
all the people shall say, 'Amen.'

[18] "'Cursed be he who misleads a blind man on the road.' And
all the people shall say, 'Amen.'

[19] "'Cursed be he who perverts the justice due to the sojourner,
the fatherless, and the widow.' And all the people shall say,
'Amen.'

[20] "'Cursed be he who lies with his father's wife, because he has
uncovered her who is his father's.' [w] And all the people shall
say, 'Amen.'

[21] "'Cursed be he who lies with any kind of beast.' And all the
people shall say, 'Amen.'

[22] "'Cursed be he who lies with his sister, whether the daughter
of his father or the daughter of his mother.' And all the people
shall say, 'Amen.'

[23] "'Cursed be he who lies with his mother-in-law.' And all the
people shall say, 'Amen.'

[24] "'Cursed be he who slays his neighbor in secret.' And all the
people shall say, 'Amen.'

[25] "'Cursed be he who takes a bribe to slay an innocent person.'
And all the people shall say, 'Amen.'

[26] "'Cursed be he who does not confirm the words of this law
by doing them.' And all the people shall say, 'Amen.'

Blessings and Curses

28 "And if you obey the voice of the LORD your God, being
careful to do all his commandments which I command you
this day, the LORD your God will set you high above all the
[2] nations of the earth. And all these blessings shall come upon
you and overtake you, if you obey the voice of the LORD your
[3] God. Blessed shall you be in the city, and blessed shall you be
[4] in the field. Blessed shall be the fruit of your body, and the
fruit of your ground, and the fruit of your beasts, the increase
[5] of your cattle, and the young of your flock. Blessed shall be
[6] your basket and your kneading-trough. Blessed shall you be
when you come in, and blessed shall you be when you go out.
[7] "The LORD will cause your enemies who rise against you to be
defeated before you; they shall come out against you one way,
[8] and flee before you seven ways. The LORD will command the
blessing upon you in your barns, and in all that you undertake; and he will bless you in the land which the LORD your God
[9] gives you. The LORD will establish you as a people holy to himself, as he has sworn to you, if you keep the commandments
[10] of the LORD your God, and walk in his ways. And all the
peoples of the earth shall see that you are called by the name
[11] of the LORD; and they shall be afraid of you. And the LORD will
make you abound in prosperity, in the fruit of your body, and
in the fruit of your cattle, and in the fruit of your ground,
within the land which the LORD swore to your fathers to give
[12] you. The LORD will open to you his good treasury the heavens,
to give the rain of your land in its season and to bless all the
work of your hands; and you shall lend to many nations, but
[13] you shall not borrow. And the LORD will make you the head,
and not the tail; and you shall tend upward only, and not
downward; if you obey the commandments of the LORD your
God, which I command you this day, being careful to do them,
[14] and if you do not turn aside from any of the words which I
command you this day, to the right hand or to the left, to go
after other gods to serve them.

[15] "But if you will not obey the voice of the LORD your God or
be careful to do all his commandments and his statutes which I
command you this day, then all these curses shall came upon
[16] you and overtake you. Cursed shall you be in the city, and
[17] cursed shall you be in the field. Cursed shall be your basket
[18] and your kneading-trough. Cursed shall be the fruit of your
body, and the fruit of your ground, the increase of your cattle,
[19] and the young of your flock. Cursed shall you be when you
come in, and cursed shall you be when you go out.
[20] "The LORD will send upon you curses, confusion, and frustra-

[v] Heb *whole*   [w] Heb *uncovered his father's skirt*

123

tion, in all that you undertake to do, until you are destroyed and perish quickly, on account of the evil of your doings, be-
21 cause you have forsaken me. The LORD will make the pestilence cleave to you until he has consumed you off the land which
22 you are entering to take possession of it. The LORD will smite you with consumption, and with fever, inflammation, and fiery heat, and with drought,[x] and with blasting, and with mildew;
23 they shall pursue you until you perish. And the heavens over your head shall be brass, and the earth under you shall be iron.
24 The LORD will make the rain of your land powder and dust; from heaven it shall come down upon you until you are destroyed.
25 "The LORD will cause you to be defeated before your enemies; you shall go out one way against them, and flee seven ways before them; and you shall be a horror to all the kingdoms of
26 the earth. And your dead body shall be food for all birds of the air, and for the beasts of the earth; and there shall be no one
27 to frighten them away. The LORD will smite you with the boils of Egypt, and with the ulcers and the scurvy and the itch, of
28 which you cannot be healed. The LORD will smite you with mad-
29 ness and blindness and confusion of mind; and you shall grope at noonday, as the blind grope in darkness, and you shall not prosper in your ways; and you shall be only oppressed and
30 robbed continually, and there shall be no one to help you. You shall betroth a wife, and another man shall lie with her; you shall build a house, and you shall not dwell in it; you shall plant
31 a vineyard, and you shall not use the fruit of it. Your ox shall be slain before your eyes, and you shall not eat of it; your ass shall be violently taken away before your face, and shall not be restored to you; your sheep shall be given to your enemies,
32 and there shall be no one to help you. Your sons and your daughters shall be given to another people, while your eyes look on and fail with longing for them all the day; and it shall
33 not be in the power of your hand to prevent it. A nation which you have not known shall eat up the fruit of your ground and of all your labors; and you shall be only oppressed and crushed
34 continually; so that you shall be driven mad by the sight which
35 your eyes shall see. The LORD will smite you on the knees and on the legs with grievous boils of which you cannot be healed, from the sole of your foot to the crown of your head.
36 "The LORD will bring you, and your king whom you set over you, to a nation that neither you nor your fathers have known; and there you shall serve other gods, of wood and stone.
37 And you shall become a horror, a proverb, and a byword, among all the peoples where the LORD will lead you away.
38 You shall carry much seed into the field, and shall gather little
39 in; for the locust shall consume it. You shall plant vineyards and dress them, but you shall neither drink of the wine nor gather
40 the grapes; for the worm shall eat them. You shall have olive trees throughout all your territory, but you shall not anoint
41 yourself with the oil; for your olives shall drop off. You shall beget sons and daughters, but they shall not be yours; for they
42 shall go into captivity. All your trees and the fruit of your
43 ground the locust shall possess. The sojourner who is among you shall mount above you higher and higher; and you shall come
44 down lower and lower. He shall lend to you, and you shall not lend to him; he shall be the head, and you shall be the tail.
45 All these curses shall come upon you and pursue you and over-take you, till you are destroyed, because you did not obey the voice of the LORD your God, to keep his commandments and his
46 statutes which he commanded you. They shall be upon you as a sign and a wonder, and upon your descendants for ever.
47 "Because you did not serve the LORD your God with joyfulness and gladness of heart, by reason of the abundance of all things,
48 therefore you shall serve your enemies whom the LORD will send against you, in hunger and thirst, in nakedness, and in want of all things; and he will put a yoke of iron upon your neck, until
49 he has destroyed you. The LORD will bring a nation against you from afar, from the end of the earth, as swift as the eagle flies,
50 a nation whose language you do not understand, a nation of stern countenance, who shall not regard the person of the old
51 or show favor to the young, and shall eat the offspring of your cattle and the fruit of your ground, until you are destroyed; who also shall not leave you grain, wine, or oil, the increase of your cattle or the young of your flock, until they have caused
52 you to perish. They shall besiege you in all your towns, until your high and fortified walls, in which you trusted, come down throughout all your land; and they shall besiege you in all your towns throughout all your land, which the LORD your God has
53 given you. And you shall eat the offspring of your own body,

the flesh of your sons and daughters, whom the LORD your God has given you, in the siege and in the distress with which your
54 enemies shall distress you. The man who is the most tender and delicately bred among you will grudge food to his brother, to the wife of his bosom, and to the last of the children who
55 remain to him; so that he will not give to any of them any of the flesh of his children whom he is eating, because he has nothing left him, in the siege and in the distress with which
56 your enemy shall distress you in all your towns. The most tender and delicately bred woman among you, who would not venture to set the sole of her foot upon the ground because she is so delicate and tender, will grudge to the husband of her
57 bosom, to her son and to her daughter, her afterbirth that comes out from between her feet and her children whom she bears, because she will eat them secretly, for want of all things, in the siege and in the distress with which your enemy shall distress you in your towns.
58 "If you are not careful to do all the words of this law which are written in this book, that you may fear this glorious and
59 awful name, the LORD your God, then the LORD will bring on you and your offspring extraordinary afflictions, afflictions severe and
60 lasting, and sicknesses grievous and lasting. And he will bring upon you again all the diseases of Egypt, which you were
61 afraid of; and they shall cleave to you. Every sickness also, and every affliction which is not recorded in the book of this law, the LORD will bring upon you, until you are destroyed.
62 Whereas you were as the stars of heaven for multitude, you shall be left few in number; because you did not obey the voice
63 of the LORD your God. And as the LORD took delight in doing you good and multiplying you, so the LORD will take delight in bringing ruin upon you and destroying you; and you shall be plucked off the land which you are entering to take possession
64 of it. And the LORD will scatter you among all peoples, from one end of the earth to the other; and there you shall serve other gods, of wood and stone, which neither you nor your fathers
65 have known. And among these nations you shall find no ease, and there shall be no rest for the sole of your foot; but the LORD will give you there a trembling heart, and failing eyes,
66 and a languishing soul; your life shall hang in doubt before you; night and day you shall be in dread, and have no assur-
67 ance of your life. In the morning you shall say, 'Would it were evening!' and at evening you shall say, 'Would it were morn-
68 ing!' because of the dread which your heart shall fear, and the sights which your eyes shall see. And the LORD will bring you back in ships to Egypt, a journey which I promised that you should never make again; and there you shall offer your-selves for sale to your enemies as male and female slaves, but no man will buy you."

AN ADDRESS ABOUT THE COVENANT

29 [y] These are the words of the covenant which the LORD commanded Moses to make with the people of Israel in the land of Moab, besides the covenant which he had made with them at Horeb.
2 [z] And Moses summoned all Israel and said to them: "You have seen all that the LORD did before your eyes in the land of Egypt, to Pharaoh and to all his servants and to all his land,
3 the great trials which your eyes saw, the signs, and those great
4 wonders; but to this day the LORD has not given you a mind to
5 understand, or eyes to see, or ears to hear. I have led you forty years in the wilderness; your clothes have not worn out upon you, and your sandals have not worn off your feet;
6 you have not eaten bread, and you have not drunk wine or strong drink; that you may know that I am the LORD your God.
7 And when you came to this place, Sihon the king of Heshbon and Og the king of Bashan came out against us to battle, but
8 we defeated them; we took their land, and gave it for an inheritance to the Reubenites, the Gadites, and the half-tribe of
9 the Manas'sites. Therefore be careful to do the words of this covenant, that you may prosper [a] in all that you do.
10 "You stand this day all of you before the LORD your God; the heads of your tribes,[b] your elders, and your officers, all the
11 men of Israel, your little ones, your wives, and the sojourner who is in your camp, both he who hews your wood and he
12 who draws your water, that you may enter into the sworn covenant of the LORD your God, which the LORD your God makes
13 with you this day; that he may establish you this day as his people, and that he may be your God, as he promised you, and as he swore to your fathers, to Abraham, to Isaac, and to Jacob.

<hr>

[x] Another reading is *sword*   [y] Ch 28. 69 in Heb   [z] Ch 29. 1 in Heb   [a] Or *deal wisely*
[b] Gk Syr: Heb *your heads, your tribes*

¹⁴, ¹⁵ Nor is it with you only that I make this sworn covenant, but with him who is not here with us this day as well as with him who stands here with us this day before the LORD our God.

¹⁶ "You know how we dwelt in the land of Egypt, and how we came through the midst of the nations through which you ¹⁷ passed; and you have seen their detestable things, their idols of wood and stone, of silver and gold, which were among them. ¹⁸ Beware lest there be among you a man or woman or family or tribe, whose heart turns away this day from the LORD our God to go and serve the gods of those nations; lest there be among ¹⁹ you a root bearing poisonous and bitter fruit, one who, when he hears the words of this sworn covenant, blesses himself in his heart, saying, 'I shall be safe, though I walk in the stubbornness of my heart.' This would lead to the sweeping away ²⁰ of moist and dry alike. The LORD would not pardon him, but rather the anger of the LORD and his jealousy would smoke against that man, and the curses written in this book would settle upon him, and the LORD would blot out his name from ²¹ under heaven. And the LORD would single him out from all the tribes of Israel for calamity, in accordance with all the curses ²² of the covenant written in this book of the law. And the generation to come, your children who rise up after you, and the foreigner who comes from a far land, would say, when they see the afflictions of that land and the sicknesses with which ²³ the LORD has made it sick—the whole land brimstone and salt, and a burnt-out waste, unsown, and growing nothing, where no grass can sprout, an overthrow like that of Sodom and Gomor'rah, Admah and Zeboi'im, which the LORD overthrew in his ²⁴ anger and wrath—yea, all the nations would say, 'Why has the LORD done thus to this land? What means the heat of this great ²⁵ anger?' Then men would say, 'It is because they forsook the covenant of the LORD, the God of their fathers, which he made with them when he brought them out of the land of Egypt, ²⁶ and went and served other gods and worshiped them, gods whom they had not known and whom he had not allotted to ²⁷ them; therefore the anger of the LORD was kindled against this ²⁸ land, bringing upon it all the curses written in this book; and the LORD uprooted them from their land in anger and fury and great wrath, and cast them into another land, as at this day.' ²⁹ "The secret things belong to the LORD our God; but the things that are revealed belong to us and to our children for ever, that we may do all the words of this law.

30 "And when all these things come upon you, the blessing and the curse, which I have set before you, and you call them to mind among all the nations where the LORD your ² God has driven you, and return to the LORD your God, you and your children, and obey his voice in all that I command you ³ this day, with all your heart and with all your soul; then the LORD your God will restore your fortunes, and have compassion upon you, and he will gather you again from all the peoples ⁴ where the LORD your God has scattered you. If your outcasts are in the uttermost parts of heaven, from there the LORD your God will gather you, and from there he will fetch you; ⁵ and the LORD your God will bring you into the land which your fathers possessed, that you may possess it; and he will make you more prosperous and numerous than your fathers. ⁶ And the LORD your God will circumcise your heart and the heart of your offspring, so that you will love the LORD your God with all your heart and with all your soul, that you may ⁷ live. And the LORD your God will put all these curses upon ⁸ your foes and enemies who persecuted you. And you shall again obey the voice of the LORD, and keep all his commandments

ᶜ Gk: Heb lacks If you obey the commandments of the LORD your God

⁹ which I command you this day. The LORD your God will make you abundantly prosperous in all the work of your hand, in the fruit of your body, and in the fruit of your cattle, and in the fruit of your ground; for the LORD will again take delight in ¹⁰ prospering you, as he took delight in your fathers, if you obey the voice of the LORD your God, to keep his commandments and his statutes which are written in this book of the law, if you turn to the LORD your God with all your heart and with all your soul.

¹¹ "For this commandment which I command you this day is ¹² not too hard for you, neither is it far off. It is not in heaven, that you should say, 'Who will go up for us to heaven, and ¹³ bring it to us, that we may hear it and do it?' Neither is it beyond the sea, that you should say, 'Who will go over the sea for us, and bring it to us, that we may hear it and do it?' ¹⁴ But the word is very near you; it is in your mouth and in your heart, so that you can do it.

¹⁵ "See, I have set before you this day life and good, death and ¹⁶ evil. If you obey the commandments of the LORD your God ᶜ which I command you this day, by loving the LORD your God, by walking in his ways, and by keeping his commandments and his statutes and his ordinances, then you shall live and multiply, and the LORD your God will bless you in the land which ¹⁷ you are entering to take possession of it. But if your heart turns away, and you will not hear, but are drawn away to ¹⁸ worship other gods and serve them, I declare to you this day, that you shall perish; you shall not live long in the land which ¹⁹ you are going over the Jordan to enter and possess. I call heaven and earth to witness against you this day, that I have set before you life and death, blessing and curse; therefore ²⁰ choose life, that you and your descendants may live, loving the LORD your God, obeying his voice, and cleaving to him; for that means life to you and length of days, that you may dwell in the land which the LORD swore to your fathers, to Abraham, to Isaac, and to Jacob, to give them."

THE PARTING WORDS OF MOSES

31 So Moses continued to speak these words to all ² Israel. And he said to them, "I am a hundred and twenty years old this day; I am no longer able to go out and come in. The LORD has said to me, 'You shall not go ³ over this Jordan.' The LORD your God himself will go over before you; he will destroy these nations before you, so that you shall dispossess them; and Joshua will go ⁴ over at your head, as the LORD has spoken. And the LORD will do to them as he did to Sihon and Og, the kings of the Amorites, and to their land, when he destroyed them. ⁵ And the LORD will give them over to you, and you shall do to them according to all the commandment which I ⁶ have commanded you. Be strong and of good courage, do not fear or be in dread of them: for it is the LORD your God who goes with you; he will not fail you or forsake you."

⁷ Then Moses summoned Joshua, and said to him in the sight of all Israel, "Be strong and of good courage: for you shall go with this people into the land which the LORD has sworn to their fathers to give them; and you ⁸ shall put them in possession of it. It is the LORD who goes before you; he will be with you, he will not fail you or forsake you; do not fear or be dismayed."

⁹ And Moses wrote this law, and gave it to the priests the sons of Levi, who carried the ark of the covenant of ¹⁰ the LORD, and to all the elders of Israel. And Moses commanded them, "At the end of every seven years, at the set time of the year of release, at the feast of booths,

11 when all Israel comes to appear before the LORD your God at the place which he will choose, you shall read this law 12 before all Israel in their hearing. Assemble the people, men, women, and little ones, and the sojourner within your towns, that they may hear and learn to fear the LORD your God, and be careful to do all the words of 13 this law, and that their children, who have not known it, may hear and learn to fear the LORD your God, as long as you live in the land which you are going over the Jordan to possess."

14 And the LORD said to Moses, "Behold, the days approach when you must die; call Joshua, and present yourselves in the tent of meeting, that I may commission him." And Moses and Joshua went and presented them- 15 selves in the tent of meeting. And the LORD appeared in the tent in a pillar of cloud; and the pillar of cloud stood by the door of the tent.

16 And the LORD said to Moses, "Behold, you are about to sleep with your fathers; then this people will rise and play the harlot after the strange gods of the land, where they go to be among them, and they will forsake me and 17 break my covenant which I have made with them. Then my anger will be kindled against them in that day, and I will forsake them and hide my face from them, and they will be devoured; and many evils and troubles will come upon them, so that they will say in that day, 'Have not these evils come upon us because our God is not among 18 us?' And I will surely hide my face in that day on account of all the evil which they have done, because they have 19 turned to other gods. Now therefore write this song, and teach it to the people of Israel; put it in their mouths, that this song may be a witness for me against the people 20 of Israel. For when I have brought them into the land flowing with milk and honey, which I swore to give to their fathers, and they have eaten and are full and grown fat, they will turn to other gods and serve them, and 21 despise me and break my covenant. And when many evils and troubles have come upon them, this song shall confront them as a witness (for it will live unforgotten in the mouths of their descendants); for I know the purposes which they are already forming, before I have brought 22 them into the land that I swore to give." So Moses wrote this song the same day, and taught it to the people of Israel.

23 And the LORD commissioned Joshua the son of Nun and said, "Be strong and of good courage; for you shall bring the children of Israel into the land which I swore to give them: I will be with you."

24 When Moses had finished writing the words of this 25 law in a book, to the very end, Moses commanded the Levites who carried the ark of the covenant of the LORD, 26 "Take this book of the law, and put it by the side of the ark of the covenant of the LORD your God, that it may be

d Compare Gk: Heb Israel

27 there for a witness against you. For I know how rebellious and stubborn you are; behold, while I am yet alive with you, today you have been rebellious against 28 the LORD; how much more after my death! Assemble to me all the elders of your tribes, and your officers, that I may speak these words in their ears and call heaven and 29 earth to witness against them. For I know that after my death you will surely act corruptly, and turn aside from the way which I have commanded you; and in the days to come evil will befall you, because you will do what is evil in the sight of the LORD, provoking him to anger through the work of your hands."

The Song of Moses

30 Then Moses spoke the words of this song until they were finished, in the ears of all the assembly of Israel:

32 "Give ear, O heavens, and I will speak;
  and let the earth hear the words of my mouth.
2 May my teaching drop as the rain,
  my speech distil as the dew,
 as the gentle rain upon the tender grass,
  and as the showers upon the herb.
3 For I will proclaim the name of the LORD.
  Ascribe greatness to our God!
4 "The Rock, his work is perfect;
  for all his ways are justice.
 A God of faithfulness and without iniquity,
  just and right is he.
5 They have dealt corruptly with him,
  they are no longer his children because of their
    blemish;
 they are a perverse and crooked generation.
6 Do you thus requite the LORD,
  you foolish and senseless people?
 Is not he your father, who created you,
  who made you and established you?
7 Remember the days of old,
  consider the years of many generations;
 ask your father, and he will show you;
  your elders, and they will tell you.
8 When the Most High gave to the nations their inheritance,
  when he separated the sons of men,
 he fixed the bounds of the peoples
  according to the number of the sons of God.d
9 For the LORD's portion is his people.
  Jacob his allotted heritage.

10 "He found him in a desert land,
  and in the howling waste of the wilderness;
 he encircled him, he cared for him,
  he kept him as the apple of his eye.
11 Like an eagle that stirs up its nest,
  that flutters over its young,
 spreading out its wings, catching them,

bearing them on its pinions,
[12] the LORD alone did lead him,
and there was no foreign god with him.
[13] He made him ride on the high places of the earth,
and he ate the produce of the field;
and he made him suck honey out of the rock,
and oil out of the flinty rock.
[14] Curds from the herd, and milk from the flock,
with fat of lambs and rams,
herds of Bashan and goats,
with the finest of the wheat—
and of the blood of the grape you drank wine.

[15] "But Jesh'urun waxed fat, and kicked;
you waxed fat, you grew thick, you became sleek;
then he forsook God who made him,
and scoffed at the Rock of his salvation.
[16] They stirred him to jealousy with strange gods;
with abominable practices they provoked him to anger.
[17] They sacrificed to demons which were no gods,
to gods they had never known,
to new gods that had come in of late,
whom your fathers had never dreaded.
[18] You were unmindful of the Rock that begot [e] you,
and you forgot the God who gave you birth.

[19] "The LORD saw it, and spurned them,
because of· the provocation of his sons and his daughters.
[20] And he said, 'I will hide my face from them,
I will see what their end will be,
for they are a perverse generation,
children in whom is no faithfulness.
[21] They have stirred me to jealousy with what is no god;
they have provoked me with their idols.
So I will stir them to jealousy with those who are no people;
I will provoke them with a foolish nation.
[22] For a fire is kindled by my anger
and it burns to the depths of Sheol,
devours the earth and its increase,
and sets on fire the foundations of the mountains.

[23] " 'And I will heap evils upon them;
I will spend my arrows upon them;
[24] they shall be wasted with hunger,
and devoured with burning heat
and poisonous pestilence;
and I will send the teeth of beasts against them,
with venom of crawling things of the dust.
[25] In the open the sword shall bereave,
and in the chambers shall be terror,
destroying both young man and virgin,

the sucking child with the man of gray hairs.
[26] I would have said, "I will scatter them afar,
I will make the remembrance of them cease from among men,"
[27] had I not feared provocation by the enemy,
lest their adversaries should judge amiss,
lest they should say, "Our hand is triumphant,
the LORD has not wrought all this." '

[28] "For they are a nation void of counsel,
and there is no understanding in them.
[29] If they were wise, they would understand this,
they would discern their latter end!
[30] How should one chase a thousand,
and two put ten thousand to flight,
unless their Rock had sold them,
and the LORD had given them up?
[31] For their rock is not as our Rock,
even our enemies themselves being judges.
[32] For their vine comes from the vine of Sodom,
and from the fields of Gomor'rah;
their grapes are grapes of poison,
their clusters are bitter;
[33] their wine is the poison of serpents,
and the cruel venom of asps.

[34] "Is not this laid up in store with me,
sealed up in my treasuries?
[35] Vengeance is mine, and recompense,
for the time when their foot shall slip;
for the day of their calamity is at hand,
and their doom comes swiftly.
[36] For the LORD will vindicate his people
and have compassion on his servants,
when he sees that their power is gone,
and there is none remaining, bond or free.
[37] Then he will say, 'Where are their gods,
the rock in which they took refuge,
[38] who ate the fat of their sacrifices,
and drank the wine of their drink offering?
Let them rise up and help you,
let them be your protection!

[39] " 'See now that I, even I, am he,
and there is no god beside me;
I kill and I make alive;
I wound and I heal;
and there is none that can deliver out of my hand.
[40] For I lift up my hand to heaven,
and swear, As I live for ever,
[41] if I whet my glittering sword, [f]
and my hand takes hold on judgment,

e Or *bore*   f Heb *the lightning of my sword*

127

I will take vengeance on my adversaries,
and will requite those who hate me.
42 I will make my arrows drunk with blood,
and my sword shall devour flesh—
with the blood of the slain and the captives,
from the long-haired heads of the enemy.'

43 "Praise his people, O you nations;
for he avenges the blood of his servants,
and takes vengeance on his adversaries,
and makes expiation for the land of his people." g

44 Moses came and recited all the words of this song in
the hearing of the people, he and Joshua h the son of

with flaming fire j at his right hand.
3 Yea, he loved his people; k
all those consecrated to him were in his x hand;
so they followed j in thy steps,
receiving direction from thee,
4 when Moses commanded us a law,
as a possession for the assembly of Jacob.
5 Thus the LORD became king in Jesh'urun,
when the heads of the people were gathered,
all the tribes of Israel together.

6 "Let Reuben live, and not die,
nor let his men be few."

45 Nun. And when Moses had finished speaking all these
46 words to all Israel, he said to them, "Lay to heart all
the words which I enjoin upon you this day, that you
may command them to your children, that they may be
47 careful to do all the words of this law. For it is no trifle
for you, but it is your life, and thereby you shall live
long in the land which you are going over the Jordan to
possess."
48, 49 And the LORD said to Moses that very day, "Ascend
this mountain of the Ab'arim, Mount Nebo, which is in
the land of Moab, opposite Jericho; and view the land
of Canaan, which I give to the people of Israel for a
50 possession; and die on the mountain which you ascend,
and be gathered to your people, as Aaron your brother
51 died in Mount Hor and was gathered to his people; because you broke faith with me in the midst of the people
of Israel at the waters of Mer'i-bath-ka'desh, in the wilderness of Zin; because you did not revere me as holy
52 in the midst of the people of Israel. For you shall see the
land before you; but you shall not go there, into the
land which I give to the people of Israel."

The Blessing of Moses

33 This is the blessing with which Moses the man of
God blessed the children of Israel before his death.
2 He said,
"The LORD came from Sinai,
and dawned from Se'ir upon us; i
he shone forth from Mount Paran,
he came from the ten thousands of holy ones,

7 And this he said of Judah:
"Hear, O LORD, the voice of Judah,
and bring him in to his people.
With thy hands contend l for him,
and be a help against his adversaries."

8 And of Levi he said,
"Give to Levi m thy Thummim,
and thy Urim to thy godly one,
whom thou didst test at Massah,
with whom thou didst strive at the waters of Mer'ibah;
9 who said of his father and mother,
'I regard them not';
he disowned his brothers,
and ignored his children.
For they observed thy word,
and kept thy covenant.
10 They shall teach Jacob thy ordinances,
and Israel thy law;
they shall put incense before thee,
and whole burnt offering upon thy altar.
11 Bless, O LORD, his substance,
and accept the work of his hands;
crush the loins of his adversaries,
of those that hate him, that they rise not again."

12 Of Benjamin he said,
"The beloved of the LORD,
he dwells in safety by him;

g Gk Vg: Heb *his land his people*   h Gk Syr Vg: Heb *Hoshea*
j The meaning of the Hebrew word is uncertain   k Gk: Heb *peoples*
m Gk: Heb lacks *Give to Levi*

l Gk Syr Vg: Heb *them*
x Heb *thy*   l Cn: Heb *with his hands he contended*

he encompasses him all the day long,
and makes his dwelling between his shoulders."

13 And of Joseph he said,
"Blessed by the LORD be his land,
with the choicest gifts of heaven above,[n]
and of the deep that couches beneath,
14 with the choicest fruits of the sun,
and the rich yield of the months,
15 with the finest produce of the ancient mountains,
and the abundance of the everlasting hills,
16 with the best gifts of the earth and its fulness,
and the favor of him that dwelt in the bush.
Let these come upon the head of Joseph,
and upon the crown of the head of him that is prince
among his brothers.
17 His firstling bull has majesty,
and his horns are the horns of a wild ox;
with them he shall push the peoples,
all of them, to the ends of the earth;
such are the ten thousands of E'phraim,
and such are the thousands of Manas'seh."

18 And of Zeb'ulun he said,
"Rejoice, Zeb'ulun, in your going out;
and Is'sachar, in your tents.
19 They shall call peoples to their mountain;
there they offer right sacrifices;
for they suck the affluence of the seas
and the hidden treasures of the sand."

20 And of Gad he said,
"Blessed be he who enlarges Gad!
Gad couches like a lion,
he tears the arm, and the crown of the head.
21 He chose the best of the land for himself,
for there a commander's portion was reserved;
and he came to the heads of the people,
with Israel he executed the commands
and just decrees of the LORD."

22 And of Dan he said,
"Dan is a lion's whelp,
that leaps forth from Bashan."

23 And of Naph'tali he said,
"O Naph'tali, satisfied with favor,
and full of the blessing of the LORD,
possess the lake and the south."

24 And of Asher he said,
"Blessed above sons be Asher;
let him be the favorite of his brothers,

[n] Two Heb Mss and Tg: Heb with the dew

and let him dip his foot in oil.
25 Your bars shall be iron and bronze;
and as your days, so shall your strength be.

26 "There is none like God, O Jesh'urun,
who rides through the heavens to your help,
and in his majesty through the skies.
27 The eternal God is your dwelling place,
and underneath are the everlasting arms.
And he thrust out the enemy before you,
and said, Destroy.
28 So Israel dwelt in safety,
the fountain of Jacob alone,
in a land of grain and wine;
yea, his heavens drop down dew.
29 Happy are you, O Israel! Who is like you,
a people saved by the LORD,
the shield of your help,
and the sword of your triumph!
Your enemies shall come fawning to you;
and you shall tread upon their high places."

The Death of Moses

34 And Moses went up from the plains of Moab to Mount Nebo, to the top of Pisgah, which is opposite Jericho. And the LORD showed him all the land, Gilead 2 as far as Dan, all Naph'tali, the land of E'phraim and Manas'seh, all the land of Judah as far as the Western 3 Sea, the Negeb, and the Plain, that is, the valley of Jericho 4 the city of palm trees, as far as Zo'ar. And the LORD said to him, "This is the land of which I swore to Abraham, to Isaac, and to Jacob, 'I will give it to your descendants.' I have let you see it with your eyes, but you 5 shall not go over there." So Moses the servant of the LORD died there in the land of Moab, according to the word 6 of the LORD, and he buried him in the valley in the land of Moab opposite Beth-pe'or; but no man knows the 7 place of his burial to this day. Moses was a hundred and twenty years old when he died; his eye was not dim, nor 8 his natural force abated. And the people of Israel wept for Moses in the plains of Moab thirty days; then the days of weeping and mourning for Moses were ended.

9 And Joshua the son of Nun was full of the spirit of wisdom, for Moses had laid his hands upon him; so the people of Israel obeyed him, and did as the LORD had 10 commanded Moses. And there has not arisen a prophet since in Israel like Moses, whom the LORD knew face to 11 face, none like him for all the signs and the wonders which the LORD sent him to do in the land of Egypt, to 12 Pharaoh and to all his servants and to all his land, and for all the mighty power and all the great and terrible deeds which Moses wrought in the sight of all Israel.

INTRODUCTION TO

JOSHUA

The first five books of the Bible tell the marvelous story of God's creation of the world and of the beginnings of the Hebrew people. They tell of the slavery of the Hebrews, their escape from Egypt, and their difficulties in serving the one true God. They tell how the people received the Ten Commandments and wandered in the desert many years.

The Book of Joshua begins a new series of historical stories about how the Hebrews crossed the Jordan River, captured Jericho, and began to take possession of Canaan. This book is named for the Hebrew leader who succeeded Moses when the people began their invasion and conquest of Canaan. Most of it was written about 550 B.C. It was revised and completed about 400 B.C.

This book tells how the Hebrews found that the people already living in Canaan worshiped other gods. These people had rules for living as farmers that conflicted with the Hebrews' way of living as wandering herdsmen. This book shows how the Hebrew people were tempted to be disloyal to the Lord and how close they came to rejecting God's laws for their lives.

Joshua 24 tells the thrilling story of the renewed pledging of their faith. Joshua stood before the people and challenged them by saying, "If you be unwilling to serve the Lord, choose this day whom you will serve, whether the gods your fathers served in the region beyond the River, or the gods of the Amorites in whose land you dwell; but as for me and my house, we will serve the LORD" (Joshua 24. 15).

THE BOOK OF

JOSHUA

THE CONQUEST

Joshua Assumes Command

1 After the death of Moses the servant of the LORD, the LORD said to Joshua the son of Nun, Moses' minis-
2 ter, "Moses my servant is dead; now therefore arise, go over this Jordan, you and all this people, into the land
3 which I am giving to them, to the people of Israel. Every place that the sole of your foot will tread upon I have
4 given to you, as I promised to Moses. From the wilderness and this Lebanon as far as the great river, the river Eu-phra'tes, all the land of the Hittites to the Great Sea toward the going down of the sun shall be your territory.
5 No man shall be able to stand before you all the days of your life; as I was with Moses, so I will be with you; I
6 will not fail you or forsake you. Be strong and of good courage; for you shall cause this people to inherit the
7 land which I swore to their fathers to give them. Only be strong and very courageous, being careful to do according to all the law which Moses my servant commanded you; turn not from it to the right hand or to the left, that
8 you may have good success wherever you go. This book

of the law shall not depart out of your mouth, but you shall meditate on it day and night, that you may be careful to do according to all that is written in it; for then you shall make your way prosperous, and then you shall
9 have good success. Have I not commanded you? Be strong

and of good courage; be not frightened, neither be dismayed; for the LORD your God is with you wherever you
go."

10 Then Joshua commanded the officers of the people,
11 "Pass through the camp, and command the people, 'Prepare your provisions; for within three days you are to
pass over this Jordan, to go in to take possession of the
land which the LORD your God gives you to possess.' "

12 And to the Reubenites, the Gadites, and the half-tribe
13 of Manas'seh Joshua said, "Remember the word which
Moses the servant of the LORD commanded you, saying,
'The LORD your God is providing you a place of rest, and
14 will give you this land.' Your wives, your little ones, and
your cattle shall remain in the land which Moses gave you
beyond the Jordan; but all the men of valor among you
shall pass over armed before your brethren and shall help
15 them, until the LORD gives rest to your brethren as well
as to you, and they also take possession of the land which
the LORD your God is giving them; then you shall return
to the land of your possession, and shall possess it, the
land which Moses the servant of the LORD gave you be-
16 yond the Jordan toward the sunrise." And they answered
Joshua, "All that you have commanded us we will do,
17 and wherever you send us we will go. Just as we obeyed
Moses in all things, so we will obey you; only may the
18 LORD your God be with you, as he was with Moses! Whoever rebels against your commandment and disobeys your
words, whatever you command him, shall be put to death.
Only be strong and of good courage."

2 And Joshua the son of Nun sent two men secretly
from Shittim as spies, saying, "Go, view the land, especially Jericho." And they went, and came into the house
of a harlot whose name was Rahab, and lodged there.
2 And it was told the king of Jericho, "Behold, certain
men of Israel have come here tonight to search out the
3 land." Then the king of Jericho sent to Rahab, saying,
"Bring forth the men that have come to you, who entered
your house; for they have come to search out all the
4 land." But the woman had taken the two men and hidden
them; and she said, "True, men came to me, but I did
5 not know where they came from; and when the gate was
to be closed, at dark, the men went out; where the men
went I do not know; pursue them quickly, for you will
6 overtake them." But she had brought them up to the roof,
and hid them with the stalks of flax which she had laid in
7 order on the roof. So the men pursued after them on the
way to the Jordan as far as the fords; and as soon as
the pursuers had gone out, the gate was shut.

8 Before they lay down, she came up to them on the roof,
9 and said to the men, "I know that the LORD has given
you the land, and that the fear of you has fallen upon us,
and that all the inhabitants of the land melt away before
10 you. For we have heard how the LORD dried up the water
of the Red Sea before you when you came out of Egypt,

and what you did to the two kings of the Amorites that
were beyond the Jordan, to Sihon and Og, whom you
11 utterly destroyed. And as soon as we heard it, our hearts
melted, and there was no courage left in any man, because of you; for the LORD your God is he who is God in
12 heaven above and on earth beneath. Now then, swear to
me by the LORD that as I have dealt kindly with you, you
also will deal kindly with my father's house, and give me
13 a sure sign, and save alive my father and mother, my
brothers and sisters, and all who belong to them, and
14 deliver our lives from death." And the men said to her,
"Our life for yours! If you do not tell this business of
ours, then we will deal kindly and faithfully with you
when the LORD gives us the land."

15 Then she let them down by a rope through the window,
for her house was built into the city wall, so that she
16 dwelt in the wall. And she said to them, "Go into the hills,
lest the pursuers meet you; and hide yourselves there
three days, until the pursuers have returned; then after-
17 ward you may go your way." The men said to her, "We
will be guiltless with respect to this oath of yours which
18 you have made us swear. Behold, when we come into the
land, you shall bind this scarlet cord in the window
through which you let us down; and you shall gather
into your house your father and mother, your brothers,
19 and all your father's household. If any one goes out of
the doors of your house into the street, his blood shall be
upon his head, and we shall be guiltless; but if a hand
is laid upon any one who is with you in the house, his
20 blood shall be on our head. But if you tell this business
of ours, then we shall be guiltless with respect to your
21 oath which you have made us swear." And she said, "According to your words, so be it." Then she sent them
away, and they departed; and she bound the scarlet cord
in the window.

22 They departed, and went into the hills, and remained
there three days, until the pursuers returned; for the
pursuers had made search all along the way and found
23 nothing. Then the two men came down again from the
hills, and passed over and came to Joshua the son of Nun;
24 and they told him all that had befallen them. And they
said to Joshua, "Truly the LORD has given all the land
into our hands; and moreover all the inhabitants of the
land are fainthearted because of us."

Crossing the Jordan
3 Early in the morning Joshua rose and set out from
Shittim, with all the people of Israel; and they came
to the Jordan, and lodged there before they passed over.
2 At the end of three days the officers went through the
3 camp and commanded the people, "When you see the ark
of the covenant of the LORD your God being carried by
the Levitical priests, then you shall set out from your place
4 and follow it, that you may know the way you shall go,

for you have not passed this way before. Yet there shall be a space between you and it, a distance of about two 5 thousand cubits; do not come near it." And Joshua said to the people, "Sanctify yourselves; for tomorrow the 6 LORD will do wonders among you." And Joshua said to the priests, "Take up the ark of the covenant, and pass on before the people." And they took up the ark of the covenant, and went before the people.

7 And the LORD said to Joshua, "This day I will begin to exalt you in the sight of all Israel, that they may know 8 that, as I was with Moses, so I will be with you. And you shall command the priests who bear the ark of the covenant, 'When you come to the brink of the waters of the 9 Jordan, you shall stand still in the Jordan.'" And Joshua said to the people of Israel, "Come hither, and hear the 10 words of the LORD your God." And Joshua said, "Hereby you shall know that the living God is among you, and that he will without fail drive out from before you the Canaanites, the Hittites, the Hivites, the Per'izzites, the 11 Gir'gashites, the Amorites, and the Jeb'usites. Behold, the ark of the covenant of the Lord of all the earth is to pass 12 over before you into the Jordan. Now therefore take twelve men from the tribes of Israel, from each tribe a 13 man. And when the soles of the feet of the priests who bear the ark of the LORD, the Lord of all the earth, shall rest in the waters of the Jordan, the waters of the Jordan shall be stopped from flowing, and the waters coming down from above shall stand in one heap."

14 So, when the people set out from their tents, to pass over the Jordan with the priests bearing the ark of the 15 covenant before the people, and when those who bore the ark had come to the Jordan, and the feet of the priests bearing the ark were dipped in the brink of the water (the Jordan overflows all its banks throughout the time 16 of harvest), the waters coming down from above stood and rose up in a heap far off, at Adam, the city that is beside Zar'ethan, and those flowing down toward the sea of the Arabah, the Salt Sea, were wholly cut off; and 17 the people passed over opposite Jericho. And while all Israel were passing over on dry ground, the priests who bore the ark of the covenant of the LORD stood on dry

ground in the midst of the Jordan, until all the nation finished passing over the Jordan.

4 When all the nation had finished passing over the 2 Jordan, the LORD said to Joshua, "Take twelve men 3 from the people, from each tribe a man, and command them, 'Take twelve stones from here out of the midst of the Jordan, from the very place where the priests' feet stood, and carry them over with you, and lay them down 4 in the place where you lodge tonight.'" Then Joshua called the twelve men from the people of Israel, whom he 5 had appointed, a man from each tribe; and Joshua said to them, "Pass on before the ark of the LORD your God into the midst of the Jordan, and take up each of you a stone upon his shoulder, according to the number of the 6 tribes of the people of Israel, that this may be a sign among you, when your children ask in time to come, 7 'What do those stones mean to you?' Then you shall tell them that the waters of the Jordan were cut off before the ark of the covenant of the LORD; when it passed over the Jordan, the waters of the Jordan were cut off. So these stones shall be to the people of Israel a memorial for ever."

8 And the men of Israel did as Joshua commanded, and took up twelve stones out of the midst of the Jordan, according to the number of the tribes of the people of Israel, as the LORD told Joshua; and they carried them over with them to the place where they lodged, and laid 9 them down there. And Joshua set up twelve stones in the midst of the Jordan, in the place where the feet of the priests bearing the ark of the covenant had stood; and 10 they are there to this day. For the priests who bore the ark stood in the midst of the Jordan, until everything was finished that the LORD commanded Joshua to tell the people, according to all that Moses had commanded Joshua.

11 The people passed over in haste; and when all the people had finished passing over, the ark of the LORD and 12 the priests passed over before the people. The sons of Reuben and the sons of Gad and the half-tribe of Manas'-seh passed over armed before the people of Israel, as 13 Moses had bidden them; about forty thousand ready armed for war passed over before the LORD for battle, to 14 the plains of Jericho. On that day the LORD exalted Joshua in the sight of all Israel; and they stood in awe of him, as they had stood in awe of Moses, all the days of his life. 15, 16 And the LORD said to Joshua, "Command the priests who bear the ark of the testimony to come up out of the 17 Jordan." Joshua therefore commanded the priests, "Come 18 up out of the Jordan." And when the priests bearing the ark of the covenant of the LORD came up from the midst of the Jordan, and the soles of the priests' feet were lifted up on dry ground, the waters of the Jordan returned to their place and overflowed all its banks, as before.

19 The people came up out of the Jordan on the tenth day of the first month, and they encamped in Gilgal on the 20 east border of Jericho. And those twelve stones, which they took out of the Jordan, Joshua set up in Gilgal. 21 And he said to the people of Israel, "When your children ask their fathers in time to come, 'What do these stones 22 mean?' then you shall let your children know, 'Israel 23 passed over this Jordan on dry ground.' For the LORD your God dried up the waters of the Jordan for you until you passed over, as the LORD your God did to the Red 24 Sea, which he dried up for us until we passed over, so that all the peoples of the earth may know that the hand of the LORD is mighty; that you may fear the LORD your God for ever."

5 When all the kings of the Amorites that were beyond the Jordan to the west, and all the kings of the Canaanites that were by the sea, heard that the LORD had dried up the waters of the Jordan for the people of Israel until they had crossed over, their heart melted, and there was no longer any spirit in them, because of the people of Israel.

In the Camp at Gilgal

2 At that time the LORD said to Joshua, "Make flint knives and circumcise the people of Israel again the second 3 time." So Joshua made flint knives, and circumcised the 4 people of Israel at Gibeath-haaraloth.[a] And this is the reason why Joshua circumcised them: all the males of the people who came out of Egypt, all the men of war, had died on the way in the wilderness after they had come out 5 of Egypt. Though all the people who came out had been circumcised, yet all the people that were born on the way in the wilderness after they had come out of Egypt, had 6 not been circumcised. For the people of Israel walked forty years in the wilderness, till all the nation, the men of war that came forth out of Egypt, perished, because they did not hearken to the voice of the LORD; to them the LORD swore that he would not let them see the land which the LORD had sworn to their fathers to give us, a 7 land flowing with milk and honey. So it was their children, whom he raised up in their stead, that Joshua circumcised; for they were uncircumcised, because they had not been circumcised on the way.

8 When the circumcising of all the nation was done, they remained in their places in the camp till they were healed. 9 And the LORD said to Joshua, "This day I have rolled away the reproach of Egypt from you." And so the name of that place is called Gilgal[b] to this day.

10 While the people of Israel were encamped in Gilgal they kept the passover on the fourteenth day of the month 11 at evening in the plains of Jericho. And on the morrow after the passover, on that very day, they ate of the produce of the land, unleavened cakes and parched grain. 12 And the manna ceased on the morrow, when they ate of the produce of the land; and the people of Israel had manna no more, but ate of the fruit of the land of Canaan that year.

13 When Joshua was by Jericho, he lifted up his eyes and looked, and behold, a man stood before him with his drawn sword in his hand; and Joshua went to him and said to him, "Are you for us, or for our adversaries?" 14 And he said, "No; but as commander of the army of the LORD I have now come." And Joshua fell on his face to the earth, and worshiped, and said to him, "What does 15 my lord bid his servant?" And the commander of the LORD's army said to Joshua, "Put off your shoes from your feet; for the place where you stand is holy." And Joshua did so.

The Fall of Jericho

6 Now Jericho was shut up from within and from without because of the people of Israel; none went out, 2 and none came in. And the LORD said to Joshua, "See, I have given into your hand Jericho, with its king and 3 mighty men of valor. You shall march around the city, all the men of war going around the city once. Thus shall 4 you do for six days. And seven priests shall bear seven trumpets of rams' horns before the ark; and on the seventh day you shall march around the city seven times, 5 the priests blowing the trumpets. And when they make a long blast with the ram's horn, as soon as you hear the sound of the trumpet, then all the people shall shout with a great shout; and the wall of the city will fall down flat, and the people shall go up every man straight before him." 6 So Joshua the son of Nun called the priests and said to them, "Take up the ark of the covenant, and let seven priests bear seven trumpets of rams' horns before the 7 ark of the LORD." And he said to the people, "Go forward; march around the city, and let the armed men pass on before the ark of the LORD."

8 And as Joshua had commanded the people, the seven priests bearing the seven trumpets of rams' horns before the LORD went forward, blowing the trumpets, with the 9 ark of the covenant of the LORD following them. And the armed men went before the priests who blew the trumpets, and the rear guard came after the ark, while the trumpets 10 blew continually. But Joshua commanded the people, "You shall not shout or let your voice be heard, neither shall any word go out of your mouth, until the day I bid 11 you shout; then you shall shout." So he caused the ark of the LORD to compass the city, going about it once; and they came into the camp, and spent the night in the camp.

12 Then Joshua rose early in the morning, and the priests 13 took up the ark of the LORD. And the seven priests bearing the seven trumpets of rams' horns before the ark of the LORD passed on, blowing the trumpets continually; and the armed men went before them, and the rear guard

---

[a] That is *the hill of the foreskins*   [b] From Heb *galal* to roll

came after the ark of the Lord, while the trumpets blew
14 continually. And the second day they marched around the city once, and returned into the camp. So they did for six days.

15 On the seventh day they rose early at the dawn of day, and marched around the city in the same manner seven times: it was only on that day that they marched around
16 the city seven times. And at the seventh time, when the priests had blown the trumpets, Joshua said to the people,
17 "Shout; for the Lord has given you the city. And the city and all that is within it shall be devoted to the Lord for destruction; only Rahab the harlot and all who are with her in her house shall live, because she hid the messengers
18 that we sent. But you, keep yourselves from the things

devoted to destruction, lest when you have devoted them you take any of the devoted things and make the camp of Israel a thing for destruction, and bring trouble upon
19 it. But all silver and gold, and vessels of bronze and iron, are sacred to the Lord; they shall go into the treasury of
20 the Lord." So the people shouted, and the trumpets were blown. As soon as the people heard the sound of the trumpet, the people raised a great shout, and the wall fell down flat, so that the people went up into the city, every
21 man straight before him, and they took the city. Then they utterly destroyed all in the city, both men and women, young and old, oxen, sheep, and asses, with the edge of the sword.

22 And Joshua said to the two men who had spied out the land, "Go into the harlot's house, and bring out from it the woman, and all who belong to her, as you swore to
23 her." So the young men who had been spies went in, and brought out Rahab, and her father and mother and brothers and all who belonged to her; and they brought all her kindred, and set them outside the camp of Israel.
24 And they burned the city with fire, and all within it; only the silver and gold, and the vessels of bronze and of iron,
25 they put into the treasury of the house of the Lord. But Rahab the harlot, and her father's household, and all who belonged to her, Joshua saved alive; and she dwelt in Israel to this day, because she hid the messengers whom Joshua sent to spy out Jericho.
26 Joshua laid an oath upon them at that time, saying,

"Cursed before the Lord be the man that rises up and rebuilds this city, Jericho.

At the cost of his first-born shall he lay its foundation, and at the cost of his youngest son shall he set up its gates."
27 So the Lord was with Joshua; and his fame was in all the land.

Campaign Against Ai

7 But the people of Israel broke faith in regard to the devoted things; for Achan the son of Carmi, son of Zabdi, son of Zerah, of the tribe of Judah, took some of the devoted things; and the anger of the Lord burned against the people of Israel.

2 Joshua sent men from Jericho to Ai, which is near Beth-aven, east of Bethel, and said to them, "Go up and spy out the land." And the men went up and spied out
3 Ai. And they returned to Joshua, and said to him, "Let not all the people go up, but let about two or three thousand men go up and attack Ai; do not make the
4 whole people toil up there, for they are but few." So about three thousand went up there from the people; and they
5 fled before the men of Ai, and the men of Ai killed about thirty-six men of them, and chased them before the gate as far as Sheb′arim, and slew them at the descent. And the hearts of the people melted, and became as water.

6 Then Joshua rent his clothes, and fell to the earth upon his face before the ark of the Lord until the evening, he and the elders of Israel; and they put dust upon their
7 heads. And Joshua said, "Alas, O Lord God, why hast thou brought this people over the Jordan at all, to give us into the hands of the Amorites, to destroy us? Would that we had been content to dwell beyond the Jordan!
8 O Lord, what can I say, when Israel has turned their
9 backs before their enemies! For the Canaanites and all the inhabitants of the land will hear of it, and will surround us, and cut off our name from the earth; and what wilt thou do for thy great name?"

10 The Lord said to Joshua, "Arise, why have you thus
11 fallen upon your face? Israel has sinned; they have transgressed my covenant which I commanded them; they have taken some of the devoted things; they have stolen, and
12 lied, and put them among their own stuff. Therefore the people of Israel cannot stand before their enemies; they turn their backs before their enemies, because they have become a thing for destruction. I will be with you no more, unless you destroy the devoted things from among
13 you. Up, sanctify the people, and say, 'Sanctify yourselves for tomorrow; for thus says the Lord, God of Israel, "There are devoted things in the midst of you, O Israel; you cannot stand before your enemies, until you take
14 away the devoted things from among you." In the morning therefore you shall be brought near by your tribes;

and the tribe which the LORD takes shall come near by families; and the family which the LORD takes shall come near by households; and the household which the LORD
15 takes shall come near man by man. And he who is taken with the devoted things shall be burned with fire, he and all that he has, because he has transgressed the covenant of the LORD, and because he has done a shameful thing in Israel.' "

16 So Joshua rose early in the morning, and brought Israel near tribe by tribe, and the tribe of Judah was
17 taken; and he brought near the families of Judah, and the family of the Zer'ahites was taken; and he brought near the family of the Zer'ahites man by man, and Zabdi
18 was taken; and he brought near his household man by man, and Achan the son of Carmi, son of Zabdi, son of
19 Zerah, of the tribe of Judah, was taken. Then Joshua said to Achan, "My son, give glory to the LORD God of Israel, and render praise to him; and tell me now what you
20 have done; do not hide it from me." And Achan answered Joshua, "Of a truth I have sinned against the LORD God
21 of Israel, and this is what I did: when I saw among the spoil a beautiful mantle from Shinar, and two hundred shekels of silver, and a bar of gold weighing fifty shekels, then I coveted them, and took them; and behold, they are hidden in the earth inside my tent, with the silver underneath."

22 So Joshua sent messengers, and they ran to the tent; and behold, it was hidden in his tent with the silver
23 underneath. And they took them out of the tent and brought them to Joshua and all the people of Israel; and
24 they laid them down before the LORD. And Joshua and all Israel with him took Achan the son of Zerah, and the silver and the mantle and the bar of gold, and his sons and daughters, and his oxen and asses and sheep, and his tent, and all that he had; and they brought them up to the
25 Valley of Achor. And Joshua said, "Why did you bring trouble on us? The LORD brings trouble on you today." And all Israel stoned him with stones; they burned them
26 with fire, and stoned them with stones. And they raised over him a great heap of stones that remains to this day; then the LORD turned from his burning anger. Therefore to this day the name of that place is called the Valley of Achor.ᶜ

8 And the LORD said to Joshua, "Do not fear or be dismayed; take all the fighting men with you, and arise, go up to Ai; see, I have given into your hand the
2 king of Ai, and his people, his city, and his land; and you shall do to Ai and its king as you did to Jericho and its king; only its spoil and its cattle you shall take as booty for yourselves; lay an ambush against the city, behind it."
3 So Joshua arose, and all the fighting men, to go up to Ai; and Joshua chose thirty thousand mighty men of
4 valor, and sent them forth by night. And he commanded them, "Behold, you shall lie in ambush against the city,

behind it; do not go very far from the city, but hold
5 yourselves all in readiness; and I, and all the people who are with me, will approach the city. And when they come
6 out against us, as before, we shall flee before them; and they will come out after us, till we have drawn them away from the city; for they will say, 'They are fleeing from
7 us, as before.' So we will flee from them; then you shall rise up from the ambush, and seize the city; for the LORD
8 your God will give it into your hand. And when you have taken the city, you shall set the city on fire, doing as the
9 LORD has bidden; see, I have commanded you." So Joshua sent them forth; and they went to the place of ambush, and lay between Bethel and Ai, to the west of Ai; but Joshua spent that night among the people.

10 And Joshua arose early in the morning and mustered the people, and went up, with the elders of Israel, before
11 the people to Ai. And all the fighting men who were with him went up, and drew near before the city, and encamped on the north side of Ai, with a ravine between them and
12 Ai. And he took about five thousand men, and set them in ambush between Bethel and Ai, to the west of the city.
13 So they stationed the forces, the main encampment which was north of the city and its rear guard west of the city.
14 But Joshua spent that night in the valley. And when the king of Ai saw this he and all his people, the men of the city, made haste and went out early to the descent ᵈ toward the Arabah to meet Israel in battle; but he did not know that there was an ambush against him behind the city.
15 And Joshua and all Israel made a pretense of being beaten before them, and fled in the direction of the wilderness.
16 So all the people who were in the city were called together to pursue them, and as they pursued Joshua they were
17 drawn away from the city. There was not a man left in Ai or Bethel, who did not go out after Israel; they left the city open, and pursued Israel.

18 Then the LORD said to Joshua, "Stretch out the javelin that is in your hand toward Ai; for I will give it into your hand." And Joshua stretched out the javelin that was
19 in his hand toward the city. And the ambush rose quickly out of their place, and as soon as he had stretched out his hand, they ran and entered the city and took it; and
20 they made haste to set the city on fire. So when the men of Ai looked back, behold, the smoke of the city went up to heaven; and they had no power to flee this way or that, for the people that fled to the wilderness turned back
21 upon the pursuers. And when Joshua and all Israel saw that the ambush had taken the city, and that the smoke of the city went up, then they turned back and smote the
22 men of Ai. And the others came forth from the city against them; so they were in the midst of Israel, some on this side, and some on that side; and Israel smote them, until there was left none that survived or escaped.
23 But the king of Ai they took alive, and brought him to Joshua.

ᶜ That is *Trouble*   ᵈ Cn: Heb *appointed time*

24 When Israel had finished slaughtering all the inhabitants of Ai in the open wilderness where they pursued them and all of them to the very last had fallen by the edge of the sword, all Israel returned to Ai, and smote it 25 with the edge of the sword. And all who fell that day, both men and women, were twelve thousand, all the people of 26 Ai. For Joshua did not draw back his hand, with which he stretched out the javelin, until he had utterly destroyed 27 all the inhabitants of Ai. Only the cattle and the spoil of that city Israel took as their booty, according to the 28 word of the LORD which he commanded Joshua. So Joshua burned Ai, and made it for ever a heap of ruins, as it is 29 to this day. And he hanged the king of Ai on a tree until evening; and at the going down of the sun Joshua commanded, and they took his body down from the tree, and cast it at the entrance of the gate of the city, and raised over it a great heap of stones, which stands there to this day.

30 Then Joshua built an altar in Mount Ebal to the LORD, 31 the God of Israel, as Moses the servant of the LORD had commanded the people of Israel, as it is written in the book of the law of Moses, "an altar of unhewn stones, upon which no man has lifted an iron tool"; and they offered on it burnt offerings to the LORD, and sacrificed 32 peace offerings. And there, in the presence of the people of Israel, he wrote upon the stones a copy of the law of 33 Moses, which he had written. And all Israel, sojourner as well as homeborn, with their elders and officers and their judges, stood on opposite sides of the ark before the Levitical priests who carried the ark of the covenant of the LORD, half of them in front of Mount Ger'izim and half of them in front of Mount Ebal, as Moses the servant of the LORD had commanded at the first, that they should 34 bless the people of Israel. And afterward he read all the words of the law, the blessing and the curse, according 35 to all that is written in the book of the law. There was not a word of all that Moses commanded which Joshua did not read before all the assembly of Israel, and the women, and the little ones, and the sojourners who lived among them.

Treaty With the Gibeonites

9 When all the kings who were beyond the Jordan in the hill country and in the lowland all along the coast of the Great Sea toward Lebanon, the Hittites, the Amorites, the Canaanites, the Per'izzites, the Hivites, and 2 the Jeb'usites, heard of this, they gathered together with one accord to fight Joshua and Israel.

3 But when the inhabitants of Gibeon heard what Joshua 4 had done to Jericho and to Ai, they on their part acted with cunning, and went and made ready provisions, and took worn-out sacks upon their asses, and wineskins, 5 worn-out and torn and mended, with worn-out, patched

sandals on their feet, and worn-out clothes; and all their 6 provisions were dry and moldy. And they went to Joshua in the camp at Gilgal, and said to him and to the men of Israel, "We have come from a far country; so now 7 make a covenant with us." But the men of Israel said to the Hivites, "Perhaps you live among us; then how can 8 we make a covenant with you?" They said to Joshua, "We are your servants." And Joshua said to them, "Who are 9 you? And where do you come from?" They said to him, "From a very far country your servants have come, because of the name of the LORD your God; for we have heard a report of him, and all that he did in Egypt, 10 and all that he did to the two kings of the Amorites who were beyond the Jordan, Sihon the king of Heshbon, and 11 Og king of Bashan, who dwelt in Ash'taroth. And our elders and all the inhabitants of our country said to us, 'Take provisions in your hand for the journey, and go to meet them, and say to them, "We are your servants; 12 come now, make a covenant with us." ' Here is our bread; it was still warm when we took it from our houses as our food for the journey, on the day we set forth to come to 13 you, but now, behold, it is dry and moldy; these wineskins were new when we filled them, and behold, they are burst; and these garments and shoes of ours are worn 14 out from the very long journey." So the men partook of their provisions, and did not ask direction from the LORD.

15 And Joshua made peace with them, and made a covenant with them, to let them live; and the leaders of the congregation swore to them.

16 At the end of three days after they had made a covenant with them, they heard that they were their neighbors, 17 and that they dwelt among them. And the people of Israel set out and reached their cities on the third day. Now their cities were Gibeon, Chephi'rah, Be-er'oth, and Kir'-18 iath-je'arim. But the people of Israel did not kill them, because the leaders of the congregation had sworn to them by the LORD, the God of Israel. Then all the congre-19 gation murmured against the leaders. But all the leaders said to all the congregation, "We have sworn to them by the LORD, the God of Israel, and now we may not touch 20 them. This we will do to them, and let them live, lest wrath be upon us, because of the oath which we swore to 21 them." And the leaders said to them, "Let them live." So they became hewers of wood and drawers of water for all the congregation, as the leaders had said of them.

22 Joshua summoned them, and he said to them, "Why did you deceive us, saying, 'We are very far from you,' when
23 you dwell among us? Now therefore you are cursed, and some of you shall always be slaves, hewers of wood and
24 drawers of water for the house of my God." They answered Joshua, "Because it was told to your servants for a certainty that the LORD your God had commanded his servant Moses to give you all the land, and to destroy all the inhabitants of the land from before you; so we feared greatly for our lives because of you, and did this thing.
25 And now, behold, we are in your hand: do as it seems
26 good and right in your sight to do to us." So he did to them, and delivered them out of the hand of the people
27 of Israel; and they did not kill them. But Joshua made them that day hewers of wood and drawers of water for the congregation and for the altar of the LORD, to continue to this day, in the place which he should choose.

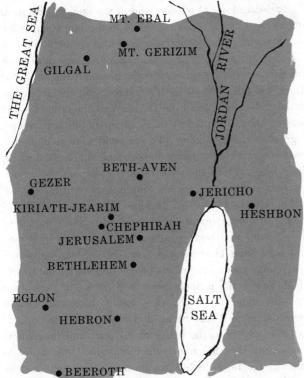

Campaigns in the South

10 When Ado'ni-ze'dek king of Jerusalem heard how Joshua had taken Ai, and had utterly destroyed it, doing to Ai and its king as he had done to Jericho and its king, and how the inhabitants of Gibeon had made
2 peace with Israel and were among them, he ˣ feared greatly, because Gibeon was a great city, like one of the royal cities, and because it was greater than Ai, and all its men
3 were mighty. So Ado'ni-ze'dek king of Jerusalem sent to Hoham king of Hebron, to Piram king of Jarmuth, to Japhi'a king of Lachish, and to Debir king of Eglon,
4 saying, "Come up to me, and help me, and let us smite Gibeon; for it has made peace with Joshua and with the

ˣ Heb *they*

5 people of Israel." Then the five kings of the Amorites, the king of Jerusalem, the king of Hebron, the king of Jarmuth, the king of Lachish, and the king of Eglon, gathered their forces, and went up with all their armies and encamped against Gibeon, and made war against it.
6 And the men of Gibeon sent to Joshua at the camp in Gilgal, saying, "Do not relax your hand from your servants; come up to us quickly, and save us, and help us; for all the kings of the Amorites that dwell in the hill
7 country are gathered against us." So Joshua went up from Gilgal, he and all the people of war with him, and
8 all the mighty men of valor. And the LORD said to Joshua, "Do not fear them, for I have given them into your hands; there shall not a man of them stand before you."
9 So Joshua came upon them suddenly, having marched
10 up all night from Gilgal. And the LORD threw them into a panic before Israel, who slew them with a great slaughter at Gibeon, and chased them by the way of the ascent of Beth-horon, and smote them as far as Aze'kah
11 and Makke'dah. And as they fled before Israel, while they were going down the ascent of Beth-horon, the LORD threw down great stones from heaven upon them as far as Aze'kah, and they died; there were more who died because of the hailstones than the men of Israel killed with the sword.
12 Then spoke Joshua to the LORD in the day when the LORD gave the Amorites over to the men of Israel; and he said in the sight of Israel,

"Sun, stand thou still at Gibeon,
    and thou Moon in the valley of Ai'jalon."
13 And the sun stood still, and the moon stayed,
    until the nation took vengeance on their enemies.

Is this not written in the Book of Jashar? The sun stayed in the midst of heaven, and did not hasten to go down
14 for about a whole day. There has been no day like it before or since, when the LORD hearkened to the voice of a man; for the LORD fought for Israel.
15 Then Joshua returned, and all Israel with him, to the camp at Gilgal.
16 These five kings fled, and hid themselves in the cave at
17 Makke'dah. And it was told Joshua, "The five kings have
18 been found, hidden in the cave at Makke'dah." And Joshua said, "Roll great stones against the mouth of the
19 cave, and set men by it to guard them; but do not stay there yourselves, pursue your enemies, fall upon their rear, do not let them enter their cities; for the LORD your God
20 has given them into your hand." When Joshua and the men of Israel had finished slaying them with a very great slaughter, until they were wiped out, and when the remnant which remained of them had entered into the
21 fortified cities, all the people returned safe to Joshua in the camp at Makke'dah; not a man moved his tongue against any of the people of Israel.

22 Then Joshua said, "Open the mouth of the cave, and
23 bring those five kings out to me from the cave." And they
did so, and brought those five kings out to him from the
cave, the king of Jerusalem, the king of Hebron, the king
of Jarmuth, the king of Lachish, and the king of Eglon.
24 And when they brought those kings out to Joshua, Joshua
summoned all the men of Israel, and said to the chiefs of
the men of war who had gone with him, "Come near, put
your feet upon the necks of these kings." Then they came
25 near, and put their feet on their necks. And Joshua said
to them, "Do not be afraid or dismayed; be strong and
of good courage; for thus the LORD will do to all your
26 enemies against whom you fight." And afterward Joshua
smote them and put them to death, and he hung them on
five trees. And they hung upon the trees until evening;
27 but at the time of the going down of the sun, Joshua commanded, and they took them down from the trees, and
threw them into the cave where they had hidden themselves, and they set great stones against the mouth of the
cave, which remain to this very day.
28 And Joshua took Makke'dah on that day, and smote it
and its king with the edge of the sword; he utterly destroyed every person in it, he left none remaining; and he
did to the king of Makke'dah as he had done to the king
of Jericho.
29 Then Joshua passed on from Makke'dah, and all Israel
30 with him, to Libnah, and fought against Libnah; and the
LORD gave it also and its king into the hand of Israel; and
he smote it with the edge of the sword, and every person
in it; he left none remaining in it; and he did to its king
as he had done to the king of Jericho.
31 And Joshua passed on from Libnah, and all Israel with
him, to Lachish, and laid siege to it, and assaulted it:
32 and the LORD gave Lachish into the hand of Israel, and
he took it on the second day, and smote it with the edge
of the sword, and every person in it, as he had done to
Libnah.
33 Then Horam king of Gezer came up to help Lachish;
and Joshua smote him and his people, until he left none
remaining.
34 And Joshua passed on with all Israel from Lachish to
35 Eglon; and they laid siege to it, and assaulted it; and
they took it on that day, and smote it with the edge of the
sword; and every person in it he utterly destroyed that
day, as he had done to Lachish.
36 Then Joshua went up with all Israel from Eglon to
37 Hebron; and they assaulted it, and took it, and smote it
with the edge of the sword, and its king and its towns,
and every person in it; he left none remaining, as he had
done to Eglon, and utterly destroyed it with every person
in it.
38 Then Joshua, with all Israel, turned back to Debir and
39 assaulted it, and he took it with its king and all its towns;

and they smote them with the edge of the sword, and
utterly destroyed every person in it; he left none remaining; as he had done to Hebron and to Libnah and its
king, so he did to Debir and to its king.
40 So Joshua defeated the whole land, the hill country and
the Negeb and the lowland and the slopes, and all their
kings; he left none remaining, but utterly destroyed all
that breathed, as the LORD God of Israel commanded.
41 And Joshua defeated them from Ka'desh-bar'nea to Gaza,
42 and all the country of Goshen, as far as Gibeon. And
Joshua took all these kings and their land at one time,
43 because the LORD God of Israel fought for Israel. Then
Joshua returned, and all Israel with him, to the camp at
Gilgal.

Victory in the North

11 When Jabin king of Hazor heard of this, he sent
   to Jobab king of Madon, and to the king of Shimron,
2 and to the king of Ach'shaph, and to the kings who were
in the northern hill country, and in the Arabah south of
Chin'neroth, and in the lowland, and in Naphothdor on
3 the west, to the Canaanites in the east and the west, the
Amorites, the Hittites, the Per'izzites, and the Jeb'usites
in the hill country, and the Hivites under Hermon in the
4 land of Mizpah. And they came out, with all their troops,
a great host, in number like the sand that is upon the
5 seashore, with very many horses and chariots. And all
these kings joined their forces, and came and encamped
together at the waters of Merom, to fight with Israel.
6 And the LORD said to Joshua, "Do not be afraid of
them, for tomorrow at this time I will give over all of
them, slain, to Israel; you shall hamstring their horses,
7 and burn their chariots with fire." So Joshua came suddenly upon them with all his people of war, by the waters
8 of Merom, and fell upon them. And the LORD gave them
into the hand of Israel, who smote them and chased
them as far as Great Sidon and Mis'rephothma'im, and
eastward as far as the valley of Mizpeh; and they smote
9 them, until they left none remaining. And Joshua did to
them as the LORD bade him; he hamstrung their horses,
and burned their chariots with fire.
10 And Joshua turned back at that time, and took Hazor,
and smote its king with the sword; for Hazor formerly
11 was the head of all those kingdoms. And they put to the
sword all who were in it, utterly destroying them; there
was none left that breathed, and he burned Hazor with
12 fire. And all the cities of those kings, and all their kings,
Joshua took, and smote them with the edge of the sword,
utterly destroying them, as Moses the servant of the
13 LORD had commanded. But none of the cities that stood
on mounds did Israel burn, except Hazor only; that
14 Joshua burned. And all the spoil of these cities and the
cattle, the people of Israel took for their booty; but every

man they smote with the edge of the sword, until they had destroyed them, and they did not leave any that 15 breathed. As the LORD had commanded Moses his servant, so Moses commanded Joshua, and so Joshua did; he left nothing undone of all that the LORD had commanded Moses.

16 So Joshua took all that land, the hill country and all the Negeb and all the land of Goshen and the lowland and the Arabah and the hill country of Israel and its 17 lowland from Mount Halak, that rises toward Se'ir, as far as Ba'al-gad in the valley of Leb'anon below Mount Hermon. And he took all their kings, and smote them, and 18 put them to death. Joshua made war a long time with all 19 those kings. There was not a city that made peace with the people of Israel, except the Hivites, the inhabitants of 20 Gibeon; they took all in battle. For it was the LORD'S doing to harden their hearts that they should come against Israel in battle, in order that they should be utterly destroyed, and should receive no mercy but be exterminated, as the LORD commanded Moses.

21 And Joshua came at that time, and wiped out the Anakim from the hill country, from Hebron, from Debir, from Anab, and from all the hill country of Judah, and from all the hill country of Israel; Joshua utterly de- 22 stroyed them with their cities. There was none of the Anakim left in the land of the people of Israel; only in 23 Gaza, in Gath, and in Ashdod, did some remain. So Joshua took the whole land, according to all that the LORD had spoken to Moses; and Joshua gave it for an inheritance to Israel according to their tribal allotments. And the land had rest from war.

CONQUESTS SUMMARIZED

12 Now these are the kings of the land, whom the people of Israel defeated, and took possession of their land beyond the Jordan toward the sunrising, from the valley of the 2 Arnon to Mount Hermon, with all the Arabah eastward: Sihon king of the Amorites who dwelt at Heshbon, and ruled from Aro'er, which is on the edge of the valley of the Arnon, and from the middle of the valley as far as the river Jabbok, the 3 boundary of the Ammonites, that is, half of Gilead, and the Arabah to the Sea of Chin'neroth eastward, and in the direction of Beth-jesh'imoth, to the sea of the Arabah, the Salt Sea, 4 southward to the foot of the slopes of Pisgah; and Og e king of Bashan, one of the remnant of the Reph'aim, who dwelt at 5 Ash'taroth and at Ed're-i and ruled over Mount Hermon and Sal'ecah and all Bashan to the boundary of the Gesh'urites and the Ma-ac'athites, and over half of Gilead to the boundary of 6 Sihon king of Heshbon. Moses, the servant of the LORD, and the people of Israel defeated them; and Moses the servant of the LORD gave their land for a possession to the Reubenites and the Gadites and the half-tribe of Manas'seh.

7 And these are the kings of the land whom Joshua and the people of Israel defeated on the west side of the Jordan, from Ba'al-gad in the valley of Lebanon to Mount Halak, that rises toward Se'ir (and Joshua gave their land to the tribes of Israel 8 as a possession according to their allotments, in the hill country, in the lowland, in the Arabah, in the slopes, in the wilderness, and in the Negeb, the land of the Hittites, the Amorites, the Canaanites, the Per'izzites, the Hivites, and the Jeb'usites):
9 the king of Jericho, one; the king of Ai, which is beside Bethel, 10 one; the king of Jerusalem, one; the king of Hebron, one; 11, 12 the king of Jarmuth, one; the king of Lachish, one; the king 13 of Eglon, one; the king of Gezer, one; the king of Debir, one;

14 the king of Geder, one; the king of Hormah, one; the king of 15 Arad, one; the king of Libnah, one; the king of Adullam, one; 16, 17 the king of Makke'dah, one; the king of Bethel, one; the king 18 of Tap'pu-ah, one; the king of Hepher, one; the king of Aphek, 19 one; the king of Lashar'on, one; the king of Madon, one; the 20 king of Hazor, one; the king of Shim'ron-me'ron, one; the king 21 of Ach'shaph, one; the king of Ta'anach, one; the king of 22 Megid'do, one; the king of Kedesh, one; the king of Jok'ne-am 23 in Carmel, one; the king of Dor in Naphath-dor, one; the king 24 of Goi'im in Galilee,f one; the king of Tirzah, one: in all, thirty-one kings.

DIVISION OF THE LAND

13 Now Joshua was old and advanced in years; and the LORD said to him, "You are old and advanced in years, and 2 there remains yet very much land to be possessed. This is the land that yet remains: all the regions of the Philistines, and all 3 those of the Gesh'urites (from the Shihor, which is east of Egypt, northward to the boundary of Ekron, it is reckoned as Canaanite; there are five rulers of the Philistines, those of Gaza, Ashdod, Ash'kelon, Gath, and Ekron), and those of the Avvim, 4 in the south, all the land of the Canaanites, and Mear'ah which belongs to the Sido'nians, to Aphek, to the boundary of the 5 Amorites, and the land of the Geb'alites, and all Lebanon, toward the sunrising, from Ba'al-gad below Mount Hermon to the 6 entrance of Hamath, all the inhabitants of the hill country from Lebanon to Mis'rephoth-ma'im, even all the Sido'nians. I will myself drive them out from before the people of Israel; only allot the land to Israel for an inheritance, as I have commanded 7 you. Now therefore divide this land for an inheritance to the nine tribes and half the tribe of Manas'seh."

8 With the other half of the tribe of Manas'seh g the Reubenites

and the Gadites received their inheritance, which Moses gave them, beyond the Jordan eastward, as Moses the servant of 9 the LORD gave them: from Aro'er, which is on the edge of the valley of the Arnon, and the city that is in the middle of the 10 valley and all the tableland of Med'eba as far as Dibon; and all the cities of Sihon king of the Amorites, who reigned in 11 Heshbon, as far as the boundary of the Ammonites; and Gilead, and the region of the Gesh'urites and Ma-ac'athites, and all 12 Mount Hermon, and all Bashan to Sal'ecah; all the kingdom of Og in Bashan, who reigned in Ash'taroth and in Ed're-i (he alone was left of the remnant of the Reph'aim); these Moses 13 had defeated and driven out. Yet the people of Israel did not drive out the Gesh'urites or the Ma-ac'athites; but Geshur and Ma'acath dwell in the midst of Israel to this day.

14 To the tribe of Levi alone Moses gave no inheritance; the offerings by fire to the LORD God of Israel are their inheritance, as he said to him.

15 And Moses gave an inheritance to the tribe of the Reubenites 16 according to their families. So their territory was from Aro'er, which is on the edge of the valley of the Arnon, and the city that is the middle of the valley, and all the tableland by Med'- 17 eba; with Heshbon, and all its cities that are in the tableland;

e Gk: Heb *the boundary of Og*　　　f Gk: Heb *Gilgal*　　　g Cn: Heb *With it*

18 Dibon, and Ba'moth-ba'al, and Beth-ba'al-me'on, and Jahaz,
19 and Ked'emoth, and Meph'a-ath, and Kir'iatha'im, and Sibmah,
20 and Zer'eth-sha'har on the hill of the valley, and Beth-pe'or, and
21 the slopes of Pisgah, and Beth-jesh'imoth, that is, all the cities of the tableland, and all the kingdom of Sihon king of the Amorites, who reigned in Heshbon, whom Moses defeated with the leaders of Mid'ian, Evi and Rekem and Zur and Hur and
22 Reba, the princes of Sihon, who dwelt in the land. Balaam also, the son of Be'or, the soothsayer, the people of Israel killed
23 with the sword among the rest of their slain. And the border of the people of Reuben was the Jordan as a boundary. This was the inheritance of the Reubenites, according to their families with their cities and villages.
24 And Moses gave an inheritance also to the tribe of the Gadites,
25 according to their families. Their territory was Jazer, and all the cities of Gilead, and half the land of the Ammonites, to
26 Aro'er, which is east of Rabbah, and from Heshbon to Ra'math-miz'peh and Bet'onim, and from Mahana'im to the territory of
27 Debir,[h] and in the valley Beth-ha'ram, Beth-nim'rah, Succoth, and Zaphon, the rest of the kingdom of Sihon king of Heshbon, having the Jordan as a boundary, to the lower end of the Sea
28 of Chin'nereth, eastward beyond the Jordan. This is the inheritance of the Gadites according to their families, with their cities and villages.
29 And Moses gave an inheritance to the half-tribe of Manas'seh; it was allotted to the half-tribe of the Manas'sites according to
30 their families. Their region extended from Mahana'im, through all Bashan, the whole kingdom of Og king of Bashan, and all
31 the towns of Ja'ir, which are in Bashan, sixty cities, and half Gilead, and Ash'taroth, and Ed're-i, the cities of the kingdom of Og in Bashan; these were allotted to the people of Machir the son of Manas'seh for the half of the Machirites according to their families.
32 These are the inheritances which Moses distributed in the
33 plains of Moab, beyond the Jordan east of Jericho. But to the tribe of Levi Moses gave no inheritance; the LORD God of Israel is their inheritance, as he said to them.

14 And these are the inheritances which the people of Israel received in the land of Canaan, which Elea'zar the priest, and Joshua the son of Nun, and the heads of the fathers' houses of the tribes of the people of Israel distributed to them.
2 Their inheritance was by lot, as the LORD had commanded Moses
3 for the nine and one-half tribes. For Moses had given an inheritance to the two and one-half tribes beyond the Jordan;
4 but to the Levites he gave no inheritance among them. For the people of Joseph were two tribes, Manas'seh and E'phraim; and no portion was given to the Levites in the land, but only cities to dwell in, with their pasture lands for their cattle and their
5 substance. The people of Israel did as the LORD commanded Moses; they allotted the land.
6 Then the people of Judah came to Joshua at Gilgal; and Caleb the son of Jephun'neh the Ken'izzite said to him, "You know what the LORD said to Moses the man of God in Ka'desh-bar'ne-a
7 concerning you and me. I was forty years old when Moses the servant of the LORD sent me from Ka'desh-bar'ne-a to spy out the land; and I brought him word again as it was in my heart.
8 But my brethren who went up with me made the heart of the
9 people melt; yet I wholly followed the LORD my God. And Moses swore on that day, saying, 'Surely the land on which your foot has trodden shall be an inheritance for you and your children for ever, because you have wholly followed the LORD my God.'
10 And now, behold, the LORD has kept me alive, as he said, these forty-five years since the time that the LORD spoke this word to Moses, while Israel walked in the wilderness; and now, lo, I am
11 this day eighty-five years old. I am still as strong to this day as I was in the day that Moses sent me; my strength now is as my
12 strength was then, for war, and for going and coming. So now give me this hill country of which the LORD spoke on that day; for you heard on that day how the Anakim were there, with great fortified cities: it may be that the LORD will be with me, and I shall drive them out as the LORD said."
13 Then Joshua blessed him; and he gave Hebron to Caleb the
14 son of Jephun'neh for an inheritance. So Hebron became the inheritance of Caleb the son of Jephun'neh the Ken'izzite to this day, because he wholly followed the LORD, the God of Israel.
15 Now the name of Hebron formerly was Kir'iath-ar'ba;[i] this Arba was the greatest man among the Anakim. And the land had rest from war.

[h] Gk Syr Vg: Heb Lidebir   [i] That is The city of Arba

Lot of Judah

15 The lot for the tribe of the people of Judah according to their families reached southward to the boundary of
2 Edom, to the wilderness of Zin at the farthest south. And their south boundary ran from the end of the Salt Sea, from the bay
3 that faces southward; it goes out southward of the ascent of Akrab'bim, passes along to Zin, and goes up south of Ka'desh-bar'ne-a, along by Hezron, up to Addar, turns about to Karka,
4 passes along to Azmon, goes out by the Brook of Egypt, and comes to its end at the sea. This shall be your south boundary.
5 And the east boundary is the Salt Sea, to the mouth of the Jordan. And the boundary on the north side runs from the bay
6 of the sea at the mouth of the Jordan; and the boundary goes up to Beth-hoglah, and passes along north of Beth-arabah; and the boundary goes up to the stone of Bohan the son of Reuben;
7 and the boundary goes up to Debir from the Valley of Achor, and so northward, turning toward Gilgal, which is opposite the ascent of Adum'mim, which is on the south side of the valley; and the boundary passes along to the waters of En-she'mesh,
8 and ends at En-ro'gel; then the boundary goes up by the valley of the son of Hinnom at the southern shoulder of the Jeb'usite (that is, Jerusalem); and the boundary goes up to the top of the mountain that lies over against the valley of Hinnom, on
9 the west, at the northern end of the valley of Reph'aim; then the boundary extends from the top of the mountain to the spring of the Waters of Nephto'ah, and from there to the cities of Mount Ephron; then the boundary bends round to Ba'alah
10 (that is, Kir'iath-je'arim); and the boundary circles west of Ba'alah to Mount Se'ir, passes along to the northern shoulder of Mount Je'arim (that is, Ches'alon), and goes down to Beth-she'-
11 mesh, and passes along by Timnah; the boundary goes out to the shoulder of the hill north of Ekron, then the boundary bends round to Shik'keron, and passes along to Mount Ba'alah, and goes out to Jabneel; then the boundary comes to an end at the
12 sea. And the west boundary was the Great Sea with its coastline. This is the boundary round about the people of Judah according to their families.
13 According to the commandment of the LORD to Joshua, he gave to Caleb the son of Jephun'neh a portion among the people of Judah, Kir'iath-ar'ba, that is, Hebron (Arba was the
14 father of Anak). And Caleb drove out from there the three sons of Anak, She'shai and Ahi'man and Talmai, the descend-
15 ants of Anak. And he went up from there against the inhabitants of Debir; now the name of Debir formerly was
16 Kir'iath-se'pher. And Caleb said, "Whoever smites Kir'iath-se'pher, and takes it, to him will I give Achsah my daughter as
17 wife." And Oth'ni-el the son of Kenaz, the brother of Caleb,
18 took it; and he gave him Achsah his daughter as wife. When she came to him, she urged him to ask her father for a field; and she alighted from her ass, and Caleb said to her, "What do you
19 wish?" She said to him, "Give me a present; since you have set me in the land of the Negeb, give me also springs of water." And Caleb gave her the upper springs and the lower springs.
20 This is the inheritance of the tribe of the people of Judah
21 according to their families. The cities belonging to the tribe of the people of Judah in the extreme South, toward the boundary
22 of Edom, were Kabzeel, Eder, Jagur, Kinah, Dimo'nah, Ada'-
23, 24, 25 dah, Kedesh, Hazor, Ithnan, Ziph, Telem, Be-a'loth, Ha'zor-
26 hadat'tah, Ker'i-oth-hezron (that is, Hazor), Amam, Shema,
27, 28 Mola'dah, Ha'zar-gad'dah, Heshmon, Beth-pel'et, Hazar-shu'al,
29, 30 Beer-sheba, Biziothi'ah, Ba'alah, I'im, Ezem, Elto'lad, Chesil,
31, 32 Hormah, Ziklag, Madman'nah, Sansan'nah, Leba'oth, Shilhim, A'in, and Rimmon: in all, twenty-nine cities, with their villages.
33, 34 And in the lowland, Eshta'ol, Zorah, Ashnah, Zano'ah, En-
35 gan'nim, Tap'pu-ah, Enam, Jarmuth, Adullam, Socoh, Aze'kah,
36 Shaara'im, Aditha'im, Gede'rah, Gederotha'im: fourteen cities with their villages.
37, 38 Zenan, Hadash'ah, Mig'dal-gad, Di'lean, Mizpeh, Jok'theel,
39, 40, 41 Lachish, Bozkath, Eglon, Cabbon, Lahmam, Chitlish, Gede'-roth, Beth-da'gon, Na'amah, and Makke'dah: sixteen cities with their villages.
42, 43, 44 Libnah, Ether, Ashan, Iphtah, Ashnah, Nezib, Kei'lah, Achzib, and Mare'shah: nine cities with their villages.
45, 46 Ekron, with its towns and its villages; from Ekron to the sea, all that were by the side of Ashdod, with their villages.
47 Ashdod, its towns and its villages; Gaza, its towns and its villages; to the Brook of Egypt, and the Great Sea with its coast-line.
48, 49 And in the hill country, Shamir, Jattir, Socoh, Dannah,
50 Kir'iath-san'nah (that is, Debir), Anab, Esh'temoh, Anim,

51 Goshen, Holon, and Giloh: eleven cities with their villages.

52, 53 Arab, Dumah, Eshan, Janim, Beth-tap′pu-ah, Aphe′kah,
54 Humtah, Kir′iath-ar′ba (that is, Hebron), and Zi′or: nine cities with their villages.

55, 56 Ma′on, Carmel, Ziph, Juttah, Jezreel, Jok′de-am, Zano′ah,
57 Kain, Gib′e-ah, and Timnah: ten cities with their villages.

58, 59 Halhul, Beth-zur, Gedor, Ma′arath, Beth-anoth, and El′tekon: six cities with their villages.

60 Kir′iath-ba′al (that is, Kir′iath-je′arim), and Rabbah: two cities with their villages.

61, 62 In the wilderness, Beth-arabah, Middin, Seca′cah, Nibshan, the City of Salt, and En-ge′di: six cities with their villages.

63 But the Jeb′usites, the inhabitants of Jerusalem, the people of Judah could not drive out; so the Jeb′usites dwell with the people of Judah at Jerusalem to this day.

Lot of Joseph

16 The allotment of the descendants of Joseph went from the Jordan by Jericho, east of the waters of Jericho, into the wilderness, going up from Jericho into the hill country to 2 Bethel; then going from Bethel to Luz, it passes along to 3 At′aroth, the territory of the Archites; then it goes down westward to the territory of the Japh′letites, as far as the territory of Lower Beth-horon, then to Gezer, and it ends at the sea.
4 The people of Joseph, Manas′seh and E′phraim, received their inheritance.
5 The territory of the E′phraimites by their families was as follows: the boundary of their inheritance on the east was 6 At′aroth-ad′dar as far as Upper Beth-horon, and the boundary goes thence to the sea; on the north is Michme′thath; then on the east the boundary turns round toward Ta′anath-shi′loh, and 7 passes along beyond it on the east to Jano′ah, then it goes down from Jano′ah to At′aroth and to Na′arah, and touches Jericho, 8 ending at the Jordan. From Tap′pu-ah the boundary goes westward to the brook Kanah, and ends at the sea. Such is the inheritance of the tribe of the E′phraimites by their families, 9 together with the towns which were set apart for the E′phraim-ites within the inheritance of the Manas′sites, all those towns 10 with their villages. However they did not drive out the Canaanites that dwelt in Gezer: so the Canaanites have dwelt in the midst of E′phraim to this day but have become slaves to do forced labor.

17 Then allotment was made to the tribe of Manas′seh, for he was the first-born of Joseph. To Machir the first-born of Manas′seh, the father of Gilead, were allotted Gilead and 2 Bashan, because he was a man of war. And allotments were made to the rest of the tribe of Manas′seh, by their families, Abie′zer, Helek, As′riel, Shechem, Hepher, and Shemi′da; these were the male descendants of Manas′seh the son of Joseph, by their families.
3 Now Zeloph′e-had the son of Hepher, son of Gilead, son of Machir, son of Manas′seh, had no sons, but only daughters; and these are the names of his daughters: Mahlah, Noah, Hoglah, 4 Milcah, and Tirzah. They came before Elea′zar the priest and Joshua the son of Nun and the leaders, and said, "The LORD commanded Moses to give us an inheritance along with our brethren." So according to the commandment of the LORD he gave them an inheritance among the brethren of their father. 5 Thus there fell to Manas′seh ten portions, besides the land of Gilead and Bashan, which is on the other side of the Jordan; 6 because the daughters of Manas′seh received an inheritance along with his sons. The land of Gilead was allotted to the rest of the Manas′sites.
7 The territory of Manas′seh reached from Asher to Michme′-thath, which is east of Shechem; then the boundary goes along 8 southward to the inhabitants of En-tap′pu-ah. The land of Tap′pu-ah belonged to Manas′seh, but the town of Tap′pu-ah on the boundary of Manas′seh belonged to the sons of E′phraim. 9 Then the boundary went down to the brook Kanah. The cities here, to the south of the brook, among the cities of Manas′seh, belong to E′phraim. Then the boundary of Manas′seh goes 10 the north side of the brook and ends at the sea; the land to the south being E′phraim's and that to the north being Manas′seh's, with the sea forming its boundary; on the north Asher is 11 reached, and on the east Is′sachar. Also in Is′sachar and in Asher Manas′seh had Beth-she′an and its villages, and Ib′le-am and its villages, and the inhabitants of Dor and its villages, and the inhabitants of En-dor and its villages, and the inhabitants of Ta′anach and its villages, and the inhabitants of Megid′do and 12 its villages; the third is Naphath.[j] Yet the sons of Manas′seh

could not take possession of those cities; but the Canaanites 13 persisted in dwelling in that land. But when the people of Israel grew strong, they put the Canaanites to forced labor, and did not utterly drive them out.
14 And the tribe of Joseph spoke to Joshua, saying, "Why have you given me but one lot and one portion as an inheritance, although I am a numerous people, since hitherto the LORD has 15 blessed me?" And Joshua said to them, "If you are a numerous people, go up to the forest, and there clear ground for yourselves in the land of the Per′izzites and the Reph′aim, since the 16 hill country of E′phraim is too narrow for you." The tribe of Joseph said, "The hill country is not enough for us; yet all the Canaanites who dwell in the plain have chariots of iron, both those in Beth-she′an and its villages and those in the Valley of 17 Jezreel." Then Joshua said to the house of Joseph, to E′phraim and Manas′seh, "You are a numerous people, and have great 18 power; you shall not have one lot only, but the hill country shall be yours, for though it is a forest, you shall clear it and possess it to its farthest borders; for you shall drive out the Canaanites, though they have chariots of iron, and though they are strong."

Lots for Other Tribes

18 Then the whole congregation of the people of Israel assembled at Shiloh, and set up the tent of meeting there; the land lay subdued before them.
2 There remained among the people of Israel seven tribes whose 3 inheritance had not yet been apportioned. So Joshua said to the people of Israel, "How long will you be slack to go in and take possession of the land, which the LORD the God of your 4 fathers, has given you? Provide three men from each tribe, and I will send them out that they may set out and go up and down the land, writing a description of it with a view to their 5 inheritances, and then come to me. They shall divide it into seven portions, Judah continuing in his territory on the south, 6 and the house of Joseph in their territory on the north. And you shall describe the land in seven divisions and bring the description here to me; and I will cast lots for you here before the 7 LORD our God. The Levites have no portion among you, for the priesthood of the LORD is their heritage; and Gad and Reuben and half the tribe of Manas′seh have received their inheritance beyond the Jordan eastward, which Moses the servant of the LORD gave them."
8 So the men started on their way; and Joshua charged those who went to write the description of the land, saying, "Go up and down and write a description of the land, and come again to me; and I will cast lots for you here before the LORD in 9 Shiloh." So the men went and passed up and down in the land and set down in a book a description of it by towns in seven divisions; then they came to Joshua in the camp at Shiloh, 10 and Joshua cast lots for them in Shiloh before the LORD; and there Joshua apportioned the land to the people of Israel, to each his portion.
11 The lot of the tribe of Benjamin according to its families came up, and the territory allotted to it fell between the tribe of 12 Judah and the tribe of Joseph. On the north side their boundary began at the Jordan; then the boundary goes up to the shoulder north of Jericho, then up through the hill country westward; 13 and it ends at the wilderness of Beth-aven. From there the boundary passes along southward in the direction of Luz, to the shoulder of Luz (the same is Bethel), then the boundary goes down to At′aroth-ad′dar, upon the mountain that lies south of 14 Lower Beth-horon. Then the boundary goes in another direction, turning on the western side southward from the mountain that lies to the south, opposite Beth-horon, and it ends at Kir′-iath-ba′al (that is, Kir′iath-je′arim), a city belonging to the 15 tribe of Judah. This forms the western side. And the southern side begins at the outskirts of Kir′iath-je′arim; and the boundary goes from there to Ephron,[k] to the spring of the Waters of 16 Nephto′ah; then the boundary goes down to the border of the mountain that overlooks the valley of the son of Hinnom, which is at the north end of the valley of Reph′aim; and it then goes down the valley of Hinnom, south of the shoulder of the Jeb′-17 usites, and downward to En-ro′gel; then it bends in a northerly direction going on to En-she′mesh, and thence goes to Geli′loth, which is opposite the ascent of Adum′mim; then it goes down 18 to the Stone of Bohan the son of Reuben; and passing on to the north of the shoulder of Beth-arabah[l] it goes down to the 19 Arabah; then the boundary passes on to the north of the shoulder of Beth-hoglah; and the boundary ends at the northern bay of the Salt Sea, at the south end of the Jordan: this is the

j Heb obscure   k Cn See 15. 9. Heb westward   l Gk: Heb to the shoulder over against the Arabah

20 southern border. The Jordan forms its boundary on the eastern side. This is the inheritance of the tribe of Benjamin, according to its families, boundary by boundary round about.

21 Now the cities of the tribe of Benjamin according to their 22 families were Jericho, Beth-hoglah, Emek-ke'ziz, Beth-arabah, 23, 24 Zemara'im, Bethel, Avvim, Parah, Ophrah, Che'phar-am'moni, 25 Ophni, Geba—twelve cities with their villages: Gibeon, Ramah, 26, 27 Be-er'oth, Mizpeh, Che-phi'rah, Mozah, Reckem, Irpeel, Tar'- 28 alah, Zela, Ha-eleph, Jebus m (that is, Jerusalem), Gib'e-ah n and Kir'iath-je'arim o—fourteen cities with their villages. This is the inheritance of the tribe of Benjamin according to its families.

19 The second lot came out for Simeon, for the tribe of Simeon, according to its families; and its inheritance was 2 in the midst of the inheritance of the tribe of Judah. And it 3 had for its inheritance Beer-sheba, Sheba, Mola'dah, Hazar- 4, 5 shu'al, Balah, Ezem, Elto'lad, Bethul, Hormah, Ziklag, Beth- 6 mar'caboth, Ha'zar-su'sah, Beth-leba'oth, and Sharu'hen—thir- 7 teen cities with their villages; En-rimmon, Ether, and Ashan— 8 four cities with their villages; together with all the villages round about these cities as far as Ba'alath-beer, Ramah of the Negeb. This was the inheritance of the tribe of Simeon accord- 9 ing to its families. The inheritance of the tribe of Simeon formed part of the territory of Judah; because the portion of the tribe of Judah was too large for them, the tribe of Simeon obtained an inheritance in the midst of their inheritance.

10 The third lot came up for the tribe of Zeb'ulun, according to its families. And the territory of its inheritance reached as far as 11 Sarid; then its boundary goes up westward, and on to Mar'eal, and touches Dab'besheth, then the brook which is east of 12 Jok'neam; from Sarid it goes in the other direction eastward toward the sunrise to the boundary of Chis'loth-ta'bor; thence 13 it goes to Dab'erath, then up to Japhi'a; from there it passes along on the east toward the sunrise to Gath-hepher, to Eth- 14 kazin, and going on to Rimmon it bends toward Ne'ah; then on the north the boundary turns about to Han'nathon, and it ends 15 at the valley of Iph'tahel; and Kattath, Nahal'al, Shimron, 16 I'dalah, and Bethlehem—twelve cities with their villages. This is the inheritance of the tribe of Zeb'ulun, according to its families—these cities with their villages.

17 The fourth lot came out for Is'sachar, for the tribe of Is'sachar, 18 according to its families. Its territory included Jez'reel, Chesul'- 19, 20 loth, Shunem, Haph'ara-im, Shion, Ana'harath, Rabbith, 21 Kish'ion, Ebez, Remeth, En-gan'nim, En-had'dah, Beth-paz'zez; 22 the boundary also touches Tabor, Shahazu'mah, and Beth-she'- mesh, and its boundary ends at the Jordan—sixteen cities with 23 their villages. This is the inheritance of the tribe of Is'sachar, according to its families—the cities with their villages.

24 The fifth lot came out for the tribe of Asher according to its 25 families. Its territory included Helkath, Hali, Beten, Ach'shaph, 26 Allam'melech, Amad, and Mishal; on the west it touches Carmel 27 and Shihor-lib'nath, then it turns eastward, it goes to Beth- dagon, and touches Zeb'ulun and the valley of Iph'tha-el north- ward to Beth-emek and Nei'el; then it continues in the north to 28 Cabul, Ebron, Rehob, Hammon, Kanah, as far as Sidon the 29 Great; then the boundary turns to Ramah, reaching to the forti- fied city of Tyre; then the boundary turns to Hosah, and it ends 30 at the sea; Mahalab,p Achzib, Ummah, Aphek and Rehob— 31 twenty-two cities with their villages. This is the inheritance of the tribe of Asher according to its families—these cities with their villages.

32 The sixth lot came out for the tribe of Naph'tali, for the tribe 33 of Naph'tali, according to its families. And its boundary ran from Heleph, from the oak in Za-anan'nim, and Ad'ami-nekeb, and Jabneel, as far as Lak-kum; and it ended at the Jordan; 34 then the boundary turns westward to Az'noth-tabor, and goes from there to Hukkok, touching Zeb'ulun at the south, and 35 Asher on the west, and Judah on the east at the Jordan. The fortified cities are Ziddim, Zer, Hammath, Rakkath, Chin'nereth, 36, 37, 38 Ad'amah, Ramah, Hazor, Kedesh, Ed're-i, En-ha'zor, Yiron, Mig'dal-el, Horem, Beth-anath, and Beth-she'mesh—nineteen 39 cities with their villages. This is the inheritance of the tribe of Naph'tali according to its families—the cities with their villages.

40 The seventh lot came out for the tribe of Dan, according to its 41 families. And the territory of its inheritance included Zorah, 42, 43 Esh'ta-ol, Ir-she'mesh, Sha-alab'bin, Ai'jalon, Ithlah, Elon, 44, 45 Timnah, Ekron, El'tekeh, Gib'bethon, Ba'alath, Jehud, Bene- 46 be'rak, Gath-rim'mon, and Me-jar'kon and Rakkon with the 47 territory over against Joppa. When the territory of the Danites

was lost to them, the Danites went up and fought against Leshem, and after capturing it and putting it to the sword they took possession of it and settled in it, calling Leshem, Dan, after 48 the name of Dan their ancestor. This is the inheritance of the tribe of Dan, according to their families—these cities with their villages.

49 When they had finished distributing the several territories of the land as inheritances, the people of Israel gave an inheri- 50 tance among them to Joshua the son of Nun. By command of the LORD they gave him the city which he asked, Tim'nath-se'- rah in the hill country of E'phraim; and he rebuilt the city, and settled in it.

51 These are the inheritances which Elea'zar the priest and Joshua the son of Nun and the heads of the fathers' houses of the tribes of the people of Israel distributed by lot at Shiloh before the LORD, at the door of the tent of meeting. So they finished dividing the land.

Assignment of Cities

20 Then the LORD said to Joshua, "Say to the people of Israel, 'Appoint the cities of refuge, of which I spoke to 3 you through Moses, that the manslayer who kills any person without intent or unwittingly may flee there; they shall be for 4 you a refuge from the avenger of blood. He shall flee to one of these cities and shall stand at the entrance of the gate of the city, and explain his case to the elders of that city; then they shall take him into the city, and give him a place, and he shall 5 remain with them. And if the avenger of blood pursues him, they shall not give up the slayer into his hand; because he killed his neighbor unwittingly, having had no enmity against 6 him in times past. And he shall remain in that city until he has stood before the congregation for judgment, until the death of him who is high priest at the time: then the slayer may go again to his own town and his own home, to the town from which he fled.'"

7 And they set apart Kedesh in Galilee in the hill country of Naph'tali, and Shechem in the hill country of E'phraim, and Kir'iath-ar'ba (that is, Hebron) in the hill country of Judah. 8 And beyond the Jordan east of Jericho, they appointed Bezer in the wilderness on the tableland, from the tribe of Reuben, and Ramoth in Gilead, from the tribe of Gad, and Golan in 9 Bashan, from the tribe of Manas'seh. These were the cities designated for all the people of Israel, and for the stranger sojourning among them, that any one who killed a person with- out intent could flee there, so that he might not die by the hand of the avenger of blood, till he stood before the congregation.

21 Then the heads of the fathers' houses of the Levites came to Elea'zar the priest and to Joshua the son of Nun and to the heads of the fathers' houses of the tribes of the people of 2 Israel; and they said to them at Shiloh in the land of Canaan, "The LORD commanded through Moses that we be given cities to dwell in, along with their pasture lands for our cattle." 3 So by command of the LORD the people of Israel gave to the Levites the following cities and pasture lands out of their inheritance.

4 The lot came out for the families of the Ko'hathites. So those Levites who were descendants of Aaron the priest received by lot from the tribes of Judah, Simeon, and Benjamin, thirteen cities.

5 And the rest of the Ko'hathites received by lot from the families of the tribe of E'phraim, from the tribe of Dan and the half-tribe of Manas'seh, ten cities.

6 The Gershonites received by lot from the families of the tribe of Is'sachar, from the tribe of Asher, from the tribe of Naph'tali, and from the half-tribe of Manas'seh in Bashan, thirteen cities.

7 The Merar'ites according to their families received from the tribe of Reuben, the tribe of Gad, and the tribe of Zeb'ulun, twelve cities.

8 These cities and their pasture lands the people of Israel gave by lot to the Levites, as the LORD had commanded through Moses.

9 Out of the tribe of Judah and the tribe of Simeon they gave 10 the following cities mentioned by name, which went to the descendants of Aaron, one of the families of the Ko'hathites who belonged to the Levites; since the lot fell to them first. 11 They gave them Kir'iath-ar'ba (Arba being the father of Anak), that is, Hebron, in the hill country of Judah, along with the 12 pasture lands round about it. But the fields of the city and its villages had been given to Caleb the son of Jephun'neh as his possession.

m Gk Syr Vg: Heb the Jebusite   n Heb Gibeath   o Gk: Heb Kiriath   p Cn Compare Gk: Heb Mehebel

¹³ And to the descendants of Aaron the priest they gave Hebron, the city of refuge for the slayer, with its pasture lands, Libnah ¹⁴ with its pasture lands, Jattir with its pasture lands, Eshtemo'a ¹⁵ with its pasture lands, Holon with its pasture lands, Debir with ¹⁶ its pasture lands, A'in with its pasture lands, Beth-she'mesh with its pasture lands—nine cities out of these two tribes; ¹⁷ then out of the tribe of Benjamin, Gibeon with its pasture ¹⁸ lands, Geba with its pasture lands, An'athoth with its pasture ¹⁹ lands, and Almon with its pasture lands—four cities. The cities of the descendants of Aaron, the priests, were in all thirteen cities with their pasture lands.

²⁰ As to the rest of the Ko'hathites belonging to the Ko'hathite families of the Levites, the cities allotted to them were out of ²¹ the tribe of E'phraim. To them were given Shechem, the city of refuge for the slayer, with its pasture lands in the hill country ²² of E'phraim, Gezer with its pasture lands, Kib'za-im with its pasture lands, Beth-horon with its pasture lands—four cities; ²³ and out of the tribe of Dan, El'teke with its pasture lands, ²⁴ Gib'bethon with its pasture lands, Ai'jalon with its pasture ²⁵ lands, Gath-rim'mon with its pasture lands—four cities; and out of the half-tribe of Manas'seh, Ta'anach with its pasture lands, ²⁶ and Gath-rim'mon with its pasture lands—two cities. The cities of the families of the rest of the Ko'hathites were ten in all with their pasture lands.

²⁷ And to the Gershonites, one of the families of the Levites, were given out of the half-tribe of Manas'seh, Golan in Bashan with its pasture lands, the city of refuge for the slayer, and ²⁸ Be-esh'terah with its pasture lands—two cities; and out of the tribe of Is'sachar, Ki'shion with its pasture lands, Dab'erath ²⁹ with its pasture lands, Jarmuth with its pasture lands, En-gan'- ³⁰ nim with its pasture lands—four cities; and out of the tribe of Asher, Mishal with its pasture lands, Abdon with its pasture ³¹ lands, Helkath with its pasture lands, and Rehob with its pasture ³² lands—four cities; and out of the tribe of Naph'tali, Kedesh in Galilee with its pasture lands, the city of refuge for the slayer, Ham'moth-dor with its pasture lands, and Kartan with its ³³ pasture lands—three cities. The cities of the several families of the Gershonites were in all thirteen cities with their pasture lands.

³⁴ And to the rest of the Levites, the Merar'ite families, were given out of the tribe of Zeb'ulun, Jok'ne-am with its pasture ³⁵ lands, Kartah with its pasture lands, Dimnah with its pasture ³⁶ lands, Na'halal with its pasture lands—four cities; and out of the tribe of Reuben, Bezer with its pasture lands, Jahaz with ³⁷ its pasture lands, Ked'emoth with its pasture lands, and Meph'- ³⁸ a-ath with its pasture lands—four cities; and out of the tribe of Gad, Ramoth in Gilead with its pasture lands, the city of refuge ³⁹ for the slayer, Mahana'im with its pasture lands, Heshbon with its pasture lands, Jazer with its pasture lands—four cities in all. ⁴⁰ As for the cities of the several Merar'ite families, that is, the remainder of the families of the Levites, those allotted to them were in all twelve cities.

⁴¹ The cities of the Levites in the midst of the possession of the people of Israel were in all forty-eight cities with their pasture ⁴² lands. These cities had each its pasture lands round about it; so it was with all these cities.

⁴³ Thus the LORD gave to Israel all the land which he swore to give to their fathers; and having taken possession of it, they ⁴⁴ settled there. And the LORD gave them rest on every side just as he had sworn to their fathers; not one of all their enemies had withstood them, for the LORD had given all their enemies ⁴⁵ into their hands. Not one of all the good promises which the LORD had made to the house of Israel had failed; all came to pass.

THE LAST DAYS OF JOSHUA

22 Then Joshua summoned the Reubenites, and the Gadites, ² and the half-tribe of Manas'seh, and said to them, "You have kept all that Moses the servant of the LORD commanded you, and have obeyed my voice in all that I have commanded ³ you; you have not forsaken your brethren these many days, down to this day, but have been careful to keep the charge of ⁴ the LORD your God. And now the LORD your God has given rest to your brethren, as he promised them; therefore turn and go to your home in the land where your possession lies, which Moses the servant of the LORD gave you on the other side of ⁵ the Jordan. Take good care to observe the commandment and the law which Moses the servant of the LORD commanded you, to love the LORD your God, and to walk in all his ways, and to keep his commandments, and to cleave to him, and to serve

⁶ him with all your heart and with all your soul." So Joshua blessed them, and sent them away; and they went to their homes.

⁷ Now to the one half of the tribe of Manas'seh Moses had given a possession in Bashan; but to the other half Joshua had given a possession beside their brethren in the land west of the Jordan. And when Joshua sent them away to their homes ⁸ and blessed them, he said to them, "Go back to your homes with much wealth, and with very many cattle, with silver, gold, bronze, and iron, and with much clothing; divide the spoil of ⁹ your enemies with your brethren." So the Reubenites and the Gadites and the half-tribe of Manas'seh returned home, parting from the people of Israel at Shiloh, which is in the land of Canaan, to go to the land of Gilead, their own land of which they had possessed themselves by command of the LORD through Moses.

¹⁰ And when they came to the region about the Jordan, that lies in the land of Canaan, the Reubenites and the Gadites and the half-tribe of Manas'seh built there an altar by the Jordan, an ¹¹ altar of great size. And the people of Israel heard say, "Behold, the Reubenites and the Gadites and the half-tribe of Manas'seh have built an altar at the frontier of the land of Canaan, in the region about the Jordan, on the side that belongs to the ¹² people of Israel." And when the people of Israel heard of it, the whole assembly of the people of Israel gathered at Shiloh, to make war against them.

¹³ Then the people of Israel sent to the Reubenites and the Gadites and the half-tribe of Manas'seh, in the land of Gilead, ¹⁴ Phin'ehas the son of Elea'zar the priest, and with him ten chiefs, one from each of the tribal families of Israel, every one of ¹⁵ them the head of a family among the clans of Israel. And they came to the Reubenites, the Gadites, and the half-tribe of ¹⁶ Manas'seh, in the land of Gilead, and they said to them, "Thus says the whole congregation of the LORD, 'What is this treachery which you have committed against the God of Israel in turning away this day from following the LORD, by building yourselves ¹⁷ an altar this day in rebellion against the LORD? Have we not had enough of the sin at Pe'or from which even yet we have not cleansed ourselves, and for which there came a plague upon ¹⁸ the congregation of the LORD, that you must turn away this day from following the LORD? And if you rebel against the LORD today he will be angry with the whole congregation of Israel ¹⁹ tomorrow. But now, if your land is unclean, pass over into the LORD's land where the LORD's tabernacle stands, and take for yourselves a possession among us; only do not rebel against the LORD, or make us as rebels by building yourselves an altar ²⁰ other than the altar of the LORD our God. Did not Achan the son of Zerah break faith in the matter of the devoted things, and wrath fell upon all the congregation of Israel? And he did not perish alone for his iniquity.'"

²¹ Then the Reubenites, the Gadites, and the half-tribe of Manas'seh said in answer to the heads of the families of Israel, ²² "The Mighty One, God, the LORD! The Mighty One, God, the LORD! He knows; and let Israel itself know! If it was in rebellion ²³ or in breach of faith toward the LORD, spare us not today for building an altar to turn away from following the LORD; or if we did so to offer burnt offerings or cereal offerings or peace ²⁴ offerings on it, may the LORD himself take vengeance. Nay, but we did it from fear that in time to come your children might say to our children, 'What have you to do with the LORD, the ²⁵ God of Israel? For the LORD has made the Jordan a boundary between us and you, you Reubenites and Gadites; you have no portion in the LORD.' So your children might make our children ²⁶ cease to worship the LORD. Therefore we said, 'Let us now build ²⁷ an altar, not for burnt offering, nor for sacrifice, but to be a witness between us and you, and between the generations after us, that we do perform the service of the LORD in his presence with our burnt offerings and sacrifices and peace offerings; lest your children say to our children in time to come, "You ²⁸ have no portion in the LORD." ' And we thought, If this should be said to us or to our descendants in time to come, we should say, 'Behold the copy of the altar of the LORD, which our fathers made, not for burnt offerings, nor for sacrifice, but to be a ²⁹ witness between us and you.' Far be it from us that we should rebel against the LORD, and turn away this day from following the LORD by building an altar for burnt offering, cereal offering, or sacrifice, other than the altar of the LORD our God that stands before his tabernacle!"

³⁰ When Phin'ehas the priest and the chiefs of the congregation,

the heads of the families of Israel who were with him, heard the words that the Reubenites and the Gadites and the Manas'-
31 sites spoke, it pleased them well. And Phin'ehas the son of Elea'zar the priest said to the Reubenites and the Gadites and the Manas'sites, "Today we know that the LORD is in the midst of us, because you have not committed this treachery against the LORD; now you have saved the people of Israel from the hand of the LORD."

32 Then Phin'ehas the son of Elea'zar the priest, and the chiefs, returned from the Reubenites and the Gadites in the land of Gilead to the land of Canaan, to the people of Israel, and
33 brought back word to them. And the report pleased the people of Israel; and the people of Israel blessed God and spoke no more of making war against them, to destroy the land where
34 the Reubenites and the Gadites were settled. The Reubenites and the Gadites called the altar Witness; "For," said they, "it is a witness between us that the LORD is God."

Farewell Address of Joshua

23 A long time afterward, when the LORD had given rest to Israel from all their enemies round about, and Joshua was old and well advanced in years,
2 Joshua summoned all Israel, their elders and heads, their judges and officers, and said to them, "I am now old and
3 well advanced in years; and you have seen all that the LORD your God has done to all these nations for your sake, for it is the LORD your God who has fought for you.
4 Behold, I have allotted to you as an inheritance for your tribes those nations that remain, along with all the nations that I have already cut off, from the Jordan to the Great
5 Sea in the west. The LORD your God will push them back before you, and drive them out of your sight; and you shall possess their land, as the LORD your God promised
6 you. Therefore be very steadfast to keep and do all that is written in the book of the law of Moses, turning aside
7 from it neither to the right hand nor to the left, that you may not be mixed with these nations left here among you, or make mention of the names of their gods, or swear by them, or serve them, or bow down yourselves to them,
8 but cleave to the LORD your God as you have done to
9 this day. For the LORD has driven out before you great and strong nations; and as for you, no man has been
10 able to withstand you to this day. One man of you puts to flight a thousand, since it is the LORD your God who
11 fights for you, as he promised you. Take good heed to
12 yourselves, therefore, to love the LORD your God. For if you turn back, and join the remnant of these nations left here among you, and make marriages with them, so that
13 you marry their women and they yours, know assuredly that the LORD your God will not continue to drive out these nations before you; but they shall be a snare and a trap for you, a scourge on your sides, and thorns in your eyes, till you perish from off this good land which the LORD your God has given you.
14 "And now I am about to go the way of all the earth, and you know in your hearts and souls, all of you, that not one thing has failed of all the good things which the LORD your God promised concerning you; all have come
15 to pass for you, not one of them has failed. But just as all

the good things which the LORD your God promised concerning you have been fulfilled for you, so the LORD will bring upon you all the evil things, until he have destroyed you from off this good land which the LORD your God
16 has given you, if you transgress the covenant of the LORD your God, which he commanded you, and go and serve other gods and bow down to them. Then the anger of the LORD will be kindled against you, and you shall perish quickly from off the good land which he has given to you."

The Covenant at Shechem

24 Then Joshua gathered all the tribes of Israel to Shechem, and summoned the elders, the heads, the judges, and the officers of Israel; and they presented
2 themselves before God. And Joshua said to all the people, "Thus says the LORD, the God of Israel, 'Your fathers lived of old beyond the Eu-phra'tes, Terah, the father of Abraham and of Nahor; and they served other gods.
3 Then I took your father Abraham from beyond the River and led him through all the land of Canaan, and made his
4 offspring many. I gave him Isaac; and to Isaac I gave Jacob and Esau. And I gave Esau the hill country of Se'ir to possess, but Jacob and his children went down to Egypt.
5 And I sent Moses and Aaron, and I plagued Egypt with what I did in the midst of it; and afterwards I brought
6 you out. Then I brought your fathers out of Egypt, and you came to the sea; and the Egyptians pursued your
7 fathers with chariots and horsemen to the Red Sea. And when they cried to the LORD, he put darkness between you and the Egyptians, and made the sea come upon them and cover them; and your eyes saw what I did to
8 Egypt; and you lived in the wilderness a long time. Then I brought you to the land of the Amorites, who lived on the other side of the Jordan; they fought with you, and I gave them into your hand, and you took possession
9 of their land, and I destroyed them before you. Then Balak the son of Zippor, king of Moab, arose and fought against Israel; and he sent and invited Balaam the son of
10 Be'or to curse you, but I would not listen to Balaam; therefore he blessed you; so I delivered you out of his
11 hand. And you went over the Jordan and came to Jericho, and the men of Jericho fought against you, and also the Amorites, the Per'izzites, the Canaanites, the Hittites, the Gir'gashites, the Hivites, and the Jeb'usites; and I gave
12 them into your hand. And I sent the hornet before you, which drove them out before you, the two kings of the
13 Amorites; it was not by your sword or by your bow. I gave you a land on which you had not labored, and cities which you had not built, and you dwell therein; you eat the fruit of vineyards and oliveyards which you did not plant.'
14 "Now therefore fear the LORD, and serve him in sincerity and in faithfulness; put away the gods which your

fathers served beyond the River, and in Egypt, and serve
15 the LORD. And if you be unwilling to serve the LORD,
choose this day whom you will serve, whether the gods
your fathers served in the region beyond the River, or
the gods of the Amorites in whose land you dwell; but as
for me and my house, we will serve the LORD."
16 Then the people answered, "Far be it from us that we
17 should forsake the LORD, to serve other gods; for it is
the LORD our God who brought us and our fathers up
from the land of Egypt, out of the house of bondage, and
who did those great signs in our sight, and preserved us
in all the way that we went, and among all the peoples
18 through whom we passed; and the LORD drove out before
us all the peoples, the Amorites who lived in the land;
therefore we also will serve the LORD, for he is our God."
19 But Joshua said to the people, "You cannot serve the
LORD; for he is a holy God; he is a jealous God; he will
20 not forgive your transgressions or your sins. If you forsake the LORD and serve foreign gods, then he will turn
and do you harm, and consume you, after having done
21 you good." And the people said to Joshua, "Nay; but we
22 will serve the LORD." Then Joshua said to the people,
"You are witnesses against yourselves that you have
chosen the LORD, to serve him." And they said, "We are
23 witnesses." He said, "Then put away the foreign gods
which are among you, and incline your heart to the
24 LORD, the God of Israel." And the people said to Joshua,
"The LORD our God we will serve, and his voice we will
25 obey." So Joshua made a covenant with the people that
day, and made statutes and ordinances for them at
26 Shechem. And Joshua wrote these words in the book of
the law of God; and he took a great stone, and set it up
27 there under the oak in the sanctuary of the LORD. And
Joshua said to all the people, "Behold, this stone shall be
a witness against us; for it has heard all the words of the
LORD which he spoke to us; therefore it shall be a witness
28 against you, lest you deal falsely with your God." So
Joshua sent the people away, every man to his inheritance.

Three Burials

29 After these things Joshua the son of Nun, the servant
of the LORD, died, being a hundred and ten years old.
30 And they buried him in his own inheritance at Tim'nath-
se'rah which is in the hill country of E'phraim, north of
the mountain of Ga'ash.
31 And Israel served the LORD all the days of Joshua, and
all the days of the elders who outlived Joshua and had
known all the work which the LORD did for Israel.
32 The bones of Joseph which the people of Israel brought
up from Egypt were buried at Shechem, in the portion of
ground which Jacob bought from the sons of Hamor the
father of Shechem for a hundred pieces of money;[q] it
became an inheritance of the descendants of Joseph.
33 And Elea'zar the son of Aaron died; and they buried
him at Gib'e-ah, the town of Phin'ehas his son, which had
been given him in the hill country of E'phraim.

[q] Heb *qesitah*

INTRODUCTION TO

JUDGES

After Joshua died the Hebrews had no one outstanding leader to keep them united. They began to follow various leaders. The Bible calls them "judges" because the people brought their disputes to them to settle. Occasionally these men and at least one woman led the people in battles with the Canaanites, who had been living in Palestine before the Hebrews came and who naturally wanted their land back.

During this period there were frequent clashes with the Canaanites. There were six serious times of crisis, and the judges who rose to leadership were Othniel, Ehud, Deborah, Gideon, Jephthah, and Samson. Their stories are told in this book. Several less important judges are also mentioned.

The writer of Judges realized that lack of a strong leader for all the people had weakened the Hebrews, so he wrote, "In those days there was no king in Israel; every man did what was right in his own eyes" (Judges 21. 25). The people began to wish for a king who would unite all the tribes into one nation.

The people learned from the Canaanites how to worship their false gods, called baals and asherahs, and began to live in ways that by their Hebrew laws were wrong. So when the Book of Judges was written, it said over and over that "the people of Israel did what was evil in the sight of the Lord" (Judges 2. 11).

This book, recounting the adventures of the "judges," was first written probably about 550 B.C. From time to time various parts were added until about 200 B.C., when it was accepted as holy Scripture.

THE BOOK OF

JUDGES

THE INVASION OF CANAAN

1 After the death of Joshua the people of Israel inquired of the LORD, "Who shall go up first for us
2 against the Canaanites, to fight against them?" The LORD

said, "Judah shall go up; behold, I have given the land
3 into his hand." And Judah said to Simeon his brother, "Come up with me into the territory allotted to me, that we may fight against the Canaanites; and I likewise will go with you into the territory allotted to you." So Simeon
4 went with him. Then Judah went up and the LORD gave

the Canaanites and the Per'izzites into their hand; and
5 they defeated ten thousand of them at Bezek. They came upon Ado'ni-be'zek at Bezek, and fought against him, and
6 defeated the Canaanites and the Per'izzites. Ado'ni-be'zek fled; but they pursued him, and caught him, and cut off
7 his thumbs and his great toes. And Ado'ni-be'zek said, "Seventy kings with their thumbs and their great toes cut off used to pick up scraps under my table; as I have done, so God has requited me." And they brought him to Jerusalem, and he died there.
8 And the men of Judah fought against Jerusalem, and took it, and smote it with the edge of the sword, and set
9 the city on fire. And afterward the men of Judah went down to fight against the Canaanites who dwelt in the hill
10 country, in the Negeb, and in the lowland. And Judah went against the Canaanites who dwelt in Hebron (now

the name of Hebron was formerly Kir′iath-ar′ba) ; and they defeated Sheshai and Ahi′man and Talmai.

11 From there they went against the inhabitants of Debir.
12 The name of Debir was formerly Kir′iath-se′pher. And Caleb said, "He who attacks Kir′iath-se′pher and takes
13 it, I will give him Achsah my daughter as wife." And Oth′ni-el the son of Kenaz, Caleb's younger brother, took
14 it; and he gave him Achsah his daughter as wife. When she came to him, she urged him to ask her father for a field; and she alighted from her ass, and Caleb said to
15 her, "What do you wish?" She said to him, "Give me a present; since you have set me in the land of the Negeb, give me also springs of water." And Caleb gave her the upper springs and the lower springs.

16 And the descendants of the Ken′ite, Moses' father-in-law, went up with the people of Judah from the city of palms into the wilderness of Judah, which lies in the Negeb near Arad; and they went and settled with the
17 people. And Judah went with Simeon his brother, and they defeated the Canaanites who inhabited Zephath, and utterly destroyed it. So the name of the city was called
18 Hormah. Judah also took Gaza with its territory, and Ash′kelon with its territory, and Ekron with its territory.
19 And the LORD was with Judah, and he took possession of the hill country, but he could not drive out the inhabitants of the plain, because they had chariots of iron.
20 And Hebron was given to Caleb, as Moses had said; and
21 he drove′ out from it the three sons of Anak. But the people of Benjamin did not drive out the Jeb′usites who dwelt in Jerusalem; so the Jeb′usites have dwelt with the people of Benjamin in Jerusalem to this day.

22 The house of Joseph also went up against Bethel; and
23 the LORD was with them. And the house of Joseph sent to spy out Bethel. (Now the name of the city was formerly
24 Luz.) And the spies saw a man coming out of the city, and they said to him, "Pray, show us the way into the
25 city, and we will deal kindly with you." And he showed them the way into the city; and they smote the city with the edge of the sword, but they let the man and all his
26 family go. And the man went to the land of the Hittites and built a city, and called its name Luz; that is its name to this day.

27 Manas′seh did not drive out the inhabitants of Beth-she′an and its villages, or Ta′a-nach and its villages, or the inhabitants of Dor and its villages, or the inhabitants of Ib′leam and its villages, or the inhabitants of Megid′do and its villages; but the Canaanites persisted in dwelling
28 in that land. When Israel grew strong, they put the Canaanites to forced labor, but did not utterly drive them out.

29 And E′phraim did not drive out the Canaanites who dwelt in Gezer; but the Cananites dwelt in Gezer among them.

30 Zeb′ulun did not drive out the inhabitants of Kitron, or the inhabitants of Na′halol; but the Canaanites dwelt among them, and became subject to forced labor.

31 Asher did not drive out the inhabitants of Acco, or the inhabitants of Sidon, or of Ahlab, or of Achzib, or of
32 Helbah, or of Aphik, or of Rehob; but the Asherites dwelt among the Canaanites, the inhabitants of the land; for they did not drive them out.

33 Naph′tali did not drive out the inhabitants of Beth-she′-mesh, or the inhabitants of Beth-anath, but dwelt among the Canaanites, the inhabitants of the land; nevertheless the inhabitants of Beth-she′mesh and of Beth-anath be-came subject to forced labor for them.

34 The Amorites pressed the Danites back into the hill country, for they did not allow them to come down to
35 the plain; the Amorites persisted in dwelling in Har-heres, in Ai′jalon, and in Sha-al′bim, but the hand of the house of Joseph rested heavily upon them, and they became
36 subject to forced labor. And the border of the Amorites ran from the ascent of Akrab′bim, from Sela and upward.

2 Now the angel of the LORD went up from Gilgal to Bochim. And he said, "I brought you up from Egypt, and brought you into the land which I swore to give to your fathers. I said, 'I will never break my covenant with
2 you, and you shall make no covenant with the inhabitants of this land; you shall break down their altars.' But you have not obeyed my command. What is this you have
3 done? So now I say, I will not drive them out before you; but they shall become adversaries a to you, and
4 their gods shall be a snare to you." When the angel of the LORD spoke these words to all the people of Israel,
5 the people lifted up their voices and wept. And they called the name of that place Bochim; b and they sacrificed there to the LORD.

THE RULE OF THE JUDGES

6 When Joshua dismissed the people, the people of Israel went each to his inheritance to take possession of the
7 land. And the people served the LORD all the days of Joshua, and all the days of the elders who outlived Joshua, who had seen all the great work which the LORD had done
8 for Israel. And Joshua the son of Nun, the servant of the
9 LORD, died at the age of one hundred and ten years. And they buried him within the bounds of his inheritance in Tim′nath-he′res, in the hill country of E′phraim, north
10 of the mountain of Ga′ash. And all that generation also were gathered to their fathers; and there arose another generation after them, who did not know the LORD or the work which he had done for Israel.

11 And the people of Israel did what was evil in the sight
12 of the LORD and served the Ba′als; and they forsook the LORD, the God of their fathers, who had brought them out of the land of Egypt; they went after other gods, from among the gods of the peoples who were round

---

a Vg Old Latin Compare Gk: Heb *sides*　　　b That is *Weepers*

about them, and bowed down to them; and they provoked
13 the LORD to anger. They forsook the LORD, and served
14 the Ba'als and the Ash'taroth. So the anger of the LORD
was kindled against Israel, and he gave them over to
plunderers, who plundered them; and he sold them into
the power of their enemies round about, so that they
15 could no longer withstand their enemies. Whenever they
marched out, the hand of the LORD was against them for
evil, as the LORD had warned, and as the LORD had sworn
to them; and they were in sore straits.
16 Then the LORD raised up judges, who saved them out
17 of the power of those who plundered them. And yet they
did not listen to their judges; for they played the harlot
after other gods and bowed down to them; they soon
turned aside from the way in which their fathers had
walked, who had obeyed the commandments of the LORD,
18 and they did not do so. Whenever the LORD raised up
judges for them, the LORD was with the judge, and he
saved them from the hand of their enemies all the days
of the judge; for the LORD was moved to pity by their
groaning because of those who afflicted and oppressed
19 them. But whenever the judge died, they turned back and
behaved worse than their fathers, going after other gods,
serving them and bowing down to them; they did not
20 drop any of their practices or their stubborn ways. So
the anger of the LORD was kindled against Israel; and he
said, "Because this people have transgressed my covenant
which I commanded their fathers, and have not obeyed
21 my voice, I will not henceforth drive out before them any
22 of the nations that Joshua left when he died, that by them
I may test Israel, whether they will take care to walk in
23 the way of the LORD as their fathers did, or not." So the
LORD left those nations, not driving them out at once, and
he did not give them into the power of Joshua.

3 Now these are the nations which the LORD left, to
test Israel by them, that is, all in Israel who had no
2 experience of any war in Canaan; it was only that the
generations of the people of Israel might know war, that
he might teach war to such at least as had not known it
3 before. These are the nations: the five lords of the Philistines, and all the Canaanites, and the Sido'nians, and the
Hivites who dwelt on Mount Lebanon, from Mount Ba'al-
4 her'mon as far as the entrance of Hamath. They were for
the testing of Israel, to know whether Israel would obey
the commandments of the LORD, which he commanded
5 their fathers by Moses. So the people of Israel dwelt
among the Canaanites, the Hittites, the Amorites, the
6 Per'izzites, the Hivites, and the Jeb'usites; and they took
their daughters to themselves for wives, and their own
daughters they gave to their sons; and they served their
gods.
7 And the people of Israel did what was evil in the sight
of the LORD, forgetting the LORD their God, and serving

8 the Ba'als and the Ashe'roth. Therefore the anger of the
LORD was kindled against Israel, and he sold them into
the hand of Cu'shan-rishatha'im king of Mesopota'mia;
and the people of Israel served Cu'shan-rishatha'im eight
9 years. But when the people of Israel cried to the LORD, the
LORD raised up a deliverer for the people of Israel, who
delivered them, Oth'ni-el the son of Kenaz, Caleb's
10 younger brother. The Spirit of the LORD came upon him,
and he judged Israel; he went out to war, and the LORD
gave Cu'shan-rishatha'im king of Mesopota'mia into his
hand; and his hand prevailed over Cu'shan-rishatha'im.
11 So the land had rest forty years. Then Oth'ni-el the son
of Kenaz died.
12 And the people of Israel again did what was evil in the
sight of the LORD; and the LORD strengthened Eglon the
king of Moab against Israel, because they had done what
13 was evil in the sight of the LORD. He gathered to himself
the Ammonites and the Amal'ekites, and went and defeated Israel; and they took possession of the city of
14 palms. And the people of Israel served Eglon the king of
Moab eighteen years.
15 But when the people of Israel cried to the LORD, the
LORD raised up for them a deliverer, Ehud, the son of
Gera, the Benjaminite, a left-handed man. The people of
Israel sent tribute by him to Eglon the king of Moab.
16 And Ehud made for himself a sword with two edges, a
cubit in length; and he girded it on his right thigh under
17 his clothes. And he presented the tribute to Eglon king
18 of Moab. Now Eglon was a very fat man. And when
Ehud had finished presenting the tribute, he sent away
19 the people that carried the tribute. But he himself turned
back at the sculptured stones near Gilgal, and said, "I
have a secret message for you, O king." And he commanded, "Silence." And all his attendants went out from
20 his presence. And Ehud came to him, as he was sitting
alone in his cool roof chamber. And Ehud said, "I have a
message from God for you." And he arose from his seat.
21 And Ehud reached with his left hand, took the sword
22 from his right thigh, and thrust it into his belly; and the
hilt also went in after the blade, and the fat closed over
the blade, for he did not draw the sword out of his belly;
23 and the dirt came out. Then Ehud went out into the
vestibule,c and closed the doors of the roof chamber upon
him, and locked them.
24 When he had gone, the servants came; and when they
saw that the doors of the roof chamber were locked they
thought, "He is only relieving himself in the closet of
25 the cool chamber." And they waited till they were utterly
at a loss; but when he still did not open the doors of the
roof chamber, they took the key and opened them; and
there lay their lord dead on the floor.
26 Ehud escaped while they delayed, and passed beyond
27 the sculptured stones, and escaped to Se-i'rah. When he

c The meaning of the Hebrew word is unknown

arrived, he sounded the trumpet in the hill country of E'phraim; and the people of Israel went down with him

28 from the hill country, having him at their head. And he said to them, "Follow after me; for the LORD has given your enemies the Moabites into your hand." So they went down after him, and seized the fords of the Jordan against

29 the Moabites, and allowed not a man to pass over. And they killed at that time about ten thousand of the Moabites, all strong, able-bodied men; not a man escaped.

30 So Moab was subdued that day under the hand of Israel. And the land had rest for eighty years.

31 After him was Shamgar the son of Anath, who killed six hundred of the Philistines with an oxgoad; and he too delivered Israel.

4 And the people of Israel again did what was evil in

2 the sight of the LORD, after Ehud died. And the LORD sold them into the hand of Jabin king of Canaan, who reigned in Hazor; the commander of his army was Sis'era,

3 who dwelt in Haro'sheth-ha-goiim. Then the people of Israel cried to the LORD for help; for he had nine hundred chariots of iron, and oppressed the people of Israel cruelly for twenty years.

Deborah and Barak

4 Now Deb'orah, a prophetess, the wife of Lapp'idoth,

5 was judging Israel at that time. She used to sit under the palm of Deb'orah between Ramah and Bethel in the hill country of E'phraim; and the people of Israel came up to

6 her for judgment. She sent and summoned Barak the son of Abin'o-am from Kedesh in Naph'tali, and said to him, "The LORD, the God of Israel, commands you, 'Go, gather your men at Mount Tabor, taking ten thousand from the tribe of Naph'tali and the tribe of Zeb'ulun.

7 And I will draw out Sis'era, the general of Jabin's army, to meet you by the river Kishon with his chariots and his

8 troops; and I will give him into your hand.' " Barak said to her, "If you will go with me, I will go; but if you will

9 not go with me, I will not go." And she said, "I will surely go with you; nevertheless, the road on which you are going will not lead to your glory, for the LORD will sell Sis'era into the hand of a woman." Then Deb'orah arose,

10 and went with Barak to Kedesh. And Barak summoned Zeb'ulun and Naph'tali to Kedesh; and ten thousand men went up at his heels; and Deb'orah went up with him.

11 Now Heber the Ken'ite had separated from the Ken'ites, the descendants of Hobab the father-in-law of Moses, and had pitched his tent as far away as the oak in Za-anan'-nim, which is near Kedesh.

12 When Sis'era was told that Barak the son of Abin'o-am

13 had gone up to Mount Tabor, Sis'era called out all his chariots, nine hundred chariots of iron, and all the men who were with him, from Haro'sheth-ha-goiim to the

14 river Kishon. And Deb'orah said to Barak, "Up! For this is the day in which the LORD has given Sis'era into your hand. Does not the LORD go out before you?" So Barak went down from Mount Tabor with ten thousand men

15 following him. And the LORD routed Sis'era and all his chariots and all his army before Barak at the edge of the sword; and Sis'era alighted from his chariot and fled

16 away on foot. And Barak pursued the chariots and the army to Haro'sheth-ha-goiim, and all the army of Sis'era fell by the edge of the sword; not a man was left.

17 But Sis'era fled away on foot to the tent of Ja'el, the wife of Heber the Ken'ite; for there was peace between Jabin the king of Hazor and the house of Heber the

18 Ken'ite. And Ja'el came out to meet Sis'era, and said to him, "Turn aside, my lord, turn aside to me; have no fear." So he turned aside to her into the tent, and she

19 covered him with a rug. And he said to her, "Pray, give me a little water to drink; for I am thirsty." So she opened a skin of milk and gave him a drink and covered

20 him. And he said to her, "Stand at the door of the tent, and if any man comes and asks you, 'Is any one here?'

21 say, No." But Ja'el the wife of Heber took a tent peg, and took a hammer in her hand, and went softly to him and drove the peg into his temple, till it went down into the ground, as he was lying fast asleep from weariness. So he

22 died. And behold, as Barak pursued Sis'era, Ja'el went out to meet him, and said to him, "Come, and I will show you the man whom you are seeking." So he went in to her tent; and there lay Sis'era dead, with the tent peg in his temple.

23 So on that day God subdued Jabin the king of Canaan

24 before the people of Israel. And the hand of the people of Israel bore harder and harder on Jabin the king of Canaan, until they destroyed Jabin king of Canaan.

The Song of Deborah

5 Then sang Deb'orah and Barak the son of Abin'-o-am on that day:

2 "That the leaders took the lead in Israel,
　　that the people offered themselves willingly,
　　bless d the LORD!

3 "Hear, O kings; give ear, O princes;
　　to the LORD I will sing,
　　I will make melody to the LORD, the God of Israel.

d Or You who offered yourselves willingly among the people, bless

149

4 "LORD, when thou didst go forth from Se'ir,
  when thou didst march from the region of Edom,
the earth trembled,
  and the heavens dropped,
  yea, the clouds dropped water.
5 The mountains quaked before the LORD,
  yon Sinai before the LORD, the God of Israel.

6 "In the days of Shamgar, son of Anath,
  in the days of Ja'el, caravans ceased
  and travelers kept to the byways.
7 The peasantry ceased in Israel, they ceased
  until you arose, Deb'orah,
  arose as a mother in Israel.
8 When new gods were chosen,
  then war was in the gates.
Was shield or spear to be seen
  among forty thousand in Israel?
9 My heart goes out to the commanders of Israel
  who offered themselves willingly among the people.
Bless the LORD.

10 "Tell of it, you who ride on tawny asses,
  you who sit on rich carpets e
  and you who walk by the way.
11 To the sound of musicians e at the watering places,
  there they repeat the triumphs of the LORD,
  the triumphs of his peasantry in Israel.

"Then down to the gates marched the people of the LORD.

12 "Awake, awake, Deb'orah!
  Awake, awake, utter a song!
Arise, Barak, lead away your captives,
  O son of Abin'o-am.
13 Then down marched the remnant of the noble;
  the people of the LORD marched down for him f against
    the mighty.
14 From E'phraim they set out thither x into the valley,g
  following you, Benjamin, with your kinsmen;
  from Machir marched down the commanders,
  and from Zeb'ulun those who bear the marshal's staff;
15 the princes of Is'sachar came with Deb'orah,
  and Is'sachar faithful to Barak;
  into the valley they rushed forth at his heels.
Among the clans of Reuben
  there were great searchings of heart.
16 Why did you tarry among the sheepfolds,
  to hear the piping for the flocks?
Among the clans of Reuben
  there were great searchings of heart.
17 Gilead stayed beyond the Jordan;
  and Dan, why did he abide with the ships?
Asher sat still at the coast of the sea,
  settling down by his landings.

18 Zeb'ulun is a people that jeoparded their lives to the
    death;
  Naph'tali too, on the heights of the field.

19 "The kings came, they fought;
  then fought the kings of Canaan,
at Ta'anach, by the waters of Megid'do;
  they got no spoils of silver.
20 From heaven fought the stars,
  from their courses they fought against Sis'era.
21 The torrent Kishon swept them away,
  the onrushing torrent, the torrent Kishon.
  March on, my soul, with might!

22 "Then loud beat the horses' hoofs
  with the galloping, galloping of his steeds.

23 "Curse Meroz, says the angel of the LORD,
  curse bitterly its inhabitants,
because they came not to the help of the LORD,
  to the help of the LORD against the mighty.

24 "Most blessed of women be Ja'el,
  the wife of Heber the Ken'ite,
  of tent-dwelling women most blessed.
25 He asked water and she gave him milk,
  she brought him curds in a lordly bowl.
26 She put her hand to the tent peg
  and her right hand to the workmen's mallet;
  she struck Sis'era a blow,
  she crushed his head,
  she shattered and pierced his temple.
27 He sank, he fell,
  he lay still at her feet;
at her feet he sank, he fell;
  where he sank, there he fell dead.

28 "Out of the window she peered,
  the mother of Sis'era gazed h through the lattice:
'Why is his chariot so long in coming?
  Why tarry the hoofbeats of his chariots?'
29 Her wisest ladies make answer,
  nay, she gives answer to herself,
30 'Are they not finding and dividing the spoil?—
  A maiden or two for every man;
spoil of dyed stuffs for Sis'era,
  spoil of dyed stuffs embroidered,
  two pieces of dyed work embroidered for my neck as
    spoil?'

31 "So perish all thine enemies,
  O LORD!
But thy friends be like the sun as he rises in his might."

And the land had rest for forty years.

---

e The meaning of the Hebrew word is uncertain   f Gk: Heb me   g Gk: Heb in Amalek
x Cn: Heb From Ephraim their root   h Gk Compare Tg: Heb exclaimed

The Story of Gideon

6 The people of Israel did what was evil in the sight of the LORD; and the LORD gave them into the hand of 2 Mid′ian seven years. And the hand of Mid′ian prevailed over Israel; and because of Mid′ian the people of Israel made for themselves the dens which are in the moun- 3 tains, and the caves and the strongholds. For whenever the Israelites put in seed the Mid′ianites and the Amal′- ekites and the people of the East would come up and 4 attack them; they would encamp against them and de- stroy the produce of the land, as far as the neighborhood of Gaza, and leave no sustenance in Israel, and no sheep 5 or ox or ass. For they would come up with their cattle and their tents, coming like locusts for number; both they and their camels could not be counted; so that they 6 wasted the land as they came in. And Israel was brought very low because of Mid′ian; and the people of Israel cried for help to the LORD.

7 When the people of Israel cried to the LORD on account 8 of the Mid′ianites, the LORD sent a prophet to the people of Israel; and he said to them, "Thus says the LORD, the God of Israel: I led you up from Egypt, and brought you 9 out of the house of bondage; and I delivered you from the hand of the Egyptians, and from the hand of all who oppressed you, and drove them out before you, and gave 10 you their land; and I said to you, 'I am the LORD your God; you shall not pay reverence to the gods of the Amorites, in whose land you dwell.' But you have not given heed to my voice."

11 Now the angel of the LORD came and sat under the oak at Ophrah, which belonged to Jo′ash the Abiez′rite, as his son Gideon was beating out wheat in the wine press, to 12 hide it from the Mid′ianites. And the angel of the LORD appeared to him and said to him, "The LORD is with you, 13 you mighty man of valor." And Gideon said to him, "Pray, sir, if the LORD is with us, why then has all this befallen us? And where are all his wonderful deeds which our fathers recounted to us, saying, 'Did not the LORD bring us up from Egypt?' But now the LORD has cast us 14 off, and given us into the hand of Mid′ian." And the LORD turned to him and said, "Go in this might of yours and deliver Israel from the hand of Mid′ian; do not I 15 send you?" And he said to him, "Pray, Lord, how can I deliver Israel? Behold, my clan is the weakest in Ma- 16 nas′seh, and I am the least in my family." And the LORD said to him, "But I will be with you, and you shall smite 17 the Mid′ianites as one man." And he said to him, "If now I have found favor with thee, then show me a sign that it 18 is thou who speakest with me. Do not depart from here, I pray thee, until I come to thee, and bring out my present, and set it before thee." And he said, "I will stay till you return."

19 So Gideon went into his house and prepared a kid, and unleavened cakes from an ephah of flour; the meat he put in a basket, and the broth he put in a pot, and brought 20 them to him under the oak and presented them. And the angel of God said to him, "Take the meat and the un- leavened cakes, and put them on this rock, and pour the 21 broth over them." And he did so. Then the angel of the LORD reached out the tip of the staff that was in his hand, and touched the meat and the unleavened cakes; and there sprang up fire from the rock and consumed the flesh and the unleavened cakes; and the angel of the 22 LORD vanished from his sight. Then Gideon perceived that he was the angel of the LORD; and Gideon said, "Alas, O Lord GOD! For now I have seen the angel of 23 the Lord face to face." But the LORD said to him, "Peace 24 be to you; do not fear, you shall not die." Then Gideon built an altar there to the LORD, and called it, The LORD is peace. To this day it still stands at Ophrah, which be- longs to the Abiez′rites.

25 That night the LORD said to him, "Take your father's bull, the second bull seven years old, and pull down the altar of Ba′al which your father has, and cut down the 26 Ashe′rah that is beside it; and build an altar to the LORD your God on the top of the stronghold here, with stones laid in due order; then take the second bull, and offer it as a burnt offering with the wood of the Ashe′rah which you 27 shall cut down." So Gideon took ten men of his servants, and did as the LORD had told him; but because he was too afraid of his family and the men of the town to do it by day, he did it by night.

28 When the men of the town rose early in the morning, behold, the altar of Ba′al was broken down, and the Ashe′rah beside it was cut down, and the second bull was 29 offered upon the altar which had been built. And they said to one another, "Who has done this thing?" And after they had made search and inquired, they said, "Gid- 30 eon the son of Jo′ash has done this thing." Then the men of the town said to Jo′ash, "Bring out your son, that he may die, for he has pulled down the altar of Ba′al and 31 cut down the Ashe′rah beside it." But Jo′ash said to all who were arrayed against him, "Will you contend for Ba′al? Or will you defend his cause? Whoever contends for him shall be put to death by morning. If he is a god, let him contend for himself, because his altar has been 32 pulled down." Therefore on that day he was called Jerub- ba′al, that is to say, "Let Ba′al contend against him," because he pulled down his altar.

33 Then all the Mid′ianites and the Amal′ekites and the people of the East came together, and crossing the Jordan 34 they encamped in the Valley of Jezreel. But the Spirit of the LORD took possession of Gideon; and he sounded the trumpet, and the Abiez′rites were called out to follow him. 35 And he sent messengers throughout all Manas′seh; and they too were called out to follow him. And he sent

messengers to Asher, Zeb'ulun, and Naph'tali; and they went up to meet them.

36 Then Gideon said to God, "If thou wilt deliver Israel 37 by my hand, as thou hast said, behold, I am laying a fleece of wool on the threshing floor; if there is dew on the fleece alone, and it is dry on all the ground, then I shall know that thou wilt deliver Israel by my hand, as 38 thou hast said." And it was so. When he rose early next morning and squeezed the fleece, he wrung enough dew 39 from the fleece to fill a bowl with water. Then Gideon said to God, "Let not thy anger burn against me, let me speak but this once; pray, let me make trial only this once with the fleece; pray, let it be dry only on the fleece, and on 40 all the ground let there be dew." And God did so that night; for it was dry on the fleece only, and on all the ground there was dew.

7 Then Jerubba'al (that is, Gideon) and all the people who were with him rose early and encamped beside the spring of Harod; and the camp of Mid'ian was north of them, by the hill of Moreh, in the valley. 2 The LORD said to Gideon, "The people with you are too many for me to give the Mid'ianites into their hand, lest Israel vaunt themselves against me, saying, 'My own 3 hand has delivered me.' Now therefore proclaim in the ears of the people, saying, 'Whoever is fearful and trembling, let him return home.'" And Gideon tested them;[i] twenty-two thousand returned, and ten thousand remained.

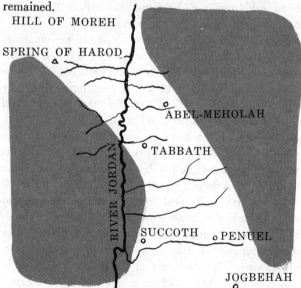

HILL OF MOREH

SPRING OF HAROD

ABEL-MEHOLAH

TABBATH

RIVER JORDAN

SUCCOTH   PENUEL

JOGBEHAH

4 And the LORD said to Gideon, "The people are still too many; take them down to the water and I will test them for you there; and he of whom I say to you, 'This man shall go with you,' shall go with you; and any of whom I say to you, 'This man shall not go with you,' shall not 5 go." So he brought the people down to the water; and the LORD said to Gideon, "Every one that laps the water with his tongue, as a dog laps, you shall set by himself; 6 likewise every one that kneels down to drink." And the

number of those that lapped, putting their hands to their mouths, was three hundred men; but all the rest of the 7 people knelt down to drink water. And the LORD said to Gideon, "With the three hundred men that lapped I will deliver you, and give the Mid'ianites into your hand; and 8 let all the others go every man to his home." So he took the jars of the people from their hands,[j] and their trumpets; and he sent all the rest of Israel every man to his tent, but retained the three hundred men; and the camp of Mid'ian was below him in the valley.

9 That same night the LORD said to him, "Arise, go down against the camp; for I have given it into your hand. 10 But if you fear to go down, go down to the camp with 11 Purah your servant; and you shall hear what they say, and afterward your hands shall be strengthened to go down against the camp." Then he went down with Purah his servant to the outposts of the armed men that were in 12 the camp. And the Mid'ianites and the Amal'ekites and all the people of the East lay along the valley like locusts for multitude; and their camels were without number, as 13 the sand which is upon the seashore for multitude. When Gideon came, behold, a man was telling a dream to his comrade; and he said, "Behold, I dreamed a dream; and lo, a cake of barley bread tumbled into the camp of Mid'ian, and came to the tent, and struck it so that it fell, 14 and turned it upside down, so that the tent lay flat." And his comrade answered, "This is no other than the sword of Gideon the son of Jo'ash, a man of Israel; into his hand God has given Mid'ian and all the host."

15 When Gideon heard the telling of the dream and its interpretation, he worshiped; and he returned to the camp of Israel, and said, "Arise; for the LORD has given the 16 host of Mid'ian into your hand." And he divided the three hundred men into three companies, and put trumpets into the hands of all of them and empty jars, with torches 17 inside the jars. And he said to them, "Look at me, and do likewise; when I come to the outskirts of the camp, do as 18 I do. When I blow the trumpet, I and all who are with me, then blow the trumpets also on every side of all the camp, and shout, 'For the LORD and for Gideon.'"

19 So Gideon and the hundred men who were with him came to the outskirts of the camp at the beginning of the middle watch, when they had just set the watch; and they blew the trumpets and smashed the jars that were in their 20 hands. And the three companies blew the trumpets and broke the jars, holding in their left hands the torches, and in their right hands the trumpets to blow; and they cried, 21 "A sword for the LORD and for Gideon!" They stood every man in his place round about the camp, and all the 22 army ran; they cried out and fled. When they blew the three hundred trumpets, the LORD set every man's sword against his fellow and against all the army; and the army fled as far as Beth-shit'tah toward Zer'erah,[k] as far as the

[i] Cn: Heb *and depart from Mount Gilead*   [j] Cn: Heb *the people took provisions in their hands*   [k] Another reading is *Zeredah*

23 border of A'bel-meho'lah, by Tabbath. And the men of Israel were called out from Naph'tali and from Asher and from all Manas'seh, and they pursued after Mid'ian.
24 And Gideon sent messengers throughout all the hill country of E'phraim, saying, "Come down against the Mid'ianites and seize the waters against them, as far as Beth-bar'ah, and also the Jordan." So all the men of E'phraim were called out, and they seized the waters as
25 far as Beth-bar'ah, and also the Jordan. And they took the two princes of Mid'ian, Oreb and Zeeb; they killed Oreb at the rock of Oreb, and Zeeb they killed at the wine press of Zeeb, as they pursued Mid'ian; and they brought the heads of Oreb and Zeeb to Gideon beyond the Jordan.

8 And the men of E'phraim said to him, "What is this that you have done to us, not to call us when you went to fight with Mid'ian?" And they upbraided him
2 violently. And he said to them, "What have I done now in comparison with you? Is not the gleaning of the grapes
3 of E'phraim better than the vintage of Abie'zer? God has given into your hands the princes of Mid'ian, Oreb and Zeeb; what have I been able to do in comparison with you?" Then their anger against him was abated, when he had said this.
4 And Gideon came to the Jordan and passed over, he and the three hundred men who were with him, faint yet
5 pursuing. So he said to the men of Succoth, "Pray, give loaves of bread to the people who follow me; for they are faint, and I am pursuing after Zebah and Zalmun'na,
6 the kings of Mid'ian." And the officials of Succoth said, "Are Zebah and Zalmun'na already in your hand, that we
7 should give bread to your army?" And Gideon said, "Well then, when the LORD has given Zebah and Zalmun'-na into my hand, I will flail your flesh with the thorns of
8 the wilderness and with briers." And from there he went up to Penu'el, and spoke to them in the same way; and the men of Penu'el answered him as the men of Succoth
9 had answered. And he said to the men of Penu'el, "When I come again in peace, I will break down this tower."
10 Now Zebah and Zalmun'na were in Karkor with their army, about fifteen thousand men, all who were left of all the army of the people of the East; for there had fallen a hundred and twenty thousand men who drew the sword.
11 And Gideon went up by the caravan route east of Nobah and Jog'behah, and attacked the army; for the army was
12 off its guard. And Zebah and Zalmun'na fled; and he pursued them and took the two kings of Mid'ian, Zebah and Zalmun'na, and he threw all the army into a panic.
13 Then Gideon the son of Jo'ash returned from the battle
14 by the ascent of Heres. And he caught a young man of Succoth, and questioned him; and he wrote down for him the officials and elders of Succoth, seventy-seven men.
15 And he came to the men of Succoth, and said, "Behold Zebah and Zalmun'na, about whom you taunted me,

saying, 'Are Zebah and Zalmun'na already in your hand, that we should give bread to your men who are faint?'"
16 And he took the elders of the city and he took thorns of the wilderness and briers and with them taught the men
17 of Succoth. And he broke down the tower of Penu'el, and slew the men of the city.

18 Then he said to Zebah and Zalmun'na, "Where are the men whom you slew at Tabor?" They answered, "As you are, so were they, every one of them; they resembled the
19 sons of a king." And he said, "They were my brothers, the sons of my mother; as the LORD lives, if you had saved
20 them alive, I would not slay you." And he said to Jether his first-born, "Rise, and slay them." But the youth did not draw his sword; for he was afraid, because he was
21 still a youth. Then Zebah and Zalmun'na said, "Rise yourself, and fall upon us; for as the man is, so is his strength." And Gideon arose and slew Zebah and Zal-mun'na; and he took the crescents that were on the necks of their camels.
22 Then the men of Israel said to Gideon, "Rule over us, you and your son and your grandson also; for you have
23 delivered us out of the hand of Mid'ian." Gideon said to them, "I will not rule over you, and my son will not rule
24 over you; the LORD will rule over you." And Gideon said to them, "Let me make a request of you; give me every man of you the earrings of his spoil." (For they had
25 golden earrings, because they were Ish'maelites.) And they answered, "We will willingly give them." And they spread a garment, and every man cast in it the earrings
26 of his spoil. And the weight of the golden earrings that he requested was one thousand seven hundred shekels of gold; besides the crescents and the pendants and the purple garments worn by the kings of Mid'ian, and besides the collars that were about the necks of their camels.
27 And Gideon made an ephod of it and put it in his city, in Ophrah; and all Israel played the harlot after it there,
28 and it became a snare to Gideon and to his family. So Mid'ian was subdued before the people of Israel, and they lifted up their heads no more. And the land had rest forty years in the days of Gideon.
29 Jerubba'al the son of Jo'ash went and dwelt in his own
30 house. Now Gideon had seventy sons, his own offspring,
31 for he had many wives. And his concubine who was in Shechem also bore him a son, and he called his name

32 Abim′elech. And Gideon the son of Jo′ash died in a good old age, and was buried in the tomb of Jo′ash his father, at Ophrah of the Abiez′rites.

33 As soon as Gideon died, the people of Israel turned again and played the harlot after the Ba′als, and made 34 Ba′al-be′rith their god. And the people of Israel did not remember the LORD their God, who had rescued them 35 from the hand of all their enemies on every side; and they did not show kindness to the family of Jerubba′al (that is, Gideon) in return for all the good that he had done to Israel.

The Story of Abimelech

9 Now Abim′elech the son of Jerubba′al went to She-chem to his mother's kinsmen and said to them and to 2 the whole clan of his mother's family, "Say in the ears of all the citizens of Shechem, 'Which is better for you, that all seventy of the sons of Jerubba′al rule over you, or that one rule over you?' Remember also that I am your 3 bone and your flesh." And his mother's kinsmen spoke all these words on his behalf in the ears of all the men of Shechem; and their hearts inclined to follow Abim′- 4 elech, for they said, "He is our brother." And they gave him seventy pieces of silver out of the house of Ba′al-be′rith with which Abim′elech hired worthless and reck- 5 less fellows, who followed him. And he went to his father's house at Ophrah, and slew his brothers the sons of Jerubba′al, seventy men, upon one stone; but Jotham the youngest son of Jerubba′al was left, for he hid himself. 6 And all the citizens of Shechem came together, and all Beth-millo, and they went and made Abim′elech king, by the oak of the pillar at Shechem.

7 When it was told to Jotham, he went and stood on the top of Mount Ger′izim, and cried aloud and said to them, "Listen to me, you men of Shechem, that God may listen 8 to you. The trees once went forth to anoint a king over them; and they said to the olive tree, 'Reign over us.' 9 But the olive tree said to them, 'Shall I leave my fatness, by which gods and men are honored, and go to sway over 10 the trees?' And the trees said to the fig tree, 'Come you, 11 and reign over us.' But the fig tree said to them, 'Shall I leave my sweetness and my good fruit, and go to sway 12 over the trees?' And the trees said to the vine, 'Come you, 13 and reign over us.' But the vine said to them, 'Shall I leave my wine which cheers gods and men, and go to 14 sway over the trees?' Then all the trees said to the 15 bramble, 'Come you, and reign over us.' And the bramble said to the trees, 'If in good faith you are anointing me king over you, then come and take refuge in my shade; but if not, let fire come out of the bramble and devour the cedars of Lebanon.'

16 "Now therefore, if you acted in good faith and honor when you made Abim′elech king, and if you have dealt well with Jerubba′al and his house, and have done to 17 him as his deeds deserved—for my father fought for you, and risked his life, and rescued you from the hand of 18 Mid′ian; and you have risen up against my father's house this day, and have slain his sons, seventy men on one stone, and have made Abim′elech, the son of his maid-servant, king over the citizens of Shechem, because he is 19 your kinsman—if you then have acted in good faith and honor with Jerubba′al and with his house this day, then rejoice in Abim′elech, and let him also rejoice in you; 20 but if not, let fire come out from Abim′elech, and devour the citizens of Shechem, and Beth-millo; and let fire come out from the citizens of Shechem, and from Beth-millo, 21 and devour Abim′elech." And Jotham ran away and fled, and went to Beer and dwelt there, for fear of Abim′-elech his brother.

22, 23 Abim′elech ruled over Israel three years. And God sent an evil spirit between Abim′elech and the men of Shechem; and the men of Shechem dealt treacherously 24 with Abim′elech; that the violence done to the seventy sons of Jerubba′al might come and their blood be laid upon Abim′elech their brother, who slew them, and upon the men of Shechem, who strengthened his hands to slay 25 his brothers. And the men of Shechem put men in ambush against him on the mountain tops, and they robbed all who passed by them along that way; and it was told Abim′elech.

26 And Ga′al the son of Ebed moved into Shechem with his kinsmen; and the men of Shechem put confidence in 27 him. And they went out into the field, and gathered the grapes from their vineyards and trod them, and held festival, and went into the house of their god, and ate 28 and drank and reviled Abim′elech. And Ga′al the son of Ebed said, "Who is Abim′elech, and who are we of Shechem, that we should serve him? Do not the son of Jerubba′al and Zebul his officer serve the men of Hamor the father of Shechem? Why then should we serve him? 29 Would that this people were under my hand! then I would remove Abim′elech. I would say[1] to Abim′elech, 'Increase your army, and come out.' "

30 When Zebul the ruler of the city heard the words of 31 Ga′al the son of Ebed, his anger was kindled. And he sent messengers to Abim′elech at Aru′mah,[m] saying, "Behold, Ga′al the son of Ebed and his kinsmen have come to Shechem, and they are stirring up[n] the city 32 against you. Now therefore, go by night, you and the 33 men that are with you, and lie in wait in the fields. Then in the morning, as soon as the sun is up, rise early and rush upon the city; and when he and the men that are with him come out against you, you may do to them as occasion offers."

34 And Abim′elech and all the men that were with him rose up by night, and laid wait against Shechem in four 35 companies. And Ga′al the son of Ebed went out and stood in the entrance of the gate of the city; and Abim′elech

---

[1] Gk: Heb *and he said*   [m] Cn See 9. 41. Heb *Tormah*   [n] Cn: Heb *besieging*

and the men that were with him rose from the ambush. ³⁶ And when Ga'al saw the men, he said to Zebul, "Look, men are coming down from the mountain tops!" And Zebul said to him, "You see the shadow of the mountains ³⁷ as if they were men." Ga'al spoke again and said, "Look, men are coming down from the center of the land, and one company is coming from the direction of the Diviners' ³⁸ Oak." Then Zebul said to him, "Where is your mouth now, you who said, 'Who is Abim'elech, that we should serve him?' Are not these the men whom you despised? ³⁹ Go out now and fight with them." And Ga'al went out at the head of the men of Shechem, and fought with ⁴⁰ Abim'elech. And Abim'elech chased him, and he fled before him; and many fell wounded, up to the entrance of ⁴¹ the gate. And Abim'elech dwelt at Aru'mah; and Zebul drove out Ga'al and his kinsmen, so that they could not live on at Shechem.

⁴² On the following day the men went out into the fields. ⁴³ And Abim'elech was told. He took his men and divided them into three companies, and laid wait in the fields; and he looked and saw the men coming out of the city, and ⁴⁴ he rose against them and slew them. Abim'elech and the company ° that was with him rushed forward and stood at the entrance of the gate of the city, while the two companies rushed upon all who were in the fields and slew ⁴⁵ them. And Abim'elech fought against the city all that day; he took the city, and killed the people that were in it; and he razed the city and sowed it with salt.

⁴⁶ When all the people of the Tower of Shechem heard of it, they entered the stronghold of the house of El-be'rith. ⁴⁷ Abim'elech was told that all the people of the Tower of ⁴⁸ Shechem were gathered together. And Abim'elech went up to Mount Zalmon, he and all the men that were with him; and Abim'elech took an axe in his hand, and cut down a bundle of brushwood, and took it up and laid it on his shoulder. And he said to the men that were with him, "What you have seen me do, make haste to do, as I ⁴⁹ have done." So every one of the people cut down his bundle and following Abim'elech put it against the stronghold, and they set the stronghold on fire over them, so that all the people of the Tower of Shechem also died, about a thousand men and women.

⁵⁰ Then Abim'elech went to Thebez, and encamped against ⁵¹ Thebez, and took it. But there was a strong tower within the city, and all the people of the city fled to it, all the men and women, and shut themselves in; and they went ⁵² to the roof of the tower. And Abim'elech came to the tower, and fought against it, and drew near to the door ⁵³ of the tower to burn it with fire. And a certain woman threw an upper millstone upon Abim'elech's head, and ⁵⁴ crushed his skull. Then he called hastily to the young man his armorbearer, and said to him, "Draw your sword and kill me, lest men say of me, 'A woman killed him.' " And his young man thrust him through, and he died.

⁵⁵ And when the men of Israel saw that Abim'elech was ⁵⁶ dead, they departed every man to his home. Thus God requited the crime of Abim'elech, which he committed ⁵⁷ against his father in killing his seventy brothers; and God also made all the wickedness of the men of Shechem fall back upon their heads, and upon them came the curse of Jotham the son of Jerubba'al.

Other Judges

10 After Abim'elech there arose to deliver Israel Tola the son of Pu'ah, son of Dodo, a man of Is'sachar; and he lived at Shamir in the hill country of E'phraim. ² And he judged Israel twenty-three years. Then he died, and was buried at Shamir.

³ After him arose Ja'ir the Gileadite, who judged Israel ⁴ twenty-two years. And he had thirty sons who rode on thirty asses; and they had thirty cities, called Hav'voth-⁵ja'ir to this day, which are in the land of Gilead. And Ja'ir died, and was buried in Kamon.

⁶ And the people of Israel again did what was evil in the sight of the LORD, and served the Ba'als and the Ash'taroth, the gods of Syria, the gods of Sidon, the gods of Moab, the gods of the Ammonites, and the gods of the Philistines; and they forsook the LORD, and did not serve ⁷ him. And the anger of the LORD was kindled against Israel, and he sold them into the hand of the Philistines ⁸ and into the hand of the Ammonites, and they crushed and oppressed the children of Israel that year. For eighteen years they oppressed all the people of Israel that were beyond the Jordan in the land of the Amorites, ⁹ which is in Gilead. And the Ammonites crossed the Jordan to fight also against Judah and against Benjamin and against the house of E'phraim; so that Israel was sorely distressed.

¹⁰ And the people of Israel cried to the LORD, saying, "We have sinned against thee, because we have forsaken our ¹¹ God and have served the Ba'als." And the LORD said to the people of Israel, "Did I not deliver you from the Egyptians and from the Amorites, from the Ammonites ¹² and from the Philistines? The Sido'nians also, and the Amal'ekites, and the Ma'onites, oppressed you; and you ¹³ cried to me, and I delivered you out of their hand. Yet you have forsaken me and served other gods; therefore I ¹⁴ will deliver you no more. Go and cry to the gods whom you have chosen; let them deliver you in the time of your ¹⁵ distress." And the people of Israel said to the LORD, "We have sinned; do to us whatever seems good to thee; only ¹⁶ deliver us, we pray thee, this day." So they put away the foreign gods from among them and served the LORD; and he became indignant over the misery of Israel.

¹⁷ Then the Ammonites were called to arms, and they encamped in Gilead; and the people of Israel came to-¹⁸gether, and they encamped at Mizpah. And the people, the leaders of Gilead, said one to another, "Who is the

° Vg and some Mss of Gk: Heb *companies*

man that will begin to fight against the Ammonites? He shall be head over all the inhabitants of Gilead."

11 Now Jephthah the Gileadite was a mighty warrior, but he was the son of a harlot. Gilead was the father ² of Jephthah. And Gilead's wife also bore him sons; and when his wife's sons grew up, they thrust Jephthah out, and said to him, "You shall not inherit in our father's ³ house; for you are the son of another woman." Then Jephthah fled from his brothers, and dwelt in the land of Tob; and worthless fellows collected round Jephthah, and went raiding with him.

⁴ After a time the Ammonites made war against Israel. ⁵ And when the Ammonites made war against Israel, the elders of Gilead went to bring Jephthah from the land of ⁶ Tob; and they said to Jephthah, "Come and be our leader, ⁷ that we may fight with the Ammonites." But Jephthah said to the elders of Gilead, "Did you not hate me, and drive me out of my father's house? Why have you come ⁸ to me now when you are in trouble?" And the elders of Gilead said to Jephthah, "That is why we have turned to you now, that you may go with us and fight with the Ammonites, and be our head over all the inhabitants of ⁹ Gilead." Jephthah said to the elders of Gilead, "If you bring me home again to fight with the Ammonites, and the LORD gives them over to me, I will be your head." ¹⁰ And the elders of Gilead said to Jephthah, "The LORD will be witness between us; we will surely do as you say." ¹¹ So Jephthah went with the elders of Gilead, and the people made him head and leader over them; and Jephthah spoke all his words before the LORD at Mizpah.

¹² Then Jephthah sent messengers to the king of the Ammonites and said, "What have you against me, that you ¹³ come to me to fight against my land?" And the king of the Ammonites answered the messengers of Jephthah, "Because Israel on coming from Egypt took away my land, from the Arnon to the Jabbok and to the Jordan; ¹⁴ now therefore restore it peaceably." And Jephthah sent ¹⁵ messengers again to the king of the Ammonites and said to him, "Thus says Jephthah: Israel did not take away ¹⁶ the land of Moab or the land of the Ammonites, but when they came up from Egypt, Israel went through the wil- ¹⁷ derness to the Red Sea and came to Kadesh. Israel then sent messengers to the king of Edom, saying, 'Let us pass, we pray, through your land'; but the king of Edom would not listen. And they sent also to the king of Moab, but he would not consent. So Israel remained at Kadesh. ¹⁸ Then they journeyed through the wilderness, and went around the land of Edom and the land of Moab, and arrived on the east side of the land of Moab, and camped on the other side of the Arnon; but they did not enter the territory of Moab, for the Arnon was the boundary ¹⁹ of Moab. Israel then sent messengers to Sihon king of the Amorites, king of Heshbon; and Israel said to him, 'Let us pass, we pray, through your land to our country.'

²⁰ But Sihon did not trust Israel to pass through his territory; so Sihon gathered all his people together, and en- ²¹ camped at Jahaz, and fought with Israel. And the LORD, the God of Israel, gave Sihon and all his people into the hand of Israel, and they defeated them; so Israel took possession of all the land of the Amorites, who inhabited ²² that country. And they took possession of all the territory of the Amorites from the Arnon to the Jabbok and from ²³ the wilderness to the Jordan. So then the LORD, the God of Israel, dispossessed the Amorites from before his people ²⁴ Israel; and are you to take possession of them? Will you not possess what Chemosh your god gives you to possess? And all that the LORD our God has dispossessed before us, ²⁵ we will possess. Now are you any better than Balak the son of Zippor, king of Moab? Did he ever strive against ²⁶ Israel, or did he ever go to war with them? While Israel dwelt in Heshbon and its villages, and in Aro'er and its villages, and in all the cities that are on the banks of the Arnon, three hundred years, why did you not recover ²⁷ them within that time? I therefore have not sinned against you, and you do me wrong by making war on me; the LORD, the Judge, decide this day between the people of ²⁸ Israel and the people of Ammon." But the king of the Ammonites did not heed the message of Jephthah which he sent to him.

²⁹ Then the Spirit of the LORD came upon Jephthah, and he passed through Gilead and Manas'seh, and passed on to Mizpah of Gilead, and from Mizpah of Gilead he passed ³⁰ on to the Ammonites. And Jephthah made a vow to the LORD, and said, "If thou wilt give the Ammonites into my ³¹ hand, then whoever comes forth from the doors of my house to meet me, when I return victorious from the Ammonites, shall be the LORD's, and I will offer him up for ³² a burnt offering." So Jephthah crossed over to the Ammonites to fight against them; and the LORD gave them ³³ into his hand. And he smote them from Aro'er to the neighborhood of Minnith, twenty cities, and as far as Abel-keramim, with a very great slaughter. So the Ammonites were subdued before the people of Israel.

³⁴ Then Jephthah came to his home at Mizpah; and behold, his daughter came out to meet him with timbrels and with dances; she was his only child; beside her he ³⁵ had neither son nor daughter. And when he saw her, he rent his clothes, and said, "Alas, my daughter! you have brought me very low, and you have become the cause of great trouble to me; for I have opened my mouth to the ³⁶ LORD, and I cannot take back my vow." And she said to him, "My father, if you have opened your mouth to the LORD, do to me according to what has gone forth from your mouth, now that the LORD has avenged you on your ³⁷ enemies, on the Ammonites." And she said to her father, "Let this thing be done for me; let me alone two months, that I may go and wander ^P on the mountains, and bewail ³⁸ my virginity, I and my companions." And he said, "Go."

^P Cn: Heb *go down*

And he sent her away for two months; and she departed, she and her companions, and bewailed her virginity upon 39 the mountains. And at the end of two months, she returned to her father, who did with her according to his vow which he had made. She had never known a man. 40 And it became a custom in Israel that the daughters of Israel went year by year to lament the daughter of Jephthah the Gileadite four days in the year.

12 The men of E'phraim were called to arms, and they crossed the Zaphon and said to Jephthah, "Why did you cross over to fight against the Ammonites, and did not call us to go with you? We will burn your house over 2 you with fire." And Jephthah said to them, "I and my people had a great feud with the Ammonites; and when I called you, you did not deliver me from their hand. 3 And when I saw that you would not deliver me, I took my life in my hand, and crossed over against the Ammonites, and the LORD gave them into my hand; why then have you come up to me this day, to fight against me?" 4 Then Jephthah gathered all the men of Gilead and fought with E'phraim; and the men of Gilead smote E'phraim, because they said, "You are fugitives of E'phraim, you Gileadites, in the midst of E'phraim and Manas'seh." 5 And the Gileadites took the fords of the Jordan against the E'phraimites. And when any of the fugitives of E'phraim said, "Let me go over," the men of Gilead said to him, "Are you an E'phraimite?" When he said, "No," 6 they said to him, "Then say Shibboleth," and he said, "Sibboleth," for he could not pronounce it right; then they seized him and slew him at the fords of the Jordan. And there fell at that time forty-two thousand of the E'phraimites.

7 Jephthah judged Israel six years. Then Jephthah the Gileadite died, and was buried in his city in Gilead q.

8, 9 After him Ibzan of Bethlehem judged Israel. He had thirty sons; and thirty daughters he gave in marriage outside his clan, and thirty daughters he brought in from outside for his sons. And he judged Israel seven years. 10 Then Ibzan died, and was buried at Bethlehem.

11 After him Elon the Zeb'ulunite judged Israel; and he 12 judged Israel ten years. Then Elon the Zeb'ulunite died, and was buried at Ai'jalon in the land of Zeb'ulun.

13 After him Abdon the son of Hillel the Pir'athonite 14 judged Israel. He had forty sons and thirty grandsons, who rode on seventy asses; and he judged Israel eight 15 years. Then Abdon the son of Hillel the Pir'athonite died, and was buried at Pir'athon in the land of E'phraim, in the hill country of the Amal'ekites.

The Story of Samson

13 And the people of Israel again did what was evil in the sight of the LORD; and the LORD gave them into the hand of the Philistines for forty years.

2 And there was a certain man of Zorah, of the tribe of the Danites, whose name was Mano'ah; and his wife was 3 barren and had no children. And the angel of the LORD appeared to the woman and said to her, "Behold, you are barren and have no children; but you shall conceive and 4 bear a son. Therefore beware, and drink no wine or 5 strong drink, and eat nothing unclean, for lo, you shall conceive and bear a son. No razor shall come upon his head, for the boy shall be a Nazirite to God from birth; and he shall begin to deliver Israel from the hand of the 6 Philistines." Then the woman came and told her husband, "A man of God came to me, and his countenance was like the countenance of the angel of God, very terrible; I did not ask him whence he was, and he did not tell me his 7 name; but he said to me, 'Behold, you shall conceive and bear a son; so then drink no wine or strong drink, and eat nothing unclean, for the boy shall be a Nazirite to God from birth to the day of his death.' "

8 Then Mano'ah entreated the LORD, and said, "O, LORD, I pray thee, let the man of God whom thou didst send come again to us, and teach us what we are to do with 9 the boy that will be born." And God listened to the voice of Mano'ah, and the angel of God came again to the woman as she sat in the field; but Mano'ah her husband 10 was not with her. And the woman ran in haste and told her husband, "Behold, the man who came to me the other 11 day has appeared to me." And Mano'ah arose and went after his wife, and came to the man and said to him, "Are you the man who spoke to this woman?" And he said, 12 "I am." And Mano'ah said, "Now when your words come true, what is to be the boy's manner of life, and what is 13 he to do?" And the angel of the LORD said to Mano'ah, 14 "Of all that I said to the woman let her beware. She may not eat of anything that comes from the vine, neither let her drink wine or strong drink, or eat any unclean thing; all that I commanded her let her observe."

15 Mano'ah said to the angel of the LORD, "Pray, let us 16 detain you, and prepare a kid for you." And the angel of the LORD said to Mano'ah, "If you detain me, I will not eat of your food; but if you make ready a burnt offering, then offer it to the LORD." (For Mano'ah did not 17 know that he was the angel of the LORD.) And Mano'ah said to the angel of the LORD, "What is your name, so that, when your words come true, we may honor you?" 18 And the angel of the LORD said to him, "Why do you ask 19 my name, seeing it is wonderful?" So Mano'ah took the kid with the cereal offering, and offered it upon the rock 20 to the LORD, to him who works r wonders s. And when the flame went up toward heaven from the altar, the angel of the LORD ascended in the flame of the altar while Mano'ah and his wife looked on; and they fell on their faces to the ground.

21 The angel of the LORD appeared no more to Mano'ah

q Gk: Heb *in the cities of Gilead*   r Gk Vg: Heb *and working*   s Heb *wonders, while Manoah and his wife looked on*

and to his wife. Then Mano'ah knew that he was the
²² angel of the LORD. And Mano'ah said to his wife, "We
²³ shall surely die, for we have seen God." But his wife said
to him, "If the LORD had meant to kill us, he would not
have accepted a burnt offering and a cereal offering at
our hands, or shown us all these things, or now an-
²⁴ nounced to us such things as these." And the woman
bore a son, and called his name Samson; and the boy
²⁵ grew, and the LORD blessed him. And the Spirit of the
LORD began to stir him in Ma'haneh-dan, between Zorah
and Esh'ta-ol.

14 Samson went down to Timnah, and at Timnah he
² saw one of the daughters of the Philistines. Then he
came up, and told his father and mother, "I saw one of
the daughters of the Philistines at Timnah; now get her
³ for me as my wife." But his father and mother said to
him, "Is there not a woman among the daughters of your
kinsmen, or among all our people, that you must go to
take a wife from the uncircumcised Philistines?" But
Samson said to his father, "Get her for me; for she pleases
me well."

⁴ His father and mother did not know that it was from
the LORD; for he was seeking an occasion against the
Philistines. At that time the Philistines had dominion
over Israel.

⁵ Then Samson went down with his father and mother
to Timnah, and he came to the vineyards of Timnah. And
⁶ behold, a young lion roared against him; and the Spirit
of the LORD came mightily upon him, and he tore the lion
asunder as one tears a kid; and he had nothing in his
hand. But he did not tell his father or his mother what
⁷ he had done. Then he went down and talked with the
⁸ woman; and she pleased Samson well. And after a while
he returned to take her; and he turned aside to see the
carcass of the lion, and behold, there was a swarm of
⁹ bees in the body of the lion, and honey. He scraped it out
into his hands, and went on, eating as he went; and he
came to his father and mother, and gave some to them,
and they ate. But he did not tell them that he had taken
the honey from the carcass of the lion.

¹⁰ And his father went down to the woman, and Samson
made a feast there; for so the young men used to do.
¹¹ And when the people saw him, they brought thirty com-
¹² panions to be with him. And Samson said to them, "Let
me now put a riddle to you; if you can tell me what it
is, within the seven days of the feast, and find it out, then
I will give you thirty linen garments and thirty festal
¹³ garments; but if you cannot tell me what it is, then you
shall give me thirty linen garments and thirty festal gar-

ᵗ Gk Syr: Heb *seventh*

ments." And they said to him, "Put your riddle, that we
¹⁴ may hear it." And he said to them,

"Out of the eater came something to eat.
Out of the strong came something sweet."

And they could not in three days tell what the riddle was.
¹⁵ On the fourth ᵗ day they said to Samson's wife, "Entice
your husband to tell us what the riddle is, lest we burn
you and your father's house with fire. Have you invited
¹⁶ us here to impoverish us?" And Samson's wife wept before him, and said, "You only hate me, you do not love
me; you have put a riddle to my countrymen, and you
have not told me what it is." And he said to her, "Behold,
I have not told my father nor my mother, and shall I tell
¹⁷ you?" She wept before him the seven days that their
feast lasted; and on the seventh day he told her, because
she pressed him hard. Then she told the riddle to her
¹⁸ countrymen. And the men of the city said to him on the
seventh day before the sun went down,

"What is sweeter than honey?
What is stronger than a lion?"

And he said to them,

"If you had not plowed with my heifer,
you would not have found out my riddle."

¹⁹ And the Spirit of the LORD came mightily upon him, and
he went down to Ash'kelon and killed thirty men of the
town, and took their spoil and gave the festal garments
to those who had told the riddle. In hot anger he went
²⁰ back to his father's house. And Samson's wife was given
to his companion, who had been his best man.

15 After a while, at the time of wheat harvest, Samson went to visit his wife with a kid; and he said, "I
will go in to my wife in the chamber." But her father
² would not allow him to go in. And her father said, "I
really thought that you utterly hated her; so I gave her
to your companion. Is not her younger sister fairer than
³ she? Pray take her instead." And Samson said to them,
"This time I shall be blameless in regard to the Philis-
⁴ tines, when I do them mischief." So Samson went and
caught three hundred foxes, and took torches; and he
turned them tail to tail, and put a torch between each pair
⁵ of tails. And when he had set fire to the torches, he let
the foxes go into the standing grain of the Philistines,
and burned up the shocks and the standing grain, as well
⁶ as the olive orchards. Then the Philistines said, "Who
has done this?" And they said, "Samson, the son-in-law
of the Timnite, because he has taken his wife and given
her to his companion." And the Philistines came up, and
⁷ burned her and her father with fire. And Samson said
to them, "If this is what you do, I swear I will be avenged
⁸ upon you, and after that I will quit." And he smote them
hip and thigh with great slaughter; and he went down
and stayed in the cleft of the rock of Etam.

⁹ Then the Philistines came up and encamped in Judah,
¹⁰ and made a raid on Lehi. And the men of Judah said,

"Why have you come up against us?" They said, "We have come up to bind Samson, to do to him as he did to 11 us." Then three thousand men of Judah went down to the cleft of the rock of Etam, and said to Samson, "Do you not know that the Philistines are rulers over us? What then is this that you have done to us?" And he said to 12 them, "As they did to me, so have I done to them." And they said to him, "We have come down to bind you, that we may give you into the hands of the Philistines." And Samson said to them, "Swear to me that you will not fall 13 upon me yourselves." They said to him, "No; we will only bind you and give you into their hands; we will not kill you." So they bound him with two new ropes, and brought him up from the rock.

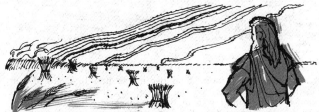

14 When he came to Lehi, the Philistines came shouting to meet him; and the Spirit of the LORD came mightily upon him, and the ropes which were on his arms became as flax that has caught fire, and his bonds melted off his 15 hands. And he found a fresh jawbone of an ass, and put out his hand and seized it, and with it he slew a thousand 16 men. And Samson said,

"With the jawbone of an ass,
    heaps upon heaps,
with the jawbone of an ass
    have I slain a thousand men."

17 When he had finished speaking, he threw away the jawbone out of his hand; and that place was called Ra'math-le'hi.[u]

18 And he was very thirsty, and he called on the LORD and said, "Thou hast granted this great deliverance by the hand of thy servant; and shall I now die of thirst, and 19 fall into the hands of the uncircumcised?" And God split open the hollow place that is at Lehi, and there came water from it; and when he drank, his spirit returned, and he revived. Therefore the name of it was called En-20 hakkor'e;[v] it is at Lehi to this day. And he judged Israel in the days of the Philistines twenty years.

16 Samson went to Gaza, and there he saw a harlot, 2 and he went in to her. The Gazites were told, "Samson has come here," and they surrounded the place and lay in wait for him all night at the gate of the city. They kept quiet all night, saying, "Let us wait till the light of 3 the morning; then we will kill him." But Samson lay till midnight, and at midnight he arose and took hold of the doors of the gate of the city and the two posts, and pulled them up, bar and all, and put them on his shoulders and carried them to the top of the hill that is before Hebron.

4 After this he loved a woman in the valley of Sorek, 5 whose name was Deli'lah. And the lords of the Philistines came to her and said to her, "Entice him, and see wherein his great strength lies, and by what means we may overpower him, that we may bind him to subdue him; and we 6 will each give you eleven hundred pieces of silver." And Deli'lah said to Samson, "Please tell me wherein your great strength lies, and how you might be bound, that one 7 could subdue you." And Samson said to her, "If they bind me with seven fresh bowstrings which have not been dried, then I shall become weak, and be like any other 8 man." Then the lords of the Philistines brought her seven fresh bowstrings which had not been dried, and she 9 bound him with them. Now she had men lying in wait in an inner chamber. And she said to him, "The Philistines are upon you, Samson!" But he snapped the bowstrings, as a string of tow snaps when it touches the fire. So the secret of his strength was not known.

10 And Deli'lah said to Samson, "Behold, you have mocked me, and told me lies; please tell me how you might be 11 bound." And he said to her, "If they bind me with new ropes that have not been used, then I shall become weak, 12 and be like any other man." So Deli'lah took new ropes and bound him with them, and said to him, "The Philistines are upon you, Samson!" And the men lying in wait were in an inner chamber. But he snapped the ropes off his arms like a thread.

13 And Deli'lah said to Samson, "Until now you have mocked me, and told me lies; tell me how you might be bound." And he said to her, "If you weave the seven locks of my head with the web and make it tight with the pin, then I shall become weak, and be like any other man." 14 So while he slept, Deli'lah took the seven locks of his head and wove them into the web.[w] And she made them tight with the pin, and said to him, "The Philistines are upon you, Samson!" But he awoke from his sleep, and pulled away the pin, the loom, and the web.

15 And she said to him, "How can you say, 'I love you,' when your heart is not with me? You have mocked me these three times, and you have not told me wherein your 16 great strength lies." And when she pressed him hard with her words day after day, and urged him, his soul was 17 vexed to death. And he told her all his mind, and said to her, "A razor has never come upon my head; for I have been a Nazirite to God from my mother's womb. If I be shaved, then my strength will leave me, and I shall become weak, and be like any other man."

18 When Deli'lah saw that he had told her all his mind, she sent and called the lords of the Philistines, saying, "Come up this once, for he has told me all his mind." Then the lords of the Philistines came up to her, and 19 brought the money in their hands. She made him sleep upon her knees; and she called a man, and had him shave off the seven locks of his head. Then she began to

[u] That is *The hill of the jawbone*   [v] That is *The spring of him who called*
[w] Compare Gk: Heb lacks *and make it tight . . . into the web*

20 torment him, and his strength left him. And she said, "The Philistines are upon you, Samson!" And he awoke from his sleep, and said, "I will go out as at other times, and shake myself free." And he did not know that the LORD

21 had left him. And the Philistines seized him and gouged out his eyes, and brought him down to Gaza, and bound him with bronze fetters; and he ground at the mill in the

22 prison. But the hair of his head began to grow again after it had been shaved.

23 Now the lords of the Philistines gathered to offer a great sacrifice to Dagon their god, and to rejoice; for they said, "Our god has given Samson our enemy into

24 our hand." And when the people saw him, they praised their god; for they said, "Our god has given our enemy into our hand, the ravager of our country, who has slain

25 many of us." And when their hearts were merry, they said, "Call Samson, that he may make sport for us." So they called Samson out of the prison, and he made sport before them. They made him stand between the pillars;

26 and Samson said to the lad who held him by the hand, "Let me feel the pillars on which the house rests, that I

27 may lean against them." Now the house was full of men and women; all the lords of the Philistines were there, and on the roof there were about three thousand men and women, who looked on while Samson made sport.

28 Then Samson called to the LORD and said, "O Lord GOD, remember me, I pray thee, and strengthen me, I pray thee, only this once, O God, that I may be avenged upon

29 the Philistines for one of my two eyes." And Samson grasped the two middle pillars upon which the house rested, and he leaned his weight upon them, his right hand

30 on the one and his left hand on the other. And Samson said, "Let me die with the Philistines." Then he bowed with all his might; and the house fell upon the lords and upon all the people that were in it. So the dead whom he slew at his death were more than those whom he had slain

31 during his life. Then his brothers and all his family came down and took him and brought him up and buried him between Zorah and Esh'ta-ol in the tomb of Mano'ah his father. He had judged Israel twenty years.

ADDITIONAL STORIES

17 There was a man of the hill country of E'phraim, whose
2 name was Micah. And he said to his mother, "The eleven hundred pieces of silver which were taken from you, about which you uttered a curse, and also spoke it in my ears, behold, the silver is with me; I took it." And his mother said, "Blessed

3 be my son by the LORD." And he restored the eleven hundred pieces of silver to his mother; and his mother said, "I consecrate the silver to the LORD from my hand for my son, to make a graven image and a molten image; now therefore I will restore

4 it to you." So when he restored the money to his mother, his mother took two hundred pieces of silver, and gave it to the silversmith, who made it into a graven image and a molten

5 image; and it was in the house of Micah. And the man Micah had a shrine, and he made an ephod and teraphim, and installed

6 one of his sons, who became his priest. In those days there was no king in Israel; every man did what was right in his own eyes.

7 Now there was a young man of Bethlehem in Judah, of the

family of Judah, who was a Levite; and he sojourned there.

8 And the man departed from the town of Bethlehem in Judah, to live where he could find a place; and as he journeyed, he came to the hill country of E'phraim to the house of Micah.

9 And Micah said to him, "From where do you come?" And he said to him, "I am a Levite of Bethlehem in Judah, and I am

10 going to sojourn where I may find a place." And Micah said to him, "Stay with me, and be to me a father and a priest, and I will give you ten pieces of silver a year, and a suit of apparel,

11 and your living." x And the Levite was content to dwell with

the man; and the young man became to him like one of his
12 sons. And Micah installed the Levite, and the young man be-
13 came his priest, and was in the house of Micah. Then Micah said, "Now I know that the LORD will prosper me, because I have a Levite as priest."

The Danites Relocate

18 In those days there was no king in Israel. And in those days the tribe of the Danites was seeking for itself an inheritance to dwell in; for until then no inheritance among the
2 tribes of Israel had fallen to them. So the Danites sent five able men from the whole number of their tribe, from Zorah and from Esh'ta-ol, to spy out the land and to explore it; and they said to them, "Go and explore the land." And they came to the hill country of E'phraim, to the house of Micah, and
3 lodged there. When they were by the house of Micah, they recognized the voice of the young Levite; and they turned aside and said to him, "Who brought you here? What are you
4 doing in this place? What is your business here?" And he said to them, "Thus and thus has Micah dealt with me: he has hired
5 me, and I have become his priest." And they said to him, "Inquire of God, we pray thee, that we may know whether the
6 journey on which we are setting out will succeed." And the priest said to them, "Go in peace. The journey on which you go is under the eye of the LORD."

7 Then the five men departed, and came to La'ish, and saw the people who were there, how they dwelt in security, after the manner of the Sido'nians, quiet and unsuspecting, lacking y nothing that is in the earth, and possessing wealth, and how they were far from the Sido'nians and had no dealings with
8 any one. And when they came to their brethren at Zorah and Esh'ta-ol, their brethren said to them, "What do you report?"
9 They said, "Arise, and let us go up against them; for we have seen the land, and behold, it is very fertile. And will you do nothing? Do not be slow to go, and enter in and possess the
10 land. When you go, you will come to an unsuspecting people. The land is broad; yea, God has given it into your hands, a place where there is no lack of anything that is in the earth."

11 And six hundred men of the tribe of Dan, armed with
12 weapons of war, set forth from Zorah and Esh'ta-ol, and went up and encamped at Kir'iath-je'arim in Judah. On this account that place is called Ma'haneh-dan z to this day; behold, it is
13 west of Kir'iath-je'arim. And they passed on from there to the hill country of E'phraim, and came to the house of Micah.

14 Then the five men who had gone to spy out the country of La'ish said to their brethren, "Do you know that in these houses there are an ephod, teraphim, a graven image, and a molten image? Now therefore consider what you will do."

15 And they turned aside thither, and came to the house of the young Levite, at the home of Micah, and asked him of his
16 welfare. Now the six hundred men of the Danites, armed with
17 their weapons of war, stood by the entrance of the gate; and the

---

x Heb *living, and the Levite went*   y Cn Compare 18. 10. The Hebrew text is uncertain   z That is *Camp of Dan* five men who had gone to spy out the land went up, and entered and took the graven image, the ephod, the teraphim, and the molten image, while the priest stood by the entrance of the 18 gate with the six hundred men armed with weapons of war. And when these went into Micah's house and took the graven image, the ephod, the teraphim, and the molten image, the priest said 19 to them, "What are you doing?" And they said to him, "Keep quiet, put your hand upon your mouth, and come with us, and be to us a father and a priest. Is it better for you to be priest to the house of one man, or to be priest to a tribe and 20 family in Israel?" And the priest's heart was glad; he took the ephod, and the teraphim, and the graven image, and went in the midst of the people.

21 So they turned and departed, putting the little ones and the 22 cattle and the goods in front of them. When they were a good way from the home of Micah, the men who were in the houses near Micah's house were called out, and they overtook the 23 Danites. And they shouted to the Danites, who turned round and said to Micah, "What ails you that you come with such a 24 company?" And he said, "You take my gods which I made, and the priest, and go away, and what have I left? How then do 25 you ask me, 'What ails you?' " And the Danites said to him, "Do not let your voice be heard among us, lest angry fellows fall upon you, and you lose your life with the lives of your 26 household." Then the Danites went their way; and when Micah saw that they were too strong for him, he turned and went back to his home.

27 And taking what Micah had made, and the priest who belonged to him, the Danites came to La'ish, to a people quiet and unsuspecting, and smote them with the edge of the sword, 28 and burned the city with fire. And there was no deliverer because it was far from Sidon, and they had no dealings with any one. It was in the valley which belongs to Beth-rehob. 29 And they rebuilt the city, and dwelt in it. And they named the city Dan, after the name of Dan their ancestor, who was born to Israel; but the name of the city was La'ish at the first. 30 And the Danites set up the graven image for themselves; and Jonathan the son of Gershom, son of Moses,[a] and his sons were priests to the tribe of the Danites until the day of the captivity 31 of the land. So they set up Micah's graven image which he made, so long as the house of God was at Shiloh.

The Offense of Gibeah

19 In those days, when there was no king in Israel, a certain Levite was sojourning in the remote parts of the hill country of E'phraim, who took to himself a concubine from Bethle-2 hem in Judah. And his concubine became angry with[b] him, and she went away from him to her father's house at Bethlehem 3 in Judah, and was there some four months. Then her husband arose and went after her, to speak kindly to her and bring her back. He had with him his servant and a couple of asses. And he came[c] to her father's house; and when the girl's father saw 4 him, he came with joy to meet him. And his father-in-law, the girl's father, made him stay, and he remained with him three 5 days; so they ate and drank, and lodged there. And on the fourth day they arose early in the morning, and he prepared to go; but the girl's father said to his son-in-law, "Strengthen your heart with a morsel of bread, and after that you may go." 6 So the two men sat and ate and drank together; and the girl's father said to the man, "Be pleased to spend the night, and let 7 your heart be merry." And when the man rose up to go, his 8 father-in-law urged him, till he lodged there again. And on the fifth day he arose early in the morning to depart; and the girl's father said, "Strengthen your heart, and tarry until the day 9 declines." So they ate, both of them. And when the man and his concubine and his servant rose up to depart, his father-in-law, the girl's father, said to him, "Behold, now the day has waned toward evening; pray tarry all night. Behold, the day draws to its close; lodge here and let your heart be merry; and tomorrow you shall arise early in the morning for your journey, and go home." 10 But the man would not spend the night; he rose up and departed, and arrived opposite Jebus (that is, Jerusalem). He had with him a couple of saddled asses, and his concubine 11 was with him. When they were near Jebus, the day was far spent, and the servant said to his master, "Come now, let us turn aside to the city of the Jeb'usites, and spend the night 12 in it." And his master said to him, "We will not turn aside into the city of foreigners, who do not belong to the people of 13 Israel; but we will pass on to Gib'e-ah." And he said to his

servant, "Come and let us draw near to one of these places, 14 and spend the night at Gib'e-ah or at Ramah." So they passed on and went their way; and the sun went down on them near 15 Gib'e-ah, which belongs to Benjamin, and they turned aside there, to go in and spend the night at Gib'e-ah. And he went in and sat down in the open square of the city; for no man took them into his house to spend the night.

16 And behold, an old man was coming from his work in the field at evening; the man was from the hill country of E'phraim, and he was sojourning in Gib'e-ah; the men of the place were 17 Benjaminites. And he lifted up his eyes, and saw the wayfarer in the open square of the city; and the old man said, 18 "Where are you going? and whence do you come?" And he said to him, "We are passing from Bethlehem in Judah to the remote parts of the hill country of E'phraim, from which I come. I went to Bethlehem in Judah; and I am going to my home;[d] 19 and nobody takes me into his house. We have straw and provender for our asses, with bread and wine for me and your maidservant and the young man with your servants; there is no 20 lack of anything." And the old man said, "Peace be to you; I will care for all your wants; only, do not spend the night in 21 the square." So he brought him into his house, and gave the asses provender; and they washed their feet, and ate and drank.

22 As they were making their hearts merry, behold, the men of the city, base fellows, beset the house round about, beating on the door; and they said to the old man, the master of the house, "Bring out the man who came into your house, that we may 23 know him." And the man, the master of the house, went out to them and said to them, "No, my brethren, do not act so wickedly; seeing that this man has come into my house, do not do 24 this vile thing. Behold, here are my virgin daughter and his concubine; let me bring them out now. Ravish them and do with them what seems good to you; but against this man do not do so 25 vile a thing." But the men would not listen to him. So the man seized his concubine, and put her out to them; and they knew her, and abused her all night until the morning. And as the 26 dawn began to break, they let her go. And as morning appeared, the woman came and fell down at the door of the man's house where her master was, till it was light.

27 And her master rose up in the morning, and when he opened the doors of the house and went out to go on his way, behold, there was his concubine lying at the door of the house, with her 28 hands on the threshold. He said to her, "Get up, let us be going." But there was no answer. Then he put her upon the ass; and 29 the man rose up and went away to his home. And when he entered his house, he took a knife, and laying hold of his concubine he divided her, limb by limb, into twelve pieces, and 30 sent her throughout all the territory of Israel. And all who saw it said, "Such a thing has never happened or been seen from the day that the people of Israel came up out of the land of Egypt until this day; consider it, take counsel, and speak."

20 Then all the people of Israel came out, from Dan to Beersheba, including the land of Gilead, and the congre-2 gation assembled as one man to the LORD at Mizpah. And the chiefs of all the people, of all the tribes of Israel, presented themselves in the assembly of the people of God, four hundred 3 thousand men on foot that drew the sword. (Now the Benjaminites heard that the people of Israel had gone up to Mizpah.) And the people of Israel said, "Tell us, how was this wickedness 4 brought to pass?" And the Levite, the husband of the woman who was murdered, answered and said, "I came to Gib'e-ah that belongs to Benjamin, I and my concubine, to spend the 5 night. And the men of Gib'e-ah rose against me, and beset the house round about me by night; they meant to kill me, and 6 they ravished my concubine, and she is dead. And I took my concubine and cut her in pieces, and sent her throughout all the country of the inheritance of Israel; for they have com-7 mitted abomination and wantonness in Israel. Behold, you people of Israel, all of you, give your advice and counsel here." 8 And all the people arose as one man, saying, "We will not any of us go to his tent, and none of us will return to his 9 house. But now this is what we will do to Gib'e-ah: we will go 10 up against it by lot, and we will take ten men of a hundred throughout all the tribes of Israel, and a hundred of a thousand, and a thousand of ten thousand, to bring provisions for the people, that when they come they may requite Gib'e-ah of Benjamin, for all the wanton crime which they have com-11 mitted in Israel." So all the men of Israel gathered against the city, united as one man.

12 And the tribes of Israel sent men through all the tribe of

---

[a] Another reading is *Manasseh*   [b] Gk Old Latin: Heb *played the harlot against*   [c] Gk: Heb *she brought him*
[d] Gk Compare 19. 29. Heb *to the house of the* LORD

Benjamin, saying, "What wickedness is this that has taken
13 place among you? Now therefore give up the men, the base fellows in Gib'e-ah, that we may put them to death, and put away evil from Israel." But the Benjaminites would not listen
14 to the voice of their brethren, the people of Israel. And the Benjaminites came together out of the cities to Gib'e-ah, to go
15 out to battle against the people of Israel. And the Benjaminites mustered out of their cities on that day twenty-six thousand men that drew the sword, besides the inhabitants of Gib'e-ah,
16 who mustered seven hundred picked men. Among all these were seven hundred picked men who were left-handed; every one
17 could sling a stone at a hair, and not miss. And the men of Israel, apart from Benjamin, mustered four hundred thousand men that drew sword; all these were men of war.
18 The people of Israel arose and went up to Bethel, and inquired of God, "Which of us shall go up first to battle against the Benjaminites?" And the Lord said, "Judah shall go up first."
19 Then the people of Israel rose in the morning, and encamped
20 against Gib'e-ah. And the men of Israel went out to battle against Benjamin; and the men of Israel drew up the battle
21 line against them at Gib'e-ah. The Benjaminites came out of Gib'e-ah, and felled to the ground on that day twenty-two
22 thousand men of the Israelites. But the people, the men of Israel, took courage, and again formed the battle line in the
23 same place where they had formed it on the first day. And the people of Israel went up and wept before the Lord until the evening; and they inquired of the Lord, "Shall we again draw near to battle against our brethren the Benjaminites?" And the Lord said, "Go up against them."
24 So the people of Israel came near against the Benjaminites
25 the second day. And Benjamin went against them out of Gib'e-ah the second day, and felled to the ground eighteen thousand men of the people of Israel; all these were men who
26 drew the sword. Then all the people of Israel, the whole army, went up and came to Bethel and wept; they sat there before the Lord, and fasted that day until evening, and offered burnt
27 offerings and peace offerings before the Lord. And the people of Israel inquired of the Lord (for the ark of the covenant of God
28 was there in those days, and Phin'ehas the son of Elea'zar, son of Aaron, ministered before it in those days), saying, "Shall we yet again go out to battle against our brethren the Benjaminites, or shall we cease?" And the Lord said, "Go up; for tomorrow I will give them into your hand."
29, 30 So Israel set men in ambush round about Gib'e-ah. And the people of Israel went up against the Benjaminites on the third day, and set themselves in array against Gib'e-ah, as at other
31 times. And the Benjaminites went out against the people and were drawn away from the city; and as at other times they began to smite and kill some of the people, in the highways, one of which goes up to Bethel and the other to Gib'e-ah, and in
32 the open country, about thirty men of Israel. And the Benjaminites said, "They are routed before us, as at the first." But the men of Israel said, "Let us flee, and draw them away from
33 the city to the highways." And all the men of Israel rose up out of their place, and set themselves in array at Ba'al-ta'mar; and the men of Israel who were in ambush rushed out of their
34 place west e of Geba. And there came against Gib'e-ah ten thousand picked men out of all Israel, and the battle was hard; but the Benjaminites did not know that disaster was close upon
35 them. And the Lord defeated Benjamin before Israel; and the men of Israel destroyed twenty-five thousand one hundred men of Benjamin that day; all these were men who drew the sword.
36 So the Benjaminites saw that they were defeated.
The men of Israel gave ground to Benjamin, because they trusted to the men in ambush whom they had set against
37 Gib'e-ah. And the men in ambush made haste and rushed upon Gib'e-ah; the men in ambush moved out and smote all the city
38 with the edge of the sword. Now the appointed signal between the men of Israel and the men in ambush was that when they
39 made a great cloud of smoke rise up out of the city the men of Israel should turn in battle. Now Benjamin had begun to smite and kill about thirty men of Israel; they said, "Surely
40 they are smitten down before us, as in the first battle." But when the signal began to rise out of the city in a column of smoke, the Benjaminites looked behind them; and behold, the
41 whole of the city went up in smoke to heaven. Then the men of Israel turned, and the men of Benjamin were dismayed, for
42 they saw that disaster was close upon them. Therefore they turned their backs before the men of Israel in the direction of the wilderness; but the battle overtook them, and those who

came out of the cities destroyed them in the midst of them.
43 Cutting down f the Benjaminites, they pursued them and trod them down from Nohah g as far as opposite Gib'e-ah on the
44 east. Eighteen thousand men of Benjamin fell, all of them men
45 of valor. And they turned and fled toward the wilderness to the rock of Rimmon; five thousand men of them were cut down in the highways, and they were pursued hard to Gidom, and two
46 thousand men of them were slain. So all who fell that day of Benjamin were twenty-five thousand men that drew the sword,
47 all of them men of valor. But six hundred men turned and fled toward the wilderness to the rock of Rimmon, and abode at the
48 rock of Rimmon four months. And the men of Israel turned back against the Benjaminites, and smote them with the edge of the sword, men and beasts and all that they found. And all the towns which they found they set on fire.

21 Now the men of Israel had sworn at Mizpah, "No one of us shall give his daughter in marriage to Benjamin."
2 And the people came to Bethel, and sat there till evening before
3 God, and they lifted up their voices and wept bitterly. And they said, "O Lord, the God of Israel, why has this come to pass in Israel, that there should be today one tribe lacking in Israel?"
4 And on the morrow the people rose early, and built there an
5 altar, and offered burnt offerings and peace offerings. And the people of Israel said, "Which of all the tribes of Israel did not come up in the assembly to the Lord?" For they had taken a great oath concerning him who did not come up to the Lord to
6 Mizpah, saying, "He shall be put to death." And the people of Israel had compassion for Benjamin their brother, and said,
7 "One tribe is cut off from Israel this day. What shall we do for wives for those who are left, since we have sworn by the Lord that we will not give them any of our daughters for wives?"
8 And they said, "What one is there of the tribes of Israel that did not come up to the Lord to Mizpah?" And behold, no one had come to the camp from Ja'besh-gil'ead, to the assembly.
9 For when the people were mustered, behold, not one of the
10 inhabitants of Ja'besh-gil'ead was there. So the congregation sent thither twelve thousand of their bravest men, and commanded them, "Go and smite the inhabitants of Ja'besh-gil'ead with the edge of the sword; also the women and the little ones.
11 This is what you shall do; every male and every woman that
12 has lain with a male you shall utterly destroy." And they found among the inhabitants of Ja'besh-gil'ead four hundred young virgins who had not known man by lying with him; and they brought them to the camp at Shiloh, which is in the land of Canaan.
13 Then the whole congregation sent word to the Benjaminites who were at the rock of Rimmon, and proclaimed peace to
14 them. And Benjamin returned at that time; and they gave them the women whom they had saved alive of the women of
15 Ja'besh-gil'ead; but they did not suffice for them. And the people had compassion on Benjamin because the Lord had made a breach in the tribes of Israel.
16 Then the elders of the congregation said, "What shall we do for wives for those who are left, since the women are destroyed
17 out of Benjamin?" And they said, "There must be an inheritance for the survivors of Benjamin, that a tribe be not blotted
18 out from Israel. Yet we cannot give them wives of our daughters." For the people of Israel had sworn, "Cursed be
19 he who gives a wife to Benjamin." So they said, "Behold, there is the yearly feast of the Lord at Shiloh, which is north of Bethel, on the east of the highway that goes up from Bethel
20 to Shechem, and south of Lebo'nah." And they commanded the
21 Benjaminites, saying, "Go and lie in wait in the vineyards, and watch; if the daughters of Shiloh come out to dance in the dances, then come out of the vineyards and seize each man his wife from the daughters of Shiloh, and go to the land of
22 Benjamin. And when their fathers or their brothers come to complain to us, we will say to them, 'Grant them graciously to us; because we did not take for each man of them his wife in battle, neither did you give them to them, else you would now
23 be guilty.'" And the Benjaminites did so, and took their wives, according to their number, from the dancers whom they carried off; then they went and returned to their inheritance, and
24 rebuilt the towns, and dwelt in them. And the people of Israel departed from there at that time, every man to his tribe and family, and they went out from there every man to his inheritance.
25 In those days there was no king in Israel; every man did what was right in his own eyes.

e Gk Vg: Heb *in the plain*   f Gk: Heb *surrounding*   g Gk: Heb *(at their) resting place*

INTRODUCTION TO

RUTH

The Book of Ruth tells the love story of a man and a woman from different backgrounds. Ruth, from the land of Moab, and Boaz, a Hebrew, fell in love and married. The setting of the story is during the period of the judges, told about in the Book of Judges.

When Ruth was written, there was a drive to keep Jews from marrying foreigners. The Bible books of Ezra and Nehemiah show this. The writer used the beautiful story of the Book of Ruth to show that marriage with foreigners had long been accepted among the Hebrews. Ruth is really a plea for good will among all sorts of people, however different they may be. In the story of Ruth, a foreigner whose great-grandson became the popular King David, the writer was pleading for the acceptance of foreigners at a time when many Jews would have nothing to do with persons of other nations.

It was Ruth, the Moabitess, who said to Naomi, the Hebrew, "Entreat me not to leave you . . . for where you go I will go, and where you lodge I will lodge; your people shall be my people, and your God my God . . ." (Ruth 1.16).

It is interesting that the Gospel of Matthew also traces "the genealogy of Jesus Christ, the son of David, the son of Abraham," through Boaz and Ruth, the Moabitess, to "Joseph the husband of Mary, of whom Jesus was born, who is called Christ" (1.1-16).

The Book of Ruth was written about 400 B.C., after the Jews, who had been exiled in Babylon, had returned to Judah.

Ru

THE BOOK OF

RUTH

IN MOAB

1 In the days when the judges ruled there was a famine in the land, and a certain man of Bethlehem in Judah went to sojourn in the country of Moab, he and his wife 2 and his two sons. The name of the man was Elim'elech and the name of his wife Na'omi, and the names of his two sons were Mahlon and Chil'ion; they were Eph'-rathites from Bethlehem in Judah. They went into the 3 country of Moab and remained there. But Elim'elech, the husband of Na'omi, died, and she was left with her two 4 sons. These took Moabite wives; the name of the one was Orpah and the name of the other Ruth. They lived there 5 about ten years; and both Mahlon and Chil'ion died, so that the woman was bereft of her two sons and her husband.

6 Then she started with her daughters-in-law to return from the country of Moab, for she had heard in the country of Moab that the LORD had visited his people and 7 given them food. So she set out from the place where she was, with her two daughters-in-law, and they went on the 8 way to return to the land of Judah. But Na'omi said to her two daughters-in-law, "Go, return each of you to her mother's house. May the LORD deal kindly with you, as 9 you have dealt with the dead and with me. The LORD grant that you may find a home, each of you in the house of her husband!" Then she kissed them, and they lifted up 10 their voices and wept. And they said to her, "No, we 11 will return with you to your people." But Na'omi said, "Turn back, my daughters, why will you go with me? Have I yet sons in my womb that they may become your

163

¹² husbands? Turn back, my daughters, go your way, for I am too old to have a husband. If I should say I have hope, even if I should have a husband this night and ¹³ should bear sons, would you therefore wait till they were grown? Would you therefore refrain from marrying? No, my daughters, for it is exceedingly bitter to me for your sake that the hand of the LORD has gone forth against ¹⁴ me." Then they lifted up their voices and wept again; and Orpah kissed her mother-in-law, but Ruth clung to her.

¹⁵ And she said, "See, your sister-in-law has gone back to her people and to her gods; return after your sister-in-¹⁶ law." But Ruth said, "Entreat me not to leave you or to return from following you; for where you go I will go, and where you lodge I will lodge; your people shall be ¹⁷ my people, and your God my God; where you die I will die, and there will I be buried. May the LORD do so to me and more also if even death parts me from you." ¹⁸ And when Na'omi saw that she was determined to go with her, she said no more.

BETHLEHEM

¹⁹ So the two of them went on until they came to Bethlehem. And when they came to Bethlehem, the whole town was stirred because of them; and the women said, "Is this ²⁰ Na'omi?" She said to them, "Do not call me Na'omi,ᵃ call me Mara,ᵇ for the Almighty has dealt very bitterly ²¹ with me. I went away full, and the LORD has brought me back empty. Why call me Na'omi, when the LORD has afflictedᶜ me and the Almighty has brought calamity upon me?"

²² So Na'omi returned, and Ruth the Moabitess her daughter-in-law with her, who returned from the country of Moab. And they came to Bethlehem at the beginning of barley harvest.

The Harvest Field

2 Now Na'omi had a kinsman of her husband's, a man of wealth, of the family of Elim'elech, whose name ² was Bo'az. And Ruth the Moabitess said to Na'omi, "Let me go to the field, and glean among the ears of grain after him in whose sight I shall find favor." And she said ³ to her, "Go, my daughter." So she set forth and went and gleaned in the field after the reapers; and she happened to come to the part of the field belonging to Bo'az, who ⁴ was of the family of Elim'elech. And behold, Bo'az came from Bethlehem; and he said to the reapers, "The LORD be with you!" And they answered, "The LORD bless you." ⁵ Then Bo'az said to his servant who was in charge of the ⁶ reapers, "Whose maiden is this?" And the servant who was in charge of the reapers answered, "It is the Moabite maiden, who came back with Na'omi from the country of ⁷ Moab. She said, 'Pray, let me glean and gather among the sheaves after the reapers.' So she came, and she has continued from early morning until now, without resting even for a moment." ᵈ

⁸ Then Bo'az said to Ruth, "Now, listen, my daughter, do not go to glean in another field or leave this one, but keep ⁹ close to my maidens. Let your eyes be upon the field which they are reaping, and go after them. Have I not charged the young men not to molest you? And when you are thirsty, go to the vessels and drink what the young ¹⁰ men have drawn." Then she fell on her face, bowing to the ground, and said to him, "Why have I found favor in your eyes, that you should take notice of me, when I am ¹¹ a foreigner?" But Bo'az answered her, "All that you have done for your mother-in-law since the death of your husband has been fully told me, and how you left your father and mother and your native land and came to a ¹² people that you did not know before. The LORD recompense you for what you have done, and a full reward be given you by the LORD, the God of Israel, under whose ¹³ wings you have come to take refuge!" Then she said, "You are most gracious to me, my lord, for you have comforted me and spoken kindly to your maidservant, though I am not one of your maidservants."

¹⁴ And at mealtime Bo'az said to her, "Come here, and eat some bread, and dip your morsel in the wine." So she sat beside the reapers, and he passed to her parched grain; and she ate until she was satisfied, and she had ¹⁵ some left over. When she rose to glean, Bo'az instructed his young men, saying, "Let her glean even among the ¹⁶ sheaves, and do not reproach her. And also pull out some from the bundles for her, and leave it for her to glean, and do not rebuke her."

¹⁷ So she gleaned in the field until evening; then she beat out what she had gleaned, and it was about an ephah ¹⁸ of barley. And she took it up and went into the city; she showed her mother-in-law what she had gleaned, and she also brought out and gave her what food she had left over ¹⁹ after being satisfied. And her mother-in-law said to her, "Where did you glean today? And where have you worked? Blessed be the man who took notice of you."

ᵃ That is *Pleasant* ᵇ That is *Bitter* ᶜ Gk Syr Vg: Heb *testified against*
ᵈ Compare Gk Vg: the meaning of the Hebrew text is uncertain

So she told her mother-in-law with whom she had worked, and said, "The man's name with whom I worked today 20 is Bo'az." And Na'omi said to her daughter-in-law, "Blessed be he by the LORD, whose kindness has not forsaken the living or the dead!" Na'omi also said to her, "The man is a relative of ours, one of our nearest kin." 21 And Ruth the Moabitess said, "Besides, he said to me, 'You shall keep close by my servants, till they have 22 finished all my harvest.'" And Na'omi said to Ruth, her daughter-in-law, "It is well, my daughter, that you go out with his maidens, lest in another field you be molested." 23 So she kept close to the maidens of Bo'az, gleaning until the end of the barley and wheat harvests; and she lived with her mother-in-law.

The Threshing Floor

3 Then Na'omi her mother-in-law said to her, "My daughter, should I not seek a home for you, that it may 2 be well with you? Now is not Bo'az our kinsman, with whose maidens you were? See, he is winnowing barley 3 tonight at the threshing floor. Wash therefore and anoint yourself, and put on your best clothes and go down to the threshing floor; but do not make yourself known to 4 the man until he has finished eating and drinking. But when he lies down, observe the place where he lies; then, go and uncover his feet and lie down, and he will tell 5 you what to do." And she replied, "All that you say I will do."

6 So she went down to the threshing floor and did just 7 as her mother-in-law had told her. And when Bo'az had eaten and drunk, and his heart was merry, he went to lie down at the end of the heap of grain. Then she came 8 softly, and uncovered his feet, and lay down. At midnight the man was startled, and turned over, and behold, a 9 woman lay at his feet! He said, "Who are you?" And she answered, "I am Ruth, your maidservant; spread your skirt over your maidservant, for you are next of 10 kin." And he said, "May you be blessed by the LORD, my daughter; you have made this last kindness greater than the first, in that you have not gone after young men, 11 whether poor or rich. And now, my daughter, do not fear, I will do for you all that you ask, for all my fellow 12 townsmen know that you are a woman of worth. And now it is true that I am a near kinsman, yet there is a kinsman 13 nearer than I. Remain this night, and in the morning, if he will do the part of the next of kin for you, well; let him do it; but if he is not willing to do the part of the next of kin for you, then, as the LORD lives, I will do the part of the next of kin for you. Lie down until the morning."

14 So she lay at his feet until the morning, but arose before one could recognize another; and he said, "Let it not be known that the woman came to the threshing floor."

15 And he said, "Bring the mantle you are wearing and hold it out." So she held it, and he measured out six measures of barley, and laid it upon her; then she went into the 16 city. And when she came to her mother-in-law, she said, "How did you fare, my daughter?" Then she told her 17 all that the man had done for her, saying, "These six measures of barley he gave to me, for he said, 'You must 18 not go back empty-handed to your mother-in-law.'" She replied, "Wait, my daughter, until you learn how the matter turns out, for the man will not rest, but will settle the matter today."

At the Gate

4 And Bo'az went up to the gate and sat down there; and behold, the next of kin, of whom Bo'az had spoken, came by. So Bo'az said, "Turn aside, friend; sit 2 down here"; and he turned aside and sat down. And he took ten men of the elders of the city, and said, "Sit 3 down here"; so they sat down. Then he said to the next of kin, "Na'omi, who has come back from the country of Moab, is selling the parcel of land which belonged to 4 our kinsman Elim'elech. So I thought I would tell you of it, and say, Buy it in the presence of those sitting here, and in the presence of the elders of my people. If you will redeem it, redeem it; but if you will not, tell me, that I may know, for there is no one besides you to redeem it, and I come after you." And he said, "I will redeem it." 5 Then Bo'az said, "The day you buy the field from the hand of Na'omi, you are also buying Ruth e the Moabitess, the widow of the dead, in order to restore the name of 6 the dead to his inheritance." Then the next of kin said, "I cannot redeem it for myself, lest I impair my own inheritance. Take my right of redemption yourself, for I cannot redeem it."

7 Now this was the custom in former times in Israel concerning redeeming and exchanging: to confirm a transaction, the one drew off his sandal and gave it to the other, and this was the manner of attesting in Israel. 8 So when the next of kin said to Bo'az, "Buy it for your- 9 self," he drew off his sandal. Then Bo'az said to the elders and all the people, "You are witnesses this day that I have bought from the hand of Na'omi all that belonged to Elim'elech and all that belonged to Chil'ion and to Mah- 10 lon. Also Ruth the Moabitess, the widow of Mahlon, I have bought to be my wife, to perpetuate the name of the dead in his inheritance, that the name of the dead may not be cut off from among his brethren and from the gate 11 of his native place; you are witnesses this day." Then all the people who were at the gate, and the elders, said, "We are witnesses. May the LORD make the woman, who is coming into your house, like Rachel and Leah, who together built up the house of Israel. May you prosper in 12 Eph'rathah and be renowned in Bethlehem; and may your

e Old Latin Vg: Heb of Naomi and from Ruth

house be like the house of Perez, whom Tamar bore to Judah, because of the children that the LORD will give you by this young woman."

An Heir

13 So Bo'az took Ruth and she became his wife; and he went in to her, and the LORD gave her conception, and 14 she bore a son. Then the women said to Na'omi, "Blessed be the LORD, who has not left you this day without next 15 of kin; and may his name be renowned in Israel! He shall be to you a restorer of life and a nourisher of your old age; for your daughter-in-law who loves you, who is 16 more to you than seven sons, has borne him." Then Na'omi took the child and laid him in her bosom, and 17 became his nurse. And the women of the neighborhood gave him a name, saying, "A son has been born to Na'-omi." They named him Obed; he was the father of Jesse, the father of David.

18 Now these are the descendants of Perez: Perez was the 19 father of Hezron, Hezron of Ram, Ram of Ammin'adab, 20, 21 Ammin'adab of Nahshon, Nahshon of Salmon, Salmon 22 of Bo'az, Bo'az of Obed, Obed of Jesse, and Jesse of David.

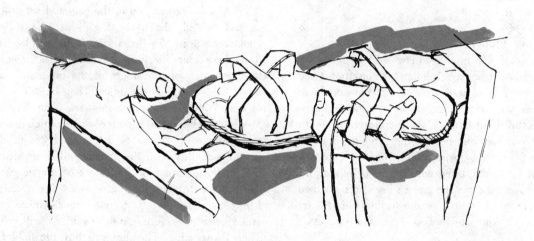

INTRODUCTION TO

THE FIRST BOOK OF

SAMUEL

Samuel was a great leader of the Hebrews—a priest, judge, and prophet or preacher, who lived about 1000 B.C. His training for leadership began when he was a boy, and when he grew up, God used him to select and anoint two kings, Saul and David.

This book tells of the battles, the victories, and the sins of the people and their leaders during Samuel's lifetime. The writers were trying to teach the people the meaning of the events in their own history. When men are not faithful to God and do wrong, history teaches that they bring trouble upon their whole nation and God does not bless them.

Like most of the history books of the Bible, this one was not completed until many years after the events it tells about. The account was not finished until about 550 B.C.

First Samuel is named for its most important character, Samuel, who lived some 450 years before the whole record was assembled. Second Samuel continues the story started in this book.

THE FIRST BOOK OF

SAMUEL

THE CHILDHOOD OF SAMUEL

1 There was a certain man of Ramatha'im-zo'phim of the hill country of E'phraim, whose name was Elka'nah the son of Jero'ham, son of Eli'hu, son of Tohu, son of 2 Zuph, an E'phraimite. He had two wives; the name of the one was Hannah, and the name of the other Penin'nah. And Penin'nah had children, but Hannah had no children. 3 Now this man used to go up year by year from his city to worship and to sacrifice to the LORD of hosts at Shiloh, where the two sons of Eli, Hophni and Phin'ehas, were 4 priests of the LORD. On the day when Elka'nah sacrificed, he would give portions to Penin'nah his wife and to all 5 her sons and daughters; and, although a he loved Hannah, he would give Hannah only one portion, because the LORD 6 had closed her womb. And her rival used to provoke her sorely, to irritate her, because the LORD had closed 7 her womb. So it went on year by year; as often as she went up to the house of the LORD, she used to provoke 8 her. Therefore Hannah wept and would not eat. And Elka'nah, her husband, said to her, "Hannah, why do you weep? And why do you not eat? And why is your heart sad? Am I not more to you than ten sons?"

9 After they had eaten and drunk in Shiloh, Hannah rose. Now Eli the priest was sitting on the seat beside the door- 10 post of the temple of the LORD. She was deeply distressed 11 and prayed to the LORD, and wept bitterly. And she vowed a vow and said, "O LORD of hosts, if thou wilt indeed look on the affliction of thy maidservant, and remember me, and not forget thy maidservant, but wilt give to thy maidservant a son, then I will give him to the LORD all the days of his life, and no razor shall touch his head." 12 As she continued praying before the LORD, Eli observed 13 her mouth. Hannah was speaking in her heart; only her lips moved, and her voice was not heard; therefore Eli 14 took her to be a drunken woman. And Eli said to her, "How long will you be drunken? Put away your wine 15 from you." But Hannah answered, "No, my lord, I am a woman sorely troubled; I have drunk neither wine nor strong drink, but I have been pouring out my soul before 16 the LORD. Do not regard your maidservant as a base woman, for all along I have been speaking out of my 17 great anxiety and vexation." Then Eli answered, "Go in peace, and the God of Israel grant your petition which 18 you have made to him." And she said, "Let your maid-

a Gk: Heb obscure

167

servant find favor in your eyes." Then the woman went her way and ate, and her countenance was no longer sad.

19 They rose early in the morning and worshiped before the Lord; then they went back to their house at Ramah. And Elka'nah knew Hannah his wife, and the Lord 20 remembered her; and in due time Hannah conceived and bore a son, and she called his name Samuel, for she said, "I have asked him of the Lord."

21 And the man Elka'nah and all his house went up to offer to the Lord the yearly sacrifice, and to pay his vow. 22 But Hannah did not go up, for she said to her husband, "As soon as the child is weaned, I will bring him, that he may appear in the presence of the Lord, and abide 23 there for ever." Elka'nah her husband said to her, "Do what seems best to you, wait until you have weaned him; only, may the Lord establish his word." So the woman remained and nursed her son, until she weaned him. 24 And when she had weaned him, she took him up with her, along with a three-year-old bull,[b] an ephah of flour, and a

skin of wine; and she brought him to the house of the 25 Lord at Shiloh; and the child was young. Then they slew 26 the bull, and they brought the child to Eli. And she said, "Oh, my lord! As you live, my lord, I am the woman who was standing here in your presence, praying to the 27 Lord. For this child I prayed; and the Lord has granted 28 me my petition which I made to him. Therefore I have lent him to the Lord; as long as he lives, he is lent to the Lord."

And [x] they worshiped the Lord there.

The Song of Hannah

2 Hannah also prayed and said,
"My heart exults in the Lord;
my strength is exalted in the Lord.
My mouth derides my enemies,
because I rejoice in thy salvation.

2 "There is none holy like the Lord,
there is none besides thee;
there is no rock like our God.
3 Talk no more so very proudly,
let not arrogance come from your mouth;
for the Lord is a God of knowledge,
and by him actions are weighed.

4 The bows of the mighty are broken,
but the feeble gird on strength.
5 Those who were full have hired themselves out for bread.
but those who were hungry have ceased to hunger.
The barren has borne seven,
but she who has many children is forlorn.
6 The Lord kills and brings to life;
he brings down to Sheol and raises up.
7 The Lord makes poor and makes rich;
he brings low, he also exalts.
8 He raises up the poor from the dust;
he lifts the needy from the ash heap,
to make them sit with princes
and inherit a seat of honor.
For the pillars of the earth are the Lord's,
and on them he has set the world.

9 "He will guard the feet of his faithful ones;
but the wicked shall be cut off in darkness;
for not by might shall a man prevail.
10 The adversaries of the Lord shall be broken to pieces;
against them he will thunder in heaven.
The Lord will judge the ends of the earth;
he will give strength to his king,
and exalt the power of his anointed."

11 Then Elka'nah went home to Ramah. And the boy ministered to the Lord, in the presence of Eli the priest. 12 Now the sons of Eli were worthless men; they had no 13 regard for the Lord. The custom of the priests with the people was that when any man offered sacrifice, the priest's servant would come, while the meat was boiling, 14 with a three-pronged fork in his hand, and he would thrust it into the pan, or kettle, or caldron, or pot; all that the fork brought up the priest would take for himself.[c] So they did at Shiloh to all the Israelites who came 15 there. Moreover, before the fat was burned, the priest's servant would come and say to the man who was sacrificing, "Give meat for the priest to roast; for he will not 16 accept boiled meat from you, but raw." And if the man said to him, "Let them burn the fat first, and then take as much as you wish," he would say, "No, you must give 17 it now; and if not, I will take it by force." Thus the sin of the young men was very great in the sight of the Lord; for the men treated the offering of the Lord with contempt.

18 Samuel was ministering before the Lord, a boy girded 19 with a linen ephod. And his mother used to make for him a little robe and take it to him each year, when she went up with her husband to offer the yearly sacrifice. 20 Then Eli would bless Elka'nah and his wife, and say, "The Lord give you children by this woman for the loan which she lent to [d] the Lord"; so then they would return to their home.

b Gk Syr: Heb three bulls   x Heb he   c Gk Syr Vg: Heb with it   d Or for the petition which she asked of

21 And the LORD visited Hannah, and she conceived and bore three sons and two daughters. And the boy Samuel grew in the presence of the LORD.

22 Now Eli was very old, and he heard all that his sons were doing to all Israel, and how they lay with the women 23 who served at the entrance to the tent of meeting. And he said to them, "Why do you do such things? For I hear of 24 your evil dealings from all the people. No, my sons; it is no good report that I hear the people of the LORD spread- 25 ing abroad. If a man sins against a man, God will mediate for him; but if a man sins against the LORD, who can intercede for him?" But they would not listen to the voice of their father; for it was the will of the LORD to slay them.

26 Now the boy Samuel continued to grow both in stature and in favor with the LORD and with men.

27 And there came a man of God to Eli, and said to him, "Thus the LORD has said, 'I revealed e myself to the house of your father when they were in Egypt subject to 28 the house of Pharaoh. And I chose him out of all the tribes of Israel to be my priest, to go up to my altar, to burn incense, to wear an ephod before me; and I gave to the house of your father all my offerings by fire from 29 the people of Israel. Why then look with greedy eye at f my sacrifices and my offerings which I commanded, and honor your sons above me by fattening yourselves upon the choicest parts of every offering of my people Israel?' 30 Therefore the LORD the God of Israel declares: 'I promised that your house and the house of your father should go in and out before me for ever'; but now the LORD declares: 'Far be it from me; for those who honor me I will honor, and those who despise me shall be lightly 31 esteemed. Behold, the days are coming, when I will cut off your strength and the strength of your father's house, 32 so that there will not be an old man in your house. Then in distress you will look with envious eye on all the prosperity which shall be bestowed upon Israel; and there 33 shall not be an old man in your house for ever. The man of you whom I shall not cut off from my altar shall be spared to weep out his g eyes and grieve his g heart; and all the increase of your house shall die by the sword of 34 men. h And this which shall befall your two sons, Hophni and Phin'ehas, shall be the sign to you: both of them 35 shall die on the same day. And I will raise up for myself a faithful priest, who shall do according to what is in my heart and in my mind; and I will build him a sure house, and he shall go in and out before my anointed for ever. 36 And every one who is left in your house shall come to implore him for a piece of silver or a loaf of bread, and shall say, "Put me, I pray you, in one of the priest's places, that I may eat a morsel of bread."'"

3 Now the boy Samuel was ministering to the LORD under Eli. And the word of the LORD was rare in those days; there was no frequent vision.

2 At that time Eli, whose eyesight had begun to grow dim, so that he could not see, was lying down in his own place; 3 the lamp of God had not yet gone out, and Samuel was lying down within the temple of the LORD, where the ark 4 of God was. Then the LORD called, "Samuel! Samuel!" i 5 and he said, "Here I am!" and ran to Eli, and said, "Here I am, for you called me." But he said, "I did not 6 call; lie down again." So he went and lay down. And the LORD called again, "Samuel!" And Samuel arose and went to Eli, and said, "Here I am, for you called me." But he said, "I did not call, my son; lie down again." 7 Now Samuel did not yet know the LORD, and the word of 8 the LORD had not yet been revealed to him. And the LORD called Samuel again the third time. And he arose and went to Eli, and said, "Here I am, for you called me." Then Eli perceived that the LORD was calling the boy. 9 Therefore Eli said to Samuel, "Go, lie down; and if he calls you, you shall say, 'Speak, LORD, for thy servant hears.'" So Samuel went and lay down in his place.

10 And the LORD came and stood forth, calling as at other times, "Samuel! Samuel!" And Samuel said, "Speak, for 11 thy servant hears." Then the LORD said to Samuel, "Behold, I am about to do a thing in Israel, at which the 12 two ears of every one that hears it will tingle. On that day I will fulfil against Eli all that I have spoken concerning

13 his house, from beginning to end. And I tell him that I am about to punish his house for ever, for the iniquity which he knew, because his sons were blaspheming God, j 14 and he did not restrain them. Therefore I swear to the house of Eli that the iniquity of Eli's house shall not be expiated by sacrifice or offering for ever."

15 Samuel lay until morning; then he opened the doors of the house of the LORD. And Samuel was afraid to tell 16 the vision to Eli. But Eli called Samuel and said, "Samuel, 17 my son." And he said, "Here I am." And Eli said, "What was it that he told you? Do not hide it from me. May God do so to you and more also, if you hide anything 18 from me of all that he told you." So Samuel told him everything and hid nothing from him. And he said, "It is the LORD; let him do what seems good to him."

19 And Samuel grew, and the LORD was with him and let 20 none of his words fall to the ground. And all Israel from Dan to Beer-sheba knew that Samuel was established as a 21 prophet of the LORD. And the LORD appeared again at Shiloh, for the LORD revealed himself to Samuel at Shiloh

e Gk Tg: Heb *Did I reveal*   f Or *treat with scorn* Gk: Heb *kick at*   g Gk: Heb *your*   h Gk: Heb *die as men*
i Gk See 3. 10: Heb *the LORD called Samuel*   j Gk: Heb Another reading is *for themselves*

THE CAPTURE OF THE ARK

4 by the word of the Lord. And the word of Samuel came to all Israel.

Now Israel went out to battle against the Philistines; they encamped at Ebene'zer, and the Philistines encamped 2 at Aphek. The Philistines drew up in line against Israel, and when the battle spread, Israel was defeated

by the Philistines, who slew about four thousand men on 3 the field of battle. And when the troops came to the camp, the elders of Israel said, "Why has the Lord put us to rout today before the Philistines? Let us bring the ark of the covenant of the Lord here from Shiloh, that he may come among us and save us from the power of our 4 enemies." So the people sent to Shiloh, and brought from there the ark of the covenant of the Lord of hosts, who is enthroned on the cherubim; and the two sons of Eli, Hophni and Phin'ehas, were there with the ark of the covenant of God.

5 When the ark of the covenant of the Lord came into the camp, all Israel gave a mighty shout, so that the earth 6 resounded. And when the Philistines heard the noise of the shouting, they said, "What does this great shouting in the camp of the Hebrews mean?" And when they learned 7 that the ark of the Lord had come to the camp, the Philistines were afraid; for they said, "A god has come into the camp." And they said, "Woe to us! For nothing 8 like this has happened before. Woe to us! Who can deliver us from the power of these mighty gods? These are the gods who smote the Egyptians with every sort of 9 plague in the wilderness. Take courage, and acquit yourselves like men, O Philistines, lest you become slaves to the Hebrews as they have been to you; acquit yourselves like men and fight."

10 So the Philistines fought, and Israel was defeated, and they fled, every man to his home; and there was a very great slaughter, for there fell of Israel thirty thousand foot 11 soldiers. And the ark of God was captured; and the two sons of Eli, Hophni and Phin'ehas, were slain.

12 A man of Benjamin ran from the battle line, and came to Shiloh the same day, with his clothes rent and with 13 earth upon his head. When he arrived, Eli was sitting upon his seat by the road watching, for his heart trembled for the ark of God. And when the man came into the 14 city and told the news, all the city cried out. When Eli heard the sound of the outcry, he said, "What is this uproar?" Then the man hastened and came and told Eli.

15 Now Eli was ninety-eight years old and his eyes were set, 16 so that he could not see. And the man said to Eli, "I am he who has come from the battle; I fled from the battle 17 today." And he said, "How did it go, my son?" He who brought the tidings answered and said, "Israel has fled before the Philistines, and there has also been a great slaughter among the people; your two sons also, Hophni and Phin'ehas, are dead, and the ark of God has been 18 captured." When he mentioned the ark of God, Eli fell over backward from his seat by the side of the gate; and his neck was broken and he died, for he was an old man, and heavy. He had judged Israel forty years.

19 Now his daughter-in-law, the wife of Phin'ehas, was with child, about to give birth. And when she heard the tidings that the ark of God was captured, and that her father-in-law and her husband were dead, she bowed and 20 gave birth; for her pains came upon her. And about the time of her death the women attending her said to her, "Fear not, for you have borne a son." But she did not 21 answer or give heed. And she named the child Ich'abod, saying, "The glory has departed from Israel!" because the ark of God had been captured and because of her 22 father-in-law and her husband. And she said, "The glory has departed from Israel, for the ark of God has been captured."

5 When the Philistines captured the ark of God, they 2 carried it from Ebene'zer to Ashdod; then the Philistines took the ark of God and brought it into the house 3 of Dagon and set it up beside Dagon. And when the people of Ashdod rose early the next day, behold, Dagon had fallen face downward on the ground before the ark of the Lord. So they took Dagon and put him back in his 4 place. But when they rose early on the next morning, behold, Dagon had fallen face downward on the ground before the ark of the Lord, and the head of Dagon and both his hands were lying cut off upon the threshold; 5 only the trunk of Dagon was left to him. This is why the priests of Dagon and all who enter the house of Dagon do not tread on the threshold of Dagon in Ashdod to this day.

6 The hand of the Lord was heavy upon the people of Ashdod, and he terrified and afflicted them with tumors, 7 both Ashdod and its territory. And when the men of Ashdod saw how things were, they said, "The ark of the God of Israel must not remain with us; for his hand is 8 heavy upon us and upon Dagon our god." So they sent and gathered together all the lords of the Philistines, and said, "What shall we do with the ark of the God of Israel?" They answered, "Let the ark of the God of Israel be brought around to Gath." So they brought the ark of 9 the God of Israel there. But after they had brought it around, the hand of the Lord was against the city, causing a very great panic, and he afflicted the men of the city, both young and old, so that tumors broke out upon 10 them. So they sent the ark of God to Ekron. But when

the ark of God came to Ekron, the people of Ekron cried out, "They have brought around to us the ark of the
11 God of Israel to slay us and our people." They sent therefore and gathered together all the lords of the Philistines, and said, "Send away the ark of the God of Israel, and let it return to its own place, that it may not slay us and our people." For there was a deathly panic throughout the whole city. The hand of God was very heavy there;
12 the men who did not die were stricken with tumors, and the cry of the city went up to heaven.

6 The ark of the LORD was in the country of the Phi-
2 listines seven months. And the Philistines called for the priests and the diviners and said, "What shall we do with the ark of the LORD? Tell us with what we shall
3 send it to its place." They said, "If you send away the ark of the God of Israel, do not send it empty, but by all means return him a guilt offering. Then you will be healed, and it will be known to you why his hand does
4 not turn away from you." And they said, "What is the guilt offering that we shall return to him?" They answered, "Five golden tumors and five golden mice, according to the number of the lords of the Philistines; for the same plague was upon all of you and upon your lords.
5 So you must make images of your tumors and images of your mice that ravage the land, and give glory to the God of Israel; perhaps he will lighten his hand from off you
6 and your gods and your land. Why should you harden your hearts as the Egyptians and Pharaoh hardened their hearts? After he had made sport of them, did not
7 they let the people go, and they departed? Now then, take and prepare a new cart and two milch cows upon which there has never come a yoke, and yoke the cows to the
8 cart, but take their calves home, away from them. And take the ark of the LORD and place it on the cart, and put in a box at its side the figures of gold, which you are returning to him as a guilt offering. Then send it off, and
9 let it go its way. And watch; if it goes up on the way to its own land, to Beth-she'mesh, then it is he who has done us this great harm; but if not, then we shall know that it is not his hand that struck us, it happened to us by chance."
10 The men did so, and took two milch cows and yoked
11 them to the cart, and shut up their calves at home. And they put the ark of the LORD on the cart, and the box with
12 the golden mice and the images of their tumors. And the cows went straight in the direction of Beth-she'mesh along one highway, lowing as they went; they turned neither to the right nor to the left, and the lords of the Philistines went after them as far as the border of Beth-
13 she'mesh. Now the people of Beth-she'mesh were reaping their wheat harvest in the valley; and when they lifted up their eyes and saw the ark, they rejoiced to see it.
14 The cart came into the field of Joshua of Beth-she'mesh, and stopped there. A great stone was there; and they

split up the wood of the cart and offered the cows as a
15 burnt offering to the LORD. And the Levites took down the ark of the LORD and the box that was beside it, in which were the golden figures, and set them upon the great stone; and the men of Beth-she'mesh offered burnt offerings and sacrificed sacrifices on that day to the LORD.
16 And when the five lords of the Philistines saw it, they returned that day to Ekron.
17 These are the golden tumors, which the Philistines returned as a guilt offering to the LORD: one for Ashdod, one for Gaza, one for Ash'kelon, one for Gath, one for
18 Ekron; also the golden mice, according to the number of all the cities of the Philistines belonging to the five lords, both fortified cities and unwalled villages. The great stone, beside which they set down the ark of the LORD, is a witness to this day in the field of Joshua of Beth-she'mesh.
19 And he slew some of the men of Beth-she'mesh, because they looked into the ark of the LORD; he slew seventy men of them,[k] and the people mourned because the LORD
20 had made a great slaughter among the people. Then the men of Beth-she'mesh said, "Who is able to stand before the LORD, this holy God? And to whom shall he go up
21 away from us?" So they sent messengers to the inhabitants of Kir'iath-je'arim, saying, "The Philistines have returned the ark of the LORD. Come down and take it up
1 7 to you." And the men of Kir'iath-je'arim came and took up the ark of the LORD, and brought it to the house of Abin'adab on the hill; and they consecrated his
2 son, Elea'zar, to have charge of the ark of the LORD. From the day that the ark was lodged at Kir'iath-je'arim, a long time passed, some twenty years, and all the house of Israel lamented after the LORD.

A KING FOR ISRAEL

3 Then Samuel said to all the house of Israel, "If you are returning to the LORD with all your heart, then put away the foreign gods and the Ash'taroth from among you, and direct your heart to the LORD, and serve him only, and he will deliver you out of the hand of the
4 Philistines." So Israel put away the Ba'als and the Ash'taroth, and they served the LORD only.
5 Then Samuel said, "Gather all Israel at Mizpah, and I
6 will pray to the LORD for you." So they gathered at Mizpah, and drew water and poured it out before the LORD, and fasted on that day, and said there, "We have sinned against the LORD." And Samuel judged the people of
7 Israel at Mizpah. Now when the Philistines heard that the people of Israel had gathered at Mizpah, the lords of the Philistines went up against Israel. And when the people of Israel heard of it they were afraid of the Philistines.
8 And the people of Israel said to Samuel, "Do not cease to cry to the LORD our God for us, that he may save us
9 from the hand of the Philistines." So Samuel took a suck-

k Cn: Heb of the people seventy men, fifty thousand men

ing lamb and offered it as a whole burnt offering to the LORD; and Samuel cried to the LORD for Israel, and the 10 LORD answered him. As Samuel was offering up the burnt offering, the Philistines drew near to attack Israel; but the LORD thundered with a mighty voice that day against the Philistines and threw them into confusion; and they 11 were routed before Israel. And the men of Israel went out of Mizpah and pursued the Philistines, and smote them, as far as below Beth-car.

12 Then Samuel took a stone and set it up between Mizpah and Jesha'nah,[1] and called its name Eben-e'zer;[m] for he

13 said, "Hitherto the LORD has helped us." So the Philistines were subdued and did not again enter the territory of Israel. And the hand of the LORD was against the Phi- 14 listines all the days of Samuel. The cities which the Philistines had taken from Israel were restored to Israel, from Ekron to Gath; and Israel rescued the territory from the hand of the Philistines. There was peace also between Israel and the Amorites.

15, 16 Samuel judged Israel all the days of his life. And he went on a circuit year by year to Bethel, Gilgal, and 17 Mizpah; and he judged Israel in all these places. Then he would come back to Ramah, for his home was there, and there also he administered justice to Israel. And he built there an altar to the LORD.

8 When Samuel became old, he made his sons judges 2 over Israel. The name of his first-born son was Jo'el, the name of his second, Abi'jah; they were judges in 3 Beer-sheba. Yet his sons did not walk in his ways, but turned aside after gain; they took bribes and perverted justice.

4 Then all the elders of Israel gathered together and 5 came to Samuel at Ramah, and said to him, "Behold, you are old and your sons do not walk in your ways; now appoint for us a king to govern us like all the nations." 6 But the thing displeased Samuel when they said, "Give us a king to govern us." And Samuel prayed to the LORD. 7 And the LORD said to Samuel, "Hearken to the voice of the people in all that they say to you; for they have not rejected you, but they have rejected me from being king 8 over them. According to all the deeds which they have done to me,[n] from the day I brought them up out of

Egypt even to this day, forsaking me and serving other 9 gods, so they are also doing to you. Now then, hearken to their voice; only, you shall solemnly warn them, and show them the ways of the king who shall reign over them."

10 So Samuel told all the words of the LORD to the people 11 who were asking a king from him. He said, "These will be the ways of the king who will reign over you: he will take your sons and appoint them to his chariots and to 12 be his horsemen, and to run before his chariots; and he will appoint for himself commanders of thousands and commanders of fifties, and some to plow his ground and to reap his harvest, and to make his implements of war 13 and the equipment of his chariots. He will take your 14 daughters to be perfumers and cooks and bakers. He will take the best of your fields and vineyards and olive or- 15 chards and give them to his servants. He will take the tenth of your grain and of your vineyards and give it to 16 his officers and to his servants. He will take your menservants and maidservants, and the best of your cattle[o] 17 and your asses, and put them to his work. He will take 18 the tenth of your flocks, and you shall be his slaves. And in that day you will cry out because of your king, whom you have chosen for yourselves; but the LORD will not answer you in that day."

19 But the people refused to listen to the voice of Samuel; 20 and they said, "No! but we will have a king over us, that we also may be like all the nations, and that our king may govern us and go out before us and fight our battles." 21 And when Samuel had heard all the words of the people, 22 he repeated them in the ears of the LORD. And the LORD said to Samuel, "Hearken to their voice, and make them a king." Samuel then said to the men of Israel, "Go every man to his city."

9 There was a man of Benjamin whose name was Kish, the son of Abi'el, son of Zeror, son of Beco'rath, 2 son of Aphi'ah, a Benjaminite, a man of wealth; and he had a son whose name was Saul, a handsome young man. There was not a man among the people of Israel more handsome than he; from his shoulders upward he was taller than any of the people.

3 Now the asses of Kish, Saul's father, were lost. So Kish said to Saul his son, "Take one of the servants with you, 4 and arise, go and look for the asses." And they[p] passed through the hill country of E'phraim and passed through the land of Shal'ishah, but they did not find them. And they passed through the land of Sha'alim, but they were not there. Then they passed through the land of Benjamin, but did not find them.

5 When they came to the land of Zuph, Saul said to his servant who was with him, "Come, let us go back, lest my father cease to care about the asses and become 6 anxious about us." But he said to him, "Behold, there is a man of God in this city, and he is a man that is held

---

[1] Gk Syr: Heb Shen   [m] That is Stone of help   [n] Gk: Heb lacks to me   [o] Gk: Heb young men   [p] Gk Vg: Heb he

in honor; all that he says comes true. Let us go there; perhaps he can tell us about the journey on which we 7 have set out." Then Saul said to his servant, "But if we go, what can we bring the man? For the bread in our sacks is gone, and there is no present to bring to the man 8 of God. What have we?" The servant answered Saul again, "Here, I have with me the fourth part of a shekel of silver, and I will give it to the man of God, to tell us 9 our way." (Formerly in Israel, when a man went to inquire of God, he said, "Come, let us go to the seer"; for he who is now called a prophet was formerly called a 10 seer.) And Saul said to his servant, "Well said; come, let us go." So they went to the city where the man of God was.

11 As they went up the hill to the city, they met young maidens coming out to draw water, and said to them, "Is 12 the seer here?" They answered, "He is; behold, he is just ahead of you. Make haste; he has come just now to the city, because the people have a sacrifice today on the 13 high place. As soon as you enter the city, you will find him, before he goes up to the high place to eat; for the people will not eat till he comes, since he must bless the sacrifice; afterward those eat who are invited. Now go up, 14 for you will meet him immediately." So they went up to the city. As they were entering the city, they saw Samuel coming out toward them on his way up to the high place.

15 Now the day before Saul came, the LORD had revealed 16 to Samuel: "Tomorrow about this time I will send to you a man from the land of Benjamin, and you shall anoint him to be prince over my people Israel. He shall save my people from the hand of the Philistines; for I have seen the affliction of [q] my people, because their cry 17 has come to me." When Samuel saw Saul, the LORD told him, "Here is the man of whom I spoke to you! He it is 18 who shall rule over my people." Then Saul approached Samuel in the gate, and said, "Tell me where is the house 19 of the seer?" Samuel answered Saul, "I am the seer; go up before me to the high place, for today you shall eat with me, and in the morning I will let you go and will 20 tell you all that is on your mind. As for your asses that were lost three days ago, do not set your mind on them, for they have been found. And for whom is all that is desirable in Israel? Is it not for you and for all your 21 father's house?" Saul answered, "Am I not a Benjaminite, from the least of the tribes of Israel? And is not my family the humblest of all the families of the tribe of Benjamin? Why then have you spoken to me in this way?"

22 Then Samuel took Saul and his servant and brought them into the hall and gave them a place at the head of those who had been invited, who were about thirty per- 23 sons. And Samuel said to the cook, "Bring the portion 24 I gave you, of which I said to you, 'Put it aside.'" So

the cook took up the leg and the upper portion [r] and set them before Saul; and Samuel said, "See, what was kept is set before you. Eat; because it was kept for you until the hour appointed, that you might eat with the guests." [s]

25 So Saul ate with Samuel that day. And when they came down from the high place into the city, a bed was spread 26 for Saul [t] upon the roof, and he lay down to sleep. Then at the break of dawn [u] Samuel called to Saul upon the roof, "Up, that I may send you on your way." So Saul arose, and both he and Samuel went out into the street. 27 As they were going down to the outskirts of the city, Samuel said to Saul, "Tell the servant to pass on before us, and when he has passed on stop here yourself for a while, that I may make known to you the word of God."

10 Then Samuel took a vial of oil and poured it on his head, and kissed him and said, "Has not the LORD anointed you to be prince over his people Israel? And you shall reign over the people of the LORD and you will save them from the hand of their enemies round about. And this shall be the sign to you that the LORD has 2 anointed you to be prince [w] over his heritage. When you depart from me today you will meet two men by Rachel's tomb in the territory of Benjamin at Zelzah, and they will say to you, 'The asses which you went to seek are found, and now your father has ceased to care about the asses and is anxious about you, saying, "What shall I do 3 about my son?"' Then you shall go on from there further and come to the oak of Tabor; three men going up to God at Bethel will meet you there, one carrying three kids, another carrying three loaves of bread, and another 4 carrying a skin of wine. And they will greet you and give you two loaves of bread, which you shall accept from 5 their hand. After that you shall come to Gib'eathelohim,[x] where there is a garrison of the Philistines; and there, as you come to the city, you will meet a band of prophets coming down from the high place with harp, tambourine, 6 flute, and lyre before them, prophesying. Then the spirit of the LORD will come mightily upon you, and you shall 7 prophesy with them and be turned into another man. Now when these signs meet you, do whatever your hand finds 8 to do, for God is with you. And you shall go down before me to Gilgal; and behold, I am coming to you to offer burnt offerings and to sacrifice peace offerings. Seven

q Gk: Heb lacks *the affliction of*   r Heb obscure   s Cn: Heb *saying, I have invited the people*
t Gk: Heb *and he spoke with Saul*   u Gk: Heb *and they arose early and at break of dawn*
w Gk: Heb lacks *over his people Israel? And you shall . . . to be prince*   x Or *the hill of God*

days you shall wait, until I come to you and show you what you shall do."

9 When he turned his back to leave Samuel, God gave him another heart; and all these signs came to pass that 10 day. When they came to Gib'e-ah,[z] behold, a band of prophets met him; and the spirit of God came mightily 11 upon him, and he prophesied among them. And when all who knew him before saw how he prophesied with the prophets, the people said to one another, "What has come over the son of Kish? Is Saul also among the 12 prophets?" And a man of the place answered, "And who is their father?" Therefore it became a proverb, "Is Saul 13 also among the prophets?" When he had finished prophesying, he came to the high place.

14 Saul's uncle said to him and to his servant, "Where did you go?" And he said, "To seek the asses; and when we saw they were not to be found, we went to Samuel." 15 And Saul's uncle said, "Pray, tell me what Samuel said 16 to you." And Saul said to his uncle, "He told us plainly that the asses had been found." But about the matter of the kingdom, of which Samuel had spoken, he did not tell him anything.

17 Now Samuel called the people together to the LORD 18 at Mizpah; and he said to the people of Israel, "Thus says the LORD, the God of Israel, 'I brought up Israel out of Egypt, and I delivered you from the hand of the Egyptians and from the hand of all the kingdoms that 19 were oppressing you.' But you have this day rejected your God, who saves you from all your calamities and your distresses; and you have said, 'No! but set a king over us.' Now therefore present yourselves before the LORD by your tribes and by your thousands."

20 Then Samuel brought all the tribes of Israel near, and 21 the tribe of Benjamin was taken by lot. He brought the tribe of Benjamin near by its families, and the family of the Matrites was taken by lot; finally he brought the family of the Matrites near man by man,[a] and Saul the son of Kish was taken by lot. But when they sought him, 22 he could not be found. So they inquired again of the LORD, "Did the man come hither?"[b] and the LORD said, 23 "Behold, he has hidden himself among the baggage." Then they ran and fetched him from there; and when he stood among the people, he was taller than any of the people 24 from his shoulders upward. And Samuel said to all the people, "Do you see him whom the LORD has chosen? There is none like him among all the people." And all the people shouted, "Long live the king!"

25 Then Samuel told the people the rights and duties of the kingship; and he wrote them in a book and laid it up before the LORD. Then Samuel sent all the people away, 26 each one to his home. Saul also went to his home at Gib'e-ah, and with him went men of valor whose hearts 27 God had touched. But some worthless fellows said, "How can this man save us?" And they despised him, and brought him no present. But he held his peace.

11 Then Nahash the Ammonite went up and besieged Ja'besh-gil'ead; and all the men of Jabesh said to Nahash, "Make a treaty with us, and we will serve you." 2 But Nahash the Ammonite said to them, "On this condition I will make a treaty with you, that I gouge out all your right eyes, and thus put disgrace upon all Israel." 3 The elders of Jabesh said to him, "Give us seven days respite that we may send messengers through all the territory of Israel. Then, if there is no one to save us, we 4 will give ourselves up to you." When the messengers came to Gib'e-ah of Saul, they reported the matter in the ears of the people; and all the people wept aloud.

5 Now Saul was coming from the field behind the oxen; and Saul said, "What ails the people, that they are weeping?" So they told him the tidings of the men of Jabesh. 6 And the spirit of God came mightily upon Saul when he heard these words, and his anger was greatly kindled. 7 He took a yoke of oxen, and cut them in pieces and sent them throughout all the territory of Israel by the hand of messengers, saying, "Whoever does not come out after Saul and Samuel, so shall it be done to his oxen!" Then the dread of the LORD fell upon the people, and they came 8 out as one man. When he mustered them at Bezek, the men of Israel were three hundred thousand, and the men 9 of Judah thirty thousand. And they said to the messengers who had come, "Thus shall you say to the men of Ja'besh-gil'ead: 'Tomorrow, by the time the sun is hot, you shall have deliverance.'" When the messengers came and told 10 the men of Jabesh, they were glad. Therefore the men of Jabesh said, "Tomorrow we will give ourselves up to you, and you may do to us whatever seems good to you."

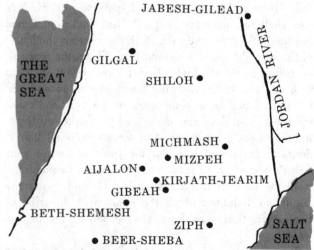

11 And on the morrow Saul put the people in three companies; and they came into the midst of the camp in the morning watch, and cut down the Ammonites until the heat of the day; and those who survived were scattered, so that no two of them were left together.

12 Then the people said to Samuel, "Who is it that said, 'Shall Saul reign over us?' Bring the men, that we may 13 put them to death." But Saul said, "Not a man shall be put to death this day, for today the LORD has wrought 14 deliverance in Israel." Then Samuel said to the people, "Come, let us go to Gilgal and there renew the kingdom." 15 So all the people went to Gilgal, and there they made Saul king before the LORD in Gilgal. There they sacrificed peace offerings before the LORD, and there Saul and all the men of Israel rejoiced greatly.

12 And Samuel said to all Israel, "Behold, I have hearkened to your voice in all that you have said to 2 me, and have made a king over you. And now, behold, the king walks before you; and I am old and gray, and behold, my sons are with you; and I have walked before 3 you from my youth until this day. Here I am; testify against me before the LORD and before his anointed. Whose ox have I taken? Or whose ass have I taken? Or whom have I defrauded? Whom have I oppressed? Or from whose hand have I taken a bribe to blind my eyes with it? Testify against me c and I will restore it to you." 4 They said, "You have not defrauded us or oppressed us or 5 taken anything from any man's hand." And he said to them, "The LORD is witness against you, and his anointed is witness this day, that you have not found anything in my hand." And they said, "He is witness."

6 And Samuel said to the people, "The LORD is witness,d who appointed Moses and Aaron and brought your fathers 7 up out of the land of Egypt. Now therefore stand still, that I may plead with you before the LORD concerning all the saving deeds of the LORD which he performed for you 8 and for your fathers. When Jacob went into Egypt and the Egyptians oppressed them,e then your fathers cried to the LORD and the LORD sent Moses and Aaron, who brought forth your fathers out of Egypt, and made them 9 dwell in this place. But they forgot the LORD their God; and he sold them into the hand of Sis'era, commander of the army of Jabin king of f Hazor, and into the hand of the Philistines, and into the hand of the king of Moab; 10 and they fought against them. And they cried to the LORD, and said, 'We have sinned, because we have forsaken the LORD, and have served the Ba'als and the Ash'taroth; but now deliver us out of the hand of our enemies, and we 11 will serve thee.' And the LORD sent Jerubba'al and Barak, g and Jephthah, and Samuel, and delivered you out of the hand of your enemies on every side; and you dwelt in 12 safety. And when you saw that Nahash the king of the Ammonites came against you, you said to me, 'No, but a king shall reign over us,' when the LORD your God was 13 your king. And now behold the king whom you have chosen, for whom you have asked; behold, the LORD has 14 set a king over you. If you will fear the LORD and serve him and hearken to his voice and not rebel against the commandment of the LORD, and if both you and the king who reigns over you will follow the LORD your God, it 15 will be well; but if you will not hearken to the voice of the LORD, but rebel against the commandment of the LORD, then the hand of the LORD will be against you and 16 your king.h Now therefore stand still and see this great 17 thing, which the LORD will do before your eyes. Is it not wheat harvest today? I will call upon the LORD, that he may send thunder and rain; and you shall know and see that your wickedness is great, which you have done in the 18 sight of the LORD, in asking for yourselves a king." So Samuel called upon the LORD, and the LORD sent thunder and rain that day; and all the people greatly feared the LORD and Samuel.

19 And all the people said to Samuel, "Pray for your servants to the LORD your God, that we may not die; for we have added to all our sins this evil, to ask for ourselves 20 a king." And Samuel said to the people, "Fear not; you have done all this evil, yet do not turn aside from follow-21 ing the LORD, but serve the LORD with all your heart; and do not turn aside after i vain things which cannot profit 22 or save, for they are vain. For the LORD will not cast away his people, for his great name's sake, because it has 23 pleased the LORD to make you a people for himself. Moreover as for me, far be it from me that I should sin against the LORD by ceasing to pray for you; and I will instruct 24 you in the good and the right way. Only fear the LORD, and serve him faithfully with all your heart; for consider 25 what great things he has done for you. But if you still do wickedly, you shall be swept away, both you and your king."

THE WAR OF INDEPENDENCE

13 Saul was . . .j years old when he began to reign; and he reigned . . . and two k years over Israel. 2 Saul chose three thousand men of Israel; two thousand were with Saul in Michmash and the hill country of Bethel, and a thousand were with Jonathan in Gib'e-ah of Benjamin; the rest of the people he sent home, every man 3 to his tent. Jonathan defeated the garrison of the Philistines which was at Geba; and the Philistines heard of it. And Saul blew the trumpet throughout all the land, say-4 ing, "Let the Hebrews hear." And all Israel heard it said that Saul had defeated the garrison of the Philistines, and also that Israel had become odious to the Philistines. And the people were called out to join Saul at Gilgal.

c Gk: Heb lacks *Testify against me*   d Gk: Heb lacks *is witness*   e Gk: Heb lacks *and the Egyptians oppressed them*
f Gk: Heb lacks *Jabin king of*   g Gk Syr: Heb *Bedan*   h Gk: Heb *fathers*   i Gk Syr Tg Vg: Heb *because after*
j The number is lacking in Heb   k Two is not the entire number. Something has dropped out.

5 And the Philistines mustered to fight with Israel, thirty thousand chariots, and six thousand horsemen, and troops like the sand on the seashore in multitude; they came up and encamped in Michmash, to the east of Beth-a'ven. 6 When the men of Israel saw that they were in straits (for the people were hard pressed), the people hid themselves in caves and in holes and in rocks and in tombs and in 7 cisterns, or crossed the fords of the Jordan[1] to the land of Gad and Gilead. Saul was still at Gilgal, and all the people followed him trembling.

8 He waited seven days, the time appointed by Samuel; but Samuel did not come to Gilgal, and the people were 9 scattering from him. So Saul said, "Bring the burnt offering here to me, and the peace offerings." And he 10 offered the burnt offering. As soon as he had finished offering the burnt offering, behold, Samuel came; and 11 Saul went out to meet him and salute him. Samuel said, "What have you done?" And Saul said, "When I saw that the people were scattering from me, and that you did not come within the days appointed, and that the Philistines 12 had mustered at Michmash, I said, 'Now the Philistines will come down upon me at Gilgal, and I have not entreated the favor of the LORD'; so I forced myself, and 13 offered the burnt offering." And Samuel said to Saul, "You have done foolishly; you have not kept the commandment of the LORD your God, which he commanded you; for now the LORD would have established your 14 kingdom over Israel for ever. But now your kingdom shall not continue; the LORD has sought out a man after his own heart; and the LORD has appointed him to be prince over his people, because you have not kept what 15 the LORD commanded you." And Samuel arose, and went up from Gilgal to Gib'e-ah of Benjamin.

And Saul numbered the people who were present with 16 him, about six hundred men. And Saul, and Jonathan his son, and the people who were present with them, stayed in Geba of Benjamin; but the Philistines en- 17 camped in Michmash. And raiders came out of the camp of the Philistines in three companies; one company 18 turned toward Ophrah, to the land of Shu'al, another company turned toward Beth-hor'on, and another company turned toward the border that looks down upon the valley of Zebo'im toward the wilderness.

19 Now there was no smith to be found throughout all the land of Israel; for the Philistines said, "Lest the Hebrews 20 make themselves swords or spears"; but every one of the Israelites went down to the Philistines to sharpen his 21 plowshare, his mattock, his axe, or his sickle;[m] and the charge was a pim for the plowshares and for the mattocks, and a third of a shekel for sharpening the axes and for 22 setting the goads.[n] So on the day of the battle there was neither sword nor spear found in the hand of any of the people with Saul and Jonathan; but Saul and Jonathan

23 his son had them. And the garrison of the Philistines went out to the pass of Michmash.

14 One day Jonathan the son of Saul said to the young man who bore his armor, "Come, let us go over to the Philistine garrison on yonder side." But he did not 2 tell his father. Saul was staying in the outskirts of Gib'e-ah under the pomegranate tree which is at Migron; the people who were with him were about six hundred men, 3 and Ahi'jah the son of Ahi'tub, Ich'abod's brother, son of Phin'ehas, son of Eli, the priest of the LORD in Shiloh, wearing an ephod. And the people did not know that 4 Jonathan had gone. In the pass,[o] by which Jonathan sought to go over to the Philistine garrison, there was a rocky crag on the one side and a rocky crag on the other side; the name of the one was Bozez, and the name of the 5 other Seneh. The one crag rose on the north in front of Michmash, and the other on the south in front of Geba.

6 And Jonathan said to the young man who bore his armor, "Come, let us go over to the garrison of these uncircumcised; it may be that the LORD will work for us; for nothing can hinder the LORD from saving by many or 7 by few." And his armor-bearer said to him, "Do all that your mind inclines to;[p] behold, I am with you, as is your 8 mind so is mine."[q] Then said Jonathan, "Behold, we will cross over to the men, and we will show ourselves to them. 9 If they say to us, 'Wait until we come to you,' then we will stand still in our place, and we will not go up to them. 10 But if they say, 'Come up to us,' then we will go up; for the LORD has given them into our hand. And this shall be

11 the sign to us." So both of them showed themselves to the garrison of the Philistines; and the Philistines said, "Look, Hebrews are coming out of the holes where they 12 have hid themselves." And the men of the garrison hailed Jonathan and his armor-bearer, and said, "Come up to us, and we will show you a thing." And Jonathan said to his armor-bearer, "Come up after me; for the LORD has 13 given them into the hand of Israel." Then Jonathan climbed up on his hands and feet, and his armor-bearer after him. And they fell before Jonathan, and his armor- 14 bearer killed them after him; and that first slaughter, which Jonathan and his armor-bearer made, was of about twenty men within as it were half a furrow's length in an 15 acre[r] of land. And there was a panic in the camp, in the

1 Cn: Heb *Hebrews crossed the Jordan*   m Gk: Heb *plowshare*   n The Heb of this verse is obscure
o Heb *between the passes*   p Gk: Heb *Do all that is in your mind. Turn*   q Gk: Heb lacks *so is mine*   r Heb *yoke*

field, and among all the people; the garrison and even the raiders trembled; the earth quaked; and it became a very great panic.

16 And the watchmen of Saul in Gib'e-ah of Benjamin looked; and behold, the multitude was surging hither
17 and thither.[s] Then Saul said to the people who were with him, "Number and see who has gone from us." And when they had numbered, behold, Jonathan and his armor-
18 bearer were not there. And Saul said to Ahi'jah, "Bring hither the ark of God." For the ark of God went at that
19 time with the people of Israel. And while Saul was talking to the priest, the tumult in the camp of the Philistines increased more and more; and Saul said to the priest,
20 "Withdraw your hand." Then Saul and all the people who were with him rallied and went into the battle; and behold, every man's sword was against his fellow, and
21 there was very great confusion. Now the Hebrews who had been with the Philistines before that time and who had gone up with them into the camp, even they also turned to be with[t] the Israelites who were with Saul and
22 Jonathan. Likewise, when all the men of Israel who had hid themselves in the hill country of E'phraim heard that the Philistines were fleeing, they too followed hard after
23 them in the battle. So the LORD delivered Israel that day; and the battle passed beyond Beth-a'ven.

24 And the men of Israel were distressed that day; for Saul laid an oath on the people, saying, "Cursed be the man who eats food until it is evening and I am avenged
25 on my enemies." So none of the people tasted food. And all the people[u] came into the forest; and there was honey
26 on the ground. And when the people entered the forest, behold, the honey was dropping, but no man put his hand
27 to his mouth; for the people feared the oath. But Jonathan had not heard his father charge the people with the oath; so he put forth the tip of the staff that was in his hand, and dipped it in the honeycomb, and put his hand to his
28 mouth; and his eyes became bright. Then one of the people said, "Your father strictly charged the people with an oath, saying, 'Cursed be the man who eats food this
29 day.'" And the people were faint. Then Jonathan said, "My father has troubled the land; see how my eyes have become bright, because I tasted a little of this honey.
30 How much better if the people had eaten freely today of the spoil of their enemies which they found; for now the slaughter among the Philistines has not been great."
31 They struck down the Philistines that day from Mich-
32 mash to Ai'jalon. And the people were very faint; the people flew upon the spoil, and took sheep and oxen and calves, and slew them on the ground; and the people
33 ate them with the blood. Then they told Saul, "Behold, the people are sinning against the LORD, by eating with the blood." And he said, "You have dealt treacherously; roll
34 a great stone to me here."[v] And Saul said, "Disperse yourselves among the people, and say to them, 'Let every man bring his ox or his sheep, and slay them here, and eat; and do not sin against the LORD by eating with the blood.'" So every one of the people brought his ox with
35 him that night, and slew them there. And Saul built an altar to the LORD; it was the first altar that he built to the LORD.

36 Then Saul said, "Let us go down after the Philistines by night and despoil them until the morning light; let us not leave a man of them." And they said, "Do whatever seems good to you." But the priest said, "Let us draw near
37 hither to God." And Saul inquired of God, "Shall I go down after the Philistines? Wilt thou give them into the hand of Israel?" But he did not answer him that day.
38 And Saul said, "Come hither, all you leaders of the people; and know and see how this sin has arisen today.
39 For as the LORD lives who saves Israel, though it be in Jonathan my son, he shall surely die." But there was not
40 a man among all the people that answered him. Then he said to all Israel, "You shall be on one side, and I and Jonathan my son will be on the other side." And the people said to Saul, "Do what seems good to you."
41 Therefore Saul said, "O LORD God of Israel, why hast thou not answered thy servant this day? If this guilt is in me or in Jonathan my son, O LORD, God of Israel, give Urim; but if this guilt is in thy people Israel,[w] give Thummim." And Jonathan and Saul were taken, but the
42 people escaped. Then Saul said, "Cast the lot between me and my son Jonathan." And Jonathan was taken.
43 Then Saul said to Jonathan, "Tell me what you have done." And Jonathan told him, "I tasted a little honey with the tip of the staff that was in my hand; here I am,
44 I will die." And Saul said, "God do so to me and more
45 also; you shall surely die, Jonathan." Then the people said to Saul, "Shall Jonathan die, who has wrought this great victory in Israel? Far from it! As the LORD lives, there shall not one hair of his head fall to the ground; for he has wrought with God this day." So the people ran-
46 somed Jonathan, that he did not die. Then Saul went up from pursuing the Philistines; and the Philistines went to their own place.

47 When Saul had taken the kingship over Israel, he fought against all his enemies on every side, against Moab, against the Ammonites, against Edom, against the kings of Zobah, and against the Philistines; wherever he turned
48 he put them to the worse. And he did valiantly, and smote the Amal'ekites, and delivered Israel out of the hands of those who plundered them.

49 Now the sons of Saul were Jonathan, Ishvi, and Mal'-chishu'a; and the names of his two daughters were these: the name of the first-born was Merab, and the name of
50 the younger Michal; and the name of Saul's wife was Ahin'o-am the daughter of Ahim'a-az. And the name of the commander of his army was Abner the son of Ner,
51 Saul's uncle; Kish was the father of Saul, and Ner the

---

[s] Gk: Heb *they went and thither*   [t] Gk Syr Vg Tg: Heb *round about, they also, to be with*   [u] Heb *land*
[v] Gk: Heb *this day*   [w] Vg Compare Gk: Heb *Saul said to the LORD, the God of Israel*

father of Abner was the son of Abi'el.

52 There was hard fighting against the Philistines all the days of Saul; and when Saul saw any strong man, or any valiant man, he attached him to himself.

THE RISE OF DAVID

15 And Samuel said to Saul, "The LORD sent me to anoint you king over his people Israel; now there-
2 fore hearken to the words of the LORD. Thus says the LORD of hosts, 'I will punish what Am'alek did to Israel in opposing them on the way, when they came up out of
3 Egypt. Now go and smite Am'alek, and utterly destroy all that they have; do not spare them, but kill both man and woman, infant and suckling, ox and sheep, camel and ass.' "

4 So Saul summoned the people, and numbered them in Tela'im, two hundred thousand men on foot, and ten
5 thousand men of Judah. And Saul came to the city of
6 Am'alek, and lay in wait in the valley. And Saul said to the Ken'ites, "Go, depart, go down from among the Amal'ekites, lest I destroy you with them; for you showed kindness to all the people of Israel when they came up out of Egypt." So the Ken'ites departed from among the
7 Amal'ekites. And Saul defeated the Amal'ekites, from
8 Hav'i-lah as far as Shur, which is east of Egypt. And he took Agag the king of the Amal'ekites alive, and utterly
9 destroyed all the people with the edge of the sword. But Saul and the people spared Agag, and the best of the sheep and of the oxen and of the fatlings, and the lambs, and all that was good, and would not utterly destroy them; all that was despised and worthless they utterly destroyed.
10, 11 The word of the LORD came to Samuel: "I repent that I have made Saul king; for he has turned back from following me, and has not performed my commandments." And Samuel was angry; and he cried to the LORD all
12 night. And Samuel rose early to meet Saul in the morning; and it was told Samuel, "Saul came to Carmel, and behold, he set up a monument for himself and turned,
13 and passed on, and went down to Gilgal." And Samuel came to Saul, and Saul said to him, "Blessed be you to the LORD; I have performed the commandment of the
14 LORD." And Samuel said, "What then is this bleating of the sheep in my ears, and the lowing of the oxen which I
15 hear?" Saul said, "They have brought them from the Amal'ekites; for the people spared the best of the sheep and of the oxen, to sacrifice to the LORD your God; and
16 the rest we have utterly destroyed." Then Samuel said to Saul, "Stop! I will tell you what the LORD said to me this night." And he said to him, "Say on."

17 And Samuel said, "Though you are little in your own eyes, are you not the head of the tribes of Israel? The
18 LORD anointed you king over Israel. And the LORD sent you on a mission, and said, 'Go, utterly destroy the sinners, the Amal'ekites, and fight against them until they

19 are consumed.' Why then did you not obey the voice of the LORD? Why did you swoop on the spoil, and do what
20 was evil in the sight of the LORD?" And Saul said to Samuel, "I have obeyed the voice of the LORD, I have gone on the mission on which the LORD sent me, I have brought Agag the king of Am'alek, and I have utterly
21 destroyed the Amal'ekites. But the people took of the spoil, sheep and oxen, the best of the things devoted to destruction, to sacrifice to the LORD your God in Gilgal."
22 And Samuel said,

"Has the LORD as great delight in burnt offerings and sacrifices,
  as in obeying the voice of the LORD?
Behold, to obey is better than sacrifice,
  and to hearken than the fat of rams.
23 For rebellion is as the sin of divination,
  and stubbornness is as iniquity and idolatry.

Because you have rejected the word of the LORD,
  he has also rejected you from being king."

24 And Saul said to Samuel, "I have sinned; for I have trangressed the commandment of the LORD and your words, because I feared the people and obeyed their voice.
25 Now therefore, I pray, pardon my sin, and return with
26 me, that I may worship the LORD." And Samuel said to Saul, "I will not return with you; for you have rejected the word of the LORD, and the LORD has rejected you from
27 being king over Israel." As Samuel turned to go away, Saul laid hold upon the skirt of his robe, and it tore.
28 And Samuel said to him, "The LORD has torn the kingdom of Israel from you this day, and has given it to a neighbor
29 of yours, who is better than you. And also the Glory of Israel will not lie or repent; for he is not a man, that he
30 should repent." Then he said, "I have sinned; yet honor me now before the elders of my people and before Israel, and return with me, that I may worship the LORD your
31 God." So Samuel turned back after Saul; and Saul worshiped the LORD.

32 Then Samuel said, "Bring here to me Agag the king of the Amal'ekites." And Agag came to him cheerfully.
33 Agag said, "Surely the bitterness of death is past." And Samuel said, "As your sword has made women childless, so shall your mother be childless among women." And Samuel hewed Agag in pieces before the LORD in Gilgal.
34 Then Samuel went to Ramah; and Saul went up to his
35 house in Gib'e-ah of Saul. And Samuel did not see Saul again until the day of his death, but Samuel grieved over

Saul. And the LORD repented that he had made Saul king over Israel.

16 The LORD said to Samuel, "How long will you grieve over Saul, seeing I have rejected him from being king over Israel? Fill your horn with oil, and go; I will send you to Jesse the Bethlehemite, for I have ² provided for myself a king among his sons." And Samuel said, "How can I go? If Saul hears it, he will kill me." And the LORD said, "Take a heifer with you, and say, 'I ³ have come to sacrifice to the LORD.' And invite Jesse to the sacrifice, and I will show you what you shall do; and you shall anoint for me him whom I name to you." ⁴ Samuel did what the LORD commanded, and came to Bethlehem. The elders of the city came to meet him ⁵ trembling, and said, "Do you come peaceably?" And he said, "Peaceably; I have come to sacrifice to the LORD; consecrate yourselves, and come with me to the sacrifice." And he consecrated Jesse and his sons, and invited them to the sacrifice.

⁶ When they came, he looked on Eli'ab and thought, ⁷ "Surely the LORD's anointed is before him." But the LORD said to Samuel, "Do not look on his appearance or on the height of his stature, because I have rejected him; for the LORD sees not as man sees; man looks on the outward ⁸ appearance, but the LORD looks on the heart." Then Jesse called Abin'adab, and made him pass before Samuel. And ⁹ he said, "Neither has the LORD chosen this one." Then Jesse made Shammah pass by. And he said, "Neither ¹⁰ has the LORD chosen this one." And Jesse made seven of his sons pass before Samuel. And Samuel said to Jesse, ¹¹ "The LORD has not chosen these." And Samuel said to Jesse, "Are all your sons here?" And he said, "There remains yet the youngest, but behold, he is keeping the sheep." And Samuel said to Jesse, "Send and fetch him; ¹² for we will not sit down till he comes here." And he sent, and brought him in. Now he was ruddy, and had beautiful eyes, and was handsome. And the LORD said, "Arise, ¹³ anoint him; for this is he." Then Samuel took the horn of oil, and anointed him in the midst of his brothers; and the Spirit of the LORD came mightily upon David from that day forward. And Samuel rose up, and went to Ramah.

¹⁴ Now the Spirit of the LORD departed from Saul, and ¹⁵ an evil spirit from the LORD tormented him. And Saul's servants said to him, "Behold now, an evil spirit from ¹⁶ God is tormenting you. Let our lord now command your servants, who are before you, to seek out a man who is skilful in playing the lyre; and when the evil spirit from God is upon you, he will play it, and you will be well." ¹⁷ So Saul said to his servants, "Provide for me a man who ¹⁸ can play well, and bring him to me." One of the young men answered, "Behold, I have seen a son of Jesse the Bethlehemite, who is skilful in playing, a man of valor, a man of war, prudent in speech, and a man of good

¹⁹ presence; and the LORD is with him." Therefore Saul sent messengers to Jesse, and said, "Send me David your ²⁰ son, who is with the sheep." And Jesse took an ass laden with bread, and a skin of wine and a kid, and sent them ²¹ by David his son to Saul. And David came to Saul, and entered his service. And Saul loved him greatly, and he ²² became his armor-bearer. And Saul sent to Jesse, saying, "Let David remain in my service, for he has found favor ²³ in my sight." And whenever the evil spirit from God was upon Saul, David took the lyre and played it with his hand; so Saul was refreshed, and was well, and the evil spirit departed from him.

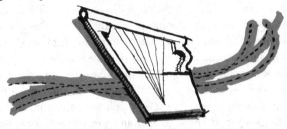

17 Now the Philistines gathered their armies for battle; and they were gathered at Socoh, which belongs to Judah, and encamped between Socoh and ² Aze'kah, in E'phes-dam'min. And Saul and the men of Israel were gathered, and encamped in the valley of Elah, ³ and drew up in line of battle against the Philistines. And the Philistines stood on the mountain on the one side, and Israel stood on the mountain on the other side, with ⁴ a valley between them. And there came out from the camp of the Philistines a champion named Goliath, of Gath, ⁵ whose height was six cubits and a span. He had a helmet of bronze on his head, and he was armed with a coat of mail, and the weight of the coat was five thousand shekels ⁶ of bronze. And he had greaves of bronze upon his legs, ⁷ and a javelin of bronze slung between his shoulders. And the shaft of his spear was like a weaver's beam, and his spear's head weighed six hundred shekels of iron; and ⁸ his shield-bearer went before him. He stood and shouted to the ranks of Israel, "Why have you come out to draw up for battle? Am I not a Philistine, and are you not servants of Saul? Choose a man for yourselves, and let ⁹ him come down to me. If he is able to fight with me and kill me, then we will be your servants; but if I prevail against him and kill him, then you shall be our servants ¹⁰ and serve us." And the Philistine said, "I defy the ranks of Israel this day; give me a man, that we may fight ¹¹ together." When Saul and all Israel heard these words of the Philistine, they were dismayed and greatly afraid.

¹² Now David was the son of an Eph'rathite of Bethlehem in Judah, named Jesse, who had eight sons. In the days of Saul the man was already old and advanced in years.ˣ ¹³ The three eldest sons of Jesse had followed Saul to the battle; and the names of his three sons who went to the battle were Eli'ab the first-born, and next to him Abin'-

ˣ Gk Syr: Heb *among men*

14 adab, and the third Shammah. David was the youngest;
15 the three eldest followed Saul, but David went back and forth from Saul to feed his father's sheep at Bethlehem.
16 For forty days the Philistine came forward and took his stand, morning and evening.
17 And Jesse said to David his son, "Take for your brothers an ephah of this parched grain, and these ten loaves, and carry them quickly to the camp to your
18 brothers; also take these ten cheeses to the commander of their thousand. See how your brothers fare, and bring some token from them."
19 Now Saul, and they, and all the men of Israel, were in
20 the valley of Elah, fighting with the Philistines. And David rose early in the morning, and left the sheep with a keeper, and took the provisions, and went, as Jesse had commanded him; and he came to the encampment as the host was going forth to the battle line, shouting the war
21 cry. And Israel and the Philistines drew up for battle,
22 army against army. And David left the things in charge of the keeper of the baggage, and ran to the ranks, and
23 went and greeted his brothers. As he talked with them, behold, the champion, the Philistine of Gath, Goliath by name, came up out of the ranks of the Philistines, and spoke the same words as before. And David heard him.
24 All the men of Israel, when they saw the man, fled
25 from him, and were much afraid. And the men of Israel said, "Have you seen this man who has come up? Surely he has come up to defy Israel; and the man who kills him, the king will enrich with great riches, and will give him his daughter, and make his father's house free in Israel."
26 And David said to the men who stood by him, "What shall be done for the man who kills this Philistine, and takes away the reproach from Israel? For who is this uncircumcised Philistine, that he should defy the armies
27 of the living God?" And the people answered him in the same way, "So shall it be done to the man who kills him."
28 Now Eli'ab his eldest brother heard when he spoke to the men; and Eli'ab's anger was kindled against David, and he said, "Why have you come down? And with whom have you left those few sheep in the wilderness? I know your presumption, and the evil of your heart; for
29 you have come down to see the battle." And David said,
30 "What have I done now? Was it not but a word?" And he turned away from him toward another, and spoke in the same way; and the people answered him again as before.
31 When the words which David spoke were heard, they
32 repeated them before Saul; and he sent for him. And David said to Saul, "Let no man's heart fail because of him; your servant will go and fight with this Philistine."
33 And Saul said to David, "You are not able to go against this Philistine to fight with him; for you are but a youth,
34 and he has been a man of war from his youth." But

David said to Saul, "Your servant used to keep sheep for his father; and when there came a lion, or a bear, and
35 took a lamb from the flock, I went after him and smote him and delivered it out of his mouth; and if he arose against me, I caught him by his beard, and smote him and
36 killed him. Your servant has killed both lions and bears; and this uncircumcised Philistine shall be like one of them, seeing he has defied the armies of the living God."
37 And David said, "The Lord who delivered me from the paw of the lion and from the paw of the bear, will deliver me from the hand of this Philistine." And Saul said to
38 David, "Go, and the Lord be with you!" Then Saul clothed David with his armor; he put a helmet of bronze
39 on his head, and clothed him with a coat of mail. And David girded his sword over his armor, and he tried in vain to go, for he was not used to them. Then David said to Saul, "I cannot go with these; for I am not used to
40 them." And David put them off. Then he took his staff in his hand, and chose five smooth stones from the brook, and put them in his shepherd's bag or wallet; his sling was in his hand, and he drew near to the Philistine.
41 And the Philistine came on and drew near to David,
42 with his shield-bearer in front of him. And when the Philistine looked, and saw David, he disdained him; for he was but a youth, ruddy and comely in appearance.
43 And the Philistine said to David, "Am I a dog, that you come to me with sticks?" And the Philistine cursed David
44 by his gods. The Philistine said to David, "Come to me, and I will give your flesh to the birds of the air and to the
45 beasts of the field." Then David said to the Philistine,

"You come to me with a sword and with a spear and with a javelin; but I come to you in the name of the Lord of hosts, the God of the armies of Israel, whom you have
46 defied. This day the Lord will deliver you into my hand, and I will strike you down, and cut off your head; and I will give the dead bodies of the host of the Philistines this day to the birds of the air and the wild beasts of the earth; that all the earth may know that there is a God
47 in Israel, and that all this assembly may know that the Lord saves not with sword and spear; for the battle is the Lord's and he will give you into our hand."
48 When the Philistine arose and came and drew near to meet David, David ran quickly toward the battle line to
49 meet the Philistine. And David put his hand in his bag and took out a stone, and slung it, and struck the Philistine on his forehead; the stone sank into his fore-

head, and he fell on his face to the ground.

50 So David prevailed over the Philistine with a sling and with a stone, and struck the Philistine, and killed him; 51 there was no sword in the hand of David. Then David ran and stood over the Philistine, and took his sword and drew it out of its sheath, and killed him, and cut off his head with it. When the Philistines saw that their 52 champion was dead, they fled. And the men of Israel and Judah rose with a shout and pursued the Philistines as far as Gath ʸ and the gates of Ekron, so that the wounded Philistines fell on the way from Sha-ara′im as far as Gath 53 and Ekron. And the Israelites came back from chasing 54 the Philistines, and they plundered their camp. And David took the head of the Philistine and brought it to Jerusalem; but he put his armor in his tent.

55 When Saul saw David go forth against the Philistine, he said to Abner, the commander of the army, "Abner, whose son is this youth?" And Abner said, "As your soul 56 lives, O king, I cannot tell." And the king said, "Inquire 57 whose son the stripling is." And as David returned from the slaughter of the Philistine, Abner took him, and brought him before Saul with the head of the Philistine 58 in his hand. And Saul said to him, "Whose son are you, young man?" And David answered, "I am the son of your servant Jesse the Bethlehemite."

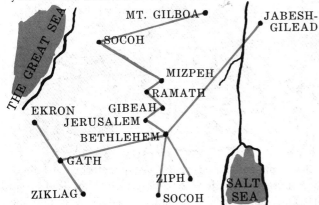

18 When he had finished speaking to Saul, the soul of Jonathan was knit to the soul of David, and 2 Jonathan loved him as his own soul. And Saul took him that day, and would not let him return to his father's 3 house. Then Jonathan made a covenant with David, be- 4 cause he loved him as his own soul. And Jonathan stripped himself of the robe that was upon him, and gave it to David, and his armor, and even his sword and his 5 bow and his girdle. And David went out and was successful wherever Saul sent him; so that Saul set him over the men of war. And this was good in the sight of all the people and also in the sight of Saul's servants.

6 As they were coming home, when David returned from slaying the Philistine, the women came out of all the cities of Israel, singing and dancing, to meet King Saul, with timbrels, with songs of joy, and with instruments ᶻ

7 of music. And the women sang to one another as they made merry,

"Saul has slain his thousands,
and David his ten thousands."

8 And Saul was very angry, and this saying displeased him; he said, "They have ascribed to David ten thousands, and to me they have ascribed thousands; and what 9 more can he have but the kingdom?" And Saul eyed David from that day on.

10 And on the morrow an evil spirit from God rushed upon Saul, and he raved within his house, while David was playing the lyre, as he did day by day. Saul had his 11 spear in his hand; and Saul cast the spear, for he thought, "I will pin David to the wall." But David evaded him twice.

12 Saul was afraid of David, because the LORD was with 13 him but had departed from Saul. So Saul removed him from his presence, and made him a commander of a thousand; and he went out and came in before the people. 14 And David had success in all his undertakings; for the 15 LORD was with him. And when Saul saw that he had great 16 success, he stood in awe of him. But all Israel and Judah loved David; for he went out and came in before them.

17 Then Saul said to David, "Here is my elder daughter Merab; I will give her to you for a wife; only be valiant for me and fight the LORD's battles." For Saul thought, "Let not my hand be upon him, but let the hand of the 18 Philistines be upon him." And David said to Saul, "Who am I, and who are my kinsfolk, my father's family in 19 Israel, that I should be son-in-law to the king?" But at the time when Merab, Saul's daughter, should have been given to David, she was given to A′driel the Meho′lathite for a wife.

20 Now Saul's daughter Michal loved David; and they told 21 Saul, and the thing pleased him. Saul thought, "Let me give her to him, that she may be a snare for him, and that the hand of the Philistines may be against him." Therefore Saul said to David a second time,ᵃ "You shall 22 now be my son-in-law." And Saul commanded his servants, "Speak to David in private and say, 'Behold, the king has delight in you, and all his servants love you; 23 now then become the king's son-in-law.'" And Saul's servants spoke those words in the ears of David. And David said, "Does it seem to you a little thing to become the king's son-in-law, seeing that I am a poor man and of no 24 repute?" And the servants of Saul told him, "Thus and 25 so did David speak." Then Saul said, "Thus shall you say to David, 'The king desires no marriage present except a hundred foreskins of the Philistines, that he may be avenged of the king's enemies.'" Now Saul thought 26 to make David fall by the hand of the Philistines. And when his servants told David these words, it pleased David well to be the king's son-in-law. Before the time had 27 expired, David arose and went, along with his men, and

ʸ Gk: Heb Gai   ᶻ Or triangles, or three-stringed instruments   ᵃ Heb by two

killed two hundred of the Philistines; and David brought their foreskins, which were given in full number to the king, that he might become the king's son-in-law. And
28 Saul gave him his daughter Michal for a wife. But when Saul saw and knew that the Lord was with David, and
29 that all Israel[b] loved him, Saul was still more afraid of David. So Saul was David's enemy continually.

30 Then the princes of the Philistines came out to battle, and as often as they came out David had more success than all the servants of Saul; so that his name was highly esteemed.

SAUL SEEKS TO KILL DAVID

19 And Saul spoke to Jonathan his son and to all his servants, that they should kill David. But Jonathan,
2 Saul's son, delighted much in David. And Jonathan told David, "Saul my father seeks to kill you; therefore take heed to yourself in the morning, stay in a secret place and
3 hide yourself; and I will go out and stand beside my father in the field where you are, and I will speak to my father about you; and if I learn anything I will tell you."
4 And Jonathan spoke well of David to Saul his father, and said to him, "Let not the king sin against his servant David; because he has not sinned against you, and be-
5 cause his deeds have been of good service to you; for he took his life in his hand and he slew the Philistine, and the Lord wrought a great victory for all Israel. You saw it, and rejoiced; why then will you sin against innocent
6 blood by killing David without cause?" And Saul hearkened to the voice of Jonathan; Saul swore, "As the Lord
7 lives, he shall not be put to death." And Jonathan called David, and Jonathan showed him all these things. And Jonathan brought David to Saul, and he was in his presence as before.

8 And there was war again; and David went out and fought with the Philistines, and made a great slaughter
9 among them, so that they fled before him. Then an evil spirit from the Lord came upon Saul, as he sat in his house with his spear in his hand; and David was playing
10 the lyre. And Saul sought to pin David to the wall with the spear; but he eluded Saul, so that he struck the spear into the wall. And David fled, and escaped.

11 That night Saul[x] sent messengers to David's house to watch him, that he might kill him in the morning. But Michal, David's wife, told him, "If you do not save your
12 life tonight, tomorrow you will be killed." So Michal let David down through the window; and he fled away and
13 escaped. Michal took an image[c] and laid it on the bed and put a pillow[d] of goats' hair at its head, and covered
14 it with the clothes. And when Saul sent messengers to
15 take David, she said, "He is sick." Then Saul sent the messengers to see David, saying, "Bring him up to me
16 in the bed, that I may kill him." And when the messengers came in, behold, the image[c] was in the bed, with

17 the pillow[d] of goats' hair at its head. Saul said to Michal, "Why have you deceived me thus, and let my enemy go, so that he has escaped?" And Michal answered Saul, "He said to me, 'Let me go; why should I kill you?'"
18 Now David fled and escaped, and he came to Samuel at Ramah, and told him all that Saul had done to him.
19 And he and Samuel went and dwelt at Nai'oth. And it was told Saul, "Behold, David is at Nai'oth in Ramah."
20 Then Saul sent messengers to take David; and when they saw the company of the prophets prophesying, and Samuel standing as head over them, the Spirit of God came upon the messengers of Saul, and they also prophe-
21 sied. When it was told Saul, he sent other messengers, and they also prophesied. And Saul sent messengers again
22 the third time, and they also prophesied. Then he himself went to Ramah, and came to the great well that is in Secu; and he asked, "Where are Samuel and David?" And one said, "Behold, they are at Nai'oth in Ramah."
23 And he went from[f] there to Nai'oth in Ramah; and the Spirit of God came upon him also, and as he went he
24 prophesied, until he came to Nai'oth in Ramah. And he too stripped off his clothes, and he too prophesied before Samuel, and lay naked all that day and all that night. Hence it is said, "Is Saul also among the prophets?"

20 Then David fled from Nai'oth in Ramah, and came and said before Jonathan, "What have I done?

What is my guilt? And what is my sin before your father,
2 that he seeks my life?" And he said to him, "Far from it! You shall not die. Behold, my father does nothing either great or small without disclosing it to me; and why should my father hide this from me? It is not so."
3 But David replied,[g] "Your father knows well that I have found favor in your eyes; and he thinks, 'Let not Jonathan know this, lest he be grieved.' But truly, as the Lord lives and as your soul lives, there is but a step between
4 me and death." Then said Jonathan to David, "Whatever
5 you say, I will do for you." David said to Jonathan, "Behold, tomorrow is the new moon, and I should not fail to sit at table with the king; but let me go, that I may hide
6 myself in the field till the third day at evening. If your father misses me at all, then say, 'David earnestly asked leave of me to run to Bethlehem his city; for there is a
7 yearly sacrifice there for all the family.' If he says, 'Good!' it will be well with your servant; but if he is
8 angry, then know that evil is determined by him. There-

[b] Gk: Heb Michal, Saul's daughter   [x] Gk Old Latin: Heb escaped that night. [11] And Saul   [c] Heb teraphim
[d] The meaning of the Hebrew word is uncertain   [f] Gk: Heb lacks from   [g] Gk: Heb swore again

fore deal kindly with your servant, for you have brought your servant into a sacred covenant[h] with you. But if there is guilt in me, slay me yourself; for why should 9 you bring me to your father?" And Jonathan said, "Far be it from you! If I knew that it was determined by my father that evil should come upon you, would I not tell 10 you?" Then said David to Jonathan, "Who will tell me 11 if your father answers you roughly?" And Jonathan said to David, "Come, let us go out into the field." So they both went out into the field.

12 And Jonathan said to David, "The LORD, the God of Israel, be witness![i] When I have sounded my father, about this time tomorrow, or the third day, behold, if he is well disposed toward David, shall I not then send 13 and disclose it to you? But should it please my father to do you harm, the LORD do so to Jonathan, and more also, if I do not disclose it to you, and send you away, that you may go in safety. May the LORD be with you, as 14 he has been with my father. If I am still alive, show me 15 the loyal love of the LORD, that I may not die;[j] and do not cut off your loyalty from my house for ever. When the LORD cuts off every one of the enemies of David from 16 the face of the earth, let not the name of Jonathan be cut off from the house of David.[k] And may the LORD take 17 vengeance on David's enemies." And Jonathan made David swear again by his love for him; for he loved him as he loved his own soul.

18 Then Jonathan said to him, "Tomorrow is the new moon; and you will be missed, because your seat will be 19 empty. And on the third day you will be greatly missed;[l] then go to the place where you hid yourself when the matter was in hand, and remain beside yonder stone 20 heap.[m] And I will shoot three arrows to the side of it, as 21 though I shot at a mark. And behold, I will send the lad, saying, 'Go, find the arrows.' If I say to the lad, 'Look, the arrows are on this side of you, take them,' then you are to come, for, as the LORD lives, it is safe for you and 22 there is no danger. But if I say to the youth, 'Look, the arrows are beyond you,' then go; for the LORD has sent 23 you away. And as for the matter of which you and I have spoken, behold, the LORD is between you and me for ever."

24 So David hid himself in the field; and when the new 25 moon came, the king sat down to eat food. The king sat upon his seat, as at other times, upon the seat by the wall; Jonathan sat opposite,[n] and Abner sat by Saul's side, but David's place was empty.

26 Yet Saul did not say anything that day; for he thought, "Something has befallen him; he is not clean, surely he 27 is not clean." But on the second day, the morrow after the new moon, David's place was empty. And Saul said to Jonathan his son, "Why has not the son of Jesse come 28 to the meal, either yesterday or today?" Jonathan an-

swered Saul, "David earnestly asked leave of me to go 29 to Bethlehem; he said, 'Let me go; for our family holds a sacrifice in the city, and my brother has commanded me to be there. So now, if I have found favor in your eyes, let me get away, and see my brothers.' For this reason he has not come to the king's table."

30 Then Saul's anger was kindled against Jonathan, and he said to him, "You son of a perverse, rebellious woman, do I not know that you have chosen the son of Jesse to your own shame, and to the shame of your mother's 31 nakedness? For as long as the son of Jesse lives upon the earth, neither you nor your kingdom shall be established. Therefore send and fetch him to me, for 32 he shall surely die." Then Jonathan answered Saul his father, "Why should he be put to death? What has he 33 done?" But Saul cast his spear at him to smite him; so Jonathan knew that his father was determined to put 34 David to death. And Jonathan rose from the table in fierce anger and ate no food the second day of the month, for he was grieved for David, because his father had disgraced him.

35 In the morning Jonathan went out into the field to the 36 appointment with David, and with him a little lad. And he said to his lad, "Run and find the arrows which I 37 shoot." As the lad ran, he shot an arrow beyond him. And when the lad came to the place of the arrow which Jonathan had shot, Jonathan called after the lad and said, "Is 38 not the arrow beyond you?" And Jonathan called after the lad, "Hurry, make haste, stay not." So Jonathan's 39 lad gathered up the arrows, and came to his master. But

the lad knew nothing; only Jonathan and David knew 40 the matter. And Jonathan gave his weapons to his lad, 41 and said to him, "Go and carry them to the city." And as soon as the lad had gone, David rose from beside the stone heap[o] and fell on his face to the ground, and bowed three times; and they kissed one another, and wept with 42 one another, until David recovered himself.[p] Then Jona-

h Heb a covenant of the LORD   i Heb lacks be witness   j Heb uncertain
k Gk: Heb earth, and Jonathan made a covenant with the house of David   l Gk: Heb go down quickly
m Gk: Heb the stone Ezel   n Cn See Gk: Heb stood up   o Gk: Heb from beside the south   p Or exceeded

than said to David, "Go in peace, forasmuch as we have sworn both of us in the name of the LORD, saying, 'The LORD shall be between me and you, and between my descendants and your descendants, for ever.'" And he rose and departed; and Jonathan went into the city.[q]

CIVIL WAR: SAUL VS. DAVID

21 [r] Then came David to Nob to Ahim'elech the priest; and Ahim'elech came to meet David trembling, and said to him, "Why are you alone, and no one with you?" [2] And David said to Ahim'elech the priest, "The king has charged me with a matter, and said to me, 'Let no one know anything of the matter about which I send you, and with which I have charged you.' I have made an appointment with the young men for such and such a [3] place. Now then, what have you at hand? Give me five [4] loaves of bread, or whatever is here." And the priest answered David, "I have no common bread at hand, but there is holy bread; if only the young men have kept [5] themselves from women." And David answered the priest, "Of a truth women have been kept from us as always when I go on an expedition; the vessels of the young men are holy, even when it is a common journey; how [6] much more today will their vessels be holy?" So the priest gave him the holy bread; for there was no bread there but the bread of the Presence, which is removed from before the LORD, to be replaced by hot bread on the day it is taken away.

[7] Now a certain man of the servants of Saul was there that day, detained before the LORD; his name was Do'eg the E'domite, the chief of Saul's herdsmen.

[8] And David said to Ahim'elech, "And have you not here a spear or a sword at hand? For I have brought neither my sword nor my weapons with me, because the [9] king's business required haste." And the priest said, "The sword of Goliath the Philistine, whom you killed in the valley of Elah, behold, it is here wrapped in a cloth behind the ephod; if you will take that, take it, for there is none but that here." And David said, "There is none like that; give it to me."

[10] And David rose and fled that day from Saul, and went [11] to A'chish the king of Gath. And the servants of A'chish said to him, "Is not this David the king of the land? Did they not sing to one another of him in dances,

'Saul has slain his thousands,
and David his ten thousands'?"

[12] And David took these words to heart, and was much [13] afraid of A'chish the king of Gath. So he changed his behavior before them, and feigned himself mad in their hands, and made marks on the doors of the gate, and let [14] his spittle run down his beard. Then said A'chish to his servants, "Lo, you see the man is mad; why then have [15] you brought him to me? Do I lack madmen, that you

have brought this fellow to play the madman in my presence? Shall this fellow come into my house?"

22 David departed from there and escaped to the cave of Adullam; and when his brothers and all his [2] father's house heard it, they went down there to him. And every one who was in distress, and every one who was in debt, and every one who was discontented, gathered to him; and he became captain over them. And there were with him about four hundred men.

[3] And David went from there to Mizpeh of Moab; and he said to the king of Moab, "Pray let my father and my mother stay[s] with you, till I know what God will do

[4] for me." And he left them with the king of Moab, and they stayed with him all the time that David was in the [5] stronghold. Then the prophet Gad said to David, "Do not remain in the stronghold; depart, and go into the land of Judah." So David departed, and went into the forest of Hereth.

[6] Now Saul heard that David was discovered, and the men who were with him. Saul was sitting at Gib'e-ah, under the tamarisk tree on the height, with his spear in his hand, and all his servants were standing about him. [7] And Saul said to his servants who stood about him, "Hear now, you Benjaminites; will the son of Jesse give every one of you fields and vineyards, will he make you all commanders of thousands and commanders of hun- [8] dreds, that all of you have conspired against me? No one discloses to me when my son makes a league with the son of Jesse, none of you is sorry for me or discloses to me that my son has stirred up my servant against me, to [9] lie in wait, as at this day." Then answered Do'eg the E'domite, who stood by the servants of Saul, "I saw the son of Jesse coming to Nob, to Ahim'elech the son of [10] Ahi'tub, and he inquired of the LORD for him, and gave him provisions, and gave him the sword of Goliath the Philistine."

[11] Then the king sent to summon Ahim'elech the priest, the son of Ahi'tub, and all his father's house, the priests who were at Nob; and all of them came to the king. [12] And Saul said, "Hear now, son of Ahi'tub." And he an- [13] swered, "Here I am, my lord." And Saul said to him, "Why have you conspired against me, you and the son of Jesse, in that you have given him bread and a sword, and have inquired of God for him, so that he has risen [14] against me, to lie in wait, as at this day?" Then Ahim'-elech answered the king, "And who among all your ser-

[q] This sentence is 21.1 in Heb   [r] Ch 21.2 in Heb   [s] Syr Vg: Heb *come out*

vants is so faithful as David, who is the king's son-in-law, and captain over [t] your bodyguard, and honored in your 15 house? Is today the first time that I have inquired of God for him? No! Let not the king impute anything to his servant or to all the house of my father; for your servant has known nothing of all this, much or little." 16 And the king said, "You shall surely die, Ahim'elech, you 17 and all your father's house." And the king said to the guard who stood about him, "Turn and kill the priests of the LORD; because their hand also is with David, and they knew that he fled, and did not disclose it to me." But the servants of the king would not put forth their 18 hand to fall upon the priests of the LORD. Then the king said to Do'eg, "You turn and fall upon the priests." And Do'eg the E'domite turned and fell upon the priests, and he killed on that day eighty-five persons who wore the 19 linen ephod. And Nob, the city of the priests, he put to the sword; both men and women, children and sucklings, oxen, asses and sheep, he put to the sword.

20 But one of the sons of Ahim'elech the son of Ahi'tub, 21 named Abi'athar, escaped and fled after David. And Abi'athar told David that Saul had killed the priests of 22 the LORD. And David said to Abi'athar, "I knew on that day, when Do'eg the E'domite was there, that he would surely tell Saul. I have occasioned the death of all the 23 persons of your father's house. Stay with me, fear not; for he that seeks my life seeks your life; with me you shall be in safekeeping."

23 Now they told David, "Behold, the Philistines are fighting against Kei'lah, and are robbing the thresh- 2 ing floors." Therefore David inquired of the LORD, "Shall I go and attack these Philistines?" And the LORD said to David, "Go and attack the Philistines and save Kei'lah." 3 But David's men said to him, "Behold, we are afraid here in Judah; how much more then if we go to Kei'lah 4 against the armies of the Philistines?" Then David inquired of the LORD again. And the LORD answered him, "Arise, go down to Kei'lah; for I will give the Philistines 5 into your hand." And David and his men went to Kei'lah, and fought with the Philistines, and brought away their cattle, and made a great slaughter among them. So David delivered the inhabitants of Kei'lah.

6 When Abi'athar the son of Ahim'elech fled to David to Kei'lah, he came down with an ephod in his hand. 7 Now it was told Saul that David had come to Kei'lah. And Saul said, "God has given him into my hand; for he has shut himself in by entering a town that has gates and 8 bars." And Saul summoned all the people to war, to go 9 down to Kei'lah, to besiege David and his men. David knew that Saul was plotting evil against him; and he said 10 to Abi'athar the priest, "Bring the ephod here." Then said David, "O LORD, the God of Israel, thy servant has surely heard that Saul seeks to come to Kei'lah, to destroy 11 the city on my account. Will the men of Kei'lah surrender me into his hand? Will Saul come down, as thy servant has heard? O LORD, the God of Israel, I beseech thee, tell thy servant." And the LORD said, "He will come 12 down." Then said David, "Will the men of Kei'lah surrender me and my men into the hand of Saul?" And the 13 LORD said, "They will surrender you." Then David and his men, who were about six hundred, arose and departed from Kei'lah, and they went wherever they could go. When Saul was told that David had escaped from Kei'lah, 14 he gave up the expedition. And David remained in the strongholds in the wilderness, in the hill country of the Wilderness of Ziph. And Saul sought him every day, but God did not give him into his hand.

15 And David was afraid because [u] Saul had come out to seek his life. David was in the Wilderness of Ziph at 16 Horesh. And Jonathan, Saul's son, rose, and went to David at Horesh, and strengthened his hand in God. 17 And he said to him, "Fear not; for the hand of Saul my father shall not find you; you shall be king over Israel, and I shall be next to you; Saul my father also knows 18 this." And the two of them made a covenant before the LORD; David remained at Horesh, and Jonathan went home.

19 Then the Ziphites went up to Saul at Gib'e-ah, saying, "Does not David hide among us in the strongholds at Horesh, on the hill of Hachi'lah, which is south of Jeshi'- 20 mon? Now come down, O king, according to all your heart's desire to come down; and our part shall be to 21 surrender him into the king's hand." And Saul said, "May you be blessed by the LORD; for you have had 22 compassion on me. Go, make yet more sure; know and see the place where his haunt is, and who has seen him 23 there; for it is told me that he is very cunning. See therefore, and take note of all the lurking places where he hides, and come back to me with sure information. Then I will go with you; and if he is in the land, I will search 24 him out among all the thousands of Judah." And they arose, and went to Ziph ahead of Saul.

Now David and his men were in the wilderness of 25 Ma'on, in the Arabah to the south of Jeshi'mon. And Saul and his men went to seek him. And David was told; therefore he went down to the rock which is [v] in the wilderness of Ma'on. And when Saul heard that, he pur- 26 sued after David in the wilderness of Ma'on. Saul went on one side of the mountain, and David and his men on the other side of the mountain; and David was making haste to get away from Saul, as Saul and his men were closing in upon David and his men to capture them, 27 when a messenger came to Saul, saying, "Make haste and come; for the Philistines have made a raid upon the 28 land." So Saul returned from pursuing after David, and went against the Philistines; therefore that place was 29 [w] called the Rock of Escape. And David went up from there, and dwelt in the strongholds of Enge'di.

---

[t] Gk Tg: Heb *and has turned aside to*   [u] Or *saw that*   [v] Gk: Heb *and dwelt*   [w] Ch 24. 1 in Heb

24 When Saul returned from following the Philistines, he was told, "Behold, David is in the wilderness of [2] Enge'di." Then Saul took three thousand chosen men out of all Israel, and went to seek David and his men in [3] front of the Wildgoats' Rocks. And he came to the sheepfolds by the way, where there was a cave; and Saul went in to relieve himself. Now David and his men were sitting [4] in the innermost parts of the cave. And the men of David said to him, "Here is the day of which the LORD said to you, 'Behold, I will give your enemy into your hand, and you shall do to him as it shall seem good to you.'" Then David arose and stealthily cut off the skirt of Saul's [5] robe. And afterward David's heart smote him, because [6] he had cut off Saul's skirt. He said to his men, "The LORD forbid that I should do this thing to my lord, the LORD's anointed, to put forth my hand against him, seeing he is [7] the LORD's anointed." So David persuaded his men with these words, and did not permit them to attack Saul. And Saul rose up and left the cave, and went upon his way.

[8] Afterward David also arose, and went out of the cave, and called after Saul, "My lord the king!" And when Saul looked behind him, David bowed with his face to [9] the earth, and did obeisance. And David said to Saul, "Why do you listen to the words of men who say, 'Be-[10] hold, David seeks your hurt'? Lo, this day your eyes have seen how the LORD gave you today into my hand in the cave; and some bade me kill you, but I[x] spared you. I said, 'I will not put forth my hand against my lord; for [11] he is the LORD's anointed.' See, my father, see the skirt of your robe in my hand; for by the fact that I cut off the skirt of your robe, and did not kill you, you may know and see that there is no wrong or treason in my hands. I have not sinned against you, though you hunt [12] my life to take it. May the LORD judge between me and

you, may the LORD avenge me upon you; but my hand [13] shall not be against you. As the proverb of the ancients says, 'Out of the wicked comes forth wickedness'; but [14] my hand shall not be against you. After whom has the king of Israel come out? After whom do you pursue? [15] After a dead dog! After a flea! May the LORD therefore be judge, and give sentence between me and you, and see to it, and plead my cause, and deliver me from your hand."

[16] When David had finished speaking these words to Saul, Saul said, "Is this your voice, my son David?" And [17] Saul lifted up his voice and wept. He said to David, "You are more righteous than I; for you have repaid me good,

[18] whereas I have repaid you evil. And you have declared this day how you have dealt well with me, in that you did not kill me when the LORD put me into your hands. [19] For if a man finds his enemy, will he let him go away safe? So may the LORD reward you with good for what [20] you have done to me this day. And now, behold, I know that you shall surely be king, and that the kingdom of [21] Israel shall be established in your hand. Swear to me therefore by the LORD that you will not cut off my descendants after me, and that you will not destroy my [22] name out of my father's house." And David swore this to Saul. Then Saul went home; but David and his men went up to the stronghold.

25 Now Samuel died; and all Israel assembled and mourned for him, and they buried him in his house at Ramah.

Then David rose and went down to the wilderness of [2] Paran. And there was a man in Ma'on, whose business was in Carmel. The man was very rich; he had three thousand sheep and a thousand goats. He was shearing [3] his sheep in Carmel. Now the name of the man was Nabal, and the name of his wife Ab'igail. The woman was of good understanding and beautiful, but the man [4] was churlish and ill-behaved; he was a Calebite. David heard in the wilderness that Nabal was shearing his [5] sheep. So David sent ten young men; and David said to the young men, "Go up to Carmel, and go to Nabal, and [6] greet him in my name. And thus you shall salute him: 'Peace be to you, and peace be to your house, and peace [7] be to all that you have. I hear that you have shearers; now your shepherds have been with us, and we did them no harm, and they missed nothing, all the time they were [8] in Carmel. Ask your young men, and they will tell you. Therefore let my young men find favor in your eyes; for we come on a feast day. Pray, give whatever you have at hand to your servants and to your son David.'"

[9] When David's young men came, they said all this to [10] Nabal in the name of David; and then they waited. And Nabal answered David's servants, "Who is David? Who is the son of Jesse? There are many servants nowadays [11] who are breaking away from their masters. Shall I take my bread and my water and my meat that I have killed for my shearers, and give it to men who come from I do [12] not know where?" So David's young men turned away, [13] and came back and told him all this. And David said to his men, "Every man gird on his sword!" And every man of them girded on his sword; David also girded on his sword; and about four hundred men went up after David, while two hundred remained with the baggage.

[14] But one of the young men told Ab'igail, Nabal's wife, "Behold, David sent messengers out of the wilderness to [15] salute our master; and he railed at them. Yet the men were very good to us, and we suffered no harm, and we did not miss anything when we were in the fields, as long

16 as we went with them; they were a wall to us both by night and by day, all the while we were with them keep-
17 ing the sheep. Now therefore know this and consider what you should do; for evil is determined against our master and against all his house, and he is so ill-natured that one cannot speak to him."
18 Then Ab'igail made haste, and took two hundred loaves, and two skins of wine, and five sheep ready dressed, and five measures of parched grain, and a hundred clusters of raisins, and two hundred cakes of figs,
19 and laid them on asses. And she said to her young men, "Go on before me; behold, I come after you." But she
20 did not tell her husband Nabal. And as she rode on the

ass, and came down under cover of the mountain, behold, David and his men came down toward her; and she met
21 them. Now David had said, "Surely in vain have I guarded all that this fellow has in the wilderness, so that nothing was missed of all that belonged to him; and he
22 has returned me evil for good. God do so to David[y] and more also, if by morning I leave so much as one male of all who belong to him."
23 When Ab'igail saw David, she made haste, and alighted from the ass, and fell before David on her face, and
24 bowed to the ground. She fell at his feet and said, "Upon me alone, my lord, be the guilt; pray let your handmaid speak in your ears, and hear the words of your hand-
25 maid. Let not my lord regard this ill-natured fellow, Nabal; for as his name is, so is he; Nabal[z] is his name, and folly is with him; but I your handmaid did not see
26 the young men of my lord, whom you sent. Now then, my lord, as the LORD lives, and as your soul lives, seeing the LORD has restrained you from bloodguilt, and from taking vengeance with your own hand, now then let your enemies and those who seek to do evil to my lord be as
27 Nabal. And now let this present which your servant has brought to my lord be given to the young men who follow
28 my lord. Pray forgive the trespass of your handmaid; for the LORD will certainly make my lord a sure house, because my lord is fighting the battles of the LORD; and evil shall not be found in you so long as you
29 live. If men rise up to pursue you and to seek your life, the life of my lord shall be bound in the bundle of the living in the care of the LORD your God; and the lives of your enemies he shall sling out as from the hollow of a
30 sling. And when the LORD has done to my lord according

to all the good that he has spoken concerning you, and
31 has appointed you prince over Israel, my lord shall have no cause of grief, or pangs of conscience, for having shed blood without cause or for my lord taking vengeance himself. And when the LORD has dealt well with my lord, then remember your handmaid."
32 And David said to Ab'igail, "Blessed be the LORD, the
33 God of Israel, who sent you this day to meet me! Blessed be your discretion, and blessed be you, who have kept me this day from bloodguilt and from avenging myself
34 with my own hand! For as surely as the LORD the God of Israel lives, who has restrained me from hurting you, unless you had made haste and come to meet me, truly by morning there had not been left to Nabal so much as
35 one male." Then David received from her hand what she had brought him; and he said to her, "Go up in peace to your house; see, I have hearkened to your voice, and I have granted your petition."
36 And Ab'igail came to Nabal; and, lo, he was holding a feast in his house, like the feast of a king. And Nabal's heart was merry within him, for he was very drunk; so
37 she told him nothing at all until the morning light. And in the morning, when the wine had gone out of Nabal, his wife told him these things, and his heart died within
38 him, and he became as a stone. And about ten days later the LORD smote Nabal; and he died.
39 When David heard that Nabal was dead, he said, "Blessed be the LORD who has avenged the insult I received at the hand of Nabal, and has kept back his servant from evil; the LORD has returned the evil-doing of Nabal upon his own head." Then David sent and wooed
40 Ab'igail, to make her his wife. And when the servants of David came to Ab'igail at Carmel, they said to her, "David has sent us to you to take you to him as his wife."
41 And she rose and bowed with her face to the ground, and said, "Behold, your handmaid is a servant to wash
42 the feet of the servants of my lord." And Ab'igail made haste and rose and mounted on an ass, and her five maidens attended her; she went after the messengers of David, and became his wife.
43 David also took Ahin'o-am of Jezreel; and both of
44 them became his wives. Saul had given Michal his daughter, David's wife, to Palti the son of La'ish, who was of Gallim.

26 Then the Ziphites came to Saul at Gib'e-ah, saying, "Is not David hiding himself on the hill of

2 Hachi'lah, which is on the east of Jeshi'mon?" So Saul arose and went down to the wilderness of Ziph, with three thousand chosen men of Israel, to seek David in the 3 wilderness of Ziph. And Saul encamped on the hill of Hachi'lah, which is beside the road on the east of Jeshi'-mon. But David remained in the wilderness; and when he 4 saw that Saul came after him into the wilderness, David sent out spies, and learned of a certainty that Saul had 5 come. Then David rose and came to the place where Saul had encamped; and David saw the place where Saul lay, with Abner the son of Ner, the commander of his army; Saul was lying within the encampment, while the army was encamped around him.

6 Then David said to Ahim'elech the Hittite, and to Jo'ab's brother Abi'shai the son of Zeru'iah, "Who will go down with me into the camp to Saul?" And Abi'shai 7 said, "I will go down with you." So David and Abi'shai went to the army by night; and there lay Saul sleeping within the encampment, with his spear stuck in the ground at his head; and Abner and the army lay around 8 him. Then said Abi'shai to David, "God has given your enemy into your hand this day; now therefore let me pin him to the earth with one stroke of the spear, and I will 9 not strike him twice." But David said to Abi'shai, "Do not destroy him; for who can put forth his hand against 10 the LORD's anointed, and be guiltless?" And David said, "As the LORD lives, the LORD will smite him; or his day shall come to die; or he shall go down into battle and 11 perish. The LORD forbid that I should put forth my hand against the LORD's anointed; but take now the spear that 12 is at his head, and the jar of water, and let us go." So David took the spear and the jar of water from Saul's head; and they went away. No man saw it, or knew it, nor did any awake; for they were all asleep, because a deep sleep from the LORD had fallen upon them.

13 Then David went over to the other side, and stood afar off on the top of the mountain, with a great space between 14 them; and David called to the army, and to Abner the son of Ner, saying, "Will you not answer, Abner?" Then Abner answered, "Who are you that calls to the 15 king?" And David said to Abner, "Are you not a man? Who is like you in Israel? Why then have you not kept watch over your lord the king? For one of the people 16 came in to destroy the king your lord. This thing that you have done is not good. As the LORD lives, you deserve to die, because you have not kept watch over your lord, the LORD's anointed. And now see where the king's spear is, and the jar of water that was at his head."

17 Saul recognized David's voice, and said, "Is this your voice, my son David?" And David said, "It is my voice, 18 my lord, O king." And he said, "Why does my lord pursue after his servant? For what have I done? What 19 guilt is on my hands? Now therefore let my lord the king hear the words of his servant. If it is the LORD who has

stirred you up against me, may he accept an offering; but if it is men, may they be cursed before the LORD, for they have driven me out this day that I should have no share in the heritage of the LORD, saying, 'Go, serve 20 other gods.' Now therefore, let not my blood fall to the earth away from the presence of the LORD; for the king of Israel has come out to seek my life,[a] like one who hunts a partridge in the mountains."

21 Then Saul said, "I have done wrong; return, my son David, for I will no more do you harm, because my life was precious in your eyes this day; behold, I have played 22 the fool, and have erred exceedingly." And David made answer, "Here is the spear, O king! Let one of the young 23 men come over and fetch it. The LORD rewards every man for his righteousness and his faithfulness; for the LORD gave you into my hand today, and I would not put forth 24 my hand against the LORD's anointed. Behold, as your life was precious this day in my sight, so may my life be precious in the sight of the LORD, and may he deliver 25 me out of all tribulation." Then Saul said to David, "Blessed be you, my son David! You will do many things and will succeed in them." So David went his way, and Saul returned to his place.

PHILISTINES WAR AGAINST SAUL

27 And David said in his heart, "I shall now perish one day by the hand of Saul; there is nothing better for me than that I should escape to the land of the Philistines; then Saul will despair of seeking me any longer within the borders of Israel, and I shall escape 2 out of his hand." So David arose and went over, he and the six hundred men who were with him, to A'chish the 3 son of Ma'och, king of Gath. And David dwelt with A'chish at Gath, he and his men, every man with his household, and David with his two wives, Ahin'o-am of 4 Jezreel, and Ab'igail of Carmel, Nabal's widow. And when it was told Saul that David had fled to Gath, he sought for him no more.

5 Then David said to A'chish, "If I have found favor in your eyes, let a place be given me in one of the country towns, that I may dwell there; for why should your 6 servant dwell in the royal city with you?" So that day A'chish gave him Ziklag; therefore Ziklag has belonged 7 to the kings of Judah to this day. And the number of the days that David dwelt in the country of the Philistines was a year and four months.

8 Now David and his men went up, and made raids upon the Gesh'urites, the Gir'zites, and the Amal'ekites; for these were the inhabitants of the land from of old, as 9 far as Shur, to the land of Egypt. And David smote the land, and left neither man nor woman alive, but took away the sheep, the oxen, the asses, the camels, and the 10 garments, and came back to A'chish. When A'chish asked, "Against whom[b] have you made a raid today?" David

---

[a] Gk: Heb a flea (as in 24. 14)   [b] Gk Vg: Heb lacks whom

would say, "Against the Negeb of Judah," or "Against the Negeb of the Jerah'meelites," or, "Against the Negeb
11 of the Ken'ites." And David saved neither man nor woman alive, to bring tidings to Gath, thinking, "Lest they should tell about us, and say, 'So David has done.' " Such was his custom all the while he dwelt in the country
12 of the Philistines. And A'chish trusted David, thinking, "He has made himself utterly abhorred by his people Israel; therefore he shall be my servant always."

28 In those days the Philistines gathered their forces for war, to fight against Israel. And A'chish said to David, "Understand that you and your men are to go
2 out with me in the army." David said to A'chish, "Very well, you shall know what your servant can do." And A'chish said to David, "Very well, I will make you my bodyguard for life."
3 Now Samuel had died, and all Israel had mourned for him and buried him in Ramah, his own city. And Saul had put the mediums and the wizards out of the land.
4 The Philistines assembled, and came and encamped at Shunem; and Saul gathered all Israel, and they encamped
5 at Gilbo'a. When Saul saw the army of the Philistines, he
6 was afraid, and his heart trembled greatly. And when Saul inquired of the LORD, the LORD did not answer him,
7 either by dreams, or by Urim, or by prophets. Then Saul said to his servants, "Seek out for me a woman who is a medium, that I may go to her and inquire of her." And his servants said to him, "Behold, there is a medium at Endor."
8 So Saul disguised himself and put on other garments, and went, he and two men with him; and they came to the woman by night. And he said, "Divine for me by a spirit, and bring up for me whomever I shall name to
9 you." The woman said to him, "Surely you know what Saul has done, how he has cut off the mediums and the wizards from the land. Why then are you laying a snare
10 for my life to bring about my death?" But Saul swore to her by the LORD, "As the LORD lives, no punishment shall
11 come upon you for this thing." Then the woman said, "Whom shall I bring up for you?" He said, "Bring up
12 Samuel for me." When the woman saw Samuel, she cried out with a loud voice; and the woman said to Saul, "Why
13 have you deceived me? You are Saul." The king said to her, "Have no fear; what do you see?" And the woman said to Saul, "I see a god coming up out of the earth."
14 He said to her, "What is his appearance?" And she said, "An old man is coming up; and he is wrapped in a robe." And Saul knew that it was Samuel, and he bowed with his face to the ground, and did obeisance.
15 Then Samuel said to Saul, "Why have you disturbed me by bringing me up?" Saul answered, "I am in great distress; for the Philistines are warring against me, and God has turned away from me and answers me no more, either by prophets or by dreams; therefore I have sum-

16 moned you to tell me what I shall do." And Samuel said, "Why then do you ask me, since the LORD has turned
17 from you and become your enemy? The LORD has done to you as he spoke by me; for the LORD has torn the kingdom out of your hand, and given it to your neighbor,
18 David. Because you did not obey the voice of the LORD, and did not carry out his fierce wrath against Am'alek, therefore the LORD has done this thing to you this day.
19 Moreover the LORD will give Israel also with you into the hand of the Philistines; and tomorrow you and your sons shall be with me; the LORD will give the army of Israel also into the hand of the Philistines."
20 Then Saul fell at once full length upon the ground, filled with fear because of the words of Samuel; and there was no strength in him, for he had eaten nothing all day
21 and all night. And the woman came to Saul, and when she saw that he was terrified, she said to him, "Behold, your handmaid has hearkened to you; I have taken my life in my hand, and have hearkened to what you have
22 said to me. Now therefore, you also hearken to your handmaid; let me set a morsel of bread before you; and eat, that you may have strength when you go on your
23 way." He refused, and said, "I will not eat." But his servants, together with the woman, urged him; and he hearkened to their words. So he arose from the earth,
24 and sat upon the bed. Now the woman had a fatted calf in the house, and she quickly killed it, and she took flour,
25 and kneaded it and baked unleavened bread of it, and she put it before Saul and his servants; and they ate. Then they rose and went away that night.

29 Now the Philistines gathered all their forces at Aphek; and the Israelites were encamped by the
2 fountain which is in Jezreel. As the lords of the Philistines were passing on by hundreds and by thousands, and David and his men were passing on in the rear with
3 A'chish, the commanders of the Philistines said, "What are these Hebrews doing here?" And A'chish said to the commanders of the Philistines, "Is not this David, the servant of Saul, king of Israel, who has been with me now for days and years, and since he deserted to me I
4 have found no fault in him to this day." But the commanders of the Philistines were angry with him; and the commanders of the Philistines said to him, "Send the man back, that he may return to the place to which you have assigned him; he shall not go down with us to battle, lest in the battle he become an adversary to us. For how

could this fellow reconcile himself to his lord? Would it
5 not be with the heads of the men here? Is not this David, of whom they sing to one another in dances,

'Saul has slain his thousands,
and David his ten thousands'?"

6 Then A'chish called David and said to him, "As the LORD lives, you have been honest, and to me it seems right that you should march out and in with me in the campaign; for I have found nothing wrong in you from the day of your coming to me to this day. Nevertheless
7 the lords do not approve of you. So go back now; and go peaceably, that you may not displease the lords of the
8 Philistines." And David said to A'chish, "But what have I done? What have you found in your servant from the day I entered your service until now, that I may not go
9 and fight against the enemies of my lord the king?" And A'chish made answer to David, "I know that you are as blameless in my sight as an angel of God; nevertheless the commanders of the Philistines have said, 'He shall not
10 go up with us to the battle.' Now then rise early in the morning with the servants of your lord who came with you; and start early in the morning, and depart as soon
11 as you have light." So David set out with his men early in the morning, to return to the land of the Philistines. But the Philistines went up to Jezreel.

30 Now when David and his men came to Ziklag on the third day, the Amal'ekites had made a raid upon the Negeb and upon Ziklag. They had overcome Ziklag,
2 and burned it with fire, and taken captive the women and all c who were in it, both small and great; they killed no
3 one, but carried them off, and went their way. And when David and his men came to the city, they found it burned with fire, and their wives and sons and daughters taken
4 captive. Then David and the people who were with him raised their voices and wept, until they had no more
5 strength to weep. David's two wives also had been taken captive, Ahin'o-am of Jezreel, and Ab'igail the widow of
6 Nabal of Carmel. And David was greatly distressed; for the people spoke of stoning him, because all the people were bitter in soul, each for his sons and daughters. But David strengthened himself in the LORD his God.
7 And David said to Abi'athar the priest, the son of Ahim'elech, "Bring me the ephod." So Abi'athar brought
8 the ephod to David. And David inquired of the LORD, "Shall I pursue after this band? Shall I overtake them?" He answered him, "Pursue; for you shall surely over-
9 take and shall surely rescue." So David set out, and the six hundred men who were with him, and they came to the brook Besor, where those stayed who were left be-
10 hind. But David went on with the pursuit, he and four hundred men; two hundred stayed behind, who were too exhausted to cross the brook Besor.
11 They found an Egyptian in the open country, and brought him to David; and they gave him bread and he

12 ate, they gave him water to drink, and they gave him a piece of a cake of figs and two clusters of raisins. And when he had eaten, his spirit revived; for he had not eaten bread or drunk water for three days and three nights.
13 And David said to him, "To whom do you belong? And where are you from?" He said, "I am a young man of Egypt, servant to an Amal'ekite; and my master left me
14 behind because I fell sick three days ago. We had made a raid upon the Negeb of the Cher'ethites and upon that which belongs to Judah and upon the Negeb of Caleb;
15 and we burned Ziklag with fire." And David said to him, "Will you take me down to this band?" And he said, "Swear to me by God, that you will not kill me, or deliver me into the hands of my master, and I will take you down to this band."
16 And when he had taken him down, behold, they were spread abroad over all the land, eating and drinking and dancing, because of all the great spoil they had taken from the land of the Philistines and from the land of
17 Judah. And David smote them from twilight until the evening of the next day; and not a man of them escaped, except four hundred young men, who mounted camels
18 and fled. David recovered all that the Amal'ekites had
19 taken; and David rescued his two wives. Nothing was missing, whether small or great, sons or daughters, spoil or anything that had been taken; David brought back all.
20 David also captured all the flocks and herds; and the people drove those cattle before him,d and said, "This is David's spoil."
21 Then David came to the two hundred men, who had been too exhausted to follow David, and who had been left at the brook Besor; and they went out to meet David and to meet the people who were with him; and when
22 David drew near to the people he saluted them. Then all the wicked and base fellows among the men who had gone with David said, "Because they did not go with us, we will not give them any of the spoil which we have re-covered, except that each man may lead away his wife
23 and children, and depart." But David said, "You shall not do so, my brothers, with what the LORD has given us; he has preserved us and given into our hand the band
24 that came against us. Who would listen to you in this matter? For as his share is who goes down into the battle, so shall his share be who stays by the baggage;
25 they shall share alike." And from that day forward he made it a statute and an ordinance for Israel to this day.
26 When David came to Ziklag, he sent part of the spoil to his friends, the elders of Judah, saying, "Here is a present for you from the spoil of the enemies of the
27 LORD;" it was for those in Bethel, in Ramoth of the
28 Negeb, in Jattir, in Aro'er, in Siphmoth, in Eshtemo'a,
29 in Racal, in the cities of the Jerah'meelites, in the cities
30 of the Ken'ites, in Hormah, in Borash'an, in A'thach,

---

c Gk: Heb lacks and all   d Cn: Heb they drove before those cattle

31 in Hebron, for all the places where David and his men had roamed.

31 Now the Philistines fought against Israel; and the men of Israel fled before the Philistines, and fell 2 slain on Mount Gilbo'a. And the Philistines overtook Saul and his sons; and the Philistines slew Jonathan and 3 Abin'adab and Mal'chishu'a, the sons of Saul. The battle pressed hard upon Saul, and the archers found him; and 4 he was badly wounded by the archers. Then Saul said to his armor-bearer, "Draw your sword, and thrust me through with it, lest these uncircumcised come and thrust me through, and make sport of me." But his armor-bearer would not; for he feared greatly. Therefore Saul 5 took his own sword, and fell upon it. And when his armor-bearer saw that Saul was dead, he also fell upon 6 his sword, and died with him. Thus Saul died, and his three sons, and his armor-bearer, and all his men, on the 7 same day together. And when the men of Israel who were on the other side of the valley and those beyond the Jordan saw that the men of Israel had fled and that Saul and his sons were dead, they forsook their cities and fled; and the Philistines came and dwelt in them.

8 On the morrow, when the Philistines came to strip the slain, they found Saul and his three sons fallen on Mount 9 Gilbo'a. And they cut off his head, and stripped off his armor, and sent messengers throughout the land of the Philistines, to carry the good news to their idols [e] and 10 to the people. They put his armor in the temple of Ash'taroth; and they fastened his body to the wall of Beth-11 shan. But when the inhabitants of Ja'besh-gil'ead heard 12 what the Philistines had done to Saul, all the valiant men arose, and went all night, and took the body of Saul and the bodies of his sons from the wall of Beth-shan; and 13 they came to Jabesh and burnt them there. And they took their bones and buried them under the tamarisk tree in Jabesh, and fasted seven days.

e Gk Compare 1 Ch 10. 9: Heb *to the house of their idols*

INTRODUCTION TO

THE SECOND BOOK OF

SAMUEL

The Second Book of Samuel tells how the handsome hero David, anointed by Samuel, became king of Israel. As a lad David used to sing and play music for King Saul when he was ill. Second Samuel also contains the beautiful but sad song of David about the death of Saul and Jonathan (2 Samuel 1. 17-27). This book tells of many daring adventures of David, including the story of how he captured Jerusalem and made it the capital city of his kingdom.

The writer does not hide the evil-doing of King David, but he also tells how David sought God's forgiveness when the brave prophet Nathan condemned him for his sin. When he repented, God enabled him to do many good things for his people. Many of the songs in the Book of Psalms are attributed to David. Psalm 32 is believed to be the prayer of repentance King David offered after the prophet Nathan had confronted him.

The stories told in First and Second Samuel were gathered into their present form probably about 550 B.C. They are really one continuous account of the early Hebrew kingdom. The writing was divided because the scroll or sheepskin on which it was written would have been too large to handle all in one roll.

THE SECOND BOOK OF

SAMUEL

DAVID, KING AT HEBRON

1 After the death of Saul, when David had returned from the slaughter of the Amal'ekites, David remained ² two days in Ziklag; and on the third day, behold, a man came from Saul's camp, with his clothes rent and earth upon his head. And when he came to David, he fell to the ³ ground and did obeisance. David said to him, "Where do you come from?" And he said to him, "I have escaped ⁴ from the camp of Israel." And David said to him, "How did it go? Tell me." And he answered, "The people have fled from the battle, and many of the people also have fallen and are dead; and Saul and his son Jonathan are ⁵ also dead." Then David said to the young man who told him, "How do you know that Saul and his son Jonathan ⁶ are dead?" And the young man who told him said, "By chance I happened to be on Mount Gilbo'a; and there was Saul leaning upon his spear; and lo, the chariots and ⁷ the horsemen were close upon him. And when he looked behind him, he saw me, and called to me. And I answered, ⁸ 'Here I am.' And he said to me, 'Who are you?' I an- ⁹ swered him, 'I am an Amal'ekite.' And he said to me,

'Stand beside me and slay me; for anguish has seized ¹⁰ me, and yet my life still lingers.' So I stood beside him, and slew him, because I was sure that he could not live after he had fallen; and I took the crown which was on his head and the armlet which was on his arm, and I have brought them here to my lord."

11 Then David took hold of his clothes, and rent them; ¹² and so did all the men who were with him; and they mourned and wept and fasted until evening for Saul and for Jonathan his son and for the people of the Lord and for the house of Israel, because they had fallen by the ¹³ sword. And David said to the young man who told him, "Where do you come from?" And he answered, "I am ¹⁴ the son of a sojourner, an Amal'ekite." David said to him, "How is it you were not afraid to put forth your hand ¹⁵ to destroy the Lord's anointed?" Then David called one of the young men and said, "Go, fall upon him." And he ¹⁶ smote him so that he died. And David said to him, "Your blood be upon your head; for your own mouth has testified against you, saying, 'I have slain the Lord's anointed.'"

David's Dirge

17 And David lamented with this lamentation over Saul
18 and Jonathan his son, and he said it ᵃ should be taught
to the people of Judah; behold, it is written in the Book
of Jashar.ᵇ He said:
19 "Thy glory, O Israel, is slain upon thy high places!
  How are the mighty fallen!
20 Tell it not in Gath,
    publish it not in the streets of Ash′kelon;
  lest the daughters of the Philistines rejoice,
    lest the daughters of the uncircumcised exult.

21 "Ye mountains of Gilbo′a,
    let there be no dew or rain upon you,
    nor upsurging of the deep! ᶜ
  For there the shield of the mighty was defiled,
    the shield of Saul, not anointed with oil.

22 "From the blood of the slain,
    from the fat of the mighty,
  the bow of Jonathan turned not back,
    and the sword of Saul returned not empty.

23 "Saul and Jonathan, beloved and lovely!
    In life and in death they were not divided;
  they were swifter than eagles,
    they were stronger than lions.

24 "Ye daughters of Israel, weep over Saul,
    who clothed you daintily in scarlet,
  who put ornaments of gold upon your apparel.

25 "How are the mighty fallen
    in the midst of the battle!

  "Jonathan lies slain upon thy high places.
26 I am distressed for you, my brother Jonathan;
  very pleasant have you been to me;
    your love to me was wonderful,
    passing the love of women.

27 "How are the mighty fallen,
    and the weapons of war perished!"

2 After this David inquired of the LORD, "Shall I go
up into any of the cities of Judah?" And the LORD
said to him, "Go up." David said, "To which shall I go
2 up?" And he said, "To Hebron." So David went up
there, and his two wives also, Ahin′o-am of Jezreel, and
3 Ab′igail the widow of Nabal of Carmel. And David
brought up his men who were with him, every one with
his household; and they dwelt in the towns of Hebron.
4 And the men of Judah came, and there they anointed
David king over the house of Judah.

When they told David, "It was the men of Ja′besh-gil′-
5 ead who buried Saul," David sent messengers to the men
of Ja′besh-gil′ead, and said to them, "May you be blessed
by the LORD, because you showed this loyalty to Saul
6 your lord, and buried him! Now may the LORD show
steadfast love and faithfulness to you! And I will do
7 good to you because you have done this thing. Now
therefore let your hands be strong, and be valiant; for
Saul your lord is dead, and the house of Judah has
anointed me king over them."

8 Now Abner the son of Ner, commander of Saul's army,
had taken Ish-bo′sheth the son of Saul, and brought him
9 over to Mahana′im; and he made him king over Gilead
and the Ash′urites and Jezreel and E′phraim and Benja-
10 min and all Israel. Ish-bo′sheth, Saul's son, was forty
years old when he began to reign over Israel, and he
reigned two years. But the house of Judah followed
11 David. And the time that David was king in Hebron over
the house of Judah was seven years and six months.
12 Abner the son of Ner, and the servants of Ish-bo′sheth
the son of Saul, went out from Mahana′im to Gibeon.
13 And Jo′ab the son of Zeru′iah, and the servants of David,
went out and met them at the pool of Gibeon; and they
sat down, the one on the one side of the pool, and the
14 other on the other side of the pool. And Abner said to
Jo′ab, "Let the young men arise and play before us."
15 And Jo′ab said, "Let them arise." Then they arose and
passed over by number, twelve for Benjamin and Ish-bo′-
sheth the son of Saul, and twelve of the servants of David.
16 And each caught his opponent by the head, and thrust
his sword in his opponent's side; so they fell down together. Therefore that place was called Hel′kath-hazzu′-
17 rim,ᵈ which is at Gibeon. And the battle was very fierce
that day; and Abner and the men of Israel were beaten
before the servants of David.
18 And the three sons of Zeru′iah were there, Jo′ab, Abi′-
shai, and As′ahel. Now As′ahel was as swift of foot as a
19 wild gazelle; and As′ahel pursued Abner, and as he went
he turned neither to the right hand nor to the left from
20 following Abner. Then Abner looked behind him and
said, "Is it you, As′ahel?" And he answered, "It is I."
21 Abner said to him, "Turn aside to your right hand or to
your left, and seize one of the young men, and take his
spoil." But As′ahel would not turn aside from following

ᵃ Gk: Heb *the Bow*   ᵇ Or *The upright*   ᶜ Cn: Heb *fields of offerings*   ᵈ That is *the field of sword-edges*

22 him. And Abner said again to As'ahel, "Turn aside from following me; why should I smite you to the ground? How then could I lift up my face to your brother Jo'ab?" 23 But he refused to turn aside; therefore Abner smote him in the belly with the butt of his spear, so that the spear came out at his back; and he fell there, and died where he was. And all who came to the place where As'ahel had fallen and died, stood still.

24 But Jo'ab and Abi'shai pursued Abner; and as the sun was going down they came to the hill of Ammah, which lies before Gi'ah on the way to the wilderness of Gibeon. 25 And the Benjaminites gathered themselves together behind Abner, and became one band, and took their stand 26 on the top of a hill. Then Abner called to Jo'ab, "Shall the sword devour for ever? Do you not know that the end will be bitter? How long will it be before you bid your 27 people turn from the pursuit of their brethren?" And Jo'ab said, "As God lives, if you had not spoken, surely the men would have given up the pursuit of their brethren 28 in the morning." So Jo'ab blew the trumpet; and all the men stopped, and pursued Israel no more, nor did they fight any more.

29 And Abner and his men went all that night through the Arabah; they crossed the Jordan, and marching the 30 whole forenoon they came to Mahana'im. Jo'ab returned from the pursuit of Abner; and when he had gathered all the people together, there were missing of David's 31 servants nineteen men besides As'ahel. But the servants of David had slain of Benjamin three hundred and sixty of 32 Abner's men. And they took up As'ahel, and buried him in the tomb of his father, which was at Bethlehem. And Jo'ab and his men marched all night, and the day broke upon them at Hebron.

3 There was a long war between the house of Saul and the house of David; and David grew stronger and stronger, while the house of Saul became weaker and weaker.

2 And sons were born to David at Hebron: his first-born 3 was Amnon, of Ahin'o-am of Jezreel; and his second, Chil'e-ab, of Ab'igail the widow of Nabal of Carmel; and the third, Ab'salom the son of Ma'acah the daughter of 4 Talmai king of Geshur; and the fourth, Adoni'jah the son of Haggith; and the fifth, Shephati'ah the son of 5 Abi'tal; and the sixth, Ith're-am, of Eglah, David's wife. These were born to David in Hebron.

6 While there was war between the house of Saul and the house of David, Abner was making himself strong in 7 the house of Saul. Now Saul had a concubine, whose name was Rizpah, the daughter of Ai'ah; and Ish-bo'-sheth said to Abner, "Why have you gone in to my 8 father's concubine?" Then Abner was very angry over the words of Ish-bo'sheth, and said, "Am I a dog's head of Judah? This day I keep showing loyalty to the house

e Gk: Heb *where he was*

of Saul your father, to his brothers, and to his friends, and have not given you into the hand of David; and yet you charge me today with a fault concerning a woman. 9 God do so to Abner, and more also, if I do not accomplish 10 for David what the LORD has sworn to him, to transfer the kingdom from the house of Saul, and set up the throne of David over Israel and over Judah, from Dan 11 to Beer-sheba." And Ish-bo'sheth could not answer Abner another word, because he feared him.

12 And Abner sent messengers to David at Hebron,e saying, "To whom does the land belong? Make your covenant with me, and behold, my hand shall be with 13 you to bring over all Israel to you." And he said, "Good; I will make a covenant with you; but one thing I require of you; that is, you shall not see my face, unless you first bring Michal, Saul's daughter, when you come to see my 14 face." Then David sent messengers to Ish-bo'sheth Saul's son, saying, "Give me my wife Michal, whom I betrothed at the price of a hundred foreskins of the Philistines." 15 And Ish-bo'sheth sent, and took her from her husband 16 Pal'ti-el the son of La'ish. But her husband went with her, weeping after her all the way to Bahu'rim. Then Abner said to him, "Go, return"; and he returned.

17 And Abner conferred with the elders of Israel, saying, "For some time past you have been seeking David as 18 king over you. Now then bring it about; for the LORD has promised David, saying, 'By the hand of my servant David I will save my people Israel from the hand of the Philistines, and from the hand of all their enemies.'" 19 Abner also spoke to Benjamin; and then Abner went to tell David at Hebron all that Israel and the whole house of Benjamin thought good to do.

20 When Abner came with twenty men to David at Hebron, David made a feast for Abner and the men who 21 were with him. And Abner said to David, "I will arise and go, and will gather all Israel to my lord the king, that they may make a covenant with you, and that you may reign over all that your heart desires." So David sent Abner away; and he went in peace.

22 Just then the servants of David arrived with Jo'ab from a raid, bringing much spoil with them. But Abner was not with David at Hebron, for he had sent him away, 23 and he had gone in peace. When Jo'ab and all the army that was with him came, it was told Jo'ab, "Abner the son of Ner came to the king, and he has let him go, and

24 he has gone in peace." Then Jo'ab went to the king and said, "What have you done? Behold, Abner came to you; why is it that you have sent him away, so that he 25 is gone? You know that Abner the son of Ner came to deceive you, and to know your going out and your coming in, and to know all that you are doing."

26 When Jo'ab came out from David's presence, he sent messengers after Abner, and they brought him back from the cistern of Sirah; but David did not know about it. 27 And when Abner returned to Hebron, Jo'ab took him aside into the midst of the gate to speak with him private- ly, and there he smote him in the belly, so that he died, 28 for the blood of As'ahel his brother. Afterward, when David heard of it, he said, "I and my kingdom are for ever guiltless before the LORD for the blood of Abner the 29 son of Ner. May it fall upon the head of Jo'ab, and upon all his father's house; and may the house of Jo'ab never be without one who has a discharge, or who is leprous, or who holds a spindle, or who is slain by the sword, or 30 who lacks bread!" So Jo'ab and Abi'shai his brother slew Abner, because he had killed their brother As'ahel in the battle at Gibeon.

31 Then David said to Jo'ab and to all the people who were with him, "Rend your clothes, and gird on sack- cloth, and mourn before Abner." And King David 32 followed the bier. They buried Abner at Hebron; and the king lifted up his voice and wept at the grave of 33 Abner; and all the people wept. And the king lamented for Abner, saying,

"Should Abner die as a fool dies?
34 Your hands were not bound,
  your feet were not fettered;
as one falls before the wicked
  you have fallen."

35 And all the people wept again over him. Then all the people came to persuade David to eat bread while it was yet day; but David swore, saying, "God do so to me and more also, if I taste bread or anything else till the sun 36 goes down!" And all the people took notice of it, and it pleased them; as everything that the king did pleased all 37 the people. So all the people and all Israel understood that day that it had not been the king's will to slay Abner 38 the son of Ner. And the king said to his servants, "Do you not know that a prince and a great man has fallen 39 this day in Israel? And I am this day weak, though anointed king; these men the sons of Zeru'iah are too hard for me. The LORD requite the evildoer according to his wickedness!"

4 When Ish-bo'sheth, Saul's son, heard that Abner had died at Hebron, his courage failed, and all Israel 2 was dismayed. Now Saul's son had two men who were captains of raiding bands; the name of the one was Ba'anah, and the name of the other Rechab, sons of Rimmon a man of Benjamin from Be-er'oth (for Be-er'- 3 oth also is reckoned to Benjamin; the Be-er'othites fled to Gitta'im, and have been sojourners there to this day). 4 Jonathan, the son of Saul, had a son who was crippled in his feet. He was five years old when the news about Saul and Jonathan came from Jezreel; and his nurse took him up, and fled; and, as she fled in her haste, he fell, and became lame. And his name was Mephib'osheth. 5 Now the sons of Rimmon the Be-er'othite, Rechab and Ba'anah, set out, and about the heat of the day they came to the house of Ish-bo'sheth, as he was taking his noon- 6 day rest. And behold, the doorkeeper of the house had been cleaning wheat, but she grew drowsy and slept; so 7 Rechab and Ba'anah his brother slipped in.f When they came into the house, as he lay on his bed in his bed- chamber, they smote him, and slew him, and beheaded him. They took his head, and went by the way of the 8 Arabah all night, and brought the head of Ish-bo'sheth to David at Hebron. And they said to the king, "Here is the head of Ish-bo'sheth, the son of Saul, your enemy, who sought your life; the LORD has avenged my lord the 9 king this day on Saul and on his offspring." But David answered Rechab and Ba'anah his brother, the sons of Rimmon the Be-er'othite, "As the LORD lives, who has 10 redeemed my life out of every adversity, when one told me, 'Behold, Saul is dead,' and thought he was bringing good news, I seized him and slew him at Ziklag, which 11 was the reward I gave him for his news. How much more, when wicked men have slain a righteous man in his own house upon his bed, shall I not now require his blood at

12 your hand, and destroy you from the earth?" And David commanded his young men, and they killed them, and cut off their hands and feet, and hanged them beside the pool at Hebron. But they took the head of Ish-bo'sheth, and buried it in the tomb of Abner at Hebron.

DAVID, KING AT JERUSALEM

5 Then all the tribes of Israel came to David at Hebron, and said, "Behold, we are your bone and 2 flesh. In times past, when Saul was king over us, it was you that led out and brought in Israel; and the LORD said to you, 'You shall be shepherd of my people Israel, and 3 you shall be prince over Israel.'" So all the elders of Israel came to the king at Hebron; and King David made a covenant with them at Hebron before the LORD, and

f Gk: Heb 6 And hither they came into the midst of the house fetching wheat; and they smote him in the belly; and Rechab and Baanah his brother escaped

4 they anointed David king over Israel. David was thirty years old when he began to reign, and he reigned forty 5 years. At Hebron he reigned over Judah seven years and six months; and at Jerusalem he reigned over all Israel and Judah thirty-three years.

6 And the king and his men went to Jerusalem against the Jeb'usites, the inhabitants of the land, who said to David, "You will not come in here, but the blind and the lame will ward you off"—thinking, "David cannot come 7 in here." Nevertheless David took the stronghold of Zion, 8 that is, the city of David. And David said on that day, "Whoever would smite the Jeb'usites, let him get up the water shaft to attack the lame and the blind, who are

hated by David's soul." Therefore it is said, "The blind 9 and the lame shall not come into the house." And David dwelt in the stronghold, and called it the city of David. And David built the city round about from the Millo 10 inward. And David became greater and greater, for the LORD, the God of hosts, was with him.

11 And Hiram king of Tyre sent messengers to David, and cedar trees, also carpenters and masons who built David 12 a house. And David perceived that the LORD had established him king over Israel, and that he had exalted his kingdom for the sake of his people Israel.

13 And David took more concubines and wives from Jerusalem, after he came from Hebron; and more sons 14 and daughters were born to David. And these are the names of those who were born to him in Jerusalem: 15 Sham'mu-a, Shobab, Nathan, Solomon, Ibhar, Eli'shu-a, 16 Nepheg, Japhi'a, Elish'ama, Eli'ada, and Eliph'elet.

17 When the Philistines heard that David had been anointed king over Israel, all the Philistines went up in search of David; but David heard of it and went down 18 to the stronghold. Now the Philistines had come and 19 spread out in the valley of Reph'aim. And David inquired of the LORD, "Shall I go up against the Philistines? Wilt thou give them into my hand?" And the LORD said to David, "Go up; for I will certainly give the Philistines 20 into your hand." And David came to Ba'al-pera'zim, and David defeated them there; and he said, "The LORD has broken through[g] my enemies before me, like a bursting flood." Therefore the name of that place is called Ba'al-21 pera'zim.[h] And the Philistines left their idols there, and David and his men carried them away.

22 And the Philistines came up yet again, and spread

23 out in the valley of Reph'aim. And when David inquired of the LORD, he said, "You shall not go up; go around to their rear, and come upon them opposite the balsam 24 trees. And when you hear the sound of marching in the tops of the balsam trees, then bestir yourself; for then the LORD has gone out before you to smite the army of 25 the Philistines." And David did as the LORD commanded him, and smote the Philistines from Geba to Gezer.

The Ark Brought to Jerusalem

6 David again gathered all the chosen men of Israel, 2 thirty thousand. And David arose and went with all the people who were with him from Ba'ale-judah, to bring up from there the ark of God, which is called by the name of the LORD of hosts who sits enthroned on the 3 cherubim. And they carried the ark of God upon a new cart, and brought it out of the house of Abin'adab which was on the hill; and Uzzah and Ahi'o,[i] the sons of 4 Abin'adab, were driving the new cart[j] with the ark of 5 God; and Ahi'o[i] went before the ark. And David and all the house of Israel were making merry before the LORD with all their might, with songs[k] and lyres and harps and tambourines and castanets and cymbals.

6 And when they came to the threshing floor of Nacon, Uzzah put out his hand to the ark of God and took hold 7 of it, for the oxen stumbled. And the anger of the LORD was kindled against Uzzah; and God smote him there because he put forth his hand to the ark;[l] and he died 8 there beside the ark of God. And David was angry because the LORD had broken forth upon Uzzah; and that 9 place is called Pe'rez-uz'zah,[m] to this day. And David was afraid of the LORD that day; and he said, "How can the 10 ark of the LORD come to me?" So David was not willing to take the ark of the LORD into the city of David; but David took it aside to the house of O'bed-e'dom the 11 Gittite. And the ark of the LORD remained in the house of O'bed-e'dom the Gittite three months; and the LORD blessed O'bed-e'dom and all his household.

12 And it was told King David, "The LORD has blessed the household of O'bed-e'dom and all that belongs to him, because of the ark of God." So David went and brought up the ark of God from the house of O'bed-e'dom to the 13 city of David with rejoicing; and when those who bore the ark of the LORD had gone six paces, he sacrificed an 14 ox and a fatling. And David danced before the LORD with all his might; and David was girded with a linen 15 ephod. So David and all the house of Israel brought up the ark of the LORD with shouting, and with the sound of the horn.

16 As the ark of the LORD came into the city of David, Michal the daughter of Saul looked out of the window, and saw King David leaping and dancing before the 17 LORD; and she despised him in her heart. And they

g Heb *paraz*   h That is *Lord of breaking through*   i Or *and his brother*
j Compare Gk: Heb *the new cart, and brought it out of the house of Abinadab which was on the hill*   k Gk 1 Ch 13. 8: Heb *fir-trees*
l 1 Ch 13. 10: Heb uncertain   m That is *The breaking forth upon Uzzah*

brought in the ark of the LORD, and set it in its place, inside the tent which David had pitched for it; and David offered burnt offerings and peace offerings before 18 the LORD. And when David had finished offering the burnt offerings and the peace offerings, he blessed the 19 people in the name of the LORD of hosts, and distributed among all the people, the whole multitude of Israel, both men and women, to each a cake of bread, a portion of meat,[n] and a cake of raisins. Then all the people departed, each to his house.

20 And David returned to bless his household. But Michal the daughter of Saul came out to meet David, and said, "How the king of Israel honored himself today, uncovering himself today before the eyes of his servants' maids, as one of the vulgar fellows shamelessly uncovers 21 himself!" And David said to Michal, "It was before the LORD, who chose me above your father, and above all his house, to appoint me as prince over Israel, the people of the LORD—and I will make merry before the LORD. 22 I will make myself yet more contemptible than this, and I will be abased in your[o] eyes; but by the maids of whom you have spoken, by them I shall be held in 23 honor." And Michal the daughter of Saul had no child to the day of her death.

Nathan's Prophecy

7 Now when the king dwelt in his house, and the LORD had given him rest from all his enemies round about, 2 the king said to Nathan the prophet, "See now, I dwell in a house of cedar, but the ark of God dwells in a tent." 3 And Nathan said to the king, "Go, do all that is in your heart; for the LORD is with you."

4 But that same night the word of the LORD came to 5 Nathan, "Go and tell my servant David, 'Thus says the 6 LORD: Would you build me a house to dwell in? I have not dwelt in a house since the day I brought up the people of Israel from Egypt to this day, but I have been 7 moving about in a tent for my dwelling. In all places where I have moved with all the people of Israel, did I speak a word with any of the judges[p] of Israel, whom I commanded to shepherd my people Israel, saying, "Why

8 have you not built me a house of cedar?"' Now therefore thus you shall say to my servant David, 'Thus says the LORD of hosts, I took you from the pasture, from following the sheep, that you should be prince over my people 9 Israel; and I have been with you wherever you went, and have cut off all your enemies from before you; and I will make for you a great name, like the name of the 10 great ones of the earth. And I will appoint a place for my people Israel, and will plant them, that they may dwell in their own place, and be disturbed no more; and 11 violent men shall afflict them no more, as formerly, from the time that I appointed judges over my people Israel; and I will give you rest from all your enemies. Moreover the LORD declares to you that the LORD will make you a 12 house. When your days are fulfilled and you lie down with your fathers, I will raise up your offspring after you, who shall come forth from your body, and I will 13 establish his kingdom. He shall build a house for my name, and I will establish the throne of his kingdom for 14 ever. I will be his father, and he shall be my son. When he commits iniquity, I will chasten him with the rod of 15 men, with the stripes of the sons of men; but I will not take[q] my steadfast love from him, as I took it from Saul, 16 whom I put away from before you. And your house and your kingdom shall be made sure for ever before me; 17 your throne shall be established for ever.'" In accordance with all these words, and in accordance with all this vision, Nathan spoke to David.

18 Then King David went in and sat before the LORD, and said, "Who am I, O Lord GOD, and what is my house, 19 that thou hast brought me thus far? And yet this was a small thing in thy eyes, O Lord GOD; thou hast spoken also of thy servant's house for a great while to come, and 20 hast shown me future generations,[r] O Lord GOD! And what more can David say to thee? For thou knowest thy 21 servant, O Lord GOD! Because of thy promise, and according to thy own heart, thou hast wrought all this 22 greatness, to make thy servant know it. Therefore thou art great, O Lord God; for there is none like thee, and there is no God besides thee, according to all that we 23 have heard with our ears. What other[s] nation on earth is like thy people Israel, whom God went to redeem to be his people, making himself a name, and doing for them[t] great and terrible things, by driving out[u] before his peo- 24 ple a nation and its gods?[v] And thou didst establish for thyself thy people Israel to be thy people for ever; and 25 thou, O LORD, didst become their God. And now, O LORD God, confirm for ever the word which thou hast spoken concerning thy servant and concerning his house, and 26 do as thou hast spoken; and thy name will be magnified for ever, saying, 'The LORD of hosts is God over Israel,' and the house of thy servant David will be established 27 before thee. For thou, O LORD of hosts, the God of

n Vg: Heb uncertain   o Gk: Heb my   p 1 Ch 17. 6: Heb tribes   q Gk Syr Vg 1 Ch 17. 13: Heb shall not depart
r Cn: Heb this is the law for man   s Gk: Heb one   t Heb you   u Gk 1 Ch 17. 21: Heb for your land
v Heb before thy people, whom thou didst redeem for thyself from Egypt, nations and its gods

Israel, hast made this revelation to thy servant, saying, 'I will build you a house'; therefore thy servant has 28 found courage to pray this prayer to thee. And now, O Lord GOD, thou art God, and thy words are true, and 29 thou hast promised this good thing to thy servant; now therefore may it please thee to bless the house of thy servant, that it may continue for ever before thee; for thou, O Lord GOD, hast spoken, and with thy blessing shall the house of thy servant be blessed for ever."

8 After this David defeated the Philistines and subdued them, and David took Meth'eg-am'mah out of the hand of the Philistines.

2 And he defeated Moab, and measured them with a line, making them lie down on the ground; two lines he measured to be put to death, and one full line to be spared. And the Moabites became servants to David and brought tribute.

3 David also defeated Hadade'zer the son of Rehob, king of Zobah, as he went to restore his power at the 4 river Eu-phra'tes. And David took from him a thousand and seven hundred horsemen, and twenty thousand foot soldiers; and David hamstrung all the chariot horses, 5 but left enough for a hundred chariots. And when the Syrians of Damascus came to help Hadade'zer king of Zobah, David slew twenty-two thousand men of the 6 Syrians. Then David put garrisons in Aram of Damascus; and the Syrians became servants to David and brought tribute. And the LORD gave victory to David 7 wherever he went. And David took the shields of gold which were carried by the servants of Hadade'zer, and 8 brought them to Jerusalem. And from Betah and from Bero'thai, cities of Hadade'zer, King David took very much bronze.

9 When To'i king of Hamath heard that David had de10 feated the whole army of Hadade'zer, To'i sent his son Joram to King David, to greet him, and to congratulate him because he had fought against Hadade'zer and defeated him; for Hadade'zer had often been at war with To'i. And Joram brought with him articles of 11 silver, of gold, and of bronze; these also King David dedicated to the LORD, together with the silver and gold which he dedicated from all the nations he subdued, 12 from Edom, Moab, the Ammonites, the Philistines, Am'alek, and from the spoil of Hadade'zer the son of Rehob, king of Zobah.

13 And David won a name for himself. When he returned, he slew eighteen thousand Edomites [w] in the Valley of 14 Salt. And he put garrisons in Edom; throughout all Edom he put garrisons, and all the Edomites became David's servants. And the LORD gave victory to David wherever he went.

15 So David reigned over all Israel; and David admin16 istered justice and equity to all his people. And Jo'ab the son of Zeru'iah was over the army; and Jehosh'17 aphat the son of Ahi'lud was recorder; and Zadok the son of Ahi'tub and Ahim'elech the son of Abi'athar 18 were priests; and Serai'ah was secretary; and Bena'iah the son of Jehoi'ada was over [x] the Cher'ethites and the Pel'ethites; and David's sons were priests.

DAVID'S PERSONAL LIFE

9 And David said, "Is there still any one left of the house of Saul, that I may show him kindness for 2 Jonathan's sake?" Now there was a servant of the house of Saul whose name was Ziba, and they called him to David; and the king said to him, "Are you Ziba?" And 3 he said, "Your servant is he." And the king said, "Is there not still some one of the house of Saul, that I may show the kindness of God to him?" Ziba said to the king, "There is still a son of Jonathan; he is crippled 4 in his feet." The king said to him, "Where is he?" And Ziba said to the king, "He is in the house of Machir the 5 son of Am'miel, at Lo-debar." Then King David sent and brought him from the house of Machir the son of 6 Am'miel, at Lo-debar. And Mephib'osheth the son of Jonathan, son of Saul, came to David, and fell on his face and did obeisance. And David said, "Mephib'7 osheth!" And he answered, "Behold, your servant." And David said to him, "Do not fear; for I will show you kindness for the sake of your father Jonathan, and I will restore to you all the land of Saul your father; 8 and you shall eat at my table always." And he did obeisance, and said, "What is your servant, that you should look upon a dead dog such as I?"

9 Then the king called Ziba, Saul's servant, and said to him, "All that belonged to Saul and to all his house 10 I have given to your master's son. And you and your sons and your servants shall till the land for him, and shall bring in the produce, that your master's son may have bread to eat; but Mephib'osheth your master's son shall always eat at my table." Now Ziba had fifteen sons 11 and twenty servants. Then Ziba said to the king, "According to all that my lord the king commands his servant, so will your servant do." So Mephib'osheth ate at 12 David's [y] table, like one of the king's sons. And Mephib'osheth had a young son, whose name was Mica. And all who dwelt in Ziba's house became Mephib'osheth's ser13 vants. So Mephib'osheth dwelt in Jerusalem; for he ate always at the king's table. Now he was lame in both his feet.

10 After this the king of the Ammonites died, and 2 Hanun his son reigned in his stead. And David said, "I will deal loyally with Hanun the son of Nahash, as his father dealt loyally with me." So David sent by his servants to console him concerning his father. And David's servants came into the land of the Ammonites. 3 But the princes of the Ammonites said to Hanun their

---

[w] Gk: Heb *returned from smiting eighteen thousand Syrians*   [x] Syr Tg Vg 20. 23; 1 Ch 18. 17: Heb lacks *was over*   [y] Gk: Heb *my*

lord, "Do you think, because David has sent comforters to you, that he is honoring your father? Has not David sent his servants to you to search the city, and to spy 4 it out, and to overthrow it?" So Hanun took David's servants, and shaved off half the beard of each, and cut off their garments in the middle, at their hips, and 5 sent them away. When it was told David, he sent to meet them, for the men were greatly ashamed. And the king said, "Remain at Jericho until your beards have grown, and then return."

6 When the Ammonites saw that they had become odious to David, the Ammonites sent and hired the Syrians of Beth-re'hob, and the Syrians of Zobah, twenty thousand foot soldiers, and the king of Ma'acah with a thousand men, and the men of Tob, twelve thou-7 sand men. And when David heard of it, he sent Jo'ab 8 and all the host of the mighty men. And the Ammonites came out and drew up in battle array at the entrance of the gate; and the Syrians of Zobah and of Rehob, and the men of Tob and Ma'acah, were by themselves in the open country.

9 When Jo'ab saw that the battle was set against him both in front and in the rear, he chose some of the picked men of Israel, and arrayed them against the 10 Syrians; the rest of his men he put in the charge of Abi'shai his brother, and he arrayed them against the 11 Ammonites. And he said, "If the Syrians are too strong for me, then you shall help me; but if the Ammonites are too strong for you, then I will come and help you. 12 Be of good courage, and let us play the man for our people, and for the cities of our God; and may the 13 LORD do what seems good to him." So Jo'ab and the people who were with him drew near to battle against 14 the Syrians; and they fled before him. And when the Ammonites saw that the Syrians fled, they likewise fled before Abi'shai, and entered the city. Then Jo'ab returned from fighting against the Ammonites, and came to Jerusalem.

15 But when the Syrians saw that they had been de-16 feated by Israel, they gathered themselves together. And Hadade'zer sent, and brought out the Syrians who were beyond the Eu-phra'tes;ᶻ and they came to Helam, with Shobach the commander of the army of Hadade'zer at 17 their head. And when it was told David, he gathered all Israel together, and crossed the Jordan, and came to Helam. And the Syrians arrayed themselves against 18 David, and fought with him. And the Syrians fled before Israel; and David slew of the Syrians the men of seven hundred chariots, and forty thousand horsemen, and wounded Shobach the commander of their army, 19 so that he died there. And when all the kings who were servants of Hadade'zer saw that they had been defeated by Israel, they made peace with Israel, and became sub-

ᶻ Heb *river*

ject to them. So the Syrians feared to help the Ammonites any more.

David and Bathsheba

11 In the spring of the year, the time when kings go forth to battle, David sent Jo'ab, and his servants with him, and all Israel; and they ravaged the Ammonites, and besieged Rabbah. But David remained at Jerusalem.

2 It happened, late one afternoon, when David arose from his couch and was walking upon the roof of the king's house, that he saw from the roof a woman bath-3 ing; and the woman was very beautiful. And David sent and inquired about the woman. And one said, "Is not this Bathshe'ba, the daughter of Eli'am, the wife of 4 Uri'ah the Hittite?" So David sent messengers, and took her; and she came to him, and he lay with her. (Now she was purifying herself from her uncleanness.) Then 5 she returned to her house. And the woman conceived; and she sent and told David, "I am with child."

6 So David sent word to Jo'ab, "Send me Uri'ah the 7 Hittite." And Jo'ab sent Uri'ah to David. When Uri'ah came to him, David asked how Jo'ab was doing, and how the people fared, and how the war prospered. 8 Then David said to Uri'ah, "Go down to your house, and wash your feet." And Uri'ah went out of the king's house, and there followed him a present from the king. 9 But Uri'ah slept at the door of the king's house with all the servants of his lord, and did not go down to his 10 house. When they told David, "Uri'ah did not go down to his house," David said to Uri'ah, "Have you not come from a journey? Why did you not go down to 11 your house?" Uri'ah said to David, "The ark and Israel and Judah dwell in booths; and my lord Jo'ab and the servants of my lord are camping in the open field; shall I then go to my house, to eat and to drink, and to lie with my wife? As you live, and as your soul lives, I 12 will not do this thing." Then David said to Uri'ah, "Remain here today also, and tomorrow I will let you de-13 part." So Uri'ah remained in Jerusalem that day, and the next. And David invited him, and he ate in his presence and drank, so that he made him drunk; and in the evening he went out to lie on his couch with the servants of his lord, but he did not go down to his house.

14 In the morning David wrote a letter to Jo'ab, and 15 sent it by the hand of Uri'ah. In the letter he wrote, "Set Uriah in the forefront of the hardest fighting, and then draw back from him, that he may be struck down, 16 and die." And as Jo'ab was besieging the city, he assigned Uriah to the place where he knew there were 17 valiant men. And the men of the city came out and fought with Jo'ab; and some of the servants of David among the people fell. Uriah the Hittite was slain also. 18 Then Jo'ab sent and told David all the news about the

19 fighting; and he instructed the messenger, "When you have finished telling all the news about the fighting to
20 the king, then, if the king's anger arises, and if he says to you, 'Why did you go so near the city to fight? Did you not know that they would shoot from the wall?
21 Who killed Abim'elech the son of Jerub'besheth? Did not a woman cast an upper millstone upon him from the wall, so that he died at Thebez? Why did you go so near the wall?' then you shall say, 'Your servant Uri'ah the Hittite is dead also.'"

22 So the messenger went, and came and told David all
23 that Jo'ab had sent him to tell. The messenger said to David, "The men gained an advantage over us, and came out against us in the field; but we drove them
24 back to the entrance of the gate. Then the archers shot at your servants from the wall; some of the king's servants are dead; and your servant Uri'ah the Hittite is
25 dead also." David said to the messenger, "Thus shall you say to Jo'ab, 'Do not let this matter trouble you, for the sword devours now one and now another; strengthen your attack upon the city, and overthrow it.' And encourage him."

26 When the wife of Uri'ah heard that Uri'ah her husband was dead, she made lamentation for her husband.

27 And when the mourning was over, David sent and brought her to his house, and she became his wife, and bore him a son. But the thing that David had done displeased the LORD.

Nathan Rebukes the King

12 And the LORD sent Nathan to David. He came to him, and said to him, "There were two men in a
2 certain city, the one rich and the other poor. The rich
3 man had very many flocks and herds; but the poor man had nothing but one little ewe lamb, which he had bought. And he brought it up, and it grew up with him and with his children; it used to eat of his morsel, and drink from his cup, and lie in his bosom, and it was
4 like a daughter to him. Now there came a traveler to the rich man, and he was unwilling to take one of his own flock or herd to prepare for the wayfarer who had come to him, but he took the poor man's lamb, and pre-
5 pared it for the man who had come to him." Then David's anger was greatly kindled against the man; and

a Heb the enemies of the LORD

he said to Nathan, "As the LORD lives, the man who has
6 done this deserves to die; and he shall restore the lamb fourfold, because he did this thing, and because he had no pity."

7 Nathan said to David, "You are the man. Thus says the LORD, the God of Israel, 'I anointed you king over Israel, and I delivered you out of the hand of Saul;
8 and I gave you your master's house, and your master's wives into your bosom, and gave you the house of Israel and of Judah; and if this were too little, I would add to
9 you as much more. Why have you despised the word of the LORD, to do what is evil in his sight? You have smitten Uri'ah the Hittite with the sword, and have taken his wife to be your wife, and have slain him with the
10 sword of the Ammonites. Now therefore the sword shall never depart from your house, because you have despised me, and have taken the wife of Uri'ah the Hittite
11 to be your wife.' Thus says the LORD, 'Behold, I will raise up evil against you out of your own house; and I will take your wives before your eyes, and give them to your neighbor, and he shall lie with your wives in
12 the sight of this sun. For you did it secretly; but I will do this thing before all Israel, and before the sun.'"
13 David said to Nathan, "I have sinned against the LORD." And Nathan said to David, "The LORD also has put away
14 your sin; you shall not die. Nevertheless, because by this deed you have utterly scorned the LORD,a the child
15 that is born to you shall die." Then Nathan went to his house.

And the LORD struck the child that Uri'ah's wife bore
16 to David, and it became sick. David therefore besought God for the child; and David fasted, and went in and
17 lay all night upon the ground. And the elders of his house stood beside him, to raise him from the ground;
18 but he would not, nor did he eat food with them. On the seventh day the child died. And the servants of David feared to tell him that the child was dead; for they said, "Behold, while the child was yet alive, we spoke to him, and he did not listen to us; how then can we say to him
19 the child is dead? He may do himself some harm." But when David saw that his servants were whispering together, David perceived that the child was dead; and David said to his servants, "Is the child dead?" They
20 said, "He is dead." Then David arose from the earth, and washed, and anointed himself, and changed his clothes; and he went into the house of the LORD, and worshiped; he then went to his own house; and when he
21 asked, they set food before him, and he ate. Then his servants said to him, "What is this thing that you have done? You fasted and wept for the child while it was alive; but when the child died, you arose and ate food."
22 He said, "While the child was still alive, I fasted and wept; for I said, 'Who knows whether the LORD will be

23 gracious to me, that the child may live?' But now he is dead; why should I fast? Can I bring him back again? I shall go to him, but he will not return to me."

24 Then David comforted his wife, Bathshe'ba, and went in to her, and lay with her; and she bore a son, and he 25 called his name Solomon. And the LORD loved him, and sent a message by Nathan the prophet; so he called his name Jedidi'ah,[b] because of the LORD.

26 Now Jo'ab fought against Rabbah of the Ammonites 27 and took the royal city. And Jo'ab sent messengers to David, and said, "I have fought against Rabbah; more-28 over, I have taken the city of waters. Now, then, gather the rest of the people together, and encamp against the city, and take it; lest I take the city, and it be called by 29 my name." So David gathered all the people together and went to Rabbah, and fought against it and took it. 30 And he took the crown of their king[c] from his head; the weight of it was a talent of gold, and in it was a precious stone; and it was placed on David's head. And he brought forth the spoil of the city, a very great 31 amount. And he brought forth the people who were in it, and set them to labor with saws and iron picks and iron axes, and made them toil at[d] the brickkilns; and

to see him, Amnon said to the king, "Pray let my sister Tamar come and make a couple of cakes in my sight, that I may eat from her hand."

7 Then David sent home to Tamar, saying, "Go to your 8 brother Amnon's house, and prepare food for him." So Tamar went to her brother Amnon's house, where he was lying down. And she took dough, and kneaded it, 9 and made cakes in his sight, and baked the cakes. And she took the pan and emptied it out before him, but he refused to eat. And Amnon said, "Send out every one 10 from me." So every one went out from him. Then Amnon said to Tamar, "Bring the food into the chamber, that I may eat from your hand." And Tamar took the cakes she had made, and brought them into the chamber 11 to Amnon her brother. But when she brought them near him to eat, he took hold of her, and said to her, "Come, 12 lie with me, my sister." She answered him, "No, my brother, do not force me; for such a thing is not done in 13 Israel; do not do this wanton folly. As for me, where could I carry my shame? And as for you, you would be as one of the wanton fools in Israel. Now therefore, I pray you, speak to the king; for he will not withhold me 14 from you." But he would not listen to her; and being

thus he did to all the cities of the Ammonites. Then David and all the people returned to Jerusalem.

TROUBLES IN DAVID'S COURT

13 Now Ab'salom, David's son, had a beautiful sister, whose name was Tamar; and after a time Amnon, 2 David's son, loved her. And Amnon was so tormented that he made himself ill because of his sister Tamar; for she was a virgin, and it seemed impossible to Amnon to 3 do anything to her. But Amnon had a friend, whose name was Jon'adab, the son of Shim'e-ah, David's 4 brother; and Jon'adab was a very crafty man. And he said to him, "O son of the king, why are you so haggard morning after morning? Will you not tell me?" Amnon said to him, "I love Tamar, my brother Ab'salom's sis-5 ter." Jon'adab said to him, "Lie down on your bed, and pretend to be ill; and when your father comes to see you, say to him, 'Let my sister Tamar come and give me bread to eat, and prepare the food in my sight, that I 6 may see it, and eat it from her hand.'" So Amnon lay down, and pretended to be ill; and when the king came

stronger than she, he forced her, and lay with her.

15 Then Amnon hated her with very great hatred; so that the hatred with which he hated her was greater than the love with which he had loved her. And Amnon said 16 to her, "Arise, be gone." But she said to him, "No, my brother; for this wrong in sending me away is greater than the other which you did to me."[e] But he would not 17 listen to her. He called the young man who served him and said, "Put this woman out of my presence, and bolt 18 the door after her." Now she was wearing a long robe with sleeves; for thus were the virgin daughters of the king clad of old.[f] So his servant put her out, and bolted 19 the door after her. And Tamar put ashes on her head, and rent the long robe which she wore; and she laid her hand on her head, and went away, crying aloud as she went.

20 And her brother Ab'salom said to her, "Has Amnon your brother been with you? Now hold your peace, my sister; he is your brother; do not take this to heart." So Tamar dwelt, a desolate woman, in her brother Ab'-21 salom's house. When King David heard of all these

b That is beloved of the LORD   c Or Milcom See Zp 1. 5   d Cn: Heb pass through
e Cn Compare Gk Vg: Heb No, for this great wrong in sending me away is (worse) than the other which you did to me
f Cn: Heb clad in robes

22 things, he was very angry. But Ab'salom spoke to Amnon neither good nor bad; for Ab'salom hated Amnon, because he had forced his sister Tamar.

23 After two full years Ab'salom had sheepshearers at Bal'al-ha'zor, which is near E'phraim, and Ab'salom in- 24 vited all the king's sons. And Ab'salom came to the king, and said, "Behold, your servant has sheepshearers; pray let the king and his servants go with your servant." 25 But the king said to Ab'salom, "No, my son, let us not all go, lest we be burdensome to you." He pressed him, 26 but he would not go but gave him his blessing. Then Ab'salom said, "If not, pray let my brother Amnon go with us." And the king said to him, "Why should he go 27 with you?" But Ab'salom pressed him until he let Am- 28 non and all the king's sons go with him. Then Ab'salom commanded his servants, "Mark when Amnon's heart is merry with wine, and when I say to you, 'Strike Amnon,' then kill him. Fear not; have I not commanded you? Be 29 courageous and be valiant." So the servants of Ab'salom did to Amnon as Ab'salom had commanded. Then all the king's sons arose, and each mounted his mule and fled.

30 While they were on the way, tidings came to David, "Ab'salom has slain all the king's sons, and not one of 31 them is left." Then the king arose, and rent his garments, and lay on the earth; and all his servants who were 32 standing by rent their garments. But Jon'adab the son of Shim'e-ah, David's brother, said, "Let not my lord suppose that they have killed all the young men the king's sons, for Amnon alone is dead, for by the command of Ab'salom this has been determined from the 33 day he forced his sister Tamar. Now therefore let not my lord the king so take it to heart as to suppose that all the king's sons are dead; for Amnon alone is dead." 34 But Ab'salom fled. And the young man who kept the watch lifted up his eyes, and looked, and behold, many people were coming from the Horona'im road g by the 35 side of the mountain. And Jon'adab said to the king, "Behold, the king's sons have come; as your servant 36 said, so it has come about." And as soon as he had finished speaking, behold, the king's sons came, and lifted up their voice and wept; and the king also and all his servants wept very bitterly.

37 But Ab'salom fled, and went to Talmai the son of Ammi'hud, king of Geshur. And David mourned for his 38 son day after day. So Ab'salom fled, and went to Geshur, 39 and was there three years. And the spirit h of the king longed to go forth to Ab'salom; for he was comforted about Amnon, seeing he was dead.

14 Now Jo'ab the son of Zeru'iah perceived that the 2 king's heart went out to Ab'salom. And Jo'ab sent to Teko'a, and fetched from there a wise woman, and said to her, "Pretend to be a mourner, and put on mourning garments; do not anoint yourself with oil, but behave like a woman who has been mourning many days for the 3 dead; and go to the king, and speak thus to him." So Jo'ab put the words in her mouth.

4 When the woman of Teko'a came to the king, she fell on her face to the ground, and did obeisance, and said, 5 "Help, O king." And the king said to her, "What is your trouble?" she answered, "Alas, I am a widow; my hus- 6 band is dead. And your handmaid had two sons, and they quarreled with one another in the field; there was no one to part them, and one struck the other and killed 7 him. And now the whole family has risen against your handmaid, and they say, 'Give up the man who struck his brother, that we may kill him for the life of his brother whom he slew'; and so they would destroy the heir also. Thus they would quench my coal which is left, and leave to my husband neither name nor remnant upon the face of the earth."

8 Then the king said to the woman, "Go to your house, 9 and I will give orders concerning you." And the woman of Teko'a said to the king, "On me be the guilt, my lord the king, and on my father's house; let the king and his 10 throne be guiltless." The king said, "If any one says anything to you, bring him to me, and he shall never 11 touch you again." Then she said, "Pray let the king invoke the LORD your God, that the avenger of blood slay no more, and my son be not destroyed." He said, "As the LORD lives, not one hair of your son shall fall to the ground."

12 Then the woman said, "Pray let your handmaid speak 13 a word to my lord the king." He said, "Speak." And the woman said, "Why then have you planned such a thing against the people of God? For in giving this decision the king convicts himself, inasmuch as the king 14 does not bring his banished one home again. We must all die, we are like water spilt on the ground, which cannot be gathered up again; but God will not take away the life of him who devises i means not to keep his 15 banished one an outcast. Now I have come to say this to my lord the king because the people have made me afraid; and your handmaid thought, 'I will speak to the king; it may be that the king will perform the request 16 of his servant. For the king will hear, and deliver his servant from the hand of the man who would destroy 17 me and my son together from the heritage of God.' And your handmaid thought, 'The word of my lord the king will set me at rest'; for my lord the king is like the angel of God to discern good and evil. The LORD your God be with you!"

18 Then the king answered the woman, "Do not hide from me anything I ask you." And the woman said, 19 "Let my lord the king speak." The king said, "Is the hand of Jo'ab with you in all this?" The woman answered and said, "As surely as you live, my lord the king, one cannot turn to the right hand or to the left

g Cn Compare Gk: Heb the road behind him   h Gk: Heb David   i Cn: Heb and he devises

from anything that my lord the king has said. It was your servant Jo'ab who bade me; it was he who put all ²⁰ these words in the mouth of your handmaid. In order to change the course of affairs your servant Jo'ab did this. But my lord has wisdom like the wisdom of the angel of God to know all things that are on the earth."

²¹ Then the king said to Jo'ab, "Behold now, I grant ²² this; go, bring back the young man Ab'salom." And Jo'ab fell on his face to the ground, and did obeisance, and blessed the king; and Jo'ab said, "Today your servant knows that I have found favor in your sight, my lord the king, in that the king has granted the request ²³ of his servant." So Jo'ab arose and went to Geshur, and ²⁴ brought Ab'salom to Jerusalem. And the king said, "Let him dwell apart in his own house; he is not to come into my presence." So Ab'salom dwelt apart in his own house, and did not come into the king's presence.

²⁵ Now in all Israel there was no one so much to be praised for his beauty as Ab'salom; from the sole of his foot to the crown of his head there was no blemish ²⁶ in him. And when he cut the hair of his head (for at the end of every year he used to cut it; when it was heavy on him, he cut it), he weighed the hair of his head, ²⁷ two hundred shekels by the king's weight. There were born to Ab'salom three sons, and one daughter whose name was Tamar; she was a beautiful woman.

²⁸ So Ab'salom dwelt two full years in Jerusalem, with- ²⁹ out coming into the king's presence. Then Ab'salom sent for Jo'ab, to send him to the king; but Jo'ab would not come to him. And he sent a second time, but Jo'ab ³⁰ would not come. Then he said to his servants, "See, Jo'ab's field is next to mine, and he has barley there; go and set it on fire." So Ab'salom's servants set the field ³¹ on fire. Then Jo'ab arose and went to Ab'salom at his house, and said to him, "Why have your servants set ³² my field on fire?" Ab'salom answered Jo'ab, "Behold, I sent word to you, 'Come here, that I may send you to the king, to ask, "Why have I come from Geshur? It would be better for me to be there still." Now therefore let me go into the presence of the king; and if there is ³³ guilt in me, let him kill me.'" Then Jo'ab went to the king, and told him; and he summoned Ab'salom. So he came to the king, and bowed himself on his face to the ground before the king; and the king kissed Ab'salom.

Absalom's Rebellion

15 After this Ab'salom got himself a chariot and ² horses, and fifty men to run before him. And Ab'salom used to rise early and stand beside the way of the gate; and when any man had a suit to come before the king for judgment, Ab'salom would call to him, and say, "From what city are you?" And when he said, "Your servant is of such and such a tribe in Israel,"

³ Ab'salom would say to him, "See, your claims are good and right; but there is no man deputed by the king to ⁴ hear you." Ab'salom said moreover, "Oh that I were judge in the land! Then every man with a suit or cause ⁵ might come to me, and I would give him justice." And whenever a man came near to do obeisance to him, he

would put out his hand, and take hold of him, and kiss ⁶ him. Thus Ab'salom did to all of Israel who came to the king for judgment; so Ab'salom stole the hearts of the men of Israel.

⁷ And at the end of four ʲ years Ab'salom said to the king, "Pray let me go and pay my vow, which I have ⁸ vowed to the LORD, in Hebron. For your servant vowed a vow while I dwelt at Geshur in Aram, saying, 'If the LORD will indeed bring me back to Jerusalem, then I ⁹ will offer worship to the LORD.'" The king said to him, ¹⁰ "Go in peace." So he arose, and went to Hebron. But Ab'salom sent secret messengers throughout all the tribes of Israel, saying, "As soon as you hear the sound of the trumpet, then say, 'Ab'salom is king at Hebron!'" ¹¹ With Ab'salom went two hundred men from Jerusalem who were invited guests, and they went in their sim- ¹² plicity, and knew nothing. And while Ab'salom was offering the sacrifices, he sent for ᵏ Ahith'ophel the Gi'lonite, David's counselor, from his city Giloh. And the conspiracy grew strong, and the people with Ab'- salom kept increasing.

¹³ And a messenger came to David, saying, "The hearts ¹⁴ of the men of Israel have gone after Ab'salom." Then David said to all his servants who were with him at Jerusalem, "Arise, and let us flee; or else there will be no escape for us from Ab'salom; go in haste, lest he overtake us quickly, and bring down evil upon us, and ¹⁵ smite the city with the edge of the sword." And the king's servants said to the king, "Behold, your servants are ready to do whatever my lord the king decides." ¹⁶ So the king went forth, and all his household after him. ¹⁷ And the king left ten concubines to keep the house. And the king went forth, and all the people after him; and ¹⁸ they halted at the last house. And all his servants passed by him; and all the Cher'ethites, and all the Pel'ethites, and all the six hundred Gittites who had followed him from Gath, passed on before the king.

¹⁹ Then the king said to It'tai the Gittite, "Why do you

ʲ Gk Syr: Heb forty   ᵏ Or sent

also go with us? Go back, and stay with the king; for you are a foreigner, and also an exile from[1] your home.
20 You came only yesterday, and shall I today make you wander about with us, seeing I go I know not where? Go back, and take your brethren with you; and may the LORD show[m] steadfast love and faithfulness to you."
21 But It'tai answered the king, "As the LORD lives, and as my lord the king lives, wherever my lord the king shall be, whether for death or for life, there also will
22 your servant be." And David said to It'tai, "Go then, pass on." So It'tai the Gittite passed on, with all his
23 men and all the little ones who were with him. And all the country wept aloud as all the people passed by, and the king crossed the brook Kidron, and all the people passed on toward the wilderness.
24 And Abi'athar came up, and lo, Zadok came also, with all the Levites, bearing the ark of the covenant of God; and they set down the ark of God, until the people
25 had all passed out of the city. Then the king said to Zadok, "Carry the ark of God back into the city. If I find favor in the eyes of the LORD, he will bring me
26 back and let me see both it and his habitation; but if he says, 'I have no pleasure in you,' behold, here I am,
27 let him do to me what seems good to him." The king also said to Zadok the priest, "Look,[n] go back to the city in peace, you and Abi'athar,[o] with your two sons, Ahim'a-az your son, and Jonathan the son of Abi'athar.
28 See, I will wait at the fords of the wilderness, until word
29 comes from you to inform me." So Zadok and Abi'athar carried the ark of God back to Jerusalem; and they remained there.
30 But David went up the ascent of the Mount of Olives, weeping as he went, barefoot and with his head covered; and all the people who were with him covered their
31 heads, and they went up, weeping as they went. And it was told David, "Ahith'ophel is among the conspirators with Ab'salom." And David said, "O LORD, I pray thee, turn the counsel of Ahith'ophel into foolishness."
32 When David came to the summit, where God was worshiped, behold, Hushai the Archite came to meet
33 him with his coat rent and earth upon his head. David said to him, "If you go on with me, you will be a
34 burden to me. But if you return to the city, and say to Ab'salom, 'I will be your servant, O king; as I have been your father's servant in time past, so now I will be your servant,' then you will defeat for me the counsel
35 of Ahith'ophel. Are not Zadok and Abi'athar the priests with you there? So whatever you hear from the king's
36 house, tell it to Zadok and Abi'athar the priests. Behold, their two sons are with them there, Ahim'a-az, Zadok's son, and Jonathan, Abi'athar's son; and by them you
37 shall send to me everything you hear." So Hushai, David's friend, came into the city, just as Ab'salom was entering Jerusalem.

16 When David had passed a little beyond the summit, Ziba the servant of Mephib'osheth met him, with a couple of asses saddled, bearing two hundred loaves of bread, a hundred bunches of raisins,
2 a hundred of summer fruits, and a skin of wine. And the king said to Ziba, "Why have you brought these?" Ziba answered, "The asses are for the king's household to ride on, the bread and summer fruit for the young men to eat, and the wine for those who faint in the
3 wilderness to drink." And the king said, "And where is your master's son?" Ziba said to the king, "Behold, he remains in Jerusalem; for he said, 'Today the house of Israel will give me back the kingdom of my father.' "
4 Then the king said to Ziba, "Behold, all that belonged to Mephib'osheth is now yours." And Ziba said, "I do obeisance; let me ever find favor in your sight, my lord the king."
5 When King David came to Bahu'rim, there came out a man of the family of the house of Saul, whose name was Shim'e-i, the son of Gera; and as he came he cursed
6 continually. And he threw stones at David, and at all the servants of King David; and all the people and all the mighty men were on his right hand and on his left.
7 And Shim'e-i said as he cursed, "Begone, begone, you

8 man of blood, you worthless fellow! The LORD has avenged upon you all the blood of the house of Saul, in whose place you have reigned; and the LORD has given the kingdom into the hand of your son Ab'salom. See, your ruin is on you; for you are a man of blood."
9 Then Abi'shai the son of Zeru'iah said to the king, "Why should this dead dog curse my lord the king? Let
10 me go over and take off his head." But the king said, "What have I to do with you, you sons of Zeru'iah? If he is cursing because the LORD has said to him, 'Curse David,' who then shall say, 'Why have you done so?' "
11 And David said to Abi'shai and to all his servants, "Behold, my own son seeks my life; how much more now may this Benjaminite! Let him alone, and let him curse;
12 for the LORD has bidden him. It may be that the LORD will look upon my affliction,[p] and that the LORD will repay
13 me with good for this cursing of me today." So David and his men went on the road, while Shim'e-i went along on the hillside opposite him and cursed as he went, and
14 threw stones at him and flung dust. And the king, and all the people who were with him, arrived weary at the Jordan;[q] and there he refreshed himself.

1 Gk Syr Vg: Heb to   m Gk: Heb lacks may the LORD show
o Cn: Heb lacks and Abiathar   p Gk Vg: Heb iniquity

n Gk: Heb Are you a seer or Do you see?
q Gk: Heb lacks at the Jordan

15 Now Ab'salom and all the people, the men of Israel,
16 came to Jerusalem, and Ahith'ophel with him. And when
Hushai the Archite, David's friend, came to Ab'salom,
Hushai said to Ab'salom, "Long live the king! Long live
17 the king!" And Ab'salom said to Hushai, "Is this your
loyalty to your friend? Why did you not go with your
18 friend?" And Hushai said to Ab'salom, "No; for whom
the Lord and this people and all the men of Israel have
19 chosen, his I will be, and with him I will remain. And
again, whom should I serve? Should it not be his son?
As I have served your father, so I will serve you."

20 Then Ab'salom said to Ahith'ophel, "Give your coun-
21 sel; what shall we do?" Ahith'ophel said to Ab'salom,
"Go in to your father's concubines, whom he has left to
keep the house; and all Israel will hear that you have
made yourself odious to your father, and the hands of all
22 who are with you will be strengthened." So they pitched
a tent for Ab'salom upon the roof; and Ab'salom went
in to his father's concubines in the sight of all Israel.
23 Now in those days the counsel which Ahith'ophel gave
was as if one consulted the oracle r of God; so was all
the counsel of Ahith'ophel esteemed, both by David and
by Ab'salom.

17 Moreover Ahith'ophel said to Ab'salom, "Let me
choose twelve thousand men, and I will set out and
2 pursue David tonight. I will come upon him while he is
weary and discouraged, and throw him into a panic; and
all the people who are with him will flee. I will strike
3 down the king only, and I will bring all the people back
to you as a bride comes home to her husband. You seek
the life of only one man, s and all the people will be at
4 peace." And the advice pleased Ab'salom and all the
elders of Israel.

5 Then Ab'salom said, "Call Hushai the Archite also, and
6 let us hear what he has to say." And when Hushai came
to Ab'salom, Ab'salom said to him, "Thus has Ahith'-
ophel spoken; shall we do as he advises? If not, you
7 speak." Then Hushai said to Ab'salom, "This time the
counsel which Ahith'ophel has given is not good."
8 Hushai said moreover, "You know that your father and
his men are mighty men, and that they are enraged, like
a bear robbed of her cubs in the field. Besides, your father
is expert in war; he will not spend the night with the
9 people. Behold, even now he has hidden himself in one of
the pits, or in some other place. And when some of the
people fall t at the first attack, whoever hears it will say,
'There has been a slaughter among the people who follow
10 Ab'salom.' Then even the valiant man, whose heart is
like the heart of a lion, will utterly melt with fear; for
all Israel knows that your father is a mighty man, and that
11 those who are with him are valiant men. But my counsel
is that all Israel be gathered to you, from Dan to Beer-
sheba, as the sand by the sea for multitude, and that you

12 go to battle in person. So we shall come upon him in some
place where he is to be found, and we shall light upon
him as the dew falls on the ground; and of him and all
13 the men with him not one will be left. If he withdraws
into a city, then all Israel will bring ropes to that city,
and we shall drag it into the valley, until not even a
14 pebble is to be found there." And Ab'salom and all the
men of Israel said, 'The counsel of Hushai the Archite is
better than the counsel of Ahith'ophel." For the Lord had
ordained to defeat the good counsel of Ahith'ophel, so
that the Lord might bring evil upon Ab'salom.

15 Then Hushai said to Zadok and Abi'athar the priests,
"Thus and so did Ahith'ophel counsel Ab'salom and the
16 elders of Israel; and thus and so have I counseled. Now
therefore send quickly and tell David, 'Do not lodge
tonight at the fords of the wilderness, but by all means
pass over; lest the king and all the people who are with
17 him be swallowed up.' " Now Jonathan and Ahim'a-az
were waiting at En-ro'gel; a maidservant used to go and
tell them, and they would go and tell King David; for

18 they must not be seen entering the city. But a lad saw
them, and told Ab'salom; so both of them went away
quickly, and came to the house of a man at Bahu'rim,
who had a well in his courtyard; and they went down
19 into it. And the woman took and spread a covering over
the well's mouth, and scattered grain upon it; and nothing
20 was known of it. When Ab'salom's servants came to the
woman at the house, they said, "Where are Ahim'a-az
and Jonathan?" And the woman said to them, "They
have gone over the brook u of water." And when they had
sought and could not find them, they returned to Jerusalem.
21 After they had gone, the men came up out of the well,
and went and told King David. They said to David,
"Arise, and go quickly over the water; for thus and so
22 has Ahith'ophel counseled against you." Then David
arose, and all the people who were with him, and they
crossed the Jordan; by daybreak not one was left who had
not crossed the Jordan.
23 When Ahith'ophel saw that his counsel was not followed, he saddled his ass, and went off home to his own
city. And he set his house in order, and hanged himself;
and he died, and was buried in the tomb of his father.
24 Then David came to Mahana'im. And Ab'salom crossed

r Heb word   s Gk: Heb like the return of the whole (is) the man whom you seek   t Or when he falls upon them
u The meaning of the Hebrew word is uncertain

25 the Jordan with all the men of Israel. Now Ab'salom had set Ama'sa over the army instead of Jo'ab. Ama'sa was the son of a man named Ithra the Ish'maelite,ᵛ who had married Ab'igal the daughter of Nahash, sister of Zeru'- 26 iah, Jo'ab's mother. And Israel and Ab'salom encamped in the land of Gilead.

27 When David came to Mahana'im, Shobi the son of Nahash from Rabbah of the Ammonites, and Machir the son of Am'mi-el from Lo'debar, and Bar-zil'lai the 28 Gileadite from Ro'gelim, brought beds, basins, and earthen vessels, wheat, barley, meal, parched grain, beans 29 and lentils,ʷ honey and curds and sheep and cheese from the herd, for David and the people with him to eat; for they said, "The people are hungry and weary and thirsty in the wilderness."

18 Then David mustered the men who were with him, and set over them commanders of thousands and 2 commanders of hundreds. And David sent forth the army, one third under the command of Jo'ab, one third under the command of Abi'shai the son of Zeru'iah, Jo'ab's brother, and one third under the command of It'tai the Gittite. And the king said to the men, "I myself will also 3 go out with you." But the men said, "You shall not go out. For if we flee, they will not care about us. If half of us die, they will not care about us. But you are worth ten thousand of us;ˣ therefore it is better that you send 4 us help from the city." The king said to them, "Whatever seems best to you I will do." So the king stood at the side of the gate, while all the army marched out by 5 hundreds and by thousands. And the king ordered Jo'ab and Abi'shai and It'tai, "Deal gently for my sake with the young man Ab'salom." And all the people heard when the king gave orders to all the commanders about Ab'- salom.

6 So the army went out into the field against Israel; and 7 the battle was fought in the forest of E'phraim. And the men of Israel were defeated there by the servants of David, and the slaughter there was great on that day, 8 twenty thousand men. The battle spread over the face of all the country; and the forest devoured more people that day than the sword.

9 And Ab'salom chanced to meet the servants of David. Ab'salom was riding upon his mule, and the mule went under the thick branches of a great oak, and his head caught fast in the oak, and he was left hangingʸ between heaven and earth, while the mule that was under him 10 went on. And a certain man saw it, and told Jo'ab, "Be- 11 hold, I saw Ab'salom hanging in an oak." Jo'ab said to the man who told him, "What, you saw him! Why then did you not strike him there to the ground? I would have been glad to give you ten pieces of silver and a girdle." 12 But the man said to Jo'ab, "Even if I felt in my hand the weight of a thousand pieces of silver, I would not put forth my hand against the king's son; for in our hearing the king commanded you and Abi'shai and It'tai, 13 'For my sake protect the young man Ab'salom.' On the other hand, if I had dealt treacherously against his lifeᶻ (and there is nothing hidden from the king), then you 14 yourself would have stood aloof." Jo'ab said, "I will not waste time like this with you."ᵃ And he took three darts in his hand, and thrust them into the heart of Ab'salom, 15 while he was still alive in the oak. And ten young men, Jo'ab's armor-bearers, surrounded Ab'salom and struck him, and killed him.

16 Then Jo'ab blew the trumpet, and the troops came back 17 from pursuing Israel; for Jo'ab restrained them. And they took Ab'salom, and threw him into a great pit in the forest, and raised over him a very great heap of stones; 18 and all Israel fled every one to his own home. Now Ab'- salom in his lifetime had taken and set up for himself the pillar which is in the King's Valley, for he said, "I have no son to keep my name in remembrance"; he called the pillar after his own name, and it is called Ab'salom's monument to this day.

19 Then said Ahi'ma-az the son of Zadok, "Let me run, and carry tidings to the king that the LORD has delivered 20 him from the power of his enemies." And Jo'ab said to him, "You are not to carry tidings today; you may carry tidings another day, but today you shall carry no tidings, 21 because the king's son is dead." Then Jo'ab said to the Cushite, "Go, tell the king what you have seen." The 22 Cushite bowed before Jo'ab, and ran. Then Ahi'ma-az the son of Zadok said again to Jo'ab, "Come what may, let me also run after the Cushite." And Jo'ab said, "Why will you run, my son, seeing that you will have no reward 23 for the tidings?" "Come what may," he said, "I will run." So he said to him, "Run." Then Ahi'ma-az ran by the way of the plain, and outran the Cushite.

24 Now David was sitting between the two gates; and the watchman went up to the roof of the gate by the wall, and when he lifted up his eyes and looked, he saw a man 25 running alone. And the watchman called out and told the king. And the king said, "If he is alone, there are tidings 26 in his mouth." And he came apace, and drew near. And the watchman saw another man running; and the watch- man called to the gate and said, "See, another man run- ning alone!" The king said, "He also brings tidings." 27 And the watchman said, "I think the running of the foremost is like the running of Ahi'ma-az the son of Zadok." And the king said, "He is a good man, and comes with good tidings."

28 Then Ahi'ma-az cried out to the king, "All is well." And he bowed before the king with his face to the earth, and said, "Blessed be the LORD your God, who has de- livered up the men who raised their hand against my lord 29 the king." And the king said, "Is it well with the young

---

ᵛ 1 Ch 2. 17: Heb *Israelite*   ʷ Heb *lentils and parched grain*
ˣ Gk Vg Symmachus: Heb *for now there are ten thousand such as we*
ᶻ Another reading is *at the risk of my life*

ʸ Gk Syr Tg: Heb *was put*
ᵃ Or *Not so, I will pierce him in your presence*

man Ab'salom?" Ahi'ma-az answered, "When Jo'ab sent your servant,[b] I saw a great tumult, but I do not know

30 what it was." And the king said, "Turn aside, and stand here." So he turned aside, and stood still.

31 And behold, the Cushite came; and the Cushite said, "Good tidings for my lord the king! For the LORD has delivered you this day from the power of all who rose up

32 against you." The king said to the Cushite, "Is it well with the young man Ab'salom?" And the Cushite answered, "May the enemies of my lord the king, and all who rise up against you for evil, be like that young man."

33 [c] And the king was deeply moved, and went up to the

chamber over the gate, and wept; and as he went, he said, "O my son Ab'salom, my son, my son Ab'salom! Would I had died instead of you, O Ab'salom, my son, my son!"

19 It was told Jo'ab, "Behold, the king is weeping

2 and mourning for Ab'salom." So the victory that day was turned into mourning for all the people; for the people heard that day, "The king is grieving for his son."

3 And the people stole into the city that day as people steal

4 in who are ashamed when they flee in battle. The king covered his face, and the king cried with a loud voice, "O my son Ab'salom, O Ab'salom, my son, my son!"

5 Then Jo'ab came into the house to the king, and said, "You have today covered with shame the faces of all your servants, who have this day saved your life, and the lives of your sons and your daughters, and the lives of

6 your wives and your concubines, because you love those who hate you and hate those who love you. For you have made it clear today that commanders and servants are nothing to you; for today I perceive that if Ab'salom were alive and all of us were dead today, then you would

7 be pleased. Now therefore arise, go out and speak kindly to your servants; for I swear by the LORD, if you do not go, not a man will stay with you this night; and this will be worse for you than all the evil that has come upon you

8 from your youth until now." Then the king arose, and took his seat in the gate. And the people were all told, "Behold, the king is sitting in the gate"; and all the people came before the king.

9 Now Israel had fled every man to his own home. And all the people were at strife throughout all the tribes of Israel, saying, "The king delivered us from the hand of our enemies, and saved us from the hand of the Philistines; and now he has fled out of the land from Ab'salom.

10 But Ab'salom, whom we anointed over us, is dead in battle. Now therefore why do you say nothing about bringing the king back?"

11 And King David sent this message to Zadok and Abi'athar the priests, "Say to the elders of Judah, 'Why should you be the last to bring the king back to his house, when the word of all Israel has come to the king? [d]

12 You are my kinsmen, you are my bone and my flesh; why then should you be the last to bring back the king?'

13 And say to Ama'sa, 'Are you not my bone and my flesh? God do so to me, and more also, if you are not com-

14 mander of my army henceforth in place of Jo'ab.'" And he swayed the heart of all the men of Judah as one man; so that they sent word to the king. "Return, both you

15 and all your servants." So the king came back to the Jordan; and Judah came to Gilgal to meet the king and to bring the king over the Jordan.

16 And Shim'e-i the son of Gera, the Benjaminite, from Bahu'rim, made haste to come down with the men of

17 Judah to meet King David; and with him were a thousand men from Benjamin. And Ziba the servant of the house of Saul, with his fifteen sons and his twenty servants,

18 rushed down to the Jordan before the king, and they crossed the ford [e] to bring over the king's household, and to do his pleasure. And Shim'e-i the son of Gera fell down before the king, as he was about to cross the Jordan,

19 and said to the king, "Let not my lord hold me guilty or remember how your servant did wrong on the day my lord the king left Jerusalem; let not the king bear it

20 in mind. For your servant knows that I have sinned; therefore, behold, I have come this day, the first of all the house of Joseph to come down to meet my lord the

21 king." Abi'shai the son of Zeru'iah answered, "Shall not Shim'e-i be put to death for this, because he cursed the

22 LORD's anointed?" But David said, "What have I to do with you, you sons of Zeru'iah, that you should this day be as an adversary to me? Shall any one be put to death in Israel this day? For do I not know that I am this day

23 king over Israel?" And the king said to Shim'e-i, "You shall not die." And the king gave him his oath.

24 And Mephib'osheth the son of Saul came down to meet the king; he had neither dressed his feet, nor trimmed his beard, nor washed his clothes, from the day the king

25 departed until the day he came back in safety. And when he came from [f] Jerusalem to meet the king, the king said to him, "Why did you not go with me, Mephib'osheth?"

26 He answered, "My lord, O king, my servant deceived me; for your servant said to him, 'Saddle an ass for me,[g] that I may ride upon it and go with the king.' For your servant

27 is lame. He has slandered your servant to my lord the king. But my lord the king is like the angel of God; do

28 therefore what seems good to you. For all my father's house were but men doomed to death before my lord the king; but you set your servant among those who eat at your table. What further right have I, then, to cry to

[b] Heb *the king's servant, your servant*   [c] Ch 19. 1 in Heb   [d] Gk: Heb *to the king, to his house*
[e] Cn: Heb *the ford crossed*   [f] Heb *to*   [g] Gk Syr Vg: Heb *said, I will saddle an ass for myself*

29 the king?" And the king said to him, "Why speak any more of your affairs? I have decided: you and Ziba shall 30 divide the land." And Mephib'osheth said to the king, "Oh, let him take it all, since my lord the king has come safely home."

31 Now Barzil'lai the Gileadite had come down from Ro'gelim; and he went on with the king to the Jordan, 32 to escort him over the Jordan. Barzil'lai was a very aged man, eighty years old; and he had provided the king with food while he stayed at Mahana'im; for he was a very 33 wealthy man. And the king said to Barzil'lai, "Come over with me, and I will provide for you with me in Jeru-34 salem." But Barzil'lai said to the king, "How many years have I still to live, that I should go up with the king to 35 Jerusalem? I am this day eighty years old; can I discern what is pleasant and what is not? Can your servant taste what he eats or what he drinks? Can I still listen to the voice of singing men and singing women? Why then should your servant be an added burden to my lord the 36 king? Your servant will go a little way over the Jordan with the king. Why should the king recompense me with 37 such a reward? Pray let your servant return, that I may die in my own city, near the grave of my father and my mother. But here is your servant Chimham; let him go over with my lord the king; and do for him whatever 38 seems good to you." And the king answered, "Chimham shall go over with me, and I will do for him whatever seems good to you; and all that you desire of me I will 39 do for you." Then all the people went over the Jordan, and the king went over; and the king kissed Barzil'lai 40 and blessed him, and he returned to his own home. The king went on to Gilgal, and Chimham went on with him; all the people of Judah, and also half the people of Israel,

brought the king on his way.

41 Then all the men of Israel came to the king, and said to the king, "Why have our brethren the men of Judah stolen you away, and brought the king and his household 42 over the Jordan, and all David's men with him?" All the men of Judah answered the men of Israel, "Because the king is near of kin to us. Why then are you angry over this matter? Have we eaten at all at the king's expense? 43 Or has he given us any gift?" And the men of Israel answered the men of Judah, "We have ten shares in the king, and in David also we have more than you. Why

then did you despise us? Were we not the first to speak of bringing back our king?" But the words of the men of Judah were fiercer than the words of the men of Israel.

20 Now there happened to be there a worthless fellow, whose name was Sheba, the son of Bichri, a Benjaminite; and he blew the trumpet, and said,

"We have no portion in David,
and we have no inheritance in the son of Jesse;
every man to his tents, O Israel!"

2 So all the men of Israel withdrew from David, and followed Sheba the son of Bichri; but the men of Judah followed their king steadfastly from the Jordan to Jerusalem.

3 And David came to his house at Jerusalem; and the king took the ten concubines whom he had left to care for the house, and put them in a house under guard, and provided for them, but did not go in to them. So they were shut up until the day of their death, living as if in widowhood.

4 Then the king said to Ama'sa, "Call the men of Judah together to me within three days, and be here yourself." 5 So Ama'sa went to summon Judah; but he delayed be-6 yond the set time which had been appointed him. And David said to Abi'shai, "Now Sheba the son of Bichri will do us more harm than Ab'salom; take your lord's servants and pursue him, lest he get himself fortified 7 cities, and cause us trouble."ʰ And there went out after Abi'shai, Jo'abⁱ and the Cher'ethites and the Pel'ethites, and all the mighty men; they went out from Jerusalem to 8 pursue Sheba the son of Bichri. When they were at the great stone which is in Gibeon, Ama'sa came to meet them. Now Jo'ab was wearing a soldier's garment, and over it was a girdle with a sword in its sheath fastened 9 upon his loins, and as he went forward it fell out. And Jo'ab said to Ama'sa, "Is it well with you, my brother?" And Jo'ab took Ama'sa by the beard with his right hand 10 to kiss him. But Ama'sa did not observe the sword which was in Jo'ab's hand; so Jo'ab struck him with it in the body, and shed his bowels to the ground, without striking a second blow; and he died.

Then Jo'ab and Abi'shai his brother pursued Sheba 11 the son of Bichri. And one of Jo'ab's men took his stand by Ama'sa, and said, "Whoever favors Jo'ab, and who-12 ever is for David, let him follow Jo'ab." And Ama'sa lay

ʰ Tg: Heb *snatch away our eyes*   ⁱ Cn Compare Gk: Heb *after him Joab's men*

wallowing in his blood in the highway. And any one who came by, seeing him, stopped;[j] and when the man saw that all the people stopped, he carried Ama'sa out of the highway into the field, and threw a garment over him. 13 When he was taken out of the highway, all the people went on after Jo'ab to pursue Sheba the son of Bichri.

14 And Sheba passed through all the tribes of Israel to Abel of Beth-ma'acah;[k] and all the Bichrites[l] assembled, 15 and followed him in. And all the men who were with Jo'ab came and besieged him in Abel of Beth-ma'acah; they cast up a mound against the city, and it stood against the rampart; and they were battering the wall, to throw 16 it down. Then a wise woman called from the city, "Hear! Hear! Tell Jo'ab, 'Come here, that I may speak to you.'" 17 And he came near her; and the woman said, "Are you Jo'ab?" He answered, "I am." Then she said to him, "Listen to the words of your maidservant." And he 18 answered, "I am listening." Then she said, "They were wont to say in old time, 'Let them but ask counsel at 19 Abel'; and so they settled a matter. I am one of those who are peaceable and faithful in Israel; you seek to destroy a city which is a mother in Israel; why will you 20 swallow up the heritage of the LORD?" Jo'ab answered, "Far be it from me, far be it, that I should swallow up or 21 destroy! That is not true. But a man of the hill country of E'phraim, called Sheba the son of Bichri, has lifted up his hand against King David; give up him alone, and I will withdraw from the city." And the woman said to Jo'ab, "Behold, his head shall be thrown to you over the 22 wall." Then the woman went to all the people in her wisdom. And they cut off the head of Sheba the son of Bichri, and threw it out to Jo'ab. So he blew the trumpet, and they dispersed from the city, every man to his home. And Jo'ab returned to Jerusalem to the king.

23 Now Jo'ab was in command of all the army of Israel; and Benai'ah the son of Jehoi'ada was in command of 24 the Cher'ethites and the Pel'ethites; and Ador'am was in charge of the forced labor; and Jehosh'aphat the son 25 of Ahi'lud was the recorder; and Sheva was secretary; 26 and Zadok and Abi'athar were priests; and Ira the Ja'-irite was also David's priest.

ADDITIONAL DETAILS

21 Now there was a famine in the days of David for three years, year after year; and David sought the face of the LORD. And the LORD said, "There is blood-guilt on Saul and on his house, because he put the Gib'eon-2 ites to death." So the king called the Gib'eonites.[m] Now the Gib'eonites were not of the people of Israel, but of the remnant of the Amorites; although the people of Israel had sworn to spare them, Saul had sought to slay 3 them in his zeal for the people of Israel and Judah. And David said to the Gib'eonites, "What shall I do for you?

And how shall I make expiation, that you may bless the 4 heritage of the LORD?" The Gib'eonites said to him, "It is not a matter of silver or gold between us and Saul or his house; neither is it for us to put any man to death in Israel." And he said, "What do you say that I shall do 5 for you?" They said to the king, "The man who consumed us and planned to destroy us, so that we should 6 have no place in all the territory of Israel, let seven of his sons be given to us, so that we may hang them up before the LORD at Gibeon on the mountain of the LORD."[n] And the king said, "I will give them."

7 But the king spared Mephib'osheth, the son of Saul's son Jonathan, because of the oath of the LORD which was between them, between David and Jonathan the son of 8 Saul. The king took the two sons of Rizpah the daughter of Ai'ah, whom she bore to Saul, Armo'ni and Mephib'-osheth; and the five sons of Merab[o] the daughter of Saul whom she bore to A'dri-el the son of Brazil'lai the Meho'-9 lathite; and he gave them into the hands of the Gib'eonites, and they hanged them on the mountain before the LORD, and the seven of them perished together. They were put to death in the first days of harvest, at the beginning of barley harvest.

10 Then Rizpah the daughter of Ai'ah took sackcloth, and spread it for herself on the rock, from the beginning of harvest until rain fell upon them from the heavens; and she did not allow the birds of the air to come upon them 11 by day, or the beasts of the field by night. When David was told what Rizpah the daughter of Ai'ah, the concu-12 bine of Saul, had done, David went and took the bones of Saul and the bones of his son Jonathan from the men of Ja'besh-gil'ead, who had stolen them from the public square of Bethshan, where the Philistines had hanged them, on the day the Philistines killed Saul on Gilbo'a; 13 and he brought up from there the bones of Saul and the bones of his son Jonathan; and they gathered the bones 14 of those who were hanged. And they buried the bones of Saul and his son Jonathan in the land of Benjamin in Zela, in the tomb of Kish his father; and they did all that the king commanded. And after that God heeded suppli-cations for the land.

15 The Philistines had war again with Israel, and David went down together with his servants, and they fought 16 against the Philistines; and David grew weary. And Ish'-bi-be'nob, one of the descendants of the giants, whose spear weighed three hundred shekels of bronze, and who was girded with a new sword, thought to kill David. 17 But Abi'shai the son of Zeru'iah came to his aid, and attacked the Philistine and killed him. Then David's men adjured him, "You shall no more go out with us to battle, lest you quench the lamp of Israel."

18 After this there was again war with the Philistines at Gob; then Sib'becai the Hu'shathite slew Saph, who was

¹⁹ one of the descendants of the giants. And there was again war with the Philistines at Gob; and Elha'nan the son of Ja'areor'egim, the Bethlehemite, slew Goliath the Gittite, ²⁰ the shaft of whose spear was like a weaver's beam. And there was again war at Gath, where there was a man of great stature, who had six fingers on each hand, and six toes on each foot, twenty-four in number; and he also was ²¹ descended from the giants. And when he taunted Israel, Jonathan the son of Shim'e-i, David's brother, slew him. ²² These four were descended from the giants in Gath; and they fell by the hand of David and by the hand of his servants.

A Thanksgiving Psalm

22 And David spoke to the LORD the words of this song on the day when the LORD delivered him from the ² hand of all his enemies, and from the hand of Saul. He said,

"The LORD is my rock, and my fortress, and my deliverer, ³ my ^p God, my rock, in whom I take refuge,

my shield and the horn of my salvation,
my stronghold and my refuge,
my savior; thou savest me from violence.
⁴ I call upon the LORD, who is worthy to be praised,
and I am saved from my enemies.

⁵ "For the waves of death encompassed me,
the torrents of perdition assailed me;
⁶ the cords of Sheol entangled me,
the snares of death confronted me.

⁷ "In my distress I called upon the LORD;
to my God I called.
From his temple he heard my voice,
and my cry came to his ears.

⁸ "Then the earth reeled and rocked;
the foundations of the heavens trembled
and quaked, because he was angry.
⁹ Smoke went up from his nostrils,
and devouring fire from his mouth;
glowing coals flamed forth from him.
¹⁰ He bowed the heavens, and came down;
thick darkness was under his feet.
¹¹ He rode on a cherub, and flew;
he was seen upon the wings of the wind.
¹² He made darkness around him
his canopy, thick clouds, a gathering of water.

¹³ Out of the brightness before him
coals of fire flamed forth.
¹⁴ The LORD thundered from heaven,
and the Most High uttered his voice.
¹⁵ And he sent out arrows, and scattered them;
lightning, and routed them.
¹⁶ Then the channels of the sea were seen,
the foundations of the world were laid bare,
at the rebuke of the LORD,
at the blast of the breath of his nostrils.

¹⁷ "He reached from on high, he took me,
he drew me out of many waters.
¹⁸ He delivered me from my strong enemy,
from those who hated me;
for they were too mighty for me.
¹⁹ They came upon me in the day of my calamity;
but the LORD was my stay.
²⁰ He brought me forth into a broad place;
he delivered me, because he delighted in me.

²¹ "The LORD rewarded me according to my righteousness;
according to the cleanness of my hands he recompensed me.
²² For I have kept the ways of the LORD,
and have not wickedly departed from my God.
²³ For all his ordinances were before me,
and from his statutes I did not turn aside.
²⁴ I was blameless before him,
and I kept myself from guilt.
²⁵ Therefore the LORD has recompensed me according to my righteousness,
according to my cleanness in his sight.

²⁶ "With the loyal thou dost show thyself loyal;
with the blameless man thou dost show thyself blameless;
²⁷ with the pure thou dost show thyself pure,
and with the crooked thou dost show thyself perverse.
²⁸ Thou dost deliver a humble people,
but thy eyes are upon the haughty to bring them down.
²⁹ Yea, thou art my lamp, O LORD,
and my God lightens my darkness.
³⁰ Yea, by thee I can crush a troop,
and by my God I can leap over a wall.
³¹ This God—his way is perfect;
the promise of the LORD proves true;
he is a shield for all those who take refuge in him.

³² "For who is God, but the LORD?
And who is a rock, except our God?
³³ This God is my strong refuge,
and has made ^r my ^s way safe.

^p Gk Ps 18. 2: Heb lacks *my*   ^r Ps 18. 32: Heb *set free*   ^s Another reading is *his*

34 He made my [s] feet like hinds' feet,
   and set me secure on the heights.
35 He trains my hands for war,
   so that my arms can bend a bow of bronze.
36 Thou hast given me the shield of thy salvation,
   and thy help [t] made me great.

37 Thou didst give a wide place for my steps under me,
   and my feet [u] did not slip;
38 I pursued my enemies and destroyed them,
   and did not turn back until they were consumed.
39 I consumed them; I thrust them through, so that they
       did not rise;
   they fell under my feet.
40 For thou didst gird me with strength for the battle;
   thou didst make my assailants sink under me.
41 Thou didst make my enemies turn their backs to me,
   those who hated me, and I destroyed them.
42 They looked, but there was none to save;
   they cried to the LORD, but he did not answer them.
43 I beat them fine as the dust of the earth,
   I crushed them and stamped them down like the mire
       of the streets.

44 "Thou didst deliver me from strife with the peoples; [v]
   thou didst keep me as the head of the nations;
   people whom I had not known served me.
45 Foreigners came cringing to me;
   as soon as they heard of me, they obeyed me.
46 Foreigners lost heart,
   and came trembling [w] out of their fastnesses.

47 "The LORD lives; and blessed be my rock,
   and exalted be my God, the rock of my salvation,
48 the God who gave me vengeance
   and brought down peoples under me,
49 who brought me out from my enemies;
   thou didst exalt me above my adversaries,
   thou didst deliver me from men of violence.

50 "For this I will extol thee, O LORD, among the nations,
   and sing praises to thy name.
51 Great triumphs he gives [x] to his king,
   and shows steadfast love to his anointed,
   to David, and his descendants for ever."

David's Last Words

23 Now these are the last words of David:
   The oracle of David, the son of Jesse,
   the oracle of the man who was raised on high,
   the anointed of the God of Jacob,
   the sweet psalmist of Israel: [y]

2 "The Spirit of the LORD speaks by me,
   his word is upon my tongue.
3 The God of Israel has spoken,
   the Rock of Israel has said to me:
When one rules justly over men,
   ruling in the fear of God,
4 he dawns on them like the morning light,
   like the sun shining forth upon a cloudless morning,
   like rain [z] that makes grass to sprout from the earth.
5 Yea, does not my house stand so with God?
   For he has made with me an everlasting covenant,
   ordered in all things and secure.
For will he not cause to prosper
   all my help and my desire?
6 But godless men [a] are all like thorns that are thrown
       away;
   for they cannot be taken with the hand;
7 but the man who touches them
   arms himself with iron and the shaft of a spear,
   and they are utterly consumed with fire." [b]

8 These are the names of the mighty men whom David had: Josheb-basshe'beth a Tah-che'monite; he was chief of the three; [c] he wielded his spear [d] against eight hundred whom he slew at one time.
9 And next to him among the three mighty men was Elea'zar the son of Dodo, son of Aho'hi. He was with David when they defied the Philistines who were gathered
10 there for battle, and the men of Israel withdrew. He rose and struck down the Philistines until his hand was weary, and his hand cleaved to the sword; and the LORD wrought a great victory that day; and the men returned after him only to strip the slain.
11 And next to him was Shammah, the son of Agee the Har'arite. The Philistines gathered together at Lehi, where there was a plot of ground full of lentils; and the men
12 fled from the Philistines. But he took his stand in the midst of the plot, and defended it, and slew the Philistines; and the LORD wrought a great victory.
13 And three of the thirty chief men went down, and came about harvest time to David at the cave of Adullam, when a band of Philistines was encamped in the valley of Reph'-
14 aim. David was then in the stronghold; and the garrison
15 of the Philistines was then at Bethlehem. And David said longingly, "O that some one would give me water to drink
16 from the well of Bethlehem which is by the gate!" Then the three mighty men broke through the camp of the

---

[t] Or *gentleness*   [u] Heb *ankles*   [v] Gk: Heb *from strife with my people*   [w] Ps 18. 45: Heb *girded themselves*
[x] Another reading is *He is a tower of salvation*   [y] Or *the favorite of the songs of Israel*   [z] Heb *from rain*
[a] Heb *worthlessness*   [b] Heb *fire in the sitting*   [c] Or *captains*   [d] 1 Ch 11. 11: Heb *obscure*

Philistines, and drew water out of the well of Bethlehem which was by the gate, and took and brought it to David. But he would not drink of it; he poured it out to the 17 LORD, and said, "Far be it from me, O LORD, that I should do this. Shall I drink the blood of the men who went at the risk of their lives?" Therefore he would not drink it. These things did the three mighty men.

18 Now Abi'shai, the brother of Jo'ab, the son of Zeru'iah, was chief of the thirty.[e] And he wielded his spear against three hundred men and slew them, and won a name be- 19 side the three. He was the most renowned of the thirty,[f] and became their commander; but he did not attain to the three.

20 And Benai'ah the son of Jehoi'ada was a valiant man[g] of Kabzeel, a doer of great deeds; he smote two ariels[h] of Moab. He also went down and slew a lion in a pit on 21 a day when snow had fallen. And he slew an Egyptian, a handsome man. The Egyptian had a spear in his hand; but Benai'ah went down to him with a staff, and snatched the spear out of the Egyptian's hand, and slew him with 22 his own spear. These things did Benai'ah the son of Jehoi'ada, and won a name beside the three mighty men. 23 He was renowned among the thirty, but he did not attain to the three. And David set him over his bodyguard.

24 As'ahel the brother of Jo'ab was one of the thirty; 25 Elha'nan the son of Dodo of Bethlehem, Shammah of 26 Harod, Eli'ka of Harod, Helez the Paltite, Ira the son of 27 Ikkesh of Teko'a, Abi-e'zer, of An'athoth, Mebun'nai the 28 Hu'shathite, Zalmon the Aho'hite, Ma'harai of Netoph'ah, 29 Heleb the son of Ba'anah of Netoph'ah, It'tai the son of 30 Ri'bai of Gib'e-ah of the Benjaminites, Benai'ah of 31 Pira'thon, Hid'dai of the brooks of Ga'ash, Abial'bon the 32 Ar'bathite, Az'maveth of Bahu'rim, Eli'ahba of Sha-al'- 33 bon, the sons of Jashen, Jonathan, Shammah the Har'- 34 arite, Ahi'am the son of Sharar the Har'arite, Eliph'elet the son of Ahas'bai of Ma'acah, Eli'am the son of Ahith'- 35, 36 ophel of Gilo, Hezro[i] of Carmel, Pa'arai the Arbite, Igal 37 the son of Nathan of Zobah, Bani the Gadite, Zelek the Ammonite, Na'harai of Be-er'oth, the armor-bearer of 38 Jo'ab the son of Zeru'iah, Ira the Ithrite, Gareb the 39 Ithrite, Uri'ah the Hittite: thirty-seven in all.

24 Again the anger of the LORD was kindled against Israel, and he incited David against them, saying, 2 "Go, number Israel and Judah." So the king said to Jo'ab and the commanders of the army,[j] who were with him, "Go through all the tribes of Israel, from Dan to Beer-sheba, and number the people, that I may know the num- 3 ber of the people." But Jo'ab said to the king, "May the LORD your God add to the people a hundred times as many as they are, while the eyes of my lord the king still see it; but why does my lord the king delight in this 4 thing?" But the king's word prevailed against Jo'ab and

the commanders of the army. So Jo'ab and the command-ers of the army went out from the presence of the king to 5 number the people of Israel. They crossed the Jordan, and began from Aro'er,[k] and from the city that is in the mid- 6 dle of the valley, toward Gad and on to Jazer. Then they came to Gilead, and to Kadesh in the land of the Hittites;[l] and they came to Dan, and from Dan[m] they went around 7 to Sidon, and came to the fortress of Tyre and to all the cities of the Hivites and Canaanites; and they went out 8 to the Negeb of Judah at Beer-sheba. So when they had gone through all the land, they came to Jerusalem at the 9 end of nine months and twenty days. And Jo'ab gave the sum of the numbering of the people to the king: in Israel there were eight hundred thousand valiant men who drew the sword, and the men of Judah were five hundred thousand.

10 But David's heart smote him after he had numbered the people. And David said to the LORD, "I have sinned greatly in what I have done. But now, O LORD, I pray thee, take away the iniquity of thy servant; for I have 11 done very foolishly." And when David arose in the morn-ing, the word of the LORD came to the prophet Gad, 12 David's seer, saying, "Go and say to David, 'Thus says the LORD, Three things I offer[n] you; choose one of them, 13 that I may do it to you.'" So Gad came to David and told him, and said to him, "Shall three[o] years of famine come to you in your land? Or will you flee three months before your foes while they pursue you? Or shall there be three days' pestilence in your land? Now consider, and decide what answer I shall return to him who sent 14 me." Then David said to Gad, "I am in great distress; let us fall into the hand of the LORD, for his mercy is great; but let me not fall into the hand of man."

15 So the LORD sent a pestilence upon Israel from the morning until the appointed time; and there died of the people from Dan to Beer-sheba seventy thousand men. 16 And when the angel stretched forth his hand toward Jerusalem to destroy it, the LORD repented of the evil, and said to the angel who was working destruction among the people, "It is enough; now stay your hand." And the angel of the LORD was by the threshing floor of Arau'nah 17 the Jeb'usite. Then David spoke to the LORD when he saw

[e] Two Hebrew Mss Syr: MT three
[f] 1 Ch 11. 25: Heb Was he the most renowned of the three?
[g] Another reading is the son of Ish-hai
[h] The meaning of the word ariel is unknown
[i] Another reading is Hezrai
[j] 1 Ch 21. 2 Gk: Heb to Joab the commander of the army
[k] Gk: Heb encamped in Aroer
[l] Gk: Heb to the land of Tahtim-hodshi
[m] Cn Compare Gk: Heb they came to Dan-jaan and
[n] Or hold over
[o] Ch 21. 12 Gk: Heb seven

the angel who was smiting the people, and said, "Lo, I have sinned, and I have done wickedly; but these sheep, what have they done? Let thy hand, I pray thee, be against me and against my father's house."

18 And Gad came that day to David, and said to him, "Go up, rear an altar to the LORD on the threshing floor 19 of Arau'nah the Jeb'usite." So David went up at Gad's 20 word, as the LORD commanded. And when Arau'nah looked down, he saw the king and his servants coming on toward him; and Arau'nah went forth, and did obei- 21 sance to the king with his face to the ground. And Arau'- nah said, "Why has my lord the king come to his ser- vant?" David said, "To buy the threshing floor of you, in order to build an altar to the LORD, that the plague 22 may be averted from the people." Then Arau'nah said to David, "Let my lord the king take and offer up what seems good to him; here are the oxen for the burnt offer- ing, and the threshing sledges and the yokes of the oxen 23 for the wood. All this, O king, Arau'nah gives to the king." And Arau'nah said to the king, "The LORD your 24 God accept you." But the king said to Arau'nah, "No, but I will buy it of you for a price; I will not offer burnt offerings to the LORD my God which cost me nothing." So David bought the threshing floor and the oxen for 25 fifty shekels of silver. And David built there an altar to the LORD, and offered burnt offerings and peace offerings. So the LORD heeded supplications for the land, and the plague was averted from Israel.

INTRODUCTION TO

THE FIRST BOOK OF THE

KINGS

The First Book of the Kings begins its story when David was an old man about to die. After David's death his son Solomon became king. Solomon led the people in battles against their enemies. He built the Temple for worship and other fine buildings and places in Jerusalem. To pay for these expensive things, the king required the people to pay heavy taxes and forced many of them to work as carpenters and stonemasons. The writer of the book believed that in spite of his many faults God had given Solomon "a wise and discerning mind" (1 Kings 3. 12).

After King Solomon's death a quarrel among the people over the high taxes and other matters divided the Hebrews into two small rival kingdoms. Judah, the southern part, was ruled by Solomon's son Rehoboam. Israel, the northern part, was ruled by a popular hero named Jeroboam. The rest of First Kings tells of the many kings who ruled each of these two kingdoms.

One of the kings of the northern kingdom was named Ahab, who married a princess from Tyre named Jezebel. Queen Jezebel continued to worship the baals, or gods, of Tyre and even brought priests of these gods into Israel. Soon Ahab and Jezebel were challenged by Elijah, one of the greatest preachers or prophets of early Old Testament times. Elijah spoke fearlessly for God in condemning the terrible sins of Ahab and Jezebel. He demanded that Ahab decide whether he would worship many foreign gods (or baals) or the one true God.

Like the Books of Samuel, the two Books of the Kings are really one continuous history divided into two parts so that the scrolls would not be too large to handle. While David was king, records began to be kept about the nation's history. Stories of many events were written down by various leaders in different places.

Finally about 550 B.C. God inspired some thoughtful man to gather these scattered records to make a history. As we read these stories, we can see that the writer was teaching that it was important for the king himself and for all his subjects to be obedient to the true God and to him alone.

THE FIRST BOOK OF THE

KINGS

THE LAST DAYS OF DAVID

1 Now King David was old and advanced in years; and although they covered him with clothes, he could ² not get warm. Therefore his servants said to him, "Let a young maiden be sought for my lord the king, and let her wait upon the king, and be his nurse; let her lie in ³ your bosom, that my lord the king may be warm." So they sought for a beautiful maiden throughout all the territory of Israel, and found Ab'ishag the Shu'nammite, ⁴ and brought her to the king. The maiden was very beautiful; and she became the king's nurse and ministered to him; but the king knew her not.

⁵ Now Adoni'jah the son of Haggith exalted himself, saying, "I will be king"; and he prepared for himself chariots and horsemen, and fifty men to run before him. ⁶ His father had never at any time displeased him by asking, "Why have you done thus and so?" He was also a very handsome man; and he was born next after Ab'- ⁷ salom. He conferred with Jo'ab the son of Zeru'iah and with Abi'athar the priest; and they followed Adoni'jah ⁸ and helped him. But Zadok the priest, and Benai'ah the son of Jehoi'ada, and Nathan the prophet, and Shim'e-i, and Re'i, and David's mighty men were not with Adoni'jah.

9 Adoni′jah sacrificed sheep, oxen, and fatlings by the Serpent's Stone, which is beside En-ro′gel, and he invited all his brothers, the king's sons, and all the royal officials 10 of Judah, but he did not invite Nathan the prophet or Benai′ah or the mighty men or Solomon his brother.

11 Then Nathan said to Bathshe′ba the mother of Solomon, "Have you not heard that Adoni′jah the son of Haggith has become king and David our lord does not 12 know it? Now therefore come, let me give you counsel, that you may save your own life and the life of your son 13 Solomon. Go in at once to King David, and say to him, 'Did you not, my lord the king, swear to your maidservant, saying, "Solomon your son shall reign after me, and he shall sit upon my throne"? Why then is Adoni′jah 14 king?' Then while you are still speaking with the king, I also will come in after you and confirm your words."

15 So Bathshe′ba went to the king into his chamber (now the king was very old, and Ab′ishag the Shu′nammite was 16 ministering to the king). Bathshe′ba bowed and did obeisance to the king, and the king said, "What do you 17 desire?" She said to him, "My lord, you swore to your maidservant by the LORD your God, saying, 'Solomon your son shall reign after me, and he shall sit upon my 18 throne.' And now, behold, Adoni′jah is king, although 19 you, my lord the king, do not know it. He has sacrificed oxen, fatlings, and sheep in abundance, and has invited all the sons of the king, Abi′athar the priest, and Jo′ab the commander of the army; but Solomon your servant 20 he has not invited. And now, my lord the king, the eyes of all Israel are upon you, to tell them who shall sit on 21 the throne of my lord the king after him. Otherwise it will come to pass, when my lord the king sleeps with his fathers, that I and my son Solomon will be counted offenders."

22 While she was still speaking with the king, Nathan the 23 prophet came in. And they told the king, "Here is Nathan the prophet." And when he came in before the king, he 24 bowed before the king, with his face to the ground. And Nathan said, "My lord the king, have you said, 'Adoni′jah shall reign after me, and he shall sit upon my throne'? 25 For he has gone down this day, and has sacrificed oxen, fatlings, and sheep in abundance, and has invited all the king's sons, Jo′ab the commander [a] of the army, and Abi′athar the priest; and behold, they are eating and drinking before him, and saying, 'Long live King Adoni′- 26 jah!' But me, your servant, and Zadok the priest, and Benai′ah the son of Jehoi′ada, and your servant Solomon, 27 he has not invited. Has this thing been brought about by my lord the king and you have not told your servants who should sit on the throne of my lord the king after him?"

28 Then King David answered, "Call Bathshe′ba to me." So she came into the king's presence, and stood before

[a] Gk: Heb commanders

29 the king. And the king swore, saying, "As the LORD lives, 30 who has redeemed my soul out of every adversity, as I swore to you by the LORD, the God of Israel, saying, 'Solomon your son shall reign after me, and he shall sit upon my throne in my stead'; even so will I do this day." 31 Then Bathshe′ba bowed with her face to the ground, and did obeisance to the king, and said, "May my lord King David live for ever!"

32 King David said, "Call to me Zadok the priest, Nathan the prophet, and Benai′ah the son of Jehoi′ada." So they 33 came before the king. And the king said to them, "Take with you the servants of your lord, and cause Solomon my son to ride on my own mule, and bring him down to 34 Gihon; and let Zadok the priest and Nathan the prophet there anoint him king over Israel; then blow the trumpet, 35 and say, 'Long live King Solomon!' You shall then come up after him, and he shall come and sit upon my throne; for he shall be king in my stead; and I have appointed 36 him to be ruler over Israel and over Judah." And Benai′- ah the son of Jehoi′ada answered the king, "Amen! May 37 the LORD, the God of my lord the king, say so. As the LORD has been with my lord the king, even so may he be with Solomon, and make his throne greater than the throne of my lord King David."

38 So Zadok the priest, Nathan the prophet, and Benai′ah the son of Jehoi′ada, and the Cher′ethites and the Pel′- ethites, went down and caused Solomon to ride on King 39 David's mule, and brought him to Gihon. There Zadok the priest took the horn of oil from the tent, and anointed Solomon. Then they blew the trumpet; and all the people 40 said, "Long live King Solomon!" And all the people went up after him, playing on pipes, and rejoicing with great joy, so that the earth was split by their noise.

41 Adoni′jah and all the guests who were with him heard it as they finished feasting. And when Jo′ab heard the sound of the trumpet, he said, "What does this uproar in 42 the city mean?" While he was still speaking, behold, Jonathan the son of Abi′athar the priest came; and Adoni′jah said, "Come in, for you are a worthy man and 43 bring good news." Jonathan answered Adoni′jah, "No, 44 for our lord King David has made Solomon king; and the king has sent with him Zadok the priest, Nathan the prophet, and Benai′ah the son of Jehoi′ada, and the Cher′ethites and the Pel′ethites; and they have caused 45 him to ride on the king's mule; and Zadok the priest and

Nathan the prophet have anointed him king at Gihon; and they have gone up from there rejoicing, so that the city is in an uproar. This is the noise that you have heard. 46, 47 Solomon sits upon the royal throne. Moreover the king's servants came to congratulate our lord King David, saying, 'Your God make the name of Solomon more famous than yours, and make his throne greater than your 48 throne.' And the king bowed himself upon the bed. And the king also said, 'Blessed be the LORD, the God of Israel, who has granted one of my offspring b to sit on my throne this day, my own eyes seeing it.' "

49 Then all the guests of Adoni'jah trembled, and rose, 50 and each went his own way. And Adoni'jah feared Solomon; and he arose, and went, and caught hold of 51 the horns of the altar. And it was told Solomon, "Behold, Adoni'jah fears King Solomon; for, lo, he has laid hold of the horns of the altar, saying, 'Let King Solomon swear to me first that he will not slay his servant with the 52 sword.' " And Solomon said, "If he prove to be a worthy man, not one of his hairs shall fall to the earth; but if 53 wickedness is found in him, he shall die." So King Solomon sent, and they brought him down from the altar. And he came and did obeisance to King Solomon; and Solomon said to him, "Go to your house."

2 When David's time to die drew near, he charged 2 Solomon his son, saying, "I am about to go the way of all the earth. Be strong, and show yourself a man, 3 and keep the charge of the LORD your God, walking in his ways and keeping his statutes, his commandments, his ordinances, and his testimonies, as it is written in the law of Moses, that you may prosper in all that you do 4 and wherever you turn; that the LORD may establish his word which he spoke concerning me, saying, 'If your sons take heed to their way, to walk before me in faithfulness with all their heart and with all their soul, there shall not fail you a man on the throne of Israel.'

5 "Moreover you know also what Jo'ab the son of Zeru'iah did to me, how he dealt with the two commanders of the armies of Israel, Abner the son of Ner, and Ama'sa the son of Jether, whom he murdered, avenging c in time of peace blood which had been shed in war, and putting innocent blood d upon the girdle about my e loins, and 6 upon the sandals on my e feet. Act therefore according to your wisdom, but do not let his gray head go down to 7 Sheol in peace. But deal loyally with the sons of Barzil'lai the Gileadite, and let them be among those who eat at your table; for with such loyalty they met me when I 8 fled from Absalom your brother. And there is also with you Shim'e-i the son of Gera, the Benjaminite from Bahu'rim, who cursed me with a grievous curse on the day when I went to Mahana'im; but when he came down to meet me at the Jordan, I swore to him by the LORD, say-9 ing, 'I will not put you to death with the sword.' Now

therefore hold him not guiltless, for you are a wise man; you will know what you ought to do to him, and you shall bring his gray head down with blood to Sheol."

10 Then David slept with his fathers, and was buried in 11 the city of David. And the time that David reigned over Israel was forty years; he reigned seven years in Hebron, 12 and thirty-three years in Jerusalem. So Solomon sat upon the throne of David his father; and his kingdom was firmly established.

13 Then Adoni'jah the son of Haggith came to Bathshe'ba the mother of Solomon. And she said, "Do you come 14 peaceably?" He said, "Peaceably." Then he said, "I have 15 something to say to you." She said, "Say on." He said, "You know that the kingdom was mine, and that all Israel fully expected me to reign; however the kingdom has turned about and become my brother's, for it was his 16 from the LORD. And now I have one request to make of you; do not refuse me." She said to him, "Say on." 17 And he said, "Pray ask King Solomon—he will not refuse you—to give me Ab'ishag the Shu'nammite as my wife." 18 Bathshe'ba said, "Very well; I will speak for you to the king."

19 So Bathshe'ba went to King Solomon, to speak to him on behalf of Adoni'jah. And the king rose to meet her, and bowed down to her; then he sat on his throne, and had a seat brought for the king's mother; and she sat on 20 his right. Then she said, "I have one small request to make of you; do not refuse me." And the king said to her, "Make your request, my mother; for I will not refuse 21 you." She said, "Let Ab'ishag the Shu'nammite be given 22 to Adoni'jah your brother as his wife." King Solomon answered his mother, "And why do you ask Ab'ishag the Shu'nammite for Adoni'jah? Ask for him the kingdom also; for he is my elder brother, and on his side are Abi'athar f the priest and Jo'ab the son of Zeru'iah." 23 Then King Solomon swore by the LORD, saying, "God do so to me and more also if this word does not cost 24 Adoni'jah his life! Now therefore as the LORD lives, who has established me, and placed me on the throne of David my father, and who has made me a house, as he promised, 25 Adoni'jah shall be put to death this day." So King Solomon sent Benai'ah the son of Jehoi'ada; and he struck him down, and he died.

26 And to Abi'athar the priest the king said, "Go to An'athoth, to your estate; for you deserve death. But I will not at this time put you to death, because you bore the ark of the Lord GOD before David my father, and because 27 you shared in all the affliction of my father." So Solomon expelled Abi'athar from being priest to the LORD, thus fulfilling the word of the LORD which he had spoken concerning the house of Eli in Shiloh.

28 When the news came to Jo'ab—for Jo'ab had supported Adoni'jah although he had not supported Ab'-

---

b Gk: Heb one   c Gk: Heb placing   d Gk: Heb blood of war   e Gk: Heb his
f Gk Syr Vg: Heb and for him and for Abiathar

salom—Jo'ab fled to the tent of the LORD and caught hold
29 of the horns of the altar. And when it was told King
Solomon, "Jo'ab has fled to the tent of the LORD, and
behold, he is beside the altar," Solomon sent Benai'-ah
the son of Jehoi'ada, saying, "Go, strike him down."
30 So Benai'ah came to the tent of the LORD, and said to
him, "The king commands, 'Come forth.'" But he said,
"No, I will die here." Then Benai'ah brought the king
word again, saying, "Thus said Jo'ab, and thus he an-
31 swered me." The king replied to him, "Do as he has said,
strike him down and bury him; and thus take away from
me and from my father's house the guilt for the blood
32 which Jo'ab shed without cause. The LORD will bring
back his bloody deeds upon his own head, because, without the knowledge of my father David, he attacked and
slew with the sword two men more righteous and better
than himself, Abner the son of Ner, commander of the
army of Israel, and Ama'sa the son of Jether, commander
33 of the army of Judah. So shall their blood come back
upon the head of Jo'ab and upon the head of his descendants for ever; but to David, and to his descendants, and
to his house, and to his throne, there shall be peace from
34 the LORD for evermore." Then Benai'ah the son of Jehoi'-
ada went up, and struck him down and killed him; and
35 he was buried in his own house in the wilderness. The
king put Benai'ah the son of Jehoi'ada over the army in
place of Jo'ab, and the king put Zadok the priest in the
place of Abi'athar.

36 Then the king sent and summoned Shim'e-i, and said
to him, "Build yourself a house in Jerusalem, and dwell
there, and do not go forth from there to any place what-
37 ever. For on the day you go forth, and cross the brook
Kidron, know for certain that you shall die; your blood
38 shall be upon your own head." And Shim'e-i said to the
king, "What you say is good; as my lord the king has
said, so will your servant do." So Shim'e-i dwelt in
Jerusalem many days.

39 But it happened at the end of three years that two of
Shim'e-i's slaves ran away to Achish, son of Ma'acah,
king of Gath. And when it was told Shim'e-i, "Behold,
40 your slaves are in Gath," Shim'e-i arose and saddled an
ass, and went to Gath to Achish, to seek his slaves;
41 Shim'e-i went and brought his slaves from Gath. And
when Solomon was told that Shim'e-i had gone from
42 Jerusalem to Gath and returned, the king sent and summoned Shim'e-i, and said to him, "Did I not make you
swear by the LORD, and solemnly admonish you, saying,
'Know for certain that on the day you go forth and go to
any place whatever, you shall die'? And you said to me,
43 'What you say is good; I obey.' Why then have you not
kept your oath to the LORD and the commandment with
44 which I charged you?" The king also said to Shim'e-i,
"You know in your own heart all the evil that you did to

David my father; so the LORD will bring back your evil
45 upon your own head. But King Solomon shall be blessed,
and the throne of David shall be established before the
46 LORD for ever." Then the king commanded Benai'ah the
son of Jehoi'ada; and he went out and struck him down,
and he died.

THE REIGN OF SOLOMON

So the kingdom was established in the hand of Solomon.
3 Solomon made a marriage alliance with Pharaoh
king of Egypt; he took Pharaoh's daughter, and
brought her into the city of David, until he had finished
building his own house and the house of the LORD and
2 the wall around Jerusalem. The people were sacrificing
at the high places, however, because no house had yet
been built for the name of the LORD.
3 Solomon loved the LORD, walking in the statutes of
David his father; only, he sacrificed and burnt incense
4 at the high places. And the king went to Gibeon to sacrifice there, for that was the great high place; Solomon

used to offer a thousand burnt offerings upon that altar.
5 At Gibeon the LORD appeared to Solomon in a dream by
6 night; and God said, "Ask what I shall give you." And
Solomon said, "Thou hast shown great and steadfast love
to thy servant David my father, because he walked before
thee in faithfulness, in righteousness, and in uprightness
of heart toward thee; and thou hast kept for him this
great and steadfast love, and hast given him a son to sit
7 on his throne this day. And now, O LORD my God, thou
hast made thy servant king in place of David my father,
although I am but a little child; I do not know how to
8 go out or come in. And thy servant is in the midst of thy
people whom thou hast chosen, a great people, that can-
9 not be numbered or counted for multitude. Give thy servant therefore an understanding mind to govern thy people, that I may discern between good and evil; for who
is able to govern this thy great people?"
10, 11 It pleased the Lord that Solomon had asked this. And
God said to him, "Because you have asked this, and have
not asked for yourself long life or riches or the life of
your enemies, but have asked for yourself understanding
12 to discern what is right, behold, I now do according to
your word. Behold, I give you a wise and discerning
mind, so that none like you has been before you and
13 none like you shall arise after you. I give you also what
you have not asked, both riches and honor, so that no
14 other king shall compare with you, all your days. And if

you will walk in my ways, keeping my statutes and my commandments, as your father David walked, then I will lengthen your days."

15 And Solomon awoke, and behold, it was a dream. Then he came to Jerusalem, and stood before the ark of the covenant of the LORD, and offered up burnt offerings and peace offerings, and made a feast for all his servants.

16 Then two harlots came to the king, and stood before 17 him. The one woman said, "Oh, my lord, this woman and I dwell in the same house; and I gave birth to a child 18 while she was in the house. Then on the third day after I was delivered, this woman also gave birth; and we were alone; there was no one else with us in the house, only 19 we two were in the house. And this woman's son died in 20 the night, because she lay on it. And she arose at midnight, and took my son from beside me, while your maidservant slept, and laid it in her bosom, and laid her dead 21 son in my bosom. When I rose in the morning to nurse my child, behold, it was dead; but when I looked at it closely in the morning, behold, it was not the child that I had 22 borne." But the other woman said, "No, the living child is mine, and the dead child is yours." The first said, "No, the dead child is yours, and the living child is mine." Thus they spoke before the king.

23 Then the king said, "The one says, 'This is my son that is alive, and your son is dead'; and the other says, 'No; 24 but your son is dead, and my son is the living one.'" And the king said, "Bring me a sword." So a sword was 25 brought before the king. And the king said, "Divide the living child in two, and give half to the one, and half 26 to the other." Then the woman whose son was alive said to the king, because her heart yearned for her son, "Oh, my lord, give her the living child, and by no means slay it." But the other said, "It shall be neither mine nor 27 yours; divide it." Then the king answered and said, "Give the living child to the first woman, and by no means slay 28 it; she is its mother." And all Israel heard of the judgment which the king had rendered; and they stood in awe of the king, because they perceived that the wisdom of God was in him, to render justice.

4 King Solomon was king over all Israel, and these were his high officials: Azari′ah the son of Zadok was 3 the priest; Elihor′eph and Ahi′jah the sons of Shisha were secretaries; Jehosh′aphat the son of Ahi′lud was re- 4 corder; Benai′ah the son of Jehoi′ada was in command 5 of the army; Zadok and Abi′athar were priests; Azari′ah the son of Nathan was over the officers; Zabud the son 6 of Nathan was priest and king's friend; Ahi′shar was in charge of the palace; and Adoni′ram the son of Abda was in charge of the forced labor.

7 Solomon had twelve officers over all Israel, who provided food for the king and his household; each man had 8 to make provision for one month in the year. These were their names: Ben-hur, in the hill country of E′phraim;

9 Ben-deker, in Makaz, Sha-al′bim, Beth-she′mesh, and 10 E′lonbeth-ha′nan; Ben-hesed, in Arub′both (to him be- 11 longed Socoh and all the land of Hepher); Ben-abin′adab, in all Naphath-dor (he had Taphath the daughter of 12 Solomon as his wife); Ba′ana the son of Ahi′lud, in Ta′- anach, Megid′do, and all Beth-she′an which is beside Zarethan below Jezreel, and from Beth-she′an to A′bel- 13 meho′lah, as far as the other side of Jok′meam; Ben- geber, in Ra′moth-gil′ead (he had the villages of Ja′ir the son of Manas′seh, which are in Gilead, and he had the region of Argob, which is in Bashan, sixty great cities 14 with walls and bronze bars); Ahin′adab the son of Iddo, 15 in Mahana′im; Ahi′ma-az, in Naph′tali (he had taken 16 Bas′emath the daughter of Solomon as his wife); Ba′ana 17 the son of Hushai, in Asher and Bealoth; Jehosh′aphat 18 the son of Paru′ah, in Is′sachar; Shim′e-i the son of Ela, 19 in Benjamin; Geber the son of Uri, in the land of Gilead, the country of Sihon king of the Amorites and of Og king of Bashan. And there was one officer in the land of Judah.

20 Judah and Israel were as many as the sand by the sea; 21 g they ate and drank and were happy. Solomon ruled over all the kingdoms from the Eu-phra′tes to the land of the Philistines and to the border of Egypt; they brought tribute and served Solomon all the days of his life.

22 Solomon's provision for one day was thirty cors of 23 fine flour, and sixty cors of meal, ten fat oxen, and twenty pasture-fed cattle, a hundred sheep, besides harts, gazelles, 24 roebucks, and fatted fowl. For he had dominion over all the region west of the Eu-phra′tes from Tiphsah to Gaza, over all the kings west of the Eu-phra′tes; and he had 25 peace on all sides round about him. And Judah and Israel dwelt in safety, from Dan even to Beer-sheba, every man under his vine and under his fig tree, all the days of 26 Solomon. Solomon also had forty thousand stalls of horses for his chariots, and twelve thousand horsemen. 27 And those officers supplied provisions for King Solomon, and for all who came to King Solomon's table, each one 28 in his month; they let nothing be lacking. Barley also and straw for the horses and swift steeds they brought to the place where it was required, each according to his charge.

29 And God gave Solomon wisdom and understanding beyond measure, and largeness of mind like the sand on 30 the seashore, so that Solomon's wisdom surpassed the wisdom of all the people of the east, and all the wisdom 31 of Egypt. For he was wiser than all other men, wiser than Ethan the Ez′rahite, and Heman, Calcol, and Darda, the sons of Mahol; and his fame was in all the nations round 32 about. He also uttered three thousand proverbs; and his 33 songs were a thousand and five. He spoke of trees, from the cedar that is in Lebanon to the hyssop that grows out of the wall; he spoke also of beasts, and of birds, and of 34 reptiles, and of fish. And men came from all peoples to

g Ch 5. 1 in Heb

hear the wisdom of Solomon, and from all the kings of the earth, who had heard of his wisdom.

The Erection of the Temple

5 [h] Now Hiram king of Tyre sent his servants to Solomon, when he heard that they had anointed him king
2 in place of his father; for Hiram always loved David. And
3 Solomon sent word to Hiram, "You know that David my father could not build a house for the name of the LORD his God because of the warfare with which his enemies surrounded him, until the LORD put them under the soles

4 of his feet. But now the LORD my God has given me rest on every side; there is neither adversary nor misfortune.
5 And so I purpose to build a house for the name of the LORD my God, as the LORD said to David my father, 'Your son, whom I will set upon your throne in your place,
6 shall build the house for my name.' Now therefore command that cedars of Lebanon be cut for me; and my servants will join your servants, and I will pay you for your servants such wages as you set; for you know that there is no one among us who knows how to cut timber like the Sido'nians."
7 When Hiram heard the words of Solomon, he rejoiced greatly, and said, "Blessed be the LORD this day, who has given to David a wise son to be over this great peo-
8 ple." And Hiram sent to Solomon, saying, "I have heard the message which you have sent to me; I am ready to do all you desire in the matter of cedar and cypress
9 timber. My servants shall bring it down to the sea from Lebanon; and I will make it into rafts to go by sea to the place you direct, and I will have them broken up there, and you shall receive it; and you shall meet my wishes
10 by providing food for my household." So Hiram supplied Solomon with all the timber of cedar and cypress
11 that he desired, while Solomon gave Hiram twenty thousand cors of wheat as food for his household, and twenty thousand [i] cors of beaten oil. Solomon gave this to Hiram
12 year by year. And the LORD gave Solomon wisdom, as he promised him; and there was peace between Hiram and Solomon; and the two of them made a treaty.
13 King Solomon raised a levy of forced labor out of all
14 Israel; and the levy numbered thirty thousand men. And he sent them to Lebanon, ten thousand a month in relays; they would be a month in Lebanon and two months at

15 home; Adoni'ram was in charge of the levy. Solomon also had seventy thousand burden-bearers and eighty
16 thousand hewers of stone in the hill country, besides Solomon's three thousand three hundred chief officers who were over the work, who had charge of the people
17 who carried on the work. At the king's command, they quarried out great, costly stones in order to lay the foun-
18 dation of the house with dressed stones. So Solomon's builders and Hiram's builders and the men of Gebal did the hewing and prepared the timber and the stone to build the house.

6 In the four hundred and eightieth year after the people of Israel came out of the land of Egypt, in the fourth year of Solomon's reign over Israel, in the month of Ziv, which is the second month, he began to build the house of the LORD.

2 The house which King Solomon built for the LORD was sixty
3 cubits long, twenty cubits wide, and thirty cubits high. The vestibule in front of the nave of the house was twenty cubits long, equal to the width of the house, and ten cubits deep in
4 front of the house. And he made for the house windows with
5 recessed frames. He also built a structure against the wall of the house, running round the walls of the house, both the nave and the inner sanctuary; and he made side chambers all
6 around. The lowest story [j] was five cubits broad, the middle one was six cubits broad, and the third was seven cubits broad; for around the outside of the house he made offsets on the wall in order that the supporting beams should not be inserted into the walls of the house.
7 When the house was built, it was with stone prepared at the quarry; so that neither hammer nor axe nor any tool of iron was heard in the temple, while it was being built.
8 The entrance for the lowest [k] story was on the south side of the house; and one went up by stairs to the middle story, and
9 from the middle story to the third. So he built the house, and finished it; and he made the ceiling of the house of beams and
10 planks of cedar. He built the structure against the whole house, each story [l] five cubits high, and it was joined to the house with timbers of cedar.
11, 12 Now the word of the LORD came to Solomon, "Concerning this house which you are building, if you will walk in my statutes and obey my ordinances and keep all my commandments and walk in them, then I will establish my word with
13 you, which I spoke to David your father. And I will dwell among the children of Israel, and will not forsake my people Israel."
14, 15 So Solomon built the house, and finished it. He lined the walls of the house on the inside with boards of cedar; from the floor of the house to the rafters [m] of the ceiling, he covered them on the inside with wood; and he covered the floor of the house
16 with boards of cypress. He built twenty cubits of the rear of the house with boards of cedar from the floor to the rafters, [m] and he built this within as an inner sanctuary, as the most holy
17 place. The house, that is, the nave in front of the inner
18 sanctuary, was forty cubits long. The cedar within the house was carved in the form of gourds and open flowers; all was
19 cedar, no stone was seen. The inner sanctuary he prepared in the innermost part of the house, to set there the ark of the
20 covenant of the LORD. The inner sanctuary [n] was twenty cubits long, twenty cubits wide, and twenty cubits high; and he overlaid it with pure gold. He also made [o] an altar of cedar.
21 And Solomon overlaid the inside of the house with pure gold, and he drew chains of gold across, in front of the inner
22 sanctuary, and overlaid it with gold. And he overlaid the whole house with gold, until all the house was finished. Also the whole altar that belonged to the inner sanctuary he overlaid with gold.
23 In the inner sanctuary he made two cherubim of olivewood,
24 each ten cubits high. Five cubits was the length of one wing of the cherub, and five cubits the length of the other wing of the cherub; it was ten cubits from the tip of one wing to the tip

[h] Ch 5. 15 in Heb   [i] Gk: Heb twenty   [j] Gk: Heb structure   [k] Gk Tg: Heb middle   [l] Heb lacks each story
[m] Gk: Heb walls   [n] Vg: Heb and before the inner sanctuary   [o] Gk: Heb covered

25 of the other. The other cherub also measured ten cubits; both
26 cherubim had the same measure and the same form. The height
of one cherub was ten cubits, and so was that of the other
27 cherub. He put the cherubim in the innermost part of the
house; and the wings of the cherubim were spread out so that
a wing of one touched the one wall, and a wing of the other
cherub touched the other wall; their other wings touched each
28 other in the middle of the house. And he overlaid the cherubim
with gold.
29 He carved all the walls of the house round about with carved
figures of cherubim and palm trees and open flowers, in the
30 inner and outer rooms. The floor of the house he overlaid with
gold in the inner and outer rooms.
31 For the entrance to the inner sanctuary he made doors of
olivewood; the lintel and the doorposts formed a pentagon.P
32 He covered the two doors of olivewood with carvings of cherubim, palm trees, and open flowers; he overlaid them with gold,
and spread gold upon the cherubim and upon the palm trees.
33 So also he made for the entrance to the nave doorposts of
34 olivewood, in the form of a square, and two doors of cypress
wood; the two leaves of the one door were folding, and the
35 two leaves of the other door were folding. On them he carved
cherubim and palm trees and open flowers; and he overlaid
36 them with gold evenly applied upon the carved work. He built
the inner court with three courses of hewn stone and one
course of cedar beams.
37 In the fourth year the foundation of the house of the LORD
38 was laid, in the month of Ziv. And in the eleventh year, in the
month of Bul, which is the eighth month, the house was finished
in all its parts, and according to all its specifications. He was
seven years in building it.
7 Solomon was building his own house thirteen years, and
he finished his entire house.
2 He built the House of the Forest of Lebanon; its length was
a hundred cubits, and its breadth fifty cubits, and its height
thirty cubits, and it was built upon three q rows of cedar pillars,
3 with cedar beams upon the pillars. And it was covered with
cedar above the chambers that were upon the forty-five pillars,
4 fifteen in each row. There were window frames in three rows,
5 and window opposite window in three tiers. All the doorways
and windows r had square frames, and window was opposite
window in three tiers.
6 And he made the Hall of Pillars; its length was fifty cubits,
and its breadth thirty cubits; there was a porch in front with
pillars, and a canopy before them.
7 And he made the Hall of the Throne where he was to pronounce judgment, even the Hall of Judgment; it was finished
with cedar from floor to rafters.s
8 His own house where he was to dwell, in the other court back
of the hall, was of like workmanship. Solomon also made a
house like this hall for Pharaoh's daughter whom he had taken
in marriage.
9 All these were made of costly stones, hewn according to
measure, sawed with saws, back and front, even from the
foundation to the coping, and from the court of the house of
10 the LORD t to the great court. The foundation was of costly
11 stones, huge stones, stones of eight and ten cubits. And above
were costly stones, hewn according to measurement, and cedar.
12 The great court had three courses of hewn stone round about,
and a course of cedar beams; so had the inner court of the house
of the LORD, and the vestibule of the house.
13, 14 And King Solomon sent and brought Hiram from Tyre. He
was the son of a widow of the tribe of Naph'tali, and his father
was a man of Tyre, a worker in bronze; and he was full of
wisdom, understanding, and skill, for making any work in
bronze. He came to King Solomon, and did all his work.
15 He cast two pillars of bronze. Eighteen cubits was the height
of one pillar, and a line of twelve cubits measured its circumference; it was hollow, and its thickness was four fingers; the
16 second pillar was the same.u He also made two capitals of molten
bronze, to set upon the tops of the pillars; the height of the
one capital was five cubits, and the height of the other capital
17 was five cubits. Then he made two v nets of checker work with
wreaths of chain work for the capitals upon the tops of the
pillars; a net w for the one capital, and a net w for the other
18 capital. Likewise he made pomegranates;x in two rows round
about upon the one network, to cover the capital that was upon
the top of the pillar; and he did the same with the other capital.
19 Now the capitals that were upon the tops of the pillars in the

20 vestibule were of lily-work, four cubits. The capitals were
upon the two pillars and also above the rounded projection
which was beside the network; there were two hundred pomegranates, in two rows round about; and so with the other
21 capital. He set up the pillars at the vestibule of the temple;
he set up the pillar on the south and called its name Jachin;
and he set up the pillar on the north and called its name Bo'az.
22 And upon the tops of the pillars was lily-work. Thus the work
of the pillars was finished.
23 Then he made the molten sea; it was round, ten cubits from
brim to brim, and five cubits high, and a line of thirty cubits
24 measured its circumference. Under its brim were gourds, for
thirty y cubits, compassing the sea round about; the gourds were
25 in two rows, cast with it when it was cast. It stood upon twelve
oxen, three facing north, three facing west, three facing south,
and three facing east; the sea was set upon them, and all their
26 hinder parts were inward. Its thickness was a handbreadth; and
its brim was made like the brim of a cup, like the flower of a
lily; it held two thousand baths.
27 He also made the ten stands of bronze; each stand was four
28 cubits long, four cubits wide, and three cubits high. This was
the construction of the stands: they had panels, and the panels
29 were set in the frames and on the panels that were set in the
frames were lions, oxen, and cherubim. Upon the frames, both
above and below the lions and oxen, there were wreaths of
30 beveled work. Moreover each stand had four bronze wheels
and axles of bronze; and at the four corners were supports for
a laver. The supports were cast, with wreaths at the side of
31 each. Its opening was within a crown which projected upward
one cubit; its opening was round, as a pedestal is made, a cubit
and a half deep. At its opening there were carvings; and its
32 panels were square, not round. And the four wheels were
underneath the panels; the axles of the wheels were of one piece
with the stands; and the height of a wheel was a cubit and a
33 half. The wheels were made like a chariot wheel; their axles,
34 their rims, their spokes, and their hubs, were all cast. There
were four supports at the four corners of each stand; the
35 supports were of one piece with the stands. And on the top of
the stand there was a round band half a cubit high; and on the
top of the stand its stays and its panels were of one piece with
36 it. And on the surfaces of its stays and on its panels, he carved
cherubim, lions, and palm trees, according to the space of each,
37 with wreaths round about. After this manner he made the ten
stands; all of them were cast alike, of the same measure and
the same form.
38 And he made ten lavers of bronze; each laver held forty
baths, each laver measured four cubits, and there was a laver
39 for each of the ten stands. And he set the stands, five on the
south side of the house, and five on the north side of the house;
and he set the sea on the southeast corner of the house.

40 Hiram also made the pots, the shovels, and the basins. So
Hiram finished all the work that he did for King Solomon on
41 the house of the LORD: the two pillars, the two bowls of the
capitals that were on the tops of the pillars, and the two networks to cover the two bowls of the capitals that were on the
42 tops of the pillars; and the four hundred pomegranates for the
two networks, two rows of pomegranates for each network, to
cover the two bowls of the capitals that were upon the pillars;
43, 44 the ten stands, and the ten lavers upon the stands; and the
one sea, and the twelve oxen underneath the sea.
45 Now the pots, the shovels, and the basins, all these vessels in
the house of the LORD, which Hiram made for King Solomon,
46 were of burnished bronze. In the plain of the Jordan the king
cast them, in the clay ground between Succoth and Zarethan.
47 And Solomon left all the vessels unweighed, because there were
so many of them; the weight of the bronze was not found out.

P Heb obscure   q Gk: Heb four   r Gk: Heb posts   s Syr Vg: Heb floor   t With 7. 12: Heb from the outside
u Tg Syr Compare Gk and Jr 52. 21: Heb and a line of twelve cubits measured the circumference of the second pillar
v Gk: Heb lacks he made two   w Gk: Heb seven   x With 2 Mss Compare Gk: Heb pillars   y Heb ten

48 So Solomon made all the vessels that were in the house of the LORD: the golden altar, the golden table for the bread of 49 the Presence, the lampstands of pure gold, five on the south side and five on the north, before the inner sanctuary; the 50 flowers, the lamps, and the tongs, of gold; the cups, snuffers, basins, dishes for incense, and firepans, of pure gold; and the sockets of gold, for the doors of the innermost part of the house, the most holy place, and for the doors of the nave of the temple.

Dedication of the Temple

51 Thus all the work that King Solomon did on the house of the LORD was finished. And Solomon brought in the things which David his father had dedicated, the silver, the gold, and the vessels, and stored them in the treasuries of the house of the LORD.

8 Then Solomon assembled the elders of Israel and all the heads of the tribes, the leaders of the fathers' houses of the people of Israel, before King Solomon in Jerusalem, to bring up the ark of the covenant of the 2 LORD out of the city of David, which is Zion. And all the men of Israel assembled to King Solomon at the feast in 3 the month Eth'anim, which is the seventh month. And all the elders of Israel came, and the priests took up the ark. 4 And they brought up the ark of the LORD, the tent of meeting, and all the holy vessels that were in the tent; the 5 priests and the Levites brought them up. And King Solomon and all the congregation of Israel, who had assembled before him, were with him before the ark, sacrificing so many sheep and oxen that they could not be 6 counted or numbered. Then the priests brought the ark of the covenant of the LORD to its place, in the inner sanctuary of the house, in the most holy place, underneath the wings of the cherubim. For the cherubim spread out their wings over the place of the ark, so that the cherubim made a covering above the ark and its poles. 8 And the poles were so long that the ends of the poles were seen from the holy place before the inner sanctuary; but they could not be seen from outside; and they are 9 there to this day. There was nothing in the ark except the two tables of stone which Moses put there at Horeb, where the LORD made a covenant with the people of Israel, 10 when they came out of the land of Egypt. And when the priests came out of the holy place, a cloud filled the house 11 of the LORD, so that the priests could not stand to minister because of the cloud; for the glory of the LORD filled the house of the LORD.

12   Then Solomon said,

"The LORD has set the sun in the heavens,
    but [z] has said that he would dwell in thick darkness.
13 I have built thee an exalted house,
    a place for thee to dwell in for ever."

14   Then the king faced about, and blessed all the assembly 15 of Israel, while all the assembly of Israel stood. And he said, "Blessed be the LORD, the God of Israel, who with his hand has fulfilled what he promised with his mouth to 16 David my father, saying, 'Since the day that I brought my people Israel out of Egypt, I chose no city in all the tribes of Israel in which to build a house, that my name might be there; but I chose David to be over my people 17 Israel.' Now it was in the heart of David my father to build a house for the name of the LORD, the God of 18 Israel. But the LORD said to David my father, 'Whereas it was in your heart to build a house for my name, you did 19 well that it was in your heart; nevertheless you shall not build the house, but your son who shall be born to you 20 shall build the house for my name.' Now the LORD has fulfilled his promise which he made; for I have risen in the place of David my father, and sit on the throne of Israel, as the LORD promised, and I have built the house 21 for the name of the LORD, the God of Israel. And there I have provided a place for the ark, in which is the covenant of the LORD which he made with our fathers, when he brought them out of the land of Egypt."

22   Then Solomon stood before the altar of the LORD in the presence of all the assembly of Israel, and spread 23 forth his hands toward heaven; and said, "O LORD, God of Israel, there is no God like thee, in heaven above or on earth beneath, keeping covenant and showing steadfast love to thy servants who walk before thee with all 24 their heart; who hast kept with thy servant David my father what thou didst declare to him; yea, thou didst speak with thy mouth, and with thy hand hast fulfilled it 25 this day. Now therefore, O LORD, God of Israel, keep with thy servant David my father what thou hast promised him, saying, 'There shall never fail you a man before me to sit upon the throne of Israel, if only your sons take heed to their way, to walk before me as you have walked 26 before me.' Now therefore, O God of Israel, let thy word be confirmed, which thou hast spoken to thy servant David my father.

27   "But will God indeed dwell on the earth? Behold, heaven and the highest heaven cannot contain thee; how 28 much less this house which I have built! Yet have regard to the prayer of thy servant and to his supplication, O LORD my God, hearkening to the cry and to the prayer 29 which thy servant prays before thee this day; that thy eyes may be open night and day toward this house, the place of which thou hast said, 'My name shall be there,' that thou mayest hearken to the prayer which thy servant 30 offers toward this place. And hearken thou to the supplication of thy servant and of thy people Israel, when they pray toward this place; yea, hear thou in heaven thy dwelling place; and when thou hearest, forgive.

31   "If a man sins against his neighbor and is made to take an oath, and comes and swears his oath before thine 32 altar in this house, then hear thou in heaven, and act, and judge thy servants, condemning the guilty by bringing his conduct upon his own head, and vindicating the righteous by rewarding him according to his righteousness.

z Gk: Heb lacks *has set the sun in the heavens, but*

33 "When thy people Israel are defeated before the enemy because they have sinned against thee, if they turn again to thee, and acknowledge thy name, and pray and make 34 supplication to thee in this house; then hear thou in heaven, and forgive the sin of thy people Israel, and bring them again to the land which thou gavest to their fathers.

35 "When heaven is shut up and there is no rain because they have sinned against thee, if they pray toward this place, and acknowledge thy name, and turn from their 36 sin, when thou dost afflict them, then hear thou in heaven, and forgive the sin of thy servants, thy people Israel, when thou dost teach them the good way in which they should walk; and grant rain upon thy land, which thou hast given to thy people as an inheritance.

37 "If there is famine in the land, if there is pestilence or blight or mildew or locust or caterpillar; if their enemy besieges them in any a of their cities; whatever plague, 38 whatever sickness there is; whatever prayer, whatever supplication is made by any man or by all thy people Israel, each knowing the affliction of his own heart and 39 stretching out his hands toward this house; then hear thou in heaven thy dwelling place, and forgive, and act, and render to each whose heart thou knowest, according to all his ways (for thou, thou only, knowest the hearts of 40 all the children of men); that they may fear thee all the days that they live in the land which thou gavest to our fathers.

41 "Likewise when a foreigner, who is not of thy people Israel, comes from a far country for thy name's sake 42 (for they shall hear of thy great name, and thy mighty hand, and of thy outstretched arm), when he comes and 43 prays toward this house, hear thou in heaven thy dwelling place, and do according to all for which the foreigner calls to thee; in order that all the peoples of the earth may know thy name and fear thee, as do thy people Israel, and that they may know that this house which I have built is called by thy name.

44 "If thy people go out to battle against their enemy, by whatever way thou shalt send them, and they pray to the LORD toward the city which thou hast chosen and the 45 house which I have built for thy name, then hear thou in heaven their prayer and their supplication, and maintain their cause.

46 "If they sin against thee—for there is no man who does not sin—and thou art angry with them, and dost give them to an enemy, so that they are carried away 47 captive to the land of the enemy, far off or near; yet if they lay it to heart in the land to which they have been carried captive, and repent, and make supplication to thee in the land of their captors, saying, 'We have sinned, 48 and have acted perversely and wickedly'; if they repent with all their mind and with all their heart in the land of

a Gk Syr: Heb the land

their enemies, who carried them captive, and pray to thee toward their land, which thou gavest to their fathers, the city which thou hast chosen, and the house which I have 49 built for thy name; then hear thou in heaven thy dwelling place their prayer and their supplication, and main-50 tain their cause and forgive thy people who have sinned against thee, and all their transgressions which they have committed against thee; and grant them compassion in the sight of those who carried them captive, that they may 51 have compassion on them (for they are thy people, and thy heritage, which thou didst bring out of Egypt, from 52 the midst of the iron furnace). Let thy eyes be open to the supplication of thy servant, and to the supplication of thy people Israel, giving ear to them whenever they call 53 to thee. For thou didst separate them from among all the peoples of the earth, to be thy heritage, as thou didst declare through Moses, thy servant, when thou didst bring our fathers out of Egypt, O Lord GOD."

54 Now as Solomon finished offering all this prayer and supplication to the LORD, he arose from before the altar of the LORD, where he had knelt with hands outstretched 55 toward heaven; and he stood, and blessed all the as-56 sembly of Israel with a loud voice, saying, "Blessed be the LORD who has given rest to his people Israel, according to all that he promised; not one word has failed of all his good promise, which he uttered by Moses his servant. 57 The LORD our God be with us, as he was with our fathers; 58 may he not leave us or forsake us; that he may incline our hearts to him, to walk in all his ways, and to keep his commandments, his statutes, and his ordinances, which 59 he commanded our fathers. Let these words of mine, wherewith I have made supplication before the LORD, be near to the LORD our God day and night, and may he maintain the cause of his servant, and the cause of his 60 people Israel, as each day requires; that all the peoples of the earth may know that the LORD is God; there is no 61 other. Let your heart therefore be wholly true to the LORD our God, walking in his statutes and keeping his commandments, as at this day."

62 Then the king, and all Israel with him, offered sacrifice 63 before the LORD. Solomon offered as peace offerings to the LORD twenty-two thousand oxen and a hundred and twenty thousand sheep. So the king and all the people of 64 Israel dedicated the house of the LORD. The same day the king consecrated the middle of the court that was before the house of the LORD; for there he offered the burnt offering and the cereal offering and the fat pieces of the peace offerings, because the bronze altar that was before the LORD was too small to receive the burnt offering and the cereal offering and the fat pieces of the peace offerings.

65 So Solomon held the feast at that time, and all Israel with him, a great assembly, from the entrance of Hamath

to the Brook of Egypt, before the LORD our God, seven
66 days.[b] On the eighth day he sent the people away; and
they blessed the king, and went to their homes joyful and
glad of heart for all the goodness that the LORD had
shown to David his servant and to Israel his people.

Solomon's Decline

9 When Solomon had finished building the house of
the LORD and the king's house and all that Solomon de-
2 sired to build, the LORD appeared to Solomon a second
3 time, as he had appeared to him at Gibeon. And the LORD
said to him, "I have heard your prayer and your supplication, which you have made before me; I have consecrated this house which you have built, and put my name
there for ever; my eyes and my heart will be there for
4 all time. And as for you, if you will walk before me, as
David your father walked, with integrity of heart and
uprightness, doing according to all that I have commanded you, and keeping my statutes and my ordinances,
5 then I will establish your royal throne over Israel for
ever, as I promised David your father, saying, 'There
6 shall not fail you a man upon the throne of Israel.' But
if you turn aside from following me, you or your children, and do not keep my commandments and my statutes
which I have set before you, but go and serve other gods
7 and worship them, then I will cut off Israel from the land
which I have given them; and the house which I have
consecrated for my name I will cast out of my sight; and
Israel will become a proverb and a byword among all
8 peoples. And this house will become a heap of ruins;[c]
everyone passing by it will be astonished, and will hiss;
and they will say, 'Why has the LORD done thus to this
9 land and to this house?' Then they will say, 'Because
they forsook the LORD their God who brought their fathers
out of the land of Egypt, and laid hold on other gods,
and worshiped them and served them; therefore the LORD
has brought all this evil upon them.' "

10 At the end of twenty years, in which Solomon had
built the two houses, the house of the LORD and the king's
11 house, and Hiram king of Tyre had supplied Solomon
with cedar and cypress timber and gold, as much as he
desired, King Solomon gave to Hiram twenty cities in
12 the land of Galilee. But when Hiram came from Tyre to
see the cities which Solomon had given him, they did not
13 please him. Therefore he said, "What kind of cities are
these which you have given me, my brother?" So they
14 are called the land of Cabul to this day. Hiram had sent
to the king one hundred and twenty talents of gold.

15 And this is the account of the forced labor which King
Solomon levied to build the house of the LORD and his
own house and the Millo and the wall of Jerusalem and
16 Hazor and Megid'do and Gezer (Pharaoh king of Egypt
had gone up and captured Gezer and burnt it with fire,

and had slain the Canaanites who dwelt in the city, and
had given it as dowry to his daughter, Solomon's wife;
17, 18 so Solomon rebuilt Gezer) and Lower Beth-hor'on and
Ba'alath and Tamar in the wilderness, in the land of
19 Judah,[d] and all the store-cities that Solomon had, and
the cities for his chariots, and the cities for his horsemen,
and whatever Solomon desired to build in Jerusalem,
20 in Lebanon, and in all the land of his dominion. All the
people who were left of the Amorites, the Hittites, the
Per'izzites, the Hivites, and the Jeb'usites, who were not
21 of the people of Israel—their descendants who were left
after them in the land, whom the people of Israel were
unable to destroy utterly—these Solomon made a forced
22 levy of slaves, and so they are to this day. But of the
people of Israel Solomon made no slaves; they were the
soldiers, they were his officials, his commanders, his captains, his chariot commanders and his horsemen.

23 These were the chief officers who were over Solomon's
work: five hundred and fifty, who had charge of the
people who carried on the work.

24 But Pharaoh's daughter went up from the city of David
to her own house which Solomon had built for her; then
he built the Millo.

25 Three times a year Solomon used to offer up burnt
offerings and peace offerings upon the altar which he
built to the LORD, burning incense[e] before the LORD. So
he finished the house.

26 King Solomon built a fleet of ships at E'zion-ge'ber,
which is near Eloth on the shore of the Red Sea, in the
27 land of Edom. And Hiram sent with the fleet his servants,
seamen who were familiar with the sea, together with the
28 servants of Solomon; and they went to Ophir, and brought
from there gold, to the amount of four hundred and
twenty talents; and they brought it to King Solomon.

10 Now when the queen of Sheba heard of the fame of
Solomon concerning the name of the LORD, she came
2 to test him with hard questions. She came to Jerusalem
with a very great retinue, with camels bearing spices, and
very much gold, and precious stones; and when she came
3 to Solomon, she told him all that was on her mind. And
Solomon answered all her questions; there was nothing
hidden from the king which he could not explain to her.
4 And when the queen of Sheba had seen all the wisdom

[b] Gk: Heb *seven days and seven days, fourteen days*   [c] Syr Old Latin: Heb *high*   [d] Heb lacks *of Judah*
[e] Gk: Heb *burning incense with it which*

5 of Solomon, the house that he had built, the food of his table, the seating of his officials, and the attendance of his servants, their clothing, his cupbearers, and his burnt offerings which he offered at the house of the LORD, there was no more spirit in her.

6 And she said to the king, "The report was true which I heard in my own land of your affairs and of your wis-
7 dom, but I did not believe the reports until I came and my own eyes had seen it; and, behold, the half was not told me; your wisdom and prosperity surpass the re-
8 port which I heard. Happy are your wives![f] Happy are these your servants, who continually stand before you
9 and hear your wisdom! Blessed be the LORD your God, who has delighted in you and set you on the throne of Israel! Because the LORD loved Israel for ever, he has made you king, that you may execute justice and righ-
10 teousness." Then she gave the king a hundred and twenty talents of gold, and a very great quantity of spices, and precious stones; never again came such an abundance of spices as these which the queen of Sheba gave to King Solomon.

11 Moreover the fleet of Hiram, which brought gold from Ophir, brought from Ophir a very great amount of almug
12 wood and precious stones. And the king made of the almug wood supports for the house of the LORD, and for the king's house, lyres also and harps for the singers; no such almug wood has come or been seen, to this day.

13 And King Solomon gave to the queen of Sheba all that she desired, whatever she asked besides what was given her by the bounty of King Solomon. So she turned and went back to her own land, with her servants.

14 Now the weight of gold that came to Solomon in one
15 year was six hundred and sixty-six talents of gold, besides that which came from the traders and from the traffic of the merchants, and from all the kings of Arabia and from
16 the governors of the land. King Solomon made two hundred large shields of beaten gold; six hundred shekels of
17 gold went into each shield. And he made three hundred shields of beaten gold; three minas of gold went into each shield; and the king put them in the House of the Forest
18 of Lebanon. The king also made a great ivory throne,
19 and overlaid it with the finest gold. The throne had six steps, and at the back of the throne was a calf's head, and on each side of the seat were arm rests and two lions
20 standing beside the arm rests, while twelve lions stood there, one on each end of a step on the six steps. The like
21 of it was never made in any kingdom. All King Solomon's drinking vessels were of gold, and all the vessels of the House of the Forest of Lebanon were of pure gold; none were of silver, it was not considered as anything in the
22 days of Solomon. For the king had a fleet of ships of Tarshish at sea with the fleet of Hiram. Once every three years the fleet of ships of Tarshish used to come bringing

gold, silver, ivory, apes, and peacocks.[g]

23 Thus King Solomon excelled all the kings of the earth
24 in riches and in wisdom. And the whole earth sought the presence of Solomon to hear his wisdom, which God had
25 put into his mind. Every one of them brought his present, articles of silver and gold, garments, myrrh, spices, horses, and mules, so much year by year.

26 And Solomon gathered together chariots and horsemen; he had fourteen hundred chariots and twelve thousand horsemen, whom he stationed in the chariot cities
27 and with the king in Jerusalem. And the king made silver as common in Jerusalem as stone, and he made cedar as
28 plentiful as the sycamore of the Shephe'lah. And Solomon's import of horses was from Egypt and Ku'e, and the
29 king's traders received them from Ku'e at a price. A chariot could be imported from Egypt for six hundred shekels of silver, and a horse for a hundred and fifty; and so through the king's traders they were exported to all the kings of the Hittites and the kings of Syria.

11 Now King Solomon loved many foreign women: the daughter of Pharaoh, and Moabite, Ammonite,
2 Edomite, Sido'nian, and Hittite women, from the nations concerning which the LORD had said to the people of Israel, "You shall not enter into marriage with them, neither shall they with you, for surely they will turn away your heart after their gods"; Solomon clung to
3 these in love. He had seven hundred wives, princesses, and three hundred concubines; and his wives turned
4 away his heart. For when Solomon was old his wives turned away his heart after other gods; and his heart was not wholly true to the LORD his God, as was the heart of
5 David his father. For Solomon went after Ash'toreth the goddess of the Sido'nians, and after Milcom the abomina-
6 tion of the Ammonites. So Solomon did what was evil in the sight of the LORD, and did not wholly follow the
7 LORD, as David his father had done. Then Solomon built a high place for Chemosh the abomination of Moab, and for Molech the abomination of the Ammonites, on
8 the mountain east of Jerusalem. And so he did for all his foreign wives, who burned incense and sacrificed to their gods.

9 And the LORD was angry with Solomon, because his heart had turned away from the LORD, the God of Israel,
10 who had appeared to him twice, and had commanded him concerning this thing, that he should not go after other gods; but he did not keep what the LORD commanded.
11 Therefore the LORD said to Solomon, "Since this has been your mind and you have not kept my covenant and my statutes which I have commanded you, I will surely tear the kingdom from you and will give it to your servant.
12 Yet for the sake of David your father I will not do it in your days, but I will tear it out of the hand of your son.
13 However I will not tear away all the kingdom; but I will

---

[f] Gk Syr: Heb *men*   [g] Or *baboons*

give one tribe to your son, for the sake of David my servant and for the sake of Jerusalem which I have chosen."

14 And the LORD raised up an adversary against Solomon, Hadad the Edomite; he was of the royal house in Edom.
15 For when David was in Edom, and Jo'ab the commander of the army went up to bury the slain, he slew every male
16 in Edom (for Jo'ab and all Israel remained there six
17 months, until he had cut off every male in Edom); but Hadad fled to Egypt, together with certain Edomites of
18 his father's servants, Hadad being yet a little child. They set out from Mid'ian and came to Paran, and took men with them from Paran and came to Egypt, to Pharaoh king of Egypt, who gave him a house, and assigned him
19 an allowance of food, and gave him land. And Hadad found great favor in the sight of Pharaoh, so that he gave him in marriage the sister of his own wife, the sister
20 of Tah'penes the queen. And the sister of Tah'penes bore him Genu'bath his son, whom Tah'penes weaned in Pharaoh's house; and Genu'bath was in Pharaoh's house
21 among the sons of Pharaoh. But when Hadad heard in Egypt that David slept with his fathers and that Jo'ab the commander of the army was dead, Hadad said to Pharaoh, "Let me depart, that I may go to my own
22 country." But Pharaoh said to him, "What have you lacked with me that you are now seeking to go to your own country?" And he said to him, "Only let me go."

23 God also raised up as an adversary to him, Rezon the son of Eli'ada, who had fled from his master Hadad-e'zer
24 king of Zobah. And he gathered men about him and became leader of a marauding band, after the slaughter by David; and they went to Damascus, and dwelt there,
25 and made him king in Damascus. He was an adversary of Israel all the days of Solomon, doing mischief as Hadad did; and he abhorred Israel, and reigned over Syria.

26 Jerobo'am the son of Nebat, an E'phraimite of Zer'edah, a servant of Solomon, whose mother's name was Zeru'ah, a widow, also lifted up his hand against the king.
27 And this was the reason why he lifted up his hand against the king. Solomon built the Millo, and closed up the
28 breach of the city of David his father. The man Jerobo'am was very able, and when Solomon saw that the young man was industrious he gave him charge over all the forced
29 labor of the house of Joseph. And at that time, when Jerobo'am went out of Jerusalem, the prophet Ahi'jah the Shi'lonite found him on the road. Now Ahi'jah had clad himself with a new garment; and the two of them
30 were alone in the open country. Then Ahi'jah laid hold of the new garment that was on him, and tore it into twelve
31 pieces. And he said to Jerobo'am, "Take for yourself ten pieces; for thus says the LORD, the God of Israel, 'Behold, I am about to tear the kingdom from the hand of Solo-

32 mon, and will give you ten tribes (but he shall have one tribe, for the sake of my servant David and for the sake of Jerusalem, the city which I have chosen out of all the
33 tribes of Israel), because he has ʰ forsaken me, and worshiped Ash'toreth the goddess of the Sido'nians, Chemosh

the god of Moab, and Milcom the god of the Ammonites, and has ʰ not walked in my ways, doing what is right in my sight and keeping my statutes and my ordinances, as
34 David his father did. Nevertheless I will not take the whole kingdom out of his hand; but I will make him ruler all the days of his life, for the sake of David my servant whom I chose, who kept my commandments and
35 my statutes; but I will take the kingdom out of his son's
36 hand, and will give it to you, ten tribes. Yet to his son I will give one tribe, that David my servant may always have a lamp before me in Jerusalem, the city where I have
37 chosen to put my name. And I will take you, and you shall reign over all that your soul desires, and you shall
38 be king over Israel. And if you will hearken to all that I command you, and will walk in my ways, and do what is right in my eyes by keeping my statutes and my commandments, as David my servant did, I will be with you, and will build you a sure house, as I built for David, and
39 I will give Israel to you. And I will for this afflict the
40 descendants of David, but not for ever.' " Solomon sought therefore to kill Jerobo'am; but Jerobo'am arose, and fled into Egypt, to Shishak king of Egypt, and was in Egypt until the death of Solomon.

41 Now the rest of the acts of Solomon, and all that he did, and his wisdom, are they not written in the book of
42 the acts of Solomon? And the time that Solomon reigned
43 in Jerusalem over all Israel was forty years. And Solomon slept with his fathers, and was buried in the city of David his father; and Rehobo'am his son reigned in his stead.

THE TWO KINGDOMS

12 Rehobo'am went to Shechem, for all Israel had
2 come to Shechem to make him king. And when Jerobo'am the son of Nebat heard of it (for he was still in Egypt, whither he had fled from King Solomon),
3 then Jerobo'am returned from ⁱ Egypt. And they sent and called him; and Jerobo'am and all the assembly of Israel
4 came and said to Rehobo'am, "Your father made our yoke

ʰ Gk Syr Vg: Heb they have   ⁱ Gk Vg Compare 2 Ch 10. 2: Heb dwelt in

heavy. Now therefore lighten the hard service of your father and his heavy yoke upon us, and we will serve 5 you." He said to them, "Depart for three days, then come again to me." So the people went away.

6 Then King Rehobo'am took counsel with the old men, who had stood before Solomon his father while he was yet alive, saying, "How do you advise me to answer this 7 people?" And they said to him, "If you will be a servant to this people today and serve them, and speak good words to them when you answer them, then they will be 8 your servants for ever." But he forsook the counsel which the old men gave him, and took counsel with the young men who had grown up with him and stood before him. 9 And he said to them, "What do you advise that we answer this people who have said to me, 'Lighten the 10 yoke that your father put upon us'?" And the young men who had grown up with him said to him, "Thus shall you speak to this people who said to you, 'Your father made our yoke heavy, but do you lighten it for us'; thus shall you say to them, 'My little finger is thicker than my 11 father's loins. And now, whereas my father laid upon you a heavy yoke, I will add to your yoke. My father chastised you with whips, but I will chastise you with scorpions.'"

12 So Jerobo'am and all the people came to Rehobo'am the third day, as the king said, "Come to me again the 13 third day." And the king answered the people harshly, and forsaking the counsel which the old men had given 14 him, he spoke to them according to the counsel of the young men, saying, "My father made your yoke heavy, but I will add to your yoke; my father chastised you with 15 whips, but I will chastise you with scorpions." So the king did not hearken to the people; for it was a turn of affairs brought about by the LORD that he might fulfil his

word, which the LORD spoke by Ahi'jah the Shi'lonite to Jerobo'am the son of Nebat.

16 And when all Israel saw that the king did not hearken to them, the people answered the king,

"What portion have we in David?
　We have no inheritance in the son of Jesse.
To your tents, O Israel!
　Look now to your own house, David."

17 So Israel departed to their tents. But Rehobo'am reigned over the people of Israel who dwelt in the cities of Judah. 18 Then King Rehobo'am sent Ado'ram, who was taskmaster over the forced labor, and all Israel stoned him to death with stones. And King Rehobo'am made haste to mount 19 his chariot, to flee to Jerusalem. So Israel has been in 20 rebellion against the house of David to this day. And

ʲ Gk: Heb *went to the one as far as Dan*

when all Israel heard that Jerobo'am had returned, they sent and called him to the assembly and made him king over all Israel. There was none that followed the house of David, but the tribe of Judah only.

21 When Rehobo'am came to Jerusalem, he assembled all the house of Judah, and the tribe of Benjamin, a hundred and eighty thousand chosen warriors, to fight against the house of Israel, to restore the kingdom to Rehobo'am 22 the son of Solomon. But the word of God came to 23 Shemai'ah the man of God: "Say to Rehobo'am the son of Solomon, king of Judah, and to all the house of Judah 24 and Benjamin, and to the rest of the people, 'Thus says the LORD, You shall not go up or fight against your kinsmen the people of Israel. Return every man to his home, for this thing is from me.'" So they hearkened to the word of the LORD, and went home again, according to the word of the LORD.

25 Then Jerobo'am built Shechem in the hill country of E'phraim, and dwelt there; and he went out from there 26 and built Penu'el. And Jerobo'am said in his heart, "Now the kingdom will turn back to the house of David; 27 if this people go up to offer sacrifices in the house of the LORD at Jerusalem, then the heart of this people will turn again to their lord, to Rehobo'am king of Judah, and they will kill me and return to Rehobo'am king of Judah." 28 So the king took counsel, and made two calves of gold. And he said to the people, "You have gone up to Jerusalem long enough. Behold your gods, O Israel, who 29 brought you up out of the land of Egypt." And he set one 30 in Bethel, and the other he put in Dan. And this thing became a sin, for the people went to the one at Bethel and 31 to the other as far as Dan.ʲ He also made houses on high places, and appointed priests from among all the people, 32 who were not of the Levites. And Jerobo'am appointed a feast on the fifteenth day of the eighth month like the feast that was in Judah, and he offered sacrifices upon the altar; so he did in Bethel, sacrificing to the calves that he had made. And he placed in Bethel the priests of 33 the high places that he had made. He went up to the altar which he had made in Bethel on the fifteenth day in the eighth month, in the month which he had devised of his own heart; and he ordained a feast for the people of Israel, and went up to the altar to burn incense.

13 And behold, a man of God came out of Judah by the word of the LORD to Bethel. Jerobo'am was 2 standing by the altar to burn incense. And the man cried against the altar by the word of the LORD, and said, "O altar, altar, thus says the LORD: 'Behold, a son shall be born to the house of David, Josi'ah by name; and he shall sacrifice upon you the priests of the high places who burn incense upon you, and men's bones shall be 3 burned upon you.'" And he gave a sign the same day, saying, "This is the sign that the LORD has spoken: 'Be-

hold, the altar shall be torn down, and the ashes that are
4 upon it shall be poured out.' " And when the king heard
the saying of the man of God, which he cried against the
altar at Bethel, Jerobo'am stretched out his hand from the
altar, saying, "Lay hold of him." And his hand, which
he stretched out against him, dried up, so that he could
5 not draw it back to himself. The altar also was torn down,
and the ashes poured out from the altar, according to
the sign which the man of God had given by the word of
6 the LORD. And the king said to the man of God, "Entreat
now the favor of the LORD your God, and pray for me,
that my hand may be restored to me." And the man of
God entreated the LORD; and the king's hand was restored
7 to him, and became as it was before. And the king said
to the man of God, "Come home with me, and refresh
8 yourself, and I will give you a reward." And the man of
God said to the king, "If you give me half your house, I
will not go in with you. And I will not eat bread or drink
9 water in this place; for so was it commanded me by the
word of the LORD, saying, 'You shall neither eat bread,
nor drink water, nor return by the way that you came.' "
10 So he went another way, and did not return by the way
that he came to Bethel.

11 Now there dwelt an old prophet in Bethel. And his
sons[k] came and told him all that the man of God had

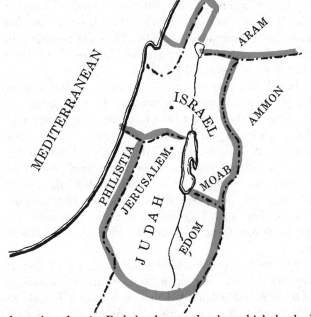

done that day in Bethel; the words also which he had
12 spoken to the king, they told to their father. And their
father said to them, "Which way did he go?" And his
sons showed him the way which the man of God who
13 came from Judah had gone. And he said to his sons,
"Saddle the ass for me." So they saddled the ass for him
14 and he mounted it. And he went after the man of God,
and found him sitting under an oak; and he said to him,
"Are you the man of God who came from Judah?" And

15 he said, "I am." Then he said to him, "Come home with
16 me and eat bread." And he said, "I may not return
with you, or go in with you; neither will I eat bread nor
17 drink water with you in this place; for it was said to me
by the word of the LORD, 'You shall neither eat bread
nor drink water there, nor return by the way that you
18 came.' " And he said to him, "I also am a prophet as
you are, and an angel spoke to me by the word of the
LORD, saying, 'Bring him back with you into your house
that he may eat bread and drink water.' " But he lied to
19 him. So he went back with him, and ate bread in his
house, and drank water.

20 And as they sat at the table, the word of the LORD
21 came to the prophet who had brought him back; and he
cried to the man of God who came from Judah, "Thus
says the LORD, 'Because you have disobeyed the word of
the LORD, and have not kept the commandment which the
22 LORD your God commanded you, but have come back,
and have eaten bread and drunk water in the place of
which he said to you, "Eat no bread, and drink no
water"; your body shall not come to the tomb of your
23 fathers.' " And after he had eaten bread and drunk, he
saddled the ass for the prophet whom he had brought
24 back. And as he went away a lion met him on the road
and killed him. And his body was thrown in the road,
and the ass stood beside it; the lion also stood beside the
25 body. And behold, men passed by, and saw the body
thrown in the road, and the lion standing by the body.
And they came and told it in the city where the old
prophet dwelt.

26 And when the prophet who had brought him back from
the way heard of it, he said, "It is the man of God, who
disobeyed the word of the LORD; therefore the LORD has
given him to the lion, which has torn him and slain him,
27 according to the word which the LORD spoke to him." And
he said to his sons, "Saddle the ass for me." And they
28 saddled it. And he went and found his body thrown in
the road, and the ass and the lion standing beside the
body. The lion had not eaten the body or torn the ass.
29 And the prophet took up the body of the man of God and
laid it upon the ass, and brought it back to the city,[l] to
30 mourn and to bury him. And he laid the body in his own
grave; and they mourned over him, saying, "Alas, my
31 brother!" And after he had buried him, he said to his
sons, "When I die, bury me in the grave in which the
man of God is buried; lay my bones beside his bones.
32 For the saying which he cried by the word of the LORD
against the altar in Bethel, and against all the houses of
the high places which are in the cities of Samar'ia, shall
surely come to pass."

33 After this thing Jerobo'am did not turn from his evil
way, but made priests for the high places again from
among all the people; any who would, he consecrated to

k Gk Syr Vg: Heb *son*   l Gk: Heb *he came to the city of the old prophet*

34 be priests of the high places. And this thing became sin to the house of Jerobo'am, so as to cut it off and to destroy it from the face of the earth.

14 At that time Abi'jah the son of Jerobo'am fell
2 sick. And Jerobo'am said to his wife, "Arise, and disguise yourself, that it be not known that you are the wife of Jerobo'am, and go to Shiloh; behold, Ahi'jah the prophet is there, who said of me that I should be king
3 over this people. Take with you ten loaves, some cakes, and a jar of honey, and go to him; he will tell you what shall happen to the child."
4 Jerobo'am's wife did so; she arose, and went to Shiloh, and came to the house of Ahi'jah. Now Ahi'jah could
5 not see, for his eyes were dim because of his age. And the LORD said to Ahi'jah, "Behold, the wife of Jerobo'am is coming to inquire of you concerning her son; for he is sick. Thus and thus shall you say to her."

When she came, she pretended to be another woman.
6 But when Ahi'jah heard the sound of her feet, as she came in at the door, he said, "Come in, wife of Jerobo'-am; why do you pretend to be another? For I am
7 charged with heavy tidings for you. Go, tell Jerobo'am, 'Thus says the LORD, the God of Israel: "Because I exalted you from among the people, and made you leader over
8 my people Israel, and tore the kingdom away from the house of David and gave it to you; and yet you have not been like my servant David, who kept my commandments, and followed me with all his heart, doing only
9 that which was right in my eyes, but you have done evil above all that were before you and have gone and made for yourself other gods, and molten images, provoking
10 me to anger, and have cast me behind your back; therefore behold, I will bring evil upon the house of Jerobo'-am, and will cut off from Jerobo'am every male, both bond and free in Israel, and will utterly consume the house of Jerobo'am, as a man burns up dung until it is
11 all gone. Any one belonging to Jerobo'am who dies in the city the dogs shall eat; and any one who dies in the open country the birds of the air shall eat; for the LORD
12 has spoken it." ' Arise therefore, go to your house. When
13 your feet enter the city, the child shall die. And all Israel shall mourn for him, and bury him; for he only of Jero-bo'am shall come to the grave, because in him there is found something pleasing to the LORD, the God of Israel,
14 in the house of Jerobo'am. Moreover the LORD will raise up for himself a king over Israel, who shall cut off the
15 house of Jerobo'am today. And henceforth m the LORD will smite Israel, as a reed is shaken in the water, and root up Israel out of this good land which he gave to their fathers, and scatter them beyond the Eu-phra'tes, because they have made their Ashe'rim, provoking the LORD to
16 anger. And he will give Israel up because of the sins of Jerobo'am, which he sinned and which he made Israel to sin."

m Heb obscure

17 Then Jerobo'am's wife arose, and departed, and came to Tirzah. And as she came to the threshold of the house,
18 the child died. And all Israel buried him and mourned for him, according to the word of the LORD, which he
19 spoke by his servant Ahi'jah the prophet. Now the rest of the acts of Jerobo'am, how he warred and how he reigned, behold, they are written in the Book of the
20 Chronicles of the Kings of Israel. And the time that Jerobo'am reigned was twenty-two years; and he slept with his fathers, and Nadab his son reigned in his stead.
21 Now Rehobo'am the son of Solomon reigned in Judah. Rehobo'am was forty-one years old when he began to reign, and he reigned seventeen years in Jerusalem, the city which the LORD had chosen out of all the tribes of Israel, to put his name there. His mother's name was

22 Na'amah the Ammonitess. And Judah did what was evil in the sight of the LORD, and they provoked him to jealousy with their sins which they committed, more than
23 all that their fathers had done. For they also built for themselves high places, and pillars, and Ashe'rim on every
24 high hill and under every green tree; and there were also male cult prostitutes in the land. They did according to all the abominations of the nations which the LORD drove out before the people of Israel.
25 In the fifth year of King Rehobo'am, Shishak king of
26 Egypt came up against Jerusalem; he took away the treasures of the house of the LORD and the treasures of the king's house; he took away everything. He also took away all the shields of gold which Solomon had made;
27 and King Rehobo'am made in their stead shields of bronze, and committed them to the hands of the officers of the guard, who kept the door of the king's house.
28 And as often as the king went into the house of the LORD, the guard bore them and brought them back to the guard-room.
29 Now the rest of the acts of Rehobo'am, and all that he did, are they not written in the Book of the Chronicles
30 of the Kings of Judah? And there was war between Reho-
31 bo'am and Jerobo'am continually. And Rehobo'am slept with his fathers and was buried with his fathers in the city of David. His mother's name was Na'amah the Ammonitess. And Abi'jam his son reigned in his stead.

Wars Between Israel and Judah

15 Now in the eighteenth year of King Jerobo'am the son of Nebat, Abi'jam began to reign over Judah.
2 He reigned for three years in Jerusalem. His mother's
3 name was Ma'acah the daughter of Abish'alom. And he

walked in all the sins which his father did before him; and his heart was not wholly true to the LORD his God, ⁴ as the heart of David his father. Nevertheless for David's sake the LORD his God gave him a lamp in Jerusalem, setting up his son after him, and establishing Jerusalem; ⁵ because David did what was right in the eyes of the LORD, and did not turn aside from anything that he commanded him all the days of his life, except in the matter of Uri'ah ⁶ the Hittite. Now there was war between Rehobo'am and ⁷ Jerobo'am all the days of his life. The rest of the acts of Abi'jam, and all that he did, are they not written in the Book of the Chronicles of the Kings of Judah? And there ⁸ was war between Abi'jam and Jerobo'am. And Abi'jam slept with his fathers; and they buried him in the city of David. And Asa his son reigned in his stead.

⁹ In the twentieth year of Jerobo'am king of Israel Asa ¹⁰ began to reign over Judah, and he reigned forty-one years in Jerusalem. His mother's name was Ma'acah the ¹¹ daughter of Abish'alom. And Asa did what was right in ¹² the eyes of the LORD, as David his father had done. He put away the male cult prostitutes out of the land, and ¹³ removed all the idols that his fathers had made. He also removed Ma'acah his mother from being queen mother because she had an abominable image made for Ashe'rah; and Asa cut down her image and burned it at the brook ¹⁴ Kidron. But the high places were not taken away. Nevertheless the heart of Asa was wholly true to the LORD all ¹⁵ his days. And he brought into the house of the LORD the votive gifts of his father and his own votive gifts, silver, and gold, and vessels.

¹⁶ And there was war between Asa and Ba'asha king of ¹⁷ Israel all their days. Ba'asha king of Israel went up against Judah, and built Ramah, that he might permit no ¹⁸ one to go out or come in to Asa king of Judah. Then Asa took all the silver and the gold that were left in the treasures of the house of the LORD and the treasures of the king's house, and gave them into the hands of his servants; and King Asa sent them to Ben-ha'dad the son of Tabrim'mon, the son of He'zi-on, king of Syria, who ¹⁹ dwelt in Damascus, saying, "Let there be a league between me and you, as between my father and your father: behold, I am sending to you a present of silver and gold; go, break your league with Ba'asha king of Israel, that he ²⁰ may withdraw from me." And Ben-ha'dad hearkened to King Asa, and sent the commanders of his armies against the cities of Israel, and conquered Ijon, Dan, A'bel-beth-ma'acah, and all Chin'neroth, with all the land of Naph'- ²¹ tali. And when Ba'asha heard of it, he stopped building ²² Ramah, and he dwelt in Tirzah. Then King Asa made a proclamation to all Judah, none was exempt, and they carried away the stones of Ramah and its timber, with which Ba'asha had been building; and with them King ²³ Asa built Geba of Benjamin and Mizpah. Now the rest

of all the acts of Asa, all his might, and all that he did, and the cities which he built, are they not written in the Book of the Chronicles of the Kings of Judah? But in his ²⁴ old age he was diseased in his feet. And Asa slept with his fathers, and was buried with his fathers in the city of David his father; and Jehosh'aphat his son reigned in his stead.

²⁵ Nadab the son of Jerobo'am began to reign over Israel in the second year of Asa king of Judah; and he reigned ²⁶ over Israel two years. He did what was evil in the sight of the LORD, and walked in the way of his father, and in his sin which he made Israel to sin.

²⁷ Ba'asha the son of Ahi'jah, of the house of Is'sachar, conspired against him; and Ba'asha struck him down at Gib'bethon, which belonged to the Philistines; for Nadab ²⁸ and all Israel were laying siege to Gib'bethon. So Ba'asha killed him in the third year of Asa king of Judah, and ²⁹ reigned in his stead. And as soon as he was king, he killed all the house of Jerobo'am; he left to the house of Jerobo'am not one that breathed, until he had destroyed it, according to the word of the LORD which he spoke by ³⁰ his servant Ahi'jah the Shi'lonite; it was for the sins of Jerobo'am which he sinned and which he made Israel to sin, and because of the anger to which he provoked the LORD, the God of Israel.

³¹ Now the rest of the acts of Nadab, and all that he did, are they not written in the Book of the Chronicles ³² of the Kings of Israel? And there was war between Asa and Ba'asha king of Israel all their days.

³³ In the third year of Asa king of Judah, Ba'asha the son of Ahi'jah began to reign over all Israel at Tirzah, and ³⁴ reigned twenty-four years. He did what was evil in the sight of the LORD, and walked in the way of Jerobo'am and in his sin which he made Israel to sin.

16 And the word of the LORD came to Jehu the son ² of Hana'ni against Ba'asha, saying, "Since I exalted you out of the dust and made you leader over my people Israel, and you have walked in the way of Jerobo'am, and have made my people Israel to sin, provoking me to anger ³ with their sins, behold, I will utterly sweep away Ba'asha and his house, and I will make your house like the house ⁴ of Jerobo'am the son of Nebat. Any one belonging to Ba'asha who dies in the city the dogs shall eat; and any one of his who dies in the field the birds of the air shall eat."

⁵ Now the rest of the acts of Ba'asha, and what he did, and his might, are they not written in the Book of the ⁶ Chronicles of the Kings of Israel? And Ba'asha slept with his fathers, and was buried at Tirzah; and Elah his son ⁷ reigned in his stead. Moreover the word of the LORD came by the prophet Jehu the son of Hana'ni against Ba'asha and his house, both because of all the evil that he did in the sight of the LORD, provoking him to anger with the

work of his hands, in being like the house of Jerobo′am, and also because he destroyed it.

8 In the twenty-sixth year of Asa king of Judah, Elah the son of Ba′asha began to reign over Israel in Tirzah, and 9 reigned two years. But his servant Zimri, commander of half his chariots, conspired against him. When he was at Tirzah, drinking himself drunk in the house of Arza, 10 who was over the household in Tirzah, Zimri came in and struck him down and killed him, in the twenty-seventh year of Asa king of Judah, and reigned in his stead.

11 When he began to reign, as soon as he had seated himself on his throne, he killed all the house of Ba′asha; he did not leave him a single male of his kinsmen or his 12 friends. Thus Zimri destroyed all the house of Ba′asha, according to the word of the LORD, which he spoke 13 against Ba′asha by Jehu the prophet, for all the sins of Ba′asha and the sins of Elah his son which they sinned, and which they made Israel to sin, provoking the LORD 14 God of Israel to anger with their idols. Now the rest of the acts of Elah, and all that he did, are they not written in the Book of the Chronicles of the Kings of Israel?

15 In the twenty-seventh year of Asa king of Judah, Zimri reigned seven days in Tirzah. Now the troops were encamped against Gib′bethon, which belonged to the Phi- 16 listines, and the troops who were encamped heard it said, "Zimri has conspired, and he has killed the king"; therefore all Israel made Omri, the commander of the army, 17 king over Israel that day in the camp. So Omri went up from Gib′bethon, and all Israel with him, and they be- 18 sieged Tirzah. And when Zimri saw that the city was taken, he went into the citadel of the king's house, and 19 burned the king's house over him with fire, and died, because of his sins which he committed, doing evil in the sight of the LORD, walking in the way of Jerobo′am, and for his sin which he committed, making Israel to sin. 20 Now the rest of the acts of Zimri, and the conspiracy which he made, are they not written in the Book of the Chronicles of the Kings of Israel?

21 Then the people of Israel were divided into two parts; half of the people followed Tibni the son of Ginath, to 22 make him king, and half followed Omri. But the people who followed Omri overcame the people who followed Tibni the son of Ginath; so Tibni died, and Omri became 23 king. In the thirty-first year of Asa king of Judah, Omri began to reign over Israel, and reigned for twelve years; 24 six years he reigned in Tirzah. He bought the hill of Samar′ia from Shemer for two talents of silver; and he fortified the hill, and called the name of the city which he built, Samar′ia, after the name of Shemer, the owner of the hill.

25 Omri did what was evil in the sight of the LORD, and 26 did more evil than all who were before him. For he walked in all the way of Jerobo′am the son of Nebat, and in the sins which he made Israel to sin, provoking the

27 LORD, the God of Israel, to anger by their idols. Now the rest of the acts of Omri which he did, and the might that he showed, are they not written in the Book of the 28 Chronicles of the Kings of Israel? And Omri slept with his fathers, and was buried in Samar′ia; and Ahab his son reigned in his stead.

King Ahab and the Prophet Elijah

29 In the thirty-eighth year of Asa king of Judah, Ahab the son of Omri began to reign over Israel, and Ahab the son of Omri reigned over Israel in Samar′ia twenty- 30 two years. And Ahab the son of Omri did evil in the sight of the LORD more than all that were before him. 31 And as if it had been a light thing for him to walk in the sins of Jerobo′am the son of Nebat, he took for wife Jez′ebel the daughter of Ethba′al king of the Sido′nians, 32 and went and served Ba′al, and worshiped him. He erected an altar for Ba′al in the house of Ba′al, which he 33 built in Samar′ia. And Ahab made an Ashe′rah. Ahab did more to provoke the LORD, the God of Israel, to anger 34 than all the kings of Israel who were before him. In his days Hi′el of Bethel built Jericho; he laid its foundation at the cost of Abi′ram his first-born, and set up its gates at the cost of his youngest son Segub, according to the word of the LORD, which he spoke by Joshua the son of Nun.

17 Now Eli′jah the Tishbite, of Tishbe[n] in Gilead, said to Ahab, "As the LORD the God of Israel lives, before whom I stand, there shall be neither dew nor rain 2 these years, except by my word." And the word of the 3 LORD came to him, "Depart from here and turn eastward, and hide yourself by the brook Cherith, that is east of 4 the Jordan. You shall drink from the brook, and I have 5 commanded the ravens to feed you there." So he went and did according to the word of the LORD; he went and dwelt by the brook Cherith that is east of the Jordan. 6 And the ravens brought him bread and meat in the morning, and bread and meat in the evening; and he 7 drank from the brook. And after a while the brook dried up, because there was no rain in the land.

8, 9 The word of the LORD came to him, "Arise, go to Zar′ephath, which belongs to Sidon, and dwell there. Behold, I have commanded a widow there to feed you." 10 So he arose and went to Zar′ephath; and when he came to the gate of the city, behold, a widow was there gathering sticks; and he called to her and said, "Bring me a 11 little water in a vessel, that I may drink." And as she was going to bring it, he called to her and said, "Bring

[n] Gk: Heb of the settlers

12 me a morsel of bread in your hand." And she said, "As the LORD your God lives, I have nothing baked, only a handful of meal in a jar, and a little oil in a cruse; and now, I am gathering a couple of sticks, that I may go in and prepare it for myself and my son, that we may eat
13 it, and die." And Eli'jah said to her, "Fear not; go and do as you have said; but first make me a little cake of it and bring it to me, and afterward make for yourself and
14 your son. For thus says the LORD the God of Israel, 'The jar of meal shall not be spent, and the cruse of oil shall not fail, until the day that the LORD sends rain upon the
15 earth.' " And she went and did as Eli'jah said; and she,
16 and he, and her household ate for many days. The jar of meal was not spent, neither did the cruse of oil fail, according to the word of the LORD which he spoke by Eli'jah.

17 After this the son of the woman, the mistress of the house, became ill; and his illness was so severe that there
18 was no breath left in him. And she said to Eli'jah, "What have you against me, O man of God? You have come to me to bring my sin to remembrance, and to cause the
19 death of my son!" And he said to her, "Give me your son." And he took him from her bosom, and carried him up into the upper chamber, where he lodged, and laid him
20 upon his own bed. And he cried to the LORD, "O LORD my God, hast thou brought calamity even upon the widow
21 with whom I sojourn, by slaying her son?" Then he stretched himself upon the child three times, and cried to the LORD, "O LORD my God, let this child's soul come
22 into him again." And the LORD hearkened to the voice of Eli'jah; and the soul of the child came into him again,
23 and he revived. And Eli'jah took the child, and brought him down from the upper chamber into the house, and delivered him to his mother; and Eli'jah said, "See, your
24 son lives." And the woman said to Eli'jah, "Now I know that you are a man of God, and that the word of the LORD in your mouth is truth."

18 After many days the word of the LORD came to Eli'jah, in the third year, saying, "Go, show your-
2 self to Ahab; and I will send rain upon the earth." So Eli'jah went to show himself to Ahab. Now the famine
3 was severe in Samar'ia. And Ahab called Obadi'ah, who was over the household. (Now Obadi'ah revered the
4 LORD greatly; and when Jez'ebel cut off the prophets of the LORD, Obadi'ah took a hundred prophets and hid them by fifties in a cave, and fed them with bread and
5 water.) And Ahab said to Obadi'ah, "Go through the land to all the springs of water and to all the valleys; perhaps we may find grass and save the horses and mules
6 alive, and not lose some of the animals." So they divided the land between them to pass through it; Ahab went in one direction by himself, and Obadi'ah went in another direction by himself.

7 And as Obadi'ah was on the way, behold, Eli'jah met him; and Obadi'ah recognized him, and fell on his face,
8 and said, "Is it you, my lord Eli'jah?" And he answered him, "It is I. Go, tell your lord, 'Behold, Eli'jah is here.' "
9 And he said, "Wherein have I sinned, that you would give your servant into the hand of Ahab, to kill me?
10 As the LORD your God lives, there is no nation or kingdom whither my lord has not sent to seek you; and when they would say, 'He is not here,' he would take an oath of the kingdom or nation, that they had not found
11 you. And now you say, 'Go, tell your lord, "Behold,
12 Eli'jah is here." ' And as soon as I have gone from you, the Spirit of the LORD will carry you whither I know not; and so, when I come and tell Ahab and he cannot find you, he will kill me, although I your servant have revered
13 the LORD from my youth. Has it not been told my lord what I did when Jez'ebel killed the prophets of the LORD, how I hid a hundred men of the LORD's prophets by fifties
14 in a cave, and fed them with bread and water? And now you say, 'Go, tell your lord, "Behold, Eli'jah is here" ';
15 and he will kill me." And Eli'jah said, "As the LORD of hosts lives, before whom I stand, I will surely show my-
16 self to him today." So Obadi'ah went to meet Ahab, and told him; and Ahab went to meet Eli'jah.

17 When Ahab saw Eli'jah, Ahab said to him, "Is it you,
18 you troubler of Israel?" And he answered, "I have not troubled Israel; but you have, and your father's house, because you have forsaken the commandments of the
19 LORD and followed the Ba'als. Now therefore send and gather all Israel to me at Mount Carmel, and the four hundred and fifty prophets of Ba'al and the four hundred prophets of Ashe'rah, who eat at Jez'ebel's table."

20 So Ahab sent to all the people of Israel, and gathered
21 the prophets together at Mount Carmel. And Eli'jah came near to all the people, and said, "How long will you go limping with two different opinions? If the LORD is God, follow him; but if Ba'al, then follow him." And the people
22 did not answer him a word. Then Eli'jah said to the people, "I, even I only, am left a prophet of the LORD; but Ba'al's prophets are four hundred and fifty men.
23 Let two bulls be given to us; and let them choose one bull for themselves, and cut it in pieces and lay it on the wood, but put no fire to it; and I will prepare the other

24 bull and lay it on the wood, and put no fire to it. And you call on the name of your god and I will call on the name of the Lord; and the God who answers by fire, he is God." And all the people answered, "It is well spoken." 25 Then Eli′jah said to the prophets of Ba′al, "Choose for yourselves one bull and prepare it first, for you are many; and call on the name of your god, but put no fire to it." 26 And they took the bull which was given them, and they prepared it, and called on the name of Ba′al from morning until noon, saying, "O Ba′al, answer us!" But there was no voice, and no one answered. And they limped 27 about the altar which they had made. And at noon Eli′jah mocked them, saying, "Cry aloud, for he is a god; either he is musing, or he has gone aside, or he is on a journey, 28 or perhaps he is asleep and must be awakened." And they cried aloud, and cut themselves after their custom with swords and lances, until the blood gushed out upon 29 them. And as midday passed, they raved on until the time of the offering of the oblation, but there was no voice; no one answered, no one heeded.

30 Then Eli′jah said to all the people, "Come near to me"; and all the people came near to him. And he repaired 31 the altar of the Lord that had been thrown down; Eli′jah took twelve stones, according to the number of the tribes of the sons of Jacob, to whom the word of the Lord came, 32 saying, "Israel shall be your name"; and with the stones he built an altar in the name of the Lord. And he made a trench about the altar, as great as would contain two 33 measures of seed. And he put the wood in order, and cut the bull in pieces and laid it on the wood. And he said, "Fill four jars with water, and pour it on the burnt 34 offering, and on the wood." And he said, "Do it a second time"; and they did it a second time. And he said, "Do it 35 a third time"; and they did it a third time. And the water ran round about the altar, and filled the trench also with water.

36 And at the time of the offering of the oblation, Eli′jah the prophet came near and said, "O Lord, God of Abraham, Isaac, and Israel, let it be known this day that thou art God in Israel, and that I am thy servant, and that I 37 have done all these things at thy word. Answer me, O Lord, answer me, that this people may know that thou, O Lord, art God, and that thou hast turned their hearts 38 back." Then the fire of the Lord fell, and consumed the burnt offering, and the wood, and the stones, and the 39 dust, and licked up the water that was in the trench. And when all the people saw it, they fell on their faces; and they said, "The Lord, he is God; the Lord, he is God." 40 And Eli′jah said to them, "Seize the prophets of Ba′al; let not one of them escape." And they seized them; and Eli′jah brought them down to the brook Kishon, and killed them there.

41 And Eli′jah said to Ahab, "Go up, eat and drink; for 42 there is a sound of the rushing of rain." So Ahab went up to eat and to drink. And Eli′jah went up to the top of Carmel; and he bowed himself down upon the earth, 43 and put his face between his knees. And he said to his servant, "Go up now, look toward the sea." And he went up and looked, and said, "There is nothing." And he said, 44 "Go again seven times." And at the seventh time he said, "Behold, a little cloud like a man's hand is rising out of the sea." And he said, "Go up, say to Ahab, 'Prepare 45 your chariot and go down, lest the rain stop you.' " And in a little while the heavens grew black with clouds and wind, and there was a great rain. And Ahab rode and 46 went to Jezreel. And the hand of the Lord was on Eli′jah; and he girded up his loins and ran before Ahab to the entrance of Jezreel.

19 Ahab told Jez′ebel all that Eli′jah had done, and how he had slain all the prophets with the sword. 2 Then Jez′ebel sent a messenger to Eli′jah, saying, "So may the gods do to me, and more also, if I do not make your life as the life of one of them by this time tomor- 3 row." Then he was afraid, and he arose and went for his life, and came to Beer-sheba, which belongs to Judah, and left his servant there.

4 But he himself went a day's journey into the wilderness, and came and sat down under a broom tree; and he asked that he might die, saying, "It is enough; now, O Lord, take away my life; for I am no better than my 5 fathers." And he lay down and slept under a broom tree; and behold, an angel touched him, and said to him, 6 "Arise and eat." And he looked, and behold, there was at his head a cake baked on hot stones and a jar of water. 7 And he ate and drank, and lay down again. And the angel of the Lord came again a second time, and touched him, and said, "Arise and eat, else the journey will be 8 too great for you." And he arose, and ate and drank, and went in the strength of that food forty days and forty nights to Horeb the mount of God.

9 And there he came to a cave, and lodged there; and behold, the word of the Lord came to him, and he said 10 to him, "What are you doing here, Eli′jah?" He said, "I have been very jealous for the Lord, the God of hosts; for the people of Israel have forsaken thy covenant, thrown down thy altars, and slain thy prophets with the sword; and I, even I only, am left; and they seek my life, 11 to take it away." And he said, "Go forth, and stand upon the mount before the Lord." And behold, the Lord passed by, and a great and strong wind rent the mountains, and broke in pieces the rocks before the Lord, but the Lord was not in the wind; and after the wind an earthquake, 12 but the Lord was not in the earthquake; and after the earthquake a fire, but the Lord was not in the fire; and 13 after the fire a still small voice. And when Eli′jah heard it, he wrapped his face in his mantle and went out and stood at the entrance of the cave. And behold, there came a voice to him, and said, "What are you doing here,

14 Elijah?" He said, "I have been very jealous for the LORD, the God of hosts; for the people of Israel have forsaken thy covenant, thrown down thy altars, and slain thy prophets with the sword; and I, even I only, am left; 15 and they seek my life, to take it away." And the LORD said to him, "Go, return on your way to the wilderness of Damascus; and when you arrive, you shall anoint 16 Haz'ael to be king over Syria; and Jehu the son of Nimshi you shall anoint to be king over Israel; and Eli'sha the son of Shaphat of A'bel-meho'lah you shall anoint 17 to be prophet in your place. And him who escapes from the sword of Haz'ael shall Jehu slay; and him who es- 18 capes from the sword of Jehu shall Eli'sha slay. Yet I will leave seven thousand in Israel, all the knees that have not bowed to Ba'al, and every mouth that has not kissed him."

19 So he departed from there, and found Eli'sha the son of Shaphat, who was plowing, with twelve yoke of oxen before him, and he was with the twelfth. Eli'jah passed 20 by him and cast his mantle upon him. And he left the oxen, and ran after Eli'jah, and said, "Let me kiss my father and my mother, and then I will follow you." And he said to him, "Go back again; for what have I done

21 to you?" And he returned from following him, and took the yoke of oxen, and slew them, and boiled their flesh with the yokes of the oxen, and gave it to the people, and they ate. Then he arose and went after Eli'jah, and ministered to him.

20 Ben-ha'dad the king of Syria gathered all his army together; thirty-two kings were with him, and horses and chariots; and he went up and besieged Samar'ia, and 2 fought against it. And he sent messengers into the city to Ahab king of Israel, and said to him, "Thus says Ben-ha'- 3 dad: 'Your silver and your gold are mine; your fairest 4 wives and children also are mine.' " And the king of Israel answered, "As you say, my lord, O king, I am yours, and 5 all that I have." The messengers came again, and said, "Thus says Ben-ha'dad: 'I sent to you, saying, "Deliver to me your silver and your gold, your wives and your 6 children"; nevertheless I will send my servants to you tomorrow about this time, and they shall search your house and the houses of your servants, and lay hands on whatever pleases them,o and take it away.' "

7 Then the king of Israel called all the elders of the land, and said, "Mark, now, and see how this man is seeking

trouble; for he sent to me for my wives and my children, and for my silver and my gold, and I did not refuse him." 8 And all the elders and all the people said to him, "Do 9 not heed or consent." So he said to the messengers of Ben-ha'dad, "Tell my lord the king, 'All that you first demanded of your servant I will do; but this thing I cannot do.' " And the messengers departed and brought him 10 word again. Ben-ha'dad sent to him and said, "The gods do so to me, and more also, if the dust of Samar'ia shall suffice for handfuls for all the people who follow me." 11 And the king of Israel answered, "Tell him, 'Let not him that girds on his armor boast himself as he that puts it 12 off.' " When Ben-ha'dad heard this message as he was drinking with the kings in the booths, he said to his men, "Take your positions." And they took their positions against the city.

13 And behold, a prophet came near to Ahab king of Israel and said, "Thus says the LORD, Have you seen all this great multitude? Behold, I will give it into your hand 14 this day; and you shall know that I am the LORD." And Ahab said, "By whom?" He said, "Thus says the LORD, By the servants of the governors of the districts." Then he said, "Who shall begin the battle?" He answered, 15 "You." Then he mustered the servants of the governors of the districts, and they were two hundred and thirty-two; and after them he mustered all the people of Israel, seven thousand.

16 And they went out at noon, while Ben-ha'dad was drinking himself drunk in the booths, he and the thirty- 17 two kings who helped him. The servants of the governors of the districts went out first. And Ben-ha'dad sent out scouts, and they reported to him, "Men are coming out 18 from Samar'ia." He said, "If they have come out for peace, take them alive; or if they have come out for war, take them alive."

19 So these went out of the city, the servants of the governors of the districts, and the army which followed them. 20 And each killed his man; the Syrians fled and Israel pursued them, but Ben-ha'dad king of Syria escaped on 21 a horse with horsemen. And the king of Israel went out, and captured p the horses and chariots, and killed the Syrians with a great slaughter.

22 Then the prophet came near to the king of Israel, and said to him, "Come, strengthen yourself, and consider well what you have to do; for in the spring the king of Syria will come up against you."

23 And the servants of the king of Syria said to him, "Their gods are gods of the hills, and so they were stronger than we; but let us fight against them in the 24 plain, and surely we shall be stronger than they. And do this: remove the kings, each from his post, and put 25 commanders in their places; and muster an army like the army that you have lost, horse for horse, and chariot for

o Gk Syr Vg: Heb *you*   p Gk: Heb *smote*

chariot; then we will fight against them in the plain, and surely we shall be stronger than they." And he hearkened to their voice, and did so.

26 In the spring Ben-ha'dad mustered the Syrians, and 27 went up to Aphek, to fight against Israel. And the people of Israel were mustered, and were provisioned, and went against them; the people of Israel encamped before them like two little flocks of goats, but the Syrians filled the 28 country. And a man of God came near and said to the king of Israel, "Thus says the LORD, 'Because the Syrians have said, "The LORD is a god of the hills but he is not a god of the valleys," therefore I will give all this great multitude into your hand, and you shall know that I am 29 the LORD.'" And they encamped opposite one another seven days. Then on the seventh day the battle was joined; and the people of Israel smote of the Syrians a hundred 30 thousand foot soldiers in one day. And the rest fled into the city of Aphek; and the wall fell upon twenty-seven thousand men that were left.

Ben-ha'dad also fled, and entered an inner chamber in 31 the city. And his servants said to him, "Behold now, we have heard that the kings of the house of Israel are merciful kings; let us put sackcloth on our loins and ropes upon our heads, and go out to the king of Israel; 32 perhaps he will spare your life." So they girded sackcloth on their loins, and put ropes on their heads, and went to the king of Israel and said, "Your servant Ben-ha'dad says, 'Pray, let me live.'" And he said, "Does he still 33 live? He is my brother." Now the men were watching for an omen, and they quickly took it up from him and said, "Yes, your brother Ben-ha'dad." Then he said, "Go and bring him." Then Ben-ha'dad came forth to him; 34 and he caused him to come up into the chariot. And Ben-ha'dad said to him, "The cities which my father took from your father I will restore; and you may establish bazaars for yourself in Damascus, as my father did in Samar'ia." And Ahab said, "I will let you go on these terms." So he made a covenant with him and let him go. 35 And a certain man of the sons of the prophets said to his fellow at the command of the LORD, "Strike me, I 36 pray." But the man refused to strike him. Then he said to him, "Because you have not obeyed the voice of the LORD, behold, as soon as you have gone from me, a lion shall kill you." And as soon as he had departed from him, 37 a lion met him and killed him. Then he found another man, and said, "Strike me, I pray." And the man struck him, 38 smiting and wounding him. So the prophet departed, and waited for the king by the way, disguising himself with 39 a bandage over his eyes. And as the king passed, he cried to the king and said, "Your servant went out into the midst of the battle; and behold, a soldier turned and brought a man to me, and said, 'Keep this man; if by any means he be missing, your life shall be for his life,

40 or else you shall pay a talent of silver.' And as your servant was busy here and there, he was gone." The king of Israel said to him, "So shall your judgment be; you your- 41 self have decided it." Then he made haste to take the bandage away from his eyes; and the king of Israel rec- 42 ognized him as one of the prophets. And he said to him, "Thus says the LORD, 'Because you have let go out of your hand the man whom I had devoted to destruction, therefore your life shall go for his life, and your people 43 for his people.'" And the king of Israel went to his house resentful and sullen, and came to Samar'ia.

21 Now Naboth the Jez'reelite had a vineyard in Jez- 2 reel, beside the palace of Ahab king of Samar'ia. And after this Ahab said to Naboth, "Give me your vineyard, that I may have it for a vegetable garden, because it is near my house; and I will give you a better vineyard for it; or, if it seems good to you, I will give you its value 3 in money." But Naboth said to Ahab, "The LORD forbid that I should give you the inheritance of my fathers." 4 And Ahab went into his house vexed and sullen because of what Naboth the Jez'reelite had said to him; for he had said, "I will not give you the inheritance of my fathers." And he lay down on his bed, and turned away his face, and would eat no food.

5 But Jez'ebel his wife came to him, and said to him, 6 "Why is your spirit so vexed that you eat no food?" And he said to her, "Because I spoke to Naboth the Jez'reelite, and said to him, 'Give me your vineyard for money; or else, if it please you, I will give you another vineyard 7 for it'; and he answered, 'I will not give you my vine- yard.'" And Jez'ebel his wife said to him, "Do you now govern Israel? Arise, and eat bread, and let your heart be cheerful; I will give you the vineyard of Naboth the Jez'reelite."

8 So she wrote letters in Ahab's name and sealed them with his seal, and she sent the letters to the elders and 9 the nobles who dwelt with Naboth in his city. And she wrote in the letters, "Proclaim a fast, and set Naboth on 10 high among the people; and set two base fellows opposite

him, and let them bring a charge against him, saying, 'You have cursed God and the king.' Then take him out, 11 and stone him to death." And the men of his city, the elders and the nobles who dwelt in his city, did as Jez'- ebel had sent word to them. As it was written in the 12 letters which she had sent to them, they proclaimed a fast, 13 and set Naboth on high among the people. And the two base fellows came in and sat opposite him; and the base fellows brought a charge against Naboth, in the presence of the people, saying, "Naboth cursed God and the king." So they took him outside the city, and stoned him to ¹⁴ death with stones. Then they sent to Jez′ebel, saying, "Naboth has been stoned; he is dead."

¹⁵ As soon as Jez′ebel heard that Naboth had been stoned and was dead, Jez′ebel said to Ahab, "Arise, take possession of the vineyard of Naboth the Jez′reelite, which he refused to give you for money; for Naboth is not alive, ¹⁶ but dead." And as soon as Ahab heard that Naboth was dead, Ahab arose to go down to the vineyard of Naboth the Jez′reelite, to take possession of it.

¹⁷ Then the word of the LORD came to Eli′jah the Tish- ¹⁸ bite, saying, "Arise, go down to meet Ahab king of Israel, who is in Samar′ia; behold, he is in the vineyard of ¹⁹ Naboth, where he has gone to take possession. And you shall say to him, 'Thus says the LORD, "Have you killed, and also taken possession?" ' And you shall say to him, 'Thus says the LORD: "In the place where dogs licked up the blood of Naboth shall dogs lick your own blood." ' "

²⁰ Ahab said to Eli′jah, "Have you found me, O my enemy?" He answered, "I have found you, because you have sold yourself to do what is evil in the sight of the ²¹ LORD. Behold, I will bring evil upon you; I will utterly sweep you away, and will cut off from Ahab every male, ²² bond or free, in Israel; and I will make your house like the house of Jerobo′am the son of Nebat, and like the house of Ba′asha the son of Ahi′jah, for the anger to which you have provoked me, and because you have made ²³ Israel to sin. And of Jez′ebel the LORD also said, 'The ²⁴ dogs shall eat Jez′ebel within the bounds of Jezreel.' Any one belonging to Ahab who dies in the city the dogs shall eat; and any one of his who dies in the open country the birds of the air shall eat."

²⁵ (There was none who sold himself to do what was evil in the sight of the LORD like Ahab, whom Jez′ebel ²⁶ his wife incited. He did very abominably in going after idols, as the Amorites had done, whom the LORD cast out before the people of Israel.)

²⁷ And when Ahab heard those words, he rent his clothes, and put sackcloth upon his flesh, and fasted and lay in ²⁸ sackcloth, and went about dejectedly. And the word of ²⁹ the LORD came to Eli′jah the Tishbite, saying, "Have you seen how Ahab has humbled himself before me? Because he has humbled himself before me, I will not bring the evil in his days; but in his son's days I will bring the evil upon his house."

22 For three years Syria and Israel continued without ² war. But in the third year Jehosh′aphat the king of ³ Judah came down to the king of Israel. And the king of Israel said to his servants, "Do you know that Ramoth-gilead belongs to us, and we keep quiet and do not take ⁴ it out of the hand of the king of Syria?" And he said to Jehosh′aphat, "Will you go with me to battle at Ramoth-gilead?" And Jehosh′aphat said to the king of Israel, "I am as you are, my people as your people, my horses as your horses."

⁵ And Jehosh′aphat said to the king of Israel, "Inquire ⁶ first for the word of the LORD." Then the king of Israel gathered the prophets together, about four hundred men, and said to them, "Shall I go to battle against Ramoth-gilead, or shall I forbear?" And they said, "Go up; for ⁷ the Lord will give it in the hand of the king." But Jehosh′-aphat said, "Is there not here another prophet of the LORD ⁸ of whom we may inquire?" And the king of Israel said to Jehosh′aphat, "There is yet one man by whom we may inquire of the LORD, Micai′ah the son of Imlah; but I hate him, for he never prophesies good concerning me, but evil." And Jehosh′aphat said, "Let not the king ⁹ say so." Then the king of Israel summoned an officer and ¹⁰ said, "Bring quickly Micai′ah the son of Imlah." Now the king of Israel and Jehosh′aphat the king of Judah were sitting on their thrones, arrayed in their robes, at the threshing floor at the entrance of the gate of Samar′-ia; and all the prophets were prophesying before them. ¹¹ And Zedeki′ah the son of Chena′anah made for himself horns of iron, and said, "Thus says the LORD, 'With these you shall push the Syrians until they are destroyed.' " ¹² And all the prophets prophesied so, and said, "Go up to Ramoth-gilead and triumph; the LORD will give it into the hand of the king."

¹³ And the messenger who went to summon Micai′ah said to him, "Behold, the words of the prophets with one accord are favorable to the king; let your word be ¹⁴ like the word of one of them, and speak favorably." But Micai′ah said, "As the LORD lives, what the LORD says ¹⁵ to me, that I will speak." And when he had come to the king, the king said to him, "Micai′ah, shall we go to Ramoth-gilead to battle, or shall we forbear?" And he answered him, "Go up and triumph; the LORD will give ¹⁶ it into the hand of the king." But the king said to him, "How many times shall I adjure you that you speak to ¹⁷ me nothing but the truth in the name of the LORD?" And he said, "I saw all Israel scattered upon the mountains, as sheep that have no shepherd; and the LORD said, 'These have no master; let each return to his home in ¹⁸ peace.' " And the king of Israel said to Jehosh′aphat, "Did I not tell you that he would not prophesy good con- ¹⁹ cerning me, but evil?" And Micai′ah said, "Therefore hear the word of the LORD: I saw the LORD sitting on his throne, and all the host of heaven standing beside him ²⁰ on his right hand and on his left; and the LORD said, 'Who will entice Ahab, that he may go up and fall at Ramoth-gilead?' And one said one thing, and another ²¹ said another. Then a spirit came forward and stood be- ²² fore the LORD, saying, 'I will entice him.' And the LORD

said to him, 'By what means?' And he said, 'I will go forth, and will be a lying spirit in the mouth of all his prophets.' And he said, 'You are to entice him, and you 23 shall succeed; go forth and do so.' Now therefore behold, the LORD has put a lying spirit in the mouth of all these your prophets; the LORD has spoken evil concerning you."

24 Then Zedeki'ah the son of Chena'anah came near and struck Micai'ah on the cheek, and said, "How did the 25 Spirit of the LORD go from me to speak to you?" And Micai'ah said, "Behold, you shall see on that day when 26 you go into an inner chamber to hide yourself." And the king of Israel said, "Seize Micai'ah, and take him back to Amon the governor of the city and to Jo'ash the king's 27 son; and say, 'Thus says the king, "Put this fellow in prison, and feed him with scant fare of bread and water, 28 until I come in peace."'" And Micai'ah said, "If you return in peace, the LORD has not spoken by me." And he said, "Hear, all you peoples!"

29 So the king of Israel and Jehosh'aphat the king of 30 Judah went up to Ramoth-gilead. And the king of Israel said to Jehosh'aphat, "I will disguise myself and go into battle, but you wear your robes." And the king of Israel 31 disguised himself and went into battle. Now the king of Syria had commanded the thirty-two captains of his chariots, "Fight with neither small nor great, but only 32 with the king of Israel." And when the captains of the chariots saw Jehosh'aphat, they said, "It is surely the king of Israel." So they turned to fight against him; and 33 Jehosh'aphat cried out. And when the captains of the chariots saw that it was not the king of Israel, they 34 turned back from pursuing him. But a certain man drew his bow at a venture, and struck the king of Israel between the scale armor and the breastplate; therefore he said to the driver of his chariot, "Turn about, and carry 35 me out of the battle, for I am wounded." And the battle grew hot that day, and the king was propped up in his chariot facing the Syrians, until at evening he died; and the blood of the wound flowed into the bottom of the 36 chariot. And about sunset a cry went through the army, "Every man to his city, and every man to his country!"

37 So the king died, and was brought to Samar'ia; and 38 they buried the king in Samar'ia. And they washed the chariot by the pool of Samar'ia, and the dogs licked up his blood, and the harlots washed themselves in it, according to the word of the LORD which he had spoken. 39 Now the rest of the acts of Ahab, and all that he did, and the ivory house which he built, and all the cities that he built, are they not written in the Book of the Chronicles 40 of the Kings of Israel? So Ahab slept with his fathers; and Ahazi'ah his son reigned in his stead.

41 Jehosh'aphat the son of Asa began to reign over Judah 42 in the fourth year of Ahab king of Israel. Jehosh'aphat was thirty-five years old when he began to reign, and he reigned twenty-five years in Jerusalem. His mother's name 43 was Azu'bah the daughter of Shilhi. He walked in all the way of Asa his father; he did not turn aside from it, doing what was right in the sight of the LORD; yet the high places were not taken away, and the people still 44 sacrificed and burned incense on the high places. Jehosh'-aphat also made peace with the king of Israel.

45 Now the rest of the acts of Jehosh'aphat, and his might that he showed, and how he warred, are they not written in the Book of the Chronicles of the Kings of Judah? 46 And the remnant of the male cult prostitutes who remained in the days of his father Asa, he exterminated from the land.

47 There was no king in Edom; a deputy was king. 48 Jehosh'aphat made ships of Tarshish to go to Ophir for gold; but they did not go, for the ships were wrecked at 49 E'zion-ge'ber. Then Ahazi'ah the son of Ahab said to Jehosh'aphat, "Let my servants go with your servants in 50 the ships," but Jehosh'aphat was not willing. And Jehosh'-aphat slept with his fathers, and was buried with his fathers in the city of David his father; and Jeho'ram his son reigned in his stead.

51 Ahazi'ah the son of Ahab began to reign over Israel in Samar'ia in the seventeenth year of Jehosh'aphat king 52 of Judah, and he reigned two years over Israel. He did what was evil in the sight of the LORD, and walked in the way of his father, and in the way of his mother, and in the way of Jerobo'am the son of Nebat, who made Israel 53 to sin. He served Ba'al and worshiped him, and provoked the LORD, the God of Israel, to anger in every way that his father had done.

THE SECOND BOOK OF THE

KINGS

The Second Book of the Kings was written at the same time as the First Book of the Kings, namely, about 550 B.C. It continues with stories about Elijah and his successor Elisha and their many wonderful deeds.

Second Kings tells briefly of many Hebrew kings during a period of over a hundred years. During this time the warlike kingdom of Assyria was becoming stronger and stronger. In 721 B.C. Assyrian armies attacked and destroyed Samaria, the capital city of Israel (Northern Kingdom), and carried away 27,000 Hebrews as captives of war. They never came back to their homeland, and so they are sometimes called "the ten lost tribes of Israel."

The Assyrians later tried to conquer Jerusalem, the capital of the Southern Kingdom of Judah. King Hezekiah of Judah, with the help of the great prophet Isaiah, resisted the Assyrians, and the city was saved. Manasseh, the son of Hezekiah, was a wicked king who ruled many long years. Not all the kings sought to serve God.

One of Manasseh's grandsons, named Josiah, became king when he was only a boy. During Josiah's reign, while repairs were being made on the Temple, a wonderful book that had been lost was found. It was the central part of the Book of Deuteronomy, now the fifth book in the Bible. (See the Introduction to Deuteronomy, page 107.) Josiah had it read aloud and ordered many reforms as a result of its teachings (2 Kings 22 and 23). While he was king, Josiah was killed in a battle with the Egyptians.

During these years the nation of Babylon, to the northeast, was growing in power and warlikeness. Babylon conquered Assyria about 605 B.C. Since Assyria had already conquered the Northern Kingdom of Israel, Babylon became its new master. Finally in 597 and again in 586 B.C. the Babylonian armies conquered Jerusalem itself and deported thousands of the people to a sort of prison camp in Babylonia, sometimes called Chaldea. Thus came the sad end of the southern Hebrew kingdom (Judah), but it was not the end of the Hebrew people.

2

THE SECOND BOOK OF THE

KINGS

King Ahaziah of Israel

1 After the death of Ahab, Moab rebelled against Israel.

2 Now Ahazi'ah fell through the lattice in his upper chamber in Samar'ia, and lay sick; so he sent messengers, telling them, "Go, inquire of Ba'al-ze'bub, the god of 3 Ekron, whether I shall recover from this sickness." But the angel of the LORD said to Eli'jah the Tishbite, "Arise, go up to meet the messengers of the king of Samar'ia, and say to them, 'Is it because there is no God in Israel that you are going to inquire of Ba'al-ze'bub, the god of 4 Ekron?' Now therefore thus says the LORD, 'You shall not

come down from the bed to which you have gone, but you shall surely die.'" So Eli'jah went.

5 The messengers returned to the king, and he said to 6 them, "Why have you returned?" And they said to him, "There came a man to meet us, and said to us, 'Go back to the king who sent you, and say to him, Thus says the LORD, Is it because there is no God in Israel that you are sending to inquire of Ba'al-ze'bub, the god of Ekron? Therefore you shall not come down from the bed to 7 which you have gone, but shall surely die.'" He said to them, "What kind of man was he who came to meet you 8 and told you these things?" They answered him, "He

237

wore a garment of haircloth, with a girdle of leather about his loins." And he said, "It is Eli'jah the Tishbite."

9 Then the king sent to him a captain of fifty men with his fifty. He went up to Eli'jah, who was sitting on the top of a hill, and said to him, "O man of God, the king

10 says, 'Come down.' " But Eli'jah answered the captain of fifty, "If I am a man of God, let fire come down from heaven and consume you and your fifty." Then fire came down from heaven, and consumed him and his fifty.

11 Again the king sent to him another captain of fifty men with his fifty. And he went up[a] and said to him, "O man

of God, this is the king's order, 'Come down quickly!' "

12 But Eli'jah answered them, "If I am a man of God, let fire come down from heaven and consume you and your fifty." Then the fire of God came down from heaven and consumed him and his fifty.

13 Again the king sent the captain of a third fifty with his fifty. And the third captain of fifty went up, and came and fell on his knees before Eli'jah, and entreated him, "O man of God, I pray you, let my life, and the life of these fifty servants of yours, be precious in your sight.

14 Lo, fire came down from heaven, and consumed the two former captains of fifty men with their fifties; but now

15 let my life be precious in your sight." Then the angel of the LORD said to Eli'jah, "Go down with him; do not be afraid of him." So he arose and went down with him to

16 the king, and said to him, "Thus says the LORD, 'Because you have sent messengers to inquire of Ba'al-ze'bub, the god of Ekron,—is it because there is no God in Israel to inquire of his word?—therefore you shall not come down from the bed to which you have gone, but you shall surely die.' "

17 So he died according to the word of the LORD which Eli'jah had spoken. Jeho'ram, his brother,[b] became king in his stead in the second year of Jeho'ram the son of Jehosh'aphat, king of Judah, because Ahazi'ah had no

18 son. Now the rest of the acts of Ahazi'ah which he did, are they not written in the Book of the Chronicles of the Kings of Israel?

Elisha Succeeds Elijah

2 Now when the LORD was about to take Eli'jah up to heaven by a whirlwind, Eli'jah and Eli'sha were on

2 their way from Gilgal. And Eli'jah said to Eli'sha, "Tarry here, I pray you; for the LORD has sent me as far as

Bethel." But Eli'sha said, "As the LORD lives, and as you yourself live, I will not leave you." So they went down

3 to Bethel. And the sons of the prophets who were in Bethel came out to Eli'sha, and said to him, "Do you know that today the LORD will take away your master from over you?" And he said, "Yes, I know it; hold your peace."

4 Eli'jah said to him, "Eli'sha, tarry here, I pray you; for the LORD has sent me to Jericho." But he said, "As the LORD lives, and as you yourself live, I will not leave

5 you." So they came to Jericho. The sons of the prophets who were at Jericho drew near to Eli'sha, and said to him, "Do you know that today the LORD will take away your master from over you?" And he answered, "Yes, I know it; hold your peace."

6 Then Eli'jah said to him, "Tarry here, I pray you; for the LORD has sent me to the Jordan." But he said, "As the LORD lives, and as you yourself live, I will not leave

7 you." So the two of them went on. Fifty men of the sons of the prophets also went, and stood at some distance from them, as they both were standing by the Jordan.

8 Then Eli'jah took his mantle, and rolled it up, and struck the water, and the water was parted to the one side and to the other, till the two of them could go over on dry ground.

9 When they had crossed, Eli'jah said to Eli'sha, "Ask what I shall do for you, before I am taken from you." And Eli'sha said, "I pray you, let me inherit a double

10 share of your spirit." And he said, "You have asked a hard thing; yet, if you see me as I am being taken from you, it shall be so for you; but if you do not see me, it

11 shall not be so." And as they still went on and talked, behold, a chariot of fire and horses of fire separated the two of them. And Eli'jah went up by a whirlwind into

12 heaven. And Eli'sha saw it and he cried, "My father, my father! the chariots of Israel and its horsemen!" And he saw him no more.

Then he took hold of his own clothes and rent them in

13 two pieces. And he took up the mantle of Eli'jah that had fallen from him, and went back and stood on the bank

14 of the Jordan. Then he took the mantle of Eli'jah that had fallen from him, and struck the water, saying, "Where is the LORD, the God of Eli'jah?" And when he had struck the water, the water was parted to the one side and to the other; and Eli'sha went over.

15 Now when the sons of the prophets who were at Jericho saw him over against them, they said, "The spirit of Eli'jah rests on Eli'sha." And they came to meet him, and

16 bowed to the ground before him. And they said to him, "Behold now, there are with your servants fifty strong men; pray, let them go, and seek your master; it may be that the Spirit of the LORD has caught him up and cast him upon some mountain or into some valley." And he

17 said, "You shall not send." But when they urged him till he was ashamed, he said, "Send." They sent therefore

[a] Gk Compare verses 9, 13: Heb *answered*   [b] Gk Syr: Heb lacks *his brother*

fifty men; and for three days they sought him but did
18 not find him. And they came back to him, while he tarried at Jericho, and he said to them, "Did I not say to you, Do not go?"

19 Now the men of the city said to Eli′sha, "Behold, the situation of this city is pleasant, as my lord sees; but the
20 water is bad, and the land is unfruitful." He said, "Bring me a new bowl, and put salt in it." So they brought it to
21 him. Then he went to the spring of water and threw salt

in it, and said, "Thus says the LORD, I have made this water wholesome; henceforth neither death nor miscar-
22 riage shall come from it." So the water has been whole-some to this day, according to the word which Eli′sha spoke.

23 He went up from there to Bethel; and while he was going up on the way, some small boys came out of the city and jeered at him, saying, "Go up, you baldhead!
24 Go up, you baldhead!" And he turned around, and when he saw them, he cursed them in the name of the LORD. And two she-bears came out of the woods and tore forty-
25 two of the boys. From there he went on to Mount Carmel, and thence he returned to Samar′ia.

3 In the eighteenth year of Jehosh′aphat king of Judah, Jeho′ram the son of Ahab became king over
2 Israel in Samar′ia, and he reigned twelve years. He did what was evil in the sight of the LORD, though not like his father and mother, for he put away the pillar of Ba′al
3 which his father had made. Nevertheless he clung to the sin of Jerobo′am the son of Nebat, which he made Israel to sin; he did not depart from it.

4 Now Mesha king of Moab was a sheep breeder; and he had to deliver annually[c] to the king of Israel a hundred thousand lambs, and the wool of a hundred thousand
5 rams. But when Ahab died, the king of Moab rebelled
6 against the king of Israel. So King Jeho′ram marched out
7 of Samar′ia at that time and mustered all Israel. And he went and sent word to Jehosh′aphat king of Judah, "The king of Moab has rebelled against me; will you go with me to battle against Moab?" And he said, "I will go; I am as you are, my people as your people, my horses as
8 your horses." Then he said, "By which way shall we march?" Jeho′ram answered, "By the way of the wilderness of Edom."

9 So the king of Israel went with the king of Judah and the king of Edom. And when they had made a circuitous march of seven days, there was no water for the army
10 or for the beasts which followed them. Then the king of

Israel said, "Alas! The LORD has called these three kings
11 to give them into the hand of Moab." And Jehosh′aphat said, "Is there no prophet of the LORD here, through whom we may inquire of the LORD?" Then one of the king of Israel's servants answered, "Eli′sha the son of Shaphat is here, who poured water on the hands of
12 Eli′jah." And Jehosh′aphat said, "The word of the LORD is with him." So the king of Israel and Jehosh′aphat and the king of Edom went down to him.

13 And Eli′sha said to the king of Israel, "What have I to do with you? Go to the prophets of your father and the prophets of your mother." But the king of Israel said to him, "No; it is the LORD who has called these three kings
14 to give them into the hand of Moab." And Eli′sha said, "As the LORD of hosts lives, whom I serve, were it not that I have regard for Jehosh′aphat the king of Judah, I
15 would neither look at you, nor see you. But now bring me a minstrel." And when the minstrel played, the power of
16 the LORD came upon him. And he said, "Thus says the LORD, 'I will make this dry stream-bed full of pools.'
17 For thus says the LORD, 'You shall not see wind or rain, but that stream-bed shall be filled with water, so that you
18 shall drink, you, your cattle, and your beasts.' This is a light thing in the sight of the LORD; he will also give the
19 Moabites into your hand, and you shall conquer every fortified city, and every choice city, and shall fell every good tree, and stop up all springs of water, and ruin every
20 good piece of land with stones." The next morning, about the time of offering the sacrifice, behold, water came from the direction of Edom, till the country was filled with water.

21 When all the Moabites heard that the kings had come up to fight against them, all who were able to put on armor, from the youngest to the oldest, were called out,
22 and were drawn up at the frontier. And when they rose early in the morning, and the sun shone upon the water, the Moabites saw the water opposite them as red as blood.
23 And they said, "This is blood; the kings have surely fought together, and slain one another. Now then, Moab,
24 to the spoil!" But when they came to the camp of Israel, the Israelites rose and attacked the Moabites, till they fled before them; and they went forward, slaughtering
25 the Moabites as they went.[d] And they overthrew the cities,

---

c Tg: Heb lacks *annually*   d Gk: Heb uncertain

and on every good piece of land every man threw a stone, until it was covered; they stopped every spring of water, and felled all the good trees; till only its stones were left in Kir-har′eseth, and the slingers surrounded and con-

26 quered it. When the king of Moab saw that the battle was going against him, he took with him seven hundred swordsmen to break through, opposite the king of Edom;

27 but they could not. Then he took his eldest son who was to reign in his stead, and offered him for a burnt offering upon the wall. And there came great wrath upon Israel; and they withdrew from him and returned to their own land.

Stories of Elisha

4 Now the wife of one of the sons of the prophets cried to Eli′sha, "Your servant my husband is dead; and you know that your servant feared the LORD, but the creditor has come to take my two children to be his

2 slaves." And Eli′sha said to her, "What shall I do for you? Tell me; what have you in the house?" And she said, "Your maidservant has nothing in the house, except

3 a jar of oil." Then he said, "Go outside, borrow vessels of all your neighbors, empty vessels and not too few.

4 Then go in, and shut the door upon yourself and your sons, and pour into all these vessels; and when one is

5 full, set it aside." So she went from him and shut the door upon herself and her sons; and as she poured they

6 brought the vessels to her. When the vessels were full, she said to her son, "Bring me another vessel." And he said to her, "There is not another." Then the oil stopped

7 flowing. She came and told the man of God, and he said, "Go, sell the oil and pay your debts, and you and your sons can live on the rest."

8 One day Eli′sha went on to Shunem, where a wealthy woman lived, who urged him to eat some food. So whenever he passed that way, he would turn in there to eat

9 food. And she said to her husband, "Behold now, I perceive that this is a holy man of God, who is continually

10 passing our way. Let us make a small roof chamber with walls, and put there for him a bed, a table, a chair, and a lamp, so that whenever he comes to us, he can go in there."

11 One day he came there, and he turned into the chamber

12 and rested there. And he said to Geha′zi his servant, "Call this Shu′nammite." When he had called her, she stood

13 before him. And he said to him, "Say now to her, See, you have taken all this trouble for us; what is to be done for you? Would you have a word spoken on your behalf to the king or to the commander of the army?" She an-

14 swered, "I dwell among my own people." And he said, "What then is to be done for her?" Geha′zi answered,

15 "Well, she has no son, and her husband is old." He said, "Call her." And when he called her, she stood in the door-

16 way. And he said, "At this season, when the time comes round, you shall embrace a son." And she said, "No, my lord, O man of God; do not lie to your maidservant."

17 But the woman conceived, and she bore a son about that time the following spring, as Eli′sha had said to her.

18 When the child had grown, he went out one day to his

19 father among the reapers. And he said to his father, "Oh, my head, my head!" The father said to his servant,

20 "Carry him to his mother." And when he had lifted him,

and brought him to his mother, the child sat on her lap

21 till noon, and then he died. And she went up and laid him on the bed of the man of God, and shut the door

22 upon him, and went out. Then she called to her husband, and said, "Send me one of the servants and one of the asses, that I may quickly go to the man of God, and come

23 back again." And he said, "Why will you go to him today? It is neither new moon nor sabbath." She said,

24 "It will be well." Then she saddled the ass, and she said to her servant, "Urge the beast on; do not slacken the

25 pace for me unless I tell you." So she set out, and came to the man of God at Mount Carmel.

When the man of God saw her coming, he said to Geha′zi his servant, "Look, yonder is the Shu′nammite;

26 run at once to meet her, and say to her, Is it well with you? Is it well with your husband? Is it well with the

27 child?" And she answered, "It is well." And when she came to the mountain to the man of God, she caught hold of his feet. And Geha′zi came to thrust her away. But the man of God said, "Let her alone, for she is in bitter distress; and the LORD has hidden it from me, and has not

28 told me." Then she said, "Did I ask my lord for a son?

29 Did I not say, Do not deceive me?" He said to Geha′zi, "Gird up your loins, and take my staff in your hand, and go. If you meet any one, do not salute him; and if any one salutes you, do not reply; and lay my staff upon the

30 face of the child." Then the mother of the child said, "As the LORD lives, and as you yourself live, I will not leave

31 you." So he arose and followed her. Geha′zi went on ahead and laid the staff upon the face of the child, but there was no sound or sign of life. Therefore he returned to meet him, and told him, "The child has not awaked."

32 When Eli′sha came into the house, he saw the child

33 lying dead on his bed. So he went in and shut the door

34 upon the two of them, and prayed to the LORD. Then he went up and lay upon the child, putting his mouth upon

his mouth, his eyes upon his eyes, and his hands upon his hands; and as he stretched himself upon him, the flesh 35 of the child became warm. Then he got up again, and walked once to and fro in the house, and went up, and stretched himself upon him; the child sneezed seven times, 36 and the child opened his eyes. Then he summoned Geha'zi and said, "Call this Shu'nammite." So he called her. And when she came to him, he said, "Take up your son." 37 She came and fell at his feet, bowing to the ground; then she took up her son and went out.

38 And Eli'sha came again to Gilgal when there was a famine in the land. And as the sons of the prophets were sitting before him, he said to his servant, "Set on the great pot, and boil pottage for the sons of the prophets." 39 One of them went out into the field to gather herbs, and found a wild vine and gathered from it his lap full of wild gourds, and came and cut them up into the pot of pottage, 40 not knowing what they were. And they poured out for the men to eat. But while they were eating of the pottage, they cried out, "O man of God, there is death in the pot!" 41 And they could not eat it. He said, "Then bring meal." And he threw it into the pot, and said, "Pour out for the men, that they may eat." And there was no harm in the pot.

42 A man came from Ba'al-shal'ishah, bringing the man of God bread of the first fruits, twenty loaves of barley, and fresh ears of grain in his sack. And Eli'sha said, 43 "Give to the men, that they may eat." But his servant said, "How am I to set this before a hundred men?" So he repeated, "Give them to the men, that they may eat, for thus says the LORD, 'They shall eat and have some 44 left.' " So he set it before them. And they ate, and had some left, according to the word of the LORD.

5 Na'aman, commander of the army of the king of Syria, was a great man with his master and in high favor, because by him the LORD had given victory to Syria. He was a mighty man of valor, but he was a leper. 2 Now the Syrians on one of their raids had carried off a little maid from the land of Israel, and she waited on 3 Na'aman's wife. She said to her mistress, "Would that my lord were with the prophet who is in Samar'ia! He 4 would cure him of his leprosy." So Na'aman went in and told his lord, "Thus and so spoke the maiden from the 5 land of Israel." And the king of Syria said, "Go now, and I will send a letter to the king of Israel."

e Another reading is Amana

So he went, taking with him ten talents of silver, six 6 thousand shekels of gold, and ten festal garments. And he brought the letter to the king of Israel, which read, "When this letter reaches you, know that I have sent to you Na'aman my servant, that you may cure him of his 7 leprosy." And when the king of Israel read the letter, he rent his clothes and said, "Am I God, to kill and to make alive, that this man sends word to me to cure a man of his leprosy? Only consider, and see how he is seeking a quarrel with me."

8 But when Eli'sha the man of God heard that the king of Israel had rent his clothes, he sent to the king, saying, "Why have you rent your clothes? Let him come now to me, that he may know that there is a prophet in Israel." 9 So Na'aman came with his horses and chariots, and halted 10 at the door of Eli'sha's house. And Eli'sha sent a messenger to him, saying, "Go and wash in the Jordan seven times, and your flesh shall be restored, and you shall be 11 clean." But Na'aman was angry, and went away, saying, "Behold, I thought that he would surely come out to me, and stand, and call on the name of the LORD his God, and 12 wave his hand over the place, and cure the leper. Are not Aba'na e and Pharpar, the rivers of Damascus, better than all the waters of Israel? Could I not wash in them, and be clean?" So he turned and went away in a rage. 13 But his servants came near and said to him, "My father, if the prophet had commanded you to do some great thing, would you not have done it? How much rather, 14 then, when he says to you, 'Wash, and be clean'?" So he went down and dipped himself seven times in the Jordan, according to the word of the man of God; and his flesh was restored like the flesh of a little child, and he was clean.

15 Then he returned to the man of God, he and all his company, and he came and stood before him; and he said, "Behold, I know that there is no God in all the earth but in Israel; so accept now a present from your 16 servant." But he said, "As the LORD lives, whom I serve, I will receive none." And he urged him to take it, but 17 he refused. Then Na'aman said, "If not, I pray you, let there be given to your servant two mules' burden of earth; for henceforth your servant will not offer burnt offering 18 or sacrifice to any god but the LORD. In this matter may the LORD pardon your servant: when my master goes into the house of Rimmon to worship there, leaning on my arm, and I bow myself in the house of Rimmon, when I bow myself in the house of Rimmon, the LORD pardon 19 your servant in this matter." He said to him, "Go in peace."

But when Na'aman had gone from him a short distance, 20 Geha'zi, the servant of Eli'sha the man of God, said, "See, my master has spared this Na'aman the Syrian, in not accepting from his hand what he brought. As the LORD

lives, I will run after him, and get something from him."
21 So Geha'zi followed Na'aman. And when Na'aman saw some one running after him, he alighted from the chariot
22 to meet him, and said, "Is all well?" And he said, "All is well. My master has sent me to say, 'There have just now come to me from the hill country of E'phraim two young men of the sons of the prophets; pray, give them
23 a talent of silver and two festal garments.'" And Na'aman said, "Be pleased to accept two talents." And he urged him, and tied up two talents of silver in two bags, with two festal garments, and laid them upon two of his
24 servants; and they carried them before Geha'zi. And when he came to the hill, he took them from their hand, and put them in the house; and he sent the men away, and
25 they departed. He went in, and stood before his master, and Eli'sha said to him, "Where have you been, Geha'-
26 zi?" And he said, "Your servant went nowhere." But he said to him, "Did I not go with you in spirit when the man turned from his chariot to meet you? Was it a time to accept money and garments, olive orchards and vine-yards, sheep and oxen, menservants and maidservants?
27 Therefore the leprosy of Na'aman shall cleave to you, and to your descendants for ever." So he went out from his presence a leper, as white as snow.

6 Now the sons of the prophets said to Eli'sha, "See, the place where we dwell under your charge is too
2 small for us. Let us go to the Jordan and each of us get there a log, and let us make a place for us to dwell there."
3 And he answered, "Go." Then one of them said, "Be pleased to go with your servants." And he answered, "I
4 will go." So he went with them. And when they came to
5 the Jordan, they cut down trees. But as one was felling a log, his axe head fell into the water; and he cried out,
6 "Alas, my master! It was borrowed." Then the man of God said, "Where did it fall?" When he showed him the place, he cut off a stick, and threw it in there, and made
7 the iron float. And he said, "Take it up." So he reached out his hand and took it.
8 Once when the king of Syria was warring against Israel, he took counsel with his servants, saying, "At such
9 and such a place shall be my camp." But the man of God sent word to the king of Israel, "Beware that you do not pass this place, for the Syrians are going down there."
10 And the king of Israel sent to the place of which the man of God told him. Thus he used to warn him, so that he saved himself there more than once or twice.
11 And the mind of the king of Syria was greatly troubled because of this thing; and he called his servants and said to them, "Will you not show me who of us is for the
12 king of Israel?" And one of his servants said, "None, my lord, O king; but Eli'sha, the prophet who is in Israel, tells the king of Israel the words that you speak in your
13 bedchamber." And he said, "Go and see where he is, that I may send and seize him." It was told him, "Behold, he

14 is in Dothan." So he sent there horses and chariots and a great army; and they came by night, and surrounded the city.
15 When the servant of the man of God rose early in the morning and went out, behold, an army with horses and chariots was round about the city. And the servant said,
16 "Alas, my master! What shall we do?" He said, "Fear not, for those who are with us are more than those who
17 are with them." Then Eli'sha prayed, and said, "O LORD, I pray thee, open his eyes that he may see." So the LORD opened the eyes of the young man, and he saw; and behold, the mountain was full of horses and chariots of
18 fire round about Eli'sha. And when the Syrians came down against him, Eli'sha prayed to the LORD, and said, "Strike this people, I pray thee, with blindness." So he struck them with blindness in accordance with the prayer
19 of Eli'sha. And Eli'sha said to them, "This is not the way, and this is not the city; follow me, and I will bring you to the man whom you seek." And he led them to Samar'ia.
20 As soon as they entered Samar'ia, Eli'sha said, "O LORD, open the eyes of these men, that they may see." So the LORD opened their eyes, and they saw; and lo,
21 they were in the midst of Samar'ia. When the king of Israel saw them he said to Eli'sha, "My father, shall I
22 slay them? Shall I slay them?" He answered, "You shall not slay them. Would you slay those whom you have taken captive with your sword and with your bow? Set bread and water before them, that they may eat and drink
23 and go to their master." So he prepared for them a great feast; and when they had eaten and drunk, he sent them away, and they went to their master. And the Syrians came no more on raids into the land of Israel.
24 Afterward Ben-ha'dad king of Syria mustered his entire
25 army, and went up, and besieged Samar'ia. And there was a great famine in Samar'ia, as they besieged it, until an ass's head was sold for eighty shekels of silver, and the fourth part of a kab of dove's dung for five shekels of
26 silver. Now as the king of Israel was passing by upon the wall, a woman cried out to him, saying, "Help, my
27 lord, O king!" And he said, "If the LORD will not help you, whence shall I help you? From the threshing floor,
28 or from the wine press?" And the king asked her, "What is your trouble?" She answered, "This woman said to me, 'Give your son, that we may eat him today, and we will
29 eat my son tomorrow.' So we boiled my son, and ate him. And on the next day I said to her, 'Give your son, that
30 we may eat him'; but she has hidden her son." When the king heard the words of the woman he rent his clothes— now he was passing by upon the wall—and the people looked, and behold, he had sackcloth beneath upon his
31 body—and he said, "May God do so to me, and more also, if the head of Eli'sha the son of Shaphat remains on his shoulders today."

³² Eli'sha was sitting in his house, and the elders were sitting with him. Now the king had dispatched a man from his presence; but before the messenger arrived Eli'sha said to the elders, "Do you see how this murderer has sent to take off my head? Look, when the messenger comes, shut the door, and hold the door fast against him. ³³ Is not the sound of his master's feet behind him?" And while he was still speaking with them, the king^f came down to him and said, "This trouble is from the LORD! Why should I wait for the LORD any longer?" But ¹ Eli'sha said, "Hear the word of the LORD: thus says the LORD, Tomorrow about this time a measure of fine meal shall be sold for a shekel, and two measures of ² barley for a shekel, at the gate of Samar'ia." Then the captain on whose hand the king leaned said to the man of God, "If the LORD himself should make windows in heaven, could this thing be?" But he said, "You shall see it with your own eyes, but you shall not eat of it."

³ Now there were four men who were lepers at the entrance to the gate; and they said to one another, "Why ⁴ do we sit here till we die? If we say, 'Let us enter the city,' the famine is in the city, and we shall die there; and if we sit here, we die also. So now come, let us go over to the camp of the Syrians; if they spare our lives ⁵ we shall live, and if they kill us we shall but die." So they arose at twilight to go to the camp of the Syrians; but when they came to the edge of the camp of the Syrians, ⁶ behold, there was no one there. For the LORD had made the army of the Syrians hear the sound of chariots, and of horses, the sound of a great army, so that they said to one another, "Behold, the king of Israel has hired against us the kings of the Hittites and the kings of Egypt to ⁷ come upon us." So they fled away in the twilight and for-

sook their tents, their horses, and their asses, leaving the ⁸ camp as it was, and fled for their lives. And when these lepers came to the edge of the camp, they went into a tent, and ate and drank, and they carried off silver and gold and clothing, and went and hid them; then they came back, and entered another tent, and carried off things from it, and went and hid them.

⁹ Then they said to one another, "We are not doing right. This day is a day of good news; if we are silent and wait until the morning light, punishment will overtake us; now therefore come, let us go and tell the king's ¹⁰ household." So they came and called to the gatekeepers of the city, and told them, "We came to the camp of the

^f See 7. 2: Heb *messenger*

Syrians, and behold, there was no one to be seen or heard there, nothing but the horses tied, and the asses tied, and ¹¹ the tents as they were." Then the gatekeepers called out, ¹² and it was told within the king's household. And the king rose in the night, and said to his servants, "I will tell you what the Syrians have prepared against us. They know that we are hungry; therefore they have gone out of the camp to hide themselves in the open country, thinking, 'When they come out of the city, we shall take them ¹³ alive and get into the city.'" And one of his servants said, "Let some men take five of the remaining horses, seeing that those who are left here will fare like the whole multitude of Israel that have already perished; let us send ¹⁴ and see." So they took two mounted men, and the king sent them after the army of the Syrians, saying, "Go and ¹⁵ see." So they went after them as far as the Jordan; and, lo, all the way was littered with garments and equipment which the Syrians had thrown away in their haste. And the messengers returned, and told the king.

¹⁶ Then the people went out, and plundered the camp of the Syrians. So a measure of fine meal was sold for a shekel, and two measures of barley for a shekel, according ¹⁷ to the word of the LORD. Now the king had appointed the captain on whose hand he leaned to have charge of the gate; and the people trod upon him in the gate, so that he died, as the man of God had said when the king came ¹⁸ down to him. For when the man of God had said to the king, "Two measures of barley shall be sold for a shekel, and a measure of fine meal for a shekel, about this time ¹⁹ tomorrow in the gate of Samar'ia," the captain had answered the man of God, "If the LORD himself should make windows in heaven, could such a thing be?" And he had said, "You shall see it with your own eyes, but you shall ²⁰ not eat of it." And so it happened to him, for the people trod upon him in the gate and he died.

⁸ Now Eli'sha had said to the woman whose son he had restored to life, "Arise, and depart with your household, and sojourn wherever you can; for the LORD has called for a famine, and it will come upon the land ² for seven years." So the woman arose, and did according to the word of the man of God; she went with her household and sojourned in the land of the Philistines seven ³ years. And at the end of the seven years, when the woman returned from the land of the Philistines, she went forth ⁴ to appeal to the king for her house and her land. Now the king was talking with Geha'zi the servant of the man of God, saying, "Tell me all the great things that Eli'sha ⁵ has done." And while he was telling the king how Eli'sha had restored the dead to life, behold, the woman whose son he had restored to life appealed to the king for her house and her land. And Geha'zi said, "My lord, O king, here is the woman, and here is her son whom Eli'sha ⁶ restored to life." And when the king asked the woman,

she told him. So the king appointed an official for her, saying, "Restore all that was hers, together with all the produce of the fields from the day that she left the land until now."

7 Now Eli'sha came to Damascus. Ben-ha'dad the king of Syria was sick; and when it was told him, "The man of 8 God has come here," the king said to Haz'ael, "Take a present with you and go to meet the man of God, and inquire of the LORD through him, saying, 'Shall I recover 9 from this sickness?'" So Haz'ael went to meet him, and took a present with him, all kinds of goods of Damascus, forty camel loads. When he came and stood before him, he said, "Your son Ben-ha'dad king of Syria has sent me to you, saying, 'Shall I recover from this sickness?'" 10 And Eli'sha said to him, "Go, say to him, 'You shall certainly recover'; but the LORD has shown me that he 11 shall certainly die." And he fixed his gaze and stared at him, until he was ashamed. And the man of God wept. 12 And Haz'ael said, "Why does my lord weep?" He answered, "Because I know the evil that you will do to the people of Israel; you will set on fire their fortresses, and you will slay their young men with the sword, and dash in pieces their little ones, and rip up their women with 13 child." And Haz'ael said, "What is your servant, who is but a dog, that he should do this great thing?" Eli'sha answered, "The LORD has shown me that you are to be 14 king over Syria." Then he departed from Eli'sha, and came to his master, who said to him, "What did Eli'sha say to you?" And he answered, "He told me that you 15 would certainly recover." But on the morrow he took the coverlet and dipped it in water and spread it over his face, till he died. And Haz'ael became king in his stead.

16 In the fifth year of Joram the son of Ahab, king of Israel,[g] Jeho'ram the son of Jehosh'aphat, king of Judah, 17 began to reign. He was thirty-two years old when he be- 18 came king, and he reigned eight years in Jerusalem. And he walked in the way of the kings of Israel, as the house of Ahab had done, for the daughter of Ahab was his wife. 19 And he did what was evil in the sight of the LORD. Yet the LORD would not destroy Judah, for the sake of David his servant, since he promised to give a lamp to him and to his sons for ever.

20 In his days Edom revolted from the rule of Judah, and 21 set up a king of their own. Then Joram passed over to Za'ir with all his chariots, and rose by night, and he and his chariot commanders smote the Edomites who had 22 surrounded him; but his army fled home. So Edom re- volted from the rule of Judah to this day. Then Libnah 23 revolted at the same time. Now the rest of the acts of Joram, and all that he did, are they not written in the 24 Book of the Chronicles of the Kings of Judah? So Joram slept with his fathers, and was buried with his fathers in the city of David; and Ahazi'ah his son reigned in his stead.

25 In the twelfth year of Joram the son of Ahab, king of Israel, Ahazi'ah the son of Jeho'ram, king of Judah, began 26 to reign. Ahazi'ah was twenty-two years old when he began to reign, and he reigned one year in Jerusalem. His mother's name was Athali'ah; she was a grand- 27 daughter of Omri king of Israel. He also walked in the way of the house of Ahab, and did what was evil in the sight of the LORD, as the house of Ahab had done, for he was son-in-law to the house of Ahab.

28 He went with Joram the son of Ahab to make war against Haz'ael king of Syria at Ramoth-gilead, where 29 the Syrians wounded Joram. And King Joram returned to be healed in Jezreel of the wounds which the Syrians had given him at Ramah, when he fought against Haz'ael king of Syria. And Ahazi'ah the son of Jeho'ram king of Judah went down to see Joram the son of Ahab in Jezreel, because he was sick.

Jehu's Revolution

9 Then Eli'sha the prophet called one of the sons of the prophets and said to him, "Gird up your loins, and take this flask of oil in your hand, and go to Ramoth- 2 gilead. And when you arrive, look there for Jehu the son of Jehosh'aphat, son of Nimshi; and go in and bid him rise from among his fellows, and lead him to an inner 3 chamber. Then take the flask of oil, and pour it on his head, and say, 'Thus says the LORD, I anoint you king over Israel.' Then open the door and flee; do not tarry." 4 So the young man, the prophet,[h] went to Ramoth-gil- 5 ead. And when he came, behold, the commanders of the army were in council; and he said, "I have an errand to you, O commander." And Jehu said, "To which of us 6 all?" And he said, "To you, O commander." So he arose, and went into the house; and the young man poured the oil on his head, saying to him, "Thus says the LORD the God of Israel, I anoint you king over the people of the 7 LORD, over Israel. And you shall strike down the house of Ahab your master, that I may avenge on Jez'ebel the blood of my servants the prophets, and the blood of all 8 the servants of the LORD. For the whole house of Ahab shall perish; and I will cut off from Ahab every male, 9 bond or free, in Israel. And I will make the house of Ahab like the house of Jerobo'am the son of Nebat, and 10 like the house of Ba'asha the son of Ahi'jah. And the dogs shall eat Jez'ebel in the territory of Jezreel, and none shall bury her." Then he opened the door, and fled.

11 When Jehu came out to the servants of his master, they said to him, "Is all well? Why did this mad fellow come to you?" And he said to them, "You know the 12 fellow and his talk." And they said, "That is not true; tell us now." And he said, "Thus and so he spoke to me, saying, 'Thus says the LORD, I anoint you king over 13 Israel.'" Then in haste every man of them took his garment, and put it under him on the bare[i] steps, and

g Gk Syr: Heb *Israel, Jehoshaphat being king of Judah*
h Gk Syr: Heb *the young man, the young man, the prophet*
i The meaning of the Hebrew word is uncertain

they blew the trumpet, and proclaimed, "Jehu is king."

14 Thus Jehu the son of Jehosh'aphat the son of Nimshi conspired against Joram. (Now Joram with all Israel had been on guard at Ramoth-gilead against Haz'ael king of 15 Syria; but King Joram had returned to be healed in Jezreel of the wounds which the Syrians had given him, when he fought with Haz'ael king of Syria.) So Jehu said, "If this is your mind, then let no one slip out of the 16 city to go and tell the news in Jezreel." Then Jehu mounted his chariot, and went to Jezreel, for Joram lay there. And Ahazi'ah king of Judah had come down to visit Joram.

17 Now the watchman was standing on the tower in Jezreel, and he spied the company of Jehu as he came, and said, "I see a company." And Joram said, "Take a horseman, and send to meet them, and let him say, 'Is 18 it peace?'" So a man on horseback went to meet him, and said, "Thus says the king, 'Is it peace?'" And Jehu said, "What have you to do with peace? Turn round and ride behind me." And the watchman reported, saying, "The messenger reached them, but he is not coming back." 19 Then he sent out a second horseman, who came to them, and said, "Thus the king has said, 'Is it peace?'" And Jehu answered, "What have you to do with peace? Turn 20 round and ride behind me." Again the watchman reported, "He reached them, but he is not coming back. And the driving is like the driving of Jehu the son of Nimshi; for he drives furiously."

21 Joram said, "Make ready." And they made ready his chariot. Then Joram king of Israel and Ahazi'ah king of Judah set out, each in his chariot, and went to meet Jehu, and met him at the property of Naboth the Jezreelite. 22 And when Joram saw Jehu, he said, "Is it peace, Jehu?" He answered, "What peace can there be, so long as the harlotries and the sorceries of your mother Jez'ebel are 23 so many?" Then Joram reined about and fled, saying 24 to Ahazi'ah, "Treachery, O Ahazi'ah!" And Jehu drew his bow with his full strength, and shot Joram between the shoulders, so that the arrow pierced his heart, and he 25 sank in his chariot. Jehu said to Bidkar his aide, "Take him up, and cast him on the plot of ground belonging to Naboth the Jezreelite, for remember, when you and I rode side by side behind Ahab his father, how the LORD 26 uttered this oracle against him: 'As surely as I saw yesterday the blood of Naboth and the blood of his sons —says the LORD—I will requite you on this plot of ground.' Now therefore take him up and cast him on the plot of ground, in accordance with the word of the LORD."

27 When Ahazi'ah the king of Judah saw this, he fled in the direction of Beth-haggan. And Jehu pursued him, and said, "Shoot him also"; and they shot him [j] in the chariot at the ascent of Gur, which is by Ibleam. And he fled to 28 Megid'do, and died there. His servants carried him in a chariot to Jerusalem, and buried him in his tomb with his fathers in the city of David.

29 In the eleventh year of Joram the son of Ahab, Ahazi'ah began to reign over Judah.

30 When Jehu came to Jezreel, Jez'ebel heard of it; and she painted her eyes, and adorned her head, and looked 31 out of the window. And as Jehu entered the gate, she said, "Is it peace, you Zimri, murderer of your master?" 32 And he lifted up his face to the window, and said, "Who is on my side? Who?" Two or three eunuchs looked out 33 at him. He said, "Throw her down." So they threw her down; and some of her blood spattered on the wall and 34 on the horses, and they trampled on her. Then he went in and ate and drank; and he said, "See now to this cursed woman, and bury her; for she is a king's daughter." 35 But when they went to bury her, they found no more of her than the skull and the feet and the palms of her hands. 36 When they came back and told him, he said, "This is the word of the LORD, which he spoke by his servant Eli'jah the Tishbite, 'In the territory of Jezreel the dogs shall eat 37 the flesh of Jez'ebel; and the corpse of Jez'ebel shall be as dung upon the face of the field in the territory of Jezreel, so that no one can say, This is Jez'ebel.'"

10 Now Ahab had seventy sons in Samar'ia. So Jehu wrote letters, and sent them to Samar'ia, to the rulers of the city,[k] to the elders, and to the guardians of the sons 2 of Ahab, saying, "Now then, as soon as this letter comes to you, seeing your master's sons are with you, and there are with you chariots and horses, fortified cities also, and 3 weapons, select the best and fittest of your master's sons and set him on his father's throne, and fight for your 4 master's house." But they were exceedingly afraid, and said, "Behold, the two kings could not stand before 5 him; how then can we stand?" So he who was over the palace, and he who was over the city, together with the elders and the guardians, sent to Jehu, saying, "We are your servants, and we will do all that you bid us. We will not make any one king; do whatever is good in your 6 eyes." Then he wrote to them a second letter, saying, "If you are on my side, and if you are ready to obey me, take the heads of your master's sons, and come to me at Jezreel tomorrow at this time." Now the king's sons, seventy persons, were with the great men of the city, who 7 were bringing them up. And when the letter came to them, they took the king's sons, and slew them, seventy persons, and put their heads in baskets, and sent them to 8 him at Jezreel. When the messenger came and told him,

---

[j] Syr Vg Compare Gk: Heb lacks *and they shot him*   [k] Gk Vg: Heb *Jezreel*

"They have brought the heads of the king's sons," he said, "Lay them in two heaps at the entrance of the gate 9 until the morning." Then in the morning, when he went out, he stood, and said to all the people, "You are innocent. It was I who conspired against my master, and 10 slew him; but who struck down all these? Know then that there shall fall to the earth nothing of the word of the LORD, which the LORD spoke concerning the house of Ahab; for the LORD has done what he said by his servant 11 Eli'jah." So Jehu slew all that remained of the house of Ahab in Jezreel, all his great men, and his familiar friends, and his priests, until he left him none remaining. 12 Then he set out and went to Samar'ia. On the way, 13 when he was at Beth-eked of the Shepherds, Jehu met the kinsmen of Ahazi'ah king of Judah, and he said, "Who are you?" And they answered, "We are the kinsmen of Ahazi'ah, and we came down to visit the royal princes 14 and the sons of the queen mother." He said, "Take them alive." And they took them alive, and slew them at the pit of Beth-eked, forty-two persons, and he spared none of them.

15 And when he departed from there, he met Jehon'adab the son of Rechab coming to meet him; and he greeted him, and said to him, "Is your heart true to my heart as mine is to yours?"[1] And Jehon'adab answered, "It is." Jehu said,[m] "If it is, give me your hand." So he gave him his hand. And Jehu took him up with him into the 16 chariot. And he said, "Come with me, and see my zeal 17 for the LORD." So he[n] had him ride in his chariot. And when he came to Samar'ia, he slew all that remained to Ahab in Samar'ia, till he had wiped them out, according to the word of the LORD which he spoke to Eli'jah.

18 Then Jehu assembled all the people, and said to them, "Ahab served Ba'al a little; but Jehu will serve him much. 19 Now therefore call to me all the prophets of Ba'al, all his worshipers and all his priests; let none be missing, for I have a great sacrifice to offer to Ba'al; whoever is missing shall not live." But Jehu did it with cunning in 20 order to destroy the worshipers of Ba'al. And Jehu ordered, "Sanctify a solemn assembly for Ba'al." So they 21 proclaimed it. And Jehu sent throughout all Israel; and all the worshipers of Ba'al came, so that there was not a man left who did not come. And they entered the house of Ba'al, and the house of Ba'al was filled from one end 22 to the other. He said to him who was in charge of the wardrobe, "Bring out the vestments for all the worshipers of Ba'al." So he brought out the vestments for them. 23 Then Jehu went into the house of Ba'al with Jehon'adab the son of Rechab; and he said to the worshipers of Ba'al, "Search, and see that there is no servant of the LORD here among you, but only the worshipers of Ba'al." 24 Then he[o] went in to offer sacrifices and burnt offerings.

Now Jehu had stationed eighty men outside, and said,

"The man who allows any of those whom I give into your 25 hands to escape shall forfeit his life." So as soon as he had made an end of offering the burnt offering, Jehu said to the guard and to the officers, "Go in and slay them; let not a man escape." So when they put them to the sword, the guard and the officers cast them out and went into the 26 inner room[p] of the house of Ba'al and they brought out

the pillar that was in the house of Ba'al, and burned it. 27 And they demolished the pillar of Ba'al, and demolished the house of Ba'al, and made it a latrine to this day.

28, 29 Thus Jehu wiped out Ba'al from Israel. But Jehu did not turn aside from the sins of Jerobo'am the son of Nebat, which he made Israel to sin, the golden calves that 30 were in Bethel, and in Dan. And the LORD said to Jehu, "Because you have done well in carrying out what is right in my eyes, and have done to the house of Ahab according to all that was in my heart, your sons of the fourth 31 generation shall sit on the throne of Israel." But Jehu was not careful to walk in the law of the LORD the God of Israel with all his heart; he did not turn from the sins of Jerobo'am, which he made Israel to sin.

32 In those days the LORD began to cut off parts of Israel. Haz'ael defeated them throughout the territory of Israel: 33 from the Jordan eastward, all the land of Gilead, the Gadites, and the Reubenites, and the Manas'sites, from Aro'er, which is by the valley of the Arnon, that is, Gilead 34 and Bashan. Now the rest of the acts of Jehu, and all that he did, and all his might, are they not written in the 35 Book of the Chronicles of the Kings of Israel? So Jehu slept with his fathers, and they buried him in Samar'ia. 36 And Jeho'ahaz his son reigned in his stead. The time that Jehu reigned over Israel in Samaria was twenty-eight years.

Revolutions in Judah

11 Now when Athali'ah the mother of Ahazi'ah saw that her son was dead, she arose and destroyed all 2 the royal family. But Jehosh'eba, the daughter of King Joram, sister of Ahazi'ah, took Jo'ash the son of Ahazi'ah, and stole him away from among the king's sons who were about to be slain, and she put[q] him and his nurse in a bedchamber. Thus she[r] hid him from Athali'ah, so that 3 he was not slain; and he remained with her six years, hid in the house of the LORD, while Athali'ah reigned over the land.

4 But in the seventh year Jehoi'ada sent and brought the captains of the Carites and of the guards, and had them come to him in the house of the LORD; and he made a

covenant with them and put them under oath in the house 5 of the LORD, and he showed them the king's son. And he commanded them, "This is the thing that you shall do: one third of you, those who come off duty on the sabbath 6 and guard the king's house (another third being at the gate Sur and a third at the gate behind the guards), shall 7 guard the palace; and the two divisions of you, which come on duty in force on the sabbath and guard the house 8 of the LORD,ˢ shall surround the king, each with his weapons in his hand; and whoever approaches the ranks is to be slain. Be with the king when he goes out and when he comes in."

9 The captains did according to all that Jehoi'ada the priest commanded, and each brought his men who were to go off duty on the sabbath, with those who were to come on duty on the sabbath, and came to Jehoi'ada the 10 priest. And the priest delivered to the captains the spears and shields that had been King David's, which were in 11 the house of the LORD; and the guards stood, every man with his weapons in his hand, from the south side of the house to the north side of the house, around the altar 12 and the house.ᵗ Then he brought out the king's son, and put the crown upon him, and gave him the testimony; and they proclaimed him king, and anointed him; and they clapped their hands, and said, "Long live the king!"

13 When Athali'ah heard the noise of the guard and of the people, she went into the house of the LORD to the 14 people; and when she looked, there was the king standing by the pillar, according to the custom, and the captains and the trumpeters beside the king, and all the people of the land rejoicing and blowing trumpets. And Athali'ah 15 rent her clothes, and cried, "Treason! Treason!" Then Jehoi'ada the priest commanded the captains who were set over the army, "Bring her out between the ranks; and slay with the sword any one who follows her." For the priest said, "Let her not be slain in the house of the 16 LORD." So they laid hands on her; and she went through the horses' entrance to the king's house, and there she was slain.

17 And Jehoi'ada made a covenant between the LORD and the king and people, that they should be the LORD's peo- 18 ple; and also between the king and the people. Then all the people of the land went to the house of Ba'al, and tore it down; his altars and his images they broke in pieces, and they slew Mattan the priest of Ba'al before the altars. And the priest posted watchmen over the house of the 19 LORD. And he took the captains, the Carites, the guards, and all the people of the land; and they brought the king down from the house of the LORD, marching through the gate of the guards to the king's house. And he took his 20 seat on the throne of the kings. So all the people of the land rejoiced; and the city was quiet after Athali'ah had been slain with the sword at the king's house.

21 u Jeho'ash was seven years old when he began to reign.

12 In the seventh year of Jehu Jeho'ash began to reign, and he reigned forty years in Jerusalem. His 2 mother's name was Zib'iah of Beer-sheba. And Jeho'ash did what was right in the eyes of the LORD all his days, 3 because Jehoi'ada the priest instructed him. Nevertheless the high places were not taken away; the people continued to sacrifice and burn incense on the high places.

4 Jeho'ash said to the priests, "All the money of the holy things which is brought into the house of the LORD, the money for which each man is assessed—the money from the assessment of persons—and the money which a man's heart prompts him to bring into the house of 5 the LORD, let the priests take, each from his acquaint- ance; and let them repair the house wherever any need 6 of repairs is discovered." But by the twenty-third year of King Jeho'ash the priests had made no repairs on the 7 house. Therefore King Jeho'ash summoned Jehoi'ada the priest and the other priests and said to them, "Why are you not repairing the house? Now therefore take no more money from your acquaintances, but hand it over for the 8 repair of the house." So the priests agreed that they should take no more money from the people, and that they should not repair the house.

9 Then Jehoi'ada the priest took a chest, and bored a hole in the lid of it, and set it beside the altar on the right side as one entered the house of the LORD; and the priests who guarded the threshold put in it all the money that 10 was brought into the house of the LORD. And whenever they saw that there was much money in the chest, the king's secretary and the high priest came up and they counted and tied up in bags the money that was found in 11 the house of the LORD. Then they would give the money that was weighed out into the hands of the workmen who had the oversight of the house of the LORD; and they paid it out to the carpenters and the builders who worked 12 upon the house of the LORD, and to the masons and the stonecutters, as well as to buy timber and quarried stone for making repairs on the house of the LORD, and for any 13 outlay upon the repairs of the house. But there were not made for the house of the LORD basins of silver, snuffers, bowls, trumpets, or any vessels of gold, or of silver, from the money that was brought into the house of the LORD, 14 for that was given to the workmen who were repairing 15 the house of the LORD with it. And they did not ask an accounting from the men into whose hand they delivered the money to pay out to the workmen, for they dealt 16 honestly. The money from the guilt offerings and the money from the sin offerings was not brought into the house of the LORD; it belonged to the priests.

17 At that time Haz'ael king of Syria went up and fought against Gath, and took it. But when Haz'ael set his face 18 to go up against Jerusalem, Jeho'ash king of Judah took all the votive gifts that Jehosh'aphat and Jeho'ram and Ahazi'ah, his fathers, the kings of Judah, had dedicated,

---

ˢ Heb the LORD to the king   ᵗ Heb the house to the king   ᵘ Ch 12. 1 in Heb

and his own votive gifts, and all the gold that was found in the treasuries of the house of the LORD and of the king's house, and sent these to Haz'ael king of Syria. Then Haz'ael went away from Jerusalem.

19 Now the rest of the acts of Jo'ash, and all that he did, are they not written in the Book of the Chronicles of the 20 Kings of Judah? His servants arose and made a conspiracy, and slew Jo'ash in the house of Millo, on the 21 way that goes down to Silla. It was Jo'zacar the son of Shim'eath and Jeho'zabad the son of Shomer, his servants, who struck him down, so that he died. And they buried him with his fathers in the city of David, and Amazi'ah his son reigned in his stead.

13 In the twenty-third year of Jo'ash the son of Ahazi'ah, king of Judah, Jeho'ahaz the son of Jehu began to reign over Israel in Samar'ia, and he reigned 2 seventeen years. He did what was evil in the sight of the LORD, and followed the sins of Jerobo'am the son of Nebat, which he made Israel to sin; he did not depart 3 from them. And the anger of the LORD was kindled against Israel, and he gave them continually into the hand of Haz'ael king of Syria and into the hand of Ben-ha'dad the 4 son of Haz'ael. Then Jeho'ahaz besought the LORD, and the LORD hearkened to him; for he saw the oppression 5 of Israel, how the king of Syria oppressed them. (Therefore the LORD gave Israel a savior, so that they escaped from the hand of the Syrians; and the people of Israel 6 dwelt in their homes as formerly. Nevertheless they did not depart from the sins of the house of Jerobo'am, which he made Israel to sin, but walked ᵛ in them; and the 7 Ashe'rah also remained in Samar'ia.) For there was not left to Jeho'ahaz an army of more than fifty horsemen and ten chariots and ten thousand footmen; for the king of Syria had destroyed them and made them like the 8 dust at threshing. Now the rest of the acts of Jeho'ahaz and all that he did, and his might, are they not written 9 in the Book of the Chronicles of the Kings of Israel? So Jeho'ahaz slept with his fathers, and they buried him in Samar'ia; and Jo'ash his son reigned in his stead.

10 In the thirty-seventh year of Jo'ash king of Judah Jeho'ash the son of Jeho'ahaz began to reign over Israel 11 in Samar'ia, and he reigned sixteen years. He also did what was evil in the sight of the LORD; he did not depart from all the sins of Jerobo'am the son of Nebat, which 12 he made Israel to sin, but he walked in them. Now the rest of the acts of Jo'ash, and all that he did, and the might with which he fought against Amazi'ah king of Judah, are they not written in the Book of the Chronicles 13 of the Kings of Israel? So Jo'ash slept with his fathers, and Jerobo'am sat upon this throne; and Jo'ash was buried in Samar'ia with the kings of Israel.

14 Now when Eli'sha had fallen sick with the illness of which he was to die, Jo'ash king of Israel went down to him, and wept before him, crying, "My father, my father!

15 The chariots of Israel and its horsemen!" And Eli'sha said to him, "Take a bow and arrows"; so he took a bow 16 and arrows. Then he said to the king of Israel, "Draw the bow"; and he drew it. And Eli'sha laid his hands 17 upon the king's hands. And he said, "Open the window eastward"; and he opened it. Then Eli'sha said, "Shoot"; and he shot. And he said, "The LORD's arrow of victory, the arrow of victory over Syria! For you shall fight the Syrians in Aphek until you have made an end of them." 18 And he said, "Take the arrows"; and he took them. And he said to the king of Israel, "Strike the ground with 19 them"; and he struck three times, and stopped. Then the man of God was angry with him, and said, "You should have struck five or six times; then you would have struck down Syria until you had made an end of it, but now you will strike down Syria only three times."

20 So Eli'sha died, and they buried him. Now bands of Moabites used to invade the land in the spring of the 21 year. And as a man was being buried, lo, a marauding band was seen and the man was cast into the grave of Eli'sha; and as soon as the man touched the bones of Eli'sha, he revived, and stood on his feet.

22 Now Haz'ael king of Syria oppressed Israel all the days 23 of Jeho'ahaz. But the LORD was gracious to them and had compassion on them, and he turned toward them, because of his covenant with Abraham, Isaac, and Jacob, and would not destroy them; nor has he cast them from his presence until now.

24 When Haz'ael king of Syria died, Ben-ha'dad his son 25 became king in his stead. Then Jeho'ash the son of Jeho'-ahaz took again from Ben-ha'dad the son of Haz'ael the cities which he had taken from Jeho'ahaz his father in war. Three times Jo'ash defeated him and recovered the cities of Israel.

14 In the second year of Jo'ash the son of Jo'ahaz, king of Israel, Amazi'ah the son of Jo'ash, king of 2 Judah, began to reign. He was twenty-five years old when he began to reign, and he reigned twenty-nine years in Jerusalem. His mother's name was Jeho-ad'din of Jerusa-3 lem. And he did what was right in the eyes of the LORD, yet not like David his father; he did in all things as Jo'ash 4 his father had done. But the high places were not removed; the people still sacrificed and burned incense on 5 the high places. And as soon as the royal power was firmly in his hand he killed his servants who had slain 6 the king his father. But he did not put to death the children of the murderers; according to what is written in the book of the law of Moses, where the LORD commanded, "The fathers shall not be put to death for the children, or the children be put to death for the fathers; but every man shall die for his own sin."

7 He killed ten thousand Edomites in the Valley of Salt and took Sela by storm, and called it Jok'the-el, which is its name to this day.

ᵛ Gk Syr Tg Vg: Heb *he walked*

8 Then Amazi'ah sent messengers to Jeho'ash the son of Jeho'ahaz, son of Jehu, king of Israel, saying, "Come, let 9 us look one another in the face." And Jeho'ash king of Israel sent word to Amazi'ah king of Judah, "A thistle on Lebanon sent to a cedar on Lebanon, saying, 'Give your daughter to my son for a wife'; and a wild beast of 10 Lebanon passed by and trampled down the thistle. You have indeed smitten Edom, and your heart has lifted you up. Be content with your glory, and stay at home; for why should you provoke trouble so that you fall, you and Judah with you?"

11 But Amazi'ah would not listen. So Jeho'ash king of Israel went up, and he and Amazi'ah king of Judah faced one another in battle at Beth-she'mesh, which belongs to 12 Judah. And Judah was defeated by Israel, and every man 13 fled to his home. And Jeho'ash king of Israel captured Amazi'ah king of Judah, the son of Jeho'ash, son of Ahazi'ah, at Beth-she'mesh, and came to Jerusalem, and broke down the wall of Jerusalem for four hundred cubits, 14 from the E'phraim Gate to the Corner Gate. And he seized

all the gold and silver, and all the vessels that were found in the house of the LORD and in the treasuries of the king's house, also hostages, and he returned to Samar'ia.
15 Now the rest of the acts of Jeho'ash which he did, and his might, and how he fought with Amazi'ah king of Judah, are they not written in the Book of the Chronicles 16 of the Kings of Israel? And Jeho'ash slept with his fathers, and was buried in Samar'ia with the kings of Israel; and Jerobo'am his son reigned in his stead.
17 Amazi'ah the son of Jo'ash, king of Judah, lived fifteen

years after the death of Jeho'ash son of Jeho'ahaz, king of 18 Israel. Now the rest of the deeds of Amazi'ah, are they not written in the Book of the Chronicles of the Kings of 19 Judah? And they made a conspiracy against him in Jerusalem, and he fled to Lachish. But they sent after him 20 to Lachish, and slew him there. And they brought him upon horses; and he was buried in Jerusalem with his 21 fathers in the city of David. And all the people of Judah took Azari'ah, who was sixteen years old, and made him 22 king instead of his father Amazi'ah. He built Elath and restored it to Judah, after the king slept with his fathers.
23 In the fifteenth year of Amazi'ah the son of Jo'ash, king of Judah, Jerobo'am the son of Jo'ash, king of Israel, began to reign in Samar'ia, and he reigned forty-one 24 years. And he did what was evil in the sight of the LORD; he did not depart from all the sins of Jerobo'am the son 25 of Nebat, which he made Israel to sin. He restored the border of Israel from the entrance of Hamath as far as the Sea of the Arabah, according to the word of the LORD, the God of Israel, which he spoke by his servant Jonah the son of Amit'tai, the prophet, who was from Gath-he'- 26 pher. For the LORD saw that the affliction of Israel was very bitter, for there was none left, bond or free, and there 27 was none to help Israel. But the LORD had not said that he would blot out the name of Israel from under heaven, so he saved them by the hand of Jerobo'am the son of Jo'ash.
28 Now the rest of the acts of Jerobo'am, and all that he did, and his might, how he fought, and how he recovered for Israel Damascus and Hamath, which had belonged to Judah, are they not written in the Book of the Chronicles 29 of the Kings of Israel? And Jerobo'am slept with his fathers, the kings of Israel, and Zechari'ah his son reigned in his stead.

15 In the twenty-seventh year of Jerobo'am king of Israel Azari'ah the son of Amazi'ah, king of Judah, 2 began to reign. He was sixteen years old when he began to reign, and he reigned fifty-two years in Jerusalem. His 3 mother's name was Jecoli'ah of Jerusalem. And he did what was right in the eyes of the LORD, according to all 4 that his father Amazi'ah had done. Nevertheless the high places were not taken away; the people still sacrificed and 5 burned incense on the high places. And the LORD smote the king, so that he was a leper to the day of his death, and he dwelt in a separate house. And Jotham the king's son was over the household, governing the people of the 6 land. Now the rest of the acts of Azari'ah, and all that he did, are they not written in the Book of the Chronicles of 7 the Kings of Judah? And Azari'ah slept with his fathers, and they buried him with his fathers in the city of David, and Jotham his son reigned in his stead.
8 In the thirty-eighth year of Azari'ah king of Judah Zechari'ah the son of Jerobo'am reigned over Israel in

Samar'ia six months. And he did what was evil in the sight of the LORD, as his fathers had done. He did not depart from the sins of Jerobo'am the son of Nebat, [10] which he made Israel to sin. Shallum the son of Jabesh conspired against him, and struck him down at Ibleam,[w] [11] and killed him, and reigned in his stead. Now the rest of the deeds of Zechari'ah, behold, they are written in the [12] Book of the Chronicles of the Kings of Israel. (This was the promise of the LORD which he gave to Jehu, "Your sons shall sit upon the throne of Israel to the fourth generation." And so it came to pass.)

[13] Shallum the son of Jabesh began to reign in the thirty-ninth year of Uzzi'ah king of Judah, and he reigned one [14] month in Samar'ia. Then Men'ahem the son of Gadi came up from Tirzah and came to Samar'ia, and he struck down Shallum the son of Jabesh in Samar'ia and slew [15] him, and reigned in his stead. Now the rest of the deeds of Shallum, and the conspiracy which he made, behold, they are written in the Book of the Chronicles of the [16] Kings of Israel. At that time Men'ahem sacked Tappuah [x] and all who were in it and its territory from Tirzah on; because they did not open it to him, therefore he sacked it, and he ripped up all the women in it who were with child.

[17] In the thirty-ninth year of Azari'ah king of Judah Men'ahem the son of Gadi began to reign over Israel, and [18] he reigned ten years in Samar'ia. And he did what was evil in the sight of the LORD; he did not depart all his days from all the sins of Jerobo'am the son of Nebat, [19] which he made Israel to sin. Pul the king of Assyria came against the land; and Men'ahem gave Pul a thousand talents of silver, that he might help him to confirm his [20] hold of the royal power. Men'ahem exacted the money from Israel, that is, from all the wealthy men, fifty shekels of silver from every man, to give to the king of Assyria. So the king of Assyria turned back, and did not stay there [21] in the land. Now the rest of the deeds of Men'ahem, and all that he did, are they not written in the Book of the [22] Chronicles of the Kings of Israel? And Men'ahem slept with his fathers, and Pekahi'ah his son reigned in his stead.

[23] In the fiftieth year of Azari'ah king of Judah Pekahi'ah the son of Men'ahem began to reign over Israel in Samar'- [24] ia, and he reigned two years. And he did what was evil in the sight of the LORD; he did not turn away from the sins of Jerobo'am the son of Nebat, which he made [25] Israel to sin. And Pekah the son of Remali'ah, his captain, conspired against him with fifty men of the Gileadites, and slew him in Samar'ia, in the citadel of the king's house;[y] he slew him, and reigned in his stead. [26] Now the rest of the deeds of Pekahi'ah, and all that he did, behold, they are written in the Book of the Chronicles of the Kings of Israel.

[27] In the fifty-second year of Azari'ah king of Judah Pekah the son of Remali'ah began to reign over Israel [28] in Samar'ia, and reigned twenty years. And he did what was evil in the sight of the LORD; he did not depart from the sins of Jerobo'am the son of Nebat, which he made Israel to sin.

[29] In the days of Pekah king of Israel Tig'lath-pile'ser king of Assyria came and captured I'jon, A'bel-beth-ma'-acah, Jano'ah, Kedesh, Hazor, Gilead, and Galilee, all the land of Naph'tali; and he carried the people captive [30] to Assyria. Then Hoshe'a the son of Elah made a conspiracy against Pekah the son of Remali'ah, and struck him down, and slew him, and reigned in his stead, in the [31] twentieth year of Jotham the son of Uzzi'ah. Now the rest of the acts of Pekah, and all that he did, behold, they are written in the Book of the Chronicles of the Kings of Israel.

[32] In the second year of Pekah the son of Remali'ah, king of Israel, Jotham the son of Uzzi'ah, king of Judah, began [33] to reign. He was twenty-five years old when he began to reign, and he reigned sixteen years in Jerusalem. His [34] mother's name was Jeru'sha the daughter of Zadok. And he did what was right in the eyes of the LORD, according [35] to all that his father Uzzi'ah had done. Nevertheless the high places were not removed; the people still sacrificed and burned incense on the high places. He built the upper [36] gate of the house of the LORD. Now the rest of the acts of Jotham, and all that he did, are they not written in [37] the Book of the Chronicles of the Kings of Judah? In those days the LORD began to send Rezin the king of Syria and Pekah the son of Remali'ah against Judah. [38] Jotham slept with his fathers, and was buried with his fathers in the city of David his father; and Ahaz his son reigned in his stead.

16 In the seventeenth year of Pekah the son of Remali'ah, Ahaz the son of Jotham, king of Judah, [2] began to reign. Ahaz was twenty years old when he began to reign, and he reigned sixteen years in Jerusalem. And he did not do what was right in the eyes of the LORD his [3] God, as his father David had done, but he walked in the way of the kings of Israel. He even burned his son as an offering,[z] according to the abominable practices of the nations whom the LORD drove out before the people of [4] Israel. And he sacrificed and burned incense on the high places, and on the hills, and under every green tree.

[5] Then Rezin king of Syria and Pekah the son of Remali'ah, king of Israel, came up to wage war on Jerusalem, [6] and they besieged Ahaz but could not conquer him. At that time [a] the king of Edom [b] recovered Elath for Edom,[b] and drove the men of Judah from Elath; and the Edom- [7] ites came to Elath, where they dwell to this day. So Ahaz sent messengers to Tig'lath-pile'ser king of Assyria, saying, "I am your servant and your son. Come up, and

---

[w] Gk Compare 9. 27: Heb *before the people*   [x] Compare Gk: Heb *Tiphsah*
[y] Heb adds *Argob and Arieh*, which probably belong to the list of places in verse 29
[z] Or *made his son to pass through the fire*   [a] Heb *At that time Rezin*   [b] Heb *Aram* (Syria)

rescue me from the hand of the king of Syria and from the hand of the king of Israel, who are attacking me."

8 Ahaz also took the silver and gold that was found in the house of the LORD and in the treasuries of the king's
9 house, and sent a present to the king of Assyria. And the king of Assyria hearkened to him; the king of Assyria marched up against Damascus, and took it, carrying its people captive to Kir, and he killed Rezin.

10 When King Ahaz went to Damascus to meet Tig′lath-pile′ser king of Assyria, he saw the altar that was at Damascus. And King Ahaz sent to Uri′ah the priest a model of the altar, and its pattern, exact in all its details.
11 And Uri′ah the priest built the altar; in accordance with all that King Ahaz had sent from Damascus, so Uri′ah the priest made it, before King Ahaz arrived from
12 Damascus. And when the king came from Damascus, the king viewed the altar. Then the king drew near to the
13 altar, and went up on it, and burned his burnt offering and his cereal offering, and poured his drink offering, and threw the blood of his peace offerings upon the altar.
14 And the bronze altar which was before the LORD he removed from the front of the house, from the place between his altar and the house of the LORD, and put it
15 on the north side of his altar. And King Ahaz commanded Uri′ah the priest, saying, "Upon the great altar burn the morning burnt offering, and the evening cereal offering, and the king's burnt offering, and his cereal offering, with the burnt offering of all the people of the land, and their cereal offering, and their drink offering; and throw upon it all the blood of the burnt offering, and all the blood of the sacrifice; but the bronze altar shall be for
16 me to inquire by." Uri′ah the priest did all this, as King Ahaz commanded.

17 And King Ahaz cut off the frames of the stands, and removed the laver from them, and he took down the sea from off the bronze oxen that were under it, and put it
18 upon a pediment of stone. And the covered way for the sabbath which had been built inside the palace, and the outer entrance for the king he removed from[c] the house
19 of the LORD, because of the king of Assyria. Now the rest of the acts of Ahaz which he did, are they not written in
20 the Book of the Chronicles of the Kings of Judah? And Ahaz slept with his fathers, and was buried with his fathers in the city of David; and Hezeki′ah his son reigned in his stead.

The Fall of the Northern Kingdom

17 In the twelfth year of Ahaz king of Judah Hoshe′a the son of Elah began to reign in Samar′ia over
2 Israel, and he reigned nine years. And he did what was evil in the sight of the LORD, yet not as the kings of Israel
3 who were before him. Against him came up Shalmane′ser king of Assyria; and Hoshe′a became his vassal, and paid
4 him tribute. But the king of Assyria found treachery in Hoshe′a; for he had sent messengers to So, king of Egypt, and offered no tribute to the king of Assyria, as he had done year by year; therefore the king of Assyria shut
5 him up, and bound him in prison. Then the king of Assyria invaded all the land and came to Samar′ia, and
6 for three years he besieged it. In the ninth year of Hoshe′a the king of Assyria captured Samar′ia, and he carried the Israelites away to Assyria, and placed them in Halah, and on the Habor, the river of Gozan, and in the cities of the Medes.

7 And this was so, because the people of Israel had sinned against the LORD their God, who had brought them up out of the land of Egypt from under the hand of Pharaoh
8 king of Egypt, and had feared other gods and walked in the customs of the nations whom the LORD drove out before the people of Israel, and in the customs which the
9 kings of Israel had introduced.[d] And the people of Israel did secretly against the LORD their God things that were not right. They built for themselves high places at all
10 their towns, from watchtower to fortified city; they set up for themselves pillars and Ashe′rim on every high hill
11 and under every green tree; and there they burned incense on all the high places, as the nations did whom the LORD carried away before them. And they did wicked
12 things, provoking the LORD to anger, and they served idols, of which the LORD had said to them, "You shall not
13 do this." Yet the LORD warned Israel and Judah by every

prophet and every seer, saying, "Turn from your evil ways and keep my commandments and my statutes, in accordance with all the law which I commanded your fathers, and which I sent to you by my servants the
14 prophets." But they would not listen, but were stubborn, as their fathers had been, who did not believe in the
15 LORD their God. They despised his statutes, and his covenant that he made with their fathers, and the warnings which he gave them. They went after false idols, and became false, and they followed the nations that were round about them, concerning whom the LORD had com-
16 manded them that they should not do like them. And they forsook all the commandments of the LORD their God, and made for themselves molten images of two calves; and they made an Ashe′rah, and worshiped all the host of
17 heaven, and served Ba′al. And they burned their sons and their daughters as offerings,[e] and used divination and

---

[c] Cn: Heb *turned to*   [d] Heb obscure   [e] Or *made their sons and their daughters pass through the fire*

sorcery, and sold themselves to do evil in the sight of the
18 LORD, provoking him to anger. Therefore the LORD was
very angry with Israel, and removed them out of his
sight; none was left but the tribe of Judah only.

19 Judah also did not keep the commandments of the LORD
their God, but walked in the customs which Israel had
20 introduced. And the LORD rejected all the descendants of
Israel, and afflicted them, and gave them into the hand
of spoilers, until he had cast them out of his sight.

21 When he had torn Israel from the house of David they
made Jerobo'am the son of Nebat king. And Jerobo'am
drove Israel from following the LORD and made them
22 commit great sin. The people of Israel walked in all the
sins which Jerobo'am did; they did not depart from them,
23 until the LORD removed Israel out of his sight, as he had
spoken by all his servants the prophets. So Israel was
exiled from their own land to Assyria until this day.

Origins of the Samaritans

24 And the king of Assyria brought people from Babylon,
Cuthah, Avva, Hamath, and Sepharva'im, and placed
them in the cities of Samar'ia instead of the people of
Israel; and they took possession of Samar'ia, and dwelt
25 in its cities. And at the beginning of their dwelling there,
they did not fear the LORD; therefore the LORD sent lions
26 among them, which killed some of them. So the king of
Assyria was told, "The nations which you have carried
away and placed in the cities of Samar'ia do not know
the law of the god of the land; therefore he has sent lions
among them, and behold, they are killing them, because
27 they do not know the law of the god of the land." Then
the king of Assyria commanded, "Send there one of the
priests whom you carried away thence; and let him [f] go
and dwell there, and teach them the law of the god of the
28 land." So one of the priests whom they had carried away
from Samar'ia came and dwelt in Bethel, and taught them
how they should fear the LORD.

29 But every nation still made gods of its own, and put
them in the shrines of the high places which the Samaritans had made, every nation in the cities in which they
30 dwelt; the men of Babylon made Suc'coth-be'noth, the
men of Cuth made Negal, the men of Hamath made
31 Ashi'ma, and the Av'vites made Nibhaz and Tartak; and
the Sephar'vites burned their children in the fire to
Adram'melech and Anam'melech, the gods of Sepharva'-
32 im. They also feared the LORD, and appointed from
among themselves all sorts of people as priests of the high
places, who sacrificed for them in the shrines of the high
33 places. So they feared the LORD but also served their
own gods, after the manner of the nations from among
34 whom they had been carried away. To this day they do
according to the former manner.

They do not fear the LORD, and they do not follow the

[f] Syr Vg: Heb *them*

statutes or the ordinances or the law or the commandment
which the LORD commanded the children of Jacob, whom
35 he named Israel. The LORD made a covenant with them,
and commanded them, "You shall not fear other gods or
bow yourselves to them or serve them or sacrifice to them;
36 but you shall fear the LORD, who brought you out of the
land of Egypt with great power and with an outstretched
arm; you shall bow yourselves to him, and to him you

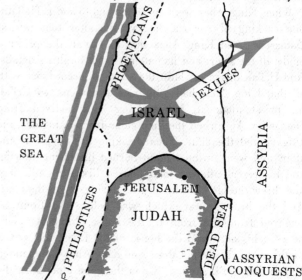

37 shall sacrifice. And the statutes and the ordinances and
the law and the commandment which he wrote for you,
you shall always be careful to do. You shall not fear other
38 gods, and you shall not forget the covenant that I have
39 made with you. You shall not fear other gods, but you
shall fear the LORD your God, and he will deliver you out
40 of the hand of all your enemies." However they would
not listen, but they did according to their former manner.
41 So these nations feared the LORD, and also served their
graven images; their children likewise, and their children's children—as their fathers did, so they do to this
day.

THE SURVIVING KINGDOM OF JUDAH
Hezekiah Becomes King

18 In the third year of Hoshe'a son of Elah, king of
Israel, Hezeki'ah the son of Ahaz, king of Judah,
2 began to reign. He was twenty-five years old when he began to reign, and he reigned twenty-nine years in Jerusalem. His mother's name was Abi the daughter of
3 Zechari'ah. And he did what was right in the eyes of the
LORD, according to all that David his father had done.
4 He removed the high places, and broke the pillars, and
cut down the Ashe'rah. And he broke in pieces the bronze
serpent that Moses had made, for until those days the
people of Israel had burned incense to it; it was called
5 Nehush'tan. He trusted in the LORD the God of Israel; so
that there was none like him among all the kings of

Judah after him, nor among those who were before him. 6 For he held fast to the LORD; he did not depart from following him, but kept the commandments which the 7 LORD commanded Moses. And the LORD was with him; wherever he went forth, he prospered. He rebelled against 8 the king of Assyria, and would not serve him. He smote the Philistines as far as Gaza and its territory, from watchtower to fortified city.

9 In the fourth year of King Hezeki'ah, which was the seventh year of Hoshe'a son of Elah, king of Israel, Shalmane'ser king of Assyria came up against Samar'ia 10 and besieged it and at the end of three years he took it. In the sixth year of Hezeki'ah, which was the ninth year 11 of Hoshe'a king of Israel, Samar'ia was taken. The king of Assyria carried the Israelites away to Assyria, and put them in Halah, and on the Habor, the river of Gozan, and 12 in the cities of the Medes, because they did not obey the voice of the LORD their God but transgressed his covenant, even all that Moses the servant of the LORD commanded; they neither listened nor obeyed.

13 In the fourteenth year of King Hezeki'ah Sennach'erib king of Assyria came up against all the fortified cities of 14 Judah and took them. And Hezeki'ah king of Judah sent to the king of Assyria at Lachish, saying, "I have done wrong; withdraw from me; whatever you impose on me I will bear." And the king of Assyria required of Hezeki'ah king of Judah three hundred talents of silver and 15 thirty talents of gold. And Hezeki'ah gave him all the silver that was found in the house of the LORD, and in the 16 treasuries of the king's house. At that time Hezeki'ah stripped the gold from the doors of the temple of the LORD, and from the doorposts which Hezeki'ah king of Judah had overlaid and gave it to the king of Assyria.

17 And the king of Assyria sent the Tartan, the Rab'saris, and the Rab'shakeh with a great army from Lachish to King Hezeki'ah at Jerusalem. And they went up and came to Jerusalem. When they arrived, they came and stood by the conduit of the upper pool, which is on the high- 18 way to the Fuller's Field. And when they called for the king, there came out to them Eli'akim the son of Hilki'ah, who was over the household, and Shebnah the secretary, and Jo'ah the son of Asaph, the recorder.

19 And the Rab'shakeh said to them, "Say to Hezeki'ah 'Thus says the great king, the king of Assyria: On what 20 do you rest this confidence of yours? Do you think that mere words are strategy and power for war? On whom 21 do you now rely, that you have rebelled against me? Behold, you are relying now on Egypt, that broken reed of a staff, which will pierce the hand of any man who leans on it. Such is Pharaoh king of Egypt to all who rely on 22 him. But if you say to me, "We rely on the LORD our God," is it not he whose high places and altars Hezeki'ah has removed, saying to Judah and to Jerusalem, "You 23 shall worship before this altar in Jerusalem"? Come now, make a wager with my master the king of Assyria: I will give you two thousand horses, if you are able on your 24 part to set riders upon them. How then can you repulse a single captain among the least of my master's servants, when you rely on Egypt for chariots and for horsemen? 25 Moreover, is it without the LORD that I have come up against this place to destroy it? The LORD said to me, Go up against this land, and destroy it.' "

26 Then Eli'akim the son of Hilki'ah, and Shebnah, and Jo'ah, said to the Rab'shakeh, "Pray, speak to your servants in the Aramaic language, for we understand it; do not speak to us in the language of Judah within the 27 hearing of the people who are on the wall." But the Rab'shakeh said to them, "Has my master sent me to speak these words to your master and to you, and not to the men sitting on the wall, who are doomed with you to eat their own dung and to drink their own urine?" 28 Then the Rab'shakeh stood and called out in a loud voice in the language of Judah: "Hear the word of the 29 great king, the king of Assyria! Thus says the king: 'Do not let Hezeki'ah deceive you, for he will not be able to 30 deliver you out of my hand. Do not let Hezeki'ah make you to rely on the LORD by saying, The LORD will surely deliver us, and this city will not be given into the hand 31 of the king of Assyria.' Do not listen to Hezeki'ah; for thus says the king of Assyria: 'Make your peace with me and come out to me; then every one of you will eat of his own vine, and every one of his own fig tree, and every 32 one of you will drink the water of his own cistern; until I come and take you away to a land like your own land, a land of grain and wine, a land of bread and vineyards, a land of olive trees and honey, that you may live, and not die. And do not listen to Hezeki'ah when he misleads 33 you by saying, The LORD will deliver us. Has any of the gods of the nations ever delivered his land out of the hand 34 of the king of Assyria? Where are the gods of Hamath and Arpad? Where are the gods of Sepharva'im, Hena, and Ivvah? Have they delivered Samar'ia out of my 35 hand? Who among all the gods of the countries have delivered their countries out of my hand, that the LORD should deliver Jerusalem out of my hand?' "

36 But the people were silent and answered him not a word, for the king's command was, "Do not answer him." 37 Then Eli'akim the son of Hilki'ah, who was over the household, and Shebna the secretary, and Jo'ah the son of Asaph, the recorder, came to Hezeki'ah with their clothes rent, and told him the words of the Rab'shakeh.

19 When King Hezeki'ah heard it, he rent his clothes, and covered himself with sackcloth, and went into the 2 house of the LORD. And he sent Eli'akim, who was over the household, and Shebnah the secretary, and the senior priests, covered with sackcloth, to the prophet Isaiah the

³ son of Amoz. They said to him, "Thus says Hezeki'ah, This day is a day of distress, of rebuke, and of disgrace; children have come to the birth, and there is no strength ⁴ to bring them forth. It may be that the LORD your God heard all the words of the Rab'shakeh, whom his master the king of Assyria has sent to mock the living God, and will rebuke the words which the LORD your God has heard; therefore lift up your prayer for the remnant that ⁵ is left." When the servants of King Hezeki'ah came to

⁶ Isaiah, Isaiah said to them, "Say to your master, 'Thus says the LORD: Do not be afraid because of the words that you have heard, with which the servants of the king ⁷ of Assyria have reviled me. Behold, I will put a spirit in him, so that he shall hear a rumor and return to his own land; and I will cause him to fall by the sword in his own land.' "

⁸ The Rab'shakeh returned, and found the king of Assyria fighting against Libnah; for he heard that the king ⁹ had left Lachish. And when the king heard concerning Tirha'kah king of Ethiopia, "Behold, he has set out to fight against you," he sent messengers again to Hezeki'ah, ¹⁰ saying, "Thus shall you speak to Hezeki'ah king of Judah: 'Do not let your God on whom you rely deceive you by promising that Jerusalem will not be given into the hand ¹¹ of the king of Assyria. Behold, you have heard what the kings of Assyria have done to all lands, destroying them ¹² utterly. And shall you be delivered? Have the gods of the nations delivered them, the nations which my fathers destroyed, Gozan, Haran, Rezeph, and the people of Eden ¹³ who were in Tel-assar? Where is the king of Hamath, the king of Arpad, the king of the city of Sepharva'im, the king of Hena, or the king of Ivvah?' "

¹⁴ Hezeki'ah received the letter from the hand of the messengers, and read it; and Hezeki'ah went up to the ¹⁵ house of the LORD, and spread it before the LORD. And Hezeki'ah prayed before the LORD, and said: "O LORD the God of Israel, who art enthroned above the cherubim, thou art the God, thou alone, of all the kingdoms of the ¹⁶ earth; thou hast made heaven and earth. Incline thy ear, O LORD, and hear; open thy eyes, O LORD, and see; and hear the words of Sennach'erib, which he has sent to ¹⁷ mock the living God. Of a truth, O LORD, the kings of ¹⁸ Assyria have laid waste the nations and their lands, and have cast their gods into the fire; for they were no gods, but the work of men's hands, wood and stone; therefore ¹⁹ they were destroyed. So now, O LORD our God, save us, I beseech thee, from his hand, that all the kingdoms of

the earth may know that thou, O LORD, art God alone."

²⁰ Then Isaiah the son of Amoz sent to Hezeki'ah, saying, "Thus says the LORD, the God of Israel: Your prayer to me about Sennach'erib king of Assyria I have heard. ²¹ This is the word that the LORD has spoken concerning him:

"She despises you, she scorns you—
the virgin daughter of Zion;
she wags her head behind you—
the daughter of Jerusalem.

²² "Whom have you mocked and reviled?
Against whom have you raised your voice
and haughtily lifted your eyes?
Against the Holy One of Israel!
²³ By your messengers you have mocked the Lord,
and you have said, 'With my many chariots
I have gone up the heights of the mountains,
to the far recesses of Lebanon;
I felled its tallest cedars,
its choicest cypresses;
I entered its farthest retreat,
its densest forest.
²⁴ I dug wells
and drank foreign waters,
and I dried up with the sole of my foot
all the streams of Egypt.'

²⁵ "Have you not heard
that I determined it long ago?
I planned from days of old
what now I bring to pass,
that you should turn fortified cities into heaps of ruins,
²⁶ while their inhabitants, shorn of strength,
are dismayed and confounded,
and have become like plants of the field,
and like tender grass,
like grass on the housetops;
blighted before it is grown?

²⁷ "But I know your sitting down
and your going out and coming in,
and your raging against me.
²⁸ Because you have raged against me
and your arrogance has come into my ears,

I will put my hook in your nose
  and my bit in your mouth,
and I will turn you back on the way
  by which you came.

29 "And this shall be the sign for you: this year you shall eat what grows of itself, and in the second year what springs of the same; then in the third year sow, and reap,
30 and plant vineyards, and eat their fruit. And the surviving remnant of the house of Judah shall again take root
31 downward, and bear fruit upward; for out of Jerusalem shall go forth a remnant, and out of Mount Zion a band of survivors. The zeal of the LORD will do this.

32 "Therefore thus says the LORD concerning the king of Assyria, He shall not come into this city or shoot an arrow there, or come before it with a shield or cast up a siege
33 mound against it. By the way that he came, by the same he shall return, and he shall not come into this city, says
34 the LORD. For I will defend this city to save it, for my own sake and for the sake of my servant David."

35 And that night the angel of the LORD went forth, and slew a hundred and eighty-five thousand in the camp of the Assyrians; and when men arose early in the morning,
36 behold, these were all dead bodies. Then Sennach'erib king of Assyria departed, and went home, and dwelt at
37 Nin'eveh. And as he was worshiping in the house of Nisroch his god, Adram'melech and Share'zer, his sons, slew him with the sword, and escaped into the land of Ararat. And Esarhad'don his son reigned in his stead.

20 In those days Hezeki'ah became sick and was at the point of death. And Isaiah the prophet the son of Amoz came to him, and said to him, "Thus says the LORD, 'Set your house in order; for you shall die, you shall not
2 recover.'" Then Hezeki'ah turned his face to the wall,
3 and prayed to the LORD, saying, "Remember now, O LORD, I beseech thee, how I have walked before thee in faithfulness and with a whole heart, and have done what
4 is good in thy sight." And Hezeki'ah wept bitterly. And before Isaiah had gone out of the middle court, the word
5 of the LORD came to him: "Turn back, and say to Hezeki'ah the prince of my people, Thus says the LORD, the God of David your father: I have heard your prayer, I have seen your tears; behold, I will heal you; on the third day
6 you shall go up to the house of the LORD. And I will add fifteen years to your life. I will deliver you and this city out of the hand of the king of Assyria, and I will defend this city for my own sake and for my servant David's
7 sake." And Isaiah said, "Bring a cake of figs. And let them take and lay it on the boil, that he may recover."

8 And Hezeki'ah said to Isaiah, "What shall be the sign that the LORD will heal me, and that I shall go up to the
9 house of the LORD on the third day?" And Isaiah said, "This is the sign to you from the LORD, that the LORD

will do the thing that he has promised: shall the shadow
10 go forward ten steps, or go back ten steps?" And Hezeki'ah answered, "It is an easy thing for the shadow to lengthen ten steps; rather let the shadow go back ten
11 steps." And Isaiah the prophet cried to the LORD; and he brought the shadow back ten steps, by which the sun [g] had declined on the dial of Ahaz.

12 At that time Mero'dach-bal'adan the son of Bal'adan, king of Babylon, sent envoys with letters and a present to Hezeki'ah; for he heard that Hezeki'ah had been sick.
13 And Hezeki'ah welcomed them, and he showed them all his treasure house, the silver, the gold, the spices, the precious oil, his armory, all that was found in his storehouses; there was nothing in his house or in all his realm
14 that Hezeki'ah did not show them. Then Isaiah the prophet came to King Hezeki'ah, and said to him, "What did these men say? And whence did they come to you?" And Hezeki'ah said, "They have come from a far country, from
15 Babylon." He said, "What have they seen in your house?" And Hezeki'ah answered, "They have seen all that is in my house; there is nothing in my storehouses that I did not show them."

16 Then Isaiah said to Hezeki'ah, "Hear the word of the
17 LORD: Behold, the days are coming, when all that is in your house, and that which your fathers have stored up till this day, shall be carried to Babylon; nothing shall
18 be left, says the LORD. And some of your own sons, who are born to you, shall be taken away; and they shall be
19 eunuchs in the palace of the king of Babylon." Then said Hezeki'ah to Isaiah, "The word of the LORD which you have spoken is good." For he thought, "Why not, if there will be peace and security in my days?"

20 The rest of the deeds of Hezeki'ah, and all his might, and how he made the pool and the conduit and brought water into the city, are they not written in the Book of the
21 Chronicles of the Kings of Judah? And Hezeki'ah slept with his fathers; and Manas'seh his son reigned in his stead.

21 Manas'seh was twelve years old when he began to reign, and he reigned fifty-five years in Jerusalem.
2 His mother's name was Heph'zibah. And he did what was evil in the sight of the LORD, according to the abominable practices of the nations whom the LORD drove out before
3 the people of Israel. For he rebuilt the high places which Hezeki'ah his father had destroyed; and he erected altars for Ba'al, and made an Ashe'rah, as Ahab king of Israel had done, and worshiped all the host of heaven, and

g Syr See Is 38. 8 and Tg: Heb lacks the sun

⁴ served them. And he built altars in the house of the LORD, of which the LORD had said, "In Jerusalem will I put my ⁵ name." And he built altars for all the host of heaven in ⁶ the two courts of the house of the LORD. And he burned his son as an offering, and practiced soothsaying and augury, and dealt with mediums and with wizards. He did much evil in the sight of the LORD, provoking him to ⁷ anger. And the graven image of Ashe'rah that he had made he set in the house of which the LORD said to David

and to Solomon his son, "In this house, and in Jerusalem, which I have chosen out of all the tribes of Israel, I will ⁸ put my name for ever; and I will not cause the feet of Israel to wander any more out of the land which I gave to their fathers, if only they will be careful to do according to all that I have commanded them, and according to all the law that my servant Moses commanded them." ⁹ But they did not listen, and Manas'seh seduced them to do more evil than the nations had done whom the LORD destroyed before the people of Israel.

^{10, 11} And the LORD said by his servants the prophets, "Because Manas'seh king of Judah has committed these abominations, and has done things more wicked than all that the Amorites did, who were before him, and has ¹² made Judah also to sin with his idols; therefore thus says the LORD, the God of Israel, Behold, I am bringing upon Jerusalem and Judah such evil that the ears of every ¹³ one who hears of it will tingle. And I will stretch over Jerusalem the measuring line of Samar'ia, and the plummet of the house of Ahab; and I will wipe Jerusalem as one wipes a dish, wiping it and turning it upside down. ¹⁴ And I will cast off the remnant of my heritage, and give them into the hand of their enemies, and they shall be- ¹⁵ come a prey and a spoil to all their enemies, because they have done what is evil in my sight and have provoked me to anger, since the day their fathers came out of Egypt, even to this day."

¹⁶ Moreover Manas'seh shed very much innocent blood, till he had filled Jerusalem from one end to another, besides the sin which he made Judah to sin so that they did what was evil in the sight of the LORD.

¹⁷ Now the rest of the acts of Manas'seh, and all that he did, and the sin that he committed, are they not written in the Book of the Chronicles of the Kings of Judah? ¹⁸ And Manas'seh slept with his fathers, and was buried in the garden of his house, in the garden of Uzza; and Amon his son reigned in his stead.

¹⁹ Amon was twenty-two years old when he began to reign, and he reigned two years in Jerusalem. His mother's name was Meshul'lemeth the daughter of Haruz ²⁰ of Jotbah. And he did what was evil in the sight of the ²¹ LORD, as Manas'seh his father had done. He walked in all the way in which his father walked, and served the idols ²² that his father served, and worshiped them; he forsook the LORD, the God of his fathers, and did not walk in the ²³ way of the LORD. And the servants of Amon conspired ²⁴ against him, and killed the king in his house. But the people of the land slew all those who had conspired against King Amon, and the people of the land made ²⁵ Josi'ah his son king in his stead. Now the rest of the acts of Amon which he did, are they not written in the Book ²⁶ of the Chronicles of the Kings of Judah? And he was buried in his tomb in the garden of Uzza; and Josi'ah his son reigned in his stead.

THE KINGDOM OF JUDAH NEARS THE END
When Josiah Was King of Judah

22 Josi'ah was eight years old when he began to reign, and he reigned thirty-one years in Jerusalem. His mother's name was Jedi'dah the daughter of Adai'ah of ² Bozkath. And he did what was right in the eyes of the LORD, and walked in all the way of David his father, and he did not turn aside to the right hand or to the left.

³ In the eighteenth year of King Josi'ah, the king sent Shaphan the son of Azali'ah, son of Meshul'lam, the sec- ⁴ retary, to the house of the LORD, saying, "Go up to Hilki'- ah the high priest, that he may reckon the amount of the money which has been brought into the house of the LORD, which the keepers of the threshold have collected

⁵ from the people; and let it be given into the hand of the workmen who have the oversight of the house of the LORD; and let them give it to the workmen who are at the ⁶ house of the LORD, repairing the house, that is, to the carpenters, and to the builders, and to the masons, as well as for buying timber and quarried stone to repair ⁷ the house. But no accounting shall be asked from them for the money which is delivered into their hand, for they deal honestly."

⁸ And Hilki'ah the high priest said to Shaphan the secretary, "I have found the book of the law in the house of the LORD." And Hilki'ah gave the book to Shaphan, and ⁹ he read it. And Shaphan the secretary came to the king,

and reported to the king, "Your servants have emptied out the money that was found in the house, and have delivered it into the hand of the workmen who have the oversight of the house of the LORD." Then Shaphan the secretary told the king, "Hilki'ah the priest has given me a book." And Shaphan read it before the king.

11 And when the king heard the words of the book of 12 the law, he rent his clothes. And the king commanded Hilki'ah the priest, and Ahi'kam the son of Shaphan, and Achbor the son of Micai'ah, and Shaphan the secretary, 13 and Asai'ah the king's servant saying, "Go, inquire of the LORD for me, and for the people, and for all Judah, concerning the words of this book that has been found; for great is the wrath of the LORD that is kindled against us, because our fathers have not obeyed the words of this book, to do according to all that is written concerning us."

14 So Hilki'ah the priest, and Ahi'kam, and Achbor, and Shaphan, and Asai'ah went to Huldah the prophetess, the wife of Shallum the son of Tikvah, son of Harhas, keeper of the wardrobe (now she dwelt in Jerusalem in 15 the Second Quarter); and they talked with her. And she said to them, "Thus says the LORD, the God of Israel: 16 'Tell the man who sent you to me, Thus says the LORD, Behold, I will bring evil upon this place and upon its inhabitants, all the words of the book which the king of 17 Judah has read. Because they have forsaken me and have burned incense to other gods, that they might provoke me to anger with all the work of their hands, therefore my wrath will be kindled against this place, and it will 18 not be quenched. But as to the king of Judah, who sent you to inquire of the LORD, thus shall you say to him, Thus says the LORD, the God of Israel: Regarding the 19 words which you have heard, because your heart was penitent, and you humbled yourself before the LORD, when you heard how I spoke against this place, and against its inhabitants, that they should become a desolation and a curse, and you have rent your clothes and wept before me, I also have heard you, says the LORD. 20 Therefore, behold, I will gather you to your fathers, and you shall be gathered to your grave in peace, and your eyes shall not see all the evil which I will bring upon this place.' " And they brought back word to the king.

23 Then the king sent, and all the elders of Judah and 2 Jerusalem were gathered to him. And the king went up to the house of the LORD, and with him all the men of Judah and all the inhabitants of Jerusalem, and the priests and the prophets, all the people, both small and great; and he read in their hearing all the words of the book of the covenant which had been found in the house 3 of the LORD. And the king stood by the pillar and made a covenant before the LORD, to walk after the LORD and to keep his commandments and his testimonies and his

statutes, with all his heart and all his soul, to perform the words of this covenant that were written in this book; and all the people joined in the covenant.

4 And the king commanded Hilki'ah, the high priest, and the priests of the second order, and the keepers of the threshold, to bring out of the temple of the LORD all the vessels made for Ba'al, for Ashe'rah, and for all

the host of heaven; he burned them outside Jerusalem in the fields of the Kidron, and carried their ashes to Bethel. 5 And he deposed the idolatrous priests whom the kings of Judah had ordained to burn incense in the high places at the cities of Judah and round about Jerusalem; those also who burned incense to Ba'al, to the sun, and the moon, and the constellations, and all the host of the 6 heavens. And he brought out the Ashe'rah from the house of the LORD, outside Jerusalem, to the brook Kidron, and burned it at the brook Kidron, and beat it to dust and cast the dust of it upon the graves of the common people. 7 And he broke down the houses of the male cult prostitutes which were in the house of the LORD, where the 8 women wove hangings for the Ashe'rah. And he brought all the priests out of the cities of Judah, and defiled the high places where the priests had burned incense, from Geba to Beer-sheba; and he broke down the high places of the gates that were at the entrance of the gate of Joshua the governor of the city, which were on one's left at the 9 gate of the city. However, the priests of the high places did not come up to the altar of the LORD in Jerusalem, but they ate unleavened bread among their brethren. 10 And he defiled To'pheth, which is in the valley of the sons of Hinnom, that no one might burn his son or his 11 daughter as an offering to Molech. And he removed the horses that the kings of Judah had dedicated to the sun, at the entrance to the house of the LORD, by the chamber of Nathan-melech the chamberlain, which was in the precincts;[h] and he burned the chariots of the sun with fire. 12 And the altars on the roof of the upper chamber of Ahaz, which the kings of Judah had made, and the altars which Manas'seh had made in the two courts of the house of the LORD, he pulled down and broke in pieces,[i] and cast the 13 dust of them into the brook Kidron. And the king defiled the high places that were east of Jerusalem, to the south of the mount of corruption, which Solomon the king of Israel had built for Ash'toreth the abomination of the

---

Sido'nians, and for Chemosh the abomination of Moab,
14 and for Milcom the abomination of the Ammonites. And he broke in pieces the pillars, and cut down the Ashe'rim, and filled their places with the bones of men.

15 Moreover the altar at Bethel, the high place erected by Jerobo'am the son of Nebat, who made Israel to sin, that altar with the high place he pulled down and he broke in pieces its stones,ʲ crushing them to dust; also he
16 burned the Ashe'rah. And as Josi'ah turned, he saw the tombs there on the mount; and he sent and took the bones out of the tombs, and burned them upon the altar, and defiled it, according to the word of the LORD which the man of God proclaimed, who had predicted these things.
17 Then he said, "What is yonder monument that I see?" And the men of the city told him, "It is the tomb of the man of God who came from Judah and predicted these things which you have done against the altar at Bethel."
18 And he said, "Let him be; let no man move his bones." So they let his bones alone, with the bones of the prophet
19 who came out of Samar'ia. And all the shrines also of the high places that were in the cities of Samar'ia, which kings of Israel had made, provoking the LORD to anger, Josi'ah removed; he did to them according to all that he
20 had done at Bethel. And he slew all the priests of the high places who were there, upon the altars, and burned the bones of men upon them. Then he returned to Jerusalem.
21 And the king commanded all the people, "Keep the passover to the LORD your God, as it is written in this
22 book of the covenant." For no such passover had been kept since the days of the judges who judged Israel, or during all the days of the kings of Israel or of the kings
23 of Judah; but in the eighteenth year of King Josi'ah this passover was kept to the LORD in Jerusalem.
24 Moreover Josi'ah put away the mediums and the wizards and the teraphim and the idols and all the abominations that were seen in the land of Judah and in Jerusalem, that he might establish the words of the law which were written in the book that Hilki'ah the priest found
25 in the house of the LORD. Before him there was no king like him, who turned to the LORD with all his heart and with all his soul and with all his might, according to all the law of Moses; nor did any like him arise after him.
26 Still the LORD did not turn from the fierceness of his great wrath, by which his anger was kindled against Judah, because of all the provocations with which Manas'-
27 seh had provoked him. And the LORD said, "I will remove Judah also out of my sight, as I have removed Israel, and I will cast off this city which I have chosen, Jerusalem, and the house of which I said, My name shall be there."
28 Now the rest of the acts of Josi'ah, and all that he did, are they not written in the Book of the Chronicles of
29 the Kings of Judah? In his days Pharaoh Neco king of Egypt went up to the king of Assyria to the river Euphra'-

ⱼ Gk: Heb *he burned the high place*

tes. King Josi'ah went to meet him; and Pharaoh Neco
30 slew him at Megid'do, when he saw him. And his servants carried him dead in a chariot from Megid'do, and brought him to Jerusalem, and buried him in his own tomb. And the people of the land took Jeho'ahaz the son of Josi'ah, and anointed him, and made him king in his father's stead.

Other Kings

31 Jeho'ahaz was twenty-three years old when he began to reign, and he reigned three months in Jerusalem. His mother's name was Hamu'tal the daughter of Jeremiah
32 of Libnah. And he did what was evil in the sight of the
33 LORD, according to all that his fathers had done. And Pharaoh Neco put him in bonds at Riblah in the land of Hamath, that he might not reign in Jerusalem, and laid upon the land a tribute of a hundred talents of silver and
34 a talent of gold. And Pharaoh Neco made Eli'akim the son of Josi'ah king in the place of Josi'ah his father, and changed his name to Jehoi'akim. But he took Jeho'ahaz
35 away; and he came to Egypt, and died there. And Jehoi'akim gave the silver and the gold to Pharaoh, but he taxed the land to give the money according to the command of Pharaoh. He exacted the silver and the gold of the people of the land, from every one according to his assessment, to give it to Pharaoh Neco.

36 Jehoi'akim was twenty-five years old when he began to reign, and he reigned eleven years in Jerusalem. His mother's name was Zebi'dah the daughter of Pedai'ah of
37 Rumah. And he did what was evil in the sight of the LORD, according to all that his fathers had done.

24 In his days Nebuchadnez'zar king of Babylon came up, and Jehoi'akim became his servant three
2 years; then he turned and rebelled against him. And the LORD sent against him bands of the Chalde'ans, and bands of the Syrians, and bands of the Moabites, and bands of the Ammonites, and sent them against Judah to destroy it, according to the word of the LORD which he
3 spoke by his servants the prophets. Surely this came upon Judah at the command of the LORD, to remove them out of his sight, for the sins of Manas'seh, according to
4 all that he had done, and also for the innocent blood that he had shed; for he filled Jerusalem with innocent blood,
5 and the LORD would not pardon. Now the rest of the deeds of Jehoi'akim, and all that he did, are they not written in
6 the Book of the Chronicles of the Kings of Judah? So Jehoi'akim slept with his fathers, and Jehoi'achin his son
7 reigned in his stead. And the king of Egypt did not come again out of his land, for the king of Babylon had taken all that belonged to the king of Egypt from the Brook of Egypt to the river Eu-phra'tes.

8 Jehoi'achin was eighteen years old when he became king, and he reigned three months in Jerusalem. His

mother's name was Nehush′ta the daughter of Elna′than of Jerusalem. And he did what was evil in the sight of the LORD, according to all that his father had done.

10 At that time the servants of Nebuchadnez′zar king of Babylon came up to Jerusalem, and the city was be-
11 sieged. And Nebuchadnez′zar king of Babylon came to
12 the city, while his servants were besieging it; and Jehoi′achin the king of Judah gave himself up to the king of Babylon, himself, and his mother, and his servants, and his princes, and his palace officials. The king of Babylon took him prisoner in the eighth year of his
13 reign, and carried off all the treasures of the house of the LORD, and the treasures of the king's house, and cut in pieces all the vessels of gold in the temple of the LORD, which Solomon king of Israel had made, as the LORD had
14 foretold. He carried away all Jerusalem, and all the princes, and all the mighty men of valor, ten thousand captives, and all the craftsmen and the smiths; none re-
15 mained, except the poorest people of the land. And he carried away Jehoi′achin to Babylon; the king's mother, the king's wives, his officials, and the chief men of the land, he took into captivity from Jerusalem to Babylon.
16 And the king of Babylon brought captive to Babylon all the men of valor, seven thousand, and the craftsmen and the smiths, one thousand, all of them strong and fit for
17 war. And the king of Babylon made Mattani′ah, Jehoi′-achin's uncle, king in his stead, and changed his name to Zedeki′ah.

18 Zedeki′ah was twenty-one years old when he became king, and he reigned eleven years in Jerusalem. His mother's name was Hamu′tal the daughter of Jeremiah of
19 Libnah. And he did what was evil in the sight of the LORD, according to all that Jehoi′akim had done.
20 For because of the anger of the LORD it came to the point in Jerusalem and Judah that he cast them out from his presence.

k Gk Compare Jr 39. 4; 52. 7: Heb lacks *the king* and *fled*

Jerusalem Burned

And Zedeki′ah rebelled against the king of Babylon.
1 And in the ninth year of his reign, in the tenth month,
25 on the tenth day of the month, Nebuchadnez′zar king of Babylon came with all his army against Jerusalem, and laid siege to it; and they built siegeworks against it
2 round about. So the city was besieged till the eleventh
3 year of King Zedeki′ah. On the ninth day of the fourth month the famine was so severe in the city that there was
4 no food for the people of the land. Then a breach was made in the city; the king with all the men of war fled k

by night by the way of the gate between the two walls, by the king's garden, though the Chalde′ans were around the city. And they went in the direction of the Arabah.
5 But the army of the Chalde′ans pursued the king, and overtook him in the plains of Jericho; and all his army
6 was scattered from him. Then they captured the king, and brought him up to the king of Babylon at Riblah, who
7 passed sentence upon him. They slew the sons of Zedeki′ah before his eyes, and put out the eyes of Zedeki′ah, and bound him in fetters, and took him to Babylon.
8 In the fifth month, on the seventh day of the month— which was the nineteenth year of King Nebuchadnez′zar, king of Babylon—Nebu′zarad′an, the captain of the bodyguard, a servant of the king of Babylon, came to
9 Jerusalem. And he burned the house of the LORD, and the king's house and all the houses of Jerusalem; every great
10 house he burned down. And all the army of the Chalde′ans, who were with the captain of the guard, broke
11 down the walls around Jerusalem. And the rest of the people who were left in the city and the deserters who had deserted to the king of Babylon, together with the rest of the multitude, Nebu′zarad′an the captain of the guard
12 carried into exile. But the captain of the guard left some of the poorest of the land to be vinedressers and plowmen.
13 And the pillars of bronze that were in the house of the LORD, and the stands and the bronze sea that were in the house of the LORD, the Chalde′ans broke in pieces,
14 and carried the bronze to Babylon. And they took away the pots, and the shovels, and the snuffers, and the dishes for incense and all the vessels of bronze used in the

15 temple service, the firepans also, and the bowls. What was of gold the captain of the guard took away as gold, 16 and what was of silver, as silver. As for the two pillars, the one sea, and the stands, which Solomon had made for the house of the LORD, the bronze of all these vessels 17 was beyond weight. The height of the one pillar was eighteen cubits, and upon it was a capital of bronze; the height of the capital was three cubits; a network and pomegranates, all of bronze, were upon the capital round about. And the second pillar had the like, with the network.

23 Shaphan, governor. Now when all the captains of the forces in the open country [1] and their men heard that the king of Babylon had appointed Gedali'ah governor, they came with their men to Gedali'ah at Mizpah, namely, Ishmael the son of Nethani'ah, and Joha'nan the son of Kare'ah, and Serai'ah the son of Tanhu'meth the Netoph'- 24 athite, and Jaazani'ah the son of Ma-ac'athite. And Gedali'ah swore to them and their men, saying, "Do not be afraid because of the Chalde'an officials; dwell in the land, and serve the king of Babylon, and it shall be well 25 with you." But in the seventh month, Ishmael the son of

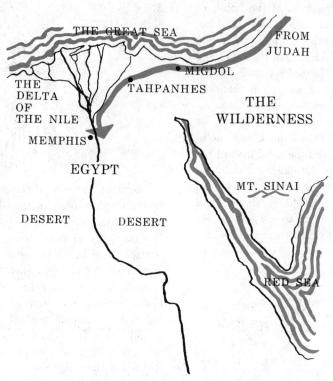

18 And the captain of the guard took Serai'ah the chief priest, and Zephani'ah the second priest, and the three 19 keepers of the threshold; and from the city he took an officer who had been in command of the men of war, and five men of the king's council who were found in the city; and the secretary of the commander of the army who mustered the people of the land; and sixty men of the 20 people of the land who were found in the city. And Nebu'zarad'an the captain of the guard took them, and 21 brought them to the king of Babylon at Riblah. And the king of Babylon smote them, and put them to death at Riblah in the land of Hamath. So Judah was taken into exile out of its land.

A Remnant to Egypt

22 And over the people who remained in the land of Judah, whom Nebuchadnez'zar king of Babylon had left, he appointed Gedali'ah the son of Ahi'kam, son of

Nethani'ah, son of Eli'shama, of the royal family, came with ten men, and attacked and killed Gedali'ah and the Jews and the Chalde'ans who were with him at Mizpah. 26 Then all the people, both small and great, and the captains of the forces arose, and went to Egypt; for they were afraid of the Chalde'ans.

27 And in the thirty-seventh year of the exile of Jehoi'-achin king of Judah, in the twelfth month, on the twenty-seventh day of the month, Evil-mero'dach king of Babylon, in the year that he began to reign, graciously freed 28 Jehoi'achin king of Judah from prison; and he spoke kindly to him, and gave him a seat above the seats of 29 the kings who were with him in Babylon. So Jehoi'achin put off his prison garments. And every day of his life he 30 dined regularly at the king's table; and for his allowance, a regular allowance was given him by the king, every day a portion, as long as he lived.

1 With Jr 40. 7: Heb lacks *in the open country*

260

INTRODUCTION TO

THE FIRST BOOK OF THE

CHRONICLES

First Chronicles is the first of a group of four books of Hebrew history which includes First and Second Chronicles, Ezra, and Nehemiah. There is uncertainty about the date of First and Second Chronicles, but they were probably written about 350 B.C.

The Chronicler, or writer, believed that when the people were faithful to God and especially to the Temple worship, they prospered. He taught that when they became careless in their worship and obedience, God punished them and the nation had trouble. To illustrate this idea, this writer used many stories and passages from the earlier books of First and Second Samuel and First and Second Kings. He also used material from Nehemiah, Ezra, and many other books. All these rewritten accounts encouraged the Hebrews of 350 B.C. to support their nation and to look to Jerusalem and to the rebuilt Temple there as their national religious center and symbol of unity.

These chronicles, or tales, of the heroes of days past were written at a time when the armies of both Persia and Egypt threatened war. These retold stories were meant to make the Jews more loyal and brave in the struggle against their enemies.

Like the series of books from Genesis through Second Kings, this set of books begins with Adam and Eve. However, First Chronicles merely mentions the names of the persons from the earlier periods of history until it comes to David. King David is really the hero of the Chronicler. He showed David as the one who had helped unify the Hebrew people by strong leadership and victorious armies, by planning the Temple worship and music, and by setting aside the Levites to be priests.

THE FIRST BOOK OF THE

CHRONICLES

ANCESTORS

2, 3 1 Adam, Seth, Enosh; Kenan, Mahal'alel, Jared; Enoch, Me-
4 thu'selah, Lamech; Noah, Shem, Ham, and Japheth.
5 The sons of Japheth: Gomer, Magog, Madai, Javan, Tubal,
6 Meshech, and Tiras. The sons of Gomer: Ash'kenaz, Diphath,
7 and Togar'mah. The sons of Javan: Eli'shah, Tarshish, Kittim, and Ro'danim.
8, 9 The sons of Ham: Cush, Egypt, Put, and Canaan. The sons of Cush: Seba, Hav'ilah, Sabta, Ra'ama, and Sab'teca. The sons of
10 Ra'amah: Sheba and Dedan. Cush was the father of Nimrod; he began to be a mighty one in the earth.
11 Egypt was the father of Ludim, An'amim, Le'habim, Naph'tu-
12 him, Pathru'sim, Caslu'him (whence came the Philis'tines), and Caph'torim.
13, 14 Canaan was the father of Sidon his first-born, and Heth, and
15 the Jeb'usites, the Am'orites, the Gir'gashites, the Hivites, the
16 Arkites, the Sinites, the Ar'vadites, the Zem'arites, and the Ha'mathites.
17 The sons of Shem: Elam, Asshur, Arpach'shad, Lud, Aram,
18 Uz, Hul, Gether, and Meshech. Arpach'shad was the father of
19 Shelah; and Shelah was the father of Eber. To Eber were born two sons: the name of the one was Peleg (for in his days the earth was divided), and the name of his brother Joktan.

20 Joktan was the father of Almo'dad, Sheleph, Hazarma'veth,
21, 22 Jerah, Hador'am, Uzal, Diklah, Ebal, Abim'a-el, Sheba,
23 Ophir, Hav'ilah, and Jobab; all these were the sons of Joktan.
24, 25, 26 Shem, Arpach'shad, Shelah; Eber, Peleg, Re'u; Serug,
27 Nahor, Terah; Abram, that is, Abraham.
28, 29 The sons of Abraham: Isaac and Ish'mael. These are their genealogies: the first-born of Ish'mael, Neba'ioth; and Kedar,
30, 31 Adbeel, Mibsam, Mishma, Dumah, Massa, Hadad, Tema, Jetur,

32 Naphish, and Ked'emah. These are the sons of Ish'mael. The sons of Ketu'rah, Abraham's concubine: she bore Zimran, Jokshan, Medan, Mid'ian, Ishbak, and Shu'ah. The sons of
33 Jokshan: Sheba and Dedan. The sons of Mid'ian: Ephah, Epher, Hanoch, Abida, and Elda'ah. All these were the descendants of Ketu'rah.

34 Abraham was the father of Isaac. The sons of Isaac: Esau and
35 Israel. The sons of Esau: Eli'phaz, Reu'el, Je'ush, Jalam, and
36 Korah. The sons of Eli'phaz: Teman, Omar, Zephi, Gatam,
37 Kenaz, Timna, and Am'alek. The sons of Reu'el: Nahath, Zerah,
Shammah, and Mizzah.
38 The sons of Se'ir: Lotan, Shobal, Zib'eon, Anah, Dishon, Ezer,
39 and Dishan. The sons of Lotan: Hori and Homam; and Lotan's
40 sister was Timna. The sons of Shobal: Al'ian, Man'ahath, Ebal,
41 Shephi, and Onam. The sons of Zib'eon: Ai'ah and Anah. The
sons of Anah: Dishon. The sons of Dishon: Hamran, Eshban,
42 Ithran, and Cheran. The sons of Ezer: Bilhan, Za'avan, and
Ja'akan. The sons of Dishan: Uz and Aran.
43 These are the kings who reigned in the land of Edom before
any king reigned over the Israelites: Bela the son of Be'or, the
44 name of whose city was Din'habah. When Bela died, Jobab the
45 son of Zerah of Bozrah reigned in his stead. When Jobab died,
46 Husham of the land of the Te'manites reigned in his stead. When
Husham died, Hadad the son of Bedad, who defeated Mid'ian in
the country of Moab, reigned in his stead; and the name of his
47 city was Avith. When Hadad died, Samlah of Masre'kah reigned
48 in his stead. When Samlah died, Sha'ul of Reho'both on the
49 Euphra'tes reigned in his stead. When Sha'ul died, Ba'al-ha'nan,
50 the son of Achbor, reigned in his stead. When Ba'al-ha'nan died,
Hadad reigned in his stead; and the name of his city was
Pa'i, and his wife's name Mehet'abel the daughter of Matred,
51 the daughter of Me'zahab. And Hadad died.
The chiefs of Edom were: chiefs Timna, Al'iah, Jetheth,
52, 53, 54 Oholiba'mah, Elah, Pinon, Kenaz, Teman, Mibzar, Mag'di-el,
and Iram; these are the chiefs of Edom.

Descendants of Judah

2 These are the sons of Israel: Reuben, Simeon, Levi, Judah,
2 Is'sachar, Zeb'ulun, Dan, Joseph, Benjamin, Naph'tali, Gad,
3 and Asher. The sons of Judah: Er, Onan, and Shelah; these
three Bath-shu'a the Canaanitess bore to him. Now Er, Judah's
first-born, was wicked in the sight of the LORD, and he slew him.
4 His daughter-in-law Tamar also bore him Perez and Zerah.
Judah had five sons in all.
5, 6 The sons of Perez: Hezron and Hamul. The sons of Zerah:
7 Zimri, Ethan, Heman, Calcol, and Dara, five in all. The sons of
Carmi: Achar, the troubler of Israel, who transgressed in the
8 matter of the devoted thing; and Ethan's son was Azari'ah.
9 The sons of Hezron, that were born to him: Jerah'meel, Ram,
10 and Chelu'bai. Ram was the father of Ammin'adab, and Ammin'adab was the father of Nahshon, prince of the sons of
11 Judah. Nahshon was the father of Salma, Salma of Bo'az,
12, 13 Bo'az of Obed, Obed of Jesse. Jesse was the father of Eli'ab
14 his first-born, Abin'adab the second, Shim'ea the third, Nethan'-
15 el the fourth, Raddai the fifth, Ozem the sixth, David the
16 seventh; and their sisters were Zeru'iah and Ab'igail. The sons
17 of Zeru'iah: Abi'shai, Jo'ab, and As'ahel, three. Ab'igail bore
Ama'sa, and the father of Ama'sa was Jether the Ish'maelite.
18 Caleb the son of Hezron had children by his wife Azu'bah, and
by Jer'ioth; and these were her sons; Jesher, Shobab, and Ardon.
19 When Azu'bah died, Caleb married Ephrath, who bore him Hur.
20 Hur was the father of Uri, and Uri was the father of Bez'alel.
21 Afterward Hezron went in to the daughter of Machir the
father of Gilead, whom he married when he was sixty years
22 old; and she bore him Segub; and Segub was the father of
23 Ja'ir, who had twenty-three cities in the land of Gilead. But
Geshur and Aram took from them Havvoth-ja'ir, Kenath and
its villages, sixty towns. All these were descendants of Machir,
24 the father of Gilead. After the death of Hezron, Caleb went in
to Eph'rathah,ᵃ the wife of Hezron his father, and she bore him
Ashhur, the father of Teko'a.
25 The sons of Jerah'meel, the first-born of Hezron: Ram, his
26 first-born, Bunah, Oren, Ozem, and Ahi'jah. Jerah'meel also had
another wife, whose name was At'arah; she was the mother of
27 Onam. The sons of Ram, the first-born of Jerah'meel: Ma'az,
28 Jamin, and Eker. The sons of Onam: Sham'mai and Jada. The
29 sons of Sham'mai: Nadab and Abi'shur. The name of Abi'shur's
30 wife was Ab'ihail, and she bore him Ahban and Molid. The
sons of Nadab: Seled and Ap'pa-im; and Seled died childless.
31 The sons of Ap'pa-im: Ishi. The sons of Ishi: Sheshan. The sons
32 of Sheshan: Ahlai. The sons of Jada, Sham'mai's brother: Jether
33 and Jonathan; and Jether died childless. The sons of Jonathan:
Peleth and Zaza. These were the descendants of Jerah'meel.
34 Now Sheshan had no sons, only daughters; but Sheshan had an
35 Egyptian slave, whose name was Jarha. So Sheshan gave his
daughter in marriage to Jarha his slave; and she bore him Attai.
36, 37 Attai was the father of Nathan and Nathan of Zabad. Zabad

38 was the father of Ephlal, and Ephlal of Obed. Obed was the
39 father of Jehu, and Jehu of Azari'ah. Azari'ah was the father
40 of Helez, and Helez of Ele-a'sah. Ele-a'sah was the father of
41 Sismai, and Sismai of Shallum. Shallum was the father of
Jekami'ah, and Jekami'ah of Elish'ama.
42 The sons of Caleb the brother of Jerah'meel: Mare'shah ᵇ his
first-born, who was the father of Ziph. The sons of Mare'shah:
43 Hebron.ᶜ The sons of Hebron: Korah, Tap'puah, Rekem, and
44 Shema. Shema was the father of Raham, the father of Jor'ke-am;
45 and Rekem was the father of Sham'mai. The son of Sham'mai:
46 Ma'on; and Ma'on was the father of Bethzur. Ephah also,
Caleb's concubine, bore Haran, Moza, and Gazez; and Haran
47 was the father of Gazez. The sons of Jah'dai: Regem, Jotham,
48 Geshan, Pelet, Ephah, and Sha'aph. Ma'acah, Caleb's concubine,
49 bore Sheber and Tir'hanah. She also bore Sha'aph the father of
Madman'nah, Sheva the father of Machbe'nah and the father of
50 Gib'e-a; and the daughter of Caleb was Achsah. These were the
descendants of Caleb.
The sons ᵈ of Hur the first-born of Eph'rathah: Shobal the
51 father of Kir'iath-je'arim, Salma, the father of Bethlehem, and
52 Hareph the father of Beth-gader. Shobal the father of Kir'iath-
53 je'arim had other sons: Haro'eh, half of the Menu'hoth. And the
families of Kir'iath-je'arim: the Ithrites, the Puthites, the Shu'-
mathites, and the Mish'ra-ites; from these came the Zo'rathites
54 and the Esh'taolites. The sons of Salma: Bethlehem, the Netoph'-
athites, At'roth-beth-jo'ab, and half of the Man'aha'thites, the
55 Zorites. The families also of the scribes that dwelt at Jabez: the
Ti'rathites, the Shim'e-athites, and the Sucathites. These are the
Ken'ites who came from Hammath, the father of the house of
Rechab.

Descendants of David

3 These are the sons of David that were born to him in
Hebron: the first-born Amnon, by Ahin'o-am the Jez'-
2 reelitess; the second Daniel, by Ab'igail the Car'melitess, the
third Ab'salom, whose mother was Ma'acah, the daughter of
Talmai, king of Geshur; the fourth Adoni'jah, whose mother
3 was Haggith; the fifth Shephati'ah, by Abi'tal; the sixth Ith'-
4 ream, by his wife Eglah; six were born to him in Hebron, where
he reigned for seven years and six months. And he reigned
5 thirty-three years in Jerusalem. These were born to him in
Jerusalem: Shim'e-a, Shobab, Nathan, and Solomon, four by
6 Bath-shu'a, the daughter of Am'mi-el; then Ibhar, Elish'ama,
7, 8 Eliph'elet, Nogah, Nepheg, Japhi'a, Elish'ama, Eli'ada, and
9 Eliph'elet, nine. All these were David's sons, besides the sons
of the concubines; and Tamar was their sister.
10 The descendants of Solomon: Rehobo'am, Abi'jah his son,
11 Asa his son, Jehosh'aphat his son, Joram his son, Ahazi'ah his
12 son, Jo'ash his son, Amazi'ah his son, Azari'ah his son, Jotham
13 his son, Ahaz his son, Hezeki'ah his son, Manas'seh his son,
14, 15 Amon his son, Josi'ah his son. The sons of Josi'ah: Joha'nan
the first-born, the second Jehoi'akim, the third Zedeki'ah, the
16 fourth Shallum. The descendants of Jehoi'akim: Jeconi'ah his
17 son, Zedeki'ah his son; and the sons of Jeconi'ah, the captive:
18 Sheal'tiel his son, Malchi'ram, Peda'iah, Shenaz'zar, Jekami'ah,
19 Hosh'ama, and Nedabi'ah; and the sons of Peda'iah: Zerub'babel
and Shim'e-i; and the sons of Zerub'babel: Meshul'lam and
20 Hanani'ah, and Shelo'mith was their sister; and Hashu'bah,
21 Ohel, Berechi'ah, Hasadi'ah, and Ju'shab-he'sed, five. The sons
of Hanani'ah: Pelati'ah and Jesha'iah, his son ᵉ Repha'iah, his
22 son ᵉ Arnan, his son ᵉ Obadi'ah, his son ᵉ Shecani'ah. The sons
of Shecani'ah: Shemai'ah. And the sons of Shemai'ah: Hattush,
23 Igal, Bari'ah, Neari'ah, and Shaphat, six. The sons of Neari'ah:
24 Eli-o-e'nai, Hizki'ah, and Azri'kam, three. The sons of Eli-o-e'-
nai: Hod'avi'ah, Eli'ashib, Pela'iah, Akkub, Joha'nan, Dela'iah,
and Ana'ni, seven.

Sons of Judah and Simeon

4 The sons of Judah: Perez, Hezron, Carmi, Hur, and
2 Shobal. Rea'iah the son of Shobal was the father of Jahath,
and Jahath was the father of Ahu'mai and Lahad. These were
3 the families of the Zo'rathites. These were the sons ᶠ of Etam:
Jezreel, Ishma, and Idbash; and the name of their sister was
4 Hazzelelpo'ni, and Penu'el was the father of Gedor, and Ezer
the father of Hushah. These were the sons of Hur, the first-born
5 of Eph'rathah, the father of Bethlehem. Ashhur, the father of
6 Teko'a, had two wives, Helah and Na'arah; Na'arah bore him
Ahuz'zam, Hepher, Te'meni, and Ha-ahash'tari. These were the
7 sons of Na'arah. The sons of Helah: Zereth, Izhar, and Ethnan.
8 Koz was the father of Anub, Zobe'bah, and the families of
9 Ahar'hel the son of Harum. Jabez was more honorable than his

ᵃ Gk Vg: Heb in Caleb Ephrathah   ᵇ Gk: Heb Mesha   ᶜ Heb the father of Hebron   ᵈ Gk Vg: Heb son
ᵉ Gk Compare Syr Vg: Heb sons of   ᶠ Gk Compare Vg: Heb father

brothers; and his mother called his name Jabez, saying, "Be-
10 cause I bore him in pain." Jabez called on the God of Israel,
saying, "Oh that thou wouldst bless me and enlarge my border,
and that thy hand might be with me, and that thou wouldst
keep me from harm so that it might not hurt me!" And God
11 granted what he asked. Chelub, the brother of Shuhah, was the
12 father of Mehir, who was the father of Eshton. Eshton was the
father of Bethra'pha, Pase'ah, and Tehin'nah the father of
13 Irna'hash. These are the men of Recah. The sons of Kenaz:
Oth'ni-el and Sera'iah; and the sons of Oth'ni-el: Hathath and
14 Meo'nothai.[g] Meo'nothai was the father of Ophrah; and Sera'iah
was the father of Jo'ab the father of Ge-har'ashim,[h] so-called
15 because they were craftsmen. The sons of Caleb the son of
Jephun'neh: Iru, Elah, and Na'am; and the sons of Elah: Kenaz.
16 The sons of Jehal'lelel: Ziph, Ziphah, Tir'i-a, and As'arel.
17 The sons of Ezrah: Jether, Mered, Epher, and Jalon. These are
the sons of Bith'i-ah, the daughter of Pharaoh, whom Mered
married;[i] and she conceived and bore[j] Miriam, Sham'mai, and
18 Ishbah, the father of Eshtemo'a. And his Jewish wife bore Jered
the father of Gedor, Heber the father of Soco, and Jeku'thiel the
19 father of Zano'ah. The sons of the wife of Hodi'ah, the sister of
Naham, were the fathers of Kei'lah the Garmite and Eshtemo'a
20 the Ma-ac'athite. The sons of Shimon: Amnon, Rinnah, Ben-
ha'nan, and Tilon. The sons of Ishi: Zoheth and Ben-zo'heth.
21 The sons of Shelah the son of Judah: Er the father of Lecah,
La'adah the father of Mare'shah, and the families of the house
22 of linen workers at Beth-ashbe'a; and Jokim, and the men of
Coze'ba, and Jo'ash, and Saraph, who ruled in Moab and re-
23 turned to Lehem[k] (now the records[l] are ancient). These were
the potters and inhabitants of Neta'im and Gede'rah; they dwelt
there with the king for his work.
24 The sons of Simeon: Nem'u-el, Jamin, Jarib, Zerah, Sha'ul;
25, 26 Shallum was his son, Mibsam his son, Mishma his son. The
sons of Mishma: Ham'mu-el his son, Zac'cur his son, Shim'e-i
27 his son. Shim'e-i had sixteen sons and six daughters; but his
brothers had not many children, nor did all their family
28 multiply like the men of Judah. They dwelt in Beer-sheba,
29, 30 Mola'dah, Ha'zar-shu'al, Bilhah, Ezem, Tolad, Bethu'el, Hor-
31 mah, Ziklag, Beth-mar'caboth, Ha'zar-su'sim, Beth-biri, and
32 Sha-ara'im. These were their cities until David reigned. And
their villages were Etam, A'in, Rimmon, Tochen, and Ashan,
33 five cities, along with all their villages which were round
about these cities as far as Ba'al. These were their settlements,
and they kept a genealogical record.
34, 35 Mesho'bab, Jamlech, Joshah the son of Amazi'ah, Jo'el, Jehu
36 the son of Joshibi'ah, son of Sera'iah, son of As'i-el, Eli-o-e'nai,
Ja-ako'bah, Jesh-ohai'ah, Asa'iah, Ad'i-el, Jesim'i-el, Benai'ah,
37 Ziza the son of Shiphi, son of Allon, son of Jeda'iah, son of
38 Shimri, son of Shemai'ah—these mentioned by name were
princes in their families, and their fathers' houses increased
39 greatly. They journeyed to the entrance of Gedor, to the east
40 side of the valley, to seek pasture for their flocks, where they
found rich, good pasture, and the land was very broad, quiet,
and peaceful; for the former inhabitants there belonged to Ham.
41 These, registered by name, came in the days of Hezeki'ah, king
of Judah, and destroyed their tents and the Me-u'nim who were
found there, and exterminated them to this day, and settled
in their place, because there was pasture there for their flocks.
42 And some of them, five hundred men of the Simeonites, went
to Mount Se'ir, having as their leaders Pelati'ah, Ne-ari'ah,
43 Repha'iah, and Uz'ziel, the sons of Ishi; and they destroyed the
remnant of the Amal'ekites that had escaped, and they have
dwelt there to this day.

Trans-Jordan Tribes

5 The sons of Reuben the first-born of Israel (for he was
the first-born; but because he polluted his father's couch,
his birthright was given to the sons of Joseph the son of Israel,
so that he is not enrolled in the genealogy according to the
2 birthright; though Judah became strong among his brothers and
a prince was from him, yet the birthright belonged to Joseph),
3 the sons of Reuben, the first-born of Israel: Hanoch, Pallu,
4 Hezron, and Carmi. The sons of Jo'el: Shemai'ah his son, Gog
5 his son, Shim'e-i his son, Micah his son, Re-a'iah his son,
6 Ba'al his son, Be-er'ah his son, whom Til'gath-pilne'ser king of
Assyria carried away into exile; he was a chieftain of the
7 Reubenites. And his kinsmen by their families, when the
genealogy of their generations was reckoned: the chief, Je-i'el,
8 and Zechari'ah, and Bela the son of Azaz, son of Shema, son
of Jo'el, who dwelt in Aro'er, as far as Nebo and Ba'al-me'on.
9 He also dwelt to the east as far as the entrance of the desert
this side of the Eu-phra'tes, because their cattle had multiplied
10 in the land of Gilead. And in the days of Saul they made war
on the Hagrites, who fell by their hand; and they dwelt in
their tents throughout all the region east of Gilead.
11 The sons of Gad dwelt over against them in the land of
12 Bashan as far as Sal'ecah: Jo'el the chief, Shapham the second,
13 Ja'nai, and Shaphat in Bashan. And their kinsmen according to
their fathers' houses: Michael, Meshul'lam, Sheba, Jo'rai, Jacan,
14 Zi'a, and Eber, seven. These were the sons of Ab'ihail the son of
Huri, son of Jaro'ah, son of Gilead, son of Michael, son of
15 Jeshish'ai, son of Jahdo, son of Buz; Ahi the son of Ab'di-el, son
16 of Guni, was chief in their fathers' houses; and they dwelt in
Gilead, in Bashan and in its towns, and in all the pasture lands
17 of Sharon to their limits. All of these were enrolled by genealogies in the days of Jotham king of Judah, and in the days of
Jerobo'am king of Israel.
18 The Reubenites, the Gadites, and the half-tribe of Manas'seh
had valiant men, who carried shield and sword, and drew the
bow, expert in war, forty-four thousand seven hundred and
19 sixty, ready for service. They made war upon the Hagrites,
20 Jetur, Naphish, and Nodab; and when they received help
against them, the Hagrites and all who were with them were
given into their hands, for they cried to God in the battle, and
21 he granted their entreaty because they trusted in him. They
carried off their livestock: fifty thousand of their camels, two
hundred and fifty thousand sheep, two thousand asses, and a
22 hundred thousand men alive. For many fell slain, because the
war was of God. And they dwelt in their place until the exile.
23 The members of the half-tribe of Manas'seh dwelt in the land;
they were very numerous from Bashan to Ba'al-her'mon, Senir,
24 and Mount Hermon. These were the heads of their fathers'
houses: Epher,[m] Ishi, Eli'el, Az'ri-el, Jeremiah, Hodavi'ah, and
Jah'di-el, mighty warriors, famous men, heads of their fathers'
25 houses. But they transgressed against the God of their fathers,
and played the harlot after the gods of the peoples of the land,
26 whom God had destroyed before them. So the God of Israel
stirred up the spirit of Pul king of Assyria, the spirit of Til'gath-
pilne'ser king of Assyria, and he carried them away, namely,
the Reubenites, the Gadites, and the half-tribe of Manas'seh,
and brought them to Halah, Habor, Hara, and the river Gozan,
to this day.

Sons of Levi

2 6[n] The sons of Levi: Gershom, Kohath, and Merar'i. The sons
3 of Kohath: Amram, Izhar, Hebron, and Uz'ziel. The children
of Amram: Aaron, Moses, and Miriam. The sons of Aaron:
4 Nadab, Abi'hu, Ele-a'zar, and Ith'amar. Ele-a'zar was the father
5 of Phin'ehas, Phin'ehas of Abishu'a, Abishu'a of Bukki, Bukki
6, 7 of Uzzi, Uzzi of Zerahi'ah, Zerahi'ah of Mera'ioth, Mera'ioth of
8 Amari'ah, Amari'ah of Ahi'tub, Ahi'tub of Zadok, Zadok of
9, 10 Ahim'a-az, Ahim'a-az of Azari'ah, Azari'ah of Joha'nan, and
Joha'nan of Azari'ah (it was he who served as priest in the
11 house that Solomon built in Jerusalem). Azari'ah was the father
12 of Amari'ah, Amari'ah of Ahi'tub, Ahi'tub of Zadok, Zadok of
13, 14 Shallum, Shallum of Hilki'ah, Hilki'ah of Azari'ah, Azari'ah of
15 Sera'iah, Sera'iah of Jehoz'adak; and Jehoz'adak went into exile
when the LORD sent Judah and Jerusalem into exile by the hand
of Nebuchadnez'zar.
16,[o] 17 The sons of Levi: Gershom, Kohath, and Merar'i. And these
18 are the names of the sons of Gershom: Libni and Shim'e-i. The
19 sons of Kohath: Amram, Izhar, Hebron, and Uz'ziel. The sons
of Merar'i: Mahli and Mushi. These are the families of the
20 Levites according to their fathers. Of Gershom: Libni his son,
21 Jahath his son, Zimmah his son, Jo'ah his son, Iddo his son,
22 Zerah his son, Je-ath'erai his son. The sons of Kohath: Ammin'-
23 adab his son, Korah his son, Assir his son, Elka'nah his son,
24 Ebi'asaph his son, Assir his son, Tahath his son, Uri'el his son,
25 Uzzi'ah his son, and Sha'ul his son. The sons of Elka'nah:
26 Ama'sai and Ahi'moth, Elka'nah his son, Zophai his son, Nahath
27 his son, Eli'ab his son, Jero'ham his son, Elka'nah his son.
28 The sons of Samuel: Jo'el[p] his first-born, the second Abi'jah.[q]
29 The sons of Merar'i: Mahli, Libni his son, Shim'e-i his son,
30 Uzzah his son, Shim'e-a his son, Haggi'ah his son, and Asa'iah
his son.
31 These are the men whom David put in charge of the service
of song in the house of the LORD, after the ark rested there.
32 They ministered with song before the tabernacle of the tent of
meeting, until Solomon had built the house of the LORD in Jeru-
33 salem; and they performed their service in due order. These are

[g] Gk Vg: Heb lacks *Meonothai*
[h] That is *Valley of craftsmen*
[i] The clause: *These are . . . married* is transposed from verse 18
[j] Heb lacks *and bore*
[k] Vg Compare Gk: Heb *and Jashubi-lahem*
[l] Or *matters*
[m] Gk Vg: Heb *and Epher*
[n] Ch 5.27 in Heb
[o] Ch 6.1 in Heb
[p] Gk Syr Compare verse 33 and 1 S 8.2: Heb lacks *Joel*
[q] Heb *and Abijah*

the men who served and their sons. Of the sons of the Ko'hathites: Heman the singer the son of Jo'el, son of Samuel, [34] son of Elka'nah, son of Jero'ham, son of Eli'el, son of To'ah, [35] son of Zuph, son of Elka'nah, son of Mahath, son of Ama'sai, [36] son of Elka'nah, son of Jo'el, son of Azari'ah, son of Zephani'ah, [37] son of Tahath, son of Assir, son of Ebi'asaph, son of Korah, [38, 39] son of Izhar, son of Kohath, son of Levi, son of Israel; and his brother Asaph, who stood on his right hand, namely, Asaph [40] the son of Berechi'ah, son of Shim'e-a, son of Michael, son of [41] Ba-ase'iah, son of Malchi'jah, son of Ethni, son of Zerah, son of [42, 43] Ada'iah, son of Ethan, son of Zimmah, son of Shim'e-i, son of [44] Jahath, son of Gershom, son of Levi. On the left hand were their brethren the sons of Merar'i: Ethan the son of Kishi, son [45] of Abdi, son of Malluch, son of Hashabi'ah, son of Amazi'ah, [46] son of Hilki'ah, son of Amzi, son of Bani, son of Shemer, [47, 48] son of Mahli, son of Mushi, son of Merar'i, son of Levi; and their brethren the Levites were appointed for all the service of the tabernacle of the house of God.

[49] But Aaron and his sons made offerings upon the altar of burnt offering and upon the altar of incense for all the work of the most holy place, and to make atonement for Israel, according to all that Moses the servant of God had commanded. [50] These are the sons of Aaron: Ele-a'zar his son, Phin'ehas his [51] son, Abishu'a his son, Bukki his son, Uzzi his son, Zerahi'ah his [52] son, Mera'ioth his son, Amari'ah his son, Ahi'tub his son, [53] Zadok his son, Ahim'a-az his son.

[54] These are their dwelling places according to their settlements within their borders: to the sons of Aaron of the families of [55] Ko'hathites, for theirs was the lot, to them they gave Hebron [56] in the land of Judah and its surrounding pasture lands, but the fields of the city and its villages they gave to Caleb the son of [57] Jephun'neh. To the sons of Aaron they gave the cities of refuge: Hebron, Libnah with its pasture lands, Jattir, Eshtemo'a with [58] its pasture lands, Hilen with its pasture lands, Debir with its [59] pasture lands, Ashan with its pasture lands, and Beth-she'mesh [60] with its pasture lands; and from the tribe of Benjamin, Geba with its pasture lands, Al'emeth with its pasture lands, and An'athoth with its pasture lands. All their cities throughout their families were thirteen.

[61] To the rest of the Ko'hathites were given by lot out of the family of the tribe, out of the half-tribe, the half of Manas'seh, [62] ten cities. To the Gershomites according to their families were allotted thirteen cities out of the tribes of Is'sachar, Asher, [63] Naph'tali, and Manas'seh in Bashan. To the Merar'ites according to their families were allotted twelve cities out of the tribes of [64] Reuben, Gad, and Zeb'ulun. So the people of Israel gave the [65] Levites the cities with their pasture lands. They also gave them by lot out of the tribes of Judah, Simeon, and Benjamin these cities which are mentioned by name.

[66] And some of the families of the sons of Kohath had cities of [67] their territory out of the tribe of E'phraim. They were given the cities of refuge: Shechem with its pasture lands in the hill [68] country of E'phraim, Gezer with its pasture lands, Jok'me-am with its pasture lands, Beth-ho'ron with its pasture lands, [69] Ai'jalon with its pasture lands, Gath-rim'mon with its pasture [70] lands, and out of the half-tribe of Manas'seh, Aner with its pasture lands, and Bil'e-am with its pasture lands, for the rest of the families of the Ko'hathites.

[71] To the Gershomites were given out of the half-tribe of Manas'seh: Golan in Bashan with its pasture lands and Ash'[72]taroth with its pasture lands; and out of the tribe of Is'sachar: Kedesh with its pasture lands, Dab'erath with its pasture lands, [73] Ramoth with its pasture lands, and Anem with its pasture lands; [74] out of the tribe of Asher: Mashal with its pasture lands, Abdon [75] with its pasture lands, Hukok with its pasture lands, and Rehob [76] with its pasture lands; and out of the tribe of Naph'tali: Kedesh in Galilee with its pasture lands, Ham'mon with its pasture [77] lands, and Kiriatha'im with its pasture lands. To the rest of the Merar'ites were allotted out of the tribe of Zeb'ulun: Rim'[78]mono with its pasture lands, Tabor with its pasture lands, [78] and beyond the Jordan at Jericho, on the east side of the Jordan, out of the tribe of Reuben: Bezer in the steppe with [79] its pasture lands, Jahzah with its pasture lands, Ked'emoth with its pasture lands, and Meph'a-ath with its pasture lands; [80] and out of the tribe of Gad: Ramoth in Gilead with its pasture [81] lands, Mahana'im with its pasture lands, Heshbon with its pasture lands, and Jazer with its pasture lands.

The Northern Tribes

7 The sons [r] of Is'sachar: Tola, Pu'ah, Jashub, and Shimron, [2] four. The sons of Tola: Uzzi, Repha'iah, Je'ri-el, Jah'mai, Ibsam, and Shem'uel, heads of their fathers' houses, namely of Tola, mighty warriors of their generations, their number in the [3] days of David being twenty-two thousand six hundred. The sons of Uzzi: Izrahi'ah. And the sons of Izrahi'ah: Michael, [4] Obadi'ah, Jo'el, and Isshi'ah, five, all of them chief men; and along with them, by their generations, according to their fathers' houses, were units of the army for war, thirty-six thousand, [5] for they had many wives and sons. Their kinsmen belonging to all the families of Is'sachar were in all eighty-seven thousand mighty warriors, enrolled by genealogy.

[6] The sons of Benjamin: Bela, Becher, and Jedi'a-el, three. [7] The sons of Bela: Ezbon, Uzzi, Uz'ziel, Jer'imoth, and Iri, five, heads of fathers' houses, mighty warriors; and their enrollment [8] by genealogies was twenty-two thousand and thirty-four. The sons of Becher: Zemi'rah, Jo'ash, Elie'zer, Eli-o-e'nai, Omri, Jer'emoth, Abi'jah, An'athoth, and Al'emeth. All these were [9] the sons of Becher; and their enrollment by genealogies, according to their generations, as heads of their fathers' houses, [10] mighty warriors, was twenty thousand two hundred. The sons of Jedi'a-el: Bilhan. And the sons of Bilhan: Je'ush, Benjamin, [11] Ehud, Chena'anah, Zethan, Tarshish, and Ahish'ahar. All these were the sons of Jedi'a-el according to the heads of their fathers' houses, mighty warriors, seventeen thousand and two [12] hundred, ready for service in war. And Shuppim and Huppim were the sons of Ir, Hushim the sons of Aher.

[13] The sons of Naph'tali: Jah'zi-el, Guni, Jezer, and Shallum, the offspring of Bilhah.

[14] The sons of Manas'seh: As'ri-el, whom his Aramean concubine [15] bore; she bore Machir the father of Gilead. And Machir took a wife for Huppim and for Shuppim. The name of his sister was Ma'acah. And the name of the second was Zeloph'ehad; and [16] Zeloph'ehad had daughters. And Ma'acah the wife of Machir bore a son, and she called his name Peresh; and the name of his brother was Sheresh; and his sons were Ulam and Rakem. [17] The sons of Ulam: Bedan. These were the sons of Gilead the [18] son of Machir, son of Manas'seh. And his sister Hammo'lecheth [19] bore Ishhod, Abie'zer, and Mahlah. The sons of Shemi'da were Ahi'an, Shechem, Likhi, and Ani'am.

[20] The sons of E'phraim: Shuthe'lah, and Bered his son, Tahath [21] his son, Ele-a'dah his son, Tahath his son, Zabad his son, Shuthe'lah his son, and Ezer and E'le-ad, whom the men of Gath who were born in the land slew, because they came down to [22] raid their cattle. And E'phraim their father mourned many days, [23] and his brothers came to comfort him. And E'phraim went in to his wife, and she conceived and bore a son; and he called his [24] name Beri'ah, because evil had befallen his house. His daughter was She'erah, who built both Lower and Upper Beth-ho'ron, [25] and Uz'zen-she'erah. Rephah was his son, Resheph his son, Telah [26] his son, Tahan his son, Ladan his son, Ammi'hud his son, Elish'[27, 28]ama his son, Nun his son, Joshua his son. Their possessions and settlements were Bethel and its towns, and eastward Na'aran, and westward Gezer and its towns, Shechem and its towns, [29] and Ayyah and its towns; also along the borders of the Manas'sites, Beth-she'an and its towns, Ta'anach and its towns, Megid'do and its towns, Dor and its towns. In these dwelt the sons of Joseph the son of Israel.

[30] The sons of Asher: Imnah, Ishvah, Ishvi, Beri'ah, and their [31] sister Serah. The sons of Beri'ah: Heber and Mal'chi-el, who [32] was the father of Bir'zaith. Heber was the father of Japhlet, [33] Shomer, Hotham, and their sister Shu'a. The sons of Japhlet: [34] Pasach, Bimhal, and Ashvath. These are the sons of Japhlet. The sons of Shemer his brother: Rohgah, Jehub'bah, and Aram. [35] The sons of Helem his brother: Zophah, Imna, Shelesh, and [36] Amal. The sons of Zophah: Su'ah, Har'nepher, Shu'al, Beri, [37] Imrah, Bezer, Hod, Shamma, Shilshah, Ithran, and Be-e'ra. [38, 39] The sons of Jether: Jephun'neh, Pispa, and Ara. The sons of [40] Ulla: Arah, Han'niel, and Rizi'a. All of these were men of Asher, heads of fathers' houses, approved, mighty warriors, chief of the princes. Their number enrolled by genealogies, for service in war, was twenty-six thousand men.

Sons of Benjamin

8 Benjamin was the father of Bela his first-born, Ashbel the [2] second, Ahar'ah the third, Nohah the fourth, and Rapha the [3, 4] fifth. And Bela had sons: Addar, Gera, Abi'hud, Abishu'a, Na'-[5, 6]aman, Aho'ah, Gera, Shephu'phan, and Huram. These are the sons of Ehud (they were heads of fathers' houses of the inhabitants of Geba, and they were carried into exile to Mana'[7]hath): Na'aman,[s] Ahi'jah, and Gera, that is, Heglam,[t] who was [8] the father of Uzza and Ahi'hud. And Shahara'im had sons in the country of Moab after he had sent away Hushim and Ba'ara

---

[r] Syr Compare Vg: Heb *and to the sons*   [s] Heb *and Naaman*   [t] Or *he carried them into exile*

9 his wives. He had sons by Hodesh his wife: Jobab, Zib′i-a, Me-
10 sha, Malcam, Je′uz, Sachi′a, and Mirmah. These were his sons,
11 heads of fathers' houses. He also had sons by Hushim: Abi′tub
12 and Elpa′al. The sons of Elpa′al: Eber, Misham, and Shemed,
13 who built Ono and Lod with its towns, and Beri′ah and Shema
(they were heads of fathers' houses of the inhabitants of
14 Ai′jalon, who put to flight the inhabitants of Gath); and Ahi′o,
15, 16 Shashak, and Jer′emoth. Zebadi′ah, Arad, Eder, Michael, Ish-
17 pah, and Joha were sons of Beri′ah. Zebadi′ah, Meshul′lam,
18 Hizki, Heber, Ish′merai, Izli′ah, and Jobab were the sons of
19, 20 Elpa′al. Jakim, Zichri, Zabdi, Eli-e′nai, Zil′le-thai, Eli′el,
21 Ada′iah, Bera′iah, and Shimrath were the sons of Shim′e-i.
22, 23, 24 Ishpan, Eber, Eli′el, Abdon, Zichri, Hanan, Hanani′ah, Elam,
25 Anthothi′jah, Iphde′iah, and Penu′el were the sons of Shashak.
26, 27 Sham′sherai, Shehari′ah, Athali′ah, Ja-areshi′ah, Eli′jah, and
28 Zichri were the sons of Jero′ham. These were the heads of
fathers' houses, according to their generations, chief men. These
dwelt in Jerusalem.
29 Je-i′el[u] the father of Gibeon dwelt in Gibeon, and the name
30 of his wife was Ma′acah. His first-born son: Abdon, then Zur,
31, 32 Kish, Ba′al, Nadab, Gedor, Ahi′o, Zecher, and Mikloth (he
was the father of Shim′e-ah). Now these also dwelt opposite
33 their kinsmen in Jerusalem, with their kinsmen. Ner was the
father of Kish, Kish of Saul, Saul of Jonathan, Mal′chishu′a,
34 Abin′adab, and Eshba′al; and the son of Jonathan was Mer′ib-
35 ba′al; and Mer′ib-ba′al was the father of Micah. The sons of
36 Micah: Pithon, Melech, Tare′a, and Ahaz. Ahaz was the father
of Jeho′addah; and Jeho′addah was the father of Al′emeth, Az′-
37 maveth, and Zimri; Zimri was the father of Moza. Moza was
the father of Bin′e-a; Raphah was his son, Ele-a′sah his son,
38 Azel his son. Azel had six sons, and these are their names:
Azri′kam, Bo′cheru, Ish′mael, She-ari′ah, Obadi′ah, and Hanan.
39 All these were the sons of Azel. The sons of Eshek his brother:
Ulam his first-born, Je′ush the second, and Eliph′elet the third.
40 The sons of Ulam were men who were mighty warriors, bowmen, having many sons and grandsons, one hundred and fifty.
All these were Benjaminites.

Jerusalem Families

9 So all Israel was enrolled by genealogies; and these are
written in the Book of the Kings of Israel. And Judah was
2 taken into exile in Babylon because of their unfaithfulness. Now
the first to dwell again in their possessions in their cities were
3 Israel, the priests, the Levites, and the temple servants. And
some of the people of Judah, Benjamin, E′phraim, and Manas′-
4 seh dwelt in Jerusalem: Uthai the son of Ammi′hud, son of
Omri, son of Imri, son of Bani, from the sons of Perez the son
5 of Judah. And of the Shi′lonites: Asa′iah the first-born, and
6 his sons. Of the sons of Zerah: Jeu′el and their kinsmen, six
7 hundred and ninety. Of the Benjaminites: Sallu the son of
8 Meshul′lam, son of Hodavi′ah, son of Hassenu′ah, Ibne′iah the
son of Jero′ham, Elah the son of Uzzi, son of Michri, and
Meshul′lam the son of Shephati′ah, son of Reu′el, son of Ibni′jah;
9 and their kinsmen according to their generations, nine hundred
and fifty-six. All these were heads of fathers' houses according
to their fathers' houses.
10, 11 Of the priests: Jeda′iah, Jehoi′arib, Jachin, and Azari′ah the
son of Hilki′ah, son of Meshul′lam, son of Zadok, son of Mera′-
ioth, son of Ahi′tub, the chief officer of the house of God;
12 and Ada′iah the son of Jero′ham, son of Pashhur, son of
Malchi′jah, and Ma′asai the son of Ad′i-el, son of Jah′zerah,
13 son of Meshul′lam, son of Meshil′lemith, son of Immer; besides
their kinsmen, heads of their fathers' houses, one thousand
seven hundred and sixty, very able men for the work of the
service of the house of God.
14 Of the Levites: Shemai′ah the son of Hasshub, son of Azri′-
15 kam, son of Hashabi′ah, of the sons of Merar′i; and Bakbak′kar,
Heresh, Galal, and Mattani′ah the son of Mica, son of Zichri,
16 son of Asaph; and Obadi′ah the son of Shemai′ah, son of Galal,
son of Jedu′thun, and Berechi′ah the son of Asa, son of Elka′nah,
who dwelt in the villages of the Netoph′athites.

Duties of the Temple Staff

17 The gatekeepers were: Shallum, Akkub, Talmon, Ahi′man,
18 and their kinsmen (Shallum being the chief), stationed hitherto in the king's gate on the east side. These were the gate-
19 keepers of the camp of the Levites. Shallum the son of Ko′re,
son of Ebi′asaph, son of Korah, and his kinsmen of his fathers'
house, the Ko′rahites, were in charge of the work of the service,
keepers of the thresholds of the tent, as their fathers had been
in charge of the camp of the LORD, keepers of the entrance.
20 And Phin′ehas the son of Elea′zar was the ruler over them in
21 time past; the LORD was with him. Zechari′ah the son of
Meshelemi′ah was gatekeeper at the entrance of the tent of
22 meeting. All these, who were chosen as gatekeepers at the
thresholds, were two hundred and twelve. They were enrolled
by genealogies in their villages. David and Samuel the seer
23 established them in their office of trust. So they and their sons
were in charge of the gates of the house of the LORD, that is,
24 the house of the tent, as guards. The gatekeepers were on the
25 four sides, east, west, north, and south; and their kinsmen who
were in their villages were obliged to come in every seven
26 days, from time to time, to be with these; for the four chief
gatekeepers, who were Levites, were in charge of the chambers
27 and the treasurers of the house of God. And they lodged round
about the house of God; for upon them lay the duty of watching, and they had charge of opening it every morning.
28 Some of them had charge of the utensils of service, for they
were required to count them when they were brought in and
29 taken out. Others of them were appointed over the furniture,
and over all the holy utensils, also over the fine flour, the wine,
30 the oil, the incense, and the spices. Others, of the sons of the
31 priests, prepared the mixing of the spices, and Mattithi′ah, one
of the Levites, the first-born of Shallum the Ko′rahite, was in
32 charge of making the flat cakes. Also some of their kinsmen of
the Ko′hathites had charge of the showbread, to prepare it
every sabbath.
33 Now these are the singers, the heads of fathers' houses of the
Levites, dwelling in the chambers of the temple free from
34 other service, for they were on duty day and night. These were
heads of fathers' houses of the Levites, according to their
generations, leaders, who lived in Jerusalem.

Ancestors of Saul

35 In Gibeon dwelt the father of Gibeon, Je-i′el, and the name
36 of his wife was Ma′acah, and his first-born son Abdon, then
37 Zur, Kish, Ba′al, Ner, Nadab, Gedor, Ahi′o, Zechari′ah, and
38 Mikloth; and Mikloth was the father of Shim′e-am; and these
also dwelt opposite their kinsmen in Jerusalem, with their
39 kinsmen. Ner was the father of Kish, Kish of Saul, Saul of
40 Jonathan, Mal′chishu′a, Abin′adab, and Eshba′al; and the son
of Jonathan was Mer′ib-ba′al; and Mer′ib-ba′al was the father
41 of Micah. The sons of Micah: Pithon, Melech, Tahr′e-a, and
42 Ahaz;[v] and Ahaz was the father of Jarah, and Jarah of Al′emeth,
43 Az′maveth, and Zimri; and Zimri was the father of Moza. Moza
was the father of Bin′e-a; and Repha′iah was his son, Ele-a′sah
44 his son, Azel his son. Azel had six sons and these are their
names: Azri′kam, Bo′cheru, Ish′mael, She-ari′ah, Obadi′ah, and
Hanan; these were the sons of Azel.

THE REIGN OF DAVID

10 Now the Philistines fought against Israel; and
the men of Israel fled before the Philistines, and fell
2 slain on Mount Gilbo′a. And the Philistines overtook Saul
and his sons; and the Philistines slew Jonathan and
3 Abin′adab and Mal′chishu′a, the sons of Saul. The battle
pressed hard upon Saul, and the archers found him; and
4 he was wounded by the archers. Then Saul said to his
armor-bearer, "Draw your sword, and thrust me through
with it, lest these uncircumcised come and make sport
of me." But his armor-bearer would not; for he feared
greatly. Therefore Saul took his own sword, and fell upon
5 it. And when his armor-bearer saw that Saul was dead, he
6 also fell upon his sword, and died. Thus Saul died; he and
7 his three sons and all his house died together. And when
all the men of Israel who were in the valley saw that the
army[w] had fled and that Saul and his sons were dead,
they forsook their cities and fled; and the Philistines
came and dwelt in them.

---

[u] Compare 9.35: Heb lacks *Jeiel*   [v] Compare 8.35: Heb lacks *and Ahaz*   [w] Heb *they*

8 On the morrow, when the Philistines came to strip the slain, they found Saul and his sons fallen on Mount 9 Gilbo′a. And they stripped him and took his head and his armor, and sent messengers throughout the land of the Philistines, to carry the good news to their idols and to 10 the people. And they put his armor in the temple of their gods, and fastened his head in the temple of Dagon. 11 But when all Ja′besh-gil′ead heard all that the Philistines 12 had done to Saul, all the valiant men arose, and took away the body of Saul and the bodies of his sons, and brought them to Jabesh. And they buried their bones under the oak in Jabesh, and fasted seven days.

13 So Saul died for his unfaithfulness; he was unfaithful to the LORD in that he did not keep the command of the LORD, and also consulted a medium, seeking guidance, 14 and did not seek guidance from the LORD. Therefore the LORD slew him, and turned the kingdom over to David the son of Jesse.

David's Triumphs

11 Then all Israel gathered together to David at Hebron, and said, "Behold, we are your bone and 2 flesh. In times past, even when Saul was king, it was you that led out and brought in Israel; and the LORD your God said to you, 'You shall be shepherd of my people Israel, and you shall be prince over my people Israel.' " 3 So all the elders of Israel came to the king at Hebron; and David made a covenant with them at Hebron before the LORD, and they anointed David king over Israel, according to the word of the LORD by Samuel.

4 And David and all Israel went to Jerusalem, that is Jebus, where the Jeb′usites were, the inhabitants of the 5 land. The inhabitants of Jebus said to David, "You will not come in here." Nevertheless David took the stronghold 6 of Zion, that is, the city of David. David said, "Whoever shall smite the Jeb′usites first shall be chief and commander." And Jo′ab the son of Zeru′iah went up first, so 7 he became chief. And David dwelt in the stronghold; 8 therefore it was called the city of David. And he built the city round about from the Millo in complete circuit; and 9 Jo′ab repaired the rest of the city. And David became greater and greater, for the LORD of hosts was with him.

10 Now these are the chiefs of David's mighty men, who gave him strong support in his kingdom, together with all Israel, to make him king, according to the word of the LORD concerning 11 Israel. This is an account of David's mighty men: Jasho′be-am, a Hach′monite, was chief of the three;ˣ he wielded his spear against three hundred whom he slew at one time. 12 And next to him among the three mighty men was Elea′zar 13 the son of Dodo, the Aho′hite. He was with David at Pas-dam′mim when the Philistines were gathered there for battle. There was a plot of ground full of barley, and the men fled from the 14 Philistines. But heʸ took hisʸ stand in the midst of the plot, and defended it, and slew the Philistines; and the LORD saved them by a great victory.

15 Three of the thirty chief men went down to the rock to David at the cave of Adul′lam, when the army of Philistines 16 was encamped in the valley of Reph′aim. David was then in the

stronghold; and the garrison of the Philistines was then at 17 Bethlehem. And David said longingly, "O that some one would give me water to drink from the well of Bethlehem which is 18 by the gate!" Then the three mighty men broke through the camp of the Philistines, and drew water out of the well of Bethlehem which was by the gate, and took and brought it to David. But David would not drink of it; he poured it out to 19 the LORD, and said, "Far be it from me before my God that I should do this. Shall I drink the lifeblood of these men? For at the risk of their lives they brought it." Therefore he would not drink it. These things did the three mighty men.

20 Now Abi′shai, the brother of Jo′ab, was chief of the thirty.ᶻ And he wielded his spear against three hundred men and slew 21 them, and won a name beside the three. He was the most renownedᵃ of the thirty,ᶻ and became their commander; but he did not attain to the three.

22 And Benai′ah the son of Jehoi′ada was a valiant manᵇ of Kabzeel, a doer of great deeds; he smote two arielsᶜ of Moab. He also went down and slew a lion in a pit on a day when 23 snow had fallen. And he slew an Egyptian, a man of great stature, five cubits tall. The Egyptian had in his hand a spear like a weaver's beam; but Benai′ah went down to him with a staff, and snatched the spear out of the Egyptian's hand, 24 and slew him with his own spear. These things did Benai′ah the son of Jehoi′ada, and won a name beside the three mighty 25 men. He was renowned among the thirty, but he did not attain to the three. And David set him over his bodyguard.

26 The mighty men of the armies were As′ahel the brother of 27 Jo′ab, Elha′nan the son of Dodo of Bethlehem, Shammoth of 28 Harod,ᵈ Helez the Pel′onite, Ira the son of Ikkesh of Teko′a, 29 Abi-e′zer of An′athoth, Sib′becai the Hu′shathite, I′lai of 30 Aho′hite, Ma′harai of Netoph′ah, Heled the son of Ba′anah of 31 Netoph′ah, Ithai the son of Ribai of Gib′e-ah of the Benjamin- 32 ites, Benai′ah of Pir′athon, Hurai of the brooks of Ga′ash, Abi′el 33 the Ar′bathite, Az′maveth of Baha′rum, Eli′ahba of Sha-al′bon, 34 Hashemᵉ the Gi′zonite, Jonathan the son of Shagee the Har′- 35 arite, Ahi′am the son of Sachar the Har′arite, Eli′phal the son 36, 37 of Ur, Hepher the Meche′rathite, Ahi′jah the Pel′onite, Hezro 38 of Carmel, Na′arai the son of Ezbai, Jo′el the brother of Nathan, 39 Mibhar the son of Hagri, Zelek the Ammonite, Na′harai of 40 Be-er′oth, the armor-bearer of Jo′ab the son of Zeru′iah, Ira the 41 Ithrite, Gareb the Ithrite, Uri′ah the Hittite, Zabad the son of 42 Ahlai, Ad′ina the son of Shiza the Reubenite, a leader of the 43 Reubenites, and thirty with him, Hanan the son of Ma′acah, and 44 Josh′aphat the Mithnite, Uzzi′a the Ash′terathite, Shama and 45 Je-i′el the sons of Hotham the Aro′erite, Jedi′a-el the son of 46 Shimri, and Joha his brother, the Tizite, Eli′el the Ma′havite, and Jer′ibai, and Joshavi′ah, the sons of El′na-am, and Ithmah 47 the Mo′abite, Eli′el, and Obed, and Ja-asi′el the Mezo′ba-ite.

12 Now these are the men who came to David at Ziklag, while he could not move about freely because of Saul the son of Kish; and they were among the mighty men who helped 2 him in war. They were bowmen, and could shoot arrows and sling stones with either the right or the left hand; they were 3 Benjaminites, Saul's kinsmen. The chief was Ahi-e′zer, then Jo′ash, both sons of Shema′ah of Gib′e-ah; also Je′zi-el and Pelet the sons of Az′maveth; Ber′acah, Jehu of An′athoth, 4 Ishma′iah of Gibeon, a mighty man among the thirty and a leader over the thirty; Jeremiah,ᶠ Jahazi′el, Joha′nan, Joz′abad 5 of Gede′rah, Elu′zai,ᵍ Jer′imoth, Beali′ah, Shemari′ah, Shephati′- 6 ah the Har′uphites; Elka′nah, Isshi′ah, Az′arel, Jo-e′zer, and 7 Jasho′be-am, the Ko′rahites; and Jo-e′lah and Zebadi′ah, the sons of Jero′ham of Gedor.

8 From the Gadites there went over to David at the stronghold in the wilderness mighty and experienced warriors, expert with shield and spear, whose faces were like the faces of lions, and 9 who were swift as gazelles upon the mountains: Ezer the chief, 10 Obadi′ah second, Eli′ab third, Mishman′nah fourth, Jeremiah fifth, 11, 12 Attai sixth, Eli′el seventh, Joha′nan eighth, Elza′bad ninth, 13, 14 Jeremiah tenth, Mach′bannai eleventh. These Gadites were officers of the army, the lesser over a hundred and the greater 15 over a thousand. These are the men who crossed the Jordan in the first month, when it was overflowing all its banks, and put to flight all those in the valleys, to the east and to the west.

16 And some of the men of Benjamin and Judah came to the 17 stronghold to David. David went out to meet them and said to them, "If you have come to me in friendship to help me, my heart will be knit to you; but if to betray me to my adversaries, although there is no wrong in my hands, then may the God of

---

ˣ Compare 2 S 23.8: Heb *thirty* or *captains*   ʸ Compare 2 S 23.12: Heb *they . . . their*   ᶻ Syr: Heb *three*
ᵃ Compare 2 S 23.19: Heb *more renowned among the two*   ᶻ Syr: Heb *three*   ᵇ Syr: Heb *the son of a valiant man*
ᶜ The meaning of the word *ariel* is unknown   ᵈ Compare 2 S 23.25: Heb *the Harorite*
ᵉ Compare Gk and 2 S 23.32: Heb *the sons of Hashem*   ᶠ Heb verse 5   ᵍ Heb verse 6

¹⁸ our fathers see and rebuke you." Then the Spirit came upon Ama'sai, chief of the thirty, and he said,

> "We are yours, O David;
> and with you, O son of Jesse!
> Peace, peace to you,
> and peace to your helpers!
> For your God helps you."

Then David received them, and made them officers of his troops. ¹⁹ Some of the men of Manas'seh deserted to David when he came with the Philistines for the battle against Saul. (Yet he did not help them, for the rulers of the Philistines took counsel and sent him away, saying, "At peril to our heads he will desert ²⁰ to his master Saul.") As he went to Ziklag these men of Manas'seh deserted to him: Adnah, Joz'abad, Jedi'a-el, Michael, Joz'abad, Eli'hu, and Zil'lethai, chiefs of thousands in Manas'seh. ²¹ They helped David against the band of raiders;^h for they were ²² all mighty men of valor, and were commanders in the army. For from day to day men kept coming to David to help him, until there was a great army, like an army of God.

²³ These are the numbers of the divisions of the armed troops, who came to David in Hebron, to turn the kingdom of Saul over ²⁴ to him, according to the word of the LORD. The men of Judah bearing shield and spear were six thousand eight hundred ²⁵ armed troops. Of the Simeonites, mighty men of valor for war, ²⁶ seven thousand one hundred. Of the Levites four thousand six ²⁷ hundred. The prince Jehoi'ada, of the house of Aaron, and with ²⁸ him three thousand seven hundred. Zadok, a young man mighty in valor, and twenty-two commanders from his own father's ²⁹ house. Of the Benjaminites, the kinsmen of Saul, three thousand, of whom the majority had hitherto kept their allegiance ³⁰ to the house of Saul. Of the E'phraimites twenty thousand eight hundred, mighty men of valor, famous men in their fathers' ³¹ houses. Of the half-tribe of Manas'seh eighteen thousand, who ³² were expressly named to come and make David king. Of Is'sachar men who had understanding of the times, to know what Israel ought to do, two hundred chiefs, and all their kinsmen ³³ under their command. Of Zeb'ulun fifty thousand seasoned troops, equipped for battle with all the weapons of war, to ³⁴ help David ⁱ with singleness of purpose. Of Naph'tali a thousand commanders with whom were thirty-seven thousand men armed ³⁵ with shield and spear. Of the Danites twenty-eight thousand ³⁶ six hundred men equipped for battle. Of Asher forty thousand ³⁷ seasoned troops ready for battle. Of the Reubenites and Gadites and the half-tribe of Manas'seh from beyond the Jordan, one hundred and twenty thousand men armed with all the weapons of war.

³⁸ All these, men of war, arrayed in battle order, came to Hebron with full intent to make David king over all Israel; likewise all the rest of Israel were of a single mind to make David king. ³⁹ And they were there with David for three days, eating and drinking, for their brethren had made preparation for them. ⁴⁰ And also their neighbors, from as far as Is'sachar and Zeb'ulun and Naph'tali, came bringing food on asses and on camels and on mules and on oxen, abundant provisions of meal, cakes of figs, clusters of raisins, and wine and oil, oxen and sheep, for there was joy in Israel.

David's Failure to Bring the Ark

13 David consulted with the commanders of thou²sands and of hundreds, with every leader. And David said to all the assembly of Israel, "If it seems good to you, and if it is the will of the LORD our God, let us send abroad to our brethren who remain in all the land of Israel, and with them to the priests and Levites in the cities that have pasture lands, that they may come together ³ to us. Then let us bring again the ark of our God to us; ⁴ for we neglected it in the days of Saul." All the assembly agreed to do so, for the thing was right in the eyes of all the people.

⁵ So David assembled all Israel from the Shihor of Egypt to the entrance of Hamath, to bring the ark of God from

⁶ Kir'iath-je'arim. And David and all Israel went up to Ba'alah, that is, to Kir'iath-je'arim which belongs to Judah, to bring up from there the ark of God, which is called by the name of the LORD who sits enthroned above ⁷ the cherubim. And they carried the ark of God upon a new cart, from the house of Abin'adab, and Uzzah and ⁸ Ahi'o ^j were driving the cart. And David and all Israel

were making merry before God with all their might, with song and lyres and harps and tambourines and cymbals and trumpets.

⁹ And when they came to the threshing floor of Chidon, Uzzah put out his hand to hold the ark, for the oxen ¹⁰ stumbled. And the anger of the LORD was kindled against Uzzah; and he smote him because he put forth his hand ¹¹ to the ark; and he died there before God. And David was angry because the LORD had broken forth upon Uzzah; ¹² and that place is called Pe'rez-uz'za ^k to this day. And David was afraid of God that day; and he said, "How can ¹³ I bring the ark of God home to me?" So David did not take the ark home into the city of David, but took it aside ¹⁴ to the house of O'bed-e'dom the Gittite. And the ark of God remained with the household of O'bed-e'dom in his house three months; and the LORD blessed the household of O'bed-e'dom and all that he had.

14 And Hiram king of Tyre sent messengers to David, and cedar trees, also masons and carpenters ² to build a house for him. And David perceived that the LORD had established him king over Israel, and that his kingdom was highly exalted for the sake of his people Israel.

³ And David took more wives in Jerusalem, and David ⁴ begot more sons and daughters. These are the names of the children whom he had in Jerusalem: Shammu'a, ⁵ Shobab, Nathan, Solomon, Ibhar, Eli'shu-a, El'pelet, ^{6,7} Nogah, Nepheg, Japhi'a, Elish'ama, Beeli'ada, and Eliph'elet.

⁸ When the Philistines heard that David had been anointed king over all Israel, all the Philistines went up in search of David; and David heard of it and went out ⁹ against them. Now the Philistines had come and made a ¹⁰ raid in the valley of Reph'aim. And David inquired of God, "Shall I go up against the Philistines? Wilt thou give them into my hand?" And the LORD said to him, "Go up,

---

^h Or *as officers of his troops* ⁱ Gk: Heb lacks *David* ^j Or *and his brother* ^k That is *The breaking forth upon Uzzah*

11 and I will give them into your hand." And he went up to Ba'al-pera'zim, and David defeated them there; and David said, "God has broken through[1] my enemies by my hand, like a bursting flood." Therefore the name of 12 that place is called Ba'al-pera'zim.[m] And they left their gods there, and David gave command, and they were burned.

13 And the Philistines yet again made a raid in the valley. 14 And when David again inquired of God, God said to him, "You shall not go up after them; go around and come 15 upon them opposite the balsam trees. And when you hear the sound of marching in the tops of the balsam trees, then go out to battle; for God has gone out before you to 16 smite the army of the Philistines." And David did as God commanded him, and they smote the Philistine army from 17 Gibeon to Gezer. And the fame of David went out into all lands, and the LORD brought the fear of him upon all nations.

The Ark in Zion

15 David built houses for himself in the city of David; and he prepared a place for the ark of God, 2 and pitched a tent for it. Then David said, "No one but the Levites may carry the ark of God, for the LORD chose them to carry the ark of the LORD and to minister to him 3 for ever." And David assembled all Israel at Jerusalem, to bring up the ark of the LORD to its place, which he had 4 prepared for it. And David gathered together the sons of 5 Aaron and the Levites: of the sons of Kohath, Uri'el the 6 chief, with a hundred and twenty of his brethren; of the sons of Merar'i, Asa'iah the chief, with two hundred and 7 twenty of his brethren; of the sons of Gershom, Jo'el the 8 chief, with a hundred and thirty of his brethren; of the sons of Eliza'phan, Shemai'ah the chief, with two hundred 9 of his brethren; of the sons of Hebron, Eli'el the chief, 10 with eighty of his brethren; of the sons of Uz'ziel, Ammin'adab the chief, with a hundred and twelve of his 11 brethren. Then David summoned the priests Zadok and Abi'athar, and the Levites Uri'el, Asa'iah, Jo'el, Shemai'- 12 ah, Eli'el, and Ammin'adab, and said to them, "You are the heads of the fathers' houses of the Levites; sanctify yourselves, you and your brethren, so that you may bring up the ark of the LORD, the God of Israel, to the place that 13 I have prepared for it. Because you did not carry it the first time,[n] the LORD our God broke forth upon us, because we did not care for it in the way that is ordained." 14 So the priests and the Levites sanctified themselves to 15 bring up the ark of the LORD, the God of Israel. And the Levites carried the ark of God upon their shoulders with the poles, as Moses had commanded according to the word of the LORD.

16 David also commanded the chiefs of the Levites to appoint their brethren as the singers who should play loudly on musical instruments, on harps and lyres and 17 cymbals, to raise sounds of joy. So the Levites appointed Heman the son of Jo'el; and of his brethren Asaph the son of Berechi'ah; and of the sons of Merar'i, their breth- 18 ren, Ethan the son of Kusha'iah; and with them their brethren of the second order, Zechari'ah, Ja-a'ziel, Shemir'amoth, Jehi'el, Unni, Eli'ab, Benai'ah, Ma-ase'iah, Mattithi'ah, Eliph'elehu, and Mik-ne'iah, and the gate- 19 keepers O'bed-e'dom and Je-i'el. The singers, Heman, Asaph, and Ethan, were to sound bronze cymbals; 20 Zechari'ah, A'zi-el, Shemir'amoth, Jehi'el, Unni, Eli'ab, Ma-ase'iah, and Benai'ah were to play harps according to 21 Al'amoth; but Mattithi'ah, Eliph'elehu, Mikne'iah, O'bed- e'dom, Je-i'el, and Azazi'ah were to lead with lyres accord- 22 ing to the Shem'inith. Chenani'ah, leader of the Levites in music, should direct the music, for he understood it. 23 Berechi'ah and Elka'nah were to be gatekeepers for the 24 ark. Shebani'ah, Josh'aphat, Nethan'el, Ama'sai, Zechari'- ah, Benai'ah, and Elie'zer, the priests, should blow the trumpets before the ark of God. O'bed-e'dom and Jehi'ah also were to be gatekeepers for the ark.

25 So David and the elders of Israel, and the commanders of thousands, went to bring up the ark of the covenant of the LORD from the house of O'bed-e'dom with rejoicing. 26 And because God helped the Levites who were carrying the ark of the covenant of the LORD, they sacrificed seven 27 bulls and seven rams. David was clothed with a robe of fine linen, as also were all the Levites who were carrying the ark, and the singers, and Chenani'ah the leader of the music of the singers; and David wore a linen ephod. 28 So all Israel brought up the ark of the covenant of the LORD with shouting, to the sound of the horn, trumpets, and cymbals, and made loud music on harps and lyres. 29 And as the ark of the covenant of the LORD came to the city of David, Michal the daughter of Saul looked out of the window, and saw King David dancing and making merry; and she despised him in her heart.

16 And they brought in the ark of God, and set it inside the tent which David had pitched for it; and they offered burnt offerings and peace offerings before 2 God. And when David had finished offering the burnt offerings and the peace offerings, he blessed the people in 3 the name of the LORD, and distributed to all Israel, both men and women, to each a loaf of bread, a portion of meat,[o] and a cake of raisins.

4 Moreover he appointed certain of the Levites as ministers before the ark of the LORD, to invoke, to thank, and 5 to praise the LORD, the God of Israel. Asaph was the chief, and second to him were Zechari'ah, Je-i'el, Shemi'ramoth, Jehi'el, Mattithi'ah, Eli'ab, Benai'ah, O'bed-e'dom, and Je-i'el, who were to play harps and lyres; Asaph was to 6 sound the cymbals, and Benai'ah and Jaha'ziel the priests were to blow trumpets continually, before the ark of the covenant of God.

[1] Heb paraz   [m] That is Lord of breaking through   [n] The meaning of the Hebrew word is uncertain
[o] Compare Gk Syr Vg: Heb uncertain

A Psalm of Thanksgiving

7 Then on that day David first appointed that thanksgiving be sung to the Lord by Asaph and his brethren.

8 O give thanks to the Lord, call on his name,
   make known his deeds among the peoples!
9 Sing to him, sing praises to him,
   tell of all his wonderful works!
10 Glory in his holy name;
   let the hearts of those who seek the Lord rejoice!
11 Seek the Lord and his strength,
   seek his presence continually!
12 Remember the wonderful works that he has done,
   the wonders he wrought, the judgments he uttered.
13 O offspring of Abraham his servant,
   sons of Jacob, his chosen ones!

14 He is the Lord our God;
   his judgments are in all the earth.
15 He is mindful of his covenant for ever,
   of the word that he commanded, for a thousand generations,
16 the covenant which he made with Abraham,
   his sworn promise to Isaac,
17 which he confirmed as a statute to Jacob,
   as an everlasting covenant to Israel,
18 saying, "To you I will give the land of Canaan,
   as your portion for an inheritance."

19 When they were few in number,
   and of little account, and sojourners in it,
20 wandering from nation to nation,
   from one kingdom to another people,
21 he allowed no one to oppress them;
   he rebuked kings on their account,
22 saying, "Touch not my anointed ones,
   do my prophets no harm!"

23 Sing to the Lord, all the earth!
   Tell of his salvation from day to day.
24 Declare his glory among the nations,
   his marvelous works among all the peoples!
25 For great is the Lord, and greatly to be praised,
   and he is to be held in awe above all gods.
26 For all the gods of the peoples are idols;
   but the Lord made the heavens.
27 Honor and majesty are before him;
   strength and joy are in his place.
28 Ascribe to the Lord, O families of the peoples,
   ascribe to the Lord glory and strength!
29 Ascribe to the Lord the glory due his name;
   bring an offering, and come before him!
   Worship the Lord in holy array;
30   tremble before him, all the earth;

p Heb their

yea, the world stands firm, never to be moved.
31 Let the heavens be glad, and let the earth rejoice,
   and let them say among the nations, "The Lord reigns!"
32 Let the sea roar, and all that fills it,
   let the field exult, and everything in it!
33 Then shall the trees of the wood sing for joy
   before the Lord, for he comes to judge the earth.
34 O give thanks to the Lord, for he is good;
   for his steadfast love endures for ever!

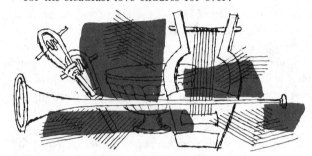

35 Say also:
   "Deliver us, O God of our salvation,
   and gather and save us from among the nations,
   that we may give thanks to thy holy name,
   and glory in thy praise.
36 Blessed be the Lord, the God of Israel,
   from everlasting to everlasting!"
   Then all the people said "Amen!" and praised the Lord.
37 So David left Asaph and his brethren there before the ark of the covenant of the Lord to minister continually
38 before the ark as each day required, and also O'bed-e'dom and his p sixty-eight brethren; while O'bed-e'dom, the son of Jedu'thun, and Hosah were to be gatekeepers.
39 And he left Zadok the priest and his brethren the priests before the tabernacle of the Lord in the high place that
40 was at Gibeon, to offer burnt offerings to the Lord upon the altar of burnt offering continually morning and evening, according to all that is written in the law of the
41 Lord which he commanded Israel. With them were Heman and Jedu'thun, and the rest of those chosen and expressly named to give thanks to the Lord, for his stead-
42 fast love endures for ever. Heman and Jedu'thun had trumpets and cymbals for the music and instruments for sacred song. The sons of Jedu'thun were appointed to the gate.
43 Then all the people departed each to his house, and David went home to bless his household.

David's Desire to Build a Temple

17 Now when David dwelt in his house, David said to Nathan the prophet, "Behold, I dwell in a house of cedar, but the ark of the covenant of the Lord is under
2 a tent." And Nathan said to David, "Do all that is in your heart, for God is with you."

3 But that same night the word of the LORD came to 4 Nathan, "Go and tell my servant David, 'Thus says the 5 LORD: You shall not build me a house to dwell in. For I have not dwelt in a house since the day I led up Israel to this day, but I have gone from tent to tent and from 6 dwelling to dwelling. In all places where I have moved with all Israel, did I speak a word with any of the judges of Israel, whom I commanded to shepherd my people, 7 saying, "Why have you not built me a house of cedar?" ' Now therefore thus shall you say to my servant David, 'Thus says the LORD of hosts, I took you from the pasture, from following the sheep, that you should be prince over 8 my people Israel; and I have been with you wherever you went, and have cut off all your enemies from before you; and I will make for you a name, like the name of the 9 great ones of the earth. And I will appoint a place for my people Israel, and will plant them, that they may dwell in their own place, and be disturbed no more; and violent 10 men shall waste them no more, as formerly, from the time that I appointed judges over my people Israel; and I will subdue all your enemies. Moreover I declare to you 11 that the LORD will build you a house. When your days are fulfilled to go to be with your fathers, I will raise up your offspring after you, one of your own sons, and I will 12 establish his kingdom. He shall build a house for me, 13 and I will establish his throne for ever. I will be his father, and he shall be my son; I will not take my steadfast love from him, as I took it from him who was before 14 you, but I will confirm him in my house and in my kingdom for ever and his throne shall be established for 15 ever.' " In accordance with all these words, and in accordance with all this vision, Nathan spoke to David.

16 Then King David went in and sat before the LORD, and said, "Who am I, O LORD God, and what is my 17 house, that thou hast brought me thus far? And this was a small thing in thy eyes, O God; thou hast also spoken of thy servant's house for a great while to come, and hast 18 shown me future generations,q O LORD God! And what more can David say to thee for honoring thy servant? 19 For thou knowest thy servant. For thy servant's sake, O LORD, and according to thy own heart, thou hast wrought all this greatness, in making known all these great things. 20 There is none like thee, O LORD, and there is no God besides thee, according to all that we have heard with our 21 ears. What otherr nation on earth is like thy people Israel, whom God went to redeem to be his people, making for thyself a name for great and terrible things, in driving out nations before thy people whom thou didst redeem 22 from Egypt? And thou didst make thy people Israel to be thy people for ever; and thou, O LORD, didst become 23 their God. And now, O LORD, let the word which thou hast spoken concerning thy servant and concerning his house be established for ever, and do as thou hast spoken; 24 and thy name will be established and magnified for ever,

saying, 'The LORD of hosts, the God of Israel, is Israel's God,' and the house of thy servant David will be estab- 25 lished before thee. For thou, my God, hast revealed to thy servant that thou wilt build a house for him; therefore thy 26 servant has found courage to pray before thee. And now, O LORD, thou art God, and thou hast promised this good 27 thing to thy servant; now therefore may it please thee to bless the house of thy servant, that it may continue for ever before thee; for what thou, O LORD, hast blessed is blessed for ever."

David's Victories

18 After this David defeated the Philistines and subdued them, and he took Gath and its villages out of the hand of the Philistines.

2 And he defeated Moab, and the Mo'abites became servants to David and brought tribute.

3 David also defeated Hadade'zer king of Zobah, toward Hamath, as he went to set up his monuments at the river 4 Eu-phra'tes. And David took from him a thousand chariots, seven thousand horsemen, and twenty thousand foot soldiers; and David hamstrung all the chariot horses, 5 but left enough for a hundred chariots. And when the Syrians of Damascus came to help Hadade'zer king of Zobah, David slew twenty-two thousand men of the 6 Syrians. Then David put garrisonst in Syria of Damascus; and the Syrians became servants to David, and brought tribute. And the LORD gave victory to David 7 wherever he went. And David took the shields of gold which were carried by the servants of Hadade'zer, and 8 brought them to Jerusalem. And from Tibhath and from Cun, cities of Hadade'zer, David took very much bronze; with it Solomon made the bronze sea and the pillars and the vessels of bronze.

9 When To'u king of Hamath heard that David had defeated the whole army of Hadade'zer, king of Zobah, 10 he sent his son Hador'am to King David, to greet him, and to congratulate him because he had fought against Hadade'zer and defeated him; for Hadade'zer had often been at war with To'u. And he sent all sorts of articles of 11 gold, of silver, and of bronze; these also King David dedicated to the LORD, together with the silver and gold which he had carried off from all the nations, from Edom, Moab, the Ammonites, the Philistines, and Am'alek.

12 And Abi'shai, the son of Zeru'iah, slew eighteen thou- 13 sand E'domites in the Valley of Salt. And he put garrisons in Edom; and all the E'domites became David's servants. And the LORD gave victory to David wherever he went.

14 So David reigned over all Israel; and he administered 15 justice and equity to all his people. And Jo'ab the son of Zeru'iah was over the army; and Jehosh'aphat the son 16 of Ahi'lud was recorder; and Zadok the son of Ahi'tub and Ahim'elech the son of Abi'athar were priests; and 17 Shavsha was secretary; and Bena'iah the son of Jehoi'ada

q Cn: Heb uncertain   r Gk Vg: Heb one   s Heb hand   t Gk Vg 2 S 8.6 Compare Syr: Heb lacks *garrisons*

was over the Cher′ethites and the Pel′ethites; and David's sons were the chief officials in the service of the king.

19 Now after this Nahash the king of the Ammonites died, and his son reigned in his stead. And David said, "I will deal loyally with Hanun the son of Nahash, for his father dealt loyally with me." So David sent messengers to console him concerning his father. And David's servants came to Hanun in the land of the Am-3 monites, to console him. But the princes of the Ammonites said to Hanun, "Do you think, because David has sent comforters to you, that he is honoring your father? Have not his servants come to you to search and to overthrow 4 and to spy out the land?" So Hanun took David's serv-ants, and shaved them, and cut off their garments in 5 the middle, at their hips, and sent them away; and they departed. When David was told concerning the men, he sent to meet them, for the men were greatly ashamed. And the king said, "Remain at Jericho until your beards have grown, and then return."

6 When the Ammonites saw that they had made them-selves odious to David, Hanun and the Ammonites sent a thousand talents of silver to hire chariots and horsemen from Mesopota′mia, from Aram-ma′acah, and from 7 Zobah. They hired thirty-two thousand chariots and the king of Ma′acah with his army, who came and encamped before Med′eba. And the Ammonites were mustered from 8 their cities and came to battle. When David heard of it, 9 he sent Jo′ab and all the army of the mighty men. And the Ammonites came out and drew up in battle array at the entrance of the city, and the kings who had come were by themselves in the open country.

10 When Jo′ab saw that the battle was set against him both in front and in the rear, he chose some of the picked men of Israel, and arrayed them against the Syrians; 11 the rest of his men he put in the charge of Abi′shai his brother, and they were arrayed against the Ammonites. 12 And he said, "If the Syrians are too strong for me, then you shall help me; but if the Ammonites are too strong 13 for you, then I will help you. Be of good courage, and let us play the man for our people, and for the cities of our God; and may the LORD do what seems good to him." 14 So Jo′ab and the people who were with him drew near before the Syrians for battle; and they fled before him. 15 And when the Ammonites saw that the Syrians fled, they likewise fled before Abi′shai, Jo′ab's brother, and entered the city. Then Jo′ab came to Jerusalem.

16 But when the Syrians saw that they had been defeated by Israel, they sent messengers and brought out the Syrians who were beyond the Eu-phra′tes, with Shophach the commander of the army of Hadade′zer at their head. 17 And when it was told David, he gathered all Israel to-gether, and crossed the Jordan, and came to them, and drew up his forces against them. And when David set the battle in array against the Syrians, they fought with him.

18 And the Syrians fled before Israel; and David slew of the Syrians the men of seven thousand chariots, and forty thousand foot soldiers, and killed also Shophach the 19 commander of their army. And when the servants of Hadade′zer saw that they had been defeated by Israel, they made peace with David, and became subject to him. So the Syrians were not willing to help the Ammonites any more.

20 In the spring of the year, the time when kings go forth to battle, Jo′ab led out the army, and ravaged the country of the Ammonites, and came and besieged Rabbah. But David remained at Jerusalem. And Jo′ab 2 smote Rabbah, and overthrew it. And David took the crown of their king ᵘ from his head; he found that it weighed a talent of gold, and in it was a precious stone; and it was placed on David's head. And he brought forth 3 the spoil of the city, a very great amount. And he brought forth the people who were in it, and set them to labor ᵛ with saws and iron picks and axes; ʷ and thus David did to all the cities of the Ammonites. Then David and all the people returned to Jerusalem.

4 And after this there arose war with the Philistines at Gezer; then Sib′becai the Hu′shathite slew Sip′pai, who was one of the descendants of the giants; and the 5 Philistines were subdued. And there was again war with the Philistines; and Elha′nan the son of Ja′ir slew Lahmi the brother of Goliath the Gittite, the shaft of whose spear 6 was like a weaver's beam. And there was again war at Gath, where there was a man of great stature, who had six fingers on each hand, and six toes on each foot, twenty-four in number; and he also was descended from the 7 giants. And when he taunted Israel, Jonathan the son of 8 Shim′e-a, David's brother, slew him. These were de-scended from the giants in Gath; and they fell by the hand of David and by the hand of his servants.

Census and Plague

21 Satan stood up against Israel, and incited David to number Israel. So David said to Jo′ab and the commanders of the army, "Go, number Israel, from Beer-sheba to Dan, and bring me a report, that I may 3 know their number." But Jo′ab said, "May the LORD add to his people a hundred times as many as they are! Are they not, my lord the king, all of them my lord's servants? Why then should my lord require this? Why should he 4 bring guilt upon Israel?" But the king's word prevailed against Jo′ab. So Jo′ab departed and went throughout all 5 Israel, and came back to Jerusalem. And Jo′ab gave the sum of the numbering of the people of David. In all Israel there were one million one hundred thousand men who drew the sword, and in Judah four hundred and 6 seventy thousand who drew the sword. But he did not include Levi and Benjamin in the numbering, for the king's command was abhorrent to Jo′ab.

ᵘ Or *Milcom* See 1 K 11.5   ᵛ Compare 2 S 12.31: Heb *he sawed*   ʷ Compare 2 S 12.31: Heb *saws*

7 But God was displeased with this thing, and he smote
8 Israel. And David said to God, "I have sinned greatly in that I have done this thing. But now, I pray thee, take away the iniquity of thy servant; for I have done very
9 foolishly." And the LORD spoke to Gad, David's seer,
10 saying, "Go and say to David, 'Thus says the LORD, Three things I offer you; choose one of them, that I may do it
11 to you.'" So Gad came to David and said to him, "Thus
12 says the LORD, 'Take which you will: either three years of famine; or three months of devastation by your foes, while the sword of your enemies overtakes you; or else three days of the sword of the LORD, pestilence upon the land, and the angel of the LORD destroying throughout all the territory of Israel.' Now decide what answer I shall
13 return to him who sent me." Then David said to Gad, "I am in great distress; let me fall into the hand of the LORD, for his mercy is very great; but let me not fall into the hand of man."

14 So the LORD sent a pestilence upon Israel; and there fell
15 seventy thousand men of Israel. And God sent the angel to Jerusalem to destroy it; but when he was about to destroy it, the LORD saw, and he repented of the evil; and he said to the destroying angel, "It is enough; now stay your hand." And the angel of the LORD was standing by
16 the threshing floor of Ornan the Jeb'usite. And David lifted his eyes and saw the angel of the LORD standing between earth and heaven, and in his hand a drawn sword stretched out over Jerusalem. Then David and the elders,
17 clothed in sackcloth, fell upon their faces. And David said to God, "Was it not I who gave command to number the people? It is I who have sinned and done very wickedly. But these sheep, what have they done? Let thy hand, I pray thee, O LORD my God, be against me and against my father's house; but let not the plague be upon thy people."

18 Then the angel of the LORD commanded Gad to say to David that David should go up and rear an altar to the LORD on the threshing floor of Ornan the Jeb'usite.
19 So David went up at Gad's word, which he had spoken
20 in the name of the LORD. Now Ornan was threshing wheat; he turned and saw the angel, and his four sons
21 who were with him hid themselves. As David came to Ornan, Ornan looked and saw David and went forth from the threshing floor, and did obeisance to David with his
22 face to the ground. And David said to Ornan, "Give me the site of the threshing floor that I may build on it an altar to the LORD—give it to me at its full price—that the
23 plague may be averted from the people." Then Ornan said to David, "Take it; and let my lord the king do what seems good to him; see, I give the oxen for burnt offerings, and the threshing sledges for the wood, and the
24 wheat for a cereal offering. I give it all." But King David said to Ornan, "No, but I will buy it for the full price; I

will not take for the LORD what is yours, nor offer burnt
25 offerings which cost me nothing." So David paid Ornan
26 six hundred shekels of gold by weight for the site. And David built there an altar to the LORD and presented burnt offerings and peace offerings, and called upon the LORD, and he answered him with fire from heaven upon the altar
27 of burnt offering. Then the LORD commanded the angel; and he put his sword back into its sheath.

28 At that time, when David saw that the LORD had answered him at the threshing floor of Ornan the Jeb'usite,
29 he made his sacrifices there. For the tabernacle of the LORD, which Moses had made in the wilderness, and the altar of burnt offering were at that time in the high place
30 at Gibeon; but David could not go before it to inquire of God, for he was afraid of the sword of the angel of the
22 1 LORD. Then David said, "Here shall be the house of the LORD God and here the altar of burnt offering for Israel."

Preparations for the Temple

2 David commanded to gather together the aliens who were in the land of Israel, and he set stonecutters to pre-
3 pare dressed stones for building the house of God. David also provided great stores of iron for nails for the doors of the gates and for clamps, as well as bronze in quantities
4 beyond weighing, and cedar timbers without number; for the Sido'nians and Tyrians brought great quantities of
5 cedar to David. For David said, "Solomon my son is young and inexperienced, and the house that is to be built for the LORD must be exceedingly magnificent, of fame and glory throughout all lands; I will therefore make preparation for it." So David provided materials in great quantity before his death.

6 Then he called for Solomon his son, and charged him
7 to build a house for the LORD, the God of Israel. David said to Solomon, "My son, I had it in my heart to build
8 a house to the name of the LORD my God. But the word of the LORD came to me, saying, 'You have shed much blood and have waged great wars; you shall not build a house to my name, because you have shed so much
9 blood before me upon the earth. Behold, a son shall be born to you; he shall be a man of peace. I will give him peace from all his enemies round about; for his name

shall be Solomon, and I will give peace and quiet to
10 Israel in his days. He shall build a house for my name.
He shall be my son, and I will be his father, and I will
11 establish his royal throne in Israel for ever.' Now, my
son, the LORD be with you, so that you may succeed in
building the house of the LORD your God, as he has
12 spoken concerning you. Only, may the LORD grant you
discretion and understanding, that when he gives you
charge over Israel you may keep the law of the LORD your
13 God. Then you will prosper if you are careful to observe
the statutes and the ordinances which the LORD commanded Moses for Israel. Be strong, and of good courage.
14 Fear not; be not dismayed. With great pains I have
provided for the house of the LORD a hundred thousand
talents of gold, a million talents of silver, and bronze and
iron beyond weighing, for there is so much of it; timber
and stone too I have provided. To these you must add.
15 You have an abundance of workmen: stonecutters,
masons, carpenters, and all kinds of craftsmen without
16 number, skilled in working gold, silver, bronze, and iron.
Arise and be doing! The LORD be with you!"
17 David also commanded all the leaders of Israel to help
18 Solomon his son, saying, "Is not the LORD your God with
you? And has he not given you peace on every side? For
he has delivered the inhabitants of the land into my hand;
and the land is subdued before the LORD and his people.
19 Now set your mind and heart to seek the LORD your God.
Arise and build the sanctuary of the LORD God, so that
the ark of the covenant of the LORD and the holy vessels
of God may be brought into a house built for the name of
the LORD."

GROUND PLAN OF SOLOMON'S TEMPLE

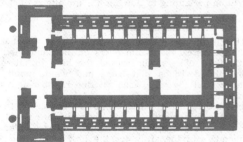

Duties of the Levites

23 When David was old and full of days, he made Solomon
his son king over Israel.
2 David assembled all the leaders of Israel and the priests and
3 the Levites. The Levites, thirty years old and upward, were
numbered, and the total was thirty-eight thousand men.
4 "Twenty-four thousand of these," David said, "shall have
charge of the work in the house of the LORD, six thousand shall
5 be officers and judges, four thousand gatekeepers, and four
thousand shall offer praises to the LORD with the instruments
6 which I have made for praise." And David organized them in
divisions corresponding to the sons of Levi: Gershom, Kohath,
and Merar'i.
7, 8 The sons of Gershom x were Ladan and Shim'e-i. The sons of
9 Ladan: Jehi'el the chief, and Zetham, and Jo'el, three. The sons
of Shim'e-i: Shelo'moth, Ha'zi-el, and Haran, three. These were
10 the heads of the fathers' houses of Ladan. And the sons of
Shim'e-i: Jahath, Zina, and Je'ush, and Beri'ah. These four were

11 the sons of Shim'e-i. Jahath was the chief, and Zizah the second;
but Je'ush and Beri'ah had not many sons, therefore they became a father's house in one reckoning.
12 The sons of Kohath: Amram, Izhar, Hebron, and Uz'ziel, four.
13 The sons of Amram: Aaron and Moses. Aaron was set apart to
consecrate the most holy things, that he and his sons for ever
should burn incense before the LORD, and minister to him and
14 pronounce blessings in his name for ever. But the sons of Moses
15 the man of God were named among the tribe of Levi. The sons
16 of Moses: Gershom and Elie'zer. The sons of Gershom: Sheb'uel
17 the chief. The sons of Elie'zer: Rehabi'ah the chief; Elie'zer had
18 no other sons, but the sons of Rehabi'ah were very many. The
19 sons of Izhar: Shelo'mith the chief. The sons of Hebron: Jeri'ah
the chief, Amari'ah the second, Jaha'ziel the third, and Jekame'-
20 am the fourth. The sons of Uz'ziel: Micah the chief and Isshi'ah
the second.
21 The sons of Merar'i: Mahli and Mushi. The sons of Mahli:
22 Elea'zar and Kish. Elea'zar died having no sons, but only
23 daughters; their kinsmen, the sons of Kish, married them. The
sons of Mushi: Mahli, Eder, and Jer'emoth, three.
24 These were the sons of Levi by their fathers' houses, the
heads of fathers' houses as they were registered according to
the number of the names of the individuals from twenty years
old and upward who were to do the work for the service of
25 the house of the LORD. For David said, "The LORD, the God of
Israel, has given peace to his people; and he dwells in Jerusalem
26 for ever. And so the Levites no longer need to carry the taber-
27 nacle or any of the things for its service"— for by the last words
of David these were the number of the Levites from twenty
28 years old and upward—"but their duty shall be to assist the
sons of Aaron for the service of the house of the LORD, having
the care of the courts and the chambers, the cleansing of all
that is holy, and any work for the service of the house of God;
29 to assist also with the showbread, the flour for the cereal offering, the wafers of unleavened bread, the baked offering, the
offering mixed with oil, and all measures of quantity or size.
30 And they shall stand every morning, thanking and praising the
31 LORD, and likewise at evening, and whenever burnt offerings are
offered to the LORD on sabbaths, new moons, and feast days,
according to the number required of them, continually before
32 the LORD. Thus they shall keep charge of the tent of meeting and
the sanctuary, and shall attend the sons of Aaron, their
brethren, for the service of the house of the LORD."

24 The divisions of the sons of Aaron were these. The
sons of Aaron: Nadab, Abi'hu, Elea'zar, and Ith'amar.
2 But Nadab and Abi'hu died before their father, and had no
3 children, so Elea'zar and Ith'amar became the priests. With the
help of Zadok of the sons of Elea'zar, and Ahim'elech of the
sons of Ith'amar, David organized them according to the ap-
4 pointed duties in their service. Since more chief men were found
among the sons of Elea'zar than among the sons of Ith'amar,
they organized them under sixteen heads of fathers' houses of
5 the sons of Elea'zar, and eight of the sons of Ith'amar. They
organized them by lot, all alike, for there were officers of the
sanctuary and officers of God among both the sons of Elea'zar
6 and the sons of Ith'amar. And the scribe Shemai'ah the son of
Nethan'el, a Levite, recorded them in the presence of the king,
and the princes, and Zadok the priest, and Ahim'elech the son
of Abi'athar, and the heads of the fathers' houses of the priests
and of the Levites; one father's house being chosen for Elea'zar
and one chosen for Ith'amar.
7, 8 The first lot fell to Jehoi'arib, the second to Jeda'iah, the
9 third to Harim, the fourth to Se-o'rim, the fifth to Malchi'jah,
10 the sixth to Mij'amin, the seventh to Hakkoz, the eighth to
11, 12 Abi'jah, the ninth to Jeshua, the tenth to Shecani'ah, the
13 eleventh to Eli'ashib, the twelfth to Jakim, the thirteenth to
14 Huppah, the fourteenth to Jesheb'e-ab, the fifteenth to Bilgah,
15 the sixteenth to Immer, the seventeenth to Hezir, the eighteenth
16 to Hap'pizzez, the nineteenth to Pethahi'ah, the twentieth to
17 Jehez'kel, the twenty-first to Jachin, the twenty-second to
18 Gamul, the twenty-third to Dela'iah, the twenty-fourth to
19 Ma-azi'ah. These had as their appointed duty in their service
to come into the house of the LORD according to the procedure
established for them by Aaron their father, as the LORD God
of Israel had commanded him.
20 And of the rest of the sons of Levi: of the sons of Amram,
21 Shu'ba-el; of the sons of Shu'ba-el, Jehde'iah. Of Rehabi'ah: of
22 the sons of Rehabi'ah, Isshi'ah, the chief. Of the Iz'harites:
23 Shelo'moth; of the sons of Shelo'moth, Jahath. The sons of
Hebron: y Jeri'ah the chief,z Amari'ah the second, Jahazi'el the

x Vg Compare Gk Syr: Heb to the Gershonite   y See 23.19: Heb lacks Hebron   z See 23.19: Heb lacks the chief

24 third, Jekame'am the fourth. The sons of Uz'ziel, Micah; of 25 the sons of Micah, Shamir. The brother of Micah, Isshi'ah; of 26 the sons of Isshi'ah, Zechari'ah. The sons of Merar'i: Mahli and 27 Mushi. The sons of Ja-azi'ah: Beno. The sons of Merar'i: of 28 Ja-azi'ah, Beno, Shoham, Zaccur, and Ibri. Of Mahli: Elea'zar, 29 who had no sons. Of Kish, the sons of Kish: Jerah'meel. 30 The sons of Mushi: Mahli, Eder, and Jer'imoth. These were 31 the sons of the Levites according to their fathers' houses. These also, the head of each father's house and his younger brother alike, cast lots, just as their brethren the sons of Aaron, in the presence of King David, Zadok, Ahim'elech, and the heads of fathers' houses of the priests and of the Levites.

25 David and the chiefs of the service also set apart for the service certain of the sons of Asaph, and of Heman, and of Jedu'thun, who should prophesy with lyres, with harps, 2 and with cymbals. The list of those who did the work and of their duties was: Of the sons of Asaph: Zaccur, Joseph, Nethani'ah, and Ashare'lah, sons of Asaph, under the direction 3 of Asaph, who prophesied under the direction of the king. Of Jedu'thun, the sons of Jedu'thun: Gedali'ah, Zeri, Jesha'iah, Shim'e-i,ᵃ Hashabi'ah, and Mattithi'ah, six, under the direction of their father Jedu'thun, who prophesied with the lyre in thanks- 4 giving and praise to the LORD. Of Heman, the sons of Heman: Bukki'ah, Mattani'ah, Uz'ziel, Shebu'el, and Jer'imoth, Hanani- ah, Hana'ni, Eli'athah, Giddal'ti, and Romam'ti-e'zer, Joshbek- 5 ash'ah, Mallo'thi, Hothir, Maha'zi-oth. All these were the sons of Heman the king's seer, according to the promise of God to exalt him; for God had given Heman fourteen sons and three 6 daughters. They were all under the direction of their father in the music in the house of the LORD with cymbals, harps, and lyres for the service of the house of God. Asaph, Jedu'thun, 7 and Heman were under the order of the king. The number of them along with their brethren, who were trained in singing to the LORD, all who were skilful, was two hundred and eighty- 8 eight. And they cast lots for their duties, small and great, teacher and pupil alike.

9 The first lot fell for Asaph to Joseph; the second to Gedali'ah, 10 to him and his brethren and his sons, twelve; the third to 11 Zaccur, his sons and his brethren, twelve; the fourth to Izri 12 his sons and his brethren, twelve; the fifth to Nethani'ah, his 13 sons and his brethren, twelve; the sixth to Bukki'ah, his sons 14 and his brethren, twelve; the seventh to Jeshare'lah, his sons 15 and his brethren, twelve; the eighth to Jesha'iah, his 16 sons and his brethren, twelve; the ninth to Mattani'ah, his sons 17 and his brethren, twelve; the tenth to Shim'e-i, his sons and his 18 brethren, twelve; the eleventh to Az'arel, his sons and his 19 brethren, twelve; the twelfth to Hashabi'ah, his sons and 20 his brethren, twelve; to the thirteenth, Shu'ba-el, his sons 21 and his brethren, twelve; to the fourteenth, Mattithi'ah, his 22 sons and his brethren, twelve; to the fifteenth, to Jer'emoth, 23 his sons and his brethren, twelve; to the sixteenth, to 24 Hanani'ah, his sons and his brethren, twelve; to the seven- teenth, to Josh-bekash'ah, his sons and his brethren, twelve; 25 to the eighteenth, to Hana'ni, his sons and his brethren, 26 twelve; to the nineteenth, to Mallo'thi, his sons and his 27 brethren, twelve; to the twentieth, to Eli'athah, his sons and 28 his brethren, twelve; to the twenty-first, to Hothir, his sons 29 and his brethren, twelve; to the twenty-second, to Giddal'ti, 30 his sons and his brethren, twelve; to the twenty-third, to 31 Maha'zi-oth, his sons and his brethren, twelve; to the twenty- fourth, to Romam'ti-e'zer, his sons and his brethren, twelve.

26 As for the divisions of the gatekeepers: of the Ko'- rahites, Meshelemi'ah the son of Ko're, of the sons of 2 Asaph. And Meshelemi'ah had sons: Zechari'ah the first-born, Jedi'a-el the second, Zebadi'ah the third, Jath'ni-el the fourth, 3 Elam the fifth, Jehoha'nan the sixth, El'ie-ho-e'nai the seventh. 4 And O'bed-e'dom had sons: Shemai'ah the first-born, Jehoz'- abad the second, Jo'ah the third, Sachar the fourth, Nethan'el 5 the fifth, Am'mi-el the sixth, Is'sachar the seventh, Pe-ul'lethai 6 the eighth; for God blessed him. Also to his son Shemai'ah were sons born who were rulers in their fathers' houses, for they 7 were men of great ability. The sons of Shemai'ah: Othni, Reph'- a-el, Obed, and Elza'bad, whose brethren were able men, Eli'hu 8 and Semachi'ah. All these were of the sons of O'bed-e'dom with their sons and brethren, able men qualified for the service; 9 sixty-two of O'bed-e'dom. And Meshelemi'ah had sons and 10 brethren, able men, eighteen. And Hosah, of the sons of Merar'i, had sons: Shimri the chief (for though he was not the first-born, 11 his father made him chief), Hilki'ah the second, Tebali'ah the third, Zechari'ah the fourth: all the sons and brethren of Hosah were thirteen.

12 These divisions of the gatekeepers, corresponding to their chief men, had duties, just as their brethren did, ministering in 13 the house of the LORD; and they cast lots by fathers' houses, 14 small and great alike, for their gates. The lot for the east fell to Shelemi'ah. They cast lots also for his son Zechari'ah, a 15 shrewd counselor, and his lot came out for the north. O'bed-e'- dom's came out for the south, and to his sons was allotted the 16 storehouse. For Shuppim and Hosah it came out for the west, at the gate of Shal'lecheth on the road that goes up. Watch 17 corresponded to watch. On the east there were six each day,ᵇ on the north four each day, on the south four each day, as well 18 as two and two at the storehouse; and for the parbar ᶜ on the 19 west there were four at the road and two at the parbar. These were the divisions of the gatekeepers among the Ko'rahites and the sons of Merar'i.

20 And of the Levites, Ahi'jah had charge of the treasuries of the 21 house of God and the treasuries of the dedicated gifts. The sons of Ladan, the sons of the Gershonites belonging to Ladan, the heads of the fathers' houses belonging to Ladan the Gershonite: Jehi'eli.ᵈ 22 The sons of Jehi'eli, Zetham and Jo'el his brother, were in 23 charge of the treasuries of the house of the LORD. Of the Am'- ramites, the Iz'harites, the He'bronites, and the Uz'zielites— 24 and Sheb'uel the son of Gershom, son of Moses, was chief officer 25 in charge of the treasuries. His brethren: from Elie'zer were his son Rehabi'ah, and his son Jesh'a-iah, and his son Joram, and 26 his son Zichri, and his son Shelo'moth. This Shelo'moth and his brethren were in charge of all the treasuries of the dedicated gifts which David the king, and the heads of the fathers' houses, and the officers of the thousands and the hundreds, and the 27 commanders of the army, had dedicated. From spoil won in battles they dedicated gifts for the maintenance of the house 28 of the LORD. Also all that Samuel the seer, and Saul the son of Kish, and Abner the son of Ner, and Jo'ab the son of Zeru'iah had dedicated—all dedicated gifts were in the care of Shelo'- moth ᵉ and his brethren. 29 Of the Iz'harites, Chenani'ah and his sons were appointed to 30 outside duties for Israel, as officers and judges. Of the He'- bronites, Hashabi'ah and his brethren, one thousand seven hun- dred men of ability, had the oversight of Israel westward of the Jordan for all the work of the LORD and for the service of the 31 king. Of the He'bronites, Jeri'jah was chief of the He'bronites of whatever genealogy or fathers' houses. (In the fortieth year of David's reign search was made and men of great ability among 32 them were found at Jazer in Gilead.) King David appointed him and his brethren, two thousand seven hundred men of ability, heads of fathers' houses, to have the oversight of the Reubenites, the Gadites, and the half-tribe of the Manas'sites for everything pertaining to God and for the affairs of the king.

Military and Civil Administration

27 This is the list of the people of Israel, the heads of fathers' houses, the commanders of thousands and hun- dreds, and their officers who served the king in all matters concerning the divisions that came and went, month after month throughout the year, each division numbering twenty- four thousand: 2 Jasho'beam the son of Zab'di-el was in charge of the first 3 division in the first month; in his division were twenty-four 4 thousand. He was a descendant of Perez, and was chief of all the commanders of the army for the first month. Dodai the Aho'hite ᶠ was in charge of the division of the second month; in 5 his division were twenty-four thousand. The third commander, for the third month was Benai'ah, the son of Jehoi'ada the priest, as chief; in his division were twenty-four thousand. 6 This is the Benai'ah who was a mighty man of the thirty and in command of the thirty; Ammiz'abad his son was in charge of 7 his division.ᵍ As'ahel the brother of Jo'ab was fourth, for the fourth month, and his son Zebadi'ah after him; in his division 8 were twenty-four thousand. The fifth commander, for the fifth month, was Shamhuth, the Iz'rahite; in his division were 9 twenty-four thousand. Sixth, for the sixth month, was Ira, the son of Ikkesh the Teko'ite; in his division were twenty-four 10 thousand. Seventh, for the seventh month, was Helez the Pel'onite, of the sons of E'phraim; in his division were twenty- 11 four thousand. Eighth, for the eighth month, was Sib'becai the Hu'shathite, of the Ze'rahites; in his division were twenty-four 12 thousand. Ninth, for the ninth month, was Abi-e'zer of An'a- thoth, a Benjaminite; in his division were twenty-four thou- 13 sand. Tenth, for the tenth month, was Ma'harai of Netoph'ah,

ᵃ One Ms: Gk: Heb lacks Shimei   ᵇ Gk: Heb Levites   ᶜ The meaning of the word parbar is unknown
ᵈ The Hebrew text of verse 21 is confused   ᵉ Heb Shelomith   ᶠ Gk: Heb Ahohite and his division and Mikloth the chief officer
ᵍ Gk Vg: Heb was his division

of the Ze′rahites; in his division were twenty-four thousand.
14 Eleventh, for the eleventh month, was Benai′ah of Pir′athon, of the sons of E′phraim; in his division were twenty-four
15 thousand. Twelfth, for the twelfth month, was Heldai the Netoph′athite, of Oth′ni-el; in his division were twenty-four thousand.
16 Over the tribes of Israel, for the Reubenites Elie′zer the son of Zichri was chief officer; for the Simeonites, Shephati′ah the
17 son of Ma′acah; for Levi, Hashabi′ah the son of Kem′uel; for
18 Aaron, Zadok; for Judah, Eli′hu, one of David's brothers; for
19 Is′sachar, Omri the son of Michael; for Zeb′ulun, Ishma′iah the son of Obadi′ah; for Naph′tali, Jer′emoth the son of Az′riel;
20 for the E′phraimites, Hoshe′a the son of Azazi′ah; for the half-
21 tribe of Manas′seh, Jo′el the son of Peda′iah; for the half-tribe of Manas′seh in Gilead, Iddo the son of Zechari′ah; for Benja-
22 min, Ja-a′si-el the son of Abner; for Dan, Az′arel the son of
23 Jero′ham. These were the leaders of the tribes of Israel. David did not number those below twenty years of age, for the LORD had promised to make Israel as many as the stars of heaven.
24 Jo′ab the son of Zeru′iah began to number, but did not finish; yet wrath came upon Israel for this, and the number was not entered in the chronicles of King David.
25 Over the king's treasuries was Az′maveth the son of Ad′i-el; and over the treasuries in the country, in the cities, in the villages and in the towers, was Jonathan the son of Uzzi′ah;
26 and over those who did the work of the field for tilling the soil
27 was Ezri the son of Chelub; and over the vineyards was Shim′-e-i the Ra′mathite; and over the produce of the vineyards for
28 the wine cellars was Zabdi the Shiphmite. Over the olive and sycamore trees in the Shephe′lah was Ba′al-ha′nan the Gede′-
29 rite; and over the stores of oil was Jo′ash. Over the herds that pastured in Sharon was Shitrai the Shar′onite; over the herds
30 in the valleys was Shaphat the son of Adlai. Over the camels was Obil the Ish′maelite; and over the she-asses was Jehde′iah
31 the Meron′othite. Over the flocks was Jaziz the Hagrite. All these were stewards of King David's property.
32 Jonathan, David's uncle, was a counselor, being a man of understanding and a scribe; he and Jehi′el the son of Hach′-
33 moni attended the king's sons. Ahith′ophel was the king's counselor, and Hushai the Archite was the king's friend.
34 Ahith′ophel was succeeded by Jehoi′ada the son of Benai′ah, and Abi′athar. Jo′ab was commander of the king's army.

David's Farewell

28 David assembled at Jerusalem all the officials of Israel, the officials of the tribes, the officers of the divisions that served the king, the commanders of thousands, the commanders of hundreds, the stewards of all the property and cattle of the king and his sons, together with the palace officials, the mighty men, and all the
2 seasoned warriors. Then King David rose to his feet and said: "Hear me, my brethren and my people. I had it in my heart to build a house of rest for the ark of the covenant of the LORD, and for the footstool of our God;
3 and I made preparations for building. But God said to me, 'You may not build a house for my name, for you
4 are a warrior and have shed blood.' Yet the LORD God of Israel chose me from all my father's house to be king over Israel for ever; for he chose Judah as leader, and in the house of Judah my father's house, and among my father's sons he took pleasure in me to make me king over
5 all Israel. And of all my sons (for the LORD has given me many sons) he has chosen Solomon my son to sit upon the throne of the kingdom of the LORD over Israel.
6 He said to me, 'It is Solomon your son who shall build my house and my courts, for I have chosen him to be
7 my son, and I will be his father. I will establish his kingdom for ever if he continues resolute in keeping my

h Cn: Heb *upon me*

8 commandments and my ordinances, as he is today.' Now therefore in the sight of all Israel, the assembly of the LORD, and in the hearing of our God, observe and seek out all the commandments of the LORD your God; that you may possess this good land, and leave it for an inheritance to your children after you for ever.
9 "And you, Solomon my son, know the God of your father, and serve him with a whole heart and with a willing mind; for the LORD searches all hearts, and understands every plan and thought. If you seek him, he will be found by you; but if you forsake him, he will cast you
10 off for ever. Take heed now, for the LORD has chosen you to build a house for the sanctuary; be strong, and do it."
11 Then David gave Solomon his son the plan of the vestibule of the temple, and of its houses, its treasuries, its upper rooms, and its inner chambers, and of the room for
12 the mercy seat; and the plan of all that he had in mind for the courts of the house of the LORD, all the surrounding chambers, the treasuries of the house of God, and the
13 treasuries for dedicated gifts; for the divisions of the priests and of the Levites, and all the work of the service in the house of the LORD; for all the vessels for the
14 service in the house of the LORD, the weight of gold for all golden vessels for each service, the weight of silver vessels
15 for each service, the weight of the golden lampstands and their lamps, the weight of gold for each lampstand and its lamps, the weight of silver for a lampstand and its lamps, according to the use of each lampstand in the
16 service, the weight of gold for each table for the show-
17 bread, the silver for the silver tables, and pure gold for the forks, the basins, and the cups; for the golden bowls and the weight of each; for the silver bowls and the
18 weight of each; for the altar of incense made of refined gold, and its weight; also his plan for the golden chariot of the cherubim that spread their wings and covered the
19 ark of the covenant of the LORD. All this he made clear by the writing from the hand of the LORD concerning it,h all the work to be done according to the plan.
20 Then David said to Solomon his son, "Be strong and of good courage, and do it. Fear not, be not dismayed; for the LORD God, even my God, is with you. He will not fail you or forsake you, until all the work for the service of the
21 house of the LORD is finished. And behold the divisions of the priests and the Levites for all the service of the house of God; and with you in all the work will be every willing man who has skill for any kind of service; also the officers and all the people will be wholly at your command."

29 And David the king said to all the assembly, "Solomon my son, whom alone God has chosen, is young and inexperienced, and the work is great; for the
2 palace will not be for man but for the LORD God. So I have provided for the house of my God, so far as I was able, the gold for the things of gold, the silver for the

things of silver, and the bronze for the things of bronze, the iron for the things of iron, and wood for the things of wood, besides great quantities of onyx and stones for setting, antimony, colored stones, all sorts of precious ³ stones, and marble. Moreover, in addition to all that I have provided for the holy house, I have a treasure of my own of gold and silver, and because of my devotion to the house of my God I give it to the house of my God: ⁴ three thousand talents of gold, of the gold of Ophir, and seven thousand talents of refined silver, for overlaying the ⁵ walls of the house, and for all the work to be done by craftsmen, gold for the things of gold and silver for the things of silver. Who then will offer willingly, consecrating himself today to the LORD?"

⁶ Then the heads of fathers' houses made their freewill offerings, as did also the leaders of the tribes, the commanders of thousands and of hundreds, and the officers ⁷ over the king's work. They gave for the service of the house of God five thousand talents and ten thousand darics of gold, ten thousand talents of silver, eighteen thousand talents of bronze, and a hundred thousand ⁸ talents of iron. And whoever had precious stones gave them to the treasury of the house of the LORD, in the care ⁹ of Jehi'el the Gershonite. Then the people rejoiced because these had given willingly, for with a whole heart they had offered freely to the LORD; David the king also rejoiced greatly.

¹⁰ Therefore David blessed the LORD in the presence of all the assembly; and David said: "Blessed art thou, O LORD, ¹¹ the God of Israel our father, for ever and ever. Thine, O LORD, is the greatness, and the power, and the glory, and the victory, and the majesty; for all that is in the heavens and in the earth is thine; thine is the kingdom, O LORD, ¹² and thou art exalted as head above all. Both riches and honor come from thee, and thou rulest over all. In thy

hand are power and might; and in thy hand it is to make ¹³ great and to give strength to all. And now we thank thee, our God, and praise thy glorious name.

¹⁴ "But who am I, and what is my people, that we should be able thus to offer willingly? For all things come from ¹⁵ thee, and of thy own have we given thee. For we are strangers before thee, and sojourners, as all our fathers were; our days on the earth are like a shadow, and there ¹⁶ is no abiding.ⁱ O LORD our God, all this abundance that we have provided for building thee a house for thy holy ¹⁷ name comes from thy hand and is all thy own. I know, my God, that thou triest the heart, and hast pleasure in uprightness; in the uprightness of my heart I have freely offered all these things, and now I have seen thy people, who are present here, offering freely and joyously to thee. ¹⁸ O LORD, the God of Abraham, Isaac, and Israel, our fathers, keep for ever such purposes and thoughts in the hearts of thy people, and direct their hearts toward thee. ¹⁹ Grant to Solomon my son that with a whole heart he may keep thy commandments, thy testimonies, and thy statutes, performing all, and that he may build the palace for which I have made provision."

²⁰ Then David said to all the assembly, "Bless the LORD your God." And all the assembly blessed the LORD, the God of their fathers, and bowed their heads, and wor- ²¹ shiped the LORD, and did obeisance to the king. And they performed sacrifices to the LORD, and on the next day offered burnt offerings to the LORD, a thousand bulls, a thousand rams, and a thousand lambs, with their drink ²² offerings, and sacrifices in abundance for all Israel; and they ate and drank before the LORD on that day with great gladness.

And they made Solomon the son of David king the second time, and they anointed him as prince for the ²³ LORD, and Zadok as priest. Then Solomon sat on the throne of the LORD as king instead of David his father; ²⁴ and he prospered, and all Israel obeyed him. All the leaders and the mighty men, and also all the sons of King ²⁵ David, pledged their allegiance to King Solomon. And the LORD gave Solomon great repute in the sight of all Israel, and bestowed upon him such royal majesty as had not been on any king before him in Israel.

²⁶ Thus David the son of Jesse reigned over all Israel. ²⁷ The time that he reigned over Israel was forty years; he reigned seven years in Hebron, and thirty-three years in ²⁸ Jerusalem. Then he died in a good old age, full of days, riches, and honor; and Solomon his son reigned in his ²⁹ stead. Now the acts of King David, from first to last, are written in the Chronicles of Samuel the seer, and in the Chronicles of Nathan the prophet, and in the Chronicles ³⁰ of Gad the seer, with accounts of all his rule and his might and of the circumstances that came upon him and upon Israel, and upon all the kingdoms of the countries.

INTRODUCTION TO

THE SECOND BOOK OF THE

CHRONICLES

First Chronicles closes with an account of the end of David's reign. Second Chronicles begins with the reign of David's son Solomon; it tells about the building and consecration of the Temple and other events of Solomon's reign.

Beginning with Chapter 10 there is an account of how the Hebrew kingdom divided after Solomon's death. Because of the heavy taxes that Solomon had demanded of the people, the ten northern tribes rebelled against Solomon's son. They set up the kingdom of Israel with Jeroboam as their king. The two southern tribes remained loyal to Solomon's son, King Rehoboam, and continued as the kingdom of Judah. Second Chronicles tells of the many kings of Judah from the death of Solomon in 931 B.C. until Judah was conquered by Babylon in 597 and destroyed in 586.

One of the greatest of those kings was the young Josiah. He realized that many people were no longer loyal to God but were worshiping the gods in whom their Canaanite and Assyrian neighbors believed. Scrolls of the central portion of the Book of Deuteronomy were discovered at the Temple (see page 256) during Josiah's reign, and he began vigorous reforms. Several prophets were active during these years, including Zephaniah, Nahum, Habakkuk, and Jeremiah.

Second Chronicles closes by telling how the Babylonians, also called Chaldeans, finally conquered Judah and forced many of its people into exile in Babylonia. The Jews remained there until Cyrus of Persia conquered Babylonia and let the Jews return to their homeland about 538 B.C.

The Chronicler was so interested in Judah and Jerusalem, where the Temple and its priests were located, that he told very little about the northern kingdom of Israel.

Second Chronicles was written by the same writer and at the same time as First Chronicles, namely, about 350 B.C. It was probably divided into two books because one scroll was not large enough to contain it all.

Like First Chronicles, this book stresses the thought that when the people were faithful to the worship of God at the Temple, they prospered, and when they became careless, the nation had trouble. The introduction to First Chronicles on page 261 tells more about the purpose of the Chronicler.

THE SECOND BOOK OF THE

CHRONICLES

THE REIGN OF SOLOMON

1 Solomon the son of David established himself in his kingdom, and the LORD his God was with him and made him exceedingly great.

2 Solomon spoke to all Israel, to the commanders of thousands and of hundreds, to the judges, and to all the 3 leaders in all Israel, the heads of fathers' houses. And Solomon, and all the assembly with him, went to the high place that was at Gibeon; for the tent of meeting of God, which Moses the servant of the LORD had made in the 4 wilderness, was there. (But David had brought up the ark of God from Kir'iath-je'arim to the place that David had prepared for it, for he had pitched a tent for it in 5 Jerusalem.) Moreover the bronze altar that Bez'alel the son of Uri, son of Hur, had made, was there before the tabernacle of the LORD. And Solomon and the assembly 6 sought the LORD. And Solomon went up there to the bronze altar before the LORD, which was at the tent of meeting, and offered a thousand burnt offerings upon it. 7 In that night God appeared to Solomon, and said to 8 him, "Ask what I shall give you." And Solomon said to God, "Thou hast shown great and steadfast love to David 9 my father, and hast made me king in his stead. O LORD God, let thy promise to David my father be now fulfilled, for thou hast made me king over a people as many as the 10 dust of the earth. Give me now wisdom and knowledge to go out and come in before this people, for who can rule 11 this thy people, that is so great?" God answered Solomon, "Because this was in your heart, and you have not asked possessions, wealth, honor, or the life of those who hate you, and have not even asked long life, but have asked wisdom and knowledge for yourself that you may rule my 12 people over whom I have made you king, wisdom and knowledge are granted to you. I will also give you riches, possessions, and honor, such as none of the kings had who were before you, and none after you shall have the like." 13 So Solomon came from [a] the high place at Gibeon, from before the tent of meeting, to Jerusalem. And he reigned over Israel.

14 Solomon gathered together chariots and horsemen; he had fourteen hundred chariots and twelve thousand horsemen, whom he stationed in the chariot cities and with the 15 king in Jerusalem. And the king made silver and gold as common in Jerusalem as stone, and he made cedar as 16 plentiful as the sycamore of the Shephe'lah. And Solomon's import of horses was from Egypt and Ku'e, and the 17 king's traders received them from Ku'e for a price. They imported a chariot from Egypt for six hundred shekels of silver, and a horse for a hundred and fifty; likewise through them these were exported to all the kings of the Hittites and the kings of Syria.

Building of the Temple

2 [b] Now Solomon purposed to build a temple for the name of the LORD, and a royal palace for himself. 2 [c] And Solomon assigned seventy thousand men to bear burdens and eighty thousand to quarry in the hill country, 3 and three thousand six hundred to oversee them. And Solomon sent word to Huram the king of Tyre: "As you dealt with David my father and sent him cedar to build 4 himself a house to dwell in, so deal with me. Behold, I am about to build a house for the name of the LORD my God and dedicate it to him for the burning of incense of sweet spices before him, and for the continual offering of the showbread, and for burnt offerings morning and evening, on the sabbaths and the new moons and the appointed feasts of the LORD our God, as ordained for ever for 5 Israel. The house which I am to build will be great, for 6 our God is greater than all gods. But who is able to build him a house, since heaven, even highest heaven, cannot contain him? Who am I to build a house for him, except 7 as a place to burn incense before him? So now send me a man skilled to work in gold, silver, bronze, and iron, and in purple, crimson, and blue fabrics, trained also in engraving, to be with the skilled workers who are with me in Judah and Jerusalem, whom David my father provided. 8 Send me also cedar, cypress, and algum timber from Lebanon, for I know that your servants know how to cut timber in Lebanon. And my servants will be with your 9 servants, to prepare timber for me in abundance, for the 10 house I am to build will be great and wonderful. I will give for your servants, the hewers who cut timber, twenty thousand cors of crushed wheat, twenty thousand cors of barley, twenty thousand baths of wine, and twenty thousand baths of oil."

11 Then Huram the king of Tyre answered in a letter which he sent to Solomon, "Because the LORD loves his 12 people he has made you king over them." Huram also said, "Blessed be the LORD God of Israel, who made heaven and earth, who has given King David a wise son, endued with discretion and understanding, who will build a temple for the LORD, and a royal palace for himself. 13 "Now I have sent a skilled man, endued with under- 14 standing, Huramabi, the son of a woman of the daughters of Dan, and his father was a man of Tyre. He is trained to work in gold, silver, bronze, iron, stone, and wood, and in purple, blue, and crimson fabrics and fine linen, and to do all sorts of engraving and execute any design

[a] Gk Vg: Heb to   [b] Ch 1.18 in Heb   [c] Ch 2.1 in Heb

that may be assigned him, with your craftsmen, the crafts-
15 men of my lord, David your father. Now therefore the
wheat and barley, oil and wine, of which my lord has
16 spoken, let him send to his servants; and we will cut
whatever timber you need from Lebanon, and bring it to
you in rafts by sea to Joppa, so that you may take it up
to Jerusalem."

17 Then Solomon took a census of all the aliens who were
in the land of Israel, after the census of them which
David his father had taken; and there were found a
18 hundred and fifty-three thousand six hundred. Seventy
thousand of them he assigned to bear burdens, eighty
thousand to quarry in the hill country, and three thousand
six hundred as overseers to make the people work.

3 Then Solomon began to build the house of the LORD
in Jerusalem on Mount Mori′ah, where the LORD had
appeared to David his father, at the place that David had
appointed, on the threshing floor of Ornan the Jeb′usite.
2 He began to build in the second month of the fourth year
of his reign.

TEMPLE MEASUREMENTS

3 These are Solomon's measurements[d] for building the house of
God: the length, in cubits of the old standard, was sixty cubits,
4 and the breadth twenty cubits. The vestibule in front of the
nave of the house was twenty cubits long, equal to the width
of the house;[e] and its height was a hundred and twenty cubits.
5 He overlaid it on the inside with pure gold. The nave he lined
with cypress, and covered it with fine gold, and made palms
6 and chains on it. He adorned the house with settings of precious
7 stones. The gold was gold of Parva′im. So he lined the house
with gold—its beams, its thresholds, its walls, and its doors;
and he carved cherubim on the walls.
8 And he made the most holy place; its length, corresponding
to the breadth of the house, was twenty cubits, and its breadth
was twenty cubits; he overlaid it with six hundred talents of
9 fine gold. The weight of the nails was one shekel[f] to fifty
shekels of gold. And he overlaid the upper chambers with gold.
10 In the most holy place he made two cherubim of wood[g]
11 and overlaid[h] them with gold. The wings of the cherubim together extended twenty cubits: one wing of the one, of five
cubits, touched the wall of the house, and its other wing, of
12 five cubits, touched the wing of the other cherub; and of this
cherub, one wing, of five cubits, touched the wall of the house,
and the other wing, also of five cubits, was joined to the wing
13 of the first cherub. The wings of these cherubim extended
twenty cubits; the cherubim[i] stood on their feet, facing the
14 nave. And he made the veil of blue and purple and crimson
fabrics and fine linen, and worked cherubim on it.
15 In front of the house he made two pillars thirty-five cubits
16 high, with a capital of five cubits on the top of each. He made
chains like a necklace[j] and put them on the tops of the pillars;
and he made a hundred pomegranates, and put them on the
17 chains. He set up the pillars in front of the temple, one on the
south, the other on the north; that on the south he called Jachin,
and that on the north Bo′az.
4 He made an altar of bronze, twenty cubits long, and
2 twenty cubits wide, and ten cubits high. Then he made the

molten sea; it was round, ten cubits from brim to brim, and
five cubits high, and a line of thirty cubits measured its cir-
3 cumference. Under it were figures of gourds,[k] for thirty[l]
cubits, compassing the sea round about; the gourds[k] were in
4 two rows, cast with it when it was cast. It stood upon twelve
oxen, three facing north, three facing west, three facing south,
and three facing east; the sea was set upon them, and all their
5 hinder parts were inward. Its thickness was a handbreadth; and
its brim was made like the brim of a cup, like the flower of a
6 lily; it held over three thousand baths. He also made ten lavers
in which to wash, and set five on the south side, and five on the
north side. In these they were to rinse off what was used
for the burnt offering, and the sea was for the priests to wash
in.
7 And he made ten golden lampstands as prescribed, and set
them in the temple, five on the south side and five on the north.
8 He also made ten tables, and placed them in the temple, five
on the south side and five on the north. And he made a hun-
9 dred basins of gold. He made the court of the priests, and the
great court, and doors for the court, and overlaid their doors
10 with bronze; and he set the sea at the southeast corner of the
house.
11 Huram also made the pots, the shovels, and the basins. So
Huram finished the work that he did for King Solomon on
12 the house of God: the two pillars, the bowls, and the two
capitals on the top of the pillars; and the two networks to cover
the two bowls of the capitals that were on the top of the pillars;
13 and the four hundred pomegranates for the two networks, two
rows of pomegranates for each network, to cover the two bowls
14 of the capitals that were upon the pillars. He made the stands
15 also, and the lavers upon the stands, and the one sea, and the
16 twelve oxen underneath it. The pots, the shovels, the forks,
and all the equipment for these Huram-abi made of burnished
17 bronze for King Solomon for the house of the LORD. In the plain of
the Jordan the king cast them, in the clay ground between
18 Succoth and Zer′edah. Solomon made all these things in great
quantities, so that the weight of the bronze was not ascertained.
19 So Solomon made all the things that were in the house of God:
the golden altar, the tables for the bread of the Presence,
20 the lampstands and their lamps of pure gold to burn before
21 the inner sanctuary, as prescribed; the flowers, the lamps, and
22 the tongs, of purest gold; the snuffers, basins, dishes for incense,
and firepans, of pure gold; and the sockets[m] of the temple, for
the inner doors to the most holy place and for the doors of the
nave of the temple were of gold.

Consecration of the Temple

5 Thus all the work that Solomon did for the house
of the LORD was finished. And Solomon brought in the
things which David his father had dedicated, and stored
the silver, the gold, and all the vessels in the treasuries of
the house of God.

2 Then Solomon assembled the elders of Israel and all
the heads of the tribes, the leaders of the fathers' houses
of the people of Israel, in Jerusalem, to bring up the ark
of the covenant of the LORD out of the city of David,
3 which is Zion. And all the men of Israel assembled before
the king at the feast which is in the seventh month.
4 And all the elders of Israel came, and the Levites took
5 up the ark. And they brought up the ark, the tent of
meeting, and all the holy vessels that were in the tent; the
6 priests and the Levites brought them up. And King Solomon and all the congregation of Israel, who had assembled
before him, were before the ark, sacrificing so many sheep
7 and oxen that they could not be counted or numbered. So
the priests brought the ark of the covenant of the LORD to
its place, in the inner sanctuary of the house, in the most
8 holy place, underneath the wings of the cherubim. For the

---

[d] Syr: Heb foundations   [e] 1 K 6.3: Heb uncertain   [f] Compare Gk: Heb lacks one shekel   [g] Gk: Heb uncertain
[h] Heb they overlaid   [i] Heb they   [j] Cn: Heb in the inner sanctuary   [k] 1 K 7.24: Heb oxen
[l] Compare verse 2: Heb ten   [m] 1 K 7.50: Heb the door of the house

cherubim spread out their wings over the place of the ark, so that the cherubim made a covering above the ark
9 and its poles. And the poles were so long that the ends of the poles were seen from the holy place before the inner sanctuary; but they could not be seen from outside;
10 and they are there to this day. There was nothing in the ark except the two tables which Moses put there at Horeb, where the LORD made a covenant with the people of
11 Israel, when they came out of Egypt. Now when the priests came out of the holy place (for all the priests who were present had sanctified themselves, without regard
12 to their divisions; and all the Levitical singers, Asaph, Heman, and Jedu'thun, their sons and kinsmen, arrayed in fine linen, with cymbals, harps, and lyres, stood east of the altar with a hundred and twenty priests who were
13 trumpeters; and it was the duty of the trumpeters and singers to make themselves heard in unison in praise and thanksgiving to the LORD), and when the song was raised, with trumpets and cymbals and other musical instruments, in praise to the LORD,

"For he is good,
for his steadfast love endures for ever,"

the house, the house of the LORD, was filled with a cloud,
14 so that the priests could not stand to minister because of the cloud; for the glory of the LORD filled the house of God.

6 Then Solomon said,
"The LORD has said that he would dwell in thick darkness.
2 I have built thee an exalted house,
a place for thee to dwell in for ever."

3 Then the king faced about, and blessed all the assembly
4 of Israel, while all the assembly of Israel stood. And he said, "Blessed be the LORD, the God of Israel, who with his hand has fulfilled what he promised with his mouth
5 to David my father, saying, 'Since the day that I brought my people out of the land of Egypt, I chose no city in all the tribes of Israel in which to build a house, that my name might be there, and I chose no man as prince over
6 my people Israel; but I have chosen Jerusalem that my name may be there and I have chosen David to be over
7 my people Israel.' Now it was in the heart of David my father to build a house for the name of the LORD, the God
8 of Israel. But the LORD said to David my father, 'Whereas it was in your heart to build a house for my name, you
9 did well that it was in your heart; nevertheless you shall not build the house, but your son who shall be born to
10 you shall build the house for my name.' Now the LORD has fulfilled his promise which he made; for I have risen in the place of David my father, and sit on the throne of Israel, as the LORD promised, and I have built the
11 house for the name of the LORD, the God of Israel. And there I have set the ark, in which is the covenant of the

LORD which he made with the people of Israel."
12 Then Solomon stood before the altar of the LORD in the presence of all the assembly of Israel, and spread forth
13 his hands. Solomon had made a bronze platform five cubits long, five cubits wide, and three cubits high, and had set it in the court; and he stood upon it. Then he knelt upon his knees in the presence of all the assembly of Israel, and spread forth his hands toward heaven;
14 and said, "O LORD, God of Israel, there is no God like thee, in heaven or on earth, keeping covenant and showing steadfast love to thy servants who walk before thee with
15 all their heart; who hast kept with thy servant David my father what thou didst declare to him; yea, thou didst speak with thy mouth, and with thy hand hast fulfilled it
16 this day. Now therefore, O LORD, God of Israel, keep with thy servant David my father what thou hast promised him, saying, 'There shall never fail you a man before me to sit upon the throne of Israel, if only your sons take heed to their way, to walk in my law as you have walked
17 before me.' Now therefore, O LORD, God of Israel, let thy word be confirmed, which thou hast spoken to thy servant David.
18 "But will God dwell indeed with man on the earth? Behold, heaven and the highest heaven cannot contain
19 thee; how much less this house which I have built! Yet have regard to the prayer of thy servant and to his supplication, O LORD my God, hearkening to the cry and to
20 the prayer which thy servant prays before thee; that thy eyes may be open day and night toward this house, the place where thou hast promised to set thy name, that thou mayest hearken to the prayer which thy servant offers
21 toward this place. And hearken thou to the supplications of thy servant and of thy people Israel, when they pray toward this place; yea, hear thou from heaven thy dwelling place; and when thou hearest, forgive.

22 "If a man sins against his neighbor and is made to take an oath, and comes and swears his oath before thy altar
23 in this house, then hear thou from heaven, and act, and judge thy servants, requiting the guilty by bringing his conduct upon his own head, and vindicating the righteous by rewarding him according to his righteousness.
24 "If thy people Israel are defeated before the enemy because they have sinned against thee, when they turn again and acknowledge thy name, and pray and make supplica-
25 tion to thee in this house, then hear thou from heaven,

and forgive the sin of thy people Israel, and bring them again to the land which thou gavest to them and to their fathers.

26 "When heaven is shut up and there is no rain because they have sinned against thee, if they pray toward this place, and acknowledge thy name, and turn from their 27 sin, when thou dost afflict them, then hear thou in heaven, and forgive the sin of thy servants, thy people Israel, when thou dost teach them the good way [n] in which they should walk; and grant rain upon thy land, which thou hast given to thy people as an inheritance.

28 "If there is famine in the land, if there is pestilence or blight or mildew or locust or caterpillar; if their enemies besiege them in any of their cities; whatever plague, what-29 ever sickness there is; whatever prayer, whatever supplication is made by any man or by all thy people Israel, each knowing his own affliction, and his own sorrow and 30 stretching out his hands toward this house; then hear thou from heaven thy dwelling place, and forgive, and render to each whose heart thou knowest, according to all his ways (for thou, thou only, knowest the hearts of the 31 children of men); that they may fear thee and walk in thy ways all the days that they live in the land which thou gavest to our fathers.

32 "Likewise when a foreigner, who is not of thy people Israel, comes from a far country for the sake of thy great name, and thy mighty hand, and thy outstretched arm, 33 when he comes and prays toward this house, hear thou from heaven thy dwelling place, and do according to all for which the foreigner calls to thee; in order that all the peoples of the earth may know thy name and fear thee, as do thy people Israel, and that they may know that this house which I have built is called by thy name.

34 "If thy people go out to battle against their enemies, by whatever way thou shalt send them, and they pray to thee toward this city which thou hast chosen and the 35 house which I have built for thy name, then hear thou from heaven their prayer and their supplication, and maintain their cause.

36 "If they sin against thee—for there is no man who does not sin—and thou art angry with them, and dost give them to an enemy, so that they are carried away captive to a 37 land far or near; yet if they lay it to heart in the land to which they have been carried captive, and repent, and make supplication to thee in the land of their captivity, saying, 'We have sinned, and have acted perversely and 38 wickedly'; if they repent with all their mind and with all their heart in the land of their captivity, to which they were carried captive, and pray toward their land, which thou gavest to their fathers, the city which thou hast chosen, and the house which I have built for thy name, 39 then hear thou from heaven thy dwelling place their prayer and their supplications, and maintain their cause and forgive thy people who have sinned against thee.

40 Now, O my God, let thy eyes be open and thy ears attentive to a prayer of this place.
41 "And now arise, O Lord God, and go to thy resting place,
   thou and the ark of thy might.
   Let thy priests, O Lord God, be clothed with salvation,
   and let thy saints rejoice in thy goodness.
42 O Lord God, do not turn away the face of thy anointed one!
   Remember thy steadfast love for David thy servant."

7 When Solomon had ended his prayer, fire came down from heaven and consumed the burnt offering and the sacrifices, and the glory of the Lord filled the 2 temple. And the priests could not enter the house of the Lord, because the glory of the Lord filled the Lord's 3 house. When all the children of Israel saw the fire come down and the glory of the Lord upon the temple, they bowed down with their faces to the earth on the pavement, and worshiped and gave thanks to the Lord, saying,
   "For he is good,
      for his steadfast love endures for ever."
4 Then the king and all the people offered sacrifice be-5 fore the Lord. King Solomon offered as a sacrifice twenty-two thousand oxen and a hundred and twenty thousand sheep. So the king and all the people dedicated the house 6 of God. The priests stood at their posts; the Levites also, with the instruments for music to the Lord which King David had made for giving thanks to the Lord—for his steadfast love endures for ever—whenever David offered praises by their ministry; opposite them the priests sounded trumpets; and all Israel stood.

7 And Solomon consecrated the middle of the court that was before the house of the Lord; for there he offered the burnt offering and the fat of the peace offerings, because the bronze altar Solomon had made could not hold the burnt offering and the cereal offering and the fat.

8 At that time Solomon held the feast for seven days, and all Israel with him, a very great congregation, from the 9 entrance of Hamath to the Brook of Egypt. And on the eighth day they held a solemn assembly; for they had kept the dedication of the altar seven days and the feast 10 seven days. On the twenty-third day of the seventh month he sent the people away to their homes, joyful and glad of heart for the goodness that the Lord had shown to David and to Solomon and to Israel his people.

11 Thus Solomon finished the house of the Lord and the king's house; all that Solomon had planned to do in the house of the Lord and in his own house he successfully 12 accomplished. Then the Lord appeared to Solomon in the night and said to him: "I have heard your prayer, and have chosen this place for myself as a house of sacrifice. 13 When I shut up the heavens so that there is no rain, or command the locust to devour the land, or send pestilence 14 among my people, if my people who are called by my name humble themselves, and pray and seek my face, and

[n] Gk Syr Vg: Heb *toward the good way*

turn from their wicked ways, then I will hear from heaven, and will forgive their sin and heal their land.
15 Now my eyes will be open and my ears attentive to the
16 prayer that is made in this place. For now I have chosen and consecrated this house that my name may be there for ever; my eyes and my heart will be there for all time.
17 And as for you, if you walk before me, as David your father walked, doing according to all that I have commanded you and keeping my statutes and my ordinances,
18 then I will establish your royal throne, as I covenanted with David your father, saying, 'There shall not fail you a man to rule Israel.'
19 "But if you o turn aside and forsake my statutes and my commandments which I have set before you, and go and
20 serve other gods and worship them, then I will pluck you p up from the land which I have given you; p and this house, which I have consecrated for my name, I will cast out of my sight, and will make it a proverb and a byword
21 among all peoples. And at this house, which is exalted, every one passing by will be astonished, and say, 'Why has the Lord done thus to this land and to this house?'
22 Then they will say, 'Because they forsook the Lord the God of their fathers who brought them out of the land of Egypt, and laid hold on other gods, and worshiped them and served them; therefore he has brought all this evil upon them.'"

Solomon Builds

8 At the end of twenty years, in which Solomon had built the house of the Lord and his own house,
2 Solomon rebuilt the cities which Huram had given to him, and settled the people of Israel in them.
3 And Solomon went to Ha'math-zo'bah, and took it.
4 He built Tadmor in the wilderness and all the store-
5 cities which he built in Hamath. He also built Upper Beth-hor'on and Lower Beth-hor'on, fortified cities with
6 walls, gates, and bars, and Ba'alath, and all the store-cities that Solomon had, and all the cities for his chariots, and the cities for his horsemen, and whatever Solomon desired to build in Jerusalem, in Lebanon, and in all the land of
7 his dominion. All the people who were left of the Hittites, the Amorites, the Per'izzites, the Hivites, and the Jeb'-
8 usites, who were not of Israel, from their descendants who were left after them in the land, whom the people of Israel had not destroyed—these Solomon made a forced levy
9 and so they are to this day. But of the people of Israel Solomon made no slaves for his work; they were soldiers, and his officers, the commanders of his chariots, and his
10 horsemen. And these were the chief officers of King Solomon, two hundred and fifty, who exercised authority over the people.
11 Solomon brought Pharaoh's daughter up from the city of David to the house which he had built for her, for he said, "My wife shall not live in the house of David king

of Israel, for the places to which the ark of the Lord has come are holy."
12 Then Solomon offered up burnt offerings to the Lord upon the altar of the Lord which he had built before the
13 vestibule, as the duty of each day required, offering according to the commandment of Moses for the sabbaths, the new moons, and the three annual feasts—the feast of unleavened bread, the feast of weeks, and the feast of
14 tabernacles. According to the ordinance of David his father, he appointed the divisions of the priests for their service, and the Levites for their offices of praise and ministry before the priests as the duty of each day required, and the gatekeepers in their divisions for the several gates; for so David the man of God had com-
15 manded. And they did not turn aside from what the king had commanded the priests and Levites concerning any matter and concerning the treasuries.

16 Thus was accomplished all the work of Solomon from q the day the foundation of the house of the Lord was laid until it was finished. So the house of the Lord was completed.
17 Then Solomon went to E'zion-ge'ber and Eloth on the
18 shore of the sea, in the land of Edom. And Huram sent him by his servants ships and servants familiar with the sea, and they went to Ophir together with the servants of Solomon, and fetched from there four hundred and fifty talents of gold and brought it to King Solomon.

Visit of Sheba's Queen

9 Now when the queen of Sheba heard of the fame of Solomon she came to Jerusalem to test him with hard questions, having a very great retinue and camels bearing spices and very much gold and precious stones. When she came to Solomon, she told him all that was on her mind.
2 And Solomon answered all her questions; there was nothing hidden from Solomon which he could not explain
3 to her. And when the queen of Sheba had seen the wisdom
4 of Solomon, the house that he had built, the food of his table, the seating of his officials, and the attendance of his servants, and their clothing, his cupbearers, and their clothing, and his burnt offerings which he offered at the house of the Lord, there was no more spirit in her.

o The word *you* is plural here   p Heb *them*   q Gk Syr Vg: Heb *to*

5 And she said to the king, "The report was true which I heard in my own land of your affairs and of your
6 wisdom, but I did not believe the ʳ reports until I came and my own eyes had seen it; and behold, half the greatness of your wisdom was not told me; you surpass the
7 report which I heard. Happy are your wives! ˢ Happy are these your servants, who continually stand before you and
8 hear your wisdom! Blessed be the Lᴏʀᴅ your God, who has delighted in you and set you on his throne as king for the Lᴏʀᴅ your God! Because your God loved Israel and would establish them for ever, he has made you king over them, that you may execute justice and righteous-
9 ness." Then she gave the king a hundred and twenty talents of gold, and a very great quantity of spices, and precious stones: there were no spices such as those which the queen of Sheba gave to King Solomon.
10 Moreover the servants of Huram and the servants of Solomon, who brought gold from Ophir, brought algum
11 wood and precious stones. And the king made of the algum wood steps ᵗ for the house of the Lᴏʀᴅ and for the

king's house, lyres also and harps for the singers; there never was seen the like of them before in the land of Judah.
12 And King Solomon gave to the queen of Sheba all that she desired, whatever she asked besides what she had brought to the king. So she turned and went back to her own land, with her servants.
13 Now the weight of gold that came to Solomon in one year was six hundred and sixty-six talents of gold,
14 besides that which the traders and merchants brought; and all the kings of Arabia and the governors of the land
15 brought gold and silver to Solomon. King Solomon made two hundred large shields of beaten gold; six hundred
16 shekels of beaten gold went into each shield. And he made three hundred shields of beaten gold; three hundred shekels of gold went into each shield; and the king put
17 them in the House of the Forest of Lebanon. The king also made a great ivory throne, and overlaid it with pure
18 gold. The throne had six steps and a footstool of gold, which were attached to the throne, and on each side of the seat were arm rests and two lions standing beside the arm
19 rests, while twelve lions stood there, one on each end of

a step on the six steps. The like of it was never made in
20 any kingdom. All King Solomon's drinking vessels were of gold, and all the vessels of the House of the Forest of Lebanon were of pure gold; silver was not considered as
21 anything in the days of Solomon. For the king's ships went to Tarshish with the servants of Huram; once every three years the ships of Tarshish used to come bringing gold, silver, ivory, apes, and peacocks.ˣ
22 Thus King Solomon excelled all the kings of the earth
23 in riches and in wisdom. And all the kings of the earth sought the presence of Solomon to hear his wisdom, which
24 God had put into his mind. Every one of them brought his present, articles of silver and of gold, garments, myrrh,
25 spices, horses, and mules, so much year by year. And Solomon had four thousand stalls for horses and chariots, and twelve thousand horsemen whom he stationed in the
26 chariot cities and with the king in Jerusalem. And he ruled over all the kings from the Eu-phra'tes to the land of the
27 Philistines, and to the border of Egypt. And the king made silver as common in Jerusalem as stone, and cedar as
28 plentiful as the sycamore of the Shephe'lah. And horses were imported for Solomon from Egypt and from all lands.
29 Now the rest of the acts of Solomon, from first to last, are they not written in the history of Nathan the prophet, and in the prophecy of Ahi'jah the Shi'lonite, and in the visions of Iddo the seer concerning Jerobo'am the son
30 of Nebat? Solomon reigned in Jerusalem over all Israel
31 forty years. And Solomon slept with his fathers, and was buried in the city of David his father; and Rehobo'am his son reigned in his stead.

THE KINGS OF JUDAH
Reign of Rehoboam

10 Rehobo'am went to Shechem, for all Israel had
2 come to Shechem to make him king. And when Jerobo'am the son of Nebat heard of it (for he was in Egypt, whither he had fled from King Solomon), then Jerobo'am
3 returned from Egypt. And they sent and called him; and Jerobo'am and all Israel came and said to Rehobo'am,
4 "Your father made our yoke heavy. Now therefore lighten the hard service of your father and his heavy yoke upon
5 us, and we will serve you." He said to them, "Come to me again in three days." So the people went away.
6 Then King Rehobo'am took counsel with the old men, who had stood before Solomon his father while he was yet alive, saying, "How do you advise me to answer this
7 people?" And they said to him, "If you will be kind to this people and please them, and speak good words to
8 them, then they will be your servants for ever." But he forsook the counsel which the old men gave him, and took counsel with the young men who had grown up with him
9 and stood before him. And he said to them, "What do you advise that we answer this people who have said to me,

ʳ Heb their   ˢ Gk Compare 1 K 10.8: Heb men   ᵗ Gk Vg: The meaning of the Hebrew word is uncertain   ˣ Or baboons

10 'Lighten the yoke that your father put upon us'?" And the young men who had grown up with him said to him, "Thus shall you speak to the people who said to you, 'Your father made our yoke heavy, but do you lighten it for us'; thus shall you say to them, 'My little finger is 11 thicker than my father's loins. And now, whereas my father laid upon you a heavy yoke, I will add to your yoke. My father chastised you with whips, but I will chastise you with scorpions.'"

12 So Jerobo'am and all the people came to Rehobo'am the third day, as the king said, "Come to me again the 13 third day." And the king answered them harshly, and 14 forsaking the counsel of the old men, King Rehobo'am spoke to them according to the counsel of the young men, saying, "My father made your yoke heavy, but I will add to it; my father chastised you with whips, but I will 15 chastise you with scorpions." So the king did not hearken to the people; for it was a turn of affairs brought about by God that the LORD might fulfil his word, which he spoke by Ahi'jah the Shi'lonite to Jerobo'am the son of Nebat.

16 And when all Israel saw that the king did not hearken to them, the people answered the king,

"What portion have we in David?
We have no inheritance in the son of Jesse.
Each of you to your tents, O Israel!
Look now to your own house, David."

17 So all Israel departed to their tents. But Rehobo'am reigned over the people of Israel who dwelt in the cities of 18 Judah. Then King Rehobo'am sent Hador'am, who was taskmaster over the forced labor, and the people of Israel stoned him to death with stones. And King Rehobo'am made haste to mount his chariot, to flee to Jerusalem. 19 So Israel has been in rebellion against the house of David to this day.

11 When Rehobo'am came to Jerusalem, he assembled the house of Judah, and Benjamin, a hundred and eighty thousand chosen warriors, to fight against Israel, 2 to restore the kingdom to Rehobo'am. But the word of the 3 LORD came to Shemai'ah the man of God: "Say to Rehobo'am the son of Solomon king of Judah, and to all Israel 4 in Judah and Benjamin, 'Thus says the LORD, You shall not go up or fight against your brethren. Return every man to his home, for this thing is from me.'" So they hearkened to the word of the LORD, and returned and did not go against Jerobo'am.

u Cn: Heb sought a multitude of wives

5 Rehobo'am dwelt in Jerusalem, and he built cities for 6, 7 defense in Judah. He built Bethlehem, Etam, Teko'a, Beth- 8, 9 zur, Soco, Adul'lam, Gath, Mare'shah, Ziph, Adora'im, 10 Lachish, Aze'kah, Zorah, Ai'jalon, and Hebron, fortified 11 cities which are in Judah and in Benjamin. He made the fortresses strong and put commanders in them, and stores 12 of food, oil, and wine. And he put shields and spears in all the cities, and made them very strong. So he held Judah and Benjamin.

13 And the priests and the Levites that were in all Israel 14 resorted to him from all places where they lived. For the Levites left their common lands and their holdings and came to Judah and Jerusalem, because Jerobo'am and his sons cast them out from serving as priests of the LORD, 15 and he appointed his own priests for the high places, and 16 for the satyrs, and for the calves which he had made. And those who had set their hearts to seek the LORD God of Israel came after them from all the tribes of Israel to Jerusalem to sacrifice to the LORD, the God of their fathers. 17 They strengthened the kingdom of Judah, and for three years they made Rehobo'am the son of Solomon secure, for they walked for three years in the way of David and Solomon.

18 Rehobo'am took as wife Ma'halath the daughter of Jer'imoth the son of David, and of Ab'ihail the daughter 19 of Eli'ab the son of Jesse; and she bore him sons, Je'ush, 20 Shemari'ah, and Zaham. After her he took Ma'acah the daughter of Ab'salom, who bore him Abi'jah, Attai, Ziza, 21 and Shelo'mith. Rehobo'am loved Ma'acah the daughter of Ab'salom above all his wives and concubines (he took eighteen wives and sixty concubines, and had twenty-eight 22 sons and sixty daughters); and Rehobo'am appointed Abi'jah the son of Ma'acah as chief prince among his 23 brothers, for he intended to make him king. And he dealt wisely, and distributed some of his sons through all the districts of Judah and Benjamin, in all the fortified cities; and he gave them abundant provisions, and procured wives for them.u

12 When the rule of Rehobo'am was established and was strong, he forsook the law of the LORD, and all 2 Israel with him. In the fifth year of King Rehobo'am, because they had been unfaithful to the LORD, Shishak 3 king of Egypt came up against Jerusalem with twelve hundred chariots and sixty thousand horsemen. And the people were without number who came with him from 4 Egypt—Libyans, Suk'ki-im, and Ethiopians. And he took the fortified cities of Judah and came as far as Jerusalem. 5 Then Shemai'ah the prophet came to Rehobo'am and to the princes of Judah, who had gathered at Jerusalem because of Shishak, and said to them, "Thus says the LORD, 'You abandoned me, so I have abandoned you to 6 the hand of Shishak.'" Then the princes of Israel and the king humbled themselves and said, "The LORD is

7 righteous." When the LORD saw that they humbled themselves, the word of the LORD came to Shemai'ah: "They have humbled themselves; I will not destroy them, but I will grant them some deliverance, and my wrath shall not be poured out upon Jerusalem by the hand of Shishak.
8 Nevertheless they shall be servants to him, that they may know my service and the service of the kingdoms of the countries."

9 So Shishak king of Egypt came up against Jerusalem; he took away the treasures of the house of the LORD and the treasures of the king's house; he took away everything. He also took away the shields of gold which Solo-
10 mon had made; and King Rehobo'am made in their stead shields of bronze, and committed them to the hands of the officers of the guard, who kept the door of the king's
11 house. And as often as the king went into the house of the LORD, the guard came and bore them, and brought them
12 back to the guardroom. And when he humbled himself the wrath of the LORD turned from him, so as not to make a complete destruction; moreover, conditions were good in Judah.

13 So King Rehobo'am established himself in Jerusalem and reigned. Rehobo'am was forty-one years old when he began to reign, and he reigned seventeen years in Jerusalem, the city which the LORD had chosen out of all the tribes of Israel to put his name there. His mother's
14 name was Na'amah the Ammonitess. And he did evil, for he did not set his heart to seek the LORD.
15 Now the acts of Rehobo'am, from first to last, are they not written in the chronicles of Shemai'ah the prophet and of Iddo the seer? ᵛ There were continual wars between
16 Rehobo'am and Jerobo'am. And Rehobo'am slept with his fathers, and was buried in the city of David; and Abi'jah his son reigned in his stead.

Reign of Abijah

13 In the eighteenth year of King Jerobo'am Abi'jah
2 began to reign over Judah. He reigned for three years in Jerusalem. His mother's name was Micai'ah the daughter of U'riel of Gib'e-ah.

Now there was war between Abi'jah and Jerobo'am.
3 Abi'jah went out to battle having an army of valiant men of war, four hundred thousand picked men; and Jerobo'am drew up his line of battle against him with eight
4 hundred thousand picked mighty warriors. Then Abi'jah stood up on Mount Zemara'im which is in the hill country of E'phraim, and said, "Hear me, O Jerobo'am and all
5 Israel! Ought you not to know that the LORD God of Israel gave the kingship over Israel for ever to David and
6 his sons by a covenant of salt? Yet Jerobo'am the son of Nebat, a servant of Solomon the son of David, rose up
7 and rebelled against his lord; and certain worthless scoundrels gathered about him and defied Rehobo'am the son of Solomon, when Rehobo'am was young and irresolute and could not withstand them.

8 "And now you think to withstand the kingdom of the LORD in the hand of the sons of David, because you are a great multitude and have with you the golden calves
9 which Jerobo'am made you for gods. Have you not driven out the priests of the LORD, the sons of Aaron, and the Levites, and made priests for yourselves like the peoples of other lands? Whoever comes to consecrate himself with a young bull or seven rams becomes a priest
10 of what are no gods. But as for us, the LORD is our God, and we have not forsaken him. We have priests ministering to the LORD who are sons of Aaron, and
11 Levites for their service. They offer to the LORD every morning and every evening burnt offerings and incense of sweet spices, set out the showbread on the table of pure gold, and care for the golden lampstand that its lamps may burn every evening; for we keep the charge of the LORD our God, but you have forsaken him.
12 Behold, God is with us at our head, and his priests with their battle trumpets to sound the call to battle against you. O sons of Israel, do not fight against the LORD, the God of your fathers; for you cannot succeed."

13 Jerobo'am had sent an ambush around to come on them from behind; thus his troops ʷ were in front of Judah,
14 and the ambush was behind them. And when Judah looked, behold, the battle was before and behind them; and they cried to the LORD, and the priests blew the
15 trumpets. Then the men of Judah raised the battle shout. And when the men of Judah shouted, God defeated
16 Jerobo'am and all Israel before Abi'jah and Judah. The men of Israel fled before Judah, and God gave them into
17 their hand. Abi'jah and his people slew them with a great slaughter; so there fell slain of Israel five hundred thou-
18 sand picked men. Thus the men of Israel were subdued at that time, and the men of Judah prevailed, because they relied upon the LORD, the God of their fathers.
19 And Abi'jah pursued Jerobo'am, and took cities from him, Bethel with its villages and Jesh'anah with its vil-
20 lages and Ephron ˣ with its villages. Jerobo'am did not recover his power in the days of Abi'jah; and the LORD
21 smote him, and he died. But Abi'jah grew mighty. And he took fourteen wives, and had twenty-two sons and
22 sixteen daughters. The rest of the acts of Abi'jah, his ways and his sayings, are written in the story of the prophet Iddo.

Reign of Asa

14 ʸ So Abi'jah slept with his fathers, and they buried him in the city of David; and Asa his son reigned in his stead. In his days the land had rest for ten years.
2 ᶻ And Asa did what was good and right in the eyes of the
3 LORD his God. He took away the foreign altars and the high places, and broke down the pillars and hewed down
4 the Ashe'rim, and commanded Judah to seek the LORD, the God of their fathers, and to keep the law and the

---

ᵛ Heb seer, to enroll oneself   ʷ Heb they   ˣ Another reading is Ephrain   ʸ Ch 13.23 in Heb   ᶻ Ch 14.1 in Heb

[5] commandment. He also took out of all the cities of Judah the high places and the incense altars. And the kingdom [6] had rest under him. He built fortified cities in Judah, for the land had rest. He had no war in those years, for the [7] LORD gave him peace. And he said to Judah, "Let us build these cities, and surround them with walls and towers, gates and bars; the land is still ours, because we have sought the LORD our God; we have sought him, and he has given us peace on every side." So they built and [8] prospered. And Asa had an army of three hundred thousand from Judah, armed with bucklers and spears, and two hundred and eighty thousand men from Benjamin, that carried shields and drew bows; all these were mighty men of valor.

[9] Zerah the Ethiopian came out against them with an army of a million men and three hundred chariots, and [10] came as far as Mare'shah. And Asa went out to meet him, and they drew up their lines of battle in the valley of [11] Zeph'athah at Mare'shah. And Asa cried to the LORD his God, "O LORD, there is none like thee to help, between the mighty and the weak. Help us, O LORD our God, for we rely on thee, and in thy name we have come against this multitude. O LORD, thou art our God; let not man [12] prevail against thee." So the LORD defeated the Ethiopians [13] before Asa and before Judah, and the Ethiopians fled. Asa and the people that were with him pursued them as far as Gerar, and the Ethiopians fell until none remained alive; for they were broken before the LORD and his army. [14] The men of Judah [a] carried away very much booty. And they smote all the cities round about Gerar, for the fear of the LORD was upon them. They plundered all the cities, [15] for there was much plunder in them. And they smote the tents of those who had cattle,[b] and carried away sheep in abundance and camels. Then they returned to Jerusalem.

[15] The Spirit of God came upon Azari'ah the son of [2] Oded, and he went out to meet Asa, and said to him, "Hear me, Asa, and all Judah and Benjamin: The LORD is with you, while you are with him. If you seek him, he will be found by you, but if you forsake him, he will [3] forsake you. For a long time Israel was without the true [4] God, and without a teaching priest, and without law; but when in their distress they turned to the LORD, the God [5] of Israel, and sought him, he was found by them. In those times there was no peace to him who went out or to him who came in, for great disturbances afflicted all the in-[6] habitants of the lands. They were broken in pieces, nation against nation and city against city, for God troubled them [7] with every sort of distress. But you, take courage! Do not let your hands be weak, for your work shall be rewarded."

[8] When Asa heard these words, the prophecy of Azari'ah the son of Oded,[c] he took courage, and put away the abominable idols from all the land of Judah and Benjamin and from the cities which he had taken in the hill country of E'phraim, and he repaired the altar of the LORD that was in front of the vestibule of the house of the LORD.[d] [9] And he gathered all Judah and Benjamin, and those from E'phraim, Manas'seh, and Simeon who were sojourning with them, for great numbers had deserted to him from Israel when they saw that the LORD his God was with him. [10] They were gathered at Jerusalem in the third month of [11] the fifteenth year of the reign of Asa. They sacrificed to the LORD on that day, from the spoil which they had brought, seven hundred oxen and seven thousand sheep. [12] And they entered into a covenant to seek the LORD, the God of their fathers, with all their heart and with all [13] their soul; and that whoever would not seek the LORD, the God of Israel, should be put to death, whether young or [14] old, man or woman. They took oath to the LORD with a loud voice, and with shouting, and with trumpets, and [15] with horns. And all Judah rejoiced over the oath; for they had sworn with all their heart, and had sought him with their whole desire, and he was found by them, and the LORD gave them rest round about.

[16] Even Ma'acah, his mother, King Asa removed from being queen mother because she had made an abominable image for Ashe'rah. Asa cut down her image, crushed it, [17] and burned it at the brook Kidron. But the high places were not taken out of Israel. Nevertheless the heart of Asa [18] was blameless all his days. And he brought into the house of God the votive gifts of his father and his own votive [19] gifts, silver, and gold, and vessels. And there was no more war until the thirty-fifth year of the reign of Asa.

[16] In the thirty-sixth year of the reign of Asa, Ba'asha king of Israel went up against Judah, and built Ramah, that he might permit no one to go out or come [2] in to Asa king of Judah. Then Asa took silver and gold from the treasures of the house of the LORD and the king's house, and sent them to Ben-ha'dad king of Syria, who [3] dwelt in Damascus, saying, "Let there be a league between me and you, as between my father and your father; behold, I am sending to you silver and gold; go, break your league with Ba'asha king of Israel, that he may with-[4] draw from me." And Ben-ha'dad hearkened to King Asa, and sent the commanders of his armies against the cities of Israel, and they conquered I'jon, Dan, A'bel-ma'im, [5] and all the store-cities of Naph'tali. And when Ba'asha heard of it, he stopped building Ramah, and let his work [6] cease. Then King Asa took all Judah, and they carried away the stones of Ramah and its timber, with which Ba'-asha had been building, and with them he built Geba and Mizpah.

[7] At that time Hana'ni the seer came to Asa king of Judah, and said to him, "Because you relied on the king of Syria, and did not rely on the LORD your God, the army [8] of the king of Syria has escaped you. Were not the Ethiopians and the Libyans a huge army with exceedingly many chariots and horsemen? Yet because you relied on [9] the LORD, he gave them into your hand. For the eyes of

---

[a] Heb they   [b] Heb obscure   [c] Compare Syr Vg: Heb the prophecy, Oded the prophet   [d] Heb the vestibule of the LORD

the LORD run to and fro throughout the whole earth, to show his might in behalf of those whose heart is blameless toward him. You have done foolishly in this; for 10 from now on you will have wars." Then Asa was angry with the seer, and put him in the stocks, in prison, for he was in a rage with him because of this. And Asa inflicted cruelties upon some of the people at the same time.

11 The acts of Asa, from first to last, are written in the 12 Book of the Kings of Judah and Israel. In the thirty-ninth year of his reign Asa was diseased in his feet, and his disease became severe; yet even in his disease he did not 13 seek the LORD, but sought help from physicians. And Asa slept with his fathers, dying in the forty-first year of his 14 reign. They buried him in the tomb which he had hewn out for himself in the city of David. They laid him on a bier which had been filled with various kinds of spices prepared by the perfumer's art; and they made a very great fire in his honor.

Reign of Jehoshaphat

17 Jehosh'aphat his son reigned in his stead, and
2 strengthened himself against Israel. He placed forces in all the fortified cities of Judah, and set garrisons in the land of Judah, and in the cities of E'phraim which 3 Asa his father had taken. The LORD was with Jehosh'-aphat, because he walked in the earlier ways of his 4 father; e he did not seek the Ba'als, but sought the God of his father and walked in his commandments, and not 5 according to the ways of Israel. Therefore the LORD established the kingdom in his hand; and all Judah brought tribute to Jehosh'aphat; and he had great riches 6 and honor. His heart was courageous in the way of the LORD; and furthermore he took the high places and the Ashe'rim out of Judah.

7 In the third year of his reign he sent his princes, Ben-hail, Obadi'ah, Zechari'ah, Nethan'el, and Micai'ah, 8 to teach in the cities of Judah; and with them the Levites, Shemai'ah, Nethani'ah, Zebadi'ah, As'ahel, Shemi'ramoth, Jehon'athan, Adoni'jah, Tobi'jah, and Tobadoni'jah; and with these Levites, the priests Elish'ama and Jeho'ram. 9 And they taught in Judah, having the book of the law of the LORD with them; they went about through all the cities of Judah and taught among the people.

10 And the fear of the LORD fell upon all the kingdoms of the lands that were round about Judah, and they made 11 no war against Jehosh'aphat. Some of the Philistines brought Jehosh'aphat presents, and silver for tribute; and the Arabs also brought him seven thousand seven hundred 12 rams and seven thousand seven hundred he-goats. And Jehosh'aphat grew steadily greater. He built in Judah 13 fortresses and store-cities, and he had great stores in the cities of Judah. He had soldiers, mighty men of valor, 14 in Jerusalem. This was the muster of them by fathers' houses: Of Judah, the commanders of thousands: Adnah the commander, with three hundred thousand mighty men

15 of valor, and next to him Jehoha'nan the commander, 16 with two hundred and eighty thousand, and next to him Amasi'ah the son of Zichri, a volunteer for the service of the LORD, with two hundred thousand mighty men of 17 valor. Of Benjamin: Eli'ada, a mighty man of valor, with two hundred thousand men armed with bow and shield, 18 and next to him Jeho'zabad with a hundred and eighty 19 thousand armed for war. These were in the service of the king, besides those whom the king had placed in the fortified cities throughout all Judah.

18 Now Jehosh'aphat had great riches and honor;
2 and he made a marriage alliance with Ahab. After some years he went down to Ahab in Samar'ia. And Ahab killed an abundance of sheep and oxen for him and for the people who were with him, and induced him to go 3 up against Ramoth-gilead. Ahab king of Israel said to Jehosh'aphat king of Judah, "Will you go with me to Ramoth-gilead?" He answered him, "I am as you are, my people as your people. We will be with you in the war."

4 And Jehosh'aphat said to the king of Israel, "Inquire 5 first for the word of the LORD." Then the king of Israel gathered the prophets together, four hundred men, and said to them, "Shall we go to battle against Ramoth-gilead, or shall I forbear?" And they said, "Go up; for 6 God will give it into the hand of the king." But Jehosh'-aphat said, "Is there not here another prophet of the 7 LORD of whom we may inquire?" And the king of Israel said to Jehosh'aphat, "There is yet one man by whom we may inquire of the LORD, Micai'ah the son of Imlah; but I hate him, for he never prophesies good concerning me, but always evil." And Jehosh'aphat said, "Let not the 8 king say so." Then the king of Israel summoned an officer 9 and said, "Bring quickly Micai'ah the son of Imlah." Now the king of Israel and Jehosh'aphat the king of Judah were sitting on their thrones, arrayed in their robes; and they were sitting at the threshing floor at the entrance of the gate of Samar'ia; and all the prophets were prophesy-10 ing before them. And Zedeki'ah the son of Chena'anah made for himself horns of iron, and said, "Thus says the LORD, 'With these you shall push the Syrians until they 11 are destroyed.'" And all the prophets prophesied so, and said, "Go up to Ramoth-gilead and triumph; the LORD will give it into the hand of the king."

12 And the messenger who went to summon Micai'ah said to him, "Behold, the words of the prophets with one accord are favorable to the king; let your word be like the 13 word of one of them, and speak favorably." But Micai'ah said, "As the LORD lives, what my God says, that I will 14 speak." And when he had come to the king, the king said to him, "Micai'ah, shall we go to Ramoth-gilead to battle, or shall I forbear?" And he answered, "Go up and 15 triumph; they will be given into your hand." But the king said to him, "How many times shall I adjure you that you speak to me nothing but the truth in the name of the

e Another reading is *his father David*

287

16 LORD?" And he said, "I saw all Israel scattered upon the mountains, as sheep that have no shepherd; and the LORD said, 'These have no master; let each return to his 17 home in peace.' " And the king of Israel said to Jehosh'-aphat, "Did I not tell you that he would not prophesy 18 good concerning me, but evil?" And Micai'ah said, "Therefore hear the word of the LORD: I saw the LORD sitting on his throne, and all the host of heaven standing 19 on his right hand and on his left; and the LORD said, 'Who will entice Ahab the king of Israel, that he may go up and fall at Ramoth-gilead?' And one said one thing, 20 and another said another. Then a spirit came forward and stood before the LORD, saying, 'I will entice him.' And the 21 LORD said to him, 'By what means?' And he said, 'I will go forth, and will be a lying spirit in the mouth of all his prophets.' And he said, 'You are to entice him, and you 22 shall succeed; go forth and do so.' Now therefore behold, the LORD has put a lying spirit in the mouth of these your prophets; the LORD has spoken evil concerning you."

23 Then Zedeki'ah the son of Chena'anah came near and struck Micai'ah on the cheek, and said, "Which way did the Spirit of the LORD go from me to speak to you?" 24 And Micai'ah said, "Behold, you shall see on that day when you go into an inner chamber to hide yourself." 25 And the king of Israel said, "Seize Micai'ah, and take him back to Amon the governor of the city and to Jo'ash the 26 king's son; and say, 'Thus says the king, Put this fellow in prison, and feed him with scant fare of bread and 27 water, until I return in peace.' " And Micai'ah said, "If you return in peace, the LORD has not spoken by me." And he said, "Hear, all you peoples!"

28 So the king of Israel and Jehosh'aphat the king of 29 Judah went up to Ramoth-gilead. And the king of Israel said to Jehosh'aphat, "I will disguise myself and go into battle, but you wear your robes." And the king of Israel 30 disguised himself; and they went into battle. Now the king of Syria had commanded the captains of his chariots, "Fight with neither small nor great, but only with the 31 king of Israel." And when the captains of the chariots saw Jehosh'aphat, they said, "It is the king of Israel." So they turned to fight against him; and Jehosh'aphat cried out, and the LORD helped him. God drew them away 32 from him, for when the captains of the chariots saw that it was not the king of Israel, they turned back from pur- 33 suing him. But a certain man drew his bow at a venture, and struck the king of Israel between the scale armor and

the breastplate; therefore he said to the driver of his chariot, "Turn about, and carry me out of the battle, for 34 I am wounded." And the battle grew hot that day, and the king of Israel propped himself up in his chariot facing the Syrians until evening; then at sunset he died.

19 Jehosh'aphat the king of Judah returned in safety 2 to his house in Jerusalem. But Jehu the son of Hana'-ni the seer went out to meet him, and said to King Jehosh'aphat, "Should you help the wicked and love those who hate the LORD? Because of this, wrath has gone out 3 against you from the LORD. Nevertheless some good is found in you, for you destroyed the Ashe'rahs out of the land and have set your heart to seek God."

4 Jehosh'aphat dwelt at Jerusalem; and he went out again among the people, from Beer-sheba to the hill country of E'phraim, and brought them back to the LORD, the God of 5 their fathers. He appointed judges in the land in all the 6 fortified cities of Judah, city by city, and said to the judges, "Consider what you do, for you judge not for man but for the LORD; he is with you in giving judgment. 7 Now then, let the fear of the LORD be upon you; take heed what you do, for there is no perversion of justice with the LORD our God, or partiality, or taking bribes."

8 Moreover in Jerusalem Jehosh'aphat appointed certain Levites and priests and heads of families of Israel, to give judgment for the LORD and to decide disputed cases. They 9 had their seat at Jerusalem. And he charged them: "Thus you shall do in the fear of the LORD, in faithfulness, and 10 with your whole heart: whenever a case comes to you from your brethren who live in their cities, concerning blood-shed, law or commandment, statutes or ordinances, then you shall instruct them, that they may not incur guilt before the LORD and wrath may not come upon you and your brethren. Thus you shall do, and you will not incur 11 guilt. And behold, Amari'ah the chief priest is over you in all matters of the LORD; and Zebadi'ah the son of Ish'-mael, the governor of the house of Judah, in all the king's matters; and the Levites will serve you as officers. Deal courageously, and may the LORD be with the up-right!"

20 After this the Moabites and Ammonites, and with them some of the Me-u'nites,[f] came against Jehosh'- 2 aphat for battle. Some men came and told Jehosh'aphat, "A great multitude is coming against you from Edom,[g] from beyond the sea; and, behold, they are in Haz'azon- 3 ta'mar" (that is, En-ge'di). Then Jehosh'aphat feared, and set himself to seek the LORD, and proclaimed a fast 4 throughout all Judah. And Judah assembled to seek help from the LORD; from all the cities of Judah they came to seek the LORD.

5 And Jehosh'aphat stood in the assembly of Judah and Jerusalem, in the house of the LORD, before the new court, 6 and said, "O LORD, God of our fathers, art thou not

f Compare 26.7: Heb Ammonites   g One Ms: Heb Aram (Syria)

God in heaven? Dost thou not rule over all the kingdoms of the nations? In thy hand are power and might, so that 7 none is able to withstand thee. Didst thou not, O our God, drive out the inhabitants of this land before thy people Israel, and give it for ever to the descendants of Abraham 8 thy friend? And they have dwelt in it, and have built 9 thee in it a sanctuary for thy name, saying, 'If evil comes upon us, the sword, judgment,[h] or pestilence, or famine, we will stand before this house, and before thee, for thy name is in this house, and cry to thee in our affliction, 10 and thou wilt hear and save.' And now behold, the men of Ammon and Moab and Mount Se'ir, whom thou wouldest not let Israel invade when they came from the land of Egypt, and whom they avoided and did not de- 11 stroy—behold, they reward us by coming to drive us out of thy possession, which thou hast given us to inherit. 12 O our God, wilt thou not execute judgment upon them? For we are powerless against this great multitude that is coming against us. We do not know what to do, but our eyes are upon thee."

13 Meanwhile all the men of Judah stood before the LORD, with their little ones, their wives, and their children. 14 And the Spirit of the LORD came upon Jahazi'el the son of Zechari'ah, son of Benai'ah, son of Je-i'el, son of Mattani'ah, a Levite of the sons of Asaph, in the midst 15 of the assembly. And he said, "Hearken, all Judah and inhabitants of Jerusalem, and King Jehosh'aphat: Thus says the LORD to you, 'Fear not, and be not dismayed at this great multitude; for the battle is not yours but God's. 16 Tomorrow go down against them; behold, they will come up by the ascent of Ziz; you will find them at the end of 17 the valley, east of the wilderness of Jeru'el. You will not need to fight in this battle; take your position, stand still, and see the victory of the LORD on your behalf, O Judah and Jerusalem.' Fear not, and be not dismayed; tomorrow go out against them, and the LORD will be with you."

18 Then Jehosh'aphat bowed his head with his face to the ground, and all Judah and the inhabitants of Jerusalem fell down before the LORD, worshiping the LORD. 19 And the Levites, of the Ko'hathites and the Kor'ahites, stood up to praise the LORD, the God of Israel, with a very loud voice.

20 And they rose early in the morning and went out into the wilderness of Teko'a; and as they went out, Jehosh'aphat stood and said, "Hear me, Judah and inhabitants of Jerusalem! Believe in the LORD your God, and you will be established; believe his prophets, and you will suc- 21 ceed." And when he had taken counsel with the people, he appointed those who were to sing to the LORD and praise him in holy array, as they went before the army, and say,

"Give thanks to the LORD,
    for his steadfast love endures for ever."

22 And when they began to sing and praise, the LORD set an ambush against the men of Ammon, Moab, and Mount Se'ir, who had come against Judah, so that they were 23 routed. For the men of Ammon and Moab rose against the inhabitants of Mount Se'ir, destroying them utterly, and when they had made an end of the inhabitants of Se'ir, they all helped to destroy one another.

24 When Judah came to the watchtower of the wilderness, they looked toward the multitude; and behold, they were dead bodies lying on the ground; none had escaped. 25 When Jehosh'aphat and his people came to take the spoil from them, they found cattle[i] in great numbers, goods, clothing, and precious things, which they took for themselves until they could carry no more. They were three 26 days in taking the spoil, it was so much. On the fourth day they assembled in the Valley of Bera'cah,[j] for there they blessed the LORD; therefore the name of that place 27 has been called the Valley of Bera'cah to this day. Then they returned, every man of Judah and Jerusalem, and Jehosh'aphat at their head, returning to Jerusalem with joy, for the LORD had made them rejoice over their ene- 28 mies. They came to Jerusalem, with harps and lyres and 29 trumpets, to the house of the LORD. And the fear of God came on all the kingdoms of the countries when they heard that the LORD had fought against the enemies of 30 Israel. So the realm of Jehosh'aphat was quiet, for his God gave him rest round about.

31 Thus Jehosh'aphat reigned over Judah. He was thirty-five years old when he began to reign, and he reigned twenty-five years in Jerusalem. His mother's name was 32 Azu'bah the daughter of Shilhi. He walked in the way of Asa his father and did not turn aside from it; he did 33 what was right in the sight of the LORD. The high places, however, were not taken away; the people had not yet set their hearts upon the God of their fathers.

34 Now the rest of the acts of Jehosh'aphat, from first to last, are written in the chronicles of Jehu the son of Hana'ni, which are recorded in the Book of the Kings of Israel.

35 After this Jehosh'aphat king of Judah joined with 36 Ahazi'ah king of Israel, who did wickedly. He joined him in building ships to go to Tarshish, and they built the 37 ships in E'zion-ge'ber. Then Elie'zer the son of Dodav'ahu of Mare'shah prophesied against Jehosh'aphat, saying, "Because you have joined with Ahazi'ah, the LORD will destroy what you have made." And the ships were wrecked and were not able to go to Tarshish.

Jehoram, Ahaziah, and Athaliah

21 Jehosh'aphat slept with his fathers, and was buried with his fathers in the city of David; and Jeho'ram 2 his son reigned in his stead. He had brothers, the sons of Jehosh'aphat: Azari'ah, Jehi'el, Zechari'ah, Azari'ah, Michael, and Shephati'ah; all these were the sons of 3 Jehosh'aphat king of Judah. Their father gave them great

[h] Or *the sword of judgment*   [i] Gk: Heb *among them*   [j] That is *Blessing*

gifts, of silver, gold, and valuable possessions, together with fortified cities in Judah; but he gave the kingdom to 4 Jeho′ram, because he was the first-born. When Jeho′ram had ascended the throne of his father and was established, he slew all his brothers with the sword, and also some of 5 the princes of Israel. Jeho′ram was thirty-two years old when he became king, and he reigned eight years in Jeru- 6 salem. And he walked in the way of the kings of Israel, as the house of Ahab had done; for the daughter of Ahab was his wife. And he did what was evil in the sight of the 7 Lord. Yet the Lord would not destroy the house of David, because of the covenant which he had made with David, and since he had promised to give a lamp to him and to his sons for ever.

8 In his days Edom revolted from the rule of Judah, and 9 set up a king of their own. Then Jeho′ram passed over with his commanders and all his chariots, and he rose by night and smote the E′domites who had surrounded 10 him and his chariot commanders. So Edom revolted from the rule of Judah to this day. At that time Libnah also revolted from his rule, because he had forsaken the Lord, the God of his fathers.

11 Moreover he made high places in the hill country of Judah, and led the inhabitants of Jerusalem into unfaith- 12 fulness, and made Judah go astray. And a letter came to him from Eli′jah the prophet, saying, "Thus says the Lord, the God of David your father, 'Because you have not walked in the ways of Jehosh′aphat your father, or 13 in the ways of Asa king of Judah, but have walked in the way of the kings of Israel, and have led Judah and the inhabitants of Jerusalem into unfaithfulness, as the house of Ahab led Israel into unfaithfulness, and also you have killed your brothers, of your father's house, who were 14 better than yourself; behold, the Lord will bring a great plague on your people, your children, your wives, and all 15 your possessions, and you yourself will have a severe sickness with a disease of your bowels, until your bowels come out because of the disease, day by day.'"

16 And the Lord stirred up against Jeho′ram the anger of the Philistines and of the Arabs who are near the 17 Ethiopians; and they came up against Judah, and invaded it, and carried away all the possessions they found that belonged to the king's house, and also his sons and his wives, so that no son was left to him except Jeho′ahaz, his youngest son.

18 And after all this the Lord smote him in his bowels 19 with an incurable disease. In course of time, at the end of two years, his bowels came out because of the disease, and he died in great agony. His people made no fire in 20 his honor, like the fires made for his fathers. He was thirty-two years old when he began to reign, and he reigned eight years in Jerusalem; and he departed with no one's regret. They buried him in the city of David, but not in the tombs of the kings.

22 And the inhabitants of Jerusalem made Ahazi′ah his youngest son king in his stead; for the band of men that came with the Arabs to the camp had slain all the older sons. So Ahazi′ah the son of Jeho′ram king 2 of Judah reigned. Ahazi′ah was forty-two years old when he began to reign, and he reigned one year in Jerusalem. His mother's name was Athali′ah, the granddaughter of 3 Omri. He also walked in the ways of the house of Ahab, 4 for his mother was his counselor in doing wickedly. He did what was evil in the sight of the Lord, as the house of Ahab had done; for after the death of his father they 5 were his counselors, to his undoing. He even followed their counsel, and went with Jeho′ram the son of Ahab king of Israel to make war against Haz′ael king of Syria 6 at Ramoth-gilead. And the Syrians wounded Joram, and he returned to be healed in Jezreel of the wounds which he had received at Ramah, when he fought against Haz′ael king of Syria. And Ahazi′ah the son of Jeho′ram king of Judah went down to see Joram the son of Ahab in Jezreel, because he was sick.

7 But it was ordained by God that the downfall of Ahazi′- ah should come about through his going to visit Joram. For when he came there he went out with Jeho′ram to meet Jehu the son of Nimshi, whom the Lord had 8 anointed to destroy the house of Ahab. And when Jehu was executing judgment upon the house of Ahab, he met the princes of Judah and the sons of Ahazi′ah's 9 brothers, who attended Ahazi′ah, and he killed them. He searched for Ahazi′ah, and he was captured while hiding in Samar′ia, and he was brought to Jehu and put to death. They buried him, for they said, "He is the grandson of Jehosh′aphat, who sought the Lord with all his heart." And the house of Ahazi′ah had no one able to rule the kingdom.

10 Now when Athali′ah the mother of Ahazi′ah saw that her son was dead, she arose and destroyed all the royal 11 family of the house of Judah. But Jeho-shab′e-ath, the daughter of the king, took Jo′ash the son of Ahazi′ah, and stole him away from among the king's sons who were about to be slain, and she put him and his nurse in a bedchamber. Thus Jeho-shab′e-ath, the daughter of King Jeho′ram and wife of Jehoi′ada the priest, because she was a sister of Ahazi′ah, hid him from Athali′ah, so that

12 she did not slay him; and he remained with them six years, hid in the house of God, while Athali'ah reigned over the land.

23 But in the seventh year Jehoi'ada took courage, and entered into a compact with the commanders of hundreds, Azari'ah the son of Jero'ham, Ish'mael the son of Jehoha'nan, Azari'ah the son of Obed, Ma-asei'ah the 2 son of Adai'ah, and Elisha'phat the son of Zichri. And they went about through Judah and gathered the Levites from all the cities of Judah, and the heads of fathers' 3 houses of Israel, and they came to Jerusalem. And all the assembly made a covenant with the king in the house of God. And Jehoi'ada [1] said to them, "Behold, the king's son! Let him reign, as the LORD spoke concerning the sons 4 of David. This is the thing that you shall do: of you priests and Levites who come off duty on the sabbath, one 5 third shall be gatekeepers, and one third shall be at the king's house and one third at the Gate of the Foundation; and all the people shall be in the courts of the house of the 6 LORD. Let no one enter the house of the LORD except the priests and ministering Levites; they may enter, for they are holy, but all the people shall keep the charge of the 7 LORD. The Levites shall surround the king, each with his weapons in his hand; and whoever enters the house shall be slain. Be with the king when he comes in, and when he goes out."

8 The Levites and all Judah did according to all that Jehoi'ada the priest commanded. They each brought his men, who were to go off duty on the sabbath, with those who were to come on duty on the sabbath; for Jehoi'ada 9 the priest did not dismiss the divisions. And Jehoi'ada the priest delivered to the captains the spears and the large and small shields that had been King David's, which were 10 in the house of God; and he set all the people as a guard for the king, every man with his weapon in his hand, from the south side of the house to the north side of the house, 11 around the altar and the house. Then he brought out the king's son, and put the crown upon him, and gave him the testimony; and they proclaimed him king, and Jehoi'- ada and his sons anointed him, and they said, "Long live the king."

12 When Athali'ah heard the noise of the people running and praising the king, she went into the house of the 13 LORD to the people; and when she looked, there was the king standing by his pillar at the entrance, and the captains and the trumpeters beside the king, and all the people of the land rejoicing and blowing trumpets, and the singers with their musical instruments leading in the celebration. And Athali'ah rent her clothes, and cried, 14 "Treason! Treason!" Then Jehoi'ada the priest brought out the captains who were set over the army, saying to them, "Bring her out between the ranks; any one who follows her is to be slain with the sword." For the priest 15 said, "Do not slay her in the house of the LORD." So they

laid hands on her; and she went into the entrance of the horse gate of the king's house, and they slew her there. 16 And Jehoi'ada made a covenant between himself and all the people and the king that they should be the LORD's 17 people. Then all the people went to the house of Ba'al, and tore it down; his altars and his images they broke in pieces, and they slew Mattan the priest of Ba'al before 18 the altars. And Jehoi'ada posted watchmen for the house of the LORD under the direction of the Levitical priests and the Levites whom David had organized to be in charge of the house of the LORD, to offer burnt offerings to the LORD, as it is written in the law of Moses, with rejoicing and with singing, according to the order of 19 David. He stationed the gatekeepers at the gates of the house of the LORD so that no one should enter who was in 20 any way unclean. And he took the captains, the nobles, the governors of the people, and all the people of the land; and they brought the king down from the house of the LORD, marching through the upper gate to the king's 21 house. And they set the king upon the royal throne. So all the people of the land rejoiced; and the city was quiet, after Athali'ah had been slain with the sword.

Reign of Joash

24 Jo'ash was seven years old when he began to reign, and he reigned forty years in Jerusalem; his 2 mother's name was Zib'iah of Beer-sheba. And Jo'ash did what was right in the eyes of the LORD all the days of 3 Jehoi'ada the priest. Jehoi'ada got for him two wives, and he had sons and daughters.

4 After this Jo'ash decided to restore the house of the 5 LORD. And he gathered the priests and the Levites, and said to them, "Go out to the cities of Judah, and gather from all Israel money to repair the house of your God from year to year; and see that you hasten the matter." 6 But the Levites did not hasten it. So the king summoned Jehoi'ada the chief, and said to him, "Why have you not required the Levites to bring in from Judah and Jerusalem the tax levied by Moses, the servant of the LORD, on [m] the congregation of Israel for the tent of testimony?" 7 For the sons of Athali'ah, that wicked woman, had broken into the house of God; and had also used all the dedicated things of the house of the LORD for the Ba'als.

8 So the king commanded, and they made a chest, and 9 set it outside the gate of the house of the LORD. And proclamation was made throughout Judah and Jerusalem, to bring in for the LORD the tax that Moses the servant of 10 God laid upon Israel in the wilderness. And all the princes and all the people rejoiced and brought their tax and 11 dropped it into the chest until they had finished. And whenever the chest was brought to the king's officers by the Levites, when they saw that there was much money in it, the king's secretary and the officer of the chief priest would come and empty the chest and take it and return it

[1] Heb he   [m] Compare Vg: Heb and

to its place. Thus they did day after day, and collected
12 money in abundance. And the king and Jehoi'ada gave
it to those who had charge of the work of the house of
the LORD, and they hired masons and carpenters to restore
the house of the LORD, and also workers in iron and
13 bronze to repair the house of the LORD. So those who were
engaged in the work labored, and the repairing went forward in their hands, and they restored the house of God
14 to its proper condition and strengthened it. And when
they had finished, they brought the rest of the money
before the king and Jehoi'ada, and with it were made
utensils for the house of the LORD, both for the service and
for the burnt offerings, and dishes for incense, and vessels
of gold and silver. And they offered burnt offerings in
the house of the LORD continually all the days of Jehoi'ada.
15 But Jehoi'ada grew old and full of days, and died; he
16 was a hundred and thirty years old at his death. And
they buried him in the city of David among the kings,
because he had done good in Israel, and toward God and
his house.
17 Now after the death of Jehoi'ada the princes of Judah
came and did obeisance to the king; then the king
18 hearkened to them. And they forsook the house of the
LORD, the God of their fathers, and served the Ashe'rim
and the idols. And wrath came upon Judah and Jerusalem
19 for this their guilt. Yet he sent prophets among them to
bring them back to the LORD; these testified against them,
but they would not give heed.
20 Then the Spirit of God took possession of n Zechari'ah
the son of Jehoi'ada the priest; and he stood above the
people, and said to them, "Thus says God, 'Why do you
transgress the commandments of the LORD, so that you
cannot prosper? Because you have forsaken the LORD,
21 he has forsaken you.'" But they conspired against him,
and by command of the king they stoned him with stones
22 in the court of the house of the LORD. Thus Jo'ash the king
did not remember the kindness which Jehoi'ada, Zechari'-
ah's father, had shown him, but killed his son. And when
he was dying, he said, "May the LORD see and avenge!"
23 At the end of the year the army of the Syrians came
up against Jo'ash. They came to Judah and Jerusalem, and
destroyed all the princes of the people from among the
people, and sent all their spoil to the king of Damascus.
24 Though the army of the Syrians had come with few men,
the LORD delivered into their hand a very great army,
because they had forsaken the LORD, the God of their
fathers. Thus they executed judgment on Jo'ash.
25 When they had departed from him, leaving him severely
wounded, his servants conspired against him because of
the blood of the son o of Jehoi'ada the priest, and slew
him on his bed. So he died; and they buried him in the
city of David, but they did not bury him in the tombs
26 of the king. Those who conspired against him were Zabad
the son of Shim'e-ath the Ammonitess, and Jeho'zabad

27 the son of Shimrith the Moabitess. Accounts of his sons,
and of the many oracles against him, and of the rebuilding p of the house of God are written in the Commentary
on the Book of the Kings. And Amazi'ah his son reigned
in his stead.

Reign of Amaziah

25 Amazi'ah was twenty-five years old when he began to reign, and he reigned twenty-nine years in
Jerusalem. His mother's name was Jeho-ad'dan of Jeru-
2 salem. And he did what was right in the eyes of the LORD,
3 yet not with a blameless heart. And as soon as the royal
power was firmly in his hand he killed his servants who
4 had slain the king his father. But he did not put their
children to death, according to what is written in the
law, in the book of Moses, where the LORD commanded,
"The fathers shall not be put to death for the children,
or the children be put to death for the fathers; but every
man shall die for his own sin."
5 Then Amazi'ah assembled the men of Judah, and set
them by fathers' houses under commanders of thousands
and of hundreds for all Judah and Benjamin. He mustered
those twenty years old and upward, and found that they
were three hundred thousand picked men, fit for war, able
6 to handle spear and shield. He hired also a hundred
thousand mighty men of valor from Israel for a hundred
7 talents of silver. But a man of God came to him and said,
"O king, do not let the army of Israel go with you, for
the LORD is not with Israel, with all these E'phraimites.
8 But if you suppose that in this way you will be strong
for war,q God will cast you down before the enemy; for
9 God has power to help or to cast down." And Amazi'ah
said to the man of God, "But what shall we do about the
hundred talents which I have given to the army of Israel?"
The man of God answered, "The LORD is able to give
10 you much more than this." Then Amazi'ah discharged
the army that had come to him from E'phraim, to go
home again. And they became very angry with Judah,
11 and returned home in fierce anger. But Amazi'ah took
courage, and led out his people, and went to the Valley of
12 Salt and smote ten thousand men of Se'ir. The men of
Judah captured another ten thousand alive, and took them
to the top of a rock and threw them down from the top
13 of the rock; and they were all dashed to pieces. But the
men of the army whom Amazi'ah sent back, not letting
them go with him to battle, fell upon the cities of Judah,
from Samar'ia to Beth-hor'on, and killed three thousand
people in them, and took much spoil.
14 After Amazi'ah came from the slaughter of the E'domites, he brought the gods of the men of Se'ir, and set them
up as his gods, and worshiped them, making offerings to
15 them. Therefore the LORD was angry with Amazi'ah and
sent to him a prophet, who said to him, "Why have you
resorted to the gods of a people, which did not deliver

n Heb *clothed itself with*   o Gk Vg: Heb *sons*   p Heb *founding*   q Gk: Heb *But if you go, act, be strong for the battle*

16 their own people from your hand?" But as he was speaking the king said to him, "Have we made you a royal counselor? Stop! Why should you be put to death?" So the prophet stopped, but said, "I know that God has determined to destroy you, because you have done this and have not listened to my counsel."

17 Then Amazi'ah king of Judah took counsel and sent to Jo'ash the son of Jeho'ahaz, son of Jehu, king of Israel,

18 saying, "Come, let us look one another in the face." And Jo'ash the king of Israel sent word to Amazi'ah king of Judah, "A thistle on Lebanon sent to a cedar on Lebanon, saying, 'Give your daughter to my son for a wife'; and a wild beast of Lebanon passed by and trampled down the

19 thistle. You say, 'See, I have smitten Edom,' and your heart has lifted you up in boastfulness. But now stay at home; why should you provoke trouble so that you fall, you and Judah with you?"

20 But Amazi'ah would not listen; for it was of God, in order that he might give them into the hand of their enemies, because they had sought the gods of Edom.

21 So Jo'ash king of Israel went up; and he and Amazi'ah king of Judah faced one another in battle at Beth-she'-

22 mesh, which belongs to Judah. And Judah was defeated

23 by Israel, and every man fled to his home. And Jo'ash king of Israel captured Amazi'ah king of Judah, the son of Jo'ash, son of Ahazi'ah, at Beth-she'mesh, and brought him to Jerusalem, and broke down the wall of Jerusalem for four hundred cubits, from the E'phraim Gate to the

24 Corner Gate. And he seized all the gold and silver, and all the vessels that were found in the house of God, and O'bed-e'dom with them; he seized also the treasuries of the king's house, and hostages, and he returned to Samar'ia.

25 Amazi'ah the son of Jo'ash king of Judah lived fifteen years after the death of Jo'ash the son of Jeho'ahaz, king

26 of Israel. Now the rest of the deeds of Amazi'ah, from first to last, are they not written in the Book of the Kings

27 of Judah and Israel? From the time when he turned away from the LORD they made a conspiracy against him in Jerusalem, and he fled to Lachish. But they sent after

28 him to Lachish, and slew him there. And they brought him upon horses; and he was buried with his fathers in the city of David.

Uzziah, Jotham, and Ahaz

26 And all the people of Judah took Uzzi'ah, who was sixteen years old, and made him king instead

2 of his father Amazi'ah. He built Eloth and restored it to

3 Judah, after the king slept with his fathers. Uzzi'ah was sixteen years old when he began to reign, and he reigned fifty-two years in Jerusalem. His mother's name was

4 Jecoli'ah of Jerusalem. And he did what was right in the eyes of the LORD, according to all that his father Amazi'-

5 ah had done. He set himself to seek God in the days of Zechari'ah, who instructed him in the fear of God; and as long as he sought the LORD, God made him prosper.

6 He went out and made war against the Philistines, and broke down the wall of Gath and the wall of Jabneh and the wall of Ashdod; and he built cities in the territory of

7 Ashdod and elsewhere among the Philistines. God helped him against the Philistines, and against the Arabs that

8 dwelt in Gurba'al, and against the Me-u'nites. The Ammonites paid tribute to Uzzi'ah, and his fame spread even

9 to the border of Egypt, for he became very strong. Moreover Uzzi'ah built towers in Jerusalem at the Corner Gate and at the Valley Gate and at the Angle, and fortified

10 them. And he built towers in the wilderness, and hewed out many cisterns, for he had large herds, both in the Shephe'lah and in the plain, and he had farmers and vinedressers in the hills and in the fertile lands, for he

11 loved the soil. Moreover Uzzi'ah had an army of soldiers, fit for war, in divisions according to the numbers in the muster made by Je-i'el the secretary and Ma-asei'ah the officer, under the direction of Hanani'ah, one of the king's

12 commanders. The whole number of the heads of fathers' houses of mighty men of valor was two thousand six

13 hundred. Under their command was an army of three hundred and seven thousand five hundred, who could make war with mighty power, to help the king against the

14 enemy. And Uzzi'ah prepared for all the army shields, spears, helmets, coats of mail, bows, and stones for sling-

15 ing. In Jerusalem he made engines, invented by skilful men, to be on the towers and the corners, to shoot arrows and great stones. And his fame spread far, for he was marvelously helped, till he was strong.

16 But when he was strong he grew proud, to his destruction. For he was false to the LORD his God, and entered the temple of the LORD to burn incense on the altar of in-

17 cense. But Azari'ah the priest went in after him, with

18 eighty priests of the LORD who were men of valor; and they withstood King Uzzi'ah, and said to him, "It is not for you, Uzzi'ah, to burn incense to the LORD, but for the priests the sons of Aaron, who are consecrated to burn incense. Go out of the sanctuary; for you have done wrong, and it will bring you no honor from the LORD

19 God." Then Uzzi'ah was angry. Now he had a censer in his hand to burn incense, and when he became angry with the priests leprosy broke out on his forehead, in the presence of the priests in the house of the LORD, by the

20 altar of incense. And Azari'ah the chief priest, and all the priests, looked at him, and behold, he was leprous in

his forehead! And they thrust him out quickly, and he himself hastened to go out, because the LORD had smitten 21 him. And King Uzzi'ah was a leper to the day of his death, and being a leper dwelt in a separate house, for he was excluded from the house of the LORD. And Jotham his son was over the king's household, governing the people of the land.

22 Now the rest of the acts of Uzzi'ah, from first to last, 23 Isaiah the prophet the son of Amoz wrote. And Uzzi'ah slept with his fathers, and they buried him with his fathers in the burial field which belonged to the kings, for they said, "He is a leper." And Jotham his son reigned in his stead.

27 Jotham was twenty-five years old when he began to reign, and he reigned sixteen years in Jerusalem. His mother's name was Jeru'shah the daughter of Zadok. 2 And he did what was right in the eyes of the LORD according to all that his father Uzzi'ah had done—only he did not invade the temple of the LORD. But the people still 3 followed corrupt practices. He built the upper gate of the house of the LORD, and did much building on the 4 wall of Ophel. Moreover he built cities in the hill country of Judah, and forts and towers on the wooded hills. 5 He fought with the king of the Ammonites and prevailed against them. And the Ammonites gave him that year a hundred talents of silver, and ten thousand cors of wheat and ten thousand of barley. The Ammonites paid him the 6 same amount in the second and the third years. So Jotham became mighty, because he ordered his ways before the 7 LORD his God. Now the rest of the acts of Jotham, and all his wars, and his ways, behold, they are written in the 8 Book of the Kings of Israel and Judah. He was twenty-five years old when he began to reign, and he reigned sixteen 9 years in Jerusalem. And Jotham slept with his fathers, and they buried him in the city of David; and Ahaz his son reigned in his stead.

28 Ahaz was twenty years old when he began to reign, and he reigned sixteen years in Jerusalem. And he did not do what was right in the eyes of the LORD, like his 2 father David, but walked in the ways of the kings of 3 Israel. He even made molten images for the Ba'als; and he burned incense in the valley of the son of Hinnom, and burned his sons as an offering, according to the abominable practices of the nations whom the LORD drove out 4 before the people of Israel. And he sacrificed and burned incense on the high places, and on the hills, and under every green tree.

5 Therefore the LORD his God gave him into the hand of the king of Syria, who defeated him and took captive a great number of his people and brought them to Damascus. He was also given into the hand of the king of 6 Israel, who defeated him with great slaughter. For Pekah the son of Remali'ah slew a hundred and twenty thousand in Judah in one day, all of them men of valor, because

they had forsaken the LORD, the God of their fathers. 7 And Zichri, a mighty man of E'phraim, slew Ma-asei'ah the king's son and Azri'kam the commander of the palace and Elka'nah the next in authority to the king.

8 The men of Israel took captive two hundred thousand of their kinsfolk, women, sons, and daughters; they also took much spoil from them and brought the spoil to 9 Samar'ia. But a prophet of the LORD was there, whose name was Oded; and he went out to meet the army that came to Samar'ia, and said to them, "Behold, because the LORD, the God of your fathers, was angry with Judah, he gave them into your hand, but you have slain them in 10 a rage which has reached up to heaven. And now you intend to subjugate the people of Judah and Jerusalem, male and female, as your slaves. Have you not sins of 11 your own against the LORD your God? Now hear me, and send back the captives from your kinsfolk whom you have 12 taken, for the fierce wrath of the LORD is upon you." Certain chiefs also of the men of E'phraim, Azari'ah the son of Joha'nan, Berechi'ah the son of Meshil'lemoth, Jehizki'-ah the son of Shallum, and Ama'sa the son of Hadlai, stood up against those who were coming from the war, 13 and said to them, "You shall not bring the captives in here, for you propose to bring upon us guilt against the LORD in addition to our present sins and guilt. For our guilt is already great, and there is fierce wrath against 14 Israel." So the armed men left the captives and the spoil 15 before the princes and all the assembly. And the men who have been mentioned by name rose and took the captives, and with the spoil they clothed all that were naked among them; they clothed them, gave them sandals, provided them with food and drink, and anointed them; and carrying all the feeble among them on asses, they brought them to their kinsfolk at Jericho, the city of palm trees. Then they returned to Samar'ia.

16 At that time King Ahaz sent to the king r of Assyria 17 for help. For the E'domites had again invaded and de-18 feated Judah, and carried away captives. And the Philistines had made raids on the cities in the Shephe'lah and the Negeb of Judah, and had taken Beth-she'mesh, Ai'jalon, Gede'roth, Soco with its villages, Timnah with its villages, and Gimzo with its villages; and they settled 19 there. For the LORD brought Judah low because of Ahaz king of Israel, for he had dealt wantonly in Judah and 20 had been faithless to the LORD. So Til'gath-pilne'ser king of Assyria came against him, and afflicted him instead of 21 strengthening him. For Ahaz took from the house of the LORD and the house of the king and of the princes, and gave tribute to the king of Assyria; but it did not help him.

22 In the time of his distress he became yet more faithless 23 to the LORD—this same King Ahaz. For he sacrificed to the gods of Damascus which had defeated him, and said, "Because the gods of the kings of Syria helped them, I

r Gk Syr Vg Compare 2 K 16.7: Heb kings

will sacrifice to them that they may help me." But they
24 were the ruin of him, and of all Israel. And Ahaz gathered
together the vessels of the house of God and cut in pieces
the vessels of the house of God, and he shut up the doors
of the house of the LORD; and he made himself altars in
25 every corner of Jerusalem. In every city of Judah he made
high places to burn incense to other gods, provoking to
26 anger the LORD, the God of his fathers. Now the rest of
his acts and all his ways, from first to last, behold, they
are written in the Book of the Kings of Judah and Israel.
27 And Ahaz slept with his fathers, and they buried him in
the city, in Jerusalem, for they did not bring him into the
tombs of the kings of Israel. And Hezeki'ah his son
reigned in his stead.

Reign of Hezekiah

29 Hezeki'ah began to reign when he was twenty-five
years old, and he reigned twenty-nine years in Jerusalem. His mother's name was Abi'jah the daughter of
2 Zechari'ah. And he did what was right in the eyes of
the LORD, according to all that David his father had done.
3   In the first year of his reign, in the first month, he
opened the doors of the house of the LORD, and repaired
4 them. He brought in the priests and the Levites, and as-
5 sembled them in the square on the east, and said to them,
"Hear me, Levites! Now sanctify yourselves, and sanctify
the house of the LORD, the God of your fathers, and carry
6 out the filth from the holy place. For our fathers have
been unfaithful and have done what was evil in the sight
of the LORD our God; they have forsaken him, and have
turned away their faces from the habitation of the LORD,
7 and turned their backs. They also shut the doors of the

vestibule and put out the lamps, and have not burned
incense or offered burnt offerings in the holy place to the
8 God of Israel. Therefore the wrath of the LORD came on
Judah and Jerusalem, and he has made them an object of
horror, of astonishment, and of hissing, as you see with
9 your own eyes. For lo, our fathers have fallen by the
sword and our sons and our daughters and our wives are
10 in captivity for this. Now it is in my heart to make a
covenant with the LORD, the God of Israel, that his fierce
11 anger may turn away from us. My sons, do not now be
negligent, for the LORD has chosen you to stand in his
presence, to minister to him, and to be his ministers and
burn incense to him."

12   Then the Levites arose, Mahath the son of Ama'sai, and
Jo'el the son of Azari'ah, of the sons of the Ko'hathites;
and of the sons of Merar'i, Kish the son of Abdi, and
Azari'ah the son of Jehal'lelel; and of the Gershonites,
13 Jo'ah the son of Zimmah, and Eden the son of Jo'ah; and
of the sons of Eliza'phan, Shimri and Jeu'el; and of the
14 sons of Asaph, Zechari'ah and Mattani'ah; and of the
sons of Heman, Jehu'el and Shim'e-i; and of the sons of
15 Pedu'thun, Shemai'ah and Uz'ziel. They gathered their
brethren, and sanctified themselves, and went in as the
king had commanded, by the words of the LORD, to cleanse
16 the house of the LORD. The priests went into the inner part
of the house of the LORD to cleanse it, and they brought
out all the uncleanness that they found in the temple of
the LORD into the court of the house of the LORD; and
the Levites took it and carried it out to the brook Kidron.
17 They began to sanctify on the first day of the first month,
and on the eighth day of the month they came to the
vestibule of the LORD; then for eight days they sanctified
the house of the LORD, and on the sixteenth day of the first
18 month they finished. Then they went in to Hezeki'ah the
king and said, "We have cleansed all the house of the
LORD, the altar of burnt offering and all its utensils, and
19 the table for the showbread and all its utensils. All the
utensils which King Ahaz discarded in his reign when
he was faithless, we have made ready and sanctified; and
behold, they are before the altar of the LORD."
20   Then Hezeki'ah the king rose early and gathered the
officials of the city, and went up to the house of the LORD.
21 And they brought seven bulls, seven rams, seven lambs,
and seven he-goats for a sin offering for the kingdom and
for the sanctuary and for Judah. And he commanded
the priests the sons of Aaron to offer them on the altar of
22 the LORD. So they killed the bulls, and the priests received
the blood and threw it against the altar; and they killed
the rams and their blood was thrown against the altar;
and they killed the lambs and their blood was thrown
23 against the altar. Then the he-goats for the sin offering
were brought to the king and the assembly, and they laid
24 their hands upon them, and the priests killed them and
made a sin offering with their blood on the altar, to make
atonement for all Israel. For the king commanded that
the burnt offering and the sin offering should be made
for all Israel.
25   And he stationed the Levites in the house of the LORD
with cymbals, harps, and lyres, according to the commandment of David and of Gad the king's seer and of
Nathan the prophet; for the commandment was from the
26 LORD through his prophets. The Levites stood with the
instruments of David, and the priests with the trumpets.
27 Then Hezeki'ah commanded that the burnt offering be
offered on the altar. And when the burnt offering began,
the song to the LORD began also, and the trumpets, ac-
28 companied by the instruments of David king of Israel. The

whole assembly worshiped, and the singers sang, and the trumpeters sounded; all this continued until the burnt
29 offering was finished. When the offering was finished, the king and all who were present with him bowed themselves
30 and worshiped. And Hezeki'ah the king and the princes commanded the Levites to sing praises to the LORD with the words of David and of Asaph the seer. And they sang praises with gladness, and they bowed down and worshiped.

31 Then Hezeki'ah said, "You have now consecrated yourselves to the LORD; come near, bring sacrifices and thank offerings to the house of the LORD." And the assembly brought sacrifices and thank offerings; and all who were
32 of a willing heart brought burnt offerings. The number of the burnt offerings which the assembly brought was seventy bulls, a hundred rams, and two hundred lambs;
33 all these were for a burnt offering to the LORD. And the consecrated offerings were six hundred bulls and three
34 thousand sheep. But the priests were too few and could not flay all the burnt offerings, so until other priests had sanctified themselves their brethren the Levites helped them, until the work was finished—for the Levites were more upright in heart than the priests in sanctifying
35 themselves. Besides the great number of burnt offerings there was the fat of the peace offerings, and there were the libations for the burnt offerings. Thus the service of
36 the house of the LORD was restored. And Hezeki'ah and all the people rejoiced because of what God had done for the people; for the thing came about suddenly.

30 Hezeki'ah sent to all Israel and Judah, and wrote letters also to E'phraim and Manas'seh, that they should come to the house of the LORD at Jerusalem, to
2 keep the passover to the LORD the God of Israel. For the king and his princes and all the assembly in Jerusalem had taken counsel to keep the passover in the second
3 month—for they could not keep it in its time because the priests had not sanctified themselves in sufficient number,
4 nor had the people assembled in Jerusalem—and the plan
5 seemed right to the king and all the assembly. So they decreed to make a proclamation throughout all Israel, from Beer-sheba to Dan, that the people should come and keep the passover to the LORD the God of Israel, at Jerusalem; for they had not kept it in great numbers as
6 prescribed. So couriers went throughout all Israel and Judah with letters from the king and his princes, as the king had commanded, saying, "O people of Israel, return to the LORD, the God of Abraham, Isaac, and Israel, that he may turn again to the remnant of you who have
7 escaped from the hand of the kings of Assyria. Do not be like your fathers and your brethren, who were faithless to the LORD God of their fathers, so that he made them a
8 desolation, as you see. Do not now be stiff-necked as your fathers were, but yield yourselves to the LORD, and come to his sanctuary, which he has sanctified for ever, and

serve the LORD your God, that his fierce anger may turn
9 away from you. For if you return to the LORD, your brethren and your children will find compassion with their captors, and return to this land. For the LORD your God is gracious and merciful, and will not turn away his face from you, if you return to him."

10 So the couriers went from city to city through the country of E'phraim and Manas'seh, and as far as Zeb'-ulun; but they laughed them to scorn, and mocked them.
11 Only a few men of Asher, of Manas'seh, and of Zeb'ulun
12 humbled themselves and came to Jerusalem. The hand of God was also upon Judah to give them one heart to do what the king and the princes commanded by the word of the LORD.
13 And many people came together in Jerusalem to keep the feast of unleavened bread in the second month, a very
14 great assembly. They set to work and removed the altars that were in Jerusalem, and all the altars for burning incense they took away and threw into the Kidron valley.
15 And they killed the passover lamb on the fourteenth day of the second month. And the priests and the Levites were put to shame, so that they sanctified themselves, and brought burnt offerings into the house of the LORD.
16 They took their accustomed posts according to the law of Moses the man of God; the priests sprinkled the blood
17 which they received from the hand of the Levites. For there were many in the assembly who had not sanctified themselves; therefore the Levites had to kill the passover lamb for every one who was not clean, to make it holy to
18 the LORD. For a multitude of the people, many of them from E'phraim, Manas'seh, Is'sachar, and Zeb'ulun, had not cleansed themselves, yet they ate the passover otherwise than as prescribed. For Hezeki'ah had prayed for
19 them, saying, "The good LORD pardon every one who sets his heart to seek God, the LORD the God of his fathers, even though not according to the sanctuary's rules of
20 cleanness." And the LORD heard Hezeki'ah, and healed
21 the people. And the people of Israel that were present at Jerusalem kept the feast of unleavened bread seven days with great gladness; and the Levites and the priests praised the LORD day by day, singing with all their
22 might [s] to the LORD. And Hezeki'ah spoke encouragingly to all the Levites who showed good skill in the service of the LORD. So the people ate the food of the festival for seven days, sacrificing peace offerings and giving thanks to the LORD the God of their fathers.

[s] Compare 1 Ch 13.8: Heb *with instruments of might*

23 Then the whole assembly agreed together to keep the feast for another seven days; so they kept it for another 24 seven days with gladness. For Hezeki'ah king of Judah gave the assembly a thousand bulls and seven thousand sheep for offerings, and the princes gave the assembly a thousand bulls and ten thousand sheep. And the priests 25 sanctified themselves in great numbers. The whole assembly of Judah, and the priests and the Levites, and the whole assembly that came out of Israel, and the sojourners who came out of the land of Israel, and the sojourners 26 who dwelt in Judah, rejoiced. So there was great joy in Jerusalem, for since the time of Solomon the son of David king of Israel there had been nothing like this in Jeru- 27 salem. Then the priests and the Levites arose and blessed the people, and their voice was heard, and their prayer came to his holy habitation in heaven.

31 Now when all this was finished, all Israel who were present went out to the cities of Judah and broke in pieces the pillars and hewed down the Ashe'rim and broke down the high places and the altars throughout all Judah and Benjamin, and in E'phraim and Manas'seh, until they had destroyed them all. Then all the people of Israel returned to their cities, every man to his possession. 2 And Hezeki'ah appointed the divisions of the priests and of the Levites, division by division, each according to his service, the priests and the Levites, for burnt offerings and peace offerings, to minister in the gates of the 3 camp of the LORD and to give thanks and praise. The contribution of the king from his own possessions was for the burnt offerings: the burnt offerings of morning and evening, and the burnt offerings for the sabbaths, the new moons, and the appointed feasts, as it is written in the 4 law of the LORD. And he commanded the people who lived in Jerusalem to give the portion due to the priests and the Levites, that they might give themselves to the 5 law of the LORD. As soon as the command was spread abroad, the people of Israel gave in abundance the first fruits of grain, wine, oil, honey, and of all the produce of the field; and they brought in abundantly the tithe of 6 everything. And the people of Israel and Judah who lived in the cities of Judah also brought in the tithe of cattle and sheep, and the dedicated things t which had been consecrated to the LORD their God, and laid them in heaps. 7 In the third month they began to pile up the heaps, and 8 finished them in the seventh month. When Hezeki'ah and the princes came and saw the heaps, they blessed the LORD 9 and his people Israel. And Hezeki'ah questioned the 10 priests and the Levites about the heaps. Azari'ah the chief priest, who was of the house of Zadok, answered him, "Since they began to bring the contributions into the house of the LORD we have eaten and had enough and have plenty left; for the LORD has blessed his people, so that we have this great store left."

11 Then Hezeki'ah commanded them to prepare chambers 12 in the house of the LORD; and they prepared them. And they faithfully brought in the contributions, the tithes and the dedicated things. The chief officer in charge of them was Conani'ah the Levite, with Shim'e-i his brother as 13 second; while Jehi'el, Azazi'ah, Nahath, As'ahel, Jer'imoth, Jo'zabad, Eli'el, Ismachi'ah, Mahath, and Benai'ah were overseers assisting Conani'ah and Shim'e-i his brother, by the appointment of Hezeki'ah the king and Azari'ah the 14 chief officer of the house of God. And Ko're the son of Imnah the Levite, keeper of the east gate, was over the freewill offerings to God, to apportion the contribution 15 reserved for the LORD and the most holy offerings. Eden, Mini'amin, Jeshua, Shemai'ah, Amari'ah, and Shecami'ah were faithfully assisting him in the cities of the priests, to distribute the portions to their brethren, old and young 16 alike, by divisions, except those enrolled by genealogy, males from three years old and upwards, all who entered the house of the LORD as the duty of each day required, for their service according to their offices, by their divi- 17 sions. The enrollment of the priests was according to their fathers' houses; that of the Levites from twenty years old and upwards was according to their offices, by their 18 divisions. The priests were enrolled with all their little children, their wives, their sons, and their daughters, the whole multitude; for they were faithful in keeping them- 19 selves holy. And for the sons of Aaron, the priests, who were in the fields of common land belonging to their cities, there were men in the several cities who were designated by name to distribute portions to every male among the priests and to every one among the Levites who was enrolled.

20 Thus Hezeki'ah did throughout all Judah; and he did what was good and right and faithful before the LORD 21 his God. And every work that he undertook in the service of the house of God and in accordance with the law and the commandments, seeking his God, he did with all his heart, and prospered.

32 After these things and these acts of faithfulness Sennach'erib king of Assyria came and invaded Judah and encamped against the fortified cities, thinking 2 to win them for himself. And when Hezeki'ah saw that Sennach'erib had come and intended to fight against Jeru- 3 salem; he planned with his officers and his mighty men to stop the water of the springs that were outside the city; 4 and they helped him. A great many people were gathered, and they stopped all the springs and the brook that flowed through the land, saying, "Why should the kings of As- 5 syria come and find much water?" He set to work resolutely and built up all the wall that was broken down, and raised towers upon it,u and outside it he built another wall; and he strengthened the Millo in the city of David. 6 He also made weapons and shields in abundance. And he

---

t Heb the tithe of the dedicated things　　u Vg: Heb and raised upon the towers

set combat commanders over the people, and gathered them together to him in the square at the gate of the city 7 and spoke encouragingly to them, saying, "Be strong and of good courage. Do not be afraid or dismayed before the king of Assyria and all the horde that is with him; for 8 there is one greater with us than with him. With him is an arm of flesh; but with us is the LORD our God, to help us and to fight our battles." And the people took confidence from the words of Hezeki'ah king of Judah.

9 After this Sennach'erib king of Assyria, who was besieging Lachish with all his forces, sent his servants to Jerusalem to Hezeki'ah king of Judah and to all the people 10 of Judah that were in Jerusalem, saying, "Thus says Sennach'erib king of Assyria, 'On what are you relying, 11 that you stand siege in Jerusalem? Is not Hezeki'ah misleading you, that he may give you over to die by famine and by thirst, when he tells you, "The LORD our God will 12 deliver us from the hand of the king of Assyria"? Has not this same Hezeki'ah taken away his high places and his altars and commanded Judah and Jerusalem, "Before one altar you shall worship, and upon it you shall burn 13 your sacrifices"? Do you not know what I and my fathers have done to all the peoples of other lands? Were the gods of the nations of those lands at all able to deliver their 14 lands out of my hand? Who among all the gods of those nations which my fathers utterly destroyed was able to deliver his people from my hand, that your God should be 15 able to deliver you from my hand? Now therefore do not let Hezeki'ah deceive you or mislead you in this fashion, and do not believe him, for no god of any nation or kingdom has been able to deliver his people from my hand or from the hand of my fathers. How much less will your God deliver you out of my hand!'"

16 And his servants said still more against the LORD God 17 and against his servant Hezeki'ah. And he wrote letters to cast contempt on the LORD the God of Israel and to speak against him, saying, "Like the gods of the nations of the lands who have not delivered their people from my hands, so the God of Hezeki'ah will not deliver his people 18 from my hand." And they shouted it with a loud voice in the language of Judah to the people of Jerusalem who were upon the wall, to frighten and terrify them, in order 19 that they might take the city. And they spoke of the God of Jerusalem as they spoke of the gods of the peoples of the earth, which are the work of men's hands.

20 Then Hezeki'ah the king and Isaiah the prophet, the son of Amoz, prayed because of this and cried to heaven. 21 And the LORD sent an angel, who cut off all the mighty warriors and commanders and officers in the camp of the king of Assyria. So he returned with shame of face to his own land. And when he came into the house of his god, some of his own sons struck him down there with 22 the sword. So the LORD saved Hezeki'ah and the inhabitants of Jerusalem from the hand of Sennach'erib king of Assyria and from the hand of all his enemies; and he gave 23 them rest on every side. And many brought gifts to the LORD to Jerusalem and precious things to Hezeki'ah king of Judah, so that he was exalted in the sight of all nations from that time onward.

24 In those days Hezeki'ah became sick and was at the point of death, and he prayed to the LORD; and he an- 25 swered him and gave him a sign. But Hezeki'ah did not make return according to the benefit done to him, for his heart was proud. Therefore wrath came upon him and 26 Judah and Jerusalem. But Hezeki'ah humbled himself for the pride of his heart, both he and the inhabitants of Jerusalem, so that the wrath of the LORD did not come upon them in the days of Hezeki'ah.

27 And Hezeki'ah had very great riches and honor; and he made for himself treasuries for silver, for gold, for precious stones, for spices, for shields, and for all kinds 28 of costly vessels; storehouses also for the yield of grain, wine, and oil; and stalls for all kinds of cattle, and sheep- 29 folds. He likewise provided cities for himself, and flocks and herds in abundance; for God had given him very 30 great possessions. This same Hezeki'ah closed the upper outlet of the waters of Gihon and directed them down to the west side of the city of David. And Hezeki'ah pros- 31 pered in all his works. And so in the matter of the envoys of the princes of Babylon, who had been sent to him to inquire about the sign that had been done in the land, God left him to himself, in order to try him and to know all that was in his heart.

32 Now the rest of the acts of Hezeki'ah, and his good deeds, behold, they are written in the vision of Isaiah the prophet the son of Amoz, in the Book of the Kings of 33 Judah and Israel. And Hezeki'ah slept with his fathers, and they buried him in the ascent of the tombs of the sons of David; and all Judah and the inhabitants of Jerusalem did him honor at his death. And Manas'seh his son reigned in his stead.

Manasseh and Amon

33 Manas'seh was twelve years old when he began to reign, and he reigned fifty-five years in Jerusa- 2 lem. He did what was evil in the sight of the LORD, according to the abominable practices of the nations whom the LORD drove out before the people of Israel. 3 For he rebuilt the high places which his father Hezeki'ah

had broken down, and erected altars to the Ba'als, and made Ashe'rahs, and worshiped all the host of heaven,
4 and served them. And he built altars in the house of the LORD, of which the LORD had said, "In Jerusalem shall
5 my name be for ever." And he built altars for all the host of heaven in the two courts of the house of the LORD.
6 And he burned his sons as an offering in the valley of the son of Hinnom, and practiced soothsaying and augury and sorcery, and dealt with mediums and with wizards. He did much evil in the sight of the LORD, provoking him
7 to anger. And the image of the idol which he had made he set in the house of God, of which God said to David and to Solomon his son, "In this house, and in Jerusalem, which I have chosen out of all the tribes of Israel, I will
8 put my name for ever; and I will no more remove the foot of Israel from the land which I appointed for your fathers, if only they will be careful to do all that I have commanded them, all the law, the statutes, and the
9 ordinances given through Moses." Manas'seh seduced Judah and the inhabitants of Jerusalem, so that they did more evil than the nations whom the LORD destroyed before the people of Israel.
10 The LORD spoke to Manas'seh and to his people, but
11 they gave no heed. Therefore the LORD brought upon them the commanders of the army of the king of Assyria, who took Manas'seh with hooks and bound him with
12 fetters of bronze and brought him to Babylon. And when he was in distress he entreated the favor of the LORD his God and humbled himself greatly before the God of his
13 fathers. He prayed to him, and God received his entreaty and heard his supplication and brought him again to Jerusalem into his kingdom. Then Manas'seh knew that the LORD was God.
14 Afterwards he built an outer wall for the city of David west of Gihon, in the valley, and for the entrance into the Fish Gate, and carried it round Ophel, and raised it to a very great height; he also put commanders of the army
15 in all the fortified cities in Judah. And he took away the foreign gods and the idol from the house of the LORD, and all the altars that he had built on the mountain of the house of the LORD and in Jerusalem, and he threw them
16 outside of the city. He also restored the altar of the LORD and offered upon it sacrifices of peace offerings and of thanksgiving; and he commanded Judah to serve the LORD
17 the God of Israel. Nevertheless the people still sacrificed at the high places, but only to the LORD their God.
18 Now the rest of the acts of Manas'seh, and his prayer to his God, and the words of the seers who spoke to him in the name of the LORD the God of Israel, behold, they
19 are in the Chronicles of the Kings of Israel. And his prayer, and how God received his entreaty, and all his sin and his faithlessness, and the sites on which he built high places and set up the Ashe'rim and the images, before he humbled himself, behold, they are written in the

20 Chronicles of the Seers.v So Manas'seh slept with his fathers, and they buried him in his house; and Amon his son reigned in his stead.
21 Amon was twenty-two years old when he began to
22 reign, and he reigned two years in Jerusalem. He did what was evil in the sight of the LORD, as Manas'seh his father had done. Amon sacrificed to all the images that Manas'-
23 seh his father had made, and served them. And he did not humble himself before the LORD, as Manas'seh his father had humbled himself, but this Amon incurred guilt
24 more and more. And his servants conspired against him
25 and killed him in his house. But the people of the land slew all those who had conspired against King Amon; and the people of the land made Josi'ah his son king in his stead.

Reign of Josiah

34 Josi'ah was eight years old when he began to reign, and he reigned thirty-one years in Jerusalem.
2 He did what was right in the eyes of the LORD, and walked in the ways of David his father; and he did not turn aside
3 to the right or to the left. For in the eighth year of his reign, while he was yet a boy, he began to seek the God of David his father; and in the twelfth year he began to purge Judah and Jerusalem of the high places, the Ashe'-
4 rim and the graven and the molten images. And they broke down the altars of the Ba'als in his presence; and he hewed down the incense altars which stood above them; and he broke in pieces the Ashe'rim and the graven and the molten images, and he made dust of them and strewed it over the graves of those who had sacrificed to
5 them. He also burned the bones of the priests on their
6 altars, and purged Judah and Jerusalem. And in the cities of Manas'seh, E'phraim, and Simeon, and as far as Naph'-
7 tali, in their ruinsw round about, he broke down the altars, and beat the Ashe'rim and the images into powder, and hewed down all the incense altars throughout all the land of Israel. Then he returned to Jerusalem.
8 Now in the eighteenth year of his reign, when he had purged the land and the house, he sent Shaphan the son of Azali'ah, and Ma-asei'ah the governor of the city, and Jo'ah the son of Jo'ahaz, the recorder, to repair the house
9 of the LORD his God. They came to Hilki'ah the high priest and delivered the money that had been brought into the house of God, which the Levites, the keepers of the threshold, had collected from Manas'seh and E'phraim and from all the remnant of Israel and from all Judah and Benjamin and from the inhabitants of Jerusalem.
10 They delivered it to the workmen who had the oversight of the house of the LORD; and the workmen who were working in the house of the LORD gave it for repairing and
11 restoring the house. They gave it to the carpenters and the builders to buy quarried stone, and timber for binders and beams for the buildings which the kings of Judah had

v One Ms: Gk: Heb *of Hozai*   w Heb uncertain

12 let go to ruin. And the men did the work faithfully. Over them were set Jahath and Obadi'ah the Levites, of the sons of Merar'i, and Zechari'ah and Meshul'lam, of the sons of the Ko'hathites, to have oversight. The Levites, all who
13 were skilful with instruments of music, were over the burden bearers and directed all who did work in every kind of service; and some of the Levites were scribes, and officials, and gatekeepers.

14 While they were bringing out the money that had been brought into the house of the LORD, Hilki'ah the priest found the book of the law of the LORD given through
15 Moses. Then Hilki'ah said to Shaphan the secretary, "I have found the book of the law in the house of the LORD";
16 and Hilki'ah gave the book to Shaphan. Shaphan brought the book to the king, and further reported to the king, "All that was committed to your servants they are doing.
17 They have emptied out the money that was found in the house of the LORD and have delivered it into the hand of
18 the overseers and the workmen." Then Shaphan the secretary told the king, "Hilki'ah the priest has given me a book." And Shaphan read it before the king.

19 When the king heard the words of the law he rent his
20 clothes. And the king commanded Hilki'ah, Ahi'kam the son of Shaphan, Abdon the son of Micah, Shaphan the
21 secretary, and Asai'ah the king's servant, saying, "Go, inquire of the LORD for me and for those who are left in Israel and in Judah, concerning the words of the book that has been found; for great is the wrath of the LORD that is poured out on us, because our fathers have not kept the word of the LORD, to do according to all that is written in this book."

22 So Hilki'ah and those whom the king had sent [x] went to Huldah the prophetess, the wife of Shallum the son of Tokhath, son of Hasrah, keeper of the wardrobe (now she dwelt in Jerusalem in the Second Quarter) and spoke to
23 her to that effect. And she said to them, "Thus says the LORD, the God of Israel: 'Tell the man who sent you to
24 me, Thus says the LORD, Behold, I will bring evil upon this place and upon its inhabitants, all the curses that are written in the book which was read before the king of
25 Judah. Because they have forsaken me and have burned incense to other gods, that they might provoke me to anger with all the works of their hands, therefore my wrath will be poured out upon this place and will not be
26 quenched. But to the king of Judah, who sent you to inquire of the LORD, thus shall you say to him, Thus says the LORD, the God of Israel: Regarding the words which
27 you have heard, because your heart was penitent and you humbled yourself before God when you heard his words against this place and its inhabitants, and you have humbled yourself before me, and have rent your clothes and wept before me, I also have heard you, says the LORD.
28 Behold, I will gather you to your fathers, and you shall be gathered to your grave in peace, and your eyes shall not

see all the evil which I will bring upon this place and its inhabitants.' " And they brought back word to the king.
29 Then the king sent and gathered together all the elders
30 of Judah and Jerusalem. And the king went up to the house of the LORD, with all the men of Judah and the inhabitants of Jerusalem and the priests and the Levites, all the people both great and small; and he read in their hearing all the words of the book of the covenant which
31 had been found in the house of the LORD. And the king stood in his place and made a covenant before the LORD, to walk after the LORD and to keep his commandments and his testimonies and his statutes, with all his heart and all his soul, to perform the words of the covenant that
32 were written in this book. Then he made all who were present in Jerusalem and in Benjamin stand to it. And the inhabitants of Jerusalem did according to the covenant of
33 God, the God of their fathers. And Josi'ah took away all the abominations from all the territory that belonged to the people of Israel, and made all who were in Israel serve the LORD their God. All his days they did not turn away from following the LORD the God of their fathers.

35 Josi'ah kept a passover to the LORD in Jerusalem; and they killed the passover lamb on the fourteenth
2 day of the first month. He appointed the priests to their offices and encouraged them in the service of the house of
3 the LORD. And he said to the Levites who taught all Israel and who were holy to the LORD, "Put the holy ark in the house which Solomon the son of David, king of Israel, built; you need no longer carry it upon your shoulders. Now serve the LORD your God and his people Israel.
4 Prepare yourselves according to your fathers' houses by your divisions, following the directions of David king of
5 Israel and the directions of Solomon his son. And stand in the holy place according to the groupings of the fathers' houses of your brethren the lay people, and let there be for
6 each a part of a father's house of the Levites.[y] And kill

the passover lamb, and sanctify yourselves, and prepare for your brethren, to do according to the word of the LORD by Moses."
7 Then Josi'ah contributed to the lay people, as passover offerings for all that were present, lambs and kids from the flock to the number of thirty thousand, and three thousand bulls; these were from the king's possessions.
8 And his princes contributed willingly to the people, to the priests, and to the Levites. Hilki'ah, Zechari'ah, and Jehi'el, the chief officers of the house of God, gave to the priests for the passover offerings two thousand six hun-

[x] Syr Vg: Heb lacks *had sent*   [y] Heb obscure

9 dred lambs and kids and three hundred bulls. Conani'ah also, and Shemai'ah and Nethan'el his brothers, and Hashabi'ah and Je-i'el and Jo'zabad, the chiefs of the Levites, gave to the Levites for the passover offerings five thousand lambs and kids and five hundred bulls.

10 When the service had been prepared for, the priests stood in their place, and the Levites in their divisions 11 according to the king's command. And they killed the passover lamb, and the priests sprinkled the blood which they received from them while the Levites flayed the 12 victims. And they set aside the burnt offerings that they might distribute them according to the groupings of the fathers' houses of the lay people, to offer to the LORD, as it is written in the book of Moses. And so they did with 13 the bulls. And they roasted the passover lamb with fire according to the ordinance; and they boiled the holy offerings in pots, in caldrons, and in pans, and carried 14 them quickly to all the lay people. And afterward they prepared for themselves and for the priests, because the priests the sons of Aaron were busied in offering the burnt offerings and the fat parts until night; so the Levites prepared for themselves and for the priests the sons of 15 Aaron. The singers, the sons of Asaph, were in their place according to the command of David, and Asaph, and Heman, and Jedu'thun the king's seer; and the gatekeepers were at each gate; they did not need to depart from their service, for their brethren the Levites prepared for them.

16 So all the service of the LORD was prepared that day, to keep the passover and to offer burnt offerings on the altar of the LORD, according to the command of King 17 Josi'ah. And the people of Israel who were present kept the passover at that time, and the feast of unleavened 18 bread seven days. No passover like it had been kept in Israel since the days of Samuel the prophet; none of the kings of Israel had kept such a passover as was kept by Josi'ah, and the priests and the Levites, and all Judah and Israel who were present, and the inhabitants of 19 Jerusalem. In the eighteenth year of the reign of Josi'ah this passover was kept.

20 After all this, when Josi'ah had prepared the temple, Neco king of Egypt went up to fight at Car'chemish on 21 the Eu-phra'tes and Josi'ah went out against him. But he sent envoys to him, saying, "What have we to do with each other, king of Judah? I am not coming against you this day, but against the house with which I am at war; and God has commanded me to make haste. Cease opposing 22 God, who is with me, lest he destroy you." Nevertheless Josi'ah would not turn away from him, but disguised himself in order to fight with him. He did not listen to the words of Neco from the mouth of God, but joined battle 23 in the plain of Megid'do. And the archers shot King Josi'ah; and the king said to his servants, "Take me away, 24 for I am badly wounded." So his servants took him out of the chariot and carried him in his second chariot and brought him to Jerusalem. And he died, and was buried in the tombs of his fathers. All Judah and Jerusalem 25 mourned for Josi'ah. Jeremiah also uttered a lament for Josi'ah; and all the singing men and singing women have spoken of Josi'ah in their laments to this day. They made these an ordinance in Israel; behold, they are written in 26 the Laments. Now the rest of the acts of Josi'ah, and his good deeds according to what is written in the law of the 27 LORD, and his acts, first and last, behold, they are written in the Book of the Kings of Israel and Judah.

Last Kings of Judah

36 The people of the land took Jeho'ahaz the son of Josi'ah and made him king in his father's stead in 2 Jerusalem. Jeho'ahaz was twenty-three years old when he began to reign; and he reigned three months in Jerusalem. 3 Then the king of Egypt deposed him in Jerusalem and laid upon the land a tribute of a hundred talents of silver 4 and a talent of gold. And the king of Egypt made Eli'akim his brother king over Judah and Jerusalem, and changed his name to Jehoi'akim; but Neco took Jeho'ahaz his brother and carried him to Egypt.

5 Jehoi'akim was twenty-five years old when he began to reign, and he reigned eleven years in Jerusalem. He did 6 what was evil in the sight of the LORD his God. Against him came up Nebuchadnez'zar king of Babylon, and 7 bound him in fetters to take him to Babylon. Nebuchadnez'zar also carried part of the vessels of the house of the LORD to Babylon and put them in his palace in 8 Babylon. Now the rest of the acts of Jehoi'akim, and the abominations which he did, and what was found against him, behold, they are written in the Book of the Kings of Israel and Judah; and Jehoi'achin his son reigned in his stead.

9 Jehoi'achin was eight years old when he began to reign, and he reigned three months and ten days in Jerusalem. 10 He did what was evil in the sight of the LORD. In the

spring of the year King Nebuchadnez′zar sent and brought him to Babylon, with the precious vessels of the house of the LORD, and made his brother Zedeki′ah king over Judah and Jerusalem.

11 Zedeki′ah was twenty-one years old when he began to 12 reign, and he reigned eleven years in Jerusalem. He did what was evil in the sight of the LORD his God. He did not humble himself before Jeremiah the prophet, who 13 spoke from the mouth of the LORD. He also rebelled against King Nebuchadnez′zar, who had made him swear by God; he stiffened his neck and hardened his heart 14 against turning to the LORD, the God of Israel. All the leading priests and the people likewise were exceedingly unfaithful, following all the abominations of the nations; and they polluted the house of the LORD which he had hallowed in Jerusalem.

15 The LORD, the God of their fathers, sent persistently to them by his messengers, because he had compassion on 16 his people and on his dwelling place; but they kept mocking the messengers of God, despising his words, and scoffing at his prophets, till the wrath of the LORD rose against his people, till there was no remedy.

17 Therefore he brought up against them the king of the Chalde′ans, who slew their young man with the sword in the house of their sanctuary, and had no compassion on young man or virgin, old man or aged; he gave them all 18 into his hand. And all the vessels of the house of God, great and small, and the treasures of the house of the LORD, and the treasures of the king and of his princes, 19 all these he brought to Babylon. And they burned the house of God, and broke down the wall of Jerusalem, and burned all its palaces with fire, and destroyed all its 20 precious vessels. He took into exile in Babylon those who had escaped from the sword, and they became servants to him and to his sons until the establishment of the kingdom

21 of Persia, to fulfil the word of the LORD by the mouth of Jeremiah, until the land had enjoyed its sabbaths. All the days that it lay desolate it kept sabbath, to fulfil seventy years.

22 Now in the first year of Cyrus king of Persia, that the word of the LORD by the mouth of Jeremiah might be accomplished, the LORD stirred up the spirit of Cyrus

king of Persia so that he made a proclamation throughout 23 all his kingdom and also put it in writing: "Thus says Cyrus king of Persia, 'The LORD, the God of heaven, has given me all the kingdoms of the earth, and he has charged me to build him a house at Jerusalem, which is in Judah. Whoever is among you of all his people, may the LORD his God be with him. Let him go up.'"

INTRODUCTION TO

EZRA

The Book of Ezra tells of the trouble and hardships of the Jews who were permitted to return from exile to their homeland after Cyrus of Persia conquered Babylonia in 538 B.C. Solomon's Temple had been destroyed many years earlier, in 586 B.C., when their nation was conquered. After Ezra returned, he served as chief priest, devoting most of his time to instructing the people and the priests in their religious rules for life and worship.

Ezra found that many of the Jews in Jerusalem had married foreigners. Therefore, he demanded that all Jews who had married foreign women divorce them regardless of the suffering and sorrow it caused. He felt that these foreign wives would corrupt the true worship of God with the pagan ideas and moral standards of the foreign gods they worshiped. However, some men did not agree with Ezra and refused to abandon their foreign wives. Indeed, the Book of Ruth seems to have been written to protest the divorcing of foreign wives. (See the Introduction to Ruth, page 163.)

The Book of Ezra was written possibly about 350 B.C. as a part of the series of books—First and Second Chronicles, Ezra, and Nehemiah. Like all the books of this series it emphasized the importance of the official Temple worship at Jerusalem. The Introduction to First Chronicles on page 261 tells more about the purpose of the Chronicler in all four of these books.

THE BOOK OF

EZRA

THE RETURN OF THE EXILES IN PERSIA

1 In the first year of Cyrus king of Persia, that the word of the LORD by the mouth of Jeremiah might be accomplished, the LORD stirred up the spirit of Cyrus king of Persia so that he made a proclamation throughout all his kingdom and also put it in writing:

2 "Thus says Cyrus king of Persia: The LORD, the God of heaven, has given me all the kingdoms of the earth, and he has charged me to build him a house at Jerusalem, 3 which is in Judah. Whoever is among you of all his people, may his God be with him, and let him go up to Jerusalem, which is in Judah, and rebuild the house of the LORD, the God of Israel—he is the God who is in 4 Jerusalem; and let each survivor, in whatever place he sojourns, be assisted by the men of his place with silver and gold, with goods and with beasts, besides freewill offerings for the house of God which is in Jerusalem."

5 Then rose up the heads of the fathers' houses of Judah and Benjamin, and the priests and the Levites, every one whose spirit God had stirred to go up to rebuild the house 6 of the LORD which is in Jerusalem; and all who were about them aided them with vessels of silver, with gold, with goods, with beasts, and with costly wares, besides 7 all that was freely offered. Cyrus the king also brought out the vessels of the house of the LORD which Nebuchadnez'zar had carried away from Jerusalem and placed in 8 the house of his gods. Cyrus king of Persia brought these out in charge of Mith'redath the treasurer, who counted 9 them out to Shesh-baz'zar the prince of Judah. And this was the number of them: a thousand[a] basins of gold, a

10 thousand basins of silver, twenty-nine censers, thirty bowls of gold, two thousand[b] four hundred and ten bowls of 11 silver, and a thousand other vessels; all the vessels of gold and of silver were five thousand four hundred and sixty-nine.[c] All these did Shesh-baz'zar bring up when the exiles were brought up from Babylonia to Jerusalem.

ᵃ 1 Esdras 2.13: Heb *thirty*   ᵇ 1 Esdras 2.13: Heb *of a second sort*   ᶜ 1 Esdras 2.14: Heb *five thousand four hundred*

2 Now these were the people of the province who came up out of the captivity of those exiles whom Nebuchadnez'zar the king of Babylon had carried captive to Babylonia; they returned to Jerusalem and Judah, each to his own town. 2 They came with Zerub'babel, Jeshua, Nehemi'ah, Serai'ah, Re-el-ai'ah, Mor'decai, Bilshan, Mispar, Big'vai, Rehum, and Ba'anah.

3 The number of the men of the people of Israel: the sons of 4 Parosh, two thousand one hundred and seventy-two. The sons 5 of Shephati'ah, three hundred and seventy-two. The sons of 6 Arah, seven hundred and seventy-five. The sons of Pa'hath- mo'ab, namely the sons of Jeshua and Jo'ab, two thousand eight 7 hundred and twelve. The sons of Elam, one thousand two 8 hundred and fifty-four. The sons of Zattu, nine hundred and 9, 10 forty-five. The sons of Zac'cai, seven hundred and sixty. The 11 sons of Bani, six hundred and forty-two. The sons of Be'bai, 12 six hundred and twenty-three. The sons of Azgad, one thousand 13 two hundred and twenty-two. The sons of Adoni'kam, six hun- 14 dred and sixty-six. The sons of Big'vai, two thousand and fifty- 15, 16 six. The sons of Adin, four hundred and fifty-four. The sons of 17 Ater, namely of Hezeki'ah, ninety-eight. The sons of 18 Be'zai, three hundred and twenty-three. The sons of Jorah, one 19 hundred and twelve. The sons of Hashum, two hundred and 20, 21 twenty-three. The sons of Gibbar, ninety-five. The sons of 22 Bethlehem, one hundred and twenty-three. The men of Neto'- 23 phah, fifty-six. The men of An'athoth, one hundred and twenty- 24, 25 eight. The sons of Az'maveth, forty-two. The sons of Kir'- iathar'im, Chephi'rah, and Be-er'oth, seven hundred and forty- 26 three. The sons of Ramah and Geba, six hundred and twenty- 27, 28 one. The men of Michmas, one hundred and twenty-two. The 29 men of Bethel and Ai, two hundred and twenty-three. The sons 30 of Nebo, fifty-two. The sons of Magbish, one hundred and fifty- 31 six. The sons of the other Elam, one thousand two hundred and 32 fifty-four. The sons of Harim, three hundred and twenty. 33 The sons of Lod, Hadid, and Ono, seven hundred and twenty- 34, 35 five. The sons of Jericho, three hundred and forty-five. The sons of Sena'ah, three thousand six hundred and thirty.

36 The priests: the sons of Jedai'ah, of the house of Jeshua, nine 37 hundred and seventy-three. The sons of Immer, one thousand 38 and fifty-two. The sons of Pashhur, one thousand two hundred 39 and forty-seven. The sons of Harim, one thousand and seventeen.

40 The Levites: the sons of Jeshua and Kad'mi-el, of the sons of 41 Hodavi'ah, seventy-four. The singers: the sons of Asaph, one 42 hundred and twenty-eight. The sons of the gatekeepers: the sons of Shallum, the sons of Ater, the sons of Talmon, the sons of Akkub, the sons of Hati'ta, and the sons of Sho'bai, in all one hundred and thirty-nine.

43 The temple servants: d the sons of Ziha, the sons of Hasu'pha, 44 the sons of Tabba'oth, the sons of Keros, the sons of Si'aha, 45 the sons of Padon, the sons of Leba'nah, the sons of 46 Hag'abah, the sons of Akkub, the sons of Hagab, the sons of 47 Shamlai, the sons of Hanan, the sons of Giddel, the sons of 48 Gahar, the sons of Re-ai'ah, the sons of Rezin, the sons of Neko'- 49 da, the sons of Gazzam, the sons of Uzza, the sons of Pase'ah, 50 the sons of Besai, the sons of Asnah, the sons of Me-u'nim, the 51 sons of Nephi'sim, the sons of Bakbuk, the sons of Haku'pha, 52 the sons of Harhur, the sons of Bazluth, the sons of Mehi'da, the 53 sons of Harsha, the sons of Barkos, the sons of Sis'era, the sons 54 of Temah, the sons of Nezi'ah, and the sons of Hati'pha.

55 The sons of Solomon's servants: the sons of So'tai, the sons 56 of Hasso'phereth, the sons of Peru'da, the sons of Ja'alah, the 57 sons of Darkon, the sons of Giddel, the sons of Shephati'ah, the sons of Hattil, the sons of Po'chereth-hazzeba'im, and the sons of Ami.

58 All the temple servants d and the sons of Solomon's servants were three hundred and ninety-two.

59 The following were those who came up from Tel-me'lah, Tel- har'sha, Cherub, Addan, and Immer, though they could not prove their fathers' houses or their descent, whether they 60 belonged to Israel: the sons of Del-ai'ah, the sons of Tobi'ah, 61 and the sons of Neko'da, six hundred and fifty-two. Also, of the sons of the priests: the sons of Habai'ah, the sons of Hak- koz, and the sons of Barzil'lai (who had taken a wife from the daughters of Barzil'lai the Gileadite, and was called by their 62 name). These sought their registration among those enrolled in the genealogies, but they were not found there, and so they 63 were excluded from the priesthood as unclean; the governor told them that they were not to partake of the most holy food, until there should be a priest to consult Urim and Thummim.

64 The whole assembly together was forty-two thousand three 65 hundred and sixty, besides their menservants and maidservants, of whom there were seven thousand three hundred and thirty- seven; and they had two hundred male and female singers. 66 Their horses were seven hundred and thirty-six, their mules 67 were two hundred and forty-five, their camels were four hundred and thirty-five, and their asses were six thousand seven hundred and twenty.

68 Some of the heads of families, when they came to the house of the LORD which is in Jerusalem, made freewill offerings for 69 the house of God, to erect it on its site; according to their ability they gave to the treasury of the work sixty-one thousand darics of gold, five thousand minas of silver, and one hundred priests' garments.

70 The priests, the Levites, and some of the people lived in Jerusalem and its vicinity; e and the singers, the gatekeepers, and the temple servants lived in their towns, and all Israel in their towns.

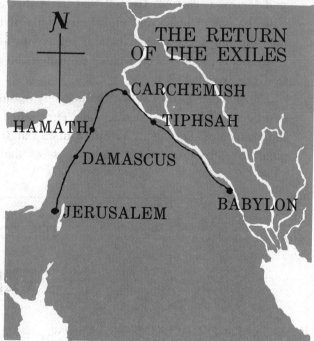

THE RETURN OF THE EXILES

CARCHEMISH
TIPHSAH
HAMATH
DAMASCUS
JERUSALEM
BABYLON

REBUILDING OF THE TEMPLE

3 When the seventh month came, and the sons of Israel were in the towns, the people gathered as one man to 2 Jerusalem. Then arose Jeshua the son of Jo'zadak, with his fellow priests, and Zerub'babel the son of She-al'ti-el with his kinsmen, and they built the altar of the God of Israel, to offer burnt offerings upon it, as it is written in 3 the law of Moses the man of God. They set the altar in its place, for fear was upon them because of the peoples of the lands, and they offered burnt offerings upon it to 4 the LORD, burnt offerings morning and evening. And they kept the feast of booths, as it is written, and offered the daily burnt offerings by number according to the ordi- 5 nance, as each day required, and after that the continual burnt offerings, the offerings at the new moon and at all the appointed feasts of the LORD, and the offerings of every one who made a freewill offering to the LORD. 6 From the first day of the seventh month they began to offer burnt offerings to the LORD. But the foundation of 7 the temple of the LORD was not yet laid. So they gave

d Heb nethinim   e 1 Esdras 5.46: Heb lacks lived in Jerusalem and its vicinity

money to the masons and the carpenters, and food, drink, and oil to the Sido'nians and the Tyrians to bring cedar trees from Lebanon to the sea, to Joppa, according to the grant which they had from Cyrus king of Persia.

8 Now in the second year of their coming to the house of God at Jerusalem, in the second month, Zerub'babel the son of She-al'ti-el and Jeshua the son of Jo'zadak made a beginning, together with the rest of their brethren, the priests and the Levites and all who had come to Jerusalem from the capitivity. They appointed the Levites, from twenty years old and upward, to have the 9 oversight of the work of the house of the LORD. And Jeshua with his sons and his kinsmen, and Kad'mi-el and his sons, the sons of Judah, together took the oversight of the workmen in the house of God, along with the sons of Hen'adad and the Levites, their sons and kinsmen.

10 And when the builders laid the foundation of the temple of the LORD, the priests in their vestments came forward with trumpets, and the Levites, the sons of Asaph, with cymbals, to praise the LORD, according to the direc- 11 tions of David king of Israel; and they sang responsively, praising and giving thanks to the LORD,

"For he is good,

for his steadfast love endures for ever toward Israel." And all the people shouted with a great shout, when they praised the LORD, because the foundation of the house of 12 the LORD was laid. But many of the priests and Levites and heads of fathers' houses, old men who had seen the first house, wept with a loud voice when they saw the foundation of this house being laid, though many shouted 13 aloud for joy; so that the people could not distinguish the sound of the joyful shout from the sound of the people's weeping, for the people shouted with a great shout, and the sound was heard afar.

4 Now when the adversaries of Judah and Benjamin heard that the returned exiles were building a temple 2 to the LORD, the God of Israel, they approached Zerub'- babel and the heads of fathers' houses and said to them, "Let us build with you; for we worship your God as you do, and we have been sacrificing to him ever since the days of E'sar-had'don king of Assyria who brought us 3 here." But Zerub'babel, Jeshua, and the rest of the heads of fathers' houses in Israel said to them, "You have noth- ing to do with us in building a house to our God; but

we alone will build to the LORD, the God of Israel, as King Cyrus the king of Persia has commanded us."

4 Then the people of the land discouraged the people of 5 Judah, and made them afraid to build, and hired counsel- ors against them to frustrate their purpose, all the days of Cyrus king of Persia, even until the reign of Darius king of Persia.

6 And in the reign of Ahasu-e'rus, in the beginning of his reign, they wrote an accusation against the inhabitants of Judah and Jerusalem.

7 And in the days of Ar-ta-xerx'es, Bishlam and Mith'- redath and Tab'eel and the rest of their associates wrote to Ar-ta-xerx'es king of Persia; the letter was written in 8 Aramaic and translated.[f] Rehum the commander and Shim'shai the scribe wrote a letter against Jerusalem to 9 Ar-ta-xerx'es the king as follows—then wrote Rehum the commander, Shim'shai the scribe, and the rest of their as- sociates, the judges, the governors, the officials, the Persians, the men of Erech, the Babylonians, the men of 10 Susa, that is, the Elamites, and the rest of the nations whom the great and noble Osnap'par deported and settled in the cities of Samar'ia and in the rest of the province 11 Beyond the River, and now this is a copy of the letter that they sent—"To Ar-ta-xerx'es the king: Your servants, the 12 men of the province Beyond the River, send greeting. And now be it known to the king that the Jews who came up from you to us have gone to Jerusalem. They are rebuild- ing that rebellious and wicked city; they are finishing the 13 walls and repairing the foundations. Now be it known to the king that, if this city is rebuilt and the walls finished, they will not pay tribute, custom, or toll, and the royal 14 revenue will be impaired. Now because we eat the salt of the palace and it is not fitting for us to witness the king's 15 dishonor, therefore we send and inform the king, in order that search may be made in the book of the records of your fathers. You will find in the book of the records and learn that this city is a rebellious city, hurtful to kings and provinces, and that sedition was stirred up in it from of 16 old. That was why this city was laid waste. We make known to the king that, if this city is rebuilt and its walls finished, you will then have no possession in the province Beyond the River."

17 The king sent an answer: "To Rehum the commander and Shim'shai the scribe and the rest of their associates who live in Samar'ia and in the rest of the province Be- 18 yond the River, greeting. And now the letter which you 19 sent to us has been plainly read before me. And I made a decree, and search has been made, and it has been found that this city from of old has risen against kings, 20 and that rebellion and sedition have been made in it. And mighty kings have been over Jerusalem, who ruled over the whole province Beyond the River, to whom tribute, 21 custom, and toll were paid. Therefore make a decree that these men be made to cease, and that this city be not re-

f Heb adds *in Aramaic,* indicating that 4.8-6.18 is in Aramaic. Another interpretation is *The letter was written in the Aramaic script and set forth in the Aramaic language*

22 built, until a decree is made by me. And take care not to be slack in this matter; why should damage grow to the hurt of the king?"

23 Then, when the copy of King Ar-ta-xerx'es' letter was read before Rehum and Shim'shai the scribe and their associates, they went in haste to the Jews at Jerusalem 24 and by force and power made them cease. Then the work on the house of God which is in Jerusalem stopped; and it ceased until the second year of the reign of Darius king of Persia.

5 Now the prophets, Hag'gai and Zechari'ah the son of Iddo, prophesied to the Jews who were in Judah and Jerusalem, in the name of the God of Israel who was over 2 them. Then Zerub'babel the son of Sheal'ti-el and Jeshua the son of Jo'zadak arose and began to rebuild the house of God which is in Jerusalem; and with them were the prophets of God, helping them. 3 At the same time Tat'tenai the governor of the province Beyond the River and She'thar-boz'enai and their associates came to them and spoke to them thus, "Who gave you a decree to build this house and to finish this struc- 4 ture?" They g also asked them this, "What are the names

5 of the men who are building this building?" But the eye of their God was upon the elders of the Jews, and they did not stop them till a report should reach Darius and then answer be returned by letter concerning it. 6 The copy of the letter which Tat'tenai the governor of the province Beyond the River and She'thar-boz'enai and his associates the governors who were in the province 7 Beyond the River sent to Darius the king; they sent him a report, in which was written as follows: "To Darius the 8 king, all peace. Be it known to the king that we went to the province of Judah, to the house of the great God. It is being built with huge stones, and timber is laid in the walls; this work goes on diligently and prospers in their 9 hands. Then we asked those elders and spoke to them thus, 'Who gave you a decree to build this house and to 10 finish this structure?' We also asked them their names, for your information, that we might write down the names 11 of the men at their head. And this was their reply to us: 'We are the servants of the God of heaven and earth, and we are rebuilding the house that was built many years ago, 12 which a great king of Israel built and finished. But because our fathers had angered the God of heaven, he gave them into the hand of Nebuchadnez'zar king of Babylon, the Chalde'an, who destroyed this house and carried away 13 the people to Babylonia. However in the first year of Cyrus

g Gk Syr: Aramaic We

king of Babylon, Cyrus the king made a decree that this 14 house of God should be rebuilt. And the gold and silver vessels of the house of God, which Nebuchadnez'zar had taken out of the temple that was in Jerusalem and brought into the temple of Babylon, these Cyrus the king took out of the temple of Babylon, and they were delivered to one whose name was Shesh-baz'zar, whom he had made 15 governor; and he said to him, "Take these vessels, go and put them in the temple which is in Jerusalem, and let the 16 house of God be rebuilt on its site." Then this Shesh-baz'zar came and laid the foundations of the house of God which is in Jerusalem; and from that time until now it has been in building, and it is not yet finished.' 17 Therefore, if it seem good to the king, let search be made in the royal archives there in Babylon, to see whether a decree was issued by Cyrus the king for the rebuilding of this house of God in Jerusalem. And let the king send us his pleasure in this matter."

6 Then Darius the king made a decree, and search was made in Babylonia, in the house of the archives 2 where the documents were stored. And in Ecbat'ana, the capital which is in the province of Media, a scroll was 3 found on which this was written: "A record. In the first year of Cyrus the king, Cyrus the king issued a decree: Concerning the house of God at Jerusalem, let the house be rebuilt, the place where sacrifices are offered and burnt offerings are brought; its height shall be sixty cubits and 4 its breadth sixty cubits, with three courses of great stones and one course of timber; let the cost be paid from the 5 royal treasury. And also let the gold and silver vessels of the house of God, which Nebuchadnez'zar took out of the temple that is in Jerusalem and brought to Babylon, be restored and brought back to the temple which is in Jerusalem, each to its place; you shall put them in the house of God."

6 "Now therefore, Tat'tenai, governor of the province Beyond the River, She'thar-boz'enai, and your associates the governors who are in the province Beyond the River, 7 keep away; let the work on this house of God alone; let the governor of the Jews and the elders of the Jews rebuild 8 this house of God on its site. Moreover I make a decree regarding what you shall do for these elders of the Jews for rebuilding of this house of God; the cost is to be paid to these men in full and without delay from the royal revenue, the tribute of the province from Beyond the 9 River. And whatever is needed—young bulls, rams, or sheep for burnt offerings to the God of heaven, wheat, salt, wine, or oil, as the priests at Jerusalem require—let 10 that be given to them day by day without fail, that they may offer pleasing sacrifices to the God of heaven, and 11 pray for the life of the king and his sons. Also I make a decree that if anyone alters this edict, a beam shall be pulled out of his house, and he shall be impaled upon it, 12 and his house shall be made a dunghill. May the God who

has caused his name to dwell there overthrow any king or people that shall put forth a hand to alter this, or to destroy this house of God which is in Jerusalem. I Darius make a decree; let it be done with all diligence."

13 Then, according to the word sent by Darius the king, Tat'tenai, the governor of the province Beyond the River, She'thar-boz'enai, and their associates did with all dili-
14 gence what Darius the king had ordered. And the elders of the Jews built and prospered, through the prophesying of Hag'gai the prophet and Zechari'ah the son of Iddo. They finished their building by command of the God of Israel and by decree of Cyrus and Darius and Ar-ta-xerx'es king
15 of Persia; and this house was finished on the third day of the month of Adar, in the sixth year of the reign of Darius the king.

16 And the people of Israel, the priests and the Levites, and the rest of the returned exiles, celebrated the dedication
17 of this house of God with joy. They offered at the dedication of this house of God one hundred bulls, two hundred rams, four hundred lambs, and as a sin offering for all Israel twelve he-goats, according to the number of the
18 tribes of Israel. And they set the priests in their divisions and the Levites in their courses, for the service of God at Jerusalem, as it is written in the book of Moses.

19 On the fourteenth day of the first month the returned
20 exiles kept the passover. For the priests and the Levites had purified themselves together; all of them were clean. So they killed the passover lamb for all the returned exiles,
21 for their fellow priests, and for themselves; it was eaten by the people of Israel who had returned from exile, and also by every one who had joined them and separated himself from the pollutions of the peoples of the land to worship
22 the LORD, the God of Israel. And they kept the feast of unleavened bread seven days with joy; for the LORD had made them joyful, and had turned the heart of the king of Assyria to them, so that he aided them in the work of the house of God, the God of Israel.

EZRA'S RETURN

7 Now after this, in the reign of Ar-ta-xerx'es king of Persia, Ezra the son of Serai'ah, son of Azari'ah, son
2 of Hilki'ah, son of Shallum, son of Zadok, son of Ahi'tub,
3, 4 son of Amari'ah, son of Azari'ah, son of Merai'oth, son of
5 Zerahi'ah, son of Uzzi, son of Bukki, son of Abi'shu-a, son of Phin'ehas, son of Elea'zar, son of Aaron the chief priest

6 —this Ezra went up from Babylonia. He was a scribe skilled in the law of Moses which the LORD the God of Israel had given; and the king granted him all that he asked, for the hand of the LORD his God was upon him.
7 And there went up also to Jerusalem, in the seventh year of Ar-ta-xerx'es the king, some of the people of Israel, and some of the priests and Levites, the singers and gate-
8 keepers, and the temple servants. And he came to Jerusalem in the fifth month, which was in the seventh year of
9 the king; for on the first day of the first month he began h to go up from Babylonia, and on the first day of the fifth month he came to Jerusalem, for the good hand of his
10 God was upon him. For Ezra had set his heart to study the law of the LORD, and to do it, and to teach his statutes and ordinances in Israel.

11 This is a copy of the letter which King Ar-ta-xerx'es gave to Ezra the priest, the scribe, learned in matters of the commandments of the LORD and his statutes for Israel:
12 "Ar-ta-xerx'es, king of kings, to Ezra the priest, the
13 scribe of the law of the God of heaven.x And now I make a decree that any one of the people of Israel or their priests or Levites in my kingdom, who freely offers to go
14 to Jerusalem, may go with you. For you are sent by the king and his seven counselors to make inquiries about Judah and Jerusalem according to the law of your God,
15 which is in your hand, and also to convey the silver and gold which the king and his counselors have freely offered to the God of Israel, whose dwelling is in Jerusalem,
16 with all the silver and gold which you shall find in the whole province of Babylonia, and with the freewill offerings of the people and the priests, vowed willingly for the
17 house of their God which is in Jerusalem. With this money, then, you shall with all diligence buy bulls, rams, and lambs, with their cereal offerings and their drink offerings, and you shall offer them upon the altar of the
18 house of your God which is in Jerusalem. Whatever seems good to you and your brethren to do with the rest of the silver and gold, you may do, according to the will of your
19 God. The vessels that have been given you for the service of the house of your God, you shall deliver before the

20 God of Jerusalem. And whatever else is required for the house of your God, which you have occasion to provide, you may provide it out of the king's treasury.
21 "And I, Ar-ta-xerx'es the king, make a decree to all the treasurers in the province Beyond the River: Whatever Ezra the priest, the scribe of the law of the God of heaven,
22 requires of you, be it done with all diligence, up to a hundred talents of silver, a hundred cors of wheat, a

h Vg See Syr: Heb *that was the foundation of the going up*   x Aram adds a word of uncertain meaning

hundred baths of wine, a hundred baths of oil, and salt
23 without prescribing how much. Whatever is commanded by the God of heaven, let it be done in full for the house of the God of heaven, lest his wrath be against the realm
24 of the king and his sons. We also notify you that it shall not be lawful to impose tribute, custom, or toll upon any one of the priests, the Levites, the singers, the door-keepers, the temple servants, or other servants of this house of God.

25 "And you, Ezra, according to the wisdom of your God which is in your hand, appoint magistrates and judges who may judge all the people in the province Beyond the River, all such as know the laws of your God; and those
26 who do not know them, you shall teach. Whoever will not obey the law of your God and the law of the king, let judgment be strictly executed upon him, whether for death or for banishment or for confiscation of his goods or for imprisonment."

27 Blessed be the LORD, the God of our fathers, who put such a thing as this into the heart of the king, to beautify
28 the house of the LORD which is in Jerusalem, and who extended to me his steadfast love before the king and his counselors, and before all the king's mighty officers. I took courage, for the hand of the LORD my God was upon me, and I gathered leading men from Israel to go up with me.

8 These are the heads of their fathers' houses, and this is
   the genealogy of those who went up with me from Baby-
2 lonia, in the reign of Ar-ta-xerx'es the king: Of the sons of Phin'ehas, Gershom. Of the sons of Ith'amar, Daniel. Of the
3 sons of David, Hattush, of the sons of Shecani'ah. Of the sons of Parosh, Zechari'ah, with whom were registered one hundred
4 and fifty men. Of the sons of Pa'hath-mo'ab, Eli-e-hoe'nai the
5 son of Zerahi'ah, and with him two hundred men. Of the sons of Zattu,¹ Shecani'ah the son of Jahazi'el, and with him three
6 hundred men. Of the sons of Adin, Ebed the son of Jonathan,
7 and with him fifty men. Of the sons of Elam, Jeshai'ah the son
8 of Athali'ah, and with him seventy men. Of the sons of Shephati'ah, Zebadi'ah the son of Michael, and with him eighty men.
9 Of the sons of Jo'ab, Obadi'ah the son of Jehi'el, and with him
10 two hundred and eighteen men. Of the sons of Bani,ʲ Shelo'-mith the son of Josiphi'ah, and with him a hundred and sixty
11 men. Of the sons of Be'bai, Zechari'ah, the son of Be'bai, and
12 with him twenty-eight men. Of the sons of Azgad, Joha'nan the son of Hak'katan, and with him a hundred and ten men.
13 Of the sons of Adoni'kam, those who came later, their names being Eliph'elet, Jeu'el, and Shemai'ah, and with them sixty
14 men. Of the sons of Bigva'i, Uthai and Zaccur, and with them seventy men.

15 I gathered them to the river that runs to Aha'va, and there we encamped three days. As I reviewed the people and the priests, I found there none of the sons of Levi.

16 Then I sent for Elie'zer, Ar'i-el, Shemai'ah, Elna'than, Jarib, Elna'than, Nathan, Zechari'ah, and Meshul'lam, leading men, and for Joi'arib and Elna'than, who were
17 men of insight, and sent them to Iddo, the leading man at the place Casiphi'a, telling them what to say to Iddo and his brethren the temple servants ᵏ at the place Casiphi'a, namely, to send us ministers for the house of our God.
18 And by the good hand of our God upon us, they brought us a man of discretion, of the sons of Mahli the son of Levi, son of Israel, namely Sherebi'ah with his sons and
19 kinsmen, eighteen; also Hashabi'ah and with him Jeshai'ah of the sons of Merar'i, with his kinsmen and
20 their sons, twenty; besides two hundred and twenty of the temple servants, whom David and his officials had set apart to attend the Levites. These were all mentioned by name.

21 Then I proclaimed a fast there, at the river Aha'va, that we might humble ourselves before our God, to seek from him a straight way for ourselves, our children, and
22 all our goods. For I was ashamed to ask the king for a band of soldiers and horsemen to protect us against the enemy on our way; since we had told the king, "The hand of our God is for good upon all that seek him, and the
23 power of his wrath is against all that forsake him." So we fasted and besought our God for this, and he listened to our entreaty.

24 Then I set apart twelve of the leading priests: Sherebi'-ah, Hashabi'ah, and ten of their kinsmen with them.
25 And I weighed out to them the silver and the gold and the vessels, the offering for the house of our God which the king and his counselors and his lords and all Israel
26 there present had offered; I weighed out into their hand six hundred and fifty talents of silver, and silver vessels worth a hundred talents, and a hundred talents of gold,
27 twenty bowls of gold worth a thousand darics, and two
28 vessels of fine bright bronze as precious as gold. And I said to them, "You are holy to the LORD, and the vessels are holy, and the silver and the gold are a freewill offering
29 to the LORD, the God of your fathers. Guard them and keep them until you weigh them before the chief priests and the Levites and the heads of fathers' houses in Israel at Jerusalem, within the chambers of the house of the LORD."
30 So the priests and the Levites took over the weight of the silver and the gold and the vessels, to bring them to Jerusalem, to the house of our God.

31 Then we departed from the river Aha'va on the twelfth day of the first month, to go to Jerusalem; the hand of our God was upon us, and he delivered us from the hand
32 of the enemy and from ambushes by the way. We came to
33 Jerusalem, and there we remained three days. On the fourth day, within the house of our God, the silver and the gold and the vessels were weighed into the hands of Mer'emoth the priest, son of Uri'ah, and with him was Elea'zar the son of Phin'ehas, and with them were the

¹ Gk 1 Esdras 8.32: Heb lacks *of Zattu*   ʲ Gk 1 Esdras 8.36: Heb lacks *Bani*   ᵏ Heb *nethinim*

Levites, Jo'zabad the son of Jeshua and No-adi'ah the son
34 of Bin'nui. The whole was counted and weighed, and the
weight of everything was recorded.

35 At that time those who had come from captivity, the
returned exiles, offered burnt offerings to the God of
Israel, twelve bulls for all Israel, ninety-six rams, seventy-
seven lambs, and as a sin offering twelve he-goats; all
36 this was a burnt offering to the LORD. They also delivered
the king's commissions to the king's satraps and to the
governors of the province Beyond the River; and they
aided the people and the house of God.

MIXED MARRIAGES

9 After these things had been done, the officials approached me and said, "The people of Israel and the
priests and the Levites have not separated themselves from
the peoples of the lands with their abominations, from the
Canaanites, the Hittites, the Per'izzites, the Jeb'usites, the
Ammonites, the Moabites, the Egyptians, and the Amo-
2 rites. For they have taken some of their daughters to be
wives for themselves and for their sons; so that the holy
race has mixed itself with the peoples of the lands. And
in this faithlessness the hand of the officials and chief men
3 has been foremost." When I heard this, I rent my
garments and my mantle, and pulled hair from my head
4 and beard, and sat appalled. Then all who trembled at the
words of the God of Israel, because of the faithlessness of
the returned exiles, gathered round me while I sat ap-
5 palled until the evening sacrifice. And at the evening
sacrifice I rose from my fasting, with my garments and
my mantle rent, and fell upon my knees and spread out my
6 hands to the LORD my God, saying:

"O my God, I am ashamed and blush to lift my face
to thee, my God, for our iniquities have risen higher than
our heads, and our guilt has mounted up to the heavens.
7 From the days of our fathers to this day we have been in
great guilt; and for our iniquities we, our kings, and our
priests have been given into the hand of the kings of the
lands, to the sword, to captivity, to plundering, and to
8 utter shame, as at this day. But now for a brief moment
favor has been shown by the LORD our God, to leave us a
remnant, and to give us a secure hold[l] within his holy
place, that our God may brighten our eyes and grant us
9 a little reviving in our bondage. For we are bondmen; yet
our God has not forsaken us in our bondage, but has
extended to us his steadfast love before the kings of Persia,
to grant us some reviving to set up the house of our God,
to repair its ruins, and to give us protection[m] in Judea
and Jerusalem.
10 "And now, O our God, what shall we say after this?
11 For we have forsaken thy commandments, which thou
didst command by thy servants the prophets, saying, 'The
land which you are entering, to take possession of it, is a

land unclean with the pollutions of the peoples of the
lands, with their abominations which have filled it from
12 end to end with their uncleanness. Therefore give not
your daughters to their sons, neither take their daughters
for your sons, and never seek their peace or prosperity,
that you may be strong, and eat the good of the land, and
13 leave it for an inheritance to your children for ever.' And
after all that has come upon us for our evil deeds and for
our great guilt, seeing that thou, our God, hast punished
us less than our iniquities deserved and hast given us such
14 a remnant as this, shall we break thy commandments
again and intermarry with the peoples who practice
these abominations? Wouldst thou not be angry with us
till thou wouldst consume us, so that there should be no
15 remnant, nor any to escape? O LORD the God of Israel,
thou art just, for we are left a remnant that has escaped,
as at this day. Behold, we are before thee in our guilt, for
none can stand before thee because of this."

10 While Ezra prayed and made confession, weeping
and casting himself down before the house of God,
a very great assembly of men, women, and children,
gathered to him out of Israel; for the people wept bitterly.
2 And Shecani'ah the son of Jehi'el, of the sons of Elam,
addressed Ezra: "We have broken faith with our God and
have married foreign women from the peoples of the
land, but even now there is hope for Israel in spite of this.
3 Therefore let us make a covenant with our God to put
away all these wives and their children, according to the
counsel of my lord and of those who tremble at the commandment of our God; and let it be done according to
4 the law. Arise, for it is your task, and we are with you;
5 be strong and do it." Then Ezra arose and made the leading priests and Levites and all Israel take oath that they
would do as had been said. So they took the oath.
6 Then Ezra withdrew from before the house of God, and
went to the chamber of Jehoha'nan the son of Eli'ashib,
where he spent the night,[n] neither eating bread nor drinking water; for he was mourning over the faithlessness of
7 the exiles. And a proclamation was made throughout
Judah and Jerusalem to all the returned exiles that they
8 should assemble at Jerusalem, and that if any one did not
come within three days, by order of the officials and the
elders all his property should be forfeited, and he himself
banned from the congregation of the exiles.
9 Then all the men of Judah and Benjamin assembled
at Jerusalem within the three days; it was the ninth
month, on the twentieth day of the month. And all the
people sat in the open square before the house of God,
trembling because of this matter and because of the
10 heavy rain. And Ezra the priest stood up and said to
them, "You have trespassed and married foreign women,
11 and so increased the guilt of Israel. Now then make confession to the LORD the God of your fathers, and do his

---

[l] Heb *nail* or *tent-pin*   [m] Heb *a wall*   [n] 1 Esdras 9.2: Heb *where he went*

will; separate yourselves from the peoples of the land
12 and from the foreign wives." Then all the assembly answered with a loud voice, "It is so; we must do as you
13 have said. But the people are many, and it is a time of
heavy rain; we cannot stand in the open. Nor is this a
work for one day or for two; for we have greatly trans-
14 gressed in this matter. Let our officials stand for the whole
assembly; let all in our cities who have taken foreign
wives come at appointed times, and with them the elders
and judges of every city, till the fierce wrath of our God
15 over this matter be averted from us." Only Jonathan the
son of As'ahel and Jahzei'ah the son of Tikvah opposed
this, and Meshul'lam and Shab'bethai the Levite supported
them.

16 Then the returned exiles did so. Ezra the priest selected
men,[o] heads of fathers' houses, according to their fathers'
houses, each of them designated by name. On the first day
of the tenth month they sat down to examine the matter;
17 and by the first day of the first month they had come to
the end of all the men who had married foreign women.
18 Of the sons of the priests who had married foreign women
were found Ma'asei-ah, Elie'zer, Jarib, and Gedali'ah, of the

19 sons of Jeshua the son of Jo'zadak and his brethren. They
pledged themselves to put away their wives, and their guilt
20 offering was a ram of the flock for their guilt. Of the sons of
21 Immer: Hana'ni and Zebadi'ah. Of the sons of Harim: Ma-asei'-
22 ah, Eli'jah, Shemai'ah, Jehi'el, and Uzzi'ah. Of the sons of
Pashhur: Eli-o-e'nai, Ma-asei'ah, Ish'mael, Nethan'el, Jo'-
zabad, and Ela'sah.
23 Of the Levites: Jo'zabad, Shi'me-i. Kelai'ah (that is, Keli'ta),
24 Petha-hi'ah, Judah, and Elie'zer. Of the singers: Eli'ashib. Of
the gatekeepers: Shallum, Telem, and Uri.
25 And of Israel: of the sons of Parosh: Rami'ah, Izzi'ah, Malchi'-
26 jah, Mi'jamin, Elea'zar, Hashabi'ah,[p] and Benai'ah. Of the sons
of Elam: Mattani'ah, Zechari'ah, Jehi'el, Abdi, Jer'emoth, and
27 Eli'jah. Of the sons of Zattu: Eli-o-e'nai, Eli'ashib, Mattani'ah,
28 Jer'emoth, Zabad, and Azi'za. Of the sons of Be'bai were
29 Jehoha'nan, Hanani'ah, Zab'bai, and Ath'lai. Of the sons of Bani
were Meshul'lam, Malluch, Adai'ah, Jashub, She'al, and Jere'-
30 moth. Of the sons of Pa'hath-mo'ab: Adna, Chelal, Benai'ah,
31 Ma-asei'ah, Mattani'ah, Bez'alel, Bin'nui, and Manas'seh. Of the
sons of Harim: Elie'zer, Isshi'jah, Malchi'jah, Shemai'ah, Shim'-
32, 33 e-on, Benjamin, Malluch, and Shemari'ah. Of the sons of
Hashum: Matte'nai, Mat'tattah, Zabad, Eliph'elet, Jer'emai,
34 Manas'seh, and Shim'e-i. Of the sons of Bani: Ma-ada'i, Am-
35, 36 ram, Uel, Be-nai'ah, Bedei'ah, Chel'uhi, Vani'ah, Mer'emoth,
37, 38 Eli'ashib, Mattani'ah, Matte'nai, Ja'asu. Of the sons of
39, 40 Bin'nui:[q] Shim'e-i, Shelemi'ah, Nathan, Adai'ah, Machnad'-
41, 42 ebai, Shashai, Sha'rai, Az'arel, Shelemi'ah, Shemari'ah, Shal-
43 lum, Amari'ah, and Joseph. Of the sons of Nebo: Je-i'el,
44 Matti-thi'ah, Zabad, Zebi'na, Jaddai, Jo'el, and Benai'ah. All
these had married foreign women, and they put them away
with their children.[r]

[o] 1 Esdras 9.16 Syr: Heb *and there were selected Ezra*, etc.   [p] 1 Esdras 9.26 Gk: Heb *Malchijah*   [q] Gk: Heb *Bani, Binnui*
[r] 1 Esdras 9.36: Heb obscure

INTRODUCTION TO

NEHEMIAH

The Book of Nehemiah is the last of four books that are best understood together: First and Second Chronicles, Ezra, and Nehemiah. All four books were probably completed by the same writer about 350 B.C., although part of the Book of Nehemiah was probably written about 444 B.C.

The Chronicler felt that it was important for all Jews to worship God at the Temple in Jerusalem. The Introduction to First Chronicles, on page 261, explains more fully his purposes.

The Book of Nehemiah is about a Jew named Nehemiah, who had come to be a trusted official of King Artaxerxes of Persia. Jerusalem had been destroyed and thousands of Jews had been deported as prisoners to Babylon about 597 and 586 B.C. However, in 538 B.C. Babylon was conquered by Persia. The Persian king, Cyrus, promptly permitted the Jews who wished to do so to return to Judah. In 444 B.C., with the permission and support of King Artaxerxes, Nehemiah went to Jerusalem and helped the returned exiles rebuild the city. Then Nehemiah returned to Persia.

Twelve years later, when Nehemiah came back to Jerusalem again, he found that the people were not keeping the laws of Moses and were marrying their pagan neighbors. He demanded changes that seem terribly strict to us. He felt that the people would lose their faith in God and their loyalty to their nation if they did not keep separated from people of other tribes and nations. Not all Jews accepted this idea, as we see in the Book of Ruth whose writer pointed out that Ruth had been a Moabite foreigner who said to her Hebrew mother-in-law, "Your people shall be my people, and your God my God."

THE BOOK OF

NEHEMIAH

BAD NEWS FROM JERUSALEM

1 The words of Nehemi'ah the son of Hacali'ah.

Now it happened in the month of Chislev, in the 2 twentieth year, as I was in Susa the capital, that Hana'ni, one of my brethren, came with certain men out of Judah; and I asked them concerning the Jews that survived, who

3 had escaped exile, and concerning Jerusalem. And they said to me, "The survivors there in the province who escaped exile are in great trouble and shame; the wall of Jerusalem is broken down, and its gates are destroyed by fire."

4 When I heard these words I sat down and wept, and mourned for days; and I continued fasting and praying 5 before the God of heaven. And I said, "O LORD God of heaven, the great and terrible God who keeps covenant and steadfast love with those who love him and keep his 6 commandments; let thy ear be attentive, and thy eyes open, to hear the prayer of thy servant which I now pray before thee day and night for the people of Israel thy servants, confessing the sins of the people of Israel, which we have sinned against thee. Yea, I and my father's house 7 have sinned. We have acted very corruptly against thee, and have not kept the commandments, the statutes, and the ordinances which thou didst command thy servant 8 Moses. Remember the word which thou didst command thy servant Moses, saying, 'If you are unfaithful, I will 9 scatter you among the peoples; but if you return to me and keep my commandments and do them, though your dispersed be under the farthest skies, I will gather them

thence and bring them to the place which I have chosen,
10 to make my name dwell there.' They are thy servants and thy people, whom thou hast redeemed by thy great power
11 and by thy strong hand. O Lord, let thy ear be attentive to the prayer of thy servant, and to the prayer of thy servants who delight to fear thy name; and give success to thy servant today, and grant him mercy in the sight of this man."

Now I was cupbearer to the king.

2 In the month of Nisan, in the twentieth year of King Ar-ta-xerx'es, when wine was before him, I took up the wine and gave it to the king. Now I had not been sad
2 in his presence. And the king said to me, "Why is your face sad, seeing you are not sick? This is nothing else but sadness of the heart." Then I was very much afraid.
3 I said to the king, "Let the king live for ever! Why should not my face be sad, when the city, the place of my fathers' sepulchres, lies waste, and its gates have been destroyed
4 by fire?" Then the king said to me, "For what do you
5 make request?" So I prayed to the God of heaven. And I said to the king, "If it pleases the king, and if your servant has found favor in your sight, that you send me to Judah, to the city of my fathers' sepulchres, that I may
6 rebuild it." And the king said to me (the queen sitting beside him), "How long will you be gone, and when will you return?" So it pleased the king to send me; and I set
7 him a time. And I said to the king, "If it pleases the king, let letters be given me to the governors of the province Beyond the River, that they may let me pass through until
8 I come to Judah; and a letter to Asaph, the keeper of the king's forest, that he may give me timber to make beams for the gates of the fortress of the temple, and for the wall of the city, and for the house which I shall occupy." And the king granted me what I asked, for the good hand of my God was upon me.

NEHEMIAH BECOMES GOVERNOR OF JUDAH

9 Then I came to the governors of the province Beyond the River, and gave them the king's letters. Now the king had sent with me officers of the army and horsemen.
10 But when Sanbal'lat the Hor'onite and Tobi'ah the servant, the Ammonite, heard this, it displeased them greatly that some one had come to seek the welfare of the children of Israel.

11 So I came to Jerusalem and was there three days.
12 Then I arose in the night, I and a few men with me; and I told no one what my God had put into my heart to do for Jerusalem. There was no beast with me but the beast
13 on which I rode. I went out by night by the Valley Gate to the Jackal's Well and to the Dung Gate, and I inspected the walls of Jerusalem which were broken down and its
14 gates which had been destroyed by fire. Then I went on to the Fountain Gate and to the King's Pool; but there was no place for the beast that was under me to pass.

15 Then I went up in the night by the valley and inspected the wall; and I turned back and entered by the Valley
16 Gate, and so returned. And the officials did not know where I had gone or what I was doing; and I had not yet told the Jews, the priests, the nobles, the officials, and the rest that were to do the work.

17 Then I said to them, "You see the trouble we are in, how Jerusalem lies in ruins with its gates burned. Come, let us build the wall of Jerusalem, that we may no longer
18 suffer disgrace." And I told them of the hand of my God which had been upon me for good, and also of the words which the king had spoken to me. And they said, "Let us rise up and build." So they strengthened their hands
19 for the good work. But when Sanbal'lat the Hor'onite and Tobi'ah the servant, the Ammonite, and Geshem the Arab heard of it, they derided us and despised us and said, "What is this thing that you are doing? Are you rebelling
20 against the king?" Then I replied to them, "The God of heaven will make us prosper, and we his servants will arise and build; but you have no portion or right or memorial in Jerusalem."

Rebuilding Jerusalem's Walls

3 Then Eli'ashib the high priest rose up with his brethren the priests and they built the Sheep Gate. They consecrated it and set its doors; they consecrated it as far as the Tower of
2 the Hundred, as far as the Tower of Hanan'el. And next to him the men of Jericho built. And next to them ᵃ Zaccur the son of Imri built.
3 And the sons of Hassena'ah built the Fish Gate; they laid its
4 beams and set its doors, its bolts, and its bars. And next to them Mer'emoth the son of Uri'ah, son of Hakkoz repaired. And next to them Meshul'lam the son of Berechi'ah, son of Meshez'abel repaired. And next to them Zadok the son of
5 Ba'ana repaired. And next to them the Teko'ites repaired; but their nobles did not put their necks to the work of their Lord.ᵇ
6 And Joi'ada the son of Pase'ah and Meshul'lam the son of Besodei'ah repaired the Old Gate; they laid its beams and set
7 its doors, its bolts, and its bars. And next to them repaired Melati'ah the Gibeonite and Jadon the Mero'nothite, the men of Gibeon and of Mizpah, who were under the jurisdiction of
8 the governor of the province Beyond the River. Next to them Uz'ziel the son of Harhai'ah, goldsmiths, repaired. Next to him Hanani'ah, one of the perfumers, repaired; and they restored ᶜ
9 Jerusalem as far as the Broad Wall. Next to them Rephai'ah the son of Hur, ruler of half the district of ᵈ Jerusalem, repaired.
10 Next to them Jedai'ah the son of Haru'maph repaired opposite his house; and next to him Hattush the son of Hashabnei'ah
11 repaired. Malchi'jah the son of Harim and Hasshub the son of Pa'hath-mo'ab repaired another section and the Tower of the
12 Ovens. Next to him Shallum the son of Hallo'hesh, ruler of half the district of ᵈ Jerusalem, repaired, he and his daughters.
13 Hanun and the inhabitants of Zano'ah repaired the Valley Gate; they rebuilt it and set its doors, its bolts, and its bars, and repaired a thousand cubits of the wall, as far as the Dung Gate.
14 Malchi'jah the son of Rechab, ruler of the district of ᵈ Beth-hac'che'rem, repaired the Dung Gate; he rebuilt it and set its doors, its bolts, and its bars.
15 And Shallum the son of Colho'zeh, ruler of the district of ᵈ

ᵃ Heb *him*   ᵇ Or *lords*   ᶜ Or *abandoned*   ᵈ Or *foreman of half the portion assigned to*
ᵈ Or *foreman of half the portion assigned to*

Mizpah, repaired the Fountain Gate; he rebuilt it and covered it and set its doors, its bolts, and its bars; and he built the wall of the Pool of Shelah of the king's garden, as far as the stairs
16 that go down from the City of David. After him Nehemi'ah the son of Azbuk, ruler of half the district of d Beth-zur, repaired to a point opposite the sepulchres of David, to the artificial
17 pool, and to the house of the mighty men. After him the Levites repaired: Rehum the son of Bani; next to him Hashabi'ah, ruler of half the district of d Kei'lah, repaired for his district.
18 After him their brethren repaired: Bav'vai the son of Hen'adad,
19 ruler of half the district of d Kei'lah; next to him Ezer the son of Jeshua, ruler of Mizpah, repaired another section opposite
20 the ascent to the armory at the Angle. After him Baruch the son of Zab'bai repaired another section from the Angle to the
21 door of the house of Eli'ashib the high priest. After him Mer'-emoth the son of Uri'ah, son of Hakkoz repaired another section from the door of the house of Eli'ashib to the end of the house
22 of Eli'ashib. After him the priests, the men of the Plain, re-
23 paired. After him Benjamin and Hasshub repaired opposite their house. After them Azari'ah the son of Ma-asei'ah, son of
24 Anani'ah repaired beside his own house. After him Bin'nui the son of Hen'adad repaired another section, from the house of
25 Azari'ah to the Angle and to the corner. Palal the son of Uzai repaired opposite the Angle and the tower projecting from the upper house of the king at the court of the guard. After him
26 Pedai'ah the son of Parosh and the temple servants living e on Ophel repaired to a point opposite the Water Gate on the east
27 and the projecting tower. After him the Teko'ites repaired another section opposite the great projecting tower as far as the wall of Ophel.
28 Above the Horse Gate the priests repaired, each one opposite
29 his own house. After them Zadok the son of Immer repaired opposite his own house. After him Shemai'ah the son of
30 Shecani'ah, the keeper of the East Gate, repaired. After him Hanani'ah the son of Shelemi'ah and Hanun the sixth son of Zalaph repaired another section. After him Meshul'lam the son
31 of Berechi'ah repaired opposite his chamber. After him Malchi'-jah, one of the goldsmiths, repaired as far as the house of the temple servants and of the merchants, opposite the Muster
32 Gate,f and to the upper chamber of the corner. And between the upper chamber of the corner and the Sheep Gate the gold-smiths and the merchants repaired.

4 g Now when Sanbal'lat heard that we were building the wall, he was angry and greatly enraged, and he
2 ridiculed the Jews. And he said in the presence of his brethren and of the army of Samar'ia, "What are these feeble Jews doing? Will they restore things? Will they sacrifice? Will they finish up in a day? Will they revive the stones out of the heaps of rubbish, and burned ones
3 at that?" Tobi'ah the Ammonite was by him, and he said, "Yes, what they are building—if a fox goes up on
4 it he will break down their stone wall!" Hear, O our God, for we are despised; turn back their taunt upon their own heads, and give them up to be plundered in a land where
5 they are captives. Do not cover their guilt, and let not their sin be blotted out from thy sight; for they have provoked thee to anger before the builders.
6 So we built the wall; and all the wall was joined to-gether to half its height. For the people had a mind to work.
7 h But when Sanbal'lat and Tobi'ah and the Arabs and the Ammonites and the Ash'dodites heard that the repair-ing of the walls of Jerusalem was going forward and that the breaches were beginning to be closed, they were very
8 angry; and they all plotted together to come and fight
9 against Jerusalem and to cause confusion in it. And we prayed to our God, and set a guard as a protection against them day and night.

10 But Judah said, "The strength of the burden-bearers is failing, and there is much rubbish; we are not able to
11 work on the wall." And our enemies said, "They will not know or see till we come into the midst of them and kill
12 them and stop the work." When the Jews who lived by them came they said to us ten times, "From all the places
13 where they live i they will come up against us." j So in the

lowest parts of the space behind the wall, in open places, I stationed the people according to their families, with
14 their swords, their spears, and their bows. And I looked, and arose, and said to the nobles and to the officials and to the rest of the people, "Do not be afraid of them. Re-member the LORD, who is great and terrible, and fight for your brethren, your sons, your daughters, your wives, and your homes."
15 When our enemies heard that it was known to us and that God had frustrated their plan, we all returned to the
16 wall, each to his work. From that day on, half of my servants worked on construction, and half held the spears, shields, bows, and coats of mail; and the leaders stood
17 behind all the house of Judah, who were building on the wall. Those who carried burdens were laden in such a way that each with one hand labored on the work and with the
18 other held his weapon. And each of the builders had his sword girded at his side while he built. The man who
19 sounded the trumpet was beside me. And I said to the nobles and to the officials and to the rest of the people, "The work is great and widely spread, and we are
20 separated on the wall, far from one another. In the place where you hear the sound of the trumpet, rally to us there. Our God will fight for us."
21 So we labored at the work, and half of them held the spears from the break of dawn till the stars came out.
22 I also said to the people at that time, "Let every man and his servant pass the night within Jerusalem, that they may be a guard for us by night and may labor by day."
23 So neither I nor my brethren nor my servants nor the men of the guard who followed me, none of us took off our clothes; each kept his weapon in his hand.k

5 Now there arose a great outcry of the people and of
2 their wives against their Jewish brethren. For there were those who said, "With our sons and our daughters, we are many; let us get grain, that we may eat and keep
3 alive." There were also those who said, "We are mortgag-ing our fields, our vineyards, and our houses to get grain

e Cn: Heb were living   f Or Hammiphkad Gate   g Ch 3.33 in Heb   h Ch 4.1 in Heb   i Cn: Heb you return
j Compare Gk Syr: Heb uncertain   k Cn: Heb each his weapon the water

4 because of the famine." And there were those who said, "We have borrowed money for the king's tax upon our 5 fields and our vineyards. Now our flesh is as the flesh of our brethren, our children are as their children; yet we are forcing our sons and our daughters to be slaves, and some of our daughters have already been enslaved; but it is not in our power to help it, for other men have our fields and our vineyards."

6 I was very angry when I heard their outcry and these 7 words. I took counsel with myself, and I brought charges against the nobles and the officials. I said to them, "You are exacting interest, each from his brother." And I held 8 a great assembly against them, and said to them, "We, as far as we are able, have bought back our Jewish brethren who have been sold to the nations; but you even sell your brethren that they may be sold to us!" They were silent, 9 and could not find a word to say. So I said, "The thing that you are doing is not good. Ought you not to walk in the fear of our God to prevent the taunts of the na- 10 tions our enemies? Moreover I and my brethren and my servants are lending them money and grain. Let us 11 leave off this interest. Return to them this very day their fields, their vineyards, their olive orchards, and their houses, and the hundredth of money, grain, wine, and oil 12 which you have been exacting of them." Then they said, "We will restore these and require nothing from them. We will do as you say." And I called the priests, and took 13 an oath of them to do as they had promised. I also shook out my lap and said, "So may God shake out every man from his house and from his labor who does not perform this promise. So may he be shaken out and emptied." And all the assembly said "Amen" and praised the Lord. And the people did as they had promised.

14 Moreover from the time that I was appointed to be their governor in the land of Judah, from the twentieth year to the thirty-second year of Ar-ta-xerx'es the king, twelve years, neither I nor my brethren ate the food 15 allowance of the governor. The former governors who were before me laid heavy burdens upon the people, and took from them food and wine, besides forty shekels of silver. Even their servants lorded it over the people. But I 16 did not do so, because of the fear of God. I also held to the work on this wall, and acquired no land; and all my 17 servants were gathered there for the work. Moreover there were at my table a hundred and fifty men, Jews and officials, besides those who came to us from the nations 18 which were about us. Now that which was prepared for one day was one ox and six choice sheep; fowls likewise were prepared for me, and every ten days skins of wine in abundance; yet with all this I did not demand the food allowance of the governor, because the servitude was 19 heavy upon this people. Remember for my good, O my God, all that I have done for this people.

6 Now when it was reported to Sanbal'lat and Tobi'ah and to Geshem the Arab and to the rest of our enemies that I had built the wall and that there was no breach left in it (although up to that time I had not set up the doors 2 in the gates), Sanbal'lat and Geshem sent to me, saying, "Come and let us meet together in one of the villages in the plain of Ono." But they intended to do me harm. 3 And I sent messengers to them, saying, "I am doing a great work and I cannot come down. Why should the work 4 stop while I leave it and come down to you?" And they sent to me four times in this way and I answered them in 5 the same manner. In the same way Sanbal'lat for the fifth time sent his servant to me with an open letter in his hand. 6 In it was written, "It is reported among the nations, and Geshem [1] also says it, that you and the Jews intend to rebel; that is why you are building the wall; and you wish 7 to become their king, according to this report. And you have also set up prophets to proclaim concerning you in Jerusalem, 'There is a king in Judah.' And now it will be reported to the king according to these words. So now 8 come, and let us take counsel together." Then I sent to him, saying, "No such things as you say have been done, for you are inventing them out of your own mind." 9 For they all wanted to frighten us, thinking, "Their hands will drop from the work, and it will not be done." But now, O God, strengthen thou my hands.

10 Now when I went into the house of Shemai'ah the son of Delai'ah, son of Mehet'abel, who was shut up, he said, "Let us meet together in the house of God, within the temple, and let us close the doors of the temple; for they are coming to kill you, at night they are coming to kill 11 you." But I said, "Should such a man as I flee? And what man such as I could go into the temple and live? [m] I

12 will not go in." And I understood, and saw that God had not sent him, but he had pronounced the prophecy against 13 me because Tobi'ah and Sanbal'lat had hired him. For this purpose he was hired, that I should be afraid and act in this way and sin, and so they could give me an evil name, 14 in order to taunt me. Remember Tobi'ah and Sanbal'lat, O my God, according to these things that they did, and also the prophetess No-adi'ah and the rest of the prophets who wanted to make me afraid.

15 So the wall was finished on the twenty-fifth day of the 16 month Elul, in fifty-two days. And when all our enemies heard of it, all the nations round about us were afraid [n]

[1] Heb Gashmu   [m] Or would go into the temple to save his life   [n] Another reading is saw

and fell greatly in their own esteem; for they perceived that this work had been accomplished with the help of our 17 God. Moreover in those days the nobles of Judah sent many letters to Tobi'ah, and Tobi'ah's letters came to 18 them. For many in Judah were bound by oath to him, because he was the son-in-law of Shecani'ah the son of Arah: and his son Jehoha'nan had taken the daughter of 19 Meshul'lam the son of Berechi'ah as his wife. Also they spoke of his good deeds in my presence, and reported my words to him. And Tobi'ah sent letters to make me afraid.

7 Now when the wall had been built and I had set up the doors, and the gatekeepers, the singers, and the 2 Levites had been appointed, I gave my brother Hana'ni and Hanani'ah the governor of the castle charge over Jerusalem, for he was a more faithful and God-fearing 3 man than many. And I said to them, "Let not the gates of Jerusalem be opened until the sun is hot; and while they are still standing guard o let them shut and bar the doors. Appoint guards from among the inhabitants of Jerusalem, each to his station and each opposite his own 4 house." The city was wide and large, but the people within it were few and no houses had been built.

5 Then God put it into my mind to assemble the nobles and the officials and the people to be enrolled by genealogy. And I found the book of the genealogy of those who came up at the first, and I found written in it:

6 These were the people of the province who came up out of the captivity of those exiles whom Nebuchadnez'zar the king of Babylon had carried into exile; they returned to Jerusalem and Judah, each to his town.

7 They came with Zerub'babel, Jeshua, Nehemi'ah, Azari'ah, Raami'ah, Naham'ani, Mor'decai, Bilshan, Mis'pereth, Big'vai, Nehum, Ba'anah.
8 The number of the men of the people of Israel: the sons of 9 Parosh, two thousand a hundred and seventy-two. The sons of 10 Shephati'ah, three hundred and seventy-two. The sons of Arah, 11 six hundred and fifty-two. The sons of Pa'hath-mo'ab, namely the sons of Jeshua and Jo'ab, two thousand eight hundred and 12 eighteen. The sons of Elam, a thousand two hundred and fifty-13, 14 four. The sons of Zattu, eight hundred and forty-five. The 15 sons of Zac'cai, seven hundred and sixty. The sons of Bin'nui, 16 six hundred and forty-eight. The sons of Be'bai, six hundred 17 and twenty-eight. The sons of Azgad, two thousand three 18 hundred and twenty-two. The sons of Adoni'kam, six hundred 19 and sixty-seven. The sons of Big'vai, two thousand and sixty-20, 21 seven. The sons of Adin, six hundred and fifty-five. The sons 22 of Ater, namely of Hezeki'ah, ninety-eight. The sons of Hashum, 23 three hundred and twenty-eight. The sons of Be'zai, three hun-24 dred and twenty-four. The sons of Hariph, a hundred and 25, 26 twelve. The sons of Gibeon, ninety-five. The men of Bethle-27 hem and Neto'phah, a hundred and eighty-eight. The men of 28 An'athoth, a hundred and twenty-eight. The men of Beth-az'-29 maveth, forty-two. The men of Kir'iath-je'arim, Chephi'rah, 30 and Be-er'oth, seven hundred and forty-three. The men of 31 Ramah and Geba, six hundred and twenty-one. The men of 32 Michmas, a hundred and twenty-two. The men of Bethel and 33 Ai, a hundred and twenty-three. The men of the other Nebo, 34 fifty-two. The sons of the other Elam, a thousand two hundred 35 and fifty-four. The sons of Harim, three hundred and twenty. 36, 37 The sons of Jericho, three hundred and forty-five. The sons 38 of Lod, Hadid, and Ono, seven hundred and twenty-one. The sons of Sena'ah, three thousand nine hundred and thirty. 39 The priests: the sons of Jedai'ah, namely the house of Jeshua,

40 nine hundred and seventy-three. The sons of Immer, a thousand 41 and fifty-two. The sons of Pashhur, a thousand two hundred and 42 forty-seven. The sons of Harim, a thousand and seventeen. 43 The Levites: the sons of Jeshua, namely of Kad'mi-el of the 44 sons of Ho'devah, seventy-four. The singers: the sons of Asaph, 45 a hundred and forty-eight. The gatekeepers: the sons of Shallum, the sons of Ater, the sons of Talmon, the sons of Akkub, the sons of Hati'ta, the sons of Sho'bai, a hundred and thirty-eight. 46 The temple servants: p the sons of Ziha, the sons of Hasu'pha, 47 the sons of Tabba'oth, the sons of Keros, the sons of Si'a, the 48 sons of Padon, the sons of Leba'na, the sons of Hag'aba, the 49 sons of Shalmai, the sons of Hanan, the sons of Giddel, 50 the sons of Gahar, the sons of Re-ai'ah, the sons of Rezin, the 51 sons of Neko'da, the sons of Gazzam, the sons of Uzza, the sons 52 of Pase'ah, the sons of Besai, the sons of Me-u'nim, the sons of 53 Nephush'esim, the sons of Bakbuk, the sons of Haku'pha, the 54 sons of Harhur, the sons of Bazlith, the sons of Mehi'da, the 55 sons of Harsha, the sons of Barkos, the sons of Sis'era, the sons 56 of Temah, the sons of Nezi'ah, the sons of Hati'pha. 57 The sons of Solomon's servants: the sons of So'tai, the sons of 58 So'phereth, the sons of Peri'da, the sons of Ja'ala, the sons 59 of Darkon, the sons of Giddel, the sons of Shephati'ah, the sons of Hattil, the sons of Po'chereth-hazzeba'im, the sons of Amon. 60 All the temple servants and the sons of Solomon's servants were three hundred and ninety-two. 61 The following were those who came up from Tel-me'lah, Tel-har'sha, Cherub, Addon, and Immer, but they could not prove their fathers' houses nor their descent, whether they belonged 62 to Israel: the sons of Delai'ah, the sons of Tobi'ah, the sons of 63 Neko'da, six hundred and forty-two. Also, of the priests: the sons of Hobai'ah, the sons of Hakkoz, the sons of Barzil'lai (who had taken a wife of the daughters of Barzil'lai the Gileadite 64 and was called by their name). These sought their registration among those enrolled in the genealogies, but it was not found there, so they were excluded from the priesthood as unclean; 65 the governor told them that they were not to partake of the most holy food, until a priest with Urim and Thummim should arise. 66 The whole assembly together was forty-two thousand three 67 hundred and sixty, besides their menservants and maidservants, of whom there were seven thousand three hundred and thirty-seven; and they had two hundred and forty-five singers, male 68 and female. Their horses were seven hundred and thirty-six, 69 their mules two hundred and forty-five,q their camels four hundred and thirty-five, and their asses six thousand seven hundred and twenty. 70 Now some of the heads of fathers' houses gave to the work. The governor gave to the treasury a thousand darics of gold, 71 fifty basins, five hundred and thirty priests' garments. And some of the heads of fathers' houses gave into the treasury of the work twenty thousand darics of gold and two thousand 72 two hundred minas of silver. And what the rest of the people gave was twenty thousand darics of gold, two thousand minas of silver, and sixty-seven priests' garments.

Ezra Reads the Law to the People

73 So the priests, the Levites, the gatekeepers, the singers, some of the people, the temple servants, and all Israel, lived in their towns.

And when the seventh month had come, the children of 8 Israel were in their towns. And all the people gathered as one man into the square before the Water Gate; and they told Ezra the scribe to bring the book of the law of 2 Moses which the LORD had given to Israel. And Ezra the priest brought the law before the assembly, both men and women and all who could hear with understanding, on 3 the first day of the seventh month. And he read from it facing the square before the Water Gate from early morning until midday, in the presence of the men and the women and those who could understand; and the ears of 4 all the people were attentive to the book of the law. And

o Heb obscure   p Heb nethinim   q Ezr 2.66 and the margins of some Hebrew Mss: Heb lacks their horses . . . forty-five

Ezra the scribe stood on a wooden pulpit which they had made for the purpose; and beside him stood Mattithi′ah, Shema, Anai′ah, Uri′ah, Hilki′ah, and Ma-asei′ah on his right hand; and Pedai′ah, Mish′a-el, Malchi′jah, Hashum, Hash-bad′danah, Zechari′ah, and Meshul′lam on his left 5 hand. And Ezra opened the book in the sight of all the people, for he was above all the people; and when he 6 opened it all the people stood. And Ezra blessed the Lord, the great God; and all the people answered, "Amen, Amen," lifting up their hands; and they bowed their heads and worshiped the Lord with their faces to the ground. 7 Also Jeshua, Bani, Sherebi′ah, Jamin, Akkub, Shab′bethai, Hodi′ah, Ma-asei′ah, Keli′ta, Azari′ah, Jo′zabad, Hanan, Pelai′ah, the Levites,ʳ helped the people to understand the 8 law, while the people remained in their places. And they read from the book, from the law of God, clearly; ˢ and they gave the sense, so that the people understood the reading.

9 And Nehemi′ah, who was the governor, and Ezra the priest and scribe, and the Levites who taught the people said to all the people, "This day is holy to the Lord your God; do not mourn or weep." For all the people wept 10 when they heard the words of the law. Then he said to them, "Go your way, eat the fat and drink sweet wine and send portions to him for whom nothing is prepared; for this day is holy to our Lord; and do not be grieved, for 11 the joy of the Lord is your strength." So the Levites stilled all the people, saying, "Be quiet, for this day is 12 holy; do not be grieved." And all the people went their way to eat and drink and to send portions and to make great rejoicing, because they had understood the words that were declared to them.

13 On the second day the heads of fathers' houses of all the people, with the priests and the Levites, came together to Ezra the scribe in order to study the words of the law. 14 And they found it written in the law that the Lord had commanded by Moses that the people of Israel should dwell in booths during the feast of the seventh month, 15 and that they should publish and proclaim in all their towns and in Jerusalem, "Go out to the hills and bring branches of olive, wild olive, myrtle, palm, and other 16 leafy trees to make booths, as it is written." So the people went out and brought them and made booths for themselves, each on his roof, and in their courts and in the courts of the house of God, and in the square at the Water Gate and in the square at the Gate of E′phraim. 17 And all the assembly of those who had returned from the captivity made booths and dwelt in the booths; for from

the days of Jeshua the son of Nun to that day the people of Israel had not done so. And there was very great re- 18 joicing. And day by day, from the first day to the last day, he read from the book of the law of God. They kept the feast seven days; and on the eighth day there was a solemn assembly, according to the ordinance.

9 Now on the twenty-fourth day of this month the people of Israel were assembled with fasting and in 2 sackcloth, and with earth upon their heads. And the Israelites separated themselves from all foreigners, and stood and confessed their sins and the iniquities of their 3 fathers. And they stood up in their place and read from the book of the law of the Lord their God for a fourth of the day; for another fourth of it they made confession 4 and worshiped the Lord their God. Upon the stairs of the Levites stood Jeshua, Bani, Kad′mi-el, Shebani′ah, Bunni, Sherebi′ah, Bani, and Chena′ni; and they cried with a 5 loud voice to the Lord their God. Then the Levites, Jeshua, Kad′mi-el, Bani, Hashabnei′ah, Sherebi′ah, Hodi′- ah, Shebani′ah, and Pethahi′ah, said, "Stand up and bless the Lord your God from everlasting to everlasting. Blessed be thy glorious name which is exalted above all blessing and praise."

Ezra's Psalm of Penitence

6 And Ezra said: ᵗ "Thou art the Lord, thou alone; thou hast made heaven, the heaven of heavens, with all their host, the earth and all that is on it, the seas and all that is in them; and thou preservest all of them; and the host 7 of heaven worships thee. Thou art the Lord, the God who didst choose Abram and bring him forth out of Ur of the 8 Chaldeans and give him the name Abraham; and thou didst find his heart faithful before thee, and didst make with him the covenant to give to his descendants the land of the Canaanite, the Hittite, the Amorite, the Per′izzite, the Jeb′usite, and the Gir′gashite; and thou hast fulfilled thy promise, for thou art righteous.

9 "And thou didst see the affliction of our fathers in 10 Egypt and hear their cry at the Red Sea, and didst per- form signs and wonders against Pharaoh and all his servants and all the people of his land, for thou knewest that they acted insolently against our fathers; and thou 11 didst get thee a name, as it is to this day. And thou didst divide the sea before them, so that they went through the midst of the sea on dry land; and thou didst cast their pursuers into the depths, as a stone into mighty waters. 12 By a pillar of cloud thou didst lead them in the day, and by a pillar of fire in the night to light for them the way 13 in which they should go. Thou didst come down upon Mount Sinai, and speak with them from heaven and give them right ordinances and true laws, good statutes and 14 commandments, and thou didst make known to them thy holy sabbath and command them commandments and 15 statutes and a law by Moses thy servant. Thou didst give

---

ʳ 1 Esdras 9.48 Vg: Heb *and the Levites*   ˢ Or *with interpretation*   ᵗ Gk: Heb lacks *and Ezra said*

them bread from heaven for their hunger and bring forth water for them from the rock for their thirst, and thou didst tell them to go in to possess the land which thou hadst sworn to give them.

16 "But they and our fathers acted presumptuously and stiffened their neck and did not obey thy commandments; 17 they refused to obey, and were not mindful of the wonders which thou didst perform among them; but they stiffened their neck and appointed a leader to return to their bondage in Egypt. But thou art a God ready to forgive, gracious and merciful, slow to anger and abounding in 18 steadfast love, and didst not forsake them. Even when they had made for themselves a molten calf and said, 'This is your God who brought you up out of Egypt,' and had 19 committed great blasphemies, thou in thy great mercies didst not forsake them in the wilderness; the pillar of cloud which led them in the way did not depart from them by day, nor the pillar of fire by night which lighted 20 for them the way by which they should go. Thou gavest thy good Spirit to instruct them, and didst not withhold thy manna from their mouth, and gavest them water for 21 their thirst. Forty years didst thou sustain them in the wilderness, and they lacked nothing; their clothes did not 22 wear out and their feet did not swell. And thou didst give them kingdoms and peoples, and didst allot to them every corner; so they took possession of the land of Sihon king 23 of Heshbon and the land of Og king of Bashan. Thou didst multiply their descendants as the stars of heaven, and thou didst bring them into the land which thou hadst 24 told their fathers to enter and possess. So the descendants went in and possessed the land, and thou didst subdue before them the inhabitants of the land, the Canaanites, and didst give them into their hands, with their kings and the peoples of the land, that they might do with them as 25 they would. And they captured fortified cities and a rich land, and took possession of houses full of all good things, cisterns hewn out, vineyards, olive orchards and fruit trees in abundance; so they ate, and were filled and became fat, and delighted themselves in thy great goodness. 26 "Nevertheless they were disobedient and rebelled against thee and cast thy law behind their back and killed thy prophets, who had warned them in order to turn them back to thee, and they committed great blas- 27 phemies. Therefore thou didst give them into the hand of their enemies, who made them suffer; and in the time of their suffering they cried to thee and thou didst hear them from heaven; and according to thy great mercies thou didst give them saviors who saved them from the 28 hand of their enemies. But after they had rest they did evil again before thee, and thou didst abandon them to the hand of their enemies, so that they had dominion over them; yet when they turned and cried to thee thou didst hear from heaven, and many times thou didst deliver

29 them according to thy mercies. And thou didst warn them in order to turn them back to thy law. Yet they acted presumptuously and did not obey thy commandments, but sinned against thy ordinances, by the observance of which a man shall live, and turned a stubborn shoulder and stiffened their neck and would not obey. 30 Many years thou didst bear with them, and didst warn them by thy Spirit through thy prophets; yet they would not give ear. Therefore thou didst give them into the 31 hand of the peoples of the lands. Nevertheless in thy great mercies thou didst not make an end of them or forsake them; for thou art a gracious and merciful God.

32 "Now therefore, our God, the great and mighty and terrible God, who keepest covenant and steadfast love, let not all the hardship seem little to thee that has come upon us, upon our kings, our princes, our priests, our prophets, our fathers, and all thy people, since the time 33 of the kings of Assyria until this day. Yet thou hast been just in all that has come upon us, for thou hast dealt 34 faithfully and we have acted wickedly; our kings, our princes, our priests, and our fathers have not kept thy law or heeded thy commandments and thy warnings 35 which thou didst give them. They did not serve thee in their kingdom, and in thy great goodness which thou gavest them, and in the large and rich land which thou didst set before them; and they did not turn from their 36 wicked works. Behold, we are slaves this day; in the land that thou gavest to our fathers to enjoy its fruit and 37 its good gifts, behold, we are slaves. And its rich yield goes to the kings whom thou hast set over us because of our sins; they have power also over our bodies and over our cattle at their pleasure, and we are in great distress." 38 u Because of all this we make a firm covenant and write it, and our princes, our Levites, and our priests set their seal to it.

Reforms Pledged

10 v Those who set their seal are Nehemi'ah the governor, 2 the son of Hacali'ah, Zedeki'ah, Serai'ah, Azari'ah, Jere- 3, 4 miah, Pashhur, Amari'ah, Malchi'jah, Hattush, Shebani'ah, 5, 6 Malluch, Harim, Mer'emoth, Obadi'ah, Daniel, Gin'nethon, 7, 8 Baruch, Meshul'lam, Abi'jah, Mi'jamin, Ma-azi'ah, Bil'gai, 9 Shemai'ah; these are the priests. And the Levites: Jeshua the son of Azani'ah, Bin'nui of the sons of Hen'adad, Kad'mi-el; 10 and their brethren, Shebani'ah, Hodi'ah, Keli'ta, Pelai'ah, 11, 12 Hanan, Mica, Rehob, Hashabi'ah, Zaccur, Sherebi'ah, Shebani'- 13, 14 ah, Hodi'ah, Bani, Beni'nu. The chiefs of the people: Parosh, 15 Pa'hath-mo'ab, Elam, Zattu, Bani, Bunni, Azgad, Be'bai, 16, 17, 18 Adoni'jah, Big'vai, Adin, Ater, Hezeki'ah, Azzur, Hodi'ah, 19, 20 Hashum, Be'zai, Hariph, An'athoth, Ne'bai, Mag'piash, 21, 22 Meshul'lam, Hezir, Meshez'abel, Zadok, Jad'du-a, Pe-lati'ah, 23, 24 Hanan, Anai'ah, Hoshe'a, Hanani'ah, Hasshub, Hallo'hesh, 25, 26 Pi'lha, Shobek, Rehum, Hashab'nah, Ma-asei'ah, Ahi'ah, 27 Hanan, Anan, Malluch, Harim, Ba'anah. 28 The rest of the people, the priests, the Levites, the gatekeepers, the singers, the temple servants, and all who have separated themselves from the peoples of the lands to the law of God, their wives, their sons, their daughters, all who have knowledge 29 and understanding, join with their brethren, their nobles, and enter into a curse and an oath to walk in God's law which was given by Moses the servant of God, and to observe and do all the commandments of the LORD our Lord and his ordinances

u Ch 10.1 in Heb   v Ch 10.2 in Heb

30 and his statutes. We will not give our daughters to the peoples 31 of the land or take their daughters for our sons; and if the peoples of the land bring in wares or any grain on the sabbath day to sell, we will not buy from them on the sabbath or on a holy day; and we will forego the crops of the seventh year and the exaction of every debt.

32 We also lay upon ourselves the obligation to charge ourselves yearly with the third part of a shekel for the service of the 33 house of our God: for the showbread, the continual cereal offering, the continual burnt offering, the sabbaths, the new moons, the appointed feasts, the holy things, and the sin offerings to make atonement for Israel, and for all the work of the 34 house of our God. We have likewise cast lots, the priests, the Levites, and the people, for the wood offering, to bring it into the house of our God, according to our fathers' houses, at times appointed, year by year, to burn upon the altar of the LORD our 35 God, as it is written in the law. We obligate ourselves to bring the first fruits of our ground and the first fruits of all fruit of 36 every tree, year by year, to the house of the LORD; also to bring to the house of our God, to the priests who minister in the house of our God, the first-born of our sons and of our cattle, as it is written in the law, and the firstlings of our herds and of 37 our flocks; and to bring the first of our coarse meal, and our contributions, the fruit of every tree, the wine and the oil, to the priests, to the chambers of the house of our God; and to bring to the Levites the tithes from our ground, for it is the 38 Levites who collect the tithes in all our rural towns. And the priest, the son of Aaron, shall be with the Levites when the Levites receive the tithes; and the Levites shall bring up the tithe of the tithes to the house of our God, to the chambers, to 39 the storehouse. For the people of Israel and the sons of Levi shall bring the contribution of grain, wine, and oil to the chambers, where are the vessels of the sanctuary, and the priests that minister, and the gatekeepers and the singers. We will not neglect the house of our God.

DISTRIBUTION OF PEOPLE

11 Now the leaders of the people lived in Jerusalem; and the rest of the people cast lots to bring one out of ten to live in Jerusalem the holy city, while nine tenths remained in 2 the other towns. And the people blessed all the men who willingly offered to live in Jerusalem.

3 These are the chiefs of the province who lived in Jerusalem; but in the towns of Judah every one lived on his property in their towns: Israel, the priests, the Levites, the temple servants, 4 and the descendants of Solomon's servants. And in Jerusalem lived certain of the sons of Judah and of the sons of Benjamin. Of the sons of Judah: Athai'ah the son of Uzzi'ah, son of Zechari'ah, son of Amari'ah, son of Shephati'ah, son of Mahal'- 5 alel of the sons of Perez; and Ma-asei'ah the son of Baruch, son of Col-ho'zeh, son of Hazai'ah, son of Adai'ah, son of Joi'arib, 6 of Zechari'ah, son of the Shilo'nite. All the sons of Perez who lived in Jerusalem were four hundred and sixty-eight valiant men.

7 And these are the sons of Benjamin: Sallu the son of Meshul'- lam, son of Jo'ed, son of Pedai'ah, son of Kolai'ah, son of Ma- 8 asei'ah, son of I'thi-el, son of Jeshai'ah. And after him Gabba'i, 9 Salla'i, nine hundred and twenty-eight. Jo'el the son of Zichri was their overseer; and Judah the son of Hassen'u-ah was second over the city.

10, 11 Of the priests: Jedai'ah the son of Joi'arib, Jachin, Serai'ah the son of Hilki'ah, son of Meshul'lam, son of Zadok, son of 12 Merai'oth, son of Ahi'tub, ruler of the house of God, and their brethren who did the work of the house, eight hundred and twenty-two; and Adai'ah the son of Jero'ham, son of Pelali'ah, son of Amzi, son of Zechari'ah, son of Pashhur, son of Malchi'- 13 jah, and his brethren, heads of fathers' houses, two hundred and forty-two; and Amash'sai, the son of Az'arel, son of Ah'zai, son 14 of Meshil'lemoth, son of Immer, and their brethren, mighty men of valor, a hundred and twenty-eight; their overseer was Zab'- diel the son of Haggedo'lim.

15 And of the Levites: Shemai'ah the son of Hasshub, son of 16 Azri'kam, son of Hashabi'ah, son of Bunni; and Shab'bethai and Jo'zabad, of the chiefs of the Levites, who were over the out- 17 side work of the house of God; and Mattani'ah the son of Mica, son of Zabdi, son of Asaph, who was the leader to begin the thanksgiving in prayer, and Bakbuki'ah, the second among his brethren; and Abda the son of Sham'mua, son of Galal, son of 18 Jedu'thun. All the Levites in the holy city were two hundred and eighty-four.

19 The gatekeepers, Akkub, Talmon and their brethren, who kept watch at the gates were a hundred and seventy-two. 20 And the rest of Israel, and of the priests and the Levites, were 21 in all the towns of Judah, every one in his inheritance. But the temple servants lived on Ophel; and Ziha and Gishpa were over the temple servants.

22 The overseer of the Levites in Jerusalem was Uzzi the son of Bani, son of Hashabi'ah, son of Mattani'ah, son of Mica, of the 23 sons of Asaph, the singers, over the work of the house of God. For there was a command from the king concerning them, and 24 a settled provision for the singers, as every day required. And Pethahi'ah the son of Meshez'abel, of the sons of Zerah the son of Judah, was at the king's hand in all matters concerning the people.

25 And as for the villages, with their fields, some of the people of Judah lived in Kir'iath-ar'ba and its villages, and in Dibon 26 and its villages, and in Jekab'zeel and its villages, and in 27 Jeshua and in Mola'dah and Beth-pelet, in Ha'zar-shu'al, in 28 Beer-sheba and its villages, in Ziklag, in Meco'nah and its 29, 30 villages, in En-rim'mon, in Zorah, in Jarmuth, Zano'ah, Adul- lam, and their villages, Lachish and its fields, and Aze'kah and its villages. So they encamped from Beer-sheba to the valley of 31 Hinnom. The people of Benjamin also lived from Geba onward, 32 at Michmash, Ai'ja, Bethel and its villages, An'athoth, Nob, 33, 34 Anani'ah, Hazor, Ramah, Git'taim, Hadid, Zebo'im, Nebal'lat, 35, 36 Lod, and Ono, the valley of craftsmen. And certain divisions of the Levites in Judah were joined to Benjamin.

CLERICAL GENEALOGIES

12 These are the priests and the Levites who came up with Zerub'babel the son of She-al'ti-el, and Jeshua: Serai'ah, 2, 3 Jeremiah, Ezra, Amari'ah, Malluch, Hattush, Shecani'ah, 4, 5 Rehum, Mer'emoth, Iddo, Gin'nethoi, Abi'jah, Mi'jamin, Ma- 6, 7 adi'ah, Balgah, Shemai'ah, Joi'arib, Jedai'ah, Sallu, Amok, Hilki'- ah, Jedai'ah. These were the chiefs of the priests and of their brethren in the days of Jeshua.

8 And the Levites: Jeshua, Bin'nui, Kad'mi-el Sherebi'ah, Judah, and Mattani'ah who with his brethren was in charge of 9 the songs of thanksgiving. And Bakbuki'ah and Unno their 10 brethren stood opposite them in the service. And Jeshua was the father of Joi'akim, Joi'akim the father of Eli'ashib, Eli'ashib the 11 father of Joi'ada, Joi'ada the father of Jonathan, and Jonathan the father of Jad'du-a.

12 And in the days of Joi'akim were priests, heads of fathers' 13 houses: of Serai'ah, Merai'ah; of Jeremiah, Hanani'ah; of Ezra, 14 Meshul'lam; of Amari'ah, Jehoha'nan; of Mal'luchi, Jonathan; 15 of Shebani'ah, Joseph; of Harim, Adna; of Merai'oth, Hel'kai; 16, 17 of Iddo, Zechari'ah; of Gin'nethon, Meshul'lam; of Abi'jah, 18 Zachri; of Mini'amin, of Moadi'ah, Pil'tai; of Bilgah, Sham'mu-a; 19 of Shemai'ah, Jehon'athan; of Joi'arib, Matte'nai; of Jedai'ah, 20, 21 Uzzi; of Sal'lai, Kal'lai; of Amok, Eber; of Hilki'ah, Hasha- bi'ah; of Jedai'ah, Nethan'el.

22 As for the Levites, in the days of Eli'ashib, Joi'ada, Joha'nan, and Jad'du-a, there were recorded the heads of fathers' houses; 23 also the priests until the reign of Darius the Persian. The sons of Levi, heads of fathers' houses, were written in the Book of the Chronicles until the days of Joha'nan the son of Eli'ashib. 24 And the chiefs of the Levites: Hashabi'ah, Sherebi'ah, and Jeshua the son of Kad'mi-el, with their brethren over against them, to praise and to give thanks, according to the command- ment of David the man of God, watch corresponding to watch.

²⁵ Mattani'ah, Bakbuki'ah, Obadi'ah, Meshul'lam, Talmon, and Akkub were gatekeepers standing guard at the storehouses of ²⁶ the gates. These were in the days of Joi'akim the son of Jeshua son of Jo'zadak, and in the days of Nehemi'ah the governor and of Ezra the priest the scribe.

JERUSALEM'S NEW WALLS DEDICATED

²⁷ And at the dedication of the wall of Jerusalem they sought the Levites in all their places, to bring them to Jerusalem to celebrate the dedication with gladness, with thanksgiving and with singing, with cymbals, harps, and ²⁸ lyres. And the sons of the singers gathered together from the circuit round Jerusalem and from the villages of the ²⁹ Netoph'athites; also from Beth-gilgal and from the region of Geba and Az'maveth; for the singers had built ³⁰ for themselves villages around Jerusalem. And the priests and the Levites purified themselves; and they purified the people and the gates and the wall.

³¹ Then I brought up the princes of Judah upon the wall, and appointed two great companies which gave thanks and went in procession. One went to the right upon the ³² wall to the Dung Gate; and after them went Hoshai'ah ³³ and half of the princes of Judah, and Azari'ah, Ezra, ³⁴ Meshul'lam, Judah, Benjamin, Shemai'ah, and Jeremiah, ³⁵ and certain of the priests' sons with trumpets: Zechari'ah the son of Jonathan, son of Shemai'ah, son of Mattani'ah, ³⁶ son of Micai'ah, son of Zaccur, son of Asaph; and his kinsmen, Shemai'ah, Az'arel, Mil'alai, Gil'alai, Ma'ai, Nethan'el, Judah, and Hana'ni, with the musical instruments of David the man of God; and Ezra the scribe went ³⁷ before them. At the Fountain Gate they went up straight before them by the stairs of the city of David, at the ascent of the wall, above the house of David, to the Water Gate on the east.

³⁸ The other company of those who gave thanks went to the left, and I followed them with half of the people, upon the wall, above the Tower of the Ovens, to the ³⁹ Broad Wall, and above the Gate of E'phraim, and by the Old Gate, and by the Fish Gate and the Tower of Hanan'el and the Tower of the Hundred, to the Sheep Gate; and ⁴⁰ they came to a halt at the Gate of the Guard. So both companies of those who gave thanks stood in the house ⁴¹ of God, and I and half of the officials with me, and the priests Eli'akim, Ma-asei'ah, Mini'amin, Micai'ah, Eli-⁴² o-e'nai, Zechari'ah, and Hanani'ah, with trumpets; and Ma-asei'ah, Shemai'ah, Elea'zar, Uzzi, Jehoha'nan, Malchi'jah, Elam, and Ezer. And the singers sang with Jez-⁴³ rahi'ah as their leader. And they offered great sacrifices that day and rejoiced, for God had made them rejoice with great joy; the women and children also rejoiced. And the joy of Jerusalem was heard afar off.

⁴⁴ On that day men were appointed over the chambers for the stores, the contributions, the first fruits, and the tithes, to gather into them the portions required by the law for the priests and for the Levites according to the fields of the towns; for Judah rejoiced over the priests ⁴⁵ and the Levites who ministered. And they performed the service of their God and the service of purification, as did the singers and the gatekeepers, according to the ⁴⁶ command of David and his son Solomon. For in the days of David and Asaph of old there was a chief of the singers, and there were songs of praise and thanksgiving ⁴⁷ to God. And all Israel in the days of Zerub'babel and in the days of Nehemi'ah gave the daily portions for the singers and the gatekeepers; and they set apart that which was for the Levites; and the Levites set apart that which was for the sons of Aaron.

13 On that day they read from the book of Moses in the hearing of the people; and in it was found written that no Ammonite or Moabite should ever enter the as-² sembly of God; for they did not meet the children of Israel with bread and water, but hired Balaam against them to curse them—yet our God turned the curse into a ³ blessing. When the people heard the law, they separated from Israel all those of foreign descent.

NEHEMIAH'S REFORMS

⁴ Now before this, Eli'ashib the priest, who was appointed over the chambers of the house of our God, and who ⁵ was connected with Tobi'ah, prepared for Tobi'ah a large chamber where they had previously put the cereal offering, the frankincense, the vessels, and the tithes of grain, wine, and oil, which were given by commandment to the Levites, singers, and gatekeepers, and the contributions for the ⁶ priests. While this was taking place I was not in Jerusalem, for in the thirty-second year of Ar-ta-xerx'es king of Babylon I went to the king. And after some time I ⁷ asked leave of the king and came to Jerusalem, and I then discovered the evil that Eli'ashib had done for Tobi'ah, preparing for him a chamber in the courts of the ⁸ house of God. And I was very angry, and I threw all the ⁹ household furniture of Tobi'ah out of the chamber. Then I gave orders and they cleansed the chambers; and I brought back thither the vessels of the house of God, with the cereal offering and the frankincense.

10 I also found out that the portions of the Levites had not been given to them; so that the Levites and the singers, 11 who did the work, had fled each to his field. So I remonstrated with the officials and said, "Why is the house of God forsaken?" And I gathered them together and set 12 them in their stations. Then all Judah brought the tithe of 13 the grain, wine, and oil into the storehouses. And I appointed as treasurers over the storehouses Shelemi'ah the priest, Zadok the scribe, and Pedai'ah of the Levites, and as their assistant Hanan the son of Zaccur, son of Mattani'ah, for they were counted faithful; and their duty 14 was to distribute to their brethren. Remember me, O my God, concerning this, and wipe not out my good deeds that I have done for the house of my God and for his service.

15 In those days I saw in Judah men treading wine presses on the sabbath, and bringing in heaps of grain and loading them on asses; and also wine, grapes, figs, and all kinds of burdens, which they brought into Jerusalem on the sabbath day; and I warned them on the day when 16 they sold food. Men of Tyre also, who lived in the city, brought in fish and all kinds of wares and sold them on the sabbath to the people of Judah, and in Jerusalem. 17 Then I remonstrated with the nobles of Judah and said to them, "What is this evil thing which you are doing 18 profaning the sabbath day? Did not your fathers act in this way, and did not our God bring all this evil on us and on this city? Yet you bring more wrath upon Israel by profaning the sabbath."

19 When it began to be dark at the gates of Jerusalem before the sabbath, I commanded that the doors should be shut and gave orders that they should not be opened until after the sabbath. And I set some of my servants over the gates, that no burden might be brought in on the 20 sabbath day. Then the merchants and sellers of all kinds

21 of wares lodged outside Jerusalem once or twice. But I warned them and said to them, "Why do you lodge before the wall? If you do so again I will lay hands on you." From that time on they did not come on the sab- 22 bath. And I commanded the Levites that they should purify themselves and come and guard the gates, to keep the sabbath day holy. Remember this also in my favor, O my God, and spare me according to the greatness of thy steadfast love.

23 In those days also I saw the Jews who had married 24 women of Ashdod, Ammon, and Moab; and half of their children spoke the language of Ashdod, and they could not speak the language of Judah, but the language 25 of each people. And I contended with them and cursed them and beat some of them and pulled out their hair; and I made them take oath in the name of God, saying, "You shall not give your daughters to their sons, or take 26 their daughters for your sons or for yourselves. Did not Solomon king of Israel sin on account of such women? Among the many nations there was no king like him, and he was beloved by his God, and God made him king over all Israel; nevertheless foreign women made even him to 27 sin. Shall we then listen to you and do all this great evil and act treacherously against our God by marrying foreign women?"

28 And one of the sons of Jehoi'ada, the son of Eli'ashib the high priest, was the son-in-law of Sanbal'lat the Hor'- 29 onite; therefore I chased him from me. Remember them, O my God, because they have defiled the priesthood and the covenant of the priesthood and the Levites.

30 Thus I cleansed them from everything foreign, and I established the duties of the priests and Levites, each in 31 his work; and I provided for the wood offering, at appointed times, and for the first fruits. Remember me, O my God, for good.

INTRODUCTION TO

ESTHER

The Book of Esther was written about 150 B.C. It tells about a time centuries earlier, about 485-465 B.C., when many Jews were living in exile in Persia. They had been taken as prisoners of war. It is thought that Esther was not written as a historical record but as a story to encourage the patriotic loyalty of Jews.

The reading of the dramatic story of Esther became a regular part of the observance of the Festival of Purim, which continues today. This festival celebrates the Jews' hope that however much they suffer, their final victory is certain. The beautiful Esther, although she became a queen of Persia, was still loyal to her own people, the Jews. The story of her personal daring would certainly strengthen the patriotism of the Jews at any time when they were in danger from their enemies. This story is more patriotic than religious. It does not mention the name of God.

THE BOOK OF

ESTHER

PERSIAN COURT LIFE AND INTRIGUES

1 In the days of Ahasu-e′rus, the Ahasu-e′rus who reigned from India to Ethiopia over one hundred and 2 twenty-seven provinces, in those days when King Ahasu- 3 e′rus sat on his royal throne in Susa the capital, in the third year of his reign he gave a banquet for all his princes and servants, the army chiefs ª of Persia and

Media and the nobles and governors of the provinces 4 being before him, while he showed the riches of his royal glory and the splendor and pomp of his majesty for many 5 days, a hundred and eighty days. And when these days were completed, the king gave for all the people present in Susa the capital, both great and small, a banquet lasting for seven days, in the court of the garden of the king's 6 palace. There were white cotton curtains and blue hangings caught up with cords of fine linen and purple to silver rings ᵇ and marble pillars, and also couches of gold and silver on a mosaic pavement of porphyry, marble, 7 mother-of-pearl and precious stones. Drinks were served in golden goblets, goblets of different kinds, and the royal wine was lavished according to the bounty of the king.

8 And drinking was according to the law, no one was compelled; for the king had given orders to all the officials of 9 his palace to do as every man desired. Queen Vashti also gave a banquet for the women in the palace which belonged to King Ahasu-e′rus.

10 On the seventh day, when the heart of the king was merry with wine, he commanded Mehu′man, Biztha, Harbo′na, Bigtha and Abag′tha, Zethar and Carkas, the seven eunuchs who served King Ahasu-e′rus as chamber- 11 lains, to bring Queen Vashti before the king with her royal crown, in order to show the peoples and the princes 12 her beauty; for she was fair to behold. But Queen Vashti refused to come at the king's command conveyed by the eunuchs. At this the king was enraged, and his anger burned within him.

13 Then the king said to the wise men who knew the times —for this was the king's procedure toward all who were 14 versed in law and judgment, the men next to him being Carshe′na, Shethar, Adma′tha, Tarshish, Meres, Marse′na, and Memu′can, the seven princes of Persia and Media, who saw the king's face, and sat first in the kingdom—: 15 "According to the law, what is to be done to Queen Vashti, because she has not performed the command of 16 King Ahasu-e′rus conveyed by the eunuchs?" Then Memu′can said in presence of the king and the princes, "Not only to the king has Queen Vashti done wrong, but also to all the princes and all the peoples who are in all 17 the provinces of King Ahasu-e′rus. For this deed of the

ª Heb *the army*   ᵇ Or *rods*

queen will be made known to all women, causing them to look with contempt upon their husbands, since they will say, 'King Ahasu-e'rus commanded Queen Vashti to
18 be brought before him, and she did not come.' This very day the ladies of Persia and Media who have heard of the queen's behavior will be telling it to all the king's princes, and there will be contempt and wrath in plenty.
19 If it please the king, let a royal order go forth from him, and let it be written among the laws of the Persians and the Medes so that it may not be altered, that Vashti is to come no more before King Ahasu-e'rus; and let the king give her royal position to another who is better than she.
20 So when the decree made by the king is proclaimed throughout all his kingdom, vast as it is, all women will
21 give honor to their husbands, high and low." This advice pleased the king and the princes, and the king did as
22 Memu'can proposed; he sent letters to all the royal provinces, to every province in its own script and to every people in its own language, that every man be lord in his own house and speak according to the language of his people.

2 After these things, when the anger of King Ahasu-e'-rus had abated, he remembered Vashti and what she
2 had done and what had been decreed against her. Then the king's servants who attended him said, "Let beautiful
3 young virgins be sought out for the king. And let the king appoint officers in all the provinces of his kingdom to gather all the beautiful young virgins to the harem in Susa the capital, under custody of Hegai the king's eunuch who is in charge of the women; let their ointments
4 be given them. And let the maiden who pleases the king be queen instead of Vashti." This pleased the king, and he did so.

Esther Becomes a Queen

5 Now there was a Jew in Susa the capital whose name was Mor'decai, the son of Ja'ir, son of Shim'e-i, son of
6 Kish, a Benjaminite, who had been carried away from Jerusalem among the captives carried away with Jeconi'-ah king of Judah, whom Nebuchadnez'zar king of Babylon
7 had carried away. He had brought up Hadas'sah, that is Esther, the daughter of his uncle, for she had neither father nor mother; the maiden was beautiful and lovely, and when her father and her mother died, Mor'decai
8 adopted her as his own daughter. So when the king's order and his edict were proclaimed, and when many maidens were gathered in Susa the capital in custody of Hegai, Esther also was taken into the king's palace and put in
9 custody of Hegai who had charge of the women. And the maiden pleased him and won his favor; and he quickly provided her with her ointments and her portion of food, and with seven chosen maids from the king's palace, and advanced her and her maids to the best place in the harem.
10 Esther had not made known her people or kindred, for

11 Mor'decai had charged her not to make it known. And every day Mor'decai walked in front of the court of the harem, to learn how Esther was and how she fared.
12 Now when the turn came for each maiden to go in to King Ahasu-e'rus, after being twelve months under the regulations for the women, since this was the regular period of their beautifying, six months with oil of myrrh and six months with spices and ointments for women—
13 when the maiden went in to the king in this way she was given whatever she desired to take with her from the
14 harem to the king's palace. In the evening she went, and in the morning she came back to the second harem in custody of Sha-ash'gaz the king's eunuch who was in charge of the concubines; she did not go in to the king again, unless the king delighted in her and she was summoned by name.
15 When the turn came for Esther the daughter of Ab'ihail the uncle of Mor'decai, who had adopted her as his own daughter, to go in to the king, she asked for nothing except what Hegai the king's eunuch, who had charge of the women, advised. Now Esther found favor in the eyes
16 of all who saw her. And when Esther was taken to King Ahasu-e'rus into his royal palace in the tenth month, which is the month of Tebeth, in the seventh year of his
17 reign, the king loved Esther more than all the women, and

she found grace and favor in his sight more than all the virgins, so that he set the royal crown on her head and
18 made her queen instead of Vashti. Then the king gave a great banquet to all his princes and servants; it was Esther's banquet. He also granted a remission of taxes [c] to the provinces and gave gifts with royal liberality.
19 When the virgins were gathered together the second
20 time, Mor'decai was sitting at the king's gate. Now Esther had not made known her kindred or her people, as Mor'-decai had charged her; for Esther obeyed Mor'decai just
21 as when she was brought up by him. And in those days, as Mor'decai was sitting at the king's gate, Bigthan and Teresh, two of the king's eunuchs, who guarded the threshold, became angry and sought to lay hands on King
22 Ahasu-e'rus. And this came to the knowledge of Mor'decai, and he told it to Queen Esther, and Esther told the king
23 in the name of Mor'decai. When the affair was investigated and found to be so, the men were both hanged on the gallows. And it was recorded in the Book of the Chronicles in the presence of the king.

c Or *a holiday*

THE HOUSES OF AMALEK AND BENJAMIN FEUD

3 After these things King Ahasu-e'rus promoted Haman the Ag'agite, the son of Hammeda'tha, and advanced him and set his seat above all the princes who ² were with him. And all the king's servants who were at the king's gate bowed down and did obeisance to Haman; for the king had so commanded concerning him. But ³ Mor'decai did not bow down or do obeisance. Then the king's servants who were at the king's gate said to Mor'- ⁴ decai, "Why do you transgress the king's command?" And when they spoke to him day after day and he would not listen to them, they told Haman, in order to see whether Mor'decai's words would avail; for he had told them ⁵ that he was a Jew. And when Haman saw that Mor'decai did not bow down or do obeisance to him, Haman was ⁶ filled with fury. But he disdained to lay hands on Mor'decai alone. So, as they had made known to him the people of Mor'decai, Haman sought to destroy all the Jews, the people of Mor'decai, throughout the whole kingdom of Ahasu-e'rus.

Haman Seeks to Destroy the Jews

7 In the first month, which is the month of Nisan, in the twelfth year of King Ahasu-e'rus, they cast Pur, that is the lot, before Haman day after day; and they cast it month after month till the twelfth month, which is the ⁸ month of Adar. Then Haman said to King Ahasu-e'rus, "There is a certain people scattered abroad and dispersed among the peoples in all the provinces of your kingdom; their laws are different from those of every other people, and they do not keep the king's laws, so that it is not for ⁹ the king's profit to tolerate them. If it please the king, let it be decreed that they be destroyed, and I will pay ten thousand talents of silver into the hands of those who have charge of the king's business, that they may ¹⁰ put it into the king's treasuries." So the king took his signet ring from his hand and gave it to Haman the Ag'agite, the son of Hammeda'tha, the enemy of the ¹¹ Jews. And the king said to Haman, "The money is given to you, the people also, to do with them as it seems good to you."

12 Then the king's secretaries were summoned on the thirteenth day of the first month, and an edict, according to all that Haman commanded, was written to the king's satraps and to the governors over all the provinces and to the princes of all the peoples, to every province in its own script and every people in its own language; it was written in the name of King Ahasu-e'rus and sealed with ¹³ the king's ring. Letters were sent by couriers to all the king's provinces, to destroy, to slay, and to annihilate all Jews, young and old, women and children, in one day, the thirteenth day of the twelfth month, which is the ¹⁴ month of Adar, and to plunder their goods. A copy of the document was to be issued as a decree in every province by proclamation to all the peoples to be ready for that ¹⁵ day. The couriers went in haste by order of the king, and the decree was issued in Susa the capital. And the king and Haman sat down to drink; but the city of Susa was perplexed.

4 When Mor'decai learned all that had been done, Mor'decai rent his clothes and put on sackcloth and ashes, and went out into the midst of the city, wailing with ² a loud and bitter cry; he went up to the entrance of the king's gate, for no one might enter the king's gate ³ clothed with sackcloth. And in every province, wherever the king's command and his decree came, there was great mourning among the Jews, with fasting and weeping and lamenting, and most of them lay in sackcloth and ashes. ⁴ When Esther's maids and her eunuchs came and told her, the queen was deeply distressed; she sent garments to clothe Mor'decai, so that he might take off his sack- ⁵ cloth, but he would not accept them. Then Esther called for Hathach, one of the king's eunuchs, who had been appointed to attend her, and ordered him to go to Mor'- ⁶ decai to learn what this was and why it was. Hathach went out to Mor'decai in the open square of the city in front of ⁷ the king's gate, and Mor'decai told him all that had happened to him, and the exact sum of money that Haman had promised to pay into the king's treasuries for the ⁸ destruction of the Jews. Mor'decai also gave him a copy of the written decree issued in Susa for their destruction, that he might show it to Esther and explain it to her and charge her to go to the king to make supplication to him ⁹ and entreat him for her people. And Hathach went and ¹⁰ told Esther what Mor'decai had said. Then Esther spoke to Hathach and gave him a message for Mor'decai, saying, ¹¹ "All the king's servants and the people of the king's provinces know that if any man or woman goes to the king inside the inner court without being called, there is but one law; all alike are to be put to death, except the one to whom the king holds out the golden scepter that he may live. And I have not been called to come in to the ¹² king these thirty days." And they told Mor'decai what ¹³ Esther had said. Then Mor'decai told them to return answer to Esther, "Think not that in the king's palace you ¹⁴ will escape any more than all the other Jews. For if you keep silence at such a time as this, relief and deliverance will rise for the Jews from another quarter, but you and your father's house will perish. And who knows whether you have not come to the kingdom for such a time as ¹⁵ this?" Then Esther told them to reply to Mor'decai,

16 "Go, gather all the Jews to be found in Susa, and hold a fast on my behalf, and neither eat nor drink for three days, night or day. I and my maids will also fast as you do. Then I will go to the king, though it is against the 17 law; and if I perish, I perish." Mor'decai then went away and did everything as Esther had ordered him.

Esther's Audience With the King

5 On the third day Esther put on her royal robes and stood in the inner court of the king's palace, opposite the king's hall. The king was sitting on his royal throne inside the palace opposite the entrance to the palace; 2 and when the king saw Queen Esther standing in the court, she found favor in his sight and he held out to Esther the golden scepter that was in his hand. Then Esther approached and touched the top of the scepter. 3 And the king said to her, "What is it, Queen Esther? What is your request? It shall be given you, even to the half of 4 my kingdom." And Esther said, "If it please the king, let the king and Haman come this day to a dinner that 5 I have prepared for the king." Then said the king, "Bring Haman quickly, that we may do as Esther desires." So the king and Haman came to the dinner that Esther had 6 prepared. And as they were drinking wine, the king said to Esther, "What is your petition? It shall be granted you. And what is your request? Even to the half of my 7 kingdom, it shall be fulfilled." But Esther said, "My peti- 8 tion and my request is: If I have found favor in the sight of the king, and if it please the king to grant my petition and fulfil my request, let the king and Haman come to- morrow[d] to the dinner which I will prepare for them, and tomorrow I will do as the king has said."

9 And Haman went out that day joyful and glad of heart. But when Haman saw Mor'decai in the king's gate, that he neither rose nor trembled before him, he was filled with 10 wrath against Mor'decai. Nevertheless Haman restrained himself, and went home; and he sent and fetched his 11 friends and his wife Zeresh. And Haman recounted to them the splendor of his riches, the number of his sons, all the promotions with which the king had honored him, and how he had advanced him above the princes and the 12 servants of the king. And Haman added, "Even Queen

Esther let no one come with the king to the banquet she prepared but myself. And tomorrow also I am invited by 13 her together with the king. Yet all this does me no good, so long as I see Mor'decai the Jew sitting at the king's 14 gate." Then his wife Zeresh and all his friends said to him, "Let a gallows fifty cubits high be made, and in the morning tell the king to have Mor'decai hanged upon it; then go merrily with the king to the dinner." This counsel pleased Haman, and he had the gallows made.

6 On that night the king could not sleep; and he gave orders to bring the book of memorable deeds, the chron- 2 icles, and they were read before the king. And it was found written how Mor'decai had told about Bigthana and Teresh, two of the king's eunuchs, who guarded the thresh- old, and who had sought to lay hands upon King Ahasu- 3 e'rus. And the king said, "What honor or dignity has been bestowed on Mor'decai for this?" The king's servants who attended him said, "Nothing has been done for him." 4 And the king said, "Who is in the court?" Now Haman had just entered the outer court of the king's palace to speak to the king about having Mor'decai hanged on the 5 gallows that he had prepared for him. So the king's servants told him, "Haman is there, standing in the court." 6 And the king said, "Let him come in." So Haman came in, and the king said to him, "What shall be done to the man whom the king delights to honor?" And Haman said to himself, "Whom would the king delight to honor more 7 than me?" And Haman said to the king, "For the man 8 whom the king delights to honor, let royal robes be brought, which the king has worn, and the horse which the king has ridden, and on whose head a royal crown is 9 set; and let the robes and the horse be handed over to one of the king's most noble princes; let him[e] array the man whom the king delights to honor, and let him[e] conduct the man on horseback through the open square of the city, proclaiming before him: 'Thus shall it be done to the man 10 whom the king delights to honor.'" Then the king said to Haman, "Make haste, take the robes and the horse, as you have said, and do so to Mor'decai the Jew who sits at the king's gate. Leave out nothing that you have mentioned." 11 So Haman took the robes and the horse, and he arrayed Mor'decai and made him ride through the open square of the city, proclaiming, "Thus shall it be done to the man whom the king delights to honor."

12 Then Mor'decai returned to the king's gate. But Haman hurried to his house, mourning and with his head covered. 13 And Haman told his wife Zeresh and all his friends every- thing that had befallen him. Then his wise men and his wife Zeresh said to him, "If Mor'decai, before whom you have begun to fall, is of the Jewish people, you will not prevail against him but will surely fall before him."

14 While they were yet talking with him, the king's eunuchs arrived and brought Haman in haste to the banquet that Esther had prepared.

[d] Gk: Heb lacks *tomorrow*   [e] Heb *them*

Haman's Downfall

7 So the king and Haman went in to feast with Queen
2 Esther. And on the second day, as they were drinking
wine, the king again said to Esther, "What is your petition, Queen Esther? It shall be granted you. And what is
your request? Even to the half of my kingdom, it shall be
3 fulfilled." Then Queen Esther answered, "If I have found
favor in your sight, O king, and if it please the king, let
my life be given me at my petition, and my people at my
4 request. For we are sold, I and my people, to be destroyed,
to be slain, and to be annihilated. If we had been sold
merely as slaves, men and women, I would have held my
peace; for our affliction is not to be compared with the
5 loss to the king." Then King Ahasu-e'rus said to Queen
Esther, "Who is he, and where is he, that would presume
6 to do this?" And Esther said, "A foe and enemy! This
wicked Haman!" Then Haman was in terror before the
7 king and the queen. And the king rose from the feast in
wrath and went into the palace garden; but Haman stayed
to beg his life from Queen Esther, for he saw that evil was
8 determined against him by the king. And the king returned from the palace garden to the place where they
were drinking wine, as Haman was falling on the couch
where Esther was; and the king said, "Will he even assault the queen in my presence, in my own house?" As
the words left the mouth of the king, they covered
9 Haman's face. Then said Harbo'na, one of the eunuchs
in attendance on the king, "Moreover, the gallows which
Haman has prepared for Mor'decai, whose word saved
the king, is standing in Haman's house, fifty cubits high."
10 And the king said, "Hang him on that." So they hanged
Haman on the gallows which he prepared for Mor'decai.
Then the anger of the king abated.

8 On that day King Ahasu-e'rus gave to Queen Esther
the house of Haman, the enemy of the Jews. And Mor'-
decai came before the king, for Esther had told what he
2 was to her; and the king took off his signet ring, which
he had taken from Haman, and gave it to Mor'decai. And
Esther set Mor'decai over the house of Haman.
3 Then Esther spoke again to the king; she fell at his
feet and besought him with tears to avert the evil design of
Haman the Ag'agite and the plot which he had devised
4 against the Jews. And the king held out the golden scepter
5 to Esther, and Esther rose and stood before the king. And
she said, "If it please the king, and if I have found favor
in his sight, and if the thing seem right before the king,
and I be pleasing in his eyes, let an order be written to
revoke the letters devised by Haman the Ag'agite, the
son of Hammeda'tha, which he wrote to destroy the Jews
6 who are in all the provinces of the king. For how can I
endure to see the calamity that is coming to my people?
Or how can I endure to see the destruction of my kin-
7 dred?" Then King Ahasu-e'rus said to Queen Esther and
to Mor'decai the Jew, "Behold, I have given Esther the
house of Haman, and they have hanged him on the gal-
8 lows, because he would lay hands on the Jews. And you
may write as you please with regard to the Jews, in the
name of the king, and seal it with the king's ring; for an
edict written in the name of the king and sealed with the
king's ring cannot be revoked."
9 The king's secretaries were summoned at that time,
in the third month, which is the month of Sivan, on the
twenty-third day; and an edict was written according to
all that Mor'decai commanded concerning the Jews to
the satraps and the governors and the princes of the
provinces from India to Ethiopia, a hundred and twenty-
seven provinces, to every province in its own script and
to every people in its own language, and also to the Jews
10 in their script and their language. The writing was in the
name of King Ahasu-e'rus and sealed with the king's ring,
and letters were sent by mounted couriers riding on swift
horses that were used in the king's service, bred from the
11 royal stud. By these the king allowed the Jews who were
in every city to gather and defend their lives, to destroy,
to slay, and to annihilate any armed force of any people
or province that might attack them, with their children
12 and women, and to plunder their goods, upon one day
throughout all the provinces of King Ahasu-e'rus, on the
thirteenth day of the twelfth month, which is the month
13 of Adar. A copy of what was written was to be issued
as a decree in every province, and by proclamation to all
peoples, and the Jews were to be ready on that day to
14 avenge themselves upon their enemies. So the couriers,
mounted on their swift horses that were used in the king's
service, rode out in haste, urged by the king's command;
and the decree was issued in Susa the capital.
15 Then Mor'decai went out from the presence of the king
in royal robes of blue and white, with a great golden
crown and a mantle of fine linen and purple, while the
16 city of Susa shouted and rejoiced. The Jews had light and
17 gladness and joy and honor. And in every province and
in every city, wherever the king's command and his edict
came, there was gladness and joy among the Jews, a
feast and a holiday. And many from the peoples of the
country declared themselves Jews, for the fear of the
Jews had fallen upon them.

The Day of Vengeance

9 Now in the twelfth month, which is the month of
Adar, on the thirteenth day of the same, when the
king's command and edict were about to be executed, on
the very day when the enemies of the Jews hoped to get
the mastery over them, but which had been changed to a
day when the Jews should get the mastery over their foes,
2 the Jews gathered in their cities throughout all the
provinces of King Ahasu-e'rus to lay hands on such as
sought their hurt. And no one could make a stand against
them, for the fear of them had fallen upon all peoples.

3 All the princes of the provinces and the satraps and the governors and the royal officials also helped the Jews, for
4 the fear of Mor'decai had fallen upon them. For Mor'decai was great in the king's house, and his fame spread throughout all the provinces; for the man Mor'decai grew
5 more and more powerful. So the Jews smote all their enemies with the sword, slaughtering, and destroying them, and did as they pleased to those who hated them.
6 In Susa the capital itself the Jews slew and destroyed five
7 hundred men, and also slew Par-shan-da'tha and Dalphon
8, 9 and Aspa'tha and Pora'tha and Ada'lia and Arida'tha and Parmash'ta and Ar'isai and Ar'idai and Vaiza'tha,
10 the ten sons of Haman the son of Hammeda'tha, the enemy of the Jews; but they laid no hand on the plunder.
11 That very day the number of those slain in Susa the
12 capital was reported to the king. And the king said to Queen Esther, "In Susa the capital the Jews have slain five hundred men and also the ten sons of Haman. What then have they done in the rest of the king's provinces! Now what is your petition? It shall be granted you. And
13 what further is your request? It shall be fulfilled." And Esther said, "If it please the king let the Jews who are in Susa be allowed tomorrow also to do according to this day's edict. And let the ten sons of Haman be hanged on
14 the gallows." So the king commanded this to be done; a decree was issued in Susa, and the ten sons of Haman
15 were hanged. The Jews who were in Susa gathered also on the fourteenth day of the month of Adar and they slew three hundred men in Susa; but they laid no hands on the plunder.
16 Now the other Jews who were in the king's provinces also gathered to defend their lives, and got relief from their enemies, and slew seventy-five thousand of those who hated them; but they laid no hands on the plunder.
17 This was on the thirteenth day of the month of Adar, and on the fourteenth day they rested and made that a day
18 of feasting and gladness. But the Jews who were in Susa gathered on the thirteenth day and on the fourteenth, and rested on the fifteenth day, making that a day of feasting
19 and gladness. Therefore the Jews of the villages, who live in the open towns, hold the fourteenth day of the month of Adar as a day for gladness and feasting and holiday-making, and a day on which they send choice portions to one another.

THE FEAST OF PURIM

20 And Mor'decai recorded these things, and sent letters to all the Jews who were in all the provinces of King
21 Ahasu-e'rus, both near and far, enjoining them that they should keep the fourteenth day of the month Adar and
22 also the fifteenth day of the same, year by year, as the days on which the Jews got relief from their enemies, and as the month that had been turned for them from sorrow into gladness and from mourning into a holiday; that they should make them days of feasting and gladness, days for sending choice portions to one another and gifts to the poor.
23 So the Jews undertook to do as they had begun, and
24 as Mor'decai had written to them. For Haman the Ag'-agite, the son of Hammeda'tha, the enemy of all the Jews, had plotted against the Jews to destroy them, and had cast Pur, that is the lot, to crush and destroy them;
25 but when Esther came before the king, he gave orders in writing that his wicked plot which he had devised against the Jews should come upon his own head, and that
26 he and his sons should be hanged on the gallows. Therefore they called these days Purim, after the term Pur. And therefore, because of all that was written in this letter, and of what they had faced in this matter, and of what
27 had befallen them, the Jews ordained and took it upon themselves and their descendants and all who joined them, that without fail they would keep these two days according to what was written and at the time appointed every
28 year, that these days should be remembered and kept throughout every generation, in every family, province, and city, and that these days of Purim should never fall into disuse among the Jews, nor should the commemoration of these days cease among their descendants.
29 Then Queen Esther, the daughter of Ab'ihail, and Mor'-decai the Jew gave full written authority, confirming this
30 second letter about Purim. Letters were sent to all the Jews, to the hundred and twenty-seven provinces of the kingdom
31 of Ahasu-e'rus, in words of peace and truth, that these days of Purim should be observed at their appointed seasons, as Mor'decai the Jew and Queen Esther enjoined upon the Jews, and as they had laid down for themselves and for their descendants, with regard to their fasts and
32 their lamenting. The command of Queen Esther fixed these practices of Purim, and it was recorded in writing.

10 King Ahasu-e'rus laid tribute on the land and on
2 the coastlands of the sea. And all the acts of his power and might, and the full account of the high honor of Mor'decai, to which the king advanced him, are they not written in the Book of the Chronicles of the kings of
3 Media and Persia? For Mor'decai the Jew was next in rank to King Ahasu-e'rus, and he was great among the Jews and popular with the multitude of his brethren, for he sought the welfare of his people and spoke peace to all his people.

JOB

The Book of Job is a poetic drama or play, written sometime between 600 B.C. and 450 B.C. It is based on the story of Job, which had been familiar to the Hebrews since before the days of King David.

The plot of the book centers around one of the hardest questions men have ever tried to answer: Why do good men suffer? Most Jews then believed that good people always prosper and bad people always suffer. The Book of Job was written to show how mistaken this popular notion is. The writer showed this by portraying Job as a righteous man who had all sorts of trouble and suffering but who never ceased to be loyal and trusting toward God.

In this play three friends argue with Job, claiming that Job must be guilty of secret sins or he wouldn't have so much sickness and trouble. Job says that he is not perfect but that he doesn't deserve so much trouble. Even though the book does not give a satisfactory answer to why good people suffer, it does make plain that Job never lost his faith in God. (See Job 13.15-18.) The Book of Job helps good persons in deep trouble to continue to trust God even when they cannot understand all the reasons for the evils and troubles of life.

THE BOOK OF

JOB

PROLOGUE IN PROSE

1 There was a man in the land of Uz, whose name was Job; and that man was blameless and upright, one who
2 feared God, and turned away from evil. There were born
3 to him seven sons and three daughters. He had seven

thousand sheep, three thousand camels, five hundred yoke of oxen, and five hundred she-asses, and very many servants; so that this man was the greatest of all the people
4 of the east. His sons used to go and hold a feast in the house of each on his day; and they would send and invite
5 their three sisters to eat and drink with them. And when the days of the feast had run their course, Job would send and sanctify them, and he would rise early in the morning and offer burnt offerings according to the number of them all; for Job said, "It may be that my sons have sinned, and cursed God in their hearts." Thus Job did continually.

First Act of the Drama

6 Now there was a day when the sons of God came to present themselves before the LORD, and Satan [a] also came
7 among them. The LORD said to Satan, "Whence have you come?" Satan answered the LORD, "From going to and fro on the earth, and from walking up and down on it."
8 And the LORD said to Satan, "Have you considered my servant Job, that there is none like him on the earth, a blameless and upright man, who fears God and turns away
9 from evil?" Then Satan answered the LORD, "Does Job
10 fear God for nought? Hast thou not put a hedge about him and his house and all that he has, on every side? Thou hast blessed the work of his hands, and his posses-
11 sions have increased in the land. But put forth thy hand now, and touch all that he has, and he will curse thee to
12 thy face." And the LORD said to Satan, "Behold, all that he has is in your power; only upon himself do not put forth your hand." So Satan went forth from the presence of the LORD.
13 Now there was a day when his sons and daughters were eating and drinking wine in their eldest brother's house;
14 and there came a messenger to Job, and said, "The oxen
15 were plowing and the asses feeding beside them; and the Sabe'ans fell upon them and took them, and slew the

[a] Heb *the adversary*

servants with the edge of the sword; and I alone have
16 escaped to tell you." While he was yet speaking, there
came another, and said, "The fire of God fell from heaven
and burned up the sheep and the servants, and consumed
17 them; and I alone have escaped to tell you." While he
was yet speaking, there came another, and said, "The
Chalde'ans formed three companies, and made a raid
upon the camels and took them, and slew the servants with
the edge of the sword; and I alone have escaped to tell
18 you." While he was yet speaking, there came another, and
said, "Your sons and daughters were eating and drinking
19 wine in their eldest brother's house; and behold, a great
wind came across the wilderness, and struck the four
corners of the house, and it fell upon the young people,
and they are dead; and I alone have escaped to tell you."
20   Then Job arose, and rent his robe, and shaved his
21 head, and fell upon the ground, and worshiped. And he
said, "Naked I came from my mother's womb, and naked
shall I return; the LORD gave, and the LORD has taken
away; blessed be the name of the LORD."
22   In all this Job did not sin or charge God with wrong.

Second Act of the Drama

2   Again there was a day when the sons of God came to
present themselves before the LORD, and Satan also
came among them to present himself before the LORD.
2 And the LORD said to Satan, "Whence have you come?"
Satan answered the LORD, "From going to and fro on
3 the earth, and from walking up and down on it." And
the LORD said to Satan, "Have you considered my servant
Job, that there is none like him on the earth, a blameless
and upright man, who fears God and turns away from
evil? He still holds fast his integrity, although you moved
4 me against him, to destroy him without cause." Then
Satan answered the LORD, "Skin for skin! All that a man
5 has he will give for his life. But put forth thy hand now,
and touch his bone and his flesh, and he will curse thee
6 to thy face." And the LORD said to Satan, "Behold, he is
in your power; only spare his life."
7   So Satan went forth from the presence of the LORD,
and afflicted Job with loathsome sores from the sole of
8 his foot to the crown of his head. And he took a potsherd
with which to scrape himself, and sat among the ashes.
9   Then his wife said to him, "Do you still hold fast your
10 integrity? Curse God, and die." But he said to her, "You
speak as one of the foolish women would speak. Shall we
receive good at the hand of God, and shall we not receive
evil?" In all this Job did not sin with his lips.
11   Now when Job's three friends heard of all this evil that
had come upon him, they came each from his own place,
Eli'phaz the Te'manite, Bildad the Shuhite, and Zophar
the Na'amathite. They made an appointment together to
12 come to condole with him and comfort him. And when
they saw him from afar, they did not recognize him; and

b Heb *come*

they raised their voices and wept; and they rent their
robes and sprinkled dust upon their heads toward heaven.
13 And they sat with him on the ground seven days and
seven nights, and no one spoke a word to him, for they
saw that his suffering was very great.

POETIC DISCUSSION
Job's Lament

3   After this Job opened his mouth and cursed the day
2   of his birth. And Job said:
3 "Let the day perish wherein I was born,
and the night which said,
'A man-child is conceived.'
4 Let that day be darkness!
May God above not seek it,
nor light shine upon it.
5 Let gloom and deep darkness claim it.
Let clouds dwell upon it;
let the blackness of the day terrify it.
6 That night—let thick darkness seize it!
let it not rejoice among the days of the year,
let it not come into the number of the months.
7 Yea, let that night be barren;
let no joyful cry be heard b in it.
8 Let those curse it who curse the day,
who are skilled to rouse up Leviathan.
9 Let the stars of its dawn be dark;
let it hope for light, but have none,
nor see the eyelids of the morning;
10 because it did not shut the doors of my mother's womb,
nor hide trouble from my eyes.

11 "Why did I not die at birth,
come forth from the womb and expire?
12 Why did the knees receive me?
Or why the breasts, that I should suck?
13 For then I should have lain down and been quiet;
I should have slept; then I should have been at rest,
14 with kings and counselors of the earth
who rebuilt ruins for themselves,
15 or with princes who had gold,
who filled their houses with silver.
16 Or why was I not as a hidden untimely birth,
as infants that never see the light?

17 There the wicked cease from troubling,
and there the weary are at rest.
18 There the prisoners are at ease together;
they hear not the voice of the taskmaster.
19 The small and the great are there,
and the slave is free from his master.

20 "Why is light given to him that is in misery,
and life to the bitter in soul,
21 who long for death, but it comes not,
and dig for it more than for hid treasures;
22 who rejoice exceedingly,
and are glad, when they find the grave?
23 Why is light given to a man whose way is hid,
whom God has hedged in?
24 For my sighing comes as c my bread,
and my groanings are poured out like water.
25 For the thing that I fear comes upon me,
and what I dread befalls me.
26 I am not at ease, nor am I quiet;
I have no rest; but trouble comes."

The First Debate

4 Then Eli'phaz the Te'manite answered:
2 "If one ventures a word with you, will you be offended?
Yet who can keep from speaking?
3 Behold, you have instructed many,
and you have strengthened the weak hands.
4 Your words have upheld him who was stumbling,
and you have made firm the feeble knees.
5 But now it has come to you, and you are impatient;
it touches you, and you are dismayed.
6 Is not your fear of God your confidence,
and the integrity of your ways your hope?

7 "Think now, who that was innocent ever perished?
Or where were the upright cut off?
8 As I have seen, those who plow iniquity
and sow trouble reap the same.
9 By the breath of God they perish,
and by the blast of his anger they are consumed.
10 The roar of the lion, the voice of the fierce lion,
the teeth of the young lions, are broken.
11 The strong lion perishes for lack of prey,
and the whelps of the lioness are scattered.

12 "Now a word was brought to me stealthily,
my ear received the whisper of it.
13 Amid thoughts from visions of the night,
when deep sleep falls on men,
14 dread came upon me, and trembling,
which made all my bones shake.
15 A spirit glided past my face;
the hair of my flesh stood up.
16 It stood still,
but I could not discern its appearance.
A form was before my eyes;
there was silence, then I heard a voice:
17 'Can mortal man be righteous before d God?
Can a man be pure before d his Maker?
18 Even in his servants he puts no trust,
and his angels he charges with error;
19 how much more those who dwell in houses of clay,
whose foundation is in the dust,
who are crushed before the moth.
20 Between morning and evening they are destroyed;
they perish for ever without any regarding it.
21 If their tent-cord is plucked up within them,
do they not die, and that without wisdom?'

5 "Call now; is there any one who will answer you?
To which of the holy ones will you turn?
2 Surely vexation kills the fool,
and jealousy slays the simple.
3 I have seen the fool taking root,
but suddenly I cursed his dwelling.
4 His sons are far from safety,
they are crushed in the gate,
and there is no one to deliver them.
5 His harvest the hungry eat,
and he takes it even out of thorns; e
and the thirsty f pant after his g wealth.
6 For affliction does not come from the dust,
nor does trouble sprout from the ground;
7 but man is born to trouble
as the sparks fly upward.

8 "As for me, I would seek God,
and to God would I commit my cause;
9 who does great things and unsearchable,
marvelous things without number:
10 he gives rain upon the earth
and sends waters upon the fields;
11 he sets on high those who are lowly,
and those who mourn are lifted to safety.
12 He frustrates the devices of the crafty,
so that their hands achieve no success.
13 He takes the wise in their own craftiness;
and the schemes of the wily are brought to a quick end.
14 They meet with darkness in the daytime,

c Heb before   d Or more than   e Heb obscure   f Aquila Symmachus Syr Vg: Heb snare   g Heb their

and grope at noonday as in the night.
15 But he saves the fatherless from their mouth,[h]
the needy from the hand of the mighty.
16 So the poor have hope,
and injustice shuts her mouth.

17 "Behold, happy is the man whom God reproves;
therefore despise not the chastening of the Almighty.
18 For he wounds, but he binds up;
he smites, but his hands heal.
19 He will deliver you from six troubles;
in seven there shall no evil touch you.
20 In famine he will redeem you from death,
and in war from the power of the sword.
21 You shall be hid from the scourge of the tongue,
and shall not fear destruction when it comes.
22 At destruction and famine you shall laugh,
and shall not fear the beasts of the earth.
23 For you shall be in league with the stones of the field,
and the beasts of the field shall be at peace with you.
24 You shall know that your tent is safe,
and you shall inspect your fold and miss nothing.
25 You shall know also that your descendants shall be many,
and your offspring as the grass of the earth.
26 You shall come to your grave in ripe old age,
as a shock of grain comes up to the threshing floor in
its season.
27 Lo, this we have searched out; it is true.
Hear, and know it for your good."[i]

6
2 Then Job answered:
"O that my vexation were weighed,
and all my calamity laid in the balances!

3 For then it would be heavier than the sand of the sea;
therefore my words have been rash.
4 For the arrows of the Almighty are in me;
my spirit drinks their poison;
the terrors of God are arrayed against me.
5 Does the wild ass bray when he has grass,
or the ox low over his fodder?
6 Can that which is tasteless be eaten without salt,
or is there any taste in the slime of the purslane?[j]
7 My appetite refuses to touch them;
they are as food that is loathsome to me.[k]

8 "O that I might have my request,
and that God would grant my desire;
9 that it would please God to crush me,

that he would let loose his hand and cut me off!
10 This would be my consolation;
I would even exult[l] in pain unsparing;
for I have not denied the words of the Holy One.
11 What is my strength, that I should wait?
And what is my end, that I should be patient?
12 Is my strength the strength of stones,
or is my flesh bronze?
13 In truth I have no help in me,
and any resource is driven from me.

14 "He who withholds[m] kindness from a friend
forsakes the fear of the Almighty.
15 My brethren are treacherous as a torrent-bed,
as freshets that pass away,
16 which are dark with ice,
and where the snow hides itself.
17 In time of heat they disappear;
when it is hot, they vanish from their place.
18 The caravans turn aside from their course;
they go up into the waste, and perish.
19 The cavarans of Tema look,
the travelers of Sheba hope.
20 They are disappointed because they were confident;
they come thither and are confounded.
21 Such you have now become to me;[n]
you see my calamity, and are afraid.
22 Have I said, 'Make me a gift'?
Or, 'From your wealth offer a bribe for me'?
23 Or, 'Deliver me from the adversary's hand'?
Or, 'Ransom me from the hand of oppressors'?

24 "Teach me, and I will be silent;
make me understand how I have erred.
25 How forceful are honest words!
But what does reproof from you reprove?
26 Do you think that you can reprove words,
when the speech of a despairing man is wind?
27 You would even cast lots over the fatherless,
and bargain over your friend.

28 "But now, be pleased to look at me;
for I will not lie to your face.
29 Turn, I pray, let no wrong be done.
Turn now, my vindication is at stake.
30 Is there any wrong on my tongue?
Cannot my taste discern calamity?

7 "Has not man a hard service upon earth,
and are not his days like the days of a hireling?
2 Like a slave who longs for the shadow,
and like a hireling who looks for his wages,
3 so I am allotted months of emptiness,
and nights of misery are apportioned to me.

---

h Cn: Heb uncertain   l Heb *for yourself*
l The meaning of the Hebrew word is uncertain

j The meaning of the Hebrew word is uncertain   k Heb obscure
m Syr Vg Compare Tg: Heb obscure   n Cn Compare Gk Syr: Heb obscure

⁴ When I lie down I say, 'When shall I arise?'
  But the night is long,
    and I am full of tossing till the dawn.
⁵ My flesh is clothed with worms and dirt;
    my skin hardens, then breaks out afresh.
⁶ My days are swifter than a weaver's shuttle,
    and come to their end without hope.

⁷ "Remember that my life is a breath;
    my eye will never again see good.
⁸ The eye of him who sees me will behold me no more;
    while thy eyes are upon me, I shall be gone.
⁹ As the cloud fades and vanishes,
    so he who goes down to Sheol does not come up;
¹⁰ he returns no more to his house,
    nor does his place know him any more.

¹¹ "Therefore I will not restrain my mouth;
    I will speak in the anguish of my spirit;
    I will complain in the bitterness of my soul.
¹² Am I the sea, or a sea monster,
    that thou settest a guard over me?
¹³ When I say, 'My bed will comfort me,
    my couch will ease my complaint,'
¹⁴ then thou dost scare me with dreams
    and terrify me with visions,
¹⁵ so that I would choose strangling
    and death rather than my bones.
¹⁶ I loathe my life; I would not live for ever.
    Let me alone, for my days are a breath.
¹⁷ What is man, that thou dost make so much of him,
    and that thou dost set thy mind upon him,
¹⁸ dost visit him every morning,
    and test him every moment?
¹⁹ How long wilt thou not look away from me,
    nor let me alone till I swallow my spittle?
²⁰ If I sin, what do I do to thee, thou watcher of men?
    Why hast thou made me thy mark?
    Why have I become a burden to thee?
²¹ Why dost thou not pardon my transgression
    and take away my inquity?
  For now I shall lie in the earth;
    thou wilt seek me, but I shall not be."

8 Then Bildad the Shuhite answered:
² "How long will you say these things,
    and the words of your mouth be a great wind?
³ Does God pervert justice?
    Or does the Almighty pervert the right?
⁴ If your children have sinned against him,
    he has delivered them into the power of their transgression.
⁵ If you will seek God
    and make supplication to the Almighty,

⁶ if you are pure and upright,
    surely then he will rouse himself for you
    and reward you with a rightful habitation.
⁷ And though your beginning was small,
    your latter days will be very great.

⁸ "For inquire, I pray you, of bygone ages,
    and consider what the fathers have found;
⁹ for we are but of yesterday, and know nothing,
    for our days on earth are a shadow.
¹⁰ Will they not teach you, and tell you,
    and utter words out of their understanding?

¹¹ "Can papyrus grow where there is no marsh?
    Can reeds flourish where there is no water?
¹² While yet in flower and not cut down,
    they wither before any other plant.
¹³ Such are the paths of all who forget God;
    the hope of the godless man shall perish.
¹⁴ His confidence breaks in sunder,
    and his trust is a spider's web.ᵒ
¹⁵ He leans against his house, but it does not stand;
    he lays hold of it, but it does not endure.
¹⁶ He thrives before the sun,
    and his shoots spread over his garden.
¹⁷ His roots twine about the stoneheap;
    he lives among the rocks.ᵖ
¹⁸ If he is destroyed from his place,
    then it will deny him, saying, 'I have never seen you.'
¹⁹ Behold, this is the joy of his way;
    and out of the earth others will spring.

²⁰ "Behold, God will not reject a blameless man,
    nor take the hand of evildoers.
²¹ He will yet fill your mouth with laughter,
    and your lips with shouting.
²² Those who hate you will be clothed with shame,
    and the tent of the wicked will be no more."

9 Then Job answered:
² "Truly I know that it is so:
  But how can a man be just before God?
³ If one wished to contend with him,
    one could not answer him once in a thousand times.
⁴ He is wise in heart, and mighty in strength
  —who has hardened himself against him, and succeeded?—
⁵ he who removes mountains, and they know it not,
    when he overturns them in his anger;

ᵒ Heb *house*   ᵖ Gk Vg: Heb uncertain

⁶who shakes the earth out of its place,
and its pillars tremble;
⁷who commands the sun, and it does not rise;
who seals up the stars;
⁸who alone stretched out the heavens,
and trampled the waves of the sea;�q
⁹who made the Bear and Orion,
the Plei′ades and the chambers of the south;
¹⁰who does great things beyond understanding,
and marvelous things without number.
¹¹Lo, he passes by me, and I see him not;
he moves on, but I do not perceive him.
¹²Behold, he snatches away; who can hinder him?
Who will say to him, 'What doest thou'?

¹³"God will not turn back his anger;
beneath him bowed the helpers of Rahab.
¹⁴How then can I answer him,
choosing my words with him?
¹⁵Though I am innocent, I cannot answer him;
I must appeal for mercy to my accuser.ʳ
¹⁶If I summoned him and he answered me,
I would not believe that he was listening to my voice.
¹⁷For he crushes me with a tempest,
and multiplies my wounds without cause;
¹⁸he will not let me get my breath,
but fills me with bitterness.
¹⁹If it is a contest of strength, behold him!
If it is a matter of justice, who can summon him?ˢ
²⁰Though I am innocent, my own mouth would condemn
me;
though I am blameless, he would prove me perverse.
²¹I am blameless; I regard not myself;
I loathe my life.
²²It is all one; therefore I say,
he destroys both the blameless and the wicked.
²³When disaster brings sudden death,
he mocks at the calamityᵗ of the innocent.
²⁴The earth is given into the hand of the wicked;
he covers the faces of its judges—
if it is not he, who then is it?

²⁵"My days are swifter than a runner;
they flee away, they see no good.
²⁶They go by like skiffs of reed,
like an eagle swooping on the prey.
²⁷If I say, 'I will forget my complaint,
I will put off my sad countenance, and be of good
cheer,'
²⁸I become afraid of all my suffering,
for I know thou wilt not hold me innocent.
²⁹I shall be condemned;
why then do I labor in vain?
³⁰If I wash myself with snow,

and cleanse my hands with lye,
³¹yet thou wilt plunge me into a pit,
and my own clothes will abhor me.
³²For he is not a man, as I am, that I might answer him,
that we should come to trial together.
³³There is noᵘ umpire between us,
who might lay his hand upon us both.
³⁴Let him take his rod away from me,
and let not dread of him terrify me.
³⁵Then I would speak without fear of him,
for I am not so in myself.

10 "I loathe my life;
I will give free utterance to my complaint;
I will speak in the bitterness of my soul.
²I will say to God, Do not condemn me;
let me know why thou dost contend against me.
³Does it seem good to thee to oppress,
to despise the work of thy hands
and favor the designs of the wicked?
⁴Hast thou eyes of flesh?
Dost thou see as man sees?
⁵Are thy days as the days of man,
or thy years as man's years,
⁶that thou dost seek out my iniquity
and search for my sin,
⁷although thou knowest that I am not guilty,
and there is none to deliver out of thy hand?
⁸Thy hands fashioned and made me;
and now thou dost turn about and destroy me.ᵛ
⁹Remember that thou hast made me of clay;ʷ
and wilt thou turn me to dust again?
¹⁰Didst thou not pour me out like milk
and curdle me like cheese?
¹¹Thou didst clothe me with skin and flesh,
and knit me together with bones and sinews.
¹²Thou hast granted me life and steadfast love;
and thy care has preserved my spirit.
¹³Yet these things thou didst hide in thy heart;
I know that this was thy purpose.
¹⁴If I sin, thou dost mark me,
and dost not acquit me of my iniquity.
¹⁵If I am wicked, woe to me!
If I am righteous, I cannot lift up my head,
for I am filled with disgrace
and look upon my affliction.
¹⁶And if I lift myself up,ˣ thou dost hunt me like a lion,
and again work wonders against me;
¹⁷thou dost renew thy witnesses against me,
and increase thy vexation toward me;
thou dost bring fresh hosts against me.ʸ
¹⁸"Why didst thou bring me forth from the womb?
Would that I had died before any eye had seen me,

---

q Or *trampled the back of the sea dragon*   r Or *for my right*   s Compare Gk: Heb *me*. The text of the verse is uncertain
t The meaning of the Hebrew word is uncertain   u Another reading is *Would that there were*
v Cn Compare Gk Syr: Heb *made me together round about and thou dost destroy me*   w Gk: Heb *like clay*
x Syr: Heb *he lifts himself up*   y Cn Compare Gk: Heb *changes and a host are with me*

¹⁹ and were as though I had not been,
  carried from the womb to the grave.
²⁰ Are not the days of my life few? ᶻ
  Let me alone, that I may find a little comfort ᵃ
²¹ before I go whence I shall not return,
  to the land of gloom and deep darkness,
²² the land of gloom ᵇ and chaos,
  where light is as darkness."

11 Then Zophar the Na'amathite answered:
² "Should a multitude of words go unanswered,
  and a man full of talk be vindicated?
³ Should your babble silence men,
  and when you mock, shall no one shame you?
⁴ For you say, 'My doctrine is pure,
  and I am clean in God's eyes.'
⁵ But oh, that God would speak,
  and open his lips to you,
⁶ and that he would tell you the secrets of wisdom!
  For he is manifold in understanding.ᶜ
  Know then that God exacts of you less than your guilt
    deserves.

⁷ "Can you find out the deep things of God?
  Can you find out the limit of the Almighty?
⁸ It is higher than heaven ᵈ—what can you do?
  Deeper than Sheol—what can you know?
⁹ Its measure is longer than the earth,
  and broader than the sea.
¹⁰ If he passes through, and imprisons,
  and calls to judgment, who can hinder him?
¹¹ For he knows worthless men;
  when he sees iniquity, will he not consider it?
¹² But a stupid man will get understanding,
  when a wild ass's colt is born a man.

¹³ "If you set your heart aright,
  you will stretch out your hands toward him.
¹⁴ If iniquity is in your hand, put it far away,
  and let not wickedness dwell in your tents.
¹⁵ Surely then you will lift up your face without blemish;
  you will be secure, and will not fear.
¹⁶ You will forget your misery;
  you will remember it as waters that have passed away.
¹⁷ And your life will be brighter than the noonday;
  its darkness will be like the morning.
¹⁸ And you will have confidence, because there is hope;
  you will be protected ᵉ and take your rest in safety.

¹⁹ You will lie down, and none will make you afraid;
  many will entreat your favor.
²⁰ But the eyes of the wicked will fail;
  all way of escape will be lost to them,
  and their hope is to breathe their last."

12 Then Job answered:
² "No doubt you are the people,
  and wisdom will die with you.
³ But I have understanding as well as you;
  I am not inferior to you.
  Who does not know such things as these?
⁴ I am a laughingstock to my friends;
  I, who called upon God and he answered me,
  a just and blameless man, am a laughingstock.
⁵ In the thought of one who is at ease there is contempt for
    misfortune;
  it is ready for those whose feet slip.
⁶ The tents of robbers are at peace,
  and those who provoke God are secure,
  who bring their god in their hand.ᶠ

⁷ "But ask the beasts, and they will teach you;
  the birds of the air, and they will tell you;
⁸ or the plants of the earth,ᵍ and they will teach you;
  and the fish of the sea will declare to you.
⁹ Who among all these does not know
  that the hand of the Lᴏʀᴅ has done this?
¹⁰ In his hand is the life of every living thing
  and the breath of all mankind.
¹¹ Does not the ear try words
  as the palate tastes food?
¹² Wisdom is with the aged,
  and understanding in length of days.

¹³ "With God ʰ are wisdom and might;
  he has counsel and understanding.
¹⁴ If he tears down, none can rebuild;
  if he shuts a man in, none can open.
¹⁵ If he withholds the waters, they dry up;
  if he sends them out, they overwhelm the land.
¹⁶ With him are strength and wisdom;
  the deceived and the deceiver are his.
¹⁷ He leads counselors away stripped,
  and judges he makes fools.
¹⁸ He looses the bonds of kings,
  and binds a waistcloth on their loins.
¹⁹ He leads priests away stripped,
  and overthrows the mighty.
²⁰ He deprives of speech those who are trusted,
  and takes away the discernment of the elders.
²¹ He pours contempt on princes,
  and looses the belt of the strong.
²² He uncovers the deeps out of darkness,

ᶻ Cn Compare Gk Syr: Heb *Are not my days few? Let him cease*   ᵃ Heb *brighten up*   ᵇ Heb *gloom as darkness, deep darkness*
ᶜ Heb *obscure*   ᵈ Heb *The heights of heaven*   ᵉ Or *you will look around*   ᶠ Hebrew uncertain
ᵍ Or *speak to the earth*   ʰ Heb *him*

and brings deep darkness to light.
²³ He makes nations great, and he destroys them:
    he enlarges nations, and leads them away.
²⁴ He takes away understanding from the chiefs of the people
      of the earth,
    and makes them wander in a pathless waste.
²⁵ They grope in the dark without light;
    and he makes them stagger like a drunken man.

13 "Lo, my eye has seen all this,
    my ear has heard and understood it.
² What you know, I also know;
    I am not inferior to you.
³ But I would speak to the Almighty,
    and I desire to argue my case with God.
⁴ As for you, you whitewash with lies;
    worthless physicians are you all.
⁵ Oh that you would keep silent,
    and it would be your wisdom!
⁶ Hear now my reasoning,
    and listen to the pleadings of my lips.
⁷ Will you speak falsely for God,
    and speak deceitfully for him?
⁸ Will you show partiality toward him,
    will you plead the case for God?
⁹ Will it be well with you when he searches you out?
    Or can you deceive him, as one deceives a man?
¹⁰ He will surely rebuke you
    if in secret you show partiality.
¹¹ Will not his majesty terrify you,
    and the dread of him fall upon you?
¹² Your maxims are proverbs of ashes,
    your defenses are defenses of clay.

¹³ "Let me have silence, and I will speak,
    and let come on me what may.
¹⁴ I will take ⁱ my flesh in my teeth,
    and put my life in my hand.
¹⁵ Behold, he will slay me; I have no hope;
    yet I will defend my ways to his face.
¹⁶ This will be my salvation,
    that a godless man shall not come before him.
¹⁷ Listen carefully to my words,
    and let my declaration be in your ears.
¹⁸ Behold, I have prepared my case;
    I know that I shall be vindicated.
¹⁹ Who is there that will contend with me?
    For then I would be silent and die.
²⁰ Only grant two things to me,
    then I will not hide myself from thy face:
²¹ withdraw thy hand far from me,
    and let not dread of thee terrify me.
²² Then call, and I will answer;
    or let me speak, and do thou reply to me.

²³ How many are my iniquities and my sins?
    Make me know my transgression and my sin.
²⁴ Why dost thou hide thy face,
    and count me as thy enemy?
²⁵ Wilt thou frighten a driven leaf and
    pursue dry chaff?
²⁶ For thou writest bitter things against me,
    and makest me inherit the iniquities of my youth.
²⁷ Thou puttest my feet in the stocks,
    and watchest all my paths;
    thou settest a bound to the soles of my feet.
²⁸ Man ʲ wastes away like a rotten thing,
    like a garment that is moth-eaten.

14 "Man that is born of a woman
    is of few days, and full of trouble.
² He comes forth like a flower, and withers;
    he flees like a shadow, and continues not.
³ And dost thou open thy eyes upon such a one
    and bring him ᵏ into judgment with thee?

⁴ Who can bring a clean thing out of an unclean?
    There is not one.
⁵ Since his days are determined,
    and the number of his months is with thee,
    and thou hast appointed his bounds that he cannot pass,
⁶ look away from him, and desist,ˡ
    that he may enjoy, like a hireling, his day.

⁷ "For there is hope for a tree,
    if it be cut down, that it will sprout again,
    and that its shoots will not cease.
⁸ Though its root grow old in the earth,
    and its stump die in the ground,
⁹ yet at the scent of water it will bud
    and put forth branches like a young plant.
¹⁰ But man dies, and is laid low;
    man breathes his last, and where is he?
¹¹ As waters fail from a lake,
    and a river wastes away and dries up,
¹² so man lies down and rises not again;
    till the heavens are no more he will not awake,
    or be roused out of his sleep.
¹³ Oh that thou wouldest hide me in Sheol,
    that thou wouldest conceal me until thy wrath be past,
    that thou wouldest appoint me a set time, and remember
      me!

ⁱ Gk: Heb *Why should I take?*   ʲ Heb *He*   ᵏ Gk Syr Vg: Heb *me*   ˡ Cn: Heb *that he may desist*

14 If a man die, shall he live again?
   All the days of my service I would wait,
      till my release should come.
15 Thou wouldest call, and I would answer thee;
   thou wouldest long for the work of thy hands.
16 For then thou wouldest number my steps,
   thou wouldest not keep watch over my sin;
17 my transgression would be sealed up in a bag,
   and thou wouldest cover over my iniquity.

18 "But the mountain falls and crumbles away,
   and the rock is removed from its place;
19 the waters wear away the stones;
   the torrents wash away the soil of the earth;
   so thou destroyest the hope of man.
20 Thou prevailest for ever against him, and he passes;
   thou changest his countenance, and sendest him away.
21 His sons come to honor, and he does not know it;
   they are brought low, and he perceives it not.
22 He feels only the pain of his own body,
   and he mourns only for himself."

The Second Debate

15 Then Eli′phaz the Te′manite answered:
2   "Should a wise man answer with windy knowledge,
   and fill himself with the east wind?
3 Should he argue in unprofitable talk,
   or in words with which he can do no good?
4 But you are doing away with the fear of God.
   and hindering meditation before God.
5 For your iniquity teaches your mouth,
   and you choose the tongue of the crafty.
6 Your own mouth condemns you, and not I;
   your own lips testify against you.

7 "Are you the first man that was born?
   Or were you brought forth before the hills?
8 Have you listened in the council of God?
   And do you limit wisdom to yourself?
9 What do you know that we do not know?
   What do you understand that is not clear to us?
10 Both the gray-haired and the aged are among us,
   older than your father.
11 Are the consolations of God too small for you,
   or the word that deals gently with you?
12 Why does your heart carry you away,
   and why do your eyes flash,
13 that you turn your spirit against God,
   and let such words go out of your mouth?
14 What is man, that he can be clean?
   Or he that is born of a woman, that he can be righteous?
15 Behold, God puts no trust in his holy ones,
   and the heavens are not clean in his sight;

16 how much less one who is abominable and corrupt,
   a man who drinks iniquity like water!

17 "I will show you, hear me;
   and what I have seen I will declare
18 (what wise men have told,
   and their fathers have not hidden,
19 to whom alone the land was given,
   and no stranger passed among them).
20 The wicked man writhes in pain all his days,
   through all the years that are laid up for the ruthless.
21 Terrifying sounds are in his ears;
   in prosperity the destroyer will come upon him.
22 He does not believe that he will return out of darkness,
   and he is destined for the sword.
23 He wanders abroad for bread, saying, 'Where is it?'
   He knows that a day of darkness is ready at his hand;
24 distress and anguish terrify him;
   they prevail against him, like a king prepared for battle.
25 Because he has stretched forth his hand against God,
   and bids defiance to the Almighty,
26 running stubbornly against him
   with a thick-bossed shield;
27 because he has covered his face with his fat,
   and gathered fat upon his loins,
28 and has lived in desolate cities,
   in houses which no man should inhabit,
   which were destined to become heaps of ruins;
29 he will not be rich, and his wealth will not endure,
   nor will he strike root in the earth; m
30 he will not escape from darkness;
   the flame will dry up his shoots,
   and his blossom n will be swept away o by the wind.
31 Let him not trust in emptiness, deceiving himself;
   for emptiness will be his recompense.
32 It will be paid in full before his time,
   and his branch will not be green.
33 He will shake off his unripe grape, like the vine,
   and cast off his blossom, like the olive tree.
34 For the company of the godless is barren,
   and fire consumes the tents of bribery.
35 They conceive mischief and bring forth evil
   and their heart prepares deceit."

16 Then Job answered:
2   "I have heard many such things;
   miserable comforters are you all.
3 Shall windy words have an end?
   Or what provokes you that you answer?
4 I also could speak as you do,
   if you were in my place;
   I could join words together against you,
   and shake my head at you.

m Vg: Heb obscure   n Gk: Heb mouth   o Cn: Heb will depart

5 I could strengthen you with my mouth,
and the solace of my lips would assuage your pain.

6 "If I speak, my pain is not assuaged,
and if I forbear, how much of it leaves me?
7 Surely now God has worn me out;
he has[p] made desolate all my company.

8 And he has[p] shriveled me up,
which is a witness against me;
and my leanness has risen up against me,
it testifies to my face.
9 He has torn me in his wrath, and hated me;
he has gnashed his teeth at me;
my adversary sharpens his eyes against me.
10 Men have gaped at me with their mouth,
they have struck me insolently upon the cheek,
they mass themselves together against me.
11 God gives me up to the ungodly,
and casts me into the hands of the wicked.
12 I was at ease, and he broke me asunder;
he seized me by the neck and dashed me to pieces;
he set me up as his target,
13 his archers surround me.
He slashes open my kidneys, and does not spare;
he pours out my gall on the ground.
14 He breaks me with breach upon breach;
he runs upon me like a warrior.
15 I have sewed sackcloth upon my skin,
and have laid my strength in the dust.
16 My face is red with weeping,
and on my eyelids is deep darkness;
17 although there is no violence in my hands,
and my prayer is pure.

18 "O earth, cover not my blood,
and let my cry find no resting place.
19 Even now, behold, my witness is in heaven,
and he that vouches for me is on high.
20 My friends scorn me;
my eye pours out tears to God,
21 that he would maintain the right of a man with God,
like[q] that of a man with his neighbor.
22 For when a few years have come
I shall go the way whence I shall not return.

17 My spirit is broken, my days are extinct,
the grave is ready for me.
2 Surely there are mockers about me,
and my eye dwells on their provocation.

3 "Lay down a pledge for me with thyself;
who is there that will give surety for me?
4 Since thou hast closed their minds to understanding,
therefore thou wilt not let them triumph.
5 He who informs against his friends to get a share of their property,
the eyes of his children will fail.

6 "He has made me a byword of the peoples,
and I am one before whom men spit.
7 My eye has grown dim from grief,
and all my members are like a shadow.
8 Upright men are appalled at this,
and the innocent stirs himself up against the godless.
9 Yet the righteous holds to his way,
and he that has clean hands grows stronger and stronger.
10 But you, come on again, all of you,
and I shall not find a wise man among you.
11 My days are past, my plans are broken off,
the desires of my heart.
12 They make night into day;
'The light,' they say, 'is near to the darkness.'[r]
13 If I look for Sheol as my house,
if I spread my couch in darkness,
14 if I say to the pit, 'You are my father,'
and to the worm, 'My mother,' or 'My sister,'
15 where then is my hope?
Who will see my hope?
16 Will it go down to the bars of Sheol?
Shall we descend together into the dust?"

18 Then Bildad the Shuhite answered:
2 "How long will you hunt for words?
Consider, and then we will speak.
3 Why are we counted as cattle?
Why are we stupid in your sight?
4 You who tear yourself in your anger,
shall the earth be forsaken for you,
or the rock be removed out of its place?

5 "Yea, the light of the wicked is put out,
and the flame of his fire does not shine.
6 The light is dark in his tent,
and his lamp above him is put out.
7 His strong steps are shortened
and his own schemes throw him down.
8 For he is cast into a net by his own feet,
and he walks on a pitfall.

[p] Heb *thou hast* [q] Syr Vg Tg: Heb *and* [r] Heb obscure

⁹ A trap seizes him by the heel,
  a snare lays hold of him.
¹⁰ A rope is hid for him in the ground,
  a trap for him in the path.
¹¹ Terrors frighten him on every side,
  and chase him at his heels.
¹² His strength is hunger-bitten,
  and calamity is ready for his stumbling.
¹³ By disease his skin is consumed,ˢ
  the first-born of death consumes his limbs.
¹⁴ He is torn from the tent in which he trusted,
  and is brought to the king of terrors.
¹⁵ In his tent dwells that which is none of his;
  brimstone is scattered upon his habitation.
¹⁶ His roots dry up beneath,
  and his branches wither above.
¹⁷ His memory perishes from the earth,
  and he has no name in the street.
¹⁸ He is thrust from light into darkness,
  and driven out of the world.
¹⁹ He has no offspring or descendant among his people,
  and no survivor where he used to live.
²⁰ They of the west are appalled at his day,
  and horror seizes them of the east.
²¹ Surely such are the dwellings of the ungodly,
  such is the place of him who knows not God.”

19 Then Job answered:
² “How long will you torment me,
  and break me in pieces with words?
³ These ten times you have cast reproach upon me;

are you not ashamed to wrong me?
⁴ And even if it be true that I have erred,
  my error remains with myself.
⁵ If indeed you magnify yourselves against me,
  and make my humiliation an argument against me,
⁶ know then that God has put me in the wrong,
  and closed his net about me.
⁷ Behold, I cry out, ‘Violence!’ but I am not answered;
  I call aloud, but there is no justice.
⁸ He has walled up my way, so that I cannot pass,
  and he has set darkness upon my paths.
⁹ He has stripped from me my glory,
  and taken the crown from my head.
¹⁰ He breaks me down on every side, and I am gone,
  and my hope has he pulled up like a tree.

¹¹ He has kindled his wrath against me,
  and counts me as his adversary.
¹² His troops come on together;
  they have cast up siegeworksᵗ against me,
  and encamp round about my tent.

¹³ “He has put my brethren far from me,
  and my acquaintances are wholly estranged from me.
¹⁴ My kinsfolk and my close friends have failed me;
¹⁵   the guests in my house have forgotten me;
  my maidservants count me as a stranger;
  I have become an alien in their eyes.
¹⁶ I call to my servant, but he gives me no answer;
  I must beseech him with my mouth.
¹⁷ I am repulsive to my wife,
  loathsome to the sons of my own mother.
¹⁸ Even young children despise me;
  when I rise they talk against me.
¹⁹ All my intimate friends abhor me,
  and those whom I loved have turned against me.
²⁰ My bones cleave to my skin and to my flesh,
  and I have escaped by the skin of my teeth.
²¹ Have pity on me, have pity on me, O you my friends,
  for the hand of God has touched me!
²² Why do you, like God, pursue me?
  Why are you not satisfied with my flesh?

²³ “Oh that my words were written!
  Oh that they were inscribed in a book!
²⁴ Oh that with an iron pen and lead
  they were graven in the rock for ever!
²⁵ For I know that my Redeemerᵘ lives,
  and at last he will stand upon the earth;ᵛ
²⁶ and after my skin has been thus destroyed,
  then fromʷ my flesh I shall see God,ˣ
²⁷ whom I shall see on my side,ʸ
  and my eyes shall behold, and not another.
  My heart faints within me!
²⁸ If you say, ‘How we will pursue him!’
  and, ‘The root of the matter is found in him’;
²⁹ be afraid of the sword,
  for wrath brings the punishment of the sword,
  that you may know there is a judgment.”

20 Then Zophar the Na'amathite answered:
² “Therefore my thoughts answer me,
  because of my haste within me.
³ I hear censure which insults me,
  and out of my understanding a spirit answers me.
⁴ Do you not know this from of old,
  since man was placed upon earth,
⁵ that the exulting of the wicked is short,
  and the joy of the godless but for a moment?
⁶ Though his height mount up to the heavens,

ˢ Cn: Heb *it consumes the limbs of his skin*   ᵗ Heb *their way*   ᵘ Or *Vindicator*   ᵛ Or *dust*   ʷ Or *without*
ˣ The meaning of this verse is uncertain   ʸ Or *for myself*

and his head reach to the clouds,
7 he will perish for ever like his own dung;
    those who have seen him will say, 'Where is he?'
8 He will fly away like a dream, and not be found;
    he will be chased away like a vision of the night.
9 The eye which saw him will see him no more,
    nor will his place any more behold him.
10 His children will seek the favor of the poor,
    and his hands will give back his wealth.
11 His bones are full of youthful vigor,
    but it will lie down with him in the dust.

12 "Though wickedness is sweet in his mouth,
    though he hides it under his tongue,
13 though he is loath to let it go,
    and holds it in his mouth,
14 yet his food is turned in his stomach;
    it is the gall of asps within him.
15 He swallows down riches and vomits them up again;
    God casts them out of his belly.
16 He will suck the poison of asps;
    the tongue of a viper will kill him.
17 He will not look upon the rivers,
    the streams flowing with honey and curds.
18 He will give back the fruit of his toil,
    and will not swallow it down;
from the profit of his trading
    he will get no enjoyment.
19 For he has crushed and abandoned the poor,
    he has seized a house which he did not build.

20 "Because his greed knew no rest,
    he will not save anything in which he delights.
21 There was nothing left after he had eaten;
    therefore his prosperity will not endure.
22 In the fulness of his sufficiency he will be in straits;
    all the force of misery will come upon him.
23 To fill his belly to the full
    God ᶻ will send his fierce anger into him,
    and rain it upon him as his food.ᵃ
24 He will flee from an iron weapon;
    a bronze arrow will strike him through.
25 It is drawn forth and comes out of his body,
    the glittering point comes out of his gall;
    terrors come upon him.
26 Utter darkness is laid up for his treasures;
    a fire not blown upon will devour him;
    what is left in his tent will be consumed.
27 The heavens will reveal his iniquity,
    and the earth will rise up against him.
28 The possessions of his house will be carried away,
    dragged off in the day of God's ᵇ wrath.
29 This is the wicked man's portion from God,
    the heritage decreed for him by God."

21 Then Job answered:
2   "Listen carefully to my words,
    and let this be your consolation.
3 Bear with me, and I will speak,
    and after I have spoken, mock on.
4 As for me, is my complaint against man?
    Why should I not be impatient?
5 Look at me, and be appalled,
    and lay your hand upon your mouth.
6 When I think of it I am dismayed,
    and shuddering seizes my flesh.
7 Why do the wicked live,
    reach old age, and grow mighty in power?
8 Their children are established in their presence,
    and their offspring before their eyes.
9 Their houses are safe from fear,
    and no rod of God is upon them.
10 Their bull breeds without fail;
    their cow calves, and does not cast her calf.
11 They send forth their little ones like a flock,
    and their children dance.
12 They sing to the tambourine and the lyre,
    and rejoice to the sound of the pipe.
13 They spend their days in prosperity,
    and in peace they go down to Sheol.
14 They say to God, 'Depart from us!
    We do not desire the knowledge of thy ways.
15 What is the Almighty, that we should serve him?
    And what profit do we get if we pray to him?'
16 Behold, is not their prosperity in their hand?
    The counsel of the wicked is far from me.

17 "How often is it that the lamp of the wicked is put out?
    That their calamity comes upon them?
    That God ᶜ distributes pains in his anger?

18 That they are like straw before the wind,
    and like chaff that the storm carries away?
19 You say, 'God stores up their iniquity for their sons.'
    Let him recompense it to themselves, that they may
      know it.
20 Let their own eyes see their destruction,
    and let them drink of the wrath of the Almighty.
21 For what do they care for their houses after them,
    when the number of their months is cut off?
22 Will any teach God knowledge,

ᶻ Heb *he*   ᵃ Cn: Heb *in his flesh*   ᵇ Heb *his*   ᶜ Heb *he*

seeing that he judges those that are on high?
²³ One dies in full prosperity,
  being wholly at ease and secure,
²⁴ his body [d] full of fat
  and the marrow of his bones moist.
²⁵ Another dies in bitterness of soul,
  never having tasted of good.
²⁶ They lie down alike in the dust,
  and the worms cover them.

²⁷ "Behold, I know your thoughts,
  and your schemes to wrong me.
²⁸ For you say, 'Where is the house of the prince?
  Where is the tent in which the wicked dwelt?'
²⁹ Have you not asked those who travel the roads,
  and do you not accept their testimony
³⁰ that the wicked man is spared in the day of calamity,
  that he is rescued in the day of wrath?
³¹ Who declares his way to his face,
  and who requites him for what he has done?
³² When he is borne to the grave,
  watch is kept over his tomb.
³³ The clods of the valley are sweet to him;
  all men follow after him,
  and those who go before him are innumerable.
³⁴ How then will you comfort me with empty nothings?
  There is nothing left of your answers but falsehood."

The Third Debate

22 Then Eli'phaz the Te'manite answered:
² "Can a man be profitable to God?
  Surely he who is wise is profitable to himself.
³ Is it any pleasure to the Almighty if you are righteous,
  or is it gain to him if you make your ways blameless?
⁴ Is it for your fear of him that he reproves you,
  and enters into judgment with you?
⁵ Is not your wickedness great?
  There is no end to your iniquities.
⁶ For you have exacted pledges of your brothers for nothing,
  and stripped the naked of their clothing.
⁷ You have given no water to the weary to drink,
  and you have withheld bread from the hungry.
⁸ The man with power possessed the land,
  and the favored man dwelt in it.
⁹ You have sent widows away empty,
  and the arms of the fatherless were crushed.
¹⁰ Therefore snares are round about you,
  and sudden terror overwhelms you;
¹¹ your light is darkened, so that [e] you cannot see,
  and a flood of water covers you.

¹² "Is not God high in the heavens?
  See the highest stars, how lofty they are!
¹³ Therefore you say, 'What does God know?

Can he judge through the deep darkness?
¹⁴ Thick clouds enwrap him, so that he does not see,
  and he walks on the vault of heaven.'
¹⁵ Will you keep to the old way
  which wicked men have trod?
¹⁶ They were snatched away before their time;
  their foundation was washed away.
¹⁷ They said to God, 'Depart from us,'
  and 'What can the Almighty do to us?' [f]
¹⁸ Yet he filled their houses with good things—
  but the counsel of the wicked is far from me.
¹⁹ The righteous see it and are glad;
  the innocent laugh them to scorn,
²⁰ saying, 'Surely our adversaries are cut off,
  and what they left the fire has consumed.'

²¹ "Agree with God, and be at peace;
  thereby good will come to you.
²² Receive instruction from his mouth,
  and lay up his words in your heart.
²³ If you return to the Almighty and humble yourself, [g]
  if you remove unrighteousness far from your tents,
²⁴ if you lay gold in the dust,
  and gold of Ophir among the stones of the torrent bed,
²⁵ and if the Almighty is your gold,
  and your precious silver;
²⁶ then you will delight yourself in the Almighty,
  and lift up your face to God.
²⁷ You will make your prayer to him, and he will hear you;
  and you will pay your vows.
²⁸ You will decide on a matter, and it will be established for you,
  and light will shine on your ways.
²⁹ For God abases the proud, [h]
  but he saves the lowly.
³⁰ He delivers the innocent man; [i]
  you will be delivered through the cleanness of your hands."

23 Then Job answered:
² "Today also my complaint is bitter, [j]
  his [k] hand is heavy in spite of my groaning.
³ Oh, that I knew where I might find him,
  that I might come even to his seat!
⁴ I would lay my case before him
  and fill my mouth with arguments.
⁵ I would learn what he would answer me,
  and understand what he would say to me.
⁶ Would he contend with me in the greatness of his power?
  No; he would give heed to me.
⁷ There an upright man could reason with him,
  and I should be acquitted for ever by my judge.

⁸ "Behold, I go forward, but he is not there;
  and backward, but I cannot perceive him;

---

[d] The meaning of the Hebrew word is uncertain   [e] Cn Compare Gk: Heb or darkness   [f] Gk Syr: Heb them
[g] Gk: Heb you will be built up   [h] Cn: Heb when they abased you said, Proud   [i] Gk Syr Vg: Heb him that is not innocent
[j] Syr Vg Tg: Heb rebellious   [k] Gk Syr: Heb my

9 on the left hand I seek him,[l] but I cannot behold him;
    I [m] turn to the right hand, but I cannot see him.
10 But he knows the way that I take;
    when he has tried me, I shall come forth as gold.
11 My foot has held fast to his steps;
    I have kept his way and have not turned aside.
12 I have not departed from the commandment of his lips;
    I have treasured in [n] my bosom the words of his mouth.
13 But he is unchangeable and who can turn him?
    What he desires, that he does.
14 For he will complete what he appoints for me;
    and many such things are in his mind.
15 Therefore I am terrified at his presence;
    when I consider, I am in dread of him.
16 God has made my heart faint;
    the Almighty has terrified me;
17 for I am [o] hemmed in by darkness,
    and thick darkness covers my face.[p]

24 "Why are not times of judgment kept by the Almighty,
    and why do those who know him never see his days?
2 Men remove landmarks;
    they seize flocks and pasture them.
3 They drive away the ass of the fatherless;
    they take the widow's ox for a pledge.
4 They thrust the poor off the road;
    the poor of the earth all hide themselves.
5 Behold, like wild asses in the desert
    they go forth to their toil,
seeking prey in the wilderness
    as food [q] for their children.
6 They gather their [r] fodder in the field

and they glean the vineyard of the wicked man.
7 They lie all night naked, without clothing,
    and have no covering in the cold.
8 They are wet with the rain of the mountains,
    and cling to the rock for want of shelter.
9 (There are those who snatch the fatherless child from the breast,
    and take in pledge the infant of the poor.)
10 They go about naked, without clothing;
    hungry, they carry the sheaves;

11 among the olive rows of the wicked [s] they make oil;
    they tread the wine presses, but suffer thirst.
12 From out of the city the dying groan,
    and the soul of the wounded cries for help;
    yet God pays no attention to their prayer.
13 "There are those who rebel against the light,
    who are not acquainted with its ways,
    and do not stay in its paths.
14 The murderer rises in the dark,[t]
    that he may kill the poor and needy;
    and in the night he is as a thief.
15 The eye of the adulterer also waits for the twilight,
    saying, 'No eye will see me';
    and he disguises his face.
16 In the dark they dig through houses;
    by day they shut themselves up;
    they do not know the light.
17 For deep darkness is morning to all of them;
    for they are friends with the terrors of deep darkness.
18 "You say, 'They are swiftly carried away upon the face of the waters;
    their portion is cursed in the land;
    no treader turns toward their vineyards.
19 Drought and heat snatch away the snow waters;
    so does Sheol those who have sinned.
20 The squares of the town [u] forget them;
    their name [v] is no longer remembered;
    so wickedness is broken like a tree.'
21 "They feed on the barren childless woman,
    and do no good to the widow.
22 Yet God [w] prolongs the life of the mighty by his power;
    they rise up when they despair of life.
23 He gives them security, and they are supported;
    and his eyes are upon their ways.
24 They are exalted a little while, and then are gone;
    they wither and fade like the mallow; [x]
    they are cut off like the heads of grain.
25 If it is not so, who will prove me a liar,
    and show that there is nothing in what I say?"

25 Then Bildad the Shuhite answered:
2 "Dominion and fear are with God; [y]
    he makes peace in his high heaven.
3 Is there any number to his armies?
    Upon whom does his light not arise?
4 How then can man be righteous before God?
    How can he who is born of woman be clean?
5 Behold, even the moon is not bright
    and the stars are not clean in his sight;
6 how much less man, who is a maggot,
    and the son of man, who is a worm!"

---

[l] Compare Syr: Heb *on the left hand when he works*   [m] Syr Vg: Heb *he*   [n] Gk Vg: Heb *from*
[o] With one Ms: Heb *am not*   [p] Vg: Heb *from my face*   [q] Heb *food to him*   [r] Heb *his*   [s] Heb *their olive rows*
[t] Cn: Heb *at the light*   [u] Cn: Heb *obscure*   [v] Cn: Heb *a worm*   [w] Heb *he*   [x] Gk: Heb *all*   [y] Heb *him*

26 Then Job answered:

2 "How you have helped him who has no power!
How you have saved the arm that has no strength!

3 How you have counseled him who has no wisdom,
and plentifully declared sound knowledge!

4 With whose help have you uttered words,
and whose spirit has come forth from you?

5 The shades below tremble,
the waters and their inhabitants.

6 Sheol is naked before God,
and Abaddon has no covering.

7 He stretches out the north over the void,
and hangs the earth upon nothing.

8 He binds up the waters in his thick clouds,
and the cloud is not rent under them.

9 He covers the face of the moon,[z]
and spreads over it his cloud.

10 He has described a circle upon the face of the waters
at the boundary between light and darkness.

11 The pillars of heaven tremble,
and are astounded at his rebuke.

12 By his power he stilled the sea;
by his understanding he smote Rahab.

13 By his wind the heavens were made fair;
his hand pierced the fleeing serpent.

14 Lo, these are but the outskirts of his ways;
and how small a whisper do we hear of him!
But the thunder of his power who can understand?"

27 And Job again took up his discourse, and said:

2 "As God lives, who has taken away my right,
and the Almighty, who has made my soul bitter;

3 as long as my breath is in me,
and the spirit of God is in my nostrils;

4 my lips will not speak falsehood,
and my tongue will not utter deceit.

5 Far be it from me to say that you are right;
till I die I will not put away my integrity from me.

6 I hold fast my righteousness, and will not let it go;
my heart does not reproach me for any of my days.

7 "Let my enemy be as the wicked,
and let him that rises up against me be as the unrighteous.

8 For what is the hope of the godless when God cuts him off,
when God takes away his life?

9 Will God hear his cry,
when trouble comes upon him?

10 Will he take delight in the Almighty?
Will he call upon God at all times?

11 I will teach you concerning the hand of God;
what is with the Almighty I will not conceal.

12 Behold, all of you have seen it yourselves;
why then have you become altogether vain?

13 "This is the portion of a wicked man with God,
and the heritage which oppressors receive from the
Almighty:

14 If his children are multiplied, it is for the sword;
and his offspring have not enough to eat.

15 Those who survive him the pestilence buries,
and their widows make no lamentation.

16 Though he heap up silver like dust,
and pile up clothing like clay;

17 he may pile it up, but the just will wear it,
and the innocent will divide the silver.

18 The house which he builds is like a spider's web,[a]

like a booth which a watchman makes.

19 He goes to bed rich, but will do so no more;[b]
he opens his eyes, and his wealth is gone.

20 Terrors overtake him like a flood;
in the night a whirlwind carries him off.

21 The east wind lifts him up and he is gone;
it sweeps him out of his place.

22 It[c] hurls at him without pity;
he flees from its[d] power in headlong flight.

23 It[c] claps its[d] hands at him,
and hisses at him from its[d] place.

Hymn on Wisdom

28 "Surely there is a mine for silver,
and a place for gold which they refine.

2 Iron is taken out of the earth,
and copper is smelted from the ore.

3 Men put an end to darkness,
and search out to the farthest bound
the ore in gloom and deep darkness.

4 They open shafts in a valley away from where men live;
they are forgotten by travelers,
they hang afar from men, they swing to and fro.

5 As for the earth, out of it comes bread;
but underneath it is turned up as by fire.

6 Its stones are the place of sapphires,[e] and it has dust of
gold.

7 "That path no bird of prey knows,
and the falcon's eye has not seen it.

8 The proud beasts have not trodden it;
the lion has not passed over it.

z Or *his throne*   a Cn Compare Gk Syr: Heb *He builds his house like the moth*   b Gk Compare Syr: Heb *shall not be gathered*
c Or *he (that is God)*   d Or *his*   e Or *lapis lazuli*

9 "Man puts his hand to the flinty rock,
  and overturns mountains by the roots.
10 He cuts out channels in the rocks,
  and his eye sees every precious thing.
11 He binds up the streams so that they do not trickle,
  and the thing that is hid he brings forth to light.

12 "But where shall wisdom be found?
  And where is the place of understanding?
13 Man does not know the way to it,[f]
  and it is not found in the land of the living.
14 The deep says, 'It is not in me,'
  and the sea says, 'It is not with me.'
15 It cannot be gotten for gold,
  and silver cannot be weighed as its price.
16 It cannot be valued in the gold of Ophir,
  in precious onyx or sapphire.[g]
17 Gold and glass cannot equal it,
  nor can it be exchanged for jewels of fine gold.
18 No mention shall be made of coral or of crystal;
  the price of wisdom is above pearls.
19 The topaz of Ethiopia cannot compare with it,
  nor can it be valued in pure gold.

20 "Whence then comes wisdom?
  And where is the place of understanding?
21 It is hid from the eyes of all living,
  and concealed from the birds of the air.
22 Abaddon and Death say,
  'We have heard a rumor of it with our ears.'

23 "God understands the way to it,
  and he knows its place.
24 For he looks to the ends of the earth,
  and sees everything under the heavens.
25 When he gave to the wind its weight,
  and meted out the waters by measure;
26 when he made a decree for the rain,
  and a way for the lightning of the thunder;
27 then he saw it and declared it;
  he established it, and searched it out.
28 And he said to man,
  'Behold, the fear of the Lord, that is wisdom;
  and to depart from evil is understanding.' "

Job Concludes His Speech

29 And Job again took up his discourse, and said:
2 "Oh, that I were as in the months of old,
  as in the days when God watched over me;
3 when his lamp shone upon my head,
  and by his light I walked through darkness;
4 as I was in my autumn days,
  when the friendship of God was upon my tent;
5 when the Almighty was yet with me,
  when my children were about me;

6 when my steps were washed with milk,
  and the rock poured out for me streams of oil!
7 When I went out to the gate of the city,
  when I prepared my seat in the square,
8 the young men saw me and withdrew,
  and the aged rose and stood;
9 the princes refrained from talking,
  and laid their hand on their mouth;
10 the voice of the nobles was hushed,
  and their tongue cleaved to the roof of their mouth.
11 When the ear heard, it called me blessed,
  and when the eye saw, it approved;
12 because I delivered the poor who cried,
  and the fatherless who had none to help him.
13 The blessing of him who was about to perish came upon me,
  and I caused the widow's heart to sing for joy.
14 I put on righteousness, and it clothed me;
  my justice was like a robe and a turban.
15 I was eyes to the blind,
  and feet to the lame.
16 I was a father to the poor,
  and I searched out the cause of him whom I did not know.
17 I broke the fangs of the unrighteous,
  and made him drop his prey from his teeth.
18 Then I thought, 'I shall die in my nest,
  and I shall multiply my days as the sand,
19 my roots spread out to the waters,
  with the dew all night on my branches,
20 my glory fresh with me,
  and my bow ever new in my hand.'

21 "Men listened to me, and waited,
  and kept silence for my counsel.
22 After I spoke they did not speak again,
  and my word dropped upon them.
23 They waited for me as for the rain;
  and they opened their mouths as for the spring rain.
24 I smiled on them when they had no confidence;
  and the light of my countenance they did not cast down.
25 I chose their way, and sat as chief,
  and I dwelt like a king among his troops,
  like one who comforts mourners.

30 "But now they make sport of me,
  men who are younger than I,
  whose fathers I would have disdained
  to set with the dogs of my flock.
2 What could I gain from the strength of their hands,
  men whose vigor is gone?
3 Through want and hard hunger
  they gnaw the dry and desolate ground;[h]

[f] Gk: Heb *its price*   [g] Or *lapis lazuli*   [h] Heb *ground yesterday waste*

⁴ they pick mallow and the leaves of bushes,
  and to warm themselves the roots of the broom.
⁵ They are driven out from among men;
  they shout after them as after a thief.
⁶ In the gullies of the torrents they must dwell,
  in holes of the earth and of the rocks.
⁷ Among the bushes they bray;
  under the nettles they huddle together.
⁸ A senseless, a disreputable brood,
  they have been whipped out of the land.

⁹ "And now I have become their song,
  I am a byword to them.
¹⁰ They abhor me, they keep aloof from me;
  they do not hesitate to spit at the sight of me.
¹¹ Because God has loosed my cord and humbled me,
  they have cast off restraint in my presence.
¹² On my right hand the rabble rise
  they drive me ⁱ forth,
  they cast up against me their ways of destruction.
¹³ They break up my path,
  they promote my calamity;
  no one restrains ʲ them.
¹⁴ As through ᵏ a wide breach they come;
  amid the crash they roll on.
¹⁵ Terrors are turned upon me;
  my honor is pursued as by the wind,
  and my prosperity has passed away like a cloud.

¹⁶ "And now my soul is poured out within me;
  days of affliction have taken hold of me.
¹⁷ The night racks my bones,
  and the pain that gnaws me takes no rest.
¹⁸ With violence it seizes my garment;ˡ
  it binds me about like the collar of my tunic.
¹⁹ God has cast me into the mire,
  and I have become like dust and ashes.
²⁰ I cry to thee and thou dost not answer me;
  I stand, and thou dost not ᵐ heed me.
²¹ Thou hast turned cruel to me;
  with the might of thy hand thou dost persecute me.
²² Thou liftest me up on the wind, thou makest me ride on it,
  and thou tossest me about in the roar of the storm.
²³ Yea, I know that thou wilt bring me to death,
  and to the house appointed for all living.

²⁴ "Yet does not one in a heap of ruins stretch out his hand,
  and in his disaster cry for help? ⁿ
²⁵ Did not I weep for him whose day was hard?
  Was not my soul grieved for the poor?
²⁶ But when I looked for good, evil came;
  and when I waited for light, darkness came.
²⁷ My heart is in turmoil, and is never still;
  days of affliction come to meet me.

²⁸ I go about blackened, but not by the sun;
  I stand up in the assembly, and cry for help.
²⁹ I am a brother of jackals,
  and a companion of ostriches.
³⁰ My skin turns black and falls from me,
  and my bones burn with heat.
³¹ My lyre is turned to mourning,
  and my pipe to the voice of those who weep.

31 "I have made a covenant with my eyes;
  how then could I look upon a virgin?
² What would be my portion from God above,
  and my heritage from the Almighty on high?
³ Does not calamity befall the unrighteous,
  and disaster the workers of iniquity?
⁴ Does not he see my ways,
  and number all my steps?

⁵ "If I have walked with falsehood,
  and my foot has hastened to deceit;
⁶ (Let me be weighed in a just balance,
  and let God know my integrity!)
⁷ if my step has turned aside from the way,
  and my heart has gone after my eyes,
  and if any spot has cleaved to my hands;
⁸ then let me sow, and another eat;
  and let what grows for me be rooted out.

⁹ "If my heart has been enticed to a woman,
  and I have lain in wait at my neighbor's door;
¹⁰ then let my wife grind for another,
  and let others bow down upon her.
¹¹ For that would be a heinous crime;
  that would be an iniquity to be punished by the judges;
¹² for that would be a fire which consumes unto Abaddon,
  and it would burn to the root all my increase.

¹³ "If I have rejected the cause of my manservant or my maidservant,
  when they brought a complaint against me;
¹⁴ what then shall I do when God rises up?
  When he makes inquiry, what shall I answer him?
¹⁵ Did not he who made me in the womb make him?
  And did not one fashion us in the womb?

¹⁶ "If I have withheld anything that the poor desired,
  or have caused the eyes of the widow to fail,
¹⁷ or have eaten my morsel alone,
  and the fatherless has not eaten of it
¹⁸ (for from his youth I reared him as a father,
  and from his mother's womb I guided him)ᵒ;
¹⁹ if I have seen any one perish for lack of clothing,
  or a poor man without covering;
²⁰ if his loins have not blessed me,
  and if he was not warmed with the fleece of my sheep;

ⁱ Heb *my feet*   ʲ Cn: Heb *helps*   ᵏ Cn: Heb *like*
ᵐ One Heb Ms and Vg: Heb lacks *not*   ⁿ Cn: Heb obscure
ᵒ Cn: Heb *for from my youth he grew up to me as a father, and from my mother's womb I guided her*

ˡ Gk: Heb *my garment is disfigured*

21 if I have raised my hand against the fatherless,
because I saw help in the gate;
22 then let my shoulder blade fall from my shoulder,
and let my arm be broken from its socket.
23 For I was in terror of calamity from God,
and I could not have faced his majesty.

24 "If I have made gold my trust,
or called fine gold my confidence;
25 if I have rejoiced because my wealth was great,
or because my hand had gotten much;
26 if I have looked at the sun[p] when it shone,
or the moon moving in splendor,
27 and my heart has been secretly enticed,
and my mouth has kissed my hand;
28 this also would be an iniquity to be punished by the judges,
for I should have been false to God above.

29 "If I have rejoiced at the ruin of him that hated me,
or exulted when evil overtook him
30 (I have not let my mouth sin
by asking for his life with a curse);
31 if the men of my tent have not said,
'Who is there that has not been filled with his meat?'
32 (the sojourner has not lodged in the street;
I have opened my doors to the wayfarer);
33 if I have concealed my trangressions from men,[q]
by hiding my iniquity in my bosom,
34 because I stood in great fear of the multitude,
and the contempt of families terrified me,
so that I kept silence, and did not go out of doors—
35 Oh, that I had one to hear me!
(Here is my signature! let the Almighty answer me!)
Oh, that I had the indictment written by my adversary!
36 Surely I would carry it on my shoulder;
I would bind it on me as a crown;
37 I would give him an account of all my steps;
like a prince I would approach him.

38 "If my land has cried out against me,
and its furrows have wept together;
39 if I have eaten its yield without payment,
and caused the death of its owners;
40 let thorns grow instead of wheat,
and foul weeds instead of barley."

The words of Job are ended.

ELIHU GIVES HIS IDEAS

32 So these three men ceased to answer Job, because
2 he was righteous in his own eyes. Then Eli'hu the
son of Bar'achel the Buzite, of the family of Ram, became
angry. He was angry at Job because he justified himself
3 rather than God; he was angry also at Job's three friends
because they had found no answer, although they had
4 declared Job to be in the wrong. Now Eli'hu had waited
5 to speak to Job because they were older than he. And
when Eli'hu saw that there was no answer in the mouth of
these three men, he became angry.

6 And Eli'hu the son of Bar'achel the Buzite answered:
"I am young in years,
and you are aged;
therefore I was timid and afraid
to declare my opinion to you.
7 I said, 'Let days speak,
and many years teach wisdom.'
8 But it is the spirit in a man,
the breath of the Almighty, that makes him understand.
9 It is not the old[r] that are wise,
nor the aged that understand what is right.
10 Therefore I say, 'Listen to me;
let me also declare my opinion.'

11 "Behold, I waited for your words,
I listened for your wise sayings,
while you searched out what to say.
12 I gave you my attention,
and, behold, there was none that confuted Job,
or that answered his words, among you.
13 Beware lest you say, 'We have found wisdom;
God may vanquish him, not man.'
14 He has not directed his words against me,
and I will not answer him with your speeches.

15 "They are discomfited, they answer no more;
they have not a word to say.
16 And shall I wait, because they do not speak,
because they stand there, and answer no more?
17 I also will give my answer;
I also will declare my opinion.
18 For I am full of words,
the spirit within me constrains me.
19 Behold, my heart is like wine that has no vent;
like new wineskins, it is ready to burst.
20 I must speak, that I may find relief;
I must open my lips and answer.
21 I will not show partiality to any person
or use flattery toward any man.
22 For I do not know how to flatter,
else would my Maker soon put an end to me.

[p] Heb *the light* [q] Cn: Heb *like men* or *like Adam* [r] Gk Syr Vg: Heb *many*

Job's Defense Refuted

33 "But now, hear my speech, O Job,
and listen to all my words.

2 Behold, I open my mouth;
the tongue in my mouth speaks.

3 My words declare the uprightness of my heart,
and what my lips know they speak sincerely.

4 The spirit of God has made me,
and the breath of the Almighty gives me life.

5 Answer me, if you can;
set your words in order before me; take your stand.

6 Behold, I am toward God as you are;
I too was formed from a piece of clay.

7 Behold, no fear of me need terrify you;
my pressure will not be heavy upon you.

8 "Surely, you have spoken in my hearing,
and I have heard the sound of your words.

9 You say, 'I am clean, without transgression;
I am pure, and there is no iniquity in me.

10 Behold, he finds occasions against me,
he counts me as his enemy;

11 he puts my feet in the stocks, and watches all my paths.'

12 "Behold, in this you are not right. I will answer you.
God is greater than man.

13 Why do you contend against him,
saying, 'He will answer none of my[s] words'?

14 For God speaks in one way,
and in two, though man does not perceive it.

15 In a dream, in a vision of the night,
when deep sleep falls upon men,
while they slumber on their beds,

16 then he opens the ears of men,
and terrifies them with warnings,

17 that he may turn man aside from his deed,
and cut off[t] pride from man;

18 he keeps back his soul from the Pit,
his life from perishing by the sword.

19 "Man is also chastened with pain upon his bed,
and with continual strife in his bones;

20 so that his life loathes bread,
and his appetite dainty food.

21 His flesh is so wasted away that it cannot be seen;
and his bones which were not seen stick out.

22 His soul draws near the Pit,
and his life to those who bring death.

23 If there be for him an angel,
a mediator, one of the thousand,
to declare to man what is right for him;

24 and he is gracious to him, and says,
'Deliver him from going down into the Pit,
I have found a ransom;

25 let his flesh become fresh with youth;
let him return to the days of his youthful vigor';

26 then man prays to God, and he accepts him,
he comes into his presence with joy.
He recounts[u] to men his salvation,

27 and he sings before men, and says:
'I sinned, and perverted what was right,
and it was not requited to me.

28 He has redeemed my soul from going down into the Pit,
and my life shall see the light.'

29 "Behold, God does all these things,
twice, three times, with a man,

30 to bring back his soul from the Pit,
that he may see the light of life.[v]

31 Give heed, O Job, listen to me;
be silent, and I will speak.

32 If you have anything to say, answer me;
speak, for I desire to justify you.

33 If not, listen to me;
be silent, and I will teach you wisdom."

34 Then Eli′hu said:

2 "Hear my words, you wise men,
and give ear to me, you who know;

3 for the ear tests words
as the palate tastes food.

4 Let us choose what is right;
let us determine among ourselves what is good.

5 For Job has said, 'I am innocent,
and God has taken away my right;

6 in spite of my right I am counted a liar;
my wound is incurable, though I am without transgression.'

7 What man is like Job,
who drinks up scoffing like water,

8 who goes in company with evildoers
and walks with wicked men?

9 For he has said, 'It profits a man nothing
that he should take delight in God.'

10 "Therefore, hear me, you men of understanding,
far be it from God that he should do wickedness,
and from the Almighty that he should do wrong.

11 For according to the work of a man he will requite him,

---

s Compare Gk: Heb *his*   t Cn: Heb *hide*   u Cn: Heb *returns*   v Syr: Heb *to be lighted with the light of life*

and according to his ways he will make it befall him.
¹² Of a truth, God will not do wickedly,
  and the Almighty will not pervert justice.
¹³ Who gave him charge over the earth
  and who laid on him ʷ the whole world?
¹⁴ If he should take back his spirit ˣ to himself,
  and gather to himself his breath,
¹⁵ all flesh would perish together,
  and man would return to dust.

¹⁶ "If you have understanding, hear this;
  listen to what I say.
¹⁷ Shall one who hates justice govern?
  Will you condemn him who is righteous and mighty,
¹⁸ who says to a king, 'Worthless one,'
  and to nobles, 'Wicked man';
¹⁹ who shows no partiality to princes,
  nor regards the rich more than the poor,
  for they are all the work of his hands?
²⁰ In a moment they die;
  at midnight the people are shaken and pass away,
  and the mighty are taken away by no human hand.

²¹ "For his eyes are upon the ways of man,
  and he sees all his steps.
²² There is no gloom or deep darkness
  where evildoers may hide themselves.
²³ For he has not appointed a time ʸ for any man
  to go before God in judgment.
²⁴ He shatters the mighty without investigation,
  and sets others in their place.
²⁵ Thus, knowing their works,
  he overturns them in the night, and they are crushed.
²⁶ He strikes them for their wickedness
  in the sight of men,
²⁷ because they turned aside from following him,
  and had no regard for any of his ways,
²⁸ so that they caused the cry of the poor to come to him,
  and he heard the cry of the afflicted—
²⁹ When he is quiet, who can condemn?
  When he hides his face, who can behold him,
  whether it be a nation or a man?—
³⁰ that a godless man should not reign,
  that he should not ensnare the people.

³¹ "For has any one said to God,
  'I have borne chastisement; I will not offend any more;
³² teach me what I do not see;
  if I have done iniquity, I will do it no more'?
³³ Will he then make requital to suit you,
  because you reject it?
For you must choose, and not I;
  therefore declare what you know.ᶻ
³⁴ Men of understanding will say to me,

and the wise man who hears me will say:
³⁵ 'Job speaks without knowledge,
  his words are without insight.'
³⁶ Would that Job were tried to the end,
  because he answers like wicked men.
³⁷ For he adds rebellion to his sin;
  he claps his hands among us,
  and multiplies his words against God."

35 And Eli′hu said:
² "Do you think this to be just?
  Do you say, 'It is my right before God,'
³ that you ask, 'What advantage have I?
  How am I better off than if I had sinned?'
⁴ I will answer you
  and your friends with you.
⁵ Look at the heavens, and see;
  and behold the clouds, which are higher than you.
⁶ If you have sinned, what do you accomplish against him?
  And if your transgressions are multiplied, what do you
    do to him?
⁷ If you are righteous, what do you give to him;
  or what does he receive from your hand?
⁸ Your wickedness concerns a man like yourself,
  and your righteousness a son of man.

⁹ "Because of the multitude of oppressions people cry out;
  they call for help because of the arm of the mighty.
¹⁰ But none says, 'Where is God my Maker,
  who gives songs in the night,
¹¹ who teaches us more than the beasts of the earth,
  and makes us wiser than the birds of the air?'
¹² There they cry out, but he does not answer,
  because of the pride of evil men.
¹³ Surely God does not hear an empty cry,
  nor does the Almighty regard it.
¹⁴ How much less when you say that you do not see him,
  that the case is before him, and you are waiting for
    him!
¹⁵ And now, because his anger does not punish,
  and he does not greatly heed transgression,ᵃ
¹⁶ Job opens his mouth in empty talk,
  he multiplies words without knowledge."

The Hidden Mercy of God

36 And Eli′hu continued, and said:
² "Bear with me a little, and I will show you,
  for I have yet something to say on God's behalf.
³ I will fetch my knowledge from afar,
  and ascribe righteousness to my Maker.
⁴ For truly my words are not false;
  one who is perfect in knowledge is with you.

⁵ "Behold, God is mighty, and does not despise any;

ʷ Heb lacks *on him*   ˣ Heb *his heart his spirit*   ʸ Cn: Heb *yet*   ᶻ The Hebrew of verses 29-33 is obscure
ᵃ Theodotion Symmachus Compare Vg: the meaning of the Hebrew word is uncertain

he is mighty in strength of understanding.
⁶ He does not keep the wicked alive,
but gives the afflicted their right.
⁷ He does not withdraw his eyes from the righteous,
but with kings upon the throne
he sets them for ever, and they are exalted.
⁸ And if they are bound in fetters
and caught in the cords of affliction,
⁹ then he declares to them their work
and their transgressions, that they are behaving arrogantly.
¹⁰ He opens their ears to instruction,
and commands that they return from iniquity.
¹¹ If they hearken and serve him,
they complete their days in prosperity,
and their years in pleasantness.
¹² But if they do not hearken, they perish by the sword,
and die without knowledge.

¹³ "The godless in heart cherish anger;
they do not cry for help when he binds them.
¹⁴ They die in youth,
and their life ends in shame.ᵇ
¹⁵ He delivers the afflicted by their affliction,
and opens their ear by adversity.
¹⁶ He also allured you out of distress
into a broad place where there was no cramping,
and what was set on your table was full of fatness.

¹⁷ "But you are full of the judgment on the wicked;
judgment and justice seize you.
¹⁸ Beware lest wrath entice you into scoffing;
and let not the greatness of the ransom turn you aside.
¹⁹ Will your cry avail to keep you from distress,
or all the force of your strength?
²⁰ Do not long for the night,
when peoples are cut off in their place.
²¹ Take heed, do not turn to iniquity,
for this you have chosen rather than affliction.
²² Behold, God is exalted in his power;
who is a teacher like him?
²³ Who has prescribed for him his way,
or who can say, 'Thou hast done wrong'?

²⁴ "Remember to extol his work,
of which men have sung.
²⁵ All men have looked on it;
man beholds it from afar.
²⁶ Behold, God is great, and we know him not;
the number of his years is unsearchable.
²⁷ For he draws up the drops of water,
he ᶜ distils his mist in rain
²⁸ which the skies pour down,
and drop upon man abundantly.

²⁹ Can any one understand the spreading of the clouds,
the thunderings of his pavilion?
³⁰ Behold, he scatters his lightning about him,
and covers the roots of the sea.
³¹ For by these he judges peoples;
he gives food in abundance.
³² He covers his hands with the lightning,
and commands it to strike the mark.

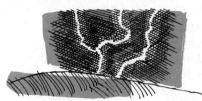

³³ Its crashing declares concerning him,
who is jealous with anger against iniquity.

37 "At this also my heart trembles,
and leaps out of its place.
² Hearken to the thunder of his voice
and the rumbling that comes from his mouth.
³ Under the whole heaven he lets it go,
and his lightning to the corners of the earth.
⁴ After it his voice roars;
he thunders with his majestic voice
and he does not restrain the lightnings ᵈ when his voice
is heard.
⁵ God thunders wondrously with his voice;
he does great things which we cannot comprehend.
⁶ For to the snow he says, 'Fall on the earth';
and to the shower and the rain,ᵉ 'Be strong.'
⁷ He seals up the hand of every man,
that all men may know his work.ᶠ
⁸ Then the beasts go into their lairs,
and remain in their dens.
⁹ From its chamber comes the whirlwind,
and cold from the scattering winds.
¹⁰ By the breath of God ice is given,
and the broad waters are frozen fast.
¹¹ He loads the thick cloud with moisture;
the clouds scatter his lightning.
¹² They turn round and round by his guidance,
to accomplish all that he commands them
on the face of the habitable world.
¹³ Whether for correction, or for his land,
or for love, he causes it to happen.

¹⁴ "Hear this, O Job;
stop and consider the wondrous works of God.
¹⁵ Do you know how God lays his command upon them,
and causes the lightning of his cloud to shine?
¹⁶ Do you know the balancings of the clouds,
the wondrous works of him who is perfect in knowledge,

ᵇ Heb *among the cult prostitutes*   ᶜ Cn: Heb *they distil*
ᵉ Cn Compare Syr: Heb *shower of rain and shower of rains*

ᵈ Heb *them*
ᶠ Vg Compare Syr Tg: Heb *that all men whom he has made may know it*

¹⁷ you whose garments are hot
  when the earth is still because of the south wind?
¹⁸ Can you, like him, spread out the skies,
  hard as a molten mirror?
¹⁹ Teach us what we shall say to him;
  we cannot draw up our case because of darkness.
²⁰ Shall it be told him that I would speak?
  Did a man ever wish that he would be swallowed up?

²¹ "And now men cannot look on the light
  when it is bright in the skies,
  when the wind has passed and cleared them.
²² Out of the north comes golden splendor;
  God is clothed with terrible majesty.
²³ The Almighty—we cannot find him;
  he is great in power and justice,
  and abundant righteousness he will not violate.
²⁴ Therefore men fear him;
  he does not regard any who are wise in their own
    conceit."

VOICE FROM THE WHIRLWIND

38 Then the Lord answered Job out of the whirlwind:
² "Who is this that darkens counsel by words without
    knowledge?
³ Gird up your loins like a man,
  I will question you, and you shall declare to me.

⁴ "Where were you when I laid the foundation of the earth?
  Tell me, if you have understanding.
⁵ Who determined its measurements—surely you know!
  Or who stretched the line upon it?
⁶ On what were its bases sunk,
  or who laid its cornerstone,
⁷ when the morning stars sang together,
  and all the sons of God shouted for joy?

⁸ "Or who shut in the sea with doors,
  when it burst forth from the womb;
⁹ when I made clouds its garment,
  and thick darkness its swaddling band,
¹⁰ and prescribed bounds for it,
  and set bars and doors,
¹¹ and said, 'Thus far shall you come, and no farther,
  and here shall your proud waves be stayed'?

¹² "Have you commanded the morning since your days
    began,
  and caused the dawn to know its place,
¹³ that it might take hold of the skirts of the earth,
  and the wicked be shaken out of it?
¹⁴ It is changed like clay under the seal,
  and it is dyed ^g like a garment.

¹⁵ From the wicked their light is withheld,
  and their uplifted arm is broken.

¹⁶ "Have you entered into the springs of the sea,
  or walked in the recesses of the deep?
¹⁷ Have the gates of death been revealed to you,
  or have you seen the gates of deep darkness?
¹⁸ Have you comprehended the expanse of the earth?
  Declare, if you know all this.

¹⁹ "Where is the way to the dwelling of light,
  and where is the place of darkness,
²⁰ that you may take it to its territory
  and that you may discern the paths to its home?
²¹ You know, for you were born then,
  and the number of your days is great!

²² "Have you entered the storehouses of the snow,
  or have you seen the storehouses of the hail,
²³ which I have reserved for the time of trouble,
  for the day of battle and war?
²⁴ What is the way to the place where the light is distributed,
  or where the east wind is scattered upon the earth?

²⁵ "Who has cleft a channel for the torrents of rain,
  and a way for the thunderbolt,
²⁶ to bring rain on a land where no man is,
  on the desert in which there is no man;
²⁷ to satisfy the waste and desolate land,
  and to make the ground put forth grass?

²⁸ "Has the rain a father,
  or who has begotten the drops of dew?
²⁹ From whose womb did the ice come forth,
  and who has given birth to the hoarfrost of heaven?
³⁰ The waters become hard like stone,
  and the face of the deep is frozen.

³¹ "Can you bind the chains of the Plei'ades,
  or loose the cords of Orion?
³² Can you lead forth the Maz'zaroth in their season,
  or can you guide the Bear with its children?
³³ Do you know the ordinances of the heavens?
  Can you establish their rule on the earth?

³⁴ "Can you lift up your voice to the clouds,
  that a flood of waters may cover you?
³⁵ Can you send forth lightnings, that they may go
  and say to you, 'Here we are'?
³⁶ Who has put wisdom in the clouds,^h
  or given understanding to the mists? ^h
³⁷ Who can number the clouds by wisdom?
  Or who can tilt the waterskins of the heavens,
³⁸ when the dust runs into a mass
  and the clods cleave fast together?

^g Cn: Heb *they stand forth*   ^h The meaning of the Hebrew word is uncertain

39 "Can you hunt the prey for the lion,
    or satisfy the appetite of the young lions,
40 when they crouch in their dens,
    or lie in wait in their covert?
41 Who provides for the raven its prey,
    when its young ones cry to God,
    and wander about for lack of food?

39 "Do you know when the mountain goats bring
    forth?
Do you observe the calving of the hinds?
2 Can you number the months that they fulfil,
    and do you know the time when they bring forth,
3 when they crouch, bring forth their offspring,
    and are delivered of their young?
4 Their young ones become strong, they grow up in the
    open;
    they go forth, and do not return to them.

5 "Who has let the wild ass go free?
    Who has loosed the bonds of the swift ass,
6 to whom I have given the steppe for his home,
    and the salt land for his dwelling place?
7 He scorns the tumult of the city;
    he hears not the shouts of the driver.
8 He ranges the mountains as his pasture,
    and he searches after every green thing.

9 "Is the wild ox willing to serve you?
    Will he spend the night at your crib?
10 Can you bind him in the furrow with ropes,
    or will he harrow the valleys after you?
11 Will you depend on him because his strength is great,
    and will you leave to him your labor?
12 Do you have faith in him that he will return,
    and bring your grain to your threshing floor? i

13 "The wings of the ostrich wave proudly;
    but are they the pinions and plumage of love? j
14 For she leaves her eggs to the earth,
    and lets them be warmed on the ground,
15 forgetting that a foot may crush them,
    and that the wild beast may trample them.
16 She deals cruelly with her young, as if they were not hers;
    though her labor be in vain, yet she has no fear;
17 because God has made her forget wisdom,
    and given her no share in understanding.
18 When she rouses herself to flee,k
    she laughs at the horse and his rider.

19 "Do you give the horse his might?
    Do you clothe his neck with strength? l
20 Do you make him leap like the locust?
    His majestic snorting is terrible.

21 He paws m in the valley, and exults in his strength;
    he goes out to meet the weapons.
22 He laughs at fear, and is not dismayed;
    he does not turn back from the sword.
23 Upon him rattle the quiver,
    the flashing spear and the javelin.
24 With fierceness and rage he swallows the ground;
    he cannot stand still at the sound of the trumpet.
25 When the trumpet sounds, he says 'Aha!'
He smells the battle from afar,
    the thunder of the captains, and the shouting.

26 "Is it by your wisdom that the hawk soars,
    and spreads his wings toward the south?
27 Is it at your command that the eagle mounts up
    and makes his nest on high?
28 On the rock he dwells and makes his home
    in the fastness of the rocky crag.
29 Thence he spies out the prey;
    his eyes behold it afar off.
30 His young ones suck up blood;
    and where the slain are, there is he."

40 And the Lord said to Job:
2   "Shall a faultfinder contend with the Almighty?
He who argues with God, let him answer it."

3 Then Job answered the Lord:
4 "Behold, I am of small account; what shall I answer thee?
    I lay my hand on my mouth.
5 I have spoken once, and I will not answer;
    twice, but I will proceed no further."

6 Then the Lord answered Job out of the whirlwind:
7 "Gird up your loins like a man;
    I will question you, and you declare to me.
8 Will you even put me in the wrong?
    Will you condemn me that you may be justified?
9 Have you an arm like God,
    and can you thunder with a voice like his?

10 "Deck yourself with majesty and dignity;
    clothe yourself with glory and splendor.
11 Pour forth the overflowings of your anger,
    and look on every one that is proud, and abase him.
12 Look on every one that is proud, and bring him low;

i Heb *your grain and your threshing floor*
l Tg: The meaning of the Hebrew word is obscure
j Heb obscure
m Gk Syr Vg: Heb *they dig*
k Heb obscure

and tread down the wicked where they stand.
13 Hide them all in the dust together;
  bind their faces in the world below.[n]
14 Then will I also acknowledge to you,
  that your own right hand can give you victory.

15 "Behold, Be′hemoth,[o]
  which I made as I made you;
  he eats grass like an ox.
16 Behold, his strength in his loins,
  and his power in the muscles of his belly.
17 He makes his tail stiff like a cedar;
  the sinews of his thighs are knit together.
18 His bones are tubes of bronze,
  his limbs like bars of iron.

19 "He is the first of the works[p] of God;
  let him who made him bring near his sword!
20 For the mountains yield food for him
  where all the wild beasts play.
21 Under the lotus plants he lies,
  in the covert of the reeds and in the marsh.
22 For his shade the lotus trees cover him;
  the willows of the brook surround him.
23 Behold, if the river is turbulent he is not frightened;
  he is confident though Jordan rushes against his mouth.
24 Can one take him with hooks,[q]
  or pierce his nose with a snare?

41[r] "Can you draw out Levi′athan[s] with a fishhook,
  or press down his tongue with a cord?

2 Can you put a rope in his nose,
  or pierce his jaw with a hook?
3 Will he make many supplications to you?
  Will he speak to you soft words?
4 Will he make a covenant with you
  to take him for your servant for ever?
5 Will you play with him as with a bird,
  or will you put him on leash for your maidens?
6 Will traders bargain over him?
  Will they divide him up among the merchants?
7 Can you fill his skin with harpoons,
  or his head with fishing spears?
8 Lay hands on him;
  think of the battle; you will not do it again!
9[t] Behold, the hope of a man is disappointed;
  he is laid low even at the sight of him.

10 No one is so fierce that he dares to stir him up.
  Who then is he that can stand before me?
11 Who has given to me,[u] that I should repay him?
  Whatever is under the whole heaven is mine.

12 "I will not keep silence concerning his limbs,
  or his mighty strength, or his goodly frame.
13 Who can strip off his outer garment?
  Who can penetrate his double coat of mail?[v]
14 Who can open the doors of his face?
  Round about his teeth is terror.
15 His back[w] is made of rows of shields,
  shut up closely as with a seal.
16 One is so near to another
  that no air can come between them.
17 They are joined one to another;
  they clasp each other and cannot be separated.
18 His sneezings flash forth light,
  and his eyes are like the eyelids of the dawn.
19 Out of his mouth go flaming torches;
  sparks of fire leap forth.
20 Out of his nostrils comes forth smoke,
  as from a boiling pot and burning rushes.
21 His breath kindles coals,
  and a flame comes forth from his mouth.
22 In his neck abides strength,
  and terror dances before him.
23 The folds of his flesh cleave together,
  firmly cast upon him and immovable.
24 His heart is hard as a stone,
  hard as the nether millstone.
25 When he raises himself up the mighty[x] are afraid;
  at the crashing they are beside themselves.
26 Though the sword reaches him, it does not avail;
  nor the spear, the dart, or the javelin.
27 He counts iron as straw,
  and bronze as rotten wood.
28 The arrow cannot make him flee;
  for him slingstones are turned to stubble.
29 Clubs are counted as stubble;
  he laughs at the rattle of javelins.
30 His underparts are like sharp potsherds;
  he spreads himself like a threshing sledge on the mire.
31 He makes the deep boil like a pot;
  he makes the sea like a pot of ointment.
32 Behind him he leaves a shining wake;
  one would think the deep to be hoary.
33 Upon earth there is not his like,
  a creature without fear.
34 He beholds everything that is high;
  he is king over all the sons of pride."

42 Then Job answered the LORD:
2 "I know that thou canst do all things,

---

n Heb *hidden place*   o Or *the hippopotamus*   p Heb *ways*   q Cn: Heb *in his eyes*   r Ch 40.25 in Heb
s Or *the crocodile*   t Ch 41.1 in Heb   u The meaning of the Hebrew is uncertain   v Gk: Heb *bridle*
w Cn Compare Gk Vg: Heb *pride*   x Or *gods*

and that no purpose of thine can be thwarted.
3 'Who is this that hides counsel without knowledge?'
Therefore I have uttered what I did not understand,
  things too wonderful for me, which I did not know.
4 'Hear, and I will speak;
  I will question you, and you declare to me.'
5 I had heard of thee by the hearing of the ear,
  but now my eye sees thee;
6 therefore I despise myself,
  and repent in dust and ashes."

EPILOGUE IN PROSE

7 After the LORD had spoken these words to Job, the LORD said to Eli'phaz the Te'manite: "My wrath is kindled against you and against your two friends; for you have not spoken of me what is right, as my servant Job 8 has. Now therefore take seven bulls and seven rams, and go to my servant Job, and offer up for yourselves a burnt offering; and my servant Job shall pray for you, for I will accept his prayer not to deal with you according to your folly; for you have not spoken of me what is right, as my 9 servant Job has." So Eli'phaz the Te'manite and Bildad

y Heb *qesitah*

the Shuhite and Zophar the Na'amathite went and did what the LORD had told them; and the LORD accepted Job's prayer.
10 And the LORD restored the fortunes of Job, when he had prayed for his friends; and the LORD gave Job twice as 11 much as he had before. Then came to him all his brothers and sisters and all who had known him before, and ate bread with him in his house; and they showed him sympathy and comforted him for all the evil that the LORD had brought upon him; and each of them gave him a piece 12 of money y and a ring of gold. And the LORD blessed the latter days of Job more than his beginning; and he had fourteen thousand sheep, six thousand camels, a thousand 13 yoke of oxen, and a thousand she-asses. He had also 14 seven sons and three daughters. And he called the name of the first Jemi'mah; and the name of the second Kezi'ah; 15 and the name of the third Ker'en-hap'puch. And in all the land there were no women so fair as Job's daughters; and their father gave them inheritance among their 16 brothers. And after this Job lived a hundred and forty years, and saw his sons, and his sons' sons, four genera-17 tions. And Job died, an old man, and full of days.

THE PSALMS

The Book of Psalms is the hymnbook of the Hebrews. Like modern hymnals it contains songs of many different writers and from many periods of history. It was completed about 100 B.C. Psalms contains five collections of hymns, including "The Songs of David" and "The Songs of the Sons of Korah."

The Hebrews did not have musical notes as we do in our songbooks, but some of the psalms include instructions to the musicians and singers.

Psalms contains hymns or poems of praise, repentance, thanksgiving, and petition. Some are very personal (Psalms 51), while some were written on behalf of a whole congregation (Psalms 90) or of the whole nation (Psalms 96). Some were planned so that one line was to be sung by the choir and the next line by the congregation. (See Psalms 95 and 100.) Some were joyful songs to be sung by groups of friends as they walked along their way to Jerusalem for some great festival. (See Psalms 120 through 134.) Others are about the wonders of God's universe (Psalms 19).

Many of the psalms are among the most familiar and best-loved portions of the Old Testament. They are regularly used in Jewish and Christian worship both as songs and as responsive readings.

The poetry of Psalms is somewhat different from our English poetry. Much of our poetry rhymes, that is, it has similar sounds at the ends of two or more lines. The writers of Hebrew songs made no effort to have the end of lines sound alike. Instead, many Hebrew songs state similar meanings in two or more successive lines. A clear example of having a second line repeat in a different way the idea of the first can be seen in these quotations:

> "The earth is the LORD's and the fulness thereof,
>   the world and those who dwell therein . . ."
>
> —Psalms 24.1

> "I will bless the LORD at all times;
>   his praise shall continually be in my mouth."
>
> —Psalms 34.1

You will notice that the first and second lines express the same idea. Sometimes a psalm may have as many as seven, eight, or even nine lines in which the same thing is said in slightly different ways!

But the fact that these poems are written so beautifully is not all that makes them important. The way they express our longings and prayers to God has made them beloved by worshipers for thousands of years.

THE PSALMS

BOOK I

1 Blessed is the man
    who walks not in the counsel of the wicked,
nor stands in the way of sinners,
    nor sits in the seat of scoffers;
2 but his delight is in the law of the LORD,
    and on his law he meditates day and night.
3 He is like a tree
    planted by streams of water,
that yields its fruit in its season,
    and its leaf does not wither.
In all that he does, he prospers.

4 The wicked are not so,
    but are like chaff which the wind drives away.
5 Therefore the wicked will not stand in the judgment,
    nor sinners in the congregation of the righteous;
6 for the LORD knows the way of the righteous,
    but the way of the wicked will perish.

2 Why do the nations conspire,
    and the peoples plot in vain?
2 The kings of the earth set themselves,
    and the rulers take counsel together,
against the LORD and his anointed, saying,
3 "Let us burst their bonds asunder,
    and cast their cords from us."

4 He who sits in the heavens laughs;
    the LORD has them in derision.
5 Then he will speak to them in his wrath,
    and terrify them in his fury, saying,
6 "I have set my king
    on Zion, my holy hill."

7 I will tell of the decree of the LORD:
He said to me, "You are my son,
    today I have begotten you.
8 Ask of me, and I will make the nations your heritage,
    and the ends of the earth your possession.
9 You shall break them with a rod of iron,
    and dash them in pieces like a potter's vessel."

10 Now therefore, O kings, be wise;
    be warned, O rulers of the earth.
11 Serve the LORD with fear,
12   with trembling kiss his feet,ᵃ

ᵃ Cn: The Hebrew of 11b and 12a is uncertain

lest he be angry, and you perish in the way;
    for his wrath is quickly kindled.

Blessed are all who take refuge in him.

A Psalm of David, when he fled from Absalom his son.

3 O LORD, how many are my foes!
    Many are rising against me;
2 many are saying of me,
    there is no help for him in God.   *Selah*

3 But thou, O LORD, art a shield about me,
    my glory, and the lifter of my head.
4 I cry aloud to the LORD,
    and he answers me from his holy hill.   *Selah*

5 I lie down and sleep;
    I wake again, for the LORD sustains me.
6 I am not afraid of ten thousands of people
    who have set themselves against me round about.

7 Arise, O LORD!
    Deliver me, O my God!
For thou dost smite all my enemies on the cheek,
    thou dost break the teeth of the wicked.
8 Deliverance belongs to the LORD;
    thy blessing be upon thy people!   *Selah*

To the choirmaster: with stringed instruments.
A Psalm of David.

4 Answer me when I call, O God of my right!
    Thou hast given me room when I was in distress.
Be gracious to me, and hear my prayer.

2 O men, who long shall my honor suffer shame?
    How long will you love vain words, and seek after lies?
    Selah
3 But know that the LORD has set apart the godly for himself;
    the LORD hears when I call to him.

4 Be angry, but sin not;
    commune with your own hearts on your beds, and be
    silent.   *Selah*
5 Offer right sacrifices,
    and put your trust in the LORD.

6 There are many who say, "O that we might see some
    good!
Lift up the light of thy countenance upon us, O LORD!"

7 Thou hast put more joy in my heart
    than they have when their grain and wine abound.

8 In peace I will both lie down and sleep;
    for thou alone, O LORD, makest me dwell in safety.

To the choirmaster: for the flutes. A Psalm of David.

5 Give ear to my words, O LORD;
    give heed to my groaning.
2 Hearken to the sound of my cry,
    my King and my God,
    for to thee do I pray.
3 O LORD, in the morning thou dost hear my voice;
    in the morning I prepare a sacrifice for thee, and watch.
4 For thou art not a God who delights in wickedness;
    evil may not sojourn with thee.
5 The boastful may not stand before thy eyes;
    thou hatest all evildoers.
6 Thou destroyest those who speak lies;
    the LORD abhors bloodthirsty and deceitful men.

7 But I through the abundance of thy steadfast love
    will enter thy house,
I will worship toward thy holy temple
    in the fear of thee.
8 Lead me, O LORD, in thy righteousness
    because of my enemies;
    make thy way straight before me.

9 For there is no truth in their mouth;
    their heart is destruction,
their throat is an open sepulchre,
    they flatter with their tongue.
10 Make them bear their guilt, O God;
    let them fall by their own counsels;
because of their many transgressions cast them out,
    for they have rebelled against thee.

11 But let all who take refuge in thee rejoice,
    let them ever sing for joy;
and do thou defend them,
    that those who love thy name may exult in thee.
12 For thou dost bless the righteous, O LORD;
    thou dost cover him with favor as with a shield.

*To the choirmaster: with stringed
instruments; according to The
Sheminith. A Psalm of David.*

6 O LORD, rebuke me not in thy anger,
    nor chasten me in thy wrath.
2 Be gracious to me, O LORD, for I am languishing;

b Or *for me*   c Cn: Heb *return*

O LORD, heal me, for my bones are troubled.
3 My soul also is sorely troubled.
    But thou, O LORD—how long?

4 Turn, O LORD, save my life;
    deliver me for the sake of thy steadfast love.
5 For in death there is no remembrance of thee;
    in Sheol who can give thee praise?

6 I am weary with my moaning;
    every night I flood my bed with tears;
    I drench my couch with my weeping.
7 My eye wastes away because of grief,
    it grows weak because of all my foes.

8 Depart from me, all you workers of evil;
    for the LORD has heard the sound of my weeping.
9 The LORD has heard my supplication;
    the LORD accepts my prayer.
10 All my enemies shall be ashamed and sorely troubled;
    they shall turn back, and be put to shame in a moment.

*A Shiggaion of David, which he sang
to the LORD concerning Cush a
Benjaminite.*

7 O LORD my God, in thee do I take refuge;
    save me from all my pursuers, and deliver me,
2 lest like a lion they rend me,
    dragging me away, with none to rescue.

3 O LORD my God, if I have done this,
    if there is wrong in my hands,
4 if I have requited my friend with evil
    or plundered my enemy without cause,
5 let the enemy pursue me and overtake me,
    and let him trample my life to the ground,
    and lay my soul in the dust.   *Selah*

6 Arise, O LORD, in thy anger,
    lift thyself up against the fury of my enemies;
    awake, O my God; b thou hast appointed a judgment.
7 Let the assembly of the peoples be gathered about thee;
    and over it take thy seat c on high.
8 The LORD judges the peoples;
    judge me, O LORD, according to my righteousness
    and according to the integrity that is in me.

9 O let the evil of the wicked come to an end,
    but establish thou the righteous,
thou, who triest the minds and hearts,
    thou righteous God.
10 My shield is with God,

who saves the upright in heart.
11 God is a righteous judge,
  and a God who has indignation every day.

12 If a man d does not repent, God d will whet his sword;
  he has bent and strung his bow;
13 he has prepared his deadly weapons,
  making his arrows fiery shafts.
14 Behold, the wicked man conceives evil,
  and is pregnant with mischief,
  and brings forth lies.
15 He makes a pit, digging it out,
  and falls into the hole which he has made.
16 His mischief returns upon his own head,
  and on his own pate his violence descends.

17 I will give to the LORD the thanks due to his righteousness,
  and I will sing praise to the name of the LORD, the Most High.

To the choirmaster: according to The Gittith. A Psalm of David.

8 O LORD, our Lord,
   how majestic is thy name in all the earth!
Thou whose glory above the heavens is chanted
2   by the mouth of babes and infants,
  thou hast founded a bulwark because of thy foes,
  to still the enemy and the avenger.

3 When I look at thy heavens, the work of thy fingers,
  the moon and the stars which thou hast established;
4 what is man that thou art mindful of him,
  and the son of man that thou dost care for him?

5 Yet thou hast made him little less than God,
  and dost crown him with glory and honor.
6 Thou hast given him dominion over the works of thy hands;
  thou hast put all things under his feet,
7 all sheep and oxen,
  and also the beasts of the field,
8 the birds of the air, and the fish of the sea,
  whatever passes along the paths of the sea.

9 O LORD, our Lord,
  how majestic is thy name in all the earth!

To the choirmaster: according to Muth-labben. A Psalm of David.

9 I will give thanks to the LORD with my whole heart;
  I will tell of all thy wonderful deeds.

d Heb *he*

2 I will be glad and exult in thee,
  I will sing praise to thy name, O Most High.

3 When my enemies turned back,
  they stumbled and perished before thee.

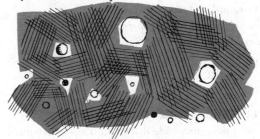

4 For thou hast maintained my just cause;
  thou hast sat on the throne giving righteous judgment.

5 Thou hast rebuked the nations, thou hast destroyed the wicked;
  thou hast blotted out their name for ever and ever.
6 The enemy have vanished in everlasting ruins;
  their cities thou hast rooted out;
  the very memory of them has perished.

7 But the LORD sits enthroned for ever,
  he has established his throne for judgment;
8 and he judges the world with righteousness,
  he judges the peoples with equity.

9 The LORD is a stronghold for the oppressed,
  a stronghold in times of trouble.
10 And those who know thy name put their trust in thee,
  for thou, O LORD, hast not forsaken those who seek thee.

11 Sing praises to the LORD, who dwells in Zion!
  Tell among the peoples his deeds!
12 For he who avenges blood is mindful of them;
  he does not forget the cry of the afflicted.

13 Be gracious to me, O LORD!
  Behold what I suffer from those who hate me,
  O thou who liftest me up from the gates of death,
14 that I may recount all thy praises,
  that in the gates of the daughter of Zion
  I may rejoice in thy deliverance.

15 The nations have sunk in the pit which they made;
  in the net which they hid has their own foot been caught.
16 The LORD has made himself known, he has executed judgment;
  the wicked are snared in the work of their own hands.
  Higgaion. Selah

17 The wicked shall depart to Sheol,
    all the nations that forget God.
18 For the needy shall not always be forgotten,
    and the hope of the poor shall not perish for ever.

19 Arise, O LORD! Let not man prevail;
    let the nations be judged before thee!
20 Put them in fear, O LORD!
    Let the nations know that they are but men!   *Selah*

10 Why dost thou stand afar off, O LORD?
    Why dost thou hide thyself in times of trouble?
2 In arrogance the wicked hotly pursue the poor;
    let them be caught in the schemes which they have
        devised.

3 For the wicked boasts of the desires of his heart,
    and the man greedy for gain curses and renounces the
        LORD.
4 In the pride of his countenance the wicked does not seek
        him;
    all his thoughts are, "There is no God."

5 His ways prosper at all times;
    thy judgments are on high, out of his sight;
    as for all his foes, he puffs at them.
6 He thinks in his heart, "I shall not be moved;
    throughout all generations I shall not meet adversity."

7 His mouth is filled with cursing and deceit and oppres-
        sion;
    under his tongue are mischief and iniquity.
8 He sits in ambush in the villages;
    in hiding places he murders the innocent.

His eyes stealthily watch for the hapless,
9   he lurks in secret like a lion in his covert;
he lurks that he may seize the poor,
    he seizes the poor when he draws him into his net.

10 The hapless is crushed, sinks down, and falls by his might.
11 He thinks in his heart, "God has forgotten,
    he has hidden his face, he will never see it."

12 Arise, O LORD; O God, lift up thy hand;
    forget not the afflicted.
13 Why does the wicked renounce God,
    and say in his heart, "Thou wilt not call to account"?

14 Thou dost see; yea, thou dost note trouble and vexation,
    that thou mayest take it into thy hands;
the hapless commits himself to thee;
    thou hast been the helper of the fatherless.

e Gk Syr Jerome Tg: Heb *flee to your mountain, O bird*

15 Break thou the arm of the wicked and evildoer;
    seek out his wickedness till thou find none.
16 The LORD is king for ever and ever;
    the nations shall perish from his land.

17 O LORD, thou wilt hear the desire of the meek;
    thou wilt strengthen their heart, thou wilt incline thy
        ear
18 to do justice to the fatherless and the oppressed,
    so that man who is of the earth may strike terror no
        more.

To the choirmaster. Of David.

11 In the LORD I take refuge;
    how can you say to me,
"Flee like a bird to the mountains; e

2 for lo, the wicked bend the bow,
    they have fitted their arrow to the string,
    to shoot in the dark at the upright in heart;
3 if the foundations are destroyed,
    what can the righteous do"?

4 The LORD is in his holy temple,
    the LORD's throne is in heaven;
    his eyes behold, his eyelids test, the children of men.
5 The LORD tests the righteous and the wicked,
    and his soul hates him that loves violence.
6 On the wicked he will rain coals of fire and brimstone;
    a scorching wind shall be the portion of their cup.
7 For the LORD is righteous, he loves righteous deeds;
    the upright shall behold his face.

To the choirmaster: according to
The Sheminith. A Psalm of David.

12 Help, LORD; for there is no longer any that is godly;
    for the faithful have vanished from among the
        sons of men.
2 Every one utters lies to his neighbor;
    with flattering lips and a double heart they speak.

3 May the LORD cut off all flattering lips,
    the tongue that makes great boasts,
4 those who say, "With our tongue we will prevail,
    our lips are with us; who is our master?"

5 "Because the poor are despoiled, because the needy groan,
    I will now arise," says the LORD;
    "I will place him in the safety for which he longs."
6 The promises of the LORD are promises that are pure,
    silver refined in a furnace on the ground,

purified seven times.
⁷ Do thou, O Lord, protect us,
　guard us ever from this generation.
⁸ On every side the wicked prowl,
　as vileness is exalted among the sons of men.

To the choirmaster. A Psalm of David.

13 How long, O Lord? Wilt thou forget me for ever?
　How long wilt thou hide thy face from me?
² How long must I bear pain ᶠ in my soul,
　and have sorrow in my heart all the day?
　How long shall my enemy be exalted over me?

³ Consider and answer me, O Lord my God;
　lighten my eyes, lest I sleep the sleep of death;
⁴ lest my enemy say, "I have prevailed over him";
　lest my foes rejoice because I am shaken.

⁵ But I have trusted in thy steadfast love;
　my heart shall rejoice in thy salvation.
⁶ I will sing to the Lord,
　because he has dealt bountifully with me.

To the choirmaster. Of David.

14 The fool says in his heart,
　"There is no God."
They are corrupt, they do abominable deeds,
　there is none that does good.

² The Lord looks down from heaven upon the children of
　　men,
　to see if there are any that act wisely,
　that seek after God.

³ They have all gone astray, they are all alike corrupt;
　there is none that does good,
　no, not one.

⁴ Have they no knowledge, all the evildoers
　who eat up my people as they eat bread,
　and do not call upon the Lord?

⁵ There they shall be in great terror,
　for God is with the generation of the righteous.
⁶ You would confound the plans of the poor,
　but the Lord is his refuge.

⁷ O that deliverance for Israel would come out of Zion!
　When the Lord restores the fortunes of his people,
　Jacob shall rejoice, Israel shall be glad.

A Psalm of David.

15 O Lord, who shall sojourn in thy tent?
　Who shall dwell on thy holy hill?

² He who walks blamelessly, and does what is right,
　and speaks truth from his heart;
³ who does not slander with his tongue,
　and does no evil to his friend,
　nor takes up a reproach against his neighbor;
⁴ in whose eyes a reprobate is despised,
　but who honors those who fear the Lord;
　who swears to his own hurt and does not change;
⁵ who does not put out his money at interest,
　and does not take a bribe against the innocent.

He who does these things shall never be moved.

A Miktam of David.

16 Preserve me, O God, for in thee I take refuge.
² 　I say to the Lord, "Thou art my Lord;
　I have no good apart from thee." ᵍ

³ As for the saints in the land, they are the noble,
　in whom is all my delight.
⁴ Those who choose another god multiply their sorrows; ʰ
　their libations of blood I will not pour out
　or take their names upon my lips.

⁵ The Lord is my chosen portion and my cup;
　thou holdest my lot.
⁶ The lines have fallen for me in pleasant places;
　yea, I have a goodly heritage.

⁷ I bless the Lord who gives me counsel;
　in the night also my heart instructs me.
⁸ I keep the Lord always before me;
　because he is at my right hand, I shall not be moved.

⁹ Therefore my heart is glad, and my soul rejoices;
　my body also dwells secure.
¹⁰ For thou dost not give me up to Sheol,
　or let thy godly one see the Pit.

¹¹ Thou dost show me the path of life;
　in thy presence there is fulness of joy,
　in thy right hand are pleasures for evermore.

A Prayer of David.

17 Hear a just cause, O Lord; attend to my cry!
　Give ear to my prayer from lips free of deceit!
² From thee let my vindication come!
　Let thy eyes see the right!

ᶠ Syr: Heb *hold counsels*　　　ᵍ Jerome Tg: The meaning of the Hebrew is uncertain　　　ʰ Cn: The meaning of the Hebrew is uncertain

³ If thou triest my heart, if thou visitest me by night,
  if thou testest me, thou wilt find no wickedness in me;
  my mouth does not transgress.
⁴ With regard to the works of men, by the word of thy lips
  I have avoided the ways of the violent.
⁵ My steps have held fast to thy paths,
  my feet have not slipped.
⁶ I call upon thee, for thou wilt answer me, O God;
  incline thy ear to me, hear my words.
⁷ Wondrously show thy steadfast love,
  O savior of those who seek refuge
  from their adversaries at thy right hand.

⁸ Keep me as the apple of the eye;
  hide me in the shadow of thy wings,
⁹ from the wicked who despoil me,
  my deadly enemies who surround me.

¹⁰ They close their hearts to pity;
  with their mouths they speak arrogantly.
¹¹ They track me down; now they surround me;
  they set their eyes to cast me to the ground.
¹² They are like a lion eager to tear,
  as a young lion lurking in ambush.

¹³ Arise, O Lord! confront them, overthrow them!
  Deliver my life from the wicked by thy sword,
¹⁴ from men by thy hand, O Lord,
  from men whose portion in life is of the world.
  May their belly be filled with what thou hast stored up
    for them;
    may their children have more than enough;
    may they leave something over to their babes.

¹⁵ As for me, I shall behold thy face in righteousness;
  when I awake, I shall be satisfied with beholding thy
    form.

*To the choirmaster. A Psalm of David the servant of the
Lord, who addressed the words of this song to the Lord
on the day when the Lord delivered him from the hand of
all his enemies, and from the hand of Saul. He said:*

18 ¹ I love thee, O Lord, my strength.
² The Lord is my rock, and my fortress, and my de-
    liverer,
  my God, my rock, in whom I take refuge,
  my shield, and the horn of my salvation, my stronghold.
³ I call upon the Lord, who is worthy to be praised,
  and I am saved from my enemies.

⁴ The cords of death encompassed me,
  the torrents of perdition assailed me;

⁵ the cords of Sheol entangled me,
  the snares of death confronted me.

⁶ In my distress I called upon the Lord;
  to my God I cried for help.
  From his temple he heard my voice,
  and my cry to him reached his ears.

⁷ Then the earth reeled and rocked;
  the foundations also of the mountains trembled
  and quaked, because he was angry.
⁸ Smoke went up from his nostrils,
  and devouring fire from his mouth;
  glowing coals flamed forth from him.
⁹ He bowed the heavens, and came down;
  thick darkness was under his feet.
¹⁰ He rode on a cherub, and flew;
  he came swiftly upon the wings of the wind.
¹¹ He made darkness his covering around him,
  his canopy thick clouds dark with water.
¹² Out of the brightness before him
  there broke through his clouds
  hailstones and coals of fire.
¹³ The Lord also thundered in the heavens,
  and the Most High uttered his voice,
  hailstones and coals of fire.
¹⁴ And he sent out his arrows, and scattered them;
  he flashed forth lightnings, and routed them.
¹⁵ Then the channels of the sea were seen,
  and the foundations of the world were laid bare,
  at thy rebuke, O Lord,
  at the blast of the breath of thy nostrils.

¹⁶ He reached from on high, he took me,
  he drew me out of many waters.
¹⁷ He delivered me from my strong enemy,
  and from those who hated me;
  for they were too mighty for me.
¹⁸ They came upon me in the day of my calamity;
  but the Lord was my stay.
¹⁹ He brought me forth into a broad place;
  he delivered me, because he delighted in me.

²⁰ The Lord rewarded me according to my righteousness;
  according to the cleanness of my hands he recompensed
    me.

THE PSALMS 19. 10

21 For I have kept the ways of the LORD,
and have not wickedly departed from my God.
22 For all his ordinances were before me,
and his statutes I did not put away from me.
23 I was blameless before him,
and I kept myself from guilt.
24 Therefore the LORD has recompensed me according to my
righteousness,
according to the cleanness of my hands in his sight.

25 With the loyal thou dost show thyself loyal;
with the blameless man thou dost show thyself blameless;
26 with the pure thou dost show thyself pure;
and with the crooked thou dost show thyself perverse.
27 For thou dost deliver a humble people;
but the haughty eyes thou dost bring down.
28 Yea, thou dost light my lamp;
the LORD my God lightens my darkness.
29 Yea, by thee I can crush a troop;
and by my God I can leap over a wall.
30 This God—his way is perfect;
the promise of the LORD proves true;
he is a shield for all those who take refuge in him.

31 For who is God, but the LORD?
And who is a rock, except our God?—
32 the God who girded me with strength,
and made my way safe.
33 He made my feet like hinds' feet,
and set me secure on the heights.
34 He trains my hands for war,
so that my arms can bend a bow of bronze.
35 Thou hast given me the shield of thy salvation,
and thy right hand supported me,
and thy help[i] made me great.
36 Thou didst give a wide place for my steps under me,
and my feet did not slip.
37 I pursued my enemies and overtook them;
and did not turn back till they were consumed.
38 I thrust them through, so that they were not able to rise;
they fell under my feet.
39 For thou didst gird me with strength for the battle;
thou didst make my assailants sink under me.
40 Thou didst make my enemies turn their backs to me,
and those who hated me I destroyed.
41 They cried for help, but there was none to save,
they cried to the LORD, but he did not answer them.
42 I beat them fine as dust before the wind;
I cast them out like the mire of the streets.

43 Thou didst deliver me from strife with the peoples;[j]
thou didst make me the head of the nations;
people whom I had not known served me.

44 As soon as they heard of me they obeyed me;
foreigners came cringing to me.
45 Foreigners lost heart,
and came trembling out of their fastnesses.

46 The LORD lives; and blessed be my rock,
and exalted be the God of my salvation,
47 the God who gave me vengeance
and subdued peoples under me;
48 who delivered me from my enemies;
yea, thou didst exalt me above my adversaries;
thou didst deliver me from men of violence.

49 For this I will extol thee, O LORD, among the nations,
and sing praises to thy name.
50 Great triumphs he gives to his king,
and shows steadfast love to his anointed,
to David and his descendants for ever.

To the choirmaster. A Psalm of David.

19 The heavens are telling the glory of God;
and the firmament proclaims his handiwork.
2 Day to day pours forth speech,
and night to night declares knowledge.
3 There is no speech, nor are there words;
their voice is not heard;
4 yet their voice[k] goes out through all the earth,
and their words to the end of the world.

In them he has set a tent for the sun,
5 which comes forth like a bridegroom leaving his chamber,
and like a strong man runs its course with joy.
6 Its rising is from the end of the heavens,
and its circuit to the end of them;
and there is nothing hid from its heat.

7 The law of the LORD is perfect,
reviving the soul;
the testimony of the LORD is sure,
making wise the simple;
8 the precepts of the LORD are right,
rejoicing the heart;
the commandment of the LORD is pure,
enlightening the eyes;
9 the fear of the LORD is clean,
enduring for ever;
the ordinances of the LORD are true,
and righteous altogether.
10 More to be desired are they than gold,
even much fine gold;
sweeter also than honey
and drippings of the honeycomb.

---

[i] Or *gentleness*   [j] Gk Tg: Heb *people*   [k] Gk Jerome Compare Syr: Heb *line*

¹¹ Moreover by them is thy servant warned;
  in keeping them there is great reward.
¹² But who can discern his errors?
  Clear thou me from hidden faults.
¹³ Keep back thy servant also from presumptuous sins;
  let them not have dominion over me!
  Then I shall be blameless,
    and innocent of great transgression.

¹⁴ Let the words of my mouth and the meditation of my heart
    be acceptable in thy sight,
  O Lord, my rock and my redeemer.

To the choirmaster. A Psalm of David.

20 The Lord answer you in the day of trouble!
    The name of the God of Jacob protect you!
² May he send you help from the sanctuary,
  and give you support from Zion!
³ May he remember all your offerings,
  and regard with favor your burnt sacrifices!   *Selah*

⁴ May he grant you your heart's desire,
  and fulfil all your plans!
⁵ May we shout for joy over your victory,
  and in the name of our God set up our banners!
  May the Lord fulfil all your petitions!

⁶ Now I know that the Lord will help his anointed;
  he will answer him from his holy heaven
  with mighty victories by his right hand.
⁷ Some boast of chariots, and some of horses;
  but we boast of the name of the Lord our God.
⁸ They will collapse and fall;
  but we shall rise and stand upright.

⁹ Give victory to the king, O Lord;
  answer us when we call.[1]

To the choirmaster. A Psalm of David.

21 In thy strength the king rejoices, O Lord;
    and in thy help how greatly he exults!
² Thou hast given him his heart's desire,
  and hast not withheld the request of his lips.   *Selah*
³ For thou dost meet him with goodly blessings;
  thou dost set a crown of fine gold upon his head.
⁴ He asked life of thee; thou gavest it to him,
  length of days for ever and ever.
⁵ His glory is great through thy help;
  splendor and majesty thou dost bestow upon him.
⁶ Yea, thou dost make him most blessed for ever;

---

[1] Gk: Heb *give victory, O Lord, let the King answer us when we call*

  thou dost make him glad with the joy of thy presence.
⁷ For the king trusts in the Lord;
  and through the steadfast love of the Most High he shall
    not be moved.

⁸ Your hand will find out all your enemies;
  your right hand will find out those who hate you.
⁹ You will make them as a blazing oven
  when you appear.
  The Lord will swallow them up in his wrath;
  and fire will consume them.
¹⁰ You will destroy their offspring from the earth,
  and their children from among the sons of men.
¹¹ If they plan evil against you,
  if they devise mischief, they will not succeed.
¹² For you will put them to flight;
  you will aim at their faces with bows.

¹³ Be exalted, O Lord, in thy strength!
  We will sing and praise thy power.

To the choirmaster: according to The Hind of the Dawn.
A Psalm of David.

22 My God, my God, why hast thou forsaken me?
    Why art thou so far from helping me, from the
    words of my groaning?
² O my God, I cry by day, but thou dost not answer;
  and by night, but find no rest.

³ Yet thou art holy,
  enthroned on the praises of Israel.
⁴ In thee our fathers trusted;
  they trusted, and thou didst deliver them.
⁵ To thee they cried, and were saved;
  in thee they trusted, and were not disappointed.

⁶ But I am a worm, and no man;
  scorned by men, and despised by the people.
⁷ All who see me mock at me,
  they make mouths at me, they wag their heads;
⁸ "He committed his cause to the Lord; let him deliver him,
  let him rescue him, for he delights in him!"

9 Yet thou art he who took me from the womb;
thou didst keep me safe upon my mother's breasts.
10 Upon thee was I cast from my birth,
and since my mother bore me thou hast been my God.
11 Be not far from me,
for trouble is near
and there is none to help.

12 Many bulls encompass me,
strong bulls of Bashan surround me;
13 they open wide their mouths at me,
like a ravening and roaring lion.

14 I am poured out like water,
and all my bones are out of joint;
my heart is like wax,
it is melted within my breast;
15 my strength is dried up like a potsherd,
and my tongue cleaves to my jaws;
thou dost lay me in the dust of death.

16 Yea, dogs are round about me;
a company of evildoers encircle me;
they have pierced[m] my hands and feet—

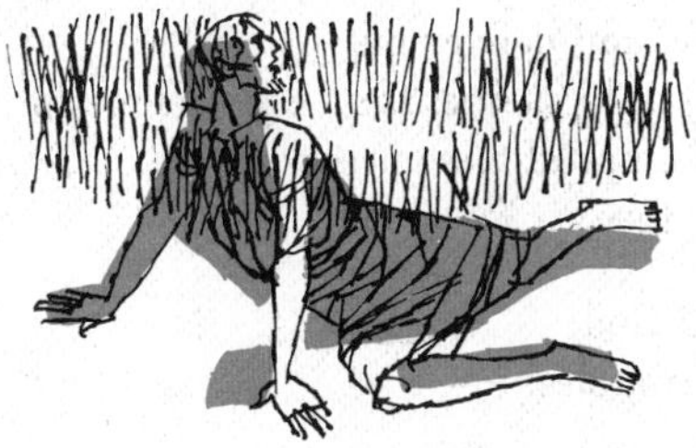

17 I can count all my bones—
they stare and gloat over me;
18 they divide my garments among them,
and for my raiment they cast lots.

19 But thou, O LORD, be not far off!
O thou my help, hasten to my aid!
20 Deliver my soul from the sword,
my life[n] from the power of the dog!
21 Save me from the mouth of the lion,
my afflicted soul[o] from the horns of the wild oxen!

22 I will tell of thy name to my brethren;
in the midst of the congregation I will praise thee:
23 You who fear the LORD, praise him!
all you sons of Jacob, glorify him,
and stand in awe of him, all you sons of Israel!
24 For he has not despised or abhorred
the affliction of the afflicted;
and he has not hid his face from him,
but has heard, when he cried to him.

25 From thee comes my praise in the great congregation;
my vows I will pay before those who fear him.
26 The afflicted[p] shall eat and be satisfied;
those who seek him shall praise the LORD!
May your hearts live for ever!

27 All the ends of the earth shall remember
and turn to the LORD;
and all the families of the nations
shall worship before him.[q]
28 For dominion belongs to the LORD,
and he rules over the nations.

29 Yea, to him[r] shall all the proud of the earth bow down;
before him shall bow all who go down to the dust,
and he who cannot keep himself alive.
30 Posterity shall serve him;
men shall tell of the LORD to the coming generation,
31 and proclaim his deliverance to a people yet unborn,
that he has wrought it.

A Psalm of David.

23 The LORD is my shepherd, I shall not want;
2 he makes me lie down in green pastures.
He leads me beside still waters;[s]
3 he restores my soul.[t]
He leads me in paths of righteousness[u]
for his name's sake.

4 Even though I walk through the valley of the shadow of death,[v]
I fear no evil;
for thou art with me;
thy rod and thy staff,
they comfort me.

5 Thou preparest a table before me
in the presence of my enemies;
thou anointest my head with oil,
my cup overflows.
6 Surely[w] goodness and mercy[x] shall follow me

all the days of my life;
and I shall dwell in the house of the LORD
for ever.[y]

[m] Gk Syr Jerome: Heb *like a lion* [n] Heb *my only one* [o] Gk Syr: Heb *thou hast answered me* [p] Or *poor*
[q] Gk Syr Jerome: Heb *thee* [r] Cn: Heb *they have eaten and* [s] Heb *the waters of rest* [t] Or *life* [u] Or *right paths*
[v] Or *the valley of deep darkness* [w] Or *only* [x] Or *kindness* [y] Or *as long as I live*

A Psalm of David.

24 The earth is the Lord's and the fulness thereof,
 the world and those who dwell therein;
2 for he has founded it upon the seas,
 and established it upon the rivers.

3 Who shall ascend the hill of the Lord?
 And who shall stand in his holy place?
4 He who has clean hands and a pure heart,
 who does not lift up his soul to what is false,
 and does not swear deceitfully.
5 He will receive blessing from the Lord,
 and vindication from the God of his salvation.
6 Such is the generation of those who seek him,
 who seek the face of the God of Jacob.ᶻ *Selah*

7 Lift up your heads, O gates!
 and be lifted up, O ancient doors!
 that the King of glory may come in.
8 Who is the King of glory?
 The Lord, strong and mighty,
 the Lord, mighty in battle!
9 Lift up your heads, O gates!
 and be lifted up,ᵃ O ancient doors!
 that the King of glory may come in.
10 Who is this King of glory?
 The Lord of hosts,
 he is the King of glory! *Selah*

A Psalm of David.

25 To thee, O Lord, I lift up my soul.
2 O my God, in thee I trust,
 let me not be put to shame;
 let not my enemies exult over me.
3 Yea, let none that wait for thee be put to shame;
 let them be ashamed who are wantonly treacherous.

4 Make me to know thy ways, O Lord;
 teach me thy paths.
5 Lead me in thy truth, and teach me,
 for thou art the God of my salvation;
 for thee I wait all the day long.

6 Be mindful of thy mercy, O Lord, and of thy steadfast love,
 for they have been from of old.
7 Remember not the sins of my youth, or my transgressions;
 according to thy steadfast love remember me,
 for thy goodness' sake, O Lord!

8 Good and upright is the Lord;
 therefore he instructs sinners in the way.

9 He leads the humble in what is right,
 and teaches the humble his way.
10 All the paths of the Lord are steadfast love and faithfulness,
 for those who keep his covenant and his testimonies.

11 For thy name's sake, O Lord,
 pardon my guilt, for it is great.
12 Who is the man that fears the Lord?
 Him will he instruct in the way that he should choose.
13 He himself shall abide in prosperity,
 and his children shall possess the land.
14 The friendship of the Lord is for those who fear him,
 and he makes known to them his covenant.
15 My eyes are ever toward the Lord,
 for he will pluck my feet out of the net.

16 Turn thou to me, and be gracious to me;
 for I am lonely and afflicted.
17 Relieve the troubles of my heart,
 and bring meᵇ out of my distresses.
18 Consider my affliction and my trouble,
 and forgive all my sins.

19 Consider how many are my foes,
 and with what violent hatred they hate me.
20 Oh guard my life, and deliver me;
 let me not be put to shame, for I take refuge in thee.
21 May integrity and uprightness preserve me,
 for I wait for thee.

22 Redeem Israel, O God,
 out of all his troubles.

A Psalm of David.

26 Vindicate me, O Lord,
 for I have walked in my integrity,
 and I have trusted in the Lord without wavering.
2 Prove me, O Lord, and try me;
 test my heart and my mind.
3 For thy steadfast love is before my eyes,
 and I walk in faithfulness to thee.ᶜ

4 I do not sit with false men,
 nor do I consort with dissemblers;
5 I hate the company of evildoers,
 and I will not sit with the wicked.

6 I wash my hands in innocence,
 and go about thy altar, O Lord,
7 singing aloud a song of thanksgiving,
 and telling all thy wondrous deeds.

8 O Lord, I love the habitation of thy house,
 and the place where thy glory dwells.

ᶻ Gk Syr: Heb *thy face, O Jacob* ᵃ Gk Syr Jerome Tg Compare verse 7: Heb *lift up*
ᵇ Or *The troubles of my heart are enlarged; bring me* ᶜ Or *in thy faithfulness*

⁹ Sweep me not away with sinners,
    nor my life with bloodthirsty men,
¹⁰ men in whose hands are evil devices,
    and whose right hands are full of bribes.

¹¹ But as for me, I walk in my integrity;
    redeem me, and be gracious to me.
¹² My foot stands on level ground;
    in the great congregation I will bless the Lord.

A Psalm of David.

27 The Lord is my light and my salvation;
    whom shall I fear?
The Lord is the stronghold ᵈ of my life;
    of whom shall I be afraid?

² When evildoers assail me,
    uttering slanders against me,ᵉ
my adversaries and foes,
    they shall stumble and fall.

³ Though a host encamp against me,
    my heart shall not fear;
though war arise against me,
    yet I will be confident.

⁴ One thing have I asked of the Lord,
    that will I seek after;
that I may dwell in the house of the Lord
    all the days of my life,
to behold the beauty of the Lord,
    and to inquire in his temple.

⁵ For he will hide me in his shelter in
    the day of trouble;
he will conceal me under the cover of his tent,
    he will set me high upon a rock.

⁶ And now my head shall be lifted up
    above my enemies round about me;
and I will offer in his tent
    sacrifices with shouts of joy;
I will sing and make melody to the Lord.

⁷ Hear, O Lord, when I cry aloud,
    be gracious to me and answer me!
⁸ Thou hast said, "Seek ye my face."
    My heart says to thee,
"Thy face, Lord, do I seek."
⁹   Hide not thy face from me.

Turn not thy servant away in anger,
    thou who hast been my help.
Cast me not off, forsake me not,
    O God of my salvation!
¹⁰ For my father and my mother have forsaken me,
    but the Lord will take me up.

¹¹ Teach me thy way, O Lord;
    and lead me on a level path
    because of my enemies.
¹² Give me not up to the will of my adversaries;
    for false witnesses have risen against me,
    and they breathe out violence.

¹³ I believe that I shall see the goodness of the Lord
    in the land of the living!
¹⁴ Wait for the Lord;
    be strong, and let your heart take courage;
    yea, wait for the Lord!

A Psalm of David.

28 To thee, O Lord, I call;
        my rock, be not deaf to me,
    lest, if thou be silent to me,
        I become like those who go down to the Pit.
² Hear the voice of my supplication,
    as I cry to thee for help,
as I lift up my hands
    toward thy most holy sanctuary.ᶠ

³ Take me not off with the wicked,
    with those who are workers of evil,
who speak peace with their neighbors,
    while mischief is in their hearts.
⁴ Requite them according to their work,
    and according to the evil of their deeds;
requite them according to the work of their hands;
    render them their due reward.
⁵ Because they do not regard the works of the Lord,
    or the work of his hands,
he will break them down and build them up no more.

⁶ Blessed be the Lord!
    for he has heard the voice of my supplications.
⁷ The Lord is my strength and my shield;
    in him my heart trusts;

ᵈ Or *refuge*   ᵉ Heb *to eat up my flesh*   ᶠ Heb *thy innermost sanctuary*

so I am helped, and my heart exults,
and with my song I give thanks to him.
8 The LORD is the strength of his people,
he is the saving refuge of his anointed.
9 O save thy people, and bless thy heritage;
be thou their shepherd, and carry them for ever.

A Psalm of David.

29 Ascribe to the LORD, O heavenly beings,[g]
ascribe to the LORD glory and strength.
2 Ascribe to the LORD the glory of his name;
worship the LORD in holy array.

3 The voice of the LORD is upon the waters;
the God of glory thunders,
the LORD, upon many waters.
4 The voice of the LORD is powerful,
the voice of the LORD is full of majesty.

5 The voice of the LORD breaks the cedars,
the LORD breaks the cedars of Lebanon.
6 He makes Lebanon to skip like a calf,
and Sir'ion like a young wild ox.

7 The voice of the LORD flashes forth flames of fire.
8 The voice of the LORD shakes the wilderness,
the LORD shakes the wilderness of Kadesh.

9 The voice of the LORD makes the oaks to whirl,[h]
and strips the forests bare;
and in his temple all cry, "Glory!"

10 The LORD sits enthroned over the flood;
the LORD sits enthroned as king for ever.
11 May the LORD give strength to his people!
May the LORD bless his people with peace!

A Psalm of David. A Song at the dedication of the Temple.

30 I will extol thee, O LORD, for thou hast drawn me up,
and hast not let my foes rejoice over me.
2 O LORD my God, I cried to thee for help,
and thou hast healed me.
3 O LORD, thou hast brought up my soul from Sheol,
restored me to life from among those gone down to the
Pit.[i]

4 Sing praises to the LORD, O you his saints,
and give thanks to his holy name.
5 For his anger is but for a moment,
and his favor is for a lifetime.
Weeping may tarry for the night,
but joy comes with the morning.

6 As for me, I said in my prosperity,
"I shall never be moved."
7 By thy favor, O Lord,
thou hadst established me as a strong mountain;
thou didst hide thy face,
I was dismayed.

8 To thee, O LORD, I cried;
and to the LORD I made supplication:
9 "What profit is there in my death,
if I go down to the Pit?
Will the dust praise thee?
Will it tell of thy faithfulness?
10 Hear, O LORD, and be gracious to me!
O LORD, be thou my helper!"

11 Thou hast turned for me my mourning into dancing;
thou hast loosed my sackcloth
and girded me with gladness,
12 that my soul[j] may praise thee and not be silent.
O LORD my God, I will give thanks to thee for ever.

To the choirmaster. A Psalm of David.

31 In thee, O LORD, do I seek refuge;
let me never be put to shame;
in thy righteousness deliver me!
2 Incline thy ear to me,
rescue me speedily!
Be thou a rock of refuge for me,
a strong fortress to save me!

3 Yea, thou art my rock and my fortress;
for thy name's sake lead me and guide me,
4 take me out of the net which is hidden for me,
for thou art my refuge.
5 Into thy hand I commit my spirit;
thou hast redeemed me, O LORD, faithful God.

6 Thou hatest[k] those who pay regard to vain idols;
but I trust in the LORD.
7 I will rejoice and be glad for thy steadfast love,
because thou hast seen my affliction,
thou hast taken heed of my adversities,
8 and hast not delivered me into the hand of the enemy;
thou hast set my feet in a broad place.

9 Be gracious to me, O LORD, for I am in distress;
my eye is wasted from grief,
my soul and my body also.
10 For my life is spent with sorrow,
and my years with sighing;
my strength fails because of my misery,[l]

g Heb *sons of gods*   h Or *makes the hinds to calve*   i Or *that I should not go down to the Pit*   j Heb *that glory*
k With one Heb Ms Gk Syr Jerome: Heb *I hate*   l Gk Syr: Heb *iniquity*

and my bones waste away.

11 I am the scorn of all my adversaries,
a horror m to my neighbors,
an object of dread to my acquaintances;
those who see me in the street flee from me.
12 I have passed out of mind like one who is dead;
I have become like a broken vessel.
13 Yea, I hear the whispering of many—
terror on every side!—
as they scheme together against me,
as they plot to take my life.

14 But I trust in thee, O Lord,
I say, "Thou art my God."
15 My times are in thy hand;
deliver me from the hand of my enemies and persecutors!
16 Let thy face shine on thy servant;
save me in thy steadfast love!
17 Let me not be put to shame, O Lord,
for I call on thee;
let the wicked be put to shame,
let them go dumbfounded to Sheol.
18 Let the lying lips be dumb,
which speak insolently against the righteous
in pride and contempt.
19 O how abundant is thy goodness,
which thou hast laid up for those who fear thee,
and wrought for those who take refuge in thee,
in the sight of the sons of men!
20 In the covert of thy presence thou hidest them
from the plots of men;
thou holdest them safe under thy shelter
from the strife of tongues.

21 Blessed be the Lord,
for he has wondrously shown his steadfast love to me
when I was beset as in a besieged city.

22 I had said in my alarm,
"I am driven far n from thy sight."
But thou didst hear my supplications,
when I cried to thee for help.

23 Love the Lord, all you his saints!
The Lord preserves the faithful,

but abundantly requites him who acts haughtily.
24 Be strong, and let your heart take courage,
all you who wait for the Lord!

A Psalm of David. A Maskil.

32 Blessed is he whose transgression is forgiven,
whose sin is covered.
2 Blessed is the man to whom the Lord imputes no iniquity,
and in whose spirit there is no deceit.

3 When I declared not my sin, my body wasted away
through my groaning all day long.
4 For day and night thy hand was heavy upon me;
my strength was dried up o as by the heat of summer.
Selah

5 I acknowledged my sin to thee,
and I did not hide my iniquity;
I said, "I will confess my transgressions to the Lord";
then thou didst forgive the guilt of my sin. *Selah*

6 Therefore let every one who is godly offer prayer to thee;
at a time of distress,p in the rush of great waters,
they shall not reach him.
7 Thou art a hiding place for me,
thou preservest me from trouble;
thou dost encompass me with deliverance.q *Selah*

8 I will instruct you and teach you the way you should go;
I will counsel you with my eye upon you.
9 Be not like a horse or a mule, without understanding,
which must be curbed with bit and bridle,
else it will not keep with you.

10 Many are the pangs of the wicked;
but steadfast love surrounds him who trusts in the
Lord.
11 Be glad in the Lord, and rejoice, O righteous,
and shout for joy, all you upright in heart!

33 Rejoice in the Lord, O you righteous!
Praise befits the upright.
2 Praise the Lord with the lyre,
make melody to him with the harp of ten strings!
3 Sing to him a new song,
play skilfully on the strings, with loud shouts.

4 For the word of the Lord is upright;
and all his work is done in faithfulness.
5 He loves righteousness and justice;
the earth is full of the steadfast love of the Lord.

---

m Cn: Heb *exceedingly*   n Another reading is *cut off*   o Heb obscure   p Cn: Heb *at a time of finding only*
q Cn: Heb *shouts of deliverance*

6 By the word of the LORD the heavens were made,
   and all their host by the breath of his mouth.
7 He gathered the waters of the sea as in a bottle;
   he put the deeps in storehouses.

8 Let all the earth fear the LORD,
   let all the inhabitants of the world stand in awe of him!
9 For he spoke, and it came to be;
   he commanded, and it stood forth.

10 The LORD brings the counsel of the nations to nought;
   he frustrates the plans of the peoples.
11 The counsel of the LORD stands for ever,
   the thoughts of his heart to all generations.
12 Blessed is the nation whose God is the LORD,
   the people whom he has chosen as his heritage!

13 The LORD looks down from heaven,
   he sees all the sons of men;
14 from where he sits enthroned he looks forth
   on all the inhabitants of the earth,
15 he who fashions the hearts of them all,
   and observes all their deeds.
16 A king is not saved by his great army;
   a warrior is not delivered by his great strength.
17 The war horse is a vain hope for victory,
   and by its great might it cannot save.

18 Behold, the eye of the LORD is on those who fear him,
   on those who hope in his steadfast love,
19 that he may deliver their soul from death,
   and keep them alive in famine.

20 Our soul waits for the LORD;
   he is our help and shield.
21 Yea, our heart is glad in him,
   because we trust in his holy name.
22 Let thy steadfast love, O LORD, be upon us,
   even as we hope in thee.

*A Psalm of David, when he feigned madness before
Abimelech, so that he drove him out, and he went away.*

34 I will bless the LORD at all times;
   his praise shall continually be in my mouth.
2 My soul makes its boast in the LORD;
   let the afflicted hear and be glad.
3 O magnify the LORD with me,
   and let us exalt his name together!

4 I sought the LORD, and he answered me,
   and delivered me from all my fears.
5 Look to him, and be radiant;
   so your r faces shall never be ashamed.

r Gk Syr Jerome: Heb *their*

6 This poor man cried, and the LORD heard him,
   and saved him out of all his troubles.
7 The angel of the LORD encamps
   around those who fear him, and delivers them.
8 O taste and see that the LORD is good!
   Happy is the man who takes refuge in him!
9 O fear the LORD, you his saints,
   for those who fear him have no want!
10 The young lions suffer want and hunger;
   but those who seek the LORD lack no good thing.

11 Come, O sons, listen to me,
   I will teach you the fear of the LORD.
12 What man is there who desires life,
   and covets many days, that he may enjoy good?
13 Keep your tongue from evil,
   and your lips from speaking deceit.
14 Depart from evil, and do good;
   seek peace, and pursue it.

15 The eyes of the LORD are toward the righteous,
   and his ears toward their cry.
16 The face of the LORD is against evildoers,
   to cut off the remembrance of them from the earth.
17 When the righteous cry for help, the LORD hears,
   and delivers them out of all their troubles.
18 The LORD is near to the brokenhearted,
   and saves the crushed in spirit.

19 Many are the afflictions of the righteous;
   but the LORD delivers him out of them all.
20 He keeps all his bones;
   not one of them is broken.
21 Evil shall slay the wicked;
   and those who hate the righteous will be condemned.
22 The LORD redeems the life of his servants;
   none of those who take refuge in him will be con-
      demned.

A Psalm of David.

35 Contend, O LORD, with those who contend with me;
   fight against those who fight against me!
2 Take hold of shield and buckler,
   and rise for my help!
3 Draw the spear and javelin
   against my pursuers!
Say to my soul,
   "I am your deliverance!"

4 Let them be put to shame and dishonor
   who seek after my life!

Let them be turned back and confounded
  who devise evil against me!
[5] Let them be like chaff before the wind,
  with the angel of the LORD driving them on!
[6] Let their way be dark and slippery,
  with the angel of the LORD pursuing them!

[7] For without cause they hid their net for me;
  without cause they dug a pit [s] for my life.
[8] Let ruin come upon them unawares!
  And let the net which they hid ensnare them;
  let them fall therein to ruin!

[9] Then my soul shall rejoice in the LORD,
  exulting in his deliverance.
[10] All my bones shall say,
  "O LORD, who is like thee,
thou who deliverest the weak
  from him who is too strong for him,
  the weak and needy from him who despoils him?"

[11] Malicious witnesses rise up;
  they ask me of things that I know not.
[12] They requite me evil for good;
  my soul is forlorn.
[13] But I, when they were sick—
  I wore sackcloth,
  I afflicted myself with fasting.
I prayed with head bowed [t] on my bosom,

[14]   as though I grieved for my friend or my brother;
I went about as one who laments his mother,
  bowed down and in mourning.

[15] But at my stumbling they gathered in glee,
  they gathered together against me;
cripples whom I knew not
  slandered me without ceasing;
[16] they impiously mocked more and more, [u]
  gnashing at me with their teeth.

[17] How long, O LORD, wilt thou look on?

Rescue me from their ravages,
  my life from the lions!
[18] Then I will thank thee in the great congregation;
  in the mighty throng I will praise thee.

[19] Let not those rejoice over me
  who are wrongfully my foes,
and let not those wink the eye
  who hate me without cause.
[20] For they do not speak peace,
  but against those who are quiet in the land
  they conceive words of deceit.
[21] They open wide their mouths against me;
  they say, "Aha, Aha!
  our eyes have seen it!"

[22] Thou hast seen, O LORD; be not silent!
  O Lord, be not far from me!
[23] Bestir thyself, and awake for my right,
  for my cause, my God and my Lord!
[24] Vindicate me, O LORD, my God, according to thy righteousness;
  and let them not rejoice over me!
[25] Let them not say to themselves,
  "Aha, we have our heart's desire!"
Let them not say, "We have swallowed him up."

[26] Let them be put to shame and confusion altogether
  who rejoice at my calamity!
Let them be clothed with shame and dishonor
  who magnify themselves against me!

[27] Let those who desire my vindication
  shout for joy and be glad,
  and say evermore,
"Great is the LORD,
  who delights in the welfare of his servant!"
[28] Then my tongue shall tell of thy righteousness
  and of thy praise all the day long.

*To the choirmaster. A Psalm of David,
the servant of the* LORD.

36 Transgression speaks to the wicked
  deep in his heart;
there is no fear of God
  before his eyes.
[2] For he flatters himself in his own eyes
  that his iniquity cannot be found out and hated.
[3] The words of his mouth are mischief and deceit;
  he has ceased to act wisely and do good.
[4] He plots mischief while on his bed;
  he sets himself in a way that is not good;
  he spurns not evil.

[s] The word *pit* is transposed from the preceding line
[u] Cn Compare Gk: Heb *like the profanest of mockers of a cake*
[t] Or *My prayer turned back*

5 Thy steadfast love, O LORD, extends to the heavens,
  thy faithfulness to the clouds.
6 Thy righteousness is like the mountains of God,
  thy judgments are like the great deep;
  man and beast thou savest, O LORD.

7 How precious is thy steadfast love, O God!
  The children of men take refuge in the shadow of thy
    wings.
8 They feast on the abundance of thy house,
  and thou givest them drink from the river of thy
    delights.
9 For with thee is the fountain of life;
  in thy light do we see light.

10 O continue thy steadfast love to those who know thee,
  and thy salvation to the upright of heart!
11 Let not the foot of arrogance come upon me,
  nor the hand of the wicked drive me away.
12 There the evildoers lie prostrate,
  they are thrust down, unable to rise.

A Psalm of David.

37 Fret not yourself because of the wicked,
    be not envious of wrongdoers!
2 For they will soon fade like the grass,
  and wither like the green herb.
3 Trust in the LORD, and do good;
  so you will dwell in the land, and enjoy security.
4 Take delight in the LORD,
  and he will give you the desires of your heart.

5 Commit your way to the LORD;
  trust in him, and he will act.
6 He will bring forth your vindication as the light,
  and your right as the noonday.

7 Be still before the LORD, and wait patiently for him;
  fret not yourself over him who prospers in his way,
  over the man who carries out evil devices!

8 Refrain from anger, and forsake wrath!
  Fret not yourself; it tends only to evil.
9 For the wicked shall be cut off;
  but those who wait for the LORD shall possess the land.

10 Yet a little while, and the wicked will be no more;
  though you look well at his place, he will not be there.
11 But the meek shall possess the land,
  and delight themselves in abundant prosperity.

12 The wicked plots against the righteous,
  and gnashes his teeth at him;
13 but the LORD laughs at the wicked,
  for he sees that his day is coming.

14 The wicked draw the sword and bend their bows,
  to bring down the poor and needy,
  to slay those who walk uprightly;
15 their sword shall enter their own heart,
  and their bows shall be broken.

16 Better is a little that the righteous has
  than the abundance of many wicked.
17 For the arms of the wicked shall be broken;
  but the LORD upholds the righteous.

18 The LORD knows the days of the blameless,
  and their heritage will abide for ever;
19 they are not put to shame in evil times,
  in the days of famine they have abundance.

20 But the wicked perish;
  the enemies of the LORD are like the glory of the
    pastures,
  they vanish—like smoke they vanish away.

21 The wicked borrows, and cannot pay back,
  but the righteous is generous and gives;
22 for those blessed by the LORD shall possess the land,
  but those cursed by him shall be cut off.

23 The steps of a man are from the LORD,
  and he establishes him in whose way he delights;
24 though he fall, he shall not be cast headlong,
  for the LORD is the stay of his hand.

25 I have been young, and now am old;
  yet I have not seen the righteous forsaken
  or his children begging bread.
26 He is ever giving liberally and lending,
  and his children become a blessing.

27 Depart from evil, and do good;
  so shall you abide for ever.
28 For the LORD loves justice;
  he will not forsake his saints.

The righteous shall be preserved for ever,
  but the children of the wicked shall be cut off.
29 The righteous shall possess the land,
  and dwell upon it for ever.

30 The mouth of the righteous utters wisdom,
  and his tongue speaks justice.

³¹ The law of his God is in his heart;
  his steps do not slip.

³² The wicked watches the righteous,
  and seeks to slay him.
³³ The LORD will not abandon him to his power,
  or let him be condemned when he is brought to trial.

³⁴ Wait for the LORD, and keep to his way,
  and he will exalt you to possess the land;
  you will look on the destruction of the wicked.

³⁵ I have seen a wicked man overbearing,
  and towering like a cedar of Lebanon.ᵛ
³⁶ Again Iʷ passed by, and, lo, he was no more;
  though I sought him, he could not be found.

³⁷ Mark the blameless man, and behold the upright,
  for there is posterity for the man of peace.
³⁸ But transgressors shall be altogether destroyed;
  the posterity of the wicked shall be cut off.

³⁹ The salvation of the righteous is from the LORD;
  he is their refuge in the time of trouble.
⁴⁰ The LORD helps them and delivers them;
  he delivers them from the wicked, and saves them,
  because they take refuge in him.

A Psalm of David, for the memorial offering.

38 O LORD, rebuke me not in thy anger,
    nor chasten me in thy wrath!
² For thy arrows have sunk into me,
  and thy hand has come down on me.

³ There is no soundness in my flesh
  because of thy indignation;
there is no health in my bones
  because of my sin.
⁴ For my iniquities have gone over my head;
  they weigh like a burden too heavy for me.

⁵ My wounds grow foul and fester
  because of my foolishness,
⁶ I am utterly bowed down and prostrate;
  all the day I go about mourning.
⁷ For my loins are filled with burning,
  and there is no soundness in my flesh.
⁸ I am utterly spent and crushed;
  I groan because of the tumult of my heart.

⁹ Lord, all my longing is known to thee,
  my sighing is not hidden from thee.

¹⁰ My heart throbs, my strength fails me;
  and the light of my eyes—it also has gone from me.
¹¹ My friends and companions stand aloof from my plague,
  and my kinsmen stand afar off.

¹² Those who seek my life lay their snares,
  those who seek my hurt speak of ruin,
  and meditate treachery all the day long.

¹³ But I am like a deaf man, I do not hear,
  like a dumb man who does not open his mouth.
¹⁴ Yea, I am like a man who does not hear,
  and in whose mouth are no rebukes.

¹⁵ But for thee, O LORD, do I wait;
  it is thou, O LORD my God, who wilt answer.
¹⁶ For I pray, "Only let them not rejoice over me,
  who boast against me when my foot slips!"

¹⁷ For I am ready to fall,
  and my pain is ever with me.
¹⁸ I confess my iniquity,
  I am sorry for my sin.
¹⁹ Those who are my foes without causeˣ are mighty,
  and many are those who hate me wrongfully.
²⁰ Those who render me evil for good
  are my adversaries because I follow after good.

²¹ Do not forsake me, O LORD!
  O my God, be not far from me!
²² Make haste to help me,
  O Lord, my salvation!

To the choirmaster: to Jeduthun. A Psalm of David.

39 I said, "I will guard my ways,
    that I may not sin with my tongue;
I will bridleʸ my mouth,
  so long as the wicked are in my presence."
² I was dumb and silent,
  I held my peace to no avail;
my distress grew worse,
³   my heart became hot within me.
As I mused, the fire burned;
  then I spoke with my tongue:

ᵛ Gk: Heb obscure   ʷ Gk Syr Jerome: Heb *he*   ˣ Cn: Heb *living*   ʸ Heb *muzzle*

4 "LORD, let me know my end,
and what is the measure of my days;
let me know how fleeting my life is!
5 Behold, thou hast made my days a few handbreadths,
and my lifetime is as nothing in thy sight.
Surely every man stands as a mere breath!   *Selah*
6   Surely man goes about as a shadow!
Surely for nought are they in turmoil;
man heaps up, and knows not who will gather!

7 "And now, Lord, for what do I wait?
My hope is in thee.
8 Deliver me from all my transgressions.
Make me not the scorn of the fool!
9 I am dumb, I do not open my mouth;
for it is thou who hast done it.
10 Remove thy stroke from me;
I am spent by the blows z of thy hand.
11 When thou dost chasten man
with rebukes for sin,
thou dost consume like a moth what is dear to him;
surely every man is a mere breath!   *Selah*

12 "Hear my prayer, O LORD,
and give ear to my cry;
hold not thy peace at my tears!
For I am thy passing guest,
a sojourner, like all my fathers.
13 Look away from me, that I may know gladness,
before I depart and be no more!"

To the choirmaster. A Psalm of David.

40 I waited patiently for the LORD;
he inclined to me and heard my cry.
2 He drew me up from the desolate pit,ᵃ
out of the miry bog,
and set my feet upon a rock,
making my steps secure.
3 He put a new song in my mouth,
a song of praise to our God.
Many will see and fear,
and put their trust in the LORD.

4 Blessed is the man who makes the LORD his trust,
who does not turn to the proud,
to those who go astray after false gods!
5 Thou hast multiplied, O LORD my God,
thy wondrous deeds and thy thoughts toward us;
none can compare with thee!
Were I to proclaim and tell of them,
they would be more than can be numbered.

6 Sacrifice and offering thou dost not desire;
but thou hast given me an open ear.ᵇ
Burnt offering and sin offering
thou hast not required.
7 Then I said, "Lo, I come;
in the roll of the book it is written of me;
8 I delight to do thy will, O my God;
thy law is within my heart."

9 I have told the glad news of deliverance
in the great congregation;
lo, I have not restrained my lips,
as thou knowest, O LORD.
10 I have not hid thy saving help within my heart,
I have spoken of thy faithfulness and thy salvation;
I have not concealed thy steadfast love and thy faithfulness
from the great congregation.

11 Do not thou, O LORD, withhold
thy mercy from me,
let thy steadfast love and thy faithfulness
ever preserve me!
12 For evils have encompassed me
without number;
my iniquities have overtaken me,
till I cannot see;
they are more than the hairs of my head;
my heart fails me.

13 Be pleased, O LORD, to deliver me!
O LORD, make haste to help me!
14 Let them be put to shame and confusion altogether
who seek to snatch away my life;
let them be turned back and brought to dishonor
who desire my hurt!
15 Let them be appalled because of their shame
who say to me, "Aha, Aha!"

16 But may all who seek thee
rejoice and be glad in thee;
may those who love thy salvation
say continually, "Great is the LORD!"
17 As for me, I am poor and needy;
but the Lord takes thought for me.
Thou art my help and my deliverer;
do not tarry, O my God!

To the choirmaster. A Psalm of David.

41 Blessed is he who considers the poor! ᶜ
The LORD delivers him in the day of trouble;
2 the LORD protects him and keeps him alive;

z Heb *hostility*   ª Cn: Heb *pit of tumult*   ᵇ Heb *ears thou hast dug for me*   ᶜ Or *weak*

he is called blessed in the land;
    thou dost not give him up to the will of his enemies.
3 The LORD sustains him on his sickbed;
    in his illness thou healest all his infirmities.d

4 As for me, I said, "O LORD, be gracious to me;
    heal me, for I have sinned against thee!"
5 My enemies say of me in malice:
    "When will he die, and his name perish?"
6 And when one comes to see me, he utters empty words,
    while his heart gathers mischief;
    when he goes out, he tells it abroad.
7 All who hate me whisper together about me;
    they imagine the worst for me.

8 They say, "A deadly thing has fastened upon him;
    he will not rise again from where he lies."
9 Even my bosom friend in whom I trusted,
    who ate of my bread, has lifted his heel against me.
10 But do thou, O LORD, be gracious to me,
    and raise me up, that I may requite them!

11 By this I know that thou art pleased with me,
    in that my enemy has not triumphed over me.
12 But thou hast upheld me because of my integrity,
    and set me in thy presence for ever.

13 Blessed be the LORD, the God of Israel,
    from everlasting to everlasting!
    Amen and Amen.

BOOK II

To the choirmaster. A Maskil of the Sons of Korah.

42 As a hart longs for flowing streams,
    so longs my soul for thee, O God.
2 My soul thirsts for God,
    for the living God.
When shall I come and behold
    the face of God?
3 My tears have been my food
    day and night,
while men say to me continually,
    "Where is your God?"

4 These things I remember,
    as I pour out my soul:
how I went with the throng,
    and led them in procession to the house of God,
with glad shouts and songs of thanksgiving,
    a multitude keeping festival.

d Heb *thou changest all his bed*

5 Why are you cast down, O my soul,
    and why are you disquieted within me?
Hope in God; for I shall again praise him,
    my help and my God.

6 My soul is cast down within me,
    therefore I remember thee
from the land of Jordan and of Hermon,
    from Mount Mizar.

7 Deep calls to deep
    at the thunder of thy cataracts;
all thy waves and thy billows
    have gone over me.
8 By day the LORD commands his steadfast love;
    and at night his song is with me,
    a prayer to the God of my life.

9 I say to God, my rock:
    "Why hast thou forgotten me?
Why go I mourning
    because of the oppression of the enemy?"
10 As with a deadly wound in my body,
    my adversaries taunt me,
while they say to me continually,
    "Where is your God?"

11 Why are you cast down, O my soul,
    and why are you disquieted within me?
Hope in God; for I shall again praise him,
    my help and my God.

43 Vindicate me, O God, and defend my cause
    against an ungodly people;
from deceitful and unjust men deliver me!
2 For thou art the God in whom I take refuge;
    why hast thou cast me off?
Why go I mourning
    because of the oppression of the enemy?

3 Oh send out thy light and thy truth;
    let them lead me,
let them bring me to thy holy hill
    and to thy dwelling!
4 Then I will go to the altar of God,

to God my exceeding joy;
and I will praise thee with the lyre,
O God, my God.

5 Why are you cast down, O my soul,
and why are you disquieted within me?
Hope in God; for I shall again praise him,
my help and my God.

To the choirmaster. A Maskil of the Sons of Korah.

44 We have heard with our ears, O God,
our fathers have told us,
what deeds thou didst perform in their days,
in the days of old:
2 thou with thy own hand didst drive out the nations,
but them thou didst plant;
thou didst afflict the peoples,
but them thou didst set free;
3 for not by their own sword did they win the land,
nor did their own arm give them victory;
but thy right hand, and thy arm,
and the light of thy countenance;
for thou didst delight in them.

4 Thou art my King and my God,
who ordainest[e] victories for Jacob.
5 Through thee we push down our foes;
through thy name we tread down our assailants.
6 For not in my bow do I trust,
nor can my sword save me.
7 But thou hast saved us from our foes,
and hast put to confusion those who hate us.
8 In God we have boasted continually,
and we will give thanks to thy name for ever.   *Selah*

9 Yet thou hast cast us off and abased us,
and hast not gone out with our armies.
10 Thou hast made us turn back from the foe;
and our enemies have gotten spoil.
11 Thou hast made us like sheep for slaughter,
and hast scattered us among the nations.
12 Thou hast sold thy people for a trifle,
demanding no high price for them.

13 Thou hast made us the taunt of our neighbors,
the derision and scorn of those about us.
14 Thou hast made us a byword among the nations,
a laughingstock[f] among the peoples.
15 All day long my disgrace is before me,
and shame has covered my face,
16 at the words of the taunters and revilers,
at the sight of the enemy and the avenger.

17 All this has come upon us,
though we have not forgotten thee,
or been false to thy covenant.
18 Our heart has not turned back,
nor have our steps departed from thy way,
19 that thou shouldst have broken us in the place of jackals,
and covered us with deep darkness.

20 If we had forgotten the name of our God,
or spread forth our hands to a strange god,
21 would not God discover this?
For he knows the secrets of the heart.
22 Nay, for thy sake we are slain all the day long,
and accounted as sheep for the slaughter.

23 Rouse thyself! Why sleepest thou, O Lord?
Awake! Do not cast us off for ever!
24 Why dost thou hide thy face?
Why dost thou forget our affliction and oppression?
25 For our soul is bowed down to the dust;
our body cleaves to the ground.
26 Rise up, come to our help!
Deliver us for the sake of thy steadfast love!

*To the choirmaster: according to Lilies.
A Maskil of the Sons of Korah; a love song.*

45 My heart overflows with a goodly theme;
I address my verses to the king;
my tongue is like the pen of a ready scribe.
2 You are the fairest of the sons of men;
grace is poured upon your lips;
therefore God has blessed you for ever.
3 Gird your sword upon your thigh, O mighty one,
in your glory and majesty!

4 In your majesty ride forth victoriously
for the cause of truth and to defend[g] the right;
let your right hand teach you dread deeds!
5 Your arrows are sharp
in the heart of the king's enemies;
the peoples fall under you.

6 Your divine throne[h] endures for ever and ever.
Your royal scepter is a scepter of equity;
7   you love righteousness and hate wickedness.
Therefore God, your God, has anointed you
with the oil of gladness above your fellows;
8   your robes are all fragrant with myrrh and aloes and
cassia.
From ivory palaces stringed instruments make you glad;
9   daughters of kings are among your ladies of honor;
at your right hand stands the queen in gold of Ophir.

---

e Gk Syr: Heb *Thou art my King, O God; ordain*   f Heb *a shaking of the head*   g Cn: Heb *and the meekness of*
h Or *Your throne is a throne of God,* or *Thy throne, O God*

¹⁰ Hear, O daughter, consider, and incline your ear;
    forget your people and your father's house;
¹¹   and the king will desire your beauty.
    Since he is your lord, bow to him;
¹²   the people[i] of Tyre will sue your favor with gifts,
¹³   the richest of the people with all kinds of wealth.

    The princess is decked in her chamber with gold-woven
        robes;[j]
¹⁴   in many-colored robes she is led to the king,
    with her virgin companions, her escort,[k] in her train.
¹⁵ With joy and gladness they are led along
    as they enter the palace of the king.

¹⁶ Instead of your fathers shall be your sons;
    you will make them princes in all the earth.
¹⁷ I will cause your name to be celebrated in all generations;
    therefore the peoples will praise you for ever and ever.

To the choirmaster. A Psalm of the
Sons of Korah. According to
Alamoth. A Song.

46 God is our refuge and strength,
    a very present[l] help in trouble.
² Therefore we will not fear though the earth should
    change,
    though the mountains shake in the heart of the sea;
³ though its waters roar and foam,
    though the mountains tremble with its tumult.   *Selah*

⁴ There is a river whose streams make glad the city of God,
    the holy habitation of the Most High.
⁵ God is in the midst of her, she shall not be moved;
    God will help her right early.
⁶ The nations rage, the kingdoms totter;
    he utters his voice, the earth melts.
⁷ The Lord of hosts is with us;
    the God of Jacob is our refuge.[m]   *Selah*

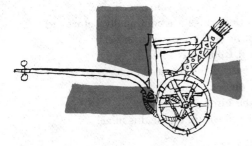

⁸ Come, behold the works of the Lord,
    how he has wrought desolations in the earth.
⁹ He makes wars cease to the end of the earth;
    he breaks the bow, and shatters the spear,
    he burns the chariots with fire!

¹⁰ "Be still, and know that I am God.
    I am exalted among the nations,
    I am exalted in the earth!"
¹¹ The Lord of hosts is with us;
    the God of Jacob is our refuge.[m]   *Selah*

To the choirmaster. A Psalm of the
Sons of Korah.

47 Clap your hands, all peoples!
    Shout to God with loud songs of joy!
² For the Lord, the Most High, is terrible,
    a great king over all the earth.
³ He subdued peoples under us,
    and nations under our feet.
⁴ He chose our heritage for us,
    the pride of Jacob whom he loves.   *Selah*

⁵ God has gone up with a shout,
    the Lord with the sound of a trumpet.
⁶ Sing praises to God, sing praises!
    Sing praises to our King, sing praises!
⁷ For God is the king of all the earth;
    sing praises with a psalm![n]

⁸ God reigns over the nations;
    God sits on his holy throne.
⁹ The princes of the peoples gather
    as the people of the God of Abraham.
    For the shields of the earth belong to God;
    he is highly exalted!

A Song. A Psalm of the Sons of Korah.

48 Great is the Lord and greatly to be praised
    in the city of our God!
² His holy mountain, beautiful in elevation,
    is the joy of all the earth,
    Mount Zion, in the far north,
    the city of the great King.
³ Within her citadels God has shown himself a sure defense.

⁴ For lo, the kings assembled,
    they came on together.
⁵ As soon as they saw it, they were astounded,
    they were in panic, they took to flight;
⁶ trembling took hold of them there,
    anguish as of a woman in travail.
⁷ By the east wind thou didst shatter the ships of Tarshish.
⁸ As we have heard, so have we seen
    in the city of the Lord of hosts,
    in the city of our God,
    which God establishes for ever.   *Selah*

---

i Heb *daughter*   j Or *people. All glorious is the princess within, gold embroidery is her clothing*   k Heb *those brought to you*
l Or *well proved*   m Or *fortress*   n Heb *Maskil*

9 We have thought on thy steadfast love, O God,
in the midst of thy temple.
10 As thy name, O God,
so thy praise reaches to the ends of the earth.
Thy right hand is filled with victory;
11 let Mount Zion be glad!
Let the daughters of Judah rejoice because of thy judgments!

12 Walk about Zion, go round about her,
number her towers,
13 consider well her ramparts,
go through her citadels;
that you may tell the next generation
14 that this is God,
our God for ever and ever.
He will be our guide for ever.

To the choirmaster. A Psalm of the Sons of Korah.

49 Hear this, all peoples!
Give ear, all inhabitants of the world,
2 both low and high,
rich and poor together!
3 My mouth shall speak wisdom;
the meditation of my heart shall be understanding.
4 I will incline my ear to a proverb;
I will solve my riddle to the music of the lyre.

5 Why should I fear in times of trouble,
when the iniquity of my persecutors surrounds me,
6 men who trust in their wealth
and boast of the abundance of their riches?
7 Truly no man can ransom himself,[o]
or give to God the price of his life,
8 for the ransom of his[p] life is costly,
and can never suffice,
9 that he should continue to live on for ever,
and never see the Pit.

10 Yea, he shall see that even the wise die,
the fool and the stupid alike must perish
and leave their wealth to others.
11 Their graves[q] are their homes for ever,
their dwelling places to all generations,
though they named lands their own.
12 Man cannot abide in his pomp,
he is like the beasts that perish.

13 This is the fate of those who have foolish confidence,
the end of those[r] who are pleased with their portion.
Selah
14 Like sheep they are appointed for Sheol;
Death shall be their shepherd;

straight to the grave they descend,[s]
and their form shall waste away;
Sheol shall be their home.[t]
15 But God will ransom my soul from the power of Sheol,
for he will receive me.
Selah

16 Be not afraid when one becomes rich,
when the glory[u] of his house increases.
17 For when he dies he will carry nothing away;
his glory[u] will not go down after him.
18 Though, while he lives, he counts himself happy,
and though a man gets praise when he does well for himself,
19 he will go to the generation of his fathers,
who will never more see the light.
20 Man cannot abide in his pomp,
he is like the beasts that perish.

A Psalm of Asaph.

50 The Mighty One, God the LORD,
speaks and summons the earth
from the rising of the sun to its setting.
2 Out of Zion, the perfection of beauty,
God shines forth.

3 Our God comes, he does not keep silence,
before him is a devouring fire,
round about him a mighty tempest.
4 He calls to the heavens above
and to the earth, that he may judge his people:
5 "Gather to me my faithful ones,
who made a covenant with me by sacrifice!"
6 The heavens declare his righteousness,
for God himself is judge!
Selah

7 "Hear, O my people, and I will speak,
O Israel, I will testify against you.
I am God, your God.
8 I do not reprove you for your sacrifices;
your burnt offerings are continually before me.
9 I will accept no bull from your house,
nor he-goat from your folds.
10 For every beast of the forest is mine,
the cattle on a thousand hills.
11 I know all the birds of the air,[v]
and all that moves in the field is mine.

12 "If I were hungry, I would not tell you;
for the world and all that is in it is mine.
13 Do I eat the flesh of bulls,
or drink the blood of goats?
14 Offer to God a sacrifice of thanksgiving,[w]

[o] Another reading is *no man can ransom his brother*   [p] Gk: Heb *their*   [q] Gk Syr Compare Tg: Heb *their inward* (thought)
[r] Tg: Heb *after them*   [s] Cn: Heb *the upright shall have dominion over them in the morning*   [t] Heb uncertain   [u] Or *wealth*
[v] Gk Syr Tg: Heb *mountains*   [w] Or *make thanksgiving your sacrifice to God*

and pay your vows to the Most High;
15 and call upon me in the day of trouble;
  I will deliver you, and you shall glorify me."

16 But to the wicked God says:
  "What right have you to recite my statutes,
    or take my covenant on your lips?
17 For you hate discipline,
    and you cast my words behind you.
18 If you see a thief, you are a friend of his;
    and you keep company with adulterers.

19 "You give your mouth free rein for evil,
    and your tongue frames deceit.
20 You sit and speak against your brother;
    you slander your own mother's son.
21 These things you have done and I have been silent;
    you thought that I was one like yourself.
  But now I rebuke you, and lay the charge before you.

22 "Mark this, then, you who forget God,
    lest I rend, and there be none to deliver!
23 He who brings thanksgiving as his sacrifice honors me;
    to him who orders his way aright
    I will show the salvation of God!"

To the choirmaster. A Psalm of David, when Nathan the prophet came to him, after he had gone in to Bathsheba.

51 Have mercy on me, O God, according to thy stead-
    fast love;
  according to thy abundant mercy blot out my transgres-
    sions.
2 Wash me thoroughly from my iniquity,
    and cleanse me from my sin!

3 For I know my transgressions,
    and my sin is ever before me.
4 Against thee, thee only, have I sinned,
    and done that which is evil in thy sight,
    so that thou art justified in thy sentence
    and blameless in thy judgment.
5 Behold, I was brought forth in iniquity,
    and in sin did my mother conceive me.

6 Behold, thou desirest truth in the inward being;
    therefore teach me wisdom in my secret heart.
7 Purge me with hyssop, and I shall be clean;
    wash me, and I shall be whiter than snow.
8 Fill ˣ me with joy and gladness;
    let the bones which thou hast broken rejoice.
9 Hide thy face from my sins,
    and blot out all my iniquities.

10 Create in me a clean heart, O God,
    and put a new and right ʸ spirit within me.
11 Cast me not away from thy presence,
    and take not thy holy Spirit from me.
12 Restore to me the joy of thy salvation,
    and uphold me with a willing spirit.
13 Then I will teach transgressors thy ways,
    and sinners will return to thee.
14 Deliver me from bloodguiltiness,ᶻ O God,
    thou God of my salvation,
    and my tongue will sing aloud of thy deliverance.

15 O Lord, open thou my lips,
    and my mouth shall show forth thy praise.
16 For thou hast no delight in sacrifice;
    were I to give a burnt offering,
    thou wouldst not be pleased.
17 The sacrifice acceptable to God ᵃ is a broken spirit;
    a broken and contrite heart, O God, thou wilt not
    despise.

18 Do good to Zion in thy good pleasure;
    rebuild the walls of Jerusalem,
19 then wilt thou delight in right sacrifices,
    in burnt offerings and whole burnt offerings;
    then bulls will be offered on thy altar.

To the choirmaster. A Maskil of David, when Doeg, the Edomite, came and told Saul, "David has come to the house of Ahimelech."

52 Why do you boast, O mighty man,
    of mischief done against the godly? ᵇ
2 All the day you are plotting destruction.
  Your tongue is like a sharp razor,
    you worker of treachery.
3 You love evil more than good,
    and lying more than speaking the truth.   *Selah*
4 You love all words that devour,
    O deceitful tongue.

5 But God will break you down for ever;
    he will snatch and tear you from your tent;
    he will uproot you from the land of the living. *Selah*

ˣ Syr: Heb *Make to hear*   ʸ Or *steadfast*   ᶻ Or *death*   ᵃ Or *My sacrifice, O God*
ᵇ Cn Compare Syr: Heb *the kindness of God*

6 The righteous shall see, and fear,
    and shall laugh at him, saying,
7 "See the man who would not make God his refuge,
  but trusted in the abundance of his riches,
    and sought refuge in his wealth!" c

8 But I am like a green olive tree
    in the house of God.
  I trust in the steadfast love of God
    for ever and ever.
9 I will thank thee for ever,
    because thou hast done it.
  I will proclaim d thy name, for it is good,
    in the presence of the godly.

*To the choirmaster: according to Mahalath. A Maskil of
David.*

53 The fool says in his heart,
      "There is no God."
  They are corrupt, doing abominable iniquity;
    there is none that does good.

2 God looks down from heaven
    upon the sons of men
  to see if there are any that are wise,
    that seek after God.

3 They have all fallen away;
    they are all alike depraved;
  there is none that does good,
    no, not one.

4 Have those who work evil no understanding,
    who eat up my people as they eat bread,
  and do not call upon God?

5 There they are, in great terror,
    in terror such as has not been!
  For God will scatter the bones of the ungodly; e
    they will be put to shame,f for God has rejected them.

6 O that deliverance for Israel would come from Zion!
    When God restores the fortunes of his people,
  Jacob will rejoice and Israel be glad.

*To the choirmaster: with stringed instruments. A Maskil
of David, when the Ziphites went and told Saul, "David
is in hiding among us."*

54 Save me, O God, by thy name,
      and vindicate me by thy might.
2 Hear my prayer, O God;
    give ear to the words of my mouth.

3 For insolent g men have risen against me,
    ruthless men seek my life;
  they do not set God before them.   Selah

4 Behold, God is my helper;
    the Lord is the upholder h of my life.
5 He will requite my enemies with evil;
    in thy faithfulness put an end to them.

6 With a freewill offering I will sacrifice to thee;
    I will give thanks to thy name, O LORD, for it is good.
7 For thou hast delivered me from every trouble,
    and my eye has looked in triumph on my enemies.

*To the choirmaster: with stringed instruments. A Maskil
of David.*

55 Give ear to my prayer, O God;
      and hide not thyself from my supplication!
2 Attend to me, and answer me;
    I am overcome by my trouble.
3 I am distraught by the noise of the enemy,
    because of the oppression of the wicked.
  For they bring i trouble upon me,
    and in anger they cherish enmity against me.

4 My heart is in anguish within me,
    the terrors of death have fallen upon me.
5 Fear and trembling come upon me,
    and horror overwhelms me.
6 And I say, "O that I had wings like a dove!
    I would fly away and be at rest;
7 yea, I would wander afar,
    I would lodge in the wilderness,   Selah
8 I would haste to find me a shelter
    from the raging wind and tempest."

9 Destroy their plans,j O Lord, confuse their tongues;
    for I see violence and strife in the city.
10 Day and night they go around it
    on its walls;
  and mischief and trouble are within it,
11   ruin is in its midst;
  oppression and fraud
    do not depart from its market place.

12 It is not an enemy who taunts me—
    then I could bear it;
  it is not an adversary who deals insolently with me—
    then I could hide from him.
13 But it is you, my equal,
    my companion, my familiar friend.
14 We used to hold sweet converse together;

c Syr Tg: Heb *his destruction*   d Cn: Heb *wait for*   e Cn Compare Gk Syr: Heb *him who encamps against you*
f Gk: Heb *you will put to shame*   g Another reading is *strangers*   h Gk Syr Jerome: Heb *of* or *with those who uphold*
i Cn Compare Gk: Heb *they cause to totter*   j Tg: Heb lacks *their plans*

within God's house we walked in fellowship.
15 Let death [k] come upon them;
  let them go down to Sheol alive;
  let them go away in terror into their graves.[l]

16 But I call upon God;
  and the LORD will save me.
17 Evening and morning and at noon
  I utter my complaint and moan,
  and he will hear my voice.
18 He will deliver my soul in safety
  from the battle that I wage,
  for many are arrayed against me.
19 God will give ear, and humble them,
  he who is enthroned from of old;
  because they keep no law,[m]
  and do not fear God.   Selah

20 My companion stretched out his hand against his friends,
  he violated his covenant.
21 His speech was smoother than butter,
  yet war was in his heart;
  his words were softer than oil,
  yet they were drawn swords.

22 Cast your burden [n] on the LORD,
  and he will sustain you;
  he will never permit
  the righteous to be moved.

23 But thou, O God, wilt cast them down
  into the lowest pit;
  men of blood and treachery
  shall not live out half their days.
  But I will trust in thee.

*To the choirmaster: according to The Dove on Far-off
Terebinths. A Miktam of David, when the Philistines
seized him in Gath.*

56 Be gracious to me, O God,
    for men trample upon me;
  all day long foemen oppress me;
2 my enemies trample upon me all day long,
  for many fight against me proudly.
3 When I am afraid,
  I put my trust in thee.
4 In God, whose word I praise,
  in God I trust without a fear.
  What can flesh do to me?

5 All day long they seek to injure my cause;
  all their thoughts are against me for evil.
6 They band themselves together, they lurk,

they watch my steps.
  As they have waited for my life,
7   so recompense [o] them for their crime;
  in wrath cast down the peoples, O God!

8 Thou hast kept count of my tossings;
  put thou my tears in thy bottle!
  Are they not in thy book?
9 Then my enemies will be turned back
  in the day when I call.
  This I know, that [p] God is for me.
10 In God, whose word I praise,
  in the LORD, whose word I praise,
11 in God I trust without a fear.
  What can man do to me?

12 My vows to thee I must perform, O God;
  I will render thank offerings to thee.
13 For thou hast delivered my soul from death,
  yea, my feet from falling,
  that I may walk before God
  in the light of life.

*To the choirmaster: according to Do Not Destroy. A
Miktam of David, when he fled from Saul, in the cave.*

57 Be merciful to me, O God, be merciful to me,
    for in thee my soul takes refuge;
  in the shadow of thy wings I will take refuge,
  till the storms of destruction pass by.
2 I cry to God Most High,
  to God who fulfils his purpose for me.
3 He will send from heaven and save me,
  he will put to shame those who trample upon me. Selah
  God will send forth his steadfast love and his faithfulness!

4 I lie in the midst of lions
  that greedily devour [q] the sons of men;
  their teeth are spears and arrows,
  their tongues sharp swords.

5 Be exalted, O God, above the heavens!
  Let thy glory be over all the earth!

6 They set a net for my steps;
  my soul was bowed down.
  They dug a pit in my way,
  but they have fallen into it themselves.   Selah

7 My heart is steadfast, O God,
  my heart is steadfast!
  I will sing and make melody!
8   Awake, my soul!
  Awake, O harp and lyre!

k Or *desolations*   l Cn: Heb *evils are in their habitation, in their midst*   m Or *do not change*   n Or *what he has given you*
o Cn: Heb *deliver*   p Or *because*   q Cn: Heb *are aflame*

I will awake the dawn!
9 I will give thanks to thee, O Lord, among the peoples;
  I will sing praises to thee among the nations.
10 For thy steadfast love is great to the heavens,
  thy faithfulness to the clouds.

11 Be exalted, O God, above the heavens!
  Let thy glory be over all the earth!

To the choirmaster: according to Do Not Destroy.
A Miktam of David.

58 Do you indeed decree what is right, you gods? [s]
  Do you judge the sons of men uprightly?
2 Nay, in your hearts you devise wrongs;
  your hands deal out violence on earth.

3 The wicked go astray from the womb,
  they err from their birth, speaking lies.
4 They have venom like the venom of a serpent,
  like the deaf adder that stops its ear,
5 so that it does not hear the voice of charmers
  or of the cunning enchanter.
6 O God, break the teeth in their mouths;
  tear out the fangs of the young lions, O Lord!
7 Let them vanish like water that runs away;
  like grass let them be trodden down and wither. [t]
8 Let them be like the snail which dissolves into slime,
  like the untimely birth that never sees the sun.
9 Sooner than your pots can feel the heat of thorns,
  whether green or ablaze, may he sweep them away!

10 The righteous will rejoice when he sees the vengeance;
  he will bathe his feet in the blood of the wicked.
11 Men will say, "Surely there is a reward for the righteous;
  surely there is a God who judges on earth."

*To the choirmaster: according to Do Not Destroy. A
Miktam of David, when Saul sent men to watch his house
in order to kill him.*

59 Deliver me from my enemies, O my God,
    protect me from those who rise up against me,
2 deliver me from those who work evil,
  and save me from bloodthirsty men.

3 For, lo, they lie in wait for my life;
  fierce men band themselves against me.
For no transgression or sin of mine, O Lord,
4 for no fault of mine, they run and make ready.

Rouse thyself, come to my help, and see!
5 Thou, Lord God of hosts, art God of Israel.
Awake to punish all the nations;
  spare none of those who treacherously plot evil. *Selah*

6 Each evening they come back,
  howling like dogs
  and prowling about the city.
7 There they are, bellowing with their mouths,
  and snarling with [u] their lips—
  for "Who," they think, "will hear us?"

8 But thou, O Lord, dost laugh at them;
  thou dost hold all the nations in derision.
9 O my Strength, I will sing praises to thee; [v]
  for thou, O God, art my fortress.
10 My God in his steadfast love will meet me;
  my God will let me look in triumph on my enemies.

11 Slay them not, lest my people forget;
  make them totter by thy power, and bring them down,
  O Lord, our shield!
12 For the sin of their mouths, the words of their lips,
  let them be trapped in their pride.
For the cursing and lies which they utter,
13 consume them in wrath,
  consume them till they are no more,
that men may know that God rules over Jacob
  to the ends of the earth.   *Selah*

14 Each evening they come back,
  howling like dogs
  and prowling about the city.
15 They roam about for food,
  and growl if they do not get their fill.

16 But I will sing of thy might;
  I will sing aloud of thy steadfast love in the morning.
For thou hast been to me a fortress
  and a refuge in the day of my distress.

s Or *mighty lords*   t Cn: Heb uncertain   u Cn: Heb *swords in*   v Syr: Heb *I will watch for thee*

17 O my Strength, I will sing praises to thee,
    for thou, O God, art my fortress,
    the God who shows me steadfast love.

To the choirmaster: according to Shushan Eduth. A
Miktam of David; for instruction; when he strove with
Aram-naharaim and with Aram-zobah, and when Joab on
his return killed twelve thousand of Edom in the Valley
of Salt.

60 O God, thou hast rejected us, broken our defenses;
    thou hast been angry; oh, restore us.
2 Thou hast made the land to quake, thou hast rent it open;
    repair its breaches, for it totters.
3 Thou hast made thy people suffer hard things;
    thou hast given us wine to drink that made us reel.

4 Thou hast set up a banner for those who fear thee,
    to rally to it from the bow.^w   *Selah*
5 That thy beloved may be delivered,
    give victory by thy right hand and answer us!

6 God has spoken in his sanctuary.^x
  "With exultation I will divide up Shechem
    and portion out the Vale of Succoth.
7 Gilead is mine; Manas′seh is mine;
  E′phraim is my helmet;
  Judah is my scepter.
8 Moab is my washbasin;
  upon Edom I cast my shoe;
  over Philistia I shout in triumph."

9 Who will bring me to the fortified city?
  Who will lead me to Edom?
10 Hast thou not rejected us, O God?
  Thou dost not go forth, O God, with our armies.
11 O grant us help against the foe,
  for vain is the help of man!
12 With God we shall do valiantly;
  it is he who will tread down our foes.

To the choirmaster: with stringed instruments. A Psalm
of David.

61 Hear my cry, O God,
    listen to my prayer;
2 from the end of the earth I call to thee,
  when my heart is faint.

Lead thou me
  to the rock that is higher than I;
3 for thou art my refuge,
  a strong tower against the enemy.

4 Let me dwell in thy tent for ever!
  Oh to be safe under the shelter of thy wings!   *Selah*
5 For thou, O God, hast heard my vows,
  thou hast given me the heritage of those who fear thy
    name.

6 Prolong the life of the king;
  may his years endure to all generations!
7 May he be enthroned for ever before God;
  bid steadfast love and faithfulness watch over him!

8 So will I ever sing praises to thy name,
  as I pay my vows day after day.

To the choirmaster: according to Jeduthun. A Psalm of
David.

62 For God alone my soul waits in silence;
    from him comes my salvation.
2 He only is my rock and my salvation,
  my fortress; I shall not be greatly moved.

3 How long will you set upon a man to shatter him, all of
    you,
  like a leaning wall, a tottering fence?
4 They only plan to thrust him down from his eminence.
  They take pleasure in falsehood.
They bless with their mouths,
  but inwardly they curse.   *Selah*

5 For God alone my soul waits in silence,
  for my hope is from him.
6 He only is my rock and my salvation,
  my fortress; I shall not be shaken.
7 On God rests my deliverance and my honor;
  my mighty rock, my refuge is God.

8 Trust in him at all times, O people;
  pour out your heart before him;
  God is a refuge for us.   *Selah*

9 Men of low estate are but a breath,
  men of high estate are a delusion;
in the balances they go up;
  they are together lighter than a breath.
10 Put no confidence in extortion,
  set no vain hopes on robbery;
  if riches increase, set not your heart on them.

11 Once God has spoken;
  twice have I heard this:
that power belongs to God;

^w Gk Syr Jerome: Heb *truth*   ^x Or *by his holiness*

¹² and that to thee, O Lord, belongs steadfast love.
For thou dost requite a man
according to his work.

*A Psalm of David, when he was in the Wilderness of
Judah.*

63 O God, thou art my God, I seek thee,
my soul thirsts for thee;
my flesh faints for thee,
as in a dry and weary land where no water is.
² So I have looked upon thee in the sanctuary,
beholding thy power and glory.
³ Because thy steadfast love is better than life,
my lips will praise thee.
⁴ So I will bless thee as long as I live;
I will lift up my hands and call on thy name.

⁵ My soul is feasted as with marrow and fat,
and my mouth praises thee with joyful lips,
⁶ when I think of thee upon my bed,
and meditate on thee in the watches of the night;
⁷ for thou hast been my help,
and in the shadow of thy wings I sing for joy.
⁸ My soul clings to thee;
thy right hand upholds me.

⁹ But those who seek to destroy my life
shall go down into the depths of the earth;
¹⁰ they shall be given over to the power of the sword,
they shall be prey for jackals.
¹¹ But the king shall rejoice in God;
all who swear by him shall glory;
for the mouths of liars will be stopped.

To the choirmaster. A Psalm of David.

64 Hear my voice, O God, in my complaint;
preserve my life from dread of the enemy,
² hide me from the secret plots of the wicked,
from the scheming of evildoers,
³ who whet their tongues like swords,
who aim bitter words like arrows,
⁴ shooting from ambush at the blameless,
shooting at him suddenly and without fear.
⁵ They hold fast to their evil purpose;

they talk of laying snares secretly,
thinking, "Who can see us? ʸ
⁶ Who can search out our crimes? ᶻ
We have thought out a cunningly conceived plot."
For the inward mind and heart of a man are deep!

⁷ But God will shoot his arrow at them;
they will be wounded suddenly.
⁸ Because of their tongue he will bring them to ruin; ᵃ
all who see them will wag their heads.
⁹ Then all men will fear;
they will tell what God has wrought,
and ponder what he has done.

¹⁰ Let the righteous rejoice in the LORD,
and take refuge in him!
Let all the upright in heart glory!

To the choirmaster. A Psalm of David. A Song.

65 Praise is due to thee,
O God, in Zion;
and to thee shall vows be performed,
² O thou who hearest prayer!
To thee shall all flesh come
³ on account of sins.
When our transgressions prevail over us,ᵇ
thou dost forgive them.
⁴ Blessed is he whom thou dost choose and bring near,
to dwell in thy courts!
We shall be satisfied with the goodness of thy house,
thy holy temple!

⁵ By dread deeds thou dost answer us with deliverance,
O God of our salvation,
who art the hope of all the ends of the earth,
and of the farthest seas;
⁶ who by thy strength hast established the mountains,
being girded with might;
⁷ who dost still the roaring of the seas,
the roaring of their waves,
the tumult of the peoples;
⁸ so that those who dwell at earth's farthest bounds
are afraid at thy signs;
thou makest the outgoings of the morning and the evening
to shout for joy.

⁹ Thou visitest the earth and waterest it,
thou greatly enrichest it;
the river of God is full of water;
thou providest their grain,
for so thou hast prepared it.

ʸ Syr: Heb *them*   ᶻ Cn: Heb *they search out crimes*   ᵃ Cn: Heb *They will bring him to ruin, their tongue being against them*
ᵇ Gk: Heb *me*

10 Thou waterest its furrows abundantly,
    settling its ridges,
  softening it with showers,
    and blessing its growth.
11 Thou crownest the year with thy bounty;
    the tracks of thy chariot drip with fatness.
12 The pastures of the wilderness drip,
    the hills gird themselves with joy,
13 the meadows clothe themselves with flocks,
    the valleys deck themselves with grain,
    they shout and sing together for joy.

To the choirmaster. A Song. A Psalm.

66 Make a joyful noise to God, all the earth;
2   sing the glory of his name;
  give to him glorious praise!
3 Say to God, "How terrible are thy deeds!
  So great is thy power that thy enemies cringe before
    thee.
4 All the earth worships thee;
  they sing praises to thee,
  sing praises to thy name."   *Selah*

5 Come and see what God has done:
  he is terrible in his deeds among men.
6 He turned the sea into dry land;
  men passed through the river on foot.
  There did we rejoice in him,
7   who rules by his might for ever,
  whose eyes keep watch on the nations—
  let not the rebellious exalt themselves.   *Selah*

8 Bless our God, O peoples,
  let the sound of his praise be heard,
9 who has kept us among the living,
  and has not let our feet slip.
10 For thou, O God, hast tested us;
  thou hast tried us as silver is tried.
11 Thou didst bring us into the net;
  thou didst lay affliction on our loins;
12 thou didst let men ride over our heads;
  we went through fire and through water;
  yet thou hast brought us forth to a spacious place.^c

c Cn Compare Gk Syr Jerome Tg: Heb *saturation*

13 I will come into thy house with burnt offerings;
  I will pay thee my vows,
14 that which my lips uttered
  and my mouth promised when I was in trouble.
15 I will offer to thee burnt offerings of fatlings,
  with the smoke of the sacrifice of rams;
  I will make an offering of bulls and goats.   *Selah*

16 Come and hear, all you who fear God,
  and I will tell what he has done for me.
17 I cried aloud to him,
  and he was extolled with my tongue.
18 If I had cherished iniquity in my heart,
  the Lord would not have listened.
19 But truly God has listened;
  he has given heed to the voice of my prayer.

20 Blessed be God,
  because he has not rejected my prayer
  or removed his steadfast love from me!

*To the choirmaster: with stringed instruments. A Psalm.
A Song.*

67 May God be gracious to us and bless us
    and make his face to shine upon us,   *Selah*
2 that thy way may be known upon earth,
  thy saving power among all nations.
3 Let the peoples praise thee, O God;
  let all the peoples praise thee!

4 Let the nations be glad and sing for joy,
  for thou dost judge the peoples with equity
  and guide the nations upon earth.   *Selah*
5 Let the peoples praise thee, O God;
  let all the peoples praise thee!

6 The earth has yielded its increase;
  God, our God, has blessed us.
7 God has blessed us;
  let all the ends of the earth fear him!

To the choirmaster. A Psalm of David. A Song.

68 Let God arise, let his enemies be scattered;
    let those who hate him flee before him!
2 As smoke is driven away, so drive them away;
  as wax melts before fire,
  let the wicked perish before God!
3 But let the righteous be joyful;
  let them exult before God;
  let them be jubilant with joy!

4 Sing to God, sing praises to his name;
    lift up a song to him who rides upon the clouds; [d]
    his name is the LORD, exult before him!

5 Father of the fatherless and protector of widows
    is God in his holy habitation.
6 God gives the desolate a home to dwell in;
    he leads out the prisoners to prosperity;
    but the rebellious dwell in a parched land.

7 O God, when thou didst go forth before thy people,
    when thou didst march through the wilderness,   *Selah*
8 the earth quaked, the heavens poured down rain,
    at the presence of God;
  yon Sinai quaked at the presence of God,
    the God of Israel.
9 Rain in abundance, O God, thou didst shed abroad;
    thou didst restore thy heritage as it languished;
10 thy flock found a dwelling in it;
    in thy goodness, O God, thou didst provide for the
    needy.

11 The Lord gives the command;
    great is the host of those who bore the tidings:
12   "The kings of the armies, they flee, they flee!"
  The women at home divide the spoil,
13   though they stay among the sheepfolds—
  the wings of a dove covered with silver,
    its pinions with green gold.
14 When the Almighty scattered kings there,
    snow fell on Zalmon.

15 O mighty mountain, mountain of Bashan;
    O many-peaked mountain, mountain of Bashan!
16 Why look you with envy, O many-peaked mountain,
    at the mount which God desired for his abode,
    yea, where the LORD will dwell for ever?

17 With mighty chariotry, twice ten thousand,
    thousands upon thousands,
    the LORD came from Sinai into the holy place. [e]
18 Thou didst ascend the high mount,
    leading captives in thy train,
    and receiving gifts among men,
  even among the rebellious, that the LORD God may dwell
    there.

19 Blessed be the Lord,
    who daily bears us up;
    God is our salvation.   *Selah*
20 Our God is a God of salvation;
    and to GOD, the Lord, belongs escape from death.

21 But God will shatter the heads of his enemies,
    the hairy crown of him who walks in his guilty ways.

22 The Lord said,
    "I will bring them back from Bashan,
    I will bring them back from the depths of the sea,
23 that you may bathe [f] your feet in blood,
    that the tongues of your dogs may have their portion
    from the foe."

24 Thy solemn processions are seen, [g] O God,
    the processions of my God, my King, into the sanc-
    tuary—
25 the singers in front, the minstrels last,
    between them maidens playing timbrels:
26 "Bless God in the great congregation,
    the LORD, O you who are of Israel's fountain!"
27 There is Benjamin, the least of them, in the lead,
    the princes of Judah in their throng,
    the princes of Zeb'ulun, the princes of Naph'tali.

28 Summon thy might, O God;
    show thy strength, O God, thou who hast wrought for
    us.
29 Because of thy temple at Jerusalem
    kings bear gifts to thee.
30 Rebuke the beasts that dwell among the reeds,
    the herd of bulls with the calves of the peoples.
  Trample [h] under foot those who lust after tribute;
    scatter the peoples who delight in war. [i]
31 Let bronze be brought from Egypt;
    let Ethiopia hasten to stretch out her hands to God.
32 Sing to God, O kingdoms of the earth;
    sing praises to the Lord,   *Selah*
33 to him who rides in the heavens, the ancient heavens;
    lo, he sends forth his voice, his mighty voice.
34 Ascribe power to God,
    whose majesty is over Israel,
    and his power is in the skies.
35 Terrible is God in his [j] sanctuary,
    the God of Israel,
    he gives power and strength to his people.

Blessed be God!

To the choirmaster: according to Lilies. A Psalm of David.

69 Save me, O God!
    For the waters have come up to my neck.
2 I sink in deep mire,
    where there is no foothold;
  I have come into deep waters,
    and the flood sweeps over me.
3 I am weary with my crying;
    my throat is parched.
  My eyes grow dim
    with waiting for my God.

[d] Or *cast up a highway for him who rides through the deserts*   [e] Cn: Heb *The Lord among them Sinai in the holy place*
[f] Gk Syr Tg: Heb *shatter*   [g] Or *have been seen*   [h] Cn: Heb *trampling*   [i] The Hebrew of verse 30 is obscure
[j] Gk: Heb *from thy*

⁴ More in number than the hairs of my head
 are those who hate me without cause;
mighty are those who would destroy me,
 those who attack me with lies.
What I did not steal
 must I now restore?
⁵ O God, thou knowest my folly;
 the wrongs I have done are not hidden from thee.

⁶ Let not those who hope in thee be put to shame through
  me,
 O Lord God of hosts;
let not those who seek thee be brought to dishonor through
  me,
 O God of Israel.
⁷ For it is for thy sake that I have borne reproach,
 that shame has covered my face.
⁸ I have become a stranger to my brethren,
 an alien to my mother's sons.

⁹ For zeal for thy house has consumed me,
 and the insults of those who insult thee have fallen on
  me.
¹⁰ When I humbled ᵏ my soul with fasting,
 it became my reproach.
¹¹ When I made sackcloth my clothing,
 I became a byword to them.
¹² I am the talk of those who sit in the gate,
 and the drunkards make songs about me.

¹³ But as for me, my prayer is to thee, O Lord.
 At an acceptable time, O God,
 in the abundance of thy steadfast love answer me.
¹⁴ With thy faithful help rescue me
 from sinking in the mire;
let me be delivered from my enemies
 and from the deep waters.
¹⁵ Let not the flood sweep over me,
 or the deep swallow me up,
 or the pit close its mouth over me.

¹⁶ Answer me, O Lord, for thy steadfast love is good;
 according to thy abundant mercy, turn to me.
¹⁷ Hide not thy face from thy servant;
 for I am in distress, make haste to answer me.
¹⁸ Draw near to me, redeem me,
 set me free because of my enemies!

¹⁹ Thou knowest my reproach,
 and my shame and my dishonor;
 my foes are all known to thee.
²⁰ Insults have broken my heart,
 so that I am in despair.
I looked for pity, but there was none;

and for comforters, but I found none.
²¹ They gave me poison for food,
 and for my thirst they gave me vinegar to drink.

²² Let their own table before them become a snare;
 let their sacrificial feasts ˡ be a trap.
²³ Let their eyes be darkened, so that they cannot see;
 and make their loins tremble continually.
²⁴ Pour out thy indignation upon them,
 and let thy burning anger overtake them.
²⁵ May their camp be a desolation,
 let no one dwell in their tents.
²⁶ For they persecute him whom thou hast smitten,
 and him ᵐ whom thou hast wounded, they afflict still
  more.ⁿ
²⁷ Add to them punishment upon punishment;
 may they have no acquittal from thee.
²⁸ Let them be blotted out of the book of the living;
 let them not be enrolled among the righteous.

²⁹ But I am afflicted and in pain;
 let thy salvation, O God, set me on high!

³⁰ I will praise the name of God with a song;
 I will magnify him with thanksgiving.
³¹ This will please the Lord more than an ox
 or a bull with horns and hoofs.
³² Let the oppressed see it and be glad;
 you who seek God, let your hearts revive.
³³ For the Lord hears the needy,
 and does not despise his own that are in bonds.

³⁴ Let heaven and earth praise him,
 the seas and everything that moves therein.
³⁵ For God will save Zion
 and rebuild the cities of Judah;
and his servants shall dwell ᵒ there and possess it;
³⁶ the children of his servants shall inherit it,
 and those who love his name shall dwell in it.

*To the choirmaster. A Psalm of David,
for the memorial offering.*

70 Be pleased, O God, to deliver me!
 O Lord, make haste to help me!
² Let them be put to shame and confusion
 who seek my life!

ᵏ Gk Syr: Heb *I wept with fasting my soul* or *I made my soul mourn with fasting*
ᵐ One Ms Tg Compare Syr: Heb *those* ⁿ Gk Syr: Heb *recount the pain of*
ˡ Tg: Heb *for security*
ᵒ Syr: Heb *and they shall dwell*

Let them be turned back and brought to dishonor
  who desire my hurt!
3 Let them be appalled because of their shame
  who say, "Aha, Aha!"

4 May all who seek thee
  rejoice and be glad in thee!
May those who love thy salvation
  say evermore, "God is great!"
5 But I am poor and needy;
  hasten to me, O God!
Thou art my help and my deliverer;
  O LORD, do not tarry!

71 In thee, O LORD, do I take refuge;
  let me never be put to shame!
2 In thy righteousness deliver me and rescue me;
  incline thy ear to me, and save me!
3 Be thou to me a rock of refuge,
  a strong fortress,p to save me,
  for thou art my rock and my fortress.

4 Rescue me, O my God, from the hand of the wicked,
  from the grasp of the unjust and cruel man.
5 For thou, O Lord, art my hope,
  my trust, O LORD, from my youth.
6 Upon thee I have leaned from my birth;
  thou art he who took me from my mother's womb.
My praise is continually of thee.

7 I have been as a portent to many;
  but thou art my strong refuge.
8 My mouth is filled with thy praise,
  and with thy glory all the day.
9 Do not cast me off in the time of old age;
  forsake me not when my strength is spent.
10 For my enemies speak concerning me,
  those who watch for my life consult together,
11 and say, "God has forsaken him;
  pursue and seize him,
  for there is none to deliver him."

12 O God, be not far from me;
  O my God, make haste to help me!
13 May my accusers be put to shame and consumed;
  with scorn and disgrace may they be covered
  who seek my hurt.
14 But I will hope continually,
  and will praise thee yet more and more.
15 My mouth will tell of thy righteous acts,
  of thy deeds of salvation all the day,
  for their number is past my knowledge.
16 With the mighty deeds of the Lord GOD I will come,
  I will praise thy righteousness, thine alone.

17 O God, from my youth thou hast taught me,
  and I still proclaim thy wondrous deeds.
18 So even to old age and gray hairs,
  O God, do not forsake me,
till I proclaim thy might to all the generations to come.q
19 Thy power and thy righteousness, O God,
  reach the high heavens.

Thou who hast done great things,
  O God, who is like thee?
20 Thou who hast made me see many sore troubles
  wilt revive me again;
from the depths of the earth
  thou wilt bring me up again.
21 Thou wilt increase my honor,
  and comfort me again.

22 I will also praise thee with the harp
  for thy faithfulness, O my God;
I will sing praises to thee with the lyre,
  O Holy One of Israel.
23 My lips will shout for joy,
  when I sing praises to thee;
  my soul also, which thou hast rescued.
24 And my tongue will talk of thy righteous help
  all the day long,
for they have been put to shame and disgraced
  who sought to do me hurt.

A Psalm of Solomon.

72 Give the king thy justice, O God,
  and thy righteousness to the royal son!
2 May he judge thy people with righteousness,
  and thy poor with justice!
3 Let the mountains bear prosperity for the people,
  and the hills, in righteousness!
4 May he defend the cause of the poor of the people,
  give deliverance to the needy,
  and crush the oppressor!

5 May he liver while the sun endures,
  and as long as the moon, throughout all generations!
6 May he be like rain that falls on the mown grass,
  like showers that water the earth!
7 In his days may righteousness flourish,
  and peace abound, till the moon be no more!

8 May he have dominion from sea to sea,
  and from the River to the ends of the earth!
9 May his foess bow down before him,
  and his enemies lick the dust!
10 May the kings of Tarshish and of the isles

p Gk Compare 31.3: Heb *to come continually thou hast commanded*
r Gk: Heb *may they fear thee*   s Cn: Heb *those who dwell in the wilderness*
q Gk Compare Syr: Heb *to a generation, to all that come*

render him tribute,
may the kings of Sheba and Seba
bring gifts!
¹¹ May all kings fall down before him,
all nations serve him!

¹² For he delivers the needy when he calls,
the poor and him who has no helper.
¹³ He has pity on the weak and the needy,
and saves the lives of the needy.
¹⁴ From oppression and violence he redeems their life;
and precious is their blood in his sight.

¹⁵ Long may he live,
may gold of Sheba be given to him!
May prayer be made for him continually,
and blessings invoked for him all the day!
¹⁶ May there be abundance of grain in the land;
on the tops of the mountains may it wave;
may its fruit be like Lebanon;
and may men blossom forth from the cities
like the grass of the field!
¹⁷ May his name endure for ever,
his fame continue as long as the sun!
May men bless themselves by him,
all nations call him blessed!

¹⁸ Blessed be the Lord, the God of Israel,
who alone does wondrous things.
¹⁹ Blessed be his glorious name for ever;
may his glory fill the whole earth!
Amen and Amen!

²⁰ The prayers of David, the son of Jesse, are ended.

BOOK III

A Psalm of Asaph.

73 Truly God is good to the upright,
to those who are pure in heart.^t
² But as for me, my feet had almost stumbled,
my steps had well nigh slipped.

³ For I was envious of the arrogant,
when I saw the prosperity of the wicked.

⁴ For they have no pangs;
their bodies are sound and sleek.
⁵ They are not in trouble as other men are;
they are not stricken like other men.
⁶ Therefore pride is their necklace;
violence covers them as a garment.
⁷ Their eyes swell out with fatness,
their hearts overflow with follies.
⁸ They scoff and speak with malice;
loftily they threaten oppression.
⁹ They set their mouths against the heavens,
and their tongue struts through the earth.

¹⁰ Therefore the people turn and praise them;^u
and find no fault in them.^v
¹¹ And they say, "How can God know?
Is there knowledge in the Most High?"
¹² Behold, these are the wicked;
always at ease, they increase in riches.
¹³ All in vain have I kept my heart clean
and washed my hands in innocence.
¹⁴ For all the day long I have been stricken,
and chastened every morning.

¹⁵ If I had said, "I will speak thus,"
I would have been untrue to the generation of thy
children.
¹⁶ But when I thought how to understand this,
it seemed to me a wearisome task,
¹⁷ until I went into the sanctuary of God;
then I perceived their end.
¹⁸ Truly thou dost set them in slippery places;
thou dost make them fall to ruin.
¹⁹ How they are destroyed in a moment,
swept away utterly by terrors!
²⁰ They are ^w like a dream when one awakes,
on awaking you despise their phantoms.

²¹ When my soul was embittered,
when I was pricked in heart,
²² I was stupid and ignorant,
I was like a beast toward thee.
²³ Nevertheless I am continually with thee;
thou dost hold my right hand.
²⁴ Thou dost guide me with thy counsel,
and afterward thou wilt receive me to glory.^x
²⁵ Whom have I in heaven but thee?
And there is nothing upon earth that I desire besides
thee.
²⁶ My flesh and my heart may fail,

^t Or *Truly God is good to Israel, to those who are pure in heart*
^v Cn: Heb *abundant waters are drained by them*
^w Cn: Heb *Lord*
^u Cn: Heb *his people return hither*
^x Or *honor*

but God is the strength ʸ of my heart and my portion
for ever.

²⁷ For lo, those who are far from thee shall perish;
thou dost put an end to those who are false to thee.
²⁸ But for me it is good to be near God;
I have made the Lord GOD my refuge,
that I may tell of all thy works.

A Maskil of Asaph.

74 O God, why dost thou cast us off for ever?
Why does thy anger smoke against the sheep of
thy pasture?
² Remember thy congregation, which thou hast gotten of
old,
which thou hast redeemed to be the tribe of thy heritage!
Remember Mount Zion, where thou hast dwelt.
³ Direct thy steps to the perpetual ruins;
the enemy has destroyed everything in the sanctuary!

⁴ Thy foes have roared in the midst of thy holy place;
they set up their own signs for signs.
⁵ At the upper entrance they hacked
the wooden trellis with axes.ᶻ
⁶ And then all its carved wood
they broke down with hatchets and hammers.
⁷ They set thy sanctuary on fire;
to the ground they desecrated the dwelling place of thy
name.
⁸ They said to themselves, "We will utterly subdue them";
they burned all the meeting places of God in the land.

⁹ We do not see our signs;
there is no longer any prophet,
and there is none among us who knows how long.
¹⁰ How long, O God, is the foe to scoff?
Is the enemy to revile thy name for ever?
¹¹ Why dost thou hold back thy hand,
why dost thou keep thy right hand in ᵃ thy bosom?

¹² Yet God my King is from of old,
working salvation in the midst of the earth.
¹³ Thou didst divide the sea by thy might;
thou didst break the heads of the dragons on the waters.
¹⁴ Thou didst crush the heads of Leviathan,
thou didst give him as food ᵇ for the creatures of the
wilderness.
¹⁵ Thou didst cleave open springs and brooks;
thou didst dry up ever-flowing streams.
¹⁶ Thine is the day, thine also the night;
thou hast established the luminaries and the sun.
¹⁷ Thou hast fixed all the bounds of the earth;

thou hast made summer and winter.

¹⁸ Remember this, O LORD, how the enemy scoffs,
and an impious people reviles thy name.
¹⁹ Do not deliver the soul of thy dove to the wild beasts;
do not forget the life of thy poor for ever.

²⁰ Have regard for thy ᶜ covenant;
for the dark places of the land are full of the habitations
of violence.
²¹ Let not the downtrodden be put to shame;
let the poor and needy praise thy name.

²² Arise, O God, plead thy cause;
remember how the impious scoff at thee all the day!
²³ Do not forget the clamor of thy foes,
the uproar of thy adversaries which goes up continually!

To the choirmaster: according to Do Not Destroy.
A Psalm of Asaph. A Song.

75 We give thanks to thee, O God; we give thanks;
we call on thy name and recount ᵈ thy wondrous
deeds.
² At the set time which I appoint
I will judge with equity.

³ When the earth totters, and all its inhabitants,
it is I who keep steady its pillars.   *Selah*
⁴ I say to the boastful, "Do not boast,"
and to the wicked, "Do not lift up your horn;
⁵ do not lift up your horn on high,
or speak with insolent neck."
⁶ For not from the east or from the west
and not from the wilderness comes lifting up;
⁷ but it is God who executes judgment,
putting down one and lifting up another.
⁸ For in the hand of the LORD there is a cup,
with foaming wine, well mixed;
and he will pour a draught from it,
and all the wicked of the earth
shall drain it down to the dregs.

⁹ But I will rejoice ᵉ for ever,
I will sing praises to the God of Jacob.
¹⁰ All the horns of the wicked he ᶠ will cut off,
but the horns of the righteous shall be exalted.

ʸ Heb *rock*   ᶻ Cn Compare Gk Syr: Heb uncertain   ᵃ Cn: Heb *consume thy right hand from*   ᵇ Heb *food for the people*
ᶜ Gk Syr: Heb *the*   ᵈ Syr Compare Gk: Heb *and near is thy name. They recount*   ᵉ Gk: Heb *declare*   ᶠ Heb *I*

To the choirmaster: with stringed instruments. A Psalm of Asaph. A Song.

76 In Judah God is known,
 his name is great in Israel.
2 His abode has been established in Salem,
 his dwelling place in Zion.
3 There he broke the flashing arrows,
 the shield, the sword, and the weapons of war. *Selah*

4 Glorious art thou, more majestic
 than the everlasting mountains.^g
5 The stouthearted were stripped of their spoil;
 they sank into sleep;
all the men of war
 were unable to use their hands.
6 At thy rebuke, O God of Jacob,
 both rider and horse lay stunned.

7 But thou, terrible art thou!
 Who can stand before thee
 when once thy anger is roused?
8 From the heavens thou didst utter judgment;
 the earth feared and was still,
9 when God arose to establish judgment
 to save all the oppressed of the earth. *Selah*

10 Surely the wrath of men shall praise thee;
 the residue of wrath thou wilt gird upon thee.
11 Make your vows to the LORD your God, and perform them;
 let all around him bring gifts to him who is to be feared,
12 who cuts off the spirit of princes,
 who is terrible to the kings of the earth.

To the choirmaster: according to Jeduthun. A Psalm of Asaph.

77 I cry aloud to God,
 aloud to God, that he may hear me.
2 In the day of my trouble I seek the Lord;
 in the night my hand is stretched out without wearying;
 my soul refuses to be comforted.

3 I think of God, and I moan;
 I meditate, and my spirit faints. *Selah*
4 Thou dost hold my eyelids from closing;
 I am so troubled that I cannot speak.
5 I consider the days of old,
 I remember the years long ago.
6 I commune ^h with my heart in the night;
 I meditate and search my spirit: ⁱ

7 "Will the Lord spurn for ever,
 and never again be favorable?
8 Has his steadfast love for ever ceased?
 Are his promises at an end for all time?
9 Has God forgotten to be gracious?
 Has he in anger shut up his compassion?" *Selah*
10 And I say, "It is my grief
 that the right hand of the Most High has changed."

11 I will call to mind the deeds of the LORD;
 yea, I will remember thy wonders of old.
12 I will meditate on all thy work,
 and muse on thy mighty deeds.
13 Thy way, O God, is holy.
 What god is great like our God?
14 Thou art the God who workest wonders,
 who hast manifested thy might among the peoples.
15 Thou didst with thy arm redeem thy people,
 the sons of Jacob and Joseph. *Selah*

16 When the waters saw thee, O God,
 when the waters saw thee, they were afraid,
 yea, the deep trembled.
17 The clouds poured out water;
 the skies gave forth thunder;
 thy arrows flashed on every side.
18 The crash of thy thunder was in the whirlwind;
 thy lightnings lighted up the world;
 the earth trembled and shook.
19 Thy way was through the sea,
 thy path through the great waters;
 yet thy footprints were unseen.
20 Thou didst lead thy people like a flock
 by the hand of Moses and Aaron.

A Maskil of Asaph.

78 Give ear, O my people, to my teaching;
 incline your ears to the words of my mouth!
2 I will open my mouth in a parable;
 I will utter dark sayings from of old,
3 things that we have heard and known,
 that our fathers have told us.
4 We will not hide them from their children,
 but tell to the coming generation
the glorious deeds of the LORD, and his might,
 and the wonders which he has wrought.

^g Gk: Heb *the mountains of prey*   ^h Gk Syr: Heb *my music*   ⁱ Syr Jerome: Heb *my spirit searches*

5 He established a testimony in Jacob,
   and appointed a law in Israel,
 which he commanded our fathers
   to teach to their children;
6 that the next generation might know them,
   the children yet unborn,
 and arise and tell them to their children,
7   so that they should set their hope in God,
 and not forget the works of God,
   but keep his commandments;
8 and that they should not be like their fathers,
   a stubborn and rebellious generation,
 a generation whose heart was not steadfast,
   whose spirit was not faithful to God.

9 The E′phraimites, armed with[j] the bow,
   turned back on the day of battle.
10 They did not keep God's covenant,
   but refused to walk according to his law.
11 They forgot what he had done,
   and the miracles that he had shown them.
12 In the sight of their fathers he wrought marvels
   in the land of Egypt, in the fields of Zo′an.
13 He divided the sea and let them pass through it,
   and made the waters stand like a heap.
14 In the daytime he led them with a cloud,
   and all the night with a fiery light.
15 He cleft rocks in the wilderness,
   and gave them drink abundantly as from the deep.
16 He made streams come out of the rock,
   and caused waters to flow down like rivers.

17 Yet they sinned still more against him,
   rebelling against the Most High in the desert.
18 They tested God in their heart
   by demanding the food they craved.
19 They spoke against God, saying,
   "Can God spread a table in the wilderness?
20 He smote the rock so that water gushed out
   and streams overflowed.
 Can he also give bread,
   or provide meat for his people?"

21 Therefore, when the LORD heard, he was full of wrath;
   a fire was kindled against Jacob,
   his anger mounted against Israel;
22 because they had no faith in God,
   and did not trust his saving power.
23 Yet he commanded the skies above,
   and opened the doors of heaven;
24 and he rained down upon them manna to eat,
   and gave them the grain of heaven.
25 Man ate of the bread of the angels;
   he sent them food in abundance.

26 He caused the east wind to blow in the heavens,
   and by his power he led out the south wind;
27 he rained flesh upon them like dust,
   winged birds like the sand of the seas;
28 he let them fall in the midst of their camp,
   all around their habitations.
29 And they ate and were well filled,
   for he gave them what they craved.
30 But before they had sated their craving,
   while the food was still in their mouths,
31 the anger of God rose against them
   and he slew the strongest of them,
   and laid low the picked men of Israel.

32 In spite of all this they still sinned;
   despite his wonders they did not believe.
33 So he made their days vanish like a breath,
   and their years in terror.
34 When he slew them, they sought for him;
   they repented and sought God earnestly.
35 They remembered that God was their rock,
   the Most High God their redeemer.
36 But they flattered him with their mouths;
   they lied to him with their tongues.
37 Their heart was not steadfast toward him;
   they were not true to his covenant.
38 Yet he, being compassionate,
   forgave their iniquity,
   and did not destroy them;
 he restrained his anger often,
   and did not stir up all his wrath.
39 He remembered that they were but flesh,
   a wind that passes and comes not again.
40 How often they rebelled against him in the wilderness
   and grieved him in the desert!
41 They tested him again and again,
   and provoked the Holy One of Israel.
42 They did not keep in mind his power,
   or the day when he redeemed them from the foe;
43 when he wrought his signs in Egypt,
   and his miracles in the fields of Zo′an.
44 He turned their rivers to blood,
   so that they could not drink of their streams.
45 He sent among them swarms of flies, which devoured them,
   and frogs, which destroyed them.
46 He gave their crops to the caterpillar,
   and the fruit of their labor to the locust.
47 He destroyed their vines with hail,
   and their sycamores with frost.
48 He gave over their cattle to the hail,
   and their flocks to thunderbolts.
49 He let loose on them his fierce anger,
   wrath, indignation, and distress,

j Heb *armed with shooting*

a company of destroying angels.
50 He made a path for his anger;
  he did not spare them from death,
  but gave their lives over to the plague.
51 He smote all the first-born in Egypt,
  the first issue of their strength in the tents of Ham.
52 Then he led forth his people like sheep,
  and guided them in the wilderness like a flock.
53 He led them in safety, so that they were not afraid;
  but the sea overwhelmed their enemies.
54 And he brought them to his holy land,
  to the mountain which his right hand had won.
55 He drove out nations before them;
  he apportioned them for a possession
  and settled the tribes of Israel in their tents.

56 Yet they tested and rebelled against the Most High God,
  and did not observe his testimonies,
57 but turned away and acted treacherously like their fathers;
  they twisted like a deceitful bow.
58 For they provoked him to anger with their high places;
  they moved him to jealousy with their graven images.

59 When God heard, he was full of wrath,
  and he utterly rejected Israel.
60 He forsook his dwelling at Shiloh,
  the tent where he dwelt among men,
61 and delivered his power to captivity,
  his glory to the hand of the foe.
62 He gave his people over to the sword,
  and vented his wrath on his heritage.
63 Fire devoured their young men,
  and their maidens had no marriage song.
64 Their priests fell by the sword,
  and their widows made no lamentation.
65 Then the Lord awoke as from sleep,
  like a strong man shouting because of wine.
66 And he put his adversaries to rout;
  he put them to everlasting shame.

67 He rejected the tent of Joseph,
  he did not choose the tribe of E'phraim;
68 but he chose the tribe of Judah,
  Mount Zion, which he loves.
69 He built his sanctuary like the high heavens,
  like the earth, which he has founded for ever.

70 He chose David his servant,
  and took him from the sheepfolds;
71 from tending the ewes that had young he brought him
  to be the shepherd of Jacob his people,
  of Israel his inheritance.
72 With upright heart he tended them,
  and guided them with skilful hand.

A Psalm of Asaph.

79 O God, the heathen have come into thy inheritance;
  they have defiled thy holy temple;
  they have laid Jerusalem in ruins.
2 They have given the bodies of thy servants
  to the birds of the air for food,
  the flesh of thy saints to the beasts of the earth.
3 They have poured out their blood like water
  round about Jerusalem,
  and there was none to bury them.
4 We have become a taunt to our neighbors,
  mocked and derided by those round about us.

5 How long, O LORD? Wilt thou be angry for ever?
  Will thy jealous wrath burn like fire?
6 Pour out thy anger on the nations that do not know thee,
  and on the kingdoms
  that do not call on thy name!
7 For they have devoured Jacob,
  and laid waste his habitation.

8 Do not remember against us the iniquities of our fore-fathers;
  let thy compassion come speedily to meet us,
  for we are brought very low.
9 Help us, O God of our salvation,
  for the glory of thy name;
  deliver us, and forgive our sins,
  for thy name's sake!
10 Why should the nations say,
  "Where is their God?"
  Let the avenging of the outpoured blood of thy servants
  be known among the nations before our eyes!

11 Let the groans of the prisoners come before thee;
  according to thy great power preserve those doomed to die!
12 Return sevenfold into the bosom of our neighbors
  the taunts with which they have taunted thee, O LORD!
13 Then we thy people, the flock of thy pasture,
  will give thanks to thee for ever;
  from generation to generation we will recount thy praise.

To the choirmaster: according to Lilies.
A Testimony of Asaph. A Psalm.

80 Give ear, O Shepherd of Israel,
thou who leadest Joseph like a flock!
Thou who art enthroned upon the cherubim, shine forth
2   before E'phraim and Benjamin and Manas'seh!
Stir up thy might,
and come to save us!

3 Restore us, O God;
let thy face shine, that we may be saved!

4 O LORD God of hosts,
how long wilt thou be angry with thy people's prayers?
5 Thou hast fed them with the bread of tears,
and given them tears to drink in full measure.
6 Thou dost make us the scorn [k] of our neighbors;
and our enemies laugh among themselves.
7 Restore us, O God of hosts;
let thy face shine, that we may be saved!

8 Thou didst bring a vine out of Egypt;
thou didst drive out the nations and plant it.
9 Thou didst clear the ground for it;
it took deep root and filled the land.
10 The mountains were covered with its shade,
the mighty cedars with its branches;
11 it sent out its branches to the sea,
and its shoots to the River.
12 Why then hast thou broken down its walls,
so that all who pass along the way pluck its fruit?
13 The boar from the forest ravages it,
and all that move in the field feed on it.

14 Turn again, O God of hosts!
Look down from heaven, and see;
have regard for this vine,
15   the stock which thy right hand planted.[l]

16 They have burned it with fire, they have cut it down;
may they perish at the rebuke of thy countenance!
17 But let thy hand be upon the man of thy right hand,
the son of man whom thou hast made strong for thyself!
18 Then we will never turn back from thee;
give us life, and we will call on thy name!

19 Restore us, O LORD God of hosts!
let thy face shine, that we may be saved!

To the choirmaster: according to The
Gittith. A Psalm of Asaph.

81 Sing aloud to God our strength;
shout for joy to the God of Jacob!
2 Raise a song, sound the timbrel,
the sweet lyre with the harp.
3 Blow the trumpet at the new moon,
at the full moon, on our feast day.
4 For it is a statute for Israel,
an ordinance of the God of Jacob.
5 He made it a decree in Joseph,
when he went out over [m] the land of Egypt.

I hear a voice I had not known:
6 "I relieved your [n] shoulder of the burden;
your [n] hands were freed from the basket.
7 In distress you called, and I delivered you;
I answered you in the secret place of thunder;
I tested you at the waters of Mer'ibah.   *Selah*
8 Hear, O my people, while I admonish you!
O Israel, if you would but listen to me!
9 There shall be no strange god among you;
you shall not bow down to a foreign god.
10 I am the LORD your God,
who brought you up out of the land of Egypt.
Open your mouth wide, and I will fill it.

11 "But my people did not listen to my voice;
Israel would have none of me.
12 So I gave them over to their stubborn hearts,
to follow their own counsels.
13 O that my people would listen to me,
that Israel would walk in my ways!
14 I would soon subdue their enemies,
and turn my hand against their foes.
15 Those who hate the LORD would cringe toward him,
and their fate would last for ever.
16 I would feed you [o] with the finest of the wheat,
and with honey from the rock I would satisfy you."

A Psalm of Asaph.

82 God has taken his place in the divine council;
in the midst of the gods he holds judgment:
2 "How long will you judge unjustly
and show partiality to the wicked?   *Selah*
3 Give justice to the weak and the fatherless;
maintain the right of the afflicted and the destitute.

4 Rescue the weak and the needy;
deliver them from the hand of the wicked."

5 They have neither knowledge nor understanding,
they walk about in darkness;
all the foundations of the earth are shaken.

6 I say, "You are gods,
sons of the Most High, all of you;
7 nevertheless, you shall die like men,
and fall like any prince." [p]

8 Arise, O God, judge the earth;
for to thee belong all the nations!

A Song. A Psalm of Asaph.

83 O God, do not keep silence;
do not hold thy peace or be still, O God!
2 For lo, thy enemies are in tumult;
those who hate thee have raised their heads.
3 They lay crafty plans against thy people;
they consult together against thy protected ones.
4 They say, "Come, let us wipe them out as a nation;
let the name of Israel be remembered no more!"
5 Yea, they conspire with one accord;
against thee they make a covenant—
6 the tents of Edom and the Ish'maelites,
Moab and the Hagrites,
7 Gebal and Ammon and Am'alek,
Philistia with the inhabitants of Tyre;
8 Assyria also has joined them;
they are the strong arm of the children of Lot. *Selah*

9 Do to them as thou didst to Mid'ian,
as to Sis'era and Jabin at the river Kishon,
10 who were destroyed at En-dor,
who became dung for the ground.
11 Make their nobles like Oreb and Zeeb,
all their princes like Zebah and Zalmun'na,
12 who said, "Let us take possession for ourselves
of the pastures of God."

13 O my God, make them like whirling dust,[q]
like chaff before the wind.
14 As fire consumes the forest,
as the flame sets the mountains ablaze,
15 so do thou pursue them with thy tempest
and terrify them with thy hurricane!
16 Fill their faces with shame,
that they may seek thy name, O LORD.
17 Let them be put to shame and dismayed for ever;
let them perish in disgrace.

18 Let them know that thou alone,
whose name is the LORD,
art the Most High over all the earth.

To the choirmaster: according to The Gittith.
A Psalm of the Sons of Korah.

84 How lovely is thy dwelling place,
O LORD of hosts!
2 My soul longs, yea, faints
for the courts of the LORD;
my heart and flesh sing for joy
to the living God.

3 Even the sparrow finds a home,
and the swallow a nest for herself,
where she may lay her young,
at thy altars, O LORD of hosts,
my King and my God.
4 Blessed are those who dwell in thy house,
ever singing thy praise! *Selah*

5 Blessed are the men whose strength is in thee,
in whose heart are the highways to Zion.[r]
6 As they go through the valley of Baca
they make it a place of springs;
the early rain also covers it with pools.
7 They go from strength to strength;
the God of gods will be seen in Zion.

8 O LORD God of hosts, hear my prayer;
give ear, O God of Jacob! *Selah*
9 Behold our shield, O God;
look upon the face of thine anointed!

10 For a day in thy courts is better
than a thousand elsewhere.
I would rather be a doorkeeper in the house of my God
than dwell in the tents of wickedness.
11 For the LORD God is a sun and shield;
he bestows favor and honor.
No good thing does the LORD withhold
from those who walk uprightly.
12 O LORD of hosts,
blessed is the man who trusts in thee!

To the choirmaster. A Psalm of the Sons of Korah.

85 LORD, thou wast favorable to thy land;
thou didst restore the fortunes of Jacob.
2 Thou didst forgive the iniquity of thy people;
thou didst pardon all their sin. *Selah*

[p] Or *fall as one man, O princes* [q] Or *a tumbleweed* [r] Heb lacks *to Zion*

3 Thou didst withdraw all thy wrath;
    thou didst turn from thy hot anger.

4 Restore us again, O God of our salvation,
    and put away thy indignation toward us!
5 Wilt thou be angry with us for ever?
    Wilt thou prolong thy anger to all generations?
6 Wilt thou not revive us again,
    that thy people may rejoice in thee?
7 Show us thy steadfast love, O LORD,
    and grant us thy salvation.

8 Let me hear what God the LORD will speak,
    for he will speak peace to his people,
    to his saints, to those who turn to him in their hearts.[s]
9 Surely his salvation is at hand for those who fear him,
    that glory may dwell in our land.

10 Steadfast love and faithfulness will meet;
    righteousness and peace will kiss each other.
11 Faithfulness will spring up from the ground,
    and righteousness will look down from the sky.
12 Yea, the LORD will give what is good,
    and our land will yield its increase.
13 Righteousness will go before him,
    and make his footsteps a way.

A Prayer of David.

86 Incline thy ear, O LORD, and answer me,
    for I am poor and needy.
2 Preserve my life, for I am godly;
    save thy servant who trusts in thee.
3 Thou art my God; be gracious to me, O Lord,
    for to thee do I cry all the day.
4 Gladden the soul of thy servant,
    for to thee, O Lord, do I lift up my soul.
5 For thou, O Lord, art good and forgiving,
    abounding in steadfast love to all who call on thee.
6 Give ear, O LORD, to my prayer;
    hearken to my cry of supplication.
7 In the day of my trouble I call on thee,
    for thou dost answer me.

8 There is none like thee among the gods, O Lord,
    nor are there any works like thine.
9 All the nations thou hast made shall come
    and bow down before thee, O Lord,
    and shall glorify thy name.
10 For thou art great and doest wondrous things,
    thou alone art God.
11 Teach me thy way, O LORD,
    that I may walk in thy truth;

unite my heart to fear thy name.
12 I give thanks to thee, O Lord my God, with my whole heart,
    and I will glorify thy name for ever.
13 For great is thy steadfast love toward me;
    thou hast delivered my soul from the depths of Sheol.

14 O God, insolent men have risen up against me;
    a band of ruthless men seek my life,
    and they do not set thee before them.
15 But thou, O Lord, art a God merciful and gracious,
    slow to anger and abounding in steadfast love and faithfulness.
16 Turn to me and take pity on me;
    give thy strength to thy servant,
    and save the son of thy handmaid.
17 Show me a sign of thy favor,
    that those who hate me may see and be put to shame
    because thou, LORD, hast helped me and comforted me.

A Psalm of the Sons of Korah. A Song.

87 On the holy mount stands the city he founded;
2   the LORD loves the gates of Zion
    more than all the dwelling places of Jacob.
3 Glorious things are spoken of you,
    O city of God.   *Selah*

4 Among those who know me I mention Rahab and Babylon;
    behold, Philistia and Tyre, with Ethiopia—
    "This one was born there," they say.
5 And of Zion it shall be said,
    "This one and that one were born in her";
    for the Most High himself will establish her.
6 The LORD records as he registers the peoples,
    "This one was born there."   *Selah*

7 Singers and dancers alike say,
    "All my springs are in you."

A Song. A Psalm of the Sons of Korah. To the choir-master: according to Mahalath Leannoth. A Maskil of Heman the Ezrahite.

88 O LORD, my God, I call for help[t] by day;
    I cry out in the night before thee.
2 Let my prayer come before thee,
    incline thy ear to my cry!

3 For my soul is full of troubles,
    and my life draws near to Sheol.
4 I am reckoned among those who go down to the Pit;

---

[s] Gk: Heb *but let them not turn back to folly*   [t] Cn: Heb *O* LORD, *God of my salvation*

I am a man who has no strength,
5 like one forsaken among the dead,
  like the slain that lie in the grave,
  like those whom thou dost remember no more,
    for they are cut off from thy hand.
6 Thou hast put me in the depths of the Pit,
  in the regions dark and deep.
7 Thy wrath lies heavy upon me,
  and thou dost overwhelm me with all thy waves. *Selah*
8 Thou hast caused my companions to shun me;
  thou hast made me a thing of horror to them.
  I am shut in so that I cannot escape;
9   my eye grows dim through sorrow.
  Every day I call upon thee, O Lord;
  I spread out my hands to thee.
10 Dost thou work wonders for the dead?
  Do the shades rise up to praise thee? *Selah*
11 Is thy steadfast love declared in the grave,
  or thy faithfulness in Abaddon?
12 Are thy wonders known in the darkness,
  or thy saving help in the land of forgetfulness?

13 But I, O Lord, cry to thee;
  in the morning my prayer comes before thee.
14 O Lord, why dost thou cast me off?
  Why dost thou hide thy face from me?
15 Afflicted and close to death from my youth up,
  I suffer thy terrors; I am helpless.[u]
16 Thy wrath has swept over me;
  thy dread assaults destroy me.
17 They surround me like a flood all day long;
  they close in upon me together.
18 Thou hast caused lover and friend to shun me;
  my companions are in darkness.

A Maskil of Ethan the Ezrahite.

89 I will sing of thy steadfast love, O Lord,[v] for ever;
    with my mouth I will proclaim thy faithfulness
  to all generations.
2 For thy steadfast love was established for ever,
  thy faithfulness is firm as the heavens.
3 Thou hast said, "I have made a covenant with my chosen
  one,
  I have sworn to David my servant:

4 'I will establish your descendants for ever,
  and build your throne for all generations.'" *Selah*

5 Let the heavens praise thy wonders, O Lord,
  thy faithfulness in the assembly of the holy ones!
6 For who in the skies can be compared to the Lord?
  Who among the heavenly beings[w] is like the Lord,
7 a God feared in the council of the holy ones,
  great and terrible[x] above all that are around about
    him?
8 O Lord God of hosts,
  who is mighty as thou art, O Lord,
  with thy faithfulness round about thee?
9 Thou dost rule the raging of the sea;
  when its waves rise, thou stillest them.
10 Thou didst crush Rahab like a carcass,
  thou didst scatter thy enemies with thy mighty arm.
11 The heavens are thine, the earth also is thine;
  the world and all that is in it, thou hast founded them.
12 The north and the south, thou hast created them;
  Tabor and Hermon joyously praise thy name.
13 Thou hast a mighty arm;
  strong is thy hand, high thy right hand.
14 Righteousness and justice are the foundation of thy
    throne;
  steadfast love and faithfulness go before thee.
15 Blessed are the people who know the festal shout,
  who walk, O Lord, in the light of thy countenance,
16 who exult in thy name all the day,
  and extol[y] thy righteousness.
17 For thou art the glory of their strength;
  by thy favor our horn is exalted.
18 For our shield belongs to the Lord,
  our king to the Holy One of Israel.

19 Of old thou didst speak in a vision
  to thy faithful one, and say:
  "I have set the crown[z] upon one who is mighty,
  I have exalted one chosen from the people.
20 I have found David, my servant;
  with my holy oil I have anointed him;
21 so that my hand shall ever abide with him,
  my arm also shall strengthen him.
22 The enemy shall not outwit him,
  the wicked shall not humble him.
23 I will crush his foes before him
  and strike down those who hate him.
24 My faithfulness and my steadfast love shall be with him,
  and in my name shall his horn be exalted.
25 I will set his hand on the sea
  and his right hand on the rivers.
26 He shall cry to me, 'Thou art my Father,
  my God, and the Rock of my salvation.'
27 And I will make him the first-born,

u The meaning of the Hebrew word is uncertain   v Gk: Heb *the steadfast love of the* Lord   w Or *sons of gods*
x Gk Syr: Heb *greatly terrible*   y Cn: Heb *are exalted in*   z Cn: Heb *help*

the highest of the kings of the earth.

28 My steadfast love I will keep for him for ever,
 and my covenant will stand firm for him.
29 I will establish his line for ever
 and his throne as the days of the heavens.
30 If his children forsake my law
 and do not walk according to my ordinances,
31 if they violate my statutes
 and do not keep my commandments,
32 then I will punish their transgression with the rod
 and their iniquity with scourges;
33 but I will not remove from him my steadfast love,
 or be false to my faithfulness.
34 I will not violate my covenant,
 or alter the word that went forth from my lips.
35 Once for all I have sworn by my holiness;
 I will not lie to David.
36 His line shall endure for ever,
 his throne as long as the sun before me.
37 Like the moon it shall be established for ever;
 it shall stand firm while the skies endure." a   *Selah*

38 But now thou hast cast off and rejected,
 thou art full of wrath against thy anointed.
39 Thou hast renounced the covenant with thy servant;
 thou hast defiled his crown in the dust.
40 Thou hast breached all his walls;
 thou hast laid his strongholds in ruins.
41 All that pass by despoil him;
 he has become the scorn of his neighbors.
42 Thou hast exalted the right hand of his foes;
 thou hast made all his enemies rejoice.
43 Yea, thou hast turned back the edge of his sword,
 and thou hast not made him stand in battle.
44 Thou hast removed the scepter from his hand,b
 and cast his throne to the ground.
45 Thou hast cut short the days of his youth;
 thou hast covered him with shame.   *Selah*

46 How long, O LORD? Wilt thou hide theyself for ever?
 How long will thy wrath burn like fire?
47 Remember, O Lord,c what the measure of life is,
 for what vanity thou hast created all the sons of men!
48 What man can live and never see death?
 Who can deliver his soul from the power of Sheol?
        Selah

49 Lord, where is thy steadfast love of old,
 which by thy faithfulness thou didst swear to David?
50 Remember, O Lord, how thy servant is scorned;
 how I bear in my bosom the insults d of the peoples,
51 with which thy enemies taunt, O LORD,
 with which they mock the footsteps of thy anointed.

52   Blessed be the LORD for ever! Amen and Amen.

BOOK IV

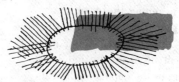

A Prayer of Moses, the man of God.

90 Lord, thou hast been our dwelling place e
 in all generations.
2 Before the mountains were brought forth,
 or ever thou hadst formed the earth and the world,
 from everlasting to everlasting thou art God.

3 Thou turnest man back to the dust,
 and sayest, "Turn back, O children of men!"
4 For a thousand years in thy sight
 are but as yesterday when it is past,
 or as a watch in the night.

5 Thou dost sweep men away; they are like a dream,
 like grass which is renewed in the morning:
6 in the morning it flourishes and is renewed;
 in the evening it fades and withers.

7 For we are consumed by thy anger;
 by thy wrath we are overwhelmed.
8 Thou hast set our iniquities before thee,
 our secret sins in the light of thy countenance.

9 For all our days pass away under thy wrath,
 our years come to an end f like a sigh.
10 The years of our life are threescore and ten,
 or even by reason of strength fourscore;
 yet their span g is but toil and trouble;
 they are soon gone, and we fly away.

11 Who considers the power of thy anger,
 and thy wrath according to the fear of thee?
12 So teach us to number our days
 that we may get a heart of wisdom.

13 Return, O LORD! How long?
 Have pity on thy servants!
14 Satisfy us in the morning with thy steadfast love,
 that we may rejoice and be glad all our days.
15 Make us glad as many days as thou hast afflicted us,
 and as many years as we have seen evil.
16 Let thy work be manifest to thy servants,
 and thy glorious power to their children.
17 Let the favor of the Lord our God be upon us,
 and establish thou the work of our hands upon us,
 yea, the work of our hands establish thou it.

---

a Cn: Heb *the witness in the skies is sure*   b Cn: Heb *removed his cleanness*   c Cn: Heb *I*   d Cn: Heb *all of many*
e Another reading is *refuge*   f Syr: Heb *we bring our years to an end*   g Cn Compare Gk Syr Jerome Tg: Heb *pride*

91 He who dwells in the shelter of the Most High,
    who abides in the shadow of the Almighty,
2 will say to the Lord, "My refuge and my fortress;
    my God, in whom I trust."
3 For he will deliver you from the snare of the fowler
    and from the deadly pestilence;
4 he will cover you with his pinions,
    and under his wings you will find refuge;
    his faithfulness is a shield and buckler.
5 You will not fear the terror of the night,
    nor the arrow that flies by day,
6 nor the pestilence that stalks in darkness,
    nor the destruction that wastes at noonday.

7 A thousand may fall at your side,
    ten thousand at your right hand;
    but it will not come near you.
8 You will only look with your eyes
    and see the recompense of the wicked.

9 Because you have made the Lord your refuge,[h]
    the Most High your habitation,
10 no evil shall befall you,
    no scourge come near your tent.

11 For he will give his angels charge of you
    to guard you in all your ways.
12 On their hands they will bear you up,
    lest you dash your foot against a stone.
13 You will tread on the lion and the adder,
    the young lion and the serpent you will trample under
      foot.

14 Because he cleaves to me in love, I will deliver him;
    I will protect him, because he knows my name.
15 When he calls to me, I will answer him;
    I will be with him in trouble,
    I will rescue him and honor him.
16 With long life I will satisfy him,
    and show him my salvation.

A Psalm. A Song for the Sabbath.

92 It is good to give thanks to the Lord,
    to sing praises to thy name, O Most High;
2 to declare thy steadfast love in the morning,
    and thy faithfulness by night,
3 to the music of the lute and the harp,
    to the melody of the lyre.
4 For thou, O Lord, hast made me glad by thy work;
    at the works of thy hands I sing for joy.

5 How great are thy works, O Lord!
    Thy thoughts are very deep!
6 The dull man cannot know,
    the stupid cannot understand this:
7 that, though the wicked sprout like grass
    and all evildoers flourish,
they are doomed to destruction for ever,
8   but thou, O Lord, art on high for ever.
9 For, lo, thy enemies, O Lord,
    for, lo, thy enemies shall perish;
    all evildoers shall be scattered.

10 But thou hast exalted my horn like that of the wild ox;
    thou hast poured over me[i] fresh oil.
11 My eyes have seen the downfall of my enemies,
    my ears have heard the doom of my evil assailants.

12 The righteous flourish like the palm tree,
    and grow like a cedar in Lebanon.
13 They are planted in the house of the Lord,
    they flourish in the courts of our God.
14 They still bring forth fruit in old age,
    they are ever full of sap and green,
15 to show that the Lord is upright;
    he is my rock, and there is no unrighteousness in him.

93 The Lord reigns; he is robed in majesty;
    the Lord is robed, he is girded with strength.
Yea, the world is established; it shall never be moved;
2   thy throne is established from of old;
    thou art from everlasting.

3 The floods have lifted up, O Lord,
    the floods have lifted up their voice,
    the floods lift up their roaring.
4 Mightier than the thunders of many waters,
    mightier than the waves[j] of the sea,
    the Lord on high is mighty!

5 Thy decrees are very sure;
    holiness befits thy house,
    O Lord, for evermore.

94 O Lord, thou God of vengeance,
    thou God of vengeance, shine forth!
2 Rise up, O judge of the earth;
    render to the proud their deserts!
3 O Lord, how long shall the wicked,
    how long shall the wicked exult?

h Cn: Heb *Because thou, Lord, art my refuge; you have made*   i Syr: Heb uncertain   j Cn: Heb *mighty the waves*

4 They pour out their arrogant words,
  they boast, all the evildoers.
5 They crush thy people, O LORD,
  and afflict thy heritage.
6 They slay the widow and the sojourner,
  and murder the fatherless;
7 and they say, "The LORD does not see;
  the God of Jacob does not perceive."

8 Understand, O dullest of the people!
  Fools, when will you be wise?
9 He who planted the ear, does he not hear?
  He who formed the eye, does he not see?
10 He who chastens the nations, does he not chastise?
  He who teaches men knowledge,
11   the LORD, knows the thoughts of man,
  that they are but a breath.

12 Blessed is the man whom thou dost chasten, O LORD,
  and whom thou dost teach out of thy law
13 to give him respite from days of trouble,
  until a pit is dug for the wicked.
14 For the LORD will not forsake his people;
  he will not abandon his heritage;
15 for justice will return to the righteous,
  and all the upright in heart will follow it.

16 Who rises up for me against the wicked?
  Who stands up for me against evildoers?
17 If the LORD had not been my help,
  my soul would soon have dwelt in the land of silence.
18 When I thought, "My foot slips,"
  thy steadfast love, O LORD, held me up.
19 When the cares of my heart are many,
  thy consolations cheer my soul.
20 Can wicked rulers be allied with thee,
  who frame mischief by statute?
21 They band together against the life of the righteous,
  and condemn the innocent to death.
22 But the LORD has become my stronghold,
  and my God the rock of my refuge.
23 He will bring back on them their iniquity
  and wipe them out for their wickedness;
  the LORD our God will wipe them out.

95 O come, let us sing to the LORD;
    let us make a joyful noise to the rock of our salvation!
2 Let us come into his presence with thanksgiving;
  let us make a joyful noise to him with songs of praise!
3 For the LORD is a great God,
  and a great King above all gods.
4 In his hand are the depths of the earth;
  the heights of the mountains are his also.

5 The sea is his, for he made it;
  for his hands formed the dry land.

6 O come, let us worship and bow down,
  let us kneel before the LORD, our Maker!
7 For he is our God,
  and we are the people of his pasture,
  and the sheep of his hand.

O that today you would hearken to his voice!
8   Harden not your hearts, as at Mer'ibah,
  as on the day at Massah in the wilderness,
9 when your fathers tested me,
  and put me to the proof, though they had seen my work.
10 For forty years I loathed that generation
  and said, "They are a people who err in heart,
  and they do not regard my ways."
11 Therefore I swore in my anger
  that they should not enter my rest.

96 O sing to the LORD a new song;
    sing to the LORD, all the earth!
2 Sing to the LORD, bless his name;
  tell of his salvation from day to day.
3 Declare his glory among the nations,
  his marvelous works among all the peoples!
4 For great is the LORD, and greatly to be praised;
  he is to be feared above all gods.
5 For all the gods of the peoples are idols;
  but the LORD made the heavens.
6 Honor and majesty are before him;
  strength and beauty are in his sanctuary.

7 Ascribe to the LORD, O families of the peoples,
  ascribe to the LORD glory and strength!
8 Ascribe to the LORD the glory due his name;
  bring an offering, and come into his courts!
9 Worship the LORD in holy array;
  tremble before him, all the earth!

10 Say among the nations, "The LORD reigns!
  Yea, the world is established, it shall never be moved;
  he will judge the peoples with equity."
11 Let the heavens be glad, and let the earth rejoice;
  let the sea roar, and all that fills it;
12   let the field exult, and everything in it!
  Then shall all the trees of the wood sing for joy
13   before the LORD, for he comes,
  for he comes to judge the earth.
  He will judge the world with righteousness,
  and the peoples with his truth.

97 The LORD reigns; let the earth rejoice;
    let the many coastlands be glad!

2 Clouds and thick darkness are round about him;
  righteousness and justice are the foundation of his
    throne.
3 Fire goes before him,
  and burns up his adversaries round about.
4 His lightnings lighten the world;
  the earth sees and trembles.
5 The mountains melt like wax before the LORD,
  before the Lord of all the earth.

6 The heavens proclaim his righteousness;
  and all the peoples behold his glory.
7 All worshipers of images are put to shame,
  who make their boast in worthless idols;
  all gods bow down before him.
8 Zion hears and is glad,
  and the daughters of Judah rejoice,
  because of thy judgments, O God.
9 For thou, O LORD, art most high over all the earth;
  thou art exalted far above all gods.

10 The LORD loves those who hate evil; [k]
  he preserves the lives of his saints;
  he delivers them from the hand of the wicked.
11 Light dawns [l] for the righteous,
  and joy for the upright in heart.
12 Rejoice in the LORD, O you righteous,
  and give thanks to his holy name!

A Psalm.

98 O sing to the LORD a new song,
    for he has done marvelous things!
  His right hand and his holy arm have gotten him victory.
2 The LORD has made known his victory,
  he has revealed his vindication in the sight of the
    nations.
3 He has remembered his steadfast love and faithfulness
  to the house of Israel.
  All the ends of the earth have seen
    the victory of our God.

4 Make a joyful noise to the LORD, all the earth;
  break forth into joyous song and sing praises!
5 Sing praises to the LORD with the lyre,
  with the lyre and the sound of melody!
6 With trumpets and the sound of the horn
  make a joyful noise before the King, the LORD!

7 Let the sea roar, and all that fills it;
  the world and those who dwell in it!
8 Let the floods clap their hands;
  let the hills sing for joy together

9 before the LORD, for he comes
  to judge the earth.
  He will judge the world with righteousness,
  and the peoples with equity.

99 The LORD reigns; let the peoples tremble!
    He sits enthroned upon the cherubim; let the earth
    quake!
2 The LORD is great in Zion;
  he is exalted over all the peoples.
3 Let them praise thy great and terrible name!
  Holy is he!
4 Mighty King, [m] lover of justice,
  thou hast established equity;
  thou hast executed justice
  and righteousness in Jacob.
5 Extol the LORD our God;
  worship at his footstool!
  Holy is he!

6 Moses and Aaron were among his priests,
  Samuel also was among those who called on his name.
  They cried to the LORD, and he answered them.
7 He spoke to them in the pillar of cloud;
  they kept his testimonies,
  and the statues that he gave them.

8 O LORD our God, thou didst answer them;
  thou wast a forgiving God to them,
  but an avenger of their wrongdoings.
9 Extol the LORD our God,
  and worship at his holy mountain;
  for the LORD our God is holy!

A Psalm for the thank offering.

100 Make a joyful noise to the LORD, all the lands! [n]
    Serve the LORD with gladness!
  Come into his presence with singing!

3 Know that the LORD is God!
  It is he that made us, and we are his; [o]
  we are his people, and the sheep of his pasture.

4 Enter his gates with thanksgiving,
  and his courts with praise!
  Give thanks to him, bless his name!

5 For the LORD is good;
  his steadfast love endures for ever,
  and his faithfulness to all generations.

k Cn: Heb *You who love the* LORD *hate evil*   l Gk Syr Jerome: Heb *is sown*   m Cn: Heb *and the king's strength*
n Heb *land or earth*   o Another reading is *and not we ourselves*

A Psalm of David.

101 I will sing of loyalty and of justice;
　　to thee, O Lord, I will sing.
2 I will give heed to the way that is blameless.
　　Oh when wilt thou come to me?

I will walk with integrity of heart
　within my house;
3 I will not set before my eyes
　anything that is base.

I hate the work of those who fall away;
　it shall not cleave to me.
4 Perverseness of heart shall be far from me;
　I will know nothing of evil.

5 Him who slanders his neighbor secretly
　I will destroy.
The man of haughty looks and arrogant heart
　I will not endure.

6 I will look with favor on the faithful in the land,
　that they may dwell with me;
he who walks in the way that is blameless
　shall minister to me.

7 No man who practices deceit shall dwell in my house;
　no man who utters lies shall continue in my presence.

8 Morning by morning I will destroy all the wicked in the
　　land,
cutting off all the evildoers
　from the city of the Lord.

*A prayer of one afflicted, when he is faint and pours out
his complaint before the Lord.*

102 Hear my prayer, O Lord;
　　let my cry come to thee!
2 Do not hide thy face from me
　in the day of my distress!
Incline thy ear to me;
　answer me speedily in the day when I call!

3 For my days pass away like smoke,
　and my bones burn like a furnace.
4 My heart is smitten like grass, and withered;
　I forget to eat my bread.
5 Because of my loud groaning
　my bones cleave to my flesh.
6 I am like a vulture ᴾ of the wilderness,
　like an owl of the waste places;
7 I lie awake,

ᴾ The meaning of the Hebrew word is uncertain

I am like a lonely bird on the housetop.
8 All the day my enemies taunt me,
　those who deride me use my name for a curse.
9 For I eat ashes like bread,
　and mingle tears with my drink,
10 because of thy indignation and anger;
　for thou hast taken me up and thrown me away.
11 My days are like an evening shadow;
　I wither away like grass.

12 But thou, O Lord, art enthroned for ever;
　thy name endures to all generations.
13 Thou wilt arise and have pity on Zion;
　it is the time to favor her;
　the appointed time has come.
14 For thy servants hold her stones dear,
　and have pity on her dust.
15 The nations will fear the name of the Lord,
　and all the kings of the earth thy glory.
16 For the Lord will build up Zion,
　he will appear in his glory;
17 he will regard the prayer of the destitute,
　and will not despise their supplication.

18 Let this be recorded for a generation to come,
　so that a people yet unborn may praise the Lord:
19 that he looked down from his holy height,
　from heaven the Lord looked at the earth,
20 to hear the groans of the prisoners,
　to set free those who were doomed to die;
21 that men may declare in Zion the name of the Lord,
　and in Jerusalem his praise,
22 when peoples gather together,
　and kingdoms, to worship the Lord.

23 He has broken my strength in mid-course;
　he has shortened my days.
24 "O my God," I say, "take me not hence
　in the midst of my days,
thou whose years endure
　throughout all generations!"

25 Of old thou didst lay the foundation of the earth,
　and the heavens are the work of thy hands.
26 They will perish, but thou dost endure;
　they will all wear out like a garment.
Thou changest them like raiment, and they pass away;
27 　but thou art the same, and thy years have no end.
28 The children of thy servants shall dwell secure;
　their posterity shall be established before thee.

A Psalm of David.

103 Bless the LORD, O my soul;
and all that is within me, bless his holy name!
2 Bless the LORD, O my soul,
and forget not all his benefits,
3 who forgives all your iniquity,
who heals all your diseases,
4 who redeems your life from the Pit,
who crowns you with steadfast love and mercy,
5 who satisfies you with good as long as you live[q]
so that your youth is renewed like the eagle's.

6 The LORD works vindication and
justice for all who are oppressed.
7 He made known his ways to Moses,
his acts to the people of Israel.
8 The LORD is merciful and gracious,
slow to anger and abounding in steadfast love.
9 He will not always chide,
nor will he keep his anger for ever.
10 He does not deal with us according to our sins,
nor requite us according to our iniquities.
11 For as the heavens are high above the earth,
so great is his steadfast love toward those who fear him;
12 as far as the east is from the west,
so far does he remove our transgressions from us.
13 As a father pities his children,
so the LORD pities those who fear him.
14 For he knows our frame;
he remembers that we are dust.

15 As for man, his days are like grass;
he flourishes like a flower of the field;
16 for the wind passes over it, and it is gone,
and its place knows it no more.
17 But the steadfast love of the LORD is from everlasting to everlasting
upon those who fear him,
and his righteousness to children's children,
18 to those who keep his covenant
and remember to do his commandments.

19 The LORD has established his throne in the heavens,
and his kingdom rules over all.
20 Bless the LORD, O you his angels,
you mighty ones who do his word,
hearkening to the voice of his word!
21 Bless the LORD, all his hosts,
his ministers that do his will!
22 Bless the LORD, all his works,
in all places of his dominion.
Bless the LORD, O my soul!

104 Bless the LORD, O my soul!
O LORD my God, thou art very great!
Thou art clothed with honor and majesty,
2 who coverest thyself with light as with a garment,
who hast stretched out the heavens like a tent,
3 who hast laid the beams of thy chambers on the waters,
who makest the clouds thy chariot,
who ridest on the wings of the wind,
4 who makest the winds thy messengers,
fire and flame thy ministers.

5 Thou didst set the earth on its foundations,
so that it should never be shaken.
6 Thou didst cover it with the deep as with a garment;
the waters stood above the mountains.
7 At thy rebuke they fled;
at the sound of thy thunder they took to flight.
8 The mountains rose, the valleys sank down
to the place which thou didst appoint for them.
9 Thou didst set a bound which they should not pass,
so that they might not again cover the earth.

10 Thou makest springs gush forth in the valleys;
they flow between the hills,
11 they give drink to every beast of the field;
the wild asses quench their thirst.
12 By them the birds of the air have their habitation;
they sing among the branches.
13 From thy lofty abode thou waterest the mountains;
the earth is satisfied with the fruit of thy work.

14 Thou dost cause the grass to grow for the cattle,
and plants for man to cultivate,[r]
that he may bring forth food from the earth,

15 and wine to gladden the heart of man,
oil to make his face shine,
and bread to strengthen man's heart.
16 The trees of the LORD are watered abundantly,
the cedars of Lebanon which he planted.
17 In them the birds build their nests;
the stork has her home in the fir trees.
18 The high mountains are for the wild goats;
the rocks are a refuge for the badgers.
19 Thou hast made the moon to mark the seasons;
the sun knows its time for setting.
20 Thou makest darkness, and it is night,
when all the beasts of the forest creep forth.
21 The young lions roar for their prey,
seeking their food from God.

[q] Heb uncertain
[r] Or *fodder for the animals that serve man*

22 When the sun rises, they get them away
  and lie down in their dens.
23 Man goes forth to his work
  and to his labor until the evening.

24 O LORD, how manifold are thy works!
  In wisdom hast thou made them all;
  the earth is full of thy creatures.
25 Yonder is the sea, great and wide,
  which teems with things innumerable,
  living things both small and great.
26 There go the ships,
  and Leviathan which thou didst form to sport in it.

27 These all look to thee,
  to give them their food in due season.
28 When thou givest to them, they gather it up;
  when thou openest thy hand, they are filled with good
    things.
29 When thou hidest thy face, they are dismayed;
  when thou takest away their breath, they die
  and return to their dust.
30 When thou sendest forth thy Spirit,ˢ they are created;
  and thou renewest the face of the ground.

31 May the glory of the LORD endure for ever,
  may the LORD rejoice in his works,
32 who looks on the earth and it trembles,
  who touches the mountains and they smoke!
33 I will sing to the LORD as long as I live;
  I will sing praise to my God while I have being.
34 May my meditation be pleasing to him,
  for I rejoice in the LORD.
35 Let sinners be consumed from the earth,
  and let the wicked be no more!
  Bless the LORD, O my soul!
  Praise the LORD!

105 O give thanks to the LORD, call on his name,
    make known his deeds among the peoples!
2 Sing to him, sing praises to him,
  tell of all his wonderful works!
3 Glory in his holy name;
  let the hearts of those who seek the LORD rejoice!
4 Seek the LORD and his strength,
  seek his presence continually!
5 Remember the wonderful works that he has done,
  his miracles, and the judgments he uttered,
6 O offspring of Abraham his servant,
  sons of Jacob, his chosen ones!

7 He is the LORD our God;
  his judgments are in all the earth.
8 He is mindful of his covenant for ever,
  of the word that he commanded, for a thousand gen-
    erations,
9 the covenant which he made with Abraham,
  his sworn promise to Isaac,
10 which he confirmed to Jacob as a statute,
  to Israel as an everlasting covenant,
11 saying, "To you I will give the land of Canaan
  as your portion for an inheritance."

12 When they were few in number,
  of little account, and sojourners in it,
13 wandering from nation to nation,
  from one kingdom to another people,
14 he allowed no one to oppress them;
  he rebuked kings on their account,
15 saying, "Touch not my anointed ones,
  do my prophets no harm!"

16 When he summoned a famine on the land,
  and broke every staff of bread,
17 he had sent a man ahead of them,
  Joseph, who was sold as a slave.
18 His feet were hurt with fetters,
  his neck was put in a collar of iron;
19 until what he had said came to pass
  the word of the LORD tested him.
20 The king sent and released him,
  the ruler of the peoples set him free;
21 he made him lord of his house,
  and ruler of all his possessions,
22 to instructᵗ his princes at his pleasure,
  and to teach his elders wisdom.

23 Then Israel came to Egypt;
  Jacob sojourned in the land of Ham.
24 And the LORD made his people very fruitful,
  and made them stronger than their foes.
25 He turned their hearts to hate his people,
  to deal craftily with his servants.

26 He sent Moses his servant,
  and Aaron whom he had chosen.
27 They wrought his signs among them,
  and miracles in the land of Ham.
28 He sent darkness, and made the land dark;
  they rebelledᵘ against his words.
29 He turned their waters into blood,
  and caused their fish to die.
30 Their land swarmed with frogs,
  even in the chambers of their kings.
31 He spoke, and there came swarms of flies,
  and gnats throughout their country.
32 He gave them hail for rain,
  and lightning that flashed through their land.

ˢ Or breath   ᵗ Gk Syr Jerome: Heb to bind   ᵘ Cn Compare Gk Syr: Heb they did not rebel

33 He smote their vines and fig trees,
  and shattered the trees of their country.
34 He spoke, and the locusts came,
  and young locusts without number;
35 which devoured all the vegetation in their land,
  and ate up the fruit of their ground.
36 He smote all the first-born in their land,
  the first issue of all their strength.

37 Then he led forth Israel with silver and gold,
  and there was none among his tribes who stumbled.
38 Egypt was glad when they departed,
  for dread of them had fallen upon it.
39 He spread a cloud for a covering,
  and fire to give light by night.
40 They asked, and he brought quails,
  and gave them bread from heaven in abundance.
41 He opened the rock, and water gushed forth;
  it flowed through the desert like a river.
42 For he remembered his holy promise,
  and Abraham his servant.

43 So he led forth his people with joy,
  his chosen ones with singing.
44 And he gave them the lands of the nations;
  and they took possession of the fruit of the peoples' toil,
45 to the end that they should keep his statutes,
  and observe his laws.
  Praise the Lord!

106 Praise the Lord!
  O give thanks to the Lord, for he is good;
  for his steadfast love endures for ever!
2 Who can utter the mighty doings of the Lord,
  or show forth all his praise?
3 Blessed are they who observe justice,
  who do righteousness at all times!

4 Remember me, O Lord, when thou showest favor to thy
    people;
  help me when thou deliverest them;
5 that I may see the prosperity of thy chosen ones,
  that I may rejoice in the gladness of thy nation,
  that I may glory with thy heritage.

6 Both we and our fathers have sinned;
  we have committed iniquity, we have done wickedly.
7 Our fathers, when they were in Egypt,
  did not consider thy wonderful works;
  they did not remember the abundance of thy steadfast
    love,
  but rebelled against the Most High v at the Red Sea.
8 Yet he saved them for his name's sake,
  that he might make known his mighty power.
9 He rebuked the Red Sea, and it became dry;

and he led them through the deep as through a desert.
10 So he saved them from the hand of the foe,
  and delivered them from the power of the enemy.
11 And the waters covered their adversaries;
  not one of them was left.
12 Then they believed his words;
  they sang his praise.

13 But they soon forgot his works;
  they did not wait for his counsel.
14 But they had a wanton craving in the wilderness,
  and put God to the test in the desert;
15 he gave them what they asked,
  but sent a wasting disease among them.

16 When men in the camp were jealous of Moses
  and Aaron, the holy one of the Lord,
17 the earth opened and swallowed up Dathan,
  and covered the company of Abi'ram.
18 Fire also broke out in their company;
  the flame burned up the wicked.

19 They made a calf in Horeb
  and worshiped a molten image.
20 They exchanged the glory of God
  for the image of an ox that eats grass.
21 They forgot God, their Savior,
  who had done great things in Egypt,
22 wondrous works in the land of Ham,
  and terrible things by the Red Sea.
23 Therefore he said he would destroy them—
  had not Moses, his chosen one,
  stood in the breach before him,
  to turn away his wrath from destroying them.

24 Then they despised the pleasant land,
  having no faith in his promise.
25 They murmured in their tents,
  and did not obey the voice of the Lord.
26 Therefore he raised his hand and swore to them
  that he would make them fall in the wilderness,
27 and would disperse w their descendants among the nations,
  scattering them over the lands.

28 Then they attached themselves to the Ba'al of Pe'or,
  and ate sacrifices offered to the dead;
29 they provoked the Lord to anger with their doings,
  and a plague broke out among them.
30 Then Phin'ehas stood up and interposed,
  and the plague was stayed.
31 And that has been reckoned to him as righteousness
  from generation to generation for ever.

32 They angered him at the waters of Mer'ibah,
  and it went ill with Moses on their account;

v Cn Compare 78.17, 56: Heb *at the sea* w Syr Compare Ezk 20.23: Heb *cause to fall*

33 for they made his spirit bitter,
and he spoke words that were rash.

34 They did not destroy the peoples,
as the LORD commanded them,
35 but they mingled with the nations
and learned to do as they did.
36 They served their idols,
which became a snare to them.
37 They sacrificed their sons and their daughters to the
demons;
38 they poured out innocent blood,
the blood of their sons and daughters,
whom they sacrificed to the idols of Canaan;
and the land was polluted with blood.
39 Thus they became unclean by their acts,
and played the harlot in their doings.

40 Then the anger of the LORD was kindled against his people,
and he abhorred his heritage;

41 he gave them into the hand of the nations,
so that those who hated them ruled over them.
42 Their enemies oppressed them,
and they were brought into subjection under their
power.
43 Many times he delivered them,
but they were rebellious in their purposes,
and were brought low through their iniquity.
44 Nevertheless he regarded their distress,
when he heard their cry.
45 He remembered for their sake his covenant,
and relented according to the abundance of his steadfast love.
46 He caused them to be pitied
by all those who held them captive.

47 Save us, O LORD our God,
and gather us from among the nations,
that we may give thanks to thy holy name
and glory in thy praise.

48 Blessed be the LORD, the God of Israel,
from everlasting to everlasting!
And let all the people say, "Amen!"
Praise the LORD!

x Cn: Heb *fools*

BOOK V

107 O give thanks to the LORD, for he is good;
for his steadfast love endures for ever!
2 Let the redeemed of the LORD say so,
whom he has redeemed from trouble
3 and gathered in from the lands,
from the east and from the west,
from the north and from the south.

4 Some wandered in desert wastes,
finding no way to a city to dwell in;
5 hungry and thirsty,
their soul fainted within them.
6 Then they cried to the LORD in their trouble,
and he delivered them from their distress;
7 he led them by a straight way,
till they reached a city to dwell in.
8 Let them thank the LORD for his steadfast love,
for his wonderful works to the sons of men!
9 For he satisfies him who is thirsty,
and the hungry he fills with good things.

10 Some sat in darkness and in gloom,
prisoners in affliction and in irons,
11 for they had rebelled against the words of God,
and spurned the counsel of the Most High.
12 Their hearts were bowed down with hard labor;
they fell down, with none to help.
13 Then they cried to the LORD in their trouble,
and he delivered them from their distress;
14 he brought them out of darkness and gloom,
and broke their bonds asunder.
15 Let them thank the LORD for his steadfast love,
for his wonderful works to the sons of men!
16 For he shatters the doors of bronze,
and cuts in two the bars of iron.

17 Some were sick x through their sinful ways,
and because of their iniquities suffered affliction;
18 they loathed any kind of food,
and they drew near to the gates of death.
19 Then they cried to the LORD in their trouble,
and he delivered them from their distress;
20 he sent forth his word, and healed them,
and delivered them from destruction.
21 Let them thank the LORD for his steadfast love,
for his wonderful works to the sons of men!
22 And let them offer sacrifices of thanksgiving,
and tell of his deeds in songs of joy!

23 Some went down to the sea in ships,
doing business on the great waters;
24 they saw the deeds of the LORD,

his wondrous works in the deep.
²⁵ For he commanded, and raised the stormy wind,
  which lifted up the waves of the sea.
²⁶ They mounted up to heaven, they went down to the
    depths;
  their courage melted away in their evil plight;
²⁷ they reeled and staggered like drunken men,
  and were at their wits' end.
²⁸ Then they cried to the LORD in their trouble,
  and he delivered them from their distress;
²⁹ he made the storm be still,
  and the waves of the sea were hushed.
³⁰ Then they were glad because they had quiet,
  and he brought them to their desired haven.
³¹ Let them thank the LORD for his steadfast love,
  for his wonderful works to the sons of men!
³² Let them extol him in the congregation of the people
  and praise him in the assembly of the elders.

³³ He turns rivers into a desert,
  springs of water into thirsty ground.
³⁴ a fruitful land into a salty waste,
  because of the wickedness of its inhabitants.
³⁵ He turns a desert into pools of water,
  a parched land into springs of water.
³⁶ And there he lets the hungry dwell,
  and they establish a city to live in;
³⁷ they sow fields, and plant vineyards,
  and get a fruitful yield.
³⁸ By his blessing they multiply greatly;
  and he does not let their cattle decrease.

³⁹ When they are diminished and brought low
  through oppression, trouble, and sorrow,
⁴⁰ he pours contempt upon princes
  and makes them wander in trackless wastes;
⁴¹ but he raises up the needy out of affliction,
  and makes their families like flocks.
⁴² The upright see it and are glad;
  and all wickedness stops its mouth.
⁴³ Whoever is wise, let him give heed to these things;
  let men consider the steadfast love of the LORD.

A Song. A Psalm of David.

108 My heart is steadfast, O God, my heart is steadfast!
  I will sing and make melody!
  Awake, my soul!
² Awake, O harp and lyre!
  I will awake the dawn!
³ I will give thanks to thee, O LORD, among the peoples,
  I will sing praises to thee among the nations.

⁴ For thy steadfast love is great above the heavens,
  thy faithfulness reaches to the clouds.

⁵ Be exalted, thyself, O God, above the heavens!
  Let thy glory be over all the earth!
⁶ That thy beloved may be delivered,
  give help by thy right hand, and answer me!

⁷ God has promised in his sanctuary:ʸ
  "With exultation I will divide up Shechem,
  and portion out the Vale of Succoth.
⁸ Gilead is mine; Manas'seh is mine;
  E'phraim is my helmet;
  Judah my scepter.
⁹ Moab is my washbasin;
  upon Edom I cast my shoe;
  over Philistia I shout in triumph."

¹⁰ Who will bring me to the fortified city?
  Who will lead me to Edom?
¹¹ Hast thou not rejected us, O God?
  Thou dost not go forth, O God, with our armies.
¹² O grant us help against the foe,
  for vain is the help of man!
¹³ With God we shall do valiantly;
  it is he who will tread down our foes.

To the choirmaster. A Psalm of David.

109 Be not silent, O God of my praise!
²   For wicked and deceitful mouths are opened against
    me,
  speaking against me with lying tongues.
³ They beset me with words of hate,
  and attack me without cause.
⁴ In return for my love they accuse me,
  even as I make prayer for them.ᶻ
⁵ So they reward me evil for good,
  and hatred for my love.

⁶ Appoint a wicked man against him;
  let an accuser bring him to trial.ᵃ
⁷ When he is tried, let him come forth guilty;
  let his prayer be counted as sin!
⁸ May his days be few;
  may another seize his goods!
⁹ May his children be fatherless,
  and his wife a widow!
¹⁰ May his children wander about and beg;
  may they be driven out ofᵇ the ruins they inhabit!
¹¹ May the creditor seize all that he has;
  may strangers plunder the fruits of his toil!
¹² Let there be none to extend kindness to him,

ʸ Or *by his holiness*   ᶻ Syr: Heb *I prayer*   ᵃ Heb *stand at his right hand*   ᵇ Gk: Heb *and seek*

nor any to pity his fatherless children!

¹³ May his posterity be cut off;
   may his name be blotted out in the second generation!
¹⁴ May the iniquity of his fathers be remembered before the
      LORD,
   and let not the sin of his mother be blotted out!
¹⁵ Let them be before the LORD continually;
   and may his ᶜ memory be cut off from the earth!

¹⁶ For he did not remember to show kindness,
   but pursued the poor and needy and the brokenhearted
      to their death.
¹⁷ He loved to curse; let curses come on him!
   He did not like blessing; may it be far from him!
¹⁸ He clothed himself with cursing as his coat,
   may it soak into his body like water,
   like oil into his bones!
¹⁹ May it be like a garment which he wraps round him,
   like a belt with which he daily girds himself!

²⁰ May this be the reward of my accusers from the LORD,
   of those who speak evil against my life!
²¹ But thou, O GOD my Lord,
   deal on my behalf for thy name's sake;
   because thy steadfast love is good, deliver me!
²² For I am poor and needy,
   and my heart is stricken within me.
²³ I am gone, like a shadow at evening;
   I am shaken off like a locust.
²⁴ My knees are weak through fasting;
   my body has become gaunt.
²⁵ I am an object of scorn to my accusers;
   when they see me, they wag their heads.

²⁶ Help me, O LORD my God!
   Save me according to thy steadfast love!
²⁷ Let them know that this is thy hand;
   thou, O LORD, hast done it!
²⁸ Let them curse, but do thou bless!
   Let my assailants be put to shame;ᵈ may thy servant be
      glad!
²⁹ May my accusers be clothed with dishonor;
   may they be wrapped in their own shame as in a
      mantle!

³⁰ With my mouth I will give great thanks to the LORD;
   I will praise him in the midst of the throng.
³¹ For he stands at the right hand of the needy,
   to save him from those who condemn him to death.

A Psalm of David.

110 The LORD says to my lord:
   "Sit at my right hand,
till I make your enemies your footstool."

² The LORD send forth from Zion
   your mighty scepter.
   Rule in the midst of your foes!
³ Your people will offer themselves freely
   on the day you lead your host
   upon the holy mountains.ᵉ
From the womb of the morning
   like dew your youth ᶠ will come to you.
⁴ The LORD has sworn
   and will not change his mind,
"You are a priest for ever
   after the order of Melchiz'edek."

⁵ The Lord is at your right hand;
   he will shatter kings on the day of his wrath.
⁶ He will execute judgment among the nations,
   filling them with corpses;
he will shatter chiefsᵍ
   over the wide earth.
⁷ He will drink from the brook by the way;
   therefore he will lift up his head.

111 Praise the LORD.
   I will give thanks to the LORD with my whole heart,
   in the company of the upright, in the congregation.
² Great are the works of the LORD,
   studied by all who have pleasure in them.
³ Full of honor and majesty is his work,
   and his righteousness endures for ever.
⁴ He has caused his wonderful works to be remembered;
   the LORD is gracious and merciful.
⁵ He provides food for those who fear him;
   he is ever mindful of his covenant.
⁶ He has shown his people the power of his works,
   in giving them the heritage of the nations.
⁷ The works of his hands are faithful and just;
   all his precepts are trustworthy,
⁸ they are established for ever and ever,
   to be performed with faithfulness and uprightness.
⁹ He sent redemption to his people;
   he has commanded his covenant for ever.
   Holy and terrible is his name!
¹⁰ The fear of the LORD is the beginning of wisdom;
   a good understanding have all those who practice it.
   His praise endures for ever!

112 Praise the LORD.
   Blessed is the man who fears the LORD,

ᶜ Gk: Heb *their*   ᵈ Gk: Heb *they have arisen and have been put to shame*   ᵉ Another reading is *in holy array*
ᶠ Cn: Heb *the dew of your youth*   ᵍ Or *the head*

who greatly delights in his commandments!
2 His descendants will be mighty in the land;
the generation of the upright will be blessed.
3 Wealth and riches are in his house;
and his righteousness endures for ever.
4 Light rises in the darkness for the upright;
the Lord h is gracious, merciful, and righteous.
5 It is well with the man who deals generously and lends,
who conducts his affairs with justice.
6 For the righteous will never be moved;
he will be remembered for ever.
7 He is not afraid of evil tidings;
his heart is firm, trusting in the Lord.
8 His heart is steady, he will not be afraid,
until he sees his desire on his adversaries.
9 He has distributed freely, he has given to the poor;
his righteousness endures for ever;
his horn is exalted in honor.
10 The wicked man sees it and is angry;
he gnashes his teeth and melts away;
the desire of the wicked man comes to nought.

113 Praise the Lord!
Praise, O servants of the Lord,
praise the name of the Lord!

2 Blessed be the name of the Lord
from this time forth and for evermore!
3 From the rising of the sun to its setting
the name of the Lord is to be praised!
4 The Lord is high above all nations,
and his glory above the heavens!

5 Who is like the Lord our God,
who is seated on high,
6 who looks far down
upon the heavens and the earth?
7 He raises the poor from the dust,
and lifts the needy from the ash heap,
8 to make them sit with princes,
with the princes of his people.
9 He gives the barren woman a home,
making her the joyous mother of children.
Praise the Lord!

114 When Israel went forth from Egypt,
the house of Jacob from a people of strange language,
2 Judah became his sanctuary,
Israel his dominion.

3 The sea looked and fled,
Jordan turned back.
4 The mountains skipped like rams,

h Gk: Heb lacks the Lord

the hills like lambs.
5 What ails you, O sea, that you flee?
O Jordan, that you turn back?
6 O mountains, that you skip like rams?
O hills, like lambs?

7 Tremble, O earth, at the presence of the Lord,
at the presence of the God of Jacob,
8 who turns the rock into a pool of water,
the flint into a spring of water.

115 Not to us, O Lord, not to us,
but to thy name give glory,
for the sake of thy steadfast love and thy faithfulness!
2 Why should the nations say,
"Where is their God?"

3 Our God is in the heavens;
he does whatever he pleases.
4 Their idols are silver and gold,
the work of men's hands.
5 They have mouths, but do not speak;
eyes, but do not see.
6 They have ears, but do not hear;
noses, but do not smell.
7 They have hands, but do not feel;
feet, but do not walk;
and they do not make a sound in their throat.
8 Those who make them are like them;
so are all who trust in them.

9 O Israel, trust in the Lord!
He is their help and their shield.
10 O house of Aaron, put your trust in the Lord!
He is their help and their shield.
11 You who fear the Lord, trust in the Lord!
He is their help and their shield.

12 The Lord has been mindful of us; he will bless us;
he will bless the house of Israel;
he will bless the house of Aaron;
13 he will bless those who fear the Lord,
both small and great.

14 May the Lord give you increase,
you and your children!
15 May you be blessed by the Lord,
who made heaven and earth!

16 The heavens are the LORD's heavens,
  but the earth he has given to the sons of men.
17 The dead do not praise the LORD,
  nor do any that go down into silence.
18 But we will bless the LORD
  from this time forth and for evermore.
  Praise the LORD!

116 I love the LORD, because he has heard
  my voice and my supplications.
2 Because he inclined his ear to me,
  therefore I will call on him as long as I live.
3 The snares of death encompassed me;
  the pangs of Sheol laid hold on me;
  I suffered distress and anguish.
4 Then I called on the name of the LORD:
  "O LORD, I beseech thee, save my life!"

5 Gracious is the LORD, and righteous;
  our God is merciful.
6 The LORD preserves the simple;
  when I was brought low, he saved me.
7 Return, O my soul, to your rest;
  for the LORD has dealt bountifully with you.

8 For thou hast delivered my soul from death,
  my eyes from tears,
  my feet from stumbling;
9 I walk before the LORD
  in the land of the living.
10 I kept my faith, even when I said,
  "I am greatly afflicted";
11 I said in my consternation,
  "Men are all a vain hope."

12 What shall I render to the LORD
  for all his bounty to me?
13 I will lift up the cup of salvation
  and call on the name of the LORD,
14 I will pay my vows to the LORD
  in the presence of all his people.
15 Precious in the sight of the LORD
  is the death of his saints.
16 O LORD, I am thy servant;
  I am thy servant, the son of thy handmaid.
  Thou hast loosed my bonds.
17 I will offer to thee the sacrifice of thanksgiving
  and call on the name of the LORD.
18 I will pay my vows to the LORD
  in the presence of all his people,
19 in the courts of the house of the LORD,
  in your midst, O Jerusalem.
  Praise the LORD!

117 Praise the LORD, all nations!
  Extol him, all peoples!
2 For great is his steadfast love toward us;
  and the faithfulness of the LORD endures for ever.
  Praise the LORD!

118 O give thanks to the LORD, for he is good;
  his steadfast love endures for ever!

2 Let Israel say,
  "His steadfast love endures for ever."
3 Let the house of Aaron say,
  "His steadfast love endures for ever."
4 Let those who fear the LORD say,
  "His steadfast love endures for ever."

5 Out of my distress I called on the LORD;
  the LORD answered me and set me free.
6 With the LORD on my side I do not fear.
  What can man do to me?
7 The LORD is on my side to help me;
  I shall look in triumph on those who hate me.
8 It is better to take refuge in the LORD
  than to put confidence in man.
9 It is better to take refuge in the LORD
  than to put confidence in princes.

10 All nations surrounded me;
  in the name of the LORD I cut them off!
11 They surrounded me, surrounded me on every side;
  in the name of the LORD I cut them off!
12 They surrounded me like bees,
  they blazed i like a fire of thorns;
  in the name of the LORD I cut them off!
13 I was pushed hard,j so that I was falling,
  but the LORD helped me.
14 The LORD is my strength and my song;
  he has become my salvation.

15 Hark, glad songs of victory
  in the tents of the righteous:
  "The right hand of the LORD does valiantly,
16   the right hand of the LORD is exalted,
  the right hand of the LORD does valiantly!"
17 I shall not die, but I shall live,
  and recount the deeds of the LORD.
18 The LORD has chastened me sorely,
  but he has not given me over to death.

19 Open to me the gates of righteousness,
  that I may enter through them
  and give thanks to the LORD.

i Gk: Heb *were extinguished*   j Gk Syr Jerome: Heb *thou didst push me hard*

²⁰ This is the gate of the LORD;
 the righteous shall enter through it.

²¹ I thank thee that thou hast answered me
 and hast become my salvation.
²² The stone which the builders rejected
 has become the head of the corner.
²³ This is the LORD's doing;
 it is marvelous in our eyes.
²⁴ This is the day which the LORD has made;
 let us rejoice and be glad in it.
²⁵ Save us, we beseech thee, O LORD!
 O LORD, we beseech thee, give us success!

²⁶ Blessed be he who enters in the name of the LORD!
 We bless you from the house of the LORD.
²⁷ The LORD is God,
 and he has given us light.
 Bind the festal procession with branches,
 up to the horns of the altar!

²⁸ Thou art my God, and I will give thanks to thee;
 thou art my God, I will extol thee.

²⁹ O give thanks to the LORD, for he is good;
 for his steadfast love endures for ever!

119 Blessed are those whose way is blameless,
 who walk in the law of the LORD!
² Blessed are those who keep his testimonies,
 who seek him with their whole heart,
³ who also do no wrong,
 but walk in his ways!
⁴ Thou hast commanded thy precepts
 to be kept diligently.
⁵ O that my ways may be steadfast
 in keeping thy statutes!
⁶ Then I shall not be put to shame,
 having my eyes fixed on all thy commandments.
⁷ I will praise thee with an upright heart,
 when I learn thy righteous ordinances.
⁸ I will observe thy statutes;
 O forsake me not utterly!

⁹ How can a young man keep his way pure?
 By guarding it according to thy word.
¹⁰ With my whole heart I seek thee;
 let me not wander from thy commandments!
¹¹ I have laid up thy word in my heart,
 that I might not sin against thee.
¹² Blessed be thou, O LORD;
 teach me thy statutes!
¹³ With my lips I declare
 all the ordinances of thy mouth.

¹⁴ In the way of thy testimonies I delight
 as much as in all riches.
¹⁵ I will meditate on thy precepts,
 and fix my eyes on thy ways.
¹⁶ I will delight in thy statutes;
 I will not forget thy word.

¹⁷ Deal bountifully with thy servant,
 that I may live and observe thy word.
¹⁸ Open my eyes, that I may behold
 wondrous things out of thy law.
¹⁹ I am a sojourner on earth;
 hide not thy commandments from me!
²⁰ My soul is consumed with longing
 for thy ordinances at all times.
²¹ Thou dost rebuke the insolent, accursed ones,
 who wander from thy commandments;
²² take away from me their scorn and contempt,
 for I have kept thy testimonies.
²³ Even though princes sit plotting against me,
 thy servant will meditate on thy statutes.
²⁴ Thy testimonies are my delight,
 they are my counselors.

²⁵ My soul cleaves to the dust;
 revive me according to thy word!
²⁶ When I told of my ways, thou didst answer me;
 teach me thy statutes!
²⁷ Make me understand the way of thy precepts,
 and I will meditate on thy wondrous works.
²⁸ My soul melts away for sorrow;
 strengthen me according to thy word!
²⁹ Put false ways far from me;
 and graciously teach me thy law!
³⁰ I have chosen the way of faithfulness,
 I set thy ordinances before me.
³¹ I cleave to thy testimonies, O LORD;
 let me not be put to shame!
³² I will run in the way of thy commandments
 when thou enlargest my understanding!

³³ Teach me, O LORD, the way of thy statutes;
 and I will keep it to the end.
³⁴ Give me understanding, that I may keep thy law
 and observe it with my whole heart.
³⁵ Lead me in the path of thy commandments,
 for I delight in it.
³⁶ Incline my heart to thy testimonies,
 and not to gain!
³⁷ Turn my eyes from looking at vanities;
 and give me life in thy ways.
³⁸ Confirm to thy servant thy promise,
 which is for those who fear thee.
³⁹ Turn away the reproach which I dread;

for thy ordinances are good.
40 Behold, I long for thy precepts;
in thy righteousness give me life!

41 Let thy steadfast love come to me, O LORD,
thy salvation according to thy promise;
42 then shall I have an answer for those who taunt me,
for I trust in thy word.
43 And take not the word of truth utterly out of my mouth,
for my hope is in thy ordinances.
44 I will keep thy law continually,
for ever and ever;
45 and I shall walk at liberty,
for I have sought thy precepts.
46 I will also speak of thy testimonies before kings,
and shall not be put to shame;
47 for I find my delight in thy commandments,
which I love.
48 I revere thy commandments, which I love,
and I will meditate on thy statutes.

49 Remember thy word to thy servant,
in which thou hast made me hope.
50 This is my comfort in my affliction
that thy promise gives me life.
51 Godless men utterly deride me,
but I do not turn away from thy law.
52 When I think of thy ordinances from of old,
I take comfort, O Lord.
53 Hot indignation seizes me because of the wicked,
who forsake thy law.
54 Thy statutes have been my songs
in the house of my pilgrimage.
55 I remember thy name in the night, O LORD,
and keep thy law.
56 This blessing has fallen to me,
that I have kept thy precepts.

57 The LORD is my portion;
I promise to keep thy words.
58 I entreat thy favor with all my heart;
be gracious to me according to thy promise.
59 When I think of thy ways,
I turn my feet to thy testimonies;
60 I hasten and do not delay
to keep thy commandments.
61 Though the cords of the wicked ensnare me,
I do not forget thy law.
62 At midnight I rise to praise thee,
because of thy righteous ordinances.
63 I am a companion of all who fear thee,
of those who keep thy precepts.
64 The earth, O LORD, is full of thy steadfast love;
teach me thy statutes!

65 Thou hast dealt well with thy servant,
O LORD, according to thy word.
66 Teach me good judgment and knowledge,
for I believe in thy commandments.
67 Before I was afflicted I went astray;
but now I keep thy word.
68 Thou art good and doest good;
teach me thy statutes.
69 The godless besmear me with lies,
but with my whole heart I keep thy precepts;
70 their heart is gross like fat,
but I delight in thy law.
71 It is good for me that I was afflicted,
that I might learn thy statutes.
72 The law of thy mouth is better to me
than thousands of gold and silver pieces.

73 Thy hands have made and fashioned me;
give me understanding that I may learn thy commandments.
74 Those who fear thee shall see me and rejoice,
because I have hoped in thy word.
75 I know, O LORD, that thy judgments are right,
and that in faithfulness thou hast afflicted me.
76 Let thy steadfast love be ready to comfort me
according to thy promise to thy servant.
77 Let thy mercy come to me, that I may live;
for thy law is my delight.
78 Let the godless be put to shame,
because they have subverted me with guile;
as for me, I will meditate on thy precepts.
79 Let those who fear thee turn to me,
that they may know thy testimonies.
80 May my heart be blameless in thy statutes,
that I may not be put to shame!

81 My soul languishes for thy salvation;
I hope in thy word.
82 My eyes fail with watching for thy promise;
I ask, "When wilt thou comfort me?"
83 For I have become like a wineskin in the smoke,
yet I have not forgotten thy statutes.
84 How long must thy servant endure?
When wilt thou judge those who persecute me?
85 Godless men have dug pitfalls for me,
men who do not conform to thy law.
86 All thy commandments are sure;
they persecute me with falsehood; help me!

87 They have almost made an end of me on earth;
  but I have not forsaken thy precepts.
88 In thy steadfast love spare my life,
  that I may keep the testimonies of thy mouth.

89 For ever, O Lord, thy word
  is firmly fixed in the heavens.
90 Thy faithfulness endures to all generations;
  thou hast established the earth, and it stands fast.
91 By thy appointment they stand this day;
  for all things are thy servants.
92 If thy law had not been my delight,
  I should have perished in my affliction.
93 I will never forget thy precepts;
  for by them thou hast given me life.

94 I am thine, save me;
  for I have sought thy precepts.
95 The wicked lie in wait to destroy me;
  but I consider thy testimonies.
96 I have seen a limit to all perfection,
  but thy commandment is exceedingly broad.

97 Oh, how I love thy law!
  It is my meditation all the day.
98 Thy commandment makes me wiser than my enemies,
  for it is ever with me.
99 I have more understanding than all my teachers,
  for thy testimonies are my meditation.
100 I understand more than the aged,
  for I keep thy precepts.
101 I hold back my feet from every evil way,
  in order to keep thy word.
102 I do not turn aside from thy ordinances,
  for thou hast taught me.
103 How sweet are thy words to my taste,
  sweeter than honey to my mouth!
104 Through thy precepts I get understanding;
  therefore I hate every false way.

105 Thy word is a lamp to my feet
  and a light to my path.
106 I have sworn an oath and confirmed it,
  to observe thy righteous ordinances.
107 I am sorely afflicted;
  give me life, O Lord, according to thy word!
108 Accept my offerings of praise, O Lord,
  and teach me thy ordinances.

k Gk Jerome: Heb uncertain

109 I hold my life in my hand continually,
  but I do not forget thy law.
110 The wicked have laid a snare for me,
  but I do not stray from thy precepts.
111 Thy testimonies are my heritage for ever;
  yea, they are the joy of my heart.
112 I incline my heart to perform thy statutes
  for ever, to the end.

113 I hate double-minded men,
  but I love thy law.
114 Thou art my hiding place and my shield;
  I hope in thy word.
115 Depart from me, you evildoers,
  that I may keep the commandments of my God.
116 Uphold me according to thy promise, that I may live,
  and let me not be put to shame in my hope!
117 Hold me up, that I may be safe
  and have regard for thy statutes continually!
118 Thou dost spurn all who go astray from thy statutes;
  yea, their cunning is in vain.
119 All the wicked of the earth thou dost count as dross;
  therefore I love thy testimonies.
120 My flesh trembles for fear of thee,
  and I am afraid of thy judgments.

121 I have done what is just and right;
  do not leave me to my oppressors.
122 Be surety for thy servant for good;
  let not the godless oppress me.
123 My eyes fail with watching for thy salvation,
  and for the fulfilment of thy righteous promise.
124 Deal with thy servant according to thy steadfast love,
  and teach me thy statutes.
125 I am thy servant; give me understanding,
  that I may know thy testimonies!
126 It is time for the Lord to act,
  for thy law has been broken.
127 Therefore I love thy commandments
  above gold, above fine gold.
128 Therefore I direct my steps by all thy precepts;k
  I hate every false way.

129 Thy testimonies are wonderful;
  therefore my soul keeps them.
130 The unfolding of thy words gives light;
  it imparts understanding to the simple.
131 With open mouth I pant,
  because I long for thy commandments.
132 Turn to me and be gracious to me,
  as is thy wont toward those who love thy name.
133 Keep steady my steps according to thy promise,
  and let no iniquity get dominion over me.

134 Redeem me from man's oppression,
   that I may keep thy precepts.
135 Make thy face shine upon thy servant,
   and teach me thy statutes.
136 My eyes shed streams of tears,
   because men do not keep thy law.

137 Righteous art thou, O LORD,
   and right are thy judgments.
138 Thou hast appointed thy testimonies in righteousness
   and in all faithfulness.
139 My zeal consumes me,
   because my foes forget thy words.
140 Thy promise is well tried,
   and thy servant loves it.
141 I am small and despised,
   yet I do not forget thy precepts.
142 Thy righteousness is righteous for ever,
   and thy law is true.
143 Trouble and anguish have come upon me,
   but thy commandments are my delight.
144 Thy testimonies are righteous for ever;
   give me understanding that I may live.

145 With my whole heart I cry; answer me, O LORD!
   I will keep thy statutes.
146 I cry to thee; save me,
   that I may observe thy testimonies.
147 I rise before dawn and cry for help;
   I hope in thy words.
148 My eyes are awake before the watches of the night,
   that I may meditate upon thy promise.
149 Hear my voice in thy steadfast love;
   O LORD, in thy justice preserve my life.
150 They draw near who persecute me with evil purpose;
   they are far from thy law.
151 But thou art near, O LORD,
   and all thy commandments are true.
152 Long have I known from thy testimonies
   that thou hast founded them for ever.
153 Look on my affliction and deliver me,
   for I do not forget thy law.
154 Plead my cause and redeem me;
   give me life according to thy promise!
155 Salvation is far from the wicked,
   for they do not seek thy statutes.
156 Great is thy mercy, O LORD;
   give me life according to thy justice.
157 Many are my persecutors and my adversaries,
   but I do not swerve from thy testimonies.
158 I look at the faithless with disgust,
   because they do not keep thy commands.
159 Consider how I love thy precepts!
   Preserve my life according to thy steadfast love.

160 The sum of thy word is truth;
   and every one of thy righteous ordinances endures for
   ever.

161 Princes persecute me without cause,
   but my heart stands in awe of thy words.
162 I rejoice at thy word
   like one who finds great spoil.
163 I hate and abhor falsehood,
   but I love thy law.
164 Seven times a day I praise thee
   for thy righteous ordinances.
165 Great peace have those who love thy law;
   nothing can make them stumble.
166 I hope for thy salvation, O LORD,
   and I do thy commandments.
167 My soul keeps thy testimonies;
   I love them exceedingly.
168 I keep thy precepts and testimonies
   for all my ways are before thee.

169 Let my cry come before thee, O LORD;
   give me understanding according to thy word!
170 Let my supplication come before thee;
   deliver me according to thy word.
171 My lips will pour forth praise
   that thou dost teach me thy statutes.
172 My tongue will sing of thy word,
   for all thy commandments are right.
173 Let thy hand be ready to help me,
   for I have chosen thy precepts.
174 I long for thy salvation, O LORD,
   and thy law is my delight.
175 Let me live, that I may praise thee,
   and let thy ordinances help me.
176 I have gone astray like a lost sheep; seek thy servant,
   for I do not forget thy commandments.

A Song of Ascents.

120 In my distress I cry to the LORD,
      that he may answer me:
2 "Deliver me, O LORD,
   from lying lips,
   from a deceitful tongue."

3 What shall be given to you?
   And what more shall be done to you,
   you deceitful tongue?
4 A warrior's sharp arrows,
   with glowing coals of the broom tree!

⁵ Woe is me, that I sojourn in Meshech,
  that I dwell among the tents of Kedar!
⁶ Too long have I had my dwelling
  among those who hate peace.
⁷ I am for peace;
  but when I speak,
  they are for war!

A Song of Ascents.

121 I lift up my eyes to the hills.
    From whence does my help come?
² My help comes from the LORD,
  who made heaven and earth.

³ He will not let your foot be moved,
  he who keeps you will not slumber.
⁴ Behold, he who keeps Israel
  will neither slumber nor sleep.

⁵ The LORD is your keeper;
  the LORD is your shade
  on your right hand.
⁶ The sun shall not smite you by day,
  nor the moon by night.

⁷ The LORD will keep you from all evil;
  he will keep your life.
⁸ The LORD will keep
  your going out and your coming in
  from this time forth and for evermore.

A Song of Ascents. Of David.

122 I was glad when they said to me,
    "Let us go to the house of the LORD!"
² Our feet have been standing
  within your gates, O Jerusalem!

³ Jerusalem, built as a city
  which is bound firmly together,
⁴ to which the tribes go up,
  the tribes of the LORD,
  as was decreed for Israel,
  to give thanks to the name of the LORD.
⁵ There thrones for judgment were set,
  the thrones of the house of David.

⁶ Pray for the peace of Jerusalem!
  "May they prosper who love you!"
⁷ Peace be within your walls,
  and security within your towers!"

⁸ For my brethren and companions' sake
  I will say, "Peace be within you!"
⁹ For the sake of the house of the LORD our God,
  I will seek your good.

A Song of Ascents.

123 To thee I lift up my eyes,
    O Thou who art enthroned in the heavens!
² Behold, as the eyes of servants
  look to the hand of their master,
  as the eyes of a maid
  to the hand of her mistress,
  so our eyes look to the LORD our God,
  till he have mercy upon us.

³ Have mercy upon us, O LORD, have mercy upon us,
  for we have had more than enough of contempt.
⁴ Too long our soul has been sated
  with the scorn of those who are at ease,
  the contempt of the proud.

A Song of Ascents. Of David.

124 If it had not been the LORD who was on our side,
    let Israel now say—
² if it had not been the LORD who was on our side,
  when men rose up against us,
³ then they would have swallowed us up alive,
  when their anger was kindled against us;
⁴ then the flood would have swept us away,
  the torrent would have gone over us;
⁵ then over us would have gone
  the raging waters.

⁶ Blessed be the LORD,
  who has not given us
  as prey to their teeth!
⁷ We have escaped as a bird
  from the snare of the fowlers;
  the snare is broken,
  and we have escaped!

⁸ Our help is in the name of the LORD,
  who made heaven and earth.

A Song of Ascents.

125 Those who trust in the LORD are like Mount Zion,
    which cannot be moved, but abides for ever.
² As the mountains are round about Jerusalem,

411

so the LORD is round about his people,
from this time forth and for evermore.
[3] For the scepter of wickedness shall not rest
upon the land allotted to the righteous,
lest the righteous put forth
their hands to do wrong.
[4] Do good, O LORD, to those who are good,
and to those who are upright in their hearts!
[5] But those who turn aside upon their crooked ways
the LORD will lead away with evildoers!
Peace be in Israel!

A Song of Ascents.

126 When the LORD restored the fortunes of Zion,[1]
we were like those who dream.
[2] Then our mouth was filled with laughter,
and our tongue with shouts of joy;
then they said among the nations,
"The LORD has done great things for them."
[3] The LORD has done great things for us;
we are glad.

[4] Restore our fortunes, O LORD,
like the watercourses in the Negeb!
[5] May those who sow in tears
reap with shouts of joy!
[6] He that goes forth weeping,
bearing the seed for sowing,
shall come home with shouts of joy,
bringing his sheaves with him.

A Song of Ascents. Of Solomon.

127 Unless the LORD builds the house,
those who build it labor in vain.
Unless the LORD watches over the city,
the watchman stays awake in vain.
[2] It is in vain that you rise up early and go late to rest,
eating the bread of anxious toil;
for [m] he gives to his beloved in sleep.

[3] Lo, sons are a heritage from the LORD,
the fruit of the womb a reward.
[4] Like arrows in the hand of a warrior
are the sons of one's youth.

[5] Happy is the man who has
his quiver full of them!
He shall not be put to shame
when he speaks with his enemies in the gate.

A Song of Ascents.

128 Blessed is every one who fears the LORD,
who walks in his ways!
[2] You shall eat the fruit of the labor of your hands;
you shall be happy, and it shall be well with you.

[3] Your wife will be like a fruitful vine
within your house;
your children will be like olive shoots
around your table.
[4] Lo, thus shall the man be blessed
who fears the LORD.

[5] The LORD bless you from Zion!
May you see the prosperity of Jerusalem
all the days of your life!
[6] May you see your children's children!
Peace be upon Israel!

A Song of Ascents.

129 "Sorely have they afflicted me from my youth,"
let Israel now say—
[2] "Sorely have they afflicted me from my youth,
yet they have not prevailed against me.
[3] The plowers plowed upon my back;
they made long their furrows."
[4] The LORD is righteous;
he has cut the cords of the wicked.
[5] May all who hate Zion
be put to shame and turned backward!
[6] Let them be like the grass on the housetops,
which withers before it grows up,
[7] with which the reaper does not fill his hand
or the binder of sheaves his bosom,
[8] while those who pass by do not say,
"The blessing of the LORD be upon you!
We bless you in the name of the LORD!"

A Song of Ascents.

130 Out of the depths I cry to thee, O LORD!
[2] Lord, hear my voice!
Let thy ears be attentive
to the voice of my supplications!

[1] Or *brought back those who returned to Zion*   [m] Another reading is *so*

³ If thou, O LORD, shouldst mark iniquities,
Lord, who could stand?
⁴ But there is forgiveness with thee,
that thou mayest be feared.

⁵ I wait for the LORD, my soul waits,
and in his word I hope;
⁶ my soul waits for the LORD
more than watchmen for the morning,
more than watchmen for the morning.

⁷ O Israel, hope in the LORD!
For with the LORD there is steadfast love,
and with him is plenteous redemption.
⁸ And he will redeem Israel
from all his iniquities.

A Song of Ascents. Of David.

131 O LORD, my heart is not lifted up,
my eyes are not raised too high;
I do not occupy myself with things
too great and too marvelous for me.
² But I have calmed and quieted my soul,
like a child quieted at its mother's breast;
like a child that is quieted is my soul.

³ O Israel, hope in the LORD
from this time forth and for evermore.

A Song of Ascents.

132 Remember, O LORD, in David's favor,
all the hardships he endured;
² how he swore to the LORD
and vowed to the Mighty One of Jacob,
³ "I will not enter my house
or get into my bed;
⁴ I will not give sleep to my eyes
or slumber to my eyelids,
⁵ until I find a place for the LORD,
a dwelling place for the Mighty One of Jacob."

⁶ Lo, we heard of it in Eph'rathah,
we found it in the fields of Ja'ar.
⁷ "Let us go to his dwelling place;
let us worship at his footstool!"

⁸ Arise, O LORD, and go to thy resting place,
thou and the ark of thy might.
⁹ Let thy priests be clothed with righteousness,
and let thy saints shout for joy.

¹⁰ For thy servant David's sake
do not turn away the face of thy anointed one.

¹¹ The LORD swore to David a sure oath
from which he will not turn back:
"One of the sons of your body
I will set on your throne.
¹² If your sons keep my covenant
and my testimonies which I shall teach them,
their sons also for ever
shall sit upon your throne."

¹³ For the LORD has chosen Zion;
he has desired it for his habitation:
¹⁴ "This is my resting place for ever;
here I will dwell, for I have desired it.
¹⁵ I will abundantly bless her provisions;
I will satisfy her poor with bread.
¹⁶ Her priests I will clothe with salvation,
and her saints will shout for joy.
¹⁷ There I will make a horn to sprout for David;
I have prepared a lamp for my anointed.
¹⁸ His enemies I will clothe with shame,
but upon himself his crown will shed its luster."

A Song of Ascents.

133 Behold, how good and pleasant it is
when brothers dwell in unity!
² It is like the precious oil upon the head,
running down upon the beard,
upon the beard of Aaron,
running down on the collar of his robes!
³ It is like the dew of Hermon,
which falls on the mountains of Zion!
For there the LORD has commanded the blessing,
life for evermore.

A Song of Ascents.

134 Come, bless the LORD,
all you servants of the LORD,
who stand by night in the house of the LORD!
² Lift up your hands to the holy place,
and bless the LORD!

³ May the LORD bless you from Zion,
he who made heaven and earth!

135 Praise the LORD.
Praise the name of the LORD,
give praise, O servants of the LORD,
² you that stand in the house of the LORD,
in the courts of the house of our God!

3 Praise the LORD, for the LORD is good;
   sing to his name, for he is gracious!
4 For the LORD has chosen Jacob for himself,
   Israel as his own possession.

5 For I know that the LORD is great,
   and that our Lord is above all gods.
6 Whatever the LORD pleases he does,
   in heaven and on earth,
   in the seas and all deeps.
7 He it is who makes the clouds rise at the end of the earth,
   who makes lightnings for the rain
   and brings forth the wind from his storehouses.

8 He it was who smote the first-born of Egypt,
   both of man and of beast;
9 who in thy midst, O Egypt,
   sent signs and wonders
   against Pharaoh and all his servants;
10 who smote many nations
   and slew mighty kings,
11 Sihon, king of the Amorites,
   and Og, king of Bashan,
   and all the kingdoms of Canaan,
12 and gave their land as a heritage,
   a heritage to his people Israel.

13 Thy name, O LORD, endures for ever,
   thy renown, O LORD, throughout all ages.
14 For the LORD will vindicate his people,
   and have compassion on his servants.

15 The idols of the nations are silver and gold,
   the work of men's hands.
16 They have mouths, but they speak not,
   they have eyes, but they see not,
17 they have ears, but they hear not,
   nor is there any breath in their mouths.
18 Like them be those who make them!—
   yea, every one who trusts in them!

19 O house of Israel, bless the LORD!
   O house of Aaron, bless the LORD!
20 O house of Levi, bless the LORD!
   You that fear the LORD, bless the LORD!
21 Blessed be the LORD from Zion,
   he who dwells in Jerusalem!
   Praise the LORD!

136 O give thanks to the LORD, for he is good,
   for his steadfast love endures for ever.
2 O give thanks to the God of gods,
   for his steadfast love endures for ever.
3 O give thanks to the Lord of lords,
   for his steadfast love endures for ever;
4 to him who alone does great wonders,

   for his steadfast love endures for ever;
5 to him who by understanding made the heavens,
   for his steadfast love endures for ever;
6 to him who spread out the earth upon the waters,
   for his steadfast love endures for ever;
7 to him who made the great lights,
   for his steadfast love endures for ever;
8 the sun to rule over the day,
   for his steadfast love endures for ever;
9 the moon and stars to rule over the night,
   for his steadfast love endures for ever;
10 to him who smote the first-born of Egypt,
   for his steadfast love endures for ever;
11 and brought Israel out from among them,
   for his steadfast love endures for ever;
12 with a strong hand and an outstretched arm,
   for his steadfast love endures for ever;
13 to him who divided the Red Sea in sunder,
   for his steadfast love endures for ever;
14 and made Israel pass through the midst of it,
   for his steadfast love endures for ever;
15 but overthrew Pharaoh and his host in the Red Sea,
   for his steadfast love endures for ever;
16 to him who led his people through the wilderness,
   for his steadfast love endures for ever;
17 to him who smote great kings,
   for his steadfast love endures for ever;
18 and slew famous kings,
   for his steadfast love endures for ever;
19 Sihon, king of the Amorites,
   for his steadfast love endures for ever;
20 and Og, king of Bashan,
   for his steadfast love endures for ever;
21 and gave their land as a heritage,
   for his steadfast love endures for ever;
22 a heritage to Israel his servant,
   for his steadfast love endures for ever.

23 It is he who remembered us in our low estate,
   for his steadfast love endures for ever;
24 and rescued us from our foes,
   for his steadfast love endures for ever;
25 he who gives food to all flesh,
   for his steadfast love endures for ever.

26 O give thanks to the God of heaven,
   for his steadfast love endures for ever.

137 By the waters ⁰ of Babylon,
   there we sat down and wept,
   when we remembered Zion.
2 On the willows ᵖ there
   we hung up our lyres.
3 For there our captors required of us songs,

⁰ Heb *streams*   ᵖ Or *poplars*

and our tormentors, mirth, saying,
"Sing us one of the songs of Zion!"

4 How shall we sing the LORD's song
in a foreign land?
5 If I forget you, O Jerusalem,
let my right hand wither!
6 Let my tongue cleave to the roof of my mouth,
if I do not remember you,
if I do not set Jerusalem
above my highest joy!

7 Remember, O LORD, against the Edomites
the day of Jerusalem,
how they said, "Rase it, rase it!
Down to its foundations!"
8 O daughter of Babylon, you devastator! q
Happy shall he be who requites you
with what you have done to us!
9 Happy shall he be who takes your little ones
and dashes them against the rock!

A Psalm of David.

138 I give thee thanks, O LORD, with my whole heart;
before the gods I sing thy praise;
2 I bow down toward thy holy temple
and give thanks to thy name for thy steadfast love and
thy faithfulness;
for thou hast exalted above everything
thy name and thy word.r
3 On the day I called, thou didst answer me,
my strength of soul thou didst increase.s

4 All the kings of the earth shall praise thee, O LORD,
for they have heard the words of thy mouth;
5 and they shall sing of the ways of the LORD,
for great is the glory of the LORD.
6 For though the LORD is high, he regards the lowly;
but the haughty he knows from afar.

7 Though I walk in the midst of trouble,
thou dost preserve my life;
thou dost stretch out thy hand against the wrath of my
enemies,
and thy right hand delivers me.
8 The LORD will fulfil his purpose for me;
thy steadfast love, O LORD, endures for ever.
Do not forsake the work of thy hands.

To the choirmaster. A Psalm of David.

139 O LORD, thou hast searched me and known me!
Thou knowest when I sit down and when I rise up;
thou discernest my thoughts from afar.

3 Thou searchest out my path and my lying down,
and art acquainted with all my ways.
4 Even before a word is on my tongue,
lo, O LORD, thou knowest it altogether.
5 Thou dost beset me behind and before,
and layest thy hand upon me.
6 Such knowledge is too wonderful for me;
it is high, I cannot attain it.

7 Whither shall I go from thy Spirit?
Or whither shall I flee from thy presence?
8 If I ascend to heaven, thou art there!
If I make my bed in Sheol, thou art there!
9 If I take the wings of the morning and dwell in the
uttermost parts of the sea,
10 even there thy hand shall lead me,
and thy right hand shall hold me.
11 If I say, "Let only darkness cover me,
and the light about me be night,"
12 even the darkness is not dark to thee,
the night is bright as the day;
for darkness is as light with thee.

13 For thou didst form my inward parts,
thou didst knit me together in my mother's womb.
14 I praise thee, for thou art fearful and wonderful.t

Wonderful are thy works!
Thou knowest me right well;
15   my frame was not hidden from thee,
when I was being made in secret,
intricately wrought in the depths of the earth.
16 Thy eyes beheld my unformed substance;
in thy book were written, every one of them,
the days that were formed for me,
when as yet there was none of them.
17 How precious to me are thy thoughts, O God!
How vast is the sum of them!
18 If I would count them, they are more than the sand.
When I awake, I am still with thee.u

19 O that thou wouldst slay the wicked, O God,
and that men of blood would depart from me,
20 men who maliciously defy thee,
who lift themselves up against thee for evil! v
21 Do I not hate them that hate thee, O LORD?
And do I not loathe them that rise up against thee?
22 I hate them with perfect hatred;
I count them my enemies.
23 Search me, O God, and know my heart!
Try me and know my thoughts!
24 And see if there be any wicked w way in me,
and lead me in the way everlasting! x

q Or *you who are devastated*   r Cn: Heb *thou hast exalted thy word above all thy name*
s Syr Compare Gk Tg: Heb *thou didst make me arrogant in my soul* with *strength*
t Cn Compare Gk Syr Jerome: Heb *fearful things I am wonderful*   u Or *were I to come to the end I would still be with thee*
v Cn: Heb uncertain   w Heb *hurtful*   x Or *the ancient way.* Compare Jr 6.16

To the choirmaster. A Psalm of David.

140 Deliver me, O Lord, from evil men;
　　preserve me from violent men,
2 who plan evil things in their heart,
　　and stir up wars continually.
3 They make their tongue sharp as a serpent's,
　　and under their lips is the poison of vipers.　　*Selah*

4 Guard me, O Lord, from the hands of the wicked;
　　preserve me from violent men,
　　who have planned to trip up my feet.
5 Arrogant men have hidden a trap for me,
　　and with cords they have spread a net,[y]
　　by the wayside they have set snares for me.　　*Selah*

6 I say to the Lord, Thou art my God;
　　give ear to the voice of my supplications, O Lord!
7 O Lord, my Lord, my strong deliverer,
　　thou hast covered my head in the day of battle.
8 Grant not, O Lord, the desires of the wicked;
　　do not further his evil plot!　　*Selah*

9 Those who surround me lift up their head,[z]
　　let the mischief of their lips overwhelm them!
10 Let burning coals fall upon them!
　　Let them be cast into pits, no more to rise!
11 Let not the slanderer be established in the land;
　　let evil hunt down the violent man speedily!

12 I know that the Lord maintains the cause of the afflicted,
　　and executes justice for the needy.
13 Surely the righteous shall give thanks to thy name;
　　the upright shall dwell in thy presence.

A Psalm of David.

141 I call upon thee, O Lord; make haste to me!
　　Give ear to my voice, when I call to thee!
2 Let my prayer be counted as incense before thee,
　　and the lifting up of my hands as an evening sacrifice!

3 Set a guard over my mouth, O Lord,
　　keep watch over the door of my lips!
4 Incline not my heart to any evil,
　　to busy myself with wicked deeds
in company with men who work iniquity;
　　and let me not eat of their dainties!

5 Let a good man strike or rebuke me in kindness,
　　but let the oil of the wicked never anoint my head;[a]
　　for my prayer is continually[b] against their wicked
　　deeds.

6 When they are given over to those who shall condemn
　　them,
　　then they shall learn that the word of the Lord is true.
7 As a rock which one cleaves and shatters on the land,
　　so shall their bones be strewn at the mouth of Sheol.[c]

8 But my eyes are toward thee, O Lord God;
　　in thee I seek refuge; leave me not defenseless!
9 Keep me from the trap which they have laid for me,
　　and from the snares of evildoers!
10 Let the wicked together fall into their own nets,
　　while I escape.

A Maskil of David, when he was in the cave. A Prayer.

142 I cry with my voice to the Lord,
　　with my voice I make supplication to the Lord,
2 I pour out my complaint before him,
　　I tell my trouble before him.
3 When my spirit is faint,
　　thou knowest my way!

In the path where I walk
　　they have hidden a trap for me.
4 I look to the right and watch,[d]
　　but there is none who takes notice of me;
no refuge remains to me,
　　no man cares for me.

5 I cry to thee, O Lord;
　　I say, Thou art my refuge,
　　my portion in the land of the living.
6 Give heed to my cry;
　　for I am brought very low!

Deliver me from my persecutors;
　　for they are too strong for me!
7 Bring me out of prison,
　　that I may give thanks to thy name!
The righteous will surround me;
　　for thou wilt deal bountifully with me.

A Psalm of David.

143 Hear my prayer, O Lord;
　　give ear to my supplications!
In thy faithfulness answer me, in thy righteousness!
2 Enter not into judgment with thy servant;
　　for no man living is righteous before thee.

3 For the enemy has pursued me;
　　he has crushed my life to the ground;
　　he has made me sit in darkness like those long dead.

---

y Or *they have spread cords as a net*　　z Cn Compare Gk: Heb *those who surround me are uplifted in head*　　a Gk: Heb obscure
b Cn: Heb *for continually and my prayer*　　c The Hebrew of verses 5-7 is obscure　　d Or *Look to the right and watch*

4 Therefore my spirit faints within me;
  my heart within me is appalled.

5 I remember the days of old,
  I meditate on all that thou hast done;
  I muse on what thy hands have wrought.
6 I stretch out my hands to thee;
  my soul thirsts for thee like a parched land.   *Selah*

7 Make haste to answer me, O Lord!
  My spirit fails!
  Hide not thy face from me,
  lest I be like those who go down to the Pit.
8 Let me hear in the morning of thy steadfast love,
  for in thee I put my trust.
  Teach me the way I should go,
  for to thee I lift up my soul.

9 Deliver me, O Lord, from my enemies!
  I have fled to thee for refuge! e
10 Teach me to do thy will,
  for thou art my God!
  Let thy good spirit lead me
  on a level path!

11 For thy name's sake, O Lord, preserve my life!
  In thy righteousness bring me out of trouble!
12 And in thy steadfast love cut off my enemies,
  and destroy all my adversaries,
  for I am thy servant.

A Psalm of David.

144 Blessed be the Lord, my rock,
      who trains my hands for war,
    and my fingers for battle;
2 my rock f and my fortress,
    my stronghold and my deliverer,
  my shield and he in whom I take refuge,
  who subdues the peoples under him.g

3 O Lord, what is man that thou dost regard him,
    or the son of man that thou dost think of him?
4 Man is like a breath,
    his days are like a passing shadow.

5 Bow thy heavens, O Lord, and come down!
  Touch the mountains that they smoke!
6 Flash forth the lightning and scatter them,
  send out thy arrows and rout them!
7 Stretch forth thy hand from on high,
  rescue me and deliver me from the many waters,
  from the hand of aliens,
8 whose mouths speak lies,
  and whose right hand is a right hand of falsehood.

9 I will sing a new song to thee, O God;
  upon a ten-stringed harp I will play to thee,
10 who givest victory to kings,
  who rescuest David thy h servant.
11 Rescue me from the cruel sword,
  and deliver me from the hand of aliens,
  whose mouths speak lies,
  and whose right hand is a right hand of falsehood.

12 May our sons in their youth
  be like plants full grown,
  our daughters like corner pillars
  cut for the structure of a palace;
13 may our garners be full,
  providing all manner of store;
  may our sheep bring forth thousands
  and ten thousands in our fields;
14 may our cattle be heavy with young,
  suffering no mischance or failure in bearing;
  may there be no cry of distress in our streets!
15 Happy the people to whom such blessings fall!
  Happy the people whose God is the Lord!

A Song of Praise. Of David.

145 I will extol thee, my God and King,
      and bless thy name for ever and ever.
2 Every day I will bless thee,
  and praise thy name for ever and ever.
3 Great is the Lord, and greatly to be praised,
  and his greatness is unsearchable.

4 One generation shall laud thy works to another,
  and shall declare thy mighty acts.
5 On the glorious splendor of thy majesty,
  and on thy wondrous works, I will meditate.
6 Men shall proclaim the might of thy terrible acts,
  and I will declare thy greatness.
7 They shall pour forth the fame of thy abundant goodness,
  and shall sing aloud of thy righteousness.

8 The Lord is gracious and merciful,
  slow to anger and abounding in steadfast love.

e One Heb Ms Gk: Heb *to thee I have hidden*   f With 18.2 2 S 22.2: Heb *my steadfast love*
g Another reading is *my people under me*   h Heb *his*

9 The LORD is good to all,
  and his compassion is over all that he has made.

10 All thy works shall give thanks to thee, O LORD,
  and all thy saints shall bless thee!
11 They shall speak of the glory of thy kingdom,
  and tell of thy power,
12 to make known to the sons of men thy [h] mighty deeds,
  and the glorious splendor of thy [h] kingdom.
13 Thy kingdom is an everlasting kingdom,
  and thy dominion endures throughout all generations.

  The LORD is faithful in all his words,
    and gracious in all his deeds.[i]
14 The LORD upholds all who are falling,
  and raises up all who are bowed down.
15 The eyes of all look to thee,
  and thou givest them their food in due season.
16 Thou openest thy hand,
  thou satisfiest the desire of every living thing.
17 The LORD is just in all his ways,
  and kind in all his doings.
18 The LORD is near to all who call upon him,
  to all who call upon him in truth.
19 He fulfils the desire of all who fear him,
  he also hears their cry, and saves them.
20 The LORD preserves all who love him;
  but all the wicked he will destroy.

21 My mouth will speak the praise of the LORD,
  and let all flesh bless his holy name for ever and ever.

146 Praise the LORD!
    Praise the LORD, O my soul!
2 I will praise the LORD as long as I live;
  I will sing praises to my God while I have being.

3 Put not your trust in princes,
  in a son of man, in whom there is no help.
4 When his breath departs he returns to his earth;
  on that very day his plans perish.

5 Happy is he whose help is the God of Jacob,
  whose hope is in the LORD his God,
6 who made heaven and earth,
  the sea, and all that is in them;
who keeps faith for ever;
7   who executes justice for the oppressed;
  who gives food to the hungry.

  The LORD sets the prisoners free;
8   the LORD opens the eyes of the blind.
  The LORD lifts up those who are bowed down;
    the LORD loves the righteous.

9 The LORD watches over the sojourners,
  he upholds the widow and the fatherless;
  but the way of the wicked he brings to ruin.

10 The LORD will reign for ever,
  thy God, O Zion, to all generations.
Praise the LORD!

147 Praise the LORD!
    For it is good to sing praises to our God;
  for he is gracious, and a song of praise is seemly.
2 The LORD builds up Jerusalem;
  he gathers the outcasts of Israel.
3 He heals the brokenhearted,
  and binds up their wounds.
4 He determines the number of the stars,
  he gives to all of them their names.
5 Great is our LORD, and abundant in power;
  his understanding is beyond measure.
6 The LORD lifts up the downtrodden,
  he casts the wicked to the ground.

7 Sing to the LORD with thanksgiving;
  make melody to our God upon the lyre!
8 He covers the heavens with clouds,
  he prepares rain for the earth,
  he makes grass grow upon the hills.
9 He gives to the beasts their food,
  and to the young ravens which cry.
10 His delight is not in the strength of the horse,
  nor his pleasure in the legs of a man;
11 but the LORD takes pleasure in those who fear him,
  in those who hope in his steadfast love.

12 Praise the LORD, O Jerusalem!
  Praise your God, O Zion!
13 For he strengthens the bars of your gates;
  he blesses your sons within you.
14 He makes peace in your borders;
  he fills you with the finest of the wheat.
15 He sends forth his command to the earth;
  his word runs swiftly.
16 He gives snow like wool;
  he scatters hoarfrost like ashes.
17 He casts forth his ice like morsels;
  who can stand before his cold?
18 He sends forth his word, and melts them;
  he makes his wind blow, and the waters flow.
19 He declares his word to Jacob,
  his statutes and ordinances to Israel.
20 He has not dealt thus with any other nation;
  they do not know his ordinances.
Praise the LORD!

[h] Heb *his*   [i] These two lines are supplied by one Hebrew Ms, Gk and Syr

148 Praise the LORD!
Praise the LORD from the heavens,
  praise him in the heights!
2 Praise him, all his angels,
  praise him, all his host!

3 Praise him, sun and moon,
  praise him, all you shining stars!
4 Praise him, you highest heavens,
  and you waters above the heavens!

5 Let them praise the name of the LORD!
  For he commanded and they were created.
6 And he established them for ever and ever;
  he fixed their bounds which cannot be passed.j

149 Praise the LORD!
Sing to the LORD a new song,
  his praise in the assembly of the faithful!
2 Let Israel be glad in his Maker,
  let the sons of Zion rejoice in their King!
3 Let them praise his name with dancing,
  making melody to him with timbrel and lyre!
4 For the LORD takes pleasure in his people;
  he adorns the humble with victory.
5 Let the faithful exult in glory;
  let them sing for joy on their couches.
6 Let the high praises of God be in their throats
  and two-edged swords in their hands,
7 to wreak vengeance on the nations
  and chastisement on the peoples,

7 Praise the LORD from the earth,
  you sea monsters and all deeps,
8 fire and hail, snow and frost,
  stormy wind fulfilling his command!

9 Mountains and all hills,
  fruit trees and all cedars!
10 Beasts and all cattle,
  creeping things and flying birds!

11 Kings of the earth and all peoples,
  princes and all rulers of the earth!
12 Young men and maidens together,
  old men and children!

13 Let them praise the name of the LORD,
  for his name alone is exalted;
  his glory is above earth and heaven.
14 He has raised up a horn for his people,
  praise for all his saints,
  for the people of Israel who are near to him.
  Praise the LORD!

j Or he set a law which cannot pass away

8 to bind their kings with chains
  and their nobles with fetters of iron,
9 to execute on them the judgment written!
  This is glory for all his faithful ones.
  Praise the LORD!

150 Praise the LORD!
Praise God in his sanctuary;
  praise him in his mighty firmament!
2 Praise him for his mighty deeds;
  praise him according to his exceeding greatness!

3 Praise him with trumpet sound;
  praise him with lute and harp!
4 Praise him with timbrel and dance;
  praise him with strings and pipe!
5 Praise him with sounding cymbals;
  praise him with loud clashing cymbals!
6 Let everything that breathes praise the LORD!
  Praise the LORD!

INTRODUCTION TO

THE PROVERBS

Proverbs is a collection of poetic sayings, many of them very short. Some of them are quite witty; others are very wise. Because Solomon was thought to be a very wise king, many of these sayings are called proverbs of Solomon. Some chapters of Proverbs are long poems. These proverbs were collected at various times over hundreds of years, and the Book of Proverbs as we now have it in the Bible was completed about 200 B.C.

Most of the proverbs are couplets or little poems of two lines each. Frequently the second line says a truth in just the opposite way from the first line, as this one does:

"A soft answer turns away wrath,

but a harsh word stirs up anger."

—Proverbs 15.1

One of the longer sections, a poem in praise of wisdom, is to be found in Proverbs 8.

THE PROVERBS

THE EXCELLENCE OF WISDOM

1 The proverbs of Solomon, son of David, king of Israel:

² That men may know wisdom and instruction,
understand words of insight,
³ receive instruction in wise dealing,
righteousness, justice, and equity;
⁴ that prudence may be given to the simple,
knowledge and discretion to the youth—
⁵ the wise man also may hear and increase in learning,
and the man of understanding acquire skill,
⁶ to understand a proverb and a figure,
the words of the wise and their riddles.

⁷ The fear of the LORD is the beginning of knowledge;
fools despise wisdom and instruction.

⁸ Hear, my son, your father's instruction,
and reject not your mother's teaching;
⁹ for they are a fair garland for your head,
and pendants for your neck.
¹⁰ My son, if sinners entice you,
do not consent.
¹¹ If they say, "Come with us, let us lie in wait for blood,
let us wantonly ambush the innocent;
¹² like Sheol let us swallow them alive
and whole, like those who go down to the Pit;
¹³ we shall find all precious goods,
we shall fill our houses with spoil;
¹⁴ throw in your lot among us,

we will all have one purse"—
¹⁵ my son, do not walk in the way with them,
hold back your foot from their paths;
¹⁶ for their feet run to evil,
and they make haste to shed blood.
¹⁷ For in vain is a net spread
in the sight of any bird;
¹⁸ but these men lie in wait for their own blood,
they set an ambush for their own lives.
¹⁹ Such are the ways of all who get gain by violence;
it takes away the life of its possessors.

²⁰ Wisdom cries aloud in the street;
in the markets she raises her voice;
²¹ on the top of the walls ᵃ she cries out;

at the entrance of the city gates she speaks:
²² "How long, O simple ones, will you love being simple?
How long will scoffers delight in their scoffing
and fools hate knowledge?
²³ Give heed ᵇ to my reproof;
behold, I will pour out my thoughts ᶜ to you;

ᵃ Heb uncertain   ᵇ Heb *Turn*   ᶜ Heb *spirit*

420

I will make my words known to you.
24 Because I have called and you refused to listen,
  have stretched out my hand and no one has heeded,
25 and you have ignored all my counsel
  and would have none of my reproof,
26 I also will laugh at your calamity;
  I will mock when panic strikes you,
27 when panic strikes you like a storm,
  and your calamity comes like a whirlwind,
  when distress and anguish come upon you.
28 Then they will call upon me, but I will not answer;
  they will seek me diligently but will not find me.
29 Because they hated knowledge
  and did not choose the fear of the LORD,
30 would have none of my counsel,
  and despised all my reproof,
31 therefore they shall eat the fruit of their way
  and be sated with their own devices.
32 For the simple are killed by their turning away,
  and the complacence of fools destroys them;
33 but he who listens to me will dwell secure
  and will be at ease, without dread of evil."

2 My son, if you receive my words
    and treasure up my commandments with you,
2 making your ear attentive to wisdom

  and inclining your heart to understanding;
3 yes, if you cry out for insight
  and raise your voice for understanding,
4 if you seek it like silver
  and search for it as for hidden treasures;
5 then you will understand the fear of the LORD
  and find the knowledge of God.
6 For the LORD gives wisdom;
  from his mouth come knowledge and understanding;
7 he stores up sound wisdom for the upright;
  he is a shield to those who walk in integrity,
8 guarding the paths of justice
  and preserving the way of his saints.
9 Then you will understand righteousness and justice
  and equity, every good path;
10 for wisdom will come into your heart,
  and knowledge will be pleasant to your soul;
11 discretion will watch over you;
  understanding will guard you;
12 delivering you from the way of evil,
  from men of perverted speech,
13 who forsake the paths of uprightness
  to walk in the ways of darkness,

14 who rejoice in doing evil
  and delight in the perverseness of evil;
15 men whose paths are crooked,
  and who are devious in their ways.

16 You will be saved from the loose [d] woman,
  from the adventuress [e] with her smooth words,
17 who forsakes the companion of her youth
  and forgets the covenant of her God;
18 for her house sinks down to death,
  and her paths to the shades;
19 none who go to her come back
  nor do they regain the paths of life.

20 So you will walk in the way of good men
  and keep to the paths of the righteous.
21 For the upright will inhabit the land,
  and men of integrity will remain in it;
22 but the wicked will be cut off from the land,
  and the treacherous will be rooted out of it.

3 My son, do not forget my teaching,
    but let your heart keep my commandments;
2 for length of days and years of life
  and abundant welfare will they give you.

3 Let not loyalty and faithfulness forsake you;
  bind them about your neck,
  write them on the tablet of your heart.
4 So you will find favor and good repute [f]
  in the sight of God and man.

5 Trust in the LORD with all your heart,
  and do not rely on your own insight.
6 In all your ways acknowledge him,
  and he will make straight your paths.
7 Be not wise in your own eyes;
  fear the LORD, and turn away from evil.
8 It will be healing to your flesh [g]
  and refreshment [h] to your bones.

9 Honor the LORD with your substance
  and with the first fruits of all your produce;
10 then your barns will be filled with plenty,
  and your vats will be bursting with wine.

11 My son, do not despise the LORD's discipline
  or be weary of his reproof,
12 for the LORD reproves him whom he loves,
  as a father the son in whom he delights.

13 Happy is the man who finds wisdom,
  and the man who gets understanding,

d Heb strange   e Heb foreign woman   f Cn: Heb understanding   g Heb navel   h Or medicine

421

14 for the gain from it is better than gain from silver
  and its profit better than gold.
15 She is more precious than jewels,
  and nothing you desire can compare with her.
16 Long life is in her right hand;
  in her left hand are riches and honor.
17 Her ways are ways of pleasantness,
  and all her paths are peace.
18 She is a tree of life to those who lay hold of her;
  those who hold her fast are called happy.

19 The LORD by wisdom founded the earth;
  by understanding he established the heavens;
20 by his knowledge the deeps broke forth,
  and the clouds drop down the dew.

21 My son, keep sound wisdom and discretion;
  let them not escape from your sight,[i]

22 and they will be life for your soul
  and adornment for your neck.
23 Then you will walk on your way securely
  and your foot will not stumble.
24 If you sit down,[j] you will not be afraid;
  when you lie down, your sleep will be sweet.
25 Do not be afraid of sudden panic,
  or of the ruin[k] of the wicked, when it comes;
26 for the LORD will be your confidence
  and will keep your foot from being caught.
27 Do not withhold good from those to whom it[l] is due,
  when it is in your power to do it.

28 Do not say to your neighbor, "Go, and come again,
  tomorrow I will give it"—when you have it with you.
29 Do not plan evil against your neighbor
  who dwells trustingly beside you.
30 Do not contend with a man for no reason,
  when he has done you no harm.
31 Do not envy a man of violence
  and do not choose any of his ways;
32 for the perverse man is an abomination to the LORD,
  but the upright are in his confidence.
33 The LORD's curse is on the house of the wicked,
  but he blesses the abode of the righteous.
34 Toward the scorners he is scornful,
  but to the humble he shows favor.
35 The wise will inherit honor,
  but fools get[m] disgrace.

4 Hear, O sons, a father's instruction,
  and be attentive, that you may gain[n] insight;
2 for I give you good precepts:
  do not forsake my teaching.
3 When I was a son with my father,
  tender, the only one in the sight of my mother,
4 he taught me, and said to me,
  "Let your heart hold fast my words;
  keep my commandments, and live;
5 do not forget, and do not turn away from the words of
    my mouth.
  Get wisdom; get insight.[o]
6 Do not forsake her, and she will keep you;
  love her, and she will guard you.
7 The beginning of wisdom is this: Get wisdom,
  and whatever you get, get insight.
8 Prize her highly,[p] and she will exalt you;
  she will honor you if you embrace her.
9 She will place on your head a fair garland;
  she will bestow on you a beautiful crown."

10 Hear, my son, and accept my words,
  that the years of your life may be many.
11 I have taught you the way of wisdom;
  I have led you in the paths of uprightness.
12 When you walk, your step will not be hampered;
  and if you run, you will not stumble.
13 Keep hold of instruction, do not let go;
  guard her, for she is your life.
14 Do not enter the path of the wicked,
  and do not walk in the way of evil men.
15 Avoid it; do not go on it;
  turn away from it and pass on.
16 For they cannot sleep unless they have done wrong;
  they are robbed of sleep unless they have made some
    one stumble.
17 For they eat the bread of wickedness
  and drink the wine of violence.
18 But the path of the righteous is like the light of dawn,
  which shines brighter and brighter until full day.
19 The way of the wicked is like deep darkness;
  they do not know over what they stumble.

20 My son, be attentive to my words;
  incline your ear to my sayings.
21 Let them not escape from your sight;
  keep them within your heart.
22 For they are life to him who finds them,
  and healing to all his flesh.
23 Keep your heart with all vigilance;
  for from it flow the springs of life.
24 Put away from you crooked speech,
  and put devious talk far from you.
25 Let your eyes look directly forward,

i Reversing the order of the clauses   j Gk: Heb lie down   k Heb storm   l Heb Do not withhold good from its owners
m Cn: Heb exalt   n Heb know   o Reversing the order of the lines   p The meaning of the Hebrew is uncertain

and your gaze be straight before you.
26 Take heed to[q] the path of your feet,
then all your ways will be sure.
27 Do not swerve to the right or to the left;
turn your foot away from evil.

5 My son, be attentive to my wisdom,
incline your ear to my understanding;
2 that you may keep discretion,
and your lips may guard knowledge.
3 For the lips of a loose woman drip honey,
and her speech[r] is smoother than oil;
4 but in the end she is bitter as wormwood,
sharp as a two-edged sword.
5 Her feet go down to death;
her steps follow the path to[s] Sheol;
6 she does not take heed to[t] the path of life;
her ways wander, and she does not know it.

7 And now, O sons, listen to me,
and do not depart from the words of my mouth.
8 Keep your way far from her,
and do not go near the door of her house;
9 lest you give your honor to others
and your years to the merciless;
10 lest strangers take their fill of your strength,[u]
and your labors go to the house of an alien;
11 and at the end of your life you groan,
when your flesh and body are consumed,
12 and you say, "How I hated discipline,
and my heart despised reproof!
13 I did not listen to the voice of my teachers
or incline my ear to my instructors.
14 I was at the point of utter ruin
in the assembled congregation."

15 Drink water from your own cistern,
flowing water from your own well.
16 Should your springs be scattered abroad,
streams of water in the streets?
17 Let them be for yourself alone,
and not for strangers with you.
18 Let your fountain be blessed,
and rejoice in the wife of your youth,
19 a lovely hind, a graceful doe.
Let her affection fill you at all times with delight,
be infatuated always with her love.
20 Why should you be infatuated, my son, with a loose woman
and embrace the bosom of an adventuress?
21 For a man's ways are before the eyes of the LORD,
and he watches[v] all his paths.
22 The iniquities of the wicked ensnare him,
and he is caught in the toils of his sin.
23 He dies for lack of discipline,
and because of his great folly he is lost.

6 My son, if you have become surety for your neighbor,
have given your pledge for a stranger;
2 if you are snared in the utterance of your lips,[w]
caught in the words of your mouth;
3 then do this, my son, and save yourself,
for you have come into your neighbor's power:
go, hasten,[x] and importune your neighbor.
4 Give your eyes no sleep
and your eyelids no slumber;
5 save yourself like a gazelle from the hunter,[y]
like a bird from the hand of the fowler.

6 Go to the ant, O sluggard;
consider her ways, and be wise.
7 Without having any chief,
officer or ruler,
8 she prepares her food in summer,
and gathers her sustenance in harvest.
9 How long will you lie there, O sluggard?
When will you arise from your sleep?
10 A little sleep, a little slumber,
a little folding of the hands to rest,
11 and poverty will come upon you like a vagabond,
and want like an armed man.

12 A worthless person, a wicked man,
goes about with crooked speech,
13 winks with his eyes, scrapes[z] with his feet,
points with his finger,
14 with perverted heart devises evil,
continually sowing discord;
15 therefore calamity will come upon him suddenly;
in a moment he will be broken beyond healing.

16 There are six things which the LORD hates,
seven which are an abomination to him:
17 haughty eyes, a lying tongue,
and hands that shed innocent blood,
18 a heart that devises wicked plans,
feet that make haste to run to evil,
19 a false witness who breathes out lies,
and a man who sows discord among brothers.

20 My son, keep your father's commandment,
and forsake not your mother's teaching.
21 Bind them upon your heart always;
tie them about your neck.
22 When you walk, they[a] will lead you;

[q] The meaning of the Hebrew word is uncertain [r] Heb *palate* [s] Heb *lay hold of*
[t] The meaning of the Hebrew word is uncertain [u] Or *wealth* [v] The meaning of the Hebrew word is uncertain
[w] Cn Compare Gk Syr: Heb *the words of your mouth* [x] Or *humble yourself* [y] Cn: Heb *hand* [z] Or *taps*
[a] Heb *it*

when you lie down, they [a] will watch over you;
and when you awake, they [a] will talk with you.
23 For the commandment is a lamp and the teaching a light,
and the reproofs of discipline are the way of life,
24 to preserve you from the evil woman,
from the smooth tongue of the adventuress.
25 Do not desire her beauty in your heart,
and do not let her capture you with her eyelashes;
26 for a harlot may be hired for a loaf of bread,[b]
but an adulteress [c] stalks a man's very life.
27 Can a man carry fire in his bosom
and his clothes not be burned?
28 Or can one walk upon hot coals
and his feet not be scorched?
29 So is he who goes in to his neighbor's wife;
none who touches her will go unpunished.
30 Do not men despise [d] a thief if he steals
to satisfy his appetite when he is hungry?
31 And if he is caught, he will pay sevenfold;
he will give all the goods of his house.
32 He who commits adultery has no sense;
he who does it destroys himself.
33 Wounds and dishonor will he get,
and his disgrace will not be wiped away.
34 For jealousy makes a man furious,
and he will not spare when he takes revenge.
35 He will accept no compensation,
nor be appeased though you multiply gifts.

7 My son, keep my words
and treasure up my commandments with you;
2 keep my commandments and live,
keep my teachings as the apple of your eye;
3 bind them on your fingers,
write them on the tablet of your heart.
4 Say to wisdom, "You are my sister,"
and call insight your intimate friend;
5 to preserve you from the loose woman,
from the adventuress with her smooth words.

6 For at the window of my house
I have looked out through my lattice,
7 and I have seen among the simple,
I have perceived among the youths,
a young man without sense,
8 passing along the street near her corner,
taking the road to her house
9 in the twilight, in the evening,
at the time of night and darkness.

10 And lo, a woman meets him,
dressed as a harlot, wily of heart.[e]
11 She is loud and wayward,
her feet do not stay at home;

12 now in the street, now in the market,
and at every corner she lies in wait.
13 She seizes him and kisses him,
and with impudent face she says to him:
14 "I had to offer sacrifices,
and today I have paid my vows;
15 so now I have come out to meet you,
to seek you eagerly, and I have found you.
16 I have decked my couch with coverings,
colored spreads of Egyptian linen;
17 I have perfumed my bed with myrrh,
aloes, and cinnamon.
18 Come, let us take our fill of love till morning;
let us delight ourselves with love.
19 For my husband is not at home;
he has gone on a long journey;
20 he took a bag of money with him;
at full moon he will come home."
21 With much seductive speech she persuades him;
with her smooth talk she compels him.
22 All at once he follows her,
as an ox goes to the slaughter,
or as a stag is caught fast [f]
23   till an arrow pierces its entrails;
as a bird rushes into a snare;
he does not know that it will cost him his life.

24 And now, O sons, listen to me,
and be attentive to the words of my mouth.
25 Let not your heart turn aside to her ways,
do not stray into her paths;
26 for many a victim has she laid low;
yea, all her slain are a mighty host.
27 Her house is the way to Sheol,
going down to the chambers of death.

8 Does not wisdom call,
does not understanding raise her voice?
2 On the heights beside the way,
in the paths she takes her stand;
3 beside the gates in front of the town,
at the entrance of the portals she cries aloud:
4 "To you, O men, I call,
and my cry is to the sons of men.
5 O simple ones, learn prudence;
O foolish men, pay attention.
6 Hear, for I will speak noble things,
and from my lips will come what is right;
7 for my mouth will utter truth;
wickedness is an abomination to my lips.
8 All the words of my mouth are righteous;
there is nothing twisted or crooked in them.
9 They are all straight to him who understands
and right to those who find knowledge.

[b] Cn Compare Gk Syr Vg Tg: Heb *for because of a harlot to a piece of bread*   [c] Heb *a man's wife*   [d] Or *Men do not despise*
[e] The meaning of the Hebrew is uncertain   [f] Cn Compare Gk: Heb uncertain

[10] Take my instruction instead of silver,
  and knowledge rather than choice gold;
[11] for wisdom is better than jewels,
  and all that you may desire cannot compare with her.
[12] I, wisdom, dwell in prudence,[g]
  and I find knowledge and discretion.
[13] The fear of the LORD is hatred of evil.
  Pride and arrogance and the way of evil
    and perverted speech I hate.
[14] I have counsel and sound wisdom,
  I have insight, I have strength.
[15] By me kings reign,
  and rulers decree what is just;
[16] by me princes rule,
  and nobles govern[h] the earth.
[17] I love those who love me,
  and those who seek me diligently find me.
[18] Riches and honor are with me,
  enduring wealth and prosperity.
[19] My fruit is better than gold, even fine gold,
  and my yield than choice silver.
[20] I walk in the way of righteousness,
  in the paths of justice,
[21] endowing with wealth those who love me,
  and filling their treasuries.

[22] The LORD created me at the beginning of his work,[i]
  the first of his acts of old.
[23] Ages ago I was set up,
  at the first, before the beginning of the earth.
[24] When there were no depths I was brought forth,
  when there were no springs abounding with water.
[25] Before the mountains had been shaped,
  before the hills, I was brought forth;
[26] before he had made the earth with its fields,[j]
  or the first of the dust[j] of the world.
[27] When he established the heavens, I was there,
  when he drew a circle on the face of the deep,
[28] when he made firm the skies above,
  when he established[j] the fountains of the deep,
[29] when he assigned to the sea its limit,
  so that the waters might not transgress his command,
  when he marked out the foundations of the earth,
[30]   then I was beside him, like a master workman;[l]
  and I was daily his[m] delight,
    rejoicing before him always,
[31] rejoicing in his inhabited world
  and delighting in the sons of men.

[32] And now, my sons, listen to me:
  happy are those who keep my ways.
[33] Hear instruction and be wise,
  and do not neglect it.
[34] Happy is the man who listens to me,
  watching daily at my gates,
  waiting beside my doors.
[35] For he who finds me finds life
  and obtains favor from the LORD;
[36] but he who misses me injures himself;
  all who hate me love death."

9 Wisdom has built her house,
  she has set up[n] her seven pillars.
[2] She has slaughtered her beasts, she has mixed her wine,
  she has also set her table.
[3] She has sent out her maids to call
  from the highest places in the town,
[4] "Whoever is simple, let him turn in here!"
  To him who is without sense she says,
[5] "Come, eat of my bread
  and drink of the wine I have mixed.
[6] Leave simpleness,[o] and live,
  and walk in the way of insight."

[7] He who corrects a scoffer gets himself abuse,
  and he who reproves a wicked man incurs injury.
[8] Do not reprove a scoffer, or he will hate you;
  reprove a wise man, and he will love you.
[9] Give instruction[p] to a wise man, and he will be still wiser;
  teach a righteous man and he will increase in learning.
[10] The fear of the LORD is the beginning of wisdom,
  and the knowledge of the Holy One is insight.
[11] For by me your days will be multiplied,
  and years will be added to your life.
[12] If you are wise, you are wise for yourself;
  if you scoff, you alone will bear it.

[13] A foolish woman is noisy;
  she is wanton[q] and knows no shame.[r]
[14] She sits at the door of her house,
  she takes a seat on the high places of the town,
[15] calling to those who pass by,
  who are going straight on their way,
[16] "Whoever is simple, let him turn in here!"
  And to him who is without sense she says,
[17] "Stolen water is sweet,
  and bread eaten in secret is pleasant."
[18] But he does not know that the dead[s] are there,
  that her guests are in the depths of Sheol.

THE PROVERBS OF SOLOMON

10 The proverbs of Solomon.

  A wise son makes a glad father,
  but a foolish son is a sorrow to his mother.
[2] Treasures gained by wickedness do not profit,
  but righteousness delivers from death.
[3] The LORD does not let the righteous go hungry,

[g] Heb obscure [h] Gk: Heb *all the governors of* [i] Heb *way* [j] The meaning of the Hebrew is uncertain
[j] The meaning of the Hebrew is uncertain [l] Another reading is *little child* [m] Gk: Heb lacks *his* [n] Gk Syr Tg: Heb *hewn*
[o] Gk Syr Vg Tg: Heb *simple ones* [p] Heb lacks *instruction* [q] Cn Compare Syr Vg: The meaning of the Hebrew is uncertain
[r] Gk Syr: The meaning of the Hebrew is uncertain [s] Heb *shades*

but he thwarts the craving of the wicked.
4 A slack hand causes poverty,
but the hand of the diligent makes rich.
5 A son who gathers in summer is prudent,
but a son who sleeps in harvest brings shame.

6 Blessings are on the head of the righteous,
but the mouth of the wicked conceals violence.
7 The memory of the righteous is a blessing,
but the name of the wicked will rot.
8 The wise of heart will heed commandments,
but a prating fool will come to ruin.
9 He who walks in integrity walks securely,
but he who perverts his ways will be found out.
10 He who winks the eye causes trouble,
but he who boldly reproves makes peace.[t]
11 The mouth of the righteous is a fountain of life,
but the mouth of the wicked conceals violence.
12 Hatred stirs up strife,
but love covers all offenses.
13 On the lips of him who has understanding wisdom is
found,
but a rod is for the back of him who lacks sense.
14 Wise men lay up knowledge,
but the babbling of a fool brings ruin near.
15 A rich man's wealth is his strong city;
the poverty of the poor is their ruin.
16 The wage of the righteous leads to life,
the gain of the wicked to sin.
17 He who heeds instruction is on the path of life,
but he who rejects reproof goes astray.
18 He who conceals hatred has lying lips,
and he who utters slander is a fool.
19 When words are many, transgression is not lacking,
but he who restrains his lips is prudent.
20 The tongue of the righteous is choice silver;
the mind of the wicked is of little worth.
21 The lips of the righteous feed many,
but fools die for lack of sense.
22 The blessing of the LORD makes rich,
and he adds no sorrow with it.[u]
23 It is like sport to a fool to do wrong,
but wise conduct is pleasure to a man of understanding.
24 What the wicked dreads will come upon him,
but the desire of the righteous will be granted.
25 When the tempest passes, the wicked is no more,
·but the righteous is established for ever.
26 Like vinegar to the teeth, and smoke to the eyes,

so is the sluggard to those who send him.
27 The fear of the LORD prolongs life,
but the years of the wicked will be short.
28 The hope of the righteous ends in gladness,
but the expectation of the wicked comes to nought.
29 The LORD is a stronghold to him whose way is upright,
but destruction to evildoers.
30 The righteous will never be removed,
but the wicked will not dwell in the land.
31 The mouth of the righteous brings forth wisdom,
but the perverse tongue will be cut off.
32 The lips of the righteous know what is acceptable,
but the mouth of the wicked, what is perverse.
11 A false balance is an abomination to the LORD,
but a just weight is his delight.
2 When pride comes, then comes disgrace;
but with the humble is wisdom.
3 The integrity of the upright guides them,
but the crookedness of the treacherous destroys them.
4 Riches do not profit in the day of wrath,
but righteousness delivers from death.
5 The righteousness of the blameless keeps his way straight,
but the wicked falls by his own wickedness.
6 The righteousness of the upright delivers them,
but the treacherous are taken captive by their lust.
7 When the wicked dies, his hope perishes,
and the expectation of the godless comes to nought.
8 The righteous is delivered from trouble,
and the wicked gets into it instead.
9 With his mouth the godless man would destroy his neighbor,
but by knowledge the righteous are delivered.
10 When it goes well with the righteous, the city rejoices;
and when the wicked perish there are shouts of gladness.
11 By the blessing of the upright a city is exalted,
but it is overthrown by the mouth of the wicked.
12 He who belittles his neighbor lacks sense,
but a man of understanding remains silent.
13 He who goes about as a talebearer reveals secrets,
but he who is trustworthy in spirit keeps a thing hidden.
14 Where there is no guidance, a people falls;
but in an abundance of counselors there is safety.
15 He who gives surety for a stranger will smart for it,
but he who hates suretyship is secure.
16 A gracious woman gets honor,
and violent men get riches.
17 A man who is kind benefits himself,
but a cruel man hurts himself.
18 A wicked man earns deceptive wages,
but one who sows righteousness gets a sure reward.
19 He who is steadfast in righteousness will live,
but he who pursues evil will die.
20 Men of perverse mind are an abomination to the LORD,

[t] Gk: Heb *but a prating fool will come to ruin*   [u] Or *and toil adds nothing to it*

but those of blameless ways are his delight.
21 Be assured, an evil man will not go unpunished,
  but those who are righteous will be delivered.
22 Like a gold ring in a swine's snout
  is a beautiful woman without discretion.
23 The desire of the righteous ends only in good;
  the expectation of the wicked in wrath.
24 One man gives freely, yet grows all the richer;
  another withholds what he should give, and only suffers
    want.
25 A liberal man will be enriched,
  and one who waters will himself be watered.
26 The people curse him who holds back grain,
  but a blessing is on the head of him who sells it.
27 He who diligently seeks good seeks favor,
  but evil comes to him who searches for it.
28 He who trusts in his riches will wither,ᵛ
  but the righteous will flourish like a green leaf.
29 He who troubles his household will inherit wind,
  and the fool will be servant to the wise.
30 The fruit of the righteous is a tree of life,
  but lawlessness ʷ takes away lives.
31 If the righteous is requited on earth,
  how much more the wicked and the sinner!

12 Whoever loves discipline loves knowledge,
  but he who hates reproof is stupid.
2 A good man obtains favor from the Lord,
  but a man of evil devices he condemns.
3 A man is not established by wickedness,
  but the root of the righteous will never be moved.
4 A good wife is the crown of her husband,
  but she who brings shame is like rottenness in his bones.
5 The thoughts of the righteous are just;
  the counsels of the wicked are treacherous.
6 The words of the wicked lie in wait for blood,
  but the mouth of the upright delivers men.
7 The wicked are overthrown and are no more,
  but the house of the righteous will stand.
8 A man is commended according to his good sense,
  but one of perverse mind is despised.
9 Better is a man of humble standing who works for himself
  than one who plays the great man but lacks bread.

10 A righteous man has regard for the life of his beast,
  but the mercy of the wicked is cruel.
11 He who tills his land will have plenty of bread,
  but he who follows worthless pursuits has no sense.

12 The strong tower of the wicked comes to ruin,
  but the root of the righteous stands firm.ˣ
13 An evil man is ensnared by the transgression of his lips,
  but the righteous escapes from trouble.
14 From the fruit of his words a man is satisfied with good,
  and the work of a man's hand comes back to him.
15 The way of a fool is right in his own eyes,
  but a wise man listens to advice.
16 The vexation of a fool is known at once,
  but the prudent man ignores an insult.
17 He who speaks the truth gives honest evidence,
  but a false witness utters deceit.
18 There is one whose rash words are like sword thrusts,
  but the tongue of the wise brings healing.
19 Truthful lips endure for ever,
  but a lying tongue is but for a moment.
20 Deceit is in the heart of those who devise evil,
  but those who plan good have joy.
21 No ill befalls the righteous,
  but the wicked are filled with trouble.
22 Lying lips are an abomination to the Lord,
  but those who act faithfully are his delight.
23 A prudent man conceals his knowledge,
  but fools ʸ proclaim their folly.
24 The hand of the diligent will rule,
  while the slothful will be put to forced labor.
25 Anxiety in a man's heart weighs him down,
  but a good word makes him glad.
26 A righteous man turns away from evil,ᶻ
  but the way of the wicked leads them astray.
27 A slothful man will not catch his prey,ᵃ
  but the diligent man will get precious wealth.ᵇ
28 In the path of righteousness is life,
  but the way of error leads to death.ᶜ

13 A wise son hears his father's instruction,
  but a scoffer does not listen to rebuke.
2 From the fruit of his mouth a good man eats good,
  but the desire of the treacherous is for violence.
3 He who guards his mouth preserves his life;
  he who opens wide his lips comes to ruin.
4 The soul of the sluggard craves, and gets nothing,
  while the soul of the diligent is richly supplied.
5 A righteous man hates falsehood,
  but a wicked man acts shamefully and disgracefully.
6 Righteousness guards him whose way is upright,
  but sin overthrows the wicked.
7 One man pretends to be rich, yet has nothing;
  another pretends to be poor, yet has great wealth.
8 The ransom of a man's life is his wealth,
  but a poor man has no means of redemption.ᵈ
9 The light of the righteous rejoices,
  but the lamp of the wicked will be put out.
10 By insolence the heedless make strife,

ᵛ Cn: Heb *fall*   ʷ Cn Compare Gk Syr: Heb *a wise man*   ˣ Cn: The Hebrew of verse 12 is obscure   ʸ Heb *the heart of fools*
ᶻ Cn: The meaning of the Hebrew is uncertain   ᵃ Cn Compare Gk Syr: The meaning of the Hebrew is uncertain
ᵇ Cn: The meaning of the Hebrew is uncertain   ᶜ Cn: The meaning of the Hebrew is uncertain   ᵈ Cn: Heb *does not hear rebuke*

but with those who take advice is wisdom.

11 Wealth hastily gotten [e] will dwindle,
    but he who gathers little by little will increase it.
12 Hope deferred makes the heart sick,
    but a desire fulfilled is a tree of life.
13 He who despises the word brings destruction on himself,
    but he who respects the commandment will be rewarded.
14 The teaching of the wise is a fountain of life,
    that one may avoid the snares of death.
15 Good sense wins favor,
    but the way of the faithless is their ruin. [f]
16 In everything a prudent man acts with knowledge,
    but a fool flaunts his folly.
17 A bad messenger plunges men into trouble,
    but a faithful envoy brings healing.
18 Poverty and disgrace come to him who ignores instruction,
    but he who heeds reproof is honored.
19 A desire fulfilled is sweet to the soul;
    but to turn away from evil is an abomination to fools.
20 He who walks with wise men becomes wise,
    but the companion of fools will suffer harm.
21 Misfortune pursues sinners,
    but prosperity rewards the righteous.
22 A good man leaves an inheritance to his children's children,
    but the sinner's wealth is laid up for the righteous.
23 The fallow ground of the poor yields much food,
    but it is swept away through injustice.
24 He who spares the rod hates his son,
    but he who loves him is diligent to discipline him.
25 The righteous has enough to satisfy his appetite,
    but the belly of the wicked suffers want.

14 Wisdom [g] builds her house,
    but folly with her own hands tears it down.
2 He who walks in uprightness fears the LORD,
    but he who is devious in his ways despises him.
3 The talk of a fool is a rod for his back, [h]
    but the lips of the wise will preserve them.
4 Where there are no oxen, there is no [i] grain;
    but abundant crops come by the strength of the ox.
5 A faithful witness does not lie,
    but a false witness breathes out lies.
6 A scoffer seeks wisdom in vain,
    but knowledge is easy for a man of understanding.
7 Leave the presence of a fool,
    for there you do not meet words of knowledge.
8 The wisdom of a prudent man is to discern his way,
    but the folly of fools is deceiving.
9 God scorns the wicked, [j]
    but the upright enjoy his favor.
10 The heart knows its own bitterness,
    and no stranger shares its joy.
11 The house of the wicked will be destroyed,

but the tent of the upright will flourish.
12 There is a way which seems right to a man,
    but its end is the way to death. [k]
13 Even in laughter the heart is sad,
    and the end of joy is grief.
14 A perverse man will be filled with the fruit of his ways,
    and a good man with the fruit of his deeds. [l]
15 The simple believes everything,
    but the prudent looks where he is going.
16 A wise man is cautious and turns away from evil,
    but a fool throws off restraint and is careless.
17 A man of quick temper acts foolishly,
    but a man of discretion is patient. [m]
18 The simple acquire folly,
    but the prudent are crowned with knowledge.
19 The evil bow down before the good,
    the wicked at the gates of the righteous.
20 The poor is disliked even by his neighbor,
    but the rich has many friends.
21 He who despises his neighbor is a sinner,
    but happy is he who is kind to the poor.
22 Do they not err that devise evil?
    Those who devise good meet loyalty and faithfulness.
23 In all toil there is profit,
    but mere talk tends only to want.
24 The crown of the wise is their wisdom, [n]
    but folly is the garland [o] of fools.
25 A truthful witness saves lives,
    but one who utters lies is a betrayer.
26 In the fear of the LORD one has strong confidence,
    and his children will have a refuge.
27 The fear of the LORD is a fountain of life,
    that one may avoid the snares of death.
28 In a multitude of people is the glory of a king,
    but without people a prince is ruined.
29 He who is slow to anger has great understanding,
    but he who has a hasty temper exalts folly.
30 A tranquil mind gives life to the flesh,
    but passion makes the bones rot.
31 He who oppresses a poor man insults his Maker,
    but he who is kind to the needy honors him.
32 The wicked is overthrown through his evil-doing,
    but the righteous finds refuge through his integrity. [p]
33 Wisdom abides in the mind of a man of understanding,
    but it is not [q] known in the heart of fools.
34 Righteousness exalts a nation,
    but sin is a reproach to any people.
35 A servant who deals wisely has the king's favor,
    but his wrath falls on one who acts shamefully.

15 A soft answer turns away wrath,
    but a harsh word stirs up anger.
2 The tongue of the wise dispenses knowledge, [r]
    but the mouths of fools pour out folly.

---

[e] Gk Vg: Heb *from vanity*   [f] Cn Compare Gk Syr Vg Tg: Heb *is enduring*   [g] Heb *Wisdom of women*
[h] Cn: Heb *a rod of pride*   [i] Cn: Heb *a manger of*   [j] Cn: Heb *obscure*   [k] Heb *ways of death*
[l] Cn: Heb *from upon him*   [m] Gk: Heb *is hated*   [n] Cn Compare Gk: Heb *riches*   [o] Cn: Heb *folly*
[p] Gk Syr: Heb *in his death*   [q] Gk Syr: Heb *lacks not*   [r] Cn: Heb *makes knowledge good*

3 The eyes of the LORD are in every place,
  keeping watch on the evil and the good.
4 A gentle tongue is a tree of life,
  but perverseness in it breaks the spirit.
5 A fool despises his father's instruction,
  but he who heeds admonition is prudent.

6 In the house of the righteous there is much treasure,
  but trouble befalls the income of the wicked.
7 The lips of the wise spread knowledge;
  not so the minds of fools.
8 The sacrifice of the wicked is an abomination to the LORD,
  but the prayer of the upright is his delight.
9 The way of the wicked is an abomination to the LORD,
  but he loves him who pursues righteousness.
10 There is severe discipline for him who forsakes the way;
  he who hates reproof will die.
11 Sheol and Abaddon lie open before the LORD,
  how much more the hearts of men!
12 A scoffer does not like to be reproved;
  he will not go to the wise.
13 A glad heart makes a cheerful countenance,
  but by sorrow of heart the spirit is broken.
14 The mind of him who has understanding seeks knowledge,
  but the mouths of fools feed on folly.
15 All the days of the afflicted are evil,
  but a cheerful heart has a continual feast.
16 Better is a little with the fear of the LORD
  than great treasure and trouble with it.
17 Better is a dinner of herbs where love is
  than a fatted ox and hatred with it.
18 A hot-tempered man stirs up strife,
  but he who is slow to anger quiets contention.
19 The way of a sluggard is overgrown with thorns,
  but the path of the upright is a level highway.
20 A wise son makes a glad father,
  but a foolish man despises his mother.
21 Folly is a joy to him who has no sense,
  but a man of understanding walks aright.
22 Without counsel plans go wrong,
  but with many advisers they succeed.
23 To make an apt answer is a joy to a man,
  and a word in season, how good it is!
24 The wise man's path leads upward to life,
  that he may avoid Sheol beneath.
25 The LORD tears down the house of the proud,

but maintains the widow's boundaries.
26 The thoughts of the wicked are an abomination to the LORD,
  the words of the pure are pleasing to him.[s]
27 He who is greedy for unjust gain makes trouble for his household,
  but he who hates bribes will live.
28 The mind of the righteous ponders how to answer,
  but the mouth of the wicked pours out evil things.
29 The LORD is far from the wicked,
  but he hears the prayer of the righteous.
30 The light of the eyes rejoices the heart,
  and good news refreshes[t] the bones.
31 He whose ear heeds wholesome admonition
  will abide among the wise.
32 He who ignores instruction despises himself,
  but he who heeds admonition gains understanding.
33 The fear of the LORD is instruction in wisdom,
  and humility goes before honor.

16 The plans of the mind belong to man,
  but the answer of the tongue is from the LORD.
2 All the ways of a man are pure in his own eyes,
  but the LORD weighs the spirit.
3 Commit your work to the LORD,
  and your plans will be established.
4 The LORD has made everything for its purpose,
  even the wicked for the day of trouble.
5 Every one who is arrogant is an abomination to the LORD;
  be assured, he will not go unpunished.
6 By loyalty and faithfulness iniquity is atoned for,
  and by the fear of the LORD a man avoids evil.
7 When a man's ways please the LORD,
  he makes even his enemies to be at peace with him.
8 Better is a little with righteousness
  than great revenues with injustice.
9 A man's mind plans his way,
  but the LORD directs his steps.
10 Inspired decisions are on the lips of a king;
  his mouth does not sin in judgment.
11 A just balance and scales are the LORD'S;
  all the weights in the bag are his work.
12 It is an abomination to kings to do evil,
  for the throne is established by righteousness.
13 Righteous lips are the delight of a king,
  and he loves him who speaks what is right.
14 A king's wrath is a messenger of death,
  and a wise man will appease it.
15 In the light of a king's face there is life,
  and his favor is like the clouds that bring the spring rain.
16 To get wisdom is better[u] than gold;
  to get understanding is to be chosen rather than silver.

s Cn Compare Gk: Heb *pleasant words are pure*   t Heb *makes fat*   u Gk Syr Vg Tg: Heb *how much better*

¹⁷ The highway of the upright turns aside from evil;
  he who guards his way preserves his life.
¹⁸ Pride goes before destruction,
  and a haughty spirit before a fall.
¹⁹ It is better to be of a lowly spirit with the poor
  than to divide the spoil with the proud.
²⁰ He who gives heed to the word will prosper,
  and happy is he who trusts in the LORD.
²¹ The wise of heart is called a man of discernment,
  and pleasant speech increases persuasiveness.
²² Wisdom is a fountain of life to him who has it,
  but folly is the chastisement of fools.
²³ The mind of the wise makes his speech judicious,
  and adds persuasiveness to his lips.
²⁴ Pleasant words are like a honeycomb,
  sweetness to the soul and health to the body.
²⁵ There is a way which seems right to a man,
  but its end is the way to death.^v
²⁶ A worker's appetite works for him;
  his mouth urges him on.
²⁷ A worthless man plots evil,
  and his speech is like a scorching fire.
²⁸ A perverse man spreads strife,
  and a whisperer separates close friends.
²⁹ A man of violence entices his neighbor
  and leads him in a way that is not good.
³⁰ He who winks his eyes plans ^w perverse things,
  he who compresses his lips brings evil to pass.
³¹ A hoary head is a crown of glory;
  it is gained in a righteous life.
³² He who is slow to anger is better than the mighty,
  and he who rules his spirit than he who takes a city.
³³ The lot is cast into the lap,
  but the decision is wholly from the LORD.

17 Better is a dry morsel with quiet
  than a house full of feasting with strife.
² A slave who deals wisely will rule over a son who acts
    shamefully,
  and will share the inheritance as one of the brothers.
³ The crucible is for silver, and the furnace is for gold,
  and the LORD tries hearts.
⁴ An evildoer listens to wicked lips;
  and a liar gives heed to a mischievous tongue.
⁵ He who mocks the poor insults his Maker;
  he who is glad at calamity will not go unpunished.
⁶ Grandchildren are the crown of the aged,

and the glory of sons is their fathers.
⁷ Fine speech is not becoming to a fool;
  still less is false speech to a prince.
⁸ A bribe is like a magic stone in the eyes of him who
    gives it;
  wherever he turns he prospers.
⁹ He who forgives an offense seeks love,
  but he who repeats a matter alienates a friend.
¹⁰ A rebuke goes deeper into a man of understanding
  than a hundred blows into a fool.
¹¹ An evil man seeks only rebellion,
  and a cruel messenger will be sent against him.
¹² Let a man meet a she-bear robbed of her cubs,
  rather than a fool in his folly.
¹³ If a man returns evil for good,
  evil will not depart from his house.
¹⁴ The beginning of strife is like letting out water;
  so quit before the quarrel breaks out.
¹⁵ He who justifies the wicked and he who condemns the
    righteous
  are both alike an abomination to the LORD.
¹⁶ Why should a fool have a price in his hand to buy wisdom,
  when he has no mind?
¹⁷ A friend loves at all times,
  and a brother is born for adversity.
¹⁸ A man without sense gives a pledge,
  and becomes surety in the presence of his neighbor.
¹⁹ He who loves transgression loves strife;
  he who makes his door high seeks destruction.
²⁰ A man of crooked mind does not prosper,
  and one with a perverse tongue falls into calamity.
²¹ A stupid son is a grief to a father;
  and the father of a fool has no joy.
²² A cheerful heart is a good medicine,
  but a downcast spirit dries up the bones.
²³ A wicked man accepts a bribe from the bosom
  to pervert the ways of justice.
²⁴ A man of understanding sets his face toward wisdom,
  but the eyes of a fool are on the ends of the earth.
²⁵ A foolish son is a grief to his father
  and bitterness to her who bore him.
²⁶ To impose a fine on a righteous man is not good;
  to flog noble men is wrong.
²⁷ He who restrains his words has knowledge,
  and he who has a cool spirit is a man of understanding.
²⁸ Even a fool who keeps silent is considered wise;
  when he closes his lips, he is deemed intelligent.

18 He who is estranged ^x seeks pretexts ^y
    to break out against all sound judgment.
² A fool takes no pleasure in understanding,
  but only in expressing his opinion.
³ When wickedness comes, contempt comes also;
  and with dishonor comes disgrace.

^v Heb *ways of death*   ^w Gk Syr Vg Tg: Heb *to plan*   ^x Heb *separated*   ^y Gk Vg: Heb *desire*

4 The words of a man's mouth are deep waters;
    the fountain of wisdom is a gushing stream.
5 It is not good to be partial to a wicked man,
    or to deprive a righteous man of justice.
6 A fool's lips bring strife,
    and his mouth invites a flogging.
7 A fool's mouth is his ruin,
    and his lips are a snare to himself.
8 The words of a whisperer are like delicious morsels;
    they go down into the inner parts of the body.
9 He who is slack in his work
    is a brother to him who destroys.
10 The name of the LORD is a strong tower;
    the righteous man runs into it and is safe.
11 A rich man's wealth is his strong city,
    and like a high wall protecting him.ᶻ
12 Before destruction a man's heart is haughty,
    but humility goes before honor.
13 If one gives answer before he hears,
    it is his folly and shame.
14 A man's spirit will endure sickness;
    but a broken spirit who can bear?
15 An intelligent mind acquires knowledge,
    and the ear of the wise seeks knowledge.
16 A man's gift makes room for him
    and brings him before great men.
17 He who states his case first seems right,
    until the other comes and examines him.
18 The lot puts an end to disputes
    and decides between powerful contenders.
19 A brother helped is like a strong city,ᵃ
    but quarreling is like the bars of a castle.
20 From the fruit of his mouth a man is satisfied;
    he is satisfied by the yield of his lips.
21 Death and life are in the power of the tongue,
    and those who love it will eat its fruits.
22 He who finds a wife finds a good thing,
    and obtains favor from the LORD.
23 The poor use entreaties,
    but the rich answer roughly.
24 There areᵇ friends who pretend to be friends,ᶜ
    but there is a friend who sticks closer than a brother.

19 Better is a poor man who walks in his integrity
        than a man who is perverse in speech, and is a
        fool.
2 It is not good for a man to be without knowledge,
    and he who makes haste with his feet misses his way.
3 When a man's folly brings his way to ruin,
    his heart rages against the LORD.
4 Wealth brings many new friends,
    but a poor man is deserted by his friend.
5 A false witness will not go unpunished,
    and he who utters lies will not escape.

6 Many seek the favor of a generous man,
    and every one is a friend to a man who gives gifts.
7 All a poor man's brothers hate him;
    how much more do his friends go far from him!
He pursues them with words, but does not have them.ᵈ
8 He who gets wisdom loves himself;
    he who keeps understanding will prosper.
9 A false witness will not go unpunished,
    and he who utters lies will perish.
10 It is not fitting for a fool to live in luxury,
    much less for a slave to rule over princes.
11 Good sense makes a man slow to anger,
    and it is his glory to overlook an offense.
12 A king's wrath is like the growling of a lion,
    but his favor is like dew upon the grass.
13 A foolish son is ruin to his father,
    and a wife's quarreling is a continual dripping of rain.
14 House and wealth are inherited from fathers,
    but a prudent wife is from the LORD.
15 Slothfulness casts into a deep sleep,
    and an idle person will suffer hunger.
16 He who keeps the commandment keeps his life;
    he who despises the wordᵉ will die.
17 He who is kind to the poor lends to the LORD,
    and he will repay him for his deed.
18 Discipline your son while there is hope;
    do not set your heart on his destruction.
19 A man of great wrath will pay the penalty;
    for if you deliver him, you will only have to do it
        again.ᶠ
20 Listen to advice and accept instruction,
    that you may gain wisdom for the future.
21 Many are the plans in the mind of a man,
    but it is the purpose of the LORD that will be estab-
        lished.
22 What is desired in a man is loyalty,
    and a poor man is better than a liar.
23 The fear of the LORD leads to life;
    and he who has it rests satisfied;
    he will not be visited by harm.
24 The sluggard buries his hand in the dish,
    and will not even bring it back to his mouth.
25 Strike a scoffer, and the simple will learn prudence;
    reprove a man of understanding, and he will gain
        knowledge.
26 He who does violence to his father and chases away his
        mother
    is a son who causes shame and brings reproach.
27 Cease, my son, to hear instruction
    only to stray from the words of knowledge.
28 A worthless witness mocks at justice,
    and the mouth of the wicked devours iniquity.
29 Condemnation is ready for scoffers,

ᶻ Or in his imagination   ᵃ Gk Syr Vg Tg: The meaning of the Hebrew is uncertain   ᵇ Syr Tg: Heb A man of
ᶜ Cn Compare Syr Vg Tg: Heb to be broken   ᵈ Heb uncertain   ᵉ Cn Compare 13.13: Heb his ways   ᶠ Heb obscure

and flogging for the backs of fools.

20 Wine is a mocker, strong drink a brawler;
and whoever is led astray by it is not wise.

2 The dread wrath of a king is like the growling of a lion;
he who provokes him to anger forfeits his life.

3 It is an honor for a man to keep aloof from strife;
but every fool will be quarreling.

4 The sluggard does not plow in the autumn;
he will seek at harvest and have nothing.

5 The purpose in a man's mind is like deep water,
but a man of understanding will draw it out.

6 Many a man proclaims his own loyalty,
but a faithful man who can find?

7 A righteous man who walks in his integrity—
blessed are his sons after him!

8 A king who sits on the throne of judgment
winnows all evil with his eyes.

9 Who can say, "I have made my heart clean;
I am pure from my sin"?

10 Diverse weights and diverse measures
are both alike an abomination to the LORD.

11 Even a child makes himself known by his acts,
whether what he does is pure and right.

12 The hearing ear and the seeing eye,
the LORD has made them both.

13 Love not sleep, lest you come to poverty;
open your eyes, and you will have plenty of bread.

14 "It is bad, it is bad," says the buyer;
but when he goes away, then he boasts.

15 There is gold, and abundance of costly stones;
but the lips of knowledge are a precious jewel.

16 Take a man's garment when he has given surety for a stranger,
and hold him in pledge when he gives surety for foreigners.

17 Bread gained by deceit is sweet to a man,
but afterward his mouth will be full of gravel.

18 Plans are established by counsel;
by wise guidance wage war.

19 He who goes about gossiping reveals secrets;
therefore do not associate with one who speaks foolishly.

20 If one curses his father or his mother,
his lamp will be put out in utter darkness.

21 An inheritance gotten hastily in the beginning
will in the end not be blessed.

22 Do not say, "I will repay evil";

g Gk: Heb loyalty

wait for the LORD, and he will help you.

23 Diverse weights are an abomination to the LORD,
and false scales are not good.

24 A man's steps are ordered by the LORD;
how then can man understand his way?

25 It is a snare for a man to say rashly, "It is holy,"
and to reflect only after making his vows.

26 A wise king winnows the wicked,
and drives the wheel over them.

27 The spirit of man is the lamp of the LORD,
searching all his innermost parts.

28 Loyalty and faithfulness preserve the king,
and his throne is upheld by righteousness.g

29 The glory of young men is their strength,
but the beauty of old men is their gray hair.

30 Blows that wound cleanse away evil;
strokes make clean the innermost parts.

21 The king's heart is a stream of water in the hand of the LORD;
he turns it wherever he will.

2 Every way of a man is right in his own eyes,
but the LORD weighs the heart.

3 To do righteousness and justice
is more acceptable to the LORD than sacrifice.

4 Haughty eyes and a proud heart,
the lamp of the wicked, are sin.

5 The plans of the diligent lead surely to abundance,
but every one who is hasty comes only to want.

6 The getting of treasures by a lying tongue
is a fleeting vapor and a snare of death.

7 The violence of the wicked will sweep them away,
because they refuse to do what is just.

8 The way of the guilty is crooked,
but the conduct of the pure is right.

9 It is better to live in a corner of the housetop
than in a house shared with a contentious woman.

10 The soul of the wicked desires evil;
his neighbor finds no mercy in his eyes.

11 When a scoffer is punished, the simple becomes wise,
when a wise man is instructed, he gains knowledge.

12 The righteous observes the house of the wicked;
the wicked are cast down to ruin.

13 He who closes his ear to the cry of the poor
will himself cry out and not be heard.

14 A gift in secret averts anger;
and a bribe in the bosom, strong wrath.

15 When justice is done, it is a joy to the righteous,
but dismay to evildoers.

16 A man who wanders from the way of understanding
will rest in the assembly of the dead.

17 He who loves pleasure will be a poor man;
he who loves wine and oil will not be rich.

18 The wicked is a ransom for the righteous,

and the faithless for the upright.
19 It is better to live in a desert land
  than with a contentious and fretful woman.
20 Precious treasure remains[h] in a wise man's dwelling,
  but a foolish man devours it.
21 He who pursues righteousness and kindness
  will find life[i] and honor.
22 A wise man scales the city of the mighty
  and brings down the stronghold in which they trust.
23 He who keeps his mouth and his tongue
  keeps himself out of trouble.
24 "Scoffer" is the name of the proud, haughty man
  who acts with arrogant pride.
25 The desire of the sluggard kills him
  for his hands refuse to labor.
26 All day long the wicked covets,[j]
  but the righteous gives and does not hold back.
27 The sacrifice of the wicked is an abomination;
  how much more when he brings it with evil intent.
28 A false witness will perish,
  but the word of a man who hears will endure.
29 A wicked man puts on a bold face,
  but an upright man considers[k] his ways.
30 No wisdom, no understanding, no counsel,
  can avail against the LORD.
31 The horse is made ready for the day of battle,
  but the victory belongs to the LORD.

22 A good name is to be chosen rather than great riches,
  and favor is better than silver or gold.
2 The rich and the poor meet together;
  the LORD is the maker of them all.
3 A prudent man sees danger and hides himself;
  but the simple go on, and suffer for it.
4 The reward for humility and fear of the LORD
  is riches and honor and life.
5 Thorns and snares are in the way of the perverse;
  he who guards himself will keep far from them.
6 Train up a child in the way he should go,
  and when he is old he will not depart from it.
7 The rich rules over the poor,
  and the borrower is the slave of the lender.
8 He who sows injustice will reap calamity,
  and the rod of his fury will fail.
9 He who has a bountiful eye will be blessed,

for he shares his bread with the poor.
10 Drive out a scoffer, and strife will go out,
  and quarreling and abuse will cease.
11 He who loves purity of heart,
  and whose speech is gracious, will have the king as his friend.
12 The eyes of the LORD keep watch over knowledge,
  but he overthrows the words of the faithless.
13 The sluggard says, "There is a lion outside!
  I shall be slain in the streets!"
14 The mouth of a loose woman is a deep pit;
  he with whom the LORD is angry will fall into it.
15 Folly is bound up in the heart of a child,
  but the rod of discipline drives it far from him.
16 He who oppresses the poor to increase his own wealth,
  or gives to the rich, will only come to want.

THE SAYINGS OF THE WISE
17 Incline your ear, and hear the words of the wise,
  and apply your mind to my knowledge;
18 for it will be pleasant if you keep them within you,
  if all of them are ready on your lips.
19 That your trust may be in the LORD,
  I have made them known to you today, even to you.

20 Have I not written for you thirty sayings
  of admonition and knowledge,
21 to show you what is right and true,
  that you may give a true answer to those who sent you?

22 Do not rob the poor, because he is poor,
  or crush the afflicted at the gate;
23 for the LORD will plead their cause
  and despoil of life those who despoil them.
24 Make no friendship with a man given to anger,
  nor go with a wrathful man,
25 lest you learn his ways
  and entangle yourself in a snare.
26 Be not one of those who give pledges,
  who become surety for debts.
27 If you have nothing with which to pay,
  why should your bed be taken from under you?
28 Remove not the ancient landmark which your fathers have set.
29 Do you see a man skilful in his work?
  he will stand before kings;
  he will not stand before obscure men.

23 When you sit down to eat with a ruler,
  observe carefully what[l] is before you;
2 and put a knife to your throat
  if you are a man given to appetite.
3 Do not desire his delicacies,

h Gk: Heb *and oil*   i Gk: Heb *life and righteousness*   j Gk: Heb *all day long he covets covetously*
k Another reading is *establishes*   l Or *who*

for they are deceptive food.
4 Do not toil to acquire wealth;
  be wise enough to desist.
5 When your eyes light upon it, it is gone;
  for suddenly it takes to itself wings,
  flying like an eagle toward heaven.
6 Do not eat the bread of a man who is stingy;
  do not desire his delicacies;
7 for he is like one who is inwardly reckoning,[m]
  "Eat and drink!" he says to you;
  but his heart is not with you.
8 You will vomit up the morsels which you have eaten,
  and waste your pleasant words.
9 Do not speak in the hearing of a fool,
  for he will despise the wisdom of your words.
10 Do not remove an ancient landmark
  or enter the fields of the fatherless;
11 for their Redeemer is strong;
  he will plead their cause against you.
12 Apply your mind to instruction
  and your ear to words of knowledge.
13 Do not withhold discipline from a child;
  if you beat him with a rod, he will not die.
14 If you beat him with the rod
  you will save his life from Sheol.
15 My son, if your heart is wise,
  my heart too will be glad.
16 My soul will rejoice
  when your lips speak what is right.
17 Let not your heart envy sinners,
  but continue in the fear of the LORD all the day.
18 Surely there is a future,
  and your hope will not be cut off.

19 Hear, my son, and be wise,
  and direct your mind in the way.
20 Be not among winebibbers,
  or among gluttonous eaters of meat;
21 for the drunkard and the glutton will come to poverty,
  and drowsiness will clothe a man with rags.

22 Hearken to your father who begot you,
  and do not despise your mother when she is old.
23 Buy truth, and do not sell it;
  buy wisdom, instruction, and understanding.
24 The father of the righteous will greatly rejoice;
  he who begets a wise son will be glad in him.
25 Let your father and mother be glad,
  let her who bore you rejoice.

26 My son, give me your heart,
  and let your eyes observe[n] my ways.
27 For a harlot is a deep pit;
  an adventuress is a narrow well.

28 She lies in wait like a robber
  and increases the faithless among men.

29 Who has woe? Who has sorrow?
  Who has strife? Who has complaining?
  Who has wounds without cause?
  Who has redness of eyes?
30 Those who tarry long over wine,
  those who go to try mixed wine.
31 Do not look at wine when it is red,
  when it sparkles in the cup
  and goes down smoothly.
32 At the last it bites like a serpent,
  and stings like an adder.
33 Your eyes will see strange things,
  and your mind utter perverse things.
34 You will be like one who lies down in the midst of the sea,
  like one who lies on the top of a mast.[o]
35 "They struck me," you will say,[p] "but I was not hurt;
  they beat me, but I did not feel it.
  When shall I awake?
  I will seek another drink."

24 Be not envious of evil men,
    nor desire to be with them;
2 for their minds devise violence,
  and their lips talk of mischief.

3 By wisdom a house is built,
  and by understanding it is established;
4 by knowledge the rooms are filled
  with all precious and pleasant riches.
5 A wise man is mightier than a strong man,[q]
  and a man of knowledge than he who has strength;
6 for by wise guidance you can wage your war,
  and in abundance of counselors there is victory.
7 Wisdom is too high for a fool;
  in the gate he does not open his mouth.

8 He who plans to do evil
  will be called a mischief-maker.
9 The devising of folly is sin,
  and the scoffer is an abomination to men.

10 If you faint in the day of adversity,
  your strength is small.
11 Rescue those who are being taken away to death;
  hold back those who are stumbling to the slaughter.
12 If you say, "Behold, we did not know this,"
  does not he who weighs the heart perceive it?
  Does not he who keeps watch over your soul know it,
  and will he not requite man according to his work?

---

m Heb obscure   n Another reading is *delight in*   o Heb obscure   p Gk Syr Vg Tg: Heb lacks *you will say*
q Gk Compare Syr Tg: Heb *is in strength*

¹³ My son, eat honey, for it is good,
and the drippings of the honeycomb are sweet to your taste.
¹⁴ Know that wisdom is such to your soul;
if you find it, there will be a future,
and your hope will not be cut off.

¹⁵ Lie not in wait as a wicked man against the dwelling of the righteous;
do not violence to his home;
¹⁶ for a righteous man falls seven times, and rises again;
but the wicked are overthrown by calamity.

¹⁷ Do not rejoice when your enemy falls,
and let not your heart be glad when he stumbles;
¹⁸ lest the LORD see it, and be displeased,
and turn away his anger from him.

¹⁹ Fret not yourself because of evildoers,
and be not envious of the wicked;
²⁰ for the evil man has no future;
the lamp of the wicked will be put out.

²¹ My son, fear the LORD and the king,
and do not disobey either of them;ʳ
²² for disaster from them will rise suddenly,
and who knows the ruin that will come from them both?

²³ These also are sayings of the wise.

Partiality in judging is not good.
²⁴ He who says to the wicked, "You are innocent,"
will be cursed by peoples, abhorred by nations;
²⁵ but those who rebuke the wicked will have delight,
and a good blessing will be upon them.
²⁶ He who gives a right answer
kisses the lips.

²⁷ Prepare your work outside,
get everything ready for you in the field;
and after that build your house.

²⁸ Be not a witness against your neighbor without cause,
and do not deceive with your lips.
²⁹ Do not say, "I will do to him as he has done to me;
I will pay the man back for what he has done."

³⁰ I passed by the field of a sluggard,
by the vineyard of a man without sense;
³¹ and lo, it was all overgrown with thorns;
the ground was covered with nettles,
and its stone wall was broken down.
³² Then I saw and considered it;
I looked and received instruction.

³³ A little sleep, a little slumber,
a little folding of the hands to rest,
³⁴ and poverty will come upon you like a robber,
and want like an armed man.

MORE PROVERBS OF SOLOMON
25 These also are proverbs of Solomon which the men of Hezekiah king of Judah copied.

² It is the glory of God to conceal things,
but the glory of kings is to search things out.
³ As the heavens for height, and the earth for depth,
so the mind of kings is unsearchable.
⁴ Take away the dross from the silver,
and the smith has material for a vessel;
⁵ take away the wicked from the presence of the king,
and his throne will be established in righteousness.
⁶ Do not put yourself forward in the king's presence
or stand in the place of the great;
⁷ for it is better to be told, "Come up here,"
than to be put lower in the presence of the prince.

What your eyes have seen
⁸ do not hastily bring into court;
forˢ what will you do in the end,
when your neighbor puts you to shame?
⁹ Argue your case with your neighbor himself,
and do not disclose another's secret;
¹⁰ lest he who hears you bring shame upon you,
and your ill repute have no end.

¹¹ A word fitly spoken
is like apples of gold in a setting of silver.
¹² Like a gold ring or an ornament of gold
is a wise reprover to a listening ear.
¹³ Like the cold of snow in the time of harvest
is a faithful messenger to those who send him,
he refreshes the spirit of his masters.
¹⁴ Like clouds and wind without rain
is a man who boasts of a gift he does not give.

¹⁵ With patience a ruler may be persuaded,
and a soft tongue will break a bone.
¹⁶ If you have found honey, eat only enough for you,
lest you be sated with it and vomit it.
¹⁷ Let your foot be seldom in your neighbor's house,
lest he become weary of you and hate you.
¹⁸ A man who bears false witness against his neighbor
is like a war club, or a sword, or a sharp arrow.
¹⁹ Trust in a faithless man in time of trouble
is like a bad tooth or a foot that slips.
²⁰ He who sings songs to a heavy heart
is like one who takes off a garment on a cold day
and like vinegar on a wound.ᵗ
²¹ If your enemy is hungry, give him bread to eat;

ʳ Gk: Heb *do not associate with those who change*   ˢ Cn: Heb *lest*   ᵗ Gk: Heb *lye*

and if he is thirsty, give him water to drink;
²² for you will heap coals of fire on his head,
and the Lord will reward you.
²³ The north wind brings forth rain;
and a backbiting tongue, angry looks.
²⁴ It is better to live in a corner of the housetop
than in a house shared with a contentious woman.
²⁵ Like cold water to a thirsty soul,
so is good news from a far country.

²⁶ Like a muddied spring or a polluted fountain
is a righteous man who gives way before the wicked.
²⁷ It is not good to eat much honey,
so be sparing of complimentary words.^u
²⁸ A man without self-control
is like a city broken into and left without walls.

26 Like snow in summer or rain in harvest,
so honor is not fitting for a fool.
² Like a sparrow in its flitting, like a swallow in its flying,
a curse that is causeless does not alight.
³ A whip for the horse, a bridle for the ass,
and a rod for the back of fools.
⁴ Answer not a fool according to his folly,
lest you be like him yourself.
⁵ Answer a fool according to his folly,
lest he be wise in his own eyes.
⁶ He who sends a message by the hand of a fool
cuts off his own feet and drinks violence.
⁷ Like a lame man's legs, which hang useless,
is a proverb in the mouth of fools.
⁸ Like one who binds the stone in the sling
is he who gives honor to a fool.
⁹ Like a thorn that goes up into the hand of a drunkard
is a proverb in the mouth of fools.
¹⁰ Like an archer who wounds everybody
is he who hires a passing fool or drunkard.^v
¹¹ Like a dog that returns to his vomit
is a fool that repeats his folly.
¹² Do you see a man who is wise in his own eyes?
There is more hope for a fool than for him.
¹³ The sluggard says, "There is a lion in the road!
There is a lion in the streets!"
¹⁴ As a door turns on its hinges,
so does a sluggard on his bed.
¹⁵ The sluggard buries his hand in the dish;
it wears him out to bring it back to his mouth.
¹⁶ The sluggard is wiser in his own eyes

than seven men who can answer discreetly.
¹⁷ He who meddles in a quarrel not his own
is like one who takes a passing dog by the ears.
¹⁸ Like a madman who throws firebrands,
arrows, and death,
¹⁹ is the man who deceives his neighbor
and says, "I am only joking!"
²⁰ For lack of wood the fire goes out;
and where there is no whisperer, quarreling ceases.
²¹ As charcoal to hot embers and wood to fire,
so is a quarrelsome man for kindling strife.
²² The words of a whisperer are like delicious morsels;
they go down into the inner parts of the body.
²³ Like the glaze^w covering an earthen vessel
are smooth^x lips with an evil heart.
²⁴ He who hates, dissembles with his lips
and harbors deceit in his heart;
²⁵ when he speaks graciously, believe him not,
for there are seven abominations in his heart;
²⁶ though his hatred be covered with guile,
his wickedness will be exposed in the assembly.
²⁷ He who digs a pit will fall into it,
and a stone will come back upon him who starts it
rolling.
²⁸ A lying tongue hates its victims,
and a flattering mouth works ruin.

27 Do not boast about tomorrow,
for you do not know what a day may bring forth.
² Let another praise you, and not your own mouth;
a stranger, and not your own lips.
³ A stone is heavy, and sand is weighty,
but a fool's provocation is heavier than both.
⁴ Wrath is cruel, anger is overwhelming;
but who can stand before jealousy?
⁵ Better is open rebuke
than hidden love.
⁶ Faithful are the wounds of a friend;
profuse are the kisses of an enemy.
⁷ He who is sated loathes honey,
but to one who is hungry everything bitter is sweet.
⁸ Like a bird that strays from its nest,
is a man who strays from his home.
⁹ Oil and perfume make the heart glad,
but the soul is torn by trouble.^y
¹⁰ Your friend, and your father's friend, do not forsake;
and do not go to your brother's house in the day of
your calamity.
Better is a neighbor who is near
than a brother who is far away.
¹¹ Be wise, my son, and make my heart glad,
that I may answer him who reproaches me.
¹² A prudent man sees danger and hides himself;
but the simple go on, and suffer for it.

^u Cn Compare Gk Syr Tg: Heb *searching out their glory is glory*
^w Cn: Heb *silver of dross*   ^x Gk: Heb *burning*

^v The Hebrew text of this verse is uncertain
^y Gk: Heb *the sweetness of his friend from hearty counsel*

13 Take a man's garment when he has given surety for a
    stranger,
    and hold him in pledge when he gives surety for
    foreigners.ᶻ
14 He who blesses his neighbor with a loud voice,
    rising early in the morning,
    will be counted as cursing.
15 A continual dripping on a rainy day
    and a contentious woman are alike;
16 to restrain her is to restrain the wind ᵃ
    or to grasp oil in his right hand.
17 Iron sharpens iron,
    and one man sharpens another.
18 He who tends a fig tree will eat its fruit,
    and he who guards his master will be honored.
19 As in water face answers to face,
    so the mind of man reflects the man.
20 Sheol and Abaddon are never satisfied,
    and never satisfied are the eyes of man.
21 The crucible is for silver, and the furnace is for gold,
    and a man is judged by his praise.
22 Crush a fool in a mortar with a pestle
    along with crushed grain,
    yet his folly will not depart from him.

23 Know well the condition of your flocks,
    and give attention to your herds;
24 for riches do not last for ever;
    and does a crown endure to all generations?
25 When the grass is gone, and the new growth appears,
    and the herbage of the mountains is gathered,
26 the lambs will provide your clothing,
    and the goats the price of a field;
27 there will be enough goats' milk for your food,
    for the food of your household
    and maintenance for your maidens.

28 The wicked flee when no one pursues,
    but the righteous are bold as a lion.
2 When a land transgresses
    it has many rulers;
    but with men of understanding and knowledge
    its stability will long continue.
3 A poor man who oppresses the poor
    is a beating rain that leaves no food.
4 Those who forsake the law praise the wicked,

but those who keep the law strive against them.
5 Evil men do not understand justice,
    but those who seek the Lord understand it completely.
6 Better is a poor man who walks in his integrity
    than a rich man who is perverse in his ways.
7 He who keeps the law is a wise son,
    but a companion of gluttons shames his father.
8 He who augments his wealth by interest and increase
    gathers it for him who is kind to the poor.
9 If one turns away his ear from hearing the law,
    even his prayer is an abomination.
10 He who misleads the upright into an evil way
    will fall into his own pit;
    but the blameless will have a goodly inheritance.
11 A rich man is wise in his own eyes,
    but a poor man who has understanding will find him
    out.
12 When the righteous triumph, there is great glory;
    but when the wicked rise, men hide themselves.
13 He who conceals his transgressions will not prosper,
    but he who confesses and forsakes them will obtain
    mercy.
14 Blessed is the man who fears the Lord always;
    but he who hardens his heart will fall into calamity.
15 Like a roaring lion or a charging bear
    is a wicked ruler over a poor people.
16 A ruler who lacks understanding is a cruel oppressor;
    but he who hates unjust gain will prolong his days.
17 If a man is burdened with the blood of another,
    let him be a fugitive until death;
    let no one help him.
18 He who walks in integrity will be delivered,
    but he who is perverse in his ways will fall into a pit.ᵇ
19 He who tills his land will have plenty of bread,
    but he who follows worthless pursuits will have plenty
    of poverty.
20 A faithful man will abound with blessings,
    but he who hastens to be rich will not go unpunished.
21 To show partiality is not good;
    but for a piece of bread a man will do wrong.
22 A miserly man hastens after wealth,
    and does not know that want will come upon him.
23 He who rebukes a man will afterward find more favor
    than he who flatters with his tongue.
24 He who robs his father or his mother
    and says, "That is no transgression,"
    is the companion of a man who destroys.
25 A greedy man stirs up strife,
    but he who trusts in the Lord will be enriched.
26 He who trusts in his own mind is a fool;
    but he who walks in wisdom will be delivered.
27 He who gives to the poor will not want,
    but he who hides his eyes will get many a curse.

ᶻ Vg and 20.16: Heb *a foreign woman*   ᵃ Heb obscure   ᵇ Syr: Heb *in one*

28 When the wicked rise, men hide themselves,
  but when they perish, the righteous increase.

29 He who is often reproved, yet stiffens his neck
  will suddenly be broken beyond healing.

2 When the righteous are in authority, the people rejoice;
  but when the wicked rule, the people groan.

3 He who loves wisdom makes his father glad,
  but one who keeps company with harlots squanders his
    substance.

4 By justice a king gives stability to the land,
  but one who exacts gifts ruins it.

5 A man who flatters his neighbor
  spreads a net for his feet.

6 An evil man is ensnared in his transgression,
  but a righteous man sings and rejoices.

7 A righteous man knows the rights of the poor;
  a wicked man does not understand such knowledge.

8 Scoffers set a city aflame,
  but wise men turn away wrath.

9 If a wise man has an argument with a fool,
  the fool only rages and laughs, and there is no quiet.

10 Bloodthirsty men hate one who is blameless,
  and the wicked c seek his life.

11 A fool gives full vent to his anger,
  but a wise man quietly holds it back.

12 If a ruler listens to falsehood,
  all his officials will be wicked.

13 The poor man and the oppressor meet together;
  the LORD gives light to the eyes of both.

14 If a king judges the poor with equity
  his throne will be established for ever.

15 The rod and reproof give wisdom,
  but a child left to himself brings shame to his mother.

16 When the wicked are in authority, transgression increases;
  but the righteous will look upon their downfall.

17 Discipline your son, and he will give you rest;
  he will give delight to your heart.

18 Where there is no prophecy the people cast off restraint,
  but blessed is he who keeps the law.

19 By mere words a servant is not disciplined,
  for though he understands, he will not give heed.

20 Do you see a man who is hasty in his words?
  There is more hope for a fool than for him.

21 He who pampers his servant from childhood,
  will in the end find him his heir.d

22 A man of wrath stirs up strife,
  and a man given to anger causes much transgression.

23 A man's pride will bring him low,
  but he who is lowly in spirit will obtain honor.

24 The partner of a thief hates his own life;
  he hears the curse, but discloses nothing.

25 The fear of man lays a snare,
  but he who trusts in the LORD is safe.

26 Many seek the favor of a ruler,
  but from the LORD a man gets justice.

27 An unjust man is an abomination to the righteous,
  but he whose way is straight is an abomination to the
    wicked.

30 The words of Agur son of Jakeh of Massa.e

The man says to Ith′i-el,
  to Ith′i-el and Ucal: f

2 Surely I am too stupid to be a man.
  I have not the understanding of a man.

3 I have not learned wisdom,
  nor have I knowledge of the Holy One.

4 Who has ascended to heaven and come down?
  Who has gathered the wind in his fists?
  Who has wrapped up the waters in a garment?
  Who has established all the ends of the earth?
  What is his name, and what is his son's name?
  Surely you know!

5 Every word of God proves true;
  he is a shield to those who take refuge in him.

6 Do not add to his words,
  lest he rebuke you, and you be found a liar.

7 Two things I ask of thee;
  deny them not to me before I die:

8 Remove far from me falsehood and lying;
  give me neither poverty nor riches;
  feed me with the food that is needful for me,

9 lest I be full, and deny thee,
  and say, "Who is the LORD?"
  or lest I be poor, and steal,
  and profane the name of my God.

10 Do not slander a servant to his master,
  lest he curse you, and you be held guilty.

11 There are those who curse their fathers
  and do not bless their mothers.

12 There are those who are pure in their own eyes
  but are not cleansed of their filth.

13 There are those—how lofty are their eyes,
  how high their eyelids lift!

14 There are those whose teeth are swords,
  whose teeth are knives,
  to devour the poor from off the earth,
  the needy from among men.

15 The leech g has two daughters;
  "Give, give," they cry.
  Three things are never satisfied;
  four never say, "Enough":

___

c Cn: Heb upright   d The meaning of the Hebrew word is uncertain   e Or the oracle
f The Hebrew of this verse is obscure   g The meaning of the Hebrew word is uncertain

16 Sheol, the barren womb,
 the earth ever thirsty for water,
 and the fire which never says, "Enough." h

17 The eye that mocks a father
 and scorns to obey a mother
 will be picked out by the ravens of the valley
 and eaten by the vultures.

18 Three things are too wonderful for me;
 four I do not understand:
19 the way of an eagle in the sky,
 the way of a serpent on a rock,
 the way of a ship on the high seas,
 and the way of a man with a maiden.

20 This is the way of an adulteress:
 she eats, and wipes her mouth,
 and says, "I have done no wrong."

21 Under three things the earth trembles;
 under four it cannot bear up:
22 a slave when he becomes king,
 and a fool when he is filled with food;
23 an unloved woman when she gets a husband,
 and a maid when she succeeds her mistress.

24 Four things on earth are small,
 but they are exceedingly wise:
25 the ants are a people not strong,
 yet they provide their food in the summer;
26 the badgers are a people not mighty,
 yet they make their homes in the rocks;
27 the locusts have no king,
 yet all of them march in rank;
28 the lizard you can take in your hands,
 yet it is in kings' palaces.

29 Three things are stately in their tread;
 four are stately in their stride:
30 the lion, which is mightiest among beasts
 and does not turn back before any;
31 the strutting cock,[i] the he-goat,
 and a king striding before[j] his people.

32 If you have been foolish, exalting yourself,
 or if you have been devising evil,
 put your hand on your mouth.
33 For pressing milk produces curds,

pressing the nose produces blood,
 and pressing anger produces strife.

31 The words of Lemuel, king of Massa,[k] which his
 mother taught him:

2 What, my son? What, son of my womb?
 What, son of my vows?
3 Give not your strength to women,
 your ways to those who destroy kings.
4 It is not for kings, O Lemuel,
 it is not for kings to drink wine,
 or for rulers to desire[l] strong drink;
5 lest they drink and forget what has been decreed,
 and pervert the rights of all the afflicted.
6 Give strong drink to him who is perishing,
 and wine to those in bitter distress;
7 let them drink and forget their poverty,
 and remember their misery no more.
8 Open your mouth for the dumb,
 for the rights of all who are left desolate.[m]
9 Open your mouth, judge righteously,
 maintain the rights of the poor and needy.

10 A good wife who can find?
 She is far more precious than jewels.
11 The heart of her husband trusts in her,
 and he will have no lack of gain.
12 She does him good, and not harm,
 all the days of her life.
13 She seeks wool and flax,
 and works with willing hands.
14 She is like the ships of the merchant,
 she brings her food from afar.
15 She rises while it is yet night
 and provides food for her household
 and tasks for her maidens.
16 She considers a field and buys it;
 with the fruit of her hands she plants a vineyard.

17 She girds her loins with strength
 and makes her arms strong.
18 She perceives that her merchandise is profitable.
 Her lamp does not go out at night.

h Heb obscure   i Gk Syr Tg Compare Vg: Heb obscure   j The meaning of the Hebrew is uncertain
k Or *King Lemuel, the oracle*   l Cn: Heb *where*   m Heb *are sons of passing away*

439

¹⁹ She puts her hands to the distaff,
  and her hands hold the spindle.
²⁰ She opens her hand to the poor,
  and reaches out her hands to the needy.
²¹ She is not afraid of snow for her household,
  for all her household are clothed in scarlet.
²² She makes herself coverings;
  her clothing is fine linen and purple.
²³ Her husband is known in the gates,
  when he sits among the elders of the land.
²⁴ She makes linen garments and sells them;
  she delivers girdles to the merchant.
²⁵ Strength and dignity are her clothing,
  and she laughs at the time to come.
²⁶ She opens her mouth with wisdom,
  and the teaching of kindness is on her tongue.
²⁷ She looks well to the ways of her household,
  and does not eat the bread of idleness.
²⁸ Her children rise up and call her blessed;
  her husband also, and he praises her:
²⁹ "Many women have done excellently,
  but you surpass them all."
³⁰ Charm is deceitful, and beauty is vain,
  but a woman who fears the Lord is to be praised.
³¹ Give her of the fruit of her hands,
  and let her works praise her in the gates.

INTRODUCTION TO

ECCLESIASTES
OR THE PREACHER

Ecclesiastes tells how hopeless a man felt who had seen his ambitions and efforts fail to bring him happiness. He tried making money; he studied to become wise; he sought for pleasure. Each of these things failed to give him real happiness, and as he told about each one, he ended by saying that it was all useless—it was futility or vanity: "and behold, all is vanity and a striving after wind" (Ecclesiastes 1.14).

He reminded the reader that youth does not last long. The last chapter contains a strangely beautiful but sad description of old age (12.1-8) which ends with his favorite refrain, "Vanity of vanities, says the Preacher; all is vanity."

This book shows over and over again how useless or vain are many things for which human beings strive. Ecclesiastes shows that life often brings doubts and problems we cannot solve. But the book ends by saying that in spite of every disappointment we should "Fear God, and keep his commandments; for this is the whole duty of man. For God will bring every deed into judgment, with every secret thing, whether good or evil." (12.13b-14.)

The word "Ecclesiastes" means the chairman of the meeting, or the preacher. The book begins by saying it was written by "the Preacher, the son of David," but there is no other hint about who the writer was. We do know that it was written about 200 B.C. when the Jews had been discouraged by many defeats and had just about given up their long-held ambition to be a powerful nation. Look at the charts on the end sheets to see how Ecclesiastes fits into the long story of the Bible and its writing.

ECCLESIASTES

OR THE PREACHER

THE PREACHER'S WORLD OUTLOOK

1 The words of the Preacher,[a] the son of David, king in Jerusalem.

2 Vanity of vanities, says the Preacher,
  vanity of vanities! All is vanity.

3 What does man gain by all the toil
  at which he toils under the sun?

4 A generation goes, and a generation comes,
  but the earth remains for ever.

5 The sun rises and the sun goes down,
  and hastens to the place where it rises.

6 The wind blows to the south,
  and goes round to the north;
round and round goes the wind,
  and on its circuits the wind returns.

7 All streams run to the sea,
  but the sea is not full;

to the place where the streams flow,
  there they flow again.

8 All things are full of weariness;
  a man cannot utter it;
the eye is not satisfied with seeing,
  nor the ear filled with hearing.

9 What has been is what will be,
  and what has been done is what will be done;
  and there is nothing new under the sun.

10 Is there a thing of which it is said,
  "See, this is new"?

a Heb *Koheleth*

It has been already,
in the ages before us.
11 There is no remembrance of former things,
nor will there be any remembrance
of later things yet to happen
among those who come after.
12 I the Preacher have been king over Israel in Jerusalem.
13 And I applied my mind to seek and to search out by
wisdom all that is done under heaven; it is an unhappy
business that God has given to the sons of men to be busy
14 with. I have seen everything that is done under the sun;
and behold, all is vanity and a striving after wind.[b]
15 What is crooked cannot be made straight,
and what is lacking cannot be numbered.
16 I said to myself, "I have acquired great wisdom, surpassing all who were over Jerusalem before me; and my
mind has had great experience of wisdom and knowledge."
17 And I applied my mind to know wisdom and to know
madness and folly. I perceived that this also is but a
striving after wind.
18 For in much wisdom is much vexation,
and he who increases knowledge increases sorrow.

2 I said to myself, "Come now, I will make a test of
pleasure; enjoy yourself." But behold, this also was
2 vanity. I said of laughter, "It is mad," and of pleasure,

3 "What use is it?" I searched with my mind how to cheer
my body with wine—my mind still guiding me with
wisdom—and how to lay hold on folly, till I might see
what was good for the sons of men to do under heaven
4 during the few days of their life. I made great works;
5 I built houses and planted vineyards for myself; I made
myself gardens and parks, and planted in them all kinds
6 of fruit trees. I made myself pools from which to water
7 the forest of growing trees. I bought male and female
slaves, and had slaves who were born in my house; I had
also great possessions of herds and flocks, more than any
8 who had been before me in Jerusalem. I also gathered for
myself silver and gold and the treasure of kings and
provinces; I got singers, both men and women, and many
concubines,[c] man's delight.
9 So I became great and surpassed all who were before
me in Jerusalem; also my wisdom remained with me.
10 And whatever my eyes desired I did not keep from them;
I kept my heart from no pleasure, for my heart found
pleasure in all my toil, and this was my reward for all my
11 toil. Then I considered all that my hands had done and

the toil I had spent in doing it, and behold, all was
vanity and a striving after wind, and there was nothing
to be gained under the sun.
12 So I turned to consider wisdom and madness and folly;
for what can the man do who comes after the king? Only
13 what he has already done. Then I saw that wisdom excels
14 folly as light excels darkness. The wise man has his eyes
in his head, but the fool walks in darkness; and yet I
15 perceived that one fate comes to all of them. Then I said
to myself, "What befalls the fool will befall me also; why
then have I been so very wise?" And I said to myself that
16 this also is vanity. For of the wise man as of the fool there
is no enduring remembrance, seeing that in the days to
come all will have been long forgotten. How the wise man
17 dies just like the fool! So I hated life, because what is
done under the sun was grievous to me; for all is vanity
and a striving after wind.
18 I hated all my toil in which I had toiled under the sun,
seeing that I must leave it to the man who will come after
19 me; and who knows whether he will be a wise man or a
fool? Yet he will be master of all for which I toiled and
20 used my wisdom under the sun. This also is vanity. So I
turned about and gave my heart up to despair over all the
21 toil of my labors under the sun, because sometimes a man
who has toiled with wisdom and knowledge and skill must
leave all to be enjoyed by a man who did not toil for it.
22 This also is vanity and a great evil. What has a man from
all the toil and strain with which he toils beneath the sun?
23 For all his days are full of pain, and his work is a vexation; even in the night his mind does not rest. This also is
vanity.
24 There is nothing better for a man than that he should
eat and drink, and find enjoyment in his toil. This also,
25 I saw, is from the hand of God; for apart from him[d] who
26 can eat or who can have enjoyment? For to the man who
pleases him God gives wisdom and knowledge and joy;
but to the sinner he gives the work of gathering and
heaping, only to give to one who pleases God. This also
is vanity and a striving after wind.

3 For everything there is a season, and a time for
every matter under heaven:
2 a time to be born, and a time to die;
a time to plant, and a time to pluck up what is planted;
3 a time to kill, and a time to heal;
a time to break down, and a time to build up;
4 a time to weep, and a time to laugh;
a time to mourn, and a time to dance;
5 a time to cast away stones, and a time to gather stones together;
a time to embrace, and a time to refrain from embracing;
6 a time to seek, and a time to lose;
a time to keep, and a time to cast away;
7 a time to rend, and a time to sew;

---

b Or *a feeding on wind*. See Ho 12.1　　　c The meaning of the Hebrew word is uncertain　　　d Gk Syr: Heb *apart from me* a time to keep silence, and a time to speak;

8 a time to love, and a time to hate;
a time for war, and a time for peace.

9 What gain has the worker from his toil?

10 I have seen the business that God has given to the sons
11 of men to be busy with. He has made everything beautiful in its time; also he has put eternity into man's mind, yet

so that he cannot find out what God has done from the
12 beginning to the end. I know that there is nothing better for them than to be happy and enjoy themselves as long
13 as they live; also that it is God's gift to man that every one should eat and drink and take pleasure in all his toil.

14 I know that whatever God does endures for ever; nothing can be added to it, nor anything taken from it; God has made it so, in order that men should fear before him.

15 That which is, already has been; that which is to be, already has been; and God seeks what has been driven away.

16 Moreover I saw under the sun that in the place of justice, even there was wickedness, and in the place of
17 righteousness, even there was wickedness. I said in my heart, God will judge the righteous and the wicked, for he has appointed a time for every matter, and for every work.

18 I said in my heart with regard to the sons of men that God is testing them to show them that they are but beasts.

19 For the fate of the sons of men and the fate of beasts is the same; as one dies, so dies the other. They all have the same breath, and man has no advantage over the beasts;
20 for all is vanity. All go to one place; all are from the
21 dust, and all turn to dust again. Who knows whether the spirit of man goes upward and the spirit of the beast goes
22 down to the earth? So I saw that there is nothing better than that a man should enjoy his work, for that is his lot; who can bring him to see what will be after him?

4 Again I saw all the oppressions that are practiced under the sun. And behold, the tears of the oppressed, and they had no one to comfort them! On the side of their oppressors there was power, and there was no one to
2 comfort them. And I thought the dead who are already dead more fortunate than the living who are still alive;
3 but better than both is he who has not yet been, and has not seen the evil deeds that are done under the sun.

A WISE MAN'S EXPERIENCES

4 Then I saw that all toil and all skill in work come from a man's envy of his neighbor. This also is vanity and a striving after wind.

5 The fool folds his hands, and eats his own flesh.

6 Better is a handful of quietness than two hands full of toil and a striving after wind.

7, 8 Again, I saw vanity under the sun: a person who has no one, either son or brother, yet there is no end to all his toil, and his eyes are never satisfied with riches, so that he never asks, "For whom am I toiling and depriving myself of pleasure?" This also is vanity and an unhappy business.

9 Two are better than one, because they have a good
10 reward for their toil. For if they fall, one will lift up his fellow; but woe to him who is alone when he falls and
11 has not another to lift him up. Again, if two lie together,
12 they are warm; but how can one be warm alone? And though a man might prevail against one who is alone, two will withstand him. A threefold cord is not quickly broken.

13 Better is a poor and wise youth than an old and foolish
14 king, who will no longer take advice, even though he had gone from prison to the throne or in his own king-
15 dom had been born poor. I saw all the living who move about under the sun, as well as that f youth, who was to
16 stand in his place; there was no end of all the people; he was over all of them. Yet those who come later will not rejoice in him. Surely this also is vanity and a striving after wind.

5 g Guard your steps when you go to the house of God; to draw near to listen is better than to offer the sacrifice of fools; for they do not know that they are
2 h doing evil. Be not rash with your mouth, nor let your heart be hasty to utter a word before God, for God is in heaven, and you upon earth; therefore let your words be few.

3 For a dream comes with much business, and a fool's voice with many words.

4 When you vow a vow to God, do not delay paying it;
5 for he has no pleasure in fools. Pay what you vow. It is better that you should not vow than that you should
6 vow and not pay. Let not your mouth lead you into sin, and do not say before the messenger i that it was a mistake; why should God be angry at your voice, and destroy the work of your hands?

7 For when dreams increase, empty words grow many; j but do you fear God.

8 If you see in a province the poor oppressed and justice and right violently taken away, do not be amazed at the matter; for the high official is watched by a higher, and
9 there are yet higher ones over them. But in all, a king is an advantage to a land with cultivated fields. k

---

f Heb *the second*   g Ch 4.17 in Heb   h Ch 5.1 in Heb   i Or *angel*
j Or *For in a multitude of dreams there is futility, and ruin in a flood of words*
k Or *The profit of the land is among all of them; a cultivated field has a king*

10 He who loves money will not be satisfied with money; nor he who loves wealth, with gain: this also is vanity.

11 When goods increase, they increase who eat them; and what gain has their owner but to see them with his eyes?

12 Sweet is the sleep of a laborer, whether he eats little or much; but the surfeit of the rich will not let him sleep.

13 There is a grievous evil which I have seen under the
14 sun: riches were kept by their owner to his hurt, and those riches were lost in a bad venture; and he is father
15 of a son, but he has nothing in his hand. As he came from his mother's womb he shall go again, naked as he came, and shall take nothing for his toil, which he may
16 carry away in his hand. This also is a grievous evil: just as he came, so shall he go; and what gain has he that he
17 toiled for the wind, and spent all his days in darkness and grief,[1] in much vexation and sickness and resentment?

18 Behold, what I have seen to be good and to be fitting is to eat and drink and find enjoyment in all the toil with which one toils under the sun the few days of his
19 life which God has given him, for this is his lot. Every man also to whom God has given wealth and possessions and power to enjoy them, and to accept his lot and find
20 enjoyment in his toil—this is the gift of God. For he will not much remember the days of his life because God keeps him occupied with joy in his heart.

6 There is an evil which I have seen under the sun,
2 and it lies heavy upon men: a man to whom God gives wealth, possessions, and honor, so that he lacks nothing of all that he desires, yet God does not give him power to enjoy them, but a stranger enjoys them; this
3 is vanity; it is a sore affliction. If a man begets a hundred children, and lives many years, so that the days of his years are many, but he does not enjoy life's good things, and also has no burial, I say that an untimely birth is
4 better off than he. For it comes into vanity and goes into
5 darkness, and in darkness its name is covered; moreover it has not seen the sun or known anything; yet it finds
6 rest rather than he. Even though he should live a thousand years twice told, yet enjoy no good—do not all go to the one place?

7 All the toil of man is for his mouth, yet his appetite is
8 not satisfied. For what advantage has the wise man over the fool? And what does the poor man have who knows
9 how to conduct himself before the living? Better is the sight of the eyes than the wandering of desire; this also is vanity and a striving after wind.

10 Whatever has come to be has already been named, and it is known what man is, and that he is not able to dispute
11 with one stronger than he. The more words, the more
12 vanity, and what is man the better? For who knows

what is good for man while he lives the few days of his vain life, which he passes like a shadow? For who can tell man what will be after him under the sun?

7 A good name is better than precious ointment;
and the day of death, than the day of birth.

2 It is better to go to the house of mourning
than to go to the house of feasting;
for this is the end of all men,
and the living will lay it to heart.

3 Sorrow is better than laughter,
for by sadness of countenance the heart is made glad.

4 The heart of the wise is in the house of mourning;
but the heart of fools is in the house of mirth.

5 It is better for a man to hear the rebuke of the wise
than to hear the song of fools.

6 For as the crackling of thorns under a pot,
so is the laughter of the fools;
this also is vanity.

7 Surely oppression makes the wise man foolish,
and a bribe corrupts the mind.

8 Better is the end of a thing than its beginning;
and the patient in spirit is better than the proud in spirit.

9 Be not quick to anger,
for anger lodges in the bosom of fools.

10 Say not, "Why were the former days better than these?"
For it is not from wisdom that you ask this.

11 Wisdom is good with an inheritance,
an advantage to those who see the sun.

12 For the protection of wisdom is like the protection of money;
and the advantage of knowledge is that wisdom preserves the life of him who has it.

13 Consider the work of God;
who can make straight what he has made crooked?

14 In the day of prosperity be joyful, and in the day of adversity consider; God has made the one as well as the other, so that man may not find out anything that will be after him.

15 In my vain life I have seen everything; there is a righteous man who perishes in his righteousness, and there is a wicked man who prolongs his life in his evil-
16 doing. Be not righteous overmuch, and do not make
17 yourself overwise; why should you destroy yourself? Be not wicked overmuch, neither be a fool; why should you
18 die before your time? It is good that you should take hold of this, and from that withhold not your hand; for he who fears God shall come forth from them all.

19 Wisdom gives strength to the wise man more than ten rulers that are in a city.

20 Surely there is not a righteous man on earth who does good and never sins.

21 Do not give heed to all the things that men say, lest you

---

[1] Gk: Heb all his days also he eats in darkness

22 hear your servant cursing you; your heart knows that many times you have yourself cursed others.

23 All this I have tested by wisdom; I said, "I will be

24 wise"; but it was far from me. That which is, is far off,

25 and deep, very deep; who can find it out? I turned my mind to know and to search out and to seek wisdom and the sum of things, and to know the wickedness of folly

26 and the foolishness which is madness. And I found more bitter than death the woman whose heart is snares and nets, and whose hands are fetters; he who pleases God

27 escapes her, but the sinner is taken by her. Behold, this is what I found, says the Preacher, adding one thing to

28 another to find the sum, which my mind has sought

repeatedly, but I have not found. One man among a thousand I found, but a woman among all these I have

29 not found. Behold, this alone I found, that God made man upright, but they have sought out many devices.

8 Who is like the wise man?

And who knows the interpretation of a thing?
A man's wisdom makes his face shine,
and the hardness of his countenance is changed.

2 Keep ^m the king's command, and because of your sacred

3 oath be not dismayed; go from his presence, do not delay when the matter is unpleasant, for he does what-

4 ever he pleases. For the word of the king is supreme, and

5 who may say to him, "What are you doing?" He who obeys a command will meet no harm, and the mind of a

6 wise man will know the time and way. For every matter has its time and way, although man's trouble lies heavy

7 upon him. For he does not know what is to be, for who

8 can tell him how it will be? No man has power to retain the spirit, or authority over the day of death; there is no discharge from war, nor will wickedness deliver those

9 who are given to it. All this I observed while applying my mind to all that is done under the sun, while man lords it over man to his hurt.

10 Then I saw the wicked buried; they used to go in and out of the holy place, and were praised in the city where

11 they had done such things. This also is vanity. Because sentence against an evil deed is not executed speedily, the heart of the sons of men is fully set to do evil.

12 Though a sinner does evil a hundred times and prolongs his life, yet I know that it will be well with those who fear

13 God, because they fear before him; but it will not be well with the wicked, neither will he prolong his days like a shadow, because he does not fear before God.

14 There is a vanity which takes place on earth, that there are righteous men to whom it happens according

to the deeds of the wicked, and there are wicked men to whom it happens according to the deeds of the righteous.

15 I said that this also is vanity. And I commend enjoyment, for man has no good thing under the sun but to eat, and drink, and enjoy himself, for this will go with him in his toil through the days of life which God gives him under the sun.

16 When I applied my mind to know wisdom, and to see the business that is done on earth, how neither day nor

17 night one's eyes see sleep; then I saw all the work of God, that man cannot find out the work that is done under the sun. However much man may toil in seeking, he will not find it out; even though a wise man claims to know, he cannot find it out.

9 But all this I laid to heart, examining it all, how the righteous and the wise and their deeds are in the hand of God; whether it is love or hate man does not

2 know. Everything before them is vanity,ⁿ since one fate comes to all, to the righteous and the wicked, to the good and the evil,^o to the clean and the unclean, to him who sacrifices and him who does not sacrifice. As is the good man, so is the sinner; and he who swears is as he

3 who shuns an oath. This is an evil in all that is done under the sun, that one fate comes to all; also the hearts of men are full of evil, and madness is in their hearts while they live, and after that they go to the dead.

4 But he who is joined with all the living has hope, for a

5 living dog is better than a dead lion. For the living know that they will die, but the dead know nothing, and they have no more reward; but the memory of them is lost.

6 Their love and their hate and their envy have already perished, and they have no more for ever any share in all that is done under the sun.

7 Go, eat your bread with enjoyment, and drink your wine with a merry heart; for God has already approved what you do.

8 Let your garments be always white; let not oil be lacking on your head.

9 Enjoy life with the wife whom you love, all the days of your vain life which he has given you under the sun, because that is your portion in life and in your toil at

10 which you toil under the sun. Whatever your hand finds to do, do it with your might; for there is no work or thought or knowledge or wisdom in Sheol, to which you are going.

11 Again I saw that under the sun the race is not to the swift, nor the battle to the strong, nor bread to the wise, nor riches to the intelligent, nor favor to the men of skill;

12 but time and chance happen to them all. For man does not know his time. Like fish which are taken in an evil net, and like birds which are caught in a snare, so the sons of men are snared at an evil time, when it suddenly falls upon them.

^m Heb inserts an *I*   ⁿ Syr Compare Gk: Heb *Everything before them is everything*   ^o Gk Syr Vg: Heb lacks *and the evil*

13 I have also seen this example of wisdom under the
14 sun, and it seemed great to me. There was a little city
with few men in it; and a great king came against it and
15 besieged it, building great siegeworks against it. But
there was found in it a poor wise man, and he by his
wisdom delivered the city. Yet no one remembered that
16 poor man. But I say that wisdom is better than might,
though the poor man's wisdom is despised, and his words
are not heeded.

CONCLUDING ADVICE TO DISCIPLES

17 The words of the wise heard in quiet are better than
18 the shouting of a ruler among fools. Wisdom is better
than weapons of war, but one sinner destroys much good.

10 Dead flies make the perfumer's ointment give off an
evil odor;
so a little folly outweighs wisdom and honor.
2 A wise man's heart inclines him toward the right,
but a fool's heart toward the left.
3 Even when the fool walks on the road, he lacks sense,
and he says to every one that he is a fool.
4 If the anger of the ruler rises against you, do not leave
your place,
for deference will make amends for great offenses.
5 There is an evil which I have seen under the sun, as

6 it were an error proceeding from the ruler: folly is set in
7 many high places, and the rich sit in a low place. I have
seen slaves on horses, and princes walking on foot like
slaves.
8 He who digs a pit will fall into it;
and a serpent will bite him who breaks through a wall.
9 He who quarries stones is hurt by them;
and he who splits logs is endangered by them.
10 If the iron is blunt, and one does not whet the edge,
he must put forth more strength;
but wisdom helps one to succeed.
11 If the serpent bites before it is charmed,
there is no advantage in a charmer.
12 The words of a wise man's mouth win him favor,
but the lips of a fool consume him.
13 The beginning of the words of his mouth is foolishness,
and the end of his talk is wicked madness.
14 A fool multiplies words,

though no man knows what is to be,
and who can tell him what will be after him?
15 The toil of a fool wearies him,
so that he does not know the way to the city.

16 Woe to you, O land, when your king is a child,
and your princes feast in the morning!
17 Happy are you, O land, when your king is the son of
free men,
and your princes feast at the proper time,
for strength, and not for drunkenness!
18 Through sloth the roof sinks in,
and through indolence the house leaks.
19 Bread is made for laughter,
and wine gladdens life,
and money answers everything.
20 Even in your thought, do not curse the king,
nor in your bedchamber curse the rich;
for a bird of the air will carry your voice,
or some winged creature tell the matter.

11 Cast your bread upon the waters,
for you will find it after many days.
2 Give a portion to seven, or even to eight,
for you know not what evil may happen on earth.
3 If the clouds are full of rain,
they empty themselves on the earth;
and if a tree falls to the south or to the north,
in the place where the tree falls, there it will lie.
4 He who observes the wind will not sow;
and he who regards the clouds will not reap.
5 As you do not know how the spirit comes to the bones
in the womb[p] of a woman with child, so you do not
know the work of God who makes everything.
6 In the morning sow your seed, and at evening withhold not your hand; for you do not know which will
prosper, this or that, or whether both alike will be good.
7 Light is sweet, and it is pleasant for the eyes to behold
the sun.
8 For if a man lives many years, let him rejoice in them
all; but let him remember that the days of darkness will
be many. All that comes is vanity.
9 Rejoice, O young man, in your youth, and let your
heart cheer you in the days of your youth; walk in the
ways of your heart and the sight of your eyes. But know
that for all these things God will bring you into judgment.
10 Remove vexation from your mind, and put away pain
from your body; for youth and the dawn of life are
vanity.

12 Remember also your Creator in the days of your
youth, before the evil days come, and the years draw
nigh, when you will say, "I have no pleasure in them";

p Or *As you do not know the way of the wind, or how the bones grow in the womb*

2 before the sun and the light and the moon and the stars
3 are darkened and the clouds return after the rain; in the day when the keepers of the house tremble, and the strong men are bent, and the grinders cease because they are few, and those that look through the windows are
4 dimmed, and the doors on the street are shut; when the sound of the grinding is low, and one rises up at the voice of a bird, and all the daughters of song are brought
5 low; they are afraid also of what is high, and terrors are in the way; the almond tree blossoms, the grasshopper drags itself along q and desire fails; because man goes to his eternal home, and the mourners go about the streets;
6 before the silver cord is snapped,r or the golden bowl is broken, or the pitcher is broken at the fountain, or the
7 wheel broken at the cistern, and the dust returns to the earth as it was, and the spirit returns to God who gave it.
8 Vanity of vanities, says the Preacher; all is vanity.

9 Besides being wise, the Preacher also taught the people knowledge, weighing and studying and arranging proverbs
10 with great care. The Preacher sought to find pleasing words, and uprightly he wrote words of truth.

11 The sayings of the wise are like goads, and like nails firmly fixed are the collected sayings which are given by
12 one Shepherd. My son, beware of anything beyond these. Of making many books there is no end, and much study is a weariness of the flesh.

13 The end of the matter; all has been heard. Fear God, and keep his commandments; for this is the whole duty
14 of man.s For God will bring every deed into judgment, with t every secret thing, whether good or evil.

q Or *is a burden*   r Syr Vg Compare Gk: Heb *is removed*

s Or *the duty of all men*   t Or *into the judgment on*

THE SONG OF SOLOMON

This book is a series of ancient Hebrew wedding songs, including parts to be sung by the bride, the groom, and the chorus of villagers. Such wedding festivities with singing and dancing are still carried on at marriages in the Middle East today.

The Song of Solomon was probably included in the Bible on the theory that the love of the new husband and wife in these songs was meant to remind us of the love of Christ for the church. However, the book really celebrates the joyful love of a groom and a bride for each other as something wholesome, beautiful, and good.

Scholars think the songs that compose this book were compiled about 300 B.C. and were probably used in the wedding celebrations of the Jews. While Solomon's name was given to the book, the real author or authors are unknown.

THE SONG OF SOLOMON

1 The Song of Songs, which is Solomon's.

2 O that you[a] would kiss me with the kisses of your[b] mouth!
For your love is better than wine,
3   your anointing oils are fragrant,
your name is oil poured out;
  therefore the maidens love you.
4 Draw me after you, let us make haste.
  The king has brought me into his chambers.
We will exult and rejoice in you;
  we will extol your love more than wine;
  rightly do they love you.

5 I am very dark, but comely,
  O daughters of Jerusalem,
like the tents of Kedar,
  like the curtains of Solomon.
6 Do not gaze at me because I am swarthy,
  because the sun has scorched me.
My mother's sons were angry with me,
  they made me keeper of the vineyards;
  but, my own vineyard I have not kept!
7 Tell me, you whom my soul loves,
  where you pasture your flock,
  where you make it lie down at noon;

for why should I be like one who wanders[c]
  beside the flocks of your companions?

8 If you do not know,
  O fairest among women,
follow in the tracks of the flock,
  and pasture your kids
  beside the shepherds' tents.

9 I compare you, my love,
  to a mare of Pharaoh's chariots.
10 Your cheeks are comely with ornaments,
  your neck with strings of jewels.
11 We will make you ornaments of gold,
  studded with silver.

12 While the king was on his couch,
  my nard gave forth its fragrance.
13 My beloved is to me a bag of myrrh,
  that lies between my breasts.
14 My beloved is to me a cluster of henna blossoms
  in the vineyards of Enge'di.

15 Behold, you are beautiful, my love;
  behold, you are beautiful;

a Heb he   b Heb his   c Gk Syr Vg: Heb is veiled

your eyes are doves.
16 Behold, you are beautiful, my beloved,
truly lovely.
  Our couch is green;
17   the beams of our house are cedar,
    our rafters d are pine.

2 I am a rose e of Sharon,
    a lily of the valleys.

2 As a lily among brambles,
    so is my love among maidens.

3 As an apple tree among the trees of the wood,
    so is my beloved among young men.
  With great delight I sat in his shadow,
    and his fruit was sweet to my taste.
4 He brought me to the banqueting house,
    and his banner over me was love.
5 Sustain me with raisins,
    refresh me with apples;
    for I am sick with love.
6 O that his left hand were under my head,
    and that his right hand embraced me!
7 I adjure you, O daughters of Jerusalem,
    by the gazelles or the hinds of the field,
  that you stir not up nor awaken love
    until it please.

8 The voice of my beloved!
    Behold, he comes,
  leaping upon the mountains,
    bounding over the hills.
9 My beloved is like a gazelle,
    or a young stag.
  Behold, there he stands
    behind our wall,
  gazing in at the windows,
    looking through the lattice.
10 My beloved speaks and says to me:
  "Arise, my love, my fair one,
    and come away;
11 for lo, the winter is past,
    the rain is over and gone.
12 The flowers appear on the earth,
    the time of singing has come,
  and the voice of the turtledove
    is heard in our land.
13 The fig tree puts forth its figs,
    and the vines are in blossom;
    they give forth fragrance.
  Arise, my love, my fair one,
    and come away.
14 O my dove, in the clefts of the rock,

in the covert of the cliff,
  let me see your face,
    let me hear your voice,
  for your voice is sweet,
    and your face is comely.
15 Catch us the foxes,
    the little foxes,
  that spoil the vineyards,
    for our vineyards are in blossom."

16 My beloved is mine and I am his,
    he pastures his flock among the lilies.
17 Until the day breathes
    and the shadows flee,
  turn, my beloved, be like a gazelle,
    or a young stag upon rugged f mountains.

3 Upon my bed by night
    I sought him whom my soul loves;
  I sought him, but found him not;
    I called him, but he gave no answer. g
2 "I will rise now and go about the city,
    in the streets and in the squares;
  I will seek him whom my soul loves."
    I sought him, but found him not.
3 The watchmen found me,
    as they went about in the city.
  "Have you seen him whom my soul loves?"
4 Scarcely had I passed them,
    when I found him whom my soul loves.
  I held him, and would not let him go
    until I had brought him into my mother's house,
    and into the chamber of her that conceived me.
5 I adjure you, O daughters of Jerusalem,
    by the gazelles or the hinds of the field,
  that you stir not up nor awaken love until it please.

6 What is that coming up from the wilderness,
    like a column of smoke,
  perfumed with myrrh and frankincense,
    with all the fragrant powders of the merchant?
7 Behold, it is the litter of Solomon!
  About it are sixty mighty men
    of the mighty men of Israel,
8 all girt with swords
    and expert in war,
  each with his sword at his thigh,
    against alarms by night.
9 King Solomon made himself a palanquin
    from the wood of Lebanon.
10 He made its posts of silver,
    its back of gold, its seat of purple;
  it was lovingly wrought within h

d The meaning of the Hebrew word is uncertain   e Heb crocus   f The meaning of the Hebrew word is unknown
g Gk: Heb lacks this line   h The meaning of the Hebrew is uncertain

by the daughters of Jerusalem.
¹¹ Go forth, O daughters of Zion,
  and behold King Solomon,
 with the crown with which his mother crowned him
  on the day of his wedding,
  on the day of the gladness of his heart.

4 Behold, you are beautiful, my love,
   behold, you are beautiful!
 Your eyes are doves
  behind your veil.
 Your hair is like a flock of goats,
  moving down the slopes of Gilead.
² Your teeth are like a flock of shorn ewes
  that have come up from the washing,
 all of which bear twins,
  and not one among them is bereaved.
³ Your lips are like a scarlet thread,
  and your mouth is lovely.
 Your cheeks are like halves of a pomegranate
  behind your veil.
⁴ Your neck is like the tower of David,
  built for an arsenal,ⁱ

whereon hang a thousand bucklers,
  all of them shields of warriors.
⁵ Your two breasts are like two fawns,
  twins of a gazelle,
  that feed among the lilies.
⁶ Until the day breathes
  and the shadows flee,
 I will hie me to the mountain of myrrh
  and the hill of frankincense.
⁷ You are all fair, my love;
  there is no flaw in you.
⁸ Come with me from Lebanon, my bride;
  come with me from Lebanon.
 Depart ʲ from the peak of Ama'na,
  from the peak of Senir and Hermon,
 from the dens of lions,
  from the mountains of leopards.

⁹ You have ravished my heart, my sister, my bride,
  you have ravished my heart with a glance of your eyes,
  with one jewel of your necklace.
¹⁰ How sweet is your love, my sister, my bride!
  how much better is your love than wine,
  and the fragrance of your oils than any spice!

¹¹ Your lips distil nectar, my bride;
  honey and milk are under your tongue;
 the scent of your garments is like the scent of Lebanon.
¹² A garden locked is my sister, my bride,
  a garden locked, a fountain sealed.
¹³ Your shoots are an orchard of pomegranates
  with all choicest fruits,
  henna with nard,
¹⁴ nard and saffron, calamus and cinnamon,
  with all trees of frankincense,
 myrrh and aloes,
  with all chief spices—
¹⁵ a garden fountain, a well of living water,
  and flowing streams from Lebanon.

¹⁶ Awake, O north wind,
  and come, O south wind!
 Blow upon my garden,
  let its fragrance be wafted abroad.
 Let my beloved come to his garden,
  and eat its choicest fruits.

5 I come to my garden, my sister, my bride,
   I gather my myrrh with my spice,
 I eat my honeycomb with my honey,
  I drink my wine with my milk.

 Eat, O friends, and drink:
  drink deeply, O lovers!

² I slept, but my heart was awake.
 Hark! my beloved is knocking.
 "Open to me, my sister, my love,
  my dove, my perfect one;
 for my head is wet with dew,
  my locks with the drops of the night."
³ I had put off my garment,
  how could I put it on?
 I had bathed my feet,
  how could I soil them?
⁴ My beloved put his hand to the latch,
  and my heart was thrilled within me.
⁵ I arose to open to my beloved,
  and my hands dripped with myrrh,
 my fingers with liquid myrrh,
  upon the handles of the bolt.
⁶ I opened to my beloved,
  but my beloved had turned and gone.
 My soul failed me when he spoke.
 I sought him, but found him not;
  I called him, but he gave no answer.
⁷ The watchmen found me,
  as they went about in the city;
 they beat me, they wounded me,

ⁱ The meaning of the Hebrew word is uncertain   ʲ Or *Look*

they took away my mantle,
    those watchmen of the walls.
8 I adjure you, O daughters of Jerusalem,
    if you find my beloved,
that you tell him
    I am sick with love.

9 What is your beloved more than another beloved,
    O fairest among women?
What is your beloved more than another beloved,
    that you thus adjure us?

10 My beloved is all radiant and ruddy,
    distinguished among ten thousand.
11 His head is the finest gold;
    his locks are wavy,
    black as a raven.
12 His eyes are like doves
    beside springs of water,
bathed in milk,
    fitly set.[k]
13 His cheeks are like beds of spices,
    yielding fragrance.
His lips are lilies,
    distilling liquid myrrh.
14 His arms are rounded gold,
    set with jewels.
His body is ivory work,[l]
    encrusted with sapphires.[m]
15 His legs are alabaster columns,
    set upon bases of gold.
His appearance is like Lebanon,
    choice as the cedars.
16 His speech is most sweet,
    and he is altogether desirable.
This is my beloved and this is my friend,
    O daughters of Jerusalem.

6 Whither has your beloved gone,
    O fairest among women?
Whither has your beloved turned,
    that we may seek him with you?

2 My beloved has gone down to his garden,
    to the beds of spices,
to pasture his flock in the gardens,
    and to gather lilies.
3 I am my beloved's and my beloved is mine;
    he pastures his flock among the lilies.

4 You are beautiful as Tirzah, my love,
    comely as Jerusalem,
    terrible as an army with banners.
5 Turn away your eyes from me,

for they disturb me—
Your hair is like a flock of goats,
    moving down the slopes of Gilead.
6 Your teeth are like a flock of ewes,
    that have come up from the washing,
all of them bear twins,
    not one among them is bereaved.
7 Your cheeks are like halves of a pomegranate
    behind your veil.
8 There are sixty queens and eighty concubines,
    and maidens without number.
9 My dove, my perfect one, is only one,
    the darling of her mother,
    flawless to her that bore her.
The maidens saw her and called her happy;
    the queens and concubines also, and they praised her.
10 "Who is this that looks forth like the dawn,
    fair as the moon, bright as the sun,
    terrible as an army with banners?"

11 I went down to the nut orchard,
    to look at the blossoms of the valley,
to see whether the vines had budded,
    whether the pomegranates were in bloom.
12 Before I was aware, my fancy set me
    in a chariot beside my prince.[n]

13 o Return, return, O Shu'lammite,
    return, return, that we may look upon you.

Why should you look upon the Shu'lammite,
    as upon a dance before two armies? [p]

7 How graceful are your feet in sandals,
    O queenly maiden!
Your rounded thighs are like jewels,
    the work of a master hand.
2 Your navel is a rounded bowl
    that never lacks mixed wine.
Your belly is a heap of wheat,
    encircled with lilies.
3 Your two breasts are like two fawns,
    twins of a gazelle.
4 Your neck is like an ivory tower.
Your eyes are pools in Heshbon,
    by the gate of Bath-rab'bim.
Your nose is like a tower of Lebanon,
    overlooking Damascus.
5 Your head crowns you like Carmel,
    and your flowing locks are like purple;
    a king is held captive in the tresses.[q]

6 How fair and pleasant you are,
    O loved one, delectable maiden! [r]
7 You are stately [s] as a palm tree,

---

k The meaning of the Hebrew is uncertain
l The meaning of the Hebrew word is uncertain
m Heb lapis lazuli
n Cn: The meaning of the Hebrew is uncertain
o Ch 7.1 in Heb
p Or dance of Mahanaim
q The meaning of the Hebrew word is uncertain
r Syr: Heb in delights
s Heb This your stature is

and your breasts are like its clusters.
⁸ I say I will climb the palm tree
  and lay hold of its branches.
Oh, may your breasts be like clusters of the vine,
  and the scent of your breath like apples,
⁹ and your kisses ᵗ like the best wine
  that goes down ᵘ smoothly,
  gliding over lips and teeth.ᵛ

¹⁰ I am my beloved's,
  and his desire is for me.
¹¹ Come, my beloved,
  let us go forth into the fields,
  and lodge in the villages;
¹² let us go out early to the vineyards,
  and see whether the vines have budded,
  whether the grape blossoms have opened
  and the pomegranates are in bloom.
There I will give you my love.
¹³ The mandrakes give forth fragrance,
  and over our doors are all choice fruits,
new as well as old,
  which I have laid up for you, O my beloved.

8 O that you were like a brother to me,
    that nursed at my mother's breast!
If I met you outside, I would kiss you,
  and none would despise me.
² I would lead you and bring you
  into the house of my mother,
  and into the chamber of her that conceived me.ʷ
I would give you spiced wine to drink,
  the juice of my pomegranates.
³ O that his left hand were under my head,
  and that his right hand embraced me!
⁴ I adjure you, O daughters of Jerusalem,
  that you stir not up nor awaken love
  until it please.

⁵ Who is that coming up from the wilderness,
  leaning upon her beloved?

Under the apple tree I awakened you.
There your mother was in travail with you,
  there she who bore you was in travail.

⁶ Set me as a seal upon your heart,
  as a seal upon your arm;
for love is strong as death,
  jealousy is cruel as the grave.
Its flashes are flashes of fire,
  a most vehement flame.
⁷ Many waters cannot quench love,

neither can floods drown it.
If a man offered for love
  all the wealth of his house,
  it would be utterly scorned.

⁸ We have a little sister,
  and she has no breasts.
What shall we do for our sister,
  on the day when she is spoken for?
⁹ If she is a wall,
  we will build upon her a battlement of silver;
but if she is a door,
  we will enclose her with boards of cedar.
¹⁰ I was a wall,
  and my breasts were like towers;
then I was in his eyes
  as one who brings ˣ peace.

¹¹ Solomon had a vineyard at Ba'al-ha'mon;
  he let out the vineyard to keepers;
  each one was to bring for its fruit a thousand pieces of
    silver.
¹² My vineyard, my very own, is for myself;
  you, O Solomon, may have the thousand,
  and the keepers of the fruit two hundred.

¹³ O you who dwell in the gardens,
  my companions are listening for your voice;
  let me hear it.

¹⁴ Make haste, my beloved,
  and be like a gazelle
or a young stag
  upon the mountains of spices.

ᵗ Heb *palate*   ᵘ Heb *down for my lover*   ᵛ Gk Syr Vg: Heb *lips of sleepers*
ʷ Gk Syr: Heb *mother; she* (or *you*) *will teach me*   ˣ Or *finds*

INTRODUCTION TO

ISAIAH

PART I, CHAPTERS 1 THROUGH 39

One of the greatest prophets or preachers of Israel lived during the years from 740 to 700 years before Christ. His name was Isaiah. His messages are to be found in Chapters 1 through 39 of the Book of Isaiah along with other writings added later.

Isaiah was from an influential family, so the rulers paid attention to his advice, even though what he told them was not always pleasant to hear.

In Chapter 6 he tells how God called him to preach while he was praying in the Temple one day during the last year of the reign of King Uzziah.

In the very first chapter of the book he spoke out against the sins and injustice of the people and warned that God would not let such evil go unchallenged. He pleaded with the people and their leaders to repent of their sins and said that God would forgive them if they were truly penitent. The kingdom of Assyria was threatening to destroy Judah and Jerusalem. Isaiah taught that God would use Assyria to punish the Jews if they did not repent. Throughout his speeches Isaiah stressed the greatness and majesty of God as well as his justice toward all men and all nations.

PART II, CHAPTERS 40 THROUGH 66

The sermons and poems of Isaiah 40 through 55 were written by an unknown prophet of the Jewish exiles in Babylon about 540 B.C. These chapters are often spoken of as "Second Isaiah" because they were written about 150 years after the Isaiah of Jerusalem, who wrote most of the first thirty-nine chapters.

The kingdom of Judah had been conquered by Babylon about 597 B.C. and again in 586 B.C., and thousands of the leading Jews were carried into exile in Babylon. During the long years the Jews spent in that foreign land, there was a pastor among them who wrote much of what is now Isaiah 40 through 55. This "Isaiah of Babylon" was one of the greatest of the prophets. His chapters announce the joyful news that the Jews will soon be set free and allowed to return to Jerusalem, even though most of that beloved city had been destroyed by conquering armies.

Probably still other writers wrote Chapters 56 through 66 a few years after Chapters 40 through 55. Jesus quoted, with a few changes, the opening verses of Isaiah 61 in the synagogue in Nazareth as he began his ministry.

> "The Spirit of the Lord is upon me,
>> because he has anointed me to preach good news to the poor.
>> He has sent me to proclaim release to the captives
>> and recovering of sight to the blind,
>> to set at liberty those who are oppressed,
>> to proclaim the acceptable year of the Lord."
> —Luke 4.18-19

This great book contains some of the most beautiful poetry in the Old Testament. It teaches that God wanted the Jews to help all nations by leading them to love and serve the one true God. Israel, the Jewish nation, was to be a servant of God who was willing to suffer in order to help achieve God's purpose for mankind. The messages were so wonderful that, over five hundred years later, Christians felt they were surely intended to describe the loving, sacrificial life of Christ. Jesus Christ was indeed the One of whom it might be said:

"Surely he has borne our griefs
and carried our sorrows
yet we esteemed him stricken,
smitten by God, and afflicted.
But he was wounded for our transgressions,
he was bruised for our iniquities . . ."
—Isaiah 53.4-5a

THE BOOK OF

ISAIAH

"THEY HAVE REBELLED AGAINST ME"

1 The vision of Isaiah the son of Amoz, which he saw concerning Judah and Jerusalem in the days of Uzzi'ah, Jotham, Ahaz, and Hezeki'ah, kings of Judah.
2 Hear, O heavens, and give ear, O earth;
  for the Lord has spoken:
"Sons have I reared and brought up,
  but they have rebelled against me.
3 The ox knows its owner,
  and the ass its master's crib;
but Israel does not know,
  my people does not understand."

4 Ah, sinful nation,
  a people laden with iniquity,
offspring of evildoers,
  sons who deal corruptly!
They have forsaken the Lord,
  they have despised the Holy One of Israel,
  they are utterly estranged.

5 Why will you still be smitten,
  that you continue to rebel?
The whole head is sick,
  and the whole heart faint.
6 From the sole of the foot even to the head,
  there is no soundness in it,
but bruises and sores

and bleeding wounds;
they are not pressed out, or bound up,
  or softened with oil.

7 Your country lies desolate,
  your cities are burned with fire;
in your very presence
  aliens devour your land;
  it is desolate, as overthrown by aliens.
8 And the daughter of Zion is left
  like a booth in a vineyard,
  like a lodge in a cucumber field,
  like a besieged city.

9 If the Lord of hosts
  had not left us a few survivors,
we should have been like Sodom,
  and become like Gomor'rah.

10 Hear the word of the Lord,
  you rulers of Sodom!
Give ear to the teaching of our God,
  you people of Gomor'rah!
11 "What to me is the multitude of your sacrifices?
  says the Lord;
I have had enough of burnt offerings of rams
  and the fat of fed beasts;
I do not delight in the blood of bulls,
  or of lambs, or of he-goats.

12 "When you come to appear before me,
  who requires of you
  this trampling of my courts?
13 Bring no more vain offerings;
  incense is an abomination to me.

New moon and sabbath and the calling of assemblies—
   I cannot endure iniquity and solemn assembly.
14 Your new moons and your appointed feasts
   my soul hates;
they have become a burden to me,
   I am weary of bearing them.
15 When you spread forth your hands,
   I will hide my eyes from you;
even though you make many prayers,
   I will not listen;
   your hands are full of blood.
16 Wash yourselves; make yourselves clean;
   remove the evil of your doings
   from before my eyes;
cease to do evil,
17   learn to do good;
seek justice,
   correct oppression;
defend the fatherless,
   plead for the widow.

18 "Come now, let us reason together,
   says the LORD:
though your sins are like scarlet,
   they shall be as white as snow;
though they are red like crimson,
   they shall become like wool.
19 If you are willing and obedient,
   you shall eat the good of the land;
20 But if you refuse and rebel,
   you shall be devoured by the sword;
   for the mouth of the LORD has spoken."

21 How the faithful city
   has become a harlot,
   she that was full of justice!
Righteousness lodged in her,
   but now murderers.
22 Your silver has become dross,
   your wine mixed with water.
23 Your princes are rebels
   and companions of thieves.
Every one loves a bribe
   and runs after gifts.
They do not defend the fatherless,
   and the widow's cause does not come to them.

24 Therefore the Lord says,
   the LORD of hosts,
   the Mighty One of Israel:
"Ah, I will vent my wrath on my enemies,
   and avenge myself on my foes.
25 I will turn my hand against you
   and will smelt away your dross as with lye

and remove all your alloy.
26 And I will restore your judges as at the first,
   and your counselors as at the beginning.
Afterward you shall be called the city of righteousness,
   the faithful city."

27 Zion shall be redeemed by justice,
   and those in her who repent, by righteousness.
28 But rebels and sinners shall be destroyed together,
   and those who forsake the LORD shall be consumed.
29 For you shall be ashamed of the oaks
   in which you delighted;
and you shall blush for the gardens
   which you have chosen.
30 For you shall be like an oak
   whose leaf withers,
   and like a garden without water.
31 And the strong shall become tow,
   and his work a spark,
and both of them shall burn together,
   with none to quench them.

2   The word which Isaiah the son of Amoz saw concerning Judah and Jerusalem.
2 It shall come to pass in the latter days
   that the mountain of the house of the LORD
shall be established as the highest of the mountains,
   and shall be raised above the hills;
and all the nations shall flow to it,
3   and many peoples shall come, and say:
"Come, let us go up to the mountain of the LORD,
   to the house of the God of Jacob;
that he may teach us his ways
   and that we may walk in his paths."
For out of Zion shall go forth the law,
   and the word of the LORD from Jerusalem.
4 He shall judge between the nations,
   and shall decide for many peoples;
and they shall beat their swords into plowshares,
   and their spears into pruning hooks;
nation shall not lift up sword against nation,
   neither shall they learn war any more.

5 O house of Jacob,
   come, let us walk
   in the light of the LORD.

6 For thou hast rejected thy people,
   the house of Jacob,
because they are full of diviners a from the east
   and of soothsayers like the Philistines,
   and they strike hands with foreigners.
7 Their land is filled with silver and gold,
   and there is no end to their treasures;

a Cn: Heb lacks *of diviners*

their land is filled with horses,
    and there is no end to their chariots.
[8] Their land is filled with idols;
    they bow down to the work of their hands,
    to what their own fingers have made.
[9] So man is humbled,
    and men are brought low—
    forgive them not!
[10] Enter into the rock,
    and hide in the dust
from before the terror of the LORD,
    and from the glory of his majesty.
[11] The haughty looks of man shall be brought low,
    and the pride of men shall be humbled;
and the LORD alone will be exalted in that day.

[12] For the LORD of hosts has a day
    against all that is proud and lofty,
    against all that is lifted up and high; [b]
[13] against all the cedars of Lebanon,
    lofty and lifted up;
    and against all the oaks of Bashan;
[14] against all the high mountains,
    and against all the lofty hills;
[15] against every high tower,
    and against every fortified wall;
[16] against all the ships of Tarshish,
    and against all the beautiful craft.
[17] And the haughtiness of man shall be humbled,
    and the pride of men shall be brought low;
    and the LORD alone will be exalted in that day.
[18] And the idols shall utterly pass away.
[19] And men shall enter the caves of the rocks
    and the holes of the ground,
from before the terror of the LORD,
    and from the glory of his majesty,
    when he rises to terrify the earth.

[20] In that day men will cast forth
    their idols of silver and their idols of gold,
which they made for themselves to worship,
    to the moles and to the bats,
[21] to enter the caverns of the rocks
    and the clefts of the cliffs,
from before the terror of the LORD,
    and from the glory of his majesty,
    when he rises to terrify the earth.
[22] Turn away from man
    in whose nostrils is breath,
    for of what account is he?

3 For, behold, the Lord, the LORD of hosts,
    is taking away from Jerusalem and from Judah
stay and staff,

the whole stay of bread,
    and the whole stay of water;
[2] the mighty man and the soldier,
    the judge and the prophet,
    the diviner and the elder,
[3] the captain of fifty
    and the man of rank,
the counselor and the skilful magician
    and the expert in charms.
[4] And I will make boys their princes,
    and babes shall rule over them.
[5] And the people will oppress one another,
    every man his fellow
    and every man his neighbor;
the youth will be insolent to the elder,
    and the base fellow to the honorable.

[6] When a man takes hold of his brother
    in the house of his father, saying:
"You have a mantle;
    you shall be our leader,
and this heap of ruins
    shall be under your rule";
[7] in that day he will speak out, saying:
"I will not be a healer;
    in my house there is neither bread nor mantle;
you shall not make me
    leader of the people."
[8] For Jerusalem has stumbled,
    and Judah has fallen;
because their speech and their deeds are against the LORD,
    defying his glorious presence.

[9] Their partiality witnesses against them;
    they proclaim their sin like Sodom,
    they do not hide it.
Woe to them!
    For they have brought evil upon themselves.
[10] Tell the righteous that it shall be well with them,
    for they shall eat the fruit of their deeds.
[11] Woe to the wicked! It shall be ill with him,
    for what his hands have done shall be done to him.
[12] My people—children are their oppressors,
    and women rule over them.
O my people, your leaders mislead you,
    and confuse the course of your paths.

[13] The LORD has taken his place to contend,
    he stands to judge his people.[d]
[14] The LORD enters into judgment
    with the elders and princes of his people:
"It is you who have devoured the vineyard,
    the spoil of the poor is in your houses.
[15] What do you mean by crushing my people,

[b] Cn Compare Gk: Heb low   [d] Gk Syr: Heb *judge peoples*

by grinding the face of the poor?" says the Lord GOD
  of hosts.

16 The LORD said:
  Because the daughters of Zion are haughty
    and walk with outstretched necks,
    glancing wantonly with their eyes,
  mincing along as they go,
    tinkling with their feet;
17 the Lord will smite with a scab
    the heads of the daughters of Zion,
    and the LORD will lay bare their secret parts.

18   In that day the Lord will take away the finery of the
19 anklets, the headbands, and the crescents; the pendants,
20 the bracelets, and the scarfs; the headdresses, the armlets,
21 the sashes, the perfume boxes, and the amulets; the signet
22 rings and nose rings; the festal robes, the mantles, the
23 cloaks, and the handbags; the garments of gauze, the
  linen garments, the turbans, and the veils.
24 Instead of perfume there will be rottenness;
    and instead of a girdle, a rope;
  and instead of well-set hair, baldness;
    and instead of a rich robe, a girding of sackcloth;
    instead of beauty, shame.[e]

25 Your men shall fall by the sword
    and your mighty men in battle.
26 And her gates shall lament and mourn;
    ravaged, she shall sit upon the ground.
4   And seven women shall take hold of one man in
    that day, saying, "We will eat our own bread and
wear our own clothes, only let us be called by your name;
take away our reproach."

2   In that day the branch of the LORD shall be beautiful
and glorious, and the fruit of the land shall be the pride
3 and glory of the survivors of Israel. And he who is left
in Zion and remains in Jerusalem will be called holy,
every one who has been recorded for life in Jerusalem,
4 when the Lord shall have washed away the filth of the
daughters of Zion and cleansed the bloodstains of Jerusalem from its midst by a spirit of judgment and by a spirit
5 of burning. Then the LORD will create over the whole site
of Mount Zion and over her assemblies a cloud by day,
and smoke and the shining of a flaming fire by night; for
over all the glory there will be a canopy and a pavilion.
6 It will be for a shade by day from the heat, and for a
refuge and a shelter from the storm and rain.

e One ancient Ms: Heb lacks *shame*

Parable of the Vineyard
5 Let me sing for my beloved
    a love song concerning his vineyard:
  My beloved had a vineyard
    on a very fertile hill.
2 He digged it and cleared it of stones,
    and planted it with choice vines;
  he built a watchtower in the midst of it,
    and hewed out a wine vat in it;
  and he looked for it to yield grapes,
    but it yielded wild grapes.

3 And now, O inhabitants of Jerusalem
    and men of Judah,
  judge, I pray you, between me
    and my vineyard.
4 What more was there to do for my vineyard,
    that I have not done in it?
  When I looked for it to yield grapes,
    why did it yield wild grapes?

5 And now I will tell you
    what I will do to my vineyard.
  I will remove its hedge,
    and it shall be devoured;
  I will break down its wall,
    and it shall be trampled down.
6 I will make it a waste;
    it shall not be pruned or hoed,
    and briers and thorns shall grow up;
  I will also command the clouds
    that they rain no rain upon it.

7 For the vineyard of the LORD of hosts
    is the house of Israel,
  and the men of Judah
    are his pleasant planting;
  and he looked for justice,
    but behold, bloodshed;
  for righteousness,
    but behold, a cry!

8 Woe to those who join house to house,
    who add field to field,
  until there is no more room,
    and you are made to dwell alone
    in the midst of the land.
9 The LORD of hosts has sworn in my hearing:
  "Surely many houses shall be desolate,
    large and beautiful houses, without inhabitant.
10 For ten acres of vineyard shall yield but one bath,
    and a homer of seed shall yield but an ephah."

11 Woe to those who rise early in the morning,
　that they may run after strong drink,
who tarry late into the evening
　till wine inflames them!
12 They have lyre and harp,
　timbrel and flute and wine at their feasts;
but they do not regard the deeds of the LORD,
　or see the work of his hands.

13 Therefore my people go into exile for want of knowledge;
　their honored men are dying of hunger,
　and their multitude is parched with thirst.
14 Therefore Sheol has enlarged its appetite
　and opened its mouth beyond measure,
and the nobility of Jerusalem f and her multitude go down,
　her throng and he who exults in her.
15 Man is bowed down, and men are brought low,
　and the eyes of the haughty are humbled.
16 But the LORD of hosts is exalted in justice,
　and the Holy God shows himself holy in righteousness.
17 Then shall the lambs graze as in their pasture,
　fatlings and kids g shall feed among the ruins.

18 Woe to those who draw iniquity with cords of falsehood,
　who draw sin as with cart ropes,
19 who say: "Let him make haste,
　let him speed his work
　that we may see it;
let the purpose of the Holy One of Israel draw near,
　and let it come, that we may know it!"
20 Woe to those who call evil good
　and good evil,
who put darkness for light
　and light for darkness,
who put bitter for sweet
　and sweet for bitter!
21 Woe to those who are wise in their own eyes,
　and shrewd in their own sight!
22 Woe to those who are heroes at drinking wine,
　and valiant men in mixing strong drink,
23 who acquit the guilty for a bribe,
　and deprive the innocent of his right!

24 Therefore, as the tongue of fire devours the stubble,
　and as dry grass sinks down in the flame,
so their root will be as rottenness,
　and their blossom go up like dust;

f Heb her nobility　　g Cn Compare Gk: Heb aliens

for they have rejected the law of the LORD of hosts,
　and have despised the word of the Holy One of Israel.
25 Therefore the anger of the LORD was kindled against his people,
　and he stretched out his hand against them and smote them,
　and the mountains quaked;
and their corpses were as refuse
　in the midst of the streets.
For all this his anger is not turned away
　and his hand is stretched out still.

26 He will raise a signal for a nation afar off,
　and whistle for it from the ends of the earth;
and lo, swiftly, speedily it comes!
27 None is weary, none stumbles,
　none slumbers or sleeps,
not a waistcloth is loose,
　not a sandal-thong broken;
28 their arrows are sharp,
　all their bows bent,
their horses' hoofs seem like flint,
　and their wheels like the whirlwind.
29 Their roaring is like a lion,
　like young lions they roar;
they growl and seize their prey,
　they carry it off, and none can rescue.
30 They will growl over it on that day,
　like the roaring of the sea.
And if one look to the land,
　behold, darkness and distress;
and the light is darkened by its clouds.

ISAIAH'S VISION

6 In the year that King Uzzi'ah died I saw the Lord sitting upon a throne, high and lifted up; and his train 2 filled the temple. Above him stood the seraphim; each had six wings: with two he covered his face, and with 3 two he covered his feet, and with two he flew. And one called to another and said:
　"Holy, holy, holy is the LORD of hosts;
　the whole earth is full of his glory."
4 And the foundations of the thresholds shook at the voice of him who called, and the house was filled with smoke. 5 And I said: "Woe is me! For I am lost; for I am a man of unclean lips, and I dwell in the midst of a people of unclean lips; for my eyes have seen the King, the LORD of hosts!"
6 Then flew one of the seraphim to me, having in his hand a burning coal which he had taken with tongs from 7 the altar. And he touched my mouth, and said: "Behold, this has touched your lips; your guilt is taken away, and 8 your sin forgiven." And I heard the voice of the Lord saying, "Whom shall I send, and who will go for us?"

9 Then I said, "Here am I! Send me." And he said, "Go, and say to this people:

'Hear and hear, but do not understand;
see and see, but do not perceive.'
10 Make the heart of this people fat,
    and their ears heavy,
    and shut their eyes;
lest they see with their eyes,
    and hear with their ears,
and understand with their hearts,
    and turn and be healed."
11 Then I said, "How long, O Lord?" And he said:
"Until cities lie waste
    without inhabitant,
and houses without men,
    and the land is utterly desolate,
12 and the LORD removes men far away,
    and the forsaken places are many in the midst of the
        land.
13 And though a tenth remain in it,
    it will be burned again,
like a terebinth or an oak,
    whose stump remains standing
    when it is felled."
The holy seed is its stump.

7 In the days of Ahaz the son of Jotham, son of Uzzi′ah, king of Judah, Rezin the king of Syria and Pekah the son of Remali′ah the king of Israel came up to Jerusalem to wage war against it, but they could not 2 conquer it. When the house of David was told, "Syria is in league with E′phraim," his heart and the heart of his people shook as the trees of the forest shake before the wind.

3 And the LORD said to Isaiah, "Go forth to meet Ahaz, you and She′ar-jash′ub[h] your son, at the end of the conduit of the upper pool on the highway to the Fuller's 4 Field, and say to him, 'Take heed, be quiet, do not fear, and do not let your heart be faint because of these two smoldering stumps of firebrands, at the fierce anger of 5 Rezin and Syria and the son of Remali′ah. Because Syria, with E′phraim and the son of Remali′ah, has devised evil 6 against you, saying, "Let us go up against Judah and terrify it, and let us conquer it for ourselves, and set up 7 the son of Ta′be-el as king in the midst of it," thus says the Lord GOD:

It shall not stand,
    and it shall not come to pass.
8 For the head of Syria is Damascus,
    and the head of Damascus is Rezin.
(Within sixty-five years E′phraim will be broken to pieces so that it will no longer be a people.)
9 And the head of E′phraim is Samar′ia,

and the head of Samar′ia is the son of Remali′ah.
If you will not believe,
    surely you shall not be established.' "

10, 11 Again the LORD spoke to Ahaz, "Ask a sign of the LORD your God; let it be deep as Sheol or high as heaven." 12 But Ahaz said, "I will not ask, and I will not put the LORD 13 to the test." And he said, "Hear then, O house of David! Is it too little for you to weary men, that you weary my 14 God also? Therefore the Lord himself will give you a sign. Behold, a young woman[i] shall conceive and bear[j] 15 a son, and shall call his name Imman′u-el.[k] He shall eat curds and honey when he knows how to refuse the evil 16 and choose the good. For before the child knows how to refuse the evil and choose the good, the land before whose 17 two kings you are in dread will be deserted. The LORD will bring upon you and upon your people and upon your father's house such days as have not come since the day that E′phraim departed from Judah—the king of Assyria."

18 In that day the LORD will whistle for the fly which is at the sources of the streams of Egypt, and for the bee 19 which is in the land of Assyria. And they will all come and settle in the steep ravines, and in the clefts of the rocks, and on all the thornbushes, and on all the pastures.

20 In that day the Lord will shave with a razor which is hired beyond the River—with the king of Assyria—the head and the hair of the feet, and it will sweep away the beard also.

21 In that day a man will keep alive a young cow and two 22 sheep; and because of the abundance of milk which they give, he will eat curds; for every one that is left in the land will eat curds and honey.

23 In that day every place where there used to be a thousand vines, worth a thousand shekels of silver, will 24 become briers and thorns. With bow and arrows men will come there, for all the land will be briers and thorns; 25 and as for all the hills which used to be hoed with a hoe, you will not come there for fear of briers and thorns; but they will become a place where cattle are let loose and where sheep tread.

8 Then the LORD said to me, "Take a large tablet and write upon it in common characters, 'Belonging to 2 Ma′her-shal′al-hash′baz.' "[l] And I got reliable witnesses, Uri′ah the priest and Zechari′ah the son of Jeberechi′ah, 3 to attest for me. And I went to the prophetess, and she conceived and bore a son. Then the LORD said to me, 4 "Call his name Ma′her-shal′al-hash′baz; for before the child knows how to cry 'My father' or 'My mother,' the wealth of Damascus and the spoil of Samar′ia will be carried away before the king of Assyria."

5, 6 The LORD spoke to me again: "Because this people have refused the waters of Shilo′ah that flow gently, and melt

---

h That is *A remnant shall return*   i Or *virgin*   j Or *is with child and shall bear*   k That is *God is with us*
l That is *The spoil speeds, the prey hastes*

7 in fear before[m] Rezin and the son of Remali'ah; therefore, behold, the Lord is bringing up against them the waters of the River, mighty and many, the king of Assyria and all his glory; and it will rise over all its channels and
8 go over all its banks; and it will sweep on into Judah, it will overflow and pass on, reaching even to the neck; and its outspread wings will fill the breadth of your land, O Imman'u-el."

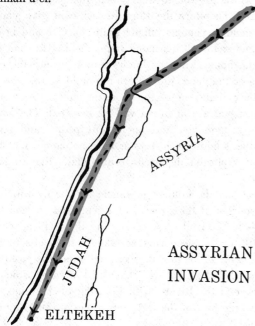

ASSYRIAN
INVASION

9 Be broken, you peoples, and be dismayed;
    give ear, all you far countries;
gird yourselves and be dismayed;
    gird yourselves and be dismayed.
10 Take counsel together, but it will come to nought;
    speak a word, but it will not stand,
    for God is with us.[x]
11 For the Lord spoke thus to me with his strong hand upon me, and warned me not to walk in the way of this
12 people, saying: "Do not call conspiracy all that this people call conspiracy, and do not fear what they fear, nor be in
13 dread. But the Lord of hosts, him you shall regard as holy; let him be your fear, and let him be your dread.
14 And he will become a sanctuary, and a stone of offense, and a rock of stumbling to both houses of Israel, a trap
15 and a snare to the inhabitants of Jerusalem. And many shall stumble thereon; they shall fall and be broken; they shall be snared and taken."

"HIS ANGER IS NOT TURNED AWAY"

16 Bind up the testimony, seal the teaching among my
17 disciples. I will wait for the Lord, who is hiding his face
18 from the house of Jacob, and I will hope in him. Behold, I and the children whom the Lord has given me are signs and portents in Israel from the Lord of hosts, who dwells

19 on Mount Zion. And when they say to you, "Consult the mediums and the wizards who chirp and mutter," should not a people consult their God? Should they consult the
20 dead on behalf of the living? To the teaching and to the testimony! Surely for this word which they speak there is
21 no dawn. They will pass through the land,[n] greatly distressed and hungry; and when they are hungry, they will be enraged and will curse[o] their king and their God,
22 and turn their faces upward; and they will look to the earth, but behold, distress and darkness, the gloom of anguish; and they will be thrust into thick darkness.

The Prince of Peace

9[p] But there will be no gloom for her that was in anguish. In the former time he brought into contempt the land of Zeb'ulun and the land of Naph'tali, but in the latter time he will make glorious the way of the sea, the land beyond the Jordan, Galilee of the nations.
2[q] The people who walked in darkness
    have seen a great light;
those who dwelt in a land of deep darkness,
    on them has light shined.
3 Thou hast multiplied the nation,
    thou hast increased its joy;
they rejoice before thee
    as with joy at the harvest,
    as men rejoice when they divide the spoil.
4 For the yoke of his burden,
    and the staff for his shoulder,
    the rod of his oppressor,
    thou hast broken as on the day of Mid'ian.
5 For every boot of the tramping warrior in battle tumult
    and every garment rolled in blood
    will be burned as fuel for the fire.
6 For to us a child is born,
    to us a son is given;
and the government will be upon his shoulder,
    and his name will be called
"Wonderful Counselor, Mighty God,
    Everlasting Father, Prince of Peace."
7 Of the increase of his government and of peace
    there will be no end,
upon the throne of David, and over his kingdom,
    to establish it, and to uphold it
with justice and with righteousness
    from this time forth and for evermore.
The zeal of the Lord of hosts will do this.

8 The Lord has sent a word against Jacob,
    and it will light upon Israel;
9 and all the people will know,
    E'phraim and the inhabitants of Samar'ia,
    who say in pride and in arrogance of heart:

[m] Cn: Heb *rejoices in*   [x] Heb *immanu el*   [n] Heb *it*   [o] Or *curse by*   [p] Ch 8.23 in Heb   [q] Ch 9.1 in Heb

¹⁰ "The bricks have fallen,
  but we will build with dressed stones;
the sycamores have been cut down,
  but we will put cedars in their place."
¹¹ So the LORD raises adversaries ʳ against them,
  and stirs up their enemies.
¹² The Syrians on the east and the Philistines on the west
  devour Israel with open mouth.
For all this his anger is not turned away
  and his hand is stretched out still.

¹³ The people did not turn to him who smote them,
  nor seek the LORD of hosts.
¹⁴ So the LORD cut off from Israel head and tail,
  palm branch and reed in one day—
¹⁵ the elder and honored man is the head,
  and the prophet who teaches lies is the tail;
¹⁶ for those who lead this people lead them astray,
  and those who are led by them are swallowed up.
¹⁷ Therefore the Lord does not rejoice over their young men,
  and has no compassion on their fatherless and widows;
for every one is godless and an evildoer,
  and every mouth speaks folly.
For all this his anger is not turned away
  and his hand is stretched out still.

¹⁸ For wickedness burns like a fire,
  it consumes briers and thorns;
it kindles the thickets of the forest,
  and they roll upward in a column of smoke.
¹⁹ Through the wrath of the LORD of hosts
  the land is burned,
and the people are like fuel for the fire;
  no man spares his brother.
²⁰ They snatch on the right, but are still hungry,
  and they devour on the left, but are not satisfied;
each devours his neighbor's ˢ flesh,
²¹ Manas'seh E'phraim, and E'phraim Manas'seh,
  and together they are against Judah.
For all this his anger is not turned away
  and his hand is stretched out still.

10 Woe to those who decree iniquitous decrees,
    and the writers who keep writing oppression,
² to turn aside the needy from justice
  and to rob the poor of my people of their right,
that widows may be their spoil,
  and that they may make the fatherless their prey!
³ What will you do on the day of punishment,
  in the storm which will come from afar?
To whom will you flee for help,
  and where will you leave your wealth?
⁴ Nothing remains but to crouch among the prisoners
  or fall among the slain.

For all this his anger is not turned away
  and his hand is stretched out still.

"BE NOT AFRAID OF THE ASSYRIAN"

⁵ Ah, Assyria, the rod of my anger,
  the staff of my fury! ᵗ
⁶ Against a godless nation I send him,
  and against the people of my wrath I command him,
to take spoil and seize plunder,
  and to tread them down like the mire of the streets.
⁷ But he does not so intend,
  and his mind does not so think;
but it is in his mind to destroy,
  and to cut off nations not a few;
⁸ for he says:
"Are not my commanders all kings?
⁹ Is not Calno like Car'chemish?
  Is not Hamath like Arpad?
  Is not Samar'ia like Damascus?
¹⁰ As my hand has reached to the kingdoms of the idols
    whose graven images were greater than those of Jerusa-
    lem and Samar'ia,
¹¹ shall I not do to Jerusalem and her idols
    as I have done to Samar'ia and her images?"

¹² When the Lord has finished all his work on Mount Zion and on Jerusalem he ᵘ will punish the arrogant boast-
¹³ ing of the king of Assyria and his haughty pride. For he says:
"By the strength of my hand I have done it,
  and by my wisdom, for I have understanding;
I have removed the boundaries of peoples,
  and have plundered their treasures;
    like a bull I have brought down those who sat on
    thrones.
¹⁴ My hand has found like a nest
  the wealth of the peoples;
and as men gather eggs that have been forsaken
  so I have gathered all the earth;
and there was none that moved a wing,
  or opened the mouth, or chirped."

¹⁵ Shall the axe vaunt itself over him who hews with it,
  or the saw magnify itself against him who wields it?
As if a rod should wield him who lifts it,
  or as if a staff should lift him who is not wood!
¹⁶ Therefore the Lord, the LORD of hosts,
  will send wasting sickness among his stout warriors,
and under his glory a burning will be kindled,

ʳ Cn: Heb *the adversaries of Rezin*   ˢ Tg Compare Gk: Heb *the flesh of his arm*   ᵗ Heb *a staff it is in their hand my fury*
ᵘ Heb *I*

461

like the burning of fire.
17 The light of Israel will become a fire,
and his Holy One a flame;
and it will burn and devour
his thorns and briers in one day.
18 The glory of his forest and of his fruitful land
the LORD will destroy, both soul and body,
and it will be as when a sick man wastes away.
19 The remnant of the trees of his forest will be so few
that a child can write them down.

20   In that day the remnant of Israel and the survivors of the house of Jacob will no more lean upon him that smote them, but will lean upon the LORD, the Holy One of Israel, 21 in truth. A remnant will return, the remnant of Jacob, to 22 the mighty God. For though your people Israel be as the sand of the sea, only a remnant of them will return. Destruction is decreed, overflowing with righteousness. 23 For the Lord, the LORD of hosts, will make a full end, as decreed, in the midst of all the earth.

24   Therefore thus says the Lord, the LORD of hosts: "O my people, who dwell in Zion, be not afraid of the Assyrians when they smite with the rod and lift up their 25 staff against you as the Egyptians did. For in a very little while my indignation will come to an end, and my 26 anger will be directed to their destruction. And the LORD of hosts will wield against them a scourge, as when he smote Mid'ian at the rock of Oreb; and his rod will be 27 over the sea, and he will lift it as he did in Egypt. And in that day his burden will depart from your shoulder, and his yoke will be destroyed from your neck."

He has gone up from Rimmon,[v]
28   he has come to Ai'ath;
he has passed through Migron,
at Michmash he stores his baggage;
29 they have crossed over the pass,
at Geba they lodge for the night;
Ramah trembles,
Gib'e-ah of Saul has fled.
30 Cry aloud, O daughter of Gallim!
Hearken, O La'ishah!
Answer her, O An'athoth!
31 Madme'nah is in flight,
the inhabitants of Gebim flee for safety.
32 This very day he will halt at Nob,
he will shake his fist
at the mount of the daughter of Zion,
the hill of Jerusalem.

33 Behold, the Lord, the LORD of hosts
will lop the boughs with terrifying power;
the great in height will be hewn down,
and the lofty will be brought low.

34 He will cut down the thickets of the forest with an axe,
and Lebanon with its majestic trees[w] will fall.

The Messianic Age

11 There shall come forth a shoot from the stump of Jesse,
and a branch shall grow out of his roots.
2 And the Spirit of the LORD shall rest upon him,
the spirit of wisdom and understanding,
the spirit of counsel and might,
the spirit of knowledge and the fear of the LORD.
3 And his delight shall be in the fear of the LORD.

He shall not judge by what his eyes see,
or decide by what his ears hear;
4 but with righteousness he shall judge the poor,
and decide with equity for the meek of the earth;
and he shall smite the earth with the rod of his mouth,
and with the breath of his lips he shall slay the wicked.
5 Righteousness shall be the girdle of his waist,
and faithfulness the girdle of his loins.

6 The wolf shall dwell with the lamb,
and the leopard shall lie down with the kid,
and the calf and the lion and the fatling together,
and a little child shall lead them.
7 The cow and the bear shall feed;
their young shall lie down together;
and the lion shall eat straw like the ox.
8 The sucking child shall play over the hole of the asp,
and the weaned child shall put his hand on the adder's den.
9 They shall not hurt or destroy
in all my holy mountain;
for the earth shall be full of the knowledge of the LORD
as the waters cover the sea.

10   In that day the root of Jesse shall stand as an ensign to the peoples; him shall the nations seek, and his dwellings shall be glorious.

11   In that day the Lord will extend his hand yet a second time to recover the remnant which is left of his people, from Assyria, from Egypt, from Pathros, from Ethiopia, from Elam, from Shinar, from Hamath, and from the coastlands of the sea.

v Cn: Heb *and his yoke from your neck, and a yoke will be destroyed because of fatness*   w Cn Compare Gk Vg: Heb *with a majestic one*

12 He will raise an ensign for the nations,
 and will assemble the outcasts of Israel,
and gather the dispersed of Judah
 from the four corners of the earth.
13 The jealousy of E'phraim shall depart,
 and those who harass Judah shall be cut off;
E'phraim shall not be jealous of Judah,
 and Judah shall not harass E'phraim.
14 But they shall swoop down upon the shoulder of the
 Philistines in the west,
 and together they shall plunder the people of the east.
They shall put forth their hand against Edom and Moab,
 and the Ammonites shall obey them.
15 And the Lord will utterly destroy
 the tongue of the sea of Egypt;
and will wave his hand over the River
 with his scorching wind,
and smite it into seven channels
 that men may cross dryshod.
16 And there will be a highway from Assyria
 for the remnant which is left of his people,
as there was for Israel
 when they came up from the land of Egypt.

12 You will say in that day:
 "I will give thanks to thee, O Lord,
for though thou wast angry with me,
thy anger turned away,
 and thou didst comfort me.

2 "Behold, God is my salvation;
 I will trust, and will not be afraid;
for the Lord God is my strength and my song,
 and he has become my salvation."

3 With joy you will draw water from the wells of salva-
4 tion. And you will say in that day:
"Give thanks to the Lord,
 call upon his name;
make known his deeds among the nations,
 proclaim that his name is exalted.

5 "Sing praises to the Lord, for he has done gloriously;
 let this be known ˣ in all the earth.
6 Shout, and sing for joy, O inhabitant of Zion,
 for great in your midst is the Holy One of Israel."

"THE UPROAR OF MANY PEOPLES"

13 The oracle concerning Babylon which Isaiah the
 son of Amoz saw.
2 On a bare hill raise a signal,
 cry aloud to them;

wave the hand for them to enter
 the gates of the nobles.
3 I myself have commanded my consecrated ones,
 have summoned my mighty men to execute my anger,
 my proudly exulting ones.

4 Hark, a tumult on the mountains
 as of a great multitude!
Hark, an uproar of kingdoms,
 of nations gathering together!
The Lord of hosts is mustering
 a host for battle.
5 They come from a distant land,
 from the end of the heavens,
the Lord and the weapons of his indignation,
 to destroy the whole earth.

6 Wail, for the day of the Lord is near;
 as destruction from the Almighty it will come!
7 Therefore all hands will be feeble,
 and every man's heart will melt,
8 and they will be dismayed.
Pangs and agony will seize them;
 they will be in anguish like a woman in travail.
They will look aghast at one another;
 their faces will be aflame.

9 Behold, the day of the Lord comes,
 cruel, with wrath and fierce anger,
to make the earth a desolation
 and to destroy its sinners from it.
10 For the stars of the heavens and their constellations
 will not give their light;
the sun will be dark at its rising
 and the moon will not shed its light.
11 I will punish the world for its evil,
 and the wicked for their iniquity;
I will put an end to the pride of the arrogant,
 and lay low the haughtiness of the ruthless.
12 I will make men more rare than fine gold,
 and mankind than the gold of Ophir.
13 Therefore I will make the heavens tremble,
 and the earth will be shaken out of its place,
at the wrath of the Lord of hosts
 in the day of his fierce anger.
14 And like a hunted gazelle,
 or like sheep with none to gather them,
every man will turn to his own people,
 and every man will flee to his own land.
15 Whoever is found will be thrust through,
 and whoever is caught will fall by the sword.
16 Their infants will be dashed in pieces
 before their eyes;

ˣ Or this is made known

their houses will be plundered
and their wives ravished.

17 Behold, I am stirring up the Medes against them,
who have no regard for silver
and do not delight in gold.
18 Their bows will slaughter the young men;
they will have no mercy on the fruit of the womb;
their eyes will not pity children.
19 And Babylon, the glory of kingdoms,
the splendor and pride of the Chalde'ans,
will be like Sodom and Gomor'rah
when God overthrew them.
20 It will never be inhabited
or dwelt in for all generations;
no Arab will pitch his tent there,
no shepherds will make their flocks lie down there.
21 But wild beasts will lie down there,
and its houses will be full of howling creatures;
there ostriches will dwell,
and there satyrs will dance.
22 Hyenas will cry in its towers,
and jackals in the pleasant palaces;
its time is close at hand
and its days will not be prolonged.

14 The LORD will have compassion on Jacob and will
again choose Israel, and will set them in their own
land, and aliens will join them and will cleave to the house
2 of Jacob. And the peoples will take them and bring them
to their place, and the house of Israel will possess them in
the LORD's land as male and female slaves; they will take
captive those who were their captors, and rule over those
who oppressed them.
3 When the LORD has given you rest from your pain and
turmoil and the hard service with which you were made
4 to serve, you will take up this taunt against the king of
Babylon:
"How the oppressor has ceased,
the insolent fury y ceased!
5 The LORD has broken the staff of the wicked,
the scepter of rulers,
6 that smote the peoples in wrath
with unceasing blows,
that ruled the nations in anger
with unrelenting persecution.
7 The whole earth is at rest and quiet;
they break forth into singing.
8 The cypresses rejoice at you,
the cedars of Lebanon, saying,
'Since you were laid low,
no hewer comes up against us.'
9 Sheol beneath is stirred up

to meet you when you come,
it rouses the shades to greet you,
all who were leaders of the earth;
it raises from their thrones
all who were kings of the nations.
10 All of them will speak
and say to you:
'You too have become as weak as we!
You have become like us!'
11 Your pomp is brought down to Sheol,
the sound of your harps;
maggots are the bed beneath you,
and worms are your covering.

12 "How you are fallen from heaven,
O Day Star, son of Dawn!
How you are cut down to the ground,
you who laid the nations low!
13 You said in your heart,
'I will ascend to heaven;
above the stars of God
I will set my throne on high;
I will sit on the mount of assembly
in the far north;
14 I will ascend above the heights of the clouds,
I will make myself like the Most High.'
15 But you are brought down to Sheol,
to the depths of the Pit.
16 Those who see you will stare at you,
and ponder over you:
'Is this the man who made the earth tremble,
who shook kingdoms,
17 who made the world like a desert
and overthrew its cities,
who did not let his prisoners go home?'
18 All the kings of the nations lie in glory,
each in his own tomb;
19 but you are cast out, away from your sepulchre,
like a loathed untimely birth,z
clothed with the slain, those pierced by the sword,
who go down to the stones of the Pit,
like a dead body trodden under foot.
20 You will not be joined with them in burial,
because you have destroyed your land,
you have slain your people.

"May the descendants of evildoers
nevermore be named!
21 Prepare slaughter for his sons
because of the guilt of their fathers,
lest they rise and possess the earth,
and fill the face of the world with cities."

y One ancient Ms Compare Gk Syr Vg: The meaning of the Hebrew word is uncertain   z Cn Compare Tg Symmachus: Heb *a loathed branch*

22 "I will rise up against them," says the LORD of hosts, "and will cut off from Babylon name and remnant, off-
23 spring and posterity, says the LORD. And I will make it a possession of the hedgehog, and pools of water, and I will sweep it with the broom of destruction, says the LORD of hosts."

24 The LORD of hosts has sworn:
"As I have planned,
    so shall it be,
and as I have purposed,
    so shall it stand,
25 that I will break the Assyrian in my land,
    and upon my mountains trample him under foot;
and his yoke shall depart from them,
    and his burden from their shoulder."
26 This is the purpose that is purposed
    concerning the whole earth;
and this is the hand that is stretched out
    over all the nations.
27 For the LORD of hosts has purposed,
    and who will annul it?
His hand is stretched out,
    and who will turn it back?

28 In the year that King Ahaz died came this oracle:
29 "Rejoice not, O Philistia, all of you,
    that the rod which smote you is broken,
for from the serpent's root will come forth an adder,
    and its fruit will be a flying serpent.
30 And the first-born of the poor will feed,
    and the needy lie down in safety;
but I will kill your root with famine,
    and your remnant I a will slay.
31 Wail, O gate; cry, O city;
    melt in fear, O Philistia, all of you!
For smoke comes out of the north,
    and there is no straggler in his ranks."

32 What will one answer the messengers of the nation?
"The LORD has founded Zion,
    and in her the afflicted of his people find refuge."

15 An oracle concerning Moab.
    Because Ar is laid waste in a night
Moab is undone;
because Kir is laid waste in a night
Moab is undone.
2 The daughter of Dibon b has gone up

to the high places to weep;
over Nebo and over Med'eba
    Moab wails.
On every head is baldness,
    every beard is shorn;
3 in the streets they gird on sackcloth;
    on the housetops and in the squares
    every one wails and melts in tears.
4 Heshbon and Elea'leh cry out,
    their voice is heard as far as Jahaz;
therefore the armed men of Moab cry aloud;
    his soul trembles.
5 My heart cries out for Moab;
    his fugitives flee to Zo'ar,
    to Eg'lath-shelish'iyah.
For at the ascent of Luhith
    they go up weeping;
on the road to Horona'im
    they raise a cry of destruction;
6 the waters of Nimrim
    are a desolation;
the grass is withered, the new growth fails,
    the verdure is no more.
7 Therefore the abundance they have gained
    and what they have laid up
they carry away
    over the Brook of the Willows.
8 For a cry has gone
    round the land of Moab;
the wailing reaches to Egla'im,
    the wailing reaches to Beer-e'lim.
9 For the waters of Dibon c are full of blood;
    yet I will bring upon Dibon c even more,
a lion for those of Moab who escape,
    for the remnant of the land.

16 They have sent lambs
        to the ruler of the land,
from Sela, by way of the desert,
    to the mount of the daughter of Zion.
2 Like fluttering birds,
    like scattered nestlings,
so are the daughters of Moab
    at the fords of the Arnon.
3 "Give counsel,
    grant justice;
make your shade like night
    at the height of noon;
hide the outcasts,
    betray not the fugitive;
4 let the outcasts of Moab
    sojourn among you;
be a refuge to them

a One ancient Ms Vg: Heb he   b Cn: Heb the house and Dibon   c One ancient Ms Vg Compare Syr: Heb Dimon

from the destroyer.
When the oppressor is no more,
  and destruction has ceased,
and he who tramples under foot
  has vanished from the land,
5 then a throne will be established in steadfast love
  and on it will sit in faithfulness
  in the tent of David
one who judges and seeks justice
  and is swift to do righteousness."

6 We have heard of the pride of Moab,
  how proud he was;
of his arrogance, his pride, and his insolence—
  his boasts are false.
7 Therefore let Moab wail,
  let every one wail for Moab.
Mourn, utterly stricken,
  for the raisin-cakes of Kir-har′eseth.

8 For the fields of Heshbon languish,
  and the vine of Sibmah;
the lords of the nations
  have struck down its branches,
which reached to Jazer
  and strayed to the desert;
its shoots spread abroad
  and passed over the sea.
9 Therefore I weep with the weeping of Jazer
  for the vine of Sibmah;
I drench you with my tears,
  O Heshbon and Elea′leh;
for upon your fruit and your harvest
  the battle shout has fallen.
10 And joy and gladness are taken away
  from the fruitful field;
and in the vineyards no songs are sung,
  no shouts are raised;
no treader treads out wine in the presses;
  the vintage shout is hushed.d
11 Therefore my soul moans like a lyre for Moab,
  and my heart for Kir-he′res.
12   And when Moab presents himself, when he wearies
himself upon the high place, when he comes to his sanctuary to pray, he will not prevail.
13   This is the word which the LORD spoke concerning
14 Moab in the past. But now the LORD says, "In three years,
like the years of a hireling, the glory of Moab will be
brought into contempt, in spite of all his great multitude,
and those who survive will be very few and feeble."

17   An oracle concerning Damascus.
    Behold, Damascus will cease to be a city,
    and will become a heap of ruins.

2 Her cities will be deserted for ever; e
  they will be for flocks,
  which will lie down, and none will make them afraid.
3 The fortress will disappear from E′phraim,
  and the kingdom from Damascus;
and the remnant of Syria will be
  like the glory of the children of Israel,
            says the LORD of hosts.

4 And in that day
  the glory of Jacob will be brought low,
  and the fat of his flesh will grow lean.
5 And it shall be as when the reaper gathers standing grain
  and his arm harvests the ears,
and as when one gleans the ears of grain
  in the Valley of Reph′aim.
6 Gleanings will be left in it,
  as when an olive tree is beaten—
two or three berries
  in the top of the highest bough,
four or five
  on the branches of a fruit tree,
            says the LORD God of Israel.

7   In that day men will regard their Maker, and their
8 eyes will look to the Holy One of Israel; they will not
have regard for the altars, the work of their hands, and
they will not look to what their own fingers have made,
either the Ashe′rim or the altars of incense.
9   In that day their strong cities will be like the deserted
places of the Hivites and the Amorites,f which they deserted because of the children of Israel, and there will be
desolation.

10 For you have forgotten the God of your salvation,
  and have not remembered the Rock of your refuge;
therefore, though you plant pleasant plants
  and set out slips of an alien god,
11 though you make them grow on the day that you plant
    them,
  and make them blossom in the morning that you sow;
yet the harvest will flee away
  in a day of grief and incurable pain.
12 Ah, the thunder of many peoples,
  they thunder like the thundering of the sea!
Ah, the roar of nations,
  they roar like the roaring of mighty waters!
13 The nations roar like the roaring of many waters,
  but he will rebuke them, and they will flee far away,
chased like chaff on the mountains before the wind
  and whirling dust before the storm.
14 At evening time, behold, terror!
  Before morning, they are no more!

d Gk: Heb I have hushed   e Cn Compare Gk: Heb the cities of Aroer are deserted
f Cn Compare Gk: Heb the wood and the highest bough

This is the portion of those who despoil us,
  and the lot of those who plunder us.

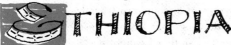THIOPIA

18 Ah, land of whirring wings
      which is beyond the rivers of Ethiopia;
2 which sends ambassadors by the Nile,
    in vessels of papyrus upon the waters!
  Go, you swift messengers,
    to a nation, tall and smooth,
  to a people feared near and far,
    a nation mighty and conquering,
  whose land the rivers divide.

3 All you inhabitants of the world,
    you who dwell on the earth,
  when a signal is raised on the mountains, look!
    When a trumpet is blown, hear!
4 For thus the LORD said to me:
  "I will quietly look from my dwelling
    like clear heat in sunshine,
    like a cloud of dew in the heat of harvest."
5 For before the harvest, when the blossom is over,
    and the flower becomes a ripening grape,
  he will cut off the shoots with pruning hooks,
    and the spreading branches he will hew away.
6 They shall all of them be left
    to the birds of prey of the mountains
    and to the beasts of the earth.
  And the birds of prey will summer upon them,
    and all the beasts of the earth will winter upon them.

7   At that time gifts will be brought to the LORD of hosts
  from a people tall and smooth,
    from a people feared near and far,
  a nation mighty and conquering,
    whose land the rivers divide,
  to Mount Zion, the place of the name of the LORD of hosts.

GYPT

19   An oracle concerning Egypt.
      Behold, the LORD is riding on a swift cloud
      and comes to Egypt;
  and the idols of Egypt will tremble at his presence,
    and the heart of the Egyptians will melt within them.
2 And I will stir up Egyptians against Egyptians,
    and they will fight, every man against his brother
  and every man against his neighbor,
    city against city, kingdom against kingdom;
3 and the spirit of the Egyptians within them will be emptied
      out,
    and I will confound their plans;

and they will consult the idols and the sorcerers,
    and the mediums and the wizards;
4 and I will give over the Egyptians
    into the hand of a hard master;
  and a fierce king will rule over them,
    says the Lord, the LORD of hosts.

5 And the waters of the Nile will be dried up,
    and the river will be parched and dry;
6 and its canals will become foul,
    and the branches of Egypt's Nile will diminish and dry
      up,
  reeds and rushes will rot away.
7 There will be bare places by the Nile,
    on the brink of the Nile,
  and all that is sown by the Nile will dry up,
    be driven away, and be no more.
8 The fishermen will mourn and lament,
    all who cast hook in the Nile;
  and they will languish
    who spread nets upon the water.
9 The workers in combed flax will be in despair,
    and the weavers of white cotton.
10 Those who are the pillars of the land will be crushed,
    and all who work for hire will be grieved.

11 The princes of Zo'an are utterly foolish;
    the wise counselors of Pharaoh give stupid counsel.
  How can you say to Pharaoh,
    "I am a son of the wise,
    a son of ancient kings"?
12 Where then are your wise men?
    Let them tell you and make known
    what the LORD of hosts has purposed against Egypt.
13 The princes of Zo'an have become fools,
    and the princes of Memphis are deluded;
  those who are the cornerstones of her tribes
    have led Egypt astray.
14 The LORD has mingled within her a spirit of confusion;
    and they have made Egypt stagger in all her doings
    as a drunken man staggers in his vomit.
15 And there will be nothing for Egypt
    which head or tail, palm branch or reed, may do.

16   In that day the Egyptians will be like women, and
    tremble with fear before the hand which the LORD of hosts
17 shakes over them. And the land of Judah will become a
    terror to the Egyptians; every one to whom it is men-
    tioned will fear because of the purpose which the LORD of
    hosts has purposed against them.
18   In that day there will be five cities in the land of Egypt
    which speak the language of Canaan and swear allegiance
    to the LORD of hosts. One of these will be called the City
    of the Sun.

19 In that day there will be an altar to the LORD in the midst of the land of Egypt, and a pillar to the LORD at its 20 border. It will be a sign and a witness to the LORD of hosts in the land of Egypt; when they cry to the LORD because of oppressors he will send them a savior, and will 21 defend and deliver them. And the LORD will make himself known to the Egyptians; and the Egyptians will know the LORD in that day and worship with sacrifice and burnt offering, and they will make vows to the LORD and per- 22 form them. And the LORD will smite Egypt, smiting and healing, and they will return to the LORD, and he will heed their supplications and heal them.

23 In that day there will be a highway from Egypt to Assyria, and the Assyrian will come into Egypt, and the Egyptian into Assyria, and the Egyptians will worship with the Assyrians. 24 In that day Israel will be the third with Egypt and 25 Assyria, a blessing in the midst of the earth, whom the LORD of hosts has blessed, saying, "Blessed be Egypt my people, and Assyria the work of my hands, and Israel my heritage."

20 In the year that the commander in chief, who was sent by Sargon the king of Assyria, came to Ashdod 2 and fought against it and took it,—at that time the LORD had spoken by Isaiah the son of Amoz, saying, "Go, and loose the sackcloth from your loins and take off your shoes from your feet," and he had done so, walking naked 3 and barefoot—the LORD said, "As my servant Isaiah has walked naked and barefoot for three years as a sign and 4 a portent against Egypt and Ethiopia, so shall the king of Assyria lead away the Egyptians captives and the Ethi-opians exiles, both the young and the old, naked and barefoot, with buttocks uncovered, to the shame of Egypt. 5 Then they shall be dismayed and confounded because of 6 Ethiopia their hope and of Egypt their boast. And the inhabitants of this coastland will say in that day, 'Behold, this is what has happened to those in whom we hoped and to whom we fled for help to be delivered from the king of Assyria! And we, how shall we escape?'"

21 The oracle concerning the wilderness of the sea.
  As whirlwinds in the Negeb sweep on,
  it comes from the desert,
  from a terrible land.
2 A stern vision is told to me;
  the plunderer plunders,
  and the destroyer destroys.
Go up, O Elam,
  lay siege, O Media;
all the sighing she has caused
  I bring to an end.

3 Therefore my loins are filled with anguish;
  pangs have seized me,
  like the pangs of a woman in travail;
I am bowed down so that I cannot hear,
  I am dismayed so that I cannot see.
4 My mind reels, horror has appalled me;
  the twilight I longed for
  has been turned for me into trembling.
5 They prepare the table,
  they spread the rugs,
  they eat, they drink.
Arise, O princes,
  oil the shield!
6 For thus the Lord said to me:
"Go, set a watchman,
  let him announce what he sees.
7 When he sees riders, horsemen in pairs,
  riders on asses, riders on camels,
let him listen diligently,
  very diligently."
8 Then he who saw g cried:
"Upon a watch tower I stand, O Lord,
  continually by day,
and at my post I am stationed
  whole nights.
9 And, behold, here come riders,
  horsemen in pairs!"
And he answered,
  "Fallen, fallen is Babylon;
and all the images of her gods
  he has shattered to the ground."
10 O my threshed and winnowed one,
  what I have heard from the LORD of hosts,
  the God of Israel, I announce to you.

11 The oracle concerning Dumah.
One is calling to me from Se'ir,
  "Watchman, what of the night?
  Watchman, what of the night?"
12 The watchman says:
"Morning comes, and also the night.
  If you will inquire, inquire;
  come back again."

13 The oracle concerning Arabia.
In the thickets in Arabia you will lodge,
  O caravans of De'danites.
14 To the thirsty bring water,
  meet the fugitive with bread,
  O inhabitants of the land of Tema.
15 For they have fled from the swords,
  from the drawn sword,
from the bent bow,
  and from the press of battle.

g One ancient Ms: Heb a lion

16 For thus the Lord said to me, "Within a year, according to the years of a hireling, all the glory of Kedar will come 17 to an end; and the remainder of the archers of the mighty men of the sons of Kedar will be few; for the LORD, the God of Israel, has spoken."

22 The oracle concerning the valley of vision.
What do you mean that you have gone up,
all of you, to the housetops,
2 you who are full of shoutings,
tumultuous city, exultant town?
Your slain are not slain with the sword
or dead in battle.
3 All your rulers have fled together,
without the bow they were captured.
All of you who were found were captured,
though they had fled far away.h
4 Therefore I said:
"Look away from me,
let me weep bitter tears;
do not labor to comfort me
for the destruction of the daughter of my people."

5 For the Lord GOD of hosts has a day
of tumult and trampling and confusion
in the valley of vision,
a battering down of walls
and a shouting to the mountains.
6 And Elam bore the quiver
with chariots and horsemen,i
and Kir uncovered the shield.
7 Your choicest valleys were full of chariots,
and the horsemen took their stand at the gates.
8 He has taken away the covering of Judah.

In that day you looked to the weapons of the House 9 of the Forest, and you saw that the breaches of the city of David were many, and you collected the waters of 10 the lower pool, and you counted the houses of Jerusalem, 11 and you broke down the houses to fortify the wall. You made a reservoir between the two walls for the water of the old pool. But you did not look to him who did it, or have regard for him who planned it long ago.

12 In that day the Lord GOD of hosts
called to weeping and mourning,
to baldness and girding with sackcloth;
13 and behold, joy and gladness,
slaying oxen and killing sheep,
eating flesh and drinking wine.

"Let us eat and drink,
for tomorrow we die."
14 The LORD of hosts has revealed himself in my ears:
"Surely this iniquity will not be forgiven you
till you die,"
says the Lord GOD of hosts.

15 Thus says the Lord GOD of hosts, "Come, go to this steward, to Shebna, who is over the household, and say 16 to him: What have you to do here and whom have you here, that you have hewn here a tomb for yourself, you who hew a tomb on the height, and carve a habitation for 17 yourself in the rock? Behold, the LORD will hurl you away violently, O you strong man. He will seize firm hold 18 on you, and whirl you round and round, and throw you like a ball into a wide land; there you shall die, and there shall be your splendid chariots, you shame of your 19 master's house. I will thrust you from your office, and you 20 will be cast down from your station. In that day I will 21 call my servant Eli'akim the son of Hilki'ah, and I will clothe him with your robe, and will bind your girdle on him, and will commit your authority to his hand; and he shall be a father to the inhabitants of Jerusalem and to the 22 house of Judah. And I will place on his shoulder the key of the house of David; he shall open, and none shall shut; 23 and he shall shut, and none shall open. And I will fasten him like a peg in a sure place, and he will become a 24 throne of honor to his father's house. And they will hang on him the whole weight of his father's house, the offspring and issue, every small vessel, from the cups to all 25 the flagons. In that day, says the LORD of hosts, the peg that was fastened in a sure place will give way; and it will be cut down and fall, and the burden that was upon it will be cut off, for the LORD has spoken."

23 The oracle concerning Tyre.
Wail, O ships of Tarshish,
for Tyre is laid waste, without house or haven!
From the land of Cyprus
it is revealed to them.
2 Be still, O inhabitants of the coast,
O merchants of Sidon;
your messengers passed over the sea j
3 and were on many waters;
your revenue was the grain of Shihor,
the harvest of the Nile;
you were the merchant of the nations.
4 Be ashamed, O Sidon, for the sea has spoken,
the stronghold of the sea, saying:

h Gk Syr Vg: Heb *from far away*   i The Hebrew of this line is obscure
j One ancient Ms: Heb *who passed over the sea, they replenished you*

"I have neither travailed nor given birth,
　I have neither reared young men
　　nor brought up virgins."
⁵ When the report comes to Egypt,
　they will be in anguish over the report about Tyre.
⁶ Pass over to Tarshish,
　wail, O inhabitants of the coast!
⁷ Is this your exultant city
　whose origin is from days of old,
whose feet carried her
　to settle afar?
⁸ Who has purposed this
　against Tyre, the bestower of crowns,
whose merchants were princes,
　whose traders were the honored of the earth?
⁹ The Lord of hosts has purposed it,
　to defile the pride of all glory,
　to dishonor all the honored of the earth.
¹⁰ Overflow your land like the Nile,
　O daughter of Tarshish;
　there is no restraint any more.
¹¹ He has stretched out his hand over the sea,
　he has shaken the kingdoms;
the Lord has given command concerning Canaan
　to destroy its strongholds.
¹² And he said:
"You will no more exult,
　O oppressed virgin daughter of Sidon;
arise, pass over to Cyprus,
　even there you will have no rest."

¹³　Behold the land of the Chalde'ans! This is the people; it was not Assyria. They destined Tyre for wild beasts. They erected their siege towers, they razed her palaces, they made her a ruin.ᵏ
¹⁴ Wail, O ships of Tarshish,
　for your stronghold is laid waste.
¹⁵ In that day Tyre will be forgotten for seventy years, like the days of one king. At the end of seventy years, it will happen to Tyre as in the song of the harlot:
¹⁶ "Take a harp,
　go about the city,
　O forgotten harlot!
Make sweet melody,
　sing many songs,
　that you may be remembered."
¹⁷ At the end of seventy years, the Lord will visit Tyre, and she will return to her hire, and will play the harlot with all the kingdoms of the world upon the face of the earth. ¹⁸ Her merchandise and her hire will be dedicated to the Lord; it will not be stored or hoarded, but her merchandise will supply abundant food and fine clothing for those who dwell before the Lord.

ᵏ The Hebrew of this verse is obscure

"YE THAT DWELL IN THE DUST"

24 Behold, the Lord will lay waste the earth and make
　　it desolate,
　and he will twist its surface and scatter its inhabitants.

² And it shall be, as with the people, so with the priest;
　as with the slave, so with his master;
　as with the maid, so with her mistress;
as with the buyer, so with the seller;
　as with the lender, so with the borrower;
　as with the creditor, so with the debtor.
³ The earth shall be utterly laid waste
　and utterly despoiled;
　for the Lord has spoken this word.

⁴ The earth mourns and withers,
　the world languishes and withers;
　the heavens languish together with the earth.
⁵ The earth lies polluted
　under its inhabitants;
for they have transgressed the laws,
　violated the statutes,
　broken the everlasting covenant.
⁶ Therefore a curse devours the earth,
　and its inhabitants suffer for their guilt;
therefore the inhabitants of the earth are scorched,
　and few men are left.
⁷ The wine mourns,
　the vine languishes,
　all the merry-hearted sigh.
⁸ The mirth of the timbrels is stilled,
　the noise of the jubilant has ceased,
　the mirth of the lyre is stilled.
⁹ No more do they drink wine with singing;
　strong drink is bitter to those who drink it.
¹⁰ The city of chaos is broken down,
　every house is shut up so that none can enter.
¹¹ There is an outcry in the streets for lack of wine;
　all joy has reached its eventide;
　the gladness of the earth is banished.
¹² Desolation is left in the city,
　the gates are battered into ruins.
¹³ For thus it shall be in the midst of the earth
　among the nations,
as when an olive tree is beaten,
　as at the gleaning when the vintage is done.

14 They lift up their voices, they sing for joy;
  over the majesty of the LORD they shout from the west.
15 Therefore in the east give glory to the LORD;
  in the coastlands of the sea, to the name of the LORD, the
    God of Israel.
16 From the ends of the earth we hear songs of praise,
  of glory to the Righteous One.
But I say, "I pine away,
  I pine away. Woe is me!
For the treacherous deal treacherously,
  the treacherous deal very treacherously."

17 Terror, and the pit, and the snare
  are upon you, O inhabitant of the earth!
18 He who flees at the sound of the terror
  shall fall into the pit;
and he who climbs out of the pit
  shall be caught in the snare.
For the windows of heaven are opened,
  and the foundations of the earth tremble.
19 The earth is utterly broken,
  the earth is rent asunder,
  the earth is violently shaken.
20 The earth staggers like a drunken man,
  it sways like a hut;
its transgression lies heavy upon it,
  and it falls, and will not rise again.

21 On that day the LORD will punish
  the host of heaven, in heaven,
  and the kings of the earth, on the earth.
22 They will be gathered together
  as prisoners in a pit;
they will be shut up in a prison,
  and after many days they will be punished.
23 Then the moon will be confounded,
  and the sun ashamed;
for the LORD of hosts will reign
  on Mount Zion and in Jerusalem
and before his elders he will manifest his glory.

Songs of Deliverance

25 O LORD, thou art my God;
  I will exalt thee, I will praise thy name;
for thou hast done wonderful things,
  plans formed of old, faithful and sure.
2 For thou hast made the city a heap,
  the fortified city a ruin;
the palace of aliens is a city no more,

1 The meaning of the Hebrew word is uncertain

it will never be rebuilt.
3 Therefore strong peoples will glorify thee;
  cities of ruthless nations will fear thee.
4 For thou hast been a stronghold to the poor,
  a stronghold to the needy in his distress,
  a shelter from the storm and a shade from the heat;
for the blast of the ruthless is like a storm against a wall,
5   like heat in a dry place.
Thou dost subdue the noise of the aliens;
  as heat by the shade of a cloud,
  so the song of the ruthless is stilled.

6 On this mountain the LORD of hosts will make for all peoples a feast of fat things, a feast of wine on the lees, of fat things full of marrow, of wine on the lees well re-7 fined. And he will destroy on this mountain the covering that is cast over all peoples, the veil that is spread over 8 all nations. He will swallow up death for ever, and the Lord GOD will wipe away tears from all faces, and the reproach of his people he will take away from all the earth; for the LORD has spoken. 9 It will be said on that day, "Lo, this is our God; we have waited for him, that he might save us. This is the LORD; we have waited for him; let us be glad and rejoice in his salvation." 10 For the hand of the LORD will rest on this mountain, and Moab shall be trodden down in his place, as straw is 11 trodden down in a dung-pit. And he will spread out his hands in the midst of it as a swimmer spreads his hands out to swim; but the LORD will lay low his pride together 12 with the skill 1 of his hands. And the high fortifications of his walls he will bring down, lay low, and cast to the ground, even to the dust.

26 In that day this song will be sung in the land of Judah:
"We have a strong city;
  he sets up salvation
  as walls and bulwarks.
2 Open the gates,
  that the righteous nation which keeps faith
  may enter in.
3 Thou dost keep him in perfect peace,
  whose mind is stayed on thee,
  because he trusts in thee.
4 Trust in the LORD for ever,
  for the LORD GOD
  is an everlasting rock.
5 For he has brought low
  the inhabitants of the height,
  the lofty city.
He lays it low, lays it low to the ground,
  casts it to the dust.

6 The foot tramples it,
the feet of the poor,
the steps of the needy."

7 The way of the righteous is level;
thou[m] dost make smooth the path of the righteous.
8 In the path of thy judgments,
O LORD, we wait for thee;
thy memorial name
is the desire of our soul.
9 My soul yearns for thee in the night,
my spirit within me earnestly seeks thee.
For when thy judgments are in the earth,
the inhabitants of the world learn righteousness.
10 If favor is shown to the wicked,
he does not learn righteousness;
in the land of uprightness he deals perversely
and does not see the majesty of the LORD.
11 O LORD, thy hand is lifted up,
but they see it not.
Let them see thy zeal for thy people, and be ashamed.
Let the fire for thy adversaries consume them.
12 O LORD, thou wilt ordain peace for us,
thou hast wrought for us all our works.
13 O LORD our God,
other lords besides thee have ruled over us,
but thy name alone we acknowledge.
14 They are dead, they will not live;
they are shades, they will not arise;
to that end thou hast visited them with destruction
and wiped out all remembrance of them.
15 But thou hast increased the nation, O LORD,
thou hast increased the nation; thou art glorified;
thou hast enlarged all the borders of the land.

16 O LORD, in distress they sought thee,
they poured out a prayer[n]
when thy chastening was upon them.
17 Like a woman with child,
who writhes and cries out in her pangs,
when she is near her time,
so were we because of thee, O LORD;
18 we were with child, we writhed,
we have as it were brought forth wind.
We have wrought no deliverance in the earth,
and the inhabitants of the world have not fallen.
19 Thy dead shall live, their bodies[o] shall rise.
O dwellers in the dust, awake and sing for joy!
For thy dew is a dew of light,
and on the land of the shades thou wilt let it fall.

20 Come, my people, enter your chambers,
and shut your doors behind you;
hide yourselves for a little while
until the wrath is past.
21 For behold, the LORD is coming forth out of his place
to punish the inhabitants of the earth for their iniquity,
and the earth will disclose the blood shed upon her,
and will no more cover her slain.

27 In that day the LORD with his hard and great and
strong sword will punish Leviathan the fleeing
serpent, Leviathan the twisting serpent, and he will slay
the dragon that is in the sea.

2 In that day:
"A pleasant vineyard, sing of it!
3 I, the LORD, am its keeper;
every moment I water it.
Lest any one harm it,
I guard it night and day;
4 I have no wrath.
Would that I had thorns and briers to battle!
I would set out against them,
I would burn them up together.
5 Or let them lay hold of my protection,
let them make peace with me,
let them make peace with me."

6 In days to come[q] Jacob shall take root,
Israel shall blossom and put forth shoots,
and fill the whole world with fruit.

7 Has he smitten them as he smote those who smote them?
or have they been slain as their slayers were slain?
8 Measure by measure,[r] by exile thou didst contend with
them;
he removed them with his fierce blast in the day of the
east wind.
9 Therefore by this the guilt of Jacob will be expiated,
and this will be the full fruit of the removal of his sin:
when he makes all the stones of the altars
like chalkstones crushed to pieces,
no Ashe'rim or incense altars will remain standing.
10 For the fortified city is solitary,
a habitation deserted and forsaken, like the wilderness;
there the calf grazes,
there he lies down, and strips its branches.
11 When its boughs are dry, they are broken;
women come and make a fire of them.
For this is a people without discernment;
therefore he who made them will not have compassion
on them,
he that formed them will show them no favor.

12 In that day from the river Euphra'tes to the Brook of
Egypt the LORD will thresh out the grain, and you will be
13 gathered one by one, O people of Israel. And in that day

[m] Cn Compare Gk: Heb *thou (that art) upright* [n] Heb uncertain [o] Cn Compare Syr Tg: Heb *my body*
[q] Heb *Those to come* [r] Compare Syr Vg Tg: The meaning of the Hebrew word is unknown

a great trumpet will be blown, and those who were lost in the land of Assyria and those who were driven out to the land of Egypt will come and worship the LORD on the holy mountain at Jerusalem.

"BE NOT SCOFFERS"

28 Woe to the proud crown of the drunkards of E'phraim,
and to the fading flower of its glorious beauty,
which is on the head of the rich valley of those overcome with wine!
2 Behold, the Lord has one who is mighty and strong;
like a storm of hail, a destroying tempest,
like a storm of mighty, overflowing waters,
he will cast down to the earth with violence.
3 The proud crown of the drunkards of E'phraim
will be trodden under foot;
4 and the fading flower of its glorious beauty,
which is on the head of the rich valley,
will be like a first-ripe fig before the summer:
when a man sees it, he eats it up
as soon as it is in his hand.

5 In that day the LORD of hosts will be a crown of glory,
and a diadem of beauty, to the remnant of his people;
6 and a spirit of justice to him who sits in judgment,
and strength to those who turn back the battle at the gate.

7 These also reel with wine
and stagger with strong drink;
the priest and the prophet reel with strong drink,
they are confused with wine,
they stagger with strong drink;
they err in vision,
they stumble in giving judgment.
8 For all tables are full of vomit,
no place is without filthiness.

9 "Whom will he teach knowledge,
and to whom will he explain the message?
Those who are weaned from the milk,
those taken from the breast?
10 For it is precept upon precept, precept upon precept,
line upon line, line upon line,
here a little, there a little."

11 Nay, but by men of strange lips
and with an alien tongue
the LORD will speak to this people,
12 to whom he has said,
"This is rest;
give rest to the weary;
and this is repose";
yet they would not hear.

13 Therefore the word of the LORD will be to them
precept upon precept, precept upon precept,
line upon line, line upon line,
here a little, there a little;
that they may go, and fall backward,
and be broken, and snared, and taken.

14 Therefore hear the word of the LORD, you scoffers,
who rule this people in Jerusalem!
15 Because you have said, "We have made a covenant with death,
and with Sheol we have an agreement;
when the overwhelming scourge passes through
it will not come to us;
for we have made lies our refuge,
and in falsehood we have taken shelter";
16 therefore thus says the Lord GOD,
"Behold, I am laying in Zion for a foundation
a stone, a tested stone,
a precious cornerstone, of a sure foundation:
'He who believes will not be in haste.'
17 And I will make justice the line,
and righteousness the plummet;
and hail will sweep away the refuge of lies,
and waters will overwhelm the shelter."
18 Then your covenant with death will be annulled,
and your agreement with Sheol will not stand;
when the overwhelming scourge passes through
you will be beaten down by it.
19 As often as it passes through it will take you;
for morning by morning it will pass through,
by day and by night;
and it will be sheer terror to understand the message.
20 For the bed is too short to stretch oneself on it,
and the covering too narrow to wrap oneself in it.
21 For the LORD will rise up as on Mount Pera'zim,
he will be wroth as in the valley of Gibeon;
to do his deed—strange is his deed!
and to work his work—alien is his work!
22 Now therefore do not scoff,
lest your bonds be made strong;
for I have heard a decree of destruction
from the Lord GOD of hosts upon the whole land.

23 Give ear, and hear my voice;
hearken, and hear my speech.
24 Does he who plows for sowing plow continually?
does he continually open and harrow his ground?
25 When he has leveled its surface,
does he not scatter dill, sow cummin,
and put in wheat in rows
and barley in its proper place,
and spelt as the border?

26 For he is instructed aright;
   his God teaches him.

27 Dill is not threshed with a threshing sledge,
   nor is a cart wheel rolled over cummin;
but dill is beaten out with a stick,
   and cummin with a rod.
28 Does one crush bread grain?
   No, he does not thresh it for ever;
when he drives his cart wheel over it
with his horses, he does not crush it.
29 This also comes from the LORD of hosts;
   he is wonderful in counsel,
   and excellent in wisdom.

29 Ho Ariel, Ariel,
   the city where David encamped!
Add year to year;
   let the feasts run their round.
2 Yet I will distress Ariel,
   and there shall be moaning and lamentation,
   and she shall be to me like an Ariel.
3 And I will encamp against you round about,
   and will besiege you with towers
   and I will raise siegeworks against you.
4 Then deep from the earth you shall speak,
   from low in the dust your words shall come;
your voice shall come from the ground like the voice of a
      ghost,
   and your speech shall whisper out of the dust.

5 But the multitude of your foes⁵ shall be like small dust,
   and the multitude of the ruthless like passing chaff.
And in an instant, suddenly,
6   you will be visited by the LORD of hosts
with thunder and with earthquake and great noise,
   with whirlwind and tempest, and the flame of a devour-
      ing fire.
7 And the multitude of all the nations that fight against
      Ariel,
   all that fight against her and her stronghold and dis-
      tress her,
   shall be like a dream, a vision of the night.
8 As when a hungry man dreams he is eating

and awakes with his hunger not satisfied,
   or as when a thirsty man dreams he is drinking
   and awakes faint, with his thirst not quenched,
so shall the multitude of all the nations be
   that fight against Mount Zion.

9 Stupefy yourselves and be in a stupor,
   blind yourselves and be blind!
Be drunk, but not with wine;
   stagger, but not with strong drink!
10 For the LORD has poured out upon you
   a spirit of deep sleep,
and has closed your eyes, the prophets,
   and covered your heads, the seers.
11   And the vision of all this has become to you like the
words of a book that is sealed. When men give it to one
who can read, saying, "Read this," he says, "I cannot,
12 for it is sealed." And when they give the book to one who
cannot read, saying, "Read this," he says, "I cannot
read."

13 And the Lord said:
"Because this people draw near with their mouth
   and honor me with their lips,
   while their hearts are far from me,
and their fear of me is a commandment of men learned
      by rote;
14 therefore, behold, I will again
   do marvelous things with this people,
   wonderful and marvelous;
and the wisdom of their wise men shall perish,
   and the discernment of their discerning men shall be
      hid."

15 Woe to those who hide deep from the LORD their counsel,
   whose deeds are in the dark,
   and who say, "Who sees us? Who knows us?"
16 You turn things upside down!
   Shall the potter be regarded as the clay;
that the thing made should say of its maker,
   "He did not make me";
or the thing formed say of him who formed it,
   "He has no understanding"?

17 Is it not yet a very little while
   until Lebanon shall be turned into a fruitful field,
   and the fruitful field shall be regarded as a forest?
18 In that day the deaf shall hear
   the words of a book,
and out of their gloom and darkness
   the eyes of the blind shall see.
19 The meek shall obtain fresh joy in the LORD,
   and the poor among men shall exult in the Holy One
      of Israel.

⁵ Cn: Heb strangers

20 For the ruthless shall come to nought and the scoffer
cease,
and all who watch to do evil shall be cut off,
21 who by a word make a man out to be an offender,
and lay a snare for him who reproves in the gate,
and with an empty plea turn aside him who is in the
right.

22 Therefore thus says the LORD, who redeemed Abraham,
concerning the house of Jacob:
"Jacob shall no more be ashamed,
no more shall his face grow pale.
23 For when he sees his children,
the work of my hands, in his midst,
they will sanctify my name;
they will sanctify the Holy One of Jacob,
and will stand in awe of the God of Israel.
24 And those who err in spirit will come to understanding,
and those who murmur will accept instruction."

30 "Woe to the rebellious children," says the LORD,
"who carry out a plan, but not mine;
and who make a league, but not of my spirit,
that they may add sin to sin;
2 who set out to go down to Egypt,
without asking for my counsel,
to take refuge in the protection of Pharaoh,
and to seek shelter in the shadow of Egypt!
3 Therefore shall the protection of Pharaoh turn to your
shame,
and the shelter in the shadow of Egypt to your humiliation.
4 For though his officials are at Zo'an
and his envoys reach Ha'nes,
5 every one comes to shame
through a people that cannot profit them,
that brings neither help nor profit,
but shame and disgrace."

6 An oracle on the beasts of the Negeb.
Through a land of trouble and anguish,
from where come the lioness and the lion,
the viper and the flying serpent,
they carry their riches on the backs of asses,
and their treasures on the humps of camels,
to a people that cannot profit them.
7 For Egypt's help is worthless and empty,
therefore I have called her
"Rahab who sits still."

8 And now, go, write it before them on a tablet,
and inscribe it in a book,
that it may be for the time to come
as a witness for ever.

9 For they are a rebellious people,
lying sons,
sons who will not hear
the instruction of the LORD;
10 who say to the seers, "See not";
and to the prophets, "Prophesy not to us what is right;
speak to us smooth things,
prophesy illusions,
11 leave the way, turn aside from the path,
let us hear no more of the Holy One of Israel."
12 Therefore thus says the Holy One of Israel,
"Because you despise this word,
and trust in oppression and perverseness,
and rely on them;
13 therefore this iniquity shall be to you
like a break in a high wall, bulging out, and about to
collapse,
whose crash comes suddenly, in an instant;
14 and its breaking is like that of a potter's vessel
which is smashed so ruthlessly
that among its fragments not a sherd is found
with which to take fire from the hearth,
or to dip up water out of the cistern."

15 For thus said the Lord GOD, the Holy One of Israel,
"In returning and rest you shall be saved;
in quietness and in trust shall be your strength."
16 And you would not, but you said,
"No! We will speed upon horses,"
therefore you shall speed away;
and, "We will ride upon swift steeds,"
therefore your pursuers shall be swift.
17 A thousand shall flee at the threat of one,
at the threat of five you shall flee,
till you are left
like a flagstaff on the top of a mountain,
like a signal on a hill.
18 Therefore the LORD waits to be gracious to you;
therefore he exalts himself to show mercy to you.
For the LORD is a God of justice;
blessed are all those who wait for him.
19 Yea, O people in Zion who dwell at Jerusalem; you
shall weep no more. He will surely be gracious to you at
the sound of your cry; when he hears it, he will answer
20 you. And though the Lord give you the bread of adversity and the water of affliction, yet your Teacher will not
hide himself any more, but your eyes shall see your
21 Teacher. And your ears shall hear a word behind you,
saying, "This is the way, walk in it," when you turn to
22 the right or when you turn to the left. Then you will
defile your silver-covered graven images and your gold-
plated molten images. You will scatter them as unclean
things; you will say to them, "Begone!"

23 And he will give rain for the seed with which you sow the ground, and grain, the produce of the ground, which will be rich and plenteous. In that day your cattle will 24 graze in large pastures; and the oxen and the asses that till the ground will eat salted provender, which has been 25 winnowed with shovel and fork. And upon every lofty mountain and every high hill there will be brooks running with water, in the day of the great slaughter, when 26 the towers fall. Moreover the light of the moon will be as the light of the sun, and the light of the sun will be sevenfold, as the light of seven days, in the day when the LORD binds up the hurt of his people, and heals the wounds inflicted by his blow.

27 Behold, the name of the LORD comes from far,
   burning with his anger, and in thick rising smoke;
 his lips are full of indignation,
   and his tongue is like a devouring fire;
28 his breath is like an overflowing stream
   that reaches up to the neck;
 to sift the nations with the sieve of destruction,
   and to place on the jaws of the peoples a bridle that
     leads astray.

29 You shall have a song as in the night when a holy feast is kept; and gladness of heart, as when one sets out to the sound of the flute to go to the mountain of the 30 LORD, to the Rock of Israel. And the LORD will cause his majestic voice to be heard and the descending blow of his arm to be seen, in furious anger and a flame of devouring fire, with a cloudburst and tempest and hailstones. 31 The Assyrians will be terror-stricken at the voice of the 32 LORD, when he smites with his rod. And every stroke of the staff of punishment which the LORD lays upon them will be to the sound of timbrels and lyres; battling with 33 brandished arm he will fight with them. For a burning place^t has long been prepared; yea, for the king^u it is made ready, its pyre made deep and wide, with fire and wood in abundance; the breath of the LORD, like a stream of brimstone, kindles it.

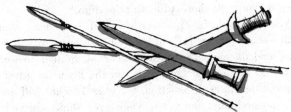

31 Woe to those who go down to Egypt for help
     and rely on horses,
 who trust in chariots because they are many
     and in horsemen because they are very strong,
 but do not look to the Holy One of Israel
     or consult the LORD!

2 And yet he is wise and brings disaster,
   he does not call back his words,
 but will arise against the house of the evildoers,
   and against the helpers of those who work iniquity.
3 The Egyptians are men, and not God;
   and their horses are flesh, and not spirit.
 When the LORD stretches out his hand,
   the helper will stumble, and he who is helped will fall,
   and they will all perish together.

4 For thus the LORD said to me,
 As a lion or a young lion growls over his prey,
   and when a band of shepherds is called forth against
     him
 is not terrified by their shouting
   or daunted at their noise,
 so the LORD of hosts will come down
   to fight upon Mount Zion and upon its hill.
5 Like birds hovering, so the LORD of hosts
   will protect Jerusalem;
 he will protect and deliver it,
   he will spare and rescue it.

6 Turn to him from whom you^v have deeply revolted, 7 O people of Israel. For in that day every one shall cast away his idols of silver and his idols of gold, which your hands have sinfully made for you. 8 "And the Assyrian shall fall by a sword, not of man; and a sword, not of man, shall devour him; and he shall flee from the sword, and his young men shall be put to forced labor. 9 His rock shall pass away in terror, and his officers desert the standard in panic," says the LORD, whose fire is in Zion, and whose furnace is in Jerusalem.

32 Behold, a king will reign in righteousness,
     and princes will rule in justice.
2 Each will be like a hiding place from the wind,
   a covert from the tempest,
 like streams of water in a dry place,
   like the shade of a great rock in a weary land.
3 Then the eyes of those who see will not be closed,
   and the ears of those who hear will hearken.
4 The mind of the rash will have good judgment,
   and the tongue of the stammerers will speak readily
     and distinctly.
5 The fool will no more be called noble,
   nor the knave said to be honorable.
6 For the fool speaks folly,
   and his mind plots iniquity:
 to practice ungodliness,
   to utter error concerning the LORD,
 to leave the craving of the hungry unsatisfied,

^t Or *Topheth*   ^u Or *Molech*   ^v Heb *they*

and to deprive the thirsty of drink.
7 The knaveries of the knave are evil;
   he devises wicked devices
to ruin the poor with lying words,
   even when the plea of the needy is right.
8 But he who is noble devises noble things,
   and by noble things he stands.

9 Rise up, you women who are at ease, hear my voice;
   you complacent daughters, give ear to my speech.
10 In little more than a year
   you will shudder, you complacent women;

for the vintage will fail,
   the fruit harvest will not come.
11 Tremble, you women who are at ease,
   shudder, you complacent ones;
strip, and make yourselves bare,
   and gird sackcloth upon your loins.
12 Beat upon your breasts for the pleasant fields,
   for the fruitful vine,
13 for the soil of my people
   growing up in thorns and briers;
yea, for all the joyous houses
   in the joyful city.
14 For the palace will be forsaken,
   the populous city deserted;
the hill and the watchtower
   will become dens for ever,
a joy of wild asses,
   a pasture of flocks;
15 until the Spirit is poured upon us from on high,
   and the wilderness becomes a fruitful field,
   and the fruitful field is deemed a forest.
16 Then justice will dwell in the wilderness,
   and righteousness abide in the fruitful field.
17 And the effect of righteousness will be peace,
   and the result of righteousness, quietness and trust for
      ever.
18 My people will abide in a peaceful habitation,
   in secure dwellings, and in quiet resting places.
19 And the forest will utterly go down,w
   and the city will be utterly laid low.
20 Happy are you who sow beside all waters,
   who let the feet of the ox and the ass range free.

w Cn: Heb *And it will hail when the forest comes down*
z One ancient Ms: Heb *cities*

"THE RECOMPENSE OF GOD"

33 Woe to you, destroyer,
      who yourself have not been destroyed;
   you treacherous one,
      with whom none has dealt treacherously!
   When you have ceased to destroy,
      you will be destroyed;
   and when you have made an end of dealing treacher-
         ously,
      you will be dealt with treacherously.

2 O LORD, be gracious to us; we wait for thee.
   Be our arm every morning,
      our salvation in the time of trouble.
3 At the thunderous noise peoples flee,
   at the lifting up of thyself nations are scattered;
4 and spoil is gathered as the caterpillar gathers;
   as locusts leap, men leap upon it.

5 The LORD is exalted, for he dwells on high;
   he will fill Zion with justice and righteousness;
6 and he will be the stability of your times,
   abundance of salvation, wisdom, and knowledge;
   the fear of the LORD is his treasure.

7 Behold, the valiant onesy cry without;
   the envoys of peace weep bitterly.
8 The highways lie waste,
   the wayfaring man ceases.
Covenants are broken,
   witnessesz are despised,
   there is no regard for man.
9 The land mourns and languishes;
   Lebanon is confounded and withers away;
Sharon is like a desert;
   and Bashan and Carmel shake off their leaves.

10 "Now I will arise," says the LORD,
   "now I will lift myself up;
   now I will be exalted.
11 You conceive chaff, you bring forth stubble;
   your breath is a fire that will consume you.
12 And the peoples will be as if burned to lime,
   like thorns cut down, that are burned in the fire."

13 Hear, you who are far off, what I have done;
   and you who are near, acknowledge my might.
14 The sinners in Zion are afraid;
   trembling has seized the godless:
"Who among us can dwell with the devouring fire?
   Who among us can dwell with everlasting burnings?"
15 He who walks righteously and speaks uprightly,
   who despises the gain of oppressions,
who shakes his hands, lest they hold a bribe,
   who stops his ears from hearing of bloodshed

y The meaning of the Hebrew word is uncertain

and shuts his eyes from looking upon evil,
¹⁶ he will dwell on the heights;
    his place of defense will be the fortresses of rocks;
    his bread will be given him, his water will be sure.

¹⁷ Your eyes will see the king in his beauty;
    they will behold a land that stretches afar.
¹⁸ Your mind will muse on the terror:
    "Where is he who counted, where is he who weighed
        the tribute?
    Where is he who counted the towers?"
¹⁹ You will see no more the insolent people,
    the people of an obscure speech which you cannot
        comprehend,
    stammering in a tongue which you cannot understand.
²⁰ Look upon Zion, the city of our appointed feasts!
    Your eyes will see Jerusalem,
    a quiet habitation, an immovable tent,
    whose stakes will never be plucked up,
    nor will any of its cords be broken.
²¹ But there the LORD in majesty will be for us
    a place of broad rivers and streams,
    where no galley with oars can go,
    nor stately ship can pass.
²² For the LORD is our judge, the LORD is our ruler,
    the LORD is our king; he will save us.

²³ Your tackle hangs loose;
    it cannot hold the mast firm in its place,
    or keep the sail spread out.

Then prey and spoil in abundance will be divided;
    even the lame will take the prey.
²⁴ And no inhabitant will say, "I am sick";
    the people who dwell there will be forgiven their
        iniquity.

34 Draw near, O nations, to hear,
    and hearken, O peoples!
Let the earth listen, and all that fills it;
    the world, and all that comes from it.
² For the LORD is enraged against all the nations,
    and furious against all their host,
    he has doomed them, has given them over for slaughter.
³ Their slain shall be cast out,
    and the stench of their corpses shall rise;
    the mountains shall flow with their blood.

⁴ All the host of heaven shall rot away,
    and the skies roll up like a scroll.
All their host shall fall,
    as leaves fall from the vine,
    like leaves falling from the fig tree.

⁵ For my sword has drunk its fill in the heavens;
    behold, it descends for judgment upon Edom,
    upon the people I have doomed.
⁶ The LORD has a sword; it is sated with blood,
    it is gorged with fat,
    with the blood of lambs and goats,
    with the fat of the kidneys of rams.
For the LORD has a sacrifice in Bozrah,
    a great slaughter in the land of Edom.
⁷ Wild oxen shall fall with them,
    and young steers with the mighty bulls.
Their land shall be soaked with blood,
    and their soil made rich with fat.

⁸ For the LORD has a day of vengeance,
    a year of recompense for the cause of Zion.
⁹ And the streams of Edom[a] shall be turned into pitch,
    and her soil into brimstone;
    her land shall become burning pitch.
¹⁰ Night and day it shall not be quenched;
    its smoke shall go up for ever.
From generation to generation it shall lie waste;
    none shall pass through it for ever and ever.
¹¹ But the hawk and the porcupine shall possess it,
    the owl and the raven shall dwell in it.
He shall stretch the line of confusion over it,
    and the plummet of chaos over[b] its nobles.
¹² They shall name it No Kingdom There,
    and all its princes shall be nothing.

¹³ Thorns shall grow over its strongholds,
    nettles and thistles in its fortresses.
It shall be the haunt of jackals,
    an abode for ostriches.
¹⁴ And wild beasts shall meet with hyenas,
    the satyr shall cry to his fellow;
    yea, there shall the night hag alight,
    and find for herself a resting place.

¹⁵ There shall the owl nest and lay
    and hatch and gather her young in her shadow;
    yea, there shall the kites be gathered,
    each one with her mate.
¹⁶ Seek and read from the book of the LORD:
    Not one of these shall be missing;
    none shall be without her mate.
For the mouth of the LORD has commanded,
    and his Spirit has gathered them.

^a Heb *her streams*   ^b Heb lacks *over*

[17] He has cast the lot for them,
  his hand has portioned it out to them with the line;
they shall possess it for ever,
  from generation to generation they shall dwell in it.

35 The wilderness and the dry land shall be glad,
  the desert shall rejoice and blossom;
[2] like the crocus it shall blossom abundantly,
  and rejoice with joy and singing.
The glory of Lebanon shall be given to it,
  the majesty of Carmel and Sharon.
They shall see the glory of the LORD,
  the majesty of our God.

[3] Strengthen the weak hands,
  and make firm the feeble knees.
[4] Say to those who are of a fearful heart,
  "Be strong, fear not!
Behold, your God
  will come with vengeance,
with the recompense of God.
  He will come and save you."

[5] Then the eyes of the blind shall be opened,
  and the ears of the deaf unstopped;
[6] then shall the lame man leap like a hart,
  and the tongue of the dumb sing for joy.
For waters shall break forth in the wilderness,
  and streams in the desert;
[7] the burning sand shall become a pool,
  and the thirsty ground springs of water;
the haunt of jackals shall become a swamp,[c]
  the grass shall become reeds and rushes.

[8] And a highway shall be there,
  and it shall be called the Holy Way;
the unclean shall not pass over it,[d]
  and fools shall not err therein.
[9] No lion shall be there,
  nor shall any ravenous beast come up on it;
they shall not be found there,
  but the redeemed shall walk there.
[10] And the ransomed of the LORD shall return,
  and come to Zion with singing;
everlasting joy shall be upon their heads;
  they shall obtain joy and gladness,
  and sorrow and sighing shall flee away.

ISAIAH AND HEZEKIAH

36 In the fourteenth year of King Hezeki'ah, Sennach'erib king of Assyria came up against all the [2] fortified cities of Judah and took them. And the king of Assyria sent the Rab'shakeh from Lachish to King Hezeki'ah at Jerusalem, with a great army. And he stood by the conduit of the upper pool on the highway to the [3] Fuller's Field. And there came out to him Eli'akim the son of Hilki'ah, who was over the household, and Shebna the secretary, and Jo'ah the son of Asaph, the recorder.

[4] And the Rab'shakeh said to them, "Say to Hezeki'ah, 'Thus says the great king, the king of Assyria: On what [5] do you rest this confidence of yours? Do you think that mere words are strategy and power for war? On whom do you now rely, that you have rebelled against me? [6] Behold, you are relying on Egypt, that broken reed of a staff, which will pierce the hand of any man who leans on it. Such is Pharaoh king of Egypt to all who rely on [7] him. But if you say to me, "We rely on the LORD our God," is it not he whose high places and altars Hezeki'ah has removed, saying to Judah and to Jerusalem, [8] "You shall worship before this altar"? Come now, make a wager with my master the king of Assyria: I will give you two thousand horses, if you are able on your part to [9] set riders upon them. How then can you repulse a single captain among the least of my master's servants, when [10] you rely on Egypt for chariots and for horsemen? Moreover, is it without the LORD that I have come up against this land to destroy it? The LORD said to me, Go up against this land, and destroy it.' "

[11] Then Eli'akim, Shebna, and Jo'ah said to the Rab'shakeh, "Pray, speak to your servants in Aramaic, for we understand it; do not speak to us in the language of Judah within the hearing of the people who are on the [12] wall." But the Rab'shakeh said, "Has my master sent me to speak these words to your master and to you, and not to the men sitting on the wall, who are doomed with you to eat their own dung and drink their own urine?"

[13] Then the Rab'shakeh stood and called out in a loud voice in the language of Judah: "Hear the words of the [14] great king, the king of Assyria! Thus says the king: 'Do not let Hezeki'ah deceive you, for he will not be able to [15] deliver you. Do not let Hezeki'ah make you rely on the LORD by saying, "The LORD will surely deliver us; this city will not be given into the hand of the king of As-[16] syria." Do not listen to Hezeki'ah; for thus says the king of Assyria: Make your peace with me and come out to me; then every one of you will eat of his own vine, and every one of his own fig tree, and every one of you will [17] drink the water of his own cistern; until I come and take you away to a land like your own land, a land of [18] grain and wine, a land of bread and vineyards. Beware lest Hezeki'ah mislead you by saying, "The LORD will deliver us." Has any of the gods of the nations delivered [19] his land out of the hand of the king of Assyria? Where are the gods of Hamath and Arpad? Where are the gods of Sepharva'im? Have they delivered Samar'ia out of my [20] hand? Who among all the gods of these countries have delivered their countries out of my hand, that the LORD

---

[c] Cn: Heb *in the haunt of jackals is her resting place*   [d] Heb *it and he is for them a wayfarer*

should deliver Jerusalem out of my hand?'"

21 But they were silent and answered him not a word, for
22 the king's command was, "Do not answer him." Then Eli'akim the son of Hilki'ah, who was over the household, and Shebna the secretary, and Jo'ah the son of Asaph, the recorder, came to Hezeki'ah with their clothes rent, and told him the words of the Rab'shakeh.

37 When King Hezeki'ah heard it, he rent his clothes, and covered himself with sackcloth, and went into
2 the house of the LORD. And he sent Eli'akim, who was over the household, and Shebna the secretary, and the senior priests, clothed with sackcloth, to the prophet
3 Isaiah the son of Amoz. They said to him, "Thus says Hezeki'ah, 'This day is a day of distress, of rebuke, and of disgrace; children have come to the birth, and there
4 is no strength to bring them forth. It may be that the LORD your God heard the words of the Rab'shakeh, whom his master the king of Assyria has sent to mock the living God, and will rebuke the words which the LORD your God has heard; therefore lift up your prayer for the remnant that is left.'"
5 When the servants of King Hezeki'ah came to Isaiah,
6 Isaiah said to them, "Say to your master, 'Thus says the LORD: Do not be afraid because of the words that you have heard, with which the servants of the king of As-
7 syria have reviled me. Behold, I will put a spirit in him, so that he shall hear a rumor, and return to his own land; and I will make him fall by the sword in his own land.'"
8 The Rab'shakeh returned, and found the king of Assyria fighting against Libnah; for he had heard that the
9 king had left Lachish. Now the king heard concerning Tirha'kah king of Ethiopia, "He has set out to fight against you." And when he heard it, he sent messengers
10 to Hezeki'ah saying, "Thus shall you speak to Hezeki'ah king of Judah: 'Do not let your God on whom you rely deceive you by promising that Jerusalem will not be given
11 into the hand of the king of Assyria. Behold, you have heard what the kings of Assyria have done to all lands, destroying them utterly. And shall you be delivered?
12 Have the gods of the nations delivered them, the nations which my fathers destroyed, Gozan, Haran, Rezeph, and
13 the people of Eden who were in Telas'sar? Where is the king of Hamath, the king of Arpad, the king of the city of Sepharva'im, the king of Hena, or the king of Ivvah?'"

Hezekiah's Prayer

14 Hezeki'ah received the letter from the hand of the messengers, and read it; and Hezeki'ah went up to the house of the LORD, and spread it before the LORD.
15, 16 And Hezeki'ah prayed to the LORD: "O LORD of hosts, God of Israel, who art enthroned above the cherubim, thou art the God, thou alone, of all the kingdoms of the
17 earth; thou hast made heaven and earth. Incline thy ear,

O LORD, and hear; open thy eyes, O LORD, and see; and hear all the words of Sennach'erib, which he has sent to
18 mock the living God. Of a truth, O LORD, the kings of Assyria have laid waste all the nations and their lands,
19 and have cast their gods into the fire; for they were no gods, but the work of men's hands, wood and stone;
20 therefore they were destroyed. So now, O LORD our God, save us from his hand, that all the kingdoms of the earth may know that thou alone art the LORD."
21 Then Isaiah the son of Amoz sent to Hezeki'ah, saying, "Thus says the LORD, the God of Israel: Because you have prayed to me concerning Sennach'erib king of
22 Assyria, this is the word that the LORD has spoken concerning him:

'She despises you, she scorns you—
  the virgin daughter of Zion;
she wags her head behind you—
  the daughter of Jerusalem.

23 'Whom have you mocked and reviled?
  Against whom have you raised your voice
and haughtily lifted your eyes?
  Against the Holy One of Israel!
24 By your servants you have mocked the Lord,
  and you have said, With my many chariots
I have gone up the heights of the mountains,
  to the far recesses of Lebanon;
I felled its tallest cedars,
  its choicest cypresses;
I came to its remotest height,
  its densest forest.
25 I dug wells
  and drank waters,
and I dried up with the sole of my foot
  all the streams of Egypt.

26 'Have you not heard
  that I determined it long ago?
I planned from days of old
  what now I bring to pass,
that you should make fortified cities
  crash into heaps of ruins,
27 while their inhabitants, shorn of strength,
  are dismayed and confounded,
and have become like plants of the field
  and like tender grass,
like grass on the housetops,
  blighted e before it is grown.

28 'I know your sitting down
  and your going out and coming in,
  and your raging against me.
29 Because you have raged against me
  and your arrogance has come to my ears,

e With 2 K 19.26: Heb field

I will put my hook in your nose
  and my bit in your mouth,
and I will turn you back on the way
  by which you came.'

30 "And this shall be the sign for you: this year eat what grows of itself, and in the second year what springs of the same; then in the third year sow and reap, and plant 31 vineyards, and eat their fruit. And the surviving remnant of the house of Judah shall again take root downward, and 32 bear fruit upward; for out of Jerusalem shall go forth a remnant, and out of Mount Zion a band of survivors. The zeal of the LORD of hosts will accomplish this.

33 "Therefore thus says the LORD concerning the king of Assyria: He shall not come into this city, or shoot an arrow there, or come before it with a shield, or cast up 34 a siege mound against it. By the way that he came, by the same he shall return, and he shall not come into this 35 city, says the LORD. For I will defend this city to save it, for my own sake and for the sake of my servant David."

36 And the angel of the LORD went forth, and slew a hundred and eighty-five thousand in the camp of the Assyrians; and when men arose early in the morning, 37 behold, these were all dead bodies. Then Sennach'erib king of Assyria departed, and went home and dwelt at 38 Nin'eveh. And as he was worshiping in the house of Nisroch his god, Adram'melech and Share'zer, his sons, slew him with the sword, and escaped into the land of Ararat. And E'sar-had'don his son reigned in his stead.

Hezekiah's Sickness

38 In those days Hezeki'ah became sick and was at the point of death. And Isaiah the prophet the son of Amoz came to him, and said to him, "Thus says the

LORD: Set your house in order; for you shall die, you shall 2 not recover." Then Hezeki'ah turned his face to the wall, 3 and prayed to the LORD, and said, "Remember now, O LORD, I beseech thee, how I have walked before thee in faithfulness and with a whole heart, and have done what is good in thy sight." And Hezeki'ah wept bitterly. 4, 5 Then the word of the LORD came to Isaiah: "Go and say to Hezeki'ah, Thus says the LORD, the God of David your father: I have heard your prayer, I have seen your tears; 6 behold, I will add fifteen years to your life. I will deliver you and this city out of the hand of the king of Assyria, and defend this city.

7 "This is the sign to you from the LORD, that the LORD 8 will do this thing that he has promised: Behold, I will make the shadow cast by the declining sun on the dial of Ahaz turn back ten steps." So the sun turned back on the dial the ten steps by which it had declined.[f]

Hymn of Thanksgiving

9 A writing of Hezeki'ah king of Judah, after he had been sick and had recovered from his sickness:

10 I said, In the noontide of my days I must depart;
  I am consigned to the gates of Sheol for the rest of my
    years.
11 I said, I shall not see the LORD
  in the land of the living;
I shall look upon man no more
  among the inhabitants of the world.
12 My dwelling is plucked up and removed from me
  like a shepherd's tent;
like a weaver I have rolled up my life;
  he cuts me off from the loom;
from day to night thou dost bring me to an end;[g]
13   I cry for help[h] until morning;
like a lion he breaks all my bones;
  from day to night thou dost bring me to an end.[g]

14 Like a swallow or a crane[i] I clamor,
  I moan like a dove.
My eyes are weary with looking upward.
  O Lord, I am oppressed; be thou my security!
15 But what can I say? For he has spoken to me,
  and he himself has done it.
All my sleep has fled[j]
  because of the bitterness of my soul.

16 O Lord, by these things men live,
  and in all these is the life of my spirit.[k]
Oh, restore me to health and make me live!
17 Lo, it was for my welfare
  that I had great bitterness;
but thou hast held back[l] my life
  from the pit of destruction,
for thou hast cast all my sins
  behind thy back.
18 For Sheol cannot thank thee,
  death cannot praise thee;
those who go down to the pit cannot hope
  for thy faithfulness.
19 The living, the living, he thanks thee,
  as I do this day;
the father makes known to the children
  thy faithfulness.

20 The LORD will save me,
  and we will sing to stringed instruments[m]

f The Hebrew of this verse is obscure   g Heb uncertain   h Cn: Heb obscure   i Heb uncertain
j Cn Compare Syr: Heb *I will walk slowly all my years*   k Heb uncertain   l Cn Compare Gk Vg: Heb *loved*
m Heb *my stringed instruments*

all the days of our life,
at the house of the LORD.

21 Now Isaiah had said, "Let them take a cake of figs,
22 and apply it to the boil, that he may recover." Hezeki'ah
also had said, "What is the sign that I shall go up to the
house of the LORD?"

39 At that time Mer'odach-bal'adan the son of Bal'-
adan, king of Babylon, sent envoys with letters and
a present to Hezeki'ah, for he heard that he had been sick
2 and had recovered. And Hezeki'ah welcomed them; and he
showed them his treasure house, the silver, the gold, the
spices, the precious oil, his whole armory, all that was
found in his storehouses. There was nothing in his house
or in all his realm that Hezeki'ah did not show them.
3 Then Isaiah the prophet came to King Hezeki'ah, and said
to him, "What did these men say? And whence did they
come to you?" Hezeki'ah said, "They have come to me
4 from a far country, from Babylon." He said, "What have
they seen in your house?" Hezeki'ah answered, "They
have seen all that is in my house; there is nothing in my
storehouses that I did not show them."
5 Then Isaiah said to Hezeki'ah, "Hear the word of the
6 LORD of hosts: Behold, the days are coming, when all
that is in your house, and that which your fathers have
stored up till this day, shall be carried to Babylon;
7 nothing shall be left, says the LORD. And some of your own
sons, who are born to you, shall be taken away; and they
shall be eunuchs in the palace of the king of Babylon."
8 Then said Hezeki'ah to Isaiah, "The word of the LORD
which you have spoken is good." For he thought, "There
will be peace and security in my days."

THE COMING OF THE LORD

40 Comfort, comfort my people,
says your God.
2 Speak tenderly to Jerusalem,
and cry to her
that her warfare[n] is ended,
that her iniquity is pardoned,
that she has received from the LORD's hand
double for all her sins.

3 A voice cries:
"In the wilderness prepare the way of the LORD,
make straight in the desert a highway for our God.
4 Every valley shall be lifted up,
and every mountain and hill be made low;
the uneven ground shall become level,
and the rough places a plain.
5 And the glory of the LORD shall be revealed,
and all flesh shall see it together,
for the mouth of the LORD has spoken."

6 A voice says, "Cry!"
And I said, "What shall I cry?"
All flesh is grass,
and all its beauty is like the flower of the field.
7 The grass withers, the flower fades,
when the breath of the LORD blows upon it;
surely the people is grass.
8 The grass withers, the flower fades;
but the word of our God will stand for ever.

9 Get you up to a high mountain,
O Zion, herald of good tidings,[o]
lift up your voice with strength,
O Jerusalem, herald of good tidings,[p]
lift it up, fear not;
say to the cities of Judah,
"Behold your God!"
10 Behold, the Lord GOD comes with might,
and his arm rules for him;
behold, his reward is with him,
and his recompense before him.
11 He will feed his flock like a shepherd,
he will gather the lambs in his arms,
he will carry them in his bosom,
and gently lead those that are with young.

The Creator

12 Who has measured the waters in the hollow of his hand
and marked off the heavens with a span,
enclosed the dust of the earth in a measure
and weighed the mountains in scales
and the hills in a balance?
13 Who has directed the Spirit of the LORD,
or as his counselor has instructed him?
14 Whom did he consult for his enlightenment,
and who taught him the path of justice,
and taught him knowledge,
and showed him the way of understanding?
15 Behold, the nations are like a drop from a bucket,
and are accounted as the dust on the scales;
behold, he takes up the isles like fine dust.
16 Lebanon would not suffice for fuel,
nor are its beasts enough for a burnt offering.
17 All the nations are as nothing before him,
they are accounted by him as less than nothing and
emptiness.

18 To whom then will you liken God,
or what likeness compare with him?
19 The idol! a workman casts it,
and a goldsmith overlays it with gold,
and casts for it silver chains.
20 He who is impoverished[q] chooses for an offering
wood that will not rot;

[n] Or *time of service*
[o] Or *O herald of good tidings to Zion*
[p] Or *O herald of good tidings to Jerusalem*
[q] Heb uncertain

he seeks out a skilful craftsman
to set up an image that will not move.

²¹ Have you not known? Have you not heard?
Has it not been told you from the beginning?
Have you not understood from the foundations of the
earth?
²² It is he who sits above the circle of the earth,
and its inhabitants are like grasshoppers;
who stretches out the heavens like a curtain,
and spreads them like a tent to dwell in;
²³ who brings princes to nought,
and makes the rulers of the earth as nothing.

²⁴ Scarcely are they planted, scarcely sown,
scarcely has their stem taken root in the earth,
when he blows upon them, and they wither,
and the tempest carries them off like stubble.

²⁵ To whom then will you compare me,
that I should be like him? says the Holy One.
²⁶ Lift up your eyes on high and see:
who created these?
He who brings out their host by number,
calling them all by name;
by the greatness of his might,
and because he is strong in power
not one is missing.

²⁷ Why do you say, O Jacob,
and speak, O Israel,
"My way is hid from the LORD,
and my right is disregarded by my God"?
²⁸ Have you not known? Have you not heard?
The LORD is the everlasting God,
the Creator of the ends of the earth.
He does not faint or grow weary,
his understanding is unsearchable.

²⁹ He gives power to the faint,
and to him who has no might he increases strength.
³⁰ Even youths shall faint and be weary,
and young men shall fall exhausted;
³¹ but they who wait for the LORD shall renew their strength,
they shall mount up with wings like eagles,
they shall run and not be weary,
they shall walk and not faint.

The Trial of the Nations

⁴¹ Listen to me in silence, O coastlands;
let the peoples renew their strength;
let them approach, then let them speak;
let us together draw near for judgment.

² Who stirred up one from the east
whom victory meets at every step?
He gives up nations before him,
so that he tramples kings under foot;
he makes them like dust with his sword,
like driven stubble with his bow.
³ He pursues them and passes on safely,
by paths his feet have not trod.
⁴ Who has performed and done this,
calling the generations from the beginning?
I, the LORD, the first,
and with the last; I am He.

⁵ The coastlands have seen and are afraid,
the ends of the earth tremble;
they have drawn near and come.
⁶ Every one helps his neighbor,
and says to his brother, "Take courage!"
⁷ The craftsman encourages the goldsmith,
and he who smooths with the hammer him who strikes
the anvil,
saying of the soldering, "It is good";
and they fasten it with nails so that it cannot be moved.

⁸ But you, Israel, my servant,
Jacob, whom I have chosen,
the offspring of Abraham, my friend;
⁹ you whom I took from the ends of the earth,
and called from its farthest corners,
saying to you, "You are my servant,
I have chosen you and not cast you off";
¹⁰ fear not, for I am with you,
be not dismayed, for I am your God;
I will strengthen you, I will help you,
I will uphold you with my victorious right hand.

¹¹ Behold, all who are incensed against you
shall be put to shame and confounded;
those who strive against you
shall be as nothing and shall perish.
¹² You shall seek those who contend with you,
but you shall not find them;
those who war against you
shall be as nothing at all.
¹³ For I, the LORD your God,
hold your right hand;
it is I who say to you, "Fear not,
I will help you."

14 Fear not, you worm Jacob,
  you men of Israel!
 I will help you, says the LORD;
  your Redeemer is the Holy One of Israel.
15 Behold, I will make of you a threshing sledge,
  new, sharp, and having teeth;
 you shall thresh the mountains and crush them,
  and you shall make the hills like chaff;
16 you shall winnow them and the wind shall carry them
    away,
  and the tempest shall scatter them.
 And you shall rejoice in the LORD;
  in the Holy One of Israel you shall glory.

17 When the poor and needy seek water,
  and there is none,
  and their tongue is parched with thirst,
 I the LORD will answer them,
  I the God of Israel will not forsake them.
18 I will open rivers on the bare heights,
  and fountains in the midst of the valleys;
 I will make the wilderness a pool of water,
  and the dry land springs of water.
19 I will put in the wilderness the cedar,
  the acacia, the myrtle, and the olive;
 I will set in the desert the cypress,
  the plane and the pine together;
20 that men may see and know,
  may consider and understand together,
 that the hand of the LORD has done this,
  the Holy One of Israel has created it.

21 Set forth your case, says the LORD;
  bring your proofs, says the King of Jacob.
22 Let them bring them, and tell us
  what is to happen.
 Tell us the former things, what they are,
  that we may consider them,
 that we may know their outcome;
  or declare to us the things to come.
23 Tell us what is to come hereafter,
  that we may know that you are gods;
 do good, or do harm,
  that we may be dismayed and terrified.
24 Behold, you are nothing,
  and your work is nought;
  an abomination is he who chooses you.

25 I stirred up one from the north, and he has come,
  from the rising of the sun, and he shall call on my
    name;
 he shall trample ʳ on rulers as on mortar,
  as the potter treads clay.
26 Who declared it from the beginning, that we might know,

and beforetime, that we might say, "He is right"?
 There was none who declared it, none who proclaimed,
  none who heard your words.
27 I first have declared it to Zion,ˢ
  and I give to Jerusalem a herald of good tidings.
28 But when I look there is no one;
  among these there is no counselor
  who, when I ask, gives an answer.
29 Behold, they are all a delusion;
  their works are nothing;
  their molten images are empty wind.

42 Behold my servant, whom I uphold,
   my chosen, in whom my soul delights;
 I have put my Spirit upon him,
  he will bring forth justice to the nations.
2 He will not cry or lift up his voice,
  or make it heard in the street;
3 a bruised reed he will not break,
  and a dimly burning wick he will not quench;
  he will faithfully bring forth justice.
4 He will not fail ᵗ or be discouraged ᵘ
  till he has established justice in the earth;
  and the coastlands wait for his law.

5 Thus says God, the LORD,
  who created the heavens and stretched them out,
  who spread forth the earth and what comes from it,
 who gives breath to the people upon it
  and spirit to those who walk in it:
6 "I am the LORD, I have called you in righteousness,
  I have taken you by the hand and kept you;
 I have given you as a covenant to the people,
  a light to the nations,
7 to open the eyes that are blind,
 to bring out the prisoners from the dungeon,
  from the prison those who sit in darkness.
8 I am the LORD, that is my name;
  my glory I give to no other,
  nor my praise to graven images.
9 Behold, the former things have come to pass,
  and new things I now declare;
 before they spring forth
  I tell you of them."

10 Sing to the LORD a new song,
  his praise from the end of the earth!
 Let the sea roar ᵛ and all that fills it,

ʳ Cn: Heb come   ˢ Cn: Heb first to Zion, Behold, behold them
ᵛ Cn Compare Ps 96.11; 98.7: Heb Those who go down to the sea

ᵗ Or burn dimly   ᵘ Or bruised

the coastlands and their inhabitants.
¹¹ Let the desert and its cities lift up their voice,
  the villages that Kedar inhabits;
let the inhabitants of Sela sing for joy,
  let them shout from the top of the mountains.
¹² Let them give glory to the LORD,
  and declare his praise in the coastlands.
¹³ The LORD goes forth like a mighty man,
  like a man of war he stirs up his fury;
he cries out, he shouts aloud,
  he shows himself mighty against his foes.

¹⁴ For a long time I have held my peace,
  I have kept still and restrained myself;
now I will cry out like a woman in travail,
  I will gasp and pant.
¹⁵ I will lay waste mountains and hills,
  and dry up all their herbage;
I will turn the rivers into islands,
  and dry up the pools.
¹⁶ And I will lead the blind
  in a way that they know not,
in paths that they have not known
  I will guide them.
I will turn the darkness before them into light,
  the rough places into level ground.
These are the things I will do,
  and I will not forsake them.
¹⁷ They shall be turned back and utterly put to shame,
  who trust in graven images,
who say to molten images,
  "You are our gods."

¹⁸ Hear, you deaf;
  and look, you blind, that you may see!
¹⁹ Who is blind but my servant,
  or deaf as my messenger whom I send?
Who is blind as my dedicated one,
  or blind as the servant of the LORD?
²⁰ He sees ʷ many things, but does not observe them;
  his ears are open, but he does not hear.
²¹ The LORD was pleased, for his righteousness' sake.
  to magnify his law and make it glorious.
²² But this is a people robbed and plundered,
  they are all of them trapped in holes
  and hidden in prisons;
they have become a prey with none to rescue,
  a spoil with none to say, "Restore!"
²³ Who among you will give ear to this,
  will attend and listen for the time to come?
²⁴ Who gave up Jacob to the spoiler,
  and Israel to the robbers?
Was it not the LORD, against whom we have sinned,

ʷ Heb *you see*

in whose ways they would not walk,
  and whose law they would not obey?
²⁵ So he poured upon him the heat of his anger
  and the might of battle;
it set him on fire round about, but he did not understand;
  it burned him, but he did not take it to heart.

43 But now thus says the LORD, he who created you,
  O Jacob, he who formed you, O Israel:
"Fear not, for I have redeemed you;
  I have called you by name, you are mine.
² When you pass through the waters I will be with you;
  and through the rivers, they shall not overwhelm you;
when you walk through fire you shall not be burned,
  and the flame shall not consume you.
³ For I am the LORD your God,
  the Holy One of Israel, your Savior.
I give Egypt as your ransom,
  Ethiopia and Seba in exchange for you.
⁴ Because you are precious in my eyes,
  and honored, and I love you,
I give men in return for you,
  peoples in exchange for your life.
⁵ Fear not, for I am with you;
  I will bring your offspring from the east,
  and from the west I will gather you;
⁶ I will say to the north, Give up,
  and to the south, Do not withhold;
bring my sons from afar
  and my daughters from the end of the earth,
⁷ every one who is called by my name,
  whom I created for my glory,
  whom I formed and made."
⁸ Bring forth the people who are blind, yet have eyes,
  who are deaf, yet have ears!
⁹ Let all the nations gather together,
  and let the peoples assemble.
Who among them can declare this,
  and show us the former things?
Let them bring their witnesses to justify them.
  and let them hear and say, It is true.
¹⁰ "You are my witnesses," says the LORD,
  "and my servant whom I have chosen,
that you may know and believe me
  and understand that I am He.
Before me no god was formed,
  nor shall there be any after me.
¹¹ I, I am the LORD,
  and besides me there is no savior.
¹² I declared and saved and proclaimed,
  when there was no strange god among you;
  and you are my witnesses," says the LORD.
¹³ "I am God, and also henceforth I am He;

there is none who can deliver from my hand;
I work and who can hinder it?"

14 Thus says the LORD,
    your Redeemer, the Holy One of Israel:
"For your sake I will send to Babylon
    and break down all the bars,
    and the shouting of the Chalde'ans will be turned to
        lamentations.ˣ
15 I am the LORD, your Holy One,
    the Creator of Israel, your King."
16 Thus says the LORD,
    who makes a way in the sea,
    a path in the mighty waters,
17 who brings forth chariot and horse,
    army and warrior;
they lie down, they cannot rise,
    they are extinguished, quenched like a wick:
18 "Remember not the former things,
    nor consider the things of old.
19 Behold, I am doing a new thing;
    now it springs forth, do you not perceive it?
I will make a way in the wilderness
    and rivers in the desert.
20 The wild beasts will honor me,
    the jackals and the ostriches;
for I give water in the wilderness,
    rivers in the desert,
to give drink to my chosen people,
21   the people whom I formed for myself
    that they might declare my praise.

22 "Yet you did not call upon me, O Jacob;
    but you have been weary of me, O Israel!
23 You have not brought me your sheep for burnt offerings,
    or honored me with your sacrifices.
I have not burdened you with offerings,
    or wearied you with frankincense.
24 You have not bought me sweet cane with money,
    or satisfied me with the fat of your sacrifices.
But you have burdened me with your sins,
    you have wearied me with your iniquities.

25 "I, I am He
    who blots out your transgressions for my own sake,
    and I will not remember your sins.
26 Put me in remembrance, let us argue together;
    set forth your case, that you may be proved right.
27 Your first father sinned,
    and your mediators transgressed against me.
28 Therefore I profaned the princes of the sanctuary,
    I delivered Jacob to utter destruction
    and Israel to reviling.

44 "But now hear, O Jacob my servant,
    Israel whom I have chosen!
2 Thus says the LORD who made you,
    who formed you from the womb and will help you:
Fear not, O Jacob my servant,
    Jeshu'run whom I have chosen.
3 For I will pour water on the thirsty land,
    and streams on the dry ground;
I will pour my Spirit upon your descendants,
    and my blessing on your offspring.
4 They shall spring up like grass amid waters,ʸ

like willows by flowing streams.
5 This one will say, 'I am the LORD's,'
    another will call himself by the name of Jacob,
and another will write on his hand, 'The LORD's,'
    and surname himself by the name of Israel."

6 Thus says the LORD, the King of Israel
    and his Redeemer, the LORD of hosts:
"I am the first and I am the last;
    besides me there is no god.
7 Who is like me? Let him proclaim it,
    let him declare and set it forth before me.
Who has announced from of old the things to come?ᶻ
    Let them tell usᵃ what is yet to be.
8 Fear not, nor be afraid;
    have I not told you from of old and declared it?
    And you are my witnesses!
Is there a God besides me?
    There is no Rock; I know not any."

9   All who make idols are nothing, and the things they
delight in do not profit; their witnesses neither see nor
10 know, that they may be put to shame. Who fashions a
god or casts an image, that is profitable for nothing?
11 Behold, all his fellows shall be put to shame, and the
craftsmen are but men; let them all assemble, let them
stand forth, they shall be terrified, they shall be put to
shame together.
12   The ironsmith fashions itᵇ and works it over the coals;
he shapes it with hammers, and forges it with his strong
arm; he becomes hungry and his strength fails, he drinks
13 no water and is faint. The carpenter stretches a line,
he marks it out with a pencil; he fashions it with
planes, and marks it with a compass; he shapes it into
the figure of a man, with the beauty of a man, to dwell
14 in a house. He cuts down cedars; or he chooses a holm
tree or an oak and lets it grow strong among the trees of
the forest; he plants a cedar and the rain nourishes it.
15 Then it becomes fuel for a man; he takes a part of it and
warms himself, he kindles a fire and bakes bread; also

ˣ Heb obscure   ʸ Gk Compare Tg: Heb *They shall spring up in among grass*
    ᶻ Cn: Heb *from my placing an eternal people and things to come*   ᵃ Tg: Heb *them*   ᵇ Cn: Heb *an axe*

he makes a god and worships it, he makes it a graven
16 image and falls down before it. Half of it he burns in the
fire; over the half he eats flesh, he roasts meat and is
satisfied; also he warms himself and says, "Aha, I am
17 warm, I have seen the fire!" And the rest of it he makes
into a god, his idol; and falls down to it and worships it;
he prays to it and says, "Deliver me, for thou art my
god!"
18 They know not, nor do they discern; for he has shut
their eyes, so that they cannot see, and their minds, so
19 that they cannot understand. No one considers, nor is
there knowledge or discernment to say, "Half of it I
burned in the fire, I also baked bread on its coals, I
roasted flesh and have eaten; and shall I make the residue
of it an abomination? Shall I fall down before a block of
20 wood?" He feeds on ashes; a deluded mind has led him
astray, and he cannot deliver himself or say, "Is there not
a lie in my right hand?"

21 Remember these things, O Jacob,
   and Israel, for you are my servant;
 I formed you, you are my servant;
   O Israel, you will not be forgotten by me.
22 I have swept away your transgressions like a cloud,
   and your sins like mist;
 return to me, for I have redeemed you.

23 Sing, O heavens, for the LORD has done it;
   shout, O depths of the earth;
 break forth into singing, O mountains,
   O forest, and every tree in it!
 For the LORD has redeemed Jacob,
   and will be glorified in Israel.

24 Thus says the LORD, your Redeemer,
   who formed you from the womb:
 "I am the LORD, who made all things,
   who stretched out the heavens alone,
   who spread out the earth—Who was with me? c—
25 who frustrates the omens of liars,
   and makes fools of diviners;
 who turns wise men back,
   and makes their knowledge foolish;
26 who confirms the word of his servant,
   and performs the counsel of his messengers;
 who says of Jerusalem, 'She shall be inhabited,'
   and of the cities of Judah, 'They shall be built,
   and I will raise up their ruins';
27 who says to the deep, 'Be dry,
   I will dry up your rivers';
28 who says of Cyrus, 'He is my shepherd,
   and he shall fulfil all my purpose';
 saying of Jerusalem, 'She shall be built,'
   and of the temple, 'Your foundation shall be laid.'"

45 Thus says the LORD to his anointed, to Cyrus,
   whose right hand I have grasped,
 to subdue nations before him
   and ungird the loins of kings,
 to open doors before him
   that gates may not be closed:
2 "I will go before you
   and level the mountains,d
 I will break in pieces the doors of bronze
   and cut asunder the bars of iron,
3 I will give you the treasures of darkness
   and the hoards in secret places,
 that you may know that it is I, the LORD,
   the God of Israel, who call you by your name.
4 For the sake of my servant Jacob,
   and Israel my chosen,
 I call you by your name,
   I surname you, though you do not know me.
5 I am the LORD, and there is no other,
   besides me there is no God;
 I gird you, though you do not know me,
6 that men may know, from the rising of the sun
   and from the west, that there is none besides me;
 I am the LORD, and there is no other.
7 I form light and create darkness,
   I make weal and create woe,
 I am the LORD, who do all these things.

8 "Shower, O heavens, from above,
   and let the skies rain down righteousness;
 let the earth open, that salvation may sprout forth,e
   and let it cause righteousness to spring up also;
 I the LORD have created it.

9 "Woe to him who strives with his Maker,
   an earthen vessel with the potter! f
 Does the clay say to him who fashions it, 'What are you
   making'?
   or 'Your work has no handles'?
10 Woe to him who says to a father, 'What are you beget-
   ting?'
   or to a woman, 'With what are you in travail?'"
11 Thus says the LORD,
   the Holy One of Israel, and his Maker:
 "Will you question me g about my children,
   or command me concerning the work of my hands?
12 I made the earth,
   and created man upon it;
 it was my hands that stretched out the heavens,
   and I commanded all their host.
13 I have aroused him in righteousness,
   and I will make straight all his ways;
 he shall build my city
   and set my exiles free,

---

c Another reading is *who spread out the earth by myself*   d One ancient Ms Gk: Heb *the swellings*
e One ancient Ms: Heb *that they may bring forth salvation*   f Cn: Heb *potsherds* or *potters*   g Cn: Heb *Ask me of things to come*

not for price or reward,"
  says the LORD of hosts.

14 Thus says the LORD:
  "The wealth of Egypt and the merchandise of Ethiopia,
    and the Sabe′ans, men of stature,
  shall come over to you and be yours,

  they shall follow you;
  they shall come over in chains and bow down to you.
  They will make supplication to you, saying:
    'God is with you only, and there is no other,
    no god besides him.' "
15 Truly, thou art a God who hidest thyself,
  O God of Israel, the Savior.
16 All of them are put to shame and confounded,
  the makers of idols go in confusion together.
17 But Israel is saved by the LORD
  with everlasting salvation;
you shall not be put to shame or confounded
  to all eternity.

18 For thus says the LORD,
who created the heavens
  (he is God!),
who formed the earth and made it
  (he established it;
he did not create it a chaos,
  he formed it to be inhabited!):
"I am the LORD, and there is no other.
19 I did not speak in secret,
  in a land of darkness;
I did not say to the offspring of Jacob,
  'Seek me in chaos.'
I the LORD speak the truth,
  I declare what is right.

20 "Assemble yourselves and come,
  draw near together,
  you survivors of the nations!
They have no knowledge
  who carry about their wooden idols,
and keep on praying to a god
  that cannot save.
21 Declare and present your case;
  let them take counsel together!

Who told this long ago?
  Who declared it of old?
Was it not I, the LORD?
  And there is no other god besides me,
a righteous God and a Savior;
  there is none besides me.

22 "Turn to me and be saved,
  all the ends of the earth!
For I am God, and there is no other.
23 By myself I have sworn,
  from my mouth has gone forth in righteousness
  a word that shall not return:
'To me every knee shall bow,
  every tongue shall swear.'

24 "Only in the LORD, it shall be said of me,
  are righteousness and strength;
to him shall come and be ashamed,
  all who were incensed against him.
25 In the LORD all the offspring of Israel
  shall triumph and glory."

46 Bel bows down, Nebo stoops,
    their idols are on beasts and cattle;
these things you carry are loaded
  as burdens on weary beasts.
2 They stoop, they bow down together,
  they cannot save the burden,
  but themselves go into captivity.

3 "Hearken to me, O house of Jacob,
  all the remnant of the house of Israel,
who have been borne by me from your birth,
  carried from the womb;
4 even to your old age I am He,
  and to gray hairs I will carry you.
I have made, and I will bear;
  I will carry and will save.

5 "To whom will you liken me and make me equal,
  and compare me, that we may be alike?
6 Those who lavish gold from the purse,
  and weigh out silver in the scales,
hire a goldsmith, and he makes it into a god;
  then they fall down and worship!
7 They lift it upon their shoulders, they carry it,
  they set it in its place, and it stands there;
  it cannot move from its place.
If one cries to it, it does not answer
  or save him from his trouble.

8 "Remember this and consider,
  recall it to mind, you transgressors,
9   remember the former things of old;

for I am God, and there is no other;
    I am God, and there is none like me,
10 declaring the end from the beginning
    and from ancient times things not yet done,
saying, 'My counsel shall stand,
    and I will accomplish all my purpose,'
11 calling a bird of prey from the east,
    the man of my counsel from a far country.
I have spoken, and I will bring it to pass;
    I have purposed, and I will do it.

12 "Hearken to me, you stubborn of heart,
    you who are far from deliverance:
13 I bring near my deliverance, it is not far off,
    and my salvation will not tarry;
I will put salvation in Zion,
    for Israel my glory."

47 Come down and sit in the dust,
    O virgin daughter of Babylon;
sit on the ground without a throne,
    O daughter of the Chalde′ans!
For you shall no more be called tender and delicate.
2 Take the millstones and grind meal,
    put off your veil,
strip off your robe, uncover your legs,
    pass through the rivers.
3 Your nakedness shall be uncovered,
    and your shame shall be seen.
I will take vengeance,
    and I will spare no man.
4 Our Redeemer—the LORD of hosts is his name—
    is the Holy One of Israel.

5 Sit in silence, and go into darkness,
    O daughter of the Chalde′ans;
for you shall no more be called
    the mistress of kingdoms.
6 I was angry with my people,
    I profaned my heritage;
I gave them into your hand,
    you showed them no mercy;
on the aged you made your yoke exceedingly heavy.
7 You said, "I shall be mistress for ever,"
    so that you did not lay these things to heart
    or remember their end.

8 Now therefore hear this, you lover of pleasures,
    who sit securely,
who say in your heart,
    "I am, and there is no one besides me;
I shall not sit as a widow
    or know the loss of children":
9 These two things shall come to you

in a moment, in one day;
the loss of children and widowhood
    shall come upon you in full measure,
in spite of your many sorceries
    and the great power of your enchantments.

10 You felt secure in your wickedness,
    you said, "No one sees me";
your wisdom and your knowledge
    led you astray,
and you said in your heart,
    "I am, and there is no one besides me."
11 But evil shall come upon you,
    for which you cannot atone;
disaster shall fall upon you,
    which you will not be able to expiate;
and ruin shall come on you suddenly,
    of which you know nothing.

12 Stand fast in your enchantments
    and your many sorceries,
    with which you have labored from your youth;
perhaps you may be able to succeed,
    perhaps you may inspire terror.
13 You are wearied with your many counsels;
    let them stand forth and save you,
those who divide the heavens,
    who gaze at the stars,
who at the new moons predict
    what h shall befall you.

14 Behold, they are like stubble,
    the fire consumes them;
they cannot deliver themselves
    from the power of the flame.
No coal for warming oneself is this,
    no fire to sit before!
15 Such to you are those with whom you have labored,
    who have trafficked with you from your youth;
they wander about each in his own direction;
    there is no one to save you.

48 Hear this, O house of Jacob,
    who are called by the name of Israel,
    and who came forth from the loins i of Judah;
who swear by the name of the LORD,
    and confess the God of Israel,
    but not in truth or right.
2 For they call themselves after the holy city,
    and stay themselves on the God of Israel;
    the LORD of hosts is his name.

3 "The former things I declared of old,
    they went forth from my mouth and I made them
    known;

h Gk Syr Compare Vg: Heb *from what*   i Cn: Heb *waters* then suddenly I did them and they came to pass.

4 Because I know that you are obstinate,
  and your neck is an iron sinew
  and your forehead brass,
5 I declared them to you from of old,
  before they came to pass I announced them to you,
lest you should say, 'My idol did them,
  my graven image and my molten image commanded
    them.'

6 "You have heard; now see all this;
  and will you not declare it?
From this time forth I make you hear new things,
  hidden things which you have not known.
7 They are created now, not long ago;
  before today you have never heard of them,
lest you should say, 'Behold, I knew them.'
8 You have never heard, you have never known,
  from of old your ear has not been opened.
For I knew that you would deal very treacherously,
  and that from birth you were called a rebel.

9 "For my name's sake I defer my anger,
  for the sake of my praise I restrain it for you,
  that I may not cut you off.
10 Behold, I have refined you, but not like[j] silver;
  I have tried you in the furnace of affliction.
11 For my own sake, for my own sake, I do it,
  for how should my name[k] be profaned?
  My glory I will not give to another.

12 "Hearken to me, O Jacob,
  and Israel, whom I called!
I am He, I am the first,
  and I am the last.
13 My hand laid the foundation of the earth,
  and my right hand spread out the heavens;
when I call to them,
  they stand forth together.

14 "Assemble, all of you, and hear!
  Who among them has declared these things?
The LORD loves him;
  he shall perform his purpose on Babylon,
  and his arm shall be against the Chalde′ans.
15 I, even I, have spoken and called him,
  I have brought him, and he will prosper in his way.
16 Draw near to me, hear this:
  from the beginning I have not spoken in secret,
  from the time it came to be I have been there."
And now the Lord GOD has sent me and his Spirit.

17 Thus says the LORD,
  your Redeemer, the Holy One of Israel:

j Cn: Heb *with*   k Gk Old Latin: Heb lacks *my name*

"I am the LORD your God,
  who teaches you to profit,
  who leads you in the way you should go.
18 O that you had hearkened to my commandments!
  Then your peace would have been like a river,
  and your righteousness like the waves of the sea;
19 your offspring would have been like the sand,
  and your descendants like its grains;
their name would never be cut off
  or destroyed from before me."

20 Go forth from Babylon, flee from Chalde′a,
  declare this with a shout of joy, proclaim it,
send it forth to the end of the earth;
  say, "The LORD has redeemed his servant Jacob!"
21 They thirsted not when he led them through the deserts;
  he made water flow for them from the rock;
  he cleft the rock and the water gushed out.
22 "There is no peace," says the LORD, "for the wicked."

THE REDEMPTION OF ISRAEL

49 Listen to me, O coastlands,
  and hearken, you peoples from afar.
The LORD called me from the womb,
  from the body of my mother he named my name.
2 He made my mouth like a sharp sword,
  in the shadow of his hand he hid me;
he made me a polished arrow,
  in his quiver he hid me away.
3 And he said to me, "You are my servant,
  Israel, in whom I will be glorified."
4 But I said, "I have labored in vain,
  I have spent my strength for nothing and vanity;
yet surely my right is with the LORD,
  and my recompense with my God."

5 And now the LORD says,
  who formed me from the womb to be his servant,
to bring Jacob back to him,
  and that Israel might be gathered to him,
for I am honored in the eyes of the LORD,
  and my God has become my strength—

6 he says:
"It is too light a thing that you should be my servant
  to raise up the tribes of Jacob
  and to restore the preserved of Israel;

I will give you as a light to the nations,
 that my salvation may reach to the end of the earth."

[7] Thus says the LORD,
 the Redeemer of Israel and his Holy One,
to one deeply despised, abhorred by the nations,
 the servant of rulers:
"Kings shall see and arise;
 princes, and they shall prostrate themselves;
because of the LORD, who is faithful,
 the Holy One of Israel, who has chosen you."

[8] Thus says the LORD:
"In a time of favor I have answered you,
 in a day of salvation I have helped you;
I have kept you and given you
 as a covenant to the people,
to establish the land,
 to apportion the desolate heritages;
[9] saying to the prisoners, 'Come forth,'
 to those who are in darkness, 'Appear.'
They shall feed along the ways,
 on all bare heights shall be their pasture;
[10] they shall not hunger or thirst,
 neither scorching wind nor sun shall smite them,
for he who has pity on them will lead them,
 and by springs of water will guide them.
[11] And I will make all my mountains a way,
 and my highways shall be raised up.
[12] Lo, these shall come from afar,
 and lo, these from the north and from the west,
 and these from the land of Syene."[1]
[13] Sing for joy, O heavens, and exult, O earth;
 break forth, O mountains, into singing!
For the LORD has comforted his people,
 and will have compassion on his afflicted.

[14] But Zion said, "The LORD has forsaken me,
 my Lord has forgotten me."
[15] "Can a woman forget her sucking child,
 that she should have no compassion on the son of
  her womb?
Even these may forget,
 yet I will not forget you.
[16] Behold, I have graven you on the palms of my hands;
 your walls are continually before me.
[17] Your builders outstrip your destroyers,
 and those who laid you waste go forth from you.
[18] Lift up your eyes round about and see;
 they all gather, they come to you.
As I live, says the LORD,
 you shall put them all on as an ornament,
 you shall bind them on as a bride does.

[19] "Surely your waste and your desolate places
 and your devastated land—
surely now you will be too narrow for your inhabitants,
 and those who swallowed you up will be far away.
[20] The children born in the time of your bereavement
 will yet say in your ears:
'The place is too narrow for me;
 make room for me to dwell in.'
[21] Then you will say in your heart:
 'Who has borne me these?
I was bereaved and barren,
 exiled and put away,
 but who has brought up these?
Behold, I was left alone;
 whence then have these come?' "

[22] Thus says the Lord GOD:
"Behold, I will lift up my hand to the nations,
 and raise my signal to the peoples;
and they shall bring your sons in their bosom,
 and your daughters shall be carried on their shoulders.
[23] Kings shall be your foster fathers,
 and their queens your nursing mothers.
With their faces to the ground they shall bow down to you,
 and lick the dust of your feet.
Then you will know that I am the LORD;
 those who wait for me shall not be put to shame."

[24] Can the prey be taken from the mighty,
 or the captives of a tyrant[m] be rescued?
[25] Surely, thus says the LORD:
"Even the captives of the mighty shall be taken,
 and the prey of the tyrant be rescued,
for I will contend with those who contend with you,
 and I will save your children.
[26] I will make your oppressors eat their own flesh,
 and they shall be drunk with their own blood as with
  wine.
Then all flesh shall know
 that I am the LORD your Savior,
 and your Redeemer, the Mighty One of Jacob."

50 Thus says the LORD:
 "Where is your mother's bill of divorce,
 with which I put her away?
Or which of my creditors is it
 to whom I have sold you?
Behold, for your iniquities you were sold,
 and for your transgressions your mother was put away.
[2] Why, when I came, was there no man?
 When I called, was there no one to answer?
Is my hand shortened, that it cannot redeem?
 Or have I no power to deliver?
Behold, by my rebuke I dry up the sea,

[1] Cn: Heb Sinim   [m] One ancient Ms Syr Vg: Heb righteous man

I make the rivers a desert;
their fish stink for lack of water,
and die of thirst.
3 I clothe the heavens with blackness,
and make sackcloth their covering."

4 The Lord GOD has given me
the tongue of those who are taught,
that I may know how to sustain with a word
him that is weary.
Morning by morning he wakens,
he wakens my ear
to hear as those who are taught.
5 The Lord GOD has opened my ear,
and I was not rebellious,
I turned not backward.
6 I gave my back to the smiters,
and my cheeks to those who pulled out the beard:
I hid not my face
from shame and spitting.

7 For the Lord GOD helps me;
therefore I have not been confounded:
therefore I have set my face like a flint,
and I know that I shall not be put to shame;
8   he who vindicates me is near.
Who will contend with me?
Let us stand up together.
Who is my adversary?
Let him come near to me.
9 Behold, the Lord GOD helps me;
who will declare me guilty?
Behold, all of them will wear out like a garment;
the moth will eat them up.

10 Who among you fears the LORD
and obeys the voice of his servant,
who walks in darkness
and has no light,
yet trusts in the name of the LORD
and relies upon his GOD?
11 Behold, all you who kindle a fire,
who set brands alight! n
Walk by the light of your fire,
and by the brands which you have kindled!
This shall you have from my hand:
you shall lie down in torment.

The Coming Salvation

51 "Hearken to me, you who pursue deliverance,
you who seek the LORD;
look to the rock from which you were hewn,
and to the quarry from which you were digged.
2 Look to Abraham your father
and to Sarah who bore you;

for when he was but one I called him,
and I blessed him and made him many.
3 For the LORD will comfort Zion;
he will comfort all the waste places,
and will make her wilderness like Eden,
her desert like the garden of the LORD;
joy and gladness will be found in her,
thanksgiving and the voice of song.

4 "Listen to me, my people,
and give ear to me, my nation;
for a law will go forth from me,
and my justice for a light to the peoples.
5 My deliverance draws near speedily,
my salvation has gone forth,
and my arms will rule the peoples;
the coastlands wait for me,
and for my arm they hope.
6 Lift up your eyes to the heavens,
and look at the earth beneath;
for the heavens will vanish like smoke,
the earth will wear out like a garment,
and they who dwell in it will die like gnats; o
but my salvation will be for ever,
and my deliverance will never be ended.

7 "Hearken to me, you who know righteousness,
the people in whose heart is my law;
fear not the reproach of men,
and be not dismayed at their revilings.
8 For the moth will eat them up like a garment,
and the worm will eat them like wool;
but my deliverance will be for ever,
and my salvation to all generations."

9 Awake, awake, put on strength,
O arm of the LORD;
awake, as in days of old,
the generations of long ago.
Was it not thou that didst cut Rahab in pieces,
that didst pierce the dragon?
10 Was it not thou that didst dry up the sea,
the waters of the great deep;
that didst make the depths of the sea a way
for the redeemed to pass over?
11 And the ransomed of the LORD shall return,
and come to Zion with singing;
everlasting joy shall be upon their heads;
they shall obtain joy and gladness,
and sorrow and sighing shall flee away.

12 "I, I am he that comforts you;
who are you that you are afraid of man who dies,
of the son of man who is made like grass,

n Syr: Heb *gird yourselves with brands*   o Or *in like manner*

13 and have forgotten the LORD, your Maker,
who stretched out the heavens
and laid the foundations of the earth,
and fear continually all the day
because of the fury of the oppressor,
when he sets himself to destroy?
And where is the fury of the oppressor?
14 He who is bowed down shall speedily be released;
he shall not die and go down to the Pit,
neither shall his bread fail.
15 For I am the LORD your God,
who stirs up the sea so that its waves roar—
the LORD of hosts is his name.
16 And I have put my words in your mouth,
and hid you in the shadow of my hand,
stretching out[p] the heavens

and laying the foundations of the earth,
and saying to Zion, 'You are my people.' "

17 Rouse yourself, rouse yourself,
stand up, O Jerusalem,
you who have drunk at the hand of the LORD
the cup of his wrath,
who have drunk to the dregs
the bowl of staggering.
18 There is none to guide her
among all the sons she has borne;
there is none to take her by the hand
among all the sons she has brought up.
19 These two things have befallen you—
who will condole with you?—
devastation and destruction, famine and sword;
who will comfort you?[q]
20 Your sons have fainted,
they lie at the head of every street
like an antelope in a net;
they are full of the wrath of the LORD,
the rebuke of your God.

21 Therefore hear this, you who are afflicted,
who are drunk, but not with wine:
22 Thus says your Lord, the LORD,
your God who pleads the cause of his people:
"Behold, I have taken from your hand
the cup of staggering;
the bowl of my wrath
you shall drink no more;
23 and I will put it into the hand of your tormentors,
who have said to you,
'Bow down, that we may pass over';
and you have made your back like the ground
and like the street for them to pass over."

52 Awake, awake,
put on your strength, O Zion;
put on your beautiful garments,
O Jerusalem, the holy city;
for there shall no more come into you
the uncircumcised and the unclean.
2 Shake yourself from the dust, arise,
O captive[r] Jerusalem;
loose the bonds from your neck,
O captive daughter of Zion.

3 For thus says the LORD: "You were sold for nothing,
4 and you shall be redeemed without money. For thus says
the Lord GOD: My people went down at the first into
Egypt to sojourn there, and the Assyrian oppressed them
5 for nothing. Now therefore what have I here, says the
LORD, seeing that my people are taken away for nothing?
Their rulers wail, says the LORD, and continually all the
6 day my name is despised. Therefore my people shall
know my name; therefore in that day they shall know
that it is I who speak; here am I."

7 How beautiful upon the mountains
are the feet of him who brings good tidings,
who publishes peace, who brings good tidings of good,
who publishes salvation,
who says to Zion, "Your God reigns."
8 Hark, your watchmen lift up their voice,
together they sing for joy;
for eye to eye they see
the return of the LORD to Zion.
9 Break forth together into singing,
you waste places of Jerusalem;
for the LORD has comforted his people,
he has redeemed Jerusalem.
10 The LORD has bared his holy arm
before the eyes of all the nations;
and all the ends of the earth shall see
the salvation of our God.

11 Depart, depart, go out thence,
touch no unclean thing;
go out from the midst of her, purify yourselves,
you who bear the vessels of the LORD.
12 For you shall not go out in haste,
and you shall not go in flight,
for the LORD will go before you,
and the God of Israel will be your rear guard.

[p] Syr: Heb *plant* [q] One ancient Ms Gk Syr Vg: Heb *how may I comfort you* [r] Cn: Heb *sit*

The Suffering Servant

13 Behold, my servant shall prosper,
  he shall be exalted and lifted up
  and shall be very high.
14 As many were astonished at him [s]—
  his appearance was so marred, beyond human semblance
  and his form beyond that of the sons of men—
15 so shall he startle [t] many nations;
  kings shall shut their mouths because of him;
  for that which has not been told them they shall see,
  and that which they have not heard they shall understand.

53 Who has believed what we have heard?
  And to whom has the arm of the LORD been revealed?
2 For he grew up before him like a young plant,
  and like a root out of dry ground;
  he had no form or comeliness that we should look at him,
  and no beauty that we should desire him.
3 He was despised and rejected [u] by men;
  a man of sorrows, [v] and acquainted with grief; [w]
  and as one from whom men hide their faces
  he was despised, and we esteemed him not.

4 Surely he has borne our griefs [x]
  and carried our sorrows; [y]
  yet we esteemed him stricken,
  smitten by God, and afflicted.
5 But he was wounded for our transgressions,
  he was bruised for our iniquities;
  upon him was the chastisement that made us whole,
  and with his stripes we are healed.
6 All we like sheep have gone astray;
  we have turned every one to his own way;
  and the LORD has laid on him
  the iniquity of us all.

7 He was oppressed, and he was afflicted,
  yet he opened not his mouth;
  like a lamb that is led to the slaughter,
  and like a sheep that before its shearers is dumb,
  so he opened not his mouth.
8 By oppression and judgment he was taken away;
  and as for his generation, who considered
  that he was cut off out of the land of the living,
  stricken for the transgression of my people?
9 And they made his grave with the wicked
  and with a rich man in his death,
  although he had done no violence,
  and there was no deceit in his mouth.

10 Yet it was the will of the LORD to bruise him;
  he has put him to grief; [z]
  when he makes himself [a] an offering for sin,
  he shall see his offspring, he shall prolong his days;
  the will of the LORD shall prosper in his hand;
11 he shall see the fruit of the travail of his soul and be satisfied;
  by his knowledge shall the righteous one, my servant,
  make many to be accounted righteous;
  and he shall bear their iniquities.
12 Therefore I will divide him a portion with the great,
  and he shall divide the spoil with the strong;
  because he poured out his soul to death,
  and was numbered with the transgressors;
  yet he bore the sin of many,
  and made intercession for the transgressors.

The Consolation of Israel

54 "Sing, O barren one, who did not bear;
  break forth into singing and cry aloud,
  you who have not been in travail!
For the children of the desolate one will be more
  than the children of her that is married, says the LORD.
2 Enlarge the place of your tent,
  and let the curtains of your habitations be stretched out;
  hold not back, lengthen your cords
  and strengthen your stakes.
3 For you will spread abroad to the right and to the left,
  and your descendants will possess the nations
  and will people the desolate cities.

4 "Fear not, for you will not be ashamed;
  be not confounded, for you will not be put to shame;
  for you will forget the shame of your youth,
  and the reproach of your widowhood you will remember no more.
5 For your Maker is your husband,
  the LORD of hosts is his name;
  and the Holy One of Israel is your Redeemer,
  the God of the whole earth he is called.

6 For the LORD has called you
  like a wife forsaken and grieved in spirit,
  like a wife of youth when she is cast off,
  says your God.

[s] Syr Tg: Heb you   [t] The meaning of the Hebrew word is uncertain   [u] Or forsaken   [v] Or pains
[w] Or sickness   [x] Or sicknesses   [y] Or pains   [z] Heb made him sick   [a] Vg: Heb thou makest his soul

7 For a brief moment I forsook you,
  but with great compassion I will gather you.
8 In overflowing wrath for a moment
  I hid my face from you,
but with everlasting love I will have compassion on you,
  says the LORD, your Redeemer.

9 "For this is like the days of Noah to me:
  as I swore that the waters of Noah
  should no more go over the earth,
so I have sworn that I will not be angry with you
  and will not rebuke you.
10 For the mountains may depart
  and the hills be removed,
but my steadfast love shall not depart from you,
  and my covenant of peace shall not be removed,
  says the LORD, who has compassion on you.

11 "O afflicted one, storm-tossed, and not comforted,
  behold, I will set your stones in antimony,
  and lay your foundations with sapphires,b
12 I will make your pinnacles of agate,
  your gates of carbuncles,
  and all your wall of precious stones.
13 All your sons shall be taught by the LORD,
  and great shall be the prosperity of your sons.
14 In righteousness you shall be established;
  you shall be far from oppression, for you shall not fear;
  and from terror, for it shall not come near you.
15 If any one stirs up strife,
  it is not from me;
whoever stirs up strife with you
  shall fall because of you.
16 Behold, I have created the smith
  who blows the fire of coals,
  and produces a weapon for its purpose.
I have also created the ravager to destroy;
  no weapon that is fashioned against you shall prosper,
and you shall confute every tongue that rises against you
  in judgment.
This is the heritage of the servants of the LORD
  and their vindication from me, says the LORD."

55 "Ho, every one who thirsts,
    come to the waters;
and he who has no money,
  come, buy and eat!
Come, buy wine and milk
  without money and without price.
2 Why do you spend your money for that which is not
    bread,
  and your labor for that which does not satisfy?
Hearken diligently to me, and eat what is good,
  and delight yourselves in fatness.

b Or lapis lazuli

3 Incline your ear, and come to me;
  hear, that your soul may live;
and I will make with you an everlasting covenant,
  my steadfast, sure love for David.
4 Behold, I made him a witness to the peoples,
  a leader and commander for the peoples.
5 Behold, you shall call nations that you know not,
  and nations that knew you not shall run to you,
because of the LORD your God, and of the Holy One of
    Israel,
  for he has glorified you.

6 "Seek the LORD while he may be found,
  call upon him while he is near;
7 let the wicked forsake his way,
  and the unrighteous man his thoughts;
let him return to the LORD, that he may have mercy on
    him,
  and to our God, for he will abundantly pardon.
8 For my thoughts are not your thoughts,
  neither are your ways my ways, says the LORD.
9 For as the heavens are higher than the earth,
  so are my ways higher than your ways
  and my thoughts than your thoughts.

10 "For as the rain and the snow come down from heaven,
  and return not thither but water the earth,
making it bring forth and sprout,
  giving seed to the sower and bread to the eater,
11 so shall my word be that goes forth from my mouth;
  it shall not return to me empty,
but it shall accomplish that which I purpose,
  and prosper in the thing for which I sent it.

12 "For you shall go out in joy,
  and be led forth in peace;
the mountains and the hills before you
  shall break forth into singing,
  and all the trees of the field shall clap their hands.
13 Instead of the thorn shall come up the cypress;
  instead of the brier shall come up the myrtle;
and it shall be to the LORD for a memorial,
  for an everlasting sign which shall not be cut off."

ADMONITIONS AND PROMISES
56 Thus says the LORD:
    "Keep justice, and do righteousness,
for soon my salvation will come,
  and my deliverance be revealed.
2 Blessed is the man who does this,

and the son of man who holds it fast,
who keeps the sabbath, not profaning it,
and keeps his hand from doing any evil."

3 Let not the foreigner who has joined himself to the LORD
say,
"The LORD will surely separate me from his people";
and let not the eunuch say,
"Behold, I am a dry tree."
4 For thus says the LORD:
"To the eunuchs who keep my sabbaths,
who choose the things that please me
and hold fast my covenant,
5 I will give in my house and within my walls
a monument and a name
better than sons and daughters;
I will give them an everlasting name
which shall not be cut off.

6 "And the foreigners who join themselves to the LORD,
to minister to him, to love the name of the LORD,
and to be his servants,
every one who keeps the sabbath, and does not profane it,
and holds fast my covenant—
7 these I will bring to my holy mountain,
and make them joyful in my house of prayer;
their burnt offerings and their sacrifices
will be accepted on my altar;
for my house shall be called a house of prayer
for all peoples.
8 Thus says the Lord GOD,
who gathers the outcasts of Israel,
I will gather yet others to him
besides those already gathered." c

Blind Leaders—Corrupt Worship
9 All you beasts of the field, come to devour—
all you beasts in the forest.
10 His watchmen are blind,
they are all without knowledge;
they are all dumb dogs,
they cannot bark;
dreaming, lying down,
loving to slumber.
11 The dogs have a mighty appetite;
they never have enough.
The shepherds also have no understanding;
they have all turned to their own way,
each to his own gain, one and all.
12 "Come," they say, "let us d get wine,
let us fill ourselves with strong drink;
and tomorrow will be like this day,
great beyond measure."

57 The righteous man perishes,
and no one lays it to heart;
devout men are taken away,
while no one understands.
For the righteous man is taken away from calamity,
2 he enters into peace;
they rest in their beds
who walk in their uprightness.
3 But you, draw near hither,
sons of the sorceress,
offspring of the adulterer and the harlot.
4 Of whom are you making sport?
Against whom do you open your mouth wide
and put out your tongue?
Are you not children of transgression,
the offspring of deceit,
5 you who burn with lust among the oaks,
under every green tree;
who slay your children in the valleys,
under the clefts of the rocks?
6 Among the smooth stones of the valley is your portion;
they, they, are your lot;
to them you have poured out a drink offering,
you have brought a cereal offering.
Shall I be appeased for these things?
7 Upon a high and lofty mountain
you have set your bed,
and thither you went up to offer sacrifice.
8 Behind the door and the doorpost
you have set up your symbol;
for, deserting me, you have uncovered your bed,
you have gone up to it,
you have made it wide;
and you have made a bargain for yourself with them,
you have loved their bed,
you have looked on nakedness. e
9 You journeyed to Molech f with oil
and multiplied your perfumes;
you sent your envoys far off,
and sent down even to Sheol.
10 You were wearied with the length of your way,
but you did not say, "It is hopeless";
you found new life for your strength,
and so you were not faint.

11 Whom did you dread and fear,
so that you lied,
and did not remember me,
did not give me a thought?
Have I not held my peace, even for a long time,
and so you do not fear me?
12 I will tell of your righteousness and your doings,
but they will not help you.

c Heb his gathered ones   d One ancient Ms Syr Vg Tg: Heb me   e The meaning of the Hebrew is uncertain   f Or the king

¹³ When you cry out, let your collection of idols deliver you!
    The wind will carry them off,
    a breath will take them away.
But he who takes refuge in me shall possess the land,
    and shall inherit my holy mountain.

¹⁴ And it shall be said,
    "Build up, build up, prepare the way,
    remove every obstruction from my people's way."
¹⁵ For thus says the high and lofty One
    who inhabits eternity, whose name is Holy:
"I dwell in the high and holy place,
    and also with him who is of a contrite and humble
        spirit,
    to revive the spirit of the humble,
    and to revive the heart of the contrite.
¹⁶ For I will not contend for ever,
    nor will I always be angry;
for from me proceeds the spirit,
    and I have made the breath of life.
¹⁷ Because of the iniquity of his covetousness I was angry,
    I smote him, I hid my face and was angry;
    but he went on backsliding in the way of his own heart.
¹⁸ I have seen his ways, but I will heal him;
    I will lead him and requite him with comfort,
    creating for his mourners the fruit of the lips.
¹⁹ Peace, peace, to the far and to the near, says the LORD;
    and I will heal him.
²⁰ But the wicked are like the tossing sea;
    for it cannot rest,
    and its waters toss up mire and dirt.
²¹ There is no peace, says my God, for the wicked."

The Service Pleasing to God

58 "Cry aloud, spare not,
        lift up your voice like a trumpet;
    declare to my people their transgression,
        to the house of Jacob their sins.
² Yet they seek me daily,
    and delight to know my ways,
as if they were a nation that did righteousness
    and did not forsake the ordinance of their God;
they ask of me righteous judgments,
    they delight to draw near to God.
³ 'Why have we fasted, and thou seest it not?
    Why have we humbled ourselves, and thou takest no
        knowledge of it?'
Behold, in the day of your fast you seek your own
        pleasure,ᵍ
    and oppress all your workers.
⁴ Behold, you fast only to quarrel and to fight
    and to hit with wicked fist.
Fasting like yours this day

will not make your voice to be heard on high.
⁵ Is such the fast that I choose,
    a day for a man to humble himself?
Is it to bow down his head like a rush,
    and to spread sackcloth and ashes under him?
Will you call this a fast,
    and a day acceptable to the LORD?

⁶ "Is not this the fast that I choose:
    to loose the bonds of wickedness,
    to undo the thongs of the yoke,
to let the oppressed go free,
    and to break every yoke?
⁷ Is it not to share your bread with the hungry,
    and bring the homeless poor into your house;
when you see the naked, to cover him,
    and not to hide yourself from your own flesh?
⁸ Then shall your light break forth like the dawn,
    and your healing shall spring up speedily;
your righteousness shall go before you,
    the glory of the LORD shall be your rear guard.
⁹ Then you shall call, and the LORD will answer;
    you shall cry, and he will say, Here I am.

"If you take away from the midst of you the yoke,
    the pointing of the finger, and speaking wickedness,
¹⁰ if you pour yourself out for the hungry
    and satisfy the desire of the afflicted,
then shall your light rise in the darkness
    and your gloom be as the noonday.
¹¹ And the LORD will guide you continually,
    and satisfy your desire with good things,ʰ
    and make your bones strong;
and you shall be like a watered garden,
    like a spring of water,
    whose waters fail not.
¹² And your ancient ruins shall be rebuilt;
    you shall raise up the foundations of many generations;
you shall be called the repairer of the breach,
    the restorer of streets to dwell in.

¹³ "If you turn back your foot from the sabbath,
    from doing your pleasureⁱ on my holy day,

and call the sabbath a delight
    and the holy day of the LORD honorable;
if you honor it, not going your own ways,
    or seeking your own pleasure,ʲ or talking idly;

ᵍ Or *pursue your own business*
ʲ Or *pursuing your own business*   ʰ The meaning of the Hebrew word is uncertain   ⁱ Or *business*

¹⁴ then you shall take delight in the LORD,
    and I will make you ride upon the heights of the earth;
I will feed you with the heritage of Jacob your father,
    for the mouth of the LORD has spoken.''

God's Intervention

59 Behold, the LORD's hand is not shortened, that it
        cannot save,
    or his ear dull, that it cannot hear;
² but your iniquities have made a separation
        between you and your God,
    and your sins have hid his face from you
        so that he does not hear.
³ For your hands are defiled with blood
        and your fingers with iniquity;
    your lips have spoken lies,
        your tongue mutters wickedness.
⁴ No one enters suit justly,
        no one goes to law honestly;
    they rely on empty pleas, they speak lies,
        they conceive mischief and bring forth iniquity.
⁵ They hatch adders' eggs,
        they weave the spider's web;
    he who eats their eggs dies,
        and from one which is crushed a viper is hatched.
⁶ Their webs will not serve as clothing;
        men will not cover themselves with what they make.
    Their works are works of iniquity,
        and deeds of violence are in their hands.
⁷ Their feet run to evil,
        and they make haste to shed innocent blood;
    their thoughts are thoughts of iniquity,
        desolation and destruction are in their highways.
⁸ The way of peace they know not,
        and there is no justice in their paths;
    they have made their roads crooked,
        no one who goes in them knows peace.

⁹ Therefore justice is far from us,
        and righteousness does not overtake us;
    we look for light, and behold, darkness,
        and for brightness, but we walk in gloom.
¹⁰ We grope for the wall like the blind,
        we grope like those who have no eyes;
    we stumble at noon as in the twilight,
        among those in full vigor we are like dead men.
¹¹ We all growl like bears,
        we moan and moan like doves;
    we look for justice, but there is none;
        for salvation, but it is far from us.
¹² For our transgressions are multiplied before thee,
        and our sins testify against us;
    for our transgressions are with us,
        and we know our iniquities:

ᵏ Heb *be enlarged*

¹³ transgressing, and denying the LORD,
        and turning away from following our God,
    speaking oppression and revolt,
        conceiving and uttering from the heart lying words.
¹⁴ Justice is turned back,
        and righteousness stands afar off;
    for truth has fallen in the public squares,
        and uprightness cannot enter.
¹⁵ Truth is lacking,
        and he who departs from evil makes himself a prey.

    The LORD saw it, and it displeased him
        that there was no justice.
¹⁶ He saw that there was no man,
        and wondered that there was no one to intervene;
    then his own arm brought him victory,
        and his righteousness upheld him.
¹⁷ He put on righteousness as a breastplate,
        and a helmet of salvation upon his head;
    he put on garments of vengeance for clothing,
        and wrapped himself in fury as a mantle.
¹⁸ According to their deeds, so will he repay,
        wrath to his adversaries, requital to his enemies;
    to the coastlands he will render requital.
¹⁹ So they shall fear the name of the LORD from the west,
        and his glory from the rising of the sun;
    for he will come like a rushing stream,
        which the wind of the LORD drives.

²⁰ ''And he will come to Zion as Redeemer,
        to those in Jacob who turn from transgression, says the
        LORD.
²¹ ''And as for me, this is my covenant with them, says the
    LORD: my spirit which is upon you, and my words which
    I have put in your mouth, shall not depart out of your
    mouth, or out of the mouth of your children, or out of
    the mouth of your children's children, says the LORD,
    from this time forth and for evermore.''

The New Jerusalem

60 Arise, shine; for your light has come,
        and the glory of the LORD has risen upon you.
² For behold, darkness shall cover the earth,
        and thick darkness the peoples;
    but the LORD will arise upon you,
        and his glory will be seen upon you.
³ And nations shall come to your light,
        and kings to the brightness of your rising.

⁴ Lift up your eyes round about, and see;
        they all gather together, they come to you;
    your sons shall come from far,
        and your daughters shall be carried in the arms.
⁵ Then you shall see and be radiant,
        your heart shall thrill and rejoice; ᵏ

because the abundance of the sea shall be turned to you,
    the wealth of the nations shall come to you.
6 A multitude of camels shall cover you,
    the young camels of Mid'ian and Ephah;
    all those from Sheba shall come.
They shall bring gold and frankincense,
    and shall proclaim the praise of the LORD.
7 All the flocks of Kedar shall be gathered to you,
    the rams of Nebai'oth shall minister to you;
they shall come up with acceptance on my altar,
    and I will glorify my glorious house.

8 Who are these that fly like a cloud,
    and like doves to their windows?
9 For the coastlands shall wait for me,
    the ships of Tarshish first,
to bring your sons from far,
    their silver and gold with them,
for the name of the LORD your God,
    and for the Holy One of Israel,
    because he has glorified you.

10 Foreigners shall build up your walls,
    and their kings shall minister to you;
for in my wrath I smote you,
    but in my favor I have had mercy on you.
11 Your gates shall be open continually;
    day and night they shall not be shut;
that men may bring to you the wealth of the nations,
    with their kings led in procession.
12 For the nation and kingdom
    that will not serve you shall perish;
    those nations shall be utterly laid waste.
13 The glory of Lebanon shall come to you,
    the cypress, the plane, and the pine,
to beautify the place of my sanctuary;
    and I will make the place of my feet glorious.
14 The sons of those who oppressed you
    shall come bending low to you;
and all who despised you
    shall bow down at your feet;
they shall call you the City of the LORD,
    the Zion of the Holy One of Israel.

15 Whereas you have been forsaken and hated,
    with no one passing through,
I will make you majestic for ever,
    a joy from age to age.
16 You shall suck the milk of nations,
    you shall suck the breast of kings;
and you shall know that I, the LORD, am your Savior
    and your Redeemer, the Mighty One of Jacob.

17 Instead of bronze I will bring gold,
    and instead of iron I will bring silver;
instead of wood, bronze,
    instead of stones, iron.
I will make your overseers peace
    and your taskmasters righteousness.
18 Violence shall no more be heard in your land,
    devastation or destruction within your borders;
you shall call your walls Salvation,
    and your gates Praise.

19 The sun shall be no more
    your light by day,
nor for brightness shall the moon
    give light to you by night; 1
but the LORD will be your everlasting light,
    and your God will be your glory.
20 Your sun shall no more go down,
    nor your moon withdraw itself;
for the LORD will be your everlasting light,
    and your days of mourning shall be ended.
21 Your people shall all be righteous;
    they shall possess the land for ever,
the shoot of my planting, the work of my hands,
    that I might be glorified.
22 The least one shall become a clan,
    and the smallest one a mighty nation;
I am the LORD;
    in its time I will hasten it.

The Lord's Anointed

61 The Spirit of the Lord GOD is upon me,
    because the LORD has anointed me
to bring good tidings to the afflicted; m
    he has sent me to bind up the brokenhearted,
to proclaim liberty to the captives,
    and the opening of the prison n to those who are bound;
2 to proclaim the year of the LORD's favor,
    and the day of vengeance of our God;
    to comfort all who mourn;
3 to grant to those who mourn in Zion—
    to give them a garland instead of ashes,
the oil of gladness instead of mourning,
    the mantle of praise instead of a faint spirit;
that they may be called oaks of righteousness,

1 One ancient Ms Gk Old Latin Tg: Heb lacks *by night*   m Or *poor*   n Or *the opening of the eyes:* Heb *the opening*

the planting of the LORD, that he may be glorified.
4 They shall build up the ancient ruins,
  they shall raise up the former devastations;
they shall repair the ruined cities,
  the devastations of many generations.

5 Aliens shall stand and feed your flocks,
  foreigners shall be your plowmen and vinedressers;
6 but you shall be called the priests of the LORD,
  men shall speak of you as the ministers of our God;
you shall eat the wealth of the nations,
  and in their riches you shall glory.
7 Instead of your shame you shall have a double portion,
  instead of dishonor you o shall rejoice in your p lot;
therefore in your p land you o shall possess a double portion;
  yours q shall be everlasting joy.

8 For I the LORD love justice,
  I hate robbery and wrong; r
I will faithfully give them their recompense,
  and I will make an everlasting covenant with them.
9 Their descendants shall be known among the nations,
  and their offspring in the midst of the peoples;
all who see them shall acknowledge them,
  that they are a people whom the LORD has blessed.

10 I will greatly rejoice in the LORD,
  my soul shall exult in my God;
for he has clothed me with the garments of salvation,
  he has covered me with the robe of righteousness,
as a bridegroom decks himself with a garland,
  and as a bride adorns herself with her jewels.
11 For as the earth brings forth its shoots,
  and as a garden causes what is sown in it to spring up,
so the Lord GOD will cause righteousness and praise
  to spring forth before all the nations.

A Chosen People

62 For Zion's sake I will not keep silent,
    and for Jerusalem's sake I will not rest,
until her vindication goes forth as brightness,
  and her salvation as a burning torch.
2 The nations shall see your vindication,
  and all the kings your glory;
and you shall be called by a new name
  which the mouth of the LORD will give.
3 You shall be a crown of beauty in the hand of the LORD,
  and a royal diadem in the hand of your God.
4 You shall no more be termed Forsaken, s
  and your land shall no more be termed Desolate; t
but you shall be called My delight is in her, u
  and your land Married; v
for the LORD delights in you,
  and your land shall be married.

5 For as a young man marries a virgin,
  so shall your sons marry you,
and as the bridegroom rejoices over the bride,
  so shall your God rejoice over you.

6 Upon your walls, O Jerusalem,
  I have set watchmen;
all the day and all the night
  they shall never be silent.
You who put the LORD in remembrance,
  take no rest,
7 and give him no rest
  until he establishes Jerusalem
  and makes it a praise in the earth.
8 The LORD has sworn by his right hand
  and by his mighty arm:
"I will not again give your grain
  to be food for your enemies,
and foreigners shall not drink your wine
  for which you have labored;
9 but those who garner it shall eat it and praise the LORD,
  and those who gather it shall drink it
  in the courts of my sanctuary."

10 Go through, go through the gates,
  prepare the way for the people;
build up, build up the highway,
  clear it of stones,
  lift up an ensign over the peoples.
11 Behold, the LORD has proclaimed
  to the end of the earth:
Say to the daughter of Zion,
  "Behold, your salvation comes;
behold, his reward is with him,
  and his recompense before him."
12 And they shall be called The holy people,
  The redeemed of the LORD;
and you shall be called Sought out,
  a city not forsaken.

63 Who is this that comes from Edom,
    in crimsoned garments from Bozrah,
he that is glorious in his apparel,
  marching in the greatness of his strength?

"It is I, announcing vindication,
  mighty to save."

2 Why is thy apparel red,
  and thy garments like his that treads in the wine press?

3 "I have trodden the wine press alone,
  and from the peoples no one was with me;
I trod them in my anger
  and trampled them in my wrath;

---

o Heb they   p Heb their   q Heb theirs   r Or robbery with a burnt offering   s Heb Azubah
t Heb Shemamah   u Heb Hephzibah   v Heb Beulah

their lifeblood is sprinkled upon my garments,
and I have stained all my raiment.
4 For the day of vengeance was in my heart,
and my year of redemption [w] has come.
5 I looked, but there was no one to help;
I was appalled, but there was no one to uphold;
so my own arm brought me victory,
and my wrath upheld me.
6 I trod down the peoples in my anger,
I made them drunk in my wrath,
and I poured out their lifeblood on the earth."

7 I will recount the steadfast love of the LORD,
the praises of the LORD,
according to all that the LORD has granted us,
and the great goodness to the house of Israel
which he has granted them according to his mercy,
according to the abundance of his steadfast love.
8 For he said, Surely they are my people,
sons who will not deal falsely;
and he became their Savior.
9 In all their affliction he was afflicted,[x]
and the angel of his presence saved them;
in his love and in his pity he redeemed them;
he lifted them up and carried them all the days of old.

10 But they rebelled
and grieved his holy Spirit;
therefore he turned to be their enemy,
and himself fought against them.
11 Then he remembered the days of old,
of Moses his servant.
Where is he who brought up out of the sea
the shepherds of his flock?
Where is he who put in the midst of them
his holy Spirit,
12 who caused his glorious arm
to go at the right hand of Moses,
who divided the waters before them
to make for himself an everlasting name,
13 who led them through the depths?
Like a horse in the desert,
they did not stumble.
14 Like cattle that go down into the valley,
the Spirit of the LORD gave them rest.
So thou didst lead thy people,
to make for thyself a glorious name.

15 Look down from heaven and see,
from thy holy and glorious habitation.
Where are thy zeal and thy might?
The yearning of thy heart and thy compassion
are withheld from me.
16 For thou art our Father,

though Abraham does not know us
and Israel does not acknowledge us;
thou, O Lord, art our Father,
our Redeemer from of old is thy name.
17 O LORD, why dost thou make us err from thy ways
and harden our heart, so that we fear thee not?
Return for the sake of thy servants,
the tribes of thy heritage.
18 Thy holy people possessed thy sanctuary a little while;
our adversaries have trodden it down.
19 We have become like those over whom thou hast never
ruled,
like those who are not called by thy name.

64 O that thou wouldst rend the heavens and come
down,
that the mountains might quake at thy presence—
2 [y] as when fire kindles brushwood
and the fire causes water to boil—
to make thy name known to thy adversaries,
and that the nations might tremble at thy presence!
3 When thou didst terrible things which we looked not for,
thou camest down, the mountains quaked at thy presence.
4 From of old no one has heard
or perceived by the ear,
no eye has seen a God besides thee,
who works for those who wait for him.
5 Thou meetest him that joyfully works righteousness,
those that remember thee in thy ways.
Behold, thou wast angry, and we sinned;
in our sins we have been a long time, and shall we be
saved? [z]
6 We have all become like one who is unclean,
and all our righteous deeds are like a polluted garment.
We all fade like a leaf,
and our iniquities, like the wind, take us away.
7 There is no one that calls upon thy name,
that bestirs himself to take hold of thee;
for thou hast hid thy face from us,
and hast delivered [a] us into the hand of our iniquities.

8 Yet, O LORD, thou art our Father;
we are the clay, and thou art our potter;
we are all the work of thy hand.
9 Be not exceedingly angry, O LORD,
and remember not iniquity for ever.

w Or *the year of my redeemed*   x Another reading is *he did not afflict*   y Ch 64.1 Heb   z Hebrew obscure
a Gk Syr Old Latin Tg: Heb *melted*

Behold, consider, we are all thy people.
10 Thy holy cities have become a wilderness,
　Zion has become a wilderness,
　　Jerusalem a desolation.
11 Our holy and beautiful house,
　where our fathers praised thee,
has been burned by fire,
　and all our pleasant places have become ruins.
12 Wilt thou restrain thyself at these things, O Lord?
　Wilt thou keep silent, and afflict us sorely?

Judgment and Salvation

65 I was ready to be sought by those who did not ask
　　　for me;
　I was ready to be found by those who did not seek me.
I said, "Here am I, here am I,"
　to a nation that did not call on my name.
2 I spread out my hands all the day
　to a rebellious people,
who walk in a way that is not good,
　following their own devices;
3 a people who provoke me
　to my face continually,
sacrificing in gardens
　and burning incense upon bricks;
4 who sit in tombs,
　and spend the night in secret places;
who eat swine's flesh,
　and broth of abominable things is in their vessels;
5 who say, "Keep to yourself,
　do not come near me, for I am set apart from you."
These are a smoke in my nostrils,
　a fire that burns all the day.
6 Behold, it is written before me:
　"I will not keep silent, but I will repay,
yea, I will repay into their bosom
7 　their [b] iniquities and their [b] fathers' iniquities together,
　　　　says the Lord;
because they burned incense upon the mountains
　and reviled me upon the hills,
I will measure into their bosom
　payment for their former doings."

8 Thus says the Lord:
　"As the wine is found in the cluster,
　　and they say, 'Do not destroy it,
　　for there is a blessing in it,'
　so I will do for my servants' sake,
　　and not destroy them all.
9 I will bring forth descendants from Jacob,
　　and from Judah inheritors of my mountains;
　my chosen shall inherit it,
　　and my servants shall dwell there.

[b] Gk Syr: Heb *your*

10 Sharon shall become a pasture for flocks,
　and the Valley of Achor a place for herds to lie down,
　　for my people who have sought me.
11 But you who forsake the Lord,
　who forget my holy mountain,
who set a table for Fortune
　and fill cups of mixed wine for Destiny;
12 I will destine you to the sword,
　and all of you shall bow down to the slaughter;
because, when I called, you did not answer,
　when I spoke, you did not listen,
but you did what was evil in my eyes,
　and chose what I did not delight in."

13 Therefore thus says the Lord God:
　"Behold, my servants shall eat,
　　but you shall be hungry;
　behold, my servants shall drink,
　　but you shall be thirsty;
　behold, my servants shall rejoice,
　　but you shall be put to shame;
14 behold, my servants shall sing for gladness of heart,
　　but you shall cry out for pain of heart,
　　and shall wail for anguish of spirit.
15 You shall leave your name to my chosen for a curse,
　　and the Lord God will slay you;
　but his servants he will call by a different name.
16 So that he who blesses himself in the land
　　shall bless himself by the God of truth,
and he who takes an oath in the land
　　shall swear by the God of truth;
because the former troubles are forgotten
　　and are hid from my eyes.

17 "For behold, I create new heavens and a new earth;
　and the former things shall not be remembered
　　or come into mind.
18 But be glad and rejoice for ever
　　in that which I create;
　for behold, I create Jerusalem a rejoicing,
　　and her people a joy.
19 I will rejoice in Jerusalem,
　　and be glad in my people;
　no more shall be heard in it the sound of weeping
　　and the cry of distress.

²⁰ No more shall there be in it
  an infant that lives but a few days,
  or an old man who does not fill out his days,
for the child shall die a hundred years old,
  and the sinner a hundred years old shall be accursed.
²¹ They shall build houses and inhabit them;
  they shall plant vineyards and eat their fruit.
²² They shall not build and another inhabit;
  they shall not plant and another eat;
for like the days of a tree shall the days of my people be,
  and my chosen shall long enjoy the work of their hands.
²³ They shall not labor in vain,
  or bear children for calamity;^c
for they shall be the offspring of the blessed of the LORD,
  and their children with them.
²⁴ Before they call I will answer,
  while they are yet speaking I will hear.
²⁵ The wolf and the lamb shall feed together,
  the lion shall eat straw like the ox;
  and dust shall be the serpent's food.
They shall not hurt or destroy
  in all my holy mountain,

                                    says the LORD."

New Birth and Judgment

66 Thus says the LORD:
  "Heaven is my throne
  and the earth is my footstool;
what is the house which you would build for me,
  and what is the place of my rest?
² All these things my hand has made,
  and so all these things are mine,^d

                                    says the LORD.

But this is the man to whom I will look,
  he that is humble and contrite in spirit,
  and trembles at my word.

³ "He who slaughters an ox is like him who kills a man;
  he who sacrifices a lamb, like him who breaks a dog's
    neck;
he who presents a cereal offering, like him who offers
    swine's blood;
  he who makes a memorial offering of frankincense,
    like him who blesses an idol.
These have chosen their own ways,
  and their soul delights in their abominations;
⁴ I also will choose affliction for them,

^c Or *sudden terror*   ^d Gk Syr: Heb *came to be*

and bring their fears upon them;
because, when I called, no one answered,
  when I spoke they did not listen;
but they did what was evil in my eyes,
  and chose that in which I did not delight."

⁵ Hear the word of the LORD,
  you who tremble at his word:
"Your brethren who hate you
  and cast you out for my name's sake
have said, 'Let the LORD be glorified,
  that we may see your joy';
  but it is they who shall be put to shame.

⁶ "Hark, an uproar from the city!
  A voice from the temple!
The voice of the LORD,
  rendering recompense to his enemies!

⁷ "Before she was in labor
  she gave birth;
before her pain came upon her
  she was delivered of a son.
⁸ Who has heard such a thing?
  Who has seen such things?
Shall a land be born in one day?
  Shall a nation be brought forth in one moment?
For as soon as Zion was in labor
  she brought forth her sons.
⁹ Shall I bring to the birth and not cause to bring forth?
                                    says the LORD;
shall I, who cause to bring forth, shut the womb?
                                    says your God.

¹⁰ "Rejoice with Jerusalem, and be glad for her,
  all you who love her;
rejoice with her in joy,
  all you who mourn over her;
¹¹ that you may suck and be satisfied with her consoling
    breasts;
that you may drink deeply with delight
  from the abundance of her glory."

¹² For thus says the LORD:
"Behold, I will extend prosperity to her like a river,
  and the wealth of the nations like an overflowing
    stream;
and you shall suck, you shall be carried upon her hip,
  and dandled upon her knees.
¹³ As one whom his mother comforts,
  so I will comfort you;
  you shall be comforted in Jerusalem.
¹⁴ You shall see, and your heart shall rejoice;
  your bones shall flourish like the grass;

and it shall be known that the hand of the LORD is with his
servants,
and his indignation is against his enemies.

15 "For behold, the LORD will come in fire,
and his chariots like the stormwind,
to render his anger in fury,
and his rebuke with flames of fire.
16 For by fire will the LORD execute judgment,
and by his sword, upon all flesh;
and those slain by the LORD shall be many.

A Summary

17 "Those who sanctify and purify themselves to go into
the gardens, following one in the midst, eating swine's
flesh and the abomination and mice, shall come to an end
together, says the LORD.

18 "For I know e their works and their thoughts, and I
am f coming to gather all nations and tongues; and they
19 shall come and shall see my glory, and I will set a sign
among them. And from them I will send survivors to the
nations, to Tarshish, Put,g and Lud, who draw the bow,

to Tubal and Javan, to the coastlands afar off, that have
not heard my fame or seen my glory; and they shall de-
20 clare my glory among the nations. And they shall bring all
your brethren from all the nations as an offering to the
LORD, upon horses, and in chariots, and in litters, and
upon mules, and upon dromedaries, to my holy mountain
Jerusalem, says the LORD, just as the Israelites bring their
cereal offering in a clean vessel to the house of the LORD.
21 And some of them also I will take for priests and for
Levites, says the LORD.

22 "For as the new heavens and the new earth
which I will make
shall remain before me, says the LORD;
so shall your descendants and your name remain.
23 From new moon to new moon,
and from sabbath to sabbath,
all flesh shall come to worship before me,
says the LORD.

24 "And they shall go forth and look on the dead bodies of
the men that have rebelled against me; for their worm
shall not die, their fire shall not be quenched, and they
shall be an abhorrence to all flesh."

e Gk Syr: Heb lacks *know*   f Gk Syr Vg Tg: Heb *it is*   g Gk: Heb *Pul*

INTRODUCTION TO

JEREMIAH

The Book of Jeremiah tells of the deeds and sermons of one of the bravest prophets of Judah. He was preaching from 626 B.C. to 586 B.C. during a period when Babylonia controlled Judah. In 621 B.C. he supported the reforms begun when King Josiah read some scrolls from Deuteronomy that had been found during repairs to the Temple.

For a number of years Jeremiah taught that the Babylonian rule over Judah was caused by the sins of the people. Because of this unpopular preaching he had to go into hiding. In 605 B.C. he had his secretary, Baruch, write his message to the people and read it in public (Jeremiah 36). King Jehoiakim was so angered that he cut the scroll to pieces and burned it. In 593 B.C., under the new king, Zedekiah, he again preached against rebellion against Babylonia and called the Jews to repentance for their sins. For this he was imprisoned. After Jerusalem fell (586 B.C.), he was forced to go with some revolutionaries as they fled to Egypt.

Because Jeremiah's name was linked with the sad songs called "The Lamentations of Jeremiah," he has been called the weeping prophet. The truth is that Jeremiah was hopeful about the future of the Jews. Even while the Babylonian army threatened Jerusalem, he bought some land to assure the people that he believed in the future of the Jewish nation.

Jeremiah taught that serving God is a very personal matter and that each of us must take personal responsibility for serving him. Jeremiah looked forward to a new day when religion would be more than a set of outward rules to be kept. Religion must be deep within our hearts and lives. This was what Jeremiah meant when he wrote that God said, "I will put my law within them, and I will write it upon their hearts" (Jeremiah 31.33).

THE BOOK OF

JEREMIAH

JEREMIAH'S CALL AND VISIONS

1 The words of Jeremiah, the son of Hilki'ah, of the priests who were in An'athoth in the land of Benjamin, ² to whom the word of the LORD came in the days of Josi'ah the son of Amon, king of Judah, in the thirteenth year ³ of his reign. It came also in the days of Jehoi'akim the son of Josi'ah, king of Judah, and until the end of the eleventh year of Zedeki'ah, the son of Josi'ah, king of Judah, until the captivity of Jerusalem in the fifth month.

⁴ Now the word of the LORD came to me saying,

⁵ "Before I formed you in the womb I knew you,
and before you were born I consecrated you;
I appointed you a prophet to the nations."

⁶ Then I said, "Ah, Lord GOD! Behold, I do not know how ⁷ to speak, for I am only a youth." But the LORD said to me,

"Do not say, 'I am only a youth';
for to all to whom I send you you shall go,
and whatever I command you you shall speak.
⁸ Be not afraid of them,
for I am with you to deliver you,

says the LORD."

⁹ Then the LORD put forth his hand and touched my mouth;
and the LORD said to me,
"Behold, I have put my words in your mouth.
¹⁰ See, I have set you this day over nations and over kingdoms,
to pluck up and to break down,
to destroy and to overthrow,
to build and to plant."

¹¹ And the word of the LORD came to me, saying, "Jeremiah, what do you see?" And I said, "I see a rod of

12 almond." [a] Then the LORD said to me, "You have seen well, for I am watching [b] over my word to perform it."
13 The word of the LORD came to me a second time, saying, "What do you see?" And I said, "I see a boiling
14 pot, facing away from the north." Then the LORD said to me, "Out of the north evil shall break forth upon all the
15 inhabitants of the land. For, lo, I am calling all the tribes of the kingdoms of the north, says the LORD; and they shall come and every one shall set his throne at the entrance of the gates of Jerusalem, against all its walls
16 round about, and against all the cities of Judah. And I will utter my judgments against them, for all their wickedness in forsaking me; they have burned incense to other gods, and worshiped the works of their own hands.
17 But you, gird up your loins; arise, and say to them everything that I command you. Do not be dismayed
18 by them, lest I dismay you before them. And I, behold, I make you this day a fortified city, an iron pillar, and bronze walls, against the whole land, against the kings of Judah, its princes, its priests, and the people of the
19 land. They will fight against you; but they shall not prevail against you, for I am with you, says the LORD, to deliver you."

JEREMIAH'S SERMONS

2 2 The word of the LORD came to me, saying, "Go and proclaim in the hearing of Jerusalem, Thus says the LORD,
I remember the devotion of your youth,
    your love as a bride,
how you followed me in the wilderness,
    in a land not sown.
3 Israel was holy to the LORD,
    the first fruits of his harvest.
All who ate of it became guilty;
    evil came upon them,

says the LORD."

4 Hear the word of the LORD, O house of Jacob, and all
5 the families of the house of Israel. Thus says the LORD:
"What wrong did your fathers find in me
    that they went far from me,
and went after worthlessness, and became worthless?
6 They did not say, 'Where is the LORD
    who brought us up from the land of Egypt,
who led us in the wilderness,
    in a land of deserts and pits,
in a land of drought and deep darkness,
    in a land that none passes through,
    where no man dwells?'
7 And I brought you into a plentiful land
    to enjoy its fruits and its good things.
But when you came in you defiled my land,

and made my heritage an abomination.
8 The priests did not say, 'Where is the LORD?'
    Those who handle the law did not know me;
the rulers [c] transgressed against me;
    the prophets prophesied by Ba'al,
    and went after things that do not profit.

9 "Therefore I still contend with you,
                                    says the LORD,
    and with your children's children I will contend.
10 For cross to the coasts of Cyprus and see,
    or send to Kedar and examine with care;
    see if there has been such a thing.
11 Has a nation changed its gods?
    even though they are no gods?
But my people have changed their glory
    for that which does not profit.
12 Be appalled, O heavens, at this,
    be shocked, be utterly desolate,
                                    says the LORD,
13 for my people have committed two evils:
    they have forsaken me,
the fountain of living waters,
    and hewed out cisterns for themselves,
broken cisterns,
    that can hold no water.

14 "Is Israel a slave? Is he a homeborn servant?
    Why then has he become a prey?
15 The lions have roared against him,
    they have roared loudly.
They have made his land a waste;
    his cities are in ruins, without inhabitant.
16 Moreover, the men of Memphis and Tah'panhes
    have broken the crown of your head.
17 Have you not brought this upon yourself
    by forsaking the LORD your God,
    when he led you in the way?

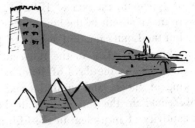

18 And now what do you gain by going to Egypt,
    to drink the waters of the Nile?
Or what do you gain by going to Assyria,
    to drink the waters of the Euphra'tes?
19 Your wickedness will chasten you,
    and your apostasy will reprove you.
Know and see that it is evil and bitter

---

[a] Heb shaqed   [b] Heb shoqed   [c] Heb shepherds

for you to forsake the LORD your God;
    the fear of me is not in you,
                    says the Lord GOD of hosts.

20 "For long ago you broke your yoke
    and burst your bonds;
    and you said, 'I will not serve.'
Yea, upon every high hill
    and under every green tree
    you bowed down as a harlot.
21 Yet I planted you a choice vine,
    wholly of pure seed.
How then have you turned degenerate
    and become a wild vine?
22 Though you wash yourself with lye
    and use much soap,
    the stain of your guilt is still before me,
                    says the Lord GOD.
23 How can you say, 'I am not defiled,
    I have not gone after the Ba′als'?
Look at your way in the valley;
    know what you have done—
a restive young camel interlacing her tracks,
24   a wild ass used to the wilderness,
in her heat sniffing the wind!
    Who can restrain her lust?
None who seek her need weary themselves;
    in her month they will find her.
25 Keep your feet from going unshod
    and your throat from thirst.
But you said, 'It is hopeless,
    for I have loved strangers,
    and after them I will go.'

26 "As a thief is shamed when caught,
    so the house of Israel shall be shamed:
they, their kings, their princes,
    their priests, and their prophets,
27 who say to a tree, 'You are my father,'
    and to a stone, 'You gave me birth.'
For they have turned their back to me,
    and not their face.
But in the time of their trouble they say,
    'Arise and save us!'
28 But where are your gods
    that you made for yourself?
Let them arise, if they can save you,
    in your time of trouble;
for as many as your cities
    are your gods, O Judah.

29 "Why do you complain against me?
    You have all rebelled against me,
                    says the LORD.

30 In vain have I smitten your children,
    they took no correction;
your own sword devoured your prophets
    like a ravening lion.
31 And you, O generation, heed the word of the LORD.
Have I been a wilderness to Israel,
    or a land of thick darkness?
Why then do my people say, 'We are free,
    we will come no more to thee'?
32 Can a maiden forget her ornaments,
    or a bride her attire?
Yet my people have forgotten me
    days without number.

33 "How well you direct your course
    to seek lovers!
So that even to wicked women
    you have taught your ways.
34 Also on your skirts is found
    the lifeblood of guiltless poor;
you did not find them breaking in.
    Yet in spite of all these things
35 you say, 'I am innocent;
    surely his anger has turned from me.'
Behold, I will bring you to judgment
    for saying, 'I have not sinned.'
36 How lightly you gad about,
    changing your way!
You shall be put to shame by Egypt
    as you were put to shame by Assyria.
37 From it too you will come away
    with your hands upon your head,
for the LORD has rejected those in whom you trust,
    and you will not prosper by them.

3 "If d a man divorces his wife
    and she goes from him
and becomes another man's wife,
    will he return to her?
Would not that land be greatly polluted?
You have played the harlot with many lovers;
    and would you return to me?
                  says the LORD.
2 Lift up your eyes to the bare heights, and see!
    Where have you not been lain with?
By the waysides you have sat awaiting lovers
    like an Arab in the wilderness.
You have polluted the land
    with your vile harlotry.
3 Therefore the showers have been withheld,
    and the spring rain has not come;
yet you have a harlot's brow,
    you refuse to be ashamed.
4 Have you not just now called to me,

d Gk Syr: Heb *Saying, If*

507

'My father, thou art the friend of my youth—
5 will he be angry for ever,
    will he be indignant to the end?'
Behold, you have spoken,
    but you have done all the evil that you could."

6 The LORD said to me in the days of King Josi'ah:
"Have you seen what she did, that faithless one, Israel,
how she went up on every high hill and under every
7 green tree, and there played the harlot? And I thought,
'After she has done all this she will return to me'; but
she did not return, and her false sister Judah saw it.
8 She saw that for all the adulteries of that faithless one,
Israel, I had sent her away with a decree of divorce; yet
her false sister Judah did not fear, but she too went and
9 played the harlot. Because harlotry was so light to her,
she polluted the land, committing adultery with stone and
10 tree. Yet for all this her false sister Judah did not return
to me with her whole heart, but in pretense, says the
LORD."

11 And the LORD said to me, "Faithless Israel has shown
12 herself less guilty than false Judah. Go, and proclaim
these words toward the north, and say,
'Return, faithless Israel,
                                        says the LORD.

I will not look on you in anger,
    for I am merciful,
                                        says the LORD;
I will not be angry for ever.
13 Only acknowledge your guilt,
    that you rebelled against the LORD your God
and scattered your favors among strangers under every
        green tree,
    and that you have not obeyed my voice,
                                        says the LORD.
14 Return, O faithless children,
                                        says the LORD;
    for I am your master;
I will take you, one from a city and two from a family,
    and I will bring you to Zion.
15 " 'And I will give you shepherds after my own heart,
16 who will feed you with knowledge and understanding.
And when you have multiplied and increased in the land,
in those days, says the LORD, they shall no more say, "The
ark of the covenant of the LORD." It shall not come to
mind, or be remembered, or missed; it shall not be made
17 again. At that time Jerusalem shall be called the throne
of the LORD, and all nations shall gather to it, to the
presence of the LORD in Jerusalem, and they shall no
18 more stubbornly follow their own evil heart. In those
days the house of Judah shall join the house of Israel,
and together they shall come from the land of the north
to the land that I gave your fathers for a heritage.

19 " 'I thought
    how I would set you among my sons,
and give you a pleasant land,
    a heritage most beauteous of all nations.
And I thought you would call me, My Father,
    and would not turn from following me.
20 Surely, as a faithless wife leaves her husband,
    so have you been faithless to me, O house of Israel,
                                        says the LORD.' "

21 A voice on the bare heights is heard,
    the weeping and pleading of Israel's sons,
because they have perverted their way,
    they have forgotten the LORD their God.
22 "Return, O faithless sons,
    I will heal your faithlessness."
"Behold, we come to thee;
    for thou art the LORD our God
23 Truly the hills are a delusion,
    the orgies on the mountains.
Truly in the LORD our God
    is the salvation of Israel.
24 "But from our youth the shameful thing has devoured
all for which our fathers labored, their flocks and their
25 herds, their sons and their daughters. Let us lie down
in our shame, and let our dishonor cover us; for we have
sinned against the LORD our God, we and our fathers,
from our youth even to this day; and we have not obeyed
the voice of the LORD our God."

4 "If you return, O Israel,
                                        says the LORD,
    to me you should return.
If you remove your abominations from my presence,
    and do not waver,
2 and if you swear, 'As the LORD lives,'
    in truth, in justice, and in uprightness,
then nations shall bless themselves in him,
    and in him shall they glory."
3 For thus says the LORD to the men of Judah and to
the inhabitants of Jerusalem:
"Break up your fallow ground,
    and sow not among thorns.
4 Circumcise yourselves to the LORD,
    remove the foreskin of your hearts,
    O men of Judah and inhabitants of Jerusalem;
lest my wrath go forth like fire,
    and burn with none to quench it,
    because of the evil of your doings."

5 Declare in Judah, and proclaim in Jerusalem, and say,
"Blow the trumpet through the land;
    cry aloud and say,
'Assemble, and let us go
    into the fortified cities!'

⁶ Raise a standard toward Zion,
  flee for safety, stay not,
for I bring evil from the north,
  and great destruction.
⁷ A lion has gone up from his thicket,

a destroyer of nations has set out;
  he has gone forth from his place
to make your land a waste;
  your cities will be ruins
  without inhabitant.
⁸ For this gird you with sackcloth,
  lament and wail;
for the fierce anger of the LORD has not turned back
  from us."

⁹ "In that day, says the LORD, courage shall fail both king and princes; the priests shall be appalled and the
¹⁰ prophets astounded." Then I said, "Ah, Lord GOD, surely thou hast utterly deceived this people and Jerusalem, saying, 'It shall be well with you'; whereas the sword has reached their very life."
¹¹ At that time it will be said to this people and to Jerusalem, "A hot wind from the bare heights in the desert toward the daughter of my people, not to winnow
¹² or cleanse, a wind too full for this comes for me. Now it is I who speak in judgment upon them."
¹³ Behold, he comes up like clouds,
  his chariots like the whirlwind;
his horses are swifter than eagles—
  woe to us, for we are ruined!
¹⁴ O Jerusalem, wash your heart from wickedness,
  that you may be saved.
How long shall your evil thoughts
  lodge within you?
¹⁵ For a voice declares from Dan
  and proclaims evil from Mount E′phraim.
¹⁶ Warn the nations that he is coming;
  announce to Jerusalem,
"Besiegers come from a distant land;
  they shout against the cities of Judah.
¹⁷ Like keepers of a field are they against her round about,
  because she has rebelled against me,
                          says the LORD.
¹⁸ Your ways and your doings
  have brought this upon you.
This is your doom, and it is bitter;
  it has reached your very heart."

¹⁹ My anguish, my anguish! I writhe in pain!
  Oh, the walls of my heart!
My heart is beating wildly;
  I cannot keep silent;
for I hear the sound of the trumpet,
  the alarm of war.
²⁰ Disaster follows hard on disaster,
  the whole land is laid waste.
Suddenly my tents are destroyed,
  my curtains in a moment.
²¹ How long must I see the standard,
  and hear the sound of the trumpet?
²² "For my people are foolish,
  they know me not;
they are stupid children,
  they have no understanding.
They are skilled in doing evil,
  but how to do good they know not."

²³ I looked on the earth, and lo, it was waste and void;
  and to the heavens, and they had no light.
²⁴ I looked on the mountains, and lo, they were quaking,
  and all the hills moved to and fro.
²⁵ I looked, and lo, there was no man,
  and all the birds of the air had fled.
²⁶ I looked, and lo, the fruitful land was a desert,
  and all its cities were laid in ruins
  before the LORD, before his fierce anger.
²⁷ For thus says the LORD, "The whole land shall be a desolation; yet I will not make a full end.
²⁸ For this the earth shall mourn,
  and the heavens above be black;
for I have spoken, I have purposed;
  I have not relented nor will I turn back."

²⁹ At the noise of horseman and archer
  every city takes to flight;
they enter thickets; they climb among rocks;
  all the cities are forsaken,
  and no man dwells in them.
³⁰ And you, O desolate one,
  what do you mean that you dress in scarlet,
  that you deck yourself with ornaments of gold,
  that you enlarge your eyes with paint?
In vain you beautify yourself.
  Your lovers despise you;
  they seek your life.
³¹ For I heard a cry as of a woman in travail,
  anguish as of one bringing forth her first child,
the cry of the daughter of Zion gasping for breath,
  stretching out her hands,
"Woe is me! I am fainting before murderers."

5 Run to and fro through the streets of Jerusalem,
　　look and take note!
Search her squares to see
　　if you can find a man,

one who does justice
　　and seeks truth;
that I may pardon her.
2 Though they say, "As the LORD lives,"
　　yet they swear falsely.
3 O LORD, do not thy eyes look for truth?
Thou hast smitten them,
　　but they felt no anguish;
thou hast consumed them,
　　but they refused to take correction.
They have made their faces harder than rock;
　　they have refused to repent.

4 Then I said, "These are only the poor,
　　they have no sense;
for they do not know the way of the LORD,
　　the law of their God.
5 I will go to the great,
　　and will speak to them;
for they know the way of the LORD,
　　the law of their God."
But they all alike had broken the yoke,
　　they had burst the bonds.

6 Therefore a lion from the forest shall slay them,
　　a wolf from the desert shall destroy them.
A leopard is watching against their cities,
　　every one who goes out of them shall be torn in pieces;
because their transgressions are many,
　　their apostasies are great.

7 "How can I pardon you?
　　Your children have forsaken me,
　　and have sworn by those who are no gods.
When I fed them to the full,
　　they committed adultery
　　and trooped to the houses of harlots.
8 They were well-fed lusty stallions,
　　each neighing for his neighbor's wife.
9 Shall I not punish them for these things?
　　　　　　　　　　　　　　says the LORD;

and shall I not avenge myself
　　on a nation such as this?

10 "Go up through her vine-rows and destroy,
　　but make not a full end;
strip away her branches,
　　for they are not the LORD's.
11 For the house of Israel and the house of Judah
　　have been utterly faithless to me,
　　　　　　　　　　　　　　says the LORD.
12 They have spoken falsely of the LORD,
　　and have said, 'He will do nothing;
no evil will come upon us,
　　nor shall we see sword or famine.
13 The prophets will become wind;
　　the word is not in them.
Thus shall it be done to them!' "

14 Therefore thus says the LORD, the God of hosts:
"Because they e have spoken this word,
behold, I am making my words in your mouth a fire,
　　and this people wood, and the fire shall devour them.
15 Behold, I am bringing upon you
　　a nation from afar, O house of Israel,
　　　　　　　　　　　　　　says the LORD.

It is an enduring nation,
　　it is an ancient nation,
a nation whose language you do not know,
　　nor can you understand what they say.
16 Their quiver is like an open tomb,
　　they are all mighty men.
17 They shall eat up your harvest and your food;
　　they shall eat up your sons and your daughters;
they shall eat up your flocks and your herds;
　　they shall eat up your vines and your fig trees;
your fortified cities in which you trust
　　they shall destroy with the sword."

18 "But even in those days, says the LORD, I will not make
19 a full end of you. And when your people say, 'Why has
the LORD our God done all these things to us?' you shall
say to them, 'As you have forsaken me and served foreign
gods in your land, so you shall serve strangers in a land
that is not yours.' "

20 Declare this in the house of Jacob,
　　proclaim it in Judah:
21 "Hear this, O foolish and senseless people,
　　who have eyes, but see not,
　　who have ears, but hear not.
22 Do you not fear me? says the LORD;
　　Do you not tremble before me?
I placed the sand as the bound for the sea,
　　a perpetual barrier which it cannot pass;
though the waves toss, they cannot prevail,

e Heb you

510

though they roar, they cannot pass over it.
23 But this people has a stubborn and rebellious heart;
    they have turned aside and gone away.
24 They do not say in their hearts,
    'Let us fear the LORD our God,
who gives the rain in its season,
    the autumn rain and the spring rain,
and keeps for us
    the weeks appointed for the harvest.'
25 Your iniquities have turned these away,
    and your sins have kept good from you.
26 For wicked men are found among my people;
    they lurk like fowlers lying in wait.ᶠ
They set a trap;
    they catch men.
27 Like a basket full of birds,
    their houses are full of treachery;
therefore they have become great and rich,
28   they have grown fat and sleek.
They know no bounds in deeds of wickedness;
    they judge not with justice
the cause of the fatherless, to make it prosper,
    and they do not defend the rights of the needy.
29 Shall I not punish them for these things?

                                    says the LORD,

    and shall I not avenge myself
    on a nation such as this?"

30 An appalling and horrible thing
    has happened in the land:
31 the prophets prophesy falsely,
    and the priests rule at their direction;
my people love to have it so,
    but what will you do when the end comes?

6 Flee for safety, O people of Benjamin,
    from the midst of Jerusalem!
Blow the trumpet in Teko'a,
    and raise a signal on Beth-hacche'rem;
for evil looms out of the north,
    and great destruction.
2 The comely and delicately bred I will destroy,
    the daughter of Zion.
3 Shepherds with their flocks shall come against her;
    they shall pitch their tents around her,
    they shall pasture, each in his place.
4 "Prepare war against her;
    up, and let us attack at noon!"
"Woe to us, for the day declines,
    for the shadows of evening lengthen!"
5 "Up, and let us attack by night,
    and destroy her palaces!"

6 For thus says the LORD of hosts:

"Hew down her trees;
    cast up a siege mound against Jerusalem.
This is the city which must be punished;
    there is nothing but oppression within her.
7 As a well keeps its water fresh,
    so she keeps fresh her wickedness;
violence and destruction are heard within her;
    sickness and wounds are ever before me.
8 Be warned, O Jerusalem,
    lest I be alienated from you;
lest I make you a desolation,
    an uninhabited land."

9 Thus says the LORD of hosts:
Glean ᵍ thoroughly as a vine
    the remnant of Israel;
like a grape-gatherer pass your hand again
    over its branches."
10 To whom shall I speak and give warning,
    that they may hear?
Behold, their ears are closed,ʰ
    they cannot listen;
behold, the word of the LORD is to them an object of scorn,
    they take no pleasure in it.
11 Therefore I am full of the wrath of the LORD;
    I am weary of holding it in.
"Pour it out upon the children in the street,
    and upon the gatherings of young men, also;
both husband and wife shall be taken,
    the old folk and the very aged.
12 Their houses shall be turned over to others,
    their fields and wives together;
for I will stretch out my hand
    against the inhabitants of the land,"

                                    says the LORD.

13 "For from the least to the greatest of them,
    every one is greedy for unjust gain;
and from prophet to priest,
    every one deals falsely.
14 They have healed the wound of my people lightly,
    saying, 'Peace, peace,'
when there is no peace.
15 Were they ashamed when they committed abomination?
    No, they were not at all ashamed;
    they did not know how to blush.
Therefore they shall fall among those who fall;
    at the time that I punish them, they shall be over-
        thrown,"

                                    says the LORD.

16 Thus says the LORD:
"Stand by the roads, and look,
    and ask for the ancient paths,
where the good way is; and walk in it,

ᶠ Heb uncertain   ᵍ Cn: Heb *they shall glean*   ʰ Heb *uncircumcised*

and find rest for your souls.
But they said, 'We will not walk in it.'
17 I set watchmen over you, saying,
'Give heed to the sound of the trumpet!'
But they said, 'We will not give heed.'
18 Therefore hear, O nations,
and know, O congregation, what will happen to them.
19 Hear, O earth; behold, I am bringing evil upon this
people,
the fruit of their devices,
because they have not given heed to my words;
and as for my law, they have rejected it.
20 To what purpose does frankincense come to me from
Sheba,
or sweet cane from a distant land?
Your burnt offerings are not acceptable,
nor your sacrifices pleasing to me.
21 Therefore thus says the LORD:
'Behold, I will lay before this people
stumbling blocks against which they shall stumble;
fathers and sons together,
neighbor and friend shall perish.' "

22 Thus says the LORD:
"Behold, a people is coming from the north country,
a great nation is stirring from the
farthest parts of the earth.
23 They lay hold on bow and spear,
they are cruel and have no mercy,
the sound of them is like the roaring sea;
they ride upon horses,
set in array as a man for battle,
against you, O daughter of Zion!"
24 We have heard the report of it,
our hands fall helpless;
anguish has taken hold of us,
pain as of a woman in travail.
25 Go not forth into the field,
nor walk on the road;
for the enemy has a sword,
terror is on every side.
26 O daughter of my people, gird on sackcloth,
and roll in ashes;
make mourning as for an only son,
most bitter lamentation;
for suddenly the destroyer
will come upon us.

27 "I have made you an assayer and tester among my people,
that you may know and assay their ways.
28 They are all stubbornly rebellious,
going about with slanders;
they are bronze and iron,
all of them act corruptly.
29 The bellows blow fiercely,
the lead is consumed by the fire;
in vain the refining goes on,
for the wicked are not removed.
30 Refuse silver they are called,
for the LORD has rejected them."

7 The word that came to Jeremiah from the LORD:
2 "Stand in the gate of the LORD's house, and proclaim

there this word, and say, Hear the word of the LORD, all
you men of Judah who enter these gates to worship the
3 LORD. Thus says the LORD of hosts, the God of Israel,
Amend your ways and your doings, and I will let you
4 dwell in this place. Do not trust in these deceptive words:
'This is the temple of the LORD, the temple of the LORD,
the temple of the LORD.'
5 "For if you truly amend your ways and your doings,
6 if you truly execute justice one with another, if you do
not oppress the alien, the fatherless or the widow, or
shed innocent blood in this place, and if you do not go
7 after other gods to your own hurt, then I will let you
dwell in this place, in the land that I gave of old to your
fathers for ever.
8 "Behold, you trust in deceptive words to no avail.
9 Will you steal, murder, commit adultery, swear falsely,
burn incense to Ba'al, and go after other gods that you
10 have not known, and then come and stand before me in
this house, which is called by my name, and say, 'We
are delivered!'—only to go on doing all these abomina-
11 tions? Has this house, which is called by my name, become a den of robbers in your eyes? Behold, I myself
12 have seen it, says the LORD. Go now to my place that was
in Shiloh, where I made my name dwell at first, and
see what I did to it for the wickedness of my people
13 Israel. And now, because you have done all these things,
says the LORD, and when I spoke to you persistently you
did not listen, and when I called you, you did not an-
14 swer, therefore I will do to the house which is called by
my name, and in which you trust, and to the place which
I gave to you and to your fathers, as I did to Shiloh.
15 And I will cast you out of my sight, as I cast out all your
kinsmen, all the offspring of E'phraim.
16 "As for you, do not pray for this people, or lift up cry
or prayer for them, and do not intercede with me, for I
17 do not hear you. Do you not see what they are doing in

18 the cities of Judah and in the streets of Jerusalem? The children gather wood, the fathers kindle fire, and the women knead dough, to make cakes for the queen of heaven; and they pour out drink offerings to other gods, 19 to provoke me to anger. Is it I whom they provoke? says the LORD. Is it not themselves, to their own confusion? 20 Therefore thus says the Lord GOD: Behold, my anger and my wrath will be poured out on this place, upon man and beast, upon the trees of the field and the fruit of the ground; it will burn and not be quenched."

21 Thus says the LORD of hosts, the God of Israel: "Add your burnt offerings to your sacrifices, and eat the flesh. 22 For in the day that I brought them out of the land of Egypt, I did not speak to your fathers or command them 23 concerning burnt offerings and sacrifices. But this command I gave them, 'Obey my voice, and I will be your God, and you shall be my people; and walk in all the way that I command you, that it may be well with 24 you.' But they did not obey or incline their ear, but walked in their own counsels and the stubbornness of their evil hearts, and went backward and not forward. 25 From the day that your fathers came out of the land of Egypt to this day, I have persistently sent all my servants 26 the prophets to them, day after day; yet they did not listen to me, or incline their ear, but stiffened their neck. They did worse than their fathers.

27 "So you shall speak all these words to them, but they will not listen to you. You shall call to them, but they will 28 not answer you. And you shall say to them, 'This is the nation that did not obey the voice of the LORD their God, and did not accept discipline; truth has perished; it is cut off from their lips.

29 Cut off your hair and cast it away;
    raise a lamentation on the bare heights,
for the LORD has rejected and forsaken
    the generation of his wrath.'

30 "For the sons of Judah have done evil in my sight, says the LORD; they have set their abominations in the 31 house which is called by my name, to defile it. And they have built the high place[i] of Topheth, which is in the valley of the son of Hinnom, to burn their sons and their daughters in the fire; which I did not command, nor did 32 it come into my mind. Therefore, behold, the days are coming, says the LORD, when it will no more be called Topheth, or the valley of the son of Hinnom, but the valley of Slaughter: for they will bury Topheth, because 33 there is no room elsewhere. And the dead bodies of this people will be food for the birds of the air, and for the beasts of the earth; and none will frighten them away. 34 And I will make to cease from the cities of Judah and from the streets of Jerusalem the voice of mirth and the voice of gladness, the voice of the bridegroom and the voice of the bride; for the land shall become a waste.

8 "At that time, says the LORD, the bones of the kings of Judah, the bones of its princes, the bones of the priests, the bones of the prophets, and the bones of the inhabitants of Jerusalem shall be brought out of their 2 tombs; and they shall be spread before the sun and the moon and all the host of heaven, which they have loved and served, which they have gone after, and which they have sought and worshiped; and they shall not be gathered or buried; they shall be as dung on the surface of 3 the ground. Death shall be preferred to life by all the remnant that remains of this evil family in all the places where I have driven them, says the LORD of hosts.

4 "You shall say to them, Thus says the LORD:
When men fall, do they not rise again?
    If one turns away, does he not return?
5 Why then has this people turned away
    in perpetual backsliding?
They hold fast to deceit,
    they refuse to return.
6 I have given heed and listened,
    but they have not spoken aright;
no man repents of his wickedness,
    saying, 'What have I done?'
Every one turns to his own course,
    like a horse plunging headlong into battle.
7 Even the stork in the heavens
    knows her times;
and the turtledove, swallow, and crane[j]
    keep the time of their coming;
but my people know not
    the ordinance of the LORD.

8 "How can you say, 'We are wise,
    and the law of the LORD is with us'?
But, behold, the false pen of the scribes
    has made it into a lie.
9 The wise men shall be put to shame,
    they shall be dismayed and taken;
lo, they have rejected the word of the LORD,
    and what wisdom is in them?
10 Therefore I will give their wives to others
    and their fields to conquerors,
because from the least to the greatest
    every one is greedy for unjust gain;
from prophet to priest
    every one deals falsely.
11 They have healed the wound of my people lightly,
    saying, 'Peace, peace,'
    when there is no peace.
12 Were they ashamed when they committed abomination?
    No, they were not at all ashamed;
    they did not know how to blush.

i Gk Tg: Heb high places   j The meaning of the Hebrew word is uncertain

513

Therefore they shall fall among the fallen;
    when I punish them, they shall be overthrown,
                        says the LORD.

13 When I would gather them, says the LORD,
    there are no grapes on the vine,
    nor figs on the fig tree;
even the leaves are withered,
    and what I gave them has passed away from them." k

14 Why do we sit still?
    Gather together, let us go into the fortified cities
    and perish there;
for the LORD our God has doomed us to perish,
    and has given us poisoned water to drink,
    because we have sinned against the LORD.
15 We looked for peace, but no good came,
    for a time of healing, but behold, terror.

16 "The snorting of their horses is heard from Dan;
    at the sound of the neighing of their stallions
    the whole land quakes.
They come and devour the land and all that fills it,
    the city and those who dwell in it.
17 For behold, I am sending among you serpents,
    adders which cannot be charmed,
    and they shall bite you,"
                        says the LORD.

18 My grief is beyond healing,[1]
    my heart is sick within me.
19 Hark, the cry of the daughter of my people
    from the length and breadth of the land:
"Is the LORD not in Zion?
Is her King not in her?"
"Why have they provoked me to anger with their graven
    images,
    and with their foreign idols?"

20 "The harvest is past, the summer is ended,
    and we are not saved."
21 For the wound of the daughter of my people is my heart
    wounded,
    I mourn, and dismay has taken hold on me.

22 Is there no balm in Gilead?
    Is there no physician there?
Why then has the health of the daughter of my people
    not been restored?
9[m] O that my head were waters,
    and my eyes a fountain of tears,
that I might weep day and night
    for the slain of the daughter of my people!
2[n] O that I had in the desert
    a wayfarers' lodging place,
that I might leave my people
    and go away from them!
For they are all adulterers,
    a company of treacherous men.
3 They bend their tongue like a bow;
    falsehood and not truth has grown strong [o] in the land;
for they proceed from evil to evil,
    and they do not know me,
                        says the LORD.

4 Let every one beware of his neighbor,
    and put no trust in any brother;
for every brother is a supplanter,
    and every neighbor goes about as a slanderer.
5 Every one deceives his neighbor,
    and no one speaks the truth;
they have taught their tongue to speak lies;
    they commit iniquity and are too weary to repent.[p]
6 Heaping oppression upon oppression, and deceit upon
    deceit,
    they refuse to know me,
                        says the LORD.

7 Therefore thus says the LORD of hosts:
    "Behold, I will refine them and test them,
    for what else can I do, because of my people?
8 Their tongue is a deadly arrow;
    it speaks deceitfully;
with his mouth each speaks peaceably to his neighbor,
    but in his heart he plans an ambush for him.
9 Shall I not punish them for these things? says the LORD;
    and shall I not avenge myself
    on a nation such as this?

10 "Take up [q] weeping and wailing for the mountains,
    and a lamentation for the pastures of the wilderness,
because they are laid waste so that no one passes through,
    and the lowing of cattle is not heard;
both the birds of the air and the beasts
    have fled and are gone.
11 I will make Jerusalem a heap of ruins,
    a lair of jackals;
and I will make the cities of Judah a desolation,
    without inhabitant."

---

k Heb uncertain   l Cn Compare Gk: Heb uncertain   m Ch 8.23 in Heb   n Ch 9.1 in Heb
o Gk: Heb *and not for truth they have grown strong*   p Cn Compare Gk: Heb *your dwelling*   q Gk Syr: Heb *I will take up*

12 Who is the man so wise that he can understand this? To whom has the mouth of the LORD spoken, that he may declare it? Why is the land ruined and laid waste like a 13 wilderness, so that no one passes through? And the LORD says: "Because they have forsaken my law which I set before them, and have not obeyed my voice, or walked 14 in accord with it, but have stubbornly followed their own hearts and have gone after the Ba'als, as their fathers 15 taught them. Therefore thus says the LORD of hosts, the God of Israel: Behold, I will feed this people with worm- 16 wood, and give them poisonous water to drink. I will scatter them among the nations whom neither they nor their fathers have known; and I will send the sword after them, until I have consumed them."

17 Thus says the LORD of hosts:
"Consider, and call for the mourning women to come;
  send for the skilful women to come;
18 let them make haste and raise a wailing over us,
  that our eyes may run down with tears,
  and our eyelids gush with water.
19 For a sound of wailing is heard from Zion:
  'How we are ruined!
We are utterly shamed,
  because we have left the land,
  because they have cast down our dwellings.' "

20 Hear, O women, the word of the LORD,
  and let your ear receive the word of his mouth;
teach to your daughters a lament,
  and each to her neighbor a dirge.
21 For death has come up into our windows,
  it has entered our palaces,
cutting off the children from the streets
  and the young men from the squares.
22 Speak, "Thus says the LORD:
  'The dead bodies of men shall fall
  like dung upon the open field,
like sheaves after the reaper,
  and none shall gather them.' "

23 Thus says the LORD: "Let not the wise man glory in his wisdom, let not the mighty man glory in his might, let 24 not the rich man glory in his riches; but let him who glories glory in this, that he understands and knows me, that I am the LORD who practice steadfast love, justice, and righteousness in the earth; for in these things I de-light, says the LORD."
25 "Behold, the days are coming, says the LORD, when I will punish all those who are circumcised but yet un- 26 circumcised—Egypt, Judah, Edom, the sons of Ammon, Moab, and all who dwell in the desert that cut the corners of their hair; for all these nations are uncircumcised, and all the house of Israel is uncircumcised in heart."

r Heb *They*   s This verse is in Aramaic

10 Hear the word which the LORD speaks to you, O house of Israel.
2 Thus says the LORD:
"Learn not the way of the nations,
  nor be dismayed at the signs of the heavens
  because the nations are dismayed at them,
3 for the customs of the peoples are false.
A tree from the forest is cut down,
  and worked with an axe by the hands of a craftsman.
4 Men deck it with silver and gold;
  they fasten it with hammer and nails
  so that it cannot move.
5 Their idols r are like scarecrows in a cucumber field,
  and they cannot speak;
they have to be carried,
  for they cannot walk.
Be not afraid of them,
  for they cannot do evil,
  neither is it in them to do good."

6 There is none like thee, O LORD;
  thou art great, and thy name is great in might.
7 Who would not fear thee, O King of the nations?
  For this is thy due;
for among all the wise ones of the nations
  and in all their kingdoms
  there is none like thee.
8 They are both stupid and foolish;
  the instruction of idols is but wood!
9 Beaten silver is brought from Tarshish,
  and gold from Uphaz.
They are the work of the craftsman
  and of the hands of the goldsmith;
  their clothing is violet and purple;
  they are all the work of skilled men.
10 But the LORD is the true God;
  he is the living God and the everlasting King.
At his wrath the earth quakes,
  and the nations cannot endure his indignation.

11 Thus shall you say to them: "The gods who did not make the heavens and the earth shall perish from the earth and from under the heavens." s

12 It is he who made the earth by his power,
  who established the world by his wisdom,
  and by his understanding stretched out the heavens.
13 When he utters his voice there is a tumult of waters in
    the heavens,
  and he makes the mist rise from the ends of the earth.
He makes lightnings for the rain,
  and he brings forth the wind from his storehouses.
14 Every man is stupid and without knowledge;
  every goldsmith is put to shame by his idols;

for his images are false,
  and there is no breath in them.
15 They are worthless, a work of delusion;
  at the time of their punishment they shall perish.
16 Not like these is he who is the portion of Jacob,
  for he is the one who formed all things,
and Israel is the tribe of his inheritance;
  the Lord of hosts is his name.

17 Gather up your bundle from the ground,
  O you who dwell under siege!
18 For thus says the Lord:
  "Behold, I am slinging out the inhabitants of the land
    at this time,
  and I will bring distress on them,
    that they may feel it."

19 Woe is me because of my hurt!
  My wound is grievous.
But I said, "Truly this is an affliction,
  and I must bear it."
20 My tent is destroyed,
  and all my cords are broken;
my children have gone from me,
  and they are not;
there is no one to spread my tent again,
  and to set up my curtains.
21 For the shepherds are stupid,
  and do not inquire of the Lord;
therefore they have not prospered,
  and all their flock is scattered.

22 Hark, a rumor! Behold, it comes!—
  a great commotion out of the north country
to make the cities of Judah a desolation,
  a lair of jackals.

23 I know, O Lord, that the way of man is not in himself,
  that it is not in man who walks to direct his steps.
24 Correct me, O Lord, but in just measure;
  not in thy anger, lest thou bring me to nothing.

25 Pour out thy wrath upon the nations that know thee not,
  and upon the peoples that call not on thy name;
for they have devoured Jacob;
  they have devoured him and consumed him,
  and have laid waste his habitation.

EVENTS IN JEREMIAH'S LIFE

11 The word that came to Jeremiah from the Lord:
2 "Hear the words of this covenant, and speak to the
3 men of Judah and the inhabitants of Jerusalem. You shall
say to them, Thus says the Lord, the God of Israel:
Cursed be the man who does not heed the words of this

t Gk: Heb many

4 covenant which I commanded your fathers when I brought
them out of the land of Egypt, from the iron furnace,
saying, Listen to my voice, and do all that I command
you. So shall you be my people, and I will be your God,
5 that I may perform the oath which I swore to your fathers,
to give them a land flowing with milk and honey, as at
this day." Then I answered, "So be it, Lord."

6 And the Lord said to me, "Proclaim all these words in
the cities of Judah, and in the streets of Jerusalem: Hear
7 the words of this covenant and do them. For I solemnly
warned your fathers when I brought them up out of the
land of Egypt, warning them persistently, even to this
8 day, saying, Obey my voice. Yet they did not obey or
incline their ear, but every one walked in the stubbornness
of his evil heart. Therefore I brought upon them all the
words of this covenant, which I commanded them to do,
but they did not."
9 Again the Lord said to me, "There is revolt among
10 the men of Judah and the inhabitants of Jerusalem. They
have turned back to the iniquities of their forefathers, who
refused to hear my words; they have gone after other
gods to serve them; the house of Israel and the house of
Judah have broken my covenant which I made with their
11 fathers. Therefore, thus says the Lord, Behold, I am
bringing evil upon them which they cannot escape; though
12 they cry to me, I will not listen to them. Then the cities
of Judah and the inhabitants of Jerusalem will go and
cry to the gods to whom they burn incense, but they
13 cannot save them in the time of their trouble. For your
gods have become as many as your cities, O Judah; and
as many as the streets of Jerusalem are the altars you
have set up to shame, altars to burn incense to Ba'al.
14 "Therefore do not pray for this people, or lift up a cry
or prayer on their behalf, for I will not listen when they
15 call to me in the time of their trouble. What right has my
beloved in my house, when she has done vile deeds? Can
vows t and sacrificial flesh avert your doom? Can you
16 then exult? The Lord once called you, 'A green olive tree,
fair with goodly fruit'; but with the roar of a great
tempest he will set fire to it, and its branches will be
17 consumed. The Lord of hosts, who planted you, has
pronounced evil against you, because of the evil which
the house of Israel and the house of Judah have done,
provoking me to anger by burning incense to Ba'al."

18 The LORD made it known to me and I knew;
  then thou didst show me their evil deeds.
19 But I was like a gentle lamb
  led to the slaughter.
I did not know it was against me
  they devised schemes, saying,
"Let us destroy the tree with its fruit,
  let us cut him off from the land of the living,
  that his name be remembered no more."
20 But, O LORD of hosts, who judgest righteously,
  who triest the heart and the mind,
let me see thy vengeance upon them,
  for to thee have I committed my cause.
21 Therefore thus says the LORD concerning the men of An'athoth, who seek your life, and say, "Do not prophesy in the name of the LORD, or you will die by our hand"— 22 therefore thus says the LORD of hosts: "Behold, I will punish them; the young men shall die by the sword; their 23 sons and their daughters shall die by famine; and none of them shall be left. For I will bring evil upon the men of An'athoth, the year of their punishment."

12 Righteous art thou, O LORD,
  when I complain to thee;
  yet I would plead my case before thee.
Why does the way of the wicked prosper?
  Why do all who are treacherous thrive?
2 Thou plantest them, and they take root;
  they grow and bring forth fruit;
thou art near in their mouth
  and far from their heart.
3 But thou, O LORD, knowest me;
  thou seest me, and triest my mind toward thee.
Pull them out like sheep for the slaughter,
  and set them apart for the day of slaughter.
4 How long will the land mourn,
  and the grass of every field wither?
For the wickedness of those who dwell in it
  the beasts and the birds are swept away,
  because men said, "He will not see our latter end."

5 "If you have raced with men on foot, and they have
    wearied you,
  how will you compete with horses?
And if in a safe land you fall down,
  how will you do in the jungle of the Jordan?
6 For even your brothers and the house of your father,
  even they have dealt treacherously with you;
  they are in full cry after you;
believe them not,
  though they speak fair words to you."

7 "I have forsaken my house,
  I have abandoned my heritage;

I have given the beloved of my soul
  into the hands of her enemies.
8 My heritage has become to me
  like a lion in the forest,
she has lifted up her voice against me;
  therefore I hate her.
9 Is my heritage to me like a speckled bird of prey?
  Are the birds of prey against her round about?
Go, assemble all the wild beasts;
  bring them to devour.
10 Many shepherds have destroyed my vineyard,
  they have trampled down my portion,
they have made my pleasant portion
  a desolate wilderness.
11 They have made it a desolation;
  desolate, it mourns to me.
The whole land is made desolate,
  but no man lays it to heart.
12 Upon all the bare heights in the desert
  destroyers have come;
for the sword of the LORD devours
  from one end of the land to the other;
  no flesh has peace.
13 They have sown wheat and have reaped thorns,
  they have tired themselves out but profit nothing.
They shall be ashamed of their u harvests
  because of the fierce anger of the LORD."

THE WORD OF THE LORD

14 Thus says the LORD concerning all my evil neighbors who touch the heritage which I have given my people Israel to inherit: "Behold, I will pluck them up from their land, and I will pluck up the house of Judah from among 15 them. And after I have plucked them up, I will again have compassion on them, and I will bring them again each 16 to his heritage and each to his land. And it shall come to pass, if they will diligently learn the ways of my people, to swear by my name, 'As the LORD lives,' even as they taught my people to swear by Ba'al, then they shall be 17 built up in the midst of my people. But if any nation will not listen, then I will utterly pluck it up and destroy it, says the LORD."

Parable of the Waistcloth

13 Thus said the LORD to me, "Go and buy a linen waistcloth, and put it on your loins, and do not dip 2 it in water." So I bought a waistcloth according to the 3 word of the LORD, and put it on my loins. And the word 4 of the LORD came to me a second time, "Take the waist-cloth which you have bought, which is upon your loins, and arise, go to the Eu-phra'tes, and hide it there in a 5 cleft of the rock." So I went, and hid it by the Eu-phra'-6 tes, as the LORD commanded me. And after many days the

u Heb *your*

LORD said to me, "Arise, go to the Eu-phra'tes, and take from there the waistcloth which I commanded you to hide 7 there." Then I went to the Eu-phra'tes, and dug, and I took the waistcloth from the place where I had hidden it. And behold, the waistcloth was spoiled; it was good for nothing.

8, 9 Then the word of the LORD came to me: "Thus says the LORD: Even so will I spoil the pride of Judah and the 10 great pride of Jerusalem. This evil people, who refuse to hear my words, who stubbornly follow their own heart and have gone after other gods to serve them and worship them, shall be like this waistcloth, which is good for 11 nothing. For as the waistcloth clings to the loins of a man, so I made the whole house of Israel and the whole house of Judah cling to me, says the LORD, that they might be for me a people, a name, a praise, and a glory, but they would not listen.

12 "You shall speak to them this word: 'Thus says the LORD, the God of Israel, "Every jar shall be filled with wine." ' And they will say to you, 'Do we not indeed know 13 that every jar will be filled with wine?' Then you shall say to them, 'Thus says the LORD: Behold, I will fill with drunkenness all the inhabitants of this land: the kings who sit on David's throne, the priests, the prophets, and 14 all the inhabitants of Jerusalem. And I will dash them one against another, fathers and sons together, says the LORD. I will not pity or spare or have compassion, that I should not destroy them.' "

15 Hear and give ear; be not proud,
  for the LORD has spoken.
16 Give glory to the LORD your God
  before he brings darkness,
before your feet stumble
  on the twilight mountains,
and while you look for light
  he turns it into gloom
  and makes it deep darkness.
17 But if you will not listen,
  my soul will weep in secret for your pride;
my eyes will weep bitterly and run down with tears,
  because the LORD's flock has been taken captive.

18 Say to the king and the queen mother:
  "Take a lowly seat,
for your beautiful crown
  has come down from your head." v
19 The cities of the Negeb are shut up,

with none to open them;
all Judah is taken into exile,
  wholly taken into exile.

20 "Lift up your eyes and see
  those who come from the north.
Where is the flock that was given you,
  your beautiful flock?
21 What will you say when they set as head over you
  those whom you yourself have taught
  to be friends to you?
Will not pangs take hold of you,
  like those of a woman in travail?
22 And if you say in your heart,
  'Why have these things come upon me?'
it is for the greatness of your iniquity
  that your skirts are lifted up,
  and you suffer violence.
23 Can the Ethiopian change his skin
  or the leopard his spots?
Then also you can do good
  who are accustomed to do evil.
24 I will scatter you w like chaff
  driven by the wind from the desert.
25 This is your lot,
  the portion I have measured out to you, says the LORD,
because you have forgotten me
  and trusted in lies.
26 I myself will lift up your skirts over your face,
  and your shame will be seen.
27 I have seen your abominations,
  your adulteries and neighings, your lewd harlotries,
  on the hills in the field.
Woe to you, O Jerusalem!
  How long will it be
  before you are made clean?"

The Drought

14 The word of the LORD which came to Jeremiah concerning the drought:

2 "Judah mourns
  and her gates languish;
her people lament on the ground,
  and the cry of Jerusalem goes up.
3 Her nobles send their servants for water;
  they come to the cisterns,
they find no water,
  they return with their vessels empty;
they are ashamed and confounded
  and cover their heads.
4 Because of the ground which is dismayed,
  since there is no rain on the land,
the farmers are ashamed,

v Gk Syr Vg: Heb obscure   w Heb them

they cover their heads.

5 Even the hind in the field forsakes her newborn calf
  because there is no grass.
6 The wild asses stand on the bare heights,
  they pant for air like jackals;
their eyes fail
  because there is no herbage.

7 "Though our iniquities testify against us,
  act, O LORD, for thy name's sake;
for our backslidings are many,
  we have sinned against thee.
8 O thou hope of Israel,
  its savior in time of trouble,
why shouldst thou be like a stranger in the land,
  like a wayfarer who turns aside to tarry for a night?
9 Why shouldst thou be like a man confused,
  like a mighty man who cannot save?
Yet thou, O LORD, art in the midst of us,
  and we are called by thy name;
    leave us not."

10 Thus says the LORD concerning this people:
"They have loved to wander thus,
  they have not restrained their feet;
therefore the LORD does not accept them,
  now he will remember their iniquity
  and punish their sins."

11 The LORD said to me: "Do not pray for the welfare of
12 this people. Though they fast, I will not hear their cry,
and though they offer burnt offering and cereal offering,
I will not accept them; but I will consume them by the
sword, by famine, and by pestilence."
13 Then I said: "Ah, Lord GOD, behold, the prophets say
to them, 'You shall not see the sword, nor shall you have
famine, but I will give you assured peace in this place.'"
14 And the LORD said to me: "The prophets are prophesying
lies in my name; I did not send them, nor did I command
them or speak to them. They are prophesying to you a
lying vision, worthless divination, and the deceit of their
15 own minds. Therefore thus says the LORD concerning the
prophets who prophesy in my name although I did not
send them, and who say, 'Sword and famine shall not
come on this land': By sword and famine those prophets
16 shall be consumed. And the people to whom they prophesy
shall be cast out in the streets of Jerusalem, victims of
famine and sword, with none to bury them—them, their
wives, their sons, and their daughters. For I will pour out
their wickedness upon them.

17 "You shall say to them this word:
'Let my eyes run down with tears night and day,
  and let them not cease,
for the virgin daughter of my people is smitten with a
great wound,
  with a very grievous blow.
18 If I go out into the field,
  behold, those slain by the sword!
And if I enter the city,
  behold, the diseases of famine!
For both prophet and priest ply their trade through the
    land,
  and have no knowledge.'"

19 Hast thou utterly rejected Judah?
  Does thy soul loathe Zion?
Why hast thou smitten us
  so that there is no healing for us?
We looked for peace, but no good came;
  for a time of healing, but behold, terror.
20 We acknowledge our wickedness, O LORD,
  and the iniquity of our fathers,
  for we have sinned against thee.
21 Do not spurn us, for thy name's sake;
  do not dishonor thy glorious throne;
  remember and do not break thy covenant with us.
22 Are there any among the false gods of the nations that
    can bring rain?
  Or can the heavens give showers?
Art thou not he, O LORD our God?
  We set our hope on thee,
  for thou doest all these things.

15 Then the LORD said to me, "Though Moses and
Samuel stood before me, yet my heart would not
turn toward this people. Send them out of my sight, and
2 let them go! And when they ask you, 'Where shall we go?'
you shall say to them, 'Thus says the LORD:
"Those who are for pestilence, to pestilence,
  and those who are for the sword, to the sword;
those who are for famine, to famine,
  and those who are for captivity, to captivity."'
3 "I will appoint over them four kinds of destroyers, says
the LORD: the sword to slay, the dogs to tear, and the
birds of the air and the beasts of the earth to devour and
4 destroy. And I will make them a horror to all the kingdoms of the earth because of what Manas'seh the son of
Hezeki'ah, king of Judah, did in Jerusalem.

Lamentations
5 "Who will have pity on you, O Jerusalem,
  or who will bemoan you?
Who will turn aside
  to ask about your welfare?
6 You have rejected me,
                                              says the LORD,
  you keep going backward;
so I have stretched out my hand against you and destroyed
    you;—

519

I am weary of relenting.
⁷ I have winnowed them with a winnowing fork
   in the gates of the land;
I have bereaved them, I have destroyed my people;
   they did not turn from their ways.
⁸ I have made their widows more in number
   than the sand of the seas;
I have brought against the mothers of young men
   a destroyer at noonday;
I have made anguish and terror
   fall upon them suddenly.
⁹ She who bore seven has languished;
   she has swooned away;
her sun went down while it was yet day;
   she has been shamed and disgraced.
And the rest of them I will give to the sword
   before their enemies,

                                 says the LORD."

¹⁰   Woe is me, my mother, that you bore me, a man of
strife and contention to the whole land! I have not lent,
¹¹ nor have I borrowed, yet all of them curse me. So let it be,
O LORD,ˣ if I have not entreated ʸ thee for their good, if
I have not pleaded with thee on behalf of the enemy in
¹² the time of trouble and in the time of distress! Can one
break iron, iron from the north, and bronze?
¹³   "Your wealth and your treasures I will give as spoil,
without price, for all your sins, throughout all your ter-
¹⁴ ritory. I will make you serve your enemies in a land which
you do not know, for in my anger a fire is kindled which
shall burn for ever."

¹⁵ O LORD, thou knowest;
   remember me and visit me,
   and take vengeance for me on my persecutors.
In thy forbearance take me not away;
   know that for thy sake I bear reproach.
¹⁶ Thy words were found, and I ate them,
   and thy words became to me a joy
   and the delight of my heart;
for I am called by thy name,
   O LORD, God of hosts.
¹⁷ I did not sit in the company of merrymakers,
   nor did I rejoice;
I sat alone, because thy hand was upon me,
   for thou hadst filled me with indignation.
¹⁸ Why is my pain unceasing,
   my wound incurable,
   refusing to be healed?
Wilt thou be to me like a deceitful brook,
   like waters that fail?

¹⁹ Therefore thus says the LORD:
   "If you return, I will restore you,

ˣ Gk Old Latin: Heb *the* LORD *said*   ʸ Cn: Heb obscure

and you shall stand before me.
If you utter what is precious, and not what is worthless,
   you shall be as my mouth.
They shall turn to you,
   but you shall not turn to them.
²⁰ And I will make you to this people
   a fortified wall of bronze;
they will fight against you,
   but they shall not prevail over you,
for I am with you
   to save you and deliver you,

                                 says the LORD.
²¹ I will deliver you out of the hand of the wicked,
   and redeem you from the grasp of the ruthless."

² 16   The word of the LORD came to me: "You shall not
take a wife, nor shall you have sons or daughters in
³ this place. For thus says the LORD concerning the sons and
daughters who are born in this place, and concerning the
mothers who bore them and the fathers who begot them
⁴ in this land: They shall die of deadly diseases. They shall
not be lamented, nor shall they be buried; they shall be
as dung on the surface of the ground. They shall perish
by the sword and by famine, and their dead bodies shall
be food for the birds of the air and for the beasts of the
earth.
⁵   "For thus says the LORD: Do not enter the house of
mourning, or go to lament, or bemoan them; for I have
taken away my peace from this people, says the LORD, my
⁶ steadfast love and mercy. Both great and small shall die
in this land; they shall not be buried, and no one shall
lament for them or cut himself or make himself bald for
⁷ them. No one shall break bread for the mourner, to
comfort him for the dead; nor shall any one give him the
cup of consolation to drink for his father or his mother.
⁸ You shall not go into the house of feasting to sit with
⁹ them, to eat and drink. For thus says the LORD of hosts,
the God of Israel: Behold, I will make to cease from this
place, before your eyes and in your days, the voice of
mirth and the voice of gladness, the voice of the bridegroom and the voice of the bride.
¹⁰   "And when you tell this people all these words, and
they say to you, 'Why has the LORD pronounced all this
great evil against us? What is our iniquity? What is the
sin that we have committed against the LORD our God?'
¹¹ then you shall say to them: 'Because your fathers have
forsaken me, says the LORD, and have gone after other
gods and have served and worshiped them, and have
¹² forsaken me and have not kept my law, and because you
have done worse than your fathers, for behold, every one
of you follows his stubborn evil will, refusing to listen to
¹³ me; therefore I will hurl you out of this land into a land
which neither you nor your fathers have known, and

there you shall serve other gods day and night, for I will show you no favor.'

14 "Therefore, behold, the days are coming, says the LORD, when it shall no longer be said, 'As the LORD lives who brought up the people of Israel out of the land of 15 Egypt,' but 'As the LORD lives who brought up the people of Israel out of the north country and out of all the countries where he had driven them.' For I will bring them back to their own land which I gave to their fathers.

16 "Behold, I am sending for many fishers, says the LORD, and they shall catch them; and afterwards I will send for many hunters, and they shall hunt them from every mountain and every hill, and out of the clefts of the rocks. 17 For my eyes are upon all their ways; they are not hid from me, nor is their iniquity concealed from my eyes. 18 And ᶻ I will doubly recompense their iniquity and their sin, because they have polluted my land with the carcasses of their detestable idols, and have filled my inheritance with their abominations."

19 O LORD, my strength and my stronghold,
      my refuge in the day of trouble,
to thee shall the nations come
      from the ends of the earth and say:
"Our fathers have inherited nought but lies,
      worthless things in which there is no profit.
20 Can man make for himself gods?
      Such are no gods!"

21 "Therefore, behold, I will make them know, this once I will make them know my power and my might, and they shall know that my name is the LORD."

17 "The sin of Judah is written with a pen of iron; with a point of diamond it is engraved on the tablet 2 of their heart, and on the horns of their altars, while their children remember their altars and their Ashe′rim, beside 3 every green tree, and on the high hills, on the mountains in the open country. Your wealth and all your treasures I will give for spoil as the price of your sin ᵃ throughout 4 all your territory. You shall loosen your hand ᵇ from your

heritage which I gave to you, and I will make you serve your enemies in a land which you do not know, for in my anger a fire is kindled which shall burn for ever."

Trust in the Lord

5 Thus says the LORD:
"Cursed is the man who trusts in man and makes flesh his arm,
      whose heart turns away from the LORD.
6 He is like a shrub in the desert,
      and shall not see any good come.
He shall dwell in the parched places of the wilderness,
      in an uninhabited salt land.

7 "Blessed is the man who trusts in the LORD,
      whose trust is the LORD.
8 He is like a tree planted by water,
      that sends out its roots by the stream,
and does not fear when heat comes,
      for its leaves remain green,
and is not anxious in the year of drought,
      for it does not cease to bear fruit."

9 The heart is deceitful above all things,
      and desperately corrupt;
who can understand it?
10 "I the LORD search the mind
      and try the heart,
to give to every man according to his ways,
      according to the fruit of his doings."

11 Like the partridge that gathers a brood which she did not hatch,
      so is he who gets riches but not by right;
in the midst of his days they will leave him,
      and at his end he will be a fool.

12 A glorious throne set on high from the beginning
      is the place of our sanctuary.
13 O LORD, the hope of Israel,
      all who forsake thee shall be put to shame;
those who turn away from thee ᶜ shall be written in the earth,
      for they have forsaken the LORD, the fountain of living water.

14 Heal me, O LORD, and I shall be healed;
      save me, and I shall be saved;
      for thou art my praise.
15 Behold, they say to me,
      "Where is the word of the LORD?
      Let it come!"
16 I have not pressed thee to send evil,
      nor have I desired the day of disaster,
      thou knowest;
that which came out of my lips
      was before thy face.
17 Be not a terror to me;
      thou art my refuge in the day of evil.
18 Let those be put to shame who persecute me,

ᶻ Gk: Heb *And first*   ᵃ Cn: Heb *your high places for sin*   ᵇ Cn: Heb *and in you*   ᶜ Heb *me*

but let me not be put to shame;
let them be dismayed,
   but let me not be dismayed;
bring upon them the day of evil;
   destroy them with double destruction!

19 Thus said the LORD to me: "Go and stand in the Benjamin [d] Gate, by which the kings of Judah enter and by
20 which they go out, and in all the gates of Jerusalem, and say: 'Hear the word of the LORD, you kings of Judah, and all Judah, and all the inhabitants of Jerusalem, who
21 enter by these gates. Thus says the LORD: Take heed for the sake of your lives, and do not bear a burden on the
22 sabbath day or bring it in by the gates of Jerusalem. And do not carry a burden out of your houses on the sabbath or do any work, but keep the sabbath day holy, as I
23 commanded your fathers. Yet they did not listen or incline their ear, but stiffened their neck, that they might not hear and receive instruction.

24 " 'But if you listen to me, says the LORD, and bring in no burden by the gates of this city on the sabbath day, but keep the sabbath day holy and do no work on
25 it, then there shall enter by the gates of this city kings [e] who sit on the throne of David, riding in chariots and on horses, they and their princes, the men of Judah and the inhabitants of Jerusalem; and this city shall be
26 inhabited for ever. And people shall come from the cities of Judah and the places round about Jerusalem, from the land of Benjamin, from the Shephe'lah, from the hill country, and from the Negeb, bringing burnt offerings and sacrifices, cereal offerings and frankincense, and
27 bringing thank offerings to the house of the LORD. But if you do not listen to me, to keep the sabbath day holy, and not to bear a burden and enter by the gates of Jerusalem on the sabbath day, then I will kindle a fire in its gates, and it shall devour the palaces of Jerusalem and shall not be quenched.' "

Parable of the Potter

18 The word that came to Jeremiah from the LORD:
2 "Arise, and go down to the potter's house, and there
3 I will let you hear my words." So I went down to the potter's house, and there he was working at his wheel.
4 And the vessel he was making of clay was spoiled in the potter's hand, and he reworked it into another vessel, as it seemed good to the potter to do.

5, 6 Then the word of the LORD came to me: "O house of Israel, can I not do with you as this potter has done?

says the LORD. Behold, like the clay in the potter's hand,
7 so are you in my hand, O house of Israel. If at any time I declare concerning a nation or a kingdom, that I will
8 pluck up and break down and destroy it, and if that nation, concerning which I have spoken, turns from its evil, I will repent of the evil that I intended to do to it.
9 And if at any time I declare concerning a nation or a
10 kingdom that I will build and plant it, and if it does evil in my sight, not listening to my voice, then I will repent of the good which I had intended to do to it.
11 Now, therefore, say to the men of Judah and the inhabitants of Jerusalem: 'Thus says the LORD, Behold, I am shaping evil against you and devising a plan against you. Return, every one from his evil way, and amend your ways and your doings.'
12 "But they say, 'That is in vain! We will follow our own plans, and will every one act according to the stubbornness of his evil heart.'

13 "Therefore thus says the LORD:
Ask among the nations,
   who has heard the like of this?
The virgin Israel
   has done a very horrible thing.
14 Does the snow of Lebanon leave
   the crags of Sirion? [f]
Do the mountain [g] waters run dry, [h]
   the cold flowing streams?
15 But my people have forgotten me,
   they burn incense to false gods;
they have stumbled [i] in their ways,
   in the ancient roads,
and have gone into bypaths,
   not the highway,
16 making their land a horror,
   a thing to be hissed at for ever.
Every one who passes by it is horrified
   and shakes his head.
17 Like the east wind I will scatter them
   before the enemy.
I will show them my back, not my face,
   in the day of their calamity."

A PLOT AGAINST JEREMIAH
18 Then they said, "Come, let us make plots against Jeremiah, for the law shall not perish from the priest, nor counsel from the wise, nor the word from the prophet. Come, let us smite him with the tongue, and let us not heed any of his words."

19 Give heed to me, O LORD,
   and hearken to my plea. [j]
20 Is evil a recompense for good?
   Yet they have dug a pit for my life.

---

[d] Cn: Heb *sons of people*   [e] Cn: Heb *kings and princes*   [f] Cn: Heb *the field*   [g] Cn: Heb *foreign*
[h] Cn: Heb *Are . . . plucked up?*   [i] Gk Syr Vg: Heb *they made them stumble*   [j] Gk Compare Syr Tg: Heb *my adversaries*

Remember how I stood before thee
  to speak good for them,
  to turn away thy wrath from them.
21 Therefore deliver up their children to famine;
  give them over to the power of the sword,
let their wives become childless and widowed.
  May their men meet death by pestilence,
  their youths be slain by the sword in battle.
22 May a cry be heard from their houses,
  when thou bringest the marauder suddenly upon them!
For they have dug a pit to take me,
  and laid snares for my feet.
23 Yet, thou, O Lord, knowest
  all their plotting to slay me.
Forgive not their iniquity,
  nor blot out their sin from thy sight.
Let them be overthrown before thee;
  deal with them in the time of thine anger.

19 Thus said the Lord, "Go, buy a potter's earthen flask, and take some of the elders of the people and 2 some of the senior priests, and go out to the valley of the son of Hinnom at the entry of the Potsherd Gate, and 3 proclaim there the words that I tell you. You shall say, 'Hear the word of the Lord, O kings of Judah and inhabitants of Jerusalem. Thus says the Lord of hosts, the God of Israel, Behold, I am bringing such evil upon this place that the ears of every one who hears of it will tingle. 4 Because the people have forsaken me, and have profaned this place by burning incense in it to other gods whom neither they nor their fathers nor the kings of Judah have known; and because they have filled this place with 5 the blood of innocents, and have built the high places of Ba'al to burn their sons in the fire as burnt offerings to Ba'al, which I did not command or decree, nor did it 6 come into my mind; therefore, behold, days are coming, says the Lord, when this place shall no more be called Topheth, or the valley of the son of Hinnom, but the 7 valley of Slaughter. And in this place I will make void the plans of Judah and Jerusalem, and will cause their people to fall by the sword before their enemies, and by the hand of those who seek their life. I will give their dead bodies for food to the birds of the air and to the 8 beasts of the earth. And I will make this city a horror, a thing to be hissed at; every one who passes by it will be horrified and will hiss because of all its disasters. 9 And I will make them eat the flesh of their sons and their daughters, and every one shall eat the flesh of his neighbor in the siege and in the distress, with which their enemies and those who seek their life afflict them.' 10 "Then you shall break the flask in the sight of the men 11 who go with you, and shall say to them, 'Thus says the Lord of hosts: So will I break this people and this city, as one breaks a potter's vessel, so that it can never be

mended. Men shall bury in Topheth because there will be 12 no place else to bury. Thus will I do to this place, says the Lord, and to its inhabitants, making this city like 13 Topheth. The houses of Jerusalem and the houses of the kings of Judah—all the houses upon whose roofs incense has been burned to all the host of heaven, and drink offerings have been poured out to other gods—shall be defiled like the place of Topheth.' "

14 Then Jeremiah came from Topheth, where the Lord had sent him to prophesy, and he stood in the court of 15 the Lord's house, and said to all the people: "Thus says the Lord of hosts, the God of Israel, Behold, I am bringing upon this city and upon all its towns all the evil that I have pronounced against it, because they have stiffened their neck, refusing to hear my words."

20 Now Pashhur the priest, the son of Immer, who was chief officer in the house of the Lord, heard Jeremiah prophesying these things. Then Pashhur beat Jeremiah the prophet, and put him in the stocks that were in 3 the upper Benjamin Gate of the house of the Lord. On the morrow, when Pashhur released Jeremiah from the stocks, Jeremiah said to him, "The Lord does not call 4 your name Pashhur, but Terror on every side. For thus says the Lord: Behold, I will make you a terror to yourself and to all your friends. They shall fall by the sword of their enemies while you look on. And I will give all Judah into the hand of the king of Babylon; he shall carry them captive to Babylon, and shall slay them with 5 the sword. Moreover, I will give all the wealth of the city, all its gains, all its prized belongings, and all the treasures of the kings of Judah into the hand of their enemies, who shall plunder them, and seize them, and carry them to 6 Babylon. And you, Pashhur, and all who dwell in your house, shall go into captivity; to Babylon you shall go; and there you shall die, and there you shall be buried, you and all your friends, to whom you have prophesied falsely."

7 O Lord, thou hast deceived me,
  and I was deceived;
thou art stronger than I,
  and thou hast prevailed.
I have become a laughingstock all the day;
  every one mocks me.
8 For whenever I speak, I cry out,
  I shout, "Violence and destruction!"

For the word of the LORD has become for me
  a reproach and derision all day long.
⁹ If I say, "I will not mention him,
  or speak any more in his name,"
there is in my heart as it were a burning fire
  shut up in my bones,
and I am weary with holding it in,
  and I cannot.
¹⁰ For I hear many whispering.
  Terror is on every side!

"Denounce him! Let us denounce him!"
  say all my familiar friends,
  watching for my fall.
"Perhaps he will be deceived,
  then we can overcome him,
  and take our revenge on him."
¹¹ But the LORD is with me as a dread warrior;
  therefore my persecutors will stumble,
  they will not overcome me.
They will be greatly shamed,
  for they will not succeed.
Their eternal dishonor
  will never be forgotten.
¹² O LORD of hosts, who triest the righteous,
  who seest the heart and the mind,
let me see thy vengeance upon them,
  for to thee have I committed my cause.

¹³ Sing to the LORD;
  praise the LORD!
For he has delivered the life of the needy
  from the hand of evildoers.

¹⁴ Cursed be the day
  on which I was born!
The day when my mother bore me,
  let it not be blessed!
¹⁵ Cursed be the man
  who brought the news to my father,
"A son is born to you,"
  making him very glad.
¹⁶ Let that man be like the cities
  which the LORD overthrew without pity;
let him hear a cry in the morning
  and an alarm at noon,
¹⁷ because he did not kill me in the womb;
  so my mother would have been my grave,
  and her womb for ever great.

¹⁸ Why did I come forth from the womb
  to see toil and sorrow,
  and spend my days in shame?

ORACLES CONCERNING KINGS OF JUDAH

21 This is the word which came to Jeremiah from the LORD, when King Zedeki'ah sent to him Pashhur the son of Malchi'ah and Zephani'ah the priest, the son of ² Ma-asei'ah, saying, "Inquire of the LORD for us, for Nebuchadrez'zar king of Babylon is making war against us; perhaps the LORD will deal with us according to all his wonderful deeds, and will make him withdraw from us."

³,⁴ Then Jeremiah said to them: "Thus you shall say to Zedeki'ah, 'Thus says the LORD, the God of Israel: Behold, I will turn back the weapons of war which are in your hands and with which you are fighting against the king of Babylon and against the Chalde'ans who are besieging you outside the walls; and I will bring them ⁵ together into the midst of this city. I myself will fight against you with outstretched hand and strong arm, in ⁶ anger, and in fury, and in great wrath. And I will smite the inhabitants of this city, both man and beast; they shall ⁷ die of a great pestilence. Afterward, says the LORD, I will give Zedeki'ah king of Judah, and his servants, and the people in this city who survive the pestilence, sword, and famine, into the hand of Nebuchadrez'zar king of Babylon and into the hand of their enemies, into the hand of those who seek their lives. He shall smite them with the edge of the sword; he shall not pity them, or spare them, or have compassion.'

⁸ "And to this people you shall say: 'Thus says the LORD: Behold, I set before you the way of life and the way of ⁹ death. He who stays in this city shall die by the sword, by famine, and by pestilence; but he who goes out and surrenders to the Chalde'ans who are besieging you shall ¹⁰ live and shall have his life as a prize of war. For I have set my face against this city for evil and not for good, says the LORD: it shall be given into the hand of the king of Babylon, and he shall burn it with fire.'

¹¹ "And to the house of the king of Judah say, 'Hear the ¹² word of the LORD, O house of David! Thus says the LORD:

" 'Execute justice in the morning,
  and deliver from the hand of the oppressor
  him who has been robbed,
lest my wrath go forth like fire,
  and burn with none to quench it,
  because of your evil doings.' "

¹³ "Behold, I am against you, O inhabitant of the valley,
  O rock of the plain,

                 says the LORD;

you who say, 'Who shall come down against us,
 or who shall enter our habitations?'
14 I will punish you according to the fruit of your doings,
 says the LORD;

I will kindle a fire in her forest,
 and it shall devour all that is round about her."

22 Thus says the LORD: "Go down to the house of
2 the king of Judah, and speak there this word, and
say, 'Hear the word of the LORD, O King of Judah, who sit
on the throne of David, you, and your servants, and your
3 people who enter these gates. Thus says the LORD: Do
justice and righteousness, and deliver from the hand of the
oppressor him who has been robbed. And do no wrong or
violence to the alien, the fatherless, and the widow, nor
4 shed innocent blood in this place. For if you will indeed
obey this word, then there shall enter the gates of this
house kings who sit on the throne of David, riding in
chariots and on horses, they, and their servants, and their
5 people. But if you will not heed these words, I swear by
myself, says the LORD, that this house shall become a
6 desolation. For thus says the LORD concerning the house of
the king of Judah:

" 'You are as Gilead to me,
 as the summit of Lebanon,
yet surely I will make you a desert,
 an uninhabited city.ᵏ
7 I will prepare destroyers against you,
 each with his weapons;
and they shall cut down your choicest cedars,
 and cast them into the fire.
8 " 'And many nations will pass by this city, and every
man will say to his neighbor, "Why has the LORD dealt
9 thus with this great city?" And they will answer, "Because they forsook the covenant of the LORD their God,
and worshiped other gods and served them." ' "

10 Weep not for him who is dead,
 nor bemoan him;
but weep bitterly for him who goes away,
 for he shall return no more
 to see his native land.

11 For thus says the LORD concerning Shallum the son of
Josi'ah, king of Judah, who reigned instead of Josi'ah
his father, and who went away from this place: "He shall
12 return here no more; but in the place where they have
carried him captive, there shall he die, and he shall never
see this land again."

13 "Woe to him who builds his house by unrighteousness,
 and his upper rooms by injustice;
who makes his neighbor serve him for nothing,
 and does not give him his wages;

14 who says, 'I will build myself a great house
 with spacious upper rooms,'
and cuts out windows for it,
 paneling it with cedar,
 and painting it with vermilion.
15 Do you think you are a king
 because you compete in cedar?
Did not your father eat and drink
 and do justice and righteousness?
 Then it was well with him.
16 He judged the cause of the poor and needy;
 then it was well.
Is not this to know me?
 says the LORD.
17 But you have eyes and heart
 only for your dishonest gain,
for shedding innocent blood,
 and for practicing oppression and violence."
18 Therefore thus says the LORD concerning Jehoi'akim
the son of Josi'ah, king of Judah:
"They shall not lament for him, saying,
 'Ah my brother!' or 'Ah sister!'
They shall not lament for him, saying,
 'Ah lord!' or 'Ah his majesty!'
19 With the burial of an ass he shall be buried,
 dragged and cast forth beyond the gates of Jerusalem."

20 "Go up to Lebanon, and cry out,
 and lift up your voice in Bashan;
cry from Ab'arim,
 for all your lovers are destroyed.
21 I spoke to you in your prosperity,
 but you said, 'I will not listen.'
This has been your way from your youth,
 that you have not obeyed my voice.
22 The wind shall shepherd all your shepherds,
 and your lovers shall go into captivity;
then you will be ashamed and confounded
 because of all your wickedness.
23 O inhabitant of Lebanon,
 nested among the cedars,
how you will groanˡ when pangs come upon you,
 pain as of a woman in travail!"

24 "As I live, says the LORD, though Coni'ah the son of
Jehoi'akim, king of Judah, were the signet ring on my
25 right hand, yet I would tear you off and give you into

ᵏ Cn: Heb *cities*   ˡ Gk Vg Syr: Heb *be pitied*

the hand of those who seek your life, into the hand of those of whom you are afraid, even into the hand of Nebuchadrez′zar king of Babylon and into the hand of 26 the Chalde′ans. I will hurl you and the mother who bore you into another country, where you were not born, and 27 there you shall die. But to the land to which they will long to return, there they shall not return."

28 Is this man Coni′ah a despised, broken pot,
  a vessel no one cares for?
Why are he and his children hurled and cast
  into a land which they do not know?
29 O land, land, land,
  hear the word of the LORD!
30 Thus says the LORD:
"Write this man down as childless,
  a man who shall not succeed in his days;
for none of his offspring shall succeed
  in sitting on the throne of David,
  and ruling again in Judah."

23 "Woe to the shepherds who destroy and scatter the sheep of my pasture!" says the LORD. Therefore thus says the LORD, the God of Israel, concerning the shepherds who care for my people: "You have scattered my flock, and have driven them away, and you have not attended to them. Behold, I will attend to you for your 3 evil doings, says the LORD. Then I will gather the remnant of my flock out of all the countries where I have driven them, and I will bring them back to their fold, and they 4 shall be fruitful and mulitiply. I will set shepherds over them who will care for them, and they shall fear no more, nor be dismayed, neither shall any be missing, says the LORD.

5 "Behold, the days are coming, says the LORD, when I will raise up for David a righteous Branch, and he shall reign as king and deal wisely, and shall execute justice 6 and righteousness in the land. In his days Judah will be saved, and Israel will dwell securely. And this is the name by which he will be called: 'The LORD is our righteousness.'

7 "Therefore, behold, the days are coming, says the LORD, when men shall no longer say, 'As the Lord lives who brought up the people of Israel out of the land of 8 Egypt,' but 'As the LORD lives who brought up and led the descendants of the house of Israel out of the north country and out of all the countries where he^m had driven them.' Then they shall dwell in their own land."

ORACLES CONCERNING THE PROPHETS

9 Concerning the prophets:
My heart is broken within me,
  all my bones shake;
I am like a drunken man,
  like a man overcome by wine,

m Gk: Heb I

because of the LORD
  and because of his holy words.
10 For the land is full of adulterers;
  because of the curse the land mourns,
  and the pastures of the wilderness are dried up.
Their course is evil,
  and their might is not right.
11 "Both prophet and priest are ungodly;
  even in my house I have found their wickedness,
                                              says the LORD.
12 Therefore their way shall be to them
  like slippery paths in the darkness,
  into which they shall be driven and fall;
for I will bring evil upon them
  in the year of their punishment,
                                              says the LORD.
13 In the prophets of Samar′ia
  I saw an unsavory thing:
they prophesied by Ba′al
  and led my people Israel astray.
14 But in the prophets of Jerusalem
  I have seen a horrible thing:
they commit adultery and walk in lies;
  they strengthen the hands of evildoers,
  so that no one turns from his wickedness;
all of them have become like Sodom to me,
  and its inhabitants like Gomor′rah."
15 Therefore thus says the LORD of hosts concerning the prophets:
"Behold, I will feed them with wormwood,
  and give them poisoned water to drink;
for from the prophets of Jerusalem
  ungodliness has gone forth into all the land."

16 Thus says the LORD of hosts: "Do not listen to the words of the prophets who prophesy to you, filling you with vain hopes; they speak visions of their own minds, not from 17 the mouth of the LORD. They say continually to those who despise the word of the LORD, 'It shall be well with you'; and to every one who stubbornly follows his own heart, they say, 'No evil shall come upon you.' "

18 For who among them has stood in the council of the LORD
  to perceive and to hear his word,
  or who has given heed to his word and listened?
19 Behold, the storm of the LORD!
  Wrath has gone forth,
  a whirling tempest;
  it will burst upon the head of the wicked.
20 The anger of the LORD will not turn back
  until he has executed and accomplished
  the intents of his mind.
In the latter days you will understand it clearly.

21 "I did not send the prophets,

yet they ran;
I did not speak to them,
  yet they prophesied.
²² But if they had stood in my council,
  then they would have proclaimed my words to my
    people,
  and they would have turned them from their evil way,
    and from the evil of their doings.

²³ "Am I a God at hand, says the LORD, and not a God afar
²⁴ off? Can a man hide himself in secret places so that I
cannot see him? says the LORD. Do I not fill heaven and
²⁵ earth? says the LORD. I have heard what the prophets
have said who prophesy lies in my name, saying, 'I have
²⁶ dreamed, I have dreamed!' How long shall there be lies [n]
in the heart of the prophets who prophesy lies, and who
²⁷ prophesy the deceit of their own heart, who think to make
my people forget my name by their dreams which they
tell one another, even as their fathers forgot my name for
²⁸ Ba'al? Let the prophet who has a dream tell the dream,
but let him who has my word speak my word faithfully.
What has straw in common with wheat? says the LORD.
²⁹ Is not my word like fire, says the LORD, and like a
³⁰ hammer which breaks the rock in pieces? Therefore,
behold, I am against the prophets, says the LORD, who
³¹ steal my words from one another. Behold, I am against
the prophets, says the LORD, who use their tongues and
³² say, 'Says the LORD.' Behold, I am against those who
prophesy lying dreams, says the LORD, and who tell them
and lead my people astray by their lies and their reckless-
ness, when I did not send them or charge them; so they
do not profit this people at all, says the LORD.
³³ "When one of this people, or a prophet, or a priest
asks you, 'What is the burden of the LORD?' you shall
say to them, 'You are the burden,[o] and I will cast you off,
³⁴ says the LORD.' And as for the prophet, priest, or one of
the people who says, 'The burden of the LORD,' I will
³⁵ punish that man and his household. Thus shall you say,
every one to his neighbor and every one to his brother,
'What has the LORD answered?' or 'What has the LORD
³⁶ spoken?' But 'the burden of the LORD' you shall mention
no more, for the burden is every man's own word, and
you pervert the words of the living God, the LORD of
³⁷ hosts, our God. Thus you shall say to the prophet, 'What
has the LORD answered you?' or 'What has the LORD
³⁸ spoken?' But if you say, 'The burden of the LORD,' thus
says the LORD, 'Because you have said these words, "The
burden of the LORD," when I sent to you, saying, "You
³⁹ shall not say, 'The burden of the LORD,'" therefore, be-
hold, I will surely lift you up and cast you away from my
presence, you and the city which I gave to you and your
⁴⁰ fathers. And I will bring upon you everlasting reproach
and perpetual shame, which shall not be forgotten.'"

[n] Cn Compare Syr: Heb obscure   [o] Gk Vg: Heb *What burden*

VISION OF THE FIGS

24 After Nebuchadrez'zar king of Babylon had taken
into exile from Jerusalem Jeconi'ah the son of
Jehoi'akim, king of Judah, together with the princes of
Judah, the craftsmen, and the smiths, and had brought
them to Babylon, the LORD showed me this vision: Behold, two baskets of figs placed before the temple of the
² LORD. One basket had very good figs, like first-ripe figs,
but the other basket had very bad figs, so bad that they
³ could not be eaten. And the LORD said to me, "What do
you see, Jeremiah?" I said, "Figs, the good figs very
good, and the bad figs very bad, so bad that they cannot
be eaten."
^{4, 5} Then the word of the LORD came to me: "Thus says
the LORD, the God of Israel: Like these good figs, so I
will regard as good the exiles from Judah, whom I have
sent away from this place to the land of the Chalde'ans.
⁶ I will set my eyes upon them for good, and I will bring
them back to this land. I will build them up, and not
tear them down; I will plant them, and not uproot them.
⁷ I will give them a heart to know that I am the LORD;
and they shall be my people and I will be their God, for
they shall return to me with their whole heart.
⁸ "But thus says the LORD: Like the bad figs which are so
bad they cannot be eaten, so will I treat Zedeki'ah the
king of Judah, his princes, the remnant of Jerusalem
who remain in this land, and those who dwell in the land
⁹ of Egypt. I will make them a horror [p] to all the kingdoms

of the earth, to be a reproach, a byword, a taunt, and a
¹⁰ curse in all the places where I shall drive them. And I
will send sword, famine, and pestilence upon them, until
they shall be utterly destroyed from the land which I gave
to them and their fathers."

JUDAH'S DISOBEDIENCE—GOD'S WRATH

25 The word that came to Jeremiah concerning all
the people of Judah, in the fourth year of Jehoi'akim
the son of Josi'ah, king of Judah (that was the first year
² of Nebuchadrez'zar king of Babylon), which Jeremiah
the prophet spoke to all the people of Judah and all the
³ inhabitants of Jerusalem: "For twenty-three years, from
the thirteenth year of Josi'ah the son of Amon, king of
Judah, to this day, the word of the LORD has come to me,
and I have spoken persistently to you, but you have not
⁴ listened. You have neither listened nor inclined your ears
to hear, although the LORD persistently sent to you all his

[p] Compare Gk: Heb *horror for evil*

5 servants the prophets, saying, 'Turn now, every one of
you, from his evil way and wrong doings, and dwell upon
the land which the LORD has given to you and your fathers
6 from of old and for ever; do not go after other gods to
serve and worship them, or provoke me to anger with the
7 work of your hands. Then I will do you no harm.' Yet
you have not listened to me, says the LORD, that you might
provoke me to anger with the work of your hands to your
own harm.
8 "Therefore thus says the LORD of hosts: Because you
9 have not obeyed my words, behold, I will send for all the
tribes of the north, says the LORD, and for Nebuchadrez'-
zar the king of Babylon, my servant, and I will bring
them against this land and its inhabitants, and against all
these nations round about; I will utterly destroy them,
and make them a horror, a hissing, and an everlasting
10 reproach.[q] Moreover, I will banish from them the voice of
mirth and the voice of gladness, the voice of the bridegroom and the voice of the bride, the grinding of the mill-
11 stones and the light of the lamp. This whole land shall
become a ruin and a waste, and these nations shall serve
12 the king of Babylon seventy years. Then after seventy
years are completed, I will punish the king of Babylon
and that nation, the land of the Chalde'ans, for their
iniquity, says the LORD, making the land an everlasting
13 waste. I will bring upon that land all the words which I
have uttered against it, everything written in this book,
14 which Jeremiah prophesied against all the nations. For
many nations and great kings shall make slaves even of
them; and I will recompense them according to their deeds
and the work of their hands."
15 Thus the LORD, the God of Israel, said to me: "Take
from my hand this cup of the wine of wrath, and make all
16 the nations to whom I send you drink it. They shall drink
and stagger and be crazed because of the sword which I
am sending among them."
17 So I took the cup from the LORD's hand, and made all
18 the nations to whom the Lord sent me drink it: Jerusalem
and the cities of Judah, its kings and princes, to make
them a desolation and a waste, a hissing and a curse, as
19 at this day; Pharaoh king of Egypt, his servants, his
20 princes, all his people, and all the foreign folk among
them; all the kings of the land of Uz and all the kings of
the land of the Philistines (Ash'kelon, Gaza, Ekron, and
21 the remnant of Ashdod); Edom, Moab, and the sons of
22 Ammon; all the kings of Tyre, all the kings of Sidon, and
23 the kings of the coastland across the sea; Dedan, Tema,
24 Buz, and all who cut the corners of their hair; all the kings
of Arabia and all the kings of the mixed tribes that dwell
25 in the desert; all the kings of Zimri, all the kings of Elam,
26 and all the kings of Media; all the kings of the north, far
and near, one after another, and all the kingdoms of the
world which are on the face of the earth. And after them
the king of Babylon[r] shall drink.
27 "Then you shall say to them, 'Thus says the LORD of
hosts, the God of Israel: Drink, be drunk and vomit, fall
and rise no more, because of the sword which I am
sending among you.'
28 "And if they refuse to accept the cup from your hand
to drink, then you shall say to them, 'Thus says the LORD
29 of hosts: You must drink! For behold, I begin to work
evil at the city which is called by my name, and shall you
go unpunished? You shall not go unpunished, for I am
summoning a sword against all the inhabitants of the
earth, says the LORD of hosts.'

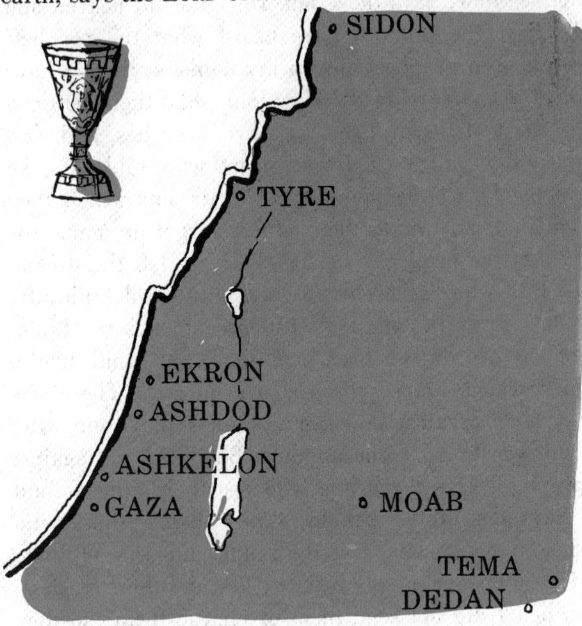

30 "You, therefore, shall prophesy against them all these
words, and say to them:
'The LORD will roar from on high,
and from his holy habitation utter his voice;
he will roar mightily against his fold,
and shout, like those who tread grapes,
against all the inhabitants of the earth.
31 The clamor will resound to the ends of the earth,
for the LORD has an indictment against the nations;
he is entering into judgment with all flesh,
and the wicked he will put to the sword,
says the LORD.'

32 "Thus says the LORD of hosts:
Behold, evil is going forth
from nation to nation,
and a great tempest is stirring
from the farthest parts of the earth!
33 "And those slain by the LORD on that day shall extend
from one end of the earth to the other. They shall not
be lamented, or gathered, or buried; they shall be dung
on the surface of the ground.

[q] Gk Compare Syr: Heb *desolations*
[r] Heb *Sheshach*, a cipher for Babylon

34 "Wail, you shepherds, and cry,
   and roll in ashes, you lords of the flock,
 for the days of your slaughter and dispersion have come,
   and you shall fall like choice rams.ˢ
35 No refuge will remain for the shepherds,
   nor escape for the lords of the flock.
36 Hark, the cry of the shepherds,
   and the wail of the lords of the flock!
 For the LORD is despoiling their pasture,
37   and the peaceful folds are devastated,
   because of the fierce anger of the LORD.
38 Like a lion he has left his covert,
   for their land has become a waste
 because of the sword of the oppressor,
   and because of his fierce anger."

JEREMIAH'S LIFE AS A PROPHET
Attacked in the Temple

26 In the beginning of the reign of Jehoi'akim the son of Josi'ah, king of Judah, this word came from 2 the LORD. "Thus says the LORD: Stand in the court of the LORD's house, and speak to all the cities of Judah which come to worship in the house of the LORD all the words that I command you to speak to them; do not hold 3 back a word. It may be they will listen, and every one turn from his evil way, that I may repent of the evil which 4 I intend to do to them because of their evil doings. You shall say to them, 'Thus says the LORD: If you will not listen to me, to walk in my law which I have set before 5 you, and to heed the words of my servants the prophets whom I send to you urgently, though you have not heeded, 6 then I will make this house like Shiloh, and I will make this city a curse for all the nations of the earth.'"

7 The priests and the prophets and all the people heard Jeremiah speaking these words in the house of the LORD. 8 And when Jeremiah had finished speaking all that the LORD had commanded him to speak to all the people, then the priests and the prophets and all the people laid hold 9 of him, saying, "You shall die! Why have you prophesied in the name of the LORD, saying, 'This house shall be like Shiloh, and this city shall be desolate, without inhabitant'?" And all the people gathered about Jeremiah in the house of the LORD.

10 When the princes of Judah heard these things, they came up from the king's house to the house of the LORD and took their seat in the entry of the New Gate of the 11 house of the LORD. Then the priests and the prophets said to the princes and to all the people, "This man deserves the sentence of death, because he has prophesied against this city, as you have heard with your own ears."

12 Then Jeremiah spoke to all the princes and all the people, saying, "The LORD sent me to prophesy against this house and this city and all the words you have heard.

13 Now therefore amend your ways and your doings, and obey the voice of the LORD your God, and the LORD will repent of the evil which he has pronounced against you. 14 But as for me, behold, I am in your hands. Do with me 15 as seems good and right to you. Only know for certain that if you put me to death, you will bring innocent blood upon yourselves and upon this city and its inhabitants, for in truth the LORD sent me to you to speak all these words in your ears."

16 Then the princes and all the people said to the priests and the prophets, "This man does not deserve the sentence of death, for he has spoken to us in the name of the LORD 17 our God." And certain of the elders of the land arose and 18 spoke to all the assembled people, saying, "Micah of More'sheth prophesied in the days of Hezeki'ah king of Judah, and said to all the people of Judah: 'Thus says the LORD of hosts,
Zion shall be plowed as a field;
   Jerusalem shall become a heap of ruins,
   and the mountain of the house a wooded height.'
19 Did Hezeki'ah king of Judah and all Judah put him to death? Did he not fear the LORD and entreat the favor of the LORD, and did not the LORD repent of the evil which he had pronounced against them? But we are about to bring great evil upon ourselves."

20 There was another man who prophesied in the name of the LORD, Uri'ah the son of Shemai'ah from Kir'iath-je'arim. He prophesied against this city and against this 21 land in words like those of Jeremiah. And when King Jehoi'akim, with all his warriors and all the princes, heard his words, the king sought to put him to death; but when Uri'ah heard of it, he was afraid and fled and escaped to 22 Egypt. Then King Jehoi'akim sent to Egypt certain men, 23 Elna'than the son of Achbor and others with him, and they fetched Uri'ah from Egypt and brought him to King Jehoi'akim, who slew him with the sword and cast his dead body into the burial place of the common people. 24 But the hand of Ahi'kam the son of Shaphan was with Jeremiah so that he was not given over to the people to be put to death.

The Yoke of Babylon

27 In the beginning of the reign of Zedeki'ahᵘ the son of Josi'ah, king of Judah, this word came to 2 Jeremiah from the LORD. Thus the LORD said to me: "Make yourself thongs and yoke-bars, and put them on your 3 neck. Send wordᵛ to the king of Edom, the king of Moab, the king of the sons of Ammon, the king of Tyre, and the king of Sidon by the hand of the envoys who have come to 4 Jerusalem to Zedeki'ah king of Judah. Give them this charge for their masters: 'Thus says the LORD of hosts, the God of Israel: This is what you shall say to your masters: 5 "It is I who by my great power and my outstretched arm

---

ˢ Gk: Heb *a choice vessel*   ᵘ Another reading is *Jehoiakim*   ᵛ Cn: Heb *send them*

have made the earth, with the men and animals that are on the earth, and I give it to whomever it seems right to 6 me. Now I have given all these lands into the hand of Nebuchadnez'zar, the king of Babylon, my servant, and I have given him also the beasts of the field to serve him. 7 All the nations shall serve him and his son and his grandson, until the time of his own land comes; then many nations and great kings shall make him their slave.

8 " ' "But if any nation or kingdom will not serve this Nebuchadnez'zar king of Babylon, and put its neck under the yoke of the king of Babylon, I will punish that nation with the sword, with famine, and with pestilence, says the 9 LORD, until I have consumed it by his hand. So do not listen to your prophets, your diviners, your dreamers,ʷ

your soothsayers, or your sorcerers, who are saying to 10 you, 'You shall not serve the king of Babylon.' For it is a lie which they are prophesying to you, with the result that you will be removed far from your land, and I will 11 drive you out, and you will perish. But any nation which will bring its neck under the yoke of the king of Babylon and serve him, I will leave on its own land, to till it and dwell there, says the LORD.' ' "

12 To Zedeki'ah king of Judah I spoke in like manner: "Bring your necks under the yoke of the king of Babylon, 13 and serve him and his people, and live. Why will you and your people die by the sword, by famine, and by pestilence, as the LORD has spoken concerning any nation 14 which will not serve the king of Babylon? Do not listen to the words of the prophets who are saying to you, 'You shall not serve the king of Babylon,' for it is a lie which 15 they are prophesying to you. I have not sent them, says the LORD, but they are prophesying falsely in my name, with the result that I will drive you out and you will perish, you and the prophets who are prophesying to you."

16 Then I spoke to the priests and to all this people, saying, "Thus says the LORD: Do not listen to the words of your prophets who are prophesying to you, saying, 'Behold, the vessels of the LORD's house will now shortly be brought back from Babylon,' for it is a lie which they are prophesy-17 ing to you. Do not listen to them; serve the king of Baby-lon and live. Why should this city become a desolation? 18 If they are prophets, and if the word of the LORD is with them, then let them intercede with the LORD of hosts, that the vessels which are left in the house of the LORD, in the

house of the king of Judah, and in Jerusalem may not go 19 to Babylon. For thus says the LORD of hosts concerning the pillars, the sea, the stands, and the rest of the vessels 20 which are left in this city, which Nebuchadnez'zar king of Babylon did not take away, when he took into exile from Jerusalem to Babylon Jeconi'ah the son of Jehoi'-akim, king of Judah, and all the nobles of Judah and 21 Jerusalem—thus says the LORD of hosts, the God of Israel, concerning the vessels which are left in the house of the LORD, in the house of the king of Judah, and in 22 Jerusalem: They shall be carried to Babylon and remain there until the day when I give attention to them, says the LORD. Then I will bring them back and restore them to this place."

28 In that same year, at the beginning of the reign of Zedeki'ah king of Judah, in the fifth month of the fourth year, Hanani'ah the son of Azzur, the prophet from Gib'eon, spoke to me in the house of the LORD, in the 2 presence of the priests and all the people, saying, "Thus says the LORD of hosts, the God of Israel: I have broken 3 the yoke of the king of Babylon. Within two years I will bring back to this place all the vessels of the LORD's house, which Nebuchadnez'zar king of Babylon took away from 4 this place and carried to Babylon. I will also bring back to this place Jeconi'ah the son of Jehoi'akim, king of Judah, and all the exiles from Judah who went to Babylon, says the LORD, for I will break the yoke of the king of Babylon."

5 Then the prophet Jeremiah spoke to Hanani'ah the prophet in the presence of the priests and all the people 6 who were standing in the house of the LORD; and the prophet Jeremiah said, "Amen! May the LORD do so; may the LORD make the words which you have prophesied come true, and bring back to this place from Babylon the vessels 7 of the house of the LORD, and all the exiles. Yet hear now this word which I speak in your hearing and in the hearing 8 of all the people. The prophets who preceded you and me from ancient times prophesied war, famine, and pestilence 9 against many countries and great kingdoms. As for the prophet who prophesies peace, when the word of that prophet comes to pass, then it will be known that the LORD has truly sent the prophet."

10 Then the prophet Hanani'ah took the yoke-bars from the neck of Jeremiah the prophet, and broke them. 11 And Hanani'ah spoke in the presence of all the people, saying, "Thus says the LORD: Even so will I break the yoke of Nebuchadnez'zar king of Babylon from the neck of all the nations within two years." But Jeremiah the prophet went his way.

12 Sometime after the prophet Hanani'ah had broken the yoke-bars from off the neck of Jeremiah the prophet, the 13 word of the LORD came to Jeremiah: "Go, tell Hanani'ah, 'Thus says the LORD: You have broken wooden bars, but

ʷ Gk Syr Vg: Heb dreams

14 I ^x will make in their place bars of iron. For thus says the LORD of hosts, the God of Israel: I have put upon the neck of all these nations an iron yoke of servitude to Nebuchadnez'zar king of Babylon, and they shall serve him, for I have given to him even the beasts of the field.' "

15 And Jeremiah the prophet said to the prophet Hanani'ah, "Listen, Hanani'ah, the LORD has not sent you, and you

16 have made this people trust in a lie. Therefore thus says the LORD: 'Behold, I will remove you from the face of the earth. This very year you shall die, because you have uttered rebellion against the LORD.' "

17 In that same year, in the seventh month, the prophet Hanani'ah died.

Letters to Babylon

29 These are the words of the letter which Jeremiah the prophet sent from Jerusalem to the elders ^y of

the exiles, and to the priests, the prophets, and all the people, whom Nebuchadnez'zar had taken into exile from

2 Jerusalem to Babylon. This was after King Jeconi'ah, and the queen mother, the eunuchs, the princes of Judah and Jerusalem, the craftsmen, and the smiths had departed

3 from Jerusalem. The letter was sent by the hand of Ela'sah the son of Shaphan and Gemari'ah the son of Hilki'ah, whom Zedeki'ah king of Judah sent to Babylon to Nebu-

4 chadnez'zar king of Babylon. It said: "Thus says the LORD of hosts, the God of Israel, to all the exiles whom I have

5 sent into exile from Jerusalem to Babylon: Build houses and live in them; plant gardens and eat their produce.

6 Take wives and have sons and daughters; take wives for your sons, and give your daughters in marriage, that they may bear sons and daughters; multiply there, and do not

7 decrease. But seek the welfare of the city where I have sent you into exile, and pray to the LORD on its behalf, for in its

8 welfare you will find your welfare. For thus says the LORD of hosts, the God of Israel: Do not let your prophets and your diviners who are among you deceive you, and do not

9 listen to the dreams which they dream,^z for it is a lie which they are prophesying to you in my name; I did not send them, says the LORD.

10 "For thus says the LORD: When seventy years are completed for Babylon, I will visit you, and I will fulfil to you

11 my promise and bring you back to this place. For I know the plans I have for you, says the LORD, plans for welfare

12 and not for evil, to give you a future and a hope. Then you will call upon me and come and pray to me, and I

13 will hear you. You will seek me and find me; when you

14 seek me with all your heart, I will be found by you, says the LORD, and I will restore your fortunes and gather you from all the nations and all the places where I have driven you, says the LORD, and I will bring you back to the place from which I sent you into exile.

15 "Because you have said, 'The LORD has raised up

16 prophets for us in Babylon,'—Thus says the LORD concerning the king who sits on the throne of David, and concerning all the people who dwell in this city, your kinsmen

17 who did not go out with you into exile: 'Thus says the LORD of hosts, Behold, I am sending on them sword, famine, and pestilence, and I will make them like vile

18 figs which are so bad they cannot be eaten. I will pursue them with sword, famine, and pestilence, and will make them a horror to all the kingdoms of the earth, to be a curse, a terror, a hissing, and a reproach among all the

19 nations where I have driven them, because they did not heed my words, says the LORD, which I persistently sent to you by my servants the prophets, but you would not

20 listen, says the LORD.'—Hear the word of the LORD, all you exiles whom I sent away from Jerusalem to Babylon:

21 'Thus says the LORD of hosts, the God of Israel, concerning Ahab the son of Kola'iah and Zedeki'ah the son of Ma-asei'ah, who are prophesying a lie to you in my name: Behold, I will deliver them into the hand of Nebuchadrez'-zar king of Babylon, and he shall slay them before your

22 eyes. Because of them this curse shall be used by all the exiles from Judah in Babylon: "The LORD make you like Zedeki'ah and Ahab, whom the king of Babylon roasted

23 in the fire," because they have committed folly in Israel, they have committed adultery with their neighbors' wives, and they have spoken in my name lying words which I did not command them. I am the one who knows, and I am witness, says the LORD.' "

24, 25 To Shemai'ah of Nehel'am you shall say: "Thus says the LORD of hosts, the God of Israel: You have sent letters in your name to all the people who are in Jerusalem, and to Zephani'ah the son of Ma-asei'ah the priest, and to all

26 the priests, saying, 'The LORD has made you priest instead of Jehoi'ada the priest, to have charge in the house of the LORD over every madman who prophesies, to put him in

27 the stocks and collar. Now why have you not rebuked Jeremiah of An'athoth who is prophesying to you?

28 For he has sent to us in Babylon, saying, "Your exile will be long; build houses and live in them and plant gardens and eat their produce." ' "

29 Zephani'ah the priest read this letter in the hearing of

30 Jeremiah the prophet. Then the word of the LORD came

31 to Jeremiah: "Send to all the exiles, saying, 'Thus says the LORD concerning Shemai'ah of Nehel'am: Because She-mai'ah has prophesied to you when I did not send him and has made you trust in a lie, therefore thus says the LORD:

32 Behold, I will punish Shemai'ah of Nehel'am and his de-

scendants; he shall not have any one living among this people to see[a] the good that I will do to my people, says the LORD, for he has talked rebellion against the LORD.'"

The Book of Comfort

30 The word that came to Jeremiah from the LORD:
2 "Thus says the LORD, the God of Israel: Write in a
3 book all the words that I have spoken to you. For behold, days are coming, says the LORD, when I will restore the fortunes of my people, Israel and Judah, says the LORD, and I will bring them back to the land which I gave to their fathers, and they shall take possession of it."

4 These are the words which the LORD spoke concerning Israel and Judah:

5 "Thus says the LORD:
We have heard a cry of panic,
    of terror, and no peace.
6 Ask now, and see,
    can a man bear a child?
Why then do I see every man
    with his hands on his loins like a woman in labor?
    Why has every face turned pale?
7 Alas! that day is so great
    there is none like it;
it is a time of distress for Jacob;
    yet he shall be saved out of it.

8 "And it shall come to pass in that day, says the LORD of hosts, that I will break the yoke from off their[b] neck, and I will burst their[b] bonds, and strangers shall no more
9 make servants of them.[c] But they shall serve the LORD their God and David, their king, whom I will raise up for them.

10 "Then fear not, O Jacob my servant, says the LORD,
    nor be dismayed, O Israel;
for lo, I will save you from afar,
    and your offspring from the land of their captivity.
Jacob shall return and have quiet and ease,
    and none shall make him afraid.
11 For I am with you to save you,

                                            says the LORD;

I will make a full end of all the nations
    among whom I scattered you,
    but of you I will not make a full end.
I will chasten you in just measure,
    and I will by no means leave you unpunished.

12 "For thus says the LORD:
Your hurt is incurable,
    and your wound is grievous.

13 There is none to uphold your cause,
    no medicine for your wound,
    no healing for you.
14 All your lovers have forgotten you;
    they care nothing for you;
for I have dealt you the blow of an enemy,
    the punishment of a merciless foe,
because your guilt is great,
    because your sins are flagrant.
15 Why do you cry out over your hurt?
    Your pain is incurable.
Because your guilt is great,
    because your sins are flagrant,
    I have done these things to you.
16 Therefore all who devour you shall be devoured,
    and all your foes, every one of them, shall go into captivity;
those who despoil you shall become a spoil,
    and all who prey on you I will make a prey.
17 For I will restore health to you,
    and your wounds I will heal,

                                            says the LORD,

because they have called you an outcast:
    'It is Zion, for whom no one cares!'

18 "Thus says the LORD:
Behold, I will restore the fortunes of the tents of Jacob,
    and have compassion on his dwellings;
the city shall be rebuilt upon its mound,
    and the palace shall stand where it used to be.
19 Out of them shall come songs of thanksgiving,
    and the voices of those who make merry.
I will multiply them, and they shall not be few;
    I will make them honored, and they shall not be small.
20 Their children shall be as they were of old,
    and their congregation shall be established before me;
    and I will punish all who oppress them.
21 Their prince shall be one of themselves,
    their ruler shall come forth from their midst;
I will make him draw near, and he shall approach me,
    for who would dare of himself to approach me?
                                            says the LORD.

22 And you shall be my people,
    and I will be your God."

23 Behold the storm of the LORD!
    Wrath has gone forth,
a whirling tempest;
    it will burst upon the head of the wicked.
24 The fierce anger of the LORD will not turn back
    until he has executed and accomplished
    the intents of his mind.
In the latter days you will understand this.

[a] Gk: Heb *and he shall not see*   [b] Gk Old Latin: Heb *your*   [c] Heb *make a servant of him*

31 "At that time, says the LORD, I will be the God of all the families of Israel, and they shall be my people."

2 Thus says the LORD:

"The people who survived the sword
  found grace in the wilderness;
when Israel sought for rest,
3 the LORD appeared to him d from afar.
I have loved you with an everlasting love;
  therefore I have continued my faithfulness to you.
4 Again I will build you, and you shall be built,
  O virgin Israel!
Again you shall adorn yourself with timbrels,
  and shall go forth in the dance of the merrymakers.
5 Again you shall plant vineyards
  upon the mountains of Samar'ia;
the planters shall plant,
  and shall enjoy the fruit.
6 For there shall be a day when watchmen will call
  in the hill country of E'phraim:
'Arise, and let us go up to Zion,
  to the LORD our God.' "

7 For thus says the LORD:

"Sing aloud with gladness for Jacob,
  and raise shouts for the chief of the nations;
proclaim, give praise, and say,
  'The LORD has saved his people,
  the remnant of Israel.'
8 Behold, I will bring them from the north country,
  and gather them from the farthest parts of the earth,
among them the blind and the lame,
  the woman with child and her who is in travail,
    together;
  a great company, they shall return here.
9 With weeping they shall come,
  and with consolations e I will lead them back,
I will make them walk by brooks of water,
  in a straight path in which they shall not stumble;
for I am a father to Israel,
  and E'phraim is my first-born.

10 "Hear the word of the LORD, O nations,
  and declare it in the coastlands afar off;
say, 'He who scattered Israel will gather him,
  and will keep him as a shepherd keeps his flock.'
11 For the LORD has ransomed Jacob,
  and has redeemed him from hands too strong for him.
12 They shall come and sing aloud on the height of Zion,
  and they shall be radiant over the goodness of the LORD,
over the grain, the wine, and the oil,
  and over the young of the flock and the herd;
their life shall be like a watered garden,
  and they shall languish no more.

13 Then shall the maidens rejoice in the dance,
  and the young men and the old shall be merry.
I will turn their mourning into joy,
  I will comfort them, and give them gladness for sorrow.
14 I will feast the soul of the priests with abundance,
  and my people shall be satisfied with my goodness,
                    says the LORD."

15 Thus says the LORD:

"A voice is heard in Ramah,
  lamentation and bitter weeping.
Rachel is weeping for her children;
  she refuses to be comforted for her children,
  because they are not."

16 Thus says the LORD:

"Keep your voice from weeping,
  and your eyes from tears;
for your work shall be rewarded,
                    says the LORD,
  and they shall come back from the land of the enemy.
17 There is hope for your future,
                    says the LORD,
  and your children shall come back to their own country.
18 I have heard E'phraim bemoaning,
  'Thou hast chastened me, and I was chastened,
    like an untrained calf;
bring me back that I may be restored,
  for thou art the LORD my God.
19 For after I had turned away I repented;
  and after I was instructed, I smote upon my thigh;
I was ashamed, and I was confounded,
  because I bore the disgrace of my youth.'
20 Is E'phraim my dear son?
  Is he my darling child?
For as often as I speak against him,
  I do remember him still.
Therefore my heart yearns for him;
  I will surely have mercy on him,
                    says the LORD.

21 "Set up waymarks for yourself,
  make yourself guideposts;
consider well the highway,
  the road by which you went.
Return, O virgin Israel,
  return to these your cities.
22 How long will you waver,
  O faithless daughter?
For the LORD has created a new thing on the earth:
  a woman protects a man."

23 Thus says the LORD of hosts, the God of Israel: "Once more they shall use these words in the land of Judah and in its cities, when I restore their fortunes:

d Gk: Heb me   e Gk Compare Vg Tg: Heb supplications

'The LORD bless you, O habitation of righteousness,
O holy hill!'

24 And Judah and all its cities shall dwell there together, and the farmers and those who wander ^f with their flocks.

25 For I will satisfy the weary soul, and every languishing soul I will replenish."

26 Thereupon I awoke and looked, and my sleep was pleasant to me.

27 "Behold, the days are coming, says the LORD, when I will sow the house of Israel and the house of Judah with

28 the seed of man and the seed of beast. And it shall come to pass that as I have watched over them to pluck up and break down, to overthrow, destroy, and bring evil, so I will watch over them to build and to plant, says the LORD.

29 In those days they shall no longer say:

'The fathers have eaten sour grapes,
and the children's teeth are set on edge.'

30 But every one shall die for his own sin; each man who eats sour grapes, his teeth shall be set on edge.

A New Covenant

31 "Behold, the days are coming, says the LORD, when I will make a new covenant with the house of Israel and the

32 house of Judah, not like the covenant which I made with their fathers when I took them by the hand to bring them out of the land of Egypt, my covenant which they broke,

33 though I was their husband, says the LORD. But this is the covenant which I will make with the house of Israel after those days, says the LORD: I will put my law within them, and I will write it upon their hearts; and I will be

34 their God, and they shall be my people. And no longer shall each man teach his neighbor and each his brother, saying, 'Know the LORD,' for they shall all know me, from the least of them to the greatest, says the LORD; for I will forgive their iniquity, and I will remember their sin no more."

35 Thus says the LORD,
who gives the sun for light by day
and the fixed order of the moon and the stars for light
by night,
who stirs up the sea so that its waves roar—
the LORD of hosts is his name:

36 "If this fixed order departs
from before me, says the LORD,
then shall the descendants of Israel cease
from being a nation before me for ever."

^f Cn Compare Syr Vg Tg: Heb *and they shall wander*

37 Thus says the LORD:

"If the heavens above can be measured,
and the foundations of the earth below can be explored,
then I will cast off all the descendants of Israel
for all that they have done,

says the LORD."

38 "Behold, the days are coming, says the LORD, when the city shall be rebuilt for the LORD from the tower of

39 Han'anel to the Corner Gate. And the measuring line shall go out farther, straight to the hill Gareb, and shall then

40 turn to Go'ah. The whole valley of the dead bodies and the ashes, and all the fields as far as the brook Kidron, to the corner of the Horse Gate toward the east, shall be sacred to the LORD. It shall not be uprooted or overthrown any more for ever."

Jeremiah Buys a Field

32 The word that came to Jeremiah from the LORD in the tenth year of Zedeki'ah king of Judah, which

2 was the eighteenth year of Nebuchadrez'zar. At that time the army of the king of Babylon was besieging Jerusalem, and Jeremiah the prophet was shut up in the court of the

3 guard which was in the palace of the king of Judah. For Zedeki'ah king of Judah had imprisoned him, saying, "Why do you prophesy and say, 'Thus says the LORD: Behold, I am giving this city into the hand of the king of

4 Babylon, and he shall take it; Zedeki'ah king of Judah shall not escape out of the hand of the Chalde'ans, but shall surely be given into the hand of the king of Babylon, and shall speak with him face to face and see him eye

5 to eye; and he shall take Zedeki'ah to Babylon, and there he shall remain until I visit him, says the LORD; though you fight against the Chalde'ans, you shall not succeed'?"

6 Jeremiah said, "The word of the LORD came to me:

7 Behold, Han'amel the son of Shallum your uncle will come to you and say, 'Buy my field which is at An'athoth, for

8 the right of redemption by purchase is yours.' Then Han'amel my cousin came to me in the court of the guard, in accordance with the word of the LORD, and said to me, 'Buy my field which is at An'athoth in the land of Benjamin, for the right of possession and redemption is yours; buy it for yourself.' Then I knew that this was the word of the LORD.

9 "And I bought the field at An'athoth from Han'amel my cousin, and weighed out the money to him, seventeen

10 shekels of silver. I signed the deed, sealed it, got witnesses,

11 and weighed the money on scales. Then I took the sealed deed of purchase, containing the terms and conditions,

12 and the open copy; and I gave the deed of purchase to Baruch the son of Neri'ah son of Mahsei'ah, in the presence of Han'amel my cousin, in the presence of the witnesses who signed the deed of purchase, and in the presence of all the Jews who were sitting in the court of the

13 guard. I charged Baruch in their presence, saying,
14 'Thus says the LORD of hosts, the God of Israel: Take these deeds, both this sealed deed of purchase and this open deed, and put them in an earthenware vessel, that
15 they may last for a long time. For thus says the LORD of hosts, the God of Israel: Houses and fields and vineyards shall again be bought in this land.'

16 "After I had given the deed of purchase to Baruch the
17 son of Neri'ah, I prayed to the LORD, saying: 'Ah Lord GOD! It is thou who hast made the heavens and the earth by thy great power and by thy outstretched arm! Nothing
18 is too hard for thee, who showest steadfast love to thousands, but dost requite the guilt of fathers to their children after them, O great and mighty God whose name
19 is the LORD of hosts, great in counsel and mighty in deed; whose eyes are open to all the ways of men, rewarding every man according to his ways and according to the
20 fruit of his doings; who hast shown signs and wonders in the land of Egypt, and to this day in Israel and among all mankind, and hast made thee a name, as at this day.
21 Thou didst bring thy people Israel out of the land of Egypt with signs and wonders, with a strong hand and out-
22 stretched arm, and with great terror; and thou gavest them this land, which thou didst swear to their fathers to
23 give them, a land flowing with milk and honey; and they entered and took possession of it. But they did not obey thy voice or walk in thy law; they did nothing of all thou didst command them to do. Therefore thou hast made
24 all this evil come upon them. Behold, the siege mounds have come up to the city to take it, and because of sword and famine and pestilence the city is given into the hands of the Chalde'ans who are fighting against it. What thou didst speak has come to pass, and behold, thou seest it.
25 Yet thou, O Lord GOD, hast said to me, "Buy the field for money and get witnesses"—though the city is given into the hands of the Chalde'ans.' "

26, 27 The word of the LORD came to Jeremiah: "Behold, I am the LORD, the God of all flesh; is anything too hard
28 for me? Therefore, thus says the LORD: Behold, I am giving this city into the hands of the Chalde'ans and into the hand of Nebuchadrez'zar king of Babylon, and he
29 shall take it. The Chalde'ans who are fighting against this city shall come and set this city on fire, and burn it, with the houses on whose roofs incense has been offered to Ba'al and drink offerings have been poured out to other
30 gods, to provoke me to anger. For the sons of Israel and the sons of Judah have done nothing but evil in my sight from their youth; the sons of Israel have done nothing but provoke me to anger by the work of their hands, says
31 the LORD. This city has aroused my anger and wrath, from the day it was built to this day, so that I will remove it
32 from my sight because of all the evil of the sons of Israel and the sons of Judah which they did to provoke me to

anger—their kings and their princes, their priests and their prophets, the men of Judah and the inhabitants of
33 Jerusalem. They have turned to me their back and not their face; and though I have taught them persistently
34 they have not listened to receive instruction. They set up their abominations in the house which is called by my
35 name, to defile it. They built the high places of Ba'al in the valley of the son of Hinnom, to offer up their sons and daughters to Molech, though I did not command them, nor did it enter into my mind, that they should do this abomination, to cause Judah to sin.

36 "Now therefore thus says the LORD, the God of Israel, concerning this city of which you say, 'It is given into the hand of the king of Babylon by sword, by famine,
37 and by pestilence': Behold, I will gather them from all the countries to which I drove them in my anger and my wrath and in great indignation; I will bring them back
38 to this place, and I will make them dwell in safety. And
39 they shall be my people, and I will be their God. I will give them one heart and one way, that they may fear me for ever, for their own good and the good of their children
40 after them. I will make with them an everlasting covenant, that I will not turn away from doing good to them; and I will put the fear of me in their hearts, that they may not
41 turn from me. I will rejoice in doing them good, and I will plant them in this land in faithfulness, with all my heart and all my soul.

42 "For thus says the LORD: Just as I have brought all this great evil upon this people, so I will bring upon them all
43 the good that I promise them. Fields shall be bought in this land of which you are saying, It is a desolation, without man or beast; it is given into the hands of the
44 Chalde'ans. Fields shall be bought for money, and deeds shall be signed and sealed and witnessed, in the land of Benjamin, in the places about Jerusalem, and in the cities of Judah, in the cities of the hill country, in the cities of the Shephe'lah, and in the cities of the Negeb; for I will restore their fortunes, says the LORD."

Hope in Prison

33 The word of the LORD came to Jeremiah a second time, while he was still shut up in the court of the
2 guard: "Thus says the LORD who made the earth,[g] the LORD who formed it to establish it—the LORD is his name:
3 Call to me and I will answer you, and will tell you great
4 and hidden things which you have not known. For thus says the LORD, the God of Israel, concerning the houses of this city and the houses of the kings of Judah which were torn down to make a defense against the siege mounds
5 and before the sword: [h] The Chalde'ans are coming in to fight [i] and to fill them with the dead bodies of men whom I shall smite in my anger and my wrath, for I have hidden my face from this city because of all their wickedness.

g Gk: Heb *it*   h Heb obscure   i Cn: Heb *They are coming in to fight against the Chaldeans*

6 Behold, I will bring to it health and healing, and I will heal them and reveal to them abundance [j] of prosperity 7 and security. I will restore the fortunes of Judah and the fortunes of Israel, and rebuild them as they were at first. 8 I will cleanse them from all the guilt of their sin against me, and I will forgive all the guilt of their sin and 9 rebellion against me. And this city [k] shall be to me a name of joy, a praise and a glory before all the nations of

the earth who shall hear of all the good that I 'do for them; they shall fear and tremble because of all the good and all the prosperity I provide for it.

10 "Thus says the LORD: In this place of which you say, 'It is a waste without man or beast,' in the cities of Judah and the streets of Jerusalem that are desolate, without man or inhabitant or beast, there shall be heard again 11 the voice of mirth and the voice of gladness, the voice of the bridegroom and the voice of the bride, the voices of those who sing, as they bring thank offerings to the house of the LORD:

'Give thanks to the LORD of hosts,
    for the LORD is good,
    for his steadfast love endures for ever!'

For I will restore the fortunes of the land as at first, says the LORD.

12 "Thus says the LORD of hosts: In this place which is waste, without man or beast, and in all of its cities, there shall again be habitations of shepherds resting their 13 flocks. In the cities of the hill country, in the cities of the Shephe'lah, and in the cities of the Negeb, in the land of Benjamin, the places about Jerusalem, and in the cities of Judah, flocks shall again pass under the hands of the one who counts them, says the LORD.

14 "Behold, the days are coming, says the LORD, when I will fulfil the promise I made to the house of Israel and 15 the house of Judah. In those days and at that time I will cause a righteous Branch to spring forth for David; and he shall execute justice and righteousness in the land. 16 In those days Judah will be saved and Jerusalem will dwell securely. And this is the name by which it will be called: 'The LORD is our righteousness.'

17 "For thus says the LORD: David shall never lack a 18 man to sit on the throne of the house of Israel, and the Levitical priests shall never lack a man in my presence to offer burnt offerings, to burn cereal offerings, and to make sacrifices for ever."

19, 20 The word of the LORD came to Jeremiah: "Thus says the LORD: If you can break my covenant with the day and my covenant with the night, so that day and night will not 21 come at their appointed time, then also my covenant with

David my servant may be broken, so that he shall not have a son to reign on his throne, and my covenant with 22 the Levitical priests my ministers. As the host of heaven cannot be numbered and the sands of the sea cannot be measured, so I will multiply the descendants of David my servant, and the Levitical priests who minister to me."

23, 24 The word of the LORD came to Jeremiah: "Have you not observed what these people are saying, 'The LORD has rejected the two families which he chose'? Thus they have despised my people so that they are no longer a nation in 25 their sight. Thus says the LORD: If I have not established my covenant with day and night and the ordinances of 26 heaven and earth, then I will reject the descendants of Jacob and David my servant and will not choose one of his descendants to rule over the seed of Abraham, Isaac, and Jacob. For I will restore their fortunes, and will have mercy upon them."

Jeremiah Rebukes the King

34 The word which came to Jeremiah from the LORD, when Nebuchadrez'zar king of Babylon and all his army and all the kingdoms of the earth under his dominion and all the peoples were fighting against 2 Jerusalem and all of its cities: "Thus says the LORD, the God of Israel: Go and speak to Zedeki'ah king of Judah and say to him, 'Thus says the LORD: Behold, I am giving this city into the hand of the king of Babylon, and he 3 shall burn it with fire. You shall not escape from his hand, but shall surely be captured and delivered into his hand; you shall see the king of Babylon eye to eye and speak with him face to face; and you shall go to Babylon.' 4 Yet hear the word of the LORD, O Zedeki'ah king of Judah! Thus says the LORD concerning you: 'You shall 5 not die by the sword. You shall die in peace. And as spices were burned for your fathers, the former kings who were before you, so men shall burn spices for you and lament for you, saying, "Alas, lord!"' For I have spoken the word, says the LORD."

6 Then Jeremiah the prophet spoke all these words to 7 Zedeki'ah king of Judah, in Jerusalem, when the army of the king of Babylon was fighting against Jerusalem and against all the cities of Judah that were left, Lachish and Aze'kah; for these were the only fortified cities of Judah that remained.

8 The word which came to Jeremiah from the LORD, after King Zedeki'ah had made a covenant with all the people in Jerusalem to make a proclamation of liberty to them, 9 that every one should set free his Hebrew slaves, male and female, so that no one should enslave a Jew, his 10 brother. And they obeyed, all the princes and all the people who had entered into the covenant that every one would set free his slave, male or female, so that they would not be enslaved again; they obeyed and set them

j Heb uncertain   k Heb and it

11 free. But afterward they turned around and took back the male and female slaves they had set free, and brought 12 them into subjection as slaves. The word of the LORD 13 came to Jeremiah from the LORD: "Thus says the LORD, the God of Israel: I made a covenant with your fathers when I brought them out of the land of Egypt, out of the 14 house of bondage, saying, 'At the end of six[1] years each of you must set free the fellow Hebrew who has been sold to you and has served you six years; you must set him free from your service.' But your fathers did not listen 15 to me or incline their ears to me. You recently repented and did what was right in my eyes by proclaiming liberty, each to his neighbor, and you made a covenant before 16 me in the house which is called by my name; but then you turned around and profaned my name when each of you took back his male and female slaves, whom you had set free according to their desire, and you brought 17 them into subjection to be your slaves. Therefore, thus says the LORD: You have not obeyed me by proclaiming liberty, every one to his brother and to his neighbor; behold, I proclaim to you liberty to the sword, to pestilence, and to famine, says the LORD. I will make you 18 a horror to all the kingdoms of the earth. And the men who transgressed my covenant and did not keep the terms of the covenant which they made before me, I will make like[m] the calf which they cut in two and passed 19 between its parts—the princes of Judah, the princes of Jerusalem, the eunuchs, the priests, and all the people of the land who passed between the parts of the calf; 20 and I will give them into the hand of their enemies and into the hand of those who seek their lives. Their dead bodies shall be food for the birds of the air and the beasts 21 of the earth. And Zedeki'ah king of Judah, and his princes I will give into the hand of their enemies and into the hand of those who seek their lives, into the hand of the army of the king of Babylon which has withdrawn from 22 you. Behold, I will command, says the LORD, and will bring them back to this city; and they will fight against it, and take it, and burn it with fire. I will make the cities of Judah a desolation without inhabitant."

35 The word which came to Jeremiah from the LORD in the days of Jehoi'akim the son of Josi'ah, king 2 of Judah: "Go to the house of the Re'chabites, and speak with them, and bring them to the house of the LORD, into one of the chambers; then offer them wine to drink." 3 So I took Ja-azani'ah the son of Jeremiah, son of Habaz-zini'ah, and his brothers, and all his sons, and the whole 4 house of the Re'chabites. I brought them to the house of the LORD into the chamber of the sons Hanan the son of Igdali'ah, the man of God, which was near the chamber of the princes, above the chamber of Ma-asei'ah the son of 5 Shallum, keeper of the threshold. Then I set before the

Re'chabites pitchers full of wine, and cups; and I said 6 to them, "Drink wine." But they answered, "We will drink no wine, for Jon'adab the son of Rechab, our father, commanded us, 'You shall not drink wine, neither 7 you nor your sons for ever; you shall not build a house; you shall not sow seed; you shall not plant or have a vineyard; but you shall live in tents all your days, that you may live many days in the land where you sojourn.' 8 We have obeyed the voice of Jon'adab the son of Rechab, our father, in all that he commanded us, to drink no wine all our days, ourselves, our wives, our sons, or our 9 daughters, and not to build houses to dwell in. We have 10 no vineyard or field or seed; but we have lived in tents, and have obeyed and done all that Jon'adab our father 11 commanded us. But when Nebuchadrez'zar king of Baby-lon came up against the land, we said, 'Come, and let us go to Jerusalem for fear of the army of the Chalde'ans and the army of the Syrians.' So we are living in Jerusalem."

12, 13 Then the word of the LORD came to Jeremiah: "Thus says the LORD of hosts, the God of Israel: Go and say to the men of Judah and the inhabitants of Jerusalem, Will you not receive instruction and listen to my words? 14 says the LORD. The command which Jon'adab the son of Rechab gave to his sons, to drink no wine, has been kept; and they drink none to this day, for they have obeyed their father's command. I have spoken to you 15 persistently, but you have not listened to me. I have sent to you all my servants the prophets, sending them persist-ently, saying, 'Turn now every one of you from his evil way, and amend your doings, and do not go after other gods to serve them, and then you shall dwell in the land which I gave to you and your fathers.' But you did not 16 incline your ear or listen to me. The sons of Jon'adab the son of Rechab have kept the command which their father 17 gave them, but this people has not obeyed me. Therefore, thus says the LORD, the God of hosts, the God of Israel: Behold, I am bringing on Judah and all the inhabitants of Jerusalem all the evil that I have pronounced against them; because I have spoken to them and they have not listened, I have called to them and they have not an-swered."

18 But to the house of the Re'chabites Jeremiah said, "Thus says the LORD of hosts, the God of Israel: Because you have obeyed the command of Jon'adab your father, and kept all his precepts, and done all that he commanded 19 you, therefore thus says the LORD of hosts, the God of Israel: Jon'adab the son of Rechab shall never lack a man to stand before me."

The Burning of the Scroll

36 In the fourth year of Jehoi'akim the son of Josi'ah, king of Judah, this word came to Jeremiah from the

[1] Gk: Heb *seven*   [m] Cn: Heb lacks *like*

2 LORD: "Take a scroll and write on it all the words that I have spoken to you against Israel and Judah and all the nations, from the day I spoke to you, from the days of 3 Josi'ah until today. It may be that the house of Judah will hear all the evil which I intend to do to them, so that every one may turn from his evil way, and that I may forgive their iniquity and their sin."

4 Then Jeremiah called Baruch the son of Neri'ah, and Baruch wrote upon a scroll at the dictation of Jeremiah all the words of the LORD which he had spoken to him. 5 And Jeremiah ordered Baruch, saying, "I am debarred 6 from going to the house of the LORD; so you are to go, and on a fast day in the hearing of all the people in the LORD's house you shall read the words of the LORD from the scroll which you have written at my dictation. You shall read them also in the hearing of all the men of 7 Judah who come out of their cities. It may be that their supplication will come before the LORD, and that every one will turn from his evil way, for great is the anger and wrath that the LORD has pronounced against this 8 people." And Baruch the son of Neri'ah did all that Jeremiah the prophet ordered him about reading from the scroll the words of the LORD in the LORD's house.

9 In the fifth year of Jehoi'akim the son of Josi'ah, king of Judah, in the ninth month, all the people in Jerusalem and all the people who came from the cities of Judah to 10 Jerusalem proclaimed a fast before the LORD. Then, in the hearing of all the people, Baruch read the words of Jeremiah from the scroll, in the house of the LORD, in the chamber of Gemari'ah the son of Shaphan the secretary, which was in the upper court, at the entry of the New Gate of the LORD's house.

11 When Micai'ah the son of Gemari'ah, son of Shaphan, 12 heard all the words of the LORD from the scroll, he went down to the king's house, into the secretary's chamber; and all the princes were sitting there: Eli'shama the secretary, Delai'ah the son of Shemai'ah, Elna'than the son of Achbor, Gemari'ah the son of Shaphan, Zedeki'ah 13 the son of Hanani'ah, and all the princes. And Micai'ah told them all the words that he had heard, when Baruch 14 read the scroll in the hearing of the people. Then all the princes sent Jehu'di the son of Nethani'ah, son of Shelemi'ah, son of Cushi, to say to Baruch, "Take in your hand the scroll that you read in the hearing of the people, and come." So Baruch the son of Neri'ah took the scroll in

15 his hand and came to them. And they said to him, "Sit 16 down and read it." So Baruch read it to them. When they heard all the words, they turned one to another in fear; and they said to Baruch, "We must report all these words 17 to the king." Then they asked Baruch, "Tell us, how did you write all these words? Was it at his dictation?" 18 Baruch answered them, "He dictated all these words to 19 me, while I wrote them with ink on the scroll." Then the princes said to Baruch, "Go and hide, you and Jeremiah, and let no one know where you are."

20 So they went into the court to the king, having put the scroll in the chamber of Eli'shama the secretary; and they 21 reported all the words to the king. Then the king sent Jehu'di to get the scroll, and he took it from the chamber of Eli'shama the secretary; and Jehu'di read it to the 22 king and all the princes who stood beside the king. It was the ninth month, and the king was sitting in the winter house and there was a fire burning in the brazier before 23 him. As Jehu'di read three or four columns, the king would cut them off with a penknife and throw them into the fire in the brazier, until the entire scroll was con- 24 sumed in the fire that was in the brazier. Yet neither the king, nor any of his servants who heard all these words, 25 was afraid, nor did they rend their garments. Even when Elna'than and Delai'ah and Gemari'ah urged the king not 26 to burn the scroll, he would not listen to them. And the king commanded Jerah'meel the king's son and Serai'ah the son of Az'ri-el and Shelemi'ah the son of Abdeel to seize Baruch the secretary and Jeremiah the prophet, but the LORD hid them.

27 Now, after the king had burned the scroll with the words which Baruch wrote at Jeremiah's dictation, the 28 word of the LORD came to Jeremiah: "Take another scroll and write on it all the former words that were in the first scroll, which Jehoi'akim the king of Judah has 29 burned. And concerning Jehoi'akim king of Judah you shall say, 'Thus says the LORD, You have burned this scroll, saying, "Why have you written in it that the king of Babylon will certainly come and destroy this land, and 30 will cut off from it man and beast?" Therefore thus says the LORD concerning Jehoi'akim king of Judah, He shall have none to sit upon the throne of David, and his dead body shall be cast out to the heat by day and the frost by 31 night. And I will punish him and his offspring and his servants for their iniquity; I will bring upon them, and upon the inhabitants of Jerusalem, and upon the men of Judah, all the evil that I have pronounced against them, but they would not hear.'"

32 Then Jeremiah took another scroll and gave it to Baruch the scribe, the son of Neri'ah, who wrote on it at the dictation of Jeremiah all the words of the scroll which Jehoi'akim king of Judah had burned in the fire; and many similar words were added to them.

Jeremiah Imprisoned, Condemned

37 Zedeki'ah the son of Josi'ah, whom Nebuchadrez'zar king of Babylon made king in the land of Judah, reigned instead of Coni'ah the son of Jehoi'akim. [2] But neither he nor his servants nor the people of the land listened to the words of the LORD which he spoke through Jeremiah the prophet.

[3] King Zedeki'ah sent Jehu'cal the son of Shelemi'ah, and Zephani'ah the priest, the son of Ma-asei'ah, to Jeremiah the prophet, saying, "Pray for us to the LORD our God." [4] Now Jeremiah was still going in and out among the [5] people, for he had not yet been put in prison. The army of Pharaoh had come out of Egypt; and when the Chalde'ans who were besieging Jerusalem heard news of them, they withdrew from Jerusalem.

[6] Then the word of the LORD came to Jeremiah the [7] prophet: "Thus says the LORD, God of Israel: Thus shall you say to the king of Judah who sent you to me to inquire of me, 'Behold, Pharaoh's army which came to help you is about to return to Egypt, to its own land. [8] And the Chalde'ans shall come back and fight against [9] this city; they shall take it and burn it with fire. Thus says the LORD, Do not deceive yourselves, saying, "The Chalde'ans will surely stay away from us," for they will not stay [10] away. For even if you should defeat the whole army of Chalde'ans who are fighting against you, and there remained of them only wounded men, every man in his tent, they would rise up and burn this city with fire.' "

[11] Now when the Chalde'an army had withdrawn from [12] Jerusalem at the approach of Pharaoh's army, Jeremiah set out from Jerusalem to go to the land of Benjamin to [13] receive his portion [n] there among the people. When he was at the Benjamin Gate, a sentry there named Iri'jah the son of Shelemi'ah, son of Hanani'ah, seized Jeremiah the prophet, saying, "You are deserting to the Chalde'ans." [14] And Jeremiah said, "It is false; I am not deserting to the Chalde'ans." But Iri'jah would not listen to him, and [15] seized Jeremiah and brought him to the princes. And the princes were enraged at Jeremiah, and they beat him and imprisoned him in the house of Jonathan the secretary, for it had been made a prison.

A Secret Interview

[16] When Jeremiah had come to the dungeon cells, and [17] remained there many days, King Zedeki'ah sent for him, and received him. The king questioned him secretly in his house, and said, "Is there any word from the LORD?" Jeremiah said, "There is." Then he said, "You shall be [18] delivered into the hand of the king of Babylon." Jeremiah also said to King Zedeki'ah, "What wrong have I done to you or your servants or this people, that you have put [19] me in prison? Where are your prophets who prophesied to you, saying, 'The king of Babylon will not come against [20] you and against this land'? Now hear, I pray you, O my lord the king: let my humble plea come before you, and do not send me back to the house of Jonathan the secre- [21] tary, lest I die there." So King Zedeki'ah gave orders, and they committed Jeremiah to the court of the guard; and a loaf of bread was given him daily from the bakers' street, until all the bread of the city was gone. So Jeremiah remained in the court of the guard.

38 Now Shephati'ah the son of Mattan, Gedali'ah the son of Pashhur, Jucal the son of Shelemi'ah, and Pashhur the son of Malchi'ah heard the words that Jere- [2] miah was saying to all the people, "Thus says the LORD, He who stays in this city shall die by the sword, by famine, and by pestilence; but he who goes out to the Chalde'ans shall live; he shall have his life as a prize of [3] war, and live. Thus says the LORD, This city shall surely be given into the hand of the army of the king of Baby- [4] lon and be taken." Then the princes said to the king, "Let this man be put to death, for he is weakening the hands of the soldiers who are left in this city, and the hands of all the people, by speaking such words to them. For this man is not seeking the welfare of this people, but [5] their harm." King Zedeki'ah said, "Behold, he is in your [6] hands; for the king can do nothing against you." So they took Jeremiah and cast him into the cistern of Malchi'ah, the king's son, which was in the court of the guard, letting Jeremiah down by ropes. And there was no water in the cistern, but only mire, and Jeremiah sank in the mire.

Rescued From Death

[7] When E'bed-mel'ech the Ethiopian, a eunuch, who was in the king's house, heard that they had put Jeremiah into the cistern—the king was sitting in the Benjamin Gate— [8] E'bed-mel'ech went from the king's house and said to [9] the king, "My lord the king, these men have done evil in all that they did to Jeremiah the prophet by casting him into the cistern; and he will die there of hunger, for there [10] is no bread left in the city." Then the king commanded E'bed-mel'ech, the Ethiopian, "Take three men with you from here, and lift Jeremiah the prophet out of the cistern [11] before he dies." So E'bed-mel'ech took the men with him and went to the house of the king, to a wardrobe of [o] the storehouse, and took from there old rags and worn-out clothes, which he let down to Jeremiah in the cistern by [12] ropes. Then E'bed-mel'ech the Ethiopian said to Jeremiah, "Put the rags and clothes between your armpits and the [13] ropes." Jeremiah did so. Then they drew Jeremiah up with ropes and lifted him out of the cistern. And Jeremiah remained in the court of the guard.

[14] King Zedeki'ah sent for Jeremiah the prophet and received him at the third entrance of the temple of the LORD. The king said to Jeremiah, "I will ask you a ques- [15] tion; hide nothing from me." Jeremiah said to Zedeki'ah,

[n] Heb obscure   [o] Cn: Heb to under

539

"If I tell you, will you not be sure to put me to death? And if I give you counsel, you will not listen to me." [16] Then King Zedeki'ah swore secretly to Jeremiah, "As the Lord lives, who made our souls, I will not put you to death or deliver you into the hand of these men who seek your life."

[17] Then Jeremiah said to Zedeki'ah, "Thus says the Lord, the God of hosts, the God of Israel, If you will surrender to the princes of the king of Babylon, then your life shall be spared, and this city shall not be burned with [18] fire, and you and your house shall live. But if you do not surrender to the princes of the king of Babylon, then this city shall be given into the hand of the Chalde'ans, and they shall burn it with fire, and you shall not escape from [19] their hand." King Zedeki'ah said to Jeremiah, "I am afraid of the Jews who have deserted to the Chalde'ans, [20] lest I be handed over to them and they abuse me." Jeremiah said, "You shall not be given to them. Obey now the voice of the Lord in what I say to you, and it shall be [21] well with you, and your life shall be spared. But if you refuse to surrender, this is the vision which the Lord has [22] shown to me: Behold, all the women left in the house of the king of Judah were being led out to the princes of the king of Babylon and were saying,

'Your trusted friends have deceived you
and prevailed against you;

now that your feet are sunk in the mire,
they turn away from you.'

[23] All your wives and your sons shall be led out to the Chalde'ans, and you yourself shall not escape from their hand, but shall be seized by the king of Babylon; and this city shall be burned with fire."

[24] Then Zedeki'ah said to Jeremiah, "Let no one know [25] of these words and you shall not die. If the princes hear that I have spoken with you and come to you and say to you, 'Tell us what you said to the king and what the king said to you; hide nothing from us and we will not [26] put you to death,' then you shall say to them, 'I made a humble plea to the king that he would not send me back [27] to the house of Jonathan to die there.'" Then all the princes came to Jeremiah and asked him, and he answered them as the king had instructed him. So they left off speaking with him, for the conversation had not been [28] overheard. And Jeremiah remained in the court of the guard until the day that Jerusalem was taken.

p This clause has been transposed from the end of Chapter 38

Jerusalem Destroyed

39 In the ninth year of Zedeki'ah king of Judah, in the tenth month, Nebuchadrez'zar king of Babylon and all his army came against Jerusalem and besieged it; [2] in the eleventh year of Zedeki'ah, in the fourth month, on the ninth day of the month, a breach was made in the [3] city. When Jerusalem was taken,p all the princes of the king of Babylon came and sat in the middle gate: Ner'-gal-share'zer, Sam'gar-ne'bo, Sar'sechim the Rab'saris, Ner'gal-share'zer the Rabmag, with all the rest of the [4] officers of the king of Babylon. When Zedeki'ah king of Judah and all the soldiers saw them, they fled, going out of the city at night by way of the king's garden through the gate between the two walls; and they went toward the [5] Arabah. But the army of the Chalde'ans pursued them, and overtook Zedeki'ah in the plains of Jericho; and when they had taken him, they brought him up to Nebuchadrez'-zar king of Babylon, at Riblah, in the land of Hamath; [6] and he passed sentence upon him. The king of Babylon slew the sons of Zedeki'ah at Riblah before his eyes; and [7] the king of Babylon slew all the nobles of Judah. He put out the eyes of Zedeki'ah, and bound him in fetters to take [8] him to Babylon. The Chalde'ans burned the king's house and the house of the people, and broke down the walls of [9] Jerusalem. Then Nebu'zarad'an, the captain of the guard, carried into exile to Babylon the rest of the people who were left in the city, those who had deserted to him, and [10] the people who remained. Nebu'zarad'an, the captain of the guard, left in the land of Judah some of the poor people who owned nothing, and gave them vineyards and fields at the same time.

Jeremiah Spared

[11] Nebuchadrez'zar king of Babylon gave command concerning Jeremiah through Nebu'zarad'an, the captain of [12] the guard, saying, "Take him, look after him well and do [13] him no harm, but deal with him as he tells you." So Nebu'zarad'an the captain of the guard, Nebushaz'ban the Rab'saris, Ner'gal-share'zer the Rabmag, and all the [14] chief officers of the king of Babylon sent and took Jeremiah from the court of the guard. They entrusted him to Gedali'ah the son of Ahi'kam, son of Shaphan, that he should take him home. So he dwelt among the people.

[15] The word of the Lord came to Jeremiah while he was [16] shut up in the court of the guard: "Go, and say to E'bed-mel'ech the Ethiopian, 'Thus says the Lord of hosts, the God of Israel: Behold, I will fulfil my words against this city for evil and not for good, and they shall be ac- [17] complished before you on that day. But I will deliver you on that day, says the Lord, and you shall not be given into [18] the hand of the men of whom you are afraid. For I will surely save you, and you shall not fall by the sword; but you shall have your life as a prize of war, because you have put your trust in me, says the Lord.'"

Stays With the Remnant

40 The word that came to Jeremiah from the LORD after Nebu'zarad'an the captain of the guard had let him go from Ramah, when he took him bound in chains along with all the captives of Jerusalem and Judah 2 who were being exiled to Babylon. The captain of the guard took Jeremiah and said to him, "The LORD your 3 God pronounced this evil against this place; the LORD has brought it about, and has done as he said. Because you sinned against the LORD, and did not obey his voice, this 4 thing has come upon you. Now, behold, I release you today from the chains on your hands. If it seems good to you to come with me to Babylon, come, and I will look after you well; but if it seems wrong to you to come with me to Babylon, do not come. See, the whole land is before you; go wherever you think it good and right 5 to go. If you remain,*q* then return to Gedali'ah the son of Ahi'kam, son of Shaphan, whom the king of Babylon appointed governor of the cities of Judah, and dwell with him among the people; or go wherever you think it right to go." So the captain of the guard gave him an allowance 6 of food and a present, and let him go. Then Jeremiah went to Gedali'ah the son of Ahi'kam, at Mizpah, and dwelt with him among the people who were left in the land.

7 When all the captains of the forces in the open country and their men heard that the king of Babylon had appointed Gedali'ah the son of Ahi'kam governor in the land, and had committed to him men, women, and children, those of the poorest of the land who had not been taken in- 8 to exile to Babylon, they went to Gedali'ah at Mizpah— Ish'mael the son of Nethani'ah, Joha'nan the son of Kare'- ah, Serai'ah the son of Tanhu'meth, the sons of Ephai the Netoph'athite, Jezani'ah the son of the Ma-ac'athite, they 9 and their men. Gedali'ah the son of Ahi'kam, son of Shaphan, swore to them and their men, saying, "Do not be afraid to serve the Chalde'ans. Dwell in the land, and serve the king of Babylon, and it shall be well with you. 10 As for me, I will dwell at Mizpah, to stand for you before the Chalde'ans who will come to us; but as for you, gather wine and summer fruits and oil, and store them in your vessels, and dwell in your cities that you have taken." 11 Likewise, when all the Jews who were in Moab and among the Ammonites and in Edom and in other lands heard that the king of Babylon had left a remnant in Judah and had appointed Gedali'ah the son of Ahi'kam, son of 12 Shaphan, as governor over them, then all the Jews returned from all the places to which they had been driven and came to the land of Judah, to Gedali'ah at Mizpah; and they gathered wine and summer fruits in great abundance.

Murder of the Governor

13 Now Joha'nan the son of Kare'ah and all the leaders of the forces in the open country came to Gedali'ah at 14 Mizpah and said to him, "Do you know that Ba'alis the king of the Ammonites has sent Ish'mael the son of Nethani'ah to take your life?" But Gedali'ah the son of 15 Ahi'kam would not believe them. Then Joha'nan the son of Kare'ah spoke secretly to Gedali'ah at Mizpah, "Let me go and slay Ish'mael the son of Nethani'ah, and no one will know it. Why should he take your life, so that all the Jews who are gathered about you would be scattered, 16 and the remnant of Judah would perish?" But Gedali'ah son of Ahi'kam said to Joha'nan the son of Kare'ah, "You shall not do this thing, for you are speaking falsely of Ish'mael."

41 In the seventh month, Ish'mael the son of Nethani'- ah, son of Eli'shama, of the royal family, one of the chief officers of the king, came with ten men to Gedali'ah the son of Ahi'kam, at Mizpah. As they ate 2 bread together there at Mizpah, Ish'mael the son of Nethani'ah and the ten men with him rose up and struck down Gedali'ah the son of Ahi'kam, son of Shaphan, with the sword, and killed him, whom the king of Babylon 3 had appointed governor in the land. Ish'mael also slew all the Jews who were with Gedali'ah at Mizpah, and the Chalde'an soldiers who happened to be there.

4 On the day after the murder of Gedali'ah, before any 5 one knew of it, eighty men arrived from Shechem and Shiloh and Samar'ia, with their beards shaved and their clothes torn, and their bodies gashed, bringing cereal offerings and incense to present at the temple of the LORD. 6 And Ish'mael the son of Nethani'ah came out from Mizpah to meet them, weeping as he came. As he met them, he said to them, "Come in to Gedali'ah the son of Ahi'kam." 7 When they came into the city, Ish'mael the son of Nethani'ah and the men with him slew them, and cast them 8 into a cistern. But there were ten men among them who said to Ish'mael, "Do not kill us, for we have stores of wheat, barley, oil, and honey hidden in the fields." So he refrained and did not kill them with their companions.

9 Now the cistern into which Ish'mael cast all the bodies of the men whom he had slain was the large cistern*r* which King Asa had made for defense against Ba'asha king of Israel; Ish'mael the son of Nethani'ah filled it 10 with the slain. Then Ish'mael took captive all the rest of the people who were in Mizpah, the king's daughters and all the people who were left at Mizpah, whom Nebu'- zarad'an, the captain of the guard, had committed to Gedali'ah the son of Ahi'kam. Ish'mael the son of Nethani'- ah took them captive and set out to cross over to the Ammonites.

11 But when Joha'nan the son of Kare'ah and all the leaders of the forces with him heard of all the evil which 12 Ish'mael the son of Nethani'ah had done, they took all their men and went to fight against Ish'mael the son of

---

q Syr: Heb obscure   *r* Gk: Heb *he had slain by the hand of Gedaliah*

Nethani'ah. They came upon him at the great pool which
13 is in Gib'eon. And when all the people who were with
Ish'mael saw Joha'nan the son of Kare'ah and all the
14 leaders of the forces with him, they rejoiced. So all the
people whom Ish'mael had carried away captive from
Mizpah turned about and came back, and went to Joha'-
15 nan the son of Kare'ah. But Ish'mael the son of Nethani'-
ah escaped from Joha'nan with eight men, and went to
16 the Ammonites. Then Joha'nan the son of Kare'ah and
all the leaders of the forces with him took all the rest of
the people whom Ish'mael the son of Nethani'ah had
carried away captive [s] from Mizpah after he had slain

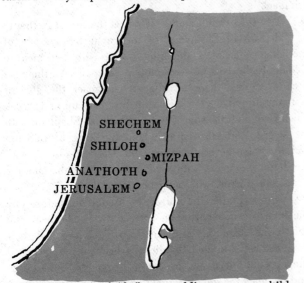

SHECHEM
SHILOH MIZPAH
ANATHOTH
JERUSALEM

Gedali'ah the son of Ahi'kam—soldiers, women, children,
and eunuchs, whom Joha'nan brought back from Gib'eon.
17 And they went and stayed at Geruth Chimham near Beth-
18 lehem, intending to go to Egypt because of the Chalde'ans;
for they were afraid of them, because Ish'mael the son
of Nethani'ah had slain Gedali'ah the son of Ahi'kam,
whom the king of Babylon had made governor over the
land.

Flight to Egypt

42 Then all the commanders of the forces, and Joha'-
nan the son of Kare'ah and Azari'ah [t] the son of
Hoshai'ah, and all the people from the least to the greatest,
2 came near and said to Jeremiah the prophet, "Let our
supplication come before you, and pray to the LORD your
God for us, for all this remnant (for we are left but a few
3 of many, as your eyes see us), that the LORD your God
may show us the way we should go, and the thing that we
4 should do." Jeremiah the prophet said to them, "I have
heard you; behold, I will pray to the LORD your God
according to your request, and whatever the LORD answers
you I will tell you: I will keep nothing back from you."
5 Then they said to Jeremiah, "May the LORD be a true
and faithful witness against us if we do not act according

to all the word with which the LORD your God sends you
6 to us. Whether it is good or evil, we will obey the voice
of the LORD our God to whom we are sending you, that
it may be well with us when we obey the voice of the
LORD our God."

7 At the end of ten days the word of the LORD came to
8 Jeremiah. Then he summoned Joha'nan the son of Kare'ah
and all the commanders of the forces who were with him,
9 and all the people from the least to the greatest, and said
to them, "Thus says the LORD, the God of Israel, to whom
you sent me to present your supplication before him:
10 If you will remain in this land, then I will build you up
and not pull you down; I will plant you, and not pluck
you up; for I repent of the evil which I did to you.
11 Do not fear the king of Babylon, of whom you are afraid;
do not fear him, says the LORD, for I am with you, to save
12 you and to deliver you from his hand. I will grant you
mercy, that he may have mercy on you and let you remain
13 in your own land. But if you say, 'We will not remain in
this land,' disobeying the voice of the LORD your God
14 and saying, 'No, we will go to the land of Egypt, where
we shall not see war, or hear the sound of the trumpet,
15 or be hungry for bread, and we will dwell there,' then
hear the word of the LORD, O remnant of Judah. Thus
says the LORD of hosts, the God of Israel: If you set your
16 faces to enter Egypt and go to live there, then the sword
which you fear shall overtake you there in the land of
Egypt; and the famine of which you are afraid shall
follow hard after you to Egypt; and there you shall die.
17 All the men who set their faces to go to Egypt to live
there shall die by the sword, by famine, and by pestilence;
they shall have no remnant or survivor from the evil
which I will bring upon them.

18 "For thus says the LORD of hosts, the God of Israel:
As my anger and my wrath were poured out on the inhabitants of Jerusalem, so my wrath will be poured out on
you when you go to Egypt. You shall become an execration, a horror, a curse, and a taunt. You shall see this
19 place no more. The LORD has said to you, O remnant of
Judah, 'Do not go to Egypt.' Know for a certainty that
20 I have warned you this day that you have gone astray at
the cost of your lives. For you sent me to the LORD your
God, saying, 'Pray for us to the LORD our God, and
whatever the LORD our God says declare to us and we will
21 do it.' And I have this day declared it to you, but you
have not obeyed the voice of the LORD your God in any-
22 thing that he sent me to tell you. Now therefore know for
a certainty that you shall die by the sword, by famine,
and by pestilence in the place where you desire to go to
live."

43 When Jeremiah finished speaking to all the people
all these words of the LORD their God, with which
2 the LORD their God had sent him to them, Azari'ah the

son of Hoshai'ah and Joha'nan the son of Kare'ah and all the insolent men said to Jeremiah, "You are telling a lie. The LORD our God did not send you to say, 'Do not
3 go to Egypt to live there'; but Baruch the son of Neri'ah has set you against us, to deliver us into the hand of the Chalde'ans, that they may kill us or take us into exile in
4 Babylon." So Joha'nan the son of Kare'ah and all the commanders of the forces and all the people did not obey the voice of the LORD, to remain in the land of Judah.
5 But Joha'nan the son of Kare'ah and all the commanders of the forces took all the remnant of Judah who had returned to live in the land of Judah from all the nations
6 to which they had been driven—the men, the women, the children, the princesses, and every person whom Nebu'zarad'an the captain of the guard had left with Gedali'ah the son of Ahi'kam, son of Shaphan; also Jeremiah the
7 prophet and Baruch the son of Neri'ah. And they came into the land of Egypt, for they did not obey the voice of the LORD. And they arrived at Tah'panhes.

8 Then the word of the LORD came to Jeremiah in Tah'-
9 panhes: "Take in your hands large stones, and hide them in the mortar in the pavement which is at the entrance to Pharaoh's palace in Tah'panhes, in the sight of the men
10 of Judah, and say to them, 'Thus says the LORD of hosts, the God of Israel: Behold, I will send and take Nebuchadrez'zar the king of Babylon, my servant, and he u will set his throne above these stones which I have hid, and he
11 will spread his royal canopy over them. He shall come and smite the land of Egypt, giving to the pestilence those who are doomed to the pestilence, to captivity those who are doomed to captivity, and to the sword those who are
12 doomed to the sword. He v shall kindle a fire in the temples of the gods of Egypt; and he shall burn them and carry them away captive; and he shall clean the land of Egypt, as a shepherd cleans his cloak of vermin; and he
13 shall go away from there in peace. He shall break the obelisks of Heliop'olis which is in the land of Egypt; and the temples of the gods of Egypt he shall burn with fire.'"

44 The word that came to Jeremiah concerning all the Jews that dwelt in the land of Egypt, at Migdol, at Tah'panhes, at Memphis, and in the land of Pathros,
2 "Thus says the LORD of hosts, the God of Israel: You have seen all the evil that I brought upon Jerusalem and upon all the cities of Judah. Behold, this day they are a desola-
3 tion, and no one dwells in them, because of the wickedness which they committed, provoking me to anger, in that they went to burn incense and serve other gods that they
4 knew not, neither they, nor you, nor your fathers. Yet I persistently sent to you all my servants the prophets, saying, 'Oh, do not do this abominable thing that I hate!'
5 But they did not listen or incline their ear, to turn from
6 their wickedness and burn no incense to other gods. There-

fore my wrath and my anger were poured forth and kindled in the cities of Judah and in the streets of Jerusalem; and they became a waste and a desolation,
7 as at this day. And now thus says the LORD God of hosts, the God of Israel: Why do you commit this great evil against yourselves, to cut off from you man and woman, infant and child, from the midst of Judah, leaving you no
8 remnant? Why do you provoke me to anger with the works of your hands, burning incense to other gods in the land of Egypt where you have come to live, that you may be cut off and become a curse and a taunt among all
9 the nations of the earth? Have you forgotten the wickedness of your fathers, the wickedness of the kings of Judah, the wickedness of their w wives, your own wickedness, and the wickedness of your wives, which they committed in the land of Judah and in the streets of Jerusa-
10 lem? They have not humbled themselves even to this day, nor have they feared, nor walked in my law and my statutes which I set before you and before your fathers.

11 "Therefore thus says the LORD of hosts, the God of Israel: Behold, I will set my face against you for evil, to
12 cut off all Judah. I will take the remnant of Judah who have set their faces to come to the land of Egypt to live, and they shall all be consumed; in the land of Egypt they shall fall; by the sword and by famine they shall be consumed; from the least to the greatest, they shall die by the sword and by famine; and they shall become an
13 execration, a horror, a curse, and a taunt. I will punish those who dwell in the land of Egypt, as I have punished Jerusalem, with the sword, with famine, and with pesti-
14 lence, so that none of the remnant of Judah who have come to live in the land of Egypt shall escape or survive or return to the land of Judah, to which they desire to return to dwell there; for they shall not return, except some fugitives."

15 Then all the men who knew that their wives had offered incense to other gods, and all the women who stood by, a great assembly, all the people who dwelt in Pathros in
16 the land of Egypt, answered Jeremiah: "As for the word which you have spoken to us in the name of the LORD, we
17 will not listen to you. But we will do everything that we have vowed, burn incense to the queen of heaven and pour out libations to her, as we did, both we and our fathers, our kings and our princes, in the cities of Judah and in the streets of Jerusalem; for then we had plenty of
18 food, and prospered, and saw no evil. But since we left off burning incense to the queen of heaven and pouring out libations to her, we have lacked everything and have been
19 consumed by the sword and by famine." And the women said, x "When we burned incense to the queen of heaven and poured out libations to her, was it without our husbands' approval that we made cakes for her bearing her image and poured out libations to her?"

u Gk Syr: Heb I   v Gk Syr Vg: Heb I   w Heb his   x Compare Syr: Heb lacks And the women said

20 Then Jeremiah said to all the people, men and women,
21 all the people who had given him this answer: "As for the incense that you burned in the cities of Judah and in the streets of Jerusalem, you and your fathers, your kings and your princes, and the people of the land, did not the LORD remember it?ʸ Did it not come into his mind?
22 The LORD could no longer bear your evil doings and the abominations which you committed; therefore your land has become a desolation and a waste and a curse, without
23 inhabitant, as it is this day. It is because you burned incense, and because you sinned against the LORD and did not obey the voice of the LORD or walk in his law and in his statutes and in his testimonies, that this evil has befallen you, as at this day."

24 Jeremiah said to all the people and all the women, "Hear the word of the LORD, all you of Judah who are in
25 the land of Egypt, Thus says the LORD of hosts, the God of Israel: You and your wives have declared with your mouths, and have fulfilled it with your hands, saying, 'We will surely perform our vows that we have made, to burn incense to the queen of heaven and to pour out libations to her.' Then confirm your vows and perform
26 your vows! Therefore hear the word of the LORD, all you of Judah who dwell in the land of Egypt: Behold, I have sworn by my great name, says the LORD, that my name shall no more be invoked by the mouth of any man of Judah in all the land of Egypt, saying, 'As the Lord GOD
27 lives.' Behold, I am watching over them for evil and not for good; all the men of Judah who are in the land of Egypt shall be consumed by the sword and by famine,
28 until there is an end of them. And those who escape the sword shall return from the land of Egypt to the land of Judah, few in number; and all the remnant of Judah, who came to the land of Egypt to live, shall know whose word
29 will stand, mine or theirs. This shall be the sign to you, says the LORD, that I will punish you in this place, in order that you may know that my words will surely stand
30 against you for evil: Thus says the LORD, Behold, I will give Pharaoh Hophra king of Egypt into the hand of his enemies and into the hand of those who seek his life, as I gave Zedeki'ah king of Judah into the hand of Nebuchadrez'zar king of Babylon, who was his enemy and sought his life."

45 The word that Jeremiah the prophet spoke to Baruch the son of Neri'ah, when he wrote these words in a book at the dictation of Jeremiah, in the fourth year of Jehoi'akim the son of Josi'ah, king of Judah:
2 "Thus says the LORD, the God of Israel, to you, O Baruch:
3 You said, 'Woe is me! for the LORD has added sorrow to my pain; I am weary with my groaning, and I find no
4 rest.' Thus shall you say to him, Thus says the LORD: Behold, what I have built I am breaking down, and what I

have planted I am plucking up—that is, the whole land.
5 And do you seek great things for yourself? Seek them not; for, behold, I am bringing evil upon all flesh, says the LORD; but I will give you your life as a prize of war in all places to which you may go."

ORACLES AGAINST THE NATIONS

46 The word of the LORD which came to Jeremiah the prophet concerning the nations.
2 About Egypt. Concerning the army of Pharaoh Neco, king of Egypt, which was by the river Eu-phra'tes at Car'chemish and which Nebuchadrez'zar king of Babylon defeated in the fourth year of Jehoi'akim the son of Josi'ah, king of Judah:

3 "Prepare buckler and shield,
    and advance for battle!
4 Harness the horses;
    mount, O horsemen!
Take your stations with your helmets,
    polish your spears,
    put on your coats of mail!
5 Why have I seen it?
They are dismayed
    and have turned backward.
Their warriors are beaten down,
    and have fled in haste;
they look not back—
    terror on every side!

                                    says the LORD.

6 The swift cannot flee away,
    nor the warrior escape;
in the north by the river Eu-phra'tes
    they have stumbled and fallen.

7 "Who is this, rising like the Nile,
    like rivers whose waters surge?
8 Egypt rises like the Nile,
    like rivers whose waters surge.
He said, I will rise, I will cover the earth,
    I will destroy cities and their inhabitants.
9 Advance, O horses,
    and rage, O chariots!
Let the warriors go forth:
    men of Ethiopia and Put who handle the shield,
    men of Lud, skilled in handling the bow.

ʸ Syr: Heb them

[10] That day is the day of the Lord GOD of hosts,
    a day of vengeance,
    to avenge himself on his foes.
The sword shall devour and be sated,
    and drink its fill of their blood.
For the Lord GOD of hosts holds a sacrifice
    in the north country by the river Eu-phra'tes.
[11] Go up to Gilead, and take balm,
    O virgin daughter of Egypt!
In vain you have used many medicines;
    there is no healing for you.
[12] The nations have heard of your shame,
    and the earth is full of your cry;
for warrior has stumbled against warrior;
    they have both fallen together."

[13] The word which the LORD spoke to Jeremiah the prophet about the coming of Nebuchadrez'zar king of Babylon to smite the land of Egypt:

[14] "Declare in Egypt, and proclaim in Migdol;
    proclaim in Memphis and Tah'panhes;
Say, 'Stand ready and be prepared,
    for the sword shall devour round about you.'
[15] Why has Apis fled? [z]
    Why did not your bull stand?
    Because the LORD thrust him down.
[16] Your multitude stumbled [a] and fell,
    and they said one to another,
'Arise, and let us go back to our own people
    and to the land of our birth,
    because of the sword of the oppressor.'
[17] Call the name of Pharaoh, king of Egypt,
    'Noisy one who lets the hour go by.'

[18] "As I live, says the King,
    whose name is the LORD of hosts,
like Tabor among the mountains,
    and like Carmel by the sea, shall one come.
[19] Prepare yourselves baggage for exile,
    O inhabitants of Egypt!
For Memphis shall become a waste,
    a ruin, without inhabitant.

[20] "A beautiful heifer is Egypt,
    but a gadfly from the north has come upon her.
[21] Even her hired soldiers in her midst
    are like fatted calves;
yea, they have turned and fled together,
    they did not stand;
for the day of their calamity has come upon them,
    the time of their punishment.

[22] "She makes a sound like a serpent gliding away;
    for her enemies march in force,
and come against her with axes,
    like those who fell trees.
[23] They shall cut down her forest,

says the LORD,

    though it is impenetrable,
because they are more numerous than locusts;
    they are without number.
[24] The daughter of Egypt shall be put to shame,
    she shall be delivered into the hand of a people from
    the north."

[25] The LORD of hosts, the God of Israel, said: "Behold, I am bringing punishment upon Amon of Thebes, and Pharaoh, and Egypt and her gods and her kings, upon [26] Pharaoh and those who trust in him. I will deliver them into the hand of those who seek their life, into the hand of Nebuchadrez'zar king of Babylon and his officers. Afterward Egypt shall be inhabited as in the days of old, says the LORD.

[27] "But fear not, O Jacob my servant,
    nor be dismayed, O Israel;
for lo, I will save you from afar,
    and your offspring from the land of their captivity.
Jacob shall return and have quiet and ease,
    and none shall make him afraid.
[28] Fear not, O Jacob my servant,

says the LORD,

    for I am with you.
I will make a full end of all the nations
    to which I have driven you,
    but of you I will not make a full end.
I will chasten you in just measure,
    and I will by no means leave you unpunished."

47 The word of the LORD that came to Jeremiah the prophet concerning the Philistines, before Pharaoh smote Gaza.
[2] "Thus says the LORD:
Behold, waters are rising out of the north,
    and shall become an overflowing torrent;
they shall overflow the land and all that fills it,
    the city and those who dwell in it.
Men shall cry out,
    and every inhabitant of the land shall wail.
[3] At the noise of the stamping of the hoofs of his stallions,
    at the rushing of his chariots, at the rumbling of their
        wheels,
the fathers look not back to their children,
    so feeble are their hands,
[4] because of the day that is coming to destroy
    all the Philistines,
to cut off from Tyre and Sidon
    every helper that remains.

[z] Gk: Heb *Why was it swept away*   [a] Gk: Heb *He made many stumble*

545

For the Lord is destroying the Philistines,
the remnant of the coastland of Caphtor.
5 Baldness has come upon Gaza,
Ash'kelon has perished.
O remnant of the Anakim,[b]
how long will you gash yourselves?
6 Ah, sword of the Lord!
How long till you are quiet?
Put yourself into your scabbard,
rest and be still!
7 How can it[c] be quiet,
when the Lord has given it a charge?
Against Ash'kelon and against the seashore
he has appointed it."

48 Concerning Moab.
Thus says the Lord of hosts, the God of Israel:
"Woe to Nebo, for it is laid waste!
Kiriatha'im is put to shame, it is taken;
the fortress is put to shame and broken down;
2 the renown of Moab is no more.
In Heshbon they planned evil against her:
'Come, let us cut her off from being a nation!'
You also, O Madmen, shall be brought to silence;
the sword shall pursue you.

3 "Hark! a cry from Horona'im,
'Desolation and great destruction!'
4 Moab is destroyed;
a cry is heard as far as Zo'ar.[d]
5 For at the ascent of Luhith
they go up weeping;[e]
for at the descent of Horona'im
they have heard the cry[f] of destruction.
6 Flee! Save yourselves!
Be like a wild ass[g] in the desert!
7 For, because you trusted in your strongholds[h] and your treasures,
you also shall be taken;
and Chemosh shall go forth into exile,
with his priests and his princes.
8 The destroyer shall come upon every city,
and no city shall escape;
the valley shall perish,
and the plain shall be destroyed, as the Lord has spoken.

9 "Give wings to Moab,
for she would fly away;
her cities shall become a desolation,
with no inhabitant in them.

10 "Cursed is he who does the work of the Lord with slackness; and cursed is he who keeps back his sword from bloodshed.

11 "Moab has been at ease from his youth
and has settled on his lees;
he has not been emptied from vessel to vessel,
nor has he gone into exile;
so his taste remains in him,
and his scent is not changed.

12 "Therefore, behold, the days are coming, says the Lord, when I shall send to him tilters who will tilt him, and empty his vessels, and break his[i] jars in pieces. 13 Then Moab shall be ashamed of Chemosh, as the house of Israel was ashamed of Bethel, their confidence.

14 "How do you say, 'We are heroes
and mighty men of war'?
15 The destroyer of Moab and his cities has come up,
and the choicest of his young men have gone down to slaughter,
says the King, whose name is the Lord of hosts.
16 The calamity of Moab is near at hand
and his affliction hastens apace.
17 Bemoan him, all you who are round about him,
and all who know his name;
say, 'How the mighty scepter is broken,
the glorious staff.'

18 "Come down from your glory,
and sit on the parched ground,
O inhabitant of Dibon!
For the destroyer of Moab has come up against you;
he has destroyed your strongholds.
19 Stand by the way and watch,
O inhabitant of Aro'er!
Ask him who flees and her who escapes;
say, 'What has happened?'
20 Moab is put to shame, for it is broken;
wail and cry!
Tell it by the Arnon,
that Moab is laid waste.

21 "Judgment has come upon the tableland, upon Holon, 22 and Jahzah, and Meph'a-ath, and Dibon, and Nebo, and 23 Beth-diblatha'im, and Kiriatha'im, and Beth-ga'mul, and 24 Beth-me'on, and Ker'i-oth, and Bozrah, and all the cities 25 of the land of Moab, far and near. The horn of Moab is cut off, and his arm is broken, says the Lord.

26 "Make him drunk, because he magnified himself against the Lord; so that Moab shall wallow in his vomit, and he 27 too shall be held in derision. Was not Israel a derision to you? Was he found among thieves, that whenever you spoke of him you wagged your head?

28 "Leave the cities, and dwell in the rock,
O inhabitants of Moab!
Be like the dove that nests

---

b Gk: Heb their valley   c Gk Vg: Heb you   d Gk: Heb her little ones   e Cn: Heb weeping goes up with weeping
f Gk Compare Is 15.5: Heb the distress of the cry   g Gk Aquila: Heb like Aroer   h Gk: Heb works   i Gk Aquila: Heb their

in the sides of the mouth of a gorge.
29 We have heard of the pride of Moab—
    he is very proud—
of his loftiness, his pride, and his arrogance,
    and the haughtiness of his heart.
30 I know his insolence, says the LORD;
    his boasts are false,
    his deeds are false.
31 Therefore I wail for Moab;
    I cry out for all Moab;
    for the men of Kir-he′res I mourn.
32 More than for Jazer I weep for you,
    O vine of Sibmah!
Your branches passed over the sea,
    reached as far as Jazer;ʲ
upon your summer fruits and your vintage
    the destroyer has fallen.
33 Gladness and joy have been taken away
    from the fruitful land of Moab;
I have made the wine cease from the wine presses;
    no one treads them with shouts of joy;
    the shouting is not the shout of joy.

34   "Heshbon and Ele-a′leh cry out;ᵏ as far as Jahaz they
utter their voice, from Zo′ar to Horona′im and Eg′lath-
shelish′iyah. For the waters of Nimrim also have become
35 desolate. And I will bring to an end in Moab, says the
LORD, him who offers sacrifice in the high place and burns
36 incense to his god. Therefore my heart moans for Moab
like a flute, and my heart moans like a flute for the men
of Kir-he′res; therefore the riches they gained have
perished.
37   "For every head is shaved and every beard cut off;
upon all the hands are gashes, and on the loins is sack-
38 cloth. On all the housetops of Moab and in the squares
there is nothing but lamentation; for I have broken Moab
like a vessel for which no one cares, says the LORD.
39 How it is broken! How they wail! How Moab has turned
his back in shame! So Moab has become a derision
and a horror to all that are round about him."
40 For thus says the LORD:
"Behold, one shall fly swiftly like an eagle,
    and spread his wings against Moab;
41 the cities shall be taken
    and the strongholds seized.
The heart of the warriors of Moab shall be in that day
    like the heart of a woman in her pangs;
42 Moab shall be destroyed and be no longer a people,
    because he magnified himself against the LORD.
43 Terror, pit, and snare
    are before you, O inhabitant of Moab!
                  says the LORD.
44 He who flees from the terror

shall fall into the pit,
and he who climbs out of the pit
    shall be caught in the snare.
For I will bring these thingsˡ upon Moab
    in the year of their punishment,

                  says the LORD.

45 "In the shadow of Heshbon
    fugitives stop without strength;
for a fire has gone forth from Heshbon,
    a flame from the house of Sihon;
it has destroyed the forehead of Moab,
    the crown of the sons of tumult.
46 Woe to you, O Moab!
    The people of Chemosh is undone;
for your sons have been taken captive
    and your daughters into captivity.
47 Yet I will restore the fortunes of Moab
    in the latter days,

                  says the LORD."

Thus far is the judgment on Moab.

49   Concerning the Ammonites.
    Thus says the LORD:
"Has Israel no sons?
    Has he no heir?
Why then has Milcom dispossessed Gad,
    and his people settled in its cities?
2 Therefore, behold, the days are coming,
    says the LORD,
when I will cause the battle cry to be heard
    against Rabbah of the Ammonites;
it shall become a desolate mound,
    and its villages shall be burned with fire;
then Israel shall dispossess those who dispossessed him,
                  says the LORD.

3 "Wail, O Heshbon, for Ai is laid waste!
    Cry, O daughters of Rabbah!
Gird yourselves with sackcloth,
    lament, and run to and fro among the hedges!
For Milcom shall go into exile,
    with his priests and his princes.
4 Why do you boast of your valleys,ᵐ

ʲCn: Heb *the sea of Jazer*   ᵏ Cn: Heb *From the cry of Heshbon to Elealeh*   ˡ Gk Syr: Heb *to her*
ᵐ Heb *valleys, your valley flows*

O faithless daughter,
who trusted in her treasures, saying,
'Who will come against me?'
[5] Behold, I will bring terror upon you,
says the Lord GOD of hosts,
from all who are round about you,
and you shall be driven out, every man straight before
him,
with none to gather the fugitives.
[6] But afterward I will restore the fortunes of the Ammonites, says the LORD."

[7] Concerning Edom.
Thus says the LORD of hosts:
"Is wisdom no more in Teman?
Has counsel perished from the prudent?
Has their wisdom vanished?
[8] Flee, turn back, dwell in the depths,
O inhabitants of Dedan!
For I will bring the calamity of Esau upon him,
the time when I punish him.
[9] If grape-gatherers came to you,
would they not leave gleanings?
If thieves came by night,
would they not destroy only enough for themselves?
[10] But I have stripped Esau bare,
I have uncovered his hiding places,
and he is not able to conceal himself.
His children are destroyed, and his brothers,
and his neighbors; and he is no more.
[11] Leave your fatherless children, I will keep them alive;
and let your widows trust in me."
[12] For thus says the LORD: "If those who did not deserve
to drink the cup must drink it, will you go unpunished?
[13] You shall not go unpunished, but you must drink. For I
have sworn by myself, says the LORD, that Bozrah .shall
become a horror, a taunt, a waste, and a curse; and all
her cities shall be perpetual wastes."
[14] I have heard tidings from the LORD,
and a messenger has been sent among the nations:
"Gather yourselves together and come against her,
and rise up for battle!"
[15] For behold, I will make you small among the nations,
despised among men.
[16] The horror you inspire has deceived you,
and the pride of your heart,
you who live in the clefts of the rock,[n]
who hold the height of the hill.
Though you make your nest as high as the eagle's,
I will bring you down from there,
says the LORD.
[17] "Edom shall become a horror; every one who passes
by it will be horrified and will hiss because of all its

[18] disasters. As when Sodom and Gomor'rah and their
neighbor cities were overthrown, says the LORD, no man
[19] shall dwell there, no man shall sojourn in her. Behold,
like a lion coming up from the jungle of the Jordan
against a strong sheepfold, I will suddenly make them[o]
run away from her; and I will appoint over her whomever I choose. For who is like me? Who will summon
[20] me? What shepherd can stand before me? Therefore hear
the plan which the LORD has made against Edom and the
purposes which he has formed against the inhabitants of
Teman: Even the little ones of the flock shall be dragged
away; surely their fold shall be appalled at their fate.
[21] At the sound of their fall the earth shall tremble; the
[22] sound of their cry shall be heard at the Red Sea. Behold,
one shall mount up and fly swiftly like an eagle, and
spread his wings against Bozrah, and the heart of the
warriors of Edom shall be in that day like the heart of a
woman in her pangs."

[23] Concerning Damascus.
"Hamath and Arpad are confounded,
for they have heard evil tidings;
they melt in fear, they are troubled like the sea[p]
which cannot be quiet.
[24] Damascus has become feeble, she turned to flee,
and panic seized her;
anguish and sorrows have taken hold of her,
as of a woman in travail.
[25] How the famous city is forsaken,[q] the joyful city![r]
[26] Therefore her young men shall fall in her squares,
and all her soldiers shall be destroyed in that day,
says the LORD of hosts.
[27] And I will kindle a fire in the wall of Damascus,
and it shall devour the strongholds of Ben-ha'dad."

[28] Concerning Kedar and the kingdoms of Hazor which
Nebuchadrez'zar king of Babylon smote.
Thus says the LORD:
"Rise up, advance against Kedar!
Destroy the people of the east!
[29] Their tents and their flocks shall be taken,
their curtains and all their goods;
their camels shall be borne away from them,
and men shall cry to them: 'Terror on every side!'
[30] Flee, wander far away, dwell in the depths,
O inhabitants of Hazor!
says the LORD.

For Nebuchadrez'zar king of Babylon
has made a plan against you,
and formed a purpose against you.
[31] "Rise up, advance against a nation at ease,
that dwells securely,
says the LORD.

[n] Or Sela   [o] Gk Syr: Heb him   [p] Cn: Heb there is trouble in the sea   [q] Vg: Heb not forsaken
[r] Syr Vg Tg: Heb city of my joy

that has no gates or bars,
  that dwells alone.
32 Their camels shall become booty,
  their herds of cattle a spoil.
I will scatter to every wind
  those who cut the corners of their hair,
and I will bring their calamity
  from every side of them,

  says the LORD.

33 Hazor shall become a haunt of jackals,
  an everlasting waste;
no man shall dwell there,
  no man shall sojourn in her."

34 The word of the LORD that came to Jeremiah the prophet concerning Elam, in the beginning of the reign of Zedeki'ah king of Judah.

35 Thus says the LORD of hosts: "Behold, I will break the
36 bow of Elam, the mainstay of their might; and I will bring upon Elam the four winds from the four quarters of heaven; and I will scatter them to all those winds, and there shall be no nation to which those driven out of
37 Elam shall not come. I will terrify Elam before their enemies, and before those who seek their life; I will bring evil upon them, my fierce anger, says the LORD. I will send the sword after them, until I have consumed them;
38 and I will set my throne in Elam, and destroy their king and princes, says the LORD.

39 "But in the latter days I will restore the fortunes of Elam, says the LORD."

50 The word which the LORD spoke concerning Babylon, concerning the land of the Chalde'ans, by Jeremiah the prophet:
2 "Declare among the nations and proclaim,
  set up a banner and proclaim,
  conceal it not, and say:
'Babylon is taken,
  Bel is put to shame,
  Mer'odach is dismayed.
Her images are put to shame,
  her idols are dismayed.'

3 "For out of the north a nation has come up against her, which shall make her land a desolation, and none shall dwell in it; both man and beast shall flee away.

4 "In those days and in that time, says the LORD, the people of Israel and the people of Judah shall come together, weeping as they come; and they shall seek the
5 LORD their God. They shall ask the way to Zion, with faces turned toward it, saying, 'Come, let us join ourselves to the LORD in an everlasting covenant which will never be forgotten.'

6 "My people have been lost sheep; their shepherds have led them astray, turning them away on the mountains; from mountain to hill they have gone, they have forgotten
7 their fold. All who found them have devoured them, and their enemies have said, 'We are not guilty, for they have sinned against the LORD, their true habitation, the LORD, the hope of their fathers.'

8 "Flee from the midst of Babylon, and go out of the land of the Chalde'ans, and be as he-goats before the flock.
9 For behold, I am stirring up and bringing against Babylon a company of great nations, from the north country; and they shall array themselves against her; from there she shall be taken. Their arrows are like a skilled warrior
10 who does not return empty-handed. Chalde'a shall be plundered; all who plunder her shall be sated, says the LORD.

11 "Though you rejoice, though you exult,
  O plunderers of my heritage,
though you are wanton as a heifer at grass,
  and neigh like stallions,
12 your mother shall be utterly shamed,
  and she who bore you shall be disgraced.
Lo, she shall be the last of the nations,
  a wilderness dry and desert.
13 Because of the wrath of the LORD she shall not be inhabited,
  but shall be an utter desolation;
every one who passes by Babylon shall be appalled,
  and hiss because of all her wounds.
14 Set yourselves in array against Babylon round about,
  all you that bend the bow;
shoot at her, spare no arrows,
  for she has sinned against the LORD.
15 Raise a shout against her round about,
  she has surrendered;
her bulwarks have fallen,
  her walls are thrown down.

For this is the vengeance of the LORD:
  take vengeance on her,
  do to her as she has done.
16 Cut off from Babylon the sower,
  and the one who handles the sickle in time of harvest;

because of the sword of the oppressor,
 every one shall turn to his own people,
 and every one shall flee to his own land.

17 "Israel is a hunted sheep driven away by lions. First the king of Assyria devoured him, and now at last Nebuchadrez'zar king of Babylon has gnawed his bones. 18 Therefore, thus says the LORD of hosts, the God of Israel: Behold, I am bringing punishment on the king of Babylon and his land, as I punished the king of Assyria. 19 I will restore Israel to his pasture, and he shall feed on Carmel and in Bashan, and his desire shall be satisfied 20 on the hills of E'phraim and in Gilead. In those days and in that time, says the LORD, iniquity shall be sought in Israel, and there shall be none; and sin in Judah, and none shall be found; for I will pardon those whom I leave as a remnant.

21 "Go up against the land of Mera-tha'im,ˢ
 and against the inhabitants of Pekod.ᵗ
Slay, and utterly destroy after them,
       says the LORD,
 and do all that I have commanded you.
22 The noise of battle is in the land,
 and great destruction!
23 How the hammer of the whole earth
 is cut down and broken!
How Babylon has become
 a horror among the nations!
24 I set a snare for you and you were taken, O Babylon,
 and you did not know it;
you were found and caught,
 because you strove against the LORD.
25 The LORD has opened his armory,
 and brought out the weapons of his wrath,
for the Lord GOD of hosts has a work to do
 in the land of the Chalde'ans.
26 Come against her from every quarter;
 open her granaries;
pile her up like heaps of grain, and destroy her utterly;
 let nothing be left of her.
27 Slay all her bulls,
 let them go down to the slaughter.
Woe to them, for their day has come,
 the time of their punishment.

28 "Hark! they flee and escape from the land of Babylon, to declare in Zion the vengeance of the LORD our God, vengeance for his temple.

29 "Summon archers against Babylon, all those who bend the bow. Encamp round about her; let no one escape. Requite her according to her deeds, do to her according to all that she has done; for she has proudly defied the 30 LORD, the Holy One of Israel. Therefore her young men shall fall in her squares, and all her soldiers shall be destroyed on that day, says the LORD.

31 "Behold, I am against you, O proud one,
 says the Lord GOD of hosts;
for your day has come,
 the time when I will punish you.
32 The proud one shall stumble and fall,
 with none to raise him up,
and I will kindle a fire in his cities,
 and it will devour all that is round about him.

33 "Thus says the LORD of hosts: The people of Israel are oppressed, and the people of Judah with them; all who took them captive have held them fast, they refuse to 34 let them go. Their Redeemer is strong; the LORD of hosts is his name. He will surely plead their cause, that he may give rest to the earth, but unrest to the inhabitants of Babylon.

35 "A sword upon the Chalde'ans, says the LORD,
 and upon the inhabitants of Babylon,
 and upon her princes and her wise men!
36 A sword upon the diviners,
 that they may become fools!
A sword upon her warriors,
 that they may be destroyed!
37 A sword upon her horses and upon her chariots,
 and upon all the foreign troops in her midst,
 that they may become women!
A sword upon all her treasures,
 that they may be plundered!
38 A drought upon her waters,
 that they may be dried up!
For it is a land of images,
 and they are mad over idols.

39 "Therefore wild beasts shall dwell with hyenas in Babylon, and ostriches shall dwell in her; she shall be peopled no more for ever, nor inhabited for all genera- 40 tions. As when God overthrew Sodom and Gomor'rah and their neighbor cities, says the LORD, so no man shall dwell there, and no son of man shall sojourn in her.

41 "Behold, a people comes from the north;
 a mighty nation and many kings
 are stirring from the farthest parts of the earth.
42 They lay hold of bow and spear;
 they are cruel, and have no mercy.
The sound of them is like the roaring of the sea;
 they ride upon horses,
arrayed as a man for battle
 against you, O daughter of Babylon!

ˢ Or *Double Rebellion*   ᵗ Or *Punishment*

43 "The king of Babylon heard the report of them,
    and his hands fell helpless;
anguish seized him,
    pain as of a woman in travail.

44   "Behold, like a lion coming up from the jungle of the Jordan against a strong sheepfold, I will suddenly make them run away from her; and I will appoint over her whomever I choose. For who is like me? Who will sum-
45 mon me? What shepherd can stand before me? Therefore hear the plan which the LORD has made against Babylon, and the purposes which he has formed against the land of the Chalde'ans: Surely the little ones of their flock shall be dragged away; surely their fold shall be appalled at
46 their fate. At the sound of the capture of Babylon the earth shall tremble, and her cry shall be heard among the nations."

51 Thus says the LORD:
    "Behold, I will stir up the spirit of a destroyer against Babylon,
    against the inhabitants of Chalde'a; u
2 and I will send to Babylon winnowers,
    and they shall winnow her,
and they shall empty her land,
    when they come against her from every side
    on the day of trouble.
3 Let not the archer bend his bow,
    and let him not stand up in his coat of mail.
Spare not her young men;
    utterly destroy all her host.
4 They shall fall down slain in the land of the Chalde'ans,
    and wounded in her streets.
5 For Israel and Judah have not been forsaken
    by their God, the LORD of hosts;
but the land of the Chalde'ans v is full of guilt
    against the Holy One of Israel.

6 "Flee from the midst of Babylon,
    let every man save his life!
Be not cut off in her punishment,
    for this is the time of the LORD's vengeance,
    the requital he is rendering her.
7 Babylon was a golden cup in the LORD's hand,
    making all the earth drunken;
the nations drank of her wine,
    therefore the nations went mad.
8 Suddenly Babylon has fallen and been broken;
    wail for her!
Take balm for her pain;
    perhaps she may be healed.
9 We would have healed Babylon,
    but she was not healed.
Forsake her, and let us go

each to his own country;
    for her judgment has reached up to heaven
    and has been lifted up even to the skies.
10 The LORD has brought forth our vindication;
    come, let us declare in Zion
    the work of the LORD our God.

11 "Sharpen the arrows!
    Take up the shields!
The LORD has stirred up the spirit of the kings of the Medes, because his purpose concerning Babylon is to destroy it, for that is the vengeance of the LORD, the vengeance for his temple.
12 Set up a standard against the walls of Babylon;
    make the watch strong;
set up watchmen;
    prepare the ambushes;
for the LORD has both planned and done
    what he spoke concerning the inhabitants of Babylon.
13 O you who dwell by many waters,
    rich in treasures,
your end has come,
    the thread of your life is cut.
14 The LORD of hosts has sworn by himself:
Surely I will fill you with men, as many as locusts,
    and they shall raise the shout of victory over you.

15 "It is he who made the earth by his power,
    who established the world by his wisdom,
and by his understanding
    stretched out the heavens.
16 When he utters his voice there is a tumult of waters in
        the heavens,
    and he makes the mist rise from the ends of the earth.
He makes lightnings for the rain,
    and he brings forth the wind from his storehouses.

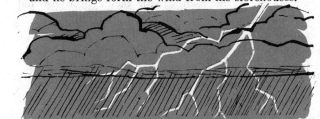

17 Every man is stupid and without knowledge;
    every goldsmith is put to shame by his idols;
for his images are false,
    and there is no breath in them.
18 They are worthless, a work of delusion;
    at the time of their punishment they shall perish.
19 Not like these is he who is the portion of Jacob,
    for he is the one who formed all things,
and Israel is the tribe of his inheritance;
    the LORD of hosts is his name.

u Heb Leb-qamai, a cipher for Chaldea   v Heb their land

20 "You are my hammer and weapon of war:
with you I break nations in pieces;
with you I destroy kingdoms;
21 with you I break in pieces the horse and his rider;
with you I break in pieces the chariot and the
charioteer;
22 with you I break in pieces man and woman;
with you I break in pieces the old man and the youth;
with you I break in pieces the young man and the maiden;
23 with you I break in pieces the shepherd and his flock;
with you I break in pieces the farmer and his team;
with you I break in pieces governors and commanders.

24 "I will requite Babylon and all the inhabitants of
Chalde'a before your very eyes for all the evil that they
have done in Zion, says the LORD.

25 "Behold, I am against you, O destroying mountain,
says the LORD,

which destroys the whole earth;
I will stretch out my hand against you,
and roll you down from the crags,
and make you a burnt mountain.
26 No stone shall be taken from you for a corner
and no stone for a foundation,
but you shall be a perpetual waste,
says the LORD.

27 "Set up a standard on the earth,
blow the trumpet among the nations;
prepare the nations for war against her,
summon against her the kingdoms,
Ar'arat, Minni, and Ash'kenaz;
appoint a marshal against her,
bring up horses like bristling locusts.
28 Prepare the nations for war against her,
the kings of the Medes, with their governors and
deputies,
and every land under their dominion.
29 The land trembles and writhes in pain,
for the LORD's purposes against Babylon stand,
to make the land of Babylon a desolation,
without inhabitant.
30 The warriors of Babylon have ceased fighting,
they remain in their strongholds;
their strength has failed,
they have become women;
her dwellings are on fire,
her bars are broken.
31 One runner runs to meet another,
and one messenger to meet another,
to tell the king of Babylon
that his city is taken on every side;
32 the fords have been seized,

the bulwarks are burned with fire,
and the soldiers are in panic.
33 For thus says the LORD of hosts, the God of Israel:
The daughter of Babylon is like a threshing floor
at the time when it is trodden;
yet a little while
and the time of her harvest will come."

34 "Nebuchadrez'zar the king of Babylon has devoured me,
he has crushed me;
he has made me an empty vessel,
he has swallowed me like a monster;
he has filled his belly with my delicacies,
he has rinsed me out.
35 The violence done to me and to my kinsmen be upon
Babylon,"
let the inhabitant of Zion say.
"My blood be upon the inhabitants of Chalde'a,"
let Jerusalem say.
36 Therefore thus says the LORD:
"Behold, I will plead your cause
and take vengeance for you.
I will dry up her sea
and make her fountain dry;
37 and Babylon shall become a heap of ruins,
the haunt of jackals,
a horror and a hissing,
without inhabitant.

38 "They shall roar together like lions;
they shall growl like lions' whelps.
39 While they are inflamed I will prepare them a feast
and make them drunk, till they swoon away [w]
and sleep a perpetual sleep
and not wake, says the LORD.
40 I will bring them down like lambs to the slaughter,
like rams and he-goats.

41 "How Babylon [x] is taken,
the praise of the whole earth seized!
How Babylon has become
a horror among the nations!
42 The sea has come up on Babylon;
she is covered with its tumultuous waves.
43 Her cities have become a horror,
a land of drought and a desert,
a land in which no one dwells,
and through which no son of man passes.
44 And I will punish Bel in Babylon,
and take out of his mouth what he has swallowed.
The nations shall no longer flow to him;
the wall of Babylon has fallen.

45 "Go out of the midst of her, my people!

w Gk Vg: Heb *rejoice*   x Heb *Sheshach*, a cipher for Babylon

Let every man save his life
from the fierce anger of the LORD!
⁴⁶ Let not your heart faint, and be not fearful
at the report heard in the land,
when a report comes in one year
and afterward a report in another year,
and violence is in the land,
and ruler is against ruler.

⁴⁷ "Therefore, behold, the days are coming
when I will punish the images of Babylon;
her whole land shall be put to shame,
and all her slain shall fall in the midst of her.
⁴⁸ Then the heavens and the earth,
and all that is in them,
shall sing for joy over Babylon;
for the destroyers shall come against them out of the
north,

says the LORD.

⁴⁹ Babylon must fall for the slain of Israel,
as for Babylon have fallen the slain of all the earth.

⁵⁰ "You that have escaped from the sword,
go, stand not still!
Remember the LORD from afar,
and let Jerusalem come into your mind:
⁵¹ 'We are put to shame, for we have heard reproach;
dishonor has covered our face,
for aliens have come
into the holy places of the LORD's house.'

⁵² "Therefore, behold, the days are coming, says the LORD,
when I will execute judgment upon her images,
and through all her land
the wounded shall groan.
⁵³ Though Babylon should mount up to heaven,
and though she should fortify her strong height,
yet destroyers would come from me upon her,

says the LORD.

⁵⁴ "Hark! a cry from Babylon!
The noise of great destruction from the land of the
Chalde'ans!
⁵⁵ For the LORD is laying Babylon waste,
and stilling her mighty voice.
Their waves roar like many waters,
the noise of their voice is raised;
⁵⁶ for a destroyer has come upon her,
upon Babylon;
her warriors are taken,
their bows are broken in pieces;
for the LORD is a God of recompense,
he will surely requite.

ʸ Gk: Heb *upon her. And they shall weary themselves*

⁵⁷ I will make drunk her princes and her wise men,
her governors, her commanders, and her warriors;
they shall sleep a perpetual sleep and not wake,
says the King, whose name is the LORD of hosts.

⁵⁸ "Thus says the LORD of hosts:
The broad wall of Babylon
shall be leveled to the ground
and her high gates
shall be burned with fire.
The peoples labor for nought,
and the nations weary themselves only for fire."

⁵⁹ The word which Jeremiah the prophet commanded Serai'ah the son of Neri'ah, son of Mahsei'ah, when he went with Zedeki'ah king of Judah to Babylon, in the fourth year of his reign. Serai'ah was the quartermaster. ⁶⁰ Jeremiah wrote in a book all the evil that should come upon Babylon, all these words that are written concerning Babylon. ⁶¹ And Jeremiah said to Serai'ah: "When you come to Babylon, see that you read all these words, ⁶² and say, 'O LORD, thou hast said concerning this place

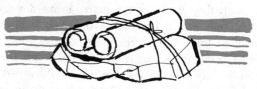

that thou wilt cut it off, so that nothing shall dwell in it, neither man nor beast, and it shall be desolate for ever.' ⁶³ When you finish reading this book, bind a stone to it, ⁶⁴ and cast it into the midst of the Eu-phra'tes, and say, 'Thus shall Babylon sink, to rise no more, because of the evil that I am bringing upon her.' " ʸ

Thus far are the words of Jeremiah.

ADDITIONAL DETAILS

52 Zedeki'ah was twenty-one years old when he became king; and he reigned eleven years in Jerusalem. His mother's name was Hamu'tal the daughter of Jeremiah ² of Libnah. And he did what was evil in the sight of the ³ LORD, according to all that Jehoi'a-kim had done. Surely because of the anger of the LORD things came to such a pass in Jerusalem and Judah that he cast them out from his presence.

And Zedeki'ah rebelled against the king of Babylon. ⁴ And in the ninth year of his reign, in the tenth month, on the tenth day of the month, Nebuchadrez'zar king of Babylon came with all his army against Jerusalem, and they laid siege to it and built siegeworks against it round ⁵ about. So the city was besieged till the eleventh year of ⁶ King Zedeki'ah. On the ninth day of the fourth month the famine was so severe in the city, that there was no

7 food for the people of the land. Then a breach was made in the city; and all the men of war fled and went out from the city by night by the way of a gate between the two walls, by the king's garden, while the Chalde'ans were round about the city. And they went in the direction of
8 the Arabah. But the army of the Chalde'ans pursued the king, and overtook Zedeki'ah in the plains of Jericho; and
9 all his army was scattered from him. Then they captured the king, and brought him up to the king of Babylon at Riblah in the land of Hamath, and he passed sentence
10 upon him. The king of Babylon slew the sons of Zedeki'ah before his eyes, and also slew all the princes of Judah
11 at Riblah. He put out the eyes of Zedeki'ah, and bound him in fetters, and the king of Babylon took him to Babylon, and put him in prison till the day of his death.
12 In the fifth month, on the tenth day of the month— which was the nineteenth year of King Nebuchadrez'zar, king of Babylon—Nebu'zarad'an the captain of the body- guard who served the king of Babylon, entered Jerusalem.
13 And he burned the house of the LORD, and the king's house and all the houses of Jerusalem; every great house
14 he burned down. And all the army of the Chalde'ans, who were with the captain of the guard, broke down all the
15 walls round about Jerusalem. And Nebu'zarad'an the captain of the guard carried away captive some of the poorest of the people and the rest of the people who were left in the city and the deserters who had deserted to the king of Babylon, together with the rest of the artisans.
16 But Nebu'zarad'an the captain of the guard left some of the poorest of the land to be vinedressers and plowmen.
17 And the pillars of bronze that were in the house of the LORD, and the stands and the bronze sea that were in the house of the LORD, the Chalde'ans broke in pieces, and
18 carried all the bronze to Babylon. And they took away the pots, and the shovels, and the snuffers, and the basins, and the dishes for incense, and all the vessels of bronze
19 used in the temple service; also the small bowls, and the firepans, and the basins, and the pots, and the lampstands, and the dishes for incense, and the bowls for libation. What was of gold the captain of the guard took away as
20 gold, and what was of silver, as silver. As for the two pillars, the one sea, the twelve bronze bulls which were under the sea,^z and the stands, which Solomon the king had made for the house of the LORD, the bronze of all
21 these things was beyond weight. As for the pillars, the height of the one pillar was eighteen cubits, its circum- ference was twelve cubits, and its thickness was four
22 fingers, and it was hollow. Upon it was a capital of bronze; the height of the one capital was five cubits; a network and pomegranates, all of bronze, were upon the capital round about. And the second pillar had the like,
23 with pomegranates. There were ninety-six pomegranates on the sides; all the pomegranates were a hundred upon

the network round about.
24 And the captain of the guard took Serai'ah the chief priest, and Zephani'ah the second priest, and the three
25 keepers of the threshold; and from the city he took an officer who had been in command of the men of war, and seven men of the king's council, who were found in the city; and the secretary of the commander of the army who mustered the people of the land; and sixty men of the people of the land, who were found in the midst of
26 the city. And Nebu'zarad'an the captain of the guard took them, and brought them to the king of Babylon at Riblah.
27 And the king of Babylon smote them, and put them to death at Riblah in the land of Hamath. So Judah was carried captive out of its land.
28 This is the number of the people whom Nebuchadrez'- zar carried away captive: in the seventh year, three thou-
29 sand and twenty-three Jews; in the eighteenth year of Nebuchadrez'zar he carried away captive from Jerusalem
30 eight hundred and thirty-two persons; in the twenty- third year of Nebuchadrez'zar, Nebu'zarad'an the captain of the guard carried away captive of the Jews seven hundred and forty-five persons; all the persons were four thousand and six hundred.
31 And in the thirty-seventh year of the captivity of Jehoi'achin king of Judah, in the twelfth month, on the twenty-fifth day of the month, E'vil-mer'odach king of Babylon, in the year that he became king, lifted up the head of Jeoi'achin king of Judah and brought him out of
32 prison; and he spoke kindly to him, and gave him a seat above the seats of the kings who were with him in
33 Babylon. So Jehoi'achin put off his prison garments. And every day of his life he dined regularly at the king's
34 table; as for his allowance, a regular allowance was given him by the king according to his daily need, until the day of his death as long as he lived.

^z Heb lacks the sea

— INTRODUCTION TO —

THE LAMENTATIONS
OF JEREMIAH

When Jerusalem was conquered for the second time by the Babylonians in 586 B.C., most of the Jewish leaders were taken prisoners to Babylon. The Lamentations are songs of sorrow for the Jewish nation. We do not know which songs if any, Jeremiah wrote, but we know that they describe the sorrow of the people over the destruction of their beloved city of Jerusalem. Lamentations was probably completed by about 300 B.C.

The song in Chapter 3 calls for penitence for the sins of the people, which had caused all their troubles. This song also expresses unshakable trust in God and in his love and forgiveness for his people. As Chapter 3.21-22 says:

> "But this I call to mind,
>   and therefore I have hope:
> The steadfast love of the LORD never ceases,
>   his mercies never come to an end;...."

THE LAMENTATIONS
OF JEREMIAH

THE MISERY OF JERUSALEM

1 How lonely sits the city
  that was full of people!
How like a widow has she become,
  she that was great among the nations!
She that was a princess among the cities
  has become a vassal.

2 She weeps bitterly in the night,
  tears on her cheeks;
among all her lovers
  she has none to comfort her;
all her friends have dealt treacherously with her,
  they have become her enemies.

3 Judah has gone into exile because of affliction
  and hard servitude;
she dwells now among the nations,
  but finds no resting place;
her pursuers have all overtaken her
  in the midst of her distress.

4 The roads to Zion mourn,
  for none come to the appointed feasts;
all her gates are desolate,
  her priests groan;

her maidens have been dragged away,[a]
  and she herself suffers bitterly.

5 Her foes have become the head,
  her enemies prosper,
because the LORD has made her suffer
  for the multitude of her transgressions;
her children have gone away,
  captives before the foe.

6 From the daughter of Zion has departed
  all her majesty.
Her princes have become like harts
  that find no pasture;
they fled without strength
  before the pursuer.

7 Jerusalem remembers
  in the days of her affliction and bitterness[b]
all the precious things
  that were hers from days of old.

[a] Gk Old Latin: Heb *afflicted*   [b] Cn: Heb *wandering*

555

When her people fell into the hand of the foe,
   and there was none to help her,
the foe gloated over her,
   mocking at her downfall.

8 Jerusalem sinned grievously,
   therefore she became filthy;
all who honored her despise her,
   for they have seen her nakedness;
yea, she herself groans,
   and turns her face away.

9 Her uncleanness was in her skirts;
   she took no thought of her doom;
therefore her fall is terrible,
   she has no comforter.
"O Lord, behold my affliction,
   for the enemy has triumphed!"

10 The enemy has stretched out his hands
   over all her precious things;
yea, she has seen the nations
   invade her sanctuary,
those whom thou didst forbid
   to enter thy congregation.

11 All her people groan
   as they search for bread;
they trade their treasures for food
   to revive their strength.
"Look, O Lord, and behold,
   for I am despised."

12 "Is it nothing to you,[c] all you who pass by?
   Look and see
if there is any sorrow like my sorrow
   which was brought upon me,
which the Lord inflicted
   on the day of his fierce anger.

13 "From on high he sent fire;
   into my bones[d] he made it descend;
he spread a net for my feet;
   he turned me back;
he has left me stunned,
   faint all the day long.

14 "My transgressions were bound[e] into a yoke;
   by his hand they were fastened together;
they were set upon my neck;
   he caused my strength to fail;
the Lord gave me into the hands
   of those whom I cannot withstand.

15 "The Lord flouted all my mighty men
   in the midst of me;
he summoned an assembly against me
   to crush my young men;
the Lord has trodden as in a wine press
   the virgin daughter of Judah.

16 "For these things I weep;
   my eyes flow with tears;
for a comforter is far from me,
   one to revive my courage;
my children are desolate,
   for the enemy has prevailed."

17 Zion stretches out her hands,
   but there is none to comfort her;
the Lord has commanded against Jacob
   that his neighbors should be his foes;
Jerusalem has become
   a filthy thing among them.

18 "The Lord is in the right,
   for I have rebelled against his word;
but hear, all you peoples,
   and behold my suffering;
my maidens and my young men
   have gone into captivity.

19 "I called to my lovers
   but they deceived me;
my priests and elders
   perished in the city,
while they sought food
   to revive their strength.

20 "Behold, O Lord, for I am in distress,
   my soul is in tumult,
my heart is wrung within me,
   because I have been very rebellious.
In the street the sword bereaves;
   in the house it is like death.

21 "Hear[f] how I groan;
   there is none to comfort me.
All my enemies have heard of my trouble;
   they are glad that thou hast done it.
Bring thou[g] the day thou hast announced,
   and let them be as I am.

22 "Let all their evil doing come before thee;
   and deal with them
as thou hast dealt with me
   because of all my transgressions;
for my groans are many
   and my heart is faint."

c Heb uncertain   d Gk: Heb *bones and*   e Cn: Heb uncertain   f Gk Syr: Heb *they heard*
g Syr: Heb *thou hast brought*

GOD'S JUDGMENT UPON THE CITY

2 How the Lord in his anger
      has set the daughter of Zion under a cloud!
He has cast down from heaven to earth
    the splendor of Israel;
he has not remembered his footstool
    in the day of his anger.

2 The Lord has destroyed without mercy
    all the habitations of Jacob;
in his wrath he has broken down
    the strongholds of the daughter of Judah;
he has brought down to the ground in dishonor
    the kingdom and its rulers.

3 He has cut down in fierce anger
    all the might of Israel;
he has withdrawn from them his right hand
    in the face of the enemy;
he has burned like a flaming fire in Jacob,
    consuming all around.

4 He has bent his bow like an enemy,
    with his right hand set like a foe;
and he has slain all the pride of our eyes
    in the tent of the daughter of Zion;
he has poured out his fury like fire.

5 The Lord has become like an enemy,
    he has destroyed Israel;
he has destroyed all its palaces,
    laid in ruins its strongholds;
and he has multiplied in the daughter of Judah
    mourning and lamentation.

6 He has broken down his booth like that of a garden,
laid in ruins the place of his appointed feasts;
the LORD has brought to an end in Zion
    appointed feast and sabbath,
and in his fierce indignation has spurned
    king and priest.

7 The Lord has scorned his altar,
    disowned his sanctuary;

h Heb *to the ground*

he has delivered into the hand of the enemy
    the walls of her palaces;
a clamor was raised in the house of the LORD
    as on the day of an appointed feast.

8 The LORD determined to lay in ruins
    the wall of the daughter of Zion;
he marked it off by the line;
    he restrained not his hand from destroying;
he caused rampart and wall to lament,
    they languish together.

9 Her gates have sunk into the ground;
    he has ruined and broken her bars;
her king and princes are among the nations;
    the law is no more,
and her prophets obtain
    no vision from the LORD.

10 The elders of the daughter of Zion
    sit on the ground in silence;
they have cast dust on their heads
    and put on sackcloth;
the maidens of Jerusalem
    have bowed their heads to the ground.

11 My eyes are spent with weeping;
    my soul is in tumult;
my heart is poured out in grief h
    because of the destruction of the daughter of my
      people,
because infants and babes faint
    in the streets of the city.

12 They cry to their mothers,
    "Where is bread and wine?"
as they faint like wounded men
    in the streets of the city,
as their life is poured out
    on their mothers' bosom.

13 What can I say for you, to what compare you.
    O daughter of Jerusalem?
What can I liken to you, that I may comfort you,
    O virgin daughter of Zion?
For vast as the sea is your ruin;
    who can restore you?

14 Your prophets have seen for you
    false and deceptive visions;
they have not exposed your iniquity
    to restore your fortunes,
but have seen for you oracles
    false and misleading.

15 All who pass along the way
    clap their hands at you;
they hiss and wag their heads
    at the daughter of Jerusalem;
"Is this the city which was called
    the perfection of beauty,
    the joy of all the earth?"

16 All your enemies
    rail against you;
they hiss, they gnash their teeth,
    they cry: "We have destroyed her!
Ah, this is the day we longed for;
    now we have it; we see it!"

17 The LORD has done what he purposed,
    has carried out his threat;
as he ordained long ago,
    he has demolished without pity;
he has made the enemy rejoice over you,
    and exalted the might of your foes.

18 Cry aloud[i] to the Lord!
    O[j] daughter of Zion!
Let tears stream down like a torrent
    day and night!
Give yourself no rest,
    your eyes no respite!

19 Arise, cry out in the night,
    at the beginning of the watches!
Pour out your heart like water
    before the presence of the Lord!
Lift your hands to him
    for the lives of your children,
who faint for hunger
    at the head of every street.

20 Look, O LORD, and see!
    With whom hast thou dealt thus?
Should women eat their offspring,
    the children of their tender care?
Should priest and prophet be slain
    in the sanctuary of the Lord?

21 In the dust of the streets
    lie the young and the old;
my maidens and my young men
    have fallen by the sword;
in the day of thy anger thou hast slain them,
    slaughtering without mercy.

22 Thou didst invite as to the day of an appointed feast
    my terrors on every side;

i Cn: Heb *Their heart cried*   j Cn: Heb *O wall of*

and on the day of the anger of the LORD
    none escaped or survived;
those whom I dandled and reared
    my enemy destroyed.

A PERSONAL LAMENT AND PRAYER

3 I am the man who has seen affliction
    under the rod of his wrath;
2 he has driven and brought me
    into darkness without any light;
3 surely against me he turns his hand
    again and again the whole day long.

4 He has made my flesh and my skin waste away,
    and broken my bones;
5 he has besieged and enveloped me
    with bitterness and tribulation;
6 he has made me dwell in darkness
    like the dead of long ago.

7 He has walled me about so that I cannot escape;
    he has put heavy chains on me;
8 though I call and cry for help,
    he shuts out my prayer;
9 he has blocked my ways with hewn stones,
    he has made my paths crooked.

10 He is to me like a bear lying in wait,
    like a lion in hiding;
11 he led me off my way and tore me to pieces;
    he has made me desolate;
12 he bent his bow and set me
    as a mark for his arrow.

13 He drove into my heart
    the arrows of his quiver;
14 I have become the laughingstock of all peoples,
    the burden of their songs all day long.
15 He has filled me with bitterness,
    he has sated me with wormwood.

16 He has made my teeth grind on gravel,
    and made me cower in ashes;
17 my soul is bereft of peace,
    I have forgotten what happiness is;

18 so I say, "Gone is my glory,
and my expectation from the Lord."

19 Remember my affliction and my bitterness,[k]
the wormwood and the gall!
20 My soul continually thinks of it
and is bowed down within me.
21 But this I called to mind,
and therefore I have hope:

22 The steadfast love of the Lord never ceases,[l]
his mercies never come to an end;
23 they are new every morning;
great is thy faithfulness.
24 "The Lord is my portion," says my soul,
"therefore I will hope in him."

25 The Lord is good to those who wait for him,
to the soul that seeks him.
26 It is good that one should wait quietly
for the salvation of the Lord.
27 It is good for a man that he bear
the yoke in his youth.

28 Let him sit alone in silence
when he has laid it on him;
29 let him put his mouth in the dust—
there may yet be hope;
30 let him give his cheek to the smiter,
and be filled with insults.

31 For the Lord will not
cast off for ever,
32 but, though he cause grief, he will have compassion
according to the abundance of his steadfast love;
33 for he does not willingly afflict
or grieve the sons of men.

34 To crush under foot
all the prisoners of the earth,
35 to turn aside the right of a man
in the presence of the Most High,
36 to subvert a man in his cause,
the Lord does not approve.

37 Who has commanded and it came to pass,
unless the Lord has ordained it?
38 Is it not from the mouth of the Most High
that good and evil come?
39 Why should a living man complain,
a man, about the punishment of his sins?

40 Let us test and examine our ways,
and return to the Lord!
41 Let us lift up our hearts and hands
to God in heaven:
42 "We have transgressed and rebelled,
and thou hast not forgiven.

43 "Thou hast wrapped thyself with anger and pursued us,
slaying without pity;
44 thou hast wrapped thyself with a cloud
so that no prayer can pass through.
45 Thou hast made us offscouring and refuse
among the peoples.

46 "All our enemies
rail against us;
47 panic and pitfall have come upon us,
devastation and destruction;
48 my eyes flow with rivers of tears
because of the destruction of the daughter of my people.

49 "My eyes will flow without ceasing,
without respite,
50 until the Lord from heaven
looks down and sees;
51 my eyes cause me grief
at the fate of all the maidens of my city.

52 "I have been hunted like a bird
by those who were my enemies without cause;
53 they flung me alive into the pit
and cast stones on me;
54 water closed over my head;
I said, 'I am lost.'

55 "I called on thy name, O Lord,
from the depths of the pit;
56 thou didst hear my plea, 'Do not
close thine ear to my cry for help!'[m]
57 Thou didst come near when I called on thee;
thou didst say, 'Do not fear!'

58 "Thou hast taken up my cause, O Lord,
thou hast redeemed my life.
59 Thou hast seen the wrong done to me, O Lord;
judge thou my cause.
60 Thou hast seen all their vengeance,
all their devices against me.

61 "Thou hast heard their taunts, O Lord,
all their devices against me.
62 The lips and thoughts of my assailants
are against me all the day long.
63 Behold their sitting and their rising;
I am the burden of their songs.

k Cn: Heb *wandering*   l Syr Tg: Heb *we are not cut off*   m Heb uncertain

64 "Thou wilt requite them, O Lord,
 according to the work of their hands.
65 Thou wilt give them dullness of heart;
 thy curse will be on them.
66 Thou wilt pursue them in anger and destroy them
 from under thy heavens, O Lord." [n]

JERUSALEM PAST AND PRESENT

4 How the gold has grown dim,
 how the pure gold is changed!
The holy stones lie scattered
 at the head of every street.

2 The precious sons of Zion,
 worth their weight in fine gold,
how they are reckoned as earthen pots,
 the work of a potter's hands!

3 Even the jackals give the breast
 and suckle their young,
but the daughter of my people has become cruel,
 like the ostriches in the wilderness.

4 The tongue of the nursling cleaves
 to the roof of its mouth for thirst;
the children beg for food,
 but no one gives to them.

5 Those who feasted on dainties
 perish in the streets;
those who were brought up in purple
 lie on ash heaps.

6 For the chastisement [o] of the daughter of my people has
 been greater
 than the punishment [p] of Sodom,
which was overthrown in a moment,
 no hand being laid on it. [q]

7 Her princes were purer than snow,
 whiter than milk;
their bodies were more ruddy than coral,
 the beauty of their form [r] was like sapphire. [s]

8 Now their visage is blacker than soot,
 they are not recognized in the streets;
their skin has shriveled upon their bones,
 it has become as dry as wood.

9 Happier were the victims of the sword
 than the victims of hunger,
who pined away, stricken
 by want of the fruits of the field.

10 The hands of compassionate women
 have boiled their own children;
they became their food
 in the destruction of the daughter of my people.

11 The Lord gave full vent to his wrath,
 he poured out his hot anger;
and he kindled a fire in Zion,
 which consumed its foundations.

12 The kings of the earth did not believe,
 or any of the inhabitants of the world,
that foe or enemy could enter
 the gates of Jerusalem.

13 This was for the sins of her prophets
 and the iniquities of her priests,
who shed in the midst of her
 the blood of the righteous.

14 They wandered, blind, through the streets,
 so defiled with blood
that none could touch
 their garments.

15 "Away! Unclean!" men cried at them;
 "Away! Away! Touch not!"
So they became fugitives and wanderers;
 men said among the nations,
 "They shall stay with us no longer."

16 The Lord himself has scattered them,
 he will regard them no more;
no honor was shown to the priests,
 no favor to the elders.

17 Our eyes failed, ever watching
 vainly for help;
in our watching [t] we watched
 for a nation which could not save.

18 Men dogged our steps
 so that we could not walk in our streets;
our end drew near; our days were numbered;
 for our end had come.

[n] Syr Compare Gk Vg: Heb *the heavens of the* Lord   [o] Or *iniquity*   [p] Or *sin*   [q] Heb uncertain   [r] Heb uncertain
[s] Heb *lapis lazuli*   [t] Heb uncertain

19 Our pursuers were swifter
   than the vultures in the heavens;
they chased us on the mountains,
   they lay in wait for us in the wilderness.

20 The breath of our nostrils, the LORD's anointed,
   was taken in their pits,
he of whom we said, "Under his shadow
   we shall live among the nations."

21 Rejoice and be glad, O daughter of Edom,
   dweller in the land of Uz;
but to you also the cup shall pass;
   you shall become drunk and strip yourself bare.

22 The punishment of your iniquity,
   O daughter of Zion, is accomplished,
he will keep you in exile no longer;
   but your iniquity, O daughter of Edom, he will punish,
   he will uncover your sins.

PRAYER FOR MERCY

5 Remember, O LORD, what has befallen us;
   behold, and see our disgrace!
2 Our inheritance has been turned over to strangers,
   our homes to aliens.
3 We have become orphans, fatherless;
   our mothers are like widows.
4 We must pay for the water we drink,
   the wood we get must be bought.
5 With a yoke ᵘ on our necks we are hard driven;
   we are weary, we are given no rest.
6 We have given the hand to Egypt,
   and to Assyria, to get bread enough.

ᵘ Symmachus: Heb lacks *with a yoke*

7 Our fathers sinned, and are no more;
   and we bear their iniquities.
8 Slaves rule over us;
   there is none to deliver us from their hand.
9 We get our bread at the peril of our lives,
   because of the sword in the wilderness.
10 Our skin is hot as an oven
   with the burning heat of famine.
11 Women are ravished in Zion,
   virgins in the towns of Judah.
12 Princes are hung up by their hands;
   no respect is shown to the elders.
13 Young men are compelled to grind at the mill;
   and boys stagger under loads of wood.
14 The old men have quit the city gate,
   the young men their music.
15 The joy of our hearts has ceased;
   our dancing has been turned to mourning.
16 The crown has fallen from our head;
   woe to us, for we have sinned!
17 For this our heart has become sick,
   for these things our eyes have grown dim,
18 for Mount Zion which lies desolate;
   jackals prowl over it.

19 But thou, O LORD, dost reign for ever;
   thy throne endures to all generations.
20 Why dost thou forget us for ever,
   why dost thou so long forsake us?
21 Restore us to thyself, O LORD, that we may be restored!
   Renew our days as of old!
22 Or hast thou utterly rejected us?
   Art thou exceedingly angry with us?

INTRODUCTION TO

EZEKIEL

Jewish priests were not usually challenging preachers or prophets. They were not great preachers because they were so concerned about the details of worship and about all sorts of rules they had to obey. Ezekiel was a most unusual priest because he was also a preacher. At least part of the time while the Jews were living in exile in Babylon, after 597 B.C., Ezekiel was with them and seems to have been their spiritual leader. Most of the Book of Ezekiel was completed by 550 B.C.

This book contains some of Ezekiel's speeches or sermons, but it also contains some symbolic passages that are hard to understand today. Ezekiel and other symbolic books, such as Daniel and Revelation, have sometimes been used to try to predict future events or even the end of the world. Jesus cautioned against such efforts, saying, "But of that day or that hour no one knows, not even the angels in heaven, nor the Son, but only the Father" (Mark 13.32).

This book also contains a careful plan (Chapters 40 through 48) to help the Jews rebuild their nation when they were freed from captivity in Babylon to return home to Jerusalem. Ezekiel's idea was that the Temple was to be the center of their whole national life.

Ezekiel's strict rules did help keep the Jews from falling into pagan ways while they were living in Babylon. Moreover, as the people listened to Ezekiel preach and read his plans, their hope of restoring their nation and their religion revived.

As the prophet thought about the purity and goodness of God, he realized that the people were desperately wicked and must repent. He did not give up hope for he believed the people would repent. He believed his nation would be restored and the people would have "a new heart and a new spirit."

Some Jews thought that just because they were Jews, God would favor them; but Ezekiel taught that each person is individually responsible to God for living a godly, righteous life.

THE BOOK OF

EZEKIEL

JUDGMENT ON JUDAH AND JERUSALEM

1 In the thirtieth year, in the fourth month, on the fifth day of the month, as I was among the exiles by the river Chebar, the heavens were opened, and I saw 2 visions of God. On the fifth day of the month (it was the 3 fifth year of the exile of King Jehoi'achin), the word of the LORD came to Ezekiel the priest, the son of Buzi, in the land of the Chalde'ans by the river Chebar; and the hand of the LORD was upon him there.

4 As I looked, behold, a stormy wind came out of the north, and a great cloud, with brightness round about it, and fire flashing forth continually, and in the midst of the 5 fire, as it were gleaming bronze. And from the midst of it came the likeness of four living creatures. And this 6 was their appearance: they had the form of men, but each had four faces, and each of them had four wings. 7 Their legs were straight, and the soles of their feet were like the sole of a calf's foot; and they sparkled like 8 burnished bronze. Under their wings on their four sides they had human hands. And the four had their faces and 9 their wings thus: their wings touched one another; they went every one straight forward, without turning as they

10 went. As for the likeness of their faces, each had the face of a man in front; [a] the four had the face of a lion

---

[a] Cn: Heb lacks in front

on the right side, the four had the face of an ox on the left side, and the four had the face of an eagle at the
11 back.[b] Such were their faces. And their wings were spread out above; each creature had two wings, each of which touched the wing of another, while two covered
12 their bodies. And each went straight forward; wherever the spirit would go, they went, without turning as they
13 went. In the midst of [c] the living creatures there was something that looked like burning coals of fire, like torches moving to and fro among the living creatures; and the fire was bright, and out of the fire went forth lightning.
14 And the living creatures darted to and fro, like a flash of lightning.

15 Now as I looked at the living creatures, I saw a wheel upon the earth beside the living creatures, one for each
16 of the four of them.[d] As for the appearance of the wheels and their construction: their appearance was like the gleaming of a chrysolite; and the four had the same likeness, their construction being as it were a wheel with-
17 in a wheel. When they went, they went in any of their
18 four directions[e] without turning as they went. The four wheels had rims and they had spokes;[f] and their rims
19 were full of eyes round about. And when the living creatures went, the wheels went beside them; and when the living creatures rose from the earth, the wheels rose.
20 Wherever the spirit would go, they went, and the wheels rose along with them; for the spirit of the living creatures
21 was in the wheels. When those went, these went; and when those stood, these stood; and when those rose from the earth, the wheels rose along with them; for the spirit of the living creatures was in the wheels.
22 Over the heads of the living creatures there was the likeness of a firmament, shining like crystal,[g] spread out
23 above their heads. And under the firmament their wings were stretched out straight, one toward another; and each
24 creature had two wings covering its body. And when they went, I heard the sound of their wings like the sound of many waters, like the thunder of the Almighty, a sound of tumult like the sound of a host; when they stood still,
25 they let down their wings. And there came a voice from above the firmament over their heads; when they stood still, they let down their wings.
26 And above the firmament over their heads there was the likeness of a throne, in appearance like sapphire;[h] and seated above the likeness of a throne was a likeness as it
27 were of a human form. And upward from what had the appearance of his loins I saw as it were gleaming bronze, like the appearance of fire enclosed round about; and downward from what had the appearance of his loins I saw as it were the appearance of fire, and there was bright-
28 ness round about him.[i] Like the appearance of the bow that is in the cloud on the day of rain, so was the appearance of the brightness round about.

Such was the appearance of the likeness of the glory of the LORD. And when I saw it, I fell upon my face, and I heard the voice of one speaking.

The Five Commissions

2 And he said to me, "Son of man, stand upon your
2 feet, and I will speak with you." And when he spoke to me, the Spirit entered into me and set me upon my
3 feet; and I heard him speaking to me. And he said to me, "Son of man, I send you to the people of Israel, to a nation [j] of rebels, who have rebelled against me; they and their fathers have transgressed against me to this very
4 day. The people also are impudent and stubborn: I send you to them; and you shall say to them, 'Thus says the
5 Lord GOD.' And whether they hear or refuse to hear (for they are a rebellious house) they will know that there has
6 been a prophet among them. And you, son of man, be not afraid of them, nor be afraid of their words, though briers and thorns are with you and you sit upon scorpions; be not afraid of their words, nor be dismayed at their
7 looks, for they are a rebellious house. And you shall speak my words to them, whether they hear or refuse to hear; for they are a rebellious house.
8 "But you, son of man, hear what I say to you; be not rebellious like that rebellious house; open your mouth,
9 and eat what I give you." And when I looked, behold, a hand was stretched out to me, and, lo, a written scroll
10 was in it; and he spread it before me; and it had writing on the front and on the back, and there were written on it
3 words of lamentation and mourning and woe. And he said to me, "Son of man, eat what is offered to you; eat this scroll, and go, speak to the house of Israel."
2 So I opened my mouth, and he gave me the scroll to eat.
3 And he said to me, "Son of man, eat this scroll that I give you and fill your stomach with it." Then I ate it; and it was in my mouth as sweet as honey.
4 And he said to me, "Son of man, go, get you to the house of Israel, and speak with my words to them.
5 For you are not sent to a people of foreign speech and a
6 hard language, but to the house of Israel—not to many peoples of foreign speech and a hard language, whose words you cannot understand. Surely, if I sent you to
7 such, they would listen to you. But the house of Israel will not listen to you; for they are not willing to listen to me; because all the house of Israel are of a
8 hard forehead and of a stubborn heart. Behold, I have made your face hard against their faces, and your fore-
9 head hard against their foreheads. Like adamant harder than flint have I made your forehead; fear them not, nor be dismayed at their looks, for they are a rebellious
10 house." Moreover he said to me, "Son of man, all my words that I shall speak to you receive in your heart, and
11 hear with your ears. And go, get you to the exiles, to your

---

[b] Cn: Heb lacks *at the back*   [c] Gk Old Latin: Heb *And the likeness of*   [d] Heb *of their faces*   [e] Heb *on their four sides*
[f] Cn: Heb uncertain   [g] Gk: Heb *awesome crystal*   [h] Heb *lapis lazuli*   [i] Or *it*   [j] Syr: Heb *nations*

people, and say to them, 'Thus says the Lord GOD'; whether they hear or refuse to hear."

12 Then the Spirit lifted me up, and as the glory of the LORD arose [k] from its place, I heard behind me the sound 13 of a great earthquake; it was the sound of the wings of the living creatures as they touched one another, and the sound of the wheels beside them, that sounded like a great 14 earthquake. The Spirit lifted me up and took me away, and I went in bitterness in the heat of my spirit, the hand 15 of the LORD being strong upon me; and I came to the exiles at Tela'bib, who dwelt by the river Chebar.[l] And I sat there overwhelmed among them seven days.

16 And at the end of seven days, the word of the LORD came 17 to me: "Son of man, I have made you a watchman for the house of Israel; whenever you hear a word from my 18 mouth, you shall give them warning from me. If I say to the wicked, 'You shall surely die,' and you give him no warning, nor speak to warn the wicked from his wicked way, in order to save his life, that wicked man shall die in his iniquity; but his blood I will require at your hand. 19 But if you warn the wicked, and he does not turn from his wickedness, or from his wicked way, he shall die in 20 his iniquity; but you will have saved your life. Again, if a righteous man turns from his righteousness and commits iniquity, and I lay a stumbling block before him, he shall die; because you have not warned him, he shall die for his sin, and his righteous deeds which he has done shall not be remembered; but his blood I will require at 21 your hand. Nevertheless if you warn the righteous man not to sin, and he does not sin, he shall surely live, because he took warning; and you will have saved your life."

22 And the hand of the LORD was there upon me; and he said to me, "Arise, go forth into the plain,[m] and there I

23 will speak with you." So I arose and went forth into the plain; [m] and, lo, the glory of the LORD stood there, like the glory which I had seen by the river Chebar; and I fell on 24 my face. But the Spirit entered into me, and set me upon my feet; and he spoke with me and said to me, "Go, shut 25 yourself within your house. And you, O son of man, behold, cords will be placed upon you, and you shall be bound with them, so that you cannot go out among the 26 people; and I will make your tongue cleave to the roof of your mouth, so that you shall be dumb and unable to 27 reprove them; for they are a rebellious house. But when

I speak with you, I will open your mouth, and you shall say to them, 'Thus says the Lord GOD'; he that will hear, let him hear; and he that will refuse to hear, let him refuse; for they are a rebellious house.

The Fate of Jerusalem

4 "And you, O son of man, take a brick and lay it before you, and portray upon it a city, even Jerusalem; 2 and put siegeworks against it, and build a siege wall against it, and cast up a mound against it; set camps also against it, and plant battering rams against it round 3 about. And take an iron plate, and place it as an iron wall between you and the city; and set your face toward it, and let it be in a state of siege, and press the siege against it. This is a sign for the house of Israel.

4 "Then lie upon your left side, and I will lay the punishment of the house of Israel upon you; [n] for the number of the days that you lie upon it, you shall bear their 5 punishment. For I assign to you a number of days, three hundred and ninety days, equal to the number of the years of their punishment; so long shall you bear the punish- 6 ment of the house of Israel. And when you have completed these, you shall lie down a second time, but on your right side, and bear the punishment of the house of Judah; forty days I assign you, a day for each year. 7 And you shall set your face toward the siege of Jerusalem, with your arm bared; and you shall prophesy against the 8 city. And, behold, I will put cords upon you, so that you cannot turn from one side to the other, till you have completed the days of your siege.

9 "And you, take wheat and barley, beans and lentils, millet and spelt, and put them into a single vessel, and make bread of them. During the number of days that you lie upon your side, three hundred and ninety days, you 10 shall eat it. And the food which you eat shall be by weight, twenty shekels a day; once a day you shall eat it. 11 And water you shall drink by measure, the sixth part of 12 a hin; once a day you shall drink. And you shall eat it as a barley cake, baking it in their sight on human dung." 13 And the LORD said, "Thus shall the people of Israel eat their bread unclean, among the nations whither I will 14 drive them." Then I said, "Ah Lord GOD! behold, I have never defiled myself; from my youth up till now I have never eaten what died of itself or was torn by beasts, nor 15 has foul flesh come into my mouth." Then he said to me, "See, I will let you have cow's dung instead of human 16 dung, on which you may prepare your bread." Moreover he said to me, "Son of man, behold, I will break the staff of bread in Jerusalem; they shall eat bread by weight and with fearfulness; and they shall drink water by 17 measure and in dismay. I will do this that they may lack bread and water, and look at one another in dismay, and waste away under their punishment.

[k] Cn: Heb *blessed be the glory of the* LORD   [l] Heb *Chebar, and to where they dwelt.* Another reading is *Chebar, and I sat where they sat*
[m] Or *valley*   [n] Cn: Heb *you shall lay . . . upon it*

5 "And you, O son of man, take a sharp sword; use it
as a barber's razor and pass it over your head and your
beard; then take balances for weighing, and divide the
2 hair. A third part you shall burn in the fire in the midst
of the city, when the days of the siege are completed; and
a third part you shall take and strike with the sword
round about the city; and a third part you shall scatter
to the wind, and I will unsheathe the sword after them.

3 And you shall take from these a small number, and bind
4 them in the skirts of your robe. And of these again you
shall take some, and cast them into the fire, and burn
them in the fire; from there a fire will come forth into all
5 the house of Israel. Thus says the Lord GOD: This is
Jerusalem; I have set her in the center of the nations, with
6 countries round about her. And she has wickedly rebelled
against my ordinances [o] more than the nations, and against
my statutes more than the countries round about her, by
rejecting my ordinances and not walking in my statutes.
7 Therefore thus says the Lord GOD: Because you are more
turbulent than the nations that are round about you, and
have not walked in my statutes or kept my ordinances, but
have acted [p] according to the ordinances of the nations
8 that are round about you; therefore thus says the Lord
GOD: Behold, I, even I, am against you; and I will
execute judgments in the midst of you in the sight of the
9 nations. And because of all your abominations I will do
with you what I have never yet done, and the like of which
10 I will never do again. Therefore fathers shall eat their
sons in the midst of you, and sons shall eat their fathers;
and I will execute judgments on you, and any of you who
11 survive I will scatter to all the winds. Wherefore, as I live,
says the Lord GOD, surely, because you have defiled my
sanctuary with all your detestable things and with all your
abominations, therefore I will cut you down; [q] my eye will
12 not spare, and I will have no pity. A third part of you
shall die of pestilence and be consumed with famine in
the midst of you; a third part shall fall by the sword
round about you; and a third part I will scatter to all
the winds and will unsheathe the sword after them.
13 "Thus shall my anger spend itself, and I will vent my
fury upon them and satisfy myself; and they shall know
that I, the LORD, have spoken in my jealousy, when I
14 spend my fury upon them. Moreover I will make you a
desolation and an object of reproach among the nations
round about you and in the sight of all that pass by.
15 You shall be [r] a reproach and a taunt, a warning and a
horror, to the nations round about you, when I execute
judgments on you in anger and fury, and with furious
16 chastisements—I, the LORD, have spoken—when I loose
against you [s] my deadly arrows of famine, arrows for
destruction, which I will loose to destroy you, and when
I bring more and more famine upon you, and break your
17 staff of bread. I will send famine and wild beasts against
you, and they will rob you of your children; pestilence
and blood shall pass through you; and I will bring the
sword upon you. I, the LORD, have spoken."

6 The word of the LORD came to me: "Son of man,
set your face toward the mountains of Israel, and
3 prophesy against them, and say, You mountains of Israel,
hear the word of the Lord GOD! Thus says the Lord GOD
to the mountains and the hills, to the ravines and the
valleys: Behold, I, even I, will bring a sword upon you,
4 and I will destroy your high places. Your altars shall
become desolate, and your incense altars shall be broken;
5 and I will cast down your slain before your idols. And I
will lay the dead bodies of the people of Israel before their
idols; and I will scatter your bones round about your
6 altars. Wherever you dwell your cities shall be waste and
your high places ruined, so that your altars will be waste
and ruined,[t] your idols broken and destroyed, your in-
7 cense altars cut down, and your works wiped out. And the
slain shall fall in the midst of you, and you shall know
that I am the LORD.
8 "Yet I will leave some of you alive. When you have
among the nations some who escape the sword, and when
9 you are scattered through the countries, then those of you
who escape will remember me among the nations where
they are carried captive, when I have broken [u] their
wanton heart which has departed from me, and blinded
their eyes which turn wantonly after their idols; and they
will be loathsome in their own sight for the evils which
10 they have committed, for all their abominations. And they
shall know that I am the LORD; I have not said in vain
that I would do this evil to them."
11 Thus says the Lord GOD: "Clap your hands, and stamp
your foot, and say, Alas! because of all the evil abominations of the house of Israel; for they shall fall by the
12 sword, by famine, and by pestilence. He that is far off
shall die of pestilence; and he that is near shall fall by
the sword; and he that is left and is preserved shall die
13 of famine. Thus I will spend my fury upon them. And you
shall know that I am the LORD, when their slain lie among
their idols round about their altars, upon every high hill,
on all the mountaintops, under every green tree, and
under every leafy oak, wherever they offered pleasing
14 odor to all their idols. And I will stretch out my hand
against them, and make the land desolate and waste,
throughout all their habitations, from the wilderness to
Riblah.[v] Then they will know that I am the LORD."

[o] Or *changed my ordinances into wickedness* [p] Another reading is *and have not acted* [q] Another reading is *I will withdraw*
[r] Gk Syr Vg Tg: Heb *And it shall be* [s] Heb *them* [t] Syr Vg Tg: Heb *and be made guilty*
[u] Syr Vg Tg: Heb *I have been broken* [v] Another reading is *Diblah*

7 ² The word of the LORD came to me: "And you, O son of man, thus says the Lord GOD to the land of Israel: An end! The end has come upon the four corners ³ of the land. Now the end is upon you, and I will let loose my anger upon you, and will judge you according to your ways; and I will punish you for all your abominations. ⁴ And my eye will not spare you, nor will I have pity; but I will punish you for your ways, while your abominations are in your midst. Then you will know that I am the LORD.

⁵ "Thus says the Lord GOD: Disaster after disaster! ⁶ Behold, it comes. An end has come, the end has come; ⁷ it has awakened against you. Behold, it comes. Your doom^w has come to you, O inhabitant of the land; the time has come, the day is near, a day of tumult, and not ⁸ of joyful shouting upon the mountains. Now I will soon pour out my wrath upon you, and spend my anger against you, and judge you according to your ways; and I will ⁹ punish you for all your abominations. And my eye will not spare, nor will I have pity; I will punish you according to your ways, while your abominations are in your midst. Then you will know that I am the LORD, who smite.

¹⁰ "Behold, the day! Behold, it comes! Your doom^w has come, injustice^x has blossomed, pride has budded. ¹¹ Violence has grown up into a rod of wickedness; none of them shall remain, nor their abundance, nor their wealth; ¹² neither shall there be pre-eminence among them.^y The time has come, the day draws near. Let not the buyer rejoice, nor the seller mourn, for wrath is upon all their ¹³ multitude. For the seller shall not return to what he has sold, while they live. For wrath^z is upon all their multitude; it shall not turn back; and because of his iniquity, none can maintain his life.^a

¹⁴ "They have blown the trumpet and made all ready; but none goes to battle, for my wrath is upon all their ¹⁵ multitude. The sword is without, pestilence and famine are within; he that is in the field dies by the sword; and him that is in the city famine and pestilence devour. ¹⁶ And if any survivors escape, they will be on the mountains, like doves of the valleys, all of them moaning, every ¹⁷ one over his iniquity. All hands are feeble, and all knees ¹⁸ weak as water. They gird themselves with sackcloth, and horror covers them; shame is upon all faces, and baldness ¹⁹ on all their heads. They cast their silver into the streets, and their gold is like an unclean thing; their silver and gold are not able to deliver them in the day of the wrath of the LORD; they cannot satisfy their hunger or fill their stomachs with it. For it was the stumbling block of their ²⁰ iniquity. Their^b beautiful ornament they used for vainglory, and they made their abominable images and their detestable things of it; therefore I will make it an unclean ²¹ thing to them. And I will give it into the hands of foreigners for a prey, and to the wicked of the earth for ²² a spoil; and they shall profane it. I will turn my face from them, that they may profane my precious^c place; robbers ²³ shall enter and profane it, and make a desolation.^d

"Because the land is full of bloody crimes and the city ²⁴ is full of violence, I will bring the worst of the nations to take possession of their houses; I will put an end to their proud might, and their holy places shall be profaned. ²⁵ When anguish comes, they will seek peace, but there shall ²⁶ be none. Disaster comes upon disaster, rumor follows rumor; they seek a vision from the prophet, but the law perishes from the priest, and counsel from the elders. ²⁷ The king mourns, the prince is wrapped in despair, and the hands of the people of the land are palsied by terror. According to their way I will do to them, and according to their own judgments I will judge them; and they shall know that I am the LORD."

The Visit to the Temple

8 In the sixth year, in the sixth month, on the fifth day of the month, as I sat in my house, with the elders of Judah sitting before me, the hand of the Lord GOD ² fell there upon me. Then I beheld, and, lo, a form that had the appearance of a man;^e below what appeared to

be his loins it was fire, and above his loins it was like the ³ appearance of brightness, like gleaming bronze. He put forth the form of a hand, and took me by a lock of my head; and the Spirit lifted me up between earth and heaven, and brought me in visions of God to Jerusalem, to the entrance of the gateway of the inner court that faces north, where was the seat of the image of jealousy, which ⁴ provokes to jealousy. And behold, the glory of the God of Israel was there, like the vision that I saw in the plain.

⁵ Then he said to me, "Son of man, lift up your eyes now in the direction of the north." So I lifted up my eyes toward the north, and behold, north of the altar gate, in ⁶ the entrance, was this image of jealousy. And he said to me, "Son of man, do you see what they are doing, the great abominations that the house of Israel are committing here, to drive me far from my sanctuary? But you will see still greater abominations."

⁷ And he brought me to the door of the court; and when ⁸ I looked, behold, there was a hole in the wall. Then said he to me, "Son of man, dig in the wall"; and when I dug ⁹ in the wall, lo, there was a door. And he said to me, "Go in, and see the vile abominations that they are committing ¹⁰ here." So I went in and saw; and there, portrayed upon the wall round about, were all kinds of creeping things,

---

^w The meaning of the Hebrew word is uncertain   ^x Or *the rod*
^a Heb *obscure*   ^b Syr Symmachus: Heb *Its*   ^c Or *secret*
^y The Hebrew of verse 11 is uncertain   ^z Cn: Heb *vision*
^d Cn: Heb *make the chain*   ^e Gk: Heb *fire*

and loathsome beasts, and all the idols of the house of
11 Israel. And before them stood seventy men of the elders
of the house of Israel, with Ja-azani'ah the son of Shaphan
standing among them. Each had his censer in his hand,
12 and the smoke of the cloud of incense went up. Then he
said to me, "Son of man, have you seen what the elders
of the house of Israel are doing in the dark, every man in
his room f of pictures? For they say, 'The LORD does not
13 see us, the LORD has forsaken the land.'" He said also
to me, "You will see still greater abominations which they
commit."
14 Then he brought me to the entrance of the north gate of
the house of the LORD; and behold, there sat women weep-
15 ing for Tammuz. Then he said to me, "Have you seen
this, O son of man? You will see still greater abominations than these."
16 And he brought me into the inner court of the house
of the LORD; and behold, at the door of the temple of the
LORD, between the porch and the altar, were about twenty-
five men, with their backs to the temple of the LORD. and
their faces toward the east, worshiping the sun toward the
17 east. Then he said to me, "Have you seen this, O son of
man? Is it too slight a thing for the house of Judah to
commit the abominations which they commit here, that
they should fill the land with violence, and provoke me
further to anger? Lo, they put the branch to their nose.
18 Therefore I will deal in wrath; my eye will not spare, nor
will I have pity; and though they cry in my ears with a
loud voice, I will not hear them."

9 Then he cried in my ears with a loud voice, saying,
"Draw near, you executioners of the city, each with
2 his destroying weapon in his hand." And lo, six men came
from the direction of the upper gate, which faces north,
every man with his weapon for slaughter in his hand, and
with them was a man clothed in linen, with a writing case
at his side. And they went in and stood beside the bronze
altar.
3 Now the glory of the God of Israel had gone up from
the cherubim on which it rested to the threshold of the
house; and he called to the man clothed in linen, who
4 had the writing case at his side. And the LORD said to
him, "Go through the city, through Jerusalem, and put a
mark upon the foreheads of the men who sigh and groan
5 over all the abominations that are committed in it." And
to the others he said in my hearing, "Pass through the
city after him, and smite; your eye shall not spare, and
6 you shall show no pity; slay old men outright, young
men and maidens, little children and women, but touch
no one upon whom is the mark. And begin at my
sanctuary." So they began with the elders who were
7 before the house. Then he said to them, "Defile the house,
and fill the courts with the slain. Go forth." So they went
8 forth, and smote in the city. And while they were smiting,

and I was left alone, I fell upon my face, and cried, "Ah
Lord GOD! wilt thou destroy all that remains of Israel
in the outpouring of thy wrath upon Jerusalem?"
9 Then he said to me, "The guilt of the house of Israel
and Judah is exceedingly great; the land is full of blood,
and the city full of injustice; for they say, 'The LORD has
10 forsaken the land, and the LORD does not see.' As for me,
my eye will not spare, nor will I have pity, but I will
requite their deeds upon their heads."
11 And lo, the man clothed in linen, with the writing case
at his side, brought back word, saying, "I have done as
thou didst command me."

10 Then I looked, and behold, on the firmament that
was over the heads of the cherubim there appeared
above them something like a sapphire, in form resembling
2 a throne. And he said to the man clothed in linen, "Go in
among the whirling wheels underneath the cherubim; fill
your hands with burning coals from between the cherubim, and scatter them over the city."
3 And he went in before my eyes. Now the cherubim were
standing on the south side of the house, when the man
4 went in; and a cloud filled the inner court. And the glory
of the LORD went up from the cherubim to the threshold of
the house; and the house was filled with the cloud, and the
court was full of the brightness of the glory of the LORD.
5 And the sound of the wings of the cherubim was heard
as far as the outer court, like the voice of God Almighty
when he speaks.
6 And when he commanded the man clothed in linen,
"Take fire from between the whirling wheels, from between the cherubim," he went in and stood beside a wheel.
7 And a cherub stretched forth his hand from between the
cherubim to the fire that was between the cherubim, and
took some of it, and put it into the hands of the man
8 clothed in linen, who took it and went out. The cherubim
appeared to have the form of a human hand under their
wings.
9 And I looked, and behold, there were four wheels
beside the cherubim, one beside each cherub; and the
appearance of the wheels was like sparkling chrysolite.
10 And as for their appearance, the four had the same like-
11 ness, as if a wheel were within a wheel. When they went,
they went in any of their four directions g without turning
as they went, but in whatever direction the front wheel
faced the others followed without turning as they went.
12 And h their rims, and their spokes, i and the wheels were
full of eyes round about—the wheels that the four of them
13 had. As for the wheels, they were called in my hearing
14 the whirling wheels. And every one had four faces: the
first face was the face of the cherub, and the second face
was the face of a man, and the third the face of a lion,
and the fourth the face of an eagle.
15 And the cherubim mounted up. These were the living

f Gk Syr Vg Tg: Heb *rooms*   g Heb *on their four sides*   h Gk: Heb *And their whole body and*
i Heb *spokes and their wings*

16 creatures that I saw by the river Chebar. And when the cherubim went, the wheels went beside them; and when the cherubim lifted up their wings to mount up from the 17 earth, the wheels did not turn from beside them. When they stood still, these stood still, and when they mounted up, these mounted up with them; for the spirit of the living creatures [j] was in them.

18 Then the glory of the Lord went forth from the thresh-19 old of the house, and stood over the cherubim. And the cherubim lifted up their wings and mounted up from the earth in my sight as they went forth, with the wheels beside them; and they stood at the door of the east gate of the house of the Lord; and the glory of the God Israel was over them.

20 These were the living creatures that I saw underneath the God of Israel by the river Chebar; and I knew that 21 they were cherubim. Each had four faces, and each four wings, and underneath their wings the semblance of 22 human hands. And as for the likeness of their faces, they were the very faces whose appearance I had seen by the river Chebar. They went every one straight forward.

11 The Spirit lifted me up, and brought me to the east gate of the house of the Lord, which faces east. And behold, at the door of the gateway there were twenty-five men; and I saw among them Ja-azani′ah the son of Azzur, and Pelati′ah the son of Benai′ah, princes of the people. 2 And he said to me, "Son of man, these are the men who devise iniquity and who give wicked counsel in this city; 3 who say, 'The time is not near [k] to build houses; this city 4 is the caldron, and we are the flesh.' Therefore prophesy against them, prophesy, O son of man."

5 And the Spirit of the Lord fell upon me, and he said to me, "Say, Thus says the Lord: So you think, O house of Israel; for I know the things that come into your mind. 6 You have multiplied your slain in this city, and have 7 filled its streets with the slain. Therefore thus says the Lord God: Your slain whom you have laid in the midst of it, they are the flesh, and this city is the caldron; but 8 you shall be brought forth out of the midst of it. You have feared the sword; and I will bring the sword upon you, 9 says the Lord God. And I will bring you forth out of the midst of it, and give you into the hands of foreigners, and 10 execute judgments upon you. You shall fall by the sword; I will judge you at the border of Israel; and you shall 11 know that I am the Lord. This city shall not be your caldron, nor shall you be the flesh in the midst of it; I 12 will judge you at the border of Israel; and you shall know that I am the Lord; for you have not walked in my statutes, nor executed my ordinances, but have acted according to the ordinances of the nations that are round about you."

13 And it came to pass, while I was prophesying, that Pelati′ah the son of Benai′ah died. Then I fell down upon my face, and cried with a loud voice, and said, "Ah Lord God! wilt thou make a full end of the remnant of Israel?"

14, 15 And the word of the Lord came to me: "Son of man, your brethren, even your brethren, your fellow exiles,[l] the whole house of Israel, all of them, are those of whom the inhabitants of Jerusalem have said, 'They have gone far from the Lord; to us this land is given for a posses-16 sion.' Therefore say, 'Thus says the Lord God: Though I removed them far off among the nations, and though I scattered them among the countries, yet I have been a sanctuary to them for a while [m] in the countries where 17 they have gone.' Therefore say, 'Thus says the Lord God: I will gather you from the peoples, and assemble you out of the countries where you have been scattered, and I will 18 give you the land of Israel.' And when they come there, they will remove from it all its detestable things and all 19 its abominations. And I will give them one [n] heart, and put a new spirit within them; I will take the stony heart 20 out of their flesh and give them a heart of flesh, that they may walk in my statutes and keep my ordinances and obey them; and they shall be my people, and I will be their 21 God. But as for those [o] whose heart goes after their detestable things and their abominations, I will requite their deeds upon their own heads, says the Lord God."

22 Then the cherubim lifted up their wings, with the wheels beside them; and the glory of the God of Israel 23 was over them. And the glory of the Lord went up from the midst of the city, and stood upon the mountain which 24 is on the east side of the city. And the Spirit lifted me up and brought me in the vision by the Spirit of God into Chalde′a, to the exiles. Then the vision that I had seen 25 went up from me. And I told the exiles all the things that the Lord had showed me.

The March of Exiles

12 The word of the Lord came to me: "Son of man, 2 you dwell in the midst of a rebellious house, who have eyes to see, but see not, who have ears to hear, but 3 hear not; for they are a rebellious house. Therefore, son of man, prepare for yourself an exile's baggage, and go into exile by day in their sight; you shall go like an exile from your place to another place in their sight.

Perhaps they will understand, though [p] they are a rebel-4 lious house. You shall bring out your baggage by day in their sight, as baggage for exile; and you shall go forth yourself at evening in their sight, as men do who must go 5 into exile. Dig through the wall in their sight, and go [q]

---

[j] Or of life   [k] Or Is not the time near . . . ?   [l] Gk Syr: Heb men of your kindred   [m] Or in small measure
[n] Another reading is a new   [o] Cn: Heb To the heart of their detestable things and their abominations their heart goes
[p] Or will see that   [q] Gk Syr Vg Tg: Heb bring

⁶out through it. In their sight you shall lift the baggage upon your shoulder, and carry it out in the dark; you shall cover your face, that you may not see the land; for I have made you a sign for the house of Israel."

⁷ And I did as I was commanded. I brought out my baggage by day, as baggage for exile, and in the evening I dug through the wall with my own hands; I went forth in the dark, carrying my outfit upon my shoulder in their sight.

⁸ In the morning the word of the LORD came to me: ⁹"Son of man, has not the house of Israel, the rebellious ¹⁰house, said to you, 'What are you doing?' Say to them, 'Thus says the Lord GOD: This oracle concerns the prince in Jerusalem and all the house of Israel who are in it.'^r ¹¹Say, 'I am a sign for you: as I have done, so shall it be done to them; they shall go into exile, into captivity.' ¹²And the prince who is among them shall lift his baggage upon his shoulder in the dark, and shall go forth; he^s shall dig through the wall and go^t out through it; he shall cover his face, that he may not see the land with ¹³his eyes. And I will spread my net over him, and he shall be taken in my snare; and I will bring him to Babylon in the land of the Chalde'ans, yet he shall not see it; and ¹⁴he shall die there. And I will scatter toward every wind all who are round about him, his helpers^u and all his ¹⁵troops; and I will unsheathe the sword after them. And they shall know that I am the LORD, when I disperse them among the nations and scatter them through the countries. ¹⁶But I will let a few of them escape from the sword, from famine and pestilence, that they may confess all their abominations among the nations where they go, and may know that I am the LORD."

^{17, 18} Moreover the word of the LORD came to me: "Son of man, eat your bread with quaking, and drink water with ¹⁹trembling and with fearfulness; and say of the people of the land, Thus says the Lord GOD concerning the inhabitants of Jerusalem in the land of Israel: They shall eat their bread with fearfulness, and drink water in dismay, because their land will be stripped of all it contains, on account of the violence of all those who dwell ²⁰in it. And the inhabited cities shall be laid waste, and the land shall become a desolation; and you shall know that I am the LORD."

^{21, 22} And the word of the LORD came to me: "Son of man, what is this proverb that you have about the land of Israel, saying, 'The days grow long, and every vision ²³comes to nought'? Tell them therefore, 'Thus says the Lord GOD: I will put an end to this proverb, and they shall no more use it as a proverb in Israel.' But say to them, The days are at hand, and the fulfilment^v of every ²⁴vision. For there shall be no more any false vision or ²⁵flattering divination within the house of Israel. But I the LORD will speak the word which I will speak, and it will be performed. It will no longer be delayed, but in your days, O rebellious house, I will speak the word and perform it, says the Lord GOD."

^{26, 27} Again the word of the LORD came to me: "Son of man, behold, they of the house of Israel say, 'The vision that he sees is for many days hence, and he prophesies of ²⁸times far off.' Therefore say to them, Thus says the Lord GOD: None of my words will be delayed any longer, but the word which I speak will be performed, says the Lord GOD."

Woe to False Prophets

13 ² The word of the LORD came to me: "Son of man, prophesy against the prophets of Israel, prophesy^w and say to those who prophesy out of their own minds: ³'Hear the word of the LORD!' Thus says the Lord GOD, Woe to the foolish prophets who follow their own spirit, ⁴and have seen nothing! Your prophets have been like ⁵foxes among ruins, O Israel. You have not gone up into the breaches, or built up a wall for the house of Israel, that it might stand in battle in the day of the LORD. ⁶They have spoken falsehood and divined a lie; they say, 'Says the LORD,' when the LORD has not sent them, and ⁷yet they expect him to fulfil their word. Have you not seen a delusive vision, and uttered a lying divination, whenever you have said, 'Says the LORD,' although I have not spoken?"

⁸ Therefore thus says the Lord GOD: "Because you have uttered delusions and seen lies, therefore behold, I am ⁹against you, says the Lord GOD. My hand will be against the prophets who see delusive visions and who give lying divinations; they shall not be in the council of my people, nor be enrolled in the register of the house of Israel, nor shall they enter the land of Israel; and you shall know ¹⁰that I am the Lord GOD. Because, yea, because they have misled my people, saying, 'Peace,' when there is no peace; and because, when the people build a wall, these prophets ¹¹daub it with whitewash; say to those who daub it with whitewash that it shall fall! There will be a deluge of rain,^x great hailstones will fall, and a stormy wind break ¹²out; and when the wall falls, will it not be said to you, ¹³'Where is the daubing with which you daubed it?' Therefore thus says the Lord GOD: I will make a stormy wind break out in my wrath; and there shall be a deluge of rain in my anger, and great hailstones in wrath to destroy ¹⁴it. And I will break down the wall that you have daubed with whitewash, and bring it down to the ground, so that its foundation will be laid bare; when it falls, you shall perish in the midst of it; and you shall know that I am ¹⁵the LORD. Thus will I spend my wrath upon the wall, and upon those who have daubed it with whitewash; and I will say to you, The wall is no more, nor those who ¹⁶daubed it, the prophets of Israel who prophesied concern-

^r Heb *in the midst of them*   ^s Gk Syr: Heb *they*   ^t Gk Syr Tg: Heb *bring*   ^u Gk Syr Tg: Heb *his help*
^w Gk: Heb *who prophesy*   ^x Heb *rain and you*   ^v Heb *word*

ing Jerusalem and saw visions of peace for her, when there was no peace, says the Lord GOD.

17 "And you, son of man, set your face against the daughters of your people, who prophesy out of their own
18 minds; prophesy against them and say, Thus says the Lord GOD: Woe to the women who sew magic bands upon all wrists, and make veils for the heads of persons of every stature, in the hunt for souls! Will you hunt down souls belonging to my people, and keep other souls alive for
19 your profit? You have profaned me among my people for handfuls of barley and for pieces of bread, putting to death persons who should not die and keeping alive persons who should not live, by your lies to my people, who listen to lies.

20 "Wherefore thus says the Lord GOD: Behold, I am against your magic bands with which you hunt the souls,[y] and I will tear them from your arms; and I will let the
21 souls that you hunt go free[z] like birds. Your veils also I will tear off, and deliver my people out of your hand, and they shall be no more in your hand as prey; and you
22 shall know that I am the LORD. Because you have disheartened the righteous falsely, although I have not disheartened him, and you have encouraged the wicked, that he should not turn from his wicked way to save his life;
23 therefore you shall no more see delusive visions nor practice divination; I will deliver my people out of your hand. Then you will know that I am the LORD."

The Certainty of Judgment

14 Then came certain of the elders of Israel to me,
2 and sat before me. And the word of the LORD came
3 to me: "Son of man, these men have taken their idols into their hearts, and set the stumbling block of their iniquity before their faces; should' I let myself be inquired of at
4 all by them? Therefore speak to them, and say to them, Thus says the Lord GOD: Any man of the house of Israel who takes his idols into his heart and sets the stumbling block of his iniquity before his face, and yet comes to the prophet, I the LORD will answer him myself[a] because of
5 the multitude of his idols, that I may lay hold of the hearts of the house of Israel, who are all estranged from me through their idols.

6 "Therefore say to the house of Israel, Thus says the Lord GOD: Repent and turn away from your idols; and
7 turn away your faces from all your abominations. For any one of the house of Israel, or of the strangers that sojourn in Israel, who separates himself from me, taking his idols into his heart and putting the stumbling block of his iniquity before his face, and yet comes to a prophet to inquire for himself of me, I the LORD will answer him
8 myself; and I will set my face against that man, I will make him a sign and a byword and cut him off from the midst of my people; and you shall know that I am the

9 LORD. And if the prophet be deceived and speak a word, I, the LORD, have deceived that prophet, and I will stretch out my hand against him, and will destroy him from the
10 midst of my people Israel. And they shall bear their punishment—the punishment of the prophet and the
11 punishment of the inquirer shall be alike—that the house of Israel may go no more astray from me, nor defile themselves any more with all their transgressions, but that they may be my people and I may be their God, says the Lord GOD."

12, 13 And the word of the LORD came to me: "Son of man, when a land sins against me by acting faithlessly, and I stretch out my hand against it, and break its staff of bread and send famine upon it, and cut off from it man and
14 beast, even if these three men, Noah, Daniel, and Job, were in it, they would deliver but their own lives by their
15 righteousness, says the Lord GOD. If I cause wild beasts to pass through the land, and they ravage it, and it be made desolate, so that no man may pass through because of
16 the beasts; even if these three men were in it, as I live, says the Lord GOD, they would deliver neither sons nor daughters; they alone would be delivered, but the land
17 would be desolate. Or if I bring a sword upon that land, and say, Let a sword go through the land; and I cut off
18 from it man and beast; though these three men were in it, as I live, says the Lord GOD, they would deliver neither sons nor daughters, but they alone would be delivered.
19 Or if I send a pestilence into that land, and pour out my wrath upon it with blood, to cut off from it man and
20 beast; even if Noah, Daniel, and Job were in it, as I live, says the Lord GOD, they would deliver neither son nor daughter; they would deliver but their own lives by their righteousness.

21 "For thus says the Lord GOD: How much more when I send upon Jerusalem my four sore acts of judgment, sword, famine, evil beasts, and pestilence, to cut off from
22 it man and beast! Yet, if there should be left in it any survivors to lead out sons and daughters, when they come forth to you, and you see their ways and their doings, you will be consoled for the evil that I have brought upon
23 Jerusalem, for all that I have brought upon it. They will console you, when you see their ways and their doings; and you shall know that I have not done without cause all that I have done in it, says the Lord GOD."

Jerusalem a Fruitless Vine

15 And the word of the LORD came to me: "Son of
2 man, how does the wood of the vine surpass any wood, the vine branch which is among the trees of the
3 forest? Is wood taken from it to make anything? Do men
4 take a peg from it to hang any vessel on? Lo, it is given to the fire for fuel; when the fire has consumed both ends of it, and the middle of it is charred, is it useful for any-

---

y Gk Syr: Heb souls for birds   z Cn: Heb the souls   a Cn Compare Tg: Heb uncertain

⁵ thing? Behold, when it was whole, it was used for nothing; how much less, when the fire has consumed it and ⁶ it is charred, can it ever be used for anything! Therefore thus says the Lord God: Like the wood of the vine among the trees of the forest, which I have given to the fire for ⁷ fuel, so will I give up the inhabitants of Jerusalem. And I will set my face against them; though they escape from the fire, the fire shall yet consume them; and you will know that I am the Lord, when I set my face against ⁸ them. And I will make the land desolate, because they have acted faithlessly, says the Lord God."

A Foundling

²**16** Again the word of the Lord came to me: "Son of man, make known to Jerusalem her abominations, ³ and say, Thus says the Lord God to Jerusalem: Your origin and your birth are of the land of the Canaanites; your father was an Amorite, and your mother a Hittite. ⁴ And as for your birth, on the day you were born your navel string was not cut, nor were you washed with water to cleanse you, nor rubbed with salt, nor swathed with ⁵ bands. No eye pitied you, to do any of these things to you out of compassion for you; but you were cast out on the open field, for you were abhorred, on the day that you were born.

⁶ "And when I passed by you, and saw you weltering in ⁷ your blood, I said to you in your blood, 'Live, and grow up ᵇ like a plant of the field.' And you grew up and became tall and arrived at full maidenhood; ᶜ your breasts were formed, and your hair had grown; yet you were naked and bare.

⁸ "When I passed by you again and looked upon you, behold, you were at the age for love; and I spread my skirt over you, and covered your nakedness: yea, I plighted my troth to you and entered into a covenant with you, ⁹ says the Lord God, and you became mine. Then I bathed you with water and washed off your blood from you, and ¹⁰ anointed you with oil. I clothed you also with embroidered cloth and shod you with leather, I swathed you in fine ¹¹ linen and covered you with silk. And I decked you with ornaments, and put bracelets on your arms, and a chain ¹² on your neck. And I put a ring on your nose, and earrings in your ears, and a beautiful crown upon your head. ¹³ Thus you were decked with gold and silver; and your raiment was of fine linen, and silk, and embroidered cloth; you ate fine flour and honey and oil. You grew exceed- ¹⁴ ingly beautiful, and came to regal estate. And your renown went forth among the nations because of your beauty, for it was perfect through the splendor which I had bestowed upon you, says the Lord God.

¹⁵ "But you trusted in your beauty, and played the harlot because of your renown, and lavished your harlotries on ¹⁶ any passer-by. You took some of your garments, and made for yourself gaily decked shrines, and on them played the harlot; the like has never been, nor ever shall ¹⁷ be. You also took your fair jewels of my gold and of my silver, which I had given you, and made for yourself ¹⁸ images of men, and with them played the harlot; and you took your embroidered garments to cover them, and set ¹⁹ my oil and my incense before them. Also my bread which I gave you—I fed you with fine flour and oil and honey— you set before them for a pleasing odor, says the Lord ²⁰ God.ᵈ And you took your sons and your daughters, whom

you had borne to me, and these you sacrificed to them to be devoured. Were your harlotries so small a matter ²¹ that you slaughtered my children and delivered them up ²² as an offering by fire to them? And in all your abominations and your harlotries you did not remember the days of your youth, when you were naked and bare, weltering in your blood.

²³ "And after all your wickedness (woe, woe to you! says ²⁴ the Lord God), you built yourself a vaulted chamber, and ²⁵ made yourself a lofty place in every square; at the head of every street you built your lofty place and prostituted your beauty, offering yourself to any passer-by, and ²⁶ multiplying your harlotry. You also played the harlot with the Egyptians, your lustful neighbors, multiplying ²⁷ your harlotry, to provoke me to anger. Behold, therefore, I stretched out my hand against you, and diminished your allotted portion, and delivered you to the greed of your enemies, the daughters of the Philistines, who were ²⁸ ashamed of your lewd behavior. You played the harlot also with the Assyrians, because you were insatiable; yea, you played the harlot with them, and still you were not ²⁹ satisfied. You multiplied your harlotry also with the trading land of Chalde'a; and even with this you were not satisfied.

³⁰ "How lovesick is your heart, says the Lord God, seeing you did all these things, the deeds of a brazen harlot; ³¹ building your vaulted chamber at the head of every street, and making your lofty place in every square. Yet you ³² were not like a harlot, because you scorned hire. Adulterous wife, who receives strangers instead of her husband! ³³ Men give gifts to all harlots; but you gave your gifts to all your lovers, bribing them to come to you from every ³⁴ side for your harlotries. So you were different from other women in your harlotries: none solicited you to play the harlot; and you gave hire, while no hire was given to you; therefore you were different.

³⁵ "Wherefore, O harlot, hear the word of the Lord: ³⁶ Thus says the Lord God, Because your shame was laid

---

ᵇ Gk Syr: Heb *I made you a myriad*   ᶜ Cn: Heb *ornament of ornaments*   ᵈ Syr: Heb *and it was, says the Lord God*

bare and your nakedness uncovered in your harlotries with your lovers, and because of all your idols, and because of the blood of your children that you gave to
37 them, therefore, behold, I will gather all your lovers, with whom you took pleasure, all those you loved and all those you loathed; I will gather them against you from every side, and will uncover your nakedness to them, that they
38 may see all your nakedness. And I will judge you as women who break wedlock and shed blood are judged, and bring upon you the blood of wrath and jealousy.
39 And I will give you into the hand of your lovers, and they shall throw down your vaulted chamber and break down your lofty places; they shall strip you of your clothes and take your fair jewels, and leave you naked
40 and bare. They shall bring up a host against you, and they shall stone you and cut you to pieces with their
41 swords. And they shall burn your houses and execute judgments upon you in the sight of many women; I will make you stop playing the harlot, and you shall also give
42 hire no more. So will I satisfy my fury on you, and my jealousy shall depart from you; I will be calm, and will
43 no more be angry. Because you have not remembered the days of your youth, but have enraged me with all these things; therefore, behold, I will requite your deeds upon your head, says the Lord GOD.

"Have you not committed lewdness in addition to all
44 your abominations? Behold, every one who uses proverbs will use this proverb about you, 'Like mother, like daugh-
45 ter.' You are the daughter of your mother, who loathed her husband and her children; and you are the sister of your sisters, who loathed their husbands and their children. Your mother was a Hittite and your father an
46 Amorite. And your elder sister is Samar'ia, who lived with her daughters to the north of you; and your younger sister, who lived to the south of you, is Sodom with her
47 daughters. Yet you were not content to walk in their ways, or do according to their abominations; within a very little time you were more corrupt than they in all
48 your ways. As I live, says the Lord GOD, your sister Sodom and her daughters have not done as you and
49 your daughters have done. Behold, this was the guilt of your sister Sodom: she and her daughters had pride, surfeit of food, and prosperous ease, but did not aid
50 the poor and needy. They were haughty, and did abominable things before me; therefore I removed them, when
51 I saw it. Samar'ia has not committed half your sins; you have committed more abominations than they, and have made your sisters appear righteous by all the abomina-
52 tions which you have committed. Bear your disgrace, you also, for you have made judgment favorable to your sisters; because of your sins in which you acted more abominably than they, they are more in the right than you. So be ashamed, you also, and bear your disgrace,

for you have made your sisters appear righteous.
53 "I will restore their fortunes, both the fortunes of Sodom and her daughters, and the fortunes of Samar'ia and her daughters, and I will restore your own fortunes
54 in the midst of them, that you may bear your disgrace and be ashamed of all that you have done, becoming a
55 consolation to them. As for your sisters, Sodom and her daughters shall return to their former estate, and Samar'ia and her daughters shall return to their former estate; and you and your daughters shall return to your former
56 estate. Was not your sister Sodom a byword in your
57 mouth in the day of your pride, before your wickedness was uncovered? Now you have become like her e an object of reproach for the daughters of Edom f and all her neighbors, and for the daughters of the Philistines, those
58 round about who despise you. You bear the penalty of your lewdness and your abominations, says the LORD.
59 "Yea, thus says the Lord GOD: I will deal with you as you have done, who have despised the oath in break-
60 ing the covenant, yet I will remember my covenant with you in the days of your youth, and I will establish with
61 you an everlasting covenant. Then you will remember your ways, and be ashamed when I g take your sisters, both your elder and your younger, and give them to you as daughters, but not on account of the covenant with
62 you. I will establish my covenant with you, and you shall
63 know that I am the LORD, that you may remember and be confounded, and never open your mouth again because of your shame, when I forgive you all that you have done, says the Lord GOD."

Two Eagles and the Cedar
2 **17** The word of the LORD came to me: "Son of man, propound a riddle, and speak an allegory to the house
3 of Israel; say, Thus says the Lord GOD: A great eagle with great wings and long pinions, rich in plumage of many colors, came to Lebanon and took the top of the cedar;

4 he broke off the topmost of its young twigs and carried it to a land of trade, and set it in a city of merchants.
5 Then he took of the seed of the land and planted it in fertile soil; he placed it beside abundant waters. He set it
6 like a willow twig, and it sprouted and became a low spreading vine, and its branches turned toward him, and its roots remained where it stood. So it became a vine, and brought forth branches and put forth foliage.
7 "But there was another great eagle with great wings and much plumage; and behold, this vine bent its roots

toward him, and shot forth its branches toward him that he might water it. From the bed where it was planted

8 he transplanted it [h] to good soil by abundant waters, that it might bring forth branches, and bear fruit, and become

9 a noble vine. Say, Thus says the Lord GOD: Will it thrive? Will he not pull up its roots and cut off its branches,[i] so that all its fresh sprouting leaves wither? It will not take a strong arm or many people to pull it

10 from its roots. Behold, when it is transplanted, will it thrive? Will it not utterly wither when the east wind strikes it—wither away on the bed where it grew?"

11, 12 Then the word of the LORD came to me: "Say now to the rebellious house, Do you not know what these things mean? Tell them, Behold, the king of Babylon came to Jerusalem, and took her king and her princes and brought

13 them to him to Babylon. And he took one of the seed royal and made a covenant with him, putting him under

14 oath. (The chief men of the land he had taken away, that the kingdom might be humble and not lift itself up, and

15 that by keeping his covenant it might stand.) But he rebelled against him by sending ambassadors to Egypt, that they might give him horses and a large army. Will he succeed? Can a man escape who does such things?

16 Can he break the covenant and yet escape? As I live, says the Lord GOD, surely in the place where the king dwells who made him king, whose oath he despised, and whose covenant with him he broke, in Babylon he shall

17 die. Pharaoh with his mighty army and great company will not help him in war, when mounds are cast up and

18 siege walls built to cut off many lives. Because he despised the oath and broke the covenant, because he gave his hand and yet did all these things, he shall not escape.

19 Therefore thus says the Lord GOD: As I live, surely my oath which he despised, and my covenant which he broke,

20 I will requite upon his head. I will spread my net over him, and he shall be taken in my snare, and I will bring him to Babylon and enter into judgment with him there

21 for the treason he has committed against me. And all the pick [j] of his troops shall fall by the sword, and the survivors shall be scattered to every wind; and you shall know that I, the LORD, have spoken."

22 Thus says the Lord GOD: "I myself will take a sprig from the lofty top of the cedar, and will set it out; I will break off from the topmost of its young twigs a tender one, and I myself will plant it upon a high and lofty

23 mountain; on the mountain height of Israel will I plant it, that it may bring forth boughs and bear fruit, and become a noble cedar; and under it will dwell all kinds of beasts;[k] in the shade of its branches birds of every sort

24 will nest. And all the trees of the field shall know that I the LORD bring low the high tree, and make high the low tree, dry up the green tree, and make the dry tree flourish. I the LORD have spoken, and I will do it."

Personal Responsibility

2 **18** The word of the LORD came to me again: "What do you mean by repeating this proverb concerning the land of Israel, 'The fathers have eaten sour grapes,

3 and the children's teeth are set on edge'? As I live, says the Lord GOD, this proverb shall no more be used by you

4 in Israel. Behold, all souls are mine; the soul of the father as well as the soul of the son is mine: the soul that sins shall die.

5 "If a man is righteous and does what is lawful and

6 right—if he does not eat upon the mountains or lift up his eyes to the idols of the house of Israel, does not defile his neighbor's wife or approach a woman in her time

7 of impurity, does not oppress any one, but restores to the debtor his pledge, commits no robbery, gives his bread to the hungry and covers the naked with a garment,

8 does not lend at interest or take any increase, withholds his hand from iniquity, executes true justice between

9 man and man, walks in my statutes, and is careful to observe my ordinances [l]—he is righteous, he shall surely live, says the Lord GOD.

10 "If he begets a son who is a robber, a shedder of

11 blood,[m] who does none of these duties, but eats upon the

12 mountains, defiles his neighbor's wife, oppresses the poor and needy, commits robbery, does not restore the pledge, lifts up his eyes to the idols, commits abomination,

13 lends at interest, and takes increase; shall he then live? He shall not live. He has done all these abominable things; he shall surely die; his blood shall be upon himself.

14 "But if this man begets a son who sees all the sins which his father has done, and fears, and does not do

15 likewise, who does not eat upon the mountains or lift up his eyes to the idols of the house of Israel, does not defile

16 his neighbor's wife, does not wrong any one, exacts no pledge, commits no robbery, but gives his bread to the

17 hungry and covers the naked with a garment, withholds his hand from iniquity,[n] takes no interest or increase, observes my ordinances, and walks in my statutes; he shall not die for his father's iniquity; he shall surely

18 live. As for his father, because he practiced extortion, robbed his brother, and did what is not good among his people, behold, he shall die for his iniquity.

19 "Yet you say, 'Why should not the son suffer for the iniquity of the father?' When the son has done what is lawful and right, and has been careful to observe all my

20 statutes, he shall surely live. The soul that sins shall die. The son shall not suffer for the iniquity of the father, nor the father suffer for the iniquity of the son; the righteousness of the righteous shall be upon himself, and the wickedness of the wicked shall be upon himself.

21 "But if a wicked man turns away from all his sins which he has committed and keeps all my statutes and does what is lawful and right, he shall surely live; he

---

[h] Cn: Heb *it was transplanted*   [i] Cn: Heb *fruit*   [j] Another reading is *fugitives*   [k] Gk: Heb lacks *all kinds of beasts*
[l] Gk: Heb *has kept my ordinances, to deal truly*   [m] Heb *blood, and he does any one of these things*   [n] Gk: Heb *the poor*

22 shall not die. None of the transgressions which he has committed shall be remembered against him; for the
23 righteousness which he has done he shall live. Have I any pleasure in the death of the wicked, says the Lord GOD, and not rather that he should turn from his way and
24 live? But when a righteous man turns away from his righteousness and commits iniquity and does the same abominable things that the wicked man does, shall he live? None of the righteous deeds which he has done shall be remembered; for the treachery of which he is guilty and the sin he has committed, he shall die.
25 "Yet you say, 'The way of the Lord is not just.' Hear now, O house of Israel: Is my way not just? Is it not
26 your ways that are not just? When a righteous man turns away from his righteousness and commits iniquity, he shall die for it; for the iniquity which he has committed
27 he shall die. Again, when a wicked man turns away from the wickedness he has committed and does what is lawful
28 and right, he shall save his life. Because he considered and turned away from all the transgressions which he
29 had committed, he shall surely live, he shall not die. Yet the house of Israel says, 'The way of the Lord is not just.' O house of Israel, are my ways not just? Is it not your ways that are not just?
30 "Therefore I will judge you, O house of Israel, every one according to his ways, say the Lord GOD. Repent and turn from all your transgressions, lest iniquity be
31 your ruin.° Cast away from you all the transgressions which you have committed against me, and get yourselves a new heart and a new spirit! Why will you die,
32 O house of Israel? For I have no pleasure in the death of any one, says the Lord GOD; so turn, and live."

A Lamentation

19 And you, take up a lamentation for the princes of
2 Israel, and say:
What a lioness was your mother
    among lions!
She couched in the midst of young lions,
    rearing her whelps.
3 And she brought up one of her whelps;
    he became a young lion,
and he learned to catch prey;
    he devoured men.
4 The nations sounded an alarm against him;
    he was taken in their pit;
and they brought him with hooks
    to the land of Egypt.
5 When she saw that she was baffled,ᵖ
    that her hope was lost,
she took another of her whelps
    and made him a young lion.
6 He prowled among the lions;

he became a young lion,
    and he learned to catch prey;
he devoured men.
7 And he ravaged their strongholds, q
    and laid waste their cities;
and the land was appalled and all who were in it
    at the sound of his roaring.
8 Then the nations set against him
    snares ʳ on every side;
they spread their net over him;
    he was taken in their pit.
9 With hooks they put him in a cage,
    and brought him to the king of Babylon;
they brought him into custody,
    that his voice should no more be heard
    upon the mountains of Israel.

10 Your mother was like a vine in a vineyard ˢ
    transplanted by the water,
fruitful and full of branches
    by reason of abundant water.
11 Its strongest stem became
    a ruler's scepter;
it towered aloft
    among the thick boughs;
it was seen in its height
    with the mass of its branches.
12 But the vine was plucked up in fury,
    cast down to the ground;
the east wind dried it up;
    its fruit was stripped off,
its strong stem was withered;
    the fire consumed it.
13 Now it is transplanted in the wilderness,
    in a dry and thirsty land.
14 And fire has gone out from its stem,
    has consumed its branches and fruit,
so that there remains in it no strong stem,
    no scepter for a ruler.

This is a lamentation, and has become a lamentation.

A Long Record of Sin

20 In the seventh year, in the fifth month, on the tenth day of the month, certain of the elders of Israel
2 came to inquire of the LORD, and sat before me. And the
3 word of the LORD came to me: "Son of man, speak to the elders of Israel, and say to them, Thus says the Lord GOD, Is it to inquire of me that you come? As I live, says the Lord GOD, I will not be inquired of by you.
4 Will you judge them, son of man, will you judge them? Then let them know the abominations of their fathers,
5 and say to them, Thus says the Lord GOD: On the day when I chose Israel, I swore to the seed of the house of Jacob, making myself known to them in the land of

---

° Or so that they shall not be a stumbling block of iniquity to you
ᵖ Heb had waited   q Tg Compare Theodotion: Heb knew his widows
ʳ Cn: Heb from the provinces   ˢ Cn: Heb in your blood

Egypt, I swore to them, saying, I am the Lord your God.
⁶ On that day I swore to them that I would bring them out of the land of Egypt into a land that I had searched out for them, a land flowing with milk and honey, the
⁷ most glorious of all lands. And I said to them, Cast away the detestable things your eyes feast on, every one of you, and do not defile yourselves with the idols of Egypt;
⁸ I am the Lord your God. But they rebelled against me and would not listen to me; they did not every man cast away the detestable things their eyes feasted on, nor did they forsake the idols of Egypt.

"Then I thought I would pour out my wrath upon them and spend my anger against them in the midst of
⁹ the land of Egypt. But I acted for the sake of my name, that it should not be profaned in the sight of the nations among whom they dwelt, in whose sight I made myself known to them in bringing them out of the land of
¹⁰ Egypt. So I led them out of the land of Egypt and
¹¹ brought them into the wilderness. I gave them my statutes and showed them my ordinances, by whose observance
¹² man shall live. Moreover I gave them my sabbaths, as a sign between me and them, that they might know that I
¹³ the Lord sanctify them. But the house of Israel rebelled against me in the wilderness; they did not walk in my statutes but rejected my ordinances, by whose observance man shall live; and my sabbaths they greatly profaned.

"Then I thought I would pour out my wrath upon
¹⁴ them in the wilderness, to make a full end of them. But I acted for the sake of my name, that it should not be profaned in the sight of the nations, in whose sight I had
¹⁵ brought them out. Moreover I swore to them in the wilderness that I would not bring them into the land which I had given them, a land flowing with milk and
¹⁶ honey, the most glorious of all lands, because they rejected my ordinances and did not walk in my statutes, and profaned my sabbaths; for their heart went after their
¹⁷ idols. Nevertheless my eye spared them, and I did not destroy them or make a full end of them in the wilderness.
¹⁸ "And I said to their children in the wilderness, Do not walk in the statutes of your fathers, nor observe their
¹⁹ ordinances, nor defile yourselves with their idols. I the Lord am your God; walk in my statutes, and be careful
²⁰ to observe my ordinances, and hallow my sabbaths that they may be a sign between me and you, that you may
²¹ know that I the Lord am your God. But the children rebelled against me; they did not walk in my statutes, and were not careful to observe my ordinances, by whose observance man shall live; they profaned my sabbaths.

"Then I thought I would pour out my wrath upon them and spend my anger against them in the wilderness.
²² But I withheld my hand, and acted for the sake of my name, that it should not be profaned in the sight of the
²³ nations, in whose sight I had brought them out. More-

over I swore to them in the wilderness that I would scatter them among the nations and disperse them
²⁴ through the countries, because they had not executed my ordinances, but had rejected my statutes and profaned my sabbaths, and their eyes were set on their fathers'
²⁵ idols. Moreover I gave them statutes that were not good
²⁶ and ordinances by which they could not have life; and I defiled them through their very gifts in making them offer by fire all their firstborn, that I might horrify them; I did it that they might know that I am the Lord.
²⁷ "Therefore, son of man, speak to the house of Israel and say to them, Thus says the Lord God: In this again your fathers blasphemed me, by dealing treacherously
²⁸ with me. For when I had brought them into the land which I swore to give them, then wherever they saw any high hill or any leafy tree, there they offered their sacrifices and presented the provocation of their offering; there they sent up their soothing odors, and there they
²⁹ poured out their drink offerings. (I said to them, What is the high place to which you go? So its name is called
³⁰ Bamah ᵗ to this day.) Wherefore say to the house of

Israel, Thus says the Lord God: Will you defile yourselves after the manner of your fathers and go astray
³¹ after their detestable things? When you offer your gifts and sacrifice your sons by fire, you defile yourselves with all your idols to this day. And shall I be inquired of by you, O house of Israel? As I live, says the Lord God, I will not be inquired of by you.
³² "What is in your mind shall never happen—the thought, 'Let us be like the nations, like the tribes of the countries, and worship wood and stone.'
³³ "As I live, says the Lord God, surely with a mighty hand and an outstretched arm, and with wrath poured
³⁴ out, I will be king over you. I will bring you out from the peoples and gather you out of the countries where you are scattered, with a mighty hand and an outstretched
³⁵ arm, and with wrath poured out; and I will bring you into the wilderness of the peoples, and there I will enter
³⁶ into judgment with you face to face. As I entered into judgment with your fathers in the wilderness of the land of Egypt, so I will enter into judgment with you, says
³⁷ the Lord God. I will make you pass under the rod, and I
³⁸ will let you go in by number.ᵘ I will purge out the rebels from among you, and those who transgress against me; I will bring them out of the land where they sojourn, but they shall not enter the land of Israel. Then you will know that I am the Lord.
³⁹ "As for you, O house of Israel, thus says the Lord

ᵗ That is *High Place*   ᵘ Gk: Heb *bring you into the bond of the covenant*

GOD: Go serve every one of you his idols, now and here-after, if you will not listen to me; but my holy name you shall no more profane with your gifts and your idols.

40 "For on my holy mountain, the mountain height of Israel, says the Lord GOD, there all the house of Israel, all of them, shall serve me in the land; there I will ac-cept them, and there I will require your contributions and the choicest of your gifts, with all your sacred offer-
41 ings. As a pleasing odor I will accept you, when I bring you out from the peoples, and gather you out of the coun-tries where you have been scattered; and I will manifest my holiness among you in the sight of the nations.
42 And you shall know that I am the LORD, when I bring you into the land of Israel, the country which I swore to
43 give to your fathers. And there you shall remember your ways and all the doings with which you have polluted yourselves; and you shall loathe yourselves for all the
44 evils that you have committed. And you shall know that I am the LORD, when I deal with you for my name's sake, not according to your evil ways, nor according to your corrupt doings, O house of Israel, says the Lord GOD."
45,v 46 And the word of the LORD came to me: "Son of man, set your face toward the south, preach against the south, and prophesy against the forest land in the Negeb:
47 say to the forest of the Negeb, Hear the word of the LORD: Thus says the Lord GOD, Behold, I will kindle a fire in you, and it shall devour every green tree in you and every dry tree; the blazing flame shall not be quenched, and all faces from south to north shall be scorched by it.
48 All flesh shall see that I the LORD have kindled it; it shall
49 not be quenched." Then I said, "Ah Lord GOD! they are saying of me, 'Is he not a maker of allegories?'"

The Sword of Justice

2 21ʷ The word of the LORD came to me: "Son of man, set your face toward Jerusalem and preach against
3 the sanctuaries; prophesy against the land of Israel and say to the land of Israel, Thus says the LORD: Behold, I am against you, and will draw forth my sword out of its sheath, and will cut off from you both righteous and
4 wicked. Because I will cut off from you both righteous and wicked, therefore my sword shall go out of its sheath
5 against all flesh from south to north; and all flesh shall know that I the LORD have drawn my sword out of its
6 sheath; it shall not be sheathed again. Sigh therefore, son of man; sigh with breaking heart and bitter grief before
7 their eyes. And when they say to you, 'Why do you sigh?' you shall say, 'Because of the tidings. When it comes, every heart will melt and all hands will be feeble, every spirit will faint and all knees will be weak as water. Behold, it comes and it will be fulfilled,'" says the Lord GOD.
8, 9 And the word of the LORD came to me: "Son of man,

prophesy and say, Thus says the Lord, Say:
A sword, a sword is sharpened
and also polished,
10 sharpened for slaughter,
polished to flash like lightning!
Or do we make mirth? You have despised the rod, my
11 son, with everything of wood. So the sword is given to be polished, that it may be handled; it is sharpened and
12 polished to be given into the hand of the slayer. Cry and wail, son of man, for it is against my people; it is against all the princes of Israel; they are delivered over to the sword with my people. Smite therefore upon your
13 thigh. For it will not be a testing—what could it do if you despise the rod?" says the Lord GOD.
14 "Prophesy therefore, son of man; clap your hands and let the sword come down twice, yea thrice, the sword for those to be slain; it is the sword for the great slaugh-
15 ter, which encompasses them, that their hearts may melt, and many fall at all their gates. I have given the glittering sword; ah! it is made like lightning, it is polished ˣ for

16 slaughter. Cut sharply to right ʸ and left where your edge
17 is directed. I also will clap my hands, and I will satisfy my fury; I the LORD have spoken."
18, 19 The word of the LORD came to me again: "Son of man, mark two ways for the sword of the king of Babylon to come; both of them shall come forth from the same land. And make a signpost, make it at the head of the
20 way to a city; mark a way for the sword to come to Rabbah of the Ammonites and to Judah and to ᶻ Jeru-
21 salem the fortified. For the king of Babylon stands at the parting of the way, at the head of the two ways, to use divination; he shakes the arrows, he consults the teraphim,
22 he looks at the liver. Into his right hand comes the lot for Jerusalem,ᵃ to open the mouth with a cry,ᵇ to lift up the voice with shouting, to set battering rams against the
23 gates, to cast up mounds, to build siege towers. But to them it will seem like a false divination; they have sworn solemn oaths; but he brings their guilt to remembrance, that they may be captured.
24 "Therefore thus says the Lord GOD: Because you have made your guilt to be remembered, in that your trans-gressions are uncovered, so that in all your doings your sins appear—because you have come to remembrance,
25 you shall be taken in them.ᶜ And you, O unhallowed wicked one, prince of Israel, whose day has come, the
26 time of your final punishment, thus says the Lord GOD: Remove the turban, and take off the crown; things shall not remain as they are; exalt that which is low, and abase
27 that which is high. A ruin, ruin, ruin I will make it;

ᵛ Ch 21.1 in Heb   ʷ Ch 21.6 in Heb   ˣ Tg: Heb *wrapped up*   ʸ Gk Syr Vg: Heb *right, set*   ᶻ Gk Syr: Heb *in*
ᵃ Heb *Jerusalem, to set battering rams*   ᵇ Gk: Heb *with slaughter*   ᶜ Gk: Heb *with the hand*

there shall not be even a trace d of it until he comes whose right it is; and to him I will give it.

28 "And you, son of man, prophesy, and say, Thus says the Lord GOD concerning the Ammonites, and concerning their reproach; say, A sword, a sword is drawn for the slaughter, it is polished to glitter e and to flash like light-
29 ning—while they see for you false visions, while they divine lies for you—to be laid on the necks of the un-hallowed wicked, whose day has come, the time of their
30 final punishment. Return it to its sheath. In the place where you were created, in the land of your origin, I
31 will judge you. And I will pour out my indignation upon you; I will blow upon you with the fire of my wrath; and I will deliver you into the hands of brutal men,
32 skilful to destroy. You shall be fuel for the fire; your blood shall be in the midst of the land; you shall be no more remembered; for I the LORD have spoken."

The City of Blood

22 Moreover the word of the LORD came to me, say-
2 ing, "And you, son of man, will you judge, will you judge the bloody city? Then declare to her all her abom-
3 inable deeds. You shall say, Thus says the Lord GOD: A city that sheds blood in the midst of her, that her time
4 may come, and that makes idols to defile herself! You have become guilty by the blood which you have shed, and defiled by the idols which you have made; and you have brought your day near, the appointed time f of your years has come. Therefore I have made you a re-proach to the nations, and a mocking to all the countries.
5 Those who are near and those who are far from you will mock you, you infamous one, full of tumult.
6 "Behold, the princes of Israel in you, every one ac-cording to his power, have been bent on shedding blood.
7 Father and mother are treated with contempt in you; the sojourner suffers extortion in your midst; the fatherless
8 and the widow are wronged in you. You have despised
9 my holy things, and profaned my sabbaths. There are men in you who slander to shed blood, and men in you who eat upon the mountains; men commit lewdness in
10 your midst. In you men uncover their fathers' nakedness; in you they humble women who are unclean in their
11 impurity. One commits abomination with his neighbor's wife; another lewdly defiles his daughter-in-law; another
12 in you defiles his sister, his father's daughter. In you men take bribes to shed blood; you take interest and increase and make gain of your neighbors by extortion; and you have forgotten me, says the Lord GOD.
13 "Behold, therefore, I strike my hands together at the dishonest gain which you have made, and at the blood
14 which has been in the midst of you. Can your courage endure, or can your hands be strong, in the days that I shall deal with you? I the LORD have spoken, and I will

15 do it. I will scatter you among the nations and disperse you through the countries, and I will consume your
16 filthiness out of you. And I g shall be profaned through you in the sight of the nations; and you shall know that I am the LORD."

17, 18 And the word of the LORD came to me: "Son of man, the house of Israel has become dross to me; all of them, silver h and bronze and tin and iron and lead in the
19 furnace, have become dross. Therefore thus says the Lord GOD: Because you have all become dross, therefore,
20 behold, I will gather you into the midst of Jerusalem. As men gather silver and bronze and iron and lead and tin into a furnace, to blow the fire upon it in order to melt it; so I will gather you in my anger and in my wrath,
21 and I will put you in and melt you. I will gather you and blow upon you with the fire of my wrath, and you shall
22 be melted in the midst of it. As silver is melted in a fur-nace, so you shall be melted in the midst of it; and you shall know that I the LORD have poured out my wrath upon you."

23, 24 And the word of the LORD came to me: "Son of man, say to her, You are a land that is not cleansed, or rained
25 upon in the day of indignation. Her princes i in the midst of her are like a roaring lion tearing the prey; they have devoured human lives; they have taken treasure and precious things; they have made many widows in the
26 midst of her. Her priests have done violence to my law and have profaned my holy things; they have made no distinction between the holy and the common, neither have they taught the difference between the unclean and the clean, and they have disregarded my sabbaths, so that
27 I am profaned among them. Her princes in the midst of her are like wolves tearing the prey, shedding blood,
28 destroying lives to get dishonest gain. And her prophets have daubed for them with whitewash, seeing false visions and divining lies for them, saying, 'Thus says the Lord
29 GOD,' when the LORD has not spoken. The people of the land have practiced extortion and committed robbery; they have oppressed the poor and needy, and have ex-
30 torted from the sojourner without redress. And I sought for a man among them who should build up the wall and stand in the breach before me for the land, that I should
31 not destroy it; but I found none. Therefore I have poured out my indignation upon them; I have consumed them with the fire of my wrath; their way have I requited upon their heads, says the Lord GOD."

The Two Sisters

23 The word of the LORD came to me: "Son of man,
2 there were two women, the daughters of one mother;
3 they played the harlot in Egypt; they played the harlot in their youth; there their breasts were pressed and their
4 virgin bosoms handled. Oho'lah was the name of the elder

---

d Cn: Heb not even this   e Cn: Heb to contain   f Two Mss Gk Syr Vg Tg: Heb until   g Gk Syr Vg: Heb you
h Transposed from the end of the verse. Compare verse 20   i Gk: Heb a conspiracy of her prophets

and Ohol'ibah the name of her sister. They became mine, and they bore sons and daughters. As for their names, Oho'lah is Samar'ia, and Ohol'ibah is Jerusalem.

5 "Oho'lah played the harlot while she was mine; and 6 she doted on her lovers the Assyrians, warriors clothed in purple, governors and commanders, all of them desir- 7 able young men, horsemen riding on horses. She bestowed her harlotries upon them, the choicest men of Assyria all of them; and she defiled herself with all the 8 idols of every one on whom she doted. She did not give up her harlotry which she had practiced since her days in Egypt; for in her youth men had lain with her and handled her virgin bosom and poured out their lust upon 9 her. Therefore I delivered her into the hands of her lovers, into the hands of the Assyrians, upon whom she 10 doted. These uncovered her nakedness; they seized her sons and her daughters; and her they slew with the sword; and she became a byword among women, when judgment had been executed upon her.

11 "Her sister Ohol'ibah saw this, yet she was more corrupt than she in her doting and in her harlotry, which 12 was worse than that of her sister. She doted upon the Assyrians, governors and commanders, warriors clothed in full armor, horsemen riding on horses, all of them 13 desirable young men. And I saw that she was defiled; 14 they both took the same way. But she carried her harlotry further; she saw men portrayed upon the wall, the images 15 of the Chalde'ans portrayed in vermilion, girded with belts on their loins, with flowing turbans on their heads, all of them looking like officers, a picture of Babylonians 16 whose native land was Chalde'a. When she saw them she doted upon them, and sent messengers to them in Chalde'a. 17 And the Babylonians came to her into the bed of love, and they defiled her with their lust; and after she was polluted 18 by them, she turned from them in disgust. When she carried on her harlotry so openly and flaunted her nakedness, I turned in disgust from her, as I had turned from 19 her sister. Yet she increased her harlotry, remembering the days of her youth, when she played the harlot in the 20 land of Egypt and doted upon her paramours there, whose members were like those of asses, and whose issue was like 21 that of horses. Thus you longed for the lewdness of your youth, when the Egyptians j handled your bosom and pressed k your young breasts."

22 Therefore, O Ohol'ibah, thus says the Lord GOD: "Behold, I will rouse against you your lovers from whom you turned in disgust, and I will bring them against you 23 from every side: the Babylonians and all the Chalde'ans, Pekod and Sho'a and Ko'a, and all the Assyrians with them, desirable young men, governors and commanders all of them, officers and warriors, l all of them riding on 24 horses. And they shall come against you from the north m with chariots and wagons and a host of peoples; they

shall set themselves against you on every side with buckler, shield, and helmet, and I will commit the judgment to them, and they shall judge you according to their 25 judgments. And I will direct my indignation against you, that they may deal with you in fury. They shall cut off your nose and your ears, and your survivors shall fall by the sword. They shall seize your sons and your daughters, and your survivors shall be devoured by fire. 26 They shall also strip you of your clothes and take away 27 your fine jewels. Thus I will put an end to your lewdness and your harlotry brought from the land of Egypt; so that you shall not lift up your eyes to the Egyptians or 28 remember them any more. For thus says the Lord GOD: Behold, I will deliver you into the hands of those whom you hate, into the hands of those from whom you turned 29 in disgust; and they shall deal with you in hatred, and take away all the fruit of your labor, and leave you naked and bare, and the nakedness of your harlotry shall be 30 uncovered. Your lewdness and your harlotry have brought this upon you, because you played the harlot with the 31 nations, and polluted yourself with their idols. You have gone the way of your sister; therefore I will give her cup 32 into your hand. Thus says the Lord GOD:

"You shall drink your sister's cup
  which is deep and large;
you shall be laughed at and held in derision,
  for it contains much;
33 you will be filled with drunkenness and sorrow.
A cup of horror and desolation,
  is the cup of your sister Samar'ia;
34 you shall drink it and drain it out,
  and pluck out your hair, n
  and tear your breasts;

35 for I have spoken, says the Lord GOD. Therefore thus says the Lord GOD: Because you have forgotten me and cast me behind your back, therefore bear the consequences of your lewdness and harlotry."

36 The LORD said to me: "Son of man, will you judge Oho'lah and Ohol'ibah? Then declare to them their 37 abominable deeds. For they have committed adultery, and blood is upon their hands; with their idols they have committed adultery; and they have even offered up to them for food the sons whom they had borne to 38 me. Moreover this they have done to me: they have defiled my sanctuary on the same day and profaned my 39 sabbaths. For when they had slaughtered their children in sacrifice to their idols, on the same day they came into my sanctuary to profane it. And lo, this is what 40 they did in my house. They even sent for men to come from far, to whom a messenger was sent, and lo, they came. For them you bathed yourself, painted your eyes, 41 and decked yourself with ornaments; you sat upon a stately couch, with a table spread before it on which you

j Two Mss: Heb _from Egypt_   k Cn: Heb _for the sake of_   l Compare verses 6 and 12: Heb _called_
m Gk: The meaning of the Hebrew word is unknown   n Compare Syr: Heb _gnaw its sherds_

42 had placed my incense and my oil. The sound of a care-
free multitude was with her; and with men of the common sort drunkards[o] were brought from the wilderness;
and they put bracelets upon the hands of the women, and
beautiful crowns upon their heads.
43 "Then I said, Do not men now commit adultery[p] when
44 they practice harlotry with her? For they have gone in to
her, as men go in to a harlot. Thus they went in to
45 Oho'lah and to Ohol'ibah to commit lewdness.[q] But
righteous men shall pass judgment on them with the
sentence of adulteresses, and with the sentence of women
that shed blood; because they are adulteresses, and blood
is upon their hands."
46 For thus says the Lord GOD: "Bring up a host against
47 them, and make them an object of terror and a spoil. And
the host shall stone them and dispatch them with their
swords; they shall slay their sons and their daughters,
48 and burn up their houses. Thus will I put an end to
lewdness in the land, that all women may take warning
49 and not commit lewdness as you have done. And your
lewdness shall be requited upon you, and you shall bear
the penalty for your sinful idolatry; and you shall know
that I am the Lord GOD."

The End of the Siege

24 In the ninth year, in the tenth month, on the tenth
day of the month, the word of the LORD came to
2 me: "Son of man, write down the name of this day, this
very day. The king of Babylon has laid siege to Jerusalem

3 this very day. And utter an allegory to the rebellious house
and say to them, Thus says the Lord GOD:
Set on the pot, set it on,
  pour in water also;
4 put in it the pieces of flesh,
  all the good pieces, the thigh and the shoulder;
  fill it with choice bones.
5 Take the choicest one of the flock,
  pile the logs[r] under it;
boil its pieces,[s]
  seethe[t] also its bones in it.
6 "Therefore thus says the Lord GOD: Woe to the bloody
city, to the pot whose rust is in it, and whose rust has
not gone out of it! Take out of it piece after piece, with-
7 out making any choice.[u] For the blood she has shed is
still in the midst of her; she put it on the bare rock,
she did not pour it upon the ground to cover it with dust.
8 To rouse my wrath, to take vengeance, I have set on
the bare rock the blood she has shed, that it may not be
9 covered. Therefore thus says the Lord GOD: Woe to the
10 bloody city! I also will make the pile great. Heap on
the logs, kindle the fire, boil well the flesh, and empty
11 out the broth,[v] and let the bones be burned up. Then set
it empty upon the coals, that it may become hot, and
its copper may burn, that its filthiness may be melted in
12 it, its rust consumed. In vain I have wearied myself;[w]
13 its thick rust does not go out of it by fire. Its rust is
your filthy lewdness. Because I would have cleansed you
and you were not cleansed from your filthiness, you shall
not be cleansed any more till I have satisfied my fury
14 upon you. I the LORD have spoken; it shall come to pass,
I will do it; I will not go back, I will not spare, I will
not repent; according to your ways and your doings I
will judge you, says the Lord GOD."
15, 16 Also the word of the LORD came to me: "Son of
man, behold, I am about to take the delight of your eyes
away from you at a stroke; yet you shall not mourn or
17 weep nor shall your tears run down. Sigh, but not
aloud; make no mourning for the dead. Bind on your
turban, and put your shoes on your feet; do not cover
18 your lips, nor eat the bread of mourners.[x]" So I spoke
to the people in the morning, and at evening my wife
died. And on the next morning I did as I was commanded.
19 And the people said to me, "Will you not tell us what
these things mean for us, that you are acting thus?"
20 Then I said to them, "The word of the LORD came to me:
21 'Say to the house of Israel, Thus says the Lord GOD:
Behold, I will profane my sanctuary, the pride of your
power, the delight of your eyes, and the desire of your
soul; and your sons and your daughters whom you left
22 behind shall fall by the sword. And you shall do as I
have done; you shall not cover your lips, nor eat the
23 bread of mourners.[x] Your turbans shall be on your
heads and your shoes on your feet; you shall not mourn
or weep, but you shall pine away in your iniquities and
24 groan to one another. Thus shall Ezekiel be to you a
sign; according to all that he has done you shall do.
When this comes, then you will know that I am the
Lord GOD.'
25 "And you, son of man, on the day when I take from
them their stronghold, their joy and glory, the delight of
their eyes and their heart's desire, and also their sons
26 and daughters, on that day a fugitive will come to you
27 to report to you the news. On that day your mouth will
be opened to the fugitive, and you shall speak and be no
longer dumb. So you will be a sign to them; and they
will know that I am the LORD."

o Heb uncertain   p Compare Gk: Heb obscure   q Gk: Heb *a woman of lewdness*   r Compare verse 10: Heb *the bones*
s Two Mss: Heb *its boilings*   t Cn: Heb *its bones seethe*   u Heb *no lot has fallen upon it*
v Compare Gk: Heb *mix the spices*   w Cn: Heb uncertain   x Vg Tg: Heb *men*

JUDGMENT UPON THE NATIONS

25 [2] The word of the LORD came to me: "Son of man, set your face toward the Ammonites, and prophesy [3] against them. Say to the Ammonites, Hear the word of the Lord GOD: Thus says the Lord GOD, Because you said, 'Aha!' over my sanctuary when it was profaned, and over the land of Israel when it was made desolate, and [4] over the house of Judah when it went into exile; therefore I am handing you over to the people of the East for a possession, and they shall set their encampments among you and make their dwellings in your midst; they shall [5] eat your fruit, and they shall drink your milk. I will make Rabbah a pasture for camels and the cities of the Ammonites[y] a fold for flocks. Then you will know that I [6] am the LORD. For thus says the Lord GOD: Because you have clapped your hands and stamped your feet and rejoiced with all the malice within you against the land [7] of Israel, therefore, behold, I have stretched out my hand against you, and will hand you over as spoil to the nations; and I will cut you off from the peoples and will make you perish out of the countries; I will destroy you. Then you will know that I am the LORD.

Moab

[8] "Thus says the Lord GOD: Because Moab[z] said, Behold, the house of Judah is like all the other nations, [9] therefore I will lay open the flank of Moab from the cities[a] on its frontier, the glory of the country, Beth-[10]jesh'imoth, Ba'al-me'on, and Kiriatha'im. I will give it along with the Ammonites to the people of the East as a possession, that it[b] may be remembered no more among [11] the nations, and I will execute judgments upon Moab. Then they will know that I am the LORD.

Edom

[12] "Thus says the Lord GOD: Because Edom acted revengefully against the house of Judah and has grievously [13] offended in taking vengeance upon them, therefore thus says the Lord GOD, I will stretch out my hand against Edom, and cut off from it man and beast; and I will make it desolate; from Teman even to Dedan they shall fall [14] by the sword. And I will lay my vengeance upon Edom by the hand of my people Israel; and they shall do in Edom according to my anger and according to my wrath; and they shall know my vengeance, says the Lord GOD.

Philistia

[15] "Thus says the Lord GOD: Because the Philistines acted revengefully and took vengeance with malice of [16] heart to destroy in never-ending enmity; therefore thus says the Lord GOD, Behold, I will stretch out my hand against the Philistines, and I will cut off the Cher'ethites, [17] and destroy the rest of the seacoast. I will execute great vengeance upon them with wrathful chastisements. Then

they will know that I am the LORD, when I lay my vengeance upon them."

Tyre

26 In the eleventh year, on the first day of the month, [2] the word of the LORD came to me: "Son of man, because Tyre said concerning Jerusalem, 'Aha, the gate of the peoples is broken, it has swung open to me; I shall [3] be replenished, now that she is laid waste,' therefore thus says the Lord GOD: Behold, I am against you, O Tyre, and will bring up many nations against you, as the sea [4] brings up its waves. They shall destroy the walls of Tyre, and break down her towers; and I will scrape her soil [5] from her, and make her a bare rock. She shall be in the midst of the sea a place for the spreading of nets; for I have spoken, says the Lord GOD; and she shall become a [6] spoil to the nations; and her daughters on the mainland shall be slain by the sword. Then they will know that I am the LORD.

[7] "For thus says the Lord GOD: Behold, I will bring upon Tyre from the north Nebuchadrez'zar king of Babylon, king of kings, with horses and chariots, and with [8] horsemen and a host of many soldiers. He will slay with the sword your daughters on the mainland; he will set up a siege wall against you, and throw up a mound against [9] you, and raise a roof of shields against you. He will direct the shock of his battering rams against your walls, [10] and with his axes he will break down your towers. His horses will be so many that their dust will cover you; your walls will shake at the noise of the horsemen and wagons and chariots, when he enters your gates as one [11] enters a city which has been breached. With the hoofs of his horses he will trample all your streets; he will slay your people with the sword; and your mighty pillars will [12] fall to the ground. They will make a spoil of your riches and a prey of your merchandise; they will break down your walls and destroy your pleasant houses; your stones and timber and soil they will cast into the midst of the [13] waters. And I will stop the music of your songs, and the [14] sound of your lyres shall be heard no more. I will make you a bare rock; you shall be a place for the spreading of nets; you shall never be rebuilt; for I the LORD have spoken, says the Lord GOD.

[15] "Thus says the Lord GOD to Tyre: Will not the coastlands shake at the sound of your fall, when the wounded groan, when slaughter is made in the midst of you? [16] Then all the princes of the sea will step down from their thrones, and remove their robes, and strip off their embroidered garments; they will clothe themselves with trembling; they will sit upon the ground and tremble [17] every moment, and be appalled at you. And they will raise a lamentation over you, and say to you,

'How you have vanished[c] from the seas,

---

[y] Cn: Heb lacks *the cities of*   [z] Gk Old Latin: Heb *Moab and Seir*
[c] Gk Old Latin Aquila: Heb *vanished, O inhabited one,*   [a] Heb *cities from its cities*   [b] Cn: Heb *the Ammonites*

O city renowned,
  that was mighty on the sea,
    you and your inhabitants,
  who imposed your terror
    on all the mainland! d
18 Now the isles tremble
    on the day of your fall;
  yea, the isles that are in the sea
    are dismayed at your passing.'

19 "For thus says the Lord GOD: When I make you a city laid waste, like the cities that are not inhabited, when I bring up the deep over you, and the great waters 20 cover you, then I will thrust you down with those who descend into the Pit, to the people of old, and I will make you to dwell in the nether world, among primeval ruins, with those who go down to the Pit, so that you will not be inhabited or have a place e in the land of the living. 21 I will bring you to a dreadful end, and you shall be no more; though you be sought for, you will never be found again, says the Lord GOD."

27 2 The word of the LORD came to me: "Now you, son 3 of man, raise a lamentation over Tyre, and say to Tyre, who dwells at the entrance to the sea, merchant of the peoples on many coastlands, thus says the Lord GOD:

"O Tyre, you have said,
  'I am perfect in beauty.'
4 Your borders are in the heart of the seas;
  your builders made perfect your beauty.
5 They made all your planks
  of fir trees from Senir;
  they took a cedar from Lebanon
    to make a mast for you.
6 Of oaks of Bashan
  they made your oars;
  they made your deck of pines
    from the coasts of Cyprus,
    inlaid with ivory.
7 Of fine embroidered linen from Egypt

was your sail,
  serving as your ensign;
  blue and purple from the coasts of Eli'shah
    was your awning.
8 The inhabitants of Sidon and Arvad
  were your rowers;
  skilled men of Zemer f were in you,
    they were your pilots.

9 The elders of Gebal and her skilled men were in you,
  caulking your seams;
  all the ships of the sea with their mariners were in you,
    to barter for your wares.

10 "Persia and Lud and Put were in your army as your men of war; they hung the shield and helmet in you; 11 they gave you splendor. The men of Arvad and Helech g were upon your walls round about, and men of Gamad were in your towers; they hung their shields upon your walls round about; they made perfect your beauty.

12 "Tarshish trafficked with you because of your great wealth of every kind; silver, iron, tin, and lead they ex- 13 changed for your wares. Javan, Tubal, and Meshech traded with you; they exchanged the persons of men and 14 vessels of bronze for your merchandise. Beth-togar'mah exchanged for your wares horses, war horses, and mules. 15 The men of Rhodes h traded with you; many coastlands were your own special markets, they brought you in pay- 16 ment ivory tusks and ebony. Edom i trafficked with you because of your abundant goods; they exchanged for your wares emeralds, purple, embroidered work, fine 17 linen, coral, and agate. Judah and the land of Israel traded with you; they exchanged for your merchandise wheat, olives and early figs,j honey, oil, and balm. 18 Damascus trafficked with you for your abundant goods, because of your great wealth of every kind; wine of Hel- 19 bon, and white wool, and wine k from Uzal they ex- changed for your wares; wrought iron, cassia, and 20 calamus were bartered for your merchandise. Dedan 21 traded with you in saddlecloths for riding. Arabia and all the princes of Kedar were your favored dealers in lambs, rams, and goats; in these they trafficked with you. 22 The traders of Sheba and Ra'amah traded with you; they exchanged for your wares the best of all kinds of spices, 23 and all precious stones, and gold. Haran, Canneh, Eden,l 24 Asshur, and Chilmad traded with you. These traded with you in choice garments, in clothes of blue and embroid- ered work, and in carpets of colored stuff, bound with cords and made secure; in these they traded with you.m 25 The ships of Tarshish traveled for you with your mer- chandise.n

"So you were filled and heavily laden
  in the heart of the seas.
26 Your rowers have brought you out
  into the high seas.
The east wind has wrecked you
  in the heart of the seas.
27 Your riches, your wares, your merchandise,
  your mariners and your pilots,
  your caulkers, your dealers in merchandise,
    and all your men of war who are in you,
  with all your company
    that is in your midst,

---

d Cn: Heb her inhabitants   e Gk: Heb I will give beauty   f Compare Gn 10.18: Heb your skilled men, O Tyre
g Or and your army   h Gk: Heb Dedan   i Another reading is Aram   j Cn: Heb wheat of minnith and pannag
k Gk: Heb Vedan and Javan   l Cn: Heb Eden the traders of Sheba   m Cn: Heb in your market
n Cn: Heb your travelers your merchandise

sink into the heart of the seas
    on the day of your ruin.
28 At the sound of the cry of your pilots
    the countryside shakes,
29 and down from their ships
    come all that handle the oar.
The mariners and all the pilots of the sea
    stand on the shore
30 and wail aloud over you,
    and cry bitterly.
They cast dust on their heads
    and wallow in ashes;
31 they make themselves bald for you,
    and gird themselves with sackcloth,
and they weep over you in bitterness of soul,
    with bitter mourning.
32 In their wailing they raise a lamentation for you,
    and lament over you:
'Who was ever destroyed o like Tyre
    in the midst of the sea?
33 When your wares came from the seas,
    you satisfied many peoples;
with your abundant wealth and merchandise
    you enriched the kings of the earth.
34 Now you are wrecked by the seas,
    in the depths of the waters;
your merchandise and all your crew
    have sunk with you.
35 All the inhabitants of the coastlands
    are appalled at you;
and their kings are horribly afraid,
    their faces are convulsed.
36 The merchants among the peoples hiss at you;
    you have come to a dreadful end
    and shall be no more for ever.' "

The Prince of Tyre

28 2 The word of the LORD came to me: "Son of man,
    say to the prince of Tyre, Thus says the Lord GOD:
"Because your heart is proud,
    and you have said, 'I am a god,
I sit in the seat of the gods,
    in the heart of the seas,
yet you are but a man, and no god,
    though you consider yourself as wise as a god—
3 you are indeed wiser than Daniel;
    no secret is hidden from you;
4 by your wisdom and your understanding
    you have gotten wealth for yourself,
and have gathered gold and silver
    into your treasuries;
5 by your great wisdom in trade
    you have increased your wealth,

and your heart has become proud in your wealth—
6 therefore thus says the Lord GOD:
"Because you consider yourself
    as wise as a god,
7 therefore, behold, I will bring strangers upon you,
    the most terrible of the nations;
and they shall draw their swords against the beauty of
        your wisdom
    and defile your splendor.
8 They shall thrust you down into the Pit,
    and you shall die the death of the slain
    in the heart of the seas.
9 Will you still say, 'I am a god,'
    in the presence of those who slay you,
though you are but a man, and no god,
    in the hands of those who wound you?
10 You shall die the death of the uncircumcised
    by the hand of foreigners;
    for I have spoken, says the Lord GOD."

11, 12   Moreover the word of the LORD came to me: "Son
of man, raise a lamentation over the king of Tyre, and
say to him, Thus says the Lord GOD:
"You were the signet of perfection, p
    full of wisdom
    and perfect in beauty.
13 You were in Eden, the garden of God;
    every precious stone was your covering,
carnelian, topaz, and jasper,
    chrysolite, beryl, and onyx,
sapphire, q carbuncle, and emerald;
    and wrought in gold were your settings
    and your engravings. r
On the day that you were created
    they were prepared.
14 With an anointed guardian cherub
        I placed you; s
    you were on the holy mountain of God;
    in the midst of the stones of fire you walked.
15 You were blameless in your ways
    from the day you were created,
    till iniquity was found in you.
16 In the abundance of your trade
    you were filled with violence, and you sinned;
so I cast you as a profane thing from the mountain of God,
    and the guardian cherub drove you out
    from the midst of the stones of fire.
17 Your heart was proud because of your beauty;
    you corrupted your wisdom for the sake of your
        splendor.
I cast you to the ground;
    I exposed you before kings,
    to feast their eyes on you.
18 By the multitude of your iniquities,

o Tg Vg: Heb *like silence*   p Heb obscure   q Or *lapis lazuli*   r Heb uncertain   s Heb uncertain

in the unrighteousness of your trade
  you profaned your sanctuaries;
so I brought forth fire from the midst of you;
  it consumed you,
and I turned you to ashes upon the earth
  in the sight of all who saw you.
¹⁹ All who know you among the peoples
  are appalled at you;
you have come to a dreadful end
  and shall be no more for ever."

²⁰,²¹ The word of the LORD came to me: "Son of man, set your face toward Sidon, and prophesy against her ²² and say, Thus says the Lord GOD:

"Behold, I am against you, O Sidon,
  and I will manifest my glory in the midst of you.
And they shall know that I am the LORD
  when I execute judgments in her,
  and manifest my holiness in her;
²³ for I will send pestilence into her,
  and blood into her streets;
and the slain shall fall in the midst of her,
  by the sword that is against her on every side.
Then they will know that I am the LORD.

²⁴ "And for the house of Israel there shall be no more a brier to prick or a thorn to hurt them among all their neighbors who have treated them with contempt. Then they will know that I am the Lord GOD.

²⁵ "Thus says the Lord GOD: When I gather the house of Israel from the peoples among whom they are scattered, and manifest my holiness in them in the sight of the nations, then they shall dwell in their own land which I ²⁶ gave to my servant Jacob. And they shall dwell securely in it, and they shall build houses and plant vineyards. They shall dwell securely, when I execute judgments upon all their neighbors who have treated them with contempt. Then they will know that I am the LORD their God."

Prophecy Against Egypt

29 In the tenth year, in the tenth month, on the twelfth day of the month, the word of the LORD came to me: ² Son of man, set your face against Pharaoh king of Egypt, ³ and prophesy against him and against all Egypt; speak,

and say, Thus says the Lord GOD:
"Behold, I am against you,
  Pharaoh king of Egypt,
the great dragon that lies
  in the midst of his streams,
that says, 'My Nile is my own;

I made it.' ᵗ
⁴ I will put hooks in your jaws,
  and make the fish of your streams stick to your scales;
and I will draw you up out of the midst of your streams,
  with all the fish of your streams
  which stick to your scales.
⁵ And I will cast you forth into the wilderness,
  you and all the fish of your streams;
you shall fall upon the open field,
  and not be gathered and buried.
To the beasts of the earth and to the birds of the air
  I have given you as food.

⁶ "Then all the inhabitants of Egypt shall know that I am the LORD. Because you ᵘ have been a staff of reed to ⁷ the house of Israel; when they grasped you with the hand, you broke, and tore all their shoulders; and when they leaned upon you, you broke, and made all their loins to ⁸ shake; ᵛ therefore thus says the Lord GOD: Behold, I will bring a sword upon you, and will cut off from you man ⁹ and beast; and the land of Egypt shall be a desolation and a waste. Then they will know that I am the LORD.

"Because you ʷ said, 'The Nile is mine, and I made it,' ¹⁰ therefore, behold, I am against you, and against your streams, and I will make the land of Egypt an utter waste and desolation, from Migdol to Syene, as far as the ¹¹ border of Ethiopia. No foot of man shall pass through it, and no foot of beast shall pass through it; it shall be un-¹² inhabited forty years. And I will make the land of Egypt a desolation in the midst of desolated countries; and her cities shall be a desolation forty years among cities that are laid waste. I will scatter the Egyptians among the nations, and disperse them among the countries.

¹³ "For thus says the Lord GOD: At the end of forty years I will gather the Egyptians from the peoples among whom ¹⁴ they were scattered; and I will restore the fortunes of Egypt, and bring them back to the land of Pathros, the land of their origin; and there they shall be a lowly ¹⁵ kingdom. It shall be the most lowly of the kingdoms, and never again exalt itself above the nations; and I will make them so small that they will never again rule over ¹⁶ the nations. And it shall never again be the reliance of the house of Israel, recalling their iniquity, when they turn to them for aid. Then they will know that I am the Lord GOD."

¹⁷ In the twenty-seventh year, in the first month, on the first day of the month, the word of the LORD came to me: ¹⁸ "Son of man, Nebuchadrez′zar king of Babylon made his army labor hard against Tyre; every head was made bald and every shoulder was rubbed bare; yet neither he nor his army got anything from Tyre to pay for the labor ¹⁹ that he had performed against it. Therefore thus says the Lord GOD: Behold, I will give the land of Egypt to Nebuchadrez′zar king of Babylon; and he shall carry off

ᵗ Syr Compare Gk: Heb *I have made myself*   ᵘ Gk Syr Vg: Heb *they*   ᵛ Syr: Heb *stand*   ʷ Gk Syr Vg: Heb *he*

its wealth ˣ and despoil it and plunder it; and it shall be
20 the wages for his army. I have given him the land of
Egypt as his recompense for which he labored, because
they worked for me, says the Lord GOD.
21 "On that day I will cause a horn to spring forth to the
house of Israel, and I will open your lips among them.
Then they will know that I am the LORD."
² 30   The word of the LORD came to me: "Son of man,
      prophesy, and say, Thus says the Lord GOD:
"Wail, 'Alas for the day!'
3   For the day is near,
    the day of the LORD is near;
it will be a day of clouds,
    a time of doom for the nations.
⁴ A sword shall come upon Egypt,
    and anguish shall be in Ethiopia,
when the slain fall in Egypt,
    and her wealth is carried away,
    and her foundations are torn down.
⁵ Ethiopia, and Put, and Lud, and all Arabia, and Libya,ʸ
and the people of the land that is in league, shall fall with
them by the sword.

6   "Thus says the LORD:
Those who support Egypt shall fall,
    and her proud might shall come down;
from Migdol to Syene
    they shall fall within her by the sword.
says the Lord GOD.
⁷ And she ᶻ shall be desolated in the midst of desolated
    countries
    and her cities shall be in the midst of cities that are
      laid waste.
⁸ Then they will know that I am the LORD.
    when I have set fire to Egypt,
    and all her helpers are broken.
9   "On that day swift ᵃ messengers shall go forth from
me to terrify the unsuspecting Ethiopians; and anguish
shall come upon them on the day of Egypt's doom; for,
lo, it comes!

10   "Thus says the Lord GOD:
I will put an end to the wealth ᵇ of Egypt,
    by the hand of Nebuchadrez'zar king of Babylon.
¹¹ He and his people with him, the most terrible of the
    nations,
    shall be brought in to destroy the land;
and they shall draw their swords against Egypt,
    and fill the land with the slain.
¹² And I will dry up the Nile,
    and will sell the land into the hand of evil men;
I will bring desolation upon the land and everything in it.
    by the hand of foreigners;
I, the LORD, have spoken.

13   "Thus says the Lord GOD:
I will destroy the idols,
    and put an end to the images, in Memphis;
there shall no longer be a prince in the land of Egypt;
    so I will put fear in the land of Egypt.
¹⁴ I will make Pathros a desolation,
    and will set fire to Zo'an,
    and will execute acts of judgment upon Thebes.
¹⁵ And I will pour my wrath upon Pelusium,
    the stronghold of Egypt,
    and cut off the multitude of Thebes.
¹⁶ And I will set fire to Egypt;
    Pelusium shall be in great agony;
Thebes shall be breached,
    and its walls broken down.ᶜ
¹⁷ The young men of On and of Pibe'seth shall fall by the
    sword;
    and the women shall go into captivity.
¹⁸ At Tehaph'nehes the day shall be dark,
    when I break there the dominion of Egypt,
and her proud might shall come to an end;
    she shall be covered by a cloud,
    and her daughters shall go into captivity.
¹⁹ Thus I will execute acts of judgment upon Egypt.
    Then they will know that I am the LORD."
20   In the eleventh year, in the first month, on the seventh
day of the month, the word of the LORD came to me:
21 "Son of man, I have broken the arm of Pharaoh king of
Egypt; and lo, it has not been bound up, to heal it by
binding it with a bandage, so that it may become strong
22 to wield the sword. Therefore thus says the Lord GOD:
Behold, I am against Pharaoh king of Egypt, and will
break his arms, both the strong arm and the one that
was broken; and I will make the sword fall from his
23 hand. I will scatter the Egyptians among the nations, and
24 disperse them throughout the lands. And I will strengthen
the arms of the king of Babylon, and put my sword in
his hand; but I will break the arms of Pharaoh, and he
will groan before him like a man mortally wounded.
25 I will strengthen the arms of the king of Babylon, but
the arms of Pharaoh shall fall; and they shall know that
I am the LORD. When I put my sword into the hand of
the king of Babylon, he shall stretch it out against the
26 land of Egypt; and I will scatter the Egyptians among
the nations and disperse them throughout the countries.
Then they will know that I am the LORD."
31   In the eleventh year, in the third month, on the
    first day of the month, the word of the LORD came to
² me: "Son of man, say to Pharaoh king of Egypt and to
his multitude:
"Whom are you like in your greatness?
3   Behold, I will liken you to ᵈ a cedar in Lebanon,
with fair branches and forest shade,

ˣ Or multitude   ʸ Gk Compare Syr Vg: Heb Cub   ᶻ Gk: Heb they   ᵃ Gk Syr: Heb in ships   ᵇ Or multitude
ᶜ Cn: Heb and Memphis' distresses by day   ᵈ Cn: Heb Behold, Assyria

and of great height,
its top among the clouds.[e]
4 The waters nourished it,
the deep made it grow tall,
making its rivers flow [f]
round the place of its planting,
sending forth its streams
to all the trees of the forest.
5 So it towered high
above all the trees of the forest;
its boughs grew large
and its branches long,
from abundant water in its shoots.
6 All the birds of the air
made their nests in its boughs;
under its branches all the beasts of the field
brought forth their young;
and under its shadow
dwelt all great nations.
7 It was beautiful in its greatness,
in the length of its branches;
for its roots went down
to abundant waters.
8 The cedars in the garden of God could not rival it,
nor the fir trees equal its boughs;
the plane trees were as nothing
compared with its branches;
no tree in the garden of God
was like it in beauty.
9 I made it beautiful
in the mass of its branches,
and all the trees of Eden envied it,
that were in the garden of God.
10 "Therefore thus says the Lord GOD: Because it [g] towered high and set its top among the clouds,[h] and its
11 heart was proud of its height, I will give it into the hand of a mighty one of the nations; he shall surely deal with
12 it as its wickedness deserves. I have cast it out. Foreigners, the most terrible of the nations, will cut it down and leave it. On the mountains and in all the valleys its branches will fall, and its boughs will lie broken in all the watercourses of the land; and all the peoples of the
13 earth will go from its shadow and leave it. Upon its ruin will dwell all the birds of the air, and upon its branches
14 will be all the beasts of the field. All this is in order that no trees by the waters may grow to lofty height or set their tops among the clouds,[h] and that no trees that drink water may reach up to them in height; for they are all given over to death, to the nether world among mortal men, with those who go down to the Pit.
15 "Thus says the Lord GOD: When it goes down to Sheol I will make the deep mourn for [i] it, and restrain its rivers, and many waters shall be stopped; I will clothe Lebanon

in gloom for it, and all the trees of the field shall faint
16 because of it. I will make the nations quake at the sound of its fall, when I cast it down to Sheol with those who go down to the Pit; and all the trees of Eden, the choice and best of Lebanon, all that drink water, will be com-
17 forted in the nether world. They also shall go down to Sheol with it, to those who are slain by the sword; yea, those who dwelt under its shadow among the nations
18 shall perish.[j] Whom are you thus like in glory and in greatness among the trees of Eden? You shall be brought down with the trees of Eden to the nether world; you shall lie among the uncircumcised, with those who are slain by the sword.

"This is Pharaoh and all his multitude, says the Lord GOD."

32 In the twelfth year, in the twelfth month, on the first day of the month, the word of the LORD came to
2 me: "Son of man, raise a lamentation over Pharaoh king of Egypt, and say to him:

"You consider yourself a lion among the nations,
but you are like a dragon in the seas;
you burst forth in your rivers,
trouble the waters with your feet,
and foul their rivers.
3 Thus says the Lord GOD:
I will throw my net over you
with a host of many peoples;
and I [k] will haul you up in my dragnet.
4 And I will cast you on the ground,
on the open field I will fling you,
and will cause all the birds of the air to settle on you.
and I will gorge the beasts of the whole earth with you.
5 I will strew your flesh upon the mountains,
and fill the valleys with your carcass.[l]

6 I will drench the land even to the mountains
with your flowing blood;
and the watercourses will be full of you.
7 When I blot you out, I will cover the heavens,
and make their stars dark;
I will cover the sun with a cloud,
and the moon shall not give its light.
8 All the bright lights of heaven
will I make dark over you,
and put darkness upon your land,
says the Lord GOD.

e Gk: Heb *thick boughs*   f Gk: Heb *going*   g Syr Vg: Heb *you*   h Gk: Heb *thick boughs*
i Gk: Heb *mourn for, I have covered*   j Compare Gk: Heb obscure   k Gk Vg: Heb *they*
l Symmachus Syr Vg: Heb *your height*

9 "I will trouble the hearts of many peoples, when I carry you captive [m] among the nations, into the coun-
10 tries which you have not known. I will make many peoples appalled at you, and their kings shall shudder because of you, when I brandish my sword before them; they shall tremble every moment, every one for his own
11 life, on the day of your downfall. For thus says the Lord GOD: The sword of the king of Babylon shall come upon
12 you. I will cause your multitude to fall by the swords of mighty ones, all of them most terrible among the nations.

"They shall bring to nought the pride of Egypt,
and all its multitude shall perish.
13 I will destroy all its beasts
from beside many waters;
and no foot of man shall trouble them any more,
nor shall the hoofs of beasts trouble them.
14 Then I will make their waters clear,
and cause their rivers to run like oil, says the Lord GOD.
15 When I make the land of Egypt desolate
and when the land is stripped of all that fills it,
when I smite all who dwell in it,
then they will know that I am the LORD.
16 This is a lamentation which shall be chanted; the daughters of the nations shall chant it; over Egypt, and over all her multitude, shall they chant it, says the Lord GOD."

17 In the twelfth year, in the first month,[n] on the fifteenth day of the month, the word of the LORD came to me:
18 "Son of man, wail over the multitude of Egypt, and send them down, her and the daughters of majestic nations, to the nether world, to those who have gone down to the Pit:
19 'Whom do you surpass in beauty?
Go down, and be laid with the uncircumcised.'
20 They shall fall amid those who are slain by the sword,[o]
21 and with her shall lie all her multitudes.[p] The mighty chiefs shall speak of them, with their helpers, out of the midst of Sheol: 'They have come down, they lie still, the uncircumcised, slain by the sword.'
22 "Assyria is there, and all her company, their graves round about her, all of them slain, fallen by the sword;
23 whose graves are set in the uttermost parts of the Pit, and her company is round about her grave; all of them slain, fallen by the sword, who spread terror in the land of the living.
24 "Elam is there, and all her multitude about her grave; all of them slain, fallen by the sword, who went down uncircumcised into the nether world, who spread terror in the land of the living, and they bear their shame with
25 those who go down to the Pit. They have made her a bed among the slain with all her multitude, their graves round about her, all of them uncircumcised, slain by the

sword; for terror of them was spread in the land of the living, and they bear their shame with those who go down to the Pit; they are placed among the slain.
26 "Meshech and Tubal are there, and all their multitude, their graves round about them, all of them uncircumcised, slain by the sword; for they spread terror in the land of
27 the living. And they do not lie with the fallen mighty men of old [q] who went down to Sheol with their weapons of war, whose swords were laid under their heads, and whose shields [r] are upon their bones; for the terror of the
28 mighty men was in the land of the living. So you shall be broken and lie among the uncircumcised, with those who are slain by the sword.
29 "Edom is there, her kings and all her princes, who for all their might are laid with those who are slain by the sword; they lie with the uncircumcised, with those who go down to the Pit.
30 "The princes of the north are there, all of them, and all the Sido'nians, who have gone down in shame with the slain, for all the terror which they caused by their might; they lie uncircumcised with those who are slain by the sword, and bear their shame with those who go down to the Pit.
31 "When Pharaoh sees them, he will comfort himself for all his multitude, Pharaoh and all his army, slain
32 by the sword, says the Lord GOD. For he [s] spread terror in the land of the living; therefore he shall be laid among the uncircumcised, with those who are slain by the sword, Pharaoh and all his multitude, says the Lord GOD."

RESTORATION OF ISRAEL

33 The word of the LORD came to me: "Son of man, speak to your people and say to them, If I bring the sword upon a land, and the people of the land take a man
3 from among them, and make him their watchman; and if he sees the sword coming upon the land and blows the
4 trumpet and warns the people; then if any one who hears

the sound of the trumpet does not take warning, and the sword comes and takes him away, his blood shall be upon
5 his own head. He heard the sound of the trumpet, and did not take warning; his blood shall be upon himself. But if he had taken warning, he would have saved his
6 life. But if the watchman sees the sword coming and

m Gk: Heb *bring your destruction*   n Gk: Heb lacks *in the first month*   o Gk Syr: Heb *sword, the sword is delivered*
p Gk: Heb *they have drawn her away and all her multitudes*   q Gk Old Latin: Heb *of the uncircumcised*   r Cn: Heb *iniquities*
s Cn: Heb *I*

does not blow the trumpet, so that the people are not warned, and the sword comes, and takes any one of them; that man is taken away in his iniquity, but his blood I will require at the watchman's hand.

7 "So you, son of man, I have made a watchman for the house of Israel; whenever you hear a word from my 8 mouth, you shall give them warning from me. If I say to the wicked, O wicked man, you shall surely die, and you do not speak to warn the wicked to turn from his way, that wicked man shall die in his iniquity, but his blood I will 9 require at your hand. But if you warn the wicked to turn from his way, and he does not turn from his way; he shall die in his iniquity, but you will have saved your life.

10 "And you, son of man, say to the house of Israel, Thus have you said: 'Our transgressions and our sins are upon us, and we waste away because of them; how then 11 can we live?' Say to them, As I live, says the Lord God, I have no pleasure in the death of the wicked, but that the wicked turn from his way and live; turn back, turn back from your evil ways; for why will you die, O house 12 of Israel? And you, son of man, say to your people, The righteousness of the righteous shall not deliver him when he transgresses; and as for the wickedness of the wicked, he shall not fall by it when he turns from his wickedness; and the righteous shall not be able to live 13 by his righteousness t when he sins. Though I say to the righteous that he shall surely live, yet if he trusts in his righteousness and commits iniquity, none of his righteous deeds shall be remembered; but in the iniquity that he 14 has committed he shall die. Again, though I say to the wicked, 'You shall surely die,' yet if he turns from his 15 sin and does what is lawful and right, if the wicked restores the pledge, gives back what he has taken by robbery, and walks in the statutes of life, committing no 16 iniquity; he shall surely live, he shall not die. None of the sins that he has committed shall be remembered against him; he has done what is lawful and right, he shall surely live.

17 "Yet your people say, 'The way of the Lord is not just'; 18 when it is their own way that is not just. When the righteous turns from his righteousness, and commits 19 iniquity, he shall die for it. And when the wicked turns from his wickedness, and does what is lawful and right, 20 he shall live by it. Yet you say, 'The way of the Lord is not just.' O house of Israel, I will judge each of you according to his ways."

21 In the twelfth year of our exile, in the tenth month, on the fifth day of the month, a man who had escaped from Jerusalem came to me and said, "The city has 22 fallen." Now the hand of the Lord had been upon me the evening before the fugitive came; and he had opened my mouth by the time the man came to me in the morning; so my mouth was opened, and I was no longer dumb.

23, 24 The word of the Lord came to me: "Son of man, the inhabitants of these waste places in the land of Israel keep saying, 'Abraham was only one man, yet he got possession of the land; but we are many; the land is 25 surely given us to possess.' Therefore say to them, Thus says the Lord God: You eat flesh with the blood, and lift up your eyes to your idols, and shed blood; shall you 26 then possess the land? You resort to the sword, you commit abominations and each of you defiles his 27 neighbor's wife; shall you then possess the land? Say this to them, Thus says the Lord God: As I live, surely those who are in the waste places shall fall by the sword; and him that is in the open field I will give to the beasts to be devoured; and those who are in strongholds and 28 in caves shall die by pestilence. And I will make the land a desolation and a waste; and her proud might shall come to an end; and the mountains of Israel shall 29 be so desolate that none will pass through. Then they will know that I am the Lord, when I have made the land a desolation and a waste because of all their abominations which they have committed.

30 "As for you, son of man, your people who talk together about you by the walls and at the doors of the houses, say to one another, each to his brother, 'Come, and hear what the word is that comes forth from the 31 Lord.' And they come to you as people come, and they sit before you as my people, and they hear what you say but they will not do it; for with their lips they show much 32 love, but their heart is set on their gain. And, lo, you are to them like one who sings love songs u with a beautiful voice and plays well on an instrument, for they hear 33 what you say, but they will not do it. When this comes —and come it will!—then they will know that a prophet has been among them."

Government to Be Replaced

34 2 The word of the Lord came to me: "Son of man, prophesy against the shepherds of Israel, prophesy, and say to them, even to the shepherds, Thus says the Lord God: Ho, shepherds of Israel who have been feeding 3 yourselves! Should not shepherds feed the sheep? You eat the fat, you clothe yourselves with the wool, you slaughter the fatlings; but you do not feed the sheep. 4 The weak you have not strengthened, the sick you have not healed, the crippled you have not bound up, the strayed you have not brought back, the lost you have not sought, and with force and harshness you have ruled 5 them. So they were scattered, because there was no shepherd; and they became food for all the wild beasts. 6 My sheep were scattered, they wandered over all the mountains and on every high hill; my sheep were scattered over all the face of the earth, with none to search or seek for them.

t Heb *by it* u Cn: Heb *like a love song*

7 "Therefore, you shepherds, hear the word of the LORD:
8 As I live, says the Lord GOD, because my sheep have become a prey, and my sheep have become food for all the wild beasts, since there was no shepherd; and because my shepherds have not searched for my sheep, but the shepherds have fed themselves, and have not fed my
9 sheep; therefore, you shepherds, hear the word of the
10 LORD: Thus says the Lord GOD, Behold, I am against the shepherds; and I will require my sheep at their hand, and put a stop to their feeding the sheep; no longer shall the shepherds feed themselves. I will rescue my sheep from their mouths, that they may not be food for them.

11 "For thus says the Lord GOD: Behold, I, I myself will
12 search for my sheep, and will seek them out. As a shepherd seeks out his flock when some of his sheep[v] have been scattered abroad, so will I seek out my sheep; and I will rescue them from all places where they have been scattered on a day of clouds and thick darkness.
13 And I will bring them out from the peoples, and gather them from the countries, and will bring them into their own land; and I will feed them on the mountains of Israel, by the fountains, and in all the inhabited places of
14 the country. I will feed them with good pasture, and upon the mountain heights of Israel shall be their pasture; there they shall lie down in good grazing land, and on fat pasture they shall feed on the mountains of Israel.
15 I myself will be the shepherd of my sheep, and I will
16 make them lie down, says the Lord GOD. I will seek the lost, and I will bring back the strayed, and I will bind up the crippled, and I will strengthen the weak, and the fat and the strong I will watch over;[w] I will feed them in justice.
17 "As for you, my flock, thus says the Lord GOD: Behold, I judge between sheep and sheep, rams and he-goats.
18 Is it not enough for you to feed on the good pasture, that you must tread down with your feet the rest of your pasture; and to drink of clear water, that you must foul
19 the rest with your feet? And must my sheep eat what you have trodden with your feet, and drink what you have fouled with your feet?
20 "Therefore, thus says the Lord GOD to them: Behold, I, I myself will judge between the fat sheep and the lean
21 sheep. Because you push with side and shoulder, and thrust at all the weak with your horns, till you have
22 scattered them abroad, I will save my flock, they shall no longer be a prey; and I will judge between sheep and
23 sheep. And I will set up over them one shepherd, my servant David, and he shall feed them: he shall feed them
24 and be their shepherd. And I, the LORD, will be their God, and my servant David shall be prince among them; I, the LORD, have spoken.
25 "I will make with them a covenant of peace and banish wild beasts from the land, so that they may dwell securely
26 in the wilderness and sleep in the woods. And I will make them and the places round about my hill a blessing; and I will send down the showers in their season; they shall
27 be showers of blessing. And the trees of the field shall yield their fruit, and the earth shall yield its increase, and they shall be secure in their land; and they shall know that I am the Lord, when I break the bars of their yoke, and deliver them from the hand of those who enslaved
28 them. They shall no more be a prey to the nations, nor shall the beasts of the land devour them; they shall dwell
29 securely, and none shall make them afraid. And I will provide for them prosperous[x] plantations so that they shall no more be consumed with hunger in the land,
30 and no longer suffer the reproach of the nations. And they shall know that I, the LORD their God, am with them, and that they, the house of Israel, are my people, says
31 the Lord GOD. And you are my sheep, the sheep of my pasture,[y] and I am your God, says the Lord GOD."

35 ²The word of the LORD came to me: "Son of man, set your face against Mount Se'ir, and prophesy
3 against it, and say to it, Thus says the Lord GOD: Behold, I am against you, Mount Se'ir, and I will stretch out my hand against you, and I will make you a desolation and
4 a waste. I will lay your cities waste, and you shall become a desolation; and you shall know that I am the LORD.
5 Because you cherished perpetual enmity, and gave over the people of Israel to the power of the sword at the time of their calamity, at the time of their final punish-
6 ment; therefore, as I live, says the Lord GOD, I will prepare you for blood, and blood shall pursue you; because you are guilty of blood,[z] therefore blood shall
7 pursue you. I will make Mount Se'ir a waste and a desolation; and I will cut off from it all who come and
8 go. And I will fill your mountains with the slain; on your hills and in your valleys and in all your ravines
9 those slain with the sword shall fall. I will make you a perpetual desolation, and your cities shall not be inhabited. Then you will know that I am the LORD.
10 "Because you said, 'These two nations and these two countries shall be mine, and we will take possession of
11 them,'—although the LORD was there—therefore, as I live, says the Lord GOD, I will deal with you according to the anger and envy which you showed because of your hatred against them; and I will make myself known
12 among you,[a] when I judge you. And you shall know that I, the LORD, have heard all the revilings which you

---

v Cn: Heb *when he is among his sheep*   w Gk Syr Vg: Heb *destroy*   x Gk Syr Old Latin: Heb *for renown*
y Gk Old Latin: Heb *pasture you are men*   z Gk: Heb *you have hated blood*   a Gk: Heb *them*

588

uttered against the mountains of Israel, saying, 'They are
13 laid desolate, they are given us to devour.' And you magnified yourselves against me with your mouth, and
14 multiplied your words against me; I heard it. Thus says the Lord GOD: For the rejoicing of the whole earth I
15 will make you desolate. As you rejoiced over the inheritance of the house of Israel, because it was desolate, so I will deal with you; you shall be desolate, Mount Se'ir, and all Edom, all of it. Then they will know that I am the LORD.

36 "And you, son of man, prophesy to the mountains of Israel, and say, O mountains of Israel, hear the
2 word of the LORD. Thus says the Lord GOD: Because the enemy said of you, 'Aha!' and, 'The ancient heights
3 have become our possession,' therefore prophesy, and say, Thus says the Lord GOD: Because, yea, because they made you desolate, and crushed you from all sides, so that you became the possession of the rest of the nations, and you became the talk and evil gossip of the people;
4 therefore, O mountains of Israel, hear the word of the Lord GOD: Thus says the Lord GOD to the mountains and the hills, the ravines and the valleys, the desolate wastes and the deserted cities, which have become a prey and
5 derision to the rest of the nations round about; therefore thus says the Lord GOD: I speak in my hot jealousy against the rest of the nations, and against all Edom, who gave my land to themselves as a possession with wholehearted joy and utter contempt, that they might
6 possess b it and plunder it. Therefore prophesy concerning the land of Israel, and say to the mountains and hills, to the ravines and valleys, Thus says the Lord GOD: Behold, I speak in my jealous wrath, because you
7 have suffered the reproach of the nations; therefore thus says the Lord GOD: I swear that the nations that are round about you shall themselves suffer reproach.

8 "But you, O mountains of Israel, shall shoot forth your branches, and yield your fruit to my people Israel;
9 for they will soon come home. For, behold, I am for you, and I will turn to you, and you shall be tilled and
10 sown; and I will multiply men upon you, the whole house of Israel, all of it; the cities shall be inhabited and
11 the waste places rebuilt; and I will multiply upon you man and beast; and they shall increase and be fruitful; and I will cause you to be inhabited as in your former times, and will do more good to you than ever before.
12 Then you will know that I am the LORD. Yea, I will let men walk upon you, even my people Israel; and they shall possess you, and you shall be their inheritance, and
13 you shall no longer bereave them of children. Thus says the Lord GOD: Because men say to you, 'You devour
14 men, and you bereave your nation of children,' therefore you shall no longer devour men and no longer bereave
15 your nation of children, says the Lord GOD; and I will

b One Ms: Heb drive out

not let you hear any more the reproach of the nations, and you shall no longer bear the disgrace of the peoples and no longer cause your nation to stumble, says the Lord GOD."

A New Heart and a New Spirit

16, 17 The word of the LORD came to me: "Son of man, when the house of Israel dwelt in their own land, they defiled it by their ways and their doings; their conduct before me was like the uncleanness of a woman in her
18 impurity. So I poured out my wrath upon them for the blood which they had shed in the land, for the idols
19 with which they had defiled it. I scattered them among the nations, and they were dispersed through the countries; in accordance with their conduct and their deeds
20 I judged them. But when they came to the nations, wherever they came, they profaned my holy name, in that men said of them, 'These are the people of the LORD,
21 and yet they had to go out of his land.' But I had concern for my holy name, which the house of Israel caused to be profaned among the nations to which they came.

22 "Therefore say to the house of Israel, Thus says the Lord GOD: It is not for your sake, O house of Israel, that I am about to act, but for the sake of my holy name, which you have profaned among the nations to which
23 you came. And I will vindicate the holiness of my great name, which has been profaned among the nations, and which you have profaned among them; and the nations will know that I am the LORD, says the Lord GOD, when
24 through you I vindicate my holiness before their eyes. For I will take you from the nations, and gather you from all the countries, and bring you into your own land.
25 I will sprinkle clean water upon you, and you shall be clean from all your uncleannesses, and from all your
26 idols I will cleanse you. A new heart I will give you, and a new spirit I will put within you; and I will take out of your flesh the heart of stone and give you a heart of
27 flesh. And I will put my spirit within you, and cause you to walk in my statutes and be careful to observe my
28 ordinances. You shall dwell in the land which I gave to your fathers; and you shall be my people, and I will be
29 your God. And I will deliver you from all your uncleannesses; and I will summon the grain and make it
30 abundant and lay no famine upon you. I will make the fruit of the tree and the increase of the field abundant, that you may never again suffer the disgrace of famine
31 among the nations. Then you will remember your evil ways, and your deeds that were not good; and you will loathe yourselves for your iniquities and your abominable
32 deeds. It is not for your sake that I will act, says the Lord GOD; let that be known to you. Be ashamed and confounded for your ways, O house of Israel.

33 "Thus says the Lord GOD: On the day that I cleanse you

from all your iniquities, I will cause the cities to be
34 inhabited, and the waste places shall be rebuilt. And the
land that was desolate shall be tilled, instead of being the
desolation that it was in the sight of all who passed by.
35 And they will say, 'This land that was desolate has
become like the garden of Eden; and the waste and
desolate and ruined cities are now inhabited and fortified.'
36 Then the nations that are left round about you shall know
that I, the LORD, have rebuilt the ruined places, and re-
planted that which was desolate; I, the LORD, have spoken,
and I will do it.

37 "Thus says the Lord GOD: This also I will let the
house of Israel ask me to do for them: to increase their
38 men like a flock. Like the flock for sacrifices,[c] like the
flock at Jerusalem during her appointed feasts, so shall the
waste cities be filled with flocks of men. Then they will
know that I am the LORD."

God's Spirit for Dry Bones

37 The hand of the LORD was upon me, and he
brought me out by the Spirit of the LORD, and set
me down in the midst of the valley;[d] it was full of bones.
2 And he led me round among them; and behold, there
were very many upon the valley;[d] and lo, they were
3 very dry. And he said to me, "Son of man, can these
bones live?" And I answered, "O Lord GOD, thou know-
4 est." Again he said to me, "Prophesy to these bones, and
say to them, O dry bones, hear the word of the LORD.
5 Thus says the Lord GOD to these bones: Behold, I will
6 cause breath[e] to enter you, and you shall live. And I
will lay sinews upon you, and will cause flesh to come
upon you, and cover you with skin, and put breath[e] in
you, and you shall live; and you shall know that I am
the LORD."

7 So I prophesied as I was commanded; and as I
prophesied, there was a noise, and behold, a rattling;
8 and the bones came together, bone to its bone. And as I
looked, there were sinews on them, and flesh had come
upon them, and skin had covered them; but there was no
9 breath in them. Then he said to me, "Prophesy to the
breath, prophesy, son of man, and say to the breath,[f]
Thus says the Lord GOD: Come from the four winds, O
breath,[f] and breathe upon these slain, that they may live."
10 So I prophesied as he commanded me, and and the breath
came into them, and they lived, and stood upon their feet,
an exceedingly great host.

11 Then he said to me, "Son of man, these bones are the
whole house of Israel. Behold, they say, 'Our bones are
dried up, and our hope is lost; we are clean cut off.'
12 Therefore prophesy, and say to them, Thus says the Lord
GOD: Behold, I will open your graves, and raise you
from your graves, O my people; and I will bring you
13 home into the land of Israel. And you shall know that I

am the LORD, when I open your graves, and raise you
14 from your graves, O my people. And I will put my Spirit
within you, and you shall live, and I will place you in
your own land; then you shall know that I, the LORD,
have spoken and I have done it, says the LORD."

15, 16 The word of the LORD came to me: "Son of man,
take a stick and write on it, 'For Judah, and the children
of Israel associated with him'; then take another stick
and write upon it, 'For Joseph (the stick of E'phraim)
17 and all the house of Israel associated with him'; and join
them together into one stick, that they may become one
18 in your hand. And when your people say to you, 'Will
19 you not show us what you mean by these?' say to them,
Thus says the Lord GOD: Behold, I am about to take the
stick of Joseph (which is in the hand of E'phraim) and
the tribes of Israel associated with him; and I will join[g]
with it the stick of Judah, and make them one stick, that
20 they may be one in my hand. When the sticks on which
21 you write are in your hand before their eyes, then say
to them, Thus says the Lord GOD: Behold, I will take the
people of Israel from the nations among which they have
gone, and will gather them from all sides, and bring them
22 to their own land; and I will make them one nation in
the land, upon the mountains of Israel; and one king
shall be king over them all; and they shall be no longer
two nations, and no longer divided into two kingdoms.
23 They shall not defile themselves any more with their
idols and their detestable things, or with any of their
transgressions; but I will save them from all the backslidings in which they have sinned, and will cleanse them;
and they shall be my people, and I will be their God.

24 "My servant David shall be king over them; and they
shall all have one shepherd. They shall follow my ordi-
25 nances and be careful to observe my statutes. They shall
dwell in the land where your fathers dwelt that I gave to
my servant Jacob; they and their children and their
children's children shall dwell there for ever; and
26 David my servant shall be their prince for ever. I
will make a covenant of peace with them; it shall be
an everlasting covenant with them; and I will bless[h]
them and multiply them, and will set my sanctuary
27 in the midst of them for evermore. My dwelling place
shall be with them; and I will be their God, and they shall
28 be my people. Then the nations will know that I the
LORD sanctify Israel, when my sanctuary is in the midst
of them for evermore."

---

[c] Heb *flock of holy things*   [d] Or *plain*   [e] Or *spirit*   [f] Or *wind* or *spirit*   [g] Heb *join them*   [h] Tg: Heb *give*

38 The word of the LORD came to me: "Son of man, set your face toward Gog, of the land of Magog, the chief prince of Meshech and Tubal, and prophesy against ³ him and say, Thus says the Lord GOD: Behold, I am against you, O Gog, chief prince of Meshech and Tubal; ⁴ and I will turn you about, and put hooks into your jaws, and I will bring you forth, and all your army, horses and horsemen, all of them clothed in full armor, a great company, all of them with buckler and shield, wielding ⁵ swords; Persia, Cush, and Put are with them, all of them ⁶ with shield and helmet; Gomer and all his hordes; Beth-togar′mah from the uttermost parts of the north with all his hordes—many peoples are with you.

⁷ "Be ready and keep ready, you and all the hosts that are assembled about you, and be a guard for them. ⁸ After many days you will be mustered; in the latter years you will go against the land that is restored from war, the land where people were gathered from many nations upon the mountains of Israel, which had been a continual waste; its people were brought out from the ⁹ nations and now dwell securely, all of them. You will advance, coming on like a storm, you will be like a cloud covering the land, you and all your hordes, and many peoples with you.

¹⁰ "Thus says the Lord GOD: On that day thoughts will come into your mind, and you will devise an evil scheme ¹¹ and say, 'I will go up against the land of unwalled villages; I will fall upon the quiet people who dwell securely, all of them dwelling without walls, and having ¹² no bars or gates'; to seize spoil and carry off plunder; to assail the waste places which are now inhabited, and the people who were gathered from the nations, who have gotten cattle and goods, who dwell at the center of the ¹³ earth. Sheba and Dedan and the merchants of Tarshish and all its villages will say to you, 'Have you come to seize spoil? Have you assembled your hosts to carry off plunder, to carry away silver and gold, to take away cattle and goods, to seize great spoil?'

¹⁴ "Therefore, son of man, prophesy, and say to Gog, Thus says the Lord GOD: On that day when my people Israel are dwelling securely, you will bestir yourself ⁱ ¹⁵ and come from your place out of the uttermost parts of the north, you and many peoples with you, all of them ¹⁶ riding on horses, a great host, a mighty army; you will come up against my people Israel, like a cloud covering the land. In the latter days I will bring you against my land, that the nations may know me, when through you, O Gog, I vindicate my holiness before their eyes.

¹⁷ "Thus says the Lord GOD: Are you he of whom I spoke in former days by my servants the prophets of Israel, who in those days prophesied for years that I would ¹⁸ bring you against them? But on that day, when Gog shall come against the land of Israel, says the Lord GOD, my

¹⁹ wrath will be roused. For in my jealousy and in my blazing wrath I declare, On that day there shall be a great ²⁰ shaking in the land of Israel; the fish of the sea, and the birds of the air, and the beasts of the field, and all creeping things that creep on the ground, and all the men that are upon the face of the earth, shall quake at my presence, and the mountains shall be thrown down, and the cliffs shall fall, and every wall shall tumble to the ²¹ ground. I will summon every kind of terror ʲ against Gog,ᵏ says the Lord GOD; every man's sword will be ²² against his brother. With pestilence and bloodshed I will enter into judgment with him; and I will rain upon him and his hordes and the many peoples that are with him, torrential rains and hailstones, fire and brimstone. ²³ So I will show my greatness and my holiness and make myself known in the eyes of many nations. Then they will know that I am the LORD.

39 "And you, son of man, prophesy against Gog, and say, Thus says the Lord GOD: Behold, I am against ² you, O Gog, chief prince of Meshech and Tubal; and I will turn you about and drive you forward, and bring you up from the uttermost parts of the north, and lead ³ you against the mountains of Israel; then I will strike your bow from your left hand, and will make your arrows ⁴ drop out of your right hand. You shall fall upon the mountains of Israel, you and all your hordes and the peoples that are with you; I will give you to birds of prey of every sort and to the wild beasts to be devoured. ⁵ You shall fall in the open field; for I have spoken, says ⁶ the Lord GOD. I will send fire on Magog and on those who dwell securely in the coastlands; and they shall know that I am the LORD.

⁷ "And my holy name I will make known in the midst of my people Israel; and I will not let my holy name be profaned any more; and the nations shall know that ⁸ I am the LORD, the Holy One in Israel. Behold, it is coming and it will be brought about, says the Lord GOD. That is the day of which I have spoken.

⁹ "Then those who dwell in the cities of Israel will go forth and make fires of the weapons and burn them, shields and bucklers, bows and arrows, handpikes and spears, and they will make fires of them for seven years; ¹⁰ so that they will not need to take wood out of the field or cut down any out of the forests, for they will make their fires of the weapons; they will despoil those who despoiled them, and plunder those who plundered them, says the Lord GOD.

¹¹ "On that day I will give to Gog a place for burial in Israel, the Valley of the Travelers ˡ east of the sea; it will block the travelers, for there Gog and all his multitude will be buried; it will be called the Valley of Hamon-gog.ᵐ ¹² For seven months the house of Israel will be burying ¹³ them, in order to cleanse the land. All the people of the

ⁱ Gk: Heb *will you not know?* ʲ Gk: Heb *a sword to all my mountains* ᵏ Heb *him* ˡ Or *Abarim*
ᵐ That is *the multitude of Gog*

land will bury them; and it will redound to their honor on the day that I show my glory, says the Lord GOD. [14] They will set apart men to pass through the land continually and bury [n] those remaining upon the face of the land, so as to cleanse it; at the end of seven months they [15] will make their search. And when these pass through the land and any one sees a man's bone, then he shall set up a sign by it, till the buriers have buried it in the [16] Valley of Hamon-gog. (A city Hamo'nah [o] is there also.) Thus shall they cleanse the land.

[17] "As for you, son of man, thus says the Lord GOD: Speak to the birds of every sort and to all beasts of the field, 'Assemble and come, gather from all sides to the sacrificial feast which I am preparing for you, a great sacrificial feast upon the mountains of Israel, and you [18] shall eat flesh and drink blood. You shall eat the flesh of the mighty, and drink the blood of the princes of the earth—of rams, of lambs, and of goats, of bulls, all of [19] them fatlings of Bashan. And you shall eat fat till you are filled, and drink blood till you are drunk, at the [20] sacrificial feast which I am preparing for you. And you shall be filled at my table with horses and riders, with mighty men and all kinds of warriors,' says the Lord GOD.

[21] "And I will set my glory among the nations; and all the nations shall see my judgment which I have executed, [22] and my hand which I have laid on them. The house of Israel shall know that I am the LORD their God, from that [23] day forward. And the nations shall know that the house of Israel went into captivity for their iniquity, because they dealt so treacherously with me that I hid my face from them and gave them into the hand of their [24] adversaries, and they all fell by the sword. I dealt with them according to their uncleanness and their transgressions, and hid my face from them.

[25] "Therefore thus says the Lord GOD: Now I will restore the fortunes of Jacob, and have mercy upon the whole house of Israel; and I will be jealous for my holy name. [26] They shall forget their shame, and all the treachery they have practiced against me, when they dwell securely in [27] their land with none to make them afraid, when I have brought them back from the peoples and gathered them from their enemies' lands, and through them have vindi- [28] cated my holiness in the sight of many nations. Then they shall know that I am the LORD their God because I sent them into exile among the nations, and then gathered them into their own land. I will leave none of them [29] remaining among the nations any more; and I will not hide my face any more from them, when I pour out my Spirit upon the house of Israel, says the Lord GOD."

VISION OF THE RESTORED COMMUNITY

40 In the twenty-fifth year of our exile, at the beginning of the year, on the tenth day of the month, in the fourteenth year after the city was conquered, on that [2] very day, the hand of the LORD was upon me, and brought me in the visions of God into the land of Israel, and set me down upon a very high mountain, on which was a [3] structure like a city opposite me. [p] When he brought me there, behold, there was a man, whose appearance was like bronze, with a line of flax and a measuring reed in [4] his hand; and he was standing in the gateway. And the man said to me, "Son of man, look with your eyes, and hear with your ears, and set your mind upon all that I shall show you, for you were brought here in order that I might show it to you; declare all that you see to the house of Israel."

THE TEMPLE BUILDINGS

[5] And behold, there was a wall all around the outside of the temple area, and the length of the measuring reed in the man's hand was six long cubits, each being a cubit and a handbreadth in length; so he measured the thickness of the wall, one reed; [6] and the height, one reed. Then he went into the gateway facing east, going up its steps, and measured the threshold of the gate, [7] one reed deep; [q] and the side rooms, one reed long, and one reed broad; and the space between the side rooms, five cubits; and the threshold of the gate by the vestibule of the gate at [8] the inner end, one reed. Then he measured the vestibule of the [9] gateway, eight cubits; and its jambs, two cubits; and the vesti- [10] bule of the gate was at the inner end. And there were three side rooms on either side of the east gate; the three were of the same size; and the jambs on either side were of the same size. [11] Then he measured the breadth of the opening of the gateway, ten cubits; and the breadth of the gateway, thirteen cubits. [12] There was a barrier before the side rooms, one cubit on either [13] side; and the side rooms were six cubits on either side. Then he measured the gate from the back [r] of the one side room to the back [r] of the other, a breadth of five and twenty cubits, [14] from door to door. He measured also the vestibule, twenty cubits; and round about the vestibule of the gateway was the [15] court. [s] From the front of the gate at the entrance to the end [16] of the inner vestibule of the gate was fifty cubits. And the gateway had windows round about, narrowing inwards into their jambs in the side rooms, and likewise the vestibule had windows round about inside, and on the jambs were palm trees. [17] Then he brought me into the outer court; and behold, there were chambers and pavement, round about the court; thirty [18] chambers fronted on the pavement. And the pavement ran along the side of the gates, corresponding to the length of the gates; [19] this was the lower pavement. Then he measured the distance from the inner front of [t] the lower gate to the outer front of the inner court, a hundred cubits.

[20] Then he went before me to the north, and behold, there was a gate [u] which faced toward the north, belonging to the outer [21] court. He measured its length and its breadth. Its side rooms, three on either side, and its jambs and its vestibule were of the same size as those of the first gate; its length was fifty cubits, [22] and its breadth twenty-five cubits. And its windows, its vestibule, and its palm trees were of the same size as those of the gate which faced toward the east; and seven steps led up [23] to it; and its vestibule was on the inside. And opposite the gate on the north, as on the east, was a gate to the inner court; and he measured from gate to gate, a hundred cubits.

[24] And he led me toward the south, and behold, there was a gate on the south; and he measured its jambs and its vestibule; they [25] had the same size as the others. And there were windows round about in it and in its vestibule, like the windows of the others; its length was fifty cubits, and its breadth twenty-five cubits. [26] And there were seven steps leading up to it, and its vestibule was on the inside; and it had palm trees on its jambs, one on [27] either side. And there was a gate on the south of the inner court; and he measured from gate to gate toward the south, a hundred cubits.

[28] Then he brought me to the inner court by the south gate, and he measured the south gate; it was of the same size as the [29] others. Its side rooms, its jambs, and its vestibule were of the

[n] Gk Syr: Heb *bury the travelers*   [o] That is *Multitude*   [p] Gk: Heb *on the south*   [q] Heb *deep, and one threshold, one reed deep*
[r] Compare Gk: Heb *roof*   [s] Compare Gk: Heb *and he made the jambs sixty cubits, and to the jamb of the court was the gateway round about*
[t] Compare Gk: Heb *from before*   [u] Gk: Heb *a hundred cubits on the east and on the north.* [20] *And the gate*

same size as the others; and there were windows round about in it and in its vestibule; its length was fifty cubits, and its
[30] breadth twenty-five cubits. And there were vestibules round
[31] about, twenty-five cubits long and five cubits broad. Its vestibule faced the outer court, and palm trees were on its jambs, and its stairway had eight steps.

[32] Then he brought me to the inner court on the east side, and he measured the gate; it was of the same size as the others.
[33] Its side rooms, its jambs, and its vestibule were of the same size as the others; and there were windows round about in it and in its vestibule; its length was fifty cubits, and its breadth
[34] twenty-five cubits. Its vestibule faced the outer court, and it had palm trees on its jambs, one on either side; and its stairway had eight steps.

[35] Then he brought me to the north gate, and he measured it; it
[36] had the same size as the others. Its side rooms, its jambs, and its vestibule were of the same size as the others; [v] and it had windows round about; its length was fifty cubits, and its breadth
[37] twenty-five cubits. Its vestibule [w] faced the outer court, and it had palm trees on its jambs, one on either side; and its stairway had eight steps.

[38] There was a chamber with its door in the vestibule of the
[39] gate,[x] where the burnt offering was to be washed. And in the vestibule of the gate were two tables on either side, on which the burnt offering and the sin offering and the guilt offering
[40] were to be slaughtered. And on the outside of the vestibule [y] at the entrance of the north gate were two tables; and on the
[41] other side of the vestibule of the gate were two tables. Four tables were on the inside, and four tables on the outside of the gate, eight tables, on which the sacrifices were to be slaughtered.
[42] And there were also four tables of hewn stone for the burnt offering, a cubit and a half long, and a cubit and a half broad, and one cubit high, on which the instruments were to be laid with which the burnt offerings and the sacrifices were
[43] slaughtered. And hooks, a hand-breadth long, were fastened round about within. And on the tables the flesh of the offering was to be laid.

[44] Then he brought me from without into the inner court, and behold, there were two chambers [z] in the inner court, one [a] at the side of the north gate facing south, the other at the side of
[45] the south [b] gate facing north. And he said to me, This chamber which faces south is for the priests who have charge of the
[46] temple, and the chamber which faces north is for the priests who have charge of the altar; these are the sons of Zadok, who alone among the sons of Levi may come near to the
[47] Lord to minister to him. And he measured the court, a hundred cubits long, and a hundred cubits broad, foursquare; and the altar was in front of the temple.

[48] Then he brought me to the vestibule of the temple and measured the jambs of the vestibule, five cubits on either side; and the breadth of the gate was fourteen cubits; and the side-
[49] walls of the gate were three cubits [c] on either side. The length of the vestibule was twenty cubits, and the breadth twelve [d] cubits; and ten steps led up [e] to it; and there were pillars beside the jambs on either side.

The Nave

41 Then he brought me to the nave, and measured the jambs; on each side six cubits was the breadth of the
[2] jambs.[f] And the breadth of the entrance was ten cubits; and the sidewalls of the entrance were five cubits on either side; and he measured the length of the nave forty cubits, and its
[3] breadth, twenty cubits. Then he went into the inner room and measured the jambs of the entrance, two cubits; and the breadth of the entrance, six cubits; and the sidewalls [g] of the
[4] entrance, seven cubits. And he measured the length of the room, twenty cubits, and its breadth, twenty cubits, beyond the nave. And he said to me, This is the most holy place.
[5] Then he measured the wall of the temple, six cubits thick; and the breadth of the side chambers, four cubits, round about
[6] the temple. And the side chambers were in three stories, one over another, thirty in each story. There were offsets [h] all

around the wall of the temple to serve as supports for the side chambers, so that they should not be supported by the wall of
[7] the temple. And the side chambers became broader as they rose [i] from story to story, corresponding to the enlargement of the offset [j] from story to story round about the temple; on the side of the temple a stairway led upward, and thus one went up from the lowest story to the top story through the middle
[8] story. I saw also that the temple had a raised platform round about; the foundations of the side chambers measured a full
[9] reed of six long cubits. The thickness of the outer wall of the side chambers was five cubits; and the part of the platform which was left free was five cubits.[k] Between the platform [l] of
[10] the temple and the chambers of the court was a breadth of
[11] twenty cubits round about the temple on every side. And the doors of the side chambers opened on the part of the platform that was left free, one door toward the north, and another door toward the south; and the breadth of the part that was left free was five cubits round about.
[12] The building that was facing the temple yard on the west side was seventy cubits broad; and the wall of the building was five cubits thick round about, and its length ninety cubits.
[13] Then he measured the temple, a hundred cubits long; and the yard and the building with its walls, a hundred cubits long;
[14] also the breadth of the east front of the temple and the yard, a hundred cubits.
[15] Then he measured the length of the building facing the yard which was at the west and its walls [m] on either side, a hundred cubits.

The nave of the temple and the inner room and the outer [n]
[16] vestibule were paneled [o] and round about all three had windows with recessed [p] frames. Over against the threshold the temple was paneled with wood round about, from the floor up to the
[17] windows (now the windows were covered), to the space above the door, even to the inner room, and on the outside. And on all the walls round about in the inner room and the nave were
[18] carved likenesses [q] of cherubim and palm trees, a palm tree between cherub and cherub. Every cherub had two faces:
[19] the face of a man toward the palm tree on the one side, and the face of a young lion toward the palm tree on the other
[20] side. They were carved on the whole temple round about; from the floor to above the door cherubim and palm trees were carved on the wall.[r]
[21] The doorposts of the nave were squared; and in front of the
[22] holy place was something resembling an altar of wood, three cubits high, two cubits long, and two cubits broad; [s] its corners, its base,[t] and its walls were of wood. He said to me, "This
[23] is the table which is before the Lord." The nave and the
[24] holy place had each a double door. The doors had two leaves
[25] apiece, two swinging leaves for each door. And on the doors of the nave were carved cherubim and palm trees, such as were carved on the walls; and there was a canopy of wood in front
[26] of the vestibule outside. And there were recessed windows and palm trees on either side, on the sidewalls of the vestibule.[u]

The Priest's Chambers

42 Then he led me out into the inner [v] court, toward the north, and he brought me to the chambers which were opposite the temple yard and opposite the building on the north.
[2] The length of the building which was on the north side [w] was [x]
[3] a hundred cubits, and the breadth fifty cubits. Adjoining the twenty cubits which belonged to the inner court, and facing the pavement which belonged to the outer court, was gallery [y]
[4] against gallery [x] in three stories. And before the chambers was a passage inward, ten cubits wide and a hundred cubits long,[z]

[v] One Ms Compare verses 29 and 33: Heb lacks *were of the same size as the others*
[x] Cn: Heb *at the jambs of the gates*   [y] Cn: Heb *to him who goes up*   [w] Gk Vg Compare verses 26, 31, 34: Heb *jambs*
[z] Gk: Heb *and from without to the inner gate were chambers for singers*   [a] Gk: Heb *which*   [b] Gk: Heb *east*
[c] Gk: Heb *and the breadth of the gate was three cubits*   [d] Gk: Heb *eleven*   [e] Gk: Heb *and by steps which went up*
[f] Compare Gk: Heb *tent*   [g] Gk: Heb *breadth*   [h] Gk Compare 1 K 6.6: Heb *they entered*   [i] Cn: Heb *it was surrounded*
[j] Gk: Heb *for the encompassing of the temple*   [k] Syr: Heb lacks *five cubits*   [l] Cn: Heb *house of the side chambers*
[m] Cn: The meaning of the Hebrew term is unknown   [n] Gk: Heb *of the court*   [o] Gk: Heb *the thresholds*
[p] Cn Compare Gk 1 K 6.4: The meaning of the Hebrew term is unknown   [q] Cn: Heb *measures and carved*
[r] Cn Compare verse 25: Heb *and the wall*   [s] Gk: Heb lacks *two cubits broad*   [t] Gk: Heb *length*
[u] Cn: Heb *vestibule. And the side chambers of the temple and the canopies*   [v] Gk: Heb *outer*   [w] Gk: Heb *door*
[x] Gk: Heb *before the length*   [y] The meaning of the Hebrew word is unknown   [z] Gk Syr: Heb *a way of one cubit*

5 and their doors were on the north. Now the upper chambers were narrower, for the galleries [y] took more away from them than from the lower and middle chambers in the building. 6 For they were in three stories, and they had no pillars like the pillars of the outer [a] court; hence the upper chambers were set back from the ground more than the lower and the middle 7 ones. And there was a wall outside parallel to the chambers, toward the outer court, opposite the chambers, fifty cubits long. 8 For the chambers on the outer court were fifty cubits long, while those opposite the temple were a hundred cubits long. 9 Below these chambers was an entrance on the east side, as one 10 enters them from the outer court, where the outside wall begins.[b]

On the south [c] also, opposite the yard and opposite the 11 building, there were chambers with a passage in front of them; they were similar to the chambers on the north, of the same length and breadth, with the same exits [d] and arrangements and 12 doors. And below the south chambers was an entrance on the east side, where one enters the passage, and opposite them was a dividing wall.[e]

13 Then he said to me, "The north chambers and the south chambers opposite the yard are the holy chambers, where the priests who approach the Lord shall eat the most holy offerings; there they shall put the most holy offerings—the cereal offering, the sin offering, and the guilt offering, for the place is holy. 14 When the priests enter the holy place, they shall not go out of it into the outer court without laying there the garments in which they minister, for these are holy; they shall put on other garments before they go near to that which is for the people."

15 Now when he had finished measuring the interior of the temple area, he led me out by the gate which faced east, and 16 measured the temple area round about. He measured the east side with the measuring reed, five hundred cubits by the 17 measuring reed. Then he turned and measured [f] the north side, 18 five hundred cubits by the measuring reed. Then he turned and measured [f] the south side, five hundred cubits by the measuring 19 reed. Then he turned to the west side and measured, five 20 hundred cubits by the measuring reed. He measured it on the four sides. It had a wall around it, five hundred cubits long and five hundred cubits broad, to make a separation between the holy and the common.

The Altar of Burnt Offering

43 Afterward he brought me to the gate, the gate facing east. And behold, the glory of the God of Israel came from the east; and the sound of his coming was like the sound of 3 many waters; and the earth shone with his glory. And [g] the vision I saw was like the vision which I had seen when he came to destroy the city, and [h] like the vision which I had 4 seen by the river Chebar; and I fell upon my face. As the glory 5 of the Lord entered the temple by the gate facing east, the Spirit lifted me up, and brought me into the inner court; and behold, the glory of the Lord filled the temple.

6 While the man was standing beside me, I heard one speaking 7 to me out of the temple; and he said to me, "Son of man, this is the place of my throne and the place of the soles of my feet, where I will dwell in the midst of the people of Israel for ever. And the house of Israel shall no more defile my holy name, neither they, nor their kings, by their harlotry, and by 8 the dead bodies [i] of their kings, by setting their threshold by my threshold and their doorposts beside my doorposts, with only a wall between me and them. They have defiled my holy name by their abominations which they have committed, so I have 9 consumed them in my anger. Now let them put away their idolatry and the dead bodies [i] of their kings far from me, and I will dwell in their midst for ever.

10 "And you, son of man, describe to the house of Israel the temple and its appearance and plan,[j] that they may be ashamed 11 of their iniquities. And if they are ashamed of all that they have done, portray [k] the temple, its arrangement, its exits and its entrances, and its whole form; and make known to them all its ordinances and all its laws; and write it down in their sight, so that they may observe and perform all its laws [l] and 12 all its ordinances. This is the law of the temple: the whole territory round about upon the top of the mountain shall be most holy. Behold, this is the law of the temple.

13 "These are the dimensions of the altar by cubits (the cubit being a cubit and a handbreadth): its base shall be one cubit high,[m] and one cubit broad, with a rim of one span around its 14 edge. And this shall be the height [x] of the altar: from the base on the ground to the lower ledge, two cubits, with a breadth of one cubit; and from the smaller ledge to the larger ledge, four 15 cubits, with a breadth of one cubit; and the altar hearth, four cubits; and from the altar hearth projecting upward, four 16 horns, one cubit high.[n] The altar hearth shall be square, twelve 17 cubits long by twelve broad. The ledge also shall be square, fourteen cubits long by fourteen broad, with a rim around it half a cubit broad, and its base one cubit round about. The steps of the altar shall face east."

18 And he said to me, "Son of man, thus says the Lord God: These are the ordinances for the altar: On the day when it is erected for offering burnt offerings upon it and for throwing 19 blood against it, you shall give to the Levitical priests of the family of Zadok, who draw near to me to minister to me, says 20 the Lord God, a bull for a sin offering. And you shall take some of its blood, and put it on the four horns of the altar, and on the four corners of the ledge, and upon the rim round about; thus 21 you shall cleanse the altar and make atonement for it. You shall also take the bull of the sin offering, and it shall be burnt in the appointed place belonging to the temple, outside the 22 sacred area. And on the second day you shall offer a he-goat without blemish for a sin offering; and the altar shall be 23 cleansed, as it was cleansed with the bull. When you have finished cleansing it, you shall offer a bull without blemish 24 and a ram from the flock without blemish. You shall present them before the Lord, and the priests shall sprinkle salt upon 25 them and offer them up as a burnt offering to the Lord. For seven days you shall provide daily a goat for a sin offering; also a bull and a ram from the flock, without blemish, shall 26 be provided. Seven days they shall make atonement for the 27 altar and purify it, and so consecrate it. And when they have completed these days, then from the eighth day onward the priests shall offer upon the altar your burnt offerings and your peace offerings; and I will accept you, says the Lord God."

Rules of the Sanctuary

44 Then he brought me back to the outer gate of the sanctuary, which faces east; and it was shut. And he [o] said to me, "This gate shall remain shut; it shall not be opened, and no one shall enter by it; for the Lord, the God of 3 Israel, has entered by it; therefore it shall remain shut. Only the prince may sit in it to eat bread before the Lord; he shall enter by way of the vestibule of the gate, and shall go out by the same way."

4 Then he brought me by way of the north gate to the front of the temple; and I looked, and behold, the glory of the Lord 5 filled the temple of the Lord; and I fell upon my face. And the Lord said to me, "Son of man, mark well, see with your eyes, and hear with your ears all that I shall tell you concerning all the ordinances of the temple of the Lord and all its laws; and mark well those who may be admitted to [p] the temple and all 6 those who are to be excluded from the sanctuary. And say to the rebellious house,[q] to the house of Israel, Thus says the Lord God: O house of Israel, let there be an end to all your 7 abominations, in admitting foreigners, uncircumcised in heart and flesh, to be in my sanctuary, profaning it,[r] when you offer to me my food, the fat and the blood. You [s] have broken my 8 covenant, in addition to all your abominations. And you have not kept charge of my holy things; but you have set foreigners to keep my charge in my sanctuary.

9 "Therefore [t] thus says the Lord God: No foreigner, uncircumcised in heart and flesh, of all the foreigners who are among 10 the people of Israel, shall enter my sanctuary. But the Levites who went far from me, going astray from me after their idols 11 when Israel went astray, shall bear their punishment. They shall be ministers in my sanctuary, having oversight at the gates of the temple, and serving in the temple; they shall slay the burnt offering and the sacrifice for the people, and they 12 shall attend on the people, to serve them. Because they ministered to them before their idols and became a stumbling block of iniquity to the house of Israel, therefore I have sworn concerning them, says the Lord God, that they shall bear their

---

[a] Gk: Heb lacks outer   [b] Cn Compare Gk: Heb in the breadth of the wall of the court   [c] Gk: Heb east   [d] Heb and all their exits
[e] Cn: Heb And according to the entrances of the chambers that were toward the south was an entrance at the head of the way, the way before the dividing wall toward the east as one enters them   [f] Gk: Heb measuring reed round about. He measured
[g] Gk: Heb And like the vision   [h] Syr: Heb and the visions   [i] Or the monuments
[j] Gk: Heb the temple that they may measure the pattern   [k] Gk: Heb the form of   [l] Compare Gk: Heb its whole form
[m] Gk: Heb lacks high   [x] Gk: Heb back   [n] Gk: Heb lacks one cubit high   [o] Cn: Heb the Lord   [p] Cn: Heb the entrance of
[q] Gk: Heb lacks house   [r] Gk: Heb it my temple   [s] Gk Syr Vg: Heb they   [t] Gk: Heb for you

13 punishment. They shall not come near to me, to serve me as priest, nor come near any of my sacred things and the things that are most sacred; but they shall bear their shame, because 14 of the abominations which they have committed. Yet I will appoint them to keep charge of the temple, to do all its service and all that is to be done in it.

15 "But the Levitical priests, the sons of Zadok, who kept the charge of my sanctuary when the people of Israel went astray from me, shall come near to me to minister to me; and they shall attend on me to offer me the fat and the blood, says the 16 Lord GOD; they shall enter my sanctuary, and they shall approach my table, to minister to me, and they shall keep my 17 charge. When they enter the gates of the inner court, they shall wear linen garments; they shall have nothing of wool on them, while they minister at the gates of the inner court, 18 and within. They shall have linen turbans upon their heads, and linen breeches upon their loins; they shall not gird them- 19 selves with anything that causes sweat. And when they go out into the outer court to the people, they shall put off the garments in which they have been ministering, and lay them in the holy chambers; and they shall put on other garments, lest they communicate holiness to the people with their 20 garments. They shall not shave their heads or let their locks grow long; they shall only trim the hair of their heads. 21 No priest shall drink wine, when he enters the inner court. 22 They shall not marry a widow, or a divorced woman, but only a virgin of the stock of the house of Israel, or a widow who 23 is the widow of a priest. They shall teach my people the difference between the holy and the common, and show them 24 how to distinguish between the unclean and the clean. In a controversy they shall act as judges, and they shall judge it according to my judgments. They shall keep my laws and my statutes in all my appointed feasts, and they shall keep my 25 sabbaths holy. They shall not defile themselves by going near to a dead person; however, for father or mother, for son or daughter, for brother or unmarried sister they may defile 26 themselves. After he is defiled,u he shall count for himself seven 27 days, and then he shall be clean.v And on the day that he goes into the holy place, into the inner court, to minister in the holy place, he shall offer his sin offering, says the Lord GOD.

28 "They shall have no w inheritance; I am their inheritance: and you shall give them no possession in Israel; I am their 29 possession. They shall eat the cereal offering, the sin offering, and the guilt offering; and every devoted thing in Israel shall be 30 theirs. And the first of all the first fruits of all kinds, and every offering of all kinds from all your offerings, shall belong to the priests; you shall also give to the priests the first of your 31 coarse meal, that a blessing may rest on your house. The priests shall not eat of anything, whether bird or beast, that has died of itself or is torn.

The Sacred District

45 "When you allot the land as a possession, you shall set apart for the LORD a portion of the land as a holy district, twenty-five thousand cubits long and twenty x thousand cubits 2 broad; it shall be holy throughout its whole extent. Of this a square plot of five hundred by five hundred cubits shall be for the sanctuary, with fifty cubits for an open space around it. 3 And in the holy district you shall measure off a section twenty-five thousand cubits long and ten thousand broad, in which 4 shall be the sanctuary, the most holy place. It shall be the holy portion of the land; it shall be for the priests, who minister in the sanctuary and approach the LORD to minister to him; and it shall be a place for their houses and a holy place for the 5 sanctuary. Another section, twenty-five thousand cubits long and ten thousand cubits broad, shall be for the Levites who minister at the temple, as their possession for cities to live in.y 6 "Alongside the portion set apart as the holy district you shall assign for the possession of the city an area five thousand cubits broad, and twenty-five thousand cubits long; it shall belong to the whole house of Israel.

7 "And to the prince shall belong the land on both sides of the holy district and the property of the city, alongside the holy district and the property of the city, on the west and on the east, corresponding in length to one of the tribal portions, and extending from the western to the eastern boundary of the 8 land. It is to be his property in Israel. And my princes shall no more oppress my people; but they shall let the house of Israel have the land according to their tribes.

9 "Thus says the Lord GOD: Enough, O princes of Israel! Put away violence and oppression, and execute justice and righteousness; cease your evictions of my people, says the Lord GOD. 10 "You shall have just balances, a just ephah, and a just bath. 11 The ephah and the bath shall be of the same measure, the bath containing one tenth of a homer, and the ephah one tenth of a 12 homer; the homer shall be the standard measure. The shekel shall be twenty gerahs; five shekels shall be five shekels, and ten shekels shall be ten shekels, and your mina shall be fifty shekels.z

13 "This is the offering which you shall make: one sixth of an ephah from each homer of wheat, and one sixth of an ephah 14 from each homer of barley, and as the fixed portion of oil,a one tenth of a bath from each cor (the cor,b like the homer, 15 contains ten baths); and one sheep from every flock of two hundred, from the familiesc of Israel. This is the offering for 16 cereal offerings, burnt offerings, and peace offerings, to make atonement for them, says the Lord GOD. All the people of the 17 land shall give d this offering to the prince in Israel. It shall be the prince's duty to furnish the burnt offerings, cereal offerings, and drink offerings, at the feasts, the new moons, and the sabbaths, all the appointed feasts of the house of Israel: he shall provide the sin offerings, cereal offerings, burnt offerings, and peace offerings, to make atonement for the house of Israel.

18 "Thus says the Lord GOD: In the first month, on the first day of the month, you shall take a young bull without blemish, 19 and cleanse the sanctuary. The priest shall take some of the blood of the sin offering and put it on the doorposts of the temple, the four corners of the ledge of the altar, and the posts 20 of the gate of the inner court. You shall do the same on the seventh day of the month for any one who has sinned through error or ignorance; so you shall make atonement for the temple.

21 "In the first month, on the fourteenth day of the month, you shall celebrate the feast of the passover, and for seven days 22 unleavened bread shall be eaten. On that day the prince shall provide for himself and all the people of the land a young bull 23 for a sin offering. And on the seven days of the festival he shall provide as a burnt offering to the LORD seven young bulls and seven rams without blemish, on each of the seven days; and a 24 he-goat daily for a sin offering. And he shall provide as a cereal offering an ephah for each bull, an ephah for each ram, 25 and a hin of oil to each ephah. In the seventh month, on the fifteenth day of the month and for the seven days of the feast, he shall make the same provision for sin offerings, burnt offerings, and cereal offerings, and for the oil.

Regulations

46 "Thus says the Lord GOD: The gate of the inner court that faces east shall be shut on the six working days; but on the sabbath day it shall be opened and on the day of the new 2 moon it shall be opened. The prince shall enter by the vestibule of the gate from without, and shall take his stand by the post of the gate. The priest shall offer his burnt offering and his peace offerings, and he shall worship at the threshold of the gate. Then he shall go out, but the gate shall not be shut until 3 evening. The people of the land shall worship at the entrance of that gate before the LORD on the sabbaths and on the new 4 moons. The burnt offering that the prince offers to the LORD on the sabbath day shall be six lambs without blemish and a ram 5 without blemish; and the cereal offering with the ram shall be

u Syr: Heb cleansed   v Syr: Heb lacks and then he shall be clean
y Gk: Heb twenty chambers   z Gk: Heb twenty shekels, twenty-five shekels, fifteen shekels shall be your mina
a Cn: Heb oil, the bath the oil   b Vg: Heb homer   c Gk: Heb watering places   d Gk Compare Syr: Heb shall be to
w Vg: Heb as an   x Gk: Heb ten

an ephah, and the cereal offering with the lambs shall be as much as he is able, together with a hin of oil to each ephah.

6 On the day of the new moon he shall offer a young bull without blemish, and six lambs and a ram, which shall be without 7 blemish; as a cereal offering he shall provide an ephah with the bull and an ephah with the ram, and with the lambs as much 8 as he is able, together with a hin of oil to each ephah. When the prince enters, he shall go in by the vestibule of the gate, and he shall go out by the same way.

9 "When the people of the land come before the LORD at the appointed feasts, he who enters by the north gate to worship shall go out by the south gate; and he who enters by the south gate shall go out by the north gate: no one shall return by way of the gate by which he entered, but each shall go out straight 10 ahead. When they go in, the prince shall go in with them; and when they go out, he shall go out.

11 "At the feasts and the appointed seasons the cereal offering with a young bull shall be an ephah, and with a ram an ephah, and with the lambs as much as one is able to give, 12 together with a hin of oil to an ephah. When the prince provides a freewill offering, either a burnt offering or peace offerings as a freewill offering to the LORD, the gate facing east shall be opened for him; and he shall offer his burnt offering or his peace offerings as he does on the sabbath day. Then he shall go out, and after he has gone out the gate shall be shut.

13 "He shall provide a lamb a year old without blemish for a burnt offering to the LORD daily; morning by morning he shall 14 provide it. And he shall provide a cereal offering with it morning by morning, one sixth of an ephah, and one third of a hin of oil to moisten the flour, as a cereal offering to the LORD; 15 this is the ordinance for the continual burnt offering.[e] Thus the lamb and the meal offering and the oil shall be provided, morning by morning, for a continual burnt offering.

16 "Thus says the Lord GOD: If the prince makes a gift to any of his sons out of[f] his inheritance, it shall belong to his sons, 17 it is their property by inheritance. But if he makes a gift out of his inheritance to one of his servants, it shall be his to the year of liberty; then it shall revert to the prince; only his sons 18 may keep a gift from his inheritance. The prince shall not take any of the inheritance of the people, thrusting them out of their property; he shall give his sons their inheritance out of his own property, so that none of my people shall be dispossessed of his property."

19 Then he brought me through the entrance, which was at the side of the gate, to the north row of the holy chambers for the priests; and there I saw a place at the extreme western end of 20 them. And he said to me, "This is the place where the priests shall boil the guilt offering and the sin offering, and where they shall bake the cereal offering, in order not to bring them out into the outer court and so communicate holiness to the people."

21 Then he brought me forth to the outer court, and led me to the four corners of the court; and in each corner of the court 22 there was a court—in the four corners of the court were small[g] courts, forty cubits long and thirty broad; the four were of the 23 same size. On the inside, around each of the four courts was a row of masonry, with hearths made at the bottom of the rows 24 round about. Then he said to me, "These are the kitchens where those who minister at the temple shall boil the sacrifices of the people."

The Sacred River

47 Then he brought me back to the door of the temple; and behold, water was issuing from below the threshold of the temple toward the east (for the temple faced east); and the water was flowing down from below the south end of the 2 threshold of the temple, south of the altar. Then he brought me out by way of the north gate, and led me round on the outside to the outer gate, that faces toward the east;[h] and the water was coming out on the south side.

3 Going on eastward with a line in his hand, the man measured a thousand cubits, and then led me through the water; and it 4 was ankle-deep. Again he measured a thousand, and led me through the water; and it was knee-deep. Again he measured a thousand, and led me through the water; and it was up to the 5 loins. Again he measured a thousand, and it was a river that I could not pass through, for the water had risen; it was deep

enough to swim in, a river that could not be passed through.
6 And he said to me, "Son of man, have you seen this?"

7 Then he led me back along the bank of the river. As I went back, I saw upon the bank of the river very many trees on the 8 one side and on the other. And he said to me, "This water flows toward the eastern region and goes down into the Arabah; and when it enters the stagnant waters of the sea,[i] the water will 9 become fresh. And wherever the river[j] goes every living creature which swarms will live, and there will be very many fish; for this water goes there, that the waters of the sea[k] may become fresh; so everything will live where the river goes. 10 Fishermen will stand beside the sea; from En-ge'di to En-eg'laim it will be a place for the spreading of nets; its fish will be of 11 very many kinds, like the fish of the Great Sea. But its swamps and marshes will not become fresh; they are to be left for salt. 12 And on the banks, on both sides of the river, there will grow all kinds of trees for food. Their leaves will not wither nor their fruit fail, but they will bear fresh fruit every month, because the water for them flows from the sanctuary. Their fruit will be for food, and their leaves for healing."

13 Thus says the Lord GOD: "These are the boundaries by which you shall divide the land for inheritance among the twelve 14 tribes of Israel. Joseph shall have two portions. And you shall divide it equally; I swore to give it to your fathers, and this land shall fall to you as your inheritance.

15 "This shall be the boundary of the land: On the north side, from the Great Sea by way of Hethlon to the entrance of 16 Hamath, and on to Zedad,[l] Bero'thah, Sib'raim (which lies on the border between Damascus and Hamath), as far as Hazer- 17 hatticon, which is on the border of Hauran. So the boundary shall run from the sea to Hazar-e'non, which is on the northern border of Damascus, with the border of Hamath to the north.[m] This shall be the north side.

18 "On the east side, the boundary shall run from Hazar-e'non[n] between Hauran and Damascus;[m] along the Jordan between Gilead and the land of Israel; to the eastern sea and as far as Tamar.[o] This shall be the east side.

19 "On the south side, it shall run from Tamar as far as the waters of Meribath-ka'desh, thence along the Brook of Egypt to the Great Sea. This shall be the south side.

20 "On the west side, the Great Sea shall be the boundary to a point opposite the entrance of Hamath. This shall be the west side.

21 "So you shall divide this land among you according to the 22 tribes of Israel. You shall allot it as an inheritance for yourselves and for the aliens who reside among you and have begotten children among you. They shall be to you as native-born sons of Israel; with you they shall be allotted an inheri- 23 tance among the tribes of Israel. In whatever tribe the alien resides, there you shall assign him his inheritance, says the Lord GOD.

Tribal Territories

48 "These are the names of the tribes: Beginning at the northern border, from the sea by way[p] of Hethlon to the entrance of Hamath, as far as Hazar-e'non (which is on the northern border of Damascus over against Hamath), and[q] extending from the east side to the west,[r] Dan, one portion. 2 Adjoining the territory of Dan, from the east side to the west, 3 Asher, one portion. Adjoining the territory of Asher, from the 4 east side to the west, Naph'tali, one portion. Adjoining the territory of Naph'tali, from the east side to the west, Manas'- 5 seh, one portion. Adjoining the territory of Manas'seh, from the 6 east side to the west, E'phraim, one portion. Adjoining the territory of E'phraim, from the east side to the west, Reuben, 7 one portion. Adjoining the territory of Reuben, from the east side to the west, Judah, one portion.

8 "Adjoining the territory of Judah, from the east side to the west, shall be the portion which you shall set apart, twenty-five thousand cubits in breadth, and in length equal to one of the tribal portions, from the east side to the west, with the 9 sanctuary in the midst of it. The portion which you shall set apart for the LORD shall be twenty-five thousand cubits in length, 10 and twenty[s] thousand in breadth. These shall be the allotments of the holy portion: the priests shall have an allotment measuring twenty-five thousand cubits on the northern side, ten thousand cubits in breadth on the western side, ten thousand

---

e Cn: Heb *perpetual ordinances continually*   f Gk: Heb *it is his inheritance*
g Gk Syr Vg: The meaning of the Hebrew word is uncertain   h Heb obscure
i Compare Syr: Heb *into the sea to the sea those that were made to issue forth*   j Gk Syr Vg Tg: Heb *two rivers*
k Compare Syr: Heb lacks *the waters of the sea*   l Gk: Heb *the entrance of Zedad, Hamath*   m Heb obscure
n Cn: Heb lacks *Hazar-enon*   o Compare Syr: Heb *you shall measure*   p Compare 47.15: Heb *by the side of the way*
q Cn: Heb *and they shall be his*   r Gk Compare verses 2-8: Heb *the east side the west*   s Compare 45.1: Heb *ten*

in breath on the eastern side, and twenty-five thousand in length on the southern side, with the sanctuary of the Lord in ¹¹ the midst of it. This shall be for the consecrated priests, the sons[t] of Zadok, who kept my charge, who did not go astray when the people of Israel went astray, as the Levites did. ¹² And it shall belong to them as a special portion from the holy portion of the land, a most holy place, adjoining the territory ¹³ of the Levites. And alongside the territory of the priests, the Levites shall have an allotment twenty-five thousand cubits in length and ten thousand in breadth. The whole length shall be twenty-five thousand cubits and the breadth twenty[u] thousand. ¹⁴ They shall not sell or exchange any of it; they shall not alienate this choice portion of the land, for it is holy to the Lord. ¹⁵ "The remainder, five thousand cubits in breadth and twenty-five thousand in length, shall be for ordinary use for the city, for dwellings and for open country. In the midst of it shall ¹⁶ be the city; and these shall be its dimensions: the north side four thousand five hundred cubits, the south side four thousand five hundred, the east side four thousand five hundred, and the ¹⁷ west side four thousand and five hundred. And the city shall have open land: on the north two hundred and fifty cubits, on the south two hundred and fifty, on the east two hundred and ¹⁸ fifty, and on the west two hundred and fifty. The remainder of the length alongside the holy portion shall be ten thousand cubits to the east, and ten thousand to the west, and it shall be alongside the holy portion. Its produce shall be food for the ¹⁹ workers of the city. And the workers of the city, from all the ²⁰ tribes of Israel, shall till it. The whole portion which you shall set apart shall be twenty-five thousand cubits square, that is, the holy portion together with the property of the city. ²¹ "What remains on both sides of the holy portion and of the property of the city shall belong to the prince. Extending from the twenty-five thousand cubits of the holy portion to the east border, and westward from the twenty-five housand cubits to the west border, parallel to the tribal portions, it shall belong to the prince. The holy portion with the sanctuary of the temple ²² in its midst, and the property of the Levites and the property of the city,[v] shall be in the midst of that which belongs to the prince. The portion of the prince shall lie between the territory of Judah and the territory of Benjamin.

²³ "As for the rest of the tribes: from the east side to the ²⁴ west, Benjamin, one portion. Adjoining the territory of Benjamin, from the east side to the west, Simeon, one portion. ²⁵ Adjoining the territory of Simeon, from the east side to ²⁶ west, Is'sachar, one portion. Adjoining the territory of Is'sachar, ²⁷ from the east side to the west, Zeb'ulun, one portion. Adjoining the territory of Zeb'ulun, from the east side to the west, Gad, ²⁸ one portion. And adjoining the territory of Gad to the south, the boundary shall run from Tamar to the waters of Meribath-ka'desh, thence along the Brook of Egypt to the Great Sea. ²⁹ This is the land which you shall allot as an inheritance among the tribes of Israel, and these are their several portions, says the Lord God.

³⁰ "These shall be the exits of the city: On the north side, which is to be four thousand five hundred cubits by measure, ³¹ three gates, the gate of Reuben, the gate of Judah, and the gate of Levi, the gates of the city being named after the tribes ³² of Israel. On the east side, which is to be four thousand five hundred cubits, three gates, the gate of Joseph, the gate of ³³ Benjamin, and the gate of Dan. On the south side, which is to be four thousand five hundred cubits by measure, three gates, the gate of Simeon, the gate of Is'sachar, and the gate of Zeb'- ³⁴ ulun. On the west side, which is to be four thousand five hundred cubits, three gates,[w] the gate of Gad, the gate of ³⁵ Asher, and the gate of Naph'tali. The circumference of the city shall be eighteen thousand cubits. And the name of the city henceforth shall be, The Lord is there."

---

[t] One Ms Gk: Heb *of the sons*   [u] Gk: Heb *ten*   [v] Cn: Heb *and from the property of the Levites and from the property of the city*
[w] One Ms Gk Syr: Heb *their gates three*

INTRODUCTION TO

DANIEL

Less than two hundred years before the birth of Jesus, a Greek king living in Syria, a country north of Palestine, controlled Judah. The king, named Antiochus Epiphanes, tried to destroy the Jewish religion so that the people would accept Greek ideas and religion. The Book of Daniel was written to encourage Jews to be faithful to their God and to their own people. It was written about 166 B.C.

The book tells the story of Daniel and his courageous resistance to the tyranny of Babylonia hundreds of years earlier, between 597 B.C. and 538 B.C. Chapters 1 through 6 contain stories of Daniel and his friends. Chapters 7 through 12 contain strange visions with symbolic pictures by which the writer encouraged his fellow Jews to resist the tyranny of Antiochus Epiphanes. For instance, in Chapter 7 the writer uses a lion, a leopard, a bear, and a goat as symbols for certain nations which had been unable to destroy the Jewish faith and the Jewish people.

Daniel and other symbolic books, such as Ezekiel and Revelation, have sometimes been used to try to predict future events or even the end of the world. Jesus cautioned against such efforts, saying, "But of that day or that hour no one knows, not even the angels in heaven, nor the Son, but only the Father" (Mark 13.32).

This is a book to which both Jews and Christians have turned whenever they have been persecuted for their faith. Daniel reminded them that God gives men the courage to be loyal to the right even when there is cruel opposition. Daniel stirred the Jews to resist oppression even to death if necessary.

Although the belief is not prominent in much of the Old Testament, there is a notable passage setting forth faith in life after death in this book (Daniel 12.2).

THE BOOK OF

DANIEL

EXILED TO THE KING'S PALACE

1 In the third year of the reign of Jehoi'akim king of Judah, Nebuchadnez'zar king of Babylon came to ² Jerusalem and besieged it. And the Lord gave Jehoi'akim king of Judah into his hand, with some of the vessels of the house of God; and he brought them to the land of Shinar, to the house of his god, and placed the vessels in ³ the treasury of his god. Then the king commanded Ash'penaz, his chief eunuch, to bring some of the people of Israel, both of the royal family and of the nobility, ⁴ youths without blemish, handsome and skilful in all wisdom, endowed with knowledge, understanding learning, and competent to serve in the king's palace, and to teach ⁵ them the letters and language of the Chalde'ans. The king assigned them a daily portion of the rich food which the king ate, and of the wine which he drank. They were to be educated for three years, and at the end of that time ⁶ they were to stand before the king. Among these were Daniel, Hanani'ah, Mish'a-el, and Azari'ah of the tribe ⁷ of Judah. And the chief of the eunuchs gave them names: Daniel he called Belteshaz'zar, Hanani'ah he called Shadrach, Mish'a-el he called Meshach, and Azari'ah he called Abed'nego.

⁸ But Daniel resolved that he would not defile himself with the king's rich food, or with the wine which he drank; therefore he asked the chief of the eunuchs to allow ⁹ him not to defile himself. And God gave Daniel favor and ¹⁰ compassion in the sight of the chief of the eunuchs; and the chief of the eunuchs said to Daniel, "I fear lest my

lord the king, who appointed your food and your drink, should see that you were in poorer condition than the youths who are of your own age. So you would endanger ¹¹ my head with the king." Then Daniel said to the steward whom the chief of the eunuchs had appointed over Daniel, ¹² Hanani′ah, Mish′a-el, and Azari′ah; "Test your servants for ten days; let us be given vegetables to eat and water ¹³ to drink. Then let our appearance and the appearance of the youths who eat the king's rich food be observed by you, and according to what you see deal with your ¹⁴ servants." So he hearkened to them in this matter, and ¹⁵ tested them for ten days. At the end of ten days it was seen that they were better in appearance and fatter in ¹⁶ flesh than all the youths who ate the king's rich food. So the steward took away their rich food and the wine they were to drink, and gave them vegetables.

¹⁷ As for these four youths, God gave them learning and skill in all letters and wisdom; and Daniel had under- ¹⁸ standing in all visions and dreams. At the end of the time, when the king had commanded that they should be brought in, the chief of the eunuchs brought them in ¹⁹ before Nebuchadnez′zar. And the king spoke with them, and among them all none was found like Daniel, Hanani′ah, Mish′a-el, and Azari′ah; therefore they stood ²⁰ before the king. And in every matter of wisdom and understanding concerning which the king inquired of them, he found them ten times better than all the magi- ²¹ cians and enchanters that were in all his kingdom. And Daniel continued until the first year of King Cyrus.

Nebuchadnezzar's Dream

2 In the second year of the reign of Nebuchadnez′zar, Nebuchadnez′zar had dreams; and his spirit was ² troubled, and his sleep left him. Then the king commanded that the magicians, the enchanters, the sorcerers, and the Chalde′ans be summoned, to tell the king his ³ dreams. So they came in and stood before the king. And the king said to them, "I had a dream, and my spirit is ⁴ troubled to know the dream." Then the Chalde′ans said to the king,ᵃ "O king, live for ever! Tell your servants ⁵ the dream, and we will show the interpretation." The king answered the Chalde′ans, "The word from me is sure: if you do not make known to me the dream and its in- terpretation, you shall be torn limb from limb, and your ⁶ houses shall be laid in ruins. But if you show the dream and its interpretation, you shall receive from me gifts and rewards and great honor. Therefore show me the dream ⁷ and its interpretation." They answered a second time, "Let the king tell his servants the dream, and we will ⁸ show its interpretation." The king answered, "I know with certainty that you are trying to gain time, because you ⁹ see that the word from me is sure that if you do not make the dream known to me, there is but one sentence for you.

You have agreed to speak lying and corrupt words before me till the times change. Therefore tell me the dream, and ¹⁰ I shall know that you can show me its interpretation." The Chalde′ans answered the king, "There is not a man on earth who can meet the king's demand; for no great and powerful king has asked such a thing of any magician or ¹¹ enchanter or Chalde′an. The thing that the king asks is difficult, and none can show it to the king except the gods, whose dwelling is not with flesh."

¹² Because of this the king was angry and very furious, and commanded that all the wise men of Babylon be ¹³ destroyed. So the decree went forth that the wise men were to be slain, and they sought Daniel and his com- ¹⁴ panions, to slay them. Then Daniel replied with prudence and discretion to Ar′i-och, the captain of the king's guard, who had gone out to slay the wise men of Babylon; ¹⁵ he said to Ar′i-och, the king's captain, "Why is the decree of the king so severe?" Then Ar′i-och made the matter ¹⁶ known to Daniel. And Daniel went in and besought the king to appoint him a time, that he might show to the king the interpretation.

¹⁷ Then Daniel went to his house and made the matter known to Hanani′ah, Mish′a-el, and Azari′ah, his com- ¹⁸ panions, and told them to seek mercy of the God of heaven concerning this mystery, so that Daniel and his companions might not perish with the rest of the wise ¹⁹ men of Babylon. Then the mystery was revealed to Daniel in a vision of the night. Then Daniel blessed the God of ²⁰ heaven. Daniel said:

"Blessed be the name of God for ever and ever,
    to whom belong wisdom and might.
²¹ He changes times and seasons;
    he removes kings and sets up kings;
he gives wisdom to the wise
    and knowledge to those who have understanding;
²² he reveals deep and mysterious things;
    he knows what is in the darkness,
    and the light dwells with him.
²³ To thee, O God of my fathers,
    I give thanks and praise,
for thou hast given me wisdom and strength,
    and hast now made known to me what we asked of thee,
    for thou hast made known to us the king's matter."

²⁴ Therefore Daniel went in to Ar′i-och, whom the king had appointed to destroy the wise men of Babylon; he went and said thus to him, "Do not destroy the wise men of Babylon; bring me in before the king, and I will show the king the interpretation."

²⁵ Then Ar′i-och brought in Daniel before the king in haste, and said thus to him: "I have found among the exiles from Judah a man who can make known to the ²⁶ king the interpretation." The king said to Daniel, whose name was Belteshaz′zar, "Are you able to make known to

ᵃ Heb adds *in Aramaic*, indicating that the text from this point to the end of chapter 7 is in Aramaic

me the dream that I have seen and its interpretation?" ²⁷ Daniel answered the king, "No wise men, enchanters, magicians, or astrologers can show to the king the mystery ²⁸ which the king has asked, but there is a God in heaven who reveals mysteries, and he has made known to King Nebuchadnez'zar what will be in the latter days. Your dream and the visions of your head as you lay in bed are ²⁹ these: To you, O king, as you lay in bed came thoughts of what would be hereafter, and he who reveals mysteries ³⁰ made known to you what is to be. But as for me, not because of any wisdom that I have more than all the living has this mystery been revealed to me, but in order that the interpretation may be made known to the king, and that you may know the thoughts of your mind.

³¹ "You saw, O king, and behold, a great image. This image, mighty and of exceeding brightness, stood before ³² you, and its appearance was frightening. The head of this image was of fine gold, its breast and arms of silver, its ³³ belly and thighs of bronze, its legs of iron, its feet partly ³⁴ of iron and partly of clay. As you looked, a stone was cut out by no human hand, and it smote the image on its ³⁵ feet of iron and clay, and broke them in pieces; then the iron, the clay, the bronze, the silver, and the gold, all together were broken in pieces, and became like the chaff of the summer threshing floors; and the wind carried them away, so that not a trace of them could be found. But the stone that struck the image became a great mountain and filled the whole earth.

³⁶ "This was the dream; now we will tell the king its ³⁷ interpretation. You, O king, the king of kings, to whom the God of heaven has given the kingdom, the power, and ³⁸ the might, and the glory, and into whose hand he has given, wherever they dwell, the sons of men, the beasts of the field, and the birds of the air, making you rule ³⁹ over them all—you are the head of gold. After you shall rise another kingdom inferior to you, and yet a third kingdom of bronze, which shall rule over all the earth. ⁴⁰ And there shall be a fourth kingdom, strong as iron, because iron breaks to pieces and shatters all things; and like iron which crushes, it shall break and crush all these. ⁴¹ And as you saw the feet and toes partly of potter's clay and partly of iron, it shall be a divided kingdom; but some of the firmness of iron shall be in it, just as you ⁴² saw iron mixed with the miry clay. And as the toes of the feet were partly iron and partly clay, so the kingdom ⁴³ shall be partly strong and partly brittle. As you saw the iron mixed with miry clay, so they will mix with one another in marriage,[b] but they will not hold together, ⁴⁴ just as iron does not mix with clay. And in the days of those kings the God of heaven will set up a kingdom which shall never be destroyed, nor shall its sovereignty be left to another people. It shall break in pieces all these kingdoms and bring them to an end, and it shall stand

[b] Aram *by the seed of men*

⁴⁵ for ever; just as you saw that a stone was cut from a mountain by no human hand, and that it broke in pieces the iron, the bronze, the clay, the silver, and the gold. A great God has made known to the king what shall be hereafter. The dream is certain, and its interpretation sure."

⁴⁶ Then King Nebuchadnez'zar fell upon his face, and did homage to Daniel, and commanded that an offering ⁴⁷ and incense be offered up to him. The king said to Daniel, "Truly, your God is God of gods and Lord of kings, and a revealer of mysteries, for you have been ⁴⁸ able to reveal this mystery." Then the king gave Daniel high honors and many great gifts, and made him ruler over the whole province of Babylon, and chief prefect ⁴⁹ over all the wise men of Babylon. Daniel made request of the king, and he appointed Shadrach, Meshach, and Abed'nego over the affairs of the province of Babylon; but Daniel remained at the king's court.

The Fiery Furnace

³ King Nebuchadnez'zar made an image of gold, whose height was sixty cubits and its breadth six cubits. He set it up on the plain of Dura, in the province ² of Babylon. Then King Nebuchadnez'zar sent to assemble

the satraps, the prefects, and the governors, the counselors, the treasurers, the justices, the magistrates, and all the officials of the provinces to come to the dedication of the ³ image which King Nebuchadnez'zar had set up. Then the satraps, the prefects, and the governors, the counselors, the treasurers, the justices, the magistrates, and all the officials of the provinces, were assembled for the dedication of the image that King Nebuchadnez'zar had set up; and they stood before the image that Nebuchadnez'zar had ⁴ set up. And the herald proclaimed aloud, "You are com- ⁵ manded, O peoples, nations, and languages, that when you hear the sound of the horn, pipe, lyre, trigon, harp, bagpipe, and every kind of music, you are to fall down and worship the golden image that King Nebuchadnez'zar has ⁶ set up; and whoever does not fall down and worship shall ⁷ immediately be cast into a burning fiery furnace." Therefore, as soon as all the peoples heard the sound of the horn, pipe, lyre, trigon, harp, bagpipe, and every kind of music, all the peoples, nations, and languages fell down and worshiped the golden image which King Nebuchadnez'zar had set up.

8 Therefore at that time certain Chalde'ans came forward 9 and maliciously accused the Jews. They said to King 10 Nebuchadnez'zar, "O king, live for ever! You, O king, have made a decree, that every man who hears the sound of the horn, pipe, lyre, trigon, harp, bagpipe, and every kind of music, shall fall down and worship the golden 11 image; and whoever does not fall down and worship shall 12 be cast into a burning fiery furnace. There are certain Jews whom you have appointed over the affairs of the province of Babylon: Shadrach, Meshach, and Abed'nego. These men, O king, pay no heed to you; they do not serve your gods or worship the golden image which you have set up."

13 Then Nebuchadnez'zar in furious rage commanded that Shadrach, Meshach, and Abed'nego be brought. Then 14 they brought these men before the king. Nebuchadnez'zar said to them, "Is it true, O Shadrach, Meshach, and Abed'nego, that you do not serve my gods or worship the 15 golden image which I have set up? Now if you are ready when you hear the sound of the horn, pipe, lyre, trigon, harp, bagpipe, and every kind of music, to fall down and worship the image which I have made, well and good; but if you do not worship, you shall immediately be cast into a burning fiery furnace; and who is the god that will deliver you out of my hands?"

16 Shadrach, Meshach, and Abed'nego answered the king, "O Nebuchadnez'zar, we have no need to answer you 17 in this matter. If it be so, our God whom we serve is able to deliver us from the burning fiery furnace; and he will 18 deliver us out of your hand, O king.c But if not, be it known to you, O king, that we will not serve your gods or worship the golden image which you have set up."

19 Then Nebuchadnez'zar was full of fury, and the expression of his face was changed against Shadrach, Meshach, and Abed'nego. He ordered the furnace heated 20 seven times more than it was wont to be heated. And he ordered certain mighty men of his army to bind Shadrach, Meshach, and Abed'nego, and to cast them into the 21 burning fiery furnace. Then these men were bound in their mantles,d their tunics,d their hats, and their other garments, and they were cast into the burning fiery 22 furnace. Because the king's order was strict and the furnace very hot, the flame of the fire slew those men 23 who took up Shadrach, Meshach, and Abed'nego. And these three men, Shadrach, Meshach, and Abed'nego, fell bound into the burning fiery furnace.

24 Then King Nebuchadnez'zar was astonished and rose up in haste. He said to his counselors, "Did we not cast three men bound into the fire?" They answered the king, 25 "True, O king." He answered, "But I see four men loose, walking in the midst of the fire, and they are not hurt; and the appearance of the fourth is like a son of the gods." 26 Then Nebuchadnez'zar came near to the door of the burning fiery furnace and said, "Shadrach, Meshach, and Abed'nego, servants of the Most High God, come forth, and come here!" Then Shadrach, Meshach, and Abed'nego 27 came out from the fire. And the satraps, the prefects, the governors, and the king's counselors gathered together and saw that the fire had not had any power over the bodies of those men; the hair of their heads was not singed, their mantles d were not harmed, and no smell of fire had 28 come upon them. Nebuchadnez'zar said, "Blessed be the God of Shadrach, Meshach, and Abed'nego, who has sent his angel and delivered his servants, who trusted in him, and set at nought the king's command, and yielded up their bodies rather than serve and worship any god 29 except their own God. Therefore I make a decree: Any people, nation, or language that speaks anything against the God of Shadrach, Meshach, and Abed'nego shall be torn limb from limb, and their houses laid in ruins; for there is no other god who is able to deliver in this way." 30 Then the king promoted Shadrach, Meshach, and Abed'-nego in the province of Babylon.

The King's Madness

4e King Nebuchadnez'zar to all peoples, nations, and languages, that dwell in all the earth: Peace be multi- 2 plied to you! It has seemed good to me to show the signs and wonders that the Most High God has wrought toward me.

3 How great are his signs,
  how mighty his wonders!
His kingdom is an everlasting kingdom,
  and his dominion is from generation to generation.

4 f I, ·Nebuchadnez'zar, was at ease in my house and 5 prospering in my palace. I had a dream which made me afraid; as I lay in bed the fancies and the visions of my 6 head alarmed me. Therefore I made a decree that all the wise men of Babylon should be brought before me, that they might make known to me the interpretation of the 7 dream. Then the magicians, the enchanters, the Chalde'ans, and the astrologers came in; and I told them the dream, but they could not make known to me its interpretation. 8 At last Daniel came in before me—he who was named Belteshaz'zar after the name of my god, and in whom is the spirit of the holy gods g—and I told him the dream, 9 saying, "O Belteshaz'zar, chief of the magicians, because I know that the spirit of the holy gods g is in you and that no mystery is difficult for you, here is h the dream 10 which I saw; tell me its interpretation. The visions of my head as I lay in bed were these: I saw, and behold, a tree in the midst of the earth; and its height was great. 11 The tree grew and became strong, and its top reached to heaven, and it was visible to the end of the whole earth. 12 Its leaves were fair and its fruit abundant, and in it was food for all. The beasts of the field found shade under it,

---

c Or *Behold, our God . . . king.* Or *If our God is able to deliver us, he will deliver us from the burning fiery furnace and out of your hand, O king.*
d The meaning of the Aramaic word is uncertain   e Ch 3.31 in Aram   f Ch 4.1 in Aram   g Or *Spirit of the holy God*
h Cn: Aram *visions of*

and the birds of the air dwelt in its branches, and all flesh was fed from it.

13 "I saw in the visions of my head as I lay in bed, and behold, a watcher, a holy one, came down from heaven.
14 He cried aloud and said thus, 'Hew down the tree and cut off its branches, strip off its leaves and scatter its fruit; let the beasts flee from under it and the birds from
15 its branches. But leave the stump of its roots in the earth, bound with a band of iron and bronze, amid the tender

grass of the field. Let him be wet with the dew of heaven; let his lot be with the beasts in the grass of the earth;
16 let his mind be changed from a man's, and let a beast's mind be given to him; and let seven times pass over
17 him. The sentence is by the decree of the watchers, the decision by the word of the holy ones, to the end that the living may know that the Most High rules the kingdom of men, and gives it to whom he will, and sets over it the
18 lowliest of men.' This dream I, King Nebuchadnez'zar, saw. And you, O Belteshaz'zar, declare the interpretation, because all the wise men of my kingdom are not able to make known to me the interpretation, but you are able, for the spirit of the holy gods[i] is in you."

19 Then Daniel, whose name was Belteshaz'zar, was dismayed for a moment, and his thoughts alarmed him. The king said, "Belteshaz'zar, let not the dream or the interpretation alarm you." Belteshaz'zar answered, "My lord, may the dream be for those who hate you and its
20 interpretation for your enemies! The tree you saw, which grew and became strong, so that its top reached to heaven,
21 and it was visible to the end of the whole earth; whose leaves were fair and its fruit abundant, and in which was food for all; under which beasts of the field found shade,
22 and in whose branches the birds of the air dwelt—it is you, O king, who have grown and become strong. Your greatness has grown and reaches to heaven, and your
23 dominion to the ends of the earth. And whereas the king saw a watcher, a holy one, coming down from heaven and saying, 'Hew down the tree and destroy it, but leave the stump of its roots in the earth, bound with a band of iron and bronze, in the tender grass of the field; and let him be wet with the dew of heaven; and let his lot be with the beasts of the field, till seven times pass over
24 him'; this is the interpretation, O king: It is a decree of the Most High, which has come upon my lord the
25 king, that you shall be driven from among men, and your dwelling shall be with the beasts of the field; you shall be made to eat grass like an ox, and you shall be

i Or *Spirit of the holy God*

wet with the dew of heaven, and seven times shall pass over you, till you know that the Most High rules the king-
26 dom of men, and gives it to whom he will. And as it was commanded to leave the stump of the roots of the tree, your kingdom shall be sure for you from the time that
27 you know that Heaven rules. Therefore, O king, let my counsel be acceptable to you; break off your sins by practicing righteousness, and your iniquities by showing mercy to the oppressed, that there may perhaps be a lengthening of your tranquillity."

28, 29 All this came upon King Nebuchadnez'zar. At the end of twelve months he was walking on the roof of the
30 royal palace of Babylon, and the king said, "Is not this great Babylon, which I have built by my mighty power as a royal residence and for the glory of my majesty?"
31 While the words were still in the king's mouth, there fell a voice from heaven, "O King Nebuchadnez'zar, to you it is spoken: The kingdom has departed from you,
32 and you shall be driven from among men, and your dwelling shall be with the beasts of the field; and you shall be made to eat grass like an ox; and seven times shall pass over you, until you have learned that the Most High rules the kingdom of men and gives it to whom he
33 will." Immediately the word was fulfilled upon Nebuchadnez'zar. He was driven from among men, and ate grass like an ox, and his body was wet with the dew of heaven till his hair grew as long as eagles' feathers, and his nails were like birds' claws.

34 At the end of the days I, Nebuchadnez'zar, lifted my eyes to heaven, and my reason returned to me, and I blessed the Most High, and praised and honored him who lives for ever;
for his dominion is an everlasting dominion,
    and his kingdom endures from generation to generation;
35 all the inhabitants of the earth are accounted as nothing;
    and he does according to his will in the host of heaven
    and among the inhabitants of the earth;
and none can stay his hand
    or say to him, "What doest thou?"
36 At the same time my reason returned to me; and for the glory of my kingdom, my majesty and splendor returned to me. My counselors and my lords sought me, and I was established in my kingdom, and still more greatness
37 was added to me. Now I, Nebuchadnez'zar, praise and extol and honor the King of heaven; for all his works are right and his ways are just; and those who walk in pride he is able to abase.

Belshazzar's Feast

5 King Belshaz'zar made a great feast for a thousand of his lords, and drank wine in front of the thousand.
2 Belshaz'zar, when he tasted the wine, commanded that

the vessels of gold and of silver which Nebuchadnez'zar his father had taken out of the temple in Jerusalem be brought, that the king and his lords, his wives, and his 3 concubines might drink from them. Then they brought in the golden and silver vessels[j] which had been taken out of the temple, the house of God in Jerusalem; and the king and his lords, his wives, and his concubines 4 drank from them. They drank wine, and praised the gods of gold and silver, bronze, iron, wood, and stone.

5 Immediately the fingers of a man's hand appeared and wrote on the plaster of the wall of the king's palace, opposite the lampstand; and the king saw the hand as it 6 wrote. Then the king's color changed, and his thoughts alarmed him; his limbs gave way, and his knees knocked 7 together. The king cried aloud to bring in the enchanters, the Chalde'ans, and the astrologers. The king said to the wise men of Babylon, "Whosoever reads this writing, and shows me its interpretation, shall be clothed with purple, and have a chain of gold about his neck, and shall be the 8 third ruler in the kingdom." Then all the king's wise men came in, but they could not read the writing or make 9 known to the king the interpretation. Then King Belshaz'-zar was greatly alarmed, and his color changed; and his lords were perplexed.

10 The queen, because of the words of the king and his lords, came into the banqueting hall; and the queen said, "O king, live for ever! Let not your thoughts alarm 11 you or your color change. There is in your kingdom a man in whom is the spirit of the holy gods.[k] In the days of your father light and understanding and wisdom, like the wisdom of the gods, were found in him, and King Nebuchadnez'zar, your father, made him chief of the 12 magicians, enchanters, Chalde'ans, and astrologers,[l] because an excellent spirit, knowledge, and understanding to interpret dreams, explain riddles, and solve problems were found in this Daniel, whom the king named Belteshaz'zar. Now let Daniel be called, and he will show the interpretation."

13 Then Daniel was brought in before the king. The king said to Daniel, "You are that Daniel, one of the exiles of Judah, whom the king my father brought from Judah. 14 I have heard of you that the spirit of the holy gods[k] is in you, and that light and understanding and excellent 15 wisdom are found in you. Now the wise men, the enchanters, have been brought in before me to read this writing and make known to me its interpretation; but they could not show the interpretation of the matter. 16 But I have heard that you can give interpretations and solve problems. Now if you can read the writing and make known to me its interpretation, you shall be clothed with purple, and have a chain of gold about your neck, and shall be the third ruler in the kingdom."

17 Then Daniel answered before the king, "Let your gifts be for yourself, and give your rewards to another; nevertheless I will read the writing to the king and make known 18 to him the interpretation. O king, the Most High God gave Nebuchadnez'zar your father kingship and greatness 19 and glory and majesty; and because of the greatness that he gave him, all peoples, nations, and languages trembled and feared before him; whom he would he slew, and whom he would he kept alive; whom he would he raised 20 up, and whom he would he put down. But when his heart was lifted up and his spirit was hardened so that he dealt proudly, he was deposed from his kingly throne, 21 and his glory was taken from him; he was driven from among men, and his mind was made like that of a beast, and his dwelling was with the wild asses; he was fed grass like an ox, and his body was wet with the dew of heaven, until he knew that the Most High God rules the 22 kingdom of men, and sets over it whom he will. And you his son, Belshaz'zar, have not humbled your heart, though 23 you knew all this, but you have lifted up yourself against the Lord of heaven; and the vessels of his house have been brought in before you, and you and your lords, your wives, and your concubines have drunk wine from them; and you have praised the gods of silver and gold, of bronze, iron, wood, and stone, which do not see or hear or know, but the God in whose hand is your breath, and whose are all your ways, you have not honored.

24 "Then from his presence the hand was sent, and this 25 writing was inscribed. And this is the writing that was 26 inscribed: MENE, MENE, TEKEL, and PARSIN. This is the interpretation of the matter: MENE, God has numbered the days of your kingdom and brought it to an end; 27 TEKEL, you have been weighed in the balances and found 28 wanting; PERES, your kingdom is divided and given to the Medes and Persians."

29 Then Belshaz'zar commanded, and Daniel was clothed with purple, a chain of gold was put about his neck, and proclamation was made concerning him, that he should be the third ruler in the kingdom.

30 That very night Belshaz'zar the Chalde'an king was 31 slain. And Darius the Mede received the kingdom, being about sixty-two years old.

In the Lion's Den

6 It pleased Darius to set over the kingdom a hundred and twenty satraps, to be throughout the whole king- 2 dom; and over them three presidents, of whom Daniel was one, to whom these satraps should give account, so 3 that the king might suffer no loss. Then this Daniel became distinguished above all the other presidents and satraps, because an excellent spirit was in him; and the 4 king planned to set him over the whole kingdom. Then the presidents and the satraps sought to find a ground for complaint against Daniel with regard to the kingdom;

---

[j] Theodotion Vg: Aram *golden vessels*   [k] Or *Spirit of the holy God*   [l] Aram repeats *the king your father*

but they could find no ground for complaint or any fault, because he was faithful, and no error or fault was found 5 in him. Then these men said, "We shall not find any ground for complaint against this Daniel unless we find it in connection with the law of his God."

6 Then these presidents and satraps came by agreement[m] to the king and said to him, "O King Darius, live for 7 ever! All the presidents of the kingdom, the prefects and the satraps, the counselors and the governors are agreed that the king should establish an ordinance and enforce an interdict, that whoever makes petition to any god or man for thirty days, except to you, O king, shall be cast into 8 the den of lions. Now, O king, establish the interdict and sign the document, so that it cannot be changed, according to the law of the Medes and the Persians, which can-9 not be revoked." Therefore King Darius signed the document and interdict.

10 When Daniel knew that the document had been signed, he went to his house where he had windows in his upper chamber open toward Jerusalem; and he got down upon his knees three times a day and prayed and gave thanks

11 before his God, as he had done previously. Then these men came by agreement[m] and found Daniel making 12 petition and supplication before his God. Then they came near and said before the king, concerning the interdict, "O king! Did you not sign an interdict, that any man who makes petition to any god or man within thirty days except to you, O king, shall be cast into the den of lions?" The king answered, "The thing stands fast, according to the law of the Medes and Persians, which can-13 not be revoked." Then they answered before the king, "That Daniel, who is one of the exiles from Judah, pays no heed to you, O king, or the interdict you have signed, but makes his petition three times a day."

14 Then the king, when he heard these words, was much distressed, and set his mind to deliver Daniel; and he 15 labored till the sun went down to rescue him. Then these men came by agreement[m] to the king, and said to the king, "Know, O king, that it is a law of the Medes and Persians that no interdict or ordinance which the king establishes can be changed."

16 Then the king commanded, and Daniel was brought and cast into the den of lions. The king said to Daniel, "May your God, whom you serve continually, deliver 17 you!" And a stone was brought and laid upon the mouth of the den, and the king sealed it with his own signet and with the signet of his lords, that nothing might be

m Or thronging

18 changed concerning Daniel. Then the king went to his palace, and spent the night fasting; no diversions were brought to him, and sleep fled from him.

19 Then, at break of day, the king arose and went in 20 haste to the den of lions. When he came near to the den where Daniel was, he cried out in a tone of anguish and said to Daniel, "O Daniel, servant of the living God, has your God, whom you serve continually, been able to de-21 liver you from the lions?" Then Daniel said to the king, 22 "O king, live for ever! My God sent his angel and shut the lions' mouths, and they have not hurt me, because I was found blameless before him; and also before you, O 23 king, I have done no wrong." Then the king was exceedingly glad, and commanded that Daniel be taken up out of the den. So Daniel was taken up out of the den, and no kind of hurt was found upon him, because he had 24 trusted in his God. And the king commanded, and those men who had accused Daniel were brought and cast into the den of lions—they, their children, and their wives; and before they reached the bottom of the den the lions overpowered them and broke all their bones in pieces.

25 Then King Darius wrote to all the peoples, nations, and languages that dwell in all the earth: "Peace be mul-26 tiplied to you. I make a decree, that in all my royal dominion men tremble and fear before the God of Daniel,

for he is the living God,
enduring for ever;
his kingdom shall never be destroyed,
and his dominion shall be to the end.

27 He delivers and rescues,
he works signs and wonders
in heaven and on earth,
he who has saved Daniel
from the power of the lions."

28 So this Daniel prospered during the reign of Darius and the reign of Cyrus the Persian.

A DREAM AND THREE VISIONS
Four Beasts

7 In the first year of Belshaz'zar king of Babylon, Daniel had a dream and visions of his head as he lay in his bed. Then he wrote down the dream, and told the 2 sum of the matter. Daniel said, "I saw in my vision by night, and behold, the four winds of heaven were stirring 3 up the great sea. And four great beasts came up out of 4 the sea, different from one another. The first was like a lion and had eagles' wings. Then as I looked its wings were plucked off, and it was lifted up from the ground and made to stand upon two feet like a man; and the 5 mind of a man was given to it. And behold, another beast, a second one, like a bear. It was raised up on one side; it had three ribs in its mouth between its teeth; 6 and it was told, 'Arise, devour much flesh.' After this I

looked, and lo, another, like a leopard, with four wings of a bird on its back; and the beast had four heads; and 7 dominion was given to it. After this I saw in the night visions, and behold, a fourth beast, terrible and dreadful and exceedingly strong; and it had great iron teeth; it devoured and broke in pieces, and stamped the residue with its feet. It was different from all the beasts that were 8 before it; and it had ten horns. I considered the horns, and behold, there came up among them another horn, a little one, before which three of the first horns were plucked up by the roots; and behold, in this horn were eyes like the eyes of a man, and a mouth speaking great 9 things. As I looked,

thrones were placed
and one that was Ancient of Days took his seat;
his raiment was white as snow,
and the hair of his head like pure wool;
his throne was fiery flames,
its wheels were burning fire.
10 A stream of fire issued
and came forth from before him;
a thousand thousands served him,
and ten thousand times ten thousand stood before
him;
the court sat in judgment,
and the books were opened.

11 I looked then because of the sound of the great words which the horn was speaking. And as I looked, the beast was slain, and its body destroyed and given over 12 to be burned with fire. As for the rest of the beasts, their dominion was taken away, but their lives were 13 prolonged for a season and a time. I saw in the night visions,

and behold, with the clouds of heaven
there came one like a son of man,
and he came to the Ancient of Days
and was presented before him.
14 And to him was given dominion
and glory and kingdom,
that all people, nations, and languages
should serve him;
his dominion is an everlasting dominion,
which shall not pass away,
and his kingdom one
that shall not be destroyed.

15 "As for me, Daniel, my spirit within me was anxious 16 and the visions of my head alarmed me. I approached one of those who stood there and asked him the truth concerning all this. So he told me, and made known to 17 me the interpretation of the things. 'These four great 18 beasts are four kings who shall arise out of the earth. But the saints of the Most High shall receive the kingdom, and possess the kingdom for ever, for ever and ever.'

19 "Then I desired to know the truth concerning the fourth beast, which was different from all the rest, exceedingly terrible, with its teeth of iron and claws of bronze; and which devoured and broke in pieces, and 20 stamped the residue with its feet; and concerning the ten horns that were on its head, and the other horn which came up and before which three of them fell, the horn which had eyes and a mouth that spoke great things, and 21 which seemed greater than its fellows. As I looked, this horn made war with the saints, and prevailed over them, 22 until the Ancient of Days came, and judgment was given for the saints of the Most High, and the time came when the saints received the kingdom.

23 "Thus he said: 'As for the fourth beast,
there shall be a fourth kingdom on earth,
which shall be different from all the kingdoms,
and it shall devour the whole earth,
and trample it down, and break it to pieces.
24 As for the ten horns,
out of this kingdom
ten kings shall arise,
and another shall arise after them;
he shall be different from the former ones,
and shall put down three kings.
25 He shall speak words against the Most High,
and shall wear out the saints of the Most High,
and shall think to change the times and the law;
and they shall be given into his hand
for a time, two times, and half a time.
26 But the court shall sit in judgment,
and his dominion shall be taken away,
to be consumed and destroyed to the end.
27 And the kingdom and the dominion
and the greatness of the kingdoms under the whole
heaven
shall be given to the people of the saints of the Most
High;
their kingdom shall be an everlasting kingdom,
and all dominions shall serve and obey them.'
28 "Here is the end of the matter. As for me, Daniel, my thoughts greatly alarmed me, and my color changed; but I kept the matter in my mind."

The Ram and the Goat

8 In the third year of the reign of King Belshaz'zar a vision appeared to me, Daniel, after that which ap-2 peared to me at the first. And I saw in the vision; and when I saw, I was in Susa the capital, which is in the province of Elam; and I saw in the vision, and I was at 3 the river U'lai. I raised my eyes and saw, and behold, a ram standing on the bank of the river. It had two horns; and both horns were high, but one was higher than the 4 other, and the higher one came up last. I saw the ram

charging westward and northward and southward; no beast could stand before him, and there was no one who could rescue from his power; he did as he pleased and magnified himself.

5 As I was considering, behold, a he-goat came from the west across the face of the whole earth, without touching the ground; and the goat had a conspicuous horn between 6 his eyes. He came to the ram with the two horns, which I had seen standing on the bank of the river, and he ran 7 at him in his mighty wrath. I saw him come close to the ram, and he was enraged against him and struck the ram and broke his two horns; and the ram had no power to stand before him, but he cast him down to the ground and trampled upon him; and there was no one who could 8 rescue the ram from his power. Then the he-goat magnified himself exceedingly; but when he was strong, the great horn was broken, and instead of it there came up four conspicuous horns toward the four winds of heaven.

9 Out of one of them came forth a little horn, which grew exceedingly great toward the south, toward the east, 10 and toward the glorious land. It grew great, even to the host of heaven; and some of the host of the stars it cast 11 down to the ground, and trampled upon them. It magnified itself, even up to the Prince of the host; and the continual burnt offering was taken away from him, and 12 the place of his sanctuary was overthrown. And the host was given over to it together with the continual burnt offering through transgression; [n] and truth was cast down to the ground, and the horn acted and prospered. 13 Then I heard a holy one speaking; and another holy one said to the one that spoke, "For how long is the vision concerning the continual burnt offering, the transgression that makes desolate, and the giving over of the sanctuary 14 and host to be trampled under foot?" [o] And he said to him,[p] "For two thousand and three hundred evenings and mornings; then the sanctuary shall be restored to its rightful state."

15 When I, Daniel, had seen the vision, I sought to understand it; and behold, there stood before me one having 16 the appearance of a man. And I heard a man's voice between the banks of the U'lai, and it called, "Gabriel, 17 make this man understand the vision." So he came near where I stood; and when he came, I was frightened and fell upon my face. But he said to me, "Understand, O son of man, that the vision is for the time of the end."

18 As he was speaking to me, I fell into a deep sleep with my face to the ground; but he touched me and set 19 me on my feet. He said, "Behold, I will make known to you what shall be at the latter end of the indignation; 20 for it pertains to the appointed time of the end. As for the ram which you saw with the two horns, these are the 21 kings of Media and Persia. And the he-goat [q] is the king of Greece; and the great horn between his eyes is the first

22 king. As for the horn that was broken, in place of which four others arose, four kingdoms shall arise from his [r] 23 nation, but not with his power. And at the latter end of their rule, when the transgressors have reached their full measure, a king of bold countenance, one who understands 24 riddles, shall arise. His power shall be great,[s] and he shall cause fearful destruction, and shall succeed in what he does, and destroy mighty men and the people of the saints. 25 By his cunning he shall make deceit prosper under his hand, and in his own mind he shall magnify himself. Without warning he shall destroy many; and he shall even rise up against the Prince of princes; but, by no 26 human hand, he shall be broken. The vision of the evenings and the mornings which has been told is true; but seal up the vision, for it pertains to many days hence."

27 And I, Daniel, was overcome and lay sick for some days; then I rose and went about the king's business; but I was appalled by the vision and did not understand it.

The Time of Restoration

9 In the first year of Darius the son of Ahasu-e'rus, by birth a Mede, who became king over the realm of the 2 Chalde'ans—in the first year of his reign, I, Daniel, perceived in the books the number of years which, according to the word of the LORD to Jeremiah the prophet, must pass before the end of the desolations of Jerusalem, namely, seventy years.

3 Then I turned my face to the Lord God, seeking him by prayer and supplications with fasting and sackcloth and 4 ashes. I prayed to the LORD my God and made confession, saying, "O Lord, the great and terrible God, who keepest covenant and steadfast love with those who love him 5 and keep his commandments, we have sinned and done wrong and acted wickedly and rebelled, turning aside 6 from thy commandments and ordinances; we have not listened to thy servants the prophets, who spoke in thy name to our kings, our princes, and our fathers, and to 7 all the people of the land. To thee, O Lord, belongs righteousness, but to us confusion of face, as at this day, to the men of Judah, to the inhabitants of Jerusalem, and to all Israel, those that are near and those that are far away, in all the lands to which thou hast driven them, because of the treachery which they have committed 8 against thee. To us, O Lord, belongs confusion of face, to our kings, to our princes, and to our fathers, because 9 we have sinned against thee. To the Lord our God belong mercy and forgiveness; because we have rebelled against 10 him, and have not obeyed the voice of the LORD our God by following his laws, which he set before us by his

[n] Heb obscure   [o] Heb obscure   [p] Theodotion Gk Syr Vg: Heb me   [q] Or shaggy he-goat
[r] Theodotion Gk Vg: Heb the   [s] Theodotion and Beatty papyrus of Gk: Heb repeats but not with his power from verse 22

[11] servants the prophets. All Israel has transgressed thy law and turned aside, refusing to obey thy voice. And the curse and oath which are written in the law of Moses the servant of God have been poured out upon us, because [12] we have sinned against him. He has confirmed his words, which he spoke against us and against our rulers who ruled us, by bringing upon us a great calamity; for under the whole heaven there has not been done the like of [13] what has been done against Jerusalem. As it is written in the law of Moses, all this calamity has come upon us, yet we have not entreated the favor of the LORD our God, turning from our iniquities and giving heed to thy truth. [14] Therefore the LORD has kept ready the calamity and has brought it upon us; for the LORD our God is righteous in all the works which he has done, and we have not obeyed [15] his voice. And now, O Lord our God, who didst bring thy people out of the land of Egypt with a mighty hand, and hast made thee a name, as at this day, we have [16] sinned, we have done wickedly. O Lord, according to all thy righteous acts, let thy anger and thy wrath turn away from thy city Jerusalem, thy holy hill; because for our sins, and for the iniquities of our fathers, Jerusalem and thy people have become a byword among all who are [17] round about us. Now therefore, O our God, hearken to the prayer of thy servant and to his supplications, and for thy own sake, O Lord,[t] cause thy face to shine upon thy [18] sanctuary, which is desolate. O my God, incline thy ear and hear; open thy eyes and behold our desolations, and the city which is called by thy name; for we do not present our supplications before thee on the ground of our righteousness, but on the ground of thy great mercy. [19] O LORD, hear; O LORD, forgive; O LORD, give heed and act; delay not, for thy own sake, O my God, because thy city and thy people are called by thy name."

[20] While I was speaking and praying, confessing my sin and the sin of my people Israel, and presenting my supplication before the LORD my God for the holy hill of my [21] God; while I was speaking in prayer, the man Gabriel, whom I had seen in the vision at the first, came to me in [22] swift flight at the time of the evening sacrifice. He came[u] and he said to me, "O Daniel, I have now come out to [23] give you wisdom and understanding. At the beginning of your supplications a word went forth, and I have come to tell it to you, for you are greatly beloved; therefore consider the word and understand the vision.

[24] "Seventy weeks of years are decreed concerning your people and your holy city, to finish the transgression, to put an end to sin, and to atone for iniquity, to bring in everlasting righteousness, to seal both vision and prophet, [25] and to anoint a most holy place.[v] Know therefore and understand that from the going forth of the word to restore and build Jerusalem to the coming of an anointed one, a prince, there shall be seven weeks. Then for sixty-two weeks it shall be built again with squares and moat, [26] but in a troubled time. And after the sixty-two weeks, an anointed one shall be cut off, and shall have nothing; and the people of the prince who is to come shall destroy the city and the sanctuary. Its[w] end shall come with a flood, and to the end there shall be war; desolations are decreed. [27] And he shall make a strong covenant with many for one week; and for half of the week he shall cause sacrifice and offering to cease; and upon the wing of abominations shall come one who makes desolate, until the decreed end is poured out on the desolator."

Conflict Between Persia and Greece

[10] In the third year of Cyrus king of Persia a word was revealed to Daniel, who was named Belteshaz'zar. And the word was true, and it was a great conflict. And he understood the word and had understanding of the vision.

[2] In those days I, Daniel, was mourning for three weeks. [3] I ate no delicacies, no meat or wine entered my mouth, nor did I anoint myself at all, for the full three weeks. [4] On the twenty-fourth day of the first month, as I was standing on the bank of the great river, that is, the Tigris, [5] I lifted up my eyes and looked, and behold, a man clothed in linen, whose loins were girded with gold of Uphaz. [6] His body was like beryl, his face like the appearance of lightning, his eyes like flaming torches, his arms and legs like the gleam of burnished bronze, and the sound of [7] his words like the noise of a multitude. And I, Daniel, alone saw the vision, for the men who were with me did not see the vision, but a great trembling fell upon them, [8] and they fled to hide themselves. So I was left alone and saw this great vision, and no strength was left in me; my radiant appearance was fearfully changed, and I retained [9] no strength. Then I heard the sound of his words; and when I heard the sound of his words, I fell on my face in a deep sleep with my face to the ground.

[10] And behold, a hand touched me and set me trembling [11] on my hands and knees. And he said to me, "O Daniel, man greatly beloved, give heed to the words that I speak to you, and stand upright, for now I have been sent to you." While he was speaking this word to me, I stood [12] up trembling. Then he said to me, "Fear not, Daniel, for from the first day that you set your mind to understand and humbled yourself before your God, your words have been heard, and I have come because of your [13] words. The prince of the kingdom of Persia withstood me twenty-one days; but Michael, one of the chief princes,

[t] Theodotion Vg Compare Syr: Heb *for the Lord's sake*   [u] Gk Syr: Heb *made to understand*   [v] Or *thing* or *one*   [w] Or *his*

came to help me, so I left him there with the prince of the

14 kingdom of Persia ˣ and came to make you understand what is to befall your people in the latter days. For the vision is for days yet to come."

15 When he had spoken to me according to these words, I
16 turned my face toward the ground and was dumb. And behold, one in the likeness of the sons of men touched my lips; then I opened my mouth and spoke. I said to him who stood before me, "O my lord, by reason of the vision pains have come upon me, and I retain no strength.
17 How can my lord's servant talk with my lord? For now no strength remains in me, and no breath is left in me."
18 Again one having the appearance of a man touched
19 me and strengthened me. And he said, "O man greatly beloved, fear not, peace be with you; be strong and of good courage." And when he spoke to me, I was strengthened and said, "Let my lord speak, for you have
20 strengthened me." Then he said, "Do you know why I have come to you? But now I will return to fight against the prince of Persia; and when I am through with him,
21 lo, the prince of Greece will come. But I will tell you what is inscribed in the book of truth: there is none who contends by my side against these except Michael, your

11 ¹ prince. And as for me, in the first year of Darius the Mede, I stood up to confirm and strengthen him.

2 "And now I will show you the truth. Behold, three more kings shall arise in Persia; and a fourth shall be far richer than all of them; and when he has become strong through his riches, he shall stir up all against the kingdom
3 of Greece. Then a mighty king shall arise, who shall rule
4 with great dominion and do according to his will. And when he has arisen, his kingdom shall be broken and divided toward the four winds of heaven, but not to his posterity, nor according to the dominion with which he ruled; for his kingdom shall be plucked up and go to others besides these.

5 "Then the king of the south shall be strong, but one of his princes shall be stronger than he and his dominion
6 shall be a great dominion. After some years they shall make an alliance, and the daughter of the king of the south shall come to the king of the north to make peace; but she shall not retain the strength of her arm, and he and his offspring shall not endure; but she shall be given up, and her attendants, her child, and he who got possession of ʸ her.

7 "In those times a branch ᶻ from her roots shall arise in his place; he shall come against the army and enter the fortress of the king of the north, and he shall deal with
8 them and shall prevail. He shall also carry off to Egypt their gods with their molten images and with their precious vessels of silver and of gold; and for some years he shall refrain from attacking the king of the north.
9 Then the latter shall come into the realm of the king of

the south but shall return into his own land.

10 "His sons shall wage war and assemble a multitude of great forces, which shall come on and overflow and pass through, and again shall carry the war as far as his
11 fortress. Then the king of the south, moved with anger, shall come out and fight with the king of the north; and he shall raise a great multitude, but it shall be given into
12 his hand. And when the multitude is taken, his heart shall be exalted, and he shall cast down tens of thousands, but
13 he shall not prevail. For the king of the north shall again raise a multitude, greater than the former; and after some years ᵃ he shall come on with a great army and abundant supplies.

14 "In those times many shall rise against the king of the south; and the men of violence among your own people shall lift themselves up in order to fulfil the vision; but
15 they shall fail. Then the king of the north shall come and throw up siegeworks, and take a well-fortified city. And the forces of the south shall not stand, or even his
16 picked troops, for there shall be no strength to stand. But he who comes against him shall do according to his own will, and none shall stand before him; and he shall stand in the glorious land, and all of it shall be in his
17 power. He shall set his face to come with the strength of his whole kingdom, and he shall bring terms of peace ᵇ and perform them. He shall give him the daughter of women to destroy the kingdom; ᶜ but it shall not stand
18 or be to his advantage. Afterward he shall turn his face to the coastlands, and shall take many of them; but a commander shall put an end to his insolence; indeed ᵈ
19 he shall turn his insolence back upon him. Then he shall turn his face back toward the fortresses of his own land; but he shall stumble and fall, and shall not be found.

20 "Then shall arise in his place one who shall send an exactor of tribute through the glory of the kingdom; but within a few days he shall be broken, neither in anger nor
21 in battle. In his place shall arise a contemptible person to whom royal majesty has not been given; he shall come in without warning and obtain the kingdom by flatteries.
22 Armies shall be utterly swept away before him and broken,
23 and the prince of the covenant also. And from the time that an alliance is made with him he shall act deceitfully;
24 and he shall become strong with a small people. Without warning he shall come into the richest parts ᵉ of the province; and he shall do what neither his fathers nor his fathers' fathers have done, scattering among them plunder, spoil, and goods. He shall devise plans against
25 strongholds, but only for a time. And he shall stir up his power and his courage against the king of the south with a great army; and the king of the south shall wage war with an exceedingly great and mighty army; but he shall not stand, for plots shall be devised against him.
26 Even those who eat his rich food shall be his undoing;

ˣ Theodotion Compare Gk: Heb *I was left there with the kings of Persia*
ᵃ Heb *at the end of the times years* ᵇ Gk: Heb *upright ones*
ᵉ Or *among the richest men*

ʸ Or *supported*
ᶜ Heb *her* or *it*

ᶻ Gk: Heb *from a branch*
ᵈ Heb obscure

his army shall be swept away, and many shall fall down
27 slain. And as for the two kings, their minds shall be bent on mischief; they shall speak lies at the same table, but to no avail; for the end is yet to be at the time appointed.
28 And he shall return to his land with great substance, but his heart shall be set against the holy covenant. And he shall work his will, and return to his own land.
29 "At the time appointed he shall return and come into the south; but it shall not be this time as it was before.
30 For ships of Kittim shall come against him, and he shall be afraid and withdraw, and shall turn back and be enraged and take action against the holy covenant. He shall turn back and give heed to those who forsake the
31 holy covenant. Forces from him shall appear and profane the temple and fortress, and shall take away the continual burnt offering. And they shall set up the abomina-
32 tion that makes desolate. He shall seduce with flattery those who violate the covenant; but the people who know
33 their God shall stand firm and take action. And those among the people who are wise shall make many understand, though they shall fall by sword and flame, by
34 captivity and plunder, for some days. When they fall, they shall receive a little help. And many shall join themselves
35 to them with flattery; and some of those who are wise shall fall, to refine and to cleanse them f and to make them white, until the time of the end, for it is yet for the time appointed.
36 "And the king shall do according to his will; he shall exalt himself and magnify himself above every god, and shall speak astonishing things against the God of gods. He shall prosper till the indignation is accomplished; for
37 what is determined shall be done. He shall give no heed to the gods of his fathers, or to the one beloved by women; he shall not give heed to any other god, for he
38 shall magnify himself above all. He shall honor the god of fortresses instead of these; a god whom his fathers did not know he shall honor with gold and silver, with
39 precious stones and costly gifts. He shall deal with the strongest fortresses by the help of a foreign god; those who acknowledge him he shall magnify with honor. He shall make them rulers over many and shall divide the land for a price.
40 "At the time of the end the king of the south shall attack g him; but the king of the north shall rush upon him like a whirlwind, with chariots and horsemen, and with many ships; and he shall come into countries and
41 shall overflow and pass through. He shall come into the glorious land. And tens of thousands shall fall, but these shall be delivered out of his hand: Edom and Moab and
42 the main part of the Ammonites. He shall stretch out his hand against the countries, and the land of Egypt shall
43 not escape. He shall become ruler of the treasures of gold and of silver, and all the precious things of Egypt;

and the Libyans and the Ethiopians shall follow in his
44 train. But tidings from the east and the north shall alarm him, and he shall go forth with great fury to exterminate
45 and utterly destroy many. And he shall pitch his palatial tents between the sea and the glorious holy mountain; yet he shall come to his end, with none to help him.

12 "At that time shall arise Michael, the great prince who has charge of your people. And there shall be a time of trouble, such as never has been since there was a nation till that time; but at that time your people shall be delivered, every one whose name shall be found written
2 in the book. And many of those who sleep in the dust of the earth shall awake, some to everlasting life, and
3 some to shame and everlasting contempt. And those who are wise shall shine like the brightness of the firmament; and those who turn many to righteousness, like the stars
4 for ever and ever. But you, Daniel, shut up the words, and seal the book, until the time of the end. Many shall run to and fro, and knowledge shall increase."
5 Then I Daniel looked, and behold, two others stood, one on this bank of the stream and one on that bank of
6 the stream. And I h said to the man clothed in linen, who

was above the waters of the stream, "How long shall it be
7 till the end of these wonders?" The man clothed in linen, who was above the waters of the stream, raised his right hand and his left hand toward heaven; and I heard him swear by him who lives for ever that it would be for a time, two times, and half a time; and that when the shattering of the power of the holy people comes to an end
8 all these things would be accomplished. I heard, but I did not understand. Then I said, "O my lord, what shall be
9 the issue of these things?" He said, "Go your way, Daniel, for the words are shut up and sealed until the time
10 of the end. Many shall purify themselves, and make themselves white, and be refined; but the wicked shall do wickedly; and none of the wicked shall understand; but
11 those who are wise shall understand. And from the time that the continual burnt offering is taken away, and the abomination that makes desolate is set up, there shall be
12 a thousand two hundred and ninety days. Blessed is he who waits and comes to the thousand three hundred and
13 thirty-five days. But go your way till the end; and you shall rest, and shall stand in your allotted place at the end of the days."

f Gk: Heb among them   g Heb thrust at   h Gk Vg: Heb he

HOSEA

About eight hundred years before Christ, Assyria was a strong nation northeast of Palestine. Because Assyria was powerful, some Hebrews wanted to worship Assyrian gods and copy Assyrian religious customs. Four prophets—Amos, Hosea, Isaiah, and Micah—began to preach against the false and wicked ways of the people.

The sermons that make up the Book of Hosea were preached in the northern kingdom, Israel, in the years following 747 B.C., probably during the same years Amos was preaching. Both these great men warned that Israel, because of its sins, would be defeated by the Assyrians. Not only were the people worshiping pagan gods, but they were being cruel and dishonest to one another, thinking only of how they might become richer.

Amos preached that the wrath of God would destroy Israel, but Hosea had a deeper insight. Hosea's wife had deserted him, but he still loved her and sought to win her back. He realized that if a man like himself could be loving and forgiving toward an unfaithful wife, God was even more patient and forgiving with his chosen people.

Like Amos, Hosea denounced the terrible sins and unfaithfulness of the people, but he also said that God was wonderfully loving and forgiving. He taught that Israel was like his own unfaithful wife. He told the people that if they would repent, God would forgive them. Many believe that Hosea reveals the highest teaching about God to be found in the Old Testament.

THE BOOK OF

HOSEA

HOSEA'S EXPERIENCES AND THEIR EFFECT

1 The word of the LORD that came to Hose'a the son of Be-e'ri, in the days of Uzzi'ah, Jotham, Ahaz, and Hezeki'ah, kings of Judah, and in the days of Jerobo'am the son of Jo'ash, king of Israel.

2 When the LORD first spoke through Hose'a, the LORD said to Hose'a, "Go, take to yourself a wife of harlotry and have children of harlotry, for the land commits 3 great harlotry by forsaking the LORD." So he went and took Gomer the daughter of Dibla'im, and she conceived and bore him a son.

4 And the LORD said to him, "Call his name Jezreel; for yet a little while, and I will punish the house of Jehu for the blood of Jezreel, and I will put an end to the kingdom 5 of the house of Israel. And on that day, I will break the bow of Israel in the valley of Jezreel."

6 She conceived again and bore a daughter. And the LORD said to him, "Call her name Not pitied, for I will no more have pity on the house of Israel, to forgive them 7 at all. But I will have pity on the house of Judah, and I will deliver them by the LORD their God; I will not deliver them by bow, nor by sword, nor by war, nor by horses, nor by horsemen."

8 When she had weaned Not pitied, she conceived and 9 bore a son. And the LORD said, "Call his name Not my people, for you are not my people and I am not your God."[a]

10 [b] Yet the number of the people of Israel shall be like the sand of the sea, which can be neither measured nor numbered; and in the place where it was said to them, "You are not my people," it shall be said to them, "Sons 11 of the living God." And the people of Judah and the people of Israel shall be gathered together, and they shall appoint for themselves one head; and they shall go up from the land, for great shall be the day of Jezreel.

2 [c] Say to your brother,[d] "My people," and to your sister,[e] "She has obtained pity."

---

[a] Heb I am not yours   [b] Ch 2.1 in Heb   [c] Ch 2.3 in Heb   [d] Gk: Heb brothers   [e] Gk Vg: Heb sisters

2 "Plead with your mother, plead—
  for she is not my wife,
  and I am not her husband—
that she put away her harlotry from her face,
  and her adultery from between her breasts;
3 lest I strip her naked
  and make her as in the day she was born,
and make her like a wilderness,
  and set her like a parched land,
  and slay her with thirst.
4 Upon her children also I will have no pity,
  because they are children of harlotry.
5 For their mother has played the harlot;
  she that conceived them has acted shamefully.
For she said, 'I will go after my lovers,
  who give me my bread and my water,
  my wool and my flax, my oil and my drink.'
6 Therefore I will hedge up her f way with thorns;

ANATHOTH (JEREMIAH)
JERUSALEM
TEKOA (ISAIAH,
(AMOS) ZEPHANIAH)
GATH
(MICAH)

HOMES OF THE PROPHETS

  and I will build a wall against her,
  so that she cannot find her paths.
7 She shall pursue her lovers,
  but not overtake them;
and she shall seek them,
  but shall not find them.
Then she shall say, 'I will go
  and return to my first husband,
  for it was better with me then than now.'
8 And she did not know
  that it was I who gave her
  the grain, the wine, and the oil,
and who lavished upon her silver
  and gold which they used for Ba'al.
9 Therefore I will take back

my grain in its time,
  and my wine in its season;
and I will take away my wool and my flax,
  which were to cover her nakedness.
10 Now I will uncover her lewdness
  in the sight of her lovers,
  and no one shall rescue her out of my hand.
11 And I will put an end to all her mirth,
  her feasts, her new moons, her sabbaths,
  and all her appointed feasts.
12 And I will lay waste her vines and her fig trees,
  of which she said,
'These are my hire,
  which my lovers have given me.'
I will make them a forest,
  and the beasts of the field shall devour them.
13 And I will punish her for the feast days of the Ba'als
  when she burned incense to them
and decked herself with her ring and jewelry,
  and went after her lovers,
  and forgot me, says the LORD.

14 "Therefore, behold, I will allure her,
  and bring her into the wilderness,
  and speak tenderly to her.
15 And there I will give her her vineyards,
  and make the Valley of Achor a door of hope.
And there she shall answer as in the days of her youth,
  as at the time when she came out of the land of Egypt.
16 "And in that day, says the LORD, you will call me, 'My husband,' and no longer will you call me, 'My Ba'al.'
17 For I will remove the names of the Ba'als from her mouth,
18 and they shall be mentioned by name no more. And I will make for you g a covenant on that day with the beasts of the field, the birds of the air, and the creeping things of the ground; and I will abolish h the bow, the sword, and war from the land; and I will make you lie down in safety.
19 And I will betroth you to me for ever; I will betroth you to me in righteousness and in justice, in steadfast love, and
20 in mercy. I will betroth you to me in faithfulness; and you shall know the LORD.
21 "And in that day, says the LORD,
  I will answer the heavens
  and they shall answer the earth;
22 and the earth shall answer the grain, the wine, and the oil,
  and they shall answer Jezreel; i
23 and I will sow him j for myself in the land.
And I will have pity on Not pitied,
  and I will say to Not my people, 'You are my people';
  and he shall say, 'Thou art my God.' "

3 And the LORD said to me, "Go again, love a woman who is beloved of a paramour and is an adulteress;

f Gk Syr: Heb your   g Heb them   h Heb break   i That is God sows   j Cn: Heb her

611

even as the LORD loves the people of Israel, though they
2 turn to other gods and love cakes of raisins." So I bought
her for fifteen shekels of silver and a homer and a lethech
3 of barley. And I said to her, "You must dwell as mine for
many days; you shall not play the harlot, or belong to
4 another man; so will I also be to you." For the children
of Israel shall dwell many days without king or prince,
without sacrifice or pillar, without ephod or teraphim.
5 Afterward the children of Israel shall return and seek
the LORD their God, and David their king; and they shall
come in fear to the LORD and to his goodness in the latter
days.

ISRAEL'S UNFAITHFULNESS TO GOD

4 Hear the word of the LORD, O people of Israel;
    for the LORD has a controversy with the inhabitants
        of the land.
There is no faithfulness or kindness,
    and no knowledge of God in the land;
2 there is swearing, lying, killing, stealing, and committing
        adultery;
    they break all bounds and murder follows murder.
3 Therefore the land mourns,
    and all who dwell in it languish,
and also the beasts of the field,
    and the birds of the air;
    and even the fish of the sea are taken away.

4 Yet let no one contend,
    and let none accuse,
    for with you is my contention, O priest.k

5 You shall stumble by day,
    the prophet also shall stumble with you by night;
    and I will destroy your mother.
6 My people are destroyed for lack of knowledge;
    because you have rejected knowledge,
    I reject you from being a priest to me.
And since you have forgotten the law of your God,
    I also will forget your children.

7 The more they increased,
    the more they sinned against me;
    I will change their glory into shame.
8 They feed on the sin of my people;
    they are greedy for their iniquity.

9 And it shall be like people, like priest;
    I will punish them for their ways,
    and requite them for their deeds.
10 They shall eat, but not be satisfied;
    they shall play the harlot, but not multiply;
because they have forsaken the LORD
    to cherish harlotry.

11 Wine and new wine
    take away the understanding.
12 My people inquire of a thing of wood,
    and their staff gives them oracles.
For a spirit of harlotry has led them astray,
    and they have left their God to play the harlot.
13 They sacrifice on the tops of the mountains,
    and make offerings upon the hills,
under oak, poplar, and terebinth,
    because their shade is good.
Therefore your daughters play the harlot,
    and your brides commit adultery.
14 I will not punish your daughters when they play the harlot,
    nor your brides when they commit adultery;
for the men themselves go aside with harlots,
    and sacrifice with cult prostitutes,
and a people without understanding shall come to ruin.

15 Though you play the harlot, O Israel,
    let not Judah become guilty.
Enter not into Gilgal,
    nor go up to Beth-a'ven,
    and swear not, "As the LORD lives."
16 Like a stubborn heifer,
    Israel is stubborn;
can the LORD now feed them
    like a lamb in a broad pasture?

17 E'phraim is joined to idols,
    let him alone.
18 A bandl of drunkards, they give themselves to harlotry;
    they love shame more than their glory.m
19 A wind has wrapped themn in its wings,
    and they shall be ashamed because of their altars.o

5 Hear this, O priests!
    Give heed, O house of Israel!
Hearken, O house of the king!
    For the judgment pertains to you;
for you have been a snare at Mizpah,
    and a net spread upon Tabor.
2 And they have made deep the pit of Shittim;p
    but I will chastise all of them.

3 I know E'phraim,
    and Israel is not hid from me;

k Cn: Heb uncertain   l Cn: Heb uncertain   m Cn Compare Gk: Heb of this line uncertain   n Heb her
o Gk Syr: Heb sacrifices   p Cn: Heb uncertain

for now, O E'phraim, you have played the harlot,
  Israel is defiled.
4 Their deeds do not permit them
    to return to their God.
  For the spirit of harlotry is within them,
    and they know not the LORD.

5 The pride of Israel testifies to his face;
    E'phraim q shall stumble in his guilt;
  Judah also shall stumble with them.
6 With their flocks and herds they shall go
    to seek the LORD,
  but they will not find him;
    he has withdrawn from them.
7 They have dealt faithlessly with the LORD;
    for they have borne alien children.
  Now the new moon shall devour them with their fields.

8 Blow the horn in Gib'e-ah,
    the trumpet in Ramah.
  Sound the alarm at Beth-a'ven;
    tremble,r O Benjamin!
9 E'phraim shall become a desolation
    in the day of punishment;
  among the tribes of Israel
    I declare what is sure.
10 The princes of Judah have become
    like those who remove the landmark;
  upon them I will pour out
    my wrath like water.
11 E'phraim is oppressed, crushed in judgment,
    because he was determined to go after vanity.s
12 Therefore I am like a moth to E'phraim,
    and like dry rot to the house of Judah.

13 When E'phraim saw his sickness,
    and Judah his wound,
  then E'phraim went to Assyria,
    and sent to the great king.t
  But he is not able to cure you
    or heal your wound.
14 For I will be like a lion to E'phraim,
    and like a young lion to the house of Judah.
  I, even I, will rend and go away,
    I will carry off, and none shall rescue.

15 I will return again to my place,
    until they acknowledge their guilt and seek my face,
    and in their distress they seek me, saying,
6 "Come, let us return to the LORD;
    for he has torn, that he may heal us;
  he has stricken, and he will bind us up.
2 After two days he will revive us;

on the third day he will raise us up,
    that we may live before him.
3 Let us know, let us press on to know the LORD;
    his going forth is sure as the dawn;
  he will come to us as the showers,
    as the spring rains that water the earth."

4 What shall I do with you, O E'phraim?
    What shall I do with you, O Judah?
  Your love is like a morning cloud,
    like the dew that goes early away.
5 Therefore I have hewn them by the prophets,
    I have slain them by the words of my mouth,
    and my judgment goes forth as the light.u
6 For I desire steadfast love and not sacrifice,
    the knowledge of God, rather than burnt offerings.

7 But at v Adam they transgressed the covenant;
    there they dealt faithlessly with me.
8 Gilead is a city of evildoers,
    tracked with blood.
9 As robbers lie in wait w for a man,
    so the priests are banded together; x
  they murder on the way to Shechem,
    yea, they commit villainy.
10 In the house of Israel I have seen a horrible thing;
    E'phraim's harlotry is there, Israel is defiled.

11 For you also, O Judah, a harvest is appointed.

When I would restore the fortunes of my people,
7   when I would heal Israel,
    the corruption of E'phraim is revealed,
    and the wicked deeds of Samar'ia;
  for they deal falsely,
    the thief breaks in,
    and the bandits raid without.
2 But they do not consider
    that I remember all their evil works.
  Now their deeds encompass them,
    they are before my face.
3 By their wickedness they make the king glad,
    and the princes by their treachery.
4 They are all adulterers;
    they are like a heated oven,
  whose baker ceases to stir the fire,
    from the kneading of the dough until it is leavened.
5 On the day of our king the princes
    became sick with the heat of wine;
    he stretched out his hand with mockers.
6 For like an oven their hearts burn y with intrigue;
    all night their anger smolders;
    in the morning it blazes like a flaming fire.

q Heb Israel and Ephraim   r Cn Compare Gk: Heb after you   s Gk: Heb a command
t Cn: Heb a king that will contend   u Gk Syr: Heb thy judgment goes forth   v Cn: Heb like   w Cn: Heb uncertain
x Syr: Heb a company   y Gk Syr: Heb brought near

7 All of them are hot as an oven,
   and they devour their rulers.
 All their kings have fallen;
   and none of them calls upon me.

8 E'phraim mixes himself with the peoples;
   E'phraim is a cake not turned.
9 Aliens devour his strength,
   and he knows it not;
 gray hairs are sprinkled upon him,
   and he knows it not.
10 The pride of Israel witnesses against him;
    yet they do not return to the LORD their God,
    nor seek him, for all this.

11 E'phraim is like a dove,
   silly and without sense,
 calling to Egypt, going to Assyria.
12 As they go, I will spread over them my net;
   I will bring them down like birds of the air;
   I will chastise them for their wicked deeds.z
13 Woe to them, for they have strayed from me!
   Destruction to them, for they have rebelled against me!
 I would redeem them,
   but they speak lies against me.

14 They do not cry to me from the heart,
   but they wail upon their beds;
 for grain and wine they gash themselves,
   they rebel against me.
15 Although I trained and strengthened their arms,
   yet they devise evil against me.
16 They turn to Ba'al; a
   they are like a treacherous bow,
 their princes shall fall by the sword
   because of the insolence of their tongue.
 This shall be their derision in the land of Egypt.

8 Set the trumpet to your lips,
    for b a vulture is over the house of the LORD,

 because they have broken my covenant,
   and transgressed my law.
2 To me they cry,
   My God, we Israel know thee.
3 Israel has spurned the good;
   the enemy shall pursue him.

4 They made kings, but not through me.
   They set up princes, but without my knowledge.
 With their silver and gold they made idols
   for their own destruction.
5 I have c spurned your calf, O Samar'ia.
   My anger burns against them.
 How long will it be
6   till they are pure in Israel? d

 A workman made it;
   it is not God.
 The calf of Samar'ia
   shall be broken to pieces.e

7 For they sow the wind,
   and they shall reap the whirlwind.
 The standing grain has no heads,
   it shall yield no meal;
 if it were to yield,
   aliens would devour it.
8 Israel is swallowed up;
   already they are among the nations
   as a useless vessel.
9 For they have gone up to Assyria,
   a wild ass wandering alone;
   E'phraim has hired lovers.
10 Though they hire allies among the nations,
    I will soon gather them up.
 And they shall cease f for a little while
   from anointing g king and princes.

11 Because E'phraim has multiplied altars for sinning,
    they have become to him altars for sinning.
12 Were I to write for him my laws by ten thousands,
    they would be regarded as a strange thing.
13 They love sacrifice; h
    they sacrifice flesh and eat it;
    but the LORD has no delight in them.
 Now he will remember their iniquity,
   and punish their sins;
   they shall return to Egypt.
14 For Israel has forgotten his Maker,
    and built palaces;
 and Judah has multiplied fortified cities;
   but I will send a fire upon his cities,
   and it shall devour his strongholds.

9 Rejoice not, O Israel!
   Exult not i like the peoples;
   for you have played the harlot, forsaking your God.
 You have loved a harlot's hire
   upon all threshing floors.
2 Threshing floor and winevat shall not feed them,
   and the new wine shall fail them.

z Cn: Heb *according to the report to their congregation*   a Cn: Heb *uncertain*   b Cn: Heb *as*   c Heb *He has*
d Gk: Heb *for from Israel*   e Or *shall go up in flames*   f Gk: Heb *begin*   g Gk: Heb *burden*
h Cn: Heb *uncertain*   i Gk: Heb *to exultation*

3 They shall not remain in the land of the LORD;
   but E'phraim shall return to Egypt,
   and they shall eat unclean food in Assyria.

4 They shall not pour libations of wine to the LORD;
   and they shall not please him with their sacrifices.
   Their bread j shall be like mourners' bread;
   all who eat of it shall be defiled;
   for their bread shall be for their hunger only;
   it shall not come to the house of the LORD.

5 What will you do on the day of appointed festival,
   and on the day of the feast of the LORD?
6 For behold, they are going to Assyria; k
   Egypt shall gather them,
   Memphis shall bury them.
   Nettles shall possess their precious things of silver;
   thorns shall be in their tents.

7 The days of punishment have come,
   the days of recompense have come;
   Israel shall know it.
   The prophet is a fool,
   the man of the spirit is mad,
   because of your great iniquity
   and great hatred.
8 The prophet is the watchman of E'phraim,
   the people of my God,
   yet a fowler's snare is on all his ways,
   and hatred in the house of his God.
9 They have deeply corrupted themselves
   as in the days of Gib'e-ah:
   he will remember their iniquity,
   he will punish their sins.

10 Like grapes in the wilderness,
   I found Israel.
   Like the first fruit on the fig tree, in its first season,
   I saw your fathers.
   But they came to Ba'al-pe'or,
   and consecrated themselves to Ba'al,¹
   and became detestable like the thing they loved.
11 E'phraim's glory shall fly away like a bird—
   no birth, no pregnancy, no conception!
12 Even if they bring up children,
   I will bereave them till none is left.
   Woe to them
   when I depart from them!
13 E'phraim's sons, as I have seen, are destined for a prey; m
   E'phraim must lead forth his sons to slaughter.
14 Give them, O LORD—
   what wilt thou give?
   Give them a miscarrying womb
   and dry breasts.

15 Every evil of theirs is in Gilgal;
   there I began to hate them.
   Because of the wickedness of their deeds
   I will drive them out of my house.
   I will love them no more;
   all their princes are rebels.

16 E'phraim is stricken,
   their root is dried up,
   they shall bear no fruit.
   Even though they bring forth,
   I will slay their beloved children.
17 My God will cast them off,
   because they have not hearkened to him;
   they shall be wanderers among the nations.

10 Israel is a luxuriant vine
      that yields its fruit.
   The more his fruit increased
      the more altars he built;
   as his country improved
      he improved his pillars.
2 Their heart is false;
   now they must bear their guilt.
   The LORD n will break down their altars,
      and destroy their pillars.

3 For now they will say:
   "We have no king,
   for we fear not the LORD,
   and a king, what could he do for us?"
4 They utter mere words;
   with empty oaths they make covenants;
   so judgment springs up like poisonous weeds
      in the furrows of the field.
5 The inhabitants of Samar'ia tremble
   for the calf o of Beth-a'ven.
   Its people shall mourn for it,
   and its idolatrous priests shall wail p over it,
   over its glory which has departed from it.
6 Yea, the thing itself shall be carried to Assyria,
   as tribute to the great king.q
   E'phraim shall be put to shame,
   and Israel shall be ashamed of his idol.r

7 Samar'ia's king shall perish,
   like a chip on the face of the waters.
8 The high places of Aven, the sin of Israel,
   shall be destroyed.
   Thorn and thistle shall grow up on their altars;
   and they shall say to the mountains, Cover us,
   and to the hills, Fall upon us.

j Cn: Heb to them   k Cn: Heb from destruction   l Heb shame   m Cn Compare Gk: Heb uncertain
n Heb he   o Gk Syr: Heb calves   p Cn: Heb exult   q Cn: Heb a king that will contend   r Cn: Heb counsel

9 From the days of Gib'e-ah, you have sinned, O Israel;
  there they have continued.
  Shall not war overtake them in Gib'e-ah?
10 I will come ˢ against the wayward people to chastise them;
  and nations shall be gathered against them
  when they are chastised ᵗ for their double iniquity.

11 E'phraim was a trained heifer
  that loved to thresh,
  and I spared her fair neck;
  but I will put E'phraim to the yoke,
  Judah must plow,
  Jacob must harrow for himself.
12 Sow for yourselves righteousness,
  reap the fruit ᵘ of steadfast love;
  break up your fallow ground,
  for it is the time to seek the LORD,
  that he may come and rain salvation upon you.

13 You have plowed iniquity,
  you have reaped injustice,
  you have eaten the fruit of lies.
  Because you have trusted in your chariots ᵛ
  and in the multitude of your warriors,
14 therefore the tumult of war shall arise among your people,
  and all your fortresses shall be destroyed,
  as Shalman destroyed Beth-ar'bel on the day of battle;
  mothers were dashed in pieces with their children.
15 Thus it shall be done to you, O house of Israel, ʷ
  because of your great wickedness.
  In the storm ˣ the king of Israel
  shall be utterly cut off.

11 When Israel was a child, I loved him,
    and out of Egypt I called my son.
2 The more I ʸ called them,
  the more they went from me; ᶻ
they kept sacrificing to the Ba'als,
  and burning incense to idols.

3 Yet it was I who taught E'phraim to walk,
  I took them up in my ᵃ arms;
  but they did not know that I healed them.
4 I led them with cords of compassion, ᵇ
  with the bands of love,
and I became to them as one
  who eases the yoke on their jaws,
  and I bent down to them and fed them.

5 They shall return to the land of Egypt,
  and Assyria shall be their king,
  because they have refused to return to me.
6 The sword shall rage against their cities,
  consume the bars of their gates,

and devour them in their fortresses. ᶜ
7 My people are bent on turning away from me; ᵈ
  so they are appointed to the yoke,
  and none shall remove it.

8 How can I give you up, O E'phraim!
  How can I hand you over, O Israel!
  How can I make you like Admah!
  How can I treat you like Zeboi'im!
My heart recoils within me,
  my compassion grows warm and tender.
9 I will not execute my fierce anger,
  I will not again destroy E'phraim;
for I am God and not man,
  the Holy One in your midst,
  and I will not come to destroy. ᵉ

10 They shall go after the LORD,
  he will roar like a lion;
yea, he will roar,
  and his sons shall come trembling from the west;
11 they shall come trembling like birds from Egypt,
  and like doves from the land of Assyria;
  and I will return them to their homes, says the LORD.
12 ᶠ E'phraim has encompassed me with lies,
  and the house of Israel with deceit;
but Judah is still known by ᵍ God,
  and is faithful to the Holy One.

12 E'phraim herds the wind,
    and pursues the east wind all day long;
they multiply falsehood and violence;
  they make a bargain with Assyria,
  and oil is carried to Egypt.

2 The LORD has an indictment against Judah,
  and will punish Jacob according to his ways,
  and requite him according to his deeds.
3 In the womb he took his brother by the heel,
  and in his manhood he strove with God.
4 He strove with the angel and prevailed,
  he wept and sought his favor.
He met God at Bethel,
  and there God spoke with him ʰ—

ˢ Cn Compare Gk: Heb in my desire   ᵗ Gk: Heb bound   ᵘ Gk: Heb according to   ᵛ Gk: Heb way   ʷ Gk: Heb O Bethel
ˣ Cn: Heb dawn   ʸ Gk: Heb they   ᶻ Gk: Heb them   ᵃ Gk Syr Vg: Heb his   ᵇ Heb man
ᶜ Cn: Heb counsels   ᵈ The meaning of the Hebrew is uncertain   ᵉ Cn: Heb into the city   ᶠ Ch 12.1 in Heb
ᵍ Cn Compare Gk: Heb roams with   ʰ Gk Syr: Heb us

[5] the LORD the God of hosts,
the LORD is his name:
[6] "So you, by the help of your God, return,
hold fast to love and justice,
and wait continually for your God."

[7] A trader, in whose hands are false balances,
he loves to oppress.
[8] E'phraim has said, "Ah, but I am rich,
I have gained wealth for myself";
but all his riches can never offset[i]
the guilt he has incurred.
[9] I am the LORD your God
from the land of Egypt;
I will again make you dwell in tents,
as in the days of the appointed feast.

[10] I spoke to the prophets;
it was I who multiplied visions,
and through the prophets gave parables.
[11] If there is iniquity in Gilead
they shall surely come to nought;
if in Gilgal they sacrifice bulls,
their altars also shall be like stone heaps
on the furrows of the field.
[12] (Jacob fled to the land of Aram,
there Israel did service for a wife,
and for a wife he herded sheep.)
[13] By a prophet the LORD brought Israel up from Egypt,
and by a prophet he was preserved.
[14] E'phraim has given bitter provocation;
so his LORD will leave his bloodguilt upon him,
and will turn back upon him his reproaches.

13 When E'phraim spoke, men trembled;
he was exalted in Israel;
but he incurred guilt through Ba'al and died.
[2] And now they sin more and more,
and make for themselves molten images,
idols skilfully made of their silver,
all of them the work of craftsmen.
Sacrifice to these, they say.[j]
Men kiss calves!
[3] Therefore they shall be like the morning mist
or like the dew that goes early away,
like the chaff that swirls from the threshing floor
or like smoke from a window.

[4] I am the LORD your God
from the land of Egypt;
you know no God but me,
and besides me there is no savior.
[5] It was I who knew you in the wilderness,
in the land of drought;
[6] but when they had fed[k] to the full,
they were filled, and their heart was lifted up;
therefore they forgot me.
[7] So I will be to them like a lion,
like a leopard I will lurk beside the way.
[8] I will fall upon them like a bear robbed of her cubs,
I will tear open their breast,
and there I will devour them like a lion,
as a wild beast would rend them.

[9] I will destroy you, O Israel;
who[l] can help you?
[10] Where[m] now is your king, to save you;
where are all[n] your princes,[o] to defend you[p]—
those of whom you said,
"Give me a king and princes"?
[11] I have given you kings in my anger,
and I have taken them away in my wrath.

[12] The iniquity of E'phraim is bound up,
his sin is kept in store.
[13] The pangs of childbirth come for him,
but he is an unwise son;
for now he does not present himself
at the mouth of the womb.

[14] Shall I ransom them from the power of Sheol?
Shall I redeem them from Death?
O Death, where[q] are your plagues?
O Sheol, where[q] is your destruction?
Compassion is hid from my eyes.

[15] Though he may flourish as the reed plant,[r]
the east wind, the wind of the LORD, shall come,
rising from the wilderness;
and his fountain shall dry up,
his spring shall be parched;
it shall strip his treasury
of every precious thing.
[16] [s] Samar'ia shall bear her guilt,
because she has rebelled against her God;
they shall fall by the sword,
their little ones shall be dashed in pieces,
and their pregnant women ripped open.

ISRAEL CALLED TO RETURN TO THE LORD

14 Return, O Israel, to the LORD your God,
for you have stumbled because of your iniquity.
[2] Take with you words
and return to the LORD;
say to him,
"Take away all iniquity;
accept that which is good
and we will render

[i] Cn Compare Gk: Heb *obscure* [j] Gk: Heb *to these they say sacrifices of* [k] Cn: Heb *according to their pasture*
[l] Gk Syr: Heb *for in me* [m] Gk Syr Vg: Heb *I will be* [n] Cn: Heb *in all* [o] Cn: Heb *cities*
[p] Cn Compare Gk: Heb *and your judges* [q] Gk Syr: Heb *I will be* [r] Cn: Heb *among brothers* [s] Ch 14.1 in Heb

the fruit[t] of our lips.
³ Assyria shall not save us,
    we will not ride upon horses;
and we will say no more, 'Our God,'
    to the work of our hands.
    In thee the orphan finds mercy."

⁴ I will heal their faithlessness;
    I will love them freely,
    for my anger has turned from them.
⁵ I will be as the dew to Israel;
    he shall blossom as the lily,
    he shall strike root as the poplar;[u]
⁶ his shoots shall spread out;
    his beauty shall be like the olive,
    and his fragrance like Lebanon.

⁷ They shall return and dwell beneath my[v] shadow,
    they shall flourish as a garden;[w]
they shall blossom as the vine,
    their fragrance shall be like the wine of Lebanon.

⁸ O E'phraim, what have I to do with idols?
    It is I who answer and look after you.[x]
I am like an evergreen cypress,
    from me comes your fruit.

⁹ Whoever is wise, let him understand these things;
    whoever is discerning, let him know them;
for the ways of the LORD are right,
    and the upright walk in them,
    but transgressors stumble in them.

[t] Gk Syr: Heb *bulls*   [u] Heb *Lebanon*   [v] Heb *his*   [w] Cn: Heb *they shall grow grain*   [x] Heb *him*

INTRODUCTION TO

JOEL

The Book of Joel was written about 400 B.C. Millions of locusts had descended upon Jerusalem. These insects moved like an army, devouring every green leaf and all the crops. Then there followed a terrible drought and famine. Joel taught that these terrible disasters were God's punishment for the sins of the people. He pleaded with them to repent and promised that God would forgive and redeem Israel.

This book tells of Joel's visions or dreams, which are something like those in the Book of Ezekiel. This kind of writing about strange visions is called apocalyptic writing. Such books usually appeared in times of great trouble and danger, and the writers used poetic, symbolic language instead of matter-of-fact prose. Sometimes this helped protect the Jews because their enemies would not know what the strange symbolic words meant. However, the symbols also made it difficult for us now to understand because we have lost the meanings the writer intended by some of the symbolic words.

Chapter 3 uses visionlike writing to describe the judgment of the nations by God and the coming of a wonderful new day. Joel and other symbolic books, such as Daniel and Revelation, have sometimes been used to try to predict future events or even the end of the world. Jesus cautioned against such efforts, saying, "But of that day or that hour no one knows, not even the angels in heaven, nor the Son, but only the Father" (Mark 13.32).

THE BOOK OF

JOEL

A CALL TO NATIONAL REPENTANCE

1 The word of the LORD that came to Joel, the son of Pethu′el:

2 Hear this, you aged men,
   give ear, all inhabitants of the land!
  Has such a thing happened in your days,
   or in the days of your fathers?
3 Tell your children of it,
   and let your children tell their children,
   and their children another generation.

4 What the cutting locust left,
   the swarming locust has eaten.
  What the swarming locust left,
   the hopping locust has eaten,
and what the hopping locust left,
   the destroying locust has eaten.

5 Awake, you drunkards, and weep;
   and wail, all you drinkers of wine,
  because of the sweet wine,
   for it is cut off from your mouth.
6 For a nation has come up against my land,
   powerful and without number;
  its teeth are lions' teeth,
   and it has the fangs of a lioness.
7 It has laid waste my vines,
   and splintered my fig trees;
  it has stripped off their bark and thrown it down;
   their branches are made white.

8 Lament like a virgin girded with sackcloth
   for the bridegroom of her youth.
9 The cereal offering and the drink offering are cut off
   from the house of the LORD.
  The priests mourn,
   the ministers of the LORD.

619

10 The fields are laid waste,
    the ground mourns;
because the grain is destroyed,
    the wine fails,
    the oil languishes.

11 Be confounded, O tillers of the soil,
    wail, O vinedressers,
for the wheat and the barley;
    because the harvest of the field has perished.
12 The vine withers,
    the fig tree languishes.
Pomegranate, palm, and apple,
    all the trees of the field are withered;
and gladness fails
    from the sons of men.

13 Gird on sackcloth and lament, O priests,
    wail, O ministers of the altar.
Go in, pass the night in sackcloth,
    O ministers of my God!
Because cereal offering and drink offering
    are withheld from the house of your God.

14 Sanctify a fast,
    call a solemn assembly.
Gather the elders
    and all the inhabitants of the land
to the house of the Lord your God;
    and cry to the Lord.

15 Alas for the day!
For the day of the Lord is near,
    and as destruction from the Almighty it comes.
16 Is not the food cut off
    before our eyes,
joy and gladness
    from the house of our God?

17 The seed shrivels under the clods,ᵃ
    the storehouses are desolate;
the granaries are ruined
    because the grain has failed.
18 How the beasts groan!
    The herds of cattle are perplexed
because there is no pasture for them;
    even the flocks of sheep are dismayed.

19 Unto thee, O Lord, I cry.
For fire has devoured
    the pastures of the wilderness,
and flame has burned
    all the trees of the field.
20 Even the wild beasts cry to thee

because the water brooks are dried up,
and fire has devoured
    the pastures of the wilderness.

2 Blow the trumpet in Zion;
    sound the alarm on my holy mountain!
Let all the inhabitants of the land tremble,
    for the day of the Lord is coming, it is near,
2 a day of darkness and gloom,
    a day of clouds and thick darkness!
Like blackness there is spread upon the mountains
    a great and powerful people;
their like has never been from of old,
    nor will be again after them
    through the years of all generations.

3 Fire devours before them,
    and behind them a flame burns.
The land is like the garden of Eden before them,
    but after them a desolate wilderness,
    and nothing escapes them.

4 Their appearance is like the appearance of horses,
    and like war horses they run.
5 As with the rumbling of chariots,
    they leap on the tops of the mountains,
like the crackling of a flame of fire
    devouring the stubble,
like a powerful army
    drawn up for battle.

6 Before them peoples are in anguish,
    all faces grow pale.
7 Like warriors they charge,
    like soldiers they scale the wall.
They march each on his way,
    they do not swerveᵇ from their paths.

8 They do not jostle one another,
    each marches in his path;
they burst through the weapons
    and are not halted.
9 They leap upon the city,
    they run upon the walls;
they climb up into the houses,
    they enter through the windows like a thief.

10 The earth quakes before them,
    the heavens tremble.
The sun and the moon are darkened,
    and the stars withdraw their shining.
11 The Lord utters his voice
    before his army,
for his host is exceedingly great;
    he that executes his word is powerful.

ᵃ Heb uncertain   ᵇ Gk Syr Vg: Heb *take a pledge*

For the day of the LORD is great and very terrible;
  who can endure it?

12 "Yet even now," says the LORD,
  "return to me with all your heart,
with fasting, with weeping, and with mourning;
13   and rend your hearts and not your garments."
Return to the LORD, your God,
  for he is gracious and merciful,
  slow to anger, and abounding in steadfast love,
    and repents of evil.
14 Who knows whether he will not turn and repent,
  and leave a blessing behind him,
a cereal offering and a drink offering
  for the LORD, your God?

15 Blow the trumpet in Zion;
  sanctify a fast;
call a solemn assembly;
16   gather the people.
Sanctify the congregation;
  assemble the elders;
gather the children,
  even nursing infants.
Let the bridegroom leave his room,
  and the bride her chamber.

17 Between the vestibule and the altar
  let the priests, the ministers of the LORD, weep
and say, "Spare thy people, O LORD,
  and make not thy heritage a reproach,
  a byword among the nations.
Why should they say among the peoples,
  'Where is their God?'"

18 Then the LORD became jealous for his land,
  and had pity on his people.
19 The LORD answered and said to his people,
  "Behold, I am sending to you
    grain, wine, and oil,
    and you will be satisfied;
  and I will no more make you
    a reproach among the nations.

20 "I will remove the northerner far from you,
  and drive him into a parched and desolate land,
his front into the eastern sea,
  and his rear into the western sea;
the stench and foul smell of him will rise,
  for he has done great things.

21 "Fear not, O land;
  be glad and rejoice,
  for the LORD has done great things!

c Ch 3.1 in Heb   d Ch 4.1 in Heb

22 Fear not, you beasts of the field,
  for the pastures of the wilderness are green;
the tree bears its fruit,
  the fig tree and vine give their full yield.

23 "Be glad, O sons of Zion,
  and rejoice in the LORD, your God;
for he has given the early rain for your vindication,
  he has poured down for you abundant rain,
  the early and the latter rain, as before.

24 "The threshing floors shall be full of grain,
  the vats shall overflow with wine and oil.
25 I will restore to you the years
  which the swarming locust has eaten,
the hopper, the destroyer, and the cutter,
  my great army, which I sent among you.

26 "You shall eat in plenty and be satisfied,
  and praise the name of the LORD your God,
  who has dealt wondrously with you.
And my people shall never again be put to shame.
27 You shall know that I am in the midst of Israel,
  and that I, the LORD, am your God and there is none
    else.
And my people shall never again be put to shame.

THE LORD'S BLESSING AND JUDGMENT
28 c "And it shall come to pass afterward,

  that I will pour out my spirit on all flesh;
your sons and your daughters shall prophesy,
  your old men shall dream dreams,
  and your young men shall see visions.
29 Even upon the menservants and maidservants
  in those days, I will pour out my spirit.

30   "And I will give portents in the heavens and on the
31 earth, blood and fire and columns of smoke. The sun
  shall be turned to darkness, and the moon to blood, be-
32 fore the great and terrible day of the LORD comes. And
  it shall come to pass that all who call upon the name of
  the LORD shall be delivered; for in Mount Zion and in
  Jerusalem there shall be those who escape, as the LORD
  has said, and among the survivors shall be those whom
  the LORD calls.

3 d "For behold, in those days and at that time, when I
2   restore the fortunes of Judah and Jerusalem, I will
  gather all the nations and bring them down to the valley

of Jehosh'aphat, and I will enter into judgment with them there, on account of my people and my heritage Israel, because they have scattered them among the nations, and ³ have divided up my land, and have cast lots for my people, and have given a boy for a harlot, and have sold a girl for wine, and have drunk it.

⁴ "What are you to me, O Tyre and Sidon, and all the regions of Philistia? Are you paying me back for something? If you are paying me back, I will requite your ⁵ deed upon your own head swiftly and speedily. For you have taken my silver and my gold, and have carried my ⁶ rich treasures into your temples.ᵉ You have sold the people of Judah and Jerusalem to the Greeks, removing them far ⁷ from their own border. But now I will stir them up from the place to which you have sold them, and I will requite ⁸ your deed upon your own head. I will sell your sons and your daughters into the hand of the sons of Judah, and they will sell them to the Sabe'ans, to a nation far off; for the LORD has spoken."

⁹ Proclaim this among the nations:
Prepare war,
    stir up the mighty men.
Let all the men of war draw near,
    let them come up.
¹⁰ Beat your plowshares into swords,
    and your pruning hooks into spears;
    let the weak say, "I am a warrior."

¹¹ Hasten and come,
    all you nations round about,
    gather yourselves there.
Bring down thy warriors, O LORD.
¹² Let the nations bestir themselves,
    and come up to the valley of Jehosh'aphat;
for there I will sit to judge
    all the nations round about.

¹³ Put in the sickle
    for the harvest is ripe.

Go in, tread,
    for the wine press is full.
The vats overflow,
    for their wickedness is great.

¹⁴ Multitudes, multitudes,
    in the valley of decision!
For the day of the LORD is near
    in the valley of decision.
¹⁵ The sun and the moon are darkened,
    and the stars withdraw their shining.

¹⁶ And the LORD roars from Zion,
    and utters his voice from Jerusalem,
    and the heavens and the earth shake.
But the LORD is a refuge to his people,
    a stronghold to the people of Israel.

¹⁷ "So you shall know that I am the LORD your God,
    who dwell in Zion, my holy mountain.
And Jerusalem shall be holy
    and strangers shall never again pass through it.

¹⁸ "And in that day
the mountains shall drip sweet wine,
    and the hills shall flow with milk,
and all the stream beds of Judah shall flow with water;
and a fountain shall come forth from the house of the
    LORD
and water the valley of Shittim.

¹⁹ "Egypt shall become a desolation
    and Edom a desolate wilderness,
for the violence done to the people of Judah,
    because they have shed innocent blood in their land.
²⁰ But Judah shall be inhabited for ever,
    and Jerusalem to all generations.
²¹ I will avenge their blood, and I will not clear the guilty,ᵍ
    for the LORD dwells in Zion."

ᵉ Or *palaces*   ᵍ Gk Syr: Heb *I will hold innocent their blood which I have not held innocent*

INTRODUCTION TO

AMOS

The Book of Amos, made up of sermons by a shepherd from Tekoa, is probably the first book of the Bible to be written down. Amos preached and wrote these sermons about 750 B.C.

This book was written during a period of great prosperity in the two Hebrew kingdoms—the southern kingdom of Judah and the northern kingdom of Israel. Even though there was prosperity, Amos, like Elijah before him, dared to challenge the sins of the people. He told them that God would punish them for their continued wrongdoing.

Some people made money by cheating the poor, and some brought fine gifts to the temple, but they continued to be cruel and unjust. Most of the people thought that Israel was God's favorite nation and that he would prosper them regardless of their sins.

When Amos realized these things, he went up to the city of Bethel, one of the two worship shrines of Israel, from his rural home down in Judah. He taught that God was a just God who should not be disobeyed. He began by preaching against the evils of enemy countries like Syria. Edom, Ammon, and Moab. He even preached against the sins of Judah, his own nation. At last, after he had the attention of his audience, he denounced Israel itself and said that it would be judged more sternly than its enemies because God had given it so many blessings.

A few years later the prophets Hosea, Isaiah, and Micah were also speaking for God in the two kingdoms. Through the inspired preaching and writing of these men, God brought the Hebrews to a higher religious life. God eventually inspired the writer of the Book of Deuteronomy to revise the Hebrew laws to include the great truths of Amos and the other great prophets of his time.

THE BOOK OF

AMOS

ORACLES AGAINST THE NATIONS

1 The words of Amos, who was among the shepherds of Teko'a, which he saw concerning Israel in the days of Uzzi'ah king of Judah and in the days of Jerobo'am the son of Jo'ash, king of Israel, two years [a] before the earth-

2 quake. And he said:
"The LORD roars from Zion,
  and utters his voice from Jerusalem;
the pastures of the shepherds mourn,
  and the top of Carmel withers."

3 Thus says the LORD:
"For three transgressions of Damascus,
  and for four, I will not revoke the punishment; [b]
because they have threshed Gilead
  with threshing sledges of iron.
4 So I will send a fire upon the house of Haz'ael,
  and it shall devour the strongholds of Ben-ha'dad.
5 I will break the bar of Damascus,
  and cut off the inhabitants from the valley of Aven, [c]
and him that holds the scepter from Beth-eden;
  and the people of Syria shall go into exile to Kir,"
                                    says the LORD.

6 Thus says the LORD:
"For three transgressions of Gaza,
  and for four, I will not revoke the punishment; [b]
because they carried into exile a whole people
  to deliver them up to Edom.
7 So I will send a fire upon the wall of Gaza,

---

[a] Or *during two years*   [b] Heb *cause it to return*   [c] Or *On*

and it shall devour her strongholds.
8 I will cut off the inhabitants from Ashdod,
    and him that holds the scepter from Ash′kelon;
I will turn my hand against Ekron;
    and the remnant of the Philistines shall perish,"
               says the Lord GOD.

9 Thus says the LORD:
"For three transgressions of Tyre,
    and for four, I will not revoke the punishment; e
because they delivered up a whole people to Edom,
    and did not remember the covenant of brotherhood.
10 So I will send a fire upon the wall of Tyre,
    and it shall devour her strongholds."

11 Thus says the LORD:
"For three transgressions of Edom,
    and for four, I will not revoke the punishment; e
because he pursued his brother with the sword,
    and cast off all pity,
and his anger tore perpetually,
    and he kept his wrath d for ever.
12 So I will send a fire upon Teman,
    and it shall devour the strongholds of Bozrah."

13 Thus says the LORD:
"For three transgressions of the Ammonites,
    and for four, I will not revoke the punishment; e
because they have ripped up women with child in Gilead,
    that they might enlarge their border.
14 So I will kindle a fire in the wall of Rabbah,
    and it shall devour her strongholds,
with shouting in the day of battle,
    with a tempest in the day of the whirlwind;
15 and their king shall go into exile,
    he and his princes together,"
               says the LORD.

2 Thus says the LORD:
"For three transgressions of Moab,
    and for four, I will not revoke the punishment; e
because he burned to lime
    the bones of the king of Edom.
2 So I will send a fire upon Moab,
    and it shall devour the strongholds of Ker′ioth,
and Moab shall die amid uproar,
    amid shouting and the sound of the trumpet;
3 I will cut off the ruler from its midst,
    and will slay all its princes with him,"
               says the LORD.

4 Thus says the LORD:
"For three transgressions of Judah,
    and for four, I will not revoke the punishment; e

because they have rejected the law of the LORD,
    and have not kept his statutes,
but their lies have led them astray,
    after which their fathers walked.
5 So I will send a fire upon Judah,
    and it shall devour the strongholds of Jerusalem."

6 Thus says the LORD:
"For three transgressions of Israel,
    and for four, I will not revoke the punishment; e
because they sell the righteous for silver,
    and the needy for a pair of shoes—
7 they that trample the head of the poor into the dust of the earth,
    and turn aside the way of the afflicted;
a man and his father go in to the same maiden,
    so that my holy name is profaned;
8 they lay themselves down beside every altar
    upon garments taken in pledge;
and in the house of their God they drink
    the wine of those who have been fined.

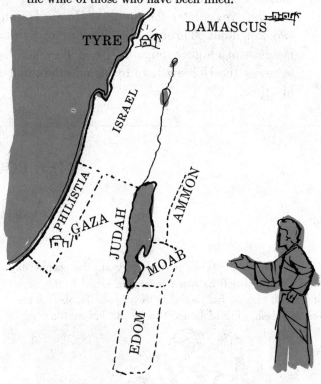

9 "Yet I destroyed the Amorite before them,
    whose height was like the height of the cedars,
    and who was as strong as the oaks;
I destroyed his fruit above,
    and his roots beneath.
10 Also I brought you up out of the land of Egypt,
    and led you forty years in the wilderness,
    to possess the land of the Amorite.

d Gk Syr Vg: Heb *his wrath kept*   e Heb *cause it to return*

11 And I raised up some of your sons for prophets,
   and some of your young men for Nazirites.
   Is it not indeed so, O people of Israel?"
                                    says the LORD.

12 "But you made the Nazirites drink wine,
   and commanded the prophets,
   saying, 'You shall not prophesy.'

13 "Behold, I will press you down in your place,
   as a cart full of sheaves presses down.
14 Flight shall perish from the swift,
   and the strong shall not retain his strength,
   nor shall the mighty save his life;
15 he who handles the bow shall not stand,
   and he who is swift of foot shall not save himself,
   nor shall he who rides the horse save his life;
16 and he who is stout of heart among the mighty
   shall flee away naked in that day,"
                                    says the LORD.

SERMONS ON THE DOOM OF ISRAEL

3 Hear this word that the LORD has spoken against
   you, O people of Israel, against the whole family which
I brought up out of the land of Egypt:
2 "You only have I known
   of all the families of the earth;
therefore I will punish you
   for all your iniquities.

3 "Do two walk together,
   unless they have made an appointment?
4 Does a lion roar in the forest,
   when he has no prey?
Does a young lion cry out from his den,
   if he has taken nothing?
5 Does a bird fall in a snare on the earth,
   when there is no trap for it?
Does a snare spring up from the ground,
   when it has taken nothing?
6 Is a trumpet blown in a city,
   and the people are not afraid?
Does evil befall a city,
   unless the LORD has done it?
7 Surely the Lord GOD does nothing,
   without revealing his secret
   to his servants the prophets.
8 The lion has roared;
   who will not fear?
The Lord GOD has spoken;
   who can but prophesy?"

9 Proclaim to the strongholds in Assyria,[f]
   and to the strongholds in the land of Egypt,

and say, "Assemble yourselves upon the mountains of
   Samar'ia,
and see the great tumults within her,
   and the oppressions in her midst."
10 "They do not know how to do right," says the LORD,
   "those who store up violence and robbery in their
   strongholds."
11 Therefore thus says the Lord GOD:
"An adversary shall surround the land,
   and bring down your defenses from you,
   and your strongholds shall be plundered."

12 Thus says the LORD: "As the shepherd rescues from the
   mouth of the lion two legs, or a piece of an ear, so shall
   the people of Israel who dwell in Samar'ia be rescued,
   with the corner of a couch and part[g] of a bed."

13 "Hear, and testify against the house of Jacob,"
   says the Lord GOD, the God of hosts,
14 "that on the day I punish Israel for his transgressions,
   I will punish the altars of Bethel,
and the horns of the altar shall be cut off
   and fall to the ground.
15 I will smite the winter house with the summer house;
   and the houses of ivory shall perish,
and the great houses[h] shall come to an end,"
                                    says the LORD.

4 "Hear this word, you cows of Bashan,
   who are in the mountain of Samar'ia,
who oppress the poor, who crush the needy,
   who say to their husbands, 'Bring, that we may drink!'
2 The Lord GOD has sworn by his holiness
   that, behold, the days are coming upon you,
when they shall take you away with hooks,
   even the last of you with fishhooks.
3 And you shall go out through the breaches,
   every one straight before her;
and you shall be cast forth into Harmon,"
                                    says the LORD.

4 "Come to Bethel, and transgress;
   to Gilgal, and multiply transgression;
bring your sacrifices every morning,
   your tithes every three days;

---

[f] Gk: Heb *Ashdod*   [g] The meaning of the Hebrew word is uncertain   [h] Or *many houses*

5 offer a sacrifice of thanksgiving of that which is leavened,
  and proclaim freewill offerings, publish them;
  for so you love to do, O people of Israel!"
                              says the Lord GOD.

6 "I gave you cleanness of teeth in all your cities,
  and lack of bread in all your places,
  yet you did not return to me,"
                              says the LORD.

7 "And I also withheld the rain from you
  when there were yet three months to the harvest;
  I would send rain upon one city,
  and send no rain upon another city;
  one field would be rained upon,
  and the field on which it did not rain withered;
8 so two or three cities wandered to one city
  to drink water, and were not satisfied;
  yet you did not return to me,"
                              says the LORD.

9 "I smote you with blight and mildew;
  I laid waste [i] your gardens and your vineyards;
  your fig trees and your olive trees the locust devoured;
  yet you did not return to me,"
                              says the LORD.

10 "I sent among you a pestilence after the manner of Egypt;
  I slew your young men with the sword;
  I carried away your horses; [j]
  and I made the stench of your camp go up into your
    nostrils;
  yet you did not return to me,"
                              says the LORD.

11 "I overthrew some of you,
  as when God overthrew Sodom and Gomor'rah,
  and you were as a brand plucked out of the burning;
  yet you did not return to me,"
                              says the LORD.

12 "Therefore thus I will do to you, O Israel;
  because I will do this to you,
  prepare to meet your God, O Israel!"

13 For lo, he who forms the mountains, and creates the wind,
  and declares to man what is his thought;
  who makes the morning darkness,
  and treads on the heights of the earth—
  the LORD, the God of hosts, is his name!

5 Hear this word which I take up over you in
  lamentation, O house of Israel:
2 "Fallen, no more to rise,

  is the virgin Israel;
forsaken on her land,
  with none to raise her up."

3 For thus says the Lord GOD:
"The city that went forth a thousand
  shall have a hundred left,
and that which went forth a hundred
  shall have ten left
  to the house of Israel."

4 For thus says the LORD to the house of Israel:
"Seek me and live;
5   but do not seek Bethel,
and do not enter into Gilgal
  or cross over to Beer-sheba;
for Gilgal shall surely go into exile,
  and Bethel shall come to nought."

6 Seek the LORD and live,
  lest he break out like fire in the house of Joseph,
  and it devour, with none to quench it for Bethel,
7 O you who turn justice to wormwood,
  and cast down righteousness to the earth!

8 He who made the Pleiades and Orion,
  and turns deep darkness into the morning,
  and darkens the day into night,
who calls for the waters of the sea,
  and pours them out upon the surface of the earth,
the LORD is his name,
9 who makes destruction flash forth against the strong,
  so that destruction comes upon the fortress.

10 They hate him who reproves in the gate,
  and they abhor him who speaks the truth.
11 Therefore because you trample upon the poor
  and take from him exactions of wheat,
you have built houses of hewn stone,
  but you shall not dwell in them;
you have planted pleasant vineyards,
  but you shall not drink their wine.
12 For I know how many are your transgressions,
  and how great are your sins—
you who afflict the righteous, who take a bribe,
  and turn aside the needy in the gate.
13 Therefore he who is prudent will keep silent in such a
    time;
  for it is an evil time.

14 Seek good, and not evil,
  that you may live;
and so the LORD, the God of hosts, will be with you,
  as you have said.

---

[i] Cn: Heb *the multitude of*   [j] Heb *with the captivity of your horses*

¹⁵ Hate evil, and love good,
    and establish justice in the gate;
it may be that the LORD, the God of hosts,
    will be gracious to the remnant of Joseph.

¹⁶ Therefore thus says the LORD, the God of hosts, the Lord:
    "In all the squares there shall be wailing;
        and in all the streets they shall say, 'Alas! alas!'
    They shall call the farmers to mourning
        and to wailing those who are skilled in lamentation,
¹⁷ and in all vineyards there shall be wailing,
    for I will pass through the midst of you,"
                                    says the LORD.

¹⁸ Woe to you who desire the day of the LORD!
    Why would you have the day of the LORD?
It is darkness, and not light;
¹⁹   as if a man fled from a lion,
        and a bear met him;
    or went into the house and leaned with his hand against
        the wall,
        and a serpent bit him.
²⁰ Is not the day of the LORD darkness, and not light,
    and gloom with no brightness in it?

²¹ "I hate, I despise your feasts,
    and I take no delight in your solemn assemblies.
²² Even though you offer me your burnt offerings and cereal
        offerings,
    I will not accept them,
and the peace offerings of your fatted beasts
    I will not look upon.
²³ Take away from me the noise of your songs;
    to the melody of your harps I will not listen.
²⁴ But let justice roll down like waters,
    and righteousness like an ever-flowing stream.

²⁵   "Did you bring to me sacrifices and offerings the forty
²⁶ years in the wilderness, O house of Israel? You shall
    take up Sakkuth your king, and Kaiwan your star-god,
²⁷ your images,ᵏ which you made for yourselves; therefore
    I will take you into exile beyond Damascus," says the
    LORD, whose name is the God of hosts.

6   "Woe to those who are at ease in Zion,
        and to those who feel secure on the mountains of
            Samar′ia,
    the notable men of the first of the nations,
        to whom the house of Israel come!
² Pass over to Calneh, and see;
    and thence go to Hamath the great;
    then go down to Gath of the Philistines.
Are they better than these kingdoms?
    Or is their territory greater than your territory,

³ O you who put far away the evil day,
    and bring near the seat of violence?

⁴ "Woe to those who lie upon beds of ivory,
    and stretch themselves upon their couches,
and eat lambs from the flock,
    and calves from the midst of the stall;
⁵ who sing idle songs to the sound of the harp,
    and like David invent for themselves instruments of
        music;
⁶ who drink wine in bowls,
    and anoint themselves with the finest oils,
    but are not grieved over the ruin of Joseph!
⁷ Therefore they shall now be the first of those to go into
        exile,
    and the revelry of those who stretch themselves shall
        pass away."

⁸ The Lord GOD has sworn by himself
    (says the LORD, the God of hosts) :
"I abhor the pride of Jacob,
    and hate his strongholds;
    and I will deliver up the city and all that is in it."

⁹   And if ten men remain in one house, they shall die.
¹⁰ And when a man's kinsman, he who burns him,¹ shall
    take him up to bring the bones out of the house, and shall
    say to him who is in the innermost parts of the house, "Is
    there still any one with you?" he shall say, "No"; and he
    shall say, "Hush! We must not mention the name of the
    LORD."

¹¹ For behold, the LORD commands,
    and the great house shall be smitten into fragments,
    and the little house into bits.
¹² Do horses run upon rocks?
    Does one plow the sea with oxen?
But you have turned justice into poison
    and the fruit of righteousness into wormwood—
¹³ you who rejoice in Lo-debar,ⁿ
    who say, "Have we not by our own strength
    taken Karnaim ° for ourselves?"
¹⁴ "For behold, I will raise up against you a nation,
    O house of Israel," says the LORD, the God of hosts;
"and they shall oppress you from the entrance of Hamath
    to the Brook of the Arabah."

THE VISIONS OF AMOS

7   Thus the Lord GOD showed me: behold, he was
    forming locusts in the beginning of the shooting up of
the latter growth; and lo, it was the latter growth after

ᵏ Heb *your images, your star-god*   ¹ Or *who makes a burning for him*   ⁿ Or *a thing of nought*   ° Or *horns*

2 the king's mowings. When they had finished eating the grass of the land, I said,
"O Lord GOD, forgive, I beseech thee!
How can Jacob stand?
He is so small!"
3 The LORD repented concerning this;
"It shall not be," said the LORD.

4 Thus the Lord GOD showed me: behold, the Lord GOD was calling for a judgment by fire, and it devoured the 5 great deep and was eating up the land. Then I said,
"O Lord GOD, cease, I beseech thee!
How can Jacob stand?
He is so small!"
6 The LORD repented concerning this;
"This also shall not be," said the Lord GOD.

7 He showed me: behold, the Lord was standing beside a wall built with a plumb line, with a plumb line in his 8 hand. And the LORD said to me, "Amos, what do you see?" And I said, "A plumb line." Then the Lord said,
"Behold, I am setting a plumb line
in the midst of my people Israel;
I will never again pass by them;
9 the high places of Isaac shall be made desolate,
and the sanctuaries of Israel shall be laid waste,
and I will rise against the house of Jerobo'am with the sword."

10 Then Amazi'ah the priest of Bethel sent to Jerobo'am king of Israel, saying, "Amos has conspired against you in the midst of the house of Israel; the land is not able to 11 bear all his words. For thus Amos has said,
'Jerobo'am shall die by the sword,
and Israel must go into exile
away from his land.' "
12 And Amazi'ah said to Amos, "O seer, go, flee away to the land of Judah, and eat bread there, and prophesy there; 13 but never again prophesy at Bethel, for it is the king's sanctuary, and it is a temple of the kingdom."
14 Then Amos answered Amazi'ah, "I am no prophet, nor a prophet's son; [p] but I am a herdsman, and a dresser of 15 sycamore trees, and the LORD took me from following the flock, and the LORD said to me, 'Go, prophesy to my people Israel.'
16 "Now therefore hear the word of the LORD.
You say, 'Do not prophesy against Israel,
and do not preach against the house of Isaac.'
17 Therefore thus says the LORD:
'Your wife shall be a harlot in the city,
and your sons and your daughters shall fall by the sword,
and your land shall be parceled out by line;
you yourself shall die in an unclean land,

and Israel shall surely go into exile away from its land.' "

8 Thus the Lord GOD showed me: behold, a basket of 2 summer fruit.[q] And he said, "Amos, what do you see?" And I said, "A basket of summer fruit."[q] Then the LORD said to me,
"The end [r] has come upon my people Israel;
I will never again pass by them.
3 The songs of the temple [s] shall become wailings in that day,"
says the Lord GOD;
"the dead bodies shall be many;
in every place they shall be cast out in silence." [t]

4 Hear this, you who trample upon the needy,
and bring the poor of the land to an end,
5 saying, "When will the new moon be over,
that we may sell grain?
And the sabbath,
that we may offer wheat for sale,
that we may make the ephah small and the shekel great,
and deal deceitfully with false balances,
6 that we may buy the poor for silver
and the needy for a pair of sandals,
and sell the refuse of the wheat?"

7 The LORD has sworn by the pride of Jacob:
"Surely I will never forget any of their deeds.
8 Shall not the land tremble on this account,
and every one mourn who dwells in it,
and all of it rise like the Nile,
and be tossed about and sink again, like the Nile of Egypt?"

9 "And on that day," says the Lord GOD,
"I will make the sun go down at noon,
and darken the earth in broad daylight.
10 I will turn your feasts into mourning,
and all your songs into lamentation;
I will bring sackcloth upon all loins,
and baldness on every head;
I will make it like the mourning for an only son,
and the end of it like a bitter day.

11 "Behold, the days are coming," says the Lord GOD,
"when I will send a famine on the land;
not a famine of bread, nor a thirst for water,
but of hearing the words of the LORD.
12 They shall wander from sea to sea,
and from north to east;
they shall run to and fro, to seek the word of the LORD,
but they shall not find it.

---

[p] Or *one of the sons of the prophets*   [q] Heb *qayits*   [r] Heb *qets*   [s] Or *palace*   [t] Or *be silent!*

13 "In that day the fair virgins and the young men
 shall faint for thirst.
14 Those who swear by Ash'imah of Samar'ia,
 and say, 'As thy god lives, O Dan,'
and, 'As the way of Beer-sheba lives,'
 they shall fall, and never rise again."

9 I saw the LORD standing beside^u the altar, and he
said:
"Smite the capitals until the thresholds shake,
 and shatter them on the heads of all the people; ^v
and what are left of them I will slay with the sword;
 not one of them shall flee away,
 not one of them shall escape.

2 "Though they dig into Sheol,
 from there shall my hand take them;
though they climb up to heaven,
 from there I will bring them down.
3 Though they hide themselves on the top of Carmel,
 from there I will search out and take them;
and though they hide from my sight at the bottom of the
 sea,
 there I will command the serpent, and it shall bite them.
4 And though they go into captivity before their enemies,
 there I will command the sword,
 and it shall slay them;
and I will set my eyes upon them
 for evil and not for good."

5 The Lord, GOD of hosts,
he who touches the earth and it melts,
 and all who dwell in it mourn,
and all of it rises like the Nile,
 and sinks again, like the Nile of Egypt;
6 who builds his upper chambers in the heavens,
 and founds his vault upon the earth;
who calls for the waters of the sea,
 and pours them out upon the surface of the earth—
the LORD is his name.

7 "Are you not like the Ethiopians to me,
 O people of Israel?" says the LORD.
"Did I not bring up Israel from the land of Egypt,
 and the Philistines from Caphtor and the Syrians from
 Kir?
8 Behold, the eyes of the Lord GOD are upon the sinful
 kingdom,
 and I will destroy it from the surface of the ground;
except that I will not utterly destroy the house of Jacob,"
 says the LORD.

9 "For lo, I will command,
 and shake the house of Israel among all the nations

u Or *upon*   v Heb *all of them*

as one shakes with a sieve,
 but no pebble shall fall upon the earth.
10 All the sinners of my people shall die by the sword,
 who say, 'Evil shall not overtake or meet us.'

11 "In that day I will raise up
 the booth of David that is fallen
and repair its breaches,
 and raise up its ruins,
 and rebuild it as in the days of old;
12 that they may possess the remnant of Edom
 and all the nations who are called by my name,"
 says the LORD who does this.

13 "Behold, the days are coming," says the LORD,
 "when the plowman shall overtake the reaper
 and the treader of grapes him who sows the seed;
the mountains shall drip sweet wine,
 and all the hills shall flow with it.
14 I will restore the fortunes of my people Israel,
 and they shall rebuild the ruined cities and inhabit
 them;
they shall plant vineyards and drink their wine,
 and they shall make gardens and eat their fruit.
15 I will plant them upon their land,
 and they shall never again be plucked up
 out of the land which I have given them,"
 says the LORD your God.

OBADIAH

Obadiah was a prophet who lived in Jerusalem about 586 B.C., during the days of the Babylonian siege of Judah, the southern kingdom. However, parts of the Book of Obadiah were added as late as 450 B.C. The Edomites, long-time enemies of the Jews, had threatened to invade Judah. At this time, however, the Edomites were also beset by enemy tribes from the Arabian desert, and Obadiah felt that the new troubles of the Edomites were a just punishment on them.

This little book, like much of the writing of the prophets, is poetry. Notice the poetic language and the parallel or similar lines so characteristic of Hebrew poetry. Beginning with verse 12 there are eight parallel lines beginning "You should not have . . ." and listing the sins of Edom.

Like Nahum forty years earlier, Obadiah was so interested in the punishment of an enemy nation that he seems unaware of the sins of his own people. He speaks only of how Jerusalem will triumph and all her enemies perish.

THE BOOK OF

OBADIAH

EDOM'S JUDGMENT

¹ The vision of Obadi'ah.

Thus says the Lord GOD concerning Edom:
We have heard tidings from the LORD,
   and a messenger has been sent among the nations:

"Rise up! let us rise against her for battle!"
² Behold, I will make you small among the nations,
   you shall be utterly despised.
³ The pride of your heart has deceived you,
   you who live in the clefts of the rock,ᵃ
   whose dwelling is high,
who say in your heart,
   "Who will bring me down to the ground?"
⁴ Though you soar aloft like the eagle,
   though your nest is set among the stars,
   thence I will bring you down,

                says the LORD.

⁵ If thieves came to you,

   ᵃ Or *Sela*

if plunderers by night—
   how you have been destroyed!—
   would they not steal only enough for themselves?
If grape gatherers came to you,
   would they not leave gleanings?
⁶ How Esau has been pillaged,
   his treasures sought out!
⁷ All your allies have deceived you,
   they have driven you to the border;
your confederates have prevailed against you;
   your trusted friends have set a trap under you—
   there is no understanding of it.
⁸ Will I not on that day, says the LORD,
   destroy the wise men out of Edom,
   and understanding out of Mount Esau?
⁹ And your mighty men shall be dismayed, O Teman,
   so that every man from Mount Esau will be cut off by
     slaughter.
¹⁰ For the violence done to your brother Jacob,
   shame shall cover you,
   and you shall be cut off for ever.
¹¹ On the day that you stood aloof,
   on the day that strangers carried off his wealth,
   and foreigners entered his gates
     and cast lots for Jerusalem,
   you were like one of them.
¹² But you should not have gloated over the day of your
    brother

in the day of his misfortune;
you should not have rejoiced over the people of Judah
 in the day of their ruin;
you should not have boasted
 in the day of distress.
13 You should not have entered the gate of my people
 in the day of his calamity;
you should not have gloated over his disaster
 in the day of his calamity;
you should not have looted his goods
 in the day of his calamity.
14 You should not have stood at the parting of the ways
 to cut off his fugitives;
you should not have delivered up his survivors
 in the day of distress.

THE DAY OF THE LORD

15 For the day of the LORD is near upon all the nations.
As you have done, it shall be done to you,
 your deeds shall return on your own head.
16 For as you have drunk upon my holy mountain,
 all the nations round about shall drink;
they shall drink, and stagger,[b]

and shall be as though they had not been.
17 But in Mount Zion there shall be those that escape,
 and it shall be holy;
and the house of Jacob shall possess their own possessions.
18 The house of Jacob shall be a fire,
 and the house of Joseph a flame,
 and the house of Esau stubble;
they shall burn them and consume them,
 and there shall be no survivor to the house of Esau;
 for the LORD has spoken.
19 Those of the Negeb shall possess Mount Esau,
 and those of the Shephe'lah the land of the Philistines;
they shall possess the land of E'phraim and the land of
 Samar'ia
 and Benjamin shall possess Gilead.
20 The exiles in Halah[c] who are of the people of Israel
 shall possess[d] Phoenicia as far as Zar'ephath;
and the exiles of Jerusalem who are in Sephar'ad
 shall possess the cities of the Negeb.
21 Saviors shall go up to Mount Zion
 to rule Mount Esau;
 and the kingdom shall be the LORD's.

[b] Cn: Heb *swallow*   [c] Cn: Heb *this army*   [d] Cn: Heb *which*

INTRODUCTION TO

JONAH

After the Jews returned from exile in Babylon, they kept to themselves and were not interested in persons who were not Jews. This was probably caused by the strict regulations their leaders developed to keep them separate from other religions while they were in Babylon. Many years after the Jews had returned from Babylonia, Ezra and Nehemiah continued to try to keep the Jewish people separate from persons of other nations. As a result the people became proud and did not want to share their faith in God with other nations.

The story of Jonah was written about 350 B.C. to try to convince the Jews that they should share their great faith with persons of other nations.

Like most of the Bible, this book was written to help men hear and do God's will rather than just to tell an event of history. Whether the story of Jonah is regarded as a historical happening or as a story to teach a lesson, the point of the book is that Jonah was required to share his faith with Nineveh, a pagan city the Jews had long despised.

This book is perhaps the first missionary pamphlet. Jonah represents self-satisfied and selfish people who did not want to share their faith in God with foreigners like the Ninevites. But no matter how Jonah tried to run from his duty to God, God found him. Even at the end of the book God reminded Jonah that he was fretting about little personal discomforts while God longed to help thousands of persons who did not know him.

The author drew a word picture that was almost as humorous as a cartoon. He wanted to show how silly and wrong it is not to be willing to share the good news of God with people who know nothing of him.

At the same time, the writer showed that God is tender and merciful even toward the Ninevites as well as toward the Jews. Whenever we are tempted to think God loves only the people of our own country, we need to read Jonah and reach out to share our faith in God with all kinds of persons in our own country and in every other country.

THE BOOK OF

JONAH

A PROPHET FLEES FROM GOD

1 Now the word of the LORD came to Jonah the son of
2 Amit'tai, saying, "Arise, go to Nin'eveh, that great city, and cry against it; for their wickedness has come
3 up before me." But Jonah rose to flee to Tarshish from the presence of the LORD. He went down to Joppa and found a ship going to Tarshish; so he paid the fare, and went on board, to go with them to Tarshish, away from the presence of the LORD.
4 But the LORD hurled a great wind upon the sea, and there was a mighty tempest on the sea, so that the ship
5 threatened to break up. Then the mariners were afraid, and each cried to his god; and they threw the wares

that were in the ship into the sea, to lighten it for them. But Jonah had gone down into the inner part of the ship
6 and had lain down, and was fast asleep. So the captain came and said to him, "What do you mean, you sleeper? Arise, call upon your god! Perhaps the god will give a thought to us, that we do not perish."

7 And they said to one another, "Come, let us cast lots, that we may know on whose account this evil has come

upon us." So they cast lots, and the lot fell upon Jonah.
8 Then they said to him, "Tell us, on whose account this evil has come upon us? What is your occupation? And whence do you come? What is your country? And of
9 what people are you?" And he said to them, "I am a Hebrew; and I fear the Lord, the God of heaven, who
10 made the sea and the dry land." Then the men were exceedingly afraid, and said to him, "What is this that you have done!" For the men knew that he was fleeing from the presence of the Lord, because he had told them.
11 Then they said to him, "What shall we do to you, that the sea may quiet down for us?" For the sea grew
12 more and more tempestuous. He said to them, "Take me up and throw me into the sea; then the sea will quiet down for you; for I know it is because of me that this
13 great tempest has come upon you." Nevertheless the men rowed hard to bring the ship back to land, but they could not, for the sea grew more and more tempestuous against
14 them. Therefore they cried to the Lord, "We beseech thee, O Lord, let us not perish for this man's life, and lay not on us innocent blood; for thou, O Lord, hast
15 done as it pleased thee." So they took up Jonah and threw him into the sea; and the sea ceased from its raging.
16 Then the men feared the Lord exceedingly, and they offered a sacrifice to the Lord and made vows.
17 a   And the Lord appointed a great fish to swallow up Jonah; and Jonah was in the belly of the fish three days and three nights.

A PSALM OF THANKSGIVING

2 Then Jonah prayed to the Lord his God from the
2 belly of the fish, saying,
"I called to the Lord, out of my distress,
    and he answered me;
out of the belly of Sheol I cried,
    and thou didst hear my voice.
3 For thou didst cast me into the deep,
    into the heart of the seas,
    and the flood was round about me;
all thy waves and thy billows
    passed over me.
4 Then I said, 'I am cast out
    from thy presence;
how shall I again look
    upon thy holy temple?'
5 The waters closed in over me,
    the deep was round about me;
weeds were wrapped about my head
6   at the roots of the mountains.
I went down to the land
    whose bars closed upon me for ever;
yet thou didst bring up my life from the Pit,
    O Lord my God.

a Ch 2.1 in Heb

7 When my soul fainted within me,
    I remembered the Lord;
and my prayer came to thee,
    into thy holy temple.
8 Those who pay regard to vain idols
    forsake their true loyalty.
9 But I with the voice of thanksgiving
    will sacrifice to thee;
what I have vowed I will pay.
    Deliverance belongs to the Lord!"
10 And the Lord spoke to the fish, and it vomited out Jonah upon the dry land.

THE RELUCTANT MISSIONARY

3 Then the word of the Lord came to Jonah the second
2 time, saying, "Arise, go to Nin'eveh, that great city,
3 and proclaim to it the message that I tell you." So Jonah arose and went to Nin'eveh, according to the word of the Lord. Now Nin'eveh was an exceedingly great city, three
4 days' journey in breadth. Jonah began to go into the city, going a day's journey. And he cried, "Yet forty days, and
5 Nin'eveh shall be overthrown!" And the people of Nin'eveh believed God; they proclaimed a fast, and put on sackcloth, from the greatest of them to the least of them.
6 Then tidings reached the king of Nin'eveh, and he arose from his throne, removed his robe, and covered
7 himself with sackcloth, and sat in ashes. And he made proclamation and published through Nin'eveh, "By the decree of the king and his nobles: Let neither man nor beast, herd nor flock, taste anything; let them not feed,
8 or drink water, but let man and beast be covered with sackcloth, and let them cry mightily to God; yea, let every one turn from his evil way and from the violence
9 which is in his hands. Who knows, God may yet repent and turn from his fierce anger, so that we perish not?"
10 When God saw what they did, how they turned from their evil way, God repented of the evil which he had said he would do to them; and he did not do it.

GOD'S MERCY WILL NOT BE LIMITED

4 But it displeased Jonah exceedingly, and he was
2 angry. And he prayed to the LORD and said, "I pray thee, LORD, is not this what I said when I was yet in my country? That is why I made haste to flee to Tarshish; for I knew that thou art a gracious God and merciful, slow to anger, and abounding in steadfast love, and re-
3 pentest of evil. Therefore now, O LORD, take my life from me, I beseech thee, for it is better for me to die than to
4 live." And the LORD said, "Do you do well to be angry?"
5 Then Jonah went out of the city and sat to the east of the city, and made a booth for himself there. He sat under it in the shade, till he should see what would become of the city.
6 And the LORD God appointed a plant,[b] and made it come up over Jonah, that it might be a shade over his head, to save him from his discomfort. So Jonah was
7 exceedingly glad because of the plant.[b] But when dawn came up the next day, God appointed a worm which at-
8 tacked the plant,[b] so that it withered. When the sun rose, God appointed a sultry east wind, and the sun beat upon the head of Jonah so that he was faint; and he asked that he might die, and said, "It is better for me to die
9 than to live." But God said to Jonah, "Do you do well to be angry for the plant?"[b] And he said, "I do well to
10 be angry, angry enough to die." And the LORD said, "You pity the plant,[b] for which you did not labor, nor did you make it grow, which came into being in a night,
11 and perished in a night. And should not I pity Nin'eveh, that great city, in which there are more than a hundred and twenty thousand persons who do not know their right hand from their left, and also much cattle?"

[b] Heb *qiqayon*, probably *the castor oil plant*

INTRODUCTION TO

MICAH

The prophet Micah lived and worked between 725 b.c. and 690 b.c. This book is a collection of his sermons prepared about 690 b.c. The Assyrian armies were destroying Samaria, capital of the northern kingdom of Israel, and were threatening to invade Jerusalem in Judah. Micah preached against the selfishness of the Jewish leaders and condemned their heartless treatment of the poor people. He has often been called "the prophet of the poor." The people had begun to worship idols on hilltops, following the customs of their pagan neighbors. Micah proclaimed that God was punishing them by letting Assyria defeat and destroy both Samaria and Jerusalem.

Beginning with Chapter 4, the sermons become more hopeful and emphasize God's forgiving mercy. They are so different from the first three chapters that some persons think writings by other prophets have been added to Micah's sermons. However that may be, Micah was a kindred spirit of Amos, Hosea, and Isaiah, who lived in the same century. The Book of Micah gives us the famous statement of the meaning of true worship:

> "He has showed you, O man, what is good;
>> and what does the LORD require of you
>> but to do justice, and to love kindness,
>> and to walk humbly with your God?"
>> —Micah 6.8

When the account of the birth of Jesus was being written hundreds of years later, these words from the Book of Micah were remembered:

> "But you, O Bethlehem Ephrathah,
>> who are little to be among the clans of Judah,
> from you shall come forth for me
>> one who is to be ruler in Israel."
>> (Micah 5.2; compare Matthew 2.6)

THE BOOK OF

MICAH

BACKGROUND TO MICAH'S PROPHECIES

1 The word of the LORD that came to Micah of Mo'-resheth in the days of Jotham, Ahaz, and Hezeki'ah, kings of Judah, which he saw concerning Samar'ia and Jerusalem.

2 Hear, you peoples, all of you;
  hearken, O earth, and all that is in it;
and let the Lord GOD be a witness against you,
  the Lord from his holy temple.

3 For behold, the LORD is coming forth out of his place,
  and will come down and tread upon the high places
    of the earth.
4 And the mountains will melt under him
  and the valleys will be cleft,
like wax before the fire,
  like waters poured down a steep place.

ABOUT THE ASSYRIAN CRISIS

5 All this is for the transgression of Jacob
  and for the sins of the house of Israel.
What is the transgression of Jacob?
  Is it not Samar'ia?
And what is the sin of the house ᵃ of Judah?

ᵃ Gk Tg Compare Syr: Heb *what are the high places*

Is it not Jerusalem?

6 Therefore I will make Samar′ia a heap in the open
  country,
  a place for planting vineyards;
and I will pour down her stones into the valley,
  and uncover her foundations.
7 All her images shall be beaten to pieces,
  all her hires shall be burned with fire,
  and all her idols I will lay waste;
for from the hire of a harlot she gathered them,
  and to the hire of a harlot they shall return.

8 For this I will lament and wail;
  I will go stripped and naked;
I will make lamentation like the jackals,
  and mourning like the ostriches.
9 For her wound b is incurable;
  and it has come to Judah,
it has reached to the gate of my people,
  to Jerusalem.

10 Tell it not in Gath,
  weep not at all;
in Beth-le-aph′rah
  roll yourselves in the dust.
11 Pass on your way,
  inhabitants of Shaphir,
  in nakedness and shame;
the inhabitants of Za′anan
  do not come forth;
the wailing of Beth-e′zel
  shall take away from you its standing place.
12 For the inhabitants of Maroth
  wait anxiously for good,
because evil has come down from the LORD
  to the gate of Jerusalem.
13 Harness the steeds to the chariots,
  inhabitants of Lachish;
you were c the beginning of sin
  to the daughter of Zion,
for in you were found
  the transgressions of Israel.
14 Therefore you shall give parting gifts
  to Mo′resheth-gath;
  the houses of Achzib shall be a deceitful thing
  to the kings of Israel.
15 I will again bring a conqueror upon you,
  inhabitants of Mare′shah;
the glory of Israel
  shall come to Adullam.
16 Make yourselves bald and cut off your hair,
  for the children of your delight;
make yourselves as bald as the eagle,
  for they shall go from you into exile.

WOE TO THOSE WHO OPPRESS

2 Woe to those who devise wickedness
  and work evil upon their beds!
When the morning dawns, they perform it,
  because it is in the power of their hand.
2 They covet fields, and seize them;
  and houses, and take them away;
they oppress a man and his house,
  a man and his inheritance.
3 Therefore thus says the LORD:
Behold, against this family I am devising evil,
  from which you cannot remove your necks;
and you shall not walk haughtily,
  for it will be an evil time.
4 In that day they shall take up a taunt song against you,
  and wail with bitter lamentation,
and say, "We are utterly ruined;
  he changes the portion of my people;
how he removes it from me!
  Among our captors d he divides our fields."
5 Therefore you will have none to cast the line by lot
  in the assembly of the LORD.

6 "Do not preach"—thus they preach—
  "one should not preach of such things;
  disgrace will not overtake us."
7 Should this be said, O house of Jacob?
  Is the Spirit of the LORD impatient?
  Are these his doings?
Do not my words do good
  to him who walks uprightly?
8 But you rise against my people e as an enemy;
  you strip the robe from the peaceful, f
from those who pass by trustingly with no thought of war.
9 The women of my people you drive out
  from their pleasant houses;
from their young children you take away
  my glory for ever.
10 Arise and go,
  for this is no place to rest;
because of uncleanness that destroys
  with a grievous destruction.
11 If a man should go about and utter wind and lies,
  saying, "I will preach to you of wine and strong
    drink,"
he would be the preacher for this people!

12 I will surely gather all of you, O Jacob,
  I will gather the remnant of Israel;
I will set them together
  like sheep in a fold,
like a flock in its pasture,
  a noisy multitude of men.

b Gk Syr Vg: Heb wounds   c Cn: Heb it was   d Cn: Heb the rebellious   e Cn: Heb yesterday my people rose
f Cn: Heb from before a garment

¹³ He who opens the breach will go up before them;
    they will break through and pass the gate,
    going out by it.
Their king will pass on before them,
    the LORD at their head.

3 And I said:
    Hear, you heads of Jacob
    and rulers of the house of Israel!
Is it not for you to know justice?—
² you who hate the good and love the evil,
who tear the skin from off my people,
    and their flesh from off their bones;
³ who eat the flesh of my people,
    and flay their skin from off them,
and break their bones in pieces,
    and chop them up like meat ᵍ in a kettle,
like flesh in a caldron.

⁴ Then they will cry to the LORD,
    but he will not answer them;
he will hide his face from them at that time,
    because they have made their deeds evil.

⁵ Thus says the LORD concerning the prophets
    who lead my people astray,
who cry "Peace"
    when they have something to eat,
but declare war against him
    who puts nothing into their mouths.
⁶ Therefore it shall be night to you, without vision,
    and darkness to you, without divination.
The sun shall go down upon the prophets,
    and the day shall be black over them;
⁷ the seers shall be disgraced,
    and the diviners put to shame;
they shall all cover their lips,
    for there is no answer from God.
⁸ But as for me, I am filled with power,
    with the Spirit of the LORD,
    and with justice and might,
to declare to Jacob his transgression
    and to Israel his sin.

⁹ Hear this, you heads of the house of Jacob
    and rulers of the house of Israel,
who abhor justice
    and pervert all equity,
¹⁰ who build Zion with blood
    and Jerusalem with wrong.
¹¹ Its heads give judgment for a bribe,
    its priests teach for hire,
    its prophets divine for money;
yet they lean upon the LORD and say,

ᵍ Gk: Heb *as*

"Is not the LORD in the midst of us?
    No evil shall come upon us."
¹² Therefore because of you
    Zion shall be plowed as a field;
Jerusalem shall become a heap of ruins,
    and the mountain of the house a wooded height.

VISIONS OF A GLORIOUS FUTURE

4 It shall come to pass in the latter days
    that the mountain of the house of the LORD
shall be established as the highest of the mountains,
    and shall be raised up above the hills;
and peoples shall flow to it,
² and many nations shall come, and say:
"Come, let us go up to the mountain of the LORD,
    to the house of the God of Jacob;

that he may teach us his ways
    and we may walk in his paths."
For out of Zion shall go forth the law,
    and the word of the LORD from Jerusalem.
³ He shall judge between many peoples,
    and shall decide for strong nations afar off;
and they shall beat their swords into plowshares,
    and their spears into pruning hooks;
nation shall not lift up sword against nation,
    neither shall they learn war any more;
⁴ but they shall sit every man under his vine and under his
        fig tree,
    and none shall make them afraid;
    for the mouth of the LORD of hosts has spoken.

⁵ For all the peoples walk
    each in the name of its god,
but we will walk in the name of the LORD our God
    for ever and ever.

⁶ In that day, says the LORD,
    I will assemble the lame
and gather those who have been driven away,
    and those whom I have afflicted;
⁷ and the lame I will make the remnant;
    and those who were cast off, a strong nation;
and the LORD will reign over them in Mount Zion
    from this time forth and for evermore.

8 And you, O tower of the flock,
　　hill of the daughter of Zion,
　to you shall it come,
　　the former dominion shall come,
　　the kingdom of the daughter of Jerusalem.
9 Now why do you cry aloud?
　　Is there no king in you?
　Has your counselor perished,
　　that pangs have seized you like a woman in travail?
10 Writhe and groan,[h] O daughter of Zion,
　　like a woman in travail;
　for now you shall go forth from the city
　　and dwell in the open country;
　you shall go to Babylon.
　There you shall be rescued,
　　there the LORD will redeem you
　　from the hand of your enemies.

11 Now many nations
　　are assembled against you,
　saying, "Let her be profaned,
　　and let our eyes gaze upon Zion."
12 But they do not know
　　the thoughts of the LORD,
　they do not understand his plan,
　　that he has gathered them as sheaves to the threshing
　　　floor.
13 Arise and thresh,
　　O daughter of Zion,
　for I will make your horn iron
　　and your hoofs bronze;
　you shall beat in pieces many peoples,
　　and shall[i] devote their gain to the LORD,
　　their wealth to the Lord of the whole earth.

5 [j] Now you are walled about with a wall;[k]
　　siege is laid against us;
　with a rod they strike upon the cheek the ruler of Israel.

2 [l] But you, O Bethlehem Eph'rathah,
　　who are little to be among the clans of Judah,
　from you shall come forth for me
　　one who is to be ruler in Israel,
　whose origin is from of old,
　　from ancient days.
3 Therefore he shall give them up until the time
　　when she who is in travail has brought forth;
　then the rest of his brethren shall return
　　to the people of Israel.
4 And he shall stand and feed his flock in the strength of the
　　LORD,
　in the majesty of the name of the LORD his God.
　And they shall dwell secure, for now he shall be great
　　to the ends of the earth.

5 And this shall be peace,
　　when the Assyrian comes into our land
　　and treads upon our soil,[m]
　that we will raise against him seven shepherds
　　and eight princes of men;
6 they shall rule the land of Assyria with the sword,
　　and the land of Nimrod with the drawn sword;[n]
　and they[o] shall deliver us from the Assyrian
　　when he comes into our land
　　and treads within our border.

7 Then the remnant of Jacob shall be
　　in the midst of many peoples
　like dew from the LORD,
　　like showers upon the grass,
　which tarry not for men
　　nor wait for the sons of men.
8 And the remnant of Jacob shall be among the nations,
　　in the midst of many peoples,
　like a lion among the beasts of the forest,
　　like a young lion among the flocks of sheep,
　which, when it goes through, treads down
　　and tears in pieces, and there is none to deliver.
9 Your hand shall be lifted up over your adversaries,
　　and all your enemies shall be cut off.

10 And in that day, says the LORD,
　　I will cut off your horses from among you
　　and will destroy your chariots;
11 and I will cut off the cities of your land
　　and throw down all your strongholds;
12 and I will cut off sorceries from your hand,
　　and you shall have no more soothsayers;
13 and I will cut off your images
　　and your pillars from among you,
　and you shall bow down no more
　　to the work of your hands;
14 and I will root out your Ashe'rim from among you
　　and destroy your cities.
15 And in anger and wrath I will execute vengeance
　　upon the nations that did not obey.

THE LORD WILL HAVE COMPASSION ON ISRAEL

6 Hear what the LORD says:
　　Arise, plead your case before the mountains,
　　and let the hills hear your voice.
2 Hear, you mountains, the controversy of the LORD,
　　and you enduring foundations of the earth;
　for the LORD has a controversy with his people,
　　and he will contend with Israel.

3 "O my people, what have I done to you?
　　In what have I wearied you? Answer me!
4 For I brought you up from the land of Egypt,

---

h Heb uncertain 　　　i Gk Syr Tg: Heb I will 　　　j Ch 4.14 in Heb 　　　k Cn Compare Gk: Heb obscure 　　　l Ch 5.1 in Heb
m Gk: Heb in our palaces 　　　n Cn: Heb in its entrances 　　　o Heb he

and redeemed you from the house of bondage;
and I sent before you Moses,
 Aaron, and Miriam.
5 O my people, remember what Balak king of Moab devised,
 and what Balaam the son of Be'or answered him,
and what happened from Shittim to Gilgal,
 that you may know the saving acts of the LORD."

6 "With what shall I come before the LORD,
 and bow myself before God on high?
Shall I come before him with burnt offerings,
 with calves a year old?
7 Will the LORD be pleased with thousands of rams,
 with ten thousands of rivers of oil?
Shall I give my first-born for my transgression,
 the fruit of my body for the sin of my soul?"
8 He has showed you, O man, what is good;
 and what does the LORD require of you
but to do justice, and to love kindness,ᵖ
 and to walk humbly with your God?

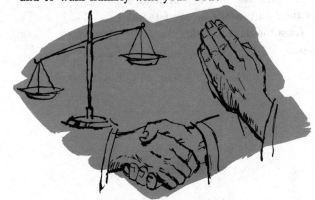

9 The voice of the LORD cries to the city—
 and it is sound wisdom to fear thy name:
"Hear, O tribe and assembly of the city! q
10 Can I forget ʳ the treasures of wickedness in the house
  of the wicked,
 and the scant measure that is accursed?
11 Shall I acquit the man with wicked scales
 and with a bag of deceitful weights?
12 Yourˢ rich men are full of violence;
 yourˢ inhabitants speak lies,
 and their tongue is deceitful in their mouth.
13 Therefore I have begunᵗ to smite you,
 making you desolate because of your sins.
14 You shall eat, but not be satisfied,
 and there shall be hunger in your inward parts;
you shall put away, but not save,
 and what you save I will give to the sword.
15 You shall sow, but not reap;
 you shall tread olives, but not anoint yourselves with
  oil;
 you shall tread grapes, but not drink wine.

16 For you have kept the statutes of Omri,ᵘ
 and all the works of the house of Ahab;
 and you have walked in their counsels;
that I may make you a desolation, and your ᵛ inhabitants
  a hissing,
 so you shall bear the scorn of the peoples." ʷ

7 Woe is me! For I have become
  as when the summer fruit has been gathered,
 as when the vintage has been gleaned:
there is no cluster to eat,
 no first-ripe fig which my soul desires.
2 The godly man has perished from the earth,
 and there is none upright among men;
they all lie in wait for blood,
 and each hunts his brother with a net.
3 Their hands are upon what is evil, to do it diligently;
 the prince and the judge ask for a bribe,
and the great man utters the evil desire of his soul;
 thus they weave it together.
4 The best of them is like a brier,
 the most upright of them a thorn hedge.
The day of their ˣ watchmen, of their ˣ punishment, has
  come;
 now their confusion is at hand.
5 Put no trust in a neighbor,
 have no confidence in a friend;
guard the doors of your mouth
 from her who lies in your bosom;
6 for the son treats the father with contempt,
 the daughter rises up against her mother,
the daughter-in-law against her mother-in-law;
 a man's enemies are the men of his own house.
7 But as for me, I will look to the LORD,
 I will wait for the God of my salvation;
 my God will hear me.

8 Rejoice not over me, O my enemy;
 when I fall, I shall rise;
when I sit in darkness,
 the LORD will be a light to me.
9 I will bear the indignation of the LORD
 because I have sinned against him,
until he pleads my cause
 and executes judgment for me.
He will bring me forth to the light;
 I shall behold his deliverance.
10 Then my enemy will see,
 and shame will cover her who said to me,
 "Where is the LORD your God?"
My eyes will gloat over her;
 now she will be trodden down
 like the mire of the streets.

ᵖ Or steadfast love q Cn Compare Gk: Heb and who has appointed it yet ʳ Cn: Heb uncertain ˢ Heb whose
ᵗ Gk Syr Vg: Heb have made sick ᵘ Gk Syr Vg Tg: Heb the statutes of Omri are kept ᵛ Heb its
ʷ Gk: Heb my people ˣ Heb your

11 A day for the building of your walls!
 In that day the boundary shall be far extended.
12 In that day they will come to you,
 from Assyria to ʸ Egypt,
 and from Egypt to the River,
 from sea to sea and from mountain to mountain.
13 But the earth will be desolate
 because of its inhabitants,
 for the fruit of their doings.

14 Shepherd thy people with thy staff,
 the flock of thy inheritance,
 who dwell alone in a forest
 in the midst of a garden land;
 let them feed in Bashan and Gilead
 as in the days of old.

15 As in the days when you came out of the land of Egypt
 I will show them ᶻ marvelous things.

16 The nations shall see and be ashamed
 of all their might;

they shall lay their hands on their mouths;
 their ears shall be deaf;
17 they shall lick the dust like a serpent,
 like the crawling things of the earth;
 they shall come trembling out of their strongholds,
 they shall turn in dread to the LORD our God,
 and they shall fear because of thee.

18 Who is a God like thee, pardoning iniquity
 and passing over transgression
 for the remnant of his inheritance?
 He does not retain his anger for ever
 because he delights in steadfast love.
19 He will again have compassion upon us,
 he will tread our iniquities under foot.
 Thou wilt cast all our ᵃ sins
 into the depths of the sea.
20 Thou wilt show faithfulness to Jacob
 and steadfast love to Abraham,
 as thou hast sworn to our fathers
 from the days of old.

ʸ Cn: Heb *and cities of*   ᶻ Heb *him*   ᵃ Gk Syr Vg Tg: Heb *their*

INTRODUCTION TO

NAHUM

The prophet Nahum was preaching between 626 and 605 B.C., and the Book of Nahum was written about the time the nation of Assyria was destroyed by the armies of Babylonia in 605 B.C. The prophets Zephaniah, Habakkuk, and Jeremiah were also active during this same period.

Assyria's armies had destroyed the northern kingdom of Israel a hundred years before, and Nineveh, the capital city of Assyria, had come to be hated and feared by the people of the southern kingdom of Judah. When Nineveh was defeated by the Babylonian armies, Nahum saw in its defeat the triumph of God over an enemy of his people.

Nahum is sometimes called a prophet of hate and vengeance. Although Nahum seems unconcerned about any sins of his own nation, he reminds us that when nations become evil, they come under God's judgment and do not endure.

THE BOOK OF

NAHUM

THE OVERTHROW OF NINEVEH

1 An oracle concerning Nin'eveh. The book of the vision of Nahum of Elkosh.
2 The LORD is a jealous God and avenging,
   the LORD is avenging and wrathful;
the LORD takes vengeance on his adversaries
   and keeps wrath for his enemies.
3 The LORD is slow to anger and of great might,
   and the LORD will by no means clear the guilty.

His way is in whirlwind and storm,
   and the clouds are the dust of his feet.
4 He rebukes the sea and makes it dry,
   he dries up all the rivers;
Bashan and Carmel wither,
   the bloom of Lebanon fades.
5 The mountains quake before him,
   the hills melt;
the earth is laid waste before him,
   the world and all that dwell therein.

6 Who can stand before his indignation?
   Who can endure the heat of his anger?
His wrath is poured out like fire,
   and the rocks are broken asunder by him.
7 The LORD is good,
   a stronghold in the day of trouble;
   he knows those who take refuge in him.
8 But with an overflowing flood
   he will make a full end of his adversaries,[a]
   and will pursue his enemies into darkness.
9 What do you plot against the LORD?
   He will make a full end;
   he will not take vengeance[b] twice on his foes.[c]
10 Like entangled thorns they are consumed,[d]
   like dry stubble.
11 Did one not[e] come out from you,
   who plotted evil against the LORD,
   and counseled villainy?

12 Thus says the LORD,
   "Though they be strong and many,[f]
   they will be cut off and pass away,
Though I have afflicted you,
   I will afflict you no more.
13 And now I will break his yoke from off you
   and will burst your bonds asunder."

14 The LORD has given commandment about you:
   "No more shall your name be perpetuated;
   from the house of your gods I will cut off

---

[a] Gk: Heb *her place*   [b] Gk: Heb *rise up*   [c] Cn: Heb *distress*   [d] Heb *are consumed, drunken as with their drink*
[e] Cn: Heb *fully*   [f] Heb uncertain

the graven image and the molten image.
I will make your grave, for you are vile."

15 g Behold, on the mountains the feet of him
  who brings good tidings,
  who proclaims peace!
Keep your feasts, O Judah,
  fulfil your vows,
for never again shall the wicked come against you,
  he is utterly cut off.

2 The shatterer has come up against you.
  Man the ramparts;
  watch the road;
gird your loins;
  collect all your strength.

2 (For the LORD is restoring the majesty of Jacob
  as the majesty of Israel,
for plunderers have stripped them
  and ruined their branches.)

3 The shield of his mighty men is red,
  his soldiers are clothed in scarlet.
The chariots flash like flame h
  when mustered in array;
  the chargers i prance.
4 The chariots rage in the streets,
  they rush to and fro through the squares;
they gleam like torches,
  they dart like lightning.
5 The officers are summoned,
  they stumble as they go,
they hasten to the wall,
  the mantelet is set up.
6 The river gates are opened,
  the palace is in dismay;
7 its mistress j is stripped, she is carried off,
  her maidens lamenting,
moaning like doves,
  and beating their breasts.
8 Nin'eveh is like a pool
  whose waters k run away.
"Halt! Halt!" they cry;
  but none turns back.
9 Plunder the silver,
  plunder the gold!
There is no end of treasure,
  or wealth of every precious thing.

10 Desolate! Desolation and ruin!
  Hearts faint and knees tremble,
anguish is on all loins,
  all faces grow pale!
11 Where is the lions' den,

the cave l of the young lions,
  where the lion brought his prey,
  where his cubs were, with none to disturb?
12 The lion tore enough for his whelps
  and strangled prey for his lionesses;
he filled his caves with prey
  and his dens with torn flesh.

13 Behold, I am against you, says the LORD of hosts, and
I will burn your m chariots in smoke, and the sword shall
devour your young lions; I will cut off your prey from
the earth, and the voice of your messengers shall no more
be heard.
3 Woe to the bloody city,
  all full of lies and booty—
  no end to the plunder!
2 The crack of whip, and rumble of wheel,
  galloping horse and bounding chariot!
3 Horsemen charging,
  flashing sword and glittering spear,
hosts of slain,
  heaps of corpses,
dead bodies without end—
  they stumble over the bodies!
4 And all for the countless harlotries of the harlot,
  graceful and of deadly charms,
who betrays nations with her harlotries,
  and peoples with her charms.

5 Behold, I am against you,
  says the LORD of hosts,
  and will lift up your skirts over your face;
and I will let nations look on your nakedness
  and kingdoms on your shame.
6 I will throw filth at you
  and treat you with contempt,
  and make you a gazingstock.
7 And all who look on you will shrink from you and say,
Wasted is Nin'eveh; who will bemoan her?
  whence shall I seek comforters for her? n

8 Are you better than Thebes o
  that sat by the Nile,
with water around her,
  her rampart a sea,
  and water her wall?
9 Ethiopia was her strength,
  Egypt too, and that without limit;
  Put and the Libyans were her p helpers.

10 Yet she was carried away,
  she went into captivity;
her little ones were dashed in pieces
  at the head of every street;

g Ch 2.1 in Heb   h Cn: The meaning of the Hebrew word is uncertain   i Cn Compare Gk Syr: Heb cypresses
j The meaning of the Hebrew is uncertain   k Cn Compare Gk: Heb from the days that she has become, and they
l Cn: Heb pasture   m Heb her   n Gk: Heb you   o Heb No-amon   p Gk: Heb your

for her honored men lots were cast,
and all her great men were bound in chains.
11 You also will be drunken,
you will be dazed;
you will seek
a refuge from the enemy.
12 All your fortresses are like fig trees
with first-ripe figs—
if shaken they fall
into the mouth of the eater.
13 Behold, your troops
are women in your midst.
The gates of your land
are wide open to your foes;
fire has devoured your bars.

14 Draw water for the siege,
strengthen your forts;
go into the clay,
tread the mortar,
take hold of the brick mold!
15 There will the fire devour you,
the sword will cut you off.
It will devour you like the locust.

q Or *marshals*

Multiply yourselves like the locust,
multiply like the grasshopper!
16 You increased your merchants
more than the stars of the heavens.
The locust spreads its wings and flies away.
17 Your princes are like grasshoppers,
your scribes q like clouds of locusts
settling on the fences
in a day of cold—
when the sun rises, they fly away;
no one knows where they are.

18 Your shepherds are asleep,
O king of Assyria;
your nobles slumber.
Your people are scattered on the mountains
with none to gather them.
19 There is no assuaging your hurt,
your wound is grievous.
All who hear the news of you
clap their hands over you.
For upon whom has not come
your unceasing evil?

INTRODUCTION TO

HABAKKUK

The Book of Habakkuk, written about 605 B.C., searches for the reason why God allows so much evil in the world. Along with the prophets Zephaniah, Nahum, and Jeremiah, the prophet Habakkuk realized that Assyria was about to fall under the military power of Babylonia and that his own small country of Judah also was in peril.

As Habakkuk the prophet thought about the history of the Hebrews, it seemed that each new enemy of his people was conquered only to make way for a more cruel overlord who in turn made prisoners of the Jews. He wondered how long his country would continue to be mistreated by large neighbor nations. He wondered how long there would be war and defeat for his people.

The answer to Habakkuk's questions is given in Chapter 2, especially verses 2-4. Habakkuk admitted that the wicked often do prosper. Nevertheless, he saw that men are able to live righteously because of the strength of their faith and loyalty to God. The song with which the book ends (Chapter 3) is one of the most beautiful in the Bible. It expresses the writer's boundless trust in God as the true source of happiness rather than trust in possessions or success.

Here in the Old Testament is clearly stated the truth that became central in Christianity—that God wants us to trust him and that we are saved by faith in him: "The righteous shall live by his faith." The answer God gave Habakkuk for all his doubts was that though oppressors continue to succeed one another, those who keep their faith in God and strive to do his will will finally overcome all their troubles.

THE BOOK OF

HABAKKUK

WHY DOES GOD PERMIT INJUSTICE?

1 The oracle of God which Habak'kuk the prophet saw.

[2] O LORD, how long shall I cry for help,
and thou wilt not hear?
Or cry to thee "Violence!"
and thou wilt not save?

[3] Why dost thou make me see wrongs
and look upon trouble?
Destruction and violence are before me;
strife and contention arise.
[4] So the law is slacked
and justice never goes forth.

For the wicked surround the righteous,
so justice goes forth perverted.

[5] Look among the nations, and see;
wonder and be astounded.
For I am doing a work in your days
that you would not believe if told.
[6] For lo, I am rousing the Chalde'ans,
that bitter and hasty nation,
who march through the breadth of the earth,
to seize habitations not their own.
[7] Dread and terrible are they;
their justice and dignity proceed from themselves.
[8] Their horses are swifter than leopards,
more fierce than the evening wolves;
their horsemen press proudly on.
Yea, their horsemen come from afar;
they fly like an eagle swift to devour.
[9] They all come for violence;
terror[a] of them goes before them.

[a] Cn: Heb uncertain

They gather captives like sand.
10 At kings they scoff,
     and of rulers they make sport.
   They laugh at every fortress,
     for they heap up earth and take it.
11 Then they sweep by like the wind and go on,
     guilty men, whose own might is their god!

12 Art thou not from everlasting,
     O LORD my God, my Holy One?
   We shall not die.
   O LORD, thou hast ordained them as a judgment;
     and thou, O Rock, hast established them for chastise-
     ment.
13 Thou who art of purer eyes than to behold evil
     and canst not look on wrong,
   why dost thou look on faithless men,
     and art silent when the wicked swallows up
     the man more righteous than he?
14 For thou makest men like the fish of the sea,
     like crawling things that have no ruler.
15 He brings all of them up with a hook,
     he drags them out with his net,
   he gathers them in his seine;
     so he rejoices and exults.
16 Therefore he sacrifices to his net
     and burns incense to his seine;
   for by them he lives in luxury,[b]
     and his food is rich.
17 Is he then to keep on emptying his net,
     and mercilessly slaying nations for ever?

2 I will take my stand to watch,
     and station myself on the tower,
   and look forth to see what he will say to me,
     and what I will answer concerning my complaint.
2 And the LORD answered me:
   "Write the vision;
     make it plain upon tablets,
     so he may run who reads it.
3 For still the vision awaits its time;
     it hastens to the end—it will not lie.
   If it seem slow, wait for it;
     it will surely come, it will not delay.
4 Behold, he whose soul is not upright in him shall fail,[c]
     but the righteous shall live by his faith.[d]
5 Moreover, wine is treacherous;
     the arrogant man shall not abide.[e]
   His greed is as wide as Sheol;
     like death he has never enough.
   He gathers for himself all nations,
     and collects as his own all peoples."

6 Shall not all these take up their taunt against him, in
     scoffing derision of him, and say,
   "Woe to him who heaps up what is not his own—
     for how long?—
     and loads himself with pledges!"
7 Will not your debtors suddenly arise,
     and those awake who will make you tremble?
   Then you will be booty for them.
8 Because you have plundered many nations,
     all the remnant of the peoples shall plunder you,
   for the blood of men and violence to the earth,
     to cities and all who dwell therein.

9 Woe to him who gets evil gain for his house,
     to set his nest on high,
     to be safe from the reach of harm!
10 You have devised shame to your house
     by cutting off many peoples;
     you have forfeited your life.
11 For the stone will cry out from the wall,
     and the beam from the woodwork respond.

12 Woe to him who builds a town with blood,
     and founds a city on iniquity!
13 Behold, is it not from the LORD of hosts
     that peoples labor only for fire,
     and nations weary themselves for nought?
14 For the earth will be filled
     with the knowledge of the glory of the LORD,
     as the waters cover the sea.

15 Woe to him who makes his neighbors drink
     of the cup of his wrath,[f] and makes them drunk,
     to gaze on their shame!
16 You will be sated with contempt instead of glory.
     Drink, yourself, and stagger![g]
   The cup in the LORD's right hand will come around to
     you,
     and shame will come upon your glory!
17 The violence done to Lebanon will overwhelm you;
     the destruction of the beasts will terrify you,[h]
   for the blood of men and violence to the earth,
     to cities and all who dwell therein.

18 What profit is an idol
  when its maker has shaped it,
  a metal image, a teacher of lies?
  For the workman trusts in his own creation
  when he makes dumb idols!
19 Woe to him who says to a wooden thing, Awake;
  to a dumb stone, Arise!
  Can this give revelation?
  Behold, it is overlaid with gold and silver,
  and there is no breath at all in it.

20 But the LORD is in his holy temple;
  let all the earth keep silence before him.

THE PSALM OF PRAISE

3 A prayer of Habak′kuk the prophet, according to
   Shigion′oth.
2 O LORD, I have heard the report of thee,
  and thy work, O LORD, do I fear.
  In the midst of the years renew it;
  in the midst of the years make it known;
  in wrath remember mercy.
3 God came from Teman,
  and the Holy One from Mount Paran.
  His glory covered the heavens,
  and the earth was full of his praise.   *Selah*
4 His brightness was like the light,
  rays flashed from his hand;
  and there he veiled his power.
5 Before him went pestilence,
  and plague followed close behind.
6 He stood and measured the earth;
  and looked and shook the nations;
  then the eternal mountains were scattered,
  the everlasting hills sank low.
  His ways were as of old.
7 I saw the tents of Cushan in affliction;
  the curtains of the land of Mid′ian did tremble.
8 Was thy wrath against the rivers, O LORD?
  Was thy anger against the rivers,
  or thy indignation against the sea,
  when thou didst ride upon thy horses,
  upon thy chariot of victory?

9 Thou didst strip the sheath from thy bow,
  and put the arrows to the string.[i]   *Selah*
  Thou didst cleave the earth with rivers.
10 The mountains saw thee, and writhed;
  the raging waters swept on;
  the deep gave forth its voice,
  it lifted its hands on high.
11 The sun and moon stood still in their habitation[j]
  at the light of thine arrows as they sped,
  at the flash of thy glittering spear.
12 Thou didst bestride the earth in fury,
  thou didst trample the nations in anger.
13 Thou wentest forth for the salvation of thy people,
  for the salvation of thy anointed.
  Thou didst crush the head of the wicked,[k]
  laying him bare from thigh to neck.[l]   *Selah*
14 Thou didst pierce with thy[m] shafts the head of his war-
    riors,[n]
  who came like a whirlwind to scatter me,
  rejoicing as if to devour the poor in secret.
15 Thou didst trample the sea with thy horses,
  the surging of mighty waters.

16 I hear, and my body trembles,
  my lips quiver at the sound;
  rottenness enters into my bones,
  my steps totter[o] beneath me.
  I will quietly wait for the day of trouble
  to come upon people who invade us.

17 Though the fig tree do not blossom,
  nor fruit be on the vines,
  the produce of the olive fail
  and the fields yield no food,
  the flock be cut off from the fold
  and there be no herd in the stalls,
18 yet I will rejoice in the LORD,
  I will joy in the God of my salvation.
19 GOD, the Lord, is my strength;
  he makes my feet like hinds' feet,
  he makes me tread upon my high places.

To the choirmaster: with stringed[p] instruments.

---

i Cn: Heb obscure   j Heb uncertain   k Cn: Heb *head from the house of the wicked*   l Heb obscure   m Heb *his*
n Vg Compare Gk Syr: Heb uncertain   o Cn Compare Gk: Heb *I tremble because*   p Heb *my stringed*

— INTRODUCTION TO —

ZEPHANIAH

The prophet Zephaniah wrote this poem-sermon about 627 B.C., six years before the young King Josiah began his reforms in the Jewish nation. Another prophet who was speaking for God in this period was Jeremiah.

The book opens with a dramatic picture of the coming of "the day of the LORD," when all nations, including the Jews, would be judged according to their loyalty and their actions. Zephaniah pleaded with the people to ask God's forgiveness for their sins. In the last chapter, beginning with verse 11, Zephaniah shows that he believes the Jews will repent and be saved by God.

THE BOOK OF

ZEPHANIAH

JUDGMENT ON JERUSALEM

1 The word of the LORD which came to Zephani'ah the son of Cushi, son of Gedali'ah, son of Amari'ah, son of Hezeki'ah, in the days of Josi'ah the son of Amon, king of Judah.

2 "I will utterly sweep away everything
    from the face of the earth," says the LORD.
3 "I will sweep away man and beast;
    I will sweep away the birds of the air
    and the fish of the sea.
I will overthrow [a] the wicked;

I will cut off mankind
    from the face of the earth," says the LORD.
4 "I will stretch out my hand against Judah,
    and against all the inhabitants of Jerusalem;
and I will cut off from this place the remnant of Ba'al
    and the name of the idolatrous priests; [b]
5 those who bow down on the roofs
    to the host of the heavens;
those who bow down and swear to the LORD
    and yet swear by Milcom;
6 those who have turned back from following the LORD,
    who do not seek the LORD or inquire of him."

7 Be silent before the Lord GOD!
    For the day of the LORD is at hand;

the LORD has prepared a sacrifice
    and consecrated his guests.
8 And on the day of the LORD's sacrifice—
    "I will punish the officials and the king's sons
    and all who array themselves in foreign attire.
9 On that day I will punish
    every one who leaps over the threshold,
    and those who fill their master's house
    with violence and fraud."

10 "On that day," says the LORD,
    "a cry will be heard from the Fish Gate,
    a wail from the Second Quarter,
    a loud crash from the hills.
11 Wail, O inhabitants of the Mortar!
    For all the traders are no more;
    all who weigh out silver are cut off.
12 At that time I will search Jerusalem with lamps,
    and I will punish the men
    who are thickening upon their lees,
    those who say in their hearts,
    'The LORD will not do good,
    nor will he do ill.'
13 Their goods shall be plundered,
    and their houses laid waste.
Though they build houses,
    they shall not inhabit them;
though they plant vineyards,
    they shall not drink wine from them."

14 The great day of the LORD is near,
    near and hastening fast;
the sound of the day of the LORD is bitter,

[a] Cn: Heb *the stumbling blocks*   [b] Compare Gk: Heb *idolatrous priests with the priests*

the mighty man cries aloud there.
15 A day of wrath is that day,
a day of distress and anguish,
a day of ruin and devastation,
a day of darkness and gloom,
a day of clouds and thick darkness,
16   a day of trumpet blast and battle cry
against the fortified cities
and against the lofty battlements.

17 I will bring distress on men,
so that they shall walk like the blind,
because they have sinned against the LORD;
their blood shall be poured out like dust,
and their flesh like dung.
18 Neither their silver nor their gold
shall be able to deliver them
on the day of the wrath of the LORD.
In the fire of his jealous wrath,
all the earth shall be consumed;
for a full, yea, sudden end
he will make of all the inhabitants of the earth.

JUDGMENT ON THE NATIONS

2 Come together and hold assembly,
O shameless nation,
2 before you are driven away
like the drifting chaff,c
before there comes upon you
the fierce anger of the LORD,
before there comes upon you
the day of the wrath of the LORD.
3 Seek the LORD, all you humble of the land,
who do his commands;
seek righteousness, seek humility;
perhaps you may be hidden
on the day of the wrath of the LORD.
4 For Gaza shall be deserted,
and Ash'kelon shall become a desolation;
Ashdod's people shall be driven out at noon,
and Ekron shall be uprooted.

5 Woe to you inhabitants of the seacoast,
you nation of the Cher'ethites!
The word of the LORD is against you,
O Canaan, land of the Philistines;
and I will destroy you till no inhabitant is left.
6 And you, O seacoast, shall be pastures,
meadows for shepherds
and folds for flocks.
7 The seacoast shall become the possession
of the remnant of the house of Judah,
on which they shall pasture,
and in the houses of Ash'kelon

they shall lie down at evening.
For the LORD their God will be mindful of them
and restore their fortunes.

8 "I have heard the taunts of Moab
and the revilings of the Ammonites,
how they have taunted my people
and made boasts against their territory.
9 Therefore, as I live," says the LORD of hosts,
the God of Israel,
"Moab shall become like Sodom,
and the Ammonites like Gomor'rah,
a land possessed by nettles and salt pits,
and a waste for ever.
The remnant of my people shall plunder them,
and the survivors of my nation shall possess them."
10 This shall be their lot in return for their pride,
because they scoffed and boasted
against the people of the LORD of hosts.
11 The LORD will be terrible against them;
yea, he will famish all the gods of the earth,
and to him shall bow down,
each in its place,
all the lands of the nations.

12 You also, O Ethiopians,
shall be slain by my sword.

13 And he will stretch out his hand against the north,
and destroy Assyria;
and he will make Nin'eveh a desolation,
a dry waste like the desert.
14 Herds shall lie down in the midst of her,
all the beasts of the field; d
the vulture e and the hedgehog
shall lodge in her capitals;
the owl f shall hoot in the window,
the raven g croak on the threshold;
for her cedar work will be laid bare.
15 This is the exultant city
that dwelt secure,
that said to herself,
"I am and there is none else."
What a desolation she has become,
a lair for wild beasts!
Every one who passes by her
hisses and shakes his fist.

THREATS AND PROMISES

3 Woe to her that is rebellious and defiled,
the oppressing city!
2 She listens to no voice,
she accepts no correction.

c Cn Compare Gk Syr: Heb *before a decree is born; like chaff a day has passed away*   d Tg Compare Gk: Heb *nation*
e The meaning of the Hebrew word is uncertain   f Cn: Heb *a voice*   g Gk Vg: Heb *desolation*

She does not trust in the LORD,
  she does not draw near to her God.
³ Her officials within her
  are roaring lions;
her judges are evening wolves
  that leave nothing till the morning.
⁴ Her prophets are wanton,
  faithless men;
her priests profane what is sacred,
  they do violence to the law.
⁵ The LORD within her is righteous,
  he does no wrong;
every morning he shows forth his justice,
  each dawn he does not fail;
but the unjust knows no shame.

⁶ "I have cut off nations;
  their battlements are in ruins;
I have laid waste their streets
  so that none walks in them;
their cities have been made desolate,
  without a man, without an inhabitant.
⁷ I said, 'Surely she will fear me,
  she will accept correction;
she will not lose sight ʰ
  of all that I have enjoined upon her.'
But all the more they were eager
  to make all their deeds corrupt."

⁸ "Therefore wait for me," says the LORD,
  "for the day when I arise as a witness.
For my decision is to gather nations,
  to assemble kingdoms,
to pour out upon them my indignation,
  all the heat of my anger;
for in the fire of my jealous wrath
  all the earth shall be consumed.

⁹ "Yea, at that time I will change the speech of the peoples
  to a pure speech,
that all of them may call on the name of the LORD
  and serve him with one accord.
¹⁰ From beyond the rivers of Ethiopia
  my suppliants, the daughter of my dispersed ones,
  shall bring my offering.

¹¹ "On that day you shall not be put to shame
  because of the deeds by which you have rebelled against
    me;

for then I will remove from your midst
  your proudly exultant ones,
and you shall no longer be haughty
  in my holy mountain.
¹² For I will leave in the midst of you
  a people humble and lowly.
They shall seek refuge in the name of the LORD,
¹³   those who are left in Israel;
they shall do no wrong
  and utter no lies,
nor shall there be found in their mouth
  a deceitful tongue.
For they shall pasture and lie down,
  and none shall make them afraid."

¹⁴ Sing aloud, O daughter of Zion;
  shout, O Israel!
Rejoice and exult with all your heart,
  O daughter of Jerusalem!
¹⁵ The LORD has taken away the judgments against you,
  he has cast out your enemies.
The King of Israel, the LORD, is in your midst;
  you shall fear evil no more.
¹⁶ On that day it shall be said to Jerusalem:
  "Do not fear, O Zion;
  let not your hands grow weak.
¹⁷ The LORD, your God, is in your midst,
  a warrior who gives victory;
he will rejoice over you with gladness,
  he will renew you ⁱ in his love;
he will exult over you with loud singing
¹⁸   as on a day of festival.ʲ
"I will remove disaster ᵏ from you,
  so that you will not bear reproach for it.
¹⁹ Behold, at that time I will deal
  with all your oppressors.
And I will save the lame
  and gather the outcast,
and I will change their shame into praise
  and renown in all the earth.
²⁰ At that time I will bring you home,
  at the time when I gather you together;
yea, I will make you renowned and praised
  among all the peoples of the earth,
when I restore your fortunes
  before your eyes," says the LORD.

ʰ Gk Syr: Heb *and her dwelling will not be cut off*   ⁱ Gk Syr: Heb *he will be silent*   ʲ Gk Syr: Heb obscure
ᵏ Cn: Heb *they were*

INTRODUCTION TO

HAGGAI

The prophet Haggai and the prophet Zechariah, who lived about the same time, are both mentioned in the Book of Ezra (5.1) as being active during the early efforts to rebuild the Temple after the Babylonian exile. The four sermons that make up this book were written about 520 B.C., the period of history told about in the Book of Ezra.

In 538 B.C., Cyrus the Great, king of Persia, had conquered the city of Babylon and freed the Jews who had been prisoners there. Soon some of the Jews who were set free went back to their country, Judah, planning to rebuild Jerusalem and the Temple. The preacher Haggai was among them.

The Book of Haggai contains some sermons in which the prophet denounced the people for working so hard to build houses for themselves but neglecting to rebuild the Temple. He has been called "a practical idealist" who helped the people begin to restore the Temple.

THE BOOK OF

HAGGAI

AN APPEAL TO REBUILD THE TEMPLE

1 In the second year of Darius the king, in the sixth month, on the first day of the month, the word of the LORD came by Haggai the prophet to Zerub'babel the son of She-al'ti-el, governor of Judah, and to Joshua the son ² of Jehoz'adak, the high priest, "Thus says the LORD of

hosts: This people say the time has not yet come to re- ³ build the house of the LORD." Then the word of the LORD ⁴ came by Haggai the prophet, "Is it a time for you your- selves to dwell in your paneled houses, while this house ⁵ lies in ruins? Now therefore thus says the LORD of hosts: ⁶ Consider how you have fared. You have sown much, and harvested little; you eat, but you never have enough; you drink, but you never have your fill; you clothe your- selves, but no one is warm; and he who earns wages earns wages to put them into a bag with holes.

⁷ "Thus says the LORD of hosts: Consider how you have ⁸ fared. Go up to the hills and bring wood and build the house, that I may take pleasure in it and that I may ap- ⁹ pear in my glory, says the LORD. You have looked for much, and, lo, it came to little; and when you brought it home, I blew it away. Why? says the LORD of hosts. Because of my house that lies in ruins, while you busy ¹⁰ yourselves each with his own house. Therefore the heavens above you have withheld the dew, and the earth has with- ¹¹ held its produce. And I have called for a drought upon the land and the hills, upon the grain, the new wine, the oil, upon what the ground brings forth, upon men and cattle, and upon all their labors."

¹² Then Zerub'babel the son of She-al'ti-el, and Joshua the son of Jehoz'adak, the high priest, with all the remnant of the people, obeyed the voice of the LORD their God, and the words of Haggai the prophet, as the LORD their God had sent him; and the people feared before the LORD. ¹³ Then Haggai, the messenger of the LORD, spoke to the people with the LORD's message, "I am with you, says ¹⁴ the LORD." And the LORD stirred up the spirit of Zerub'- babel the son of She-al'ti-el, governor of Judah, and the spirit of Joshua the son of Jehoz'adak, the high priest, and the spirit of all the remnant of the people; and they came and worked on the house of the LORD of hosts, ¹⁵ their God, on the twenty-fourth day of the month, in the sixth month.

1 **2** In the second year of Darius the king, in the seventh month, on the twenty-first day of the month, the word 2 of the LORD came by Haggai the prophet, "Speak now to Zerub'babel the son of She-al'ti-el, governor of Judah, and to Joshua the son of Jehoz'adak, the high priest, and 3 to all the remnant of the people, and say, 'Who is left among you that saw this house in its former glory? How do you see it now? Is it not in your sight as nothing? 4 Yet now take courage, O Zerub'babel, says the LORD; take courage, O Joshua, son of Jehoz'adak, the high priest; take courage, all you people of the land, says the LORD; work, for I am with you, says the LORD of hosts, 5 according to the promise that I made you when you came out of Egypt. My Spirit abides among you; fear not. 6 For thus says the LORD of hosts: Once again, in a little while, I will shake the heavens and the earth and the sea 7 and the dry land; and I will shake all nations, so that the treasures of all nations shall come in, and I will fill 8 this house with splendor, says the LORD of hosts. The silver is mine, and the gold is mine, says the LORD of 9 hosts. The latter splendor of this house shall be greater than the former, says the LORD of hosts; and in this place I will give prosperity, says the LORD of hosts.' "

HOLINESS AND UNCLEANNESS

10 On the twenty-fourth day of the ninth month, in the second year of Darius, the word of the LORD came by 11 Haggai the prophet, "Thus says the LORD of hosts: Ask 12 the priests to decide this question, 'If one carries holy flesh in the skirt of his garment, and touches with his skirt bread, or pottage, or wine, or oil, or any kind of food, does it become holy?' " The priests answered, "No."

a Gk: Heb *since they were*

13 Then said Haggai, "If one who is unclean by contact with a dead body touches any of these, does it become unclean?" The priests answered, "It does become un- 14 clean." Then Haggai said, "So is it with this people, and with this nation before me, says the LORD; and so with every work of their hands; and what they offer there is 15 unclean. Pray now, consider what will come to pass from this day onward. Before a stone was placed upon a stone 16 in the temple of the LORD, how did you fare? a When one came to a heap of twenty measures, there were but ten; when one came to the winevat to draw fifty measures, 17 there were but twenty. I smote you and all the products of your toil with blight and mildew and hail; yet you 18 did not return to me, says the LORD. Consider from this day onward, from the twenty-fourth day of the ninth month. Since the day that the foundation of the LORD's 19 temple was laid, consider: Is the seed yet in the barn? Do the vine, the fig tree, the pomegranate, and the olive tree still yield nothing? From this day on I will bless you."

20 The word of the LORD came a second time to Haggai 21 on the twenty-fourth day of the month, "Speak to Zerub'- babel, governor of Judah, saying, I am about to shake 22 the heavens and the earth, and to overthrow the throne of kingdoms; I am about to destroy the strength of the kingdoms of the nations, and overthrow the chariots and their riders; and the horses and their riders shall 23 go down, every one by the sword of his fellow. On that day, says the LORD of hosts, I will take you, O Zerub'babel my servant, the son of She-al'ti-el, says the LORD, and make you like a signet ring; for I have chosen you, says the LORD of hosts."

ZECHARIAH

Zechariah was a prophet who preached about 520 B.C., when Jews who had been permitted to return home from their Babylonian captivity were trying to rebuild Jerusalem.

Haggai's sermons during this period denounced the people for their neglect of the Temple. He and Zechariah finally persuaded them to work at rebuilding the Temple. The sermons in this book are in the form of visions that had come to Zechariah. The visions told of a time when the people would repent and, under the leadership of Joshua and Zerubbabel, would rebuild Jerusalem and the Temple.

Beginning with chapter 9, the prophecies seem to have been written by someone living at a much later time. Perhaps the most famous passage is Zechariah 9.9-10. When Jesus made his Triumphal Entry into Jerusalem, not as a warrior on a big war horse but as a prince of peace on a lowly donkey, many remembered these words of Zechariah:

> "Lo, your king comes to you;
>
> triumphant and victorious is he,
>
> humble and riding on an ass,
>
> on a colt the foal of an ass."
>
> (Zechariah 9.9, referred to
>
> in Matthew 21.4-5)

THE BOOK OF

ZECHARIAH

THE VISIONS OF ZECHARIAH

1 In the eighth month, in the second year of Darius, the word of the LORD came to Zechari'ah the son of ² Berechi'ah, son of Iddo, the prophet, saying, "The LORD ³ was very angry with your fathers. Therefore say to them, Thus says the LORD of hosts: Return to me, says the LORD

of hosts, and I will return to you, says the LORD of hosts. ⁴ Be not like your fathers, to whom the former prophets cried out, 'Thus says the LORD of hosts, Return from your evil ways and from your evil deeds.' But they did ⁵ not hear or heed me, says the LORD. Your fathers, where ⁶ are they? And the prophets, do they live for ever? But my words and my statutes, which I commanded my servants the prophets, did they not overtake your fathers? So they repented and said, As the LORD of hosts purposed to deal with us for our ways and deeds, so has he dealt with us."

⁷ On the twenty-fourth day of the eleventh month which is the month of Shebat, in the second year of Darius, the word of the LORD came to Zechari'ah the son of Berechi'ah, son of Iddo, the prophet; and Zechari'ah ⁸ said, "I saw in the night, and behold, a man riding upon a red horse! He was standing among the myrtle trees in the glen; and behind him were red, sorrel, and white ⁹ horses. Then I said, 'What are these, my lord?' The angel who talked with me said to me 'I will show you ¹⁰ what they are.' So the man who was standing among the myrtle trees answered, 'These are they whom the LORD ¹¹ has sent to patrol the earth.' And they answered the angel of the LORD who was standing among the myrtle trees, 'We have patrolled the earth, and behold, all the earth ¹² remains at rest.' Then the angel of the LORD said, 'O LORD of hosts, how long wilt thou have no mercy on Jerusalem and the cities of Judah, against which thou ¹³ hast had indignation these seventy years?' And the LORD answered gracious and comforting words to the angel ¹⁴ who talked with me. So the angel who talked with me

said to me, 'Cry out, Thus says the LORD of hosts: I am
15 exceedingly jealous for Jerusalem and for Zion. And I am very angry with the nations that are at ease; for while I was angry but a little they furthered the disaster.
16 Therefore, thus says the LORD, I have returned to Jerusalem with compassion; my house shall be built in it, says the LORD of hosts, and the measuring line shall be
17 stretched out over Jerusalem. Cry again, Thus says the LORD of hosts: My cities shall again overflow with prosperity, and the LORD will again comfort Zion and again choose Jerusalem.' "
18 a   And I lifted my eyes and saw, and behold, four
19 horns! And I said to the angel who talked with me, "What are these?" And he answered me, "These are the horns which have scattered Judah, Israel, and Jerusalem."
20, 21 Then the LORD showed me four smiths. And I said, "What are these coming to do?" He answered, "These are the horns which scattered Judah, so that no man raised his head; and these have come to terrify them, to cast down the horns of the nations who lifted up their horns against the land of Judah to scatter it."

2 b   And I lifted my eyes and saw, and behold, a man
2 with a measuring line in his hand! Then I said, "Where

are you going?" And he said to me, "To measure Jerusalem, to see what is its breadth and what is its length."
3 And behold, the angel who talked with me came forward,
4 and another angel came forward to meet him, and said to him, "Run, say to that young man, 'Jerusalem shall be inhabited as villages without walls, because of the
5 multitude of men and cattle in it. For I will be to her a wall of fire round about, says the LORD, and I will be the glory within her.' "
6   Ho! ho! Flee from the land of the north, says the LORD; for I have spread you abroad as the four winds
7 of the heavens, says the LORD. Ho! Escape to Zion, you
8 who dwell with the daughter of Babylon. For thus said the LORD of hosts, after his glory sent me to the nations who plundered you, for he who touches you touches the apple
9 of his eye: "Behold, I will shake my hand over them, and they shall become plunder for those who served them. Then you will know that the LORD of hosts has
10 sent me. Sing and rejoice, O daughter of Zion; for lo, I come and I will dwell in the midst of you, says the LORD.
11 And many nations shall join themselves to the LORD in that day, and shall be my people; and I will dwell in the midst of you, and you shall know that the LORD of hosts
12 has sent me to you. And the LORD will inherit Judah as

a Ch 2.1 in Heb   b Ch 2.5 in Heb

his portion in the holy land, and will again choose Jerusalem."
13   Be silent, all flesh, before the LORD; for he has roused himself from his holy dwelling.

3   Then he showed me Joshua the high priest standing before the angel of the LORD, and Satan standing
2 at his right hand to accuse him. And the LORD said to Satan, "The LORD rebuke you, O Satan! The LORD who has chosen Jerusalem rebuke you! Is not this a brand
3 plucked from the fire?" Now Joshua was standing before
4 the angel, clothed with filthy garments. And the angel said to those who were standing before him, "Remove the filthy garments from him." And to him he said, "Behold, I have taken your iniquity away from you, and I will
5 clothe you with rich apparel." And I said, "Let them put a clean turban on his head." So they put a clean turban on his head and clothed him with garments; and the angel of the LORD was standing by.
6, 7   And the angel of the LORD enjoined Joshua, "Thus says the LORD of hosts: If you will walk in my ways and keep my charge, then you shall rule my house and have charge of my courts, and I will give you the right of access
8 among those who are standing here. Hear now, O Joshua the high priest, you and your friends who sit before you, for they are men of good omen: behold, I will bring my
9 servant the Branch. For behold, upon the stone which I have set before Joshua, upon a single stone with seven facets, I will engrave its inscription, says the LORD of hosts, and I will remove the guilt of this land in a single
10 day. In that day, says the LORD of hosts, every one of you will invite his neighbor under his vine and under his fig tree."

4   And the angel who talked with me came again, and waked me, like a man that is wakened out of his sleep.
2 And he said to me, "What do you see?" I said, "I see, and behold, a lampstand all of gold, with a bowl on the top of it, and seven lamps on it, with seven lips on each
3 of the lamps which are on the top of it. And there are two olive trees by it, one on the right of the bowl and the
4 other on its left." And I said to the angel who talked with
5 me, "What are these, my lord?" Then the angel who talked with me answered me, "Do you not know what
6 these are?" I said, "No, my lord." Then he said to me, "This is the word of the LORD to Zerub'babel: Not by might, nor by power, but by my Spirit, says the LORD of
7 hosts. What are you, O great mountain? Before Zerub'babel you shall become a plain; and he shall bring forward the top stone amid shouts of 'Grace, grace to it!' "
8 Moreover the word of the LORD came to me, saying,
9 "The hands of Zerub'babel have laid the foundation of this house; his hands shall also complete it. Then you will know that the LORD of hosts has sent me to you.
10 For whoever has despised the day of small things shall

rejoice, and shall see the plummet in the hand of Zerub'babel.

"These seven are the eyes of the LORD, which range [11] through the whole earth." Then I said to him, "What are these two olive trees on the right and the left of the [12] lampstand?" And a second time I said to him, "What are these two branches of the olive trees, which are beside the two golden pipes from which the oil [c] is poured out?" [13] He said to me, "Do you not know what these are?" I [14] said, "No, my lord." Then he said, "These are the two anointed who stand by the Lord of the whole earth."

5 Again I lifted my eyes and saw, and behold, a flying [2] scroll! And he said to me, "What do you see?" I answered, "I see a flying scroll; its length is twenty [3] cubits, and its breadth ten cubits." Then he said to me, "This is the curse that goes out over the face of the whole land; for every one who steals shall be cut off henceforth according to it, and every one who swears [4] falsely shall be cut off henceforth according to it. I will send it forth, says the LORD of hosts, and it shall enter the house of the thief, and the house of him who swears falsely by my name; and it shall abide in his house and consume it, both timber and stones."

[5] Then the angel who talked with me came forward and said to me, "Lift your eyes, and see what this is that goes [6] forth." And I said, "What is it?" He said, "This is the ephah that goes forth." And he said, "This is their [7] iniquity [d] in all the land." And behold, the leaden cover was lifted, and there was a woman sitting in the ephah! [8] And he said, "This is Wickedness." And he thrust her back into the ephah, and thrust down the leaden weight [9] upon its mouth. Then I lifted my eyes and saw, and behold, two women coming forward! The wind was in their wings; they had wings like the wings of a stork, and they lifted up the ephah between earth and heaven. [10] Then I said to the angel who talked with me, "Where are [11] they taking the ephah?" He said to me, "To the land of Shinar, to build a house for it; and when this is prepared, they will set the ephah down there on its base."

6 And again I lifted my eyes and saw, and behold, four chariots came out from between two mountains; [2] and the mountains were mountains of bronze. The first [3] chariot had red horses, the second black horses, the third white horses, and the fourth chariot dappled gray [e] horses. [4] Then I said to the angel who talked with me, "What are [5] these, my lord?" And the angel answered me, "These are going forth to the four winds of heaven, after presenting themselves before the LORD of all the earth. [6] The chariot with the black horses goes toward the north country, the white ones go toward the west country, [f] and the dappled ones go toward the south country." [7] When the steeds came out, they were impatient to get off and patrol the earth. And he said, "Go, patrol the

[8] earth." So they patrolled the earth. Then he cried to me, "Behold, those who go toward the north country have set my Spirit at rest in the north country."

[9, 10] And the word of the LORD came to me: "Take from the exiles Heldai, Tobi'jah, and Jedai'ah, who have arrived from Babylon; and go the same day to the house [11] of Josi'ah, the son of Zephani'ah. Take from them silver and gold, and make a crown, [g] and set it upon the head [12] of Joshua, the son of Jehoz'adak, the high priest; and say to him, 'Thus says the LORD of hosts, "Behold, the man whose name is the Branch: for he shall grow up in his [13] place, and he shall build the temple of the LORD. It is he who shall build the temple of the LORD, and shall bear royal honor, and shall sit and rule upon his throne. And there shall be a priest by his throne, and peaceful under- [14] standing shall be between them both."' And the crown [h] shall be in the temple of the LORD as a reminder to Heldai, [i] Tobi'jah, Jedai'ah, and Josi'ah, [j] the son of Zephani'ah.

[15] "And those who are far off shall come and help to build the temple of the LORD; and you shall know that the LORD of hosts has sent me to you. And this shall come to pass, if you will diligently obey the voice of the LORD your God."

A DEPUTATION FROM BETHEL

7 In the fourth year of King Darius, the word of the LORD came to Zechari'ah in the fourth day of the [2] nine month, which is Chislev. Now the people of Bethel had sent Share'zer and Reg'em-mel'ech and their men, to [3] entreat the favor of the LORD, and to ask the priests of the house of the LORD of hosts and the prophets, "Should I mourn and fast in the fifth month, as I have done for [4] so many years?" Then the word of the LORD of hosts [5] came to me; "Say to all the people of the land and the priests, when you fasted and mourned in the fifth month and in the seventh, for these seventy years, was it for me [6] that you fasted? And when you eat and when you drink, do you not eat for yourselves and drink for yourselves? [7] When Jerusalem was inhabited and in prosperity, with her cities round about her, and the South and the lowland were inhabited, were not these the words which the LORD proclaimed by the former prophets?"

[8] And the word of the LORD came to Zechari'ah, saying, [9] "Thus says the LORD of hosts, Render true judgments, [10] show kindness and mercy each to his brother, do not oppress the widow, the fatherless, the sojourner, or the poor; and let none of you devise evil against his brother [11] in your heart." But they refused to hearken, and turned a stubborn shoulder, and stopped their ears that they [12] might not hear. They made their hearts like adamant lest they should hear the law and the words which the LORD of hosts had sent by his Spirit through the former prophets.

---

[c] Cn: Heb gold   [d] Gk Compare Syr: Heb eye   [e] Compare Gk: The meaning of the Hebrew word is uncertain
[f] Cn: Heb after them   [g] Gk Mss: Heb crowns   [h] Gk: Heb crowns   [i] With verse 10: Heb Helem
[j] With verse 10: Heb Hen

Therefore great wrath came from the LORD of hosts. 13 "As I called, and they would not hear, so they called, and 14 I would not hear," says the LORD of hosts, "and I scattered them with a whirlwind among all the nations which they had not known. Thus the land they left was desolate, so that no one went to and fro, and the pleasant land was made desolate."

8 And the word of the LORD of hosts came to me, 2 saying, "Thus says the LORD of hosts: I am jealous for Zion with great jealousy, and I am jealous for her 3 with great wrath. Thus says the LORD: I will return to Zion, and will dwell in the midst of Jerusalem, and Jerusalem shall be called the faithful city, and the moun- 4 tain of the LORD of hosts, the holy mountain. Thus says the LORD of hosts: Old men and old women shall again sit in the streets of Jerusalem, each with staff in hand 5 for very age. And the streets of the city shall be full of 6 boys and girls playing in its streets. Thus says the LORD of hosts: If it is marvelous in the sight of the remnant of this people in these days, should it also be marvelous 7 in my sight, says the LORD of hosts? Thus says the LORD of hosts: Behold, I will save my people from the east 8 country and from the west country; and I will bring them to dwell in the midst of Jerusalem; and they shall be my people and I will be their God, in faithfulness and in righteousness."

9 Thus says the LORD of hosts: "Let your hands be strong, you who in these days have been hearing these words from the mouth of the prophets, since the day that the foundation of the house of the LORD of hosts was laid, 10 that the temple might be built. For before those days there was no wage for man or any wage for beast, neither was there any safety from the foe for him who went out or came in; for I set every man against his fellow. 11 But now I will not deal with the remnant of this people 12 as in the former days, says the LORD of hosts. For there shall be a sowing of peace; the vine shall yield its fruit, and the ground shall give its increase, and the heavens shall give their dew; and I will cause the remnant of this 13 people to possess all these things. And as you have been a byword of cursing among the nations, O house of Judah and house of Israel, so will I save you and you shall be a blessing. Fear not, but let your hands be strong." 14 For thus says the LORD of hosts: "As I purposed to do evil to you, when your fathers provoked me to wrath, and 15 I did not relent, says the LORD of hosts, so again have I purposed in these days to do good to Jerusalem and

16 to the house of Judah; fear not. These are the things that you shall do: Speak the truth to one another, render in your gates judgments that are true and make for peace, 17 do not devise evil in your hearts against one another, and love no false oath, for all these things I hate, says the LORD."

18 And the word of the LORD of hosts came to me, saying, 19 "Thus says the LORD of hosts: The fast of the fourth month, and the fast of the fifth, and the fast of the seventh, and the fast of the tenth, shall be to the house of Judah seasons of joy and gladness, and cheerful feasts; therefore love truth and peace.

20 "Thus says the LORD of hosts: Peoples shall yet come, 21 even the inhabitants of many cities; the inhabitants of one city shall go to another, saying, 'Let us go at once to entreat the favor of the LORD, and to seek the LORD of 22 hosts; I am going.' Many peoples and strong nations shall come to seek the LORD of hosts in Jerusalem, and to 23 entreat the favor of the LORD. Thus says the LORD of hosts: In those days ten men from the nations of every tongue shall take hold of the robe of a Jew, saying, 'Let us go with you, for we have heard that God is with you.' "

9   An Oracle

The word of the LORD is against the land of Hadrach
    and will rest upon Damascus.
For to the LORD belong the cities of Aram,[k]
    even as all the tribes of Israel;
2 Hamath also, which borders thereon,
    Tyre and Sidon, though they are very wise.
3 Tyre has built herself a rampart,
    and heaped up silver like dust,
    and gold like the dirt of the streets.
4 But lo, the Lord will strip her of her possessions
    and hurl her wealth into the sea,
    and she shall be devoured by fire.

5 Ash'kelon shall see it, and be afraid;
    Gaza too, and shall writhe in anguish;
    Ekron also, because its hopes are confounded.
The king shall perish from Gaza;
    Ash'kelon shall be uninhabited;
6 a mongrel people shall dwell in Ashdod;
    and I will make an end of the pride of Philistia.
7 I will take away its blood from its mouth,
    and its abominations from between its teeth;
it too shall be a remnant for our God;
    it shall be like a clan in Judah,
    and Ekron shall be like the Jeb'usites.
8 Then I will encamp at my house as a guard,
    so that none shall march to and fro;
no oppressor shall again overrun them,
    for now I see with my own eyes.

k Cn: Heb *the eye of Adam* (or *man*)

9 Rejoice greatly, O daughter of Zion!
　　Shout aloud, O daughter of Jerusalem!
　Lo, your king comes to you;
　　triumphant and victorious is he,
　humble and riding on an ass,
　　on a colt the foal of an ass.
10 I will cut off the chariot from E′phraim
　　and the war horse from Jerusalem;
　and the battle bow shall be cut off,
　　and he shall command peace to the nations;
　his dominion shall be from sea to sea,
　　and from the River to the ends of the earth.

11 As for you also, because of the blood of my covenant
　　　with you,
　I will set your captives free from the waterless pit.
12 Return to your stronghold, O prisoners of hope;
　　today I declare that I will restore to you double.
13 For I have bent Judah as my bow;
　　I have made E′phraim its arrow.
　I will brandish your sons, O Zion,
　　over your sons, O Greece,
　　and wield you like a warrior's sword.

14 Then the LORD will appear over them,
　　and his arrow go forth like lightning;
　the Lord GOD will sound the trumpet,
　　and march forth in the whirlwinds of the south.
15 The LORD of hosts will protect them,
　　and they shall devour and tread down the slingers; [1]
　and they shall drink their blood [m] like wine,
　　and be full like a bowl,
　　drenched like the corners of the altar.

16 On that day the LORD their God will save them
　　for they are the flock of his people;
　for like the jewels of a crown
　　they shall shine on his land.
17 Yea, how good and how fair it shall be!
　　Grain shall make the young men flourish,
　　and new wine the maidens.

10 Ask rain from the LORD
　　　in the season of the spring rain,
　from the LORD who makes the storm clouds,
　　who gives men showers of rain,
　　to every one the vegetation in the field.
2 For the teraphim utter nonsense,
　　and the diviners see lies;
　the dreamers tell false dreams,
　　and give empty consolation.
　Therefore the people wander like sheep;
　　they are afflicted for want of a shepherd.

3 "My anger is hot against the shepherds,
　　and I will punish the leaders; [n]
　for the LORD of hosts cares for his flock, the house of
　　　Judah,
　　and will make them like his proud steed in battle.
4 Out of them shall come the cornerstone,
　　out of them the tent peg,
　out of them the battle bow,
　　out of them every ruler.
5 Together they shall be like mighty men in battle,
　　trampling the foe in the mud of the streets;
　they shall fight because the LORD is with them,
　　and they shall confound the riders on horses.

6 "I will strengthen the house of Judah,
　　and I will save the house of Joseph.
　I will bring them back because I have compassion on
　　　them,
　　and they shall be as though I had not rejected them;
　for I am the LORD their God and I will answer them.
7 Then E′phraim shall become like a mighty warrior,
　　and their hearts shall be glad as with wine.
　Their children shall see it and rejoice,
　　their hearts shall exult in the LORD.

8 "I will signal for them and gather them in,
　　for I have redeemed them,
　　and they shall be as many as of old.
9 Though I scattered them among the nations,
　　yet in far countries they shall remember me,
　　and with their children they shall live and return.
10 I will bring them home from the land of Egypt,
　　and gather them from Assyria;
　and I will bring them to the land of Gilead and to
　　　Lebanon,
　　till there is no room for them.
11 They shall pass through the sea of Egypt, [o]
　　and the waves of the sea shall be smitten,
　　and all the depths of the Nile dried up.
　The pride of Assyria shall be laid low,
　　and the scepter of Egypt shall depart.
12 I will make them strong in the LORD
　　and they shall glory [p] in his name," says the LORD.

11 Open your doors, O Lebanon,
　　　that the fire may devour your cedars!
2 Wail, O cypress, for the cedar has fallen,
　　for the glorious trees are ruined!
　Wail, oaks of Bashan,
　　for the thick forest has been felled!
3 Hark, the wail of the shepherds,
　　for their glory is despoiled!
　Hark, the roar of the lions,
　　for the jungle of the Jordan is laid waste!

---

[1] Cn: Heb *the slingstones*　　[m] Gk: Heb *be turbulent*　　[n] Or *he-goats*　　[o] Cn: Heb *distress*　　[p] Gk: Heb *walk*

4 Thus said the LORD my God: "Become shepherd of the
5 flock doomed to slaughter. Those who buy them slay
them and go unpunished; and those who sell them say,
'Blessed be the LORD, I have become rich'; and their own
6 shepherds have no pity on them. For I will no longer
have pity on the inhabitants of this land, says the LORD.
Lo, I will cause men to fall each into the hand of his
shepherd, and each into the hand of his king; and they
shall crush the earth, and I will deliver none from their
hand."

7 So I became the shepherd of the flock doomed to be
slain for those who trafficked in the sheep. And I took
two staffs; one I named Grace, the other I named Union.
8 And I tended the sheep. In one month I destroyed the
three shepherds. But I became impatient with them, and
9 they also detested me. So I said, "I will not be your
shepherd. What is to die, let it die; what is to be
destroyed, let it be destroyed; and let those that are left
10 devour the flesh of one another." And I took my staff
Grace, and I broke it, annulling the covenant which I
11 had made with all the peoples. So it was annulled on that
day, and the traffickers in the sheep, who were watching
12 me, knew that it was the word of the LORD. Then I said
to them, "If it seems right to you, give me my wages; but
if not, keep them." And they weighed out as my wages
13 thirty shekels of silver. Then the LORD said to me, "Cast
it into the treasury"q—the lordly price at which I was
paid off by them. So I took the thirty shekels of silver
and cast them into the treasuryq in the house of the LORD.
14 Then I broke my second staff Union, annulling the
brotherhood between Judah and Israel.
15 Then the LORD said to me, "Take once more the
16 implements of a worthless shepherd. For lo, I am raising
up in the land a shepherd who does not care for the
perishing, or seek the wandering,r or heal the maimed,
or nourish the sound, but devours the flesh of the fat
ones, tearing off even their hoofs.
17 Woe to my worthless shepherd,
  who deserts the flock!
May the sword smite his arm
  and his right eye!
Let his arm be wholly withered,
  his right eye utterly blinded!"

q Syr: Heb *to the potter*   r Syr Compare Gk Vg: Heb *the youth*

12   An Oracle

The word of the LORD concerning Israel: Thus says
the LORD, who stretched out the heavens and founded the
2 earth and formed the spirit of man within him: "Lo, I
am about to make Jerusalem a cup of reeling to all the
peoples round about; it will be against Judah also in the
3 siege against Jerusalem. On that day I will make Jerusalem a heavy stone for all the peoples; all who lift it shall
grievously hurt themselves. And all the nations of the
4 earth will come together against it. On that day, says the
LORD, I will strike every horse with panic, and its rider
with madness. But upon the house of Judah I will open
my eyes, when I strike every horse of the peoples with
5 blindness. Then the clans of Judah shall say to themselves,
'The inhabitants of Jerusalem have strength through the
LORD of hosts, their God.'
6 "On that day I will make the clans of Judah like a
blazing pot in the midst of wood, like a flaming torch
among sheaves; and they shall devour to the right and
to the left all the peoples round about, while Jerusalem
shall still be inhabited in its place, in Jerusalem.
7 "And the LORD will give victory to the tents of Judah
first, that the glory of the house of David and the glory
of the inhabitants of Jerusalem may not be exalted over
8 that of Judah. On that day the LORD will put a shield
about the inhabitants of Jerusalem so that the feeblest
among them on that day shall be like David, and the house
of David shall be like God, like the angel of the LORD, at
9 their head. And on that day I will seek to destroy all the
nations that come against Jerusalem.
10 "And I will pour out on the house of David and the
inhabitants of Jerusalem a spirit of compassion and
supplication, so that, when they look on him whom they
have pierced, they shall mourn for him, as one mourns
for an only child, and weep bitterly over him, as one
11 weeps over a first-born. On that day the mourning in
Jerusalem will be as great as the mourning for Hadad-
12 rim'mon in the plain of Megid'do. The land shall mourn,
each family by itself; the family of the house of David
by itself, and their wives by themselves; the family of the
house of Nathan by itself, and their wives by themselves;
13 the family of the house of Levi by itself, and their wives
by themselves; the family of the Shim'e-ites by itself, and
14 their wives by themselves; and all the families that are
left, each by itself, and their wives by themselves.
13 "On that day there shall be a fountain opened for
    the house of David and the inhabitants of Jerusalem
to cleanse them from sin and uncleanness.
2 "And on that day, says the LORD of hosts, I will cut
off the names of the idols from the land, so that they shall
be remembered no more; and also I will remove from
3 the land the prophets and the unclean spirit. And if any

one again appears as a prophet, his father and mother who bore him will say to him, 'You shall not live, for you speak lies in the name of the Lord'; and his father and mother who bore him shall pierce him through when 4 he prophesies. On that day every prophet will be ashamed of his vision when he prophesies; he will not put on a 5 hairy mantle in order to deceive, but he will say, 'I am no prophet, I am a tiller of the soil; for the land has 6 been my possession^t since my youth.' And if one asks him, 'What are these wounds on your back?' he will say, 'The wounds I received in the house of my friends.' "

7 "Awake, O sword, against my shepherd,
   against the man who stands next to me,"
                says the Lord of hosts.
"Strike the shepherd, that the sheep may be scattered;
   I will turn my hand against the little ones.
8 In the whole land, says the Lord,
   two thirds shall be cut off and perish,
   and one third shall be left alive.
9 And I will put this third into the fire,
   and refine them as one refines silver,
   and test them as gold is tested.
They will call on my name,
   and I will answer them.
I will say, 'They are my people';
   and they will say, 'The Lord is my God.' "

14 Behold, a day of the Lord is coming, when the spoil taken from you will be divided in the midst of 2 you. For I will gather all the nations against Jerusalem to battle, and the city shall be taken and the houses plundered and the women ravished; half of the city shall go into exile, but the rest of the people shall not be cut 3 off from the city. Then the Lord will go forth and fight against those nations as when he fights on a day of battle. 4 On that day his feet shall stand on the Mount of Olives which lies before Jerusalem on the east; and the Mount of Olives shall be split in two from east to west by a very wide valley; so that one half of the Mount shall withdraw 5 northward, and the other half southward. And the valley of my mountains shall be stopped up, for the valley of the mountains shall touch the side of it; and you shall flee as you fled from the earthquake in the days of Uzzi'ah king of Judah. Then the Lord your^u God will come, and all the holy ones with him.^v

6, 7 On that day there shall be neither cold nor frost.^w And there shall be continuous day (it is known to the Lord), not day and not night, for at evening time there shall be light.

8 On that day living waters shall flow out from Jerusalem, half of them to the eastern sea and half of them to the western sea; it shall continue in summer as in winter.

9 And the Lord will become king over all the earth; on that day the Lord will be one and his name one.

10 The whole land shall be turned into a plain from Geba to Rimmon south of Jerusalem. But Jerusalem shall remain aloft upon its site from the Gate of Benjamin to the place of the former gate, to the Corner Gate, and from 11 the Tower of Han'anel to the king's wine presses. And it shall be inhabited, for there shall be no more curse; ^x Jerusalem shall dwell in security.

12 And this shall be the plague with which the Lord will smite all the peoples that wage war against Jerusalem: their flesh shall rot while they are still on their feet, their eyes shall rot in their sockets, and their tongues shall 13 rot in their mouths. And on that day a great panic from the Lord shall fall on them, so that each will lay hold on the hand of his fellow, and the hand of the one will be 14 raised against the hand of the other; even Judah will fight against Jerusalem. And the wealth of all the nations round about shall be collected, gold, silver, and garments 15 in great abundance. And a plague like this plague shall fall on the horses, the mules, the camels, the asses, and whatever beasts may be in those camps.

16 Then every one that survives of all the nations that have come against Jerusalem shall go up year after year to worship the King, the Lord of hosts, and to keep the 17 feast of booths. And if any of the families of the earth do not go up to Jerusalem to worship the King, the Lord 18 of hosts, there will be no rain upon them. And if the family of Egypt do not go up and present themselves, then upon them shall^y come the plague with which the

Lord afflicts the nations that do not go up to keep the 19 feast of booths. This shall be the punishment to Egypt and the punishment to all the nations that do not go up to keep the feast of booths.

20 And on that day there shall be inscribed on the bells of the horses, "Holy to the Lord." And the pots in the house of the Lord shall be as the bowls before the altar; 21 and every pot in Jerusalem and Judah shall be sacred to the Lord of hosts, so that all who sacrifice may come and take of them and boil the flesh of the sacrifice in them. And there shall no longer be a trader in the house of the Lord of hosts on that day.

---

^t Cn: Heb *for man has caused me to possess*
^w Compare Gk Syr Vg Tg: Heb uncertain
^u Heb *my*
^x Or *ban of utter destruction*
^v Gk Syr Vg Tg: Heb *you*
^y Gk Syr: Heb *shall not*

INTRODUCTION TO

MALACHI

After the prophets Haggai and Zechariah succeeded in getting the returned exiles to rebuild the Temple, from 520 B.C. to 516 B.C., there was renewed interest in worship. After about sixty years the prophet Malachi was active in Jerusalem. The Book of Malachi was written about 460 B.C.

Malachi lived in Jerusalem shortly before Ezra and Nehemiah came back from Babylon to direct the restoration of the city walls. His book protested the low moral living of the people and the careless, corrupt worship at the Temple. In spite of the many evils Malachi described, the closing passages of the book show that the prophet believed the people would repent and God would save them.

THE BOOK OF

MALACHI

WHERE IS THE GOD OF JUSTICE?

1 The oracle of the word of the LORD to Israel by Mal'achi.[a]

2 "I have loved you," says the LORD. But you say, "How hast thou loved us?" "Is not Esau Jacob's brother?" says 3 the LORD. "Yet I have loved Jacob but I have hated Esau; I have laid waste his hill country and left his heritage to 4 jackals of the desert." If Edom says, "We are shattered but we will rebuild the ruins," the LORD of hosts says, "They may build, but I will tear down, till they are called the wicked country, the people with whom the LORD 5 is angry for ever." Your own eyes shall see this, and you shall say, "Great is the LORD, beyond the border of Israel!"

6 "A son honors his father, and a servant his master. If then I am a father, where is my honor? And if I am a master, where is my fear? says the LORD of hosts to you, O priests, who despise my name. You say, 'How 7 have we despised thy name?' By offering polluted food upon my altar. And you say, 'How have we polluted it?'[b]

By thinking that the LORD's table may be despised. 8 When you offer blind animals in sacrifice, is that no evil? And when you offer those that are lame or sick, is that no evil? Present that to your governor; will he be pleased with you or show you favor? says the LORD of 9 hosts. And now entreat the favor of God, that he may be gracious to us. With such a gift from your hand, will 10 he show favor to any of you? says the LORD of hosts. Oh, that there were one among you who would shut the doors, that you might not kindle fire upon my altar in vain! I have no pleasure in you, says the LORD of hosts, 11 and I will not accept an offering from your hand. For from the rising of the sun to its setting my name is great among the nations, and in every place incense is offered to my name, and a pure offering; for my name is great 12 among the nations, says the LORD of hosts. But you profane it when you say that the LORD's table is polluted, and 13 the food for it[c] may be despised. 'What a weariness this is,' you say, and you sniff at me,[d] says the LORD of hosts. You bring what has been taken by violence or is lame or sick, and this you bring as your offering! Shall I ac-14 cept that from your hand? says the LORD. Cursed be the cheat who has a male in his flock, and vows it, and yet sacrifices to the Lord what is blemished; for I am a great King, says the LORD of hosts, and my name is feared among the nations.

2 "And now, O priests, this command is for you. 2 If you will not listen, if you will not lay it to heart to give glory to my name, says the LORD of hosts, then I will send the curse upon you and I will curse your blessings; indeed I have already cursed them, because you do

---

[a] Or *my messenger*   [b] Gk: Heb *thee*   [c] Heb *its fruit, its food*   [d] Another reading is *it*

3 not lay it to heart. Behold, I will rebuke your offspring,
and spread dung upon your faces, the dung of your offer-
4 ings, and I will put you out of my presence.[e] So shall you
know that I have sent this command to you, that my
5 covenant with Levi may hold, says the LORD of hosts. My
covenant with him was a covenant of life and peace, and I
gave them to him, that he might fear; and he feared me,
6 he stood in awe of my name. True instruction[f] was in his
mouth, and no wrong was found on his lips. He walked
with me in peace and uprightness, and he turned many
7 from iniquity. For the lips of a priest should guard
knowledge, and men should seek instruction[f] from his
mouth, for he is the messenger of the LORD of hosts.
8 But you have turned aside from the way; you have
caused many to stumble by your instruction;[f] you have
corrupted the covenant of Levi, says the LORD of hosts,
9 and so I make you despised and abased before all the
people, inasmuch as you have not kept my ways but have
shown partiality in your instruction."[f]

10 Have we not all one father? Has not one God created
us? Why then are we faithless to one another, profaning
11 the covenant of our fathers? Judah has been faithless, and
abomination has been committed in Israel and in Jerusalem; for Judah has profaned the sanctuary of the LORD,
which he loves, and has married the daughter of a foreign
12 god. May the LORD cut off from the tents of Jacob, for
the man who does this, any to witness[g] or answer, or to
bring an offering to the LORD of hosts!

13 And this again you do. You cover the LORD's altar with
tears, with weeping and groaning because he no longer
regards the offering or accepts it with favor at your
14 hand. You ask, "Why does he not?" Because the
LORD was witness to the covenant between you and
the wife of your youth, to whom you have been faithless, though she is your companion and your wife
15 by covenant. Has not the one God made[h] and sustained
for us the spirit of life?[i] And what does he desire?
Godly offspring. So take heed to yourselves, and let none
16 be faithless to the wife of his youth. "For I hate[j] divorce,
says the LORD the God of Israel, and covering one's
garment with violence, says the LORD of hosts. So take
heed to yourselves and do not be faithless."

17 You have wearied the LORD with your words. Yet you
say, "How have we wearied him?" By saying, "Every
one who does evil is good in the sight of the LORD, and
he delights in them." Or by asking, "Where is the God of
justice?"

THE LORD'S MESSENGER

3 "Behold, I send my messenger to prepare the way
before me, and the Lord whom you seek will suddenly
come to his temple; the messenger of the covenant in
whom you delight, behold, he is coming, says the LORD of

2 hosts. But who can endure the day of his coming, and
who can stand when he appears?

"For he is like a refiner's fire and like fullers' soap;
3 he will sit as a refiner and purifier of silver, and he will
purify the sons of Levi and refine them like gold and
silver, till they present right offerings to the LORD.
4 Then the offering of Judah and Jerusalem will be pleasing
to the LORD as in the days of old and as in former years.
5 "Then I will draw near to you for judgment; I will be
a swift witness against the sorcerers, against the adulterers,
against those who swear falsely, against those who oppress
the hireling in his wages, the widow and the orphan,
against those who thrust aside the sojourner, and do not
fear me, says the LORD of hosts.
6 "For I the LORD do not change; therefore you, O sons
7 of Jacob, are not consumed. From the days of your fathers
you have turned aside from my statutes and have not
kept them. Return to me, and I will return to you, says
the LORD of hosts. But you say, 'How shall we return?'
8 Will man rob God? Yet you are robbing me. But you
say, 'How are we robbing thee?' In your tithes and
9 offerings. You are cursed with a curse, for you are
10 robbing me; the whole nation of you. Bring the full
tithes into the storehouse, that there may be food in my
house; and thereby put me to the test, says the LORD of
hosts, if I will not open the windows of heaven for you
11 and pour down for you an overflowing blessing. I will
rebuke the devourer[k] for you, so that it will not destroy

the fruits of your soil; and your vine in the field shall not
12 fail to bear, says the LORD of hosts. Then all nations will
call you blessed, for you will be a land of delight, says
the LORD of hosts.
13 "Your words have been stout against me, says the LORD.
14 Yet you say, 'How have we spoken against thee?' You
have said, 'It is vain to serve God. What is the good of
our keeping his charge or of walking as in mourning
15 before the LORD of hosts? Henceforth we deem the
arrogant blessed; evildoers not only prosper but when
they put God to the test they escape.'"
16 Then those who feared the LORD spoke with one another; the LORD heeded and heard them, and a book of
remembrance was written before him of those who feared
17 the LORD and thought on his name. "They shall be mine,
says the LORD of hosts, my special possession on the day
when I act, and I will spare them as a man spares his son

---

[e] Cn Compare Gk Syr: Heb *and he shall bear you to it*   [f] Or *law*
[h] Or *has he not made one?*   [i] Cn: Heb *and a remnant of spirit was his*
[f] Or *law*   [g] Cn Compare Gk: Heb *arouse*
[j] Cn: Heb *he hates*   [k] Or *devouring locust*

18 who serves him. Then once more you shall distinguish between the righteous and the wicked, between one who serves God and one who does not serve him.

4 ¹ "For behold, the day comes, burning like an oven, when all the arrogant and all evildoers will be stubble;

down the wicked, for they will be ashes under the soles of your feet, on the day when I act, says the LORD of hosts.

4 "Remember the law of my servant Moses, the statutes and ordinances that I commanded him at Horeb for all Israel.

the day that comes shall burn them up, says the LORD of hosts, so that it will leave them neither root nor branch. ² But for you who fear my name the sun of righteousness shall rise, with healing in its wings. You shall go forth ³ leaping like calves from the stall. And you shall tread

⁵ "Behold, I will send you Eli'jah the prophet before ⁶ the great and terrible day of the LORD comes. And he will turn the hearts of fathers to their children and the hearts of children to their fathers, lest I come and smite the land with a curse." ᵐ

¹ Ch 4.1-6 are Ch 3.19-24 in the Hebrew   ᵐ Or *ban of utter destruction*

NEW TESTAMENT

— INTRODUCTION TO —

MATTHEW

There are four Gospels or books of good news in the New Testament. The Gospel of Matthew was probably the third Gospel to be written. Each of the four books tells the "good news" about Jesus Christ for a different group of readers. Matthew was written especially for Jews, but it was written in the Greek language. Greek was a widely used language in all the lands where Christianity spread, so the New Testament was written in that language.

The earliest of the Gospels in the New Testament was Mark, which was written about A.D. 65-70. It contains a summary of the chief events of Jesus' life. Someone had also made a collection of Jesus' teachings. These teachings were combined with other information about Jesus to form the Gospel of Matthew about A.D. 85. It was named for Matthew because he had collected some of the information about Jesus that went into this Gospel.

When you compare Matthew with Mark, you can see that the writer of Matthew had a copy of Mark at hand and used its main outline of the events of Jesus' life. In fact, Matthew quoted much of Mark word for word.

The main purpose of the Gospel of Matthew was to persuade Jews to accept faith in Jesus as the Messiah, or the Christ, as the Greeks translated it. The Gospel of Matthew frequently pointed out that what Jesus did or said fitted teachings found in the Jewish Scriptures. Matthew often said that Jesus did certain things "in order to fulfill the scriptures."

This book contains the wonderful summary of Jesus' teachings that we call the Sermon on the Mount (Chapters 5 through 7).

THE GOSPEL ACCORDING TO

MATTHEW

GENEALOGY OF JESUS

1 The book of the genealogy of Jesus Christ, the son of David, the son of Abraham.

2 Abraham was the father of Isaac, and Isaac the father of Jacob, and Jacob the father of Judah and his brothers,
3 and Judah the father of Perez and Zerah by Tamar, and Perez the father of Hezron, and Hezron the father of
4 Ram,ᵃ and Ram ᵃ the father of Ammin'adab, and Ammin'-adab the father of Nahshon, and Nahshon the father of
5 Salmon, and Salmon the father of Bo'az by Rahab, and Bo'az the father of Obed by Ruth, and Obed the father of
6 Jesse, and Jesse the father of David the king.

And David was the father of Solomon by the wife of

7 Uri'ah, and Solomon the father of Rehobo'am, and Rehobo'am the father of Abi'jah, and Abi'jah the father
8 of Asa,ᵇ and Asa ᵇ the father of Jehosh'aphat, and Jehosh'-aphat the father of Joram, and Joram the father of
9 Uzzi'ah, and Uzzi'ah the father of Jotham, and Jotham the father of Ahaz, and Ahaz the father of Hezeki'ah,
10 and Hezeki'ah the father of Manas'seh, and Manas'seh the
11 father of Amos,ᶜ and Amos ᶜ the father of Josi'ah, and Josi'ah the father of Jechoni'ah and his brothers, at the time of the deportation to Babylon.
12 And after the deportation to Babylon: Jechoni'ah was the father of She-al'ti-el,ᵈ and She-al'ti-el ᵈ the father of
13 Zerub'babel, and Zerub'babel the father of Abi'ud, and

ᵃ Greek *Aram*   ᵇ Greek *Asaph*   ᶜ Other authorities read *Amon*   ᵈ Greek *Salathiel*

Abi'ud the father of Eli'akim, and Eli'akim the father
14 of Azor, and Azor the father of Zadok, and Zadok the
15 father of Achim, and Achim the father of Eli'ud, and
Eli'ud the father of Elea'zar, and Elea'zar the father of
16 Matthan, and Matthan the father of Jacob, and Jacob the
father of Joseph the husband of Mary, of whom Jesus
was born, who is called Christ.

17 So all the generations from Abraham to David were
fourteen generations, and from David to the deportation
to Babylon fourteen generations, and from the deportation to Babylon to the Christ fourteen generations.

JESUS' BIRTH AND CHILDHOOD

18 Now the birth of Jesus Christ *f* took place in this way.
When his mother Mary had been betrothed to Joseph,
before they came together she was found to be with child
19 of the Holy Spirit; and her husband Joseph, being a just
man and unwilling to put her to shame, resolved to
20 divorce her quietly. But as he considered this, behold, an
angel of the Lord appeared to him in a dream, saying,
"Joseph, son of David, do not fear to take Mary your wife,
for that which is conceived in her is of the Holy Spirit;
21 she will bear a son, and you shall call his name Jesus, for

22 he will save his people from their sins." All this took
place to fulfil what the Lord had spoken by the prophet:
23 "Behold, a virgin shall conceive and bear a son,
and his name shall be called Em-man'u-el"
24 (which means, God with us). When Joseph woke from
sleep, he did as the angel of the Lord commanded him;
25 he took his wife, but knew her not until she had borne a
son; and he called his name Jesus.

2 Now when Jesus was born in Bethlehem of Judea in
the days of Herod the king, behold, wise men from
2 the East came to Jerusalem, saying, "Where is he who
has been born king of the Jews? For we have seen his
3 star in the East, and have come to worship him." When
Herod the king heard this, he was troubled, and all
4 Jerusalem with him; and assembling all the chief priests
and scribes of the people, he inquired of them where the
5 Christ was to be born. They told him, "In Bethlehem of
Judea; for so it is written by the prophet:
6 'And you, O Bethlehem, in the land of Judah,
are by no means least among the rulers of Judah;
for from you shall come a ruler
who will govern my people Israel.' "

f Other ancient authorities read of the Christ

7 Then Herod summoned the wise men secretly and
ascertained from them what time the star appeared;
8 and he sent them to Bethlehem, saying, "Go and search
diligently for the child, and when you have found him
bring me word, that I too may come and worship him."
9 When they had heard the king they went their way; and
lo, the star which they had seen in the East went before

them, till it came to rest over the place where the child
10 was. When they saw the star, they rejoiced exceedingly
11 with great joy; and going into the house they saw the
child with Mary his mother, and they fell down and
worshiped him. Then, opening their treasures, they offered
12 him gifts, gold and frankincense and myrrh. And being
warned in a dream not to return to Herod, they departed
to their own country by another way.

13 Now when they had departed, behold, an angel of the
Lord appeared to Joseph in a dream and said, "Rise,
take the child and his mother, and flee to Egypt, and
remain there till I tell you; for Herod is about to search
14 for the child, to destroy him." And he rose and took the
child and his mother by night, and departed to Egypt,
15 and remained there until the death of Herod. This was
to fulfil what the Lord had spoken by the prophet, "Out
of Egypt have I called my son."

16 Then Herod, when he saw that he had been tricked by
the wise men, was in a furious rage, and he sent and killed
all the male children in Bethlehem and in all that region
who were two years old or under, according to the time
17 which he had ascertained from the wise men. Then was
fulfilled what was spoken by the prophet Jeremiah:
18 "A voice was heard in Ramah,
wailing and loud lamentation,
Rachel weeping for her children;
she refused to be consoled,
because they were no more."

19 But when Herod died, behold, an angel of the Lord
20 appeared in a dream to Joseph in Egypt, saying, "Rise,
take the child and his mother, and go to the land of
Israel, for those who sought the child's life are dead."
21 And he rose and took the child and his mother, and went
22 to the land of Israel. But when he heard that Archela'us
reigned over Judea in place of his father Herod, he was
afraid to go there, and being warned in a dream he

23 withdrew to the district of Galilee. And he went and dwelt in a city called Nazareth, that what was spoken by the prophets might be fulfilled, "He shall be called a Nazarene."

JOHN THE BAPTIST

3 In those days came John the Baptist, preaching in 2 the wilderness of Judea, "Repent, for the kingdom of 3 heaven is at hand." For this is he who was spoken of by the prophet Isaiah when he said,

"The voice of one crying in the wilderness:
Prepare the way of the Lord,
 make his paths straight."

4 Now John wore a garment of camel's hair, and a leather girdle around his waist; and his food was locusts and 5 wild honey. Then went out to him Jerusalem and all 6 Judea and all the region about the Jordan, and they were baptized by him in the river Jordan, confessing their sins.
7 But when he saw many of the Pharisees and Sad'ducees coming for baptism, he said to them, "You brood of vipers! Who warned you to flee from the wrath to come?
8, 9 Bear fruit that befits repentance, and do not presume to say to yourselves, 'We have Abraham as our father'; for I tell you, God is able from these stones to raise up chil-10 dren to Abraham. Even now the axe is laid to the root of the trees; every tree therefore that does not bear good fruit is cut down and thrown into the fire.
11 "I baptize you with water for repentance, but he who is coming after me is mightier than I, whose sandals I am not worthy to carry; he will baptize you with the 12 Holy Spirit and with fire. His winnowing fork is in his hand, and he will clear his threshing floor and gather his wheat into the granary, but the chaff he will burn with unquenchable fire."

THE BEGINNING OF JESUS' MINISTRY

13 Then Jesus came from Galilee to the Jordan to John, to 14 be baptized by him. John would have prevented him, saying, "I need to be baptized by you, and do you come 15 to me?" But Jesus answered him, "Let it be so now; for thus it is fitting for us to fulfil all righteousness." 16 Then he consented. And when Jesus was baptized, he went up immediately from the water, and behold, the heavens were opened g and he saw the Spirit of God de-17 scending like a dove, and alighting on him; and lo, a voice from heaven, saying, "This is my beloved Son,h with whom I am well pleased."

4 Then Jesus was led up by the Spirit into the wilder-2 ness to be tempted by the devil. And he fasted forty 3 days and forty nights, and afterward he was hungry. And the tempter came and said to him, "If you are the Son of God, command these stones to become loaves of bread."

4 But he answered, "It is written,
'Man shall not live by bread alone,
but by every word that proceeds from the mouth of
 God.'"
5 Then the devil took him to the holy city, and set him on 6 the pinnacle of the temple, and said to him, "If you are the Son of God, throw yourself down; for it is written,
'He will give his angels charge of you,'
and
'On their hands they will bear you up,
 lest you strike your foot against a stone.'"
7 Jesus said to him, "Again it is written, 'You shall not 8 tempt the Lord your God.'" Again, the devil took him to a very high mountain, and showed him all the kingdoms 9 of the world and the glory of them; and he said to him, "All these I will give you, if you will fall down and 10 worship me." Then Jesus said to him, "Begone, Satan! for it is written,
'You shall worship the Lord your God
and him only shall you serve.'"
11 Then the devil left him, and behold, angels came and ministered to him.
12 Now when he heard that John had been arrested, he 13 withdrew into Galilee; and leaving Nazareth he went and dwelt in Caper'na-um by the sea, in the territory of 14 Zeb'ulun and Naph'tali, that what was spoken by the prophet Isaiah might be fulfilled:
15 "The land of Zeb'ulun and the land of Naph'tali,
toward the sea, across the Jordan,
Galilee of the Gentiles—
16 the people who sat in darkness
have seen a great light,
and for those who sat in the region and shadow of death
light has dawned."

17 From that time Jesus began to preach, saying, "Repent, for the kingdom of heaven is at hand."
18 As he walked by the Sea of Galilee, he saw two brothers, Simon who is called Peter and Andrew his brother, 19 casting a net into the sea; for they were fishermen. And he said to them, "Follow me, and I will make you fishers 20 of men." Immediately they left their nets and followed 21 him. And going on from there he saw two other brothers, James the son of Zeb'edee and John his brother, in the boat with Zeb'edee their father, mending their nets, and 22 he called them. Immediately they left the boat and their father, and followed him.

g Other ancient authorities add *to him*   h Or *my Son, my* (or *the*) *Beloved*

23 And he went about all Galilee, teaching in their synagogues and preaching the gospel of the kingdom and healing every disease and every infirmity among the 24 people. So his fame spread throughout all Syria, and they brought him all the sick, those afflicted with various diseases and pains, demoniacs, epileptics, and paralytics, 25 and he healed them. And great crowds followed him from Galilee and the Decap'olis and Jerusalem and Judea and from beyond the Jordan.

JESUS TEACHES HIS DISCIPLES
The Beatitudes

5 Seeing the crowds, he went up on the mountain, and when he sat down his disciples came to him. 2 And he opened his mouth and taught them, saying:

3 "Blessed are the poor in spirit, for theirs is the kingdom of heaven.

4 "Blessed are those who mourn, for they shall be comforted.

5 "Blessed are the meek, for they shall inherit the earth.

6 "Blessed are those who hunger and thirst for righteousness, for they shall be satisfied.

7 "Blessed are the merciful, for they shall obtain mercy.

8 "Blessed are the pure in heart, for they shall see God.

9 "Blessed are the peacemakers, for they shall be called sons of God.

10 "Blessed are those who are persecuted for righteousness' sake, for theirs is the kingdom of heaven.

11 "Blessed are you when men revile you and persecute you and utter all kinds of evil against you falsely on my 12 account. Rejoice and be glad, for your reward is great in heaven, for so men persecuted the prophets who were before you.

13 "You are the salt of the earth; but if salt has lost its taste, how shall its saltness be restored? It is no longer good for anything except to be thrown out and trodden under foot by men.

14 "You are the light of the world. A city set on a hill 15 cannot be hid. Nor do men light a lamp and put it under a bushel, but on a stand, and it gives light to all in the 16 house. Let your light so shine before men, that they may see your good works and give glory to your Father who is in heaven.

The New Law and the Old

17 "Think not that I have come to abolish the law and the prophets; I have come not to abolish them but to 18 fulfil them. For truly, I say to you, till heaven and earth pass away, not an iota, not a dot, will pass from the law 19 until all is accomplished. Whoever then relaxes one of the least of these commandments and teaches men so, shall be called least in the kingdom of heaven; but he who does them and teaches them shall be called great in the king- 20 dom of heaven. For I tell you, unless your righteousness

exceeds that of the scribes and Pharisees, you will never enter the kingdom of heaven.

21 "You have heard that it was said to the men of old, 'You shall not kill; and whoever kills shall be liable to 22 judgment.' But I say to you that every one who is angry with his brother[i] shall be liable to judgment; whoever insults[j] his brother shall be liable to the council, and whoever says, 'You fool!' shall be liable to the hell[k] 23 of fire. So if you are offering your gift at the altar, and there remember that your brother has something against 24 you, leave your gift there before the altar and go; first be reconciled to your brother, and then come and offer 25 your gift. Make friends quickly with your accuser, while you are going with him to court, lest your accuser hand you over to the judge, and the judge to the guard, and you 26 be put in prison; truly, I say to you, you will never get out till you have paid the last penny.

27 "You have heard that it was said, 'You shall not com- 28 mit adultery.' But I say to you that every one who looks at a woman lustfully has already committed adultery 29 with her in his heart. If your right eye causes you to sin, pluck it out and throw it away; it is better that you lose one of your members than that your whole body be 30 thrown into hell.[k] And if your right hand causes you to sin, cut it off and throw it away; it is better that you lose one of your members than that your whole body go into hell.[k]

31 "It was also said, 'Whoever divorces his wife, let him 32 give her a certificate of divorce.' But I say to you that every one who divorces his wife, except on the ground of unchastity, makes her an adulteress; and whoever marries a divorced woman commits adultery.

33 "Again you have heard that it was said to the men of old, 'You shall not swear falsely, but shall perform to 34 the Lord what you have sworn.' But I say to you, Do not swear at all, either by heaven, for it is the throne of God, 35 or by the earth, for it is his footstool, or by Jerusalem, 36 for it is the city of the great King. And do not swear by your head, for you cannot make one hair white or black. 37 Let what you say be simply 'Yes' or 'No'; anything more than this comes from evil.[l]

38 "You have heard that it was said, 'An eye for an eye 39 and a tooth for a tooth.' But I say to you, Do not resist one who is evil. But if any one strikes you on the right 40 cheek, turn to him the other also; and if any one would sue you and take your coat, let him have your cloak as 41 well; and if any one forces you to go one mile, go with 42 him two miles. Give to him who begs from you, and do not refuse him who would borrow from you.

43 "You have heard that it was said, 'You shall love your 44 neighbor and hate your enemy.' But I say to you, Love your enemies and pray for those who persecute you, 45 so that you may be sons of your Father who is in heaven;

---

i Other ancient authorities insert *without cause* j Greek *says Raca to* (an obscure term of abuse) k Greek *Gehenna*
l Or *the evil one*

for he makes his sun rise on the evil and on the good, and
⁴⁶ sends rain on the just and on the unjust. For if you love
those who love you, what reward have you? Do not even
⁴⁷ the tax collectors do the same? And if you salute only
your brethren, what more are you doing than others? Do
⁴⁸ not even the Gentiles do the same? You, therefore, must
be perfect, as your heavenly Father is perfect.

Religious Practices of the New Life

6 "Beware of practicing your piety before men in
order to be seen by them; for then you will have no
reward from your Father who is in heaven.

² "Thus, when you give alms, sound no trumpet before
you, as the hypocrites do in the synagogues and in the
streets, that they may be praised by men. Truly, I say to
³ you, they have received their reward. But when you give
alms, do not let your left hand know what your right hand
⁴ is doing, so that your alms may be in secret; and your
Father who sees in secret will reward you.

⁵ "And when you pray, you must not be like the
hypocrites; for they love to stand and pray in the synagogues and at the street corners, that they may be seen
by men. Truly, I say to you, they have received their re-
⁶ ward. But when you pray, go into your room and shut the
door and pray to your Father who is in secret; and your
Father who sees in secret will reward you.

⁷ "And in praying do not heap up empty phrases as the
Gentiles do; for they think that they will be heard for
⁸ their many words. Do not be like them, for your Father
⁹ knows what you need before you ask him. Pray then like
this:
Our Father who art in heaven,
Hallowed be thy name.
¹⁰ Thy kingdom come,
Thy will be done,
On earth as it is in heaven.
¹¹ Give us this day our daily bread; ᵐ
¹² And forgive us our debts,
As we also have forgiven our debtors;
¹³ And lead us not into temptation,
But deliver us from evil.ⁿ
¹⁴ For if you forgive men their trespasses, your heavenly
¹⁵ Father also will forgive you; but if you do not forgive
men their trespasses, neither will your Father forgive your
trespasses.
¹⁶ "And when you fast, do not look dismal, like the
hypocrites, for they disfigure their faces that their fasting
may be seen by men. Truly, I say to you, they have re-
¹⁷ ceived their reward. But when you fast, anoint your head

¹⁸ and wash your face, that your fasting may not be seen by
men but by your Father who is in secret; and your Father
who sees in secret will reward you.

¹⁹ "Do not lay up for yourselves treasures on earth, where
moth and rust ᵒ consume and where thieves break in and
²⁰ steal, but lay up for yourselves treasures in heaven, where
neither moth nor rust ᵒ consumes and where thieves do
²¹ not break in and steal. For where your treasure is, there
will your heart be also.

²² "The eye is the lamp of the body. So, if your eye is
²³ sound, your whole body will be full of light; but if your
eye is not sound, your whole body will be full of darkness.
If then the light in you is darkness, how great is the
darkness!

²⁴ "No one can serve two masters; for either he will hate
the one and love the other, or he will be devoted to the
one and despise the other. You cannot serve God and
mammon.ˣ

²⁵ "Therefore I tell you, do not be anxious about your
life, what you shall eat or what you shall drink, nor about
your body, what you shall put on. Is not life more than
²⁶ food, and the body more than clothing? Look at the birds
of the air: they neither sow nor reap nor gather into
barns, and yet your heavenly Father feeds them. Are you
²⁷ not of more value than they? And which of you by being
²⁸ anxious can add one cubit to his span of life? ᵖ And why
are you anxious about clothing? Consider the lilies of the
²⁹ field, how they grow; they neither toil nor spin; yet I tell
you, even Solomon in all his glory was not arrayed like
³⁰ one of these. But if God so clothes the grass of the field,
which today is alive and tomorrow is thrown into the
oven, will he not much more clothe you, O men of little
³¹ faith? Therefore do not be anxious, saying, 'What shall
we eat?' or 'What shall we drink?' or 'What shall we
³² wear?' For the Gentiles seek all these things; and your
³³ heavenly Father knows that you need them all. But seek
first his kingdom and his righteousness, and all these
things shall be yours as well.

³⁴ "Therefore do not be anxious about tomorrow, for
tomorrow will be anxious for itself. Let the day's own
trouble be sufficient for the day.

² **7** "Judge not, that you be not judged. For with the
judgment you pronounce you will be judged, and the
³ measure you give will be the measure you get. Why do
you see the speck that is in your brother's eye, but do not
⁴ notice the log that is in your own eye? Or how can you
say to your brother, 'Let me take the speck out of your
⁵ eye,' when there is the log in your own eye? You
hypocrite, first take the log out of your own eye, and
then you will see clearly to take the speck out of your
brother's eye.

⁶ "Do not give dogs what is holy; and do not throw
your pearls before swine, lest they trample them under

ᵐ Or *our bread for the morrow*   ⁿ Or *the evil one.* Other authorities, some ancient, add, in some form, *For thine is the kingdom and the power*
and the glory, for ever. Amen.   ᵒ Or *worm*   ᵖ Or *to his stature*   ˣ*Mammon* is a Semitic word for money or riches

foot and turn to attack you.

7 "Ask, and it will be given you; seek, and you will find; 8 knock, and it will be opened to you. For every one who asks receives, and he who seeks finds, and to him who 9 knocks it will be opened. Or what man of you, if his son 10 asks him for bread, will give him a stone? Or if he asks 11 for a fish, will give him a serpent? If you then, who are evil, know how to give good gifts to your children, how much more will your Father who is in heaven give good 12 things to those who ask him! So whatever you wish that men would do to you, do so to them; for this is the law and the prophets.

13 "Enter by the narrow gate; for the gate is wide and the way is easy,q that leads to destruction, and those who 14 enter by it are many. For the gate is narrow and the way is hard, that leads to life, and those who find it are few.

15 "Beware of false prophets, who come to you in sheep's 16 clothing but inwardly are ravenous wolves. You will know them by their fruits. Are grapes gathered from thorns, or 17 figs from thistles? So, every sound tree bears good fruit, 18 but the bad tree bears evil fruit. A sound tree cannot bear 19 evil fruit, nor can a bad tree bear good fruit. Every tree that does not bear good fruit is cut down and thrown into 20 the fire. Thus you will know them by their fruits.

21 "Not every one who says to me, 'Lord, Lord,' shall enter the kingdom of heaven, but he who does the will of my 22 Father who is in heaven. On that day many will say to me, 'Lord, Lord, did we not prophesy in your name, and cast out demons in your name, and do many mighty works in 23 your name?' And then will I declare to them, 'I never knew you; depart from me, you evildoers.'

24 "Every one then who hears these words of mine and does them will be like a wise man who built his house 25 upon the rock; and the rain fell, and the floods came, and the winds blew and beat upon that house, but it did not 26 fall, because it had been founded on the rock. And every one who hears these words of mine and does not do them will be like a foolish man who built his house upon the 27 sand; and the rain fell, and the floods came, and the winds blew and beat against that house, and it fell; and great was the fall of it."

28 And when Jesus finished these sayings, the crowds were 29 astonished at his teaching, for he taught them as one who had authority, and not as their scribes.

JESUS' MINISTRY OF MIGHTY WORKS

8 When he came down from the mountain, great 2 crowds followed him; and behold, a leper came to him and knelt before him, saying, "Lord, if you will, you can 3 make me clean." And he stretched out his hand and touched him, saying, "I will; be clean." And immediately 4 his leprosy was cleansed. And Jesus said to him, "See that you say nothing to any one; but go, show yourself

to the priest, and offer the gift that Moses commanded, for a proof to the people." r

5 As he entered Caper'na-um, a centurion came forward 6 to him, beseeching him and saying, "Lord, my servant is 7 lying paralyzed at home, in terrible distress." And he said 8 to him, "I will come and heal him." But the centurion answered him, "Lord, I am not worthy to have you come under my roof; but only say the word, and my servant 9 will be healed. For I am a man under authority, with soldiers under me; and I say to one, 'Go,' and he goes, and to another, 'Come,' and he comes, and to my slave, 10 'Do this,' and he does it." When Jesus heard him, he marveled, and said to those who followed him, "Truly, I say to you, not even s in Israel have I found such faith. 11 I tell you, many will come from east and west and sit at table with Abraham, Isaac, and Jacob in the kingdom of 12 heaven, while the sons of the kingdom will be thrown into the outer darkness; there men will weep and gnash 13 their teeth." And to the centurion Jesus said, "Go; be it done for you as you have believed." And the servant was healed at that very moment.

14 And when Jesus entered Peter's house, he saw his 15 mother-in-law lying sick with a fever; he touched her hand, and the fever left her, and she rose and served him. 16 That evening they brought to him many who were possessed with demons; and he cast out the spirits with a 17 word, and healed all who were sick. This was to fulfil what was spoken by the prophet Isaiah, "He took our infirmities and bore our diseases."

18 Now when Jesus saw great crowds around him, he 19 gave orders to go over to the other side. And a scribe came up and said to him, "Teacher, I will follow you 20 wherever you go." And Jesus said to him, "Foxes have holes, and birds of the air have nests; but the Son of man 21 has nowhere to lay his head." Another of the disciples said 22 to him, "Lord, let me first go and bury my father." But Jesus said to him, "Follow me, and leave the dead to bury their own dead."

23 And when he got into the boat, his disciples followed 24 him. And behold, there arose a great storm on the sea, so that the boat was being swamped by the waves; but 25 he was asleep. And they went and woke him, saying, 26 "Save, Lord; we are perishing." And he said to them, "Why are you afraid, O men of little faith?" Then he rose and rebuked the winds and the sea; and there was a 27 great calm. And the men marveled, saying, "What sort of man is this, that even winds and sea obey him?"

28 And when he came to the other side, to the country of the Gadarenes,t two demoniacs met him, coming out of 29 the tombs, so fierce that no one could pass that way. And behold, they cried out, "What have you to do with us, O Son of God? Have you come here to torment us before 30 the time?" Now a herd of many swine was feeding at some

---

q Other ancient authorities read *for the way is wide and easy*   r Greek *to them*   s Other ancient authorities read *with no one*
t Other ancient authorities read *Gergesenes*; some, *Gerasenes*

31 distance from them. And the demons begged him, "If you 32 cast us out, send us away into the herd of swine." And he said to them, "Go." So they came out and went into the swine; and behold, the whole herd rushed down the steep 33 bank into the sea, and perished in the waters. The herdsmen fled, and going into the city they told everything, and 34 what had happened to the demoniacs. And behold, all the city came out to meet Jesus; and when they saw him, they begged him to leave their neighborhood.

2 9 And getting into a boat he crossed over and came to his own city. And behold, they brought to him a paralytic, lying on his bed; and when Jesus saw their faith he said to the paralytic, "Take heart, my son; your sins 3 are forgiven." And behold, some of the scribes said to 4 themselves, "This man is blaspheming." But Jesus, knowing[u] their thoughts, said, "Why do you think evil in your 5 hearts? For which is easier, to say, 'Your sins are for- 6 given,' or to say, 'Rise and walk'? But that you may know that the Son of man has authority on earth to forgive sins" —he then said to the paralytic—"Rise, take up your bed 7, 8 and go home." And he rose and went home. When the crowds saw it, they were afraid, and they glorified God, who had given such authority to men.

9 As Jesus passed on from there, he saw a man called Matthew sitting at the tax office; and he said to him, "Follow me." And he rose and followed him.

10 And as he sat at table[v] in the house, behold, many tax collectors and sinners came and sat down with Jesus and 11 his disciples. And when the Pharisees saw this, they said to his disciples, "Why does your teacher eat with tax col- 12 lectors and sinners?" But when he heard it, he said, "Those who are well have no need of a physician, but 13 those who are sick. Go and learn what this means, 'I desire mercy, and not sacrifice.' For I came not to call the righteous, but sinners."

14 Then the disciples of John came to him, saying, "Why do we and the Pharisees fast,[w] but your disciples do not 15 fast?" And Jesus said to them, "Can the wedding guests mourn as long as the bridegroom is with them? The days will come, when the bridegroom is taken away from them, 16 and then they will fast. And no one puts a piece of unshrunk cloth on an old garment, for the patch tears away 17 from the garment, and a worse tear is made. Neither is new wine put into old wineskins; if it is, the skins burst, and the wine is spilled, and the skins are destroyed; but new wine is put into fresh wineskins, and so both are preserved."

18 While he was thus speaking to them, behold, a ruler came in and knelt before him, saying, "My daughter has just died; but come and lay your hand on her, and she 19 will live." And Jesus rose and followed him, with his 20 disciples. And behold, a woman who had suffered from a hemorrhage for twelve years came up behind him and

21 touched the fringe of his garment; for she said to herself, 22 "If I only touch his garment, I shall be made well." Jesus turned, and seeing her he said, "Take heart, daughter; your faith has made you well." And instantly the woman 23 was made well. And when Jesus came to the ruler's house, and saw the flute players, and the crowd making a 24 tumult, he said, "Depart; for the girl is not dead but 25 sleeping." And they laughed at him. But when the crowd had been put outside, he went in and took her by the 26 hand, and the girl arose. And the report of this went through all that district.

27 And as Jesus passed on from there, two blind men followed him, crying aloud, "Have mercy on us, Son 28 of David." When he entered the house, the blind men

came to him; and Jesus said to them, "Do you believe that I am able to do this?" They said to him, "Yes, Lord." 29 Then he touched their eyes, saying, "According to your 30 faith be it done to you." And their eyes were opened. And Jesus sternly charged them, "See that no one knows 31 it." But they went away and spread his fame through all that district.

32 As they were going away, behold, a dumb demoniac 33 was brought to him. And when the demon had been cast out, the dumb man spoke; and the crowds marveled, saying, "Never was anything like this seen in Israel." 34 But the Pharisees said, "He casts out demons by the prince of demons."[a]

JESUS INSTRUCTS THE TWELVE

35 And Jesus went about all the cities and villages, teaching in their synagogues and preaching the gospel of the kingdom, and healing every disease and every infirmity. 36 When he saw the crowds, he had compassion for them, because they were harassed and helpless, like sheep with- 37 out a shepherd. Then he said to his disciples, "The harvest 38 is plentiful, but the laborers are few; pray therefore the Lord of the harvest to send out laborers into his harvest."

10 And he called to him his twelve disciples and gave them authority over unclean spirits, to cast them out, 2 and to heal every disease and every infirmity. The names of the twelve apostles are these: first, Simon, who is called Peter, and Andrew his brother; James the son of Zeb'edee, 3 and John his brother; Philip and Bartholomew; Thomas and Matthew the tax collector; James the son of Alphaeus, 4 and Thaddaeus;[x] Simon the Cananaean, and Judas Iscariot, who betrayed him.

5 These twelve Jesus sent out, charging them, "Go no- where among the Gentiles, and enter no town of the 6 Samaritans, but go rather to the lost sheep of the house 7 of Israel. And preach as you go, saying, 'The kingdom of

---

u Other ancient authorities read *seeing*   v Greek *reclined*
x Other ancient authorities read *Lebbaeus* or *Lebbaeus called Thaddaeus*

w Other ancient authorities add *much* or *often*
a Other ancient authorities omit this verse

8 heaven is at hand.' Heal the sick, raise the dead, cleanse lepers, cast out demons. You received without paying, 9 give without pay. Take no gold, nor silver, nor copper 10 in your belts, no bag for your journey, nor two tunics, nor sandals, nor a staff; for the laborer deserves his food. 11 And whatever town or village you enter, find out who is 12 worthy in it, and stay with him until you depart. As you 13 enter the house, salute it. And if the house is worthy, let your peace come upon it; but if it is not worthy, let your 14 peace return to you. And if any one will not receive you or listen to your words, shake off the dust from your 15 feet as you leave that house or town. Truly, I say to you, it shall be more tolerable on the day of judgment for the land of Sodom and Gomor′rah than for that town.

16 "Behold, I send you out as sheep in the midst of wolves; 17 so be wise as serpents and innocent as doves. Beware of men; for they will deliver you up to councils, and flog 18 you in their synagogues, and you will be dragged before governors and kings for my sake, to bear testimony before 19 them and the Gentiles. When they deliver you up, do not be anxious how you are to speak or what you are to say; for what you are to say will be given to you in that hour; 20 for it is not you who speak, but the Spirit of your Father 21 speaking through you. Brother will deliver up brother to death, and the father his child, and children will rise 22 against parents and have them put to death; and you will be hated by all for my name's sake. But he who 23 endures to the end will be saved. When they persecute you in one town, flee to the next; for truly, I say to you, you will not have gone through all the towns of Israel, before the Son of man comes.

24 "A disciple is not above his teacher, nor a servant [y] 25 above his master; it is enough for the disciple to be like his teacher, and the servant [y] like his master. If they have called the master of the house Be-el′zebul, how much more will they malign those of his household.

26 "So have no fear of them; for nothing is covered that will not be revealed, or hidden that will not be known. 27 What I tell you in the dark, utter in the light; and what 28 you hear whispered, proclaim upon the housetops. And do not fear those who kill the body but cannot kill the soul; rather fear him who can destroy both soul and 29 body in hell.[z] Are not two sparrows sold for a penny? And not one of them will fall to the ground without your 30 Father's will. But even the hairs of your head are all 31 numbered. Fear not, therefore; you are of more value 32 than many sparrows. So every one who acknowledges me before men, I also will acknowledge before my Father 33 who is in heaven; but whoever denies me before men, I also will deny before my Father who is in heaven.

34 "Do not think that I have come to bring peace on earth; 35 I have not come to bring peace, but a sword. For I have come to set a man against his father, and a daughter

against her mother, and a daughter-in-law against her 36 mother-in-law; and a man's foes will be those of his own 37 household. He who loves father or mother more than me is not worthy of me; and he who loves son or daughter 38 more than me is not worthy of me; and he who does not 39 take his cross and follow me is not worthy of me. He who finds his life will lose it, and he who loses his life for my sake will find it.

40 "He who receives you receives me, and he who receives 41 me receives him who sent me. He who receives a prophet because he is a prophet shall receive a prophet's reward, and he who receives a righteous man because he is a righteous man shall receive a righteous man's reward. 42 And whoever gives to one of these little ones even a cup of cold water because he is a disciple, truly, I say to you, he shall not lose his reward."

11 And when Jesus had finished instructing his twelve disciples, he went on from there to teach and preach in their cities.

SOME REJECT JESUS

2 Now when John heard in prison about the deeds of 3 the Christ, he sent word by his disciples and said to him, "Are you he who is to come, or shall we look for 4 another?" And Jesus answered them, "Go and tell John 5 what you hear and see: the blind receive their sight and the lame walk, lepers are cleansed and the deaf hear, and the dead are raised up, and the poor have good news 6 preached to them. And blessed is he who takes no offense at me."

7 As they went away, Jesus began to speak to the crowds concerning John: "What did you go out into the wilder- 8 ness to behold? A reed shaken by the wind? Why then did you go out? To see a man [a] clothed in soft raiment? Behold, those who wear soft raiment are in kings' houses. 9 Why then did you go out? To see a prophet? [b] Yes, I 10 tell you, and more than a prophet. This is he of whom it is written,

'Behold, I send my messenger before thy face,
who shall prepare thy way before thee.'

11 Truly, I say to you, among those born of women there has risen no one greater than John the Baptist; yet he who is least in the kingdom of heaven is greater than he. 12 From the days of John the Baptist until now the kingdom of heaven has suffered violence,[c] and men of violence take 13 it by force. For all the prophets and the law prophesied 14 until John; and if you are willing to accept it, he is 15 Eli′jah who is to come. He who has ears to hear,[d] let him hear.

16 "But to what shall I compare this generation? It is like children sitting in the market places and calling to their playmates,

---

[y] Or slave   [z] Greek Gehenna   [a] Or What then did you go out to see? A man . . .   [b] Other ancient authorities read What then did you go out to see? A prophet?   [c] Or has been coming violently   [d] Other ancient authorities omit to hear

17 'We piped to you, and you did not dance;
 we wailed, and you did not mourn.'
18 For John came neither eating nor drinking, and they say,
19 'He has a demon'; the Son of man came eating and
 drinking, and they say, 'Behold, a glutton and a drunkard,
 a friend of tax collectors and sinners!' Yet wisdom is
 justified by her deeds." e
20 Then he began to upbraid the cities where most of his
 mighty works had been done, because they did not re-
21 pent. "Woe to you, Chora'zin! woe to you, Beth-sa'ida!
 for if the mighty works done in you had been done in
 Tyre and Sidon, they would have repented long ago in
22 sackcloth and ashes. But I tell you, it shall be more tolerable on the day of judgment for Tyre and Sidon than
23 for you. And you, Caper'na-um, will you be exalted to
 heaven? You shall be brought down to Hades. For if the
 mighty works done in you had been done in Sodom, it
24 would have remained until this day. But I tell you that
 it shall be more tolerable on the day of judgment for
 the land of Sodom than for you."
25 At that time Jesus declared, "I thank thee, Father, Lord
 of heaven and earth, that thou hast hidden these things
 from the wise and understanding and revealed them to
26 babes; yea, Father, for such was thy gracious will.f
27 All things have been delivered to me by my Father; and
 no one knows the Son except the Father, and no one
 knows the Father except the Son and any one to whom
28 the Son chooses to reveal him. Come to me, all who labor
29 and are heavy laden, and I will give you rest. Take my
 yoke upon you, and learn from me; for I am gentle and
 lowly in heart, and you will find rest for your souls.
30 For my yoke is easy, and my burden is light."

Examples of Opposition and Rejection

12 At that time Jesus went through the grainfields on
 the sabbath; his disciples were hungry, and they be-
2 gan to pluck heads of grain and to eat. But when the
 Pharisees saw it, they said to him, "Look, your disciples are
3 doing what is not lawful to do on the sabbath." He said to
 them, "Have you not read what David did, when he was
4 hungry, and those who were with him: how he entered
 the house of God and ate the bread of the Presence, which
 it was not lawful for him to eat nor for those who were
5 with him, but only for the priests? Or have you not read
 in the law how on the sabbath the priests in the temple
6 profane the sabbath, and are guiltless? I tell you, some-
7 thing greater than the temple is here. And if you had
 known what this means, 'I desire mercy, and not sacri-
8 fice,' you would not have condemned the guiltless. For the
 Son of man is lord of the sabbath."
9 And he went on from there, and entered their syna-
10 gogue. And behold, there was a man with a withered hand.
 And they asked him, "Is it lawful to heal on the sab-

11 bath?" so that they might accuse him. He said to them,
 "What man of you, if he has one sheep and it falls into
 a pit on the sabbath, will not lay hold of it and lift it
12 out? Of how much more value is a man than a sheep!
13 So it is lawful to do good on the sabbath." Then he said
 to the man, "Stretch out your hand." And the man
 stretched it out, and it was restored, whole like the other.
14 But the Pharisees went out and took counsel against him,
 how to destroy him.
15 Jesus, aware of this, withdrew from there. And many
16 followed him, and he healed them all, and ordered them
17 not to make him known. This was to fulfil what was
 spoken by the prophet Isaiah:
18 "Behold, my servant whom I have chosen,
 my beloved with whom my soul is well pleased.
 I will put my Spirit upon him,
 and he shall proclaim justice to the Gentiles.
19 He will not wrangle or cry aloud,
 nor will any one hear his voice in the streets;
20 he will not break a bruised reed
 or quench a smoldering wick,
 till he brings justice to victory;
21 and in his name will the Gentiles hope."
22 Then a blind and dumb demoniac was brought to him,
 and he healed him, so that the dumb man spoke and
23 saw. And all the people were amazed, and said, "Can this
24 be the Son of David?" But when the Pharisees heard it
 they said, "It is only by Be-el'zebul, the prince of demons,
25 that this man casts out demons." Knowing their thoughts,
 he said to them, "Every kingdom divided against itself
 is laid waste, and no city or house divided against itself
26 will stand; and if Satan casts out Satan, he is divided
27 against himself; how then will his kingdom stand? And
 if I cast out demons by Be-el'zebul, by whom do your
 sons cast them out? Therefore they shall be your judges.
28 But if it is by the Spirit of God that I cast out demons,
29 then the kingdom of God has come upon you. Or how
 can one enter a strong man's house and plunder his goods,
 unless he first binds the strong man? Then indeed he
30 may plunder his house. He who is not with me is against
31 me, and he who does not gather with me scatters. Therefore I tell you, every sin and blasphemy will be forgiven
 men, but the blasphemy against the Spirit will not be
32 forgiven. And whoever says a word against the Son of
 man will be forgiven; but whoever speaks against the
 Holy Spirit will not be forgiven, either in this age or in
 the age to come.
33 "Either make the tree good, and its fruit good; or make
 the tree bad, and its fruit bad; for the tree is known
34 by its fruit. You brood of vipers! how can you speak
 good, when you are evil? For out of the abundance of
35 the heart the mouth speaks. The good man out of his
 good treasure brings forth good, and the evil man out

e Other ancient authorities read *children* (Lk 7.35)   f Or *so it was well-pleasing before thee*

³⁶ of his evil treasure brings forth evil. I tell you, on the day of judgment men will render account for every careless ³⁷ word they utter; for by your words you will be justified, and by your words you will be condemned."

³⁸ Then some of the scribes and Pharisees said to him, ³⁹ "Teacher, we wish to see a sign from you." But he answered them, "An evil and adulterous generation seeks for a sign; but no sign shall be given to it except the ⁴⁰ sign of the prophet Jonah. For as Jonah was three days and three nights in the belly of the whale, so will the Son of man be three days and three nights in the heart of ⁴¹ the earth. The men of Nin′eveh will arise at the judgment with this generation and condemn it; for they repented at the preaching of Jonah, and behold, something ⁴² greater than Jonah is here. The queen of the South will arise at the judgment with this generation and condemn it; for she came from the ends of the earth to hear the wisdom of Solomon, and behold, something greater than Solomon is here.

⁴³ "When the unclean spirit has gone out of a man, he passes through waterless places seeking rest, but he finds ⁴⁴ none. Then he says, 'I will return to my house from which I came.' And when he comes he finds it empty, ⁴⁵ swept, and put in order. Then he goes and brings with him seven other spirits more evil than himself, and they enter and dwell there; and the last state of that man becomes worse than the first. So shall it be also with this evil generation."

⁴⁶ While he was still speaking to the people, behold, his mother and his brothers stood outside, asking to speak ⁴⁸ to him.ᵍ But he replied to the man who told him, "Who is

⁴⁹ my mother, and who are my brothers?" And stretching out his hand toward his disciples, he said, "Here are my ⁵⁰ mother and my brothers! For whoever does the will of my Father in heaven is my brother, and sister, and mother."

JESUS TEACHES ABOUT THE KINGDOM OF HEAVEN

13 That same day Jesus went out of the house and sat ² beside the sea. And great crowds gathered about him, so that he got into a boat and sat there; and the whole ³ crowd stood on the beach. And he told them many things ⁴ in parables, saying: "A sower went out to sow. And as he sowed, some seeds fell along the path, and the birds ⁵ came and devoured them. Other seeds fell on rocky ground, where they had not much soil, and immediately ⁶ they sprang up, since they had no depth of soil, but when the sun rose they were scorched; and since they had no

⁷ root they withered away. Other seeds fell upon thorns, ⁸ and the thorns grew up and choked them. Other seeds fell on good soil and brought forth grain, some a hundred-⁹ fold, some sixty, some thirty. He who has ears,ʰ let him hear."

¹⁰ Then the disciples came and said to him, "Why do you ¹¹ speak to them in parables?" And he answered them, "To you it has been given to know the secrets of the kingdom ¹² of heaven, but to them it has not been given. For to him who has will more be given, and he will have abundance; but from him who has not, even what he has will ¹³ be taken away. This is why I speak to them in parables, because seeing they do not see, and hearing they do not ¹⁴ hear, nor do they understand. With them indeed is fulfilled the prophecy of Isaiah which says:

'You shall indeed hear but never understand,
    and you shall indeed see but never perceive.
¹⁵ For this people's heart has grown dull,
    and their ears are heavy of hearing,
    and their eyes they have closed,
lest they should perceive with their eyes,
    and hear with their ears,
and understand with their heart,
    and turn for me to heal them.'

¹⁶ But blessed are your eyes, for they see, and your ears, for ¹⁷ they hear. Truly, I say to you, many prophets and righteous men longed to see what you see, and did not see it, and to hear what you hear, and did not hear it.

¹⁸,¹⁹ "Hear then the parable of the sower. When any one hears the word of the kingdom and does not understand it, the evil one comes and snatches away what is sown in ²⁰ his heart; this is what was sown along the path. As for what was sown on rocky ground, this is he who hears ²¹ the word and immediately receives it with joy; yet he has no root in himself, but endures for a while, and when tribulation or persecution arises on account of the word, ²² immediately he falls away.ⁱ As for what was sown among thorns, this is he who hears the word, but the cares of the world and the delight in riches choke the word, and ²³ it proves unfruitful. As for what was sown on good soil, this is he who hears the word and understands it; he indeed bears fruit, and yields, in one case a hundredfold, in another sixty, and in another thirty."

²⁴ Another parable he put before them, saying, "The kingdom of heaven may be compared to a man who ²⁵ sowed good seed in his field; but while men were sleeping, his enemy came and sowed weeds among the wheat, ²⁶ and went away. So when the plants came up and bore ²⁷ grain then the weeds appeared also. And the servants ʲ of the householder came and said to him, 'Sir, did you not sow good seed in your field? How then has it weeds?' ²⁸ He said to them, 'An enemy has done this.' The servants ʲ said to him, 'Then do you want us to go and gather

ᵍ Other ancient authorities insert verse 47, *Some one told him, "Your mother and your brothers are standing outside, asking to speak to you"*
ʰ Other ancient authorities add here and in verse 43 *to hear*   ⁱ Or *stumbles*   ʲ Or *slaves*

29 them?' But he said, 'No; lest in gathering the weeds you
30 root up the wheat along with them. Let both grow together until the harvest; and at harvest time I will tell the reapers, Gather the weeds first and bind them in bundles to be burned, but gather the wheat into my barn.' "

31 Another parable he put before them, saying, "The kingdom of heaven is like a grain of mustard seed which a
32 man took and sowed in his field; it is the smallest of all seeds, but when it has grown it is the greatest of shrubs and becomes a tree, so that the birds of the air come and make nests in its branches."

33 He told them another parable. "The kingdom of heaven is like leaven which a woman took and hid in three measures of flour, till it was all leavened."

34 All this Jesus said to the crowds in parables; indeed
35 he said nothing to them without a parable. This was to fulfil what was spoken by the prophet: k

"I will open my mouth in parables,
I will utter what has been hidden since the foundation of the world."

36 Then he left the crowds and went into the house. And his disciples came to him, saying, "Explain to us the
37 parable of the weeds of the field." He answered, "He
38 who sows the good seed is the Son of man; the field is the world, and the good seed means the sons of the
39 kingdom; the weeds are the sons of the evil one, and the enemy who sowed them is the devil; the harvest is the
40 close of the age, and the reapers are angels. Just as the weeds are gathered and burned with fire, so will it be at
41 the close of the age. The Son of man will send his angels, and they will gather out of his kingdom all causes of sin
42 and all evildoers, and throw them into the furnace of
43 fire; there men will weep and gnash their teeth. Then the righteous will shine like the sun in the kingdom of their Father. He who has ears, let him hear.

44 "The kingdom of heaven is like treasure hidden in a field, which a man found and covered up; then in his joy he goes and sells all that he has and buys that field.
45 "Again, the kingdom of heaven is like a merchant in
46 search of fine pearls, who, on finding one pearl of great value, went and sold all that he had and bought it.

47 "Again, the kingdom of heaven is like a net which was thrown into the sea and gathered fish of every kind;
48 when it was full, men drew it ashore and sat down and sorted the good into vessels but threw away the bad.

49 So it will be at the close of the age. The angels will come
50 out and separate the evil from the righteous, and throw them into the furnace of fire; there men will weep and gnash their teeth.

51 "Have you understood all this?" They said to him,
52 "Yes." And he said to them, "Therefore every scribe who has been trained for the kingdom of heaven is like a householder who brings out of his treasure what is new and what is old."

53 And when Jesus had finished these parables, he went
54 away from there, and coming to his own country he taught them in their synagogue, so that they were astonished, and said, "Where did this man get this wisdom
55 and these mighty works? Is not this the carpenter's son? Is not his mother called Mary? And are not his brothers
56 James and Joseph and Simon and Judas? And are not all his sisters with us? Where then did this man get
57 all this?" And they took offense at him. But Jesus said to them, "A prophet is not without honor except in his
58 own country and in his own house." And he did not do many mighty works there, because of their unbelief.

JESUS' FAME SPREADS

14 At that time Herod the tetrarch heard about the
2 fame of Jesus; and he said to his servants, "This is John the Baptist, he has been raised from the dead; that is
3 why these powers are at work in him." For Herod had seized John and bound him and put him in prison, for the
4 sake of Hero'di-as, his brother Philip's wife; l because John said to him, "It is not lawful for you to have her."
5 And though he wanted to put him to death, he feared the
6 people, because they held him to be a prophet. But when Herod's birthday came, the daughter of Hero'di-as danced
7 before the company, and pleased Herod, so that he promised with an oath to give her whatever she might
8 ask. Prompted by her mother, she said, "Give me the
9 head of John the Baptist here on a platter." And the king was sorry; but because of his oaths and his guests
10 he commanded it to be given; he sent and had John be-
11 headed in the prison, and his head was brought on a platter and given to the girl, and she brought it to her
12 mother. And his disciples came and took the body and buried it; and they went and told Jesus.

Mighty Acts

13 Now when Jesus heard this, he withdrew from there in a boat to a lonely place apart. But when the crowds heard it, they followed him on foot from the towns.
14 As he went ashore he saw a great throng; and he had
15 compassion on them, and healed their sick. When it was evening, the disciples came to him and said, "This is a lonely place, and the day is now over; send the crowds away to go into the villages and buy food for themselves."
16 Jesus said, "They need not go away; you give them some-

---

k Other ancient authorities read *the prophet Isaiah*   l Other ancient authorities read *his brother's wife*

17 thing to eat." They said to him, "We have only five loaves
18 here and two fish." And he said, "Bring them here to me."
19 Then he ordered the crowds to sit down on the grass; and taking the five loaves and the two fish he looked up to heaven, and blessed, and broke and gave the loaves to the disciples, and the disciples gave them to the crowds.

20 And they all ate and were satisfied. And they took up
21 twelve baskets full of the broken pieces left over. And those who ate were about five thousand men, besides women and children.

22 Then he made the disciples get into the boat and go before him to the other side, while he dismissed the
23 crowds. And after he had dismissed the crowds, he went up on the mountain by himself to pray. When evening
24 came, he was there alone, but the boat by this time was many furlongs distant from the land,[m] beaten by the
25 waves; for the wind was against them. And in the fourth
26 watch of the night he came to them, walking on the sea. But when the disciples saw him walking on the sea, they were terrified, saying, "It is a ghost!" And they cried out
27 for fear. But immediately he spoke to them, saying, "Take heart, it is I; have no fear."

28 And Peter answered him, "Lord, if it is you, bid me
29 come to you on the water." He said, "Come." So Peter got out of the boat and walked on the water and came
30 to Jesus; but when he saw the wind,[n] he was afraid, and
31 beginning to sink he cried out, "Lord, save me." Jesus immediately reached out his hand and caught him, saying to him, "O man of little faith, why did you doubt?"
32 And when they got into the boat, the wind ceased.
33 And those in the boat worshiped him, saying, "Truly you are the Son of God."

34 And when they had crossed over, they came to land
35 at Gennes'aret. And when the men of that place recognized him, they sent round to all that region and brought to
36 him all that were sick, and besought him that they might only touch the fringe of his garment; and as many as touched it were made well.

Controversy Over Ritual Cleanliness

15 Then Pharisees and scribes came to Jesus from
2 Jerusalem and said, "Why do your disciples transgress the tradition of the elders? For they do not wash
3 their hands when they eat." He answered them, "And why do you transgress the commandment of God for the
4 sake of your tradition? For God commanded, 'Honor your father and your mother,' and, 'He who speaks evil

5 of father or mother, let him surely die.' But you say, 'If any one tells his father or his mother, What you would have gained from me is given to God,[o] he need not honor
6 his father.' So, for the sake of your tradition, you have
7 made void the word[p] of God. You hypocrites! Well did Isaiah prophesy of you, when he said:
8 'This people honors me with their lips, but their heart is far from me;
9 in vain do they worship me, teaching as doctrines the precepts of men.' "
10 And he called the people to him and said to them,
11 "Hear and understand: not what goes into the mouth defiles a man, but what comes out of the mouth, this
12 defiles a man." Then the disciples came and said to him, "Do you know that the Pharisees were offended
13 when they heard this saying?" He answered, "Every plant which my heavenly Father has not planted will be rooted
14 up. Let them alone; they are blind guides. And if a blind man leads a blind man, both will fall into a pit."
15 But Peter said to him, "Explain the parable to us."
16 And he said, "Are you also still without understanding?
17 Do you not see that whatever goes into the mouth passes
18 into the stomach, and so passes on?[q] But what comes out of the mouth proceeds from the heart, and this defiles a
19 man. For out of the heart come evil thoughts, murder,
20 adultery, fornication, theft, false witness, slander. These are what defile a man; but to eat with unwashed hands does not defile a man."

Jesus Ministers to Gentiles

21 And Jesus went away from there and withdrew to the
22 district of Tyre and Sidon. And behold, a Canaanite woman from that region came out and cried, "Have mercy on me, O Lord, Son of David; my daughter is severely
23 possessed by a demon." But he did not answer her a word. And his disciples came and begged him, saying,
24 "Send her away, for she is crying after us." He answered, "I was sent only to the lost sheep of the house of Israel."
25 But she came and knelt before him, saying, "Lord, help
26 me." And he answered, "It is not fair to take the children's
27 bread and throw it to the dogs." She said, "Yes, Lord, yet even the dogs eat the crumbs that fall from their
28 masters' table." Then Jesus answered her, "O woman, great is your faith! Be it done for you as you desire." And her daughter was healed instantly.

29 And Jesus went on from there and passed along the Sea of Galilee. And he went up on the mountain, and sat
30 down there. And great crowds came to him, bringing with them the lame, the maimed, the blind, the dumb, and many others, and they put them at his feet, and he healed
31 them, so that the throng wondered, when they saw the dumb speaking, the maimed whole, the lame walking, and the blind seeing; and they glorified the God of Israel.

---

[m] Other ancient authorities read *was out on the sea*   [n] Other ancient authorities read *strong wind*   [o] Or *an offering*
[p] Other ancient authorities read *law*   [q] Or *is evacuated*

³² Then Jesus called his disciples to him and said, "I have compassion on the crowd, because they have been with me now three days, and have nothing to eat; and I am unwilling to send them away hungry, lest they faint ³³ on the way." And the disciples said to him, "Where are we to get bread enough in the desert to feed so great a ³⁴ crowd?" And Jesus said to them, "How many loaves ³⁵ have you?" They said, "Seven, and a few small fish." And ³⁶ commanding the crowd to sit down on the ground, he took the seven loaves and the fish, and having given thanks he broke them and gave them to the disciples, and ³⁷ the disciples gave them to the crowds. And they all ate and were satisfied; and they took up seven baskets full ³⁸ of the broken pieces left over. Those who ate were four ³⁹ thousand men, besides women and children. And sending away the crowds, he got into the boat and went to the region of Mag'adan.

Teachings of Pharisees Rejected

16 And the Pharisees and Sad'ducees came, and to test him they asked him to show them a sign from ² heaven. He answered them,^r "When it is evening, you ³ say, 'It will be fair weather; for the sky is red.' And in the morning, 'It will be stormy today, for the sky is red and threatening.' You know how to interpret the appearance of the sky, but you cannot interpret the signs of the ⁴ times. An evil and adulterous generation seeks for a sign, but no sign shall be given to it except the sign of Jonah." So he left them and departed.

⁵ When the disciples reached the other side, they had ⁶ forgotten to bring any bread. Jesus said to them, "Take heed and beware of the leaven of the Pharisees and ⁷ Sad'ducees." And they discussed it among themselves, ⁸ saying, "We brought no bread." But Jesus, aware of this, said, "O men of little faith, why do you discuss among ⁹ yourselves the fact that you have no bread? Do you not yet perceive? Do you not remember the five loaves of the five thousand, and how many baskets you gathered? ¹⁰ Or the seven loaves of the four thousand, and how many ¹¹ baskets you gathered? How is it that you fail to perceive that I did not speak about bread? Beware of the leaven ¹² of the Pharisees and Sad'ducees." Then they understood that he did not tell them to beware of the leaven of bread, but of the teaching of the Pharisees and Sad'ducees.

Jesus the Christ Founds His Church

¹³ Now when Jesus came into the district of Caesare'a Philippi, he asked his disciples, "Who do men say that ¹⁴ the Son of man is?" And they said, "Some say John the Baptist, others say Eli'jah, and others Jeremiah or one ¹⁵ of the prophets." He said to them, "But who do you say ¹⁶ that I am?" Simon Peter replied, "You are the Christ, ¹⁷ the Son of the living God." And Jesus answered him,

"Blessed are you, Simon Bar-Jona! For flesh and blood has not revealed this to you, but my Father who is in ¹⁸ heaven. And I tell you, you are Peter,^s and on this rock^t I will build my church, and the powers of death^u shall ¹⁹ not prevail against it. I will give you the keys of the kingdom of heaven, and whatever you bind on earth shall be bound in heaven, and whatever you loose on earth ²⁰ shall be loosed in heaven." Then he strictly charged the disciples to tell no one that he was the Christ.

²¹ From that time Jesus began to show his disciples that he must go to Jerusalem and suffer many things from the elders and chief priests and scribes, and be killed, ²² and on the third day be raised. And Peter took him and began to rebuke him, saying, "God forbid, Lord! This ²³ shall never happen to you." But he turned and said to Peter, "Get behind me, Satan! You are a hindrance^v to me; for you are not on the side of God, but of men."

²⁴ Then Jesus told his disciples, "If any man would come after me, let him deny himself and take up his cross ²⁵ and follow me. For whoever would save his life will lose it, and whoever loses his life for my sake will find it. ²⁶ For what will it profit a man, if he gains the whole world and forfeits his life? Or what shall a man give in return ²⁷ for his life? For the Son of man is to come with his angels in the glory of his Father, and then he will repay ²⁸ every man for what he has done. Truly, I say to you, there are some standing here who will not taste death before they see the Son of man coming in his kingdom."

The Transfiguration

17 And after six days Jesus took with him Peter and James and John his brother, and led them up a ² high mountain apart. And he was transfigured before them, and his face shone like the sun, and his garments ³ became white as light. And behold, there appeared to ⁴ them Moses and Eli'jah, talking with him. And Peter said to Jesus, "Lord, it is well that we are here; if you wish, I will make three booths here, one for you and

⁵ one for Moses and one for Eli'jah." He was still speaking, when lo, a bright cloud overshadowed them, and a voice from the cloud said, "This is my beloved Son,^w with

6 whom I am well pleased; listen to him." When the disciples heard this, they fell on their faces, and were 7 filled with awe. But Jesus came and touched them, saying, 8 "Rise, and have no fear." And when they lifted up their eyes, they saw no one but Jesus only.

9 And as they were coming down the mountain, Jesus commanded them, "Tell no one the vision, until the Son 10 of man is raised from the dead." And the disciples asked him, "Then why do the scribes say that first Eli′jah must 11 come?" He replied, "Eli′jah does come, and he is to 12 restore all things; but I tell you that Eli′jah has already come, and they did not know him, but did to him whatever they pleased. So also the Son of man will suffer at 13 their hands." Then the disciples understood that he was speaking to them of John the Baptist.

14 And when they came to the crowd, a man came up 15 to him and kneeling before him said, "Lord, have mercy on my son, for he is an epileptic and he suffers terribly; for often he falls into the fire, and often into the water. 16 And I brought him to your disciples, and they could not 17 heal him." And Jesus answered, "O faithless and perverse generation, how long am I to be with you? How long am 18 I to bear with you? Bring him here to me." And Jesus rebuked him, and the demon came out of him, and the 19 boy was cured instantly. Then the disciples came to Jesus privately and said, "Why could we not cast it out?" 20 He said to them, "Because of your little faith. For truly, I say to you, if you have faith as a grain of mustard seed, you will say to this mountain, 'Move from here to there,' and it will move; and nothing will be impossible to you." x

22 As they were gathering y in Galilee, Jesus said to them, "The Son of man is to be delivered into the hands of 23 men, and they will kill him, and he will be raised on the third day." And they were greatly distressed.

24 When they came to Caper′na-um, the collectors of the half-shekel tax went up to Peter and said, "Does not your 25 teacher pay the tax?" He said, "Yes." And when he came home, Jesus spoke to him first, saying, "What do you think, Simon? From whom do kings of the earth take 26 toll or tribute? From their sons or from others?" And when he said, "From others," Jesus said to him, "Then 27 the sons are free. However, not to give offense to them, go to the sea and cast a hook, and take the first fish that comes up, and when you open its mouth you will find a shekel; take that and give it to them for me and for yourself."

JESUS TEACHES HIS DISCIPLES

18 At that time the disciples came to Jesus, saying, "Who is the greatest in the kingdom of heaven?" 2 And calling to him a child, he put him in the midst of 3 them, and said, "Truly, I say to you, unless you turn

and become like children, you will never enter the 4 kingdom of heaven. Whoever humbles himself like this child, he is the greatest in the kingdom of heaven.

5 "Whoever receives one such child in my name receives 6 me; but whoever causes one of these little ones who believe in me to sin,z it would be better for him to have a great millstone fastened round his neck and to be drowned in the depth of the sea.

7 "Woe to the world for temptations to sin! a For it is

necessary that temptations come, but woe to the man by 8 whom the temptation comes! And if your hand or your foot causes you to sin,z cut it off and throw it away; it is better for you to enter life maimed or lame than with two hands or two feet to be thrown into the eternal 9 fire. And if your eye causes you to sin,z pluck it out and throw it away; it is better for you to enter life with one eye than with two eyes to be thrown into the hell b of fire.

10 "See that you do not despise one of these little ones; for I tell you that in heaven their angels always behold 12 the face of my Father who is in heaven.c What do you think? If a man has a hundred sheep, and one of them has gone astray, does he not leave the ninety-nine on the hills and go in search of the one that went astray? 13 And if he finds it, truly, I say to you, he rejoices over mountains and go in search of the one that went astray? 14 So it is not the will of my d Father who is in heaven that one of these little ones should perish.

15 "If your brother sins against you, go and tell him his fault, between you and him alone. If he listens to 16 you, you have gained your brother. But if he does not listen, take one or two others along with you, that every word may be confirmed by the evidence of two or three 17 witnesses. If he refuses to listen to them, tell it to the church; and if he refuses to listen even to the church, let 18 him be to you as a Gentile and a tax collector. Truly, I say to you, whatever you bind on earth shall be bound in heaven, and whatever you loose on earth shall be 19 loosed in heaven. Again I say to you, if two of you agree on earth about anything they ask, it will be done for 20 them by my Father in heaven. For where two or three are gathered in my name, there am I in the midst of them."

21 Then Peter came up and said to him, "Lord, how often

---

x Other ancient authorities insert verse 21, "But this kind never comes out except by prayer and fasting"
y Other ancient authorities read abode   z Greek causes . . . to stumble   a Greek stumbling blocks   b Greek Gehenna
c Other ancient authorities add verse 11, For the Son of man came to save the lost   d Other ancient authorities read your

shall my brother sin against me, and I forgive him? As

22 many as seven times?" Jesus said to him, "I do not say to you seven times, but seventy times seven.e

23 "Therefore the kingdom of heaven may be compared to a king who wished to settle accounts with his servants.

24 When he began the reckoning, one was brought to him

25 who owed him ten thousand talents;f and as he could not pay, his lord ordered him to be sold, with his wife and children and all that he had, and payment to be made.

26 So the servant fell on his knees, imploring him, 'Lord, have patience with me, and I will pay you everything.'

27 And out of pity for him the lord of that servant released

28 him and forgave him the debt. But that same servant, as he went out, came upon one of his fellow servants who owed him a hundred denarii;g and seizing him by the

29 throat he said, 'Pay what you owe.' So his fellow servant fell down and besought him, 'Have patience with me, and

30 I will pay you.' He refused and went and put him in

31 prison till he should pay the debt. When his fellow servants saw what had taken place, they were greatly distressed, and they went and reported to their lord all that had

32 taken place. Then his lord summoned him and said to him, 'You wicked servant! I forgave you all that debt because

33 you besought me; and should not you have had mercy

34 on your fellow servant, as I had mercy on you?' And in anger his lord delivered him to the jailers,h till he should

35 pay all his debt. So also my heavenly Father will do to every one of you, if you do not forgive your brother from your heart."

JESUS HEADS FOR JERUSALEM

19 Now when Jesus had finished these sayings, he went away from Galilee and entered the region of

2 Judea beyond the Jordan; and large crowds followed him, and he healed them there.

man put asunder." They said to him, "Why then did Moses command one to give a certificate of divorce,

8 and to put her away?" He said to them, "For your hardness of heart Moses allowed you to divorce your wives,

9 but from the beginning it was not so. And I say to you: whoever divorces his wife, except for unchastity,j and marries another, commits adultery." k

10 The disciples said to him, "If such is the case of a man

11 with his wife, it is not expedient to marry." But he said to them, "Not all men can receive this saying, but only

12 those to whom it is given. For there are eunuchs who have been so from birth, and there are eunuchs who have been made eunuchs by men, and there are eunuchs who have made themselves eunuchs for the sake of the kingdom of heaven. He who is able to receive this, let him receive it."

13 Then children were brought to him that he might lay his hands on them and pray. The disciples rebuked the

14 people; but Jesus said, "Let the children come to me, and do not hinder them; for to such belongs the kingdom

15 of heaven." And he laid his hands on them and went away.

16 And behold, one came up to him, saying, "Teacher,

17 what good deed must I do, to have eternal life?" And he said to him, "Why do you ask me about what is good? One there is who is good. If you would enter

18 life, keep the commandments." He said to him, "Which?" And Jesus said, "You shall not kill, You shall not commit adultery, You shall not steal, You shall not bear false

19 witness, Honor your father and mother, and, You shall

20 love your neighbor as yourself." The young man said to him, "All these I have observed; what do I still lack?"

21 Jesus said to him, "If you would be perfect, go, sell what you possess and give to the poor, and you will have

22 treasure in heaven; and come, follow me." When the

Demands and Rewards for His Followers

3 And Pharisees came up to him and tested him by asking, "Is it lawful to divorce one's wife for any cause?"

4 He answered, "Have you not read that he who made them from the beginning made them male and female,

5 and said, 'For this reason a man shall leave his father and mother and be joined to his wife, and the two shall

6 become one flesh'? So they are no longer two but one flesh. What therefore God has joined together, let not

young man heard this he went away sorrowful; for he had great possessions.

23 And Jesus said to his disciples, "Truly, I say to you, it will be hard for a rich man to enter the kingdom of

24 heaven. Again I tell you, it is easier for a camel to go through the eye of a needle than for a rich man to enter

25 the kingdom of God." When the disciples heard this they were greatly astonished, saying, "Who then can be

26 saved?" But Jesus looked at them and said to them, "With men this is impossible, but with God all things are

e Or *seventy-seven times*   f This talent was more than fifteen years' wages of a laborer   g The denarius was a day's wage for a laborer
h Greek *torturers*   i Greek *one flesh*   j Other ancient authorities, after *unchastity*, read *makes her commit adultery*
k Other ancient authorities insert *and he who marries a divorced woman commits adultery*

27 possible." Then Peter said in reply, "Lo, we have left everything and followed you. What then shall we have?" 28 Jesus said to them, "Truly, I say to you, in the new world, when the Son of man shall sit on his glorious throne, you who have followed me will also sit on twelve thrones, 29 judging the twelve tribes of Israel. And every one who has left houses or brothers or sisters or father or mother or children or lands, for my name's sake, will receive a 30 hundredfold,[1] and inherit eternal life. But many that are first will be last, and the last first.

20 "For the kingdom of heaven is like a householder who went out early in the morning to hire laborers 2 for his vineyard. After agreeing with the laborers for a 3 denarius[m] a day, he sent them into his vineyard. And going out about the third hour he saw others standing 4 idle in the market place; and to them he said, 'You go into the vineyard too, and whatever is right I will give 5 you.' So they went. Going out again about the sixth hour 6 and the ninth hour, he did the same. And about the eleventh hour he went out and found others standing; and 7 he said to them, 'Why do you stand here idle all day?' They said to him, 'Because no one has hired us.' He said to 8 them, 'You go into the vineyard too.' And when evening came, the owner of the vineyard said to his steward, 'Call the laborers and pay them their wages, beginning with the 9 last, up to the first.' And when those hired about the eleventh hour came, each of them received a denarius. 10 Now when the first came, they thought they would receive more; but each of them also received a denarius. 11 And on receiving it they grumbled at the householder, 12 saying, 'These last worked only one hour, and you have made them equal to us who have borne the burden of 13 the day and the scorching heat.' But he replied to one of them, 'Friend, I am doing you no wrong; did you not 14 agree with me for a denarius? Take what belongs to you, and go; I choose to give to this last as I give to you. 15 Am I not allowed to do what I choose with what belongs 16 to me? Or do you begrudge my generosity?'[n] So the last will be first, and the first last."

17 And as Jesus was going up to Jerusalem, he took the twelve disciples aside, and on the way he said to them, 18 "Behold, we are going up to Jerusalem; and the Son of man will be delivered to the chief priests and scribes, and 19 they will condemn him to death, and deliver him to the Gentiles to be mocked and scourged and crucified, and he will be raised on the third day."

20 Then the mother of the sons of Zeb'edee came up to him, with her sons, and kneeling before him she asked 21 him for something. And he said to her, "What do you want?" She said to him, "Command that these two sons of mine may sit, one at your right hand and one at your 22 left, in your kingdom." But Jesus answered, "You do not know what you are asking. Are you able to drink the cup that I am to drink?" They said to him, "We are able." 23 He said to them, "You will drink my cup, but to sit at my right hand and at my left is not mine to grant, but it is for those for whom it has been prepared by my Father." 24 And when the ten heard it, they were indignant at the two 25 brothers. But Jesus called them to him and said, "You know that the rulers of the Gentiles lord it over them, and 26 their great men exercise authority over them. It shall not be so among you; but whoever would be great among you 27 must be your servant, and whoever would be first among 28 you must be your slave; even as the Son of man came not to be served but to serve, and to give his life as a ransom for many."

29 And as they went out of Jericho, a great crowd followed 30 him. And behold, two blind men sitting by the roadside, when they heard that Jesus was passing by, cried out,[o] 31 "Have mercy on us, Son of David!" The crowd rebuked them, telling them to be silent; but they cried out the 32 more, "Lord, have mercy on us, Son of David!" And Jesus stopped and called them, saying, "What do you want 33 me to do for you?" They said to him, "Lord, let our eyes 34 be opened." And Jesus in pity touched their eyes, and immediately they received their sight and followed him.

EVENTS IN JERUSALEM

21 And when they drew near to Jerusalem and came to Beth'phage, to the Mount of Olives, then Jesus 2 sent two disciples, saying to them, "Go into the village opposite you, and immediately you will find an ass tied, and a colt with her; untie them and bring them to me. 3 If any one says anything to you, you shall say, 'The Lord has need of them,' and he will send them immediately." 4 This took place to fulfil what was spoken by the prophet, saying,

5 "Tell the daughter of Zion,
Behold, your king is coming to you,
humble, and mounted on an ass,
and on a colt, the foal of an ass."

6 The disciples went and did as Jesus had directed them; 7 they brought the ass and the colt, and put their garments 8 on them, and he sat thereon. Most of the crowd spread their garments on the road, and others cut branches from 9 the trees and spread them on the road. And the crowds that went before him and that followed him shouted, "Hosanna to the Son of David! Blessed is he who comes in the name of the Lord! Hosanna in the highest!" 10 And when he entered Jerusalem, all the city was stirred, 11 saying, "Who is this?" And the crowds said, "This is the prophet Jesus from Nazareth of Galilee."

Cleansing of the Temple

12 And Jesus entered the temple of God[p] and drove out all who sold and bought in the temple, and he overturned

---

[1] Other ancient authorities read *manifold*
[o] Other ancient authorities insert *Lord*
[m] The denarius was a day's wage for a laborer
[p] Other ancient authorities omit *of God*
[n] Or *is your eye evil because I am good?*

the tables of the money-changers and the seats of those
13 who sold pigeons. He said to them, "It is written, 'My house shall be called a house of prayer'; but you make it a den of robbers."

14 And the blind and the lame came to him in the temple,
15 and he healed them. But when the chief priests and the scribes saw the wonderful things that he did, and the children crying out in the temple, "Hosanna to the Son
16 of David!" they were indignant; and they said to him, "Do you hear what these are saying?" And Jesus said to them, "Yes; have you never read,

'Out of the mouth of babes and sucklings
thou hast brought perfect praise'?"

17 And leaving them, he went out of the city to Bethany and lodged there.

The Fig Tree

18 In the morning, as he was returning to the city, he was
19 hungry. And seeing a fig tree by the wayside he went to it, and found nothing on it but leaves only. And he said to it, "May no fruit ever come from you again!" And
20 the fig tree withered at once. When the disciples saw it they marveled, saying, "How did the fig tree wither at
21 once?" And Jesus answered them, "Truly, I say to you, if you have faith and never doubt, you will not only do what has been done to the fig tree, but even if you say to this mountain, 'Be taken up and cast into the sea,'
22 it will be done. And whatever you ask in prayer, you will receive, if you have faith."

Discussions and Controversies

23 And when he entered the temple, the chief priests and the elders of the people came up to him as he was teaching, and said, "By what authority are you doing these
24 things, and who gave you this authority?" Jesus answered them, "I also will ask you a question; and if you tell me the answer, then I also will tell you by what
25 authority I do these things. The baptism of John, whence was it? From heaven or from men?" And they argued with one another, "If we say, 'From heaven,' he will say
26 to us, 'Why then did you not believe him?' But if we say,

'From men,' we are afraid of the multitude; for all hold
27 that John was a prophet." So they answered Jesus, "We do not know." And he said to them, "Neither will I tell you by what authority I do these things.

28 "What do you think? A man had two sons; and he went to the first and said, 'Son, go and work in the vine-
29 yard today.' And he answered, 'I will not'; but afterward
30 he repented and went. And he went to the second and said the same; and he answered, 'I go, sir,' but did not
31 go. Which of the two did the will of his father?" They said, "The first." Jesus said to them, "Truly, I say to you, the tax collectors and the harlots go into the kingdom of
32 God before you. For John came to you in the way of righteousness, and you did not believe him, but the tax collectors and the harlots believed him; and even when you saw it, you did not afterward repent and believe him.

33 "Hear another parable. There was a householder who planted a vineyard, and set a hedge around it, and dug a wine press in it, and built a tower, and let it out to
34 tenants, and went into another country. When the season of fruit drew near, he sent his servants to the tenants, to
35 get his fruit; and the tenants took his servants and beat
36 one, killed another, and stoned another. Again he sent other servants, more than the first; and they did the same
37 to them. Afterward he sent his son to them, saying, 'They
38 will respect my son.' But when the tenants saw the son, they said to themselves, 'This is the heir; come, let us
39 kill him and have his inheritance.' And they took him and
40 cast him out of the vineyard, and killed him. When therefore the owner of the vineyard comes, what will he do to
41 those tenants?" They said to him, "He will put those wretches to a miserable death, and let out the vineyard to other tenants who will give him the fruits in their seasons."

42 Jesus said to them, "Have you never read in the scriptures:
'The very stone which the builders rejected
has become the head of the corner;
this was the Lord's doing,
and it is marvelous in our eyes'?
43 Therefore I tell you, the kingdom of God will be taken away from you and given to a nation producing the fruits of it." q

45 When the chief priests and the Pharisees heard his parables, they perceived that he was speaking about them.
46 But when they tried to arrest him, they feared the multitudes, because they held him to be a prophet.

22 And again Jesus spoke to them in parables, saying,
2 "The kingdom of heaven may be compared to a king
3 who gave a marriage feast for his son, and sent his servants to call those who were invited to the marriage
4 feast; but they would not come. Again he sent other servants, saying, 'Tell those who are invited, Behold, I

q Other ancient authorities add verse 44, *And he who falls on this stone will be broken to pieces; but when it falls on any one, it will crush him*

have made ready my dinner, my oxen and my fat calves
are killed, and everything is ready; come to the marriage
⁵ feast.' But they made light of it and went off, one to his
⁶ farm, another to his business, while the rest seized his
⁷ servants, treated them shamefully, and killed them. The
king was angry, and he sent his troops and destroyed
⁸ those murderers and burned their city. Then he said to
his servants, 'The wedding is ready, but those invited
⁹ were not worthy. Go therefore to the thoroughfares, and
¹⁰ invite to the marriage feast as many as you find.' And
those servants went out into the streets and gathered all
whom they found, both bad and good; so the wedding hall
was filled with guests.

¹¹ "But when the king came in to look at the guests, he
saw there a man who had no wedding garment;
¹² and he said to him, 'Friend, how did you get in here
without a wedding garment?' And he was speechless.
¹³ Then the king said to the attendants, 'Bind him hand and
foot, and cast him into the outer darkness; there men will
¹⁴ weep and gnash their teeth.' For many are called, but few
are chosen."

¹⁵ Then the Pharisees went and took counsel how to
¹⁶ entangle him in his talk. And they sent their disciples to
him, along with the Hero′di-ans, saying, "Teacher, we
know that you are true, and teach the way of God truth-
fully, and care for no man; for you do not regard the
¹⁷ position of men. Tell us, then, what you think. Is it lawful
¹⁸ to pay taxes to Caesar, or not?" But Jesus, aware of their
malice, said, "Why put me to the test, you hypocrites?
¹⁹ Show me the money for the tax." And they brought him
²⁰ a coin.ʳ And Jesus said to them, "Whose likeness and
²¹ inscription is this?" They said, "Caesar's." Then he said
to them, "Render therefore to Caesar the things that are
²² Caesar's, and to God the things that are God's." When
they heard it, they marveled; and they left him and went
away.

²³ The same day Sad′ducees came to him, who say that
there is no resurrection; and they asked him a question,
²⁴ saying, "Teacher, Moses said, 'If a man dies, having no
children, his brother must marry the widow, and raise
²⁵ up children for his brother.' Now there were seven
brothers among us; the first married, and died, and hav-
²⁶ ing no children left his wife to his brother. So too the
²⁷ second and third, down to the seventh. After them all,
²⁸ the woman died. In the resurrection, therefore, to which of
the seven will she be wife? For they all had her."

²⁹ But Jesus answered them, "You are wrong, because
you know neither the scriptures nor the power of God.
³⁰ For in the resurrection they neither marry nor are given
³¹ in marriage, but are like angels ˢ in heaven. And as for
the resurrection of the dead, have you not read what was
³² said to you by God, 'I am the God of Abraham, and the
God of Isaac, and the God of Jacob'? He is not God of

³³ the dead, but of the living." And when the crowd heard
it, they were astonished at his teaching.

³⁴ But when the Pharisees heard that he had silenced the
³⁵ Sad′ducees, they came together. And one of them, a
³⁶ lawyer, asked him a question, to test him. "Teacher, which
³⁷ is the great commandment in the law?" And he said to
him, "You shall love the Lord your God with all your
heart, and with all your soul, and with all your mind.
³⁸, ³⁹ This is the great and first commandment. And a second
⁴⁰ is like it, You shall love your neighbor as yourself. On
these two commandments depend all the law and the
prophets."

⁴¹ Now while the Pharisees were gathered together, Jesus
⁴² asked them a question, saying, "What do you think of
the Christ? Whose son is he?" They said to him, "The
⁴³ son of David." He said to them, "How is it then that
David, inspired by the Spirit,ᵗ calls him Lord, saying,

⁴⁴ 'The Lord said to my Lord,
Sit at my right hand,
till I put thy enemies under thy feet'?
⁴⁵ If David thus calls him Lord, how is he his son?"
⁴⁶ And no one was able to answer him a word, nor from
that day did any one dare to ask him any more questions.

Scribes and Pharisees Denounced

23 Then said Jesus to the crowds and to his disciples,
² "The scribes and the Pharisees sit on Moses' seat;
³ so practice and observe whatever they tell you, but not
what they do; for they preach, but do not practice.
⁴ They bind heavy burdens, hard to bear,ᵘ and lay them
on men's shoulders; but they themselves will not move
⁵ them with their finger. They do all their deeds to be seen
by men; for they make their phylacteries broad and their
⁶ fringes long, and they love the place of honor at feasts
⁷ and the best seats in the synagogues, and salutations in
⁸ the market places, and being called rabbi by men. But you
are not to be called rabbi, for you have one teacher, and
⁹ you are all brethren. And call no man your father on
¹⁰ earth, for you have one Father, who is in heaven. Neither
be called masters, for you have one master, the Christ.
¹¹ He who is greatest among you shall be your servant;
¹² whoever exalts himself will be humbled, and whoever

ʳ Greek *a denarius*   ˢ Other ancient authorities add *of God*
ᵘ Other ancient authorities omit *hard to bear*

ᵗ Or *David in the Spirit*

humbles himself will be exalted.

13 "But woe to you, scribes and Pharisees, hypocrites! because you shut the kingdom of heaven against men; for you neither enter yourselves, nor allow those who 15 would enter to go in.ᵛ Woe to you, scribes and Pharisees, hypocrites! for you traverse sea and land to make a single proselyte, and when he becomes a proselyte, you make him twice as much a child of hell ʷ as yourselves.

16 "Woe to you, blind guides, who say, 'If any one swears by the temple, it is nothing; but if any one swears by the 17 gold of the temple, he is bound by his oath.' You blind fools! For which is greater, the gold or the temple that 18 has made the gold sacred? And you say, 'If any one swears by the altar, it is nothing; but if any one swears by the gift that is on the altar, he is bound by his oath.' 19 You blind men! For which is greater, the gift or the altar 20 that makes the gift sacred? So he who swears by the 21 altar, swears by it and by everything on it; and he who swears by the temple, swears by it and by him who dwells 22 in it; and he who swears by heaven, swears by the throne of God and by him who sits upon it.

23 "Woe to you, scribes and Pharisees, hypocrites! for you tithe mint and dill and cummin, and have neglected the weightier matters of the law, justice and mercy and faith; these you ought to have done, without neglecting 24 the others. You blind guides, straining out a gnat and swallowing a camel!

25 "Woe to you, scribes and Pharisees, hypocrites! for you cleanse the outside of the cup and of the plate, but 26 inside they are full of extortion and rapacity. You blind Pharisee! first cleanse the inside of the cup and of the plate, that the outside also may be clean.

27 "Woe to you, scribes and Pharisees, hypocrites! for you are like whitewashed tombs, which outwardly appear beautiful, but within they are full of dead men's bones 28 and all uncleanness. So you also outwardly appear righteous to men, but within you are full of hypocrisy and iniquity.

29 "Woe to you, scribes and Pharisees, hypocrites! for you build the tombs of the prophets and adorn the monu- 30 ments of the righteous, saying, 'If we had lived in the days of our fathers, we would not have taken part with 31 them in shedding the blood of the prophets.' Thus you witness against yourselves, that you are sons of those who 32 murdered the prophets. Fill up, then, the measure of your 33 fathers. You serpents, you brood of vipers, how are you 34 to escape being sentenced to hell? ʷ Therefore I send you prophets and wise men and scribes, some of whom you will kill and crucify, and some you will scourge in your 35 synagogues and persecute from town to town, that upon you may come all the righteous blood shed on earth, from the blood of innocent Abel to the blood of Zechari′ah the son of Barachi′ah, whom you murdered between the

36 sanctuary and the altar. Truly, I say to you, all this will come upon this generation.

37 "O Jerusalem, Jerusalem, killing the prophets and stoning those who are sent to you! How often would I have gathered your children together as a hen gathers 38 her brood under her wings, and you would not! Behold, 39 your house is forsaken and desolate.ˣ For I tell you, you will not see me again, until you say, 'Blessed is he who comes in the name of the Lord.' "

JESUS TELLS HIS DISCIPLES OF THE END OF THE AGE

24 Jesus left the temple and was going away, when his disciples came to point out to him the buildings 2 of the temple. But he answered them, "You see all these, do you not? Truly, I say to you, there will not be left here one stone upon another, that will not be thrown down."

3 As he sat on the Mount of Olives, the disciples came to him privately, saying, "Tell us, when will this be, and what will be the sign of your coming and of the 4 close of the age?" And Jesus answered them, "Take heed 5 that no one leads you astray. For many will come in my name, saying, 'I am the Christ,' and they will lead 6 many astray. And you will hear of wars and rumors of wars; see that you are not alarmed; for this must take 7 place, but the end is not yet. For nation will rise against nation, and kingdom against kingdom, and there will be 8 famines and earthquakes in various places: all this is but the beginning of the birth-pangs.

9 "Then they will deliver you up to tribulation, and put you to death; and you will be hated by all nations for 10 my name's sake. And then many will fall away,ʸ and 11 betray one another, and hate one another. And many false 12 prophets will arise and lead many astray. And because wickedness is multiplied, most men's love will grow cold. 13, 14 But he who endures to the end will be saved. And this gospel of the kingdom will be preached throughout the whole world, as a testimony to all nations; and then the end will come.

15 "So when you see the desolating sacrilege spoken of by the prophet Daniel, standing in the holy place (let the 16 reader understand), then let those who are in Judea flee 17 to the mountains; let him who is on the housetop not 18 go down to take what is in his house; and let him who 19 is in the field not turn back to take his mantle. And alas for those who are with child and for those who give 20 suck in those days! Pray that your flight may not be in 21 winter or on a sabbath. For then there will be great tribulation, such as has not been from the beginning of 22 the world until now, no, and never will be. And if those days had not been shortened, no human being would be saved; but for the sake of the elect those days will be

ᵛ Other authorities add here (or after verse 12) verse 14, *Woe to you, scribes and Pharisees, hypocrites! for you devour widows' houses and for a pretense you make long prayers; therefore you will receive the greater condemnation* ʷ Greek *Gehenna* ˣ Other ancient authorities omit *and desolate* ʸ Or *stumble*

23 shortened. Then if any one says to you, 'Lo, here is
24 the Christ!' or 'There he is!' do not believe it. For false
Christs and false prophets will arise and show great signs
and wonders, so as to lead astray, if possible, even the
25, 26 elect. Lo, I have told you beforehand. So, if they say to
you, 'Lo, he is in the wilderness,' do not go out; if they
say, 'Lo, he is in the inner rooms,' do not believe it.
27 For as the lightning comes from the east and shines as
far as the west, so will be the coming of the Son of man.
28 Wherever the body is, there the eagles[z] will be gathered
together.

29 "Immediately after the tribulation of those days the
sun will be darkened, and the moon will not give its
light, and the stars will fall from heaven, and the powers
30 of the heavens will be shaken; then will appear the sign
of the Son of man in heaven, and then all the tribes of the
earth will mourn, and they will see the Son of man coming on the clouds of heaven with power and great glory;
31 and he will send out his angels with a loud trumpet call,
and they will gather his elect from the four winds, from
one end of heaven to the other.

32 "From the fig tree learn its lesson: as soon as its branch
becomes tender and puts forth its leaves, you know that
33 summer is near. So also, when you see all these things,
34 you know that he is near, at the very gates. Truly, I say
to you, this generation will not pass away till all these
35 things take place. Heaven and earth will pass away, but
my words will not pass away.

36 "But of that day and hour no one knows, not even
the angels of heaven, nor the Son,[a] but the Father only.
37 As were the days of Noah, so will be the coming of the
38 Son of man. For as in those days before the flood they
were eating and drinking, marrying and giving in mar-
39 riage, until the day when Noah entered the ark, and they
did not know until the flood came and swept them all
40 away, so will be the coming of the Son of man. Then two
41 men will be in the field; one is taken and one is left. Two
women will be grinding at the mill; one is taken and
42 one is left. Watch therefore, for you do not know on what
43 day your Lord is coming. But know this, that if the householder had known in what part of the night the thief
was coming, he would have watched and would not have
44 let his house be broken into. Therefore you also must be
ready; for the Son of man is coming at an hour you do
not expect.

45 "Who then is the faithful and wise servant, whom his
master has set over his household, to give them their
46 food at the proper time? Blessed is that servant whom
47 his master when he comes will find so doing. Truly, I
48 say to you, he will set him over all his possessions. But if
that wicked servant says to himself, 'My master is
49 delayed,' and begins to beat his fellow servants, and eats
50 and drinks with the drunken, the master of that servant

will come on a day when he does not expect him and at
51 an hour he does not know, and will punish[b] him, and put
him with the hypocrites; there men will weep and gnash
their teeth.

25 "Then the kingdom of heaven shall be compared
to ten maidens who took their lamps and went to
2 meet the bridegroom.[c] Five of them were foolish, and
3 five were wise. For when the foolish took their lamps,
4 they took no oil with them; but the wise took flasks of
5 oil with their lamps. As the bridegroom was delayed, they
6 all slumbered and slept. But at midnight there was a cry,
7 'Behold, the bridegroom! Come out to meet him.' Then
8 all those maidens rose and trimmed their lamps. And the
foolish said to the wise, 'Give us some of your oil, for
9 our lamps are going out.' But the wise replied, 'Perhaps
there will not be enough for us and for you; go rather to
10 the dealers and buy for yourselves.' And while they went
to buy, the bridegroom came, and those who were ready
went in with him to the marriage feast; and the door was
11 shut. Afterward the other maidens came also, saying,
12 'Lord, lord, open to us.' But he replied, 'Truly, I say to
13 you, I do not know you.' Watch therefore, for you know
neither the day nor the hour.

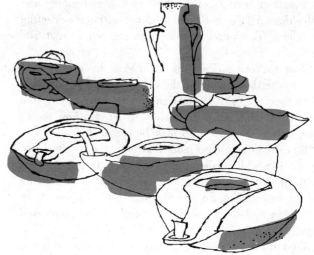

14 "For it will be as when a man going on a journey called
15 his servants and entrusted to them his property; to one
he gave five talents,[d] to another two, to another one, to
16 each according to his ability. Then he went away. He
who had received the five talents went at once and traded
17 with them; and he made five talents more. So also, he who
18 had the two talents made two talents more. But he who
had received the one talent went and dug in the ground
19 and hid his master's money. Now after a long time the
master of those servants came and settled accounts with
20 them. And he who had received the five talents came
forward, bringing five talents more, saying, 'Master, you
delivered to me five talents; here I have made five talents

---

[z] Or *vultures*   [a] Other ancient authorities omit *nor the Son*   [b] Or *cut him in pieces*
[c] Other ancient authorities add *and the bride*   [d] This talent was more than fifteen years' wages of a laborer

21 more.' His master said to him, 'Well done, good and faithful servant; you have been faithful over a little, I will set you over much; enter into the joy of your master.'
22 And he also who had the two talents came forward, saying, 'Master, you delivered to me two talents; here I
23 have made two talents more.' His master said to him, 'Well done, good and faithful servant; you have been faithful over a little, I will set you over much; enter into
24 the joy of your master.' He also who had received the one talent came forward, saying, 'Master, I knew you to be a hard man, reaping where you did not sow, and
25 gathering where you did not winnow; so I was afraid, and I went and hid your talent in the ground. Here you
26 have what is yours.' But his master answered him, 'You wicked and slothful servant! You knew that I reap where I have not sowed, and gather where I have not winnowed?
27 Then you ought to have invested my money with the bankers, and at my coming I should have received what
28 was my own with interest. So take the talent from him,
29 and give it to him who has the ten talents. For to every one who has will more be given, and he will have abundance; but from him who has not, even what he
30 has will be taken away. And cast the worthless servant into the outer darkness; there men will weep and gnash their teeth.'
31 "When the Son of man comes in his glory, and all the angels with him, then he will sit on his glorious throne.
32 Before him will be gathered all the nations, and he will separate them one from another as a shepherd separates
33 the sheep from the goats, and he will place the sheep at
34 his right hand, but the goats at the left. Then the King will say to those at his right hand, 'Come, O blessed of my Father, inherit the kingdom prepared for you from
35 the foundation of the world; for I was hungry and you gave me food, I was thirsty and you gave me drink,
36 I was a stranger and you welcomed me, I was naked and you clothed me, I was sick and you visited
37 me, I was in prison and you came to me.' Then the righteous will answer him, 'Lord, when did we see thee hungry and feed thee, or thirsty and give thee drink?
38 And when did we see thee a stranger and welcome thee,
39 or naked and clothe thee? And when did we see thee
40 sick or in prison and visit thee?' And the King will answer them, 'Truly, I say to you, as you did it to one of the
41 least of these my brethren, you did it to me.' Then he will say to those at his left hand, 'Depart from me, you cursed, into the eternal fire prepared for the devil and
42 his angels; for I was hungry and you gave me no food,
43 I was thirsty and you gave me no drink, I was a stranger and you did not welcome me, naked and you did not clothe me, sick and in prison and you did not visit me.'
44 Then they also will answer, 'Lord, when did we see thee hungry or thirsty or a stranger or naked or sick or in
45 prison, and did not minister to thee?' Then he will answer them, 'Truly, I say to you, as you did it not to one of the
46 least of these, you did it not to me.' And they will go away into eternal punishment, but the righteous into eternal life."

26 When Jesus had finished all these sayings, he said
2 to his disciples, "You know that after two days the Passover is coming, and the Son of man will be delivered up to be crucified."

THE EVENTS LEADING TO JESUS' DEATH

3 Then the chief priests and the elders of the people gathered in the palace of the high priest, who was called
4 Ca'iaphas, and took counsel together in order to arrest
5 Jesus by stealth and kill him. But they said, "Not during the feast, lest there be a tumult among the people."
6 Now when Jesus was at Bethany in the house of Simon
7 the leper, a woman came up to him with an alabaster flask of very expensive ointment, and she poured it on his
8 head, as he sat at table. But when the disciples saw it,
9 they were indignant, saying, "Why this waste? For this ointment might have been sold for a large sum, and given
10 to the poor." But Jesus, aware of this, said to them, "Why do you trouble the woman? For she has done a beautiful
11 thing to me. For you always have the poor with you, but
12 you will not always have me. In pouring this ointment on
13 my body she has done it to prepare me for burial. Truly, I say to you, wherever this gospel is preached in the whole world, what she has done will be told in memory of her."
14 Then one of the twelve, who was called Judas Iscariot,
15 went to the chief priests and said, "What will you give me if I deliver him to you?" And they paid him thirty
16 pieces of silver. And from that moment he sought an opportunity to betray him.
17 Now on the first day of Unleavened Bread the disciples came to Jesus, saying, "Where will you have us prepare
18 for you to eat the passover?" He said, "Go into the city to a certain one, and say to him, 'The Teacher says, My time is at hand; I will keep the passover at your
19 house with my disciples.'" And the disciples did as Jesus had directed them, and they prepared the passover.
20 When it was evening, he sat at table with the twelve
21 disciples; e and as they were eating, he said, "Truly, I
22 say to you, one of you will betray me." And they were very sorrowful, and began to say to him one after another,
23 "Is it I, Lord?" He answered, "He who has dipped his
24 hand in the dish with me, will betray me. The Son of man goes as it is written of him, but woe to that man by whom the Son of man is betrayed! It would have been better
25 for that man if he had not been born." Judas, who betrayed him, said, "Is it I, Master?" f He said to him, "You have said so."

e Other authorities omit *disciples*   f Or *Rabbi*

26 Now as they were eating, Jesus took bread, and blessed, and broke it, and gave it to the disciples and said, "Take,
27 eat; this is my body." And he took a cup, and when he had given thanks he gave it to them, saying, "Drink
28 of it, all of you; for this is my blood of the g covenant, which is poured out for many for the forgiveness of sins.
29 I tell you I shall not drink again of this fruit of the vine until that day when I drink it new with you in my Father's kingdom."
30 And when they had sung a hymn, they went out to the
31 Mount of Olives. Then Jesus said to them, "You will all fall away because of me this night; for it is written, 'I will strike the shepherd, and the sheep of the flock will
32 be scattered.' But after I am raised up, I will go before

33 you to Galilee." Peter declared to him, "Though they all fall away because of you, I will never fall away."
34 Jesus said to him, "Truly, I say to you, this very night, before the cock crows, you will deny me three times."
35 Peter said to him, "Even if I must die with you, I will not deny you." And so said all the disciples.
36 Then Jesus went with them to a place called Geth-sem'ane, and he said to his disciples, "Sit here, while I
37 go yonder and pray." And taking with him Peter and the two sons of Zeb'edee, he began to be sorrowful and
38 troubled. Then he said to them, "My soul is very sorrow-ful, even to death; remain here, and watch h with me."
39 And going a little farther he fell on his face and prayed, "My Father, if it be possible, let this cup pass from me;
40 nevertheless, not as I will, but as thou wilt." And he came to the disciples and found them sleeping; and he said to Peter, "So, could you not watch h with me one hour?
41 Watch h and pray that you may not enter into tempta-tion; the spirit indeed is willing, but the flesh is weak."
42 Again, for the second time, he went away and prayed, "My Father, if this cannot pass unless I drink it, thy
43 will be done." And again he came and found them
44 sleeping, for their eyes were heavy. So, leaving them again, he went away and prayed for the third time,
45 saying the same words. Then he came to the disciples and said to them, "Are you still sleeping and taking your rest? Behold, the hour is at hand, and the Son of man is
46 betrayed into the hands of sinners. Rise, let us be going; see, my betrayer is at hand."
47 While he was still speaking, Judas came, one of the twelve, and with him a great crowd with swords and clubs,

48 from the chief priests and the elders of the people. Now the betrayer had given them a sign, saying, "The one I
49 shall kiss is the man; seize him." And he came up to Jesus at once and said, "Hail, Master!" i And he kissed
50 him. Jesus said to him, "Friend, why are you here?" j Then they came up and laid hands on Jesus and seized
51 him. And behold, one of those who were with Jesus stretched out his hand and drew his sword, and struck
52 the slave of the high priest, and cut off his ear. Then Jesus said to him, "Put your sword back into its place; for all who take the sword will perish by the sword.
53 Do you think that I cannot appeal to my Father, and he will at once send me more than twelve legions of angels?
54 But how then should the scriptures be fulfilled, that it
55 must be so?" At that hour Jesus said to the crowds, "Have you come out as against a robber, with swords and clubs to capture me? Day after day I sat in the temple teaching,
56 and you did not seize me. But all this has taken place, that the scriptures of the prophets might be fulfilled." Then all the disciples forsook him and fled.
57 Then those who had seized Jesus led him to Ca'iaphas the high priest, where the scribes and the elders had
58 gathered. But Peter followed him at a distance, as far as the courtyard of the high priest, and going inside he
59 sat with the guards to see the end. Now the chief priests and the whole council sought false testimony against
60 Jesus that they might put him to death, but they found none, though many false witnesses came forward. At last
61 two came forward and said, "This fellow said, 'I am able to destroy the temple of God, and to build it in three
62 days.'" And the high priest stood up and said, "Have you no answer to make? What is it that these men
63 testify against you?" But Jesus was silent. And the high priest said to him, "I adjure you by the living God, tell
64 us if you are the Christ, the Son of God." Jesus said to him, "You have said so. But I tell you, hereafter you will see the Son of man seated at the right hand of Power,
65 and coming on the clouds of heaven." Then the high priest tore his robes, and said, "He has uttered blasphemy. Why do we still need witnesses? You have now heard his
66 blasphemy. What is your judgment?" They answered, "He
67 deserves death." Then they spat in his face, and struck
68 him; and some slapped him, saying, "Prophesy to us, you Christ! Who is it that struck you?"
69 Now Peter was sitting outside in the courtyard. And a maid came up to him, and said, "You also were with
70 Jesus the Galilean." But he denied it before them all,
71 saying, "I do not know what you mean." And when he went out to the porch, another maid saw him, and she said to the bystanders, "This man was with Jesus of Naza-
72 reth." And again he denied it with an oath, "I do not
73 know the man." After a little while the bystanders came up and said to Peter, "Certainly you are also one of them,

g Other ancient authorities insert *new*   h Or *keep awake*   i Or *Rabbi*   j Or *do that for which you have come*

74 for your accent betrays you." Then he began to invoke
a curse on himself and to swear, "I do not know the
75 man." And immediately the cock crowed. And Peter
remembered the saying of Jesus, "Before the cock crows,
you will deny me three times." And he went out and
wept bitterly.

27 When morning came, all the chief priests and the
elders of the people took counsel against Jesus to put
2 him to death; and they bound him and led him away
and delivered him to Pilate the governor.

3 When Judas, his betrayer, saw that he was condemned,
he repented and brought back the thirty pieces of silver
4 to the chief priests and the elders, saying, "I have sinned
in betraying innocent blood." They said, "What is that
5 to us? See to it yourself." And throwing down the pieces
of silver in the temple, he departed; and he went and
6 hanged himself. But the chief priests, taking the pieces of
silver, said, "It is not lawful to put them into the treasury,
7 since they are blood money." So they took counsel, and
bought with them the potter's field, to bury strangers in.
8 Therefore that field has been called the Field of Blood to
9 this day. Then was fulfilled what had been spoken by the
prophet Jeremiah, saying, "And they took the thirty
pieces of silver, the price of him on whom a price had
10 been set by some of the sons of Israel, and they gave
them for the potter's field, as the Lord directed me."

11 Now Jesus stood before the governor; and the governor
asked him, "Are you the King of the Jews?" Jesus said,
12 "You have said so." But when he was accused by the
13 chief priests and elders, he made no answer. Then
Pilate said to him, "Do you not hear how many things
14 they testify against you?" But he gave him no answer,
not even to a single charge; so that the governor wondered
greatly.

15 Now at the feast the governor was accustomed to release for the crowd any one prisoner whom they wanted.
16 And they had then a notorious prisoner, called Barab'-
17 bas.k So when they had gathered, Pilate said to them,
"Whom do you want me to release for you, Barab'bas k
18 or Jesus who is called Christ?" For he knew that it was
19 out of envy that they had delivered him up. Besides,
while he was sitting on the judgment seat, his wife sent
word to him, "Have nothing to do with that righteous
man, for I have suffered much over him today in a
20 dream." Now the chief priests and the elders persuaded
21 the people to ask for Barab'bas and destroy Jesus. The
governor again said to them, "Which of the two do you
want me to release for you?" And they said, "Barab'bas."
22 Pilate said to them, "Then what shall I do with Jesus
who is called Christ?" They all said, "Let him be
23 crucified." And he said, "Why, what evil has he done?"
But they shouted all the more, "Let him be crucified."

24 So when Pilate saw that he was gaining nothing, but

rather that a riot was beginning, he took water and
washed his hands before the crowd, saying, "I am innocent of this man's blood;l see to it yourselves."
25 And all the people answered, "His blood be on us and
26 on our children!" Then he released for them Barab'bas,
and having scourged Jesus, delivered him to be crucified.

THE CRUCIFIXION

27 Then the soldiers of the governor took Jesus into the
praetorium, and they gathered the whole battalion before
28 him. And they stripped him and put a scarlet robe upon
29 him, and plaiting a crown of thorns they put it on his
head, and put a reed in his right hand. And kneeling
before him they mocked him, saying, "Hail, King of

30 the Jews!" And they spat upon him, and took the reed
31 and struck him on the head. And when they had mocked
him, they stripped him of the robe, and put his own
clothes on him, and led him away to crucify him.

32 As they went out, they came upon a man of
Cyre'ne, Simon by name; this man they compelled to
33 carry his cross. And when they came to a place called
34 Gol'gotha (which means the place of a skull), they offered
him wine to drink, mingled with gall; but when he
35 tasted it, he would not drink it. And when they had
crucified him, they divided his garments among them by
36 casting lots; then they sat down and kept watch over
37 him there. And over his head they put the charge against
him, which read, "This is Jesus the King of the Jews."
38 Then two robbers were crucified with him, one on the
39 right and one on the left. And those who passed by
40 derided him, wagging their heads and saying, "You who
would destroy the temple and build it in three days, save
yourself! If you are the Son of God, come down from
41 the cross." So also the chief priests, with the scribes and
42 elders, mocked him, saying, "He saved others; he cannot
save himself. He is the King of Israel; let him come down
43 now from the cross, and we will believe in him. He trusts
in God; let God deliver him now, if he desires him; for
44 he said, 'I am the Son of God.'" And the robbers who
were crucified with him also reviled him in the same way.

45 Now from the sixth hour there was darkness over all
46 the land m until the ninth hour. And about the ninth hour

k Other ancient authorities read *Jesus Barabbas*   l Other authorities read *this righteous blood* or *this righteous man's blood*
m Or *earth*

Jesus cried with a loud voice, "Eli, Eli, la'ma sabach-tha'-ni?" that is, "My God, my God, why hast thou forsaken 47 me?" And some of the bystanders hearing it said, "This 48 man is calling Eli'jah." And one of them at once ran and took a sponge, filled it with vinegar, and put it on a reed, 49 and gave it to him to drink. But the others said, "Wait, let us see whether Eli'jah will come to save him." n 50 And Jesus cried again with a loud voice and yielded up his spirit.

51 And behold, the curtain of the temple was torn in two, from top to bottom; and the earth shook, and the rocks 52 were split; the tombs also were opened, and many bodies 53 of the saints who had fallen asleep were raised, and coming out of the tombs after his resurrection they went 54 into the holy city and appeared to many. When the centurion and those who were with him, keeping watch over Jesus, saw the earthquake and what took place, they were filled with awe, and said, "Truly this was the Son x of God!"

55 There were also many women there, looking on from afar, who had followed Jesus from Galilee, ministering to 56 him; among whom were Mary Mag'dalene, and Mary the mother of James and Joseph, and the mother of the sons of Zeb'edee.

THE BURIAL OF JESUS

57 When it was evening, there came a rich man from Arimathe'a, named Joseph, who also was a disciple of 58 Jesus. He went to Pilate and asked for the body of Jesus. 59 Then Pilate ordered it to be given to him. And Joseph took the body, and wrapped it in a clean linen shroud, 60 and laid it in his own new tomb, which he had hewn in the rock; and he rolled a great stone to the door of the 61 tomb, and departed. Mary Mag'dalene and the other Mary were there, sitting opposite the sepulchre.

62 Next day, that is, after the day of Preparation, the chief priests and the Pharisees gathered before Pilate 63 and said, "Sir, we remember how that impostor said, while he was still alive, 'After three days I will rise again.' 64 Therefore order the sepulchre to be made secure until the third day, lest his disciples go and steal him away, and tell the people, 'He has risen from the dead,' and 65 the last fraud will be worse than the first." Pilate said to them, "You have a guard o of soldiers; go, make it as 66 secure as you can." p So they went and made the sepulchre secure by sealing the stone and setting a guard.

THE RESURRECTION

28 Now after the sabbath, toward the dawn of the first day of the week, Mary Mag'dalene and the 2 other Mary went to see the sepulchre. And behold, there was a great earthquake; for an angel of the Lord descended from heaven and came and rolled back the 3 stone, and sat upon it. His appearance was like lightning, 4 and his raiment white as snow. And for fear of him the 5 guards trembled and became like dead men. But the angel said to the women, "Do not be afraid; for I know 6 that you seek Jesus who was crucified. He is not here; for he has risen, as he said. Come, see the place where he q 7 lay. Then go quickly and tell his disciples that he has risen from the dead, and behold, he is going before you to Galilee; there you will see him. Lo, I have told you." 8 So they departed quickly from the tomb with fear and 9 great joy, and ran to tell his disciples. And behold, Jesus met them and said, "Hail!" And they came up and took 10 hold of his feet and worshiped him. Then Jesus said to them, "Do not be afraid; go and tell my brethren to go to Galilee, and there they will see me."

11 While they were going, behold, some of the guard went into the city and told the chief priests all that had taken 12 place. And when they had assembled with the elders and taken counsel, they gave a sum of money to the soldiers 13 and said, "Tell people, 'His disciples came by night and 14 stole him away while we were asleep.' And if this comes to the governor's ears, we will satisfy him and keep you 15 out of trouble." So they took the money and did as they were directed; and this story has been spread among the Jews to this day.

16 Now the eleven disciples went to Galilee, to the moun- 17 tain to which Jesus had directed them. And when they 18 saw him they worshiped him; but some doubted. And Jesus came and said to them, "All authority in heaven 19 and on earth has been given to me. Go therefore and make disciples of all nations, baptizing them in the name of the Father and of the Son and of the Holy Spirit, 20 teaching them to observe all that I have commanded you; and lo, I am with you always, to the close of the age."

n Other ancient authorities insert *And another took a spear and pierced his side, and out came water and blood*   o Or *Take a guard*
x Or *a son*   p Greek *know*   q Other ancient authorities read *the Lord*

INTRODUCTION TO

MARK

The Gospel According to Mark was written sometime between A.D. 65 and A.D. 70, before any of the other Gospels in the New Testament.

John Mark was not one of the twelve apostles, but it was in his mother's house that Christians sometimes met. Probably it was there that Jesus and the twelve apostles ate the Last Supper together. Ancient writings from the early church tell us that Mark was with Peter when he went to Rome and that much that Mark wrote about Jesus came from Peter's sermons and conversations about Jesus.

There is nothing in Mark about Jesus' birth or boyhood. The account begins with Jesus going to John the Baptist to be baptized by him. It shows Jesus as a man of action and authority, and it was probably written for the Christians at Rome. It is plainly for Gentiles (non-Jews) and would certainly appeal to Romans, who admired men of power and action.

Because Mark's was the first story of Jesus to be written, copies were sent to various churches. It was one of the main sources used by other writers who prepared fuller accounts of the good news that Jesus was the long awaited Christ or Messiah. When you read the Gospel of Matthew and the Gospel of Luke, you will find much of Mark included.

THE GOSPEL ACCORDING TO

MARK

JOHN THE BAPTIZER AND JESUS

1 The beginning of the gospel of Jesus Christ, the Son of God.[a]

2 As it is written in Isaiah the prophet,[b]
"Behold, I send my messenger before thy face,
who shall prepare thy way;

3 the voice of one crying in the wilderness:
Prepare the way of the Lord,
make his paths straight—"

4 John the baptizer appeared[c] in the wilderness, preaching a baptism of repentance for the forgiveness of sins. 5 And there went out to him all the country of Judea, and all the people of Jerusalem; and they were baptized by 6 him in the river Jordan, confessing their sins. Now John was clothed with camel's hair, and had a leather girdle 7 around his waist, and ate locusts and wild honey. And he preached, saying, "After me comes he who is mightier than I, the thong of whose sandals I am not worthy to 8 stoop down and untie. I have baptized you with water; but he will baptize you with the Holy Spirit."

9 In those days Jesus came from Nazareth of Galilee and 10 was baptized by John in the Jordan. And when he came up out of the water, immediately he saw the heavens opened and the Spirit descending upon him like a dove; 11 and a voice came from heaven, "Thou art my beloved Son;[d] with thee I am well pleased."

12 The Spirit immediately drove him out into the wilder- 13 ness. And he was in the wilderness forty days, tempted by Satan; and he was with the wild beasts; and the angels ministered to him.

JESUS IN GALILEE

14 Now after John was arrested, Jesus came into Galilee, 15 preaching the gospel of God, and saying, "The time is fulfilled, and the kingdom of God is at hand; repent, and believe in the gospel."

16 And passing along by the Sea of Galilee, he saw Simon and Andrew the brother of Simon casting a net 17 in the sea; for they were fishermen. And Jesus said to them, "Follow me and I will make you become fishers 18 of men." And immediately they left their nets and fol- 19 lowed him. And going on a little farther, he saw James the son of Zeb'edee and John his brother, who were in 20 their boat mending the nets. And immediately he called them; and they left their father Zeb'edee in the boat with the hired servants, and followed him.

21 And they went into Caper'na-um; and immediately on 22 the sabbath he entered the synagogue and taught. And

---

[a] Other ancient authorities omit *the Son of God*   [b] Other ancient authorities read *in the prophets*
[c] Other ancient authorities read *John was baptizing*   [d] Or *my Son, my* (or *the*) *Beloved*

they were astonished at his teaching, for he taught them
23 as one who had authority, and not as the scribes. And
immediately there was in their synagogue a man with
24 an unclean spirit; and he cried out, "What have you to
do with us, Jesus of Nazareth? Have you come to destroy
25 us? I know who you are, the Holy One of God." But
Jesus rebuked him, saying, "Be silent, and come out of
26 him!" And the unclean spirit, convulsing him and crying
27 with a loud voice, came out of him. And they were all
amazed, so that they questioned among themselves, saying, "What is this? A new teaching! With authority he
commands even the unclean spirits, and they obey him."
28 And at once his fame spread everywhere throughout all
the surrounding region of Galilee.
29 And immediately he e left the synagogue, and entered

the house of Simon and Andrew, with James and John.
30 Now Simon's mother-in-law lay sick with a fever, and
31 immediately they told him of her. And he came and took
her by the hand and lifted her up, and the fever left her;
and she served them.
32 That evening, at sundown, they brought to him all who
33 were sick or possessed with demons. And the whole city
34 was gathered together about the door. And he healed
many who were sick with various diseases, and cast out
many demons; and he would not permit the demons to
speak, because they knew him.
35 And in the morning, a great while before day, he rose
and went out to a lonely place, and there he prayed.
36 And Simon and those who were with him pursued him,
37 and they found him and said to him, "Every one is
38 searching for you." And he said to them, "Let us go on
to the next towns, that I may preach there also; for that
39 is why I came out." And he went throughout all Galilee,
preaching in their synagogues and casting out demons.
40 And a leper came to him beseeching him, and kneeling
said to him, "If you will, you can make me clean."
41 Moved with pity, he stretched out his hand and touched
42 him, and said to him, "I will; be clean." And immediately the leprosy left him, and he was made clean.
43 And he sternly charged him, and sent him away at once,
44 and said to him, "See that you say nothing to any one;
but go, show yourself to the priest, and offer for your
cleansing what Moses commanded, for a proof to the
45 people." f But he went out and began to talk freely about

it, and to spread the news, so that Jesus g could no longer
openly enter a town, but was out in the country; and
people came to him from every quarter.
2 And when he returned to Caper'na-um after some
2 days, it was reported that he was at home. And many
were gathered together, so that there was no longer
room for them, not even about the door; and he was
3 preaching the word to them. And they came, bringing to
4 him a paralytic carried by four men. And when they
could not get near him because of the crowd, they
removed the roof above him; and when they had made
an opening, they let down the pallet on which the
5 paralytic lay. And when Jesus saw their faith, he said
to the paralytic, "My son, your sins are forgiven."
6 Now some of the scribes were sitting there, questioning
7 in their hearts, "Why does this man speak thus? It is
8 blasphemy! Who can forgive sins but God alone?" And
immediately Jesus, perceiving in his spirit that they thus
questioned within themselves, said to them, "Why do you
9 question thus in your hearts? Which is easier, to say to
the paralytic, 'Your sins are forgiven,' or to say, 'Rise,
10 take up your pallet and walk'? But that you may know
that the Son of man has authority on earth to forgive
11 sins"—he said to the paralytic—"I say to you, rise, take
12 up your pallet and go home." And he rose, and immediately took up the pallet and went out before them all;
so that they were all amazed and glorified God, saying,
"We never saw anything like this!"
13 He went out again beside the sea; and all the crowd
14 gathered about him, and he taught them. And as he
passed on, he saw Levi the son of Alphaeus sitting at
the tax office, and he said to him, "Follow me." And he
rose and followed him.
15 And as he sat at table in his house, many tax collectors
and sinners were sitting with Jesus and his disciples; for
16 there were many who followed him. And the scribes of h

the Pharisees, when they saw that he was eating with
sinners and tax collectors, said to his disciples, "Why does
17 he eat i with tax collectors and sinners?" And when Jesus
heard it, he said to them, "Those who are well have no
need of a physician, but those who are sick; I came not
to call the righteous, but sinners."
18 Now John's disciples and the Pharisees were fasting;
and people came and said to him, "Why do John's
disciples and the disciples of the Pharisees fast, but your

e Other ancient authorities read *they*   f Greek *to them*   g Greek *he*   h Other ancient authorities read *and*
i Other ancient authorities add *and drink*

19 disciples do not fast?" And Jesus said to them, "Can the wedding guests fast while the bridegroom is with them? As long as they have the bridegroom with them, 20 they cannot fast. The days will come, when the bridegroom is taken away from them, and then they will fast 21 in that day. No one sews a piece of unshrunk cloth on an old garment; if he does, the patch tears away from it, the 22 new from the old, and a worse tear is made. And no one puts new wine into old wineskins; if he does, the wine will burst the skins, and the wine is lost, and so are the skins; but new wine is for fresh skins." [j]

23 One sabbath he was going through the grainfields; and as they made their way his disciples began to pluck heads 24 of grain. And the Pharisees said to him, "Look, why are 25 they doing what is not lawful on the sabbath?" And he said to them, "Have you never read what David did, when he was in need and was hungry, he and those who 26 were with him: how he entered the house of God, when Abi'athar was high priest, and ate the bread of the Presence, which it is not lawful for any but the priests to eat, and also gave it to those who were with him?" 27 And he said to them, "The sabbath was made for man, 28 not man for the sabbath; so the Son of man is lord even of the sabbath."

3 Again he entered the synagogue, and a man was 2 there who had a withered hand. And they watched him, to see whether he would heal him on the sabbath, so 3 that they might accuse him. And he said to the man who 4 had the withered hand, "Come here." And he said to them, "Is it lawful on the sabbath to do good or to do 5 harm, to save life or to kill?" But they were silent. And he looked around at them with anger, grieved at their hardness of heart, and said to the man, "Stretch out your hand." He stretched it out, and his hand was restored. 6 The Pharisees went out, and immediately held counsel with the Hero'di-ans against him, how to destroy him.

The Multitudes Hear Jesus

7 Jesus withdrew with his disciples to the sea, and a great 8 multitude from Galilee followed; also from Judea and Jerusalem and Idume'a and from beyond the Jordan and from about Tyre and Sidon a great multitude, hear- 9 ing all that he did, came to him. And he told his disciples to have a boat ready for him because of the crowd, lest 10 they should crush him; for he had healed many, so that all who had diseases pressed upon him to touch him. 11 And whenever the unclean spirits beheld him, they fell down before him and cried out, "You are the Son of 12 God." And he strictly ordered them not to make him known.

Jesus Appoints the Twelve

13 And he went up on the mountain, and called to him 14 those whom he desired; and they came to him. And he appointed twelve,[k] to be with him, and to be sent out to 15, 16 preach and have authority to cast out demons: Simon [x] 17 whom he surnamed Peter; James the son of Zeb'edee and John the brother of James, whom he surnamed Bo-aner'- 18 ges, that is, sons of thunder; Andrew, and Philip, and Bartholomew, and Matthew, and Thomas, and James the son of Alphaeus, and Thaddaeus, and Simon the Cana- 19 naean, and Judas Iscariot, who betrayed him.

20 Then he went home; and the crowd came together 21 again, so that they could not even eat. And when his family heard it, they went out to seize him, for people 22 were saying, "He is beside himself." And the scribes who came down from Jerusalem said, "He is possessed by Be-el'zebul, and by the prince of demons he casts out the 23 demons." And he called them to him, and said to them in 24 parables, "How can Satan cast out Satan? If a kingdom 25 is divided against itself, that kingdom cannot stand. And if a house is divided against itself, that house will not be 26 able to stand. And if Satan has risen up against himself and is divided, he cannot stand, but is coming to an end. 27 But no one can enter a strong man's house and plunder his goods, unless he first binds the strong man; then indeed he may plunder his house.

28 "Truly, I say to you, all sins will be forgiven the sons 29 of men, and whatever blasphemies they utter; but whoever blasphemes against the Holy Spirit never has for- 30 giveness, but is guilty of an eternal sin"—for they had said, "He has an unclean spirit."

31 And his mother and his brothers came; and standing 32 outside they sent to him and called him. And a crowd was sitting about him; and they said to him, "Your mother and your brothers[l] are outside, asking for you." 33 And he replied, "Who are my mother and my brothers?" 34 And looking around on those who sat about him, he 35 said, "Here are my mother and my brothers! Whoever does the will of God is my brother, and sister, and mother."

Jesus Teaches in Parables

4 Again he began to teach beside the sea. And a very large crowd gathered about him, so that he got into a boat and sat in it on the sea; and the whole crowd was 2 beside the sea on the land. And he taught them many things in parables, and in his teaching he said to them: 3, 4 "Listen! A sower went out to sow. And as he sowed, some seed fell along the path, and the birds came and de-

J Other ancient authorities omit *but new wine is for fresh skins*
l Other early authorities add *and your sisters*
k Other ancient authorities add *whom also he named apostles*
x Other authorities read *demons*. 16 *So he appointed the twelve: Simon*

5 voured it. Other seed fell on rocky ground, where it had
not much soil, and immediately it sprang up, since it
6 had no depth of soil; and when the sun rose it was
7 scorched, and since it had no root it withered away. Other
seed fell among thorns and the thorns grew up and
8 choked it, and it yielded no grain. And other seeds fell
into good soil and brought forth grain, growing up and
increasing and yielding thirtyfold and sixtyfold and a
9 hundredfold." And he said, "He who has ears to hear,
let him hear."
10 And when he was alone, those who were about him
with the twelve asked him concerning the parables.
11 And he said to them, "To you has been given the secret

of the kingdom of God, but for those outside everything
12 is in parables; so that they may indeed see but not
perceive, and may indeed hear but not understand; lest
13 they should turn again, and be forgiven." And he said
to them, "Do you not understand this parable? How then
14 will you understand all the parables? The sower sows
15 the word. And these are the ones along the path, where
the word is sown; when they hear, Satan immediately
comes and takes away the word which is sown in them.
16 And these in like manner are the ones sown upon rocky
ground, who, when they hear the word, immediately
17 receive it with joy; and they have no root in themselves,
but endure for a while; then, when tribulation or persecution arises on account of the word, immediately they
18 fall away.m And others are the ones sown among thorns;
19 they are those who hear the word, but the cares of the
world, and the delight in riches, and the desire for other
things, enter in and choke the word, and it proves un-
20 fruitful. But those that were sown upon the good soil
are the ones who hear the word and accept it and bear
fruit, thirtyfold and sixtyfold and a hundredfold."
21 And he said to them, "Is a lamp brought in to be put
under a bushel, or under a bed, and not on a stand?
22 For there is nothing hid, except to be made manifest;
23 nor is anything secret, except to come to light. If any
24 man has ears to hear, let him hear." And he said to them,
"Take heed what you hear; the measure you give will
be the measure you get, and still more will be given you.
25 For to him who has will more be given; and from him
who has not, even what he has will be taken away."
26 And he said, "The kingdom of God is as if a man
27 should scatter seed upon the ground, and should sleep

and rise night and day, and the seed should sprout and
28 grow, he knows not how. The earth produces of itself,
first the blade, then the ear, then the full grain in the
29 ear. But when the grain is ripe, at once he puts in the
sickle, because the harvest has come."
30 And he said, "With what can we compare the kingdom
31 of God, or what parable shall we use for it? It is like
a grain of mustard seed, which, when sown upon the
32 ground, is the smallest of all the seeds on earth; yet when
it is sown it grows up and becomes the greatest of all
shrubs, and puts forth large branches, so that the birds
of the air can make nests in its shade."
33 With many such parables he spoke the word to them, as
34 they were able to hear it; he did not speak to them without a parable, but privately to his own disciples he
explained everything.
35 On that day, when evening had come, he said to them,
36 "Let us go across to the other side." And leaving the
crowd, they took him with them in the boat, just as he
37 was. And other boats were with him. And a great storm
of wind arose, and the waves beat into the boat, so that
38 the boat was already filling. But he was in the stern,
asleep on the cushion; and they woke him and said to
39 him, "Teacher, do you not care if we perish?" And he
awoke and rebuked the wind, and said to the sea, "Peace!
Be still!" And the wind ceased, and there was a great
40 calm. He said to them, "Why are you afraid? Have you
41 no faith?" And they were filled with awe, and said to
one another, "Who then is this, that even wind and sea
obey him?"

5 They came to the other side of the sea, to the country
2 of the Ger'asenes.n And when he had come out of
the boat, there met him out of the tombs a man with an
3 unclean spirit, who lived among the tombs; and no one
4 could bind him any more, even with a chain; for he had
often been bound with fetters and chains, but the chains
he wrenched apart, and the fetters he broke in pieces; and
5 no one had the strength to subdue him. Night and day
among the tombs and on the mountains he was always
6 crying out, and bruising himself with stones. And when
7 he saw Jesus from afar, he ran and worshiped him; and
crying out with a loud voice, he said, "What have you
to do with me, Jesus, Son of the Most High God? I adjure
8 you by God, do not torment me." For he had said to
9 him, "Come out of the man, you unclean spirit!" And

m Or stumble   n Other ancient authorities read Gergesenes, some Gadarenes

Jesus[o] asked him, "What is your name?" He replied,
10 "My name is Legion; for we are many." And he begged
him eagerly not to send them out of the country.
11 Now a great herd of swine was feeding there on the
12 hillside; and they begged him, "Send us to the swine,
13 let us enter them." So he gave them leave. And the
unclean spirits came out, and entered the swine; and the
herd, numbering about two thousand, rushed down the
steep bank into the sea, and were drowned in the sea.
14 The herdsmen fled, and told it in the city and in the
country. And people came to see what it was that had
15 happened. And they came to Jesus, and saw the demoniac
sitting there, clothed and in his right mind, the man who
16 had had the legion; and they were afraid. And those who
had seen it told what had happened to the demoniac and
17 to the swine. And they began to beg Jesus[p] to depart
18 from their neighborhood. And as he was getting into the
boat, the man who had been possessed with demons
19 begged him that he might be with him. But he refused,
and said to him, "Go home to your friends, and tell
them how much the Lord has done for you, and how
20 he has had mercy on you." And he went away and began
to proclaim in the Decap'olis how much Jesus had done
for him; and all men marveled.
21 And when Jesus had crossed again in the boat to the
other side, a great crowd gathered about him; and he was
22 beside the sea. Then came one of the rulers of the
synagogue, Ja'irus by name; and seeing him, he fell at
23 his feet, and besought him, saying, "My little daughter is
at the point of death. Come and lay your hands on her,
24 so that she may be made well, and live." And he went
with him.
And a great crowd followed him and thronged about
25 him. And there was a woman who had had a flow of
26 blood for twelve years, and who had suffered much
under many physicians, and had spent all that she had,
27 and was no better but rather grew worse. She had heard
the reports about Jesus, and came up behind him in the
28 crowd and touched his garment. For she said, "If I touch
29 even his garments, I shall be made well." And immediately the hemorrhage ceased; and she felt in her
30 body that she was healed of her disease. And Jesus,
perceiving in himself that power had gone forth from
him, immediately turned about in the crowd, and said,
31 "Who touched my garments?" And his disciples said to
him, "You see the crowd pressing around you, and yet
32 you say, 'Who touched me?' " And he looked around to
33 see who had done it. But the woman, knowing what had
been done to her, came in fear and trembling and fell
34 down before him, and told him the whole truth. And he
said to her, "Daughter, your faith has made you well; go
in peace, and be healed of your disease."
35 While he was still speaking, there came from the ruler's
house some who said, "Your daughter is dead. Why
36 trouble the Teacher any further?" But ignoring[q] what
they said, Jesus said to the ruler of the synagogue, "Do
37 not fear, only believe." And he allowed no one to follow
him except Peter and James and John the brother of
38 James. When they came to the house of the ruler of the
synagogue, he saw a tumult, and people weeping and
39 wailing loudly. And when he had entered, he said to them,
"Why do you make a tumult and weep? The child is
40 not dead but sleeping." And they laughed at him. But he
put them all outside, and took the child's father and
mother and those who were with him, and went in where
41 the child was. Taking her by the hand he said to her,
"Tal'itha cu'mi"; which means, "Little girl, I say to you,
42 arise." And immediately the girl got up and walked (she
was twelve years of age), and they were immediately
43 overcome with amazement. And he strictly charged them
that no one should know this, and told them to give her
something to eat.

Visit to Nazareth

6 He went away from there and came to his own
2 country; and his disciples followed him. And on the
sabbath he began to teach in the synagogue; and many
who heard him were astonished, saying, "Where did this
man get all this? What is the wisdom given to him?
3 What mighty works are wrought by his hands! Is not this
the carpenter, the son of Mary and brother of James and
Joses and Judas and Simon, and are not his sisters here
4 with us?" And they took offense[r] at him. And Jesus said
to them, "A prophet is not without honor, except in his
own country, and among his own kin, and in his own
5 house." And he could do no mighty work there, except
that he laid his hands upon a few sick people and healed
6 them. And he marveled because of their unbelief.
And he went about among the villages teaching.

The Mission of the Twelve

7 And he called to him the twelve, and began to send
them out two by two, and gave them authority over the
8 unclean spirits. He charged them to take nothing for their
journey except a staff; no bread, no bag, no money in
9 their belts; but to wear sandals and not put on two
10 tunics. And he said to them, "Where you enter a house,
11 stay there until you leave the place. And if any place
will not receive you and they refuse to hear you, when
you leave, shake off the dust that is on your feet for a
12 testimony against them." So they went out and preached
13 that men should repent. And they cast out many demons,
and anointed with oil many that were sick and healed
them.
14 King Herod heard of it; for Jesus'[s] name had become
known. Some[t] said, "John the baptizer has been raised
from the dead; that is why these powers are at work in

[o] Greek *he* [p] Greek *him* [q] Or *overhearing*. Other ancient authorities read *hearing* [r] Or *stumbled* [s] Greek *his*
[t] Other ancient authorities read *he*

15 him." But others said, "It is Eli'jah." And others said,
16 "It is a prophet, like one of the prophets of old." But
when Herod heard of it he said, "John, whom I beheaded,
17 has been raised." For Herod had sent and seized John,
and bound him in prison for the sake of Hero'di-as, his
18 brother Philip's wife; because he had married her. For
John said to Herod, "It is not lawful for you to have your
19 brother's wife." And Hero'di-as had a grudge against
20 him, and wanted to kill him. But she could not, for Herod
feared John, knowing that he was a righteous and holy
man, and kept him safe. When he heard him, he was
21 much perplexed; and yet he heard him gladly. But an
opportunity came when Herod on his birthday gave a
banquet for his courtiers and officers and the leading men
22 of Galilee. For when Hero'di-as' daughter came in and
danced, she pleased Herod and his guests; and the king
said to the girl, "Ask me for whatever you wish, and I
23 will grant it." And he vowed to her, "Whatever you ask
24 me, I will give you, even half of my kingdom." And she
went out, and said to her mother, "What shall I ask?" And
25 she said, "The head of John the baptizer." And she came
in immediately with haste to the king, and asked, saying,
"I want you to give me at once the head of John the
26 Baptist on a platter." And the king was exceedingly sorry;
but because of his oaths and his guests he did not want to
27 break his word to her. And immediately the king sent a
soldier of the guard and gave orders to bring his head.
28 He went and beheaded him in the prison, and brought
his head on a platter, and gave it to the girl; and the
29 girl gave it to her mother. When his disciples heard of it,
they came and took his body, and laid it in a tomb.

30 The apostles returned to Jesus, and told him all that
31 they had done and taught. And he said to them, "Come
away by yourselves to a lonely place, and rest a while."
For many were coming and going, and they had no
32 leisure even to eat. And they went away in the boat to a
33 lonely place by themselves. Now many saw them going,
and knew them, and they ran there on foot from all the
34 towns, and got there ahead of them. As he went ashore he
saw a great throng, and he had compassion on them,
because they were like sheep without a shepherd; and
35 he began to teach them many things. And when it grew
late, his disciples came to him and said, "This is a
36 lonely place, and the hour is now late; send them away,
to go into the country and villages round about and buy
37 themselves something to eat." But he answered them,
"You give them something to eat." And they said to him,
"Shall we go and buy two hundred denarii u worth of
38 bread, and give it to them to eat?" And he said to them,
"How many loaves have you? Go and see." And when
they had found out, they said, "Five, and two fish."
39 Then he commanded them all to sit down by companies
40 upon the green grass. So they sat down in groups, by

41 hundreds and by fifties. And taking the five loaves and
the two fish he looked up to heaven, and blessed, and
broke the loaves, and gave them to the disciples to set
before the people; and he divided the two fish among
42, 43 them all. And they all ate and were satisfied. And they
took up twelve baskets full of broken pieces and of the
44 fish. And those who ate the loaves were five thousand
men.

45 Immediately he made his disciples get into the boat
and go before him to the other side, to Beth-sa'ida, while
46 he dismissed the crowd. And after he had taken leave of
47 them, he went up on the mountain to pray. And when
evening came, the boat was out on the sea, and he was
48 alone on the land. And he saw that they were making
headway painfully, for the wind was against them. And
about the fourth watch of the night he came to them,
49 walking on the sea. He meant to pass by them, but when
they saw him walking on the sea they thought it was a
ghost, and cried out; but they all saw him, and were ter-
50 rified. But immediately he spoke to them and said,
51 "Take heart, it is I; have no fear." And he got into the
boat with them and the wind ceased. And they were
52 utterly astounded, for they did not understand about
the loaves, but their hearts were hardened.

53 And when they had crossed over, they came to land
54 at Gennes'aret, and moored to the shore. And when they
got out of the boat, immediately the people recognized
55 him, and ran about the whole neighborhood and began
to bring sick people on their pallets to any place where
56 they heard he was. And wherever he came, in villages,
cities, or country, they laid the sick in the market places,
and besought him that they might touch even the fringe
of his garment; and as many as touched it were made well.

The Traditions of the Elders

7 Now when the Pharisees gathered together to him,
with some of the scribes, who had come from Jeru-
2 salem, they saw that some of his disciples ate with hands
3 defiled, that is, unwashed. (For the Pharisees, and all the
Jews, do not eat unless they wash their hands,v observing
4 the tradition of the elders; and when they come from the
market place, they do not eat unless they purify w themselves;a and there are many other traditions which they
observe, the washing of cups and pots and vessels of
5 bronze.x) And the Pharisees and the scribes asked him,
"Why do your disciples not live y according to the tradi-
6 tion of the elders, but eat with hands defiled?" And he
said to them, "Well did Isaiah prophesy of you hypocrites,
as it is written,

'This people honors me with their lips,
but their heart is far from me;
7 in vain do they worship me,
teaching as doctrines the precepts of men.'

u The denarius was a day's wages for a laborer   a Other ancient authorities read *and they do not eat anything from the market unless they purify it*
v One Greek word is of uncertain meaning and is not translated   w Other ancient authorities read *baptize*
x Other ancient authorities add *and beds*   y Greek *walk*

8 You leave the commandment of God, and hold fast the tradition of men."

9 And he said to them, "You have a fine way of rejecting the commandment of God, in order to keep your tradition!

10 For Moses said, 'Honor your father and your mother'; and, 'He who speaks evil of father or mother, let him

11 surely die'; but you say, 'If a man tells his father or his mother, What you would have gained from me is

12 Corban' (that is, given to God)^z—then you no longer permit him to do anything for his father or mother,

13 thus making void the word of God through your tradition which you hand on. And many such things you do."

14 And he called the people to him again, and said to

15 them, "Hear me, all of you, and understand: there is nothing outside a man which by going into him can defile him; but the things which come out of a man are

17 what defile him."^a And when he had entered the house, and left the people, his disciples asked him about the

18 parable. And he said to them, "Then are you also without understanding? Do you not see that whatever goes into

19 a man from outside cannot defile him, since it enters, not his heart but his stomach, and so passes on?"^b (Thus he

20 declared all foods clean.) And he said, "What comes out

21 of a man is what defiles a man. For from within, out of the heart of man, come evil thoughts, fornication, theft,

22 murder, adultery, coveting, wickedness, deceit, licentious-

23 ness, envy, slander, pride, foolishness. All these evil things come from within, and they defile a man."

24 And from there he arose and went away to the region of Tyre and Sidon.^c And he entered a house, and would

through Sidon to the Sea of Galilee, through the region

32 of the Decap'olis. And they brought to him a man who was deaf and had an impediment in his speech; and they

33 besought him to lay his hand upon him. And taking him aside from the multitude privately, he put his fingers into

34 his ears, and he spat and touched his tongue; and looking up to heaven, he sighed, and said to him, "Eph'phatha,"

35 that is, "Be opened." And his ears were opened, his

36 tongue was released, and he spoke plainly. And he charged them to tell no one; but the more he charged

37 them, the more zealously they proclaimed it. And they were astonished beyond measure, saying, "He has done all things well; he even makes the deaf hear and the dumb speak."

8 In those days, when again a great crowd had gathered, and they had nothing to eat, he called his

2 disciples to him, and said to them, "I have compassion on the crowd, because they have been with me now three

3 days, and have nothing to eat; and if I send them away hungry to their homes, they will faint on the way; and

4 some of them have come a long way." And his disciples answered him, "How can one feed these men with bread

5 here in the desert?" And he asked them, "How many

6 loaves have you?" They said, "Seven." And he commanded the crowd to sit down on the ground; and he took the seven loaves, and having given thanks he broke them and gave them to his disciples to set before the

7 people; and they set them before the crowd. And they had a few small fish; and having blessed them, he commanded that these also should be set before them.

not have any one know it; yet he could not be hid.

25 But immediately a woman, whose little daughter was possessed by an unclean spirit, heard of him, and came

26 and fell down at his feet. Now the woman was a Greek, a Syrophoeni'cian by birth. And she begged him to cast

27 the demon out of her daughter. And he said to her, "Let the children first be fed, for it is not right to take the

28 children's bread and throw it to the dogs." But she answered him, "Yes, Lord; yet even the dogs under the

29 table eat the children's crumbs." And he said to her, "For this saying you may go your way; the demon has

30 left your daughter." And she went home, and found the child lying in bed, and the demon gone.

31 Then he returned from the region of Tyre, and went

8 And they ate, and were satisfied; and they took up the

9 broken pieces left over, seven baskets full. And there were

10 about four thousand people. And he sent them away; and immediately he got into the boat with his disciples, and went to the district of Dalmanu'tha.^d

11 The Pharisees came and began to argue with him, seek-

12 ing from him a sign from heaven, to test him. And he sighed deeply in his spirit, and said, "Why does this generation seek a sign? Truly, I say to you, no sign shall

13 be given to this generation." And he left them, and getting into the boat again he departed to the other side.

14 Now they had forgotten to bring bread; and they had

15 only one loaf with them in the boat. And he cautioned them, saying, "Take heed, beware of the leaven of the

16 Pharisees and the leaven of Herod." e And they discussed
17 it with one another, saying, "We have no bread." And
being aware of it, Jesus said to them, "Why do you dis-
cuss the fact that you have no bread? Do you not yet
perceive or understand? Are your hearts hardened?
18 Having eyes do you not see, and having ears do you not
19 hear? And do you not remember? When I broke the five
loaves for the five thousand, how many baskets full of

broken pieces did you take up?" They said to him,
20 "Twelve." "And the seven for the four thousand, how
many baskets full of broken pieces did you take up?"
21 And they said to him, "Seven." And he said to them, "Do
you not yet understand?"

22   And they came to Beth-sa'ida. And some people
brought to him a blind man, and begged him to touch
23 him. And he took the blind man by the hand, and led
him out of the village; and when he had spit on his eyes
and laid his hands upon him, he asked him, "Do you see
24 anything?" And he looked up and said, "I see men; but
25 they look like trees, walking." Then again he laid his
hands upon his eyes; and he looked intently and was
26 restored, and saw everything clearly. And he sent him
away to his home, saying, "Do not even enter the village."

Peter's Confession

27   And Jesus went on with his disciples, to the villages of
Caesare'a Philippi; and on the way he asked his dis-
28 ciples, "Who do men say that I am?" And they told him,
"John the Baptist; and others say, Eli'jah; and others
29 one of the prophets." And he asked them, "But who do
you say that I am?" Peter answered him, "You are the
30 Christ." And he charged them to tell no one about him.
31   And he began to teach them that the Son of man must
suffer many things, and be rejected by the elders and the
chief priests and the scribes, and be killed, and after three
32 days rise again. And he said this plainly. And Peter took
33 him, and began to rebuke him. But turning and seeing

his disciples, he rebuked Peter, and said, "Get behind
me, Satan! For you are not on the side of God, but of
men."
34   And he called to him the multitude with his disciples,
and said to them, "If any man would come after me,
let him deny himself and take up his cross and follow me.
35 For whoever would save his life will lose it; and whoever
loses his life for my sake and the gospel's will save it.
36 For what does it profit a man, to gain the whole world
37 and forfeit his life? For what can a man give in return
38 for his life? For whoever is ashamed of me and of my
words in this adulterous and sinful generation, of him
will the Son of man also be ashamed, when he comes in
19 the glory of his Father with the holy angels." And he
said to them, "Truly, I say to you, there are some
standing here who will not taste death before they see
that the kingdom of God has come with power."

The Transfiguration

2   And after six days Jesus took with him Peter and James
and John, and led them up a high mountain apart by
3 themselves; and he was transfigured before them, and his
garments became glistening, intensely white, as no fuller
4 on earth could bleach them. And there appeared to them
Eli'jah with Moses; and they were talking to Jesus.
5 And Peter said to Jesus, "Master,f it is well that we are
here; let us make three booths, one for you and one for
6 Moses and one for Eli'jah." For he did not know what
7 to say, for they were exceedingly afraid. And a cloud
overshadowed them, and a voice came out of the cloud,
8 "This is my beloved Son; g listen to him." And suddenly
looking around they no longer saw any one with them but
Jesus only.
9   And as they were coming down the mountain, he
charged them to tell no one what they had seen, until the
10 Son of man should have risen from the dead. So they
kept the matter to themselves, questioning what the rising
11 from the dead meant. And they asked him, "Why do
12 the scribes say that first Eli'jah must come?" And he
said to them, "Eli'jah does come first to restore all
things; and how is it written of the Son of man, that he
should suffer many things and be treated with contempt?
13 But I tell you that Eli'jah has come, and they did to
him whatever they pleased, as it is written of him."
14   And when they came to the disciples, they saw a great
15 crowd about them, and scribes arguing with them. And
immediately all the crowd, when they saw him, were
16 greatly amazed, and ran up to him and greeted him. And
he asked them, "What are you discussing with them?"
17 And one of the crowd answered him, "Teacher, I brought
18 my son to you, for he has a dumb spirit; and wherever it
seizes him, it dashes him down; and he foams and
grinds his teeth and becomes rigid; and I asked your

e Other ancient authorities read *the Herodians*   f Or *Rabbi*   g Or *my Son, my* (or *the*) *Beloved*

19 disciples to cast it out, and they were not able." And he answered them, "O faithless generation, how long am I to be with you? How long am I to bear with you? Bring
20 him to me." And they brought the boy to him; and when the spirit saw him, immediately it convulsed the boy, and he fell on the ground and rolled about, foaming at the
21 mouth. And Jesus [h] asked his father, "How long has he
22 had this?" And he said, "From childhood. And it has often cast him into the fire and into the water, to destroy him; but if you can do anything, have pity on us and
23 help us." And Jesus said to him, "If you can! All things
24 are possible to him who believes." Immediately the father of the child cried out [i] and said, "I believe; help my
25 unbelief!" And when Jesus saw that a crowd came running together, he rebuked the unclean spirit, saying to it, "You dumb and deaf spirit, I command you, come
26 out of him, and never enter him again." And after crying out and convulsing him terribly, it came out, and the boy was like a corpse; so that most of them said, "He is dead."
27 But Jesus took him by the hand and lifted him up, and
28 he arose. And when he had entered the house, his disciples asked him privately, "Why could we not cast it out?"
29 And he said to them, "This kind cannot be driven out by anything but prayer." [j]

30 They went on from there and passed through Galilee.
31 And he would not have any one know it; for he was teaching his disciples, saying to them, "The Son of man will be delivered into the hands of men, and they will kill him; and when he is killed, after three days he will rise."
32 But they did not understand the saying, and they were afraid to ask him.

The Question of Greatness

33 And they came to Caper'na-um; and when he was in the house he asked them, "What were you discussing
34 on the way?" But they were silent; for on the way they had discussed with one another who was the greatest.
35 And he sat down and called the twelve; and he said to them, "If any one would be first, he must be last of all
36 and servant of all." And he took a child, and put him in the midst of them; and taking him in his arms, he said
37 to them, "Whoever receives one such child in my name receives me; and whoever receives me, receives not me but him who sent me."

38 John said to him, "Teacher, we saw a man casting out demons in your name,[k] and we forbade him, because
39 he was not following us." But Jesus said, "Do not forbid him; for no one who does a mighty work in my name
40 will be able soon after to speak evil of me. For he that
41 is not against us is for us. For truly, I say to you, whoever gives you a cup of water to drink because you bear the name of Christ, will by no means lose his reward.
42 "Whoever causes one of these little ones who believe

in me to sin,[l] it would be better for him if a great millstone were hung around his neck and he were thrown
43 into the sea. And if your hand causes you to sin,[l] cut it off; it is better for you to enter life maimed than with two hands to go to hell,[m] to the unquenchable fire.[n]
45 And if your foot causes you to sin,[l] cut it off; it is better for you to enter life lame than with two feet to be thrown
47 into hell.[m, n] And if your eye causes you to sin,[l] pluck it out; it is better for you to enter the kingdom of God with one eye than with two eyes to be thrown into hell,[m]
48 where their worm does not die, and the fire is not
49, 50 quenched. For every one will be salted with fire.[o] Salt is good; but if the salt has lost its saltness, how will you season it? Have salt in yourselves, and be at peace with one another."

ON THE WAY TO JERUSALEM

10 And he left there and went to the region of Judea and beyond the Jordan, and crowds gathered to him again; and again, as his custom was, he taught them.
2 And Pharisees came up and in order to test him asked,
3 "Is it lawful for a man to divorce his wife?" He an-
4 swered them, "What did Moses command you?" They said, "Moses allowed a man to write a certificate of
5 divorce, and to put her away." But Jesus said to them, "For your hardness of heart he wrote you this com-
6 mandment. But from the beginning of creation, 'God
7 made them male and female.' 'For this reason a man shall leave his father and mother and be joined to his wife,[p]

8 and the two shall become one flesh.' So they are no longer
9 two but one flesh. What therefore God has joined together, let not man put asunder."

10 And in the house the disciples asked him again about
11 this matter. And he said to them, "Whoever divorces his wife and marries another, commits adultery against
12 her; and if she divorces her husband and marries another, she commits adultery."

13 And they were bringing children to him, that he might
14 touch them; and the disciples rebuked them. But when Jesus saw it he was indignant, and said to them, "Let the children come to me, do not hinder them; for to such
15 belongs the kingdom of God. Truly, I say to you, whoever does not receive the kingdom of God like a child
16 shall not enter it." And he took them in his arms and blessed them, laying his hands upon them.

17 And as he was setting out on his journey, a man ran

---

[h] Greek *he*   [i] Other ancient authorities add *with tears*   [j] Other ancient authorities add *and fasting*
[k] Other ancient authorities add *who does not follow us*   [l] Greek *stumble*   [m] Greek *Gehenna*
[n] Verses 44 and 46 (which are identical with verse 48) are omitted by the best ancient authorities
[o] Other ancient authorities add *and every sacrifice will be salted with salt*   [p] Other ancient authorities omit *and be joined to his wife*

up and knelt before him, and asked him, "Good Teacher,
18 what must I do to inherit eternal life?" And Jesus said
to him, "Why do you call me good? No one is good but
19 God alone. You know the commandments: 'Do not kill,
Do not commit adultery, Do not steal, Do not bear false
witness, Do not defraud, Honor your father and mother.'"
20 And he said to him, "Teacher, all these I have observed
21 from my youth." And Jesus looking upon him loved
him, and said to him, "You lack one thing; go, sell
what you have, and give to the poor, and you will have
22 treasure in heaven; and come, follow me." At that saying
his countenance fell, and he went away sorrowful; for
he had great possessions.

23 And Jesus looked around and said to his disciples,
"How hard it will be for those who have riches to enter
24 the kingdom of God!" And the disciples were amazed
at his words. But Jesus said to them again, "Children,
25 how hard it is ʳ to enter the kingdom of God! It is easier
for a camel to go through the eye of a needle than for a
26 rich man to enter the kingdom of God." And they were
exceedingly astonished, and said to him,ˢ "Then who can
27 be saved?" Jesus looked at them and said, "With men it is
impossible, but not with God; for all things are possible
28 with God." Peter began to say to him, "Lo, we have left
29 everything and followed you." Jesus said, "Truly, I say
to you, there is no one who has left house or brothers or
sisters or mother or father or children or lands, for my
30 sake and for the gospel, who will not receive a hundredfold now in this time, houses and brothers and sisters
and mothers and children and lands, with persecutions,
31 and in the age to come eternal life. But many that are
first will be last, and the last first."

32 And they were on the road, going up to Jerusalem, and
Jesus was walking ahead of them; and they were amazed,
and those who followed were afraid. And taking the
twelve again, he began to tell them what was to happen
33 to him, saying, "Behold, we are going up to Jerusalem;
and the Son of man will be delivered to the chief priests
and the scribes, and they will condemn him to death, and
34 deliver him to the Gentiles; and they will mock him, and
spit upon him, and scourge him, and kill him; and after
three days he will rise."

The Request of James and John

35 And James and John, the sons of Zeb'edee, came
forward to him, and said to him, "Teacher, we want you
36 to do for us whatever we ask of you." And he said to
37 them, "What do you want me to do for you?" And they
said to him, "Grant us to sit, one at your right hand and
38 one at your left, in your glory." But Jesus said to them,
"You do not know what you are asking. Are you able to
drink the cup that I drink, or to be baptized with the
39 baptism with which I am baptized?" And they said to him,

"We are able." And Jesus said to them, "The cup that
I drink you will drink; and with the baptism with which
40 I am baptized, you will be baptized; but to sit at my right
hand or at my left is not mine to grant, but it is for those
41 for whom it has been prepared." And when the ten heard
42 it, they began to be indignant at James and John. And
Jesus called them to him and said to them, "You know that
those who are supposed to rule over the Gentiles lord
it over them, and their great men exercise authority over
43 them. But it shall not be so among you; but whoever
44 would be great among you must be your servant, and
whoever would be first among you must be slave of all.
45 For the Son of man also came not to be served but to
serve, and to give his life as a ransom for many."

46 And they came to Jericho; and as he was leaving
Jericho with his disciples and a great multitude, Barti-
mae'us, a blind beggar, the son of Timae'us, was sitting
47 by the roadside. And when he heard that it was Jesus of
Nazareth, he began to cry out and say, "Jesus, Son of
48 David, have mercy on me!" And many rebuked him,
telling him to be silent; but he cried out all the more,
49 "Son of David, have mercy on me!" And Jesus stopped
and said, "Call him." And they called the blind man,
saying to him, "Take heart; rise, he is calling you."
50 And throwing off his mantle he sprang up and came to
51 Jesus. And Jesus said to him, "What do you want me to
do for you?" And the blind man said to him, "Master,ᵗ
52 let me receive my sight." And Jesus said to him, "Go your
way; your faith has made you well." And immediately
he received his sight and followed him on the way.

JESUS ENTERS JERUSALEM

11 And when they drew near to Jerusalem, to Beth'-
phage and Bethany, at the Mount of Olives, he sent
2 two of his disciples, and said to them, "Go into the
village opposite you, and immediately as you enter it you
will find a colt tied, on which no one has ever sat; untie
3 it and bring it. If any one says to you, 'Why are you
doing this?' say, 'The Lord has need of it and will send

ʳ Other ancient authorities add *for those who trust in riches*   ˢ Other ancient authorities read *to one another*   ᵗ Or *Rabbi*

4 it back here immediately.'" And they went away, and found a colt tied at the door out in the open street; and 5 they untied it. And those who stood there said to them, 6 "What are you doing, untying the colt?" And they told them what Jesus had said; and they let them go. 7 And they brought the colt to Jesus, and threw their 8 garments on it; and he sat upon it. And many spread their garments on the road, and others spread leafy 9 branches which they had cut from the fields. And those who went before and those who followed cried out, "Hosanna! Blessed is he who comes in the name of the 10 Lord! Blessed is the kingdom of our father David that is coming! Hosanna in the highest!"

11 And he entered Jerusalem, and went into the temple; and when he had looked round at everything, as it was already late, he went out to Bethany with the twelve.

12 On the following day, when they came from Bethany, 13 he was hungry. And seeing in the distance a fig tree in leaf, he went to see if he could find anything on it. When he came to it, he found nothing but leaves, for it was 14 not the season for figs. And he said to it, "May no one ever eat fruit from you again." And his disciples heard it.

15 And they came to Jerusalem. And he entered the temple and began to drive out those who sold and those who bought in the temple, and he overturned the tables of the money-changers and the seats of those who sold pigeons; 16 and he would not allow any one to carry anything 17 through the temple. And he taught, and said to them, "Is it not written, 'My house shall be called a house of prayer for all the nations'? But you have made it a den of 18 robbers." And the chief priests and the scribes heard it and sought a way to destroy him; for they feared him, because all the multitude was astonished at his teaching. 19 And when evening came they u went out of the city.

20 As they passed by in the morning, they saw the fig tree 21 withered away to its roots. And Peter remembered and said to him, "Master,v look! The fig tree which you 22 cursed has withered." And Jesus answered them, "Have 23 faith in God. Truly, I say to you, whoever says to this mountain, 'Be taken up and cast into the sea,' and does not doubt in his heart, but believes that what he says will 24 come to pass, it will be done for him. Therefore I tell you, whatever you ask in prayer, believe that you have 25 received a it, and it will be yours. And whenever you stand praying, forgive, if you have anything against any one; so that your Father also who is in heaven may forgive you your trespasses." w

27 And they came again to Jerusalem. And as he was walking in the temple, the chief priests and the scribes and 28 the elders came to him, and they said to him, "By what authority are you doing these things, or who gave you 29 this authority to do them?" Jesus said to them, "I will ask you a question; answer me, and I will tell you by

30 what authority I do these things. Was the baptism of 31 John from heaven or from men? Answer me." And they argued with one another, "If we say, 'From heaven,' he 32 will say, 'Why then did you not believe him?' But shall we say, 'From men'?"—they were afraid of the people, 33 for all held that John was a real prophet. So they answered Jesus, "We do not know." And Jesus said to them, "Neither will I tell you by what authority I do these things."

12 And he began to speak to them in parables. "A man planted a vineyard, and set a hedge around it, and dug a pit for the wine press, and built a tower, and let it out to tenants, and went into another country. 2 When the time came, he sent a servant to the tenants, to 3 get from them some of the fruit of the vineyard. And they took him and beat him, and sent him away empty-handed. 4 Again he sent to them another servant, and they wounded 5 him in the head, and treated him shamefully. And he sent another, and him they killed; and so with many 6 others, some they beat and some they killed. He had still one other, a beloved son; finally he sent him to them, 7 saying, 'They will respect my son.' But those tenants said to one another, 'This is the heir; come, let us kill him, and 8 the inheritance will be ours.' And they took him and killed 9 him, and cast him out of the vineyard. What will the owner of the vineyard do? He will come and destroy the 10 tenants, and give the vineyard to others. Have you not read this scripture:
'The very stone which the builders rejected
has become the head of the corner;
11 this was the Lord's doing,
and it is marvelous in our eyes'?"
12 And they tried to arrest him, but feared the multitude, for they perceived that he had told the parable against them; so they left him and went away.

13 And they sent to him some of the Pharisees and some 14 of the Hero'di-ans, to entrap him in his talk. And they came and said to him, "Teacher, we know that you are true, and care for no man; for you do not regard the position of men, but truly teach the way of God. Is it 15 lawful to pay taxes to Caesar, or not? Should we pay them, or should we not?" But knowing their hypocrisy, he said to them, "Why put me to the test? Bring me a 16 coin,x and let me look at it." And they brought one. And he said to them, "Whose likeness and inscription is this?" 17 They said to him, "Caesar's." Jesus said to them, "Render to Caesar the things that are Caesar's, and to God the things that are God's." And they were amazed at him.

18 And Sad'ducees came to him, who say that there is no resurrection; and they asked him a question, saying, 19 "Teacher, Moses wrote for us that if a man's brother dies and leaves a wife, but leaves no child, the man y must take 20 the wife, and raise up children for his brother. There

---

a Other ancient authorities read are receiving   v Or Rabbi   w Other ancient authorities add verse 26, But if you do not forgive, neither will your Father who is in heaven forgive your trespasses   x Greek a denarius   y Greek his brother

were seven brothers; the first took a wife, and when he
21 died left no chlidren; and the second took her, and died,
22 leaving no children; and the third likewise; and the
seven left no children. Last of all the woman also died.
23 In the resurrection whose wife will she be? For the seven
had her as wife."

24 Jesus said to them, "Is not this why you are wrong,
that you know neither the scriptures nor the power of
25 God? For when they rise from the dead, they neither
marry nor are given in marriage, but are like angels in
26 heaven. And as for the dead being raised, have you not
read in the book of Moses, in the passage about the bush,
how God said to him, 'I am the God of Abraham, and the
27 God of Isaac, and the God of Jacob'? He is not God of
the dead, but of the living; you are quite wrong."

Which Commandment Is First?

28 And one of the scribes came up and heard them
disputing with one another, and seeing that he answered
them well, asked him, "Which commandment is the first
29 of all?" Jesus answered, "The first is, 'Hear, O Israel:
30 The Lord our God, the Lord is one; and you shall love
the Lord your God with all your heart, and with all
your soul, and with all your mind, and with all your
31 strength.' The second is this, 'You shall love your
neighbor as yourself.' There is no other commandment
32 greater than these." And the scribe said to him, "You are
right, Teacher; you have truly said that he is one, and
33 there is no other but he; and to love him with all the
heart, and with all the understanding, and with all the
strength, and to love one's neighbor as oneself, is much
more than all whole burnt offerings and sacrifices."
34 And when Jesus saw that he answered wisely, he said to
him, "You are not far from the kingdom of God." And
after that no one dared to ask him any question.

35 And as Jesus taught in the temple, he said, "How can
the scribes say that the Christ is the son of David?
36 David himself, inspired by z the Holy Spirit, declared,

'The Lord said to my Lord,
Sit at my right hand,
till I put thy enemies under thy feet.'
37 David himself calls him Lord; so how is he his son?"
And the great throng heard him gladly.

38 And in his teaching he said, "Beware of the scribes,
who like to go about in long robes, and to have saluta-
39 tions in the market places and the best seats in the

z Or himself, in

40 synagogues and the places of honor at feasts, who devour
widows' houses and for a pretense make long prayers.
They will receive the greater condemnation."

41 And he sat down opposite the treasury, and watched
the multitude putting money into the treasury. Many rich
42 people put in large sums. And a poor widow came, and
43 put in two copper coins, which make a penny. And he
called his disciples to him, and said to them, "Truly, I
say to you, this poor widow has put in more than all those
44 who are contributing to the treasury. For they all con-

tributed out of their abundance; but she out of her
poverty has put in everything she had, her whole living."

SIGNS OF THE END

13 And as he came out of the temple, one of his disciples said to him, "Look, Teacher, what wonderful
2 stones and what wonderful buildings!" And Jesus said
to him, "Do you see these great buildings? There will
not be left here one stone upon another, that will not be
thrown down."

3 And as he sat on the Mount of Olives opposite the
temple, Peter and James and John and Andrew asked
4 him privately, "Tell us, when will this be, and what will
be the sign when these things are all to be accomplished?"
5 And Jesus began to say to them, "Take heed that no one
6 leads you astray. Many will come in my name, saying,
7 'I am he!' and they will lead many astray. And when you
hear of wars and rumors of wars, do not be alarmed;
8 this must take place, but the end is not yet. For nation
will rise against nation, and kingdom against kingdom;
there will be earthquakes in various places, there will be
famines; this is but the beginning of the birth-pangs.
9 "But take heed to yourselves; for they will deliver you
up to councils; and you will be beaten in synagogues;
and you will stand before governors and kings for my
10 sake, to bear testimony before them. And the gospel must
11 first be preached to all nations. And when they bring you
to trial and deliver you up, do not be anxious beforehand
what you are to say; but say whatever is given you in
that hour, for it is not you who speak, but the Holy
12 Spirit. And brother will deliver up brother to death, and
the father his child, and children will rise against parents
13 and have them put to death; and you will be hated by all
for my name's sake. But he who endures to the end will
be saved.

¹⁴ "But when you see the desolating sacrilege set up where it ought not to be (let the reader understand), then let ¹⁵ those who are in Judea flee to the mountains; let him who is on the housetop not go down, nor enter his house, ¹⁶ to take anything away; and let him who is in the field ¹⁷ not turn back to take his mantle. And alas for those who are with child and for those who give suck in those days! ^{18, 19} Pray that it may not happen in winter. For in those days there will be such tribulation as has not been from the beginning of the creation which God created until ²⁰ now, and never will be. And if the Lord had not shortened the days, no human being would be saved; but for the sake of the elect, whom he chose, he shortened the days. ²¹ And then if any one says to you, 'Look, here is the Christ!' or 'Look, there he is!' do not believe it. ²² False Christs and false prophets will arise and show signs and wonders, to lead astray, if possible, the elect. ²³ But take heed; I have told you all things beforehand.

²⁴ "But in those days, after that tribulation, the sun will ²⁵ be darkened, and the moon will not give its light, and the stars will be falling from heaven, and the powers in the ²⁶ heavens will be shaken. And then they will see the Son of man coming in clouds with great power and glory. ²⁷ And then he will send out the angels, and gather his elect from the four winds, from the ends of the earth to the ends of heaven.

²⁸ "From the fig tree learn its lesson: as soon as its branch becomes tender and puts forth its leaves, you ²⁹ know that summer is near. So also, when you see these things taking place, you know that he is near, at the ³⁰ very gates. Truly, I say to you, this generation will not ³¹ pass away before all these things take place. Heaven and earth will pass away, but my words will not pass away.

³² "But of that day or that hour no one knows, not even the angels in heaven, nor the Son, but only the Father. ³³ Take heed, watch;[a] for you do not know when the time

³⁴ will come. It is like a man going on a journey, when he leaves home and puts his servants in charge, each with his work, and commands the doorkeeper to be on the watch. ³⁵ Watch therefore—for you do not know when the master of the house will come, in the evening, or at midnight, or ³⁶ at cockcrow, or in the morning—lest he come suddenly ³⁷ and find you asleep. And what I say to you I say to all: Watch."

---

^a Other ancient authorities add *and pray*   ^b The denarius was a day's wage for a laborer

THE PLOT AGAINST JESUS

14 It was now two days before the Passover and the feast of Unleavened Bread. And the chief priests and the scribes were seeking how to arrest him by stealth, ² and kill him; for they said, "Not during the feast, lest there be a tumult of the people."

³ And while he was at Bethany in the house of Simon the leper, as he sat at table, a woman came with an alabaster flask of ointment of pure nard, very costly, and ⁴ she broke the flask and poured it over his head. But there were some who said to themselves indignantly, "Why ⁵ was the ointment thus wasted? For this ointment might have been sold for more than three hundred denarii,[b]

⁶ and given to the poor." And they reproached her. But Jesus said, "Let her alone; why do you trouble her? She ⁷ has done a beautiful thing to me. For you always have the poor with you, and whenever you will, you can do good ⁸ to them; but you will not always have me. She has done what she could; she has anointed my body beforehand ⁹ for burying. And truly, I say to you, wherever the gospel is preached in the whole world, what she has done will be told in memory of her."

¹⁰ Then Judas Iscariot, who was one of the twelve, went to the chief priests in order to betray him to them. ¹¹ And when they heard it they were glad, and promised to give him money. And he sought an opportunity to betray him.

Preparation for the Passover

¹² And on the first day of Unleavened Bread, when they sacrificed the passover lamb, his disciples said to him, "Where will you have us go and prepare for you to eat the ¹³ passover?" And he sent two of his disciples, and said to them, "Go into the city, and a man carrying a jar of ¹⁴ water will meet you; follow him, and wherever he enters, say to the householder, 'The Teacher says, Where is my guest room, where I am to eat the passover with my ¹⁵ disciples?' And he will show you a large upper room ¹⁶ furnished and ready; there prepare for us." And the disciples set out and went to the city, and found it as he had told them; and they prepared the passover.

¹⁷ And when it was evening he came with the twelve. ¹⁸ And as they were at table eating, Jesus said, "Truly, I say to you, one of you will betray me, one who is eating ¹⁹ with me." They began to be sorrowful, and to say to

20 him one after another, "Is it I?" He said to them, "It is one of the twelve, one who is dipping bread into the 21 dish with me. For the Son of man goes as it is written of him, but woe to that man by whom the Son of man is betrayed! It would have been better for that man if he had not been born."

22 And as they were eating, he took bread, and blessed, and broke it, and gave it to them, and said, "Take; this 23 is my body." And he took a cup, and when he had given thanks he gave it to them, and they all drank of it. 24 And he said to them, "This is my blood of the c covenant, 25 which is poured out for many. Truly, I say to you, I shall not drink again of the fruit of the vine until that day when I drink it new in the kingdom of God."

26 And when they had sung a hymn, they went out to the 27 Mount of Olives. And Jesus said to them, "You will all fall away; for it is written, 'I will strike the shepherd, and 28 the sheep will be scattered.' But after I am raised up, I 29 will go before you to Galilee." Peter said to him, "Even 30 though they all fall away, I will not." And Jesus said to him, "Truly, I say to you, this very night, before the 31 cock crows twice, you will deny me three times." But he said vehemently, "If I must die with you, I will not deny you." And they all said the same.

In Gethsemane

32 And they went to a place which was called Geth-sem′ane; and he said to his disciples, "Sit here, while I 33 pray." And he took with him Peter and James and John, 34 and began to be greatly distressed and troubled. And he said to them, "My soul is very sorrowful, even to death; 35 remain here, and watch." d And going a little farther, he fell on the ground and prayed that, if it were possible, 36 the hour might pass from him. And he said, "Abba, Father, all things are possible to thee; remove this cup from me; yet not what I will, but what thou wilt." 37 And he came and found them sleeping, and he said to Peter, "Simon, are you asleep? Could you not watch d 38 one hour? Watch d and pray that you may not enter into temptation; the spirit indeed is willing, but the flesh is 39 weak." And again he went away and prayed, saying the 40 same words. And again he came and found them sleeping, for their eyes were very heavy; and they did not 41 know what to answer him. And he came the third time, and said to them, "Are you still sleeping and taking your rest? It is enough; the hour has come; the Son of man 42 is betrayed into the hands of sinners. Rise, let us be going; see, my betrayer is at hand."

43 And immediately, while he was still speaking, Judas came, one of the twelve, and with him a crowd with swords and clubs, from the chief priests and the scribes 44 and the elders. Now the betrayer had given them a sign, saying, "The one I shall kiss is the man; seize him and 45 lead him away under guard." And when he came, he went

up to him at once, and said, "Master!" e And he kissed 46, 47 him. And they laid hands on him and seized him. But one of those who stood by drew his sword, and struck 48 the slave of the high priest and cut off his ear. And Jesus said to them, "Have you come out as against a robber, 49 with swords and clubs to capture me? Day after day I was with you in the temple teaching, and you did not 50 seize me. But let the scriptures be fulfilled." And they all forsook him, and fled.

51 And a young man followed him, with nothing but a 52 linen cloth about his body; and they seized him, but he left the linen cloth and ran away naked.

Before the High Priest

53 And they led Jesus to the high priest; and all the chief priests and the elders and the scribes were as-54 sembled. And Peter had followed him at a distance, right into the courtyard of the high priest; and he was sitting with the guards, and warming himself at 55 the fire. Now the chief priests and the whole council sought testimony against Jesus to put him to death; but 56 they found none. For many bore false witness against 57 him, and their witness did not agree. And some stood up 58 and bore false witness against him, saying, "We heard him say, 'I will destroy this temple that is made with hands, and in three days I will build another, not made 59 with hands.' " Yet not even so did their testimony agree. 60 And the high priest stood up in the midst, and asked Jesus, "Have you no answer to make? What is it that 61 these men testify against you?" But he was silent and made no answer. Again the high priest asked him, "Are 62 you the Christ, the Son of the Blessed?" And Jesus said, "I am; and you will see the Son of man seated at the right hand of Power, and coming with the clouds of heav-63 en." And the high priest tore his garments, and said, 64 "Why do we still need witnesses? You have heard his blasphemy. What is your decision?" And they all con-65 demned him as deserving death. And some began to spit on him, and to cover his face, and to strike him, saying to him, "Prophesy!" And the guards received him with blows.

66 And as Peter was below in the courtyard, one of the 67 maids of the high priest came; and seeing Peter warming himself, she looked at him, and said, "You also were 68 with the Nazarene, Jesus." But he denied it, saying, "I neither know nor understand what you mean." And he 69 went out into the gateway. f And the maid saw him, and began again to say to the bystanders, "This man is one 70 of them." But again he denied it. And after a little while again the bystanders said to Peter, "Certainly you are 71 one of them; for you are a Galilean." But he began to invoke a curse on himself and to swear, "I do not know 72 this man of whom you speak." And immediately the

c Other ancient authorities insert *new*   d Or *keep awake*
e Or *Rabbi*
f Or *fore-court*. Other ancient authorities add *and the cock crowed*

cock crowed a second time. And Peter remembered how Jesus had said to him, "Before the cock crows twice, you will deny me three times." And he broke down and wept.

Jesus Before Pilate

15 And as soon as it was morning the chief priests, with the elders and scribes, and the whole council held a consultation; and they bound Jesus and led him 2 away and delivered him to Pilate. And Pilate asked him, "Are you the King of the Jews?" And he answered him, 3 "You have said so." And the chief priests accused him 4 of many things. And Pilate again asked him, "Have you no answer to make? See how many charges they bring 5 against you." But Jesus made no further answer, so that Pilate wondered.

6 Now at the feast he used to release for them one 7 prisoner for whom they asked. And among the rebels in prison, who had committed murder in the insurrection, 8 there was a man called Barab'bas. And the crowd came up and began to ask Pilate to do as he was wont to do 9 for them. And he answered them, "Do you want me to 10 release for you the King of the Jews?" For he perceived that it was out of envy that the chief priests had 11 delivered him up. But the chief priests stirred up the crowd to have him release for them Barab'bas instead. 12 And Pilate again said to them, "Then what shall I do with the man whom you call the King of the Jews?" 13, 14 And they cried out again, "Crucify him." And Pilate said to them, "Why, what evil has he done?" But they 15 shouted all the more, "Crucify him." So Pilate, wishing to satisfy the crowd, released for them Barab'bas; and having scourged Jesus, he delivered him to be crucified.

16 And the soldiers led him away inside the palace (that is, the praetorium); and they called together the whole 17 battalion. And they clothed him in a purple cloak, and 18 plaiting a crown of thorns they put it on him. And they 19 began to salute him, "Hail, King of the Jews!" And they struck his head with a reed, and spat upon him, and 20 they knelt down in homage to him. And when they had mocked him, they stripped him of the purple cloak, and put his own clothes on him. And they led him out to crucify him.

THE CRUCIFIXION

21 And they compelled a passer-by, Simon of Cyre'ne, who was coming in from the country, the father of Alex-22 ander and Rufus, to carry his cross. And they brought him to the place called Gol'gotha (which means the 23 place of a skull). And they offered him wine mingled 24 with myrrh; but he did not take it. And they crucified him, and divided his garments among them, casting lots 25 for them, to decide what each should take. And it was 26 the third hour, when they crucified him. And the inscription of the charge against him read, "The King of 27 the Jews." And with him they crucified two robbers, one 29 on his right and one on his left.g And those who passed by derided him, wagging their heads, and saying, "Aha! You who would destroy the temple and build it in three 30 days, save yourself, and come down from the cross!" 31 So also the chief priests mocked him to one another with the scribes, saying, "He saved others; he cannot save 32 himself. Let the Christ, the King of Israel, come down now from the cross, that we may see and believe." Those who were crucified with him also reviled him.

33 And when the sixth hour had come, there was dark-34 ness over the whole land h until the ninth hour. And at the ninth hour Jesus cried with a loud voice, "E'lo-i, E'lo-i, la'ma sabach-tha'ni?" which means, "My God, my 35 God, why hast thou forsaken me?" And some of the bystanders hearing it said, "Behold, he is calling Eli'jah." 36 And one ran and, filling a sponge full of vinegar, put it on a reed and gave it to him to drink, saying, "Wait, let us see whether Eli'jah will come to take him down." 37 And Jesus uttered a loud cry, and breathed his last. 38 And the curtain of the temple was torn in two, from top 39 to bottom. And when the centurion, who stood facing him, saw that he thus i breathed his last, he said, "Truly this man was the Son x of God!"

40 There were also women looking on from afar, among whom were Mary Mag'dalene, and Mary the mother of 41 James the younger and of Joses, and Salo'me, who, when he was in Galilee, followed him, and ministered to him; and also many other women who came up with him to Jerusalem.

42 And when evening had come, since it was the day of 43 Preparation, that is, the day before the sabbath, Joseph of Arimathe'a, a respected member of the council, who was also himself looking for the kingdom of God, took courage and went to Pilate, and asked for the body of 44 Jesus. And Pilate wondered if he were already dead; and summoning the centurion, he asked him whether he was 45 already dead.j And when he learned from the centurion 46 that he was dead, he granted the body to Joseph. And he bought a linen shroud, and taking him down, wrapped him in the linen shroud, and laid him in a tomb which had been hewn out of the rock; and he rolled a stone

g Other ancient authorities insert verse 28, And the scripture was fulfilled which says, "He was reckoned with the transgressors"   h Or earth
i Other ancient authorities insert cried out and   x Or a son   j Other ancient authorities read whether he had been some time dead

47 against the door of the tomb. Mary Mag'dalene and Mary the mother of Joses saw where he was laid.

HE HAS RISEN

16 And when the sabbath was past, Mary Mag'dalene, and Mary the mother of James, and Salo'me, bought ² spices, so that they might go and anoint him. And very early on the first day of the week they went to the tomb ³ when the sun had risen. And they were saying to one another, "Who will roll away the stone for us from the ⁴ door of the tomb?" And looking up, they saw that the ⁵ stone was rolled back—it was very large. And entering the tomb, they saw a young man sitting on the right side, dressed in a white robe; and they were ⁶ amazed. And he said to them, "Do not be amazed; you seek Jesus of Nazareth, who was crucified. He has risen, ⁷ he is not here; see the place where they laid him. But go, tell his disciples and Peter that he is going before you to Galilee; there you will see him, as he told you." ⁸ And they went out and fled from the tomb; for trembling and astonishment had come upon them; and they said nothing to any one, for they were afraid. ⁹ Now when he rose early on the first day of the week, he appeared first to Mary Magdalene, from whom he had ¹⁰ cast out seven demons. She went and told those who had ¹¹ been with him, as they mourned and wept. But when they heard that he was alive and had been seen by her, they would not believe it.

¹² After this he appeared in another form to two of them, ¹³ as they were walking into the country. And they went back and told the rest, but they did not believe them. ¹⁴ Afterward he appeared to the eleven themselves as they sat at table; and he upbraided them for their unbelief and hardness of heart, because they had not believed ¹⁵ those who saw him after he had risen. And he said to them, "Go into all the world and preach the gospel to the ¹⁶ whole creation. He who believes and is baptized will be saved; but he who does not believe will be condemned. ¹⁷ And these signs will accompany those who believe: in my name they will cast out demons; they will speak in ¹⁸ new tongues; they will pick up serpents, and if they drink any deadly thing, it will not hurt them; they will lay their hands on the sick, and they will recover."

¹⁹ So then the Lord Jesus, after he had spoken to them, was taken up into heaven, and sat down at the right hand ²⁰ of God. And they went forth and preached everywhere, while the Lord worked with them and confirmed the message by the signs that attended it. Amen.

ᵏ Some of the most ancient authorities bring the book to a close at the end of verse 8. One authority concludes the book by adding after verse 8 the following: *But they reported briefly to Peter and those with him all that they had been told. And after this, Jesus himself sent out by means of them, from east to west, the sacred and imperishable proclamation of eternal salvation.* Other authorities include the preceding passage and continue with verses 9-20. In most authorities verses 9-20 follow immediately after verse 8; a few authorities insert additional material after verse 14.

INTRODUCTION TO

LUKE

This Gospel was written from Rome or Ephesus about A.D. 80-90. It was written in the Greek language. The author was a Gentile (non-Jewish) doctor named Luke. He was probably practicing medicine in the city of Troas when he first met the apostle-missionary Paul. In the Acts of the Apostles, we learn that Luke went with Paul on his journeys and finally to Rome, where he may have written the Gospel. Luke also wrote another book, called the Acts of the Apostles, which continued the story, telling of the beginnings of the church.

The purpose of the Gospel of Luke was to explain his faith in Jesus as the Christ to a Gentile friend, Theophilus. The phrase "most excellent Theophilus," in the opening sentence, probably indicates that he was a Roman official.

The opening words of this Gospel show something of the way in which all the Gospels came to be written. First, there were the facts about Jesus—all that he said and did. Then there were the "eyewitnesses and ministers" of the word remembering and telling others about the good news. Various persons wrote down parts of the whole wonderful story. Then Luke decided to gather everything he could learn about Jesus and prepare a more "orderly account."

To help him in his writing, Luke had the Gospel of Mark and a small collection of Jesus' sayings. We know that he also had other information about Jesus because some things are told only in his Gospel. For instance, only in Luke do we have the accounts of the birth of John the Baptist and of the visit of the shepherds and the song of the angels at the birth of Jesus. Luke is the only Gospel that tells us about the prodigal son, the shepherd who lost a sheep, and other stories.

Through the Gospel of Luke and the Acts of the Apostles Luke tells the marvelous story of God's love in Christ as the good news began to be spread to all mankind.

THE GOSPEL ACCORDING TO

LUKE

PREFACE

1 Inasmuch as many have undertaken to compile a narrative of the things which have been accomplished ² among us, just as they were delivered to us by those who from the beginning were eyewitnesses and ministers ³ of the word, it seemed good to me also, having followed all things closely[a] for some time past, to write an or-⁴ derly account for you, most excellent Theoph'ilus, that you may know the truth concerning the things of which you have been informed.

JESUS' BIRTH AND BOYHOOD

⁵ In the days of Herod, king of Judea, there was a priest named Zechari'ah,[b] of the division of Abi'jah; and he had a wife of the daughters of Aaron, and her name was ⁶ Elizabeth. And they were both righteous before God,

walking in all the commandments and ordinances of the ⁷ Lord blameless. But they had no child, because Elizabeth was barren, and both were advanced in years.

⁸ Now while he was serving as priest before God when ⁹ his division was on duty, according to the custom of the priesthood, it fell to him by lot to enter the temple of the ¹⁰ Lord and burn incense. And the whole multitude of the ¹¹ people were praying outside at the hour of incense. And there appeared to him an angel of the Lord standing on ¹² the right side of the altar of incense. And Zechari'ah was ¹³ troubled when he saw him, and fear fell upon him. But the angel said to him, "Do not be afraid, Zechari'ah, for your prayer is heard, and your wife Elizabeth will bear you a son, and you shall call his name John.

¹⁴ And you will have joy and gladness,
   and many will rejoice at his birth;

---

[a] Or accurately   [b] Greek Zacharias

15 for he will be great before the Lord,
and he shall drink no wine nor strong drink,
and he will be filled with the Holy Spirit,
even from his mother's womb.

16 And he will turn many of the sons of Israel to the Lord
their God,

17 and he will go before him in the spirit and power of
Eli′jah,
to turn the hearts of the fathers to the children,
and the disobedient to the wisdom of the just,
to make ready for the Lord a people prepared.''

18 And Zechari′ah said to the angel, "How shall I know
this? For I am an old man, and my wife is advanced in

19 years.'' And the angel answered him, "I am Gabriel, who
stand in the presence of God; and I was sent to speak

20 to you, and to bring you this good news. And behold,
you will be silent and unable to speak until the day that
these things come to pass, because you did not believe

21 my words, which will be fulfilled in their time.'' And the
people were waiting for Zechari′ah, and they wondered

22 at his delay in the temple. And when he came out, he
could not speak to them, and they perceived that he had
seen a vision in the temple; and he made signs to them

23 and remained dumb. And when his time of service was
ended, he went to his home.

24 After these days his wife Elizabeth conceived, and for

25 five months she hid herself, saying, "Thus the Lord has
done to me in the days when he looked on me, to take
away my reproach among men.''

26 In the sixth month the angel Gabriel was sent from

27 God to a city of Galilee named Nazareth, to a virgin
betrothed to a man whose name was Joseph, of the house

28 of David; and the virgin's name was Mary. And he came
to her and said, "Hail, O favored one, the Lord is with

29 you!'' c But she was greatly troubled at the saying, and
considered in her mind what sort of greeting this might

30 be. And the angel said to her, "Do not be afraid, Mary,

31 for you have found favor with God. And behold, you
will conceive in your womb and bear a son, and you
shall call his name Jesus.

32 He will be great, and will be called the Son of the Most
High;
and the Lord God will give to him the throne of his
father David,

33 and he will reign over the house of Jacob for ever;
and of his kingdom there will be no end.''

34 And Mary said to the angel, "How shall this be, since I
have no husband?''

35 And the angel said to her,
"The Holy Spirit will come upon you,
and the power of the Most High will overshadow you;
therefore the child to be born d will be called holy,
the Son of God.

36 And behold, your kinswoman Elizabeth in her old age
has also conceived a son; and this is the sixth month

37 with her who was called barren. For with God nothing

38 will be impossible.'' And Mary said, "Behold, I am the
handmaid of the Lord; let it be to me according to your
word.'' And the angel departed from her.

39 In those days Mary arose and went with haste into the

40 hill country, to a city of Judah, and she entered the

41 house of Zechari′ah and greeted Elizabeth. And when
Elizabeth heard the greeting of Mary, the babe leaped in
her womb; and Elizabeth was filled with the Holy Spirit

42 and she exclaimed with a loud cry, "Blessed are you
among women, and blessed is the fruit of your womb!

43 And why is this granted me, that the mother of my Lord

44 should come to me? For behold, when the voice of your
greeting came to my ears, the babe in my womb leaped

45 for joy. And blessed is she who believed that there would
be e a fulfilment of what was spoken to her from the

46 Lord.'' And Mary said,
"My soul magnifies the Lord,

47 and my spirit rejoices in God my Savior,

48 for he has regarded the low estate of his handmaiden.
For behold, henceforth all generations will call me
blessed;

49 for he who is mighty has done great things for me,
and holy is his name.

50 And his mercy is on those who fear him
from generation to generation.

51 He has shown strength with his arm,
he has scattered the proud in the imagination of their
hearts,

52 he has put down the mighty from their thrones,
and exalted those of low degree;

53 he has filled the hungry with good things,
and the rich he has sent empty away.

54 He has helped his servant Israel,
in remembrance of his mercy,

55 as he spoke to our fathers,
to Abraham and to his posterity for ever.''

56 And Mary remained with her about three months, and
returned to her home.

57 Now the time came for Elizabeth to be delivered, and

58 she gave birth to a son. And her neighbors and kinsfolk
heard that the Lord had shown great mercy to her, and

59 they rejoiced with her. And on the eighth day they
came to circumcise the child; and they would have named

60 him Zechari′ah after his father, but his mother said,

61 "Not so; he shall be called John.'' And they said to her,

c Other ancient authorities add *"Blessed are you among women!"*
e Or *believed, for there will be*

d Other ancient authorities add *of you*

62 "None of your kindred is called by this name." And they made signs to his father, inquiring what he would 63 have him called. And he asked for a writing tablet, and 64 wrote, "His name is John." And they all marveled. And immediately his mouth was opened and his tongue loosed, 65 and he spoke, blessing God. And fear came on all their neighbors. And all these things were talked about through 66 all the hill country of Judea; and all who heard them laid them up in their hearts, saying, "What then will this child be?" For the hand of the Lord was with him.

67 And his father Zechari'ah was filled with the Holy Spirit, and prophesied, saying,

68 "Blessed be the Lord God of Israel,
  for he has visited and redeemed his people,
69 and has raised up a horn of salvation for us
  in the house of his servant David,
70 as he spoke by the mouth of his holy prophets from of
  old,
71 that we should be saved from our enemies,
  and from the hand of all who hate us;
72 to perform the mercy promised to our fathers,
  and to remember his holy covenant,
73, 74 the oath which he swore to our father Abraham, to
  grant us
  that we, being delivered from the hand of our enemies,
  might serve him without fear,
75 in holiness and righteousness before him all the days of
  our life.
76 And you, child, will be called the prophet of the Most
  High;
  for you will go before the Lord to prepare his ways,
77 to give knowledge of salvation to his people
  in the forgiveness of their sins,
78 through the tender mercy of our God,
  when the day shall dawn upon f us from on high
79 to give light to those who sit in darkness and in the
  shadow of death,
  to guide our feet into the way of peace."

80 And the child grew and became strong in spirit, and he was in the wilderness till the day of his manifestation to Israel.

2 In those days a decree went out from Caesar Augus-
2 tus that all the world should be enrolled. This was the first enrollment, when Quirin'i-us was governor of Syria. 3, 4 And all went to be enrolled, each to his own city. And Joseph also went up from Galilee, from the city of Naza-reth, to Judea, to the city of David, which is called Beth-lehem, because he was of the house and lineage of David, 5 to be enrolled with Mary, his betrothed, who was with 6 child. And while they were there, the time came for her 7 to be delivered. And she gave birth to her first-born son and wrapped him in swaddling cloths, and laid him in a manger, because there was no place for them in the inn.

8 And in that region there were shepherds out in the 9 field, keeping watch over their flock by night. And an angel of the Lord appeared to them, and the glory of the Lord shone around them, and they were filled with 10 fear. And the angel said to them, "Be not afraid; for behold, I bring you good news of a great joy which 11 will come to all the people; for to you is born this day in the city of David a Savior, who is Christ the Lord. 12 And this will be a sign for you: you will find a babe 13 wrapped in swaddling cloths and lying in a manger." And

suddenly there was with the angel a multitude of the heavenly host praising God and saying,
14 "Glory to God in the highest,
  and on earth peace among men with whom he is
  pleased!" g
15 When the angels went away from them into heaven, the shepherds said to one another, "Let us go over to Bethlehem and see this thing that has happened, which 16 the Lord has made known to us." And they went with haste, and found Mary and Joseph, and the babe lying 17 in a manger. And when they saw it they made known the saying which had been told them concerning this child; 18 and all who heard it wondered at what the shepherds 19 told them. But Mary kept all these things, pondering 20 them in her heart. And the shepherds returned, glorifying and praising God for all they had heard and seen, as it had been told them.

21 And at the end of eight days, when he was circum-cised, he was called Jesus, the name given by the angel before he was conceived in the womb.

22 And when the time came for their purification accord-ing to the law of Moses, they brought him up to Jeru-23 salem to present him to the Lord (as it is written in the law of the Lord, "Every male that opens the womb shall 24 be called holy to the Lord") and to offer a sacrifice ac-cording to what is said in the law of the Lord, "a pair 25 of turtledoves, or two young pigeons." Now there was a man in Jerusalem, whose name was Simeon, and this man was righteous and devout, looking for the consola-26 tion of Israel, and the Holy Spirit was upon him. And

f Or *whereby the dayspring will visit.* Other ancient authorities read *since the dayspring has visited*
g Other ancient authorities read *peace, good will among men*

it had been revealed to him by the Holy Spirit that he should not see death before he had seen the Lord's Christ.
27 And inspired by the Spirit[h] he came into the temple; and when the parents brought in the child Jesus, to do
28 for him according to the custom of the law, he took him up in his arms and blessed God and said,

29 "Lord, now lettest thou thy servant depart in peace, according to thy word;
30 for mine eyes have seen thy salvation
31 which thou hast prepared in the presence of all peoples,
32 a light for revelation to the Gentiles, and for glory to thy people Israel."

33 And his father and his mother marveled at what was
34 said about him; and Simeon blessed them and said to Mary his mother,

"Behold, this child is set for the fall and rising of many in Israel,
and for a sign that is spoken against
35 (and a sword will pierce through your own soul also), that thoughts out of many hearts may be revealed."

36 And there was a prophetess, Anna, the daughter of Phan'u-el, of the tribe of Asher; she was of a great age, having lived with her husband seven years from her
37 virginity, and as a widow till she was eighty-four. She did not depart from the temple, worshiping with fasting
38 and prayer night and day. And coming up at that very hour she gave thanks to God, and spoke of him to all who were looking for the redemption of Jerusalem.

39 And when they had performed everything according to the law of the Lord, they returned into Galilee, to their
40 own city, Nazareth. And the child grew and became strong, filled with wisdom; and the favor of God was upon him.

41 Now his parents went to Jerusalem every year at the
42 feast of the Passover. And when he was twelve years old,
43 they went up according to custom; and when the feast was ended, as they were returning, the boy Jesus stayed
44 behind in Jerusalem. His parents did not know it, but supposing him to be in the company they went a day's journey, and they sought him among their kinsfolk and
45 acquaintances; and when they did not find him, they
46 returned to Jerusalem, seeking him. After three days

they found him in the temple, sitting among the teachers,
47 listening to them and asking them questions; and all who heard him were amazed at his understanding and his
48 answers. And when they saw him they were astonished;

and his mother said to him, "Son, why have you treated us so? Behold, your father and I have been looking for
49 you anxiously." And he said to them, "How is it that you sought me? Did you not know that I must be in my
50 Father's house?" And they did not understand the say-
51 ing which he spoke to them. And he went down with them and came to Nazareth, and was obedient to them; and his mother kept all these things in her heart.

52 And Jesus increased in wisdom and in stature,[i] and in favor with God and man.

INTRODUCTION TO JESUS' PUBLIC MINISTRY

John The Baptist Prepares the Way

3 In the fifteenth year of the reign of Tibe'ri-us Caesar, Pontius Pilate being governor of Judea, and Herod being tetrarch of Galilee, and his brother Philip tetrarch of the region of Iturae'a and Trachoni'tis, and
2 Lysa'ni-as tetrarch of Abile'ne, in the high-priesthood of Annas and Ca'iaphas, the word of God came to John
3 the son of Zechari'ah in the wilderness; and he went into all the region about the Jordan, preaching a baptism
4 of repentance for the forgiveness of sins. As it is written in the book of the words of Isaiah the prophet,

"The voice of one crying in the wilderness:
Prepare the way of the Lord,
make his paths straight.
5 Every valley shall be filled,
and every mountain and hill shall be brought low,
and the crooked shall be made straight,
and the rough ways shall be made smooth;
6 and all flesh shall see the salvation of God."

7 He said therefore to the multitudes that came out to be baptized by him, "You brood of vipers! Who warned
8 you to flee from the wrath to come? Bear fruits that befit repentance, and do not begin to say to yourselves, 'We have Abraham as our father'; for I tell you, God is able
9 from these stones to raise up children to Abraham. Even now the axe is laid to the root of the trees; every tree therefore that does not bear good fruit is cut down and thrown into the fire."

10 And the multitudes asked him, "What then shall we

11 do?" And he answered them, "He who has two coats, let him share with him who has none; and he who has food,
12 let him do likewise." Tax collectors also came to be baptized, and said to him, "Teacher, what shall we do?"

h Or in the Spirit   i Or years

13 And he said to them, "Collect no more than is appointed
14 you." Soldiers also asked him, "And we, what shall we do?" And he said to them, "Rob no one by violence or by false accusation, and be content with your wages."

15 As the people were in expectation, and all men questioned in their hearts concerning John, whether perhaps
16 he were the Christ, John answered them all, "I baptize you with water; but he who is mightier than I is coming, the thong of whose sandals I am not worthy to untie; he will baptize you with the Holy Spirit and with fire.
17 His winnowing fork is in his hand, to clear his threshing floor, and to gather the wheat into his granary, but the chaff he will burn with unquenchable fire."

18 So, with many other exhortations, he preached good
19 news to the people. But Herod the tetrarch, who had been reproved by him for Hero'di-as, his brother's wife,
20 and for all the evil things that Herod had done, added this to them all, that he shut up John in prison.

Jesus' Baptism

21 Now when all the people were baptized, and when Jesus also had been baptized and was praying, the heaven
22 was opened, and the Holy Spirit descended upon him in bodily form, as a dove, and a voice came from heaven, "Thou art my beloved Son;[j] with thee I am well pleased."[k]

Jesus' Genealogy

23 Jesus, when he began his ministry, was about thirty years of age, being the son (as was supposed) of Joseph,
24 the son of Heli, the son of Matthat, the son of Levi, the son of Melchi, the son of Jan'na-i, the son of Joseph,
25 the son of Mattathi'as, the son of Amos, the son of
26 Nahum, the son of Esli, the son of Nag'ga-i, the son of Ma'ath, the son of Mattathi'as, the son of Sem'e-in, the
27 son of Josech, the son of Joda, the son of Jo-an'an, the son of Rhesa, the son of Zerub'babel, the son of Sheal'ti-
28 el,[l] the son of Neri, the son of Melchi, the son of Addi, the son of Cosam, the son of Elma'dam, the son of Er, the
29 son of Joshua, the son of Elie'zer, the son of Jorim,
30 the son of Matthat, the son of Levi, the son of Simeon, the son of Judah, the son of Joseph, the son of Jonam, the
31 son of Eli'akim, the son of Me'le-a, the son of Menna, the son of Mat'tatha, the son of Nathan, the son of
32 David, the son of Jesse, the son of Obed, the son
33 of Bo'az, the son of Sala, the son of Nahshon, the son of Ammin'adab, the son of Admin, the son of Arni, the son
34 of Hezron, the son of Perez, the son of Judah, the son of Jacob, the son of Isaac, the son of Abraham, the son
35 of Terah, the son of Nahor, the son of Serug, the son of Re'u, the son of Peleg, the son of Eber, the son of
36 Shelah, the son of Ca-i'nan, the son of Arpha'xad, the son of Shem, the son of Noah, the son of Lamech,
37 the son of Methuselah, the son of Enoch, the son of
38 Jared, the son of Maha'lale-el, the son of Ca-i'nan, the son of Enos, the son of Seth, the son of Adam, the son of God.

The Temptation

4 And Jesus, full of the Holy Spirit, returned from
2 the Jordan, and was led by the Spirit for forty days in the wilderness, tempted by the devil. And he ate nothing in those days; and when they were ended, he
3 was hungry. The devil said to him, "If you are the Son
4 of God, command this stone to become bread." And Jesus answered him, "It is written, 'Man shall not live
5 by bread alone.'" And the devil took him up, and showed him all the kingdoms of the world in a moment
6 of time, and said to him, "To you I will give all this authority and their glory; for it has been delivered to
7 me, and I give it to whom I will. If you, then, will wor-
8 ship me, it shall all be yours." And Jesus answered him, "It is written,

'You shall worship the Lord your God,
and him only shall you serve.'"

9 And he took him to Jerusalem, and set him on the pinnacle of the temple, and said to him, "If you are the
10 Son of God, throw yourself down from here; for it is written,

'He will give his angels charge of you, to guard you,'
11 and

'On their hands they will bear you up
lest you strike your foot against a stone.'"
12 And Jesus answered him, "It is said, 'You shall not
13 tempt the Lord your God.'" And when the devil had ended every temptation, he departed from him until an opportune time.

JESUS' GALILEAN MINISTRY

14 And Jesus returned in the power of the Spirit into Galilee, and a report concerning him went out through
15 all the surrounding country. And he taught in their synagogues, being glorified by all.

16 And he came to Nazareth, where he had been brought up; and he went to the synagogue, as his custom was, on
17 the sabbath day. And he stood up to read; and there was given to him the book of the prophet Isaiah. He opened the book and found the place where it was written,

18 "The Spirit of the Lord is upon me,
because he has anointed me to preach good news to the poor.
He has sent me to proclaim release to the captives
and recovering of sight
to the blind,
to set at liberty those who are oppressed,
19 to proclaim the acceptable year of the Lord."

---

j Or my Son, my (or the) Beloved   k Other ancient authorities read today I have begotten thee   l Greek Salathiel

20 And he closed the book, and gave it back to the attendant, and sat down; and the eyes of all in the synagogue were 21 fixed on him. And he began to say to them, "Today this 22 scripture has been fulfilled in your hearing." And all spoke well of him, and wondered at the gracious words which proceeded out of his mouth; and they said, "Is 23 not this Joseph's son?" And he said to them, "Doubtless you will quote to me this proverb, 'Physician, heal yourself; what we have heard you did at Caper'na-um, do 24 here also in your own country.' " And he said, "Truly, I say to you, no prophet is acceptable in his own coun- 25 try. But in truth, I tell you, there were many widows in Israel in the days of Eli'jah, when the heaven was shut up three years and six months, when there came a great 26 famine over all the land; and Eli'jah was sent to none of them but only to Zar'ephath, in the land of Sidon, to a

27 woman who was a widow. And there were many lepers in Israel in the time of the prophet Eli'sha; and none of 28 them was cleansed, but only Na'aman the Syrian." When they heard this, all in the synagogue were filled with 29 wrath. And they rose up and put him out of the city, and led him to the brow of the hill on which their city was built, that they might throw him down headlong. 30 But passing through the midst of them he went away.

Visit to Capernaum

31 And he went down to Caper'na-um, a city of Galilee. 32 And he was teaching them on the sabbath; and they were astonished at his teaching, for his word was with 33 authority. And in the synagogue there was a man who had the spirit of an unclean demon; and he cried out 34 with a loud voice, "Ah!m What have you to do with us, Jesus of Nazareth? Have you come to destroy us? I 35 know who you are, the Holy One of God." But Jesus rebuked him, saying, "Be silent, and come out of him!" And when the demon had thrown him down in the midst, 36 he came out of him, having done him no harm. And they were all amazed and said to one another, "What is this word? For with authority and power he commands 37 the unclean spirits, and they come out." And reports of him went out into every place in the surrounding region. 38 And he arose and left the synagogue, and entered Simon's house. Now Simon's mother-in-law was ill with

39 a high fever, and they besought him for her. And he stood over her and rebuked the fever, and it left her; and immediately she rose and served them.

40 Now when the sun was setting, all those who had any that were sick with various diseases brought them to him; and he laid his hands on every one of them and healed 41 them. And demons also came out of many, crying, "You are the Son of God!" But he rebuked them, and would not allow them to speak, because they knew that he was the Christ.

42 And when it was day he departed and went into a lonely place. And the people sought him and came to him, and 43 would have kept him from leaving them; but he said to them, "I must preach the good news of the kingdom of God to the other cities also; for I was sent for this 44 purpose." And he was preaching in the synagogues of Judea.n

5 While the people pressed upon him to hear the word of God, he was standing by the lake of Genes'aret. And 2 he saw two boats by the lake; but the fishermen had 3 gone out of them and were washing their nets. Getting into one of the boats, which was Simon's, he asked him to put out a little from the land. And he sat down and 4 taught the people from the boat. And when he had ceased speaking, he said to Simon, "Put out into the deep and 5 let down your nets for a catch." And Simon answered, "Master, we toiled all night and took nothing! But at 6 your word I will let down the nets." And when they had done this, they enclosed a great shoal of fish; and as 7 their nets were breaking, they beckoned to their partners in the other boat to come and help them. And they came and filled both the boats, so that they began to sink. 8 But when Simon Peter saw it, he fell down at Jesus' 9 knees, saying, "Depart from me, for I am a sinful man, O Lord." For he was astonished, and all that were with 10 him, at the catch of fish which they had taken; and so also were James and John, sons of Zeb'edee, who were partners with Simon. And Jesus said to Simon, "Do not 11 be afraid; henceforth you will be catching men." And when they had brought their boats to land, they left everything and followed him.

12 While he was in one of the cities, there came a man full of leprosy; and when he saw Jesus, he fell on his face and besought him, "Lord, if you will, you can make 13 me clean." And he stretched out his hand, and touched him, saying, "I will; be clean." And immediately the 14 leprosy left him. And he charged him to tell no one; but "go and show yourself to the priest, and make an offering for your cleansing, as Moses commanded, for a 15 proof to the people."o But so much the more the report went abroad concerning him; and great multitudes gath- 16 ered to hear and to be healed of their infirmities. But he withdrew to the wilderness and prayed.

m Or *Let us alone*   n Other ancient authorities read *Galilee*   o Greek *to them*

Controversies with Pharisees

17 On one of those days, as he was teaching, there were Pharisees and teachers of the law sitting by, who had come from every village of Galilee and Judea and from Jerusalem; and the power of the Lord was with him to 18 heal.[p] And behold, men were bringing on a bed a man who was paralyzed, and they sought to bring him in and 19 lay him before Jesus;[q] but finding no way to bring him in, because of the crowd, they went up on the roof and let him down with his bed through the tiles into the midst 20 before Jesus. And when he saw their faith he said, "Man, 21 your sins are forgiven you." And the scribes and the Pharisees began to question, saying, "Who is this that speaks blasphemies? Who can forgive sins but God only?" 22 When Jesus perceived their questionings, he answered 23 them, "Why do you question in your hearts? Which is easier, to say, 'Your sins are forgiven you,' or to say, 24 'Rise and walk'? But that you may know that the Son of man has authority on earth to forgive sins"—he said to the man who was paralyzed—"I say to you, rise, take 25 up your bed and go home." And immediately he rose before them, and took up that on which he lay, and went 26 home, glorifying God. And amazement seized them all, and they glorified God and were filled with awe, saying, "We have seen strange things today."

27 After this he went out, and saw a tax collector, named Levi, sitting at the tax office; and he said to him, "Follow 28 me." And he left everything, and rose and followed him.

29 And Levi made him a great feast in his house; and there was a large company of tax collectors and others 30 sitting at table[r] with them. And the Pharisees and their scribes murmured against his disciples, saying, "Why do you eat and drink with tax collectors and sinners?" 31 And Jesus answered them, "Those who are well have no 32 need of a physician, but those who are sick; I have not come to call the righteous, but sinners to repentance."

33 And they said to him, "The disciples of John fast often and offer prayers, and so do the disciples of the 34 Pharisees, but yours eat and drink." And Jesus said to them, "Can you make wedding guests fast while the 35 bridegroom is with them? The days will come, when the bridegroom is taken away from them, and then they will 36 fast in those days." He told them a parable also: "No one tears a piece from a new garment and puts it upon an old garment; if he does, he will tear the new, and the 37 piece from the new will not match the old. And no one puts new wine into old wineskins; if he does, the new wine will burst the skins and it will be spilled, and the 38 skins will be destroyed. But new wine must be put into 39 fresh wineskins. And no one after drinking old wine desires new; for he says, 'The old is good.' "[s]

6 On a sabbath,[t] while he was going through the grainfields, his disciples plucked and ate some heads of 2 grain, rubbing them in their hands. But some of the Pharisees said, "Why are you doing what is not lawful 3 to do on the sabbath?" And Jesus answered, "Have you not read what David did when he was hungry, he and 4 those who were with him: how he entered the house of God, and took and ate the bread of the Presence, which it is not lawful for any but the priests to eat, and also 5 gave it to those with him?" And he said to them, "The Son of man is lord of the sabbath."

6 On another sabbath, when he entered the synagogue and taught, a man was there whose right hand was withered. 7 And the scribes and the Pharisees watched him, to see whether he would heal on the sabbath, so that they might 8 find an accusation against him. But he knew their thoughts, and he said to the man who had the withered hand, "Come and stand here." And he rose and stood 9 there. And Jesus said to them, "I ask you, is it lawful on the sabbath to do good or to do harm, to save life or to 10 destroy it?" And he looked around on them all, and said to him, "Stretch out your hand." And he did so, and his 11 hand was restored. But they were filled with fury and discussed with one another what they might do to Jesus.

The Twelve

12 In these days he went out to the mountain to pray; and 13 all night he continued in prayer to God. And when it was day, he called his disciples, and chose from them twelve, 14 whom he named apostles; Simon, whom he named Peter, and Andrew his brother, and James and John, and 15 Philip, and Bartholomew, and Matthew, and Thomas, and James the son of Alphaeus, and Simon who was called the 16 Zealot, and Judas the son of James, and Judas Iscariot, who became a traitor.

The Great Sermon

17 And he came down with them and stood on a level place, with a great crowd of his disciples and a great multitude of people from all Judea and Jerusalem and the seacoast of Tyre and Sidon, who came to hear him 18 and to be healed of their diseases; and those who were 19 troubled with unclean spirits were cured. And all the crowd sought to touch him, for power came forth from

---

p Other ancient authorities read *was present to heal them*   q Greek *him*   r Greek *reclining*
s Other ancient authorities read *better*   t Other ancient authorities read *On the second first sabbath* (on the second sabbath after the first)

him and healed them all.

20 And he lifted up his eyes on his disciples, and said: "Blessed are you poor, for yours is the kingdom of God.

21 "Blessed are you that hunger now, for you shall be satisfied.

"Blessed are you that weep now, for you shall laugh.

22 "Blessed are you when men hate you, and when they exclude you and revile you, and cast out your name as 23 evil, on account of the Son of man! Rejoice in that day, and leap for joy, for behold, your reward is great in heaven; for so their fathers did to the prophets.

24 "But woe to you that are rich, for you have received your consolation.

25 "Woe to you that are full now, for you shall hunger.

"Woe to you that laugh now, for you shall mourn and weep.

26 "Woe to you, when all men speak well of you, for so their fathers did to the false prophets.

27 "But I say to you that hear, Love your enemies, do 28 good to those who hate you, bless those who curse you, 29 pray for those who abuse you. To him who strikes you on the cheek, offer the other also; and from him who takes away your coat do not withhold even your shirt. 30 Give to every one who begs from you; and of him who 31 takes away your goods do not ask them again. And as you wish that men would do to you, do so to them.

32 "If you love those who love you, what credit is that to 33 you? For even sinners love those who love them. And if you do good to those who do good to you, what credit is 34 that to you? For even sinners do the same. And if you lend to those from whom you hope to receive, what credit is that to you? Even sinners lend to sinners, to receive 35 as much again. But love your enemies, and do good, and lend, expecting nothing in return; v and your reward will be great, and you will be sons of the Most High; for he 36 is kind to the ungrateful and the selfish. Be merciful, even as your Father is merciful.

37 "Judge not, and you will not be judged; condemn not, and you will not be condemned; forgive, and you will 38 be forgiven; give, and it will be given to you; good measure, pressed down, shaken together, running over, will be put into your lap. For the measure you give will be the measure you get back."

39 He also told them a parable: "Can a blind man lead 40 a blind man? Will they not both fall into a pit? A disciple is not above his teacher, but every one when he is 41 fully taught will be like his teacher. Why do you see the speck that is in your brother's eye, but do not notice the 42 log that is in your own eye? Or how can you say to your brother, 'Brother, let me take out the speck that is in your eye,' when you yourself do not see the log that is in your own eye? You hypocrite, first take the log out of your own eye, and then you will see clearly to take out the

speck that is in your brother's eye.

43 "For no good tree bears bad fruit, nor again does a bad 44 tree bear good fruit; for each tree is known by its own fruit. For figs are not gathered from thorns, nor are 45 grapes picked from a bramble bush. The good man out of the good treasure of his heart produces good, and the evil man out of his evil treasure produces evil; for out of the abundance of the heart his mouth speaks.

46 "Why do you call me 'Lord, Lord,' and not do what 47 I tell you? Every one who comes to me and hears my words and does them, I will show you what he is like: 48 he is like a man building a house, who dug deep, and laid the foundation upon rock; and when a flood arose, the stream broke against that house, and could not shake 49 it, because it had been well built.w But he who hears and does not do them is like a man who built a house on the ground without a foundation; against which the stream broke, and immediately it fell, and the ruin of that house was great."

Jesus' Healing Ministry

7 After he had ended all his sayings in the hearing of 2 the people he entered Caper′na-um. Now a centurion had a slave who was dear x to him, who was sick and at 3 the point of death. When he heard of Jesus, he sent to him elders of the Jews, asking him to come and heal his 4 slave. And when they came to Jesus, they besought him earnestly, saying, "He is worthy to have you do this for 5 him, for he loves our nation, and he built us our syna- 6 gogue." And Jesus went with them. When he was not far from the house, the centurion sent friends to him, saying to him, "Lord, do not trouble yourself, for I am not 7 worthy to have you come under my roof; therefore I did not presume to come to you. But say the word, and let 8 my servant be healed. For I am a man set under authority, with soldiers under me: and I say to one, 'Go,' and he goes; and to another, 'Come,' and he comes; and to my 9 slave, 'Do this,' and he does it." When Jesus heard this he marveled at him, and turned and said to the multitude that followed him, "I tell you, not even in Israel have I 10 found such faith." And when those who had been sent returned to the house, they found the slave well.

11 Soon afterward y he went to a city called Na′in, and his 12 disciples and a great crowd went with him. As he drew near to the gate of the city, behold, a man who had died was being carried out, the only son of his mother, and she was a widow; and a large crowd from the city was with 13 her. And when the Lord saw her, he had compassion on 14 her and said to her, "Do not weep." And he came and touched the bier, and the bearers stood still. And he said, 15 "Young man, I say to you, arise." And the dead man sat up, and began to speak. And he gave him to his 16 mother. Fear seized them all; and they glorified God,

v Other ancient authorities read *despairing of no man*   w Other ancient authorities read *founded upon the rock*   x Or *valuable*
y Other ancient authorities read *Next day*

saying, "A great prophet has arisen among us!" and
17 "God has visited his people!" And this report concerning him spread through the whole of Judea and all the surrounding country.

18 The disciples of John told him of all these things.
19 And John, calling to him two of his disciples, sent them to the Lord, saying, "Are you he who is to come, or shall
20 we look for another?" And when the men had come to him, they said, "John the Baptist has sent us to you, saying, 'Are you he who is to come, or shall we look for
21 another?'" In that hour he cured many of diseases and plagues and evil spirits, and on many that were blind he
22 bestowed sight. And he answered them, "Go and tell John what you have seen and heard: the blind receive their sight, the lame walk, lepers are cleansed, and the deaf hear, the dead are raised up, the poor have good news
23 preached to them. And blessed is he who takes no offense at me."

24 When the messengers of John had gone, he began to speak to the crowds concerning John: "What did you go out into the wilderness to behold? A reed shaken by the
25 wind? What then did you go out to see? A man clothed in soft clothing? Behold, those who are gorgeously appareled
26 and live in luxury are in kings' courts. What then did you go out to see? A prophet? Yes, I tell you, and more than
27 a prophet. This is he of whom it is written,
'Behold, I send my messenger before thy face,
who shall prepare thy way before thee.'
28 I tell you, among those born of women none is greater than John; yet he who is least in the kingdom of God is
29 greater than he." (When they heard this all the people and the tax collectors justified God, having been baptized
30 with the baptism of John; but the Pharisees and the lawyers rejected the purpose of God for themselves, not having been baptized by him.)
31 "To what then shall I compare the men of this genera-
32 tion, and what are they like? They are like children sitting in the market place and calling to one another,
'We piped to you, and you did not dance;
we wailed, and you did not weep.'
33 For John the Baptist has come eating no bread and drinking no wine; and you say, 'He has a demon.'
34 The Son of man has come eating and drinking; and you say, 'Behold, a glutton and a drunkard, a friend of tax
35 collectors and sinners!' Yet wisdom is justified by all her children."

36 One of the Pharisees asked him to eat with him, and he went into the Pharisee's house, and took his place at
37 table. And behold, a woman of the city, who was a

sinner, when she learned that he was at table in the Pharisee's house, brought an alabaster flask of ointment,
38 and standing behind him at his feet, weeping, she began to wet his feet with her tears, and wiped them with the hair of her head, and kissed his feet, and anointed them
39 with the ointment. Now when the Pharisee who had invited him saw it, he said to himself, "If this man were a prophet, he would have known who and what sort of woman this is who is touching him, for she is a sinner."
40 And Jesus answering said to him, "Simon, I have something to say to you." And he answered, "What is it,
41 Teacher?" "A certain creditor had two debtors; one
42 owed five hundred denarii, and the other fifty. When they could not pay, he forgave them both. Now which
43 of them will love him more?" Simon answered, "The one, I suppose, to whom he forgave more." And he said
44 to him, "You have judged rightly." Then turning toward the woman he said to Simon, "Do you see this woman? I entered your house, you gave me no water for my feet, but she has wet my feet with her tears and wiped them
45 with her hair. You gave me no kiss, but from the time I
46 came in she has not ceased to kiss my feet. You did not anoint my head with oil, but she has anointed my feet
47 with ointment. Therefore I tell you, her sins, which are many, are forgiven, for she loved much; but he who is
48 forgiven little, loves little." And he said to her, "Your
49 sins are forgiven." Then those who were at table with him began to say among themselves, "Who is this, who
50 even forgives sins?" And he said to the woman, "Your faith has saved you; go in peace."

Traveling Teacher and Wonder Worker

8 Soon afterward he went on through cities and villages, preaching and bringing the good news of the
2 kingdom of God. And the twelve were with him, and also some women who had been healed of evil spirits and infirmities: Mary, called Mag'dalene, from whom seven
3 demons had gone out, and Jo-an'na, the wife of Chu'za, Herod's steward, and Susanna, and many others, who provided for them z out of their means.

4 And when a great crowd came together and people from town after town came to him, he said in a parable:
5 "A sower went out to sow his seed; and as he sowed, some fell along the path, and was trodden under foot,
6 and the birds of the air devoured it. And some fell on the rock; and as it grew up, it withered away, because it
7 had no moisture. And some fell among thorns; and the
8 thorns grew with it and choked it. And some fell into good soil and grew, and yielded a hundredfold." As he said this, he called out, "He who has ears to hear, let him hear."
9 And when his disciples asked him what this parable
10 meant, he said, "To you it has been given to know the

z Other ancient authorities read him

secrets of the kingdom of God; but for others they are in parables, so that seeing they may not see, and hearing 11 they may not understand. Now the parable is this: The 12 seed is the word of God. The ones along the path are those who have heard; then the devil comes and takes away the word from their hearts, that they may not be- 13 lieve and be saved. And the ones on the rock are those who, when they hear the word, receive it with joy; but these have no root, they believe for a while and in time of 14 temptation fall away. And as for what fell among the thorns, they are those who hear, but as they go on their way they are choked by the cares and riches and pleasures 15 of life, and their fruit does not mature. And as for that

in the good soil, they are those who, hearing the word, hold it fast in an honest and good heart, and bring forth fruit with patience.

16   "No one after lighting a lamp covers it with a vessel, or puts it under a bed, but puts it on a stand, that those 17 who enter may see the light. For nothing is hid that shall not be made manifest, nor anything secret that shall not 18 be known and come to light. Take heed then how you hear; for to him who has will more be given, and from him who has not, even what he thinks that he has will be taken away."

19   Then his mother and his brothers came to him, but 20 they could not reach him for the crowd. And he was told, "Your mother and your brothers are standing outside, 21 desiring to see you." But he said to them, "My mother and my brothers are those who hear the word of God and do it."

22   One day he got into a boat with his disciples, and he said to them, "Let us go across to the other side of the 23 lake." So they set out, and as they sailed he fell asleep. And a storm of wind came down on the lake, and they 24 were filling with water, and were in danger. And they went and woke him, saying, "Master, Master, we are perish- ing!" And he awoke and rebuked the wind and the raging 25 waves; and they ceased, and there was a calm. He said to them, "Where is your faith?" And they were afraid, and they marveled, saying to one another, "Who then is this, that he commands even wind and water, and they obey him?"

26   Then they arrived at the country of the Ger'asenes,[a] 27 which is opposite Galilee. And as he stepped out on land, there met him a man from the city who had demons; for a long time he had worn no clothes, and he lived not

28 in a house but among the tombs. When he saw Jesus, he cried out and fell down before him, and said with a loud voice, "What have you to do with me, Jesus, Son of the Most High God? I beseech you, do not torment me." 29 For he had commanded the unclean spirit to come out of the man. (For many a time it had seized him; he was kept under guard, and bound with chains and fetters, but he broke the bonds and was driven by the demon 30 into the desert.) Jesus then asked him, "What is your name?" And he said, "Legion"; for many demons had 31 entered him. And they begged him not to command them 32 to depart into the abyss. Now a large herd of swine was feeding there on the hillside; and they begged him to let 33 them enter these. So he gave them leave. Then the demons came out of the man and entered the swine, and the herd rushed down the steep bank into the lake and were drowned.

34   When the herdsmen saw what had happened, they 35 fled, and told it in the city and in the country. Then people went out to see what had happened, and they came to Jesus, and found the man from whom the demons had gone, sitting at the feet of Jesus, clothed and in his right 36 mind; and they were afraid. And those who had seen it told them how he who had been possessed with demons 37 was healed. Then all the people of the surrounding country of the Ger'asenes [a] asked him to depart from them; for they were seized with great fear; so he got into 38 the boat and returned. The man from whom the demons had gone begged that he might be with him; but he sent 39 him away, saying, "Return to your home, and declare how much God has done for you." And he went away, proclaiming throughout the whole city how much Jesus had done for him.

40   Now when Jesus returned, the crowd welcomed him, 41 for they were all waiting for him. And there came a man named Ja'irus, who was a ruler of the synagogue; and falling at Jesus' feet he besought him to come to his 42 house, for he had an only daughter, about twelve years of age, and she was dying.

43   As he went, the people pressed round him. And a woman who had had a flow of blood for twelve years [b] 44 and could not be healed by any one, came up behind him, and touched the fringe of his garment; and immediately 45 her flow of blood ceased. And Jesus said, "Who was it that touched me?" When all denied it, Peter [c] said, "Master, the multitudes surround you and press upon you!"

a Other ancient authorities read *Gadarenes*, others *Gergesenes*
c Other ancient authorities add *and those who were with him*
b Other ancient authorities add *and had spent all her living upon physicians*

46 But Jesus said, "Some one touched me; for I perceive
47 that power has gone forth from me." And when the woman saw that she was not hidden, she came trembling, and falling down before him declared in the presence of all the people why she had touched him, and how she had
48 been immediately healed. And he said to her, "Daughter, your faith has made you well; go in peace."

49 While he was still speaking, a man from the ruler's house came and said, "Your daughter is dead; do not
50 trouble the Teacher any more." But Jesus on hearing this answered him, "Do not fear; only believe, and she shall
51 be well." And when he came to the house, he permitted no one to enter with him, except Peter and John and
52 James, and the father and mother of the child. And all were weeping and bewailing her; but he said, "Do not
53 weep; for she is not dead but sleeping." And they
54 laughed at him, knowing that she was dead. But taking
55 her by the hand he called, saying, "Child, arise." And her spirit returned, and she got up at once; and he
56 directed that something should be given her to eat. And her parents were amazed; but he charged them to tell no one what had happened.

Jesus and His Disciples

9 And he called the twelve together and gave them power and authority over all demons and to cure
2 diseases, and he sent them out to preach the kingdom of
3 God and to heal. And he said to them, "Take nothing for your journey, no staff, nor bag, nor bread, nor money;
4 and do not have two tunics. And whatever house you
5 enter, stay there, and from there depart. And wherever they do not receive you, when you leave that town shake off the dust from your feet as a testimony against them."
6 And they departed and went through the villages, preaching the gospel and healing everywhere.

7 Now Herod the tetrarch heard of all that was done, and he was perplexed, because it was said by some that
8 John had been raised from the dead, by some that Eli′jah

followed him; and he welcomed them and spoke to them of the kingdom of God, and cured those who had need of
12 healing. Now the day began to wear away; and the twelve came and said to him, "Send the crowd away, to go into the villages and country round about, to lodge and get
13 provisions; for we are here in a lonely place." But he said to them, "You give them something to eat." They said, "We have no more than five loaves and two fish—unless
14 we are to go and buy food for all these people." For there were about five thousand men. And he said to his disciples, "Make them sit down in companies, about fifty each."
15, 16 And they did so, and made them all sit down. And taking the five loaves and the two fish he looked up to heaven, and blessed and broke them, and gave them to
17 the disciples to set before the crowd. And all ate and were satisfied. And they took up what was left over, twelve baskets of broken pieces.

18 Now it happened that as he was praying alone the disciples were with him; and he asked them, "Who do
19 the people say that I am?" And they answered, "John the Baptist; but others say, Eli′jah; and others, that one
20 of the old prophets has risen." And he said to them, "But who do you say that I am?" And Peter answered,
21 "The Christ of God." But he charged and commanded
22 them to tell this to no one, saying, "The Son of man must suffer many things, and be rejected by the elders and chief priests and scribes, and be killed, and on the third day be raised."

23 And he said to all, "If any man would come after me, let him deny himself and take up his cross daily and
24 follow me. For whoever would save his life will lose it; and whoever loses his life for my sake, he will save it.
25 For what does it profit a man if he gains the whole world
26 and loses or forfeits himself? For whoever is ashamed of me and of my words, of him will the Son of man be ashamed when he comes in his glory and the glory of the
27 Father and of the holy angels. But I tell you truly, there are some standing here who will not taste death before

had appeared, and by others that one of the old prophets
9 had risen. Herod said, "John I beheaded; but who is this about whom I hear such things?" And he sought to see him.

10 On their return the apostles told him what they had done. And he took them and withdrew apart to a city
11 called Beth-sa′ida. When the crowds learned it, they

they see the kingdom of God."

28 Now about eight days after these sayings he took with him Peter and John and James, and went up on the
29 mountain to pray. And as he was praying, the appearance of his countenance was altered, and his raiment became
30 dazzling white. And behold, two men talked with him,
31 Moses and Eli′jah, who appeared in glory and spoke of

his departure, which he was to accomplish at Jerusalem. 32 Now Peter and those who were with him were heavy with sleep, and when they wakened they saw his glory and 33 the two men who stood with him. And as the men were parting from him, Peter said to Jesus, "Master, it is well that we are here; let us make three booths, one for you and one for Moses and one for Eli'jah"—not knowing 34 what he said. As he said this, a cloud came and overshadowed them; and they were afraid as they entered the 35 cloud. And a voice came out of the cloud, saying, "This 36 is my Son, my Chosen;[d] listen to him!" And when the voice had spoken, Jesus was found alone. And they kept silence and told no one in those days anything of what they had seen.

37 On the next day, when they had come down from the 38 mountain, a great crowd met him. And behold, a man from the crowd cried, "Teacher, I beg you to look upon 39 my son, for he is my only child; and behold, a spirit seizes him, and he suddenly cries out; it convulses him till he foams, and shatters him, and will hardly leave him. 40 And I begged your disciples to cast it out, but they could 41 not." Jesus answered, "O faithless and perverse generation, how long am I to be with you and bear with you? 42 Bring your son here." While he was coming, the demon tore him and convulsed him. But Jesus rebuked the unclean spirit, and healed the boy, and gave him back to his 43 father. And all were astonished at the majesty of God.

But while they were all marveling at everything he did, 44 he said to his disciples, "Let these words sink into your ears; for the Son of man is to be delivered into the hands 45 of men." But they did not understand this saying, and it was concealed from them, that they should not perceive it; and they were afraid to ask him about this saying.

46 And an argument arose among them as to which of 47 them was the greatest. But when Jesus perceived the thought of their hearts, he took a child and put him by 48 his side, and said to them, "Whoever receives this child in my name receives me, and whoever receives me receives him who sent me; for he who is least among you all is the one who is great."

49 John answered, "Master, we saw a man casting out demons in your name, and we forbade him, because he 50 does not follow with us." But Jesus said to him, "Do not forbid him; for he that is not against you is for you."

JESUS' JOURNEY TO JERUSALEM

51 When the days drew near for him to be received up, 52 he set his face to go to Jerusalem. And he sent messengers ahead of him, who went and entered a village of the 53 Samaritans, to make ready for him; but the people would not receive him, because his face was set toward Jerusalem. 54 And when his disciples James and John saw it, they said, "Lord, do you want us to bid fire come down from

55 heaven and consume them?"[e] But he turned and rebuked 56 them.[f] And they went on to another village.

57 As they were going along the road, a man said to him, 58 "I will follow you wherever you go." And Jesus said to him, "Foxes have holes, and birds of the air have nests; 59 but the Son of man has nowhere to lay his head." To another he said, "Follow me." But he said, "Lord, let me 60 first go and bury my father." But he said to him, "Leave the dead to bury their own dead; but as for you, go 61 and proclaim the kingdom of God." Another said, "I will follow you, Lord; but let me first say farewell to those 62 at my home." Jesus said to him, "No one who puts his hand to the plow and looks back is fit for the kingdom of God."

Mission of the Seventy

10 After this the Lord appointed seventy[g] others, and sent them on ahead of him, two by two, into every town and place where he himself was about to 2 come. And he said to them, "The harvest is plentiful, but the laborers are few; pray therefore the Lord of the 3 harvest to send out laborers into his harvest. Go your way; behold, I send you out as lambs in the midst of 4 wolves. Carry no purse, no bag, no sandals; and salute 5 no one on the road. Whatever house you enter, first say, 6 'Peace be to this house!' And if a son of peace is there, your peace shall rest upon him; but if not, it shall return 7 to you. And remain in the same house, eating and drinking what they provide, for the laborer deserves his 8 wages; do not go from house to house. Whenever you enter a town and they receive you, eat what is set before 9 you; heal the sick in it and say to them, 'The kingdom 10 of God has come near to you.' But whenever you enter a town and they do not receive you, go into its streets 11 and say, 'Even the dust of your town that clings to our feet, we wipe off against you; nevertheless know this, 12 that the kingdom of God has come near.' I tell you, it shall be more tolerable on that day for Sodom than for that town.

13 "Woe to you, Chora'zin! woe to you, Beth-sa'ida! for if the mighty works done in you had been done in Tyre and Sidon, they would have repented long ago, sitting in

[d] Other ancient authorities read *my Beloved*   [e] Other ancient authorities add *as Elijah did*
[f] Other ancient authorities add *and he said, "You do not know what manner of spirit you are of; for the Son of man came not to destroy men's lives but to save them"*   [g] Other ancient authorities read *seventy-two*

714

14 sackcloth and ashes. But it shall be more tolerable in
15 the judgment for Tyre and Sidon than for you. And you,
Caper'na-um, will you be exalted to heaven? You shall be
brought down to Hades.

16 "He who hears you hears me, and he who rejects you
rejects me, and he who rejects me rejects him who sent
me."

17 The seventy g returned with joy, saying, "Lord, even
18 the demons are subject to us in your name!" And he
said to them, "I saw Satan fall like lightning from heaven.
19 Behold, I have given you authority to tread upon serpents
and scorpions, and over all the power of the enemy; and
20 nothing shall hurt you. Nevertheless do not rejoice in
this, that the spirits are subject to you; but rejoice that
your names are written in heaven."

21 In that same hour he rejoiced in the Holy Spirit and
said, "I thank thee, Father, Lord of heaven and earth,
that thou hast hidden these things from the wise and
understanding and revealed them to babes; yea, Father,
22 for such was thy gracious will.h All things have been delivered to me by my Father; and no one knows who the
Son is except the Father, or who the Father is except the
Son and any one to whom the Son chooses to reveal him."
23 Then turning to the disciples he said privately, "Blessed
24 are the eyes which see what you see! For I tell you that
many prophets and kings desired to see what you see,
and did not see it, and to hear what you hear, and did not
hear it."

25 And behold, a lawyer stood up to put him to the test,
saying, "Teacher, what shall I do to inherit eternal life?"
26 He said to him, "What is written in the law? How do you
27 read?" And he answered, "You shall love the Lord your
God with all your heart, and with all your soul, and with
all your strength, and with all your mind; and your
28 neighbor as yourself." And he said to him, "You have
answered right; do this, and you will live."

29 But he, desiring to justify himself, said to Jesus, "And
30 who is my neighbor?" Jesus replied, "A man was going
down from Jerusalem to Jericho, and he fell among
robbers, who stripped him and beat him, and departed,
31 leaving him half dead. Now by chance a priest was going
down that road; and when he saw him he passed by on
32 the other side. So likewise a Levite, when he came to the
33 place and saw him, passed by on the other side. But a
Samaritan, as he journeyed, came to where he was; and
34 when he saw him, he had compassion, and went to him
and bound up his wounds, pouring on oil and wine; then
he set him on his own beast and brought him to an inn,
35 and took care of him. And the next day he took out two
denarii i and gave them to the innkeeper, saying, 'Take
care of him; and whatever more you spend, I will repay
36 you when I come back.' Which of these three, do you
think, proved neighbor to the man who fell among the

37 robbers?" He said, "The one who showed mercy on him."
And Jesus said to him, "Go and do likewise."

38 Now as they went on their way, he entered a village;
and a woman named Martha received him into her house.
39 And she had a sister called Mary, who sat at the Lord's
40 feet and listened to his teaching. But Martha was dis-
tracted with much serving; and she went to him and
said, "Lord, do you not care that my sister has left me
41 to serve alone? Tell her then to help me." But the Lord
answered her, "Martha, Martha, you are anxious and
42 troubled about many things; one thing is needful.j Mary
has chosen the good portion, which shall not be taken
away from her."

Teachings on Prayer

11 He was praying in a certain place, and when he
ceased, one of his disciples said to him, "Lord,
2 teach us to pray, as John taught his disciples." And he
said to them, "When you pray, say:
"Father, hallowed be thy name. Thy kingdom come.
3, 4 Give us each day our daily bread; k and forgive us our
sins, for we ourselves forgive every one who is indebted
to us; and lead us not into temptation."

5 And he said to them, "Which of you who has a friend
will go to him at midnight and say to him, 'Friend, lend
6 me three loaves; for a friend of mine has arrived on a
7 journey, and I have nothing to set before him'; and he
will answer from within, 'Do not bother me; the door is
now shut, and my children are with me in bed; I cannot
8 get up and give you anything'? I tell you, though he
will not get up and give him anything because he is his
friend, yet because of his importunity he will rise and
9 give him whatever he needs. And I tell you, Ask, and it
will be given you; seek, and you will find; knock, and it
10 will be opened to you. For every one who asks receives,
and he who seeks finds, and to him who knocks it will be
11 opened. What father among you, if his son asks for l a
12 fish, will instead of a fish give him a serpent; or if he
13 asks for an egg, will give him a scorpion? If you then,
who are evil, know how to give good gifts to your children, how much more will the heavenly Father give the
Holy Spirit to those who ask him!"

14 Now he was casting out a demon that was dumb; when
the demon had gone out, the dumb man spoke, and the
15 people marveled. But some of them said, "He casts out
16 demons by Be-el'zebul, the prince of demons"; while
others, to test him, sought from him a sign from heaven.
17 But he, knowing their thoughts, said to them, "Every
kingdom divided against itself is laid waste, and a di-
18 vided household falls. And if Satan also is divided against
himself, how will his kingdom stand? For you say that
19 I cast out demons by Be-el'zebul. And if I cast out demons
by Be-el'zebul, by whom do your sons cast them out?

---

g Other ancient authorities read *seventy-two*   h Or *so it was well-pleasing before thee*   i The denarius was a day's wages for a laborer
j Other ancient authorities read *few things are needful, or only one*   k Or *our bread for the morrow*
l Other ancient authorities insert *bread, will give him a stone; or if he asks for*

20 Therefore they shall be your judges. But if it is by the finger of God that I cast out demons, then the kingdom
21 of God has come upon you. When a strong man, fully armed, guards his own palace, his goods are in peace;
22 but when one stronger than he assails him and overcomes him, he takes away his armor in which he trusted, and
23 divides his spoil. He who is not with me is against me, and he who does not gather with me scatters.

24 "When the unclean spirit has gone out of a man, he passes through waterless places seeking rest; and finding none he says, 'I will return to my house from which I
25 came.' And when he comes he finds it swept and put in
26 order. Then he goes and brings seven other spirits more evil than himself, and they enter and dwell there; and the last state of that man becomes worse than the first."

27 As he said this, a woman in the crowd raised her voice and said to him, "Blessed is the womb that bore you, and
28 the breasts that you sucked!" But he said, "Blessed rather are those who hear the word of God and keep it!"

29 When the crowds were increasing, he began to say, "This generation is an evil generation; it seeks a sign, but no sign shall be given to it except the sign of Jonah.
30 For as Jonah became a sign to the men of Nin'eveh, so
31 will the Son of man be to this generation. The queen of the South will arise at the judgment with the men of this generation and condemn them; for she came from the ends of the earth to hear the wisdom of Solomon, and
32 behold, something greater than Solomon is here. The men of Nin'eveh will arise at the judgment with this generation and condemn it; for they repented at the preaching of Jonah, and behold, something greater than Jonah is here.

33 "No one after lighting a lamp puts it in a cellar or under a bushel, but on a stand, that those who enter may
34 see the light. Your eye is the lamp of your body; when your eye is sound, your whole body is full of light; but
35 when it is not sound, your body is full of darkness. There-
36 fore be careful lest the light in you be darkness. If then your whole body is full of light, having no part dark, it will be wholly bright, as when a lamp with its rays gives you light."

37 While he was speaking, a Pharisee asked him to dine
38 with him; so he went in and sat at table. The Pharisee was astonished to see that he did not first wash before
39 dinner. And the Lord said to him, "Now you Pharisees cleanse the outside of the cup and of the dish, but inside
40 you are full of extortion and wickedness. You fools! Did not he who made the outside make the inside also?
41 But give for alms those things which are within; and behold, everything is clean for you.

42 "But woe to you Pharisees! for you tithe mint and rue and every herb, and neglect justice and the love of God; these you ought to have done, without neglecting the
43 others. Woe to you Pharisees! for you love the best seat

in the synagogues and salutations in the market places.
44 Woe to you! for you are like graves which are not seen, and men walk over them without knowing it."

45 One of the lawyers answered him, "Teacher, in saying
46 this you reproach us also." And he said, "Woe to you lawyers also! for you load men with burdens hard to bear, and you yourselves do not touch the burdens with
47 one of your fingers. Woe to you! for you build the tombs
48 of the prophets whom your fathers killed. So you are witnesses and consent to the deeds of your fathers; for
49 they killed them, and you build their tombs. Therefore also the Wisdom of God said, 'I will send them prophets and apostles, some of whom they will kill and persecute,'
50 that the blood of all the prophets, shed from the foundation of the world, may be required of this generation,
51 from the blood of Abel to the blood of Zechari'ah, who perished between the altar and the sanctuary. Yes, I tell
52 you, it shall be required of this generation. Woe to you lawyers! for you have taken away the key of knowledge; you did not enter yourselves, and you hindered those who were entering."

53 As he went away from there, the scribes and the Pharisees began to press him hard, and to provoke him
54 to speak of many things, lying in wait for him, to catch at something he might say.

Discipleship's Privileges, Responsibilities

12 In the meantime, when so many thousands of the multitude had gathered together that they trod upon one another, he began to say to his disciples first, "Beware of the leaven of the Pharisees, which is hypocrisy.
2 Nothing is covered up that will not be revealed, or hidden
3 that will not be known. Therefore, whatever you have said in the dark shall be heard in the light, and what you have whispered in private rooms shall be proclaimed upon the housetops.

4 "I tell you, my friends, do not fear those who kill the body, and after that have no more that they can do.
5 But I will warn you whom to fear: fear him who, after he has killed, has power to cast into hell; m yes, I tell you,
6 fear him! Are not five sparrows sold for two pennies?
7 And not one of them is forgotten before God. Why, even the hairs of your head are all numbered. Fear not; you are of more value than many sparrows.

8 "And I tell you, every one who acknowledges me before men, the Son of man also will acknowledge before the
9 angels of God; but he who denies me before men will be
10 denied before the angels of God. And every one who speaks a word against the Son of man will be forgiven; but he who blasphemes against the Holy Spirit will not
11 be forgiven. And when they bring you before the synagogues and the rulers and the authorities, do not be anxious how or what you are to answer or what you are

m Greek Gehenna

12 to say; for the Holy Spirit will teach you in that very hour what you ought to say."

13 One of the multitude said to him, "Teacher, bid my 14 brother divide the inheritance with me." But he said to him, "Man, who made me a judge or divider over 15 you?" And he said to them, "Take heed, and beware of all covetousness; for a man's life does not consist in the 16 abundance of his possessions." And he told them a parable, saying, "The land of a rich man brought forth 17 plentifully; and he thought to himself, 'What shall I do, 18 for I have nowhere to store my crops?' And he said, 'I will do this: I will pull down my barns, and build larger ones; and there I will store all my grain and my goods. 19 And I will say to my soul, Soul, you have ample goods laid up for many years; take your ease, eat, drink, be 20 merry.' But God said to him, 'Fool! This night your soul is required of you; and the things you have pre- 21 pared, whose will they be?' So is he who lays up treasure for himself, and is not rich toward God."

22 And he said to his disciples, "Therefore I tell you, do not be anxious about your life, what you shall eat, nor 23 about your body, what you shall put on. For life is more 24 than food, and the body more than clothing. Consider the ravens: they neither sow nor reap, they have neither storehouse nor barn, and yet God feeds them. Of how 25 much more value are you than the birds! And which of you by being anxious can add a cubit to his span of life? n 26 If then you are not able to do as small a thing as that, 27 why are you anxious about the rest? Consider the lilies, how they grow; they neither toil nor spin; o yet I tell

you, even Solomon in all his glory was not arrayed like 28 one of these. But if God so clothes the grass which is alive in the field today and tomorrow is thrown into the oven, how much more will he clothe you, O men of little 29 faith! And do not seek what you are to eat and what you 30 are to drink, nor be of anxious mind. For all the nations of the world seek these things; and your Father knows 31 that you need them. Instead, seek his p kingdom, and these things shall be yours as well.

32 "Fear not, little flock, for it is your Father's good 33 pleasure to give you the kingdom. Sell your possessions, and give alms; provide yourselves with purses that do not grow old, with a treasure in the heavens that does not fail, where no thief approaches and no moth destroys. 34 For where your treasure is, there will your heart be also.

35 "Let your loins be girded and your lamps burning, 36 and be like men who are waiting for their master to come home from the marriage feast, so that they may open to

37 him at once when he comes and knocks. Blessed are those servants whom the master finds awake when he comes; truly, I say to you, he will gird himself and have them sit at table, and he will come and serve them. 38 If he comes in the second watch, or in the third, and finds 39 them so, blessed are those servants! But know this, that if the householder had known at what hour the thief was coming, he would have been awake and he q would not 40 have left his house to be broken into. You also must be ready; for the Son of man is coming at an unexpected hour."

41 Peter said, "Lord, are you telling this parable for us 42 or for all?" And the Lord said, "Who then is the faithful and wise steward, whom his master will set over his household, to give them their portion of food at the proper 43 time? Blessed is that servant whom his master when he 44 comes will find so doing. Truly, I say to you, he will 45 set him over all his possessions. But if that servant says to himself, 'My master is delayed in coming,' and begins to beat the menservants and the maidservants, and to eat 46 and drink and get drunk, the master of that servant will come on a day when he does not expect him and at an hour he does not know, and will punish r him, and put 47 him with the unfaithful. And that servant who knew his master's will, but did not make ready or act according 48 to his will, shall receive a severe beating. But he who did not know, and did what deserved a beating, shall receive a light beating. Every one to whom much is given, of him will much be required; and of him to whom men commit much they will demand the more.

49 "I came to cast fire upon the earth; and would that 50 it were already kindled! I have a baptism to be baptized with; and how I am constrained until it is accomplished! 51 Do you think that I have come to give peace on earth? 52 No, I tell you, but rather division; for henceforth in one house there will be five divided, three against two and 53 two against three; they will be divided, father against son and son against father, mother against daughter and daughter against her mother, mother-in-law against her daughter-in-law and daughter-in-law against her mother-in-law."

54 He also said to the multitudes, "When you see a cloud rising in the west, you say at once, 'A shower is coming'; 55 and so it happens. And when you see the south wind blowing, you say, 'There will be scorching heat'; and it 56 happens. You hypocrites! You know how to interpret the appearance of earth and sky; but why do you not know how to interpret the present time?

57 "And why do you not judge for yourselves what is 58 right? As you go with your accuser before the magistrate, make an effort to settle with him on the way, lest he drag you to the judge, and the judge hand you over to 59 the officer, and the officer put you in prison. I tell you,

---

n Or *to his stature*   o Other ancient authorities read *Consider the lilies; they neither spin nor weave*
p Other ancient authorities read *God's*   q Other ancient authorities add *would have watched and*   r Or *cut him in pieces*

you will never get out till you have paid the very last copper."

13 There were some present at that very time who told him of the Galileans whose blood Pilate had [2] mingled with their sacrifices. And he answered them, "Do you think that these Galileans were worse sinners than all the other Galileans, because they suffered thus? [3] I tell you, No; but unless you repent you will all likewise [4] perish. Or those eighteen upon whom the tower in Silo'am fell and killed them, do you think that they were worse offenders than all the others who dwelt in Jerusalem? [5] I tell you, No; but unless you repent you will all likewise perish."

[6] And he told this parable: "A man had a fig tree planted in his vineyard; and he came seeking fruit on it and [7] found none. And he said to the vinedresser, 'Lo, these three years I have come seeking fruit on this fig tree, and I find none. Cut it down; why should it use up the [8] ground?' And he answered him, 'Let it alone, sir, this [9] year also, till I dig about it and put on manure. And if it bears fruit next year, well and good; but if not, you can cut it down.' "

Teaching in a Synagogue

[10] Now he was teaching in one of the synagogues on the [11] sabbath. And there was a woman who had had a spirit of infirmity for eighteen years; she was bent over and [12] could not fully straighten herself. And when Jesus saw her, he called her and said to her, "Woman, you are [13] freed from your infirmity." And he laid his hands upon her, and immediately she was made straight, and she [14] praised God. But the ruler of the synagogue, indignant because Jesus had healed on the sabbath, said to the people, "There are six days on which work ought to be done; come on those days and be healed, and not on the [15] sabbath day." Then the Lord answered him, "You hypocrites! Does not each of you on the sabbath untie his ox or his ass from the manger, and lead it away to [16] water it? And ought not this woman, a daughter of Abraham whom Satan bound for eighteen years, be [17] loosed from this bond on the sabbath day?" As he said this, all his adversaries were put to shame; and all the people rejoiced at all the glorious things that were done by him.

The Kingdom of God

[18] He said therefore, "What is the kingdom of God like? [19] And to what shall I compare it? It is like a grain of mustard seed which a man took and sowed in his garden; and it grew and became a tree, and the birds of the air made nests in its branches."

[20] And again he said, "To what shall I compare the [21] kingdom of God? It is like leaven which a woman took

[s] Other ancient authorities read *an ass*

and hid in three measures of flour, till it was all leavened."

[22] He went on his way through towns and villages, teach-[23] ing, and journeying toward Jerusalem. And some one said to him, "Lord, will those who are saved be few?" [24] And he said to them, "Strive to enter by the narrow door; for many, I tell you, will seek to enter and will not [25] be able. When once the householder has risen up and shut the door, you will begin to stand outside and to knock at the door, saying, 'Lord, open to us.' He will answer you, 'I do not know where you come from.' [26] Then you will begin to say, 'We ate and drank in your [27] presence, and you taught in our streets.' But he will say, 'I tell you, I do not know where you come from; depart [28] from me, all you workers of iniquity!' There you will weep and gnash your teeth, when you see Abraham and Isaac and Jacob and all the prophets in the kingdom of [29] God and you yourselves thrust out. And men will come from east and west, and from north and south, and sit [30] at table in the kingdom of God. And behold, some are last who will be first, and some are first who will be last."

[31] At that very hour some Pharisees came, and said to him, "Get away from here, for Herod wants to kill you." [32] And he said to them, "Go and tell that fox, 'Behold, I cast out demons and perform cures today and tomorrow, and [33] the third day I finish my course. Nevertheless I must go on my way today and tomorrow and the day following; for it cannot be that a prophet should perish away from [34] Jerusalem.' O Jerusalem, Jerusalem, killing the prophets and stoning those who are sent to you! How often would I have gathered your children together as a hen gathers [35] her brood under her wings, and you would not! Behold, your house is forsaken. And I tell you, you will not see me until you say, 'Blessed is he who comes in the name of the Lord!' "

14 One sabbath when he went to dine at the house of a ruler who belonged to the Pharisees, they were [2] watching him. And behold, there was a man before him [3] who had dropsy. And Jesus spoke to the lawyers and Pharisees, saying, "Is it lawful to heal on the sabbath, or [4] not?" But they were silent. Then he took him and healed [5] him, and let him go. And he said to them, "Which of you, having a son[s] or an ox that has fallen into a well, will

[6] not immediately pull him out on a sabbath day?" And they could not reply to this.

[7] Now he told a parable to those who were invited, when

he marked how they chose the places of honor, saying
8 to them, "When you are invited by any one to a marriage feast, do not sit down in a place of honor, lest a more
9 eminent man than you be invited by him; and he who invited you both will come and say to you, 'Give place to this man,' and then you will begin with shame to take
10 the lowest place. But when you are invited, go and sit in the lowest place, so that when your host comes he may say to you, 'Friend, go up higher'; then you will be honored in the presence of all who sit at table with you.
11 For every one who exalts himself will be humbled, and he who humbles himself will be exalted."

12 He said also to the man who had invited him, "When you give a dinner or a banquet, do not invite your friends or your brothers or your kinsmen or rich neighbors, lest

13 they also invite you in return, and you be repaid. But when you give a feast, invite the poor, the maimed, the
14 lame, the blind, and you will be blessed, because they cannot repay you. You will be repaid at the resurrection of the just."

15 When one of those who sat at table with him heard this, he said to him, "Blessed is he who shall eat bread
16 in the kingdom of God!" But he said to him, "A man
17 once gave a great banquet, and invited many; and at the time for the banquet he sent his servant to say to those who had been invited, 'Come; for all is now ready.'
18 But they all alike began to make excuses. The first said to him, 'I have bought a field, and I must go out and see
19 it; I pray you, have me excused.' And another said, 'I have bought five yoke of oxen, and I go to examine
20 them; I pray you, have me excused.' And another said, 'I have married a wife, and therefore I cannot come.'
21 So the servant came and reported this to his master. Then the householder in anger said to his servant, 'Go out quickly to the streets and lanes of the city, and bring in
22 the poor and maimed and blind and lame.' And the servant said, "Sir, what you commanded has been done,
23 and still there is room.' And the master said to the servant, 'Go out to the highways and hedges, and compel people
24 to come in, that my house may be filled. For I tell you,[a] none of those men who were invited shall taste my banquet.' "

The Cost of Discipleship

25 Now great multitudes accompanied him; and he turned
26 and said to them, "If any one comes to me and does not hate his own father and mother and wife and children and brothers and sisters, yes, and even his own life, he cannot
27 be my disciple. Whoever does not bear his own cross and
28 come after me, cannot be my disciple. For which of you, desiring to build a tower, does not first sit down and count
29 the cost, whether he has enough to complete it? Otherwise, when he has laid a foundation, and is not able to
30 finish, all who see it begin to mock him, saying, 'This
31 man began to build, and was not able to finish.' Or what king, going to encounter another king in war, will not sit down first and take counsel whether he is able with ten thousand to meet him who comes against him with twenty
32 thousand? And if not, while the other is yet a great way
33 off, he sends an embassy and asks terms of peace. So therefore, whoever of you does not renounce all that he has cannot be my disciple.

34 "Salt is good; but if salt has lost its taste, how shall
35 its saltness be restored? It is fit neither for the land nor for the dunghill; men throw it away. He who has ears to hear, let him hear."

God's Concern for the Lost

15 Now the tax collectors and sinners were all
2 drawing near to hear him. And the Pharisees and the scribes murmured, saying, "This man receives sinners and eats with them."
3, 4 So he told them this parable: "What man of you, having a hundred sheep, if he has lost one of them, does not leave the ninety-nine in the wilderness, and go after the
5 one which is lost, until he finds it? And when he has
6 found it, he lays it on his shoulders, rejoicing. And when he comes home, he calls together his friends and his neighbors, saying to them, 'Rejoice with me, for I have
7 found my sheep which was lost.' Just so, I tell you, there will be more joy in heaven over one sinner who repents than over ninety-nine righteous persons who need no repentance.

8 "Or what woman, having ten silver coins,[t] if she loses one coin, does not light a lamp and sweep the house and
9 seek diligently until she finds it? And when she has found it, she calls together her friends and neighbors, saying, 'Rejoice with me, for I have found the coin which I had
10 lost.'" Just so, I tell you, there is joy before the angels of God over one sinner who repents."

11 And he said, "There was a man who had two sons;
12 and the younger of them said to his father, 'Father, give me the share of property that falls to me.' And he divided
13 his living between them. Not many days later, the younger son gathered all he had and took his journey into a far country, and there he squandered his property in loose

---

a The Greek word for *you* here is plural   t The drachma, rendered here by *silver coin*, was about a day's wage for a laborer

14 living. And when he had spent everything, a great famine
15 arose in that country, and he began to be in want. So he went and joined himself to one of the citizens of that country, who sent him into his fields to feed swine.
16 And he would gladly have fed on u the pods that the
17 swine ate; and no one gave him anything. But when he came to himself he said, 'How many of my father's hired servants have bread enough and to spare, but I perish
18 here with hunger! I will arise and go to my father, and I will say to him, "Father, I have sinned against heaven
19 and before you; I am no longer worthy to be called your
20 son; treat me as one of your hired servants." ' And he arose and came to his father. But while he was yet at a distance, his father saw him and had compassion, and
21 ran and embraced him and kissed him. And the son said to him, 'Father, I have sinned against heaven and before you; I am no longer worthy to be called your

called him and said to him, 'What is this that I hear about you? Turn in the account of your stewardship, for
3 you can no longer be steward.' And the steward said to himself, 'What shall I do, since my master is taking the stewardship away from me? I am not strong enough to
4 dig, and I am ashamed to beg. I have decided what to do, so that people may receive me into their houses when I am
5 put out of the stewardship.' So, summoning his master's debtors one by one, he said to the first, 'How much do
6 you owe my master?' He said, 'A hundred measures of oil.' And he said to him, 'Take your bill, and sit down
7 quickly and write fifty.' Then he said to another, 'And how much do you owe?' He said, 'A hundred measures of wheat.' He said to him, 'Take your bill, and write
8 eighty.' The master commended the dishonest steward for his shrewdness; for the sons of this world w are more shrewd in dealing with their own generation than the

22 son.' v But the father said to his servants, 'Bring quickly the best robe, and put it on him; and put a ring on his
23 hand, and shoes on his feet; and bring the fatted calf and
24 kill it, and let us eat and make merry; for this my son was dead, and is alive again; he was lost, and is found.' And they began to make merry.
25 "Now his elder son was in the field; and as he came and drew near to the house, he heard music and dancing.
26 And he called one of the servants and asked what this
27 meant. And he said to him, 'Your brother has come, and your father has killed the fatted calf, because he has
28 received him safe and sound.' But he was angry and refused to go in. His father came out and entreated him,
29 but he answered his father, 'Lo, these many years I have served you, and I never disobeyed your command; yet you never gave me a kid, that I might make merry with
30 my friends. But when this son of yours came, who has devoured your living with harlots, you killed for him the
31 fatted calf!' And he said to him, 'Son, you are always
32 with me, and all that is mine is yours. It was fitting to make merry and be glad, for this your brother was dead, and is alive; he was lost, and is found.' "

Use and Abuse of Wealth

16 He also said to the disciples, "There was a rich man who had a steward, and charges were brought
2 to him that this man was wasting his goods. And he

9 sons of light. And I tell you, make friends for yourselves by means of unrighteous mammon,a so that when it fails they may receive you into the eternal habitations.
10 "He who is faithful in a very little is faithful also in much; and he who is dishonest in a very little is dishonest
11 also in much. If then you have not been faithful in the unrighteous mammon,a who will entrust to you the true
12 riches? And if you have not been faithful in that which is another's, who will give you that which is your own?
13 No servant can serve two masters; for either he will hate the one and love the other, or he will be devoted to the one and despise the other. You cannot serve God and mammon." a
14 The Pharisees, who were lovers of money, heard all
15 this, and they scoffed at him. But he said to them, "You are those who justify yourselves before men, but God knows your hearts; for what is exalted among men is an abomination in the sight of God.
16 "The law and the prophets were until John; since then the good news of the kingdom of God is preached, and
17 every one enters it violently. But it is easier for heaven and earth to pass away, than for one dot of the law to become void.
18 "Every one who divorces his wife and marries another commits adultery, and he who marries a woman divorced from her husband commits adultery.
19 "There was a rich man, who was clothed in purple and

u Other ancient authorities read *filled his belly with*   v Other ancient authorities add *treat me as one of your hired servants*
w Greek *age*   a *Mammon* is a Semitic word for money or riches

20 fine linen and who feasted sumptuously every day. And at his gate lay a poor man named Laz′arus, full of sores,
21 who desired to be fed with what fell from the rich man's table; moreover the dogs came and licked his sores.
22 The poor man died and was carried by the angels to Abraham's bosom. The rich man also died and was
23 buried; and in Hades, being in torment, he lifted up his eyes, and saw Abraham far off and Laz′arus in his bosom.
24 And he called out, 'Father Abraham, have mercy upon me, and send Laz′arus to dip the end of his finger in water and cool my tongue; for I am in anguish in this
25 flame.' But Abraham said, 'Son, remember that you in your lifetime received your good things, and Laz′arus in like manner evil things; but now he is comforted here,
26 and you are in anguish. And besides all this, between us and you a great chasm has been fixed, in order that those who would pass from here to you may not be able, and
27 none may cross from there to us.' And he said, 'Then I
28 beg you, father, to send him to my father's house, for I have five brothers, so that he may warn them, lest they
29 also come into this place of torment.' But Abraham said, 'They have Moses and the prophets; let them hear them.'
30 And he said, 'No, father Abraham; but if some one goes
31 to them from the dead, they will repent.' He said to him, 'If they do not hear Moses and the prophets, neither will they be convinced if some one should rise from the dead.' "

Forgiveness and Faith . . .

17 And he said to his disciples, "Temptations to sin ˣ are sure to come; but woe to him by whom
2 they come! It would be better for him if a millstone were hung round his neck and he were cast into the sea, than
3 that he should cause one of these little ones to sin.ʸ Take heed to yourselves; if your brother sins, rebuke him, and
4 if he repents, forgive him; and if he sins against you seven times in the day, and turns to you seven times, and says, 'I repent,' you must forgive him."
5 The apostles said to the Lord, "Increase our faith!"
6 And the Lord said, "If you had faith as a grain of mustard seed, you could say to this sycamine tree, 'Be rooted up, and be planted in the sea,' and it would obey you.
7 "Will any one of you, who has a servant plowing or keeping sheep, say to him when he has come in from the
8 field, 'Come at once and sit down at table'? Will he not rather say to him, 'Prepare supper for me, and gird yourself and serve me, till I eat and drink; and afterward
9 you shall eat and drink'? Does he thank the servant be-
10 cause he did what was commanded? So you also, when you have done all that is commanded you, say, 'We are unworthy servants; we have only done what was our duty.' "
11 On the way to Jerusalem he was passing along between
12 Samar′ia and Galilee. And as he entered a village, he was
13 met by ten lepers, who stood at a distance and lifted up their voices and said, "Jesus, Master, have mercy on us."
14 When he saw them he said to them, "Go and show yourselves to the priests." And as they went they were cleansed.
15 Then one of them, when he saw that he was healed,
16 turned back, praising God with a loud voice; and he fell on his face at Jesus' feet, giving him thanks. Now he was
17 a Samaritan. Then said Jesus, "Were not ten cleansed?
18 Where are the nine? Was no one found to return and
19 give praise to God except this foreigner?" And he said to him, "Rise and go your way; your faith has made you well."

More About the Kingdom

20 Being asked by the Pharisees when the kingdom of God was coming, he answered them, "The kingdom of God
21 is not coming with signs to be observed; nor will they say, 'Lo, here it is!' or 'There!' for behold, the kingdom of God is in the midst of you."ᶻ
22 And he said to the disciples, "The days are coming when you will desire to see one of the days of the Son
23 of man, and you will not see it. And they will say to you, 'Lo, there!' or 'Lo, here!' Do not go, do not follow
24 them. For as the lightning flashes and lights up the sky from one side to the other, so will the Son of man be
25 in his day.ᵃ But first he must suffer many things and be
26 rejected by this generation. As it was in the days of Noah,
27 so will it be in the days of the Son of man. They ate, they drank, they married, they were given in marriage, until the day when Noah entered the ark, and the flood
28 came and destroyed them all. Likewise as it was in the days of Lot—they ate, they drank, they bought, they
29 sold, they planted, they built, but on the day when Lot went out from Sodom fire and sulphur rained from
30 heaven and destroyed them all—so will it be on the day
31 when the Son of man is revealed. On that day, let him who is on the housetop, with his goods in the house, not come down to take them away; and likewise let him
32 who is in the field not turn back. Remember Lot's wife.
33 Whoever seeks to gain his life will lose it, but whoever
34 loses his life will preserve it. I tell you, in that night there will be two in one bed; one will be taken and the
35 other left. There will be two women grinding together;
37 one will be taken and the other left." ᵇ And they said to him, "Where, Lord?" He said to them, "Where the body is, there the eagles ᶜ will be gathered together."

Parables on Prayer

18 And he told them a parable, to the effect that they
2 ought always to pray and not lose heart. He said, "In a certain city there was a judge who neither feared
3 God nor regarded man; and there was a widow in that

ˣ Greek stumbling blocks   ʸ Greek stumble   ᶻ Or within you   ᵃ Other ancient authorities omit in his day
ᵇ Other ancient authorities add verse 36, "Two men will be in the field; one will be taken and the other left"   ᶜ Or vultures

city who kept coming to him and saying, 'Vindicate me
4 against my adversary.' For a while he refused; but afterward he said to himself, 'Though I neither fear God nor
5 regard man, yet because this widow bothers me, I will
vindicate her, or she will wear me out by her continual
6 coming.' " And the Lord said, "Hear what the unrighteous
7 judge says. And will not God vindicate his elect, who
cry to him day and night? Will he delay long over them?
8 I tell you, he will vindicate them speedily. Nevertheless,
when the Son of man comes, will he find faith on earth?"

9 He also told this parable to some who trusted in themselves that they were righteous and despised others:
10 "Two men went up into the temple to pray, one a Pharisee
11 and the other a tax collector. The Pharisee stood and

prayed thus with himself, 'God, I thank thee that I am
not like other men, extortioners, unjust, adulterers, or
12 even like this tax collector. I fast twice a week, I give
13 tithes of all that I get.' But the tax collector, standing far
off, would not even lift up his eyes to heaven, but beat his
14 breast, saying, 'God, be merciful to me a sinner!' I tell
you, this man went down to his house justified rather
than the other; for every one who exalts himself will be
humbled, but he who humbles himself will be exalted."

Entrance Into the Kingdom

15 Now they were bringing even infants to him that he
might touch them; and when the disciples saw it, they
16 rebuked them. But Jesus called them to him, saying, "Let
the children come to me, and do not hinder them; for
17 to such belongs the kingdom of God. Truly, I say to you,
whoever does not receive the kingdom of God like a child
shall not enter it."

18 And a ruler asked him, "Good Teacher, what shall I do
19 to inherit eternal life?" And Jesus said to him, "Why do
you call me good? No one is good but God alone.
20 You know the commandments: 'Do not commit adultery,
Do not kill, Do not steal, Do not bear false witness, Honor
21 your father and mother.' " And he said, "All these I have
22 observed from my youth." And when Jesus heard it, he
said to him, "One thing you still lack. Sell all that you
have and distribute to the poor, and you will have treasure
23 in heaven; and come, follow me." But when he heard
24 this he became sad, for he was very rich. Jesus looking at
him said, "How hard it is for those who have riches to
25 enter the kingdom of God! For it is easier for a camel to

go through the eye of a needle than for a rich man to
26 enter the kingdom of God." Those who heard it said,
27 "Then who can be saved?" But he said, "What is im-
28 possible with men is possible with God." And Peter said,
29 "Lo, we have left our homes and followed you." And he
said to them, "Truly, I say to you, there is no man who
has left house or wife or brothers or parents or children,
30 for the sake of the kingdom of God, who will not receive
manifold more in this time, and in the age to come eternal
life."

31 And taking the twelve, he said to them, "Behold, we
are going up to Jerusalem, and everything that is written
of the Son of man by the prophets will be accomplished.
32 For he will be delivered to the Gentiles, and will be
33 mocked and shamefully treated and spit upon; they will
scourge him and kill him, and on the third day he will
34 rise." But they understood none of these things; this
saying was hid from them, and they did not grasp what
was said.

In Jericho

35 As he drew near to Jericho, a blind man was sitting
36 by the roadside begging; and hearing a multitude going
37 by, he inquired what this meant. They told him, "Jesus
38 of Nazareth is passing by." And he cried, "Jesus, Son
39 of David, have mercy on me!" And those who were in
front rebuked him, telling him to be silent; but he cried
out all the more, "Son of David, have mercy on me!"
40 And Jesus stopped, and commanded him to be brought
41 to him; and when he came near, he asked him, "What do
you want me to do for you?" He said, "Lord, let me
42 receive my sight." And Jesus said to him, "Receive your
43 sight; your faith has made you well." And immediately he
received his sight and followed him, glorifying God;
and all the people, when they saw it, gave praise to God.

19 He entered Jericho and was passing through. And
2 there was a man named Zacchae′us; he was a chief
3 tax collector, and rich. And he sought to see who Jesus
was, but could not, on account of the crowd, because he
4 was small of stature. So he ran on ahead and climbed up
into a sycamore tree to see him, for he was to pass that
5 way. And when Jesus came to the place, he looked up
and said to him, "Zacchae′us, make haste and come
6 down; for I must stay at your house today." So he made
7 haste and came down, and received him joyfully. And
when they saw it they all murmured, "He has gone in to
8 be the guest of a man who is a sinner." And Zacchae′us
stood and said to the Lord, "Behold, Lord, the half of
my goods I give to the poor; and if I have defrauded
9 any one of anything, I restore it fourfold." And Jesus
said to him, "Today salvation has come to this house,
10 since he also is a son of Abraham. For the Son of man
came to seek and to save the lost."

11 As they heard these things, he proceeded to tell a parable, because he was near to Jerusalem, and because they supposed that the kingdom of God was to appear 12 immediately. He said therefore, "A nobleman went into a far country to receive the kingdom and then return. 13 Calling ten of his servants, he gave them ten pounds,ᵉ 14 and said to them, 'Trade with these till I come.' But his citizens hated him and sent an embassy after him, saying, 15 'We do not want this man to reign over us.' When he returned, having received the kingdom, he commanded these servants, to whom he had given the money, to be called to him, that he might know what they had 16 gained by trading. The first came before him, saying, 17 'Lord, your pound has made ten pounds more.' And he said to him, 'Well done, good servant! Because you have been faithful in a very little, you shall have authority over 18 ten cities.' And the second came, saying, 'Lord, your 19 pound has made five pounds.' And he said to him, 'And 20 you are to be over five cities.' Then another came, saying, 'Lord, here is your pound, which I kept laid away in a 21 napkin; for I was afraid of you, because you are a severe man; you take up what you did not lay down, and 22 reap what you did not sow.' He said to him, 'I will condemn you out of your own mouth, you wicked servant! You knew that I was a severe man, taking up what I did 23 not lay down and reaping what I did not sow? Why then did you not put my money into the bank, and at my 24 coming I should have collected it with interest?' And he said to those who stood by, 'Take the pound from 25 him, and give it to him who has the ten pounds.' (And 26 they said to him, 'Lord, he has ten pounds!') 'I tell you, that to every one who has will more be given; but from him who has not, even what he has will be taken away. 27 But as for these enemies of mine, who did not want me to reign over them, bring them here and slay them before me.' "

JESUS' MINISTRY IN JERUSALEM

28 And when he had said this, he went on ahead, going 29 up to Jerusalem. When he drew near to Beth'phage and Bethany, at the mount that is called Olivet, he sent two 30 of the disciples, saying, "Go into the village opposite, where on entering you will find a colt tied, on which no 31 one has ever yet sat; untie it and bring it here. If any one asks you, 'Why are you untying it?' you shall say 32 this, 'The Lord has need of it.' " So those who were sent 33 went away and found it as he had told them. And as they were untying the colt, its owners said to them, "Why are 34 you untying the colt?" And they said, "The Lord has 35 need of it." And they brought it to Jesus, and throwing 36 their garments on the colt they set Jesus upon it. And as he rode along, they spread their garments on the road. 37 As he was now drawing near, at the descent of the Mount

of Olives, the whole multitude of the disciples began to rejoice and praise God with a loud voice for all the mighty 38 works that they had seen, saying, "Blessed is the King who comes in the name of the Lord! Peace in heaven and 39 glory in the highest!" And some of the Pharisees in the multitude said to him, "Teacher, rebuke your disciples." 40 He answered, "I tell you, if these were silent, the very stones would cry out."

41 And when he drew near and saw the city he wept over 42 it, saying, "Would that even today you knew the things that make for peace! But now they are hid from your 43 eyes. For the days shall come upon you, when your enemies will cast up a bank about you and surround you, 44 and hem you in on every side, and dash you to the ground, you and your children within you, and they will not leave one stone upon another in you; because you did not know the time of your visitation."

45 And he entered the temple and began to drive out those 46 who sold, saying to them, "It is written, 'My house shall be a house of prayer'; but you have made it a den of robbers."

Attempts to Incriminate Jesus

47 And he was teaching daily in the temple. The chief priests and the scribes and the principal men of the people 48 sought to destroy him; but they did not find anything they could do, for all the people hung upon his words.

20 One day, as he was teaching the people in the temple and preaching the gospel, the chief priests 2 and the scribes with the elders came up and said to him, "Tell us by what authority you do these things, or who 3 it is that gave you this authority." He answered them, 4 "I also will ask you a question; now tell me, Was the

5 baptism of John from heaven or from men?" And they discussed it with one another, saying, "If we say, 'From 6 heaven,' he will say, 'Why did you not believe him?' But if we say, 'From men,' all the people will stone us; for 7 they are convinced that John was a prophet." So they 8 answered that they did not know whence it was. And Jesus said to them, "Neither will I tell you by what authority I do these things."

9 And he began to tell the people this parable: "A man planted a vineyard, and let it out to tenants, and went 10 into another country for a long while. When the time came, he sent a servant to the tenants, that they should

ᵉ The mina, rendered here by *pound*, was about three months' wages for a laborer

give him some of the fruit of the vineyard; but the
11 tenants beat him, and sent him away empty handed. And
he sent another servant; him also they beat and treated
12 shamefully, and sent him away empty handed. And he
sent yet a third; this one they wounded and cast out.
13 Then the owner of the vineyard said, 'What shall I do?
I will send my beloved son; it may be they will respect
14 him.' But when the tenants saw him, they said to themselves, 'This is the heir; let us kill him, that the inheri-
15 tance may be ours.' And they cast him out of the vineyard
and killed him. What then will the owner of the vineyard
16 do to them? He will come and destroy those tenants, and
give the vineyard to others." When they heard this, they
17 said, "God forbid!" But he looked at them and said,
"What then is this that is written:
'The very stone which the builders rejected
has become the head of the corner'?
18 Every one who falls on that stone will be broken to pieces;
but when it falls on any one it will crush him."
19 The scribes and the chief priests tried to lay hands on
him at that very hour, but they feared the people; for
they perceived that he had told this parable against
20 them. So they watched him, and sent spies, who pretended
to be sincere, that they might take hold of what he said,
so as to deliver him up to the authority and jurisdiction
21 of the governor. They asked him, "Teacher, we know
that you speak and teach rightly, and show no partiality,
22 but truly teach the way of God. Is it lawful for us to give
23 tribute to Caesar, or not?" But he perceived their crafti-
24 ness, and said to them, "Show me a coin.^{f} Whose likeness
25 and inscription has it?" They said, "Caesar's." He said
to them, "Then render to Caesar the things that are

26 Caesar's, and to God the things that are God's." And
they were not able in the presence of the people to catch
him by what he said; but marveling at his answer they
were silent.
27 There came to him some Sad'ducees, those who say
28 that there is no resurrection, and they asked him a question, saying, "Teacher, Moses wrote for us that if a man's
brother dies, having a wife but no children, the man ^{g}
must take the wife and raise up children for his brother.
29 Now there were seven brothers; the first took a wife, and
30, 31 died without children; and the second and the third
took her, and likewise all seven left no children and died.
32, 33 Afterward the woman also died. In the resurrection,
therefore, whose wife will the woman be? For the seven

^{f} Greek *denarius* ^{g} Greek *his brother*

had her as wife."
34 And Jesus said to them, "The sons of this age marry
35 and are given in marriage; but those who are accounted
worthy to attain to that age and to the resurrection from
the dead neither marry nor are given in marriage,
36 for they cannot die any more, because they are equal to
angels and are sons of God, being sons of the resurrection.
37 But that the dead are raised, even Moses showed, in the
passage about the bush, where he calls the Lord the God
of Abraham and the God of Isaac and the God of Jacob.
38 Now he is not God of the dead, but of the living; for all
39 live to him." And some of the scribes answered, "Teacher,
40 you have spoken well." For they no longer dared to ask
him any question.
41 But he said to them, "How can they say that the Christ
42 is David's son? For David himself says in the Book of
Psalms,
'The Lord said to my Lord,
Sit at my right hand,
43 till I make thy enemies a stool for thy feet.'
44 David thus calls him Lord; so how is he his son?"
45 And in the hearing of all the people he said to his
46 disciples, "Beware of the scribes, who like to go about in
long robes, and love salutations in the market places and
the best seats in the synagogues and the places of honor
47 at feasts, who devour widows' houses and for a pretense
make long prayers. They will receive the greater condemnation."

21 He looked up and saw the rich putting their gifts
2 into the treasury; and he saw a poor widow put in
3 two copper coins. And he said, "Truly I tell you, this
4 poor widow has put in more than all of them; for they
all contributed out of their abundance, but she out of her
poverty put in all the living that she had."

The End of the Age

5 And as some spoke of the temple, how it was adorned
6 with noble stones and offerings, he said, "As for these
things which you see, the days will come when there shall
not be left here one stone upon another that will not be
7 thrown down." And they asked him, "Teacher, when will
this be, and what will be the sign when this is about to
8 take place?" And he said, "Take heed that you are not
led astray; for many will come in my name, saying, 'I am
he!' and, 'The time is at hand!' Do not go after them.
9 And when you hear of wars and tumults, do not be
terrified; for this must first take place, but the end will
not be at once."
10 Then he said to them, "Nation will rise against nation,
11 and kingdom against kingdom; there will be great earthquakes, and in various places famines and pestilences;
and there will be terrors and great signs from heaven.
12 But before all this they will lay their hands on you and

persecute you, delivering you up to the synagogues and prisons, and you will be brought before kings and [13] governors for my name's sake. This will be a time for [14] you to bear testimony. Settle it therefore in your minds, [15] not to meditate beforehand how to answer; for I will give you a mouth and wisdom, which none of your adversaries [16] will be able to withstand or contradict. You will be delivered up even by parents and brothers and kinsmen

[17] and friends, and some of you they will put to death; you [18] will be hated by all for my name's sake. But not a hair [19] of your head will perish. By your endurance you will gain your lives.

[20] "But when you see Jerusalem surrounded by armies, [21] then know that its desolation has come near. Then let those who are in Judea flee to the mountains, and let those who are inside the city depart, and let not those who are [22] out in the country enter it; for these are days of [23] vengeance, to fulfil all that is written. Alas for those who are with child and for those who give suck in those days! For great distress shall be upon the earth and wrath [24] upon this people; they will fall by the edge of the sword, and be led captive among all nations; and Jerusalem will be trodden down by the Gentiles, until the times of the Gentiles are fulfilled.

[25] "And there will be signs in sun and moon and stars, and upon the earth distress of nations in perplexity at the [26] roaring of the sea and the waves, men fainting with fear and with foreboding of what is coming on the world; [27] for the powers of the heavens will be shaken. And then they will see the Son of man coming in a cloud with [28] power and great glory. Now when these things begin to take place, look up and raise your heads, because your redemption is drawing near."

[29] And he told them a parable: "Look at the fig tree, and [30] all the trees; as soon as they come out in leaf, you see for yourselves and know that the summer is already near. [31] So also, when you see these things taking place, you know [32] that the kingdom of God is near. Truly, I say to you, this generation will not pass away till all has taken place. [33] Heaven and earth will pass away, but my words will not pass away.

[34] "But take heed to yourselves lest your hearts be weighed down with dissipation and drunkenness and cares of this life, and that day come upon you suddenly like [35] a snare; for it will come upon all who dwell upon the [36] face of the whole earth. But watch at all times, praying that you may have strength to escape all these things that will take place, and to stand before the Son of man."

[37] And every day he was teaching in the temple, but at night he went out and lodged on the mount called Olivet. [38] And early in the morning all the people came to him in the temple to hear him.

The Last Supper

22 Now the feast of Unleavened Bread drew near, [2] which is called the Passover. And the chief priests and the scribes were seeking how to put him to death; for they feared the people.

[3] Then Satan entered into Judas called Iscariot, who was [4] of the number of the twelve; he went away and conferred with the chief priests and officers how he might betray [5] him to them. And they were glad, and engaged to give him [6] money. So he agreed, and sought an opportunity to betray him to them in the absence of the multitude.

[7] Then came the day of Unleavened Bread, on which the [8] passover lamb had to be sacrificed. So Jesus[h] sent Peter and John, saying, "Go and prepare the passover for us, [9] that we may eat it." They said to him, "Where will you [10] have us prepare it?" He said to them, "Behold, when you have entered the city, a man carrying a jar of water will meet you; follow him into the house which he enters, [11] and tell the householder, 'The Teacher says to you, Where is the guest room, where I am to eat the passover with [12] my disciples?' And he will show you a large upper room [13] furnished; there make ready." And they went, and found it as he had told them; and they prepared the passover.

[14] And when the hour came, he sat at table, and the [15] apostles with him. And he said to them, "I have earnestly [16] desired to eat this passover with you before I suffer; for I tell you I shall not eat it[i] until it is fulfilled in the kingdom

[17] of God." And he took a cup, and when he had given thanks he said, "Take this, and divide it among your-[18] selves; for I tell you that from now on I shall not drink of the fruit of the vine until the kingdom of God comes." [19] And he took bread, and when he had given thanks he broke it and gave it to them, saying, "This is my body which is given for you. Do this in remembrance of me." [20] And likewise the cup after supper, saying, "This cup which is poured out for you is the new covenant in my blood.[j]

[21] But behold the hand of him who betrays me is with me on [22] the table. For the Son of man goes as it has been determined; but woe to that man by whom he is betrayed!" [23] And they began to question one another, which of them it was that would do this.

---

[h] Greek *he*   [i] Other ancient authorities read *never eat it again*

[j] Other authorities omit, in whole or in part, verses 19b-20 (*which is given . . . in my blood*).

Farewell Instructions

24 A dispute also arose among them, which of them was
25 to be regarded as the greatest. And he said to them, "The kings of the Gentiles exercise lordship over them; and those in authority over them are called benefactors.
26 But not so with you; rather let the greatest among you become as the youngest, and the leader as one who serves.
27 For which is the greater, one who sits at table, or one who serves? Is it not the one who sits at table? But I am among you as one who serves.
28 "You are those who have continued with me in my
29 trials; and I assign to you, as my Father assigned to me,
30 a kingdom, that you may eat and drink at my table in my kingdom, and sit on thrones judging the twelve tribes of Israel.
31 "Simon, Simon, behold, Satan demanded to have you,[k]
32 that he might sift you[k] like wheat, but I have prayed for you that your faith may not fail; and when you have
33 turned again, strengthen your brethren." And he said to him, "Lord, I am ready to go with you to prison and
34 to death." He said, "I tell you, Peter, the cock will not crow this day, until you three times deny that you know me."
35 And he said to them, "When I sent you out with no purse or bag or sandals, did you lack anything?" They
36 said, "Nothing." He said to them, "But now, let him who has a purse take it, and likewise a bag. And let him who
37 has no sword sell his mantle and buy one. For I tell you that this scripture must be fulfilled in me, 'And he was reckoned with transgressors'; for what is written about me
38 has its fulfilment." And they said, "Look, Lord, here are two swords." And he said to them, "It is enough."

The Arrest

39 And he came out, and went, as was his custom, to the
40 Mount of Olives; and the disciples followed him. And when he came to the place he said to them, "Pray that
41 you may not enter into temptation." And he withdrew from them about a stone's throw, and knelt down and
42 prayed, "Father, if thou art willing, remove this cup from me; nevertheless not my will, but thine, be done."[l]
45 And when he rose from prayer, he came to the disciples and found them sleeping for sorrow, and he said to them,
46 "Why do you sleep? Rise and pray that you may not enter into temptation."
47 While he was still speaking, there came a crowd, and the man called Judas, one of the twelve, was leading
48 them. He drew near to Jesus to kiss him; but Jesus said to him, "Judas, would you betray the Son of man with
49 a kiss?" And when those who were about him saw what would follow, they said, 'Lord, shall we strike with the
50 sword?" And one of them struck the slave of the high
51 priest and cut off his right ear. But Jesus said, "No more

52 of this!" And he touched his ear and healed him. Then Jesus said to the chief priests and officers of the temple and elders, who had come out against him, "Have you come out as against a robber, with swords and clubs?
53 When I was with you day after day in the temple, you did not lay hands on me. But this is your hour, and the power of darkness."

54 Then they seized him and led him away, bringing him into the high priest's house. Peter followed at a distance;
55 and when they had kindled a fire in the middle of the courtyard and sat down together, Peter sat among them.
56 Then a maid, seeing him as he sat in the light and gazing
57 at him, said, "This man also was with him." But he
58 denied it, saying, "Woman, I do not know him." And a little later some one else saw him and said, "You also are
59 one of them." But Peter said, "Man, I am not." And after an interval of about an hour still another insisted, saying, "Certainly this man also was with him; for he is a
60 Galilean." But Peter said, "Man, I do not know what you are saying." And immediately, while he was still speaking,
61 the cock crowed. And the Lord turned and looked at Peter. And Peter remembered the word of the Lord, how he had said to him, "Before the cock crows today, you will
62 deny me three times." And he went out and wept bitterly.
63 Now the men who were holding Jesus mocked him and
64 beat him; they also blindfolded him and asked him,
65 "Prophesy! Who is it that struck you?" And they spoke many other words against him, reviling him.

The Trials

66 When day came, the assembly of the elders of the people gathered together, both chief priests and scribes; and they led him away to their council, and they said,
67 "If you are the Christ, tell us." But he said to them, "If
68 I tell you, you will not believe; and if I ask you, you
69 will not answer. But from now on the Son of man shall
70 be seated at the right hand of the power of God." And they all said, "Are you the Son of God, then?" And he
71 said to them, "You say that I am." And they said, "What further testimony do we need? We have heard it ourselves from his own lips."

---

[k] The Greek word for *you* here is plural; in verse 32 it is singular

[l] Other ancient authorities add verses 43 and 44: [43] *And there appeared to him an angel from heaven, strengthening him.* [44] *And being in an agony he prayed more earnestly; and his sweat became like great drops of blood falling down upon the ground.*

23 Then the whole company of them arose, and 2 brought him before Pilate. And they began to accuse him, saying, "We found this man perverting our nation, and forbidding us to give tribute to Caesar, and saying 3 that he himself is Christ a king." And Pilate asked him, "Are you the King of the Jews?" And he answered him, 4 "You have said so." And Pilate said to the chief priests and the multitudes, "I find no crime in this man." 5 But they were urgent, saying, "He stirs up the people, teaching throughout all Judea, from Galilee even to this place."

6 When Pilate heard this, he asked whether the man was 7 a Galilean. And when he learned that he belonged to Herod's jurisdiction, he sent him over to Herod, who 8 was himself in Jerusalem at that time. When Herod saw Jesus, he was very glad, for he had long desired to see him, because he had heard about him, and he was hoping 9 to see some sign done by him. So he questioned him at 10 some length; but he made no answer. The chief priests 11 and the scribes stood by, vehemently accusing him. And Herod with his soldiers treated him with contempt and mocked him; then, arraying him in gorgeous apparel, he 12 sent him back to Pilate. And Herod and Pilate became friends with each other that very day, for before this they had been at enmity with each other.

13 Pilate then called together the chief priests and the 14 rulers and the people, and said to them, "You brought me this man as one who was perverting the people; and after examining him before you, behold, I did not find this man guilty of any of your charges against him; 15 neither did Herod, for he sent him back to us. Behold, 16 nothing deserving death has been done by him; I will therefore chastise him and release him." m

18 But they all cried out together, "Away with this man, 19 and release to us Barab'bas"—a man who had been thrown into prison for an insurrection started in the 20 city, and for murder. Pilate addressed them once more, 21 desiring to release Jesus; but they shouted out, "Crucify, 22 crucify him!" A third time he said to them, "Why, what evil has he done? I have found in him no crime deserving death; I will therefore chastise him and release 23 him." But they were urgent, demanding with loud cries that he should be crucified. And their voices prevailed. 24 So Pilate gave sentence that their demand should be 25 granted. He released the man who had been thrown into prison for insurrection and murder, whom they asked for; but Jesus he delivered up to their will.

Calvary

26 And as they led him away, they seized one Simon of Cyre'ne, who was coming in from the country, and laid 27 on him the cross, to carry it behind Jesus. And there followed him a great multitude of the people, and of 28 women who bewailed and lamented him. But Jesus turning to them said, "Daughters of Jerusalem, do not weep for me, but weep for yourselves and for your children. 29 For behold, the days are coming when they will say, 'Blessed are the barren, and the wombs that never bore, 30 and the breasts that never gave suck!' Then they will begin to say to the mountains, 'Fall on us'; and to the 31 hills, 'Cover us.' For if they do this when the wood is green, what will happen when it is dry?"

32 Two others also, who were criminals, were led away 33 to be put to death with him. And when they came to the place which is called The Skull, there they crucified him, and the criminals, one on the right and one on the 34 left. And Jesus said, "Father, forgive them; for they know not what they do." n And they cast lots to divide 35 his garments. And the people stood by, watching; but the rulers scoffed at him, saying, "He saved others; let him save himself, if he is the Christ of God, his Chosen 36 One!" The soldiers also mocked him, coming up and 37 offering him vinegar, and saying, "If you are the King 38 of the Jews, save yourself!" There was also an inscription over him,o "This is the King of the Jews."

39 One of the criminals who were hanged railed at him, saying, "Are you not the Christ? Save yourself and us!" 40 But the other rebuked him, saying, "Do you not fear God, since you are under the same sentence of condem- 41 nation? And we indeed justly; for we are receiving the due reward of our deeds; but this man has done nothing 42 wrong." And he said, "Jesus, remember me when you 43 come intop your kingdom. And he said to him, "Truly, I say to you, today you will be with me in Paradise."

44 It was now about the sixth hour, and there was dark- 45 ness over the whole land q until the ninth hour, while the sun's light failed;r and the curtain of the temple was 46 torn in two. Then Jesus, crying with a loud voice, said, "Father, into thy hands I commit my spirit!" And hav- 47 ing said this he breathed his last. Now when the centurion saw what had taken place, he praised God, and 48 said, "Certainly this man was innocent!" And all the multitudes who assembled to see the sight, when they saw what had taken place, returned home beating their 49 breasts. And all his acquaintances and the women who had followed him from Galilee stood at a distance and saw these things.

50 Now there was a man named Joseph from the Jewish town of Arimathe'a. He was a member of the council, a 51 good and righteous man, who had not consented to their purpose and deed, and he was looking for the kingdom 52 of God. This man went to Pilate and asked for the body 53 of Jesus. Then he took it down and wrapped it in a linen shroud, and laid him in a rock-hewn tomb, where no one 54 had ever yet been laid. It was the day of Preparation,

n. Here, or after verse 19, other ancient authorities add verse 17, *Now he was obliged to release one man to them at the festival*
n Other ancient authorities omit the sentence *And Jesus . . . what they do*
o Other ancient authorities add *in letters of Greek and Latin and Hebrew*   p Other ancient authorities read *in*   q Or *earth*
r Or *the sun was eclipsed*. Other ancient authorities read *the sun was darkened*

55 and the sabbath was beginning.[s] The women who had come with him from Galilee followed, and saw the tomb, 56 and how his body was laid; then they returned, and prepared spices and ointments.

On the sabbath they rested according to the commandment.

THE RISEN CHRIST

24 But on the first day of the week, at early dawn, they went to the tomb, taking the spices which they 2 had prepared. And they found the stone rolled away 3 from the tomb, but when they went in they did not find 4 the body.[t] While they were perplexed about this, behold, 5 two men stood by them in dazzling apparel; and as they were frightened and bowed their faces to the ground, the men said to them, "Why do you seek the living 6 among the dead?[u] Remember how he told you, while 7 he was still in Galilee, that the Son of man must be delivered into the hands of sinful men, and be crucified, 8 and on the third day rise." And they remembered his 9 words, and returning from the tomb they told all this to 10 the eleven and to all the rest. Now it was Mary Mag'dalene and Jo-an'na and Mary the mother of James and the other women with them who told this to the apostles; 11 but these words seemed to them an idle tale, and they did not believe them.[v]

13 That very day two of them were going to a village named Emma'us, about seven miles[w] from Jerusalem,

20 and all the people, and how our chief priests and rulers delivered him up to be condemned to death, and crucified 21 him. But we had hoped that he was the one to redeem Israel. Yes, and besides all this, it is now the third day 22 since this happened. Moreover, some women of our company amazed us. They were at the tomb early in the 23 morning and did not find his body; and they came back saying that they had even seen a vision of angels, who 24 said that he was alive. Some of those who were with us went to the tomb, and found it just as the women had said; 25 but him they did not see." And he said to them, "O foolish men, and slow of heart to believe all that the 26 prophets have spoken! Was it not necessary that the Christ should suffer these things and enter into his 27 glory?" And beginning with Moses and all the prophets, he interpreted to them in all the scriptures the things concerning himself.

28 So they drew near to the village to which they were 29 going. He appeared to be going further, but they constrained him, saying, "Stay with us, for it is toward evening and the day is now far spent." So he went in to 30 stay with them. When he was at table with them, he took the bread and blessed, and broke it, and gave it to them. 31 And their eyes were opened and they recognized him; and 32 he vanished out of their sight. They said to each other, "Did not our hearts burn within us[c] while he talked to us on the road, while he opened to us the scriptures?" 33 And they rose that same hour and returned to Jerusalem;

14 and talking with each other about all these things that 15 had happened. While they were talking and discussing together, Jesus himself drew near and went with them. 16, 17 But their eyes were kept from recognizing him. And he said to them, "What is this conversation which you are holding with each other as you walk?" And they stood 18 still, looking sad. Then one of them, named Cle'opas, answered him, "Are you the only visitor to Jerusalem who does not know the things that have happened there 19 in these days?" And he said to them, "What things?" And they said to him, "Concerning Jesus of Nazareth, who was a prophet mighty in deed and word before God

and they found the eleven gathered together and those 34 who were with them, who said, "The Lord has risen 35 indeed, and has appeared to Simon!" Then they told what had happened on the road, and how he was known to them in the breaking of the bread.

36 As they were saying this, Jesus himself stood among 37 them.[x] But they were startled and frightened, and sup- 38 posed that they saw a spirit. And he said to them, "Why are you troubled, and why do questionings rise in your 39 hearts? See my hands and my feet, that it is I myself; handle me, and see; for a spirit has not flesh and bones 41 as you see that I have."[y] And while they still disbelieved

---

[s] Greek *was dawning*   [t] Other ancient authorities add *of the Lord Jesus*   [u] Other ancient authorities add *He is not here, but has risen*
[v] Other ancient authorities add verse 12, *But Peter rose and ran to the tomb; stooping and looking in, he saw the linen cloths by themselves; and he went home wondering at what had happened*   [w] Greek *sixty stadia; some ancient authorities read a hundred and sixty stadia*
[c] Other ancient authorities omit *within us*   [x] Other ancient authorities add *and said to them, "Peace to you!"*
[y] Other ancient authorities add verse 40, *And when he had said this, he showed them his hands and his feet*

for joy, and wondered, he said to them, "Have you any-
42 thing here to eat?" They gave him a piece of broiled
43 fish, and he took it and ate before them.

44   Then he said to them, "These are my words which I
spoke to you, while I was still with you, that everything
written about me in the law of Moses and the prophets
45 and the psalms must be fulfilled." Then he opened their
46 minds to understand the scriptures, and said to them,

"Thus it is written, that the Christ should suffer and on
47 the third day rise from the dead, and that repentance and

forgiveness of sins should be preached in his name to all
48 nations,ᶻ beginning from Jerusalem. You are witnesses
49 of these things. And behold, I send the promise of my
Father upon you; but stay in the city, until you are
clothed with power from on high."
50   Then he led them out as far as Bethany, and lifting
51 up his hands he blessed them. While he blessed them,
52 he parted from them, and was carried up into heaven.ᵃ
53 And theyᵇ returned to Jerusalem with great joy, and
were continually in the temple blessing God.

ᶻ Or nations. Beginning from Jerusalem you are witnesses
ᵇ Other ancient authorities add worshiped him, and

ᵃ Other ancient authorities omit and was carried up into heaven

JOHN

This book was the last of the four Gospels to be written, and the date of its writing is sometime between A.D. 90 and A.D. 100. Just who wrote the Gospel of John is not definitely known. John was a very common name, and the book itself does not clearly state just which John actually wrote it. Whoever wrote it certainly knew and understood Jesus Christ and the meaning of his life and work.

This Gospel makes no effort to tell a connected story of the life of Jesus. The Gospels of Mark, Matthew, and Luke had already done that. The purpose of the Gospel of John was to explain the supreme importance of Jesus Christ to all mankind.

John used some of the ideas of the Greek philosophers as well as the Greek language to tell how important Jesus is. He did this to get the attention of the educated people of that time and to win them to faith in Christ. He wrote to tell the eternal meaning of Jesus Christ to all mankind.

Some of the most wonderful statements in all the Bible are to be found in the Gospel of John. Perhaps the most important of all is, "For God so loved the world that he gave his only Son, that whoever believes in him should not perish but have eternal life" (John 3.16).

THE GOSPEL ACCORDING TO

JOHN

THE PROLOGUE

1 In the beginning was the Word, and the Word was 2 with God, and the Word was God. He was in the be-3 ginning with God; all things were made through him, and without him was not anything made that was made. 4 In him was life,[a] and the life was the light of men. 5 The light shines in the darkness, and the darkness has not overcome it.

6 There was a man sent from God, whose name was 7 John. He came for testimony, to bear witness to the light, 8 that all might believe through him. He was not the light, but came to bear witness to the light.

9 The true light that enlightens every man was coming 10 into the world. He was in the world, and the world was 11 made through him, yet the world knew him not. He came to his own home, and his own people received him not. 12 But to all who received him, who believed in his name, he 13 gave power to become children of God; who were born, not of blood nor of the will of the flesh nor of the will of man, but of God.

14 And the Word became flesh and dwelt among us, full of grace and truth; we have beheld his glory, glory as of 15 the only Son from the Father. (John bore witness to him, and cried, "This was he of whom I said, 'He who comes after me ranks before me, for he was before me.' ")

16 And from his fulness have we all received, grace upon 17 grace. For the law was given through Moses; grace and 18 truth came through Jesus Christ. No one has ever seen God; the only Son,[b] who is in the bosom of the Father, he has made him known.

THE TESTIMONY

19 And this is the testimony of John, when the Jews sent priests and Levites from Jerusalem to ask him, "Who are 20 you?" He confessed, he did not deny, but confessed, "I 21 am not the Christ." And they asked him, "What then? Are you Eli'jah?" He said, "I am not." "Are you the 22 prophet?" And he answered, "No." They said to him then, "Who are you? Let us have an answer for those 23 who sent us. What do you say about yourself?" He said, "I am the voice of one crying in the wilderness, 'Make straight the way of the Lord,' as the prophet Isaiah said." 24, 25 Now they had been sent from the Pharisees. They asked him, "Then why are you baptizing, if you are 26 neither the Christ, nor Eli'jah, nor the prophet?" John answered them, "I baptize with water; but among you 27 stands one whom you do not know, even he who comes after me, the thong of whose sandal I am not worthy 28 to untie." This took place in Bethany beyond the Jordan, where John was baptizing.

[a] Or was not anything made. That which has been made was life in him

[b] Other ancient authorities read God

29 The next day he saw Jesus coming toward him, and said, "Behold, the Lamb of God, who takes away the
30 sin of the world! This is he of whom I said, 'After me comes a man who ranks before me, for he was before me.'
31 I myself did not know him; but for this I came baptizing
32 with water, that he might be revealed to Israel." And John bore witness, "I saw the Spirit descend as a dove
33 from heaven, and it remained on him. I myself did not know him; but he who sent me to baptize with water said to me, 'He on whom you see the Spirit descend and remain, this is he who baptizes with the Holy Spirit.'
34 And I have seen and have borne witness that this is the Son of God."
35 The next day again John was standing with two of his

51 saw you under the fig tree, do you believe? You shall see greater things than these." And he said to him, "Truly, truly, I say to you, you will see heaven opened, and the angels of God ascending and descending upon the Son of man."

JESUS REVEALS HIMSELF

2 On the third day there was a marriage at Cana in
2 Galilee, and the mother of Jesus was there; Jesus also
3 was invited to the marriage, with his disciples. When the wine gave out, the mother of Jesus said to him, "They
4 have no wine." And Jesus said to her, "O woman, what have you to do with me? My hour has not yet come."

36 disciples; and he looked at Jesus as he walked, and said,
37 "Behold, the Lamb of God!" The two disciples heard
38 him say this, and they followed Jesus. Jesus turned, and saw them following, and said to them, "What do you seek?" And they said to him, "Rabbi" (which means
39 Teacher), "where are you staying?" He said to them, "Come and see." They came and saw where he was staying; and they stayed with him that day, for it was
40 about the tenth hour. One of the two who heard John speak, and followed him, was Andrew, Simon Peter's
41 brother. He first found his brother Simon, and said to him, "We have found the Messiah" (which means Christ).
42 He brought him to Jesus. Jesus looked at him, and said, "So you are Simon the son of John? You shall be called Cephas" (which means Peter c).
43 The next day Jesus decided to go to Galilee. And he
44 found Philip and said to him, "Follow me." Now Philip was from Beth-sa'ida, the city of Andrew and Peter.
45 Philip found Nathan'a-el, and said to him, "We have found him of whom Moses in the law and also the prophets wrote, Jesus of Nazareth, the son of Joseph."
46 Nathan'a-el said to him, "Can anything good come out of Nazareth?" Philip said to him, "Come and see."
47 Jesus saw Nathan'a-el coming to him, and said of him, "Behold, an Israelite indeed, in whom is no guile!"
48 Nathan'a-el said to him, "How do you know me?" Jesus answered him, "Before Philip called you, when you were
49 under the fig tree, I saw you." Nathan'a-el answered him, "Rabbi, you are the Son of God! You are the King of
50 Israel!" Jesus answered him, "Because I said to you, I

5 His mother said to the servants, "Do whatever he tells
6 you." Now six stone jars were standing there, for the Jewish rites of purification, each holding twenty or thirty
7 gallons. Jesus said to them, "Fill the jars with water."
8 And they filled them up to the brim. He said to them, "Now draw some out, and take it to the steward of the
9 feast." So they took it. When the steward of the feast tasted the water now become wine, and did not know where it came from (though the servants who had drawn the water knew), the steward of the feast called the bride-
10 groom and said to him, "Every man serves the good wine first; and when men have drunk freely, then the poor wine; but you have kept the good wine until now."
11 This, the first of his signs, Jesus did at Cana in Galilee, and manifested his glory; and his disciples believed in him.
12 After this he went down to Caper'na-um, with his mother and his brothers and his disciples; and there they stayed for a few days.
13 The Passover of the Jews was at hand, and Jesus went
14 up to Jerusalem. In the temple he found those who were selling oxen and sheep and pigeons, and the money-
15 changers at their business. And making a whip of cords, he drove them all, with the sheep and oxen, out of the temple; and he poured out the coins of the money-
16 changers and overturned their tables. And he told those who sold the pigeons, "Take these things away; you shall
17 not make my Father's house a house of trade." His dis- ciples remembered that it was written, "Zeal for thy
18 house will consume me." The Jews then said to him,

c From the word for *rock* in Aramaic and Greek, respectively

"What sign have you to show us for doing this?"
19 Jesus answered them, "Destroy this temple, and in three
20 days I will raise it up." The Jews then said, "It has
taken forty-six years to build this temple, and will you
21 raise it up in three days?" But he spoke of the temple
22 of his body. When therefore he was raised from the dead,
his disciples remembered that he had said this; and
they believed the scripture and the word which Jesus had
spoken.

23 Now when he was in Jerusalem at the Passover feast,
many believed in his name when they saw signs which he
24, 25 did; but Jesus did not trust himself to them, because he
knew all men and needed no one to bear witness of man;
for he himself knew what was in man.

3 Now there was a man of the Pharisees, named
2 Nicode'mus, a ruler of the Jews. This man came to
Jesus d by night and said to him, "Rabbi, we know that
you are a teacher come from God; for no one can do
these signs that you do, unless God is with him."
3 Jesus answered him, "Truly, truly, I say to you, unless
one is born anew,e he cannot see the kingdom of God."
4 Nicode'mus said to him, "How can a man be born when
he is old? Can he enter a second time into his mother's
5 womb and be born?" Jesus answered, "Truly, truly, I
say to you, unless one is born of water and the Spirit, he
6 cannot enter the kingdom of God. That which is born of
the flesh is flesh, and that which is born of the Spirit is
7 spirit.f Do not marvel that I said to you, 'You must be
8 born anew.'e The wind f blows where it wills, and you
hear the sound of it, but you do not know whence it comes
or whither it goes; so it is with every one who is born
9 of the Spirit." Nicode'mus said to him, "How can this
10 be?" Jesus answered him, "Are you a teacher of Israel,
11 and yet you do not understand this? Truly, truly, I say
to you, we speak of what we know, and bear witness to
what we have seen; but you do not receive our testi-
12 mony. If I have told you earthly things and you do not
believe, how can you believe if I tell you heavenly things?
13 No one has ascended into heaven but he who descended
14 from heaven, the Son of man.g And as Moses lifted up
the serpent in the wilderness, so must the Son of man
15 be lifted up, that whoever believes in him may have
eternal life." h
16 For God so loved the world that he gave his only Son,
that whoever believes in him should not perish but have
17 eternal life. For God sent the Son into the world, not to

condemn the world, but that the world might be saved
18 through him. He who believes in him is not condemned;
he who does not believe is condemned already, because
he has not believed in the name of the only Son of God.
19 And this is the judgment, that the light has come into
the world, and men loved darkness rather than light,
20 because their deeds were evil. For every one who does
evil hates the light, and does not come to the light, lest
21 his deeds should be exposed. But he who does what is
true comes to the light, that it may be clearly seen that
his deeds have been wrought in God.

22 After this Jesus and his disciples went into the land of
Judea; there he remained with them and baptized.
23 John also was baptizing at Ae'non near Salim, because
there was much water there; and people came and were
24 baptized. For John had not yet been put in prison.
25 Now a discussion arose between John's disciples and a
26 Jew over purifying. And they came to John, and said to
him, "Rabbi, he who was with you beyond the Jordan, to
whom you bore witness, here he is, baptizing, and all are
27 going to him." John answered, "No one can receive any-
28 thing except what is given him from heaven. You yourselves bear me witness, that I said, I am not the Christ, but
29 I have been sent before him. He who has the bride is the
bridegroom; the friend of the bridegroom, who stands and
hears him, rejoices greatly at the bridegroom's voice;
30 therefore this joy of mine is now full. He must increase,
but I must decrease." i
31 He who comes from above is above all; he who is of
the earth belongs to the earth, and of the earth he speaks;
32 he who comes from heaven is above all. He bears witness
to what he has seen and heard, yet no one receives his
33 testimony; he who receives his testimony sets his seal to
34 this, that God is true. For he whom God has sent utters
the words of God, for it is not by measure that he gives
35 the Spirit; the Father loves the Son, and has given all
36 things into his hand. He who believes in the Son has
eternal life; he who does not obey the Son shall not see
life, but the wrath of God rests upon him.

In Samaria

4 Now when the Lord knew that the Pharisees had
heard that Jesus was making and baptizing more dis-
2 ciples than John (although Jesus himself did not baptize,
3 but only his disciples), he left Judea and departed again
4, 5 to Galilee. He had to pass through Samar'ia. So he came
to a city of Samar'ia, called Sy'char, near the field that

d Greek *him*   e Or *from above*   f The same Greek word means both *wind* and *spirit*
g Other ancient authorities add *who is in heaven*   h Some interpreters hold that the quotation continues through verse 21
i Some interpreters hold that the quotation continues through verse 36

6 Jacob gave to his son Joseph. Jacob's well was there, and so Jesus, wearied as he was with his journey, sat down beside the well. It was about the sixth hour.

7 There came a woman of Samar′ia to draw water. Jesus 8 said to her, "Give me a drink." For his disciples had 9 gone away into the city to buy food. The Samaritan woman said to him, "How is it that you, a Jew, ask a drink of me, a woman of Samar′ia?" For Jews have no 10 dealings with Samaritans. Jesus answered her, "If you knew the gift of God, and who it is that is saying to you, 'Give me a drink,' you would have asked him, and he 11 would have given you living water." The woman said to him, "Sir, you have nothing to draw with, and the well 12 is deep; where do you get that living water? Are you greater than our father Jacob, who gave us the well, and 13 drank from it himself, and his sons, and his cattle?" Jesus said to her, "Every one who drinks of this water will 14 thirst again, but whoever drinks of the water that I shall give him will never thirst; the water that I shall give him will become in him a spring of water welling up to 15 eternal life." The woman said to him, "Sir, give me this water, that I may not thirst, nor come here to draw."

16 Jesus said to her, "Go, call your husband, and come 17 here." The woman answered him, "I have no husband." Jesus said to her, "You are right in saying, 'I have no 18 husband'; for you have had five husbands, and he whom you now have is not your husband; this you said truly." 19 The woman said to him, "Sir, I perceive that you are a 20 prophet. Our fathers worshiped on this mountain; and you say that in Jerusalem is the place where men ought 21 to worship." Jesus said to her, "Woman, believe me, the hour is coming when neither on this mountain nor in 22 Jerusalem will you worship the Father. You worship what you do not know; we worship what we know, for salvation 23 is from the Jews. But the hour is coming, and now is, when the true worshipers will worship the Father in spirit and truth, for such the Father seeks to worship him. 24 God is spirit, and those who worship him must worship in 25 spirit and truth." The woman said to him, "I know that Messiah is coming (he who is called Christ); when he 26 comes, he will show us all things." Jesus said to her, "I who speak to you am he."

27 Just then his disciples came. They marveled that he was talking with a woman, but none said, "What do you 28 wish?" or "Why are you talking with her?" So the woman left her water jar, and went away into the city, and 29 said to the people, "Come, see a man who told me all that 30 I ever did. Can this be the Christ?" They went out of the city and were coming to him.

31 Meanwhile the disciples besought him, saying, "Rabbi, 32 eat." But he said to them, "I have food to eat of which 33 you do not know." So the disciples said to one another, 34 "Has any one brought him food?" Jesus said to them,

"My food is to do the will of him who sent me, and to 35 accomplish his work. Do you not say, 'There are yet four months, then comes the harvest'? I tell you, lift up your eyes, and see how the fields are already white for harvest. 36 He who reaps receives wages, and gathers fruit for eternal life, so that sower and reaper may rejoice together. 37 For here the saying holds true, 'One sows and another 38 reaps.' I sent you to reap that for which you did not labor; others have labored, and you have entered into their labor."

39 Many Samaritans from that city believed in him because of the woman's testimony, "He told me all that I 40 ever did." So when the Samaritans came to him, they asked him to stay with them; and he stayed there two 41 days. And many more believed because of his word. 42 They said to the woman, "It is no longer because of your words that we believe, for we have heard for ourselves, and we know that this is indeed the Savior of the world."

In Galilee

43, 44 After the two days he departed to Galilee. For Jesus himself testified that a prophet has no honor in his own 45 country. So when he came to Galilee, the Galileans welcomed him, having seen all that he had done in Jerusalem at the feast, for they too had gone to the feast.

46 So he came again to Cana in Galilee, where he had

made the water wine. And at Caper′na-um there was an 47 official whose son was ill. When he heard that Jesus had come from Judea to Galilee, he went and begged him to come down and heal his son, for he was at the point of 48 death. Jesus therefore said to him, "Unless you see signs 49 and wonders you will not believe." The official said to him, 50 "Sir, come down before my child dies." Jesus said to him, "Go; your son will live." The man believed the word that 51 Jesus spoke to him and went his way. As he was going down, his servants met him and told him that his son 52 was living. So he asked them the hour when he began to mend, and they said to him, "Yesterday at the seventh 53 hour the fever left him." The father knew that was the hour when Jesus had said to him, "Your son will live"; 54 and he himself believed, and all his household. This was now the second sign that Jesus did when he had come from Judea to Galilee.

SIGNS AND CONTROVERSIES

5 After this there was a feast of the Jews, and Jesus went up to Jerusalem.

2 Now there is in Jerusalem by the Sheep Gate a pool, in

Hebrew called Beth-za′tha,[j] which has five porticoes. [3] In these lay a multitude of invalids, blind, lame, [5] paralyzed.[k] One man was there who had been ill for [6] thirty-eight years. When Jesus saw him and knew that he had been lying there a long time, he said to him, "Do you [7] want to be healed?" The sick man answered him, "Sir, I have no man to put me into the pool when the water is troubled, and while I am going another steps down before [8] me." Jesus said to him, "Rise, take up your pallet, and [9] walk." And at once the man was healed, and he took up his pallet and walked.

[10] Now that day was the sabbath. So the Jews said to the man who was cured, "It is the sabbath, it is not lawful [11] for you to carry your pallet." But he answered them, "The man who healed me said to me, 'Take up your pallet, and [12] walk.'" They asked him, "Who is the man who said to [13] you, 'Take up your pallet, and walk'?" Now the man who had been healed did not know who it was, for Jesus had [14] withdrawn, as there was a crowd in the place. Afterward, Jesus found him in the temple, and said to him, "See, you are well! Sin no more, that nothing worse befall you." [15] The man went away and told the Jews that it was Jesus [16] who had healed him. And this was why the Jews perse- [17] cuted Jesus, because he did this on the sabbath. But Jesus answered them, "My Father is working still, and I [18] am working." This was why the Jews sought all the more to kill him, because he not only broke the sabbath but also called God his own Father, making himself equal with God.

[19] Jesus said to them, "Truly, truly, I say to you, the Son can do nothing of his own accord, but only what he sees the Father doing; for whatever he does, that the Son does [20] likewise. For the Father loves the Son, and shows him all that he himself is doing; and greater works than these [21] will he show him, that you may marvel. For as the Father raises the dead and gives them life, so also the Son gives [22] life to whom he will. The Father judges no one, but has [23] given all judgment to the Son, that all may honor the Son, even as they honor the Father. He who does not honor the [24] Son does not honor the Father who sent him. Truly, truly, I say to you, he who hears my word and believes him who sent me, has eternal life; he does not come into judgment, but has passed from death to life.

[25] "Truly, truly, I say to you, the hour is coming, and now is, when the dead will hear the voice of the Son of [26] God, and those who hear will live. For as the Father has life in himself, so he has granted the Son also to have life [27] in himself, and has given him authority to execute judg- [28] ment, because he is the Son of man. Do not marvel at this; for the hour is coming when all who are in the tombs will [29] hear his voice and come forth, those who have done good, to the resurrection of life, and those who have done evil, to the resurrection of judgment.

[30] "I can do nothing on my own authority; as I hear, I judge; and my judgment is just, because I seek not my [31] own will but the will of him who sent me. If I bear witness [32] to myself, my testimony is not true; there is another who bears witness to me, and I know that the testimony which [33] he bears to me is true. You sent to John, and he has borne [34] witness to the truth. Not that the testimony which I receive is from man; but I say this that you may be saved. [35] He was a burning and shining lamp, and you were willing [36] to rejoice for a while in his light. But the testimony which I have is greater than that of John; for the works which the Father has granted me to accomplish, these very works which I am doing, bear me witness that the Father has [37] sent me. And the Father who sent me has himself borne witness to me. His voice you have never heard, his form [38] you have never seen; and you do not have his word abiding in you, for you do not believe him whom he has [39] sent. You search the scriptures, because you think that in them you have eternal life; and it is they that bear witness [40] to me; yet you refuse to come to me that you may have [41, 42] life. I do not receive glory from men. But I know that [43] you have not the love of God within you. I have come in my Father's name, and you do not receive me; if another [44] comes in his own name, him you will receive. How can you believe, who receive glory from one another and do not seek the glory that comes from the only God? [45] Do not think that I shall accuse you to the Father; it is Moses who accuses you, on whom you set your hope. [46] If you believed Moses, you would believe me, for he wrote [47] of me. But if you do not believe his writings, how will you believe my words?"

Jesus; the Bread of Life

[6] After this Jesus went to the other side of the Sea of [2] Galilee, which is the Sea of Tibe′ri-as. And a multi- tude followed him, because they saw the signs which he [3] did on those who were diseased. Jesus went up on the [4] mountain, and there sat down with his disciples. Now [5] the Passover, the feast of the Jews, was at hand. Lifting up his eyes, then, and seeing that a multitude was coming to him, Jesus said to Philip, "How are we to buy bread, so [6] that these people may eat?" This he said to test him, for [7] he himself knew what he would do. Philip answered him, "Two hundred denarii[l] would not buy enough bread for [8] each of them to get a little." One of his disciples, Andrew, [9] Simon Peter's brother, said to him, "There is a lad here who has five barley loaves and two fish; but what are [10] they among so many?" Jesus said, "Make the people sit down." Now there was much grass in the place; so the [11] men sat down, in number about five thousand. Jesus then took the loaves, and when he had given thanks, he dis- tributed them to those who were seated; so also the fish, [12] as much as they wanted. And when they had eaten their

---

[j] Other ancient authorities read *Bethesda*, others *Bethsaida* of the water; [k] for an angel of the Lord went down at certain seasons into the pool, and troubled the water: whoever stepped in first after the troubling of the water was healed of whatever disease he had

[k] Other ancient authorities insert, wholly or in part, *waiting for the moving of the water: whoever stepped in first after the*

[l] The denarius was a day's wages for a laborer

fill, he told his disciples, "Gather up the fragments left
13 over, that nothing may be lost." So they gathered them
up and filled twelve baskets with fragments from the five
14 barley loaves, left by those who had eaten. When the
people saw the sign which he had done, they said, "This
is indeed the prophet who is to come into the world!"

15 Perceiving then that they were about to come and take
him by force to make him king, Jesus withdrew again to
the mountain by himself.

16 When evening came, his disciples went down to the
17 sea, got into a boat, and started across the sea to Caper'-
na-um. It was now dark, and Jesus had not yet come to
18 them. The sea rose because a strong wind was blowing.
19 When they had rowed about three or four miles,[m] they
saw Jesus walking on the sea and drawing near to the
20 boat. They were frightened, but he said to them, "It is I;
21 do not be afraid." Then they were glad to take him into
the boat, and immediately the boat was at the land to
which they were going.

22 On the next day the people who remained on the other
side of the sea saw that there had been only one boat
there, and that Jesus had not entered the boat with his
23 disciples, but that his disciples had gone away alone. However, boats from Tibe'ri-as came near the place where
they ate the bread after the Lord had given thanks.
24 So when the people saw that Jesus was not there, nor his
disciples, they themselves got into the boats and went to
Caper'na-um, seeking Jesus.

25 When they found him on the other side of the sea, they
26 said to him, "Rabbi, when did you come here?" Jesus
answered them, "Truly, truly, I say to you, you seek me,
not because you saw signs, but because you ate your fill
27 of the loaves. Do not labor for the food which perishes,
but for the food which endures to eternal life, which the
Son of man will give to you; for on him has God the
28 Father set his seal." Then they said to him, "What must
29 we do, to be doing the works of God?" Jesus answered
them, "This is the work of God, that you believe in him
30 whom he has sent." So they said to him, "Then what
sign do you do, that we may see, and believe you? What
31 work do you perform? Our fathers ate the manna in the

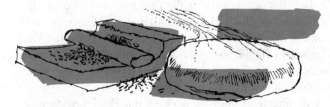

wilderness; as it is written, 'He gave them bread from
32 heaven to eat.' " Jesus then said to them, "Truly, truly,
I say to you, it was not Moses who gave you the bread
from heaven; my Father gives you the true bread from
33 heaven. For the bread of God is that which comes down

[m] Greek *twenty-five or thirty stadia*

34 from heaven, and gives life to the world." They said to
him, "Lord, give us this bread always."

35 Jesus said to them, "I am the bread of life; he who
comes to me shall not hunger, and he who believes in me
36 shall never thirst. But I said to you that you have seen
37 me and yet do not believe. All that the Father gives me
will come to me; and him who comes to me I will not
38 cast out. For I have come down from heaven, not to do
39 my own will, but the will of him who sent me; and this is
the will of him who sent me, that I should lose nothing of
all that he has given me, but raise it up at the last day.
40 For this is the will of my Father, that every one who sees
the Son and believes in him should have eternal life; and
I will raise him up at the last day."

41 The Jews then murmured at him, because he said, "I
42 am the bread which came down from heaven." They said,
"Is not this Jesus, the son of Joseph, whose father and
mother we know? How does he now say, 'I have come
43 down from heaven'?" Jesus answered them, "Do not
44 murmur among yourselves. No one can come to me unless
the Father who sent me draws him; and I will raise him
45 up at the last day. It is written in the prophets, 'And
they shall all be taught by God.' Every one who has heard
46 and learned from the Father comes to me. Not that any
one has seen the Father except him who is from God; he
47 has seen the Father. Truly, truly, I say to you, he who
48, 49 believes has eternal life. I am the bread of life. Your
fathers ate the manna in the wilderness, and they died.
50 This is the bread which comes down from heaven, that
51 a man may eat of it and not die. I am the living bread
which came down from heaven; if any one eats of this
bread, he will live for ever; and the bread which I shall
give for the life of the world is my flesh."

52 The Jews then disputed among themselves, saying,
53 "How can this man give us his flesh to eat?" So Jesus
said to them, "Truly, truly, I say to you, unless you eat
the flesh of the Son of man and drink his blood, you have
54 no life in you; he who eats my flesh and drinks my blood
has eternal life, and I will raise him up at the last day.
55 For my flesh is food indeed, and my blood is drink
56 indeed. He who eats my flesh and drinks my blood abides
57 in me, and I in him. As the living Father sent me, and I
live because of the Father, so he who eats me will live
58 because of me. This is the bread which came down from
heaven, not such as the fathers ate and died; he who eats
59 this bread will live for ever." This he said in the synagogue, as he taught at Caper'na-um.

60 Many of his disciples, when they heard it, said, "This
61 is a hard saying; who can listen to it?" But Jesus, knowing in himself that his disciples murmured at it, said to
62 them, "Do you take offense at this? Then what if you
were to see the Son of man ascending where he was be-
63 fore? It is the spirit that gives life, the flesh is of no avail;

the words that I have spoken to you are spirit and life.
64 But there are some of you that do not believe." For Jesus knew from the first who those were that did not believe,
65 and who it was that would betray him. And he said, "This is why I told you that no one can come to me unless it is granted him by the Father."

66 After this many of his disciples drew back and no
67 longer went about with him. Jesus said to the twelve,
68 "Do you also wish to go away?" Simon Peter answered him, "Lord, to whom shall we go? You have the words of
69 eternal life; and we have believed, and have come to
70 know, that you are the Holy One of God." Jesus answered them, "Did I not choose you, the twelve, and one of you
71 is a devil?" He spoke of Judas the son of Simon Iscariot, for he, one of the twelve, was to betray him.

7 After this Jesus went about in Galilee; he would not go about in Judea, because the Jews n sought to
2 kill him. Now the Jews' feast of Tabernacles was at
3 hand. So his brothers said to him, "Leave here and go to Judea, that your disciples may see the works you are
4 doing. For no man works in secret if he seeks to be known openly. If you do these things, show yourself to
5 the world." For even his brothers did not believe in him.
6 Jesus said to them, "My time has not yet come, but your
7 time is always here. The world cannot hate you, but it hates me because I testify of it that its works are evil.
8 Go to the feast yourselves; I am not o going up to this
9 feast, for my time has not yet fully come." So saying, he remained in Galilee.

10 But after his brothers had gone up to the feast, then
11 he also went up, not publicly but in private. The Jews were looking for him at the feast, and saying, "Where is
12 he?" And there was much muttering about him among the people. While some said, "He is a good man," others
13 said, "No, he is leading the people astray." Yet for fear of the Jews no one spoke openly of him.

14 About the middle of the feast Jesus went up into the
15 temple and taught. The Jews marveled at it, saying, "How is it that this man has learning,p when he has never
16 studied?" So Jesus answered them, "My teaching is not
17 mine, but his who sent me; if any man's will is to do his will, he shall know whether the teaching is from God or
18 whether I am speaking on my own authority. He who speaks on his own authority seeks his own glory; but he who seeks the glory of him who sent me is true, and in
19 him there is no falsehood. Did not Moses give you the law? Yet none of you keeps the law. Why do you seek
20 to kill me?" The people answered, "You have a demon!
21 Who is seeking to kill you?" Jesus answered them, "I
22 did one deed, and you all marvel at it. Moses gave you circumcision (not that it is from Moses, but from the
23 fathers), and you circumcise a man upon the sabbath. If on the sabbath a man receives circumcision, so that the law of Moses may not be broken, are you angry with me because on the sabbath I made a man's whole body well?
24 Do not judge by appearances, but judge with right judgment."

25 Some of the people of Jerusalem therefore said, "Is
26 not this the man whom they seek to kill? And here he is, speaking openly, and they say nothing to him! Can it be that the authorities really know that this is the Christ?
27 Yet we know where this man comes from; and when the Christ appears, no one will know where he comes from."
28 So Jesus proclaimed, as he taught in the temple, "You know me, and you know where I come from? But I have not come of my own accord; he who sent me is true, and
29 him you do not know. I know him, for I come from him,
30 and he sent me." So they sought to arrest him; but no one laid hands on him, because his hour had not yet
31 come. Yet many of the people believed in him; they said, "When the Christ appears, will he do more signs than this man has done?"

32 The Pharisees heard the crowd thus muttering about him, and the chief priests and Pharisees sent officers to
33 arrest him. Jesus then said, "I shall be with you a little
34 longer, and then I go to him who sent me; you will seek me and you will not find me; where I am you can-
35 not come." The Jews said to one another, "Where does this man intend to go that we shall not find him? Does he intend to go to the Dispersion among the Greeks and
36 teach the Greeks? What does he mean by saying, 'You will seek me and you will not find me,' and, 'Where I am you cannot come'?"

37 On the last day of the feast, the great day, Jesus stood up and proclaimed, "If any one thirst, let him come to
38 me and drink. He who believes in me, as q the scripture has said, 'Out of his heart shall flow rivers of living
39 water.'" Now this he said about the Spirit, which those who believed in him were to receive; for as yet the Spirit had not been given, because Jesus was not yet glorified.

40 When they heard these words, some of the people said,
41 "This is really the prophet." Others said, "This is the Christ." But some said, "Is the Christ to come from Gali-
42 lee? Has not the scripture said that the Christ is descended from David, and comes from Bethlehem, the vil-
43 lage where David was?" So there was a division among
44 the people over him. Some of them wanted to arrest him, but no one laid hands on him.

45 The officers then went back to the chief priests and Pharisees, who said to them, "Why did you not bring
46 him?" The officers answered, "No man ever spoke like
47 this man!" The Pharisees answered them, "Are you led
48 astray, you also? Have any of the authorities or of the
49 Pharisees believed in him? But this crowd, who do not

n Or *Judeans*   o Other ancient authorities add *yet*   p Or *this man knows his letters*
q Or *let him come to me, and let him who believes in me drink. As*

50 know the law, are accursed." Nicode'mus, who had gone to him before, and who was one of them, said to them,
51 "Does our law judge a man without first giving him a
52 hearing and learning what he does?" They replied, "Are you from Galilee too? Search and you will see that no prophet is to rise from Galilee."

Jesus; the Light of the World

53 8 They went each to his own house, but Jesus went
2 to the Mount of Olives. Early in the morning he came again to the temple; all the people came to him, and he
3 sat down and taught them. The scribes and the Pharisees brought a woman who had been caught in adultery, and
4 placing her in the midst they said to him, "Teacher, this
5 woman has been caught in the act of adultery. Now in the law Moses commanded us to stone such. What do you say
6 about her?" This they said to test him, that they might have some charge to bring against him. Jesus bent down
7 and wrote with his finger on the ground. And as they continued to ask him, he stood up and said to them, "Let him who is without sin among you be the first to throw
8 a stone at her." And once more he bent down and wrote
9 with his finger on the ground. But when they heard it, they went away, one by one, beginning with the eldest, and Jesus was left alone with the woman standing before
10 him. Jesus looked up and said to her, "Woman, where
11 are they? Has no one condemned you?" She said, "No one, Lord." And Jesus said, "Neither do I condemn you; go, and do not sin again." r

12 Again Jesus spoke to them, saying, "I am the light of the world; he who follows me will not walk in dark-
13 ness, but will have the light of life." The Pharisees then said to him, "You are bearing witness to yourself; your
14 testimony is not true." Jesus answered, "Even if I do bear witness to myself, my testimony is true, for I know whence I have come and whither I am going, but you do
15 not know whence I come or whither I am going. You
16 judge according to the flesh, I judge no one. Yet even if I do judge, my judgment is true, for it is not I alone
17 that judge, but I and he s who sent me. In your law it is
18 written that the testimony of two men is true; I bear wit- ness to myself, and the Father who sent me bears witness
19 to me." They said to him therefore, "Where is your Father?" Jesus answered, "You know neither me nor my Father; if you knew me, you would know my Father
20 also." These words he spoke in the treasury, as he taught in the temple; but no one arrested him, because his hour had not yet come.

21 Again he said to them, "I go away, and you will seek me and die in your sin; where I am going, you cannot
22 come." Then said the Jews, "Will he kill himself, since
23 he says, 'Where I am going, you cannot come'?" He said to them, "You are from below, I am from above;

24 you are of this world, I am not of this world. I told you that you would die in your sins, for you will die in your
25 sins unless you believe that I am he." They said to him, "Who are you?" Jesus said to them, "Even what I have
26 told you from the beginning.t I have much to say about you and much to judge; but he who sent me is true, and I
27 declare to the world what I have heard from him." They did not understand that he spoke to them of the Father.
28 So Jesus said, "When you have lifted up the Son of man, then you will know that I am he, and that I do nothing on my own authority but speak thus as the Father taught
29 me. And he who sent me is with me; he has not left me
30 alone, for I always do what is pleasing to him." As he spoke thus, many believed in him.

31 Jesus then said to the Jews who had believed in him, "If you continue in my word, you are truly my disciples,
32 and you will know the truth, and the truth will make you
33 free." They answered him, "We are descendants of Abra- ham, and have never been in bondage to any one. How is it that you say, 'You will be made free'?"

34 Jesus answered them, "Truly, truly, I say to you, every
35 one who commits sin is a slave to sin. The slave does not continue in the house for ever; the son continues for
36 ever. So if the Son makes you free, you will be free in-
37 deed. I know that you are descendants of Abraham; yet you seek to kill me, because my word finds no place in
38 you. I speak of what I have seen with my Father, and you do what you have heard from your father."

39 They answered him, "Abraham is our father." Jesus said to them, "If you were Abraham's children, you would
40 do what Abraham did, but now you seek to kill me, a man who has told you the truth which I heard from God;
41 this is not what Abraham did. You do what your father did." They said to him, "We were not born of fornication;
42 we have one Father, even God." Jesus said to them, "If God were your Father, you would love me, for I pro- ceeded and came forth from God; I came not of my own
43 accord, but he sent me. Why do you not understand what I say? It is because you cannot bear to hear my word.
44 You are of your father the devil, and your will is to do your father's desires. He was a murderer from the begin- ning, and has nothing to do with the truth, because there is no truth in him. When he lies, he speaks according to his own nature, for he is a liar and the father of lies.
45 But, because I tell the truth, you do not believe me.
46 Which of you convicts me of sin? If I tell the truth, why
47 do you not believe me? He who is of God hears the words of God; the reason why you do not hear them is that you are not of God."

48 The Jews answered him, "Are we not right in saying that
49 you are a Samaritan and have a demon?" Jesus answered, "I have not a demon; but I honor my Father, and you
50 dishonor me. Yet I do not seek my own glory; there is

---

r Most ancient authorities omit 7.53-8.11; other authorities add the passage here or after 7.36 or after 21.25 or after Luke 21.38, with variations of the text

s Other ancient authorities read *the Father*   t Or *Why do I talk to you at all?*

51 One who seeks it and he will be the judge. Truly, truly, I say to you, if any one keeps my word, he will never 52 see death." The Jews said to him, "Now we know that you have a demon. Abraham died, as did the prophets; and you say, 'If any one keeps my word, he will never 53 taste death.' Are you greater than our father Abraham, who died? And the prophets died! Who do you claim to 54 be?" Jesus answered, "If I glorify myself, my glory is nothing; it is my Father who glorifies me, of whom you 55 say that he is your God. But you have not known him; I know him. If I said, I do not know him, I should be a liar like you; but I do know him and I keep his word. 56 Your father Abraham rejoiced that he was to see my 57 day; he saw it and was glad." The Jews then said to him, "You are not yet fifty years old, and have you seen Abra- 58 ham?" u Jesus said to them, "Truly, truly, I say to you,

59 before Abraham was, I am." So they took up stones to throw at him; but Jesus hid himself, and went out of the temple.

9 As he passed by, he saw a man blind from his birth. 2 And his disciples asked him, "Rabbi, who sinned, this 3 man or his parents, that he was born blind?" Jesus answered, "It was not that this man sinned, or his parents, but that the works of God might be made manifest 4 in him. We must work the works of him who sent me, while it is day; night comes, when no one can work. 5 As long as I am in the world, I am the light of the 6 world." As he said this, he spat on the ground and made clay of the spittle and anointed the man's eyes with the 7 clay, saying to him, "Go, wash in the pool of Silo'am" (which means Sent). So he went and washed and came 8 back seeing. The neighbors and those who had seen him before as a beggar, said, "Is not this the man who used 9 to sit and beg?" Some said, "It is he"; others said, "No, 10 but he is like him." He said, "I am the man." They said 11 to him, "Then how were your eyes opened?" He answered, "The man called Jesus made clay and anointed my eyes and said to me, 'Go to Silo'am and wash'; so I 12 went and washed and received my sight." They said to him, "Where is he?" He said, "I do not know."

13 They brought to the Pharisees the man who had 14 formerly been blind. Now it was a sabbath day when 15 Jesus made the clay and opened his eyes. The Pharisees again asked him how he had received his sight. And he said to them, "He put clay on my eyes, and I washed, 16 and I see." Some of the Pharisees said, "This man is not from God, for he does not keep the sabbath." But others said, "How can a man who is a sinner do such signs?" 17 There was a division among them. So they again said to the blind man, "What do you say about him, since he has opened your eyes?" He said, "He is a prophet."

18 The Jews did not believe that he had been blind and had received his sight, until they called the parents of 19 the man who had received his sight, and asked them, "Is this your son, who you say was born blind? How then 20 does he now see?" His parents answered, "We know that 21 this is our son, and that he was born blind; but how he now sees we do not know, nor do we know who opened his eyes. Ask him; he is of age, he will speak for him- 22 self." His parents said this because they feared the Jews, for the Jews had already agreed that if any one should confess him to be Christ, he was to be put out of the 23 synagogue. Therefore his parents said, "He is of age, ask him."

24 So for the second time they called the man who had been blind, and said to him, "Give God the praise; we know 25 that this man is a sinner." He answered, "Whether he is a sinner, I do not know; one thing I know, that though 26 I was blind, now I see." They said to him, "What did he 27 do to you? How did he open your eyes?" He answered them, "I have told you already, and you would not listen. Why do you want to hear it again? Do you too want to 28 become his disciples?" And they reviled him, saying, 29 "You are his disciple, but we are disciples of Moses. We know that God has spoken to Moses, but as for this man, 30 we do not know where he comes from." The man an- swered, "Why, this is a marvel! You do not know where 31 he comes from, and yet he opened my eyes. We know that God does not listen to sinners, but if any one is a worshiper of God and does his will, God listens to him. 32 Never since the world began has it been heard that any 33 one opened the eyes of a man born blind. If this man 34 were not from God, he could do nothing." They an- swered him, "You were born in utter sin, and would you teach us?" And they cast him out.

35 Jesus heard that they had cast him out, and having found him he said, "Do you believe in the Son of man?" v 36 He answered, "And who is he, sir, that I may believe in 37 him?" Jesus said to him, "You have seen him, and it is 38 he who speaks to you." He said, "Lord, I believe"; and 39 he worshiped him. Jesus said, "For judgment I came into this world, that those who do not see may see, and that 40 those who see may become blind." Some of the Pharisees near him heard this, and they said to him, "Are we also 41 blind?" Jesus said to them, "If you were blind, you would have no guilt; but now that you say, 'We see,' your guilt remains.

THE SHEPHERD AND GIVER OF LIFE

10 "Truly, truly, I say to you, he who does not enter the sheepfold by the door but climbs in by another 2 way, that man is a thief and a robber; but he who enters

u Other ancient authorities read *has Abraham seen you?*   v Other ancient authorities read *the Son of God*

3 by the door is the shepherd of the sheep. To him the
gatekeeper opens; the sheep hear his voice, and he calls
4 his own sheep by name and leads them out. When he has
brought out all his own, he goes before them, and the
5 sheep follow him, for they know his voice. A stranger
they will not follow, but they will flee from him, for they
6 do not know the voice of strangers." This figure Jesus
used with them, but they did not understand what he was
saying to them.

7 So Jesus again said to them, "Truly, truly, I say to you,
8 I am the door of the sheep. All who came before me are
thieves and robbers; but the sheep did not heed them.
9 I am the door; if any one enters by me, he will be saved,
10 and will go in and out and find pasture. The thief comes
only to steal and kill and destroy; I came that they may
11 have life, and have it abundantly. I am the good shepherd. The good shepherd lays down his life for the sheep.
12 He who is a hireling and not a shepherd, whose own the
sheep are not, sees the wolf coming and leaves the sheep
and flees; and the wolf snatches them and scatters them.
13 He flees because he is a hireling and cares nothing for the
14 sheep. I am the good shepherd; I know my own and my
15 own know me, as the Father knows me and I know the
16 Father; and I lay down my life for the sheep. And I have
other sheep, that are not of this fold; I must bring them
also, and they will heed my voice. So there shall be one
17 flock, one shepherd. For this reason the Father loves me,
because I lay down my life, that I may take it again.
18 No one takes it from me, but I lay it down of my own
accord. I have power to lay it down, and I have power
to take it again; this charge I have received from my
Father."

19 There was again a division among the Jews because of
20 these words. Many of them said, "He has a demon, and
21 he is mad; why listen to him?" Others said, "These are
not the sayings of one who has a demon. Can a demon

open the eyes of the blind?"
22, 23 It was the feast of the Dedication at Jerusalem; it
was winter, and Jesus was walking in the temple, in the
24 portico of Solomon. So the Jews gathered round him and
said to him, "How long will you keep us in suspense?
25 If you are the Christ, tell us plainly." Jesus answered
them, "I told you, and you do not believe. The works
that I do in my Father's name, they bear witness to me;
26 but you do not believe, because you do not belong to my
27 sheep. My sheep hear my voice, and I know them, and
28 they follow me; and I give them eternal life, and they
shall never perish, and no one shall snatch them out of

29 my hand. My Father, who has given them to me,[w] is
greater than all, and no one is able to snatch them out of
30 the Father's hand. I and the Father are one."
31, 32 The Jews took up stones again to stone him. Jesus
answered them, "I have shown you many good works
from the Father; for which of these do you stone me?"
33 The Jews answered him, "It is not for a good work that
we stone you but for blasphemy; because you, being a
34 man, make yourself God." Jesus answered them, "Is it
35 not written in your law, 'I said, you **are gods**'? If he
called them gods to whom the word of God came (and
36 scripture cannot be broken), do you say of him whom
the Father consecrated and sent into the world, 'You are
37 blaspheming,' because I said, 'I am the Son of God'? If
38 I am not doing the works of my Father, then do not believe me; but if I do them, even though you do not believe
me, believe the works, that you may know and understand
39 that the Father is in me and I am in the Father." Again
they tried to arrest him, but he escaped from their hands.
40 He went away again across the Jordan to the place
where John at first baptized, and there he remained.
41 And many came to him; and they said, "John did no
sign, but everything that John said about this man was
42 true." And many believed in him there.

11 Now a certain man was ill, Laz'arus of Bethany,
2 the village of Mary and her sister Martha. It was
Mary who anointed the Lord with ointment and wiped
his feet with her hair, whose brother Laz'arus was ill.
3 So the sisters sent to him, saying, "Lord, he whom you
4 love is ill." But when Jesus heard it he said, "This illness is not unto death; it is for the glory of God, so that
the Son of God may be glorified by means of it."
5 Now Jesus loved Martha and her sister and Laz'arus.
6 So when he heard that he was ill, he stayed two days
7 longer in the place where he was. Then after this he said
8 to the disciples, "Let us go into Judea again." The disciples said to him, "Rabbi, the Jews were but now seeking
9 to stone you, and are you going there again?" Jesus
answered, "Are there not twelve hours in the day? If any
one walks in the day, he does not stumble, because he
10 sees the light of this world. But if any one walks in the
night, he stumbles, because the light is not in him."
11 Thus he spoke, and then he said to them, "Our friend
Laz'arus has fallen asleep, but I go to awake him out of
12 sleep." The disciples said to him, "Lord, if he has fallen
13 asleep, he will recover." Now Jesus had spoken of his
death, but they thought that he meant taking rest in
14 sleep. Then Jesus told them plainly, "Laz'arus is dead;

[w] Other ancient authorities read *What my Father has given to me*

15 and for your sake I am glad that I was not there, so that
16 you may believe. But let us go to him." Thomas, called the Twin, said to his fellow disciples, "Let us also go, that we may die with him."

17 Now when Jesus came, he found that Laz'arus[x] had
18 already been in the tomb four days. Bethany was near
19 Jerusalem, about two miles[y] off, and many of the Jews had come to Martha and Mary to console them concerning
20 their brother. When Martha heard that Jesus was coming, she went and met him, while Mary sat in the house.
21 Martha said to Jesus, "Lord, if you had been here, my
22 brother would not have died. And even now I know that
23 whatever you ask from God, God will give you." Jesus
24 said to her, "Your brother will rise again." Martha said to him, "I know that he will rise again in the resurrection
25 at the last day." Jesus said to her, "I am the resurrection and the life;[z] he who believes in me, though he die, yet

26 shall he live, and whoever lives and believes in me shall
27 never die. Do you believe this?" She said to him, "Yes, Lord; I believe that you are the Christ, the Son of God, he who is coming into the world."
28 When she had said this, she went and called her sister Mary, saying quietly, "The Teacher is here and is calling
29 for you." And when she heard it, she rose quickly and
30 went to him. Now Jesus had not yet come to the village, but was still in the place where Martha had met him.
31 When the Jews who were with her in the house, consoling her, saw Mary rise quickly and go out, they followed her, supposing that she was going to the tomb to weep there.
32 Then Mary, when she came where Jesus was and saw him, fell at his feet, saying to him, "Lord, if you had been here,
33 my brother would not have died." When Jesus saw her weeping, and the Jews who came with her also weeping,
34 he was deeply moved in spirit and troubled; and he said, "Where have you laid him?" They said to him, "Lord,
35, 36 come and see." Jesus wept. So the Jews said, "See how
37 he loved him!" But some of them said, "Could not he who opened the eyes of the blind man have kept this man from dying?"
38 Then Jesus, deeply moved again, came to the tomb; it

39 was a cave, and a stone lay upon it. Jesus said, "Take away the stone." Martha, the sister of the dead man, said to him, "Lord, by this time there will be an odor, for he
40 has been dead four days." Jesus said to her, "Did I not tell you that if you would believe you would see the glory
41 of God?" So they took away the stone. And Jesus lifted up his eyes and said, "Father, I thank thee that thou hast
42 heard me. I knew that thou hearest me always, but I have said this on account of the people standing by, that they
43 may believe that thou didst send me." When he had said this, he cried with a loud voice, "Laz'arus, come out."
44 The dead man came out, his hands and feet bound with bandages, and his face wrapped with a cloth. Jesus said to them, "Unbind him, and let him go."

45 Many of the Jews therefore, who had come with Mary
46 and had seen what he did, believed in him; but some of them went to the Pharisees and told them what Jesus had
47 done. So the chief priest and the Pharisees gathered the council, and said, "What are we to do? For this man
48 performs many signs. If we let him go on thus, every one will believe in him, and the Romans will come and destroy
49 both our holy place[a] and our nation." But one of them, Ca'iaphas, who was high priest that year, said to them,
50 "You know nothing at all; you do not understand that it is expedient for you that one man should die for the people, and that the whole nation should not perish."
51 He did not say this of his own accord, but being high priest that year he prophesied that Jesus should die for
52 the nation, and not for the nation only, but to gather into one the children of God who are scattered abroad.
53 So from that day on they took counsel how to put him to death.

54 Jesus therefore no longer went about openly among the Jews, but went from there to the country near the wilderness, to a town called E'phraim; and there he stayed with the disciples.

55 Now the Passover of the Jews was at hand, and many went up from the country to Jerusalem before the Pass-
56 over, to purify themselves. They were looking for Jesus and saying to one another as they stood in the temple, "What do you think? That he will not come to the feast?"
57 Now the chief priests and the Pharisees had given orders that if any one knew where he was, he should let them know, so that they might arrest him.

CLOSE OF THE PUBLIC MINISTRY

12 Six days before the Passover, Jesus came to Bethany, where Laz'arus was, whom Jesus had raised
2 from the dead. There they made him a supper; Martha served, and Laz'arus was one of those at table with him.
3 Mary took a pound of costly ointment of pure nard and anointed the feet of Jesus and wiped his feet with her hair; and the house was filled with the fragrance of the

---

[x] Greek *he*   [y] Greek *fifteen stadia*   [z] Other ancient authorities omit *and the life*   [a] Greek *our place*

4 ointment. But Judas Iscariot, one of his disciples (he who
5 was to betray him), said, "Why was this ointment not sold for three hundred denarii [b] and given to the poor?"
6 This he said, not that he cared for the poor but because he was a thief, and as he had the money box he used to
7 take what was put into it. Jesus said, "Let her alone, let
8 her keep it for the day of my burial. The poor you always have with you, but you do not always have me."

9 When the great crowd of the Jews learned that he was there, they came, not only on account of Jesus but also
10 to see Laz'arus, whom he had raised from the dead. So the chief priests planned to put Laz'arus also to death,
11 because on account of him many of the Jews were going away and believing in Jesus.

12 The next day a great crowd who had come to the feast
13 heard that Jesus was coming to Jerusalem. So they took branches of palm trees and went out to meet him, crying, "Hosanna! Blessed is he who comes in the name of the
14 Lord, even the King of Israel!" And Jesus found a young ass and sat upon it; as it is written,
15 "Fear not, daughter of Zion;
behold, your king is coming,
sitting on an ass's colt!"
16 His disciples did not understand this at first; but when Jesus was glorified, then they remembered that this had
17 been written of him and had been done to him. The crowd that had been with him when he called Laz'arus out of
18 the tomb and raised him from the dead bore witness. The reason why the crowd went to meet him was that they
19 heard he had done this sign. The Pharisees then said to one another, "You see that you can do nothing; look, the world has gone after him."

20 Now among those who went up to worship at the feast
21 were some Greeks. So these came to Philip, who was from Beth-sa'ida in Galilee, and said to him, "Sir, we wish to
22 see Jesus." Philip went and told Andrew; Andrew went
23 with Philip and they told Jesus. And Jesus answered them, "The hour has come for the Son of man to be glorified.
24 Truly, truly, I say to you, unless a grain of wheat falls into the earth and dies, it remains alone; but if it dies,
25 it bears much fruit. He who loves his life loses it, and he who hates his life in this world will keep it for eternal
26 life. If any one serves me, he must follow me; and where I am, there shall my servant be also; if any one serves me, the Father will honor him.
27 "Now is my soul troubled. And what shall I say? 'Father, save me from this hour'? No, for this purpose
28 I have come to this hour. Father, glorify thy name." Then a voice came from heaven, "I have glorified it, and I will
29 glorify it again." The crowd standing by heard it and said that it had thundered. Others said, "An angel has spoken
30 to him." Jesus answered, "This voice has come for your
31 sake, not for mine. Now is the judgment of this world,

b The denarius was a day's wage for a laborer

32 now shall the ruler of this world be cast out; and I, when I am lifted up from the earth, will draw all men to
33 myself." He said this to show by what death he was to
34 die. The crowd answered him, "We have heard from the law that the Christ remains for ever. How can you say that the Son of man must be lifted up? Who is this Son
35 of man?" Jesus said to them, "The light is with you for a little longer. Walk while you have the light, lest the darkness overtake you; he who walks in the darkness does not
36 know where he goes. While you have the light, believe in the light, that you may become sons of light."

When Jesus had said this, he departed and hid himself
37 from them. Though he had done so many signs before
38 them, yet they did not believe in him; it was that the word spoken by the prophet Isaiah might be fulfilled:
"Lord, who has believed our report,
and to whom has the arm of the Lord been revealed?"
39 Therefore they could not believe. For Isaiah again said,
40 "He has blinded their eyes and hardened their heart, lest they should see with their eyes and perceive with their

heart, and turn for me to heal them."
41 Isaiah said this because he saw his glory and spoke of
42 him. Nevertheless many even of the authorities believed in him, but for fear of the Pharisees they did not confess it,
43 lest they should be put out of the synagogue: for they loved the praise of men more than the praise of God.

44 And Jesus cried out and said, "He who believes in me,
45 believes not in me but in him who sent me. And he who
46 sees me sees him who sent me. I have come as light into the world, that whoever believes in me may not remain
47 in darkness. If any one hears my sayings and does not keep them, I do not judge him; for I did not come to
48 judge the world but to save the world. He who rejects me and does not receive my sayings has a judge; the word that I have spoken will be his judge on the last day.
49 For I have not spoken on my own authority; the Father who sent me has himself given me commandment what
50 to say and what to speak. And I know that his commandment is eternal life. What I say, therefore, I say as the Father has bidden me."

THE UPPER ROOM
The Last Supper

13 Now before the feast of the Passover, when Jesus knew that his hour had come to depart out of this world to the Father, having loved his own who were in
2 the world, he loved them to the end. And during supper, when the devil had already put it into the heart of Judas
3 Iscariot, Simon's son, to betray him, Jesus, knowing that the Father had given all things into his hands, and that
4 he had come from God and was going to God, rose from supper, laid aside his garments, and girded himself with
5 a towel. Then he poured water into a basin, and began to wash the disciples' feet, and to wipe them with the towel
6 with which he was girded. He came to Simon Peter; and
7 Peter said to him, "Lord, do you wash my feet?" Jesus answered him, "What I am doing you do not know now,
8 but afterward you will understand." Peter said to him, "You shall never wash my feet." Jesus answered him, "If
9 I do not wash you, you have no part in me." Simon Peter said to him, "Lord, not my feet only but also my hands
10 and my head!" Jesus said to him, "He who has bathed does not need to wash, except for his feet,c but he is clean
11 all over; and youx are clean, but not every one of you." For he knew who was to betray him; that was why he said, "You are not all clean."
12 When he had washed their feet, and taken his garments, and resumed his place, he said to them, "Do you know
13 what I have done to you? You call me Teacher and Lord;
14 and you are right, for so I am. If I then, your Lord and Teacher, have washed your feet, you also ought to wash
15 one another's feet. For I have given you an example, that
16 you also should do as I have done to you. Truly, truly, I say to you, a servantd is not greater than his master; nor is he who is sent greater than he who sent him.
17 If you know these things, blessed are you if you do them.
18 I am not speaking of you all; I know whom I have chosen; it is that the scripture may be fulfilled, 'He who
19 ate my bread has lifted his heel against me.' I tell you this now, before it takes place, that when it does take place
20 you may believe that I am he. Truly, truly, I say to you, he who receives any one whom I send receives me; and he who receives me receives him who sent me."
21 When Jesus had thus spoken, he was troubled in spirit, and testified, "Truly, truly, I say to you, one of you will
22 betray me." The disciples looked at one another, uncertain
23 of whom he spoke. One of his disciples, whom Jesus loved,
24 was lying close to the breast of Jesus; so Simon Peter beckoned to him and said, "Tell us who it is of whom he
25 speaks." So lying thus, close to the breast of Jesus, he said
26 to him, "Lord, who is it?" Jesus answered, "It is he to whom I shall give this morsel when I have dipped it." So when he had dipped the morsel, he gave it to Judas, the
27 son of Simon Iscariot. Then after the morsel, Satan

entered into him. Jesus said to him, "What you are going
28 to do, do quickly." Now no one at the table knew why he
29 said this to him. Some thought that, because Judas had the money box, Jesus was telling him, "Buy what we need for the feast"; or, that he should give something to the
30 poor. So, after receiving the morsel, he immediately went out; and it was night.

Jesus' Words of Farewell

31 When he had gone out, Jesus said, "Now is the Son of
32 man glorified, and in him God is glorified; if God is glorified in him, God will also glorify him in himself, and
33 glorify him at once. Little children, yet a little while I am with you. You will seek me; and as I said to the Jews so now I say to you, 'Where I am going you cannot come.'
34 A new commandment I give to you, that you love one another; even as I have loved you, that you also love one
35 another. By this all men will know that you are my disciples, if you have love for one another."

36 Simon Peter said to him, "Lord, where are you going?" Jesus answered, "Where I am going you cannot follow
37 me now; but you shall follow afterward." Peter said to him, "Lord, why cannot I follow you now? I will lay
38 down my life for you." Jesus answered, "Will you lay down your life for me? Truly, truly, I say to you, the cock will not crow, till you have denied me three times.

14 "Let not your hearts be troubled; believee in God,
2 believe also in me. In my Father's house are many rooms; if it were not so, would I have told you that I
3 go to prepare a place for you? And when I go and prepare a place for you, I will come again and will take you to
4 myself, that where I am you may be also. And you know
5 the way where I am going."f Thomas said to him, "Lord, we do not know where you are going; how can we know
6 the way?" Jesus said to him, "I am the way, and the truth, and the life; no one comes to the Father, but by me.
7 If you had known me, you would have known my Father also; henceforth you know him and have seen him."
8 Philip said to him, "Lord, show us the Father, and we
9 shall be satisfied." Jesus said to him, "Have I been with you so long, and yet you do not know me, Philip? He who has seen me has seen the Father; how can you say,
10 'Show us the Father'? Do you not believe that I am in the

c Other ancient authorities omit except for his feet   x The Greek word for you here is plural   d Or slave   e Or you believe
f Other ancient authorities read where I am going you know, and the way you know

Father and the Father in me? The words that I say to you I do not speak on my own authority; but the Father who
11 dwells in me does his works. Believe me that I am in the Father and the Father in me; or else believe me for the sake of the works themselves.

12 "Truly, truly, I say to you, he who believes in me will
13 also do the works that I do; and greater works than these will he do, because I go to the Father. Whatever you ask
14 in my name, I will do it, that the Father may be glorified in the Son; if you ask g anything in my name, I will do it.

15 "If you love me, you will keep my commandments.
16 And I will pray the Father, and he will give you another
17 Counselor, to be with you for ever, even the Spirit of truth, whom the world cannot receive, because it neither sees him nor knows him; you know him, for he dwells with you, and will be in you.
18 "I will not leave you desolate; I will come to you.
19 Yet a little while, and the world will see me no more, but
20 you will see me; because I live, you will live also. In that day you will know that I am in my Father, and you in me,
21 and I in you. He who has my commandments and keeps them, he it is who loves me; and he who loves me will be loved by my Father, and I will love him and manifest
22 myself to him." Judas (not Iscariot) said to him, "Lord, how is it that you will manifest yourself to us, and not to
23 the world?" Jesus answered him, "If a man loves me, he will keep my word, and my Father will love him, and we
24 will come to him and make our home with him. He who does not love me does not keep my words; and the word which you hear is not mine but the Father's who sent me.
25 "These things I have spoken to you, while I am still
26 with you. But the Counselor, the Holy Spirit, whom the Father will send in my name, he will teach you all things, and bring to your remembrance all that I have said to
27 you. Peace I leave with you; my peace I give to you; not as the world gives do I give to you. Let not your hearts be
28 troubled, neither let them be afraid. You heard me say to you, 'I go away, and I will come to you.' If you loved me, you would have rejoiced, because I go to the Father;
29 for the Father is greater than I. And now I have told you before it takes place, so that when it does take place, you
30 may believe. I will no longer talk much with you, for the ruler of this world is coming. He has no power over
31 me; but I do as the Father has commanded me, so that the world may know that I love the Father. Rise, let us go hence.

15 "I am the true vine, and my Father is the vine-
2 dresser. Every branch of mine that bears no fruit, he takes away, and every branch that does bear fruit he
3 prunes, that it may bear more fruit. You are already made
4 clean by the word which I have spoken to you. Abide in me, and I in you. As the branch cannot bear fruit by itself, unless it abides in the vine, neither can you, unless

5 you abide in me. I am the vine, you are the branches. He who abides in me, and I in him, he it is that bears much
6 fruit, for apart from me you can do nothing. If a man does not abide in me, he is cast forth as a branch and withers; and the branches are gathered, thrown into the
7 fire and burned. If you abide in me, and my words abide in you, ask whatever you will, and it shall be done for you.
8 By this my Father is glorified, that you bear much fruit,
9 and so prove to be my disciples. As the Father has loved
10 me, so have I loved you; abide in my love. If you keep my commandments, you will abide in my love, just as I have kept my Father's commandments and abide in his
11 love. These things I have spoken to you, that my joy may be in you, and that your joy may be full.
12 "This is my commandment, that you love one another
13 as I have loved you. Greater love has no man than this,
14 that a man lay down his life for his friends. You are my
15 friends if you do what I command you. No longer do I call you servants,h for the servant i does not know what his master is doing; but I have called you friends, for all that I have heard from my Father I have made known to you.
16 You did not choose me, but I chose you and appointed you that you should go and bear fruit and that your fruit should abide; so that whatever you ask the Father in my
17 name, he may give it to you. This I command you, to love one another.
18 "If the world hates you, know that it has hated me
19 before it hated you. If you were of the world, the world would love its own; but because you are not of the world, but I chose you out of the world, therefore the world hates
20 you. Remember the word that I said to you, 'A servant i is not greater than his master.' If they persecuted me, they will persecute you; if they kept my word, they will keep
21 yours also. But all this they will do to you on my account,
22 because they do not know him who sent me. If I had not come and spoken to them, they would not have sin; but
23 now they have no excuse for their sin. He who hates me
24 hates my Father also. If I had not done among them the works which no one else did, they would not have sin; but now they have seen and hated both me and my Father.
25 It is to fulfil the word that is written in their law, 'They
26 hated me without a cause.' But when the Counselor comes, whom I shall send to you from the Father, even the Spirit of truth, who proceeds from the Father, he will bear
27 witness to me; and you also are witnesses, because you have been with me from the beginning.

16 "I have said all this to you to keep you from falling
2 away. They will put you out of the synagogues; indeed, the hour is coming when whoever kills you will
3 think he is offering service to God. And they will do this
4 because they have not known the Father, nor me. But I have said these things to you, that when their hour comes you may remember that I told you of them.

g Other ancient authorities add *me*   h Or *slaves*   i Or *slave*

"I did not say these things to you from the beginning,
5 because I was with you. But now I am going to him who sent me; yet none of you asks me, 'Where are you going?'
6 But because I have said these things to you, sorrow has
7 filled your hearts. Nevertheless I tell you the truth: it is to your advantage that I go away, for if I do not go away, the Counselor will not come to you; but if I go, I will
8 send him to you. And when he comes, he will convince[x] the world concerning sin and righteousness and judg-
9, 10 ment: concerning sin, because they do not believe in me; concerning righteousness, because I go to the Father,
11 and you will see me no more; concerning judgment, because the ruler of this world is judged.

12 "I have yet many things to say to you, but you cannot
13 bear them now. When the Spirit of truth comes, he will guide you into all the truth; for he will not speak on his own authority, but whatever he hears he will speak, and he will declare to you the things that are to come.
14 He will glorify me, for he will take what is mine and
15 declare it to you. All that the Father has is mine; therefore I said that he will take what is mine and declare it to you.

16 "A little while, and you will see me no more; again a
17 little while, and you will see me." Some of his disciples said to one another, "What is this that he says to us, 'A little while, and you will not see me, and again a little while, and you will see me'; and, 'because I go to the
18 Father'?" They said, "What does he mean by 'a little

19 while'? We do not know what he means." Jesus knew that they wanted to ask him; so he said to them, "Is this what you are asking yourselves, what I meant by saying, 'A little while, and you will not see me, and again a little
20 while, and you will see me'? Truly, truly, I say to you, you will weep and lament, but the world will rejoice; you will be sorrowful, but your sorrow will turn into joy.
21 When a woman is in travail she has sorrow, because her hour has come; but when she is delivered of the child, she no longer remembers the anguish, for joy that a child[j]
22 is born into the world. So you have sorrow now, but I will see you again and your hearts will rejoice, and no one will
23 take your joy from you. In that day you will ask nothing of me. Truly, truly, I say to you, if you ask anything of
24 the Father, he will give it to you in my name. Hitherto you have asked nothing in my name; ask, and you will receive, that your joy may be full.

25 "I have said this to you in figures; the hour is coming when I shall no longer speak to you in figures but tell you
26 plainly of the Father. In that day you will ask in my

name; and I do not say to you that I shall pray the Father
27 for you; for the Father himself loves you, because you have loved me and have believed that I came from the
28 Father. I came from the Father and have come into the world; again, I am leaving the world and going to the Father."

29 His disciples said, "Ah, now you are speaking plainly,
30 not in any figure! Now we know that you know all things, and need none to question you; by this we believe that you
31 came from God." Jesus answered them, "Do you now
32 believe? The hour is coming, indeed it has come, when you will be scattered, every man to his home, and will leave me alone; yet I am not alone, for the Father is with
33 me. I have said this to you, that in me you may have peace. In the world you have tribulation; but be of good cheer, I have overcome the world."

The High-Priestly Prayer

17 When Jesus had spoken these words, he lifted up his eyes to heaven and said, "Father, the hour has come; glorify thy Son that the Son may glorify thee,
2 since thou hast given him power over all flesh, to give
3 eternal life to all whom thou hast given him. And this is eternal life, that they know thee the only true God, and
4 Jesus Christ whom thou hast sent. I glorified thee on earth, having accomplished the work which thou gavest me to
5 do; and now, Father, glorify thou me in thy own presence with the glory which I had with thee before the world was made.

6 "I have manifested thy name to the men whom thou gavest me out of the world; thine they were, and thou
7 gavest them to me, and they have kept thy word. Now they know that everything that thou hast given me is from
8 thee; for I have given them the words which thou gavest me, and they have received them and know in truth that I came from thee; and they have believed that thou didst
9 send me. I am praying for them; I am not praying for the world but for those whom thou hast given me, for they
10 are thine; all mine are thine, and thine are mine, and I
11 am glorified in them. And now I am no more in the world, but they are in the world, and I am coming to thee. Holy Father, keep them in thy name, which thou hast given me, that they may be one, even as we are one.
12 While I was with them, I kept them in thy name, which thou hast given me; I have guarded them, and none of them is lost but the son of perdition, that the scripture
13 might be fulfilled. But now I am coming to thee; and these things I speak in the world, that they may have my
14 joy fulfilled in themselves. I have given them thy word; and the world has hated them because they are not of the
15 world, even as I am not of the world. I do not pray that thou shouldst take them out of the world, but that thou
16 shouldst keep them from the evil one.[k] They are not of the

---

x Or *convict*   j Greek *a human being*   k Or *from evil*

17 world, even as I am not of the world. Sanctify them in
18 the truth; thy word is truth. As thou didst send me into
19 the world, so I have sent them into the world. And for
their sake I consecrate myself, that they also may be
consecrated in truth.

20 "I do not pray for these only, but also for those who

21 believe in me through their word, that they may all be
one; even as thou, Father, art in me, and I in thee, that
they also may be in us, so that the world may believe that
22 thou hast sent me. The glory which thou hast given me
I have given to them, that they may be one even as we
23 are one, I in them and thou in me, that they may become
perfectly one, so that the world may know that thou hast
sent me and hast loved them even as thou hast loved me.
24 Father, I desire that they also, whom thou hast given me,
may be with me where I am, to behold my glory which
thou hast given me in thy love for me before the founda-
25 tion of the world. O righteous Father, the world has not
known thee, but I have known thee; and these know that
26 thou hast sent me. I made known to them thy name, and
I will make it known, that the love with which thou hast
loved me may be in them, and I in them."

GETHSEMANE TO CALVARY

18 When Jesus had spoken these words, he went forth
with his disciples across the Kidron valley, where
there was a garden, which he and his disciples entered.
2 Now Judas, who betrayed him, also knew the place; for
3 Jesus often met there with his disciples. So Judas, procur-
ing a band of soldiers and some officers from the chief
priests and the Pharisees, went there with lanterns and
4 torches and weapons. Then Jesus, knowing all that was to
befall him, came forward and said to them, "Whom do
5 you seek?" They answered him, "Jesus of Nazareth."
Jesus said to them, "I am he." Judas, who betrayed him,
6 was standing with them. When he said to them, "I am
7 he," they drew back and fell to the ground. Again he
asked them, "Whom do you seek?" And they said, "Jesus
8 of Nazareth." Jesus answered, "I told you that I am he;
9 so, if you seek me, let these men go." This was to fulfil

1 Or *slaves*

the word which he had spoken, "Of those whom thou
10 gavest me I lost not one." Then Simon Peter, having a
sword, drew it and struck the high priest's slave and cut
11 off his right ear. The slave's name was Malchus. Jesus said
to Peter, "Put your sword into its sheath; shall I not
drink the cup which the Father has given me?"
12 So the band of soldiers and their captain and the officers
13 of the Jews seized Jesus and bound him. First they led him
to Annas; for he was the father-in-law of Ca'iaphas, who
14 was high priest that year. It was Ca'iaphas who had given
counsel to the Jews that it was expedient that one man
should die for the people.
15 Simon Peter followed Jesus, and so did another disciple. As this disciple was known to the high priest, he
16 entered the court of the high priest along with Jesus, while
Peter stood outside at the door. So the other disciple, who
was known to the high priest, went out and spoke to the
17 maid who kept the door, and brought Peter in. The maid
who kept the door said to Peter, "Are not you also one
18 of this man's disciples?" He said, "I am not." Now the
servants[1] and officers had made a charcoal fire, because it
was cold, and they were standing and warming themselves; Peter also was with them, standing and warming
himself.
19 The high priest then questioned Jesus about his dis-
20 ciples and his teaching. Jesus answered him, "I have
spoken openly to the world; I have always taught in
synagogues and in the temple, where all Jews come
21 together; I have said nothing secretly. Why do you ask
me? Ask those who have heard me, what I said to them;
22 they know what I said." When he had said this, one of the
officers standing by struck Jesus with his hand, saying,
23 "Is that how you answer the high priest?" Jesus answered
him, "If I have spoken wrongly, bear witness to the
wrong; but if I have spoken rightly, why do you strike
24 me?" Annas then sent him bound to Ca'iaphas the high
priest.
25 Now Simon Peter was standing and warming himself.
They said to him, "Are not you also one of his disciples?"
26 He denied it and said, "I am not." One of the servants[1]
of the high priest, a kinsman of the man whose ear Peter
had cut off, asked, "Did I not see you in the garden with

27 him?" Peter again denied it; and at once the cock crowed.
28 Then they led Jesus from the house of Ca'iaphas to the
praetorium. It was early. They themselves did not enter

the praetorium, so that they might not be defiled, but
29 might eat the passover. So Pilate went out to them and said, "What accusation do you bring against this man?"
30 They answered him, "If this man were not an evildoer,
31 we would not have handed him over." Pilate said to them, "Take him yourselves and judge him by your own law." The Jews said to him, "It is not lawful for us to put any
32 man to death." This was to fulfil the word which Jesus had spoken to show by what death he was to die.

33 Pilate entered the praetorium again and called Jesus, and said to him, "Are you the King of the Jews?"
34 Jesus answered, "Do you say this of your own accord, or
35 did others say it to you about me?" Pilate answered, "Am I a Jew? Your own nation and the chief priests have
36 handed you over to me; what have you done?" Jesus answered, "My kingship is not of this world; if my kingship were of this world, my servants would fight, that I might not be handed over to the Jews; but my kingship
37 is not from the world." Pilate said to him, "So you are a king?" Jesus answered, "You say that I am a king. For this I was born, and for this I have come into the world, to bear witness to the truth. Every one who is of the truth
38 hears my voice." Pilate said to him, "What is truth?"

After he had said this, he went out to the Jews again,
39 and told them, "I find no crime in him. But you have a custom that I should release one man for you at the Passover; will you have me release for you the King of
40 the Jews?" They cried out again, "Not this man, but Barab'bas!" Now Barab'bas was a robber.

2 **19** Then Pilate took Jesus and scourged him. And the soldiers plaited a crown of thorns, and put it on his
3 head, and arrayed him in a purple robe; they came up to him, saying, "Hail, King of the Jews!" and struck him
4 with their hands. Pilate went out again, and said to them, "See, I am bringing him out to you, that you may
5 know that I find no crime in him." So Jesus came out, wearing the crown of thorns and the purple robe. Pilate
6 said to them, "Behold the man!" When the chief priests and the officers saw him, they cried out, "Crucify him, crucify him!" Pilate said to them, "Take him yourselves
7 and crucify him, for I find no crime in him." The Jews answered him, "We have a law, and by that law he ought to die, because he has made himself the Son of God."
8 When Pilate heard these words, he was the more afraid;
9 he entered the praetorium again and said to Jesus, "Where
10 are you from?" But Jesus gave no answer. Pilate therefore

said to him, "You will not speak to me? Do you not know that I have power to release you, and power to
11 crucify you?" Jesus answered him, "You would have no power over me unless it had been given you from above; therefore he who delivered me to you has the greater sin."
12 Upon this Pilate sought to release him, but the Jews cried out, "If you release this man, you are not Caesar's friend; every one who makes himself a king sets himself

13 against Caesar." When Pilate heard these words, he brought Jesus out and sat down on the judgment seat at a place called The Pavement, and in Hebrew, Gab'batha.
14 Now it was the day of Preparation of the Passover; it was about the sixth hour. He said to the Jews, Behold your
15 King!" They cried out, "Away with him, away with him, crucify him!" Pilate said to them, "Shall I crucify your King?" The chief priests answered, "We have no king
16 but Caesar." Then he handed him over to them to be crucified.

17 So they took Jesus, and he went out, bearing his own cross, to the place called the place of a skull, which is
18 called in Hebrew Gol'gotha. There they crucified him, and with him two others, one on either side, and Jesus
19 between them. Pilate also wrote a title and put it on the cross; it read, "Jesus of Nazareth, the King of the Jews."
20 Many of the Jews read this title, for the place where Jesus was crucified was near the city; and it was written in
21 Hebrew, in Latin, and in Greek. The chief priests of the Jews then said to Pilate, "Do not write, 'The King of the Jews,' but 'This man said, I am King of the Jews.'"
22 Pilate answered, "What I have written I have written."
23 When the soldiers had crucified Jesus they took his garments and made four parts, one for each soldier; also his tunic. But the tunic was without seam, woven from
24 top to bottom; so they said to one another, "Let us not tear it, but cast lots for it to see whose it shall be." This was to fulfil the scripture,

"They parted my garments among them,
and for my clothing they cast lots."
25 So the soldiers did this. But standing by the cross of Jesus were his mother, and his mother's sister, Mary the
26 wife of Clopas, and Mary Mag'dalene. When Jesus saw his mother, and the disciple whom he loved standing near, he said to his mother, "Woman, behold, your son!"
27 Then he said to the disciple, "Behold, your mother!" And from that hour the disciple took her to his own home.
28 After this Jesus, knowing that all was now finished,

29 said (to fulfil the scripture), "I thirst." A bowl full of vinegar stood there; so they put a sponge full of the
30 vinegar on hyssop and held it to his mouth. When Jesus had received the vinegar, he said, "It is finished"; and he bowed his head and gave up his spirit.
31 Since it was the day of Preparation, in order to prevent the bodies from remaining on the cross on the sabbath (for that sabbath was a high day), the Jews asked Pilate that their legs might be broken, and that they might be
32 taken away. So the soldiers came and broke the legs of the first, and of the other who had been crucified with
33 him; but when they came to Jesus and saw that he was
34 already dead, they did not break his legs. But one of the soldiers pierced his side with a spear, and at once there
35 came out blood and water. He who saw it has borne witness—his testimony is true, and he knows that he tells
36 the truth—that you also may believe. For these things took place that the scripture might be fulfilled, "Not a bone of
37 him shall be broken." And again another scripture says, "They shall look on him whom they have pierced."
38 After this Joseph of Arimathe′a, who was a disciple of Jesus, but secretly, for fear of the Jews, asked Pilate that he might take away the body of Jesus, and Pilate gave
39 him leave. So he came and took away his body. Nicode′-mus also, who had at first come to him by night, came bringing a mixture of myrrh and aloes, about a hundred
40 pounds' weight. They took the body of Jesus, and bound it in linen cloths with the spices, as is the burial custom
41 of the Jews. Now in the place where he was crucified there was a garden, and in the garden a new tomb where
42 no one had ever been laid. So because of the Jewish day of Preparation, as the tomb was close at hand, they laid Jesus there.

THE RISEN LORD

20 Now on the first day of the week Mary Mag′dalene came to the tomb early, while it was still dark, and saw that the stone had been taken away from the tomb.
2 So she ran, and went to Simon Peter and the other disciple, the one whom Jesus loved, and said to them, "They have taken the Lord out of the tomb, and we do not know
3 where they have laid him." Peter then came out with the
4 other disciple, and they went toward the tomb. They both ran, but the other disciple outran Peter and reached the
5 tomb first; and stooping to look in, he saw the linen cloths
6 lying there, but he did not go in. Then Simon Peter came, following him, and went into the tomb; he saw the linen
7 cloths lying, and the napkin, which had been on his head, not lying with the linen cloths but rolled up in a place
8 by itself. Then the other disciple, who reached the tomb
9 first, also went in, and he saw and believed; for as yet they did not know the scripture, that he must rise from
10 the dead. Then the disciples went back to their homes.

11 But Mary stood weeping outside the tomb, and as she
12 wept she stooped to look into the tomb; and she saw two angels in white, sitting where the body of Jesus had
13 lain, one at the head and one at the feet. They said to her, "Woman, why are you weeping?" She said to them, "Because they have taken away my Lord, and I do not
14 know where they have laid him." Saying this, she turned round and saw Jesus standing, but she did not know that
15 it was Jesus. Jesus said to her, "Woman, why are you weeping? Whom do you seek?" Supposing him to be the gardener, she said to him, "Sir, if you have carried him away, tell me where you have laid him, and I will take
16 him away." Jesus said to her, "Mary." She turned and said to him in Hebrew, "Rab-bo′ni!" (which means
17 Teacher). Jesus said to her, "Do not hold me, for I have not yet ascended to the Father; but go to my brethren and say to them, I am ascending to my Father and your
18 Father, to my God and your God." Mary Mag′dalene went and said to the disciples, "I have seen the Lord"; and she told them that he had said these things to her.
19 On the evening of that day, the first day of the week, the doors being shut where the disciples were, for fear of the Jews, Jesus came and stood among them and said to
20 them, "Peace be with you." When he had said this, he showed them his hands and his side. Then the disciples

21 were glad when they saw the Lord. Jesus said to them again, "Peace be with you. As the Father has sent me, even
22 so I send you." And when he had said this, he breathed on them, and said to them, "Receive the Holy Spirit.
23 If you forgive the sins of any, they are forgiven; if you retain the sins of any, they are retained."
24 Now Thomas, one of the twelve, called the Twin, was
25 not with them when Jesus came. So the other disciples told him, "We have seen the Lord." But he said to them, "Unless I see in his hands the print of the nails, and place my finger in the mark of the nails, and place my hand in his side, I will not believe."
26 Eight days later, his disciples were again in the house, and Thomas was with them. The doors were shut, but Jesus came and stood among them, and said, "Peace be
27 with you." Then he said to Thomas, "Put your finger here, and see my hands; and put out your hand, and place it in
28 my side; do not be faithless, but believing." Thomas
29 answered him. "My Lord and my God!" Jesus said to him, "Have you believed because you have seen me? Blessed are those who have not seen and yet believe."

The Purpose of the Gospel

30 Now Jesus did many other signs in the presence of the
31 disciples, which are not written in this book; but these
are written that you may believe that Jesus is the Christ,
the Son of God, and that believing you may have life in
his name.

21 After this Jesus revealed himself again to the disciples by the Sea of Tibe′ri-as; and he revealed him-
2 self in this way. Simon Peter, Thomas called the Twin,
Nathan′a-el of Cana in Galilee, the sons of Zeb′edee, and
3 two others of his disciples were together. Simon Peter
said to them, "I am going fishing." They said to him,
"We will go with you." They went out and got into the
boat; but that night they caught nothing.

4 Just as day was breaking, Jesus stood on the beach;
5 yet the disciples did not know that it was Jesus. Jesus
said to them, "Children, have you any fish?" They an-
6 swered him, "No." He said to them, "Cast the net on the
right side of the boat, and you will find some." So they
cast it, and now they were not able to haul it in, for the
7 quantity of fish. That disciple whom Jesus loved said to
Peter, "It is the Lord!" When Simon Peter heard that it
was the Lord, he put on his clothes, for he was stripped
8 for work, and sprang into the sea. But the other disciples
came in the boat, dragging the net full of fish, for they
were not far from the land, but about a hundred yards[m]
off.

9 When they got out on land, they saw a charcoal fire
10 there, with fish lying on it, and bread. Jesus said to them,
11 "Bring some of the fish that you have just caught." So
Simon Peter went aboard and hauled the net ashore, full
of large fish, a hundred and fifty-three of them; and although there were so many, the net was not torn.
12 Jesus said to them, "Come and have breakfast." Now
none of the disciples dared ask him, "Who are you?"
13 They knew it was the Lord. Jesus came and took the
14 bread and gave it to them, and so with the fish. This was
now the third time that Jesus was revealed to the disciples
after he was raised from the dead.

15 When they had finished breakfast, Jesus said to Simon
Peter, "Simon, son of John, do you love me more than
these?" He said to him, "Yes, Lord; you know that I love
16 you." He said to him, "Feed my lambs." A second time
he said to him, "Simon, son of John, do you love me?"

[m] Greek *two hundred cubits*

He said to him, "Yes, Lord; you know that I love you."
17 He said to him, "Tend my sheep." He said to him the
third time, "Simon, son of John, do you love me?" Peter
was grieved because he said to him the third time, "Do
you love me?" And he said to him, "Lord, you know
everything; you know that I love you." Jesus said to him,
18 "Feed my sheep. Truly, truly, I say to you, when you
were young, you girded yourself and walked where you
would; but when you are old, you will stretch out your
hands, and another will gird you and carry you where you
19 do not wish to go." (This he said to show by what death
he was to glorify God.) And after this he said to him,
"Follow me."

20 Peter turned and saw following them the disciple whom
Jesus loved, who had lain close to his breast at the supper
and had said, "Lord, who is it that is going to betray
21 you?" When Peter saw him, he said to Jesus, "Lord,

22 what about this man?" Jesus said to him, "If it is my
will that he remain until I come, what is that to you?
23 Follow me!" The saying spread abroad among the
brethren that this disciple was not to die; yet Jesus did
not say to him that he was not to die, but, "If it is my
will that he remain until I come, what is that to you?"
24 This is the disciple who is bearing witness to these
things, and who has written these things; and we know
that his testimony is true.
25 But there are also many other things which Jesus did;
were every one of them to be written, I suppose that the
world itself could not contain the books that would be
written.

ACTS

The Acts of the Apostles was written by Luke, the same Gentile (non-Jewish) doctor who wrote the Gospel of Luke. It was written from Rome shortly after the Gospel, probably about A.D. 80. It is one of the most important books of the New Testament because it tells us so much about the early church.

Beginning with the risen Christ, Acts tells how God brought his church into being through the first Christians, who began to tell the good news of Jesus Christ and do mighty acts in his name. It tells of the struggles of the church in Jerusalem, in Syria, and in Asia, which is now Turkey. It tells how the church grew in Greece and Italy.

As the Acts of the Apostles opens, Jesus' followers still did not understand fully the meaning of Jesus' life, but they were joyful over his Resurrection. They met together to pray and study the Old Testament and think about God's will shown in Jesus' life, teachings, Crucifixion, and Resurrection. On a Jewish feast day called Pentecost they received from God the gift of his Holy Spirit, promised to them by Jesus.

In Acts 9 begins the story of Paul, the rabbi from Tarsus. It tells how he was converted and became the great missionary to the Gentiles. It was largely through Saul, called Paul by his Gentile friends, that the Christian movement broke away from the narrow limitations of Jewish religious customs and ideas. Christians began to share their faith with all sorts of persons, both Jews and non-Jews (Gentiles), slaves and free men. The good news they told changed lives.

After preaching in Syria and parts of Asia Minor, now Turkey, Paul crossed over to Europe amidst all kinds of dangers. He preached in Greece and finally in Rome, where he was taken prisoner because of his fearless preaching. There the Book of Acts ends, but the church of Jesus Christ was only just beginning its march to every nation on all the earth.

Paul was later put to death in Rome. But God had used Paul's preaching, writing, and witnessing along with the work of others. Jesus Christ, Son of God, had begun to gain followers in many places. Indeed, before Paul's death there were already churches, or groups of Christian believers, in many cities in both Europe and Asia.

THE

ACTS OF THE APOSTLES

FROM JERUSALEM TO ANTIOCH

Days of Expectation

1 In the first book, O The-oph'ilus, I have dealt with 2 all that Jesus began to do and teach, until the day when he was taken up, after he had given commandment through the Holy Spirit to the apostles whom he had 3 chosen. To them he presented himself alive after his passion by many proofs, appearing to them during forty 4 days, and speaking of the kingdom of God. And while staying ᵃ with them he charged them not to depart from Jerusalem, but to wait for the promise of the Father,

5 which, he said, "you heard from me, for John baptized with water, but before many days you shall be baptized with the Holy Spirit."

6 So when they had come together, they asked him, "Lord, will you at this time restore the kingdom to 7 Israel?" He said to them, "It is not for you to know times or seasons which the Father has fixed by his own 8 authority. But you shall receive power when the Holy Spirit has come upon you; and you shall be my witnesses in Jerusalem and in all Judea and Samar'ia and to the 9 end of the earth." And when he had said this, as they

ᵃ Or eating

were looking on, he was lifted up, and a cloud took him
10 out of their sight. And while they were gazing into heaven as he went, behold, two men stood by them in white
11 robes, and said, "Men of Galilee, why do you stand looking into heaven? This Jesus, who was taken up from you into heaven, will come in the same way as you saw him go into heaven."

12 Then they returned to Jerusalem from the mount called Olivet, which is near Jerusalem, a sabbath day's journey
13 away; and when they had entered, they went up to the upper room, where they were staying, Peter and John and James and Andrew, Philip and Thomas, Bartholomew and Matthew, James the son of Alphaeus and Simon the
14 Zealot and Judas the son of James. All these with one accord devoted themselves to prayer, together with the women and Mary the mother of Jesus, and with his brothers.

15 In those days Peter stood up among the brethren (the company of persons was in all about a hundred and
16 twenty), and said, "Brethren, the scripture had to be fulfilled, which the Holy Spirit spoke beforehand by the mouth of David, concerning Judas who was guide to
17 those who arrested Jesus. For he was numbered among us,
18 and was allotted his share in this ministry. (Now this man bought a field with the reward of his wickedness; and falling headlong [b] he burst open in the middle and all his

the lot fell on Matthi′as; and he was enrolled with the eleven apostles.

Birth of the Church

2 When the day of Pentecost had come, they were
2 all together in one place. And suddenly a sound came from heaven like the rush of a mighty wind, and it filled
3 all the house where they were sitting. And there appeared to them tongues as of fire, distributed and resting
4 on each one of them. And they were all filled with the Holy Spirit and began to speak in other tongues, as the Spirit gave them utterance.

5 Now there were dwelling in Jerusalem Jews, devout
6 men from every nation under heaven. And at this sound the multitude came together, and they were bewildered, because each one heard them speaking in his own lan-
7 guage. And they were amazed and wondered, saying,
8 "Are not all these who are speaking Galileans? And how is it that we hear, each of us in his own native language?
9 Par′thians and Medes and E′lamites and residents of Mesopota′mia, Judea and Cappado′cia, Pontus and Asia,
10 Phryg′ia and Pamphyl′ia, Egypt and the parts of Libya belonging to Cyre′ne, and visitors from Rome, both Jews
11 and proselytes, Cretans and Arabians, we hear them telling in our own tongues the mighty works of God."
12 And all were amazed and perplexed, saying to one an-

19 bowels gushed out. And it became known to all the inhabitants of Jerusalem, so that the field was called in their
20 language Akel′dama, that is, Field of Blood.) For it is written in the book of Psalms,
'Let his habitation become desolate,
and let there be no one to live in it';
and
'His office let another take.'
21 So one of the men who had accompanied us during all the time that the Lord Jesus went in and out among us,
22 beginning from the baptism of John until the day when he was taken up from us—one of these men must become
23 with us a witness to his resurrection." And they put forward two, Joseph called Barsabbas, who was sur-
24 named Justus, and Matthi′as. And they prayed and said, "Lord, who knowest the hearts of all men, show which
25 one of these two thou hast chosen to take the place in this ministry and apostleship from which Judas turned aside,
26 to go to his own place." And they cast lots for them, and

[b] Or *swelling up*

13 other, "What does this mean?" But others mocking said, "They are filled with new wine."
14 But Peter, standing with the eleven, lifted up his voice and addressed them, "Men of Judea and all who dwell in Jerusalem, let this be known to you, and give ear to
15 my words. For these men are not drunk, as you suppose,
16 since it is only the third hour of the day; but this is what was spoken by the prophet Joel:
17 'And in the last days it shall be, God declares,
that I will pour out my Spirit upon all flesh,
and your sons and your daughters shall prophesy,
and your young men shall see visions,
and your old men shall dream dreams;
18 yea, and on my menservants and my maidservants in those days
I will pour out my Spirit; and they shall prophesy.
19 And I will show wonders in the heaven above
and signs on the earth beneath,
blood, and fire, and vapor of smoke;

²⁰ the sun shall be turned into darkness
and the moon into blood,
before the day of the Lord comes,
the great and manifest day.
²¹ And it shall be that whoever calls on the name of the
Lord shall be saved.'

²² "Men of Israel, hear these words: Jesus of Nazareth,
a man attested to you by God with mighty works and
wonders and signs which God did through him in your
²³ midst, as you yourselves know—this Jesus, delivered up
according to the definite plan and foreknowledge of God,
you crucified and killed by the hands of lawless men.
²⁴ But God raised him up, having loosed the pangs of death,
because it was not possible for him to be held by it.
²⁵ For David says concerning him,
'I saw the Lord always before me,
for he is at my right hand that I may not be shaken;
²⁶ therefore my heart was glad, and my tongue rejoiced;
moreover my flesh will dwell in hope.
²⁷ For thou wilt not abandon my soul to Hades,
nor let thy Holy One see corruption.
²⁸ Thou hast made known to me the ways of life;
thou wilt make me full of gladness with thy presence.'

²⁹ "Brethren, I may say to you confidently of the patri-
arch David that he both died and was buried, and his
³⁰ tomb is with us to this day. Being therefore a prophet,
and knowing that God had sworn with an oath to him
that he would set one of his descendants upon his throne,
³¹ he foresaw and spoke of the resurrection of the Christ,
that he was not abandoned to Hades, nor did his flesh
³² see corruption. This Jesus God raised up, and of that we
³³ all are witnesses. Being therefore exalted at the right hand
of God, and having received from the Father the promise
of the Holy Spirit, he has poured out this which you see
³⁴ and hear. For David did not ascend into the heavens; but
he himself says,
'The Lord said to my Lord, Sit at my right hand,
³⁵ till I make thy enemies a stool for thy feet.'
³⁶ Let all the house of Israel therefore know assuredly that
God has made him both Lord and Christ, this Jesus whom
you crucified."

³⁷ Now when they heard this they were cut to the heart,
and said to Peter and the rest of the apostles, "Brethren,
³⁸ what shall we do?" And Peter said to them, "Repent, and
be baptized every one of you in the name of Jesus Christ
for the forgiveness of your sins; and you shall receive
³⁹ the gift of the Holy Spirit. For the promise is to you and
to your children and to all that are far off, every one
⁴⁰ whom the Lord our God calls to him." And he testified
with many other words and exhorted them, saying, "Save
⁴¹ yourselves from this crooked generation." So those who
received his word were baptized, and there were added
⁴² that day about three thousand souls. And they devoted

ᶜ Or *child*   ᵈ Greek *him*

themselves to the apostles' teaching and fellowship, to
the breaking of bread and the prayers.
⁴³ And fear came upon every soul; and many wonders
⁴⁴ and signs were done through the apostles. And all who
believed were together and had all things in common;
⁴⁵ and they sold their possessions and goods and distributed
⁴⁶ them to all, as any had need. And day by day, attending
the temple together and breaking bread in their homes,
they partook of food with glad and generous hearts,
⁴⁷ praising God and having favor with all the people. And
the Lord added to their number day by day those who
were being saved.

The Church at Jerusalem

3 Now Peter and John were going up to the temple
² at the hour of prayer, the ninth hour. And a man lame
from birth was being carried, whom they laid daily at
that gate of the temple which is called Beautiful to ask
³ alms of those who entered the temple. Seeing Peter and
John about to go into the temple, he asked for alms.
⁴ And Peter directed his gaze at him, with John, and said,
⁵ "Look at us." And he fixed his attention upon them,
⁶ expecting to receive something from them. But Peter
said, "I have no silver and gold, but I give you what
I have; in the name of Jesus Christ of Nazareth, walk."
⁷ And he took him by the right hand and raised him up;
and immediately his feet and ankles were made strong.
⁸ And leaping up he stood and walked and entered the
temple with them, walking and leaping and praising
⁹ God. And all the people saw him walking and praising
¹⁰ God, and recognized him as the one who sat for alms
at the Beautiful Gate of the temple; and they were filled
with wonder and amazement at what had happened to
him.

¹¹ While he clung to Peter and John, all the people ran
together to them in the portico called Solomon's, as-
¹² tounded. And when Peter saw it he addressed the people,
"Men of Israel, why do you wonder at this, or why do
you stare at us, as though by our own power or piety
¹³ we had made him walk? The God of Abraham and of
Isaac and of Jacob, the God of our fathers, glorified his
servant ᶜ Jesus, whom you delivered up and denied in
the presence of Pilate, when he had decided to release
¹⁴ him. But you denied the Holy and Righteous One, and
¹⁵ asked for a murderer to be granted to you, and killed
the Author of life, whom God raised from the dead. To
¹⁶ this we are witnesses. And his name, by faith in his name,
has made this man strong whom you see and know; and
the faith which is through Jesus ᵈ has given the man this
perfect health in the presence of you all.
¹⁷ "And now, brethren, I know that you acted in igno-
¹⁸ rance, as did also your rulers. But what God foretold by
the mouth of all the prophets, that his Christ should

19 suffer, he thus fulfilled. Repent therefore, and turn again, that your sins may be blotted out, that times of refresh-
20 ing may come from the presence of the Lord, and that he
21 may send the Christ appointed for you, Jesus, whom heaven must receive until the time for establishing all that God spoke by the mouth of his holy prophets from
22 of old. Moses said, 'The Lord God will raise up for you a prophet from your brethren as he raised me up. You
23 shall listen to him in whatever he tells you. And it shall be that every soul that does not listen to that prophet
24 shall be destroyed from the people.' And all the prophets who have spoken, from Samuel and those who came after-
25 wards, also proclaimed these days. You are the sons of the prophets and of the covenant which God gave to your fathers, saying to Abraham, 'And in your posterity
26 shall all the families of the earth be blessed.' God, having raised up his servant,ᶜ sent him to you first, to bless you in turning every one of you from your wickedness."

4 And as they were speaking to the people, the priests and the captain of the temple and the Sad'ducees came
2 upon them, annoyed because they were teaching the peo-ple and proclaiming in Jesus the resurrection from the
3 dead. And they arrested them and put them in custody
4 until the morrow, for it was already evening. But many of those who heard the word believed; and the number of the men came to about five thousand.

5 On the morrow their rulers and elders and scribes
6 were gathered together in Jerusalem, with Annas the high priest and Ca'iaphas and John and Alexander, and
7 all who were of the high-priestly family. And when they had set them in the midst, they inquired, "By what power
8 or by what name did you do this?" Then Peter, filled with the Holy Spirit, said to them, "Rulers of the people
9 and elders, if we are being examined today concerning a good deed done to a cripple, by what means this man
10 has been healed, be it known to you all, and to all the people of Israel, that by the name of Jesus Christ of Nazareth, whom you crucified, whom God raised from the dead, by him this man is standing before you well.

11 This is the stone which was rejected by you builders, but
12 which has become the head of the corner. And there is salvation in no one else, for there is no other name under heaven given among men by which we must be saved."
13 Now when they saw the boldness of Peter and John, and perceived that they were uneducated, common men, they wondered; and they recognized that they had been
14 with Jesus. But seeing the man that had been healed

standing beside them, they had nothing to say in op-
15 position. But when they had commanded them to go aside out of the council, they conferred with one another,
16 saying, "What shall we do with these men? For that a notable sign has been performed through them is mani-fest to all the inhabitants of Jerusalem, and we cannot
17 deny it. But in order that it may spread no further among the people, let us warn them to speak no more to
18 any one in this name." So they called them and charged them not to speak or teach at all in the name of Jesus.
19 But Peter and John answered them, "Whether it is right in the sight of God to listen to you rather than to God,
20 you must judge; for we cannot but speak of what we
21 have seen and heard." And when they had further threatened them, they let them go, finding no way to punish them, because of the people; for all men praised
22 God for what had happened. For the man on whom this sign of healing was performed was more than forty years old.
23 When they were released they went to their friends and reported what the chief priests and the elders had
24 said to them. And when they heard it, they lifted their voices together to God and said, "Sovereign Lord, who didst make the heaven and the earth and the sea and
25 everything in them, who by the mouth of our father David, thy servant,ᵉ didst say by the Holy Spirit,
    'Why did the Gentiles rage,
    and the peoples imagine vain things?
26 The kings of the earth set themselves in array,
    and the rulers were gathered together,
    against the Lord and against his Anointed'—ᵉ
27 for truly in this city there were gathered together against thy holy servantᶜ Jesus, whom thou didst anoint, both Herod and Pontius Pilate, with the Gentiles and the
28 peoples of Israel, to do whatever thy hand and thy plan
29 had predestined to take place. And now, Lord, look upon their threats, and grant to thy servantsᶠ to speak thy
30 word with all boldness, while thou stretchest out thy hand to heal, and signs and wonders are performed
31 through the name of thy holy servantᶜ Jesus." And when they had prayed, the place in which they were gathered together was shaken; and they were all filled with the Holy Spirit and spoke the word of God with boldness.
32 Now the company of those who believed were of one heart and soul, and no one said that any of the things which he possessed was his own, but they had everything
33 in common. And with great power the apostles gave their testimony to the resurrection of the Lord Jesus,
34 and great grace was upon them all. There was not a needy person among them, for as many as were posses-sors of lands or houses sold them, and brought the pro-
35 ceeds of what was sold and laid it at the apostles' feet;

ᶜ Or *child*   ᵉ Or *Christ*   ᶠ Or *slaves*

752

36 and distribution was made to each as any had need. Thus Joseph who was surnamed by the apostles Barnabas (which means, Son of encouragement), a Levite, a native 37 of Cyprus, sold a field which belonged to him, and brought the money and laid it at the apostles' feet.

5 But a man named Anani′as with his wife Sapphi′ra 2 sold a piece of property, and with his wife's knowledge he kept back some of the proceeds, and brought 3 only a part and laid it at the apostles' feet. But Peter said, "Anani′as, why has Satan filled your heart to lie to the Holy Spirit and to keep back part of the proceeds of 4 the land? While it remained unsold, did it not remain your own? And after it was sold, was it not at your dis-

posal? How is it that you have contrived this deed in 5 your heart? You have not lied to men but to God." When Anani′as heard these words, he fell down and died. And 6 great fear came upon all who heard of it. The young men rose and wrapped him up and carried him out and buried him.

7 After an interval of about three hours his wife came 8 in, not knowing what had happened. And Peter said to her, "Tell me whether you sold the land for so much." 9 And she said, "Yes, for so much." But Peter said to her, "How is it that you have agreed together to tempt the Spirit of the Lord? Hark, the feet of those that have buried your husband are at the door, and they will carry 10 you out." Immediately she fell down at his feet and died. When the young men came in they found her dead, and they carried her out and buried her beside her husband. 11 And great fear came upon the whole church, and upon all who heard of these things.

12 Now many signs and wonders were done among the people by the hands of the apostles. And they were all 13 together in Solomon's Portico. None of the rest dared join them, but the people held them in high honor. 14 And more than ever believers were added to the Lord, 15 multitudes both of men and women, so that they even carried out the sick into the streets, and laid them on beds and pallets, that as Peter came by at least his shadow 16 might fall on some of them. The people also gathered from the towns around Jerusalem, bringing the sick and those afflicted with unclean spirits, and they were all healed.

17 But the high priest rose up and all who were with him, that is, the party of the Sad′ducees, and filled with

18 jealousy they arrested the apostles and put them in the 19 common prison. But at night an angel of the Lord opened the prison doors and brought them out and said, 20 "Go and stand in the temple and speak to the people all 21 the words of this Life." And when they heard this, they entered the temple at daybreak and taught.

Now the high priest came and those who were with him and called together the council and all the senate of Israel, and sent to the prison to have them brought. 22 But when the officers came, they did not find them in 23 the prison, and they returned and reported, "We found the prison securely locked and the sentries standing at the doors, but when we opened it we found no one in-24 side." Now when the captain of the temple and the chief priests heard these words, they were much perplexed 25 about them, wondering what this would come to. And some one came and told them, "The men whom you put in prison are standing in the temple and teaching the 26 people." Then the captain with the officers went and brought them, but without violence, for they were afraid of being stoned by the people.

27 And when they had brought them, they set them before the council. And the high priest questioned them, 28 saying, "We strictly charged you not to teach in this name, yet here you have filled Jerusalem with your teaching and you intend to bring this man's blood upon 29 us." But Peter and the apostles answered, "We must 30 obey God rather than men. The God of our fathers raised Jesus whom you killed by hanging him on a tree. 31 God exalted him at his right hand as Leader and Savior, 32 to give repentance to Israel and forgiveness of sins. And we are witnesses to these things, and so is the Holy Spirit whom God has given to those who obey him."

33 When they heard this they were enraged and wanted 34 to kill them. But a Pharisee in the council named Gama′li-el, a teacher of the law, held in honor by all the people, stood up and ordered the men to be put outside for a 35 while. And he said to them, "Men of Israel, take care 36 what you do with these men. For before these days, Theu′das arose, giving himself out to be somebody, and a number of men, about four hundred, joined him; but he was slain and all who followed him were dispersed 37 and came to nothing. After him Judas the Galilean arose in the days of the census and drew away some of the people after him; he also perished, and all who followed

38 him were scattered. So in the present case I tell you, keep away from these men and let them alone; for if
39 this plan or this undertaking is of men, it will fail; but if it is of God, you will not be able to overthrow them. You might even be found opposing God!"
40 So they took his advice, and when they had called in the apostles, they beat them and charged them not to
41 speak in the name of Jesus, and let them go. Then they left the presence of the council, rejoicing that they were
42 counted worthy to suffer dishonor for the name. And every day in the temple and at home they did not cease teaching and preaching Jesus as the Christ.

Hellenistic Christianity

6 Now in these days when the disciples were increasing in number, the Hellenists murmured against the Hebrews because their widows were neglected in the
2 daily distribution. And the twelve summoned the body of the disciples and said, "It is not right that we should give up preaching the word of God to serve tables.
3 Therefore, brethren, pick out from among you seven men of good repute, full of the Spirit and of wisdom,
4 whom we may appoint to this duty. But we will devote ourselves to prayer and to the ministry of the word."
5 And what they said pleased the whole multitude, and they chose Stephen, a man full of faith and of the Holy Spirit, and Philip, and Proch'orus, and Nica'nor, and Timon, and Par'menas, and Nicola'us, a proselyte of
6 Antioch. These they set before the apostles, and they prayed and laid their hands upon them.
7 And the word of God increased; and the number of the disciples multiplied greatly in Jerusalem, and a great many of the priests were obedient to the faith.
8 And Stephen, full of grace and power, did great won-
9 ders and signs among the people. Then some of those who belonged to the synagogue of the Freedmen (as it was called), and of the Cyre'nians, and of the Alexandrians, and of those from Cili'cia and Asia, arose and disputed
10 with Stephen. But they could not withstand the wisdom
11 and the Spirit with which he spoke. Then they secretly instigated men, who said, "We have heard him speak
12 blasphemous words against Moses and God." And they stirred up the people and the elders and the scribes, and they came upon him and seized him and brought him
13 before the council, and set up false witnesses who said, "This man never ceases to speak words against this holy
14 place and the law; for we have heard him say that this Jesus of Nazareth will destroy this place, and will change
15 the customs which Moses delivered to us." And gazing at him, all who sat in the council saw that his face was like the face of an angel.
2 7 And the high priest said, "Is this so?" And Stephen said:

"Brethren and fathers, hear me. The God of glory appeared to our father Abraham, when he was in
3 Mesopota'mia, before he lived in Haran, and said to him, 'Depart from your land and from your kindred and
4 go into the land which I will show you.' Then he departed from the land of the Chalde'ans, and lived in Haran. And after his father died, God removed him from there into this land in which you are now living;
5 yet he gave him no inheritance in it, not even a foot's length, but promised to give it to him in possession and to his posterity after him, though he had no child.

6 And God spoke to this effect, that his posterity would be aliens in a land belonging to others, who would enslave
7 them and ill-treat them four hundred years. 'But I will judge the nation which they serve,' said God, 'and after that they shall come out and worship me in this place.'
8 And he gave him the covenant of circumcision. And so Abraham became the father of Isaac, and circumcised him on the eighth day; and Isaac became the father of Jacob, and Jacob of the twelve patriarchs.
9 "And the patriarchs, jealous of Joseph, sold him into
10 Egypt; but God was with him, and rescued him out of all his afflictions, and gave him favor and wisdom before Pharaoh, king of Egypt, who made him governor over
11 Egypt and over all his household. Now there came a famine throughout all Egypt and Canaan, and great afflic-
12 tion, and our fathers could find no food. But when Jacob heard that there was grain in Egypt, he sent forth
13 our fathers the first time. And at the second visit Joseph made himself known to his brothers, and Joseph's family
14 became known to Pharaoh. And Joseph sent and called to him Jacob his father and all his kindred, seventy-five
15 souls; and Jacob went down into Egypt. And he died,
16 himself and our fathers, and they were carried back to Shechem and laid in the tomb that Abraham had bought for a sum of silver from the sons of Hamor in Shechem.
17 "But as the time of the promise drew near, which God had granted to Abraham, the people grew and multiplied
18 in Egypt till there arose over Egypt another king who
19 had not known Joseph. He dealt craftily with our race and forced our fathers to expose their infants, that they
20 might not be kept alive. At this time Moses was born,

and was beautiful before God. And he was brought up
²¹ for three months in his father's house; and when he was
exposed, Pharaoh's daughter adopted him and brought
²² him up as her own son. And Moses was instructed in all
the wisdom of the Egyptians, and he was mighty in his
words and deeds.
²³ "When he was forty years old, it came into his heart
²⁴ to visit his brethren, the sons of Israel. And seeing one
of them being wronged, he defended the oppressed man
²⁵ and avenged him by striking the Egyptian. He supposed
that his brethren understood that God was giving them
²⁶ deliverance by his hand, but they did not understand. And
on the following day he appeared to them as they were
quarreling and would have reconciled them, saying, 'Men,
²⁷ you are brethren, why do you wrong each other?' But the
man who was wronging his neighbor thrust him aside,
²⁸ saying, 'Who made you a ruler and a judge over us? Do
you want to kill me as you killed the Egyptian yesterday?'
²⁹ At this retort Moses fled, and became an exile in the
land of Mid'ian, where he became the father of two sons.
³⁰ "Now when forty years had passed, an angel appeared
to him in the wilderness of Mount Sinai, in a flame of fire
³¹ in a bush. When Moses saw it he wondered at the sight;
and as he drew near to look, the voice of the Lord came,
³² 'I am the God of your fathers, the God of Abraham and
of Isaac and of Jacob.' And Moses trembled and did not
³³ dare to look. And the Lord said to him, 'Take off the
shoes from your feet, for the place where you are stand-
³⁴ ing is holy ground. I have surely seen the ill-treatment
of my people that are in Egypt and heard their groaning,
and I have come down to deliver them. And now come,
I will send you to Egypt.'
³⁵ "This Moses whom they refused, saying, 'Who made
you a ruler and a judge?' God sent as both ruler and deliverer by the hand of the angel that appeared to him in
³⁶ the bush. He led them out, having performed wonders
and signs in Egypt and at the Red Sea, and in the wil-
³⁷ derness for forty years. This is the Moses who said to
the Israelites, 'God will raise up for you a prophet from
³⁸ your brethren as he raised me up.' This is he who was in
the congregation in the wilderness with the angel who
spoke to him at Mount Sinai, and with our fathers; and
³⁹ he received living oracles to give to us. Our fathers refused to obey him, but thrust him aside, and in their
⁴⁰ hearts they turned to Egypt, saying to Aaron, 'Make for
us gods to go before us; as for this Moses who led us
out from the land of Egypt, we do not know what has
⁴¹ become of him.' And they made a calf in those days, and
offered a sacrifice to the idol and rejoiced in the works
⁴² of their hands. But God turned and gave them over to
worship the host of heaven, as it is written in the book
of the prophets:

'Did you offer to me slain beasts and sacrifices,

forty years in the wilderness, O house of Israel?
⁴³ And you took up the tent of Moloch,
and the star of the god Rephan,
the figures which you made to worship;
and I will remove you beyond Babylon.'
⁴⁴ "Our fathers had the tent of witness in the wilderness,
even as he who spoke to Moses directed him to make it,
⁴⁵ according to the pattern that he had seen. Our fathers in
turn brought it in with Joshua when they dispossessed
the nations which God thrust out before our fathers. So
⁴⁶ it was until the days of David, who found favor in the
sight of God and asked leave to find a habitation for the
⁴⁷ God of Jacob. But it was Solomon who built a house for
⁴⁸ him. Yet the Most High does not dwell in houses made
with hands; as the prophet says,
⁴⁹ 'Heaven is my throne,
and earth my footstool.
What house will you build for me, says the Lord,
or what is the place of my rest?
⁵⁰ Did not my hand make all these things?'
⁵¹ "You stiff-necked people, uncircumcised in heart and
ears, you always resist the Holy Spirit. As your fathers
⁵² did, so do you. Which of the prophets did not your
fathers persecute? And they killed those who announced
beforehand the coming of the Righteous One, whom you
⁵³ have now betrayed and murdered, you who received the

law as delivered by angels and did not keep it."
⁵⁴ Now when they heard these things they were enraged,
⁵⁵ and they ground their teeth against him. But he, full of
the Holy Spirit, gazed into heaven and saw the glory of
God, and Jesus standing at the right hand of God;
⁵⁶ and he said, "Behold, I see the heavens opened, and the
⁵⁷ Son of man standing at the right hand of God." But they
cried out with a loud voice and stopped their ears and
⁵⁸ rushed together upon him. Then they cast him out of

the city and stoned him; and the witnesses laid down their garments at the feet of a young man named Saul.
59 And as they were stoning Stephen, he prayed, "Lord
60 Jesus, receive my spirit." And he knelt down and cried with a loud voice, "Lord, do not hold this sin against
8 them." And when he had said this, he fell asleep. And Saul was consenting to his death.

And on that day a great persecution arose against the church in Jerusalem; and they were all scattered throughout the region of Judea and Samar'ia, except the apostles.
2 Devout men buried Stephen, and made great lamentation
3 over him. But Saul was ravaging the church, and entering house after house, he dragged off men and women and committed them to prison.

4 Now those who were scattered went about preaching the
5 word. Philip went down to a city of Samar'ia, and pro-
6 claimed to them the Christ. And the multitudes with one accord gave heed to what was said by Philip, when they
7 heard him and saw the signs which he did. For unclean spirits came out of many who were possessed, crying with a loud voice; and many who were paralyzed or lame
8 were healed. So there was much joy in that city.

9 But there was a man named Simon who had previously practiced magic in the city and amazed the nation of Samar'ia, saying that he himself was somebody great.
10 They all gave heed to him, from the least to the greatest, saying, "This man is that power of God which is called
11 Great." And they gave heed to him, because for a long
12 time he had amazed them with his magic. But when they believed Philip as he preached good news about the kingdom of God and the name of Jesus Christ, they were
13 baptized, both men and women. Even Simon himself believed, and after being baptized he continued with Philip. And seeing signs and great miracles performed, he was amazed.

14 Now when the apostles at Jerusalem heard that Samar'ia had received the word of God, they sent to them Peter
15 and John, who came down and prayed for them that they
16 might receive the Holy Spirit; for it had not yet fallen on any of them, but they had only been baptized in the
17 name of the Lord Jesus. Then they laid their hands on
18 them and they received the Holy Spirit. Now when Simon saw that the Spirit was given through the laying on of
19 the apostles' hands, he offered them money, saying, "Give

me also this power, that any one on whom I lay my hands
20 may receive the Holy Spirit." But Peter said to him, "Your silver perish with you, because you thought you
21 could obtain the gift of God with money! You have neither part nor lot in this matter, for your heart is not
22 right before God. Repent therefore of this wickedness of yours, and pray to the Lord that, if possible, the in-
23 tent of your heart may be forgiven you. For I see that you are in the gall of bitterness and in the bond of iniq-
24 uity." And Simon answered, "Pray for me to the Lord, that nothing of what you have said may come upon me."

25 Now when they had testified and spoken the word of the Lord, they returned to Jerusalem, preaching the gospel to many villages of the Samaritans.

26 But an angel of the Lord said to Philip, "Rise and go toward the south g to the road that goes down from Jeru-
27 salem to Gaza." This is a desert road. And he rose and went. And behold, an Ethiopian, a eunuch, a minister of the Canda'ce, queen of the Ethiopians, in charge of all
28 her treasure, had come to Jerusalem to worship and was returning; seated in his chariot, he was reading the
29 prophet Isaiah. And the Spirit said to Philip, "Go up
30 and join the chariot." So Philip ran to him, and heard him reading Isaiah the prophet, and asked, "Do you
31 understand what you are reading?" And he said, "How can I, unless some one guides me?" And he invited
32 Philip to come up and sit with him. Now the passage of the scripture which he was reading was this:

"As a sheep led to the slaughter
or a lamb before its shearer is dumb,
so he opens not his mouth.
33 In his humiliation justice was denied him.
Who can describe his generation?
For his life is taken up from the earth."

34 And the eunuch said to Philip, "About whom, pray, does the prophet say this, about himself or about some one
35 else?" Then Philip opened his mouth, and beginning with this scripture he told him the good news of Jesus.
36 And as they went along the road they came to some water, and the eunuch said, "See, here is water! What is to
38 prevent my being baptized?" h And he commanded the chariot to stop, and they both went down into the water,
39 Philip and the eunuch, and he baptized him. And when they came up out of the water, the Spirit of the Lord caught up Philip; and the eunuch saw him no more, and
40 went on his way rejoicing. But Philip was found at Azo'-tus, and passing on he preached the gospel to all the towns till he came to Caesare'a.

Conversion of Paul

9 But Saul, still breathing threats and murder against
2 the disciples of the Lord, went to the high priest and asked him for letters to the synagogues at Damascus, so

g Or at noon   h Other ancient authorities add all or most of verse 37, And Philip said, "If you believe with all your heart, you may." And he replied, "I believe that Jesus Christ is the Son of God."

that if he found any belonging to the Way, men or
³ women, he might bring them bound to Jerusalem. Now
as he journeyed he approached Damascus, and suddenly
⁴ a light from heaven flashed about him. And he fell to the
ground and heard a voice saying to him, "Saul, Saul,
⁵ why do you persecute me?" And he said, "Who are you,
Lord?" And he said, "I am Jesus, whom you are perse-
⁶ cuting; but rise and enter the city, and you will be told
⁷ what you are to do." The men who were traveling with
him stood speechless, hearing the voice but seeing no
⁸ one. Saul arose from the ground; and when his eyes
were opened, he could see nothing; so they led him by
⁹ the hand and brought him into Damascus. And for three
days he was without sight, and neither ate nor drank.
¹⁰ Now there was a disciple at Damascus named Anani′as.
The Lord said to him in a vision, "Anani′as." And he
¹¹ said, "Here I am, Lord." And the Lord said to him,
"Rise and go to the street called Straight, and inquire
in the house of Judas for a man of Tarsus named Saul;
¹² for behold, he is praying, and he has seen a man named
Anani′as come in and lay his hands on him so that he
¹³ might regain his sight." But Anani′as answered, "Lord,
I have heard from many about this man, how much evil
¹⁴ he has done to thy saints at Jerusalem; and here he has
authority from the chief priests to bind all who call upon
¹⁵ thy name." But the Lord said to him, "Go, for he is a
chosen instrument of mine to carry my name before the
¹⁶ Gentiles and kings and the sons of Israel; for I will show
him how much he must suffer for the sake of my name."
¹⁷ So Anani′as departed and entered the house. And laying
his hands on him he said, "Brother Saul, the Lord Jesus
who appeared to you on the road by which you came,
has sent me that you may regain your sight and be filled
¹⁸ with the Holy Spirit." And immediately something like
scales fell from his eyes and he regained his sight. Then
¹⁹ he rose and was baptized, and took food and was strengthened.

For several days he was with the disciples at Damas-
²⁰ cus. And in the synagogues immediately he proclaimed
²¹ Jesus, saying, "He is the Son of God." And all who heard
him were amazed, and said, "Is not this the man who
made havoc in Jerusalem of those who called on this
name? And he has come here for this purpose, to bring
²² them bound before the chief priests." But Saul increased
all the more in strength, and confounded the Jews who
lived in Damascus by proving that Jesus was the Christ.
²³ When many days had passed, the Jews plotted to kill
²⁴ him, but their plot became known to Saul. They were
²⁵ watching the gates day and night, to kill him; but his
disciples took him by night and let him down over the
wall, lowering him in a basket.
²⁶ And when he had come to Jerusalem he attempted to
join the disciples; and they were all afraid of him,

²⁷ for they did not believe that he was a disciple. But
Barnabas took him, and brought him to the apostles, and
declared to them how on the road he had seen the Lord,
who spoke to him, and how at Damascus he had preached
²⁸ boldly in the name of Jesus. So he went in and out among
²⁹ them at Jerusalem, preaching boldly in the name of the
Lord. And he spoke and disputed against the Hellenists;
³⁰ but they were seeking to kill him. And when the brethren
knew it, they brought him down to Caesare′a, and sent
him off to Tarsus.
³¹ So the church throughout all Judea and Galilee and
Samar′ia had peace and was built up; and walking in the
fear of the Lord and in the comfort of the Holy Spirit
it was multiplied.

First Missions to Gentiles

³² Now as Peter went here and there among them all, he
³³ came down also to the saints that lived at Lydda. There
he found a man named Aene′as, who had been bedridden
³⁴ for eight years and was paralyzed. And Peter said to
him, "Aene′as, Jesus Christ heals you; rise and make your
³⁵ bed." And immediately he rose. And all the residents of

Lydda and Sharon saw him, and they turned to the Lord.
³⁶ Now there was at Joppa a disciple named Tabitha,
which means Dorcas.ˣ She was full of good works
³⁷ and acts of charity. In those days she fell sick and
died; and when they had washed her, they laid her in
³⁸ an upper room. Since Lydda was near Joppa, the disciples, hearing that Peter was there, sent two men to him
³⁹ entreating him, "Please come to us without delay." So
Peter rose and went with them. And when he had come,
they took him to the upper room. All the widows stood
beside him weeping, and showing tunics and other gar-
⁴⁰ ments which Dorcas made while she was with them. But
Peter put them all outside and knelt down and prayed;
then turning to the body he said, "Tabitha, rise." And
she opened her eyes, and when she saw Peter she sat
⁴¹ up. And he gave her his hand and lifted her up. Then call-
⁴² ing the saints and widows he presented her alive. And it
became known throughout all Joppa, and many believed in

ˣ The name Tabitha in Aramaic and the name Dorcas in Greek mean *gazelle*

43 the Lord. And he stayed in Joppa for many days with one Simon, a tanner.

10 At Caesare'a there was a man named Cornelius, a centurion of what was known as the Italian Cohort, 2 a devout man who feared God with all his household, gave alms liberally to the people, and prayed constantly to 3 God. About the ninth hour of the day he saw clearly in a vision an angel of God coming in and saying to him, 4 "Cornelius." And he stared at him in terror, and said, "What is it, Lord?" And he said to him, "Your prayers and your alms have ascended as a memorial before God. 5 And now send men to Joppa, and bring one Simon who 6 is called Peter; he is lodging with Simon, a tanner, whose 7 house is by the seaside." When the angel who spoke to him had departed, he called two of his servants and a devout soldier from among those that waited on him, 8 and having related everything to them, he sent them to Joppa.

9 The next day, as they were on their journey and coming near the city, Peter went up on the housetop to pray, about 10 the sixth hour. And he became hungry and desired something to eat; but while they were preparing it, he fell into a 11 trance and saw the heaven opened, and something descending, like a great sheet, let down by four corners 12 upon the earth. In it were all kinds of animals and 13 reptiles and birds of the air. And there came a voice to 14 him, "Rise, Peter; kill and eat." But Peter said, "No, Lord; for I have never eaten anything that is common 15 or unclean." And the voice came to him again a second time, "What God has cleansed, you must not call com- 16 mon." This happened three times, and the thing was taken up at once to heaven.

17 Now while Peter was inwardly perplexed as to what the vision which he had seen might mean, behold, the men that were sent by Cornelius, having made inquiry 18 for Simon's house, stood before the gate and called out to ask whether Simon who was called Peter was lodging 19 there. And while Peter was pondering the vision, the Spirit said to him, "Behold, three men are looking for 20 you. Rise and go down, and accompany them without 21 hesitation; for I have sent them." And Peter went down to the men and said, "I am the one you are looking for; 22 what is the reason for your coming?" And they said, "Cornelius, a centurion, an upright and God-fearing man, who is well spoken of by the whole Jewish nation, was directed by a holy angel to send for you to come to his 23 house, and to hear what you have to say." So he called them in to be his guests.

The next day he rose and went off with them, and some 24 of the brethren from Joppa accompanied him. And on the following day they entered Caesare'a. Cornelius was expecting them and had called together his kinsmen and 25 close friends. When Peter entered, Cornelius met him and 26 fell down at his feet and worshiped him. But Peter lifted 27 him up, saying, "Stand up; I too am a man." And as he talked with him, he went in and found many persons 28 gathered; and he said to them, "You yourselves know how unlawful it is for a Jew to associate with or to visit any one of another nation; but God has shown me that I 29 should not call any man common or unclean. So when I was sent for, I came without objection. I ask then why you sent for me."

30 And Cornelius said, "Four days ago, about this hour, I was keeping the ninth hour of prayer in my house; and 31 behold, a man stood before me in bright apparel, saying, 'Cornelius, your prayer has been heard and your alms 32 have been remembered before God. Send therefore to Joppa and ask for Simon who is called Peter; he is lodging in the house of Simon, a tanner, by the seaside.' 33 So I sent to you at once, and you have been kind enough to come. Now therefore we are all here present in the sight of God, to hear all that you have been commanded by the Lord."

34 And Peter opened his mouth and said: "Truly I per- 35 ceive that God shows no partiality, but in every nation any one who fears him and does what is right is acceptable to 36 him. You know the word which he sent to Israel, preaching good news of peace by Jesus Christ (he is Lord of all), 37 the word which was proclaimed throughout all Judea, beginning from Galilee after the baptism which John 38 preached: how God anointed Jesus of Nazareth with the Holy Spirit and with power; how he went about doing good and healing all that were oppressed by the devil, for 39 God was with him. And we are witnesses to all that he did both in the country of the Jews and in Jerusalem. 40 They put him to death by hanging him on a tree; but God raised him on the third day and made him manifest; 41 not to all the people but to us who were chosen by God as witnesses, who ate and drank with him after he rose 42 from the dead. And he commanded us to preach to the people, and to testify that he is the one ordained by God 43 to be judge of the living and the dead. To him all the prophets bear witness that every one who believes in him receives forgiveness of sins through his name."

44 While Peter was still saying this, the Holy Spirit fell 45 on all who heard the word. And the believers from among the circumcised who came with Peter were amazed, because the gift of the Holy Spirit had been poured out 46 even on the Gentiles. For they heard them speaking in 47 tongues and extolling God. Then Peter declared, "Can any one forbid water for baptizing these people who have 48 received the Holy Spirit just as we have?" And he commanded them to be baptized in the name of Jesus Christ. Then they asked him to remain for some days.

11 Now the apostles and the brethren who were in Judea heard that the Gentiles also had received the

²word of God. So when Peter went up to Jerusalem, the
³circumcision party criticized him, saying, "Why did you
⁴go to uncircumcised men and eat with them?" But Peter
⁵began and explained to them in order: "I was in the city
of Joppa praying; and in a trance I saw a vision, something descending, like a great sheet, let down from heaven
⁶by four corners; and it came down to me. Looking at it
closely I observed animals and beasts of prey and reptiles
⁷and birds of the air. And I heard a voice saying to me,
⁸'Rise, Peter; kill and eat.' But I said, 'No, Lord; for
nothing common or unclean has ever entered my mouth.'
⁹But the voice answered a second time from heaven, 'What
¹⁰God has cleansed you must not call common.' This happened three times, and all was drawn up again into
¹¹heaven. At that very moment three men arrived at the
¹²house in which we were, sent to me from Caesare'a. And
the Spirit told me to go with them, making no distinction.
These six brethren also accompanied me, and we entered
¹³the man's house. And he told us how he had seen the
angel standing in his house and saying, 'Send to Joppa
¹⁴and bring Simon called Peter; he will declare to you a
message by which you will be saved, you and all your
¹⁵household.' As I began to speak, the Holy Spirit fell on
¹⁶them just as on us at the beginning. And I remembered
the word of the Lord, how he said, 'John baptized with
water, but you shall be baptized with the Holy Spirit.'

TARSUS.
ANTIOCH.
CYPRUS
PHOENICIA
MEDITERRANEAN SEA
CAESAREA.
•CYRENE   JOPPA.
•LYDDA
JERUSALEM.

¹⁷If then God gave the same gift to them as he gave to us
when we believed in the Lord Jesus Christ, who was I that
¹⁸I could withstand God?" When they heard this they were
silenced. And they glorified God, saying, "Then to the
Gentiles also God has granted repentance unto life."
¹⁹   Now those who were scattered because of the persecution that arose over Stephen traveled as far as Phoeni'cia
and Cyprus and Antioch, speaking the word to none except
²⁰Jews. But there were some of them, men of Cyprus and
Cyre'ne, who on coming to Antioch spoke to the Greeks ⁱ
²¹also, preaching the Lord Jesus. And the hand of the Lord

ⁱ Other ancient authorities read *Hellenists*   ʲ Or *were guests of*

was with them, and a great number that believed turned to
²²the Lord. News of this came to the ears of the church
²³in Jerusalem, and they sent Barnabas to Antioch. When
he came and saw the grace of God, he was glad; and he
exhorted them all to remain faithful to the Lord with
²⁴steadfast purpose; for he was a good man, full of the
Holy Spirit and of faith. And a large company was added
²⁵to the Lord. So Barnabas went to Tarsus to look for
²⁶Saul; and when he had found him, he brought him to
Antioch. For a whole year they met with ʲ the church, and
taught a large company of people; and in Antioch the
disciples were for the first time called Christians.
²⁷   Now in these days prophets came down from Jerusalem
²⁸to Antioch. And one of them named Ag'abus stood up and
foretold by the Spirit that there would be a great famine
over all the world; and this took place in the days of
²⁹Claudius. And the disciples determined, every one according to his ability, to send relief to the brethren who lived
³⁰in Judea; and they did so, sending it to the elders by the
hand of Barnabas and Saul.

Persecution Under Herod

12   About that time Herod the king laid violent hands
²   upon some who belonged to the church. He killed
³James the brother of John with the sword; and when he
saw that it pleased the Jews, he proceeded to arrest Peter
⁴also. This was during the days of Unleavened Bread. And
when he had seized him, he put him in prison, and
delivered him to four squads of soldiers to guard him,
intending after the Passover to bring him out to the
⁵people. So Peter was kept in prison; but earnest prayer
for him was made to God by the church.
⁶   The very night when Herod was about to bring him out,
Peter was sleeping between two soldiers, bound with two
chains, and sentries before the door were guarding the
⁷prison; and behold, an angel of the Lord appeared, and a
light shone in the cell; and he struck Peter on the side and
woke him, saying, "Get up quickly." And the chains fell
⁸off his hands. And the angel said to him, "Dress yourself
and put on your sandals." And he did so. And he said to
him, "Wrap your mantle around you and follow me."
⁹And he went out and followed him; he did not know that
what was done by the angel was real, but thought he was
¹⁰seeing a vision. When they had passed the first and the
second guard, they came to the iron gate leading into the
city. It opened to them of its own accord, and they went
out and passed on through one street; and immediately
¹¹the angel left him. And Peter came to himself, and said,
"Now I am sure that the Lord has sent his angel and
rescued me from the hand of Herod and from all that the
Jewish people were expecting."
¹²   When he realized this, he went to the house of Mary,
the mother of John whose other name was Mark, where

13 many were gathered together and were praying. And when he knocked at the door of the gateway, a maid named 14 Rhoda came to answer. Recognizing Peter's voice, in her joy she did not open the gate but ran in and told that 15 Peter was standing at the gate. They said to her, "You are mad." But she insisted that it was so. They said, "It is his 16 angel!" But Peter continued knocking; and when they 17 opened, they saw him and were amazed. But motioning to them with his hand to be silent, he described to them how the Lord had brought him out of the prison. And he said, "Tell this to James and to the brethren." Then he departed and went to another place.

18 Now when day came, there was no small stir among the 19 soldiers over what had become of Peter. And when Herod had sought for him and could not find him, he examined the sentries and ordered that they should be put to death. Then he went down from Judea to Caesare'a, and remained there.

20 Now Herod was angry with the people of Tyre and Sidon; and they came to him in a body, and having persuaded Blastus, the king's chamberlain, they asked for peace, because their country depended on the king's 21 country for food. On an appointed day Herod put on his royal robes, took his seat upon the throne, and made an 22 oration to them. And the people shouted, "The voice of a 23 god, and not of man!" Immediately an angel of the Lord smote him, because he did not give God the glory; and he was eaten by worms and died.

24 But the word of God grew and multiplied.

25 And Barnabas and Saul returned from k Jerusalem

when they had fulfilled their mission, bringing with them John whose other name was Mark.

FROM ANTIOCH TO ROME
Barnabas and Paul to the Gentiles

13 Now in the church at Antioch there were prophets and teachers, Barnabas, Simeon who was called Niger, Lucius of Cyre'ne, Man'a-en a member of the 2 court of Herod the tetrarch, and Saul. While they were worshiping the Lord and fasting, the Holy Spirit said, "Set apart for me Barnabas and Saul for the work to 3 which I have called them." Then after fasting and praying they laid their hands on them and sent them off.

4 So, being sent out by the Holy Spirit, they went down to Seleu'cia; and from there they sailed to Cyprus. 5 When they arrived at Sal'amis, they proclaimed the word of God in the synagogues of the Jews. And they had John 6 to assist them. When they had gone through the whole island as far as Paphos, they came upon a certain 7 magician, a Jewish false prophet, named Bar-Jesus. He was with the proconsul, Sergius Paulus, a man of intelligence, who summoned Barnabas and Saul and sought 8 to hear the word of God. But El'ymas the magician (for that is the meaning of his name) withstood them, seeking 9 to turn away the proconsul from the faith. But Saul, who is also called Paul, filled with the Holy Spirit, looked 10 intently at him and said, "You son of the devil, you enemy of all righteousness, full of all deceit and villainy, will you not stop making crooked the straight paths of the Lord? 11 And now, behold, the hand of the Lord is upon you, and you shall be blind and unable to see the sun for a time." Immediately mist and darkness fell upon him and he went 12 about seeking people to lead him by the hand. Then the proconsul believed, when he saw what had occurred, for he was astonished at the teaching of the Lord.

13 Now Paul and his company set sail from Paphos, and came to Perga in Pamphyl'ia. And John left them and 14 returned to Jerusalem; but they passed on from Perga and came to Antioch of Pisid'ia. And on the sabbath day 15 they went into the synagogue and sat down. After the reading of the law and the prophets, the rulers of the synagogue sent to them, saying, "Brethren, if you have 16 any word of exhortation for the people, say it." So Paul stood up, and motioning with his hand said:

17 "Men of Israel, and you that fear God, listen. The God of this people Israel chose our fathers and made the people great during their stay in the land of Egypt, and with 18 uplifted arm he led them out of it. And for about forty 19 years he bore with m them in the wilderness. And when he had destroyed seven nations in the land of Canaan, he gave them their land as an inheritance, for about four 20 hundred and fifty years. And after that he gave them 21 judges until Samuel the prophet. Then they asked for a king; and God gave them Saul the son of Kish, a man of 22 the tribe of Benjamin, for forty years. And when he had removed him, he raised up David to be their king; of whom he testified and said, 'I have found in David the son of Jesse a man after my heart, who will do all my 23 will.' Of this man's posterity God has brought to Israel

---

k Other ancient authorities read *to*   m Other ancient authorities read *cared for* (Dt 1.31)

24 a Savior, Jesus, as he promised. Before his coming John
had preached a baptism of repentance to all the people
25 of Israel. And as John was finishing his course, he said,
'What do you suppose that I am? I am not he. No, but
after me one is coming, the sandals of whose feet I am not
worthy to untie.'

26 "Brethren, sons of the family of Abraham, and those
among you that fear God, to us has been sent the message
27 of this salvation. For those who live in Jerusalem and their
rulers, because they did not recognize him nor understand
the utterances of the prophets which are read every
28 sabbath, fulfilled these by condemning him. Though they
could charge him with nothing deserving death, yet they
29 asked Pilate to have him killed. And when they had fulfilled all that was written of him, they took him down
30 from the tree, and laid him in a tomb. But God raised
31 him from the dead; and for many days he appeared to
those who came up with him from Galilee to Jerusalem,
32 who are now his witnesses to the people. And we bring you
the good news that what God promised to the fathers,
33 this he has fulfilled to us their children by raising Jesus;
as also it is written in the second psalm,
'Thou art my Son,
today I have begotten thee.'
34 And as for the fact that he raised him from the dead, no
more to return to corruption, he spoke in this way,
'I will give you the holy and sure blessings of David.'
35 Therefore he says also in another psalm,
'Thou wilt not let thy Holy One see corruption.'
36 For David, after he had served the counsel of God in his
own generation, fell asleep, and was laid with his fathers,
37 and saw corruption; but he whom God raised up saw no
38 corruption. Let it be known to you therefore, brethren,
that through this man forgiveness of sins is proclaimed
39 to you, and by him every one that believes is freed from
everything from which you could not be freed by the law
40 of Moses. Beware, therefore, lest there come upon you
what is said in the prophets:
41 'Behold, you scoffers, and wonder, and perish;
for I do a deed in your days,
a deed you will never believe, if one declares it to you.' "
42 As they went out, the people begged that these things
43 might be told them the next sabbath. And when the
meeting of the synagogue broke up, many Jews and devout
converts to Judaism followed Paul and Barnabas, who
spoke to them and urged them to continue in the grace of
God.
44 The next sabbath almost the whole city gathered to-
45 gether to hear the word of God. But when the Jews saw
the multitudes, they were filled with jealousy, and contra-
46 dicted what was spoken by Paul, and reviled him. And
Paul and Barnabas spoke out boldly, saying, "It was
necessary that the word of God should be spoken first to

you. Since you thrust it from you, and judge yourselves
unworthy of eternal life, behold, we turn to the Gentiles.
47 For so the Lord has commanded us, saying,
'I have set you to be a light for the Gentiles,
that you may bring salvation to the uttermost parts of the
earth.' "
48 And when the Gentiles heard this, they were glad and
glorified the word of God; and as many as were ordained
49 to eternal life believed. And the word of the Lord spread
50 throughout all the region. But the Jews incited the devout
women of high standing and the leading men of the city,
and stirred up persecution against Paul and Barnabas, and
51 drove them out of their district. But they shook off the
dust from their feet against them, and went to Ico'nium.
52 And the disciples were filled with joy and with the Holy
Spirit.

14 Now at Ico'nium they entered together into the
Jewish synagogue, and so spoke that a great company
2 believed, both of Jews and of Greeks. But the unbelieving
Jews stirred up the Gentiles and poisoned their minds
3 against the brethren. So they remained for a long time,
speaking boldly for the Lord, who bore witness to the
word of his grace, granting signs and wonders to be done
4 by their hands. But the people of the city were divided;
some sided with the Jews, and some with the apostles.
5 When an attempt was made by both Gentiles and Jews,
6 with their rulers, to molest them and to stone them, they

learned of it and fled to Lystra and Derbe, cities of
7 Lycao'nia, and to the surrounding country; and there they
preached the gospel.
8 Now at Lystra there was a man sitting, who could not
use his feet; he was a cripple from birth, who had never
9 walked. He listened to Paul speaking; and Paul, looking
intently at him and seeing that he had faith to be made
10 well, said in a loud voice, "Stand upright on your feet."
11 And he sprang up and walked. And when the crowds saw
what Paul had done, they lifted up their voices, saying in
Lycao'nian, "The gods have come down to us in the like-
12 ness of men!" Barnabas they called Zeus, and Paul,
13 because he was the chief speaker, they called Hermes. And
the priest of Zeus, whose temple was in front of the city,
brought oxen and garlands to the gates and wanted to
14 offer sacrifice with the people. But when the apostles

Barnabas and Paul heard of it, they tore their garments
15 and rushed out among the multitude, crying, "Men, why
are you doing this? We also are men, of like nature with
you, and bring you good news, that you should turn from
these vain things to a living God who made the heaven and
16 the earth and the sea and all that is in them. In past
generations he allowed all the nations to walk in their own
17 ways; yet he did not leave himself without witness, for he
did good and gave you from heaven rains and fruitful
seasons, satisfying your hearts with food and gladness."
18 With these words they scarcely restrained the people from
offering sacrifice to them.

19 But Jews came there from Antioch and Ico′nium; and
having persuaded the people, they stoned Paul and
dragged him out of the city, supposing that he was dead.
20 But when the disciples gathered about him, he rose up
and entered the city; and on the next day he went on with
21 Barnabas to Derbe. When they had preached the gospel
to that city and had made many disciples, they returned to
22 Lystra and to Ico′nium and to Antioch, strengthening the
souls of the disciples, exhorting them to continue in the
faith, and saying that through many tribulations we must
23 enter the kingdom of God. And when they had appointed
elders for them in every church, with prayer and fasting,
they committed them to the Lord in whom they believed.
24 Then they passed through Pisid′ia, and came to Pam-
25 phyl′ia. And when they had spoken the word in Perga,
26 they went down to Attali′a; and from there they sailed to
Antioch, where they had been commended to the grace of
27 God for the work which they had fulfilled. And when
they arrived, they gathered the church together and declared all that God had done with them, and how he had
28 opened a door of faith to the Gentiles. And they remained
no little time with the disciples.

Controversy About Gentile Freedom

15 But some men came down from Judea and were
teaching the brethren, "Unless you are circumcised
according to the custom of Moses, you cannot be saved."
2 And when Paul and Barnabas had no small dissension
and debate with them, Paul and Barnabas and some of
the others were appointed to go up to Jerusalem to the
3 apostles and the elders about this question. So, being sent
on their way by the church, they passed through both
Phoeni′cia and Samar′ia, reporting the conversion of the
Gentiles, and they gave great joy to all the brethren.
4 When they came to Jerusalem, they were welcomed by the
church and the apostles and the elders, and they declared
5 all that God had done with them. But some believers who
belonged to the party of the Pharisees rose up, and said,
"It is necessary to circumcise them, and to charge them
to keep the law of Moses."
6 The apostles and the elders were gathered together to

7 consider this matter. And after there had been much
debate, Peter rose and said to them, "Brethren, you know
that in the early days God made choice among you, that
by my mouth the Gentiles should hear the word of the
8 gospel and believe. And God who knows the heart bore
witness to them, giving them the Holy Spirit just as he
9 did to us; and he made no distinction between us and
10 them, but cleansed their hearts by faith. Now therefore
why do you make trial of God by putting a yoke upon
the neck of the disciples which neither our fathers nor
11 we have been able to bear? But we believe that we shall
be saved through the grace of the Lord Jesus, just as they
will."

12 And all the assembly kept silence; and they listened to
Barnabas and Paul as they related what signs and wonders
13 God had done through them among the Gentiles. After
they finished speaking, James replied, "Brethren, listen
14 to me. Simeon has related how God first visited the
Gentiles, to take out of them a people for his name.
15 And with this the words of the prophets agree, as it is
written,
16 'After this I will return,
and I will rebuild the dwelling of David, which has fallen;
I will rebuild its ruins,
and I will set it up,
17 that the rest of men may seek the Lord,
and all the Gentiles who are called by my name,
18 says the Lord, who has made these things known from of
old.'
19 Therefore my judgment is that we should not trouble those
20 of the Gentiles who turn to God, but should write to them
to abstain from the pollutions of idols and from unchastity
21 and from what is strangled [n] and from blood. For from
early generations Moses has had in every city those who
preach him, for he is read every sabbath in the synagogues."
22 Then it seemed good to the apostles and the elders, with
the whole church, to choose men from among them and
send them to Antioch with Paul and Barnabas. They sent
Judas called Barsabbas, and Silas, leading men among
23 the brethren, with the following letter: "The brethren,
both the apostles and the elders, to the brethren who are
of the Gentiles in Antioch and Syria and Cili′cia, greeting.
24 Since we have heard that some persons from us have
troubled you with words, unsettling your minds, although

[n] Other early authorities omit *and from what is strangled*

25 we gave them no instructions, it has seemed good to us, having come to one accord, to choose men and send them
26 to you with our beloved Barnabas and Paul, men who have
27 risked their lives for the sake of our Lord Jesus Christ. We have therefore sent Judas and Silas, who themselves
28 will tell you the same things by word of mouth. For it has seemed good to the Holy Spirit and to us to lay upon you
29 no greater burden than these necessary things: that you abstain from what has been sacrificed to idols and from blood and from what is strangled [n] and from unchasity. If you keep yourselves from these, you will do well. Farewell."

30 So when they were sent off, they went down to Antioch; and having gathered the congregation together, they
31 delivered the letter. And when they read it, they rejoiced at
32 the exhortation. And Judas and Silas, who were themselves prophets, exhorted the brethren with many words and
33 strengthened them. And after they had spent some time, they were sent off in peace by the brethren to those who
35 had sent them.[o] But Paul and Barnabas remained in Antioch, teaching and preaching the word of the Lord, with many others also.

36 And after some days Paul said to Barnabas, "Come, let us return and visit the brethren in every city where we proclaimed the word of the Lord, and see how they are."
37 And Barnabas wanted to take with them John called Mark.
38 But Paul thought best not to take with them one who had withdrawn from them in Pamphyl'ia, and had not gone
39 with them to the work. And there arose a sharp contention, so that they separated from each other; Barnabas took
40 Mark with him and sailed away to Cyprus, but Paul chose Silas and departed, being commended by the brethren to
41 the grace of the Lord. And he went through Syria and Cili'cia, strengthening the churches.

Mission of Paul to Europe

16 And he came also to Derbe and to Lystra. A disciple was there, named Timothy, the son of a Jewish woman who was a believer; but his father was a Greek.
2 He was well spoken of by the brethren at Lystra and

3 Ico'nium. Paul wanted Timothy to accompany him; and he took him and circumcised him because of the Jews that were in those places, for they all knew that his father
4 was a Greek. As they went on their way through the cities, they delivered to them for observance the decisions which had been reached by the apostles and elders who were at
5 Jerusalem. So the churches were strengthened in the faith, and they increased in numbers daily.

6 And they went through the region of Phry'gia and Galatia, having been forbidden by the Holy Spirit to
7 speak the word in Asia. And when they had come opposite My'sia, they attempted to go into Bithyn'ia, but the Spirit
8 of Jesus did not allow them; so, passing by My'sia, they
9 went down to Tro'as. And a vision appeared to Paul in the night: a man of Macedo'nia was standing beseeching him and saying, "Come over to Macedo'nia and help us."
10 And when he had seen the vision, immediately we sought to go on into Macedo'nia, concluding that God had called us to preach the gospel to them.

11 Setting sail therefore from Tro'as, we made a direct voyage to Sam'othrace, and the following day to Ne-ap'-
12 olis, and from there to Philippi, which is the leading city of the district [x] of Macedo'nia, and a Roman colony. We
13 remained in this city some days; and on the sabbath day we went outside the gate to the riverside, where we supposed there was a place of prayer; and we sat down and
14 spoke to the women who had come together. One who heard us was a woman named Lydia, from the city of Thyati'ra, a seller of purple goods, who was a worshiper of God. The Lord opened her heart to give heed to what
15 was said by Paul. And when she was baptized, with her household, she besought us, saying, "If you have judged me to be faithful to the Lord, come to my house and stay." And she prevailed upon us.

16 As we were going to the place of prayer, we were met by a slave girl who had a spirit of divination and brought
17 her owners much gain by soothsaying. She followed Paul and us, crying, "These men are servants of the Most High
18 God, who proclaim to you the way of salvation." And this she did for many days. But Paul was annoyed, and turned and said to the spirit, "I charge you in the name of Jesus Christ to come out of her." And it came out that very hour.

19 But when her owners saw that their hope of gain was gone, they seized Paul and Silas and dragged them into
20 the market place before the rulers; and when they had brought them to the magistrates they said, "These men are
21 Jews and they are disturbing our city. They advocate customs which it is not lawful for us Romans to accept or
22 practice." The crowd joined in attacking them; and the magistrates tore the garments off them and gave orders
23 to beat them with rods. And when they had inflicted many blows upon them, they threw them into prison, charging

[n] Other early authorities omit *and from what is strangled there* [x] The Greek text is uncertain [o] Other ancient authorities insert verse 34, *But it seemed good to Silas to remain*

24 the jailer to keep them safely. Having received this charge, he put them into the inner prison and fastened their feet in the stocks.

25 But about midnight Paul and Silas were praying and singing hymns to God, and the prisoners were listening to 26 them, and suddenly there was a great earthquake, so that the foundations of the prison were shaken; and immediately all the doors were opened and every one's fetters 27 were unfastened. When the jailer woke and saw that the

prison doors were open, he drew his sword and was about to kill himself, supposing that the prisoners had escaped. 28 But Paul cried with a loud voice, "Do not harm yourself, 29 for we are all here." And he called for lights and rushed in, and trembling with fear he fell down before Paul and 30 Silas, and brought them out and said, "Men, what must I 31 do to be saved?" And they said, "Believe in the Lord Jesus, and you will be saved, you and your household." 32 And they spoke the word of the Lord to him and to all 33 that were in his house. And he took them the same hour of the night, and washed their wounds, and he was bap- 34 tized at once, with all his family. Then he brought them up into his house, and set food before them; and he rejoiced with all his household that he had believed in God. 35 But when it was day, the magistrates sent the police, 36 saying, "Let those men go." And the jailer reported the words to Paul, saying, "The magistrates have sent to let you go; now therefore come out and go in peace." 37 But Paul said to them, "They have beaten us publicly, uncondemned, men who are Roman citizens, and have thrown us into prison; and do they now cast us out secretly? No! let them come themselves and take us out." 38 The police reported these words to the magistrates, and they were afraid when they heard that they were Roman

39 citizens; so they came and apologized to them. And they 40 took them out and asked them to leave the city. So they went out of the prison, and visited Lydia; and when they had seen the brethren, they exhorted them and departed.

17 Now when they had passed through Amphip'olis and Apollo'nia, they came to Thessaloni'ca, where 2 there was a synagogue of the Jews. And Paul went in, as

p Or sabbaths

was his custom, and for three weeks p he argued with them 3 from the scriptures, explaining and proving that it was necessary for the Christ to suffer and to rise from the dead, and saying, "This Jesus, whom I proclaim to you, is 4 the Christ." And some of them were persuaded, and joined Paul and Silas; as did a great many of the devout Greeks 5 and not a few of the leading women. But the Jews were jealous, and taking some wicked fellows of the rabble, they gathered a crowd, set the city in an uproar, and at- tacked the house of Jason, seeking to bring them out to 6 the people. And when they could not find them they dragged Jason and some of the brethren before the city authorities, crying, "These men who have turned the 7 world upside down have come here also, and Jason has received them; and they are all acting against the decrees 8 of Caesar, saying that there is another king, Jesus." And the people and the city authorities were disturbed when 9 they heard this. And when they had taken security from Jason and the rest, they let them go.

10 The brethren immediately sent Paul and Silas away by night to Beroe'a; and when they arrived they went into 11 the Jewish synagogue. Now these Jews were more noble than those in Thessaloni'ca, for they received the word with all eagerness, examining the scriptures daily to see 12 if these things were so. Many of them therefore believed, with not a few Greek women of high standing as well as 13 men. But when the Jews of Thessaloni'ca learned that the word of God was proclaimed by Paul at Beroe'a also, they came there too, stirring up and inciting the crowds. 14 Then the brethren immediately sent Paul off on his way 15 to the sea, but Silas and Timothy remained there. Those who conducted Paul brought him as far as Athens; and receiving a command for Silas and Timothy to come to

him as soon as possible, they departed.

16 Now while Paul was waiting for them at Athens, his spirit was provoked within him as he saw that the city was 17 full of idols. So he argued in the synagogue with the Jews and the devout persons, and in the market place every 18 day with those who chanced to be there. Some also of the Epicurean and Stoic philosophers met him. And some

said, "What would this babbler say?" Others said, "He
seems to be a preacher of foreign divinities"—because he
19 preached Jesus and the resurrection. And they took hold
of him and brought him to the Are-op′agus, saying, "May
we know what this new teaching is which you present?
20 For you bring some strange things to our ears; we wish to
21 know therefore what these things mean." Now all the
Athenians and the foreigners who lived there spent their
time in nothing except telling or hearing something new.
22 So Paul, standing in the middle of the Are-op′agus,
said: "Men of Athens, I perceive that in every way you
23 are very religious. For as I passed along, and observed
the objects of your worship, I found also an altar with
this inscription, 'To an unknown god.' What therefore you
24 worship as unknown, this I proclaim to you. The God
who made the world and everything in it, being Lord of
heaven and earth, does not live in shrines made by man,
25 nor is he served by human hands, as though he needed
anything, since he himself gives to all men life and breath

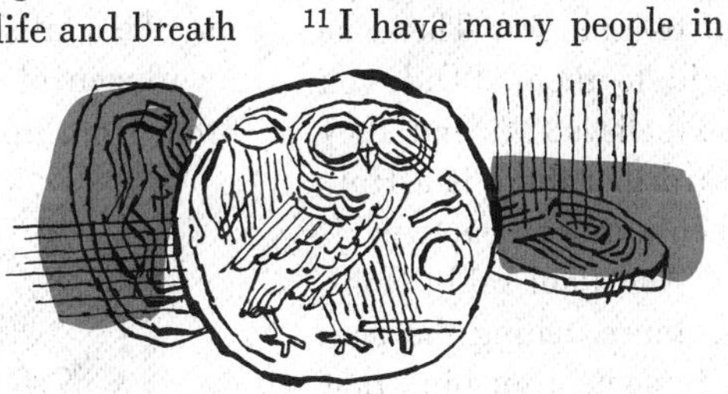

26 and everything. And he made from one every nation of
men to live on all the face of the earth, having determined allotted periods and the boundaries of their
27 habitation, that they should seek God, in the hope that
they might feel after him and find him. Yet he is not far
28 from each one of us, for
'In him we live and move and have our being';
as even some of your poets have said,
'For we are indeed his offspring.'
29 Being then God's offspring, we ought not to think that the
Deity is like gold, or silver, or stone, a representation by
30 the art and imagination of man. The times of ignorance
God overlooked, but now he commands all men every-
31 where to repent, because he has fixed a day on which he
will judge the world in righteousness by a man whom he
has appointed, and of this he has given assurance to all
men by raising him from the dead."
32 Now when they heard of the resurrection of the dead,
some mocked; but others said, "We will hear you again
33, 34 about this." So Paul went out from among them. But
some men joined him and believed, among them Dionys′-
ius the Are-op′agite and a woman named Dam′aris and
others with them.

18 After this he left Athens and went to Corinth. And
2 he found a Jew named Aquila, a native of Pontus,
lately come from Italy with his wife Priscilla, because
Claudius had commanded all the Jews to leave Rome.
3 And he went to see them; and because he was of the same
trade he stayed with them, and they worked, for by trade
4 they were tentmakers. And he argued in the synagogue
every sabbath, and persuaded Jews and Greeks.
5 When Silas and Timothy arrived from Macedo′nia,
Paul was occupied with preaching, testifying to the Jews
6 that the Christ was Jesus. And when they opposed and reviled him, he shook out his garments and said to them,
"Your blood be upon your heads! I am innocent. From
7 now on I will go to the Gentiles." And he left there and
went to the house of a man named Titius[q] Justus, a
worshiper of God; his house was next door to the syna-
8 gogue. Crispus, the ruler of the synagogue, believed in
the Lord, together with all his household; and many of
the Corinthians hearing Paul believed and were baptized.
9 And the Lord said to Paul one night in a vision, "Do
10 not be afraid, but speak and do not be silent; for I am
with you, and no man shall attack you to harm you; for
11 I have many people in this city." And he stayed a year
and six months, teaching the word of God among them.
12 But when Gallio was proconsul of Acha′ia, the Jews
made a united attack upon Paul and brought him before
13 the tribunal, saying, "This man is persuading men to
14 worship God contrary to the law." But when Paul was
about to open his mouth, Gallio said to the Jews, "If it
were a matter of wrongdoing or vicious crime, I should
15 have reason to bear with you, O Jews; but since it is a
matter of questions about words and names and your own
law, see to it yourselves; I refuse to be a judge of these
16, 17 things." And he drove them from the tribunal. And
they all seized Sos′thenes, the ruler of the synagogue, and
beat him in front of the tribunal. But Gallio paid no attention to this.
18 After this Paul stayed many days longer, and then took
leave of the brethren and sailed for Syria, and with him
Priscilla and Aquila. At Cen′chreae he cut his hair, for
19 he had a vow. And they came to Ephesus, and he left
them there; but he himself went into the synagogue and
20 argued with the Jews. When they asked him to stay for
21 a longer period, he declined; but on taking leave of them
he said, "I will return to you if God wills," and he set
sail from Ephesus.

Mission of Paul to Asia

22 When he had landed at Caesare′a, he went up and
greeted the church, and then went down to Antioch.

[q] Other early authorities read *Titus*

23 After spending some time there he departed and went from place to place through the region of Galatia and Phryg′ia, strengthening all the disciples.

24 Now a Jew named Apol′los, a native of Alexandria, came to Ephesus. He was an eloquent man, well versed 25 in the scriptures. He had been instructed in the way of the Lord; and being fervent in spirit, he spoke and taught accurately the things concerning Jesus, though he 26 knew only the baptism of John. He began to speak boldly in the synagogue; but when Priscilla and Aquila heard him, they took him and expounded to him the way of 27 God more accurately. And when he wished to cross to Acha′ia, the brethren encouraged him, and wrote to the disciples to receive him. When he arrived, he greatly 28 helped those who through grace had believed, for he powerfully confuted the Jews in public, showing by the scriptures that the Christ was Jesus.

19 While Apol′los was at Corinth, Paul passed through the upper country and came to Ephesus. There he 2 found some disciples. And he said to them, "Did you receive the Holy Spirit when you believed?" And they said, "No, we have never even heard that there is a Holy 3 Spirit." And he said, "Into what then were you baptized?" 4 They said, "Into John's baptism." And Paul said, "John baptized with the baptism of repentance, telling the people to believe in the one who was to come after him, that 5 is, Jesus." On hearing this, they were baptized in the 6 name of the Lord Jesus. And when Paul had laid his hands upon them, the Holy Spirit came on them; and they spoke 7 with tongues and prophesied. There were about twelve of them in all.

8 And he entered the synagogue and for three months spoke boldly, arguing and pleading about the kingdom of 9 God; but when some were stubborn and disbelieved, speaking evil of the Way before the congregation, he withdrew from them, taking the disciples with him, and 10 argued daily in the hall of Tyran′nus.ʳ This continued for two years, so that all the residents of Asia heard the word of the Lord, both Jews and Greeks.

11 And God did extraordinary miracles by the hands of 12 Paul, so that handkerchiefs or aprons were carried away from his body to the sick, and diseases left them and the 13 evil spirits came out of them. Then some of the itinerant Jewish exorcists undertook to pronounce the name of the Lord Jesus over those who had evil spirits, saying, "I 14 adjure you by the Jesus whom Paul preaches." Seven sons of a Jewish high priest named Sceva were doing this. 15 But the evil spirit answered them, "Jesus I know, and 16 Paul I know; but who are you?" And the man in whom the evil spirit was leaped on them, mastered all of them, and overpowered them, so that they fled out of that house 17 naked and wounded. And this became known to all residents of Ephesus, both Jews and Greeks; and fear fell

ʳ Other ancient authorities add *from the fifth hour to the tenth*

upon them all; and the name of the Lord Jesus was 18 extolled. Many also of those who were now believers 19 came, confessing and divulging their practices. And a number of those who practiced magic arts brought their books together and burned them in the sight of all; and they counted the value of them and found it came to fifty 20 thousand pieces of silver. So the word of the Lord grew and prevailed mightily.

21 Now after these events Paul resolved in the Spirit to pass through Macedo′nia and Acha′ia and go to Jerusalem, saying, "After I have been there, I must also see 22 Rome." And having sent into Macedo′nia two of his helpers, Timothy and Eras′tus, he himself stayed in Asia for a while.

23 About that time there arose no little stir concerning the 24 Way. For a man named Deme′trius, a silversmith, who made silver shrines of Ar′temis, brought no little business 25 to the craftsmen. These he gathered together, with the workmen of like occupation, and said, "Men, you know 26 that from this business we have our wealth. And you see

and hear that not only at Ephesus but almost throughout all Asia this Paul has persuaded and turned away a considerable company of people, saying that gods made with 27 hands are not gods. And there is danger not only that this trade of ours may come into disrepute but also that the temple of the great goddess Ar′temis may count for nothing, and that she may even be deposed from her magnificence, she whom all Asia and the world worship."

28 When they heard this they were enraged, and cried out, 29 "Great is Ar′temis of the Ephesians!" So the city was filled with the confusion; and they rushed together into the theater, dragging with them Ga′ius and Aristar′chus, 30 Macedo′nians who were Paul's companions in travel. Paul wished to go in among the crowd, but the disciples would 31 not let him; some of the A′si-archs also, who were friends of his, sent to him and begged him not to venture into 32 the theater. Now some cried one thing, some another; for the assembly was in confusion, and most of them did 33 not know why they had come together. Some of the crowd prompted Alexander, whom the Jews had put forward. And Alexander motioned with his hand, wishing to make 34 a defense to the people. But when they recognized that he was a Jew, for about two hours they all with one voice

35 cried out, "Great is Ar'temis of the Ephesians!" And when the town clerk had quieted the crowd, he said, "Men of Ephesus, what man is there who does not know that the city of the Ephesians is temple keeper of the great Ar'temis, and of the sacred stone that fell from the 36 sky? s Seeing then that these things cannot be contra-37 dicted, you ought to be quiet and do nothing rash. For you have brought these men here who are neither sac-38 rilegious nor blasphemers of our goddess. If therefore Deme'trius and the craftsmen with him have a complaint against any one, the courts are open, and there are pro-consuls; let them bring charges against one another. 39 But if you seek anything further,t it shall be settled in the 40 regular assembly. For we are in danger of being charged with rioting today, there being no cause that we can give 41 to justify this commotion." And when he had said this, he dismissed the assembly.

Paul's Final Visit

20 After the uproar ceased, Paul sent for the disciples and having exhorted them took leave of them and 2 departed for Macedo'nia. When he had gone through these parts and had given them much encouragement, he came 3 to Greece. There he spent three months, and when a plot was made against him by the Jews as he was about to set sail for Syria, he determined to return through Macedo'-4 nia. Sop'ater of Beroe'a, the son of Pyrrhus, accompanied him; and of the Thessalo'nians, Aristar'chus and Secun'-dus; and Ga'ius of Derbe, and Timothy; and the Asians, 5 Tych'icus and Troph'imus. These went on and were wait-6 ing for us at Tro'as, but we sailed away from Philippi after the days of Unleavened Bread, and in five days we came to them at Tro'as, where we stayed for seven days.

Return to Jerusalem

7 On the first day of the week, when we were gathered together to break bread, Paul talked with them, intending to depart on the morrow; and he prolonged his speech 8 until midnight. There were many lights in the upper 9 chamber where we were gathered. And a young man named Eu'tychus was sitting in the window. He sank into a deep sleep as Paul talked still longer; and being overcome by sleep, he fell down from the third story and 10 was taken up dead. But Paul went down and bent over him, and embracing him said, "Do not be alarmed, for 11 his life is in him." And when Paul had gone up and had broken bread and eaten, he conversed with them a long 12 while, until daybreak, and so departed. And they took the lad away alive, and were not a little comforted.

13 But going ahead to the ship, we set sail for Assos, intending to take Paul aboard there; for so he had ar-14 ranged, intending himself to go by land. And when he met us at Assos, we took him on board and came to 15 Mityle'ne. And sailing from there we came the following

day opposite Chi'os; the next day we touched at Samos; 16 and u the day after that we came to Mile'tus. For Paul had decided to sail past Ephesus, so that he might not have to spend time in Asia; for he was hastening to be at Jerusalem, if possible, on the day of Pentecost.

17 And from Mile'tus he sent to Ephesus and called to 18 him the elders of the church. And when they came to him, he said to them:

"You yourselves know how I lived among you all the 19 time from the first day that I set foot in Asia, serving the Lord with all humility and with tears and with trials 20 which befell me through the plots of the Jews; how I did not shrink from declaring to you anything that was profitable, and teaching you in public and from house to 21 house, testifying both to Jews and to Greeks of repentance 22 to God and of faith in our Lord Jesus Christ. And now, behold, I am going to Jerusalem, bound in the Spirit, not 23 knowing what shall befall me there; except that the Holy Spirit testifies to me in every city that imprisonment and 24 afflictions await me. But I do not account my life of any value nor as precious to myself, if only I may accomplish my course and the ministry which I received from the Lord Jesus, to testify to the gospel of the grace of God. 25 And now, behold, I know that all you among whom I have gone preaching the kingdom will see my face 26 no more. Therefore I testify to you this day that I am 27 innocent of the blood of all of you, for I did not shrink 28 from declaring to you the whole counsel of God. Take heed to yourselves and to all the flock, in which the Holy Spirit has made you overseers, to care for the church of 29 God v which he obtained with the blood of his own Son.w I know that after my departure fierce wolves will come in 30 among you, not sparing the flock; and from among your own selves will arise men speaking perverse things, to 31 draw away the disciples after them. Therefore be alert, re-membering that for three years I did not cease night or 32 day to admonish every one with tears. And now I com-mend you to God and to the word of his grace, which is able to build you up and to give you the inheritance 33 among all those who are sanctified. I coveted no one's 34 silver or gold or apparel. You yourselves know that these 35 hands ministered to my necessities, and to those who were with me. In all things I have shown you that by so toil-ing one must help the weak, remembering the words of the Lord Jesus, how he said, 'It is more blessed to give than to receive.' "

36 And when he had spoken thus, he knelt down and 37 prayed with them all. And they all wept and embraced 38 Paul and kissed him, sorrowing most of all because of the word he had spoken, that they should see his face no more. And they brought him to the ship.

21 And when we had parted from them and set sail, we came by a straight course to Cos, and the next

---

s The meaning of the Greek is uncertain   t Other ancient authorities read *about other matters*
u Other ancient authorities add *after remaining at Trogyllium*   v Other ancient authorities read *of the Lord*
w Greek *with the blood of his Own* or *with his own blood*

2 day to Rhodes, and from there to Pat′ara.ˣ And having found a ship crossing to Phoeni′cia, we went aboard, and

3 set sail. When we had come in sight of Cyprus, leaving it on the left we sailed to Syria, and landed at Tyre; for

4 there the ship was to unload its cargo. And having sought out the disciples, we stayed there for seven days. Through

5 the Spirit they told Paul not to go on to Jerusalem. And when our days there were ended, we departed and went on our journey; and they all, with wives and children, brought us on our way till we were outside the city; and kneeling down on the beach we prayed and bade one

6 another farewell. Then we went on board the ship, and they returned home.

7 When we had finished the voyage from Tyre, we arrived at Ptolema′is; and we greeted the brethren and stayed

8 with them for one day. On the morrow we departed and came to Caesare′a; and we entered the house of Philip the evangelist, who was one of the seven, and stayed with

9 him. And he had four unmarried daughters, who

10 prophesied. While we were staying for some days, a

11 prophet named Ag′abus came down from Judea. And coming to us he took Paul's girdle and bound his own feet and hands, and said, "Thus says the Holy Spirit, 'So shall the Jews at Jerusalem bind the man who owns this girdle and deliver him into the hands of the Gentiles.' "

12 When we heard this, we and the people there begged him

13 not to go up to Jerusalem. Then Paul answered, "What are you doing, weeping and breaking my heart? For I am ready not only to be imprisoned but even to die at

14 Jerusalem for the name of the Lord Jesus." And when he would not be persuaded, we ceased and said, "The will of the Lord be done."

15 After these days we made ready and went up to Jeru-

16 salem. And some of the disciples from Caesare′a went with us, bringing us to the house of Mnason of Cyprus, an

early disciple, with whom we should lodge.

17 When we had come to Jerusalem, the brethren received

18 us gladly. On the following day Paul went in with us to

19 James; and all the elders were present. After greeting them, he related one by one the things that God had

20 done among the Gentiles through his ministry. And when they heard it, they glorified God. And they said to him, "You see, brother, how many thousands there are among the Jews of those who have believed; they are all zealous

21 for the law, and they have been told about you that you teach all the Jews who are among the Gentiles to forsake Moses, telling them not to circumcise their children or

22 observe the customs. What then is to be done? They will

23 certainly hear that you have come. Do therefore what we

24 tell you. We have four men who are under a vow; take these men and purify yourself along with them and pay their expenses, so that they may shave their heads. Thus all will know that there is nothing in what they have been told about you but that you yourself live in observance of

25 the law. But as for the Gentiles who have believed, we have sent a letter with our judgment that they should abstain from what has been sacrificed to idols and from blood and from what is strangled ʸ and from unchastity."

26 Then Paul took the men, and the next day he purified himself with them and went into the temple, to give notice when the days of purification would be fulfilled and the offering presented for every one of them.

Paul the Prisoner

27 When the seven days were almost completed, the Jews from Asia, who had seen him in the temple, stirred up all

28 the crowd, and laid hands on him, crying out, "Men of Israel, help! This is the man who is teaching men everywhere against the people and the law and this place; moreover he also brought Greeks into the temple, and he has

29 defiled this holy place." For they had previously seen Troph′imus the Ephesian with him in the city, and they supposed that Paul had brought him into the temple.

30 Then all the city was aroused, and the people ran together; they seized Paul and dragged him out of the temple, and

31 at once the gates were shut. And as they were trying to kill him, word came to the tribune of the cohort that all

32 Jerusalem was in confusion. He at once took soldiers and centurions, and ran down to them; and when they saw the tribune and the soldiers, they stopped beating Paul.

33 Then the tribune came up and arrested him, and ordered him to be bound with two chains. He inquired who he was

34 and what he had done. Some in the crowd shouted one thing, some another; and as he could not learn the facts because of the uproar, he ordered him to be brought into

35 the barracks. And when he came to the steps, he was actually carried by the soldiers because of the violence of

36 the crowd; for the mob of the people followed, crying, "Away with him!"

37 As Paul was about to be brought into the barracks, he said to the tribune, "May I say something to you?" And

38 he said, "Do you know Greek? Are you not the Egyptian, then, who recently stirred up a revolt and led the four thousand men of the Assassins out into the wilderness?"

39 Paul replied, "I am a Jew, from Tarsus in Cili′cia, a citizen of no mean city; I beg you, let me speak to the

40 people." And when he had given him leave, Paul, standing

ˣ Other ancient authorities add *and Myra*   ʸ Other early authorities omit *and from what is strangled* on the steps, motioned with his hand to the people; and when there was a great hush, he spoke to them in the Hebrew language, saying:

22 "Brethren and fathers, hear the defense which I now make before you."

2 And when they heard that he addressed them in the Hebrew language, they were the more quiet. And he said:

3 "I am a Jew, born at Tarsus in Cili'cia, but brought up in this city at the feet of Gama'li-el, educated according to the strict manner of the law of our fathers, being zealous 4 for God as you all are this day. I persecuted this Way to the death, binding and delivering to prison both men and 5 women, as the high priest and the whole council of elders bear me witness. From them I received letters to the brethren, and I journeyed to Damascus to take those also who were there and bring them in bonds to Jerusalem to be punished.

6 "As I made my journey and drew near to Damascus, about noon a great light from heaven suddenly shone 7 about me. And I fell to the ground and heard a voice saying to me, 'Saul, Saul, why do you persecute me?' 8 And I answered, 'Who are you, Lord?' And he said to me, 'I am Jesus of Nazareth whom you are persecuting.' 9 Now those who were with me saw the light but did not 10 hear the voice of the one who was speaking to me. And I said, 'What shall I do, Lord?' And the Lord said to me, 'Rise, and go into Damascus, and there you will be told 11 all that is appointed for you to do.' And when I could not see because of the brightness of that light, I was led by the hand by those who were with me, and came into Damascus.

12 "And one Anani'as, a devout man according to the law, 13 well spoken of by all the Jews who lived there, came to me, and standing by me said to me, 'Brother Saul, receive your sight.' And in that very hour I received my sight and 14 saw him. And he said, 'The God of our fathers appointed you to know his will, to see the Just One and to hear a 15 voice from his mouth; for you will be a witness for him 16 to all men of what you have seen and heard. And now why do you wait? Rise and be baptized, and wash away your sins, calling on his name.'

17 "When I had returned to Jerusalem and was praying 18 in the temple, I fell into a trance and saw him saying to me, 'Make haste and get quickly out of Jerusalem, because 19 they will not accept your testimony about me.' And I said, 'Lord, they themselves know that in every synagogue I im- 20 prisoned and beat those who believed in thee. And when the blood of Stephen thy witness was shed, I also was standing by and approving, and keeping the garments of 21 those who killed him.' And he said to me, 'Depart; for I will send you far away to the Gentiles.'"

22 Up to this word they listened to him; then they lifted up their voices and said, "Away with such a fellow from 23 the earth! For he ought not to live." And as they cried out and waved their garments and threw dust into the 24 air, the tribune commanded him to be brought into the barracks, and ordered him to be examined by scourging, 25 to find out why they shouted thus against him. But when they had tied him up with the thongs, Paul said to the centurion who was standing by, "Is it lawful for you to scourge a man who is a Roman citizen, and uncon- 26 demned?" When the centurion heard that, he went to the tribune and said to him, "What are you about to do? For 27 this man is a Roman citizen." So the tribune came and said to him, "Tell me, are you a Roman citizen?" And

28 he said, "Yes." The tribune answered, "I bought this citizenship for a large sum." Paul said, "But I was born 29 a citizen." So those who were about to examine him withdrew from him instantly; and the tribune also was afraid, for he realized that Paul was a Roman citizen and that he had bound him.

30 But on the morrow, desiring to know the real reason why the Jews accused him, he unbound him, and commanded the chief priests and all the council to meet, and he brought Paul down and set him before them.

23 And Paul, looking intently at the council, said, "Brethren, I have lived before God in all good con- 2 science up to this day." And the high priests Anani'as commanded those who stood by him to strike him on the 3 mouth. Then Paul said to him, "God shall strike you, you whitewashed wall! Are you sitting to judge me according to the law, and yet contrary to the law you order me to be 4 struck?" Those who stood by said, "Would you revile 5 God's high priest?" And Paul said, "I did not know, brethren, that he was the high priest; for it is written, 'You shall not speak evil of a ruler of your people.'"

6 But when Paul perceived that one part were Sad'ducees and the other Pharisees, he cried out in the council, "Brethren, I am a Pharisee, a son of Pharisees; with respect to the hope and the resurrection of the dead I am 7 on trial." And when he had said this, a dissension arose between the Pharisees and the Sad'ducees; and the as- 8 sembly was divided. For the Sad'ducees say that there is no resurrection, nor angel, nor spirit; but the Pharisees 9 acknowledge them all. Then a great clamor arose; and

some of the scribes of the Pharisees' party stood up and contended, "We find nothing wrong in this man. What if
10 a spirit or an angel spoke to him?" And when the dissension became violent, the tribune, afraid that Paul would be torn in pieces by them, commanded the soldiers to go down and take him by force from among them and bring him into the barracks.

11 The following night the Lord stood by him and said, "Take courage, for as you have testified about me at

Jerusalem, so you must bear witness also at Rome."
12 When it was day, the Jews made a plot and bound themselves by an oath neither to eat nor drink till they
13 had killed Paul. There were more than forty who made
14 this conspiracy. And they went to the chief priests and elders, and said, "We have strictly bound ourselves by an
15 oath to taste no food till we have killed Paul. You therefore, along with the council, give notice now to the tribune to bring him down to you, as though you were going to determine his case more exactly. And we are ready to kill him before he comes near."
16 Now the son of Paul's sister heard of their ambush; so
17 he went and entered the barracks and told Paul. And Paul called one of the centurions and said, "Take this young man to the tribune; for he has something to tell him."
18 So he took him and brought him to the tribune and said, "Paul the prisoner called me and asked me to bring this young man to you, as he has something to say to you."
19 The tribune took him by the hand, and going aside asked him privately, "What is it that you have to tell me?"
20 And he said, "The Jews have agreed to ask you to bring

Paul down to the council tomorrow, as though they were
21 going to inquire somewhat more closely about him. But do not yield to them; for more than forty of their men lie in ambush for him, having bound themselves by an oath neither to eat nor drink till they have killed him; and now they are ready, waiting for the promise from you."
22 So the tribune dismissed the young man, charging him, "Tell no one that you have informed me of this."
23 Then he called two of the centurions and said, "At the

third hour of the night get ready two hundred soldiers with seventy horsemen and two hundred spearmen to go
24 as far as Caesare'a. Also provide mounts for Paul to ride,
25 and bring him safely to Felix the governor." And he wrote a letter to this effect:
26 "Claudius Lys'ias to his Excellency the governor Felix,
27 greeting. This man was seized by the Jews, and was about to be killed by them, when I came upon them with the soldiers and rescued him, having learned that he was a
28 Roman citizen. And desiring to know the charge on which
29 they accused him, I brought him down to their council. I found that he was accused about questions of their law, but charged with nothing deserving death or imprison-
30 ment. And when it was disclosed to me that there would be a plot against the man, I sent him to you at once, ordering his accusers also to state before you what they have against him."
31 So the soldiers, according to their instructions, took
32 Paul and brought him by night to Antip'atris. And on the morrow they returned to the barracks, leaving the
33 horsemen to go on with him. When they came to Caesare'a and delivered the letter to the governor, they presented
34 Paul also before him. On reading the letter, he asked to what province he belonged. When he learned that he was
35 from Cili'cia he said, "I will hear you when your accusers arrive." And he commanded him to be guarded in Herod's praetorium.

Paul at Caesarea
24 And after five days the high priest Anani'as came down with some elders and a spokesman, one Tertul'lus. They laid before the governor their case against
2 Paul; and when he was called, Tertul'lus began to accuse him, saying:
"Since through you we enjoy much peace, and since by your provision, most excellent Felix, reforms are intro-
3 duced on behalf of this nation, in every way and every-
4 where we accept this with all gratitude. But, to detain you no further, I beg you in your kindness to hear us
5 briefly. For we have found this man a pestilent fellow, an agitator among all the Jews throughout the world, and a
6 ringleader of the sect of the Nazarenes. He even tried to
8 profane the temple, but we seized him.z By examining him yourself you will be able to learn from him about everything of which we accuse him."
9 The Jews also joined in the charge, affirming that all this was so.
10 And when the governor had motioned to him to speak, Paul replied:
"Realizing that for many years you have been judge
11 over this nation, I cheerfully make my defense. As you may ascertain, it is not more than twelve days since I went
12 up to worship at Jerusalem; and they did not find me

z Other ancient authorities add *and we would have judged him according to our law.* 7 But the chief captain Lysias came *and with great violence took him out of our hands,* 8 commanding his accusers to come before you.

disputing with any one or stirring up a crowd, either in
13 the temple or in the synagogues, or in the city. Neither can they prove to you what they now bring up against me.
14 But this I admit to you, that according to the Way, which they call a sect, I worship the God of our fathers, believing everything laid down by the law or written in the prophets,
15 having a hope in God which these themselves accept, that there will be a resurrection of both the just and the unjust.
16 So I always take pains to have a clear conscience toward
17 God and toward men. Now after some years I came to
18 bring to my nation alms and offerings. As I was doing this, they found me purified in the temple, without any
19 crowd or tumult. But some Jews from Asia—they ought to be here before you and to make an accusation, if they
20 have anything against me. Or else let these men themselves say what wrongdoing they found when I stood before the
21 council, except this one thing which I cried out while standing among them, 'With respect to the resurrection of the dead I am on trial before you this day.' "
22 But Felix, having a rather accurate knowledge of the Way, put them off, saying, "When Lys'ias the tribune
23 comes down, I will decide your case." Then he gave orders to the centurion that he should be kept in custody but should have some liberty, and that none of his friends should be prevented from attending to his needs.
24 After some days Felix came with his wife Drusil'la, who was a Jewess; and he sent for Paul and heard him
25 speak upon faith in Christ Jesus. And as he argued about justice and self-control and future judgment, Felix was alarmed and said, "Go away for the present; when I have
26 an opportunity I will summon you." At the same time he hoped that money would be given him by Paul. So he
27 sent for him often and conversed with him. But when two years had elapsed, Felix was succeeded by Porcius Festus; and desiring to do the Jews a favor, Felix left Paul in prison.

25 Now when Festus had come into his province, after three days he went up to Jerusalem from Caesare'a.
2 And the chief priests and the principal men of the Jews
3 informed him against Paul; and they urged him, asking as a favor to have the man sent to Jerusalem, planning an
4 ambush to kill him on the way. Festus replied that Paul was being kept at Caesare'a, and that he himself intended
5 to go there shortly. "So," said he, "let the men of authority among you go down with me, and if there is anything wrong about the man, let them accuse him."
6 When he had stayed among them not more than eight or ten days, he went down to Caesare'a; and the next day he took his seat on the tribunal and ordered Paul to be
7 brought. And when he had come, the Jews who had gone down from Jerusalem stood about him, bringing against him many serious charges which they could not prove.
8 Paul said in his defense, "Neither against the law of the

Jews, against the temple, nor against Caesar have I of-
9 fended at all." But Festus, wishing to do the Jews a favor, said to Paul, "Do you wish to go up to Jerusalem, and
10 there be tried on these charges before me?" But Paul said, "I am standing before Caesar's tribunal, where I ought to be tried; to the Jews I have done no wrong, as you know
11 very well. If then I am a wrongdoer, and have committed anything for which I deserve to die, I do not seek to escape death; but if there is nothing in their charges against me,
12 no one can give me up to them. I appeal to Caesar." Then

Festus, when he had conferred with his council, answered, "You have appealed to Caesar; to Caesar you shall go."
13 Now when some days had passed, Agrippa the king and
14 Berni'ce arrived at Caesare'a to welcome Festus. And as they stayed there many days, Festus laid Paul's case before the king, saying, "There is a man left prisoner by
15 Felix; and when I was at Jerusalem, the chief priests and the elders of the Jews gave information about him, asking
16 for sentence against him. I answered them that it was not the custom of the Romans to give up any one before the accused met the accusers face to face, and had opportunity to make his defense concerning the charge laid against
17 him. When therefore they came together here, I made no delay, but on the next day took my seat on the tribunal
18 and ordered the man to be brought in. When the accusers stood up, they brought no charge in his case of such evils
19 as I supposed; but they had certain points of dispute with him about their own superstition and about one Jesus, who
20 was dead, but whom Paul asserted to be alive. Being at a loss how to investigate these questions, I asked whether he wished to go to Jerusalem and be tried there regarding

21 them. But when Paul had appealed to be kept in custody for the decision of the emperor, I commanded him to be
22 held until I could send him to Caesar." And Agrippa said to Festus, "I should like to hear the man myself." "To-morrow," said he, "you shall hear him."
23 So on the morrow Agrippa and Berni'ce came with great pomp, and they entered the audience hall with the military tribunes and the prominent men of the city. Then

24 by command of Festus Paul was brought in. And Festus said, "King Agrippa and all who are present with us, you see this man about whom the whole Jewish people petitioned me, both at Jerusalem and here, shouting that 25 he ought not to live any longer. But I found that he had done nothing deserving death; and as he himself appealed 26 to the emperor, I decided to send him. But I have nothing definite to write to my lord about him. Therefore I have brought him before you, and, especially before you, King Agrippa, that, after we have examined him, I may have 27 something to write. For it seems to me unreasonable, in sending a prisoner, not to indicate the charges against him."

26 Agrippa said to Paul, "You have permission to speak for yourself." Then Paul stretched out his hand and made his defense:

2 "I think myself fortunate that it is before you, King Agrippa, I am to make my defense today against all the 3 accusations of the Jews, because you are especially familiar with all customs and controversies of the Jews; therefore I beg you to listen to me patiently.

4 "My manner of life from my youth, spent from the beginning among my own nation and at Jerusalem, is

on the way a light from heaven, brighter than the sun, shining round me and those who journeyed with me. 14 And when we had all fallen to the ground, I heard a voice saying to me in the Hebrew language, 'Saul, Saul, why do you persecute me? It hurts you to kick against the goads.' 15 And I said, 'Who are you, Lord?' And the Lord said, 'I 16 am Jesus whom you are persecuting. But rise and stand upon your feet; for I have appeared to you for this purpose, to appoint you to serve and bear witness to the things in which you have seen me and to those in which 17 I will appear to you, delivering you from the people and 18 from the Gentiles—to whom I send you to open their eyes, that they may turn from darkness to light and from the power of Satan to God, that they may receive forgiveness of sins and a place among those who are sanctified by faith in me.'

19 "Wherefore, O King Agrippa, I was not disobedient to 20 the heavenly vision, but declared first to those at Damascus, then at Jerusalem and throughout all the country of Judea, and also to the Gentiles, that they should repent and turn to God and perform deeds worthy of their 21 repentance. For this reason the Jews seized me in the 22 temple and tried to kill me. To this day I have had the

5 known by all the Jews. They have known for a long time, if they are willing to testify, that according to the strictest 6 party of our religion I have lived as a Pharisee. And now I stand here on trial for hope in the promise made by 7 God to our fathers, to which our twelve tribes hope to attain, as they earnestly worship night and day. And for 8 this hope I am accused by Jews, O king! Why is it thought incredible by any of you that God raises the dead? 9 "I myself was convinced that I ought to do many 10 things in opposing the name of Jesus of Nazareth. And I did so in Jerusalem; I not only shut up many of the saints in prison, by authority from the chief priests, but when they were put to death I cast my vote against them. 11 And I punished them often in all the synagogues and tried to make them blaspheme; and in raging fury against them, I persecuted them even to foreign cities. 12 "Thus I journeyed to Damascus with the authority and 13 commission of the chief priests. At midday, O king, I saw

help that comes from God, and so I stand here testifying both to small and great, saying nothing but what the 23 prophets and Moses said would come to pass: that the Christ must suffer, and that, by being the first to rise from the dead, he would proclaim light both to the people and to the Gentiles."

24 And as he thus made his defense, Festus said with a loud voice, "Paul, you are mad; your great learning is 25 turning you mad." But Paul said, "I am not mad, most 26 excellent Festus, but I am speaking the sober truth. For the king knows about these things, and to him I speak freely; for I am persuaded that none of these things has escaped 27 his notice, for this was not done in a corner. King Agrippa, do you believe the prophets? I know that you 28 believe." And Agrippa said to Paul, "In a short time you 29 think to make me a Christian!" And Paul said, "Whether short or long, I would to God that not only you but also all who hear me this day might become such as I am—

except for these chains."

30 Then the king rose, and the governor and Ber'ni'ce and
31 those who were sitting with them; and when they had
withdrawn, they said to one another, "This man is doing
32 nothing to deserve death or imprisonment." And Agrippa
said to Festus, "This man could have been set free if he
had not appealed to Caesar."

Voyage to Rome

27 And when it was decided that we should sail for
Italy, they delivered Paul and some other prisoners
2 to a centurion of the Augustan Cohort, named Julius. And
embarking in a ship of Adramyt'tium, which was about
to sail to the ports along the coast of Asia, we put to
sea, accompanied by Aristar'chus, a Macedo'nian from
3 Thessaloni'ca. The next day we put in at Sidon; and
Julius treated Paul kindly, and gave him leave to go to
4 his friends and be cared for. And putting to sea from
there we sailed under the lee of Cyprus, because the winds
5 were against us. And when we had sailed across the sea
which is off Cili'cia and Pamphyl'ia, we came to Myra in
6 Ly'cia. There the centurion found a ship of Alexandria
7 sailing for Italy, and put us on board. We sailed slowly
for a number of days, and arrived with difficulty off
Cni'dus, and as the wind did not allow us to go on, we
8 sailed under the lee of Crete off Salmo'ne. Coasting along
it with difficulty, we came to a place called Fair Havens,
near which was the city of Lase'a.

9 As much time had been lost, and the voyage was already
dangerous because the fast had already gone by, Paul
10 advised them, saying, "Sirs, I perceive that the voyage
will be with injury and much loss, not only of the cargo
11 and the ship, but also of our lives." But the centurion
paid more attention to the captain and to the owner of
12 the ship than to what Paul said. And because the harbor
was not suitable to winter in, the majority advised to put
to sea from there, on the chance that somehow they could
reach Phoenix, a harbor of Crete, looking northeast and
southeast,[a] and winter there.

13 And when the south wind blew gently, supposing that
they had obtained their purpose, they weighed anchor
14 and sailed along Crete, close inshore. But soon a tempestuous wind, called the northeaster, struck down from
15 the land; and when the ship was caught and could not
16 face the wind, we gave way to it and were driven. And
running under the lee of a small island called Cauda,[b] we
17 managed with difficulty to secure the boat; after hoisting
it up, they took measures[c] to undergird the ship; then,
fearing that they should run on the Syr'tis, they lowered
18 the gear, and so were driven. As we were violently storm-
tossed, they began next day to throw the cargo overboard;
19 and the third day they cast out with their own hands the
20 tackle of the ship. And when neither sun nor stars ap-

peared for many a day, and no small tempest lay on us,
all hope of our being saved was at last abandoned.

21 As they had been long without food, Paul then came
forward among them and said, "Men, you should have
listened to me, and should not have set sail from Crete
22 and incurred this injury and loss. I now bid you take
heart; for there will be no loss of life among you, but
23 only of the ship. For this very night there stood by me an
angel of the God to whom I belong and whom I worship,
24 and he said, 'Do not be afraid, Paul; you must stand before Caesar; and lo, God has granted you all those who

25 sail with you.' So take heart, men, for I have faith in
26 God that it will be exactly as I have been told. But we
shall have to run on some island."

27 When the fourteenth night had come, as we were drifting across the sea of A'dria, about midnight the sailors
28 suspected that they were nearing land. So they sounded
and found twenty fathoms; a little farther on they sounded
29 again and found fifteen fathoms. And fearing that we
might run on the rocks, they let out four anchors from
30 the stern, and prayed for day to come. And as the sailors
were seeking to escape from the ship, and had lowered
the boat into the sea, under pretense of laying out anchors
31 from the bow, Paul said to the centurion and the soldiers,
"Unless these men stay in the ship, you cannot be saved."
32 Then the soldiers cut away the ropes of the boat, and
let it go.

33 As day was about to dawn, Paul urged them all to take
some food, saying, "Today is the fourteenth day that you
have continued in suspense and without food, having
34 taken nothing. Therefore I urge you to take some food;
it will give you strength, since not a hair is to perish from
35 the head of any of you." And when he had said this, he
took bread, and giving thanks to God in the presence of
36 all he broke it and began to eat. Then they all were en-
37 couraged and ate some food themselves. (We were in all
38 two hundred and seventy-six[d] persons in the ship.) And
when they had eaten enough, they lightened the ship,
throwing out the wheat into the sea.

39 Now when it was day, they did not recognize the land,
but they noticed a bay with a beach, on which they
40 planned if possible to bring the ship ashore. So they cast
off the anchors and left them in the sea, at the same time
loosening the ropes that tied the rudders; then hoisting
41 the foresail to the wind they made for the beach. But
striking a shoal[e] they ran the vessel aground; the bow

---

[a] Or *southwest and northwest*   [b] Other ancient authorities read *Clauda*   [c] Greek *helps*
[d] Other ancient authorities read *seventy-six* or *about seventy-six*   [e] Greek *place of two seas*

stuck and remained immovable, and the stern was broken
42 up by the surf. The soldiers' plan was to kill the prisoners,
43 lest any should swim away and escape; but the centurion,
wishing to save Paul, kept them from carrying out their
purpose. He ordered those who could swim to throw
44 themselves overboard first and make for the land, and
the rest on planks or on pieces of the ship. And so it was
that all escaped to land.

28 After we had escaped, we then learned that the is-
2 land was called Malta. And the natives showed us
unusual kindness, for they kindled a fire and welcomed
3 us all, because it had begun to rain and was cold. Paul
had gathered a bundle of sticks and put them on the fire,
when a viper came out because of the heat and fastened
4 on his hand. When the natives saw the creature hanging
from his hand, they said to one another, "No doubt this
man is a murderer. Though he has escaped from the sea,
5 justice has not allowed him to live." He, however, shook
6 off the creature into the fire and suffered no harm. They
waited, expecting him to swell up or suddenly fall down
dead; but when they had waited a long time and saw no
misfortune come to him, they changed their minds and
said that he was a god.
7 Now in the neighborhood of that place were lands
belonging to the chief man of the island, named Publius,
who received us and entertained us hospitably for three
8 days. It happened that the father of Publius lay sick with
fever and dysentery; and Paul visited him and prayed,
9 and putting his hands on him healed him. And when this
had taken place, the rest of the people on the island who
10 had diseases also came and were cured. They presented
many gifts to us;[f] and when we sailed, they put on board
whatever we needed.
11 After three months we set sail in a ship which had
wintered in the island, a ship of Alexandria, with the
12 Twin Brothers as figurehead. Putting in at Syracuse, we
13 stayed there for three days. And from there we made a
circuit and arrived at Rhe'gium; and after one day a
south wind sprang up, and on the second day we came
14 to Pute'oli. There we found brethren, and were invited
to stay with them for seven days. And so we came to
15 Rome. And the brethren there, when they heard of us,
came as far as the Forum of Ap'pius and Three Taverns
to meet us. On seeing them Paul thanked God and took
16 courage. And when we came into Rome, Paul was allowed
to stay by himself, with the soldier that guarded him.

Paul at Rome

17 After three days he called together the local leaders of
the Jews; and when they had gathered, he said to them,
"Brethren, though I had done nothing against the people
or the customs of our fathers, yet I was delivered prisoner
18 from Jerusalem into the hands of the Romans. When
they had examined me, they wished to set me at liberty,
because there was no reason for the death penalty in my
19 case. But when the Jews objected, I was compelled to
appeal to Caesar—though I had no charge to bring against
20 my nation. For this reason therefore I have asked to see
you and speak with you, since it is because of the hope of
21 Israel that I am bound with this chain." And they said
to him, "We have received no letters from Judea about
you, and none of the brethren coming here has reported
22 or spoken any evil about you. But we desire to hear from
you what your views are; for with regard to this sect we
know that everywhere it is spoken against."
23 When they had appointed a day for him, they came to
him at his lodging in great numbers. And he expounded
the matter to them from morning till evening, testifying to
the kingdom of God and trying to convince them about
Jesus both from the law of Moses and from the prophets.
24 And some were convinced by what he said, while others
25 disbelieved. So, as they disagreed among themselves, they
departed, after Paul had made one statement: "The Holy
Spirit was right in saying to your fathers through Isaiah
the prophet:
26 'Go to this people, and say,
You shall indeed hear but never understand,
and you shall indeed see but never perceive.
27 For this people's heart has grown dull,
and their ears are heavy of hearing,
and their eyes they have closed;
lest they should perceive with their eyes,
and hear with their ears,
and understand with their heart,
and turn for me to heal them.'
28 Let it be known to you then that this salvation of God
has been sent to the Gentiles; they will listen."[g]
30 And he lived there two whole years at his own expense,[h]
31 and welcomed all who came to him, preaching the kingdom of God and teaching about the Lord Jesus Christ
quite openly and unhindered.

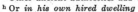

[f] Or *honored us with many honors*
[g] Other ancient authorities add verse 29, *And when he had said these words, the Jews departed, holding much dispute among themselves*
[h] Or *in his own hired dwelling*

INTRODUCTION TO

ROMANS

This book is a long letter from the apostle Paul to the Christians of the church in Rome. The story of Paul is told in the Bible book, The Acts of the Apostles. Paul wrote his Letter to the Romans about A.D. 56. He wrote from Corinth, where he had helped start a church (Acts 18.1-18). Paul was planning to take a trip to visit the Christians in Rome, so he wrote this letter ahead to explain the Christian faith as he believed it and preached it.

In this letter Paul opposed idol worship and other wrongdoing and insisted that God was displeased by such behavior. Paul's teachings about this are much like those of the Old Testament prophets. Paul then went on to explain that all men, both Jews and Gentiles, are sinful and cannot save themselves without God's help. Then he presented Jesus Christ as the Savior who is eager to save all men, saying, "While we were yet sinners Christ died for us" (Romans 5.8).

The last four chapters of the letter explain that a man's faith in Jesus Christ involves intense personal loyalty to God and his purposes. This faith-loyalty to God in Christ makes evil behavior unthinkable for a true Christian. Their new life and love for God in Christ helps Christians behave with goodness and love toward one another.

THE LETTER OF PAUL TO THE

ROMANS

INTRODUCTION

1 Paul, a servant[a] of Jesus Christ, called to be an
2 apostle, set apart for the gospel of God which he promised beforehand through his prophets in the holy
3 scriptures, the gospel concerning his Son, who was de-
4 scended from David according to the flesh and designated Son of God in power according to the Spirit of holiness by his resurrection from the dead, Jesus Christ our Lord,
5 through whom we have received grace and apostleship to bring about the obedience of faith for the sake of his name
6 among all the nations, including yourselves who are called to belong to Jesus Christ;
7 To all God's beloved in Rome, who are called to be saints:

Grace to you and peace from God our Father and the Lord Jesus Christ.

8 First, I thank my God through Jesus Christ for all of you, because your faith is proclaimed in all the world.
9 For God is my witness, whom I serve with my spirit in the gospel of his Son, that without ceasing I mention you
10 always in my prayers, asking that somehow by God's
11 will I may now at last succeed in coming to you. For I long to see you, that I may impart to you some spiritual
12 gift to strengthen you, that is, that we may be mutually

encouraged by each other's faith, both yours and mine.
13 I want you to know, brethren, that I have often intended to come to you (but thus far have been prevented), in order that I may reap some harvest among you as well as
14 among the rest of the Gentiles. I am under obligation both to Greeks and to barbarians, both to the wise and
15 to the foolish: so I am eager to preach the gospel to you also who are in Rome.
16 For I am not ashamed of the gospel: it is the power of God for salvation to every one who has faith, to the
17 Jew first and also to the Greek. For in it the righteousness of God is revealed through faith for faith; as it is written, "He who through faith is righteous shall live."[b]

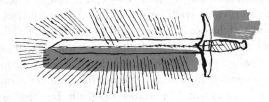

THE WORLD'S NEED OF CHRIST
18 For the wrath of God is revealed from heaven against all ungodliness and wickedness of men who by their
19 wickedness suppress the truth. For what can be known about God is plain to them, because God has shown it to
20 them. Ever since the creation of the world his invisible

nature, namely, his eternal power and deity, has been clearly perceived in the things that have been made. So 21 they are without excuse; for although they knew God they did not honor him as God or give thanks to him, but they became futile in their thinking and their senseless minds 22 were darkened. Claiming to be wise, they became fools, 23 and exchanged the glory of the immortal God for images resembling mortal man or birds or animals or reptiles.

24 Therefore God gave them up in the lusts of their hearts to impurity, to the dishonoring of their bodies among 25 themselves, because they exchanged the truth about God for a lie and worshiped and served the creature rather than the Creator, who is blessed for ever! Amen.

26 For this reason God gave them up to dishonorable passions. Their women exchanged natural relations for 27 unnatural, and the men likewise gave up natural relations with women and were consumed with passion for one another, men committing shameless acts with men and receiving in their own persons the due penalty for their error.

28 And since they did not see fit to acknowledge God, God gave them up to a base mind and to improper con- 29 duct. They were filled with all manner of wickedness, evil, covetousness, malice. Full of envy, murder, strife, deceit, 30 malignity, they are gossips, slanderers, haters of God, insolent, haughty, boastful, inventors of evil, disobedient 31, 32 to parents, foolish, faithless, heartless, ruthless. Though they know God's decree that those who do such things deserve to die, they not only do them but approve those who practice them.

2 Therefore you have no excuse, O man, whoever you are, when you judge another; for in passing judgment upon him you condemn yourself, because you, the judge, 2 are doing the very same things. We know that the judg- ment of God rightly falls upon those who do such things. 3 Do you suppose, O man, that when you judge those who do such things and yet do them yourself, you will escape 4 the judgment of God? Or do you presume upon the riches of his kindness and forbearance and patience? Do you not know that God's kindness is meant to lead you to 5 repentance? But by your hard and impenitent heart you are storing up wrath for yourself on the day of wrath when 6 God's righteous judgment will be revealed. For he will 7 render to every man according to his works: to those who by patience in well-doing seek for glory and honor and 8 immortality, he will give eternal life; but for those who are factious and do not obey the truth, but obey wicked- 9 ness, there will be wrath and fury. There will be tribula- tion and distress for every human being who does evil, 10 the Jew first and also the Greek, but glory and honor and peace for every one who does good, the Jew first and also 11 the Greek. For God shows no partiality.

12 All who have sinned without the law will also perish

without the law, and all who have sinned under the law 13 will be judged by the law. For it is not the hearers of the law who are righteous before God, but the doers of the 14 law who will be justified. When Gentiles who have not the law do by nature what the law requires, they are a law to 15 themselves, even though they do not have the law. They show that what the law requires is written on their hearts, while their conscience also bears witness and their con- 16 flicting thoughts accuse or perhaps excuse them on that day when, according to my gospel, God judges the secrets of men by Christ Jesus.

17 But if you call yourself a Jew and rely upon the law 18 and boast of your relation to God and know his will and approve what is excellent, because you are instructed 19 in the law, and if you are sure that you are a guide to 20 the blind, a light to those who are in darkness, a correc- tor of the foolish, a teacher of children, having in the 21 law the embodiment of knowledge and truth—you then who teach others, will you not teach yourself? While you

22 preach against stealing, do you steal? You who say that one must not commit adultery, do you commit adultery? 23 You who abhor idols, do you rob temples? You who boast in the law, do you dishonor God by breaking the 24 law? For, as it is written, "The name of God is blas- phemed among the Gentiles because of you."

25 Circumcision indeed is of value if you obey the law; but if you break the law, your circumcision becomes un- 26 circumcision. So, if a man who is uncircumcised keeps the precepts of the law, will not his uncircumcision be re- 27 garded as circumcision? Then those who are physically uncircumcised but keep the law will condemn you who have the written code and circumcision but break the law. 28 For he is not a real Jew who is one outwardly, nor is true 29 circumcision something external and physical. He is a Jew who is one inwardly, and real circumcision is a

matter of the heart, spiritual and not literal. His praise is not from men but from God.

3 Then what advantage has the Jew? Or what is the value of circumcision? Much in every way. To begin
³ with, the Jews are entrusted with the oracles of God. What if some were unfaithful? Does their faithlessness nullify
⁴ the faithfulness of God? By no means! Let God be true though every man be false, as it is written,
"That thou mayest be justified in thy words,
and prevail when thou art judged."
⁵ But if our wickedness serves to show the justice of God, what shall we say? That God is unjust to inflict wrath on
⁶ us? (I speak in a human way.) By no means! For then
⁷ how could God judge the world? But if through my falsehood God's truthfulness abounds to his glory, why am
⁸ I still being condemned as a sinner? And why not do evil that good may come?—as some people slanderously charge us with saying. Their condemnation is just.
⁹ What then? Are we Jews any better off? ᶜ No, not at all; for I ᵈ have already charged that all men, both Jews
¹⁰ and Greeks, are under the power of sin, as it is written:
"None is righteous, no, not one;
¹¹ no one understands, no one seeks for God.
¹² All have turned aside, together they have gone wrong;
no one does good, not even one."
¹³ "Their throat is an open grave,
they use their tongues to deceive."
"The venom of asps is under their lips."
¹⁴ "Their mouth is full of curses and bitterness."
¹⁵ "Their feet are swift to shed blood,
¹⁶ in their paths are ruin and misery,
¹⁷ and the way of peace they do not know."
¹⁸ "There is no fear of God before their eyes."
¹⁹ Now we know that whatever the law says it speaks to those who are under the law, so that every mouth may be stopped, and the whole world may be held accountable to
²⁰ God. For no human being will be justified in his sight by works of the law, since through the law comes knowledge of sin.

JUSTIFIED BY FAITH
²¹ But now the righteousness of God has been manifested apart from law, although the law and the prophets bear
²² witness to it, the righteousness of God through faith in Jesus Christ for all who believe. For there is no distinc-
²³ tion; since all have sinned and fall short of the glory of
²⁴ God, they are justified by his grace as a gift, through the
²⁵ redemption which is in Christ Jesus, whom God put forward as an expiation by his blood, to be received by faith. This was to show God's righteousness, because in his
²⁶ divine forbearance he had passed over former sins; it was to prove at the present time that he himself is righteous and that he justifies him who has faith in Jesus.

²⁷ Then what becomes of our boasting? It is excluded. On what principle? On the principle of works? No, but on
²⁸ the principle of faith. For we hold that a man is justified
²⁹ by faith apart from works of law. Or is God the God of Jews only? Is he not the God of Gentiles also? Yes, of
³⁰ Gentiles also, since God is one; and he will justify the circumcised on the ground of their faith and the uncir-
³¹ cumcised through their faith. Do we then overthrow the law by this faith? By no means! On the contrary, we uphold the law.

4 What then shall we say about ᵉ Abraham, our fore-
² father according to the flesh? For if Abraham was justified by works, he has something to boast about, but
³ not before God. For what does the scripture say? "Abraham believed God, and it was reckoned to him as right-
⁴ eousness." Now to one who works, his wages are not
⁵ reckoned as a gift but as his due. And to one who does not work but trusts him who justifies the ungodly, his
⁶ faith is reckoned as righteousness. So also David pronounces a blessing upon the man to whom God reckons righteousness apart from works:
⁷ "Blessed are those whose iniquities are forgiven, and whose sins are covered;
⁸ blessed is the man against whom the Lord will not reckon his sin."
⁹ Is this blessing pronounced only upon the circumcised, or also upon the uncircumcised? We say that faith was
¹⁰ reckoned to Abraham as righteousness. How then was it reckoned to him? Was it before or after he had been circumcised? It was not after, but before he was cir-
¹¹ cumcised. He received circumcision as a sign or seal of the righteousness which he had by faith while he was still uncircumcised. The purpose was to make him the father of all who believe without being circumcised and who thus
¹² have righteousness reckoned to them, and likewise the father of the circumcised who are not merely circumcised but also follow the example of the faith which our father Abraham had before he was circumcised.
¹³ The promise to Abraham and his descendants, that they should inherit the world, did not come through the law
¹⁴ but through the righteousness of faith. If it is the adherents of the law who are to be the heirs, faith is null and
¹⁵ the promise is void. For the law brings wrath, but where there is no law there is no transgression.
¹⁶ That is why it depends on faith, in order that the promise may rest on grace and be guaranteed to all his descendants—not only to the adherents of the law but also to those who share the faith of Abraham, for he is
¹⁷ the father of us all, as it is written, "I have made you the father of many nations"—in the presence of the God in whom he believed, who gives life to the dead and calls
¹⁸ into existence the things that do not exist. In hope he believed against hope, that he should become the father

ᶜ Or *at any disadvantage?*   ᵈ Greek *we*   ᵉ Other ancient authorities read *was gained by*

of many nations; as he had been told, "So shall your
19 descendants be." He did not weaken in faith when he considered his own body, which was as good as dead because he was about a hundred years old, or when he
20 considered the barrenness of Sarah's womb. No distrust made him waver concerning the promise of God, but he
21 grew strong in his faith as he gave glory to God, fully convinced that God was able to do what he had promised.
22 That is why his faith was "reckoned to him as righteous-
23 ness." But the words, "it was reckoned to him," were
24 written not for his sake alone, but for ours also. It will be reckoned to us who believe in him that raised from the
25 dead Jesus our Lord, who was put to death for our trespasses and raised for our justification.

THE NEW LIFE

5 Therefore, since we are justified by faith, we f have peace with God through our Lord Jesus Christ.

2 Through him we have obtained access g to this grace in which we stand, and we h rejoice in our hope of sharing
3 the glory of God. More than that, we h rejoice in our sufferings, knowing that suffering produces endurance,
4 and endurance produces character, and character pro-
5 duces hope, and hope does not disappoint us, because God's love has been poured into our hearts through the Holy Spirit which has been given to us.
6 While we were still helpless, at the right time Christ died
7 for the ungodly. Why, one will hardly die for a righteous man—though perhaps for a good man one will dare even
8 to die. But God shows his love for us in that while we
9 were yet sinners Christ died for us. Since, therefore, we are now justified by his blood, much more shall we be
10 saved by him from the wrath of God. For if while we were enemies we were reconciled to God by the death of his Son, much more, now that we are reconciled, shall we
11 be saved by his life. Not only so, but we also rejoice in God through our Lord Jesus Christ, through whom we have now received our reconciliation.
12 Therefore as sin came into the world through one man and death through sin, and so death spread to all men
13 because all men sinned—sin indeed was in the world before the law was given, but sin is not counted where
14 there is no law. Yet death reigned from Adam to Moses, even over those whose sins were not like the transgression of Adam, who was a type of the one who was to come.
15 But the free gift is not like the trespass. For if many

died through one man's trespass, much more have the grace of God and the free gift in the grace of that one man
16 Jesus Christ abounded for many. And the free gift is not like the effect of that one man's sin. For the judgment following one trespass brought condemnation, but the free
17 gift following many trespasses brings justification. If, because of one man's trespass, death reigned through that one man, much more will those who receive the abundance of grace and the free gift of righteousness reign in life through the one man Jesus Christ.
18 Then as one man's trespass led to condemnation for all men, so one man's act of righteousness leads to acquittal
19 and life for all men. For as by one man's disobedience many were made sinners, so by one man's obedience many
20 will be made righteous. Law came in, to increase the trespass; but where sin increased, grace abounded all the
21 more, so that, as sin reigned in death, grace also might reign through righteousness to eternal life through Jesus Christ our Lord.

6 What shall we say then? Are we to continue in sin
2 that grace may abound? By no means! How can we
3 who died to sin still live in it? Do you not know that all of us who have been baptized into Christ Jesus were
4 baptized into his death? We were buried therefore with him by baptism into death, so that as Christ was raised from the dead by the glory of the Father, we too might walk in newness of life.
5 For if we have been united with him in a death like his, we shall certainly be united with him in a resurrec-
6 tion like his. We know that our old self was crucified with him so that the sinful body might be destroyed, and we
7 might no longer be enslaved to sin. For he who has died
8 is freed from sin. But if we have died with Christ, we
9 believe that we shall also live with him. For we know that Christ being raised from the dead will never die again;
10 death no longer has dominion over him. The death he died he died to sin, once for all, but the life he lives he
11 lives to God. So you also must consider yourselves dead to sin and alive to God in Christ Jesus.
12 Let not sin therefore reign in your mortal bodies, to
13 make you obey their passions. Do not yield your members to sin as instruments of wickedness, but yield yourselves to God as men who have been brought from death to life, and your members to God as instruments of righteousness.
14 For sin will have no dominion over you, since you are not under law but under grace.
15 What then? Are we to sin because we are not under
16 law but under grace? By no means! Do you not know that if you yield yourselves to any one as obedient slaves, you are slaves of the one whom you obey, either of sin, which leads to death, or of obedience, which leads to
17 righteousness? But thanks be to God, that you who were once slaves of sin have become obedient from the heart

---

f Other ancient authorities read *let us*   g Other ancient authorities add *by faith*   h Or *let us*

to the standard of teaching to which you were committed,
18 and, having been set free from sin, have become slaves of
19 righteousness. I am speaking in human terms, because of your natural limitations. For just as you once yielded your members to impurity and to greater and greater iniquity, so now yield your members to righteousness for sanctification.

20 When you were slaves of sin, you were free in regard
21 to righteousness. But then what return did you get from the things of which you are now ashamed? The end of
22 those things is death. But now that you have been set free from sin and have become slaves of God, the return you
23 get is sanctification and its end, eternal life. For the wages of sin is death, but the free gift of God is eternal life in Christ Jesus our Lord.

7 Do you not know, brethren—for I am speaking to those who know the law—that the law is binding on
2 a person only during his life? Thus a married woman is bound by law to her husband as long as he lives; but if her husband dies she is discharged from the law con-
3 cerning the husband. Accordingly, she will be called an adulteress if she lives with another man while her husband is alive. But if her husband dies she is free from that law, and if she marries another man she is not an adulteress.

4 Likewise, my brethren, you have died to the law through the body of Christ, so that you may belong to another, to him who has been raised from the dead in order that
5 we may bear fruit for God. While we were living in the flesh, our sinful passions, aroused by the law, were at
6 work in our members to bear fruit for death. But now we are discharged from the law, dead to that which held us captive, so that we serve not under the old written code but in the new life of the Spirit.

7 What then shall we say? That the law is sin? By no means! Yet, if it had not been for the law, I should not have known sin. I should not have known what it is to covet if the law had not said, "You shall not covet."
8 But sin, finding opportunity in the commandment, wrought in me all kinds of covetousness. Apart from the
9 law sin lies dead. I was once alive apart from the law, but when the commandment came, sin revived and I died;
10 the very commandment which promised life proved to be
11 death to me. For sin, finding opportunity in the command-

¹ Or *and as a sin offering*

12 ment, deceived me and by it killed me. So the law is holy, and the commandment is holy and just and good.

13 Did that which is good, then, bring death to me? By no means! It was sin, working death in me through what is good, in order that sin might be shown to be sin, and through the commandment might become sinful beyond
14 measure. We know that the law is spiritual; but I am
15 carnal, sold under sin. I do not understand my own actions. For I do not do what I want, but I do the very
16 thing I hate. Now if I do what I do not want, I agree that
17 the law is good. So then it is no longer I that do it, but
18 sin which dwells within me. For I know that nothing good dwells within me, that is, in my flesh. I can will what is
19 right, but I cannot do it. For I do not do the good I want,
20 but the evil I do not want is what I do. Now if I do what I do not want, it is no longer I that do it, but sin which dwells within me.

21 So I find it to be a law that when I want to do right,
22 evil lies close at hand. For I delight in the law of God, in
23 my inmost self, but I see in my members another law at war with the law of my mind and making me captive to
24 the law of sin which dwells in my members. Wretched man that I am! Who will deliver me from this body of
25 death? Thanks be to God through Jesus Christ our Lord! So then, I of myself serve the law of God with my mind, but with my flesh I serve the law of sin.

8 There is therefore now no condemnation for those
2 who are in Christ Jesus. For the law of the Spirit of life in Christ Jesus has set me free from the law of sin and
3 death. For God has done what the law, weakened by the flesh, could not do: sending his own Son in the likeness of sinful flesh and for sin,¹ he condemned sin in the flesh,
4 in order that the just requirement of the law might be fulfilled in us, who walk not according to the flesh but
5 according to the Spirit. For those who live according to the flesh set their minds on the things of the flesh, but

those who live according to the Spirit set their minds on
6 the things of the Spirit. To set the mind on the flesh is death, but to set the mind on the Spirit is life and peace.
7 For the mind that is set on the flesh is hostile to God; it
8 does not submit to God's law, indeed it cannot; and those who are in the flesh cannot please God.

9 But you are not in the flesh, you are in the Spirit, if in fact the Spirit of God dwells in you. Any one who does
10 not have the Spirit of Christ does not belong to him. But if Christ is in you, although your bodies are dead because of sin, your spirits are alive because of righteousness.

11 If the Spirit of him who raised Jesus from the dead dwells in you, he who raised Christ Jesus from the dead will give life to your mortal bodies also through his Spirit which dwells in you.

12 So then, brethren, we are debtors, not to the flesh, to
13 live according to the flesh—for if you live according to the flesh you will die, but if by the Spirit you put to death the
14 deeds of the body you will live. For all who are led by the
15 Spirit of God are sons of God. For you did not receive the spirit of slavery to fall back into fear, but you have received the spirit of sonship. When we cry, "Abba!
16 Father!" it is the Spirit himself bearing witness with our
17 spirit that we are children of God, and if children, then heirs, heirs of God and fellow heirs with Christ, provided we suffer with him in order that we may also be glorified with him.

18 I consider that the sufferings of this present time are not worth comparing with the glory that is to be revealed
19 to us. For the creation waits with eager longing for the
20 revealing of the sons of God; for the creation was subjected to futility, not of its own will but by the will of
21 him who subjected it in hope; because the creation itself will be set free from its bondage to decay and obtain the
22 glorious liberty of the children of God. We know that the whole creation has been groaning in travail together until
23 now; and not only the creation, but we ourselves, who have the first fruits of the Spirit, groan inwardly as we wait for adoption as sons, the redemption of our bodies.
24 For in this hope we were saved. Now hope that is seen
25 is not hope. For who hopes for what he sees? But if we hope for what we do not see, we wait for it with patience.

called he also justified; and those whom he justified he also glorified.

31 What then shall we say to this? If God is for us, who is
32 against us? He who did not spare his own Son but gave him up for us all, will he not also give us all things with
33 him? Who shall bring any charge against God's elect? It
34 is God who justifies; who is to condemn? Is it Christ Jesus, who died, yes, who was raised from the dead, who is at the right hand of God, who indeed intercedes for
35 us? [m] Who shall separate us from the love of Christ? Shall tribulation, or distress, or persecution, or famine,
36 or nakedness, or peril, or sword? As it is written,
"For thy sake we are being killed all the day long;
we are regarded as sheep to be slaughtered."
37 No, in all these things we are more than conquerors
38 through him who loved us. For I am sure that neither death, nor life, nor angels, nor principalities, nor things
39 present, nor things to come, nor powers, nor height, nor depth, nor anything else in all creation, will be able to separate us from the love of God in Christ Jesus our Lord.

JEW AND GENTILE IN GOD'S PURPOSE

9 I am speaking the truth in Christ, I am not lying; my conscience bears me witness in the Holy Spirit,
2 that I have great sorrow and unceasing anguish in my
3 heart. For I could wish that I myself were accursed and cut off from Christ for the sake of my brethren, my kins-
4 men by race. They are Israelites, and to them belong the sonship, the glory, the covenants, the giving of the law,
5 the worship, and the promises; to them belong the patriarchs, and of their race, according to the flesh, is the

26 Likewise the Spirit helps us in our weakness; for we do not know how to pray as we ought, but the Spirit himself
27 intercedes for us with sighs too deep for words. And he who searches the hearts of men knows what is the mind of the Spirit, because[j] the Spirit intercedes for the saints according to the will of God.
28 We know that in everything God works for good[k] with those who love him,[l] who are called according to his
29 purpose. For those whom he foreknew he also predestined to be conformed to the image of his Son, in order that he
30 might be the firstborn among many brethren. And those whom he predestined he also called; and those whom he

Christ. God who is over all be blessed for ever.[n] Amen.
6 But it is not as though the word of God had failed. For not all who are descended from Israel belong to
7 Israel, and not all are children of Abraham because they are his descendants; but "Through Isaac shall your de-
8 scendants be named." This means that it is not the children of the flesh who are the children of God, but the children
9 of the promise are reckoned as descendants. For this is what the promise said, "About this time I will return and
10 Sarah shall have a son." And not only so, but also when Rebecca had conceived children by one man, our fore-
11 father Isaac, though they were not yet born and had done

[j] Or *that*   [k] Other ancient authorities read *in everything he works for good*, or *everything works for good*   [l] Greek *God*
[m] Or *It is Christ Jesus . . . for us*   [n] Or *Christ, who is God over all, blessed for ever*

nothing either good or bad, in order that God's purpose of election might continue, not because of works but be-
12 cause of his call, she was told, "The elder will serve the
13 younger." As it is written, "Jacob I loved, but Esau I hated."

14 What shall we say then? Is there injustice on God's
15 part? By no means! For he says to Moses, "I will have mercy on whom I have mercy, and I will have compassion
16 on whom I have compassion." So it depends not upon
17 man's will or exertion, but upon God's mercy. For the scripture says to Pharaoh, "I have raised you up for

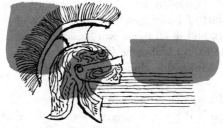

the very purpose of showing my power in you, so that my
18 name may be proclaimed in all the earth." So then he has mercy upon whomever he wills, and he hardens the heart of whomever he wills.

19 You will say to me then, "Why does he still find fault?
20 For who can resist his will?" But who are you, a man, to answer back to God? Will what is molded say to its
21 molder, "Why have you made me thus?" Has the potter no right over the clay, to make out of the same lump one
22 vessel for beauty and another for menial use? What if God, desiring to show his wrath and to make known his power, has endured with much patience the vessels of
23 wrath made for destruction, in order to make known the riches of his glory for the vessels of mercy, which he has
24 prepared beforehand for glory, even us whom he has called, not from the Jews only but also from the Gentiles?
25 As indeed he says in Hose'a,
"Those who were not my people
I will call 'my people,'
and her who was not beloved
I will call 'my beloved.' "
26 "And in the very place where it was said to them, 'You
are not my people,'
they will be called 'sons of the living God.' "
27 And Isaiah cries out concerning Israel: "Though the number of the sons of Israel be as the sand of the sea,
28 only a remnant of them will be saved; for the Lord will execute his sentence upon the earth with rigor and dis-
29 patch." And as Isaiah predicted,
"If the Lord of hosts had not left us children,
we would have fared like Sodom and been made like
Gomor'rah."
30 What shall we say, then? That Gentiles who did not pursue righteousness have attained it, that is, righteous-

31 ness through faith; but that Israel who pursued the right-eousness which is based on law did not succeed in fulfill-
32 ing that law. Why? Because they did not pursue it through faith, but as if it were based on works. They have stumbled
33 over the stumbling stone, as it is written,
"Behold, I am laying in Zion a stone that will make men
stumble,
a rock that will make them fall;
and he who believes in him will not be put to shame."

10 Brethren, my heart's desire and prayer to God for
2 them is that they may be saved. I bear them witness that they have a zeal for God, but it is not enlightened.
3 For, being ignorant of the righteousness that comes from God, and seeking to establish their own, they did not sub-
4 mit to God's righteousness. For Christ is the end of the law, that every one who has faith may be justified.
5 Moses writes that the man who practices the righteous-
6 ness which is based on the law shall live by it. But the righteousness based on faith says, Do not say in your heart, "Who will ascend into heaven?" (that is, to bring
7 Christ down) or "Who will descend into the abyss?" (that
8 is, to bring Christ up from the dead). But what does it say? The word is near you, on your lips and in your heart
9 (that is, the word of faith which we preach); because, if you confess with your lips that Jesus is Lord and believe in your heart that God raised him from the dead, you will
10 be saved. For man believes with his heart and so is justi-fied, and he confesses with his lips and so is saved.
11 The scripture says, "No one who believes in him will be
12 put to shame." For there is no distinction between Jew and Greek; the same Lord is Lord of all and bestows his
13 riches upon all who call upon him. For, "every one who calls upon the name of the Lord will be saved."

14 But how are men to call upon him in whom they have not believed? And how are they to believe in him of whom they have never heard? And how are they to hear with-
15 out a preacher? And how can men preach unless they are sent? As it is written, "How beautiful are the feet of those
16 who preach good news!" But they have not all obeyed the gospel; for Isaiah says, "Lord, who has believed what he
17 has heard from us?" So faith comes from what is heard, and what is heard comes by the preaching of Christ.
18 But I ask, have they not heard? Indeed they have; for
"Their voice has gone out to all the earth,
and their words to the ends of the world."
19 Again I ask, did Israel not understand? First Moses says,
"I will make you jealous of those who are not a nation;
with a foolish nation I will make you angry."
20 Then Isaiah is so bold as to say,
"I have been found by those who did not seek me;
I have shown myself to those who did not ask for me."
21 But of Israel he says, "All day long I have held out my
hands to a disobedient and contrary people."

11 I ask, then, has God rejected his people? By no means! I myself am an Israelite, a descendant of ² Abraham, a member of the tribe of Benjamin. God has not rejected his people whom he foreknew. Do you not know what the scripture says of Eli'jah, how he pleads with God ³ against Israel? "Lord, they have killed thy prophets, they have demolished thy altars, and I alone am left, and they

⁴ seek my life." But what is God's reply to him? "I have kept for myself seven thousand men who have not bowed ⁵ the knee to Ba'al." So too at the present time there is a ⁶ remnant, chosen by grace. But if it is by grace, it is no longer on the basis of works; otherwise grace would no longer be grace.

⁷ What then? Israel failed to obtain what it sought. The ⁸ elect obtained it, but the rest were hardened, as it is written,

"God gave them a spirit of stupor,
eyes that should not see and ears that should not hear,
down to this very day."
⁹ And David says,
"Let their table become a snare and a trap.
a pitfall and a retribution for them;
¹⁰ let their eyes be darkened so that they cannot see,
and bend their backs for ever."

¹¹ So I ask, have they stumbled so as to fall? By no means! But through their trespass salvation has come to ¹² the Gentiles, so as to make Israel jealous. Now if their trespass means riches for the world, and if their failure means riches for the Gentiles, how much more will their full inclusion mean!

¹³ Now I am speaking to you Gentiles. Inasmuch then as I am an apostle to the Gentiles, I magnify my ministry ¹⁴ in order to make my fellow Jews jealous, and thus save ¹⁵ some of them. For if their rejection means the reconciliation of the world, what will their acceptance mean but ¹⁶ life from the dead? If the dough offered as first fruits is holy, so is the whole lump; and if the root is holy, so are the branches.

¹⁷ But if some of the branches were broken off, and you, a wild olive shoot, were grafted in their place to share the ¹⁸ richness ᵒ of the olive tree, do not boast over the branches. If you do boast, remember it is not you that support ¹⁹ the root, but the root that supports you. You will say, "Branches were broken off so that I might be grafted in." ²⁰ That is true. They were broken off because of their unbelief, but you stand fast only through faith. So do not ²¹ become proud, but stand in awe. For if God did not spare

²² the natural branches, neither will he spare you. Note then the kindness and the severity of God: severity toward those who have fallen, but God's kindness to you, provided you continue in his kindness; otherwise you too will be ²³ cut off. And even the others, if they do not persist in their unbelief, will be grafted in, for God has the power to graft ²⁴ them in again. For if you have been cut from what is by nature a wild olive tree, and grafted, contrary to nature, into a cultivated olive tree, how much more will these natural branches be grafted back into their own olive tree.

²⁵ Lest you be wise in your own conceits, I want you to understand this mystery, brethren: a hardening has come upon part of Israel, until the full number of the Gentiles ²⁶ come in, and so all Israel will be saved; as it is written,
"The Deliverer will come from Zion,
he will banish ungodliness from Jacob";
²⁷ "and this will be my covenant with them
when I take away their sins."
²⁸ As regards the gospel they are enemies of God, for your sake; but as regards election they are beloved for the sake ²⁹ of their forefathers. For the gifts and the call of God are ³⁰ irrevocable. Just as you were once disobedient to God but now have received mercy because of their disobedience, ³¹ so they have now been disobedient in order that by the mercy shown to you they also may ᵖ receive mercy. ³² For God has consigned all men to disobedience, that he may have mercy upon all.

³³ O the depth of the riches and wisdom and knowledge of God! How unsearchable are his judgments and how inscrutable his ways!
³⁴ "For who has known the mind of the Lord,
or who has been his counselor?"
³⁵ "Or who has given a gift to him
that he might be repaid?"
³⁶ For from him and through him and to him are all things.
To him be glory for ever. Amen.

GOD'S WILL IS LOVE

12 I appeal to you therefore, brethren, by the mercies of God, to present your bodies as a living sacrifice, holy and acceptable to God, which is your spiritual ² worship. Do not be conformed to this world ᑫ but be transformed by the renewal of your mind, that you may prove what is the will of God, what is good and acceptable and perfect.ʳ

ᵒ Other ancient authorities read *rich root*   ᵖ Other ancient authorities add *now*   ᑫ Greek *age*
ʳ Or *what is the good and acceptable and perfect will of God*

³ For by the grace given to me I bid every one among you not to think of himself more highly than he ought to think, but to think with sober judgment, each according to the measure of faith which God has assigned him. ⁴ For as in one body we have many members, and all the ⁵ members do not have the same function, so we, though many, are one body in Christ, and individually members ⁶ one of another. Having gifts that differ according to the grace given to us, let us use them: if prophecy, in propor- ⁷ tion to our faith; if service, in our serving; he who ⁸ teaches, in his teaching; he who exhorts, in his exhorta- tion; he who contributes, in liberality; he who gives aid, with zeal; he who does acts of mercy, with cheerfulness.

⁹ Let love be genuine; hate what is evil, hold fast to ¹⁰ what is good; love one another with brotherly affection; ¹¹ outdo one another in showing honor. Never flag in zeal, ¹² be aglow with the Spirit, serve the Lord. Rejoice in your hope, be patient in tribulation, be constant in prayer. ¹³ Contribute to the needs of the saints, practice hospitality. ¹⁴ Bless those who persecute you; bless and do not curse

⁶ wrath but also for the sake of conscience. For the same reason you also pay taxes, for the authorities are ministers ⁷ of God, attending to this very thing. Pay all of them their dues, taxes to whom taxes are due, revenue to whom revenue is due, respect to whom respect is due, honor to whom honor is due.

⁸ Owe no one anything, except to love one another; for he ⁹ who loves his neighbor has fulfilled the law. The com- mandments, "You shall not commit adultery, You shall not kill, You shall not steal, You shall not covet," and any other commandment, are summed up in this sentence, ¹⁰ "You shall love your neighbor as yourself." Love does no wrong to a neighbor; therefore love is the fulfilling of the law.

¹¹ Besides this you know what hour it is, how it is full time now for you to wake from sleep. For salvation is ¹² nearer to us now than when we first believed; the night is far gone, the day is at hand. Let us then cast off the works ¹³ of darkness and put on the armor of light; let us conduct ourselves becomingly as in the day, not in reveling and

¹⁵ them. Rejoice with those who rejoice, weep with those ¹⁶ who weep. Live in harmony with one another; do not be haughty, but associate with the lowly; ^s never be conceited. ¹⁷ Repay no one evil for evil, but take thought for what ¹⁸ is noble in the sight of all. If possible, so far as it depends ¹⁹ upon you, live peaceably with all. Beloved, never avenge yourselves, but leave it ^t to the wrath of God; for it is written, "Vengeance is mine, I will repay, says the Lord." ²⁰ No, "if your enemy is hungry, feed him; if he is thirsty, give him drink; for by so doing you will heap burning ²¹ coals upon his head." Do not be overcome by evil, but overcome evil with good.

13 Let every person be subject to the governing authorities. For there is no authority except from God, and those that exist have been instituted by God. ² Therefore he who resists the authorities resists what God has appointed, and those who resist will incur judgment. ³ For rulers are not a terror to good conduct, but to bad. Would you have no fear of him who is in authority? Then ⁴ do what is good, and you will receive his approval, for he is God's servant for your good. But if you do wrong, be afraid, for he does not bear the sword in vain; he is the servant of God to execute his wrath on the wrongdoer. ⁵ Therefore one must be subject, not only to avoid God's

drunkenness, not in debauchery and licentiousness, not ¹⁴ in quarreling and jealousy. But put on the Lord Jesus Christ, and make no provision for the flesh to gratify its desires.

14 As for the man who is weak in faith, welcome him, ² but not for disputes over opinions. One believes he may eat anything, while the weak man eats only ³ vegetables. Let not him who eats despise him who ab- stains, and let not him who abstains pass judgment on ⁴ him who eats; for God has welcomed him. Who are you to pass judgment on the servant of another? It is before his own master that he stands or falls. And he will be upheld, for the Master is able to make him stand.

⁵ One man esteems one day as better than another, while another man esteems all days alike. Let every one be ⁶ fully convinced in his own mind. He who observes the day, observes it in honor of the Lord. He also who eats, eats in honor of the Lord, since he gives thanks to God; while he who abstains, abstains in honor of the Lord and ⁷ gives thanks to God. None of us lives to himself, and ⁸ none of us dies to himself. If we live, we live to the Lord, and if we die, we die to the Lord; so then, whether ⁹ we live or whether we die, we are the Lord's. For to this end Christ died and lived again, that he might be Lord

^s Or *give yourselves to humble tasks*   ^t Greek *give place*

both of the dead and of the living.

10 Why do you pass judgment on your brother? Or you, why do you despise your brother? For we shall all stand
11 before the judgment seat of God; for it is written,

"As I live, says the Lord, every knee shall bow to me,
and every tongue shall give praise[u] to God."

12 So each of us shall give account of himself to God.

13 Then let us no more pass judgment on one another, but rather decide never to put a stumbling block or hindrance
14 in the way of a brother. I know and am persuaded in the Lord Jesus that nothing is unclean in itself; but it is
15 unclean for any one who thinks it unclean. If your brother is being injured by what you eat, you are no longer walking in love. Do not let what you eat cause the ruin of one
16 for whom Christ died. So do not let your good be
17 spoken of as evil. For the kingdom of God is not food and drink but righteousness and peace and joy in the
18 Holy Spirit; he who thus serves Christ is acceptable
19 to God and approved by men. Let us then pursue what
20 makes for peace and for mutual upbuilding. Do not, for the sake of food, destroy the work of God. Everything is indeed clean, but it is wrong for any one to make others
21 fall by what he eats; it is right not to eat meat or drink wine or do anything that makes your brother stumble.[v]
22 The faith that you have, keep between yourself and God; happy is he who has no reason to judge himself for what
23 he approves. But he who has doubts is condemned, if he eats, because he does not act from faith; for whatever does not proceed from faith is sin.[w]

15 We who are strong ought to bear with the failings of the weak, and not to please ourselves; let each
2 of us please his neighbor for his good, to edify him.
3 For Christ did not please himself; but, as it is written, "The reproaches of those who reproached thee fell on me."
4 For whatever was written in former days was written for

our instruction, that by steadfastness and by the en-
5 couragement of the scriptures we might have hope. May the God of steadfastness and encouragement grant you to live in such harmony with one another, in accord with
6 Christ Jesus, that together you may with one voice glorify the God and Father of our Lord Jesus Christ.
7 Welcome one another, therefore, as Christ has wel-
8 comed you, for the glory of God. For I tell you that Christ

became a servant to the circumcised to show God's truthfulness, in order to confirm the promises given to the
9 patriarchs, and in order that the Gentiles might glorify God for his mercy. As it is written,

"Therefore I will praise thee among the Gentiles,
and sing to thy name";

10 and again it is said,

"Rejoice, O Gentiles, with his people";
11 and again,
"Praise the Lord, all Gentiles,
and let all the peoples praise him";
12 and further Isaiah says,
"The root of Jesse shall come,
he who rises to rule the Gentiles;
in him shall the Gentiles hope."
13 May the God of hope fill you with all joy and peace in believing, so that by the power of the Holy Spirit you may abound in hope.

PERSONAL AND CLOSING REMARKS

14 I myself am satisfied about you, my brethren, that you yourselves are full of goodness, filled with all knowledge,
15 and able to instruct one another. But on some points I have written to you very boldly by way of reminder,
16 because of the grace given me by God to be a minister of Christ Jesus to the Gentiles in the priestly service of the gospel of God, so that the offering of the Gentiles may be
17 acceptable, sanctified by the Holy Spirit. In Christ Jesus, then, I have reason to be proud of my work for God.
18 For I will not venture to speak of anything except what Christ has wrought through me to win obedience from the
19 Gentiles, by word and deed, by the power of signs and wonders, by the power of the Holy Spirit, so that from Jerusalem and as far round as Ilyr'icum I have fully
20 preached the gospel of Christ, thus making it my ambition to preach the gospel, not where Christ has already been named, lest I build on another man's foundation,
21 but as it is written,
"They shall see who have never been told of him,
and they shall understand who have never heard of him."
22 This is the reason why I have so often been hindered
23 from coming to you. But now, since I no longer have any room for work in these regions, and since I have longed
24 for many years to come to you, I hope to see you in passing as I go to Spain, and to be sped on my journey there by you, once I have enjoyed your company for a

u Or *confess*   v Other ancient authorities add *or be upset or be weakened*   w Other authorities, some ancient, insert here Ch. 16.25-27

784

25 little. At present, however, I am going to Jerusalem with
26 aid for the saints. For Macedo'nia and Acha'ia have been pleased to make some contribution for the poor among the
27 saints at Jerusalem; they were pleased to do it, and indeed they are in debt to them, for if the Gentiles have come to share in their spiritual blessings, they ought also to be of
28 service to them in material blessings. When therefore I have completed this, and have delivered to them what has been raised,[x] I shall go on by way of you to Spain;
29 and I know that when I come to you I shall come in the fulness of the blessing[y] of Christ.

30 I appeal to you, brethren, by our Lord Jesus Christ and by the love of the Spirit, to strive together with me in
31 your prayers to God on my behalf, that I may be delivered from the unbelievers in Judea, and that my service for
32 Jerusalem may be acceptable to the saints, so that by God's will I may come to you with joy and be refreshed in your
33 company. The God of peace be with you all. Amen.

16 I commend to you our sister Phoebe, a deaconess
2 of the church at Cen'chre-ae, that you may receive her in the Lord as befits the saints, and help her in whatever she may require from you, for she has been a helper of many and of myself as well.

3 Greet Prisca and Aquila, my fellow workers in Christ
4 Jesus, who risked their necks for my life, to whom not only I but also all the churches of the Gentiles give thanks;
5 greet also the church in their house. Greet my beloved Epae'netus, who was the first convert in Asia for Christ.
6, 7 Greet Mary, who has worked hard among you. Greet Andron'icus and Ju'nias, my kinsmen and my fellow prisoners; they are men of note among the apostles, and
8 they were in Christ before me. Greet Amplia'tus, my
9 beloved in the Lord. Greet Urba'nus, our fellow worker in
10 Christ, and my beloved Stachys. Greet Apel'les, who is approved in Christ. Greet those who belong to the family
11 of Aristob'ulus. Greet my kinsman Hero'dion. Greet those

in the Lord who belong to the family of Narcis'sus.
12 Greet those workers in the Lord, Tryphae'na and Trypho'sa. Greet the beloved Persis, who has worked hard in the
13 Lord. Greet Rufus, eminent in the Lord, also his mother
14 and mine. Greet Asyn'critus, Phlegon, Hermes, Pat'robas,
15 Hermas, and the brethren who are with them. Greet Philol'ogus, Julia, Nereus and his sister, and Olym'pas,
16 and all the saints who are with them. Greet one another with a holy kiss. All the churches of Christ greet you.

17 I appeal to you, brethren, to take note of those who create dissensions and difficulties, in opposition to the
18 doctrine which you have been taught; avoid them. For such persons do not serve our Lord Christ, but their own appetites,[z] and by fair and flattering words they deceive
19 the hearts of the simple-minded. For while your obedience is known to all, so that I rejoice over you, I would have you wise as to what is good and guileless as to what is
20 evil; then the God of peace will soon crush Satan under your feet. The grace of our Lord Jesus Christ be with you.[a]

21 Timothy, my fellow worker, greets you; so do Lucius and Jason and Sosip'ater, my kinsmen.
22 I Tertius, the writer of this letter, greet you in the Lord.
23 Ga'ius, who is host to me and to the whole church, greets you. Eras'tus, the city treasurer, and our brother Quartus, greet you.[b]

THE FINAL DOXOLOGY
25 Now to him who is able to strengthen you according to my gospel and the preaching of Jesus Christ, according to the revelation of the mystery which was kept secret for
26 long ages but is now disclosed and through the prophetic writings is made known to all nations, according to the command of the eternal God, to bring about the obedience
27 of faith—to the only wise God be glory for evermore through Jesus Christ! Amen.

---

[x] Greek *sealed to them this fruit*   [y] Other ancient authorities insert *of the gospel*   [z] Greek *their own belly* (Php 3.19)
[a] Other ancient authorities omit this sentence   [b] Other ancient authorities insert verse 24, *The grace of our Lord Jesus Christ be with you all. Amen.*

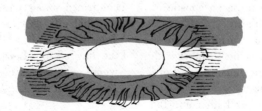

INTRODUCTION TO

THE FIRST LETTER OF PAUL TO THE
CORINTHIANS

About the year A.D. 55 Paul wrote at least four letters to the Christians of Corinth, Greece, where he had preached and founded a church. He wrote from Ephesus where he was preaching.

The two letters to the Corinthians that are in our Bible are probably made up of parts of the four letters that Paul wrote to Corinth. We do not have the original copies of them. When the letters wore out from repeated use and were being copied, they probably got rearranged and combined into the two letters First and Second Corinthians as we have them today in our Bible. This may have been the way the letters first appeared:

The earliest letter, or part of it, is found in 2 Corinthians 6.14 through 7.1.

The second letter is what we now call First Corinthians.

The third letter is now found in 2 Corinthians 10 through 13.

The fourth letter appears now in 2 Corinthians 1.1 through 6.13; 7.2 through 9.15.

In 1 Corinthians 1 through 4 Paul tried to help Christians overcome conflict and divisions among the members of the church. Some boasted because Paul or Apollos or Cephas (Peter) had baptized them. In this letter Paul says that our spiritual blessings all come from God himself and that the preacher or missionary is simply a helper for God.

The Corinthian Christians had questions and were confused about many things. In response to their questions Paul gave most careful guidance in Chapters 5 through 11.

First Corinthians 12 through 14 contains teachings about "spiritual gifts"—the ability of one Christian to teach, another to preach, another to heal the sick, and so on. In 1 Corinthians 13 Paul wrote what is really a poem about Christian love. He makes plain that it does not matter what great things we can do, for if we do not have true love in our hearts for people, our deeds count for nothing.

Chapter 15 shows Paul's triumphant faith that through the Resurrection of Jesus Christ true Christians have eternal life.

THE FIRST LETTER OF PAUL TO THE

CORINTHIANS

INTRODUCTION

1 Paul, called by the will of God to be an apostle of Christ Jesus, and our brother Sos'thenes,

2 To the church of God which is at Corinth, to those sanctified in Christ Jesus, called to be saints together with all those who in every place call on the name of our Lord Jesus Christ, both their Lord and ours:

3 Grace to you and peace from God our Father and the Lord Jesus Christ.

4 I give thanks to God [a] always for you because of the grace of God which was given you in Christ Jesus,

5 that in every way you were enriched in him with all speech

6 and all knowledge—even as the testimony to Christ was

7 confirmed among you—so that you are not lacking in any spiritual gift, as you wait for the revealing of our Lord

8 Jesus Christ; who will sustain you to the end, guiltless in

9 the day of our Lord Jesus Christ. God is faithful, by whom you were called into the fellowship of his Son, Jesus Christ our Lord.

THE PROBLEM OF FACTIONS

10 I appeal to you, brethren, by the name of our Lord Jesus Christ, that all of you agree and that there be no dissensions among you, but that you be united in the same

11 mind and the same judgment. For it has been reported

[a] Other ancient authorities read *my God*

to me by Chlo'e's people that there is quarreling among
12 you, my brethren. What I mean is that each one of you
says, "I belong to Paul," or "I belong to Apol'los," or
13 "I belong to Cephas," or "I belong to Christ." Is Christ
divided? Was Paul crucified for you? Or were you
14 baptized in the name of Paul? I am thankful[b] that I
15 baptized none of you except Crispus and Ga'ius; lest any
one should say that you were baptized in my name.
16 (I did baptize also the household of Steph'anas. Beyond
that, I do not know whether I baptized any one else.)
17 For Christ did not send me to baptize but to preach the
gospel, and not with eloquent wisdom, lest the cross of
Christ be emptied of its power.
18 For the word of the cross is folly to those who are
perishing, but to us who are being saved it is the power
19 of God. For it is written,
"I will destroy the wisdom of the wise,

4 in weakness and in much fear and trembling; and my
speech and my message were not in plausible words of
wisdom, but in demonstration of the Spirit and of power,
5 that your faith might not rest in the wisdom of men but
in the power of God.
6 Yet among the mature we do impart wisdom, although
it is not a wisdom of this age or of the rulers of this age,
7 who are doomed to pass away. But we impart a secret and
hidden wisdom of God, which God decreed before the
8 ages for our glorification. None of the rulers of this age
understood this; for if they had, they would not have
9 crucified the Lord of glory. But, as it is written,
"What no eye has seen, nor ear heard,
nor the heart of man conceived,
what God has prepared for those who love him,"
10 God has revealed to us through the Spirit. For the Spirit
11 searches everything, even the depths of God. For what

and the cleverness of the clever I will thwart."
20 Where is the wise man? Where is the scribe? Where is
the debater of this age? Has not God made foolish the
21 wisdom of the world? For since, in the wisdom of God,
the world did not know God through wisdom, it pleased
God through the folly of what we preach to save those
22 who believe. For Jews demand signs and Greeks seek
23 wisdom, but we preach Christ crucified, a stumbling
24 block to Jews and folly to Gentiles, but to those who are
called, both Jews and Greeks, Christ the power of God
25 and the wisdom of God. For the foolishness of God is
wiser than men, and the weakness of God is stronger than
men.
26 For consider your call, brethren; not many of you
were wise according to worldly standards, not many were
27 powerful, not many were of noble birth; but God chose
what is foolish in the world to shame the wise, God chose
28 what is weak in the world to shame the strong, God chose
what is low and despised in the world, even things that
29 are not, to bring to nothing things that are, so that no
30 human being might boast in the presence of God. He is
the source of your life in Christ Jesus, whom God made
our wisdom, our righteousness and sanctification and
31 redemption; therefore, as it is written, "Let him who
boasts, boast of the Lord."
2 When I came to you, brethren, I did not come proclaiming to you the testimony[c] of God in lofty words
2 or wisdom. For I decided to know nothing among you
3 except Jesus Christ and him crucified. And I was with you

person knows a man's thoughts except the spirit of the
man which is in him? So also no one comprehends the
12 thoughts of God except the Spirit of God. Now we have
received not the spirit of the world, but the Spirit which is
from God, that we might understand the gifts bestowed
13 on us by God. And we impart this in words not taught by
human wisdom but taught by the Spirit, interpreting
spiritual truths to those who possess the Spirit.[d]
14 The unspiritual[e] man does not receive the gifts of the
Spirit of God, for they are folly to him, and he is not
able to understand them because they are spiritually dis-
15 cerned. The spiritual man judges all things, but is him-
16 self to be judged by no one. "For who has known the
mind of the Lord so as to instruct him?" But we have the
mind of Christ.
3 But I, brethren, could not address you as spiritual
men, but as men of the flesh, as babes in Christ.
2 I fed you with milk, not solid food; for you were not
3 ready for it; and even yet you are not ready, for you are
still of the flesh. For while there is jealousy and strife
among you, are you not of the flesh, and behaving like
4 ordinary men? For when one says, "I belong to Paul,"
and another, "I belong to Apol'los," are you not merely
men?
5 What then is Apol'los? What is Paul? Servants through
6 whom you believed, as the Lord assigned to each. I
planted, Apol'los watered, but God gave the growth.
7 So neither he who plants nor he who waters is anything,
8 but only God who gives the growth. He who plants and he

who waters are equal, and each shall receive his wages
9 according to his labor. For we are God's fellow workers;
you are God's field, God's building.

10 According to the grace of God given to me, like a
skilled master builder I laid a foundation, and another
man is building upon it. Let each man take care how he
11 builds upon it. For no other foundation can any one lay
12 than that which is laid, which is Jesus Christ. Now if any
one builds on the foundation with gold, silver, precious
13 stones, wood, hay, straw—each man's work will become
manifest; for the Day will disclose it, because it will be
revealed with fire, and the fire will test what sort of work
14 each one has done. If the work which any man has built
on the foundation survives, he will receive a reward.
15 If any man's work is burned up, he will suffer loss, though
he himself will be saved, but only as through fire.

16 Do you not know that you are God's temple and that
17 God's Spirit dwells in you? If any one destroys God's
temple, God will destroy him. For God's temple is holy,
and that temple you are.

18 Let no one deceive himself. If any one among you
thinks that he is wise in this age, let him become a fool
19 that he may become wise. For the wisdom of this world is
folly with God. For it is written, "He catches the wise in
20 their craftiness," and again, "The Lord knows that the
21 thoughts of the wise are futile." So let no one boast of
22 men. For all things are yours, whether Paul or Apol'los
or Cephas or the world or life or death or the present or
23 the future, all are yours; and you are Christ's; and
Christ is God's.

4 This is how one should regard us, as servants of
2 Christ and stewards of the mysteries of God. Moreover
it is required of stewards that they be found trustworthy.
3 But with me it is a very small thing that I should be
judged by you or by any human court. I do not even
4 judge myself. I am not aware of anything against myself,
but I am not thereby acquitted. It is the Lord who judges
5 me. Therefore do not pronounce judgment before the time,
before the Lord comes, who will bring to light the things
now hidden in darkness and will disclose the purposes of
the heart. Then every man will receive his commendation
from God.

6 I have applied all this to myself and Apol'los for your
benefit, brethren, that you may learn by us not to go beyond what is written, that none of you may be puffed up
7 in favor of one against another. For who sees anything
different in you? What have you that you did not receive?
If then you received it, why do you boast as if it were not
a gift?

8 Already you are filled! Already you have become rich!
Without us you have become kings! And would that you
9 did reign, so that we might share the rule with you! For I
think that God has exhibited us apostles as last of all, like

men sentenced to death; because we have become a
10 spectacle to the world, to angels and to men. We are fools
for Christ's sake, but you are wise in Christ. We are
weak, but you are strong. You are held in honor, but we
11 in disrepute. To the present hour we hunger and thirst,
12 we are ill-clad and buffeted and homeless, and we labor,
working with our own hands. When reviled, we bless;
13 when persecuted, we endure; when slandered, we try to
conciliate; we have become, and are now, as the refuse
of the world, the offscouring of all things.

14 I do not write this to make you ashamed, but to
15 admonish you as my beloved children. For though you
have countless guides in Christ, you do not have many
fathers. For I became your father in Christ Jesus through
16, 17 the gospel. I urge you, then, be imitators of me. Therefore I sent g to you Timothy, my beloved and faithful child
in the Lord, to remind you of my ways in Christ, as I
18 teach them everywhere in every church. Some are arro-
19 gant, as though I were not coming to you. But I will come
to you soon, if the Lord wills, and I will find out not the
20 talk of these arrogant people but their power. For the
kingdom of God does not consist in talk but in power.
21 What do you wish? Shall I come to you with a rod, or
with love in a spirit of gentleness?

MORAL STANDARDS FOR CHRISTIANS

5 It is actually reported that there is immorality among
you, and of a kind that is not found even among
2 pagans; for a man is living with his father's wife. And you
are arrogant! Ought you not rather to mourn? Let him
who has done this be removed from among you.

3 For though absent in body I am present in spirit, and
4 as if present, I have already pronounced judgment in the
name of the Lord Jesus on the man who has done such a
thing. When you are assembled, and my spirit is present,
5 with the power of our Lord Jesus, you are to deliver this
man to Satan for the destruction of the flesh, that his spirit
may be saved in the day of the Lord Jesus.h

6 Your boasting is not good. Do you not know that a
7 little leaven leavens the whole lump? Cleanse out the old
leaven that you may be a new lump, as you really are
unleavened. For Christ, our paschal lamb, has been
8 sacrificed. Let us, therefore, celebrate the festival, not with

g Or *am sending*   h Other ancient authorities omit *Jesus* the old leaven, the leaven of malice and evil, but with the unleavened bread of sincerity and truth.

9 I wrote to you in my letter not to associate with im-
10 moral men; not at all meaning the immoral of this world, or the greedy and robbers, or idolaters, since then you
11 would need to go out of the world. But rather I wrote[1] to you not to associate with any one who bears the name of brother if he is guilty of immorality or greed, or is an idolater, reviler, drunkard, or robber—not even to eat
12 with such a one. For what have I to do with judging outsiders? Is it not those inside the church whom you are to
13 judge? God judges those outside. "Drive out the wicked person from among you."

6 When one of you has a grievance against a brother, does he dare go to law before the unrighteous instead
2 of the saints? Do you not know that the saints will judge the world? And if the world is to be judged by you, are
3 you incompetent to try trivial cases? Do you not know that we are to judge angels? How much more, matters
4 pertaining to this life! If then you have such cases, why do you lay them before those who are least esteemed by
5 the church? I say this to your shame. Can it be that there is no man among you wise enough to decide between
6 members of the brotherhood, but brother goes to law against brother, and that before unbelievers?
7 To have lawsuits at all with one another is defeat for you. Why not rather suffer wrong? Why not rather be
8 defrauded? But you yourselves wrong and defraud, and that even your own brethren.

9 Do you not know that the unrighteous will not inherit the kingdom of God? Do not be deceived; neither the immoral, nor idolaters, nor adulterers, no sexual perverts,
10 nor thieves, nor the greedy, nor drunkards, nor revilers,
11 nor robbers will inherit the kingdom of God. And such were some of you. But you were washed, you were sanctified, you were justified in the name of the Lord Jesus Christ and in the Spirit of our God.
12 "All things are lawful for me," but not all things are helpful. "All things are lawful for me," but I will not be
13 enslaved by anything. "Food is meant for the stomach and the stomach for food"—and God will destroy both one and the other. The body is not meant for immorality, but
14 for the Lord, and the Lord for the body. And God raised
15 the Lord and will also raise us up by his power. Do you not know that your bodies are members of Christ? Shall I therefore take the members of Christ and make them
16 members of a prostitute? Never! Do you not know that he who joins himself to a prostitute becomes one body with her? For, as it is written, "The two shall become
17 one flesh." But he who is united to the Lord becomes one
18 spirit with him. Shun immorality. Every other sin which a man commits is outside the body; but the immoral man
19 sins against his own body. Do you not know that your

body is a temple of the Holy Spirit within you, which you
20 have from God? You are not your own; you were bought with a price. So glorify God in your body.

7 Now concerning the matters about which you wrote.
2 It is well for a man to not touch a woman. But because of the temptation to immorality, each man should have
3 his own wife and each woman her own husband. The husband should give to his wife her conjugal rights, and
4 likewise the wife to her husband. For the wife does not rule over her own body, but the husband does; likewise the husband does not rule over his own body, but the
5 wife does. Do not refuse one another except perhaps by agreement for a season, that you may devote yourselves to prayer; but then come together again, lest Satan tempt
6 you through lack of self-control. I say this by way of
7 concession, not of command. I wish that all were as I myself am. But each has his own special gift from God, one of one kind and one of another.

8 To the unmarried and the widows I say that it is well
9 for them to remain single as I do. But if they cannot exercise self-control, they should marry. For it is better to marry than to be aflame with passion.
10 To the married I give charge, not I but the Lord, that
11 the wife should not separate from her husband (but if she does, let her remain single or else be reconciled to her husband)—and that the husband should not divorce his wife.
12 To the rest I say, not the Lord, that if any brother has a wife who is an unbeliever, and she consents to live
13 with him, he should not divorce her. If any woman has a husband who is an unbeliever, and he consents to live
14 with her, she should not divorce him. For the unbelieving husband is consecrated through his wife, and the unbelieving wife is consecrated through her husband. Otherwise, your children would be unclean, but as it is they are holy.
15 But if the unbelieving partner desires to separate, let it be so; in such a case the brother or sister is not bound.
16 For God has called us[1] to peace. Wife, how do you know whether you will save your husband? Husband, how do you know whether you will save your wife?
17 Only, let every one lead the life which the Lord has assigned to him, and in which God has called him. This
18 is my rule in all the churches. Was any one at the time of his call already circumcised? Let him not seek to remove the marks of circumcision. Was any one at the time of his call uncircumcised? Let him not seek circum-
19 cision. For neither circumcision counts for anything nor uncircumcision, but keeping the commandments of God.
20 Every one should remain in the state in which he was
21 called. Were you a slave when called? Never mind. But if you can gain your freedom, avail yourself of the oppor-
22 tunity.[x] For he who was called in the Lord as a slave is a

---

[1] Or now I write   [1] Other ancient authorities read you   [x] Or make use of your present condition instead

freedman of the Lord. Likewise he who was free when
23 called is a slave of Christ. You were bought with a price;
24 do not become slaves of men. So, brethren, in whatever
state each was called, there let him remain with God.

25   Now concerning the unmarried,[y] I have no command
of the Lord, but I give my opinion as one who by the
26 Lord's mercy is trustworthy. I think that in view of the
present [m] distress it is well for a person to remain as

27 he is. Are you bound to a wife? Do not seek to be free.
28 Are you free from a wife? Do not seek marriage. But if
you marry, you do not sin, and if a girl [z] marries she does
not sin. Yet those who marry will have worldly troubles,
29 and I would spare you that. I mean, brethren, the appointed time has grown very short; from now on, let those
30 who have wives live as though they had none, and those
who mourn as though they were not mourning, and those
who rejoice as though they were not rejoicing, and those
31 who buy as though they had no goods, and those who deal
with the world as though they had no dealings with it. For
the form of this world is passing away.
32   I want you to be free from anxieties. The unmarried
man is anxious about the affairs of the Lord, how to please
33 the Lord; but the married man is anxious about worldly
34 affairs, how to please his wife, and his interests are
divided. And the unmarried woman or girl [z] is anxious
about the affairs of the Lord, how to be holy in body and
spirit; but the married woman is anxious about worldly
35 affairs, how to please her husband. I say this for your
own benefit, not to lay any restraint upon you, but to
promote good order and to secure your undivided devotion to the Lord.
36   If any one thinks that he is not behaving properly
toward his betrothed,[z] if his passions are strong, and it
has to be, let him do as he wishes: let them marry—it is
37 no sin. But whoever is firmly established in his heart,
being under no necessity but having his desire under
control, and has determined this in his heart, to keep her
38 as his bethrothed,[z] he will do well. So that he who marries
his bethrothed [z] does well; and he who refrains from marriage will do better.
39   A wife is bound to her husband as long as he lives. If
the husband dies, she is free to be married to whom she
40 wishes, only in the Lord. But in my judgment she is
happier if she remains as she is. And I think that I have
the Spirit of God.

CHRISTIAN FREEDOM

8   Now concerning food offered to idols: we know that
"all of us possess knowledge." "Knowledge" puffs up,

2 but love builds up. If any one imagines that he knows
something, he does not yet know as he ought to know.
3 But if one loves God, one is known by him.
4   Hence, as to the eating of food offered to idols, we know
that "an idol has no real existence," and that "there is no
5 God but one." For although there may be so-called gods
in heaven or on earth—as indeed there are many "gods"
6 and many "lords"—yet for us there is one God, the
Father, from whom are all things and for whom we exist,
and one Lord, Jesus Christ, through whom are all things
and through whom we exist.
7   However, not all possess this knowledge. But some,
through being hitherto accustomed to idols, eat food as
really offered to an idol; and their conscience, being weak,
8 is defiled. Food will not commend us to God. We are no
worse off if we do not eat, and no better off if we do.
9 Only take care lest this liberty of yours somehow become
10 a stumbling block to the weak. For if any one sees you, a
man of knowledge, at table in an idol's temple, might he
not be encouraged, if his conscience is weak, to eat food
11 offered to idols? And so by your knowledge this weak
man is destroyed, the brother for whom Christ died.
12 Thus, sinning against your brethren and wounding their
conscience when it is weak, you sin against Christ.
13 Therefore, if food is a cause of my brother's falling, I will
never eat meat, lest I cause my brother to fall.

9   Am I not free? Am I not an apostle? Have I not
seen Jesus our Lord? Are not you my workmanship in
2 the Lord? If to others I am not an apostle, at least I am
to you; for you are the seal of my apostleship in the Lord.
3   This is my defense to those who would examine me.
4, 5 Do we not have the right to our food and drink? Do we
not have the right to be accompanied by a wife,[n] as the
other apostles and the brothers of the Lord and Cephas?
6 Or is it only Barnabas and I who have no right to refrain
7 from working for a living? Who serves as a soldier at his
own expense? Who plants a vineyard without eating any
of its fruit? Who tends a flock without getting some of
the milk?
8   Do I say this on human authority? Does not the law
9 say the same? For it is written in the law of Moses, "You
shall not muzzle an ox when it is treading out the grain."
10 Is it for oxen that God is concerned? Does he not speak
entirely for our sake? It was written for our sake, because
the plowman should plow in hope and the thresher thresh
11 in hope of a share in the crop. If we have sown spiritual
good among you, is it too much if we reap your material
12 benefits? If others share this rightful claim upon you, do
not we still more?
Nevertheless, we have not made use of this right, but
we endure anything rather than put an obstacle in the way
13 of the gospel of Christ. Do you not know that those who
are employed in the temple service get their food from

---

[y] Greek *virgins*   [m] Or *impending*   [z] Greek *virgin*   [n] Greek *a sister as wife*

the temple, and those who serve at the altar share in the
14 sacrificial offerings? In the same way, the Lord commanded that those who proclaim the gospel should get their living by the gospel.

15 But I have made no use of any of these rights, nor am I writing this to secure any such provision. For I would rather die than have any one deprive me of my ground
16 for boasting. For if I preach the gospel, that gives me no ground for boasting. For necessity is laid upon me. Woe
17 to me if I do not preach the gospel! For if I do this of my own will, I have a reward; but if not of my own will, I am
18 entrusted with a commission. What then is my reward? Just this: that in my preaching I may make the gospel free of charge, not making full use of my right in the gospel.

19 For though I am free from all men, I have made myself
20 a slave to all, that I might win the more. To the Jews I became as a Jew, in order to win Jews; to those under the law I became as one under the law—though not being myself under the law—that I might win those under the
21 law. To those outside the law I became as one outside the law—not being without law toward God but under the law
22 of Christ—that I might win those outside the law. To the weak I became weak, that I might win the weak. I have become all things to all men, that I might by all means
23 save some. I do it all for the sake of the gospel, that I may share in its blessings.

24 Do you not know that in a race all the runners compete, but only one receives the prize? So run that you may
25 obtain it. Every athlete exercises self-control in all things. They do it to receive a perishable wreath, but we an
26 imperishable. Well, I do not run aimlessly, I do not box
27 as one beating the air; but I pommel my body and subdue it, lest after preaching to others I myself should be disqualified.

10 I want you to know, brethren, that our fathers were all under the cloud, and all passed through the sea,
2 and all were baptized into Moses in the cloud and in the
3, 4 sea, and all ate the same supernatural o food and all drank

the same supernatural o drink. For they drank from the supernatural o Rock which followed them, and the Rock
5 was Christ. Nevertheless with most of them God was not pleased; for they were overthrown in the wilderness.

6 Now these things are warnings for us, not to desire
7 evil as they did. Do not be idolaters as some of them were; as it is written, "The people sat down to eat and
8 drink and rose up to dance." We must not indulge in immorality as some of them did, and twenty-three thousand
9 fell in a single day. We must not put the Lord p to the

test, as some of them did and were destroyed by serpents;
10 nor grumble, as some of them did and were destroyed by
11 the Destroyer. Now these things happened to them as a warning, but they were written down for our instruction,
12 upon whom the end of the ages has come. Therefore let any one who thinks that he stands take heed lest he fall.
13 No temptation has overtaken you that is not common to man. God is faithful, and he will not let you be tempted beyond your strength, but with the temptation will also provide the way of escape, that you may be able to endure it.

14, 15 Therefore, my beloved, shun the worship of idols. I speak as to sensible men; judge for yourselves what I say.
16 The cup of blessing which we bless, is it not a participation q in the blood of Christ? The bread which we break,
17 is it not a participation q in the body of Christ? Because there is one bread, we who are many are one body, for we
18 all partake of the one bread. Consider the people of Israel; a are not those who eat the sacrifices partners in the
19 altar? What do I imply then? That food offered to idols
20 is anything, or that an idol is anything? No, I imply that what pagans sacrifice they offer to demons and not to
21 God. I do not want you to be partners with demons. You cannot drink the cup of the Lord and the cup of demons.
22 You cannot partake of the table of the Lord and the table of demons. Shall we provoke the Lord to jealousy? Are we stronger than he?

23 "All things are lawful," but not all things are helpful. "All things are lawful," but not all things build up.
24 Let no one seek his own good, but the good of his
25 neighbor. Eat whatever is sold in the meat market with-
26 out raising any question on the ground of conscience. For
27 "the earth is the Lord's, and everything in it." If one of

o Greek *spiritual*   p Other ancient authorities read *Christ*   q Or *communion*   a Greek *Israel according to the flesh*

the unbelievers invites you to dinner and you are disposed to go, eat whatever is set before you without raising any

28 question on the ground of conscience. (But if some one says to you, "This has been offered in sacrifice," then out of consideration for the man who informed you, and

29 for conscience' sake—I mean his conscience, not yours—do not eat it.) For why should my liberty be determined

30 by another man's scruples? If I partake with thankfulness, why am I denounced because of that for which I give thanks?

31 So, whether you eat or drink, or whatever you do, do

32 all to the glory of God. Give no offense to Jews or to

33 Greeks or to the church of God, just as I try to please all men in everything I do, not seeking my own advantage,

11 but that of many, that they may be saved. Be imitators of me, as I am of Christ.

CHRISTIAN WORSHIP

2 I commend you because you remember me in everything and maintain the traditions even as I have delivered them

3 to you. But I want you to understand that the head of every man is Christ, the head of a woman is her husband,

4 and the head of Christ is God. Any man who prays or prophesies with his head covered dishonors his head,

5 but any woman who prays or prophesies with her head unveiled dishonors her head—it is the same as if her head

6 were shaven. For if a woman will not veil herself, then she should cut off her hair; but if it is disgraceful for a

7 woman to be shorn or shaven, let her wear a veil. For a man ought not to cover his head, since he is the image and

8 glory of God; but woman is the glory of man. (For man

9 was not made from woman, but woman from man. Neither was man created for woman, but woman for man.)

10 That is why a woman ought to have a veil r on her head,

11 because of the angels. (Nevertheless, in the Lord woman

12 is not independent of man nor man of woman; for as woman was made from man, so man is now born of

13 woman. And all things are from God.) Judge for yourselves; is it proper for a woman to pray to God with her

14 head uncovered? Does not nature itself teach you that for

15 a man to wear long hair is degrading to him, but if a woman has long hair, it is her pride? For her hair is

16 given to her for a covering. If any one is disposed to be contentious, we recognize no other practice, nor do the churches of God.

17 But in the following instructions I do not commend you, because when you come together it is not for the better

18 but for the worse. For, in the first place, when you assemble as a church, I hear that there are divisions among

19 you; and I partly believe it, for there must be factions among you in order that those who are genuine among

20 you may be recognized. When you meet together, it is

21 not the Lord's supper that you eat. For in eating, each one goes ahead with his own meal, and one is hungry and

22 another is drunk. What! Do you not have houses to eat and drink in? Or do you despise the church of God and humiliate those who have nothing? What shall I say to you? Shall I commend you in this? No, I will not.

23 For I received from the Lord what I also delivered to you, that the Lord Jesus on the night when he was betrayed

24 took bread, and when he had given thanks, he broke it, and said, "This is my body which is for s you. Do this in

25 remembrance of me." In the same way also the cup, after supper, saying, "This cup is the new covenant in my blood. Do this, as often as you drink it, in remembrance of me."

26 For as often as you eat this bread and drink the cup, you proclaim the Lord's death until he comes.

27 Whoever, therefore, eats the bread or drinks the cup of the Lord in an unworthy manner will be guilty of profan-

28 ing the body and blood of the Lord. Let a man examine himself, and so eat of the bread and drink of the cup.

29 For any one who eats and drinks without discerning the

30 body eats and drinks judgment upon himself. That is why many of you are weak and ill, and some have died.t

31 But if we judged ourselves truly, we should not be judged.

32 But when we are judged by the Lord, we are chastened u so that we may not be condemned along with the world.

33 So then, my brethren, when you come together to eat,

34 wait for one another—if any one is hungry, let him eat at home—lest you come together to be condemned. About the other things I will give directions when I come.

12 Now concerning spiritual gifts,x brethren, I do not

2 want you to be uninformed. You know that when you were heathen, you were led astray to dumb idols, however

3 you may have been moved. Therefore I want you to understand that no one speaking by the Spirit of God ever says "Jesus be cursed!" and no one can say "Jesus is Lord" except by the Holy Spirit.

4 Now there are varieties of gifts, but the same Spirit;

5 and there are varieties of service, but the same Lord;

6 and there are varieties of working, but it is the same God

7 who inspires them all in every one. To each is given the

8 manifestation of the Spirit for the common good. To one is given through the Spirit the utterance of wisdom, and

---

r Greek authority (the veil being a symbol of this)   s Other ancient authorities read broken for
t Greek have fallen asleep (as in 15.6, 20)   u Or when we are judged we are being chastened by the Lord   x Or spiritual persons

to another the utterance of knowledge according to the
9 same Spirit, to another faith by the same Spirit, to another
10 gifts of healing by the one Spirit, to another the working
of miracles, to another prophecy, to another the ability to
distinguish between spirits, to another various kinds of
11 tongues, to another the interpretation of tongues. All these
are inspired by one and the same Spirit, who apportions to
each one individually as he wills.

12 For just as the body is one and has many members,
and all the members of the body, though many, are one
13 body, so it is with Christ. For by one Spirit we were all
baptized into one body—Jews or Greeks, slaves or free—
and all were made to drink of one Spirit.

14 For the body does not consist of one member but of
15 many. If the foot should say, "Because I am not a hand,
I do not belong to the body," that would not make it any
16 less a part of the body. And if the ear should say, "Because I am not an eye, I do not belong to the body," that
17 would not make it any less a part of the body. If the whole
body were an eye, where would be the hearing? If the
whole body were an ear, where would be the sense of
18 smell? But as it is, God arranged the organs in the body,
19 each one of them, as he chose. If all were a single organ,

And I will show you a still more excellent way.

13 If I speak in the tongues of men and of angels, but
have not love, I am a noisy gong or a clanging
2 cymbal. And if I have prophetic powers, and understand
all mysteries and all knowledge, and if I have all faith,
so as to remove mountains, but have not love, I am noth-
3 ing. If I give away all I have, and if I deliver my body to
be burned,[v] but have not love, I gain nothing.

4 Love is patient and kind; love is not jealous or boastful;
5 it is not arrogant or rude. Love does not insist on its own
6 way; it is not irritable or resentful; it does not rejoice at
7 wrong, but rejoices in the right. Love bears all things,
believes all things, hopes all things, endures all things.

8 Love never ends; as for prophecies, they will pass
away; as for tongues, they will cease; as for knowledge,
9 it will pass away. For our knowledge is imperfect and our
10 prophecy is imperfect; but when the perfect comes, the
11 imperfect will pass away. When I was a child, I spoke like
a child, I thought like a child, I reasoned like a child;
12 when I became a man, I gave up childish ways. For now
we see in a mirror dimly, but then face to face. Now I
know in part; then I shall understand fully, even as I
13 have been fully understood. So faith, hope, love abide,

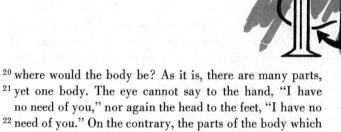

20 where would the body be? As it is, there are many parts,
21 yet one body. The eye cannot say to the hand, "I have
no need of you," nor again the head to the feet, "I have no
22 need of you." On the contrary, the parts of the body which
23 seem to be weaker are indispensable, and those parts of
the body which we think less honorable we invest with
the greater honor, and our unpresentable parts are treated
24 with greater modesty, which our more presentable parts
do not require. But God has so composed the body, giving
25 the greater honor to the inferior part, that there may be no
discord in the body, but that the members may have the
26 same care for one another. If one member suffers, all
suffer together; if one member is honored, all rejoice
together.

27 Now you are the body of Christ and individually mem-
28 bers of it. And God has appointed in the church first
apostles, second prophets, third teachers, then workers of
miracles, then healers, helpers, administrators, speakers in
29 various kinds of tongues. Are all apostles? Are all
30 prophets? Are all teachers? Do all work miracles? Do all
possess gifts of healing? Do all speak with tongues? Do
31 all interpret? But earnestly desire the higher gifts.

[v] Other ancient authorities read *body that I may glory*

these three; but the greatest of these is love.

14 Make love your aim, and earnestly desire the
spiritual gifts, especially that you may prophesy.
2 For one who speaks in a tongue speaks not to men but
to God; for no one understands him, but he utters
3 mysteries in the Spirit. On the other hand, he who prophesies speaks to men for their upbuilding and encouragement
4 and consolation. He who speaks in a tongue edifies him-
5 self, but he who prophesies edifies the church. Now I want
you all to speak in tongues, but even more to prophesy.
He who prophesies is greater than he who speaks in
tongues, unless some one interprets, so that the church
may be edified.

6 Now, brethren, if I come to you speaking in tongues,
how shall I benefit you unless I bring you some revela-
7 tion or knowledge or prophecy or teaching? If even life-
less instruments, such as the flute or the harp, do not give
distinct notes, how will any one know what is played?
8 And if the bugle gives an indistinct sound, who will get
9 ready for battle? So with yourselves; if you in a tongue
utter speech that is not intelligible, how will any one know
what is said? For you will be speaking into the air.

10 There are doubtless many different languages in the
11 world, and none is without meaning; but if I do not know
the meaning of the language, I shall be a foreigner to the
12 speaker and the speaker a foreigner to me. So with yourselves; since you are eager for manifestations of the Spirit,
strive to excel in building up the church.

13 Therefore, he who speaks in a tongue should pray for
14 the power to interpret. For if I pray in a tongue, my spirit
15 prays but my mind is unfruitful. What am I to do? I will
pray with the spirit and I will pray with the mind also;
I will sing with the spirit and I will sing with the mind
16 also. Otherwise, if you bless w with the spirit, how can
any one in the position of an outsider x say the "Amen"
to your thanksgiving when he does not know what you are
17 saying? For you may give thanks well enough, but the
18 other man is not edified. I thank God that I speak in
19 tongues more than you all; nevertheless, in church I would
rather speak five words with my mind, in order to instruct
others, than ten thousand words in a tongue.

20 Brethren, do not be children in your thinking; be babes
21 in evil, but in thinking be mature. In the law it is written,
"By men of strange tongues and by the lips of foreigners
will I speak to this people, and even then they will not
22 listen to me, says the Lord." Thus, tongues are a sign
not for believers but for unbelievers, while prophecy is
23 not for unbelievers but for believers. If, therefore, the
whole church assembles and all speak in tongues, and outsiders or unbelievers enter, will they not say that you are
24 mad? But if all prophesy, and an unbeliever or outsider
enters, he is convicted by all, he is called to account by
25 all, the secrets of his heart are disclosed; and so, falling
on his face, he will worship God and declare that God is
really among you.

26 What then, brethren? When you come together, each
one has a hymn, a lesson, a revelation, a tongue, or an
27 interpretation. Let all things be done for edification. If
any speak in a tongue, let there be only two or at most
28 three, and each in turn; and let one interpret. But if there
is no one to interpret, let each of them keep silence in
29 church and speak to himself and to God. Let two or three
prophets speak, and let the others weigh what is said.
30 If a revelation is made to another sitting by, let the first
31 be silent. For you can all prophesy one by one, so that
32 all may learn and all be encouraged; and the spirits of
33 prophets are subject to prophets. For God is not a God of
confusion but of peace.

34 As in all the churches of the saints, the women should
keep silence in the churches. For they are not permitted
to speak, but should be subordinate, as even the law says.
35 If there is anything they desire to know, let them ask their
husbands at home. For it is shameful for a woman to speak
36 in church. What! Did the word of God originate with
you, or are you the only ones it has reached?

37 If any one thinks that he is a prophet, or spiritual, he
should acknowledge that what I am writing to you is a
38 command of the Lord. If any one does not recognize this,
39 he is not recognized. So, my brethren, earnestly desire to
40 prophesy, and do not forbid speaking in tongues; but all
things should be done decently and in order.

THE RESURRECTION OF THE DEAD

15 Now I would remind you, brethren, in what terms
I preached to you the gospel, which you received, in
2 which you stand, by which you are saved, if you hold it
fast—unless you believed in vain.

3 For I delivered to you as of first importance what I
also received, that Christ died for our sins in accordance
4 with the scriptures, that he was buried, that he was raised
5 on the third day in accordance with the scriptures, and
6 that he appeared to Cephas, then to the twelve. Then he
appeared to more than five hundred brethren at one time,
most of whom are still alive, though some have fallen
7 asleep. Then he appeared to James, then to all the apostles.
8 Last of all, as to one untimely born, he appeared also to
9 me. For I am the least of the apostles, unfit to be called
10 an apostle, because I persecuted the church of God. But
by the grace of God I am what I am, and his grace toward
me was not in vain. On the contrary, I worked harder
than any of them, though it was not I, but the grace of
11 God which is with me. Whether then it was I or they, so
we preach and so you believed.

12 Now if Christ is preached as raised from the dead,
how can some of you say that there is no resurrection of
13 the dead? But if there is no resurrection of the dead, then
14 Christ has not been raised; if Christ has not been raised,
then our preaching is in vain and your faith is in vain.
15 We are even found to be misrepresenting God, because
we testified of God that he raised Christ, whom he did not
16 raise if it is true that the dead are not raised. For if the
dead are not raised, then Christ has not been raised.
17 If Christ has not been raised, your faith is futile and you

18 are still in your sins. Then those also who have fallen
19 asleep in Christ have perished. If for this life only we have
hoped in Christ, we are of all men most to be pitied.
20 But in fact Christ has been raised from the dead, the
21 first fruits of those who have fallen asleep. For as by a

w That is, *give thanks to God*   x Or *him that is without gifts*

man came death, by a man has come also the resurrection
22 of the dead. For as in Adam all die, so also in Christ shall
23 all be made alive. But each in his own order: Christ the
first fruits, then at his coming those who belong to Christ.
24 Then comes the end, when he delivers the kingdom to
God the Father after destroying every rule and every
25 authority and power. For he must reign until he has put
26 all his enemies under his feet. The last enemy to be
27 destroyed is death. "For God z has put all things in sub-

jection under his feet." But when it says, "All things are
put in subjection under him," it is plain that he is
28 excepted who put all things under him. When all things
are subjected to him, then the Son himself will also be
subjected to him who put all things under him, that God
may be everything to every one.
29   Otherwise, what do people mean by being baptized on
behalf of the dead? If the dead are not raised at all, why
30 are people baptized on their behalf? Why am I in peril
31 every hour? I protest, brethren, by my pride in you which
32 I have in Christ Jesus our Lord, I die every day! What do
I gain if, humanly speaking, I fought with beasts at
Ephesus? If the dead are not raised, "Let us eat and
33 drink, for tomorrow we die." Do not be deceived: "Bad
34 company ruins good morals." Come to your right mind,
and sin no more. For some have no knowledge of God.
I say this to your shame.
35   But some one will ask, "How are the dead raised? With
36 what kind of body do they come?" You foolish man!
37 What you sow does not come to life unless it dies. And
what you sow is not the body which is to be, but a bare
38 kernel, perhaps of wheat or of some other grain. But God
gives it a body as he has chosen, and to each kind of seed
39 its own body. For not all flesh is alike, but there is one
kind for men, another for animals, another for birds, and
40 another for fish. There are celestial bodies and there are
terrestrial bodies; but the glory of the celestial is one, and
41 the glory of the terrestrial is another. There is one glory
of the sun, and another glory of the moon, and another
glory of the stars; for star differs from star in glory.
42   So is it with the resurrection of the dead. What is sown
43 is perishable, what is raised is imperishable. It is sown in
dishonor, it is raised in glory. It is sown in weakness, it is
44 raised in power. It is sown a physical body, it is raised a
spiritual body. If there is a physical body, there is also a
45 spiritual body. Thus it is written, "The first man Adam

became a living being"; the last Adam became a lifegiving
46 spirit. But it is not the spiritual which is first but the
47 physical, and then the spiritual. The first man was from
the earth, a man of dust; the second man is from heaven.
48 As was the man of dust, so are those who are of the dust;
and as is the man of heaven, so are those who are of
49 heaven. Just as we have borne the image of the man of
dust, we shall a also bear the image of the man of heaven.
50 I tell you this, brethren: flesh and blood cannot inherit
the kingdom of God, nor does the perishable inherit the
imperishable.
51   Lo! I tell you a mystery. We shall not all sleep, but we
52 shall all be changed, in a moment, in the twinkling of an
eye, at the last trumpet. For the trumpet will sound, and
the dead will be raised imperishable, and we shall be
53 changed. For this perishable nature must put on the
imperishable, and this mortal nature must put on im-
54 mortality. When the perishable puts on the imperishable,
and the mortal puts on immortality, then shall come to
pass the saying that is written:
"Death is swallowed up in victory."
55 "O death, where is thy victory?
O death, where is thy sting?"
56 The sting of death is sin, and the power of sin is the law.
57 But thanks be to God, who gives us the victory through
our Lord Jesus Christ.
58   Therefore, my beloved brethren, be steadfast, immovable, always abounding in the work of the Lord,
knowing that in the Lord your labor is not in vain.

PERSONAL MATTERS

16   Now concerning the contribution for the saints: as
I directed the churches of Galatia, so you also are to
2 do. On the first day of every week, each of you is to put
something aside and store it up, as he may prosper, so
3 that contributions need not be made when I come. And
when I arrive, I will send those whom you accredit by
4 letter to carry your gift to Jerusalem. If it seems advisable
that I should go also, they will accompany me.
5   I will visit you after passing through Macedo'nia,
6 for I intend to pass through Macedo'nia, and perhaps I
will stay with you or even spend the winter, so that you
7 may speed me on my journey, wherever I go. For I do
not want to see you now just in passing; I hope to spend
8 some time with you, if the Lord permits. But I will stay
9 in Ephesus until Pentecost, for a wide door for effective
work has opened to me, and there are many adversaries.
10   When Timothy comes, see that you put him at ease
among you, for he is doing the work of the Lord, as I am.
11 So let no one despise him. Speed him on his way in peace,
that he may return to me; for I am expecting him with
the brethren.
12   As for our brother Apol'los, I strongly urged him to

z Greek *he*   a Other ancient authorities read *let us*

visit you with the other brethren, but it was not at all his will [b] to come. He will come when he has opportunity.

13 Be watchful, stand firm in your faith, be courageous, 14 be strong. Let all that you do be done in love.

15 Now, brethren, you know that the household of Steph'-anas were the first converts in Acha'ia, and they have 16 devoted themselves to the service of the saints; I urge you to be subject to such men and to every fellow worker and 17 laborer. I rejoice at the coming of Steph'anas and Fortuna'tus and Acha'icus, because they have made up

[b] Or *God's will for him*   [c] Greek *Maranatha*

18 for your absence; for they refreshed my spirit as well as yours. Give recognition to such men.

19 The churches of Asia send greetings. Aquila and Prisca, together with the church in their house, send you hearty 20 greetings in the Lord. All the brethren send greetings. Greet one another with a holy kiss.

21, 22 I, Paul, write this greeting with my own hand. If any one has no love for the Lord, let him be accursed. Our 23 Lord, come! [c] The grace of the Lord Jesus be with you. 24 My love be with you all in Christ Jesus. Amen.

THE SECOND LETTER OF PAUL TO THE

CORINTHIANS

Paul wrote several letters from Ephesus to the Christians at Corinth about A.D. 55. See the Introduction to First Corinthians (page 786) before you begin to read this letter.

Chapters 1 through 9 of Second Corinthians (except for 6.14 through 7.1) were written after the stern letter now found in Chapters 10 through 13. In Chapters 1.1 through 2.11 Paul told how discouraged and sad he was after he had to write the harsh letter (Chapters 10 through 13). Besides that, he was also having trouble in Ephesus, probably with the silversmiths who made idols of a goddess named Diana. (See Acts 19.23-41.)

Chapter 7 shows why Paul was so joyful as he wrote these chapters. It was because Titus had brought news that the Corinthians had repented and changed their ways when they read his letter (now 2 Corinthians 10 through 13) demanding that they repent. Paul in reply suggested that they help him with the fund he was raising for famine-stricken Jewish Christians in Jerusalem.

Chapters 10 through 13 were evidently written after a visit Timothy had made to Corinth. He had found the Corinthians quarreling and even criticizing Paul, who had first told them the good news of Christ. There were also some enemies of Christianity who followed Paul wherever he preached, telling his converts that Paul's gospel was inferior to their own ideas.

These chapters point out that we must test ourselves not by the standard of other human beings but by Jesus Christ. Paul declared that he intended to make another visit to Corinth and that he would then demand high Christian standards of all the church's members. These chapters end with the thought that this harsh letter must be but a passing unpleasantness between Paul and the Corinthians (2 Corinthians 13.10-14).

This letter clearly shows the problems the new church at Corinth had to meet and the tasks of leadership placed on the apostle Paul.

THE SECOND LETTER OF PAUL TO THE

CORINTHIANS

INTRODUCTION

1 Paul, an apostle of Christ Jesus by the will of God, and Timothy our brother.

To the church of God which is at Corinth, with all the saints who are in the whole of Acha'ia:

2 Grace to you and peace from God our Father and the Lord Jesus Christ.

3 Blessed be the God and Father of our Lord Jesus Christ,
4 the Father of mercies and God of all comfort, who comforts us in all our affliction, so that we may be able to comfort those who are in any affliction, with the comfort
5 with which we ourselves are comforted by God. For as we share abundantly in Christ's sufferings, so through Christ

6 we share abundantly in comfort too.[a] If we are afflicted, it is for your comfort and salvation; and if we are comforted, it is for your comfort, which you experience when you patiently endure the same sufferings that we suffer.
7 Our hope for you is unshaken; for we know that as you share in our sufferings, you will also share in our comfort.
8 For we do not want you to be ignorant, brethren, of the affliction we experienced in Asia; for we were so utterly,
9 unbearably crushed that we despaired of life itself. Why, we felt that we had received the sentence of death; but that was to make us rely not on ourselves but on God
10 who raises the dead; he delivered us from so deadly a peril, and he will deliver us; on him we have set our
11 hope that he will deliver us again. You also must help us

---

a Or, *For as the sufferings of Christ abound for us, so also our comfort abounds through Christ*

by prayer, so that many will give thanks on our behalf for the blessing granted us in answer to many prayers.

CHANGE IN TRAVEL PLANS

12 For our boast is this, the testimony of our conscience that we have behaved in the world, and still more toward you, with holiness and godly sincerity, not by earthly 13 wisdom but by the grace of God. For we write you nothing but what you can read and understand; I hope you will 14 understand fully, as you have understood in part, that you can be proud of us as we can be of you, on the day of the Lord Jesus.

15 Because I was sure of this, I wanted to come to you 16 first, so that you might have a double pleasure; [b] I wanted to visit you on my way to Macedo'nia, and to come back to you from Macedo'nia and have you send me on my way 17 to Judea. Was I vacillating when I wanted to do this? Do I make my plans like a worldly man, ready to say 18 Yes and No at once? As surely as God is faithful, our 19 word to you has not been Yes and No. For the Son of God, Jesus Christ, whom we preached among you, Silva'nus and Timothy and I, was not Yes and No; but in him 20 it is always Yes. For all the promises of God find their Yes in him. That is why we utter the Amen through him, 21 to the glory of God. But it is God who establishes us with 22 you in Christ, and has commissioned us; he has put his seal upon us and given us his Spirit in our hearts as a guarantee.

23 But I call God to witness against me—it was to spare 24 you that I refrained from coming to Corinth. Not that we lord it over your faith; we work with you for your joy, 2 for you stand firm in your faith. For I made up my 2 mind not to make you another painful visit. For if I cause you pain, who is there to make me glad but the one 3 whom I have pained? And I wrote as I did, so that when I came I might not suffer pain from those who should have made me rejoice, for I felt sure of all of you, that 4 my joy would be the joy of you all. For I wrote you out of much affliction and anguish of heart and with many tears, not to cause you pain but to let you know the abundant love that I have for you.

5 But if any one has caused pain, he has caused it not to me, but in some measure—not to put it too severely—to 6 you all. For such a one this punishment by the majority

7 is enough; so you should rather turn to forgive and comfort him, or he may be overwhelmed by excessive

8 sorrow. So I beg you to reaffirm your love for him. 9 For this is why I wrote, that I might test you and know 10 whether you are obedient in everything. Any one whom you forgive, I also forgive. What I have forgiven, if I have forgiven anything, has been for your sake in the 11 presence of Christ, to keep Satan from gaining the advantage over us; for we are not ignorant of his designs.

12 When I came to Tro'as to preach the gospel of Christ, 13 a door was opened for me in the Lord; but my mind could not rest because I did not find my brother Titus there. So I took leave of them and went on to Macedo'nia.

THE APOSTOLIC MINISTRY

14 But thanks be to God, who in Christ always leads us in triumph, and through us spreads the fragrance of the 15 knowledge of him everywhere. For we are the aroma of Christ to God among those who are being saved and 16 among those who are perishing, to one a fragrance from death to death, to the other a fragrance from life to life. 17 Who is sufficient for these things? For we are not, like so many, peddlers of God's word; but as men of sincerity, as commissioned by God, in the sight of God we speak in Christ.

3 Are we beginning to commend ourselves again? Or do we need, as some do, letters of recommendation to 2 you, or from you? You yourselves are our letter of recommendation, written on your [c] hearts, to be known 3 and read by all men; and you show that you are a letter from Christ delivered by us, written not with ink but with the Spirit of the living God, not on tablets of stone but on tablets of human hearts.

4 Such is the confidence that we have through Christ 5 toward God. Not that we are competent of ourselves to claim anything as coming from us; our competence is 6 from God, who has made us competent to be ministers of a new covenant, not in a written code but in the Spirit; for the written code kills, but the Spirit gives life.

7 Now if the dispensation of death, carved in letters on stone, came with such splendor that the Israelites could not look at Moses' face because of its brightness, fading 8 as this was, will not the dispensation of the Spirit be 9 attended with greater splendor? For if there was splendor in the dispensation of condemnation, the dispensation of 10 righteousness must far exceed it in splendor. Indeed, in

[b] Other ancient authorities read *favor*   [c] Other ancient authorities read *our*

this case, what once had splendor has come to have no
splendor at all, because of the splendor that surpasses it.
11 For if what faded away came with splendor, what is
permanent must have much more splendor.
12, 13 Since we have such a hope, we are very bold, not like
Moses, who put a veil over his face so that the Israelites
14 might not see the end of the fading splendor. But their
minds were hardened; for to this day, when they read the
old covenant, that same veil remains unlifted, because only
15 through Christ is it taken away. Yes, to this day whenever
16 Moses is read a veil lies over their minds; but when a
17 man turns to the Lord the veil is removed. Now the Lord
is the Spirit, and where the Spirit of the Lord is, there is
18 freedom. And we all, with unveiled face, beholding[d] the
glory of the Lord, are being changed into his likeness
from one degree of glory to another; for this comes from
the Lord who is the Spirit.

4 Therefore, having this ministry by the mercy of
2 God,[e] we do not lose heart. We have renounced disgraceful, underhanded ways; we refuse to practice
cunning or to tamper with God's word, but by the open
statement of the truth we would commend ourselves to
3 every man's conscience in the sight of God. And even
if our gospel is veiled, it is veiled only to those who are
4 perishing. In their case the god of this world has blinded
the minds of the unbelievers, to keep them from seeing
the light of the gospel of the glory of Christ, who is the
5 likeness of God. For what we preach is not ourselves, but
Jesus Christ as Lord, with ourselves as your servants[f]
6 for Jesus' sake. For it is the God who said, "Let light shine
out of darkness," who has shone in our hearts to give
the light of the knowledge of the glory of God in the face
of Christ.
7 But we have this treasure in earthen vessels, to show
that the transcendent power belongs to God and not to us.
8 We are afflicted in every way, but not crushed; perplexed,
9 but not driven to despair; persecuted, but not forsaken;
10 struck down, but not destroyed; always carrying in the
body the death of Jesus, so that the life of Jesus may also
11 be manifested in our bodies. For while we live we are
always being given up to death for Jesus' sake, so that the
life of Jesus may be manifested in our mortal flesh.
12 So death is at work in us, but life in you.
13 Since we have the same spirit of faith as he had who
wrote, "I believed, and so I spoke," we too believe, and
14 so we speak, knowing that he who raised the Lord Jesus
will raise us also with Jesus and bring us with you into
15 his presence. For it is all for your sake, so that as grace
extends to more and more people it may increase thanksgiving, to the glory of God.
16 So we do not lose heart. Though our outer nature is
wasting away, our inner nature is being renewed every
17 day. For this slight momentary affliction is preparing for
us an eternal weight of glory beyond all comparison,
18 because we look not to the things that are seen but to
the things that are unseen; for the things that are seen
are transient, but the things that are unseen are eternal.

5 For we know that if the earthly tent we live in is
destroyed, we have a building from God, a house not
2 made with hands, eternal in the heavens. Here indeed we
3 groan, and long to put on our heavenly dwelling, so that
4 by putting it on we may not be found naked. For while we
are still in this tent, we sigh with anxiety; not that we
would be unclothed, but that we would be further clothed,
so that what is mortal may be swallowed up by life.
5 He who has prepared us for this very thing is God, who
has given us the Spirit as a guarantee.
6 So we are always of good courage; we know that while
we are at home in the body we are away from the Lord,
7, 8 for we walk by faith, not by sight. We are of good courage, and we would rather be away from the body and at
9 home with the Lord. So whether we are at home or away,
10 we make it our aim to please him. For we must all appear
before the judgment seat of Christ, so that each one may
receive good or evil, according to what he has done in
the body.

11 Therefore, knowing the fear of the Lord, we persuade
men; but what we are is known to God, and I hope it is
12 known also to your conscience. We are not commending
ourselves to you again but giving you cause to be proud
of us, so that you may be able to answer those who pride
themselves on a man's position and not on his heart.
13 For if we are beside ourselves, it is for God; if we are in
14 our right mind, it is for you. For the love of Christ con-
trols us, because we are convinced that one has died for
15 all; therefore all have died. And he died for all, that
those who live might live no longer for themselves but
for him who for their sake died and was raised.
16 From now on, therefore, we regard no one from a
human point of view; even though we once regarded
Christ from a human point of view, we regard him thus no
17 longer. Therefore, if any one is in Christ, he is a new
creation;[g] the old has passed away, behold, the new has
18 come. All this is from God, who through Christ reconciled
us to himself and gave us the ministry of reconciliation;
19 that is, in Christ God was reconciling[h] the world to him-

[d] Or *reflecting* [e] Greek *as we have received mercy* [f] Or *slaves* [g] Or *creature* [h] Or *God was in Christ reconciling*

self, not counting their trespasses against them, and en-
20 trusting to us the message of reconciliation. So we are
ambassadors for Christ, God making his appeal through
us. We beseech you on behalf of Christ, be reconciled to
21 God. For our sake he made him to be sin who knew no
sin, so that in him we might become the righteousness
of God.

6 Working together with him, then, we entreat you not
2 to accept the grace of God in vain. For he says,

"At the acceptable time I have listened to you,
and helped you on the day of salvation."

Behold, now is the acceptable time; behold, now is the
3 day of salvation. We put no obstacle in any one's way,
4 so that no fault may be found with our ministry, but as
servants of God we commend ourselves in every way:
through great endurance, in afflictions, hardships, calami-
5 ties, beatings, imprisonments, tumults, labors, watching,
6 hunger; by purity, knowledge, forbearance, kindness, the
7 Holy Spirit, genuine love, truthful speech, and the power
of God; with the weapons of righteousness for the right
8 hand and for the left; in honor and dishonor, in ill repute
and good repute. We are treated as impostors, and yet are
9 true; as unknown, and yet well known; as dying, and
10 behold we live; as punished, and yet not killed; as sorrowful, yet always rejoicing; as poor, yet making many
rich; as having nothing, and yet possessing everything.

APOSTLE AND CHURCH

11 Our mouth is open to you, Corinthians; our heart is
12 wide. You are not restricted by us, but you are restricted
13 in your own affections. In return—I speak as to children
—widen your hearts also.

14 Do not be mismated with unbelievers. For what partnership have righteousness and iniquity? Or what fellowship
15 has light with darkness? What accord has Christ with
Be'lial?[i] Or what has a believer in common with an
16 unbeliever? What agreement has the temple of God with
idols? For we are the temple of the living God; as God
said,

"I will live in them and move among them,
and I will be their God,
and they shall be my people.
17 Therefore come out from them,
and be separate from them, says the Lord,
and touch nothing unclean;
then I will welcome you,
18 and I will be a father to you,
and you shall be my sons and daughters,
says the Lord Almighty."

7 Since we have these promises, beloved, let us cleanse
ourselves from every defilement of body and spirit, and
make holiness perfect in the fear of God.

[i] Greek *Beliar*

2 Open your hearts to us; we have wronged no one, we
have corrupted no one, we have taken advantage of no
3 one. I do not say this to condemn you, for I said before
that you are in our hearts, to die together and to live
4 together. I have great confidence in you; I have great
pride in you; I am filled with comfort. With all our
affliction, I am overjoyed.

5 For even when we came into Macedo'nia, our bodies
had no rest but we were afflicted at every turn—fighting
6 without and fear within. But God, who comforts the down-
7 cast, comforted us by the coming of Titus, and not only
by his coming but also by the comfort with which he was
comforted in you, as he told us of your longing, your
mourning, your zeal for me, so that I rejoiced still more.
8 For even if I made you sorry with my letter, I do not
regret it (though I did regret it), for I see that that letter
9 grieved you, though only for a while. As it is, I rejoice,
not because you were grieved, but because you were
grieved into repenting; for you felt a godly grief, so that
10 you suffered no loss through us. For godly grief produces
a repentance that leads to salvation and brings no regret,
11 but worldly grief produces death. For see what earnestness
this godly grief has produced in you, what eagerness to
clear yourselves, what indignation, what alarm, what longing, what zeal, what punishment! At every point you have
12 proved yourselves guiltless in the matter. So although I
wrote to you, it was not on account of the one who did the
wrong, nor on account of the one who suffered the wrong,
but in order that your zeal for us might be revealed to you
13 in the sight of God. Therefore we are comforted.

And besides our own comfort we rejoiced still more
at the joy of Titus, because his mind has been set at rest
14 by you all. For if I have expressed to him some pride in
you, I was not put to shame; but just as everything we
said to you was true, so our boasting before Titus has
15 proved true. And his heart goes out all the more to you,
as he remembers the obedience of you all, and the fear
16 and trembling with which you received him. I rejoice,
because I have perfect confidence in you.

COLLECTION FOR NEEDY

8 We want you to know, brethren, about the grace of
God which has been shown in the churches of Macedo'-
2 nia, for in a severe test of affliction, their abundance of
joy and their extreme poverty have overflowed in a wealth
3 of liberality on their part. For they gave according to their
means, as I can testify, and beyond their means, of their

4 own free will, begging us earnestly for the favor of taking 5 part in the relief of the saints—and this, not as we expected, but first they gave themselves to the Lord and to 6 us by the will of God. Accordingly we have urged Titus that as he had already made a beginning, he should also 7 complete among you this gracious work. Now as you excel in everything—in faith, in utterance, in knowledge, in all earnestness, and in your love for us—see that you excel in this gracious work also.

8 I say this not as a command, but to prove by the earnestness of others that your love also is genuine. 9 For you know the grace of our Lord Jesus Christ, that though he was rich, yet for your sake he became poor, so 10 that by his poverty you might become rich. And in this matter I give my advice: it is best for you now to complete what a year ago you began not only to do but to 11 desire, so that your readiness in desiring it may be matched by your completing it out of what you have. 12 For if the readiness is there, it is acceptable according to what a man has, not according to what he has not. 13 I do not mean that others should be eased and you 14 burdened, but that as a matter of equality your abundance at the present time should supply their want, so that their abundance may supply your want, that there may be 15 equality. As it is written, "He who gathered much had nothing over, and he who gathered little had no lack."

16 But thanks be to God who puts the same earnest care 17 for you into the heart of Titus. For he not only accepted our appeal, but being himself very earnest he is going to 18 you of his own accord. With him we are sending the brother who is famous among all the churches for his 19 preaching of the gospel; and not only that, but he has been appointed by the churches to travel with us in this gracious work which we are carrying on, for the glory 20 of the Lord and to show our good will. We intend that no one should blame us about this liberal gift which we 21 are administering, for we aim at what is honorable not only in the Lord's sight but also in the sight of men. 22 And with them we are sending our brother whom we have often tested and found earnest in many matters, but who is now more earnest than ever because of his great 23 confidence in you. As for Titus, he is my partner and fellow worker in your service; and as for our brethren, they are messengers j of the churches, the glory of Christ.

24 So give proof, before the churches, of your love and of our boasting about you to these men.

9 Now it is superfluous for me to write to you about 2 the offering for the saints, for I know your readiness, of which I boast about you to the people of Macedo'nia, saying that Acha'ia has been ready since last year; and 3 your zeal has stirred up most of them. But I am sending the brethren so that our boasting about you may not prove vain in this case, so that you may be ready, as I 4 said you would be; lest if some Macedo'nians come with me and find that you are not ready, we be humiliated—to 5 say nothing of you—for being so confident. So I thought it necessary to urge the brethren to go on to you before me, and arrange in advance for this gift you have promised, so that it may be ready not as an exaction but as a willing gift.

6 The point is this: he who sows sparingly will also reap sparingly, and he who sows bountifully will also reap 7 bountifully. Each one must do as he has made up his mind, not reluctantly or under compulsion, for God loves 8 a cheerful giver. And God is able to provide you with every blessing in abundance, so that you may always have enough of everything and may provide in abundance for 9 every good work. As it is written,

"He scatters abroad, he gives to the poor;
his righteousness k endures for ever."

10 He who supplies seed to the sower and bread for food will supply and multiply your resources l and increase the 11 harvest of your righteousness.k You will be enriched in every way for great generosity, which through us will 12 produce thanksgiving to God; for the rendering of this service not only supplies the wants of the saints but also 13 overflows in many thanksgivings to God. Under the test of this service, you m will glorify God by your obedience

in acknowledging the gospel of Christ, and by the generosity of your contribution for them and for all others; 14 while they long for you and pray for you, because of the 15 surpassing grace of God in you. Thanks be to God for his inexpressible gift!

---

j Greek *apostles*　　k Or *benevolence*　　l Greek *sowing*　　m Or *they*

REBUKE FOR REVOLT

10 I, Paul, myself entreat you, by the meekness and gentleness of Christ—I who am humble when face to 2 face with you, but bold to you when I am away!—I beg of you that when I am present I may not have to show boldness with such confidence as I count on showing against 3 some who suspect us of acting in worldly fashion. For though we live in the world, we are not carrying on a 4 worldly war, for the weapons of our warfare are not worldly but have divine power to destroy strongholds. 5 We destroy arguments and every proud obstacle to the knowledge of God, and take every thought captive to obey 6 Christ, being ready to punish every disobedience, when your obedience is complete.

7 Look at what is before your eyes. If any one is confident

11 I wish you would bear with me in a little foolishness. Do bear with me! I feel a divine jealousy for you, for I betrothed you to Christ to present you as a 3 pure bride to her one husband. But I am afraid that as the serpent deceived Eve by his cunning, your thoughts will be led astray from a sincere and pure devotion to 4 Christ. For if some one comes and preaches another Jesus than the one we preached, or if you receive a different spirit from the one you received, or if you accept a different gospel from the one you accepted, you submit to 5 it readily enough. I think that I am not in the least inferior 6 to these superlative apostles. Even if I am unskilled in speaking, I am not in knowledge; in every way we have made this plain to you in all things.

7 Did I commit a sin in abasing myself so that you

that he is Christ's, let him remind himself that as he is 8 Christ's, so are we. For even if I boast a little too much of our authority, which the Lord gave for building you up and not for destroying you, I shall not be put to shame. 9, 10 I would not seem to be frightening you with letters. For they say, "His letters are weighty and strong, but his bodily presence is weak, and his speech of no account." 11 Let such people understand that what we say by letter 12 when absent, we do when present. Not that we venture to class or compare ourselves with some of those who commend themselves. But when they measure themselves by one another, and compare themselves with one another, they are without understanding.

13 But we will not boast beyond limit, but will keep to the limits God has apportioned us, to reach even to you. 14 For we are not overextending ourselves, as though we did not reach you; we were the first to come all the way to 15 you with the gospel of Christ. We do not boast beyond limit, in other men's labors; but our hope is that as your faith increases, our field among you may be greatly en-16 larged, so that we may preach the gospel in lands beyond you, without boasting of work already done in another's 17, 18 field. "Let him who boasts, boast of the Lord." For it is not the man who commends himself that is accepted, but the man whom the Lord commends.

might be exalted, because I preached God's gospel with-8 out cost to you? I robbed other churches by accepting 9 support from them in order to serve you. And when I was with you and was in want, I did not burden any one, for my needs were supplied by the brethren who came from Macedo'nia. So I refrained and will refrain from burden-10 ing you in any way. As the truth of Christ is in me, this boast of mine shall not be silenced in the regions of 11 Acha'ia. And why? Because I do not love you? God knows I do!

12 And what I do I will continue to do, in order to undermine the claim of those who would like to claim that in their boasted mission they work on the same 13 terms as we do. For such men are false apostles, deceitful workmen, disguising themselves as apostles of Christ. 14 And no wonder, for even Satan disguises himself as an 15 angel of light. So it is not strange if his servants also disguise themselves as servants of righteousness. Their end will correspond to their deeds.

16 I repeat, let no one think me foolish; but even if you do, accept me as a fool, so that I too may boast a little. 17 (What I am saying I say not with the Lord's authority 18 but as a fool, in this boastful confidence; since many 19 boast of worldly things, I too will boast.) For you gladly 20 bear with fools, being wise yourselves! For you bear it if

a man makes slaves of you, or preys upon you, or takes advantage of you, or puts on airs, or strikes you in the 21 face. To my shame, I must say, we were too weak for that!

But whatever any one dares to boast of—I am speaking 22 as a fool—I also dare to boast of that. Are they Hebrews? So am I. Are they Israelites? So am I. Are they descend- 23 ants of Abraham? So am I. Are they servants of Christ? I am a better one—I am talking like a madman—with far greater labors, far more imprisonments, and countless 24 beatings, and often near death. Five times I have received 25 at the hands of the Jews the forty lashes less one. Three times I have been beaten with rods; once I was stoned. Three times I have been shipwrecked; a night and a day 26 I have been adrift at sea; on frequent journeys, in danger from rivers, danger from robbers, danger from my own people, danger from Gentiles, danger in the city, danger in the wilderness, danger at sea, danger from false breth- 27 ren; in toil and hardship, through many a sleepless night, in hunger and thirst, often without food, in cold and 28 exposure. And, apart from other things, there is the daily pressure upon me of my anxiety for all the churches. 29 Who is weak, and I am not weak? Who is made to fall, and I am not indignant?

30 If I must boast, I will boast of the things that show my 31 weakness. The God and Father of the Lord Jesus, he who 32 is blessed for ever, knows that I do not lie. At Damascus, the governor under King Ar'etas guarded the city of 33 Damascus in order to seize me, but I was let down in a basket through a window in the wall and escaped his hands.

12 I must boast; there is nothing to be gained by it, but I will go on to visions and revelations of the 2 Lord. I know a man in Christ who fourteen years ago was caught up to the third heaven—whether in the body or 3 out of the body I do not know, God knows. And I know that this man was caught up into Paradise—whether in the body or out of the body I do not know, God knows—

one may think more of me than he sees in me or hears 7 from me. And to keep me from being too elated by the abundance of revelations, a thorn was given me in the flesh, a messenger of Satan, to harass me, to keep me 8 from being too elated. Three times I besought the Lord 9 about this, that it should leave me; but he said to me, "My grace is sufficient for you, for my power is made perfect in weakness." I will all the more gladly boast of my weaknesses, that the power of Christ may rest upon 10 me. For the sake of Christ, then, I am content with weaknesses, insults, hardships, persecutions, and calamities; for when I am weak, then I am strong.

11 I have been a fool! You forced me to it, for I ought to have been commended by you. For I was not at all inferior to these superlative apostles, even though I am 12 nothing. The signs of a true apostle were performed among you in all patience, with signs and wonders and 13 mighty works. For in what were you less favored than the rest of the churches, except that I myself did not burden you? Forgive me this wrong!

14 Here for the third time I am ready to come to you. And I will not be a burden, for I seek not what is yours but you; for children ought not to lay up for their parents, 15 but parents for their children. I will most gladly spend and be spent for your souls. If I love you the more, am 16 I to be loved the less? But granting that I myself did not burden you, I was crafty, you say, and got the better of 17 you by guile. Did I take advantage of you through any 18 of those whom I sent to you? I urged Titus to go, and sent the brother with him. Did Titus take advantage of you? Did we not act in the same spirit? Did we not take the same steps?

19 Have you been thinking all along that we have been defending ourselves before you? It is in the sight of God that we have been speaking in Christ, and all for your 20 upbuilding, beloved. For I fear that perhaps I may come and find you not what I wish, and that you may find me

4 and he heard things that cannot be told, which man may 5 not utter. On behalf of this man I will boast, but on my own behalf I will not boast, except of my weaknesses. 6 Though if I wish to boast, I shall not be a fool, for I shall be speaking the truth. But I refrain from it, so that no

not what you wish; that perhaps there may be quarreling, jealousy, anger, selfishness, slander, gossip, conceit, and 21 disorder. I fear that when I come again my God may humble me before you, and I may have to mourn over many of those who sinned before and have not repented of the impurity, immorality, and licentiousness which they have practiced.

13 This is the third time I am coming to you. Any charge must be sustained by the evidence of two or ²three witnesses. I warned those who sinned before and all the others, and I warn them now while absent, as I did when present on my second visit, that if I come again I ³will not spare them—since you desire proof that Christ is speaking in me. He is not weak in dealing with you, but ⁴is powerful in you. For he was crucified in weakness, but lives by the power of God. For we are weak in him, but in dealing with you we shall live with him by the power of God.

⁵ Examine yourselves, to see whether you are holding to your faith. Test yourselves. Do you not realize that Jesus Christ is in you?—unless indeed you fail to meet the ⁶test! I hope you will find out that we have not failed. ⁷But we pray God that you may not do wrong—not that we may appear to have met the test, but that you may do ⁸what is right, though we may seem to have failed. For we cannot do anything against the truth, but only for the ⁹truth. For we are glad when we are weak and you are ¹⁰strong. What we pray for is your improvement. I write this while I am away from you in order that when I come I may not have to be severe in my use of the authority which the Lord has given me for building up and not for tearing down.

CONCLUSION

¹¹ Finally, brethren, farewell. Mend your ways, heed my appeal, agree with one another, live in peace, and the ¹²God of love and peace will be with you. Greet one an-¹³other with a holy kiss. All the saints greet you.

¹⁴ The grace of the Lord Jesus Christ and the love of God and the fellowship of ⁿ the Holy Spirit be with you all.

ⁿ Or *and participation in*

INTRODUCTION TO

GALATIANS

This letter was written to the churches in Galatia, which was located in what is now the nation called Turkey. Paul wrote it while preaching in the city of Ephesus about A.D. 52. It was intended for several churches in the province of Galatia, where he had won converts (Acts 18.23).

Paul had learned that false teachers, called Judaizers, had been talking with the newly converted Galatian Christians. The Judaizers taught that Christians must follow all the many Jewish ceremonial rules about food and other matters, such as those practiced by the Pharisees of Jesus' day.

The Letter to the Galatians was written to tell Christians that they were not required to keep all these Jewish laws and regulations. It teaches that Christians are saved through their faith and trust in God's love and forgiveness as revealed in Jesus Christ and not by the laws they keep.

This was a very important question because if Christians had to keep all the Jewish regulations, Christianity would not appeal to non-Jews. It would simply be a small sect or group among the Jews. Paul was winning many Gentiles to Christ, and their lives were truly Christian without their having known or practiced the many Jewish rules. Therefore, Paul did not wish to require Christians to practice Jewish religious customs.

In this letter Paul also told of his conversion experiences on the Damascus road and what happened to him during the following days. These experiences convinced him that Christian faith and life must be open to everyone who has received Christ with faith. The letter ends with a beautiful description of the kind of goodness that is natural for a person who truly believes in Christ and follows him.

THE LETTER OF PAUL TO THE

GALATIANS

INTRODUCTION

1 Paul an apostle—not from men nor through man, but through Jesus Christ and God the Father, who 2 raised him from the dead—and all the brethren who are with me,

To the churches of Galatia:

3 Grace to you and peace from God the Father and our 4 Lord Jesus Christ, who gave himself for our sins to deliver us from the present evil age, according to the will of 5 our God and Father; to whom be the glory for ever and ever. Amen.

DEPENDENCE ON CHRIST

6 I am astonished that you are so quickly deserting him who called you in the grace of Christ and turning to a 7 different gospel—not that there is another gospel, but there are some who trouble you and want to pervert the 8 gospel of Christ. But even if we, or an angel from heaven, should preach to you a gospel contrary to that which we 9 preached to you, let him be accursed. As we have said before, so now I say again, If any one is preaching to you a gospel contrary to that which you received, let him be accursed.

10 Am I now seeking the favor of men, or of God? Or am I trying to please men? If I were still pleasing men, I should not be a servant [a] of Christ.

11 For I would have you know, brethren, that the gospel 12 which was preached by me is not man's [b] gospel. For I did not receive it from man, nor was I taught it, but it 13 came through a revelation of Jesus Christ. For you have heard of my former life in Judaism, how I persecuted the 14 church of God violently and tried to destroy it; and I advanced in Judaism beyond many of my own age among my people, so extremely zealous was I for the traditions 15 of my fathers. But when he who had set me apart before I 16 was born, and had called me through his grace, was pleased to reveal his Son to [c] me, in order that I might

[a] Or *slave*   [b] Greek *according to man*   [c] Greek *in*

preach him among the Gentiles, I did not confer with
17 flesh and blood, nor did I go up to Jerusalem to those who were apostles before me, but I went away into Arabia; and again I returned to Damascus.

18 Then after three years I went up to Jerusalem to visit
19 Cephas, and remained with him fifteen days. But I saw none of the other apostles except James the Lord's
20 brother. (In what I am writing to you, before God, I do
21 not lie!) Then I went into the regions of Syria and
22 Cili'cia. And I was still not known by sight to the churches
23 of Christ in Judea; they only heard it said, "He who once persecuted us is now preaching the faith he once
24 tried to destroy." And they glorified God because of me.

2 Then after fourteen years I went up again to Jeru-
2 salem with Barnabas, taking Titus along with me. I went up by revelation; and I laid before them (but privately before those who were of repute) the gospel which I preach among the Gentiles, lest somehow I should be
3 running or had run in vain. But even Titus, who was with me, was not compelled to be circumcised, though he was
4 a Greek. But because of false brethren secretly brought in, who slipped in to spy out our freedom which we have in
5 Christ Jesus, that they might bring us into bondage—to them we did not yield submission even for a moment, that
6 the truth of the gospel might be preserved for you. And from those who were reputed to be something (what they were makes no difference to me; God shows no partiality) —those, I say, who were of repute added nothing to me;
7 but on the contrary, when they saw that I had been entrusted with the gospel to the uncircumcised, just as Peter had been entrusted with the gospel to the circumcised
8 (for he who worked through Peter for the mission to the circumcised worked through me also for the Gentiles),
9 and when they perceived the grace that was given to me, James and Cephas and John, who were reputed to be pillars, gave to me and Barnabas the right hand of fellowship, that we should go to the Gentiles and they to
10 the circumcised; only they would have us remember the poor, which very thing I was eager to do.

11 But when Cephas came to Antioch I opposed him to
12 his face, because he stood condemned. For before certain

men came from James, he ate with the Gentiles; but when they came he drew back and separated himself, fearing
13 the circumcision party. And with him the rest of the Jews acted insincerely, so that even Barnabas was carried
14 away by their insincerity. But when I saw that they were not straightforward about the truth of the gospel, I said to Cephas before them all, "If you, though a Jew, live like a Gentile and not like a Jew, how can you compel the
15 Gentiles to live like Jews?" We ourselves, who are Jews
16 by birth and not Gentile sinners, yet who know that a man is not justified d by works of the law but through faith in Jesus Christ, even we have believed in Christ Jesus, in order to be justified by faith in Christ, and not by works of the law, because by works of the law
17 shall no one be justified. But if, in our endeavor to be justified in Christ, we ourselves were found to be sinners,
18 is Christ then an agent of sin? Certainly not! But if I build up again those things which I tore down, then I
19 prove myself a transgressor. For I through the law died
20 to the law, that I might live to God. I have been crucified with Christ; it is no longer I who live, but Christ who lives in me; and the life I now live in the flesh I live by faith in the Son of God, who loved me and gave himself
21 for me. I do not nullify the grace of God; for if justification e were through the law, then Christ died to no purpose.

NEW STATUS FOR MEN OF FAITH

3 O foolish Galatians! Who has bewitched you, before whose eyes Jesus Christ was publicly portrayed as
2 crucified? Let me ask you only this: Did you receive the
3 Spirit by works of the law, or by hearing with faith? Are you so foolish? Having begun with the Spirit, are you
4 now ending with the flesh? Did you experience so many
5 things in vain?—if it really is in vain. Does he who supplies the Spirit to you and works miracles among you do so by works of the law, or by hearing with faith?

6 Thus Abraham "believed God, and it was reckoned to
7 him as righteousness." So you see that it is men of faith
8 who are the sons of Abraham. And the scripture, foreseeing that God would justify the Gentiles by faith, preached the gospel beforehand to Abraham, saying, "In
9 you shall all the nations be blessed." So then, those who are men of faith are blessed with Abraham who had faith.

10 For all who rely on works of the law are under a curse; for it is written, "Cursed be every one who does not abide by all things written in the book of the law, and do
11 them." Now it is evident that no man is justified before God by the law; for "He who through faith is righteous
12 shall live"; f but the law does not rest on faith, for "He
13 who does them shall live by them." Christ redeemed us from the curse of the law, having become a curse for us— for it is written, "Cursed be every one who hangs on a
14 tree"—that in Christ Jesus the blessing of Abraham might come upon the Gentiles, that we might receive the promise of the Spirit through faith.

15 To give a human example, brethren: no one annuls even a man's will,g or adds to it, once it has been ratified.
16 Now the promises were made to Abraham and to his offspring. It does not say, "And to offsprings," referring

---

d Or reckoned righteous; and so elsewhere e Or righteousness f Or the righteous shall live by faith g Or covenant (as in verse 17)

to many; but, referring to one, "And to your offspring," ¹⁷ which is Christ. This is what I mean: the law, which came four hundred and thirty years afterward, does not annul a covenant previously ratified by God, so as to ¹⁸ make the promise void. For if the inheritance is by the law, it is no longer by promise; but God gave it to Abraham by a promise.

¹⁹ Why then the law? It was added because of transgressions, till the offspring should come to whom the promise had been made; and it was ordained by angels through ²⁰ an intermediary. Now an intermediary implies more than one; but God is one.

²¹ Is the law then against the promises of God? Certainly not; for if a law had been given which could make alive, ²² then righteousness would indeed be by the law. But the scripture consigned all things to sin, that what was promised to faith in Jesus Christ might be given to those who believe.

²³ Now before faith came, we were confined under the law, kept under restraint until faith should be revealed. ²⁴ So that the law was our custodian until Christ came, that ²⁵ we might be justified by faith. But now that faith has ²⁶ come, we are no longer under a custodian; for in Christ ²⁷ Jesus you are all sons of God, through faith. For as many of you as were baptized into Christ have put on Christ. ²⁸ There is neither Jew nor Greek, there is neither slave nor free, there is neither male nor female; for you are all one ²⁹ in Christ Jesus. And if you are Christ's, then you are Abraham's offspring, heirs according to promise.

4 I mean that the heir, as long as he is a child, is no better than a slave, though he is the owner of all the ² estate; but he is under guardians and trustees until the ³ date set by the father. So with us; when we were children, we were slaves to the elemental spirits of the universe. ⁴ But when the time had fully come, God sent forth his Son, ⁵ born of woman, born under the law, to redeem those who were under the law, so that we might receive adoption as ⁶ sons. And because you are sons, God has sent the Spirit of ⁷ his Son into our hearts, crying, "Abba! Father!" So through God you are no longer a slave but a son, and if a son then an heir.

⁸ Formerly, when you did not know God, you were in ⁹ bondage to beings that by nature are no gods; but now that you have come to know God, or rather to be known by God, how can you turn back again to the weak and beggarly elemental spirits, whose slaves you want to be ¹⁰ once more? You observe days, and months, and seasons, ¹¹ and years! I am afraid I have labored over you in vain.

¹² Brethren, I beseech you, become as I am, for I also ¹³ have become as you are. You did me no wrong; you know it was because of a bodily ailment that I preached the ¹⁴ gospel to you at first; and though my condition was a trial to you, you did not scorn or despise me, but received

¹⁵ me as an angel of God, as Christ Jesus. What has become of the satisfaction you felt? For I bear you witness that, if possible, you would have plucked out your eyes and ¹⁶ given them to me. Have I then become your enemy by ¹⁷ telling you the truth? ^h They make much of you, but for no good purpose; they want to shut you out, that you may ¹⁸ make much of them. For a good purpose it is always good to be made much of, and not only when I am present with ¹⁹ you. My little children, with whom I am again in travail ²⁰ until Christ be formed in you! I could wish to be present with you now and to change my tone, for I am perplexed about you.

²¹ Tell me, you who desire to be under law, do you not ²² hear the law? For it is written that Abraham had two ²³ sons, one by a slave and one by a free woman. But the son of the slave was born according to the flesh, the son ²⁴ of the free woman through promise. Now this is an allegory: these women are two covenants. One is from Mount Sinai, bearing children for slavery; she is Hagar. ²⁵ Now Hagar is Mount Sinai in Arabia; ⁱ she corresponds to the present Jerusalem, for she is in slavery with her ²⁶ children. But the Jerusalem above is free, and she is our ²⁷ mother. For it is written,

"Rejoice, O barren one who dost not bear;
break forth and shout, you who are not in travail;
for the children of the desolate are many more
than the children of her that is married."

²⁸ Now we,^j brethren, like Isaac, are children of promise. ²⁹ But as at that time he who was born according to the flesh persecuted him who was born according to the Spirit, ³⁰ so it is now. But what does the scripture say? "Cast out the slave and her son; for the son of the slave shall not inherit with the son of the free woman." So, brethren, we are not children of the slave but of the free woman.

THE RESPONSIBILITIES OF FREEDOM

5 For freedom Christ has set us free; stand fast therefore, and do not submit again to a yoke of slavery. ² Now I, Paul, say to you that if you receive circum- ³ cision, Christ will be of no advantage to you. I testify again to every man who receives circumcision that he is ⁴ bound to keep the whole law. You are severed from Christ, you who would be justified by the law; you have fallen ⁵ away from grace. For through the Spirit, by faith, we wait ⁶ for the hope of righteousness. For in Christ Jesus neither circumcision nor uncircumcision is of any avail, but faith ⁷ working ^x through love. You were running well; who

^h Or *by dealing truly with you*
^j Other ancient authorities read *you*
ⁱ Other ancient authorities read *For Sinai is a mountain in Arabia*
^x Or *made effective*

8 hindered you from obeying the truth? This persuasion is 9 not from him who calls you. A little leaven leavens the 10 whole lump. I have confidence in the Lord that you will take no other view than mine; and he who is troubling 11 you will bear his judgment, whoever he is. But if I, brethren, still preach circumcision, why am I still persecuted? In that case the stumbling block of the cross has 12 been removed. I wish those who unsettle you would mutilate themselves!

13 For you were called to freedom, brethren; only do not use your freedom as an opportunity for the flesh, but 14 through love be servants of one another. For the whole law is fulfilled in one word, "You shall love your neighbor 15 as yourself." But if you bite and devour one another take heed that you are not consumed by one another.

16 But I say, walk by the Spirit, and do not gratify the 17 desires of the flesh. For the desires of the flesh are against the Spirit, and the desires of the Spirit are against the flesh; for these are opposed to each other, to prevent you 18 from doing what you would. But if you are led by the 19 Spirit you are not under the law. Now the works of the flesh are plain: fornication, impurity, licentiousness, 20 idolatry, sorcery, enmity, strife, jealousy, anger, selfish- 21 ness, dissension, party spirit, envy,[k] drunkenness, carousing, and the like. I warn you, as I warned you before, that those who do such things shall not inherit the kingdom of 22 God. But the fruit of the Spirit is love, joy, peace, patience, 23 kindness, goodness, faithfulness, gentleness, self-control; 24 against such there is no law. And those who belong to Christ Jesus have crucified the flesh with its passions and desires.

25 If we live by the Spirit, let us also walk by the Spirit. 26 Let us have no self-conceit, no provoking of one another, no envy of one another.

6 Brethren, if a man is overtaken in any trespass, you who are spiritual should restore him in a spirit of 2 gentleness. Look to yourself, lest you too be tempted. Bear 3 one another's burdens, and so fulfil the law of Christ. For if any one thinks he is something, when he is nothing, he 4 deceives himself. But let each one test his own work, and then his reason to boast will be in himself alone and not 5 in his neighbor. For each man will have to bear his own load.

6 Let him who is taught the word share all good things with him who teaches.

7 Do not be deceived; God is not mocked, for whatever 8 a man sows, that he will also reap. For he who sows to his own flesh will from the flesh reap corruption; but he who sows to the Spirit will from the Spirit reap eternal 9 life. And let us not grow weary in well-doing, for in due 10 season we shall reap, if we do not lose heart. So then, as we have opportunity, let us do good to all men, and especially to those who are of the household of faith.

SUMMARY

11 See with what large letters I am writing to you with 12 my own hand. It is those who want to make a good showing in the flesh that would compel you to be circumcised, and only in order that they may not be persecuted 13 for the cross of Christ. For even those who receive circumcision do not themselves keep the law, but they desire to have you circumcised that they may glory in your 14 flesh. But far be it from me to glory except in the cross of our Lord Jesus Christ, by which[l] the world has been 15 crucified to me, and I to the world. For neither circumcision counts for anything, nor uncircumcision, but a new 16 creation. Peace and mercy be upon all who walk by this rule, upon the Israel of God.

17 Henceforth let no man trouble me; for I bear on my body the marks of Jesus.

18 The grace of our Lord Jesus Christ be with your spirit, brethren. Amen.

---

k Other ancient authorities add *murder*   l Or *through whom*

EPHESIANS

This letter was written about A.D. 90. Some very old manuscript copies of this letter are not addressed to Ephesus. The Letter to the Ephesians contains no personal greetings to friends in Ephesus, although Paul had lived there for three years. Therefore, it is probable that this was a "circular" letter with copies sent to several churches rather than only to the church at Ephesus.

This letter seems to be a summary of many of Paul's important ideas, especially his teaching about the church. Possibly some friend and fellow worker gathered together in this letter many of Paul's teachings so that they might be shared with a number of churches. The Letter to the Ephesians was written especially for Gentile or non-Jewish Christians. It shows that Jesus' life and saving work on behalf of all mankind should break down all barriers between Jews and Gentiles.

THE LETTER OF PAUL TO THE

EPHESIANS

Salutation

1 Paul, an apostle of Christ Jesus by the will of God,
To the saints who are also faithful[a] in Christ Jesus:
2 Grace to you and peace from God our Father and the Lord Jesus Christ.

THANKSGIVING

3 Blessed be the God and Father of our Lord Jesus Christ, who has blessed us in Christ with every spiritual blessing 4 in the heavenly places, even as he chose us in him before the foundation of the world, that we should be holy and 5 blameless before him. He destined us in love[b] to be his sons through Jesus Christ, according to the purpose of his 6 will, to the praise of his glorious grace which he freely 7 bestowed on us in the Beloved. In him we have redemption through his blood, the forgiveness of our trespasses, 8 according to the riches of his grace which he lavished 9 upon us. For he has made known to us in all wisdom and insight the mystery of his will, according to his purpose 10 which he set forth in Christ as a plan for the fulness of time, to unite all things in him, things in heaven and things on earth.

11 In him, according to the purpose of him who accomplishes all things according to the counsel of his will, 12 we who first hoped in Christ have been destined and 13 appointed to live for the praise of his glory. In him you also, who have heard the word of truth, the gospel of your salvation, and have believed in him, were sealed with 14 the promised Holy Spirit, which is the guarantee of our inheritance until we acquire possession of it, to the praise of his glory.

PRAYER FOR READERS' ENLIGHTENMENT

15 For this reason, because I have heard of your faith in the Lord Jesus and your love[c] toward all the saints, 16 I do not cease to give thanks for you, remembering you 17 in my prayers, that the God of our Lord Jesus Christ, the Father of glory, may give you a spirit of wisdom and 18 of revelation in the knowledge of him, having the eyes of your hearts enlightened, that you may know what is the hope to which he has called you, what are the riches of 19 his glorious inheritance in the saints, and what is the immeasurable greatness of his power in us who believe, 20 according to the working of his great might which he accomplished in Christ when he raised him from the dead and made him sit at his right hand in the heavenly 21 places, far above all rule and authority and power and dominion, and above every name that is named, not only 22 in this age but also in that which is to come; and he has put all things under his feet and has made him the head 23 over all things for the church, which is his body, the fulness of him who fills all in all.

2 And you he made alive, when you were dead through 2 the trespasses and sins in which you once walked, following the course of this world, following the prince of the power of the air, the spirit that is now at work in the 3 sons of disobedience. Among these we all once lived in the passions of our flesh, following the desires of body and mind, and so we were by nature children of wrath, like the 4 rest of mankind. But God, who is rich in mercy, out of the 5 great love with which he loved us, even when we were dead through our trespasses, made us alive together with 6 Christ (by grace you have been saved), and raised us up with him, and made us sit with him in the heavenly places

---

[a] Other ancient authorities read *who are at Ephesus and faithful*
[b] Or *before him in love, having destined us*
[c] Other ancient authorities omit *your love*

7 in Christ Jesus, that in the coming ages he might show
the immeasurable riches of his grace in kindness toward
8 us in Christ Jesus. For by grace you have been saved
through faith; and this is not your own doing, it is the
9 gift of God—not because of works, lest any man should
10 boast. For we are his workmanship, created in Christ Jesus
for good works, which God prepared beforehand, that we
should walk in them.

ONE IN CHRIST

11 Therefore remember that at one time you Gentiles in the
flesh, called the uncircumcision by what is called the
circumcision, which is made in the flesh by hands—re-
12 member that you were at that time separated from Christ,
alienated from the commonwealth of Israel, and strangers
to the covenants of promise, having no hope and without
13 God in the world. But now in Christ Jesus you who once
were far off have been brought near in the blood of Christ.

fellow heirs, members of the same body, and partakers of
the promise in Christ Jesus through the gospel.
7 Of this gospel I was made a minister according to the
gift of God's grace which was given me by the working
8 of his power. To me, though I am the very least of all
the saints, this grace was given, to preach to the Gentiles
9 the unsearchable riches of Christ, and to make all men see
what is the plan of the mystery hidden for ages in d God
10 who created all things; that through the church the manifold wisdom of God might now be made known to the
11 principalities and powers in the heavenly places. This was
according to the eternal purpose which he has realized in
12 Christ Jesus our Lord, in whom we have boldness and
13 confidence of access through our faith in him. So I ask you
not to e lose heart over what I am suffering for you, which
is your glory.
14 For this reason I bow my knees before the Father,
15 from whom every family in heaven and on earth is

14 For he is our peace, who has made us both one, and has
15 broken down the dividing wall of hostility, by abolishing
in his flesh the law of commandments and ordinances,
that he might create in himself one new man in place of
16 the two, so making peace, and might reconcile us both to
God in one body through the cross, thereby bringing the
17 hostility to an end. And he came and preached peace to
you who were far off and peace to those who were near;
18 for through him we both have access in one Spirit to the
19 Father. So then you are no longer strangers and sojourners, but you are fellow citizens with the saints and
20 members of the household of God, built upon the foundation of the apostles and prophets, Christ Jesus himself
21 being the cornerstone, in whom the whole structure is
joined together and grows into a holy temple in the Lord;
22 in whom you also are built into it for a dwelling place of
God in the Spirit.

ON PAUL'S MISSION, MESSAGE

3 For this reason I, Paul, a prisoner for Christ Jesus
2 on behalf of you Gentiles—assuming that you have
heard of the stewardship of God's grace that was given to
3 me for you, how the mystery was made known to me by
4 revelation, as I have written briefly. When you read this
you can perceive my insight into the mystery of Christ,
5 which was not made known to the sons of men in other
generations as it has now been revealed to his holy apostles
6 and prophets by the Spirit; that is, how the Gentiles are

16 named, that according to the riches of his glory he may
grant you to be strengthened with might through his
17 Spirit in the inner man, and that Christ may dwell in your
hearts through faith; that you, being rooted and
18 grounded in love, may have power to comprehend with
all the saints what is the breadth and length and height
19 and depth, and to know the love of Christ which surpasses
knowledge, that you may be filled with all the fulness of
God.
20 Now to him who by the power at work within us is
able to do far more abundantly than all that we ask or
21 think, to him be glory in the church and in Christ Jesus
to all generations, for ever and ever. Amen.

PROMOTE CHURCH UNITY

4 I therefore, a prisoner for the Lord, beg you to lead
a life worthy of the calling to which you have been
2 called, with all lowliness and meekness, with patience, for-
3 bearing one another in love, eager to maintain the unity
4 of the Spirit in the bond of peace. There is one body and
one Spirit, just as you were called to the one hope that
5 belongs to your call, one Lord, one faith, one baptism,
6 one God and Father of us all, who is above all and through
7 all and in all. But grace was given to each of us according
8 to the measure of Christ's gift. Therefore it is said,
"When he ascended on high he led a host of captives,
and he gave gifts to men."
9 (In saying, "He ascended," what does it mean but that he

d Or by   e Or I ask that I may not

had also descended into the lower parts of the earth? ¹⁰ He who descended is he who also ascended far above all ¹¹ the heavens, that he might fill all things.) And his gifts were that some should be apostles, some prophets, some ¹² evangelists, some pastors and teachers, to equip the saints for the work of ministry, for building up the ¹³ body of Christ, until we all attain to the unity of the faith and of the knowledge of the Son of God, to mature manhood, to the measure of the stature of the fulness of ¹⁴ Christ; so that we may no longer be children, tossed to and fro and carried about with every wind of doctrine, by the cunning of men, by their craftiness in deceitful wiles. ¹⁵ Rather, speaking the truth in love, we are to grow up in ¹⁶ every way into him who is the head, into Christ, from whom the whole body, joined and knit together by every joint with which it is supplied, when each part is working properly, makes bodily growth and upbuilds itself in love.

PUT OFF PAGAN WAYS

¹⁷ Now this I affirm and testify in the Lord, that you must no longer live as the Gentiles do, in the futility of their ¹⁸ minds; they are darkened in their understanding, alienated from the life of God because of the ignorance that is in ¹⁹ them, due to their hardness of heart; they have become callous and have given themselves up to licentiousness, ²⁰ greedy to practice every kind of uncleanness. You did not ²¹ so learn Christ!—assuming that you have heard about him and were taught in him, as the truth is in Jesus. ²² Put off your old nature which belongs to your former manner of life and is corrupt through deceitful lusts, ^{23, 24} and be renewed in the spirit of your minds, and put on the new nature, created after the likeness of God in true righteousness and holiness.

²⁵ Therefore, putting away falsehood, let every one speak the truth with his neighbor, for we are members one of ²⁶ another. Be angry but do not sin; do not let the sun go ²⁷ down on your anger, and give no opportunity to the devil. ²⁸ Let the thief no longer steal, but rather let him labor, doing honest work with his hands, so that he may be ²⁹ able to give to those in need. Let no evil talk come out of your mouths, but only such as is good for edifying, as fits the occasion, that it may impart grace to those who hear. ³⁰ And do not grieve the Holy Spirit of God, in whom you ³¹ were sealed for the day of redemption. Let all bitterness and wrath and anger and clamor and slander be put away ³² from you, with all malice, and be kind to one another, tenderhearted, forgiving one another, as God in Christ forgave you.

⁵ Therefore be imitators of God, as beloved children. ² And walk in love, as Christ loved us and gave himself up for us, a fragrant offering and sacrifice to God.

³ But fornication and all impurity or covetousness must not even be named among you, as is fitting among saints.

⁴ Let there be no filthiness, nor silly talk, nor levity, which are not fitting; but instead let there be thanksgiving. ⁵ Be sure of this, that no fornicator or impure man, or one who is covetous (that is, an idolater), has any inheritance ⁶ in the kingdom of Christ and of God. Let no one deceive you with empty words, for it is because of these things that the wrath of God comes upon the sons of disobedi- ^{7, 8} ence. Therefore do not associate with them, for once you were darkness, but now you are light in the Lord; walk ⁹ as children of light (for the fruit of light is found in all ¹⁰ that is good and right and true), and try to learn what is ¹¹ pleasing to the Lord. Take no part in the unfruitful works ¹² of darkness, but instead expose them. For it is a shame ¹³ even to speak of the things that they do in secret; but when anything is exposed by the light it becomes visible, ¹⁴ for anything that becomes visible is light. Therefore it is said,

"Awake, O sleeper, and arise from the dead,
and Christ shall give you light."

¹⁵ Look carefully then how you walk, not as unwise men ¹⁶ but as wise, making the most of the time, because the ¹⁷ days are evil. Therefore do not be foolish, but understand ¹⁸ what the will of the Lord is. And do not get drunk with wine, for that is debauchery; but be filled with the Spirit, ¹⁹ addressing one another in psalms and hymns and spiritual songs, singing and making melody to the Lord with all ²⁰ your heart, always and for everything giving thanks in the name of our Lord Jesus Christ to God the Father.

THE CHRISTIAN FAMILY

²¹ Be subject to one another out of reverence for Christ. ^{22, 23} Wives, be subject to your husbands, as to the Lord. For the husband is the head of the wife as Christ is the head

²⁴ of the church, his body, and is himself its Savior. As the church is subject to Christ, so let wives also be subject in ²⁵ everything to their husbands. Husbands, love your wives, as Christ loved the church and gave himself up for her, ²⁶ that he might sanctify her, having cleansed her by the ²⁷ washing of water with the word, that he might present the church to himself in splendor, without spot or wrinkle or any such thing, that she might be holy and without ²⁸ blemish. Even so husbands should love their wives as their ²⁹ own bodies. He who loves his wife loves himself. For no

man ever hates his own flesh, but nourishes and cherishes
30 it, as Christ does the church, because we are members of
31 his body. "For this reason a man shall leave his father
and mother and be joined to his wife, and the two shall
32 become one flesh." This mystery is a profound one, and
33 I am saying that it refers to Christ and the church; however, let each one of you love his wife as himself, and
let the wife see that she respects her husband.

6 Children, obey your parents in the Lord, for this is
2 right. "Honor your father and mother" (this is the first

3 commandment with a promise), "that it may be well with
4 you and that you may live long on the earth." Fathers, do
not provoke your children to anger, but bring them up
in the discipline and instruction of the Lord.
5 Slaves, be obedient to those who are your earthly
masters, with fear and trembling, in singleness of heart,
6 as to Christ; not in the way of eyeservice, as men-pleasers,
but as servants f of Christ, doing the will of God from the
7 heart, rendering service with a good will as to the Lord
8 and not to men, knowing that whatever good any one
does, he will receive the same again from the Lord,
9 whether he is a slave or free. Masters, do the same to them,

f Or *slaves*

and forbear threatening, knowing that he who is both their
Master and yours is in heaven, and that there is no
partiality with him.

PUT ON GOD'S ARMOR

10 Finally, be strong in the Lord and in the strength of
11 his might. Put on the whole armor of God, that you may
12 be able to stand against the wiles of the devil. For we are
not contending against flesh and blood, but against the
principalities, against the powers, against the world rulers
of this present darkness, against the spiritual hosts of
13 wickedness in the heavenly places. Therefore take the
whole armor of God, that you may be able to withstand
14 in the evil day, and having done all, to stand. Stand therefore, having girded your loins with truth, and having put
15 on the breastplate of righteousness, and having shod your
16 feet with the equipment of the gospel of peace; besides
all these, taking the shield of faith, with which you can
17 quench all the flaming darts of the evil one. And take the
helmet of salvation, and the sword of the Spirit, which
18 is the word of God. Pray at all times in the Spirit with all
prayer and supplication. To that end keep alert with all
19 perseverance, making supplication for all the saints, and
also for me, that utterance may be given me in opening
my mouth boldly to proclaim the mystery of the gospel,
20 for which I am an ambassador in chains; that I may
declare it boldly, as I ought to speak.

21 Now that you also may know how I am and what I am
doing, Tych'icus the beloved brother and faithful minister
22 in the Lord will tell you everything. I have sent him to
you for this very purpose, that you may know how we
are, and that he may encourage your hearts.

BENEDICTION

23 Peace be to the brethren, and love with faith, from
24 God the Father and the Lord Jesus Christ. Grace be with
all who love our Lord Jesus Christ with love undying.

PHILIPPIANS

Sometime about A.D. 60-63 Paul wrote this letter to the Christians at Philippi while he was in prison in Rome (Acts 28.14, 30-31; Philippians 4.22).

The apostle Paul with his fellow missionaries Silas and Timothy had crossed over from Troas in Asia to undertake their first missionary work in Europe. Although there were only a few Jews in Philippi, Paul soon won some Christian converts. These included a woman named Lydia and the local jailer and their families. Acts 16 tells of Paul's experiences in Philippi.

The Letter to the Philippians was written to express Paul's love for the Christians at Philippi and his thanks for a gift of money they had sent for his expenses in prison. Far from dismayed by being in prison, Paul saw that it had made other Christians more bold to stand up for their faith in Jesus Christ. He gave his reasons as to why Christians do not need to keep all the Jewish regulations in order to be true Christians. Paul had also written on this subject in his Letter to the Galatians.

This letter shows Paul's strong personal faith and gives us help on how to live as Christians. As Paul wrote this letter from prison, he realized that he would probably be killed because of his faith in Christ. But Paul was not sad or afraid. He felt that if he escaped death, he would resume his missionary work; if not, he would "depart and be with Christ" (Philippians 1.23).

Paul knew that all Christians could have the deep joy he had, and so he wrote, "Rejoice in the Lord always; again I will say, Rejoice" (Philippians 4.4).

THE LETTER OF PAUL TO THE

PHILIPPIANS

Salutation and Prayer

1 Paul and Timothy, servants [a] of Christ Jesus,

To all the saints in Christ Jesus who are at Philippi, with the bishops [b] and deacons:

2 Grace to you and peace from God our Father and the Lord Jesus Christ.

3 I thank my God in all my remembrance of you, 4 always in every prayer of mine for you all making my 5 prayer with joy, thankful for your partnership in the 6 gospel from the first day until now. And I am sure that he who began a good work in you will bring it to completion 7 at the day of Jesus Christ. It is right for me to feel thus about you all, because I hold you in my heart, for you are all partakers with me of grace, both in my imprisonment 8 and in the defense and confirmation of the gospel. For God is my witness, how I yearn for you all with the 9 affection of Christ Jesus. And it is my prayer that your love may abound more and more, with knowledge and all 10 discernment, so that you may approve what is excellent, and may be pure and blameless for the day of Christ,

11 filled with the fruits of righteousness which come through Jesus Christ, to the glory and praise of God.

PAUL'S LIFE IN PRISON

12 I want you to know, brethren, that what has happened 13 to me has really served to advance the gospel, so that it has become known throughout the whole praetorian guard [c] and to all the rest that my imprisonment is for 14 Christ; and most of the brethren have been made confident in the Lord because of my imprisonment, and are much more bold to speak the word of God without fear. 15 Some indeed preach Christ from envy and rivalry, but 16 others from good will. The latter do it out of love, knowing that I am put here for the defense of the gospel; 17 the former proclaim Christ out of partisanship, not sincerely but thinking to afflict me in my imprisonment. 18 What then? Only that in every way, whether in pretense or in truth, Christ is proclaimed; and in that I rejoice.

19 Yes, and I shall rejoice. For I know that through your prayers and the help of the Spirit of Jesus Christ this 20 will turn out for my deliverance, as it is my eager expecta-

[a] Or slaves   [b] Or overseers   [c] Greek in the whole praetorium

tion and hope that I shall not be at all ashamed, but that with full courage now as always Christ will be honored in ²¹ my body, whether by life or by death. For to me to live is ²² Christ, and to die is gain. If it is to be life in the flesh, that means fruitful labor for me. Yet which I shall choose ²³ I cannot tell. I am hard pressed between the two. My desire is to depart and be with Christ, for that is far ²⁴ better. But to remain in the flesh is more necessary on ²⁵ your account. Convinced of this, I know that I shall remain and continue with you all, for your progress and joy ²⁶ in the faith, so that in me you may have ample cause to glory in Christ Jesus, because of my coming to you again.

²⁷ Only let your manner of life be worthy of the gospel of Christ, so that whether I come and see you or am absent, I may hear of you that you stand firm in one spirit, with one mind striving side by side for the faith of the gospel,

to work for his good pleasure.

¹⁴, ¹⁵ Do all things without grumbling or questioning, that you may be blameless and innocent, children of God without blemish in the midst of a crooked and perverse generation, among whom you shine as lights in the world, ¹⁶ holding fast the word of life, so that in the day of Christ I may be proud that I did not run in vain or labor in vain. ¹⁷ Even if I am to be poured as a libation upon the sacrificial offering of your faith, I am glad and rejoice with you all. ¹⁸ Likewise you also should be glad and rejoice with me.

TIMOTHY AND EPAPHRODITUS

¹⁹ I hope in the Lord Jesus to send Timothy to you soon, ²⁰ so that I may be cheered by news of you. I have no one like him, who will be genuinely anxious for your welfare. ²¹ They all look after their own interests, not those of Jesus

²⁸ and not frightened in anything by your opponents. This is a clear omen to them of their destruction, but of your ²⁹ salvation, and that from God. For it has been granted to you that fo. the sake of Christ you should not only ³⁰ believe in him but also suffer for his sake, engaged in the same conflict which you saw and now hear to be mine.

THE CHRISTIAN LIFE

2 So if there is any encouragement in Christ, any incentive of love, any participation in the Spirit, any ² affection and sympathy, complete my joy by being of the same mind, having the same love, being in full accord and ³ of one mind. Do nothing from selfishness or conceit, but ⁴ in humility count others better than yourselves. Let each of you look not only to his own interests, but also to the ⁵ interests of others. Have this mind among yourselves, ⁶ which is yours in Christ Jesus, who, though he was in the form of God, did not count equality with God a thing ⁷ to be grasped, but emptied himself, taking the form of a ⁸ servant,ᵈ being born in the likeness of men. And being found in human form he humbled himself and became ⁹ obedient unto death, even death on a cross. Therefore God has highly exalted him and bestowed on him the ¹⁰ name which is above every name, that at the name of Jesus every knee should bow, in heaven and on earth and ¹¹ under the earth, and every tongue confess that Jesus Christ is Lord, to the glory of God the Father.

¹² Therefore, my beloved, as you have always obeyed, so now, not only as in my presence but much more in my absence, work out your own salvation with fear and ¹³ trembling; for God is at work in you, both to will and

²² Christ. But Timothy's worth you know, how as a son with ²³ a father he has served with me in the gospel. I hope therefore to send him just as soon as I see how it will go ²⁴ with me; and I trust in the Lord that shortly I myself shall come also.

²⁵ I have thought it necessary to send to you Epaphrodi'tus my brother and fellow worker and fellow soldier, and ²⁶ your messenger and minister to my need, for he has been longing for you all, and has been distressed because you ²⁷ heard that he was ill. Indeed he was ill, near to death. But God had mercy on him, and not only on him but on me ²⁸ also, lest I should have sorrow upon sorrow. I am the more eager to send him, therefore, that you may rejoice at seeing him again, and that I may be less anxious. ²⁹ So receive him in the Lord with all joy; and honor such ³⁰ men, for he nearly died for the work of Christ, risking his life to complete your service to me.

PAUL'S GOAL

3 Finally, my brethren, rejoice in the Lord. To write the same things to you is not irksome to me, and is safe for you.

² Look out for the dogs, look out for the evil-workers, ³ look out for those who mutilate the flesh. For we are the true circumcision, who worship God in spirit,ᵉ and glory in Christ Jesus, and put no confidence in the flesh. ⁴ Though I myself have reason for confidence in the flesh also. If any other man thinks he has reason for confidence ⁵ in the flesh, I have more: circumcised on the eighth day; of the people of Israel, of the tribe of Benjamin, a Hebrew ⁶ born of Hebrews; as to the law a Pharisee, as to zeal a

ᵈ Or slave   ᵉ Other ancient authorities read worship by the Spirit of God

persecutor of the church, as to righteousness under the
7 law blameless. But whatever gain I had, I counted as loss
8 for the sake of Christ. Indeed I count everything as loss because of the surpassing worth of knowing Christ Jesus my Lord. For his sake I have suffered the loss of all things, and count them as refuse, in order that I may gain
9 Christ and be found in him, not having a righteousness of my own, based on law, but that which is through faith in Christ, the righteousness from God that depends on
10 faith; that I may know him and the power of his resurrection, and may share his sufferings, becoming like him
11 in his death, that if possible I may attain the resurrection from the dead.
12 Not that I have already obtained this or am already perfect; but I press on to make it my own, because Christ
13 Jesus has made me his own. Brethren, I do not consider that I have made it my own; but one thing I do, forgetting what lies behind and straining forward to what lies ahead,
14 I press on toward the goal for the prize of the upward
15 call of God in Christ Jesus. Let those of us who are mature be thus minded; and if in anything you are otherwise
16 minded, God will reveal that also to you. Only let us hold true to what we have attained.
17 Brethren, join in imitating me, and mark those who so
18 live as you have an example in us. For many, of whom I have often told you and now tell you even with tears, live
19 as enemies of the cross of Christ. Their end is destruction, their god is the belly, and they glory in their shame, with
20 minds set on earthly things. But our commonwealth is in heaven, and from it we await a Savior, the Lord Jesus
21 Christ, who will change our lowly body to be like his glorious body, by the power which enables him even to subject all things to himself.

REJOICE IN THE LORD

4 Therefore, my brethren, whom I love and long for, my joy and crown, stand firm thus in the Lord, my beloved.
2 I entreat Eu-o'dia and I entreat Syn'tyche to agree in the
3 Lord. And I ask you also, true yokefellow, help these women, for they have labored side by side with me in the gospel together with Clement and the rest of my fellow

f Other ancient authorities read *money for my needs*

workers, whose names are in the book of life.
4 Rejoice in the Lord always; again I will say, Rejoice.
5 Let all men know your forbearance. The Lord is at hand.
6 Have no anxiety about anything, but in everything by prayer and supplication with thanksgiving let your re-
7 quests be made known to God. And the peace of God, which passes all understanding, will keep your hearts and your minds in Christ Jesus.

8 Finally, brethren, whatever is true, whatever is honorable, whatever is just, whatever is pure, whatever is lovely, whatever is gracious, if there is any excellence, if there is
9 anything worthy of praise, think about these things. What you have learned and received and heard and seen in me, do; and the God of peace will be with you.

10 I rejoice in the Lord greatly that now at length you have revived your concern for me; you were indeed con-
11 cerned for me, but you had no opportunity. Not that I complain of want; for I have learned, in whatever state
12 I am, to be content. I know how to be abased, and I know how to abound; in any and all circumstances I have learned the secret of facing plenty and hunger, abundance
13 and want. I can do all things in him who strengthens me.
14, 15 Yet it was kind of you to share my trouble. And you Philippians yourselves know that in the beginning of the gospel, when I left Macedo'nia, no church entered into partnership with me in giving and receiving except you
16 only; for even in Thessaloni'ca you sent me help f once
17 and again. Not that I seek the gift; but I seek the fruit
18 which increases to your credit. I have received full payment, and more; I am filled, having received from Epaphrodi'tus the gifts you sent, a fragrant offering, a
19 sacrifice acceptable and pleasing to God. And my God will supply every need of yours according to his riches
20 in glory in Christ Jesus. To our God and Father be glory for ever and ever. Amen.

BENEDICTION
21 Greet every saint in Christ Jesus. The brethren who
22 are with me greet you. All the saints greet you, especially those of Caesar's household.
23 The grace of the Lord Jesus Christ be with your spirit.

COLOSSIANS

Paul wrote this letter from prison in Rome about A.D. 61 (Acts 28.14, 30-31). It was written to the church at Colossae, a city about one hundred miles from Ephesus in a province then called Asia. Paul had not founded the church in Colossae, but he had heard through his friend named Epaphras of the love and faith of the Christians there. He also learned that some members there claimed to have mysterious knowledge of God because they went through certain strange rituals and studied peculiar ideas. These so-called Gnostics or "wise ones" were misled about the Christian faith and so were only partly Christian in their lives and beliefs.

Paul wrote this letter to teach that true Christianity had nothing to do with the strange rituals and the peculiar ideas of the Gnostics. He explained that Christians should know the true mystery of having the very spirit of Christ in their hearts by faith. Paul spoke of it as "the riches of the glory of this mystery, which is Christ in you, the hope of glory" (Colossians 1.27).

THE LETTER OF PAUL TO THE

COLOSSIANS

Salutation and Prayer

1 Paul, an apostle of Christ Jesus by the will of God, and Timothy our brother,

2 To the saints and faithful brethren in Christ at Colos'-sae:

Grace to you and peace from our Father.

3 We always thank God, the Father of our Lord Jesus
4 Christ, when we pray for you, because we have heard of your faith in Christ Jesus and of the love which you
5 have for all the saints, because of the hope laid up for you in heaven. Of this you have heard before in the word
6 of the truth, the gospel which has come to you, as indeed in the whole world it is bearing fruit and growing—so among yourselves, from the day you heard and under-
7 stood the grace of God in truth, as you learned it from Ep'aphras our beloved fellow servant. He is a faithful
8 minister of Christ on our [a] behalf and has made known to us your love in the Spirit.

9 And so, from the day we heard of it we have not ceased to pray for you, asking that you may be filled with the knowledge of his will in all spiritual wisdom and under-
10 standing, to lead a life worthy of the Lord, fully pleasing to him, bearing fruit in every good work and increasing
11 in the knowledge of God. May you be strengthened with all power, according to his glorious might, for all en-
12 durance and patience with joy, giving thanks to the Father, who has qualified us [b] to share in the inheritance
13 of the saints in light. He has delivered us from the domin-ion of darkness and transferred us to the kingdom of his
14 beloved Son, in whom we have redemption, the forgive-ness of sins.

THE SUPREMACY OF CHRIST

15 He is the image of the invisible God the first-born of
16 all creation; for in him all things were created, in heaven and on earth, visible and invisible, whether thrones or dominions or principalities or authorities—all things
17 were created through him and for him. He is before all
18 things, and in him all things hold together. He is the head

of the body, the church; he is the beginning, the first-born from the dead, that in everything he might be pre-
19 eminent. For in him all the fulness of God was pleased to
20 dwell, and through him to reconcile to himself all things, whether on earth or in heaven, making peace by the blood of his cross.

[a] Other ancient authorities read *your*   [b] Other ancient authorities read *you*

21 And you, who once were estranged and hostile in mind,
22 doing evil deeds, he has now reconciled in his body of flesh by his death, in order to present you holy and blame-
23 less and irreproachable before him, provided that you continue in the faith, stable and steadfast, not shifting from the hope of the gospel which you heard, which has been preached to every creature under heaven, and of which I, Paul, became a minister.

24 Now I rejoice in my sufferings for your sake, and in my flesh I complete what is lacking in Christ's afflictions
25 for the sake of his body, that is, the church, of which I became a minister according to the divine office which was given to me for you, to make the word of God fully
26 known, the mystery hidden for ages and generations c
27 but now made manifest to his saints. To them God chose to make known how great among the Gentiles are the riches of the glory of this mystery, which is Christ in you,
28 the hope of glory. Him we proclaim, warning every man and teaching every man in all wisdom, that we may pre-
29 sent every man mature in Christ. For this I toil, striving with all the energy which he mightily inspires within me.

2 For I want you to know how greatly I strive for you, and for those at La-odice′a, and for all who have
2 not seen my face, that their hearts may be encouraged as they are knit together in love, to have all the riches of assured understanding and the knowledge of God's mys-
3 tery, of Christ, in whom are hid all the treasures of wis-
4 dom and knowledge. I say this in order that no one may
5 delude you with beguiling speech. For though I am ab-sent in body, yet I am with you in spirit, rejoicing to see your good order and the firmness of your faith in Christ.

6 As therefore you received Christ Jesus the Lord, so
7 live in him, rooted and built up in him and established in the faith, just as you were taught, abounding in thanks-giving.

8 See to it that no one makes a prey of you by philosophy and empty deceit, according to human tradition, accord-ing to the elemental spirits of the universe, and not ac-
9 cording to Christ. For in him the whole fulness of deity
10 dwells bodily, and you have come to fulness of life in
11 him, who is the head of all rule and authority. In him also you were circumcised with a circumcision made without hands, by putting off the body of flesh in the circumcision
12 of Christ; and you were buried with him in baptism, in which you were also raised with him through faith in the
13 working of God, who raised him from the dead. And you, who were dead in trespasses and the uncircumcision of your flesh, God made alive together with him, having
14 forgiven us all our trespasses, having canceled the bond which stood against us with its legal demands; this he set
15 aside, nailing it to the cross. He disarmed the principali-ties and powers and made a public example of them, triumphing over them in him.d

16 Therefore let no one pass judgment on you in ques-tions of food and drink or with regard to a festival or a
17 new moon or a sabbath. These are only a shadow of what
18 is to come; but the substance belongs to Christ. Let no one disqualify you, insisting on self-abasement and wor-ship of angels, taking his stand on visions, puffed up
19 without reason by his sensuous mind, and not holding fast to the Head, from whom the whole body, nourished and knit together through its joints and ligaments, grows with a growth that is from God.

20 If with Christ you died to the elemental spirits of the universe, why do you live as if you still belonged to the
21 world? Why do you submit to regulations, "Do not
22 handle, Do not taste, Do not touch" (referring to things which all perish as they are used), according to human

23 precepts and doctrines? These have indeed an appear-ance of wisdom in promoting rigor of devotion and self-abasement and severity to the body, but they are of no value in checking the indulgence of the flesh.e

3 If then you have been raised with Christ, seek the things that are above, where Christ is, seated at the
2 right hand of God. Set your minds on things that are
3 above, not on things that are on earth. For you have died,
4 and your life is hid with Christ in God. When Christ who is our life appears, then you also will appear with him in glory.

THE NEW LIFE IN CHRIST
5 Put to death therefore what is earthly in you: forni-cation, impurity, passion, evil desire, and covetousness,
6 which is idolatry. On account of these the wrath of God
7 is coming.f In these you once walked, when you lived
8 in them. But now put them all away: anger, wrath, malice,
9 slander, and foul talk from your mouth. Do not lie to one another, seeing that you have put off the old nature
10 with its practices and have put on the new nature, which is being renewed in knowledge after the image of its
11 creator. Here there cannot be Greek and Jew, circumcised and uncircumcised, barbarian, Scyth′ian, slave, free man, but Christ is all, and in all.

12 Put on then, as God's chosen ones, holy and beloved, compassion, kindness, lowliness, meekness, and patience,

---

c Or from angels and men   d Or in it (that is, the cross)
f Other ancient authorities add upon the sons of disobedience

e Or are of no value, serving only to indulge the flesh

13 forbearing one another and, if one has a complaint against another, forgiving each other; as the Lord has forgiven 14 you, so you also must forgive. And above all these put on love, which binds everything together in perfect har- 15 mony. And let the peace of Christ rule in your hearts, to which indeed you were called in the one body. And be 16 thankful. Let the word of Christ dwell in you richly, teach and admonish one another in all wisdom, and sing psalms and hymns and spiritual songs with thank- 17 fulness in your hearts to God. And whatever you do, in word or deed, do everything in the name of the Lord Jesus, giving thanks to God the Father through him.

18 Wives, be subject to your husbands, as is fitting in 19 the Lord. Husbands, love your wives, and do not be 20 harsh with them. Children, obey your parents in every- 21 thing, for this pleases the Lord. Fathers, do not provoke 22 your children, lest they become discouraged. Slaves, obey in everything those who are your earthly masters, not with eyeservice, as menpleasers, but in singleness of heart, 23 fearing the Lord. Whatever your task, work heartily, as 24 serving the Lord and not men, knowing that from the

5 Conduct yourselves wisely toward outsiders, making 6 the most of the time. Let your speech always be gracious, seasoned with salt, so that you may know how you ought to answer every one.

7 Tych'icus will tell you all about my affairs; he is a beloved brother and faithful minister and fellow servant 8 in the Lord. I have sent him to you for this very pur- pose, that you may know how we are and that he may 9 encourage your hearts, and with him Ones'imus, the faith- ful and beloved brother, who is one of yourselves. They will tell you of everything that has taken place here.

10 Aristar'chus my fellow prisoner greets you, and Mark the cousin of Barnabas (concerning whom you have re- 11 ceived instructions—if he comes to you, receive him), and Jesus who is called Justus. These are the only men of the circumcision among my fellow workers for the king- 12 dom of God, and they have been a comfort to me. Ep'- aphras, who is one of yourselves, a servant ᵍ of Christ Jesus, greets you, always remembering you earnestly in his prayers, that you may stand mature and fully assured

Lord you will receive the inheritance as your reward; 25 you are serving the Lord Christ. For the wrongdoer will be paid back for the wrong he has done, and there is no partiality.

INSTRUCTIONS, GREETINGS

4 Masters, treat your slaves justly and fairly, knowing that you also have a Master in heaven.

2 Continue steadfastly in prayer, being watchful in it 3 with thanksgiving; and pray for us also, that God may open to us a door for the word, to declare the mystery 4 of Christ, on account of which I am in prison, that I may make it clear, as I ought to speak.

ᵍ Or *slave*

13 in all the will of God. For I bear him witness that he has worked hard for you and for those in La-odice'a and in 14 Hi-erap'olis. Luke the beloved physician and Demas 15 greet you. Give my greetings to the brethren at La-odice'a, 16 and to Nympha and the church in her house. And when this letter has been read among you, have it read also in the church of the La-odice'ans; and see that you read also 17 the letter from La-odice'a. And say to Archip'pus, "See that you fulfil the ministry which you have received in the Lord."

18 I, Paul, write this greeting with my own hand. Remem- ber my fetters. Grace be with you.

INTRODUCTION TO

THE FIRST LETTER OF PAUL TO THE

THESSALONIANS

This letter was written to the Christians in Thessalonica, a city of Greece. Paul had preached there and formed a church (Acts 17.1-4). He wrote the letter about A.D. 50 from Corinth, Greece (Acts 18.1-4), where he was carrying on his missionary work.

Paul complimented the Christian Thessalonians on their faith and gave directions as to how followers of Jesus should live. Some of the members there thought that the risen Christ would return to earth any day. Therefore, they were deeply troubled when Jesus' physical return was delayed and some of their members died without witnessing that victorious event. Paul urged them to be faithful and courageous regardless of their perplexity about the Day of the Lord. He wrote more about this in the Second Letter to the Thessalonians.

THE FIRST LETTER OF PAUL TO THE

THESSALONIANS

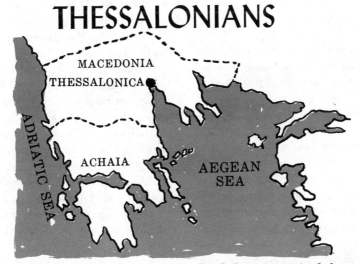

Salutation

1 Paul, Silva'nus, and Timothy,
To the church of the Thessalo'nians in God the Father and the Lord Jesus Christ:
Grace to you and peace.

REVIEW OF THE APOSTLE'S WORK

2 We give thanks to God always for you all, constantly
3 mentioning you in our prayers, remembering before our God and Father your work of faith and labor of love and
4 steadfastness of hope in our Lord Jesus Christ. For we know, brethren beloved by God, that he has chosen you;
5 for our gospel came to you not only in word, but also in power and in the Holy Spirit and with full conviction. You know what kind of men we proved to be among you
6 for your sake. And you became imitators of us and of the Lord, for you received the word in much affliction, with
7 joy inspired by the Holy Spirit; so that you became an example to all the believers in Macedo'nia and in Acha'ia.
8 For not only has the word of the Lord sounded forth from you in Macedo'nia and Acha'ia, but your faith in God has gone forth everywhere, so that we need not say any-
9 thing. For they themselves report concerning us what a welcome we had among you, and how you turned to God
10 from idols, to serve a living and true God, and to wait for his Son from heaven, whom he raised from the dead, Jesus who delivers us from the wrath to come.

2 For you yourselves know, brethren, that our visit to
2 you was not in vain; but though we had already suffered and been shamefully treated at Philippi, as you know, we had courage in our God to declare to you the
3 gospel of God in the face of great opposition. For our

appeal does not spring from error or uncleanness, nor
[4] is it made with guile; but just as we have been approved
by God to be entrusted with the gospel, so we speak,
not to please men, but to please God who tests our hearts.
[5] For we never used either words of flattery, as you know,
[6] or a cloak for greed, as God is witness; nor did we seek
glory from men, whether from you or from others,
though we might have made demands as apostles of
[7] Christ. But we were gentle[a] among you, like a nurse
[8] taking care of her children. So, being affectionately
desirous of you, we were ready to share with you not
only the gospel of God but also our own selves, because
you had become very dear to us.

[9] For you remember our labor and toil, brethren; we
worked night and day, that we might not burden any of
[10] you, while we preached to you the gospel of God. You
are witnesses, and God also, how holy and righteous and
[11] blameless was our behavior to you believers; for you
know how, like a father with his children, we exhorted
each one of you and encouraged you and charged you
[12] to lead a life worthy of God, who calls you into his own
kingdom and glory.

SUCCESS OF THE GOSPEL

[13] And we also thank God constantly for this, that when
you received the word of God which you heard from us,
you accepted it not as the word of men but as what it
really is, the word of God, which is at work in you be-
[14] lievers. For you, brethren, became imitators of the
churches of God in Christ Jesus which are in Judea; for
you suffered the same things from your own countrymen
[15] as they did from the Jews, who killed both the Lord Jesus
and the prophets, and drove us out, and displease God and
[16] oppose all men by hindering us from speaking to the
Gentiles that they may be saved—so as always to fill up
the measure of their sins. But God's wrath has come upon
them at last! [b]

[17] But since we were bereft of you, brethren, for a short
time, in person not in heart, we endeavored the more
eagerly and with great desire to see you face to face;
[18] because we wanted to come to you—I, Paul, again and
[19] again—but Satan hindered us. For what is our hope or
joy or crown of boasting before our Lord Jesus at his
[20] coming? Is it not you? For you are our glory and joy.

3 Therefore when we could bear it no longer, we were
[2] willing to be left behind at Athens alone, and we sent
Timothy, our brother and God's servant in the gospel of
Christ, to establish you in your faith and to exhort you,
[3] that no one be moved by these afflictions. You yourselves
[4] know that this is to be our lot. For when we were with
you, we told you beforehand that we were to suffer
affliction; just as it has come to pass, and as you know.
[5] For this reason, when I could bear it no longer, I sent

that I might know your faith, for fear that somehow the
tempter had tempted you and that our labor would be
in vain.

[6] But now that Timothy has come to us from you, and
has brought us the good news of your faith and love and
reported that you always remember us kindly and long to
[7] see us, as we long to see you—for this reason, brethren, in
all our distress and affliction we have been comforted
[8] about you through your faith; for now we live, if you
[9] stand fast in the Lord. For what thanksgiving can we
render to God for you, for all the joy which we feel for
[10] your sake before our God, praying earnestly night and
day that we may see you face to face and supply what is
lacking in your faith?

[11] Now may our God and Father himself, and our Lord
[12] Jesus, direct our way to you; and may the Lord make
you increase and abound in love to one another and to
[13] all men, as we do to you, so that he may establish your
hearts unblamable in holiness before our God and Father,
at the coming of our Lord Jesus with all his saints.

PLEASE GOD!

4 Finally, brethren, we beseech and exhort you in the
Lord Jesus, that as you learned from us how you ought
to live and to please God, just as you are doing, you do so
[2] more and more. For you know what instructions we gave
[3] you through the Lord Jesus. For this is the will of God,
your sanctification: that you abstain from unchastity;
[4] that each one of you know how to take a wife for himself[x]
[5] in holiness and honor, not in the passion of lust like
[6] heathen who do not know God; that no man transgress,
and wrong his brother in this matter,[c] because the Lord
is an avenger in all these things, as we solemnly fore-
[7] warned you. For God has not called us for uncleanness,
[8] but in holiness. Therefore whoever disregards this, disregards not man but God, who gives his Holy Spirit to
you.

[9] But concerning love of the brethren you have no need
to have any one write to you, for you yourselves have been
[10] taught by God to love one another; and indeed you do
love all the brethren throughout Macedo'nia. But we
[11] exhort you, brethren, to do so more and more, to aspire
to live quietly, to mind your own affairs, and to work
[12] with your hands, as we charged you; so that you may
command the respect of outsiders, and be dependent on
nobody.

THE DAY OF THE LORD

[13] But we would not have you ignorant, brethren, concerning those who are asleep, that you may not grieve as
[14] others do who have no hope. For since we believe that
Jesus died and rose again, even so, through Jesus, God
[15] will bring with him those who have fallen asleep. For this

---

[a] Other ancient authorities read *babes*　　[b] Or *completely*, or *for ever*　　[x] Or *how to control his own body*　　[c] Or *defraud his brother in business*

we declare to you by the word of the Lord, that we who are alive, who are left until the coming of the Lord, shall
16 not precede those who have fallen asleep. For the Lord himself will descend from heaven with a cry of command, with the archangel's call, and with the sound of the
17 trumpet of God. And the dead in Christ will rise first; then we who are alive, who are left, shall be caught up together with them in the clouds to meet the Lord in the air; and
18 so we shall always be with the Lord. Therefore comfort one another with these words.

5 But as to the times and the seasons, brethren, you
2 have no need to have anything written to you. For you yourselves know well that the day of the Lord will come
3 like a thief in the night. When people say, "There is peace and security," then sudden destruction will come upon them as travail comes upon a woman with child, and
4 there will be no escape. But you are not in darkness,
5 brethren, for that day to surprise you like a thief. For you are all sons of light and sons of the day; we are not of the
6 night or of darkness. So then let us not sleep, as others do,
7 but let us keep awake and be sober. For those who sleep sleep at night, and those who get drunk are drunk at night.
8 But, since we belong to the day, let us be sober, and put on the breastplate of faith and love, and for a helmet the
9 hope of salvation. For God has not destined us for wrath, but to obtain salvation through our Lord Jesus Christ,

10 who died for us so that whether we wake or sleep we might
11 live with him. Therefore encourage one another and build one another up, just as you are doing.
12 But we beseech you, brethren, to respect those who labor among you and are over you in the Lord and admonish
13 you, and to esteem them very highly in love because of
14 their work. Be at peace among yourselves. And we exhort you, brethren, admonish the idlers, encourage the faint-
15 hearted, help the weak, be patient with them all. See that none of you repays evil for evil, but always seek to do
16, 17 good to one another and to all. Rejoice always, pray
18 constantly, give thanks in all circumstances; for this is the
19 will of God in Christ Jesus for you. Do not quench the
20, 21 Spirit, do not despise prophesying, but test everything;
22 hold fast what is good, abstain from every form of evil.

BENEDICTION
23 May the God of peace himself sanctify you wholly; and may your spirit and soul and body be kept sound and
24 blameless at the coming of our Lord Jesus Christ. He who calls you is faithful, and he will do it.
25 Brethren, pray for us.
26 Greet all the brethren with a holy kiss.
27 I adjure you by the Lord that this letter be read to all the brethren.
28 The grace of our Lord Jesus Christ be with you.

THE SECOND LETTER OF PAUL TO THE

THESSALONIANS

Paul wrote this letter in A.D. 50 from Corinth shortly after the first letter to Thessalonica. (See the Introduction to the First Letter to the Thessalonians.)

Maybe the church at Thessalonica misunderstood Paul's first letter. Or perhaps someone deceived them with a letter supposedly written by Paul saying that Jesus was to return immediately. Anyway, many of the members were very upset. Some of them were even refusing to work for a living because they thought Jesus would return any day. As for those who had quit work, Paul wrote, "If any one will not work, let him not eat" (2 Thessalonians 3.10).

Paul urged the Thessalonian Christians to be loyal to the gospel he had taught them, whatever they wondered about Jesus' physical return to earth. Paul warned that they should guard against false teachings in any letters written to appear as though they were from him. At the end of the letter Paul called attention to his own personal signature and handwriting (3.17) so that they would not be misled again.

THE SECOND LETTER OF PAUL TO THE

THESSALONIANS

Greetings

1 Paul, Silva'nus, and Timothy,
To the church of the Thessalo'nians in God our Father and the Lord Jesus Christ:
2 Grace to you and peace from God the Father and the Lord Jesus Christ.

THANKSGIVING

3 We are bound to give thanks to God always for you, brethren, as is fitting, because your faith is growing abundantly, and the love of every one of you for one

4 another is increasing. Therefore we ourselves boast of you in the churches of God for your steadfastness and faith in all your persecutions and in the afflictions which you are enduring.
5 This is evidence of the righteous judgment of God, that you may be made worthy of the kingdom of God, for
6 which you are suffering—since indeed God deems it just
7 to repay with affliction those who afflict you, and to grant rest with us to you who are afflicted, when the Lord Jesus

is revealed from heaven with his mighty angels in flaming
8 fire, inflicting vengeance upon those who do not know God and upon those who do not obey the gospel of our
9 Lord Jesus. They shall suffer the punishment of eternal destruction and exclusion from the presence of the Lord
10 and from the glory of his might, when he comes on that day to be glorified in his saints, and to be marveled at in all who have believed, because our testimony to you was
11 believed. To this end we always pray for you, that our God may make you worthy of his call, and may fulfil every
12 good resolve and work of faith by his power, so that the name of our Lord Jesus may be glorified in you, and you in him, according to the grace of our God and the Lord Jesus Christ.

DO NOT BE MISLED

2 Now concerning the coming of our Lord Jesus Christ and our assembling to meet him, we beg you, brethren,
2 not to be quickly shaken in mind or excited, either by spirit or by word, or by letter purporting to be from us,
3 to the effect that the day of the Lord has come. Let no one deceive you in any way; for that day will not come, unless the rebellion comes first, and the man of lawless-
4 ness a is revealed, the son of perdition, who opposes and exalts himself against every so-called god or object of worship, so that he takes his seat in the temple of God,

a Other ancient authorities read *sin*

⁵proclaiming himself to be God. Do you not remember ⁶that when I was still with you I told you this? And you know what is restraining him now so that he may be ⁷revealed in his time. For the mystery of lawlessness is already at work; only he who now restrains it will do so ⁸until he is out of the way. And then the lawless one will be revealed, and the Lord Jesus will slay him with the breath of his mouth and destroy him by his appearing ⁹and his coming. The coming of the lawless one by the activity of Satan will be with all power and with pretended ¹⁰signs and wonders, and with all wicked deception for those who are to perish, because they refused to love the ¹¹truth and so be saved. Therefore God sends upon them a ¹²strong delusion, to make them believe what is false, so that all may be condemned who did not believe the truth but had pleasure in unrighteousness.

¹³ But we are bound to give thanks to God always for you, brethren beloved by the Lord, because God chose you from the beginning ᵇ to be saved, through sanctification by the ¹⁴Spirit ᶜ and belief in the truth. To this he called you through our gospel, so that you may obtain the glory of ¹⁵our Lord Jesus Christ. So then, brethren, stand firm and hold to the traditions which you were taught by us, either by word of mouth or by letter.

¹⁶ Now may our Lord Jesus Christ himself, and God our Father, who loved us and gave us eternal comfort and ¹⁷good hope through grace, comfort your hearts and establish them in every good work and word.

THAT THE WORD MAY TRIUMPH

3 Finally, brethren, pray for us, that the word of the Lord may speed on and triumph, as it did among you, ²and that we may be delivered from wicked and evil men; ³for not all have faith. But the Lord is faithful; he will ⁴strengthen you and guard you from evil.ᵈ And we have confidence in the Lord about you, that you are doing and ⁵will do the things which we command. May the Lord direct your hearts to the love of God and to the steadfastness of Christ.

⁶ Now we command you, brethren, in the name of our Lord Jesus Christ, that you keep away from any brother who is living in idleness and not in accord with the tradi-⁷tion that you received from us. For you yourselves know how you ought to imitate us; we were not idle when we ⁸were with you, we did not eat any one's bread without

paying, but with toil and labor we worked night and day, ⁹that we might not burden any of you. It was not because we have not that right, but to give you in our conduct an ¹⁰example to imitate. For even when we were with you, we gave you this command: If any one will not work, let him ¹¹not eat. For we hear that some of you are living in idle-¹²ness, mere busybodies, not doing any work. Now such persons we command and exhort in the Lord Jesus Christ to do their work in quietness and to earn their own living. ¹³Brethren, do not be weary in well-doing.

¹⁴ If any one refuses to obey what we say in this letter, note that man, and have nothing to do with him, that he ¹⁵may be ashamed. Do not look on him as an enemy, but warn him as a brother.

BENEDICTIONS

¹⁶ Now may the Lord of peace himself give you peace at all times in all ways. The Lord be with you all.

¹⁷ I, Paul, write this greeting with my own hand. This is the mark in every letter of mine; it is the way I write. ¹⁸The grace of our Lord Jesus Christ be with you all.

ᵇ Other ancient authorities read *as the first converts*   ᶜ Or *of spirit*   ᵈ Or *the evil one*

823

INTRODUCTION TO

THE FIRST LETTER OF PAUL TO

TIMOTHY

There is a difference of opinion about who actually wrote this letter and about when it was written. If Paul wrote it, it must be dated before he was executed by the Romans sometime about A.D. 64. There are many good reasons to think that some later Christian wrote it to give the kind of advice Paul would have given to a young pastor like Timothy. In this case, it was probably written as late as about A.D. 125.

Regardless of who wrote it, earnest Christians find that when they read it prayerfully, God speaks to them and helps them through it.

This letter reflects the kind of trust and love Paul had for his young helper and friend Timothy. It contains guidance for Christians on various subjects in language similar to that which Paul uses in other letters. Chapter 5 says that Christians should treat one another as brothers and sisters in one loving family.

THE FIRST LETTER OF PAUL TO

TIMOTHY

Salutation

1 Paul, an apostle of Christ Jesus by command of God our Savior and of Christ Jesus our hope,

2 To Timothy, my true child in the faith:

Grace, mercy, and peace from God the Father and Christ Jesus our Lord.

IN THE SERVICE OF CHRIST

3 As I urged you when I was going to Macedo'nia, remain at Ephesus that you may charge certain persons not to 4 teach any different doctrine, nor to occupy themselves with myths and endless genealogies which promote speculations rather than the divine training [a] that is in faith;

5 whereas the aim of our charge is love that issues from a pure heart and a good conscience and sincere faith. 6 Certain persons by swerving from these have wandered 7 away into vain discussion, desiring to be teachers of the law, without understanding either what they are saying or the things about which they make assertions. 8 Now we know that the law is good, if any one uses it 9 lawfully, understanding this, that the law is not laid down for the just but for the lawless and disobedient, for the ungodly and sinners, for the unholy and profane, for murderers of fathers and murderers of mothers, for man- 10 slayers, immoral persons, sodomites, kidnapers, liars, perjurers, and whatever else is contrary to sound doctrine, 11 in accordance with the glorious gospel of the blessed God with which I have been entrusted.

12 I thank him who has given me strength for this, Christ Jesus our Lord, because he judged me faithful by appoint- 13 ing me to his service, though I formerly blasphemed and persecuted and insulted him; but I received mercy be- 14 cause I had acted ignorantly in unbelief, and the grace of our Lord overflowed for me with the faith and love that 15 are in Christ Jesus. The saying is sure and worthy of full acceptance, that Christ Jesus came into the world to save 16 sinners. And I am the foremost of sinners; but I received mercy for this reason, that in me, as the foremost, Jesus Christ might display his perfect patience for an example 17 to those who were to believe in him for eternal life. To the King of ages, immortal, invisible, the only God, be honor and glory for ever and ever.[b] Amen.

18 This charge I commit to you, Timothy, my son, in accordance with the prophetic utterances which pointed

[a] Or stewardship, or order   [b] Greek to the ages of ages

to you, that inspired by them you may wage the good
19 warfare, holding faith and a good conscience. By rejecting conscience, certain persons have made shipwreck of their
20 faith, among them Hymenae′us and Alexander, whom I have delivered to Satan that they may learn not to blaspheme.

2 First of all, then, I urge that supplications, prayers, intercessions, and thanksgivings be made for all men,
2 for kings and all who are in high positions, that we may lead a quiet and peaceable life, godly and respectful in
3 every way. This is good, and it is acceptable in the sight
4 of God our Savior, who desires all men to be saved and
5 to come to the knowledge of the truth. For there is one God, and there is one mediator between God and men,
6 the man Christ Jesus, who gave himself as a ransom for all, the testimony to which was borne at the proper time.
7 For this I was appointed a preacher and apostle (I am telling the truth, I am not lying), a teacher of the Gentiles in faith and truth.

THE CHARACTER AND DUTIES OF CHRISTIANS

8 I desire then that in every place the men should pray,
9 lifting holy hands without anger or quarreling; also that women should adorn themselves modestly and sensibly in seemly apparel not with braided hair or gold or pearls
10 or costly attire but by good deeds, as befits women who
11 profess religion. Let a woman learn in silence with all
12 submissiveness. I permit no woman to teach or to have
13 authority over men; she is to keep silent. For Adam was
14 formed first, then Eve; and Adam was not deceived, but the woman was deceived and became a transgressor.
15 Yet woman will be saved through bearing children,[c] if she continues[d] in faith and love and holiness, with modesty.

3 The saying is sure: If any one aspires to the office of
2 bishop, he desires a noble task. Now a bishop must be above reproach, the husband of one wife, temperate,
3 sensible, dignified, hospitable, an apt teacher, no drunkard, not violent but gentle, not quarrelsome, and no lover
4 of money. He must manage his own household well, keeping his children submissive and respectful in every
5 way; for if a man does not know how to manage his
6 own household, how can he care for God's church? He must not be a recent convert, or he may be puffed up with conceit and fall into the condemnation of the devil;[f]
7 moreover he must be well thought of by outsiders, or he may fall into reproach and the snare of the devil.[f]

8 Deacons likewise must be serious, not double-tongued,
9 not addicted to much wine, not greedy for gain; they must hold the mystery of the faith with a clear conscience.
10 And let them also be tested first; then if they prove them-
11 selves blameless let them serve as deacons. The women likewise must be serious, no slanderers, but temperate,
12 faithful in all things. Let deacons be the husband of one

wife, and let them manage their children and their house-
13 holds well; for those who serve well as deacons gain a good standing for themselves and also great confidence in the faith which is in Christ Jesus.

14 I hope to come to you soon, but I am writing these
15 instructions to you so that, if I am delayed, you may know how one ought to behave in the household of God, which is the church of the living God, the pillar and bulwark of
16 the truth. Great indeed, we confess, is the mystery of our religion:

He[h] was manifested in the flesh,
vindicated[i] in the Spirit,
    seen by angels,
preached among the nations,
believed on in the world,
    taken up in glory.

The Good Minister

4 Now the Spirit expressly says that in later times some will depart from the faith by giving heed to
2 deceitful spirits and doctrines of demons, through the
3 pretensions of liars whose consciences are seared, who forbid marriage and enjoin abstinence from foods which God created to be received with thanksgiving by those who
4 believe and know the truth. For everything created by God is good, and nothing is to be rejected if it is received with
5 thanksgiving; for then it is consecrated by the word of God and prayer.

6 If you put these instructions before the brethren, you will be a good minister of Christ Jesus, nourished on the words of the faith and of the good doctrine which you
7 have followed. Have nothing to do with godless and silly
8 myths. Train yourself in godliness; for while bodily training is of some value, godliness is of value in every way, as it holds promise for the present life and also for the life to
9 come. The saying is sure and worthy of full acceptance.
10 For to this end we toil and strive,[j] because we have our hope set on the living God, who is the Savior of all men, especially of those who believe.

11, 12 Command and teach these things. Let no one despise your youth, but set the believers an example in speech and
13 conduct, in love, in faith, in purity. Till I come, attend to the public reading of scripture, to preaching, to teaching.
14 Do not neglect the gift you have, which was given you by prophetic utterance when the council of elders laid their
15 hands upon you. Practice these duties, devote yourself to
16 them, so that all may see your progress. Take heed to yourself and to your teaching; hold to that, for by so doing you will save both yourself and your hearers.

5 Do not rebuke an older man but exhort him as you
2 would a father; treat younger men like brothers, older

---

[c] Or by the birth of the child   [d] Greek they continue
[h] Greek Who; other ancient authorities read God; others, Which
[f] Or slanderer
[i] Or justified   [j] Other ancient authorities read suffer reproach

women like mothers, younger women like sisters, in all purity.

3, 4 Honor widows who are real widows. If a widow has children or grandchildren, let them first learn their religious duty to their own family and make some return to their parents; for this is acceptable in the sight of God. 5 She who is a real widow, and is left all alone, has set her hope on God and continues in supplications and prayers 6 night and day; whereas she who is self-indulgent is dead 7 even while she lives. Command this, so that they may be 8 without reproach. If any one does not provide for his relatives, and especially for his own family, he has disowned the faith and is worse than an unbeliever.

9 Let a widow be enrolled if she is not less than sixty years of age, having been the wife of one husband; 10 and she must be well attested for her good deeds, as one who has brought up children, shown hospitality, washed the feet of the saints, relieved the afflicted, and devoted 11 herself to doing good in every way. But refuse to enrol younger widows; for when they grow wanton against 12 Christ they desire to marry, and so they incur condemna- 13 tion for having violated their first pledge. Besides that, they learn to be idlers, gadding about from house to house, and not only idlers but gossips and busybodies, saying 14 what they should not. So I would have younger widows marry, bear children, rule their households, and give the 15 enemy no occasion to revile us. For some have already 16 strayed after Satan. If any believing woman¹ has relatives who are widows, let her assist them; let the church not be burdened, so that it may assist those who are real widows.

17 Let the elders who rule well be considered worthy of double honor, especially those who labor in preaching and 18 teaching; for the scripture says, "You shall not muzzle an ox when it is treading out the grain," and, "The laborer

19 deserves his wages." Never admit any charge against an 20 elder except on the evidence of two or three witnesses. As for those who persist in sin, rebuke them in the presence 21 of all, so that the rest may stand in fear. In the presence of God and of Christ Jesus and of the elect angels I charge you to keep these rules without favor, doing nothing from 22 partiality. Do not be hasty in the laying on of hands, nor participate in another man's sins; keep yourself pure.

23 No longer drink only water, but use a little wine for the sake of your stomach and your frequent ailments.

24 The sins of some men are conspicuous, pointing to judg- 25 ment, but the sins of others appear later. So also good deeds are conspicuous; and even when they are not, they cannot remain hidden.

6 Let all who are under the yoke of slavery regard their masters as worthy of all honor, so that the name

2 of God and the teaching may not be defamed. Those who have believing masters must not be disrespectful on the ground that they are brethren; rather they must serve all the better since those who benefit by their service are believers and beloved.

3 Teach and urge these duties. If any one teaches otherwise and does not agree with the sound words of our Lord Jesus Christ and the teaching which accords with godli- 4 ness, he is puffed up with conceit, he knows nothing; he has a morbid craving for controversy and for disputes about words, which produce envy, dissension, slander, 5 base suspicions, and wrangling among men who are depraved in mind and bereft of the truth, imagining that 6 godliness is a means of gain. There is great gain in godli- 7 ness with contentment; for we brought nothing into the world, and ᵐ we cannot take anything out of the world; 8 but if we have food and clothing, with these we shall be 9 content. But those who desire to be rich fall into tempta- tion, into a snare, into many senseless and hurtful desires 10 that plunge men into ruin and destruction. For the love of money is the root of all evils; it is through this craving that some have wandered away from the faith and pierced their hearts with many pangs.

Fight the Good Fight

11 But as for you, man of God, shun all this; aim at right- eousness, godliness, faith, love, steadfastness, gentleness. 12 Fight the good fight of the faith; take hold of the eternal life to which you were called when you made the good 13 confession in the presence of many witnesses. In the presence of God who gives life to all things, and of Christ Jesus who in his testimony before Pontius Pilate made 14 the good confession, I charge you to keep the command- ment unstained and free from reproach until the appear- 15 ing of our Lord Jesus Christ; and this will be made mani- fest at the proper time by the blessed and only Sovereign, 16 the King of kings and Lord of lords, who alone has im- mortality and dwells in unapproachable light, whom no man has ever seen or can see. To him be honor and eternal dominion. Amen.

The Use of Riches

17 As for the rich in this world, charge them not to be haughty, nor to set their hopes on uncertain riches but on God who richly furnishes us with everything to enjoy. 18 They are to do good, to be rich in good deeds, liberal 19 and generous, thus laying up for themselves a good foun- dation for the future, so that they may take hold of the life which is life indeed.

20 O Timothy, guard what has been entrusted to you. Avoid the godless chatter and contradictions of what is 21 falsely called knowledge, for by professing it some have missed the mark as regards the faith.

Grace be with you.

¹ Other ancient authorities read *man or woman*; others, simply *man*

ᵐ Other ancient authorities insert *it is certain that*

— INTRODUCTION TO —

THE SECOND LETTER OF PAUL TO

TIMOTHY

There is doubt about when this letter was written and about who wrote it. It was probably written either about A.D. 64 or about A.D. 125. (See the Introduction to the First Letter to Timothy on page 824.)

Whether Paul or some other faithful Christian leader wrote it, this tender and inspiring letter reads like a farewell message of the great apostle to his trusted helper Timothy. It certainly reflects many of Paul's ideas. It tells of what must have been the suffering and loneliness of Paul in his last days in prison, when all his helpers were preaching in faraway places and when other friends had deserted him. Through the letter runs the note of high courage and faith in spite of his loneliness, trouble and approaching death.

THE SECOND LETTER OF PAUL TO

TIMOTHY

Salutation

1 Paul, an apostle of Christ Jesus by the will of God according to the promise of the life which is in Christ Jesus,

2 To Timothy, my beloved child:

Grace, mercy, and peace from God the Father and Christ Jesus our Lord.

TESTIFY TO OUR LORD

3 I thank God whom I serve with a clear conscience, as did my fathers, when I remember you constantly in my 4 prayers. As I remember your tears, I long night and day 5 to see you, that I may be filled with joy. I am reminded of your sincere faith, a faith that dwelt first in your grandmother Lo′is and your mother Eunice and now, I 6 am sure, dwells in you. Hence I remind you to rekindle the gift of God that is within you through the laying on 7 of my hands; for God did not give us a spirit of timidity but a spirit of power and love and self-control.

8 Do not be ashamed then of testifying to our Lord, nor of me his prisoner, but share in suffering for the 9 gospel in the power of God, who saved us and called us with a holy calling, not in virtue of our works but in virtue of his own purpose and the grace which he gave 10 us in Christ Jesus ages ago, and now has manifested through the appearing of our Savior Christ Jesus, who abolished death and brought life and immortality to light 11 through the gospel. For this gospel I was appointed a 12 preacher and apostle and teacher, and therefore I suffer

ᵃ Or *what I have entrusted to him*

as I do. But I am not ashamed, for I know whom I have believed, and I am sure that he is able to guard until that 13 Day what has been entrusted to me.ᵃ Follow the pattern of the sound words which you have heard from me, in the 14 faith and love which are in Christ Jesus; guard the truth that has been entrusted to you by the Holy Spirit who dwells within us.

15 You are aware that all who are in Asia turned away from me, and among them Phy′gelus and Hermog′enes. 16 May the Lord grant mercy to the household of Onesiph′-orus, for he often refreshed me; he was not ashamed of 17 my chains, but when he arrived in Rome he searched for 18 me eagerly and found me—may the Lord grant him to

find mercy from the Lord on that Day—and you well know all the service he rendered at Ephesus.

The Minister as Christ's Soldier

2 You then, my son, be strong in the grace that is in 2 Christ Jesus, and what you have heard from me before many witnesses entrust to faithful men who will be able 3 to teach others also. Share in suffering as a good 4 soldier of Christ Jesus. No soldier on service gets entangled in civilian pursuits, since his aim is to satisfy

⁵ the one who enlisted him. An athlete is not crowned unless
⁶ he competes according to the rules. It is the hard-working farmer who ought to have the first share of the crops.
⁷ Think over what I say, for the Lord will grant you understanding in everything.

⁸ Remember Jesus Christ, risen from the dead, descended
⁹ from David, as preached in my gospel, the gospel for which I am suffering and wearing fetters like a criminal.
¹⁰ But the word of God is not fettered. Therefore I endure everything for the sake of the elect, that they also may obtain the salvation in Christ Jesus with its eternal glory.

¹¹ The saying is sure:

If we have died with him, we shall also live with him;
¹² if we endure, we shall also reign with him;
if we deny him, he also will deny us;

¹³ if we are faithless, he remains faithful—
for he cannot deny himself.

¹⁴ Remind them of this, and charge them before the Lord ᵇ to avoid disputing about words, which does no good, but
¹⁵ only ruins the hearers. Do your best to present yourself to God as one approved, a workman who has no need to
¹⁶ be ashamed, rightly handling the word of truth. Avoid such godless chatter, for it will lead people into more
¹⁷ and more ungodliness, and their talk will eat its way like gangrene. Among them are Hymenae'us and Phile'tus,
¹⁸ who have swerved from the truth by holding that the resurrection is past already. They are upsetting the faith
¹⁹ of some. But God's firm foundation stands, bearing this seal: "The Lord knows those who are his," and, "Let every one who names the name of the Lord depart from iniquity."

²⁰ In a great house there are not only vessels of gold and silver but also of wood and earthenware, and some for
²¹ noble use, some for ignoble. If any one purifies himself from what is ignoble, then he will be a vessel for noble use, consecrated and useful to the master of the house,
²² ready for any good work. So shun youthful passions and aim at righteousness, faith, love, and peace, along with
²³ those who call upon the Lord from a pure heart. Have nothing to do with stupid, senseless controversies; you
²⁴ know that they breed quarrels. And the Lord's servant must not be quarrelsome but kindly to every one, an apt
²⁵ teacher, forbearing, correcting his opponents with gentle-

ness. God may perhaps grant that they will repent and
²⁶ come to know the truth, and they may escape from the snare of the devil, after being captured by him to do his will.ᶜ

3 But understand this, that in the last days there will
² come times of stress. For men will be lovers of self, lovers of money, proud, arrogant, abusive, disobedient to
³ their parents, ungrateful, unholy, inhuman, implacable,
⁴ slanderers, profligates, fierce, haters of good, treacherous, reckless, swollen with conceit, lovers of pleasure rather
⁵ than lovers of God, holding the form of religion but
⁶ denying the power of it. Avoid such people. For among them are those who make their way into households and capture weak women, burdened with sins and swayed by
⁷ various impulses, who will listen to anybody and can
⁸ never arrive at a knowledge of the truth. As Jannes and Jambres opposed Moses, so these men also oppose the
⁹ truth, men of corrupt mind and counterfeit faith; but they will not get very far, for their folly will be plain to all, as was that of those two men.

¹⁰ Now you have observed my teaching, my conduct, my aim in life, my faith, my patience, my love, my stead-
¹¹ fastness, my persecutions, my sufferings, what befell me at Antioch, at Ico'nium, and at Lystra, what persecutions I endured; yet from them all the Lord rescued me.
¹² Indeed all who desire to live a godly life in Christ Jesus
¹³ will be persecuted, while evil men and impostors will go
¹⁴ on from bad to worse, deceivers and deceived. But as for you, continue in what you have learned and have firmly
¹⁵ believed, knowing from whom you learned it and how from childhood you have been acquainted with the sacred writings which are able to instruct you for salvation
¹⁶ through faith in Christ Jesus. All scripture is inspired by God and ᵈ profitable for teaching, for reproof, for cor-
¹⁷ rection, and for training in righteousness, that the man of God may be complete, equipped for every good work.

Fulfilling the Ministry

4 I charge you in the presence of God and of Christ Jesus who is to judge the living and the dead, and
² by his appearing and his kingdom: preach the word, be urgent in season and out of season, convince, rebuke, and
³ exhort, be unfailing in patience and in teaching. For the time is coming when people will not endure sound teach-

ᵇ Other ancient authorities read *God*   ᶜ Or *by him, to do his* (that is, God's) *will*   ᵈ Or *Every scripture inspired by God is also*

ing, but having itching ears they will accumulate for themselves teachers to suit their own likings, and will turn away from listening to the truth and wander into myths. 5 As for you, always be steady, endure suffering, do the work of an evangelist, fulfil your ministry.

6 For I am already on the point of being sacrificed; the 7 time of my departure has come. I have fought the good fight, I have finished the race, I have kept the faith. 8 Henceforth there is laid up for me the crown of righteousness, which the Lord, the righteous judge, will award to me on that Day, and not only to me but also to all who have loved his appearing.

9, 10 Do your best to come to me soon. For Demas, in love with this present world, has deserted me and gone to Thessaloni'ca; Crescens has gone to Galatia,e Titus to 11 Dalmatia. Luke alone is with me. Get Mark and bring 12 him with you; for he is very useful in serving me. Tych'- 13 icus I have sent to Ephesus. When you come, bring the cloak that I left with Carpus at Tro'as, also the books, 14 and above all the parchments. Alexander the coppersmith did me great harm; the Lord will requite him for his 15 deeds. Beware of him yourself, for he strongly opposed 16 our message. At my first defense no one took my part; all 17 deserted me. May it not be charged against them! But the

e Other ancient authorities read *Gaul*

Lord stood by me and gave me strength to proclaim the message fully, that all the Gentiles might hear it. So I 18 was rescued from the lion's mouth. The Lord will rescue me from every evil and save me for his heavenly kingdom. To him be the glory for ever and ever. Amen.

19 Greet Prisca and Aquila, and the household of One-20 siph'orus. Eras'tus remained at Corinth; Troph'imus I 21 left ill at Mile'tus. Do your best to come before winter. Eubu'lus sends greetings to you, as do Pudens and Linus and Claudia and all the brethren.

22 The Lord be with your spirit. Grace be with you.

INTRODUCTION TO

TITUS

Titus, like Timothy, was one of Paul's closest friends. Because this letter contains few of Paul's favorite teachings and varies in style and wording from Paul's letters, there is much doubt as to whether Paul actually wrote it. It was probably written by a great admirer of Paul's as late as A.D. 125. (See the Introduction to the First Letter to Timothy on page 824.)

The letter gives guidance for the church on the Mediterranean island of Crete. It holds up the highest standards of life for all who have faith in Christ.

THE LETTER OF PAUL TO

TITUS

Salutation

1 Paul, a servant[a] of God and an apostle of Jesus Christ, to further the faith of God's elect and their ² knowledge of the truth which accords with godliness, in hope of eternal life which God who never lies, promised ³ ages ago and at the proper time manifested in his word through the preaching with which I have been entrusted by command of God our Savior;

⁴ To Titus, my true child in a common faith:

Grace and peace from God the Father and Christ Jesus our Savior.

STEWARDS OF GOD

⁵ This is why I left you in Crete, that you might amend what was defective, and appoint elders in every town as ⁶ I directed you, if any man is blameless, the husband of one wife, and his children are believers and not open to ⁷ the charge of being profligate or insubordinate. For a

bishop, as God's steward, must be blameless; he must not be arrogant or quick-tempered or a drunkard or violent ⁸ or greedy for gain, but hospitable, a lover of goodness, master of himself, upright, holy, and self-controlled; ⁹ he must hold firm to the sure word as taught, so that he may be able to give instruction in sound doctrine and ¹⁰ also to confute those who contradict it. For there are many

insubordinate men, empty talkers and deceivers, espe-¹¹ cially the circumcision party; they must be silenced, since they are upsetting whole families by teaching for base ¹² gain what they have no right to teach. One of themselves, a prophet of their own, said, "Cretans are always liars, ¹³ evil beasts, lazy gluttons." This testimony is true. Therefore rebuke them sharply, that they may be sound in the ¹⁴ faith, instead of giving heed to Jewish myths or to com-¹⁵ mands of men who reject the truth. To the pure all things are pure, but to the corrupt and unbelieving nothing is pure; their very minds and consciences are corrupted. ¹⁶ They profess to know God, but they deny him by their deeds; they are detestable, disobedient, unfit for any good deed.

Duties of Ministers

2 But as for you, teach what befits sound doctrine. ² Bid the older men be temperate, serious, sensible, ³ sound in faith, in love, and in steadfastness. Bid the older women likewise to be reverent in behavior, not to be slanderers or slaves to drink; they are to teach what is ⁴ good, and so train the young women to love their hus-⁵ bands and children, to be sensible, chaste, domestic, kind, and submissive to their husbands, that the word of God ⁶ may not be discredited. Likewise urge the younger men

---

ª Or *slave*

7 to control themselves. Show yourself in all respects a model of good deeds, and in your teaching show integrity, 8 gravity, and sound speech that cannot be censured, so that an opponent may be put to shame, having nothing evil 9 to say of us. Bid slaves to be submissive to their masters and to give satisfaction in every respect; they are not to 10 be refractory, nor to pilfer, but to show entire and true fidelity, so that in everything they may adorn the doctrine of God our Savior.

11 For the grace of God has appeared for the salvation of 12 all men, training us to renounce irreligion and worldly passions, and to live sober, upright, and godly lives 13 in this world, awaiting our blessed hope, the appearing of the glory of our great God and Savior c Jesus Christ, 14 who gave himself for us to redeem us from all iniquity and to purify for himself a people of his own who are zealous for good deeds.

15 Declare these things; exhort and reprove with all authority. Let no one disregard you.

Christian Conduct

3 Remind them to be submissive to rulers and authorities, to be obedient, to be ready for any honest work, 2 to speak evil of no one, to avoid quarreling, to be gentle, 3 and to show perfect courtesy toward all men. For we ourselves were once foolish, disobedient, led astray, slaves to various passions and pleasures, passing our days in malice 4 and envy, hated by men and hating one another; but when the goodness and loving kindness of God our Savior 5 appeared, he saved us, not because of deeds done by us in righteousness, but in virtue of his own mercy, by the washing of regeneration and renewal in the Holy Spirit, 6 which he poured out upon us richly through Jesus Christ

7 our Savior, so that we might be justified by his grace and 8 become heirs in hope of eternal life. The saying is sure.

I desire you to insist on these things, so that those who have believed in God may be careful to apply themselves to good deeds; d these are excellent and profitable to men.

9 But avoid stupid controversies, genealogies, dissensions, and quarrels over the law, for they are unprofitable and 10 futile. As for a man who is factious, after admonishing him once or twice, have nothing more to do with him, 11 knowing that such a person is perverted and sinful; he is self-condemned.

12 When I send Artemas or Tych'icus to you, do your best to come to me at Nicop'olis, for I have decided to spend 13 the winter there. Do your best to speed Zenas the lawyer and Apol'los on their way; see that they lack nothing. 14 And let our people learn to apply themselves to good deeds, d so as to help cases of urgent need, and not to be unfruitful.

15 All who are with me send greetings to you. Greet those who love us in the faith.

Grace be with you all.

c Or of the great God and our Savior   d Or enter honorable occupations

INTRODUCTION TO

PHILEMON

This is one of the very short books of the Bible. Perhaps the apostle Paul wrote many such personal letters, but this is the only one, so personal in its message, that has come down to us. It is a note to Philemon, who lived in Colossae. Philemon was a friend who had been won to faith in Christ by Paul. The letter was probably written about A.D. 61 from prison in Rome (Acts 28.14, 30-31). It was probably delivered with the Letter to the Colossians by a slave named Onesimus.

Philemon had owned this slave named Onesimus, but he had run away. While Paul was in prison, he became acquainted with Onesimus, who had come to Rome when he ran away from his master. Soon Paul was telling him the good news about Jesus Christ, and Onesimus the slave became a Christian.

Onesimus decided to return to his master, and Paul gave him this letter to take back with him. In it Paul asked Philemon to receive Onesimus as a fellow Christian, "no longer as a slave but more than a slave, as a beloved brother" (verse 16).

It is possible that the runaway slave in later years became a great Christian leader. At any rate, there was a bishop named Onesimus at Ephesus about A.D. 100, some forty years after Paul sent Onesimus back to his master with the news that he had been converted to Christ. Many scholars think that this runaway slave, Bishop Onesimus, collected Paul's writings and possibly wrote the Letter to the Ephesians.

THE LETTER OF PAUL TO

PHILEMON

Salutation

1 Paul, a prisoner for Christ Jesus, and Timothy our brother,

2 To Phile′mon our beloved fellow worker and Ap′phia our sister and Archip′pus our fellow soldier, and the church in your house:

3 Grace to you and peace from God our Father and the Lord Jesus Christ.

AN APPEAL FOR ONESIMUS

4 I thank my God always when I remember you in my
5 prayers, because I hear of your love and of the faith which you have toward the Lord Jesus and all the saints,
6 and I pray that the sharing of your faith may promote the knowledge of all the good that is ours in Christ.
7 For I have derived much joy and comfort from your love, my brother, because the hearts of the saints have been refreshed through you.

8 Accordingly, though I am bold enough in Christ to
9 command you to do what is required, yet for love's sake I prefer to appeal to you—I, Paul, an ambassador ᵃ and
10 now a prisoner also for Christ Jesus—I appeal to you for my child, Ones′imus, whose father I have become in my
11 imprisonment. (Formerly he was useless to you, but now
12 he is indeed useful ᵇ to you and to me.) I am sending him
13 back to you, sending my very heart. I would have been glad to keep him with me, in order that he might serve me on your behalf during my imprisonment for the
14 gospel; but I preferred to do nothing without your consent in order that your goodness might not be by compulsion but of your own free will.

ᵃ Or *an old man*   ᵇ The name Onesimus means *useful* or (compare verse 20) *beneficial*

832

15 Perhaps this is why he was parted from you for a while,
16 that you might have him back for ever, no longer as a slave but more than a slave, as a beloved brother, especially to me but how much more to you, both in the flesh and
17 in the Lord. So if you consider me your partner, receive
18 him as you would receive me. If he has wronged you at all, or owes you anything, charge that to my account.
19 I, Paul, write this with my own hand, I will repay it— to say nothing of your owing me even your own self.
20 Yes, brother, I want some benefit from you in the Lord. Refresh my heart in Christ.
21 Confident of your obedience, I write to you, knowing
22 that you will do even more than I say. At the same time, prepare a guest room for me, for I am hoping through your prayers to be granted to you.
23 Ep'aphras, my fellow prisoner in Christ Jesus, sends
24 greetings to you, and so do Mark, Aristar'chus, Demas, and Luke, my fellow workers.
25 The grace of the Lord Jesus Christ be with your spirit.

INTRODUCTION TO

HEBREWS

This letter was written by an unnamed Christian about A.D. 85 to 95 for Christians at Rome. The Letter to Hebrews teaches that Jesus is the Jewish Messiah and that he is also the Savior of all men who have faith in him. Perhaps its purpose was to encourage Christians to be loyal to Christ even when the Roman emperor Domitian was persecuting and killing Christians.

The letter contains many references to Jewish customs and teachings. The main idea is that Jesus is the perfect high priest who offered his own life as the perfect sacrifice to overcome the sins of the world. Sacrifices conducted by a human priest had been the Jewish way of seeking God's forgiveness, so this book presents Jesus as the true high priest sent by God for all men, taking the place of all other priests and sacrifices.

Hebrews 11 tells the story of how men in ancient times were saved by their faith. This chapter reaches its climax by showing how Christians are truly saved from their sins because they have faith in Christ.

THE LETTER TO THE

HEBREWS

GOD HAS SPOKEN TO US BY A SON

1 In many and various ways God spoke of old to our 2 fathers by the prophets; but in these last days he has spoken to us by a Son, whom he appointed the heir of all things, through whom also he created the world. 3 He reflects the glory of God and bears the very stamp of his nature, upholding the universe by his word of power. When he had made purification for sins, he sat 4 down at the right hand of the Majesty on high, having become as much superior to angels as the name he has

obtained is more excellent than theirs.

5 For to what angel did God ever say,
"Thou art my Son,
today I have begotten thee"?
Or again,
"I will be to him a father,
and he shall be to me a son"?
6 And again, when he brings the firstborn into the world, he says,
"Let all God's angels worship him."

7 Of the angels he says,
"Who makes his angels winds,
and his servants flames of fire."
8 But of the Son he says,
"Thy throne, O God,[a] is for ever and ever,
the righteous scepter is the scepter of thy[b] kingdom.
9 Thou hast loved righteousness and hated lawlessness;
therefore God, thy God, has anointed thee
with the oil of gladness beyond thy comrades."
10 And,
"Thou, Lord, didst found the earth in the beginning,
and the heavens are the work of thy hands;
11 they will perish, but thou remainest;
they will all grow old like a garment,
12 like a mantle thou wilt roll them up,
and they will be changed.[c]
But thou art the same,
and thy years will never end."
13 But to what angel has he ever said,
"Sit at my right hand,
till I make thy enemies
a stool for thy feet"?
14 Are they not all ministering spirits sent forth to serve, for the sake of those who are to obtain salvation?

2 Therefore we must pay the closer attention to what 2 we have heard, lest we drift away from it. For if the message declared by angels was valid and every transgression or disobedience received a just retribution,

---

[a] Or God is thy throne   [b] Other ancient authorities read his   [c] Other ancient authorities add like a garment

³how shall we escape if we neglect such a great salvation? It was declared at first by the Lord, and it was attested ⁴to us by those who heard him, while God also bore witness by signs and wonders and various miracles and by gifts of the Holy Spirit distributed according to his own will.

⁵ For it was not to angels that God subjected the world ⁶to come, of which we are speaking. It has been testified somewhere,

"What is man that thou art mindful of him,
or the son of man, that thou carest for him?
⁷Thou didst make him for a little while lower than the
angels,
thou hast crowned him with glory and honor,ᵈ
⁸putting everything in subjection under his feet."
Now in putting everything in subjection to him, he left nothing outside his control. As it is, we do not yet see ⁹everything in subjection to him. But we see Jesus, who for a little while was made lower than the angels, crowned with glory and honor because of the suffering of death, so that by the grace of God he might taste death for every one.

¹⁰ For it was fitting that he, for whom and by whom all things exist, in bringing many sons to glory, should make the pioneer of their salvation perfect through suf-¹¹fering. For he who sanctifies and those who are sanctified have all one origin. That is why he is not ashamed to call ¹²them brethren, saying,

"I will proclaim thy name to my brethren,
in the midst of the congregation I will praise thee."
¹³And again,
"I will put my trust in him."
And again,
"Here am I, and the children God has given me."
¹⁴ Since therefore the children share in flesh and blood, he himself likewise partook of the same nature, that through death he might destroy him who has the power ¹⁵of death, that is, the devil, and deliver all those who through fear of death were subject to lifelong bondage. ¹⁶For surely it is not with angels that he is concerned but ¹⁷with the descendants of Abraham. Therefore he had to be made like his brethren in every respect, so that he might become a merciful and faithful high priest in the service of God, to make expiation for the sins of the people. ¹⁸For because he himself has suffered and been tempted, he is able to help those who are tempted.

Jesus Above Moses

3 Therefore, holy brethren, who share in a heavenly call, consider Jesus, the apostle and high priest of ²our confession. He was faithful to him who appointed him, just as Moses also was faithful in ᵉ God's house. ³Yet Jesus has been counted worthy of as much more glory than Moses as the builder of a house has more honor than ⁴the house. (For every house is built by some one, but the ⁵builder of all things is God.) Now Moses was faithful in all God's house as a servant, to testify to the things that ⁶were to be spoken later, but Christ was faithful over God's ᶠ house as a son. And we are his house if we hold fast our confidence and pride in our hope.ᵍ

⁷ Therefore, as the Holy Spirit says,
"Today, when you hear his voice,
⁸do not harden your hearts as in the rebellion,
on the day of testing in the wilderness,
⁹where your fathers put me to the test
and saw my works for forty years.
¹⁰Therefore I was provoked with that generation,
and said, 'They always go astray in their hearts;
they have not known my ways.'
¹¹As I swore in my wrath,
'They shall never enter my rest.'"
¹²Take care, brethren, lest there be in any of you an evil, unbelieving heart, leading you to fall away from the living ¹³God. But exhort one another every day, as long as it is called "today," that none of you may be hardened by ¹⁴the deceitfulness of sin. For we share in Christ, if only ¹⁵we hold our first confidence firm to the end, while it is said,

"Today, when you hear his voice,
do not harden your hearts
as in the rebellion."
¹⁶Who were they that heard and yet were rebellious? Was it not all those who left Egypt under the leadership of ¹⁷Moses? And with whom was he provoked forty years? Was it not with those who sinned, whose bodies fell in ¹⁸the wilderness? And to whom did he swear that they should never enter his rest, but to those who were dis-¹⁹obedient? So we see that they were unable to enter because of unbelief.

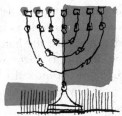

4 Therefore, while the promise of entering his rest remains, let us fear lest any of you be judged to have ²failed to reach it. For good news came to us just as to them; but the message which they heard did not benefit them, because it did not meet with faith in the hearers.ʰ ³For we who have believed enter that rest, as he has said,

"As I swore in my wrath,
'They shall never enter my rest,'"
although his works were finished from the foundation of ⁴the world. For he has somewhere spoken of the seventh

---

ᵈ Other ancient authorities insert *and didst set him over the works of thy hands*
ᶠ Greek *his*   ᵍ Other ancient authorities insert *firm to the end*
ʰ Other manuscripts read *they were not united in faith with the hearers*

ᵉ Other ancient authorities insert *all*

day in this way, "And God rested on the seventh day
5 from all his works." And again in this place he said,
"They shall never enter my rest."
6 Since therefore it remains for some to enter it, and those
who formerly received the good news failed to enter be-
7 cause of disobedience, again he sets a certain day, "Today," saying through David so long afterward, in the
words already quoted,
"Today, when you hear his voice,
  do not harden your hearts."
8 For if Joshua had given them rest, God[i] would not speak
9 later of another day. So then, there remains a sabbath rest
10 for the people of God; for whoever enters God's rest also
ceases from his labors as God did from his.
11 Let us therefore strive to enter that rest, that no one
12 fall by the same sort of disobedience. For the word of
God is living and active, sharper than any two-edged
sword, piercing to the division of soul and spirit, of joints
and marrow, and discerning the thoughts and intentions
13 of the heart. And before him no creature is hidden, but
all are open and laid bare to the eyes of him with whom
we have to do.

THE SON OF GOD OUR HIGH PRIEST

14 Since then we have a great high priest who has passed
through the heavens, Jesus, the Son of God, let us hold
15 fast our confession. For we have not a high priest who is
unable to sympathize with our weaknesses, but one who
in every respect has been tempted as we are, yet without
16 sin. Let us then with confidence draw near to the
throne of grace, that we may receive mercy and find grace
to help in time of need.

5 For every high priest chosen from among men is
appointed to act on behalf of men in relation to God,
2 to offer gifts and sacrifices for sins. He can deal gently
with the ignorant and wayward, since he himself is beset
3 with weakness. Because of this he is bound to offer
sacrifice for his own sins as well as for those of the
4 people. And one does not take the honor upon himself,
but he is called by God, just as Aaron was.
5 So also Christ did not exalt himself to be made a high
priest, but was appointed by him who said to him,
"Thou art my Son,
  today I have begotten thee";
6 as he says also in another place,
"Thou art a priest for ever,
  after the order of Melchiz'edek."
7 In the days of his flesh, Jesus[j] offered up prayers and
supplications, with loud cries and tears, to him who was
able to save him from death, and he was heard for his
8 godly fear. Although he was a Son, he learned obedience
9 through what he suffered; and being made perfect he
became the source of eternal salvation to all who obey

10 him, being designated by God a high priest after the
order of Melchiz'edek.
11 About this we have much to say which is hard to
12 explain, since you have become dull of hearing. For
though by this time you ought to be teachers, you need
some one to teach you again the first principles of God's
13 word. You need milk, not solid food; for every one who
lives on milk is unskilled in the word of righteousness,
14 for he is a child. But solid food is for the mature, for
those who have their faculties trained by practice to distinguish good from evil.

6 Therefore let us leave the elementary doctrine of
Christ and go on to maturity, not laying again a
foundation of repentance from dead works and of faith
2 toward God, with instruction[k] about ablutions, the laying

on of hands, the resurrection of the dead, and eternal
3, 4 judgment. And this we will do if God permits.[l] For it is
impossible to restore again to repentance those who have
once been enlightened, who have tasted the heavenly gift,
5 and have become partakers of the Holy Spirit, and have
tasted the goodness of the word of God and the powers of
6 the age to come, if they then commit apostasy, since they
crucify the Son of God on their own account and hold
7 him up to contempt. For land which has drunk the rain
that often falls upon it, and brings forth vegetation useful
to those for whose sake it is cultivated, receives a blessing
8 from God. But if it bears thorns and thistles, it is worthless and near to being cursed; its end is to be burned.
9 Though we speak thus, yet in your case, beloved, we
10 feel sure of better things that belong to salvation. For
God is not so unjust as to overlook your work and the
love which you showed for his sake in serving the saints,
11 as you still do. And we desire each one of you to show
the same earnestness in realizing the full assurance of
12 hope until the end, so that you may not be sluggish, but
imitators of those who through faith and patience inherit
the promises.
13 For when God made a promise to Abraham, since he
had no one greater by whom to swear, he swore by him-
14 self, saying, "Surely I will bless you and multiply you."
15 And thus Abraham,[m] having patiently endured, obtained
16 the promise. Men indeed swear by a greater than themselves, and in all their disputes an oath is final for con-
17 firmation. So when God desired to show more convinc-
ingly to the heirs of the promise the unchangeable char-
18 acter of his purpose, he interposed with an oath, so that

---

[i] Greek *he*   [j] Greek *he*   [k] Other ancient manuscripts read *of instruction*
[l] Other ancient manuscripts read *let us do this if God permits*   [m] Greek *he*

through two unchangeable things, in which it is impossible that God should prove false, we who have fled for refuge might have strong encouragement to seize the ¹⁹ hope set before us. We have this as a sure and steadfast anchor of the soul, a hope that enters into the inner ²⁰ shrine behind the curtain, where Jesus has gone as a forerunner on our behalf, having become a high priest for ever after the order of Melchiz'edek.

The Old Priesthood Imperfect

7 For this Melchiz'edek, king of Salem, priest of the Most High God, met Abraham returning from the ² slaughter of the kings and blessed him; and to him Abraham apportioned a tenth part of everything. He is first, by translation of his name, king of righteousness, and then he is also king of Salem, that is, king of peace. ³ He is without father or mother or genealogy, and has neither beginning of days nor end of life, but resembling the Son of God he continues a priest for ever.

⁴ See how great he is! Abraham the patriarch gave him ⁵ a tithe of the spoils. And those descendants of Levi who receive the priestly office have a commandment in the law to take tithes from the people, that is, from their brethren, though these also are descended from Abraham. ⁶ But this man who has not their genealogy received tithes from Abraham and blessed him who had the promises. ⁷ It is beyond dispute that the inferior is blessed by the ⁸ superior. Here tithes are received by mortal men; there, ⁹ by one of whom it is testified that he lives. One might even say that Levi himself, who receives tithes, paid ¹⁰ tithes through Abraham, for he was still in the loins of his ancestor when Melchiz'edek met him.

¹¹ Now if perfection had been attainable through the Leviti'cal priesthood (for under it the people received the

law), what further need would there have been for another priest to arise after the order of Melchiz'edek, ¹² rather than one named after the order of Aaron? For when there is a change in the priesthood, there is neces- ¹³ sarily a change in the law as well. For the one of whom these things are spoken belonged to another tribe, from ¹⁴ which no one has ever served at the altar. For it is evident that our Lord was descended from Judah, and in connection with that tribe Moses said nothing about priests.

¹⁵ This becomes even more evident when another priest ¹⁶ arises in the likeness of Melchiz'edek, who has become a priest, not according to a legal requirement concerning

ⁿ Or *tabernacle* ^o Greek *he*

bodily descent but by the power of an indestructible life. ¹⁷ For it is witnessed of him,

"Thou art a priest for ever,
after the order of Melchiz'edek."

¹⁸ On the one hand, a former commandment is set aside ¹⁹ because of its weakness and uselessness (for the law made nothing perfect); on the other hand, a better hope is introduced, through which we draw near to God.

^{20, 21} And it was not without an oath. Those who formerly became priests took their office without an oath, but this one was addressed with an oath,

"The Lord has sworn
and will not change his mind,
'Thou art a priest for ever.' "

²² This makes Jesus the surety of a better covenant.

²³ The former priests were many in number, because they were prevented by death from continuing in office; ²⁴ but he holds his priesthood permanently, because he con- ²⁵ tinues for ever. Consequently he is able for all time to save those who draw near to God through him, since he always lives to make intercession for them.

²⁶ For it was fitting that we should have such a high priest, holy, blameless, unstained, separated from sinners, ²⁷ exalted above the heavens. He has no need, like those high priests, to offer sacrifices daily, first for his own sins and then for those of the people; he did this once for all when ²⁸ he offered up himself. Indeed, the law appoints men in their weakness as high priests, but the word of the oath, which came later than the law, appoints a Son who has been made perfect for ever.

Jesus' Ministry as High Priest

8 Now the point in what we are saying is this: we have such a high priest, one who is seated at the right hand ² of the throne of the Majesty in heaven, a minister in the sanctuary and the true tent ⁿ which is set up not by man ³ but by the Lord. For every high priest is appointed to offer gifts and sacrifices; hence it is necessary for this ⁴ priest also to have something to offer. Now if he were on earth, he would not be a priest at all, since there are ⁵ priests who offer gifts according to the law. They serve a copy and shadow of the heavenly sanctuary; for when Moses was about to erect the tent, ⁿ he was instructed by God, saying, "See that you make everything according to ⁶ the pattern which was shown you on the mountain." But as it is, Christ ^o has obtained a ministry which is as much more excellent than the old as the covenant he mediates is better, since it is enacted on better promises. ⁷ For if that first covenant had been faultless, there would have been no occasion for a second.

⁸ For he finds fault with them when he says:

"The days will come, says the Lord,
when I will establish a new covenant with the house of

Israel
and with the house of Judah;
9 not like the covenant that I made with their fathers
on the day when I took them by the hand
to lead them out of the land of Egypt;
for they did not continue in my covenant,
and so I paid no heed to them, says the Lord.
10 This is the covenant that I will make with the house of
Israel
after those days, says the Lord:
I will put my laws into their minds,
and write them on their hearts,
and I will be their God,
and they shall be my people.
11 And they shall not teach every one his fellow
or every one his brother, saying, 'Know the Lord,'
for all shall know me,
from the least of them to the greatest.
12 For I will be merciful toward their iniquities,
and I will remember their sins no more."
13 In speaking of a new covenant he treats the first as
obsolete. And what is becoming obsolete and growing old
is ready to vanish away.

9 Now even the first covenant had regulations for
2 worship and an earthly sanctuary. For a tent[p] was

prepared, the outer one, in which were the lampstand and
the table and the bread of the Presence;[q] it is called the
3 Holy Place. Behind the second curtain stood a tent[p] called
4 the Holy of Holies, having the golden altar of incense and
the ark of the covenant covered on all sides with gold,
which contained a golden urn holding the manna, and
Aaron's rod that budded, and the tables of the covenant;
5 above it were the cherubim of glory overshadowing the
mercy seat. Of these things we cannot now speak in detail.
6 These preparations having thus been made, the priests
go continually into the outer tent,[p] performing their ritual
7 duties; but into the second only the high priest goes, and
he but once a year, and not without taking blood which
8 he offers for himself and for the errors of the people. By
this the Holy Spirit indicates that the way into the
sanctuary is not yet opened as long as the outer tent[p] is
9 still standing (which is symbolic for the present age).
According to this arrangement, gifts and sacrifices are
offered which cannot perfect the conscience of the wor-
10 shiper, but deal only with food and drink and various
ablutions, regulations for the body imposed until the time
of reformation.
11 But when Christ appeared as a high priest of the good
things that have come,[r] then through the greater and
more perfect tent[p] (not made with hands, that is, not of
12 this creation) he entered once for all into the Holy Place,
taking[s] not the blood of goats and calves but his own
13 blood, thus securing an eternal redemption. For if the
sprinkling of defiled persons with the blood of goats and
bulls and with the ashes of a heifer sanctifies for the
14 purification of the flesh, how much more shall the blood
of Christ, who through the eternal Spirit offered himself
without blemish to God, purify your[t] conscience from
dead works to serve the living God.
15 Therefore he is the mediator of a new covenant, so that
those who are called may receive the promised eternal
inheritance, since a death has occurred which redeems
them from the transgressions under the first covenant.[u]
16 For where a will[u] is involved, the death of the one who
17 made it must be established. For a will[u] takes effect only
at death, since it is not in force as long as the one who
18 made it is alive. Hence even the first covenant was not
19 ratified without blood. For when every commandment of
the law had been declared by Moses to all the people, he
took the blood of calves and goats, with water and scarlet
wool and hyssop, and sprinkled both the book itself and
20 all the people, saying, "This is the blood of the covenant
21 which God commanded you." And in the same way he
sprinkled with the blood both the tent[p] and all the vessels
22 used in worship. Indeed, under the law almost everything
is purified with blood, and without the shedding of blood
there is no forgiveness of sins.
23 Thus it was necessary for the copies of the heavenly
things to be purified with these rites, but the heavenly
24 things themselves with better sacrifices than these. For
Christ has entered, not into a sanctuary made with hands,
a copy of the true one, but into heaven itself, now to
25 appear in the presence of God on our behalf. Nor was it
to offer himself repeatedly, as the high priest enters the
26 Holy Place yearly with blood not his own; for then he
would have had to suffer repeatedly since the foundation
of the world. But as it is, he has appeared once for all at
the end of the age to put away sin by the sacrifice of him-
27 self. And just as it is appointed for men to die once, and
28 after that comes judgment, so Christ, having been offered

[p] Or *tabernacle* [q] Greek *the presentation of the loaves* [r] Other manuscripts read *good things to come* [s] Greek *through*
[t] Other manuscripts read *our* [u] The Greek word here used means both *covenant* and *will*

once to bear the sins of many, will appear a second time, not to deal with sin but to save those who are eagerly waiting for him.

10 For since the law has but a shadow of the good things to come instead of the true form of these realities, it can never, by the same sacrifices which are continually offered year after year, make perfect those
2 who draw near. Otherwise, would they not have ceased to be offered? If the worshipers had once been cleansed, they would no longer have any consciousness of sin.
3 But in these sacrifices there is a reminder of sin year after
4 year. For it is impossible that the blood of bulls and goats should take away sins.
5 Consequently, when Christ^v came into the world, he said,

"Sacrifices and offerings thou hast not desired,
but a body hast thou prepared for me;
6 in burnt offerings and sin offerings thou hast taken no pleasure.
7 Then I said, 'Lo, I have come to do thy will, O God,'
as it is written of me in the roll of the book."
8 When he said above, "Thou hast neither desired nor taken pleasure in sacrifices and offerings and burnt offerings and sin offerings" (these are offered according to the
9 law), then he added, "Lo, I have come to do thy will."
10 He abolishes the first in order to establish the second. And by that will we have been sanctified through the offering of the body of Jesus Christ once for all.
11 And every priest stands daily at his service, offering repeatedly the same sacrifices, which can never take
12 away sins. But when Christ^w had offered for all time a single sacrifice for sins, he sat down at the right hand of
13 God, then to wait until his enemies should be made a
14 stool for his feet. For by a single offering he has per-
15 fected for all time those who are sanctified. And the Holy Spirit also bears witness to us; for after saying,
16 "This is the covenant that I will make with them after those days, says the Lord:
I will put my laws on their hearts,
and write them on their minds,"
17 then he adds,
"I will remember their sins and their misdeeds no more."
18 Where there is forgiveness of these, there is no longer any offering for sin.

HOLD FAST BY FAITH

19 Therefore, brethren, since we have confidence to
20 enter the sanctuary by the blood of Jesus, by the new and living way which he opened for us through the cur-
21 tain, that is, through his flesh, and since we have a great
22 priest over the house of God, let us draw near with a true heart in full assurance of faith, with our hearts sprinkled clean from an evil conscience and our bodies washed

v Greek *he*   w Greek *this one*

23 with pure water. Let us hold fast the confession of our hope without wavering, for he who promised is faith-
24 ful; and let us consider how to stir up one another to
25 love and good works, not neglecting to meet together, as is the habit of some, but encouraging one another, and all the more as you see the Day drawing near.
26 For if we sin deliberately after receiving the knowledge of the truth, there no longer remains a sacrifice for
27 sins, but a fearful prospect of judgment, and a fury of
28 fire which will consume the adversaries. A man who has violated the law of Moses dies without mercy at the
29 testimony of two or three witnesses. How much worse punishment do you think will be deserved by the man who has spurned the Son of God, and profaned the blood of the covenant by which he was sanctified, and
30 outraged the Spirit of grace? For we know him who said, "Vengeance is mine, I will repay." And again,
31 "The Lord will judge his people." It is a fearful thing to fall into the hands of the living God.
32 But recall the former days when, after you were enlightened, you endured a hard struggle with sufferings,
33 sometimes being publicly exposed to abuse and affliction, and sometimes being partners with those so treated.
34 For you had compassion on the prisoners, and you joyfully accepted the plundering of your property, since you knew that you yourselves had a better possession and
35 an abiding one. Therefore do not throw away your con-
36 fidence, which has a great reward. For you have need of endurance, so that you may do the will of God and receive what is promised.
37 "For yet a little while,
and the coming one shall come and shall not tarry;
38 but my righteous one shall live by faith,
and if he shrinks back,
my soul has no pleasure in him."
39 But we are not of those who shrink back and are destroyed, but of those who have faith and keep their souls.

By Faith They Lived

11 Now faith is the assurance of things hoped for,
2 the conviction of things not seen. For by it the men
3 of old received divine approval. By faith we understand that the world was created by the word of God, so that what is seen was made out of things which do not appear.
4 By faith Abel offered to God a more acceptable sacrifice than Cain, through which he received approval as righteous, God bearing witness by accepting his gifts;
5 he died, but through his faith he is still speaking. By faith Enoch was taken up so that he should not see death; and he was not found, because God had taken him. Now before he was taken he was attested as having pleased
6 God. And without faith it is impossible to please him.

For whoever would draw near to God must believe that
7 he exists and that he rewards those who seek him. By faith Noah, being warned by God concerning events as yet unseen, took heed and constructed an ark for the saving of his household; by this he condemned the world and became an heir of the righteousness which comes by faith.

8 By faith Abraham obeyed when he was called to go out to a place which he was to receive as an inheritance;

9 and he went out, not knowing where he was to go. By faith he sojourned in the land of promise, as in a foreign land, living in tents with Isaac and Jacob, heirs with
10 him of the same promise. For he looked forward to the city which has foundations, whose builder and maker
11 is God. By faith Sarah herself received power to conceive, even when she was past the age, since she con-
12 sidered him faithful who had promised. Therefore from one man, and him as good as dead, were born descendants as many as the stars of heaven and as the innumerable grains of sand by the seashore.

13 These all died in faith, not having received what was promised, but having seen it and greeted it from afar, and having acknowledged that they were strangers and
14 exiles on the earth. For people who speak thus make it
15 clear that they are seeking a homeland. If they had been thinking of that land from which they had gone out,
16 they would have had opportunity to return. But as it is, they desire a better country, that is, a heavenly one. Therefore God is not ashamed to be called their God, for he has prepared for them a city.

17 By faith Abraham, when he was tested, offered up Isaac, and he who had received the promises was ready
18 to offer up his only son, of whom it was said, "Through
19 Isaac shall your descendants be named." He considered that God was able to raise men even from the dead;
20 hence, figuratively speaking, he did receive him back. By
21 faith Isaac invoked future blessings on Jacob and Esau. By faith Jacob, when dying, blessed each of the sons of
22 Joseph, bowing in worship over the head of his staff. By faith Joseph, at the end of his life, made mention of the exodus of the Israelites and gave directions concerning his burial.ˣ

23 By faith Moses, when he was born, was hid for three months by his parents, because they saw that the child was beautiful; and they were not afraid of the king's
24 edict. By faith Moses, when he was grown up, refused
25 to be called the son of Pharaoh's daughter, choosing rather to share ill-treatment with the people of God

26 than to enjoy the fleeting pleasures of sin. He considered abuse suffered for the Christ greater wealth than the
27 treasures of Egypt, for he looked to the reward. By faith he left Egypt, not being afraid of the anger of the king;
28 for he endured as seeing him who is invisible. By faith he kept the Passover and sprinkled the blood, so that the Destroyer of the first-born might not touch them.

29 By faith the people crossed the Red Sea as if on dry land; but the Egyptians, when they attempted to do
30 the same, were drowned. By faith the walls of Jericho fell down after they had been encircled for seven days.
31 By faith Rahab the harlot did not perish with those who were disobedient, because she had given friendly welcome to the spies.

32 And what more shall I say? For time would fail me to tell of Gideon, Barak, Samson, Jephthah, of David
33 and Samuel and the prophets—who through faith conquered kingdoms, enforced justice, received promises,
34 stopped the mouths of lions, quenched raging fire, escaped the edge of the sword, won strength out of weakness, became mighty in war, put foreign armies to flight.
35 Women received their dead by resurrection. Some were tortured, refusing to accept release, that they might rise
36 again to a better life. Others suffered mocking and
37 scourging, and even chains and imprisonment. They were stoned, they were sawn in two,ʸ they were killed with the sword; they went about in skins of sheep and goats,
38 destitute, afflicted, ill-treated—of whom the world was not worthy—wandering over deserts and mountains, and in dens and caves of the earth.

39 And all these, though well attested by their faith, did
40 not receive what was promised, since God had foreseen something better for us, that apart from us they should not be made perfect.

Looking to Jesus

12 Therefore, since we are surrounded by so great a cloud of witnesses, let us also lay aside every weight, and sin which clings so closely, and let us run with per-
2 severance the race that is set before us, looking to Jesus the pioneer and perfecter of our faith, who for the joy

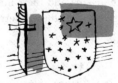

that was set before him endured the cross, despising the shame, and is seated at the right hand of the throne of God.
3 Consider him who endured from sinners such hostility against himself, so that you may not grow weary or
4 fainthearted. In your struggle against sin you have not
5 yet resisted to the point of shedding your blood. And

ˣ Greek *bones*   ʸ Other manuscripts add *they were tempted* have you forgotten the exhortation which addresses you as sons?—

"My son, do not regard lightly the discipline of the Lord, nor lose courage when you are punished by him.

[6] For the Lord disciplines him whom he loves, and chastises every son whom he receives."

[7] It is for discipline that you have to endure. God is treating you as sons; for what son is there whom his father [8] does not discipline? If you are left without discipline, in which all have participated, then you are illegitimate [9] children and not sons. Besides this, we have had earthly

fathers to discipline us and we respected them. Shall we not much more be subject to the Father of spirits and [10] live? For they disciplined us for a short time at their pleasure, but he disciplines us for our good, that we may [11] share his holiness. For the moment all discipline seems painful rather than pleasant; later it yields the peaceful fruit of righteousness to those who have been trained by it.

[12] Therefore lift your drooping hands and strengthen [13] your weak knees, and make straight paths for your feet, so that what is lame may not be put out of joint but [14] rather be healed. Strive for peace with all men, and for the holiness without which no one will see the Lord. [15] See to it that no one fail to obtain the grace of God; that no "root of bitterness" spring up and cause trouble, [16] and by it the many become defiled; that no one be immoral or irreligious like Esau, who sold his birthright [17] for a single meal. For you know that afterward, when he desired to inherit the blessing, he was rejected, for he found no chance to repent, though he sought it with tears.

[18] For you have not come to what may be touched, a [19] blazing fire, and darkness, and gloom, and a tempest, and the sound of a trumpet, and a voice whose words made the hearers entreat that no further messages be spoken to [20] them. For they could not endure the order that was given, "If even a beast touches the mountain, it shall be stoned." [21] Indeed, so terrifying was the sight that Moses said, "I [22] tremble with fear." But you have come to Mount Zion and to the city of the living God, the heavenly Jerusalem, [23] and to innumerable angels in festal gathering, and to the assembly [z] of the first-born who are enrolled in heaven,

and to a judge who is God of all, and to the spirits of [24] just men made perfect, and to Jesus, the mediator of a new covenant, and to the sprinkled blood that speaks more graciously than the blood of Abel.

[25] See that you do not refuse him who is speaking. For if they did not escape when they refused him who warned them on earth, much less shall we escape if we reject [26] him who warns from heaven. His voice then shook the earth; but now he has promised, "Yet once more I will [27] shake not only the earth but also the heaven." This phrase, "Yet once more," indicates the removal of what is shaken, as of what has been made, in order that what [28] cannot be shaken may remain. Therefore let us be grateful for receiving a kingdom that cannot be shaken, and thus let us offer to God acceptable worship, with rever- [29] ence and awe; for our God is a consuming fire.

Perfect in Every Good Work

[2] **13** Let brotherly love continue. Do not neglect to show hospitality to strangers, for thereby some have [3] entertained angels unawares. Remember those who are in prison, as though in prison with them; and those who [4] are ill-treated, since you also are in the body. Let marriage be held in honor among all, and let the marriage bed be undefiled; for God will judge the immoral and

[5] adulterous. Keep your life free from love of money, and be content with what you have; for he has said, "I will [6] never fail you nor forsake you." Hence we can confidently say,

"The Lord is my helper,
I will not be afraid;
what can man do to me?"

[7] Remember your leaders, those who spoke to you the word of God; consider the outcome of their life, and [8] imitate their faith. Jesus Christ is the same yesterday [9] and today and for ever. Do not be led away by diverse and strange teachings; for it is well that the heart be strengthened by grace, not by foods, which have not [10] benefited their adherents. We have an altar from which [11] those who serve the tent [a] have no right to eat. For the bodies of those animals whose blood is brought into the sanctuary by the high priest as a sacrifice for sin are [12] burned outside the camp. So Jesus also suffered outside the gate in order to sanctify the people through his own [13] blood. Therefore let us go forth to him outside the camp, [14] and bear the abuse he endured. For here we have no

[z] Or angels, and to the festal gathering and assembly   [a] Or tabernacle

¹⁵ lasting city, but we seek the city which is to come. Through him then let us continually offer up a sacrifice of praise to God, that is, the fruit of lips that acknowledge ¹⁶ his name. Do not neglect to do good and to share what you have, for such sacrifices are pleasing to God.

¹⁷ Obey your leaders and submit to them; for they are keeping watch over your souls, as men who will have to give account. Let them do this joyfully, and not sadly, for that would be of no advantage to you.

¹⁸ Pray for us, for we are sure that we have a clear con- ¹⁹ science, desiring to act honorably in all things. I urge you the more earnestly to do this in order that I may be restored to you the sooner.

²⁰ Now may the God of peace who brought again from

ᵇ Other ancient authorities read *us*

the dead our Lord Jesus, the great shepherd of the sheep, ²¹ by the blood of the eternal covenant, equip you with everything good that you may do his will, working in you ᵇ that which is pleasing in his sight, through Jesus Christ; to whom be glory for ever and ever. Amen.

Conclusion

²² I appeal to you, brethren, bear with my word of ex- ²³ hortation, for I have written to you briefly. You should understand that our brother Timothy has been released, ²⁴ with whom I shall see you if he comes soon. Greet all your leaders and all the saints. Those who come from ²⁵ Italy send you greeting. Grace be with all of you. Amen.

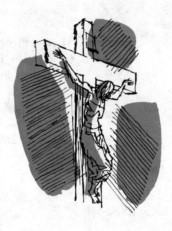

── INTRODUCTION TO ──

JAMES

This letter begins with the words "James, a servant of God and of the Lord Jesus Christ." Some think the writer was James the brother of Jesus. Today, however, most people think it was written much later and by some other man named James. It was probably written between A.D. 125 and 150.

The Letter of James is addressed to "the twelve tribes in the dispersion," referring to Christians among the Jews who had scattered throughout the empire. The chief purpose of the letter was to strengthen Christians in their times of trouble because of their faith and to insist on practical goodness in every aspect of their lives.

The theme of this book is expressed in two of the best known verses: "But be doers of the word, and not hearers only, deceiving yourselves" (1.22) and "So faith by itself, if it has no works, is dead" (2.17).

JAMES

Greeting

1 James, a servant of God and of the Lord Jesus Christ,

To the twelve tribes in the Dispersion:

Greeting.

BE DOERS OF THE WORD

2 Count it all joy, my brethren, when you meet various 3 trials, for you know that the testing of your faith pro- 4 duces steadfastness. And let steadfastness have its full effect, that you may be perfect and complete, lacking in nothing.

5 If any of you lacks wisdom, let him ask God, who gives to all men generously and without reproaching, and 6 it will be given him. But let him ask in faith, with no doubting, for he who doubts is like a wave of the sea 7, 8, that is driven and tossed by the wind. For that person must not suppose that a double-minded man, unstable in all his ways, will receive anything from the Lord.

9, 10 Let the lowly brother boast in his exaltation, and the rich in his humiliation, because like the flower of the 11 grass he will pass away. For the sun rises with its scorching heat and withers the grass; its flower falls, and its beauty perishes. So will the rich man fade away in the midst of his pursuits.

12 Blessed is the man who endures trial, for when he has stood the test he will receive the crown of life which God 13 has promised to those who love him. Let no one say when he is tempted, "I am tempted by God"; for God cannot

be tempted with evil and he himself tempts no one; 14 but each person is tempted when he is lured and enticed 15 by his own desire. Then desire when it has conceived gives birth to sin; and sin when it is full-grown brings forth death.

16, 17 Do not be deceived, my beloved brethren. Every good endowment and every perfect gift is from above, coming down from the Father of lights with whom there is no 18 variation or shadow due to change.[a] Of his own will he brought us forth by the word of truth that we should be a kind of first fruits of his creatures.

19 Know this, my beloved brethren. Let every man be 20 quick to hear, slow to speak, slow to anger, for the anger 21 of man does not work the righteousness of God. Therefore put away all filthiness and rank growth of wickedness and receive with meekness the implanted word, which is able to save your souls.

22 But be doers of the word, and not hearers only, deceiv- 23 ing yourselves. For if any one is a hearer of the word and not a doer, he is like a man who observes his natural 24 face in a mirror; for he observes himself and goes away 25 and at once forgets what he was like. But he who looks into the perfect law, the law of liberty, and perseveres, being no hearer that forgets but a doer that acts, he shall be blessed in his doing.

26 If any one thinks he is religious, and does not bridle his tongue but deceives his heart, this man's religion is 27 vain. Religion that is pure and undefiled before God and

---

a Other ancient authorities read *variation due to a shadow of turning*

the Father is this: to visit orphans and widows in their affliction, and to keep oneself unstained from the world.

FAITH AND WORKS

2 My brethren, show no partiality as you hold the faith of our Lord Jesus Christ, the Lord of glory. [2] For if a man with gold rings and in fine clothing comes into your assembly, and a poor man in shabby clothing [3] also comes in, and you pay attention to the one who wears the fine clothing and say, "Have a seat here, please," while you say to the poor man, "Stand there," or "Sit at [4] my feet," have you not made distinctions among your- [5] selves, and become judges with evil thoughts? Listen, my beloved brethren. Has not God chosen those who are poor in the world to be rich in faith and heirs of the kingdom [6] which he has promised to those who love him? But you have dishonored the poor man. Is it not the rich who oppress you, is it not they who drag you into court? [7] Is it not they who blaspheme that honorable name which was invoked over you?

[8] If you really fulfil the royal law, according to the scripture, "You shall love your neighbor as yourself," [9] you do well. But if you show partiality, you commit sin, [10] and are convicted by the law as transgressors. For who-ever keeps the whole law but fails in one point has become [11] guilty of all of it. For he who said, "Do not commit adultery," said also, "Do not kill." If you do not commit adultery but do kill, you have become a transgressor of the [12] law. So speak and so act as those who are to be judged [13] under the law of liberty. For judgment is without mercy to one who has shown no mercy; yet mercy triumphs over judgment.

[14] What does it profit, my brethren, if a man says he has [15] faith but has not works? Can his faith save him? If a [16] brother or sister is ill-clad and in lack of daily food, and one of you says to them, "Go in peace, be warmed and filled," without giving them the things needed for the [17] body, what does it profit? So faith by itself, if it has no works, is dead.

[18] But some one will say, "You have faith and I have works." Show me your faith apart from your works, and [19] I by my works will show you my faith. You believe that God is one; you do well. Even the demons believe—and [20] shudder. Do you want to be shown, you shallow fellow,

[21] that faith apart from works is barren? Was not Abraham our father justified by works, when he offered his son Isaac [22] upon the altar? You see that faith was active along with [23] his works, and faith was completed by works, and the scripture was fulfilled which says, "Abraham believed

God, and it was reckoned to him as righteousness"; and [24] he was called the friend of God. You see that a man is [25] justified by works and not by faith alone. And in the same way was not also Rahab the harlot justified by works when she received the messengers and sent them out [26] another way? For as the body apart from the spirit is dead, so faith apart from works is dead.

CHRISTIAN CONDUCT

3 Let not many of you become teachers, my brethren, for you know that we who teach shall be judged with [2] greater strictness. For we all make many mistakes, and if any one makes no mistakes in what he says he is a [3] perfect man, able to bridle the whole body also. If we put bits into the mouths of horses that they may obey us, [4] we guide their whole bodies. Look at the ships also;

though they are so great and are driven by strong winds, they are guided by a very small rudder wherever the will [5] of the pilot directs. So the tongue is a little member and boasts of great things. How great a forest is set ablaze by a small fire!

[6] And the tongue is a fire. The tongue is an unrighteous world among our members, staining the whole body, setting on fire the cycle of nature,[b] and set on fire by hell.[c] [7] For every kind of beast and bird, of reptile and sea creature, can be tamed and has been tamed by human- [8] kind, but no human being can tame the tongue—a restless [9] evil, full of deadly poison. With it we bless the Lord and Father, and with it we curse men, who are made in the [10] likeness of God. From the same mouth come blessing and [11] cursing. My brethren, this ought not to be so. Does a spring pour forth from the same opening fresh water and [12] brackish? Can a fig tree, my brethren, yield olives, or a grapevine figs? No more can salt water yield fresh.

[13] Who is wise and understanding among you? By his good life let him show his works in the meekness of [14] wisdom. But if you have bitter jealousy and selfish ambi-tion in your hearts, do not boast and be false to the truth. [15] This wisdom is not such as comes down from above, but [16] is earthly, unspiritual, devilish. For where jealousy and selfish ambition exist, there will be disorder and every [17] vile practice. But the wisdom from above is first pure, then peaceable, gentle, open to reason, full of mercy and [18] good fruits, without uncertainty or insincerity. And the harvest of righteousness is sown in peace by those who make peace.

4 What causes wars, and what causes fightings among you? Is it not your passions that are at war in your [2] members? You desire and do not have; so you kill. And

you covet[d] and cannot obtain; so you fight and wage
³ war. You do not have, because you do not ask. You ask
and do not receive, because you ask wrongly, to spend it
⁴ on your passions. Unfaithful creatures! Do you not know
that friendship with the world is enmity with God?
Therefore whoever wishes to be a friend of the world
⁵ makes himself an enemy of God. Or do you suppose it
is in vain that the scripture says, "He yearns jealously
⁶ over the spirit which he has made to dwell in us"? But he
gives more grace; therefore it says, "God opposes the
⁷ proud, but gives grace to the humble." Submit yourselves
therefore to God. Resist the devil and he will flee from
⁸ you. Draw near to God and he will draw near to you.
Cleanse your hands, you sinners, and purify your hearts,
⁹ you men of double mind. Be wretched and mourn and
weep. Let your laughter be turned to mourning and your
¹⁰ joy to dejection. Humble yourselves before the Lord
and he will exalt you.

¹¹ Do not speak evil against one another, brethren. He
that speaks evil against a brother or judges his brother,
speaks evil against the law and judges the law. But if you
judge the law, you are not a doer of the law but a judge.
¹² There is one lawgiver and judge, he who is able to save
and destroy. But who are you that you judge your
neighbor?

¹³ Come now, you who say, "Today or tomorrow we will
go into such and such a town and spend a year there and
¹⁴ trade and get gain"; whereas you do not know about
tomorrow. What is your life? For you are a mist that
¹⁵ appears for a little time and then vanishes. Instead you
ought to say, "If the Lord wills, we shall live and we
¹⁶ shall do this or that." As it is, you boast in your
¹⁷ arrogance. All such boasting is evil. Whoever knows
what is right to do and fails to do it, for him it is sin.

5 Come now, you rich, weep and howl for the miseries
² that are coming upon you. Your riches have rotted
³ and your garments are moth-eaten. Your gold and silver
have rusted, and their rust will be evidence against you
and will eat your flesh like fire. You have laid up
⁴ treasure[e] for the last days. Behold, the wages of the
laborers who mowed your fields, which you kept back
by fraud, cry out; and the cries of the harvesters have
⁵ reached the ears of the Lord of hosts. You have lived on
the earth in luxury and in pleasure; you have fattened
⁶ your hearts in a day of slaughter. You have condemned,
you have killed the righteous man; he does not resist you.

⁷ Be patient, therefore, brethren, until the coming of the
Lord. Behold, the farmer waits for the precious fruit of
the earth, being patient over it until it receives the early
⁸ and the late rain. You also be patient. Establish your
⁹ hearts, for the coming of the Lord is at hand. Do not
grumble, brethren, against one another, that you may not
be judged; behold, the Judge is standing at the doors.
¹⁰ As an example of suffering and patience, brethren, take
¹¹ the prophets who spoke in the name of the Lord. Behold,
we call those happy who were steadfast. You have heard
of the steadfastness of Job, and you have seen the purpose
of the Lord, how the Lord is compassionate and merciful.

¹² But above all, my brethren, do not swear, either by
heaven or by earth or with any other oath, but let your
yes be yes and your no be no, that you may not fall
under condemnation.

¹³ Is any one among you suffering? Let him pray. Is any
¹⁴ cheerful? Let him sing praise. Is any among you sick?
Let him call for the elders of the church, and let them
pray over him, anointing him with oil in the name of
¹⁵ the Lord; and the prayer of faith will save the sick man,
and the Lord will raise him up; and if he has committed
¹⁶ sins, he will be forgiven. Therefore confess your sins to
one another, and pray for one another, that you may be
healed. The prayer of a righteous man has great power
¹⁷ in its effects. Eli'jah was a man of like nature with ourselves and he prayed fervently that it might not rain, and
for three years and six months it did not rain on the
¹⁸ earth. Then he prayed again and the heaven gave rain,
and the earth brought forth its fruit.

¹⁹ My brethren, if any one among you wanders from the
²⁰ truth and some one brings him back, let him know that
whoever brings back a sinner from the error of his way
will save his soul from death and will cover a multitude
of sins.

---

[d] Or *you kill and you covet*   [e] Or *will eat your flesh, since you have stored up fire*

INTRODUCTION TO

THE FIRST LETTER OF

PETER

This letter was probably written about A.D. 64-67. The First Letter of Peter states that it is a message from Peter, an apostle, but that its actual writer was Silvanus (see 5.12). Peter wrote to encourage Christians who were being tempted to deny their faith because of threats, lies, and hatred by the enemies of Christ.

The letter speaks of the persecution of Christians as "fire" that will test their faith. If a Christian's faith is real, it will survive suffering just as gold is refined and made pure by fire. The letter reminded the readers that Christians were being tested everywhere. It said that "after you have suffered a little while, the God of all grace, who has called you to his eternal glory in Christ, will himself restore, establish, and strengthen you" (5.10).

THE FIRST LETTER OF

PETER

Salutation

1 Peter, an apostle of Jesus Christ, To the exiles of the Dispersion in Pontus, Galatia, Cappado'cia, Asia, and 2 Bithyn'ia, chosen and destined by God the Father and sanctified by the Spirit for obedience to Jesus Christ and for sprinkling with his blood:

May grace and peace be multiplied to you.

THE BLESSINGS OF GOD'S REDEEMED

3 Blessed be the God and Father of our Lord Jesus Christ! By his great mercy we have been born anew to a living hope through the resurrection of Jesus Christ from 4 the dead, and to an inheritance which is imperishable, 5 undefiled, and unfading, kept in heaven for you, who by God's power are guarded through faith for a salvation 6 ready to be revealed in the last time. In this you rejoice,[a] though now for a little while you may have to suffer 7 various trials, so that the genuineness of your faith, more precious than gold which though perishable is tested by fire, may redound to praise and glory and honor at the 8 revelation of Jesus Christ. Without having seen[b] him you[c] love him; though you do not now see him you[c] believe in him and rejoice with unutterable and exalted 9 joy. As the outcome of your faith you obtain the salvation of your souls.

10 The prophets who prophesied of the grace that was to be yours searched and inquired about this salvation; 11 they inquired what person or time was indicated by the Spirit of Christ within them when predicting the suffer-12 ings of Christ and the subsequent glory. It was revealed to them that they were serving not themselves but you, in the things which have now been announced to you by those who preached the good news to you through the Holy Spirit sent from heaven, things into which angels long to look.

13 Therefore gird up your minds, be sober, set your hope fully upon the grace that is coming to you at the revela-14 tion of Jesus Christ. As obedient children, do not be con-15 formed to the passions of your former ignorance, but as he who called you is holy, be holy yourselves in all your 16 conduct; since it is written, "You shall be holy, for I am 17 holy." And if you invoke as Father him who judges each one impartially according to his deeds, conduct yourselves 18 with fear throughout the time of your exile. You know that you were ransomed from the futile ways inherited from your fathers, not with perishable things such as 19 silver or gold, but with the precious blood of Christ, like 20 that of a lamb without blemish or spot. He was destined before the foundation of the world but was made manifest 21 at the end of the times for your sake. Through him you have confidence in God, who raised him from the dead and gave him glory, so that your faith and hope are in God.[d]

22 Having purified your souls by your obedience to the truth for a sincere love of the brethren, love one another 23 earnestly from the heart. You have been born anew, not of perishable seed but of imperishable, through the living 24 and abiding word of God; for

[a] Or Rejoice in this   [b] Other ancient authorities read known   [c] Or omit you   [d] Or so that your faith is hope in God

"All flesh is like grass
and all its glory like the flower of grass.
The grass withers, and the flower falls,
25 but the word of the Lord abides for ever."
That word is the good news which was preached to you.

2 So put away all malice and all guile and insincerity
2 and envy and all slander. Like newborn babes, long
for the pure spiritual milk, that by it you may grow up
3 to salvation; for you have tasted the kindness of the Lord.
4 Come to him, to that living stone, rejected by men but
5 in God's sight chosen and precious; and like living stones
be yourselves built into a spiritual house, to be a holy
priesthood, to offer spiritual sacrifices acceptable to God
6 through Jesus Christ. For it stands in scripture:

"Behold, I am laying in Zion a stone, a cornerstone
chosen and precious,
and he who believes in him will not be put to shame."

7 To you therefore who believe, he is precious, but for those
who do not believe,

"The very stone which the builders rejected
has become the head of the corner,"

8 and

"A stone that will make men stumble,
a rock that will make them fall";

for they stumble because they disobey the word, as they
were destined to do.
9 But you are a chosen race, a royal priesthood, a holy
nation, God's own people,e that you may declare the
wonderful deeds of him who called you out of darkness
10 into this marvelous light. Once you were no people but
now you are God's people; once you had not received
mercy but now you have received mercy.

CHRISTIAN DUTIES

11 Beloved, I beseech you as aliens and exiles to abstain
from the passions of the flesh that wage war against your
12 soul. Maintain good conduct among the Gentiles, so that
in case they speak against you as wrongdoers, they may
see your good deeds and glorify God on the day of
visitation.
13 Be subject for the Lord's sake to every human institu-
14 tion,f whether it be to the emperor as supreme, or to
governors as sent by him to punish those who do wrong
15 and to praise those who do right. For it is God's will that
by doing right you should put to silence the ignorance of
16 foolish men. Live as free men, yet without using your
freedom as a pretext for evil; but live as servants of God.
17 Honor all men. Love the brotherhood. Fear God. Honor
the emperor.
18 Servants, be submissive to your masters with all respect, not only to the kind and gentle but also to the
19 overbearing. For one is approved if, mindful of God, he
20 endures pain while suffering unjustly. For what credit is
it, if when you do wrong and are beaten for it you take

it patiently? But if when you do right and suffer for it
21 you take it patiently, you have God's approval. For to this
you have been called, because Christ also suffered for
you, leaving you an example, that you should follow in
22 his steps. He committed no sin; no guile was found on
23 his lips. When he was reviled, he did not revile in return;
when he suffered, he did not threaten; but he trusted to
24 him who judges justly. He himself bore our sins in his
body on the tree,g that we might die to sin and live to
25 righteousness. By his wounds you have been healed. For
you were straying like sheep, but have now returned to
the Shepherd and Guardian of your souls.

3 Likewise you wives, be submissive to your husbands, so that some, though they do not obey the
word, may be won without a word by the behavior of
2 their wives, when they see your reverent and chaste
3 behavior. Let not yours be the outward adorning with
braiding of hair, decoration of gold, and wearing of
4 fine clothing, but let it be the hidden person of the heart
with the imperishable jewel of a gentle and quite spirit,
5 which in God's sight is very precious. So once the holy
women who hoped in God used to adorn themselves and
6 were submissive to their husbands, as Sarah obeyed
Abraham, calling him lord. And you are now her children if you do right and let nothing terrify you.
7 Likewise you husbands, live considerately with your
wives, bestowing honor on the woman as the weaker sex,
since you are joint heirs of the grace of life, in order that
your prayers may not be hindered.
8 Finally, all of you, have unity of spirit, sympathy, love
of the brethren, a tender heart and a humble mind.
9 Do not return evil for evil or reviling for reviling; but on
the contrary bless, for to this you have been called, that
10 you may obtain a blessing. For

"He that would love life
and see good days,
let him keep his tongue from evil
and his lips from speaking guile;
11 let him turn away from evil and do right;

let him seek peace and pursue it.
12 For the eyes of the Lord are upon the righteous,
and his ears are open to their prayer.
But the face of the Lord is against those that do evil."
13 Now who is there to harm you if you are zealous for
14 what is right? But even if you do suffer for righteousness'
sake, you will be blessed. Have no fear of them, nor be
15 troubled, but in your hearts reverence Christ as Lord.
Always be prepared to make a defense to any one who

---

e Greek a people for his possession   f Or every institution ordained for men   g Or carried up . . . to the tree

calls you to account for the hope that is in you, yet do it
[16] with gentleness and reverence; and keep your conscience clear, so that, when you are abused, those who revile your
[17] good behavior in Christ may be put to shame. For it is better to suffer for doing right, if that should be God's
[18] will, than for doing wrong. For Christ also died[h] for sins once for all, the righteous for the unrighteous, that he might bring us to God, being put to death in the flesh
[19] but made alive in the spirit; in which he went and
[20] preached to the spirits in prison, who formerly did not obey, when God's patience waited in the days of Noah, during the building of the ark, in which a few, that is,
[21] eight persons, were saved through water. Baptism, which corresponds to this, now saves you, not as a removal of dirt from the body but as an appeal to God for a clear
[22] conscience, through the resurrection of Jesus Christ, who has gone into heaven and is at the right hand of God, with angels, authorities, and powers subject to him.

[4] Since therefore Christ suffered in the flesh,[i] arm yourselves with the same thought, for whoever has
[2] suffered in the flesh has ceased from sin, so as to live for the rest of the time in the flesh no longer by human
[3] passions but by the will of God. Let the time that is past suffice for doing what the Gentiles like to do, living in licentiousness, passions, drunkenness, revels, carousing,
[4] and lawless idolatry. They are surprised that you do not now join them in the same wild profligacy, and they
[5] abuse you; but they will give account to him who is ready
[6] to judge the living and the dead. For this is why the

gospel was preached even to the dead, that though judged in the flesh like men, they might live in the spirit like God.
[7] The end of all things is at hand; therefore keep sane
[8] and sober for your prayers. Above all hold unfailing your love for one another, since love covers a multitude
[9] of sins. Practice hospitality ungrudgingly to one another.
[10] As each has received a gift, employ it for one another, as
[11] good stewards of God's varied grace: whoever speaks, as one who utters oracles of God; whoever renders service, as one who renders it by the strength which God supplies; in order that in everything God may be glorified through

Jesus Christ. To him belong glory and dominion for ever and ever. Amen.

CHRISTIANS UNDER PERSECUTION

[12] Beloved, do not be surprised at the fiery ordeal which comes upon you to prove you, as though something
[13] strange were happening to you. But rejoice in so far as you share Christ's sufferings, that you may also rejoice
[14] and be glad when his glory is revealed. If you are reproached for the name of Christ, you are blessed, because
[15] the spirit of glory[j] and of God rests upon you. But let none of you suffer as a murderer, or a thief, or a wrong-
[16] doer, or a mischief-maker; yet if one suffers as a Christian, let him not be ashamed, but under that name let him
[17] glorify God. For the time has come for judgment to begin with the household of God; and if it begins with us, what will be the end of those who do not obey the gospel
[18] of God? And
"If the righteous man is scarcely saved,
where will the impious and sinner appear?"
[19] Therefore let those who suffer according to God's will do right and entrust their souls to a faithful Creator.

[5] So I exhort the elders among you, as a fellow elder and a witness of the sufferings of Christ as well as a
[2] partaker in the glory that is to be revealed. Tend the flock of God that is your charge,[k] not by constraint but willing-
[3] ly,[l] not for shameful gain but eagerly, not as domineering over those in your charge but being examples to the
[4] flock. And when the chief Shepherd is manifested you
[5] will obtain the unfading crown of glory. Likewise you that are younger be subject to the elders. Clothe yourselves, all of you, with humility toward one another, for "God opposes the proud, but gives grace to the humble."
[6] Humble yourselves therefore under the mighty hand
[7] of God, that in due time he may exalt you. Cast all your
[8] anxieties on him, for he cares about you. Be sober, be watchful. Your adversary the devil prowls around like a
[9] roaring lion, seeking some one to devour. Resist him, firm in your faith, knowing that the same experience of suffering is required of your brotherhood throughout the
[10] world. And after you have suffered a little while, the God of all grace, who has called you to his eternal glory in Christ, will himself restore, establish, and strengthen[m]
[11] you. To him be the dominion for ever and ever. Amen.

[12] By Silva'nus, a faithful brother as I regard him, I have written briefly to you, exhorting and declaring that this
[13] is the true grace of God; stand fast in it. She who is at Babylon, who is likewise chosen, sends you greetings;
[14] and so does my son Mark. Greet one another with the kiss of love.
Peace to all of you that are in Christ.

---

[h] Other ancient authorities read *suffered*
[j] Other ancient authorities insert *and of power*
[l] Other ancient authorities add *as God would have you*
[i] Other ancient authorities add *for us;* some *for you*
[k] Other ancient authorities add *exercising the oversight*
[m] Other ancient authorities read *restore, establish, strengthen and settle*

INTRODUCTION TO

THE SECOND LETTER OF

PETER

This letter was prepared by some unknown Christian about A.D. 125-50. It was written to strengthen Christians when they were in great danger from their enemies and also in danger of misunderstanding Christianity.

This writing is in the form of a letter from the apostle Peter. However, Peter was martyred about A.D. 64, and most scholars believe this letter was written many years later. They think this because Second Peter deals with situations Christians did not face until about A.D. 125-50.

This writer, whoever he was, intended to give the kind of advice Peter would have given had he been living then. Christians were being persecuted and murdered for their faith, and they were disturbed because Christ had not returned physically to the earth to overcome all their troubles. The letter urges Christians to trust God and live good lives whatever happens. It closes by saying, "But grow in the grace and knowledge of our Lord and Savior Jesus Christ. To him be the glory both now and to the day of eternity." (3.18)

THE SECOND LETTER OF

PETER

Salutation

1 Simeon[x] Peter, a servant and apostle of Jesus Christ,

To those who have obtained a faith of equal standing with ours in the righteousness of our God and Savior Jesus Christ:[a] 2 May grace and peace be multiplied to you in the knowledge of God and of Jesus our Lord.

SUPPLEMENT FAITH WITH VIRTUE

3 His divine power has granted to us all things that pertain to life and godliness, through the knowledge of him who called us to[b] his own glory and excellence, 4 by which he has granted to us his precious and very great promises, that through these you may escape from the corruption that is in the world because of passion, and 5 become partakers of the divine nature. For this very reason make every effort to supplement your faith with 6 virtue, and virtue with knowledge, and knowledge with self-control, and self-control with steadfastness, and stead- 7 fastness with godliness, and godliness with brotherly 8 affection, and brotherly affection with love. For if these things are yours and abound, they keep you from being ineffective or unfruitful in the knowledge of our Lord 9 Jesus Christ. For whoever lacks these things is blind and shortsighted and has forgotten that he was cleansed from 10 his old sins. Therefore, brethren, be the more zealous to confirm your call and election, for if you do this you will 11 never fall; so there will be richly provided for you an entrance into the eternal kingdom of your Lord and Savior Jesus Christ.

12 Therefore I intend always to remind you of these things, though you know them and are established in the 13 truth that you have. I think it right, as long as I am in 14 this body,[c] to arouse you by way of reminder, since I know that the putting off of my body[c] will be soon, as 15 our Lord Jesus Christ showed me. And I will see to it that after my departure you may be able at any time to recall these things.

16 For we did not follow cleverly devised myths when we made known to you the power and coming of our Lord Jesus Christ, but we were eyewitnesses of his majesty. 17 For when he received honor and glory from God the Father and the voice was borne to him by the Majestic Glory, "This is my beloved Son,[d] with whom I am well

[x] Other authorities read *Simon*   [a] Or *of our God and the Savior Jesus Christ*   [b] Or *by*   [c] Greek *tent*
[d] Or *my Son, my* (or *the*) *Beloved*

18 pleased," we heard this voice borne from heaven, for we
19 were with him on the holy mountain. And we have the prophetic word made more sure. You will do well to pay attention to this as to a lamp shining in a dark place, until the day dawns and the morning star rises in your
20 hearts. First of all you must understand this, that no prophecy of scripture is a matter of one's own interpreta-
21 tion, because no prophecy ever came by the impulse of man, but men moved by the Holy Spirit spoke from God.[e]

FALSE TEACHERS

2 But false prophets also arose among the people, just as there will be false teachers among you, who will secretly bring in destructive heresies, even denying the Master who bought them, bringing upon themselves
2 swift destruction. And many will follow their licentiousness, and because of them the way of truth will be reviled.
3 And in their greed they will exploit you with false words; from of old their condemnation has not been idle, and

their destruction has not been asleep.
4 For if God did not spare the angels when they sinned, but cast them into hell[f] and committed them to pits of
5 nether gloom to be kept until the judgment; if he did not spare the ancient world, but preserved Noah, a herald of righteousness, with seven other persons, when he brought
6 a flood upon the world of the ungodly; if by turning the cities of Sodom and Gomor'rah to ashes he condemned them to extinction and made them an example
7 to those who were to be ungodly; and if he rescued righteous Lot, greatly distressed by the licentiousness of
8 the wicked (for by what that righteous man saw and heard as he lived among them, he was vexed in his righteous soul day after day with their lawless deeds),
9 then the Lord knows how to rescue the godly from trial, and to keep the unrighteous under punishment until the
10 day of judgment, and especially those who indulge in the lust of defiling passion and despise authority.

Bold and wilful, they are not afraid to revile the
11 glorious ones, whereas angels, though greater in might and power, do not pronounce a reviling judgment upon
12 them before the Lord. But these, like irrational animals, creatures of instinct, born to be caught and killed, reviling in matters of which they are ignorant, will be de-

13 stroyed in the same destruction with them, suffering wrong for their wrongdoing. They count it pleasure to revel in the daytime. They are blots and blemishes,
14 reveling in their dissipation,[g] carousing with you. They have eyes full of adultery, insatiable for sin. They entice unsteady souls. They have hearts trained in greed. Ac-
15 cursed children! Forsaking the right way they have gone astray; they have followed the way of Balaam, the son
16 of Be'or, who loved gain from wrongdoing, but was rebuked for his own transgression; a dumb ass spoke with human voice and restrained the prophet's madness.
17 These are waterless springs and mists driven by a storm; for them the nether gloom of darkness has been
18 reserved. For, uttering loud boasts of folly, they entice with licentious passions of the flesh men who have
19 barely escaped from those who live in error. They promise them freedom, but they themselves are slaves of corruption; for whatever overcomes a man, to that he is
20 enslaved. For if, after they have escaped the defilements of the world through the knowledge of our Lord and

Savior Jesus Christ, they are again entangled in them and overpowered, the last state has become worse for them
21 than the first. For it would have been better for them never to have known the way of righteousness than after knowing it to turn back from the holy commandment
22 delivered to them. It has happened to them according to the true proverb, The dog turns back to his own vomit, and the sow is washed only to wallow in the mire.

THE COMING DAY OF THE LORD

3 This is now the second letter that I have written to you, beloved, and in both of them I have aroused
2 your sincere mind by way of reminder; that you should remember the predictions of the holy prophets and the commandment of the Lord and Savior through your
3 apostles. First of all you must understand this, that scoffers will come in the last days with scoffing, follow-
4 ing their own passions and saying, "Where is the promise of his coming? For ever since the fathers fell asleep, all things have continued as they were from the beginning of
5 creation." They deliberately ignore this fact, that by the word of God heavens existed long ago, and an earth
6 formed out of water and by means of water, through which the world that then existed was deluged with water

e Other authorities read *moved by the Holy Spirit holy men of God spoke*   f Greek *Tartarus*   g Other ancient authorities read *love feasts*

7 and perished. But by the same word the heavens and earth that now exist have been stored up for fire, being kept until the day of judgment and destruction of ungodly men.

8 But do not ignore this one fact, beloved, that with the Lord one day is as a thousand years, and a thousand years 9 as one day. The Lord is not slow about his promise as some count slowness, but is forbearing toward you,[h] not wishing that any should perish, but that all should reach 10 repentance. But the day of the Lord will come like a thief, and then the heavens will pass away with a loud noise, and the elements will be dissolved with fire, and the earth and the works that are upon it will be burned up.

11 Since all these things are thus to be dissolved, what sort of persons ought you to be in lives of holiness and godli-12 ness, waiting for and hastening[i] the coming of the day of God, because of which the heavens will be kindled and 13 dissolved, and the elements will melt with fire! But according to his promise we wait for new heavens and a new earth in which righteousness dwells.

14 Therefore, beloved, since you wait for these, be zealous to be found by him without spot or blemish, and at peace. 15 And count the forbearance of our Lord as salvation. So also our beloved brother Paul wrote to you according to 16 the wisdom given him, speaking of this as he does in all his letters. There are some things in them hard to understand, which the ignorant and unstable twist to their own 17 destruction, as they do the other scriptures. You therefore, beloved, knowing this beforehand, beware lest you be carried away with the error of lawless men and lose 18 your own stability. But grow in the grace and knowledge of our Lord and Savior Jesus Christ. To him be the glory both now and to the day of eternity. Amen.

h Other ancient authorities read *on your account*   i Or *earnestly desiring*

THE FIRST LETTER OF

JOHN

This letter was probably written by the same John who wrote the Gospel of John (see the Introduction to the Gospel of John, page 730) and written at about the same time, near A.D. 100. First John assured Christians that they could endure or overcome all their troubles and inherit eternal life by having faith in Christ.

This letter was not addressed to any particular person or group, but the writer wrote like a father or grandfather to "my little children" (2.1). He warned them not to be misled by people claiming to have certain mysterious "knowledge" of God. He taught that Christians must overcome evil and hate and must live pure, good lives if they would really know God. That is why he wrote, "Beloved, let us love one another; for love is of God, and he who loves is born of God and knows God" (4.7).

We are reminded of the Gospel of John (3.16) by these words from this letter, "In this the love of God was made manifest among us, that God sent his only Son into the world, so that we might live through him" (4.9).

THE FIRST LETTER OF

JOHN

Prologue

1 That which was from the beginning, which we have heard, which we have seen with our eyes, which we have looked upon and touched with our hands, concern-
2 ing the word of life—the life was made manifest, and we saw it, and testify to it, and proclaim to you the eternal life which was with the Father and was made manifest to
3 us—that which we have seen and heard we proclaim also to you, so that you may have fellowship with us; and our fellowship is with the Father and with his Son Jesus
4 Christ. And we are writing this that our [a] joy may be complete.

THE TEST OF FELLOWSHIP

5 This is the message we have heard from him and proclaim to you, that God is light and in him is no dark-
6 ness at all. If we say we have fellowship with him while we walk in darkness, we lie and do not live according to
7 the truth; but if we walk in the light, as he is in the light, we have fellowship with one another, and the blood of
8 Jesus his Son cleanses us from all sin. If we say we have no sin, we deceive ourselves, and the truth is not in us.
9 If we confess our sins, he is faithful and just, and will forgive our sins and cleanse us from all unrighteousness.

10 If we say we have not sinned, we make him a liar, and his word is not in us.

2 My little children, I am writing this to you so that you may not sin; but if any one does sin, we have an
2 advocate with the Father, Jesus Christ the righteous; and he is the expiation for our sins, and not for ours only but
3 also for the sins of the whole world. And by this we may be sure that we know him, if we keep his commandments.
4 He who says "I know him" but disobeys his command-
5 ments is a liar, and the truth is not in him; but whoever keeps his word, in him truly love for God is perfected.
6 By this we may be sure that we are in him: he who says he abides in him ought to walk in the same way in which he walked.

7 Beloved, I am writing you no new commandment, but an old commandment which you had from the beginning; the old commandment is the word which you have heard.
8 Yet I am writing you a new commandment, which is true in him and in you, because [b] the darkness is passing away
9 and the true light is already shining. He who says he is in the light and hates his brother is in the darkness still.
10 He who loves his brother abides in the light, and in it [c]
11 there is no cause for stumbling. But he who hates his brother is in the darkness and walks in the darkness, and

---

[a] Other ancient authorities read *your*   [b] Or *that*   [c] Or *him*

does not know where he is going, because the darkness has blinded his eyes.

12 I am writing to you, little children, because your sins 13 are forgiven for his sake. I am writing to you, fathers, because you know him who is from the beginning. I am writing to you, young men, because you have overcome the evil one. I write to you, children, because you know 14 the Father. I write to you, fathers, because you know him who is from the beginning. I write to you, young men, because you are strong, and the word of God abides in you, and you have overcome the evil one.

15 Do not love the world or the things in the world. If any one loves the world, love for the Father is not in him. 16 For all that is in the world, the lust of the flesh and the lust of the eyes and the pride of life, is not of the Father 17 but is of the world. And the world passes away, and the lust of it; but he who does the will of God abides for ever.

DENIERS OF THE FAITH

18 Children, it is the last hour; and as you have heard that antichrist is coming, so now many antichrists have come; 19 therefore we know that it is the last hour. They went out from us, but they were not of us; for if they had been of us, they would have continued with us; but they went out, 20 that it might be plain that they all are not of us. But you have been anointed by the Holy One, and you all know.[d] 21 I write to you, not because you do not know the truth, but because you know it, and know that no lie is of the 22 truth. Who is the liar but he who denies that Jesus is the Christ? This is the antichrist, he who denies the Father 23 and the Son. No one who denies the Son has the Father. 24 He who confesses the Son has the Father also. Let what you heard from the beginning abide in you. If what you heard from the beginning abides in you, then you will 25 abide in the Son and in the Father. And this is what he has promised us,[e] eternal life.

26 I write this to you about those who would deceive you; 27 but the anointing which you received from him abides in you, and you have no need that any one should teach you; as his anointing teaches you about everything, and is true, and is no lie, just as it has taught you, abide in him.

28 And now, little children, abide in him, so that when he appears we may have confidence and not shrink from him 29 in shame at his coming. If you know that he is righteous, you may be sure that every one who does right is born of him.

CHILDREN OF GOD

3 See what love the Father has given us, that we should be called children of God; and so we are. The reason why the world does not know us is that it did not 2 know him. Beloved, we are God's children now; it does not yet appear what we shall be, but we know that when he appears we shall be like him, for we shall see him as 3 he is. And every one who thus hopes in him purifies himself as he is pure.

4 Every one who commits sin is guilty of lawlessness; sin 5 is lawlessness. You know that he appeared to take away 6 sins, and in him there is no sin. No one who abides in him sins; no one who sins has either seen him or known 7 him. Little children, let no one deceive you. He who does 8 right is righteous, as he is righteous. He who commits sin is of the devil; for the devil has sinned from the beginning. The reason the Son of God appeared was to destroy 9 the works of the devil. No one born of God commits sin; for God's[f] nature abides in him, and he cannot sin 10 because he is[g] born of God. By this it may be seen who are the children of God, and who are the children of the devil: whoever does not do right is not of God, nor he who does not love his brother.

11 For this is the message which you have heard from 12 the beginning, that we should love one another, and not be like Cain who was of the evil one and murdered his brother. And why did he murder him? Because his own 13 deeds were evil and his brother's righteous. Do not 14 wonder, brethren, that the world hates you. We know that we have passed out of death into life, because we love the brethren. He who does not love abides in death. 15 Any one who hates his brother is a murderer, and you know that no murderer has eternal life abiding in him. 16 By this we know love, that he laid down his life for us; and we ought to lay down our lives for the brethren. 17 But if any one has the world's goods and sees his brother in need, yet closes his heart against him, how does God's 18 love abide in him? Little children, let us not love in word or speech but in deed and in truth.

19 By this we shall know that we are of the truth, and 20 reassure our hearts before him whenever our hearts condemn us; for God is greater than our hearts, and he 21 knows everything. Beloved, if our hearts do not condemn 22 us, we have confidence before God; and we receive from him whatever we ask, because we keep his command- 23 ments and do what pleases him. And this is his command-

ment, that we should believe in the name of his Son Jesus Christ and love one another, just as he has com- 24 manded us. All who keep his commandments abide in him, and he in them. And by this we know that he abides in us, by the Spirit which he has given us.

---

d Other ancient authorities read *you know everything*   e Other ancient authorities read *you*   f Greek *his*
g Or *for the offspring of God abide in him, and they cannot sin because they are*

TEST THE SPIRITS

4 Beloved, do not believe every spirit, but test the spirits to see whether they are of God; for many false ² prophets have gone out into the world. By this you know the Spirit of God: every spirit which confesses that Jesus ³ Christ has come in the flesh is of God, and every spirit which does not confess Jesus is not of God. This is the spirit of antichrist, of which you heard that it was com- ⁴ ing, and now it is in the world already. Little children, you are of God, and have overcome them; for he who is ⁵ in you is greater than he who is in the world. They are of the world, therefore what they say is of the world, and ⁶ the world listens to them. We are of God. Whoever knows God listens to us, and he who is not of God does not listen to us. By this we know the spirit of truth and the spirit of error.

⁷ Beloved, let us love one another; for love is of God, ⁸ and he who loves is born of God and knows God. He who ⁹ does not love does not know God; for God is love. In this the love of God was made manifest among us, that God sent his only Son into the world, so that we might ¹⁰ live through him. In this is love, not that we loved God but that he loved us and sent his Son to be the expiation ¹¹ for our sins. Beloved, if God so loved us, we also ought ¹² to love one another. No man has ever seen God; if we love one another, God abides in us and his love is perfected in us.

¹³ By this we know that we abide in him and he in us, ¹⁴ because he has given us of his own Spirit. And we have seen and testify that the Father has sent his Son as the ¹⁵ Savior of the world. Whoever confesses that Jesus is the ¹⁶ Son of God, God abides in him, and he in God. So we know and believe the love God has for us. God is love, and he who abides in love abides in God, and God abides ¹⁷ in him. In this is love perfected with us, that we may have confidence for the day of judgment, because as he is so are ¹⁸ we in this world. There is no fear in love, but perfect love casts out fear. For fear has to do with punishment, and ¹⁹ he who fears is not perfected in love. We love, because

² the child. By this we know that we love the children of God, when we love God and obey his commandments. ³ For this is the love of God, that we keep his commandments. And his commandments are not burdensome. ⁴ For whatever is born of God overcomes the world; and this is the victory that overcomes the world, our faith. ⁵ Who is it that overcomes the world but he who believes that Jesus is the Son of God?

⁶ This is he who came by water and blood, Jesus Christ, not with the water only but with the water and the blood. ⁷ And the Spirit is the witness, because the Spirit is the ⁸ truth. There are three witnesses, the Spirit, the water, and ⁹ the blood; and these three agree. If we receive the testimony of men, the testimony of God is greater; for this is the testimony of God that he has borne witness to his ¹⁰ Son. He who believes in the Son of God has the testimony in himself. He who does not believe God has made him a liar, because he has not believed in the testimony that ¹¹ God has borne to his Son. And this is the testimony, that ¹² God gave us eternal life, and this life is in his Son. He who has the Son has life; he who has not the Son of God has not life.

¹³ I write this to you who believe in the name of the Son of God, that you may know that you have eternal life. ¹⁴ And this is the confidence which we have in him, that if ¹⁵ we ask anything according to his will he hears us. And if we know that he hears us in whatever we ask, we know ¹⁶ that we have obtained the requests made of him. If any one sees his brother committing what is not a mortal sin, he will ask, and God ⁱ will give him life for those whose sin is not mortal. There is sin which is mortal; I do not ¹⁷ say that one is to pray for that. All wrongdoing is sin, but there is sin which is not mortal.

¹⁸ We know that any one born of God does not sin, but He who was born of God keeps him, and the evil one does not touch him.

²⁰ he first loved us. If any one says, "I love God," and hates his brother, he is a liar; for he who does not love his brother whom he has seen, cannot ʰ love God whom he ²¹ has not seen. And this commandment we have from him, that he who loves God should love his brother also.

5 Every one who believes that Jesus is the Christ is a child of God, and every one who loves the parent loves

¹⁹ We know that we are of God, and the whole world is in the power of the evil one.

²⁰ And we know that the Son of God has come and has given us understanding, to know him who is true; and we are in him who is true, in his Son Jesus Christ. This ²¹ is the true God and eternal life. Little children, keep yourselves from idols.

ʰ Other ancient authorities read *how can he* ⁱ Greek *he*

INTRODUCTION TO

THE SECOND LETTER OF

JOHN

This little letter is generally considered to have been written by the same John who wrote the other letters of John and the Gospel of John. (See the Introduction to the Gospel of John, page 730.) It was written about A.D. 100.

The first verse tells us it is from "The elder to the elect lady and her children." This seems to be a way of speaking of some church and its members. Most of this letter is made up of word-for-word quotations from the First Letter of John, and it contains the same warning against false teachers who do not really believe that Jesus is the Christ. It stresses love as the true mark of a Christian.

The letter ends with a friendly word from the members of the church where the writer was: "The children of your elect sister greet you" (verse 13).

THE SECOND LETTER OF

JOHN

Salutation

1 The elder to the elect lady and her children, whom I love in the truth, and not only I but also all who know 2 the truth, because of the truth which abides in us and will be with us for ever:

3 Grace, mercy, and peace will be with us, from God the Father and from Jesus Christ the Father's Son, in truth and love.

LOVE ONE ANOTHER

4 I rejoiced greatly to find some of your children following the truth, just as we have been commanded by the 5 Father. And now I beg you, lady, not as though I were writing you a new commandment, but the one we have 6 had from the beginning, that we love one another. And this is love, that we follow his commandments; this is the commandment, as you have heard from the beginning, 7 that you follow love. For many deceivers have gone out into the world, men who will not acknowledge the coming of Jesus Christ in the flesh; such a one is the deceiver 8 and the antichrist. Look to yourselves, that you may not lose what you[a] have worked for, but may win a full

[a] Other ancient authorities read *we*

9 reward. Any one who goes ahead and does not abide in the doctrine of Christ does not have God; he who abides 10 in the doctrine has both the Father and the Son. If any one comes to you and does not bring this doctrine, do not 11 receive him into the house or give him any greeting; for he who greets him shares his wicked work.

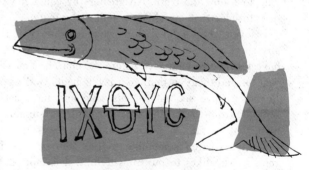

12 Though I have much to write to you, I would rather not use paper and ink, but I hope to come to see you and talk with you face to face, so that our joy may be complete.

13 The children of your elect sister greet you.

THE THIRD LETTER OF

JOHN

This letter from "The elder to the beloved Gaius" (verse 1) was written by the same person who wrote the First and Second Letters of John and the Gospel of John. (See the Introduction to the Gospel of John, page 730.) It was written about A.D. 100.

This is really a letter of introduction for a group of missionaries who probably brought the letter with them to a Christian named Gaius. John wanted Gaius, along with his Christian friends, to help these missionaries, even though Diotrephes, a leader of Gaius' church, opposed them.

John wrote as a bishop or superior officer in charge of the church to which Gaius belonged. The devotion of this great man to the Christians whom he calls his "children" shines out in these words, "No greater joy can I have than this, to hear that my children follow the truth" (Verse 4).

THE THIRD LETTER OF

JOHN

A LETTER TO GAIUS

1 The elder to the beloved Ga'ius, whom I love in the truth.

2 Beloved, I pray that all may go well with you and that you may be in health; I know that it is well with your 3 soul. For I greatly rejoiced when some of the brethren arrived and testified to the truth of your life, as indeed 4 you do follow the truth. No greater joy can I have than this, to hear that my children follow the truth.

5 Beloved, it is a loyal thing you do when you render 6 any service to the brethren, especially to strangers, who have testified to your love before the church. You will do well to send them on their journey as befits God's service. 7 For they have set out for his sake and have accepted 8 nothing from the heathen. So we ought to support such men, that we may be fellow workers in the truth.

9 I have written something to the church; but Diot'-rephes, who likes to put himself first, does not acknowl-10 edge my authority. So if I come, I will bring up what he is doing, prating against me with evil words. And not content with that, he refuses himself to welcome the brethren, and also stops those who want to welcome them and puts them out of the church.

11 Beloved, do not imitate evil but imitate good. He who does good is of God; he who does evil has not seen God.

12 Deme'trius has testimony from every one, and from the truth itself; I testify to him too, and you know my testimony is true.

13 I had much to write to you, but I would rather not 14 write with pen and ink; I hope to see you soon, and we will talk together face to face.

15 Peace be to you. The friends greet you. Greet the friends, every one of them.

INTRODUCTION TO

JUDE

This letter was written about A.D. 150 by Jude, who refers to himself as "a servant [or slave] of Jesus Christ and brother of James." We know little about the writer except that he lived over a hundred years after the death of Jesus. His letter was written to strengthen the faith of Christian converts and keep them alert to false teachers.

Jude repeats many of the ideas of the Second Letter of Peter, which was written about the same time. Most students think that it was written at a time when some Christians were being misled by false teachers who misunderstood the gospel. It is almost impossible for us to understand some parts of it today because we do not know just what some of the symbolic words meant in those troubled times.

The Letter of Jude and other symbolic books such as Daniel and Revelation have sometimes been used to try to predict future events or even the end of the world. Jesus cautioned against such efforts, saying, "But of that day or that hour no one knows, not even the angels in heaven, nor the Son, but only the Father" (Mark 13.32).

The letter reminds the reader of early Hebrew times, showing that whenever men have disobeyed God and been wicked, they have been punished. It refers to a story about how even angels could not sin without being judged by God. This story is not included in our Bible but is found in an ancient Jewish book called *The Assumption of Moses.* Some other parts of the letter refer to *The Book of Enoch,* another Jewish writing known by the readers of that day but not included in the Bible. These two old Jewish books include strange, symbolic writings that are not fully understood today. They were probably written in a secret code so that their persecutors could not understand them.

Shining through the strange symbolic language of this letter is Jude's clear message of an unshakable faith in God as revealed in Jesus Christ, who will be victorious over every evil person and nation.

THE LETTER OF

JUDE

Salutation

1 Jude, a servant of Jesus Christ and brother of James,
To those who are called, beloved in God the Father and kept for Jesus Christ:
2 May mercy, peace, and love be multiplied to you.

FALSE TEACHERS REPROVED

3 Beloved, being very eager to write to you of our common salvation, I found it necessary to write appealing to you to contend for the faith which was once for all
4 delivered to the saints. For admission has been secretly gained by some who long ago were designated for this condemnation, ungodly persons who pervert the grace of our God into licentiousness and deny our only Master and Lord, Jesus Christ.[a]

5 Now I desire to remind you, though you were once for all fully informed, that he [b] who saved a people out of the land of Egypt, afterward destroyed those who did not
6 believe. And the angels that did not keep their own position but left their proper dwelling have been kept by him in eternal chains in the nether gloom until the judgment
7 of the great day; just as Sodom and Gomor'rah and the surrounding cities, which likewise acted immorally and indulged in unnatural lust, serve as an example by undergoing a punishment of eternal fire.

8 Yet in like manner these men in their dreamings defile the flesh, reject authority, and revile the glorious ones.[c]
9 But when the archangel Michael, contending with the

---

[a] Or *the only Master and our Lord Jesus Christ*   [b] Ancient authorities read *Jesus* or *the Lord* or *God*   [c] Greek *glories*

857

devil, disputed about the body of Moses, he did not presume to pronounce a reviling judgment upon him, but 10 said, "The Lord rebuke you." But these men revile whatever they do not understand, and by those things that they know by instinct as irrational animals do, they 11 are destroyed. Woe to them! For they walk in the way of Cain, and abandon themselves for the sake of gain to 12 Balaam's error, and perish in Korah's rebellion. These are blemishes d on your love feasts, as they boldly carouse together, looking after themselves; waterless clouds, carried along by winds; fruitless trees in late autumn, 13 twice dead, uprooted; wild waves of the sea, casting up the foam of their own shame; wandering stars for whom the nether gloom of darkness has been reserved for ever. 14 It was of these also that Enoch in the seventh generation from Adam prophesied, saying, "Behold, the Lord 15 came with his holy myriads, to execute judgment on all, and to convict all the ungodly of all their deeds of ungodliness which they have committed in such an ungodly way, and of all the harsh things which ungodly 16 sinners have spoken against him." These are grumblers, malcontents, following their own passions, loud-mouthed boasters, flattering people to gain advantage.

17 But you must remember, beloved, the predictions of 18 the apostles of our Lord Jesus Christ; they said to you, "In the last time there will be scoffers, following their own 19 ungodly passions." It is these who set up divisions, world-20 ly people, devoid of the Spirit. But you, beloved, build yourselves up on your most holy faith; pray in the Holy 21 Spirit; keep yourselves in the love of God; wait for the 22 mercy of our Lord Jesus Christ unto eternal life. And 23 convince some, who doubt; save some, by snatching them out of the fire; on some have mercy with fear, hating even the garment spotted by the flesh.e

Benediction

24 Now to him who is able to keep you from falling and to present you without blemish before the presence of his 25 glory with rejoicing, to the only God, our Savior through Jesus Christ our Lord, be glory, majesty, dominion, and authority, before all time and now and for ever. Amen.

d Or *reefs*　　　e The Greek text in this sentence is uncertain at several points

INTRODUCTION TO

THE
REVELATION TO JOHN

This book was written about A.D. 95 while the Roman emperor Domitian was persecuting believers in Christ. Many Christians were imprisoned and murdered because they would not worship images of the emperor as a god. Although there is a tradition that Revelation was written by the apostle John, it is very unlikely that the apostle wrote it. The book itself does not tell which John was the author. It does say that he was an exile on the island of Patmos (1.9) in the Mediterranean Sea, not too far from Ephesus. He must have been a converted Jew, for he was very familiar with the Old Testament and with other Jewish writings.

The Revelation to John is called an apocalyptic writing because it speaks about God's victory at the end of time. It is written in picturesque language and contains many visions and symbols similar to symbolic parts of Isaiah, Ezekiel, and Daniel. It also includes ideas from another symbolic book that is not in the Bible, called *The Book of Enoch*. The Revelation to John and other symbolic books such as Daniel and Ezekiel have sometimes been used to try to predict future events or even the end of the world. Jesus cautioned against such efforts, saying, "But of that day or that hour no one knows, not even the angels in heaven, nor the Son, but only the Father" (Mark 13.32).

The Book of Revelation was written to encourage Christians of the Roman Empire, particularly in Asia Minor, to be faithful to Christ even though they had to suffer and die for their faith. John wanted them to know that the worst persecution by the Romans could not defeat God's plan for Jesus Christ and his followers. He did not criticize Rome by name, for this would have been dangerous to anyone found with such writing in his possession. He decided to refer to Rome by using the word Babylon, the ancient enemy of the Hebrews. The Romans would not know what he meant by "Babylon," but the persecuted Christians, because of their familiarity with the Old Testament writings, surely would.

In other visions John portrayed the many troubles of Christians and the final defeat of Satan and every evil thing. Because we do not always know what the symbolic expressions mean, we have trouble understanding some parts of this book.

There is no doubt about the main message of the book, however. It is that God will finally triumph over every evil here on earth and in the world to come. It says, "and God himself will be with them; he will wipe away every tear from their eyes, and death shall be no more, neither shall there be mourning nor crying nor pain any more, for the former things have passed away" (21.3-4). And men will need "no light of lamp or sun, for the Lord God will be their light . . ." (22.5).

THE

REVELATION TO JOHN

(The Apocalypse)

The Preface

1 The revelation of Jesus Christ, which God gave him to show to his servants what must soon take place; and he made it known by sending his angel to his servant ² John, who bore witness to the word of God and to the ³ testimony of Jesus Christ, even to all that he saw. Blessed

is he who reads aloud the words of the prophecy, and blessed are those who hear, and who keep what is written therein; for the time is near.

LETTERS TO THE SEVEN CHURCHES

4 John to the seven churches that are in Asia:

Grace to you and peace from him who is and who was and who is to come, and from the seven spirits who are 5 before his throne, and from Jesus Christ the faithful witness, the firstborn of the dead, and the ruler of kings on earth.

To him who loves us and has freed us from our sins 6 by his blood and made us a kingdom, priests to his God and Father, to him be glory and dominion for ever and 7 ever. Amen. Behold, he is coming with the clouds, and every eye will see him, every one who pierced him; and all tribes of the earth will wail on account of him. Even so. Amen.

8 "I am the Alpha and the Omega," says the Lord God, who is and who was and who is to come, the Almighty.

9 I John, your brother, who share with you in Jesus the tribulation and the kingdom and the patient endurance, was on the island called Patmos on account of the word 10 of God and the testimony of Jesus. I was in the Spirit on the Lord's day, and I heard behind me a loud voice like 11 a trumpet saying, "Write what you see in a book and send it to the seven churches, to Ephesus and to Smyrna and to Per'gamum and to Thyati'ra and to Sardis and to Philadelphia and to Laodice'a."

12 Then I turned to see the voice that was speaking to me, 13 and on turning I saw seven golden lampstands, and in the midst of the lampstands one like a son of man, clothed with a long robe and with a golden girdle round his 14 breast; his head and his hair were white as white wool, 15 white as snow; his eyes were like a flame of fire, his feet were like burnished bronze, refined as in a furnace, 16 and his voice was like the sound of many waters; in his right hand he held seven stars, from his mouth issued a sharp two-edged sword, and his face was like the sun shining in full strength.

17 When I saw him, I fell at his feet as though dead. But he laid his right hand upon me, saying, "Fear not, I am 18 the first and the last, and the living one; I died, and behold I am alive for evermore, and I have the keys of 19 Death and Hades. Now write what you see, what is and 20 what is to take place hereafter. As for the mystery of the seven stars which you saw in my right hand, and the seven golden lampstands, the seven stars are the angels of the seven churches and the seven lampstands are the seven churches.

2 "To the angel of the church in Ephesus write: 'The words of him who holds the seven stars in his right hand, who walks among the seven golden lampstands.

2 " 'I know your works, your toil and your patient endurance, and how you cannot bear evil men but have tested those who call themselves apostles but are not, and 3 found them to be false; I know you are enduring patiently and bearing up for my name's sake, and you 4 have not grown weary. But I have this against you, that 5 you have abandoned the love you had at first. Remember then from what you have fallen, repent and do the works you did at first. If not, I will come to you and remove 6 your lampstand from its place, unless you repent. Yet this you have, you hate the works of the Nicola'itans, which 7 I also hate. He who has an ear, let him hear what the Spirit says to the churches. To him who conquers I will grant to eat of the tree of life, which is in the paradise of God.'

8 "And to the angel of the church in Smyrna write: 'The words of the first and the last, who died and came to life.

9 " 'I know your tribulation and your poverty (but you are rich) and the slander of those who say that they are 10 Jews and are not, but are a synagogue of Satan. Do not fear what you are about to suffer. Behold, the devil is about to throw some of you into prison, that you may be tested, and for ten days you will have tribulation. Be faithful unto death, and I will give you the crown of life. 11 He who has an ear, let him hear what the Spirit says to the churches. He who conquers shall not be hurt by the second death.'

12 "And to the angel of the church in Per'gamum write: 'The words of him who has the sharp two-edged sword.

13 " 'I know where you dwell, where Satan's throne is; you hold fast my name and you did not deny my faith even in the days of An'tipas my witness, my faithful one, 14 who was killed among you, where Satan dwells. But I have a few things against you: you have some there who hold the teaching of Balaam, who taught Balak to put a stumbling block before the sons of Israel, that they might eat food sacrificed to idols and practice immorality. 15 So you also have some who hold the teaching of the 16 Nicola'itans. Repent then. If not, I will come to you soon 17 and war against them with the sword of my mouth. He who has an ear, let him hear what the Spirit says to the churches. To him who conquers I will give some of the hidden manna, and I will give him a white stone, with a new name written on the stone which no one knows except him who receives it.'

18 "And to the angel of the church in Thyati'ra write: 'The words of the Son of God, who has eyes like a flame of fire, and whose feet are like burnished bronze.

19 " 'I know your works, your love and faith and service and patient endurance, and that your latter works exceed 20 the first. But I have this against you, that you tolerate the woman Jez'ebel, who calls herself a prophetess and is teaching and beguiling my servants to practice immorality 21 and to eat food sacrificed to idols. I gave her time to repent, but she refuses to repent of her immorality. 22 Behold, I will throw her on a sickbed, and those who commit adultery with her I will throw into great tribula- 23 tion, unless they repent of her doings; and I will strike her children dead. And all the churches shall know that I am he who searches mind and heart, and I will give to 24 each of you as your works deserve. But to the rest of you in Thyati'ra, who do not hold this teaching, who have not learned what some call the deep things of Satan, to you I 25 say, I do not lay upon you any other burden; only hold 26 fast what you have, until I come. He who conquers and who keeps my works until the end, I will give him power 27 over the nations, and he shall rule them with a rod of iron, as when earthen pots are broken in pieces, even as 28 I myself have received power from my Father; and I will 29 give him the morning star. He who has an ear, let him hear what the Spirit says to the churches.'

3 "And to the angel of the church in Sardis write: 'The words of him who has the seven spirits of God and the seven stars.

" 'I know your works; you have the name of being 2 alive, and you are dead. Awake, and strengthen what remains and is on the point of death, for I have not found your works perfect in the sight of my God. 3 Remember then what you received and heard; keep that, and repent. If you will not awake, I will come like a thief, and you will not know at what hour I will come 4 upon you. Yet you have still a few names in Sardis, people who have not soiled their garments; and they 5 shall walk with me in white, for they are worthy. He who conquers shall be clad thus in white garments, and I will not blot his name out of the book of life; I will confess 6 his name before my Father and before his angels. He who has an ear, let him hear what the Spirit says to the churches.'

7 "And to the angel of the church in Philadelphia write: 'The words of the holy one, the true one, who has the key of David, who opens and no one shall shut, who shuts and no one opens.

8 " 'I know your works. Behold, I have set before you an open door, which no one is able to shut; I know that you have but little power, and yet you have kept my 9 word and have not denied my name. Behold, I will make those of the synagogue of Satan who say that they are Jews and are not, but lie—behold, I will make them come and bow down before your feet, and learn that I have 10 loved you. Because you have kept my word of patient

endurance, I will keep you from the hour of trial which is coming on the whole world, to try those who dwell upon 11 the earth. I am coming soon; hold fast what you have, 12 so that no one may seize your crown. He who conquers, I will make him a pillar in the temple of my God; never shall he go out of it, and I will write on him the name of my God, and the name of the city of my God, the new Jerusalem which comes down from my God out of heaven, 13 and my own new name. He who has an ear, let him hear what the Spirit says to the churches.'

14 "And to the angel of the church in La-odice'a write: 'The words of the Amen, the faithful and true witness, the beginning of God's creation.

15 " 'I know your works: you are neither cold nor hot. 16 Would that you were cold or hot! So, because you are lukewarm, and neither cold nor hot, I will spew you out 17 of my mouth. For you say, I am rich, I have prospered, and I need nothing; not knowing that you are wretched, 18 pitiable, poor, blind, and naked. Therefore I counsel you to buy from me gold refined by fire, that you may be rich, and white garments to clothe you and to keep the shame of your nakedness from being seen, and salve to 19 anoint your eyes, that you may see. Those whom I love, 20 I reprove and chasten; so be zealous and repent. Behold, I stand at the door and knock; if any one hears my voice and opens the door, I will come in to him and eat with 21 him, and he with me. He who conquers, I will grant him to sit with me on my throne, as I myself conquered and 22 sat down with my Father on his throne. He who has an ear, let him hear what the Spirit says to the churches.' "

VISIONS OF HEAVENLY WORSHIP

4 After this I looked, and lo, in heaven an open door! And the first voice, which I had heard speaking to me like a trumpet, said, "Come up hither, and I will 2 show you what must take place after this." At once I was in the Spirit, and lo, a throne stood in heaven, with one 3 seated on the throne! And he who sat there appeared like jasper and carnelian, and round the throne was a rainbow 4 that looked like an emerald. Round the throne were twenty-four thrones, and seated on the thrones were twenty-four elders, clad in white garments, with golden 5 crowns upon their heads. From the throne issue flashes of lightning, and voices and peals of thunder, and before the throne burn seven torches of fire, which are the seven 6 spirits of God; and before the throne there is as it were a sea of glass, like crystal.

And round the throne, on each side of the throne, are four living creatures, full of eyes in front and behind:

7 the first living creature like a lion, the second living creature like an ox, the third living creature with the face of a man, and the fourth living creature like a flying 8 eagle. And the four living creatures, each of them with six wings, are full of eyes all round and within, and day and night they never cease to sing,

"Holy, holy, holy, is the Lord God Almighty,
who was and is and is to come!"

9 And whenever the living creatures give glory and honor and thanks to him who is seated on the throne, who lives 10 for ever and ever, the twenty-four elders fall down before him who is seated on the throne and worship him who lives for ever and ever; they cast their crowns before the throne, singing,

11 "Worthy art thou, our Lord and God,
to receive glory and honor and power,
for thou didst create all things,
and by thy will they existed and were created."

5 And I saw in the right hand of him who was seated on the throne a scroll written within and on the back, 2 sealed with seven seals; and I saw a strong angel proclaiming with a loud voice, "Who is worthy to open the 3 scroll and break its seals?" And no one in heaven or on earth or under the earth was able to open the scroll or 4 to look into it, and I wept much that no one was found 5 worthy to open the scroll or to look into it. Then one of the elders said to me, "Weep not; lo, the Lion of the tribe of Judah, the Root of David, has conquered, so that he can open the scroll and its seven seals."

6 And between the throne and the four living creatures and among the elders, I saw a Lamb standing, as though it had been slain, with seven horns and with seven eyes, which are the seven spirits of God sent out into all the 7 earth; and he went and took the scroll from the right 8 hand of him who was seated on the throne. And when he had taken the scroll, the four living creatures and the twenty-four elders fell down before the Lamb, each holding a harp, and with golden bowls full of incense, which 9 are the prayers of the saints; and they sang a new song, saying,

"Worthy art thou to take the scroll and to open its seals,
for thou wast slain and by thy blood didst ransom men
for God
from every tribe and tongue and people and nation,
10 and hast made them a kingdom and priests to our God,
and they shall reign on earth."

11 Then I looked, and I heard around the throne and the living creatures and the elders the voice of many angels, numbering myriads of myriads and thousands of thou-

12 sands, saying with a loud voice, "Worthy is the Lamb who was slain, to receive power and wealth and wisdom 13 and might and honor and glory and blessing!" And I heard every creature in heaven and on earth and under the earth and in the sea, and all therein, saying, "To him who sits upon the throne and to the Lamb be blessing and 14 honor and glory and might for ever and ever!" And the four living creatures said, "Amen!" and the elders fell down and worshiped.

VISIONS OF SEVEN SEALS

6 Now I saw when the Lamb opened one of the seven seals, and I heard one of the four living creatures say, 2 as with a voice of thunder, "Come!" And I saw, and behold, a white horse, and its rider had a bow; and a crown was given to him, and he went out conquering and to conquer.

3 When he opened the second seal, I heard the second 4 living creature say, "Come!" And out came another horse, bright red; its rider was permitted to take peace from the earth, so that men should slay one another; and he was given a great sword.

5 When he opened the third seal, I heard the third living creature say, "Come!" And I saw, and behold, a black 6 horse, and its rider had a balance in his hand; and I heard what seemed to be a voice in the midst of the four living creatures saying, "A quart of wheat for a denarius,ᵃ and three quarts of barley for a denarius; ᵃ but do not harm oil and wine!"

7 When he opened the fourth seal, I heard the voice of 8 the fourth living creature say, "Come!" And I saw, and behold, a pale horse, and its rider's name was Death, and Hades followed him; and they were given power over a fourth of the earth, to kill with sword and with famine and with pestilence and by wild beasts of the earth.

9 When he opened the fifth seal, I saw under the altar the souls of those who had been slain for the word of God 10 and for the witness they had borne; they cried out with a loud voice, "O Sovereign Lord, holy and true, how long before thou wilt judge and avenge our blood on those 11 who dwell upon the earth?" Then, they were each given a white robe and told to rest a little longer, until the number of their fellow servants and their brethren should be complete, who were to be killed as they themselves had been.

12 When he opened the sixth seal, I looked, and behold, there was a great earthquake; and the sun became black 13 as sackcloth, the full moon became like blood, and the stars of the sky fell to the earth as the fig tree sheds its

ᵃ The denarius was a day's wages for a laborer

14 winter fruit when shaken by a gale; the sky vanished like a scroll that is rolled up, and every mountain and island 15 was removed from its place. Then the kings of the earth and the great men and the generals and the rich and the strong, and every one, slave and free, hid in the caves 16 and among the rocks of the mountains, calling to the mountains and rocks, "Fall on us and hide us from the face of him who is seated on the throne, and from the 17 wrath of the Lamb; for the great day of their wrath has come, and who can stand before it?"

7 After this I saw four angels standing at the four corners of the earth, holding back the four winds of the earth, that no wind might blow on earth or sea or 2 against any tree. Then I saw another angel ascend from the rising of the sun, with the seal of the living God, and he called with a loud voice to the four angels who had 3 been given power to harm earth and sea, saying, "Do not harm the earth or the sea or the trees, till we have sealed 4 the servants of our God upon their foreheads." And I heard the number of the sealed, a hundred and forty-four thousand sealed, out of every tribe of the sons of 5 Israel, twelve thousand sealed out of the tribe of Judah, twelve thousand of the tribe of Reuben, twelve thousand 6 of the tribe of Gad, twelve thousand of the tribe of Asher, twelve thousand of the tribe of Naph'tali, twelve thousand 7 of the tribe of Manas'seh, twelve thousand of the tribe of Simeon, twelve thousand of the tribe of Levi, twelve 8 thousand of the tribe of Is'sachar, twelve thousand of the tribe of Zeb'ulun, twelve thousand of the tribe of Joseph, twelve thousand sealed out of the tribe of Benjamin.

9 After this I looked, and behold, a great multitude which no man could number, from every nation, from all tribes and peoples and tongues, standing before the throne and before the Lamb, clothed in white robes, with palm 10 branches in their hands, and crying out with a loud voice, "Salvation belongs to our God who sits upon the 11 throne, and to the Lamb!" And all the angels stood round the throne and round the elders and the four living creatures, and they fell on their faces before the throne 12 and worshiped God, saying, "Amen! Blessing and glory and wisdom and thanksgiving and honor and power and might be to our God for ever and ever! Amen."

13 Then one of the elders addressed me, saying, "Who are these, clothed in white robes, and whence have they 14 come?" I said to him, "Sir, you know." And he said to me, "These are they who have come out of the great tribulation; they have washed their robes and made them white in the blood of the Lamb.

15 Therefore are they before the throne of God,
    and serve him day and night within his temple;
    and he who sits upon the throne will shelter them with
        his presence.
16 They shall hunger no more, neither thirst any more;
    the sun shall not strike them, nor any scorching heat.
17 For the Lamb in the midst of the throne will be their
        shepherd,
    and he will guide them to springs of living water;
and God will wipe away every tear from their eyes."

8 When the Lamb opened the seventh seal, there was 2 silence in heaven for about half an hour. Then I saw the seven angels who stand before God, and seven 3 trumpets were given to them. And another angel came and stood at the altar with a golden censer; and he was given much incense to mingle with the prayers of all the 4 saints upon the golden altar before the throne; and the smoke of the incense rose with the prayers of the saints 5 from the hand of the angel before God. Then the angel took the censer and filled it with fire from the altar and threw it on the earth; and there were peals of thunder, voices, flashes of lightning, and an earthquake.

SEVEN TRUMPET WOES

6 Now the seven angels who had the seven trumpets made ready to blow them.

7 The first angel blew his trumpet, and there followed hail and fire, mixed with blood, which fell on the earth; and a third of the earth was burnt up, and a third of the trees were burnt up, and all green grass was burnt up.

8 The second angel blew his trumpet, and something like

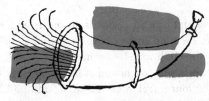

a great mountain, burning with fire, was thrown into the 9 sea; and a third of the sea became blood, a third of the living creatures in the sea died, and a third of the ships were destroyed.

10 The third angel blew his trumpet, and a great star fell from heaven, blazing like a torch, and it fell on a third of 11 the rivers and on the fountains of water. The name of the star is Wormwood. A third of the waters became wormwood, and many men died of the water, because it was made bitter.

12 The fourth angel blew his trumpet, and a third of the sun was struck, and a third of the moon, and a third of the stars, so that a third of their light was darkened; a third of the day was kept from shining, and likewise a third of the night.

13 Then I looked, and I heard an eagle crying with a loud voice, as it flew in midheaven, "Woe, woe, woe to those who dwell on the earth, at the blasts of the other trumpets which the three angels are about to blow!"

9 And the fifth angel blew his trumpet, and I saw a star fallen from heaven to earth, and he was given the

2 key of the shaft of the bottomless pit; he opened the shaft of the bottomless pit, and from the shaft rose smoke like the smoke of a great furnace, and the sun and the air 3 were darkened with the smoke from the shaft. Then from the smoke came locusts on the earth, and they were given 4 power like the power of scorpions of the earth; they were told not to harm the grass of the earth or any green growth of any tree, but only those of mankind who have 5 not the seal of God upon their foreheads; they were allowed to torture them for five months, but not to kill them, and their torture was like the torture of a scorpion, 6 when it stings a man. And in those days men will seek death and will not find it; they will long to die, and death will fly from them.

7 In appearance the locusts were like horses arrayed for battle; on their heads were what looked like crowns of 8 gold; their faces were like human faces, their hair like 9 women's hair, and their teeth like lions' teeth; they had scales like iron breastplates, and the noise of their wings was like the noise of many chariots with horses rushing 10 into battle. They have tails like scorpions, and stings, and their power of hurting men for five months lies in their 11 tails. They have as king over them the angel of the bottomless pit; his name in Hebrew is Abad′don, and in Greek he is called Apol′lyon.[b]

12 The first woe has passed; behold, two woes are still to come.

13 Then the sixth angel blew his trumpet, and I heard a voice from the four horns of the golden altar before God, 14 saying to the sixth angel who had the trumpet, "Release the four angels who are bound at the great river Eu·phra′- 15 tes." So the four angels were released, who had been held ready for the hour, the day, the month, and the year, to 16 kill a third of mankind. The number of the troops of cavalry was twice ten thousand times ten thousand; I 17 heard their number. And this was how I saw the horses in my vision: the riders wore breastplates the color of fire and of sapphire[c] and of sulphur, and the heads of the horses were like lions' heads, and fire and smoke and 18 sulphur issued from their mouths. By these three plagues a third of mankind was killed, by the fire and smoke and 19 sulphur issuing from their mouths. For the power of the horses is in their mouths and in their tails; their tails are like serpents, with heads, and by means of them they wound.

20 The rest of mankind, who were not killed by these plagues, did not repent of the works of their hands nor give up worshiping demons and idols of gold and silver and bronze and stone and wood, which cannot either see 21 or hear or walk; nor did they repent of their murders or their sorceries or their immorality or their thefts.

10 Then I saw another mighty angel coming down from heaven, wrapped in a cloud, with a rainbow

over his head, and his face was like the sun, and his legs 2 like pillars of fire. He had a little scroll open in his hand. And he set his right foot on the sea, and his left foot on 3 the land, and called out with a loud voice, like a lion roaring; when he called out, the seven thunders sounded. 4 And when the seven thunders had sounded, I was about to write, but I heard a voice from heaven saying, "Seal up what the seven thunders have said, and do not write it 5 down." And the angel whom I saw standing on sea and 6 land lifted up his right hand to heaven and swore by him who lives for ever and ever, who created heaven and what is in it, the earth and what is in it, and the sea and what 7 is in it, that there should be no more delay, but that in the days of the trumpet call to be sounded by the seventh angel, the mystery of God, as he announced to his servants the prophets, should be fulfilled.

8 Then the voice which I had heard from heaven spoke to me again, saying, "Go, take the scroll which is open in the hand of the angel who is standing on the sea and 9 on the land." So I went to the angel and told him to give me the little scroll; and he said to me, "Take it and eat; it will be bitter to your stomach, but sweet as honey 10 in your mouth." And I took the little scroll from the hand of the angel and ate it; it was sweet as honey in my mouth, but when I had eaten it my stomach was made 11 bitter. And I was told, "You must again prophesy about many peoples and nations and tongues and kings."

11 Then I was given a measuring rod like a staff, and I was told: "Rise and measure the temple of God 2 and the altar and those who worship there, but do not measure the court outside the temple; leave that out, for it is given over to the nations, and they will trample over 3 the holy city for forty-two months. And I will grant my two witnesses power to prophesy for one thousand two hundred and sixty days, clothed in sackcloth."

4 These are the two olive trees and the two lampstands 5 which stand before the Lord of the earth. And if any one would harm them, fire pours from their mouth and consumes their foes; if any one would harm them, thus he is 6 doomed to be killed. They have power to shut the sky, that no rain may fall during the days of their prophesying, and they have power over the waters to turn them into blood, and to smite the earth with every plague, as 7 often as they desire. And when they have finished their testimony, the beast that ascends from the bottomless pit will make war upon them and conquer them and kill 8 them, and their dead bodies will lie in the street of the great city which is allegorically[d] called Sodom and

b Or *Destroyer*   c Greek *hyacinth*   d Greek *spiritually*

9 Egypt, where their Lord was crucified. For three days and a half men from the peoples and tribes and tongues and nations gaze at their dead bodies and refuse to let them 10 be placed in a tomb, and those who dwell on the earth will rejoice over them and make merry and exchange presents, because these two prophets had been a torment 11 to those who dwell on the earth. But after the three and a half days a breath of life from God entered them, and they stood up on their feet, and great fear fell on those 12 who saw them. Then they heard a loud voice from heaven saying to them, "Come up hither!" And in the sight of 13 their foes they went up to heaven in a cloud. And at that hour there was a great earthquake, and a tenth of the city fell; seven thousand people were killed in the earthquake, and the rest were terrified and gave glory to the God of heaven.

14 The second woe has passed; behold, the third woe is soon to come.

15 Then the seventh angel blew his trumpet, and there were loud voices in heaven, saying, "The kingdom of the world has become the kingdom of our Lord and of his 16 Christ, and he shall reign for ever and ever." And the twenty-four elders who sit on their thrones before God fell 17 on their faces and worshiped God, saying,

"We give thanks to thee, Lord God Almighty, who art and who wast,
    that thou hast taken thy great power and begun to reign.
18 The nations raged, but thy wrath came,
    and the time for the dead to be judged,
for rewarding thy servants, the prophets and saints,
    and those who fear thy name, both small and great,
and for destroying the destroyers of the earth."

19 Then God's temple in heaven was opened, and the ark

of his covenant was seen within his temple; and there were flashes of lightning, voices, peals of thunder, an earthquake, and heavy hail.

SEVEN VISIONS OF THE DRAGON'S KINGDOM

12 And a great portent appeared in heaven, a woman clothed with the sun, with the moon under her feet, 2 and on her head a crown of twelve stars; she was with child and she cried out in her pangs of birth, in anguish 3 for delivery. And another portent appeared in heaven; behold, a great red dragon, with seven heads and ten

4 horns, and seven diadems upon his heads. His tail swept down a third of the stars of heaven, and cast them to the earth. And the dragon stood before the woman who was about to bear a child, that he might devour her child 5 when she brought it forth; she brought forth a male child, one who is to rule all the nations with a rod of iron, but 6 her child was caught up to God and to his throne, and the woman fled into the wilderness, where she has a place prepared by God, in which to be nourished for one thousand two hundred and sixty days.

7 Now war arose in heaven, Michael and his angels fighting against the dragon; and the dragon and his 8 angels fought, but they were defeated and there was no 9 longer any place for them in heaven. And the great dragon was thrown down, that ancient serpent, who is called the Devil and Satan, the deceiver of the whole world—he was thrown down to the earth, and his angels 10 were thrown down with him. And I heard a loud voice in heaven, saying, "Now the salvation and the power and the kingdom of our God and the authority of his Christ have come, for the accuser of our brethren has been thrown down, who accuses them day and night before our God. 11 And they have conquered him by the blood of the Lamb and by the word of their testimony, for they loved not 12 their lives even unto death. Rejoice then, O heaven and you that dwell therein! But woe to you, O earth and sea, for the devil has come down to you in great wrath, because he knows that his time is short!"

13 And when the dragon saw that he had been thrown down to the earth, he pursued the woman who had borne 14 the male child. But the woman was given the two wings of the great eagle that she might fly from the serpent into the wilderness, to the place where she is to be 15 nourished for a time, and times, and half a time. The serpent poured water like a river out of his mouth after 16 the woman, to sweep her away with the flood. But the earth came to the help of the woman, and the earth opened its mouth and swallowed the river which the 17 dragon had poured from his mouth. Then the dragon was angry with the woman, and went off to make war on the rest of her offspring, on those who keep the commandments of God and bear testimony to Jesus. And he stood [e] on the sand of the sea.

13 And I saw a beast rising out of the sea, with ten horns and seven heads, with ten diadems upon its 2 horns and a blasphemous name upon its heads. And the beast that I saw was like a leopard, its feet were like a bear's and its mouth was like a lion's mouth. And to it the dragon gave his power and his throne and great 3 authority. One of its heads seemed to have a mortal wound, but its mortal wound was healed, and the whole 4 earth followed the beast with wonder. Men worshiped the dragon, for he had given his authority to the beast, and

e Other ancient authorities read *And I stood*, connecting the sentence with 13.1

they worshiped the beast, saying, "Who is like the beast, and who can fight against it?"

5 And the beast was given a mouth uttering haughty and blasphemous words, and it was allowed to exercise au-
6 thority for forty-two months; it opened its mouth to utter blasphemies against God, blaspheming his name and his dwelling, that is, those who dwell in heaven.
7 Also it was allowed to make war on the saints and to conquer them.[f] And authority was given it over every
8 tribe and people and tongue and nation, and all who dwell on earth will worship it, every one whose name has not been written before the foundation of the world in
9 the book of life of the Lamb that was slain. If any one has an ear, let him hear:
10 If any one is to be taken captive,
 to captivity he goes;
 if any one slays with the sword,
 with the sword must he be slain.
Here is a call for the endurance and faith of the saints.
11 Then I saw another beast which rose out of the earth; it had two horns like a lamb and it spoke like a
12 dragon. It exercises all the authority of the first beast in its presence, and makes the earth and its inhabitants worship the first beast, whose mortal wound was healed.
13 It works great signs, even making fire come down from
14 heaven to earth in the sight of men; and by the signs which it is allowed to work in the presence of the beast, it deceives those who dwell on earth, bidding them make an image for the beast which was wounded by the sword
15 and yet lived; and it was allowed to give breath to the image of the beast so that the image of the beast should even speak, and to cause those who would not worship
16 the image of the beast to be slain. Also it causes all, both small and great, both rich and poor, both free and slave,
17 to be marked on the right hand or the forehead, so that no one can buy or sell unless he has the mark, that is,
18 the name of the beast or the number of its name. This

2 on their foreheads. And I heard a voice from heaven like the sound of many waters and like the sound of loud thunder; the voice I heard was like the sound of harpers
3 playing on their harps, and they sing a new song before the throne and before the four living creatures and before the elders. No one could learn that song except the hundred and forty-four thousand who had been redeemed
4 from the earth. It is these who have not defiled themselves with women, for they are chaste;[h] it is these who follow the Lamb wherever he goes; these have been redeemed from mankind as first fruits for God and the
5 Lamb, and in their mouth no lie was found, for they are spotless.
6 Then I saw another angel flying in midheaven, with an eternal gospel to proclaim to those who dwell on earth, to every nation and tribe and tongue and people;
7 and he said with a loud voice, "Fear God and give him glory, for the hour of his judgment has come; and worship him who made heaven and earth, the sea and the fountains of water."
8 Another angel, a second, followed, saying, "Fallen, fallen is Babylon the great, she who made all nations drink the wine of her impure passion."
9 And another angel, a third, followed them, saying with a loud voice, "If any one worships the beast and its image and receives a mark on his forehead or on his
10 hand, he also shall drink the wine of God's wrath, poured unmixed into the cup of his anger, and he shall be tormented with fire and sulphur in the presence of the
11 holy angels and in the presence of the Lamb. And the smoke of their torment goes up for ever and ever; and they have no rest, day or night, these worshipers of the beast and its image, and whoever receives the mark of its name."
12 Here is a call for the endurance of the saints, those who keep the commandments of God and the faith of Jesus.

calls for wisdom: let him who has understanding reckon the number of the beast, for it is a human number, its number is six hundred and sixty-six.[g]

SEVEN VISIONS OF WORSHIPERS

14 Then I looked, and lo, on Mount Zion stood the Lamb, and with him a hundred and forty-four thousand who had his name and his Father's name written

13 And I heard a voice from heaven saying, "Write this: Blessed are the dead who die in the Lord henceforth." "Blessed indeed," says the Spirit, "that they may rest from their labors, for their deeds follow them!"
14 Then I looked, and lo, a white cloud, and seated on the cloud one like a son of man, with a golden crown on
15 his head, and a sharp sickle in his hand. And another angel came out of the temple, calling with a loud voice

f Other ancient authorities omit this sentence   g Other ancient authorities read *six hundred and sixteen*   h Greek *virgins*

to him who sat upon the cloud, "Put in your sickle, and reap, for the hour to reap has come, for the harvest of the
16 earth is fully ripe." So he who sat upon the cloud swung his sickle on the earth, and the earth was reaped.

17 And another angel came out of the temple in heaven,
18 and he too had a sharp sickle. Then another angel came out from the altar, the angel who has power over fire, and he called with a loud voice to him who had the

sharp sickle, "Put in your sickle, and gather the clusters
19 of the vine of the earth, for its grapes are ripe." So the angel swung his sickle on the earth and gathered the vintage of the earth, and threw it into the great wine
20 press of the wrath of God; and the wine press was trodden outside the city, and blood flowed from the wine press, as high as a horse's bridle, for one thousand six hundred stadia.[i]

SEVEN VISIONS OF GOD'S WRATH

15 Then I saw another portent in heaven, great and wonderful, seven angels with seven plagues, which are the last, for with them the wrath of God is ended.

2 And I saw what appeared to be a sea of glass mingled with fire, and those who had conquered the beast and its image and the number of its name, standing beside the sea of glass with harps of God in their hands.
3 And they sing the song of Moses, the servant of God, and the song of the Lamb, saying,

"Great and wonderful are thy deeds,
O Lord God the Almighty!
Just and true are thy ways,
O King of the ages![j]
4 Who shall not fear and glorify thy name, O Lord?
For thou alone art holy.
All nations shall come and worship thee,
for thy judgments have been revealed."

5 After this I looked, and the temple of the tent of
6 witness in heaven was opened, and out of the temple came the seven angels with the seven plagues, robed in pure bright linen, and their breasts girded with golden
7 girdles. And one of the four living creatures gave the seven angels seven golden bowls full of the wrath of
8 God who lives for ever and ever; and the temple was filled with smoke from the glory of God and from his power, and no one could enter the temple until the seven plagues of the seven angels were ended.

16 Then I heard a loud voice from the temple telling the seven angels, "Go and pour out on the earth

the seven bowls of the wrath of God."
2 So the first angel went and poured his bowl on the earth, and foul and evil sores came upon the men who bore the mark of the beast and worshiped its image.
3 The second angel poured his bowl into the sea, and it became like the blood of a dead man, and every living thing died that was in the sea.
4 The third angel poured his bowl into the rivers and
5 the fountains of water, and they became blood. And I heard the angel of water say,

"Just art thou in these thy judgments,
thou who art and wast, O Holy One.
6 For men have shed the blood of saints and prophets,
and thou hast given them blood to drink.
It is their due!"
7 And I heard the altar cry,
"Yea, Lord God the Almighty,
true and just are thy judgments!"

8 The fourth angel poured his bowl on the sun, and it
9 was allowed to scorch men with fire; men were scorched by the fierce heat, and they cursed the name of God who had power over these plagues, and they did not repent and give him glory.

10 The fifth angel poured his bowl on the throne of the beast, and its kingdom was in darkness; men gnawed
11 their tongues in anguish and cursed the God of heaven for their pain and sores, and did not repent of their deeds.

12 The sixth angel poured his bowl on the great river Eu-phra′tes, and its water was dried up, to prepare the
13 way for the kings from the east. And I saw, issuing from the mouth of the dragon and from the mouth of the beast and from the mouth of the false prophet, three foul
14 spirits like frogs; for they are demonic spirits, performing signs, who go abroad to the kings of the whole world, to assemble them for battle on the great day of God the
15 Almighty. ("Lo, I am coming like a thief! Blessed is he who is awake, keeping his garments that he may not
16 go naked and be seen exposed!") And they assembled them at the place which is called in Hebrew Armaged′-don.

17 The seventh angel poured his bowl into the air, and a loud voice came out of the temple, from the throne, say-
18 ing, "It is done!" And there were flashes of lightning, voices, peals of thunder, and a great earthquake such as had never been since men were on the earth, so
19 great was that earthquake. The great city was split into three parts, and the cities of the nations fell, and God

---

i About two hundred miles   j Other ancient authorities read *the nations*

remembered great Babylon, to make her drain the cup
20 of the fury of his wrath. And every island fled away,
21 and no mountains were to be found; and great hailstones, heavy as a hundredweight, dropped on men from heaven, till men cursed God for the plague of the hail, so fearful was that plague.

SEVEN VISIONS OF THE NATIONS' FALL

17 Then one of the seven angels who had the seven bowls came and said to me, "Come, I will show you the judgment of the great harlot who is seated upon
2 many waters, with whom the kings of the earth have committed fornication, and with the wine of whose forni-
3 cation the dwellers on earth have become drunk." And he carried me away in the Spirit into a wilderness, and I saw a woman sitting on a scarlet beast which was full of blasphemous names, and it had seven heads and ten
4 horns. The woman was arrayed in purple and scarlet, and bedecked with gold and jewels and pearls, holding in her hand a golden cup full of abominations and the
5 impurities of her fornication; and on her forehead was written a name of mystery: "Babylon the great, mother
6 of harlots and of earth's abominations." And I saw the woman, drunk with the blood of the saints and the blood of the martyrs of Jesus.
7 When I saw her I marveled greatly. But the angel said to me, "Why marvel? I will tell you the mystery of the woman, and of the beast with seven heads and ten
8 horns that carries her. The beast that you saw was, and is not, and is to ascend from the bottomless pit and go to perdition; and the dwellers on earth whose names have not been written in the book of life from the foundation of the world, will marvel to behold the beast, because it
9 was and is not and is to come. This calls for a mind with wisdom: the seven heads are seven mountains on which
10 the woman is seated; they are also seven kings, five of whom have fallen, one is, the other has not yet come, and
11 when he comes he must remain only a little while. As for the beast that was and is not, it is an eighth but it
12 belongs to the seven, and it goes to perdition. And the ten horns that you saw are ten kings who have not yet received royal power, but they are to receive authority
13 as kings for one hour, together with the beast. These are of one mind and give over their power and authority to
14 the beast; they will make war on the Lamb, and the Lamb will conquer them, for he is Lord of lords and King of kings, and those with him are called and chosen and faithful."
15 And he said to me, "The waters that you saw, where the harlot is seated, are peoples and multitudes and na-
16 tions and tongues. And the ten horns that you saw, they and the beast will hate the harlot; they will make her desolate and naked, and devour her flesh and burn her

17 up with fire, for God has put it into their hearts to carry out his purpose by being of one mind and giving over their royal power to the beast, until the words of God
18 shall be fulfilled. And the woman that you saw is the great city which has dominion over the kings of the earth."

18 After this I saw another angel coming down from heaven, having great authority; and the earth was
2 made bright with his splendor. And he called out with a mighty voice,
"Fallen, fallen is Babylon the great!
It has become a dwelling place of demons,
a haunt of every foul spirit,
a haunt of every foul and hateful bird;
3 for all nations have drunk k the wine of her impure passion,
and the kings of the earth have committed fornication with her,
and the merchants of the earth have grown rich with the wealth of her wantonness."
4 Then I heard another voice from heaven saying,
"Come out of her, my people,
lest you take part in her sins,
lest you share in her plagues;
5 for her sins are heaped high as heaven,
and God has remembered her iniquities.
6 Render to her as she herself has rendered,
and repay her double for her deeds;
mix a double draught for her in the cup she mixed.
7 As she glorified herself and played the wanton,
so give her a like measure of torment and mourning.
Since in her heart she says, 'A queen I sit,
I am no widow, mourning I shall never see,'
8 so shall her plagues come in a single day,
pestilence and mourning and famine,
and she shall be burned with fire;
for mighty is the Lord God who judges her."
9 And the kings of the earth, who committed fornication and were wanton with her, will weep and wail over her
10 when they see the smoke of her burning; they will stand far off, in fear of her torment, and say,
"Alas! alas! thou great city,
thou mighty city, Babylon!
In one hour has thy judgment come."
11 And the merchants of the earth weep and mourn for
12 her, since no one buys their cargo any more, cargo of gold, silver, jewels and pearls, fine linen, purple, silk and scarlet, all kinds of scented wood, all articles of ivory, all articles of costly wood, bronze, iron and
13 marble, cinnamon, spice, incense, myrrh, frankincense, wine, oil, fine flour and wheat, cattle and sheep, horses and chariots, and slaves, that is, human souls.
14 "The fruit for which thy soul longed has gone from thee,

k Other ancient authorities read fallen by

and all thy dainties and thy splendor are lost to thee,
  never to be found again!"
15 The merchants of these wares, who gained wealth from her, will stand far off, in fear of her torment, weeping and mourning aloud,
16 "Alas, alas, for the great city
  that was clothed in fine linen, in purple and scarlet,
  bedecked with gold, with jewels, and with pearls!
17 In one hour all this wealth has been laid waste."

And all shipmasters and seafaring men, sailors and
18 all whose trade is on the sea, stood far off and cried out as they saw the smoke of her burning,
  "What city was like the great city?"
19 And they threw dust on their heads, as they wept and mourned, crying out,
  "Alas, alas, for the great city
  where all who had ships at sea grew rich by her wealth!
  In one hour she has been laid waste.
20 Rejoice over her, O heaven,
  O saints and apostles and prophets,
  for God has given judgment for you against her!"

21   Then a mighty angel took up a stone like a great millstone and threw it into the sea, saying,
  "So shall Babylon the great city be thrown down with violence,
    and shall be found no more;
22 and the sound of harpers and minstrels, of flute players and trumpeters,
    shall be heard in thee no more;
  and a craftsman of any craft
    shall be found in thee no more;
  and the sound of the millstone
    shall be heard in thee no more;
23 and the light of a lamp
    shall shine in thee no more;
  and the voice of bridegroom and bride
    shall be heard in thee no more;
  for thy merchants were the great men of the earth,
    and all nations were deceived by thy sorcery.
24 And in her was found the blood of prophets and of saints,
  and of all who have been slain on earth."

19   After this I heard what seemed to be the loud voice of a great multitude in heaven, crying,
  "Hallelujah! Salvation and glory and power belong to our God,
2 for his judgments are true and just;

he has judged the great harlot who corrupted the earth with her fornication,
  and he has avenged on her the blood of his servants."
3 Once more they cried,
  "Hallelujah! The smoke from her goes up for ever and ever."
4 And the twenty-four elders and the four living creatures fell down and worshiped God who is seated on the
5 throne, saying, "Amen. Hallelujah!" And from the throne came a voice crying,
  "Praise our God, all you his servants,
  you who fear him, small and great."
6 Then I heard what seemed to be the voice of a great multitude, like the sound of many waters and like the sound of mighty thunderpeals, crying,
  "Hallelujah! For the Lord our God the Almighty reigns.
7 Let us rejoice and exult and give him the glory,
  for the marriage of the Lamb has come,
  and his Bride has made herself ready;
8 it was granted her to be clothed with fine linen, bright and pure"—
  for the fine linen is the righteous deeds of the saints.
9   And the angel said[1] to me, "Write this: Blessed are those who are invited to the marriage supper of the Lamb." And he said to me, "These are true words of
10 God." Then I fell down at his feet to worship him, but he said to me, "You must not do that! I am a fellow servant with you and your brethren who hold the testimony of Jesus. Worship God." For the testimony of Jesus is the spirit of prophecy.

SEVEN VISIONS OF GOD'S VICTORY

11   Then I saw heaven opened, and behold, a white horse! He who sat upon it is called Faithful and True, and in
12 righteousness he judges and makes war. His eyes are like a flame of fire, and on his head are many diadems; and he has a name inscribed which no one knows but
13 himself. He is clad in a robe dipped in[m] blood, and the
14 name by which he is called is The Word of God. And the armies of heaven, arrayed in fine linen, white and
15 pure, followed him on white horses. From his mouth issues a sharp sword with which to smite the nations, and he will rule them with a rod of iron; he will tread the wine press of the fury of the wrath of God the
16 Almighty. On his robe and on his thigh he has a name inscribed, King of kings and Lord of lords.

17   Then I saw an angel standing in the sun, and with a loud voice he called to all the birds that fly in midheaven,
18 "Come, gather for the great supper of God, to eat the flesh of kings, the flesh of captains, the flesh of mighty men, the flesh of horses and their riders, and the flesh of all men, both free and slave, both small and great."
19 And I saw the beast and the kings of the earth with their

[1] Greek he said   [m] Other ancient authorities read sprinkled with

armies gathered to make war against him who sits upon
²⁰ the horse and against his army. And the beast was captured, and with it the false prophet who in its presence had worked the signs by which he deceived those who had received the mark of the beast and those who worshiped its image. These two were thrown alive into the
²¹ lake of fire that burns with sulphur. And the rest were slain by the sword of him who sits upon the horse, the sword that issues from his mouth; and all the birds were gorged with their flesh.

20 Then I saw an angel coming down from heaven, holding in his hand the key of the bottomless pit
² and a great chain. And he seized the dragon, that ancient serpent, who is the Devil and Satan, and bound
³ him for a thousand years, and threw him into the pit, and shut it and sealed it over him, that he should deceive the nations no more, till the thousand years were ended. After that he must be loosed for a little while.

⁴ Then I saw thrones, and seated on them were those to whom judgment was committed. Also I saw the souls of those who had been beheaded for their testimony to Jesus and for the word of God, and who had not worshiped the beast or its image and had not received its mark on their foreheads or their hands. They came to
⁵ life, and reigned with Christ a thousand years. The rest of the dead did not come to life until the thousand years
⁶ were ended. This is the first resurrection. Blessed and holy is he who shares in the first resurrection! Over such the second death has no power, but they shall be priests of God and of Christ, and they shall reign with him a thousand years.

⁷ And when the thousand years are ended, Satan will be
⁸ loosed from his prison and will come out to deceive the nations which are at the four corners of the earth, that is, Gog and Magog, to gather them for battle; their
⁹ number is like the sand of the sea. And they marched up over the broad earth and surrounded the camp of the saints and the beloved city; but fire came down from
¹⁰ heaven ⁿ and consumed them, and the devil who had

deceived them was thrown into the lake of fire and sulphur where the beast and the false prophet were, and they will be tormented day and night for ever and ever.
¹¹ Then I saw a great white throne and him who sat upon it; from his presence earth and sky fled away, and
¹² no place was found for them. And I saw the dead, great and small, standing before the throne, and books were

opened. Also another book was opened, which is the book of life. And the dead were judged by what was
¹³ written in the books, by what they had done. And the sea gave up the dead in it, Death and Hades gave up the dead in them, and all were judged by what they had
¹⁴ done. Then Death and Hades were thrown into the lake
¹⁵ of fire. This is the second death, the lake of fire; and if any one's name was not found written in the book of life, he was thrown into the lake of fire.

THE NEW JERUSALEM

21 Then I saw a new heaven and a new earth; for the first heaven and the first earth had passed away,
² and the sea was no more. And I saw the holy city, new Jerusalem, coming down out of heaven from God, pre-
³ pared as a bride adorned for her husband; and I heard a loud voice from the throne saying, "Behold, the dwelling of God is with men. He will dwell with them, and they shall be his people,° and God himself will be with

⁴ them; ᵖ he will wipe away every tear from their eyes, and death shall be no more, neither shall there be mourning nor crying nor pain any more, for the former things have passed away."

⁵ And he who sat upon the throne said, "Behold, I make all things new." Also he said, "Write this, for
⁶ these words are trustworthy and true." And he said to me, "It is done! I am the Alpha and the Omega, the beginning and the end. To the thirsty I will give from the
⁷ fountain of the water of life without payment. He who conquers shall have this heritage, and I will be his
⁸ God and he shall be my son. But as for the cowardly, the faithless, the polluted, as for murderers, fornicators, sorcerers, idolaters, and all liars, their lot shall be in the lake that burns with fire and sulphur, which is the second death."

⁹ Then came one of the seven angels who had the seven bowls full of the seven last plagues, and spoke to me, saying, "Come, I will show you the Bride, the wife of
¹⁰ the Lamb." And in the Spirit he carried me away to a great, high mountain, and showed me the holy city Jeru-
¹¹ salem coming down out of heaven from God, having the glory of God, its radiance like a most rare jewel, like a
¹² jasper, clear as crystal. It had a great, high wall, with twelve gates, and at the gates twelve angels, and on the

ⁿ Other ancient authorities read *from God, out of heaven,* or *out of heaven from God*
ᵖ Other ancient authorities add *and be their God*

° Other ancient authorities read *peoples*

gates the names of the twelve tribes of the sons of Israel
13 were inscribed; on the east three gates, on the north three gates, on the south three gates, and on the west
14 three gates. And the wall of the city had twelve foundations, and on them the twelve names of the twelve apostles of the Lamb.

15 And he who talked to me had a measuring rod of
16 gold to measure the city and its gates and walls. The city lies foursquare, its length the same as its breadth; and he measured the city with his rod, twelve thousand
17 stadia;q its length and breadth and height are equal. He also measured its wall, a hundred and forty-four cubits
18 by a man's measure, that is, an angel's. The wall was built of jasper, while the city was pure gold, clear as
19 glass. The foundations of the wall of the city were adorned with every jewel; the first was jasper, the second
20 sapphire, the third agate, the fourth emerald, the fifth onyx, the sixth carnelian, the seventh chrysolite, the eighth beryl, the ninth topaz, the tenth chrysoprase, the
21 eleventh jacinth, the twelfth amethyst. And the twelve gates were twelve pearls, each of the gates made of a single pearl, and the street of the city was pure gold,
22 transparent as glass. And I saw no temple in the city, for its temple is the Lord God the Almighty and the
23 Lamb. And the city has no need of sun or moon to shine upon it, for the glory of God is its light, and its lamp
24 is the Lamb. By its light shall the nations walk; and
25 the kings of the earth shall bring their glory into it, and its gates shall never be shut by day—and there shall be
26 no night there; they shall bring into it the glory and the
27 honor of the nations. But nothing unclean shall enter it, nor any one who practices abomination or falsehood, but only those who are written in the Lamb's book of life.

22 Then he showed me the river of the water of life, bright as crystal, flowing from the throne of God
2 and of the Lamb through the middle of the street of the city; also, on either side of the river, the tree of lifer with its twelve kinds of fruit, yielding its fruit each month; and the leaves of the tree were for the healing
3 of the nations. There shall no more be anything accursed, but the throne of God and of the Lamb shall be in it,
4 and his servants shall worship him; they shall see his
5 face, and his name shall be on their foreheads. And night shall be no more; they need no light of lamp or sun,

for the Lord God will be their light, and they shall reign for ever and ever.

EPILOGUE
6 And he said to me, "These words are trustworthy and true. And the Lord, the God of the spirits of the prophets, has sent his angel to show his servants what must soon
7 take place. And behold, I am coming soon."

Blessed is he who keeps the words of the prophecy of this book.

8 I John am he who heard and saw these things. And when I heard and saw them, I fell down to worship at
9 the feet of the angel who showed them to me; but he said to me, "You must not do that! I am a fellow servant with you and your brethren the prophets, and with those who keep the words of this book. Worship God."

10 And he said to me, "Do not seal up the words of the
11 prophecy of this book, for the time is near. Let the evildoer still do evil, and the filthy still be filthy, and the righteous still do right, and the holy still be holy."

12 "Behold, I am coming soon, bringing my recompense,
13 to repay every one for what he has done. I am the Alpha and the Omega, the first and the last, the beginning and the end."

14 Blessed are those who wash their robes,s that they may have the right to the tree of life and that they may enter
15 the city by the gates. Outside are the dogs and sorcerers and fornicators and murderers and idolaters, and every one who loves and practices falsehood.

16 "I Jesus have sent my angel to you with this testimony for the churches. I am the root and the offspring of David, the bright morning star."

17 The Spirit and the Bride say, "Come." And let him who hears say, "Come." And let him who is thirsty come, let him who desires take the water of life without price.

18 I warn every one who hears the words of the prophecy of this book: if any one adds to them, God will add to
19 him the plagues described in this book, and if any one takes away from the words of the book of this prophecy, God will take away his share in the tree of life and in the holy city, which are described in this book.

20 He who testifies to these things says, "Surely I am coming soon." Amen. Come, Lord Jesus!

21 The grace of the Lord Jesus be with all the saints.t Amen.

q About fifteen hundred miles   r Or the Lamb. In the midst of the street of the city, and on either side of the river, was the tree of life, etc
s Other ancient authorities read do his commandments   t Other ancient authorities omit all; others omit the saints

Maps

The Biblical World at the Time of the Patriarchs . . . . A
The Route of the Exodus and the Conquest of Canaan B-1
The Kingdoms of Israel and Judah B-2
The Assyrian Empire C-1
Great Empires of the Sixth Century B.C. C-2
The Empire of Alexander the Great and the
   Kingdoms of Alexander's Successors D-1
The Roman World in the Time of Caesar D-2
Palestine in the Time of Christ . . . . E
The Journeys of Paul F-1
The Spread of Christianity F-2
The Near East Today . . . . G
The Mediterranean World Today . . . . H

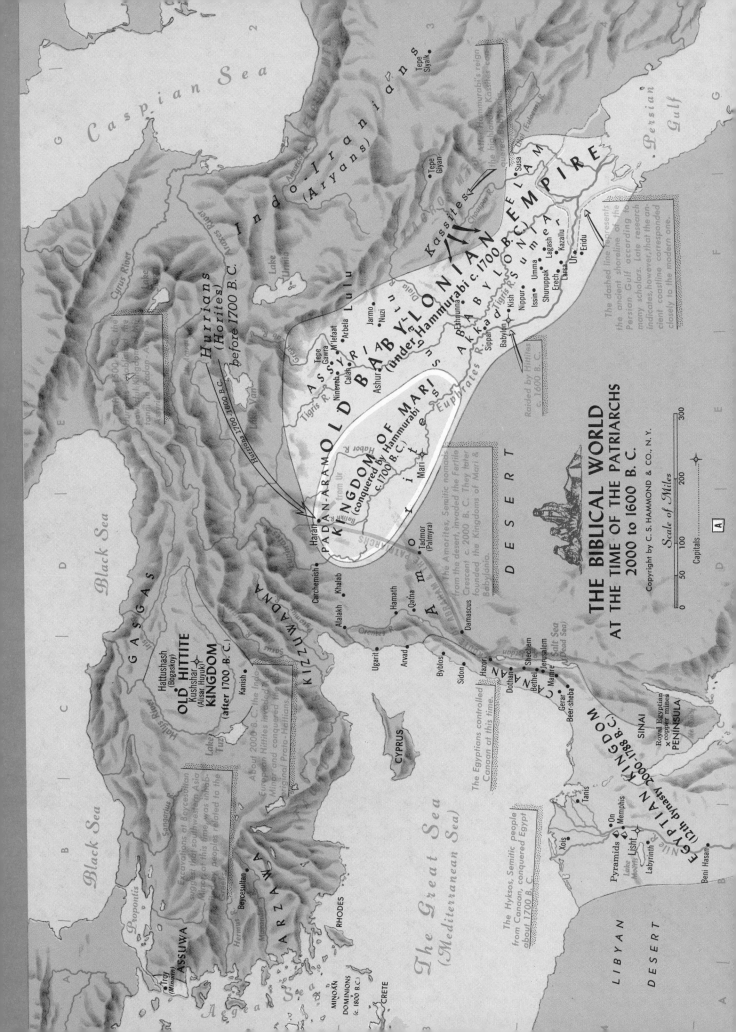

Caspian Sea

G

2

Tepe Siyalk

3

Indo-Iranians (Aryans)

Elburz Mts.

The highlands turned

H

Amadiya

Lake Urmia

Lulu

Kassites

After Hammurabi's reign the Kassites conquered.

Diala R.

Susa

ELAM

Persian Gulf

NEW BABYLONIAN EMPIRE

E L A M

F

The dashed line represents the ancient shoreline of the Persian Gulf according to many scholars. Late research indicates, however, that the ancient coastline corresponded closely to the modern one.

Hurrians (Horites) before 1700 B.C.

Lake Van

ASSYRIA

Tepe Gawra

Nineveh

Calah

Ashur

Arbela

Jarmo

Nuzi

BABYLONIA

(under Hammurabi)

S U M E R

M'lefaat

Tigris R.

Eshnunna

Sippar

Babylon

Kish

Nippur

Issin

Shuruppak

Umma

Lagash

Erech

Larsa

Kazallu

Ur

Eridu

Akkad

Raided by Hittites c. 1600 B.C.

Hurrians 1200-1600 B.C.

Cyrus River

Araxes River

Gihon

PADAN-ARAM

OLD BABYLONIAN EMPIRE

ARAM

Abraham from Ur

Euphrates R.

Harran

Haborn from Ur

Habor R.

KINGDOM OF MARI

c. 1700 B.C. (conquered by Hammurabi c. 1700 B.C.)

Mari

THE PATRIARCHS

E

D

C

Black Sea

Carchemish

Khalab

Alalakh

Tadmor (Palmyra)

A m o r i t e s

DESERT

The Amorites, Semitic nomads from the desert, invaded the Fertile Crescent c. 2000 B.C. They later founded the Kingdoms of Mari & Babylonia.

KIZZUWADNA

GASGAS

Hamath

Qatna

Damascus

Orontes

Ugarit

Arvad

Byblos

Sidon

Hazor

Dothan

Shechem

Bethel

Jerusalem

Mamre

CANAAN

Gerar

Beer-sheba

Salt Sea (Dead Sea)

THE BIBLICAL WORLD

AT THE TIME OF THE PATRIARCHS 2000 to 1600 B.C.

Copyright by C. S. HAMMOND & CO., N.Y.

Scale of Miles

0   50   100   200   300

Capitals: ✪

A

OLD HITTITE KINGDOM

Hattushash (Bogaskoy)

Kushshar (Alisar Huyuk) (after 1700 B.C.)

Kanish

About 2000 B.C. the Indo-European Hittites invaded Asia Minor and conquered the original Proto-Hittians.

Halys River

Lake Tuz

The Egyptians controlled Canaan at this time.

SINAI PENINSULA

Royal Egyptian x copper mines

EDOM

ARZAWA

ASSUWA

Troy (Minoan)

Beycesultan

Sangarios

Hermus

Maeander

Propontis

Excavations at Beycesultan 2000 ft. tell southwest of Asia Minor at this time was inhabited by a people related to the

RHODES

CYPRUS

The Great Sea (Mediterranean Sea)

B

The Hyksos, Semitic people from Canaan, conquered Egypt about 1700 B.C.

EGYPTIAN KINGDOM

(12th dynasty 2000-1788 B.C.)

On

Memphis

Pyramids

Lake Moeris

Lisht

Labyrinth

Tanis

Xois

Nile R.

Beni Hasan

LIBYAN DESERT

MINOAN DOMINIONS (c. 1800 B.C.)

CRETE

Aegean Sea

Black Sea

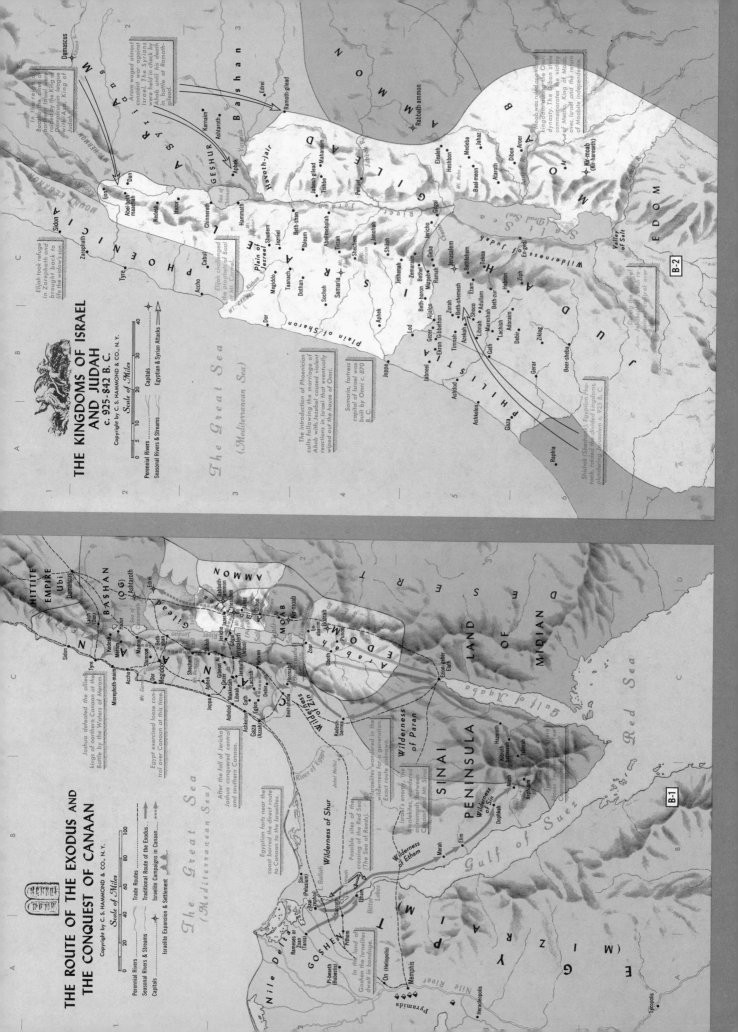

THE KINGDOMS OF ISRAEL
AND JUDAH
c. 925-842 B.C.

Copyright by C. S. HAMMOND & CO., N.Y.

Scale of Miles

0 5 10   20   30   40

Perennial Rivers ———
Seasonal Rivers & Streams ———
Capitals ✦
Egyptian & Syrian Attacks ⟶

In the reign of Baasha the cities of northern Israel were raided by the King of Damascus in league with Asa, King of Judah.

Aram waged almost constant war against Israel. The Syrians were held in check by Ahab until his death in battle of Ramoth-gilead.

Moab was ruled over by the Omri dynasty. The Dibon stele commemorates the victory of Mesha, King of Moab, over Israel and the return of Moabite independence.

Elijah took refuge in Zarephath and brought back to life the widow's son.

Elijah challenged the prophets of Baal on Mt. Carmel.

The introduction of Phoenician cults following the marriage of Ahab with Jezebel caused violent reactions in Israel that eventually wiped out the house of Omri.

Samaria, fortress capital of Israel was built by Omri c. 870 B.C.

Shishak (Sheshonk), Egyptian Pharaoh, raided the divided kingdoms, plundering Jerusalem c. 925 B.C.

The Great Sea
(Mediterranean Sea)

B-2

THE ROUTE OF THE EXODUS AND
THE CONQUEST OF CANAAN

Copyright by C. S. HAMMOND & CO., N.Y.

Scale of Miles

0   20   40   60   80   100

Perennial Rivers & Streams ———
Seasonal Rivers & Streams ———
Capitals ✦
Trade Routes ———
Traditional Route of the Exodus ⟶
Israelite Campaigns in Canaan ⟶
Israelite Expansion & Settlement ⟶

Joshua defeated the allied kings of northern Canaan at the Battle by the Waters of Meron.

Egypt exercised loose control over Canaan at this time.

After the fall of Jericho Joshua conquered central and southern Canaan.

Egyptian forts near the coast barred the direct route to Canaan to the Israelites.

Possible sites of the crossing of the Red Sea (The Sea of Reeds).

Israel's enemy, the Amalekites, wandered as nomads between Canaan and Mt. Sinai.

Israelites wandered in the wilderness for a generation. Exact route unknown.

The Great Sea
(Mediterranean Sea)

Red Sea

B-1

PALESTINE IN THE TIME OF CHRIST

Copyright by C. S. HAMMOND & CO., N. Y.

Scale of Miles

0 5 10 20 30 40

Perennial Rivers ----------
Seasonal Rivers & Streams ----------
Capitals ----------⬦
Roads & Trade Routes ----------

Tetrarchy of Lysanias
Tetrarchy of Philip
Tetrarchy of Herod Antipas
Territory under Roman procurator
Areas tributary to Salome
Decapolis *
Independent *
Roman province of Syria

Cities of the Decapolis ----------□

* The Decapolis and Ascalon retained their independence under the Roman governor of the province of Syria.

Archelaus, upon Herod's death, became ruler of Judaea, Samaria and Idumaea. His reign lasted until 6 A.D. when he was removed and exiled. His territory then was placed under a Roman procurator.

Salome, Herod's sister, was given Jamnia, Azotus and Phasaelis. They, in turn, passed to Livia, wife of Augustus and then to Emperor Tiberius.

ABILENE
Abila
Sidon
Damascus
ITURAEA
Sarepta (Zarephath)
PHOENICIA
PANIAS
Tyre
Dan Caesarea Philippi
ULATHA
TRACHONITIS
Ladder of Tyre
Cadasa (Kedesh)
Lake Semechonitis
GAULANITIS
BATANAEA
Gischala
Seleucia
Raphana
BASHAN
Horns of Hattin (Kurun Hattin) is a possible site of the Sermon on the Mount.
Chorazin
Bethsaida (Julias)
Capernaum
Ptolemais (Accho)
Jotapata
Cana
Magdala (Dalmanutha) Tabigha
Gergesa
Gamala
AURANITIS
GALILEE
Sepphoris
Sea of Galilee
Hippos
Dion
Nazareth
Tiberias
Philoteria
Abila
Edrei
Plain of Esdraelon
Nain
Gadara
Capitolias
Dora
Bethabara
The Great Sea
Caesarea
Residence of Roman procurators.
En-gannim (Ginaea)
Scythopolis (Beth-shan)
Pella
DECAPOLIS
SAMARIA
Gerasa
(Mediterranean Sea)
Samaria (Sebaste)
Shechem Sychar
Jacob's Well
Amathus
Apollonia
Mt. Gerizim
GILEAD
Antipatris
Phasaelis
PERAEA
Joppa
Archelais
Philadelphia (Rabbath-ammon)
Lydda (Diospolis)
Arimathaea (Ramathaim)
Gophna
Ephraim
Beth-nimrah
Bethel
Gezer (Gazara)
Jericho
AMMON
Jamnia
Ramah
Julias (Livias, Beth-haram)
Heshbon
Ekron
Nicopolis (Emmaus)
Emmaus
Khirbet Qumran
Azotus (Ashdod)
Jerusalem
Bethany
The Dead Sea Scrolls were found in a cave here; also the ruins of an Essene monastery.
Bethlehem
Herodium
Ascalon
Callirhoe
JUDAEA
Mareshah (Marisa)
Salt or Dead Sea (L. Asphaltitis)
Machaerus
John the Baptist was imprisoned and beheaded by order of Herod Antipas.
Gaza
Hebron
Dibon
Ziph
Wilderness of Judah
Juttah
En-gedi
Carmel
Gerar
Masada
Rabbath Moab (Areopolis, Rabba)
MOAB
Raphia
IDUMAEA
Beersheba
Kir-moab (Kir-haresheth)
ARABIA
NABATAEANS

A B C D E

THE JOURNEYS OF PAUL

THE SPREAD OF CHRISTIANITY